D1194159

ELIZABETHAN PLAYS

Elizabethan

PLAYS

Written By

SHAKESPEARE'S Friends, Colleagues, Rivals, and Successors; *to wit*:

*Christopher Marlowe, John Lyly,
Robert Greene, Thomas Kyd, Ben Jonson,
George Chapman, Thomas Dekker, John Marston,
Thomas Heywood, Francis Beaumont, John Fletcher,
John Webster, Thomas Middleton, William Rowley,
Philip Massinger, John Ford, and James Shirley.*

Edited, with new Texts *based on the* original
Folios, Quartos, *and* Octavos, *by*

HAZELTON SPENCER
Associate Professor of English in The Johns Hopkins University

D. C. Heath and Company
BOSTON

PR 1263 .S6 1933

Spencer, Hazelton, 1893-
1944.

Elizabethan plays

Ottemiller

PREFATORY NOTE

THE twenty-eight plays of this collection have been chosen primarily for their merit as master-pieces of English drama, and secondarily to represent the leading Elizabethan playwrights and the main currents of drama in Shakespeare's time and just after. The selection has been made without regard to the contents of similar anthologies; but it is a pleasant duty to acknowledge that the first of these, President Neilson's, remains, in the matter of selection, a monument to his taste and judgment.

Almost every play in the present volume, even the crude but powerful *Spanish Tragedy*, is in its way a masterpiece. *Endymion* is an exception; in none of his plays does Lyly manifest either a genuine *vis comica*, or that indispensable possession of the great serious dramatist, profound sympathy with the inner life of sensitive men and women and with its occasional revelation, under the pressure of circumstance, in the manifestations of human passion. But the court plays must be illustrated; and, superficial as Lyly is, he was one of Shakespeare's teachers. Peele on the other hand was not, and has been omitted without much regret. *The Old Wife's Tale* has a few charming passages, but most of it is sad stuff; *David and Bethsabe* opens with one of the age's most amazing bursts of lyrical genius, and then turns into an inferior history play, less dramatic than its source. *Friar Bacon and Friar Bungay* is at least sustained; and, if not quite a masterpiece, it is thoroughly delightful and shows Greene at his best. *Dr. Faustus* and *The Jew of Malta* have come down to us in forms worse than the mutilated statues of antiquity, for they have been debased by the adapter's hand. Yet, mangled as they are, they are mangled masterpieces.

Marlowe, Jonson, and the Beaumont-Fletcher collaboration are illustrated by four plays each; the last two because, except for Webster's masterpiece, their works are nearest Shakespeare's in excellence. And Marlowe's development as a dramatist is so illuminating for the student of Shakespeare's that it seems desirable to afford copious materials for tracing it. Interesting as is Jonson's *Sejanus*, his mastery was in comedy. *Every Man in His Humor* is required by historical considerations, and it seems better to give, in addition to that play, all three of the great comedies than to omit one for the sake of a second-rate tragedy. Dekker is perhaps unduly favored. *The Shoemakers' Holiday* could not be left out, though it is inferior, as a serious work of art, to *The Honest Whore*; and one part of that strangely beautiful drama is not enough. *Part II* is the masterpiece, but its power would be impaired without *Part I*. Toward the end of our period comedy becomes more significant than tragedy, both for its superior vitality, and for its greater influence on the drama of the Restoration and the eighteenth century. The selections from Massinger and Shirley have been made in accordance with this fact. The Editor thought of including less familiar examples of the lighter vein of Fletcher and of Middleton, but was forced to recognize that *The Wild-Goose Chase* and *A Trick to Catch the Old One*, while not indisputably the best of their authors' comedies, are clearly best for the purposes this volume is designed to serve.

These are, of course, chiefly to introduce university students and general readers to the riches of the non-Shakespearean drama of the English Renaissance. Yet care has been taken to make the texts as accurate as possible. For only four of these, precisely specified in the introductory notes, has the Editor been obliged to rely on reprints; and even such exceptions to the general rule of first-hand collation of the old editions have been carefully cross-checked, since for each of these four plays at least two scholarly reprints were available. In several cases (chiefly among the works of those dramatists who have not appeared in collected editions for half a century or more) the present texts, granted their "modernization", probably constitute the closest approximation to the authors' original MSS ever printed (under this category *i Honest Whore* is perhaps the most interesting example); in many others they are considerably more faithful to the earliest editions than the texts of similar undertakings; for errors arising from reliance on derivative texts, and the tampering, whether or not acknowledged, by the nineteenth-century editors, have been incorporated in anthologies to a surprising extent, the more surprising because so often silently.

Departures from the basic texts are here enclosed in square brackets. It has not been thought necessary to record such insignificant changes as "re-enter" for "enter", nor the expansion of abbreviations, nor inconsequential variations in the spelling of proper names and in speech-tags, nor altered word-order in stage directions (though in these a special effort has been made to retain the flavor of the Elizabethan theatre), nor the correction of turned letters and similarly obvious printer's blunders. Rearrangement of lines of verse has not always been indicated, nor arrangement of (printed) prose as verse, etc. It is often quite impossible to say that a given passage is one or the other. It would, however, be folly to hope that the pains taken in collation and proof-reading have eliminated error; the Editor will be grateful for corrections from users of the book. No attempt has been made to supply a complete apparatus of variant readings, but the most suggestive are given. Nor have the old texts been violated in order to wrench them into conformity with pedantic conceptions of metrical regularity. Much of the beauty of spoken blank verse depends upon slight deviations from the norm. Though editors have professed the contrary, the practice has been far too general of forcing lines into the mold of strict regularity by indicating the suppression of vowels which were probably slurred or even pronounced distinctly but rapidly on the stage, and of giving too little heed to the metrical value of dramatic pauses by insisting on the pronunciation of syllables that were probably elided. The evidence afforded by the original editions is by no means conclusive on these matters; but it is about all the evidence we have, and the Editor has followed it.

The present texts, then, are notably conservative, save in two particulars: scholars would rather read an exact reprint of an original quarto, with all variants footnoted; but it seems inadvisable to risk distracting the beginner from the plays as plays and as literature by sticking to archaic spelling and punctuation. With the same end in view, and at the cost of making the book considerably larger, a legible type (nine-point Modern Number 8 Monotype on ten-point body) has been used. The Editor hopes that the owner of this book will enjoy it and that, continuing his reading far beyond it, he will permanently join the good company of those who have found delight in these robust old plays.

The Editor has rejected the theory that annotation is necessarily a nuisance and assumed that such active and inquiring minds as choose to read this book will enjoy the plays more if they understand the meaning of the words the dramatists composed them in. It is patently impossible, however, to note within the limits of an anthology that "still" means "always" and that "friend" often means "lover", every time the words occur; such expressions are glossed scatteringly. The same principle has been adopted in noticing unfamiliar accentuation.

It remains to acknowledge the receipt of many courtesies, which have facilitated the labors of collation and annotation, from the staffs of the Harvard College Library, the Boston Public Library, the Library of Congress, and the Library of The Johns Hopkins University; from the Elizabethan Club of Yale University; and from the Supervisor of Research and his assistants at the Folger Shakespeare Library. To the last of these institutions special thanks is due for permission to reproduce its portrait of Jonson; and, as well as to several of the libraries already mentioned, the Editor is indebted for various favors (especially for the facsimiles of the old title pages) to the British Museum, the Bodleian Library, and the Huntington Library. For the constant coöperation of his publishers the Editor is particularly grateful. The format was designed by Arthur F. Williams of their staff. The coat of arms on the cover was redrawn from a copy of the Gospels bound for Queen Elizabeth and now in the British Museum. The ornaments on the shelf-back are details (cuirasses) from the elaborate design of which the coat of arms is the central feature.

So many critical, historical, and lexicographical works have been levied on that to list them is out of the question. Excellent bibliographies for this field are now so numerous and so accessible that it seems inadvisable to sacrifice precious space by including another. Yet special mention ought to be made of the help received from E. K. Chambers's *Elizabethan Stage*, W. W. Greg's *List of English Plays*, Skeat and Mayhew's *Glossary of Tudor and Stuart Words*, and, most constantly, the *New English Dictionary*. The annotation has been strengthened at a number of points by several of the Editor's colleagues at The Johns Hopkins, who have given him the benefit of their learning in a wide variety of fields. With characteristic liberality the Editor's master, George Lyman Kittredge, entered into a correspondence which continued for several months on certain problems of special difficulty. To Professor Kittredge's incomparable understanding of words and their ways in Elizabethan speech is due the illumination of a number of dark passages which all previous commentators had ignored, given up, or left in confusion worse confounded. Professor Fred N. Robinson kindly lent his aid in the handling of several Gaelic expressions. To the generosity and accuracy of Dr. W. Lee Ustick the Editor is under particular obligations, for the checking of many readings in copies of the early editions which were temporarily out of his reach. These acknowledgments would be incomplete without an allusion to prentice years under Professor John Tucker Murray, as his assistant in his course on these dramatists. The most general indebtedness, however, is to the noble army of Elizabethan play editors, both the living and the slain, to whom salute and thanks.

H. S.

CONTENTS

ELIZABETHAN PLAYS

Tamburlaine

the Great.

Who, from a Scythian Shephearde,
by his rare and woonderfull Conquests,
became a most puissant and migh-
tye Monarque.

And (for his tyranny, and terrour in
Warre)was tearmed,

The Scourge of God.

Deuided into two Tragicall Dis-
courses, as they were sundrie times
shewed vpon Stages in the Citie
of London.

By the right honorable the Lord
Admyrall, his seruantes.

Now first, and newlie published.

LONDON.
Printed by Richard Ihones: at the signe
of the Rose and Crowne neere Hol-
borne Bridge. 1590.

INTRODUCTORY NOTE

THE production of *Tamburlaine, Part I*, probably in 1587–88, definitely inaugurated the earlier of the two great ages of British drama. Never before had first-rate genius been devoted to the making of an English play. When Shakespeare came to London, a few years later, he found a highly imaginative drama, bold and passionate, and couched in a ringing blank verse, in possession of the boards. In his tragedies and histories he applied himself to perfecting what Marlowe had begun.

Though a university man, Marlowe succeeded in freeing his work from the smell of the lamp which spoils most tragedies of the 1580's. Taking his theme from the past, he swings it straight into the main current of the Renaissance; Tamburlaine personifies and voices its boundless aspiration. In fact, the form of the play suffers from the author's preoccupation with his hero; Marlowe's later works are better dramas. Outwardly, *Tamburlaine* is a ten-act history play; essentially, it is a soaring piece of almost epical poetry, often wildly extravagant, but adorned with moments of dazzling lyric beauty.[1] In *Part II* the hero extends his conquests, though he is somewhat shaken by the loss of Zenocrate and the cowardice of one of their sons. At last, glutted with blood, intoxicated with success, and broken in health, he madly orders an assault on the powers of Heaven. But now his armies are helpless; he is beaten at last; Death is the final victor.

Marlowe read widely for his materials; in *Tamburlaine* he is something of the scholar, as well as poet. His chief sources are Pedro Mexía's *Silva de Varia Lección* and Petrus Perondinus's *Magni Tamerlanis Scytharum Imperatoris Vita*. But there are many others, both geographical and historical, as Miss Ethel Seaton has shown (see introduction to Miss Ellis-Fermor's edition for references and summaries). Marlowe's great contribution is his crediting the brutal conqueror with the "undeviating pursuit of a vision"; at least this is true of *Part I*, though in the sequel there is more recognition of the horrible futility of what the hero has done.

The gigantic Edward Alleyn was famous in the title rôle, but little is known of the early stage history of the play. It was being acted with great success by the Admiral's Men in 1594 and 1595, and there are many literary allusions up to the closing of the theatres in 1642. The standard editions of Marlowe's works are those of Tucker Brooke (1910), and R. H. Case as general editor (1930–   ). *Tamburlaine* was edited for the latter by Miss U. M. Ellis-Fermor (1930). Albrecht Wagner published an edition in 1885. *Part I* originally appeared, in octavo, in 1590 (reprinted 1593?, 1597, 1605); on that text, as given by Brooke and Miss Ellis-Fermor, the present edition is based. None of the old editions ascribes the play to Marlowe, but his authorship is certain both from internal evidence and in the light of Thomas Heywood's plain statement in a prologue (1633) to *The Jew of Malta*.

---

[1] It may seem to a reader new to Marlowe that the opening lines do not bear out this statement; if so, he is advised to whet his appetite by turning to I, ii, 87, ff., or V, ii, 72, ff.

TAMBURLAINE THE GREAT

BY

CHRISTOPHER MARLOWE

THE FIRST PART

[DRAMATIS PERSONAE

MYCETES,[1] King of Persia.
COSROE, his brother.
MEANDER,
THERIDAMAS,
ORTYGIUS, } Persian lords.
CENEUS,
MENAPHON,
TAMBURLAINE, a Scythian shepherd.
TECHELLES, } his followers.
USUMCASANE,
BAJAZETH, Emperor of the Turks.
KING of FEZ.
KING of MOROCCO.
KING of ARGIER.[2]

KING of ARABIA.
SOLDAN of EGYPT.
GOVERNOR of DAMASCUS.
AGYDAS,
MAGNETES, } Median lords.
CAPOLIN, an Egyptian.
PHILEMUS, a messenger.
Bassoes, Lords, Citizens, Moors, Soldiers, and Attendants.

ZENOCRATE, daughter to the Soldan of Egypt.
ANIPPE, her maid.
ZABINA, wife to Bajazeth.
EBEA, her maid.
Virgins of Damascus.]

THE PROLOGUE

FROM jigging veins of rhyming mother wits,
And such conceits as clownage keeps in pay,
We'll lead you to the stately tent of war,
Where you shall hear the Scythian Tamburlaine
Threat'ning the world with high astounding terms,
And scourging kingdoms with his conquering sword.
View but his picture in this tragic glass,
And then applaud his fortunes as you please.

ACT I — SCENE I [3]

[*Enter*] MYCETES, COSROE, MEANDER, THERIDAMAS, ORTYGIUS, CENEUS, [MENAPHON,] *with others.*

MYC. Brother Cosroe, I find myself aggriev'd,
Yet insufficient to express the same,
For it requires a great and thund'ring speech.
Good Brother, tell the cause unto my lords;
I know you have a better wit than I.

Cos. Unhappy Persia, that in former age
Hast been the seat of mighty conquerors,
That, in their prowess and their policies,
Have triumph'd over Afric and the bounds
Of Europe,[4] where the sun dares scarce appear   10
For freezing meteors and congealed cold,
Now to be rul'd and governed by a man
At whose birthday Cynthia with Saturn join'd,
And Jove, the Sun, and Mercury denied
To shed [their][5] influence in his fickle brain.

---

[1] Some of these names are invented, some historical though unrelated to Tamburlaine, and some (like Bajazeth) both historical and related.

[2] Algiers.

[3] Unlocated by the dramatist, but presumably a camp near Persepolis.

[4] Referring to Cambyses's conquest of Egypt and the expedition of Darius I across the Danube.

[5] Emend. Dyce; old eds. *his*, which may possibly be right, referring to Jove, whose agents are the Sun and Mercury.

5

Now Turks and Tartars shake their swords at
    thee,
Meaning to mangle all thy provinces.
  MYC. Brother, I see your meaning well
    enough,
And thorough your planets I perceive you think
I am not wise enough to be a king ;   20
But I refer me to my noblemen,
That know my wit and can be witnesses.
I might command you to be slain for this ;
Meander, might I not?
  MEAND. Not for so small a fault, my sov-
    ereign Lord.
  MYC. I mean it not, but yet I know I
    might ;
Yet live ; yea, live ; Mycetes wills it so. —
Meander, thou, my faithful counsellor,
Declare the cause of my conceived grief,
Which is, God knows, about that Tambur-
    laine,   30
That, like a fox in midst of harvest time,
Doth prey upon my flocks of passengers,
And, as I hear, doth mean to pull my plumes ;
Therefore 't is good and meet for to be wise.
  MEAND. Oft have I heard your Majesty
    complain
Of Tamburlaine, that sturdy Scythian thief,
That robs your merchants of Persepolis
[Trading] [6] by land unto the Western Isles,
And in your confines with his lawless train
Daily commits incivil [7] outrages,   40
Hoping (misled by dreaming prophecies)
To reign in Asia, and with barbarous arms
To make himself the monarch of the East ;
But ere he march in Asia, or display
His vagrant ensign in the Persian fields,
Your Grace hath taken order by Theridamas,[8]
Charg'd with a thousand horse, to apprehend
And bring him captive to your Highness'
    throne.
  MYC. Full true thou speak'st, and like thy-
    self, my Lord,
Whom I may term a Damon for thy love.   50
Therefore 't is best, if so it like you all,
To send my thousand horse incontinent [9]
To apprehend that paltry Scythian.
How like you this, my honorable Lords?
Is it not a kingly resolution? [10]

  Cos. It cannot choose, because it comes
    from you.
  MYC. Then hear thy charge, valiant Theri-
    damas,
The chiefest captain of Mycetes' host,
The hope of Persia, and the very legs
Whereon our state doth lean as on a staff,   60
That holds us up, and foils our neighbor foes :
Thou shalt be leader of this thousand horse,
Whose foaming gall with rage and high disdain
Have sworn the death of wicked Tamburlaine.
Go frowning forth ; but come thou smiling
    home,
As did Sir Paris with the Grecian dame ;
Return with speed : time passeth swift away ;
Our life is frail, and we may die to-day.
  THER. Before the moon renew her borrowed
    light,
Doubt not, my lord and gracious sovereign,   70
But Tamburlaine and that Tartarian rout
Shall either perish by our warlike hands,
Or plead for mercy at your Highness' feet.
  MYC. Go, stout Theridamas ; thy words
    are swords,
And with thy looks thou conquerest all thy
    foes.
I long to see thee back return from thence,
That I may view these milk-white steeds of
    mine
All loaden with the heads of killed men,
And from their knees even to their hoofs below
Besmear'd with blood that makes a dainty
    show.   80
  THER. Then now, my Lord, I humbly take
    my leave.
  MYC. Theridamas, farewell ten thousand
    times. —   *Exit* [THERIDAMAS].
Ah, Menaphon, why stayest thou thus behind,
When other men press forward for renown?
Go, Menaphon, go into Scythia ;
And foot by foot follow Theridamas.
  Cos. Nay, pray you let him stay ; a greater
    [task] [11]
Fits Menaphon than warring with a thief.
Create him Prorex [12] of [13] Africa,
That he may win the Babylonians' hearts,   90
Which will revolt from Persian government
Unless they have a wiser king than you.
  MYC. " Unless they have a wiser king than
    you ! "
These are his words ; Meander, set them down.
  Cos. And add this to them : that all Asia
Lament to see the folly of their king.

[6] O_2 ; O_1 *treading*.   [7] Uncivilized.
[8] A twelve-syllable line, but not an Alexandrine,
the last two syllables being here lightly pronounced,
though in l. 57 (and elsewhere) the last receives a
stress.
[9] At once.
[10] "Is it not" forms the first foot of this line ;
"resolution" has five syllables. The suffix is
common as a dissyllable.

[11] Add. Robinson.
[12] Viceroy.   [13] O_4 adds *all*.

MYC. Well, here I swear by this my royal
    seat —

COS. You may do well to kiss it then.

MYC. Emboss'd with silk as best beseems
    my state,

To be reveng'd for these contemptuous words.

Oh, where is duty and allegiance now?   101

Fled to the Caspian or the Ocean main?

What shall I call thee? Brother? No, a foe,

Monster of nature, shame unto thy stock,

That dar'st presume thy sovereign for to
    mock. —

Meander, come ; I am abus'd, Meander.

[Exeunt all but] COSROE *and* MENAPHON.

MEN. How now, my Lord? What, mated [14]
    and amaz'd

To hear the King thus threaten like himself?

COS. Ah, Menaphon, I pass not for [15] his
    threats ;

The plot is laid by Persian noblemen   110

And captains of the Median garrisons

To crown me Emperor of Asia ;

But this it is that doth excruciate

The very substance of my vexed soul :

To see our neighbors, that were wont to quake

And tremble at the Persian monarch's name,

Now sits and laughs our regiment [16] to scorn ;

And, that which might resolve [17] me into tears,

Men from the farthest equinoctial line

Have swarm'd in troops into the Eastern
    India,   120

Lading their ships with gold and precious
    stones,

And made their spoils from all our provinces.

MEN. This should entreat your Highness to
    rejoice,

Since Fortune gives you opportunity

To gain the title of a conqueror

By curing of this maimed empery.

Afric and Europe bordering on your land,

And continent to your dominions,

How easily may you, with a mighty host,

Pass into Græcia,[18] as did Cyrus once,   130

And cause them to withdraw their forces home,

Lest you subdue the pride of Christendom !

COS. But, Menaphon, what means this
    trumpet's sound?

MEN. Behold, my Lord, Ortygius and the
    rest

Bringing the crown to make you emperor.

Enter ORTYGIUS *and* CENEUS *bearing a crown,
with others.*

ORTY. Magnificent and mighty Prince Cos-
    roe,

We, in the name of other Persian states [19]

And commons of this mighty monarchy,

Present thee with th' imperial diadem.

CEN. The warlike soldiers and the gentle-
    men,   140

That heretofore have fill'd Persepolis

With Afric captains taken in the field,

Whose ransom made them march in coats of
    gold,

With costly jewels hanging at their ears,

And shining stones upon their lofty crests,

Now living idle in the walled towns,

Wanting both pay and martial discipline,

Begin in troops to threaten civil war,

And openly exclaim against the King.

Therefore, to stay all sudden mutinies,   150

We will invest your Highness emperor ;

Whereat the soldiers will conceive more joy

Than did the Macedonians at the spoil

Of great Darius [20] and his wealthy host.

COS. Well, since I see the state of Persia
    droop

And languish in my brother's government,

I willingly receive th' imperial crown,

And vow to wear it for my country's good,

In spite of them shall malice my estate.   159

ORTY. And in assurance of desir'd success,

We here do crown thee monarch of the East,

Emperor of Asia and Persia,[21]

Great Lord of Media and Armenia ;

Duke of Africa and Albania,[22]

Mesopotamia and of Parthia,

East India and the late-discovered isles ;

Chief Lord of all the wide, vast Euxine sea,

And of the ever-raging Caspian lake.

Long live Cosroe, mighty emperor !

COS. And Jove may [23] never let me longer
    live   170

Than I may seek to gratify your love,

And cause the soldiers that thus honor me

To triumph over many provinces ;

By whose desires of discipline in arms

I doubt not shortly but to reign sole king,

And with the army of Theridamas

---

[14] Discomfited.

[15] Care not for, am unmoved by.

[16] Rule.

[17] Dissolve.

[18] *I.e.*, the Ionian cities of Asia Minor, reduced, after Cyrus had conquered Lydia, by his generals.

[19] Nobles, men of high estate.

[20] Darius III, defeated by Alexander the Great at Issus.

[21] "Emperor" is practically a trochee ; "Asia" and "Persia" are here trisyllables.

[22] West of the Caspian and north of the Caucasus.

[23] May Jove.

(Whither we presently will fly, my Lords)
To rest secure against my brother's force.

    ORTY. We knew, my Lord, before we
      brought the crown,
Intending your investion [24] so near   180
The residence of your despised brother,
The lords would not be too exasperate
To injure or suppress your worthy title ;
Or, if they would, there are in readiness
Ten thousand horse to carry you from hence,
In spite of all suspected enemies.

    COS. I know it well, my Lord, and thank
      you all.

    ORTY. Sound up the trumpets then. God
      save the King !   *Exeunt.*

SCENE II [25]

[*Enter*] TAMBURLAINE *leading* ZENOCRATE ;
  TECHELLES, USUMCASANE, [AGYDAS, MAG-
  NETES, *and*] *other* Lords, *and* Soldiers *loaden
  with treasure.*

    TAMB. Come, lady, let not this appall your
      thoughts ;
The jewels and the treasure we have ta'en
Shall be reserv'd, and you in better state
Than if you were arriv'd in Syria,
Even in the circle of your father's arms,
The mighty Soldan of Egyptia.

    ZENO. Ah, shepherd, pity my distressed
      plight,
If, as thou seem'st, thou art so mean a man,
And seek not to enrich thy followers
By lawless rapine from a silly [26] maid,   10
Who, travelling with these Median lords
To Memphis, from my uncle's country of
    Media,
Where all my youth I have been governed,
Have pass'd the army of the mighty Turk,
Bearing his privy signet and his hand
To safe conduct us thorough Africa.

    MAG. And since we have arriv'd in Scythia,[27]
Besides rich presents from the puissant Cham,
We have his Highness' letters to command
Aid and assistance if we stand in need.   20

    TAMB. But now you see these letters and
      commands
Are countermanded by a greater man ;
And through my provinces you must expect
Letters of conduct from my Mightiness,
If you intend to keep your treasure safe.

---

  [24] Investiture.
  [25] A hill in Scythia.
  [26] Innocent, harmless.
  [27] Part of it was north of Media, which lay between the upper Tigris and the Caspian.

But, since I love to live at liberty,
As easily may you get the Soldan's crown
As any prizes out of my precinct ;
For they are friends that help to wean [28] my
    state
Till men and kingdoms help to strengthen it,[30]
And must maintain my life exempt from servi-
    tude.
But, tell me, madam, is your Grace betroth'd ?

    ZENO. I am, my Lord, — for so you do im-
      port.

    TAMB. I am a lord, for so my deeds shall
      prove,
And yet a shepherd by my parentage.
But, lady, this fair face and heavenly hue
Must grace his bed that conquers Asia,
And means to be a terror to the world,
Measuring the limits of his empery
By east and west, as Phœbus doth his course.—
Lie here, ye weeds that I disdain to wear ;   41
This complete [29] armor and this curtle-axe [30]
Are adjuncts more beseeming Tamburlaine.
And, madam, whatsoever you esteem
Of this success and loss unvalued,[31]
Both may invest you Empress of the East ;
And these that seem but silly [32] country swains
May have the leading of so great an host
As with their weight shall make the mountains
    quake,
Even as when windy exhalations   50
Fighting for passage, tilt within the earth.

    TECH. As princely lions, when they rouse
      themselves,
Stretching their paws, and threat'ning herds of
    beasts,
So in his armor looketh Tamburlaine.
Methinks I see kings kneeling at his feet,
And he, with frowning brows and fiery looks,
Spurning their crowns from off their captive
    heads.

    USUM. And making thee and me, Techelles,
      kings,
That even to death will follow Tamburlaine.

    TAMB. Nobly resolv'd, sweet friends and
      followers.   60
These lords, perhaps, do scorn our estimates,
And think we prattle with distempered spirits ;
But since they measure our deserts so mean,
That in conceit [33] bear empires on our spears,
Affecting thoughts coequal with the clouds,

---

  [28] *I.e.,* mature.
  [29] Accented on first syllable.
  [30] Cutlass ; *i.e.,* scimitar.
  [31] Invaluable.
  [32] Simple, harmless.
  [33] Imagination.

They shall be kept our forced followers,
Till with their eyes they view us emperors.

ZENO. The gods, defenders of the innocent,
Will never prosper your intended drifts,
That thus oppress poor friendless passengers.
Therefore at least admit us liberty,   71
Even as thou hop'st to be eternized
By living Asia's mighty emperor.

AGYD. I hope our lady's treasure and our
    own
May serve for ransom to our liberties.
Return our mules and empty camels back,
That we may travel into Syria,
Where her betrothed lord, Alcidamus,
Expects th' arrival of her Highness' person.

MAG. And wheresoever we repose our-
    selves,   80
We will report but well of Tamburlaine.

TAMB. Disdains Zenocrate to live with me?
Or you, my Lords, to be my followers?
Think you I weigh this treasure more than
    you?
Not all the gold in India's wealthy arms
Shall buy the meanest soldier in my train. —
Zenocrate, lovelier than the love of Jove,
Brighter than is the silver Rhodope,[34]
Fairer than whitest snow on Scythian hills,
Thy person is more worth to Tamburlaine 90
Than the possession of the Persian crown,
Which gracious stars have promis'd at my
    birth.
A hundred Tartars shall attend on thee,
Mounted on steeds swifter than Pegasus;
Thy garments shall be made of Median silk,
Enchas'd with precious jewels of mine own,
More rich and valurous [35] than Zenocrate's.
With milk-white harts upon an ivory sled,
Thou shalt be drawn amidst the frozen pools,
And scale the icy mountains' lofty tops,   100
Which with thy beauty will be soon resolv'd.[36]
My martial prizes with five hundred men,
Won on the fifty-headed Volga's waves,
Shall all we offer to Zenocrate,
And then myself to fair Zenocrate.

TECH. What now? in love?

TAMB. Techelles, women must be flattered;
But this is she with whom I am in love.

Enter a Soldier.

SOLD. News! news!

TAMB. How now, what's the matter?   110

SOLD. A thousand Persian horsemen are at
    hand,
Sent from the King to overcome us all.

TAMB. How now, my Lords of Egypt, and
    Zenocrate!
Now must your jewels be restor'd again,
And I that triumph'd so be overcome —
How say you, lordings, is not this your hope?

AGYD. We hope yourself will willingly re-
    store them.

TAMB. Such hope, such fortune, have the
    thousand horse.
Soft ye, my Lords, and sweet Zenocrate.
You must be forced from me ere you go.   120
A thousand horsemen! We five hundred
    foot!
An odds too great for us to stand against.
But are they rich? And is their armor good?

SOLD. Their plumed helms are wrought
    with beaten gold,
Their swords enamell'd, and about their
    necks
Hangs massy chains of gold down to the waist,
In every part exceeding brave [37] and rich.

TAMB. Then shall we fight courageously
    with them,
Or look you I should play the orator?

TECH. No; cowards and faint-hearted run-
    aways   130
Look for orations when the foe is near.
Our swords shall play the orators for us.

USUM. Come, let us meet them at the
    mountain foot,[38]
And with a sudden and an hot alarm,
Drive all their horses headlong down the hill.

TECH. Come, let us march.

TAMB. Stay, Techelles, ask a parley first.

The Soldiers *enter.*

Open the mails,[39] yet guard the treasure sure;
Lay out our golden wedges to the view,   139
That their reflections may amaze the Persians;
And look we friendly on them when they come.
But if they offer word or violence,
We'll fight five hundred men at arms to one,
Before we part with our possession;
And 'gainst the general we will lift our swords,
And either lance his greedy thirsting throat,
Or take him prisoner, and his chain shall serve
For manacles, till he be ransom'd home.

TECH. I hear them come; shall we en-
    counter them?

[34] Emend. Dyce; old eds. *Rhodolfe.* These snow-
capped Thracian mountains contained silver.
[35] Valuable.
[36] Dissolved.

[37] Fine.
[38] O4 *top.*
[39] Trunks, baggage.

TAMB. Keep all your standings and not stir a foot ; 150
Myself will bide the danger of the brunt.

Enter THERIDAMAS *with others.*

THER. Where is this Scythian Tamburlaine?

TAMB. Whom seek'st thou, Persian? I am Tamburlaine.

THER. [*aside*] Tamburlaine! A Scythian shepherd so embellished
With nature's pride and richest furniture,
His looks do menace Heaven and dare the gods!
His fiery eyes are fix'd upon the earth,
As if he now devis'd some stratagem,
Or meant to pierce Avernus' darksome vaults
To pull the triple-headed dog from hell. 160

TAMB. [*aside*] Noble and mild this Persian seems to be,
If outward habit judge the inward man.

TECH. [*aside*] His deep affections [40] make him passionate.

TAMB. [*aside*] With what a majesty he rears his looks! —
In thee, thou valiant man of Persia,
I see the folly of thy emperor.
Art thou but captain of a thousand horse,
That by characters [41] graven in thy brows,
And by thy martial face and stout aspect,
Deserv'st to have the leading of an host? 170
Forsake thy king, and do but join with me,
And we will triumph over all the world.
I hold the Fates bound fast in iron chains,
And with my hand turn Fortune's wheel about ;
And sooner shall the sun fall from his sphere [42]
Than Tamburlaine be slain or overcome.
Draw forth thy sword, thou mighty man at arms,
Intending but to raze my charmed skin,
And Jove himself will stretch his hand from Heaven
To ward the blow and shield me safe from harm. 180
See how he rains down heaps of gold in showers,
As if he meant to give my soldiers pay ;
And as a sure and grounded argument
That I shall be the monarch of the East,
He sends this Soldan's daughter, rich and brave,[43]

[40] Feelings.
[41] Accented on second syllable.
[42] Marlowe's astronomy is Ptolemaic.
[43] Fine.

To be my queen and portly [44] emperess.
If thou wilt stay with me, renowmed man,
And lead thy thousand horse with my conduct,[45]
Besides thy share of this Egyptian prize,
Those thousand horse shall sweat with martial spoil 190
Of conquered kingdoms and of cities sack'd.
Both we will walk upon the lofty cliffs,[46]
And Christian merchants [47] that with Russian stems
Plough up huge furrows in the Caspian sea,
Shall vail [48] to us, as lords of all the lake.
Both we will reign as consuls of the earth,
And mighty kings shall be our senators.
Jove sometimes masked in a shepherd's weed,
And by those steps that he hath scal'd the Heavens
May we become immortal like the gods. 200
Join with me now in this my mean estate
(I call it mean because, being yet obscure,
The nations far remov'd admire me not),
And when my name and honor shall be spread
As far as Boreas claps his brazen wings,
Or fair Boötes sends his cheerful light,
Then shalt thou be competitor [49] with me,
And sit with Tamburlaine in all his majesty.

THER. Not Hermes, prolocutor to the gods,
Could use persuasions more pathetical.[50] 210

TAMB. Nor are Apollo's oracles more true
Than thou shalt find my vaunts substantial.

TECH. We are his friends, and if the Persian King
Should offer present dukedoms to our state,[51]
We think it loss to make exchange for that
We are assured of by our friend's success.

USUM. And kingdoms at the least we all expect,
Besides the honor in assured conquests,
Where kings shall crouch unto our conquering swords,
And hosts of soldiers stand amaz'd at us, 220
When with their fearful tongues they shall confess
These are the men that all the world admires.

[44] Stately. — " Renowmed " = renowned.
[45] Accented on second syllable.
[46] O₂ ; other old eds. *clifts.*
[47] Merchantmen.
[48] Strike the topsail or dip the ensign as a mark of submission.
[49] Colleague.
[50] Moving.
[51] For our rank or estate.

THER. What strong enchantments 'tice my
yielding soul?
Are these resolved [nobles] [52] Scythians?
But shall I prove a traitor to my king?
  TAMB. No, but the trusty friend of Tam-
burlaine.
  THER. Won with thy words, and conquered
with thy looks,
I yield myself, my men and horse, to thee,
To be partaker of thy good or ill,
As long as life maintains Theridamas.   230
  TAMB. Theridamas, my friend, take here
my hand,
Which is as much as if I swore by Heaven
And call'd the gods to witness of my vow.
Thus shall my heart be still combin'd with
thine
Until our bodies turn to elements,
And both our souls aspire celestial thrones.
Techelles and Casane, welcome him.
  TECH. Welcome, renowmed Persian, to us
all.
  USUM. Long may Theridamas remain with
us.
  TAMB. These are my friends, in whom I
more rejoice   240
Than doth the King of Persia in his crown;
And by the love of Pylades and Orestes,
Whose statutes [53] we adore in Scythia,
Thyself and them shall never part from me
Before I crown you kings in Asia.
Make much of them, gentle Theridamas,
And they will never leave thee till the
death.
  THER. Nor thee nor them, thrice noble
Tamburlaine,
Shall want my heart to be with gladness
pierc'd
To do you honor and security.   250
  TAMB. A thousand thanks, worthy Therida-
mas. —
And now fair madam, and my noble Lords,
If you will willingly remain with me
You shall have honors [54] as your merits be;
Or else you shall be forc'd with slavery.
  AGYD. We yield unto thee, happy Tambur-
laine.
  TAMB. For you then, madam, I am out of
doubt.
  ZENO. I must be pleas'd, perforce.
    Wretched Zenocrate!   *Exeunt.*

ACT II — SCENE I [1]

[*Enter*] COSROE, MENAPHON, ORTYGIUS, CEN-
EUS, *with other* Soldiers.

  COS. Thus far are we towards Theridamas,
And valiant Tamburlaine, the man of fame,
The man that in the forehead of his fortune
Bears figures of renown and miracle.
But tell me, that hast seen him, Menaphon,
What stature wields he, and what personage?
  MEN. Of stature tall, and straightly fash-
ioned,
Like his desire, lift upwards and divine;
So large of limbs, his joints so strongly knit,
Such breadth of shoulders as might mainly
bear   10
Old Atlas' burden; 'twixt his manly pitch,[2]
A pearl, more worth than all the world, is
plac'd,
Wherein by curious sovereignty of art
Are fix'd his piercing instruments of sight,
Whose fiery circles bear encompassed
A heaven of heavenly bodies in their spheres,
That guides his steps and actions to the throne,
Where honor sits invested royally;
Pale of complexion, wrought in him with pas-
sion,
Thirsting with sovereignty, with [3] love of
arms,   20
His lofty brows in folds do figure death,
And in their smoothness amity and life;
About them hangs a knot of amber hair,
Wrapped in curls, as fierce Achilles' was,
On which the breath of heaven delights to
play,
Making it dance with wanton majesty;
His arms and fingers long and [sinewy],[4]
Betokening valor and excess of strength:
In every part proportioned like the man
Should make the world subdued to Tambur-
laine.   30
  COS. Well hast thou portray'd in thy terms
of life
The face and personage of a wondrous man;
Nature doth strive with Fortune and his stars
To make him famous in accomplish'd worth;
And well his merits show him to be made
His fortune's master and the king of men,
That could persuade at such a sudden pinch,
With reasons of his valor and his life,

[52] Emend. Neilson; old eds. *noble.*
[53] O o 3, 4, *statues.*
[54] O1 *herors.* (Ellis-Fermor, but neither Wagner
nor Brooke.)

[1] Unlocated by the dramatist; perhaps a road in
Media.
[2] Projection of the body; here, shoulders.
[3] O o 3, 4, *and.*
[4] Emend. Dyce; old eds. *snowy.*

A thousand sworn and overmatching foes.
Then, when our powers in points of swords are
   join'd   40
And clos'd in compass of the killing bullet,
Though strait the passage and the port [5] be
   made
That leads to palace of my brother's life,
Proud is his fortune if we pierce it not.
And when the princely Persian diadem
Shall overweigh his weary, witless head,
And fall like mellowed fruit with shakes of
   death,
In fair Persia noble Tamburlaine [6]
Shall be my regent and remain as king.
    ORTY. In happy hour we have set the
      crown   50
Upon your kingly head, that seeks our honor
In joining with the man ordain'd by Heaven,
To further every action to the best.
    CEN. He that with shepherds and a little
      spoil
Durst, in disdain of wrong and tyranny,
Defend his freedom 'gainst a monarchy,
What will he do supported by a king,
Leading a troop of gentlemen and lords,
And stuff'd [7] with treasure for his highest
   thoughts !
    COS. And such shall wait on worthy Tam-
      burlaine.   60
Our army will be forty thousand strong,
When Tamburlaine and brave Theridamas
Have met us by the river Araris ; [8]
And all conjoin'd to meet the witless King,
That now is marching near to Parthia,
And with unwilling soldiers faintly arm'd,
To seek revenge on me and Tamburlaine,
To whom, sweet Menaphon, direct me straight.
    MEN. I will, my Lord.
                     Exeunt.

SCENE II [9]

[*Enter*] MYCETES, MEANDER, *with other* Lords
         and Soldiers.

    MYC. Come, my Meander, let us to this
      gear.[10]
I tell you true, my heart is swoln with wrath

---

[5] Portal.
[6] This line can be regularized by pronouncing
"fair" as a dissyllable, or "Persia" as a trisyllable
accented on the "i"; but if "fair Persia" be read
sonorously with natural emphasis, the line will give
no trouble.
[7] Supplied.
[8] Old maps show the river Araxes in Armenia;
Herodotus so calls the Oxus. (Ellis-Fermor.)
[9] A camp in Georgia.
[10] Business, affair.

On this same thievish villain, Tamburlaine,
And of that false Cosroe, my traitorous
   brother.
Would it not grieve a king to be so abus'd
And have a thousand horsemen ta'en away?
And, which is worst, to have his diadem
Sought for by such scald [11] knaves as love him
   not ?
I think it would ; well then, by Heavens I
   swear,
Aurora shall not peep out of her doors,   10
But I will have Cosroe [12] by the head,
And kill proud Tamburlaine with point of
   sword.
Tell you the rest, Meander ; I have said.
    MEAND. Then having pass'd Armenian
      deserts now,
And [pitch'd] [13] our tents under the Georgian
   hills,
Whose tops are covered with Tartarian [14]
   thieves,
That lie in ambush, waiting for a prey,
What should we do but bid them battle
   straight,
And rid the world of those detested troops,
Lest, if we let them linger here awhile,   20
They gather strength by power of fresh sup-
   plies ?
This country swarms with vile, outrageous
   men
That live by rapine and by lawless spoil,
Fit soldiers for the wicked Tamburlaine ;
And he that could with gifts and promises
Inveigle him that led a thousand horse,
And make him false his faith unto his king,
Will quickly win such as are like himself.
Therefore cheer up your minds ; prepare to
   fight ;
He that can take or slaughter Tamburlaine   30
Shall rule the province of Albania.
Who brings that traitor's head, Theridamas,
Shall have a government in Media,
Beside the spoil of him and all his train.
But if Cosroe as our spials [15] say,
And as we know, remains with Tamburlaine,
His Highness' pleasure is that he should live,
And be reclaim'd with princely lenity.

[*Enter a* Spy.]

    A SPY. An hundred horsemen of my com-
      pany

---

[11] Scurvy.
[12] Here, as often, a trisyllable.
[13] O2 ; O1 *pitch.*
[14] Scythians and Tartars are undistinguished by
Marlowe.   [15] Spies.

Scouting abroad upon these champaign plains
Have view'd the army of the Scythians, 41
Which make reports it far exceeds the King's.
  MEAND. Suppose they be in number infi-
    nite,
Yet, being void of martial discipline,
All running headlong after greedy spoils
And more regarding gain than victory,
Like to the cruel brothers of the earth,
Sprung of the teeth of dragons venomous,
Their careless swords shall lance their fellows'
    throats,
And make us triumph in their overthrow. 50
  MYC. Was there such brethren, sweet Mean-
    der, say,
That sprung of teeth of dragons venomous?
  MEAND. So poets say, my Lord.
  MYC. And 't is a pretty toy to be a poet.
Well, well, Meander, thou art deeply read ;
And, having thee, I have a jewel sure.
Go on, my Lord, and give your charge, I say ;
Thy wit will make us conquerors to-day.
  MEAND. Then, noble soldiers, to entrap
    these thieves,
That live confounded in disordered troops, 60
If wealth or riches may prevail with them,
We have our camels laden all with gold,
Which you that be but common soldiers
Shall fling in every corner of the field ;
And while the baseborn Tartars take it up,
You, fighting more for honor than for gold,
Shall massacre those greedy-minded slaves ;
And when their scattered army is subdu'd,
And you march on their slaughtered carcases,
Share equally the gold that bought their
    lives, 70
And live like gentlemen in Persia.
Strike up the drum and march courageously ;
Fortune herself doth sit upon our crests.
  MYC. He tells you true, my masters,[16] so he
    does. —
Drums, why sound ye not, when Meander
    speaks?
                                        Exeunt.

SCENE III [17]

[*Enter*] COSROE, TAMBURLAINE, THERIDAMAS,
  TECHELLES, USUMCASANE, ORTYGIUS, *with
  others.*

  COS. Now, worthy Tamburlaine, have I
    repos'd
In thy approved [18] fortunes all my hope.

What think'st thou, man, shall come of our
    attempts?
For, even as from assured oracle,
I take thy doom for satisfaction.
  TAMB. And so mistake you not a whit, my
    Lord ;
For fates and oracles [of] [19] Heaven have sworn
To royalize the deeds of Tamburlaine,
And make them blest that share in his at-
    tempts.
And doubt you not but, if you favor me 10
And let my fortunes and my valor sway
To some direction in your martial deeds,
The world will strive with hosts of men at
    arms,
To swarm unto the ensign I support.
The host of Xerxes, which by fame is said
To drink the mighty Parthian Araris,
Was but a handful to that we will have.
Our quivering lances, shaking in the air,
And bullets, like Jove's dreadful thunderbolts,
Enroll'd in flames and fiery smoldering mists,
Shall threat the gods more than Cyclopian [20]
    wars ; 21
And, with our sun-bright armor as we march,
We 'll chase the stars from Heaven and dim
    their eyes
That stand and muse at our admired arms.
  THER. You see, my Lord, what working
    words he hath ;
But when you see his actions [top] [21] his speech,
Your speech will stay or so extol his worth
As I shall be commended and excus'd
For turning my poor charge to his direction.
And these his two renowmed friends, my
    Lord, 30
Would make one thrust and strive to be re-
    tain'd
In such a great degree of amity.
  TECH. With duty [and] [22] with amity we
    yield
Our utmost service to the fair Cosroe.
  COS. Which I esteem as portion of my
    crown.
Usumcasane and Techelles both,
When she that rules in Rhamn[u]s' [23] golden
    gates,
And makes a passage for all prosperous arms,
Shall make me solely Emperor of Asia,
Then shall your meeds and valors be advanc'd
To rooms of honor and nobility. 41

---

[16] Gentlemen.
[17] Tamburlaine's camp in the Georgian hills.
[18] Tested.
[19] Add. Robinson.
[20] *I.e.*, the Titans'.
[21] Emend. Dyce ; old eds. *stop.*
[22] O₄ ; earlier eds. *not.*
[23] In Attica ; Nemesis had a temple there.

TAMB. Then haste, Cosroe, to be king alone,
That I with these, my friends, and all my men
May triumph in our long-expected fate.
The King, your brother, is now hard at hand ;
Meet with the fool, and rid your royal shoulders
Of such a burden as outweighs the sands
And all the craggy rocks of Caspia.

[*Enter a* Messenger.]

MES. My Lord, we have discovered the enemy
Ready to charge you with a mighty army. 50
   Cos. Come, Tamburlaine, now whet thy winged sword,
And lift thy lofty arm into the clouds,
That it may reach the King of Persia's crown,
And set it safe on my victorious head.
   TAMB. See where it is, the keenest cu[r]tle-axe
That e'er made passage thorough Persian arms.
These are the wings shall make it fly as swift
As doth the lightning or the breath of Heaven,
And kill as sure [24] as it swiftly flies.
   Cos. Thy words assure me of kind success ; 60
Go, valiant soldier, go before and charge
The fainting army of that foolish king.
   TAMB. Usumcasane and Techelles, come ;
We are enough to scare the enemy,
And more than needs to make an emperor.
                            [*Exeunt.*]

[SCENE IV] [25]

To the battle, and MYCETES *comes out alone with his crown in his hand, offering* [26] *to hide it.*

   MYC. Accurs'd be he that first invented war !
They knew not, ah, they knew not, simple men,
How those [27] were hit by pelting cannon shot
Stand staggering like a quivering aspen leaf
Fearing the force of Boreas' boist'rous blasts.
In what a lamentable case were I
If Nature had not given me wisdom's lore !
For kings are clouts [28] that every man shoots at,

Our crown the pin that thousands seek to cleave ;
Therefore in policy I think it good 10
To hide it close, a goodly stratagem,
And far from any man that is a fool.
So shall I not be known ; or, if I be,
They cannot take away my crown from me. —
Here will I hide it in this simple hole.

Enter TAMBURLAINE.

   TAMB. What fearful coward, straggling from the camp,
When kings themselves are present in the field?
   MYC. Thou liest.
   TAMB.   Base villain, dar'st thou give the lie?
   MYC. Away ; I am the King ; go, touch me not.
Thou break'st the law of arms unless thou kneel 20
And cry me, " Mercy, noble King."
   TAMB. Are you the witty [29] King of Persia?
   MYC. Ay, marry am I ; have you any suit to me?
   TAMB. I would entreat you speak but three wise words.
   MYC. So I can when I see my time.
   TAMB. Is this your crown?
   MYC. Ay, didst thou ever see a fairer?
   TAMB. You will not sell it, will ye?
   MYC. Such another word and I will have thee executed. Come, give it me. [30] 30
   TAMB. No ; I took it prisoner.
   MYC. You lie ; I gave it you.
   TAMB. Then 't is mine.
   MYC. No ; I mean, I let you keep it.
   TAMB. Well, I mean you shall have it again.
Here, take it for a while ; I lend it thee,
Till I may see thee hemm'd with armed men.
Then shalt thou see me pull it from thy head ;
Thou art no match for mighty Tamburlaine.
                            [*Exit.*]
   MYC. O gods ! Is this Tamburlaine the thief? 40
I marvel much he stole it not away.
Sound trumpets to the battle, and he runs in.

---

[24] Pronounce as dissyllable.
[25] A battlefield.
[26] Attempting.
[27] Understand " who."
[28] The white centres of archery targets. The *pin* was the peg at the dead centre of the target.

[29] Clever, sagacious.
[30] This departure from blank verse looks suspicious. We may have here a fragment of a longer comic scene, perhaps not composed by Marlowe ; or perhaps we have merely actors' gags here. The publisher of O₁ states that he has " left out some fond and frivolous gestures " which " were showed upon the stage in their graced deformities."

[SCENE V] [31]

[*Enter*] COSROE, TAMBURLAINE, THERIDAMAS,
  MENAPHON, MEANDER, ORTYGIUS, TECHEL-
  LES, [*and*] USUMCASANE, *with others.*

TAMB. Hold thee, Cosroe ; wear two im-
    perial crowns.
Think thee invested now as royally,
Even by the mighty hand of Tamburlaine,
As if as many kings as could encompass thee [32]
With greatest pomp, had crown'd thee em-
    peror.
  Cos. So do I, thrice renowned man at arms,
And none shall keep the crown but Tambur-
    laine :
Thee do I make my regent of Persia,
And general-lieutenant of my armies. —
Meander, you, that were our brother's guide,
And chiefest counsellor in all his acts,   11
Since he is yielded to the stroke of war,
On your submission we with thanks excuse,
And give you equal place in our affairs.
  MEAND. Most happy Emperor, in humblest
    terms,
I vow my service to your Majesty,
With utmost virtue of my faith and duty.
  Cos. Thanks, good Meander ; then, Cos-
    roe, reign
And govern Persia in her former pomp.
Now send embassage to thy neighbor kings, 20
And let them know the Persian king is
    chang'd —
From one that knew not what a king should do,
To one that can command what 'longs thereto.
And now we will to fair Persepolis,
With twenty thousand expert soldiers.
The lords and captains of my brother's camp
With little slaughter take Meander's course
And gladly yield them to my gracious rule.
Ortygius and Menaphon, my trusty friends, [33]
Now will I gratify [34] your former good,   30
And grace your calling with a greater sway.
  ORTY. And as we ever [aim'd] [35] at your
    behoof,
And sought your state [36] all honor it deserv'd,
So will we with our powers and our lives
Endeavor to preserve and prosper it.
  Cos. I will not thank thee, sweet Ortygius ;
Better replies shall prove my purposes.

[31] The same.
[32] Another "apparent" Alexandrine.
[33] Not an Alexandrine.
[34] Reward.
[35] Cor. O₃ ; Oo 1, 2, *and.*
[36] Rank, place.

And now, Lord Tamburlaine, my brother's
    camp
I leave to thee and to Theridamas,
To follow me to fair Persepolis.   40
Then will we march to all those Indian mines
My witless brother to the Christians lost,
And ransom them with fame and usury.
And till thou overtake me, Tamburlaine,
Staying to order all the scattered troops,
Farewell, Lord Regent and his happy friends !
I long to sit upon my brother's throne.
  MEAND. Your Majesty shall shortly have
    your wish,
And ride in triumph through Persepolis.
  Exeunt [*all but*] TAMBURLAINE, TECHELLES,
      THERIDAMAS, [*and*] USUMCASANE.
  TAMB. "And ride in triumph through
    Persepolis ! "   50
Is it not brave to be a king, Techelles ?
Usumcasane and Theridamas,
Is it not passing brave to be a king,
" And ride in triumph through Persepolis " ?
  TECH. Oh, my Lord, 't is sweet and full of
    pomp.
  USUM. To be a king is half to be a god.
  THER. A god is not so glorious as a king.
I think the pleasure they enjoy in Heaven
Can not compare with kingly joys in earth.
To wear a crown enchas'd with pearl and gold,
Whose virtues carry with it life and death ; 61
To ask and have, command and be obeyed ;
When looks breed love, with looks to gain the
    prize —
Such power attractive shines in princes' eyes.
  TAMB. Why say, Theridamas, wilt thou be
    a king ?
  THER. Nay, though I praise it, I can live
    without it.
  TAMB. What says my other friends ? Will
    you be kings ?
  TECH. Ay, if I could, with all my heart, my
    Lord.
  TAMB. Why, that's well said, Techelles ;
    so would I,
And so would you, my masters, would you
    not ?   70
  USUM. What then, my Lord ?
  TAMB. Why then, [Casane,] [37] shall we wish
    for aught
The world affords in greatest novelty,
And rest attemptless, faint, and destitute ?
Methinks we should not : I am strongly mov'd
That, if I should desire the Persian crown,
I could attain it with a wondrous ease.

[37] Old eds. *Casanes.*

And would not all our soldiers soon consent,
If we should aim at such a dignity?

THER. I know they would with our persua-
    sions. 80

TAMB. Why then, Theridamas, I'll first as-
    say
To get the Persian kingdom to myself;
Then thou for Parthia, they for Scythia and
    Media;
And, if I prosper, all shall be as sure
As if the Turk, the Pope, Afric, and Greece,
Came creeping to us with their crowns apace.[38]

TECH. Then shall we send to this triumph-
    ing [39] king,
And bid him battle for his novel crown?

USUM. Nay, quickly, then, before his room
    be hot.

TAMB. 'T will prove a pretty jest, in faith,
    my friends. 90

THER. A jest to charge on twenty thousand
    men?
I judge the purchase [40] more important far.

TAMB. Judge by thyself, Theridamas, not
    me;
For presently Techelles here shall haste
To bid him battle ere he pass too far,
And lose more labor than the gain will quit.[41]
Then shalt thou see the Scythian Tamburlaine
Make but a jest to win the Persian crown.
Techelles, take a thousand horse with thee,
And bid him turn [him] [42] back to war with us,
That only made him king to make us sport. 101
We will not steal upon him cowardly,
But give him warning and more warriors.
Haste thee, Techelles; we will follow thee.
What saith Theridamas?

THER.   Go on, for me.[43]
                          Exeunt.

SCENE VI [44]

[*Enter*] COSROE, MEANDER, ORTYGIUS, MENA-
PHON, *with other* Soldiers.

COS. What means this devilish shepherd to
    aspire
With such a giantly [45] presumption
To cast up hills against the face of Heaven,
And dare the force of angry Jupiter?
But as he thrust them underneath the hills

[38] Oo 3, 4, *apeece.*
[39] Accented on the second syllable.
[40] Undertaking.
[41] Repay, requite.
[42] Emend. Robinson; old eds. *his.*
[43] For all of me, as far as I'm concerned.
[44] Unlocated, but presumably on the borders of Armenia.
[45] *I.e.*, like the Titans.

And press'd out fire [46] from their burning jaws,
So will I send this monstrous slave to hell,
Where flames shall ever feed upon his soul.

MEAND. Some powers divine, or else in-
    fernal, mix'd
Their angry seeds at his conception; 10
For he was never sprung of human race,
Since with the spirit of his fearful pride
He dares so doubtlessly resolve of rule,
And by profession be ambitious.

ORTY. What god or fiend or spirit of the
    earth,
Or monster turned to a manly shape,
Or of what mold or mettle he be made,
What star or state soever govern him,
Let us put on our meet encount'ring minds
And, in detesting such a devilish thief, 20
In love of honor and defence of right,
Be arm'd against the hate of such a foe,
Whether from earth, or hell, or Heaven, he
    grow.

COS. Nobly resolv'd, my good Ortygius;
And since we all have suck'd one wholesome
    air,
And with the same proportion of elements
Resolve,[47] I hope we are resembled,
Vowing our loves to equal death and life.
Let 's cheer our soldiers to encounter him,
That grievous image of ingratitude, 30
That fiery thirster after sovereignty,
And burn him in the fury of that flame,
That none can quench but blood and empery.
Resolve, my Lords and loving soldiers, now
To save your king and country from decay.
Then strike up, drum; and all the stars that
    make
The loathsome circle of my dated life,
Direct my weapon to his barbarous heart
That thus opposeth him against the gods
And scorns the powers that govern Persia. 40
                          [*Exeunt.*]

[SCENE VII] [48]

*Enter to the battle; and after the battle, en-
ter* COSROE *wounded,* THERIDAMAS, TAM-
BURLAINE, TECHELLES, USUMCASANE, *with
others.*

COS. Barbarous and bloody Tamburlaine,
Thus to deprive me of my crown and life!
Treacherous and false Theridamas,
Even at the morning of my happy state,

[46] A dissyllable here.
[47] Dissolve; *i.e.*, when we die we shall disintegrate into the same elements.
[48] A battlefield.

Scarce being seated in my royal throne,
To work my downfall and untimely end !
An uncouth pain torments my grieved soul,
And Death arrests the organ of mv voice,
Who, ent'ring at the breach thy sword hath
    made,
Sacks every vein and artier of my heart,   10
Bloody and insatiate Tamburlaine !
    TAMB. The thirst of reign and sweetness of
       a crown,
That caus'd the eldest son of heavenly Ops
To thrust his doting father from his chair
And place himself in the imperial Heaven,
Mov'd me to manage arms against thy state.
What better precedent than mighty Jove?
Nature that fram'd us of four elements,
Warring within our breasts for regiment,[49]
Doth teach us all to have aspiring minds.   20
Our souls, whose faculties can comprehend
The wondrous architecture of the world
And measure every wand'ring planet's course,
Still climbing after knowledge infinite,
And always moving as the restless spheres,
Wills us to wear ourselves and never rest
Until we reach the ripest fruit of all,
That perfect bliss and sole felicity,
The sweet fruition of an earthly crown.
    THER. And that made me to join with Tam-
       burlaine ;   30
For he is gross and like the massy earth
That moves not upwards, nor by princely
    deeds
Doth mean to soar above the highest sort.
    TECH. And that made us the friends of
       Tamburlaine,
To lift our swords against the Persian king.
    USUM. For as, when Jove did thrust old
       Saturn down,
Neptune and Dis gain'd each of them a crown,
So do we hope to reign in Asia,
If Tamburlaine be plac'd in Persia.
    COS. The strangest men that ever nature
       made !   40
I know not how to take their tyrannies.
My bloodless body waxeth chill and cold,
And with my blood my life slides through my
    wound ;
My soul begins to take her flight to hell,
And summons all my senses to depart.
The heat and moisture, which did feed each
    other,
For want of nourishment to feed them both,
Is dry and cold ; and now doth ghastly death
With greedy talents [50] gripe my bleeding heart,

[49] Rule.   [50] Talons.

And like a harpy [51] tires [52] on my life.   50
Theridamas and Tamburlaine, I die ;
And fearful vengeance light upon you both !
       [COSROE *dies.* TAMBURLAINE] *takes*
          the crown and puts it on.
    TAMB. Not all the curses which the Furies
       breathe
Shall make me leave so rich a prize as this.
Theridamas, Techelles, and the rest,
Who think you now is King of Persia?
    ALL. Tamburlaine ! Tamburlaine !
    TAMB. Though Mars himself, the angry god
       of arms,
And all the earthly potentates, conspire
To dispossess me of this diadem,   60
Yet will I wear it in despite of them,
As great commander of this eastern world,
If you but say that Tamburlaine shall reign.
    ALL. Long live Tamburlaine and reign in
       Asia !
    TAMB. So now it is more surer on my head,
Than if the gods had held a parliament
And all pronounc'd me King of Persia.
                    [*Exeunt.*]

ACT III — SCENE I [1]

[*Enter*] BAJAZETH, *the* KINGS *of* FEZ, MOROCCO,
   and ARGIER,[2] *with others, in great pomp.*

    BAJ. Great Kings of Barbary and my portly
       bassoes,[3]
We hear the Tartars and the eastern thieves,
Under the conduct of one Tamburlaine,
Presume a bickering with your emperor,
And thinks to rouse us from our dreadful siege
Of the famous Grecian Constantinople.
You know our army is invincible ;
As many circumcised Turks we have,
And warlike bands of Christians renied,[4]
As hath the ocean or the Terrene [5] sea   10
Small drops of water when the moon begins
To join in one her semicircled horns.
Yet would we not be brav'd with foreign
    power,
Nor raise our siege before the Grecians yield,
Or breathless lie before the city walls.
    K. OF FEZ. Renowmed Emperor, and
       mighty general,
What if you sent the bassoes of your guard

[51] O₂ *Harpye;* other old eds. *Harpyr, Harper.*
[52] Preys, tears. A dissyllable here.
[1] The Turkish camp before Constantinople.
[2] Algiers.
[3] Stately pashas.
[4] Apostate ; cf. "reneged."
[5] Mediterranean.

To charge him to remain in Asia,
Or else to threaten death and deadly arms
As from the mouth of mighty Bajazeth?   20
  Baj. Hie thee, my basso, fast to Persia ;
Tell him thy lord, the Turkish Emperor,
Dread Lord of Afric, Europe, and Asia,
Great King and conqueror of Græcia,
The ocean, Terrene, and the Coal-black sea,
The high and highest monarch of the world,
Wills and commands (for say not I entreat),
Not once to set his foot in Africa,
Or spread his colors [6] in Græcia,
Lest he incur the fury of my wrath.   30
Tell him I am content to take a truce,
Because I hear he bears a valiant mind.
But if, presuming on his silly power,
He be so mad to manage arms with me,
Then stay thou with him ; say I bid thee so.
And if, before the sun have measured heaven
With triple circuit, thou regreet us not,
We mean to take his morning's next arise
For messenger he will not be reclaim'd,
And mean to fetch thee in despite of him.   40
  Bas. Most great and puissant monarch of
    the earth,
Your basso will accomplish your behest
And show your pleasure to the Persian,
As fits the legate of the stately Turk.
                 Exit Basso.
  K. of Arg. They say he is the King of
    Persia ;
But, if he dare attempt to stir your siege,
'T were requisite he should be ten times more,
For all flesh quakes at your magnificence.
  Baj. True, Argier, and tremble [7] at my
    looks.
  K. of Mor. The spring is hind'red by your
    smothering host,   50
For neither rain can fall upon the earth
Nor sun reflex his virtuous [8] beams thereon,
The ground is mantled with such multitudes.
  Baj. All this is true as holy Mahomet ;
And all the trees are blasted with our breaths.
  K. of Fez. What thinks your Greatness
    be achiev'd
In pursuit of the city's overthrow?
  Baj. I will the captive pioners of Argier
Cut off the water that by leaden pipes   59
Runs to the city from the mountain Carnon.
Two thousand horse shall forage up and down,
That no relief or succor come by land ;

---

[6] Mod. eds. add a monosyllable, but if the "r"
be rolled the metre comes right.
[7] The "r" should be rolled, or a trisyllable be
made of "Argier."
[8] Powerful.

And all the sea my galleys countermand.[9]
Then shall our footmen lie within the trench,
And with their cannons, mouth'd like Orcus'
    gulf,[10]
Batter the walls, and we will enter in ;
And thus the Grecians shall be conquered.
                 Exeunt.

Scene II [11]

[Enter] Agydas, Zenocrate, Anippe, *with
others.*

  [Agyd.] Madam Zenocrate, may I presume
To know the cause of these unquiet fits,
That work such trouble to your wonted rest?
'T is more than pity such a heavenly face
Should by heart's sorrow wax so wan and pale,
When your offensive rape [12] by Tamburlaine,
Which of your whole displeasures should be
    most,
Hath seem'd to be digested long ago.
  Zeno. Although it be digested long ago,
As his exceeding favors have deserv'd,   10
And might content the Queen of Heaven,[13] as
    well
As it hath chang'd my first conceiv'd disdain,
Yet, since, a farther passion feeds my thoughts
With ceaseless and disconsolate conceits,
Which dyes my looks so lifeless as they are,
And might, if my extremes had full events,
Make me the ghastly counterfeit of death.
  Agyd. Eternal Heaven sooner be dissolv'd,
And all that pierceth Phœbe's silver eye,
Before such hap fall to Zenocrate.   20
  Zeno. Ah, life and soul, still hover in his
    breast
And leave my body senseless as the earth ;
Or else unite you to his life and soul,
That I may live and die with Tamburlaine.

Enter [behind] Tamburlaine, *with* Techelles
and others.

  Agyd. With Tamburlaine ! Ah, fair Zeno-
    crate,
Let not a man so vile and barbarous,
That holds you from your father in despite
And keeps you from the honors of a queen,
Being suppos'd his worthless concubine,
Be honored with your love but for necessity.   30
So, now the mighty Soldan hears of you,
Your Highness needs not doubt but in short
    time

He will with Tamburlaine's destruction
Redeem you from this deadly servitude.

ZENO. [Agydas,] [14] leave to wound me with
    these words,
And speak of Tamburlaine as he deserves.
The entertainment we have had of him
Is far from villainy or servitude,
And might in noble minds be counted princely.

AGYD. How can you fancy [15] one that looks
    so fierce,   40
Only dispos'd to martial stratagems ;
Who, when he shall embrace you in his arms,
Will tell how many thousand men he slew ;
And, when you look for amorous discourse,
Will rattle forth his facts of war and blood,
Too harsh a subject for your dainty ears?

ZENO. As looks the Sun through Nilus' flow-
    ing stream,
Or when the Morning holds him in her arms,
So looks my lordly love, fair Tamburlaine ;
His talk much sweeter than the Muses' song 50
They sung for honor 'gainst Pierides, [16]
Or when Minerva did with Neptune strive [17] ;
And higher would I rear my estimate
Than Juno, sister to the highest god,
If I were match'd with mighty Tamburlaine.

AGYD. Yet be not so inconstant in your
    love,
But let the young Arabian live in hope
After your rescue to enjoy his choice.
You see, though first the King of Persia,
Being a shepherd, seem'd to love you much, 60
Now in his majesty he leaves those looks,
Those words of favor, and those comfortings,
And gives no more than common courtesies.

ZENO. Thence rise the tears that so distain
    my cheeks,
Fearing [18] his love through my unworthiness.

    TAMBURLAINE *goes to her and takes
    her away lovingly by the hand, look-
    ing wrathfully on* AGYDAS, *and says
    nothing.* [Exeunt all but AGYDAS.]

AGYD. Betray'd by fortune and suspicious
    love,
Threat'ned with frowning wrath and jealousy,
Surpris'd with fear of hideous revenge,
I stand aghast ; but most astonied [19]
To see his choler shut in secret thoughts, 70
And wrapp'd in silence of his angry soul.

Upon his brows was portray'd ugly death ;
And in his eyes the fury of his heart,
That shine as comets, menacing revenge,
And casts a pale complexion on his cheeks.
As when the seaman sees the Hyades
Gather an army of Cimmerian [20] clouds,
(Auster and Aquilon with winged steeds,
All sweating, tilt about the watery Heavens,
With shivering spears enforcing thunderclaps,
And from their shields strike flames of light-
    ening,)   81
All fearful folds his sails and sounds the main,
Lifting his prayers to the Heavens for aid
Against the terror of the winds and waves ;
So fares Agydas for the late-felt frowns,
That sent a tempest to my daunted thoughts,
And makes my soul divine her overthrow.

Re-enter TECHELLES *with a naked dagger.*

TECH. See you, Agydas, how the King
    salutes you.
He bids you prophesy what it imports.   *Exit.*[21]

AGYD. I prophesied before, and now I
    prove   90
The killing frowns of jealousy and love.
He needed not with words confirm my fear,
For words are vain where working tools pre-
    sent
The naked action of my threat'ned end :
It says, Agydas, thou shalt surely die,
And of extremities elect the least ;
More honor and less pain it may procure
To die by this resolved hand of thine,
Than stay [22] the torments he and Heaven have
    sworn.   99
Then haste, Agydas, and prevent the plagues
Which thy prolonged fates may draw on thee.
Go, wander, free from fear of tyrant's rage,
Removed from the torments and the hell
Wherewith he may excruciate thy soul ;
And let Agydas by Agydas die,
And with this stab slumber eternally.
                   [*Stabs himself.*] [23]

[*Re-enter* TECHELLES *with* USUMCASANE.] [24]

TECH. Usumcasane, see, how right the man
Hath hit the meaning of my Lord, the King.

USUM. Faith, and, Techelles, it was manly
    done ;
And since he was so wise and honorable,   110

[14] Add. Dyce.
[15] Fall in love with.
[16] The daughters of Pierus.
[17] Alluding to the strife of Athene and Poseidon
for the possession of Athens.
[18] Fearing for.
[19] Astonished.

[20] *I.e.*, black.
[21] Om. Oo[3, 4].
[22] Await.
[23] Add. O[4].
[24] Add. Neilson.

Let us afford him now the bearing hence,
And crave his triple-worthy burial.
   TECH. Agreed, Casane ; we will honor him.
              [Exeunt bearing out the body.]

SCENE III [25]

[Enter] TAMBURLAINE, TECHELLES, USUMCA-
SANE, THERIDAMAS, BASSO, ZENOCRATE,
[ANIPPE,] *with others.*

   TAMB. Basso, by this thy lord and master
    knows
I mean to meet him in Bithynia.
See how he comes ! Tush, Turks are full of
    brags,
And menace more than they can well perform.
He meet me in the field, and fetch thee hence?
Alas, poor Turk, his fortune is too weak
T' encounter with the strength of Tambur-
    laine.
View well my camp, and speak indifferently ; [26]
Do not my captains and my soldiers look
As if they meant to conquer Africa?   10
   BAS. Your men are valiant, but their num-
    ber few,
And cannot terrify his mighty host.
My lord, the great commander of the world,
Besides fifteen contributory kings
Hath now in arms ten thousand Janissaries,
Mounted on lusty Mauritanian steeds,
Brought to the war by men of Tripoli ;
Two hundred thousand footmen that have
    serv'd
In two set battles fought in Græcia ;
And, for the expedition of this war,   20
If he think good, can from his garrisons
Withdraw as many more to follow him.
   TECH. The more he brings the greater is the
    spoil ;
For, when they perish by our warlike hands,
We mean to seat our footmen on their steeds,
And rifle all those stately Janisars.
   TAMB. But will those kings accompany
    your lord?
   BAS. Such as his Highness please ; but
    some must stay
To rule the provinces he late subdu'd.
   TAMB. Then fight courageously : their
    crowns are yours.   30
This hand shall set them on your conquering
    heads,
That made me Emperor of Asia.

[25] A battlefield in Bithynia.
[26] Impartially.

   USUM. Let him bring millions infinite of
    men,
Unpeopling Western Africa and Greece ;
Yet we assure us of the victory.
   THER. Even he that in a trice vanquish'd
    two kings,
More mighty than the Turkish Emperor,
Shall rouse him out of Europe, and pursue
His scattered army till they yield or die.
   TAMB. Well said, Theridamas ; speak in
    that mood ;   40
For " will " and " shall " best fitteth Tambur-
    laine,
Whose smiling stars gives him assured hope
Of martial triumph ere he meet his foes.
I that am term'd the scourge and wrath of
    God,
The only fear and terror of the world,
Will first subdue the Turk, and then enlarge
Those Christian captives, which you keep as
    slaves,
Burdening their bodies with your heavy chains
And feeding them with thin and slender fare,
That naked row about the Terrene sea,   50
And when they chance to breathe and rest a
    space,
Are punish'd with bastones [27] so grievously
That they lie panting on the galley's side
And strive for life at every stroke they give.
These are the cruel pirates of Argier,
That damned train, the scum of Africa,
Inhabited with straggling runagates, [28]
That make quick havoc of the Christian blood ;
But, as I live, that town shall curse the time
That Tamburlaine set foot in Africa.   60

Enter BAJAZETH *with his* BASSOES *and contribu-*
   tory KINGS [*of* FEZ, MOROCCO, *and* ARGIER ;
   ZABINA *and* EBEA].

   BAJ. Bassoes and Janissaries of my guard,
Attend upon the person of your lord,
The greatest potentate of Africa.
   TAMB. Techelles and the rest, prepare your
    swords ;
I mean t' encounter with that Bajazeth.
   BAJ. Kings of Fez, Moroccus, and Argier,
He calls me Bajazeth, whom you call Lord !
Note the presumption of this Scythian slave !
I tell thee, villain, those that lead my horse
Have to their names titles of dignity ;   70
And dar'st thou bluntly call me Bajazeth?
   TAMB. And know, thou Turk, that those
    which lead my horse

[27] Sticks.
[28] Vagabonds, deserters.

Shall lead thee captive thorough Africa ;
And dar'st thou bluntly call me Tambur-
    laine?
    BAJ. By Mahomet my kinsman's sepulchre,
And by the holy Alc[o]r[a]n, I swear
He shall be made a chaste and lustless eunuch,
And in my sarell [29] tend my concubines ;
And all his captains, that thus stoutly stand,
Shall draw the chariot of my emperess,   80
Whom I have brought to see their overthrow.
    TAMB. By this my sword, that conquer'd
    Persia,
Thy fall shall make me famous through the
    world.
I will not tell thee how I 'll handle thee,
But every common soldier of my camp
Shall smile to see thy miserable state.
    K. OF FEZ. What means the mighty Turk-
    ish Emperor,
To talk with one so base as Tamburlaine?
    K. OF MOR. Ye Moors and valiant men of
    Barbary,
How can ye suffer these indignities?   90
    K. OF ARG. Leave words, and let them feel
    your lances' points,
Which glided through the bowels of the
    Greeks.
    BAJ. Well said, my stout contributory
    kings ;
Your threefold army and my hugy host
Shall swallow up these baseborn Persians.
    TECH. Puissant, renowmed, and mighty
    Tamburlaine,
Why stay we thus prolonging all their lives?
    THER. I long to see those crowns won by
    our swords,
That we may reign as kings of Africa.
    USUM. What coward would not fight for
    such a prize?   100
    TAMB. Fight all courageously and be you
    kings ;
I speak it, and my words are oracles.
    BAJ. Zabina, mother of three braver boys
Than Hercules, that in his infancy
Did pash [30] the jaws of serpents venomous ;
Whose hands are made to gripe a warlike lance,
Their shoulders broad for complete armor fit,
Their limbs more large, and of a bigger size,
Than all the brats ysprung from Typhon's
    loins ;
Who, when they come unto their father's age,
Will batter turrets with their manly fists ;   111
Sit here upon this royal chair of state,
And on thy head wear my imperial crown,

Until I bring this sturdy Tamburlaine
And all his captains bound in captive chains.
    ZAB. Such good success happen to Bajazeth.
    TAMB. Zenocrate, the loveliest maid alive,
Fairer than rocks of pearl and precious stone,
The only paragon of Tamburlaine,
Whose eyes are brighter than the lamps of
    Heaven   120
And speech more pleasant than sweet har-
    mony,
That with thy looks canst clear the darkened
    sky,
And calm the rage of thund'ring Jupiter,
Sit down by her, adorned with my crown,
As if thou wert the Empress of the world.
Stir not, Zenocrate, until thou see
Me march victoriously with all my men,
Triumphing over him and these his kings,
Which I will bring as vassals to thy feet.
Till then take thou my crown, vaunt of my
    worth,   130
And manage words with her, as we will arms.
    ZENO. And may my love, the King of Persia,
Return with victory and free from wound.
    BAJ. Now shalt thou feel the force of
    Turkish arms,
Which lately made all Europe quake for fear.
I have of Turks, Arabians, Moors, and Jews,
Enough to cover all Bithynia.
Let thousands die ; their slaughtered carcasses
Shall serve for walls and bulwarks to the rest ;
And as the heads of Hydra, so my power,   140
Subdued, shall stand as mighty as before.
If they should yield their necks unto the sword,
Thy soldiers' arms could not endure to strike
So many blows as I have heads for thee.
Thou knowest not, foolish-hardy Tamburlaine,
What 't is to meet me in the open field,
That leave no ground for thee to march upon.
    TAMB. Our conquering swords shall marshal
    us the way
We use to march upon the slaughtered foe, 149
Trampling their bowels with our horses' hoofs,
Brave horses bred on the white Tartarian hills.
My camp is like to Julius Cæsar's host,
That never fought but had the victory ;
Nor in Pharsalia was there such hot war
As these, my followers, willingly would have.
Legions of spirits fleeting [31] in the air
Direct our bullets and our weapons' points,
And make [your] [32] strokes to wound the sense-
    less [air] ; [33]

[29] Seraglio.   [30] Smash.

[31] Floating.
[32] Cor. Dyce ; old eds. *our.*
[33] Conj. Dyce ; Oo 1, 3, 4, *lure;* O₂ *lute.*

And, when she sees our bloody colors spread,
Then Victory begins to take her flight,   160
Resting herself upon my milk-white tent. —
But come, my Lords, to weapons let us fall ;
The field is ours, the Turk, his wife, and all.
                              Exit with his followers.
BAJ. Come, kings and bassoes, let us glut
      our swords,
That thirst to drink the feeble Persians' blood.
                              Exit with his followers.
ZAB. Base concubine, must thou be plac'd
      by me,
That am the empress of the mighty Turk ?
ZENO. Disdainful Turkess and unreverend
       boss,[34]
Call'st thou me concubine, that am betroth'd
Unto the great and mighty Tamburlaine ? 170
ZAB. To Tamburlaine, the great Tartarian
      thief ?
ZENO. Thou wilt repent these lavish words
       of thine,
When thy great basso-master and thyself
Must plead for mercy at his kingly feet,
And sue to me to be your advocates.
ZAB. And sue to thee ! I tell thee, shame-
      less girl,
Thou shalt be laundress to my waiting
      maid ! —
How lik'st thou her, Ebea ? Will she serve ?
EBEA. Madam, she thinks, perhaps, she is
       too fine ;
But I shall turn her into other weeds,   180
And make her dainty fingers fall to work.
ZENO. Hear'st thou, Anippe, how thy
       drudge doth talk ?
And how my slave, her mistress, menaceth ?
Both for their sauciness shall be employed
To dress the common soldiers' meat and drink,
For we will scorn they should come near our-
selves.
ANIP. Yet sometimes let your Highness
       send for them
To do the work my chambermaid disdains.
                They sound the battle within, and stay.
ZENO. Ye gods and powers that govern
       Persia,
And made my lordly love her worthy king, 190
Now strengthen him against the Turkish Baj-
      azeth,
And let his foes, like flocks of fearful roes
Pursu'd by hunters, fly his angry looks,
That I may see him issue conqueror.
ZAB. Now, Mahomet, solicit God himself,

And make him rain down murdering [35] shot
      from Heaven
To dash the Scythians' brains and strike them
      dead
That dare to manage arms with him
That offered jewels to thy sacred shrine, 199
When first he warr'd against the Christians.
                [They sound] to the battle again.
ZENO. By this the Turks lie welt'ring in
       their blood,
And Tamburlaine is Lord of Africa.
ZAB. Thou art deceiv'd. I heard the
      trumpets sound
As when my emperor overthrew the Greeks,
And led them captive into Africa.
Straight will I use thee as thy pride deserves ;
Prepare thyself to live and die my slave.
ZENO. If Mahomet should come from
       Heaven and swear
My royal lord is slain or conquered,
Yet should he not persuade me otherwise 210
But that he lives and will be conqueror.

BAJAZETH *flies and* [TAMBURLAINE] *pursues
him. The battle short, and they enter ;* BAJ-
AZETH *is overcome.*

TAMB. Now, King of bassoes, who is con-
       queror ?
BAJ. Thou, by the fortune of this damned
      [foil].[36]
TAMB. Where are your stout contributory
       kings ?

Re-enter TECHELLES, THERIDAMAS, [*and*]
USUMCASANE.

TECH. We have their crowns ; their bodies
       strow the field.
TAMB. Each man a crown ! Why, kingly
       fought, i' faith.
Deliver them into my treasury.
ZENO. Now let me offer to my gracious Lord
His royal crown again so highly won.
TAMB. Nay, take the Turkish crown from
       her, Zenocrate,   220
And crown me Emperor of Africa.
ZAB. No, Tamburlaine ; though now thou
      gat the best
Thou shalt not yet be Lord of Africa.
THER. Give her the crown, Turkess, you
       were best.
              He takes it from her, and gives it
                  ZENOCRATE.

[34] Fat woman.

[35] From "murderers", a species of small cannon
used to scatter shot at close range.
[36] Repulse ; emend. Dyce. Old eds. *soile.* Cf.
l. 235.

Zab. Injurious villains! thieves! runa-
gates!
How dare you thus abuse my Majesty?
    Ther. Here, madam, you are Empress;
    she is none.
    Tamb. Not now, Theridamas; her time is
    past.
The pillars that have bolstered up those terms
Are fall'n in clusters at my conquering feet.
    Zab. Though he be prisoner, he may be
    ransomed.   231
    Tamb. Not all the world shall ransom Baj-
    azeth.
    Baj. Ah, fair Zabina, we have lost the field;
And never had the Turkish emperor
So great a foil by any foreign foe.
Now will the Christian miscreants be glad,
Ringing with joy their superstitious bells
And making bonfires for my overthrow.
But, ere I die, those foul idolaters
Shall make me bonfires with their filthy bones;
For, though the glory of this day be lost, 241
Afric and Greece have garrisons enough
To make me sovereign of the earth again.
    Tamb. Those walled garrisons will I subdue,
And write myself great Lord of Africa.
So from the East unto the furthest West
Shall Tamburlaine extend his puissant arm.
The galleys and those pilling [37] brigandines
That yearly sail to the Venetian gulf
And hover in the Straits for Christians'
    wrack   250
Shall lie at anchor in the isle Asant,[38]
Until the Persian fleet and men-of-war,
Sailing along the oriental sea,
Have fetch'd about the Indian continent,
Even from Persepolis to Mexico
And thence unto the straits of Jubalter; [39]
Where they shall meet and join their force in
    one,
Keeping in awe the bay of Portingale,[40]
And all the ocean by the British shore;   259
And by this means I'll win the world at last.
    Baj. Yet set a ransom on me, Tamburlaine.
    Tamb. What, think'st thou Tamburlaine
    esteems thy gold?
I'll make the kings of India, ere I die,
Offer their mines, to sue for peace, to me,
And dig for treasure to appease my wrath.
Come, bind them both, and one lead in the
    Turk;
The Turkess let my love's maid lead away.
                            They bind them.

Baj. Ah, villains, dare ye touch my sacred
    arms?
O Mahomet! O sleepy Mahomet!
    Zab. O cursed Mahomet, that makest us
    thus   270
The slaves to Scythians rude and barbarous!
    Tamb. Come, bring them in; and, for this
    happy conquest,
Triumph and solemnize a martial feast.
                            Exeunt.

ACT IV — Scene I [1]

[*Enter the*] Soldan *of* Egypt, *with three or four*
    Lords, Capolin, [*and a* Messenger].

    Sold. Awake, ye men of Memphis! Hear
    the clang
Of Scythian trumpets, — hear the basilisks [2]
That, roaring, shake Damascus' turrets down.
The rogue of Volga holds Zenocrate,
The Soldan's daughter, for his concubine,
And with a troop of thieves and vagabonds
Hath spread his colors to our high disgrace;
While you faint-hearted, base Egyptians
Lie slumbering on the flow'ry banks of Nile,
As crocodiles that unaffrighted rest   10
While thund'ring cannons rattle on their skins.
    Mess. Nay, mighty Soldan, did your
    Greatness see
The frowning looks of fiery Tamburlaine,
That with his terror and imperious eyes
Commands the hearts of his associates,
It might amaze your royal Majesty.
    Sold. Villain, I tell thee, were that Tam-
    burlaine
As monstrous [3] as Gorgon,[4] prince of hell,
The Soldan would not start a foot from him.
But speak, what power [5] hath he?
    Mess.   Mighty Lord, 20
Three hundred thousand men in armor clad,
Upon their prancing steeds disdainfully
With wanton paces trampling on the ground;
Five hundred thousand footmen, threat'ning
    shot,
Shaking their swords, their spears, and iron
    bills,
Environing their standard round, that stood
As bristle-pointed as a thorny wood.

[37] Robbing, pillaging.
[38] Zante. (Bullen.)
[39] Gibraltar.
[40] Bay of Biscay.

[1] Unlocated; presumably the Soldan's palace at
Memphis.
[2] A kind of cannon.
[3] Here a trisyllable.
[4] Demogorgon.
[5] Army.

Their warlike engines and munition
Exceed the forces of their martial men.
    SOLD. Nay, could their numbers countervail
       the stars,   30
Or ever-drizzling drops of April showers,
Or withered leaves that autumn shaketh
    down,
Yet would the Soldan by his conquering power
So scatter and consume them in his rage
That not a man should live to rue their
    fall.
    CAPO. So might your Highness, had you
       time to sort
Your fighting men and raise your royal host ;
But Tamburlaine, by expedition,
Advantage takes of your unreadiness.
    SOLD. Let him take all th' advantages he
       can.   40
Were all the world conspir'd to fight for
    him,
Nay, were he devil, as he is no man,
Yet in revenge of fair Zenocrate,
Whom he detaineth in despite of us,
This arm should send him down to Erebus,
To shroud his shame in darkness of the night.
    MESS. Pleaseth your Mightiness to under-
       stand,
His resolution far exceedeth all.
The first day when he pitcheth down his tents,
White is their hue, and on his silver crest   50
A snowy feather spangled white he bears,
To signify the mildness of his mind,
That, satiate with spoil, refuseth blood.
But, when Aurora mounts the second time,
As red as scarlet is his furniture ;
Then must his kindled wrath be quench'd
    with blood,
Not sparing any that can manage arms.
But if these threats move not submission,
Black are his colors ; black, pavilion ;
His spear, his shield, his horse, his armor,
    plumes,   60
And jetty feathers menace death and hell :
Without respect of sex, degree, or age,
He razeth all his foes with fire and sword.
    SOLD. Merciless villain, peasant, ignorant
Of lawful arms or martial discipline !
Pillage and murder are his usual trades ;
The slave usurps the glorious name of war.
See, Capolin, the fair Arabian king,
That hath been disappointed by this slave
Of my fair daughter and his princely love, 70
May have fresh warning to go war with us,
And be reveng'd for her disparagement.
                       [Exeunt.]

SCENE II [6]

[Enter] TAMBURLAINE, TECHELLES, THERIDA-
MAS, USUMCASANE, ZENOCRATE, ANIPPE,
two Moors *drawing* BAJAZETH *in his cage,
and his wife* [ZABINA] *following him.*

    TAMB. Bring out my footstool.
               They take him out of the cage.
    BAJ. Ye holy priests of heavenly Mahomet,
That, sacrificing, slice and cut your flesh,
Staining his altars with your purple blood,
Make Heaven to frown and every fixed star
To suck up poison from the moorish fens
And pour it in this glorious [7] tyrant's throat.
    TAMB. The chiefest God, first mover of that
       sphere
Enchas'd with thousands ever-shining lamps,
Will sooner burn the glorious frame of Heaven
Than it should so conspire my overthrow.   11
But, villain, thou that wishest this to me,
Fall prostrate on the low disdainful earth,
And be the footstool of great Tamburlaine,
That I may rise into my royal throne.
    BAJ. First shalt thou rip my bowels with
       thy sword
And sacrifice my heart to death and hell,
Before I yield to such a slavery.
    TAMB. Base villain, vassal, slave to Tam-
       burlaine,
Unworthy to embrace or touch the ground   20
That bears the honor of my royal weight,
Stoop, villain, stoop ! — Stoop ! for so he bids [8]
That may command thee piecemeal to be
    torn,
Or scattered like the lofty cedar trees
Struck with the voice of thund'ring Jupiter.
    BAJ. Then, as I look down to the damned
       fiends,
Fiends, look on me ! and thou, dread god of
    hell,
With ebon sceptre strike this hateful earth
And make it swallow both of us at once !
        [TAMBURLAINE] gets up upon him to his chair.
    TAMB. Now clear the triple [9] region of the
       air,   30
And let the Majesty of Heaven behold
Their scourge and terror tread on emperors.
Smile, stars that reign'd at my nativity,
And dim the brightness of their neighbor
    lamps !
Disdain to borrow light of Cynthia ;

---

[6] Tamburlaine's camp before Damascus.
[7] Boastful, vainglorious.
[8] Note metrical value of pause.
[9] Upper, middle, and lower.

For I, the chiefest lamp of all the earth,
First rising in the East with mild aspect,
But fixed now in the meridian line,[10]
Will send up fire to your turning spheres,
And cause the sun to borrow light of you. 40
My sword struck fire from his coat of steel,
Even in Bithynia, when I took this Turk ;
As when a fiery exhalation,
Wrapp'd in the bowels of a freezing cloud,
Fighting for passage, [makes][11] the welkin
  crack,
And casts a flash of lightning to the earth.
But, ere I march to wealthy Persia,
Or leave Damascus and th' Egyptian fields,
As was the fame of Clymene's brainsick son,
That almost brent[12] the axletree of Heaven,
So shall our swords, our lances, and our
  shot 51
Fill all the air with fiery meteors.
Then, when the sky shall wax as red as blood,
It shall be said I made it red myself,
To make me think of naught but blood and
  war.
  ZAB. Unworthy king, that by thy cruelty
Unlawfully usurpest the Persian seat,
Dar'st thou, that never saw an emperor
Before thou met my husband in the field,
Being thy captive, thus abuse his state, 60
Keeping his kingly body in a cage,
That roofs of gold and sun-bright palaces
Should have prepar'd to entertain his Grace,
And treading him beneath thy loathsome
  feet,
Whose feet the kings of Africa have kiss'd?
  TECH. You must devise some torment
    worse, my Lord,
To make these captives rein their lavish
  tongues.
  TAMB. Zenocrate, look better to your slave.
  ZENO. She is my handmaid's slave, and she
    shall look
That these abuses flow not from her tongue.
Chide her, Anippe. 71
  ANIP. Let these be warnings for you then,
    my slave,
How you abuse the person of the King ;
Or else I swear to have you whipp'd, stark-
  nak'd.
  BAJ. Great Tamburlaine, great in my over-
    throw,
Ambitious pride shall make thee fall as low,

For treading on the back of Bajazeth,
That should be horsed on four mighty kings.
  TAMB. Thy names and titles and thy digni-
    ties 79
Are fled from Bajazeth and remain with me,
That will maintain it against a world of kings.
Put him in again.
          [*They put him into the cage.*]
  BAJ. Is this a place for mighty Bajazeth?
Confusion light on him that helps thee thus !
  TAMB. There whiles he lives, shall Bajazeth
    be kept ;
And where I go, be thus in triumph drawn ;
And thou, his wife, shalt feed him with the
  scraps
My servitors shall bring thee from my board ;
For he that gives him other food than this
Shall sit by him and starve to death himself.
This is my mind and I will have it so. 91
Not all the kings and emperors of the earth,
If they would lay their crowns before my feet,
Shall ransom him or take him from his cage.
The ages that shall talk of Tamburlaine,
Even from this day to Plato's wondrous year,[13]
Shall talk how I have handled Bajazeth ;
These Moors, that drew him from Bithynia
To fair Damascus, where we now remain,
Shall lead him with us wheresoe'er we go. —
Techelles, and my loving followers, 101
Now may we see Damascus' lofty towers,
Like to the shadows of Pyramides,
That with their beauties grac'd the Memphian
  fields.
The golden stature[14] of their feathered bird,
That spreads her wings upon the city walls,
Shall not defend it from our battering shot.
The townsmen mask in silk and cloth of gold,
And every house is as a treasury.
The men, the treasure, and the town is ours.
  THER. Your tents of white now pitch'd be-
    fore the gates, 111
And gentle flags of amity display'd,
I doubt not but the governor will yield,
Offering Damascus to your Majesty.
  TAMB. So shall he have his life, and all the
    rest.
But if he stay until the bloody flag
Be once advanc'd on my vermilion tent,
He dies, and those that kept us out so long.

---

[10] *I.e.*, now at my highest (and permanent) point.
[11] Cor. Dyce ; old eds. *make.*
[12] Burned. The allusion is to the myth of Phaëthon.

[13] Plato (*Timaeus*) refers to a perfect "year", a period at the close of which all the "seven planets" will be relatively in the same positions as at its beginning. 15,000 solar years was Cicero's estimate of its length, according to Macrobius ; but computations varied widely.
[14] Oo 3, 4, *statue.* The bird was the ibis.

And when they see me march in black array,
With mournful streamers hanging down their
    heads,   120
Were in that city all the world contain'd,
Not one should scape, but perish by our
    swords.
    ZENO. Yet would you have some pity for
    my sake,
Because it is my country's, and my father's.
    TAMB. Not for the world, Zenocrate, if I
    have sworn.
Come ; bring in the Turk.   *Exeunt.*

SCENE III [15]

[*Enter the*] SOLDAN, [*the* KING OF] ARABIA, CA-
POLIN, *with streaming colors and* Soldiers.

    SOLD. Methinks we march as Meleager did,
Environed with brave Argolian knights,
To chase the savage Cal[y]donian boar ;
Or Cephalus with lusty Theban youths
Against the wolf that angry Themis sent
To waste and spoil the sweet Aonian fields,
A monster of five hundred thousand heads,
Compact of rapine, piracy, and spoil.
The scum of men, the hate and scourge of God,
Raves in Egyptia and annoyeth us.   10
My Lord, it is the bloody Tamburlaine,
A sturdy felon and a base-bred thief,
By murder raised to the Persian crown,
That dares control us in our territories.
To tame the pride of this presumptuous beast,
Join your Arabians with the Soldan's power ;
Let us unite our royal bands in one,
And hasten to remove Damascus' siege.
It is a blemish to the majesty
And high estate of mighty emperors,   20
That such a base usurping vagabond
Should brave a king, or wear a princely crown.
    K. of ARAB. Renowmed Soldan, have ye
    lately heard
The overthrow of mighty Bajazeth
About the confines of Bithynia?
The slavery wherewith he persecutes
The noble Turk and his great emperess?
    SOLD. I have, and sorrow for his bad suc-
    cess ; [16]
But, noble Lord of great Arabia,
Be so persuaded that the Soldan is   30
No more dismay'd with tidings of his fall
Than in the haven when the pilot stands
And views a stranger's ship rent in the winds,
And shivered against a craggy rock ;

[15] Unlocated ; presumably a camp in Syria.
[16] Outcome, fortune.

Yet, in compassion of his wretched state,
A sacred vow to Heaven and him I make,
Confirming it with Ibis' holy name,
That Tamburlaine shall rue the day, the hour,
Wherein he wrought such ignominious wrong
Unto the hallowed person of a prince,   40
Or kept the fair Zenocrate so long
As concubine, I fear, to feed his lust.
    K. of ARAB. Let grief and fury hasten on re-
    venge ;
Let Tamburlaine for his offences feel
Such plagues as Heaven and we can pour on
    him.
I long to break my spear upon his crest,
And prove the weight of his victorious arm ;
For Fame, I fear, hath been too prodigal
In sounding through the world his partial
    praise.
    SOLD. Capolin, hast thou survey'd our
    powers?   50
    CAPOL. Great Emperors of Egypt and
    Arabia,
The number of your hosts united is
A hundred [17] and fifty thousand horse ;
Two hundred thousand foot, brave men at
    arms,
Courageous,[17] and full of hardiness,
As frolic as the hunters in the chase
Of savage beasts amid the desert woods.
    K. of ARAB. My mind presageth fortunate
    success ;
And, Tamburlaine, my spirit doth foresee
The utter ruin of thy men and thee.   60
    SOLD. Then rear your standards ; let your
    sounding drums
Direct our soldiers to Damascus' walls. —
Now, Tamburlaine, the mighty Soldan comes,
And leads with him the great Arabian King,
To dim thy baseness and obscurity,
Famous for nothing but for theft and spoil ;
To raze and scatter thy inglorious crew
Of Scythians and slavish Persians.   *Exeunt.*

SCENE [IV] [18]

The banquet, and to it cometh TAMBURLAINE
all in scarlet, [ZENOCRATE,] THERIDAMAS,
TECHELLES, USUMCASANE, *the* Turk [BAJA-
ZETH *in his cage,* ZABINA,] *with others.*

    TAMB. Now hang our bloody colors by Da-
    mascus,
Reflexing hues of blood upon their heads,
While they walk quivering on their city walls,

[17] Trisyllabic here.
[18] Tamburlaine's camp before Damascus.

Half dead for fear before they feel my
　　wrath.
Then let us freely banquet and carouse
Full bowls of wine unto the god of war
That means to fill your helmets full of gold,
And make Damascus spoils as rich to you
As was to Jason Colchos' golden fleece. —
And now, Bajazeth, hast thou any stomach? [19]

BAJ. Ay, such a stomach, cruel Tam- [11
burlaine, as I could willingly feed upon thy
blood-raw heart.

TAMB. Nay, thine own is easier to come by ;
pluck out that, and 't will serve thee and thy
wife. — Well, Zenocrate, Techelles, and the
rest, fall to your victuals.

BAJ. Fall to, and never may your meat digest.

Ye Furies, that can mask invisible,
Dive to the bottom of Avernus' pool　　　20
And in your hands bring hellish poison up
And squeeze it in the cup of Tamburlaine.
Or, winged snakes of Lerna, cast your stings,
And leave your venoms in this tyrant's dish.

ZAB. And may this banquet prove as
　　ominous
As Progne's to th' adulterous Thracian king,
That fed upon the substance of his child.

ZENO. My Lord, how can you [20] suffer
　　these
Outrageous curses by these slaves of yours?

TAMB. To let them see, divine Zenocrate,
I glory in the curses of my foes,　　　31
Having the power from the imperial Heaven
To turn them all upon their proper heads.

TECH. I pray you give them leave, madam ;
this speech is a goodly refreshing to them.

THER. But if his Highness would let them
be fed, it would do them more good.

TAMB. Sirrah, why fall you not to? Are
you so daintily brought up, you cannot eat
your own flesh?　　　40

BAJ. First, legions of devils shall tear thee
in pieces.

USUM. Villain, knowest thou to whom thou
speakest?

TAMB. O, let him alone. Here ; eat, sir ;
take it from my sword's point, or I 'll thrust it
to thy heart.

　　　[*Bajazeth*] *takes it and stamps upon it.*

THER. He stamps it under his feet, my Lord.

TAMB. Take it up, villain, and eat it ; [49

---

or I will make thee slice the brawns of thy arms
into carbonadoes [21] and eat them.

USUM. Nay, 't were better he kill'd his
wife, and then she shall be sure not to be
starv'd, and he be provided for a month's victual beforehand.

TAMB. Here is my dagger ; despatch her
while she is fat ; for, if she live but a while
longer, she will fall into a consumption with
fretting, and then she will not be worth the
eating.　　　60

THER. Dost thou think that Mahomet will
suffer this?

TECH. 'T is like he will when he cannot let [22]
it.

TAMB. Go to ; fall to your meat. — What,
not a bit ! Belike he hath not been watered
today ; give him some drink.

　　　*They give him water to drink, and he
　　　flings it on the ground.*

TAMB. Fast, and welcome, sir, while [23] hunger make you eat. — How now, Zenocrate, [69
doth not the Turk and his wife make a goodly
show at a banquet?

ZENO. Yes, my Lord.

THER. Methinks 't is a great deal better
than a consort [24] of music.

TAMB. Yet music would do well to cheer up
Zenocrate. — Pray thee, tell why thou art so
sad. If thou wilt have a song, the Turk shall
strain his voice. But why is it?

ZENO. My Lord, to see my father's town
　　besieg'd,　　　79
The country wasted where myself was born,
How can it but afflict my very soul?
If any love remain in you, my Lord,
Or if my love unto your Majesty
May merit favor at your Highness' hands,
Then raise your siege from fair Damascus'
　　walls,
And with my father take a friendly truce.

TAMB. Zenocrate, were Egypt Jove's own
　　land,
Yet would I with my sword make Jove to
　　stoop.
I will confute those blind geographers
That make a triple region in the world,　　　90
Excluding regions which I mean to trace
And with this pen [25] reduce them to a map,

---

[19] Appetite. Note that the comic passages which
follow are in prose. They may be non-Marlovian,
or the actors' corruption or amplification of original
verse.
[20] A short line ; Dyce adds *tamely.*

[21] Steaks.
[22] Hinder.
[23] Until.
[24] Band.
[25] *I.e.,* his sword. The " triple region " was, for
Marlowe, Eurasia, Africa, and America. " Trace "
= traverse.

Calling the provinces, cities, and towns,
After my name and thine, Zenocrate.
Here at Damascus will I make the point
That shall begin the perpendicular ; [26]
And wouldst thou have me buy thy father's
love
With such a loss?   Tell me, Zenocrate !

ZENO. Honor still wait on happy Tamburlaine !   99
Yet give me leave to plead for him, my Lord.

TAMB. Content thyself : his person shall be
safe
And all the friends of fair Zenocrate,
If with their lives they will be pleas'd to yield,
Or may be forc'd to make me Emperor ;
For Egypt and Arabia must be mine. —
Feed, you slave ! Thou mayst think thyself
happy to be fed from my trencher.

BAJ. My empty stomach, full of idle heat,
Draws bloody humors [27] from my feeble parts,
Preserving life by hasting cruel death.   110
My veins are pale, my sinews hard and dry,
My joints benumb'd ; unless I eat, I die.

ZAB. Eat, Bajazeth.   Let us live in spite of
them, looking [28] some happy power will pity
and enlarge us.

TAMB. Here, Turk ; wilt thou have a clean
trencher?

BAJ. Ay, tyrant, and more meat.

TAMB. Soft, sir ; you must be dieted ; too
much eating will make you surfeit.   120

THER. So it would, my Lord, specially having so small a walk and so little exercise.

Enter a second course of crowns.

TAMB. Theridamas, Techelles, and Casane,
here are the cates you desire to finger, are they
not?

THER. Ay, my Lord ; but none save kings
must feed with these.

TECH. 'T is enough for us to see them, and
for Tamburlaine only to enjoy them.   129

TAMB. Well, here is now to the Soldan of
Egypt, the King of Arabia, and the Governor
of Damascus. — Now take these three crowns,
and pledge me, my contributory kings. I
crown you here, Theridamas, King of Argier ;
Techelles, King of Fez ; and Usumcasane,
King of Morocous. — How say you to this,
Turk ?   These are not your contributory kings.

BAJ. Nor shall they long be thine, I warrant
them.

TAMB. Kings of Argier, Moroccus, and of
Fez,
You that have march'd with happy Tambur-
laine   140
As far as from the frozen [plage] [29] of Heaven
Unto the wat'ry morning's ruddy [bower] [30]
And thence by land unto the torrid zone,
Deserve these titles I endow you with
By [valor] [31] and by magnanimity.
Your births shall be no blemish to your fame,
For virtue [32] is the fount whence honor springs,
And they are worthy she investeth kings.

THER. And since your Highness hath so
well vouchsaf'd,   149
If we deserve them not with higher meeds
Than erst our states and actions have retain'd,
Take them away again and make us slaves.

TAMB. Well said, Theridamas ; when holy
fates
Shall 'stablish me in strong Egyptia,
We mean to travel to th' anta[rc]tic pole,
Conquering the people underneath our feet,
And be renowm'd as never emperors were. —
Zenocrate, I will not crown thee yet,
Until with greater honors I be grac'd.

                           [*Exeunt.*]

ACT V — SCENE I [1]

[*Enter*] *the* GOVERNOR *of* DAMASCO, *with three
or four* Citizens, *and four* Virgins *with
branches of laurel in their hands.*

GOV. Still doth this man, or rather god, of
war
Batter our walls and beat our turrets down ;
And to resist with longer stubbornness
Or hope of rescue from the Soldan's power,
Were but to bring our wilful overthrow
And make us desperate of our threat'ned lives.
We see his tents have now been altered
With terrors to the last and cruel'st hue.
His coal-black colors everywhere advanc'd
Threaten our city with a general spoil ;   10
And if we should with common rites of arms
Offer our safeties to his clemency,
I fear the custom, proper [2] to his sword,
Which he observes as parcel of his fame,

[29] Shore. Emend. Dyce ; old eds. *place. Plage* occurs in *Part II*, I, i, 68, in Oo 1, 2, rendered by Oo 3, 4,
place.
[30] Cor. O₃ ; Oo 1, 2, *hower.*
[31] Emend. Robinson ; old eds. *value.*
[32] Worth, ability.
[1] A holy place in Damascus.
[2] Peculiar, habitual. " Parcel " = part.

[26] *I.e.*, longitude 0°. (Ellis-Fermor.)
[27] Moistures, vapors.   [28] Expecting.

Intending so to terrify the world,
By any innovation or remorse [3]
Will never be dispens'd with till our deaths.
Therefore, for these our harmless virgins'
    sakes,
Whose honors and whose lives rely on him,
Let us have hope that their unspotted prayers,
Their blubbered cheeks, and hearty, humble
    moans,   21
Will melt his fury into some remorse,
And use us like a loving conqueror.
  [1] VIRG. If humble suits or imprecations, [4]
(Uttered with tears of wretchedness and blood
Shed from the heads and hearts of all our sex,
Some made your wives and some your children)
Might have entreated your obdurate breasts
To entertain some care of our securities
Whiles only danger beat upon our walls,   30
These more than dangerous warrants of our
    death
Had never been erected as they be,
Nor you depend on such weak helps as we.
    Gov. Well, lovely virgins, think our coun-
    try's care,
Our love of honor, loath to be enthrall'd
To foreign powers and rough imperious yokes,
Would not with too much cowardice or fear,
Before all hope of rescue were denied,
Submit yourselves and us to servitude.   39
Therefore in that your safeties and our own,
Your honors, liberties, and lives were weigh'd
In equal care and balance with our own,
Endure as we the malice of our stars,
The wrath of Tamburlaine, and power of wars ;
Or be the means the overweighing heavens
Have kept to qualify [5] these hot extremes,
And bring us pardon in your cheerful looks.
    2 VIRG. Then here before the Majesty of
    Heaven
And holy Patrons of Egyptia,
With knees and hearts submissive we entreat
Grace to our words and pity to our looks,   51
That this device may prove propitious
And through the eyes and ears of Tamburlaine
Convey events of mercy [6] to his heart ;
Grant that these signs of victory [7] we yield
May bind the temples of his conquering head,
To hide the folded furrows of his brows,
And shadow his displeased countenance
With happy looks of ruth and lenity.   59
Leave us, my Lord, and loving countrymen ;
What simple virgins may persuade, we will.

    Gov. Farewell, sweet virgins, on whose safe
    return
Depends our city, liberty, and lives.
                Exeunt [all but the Virgins].

SCENE II [8]

[*To the* Virgins *enter*] TAMBURLAINE, TECH-
ELLES, THERIDAMAS, USUMCASANE, *with
others ;* TAMBURLAINE *all in black and very
melancholy.*

    TAMB. What, are the turtles [9] fray'd [10] out
    of their nests?
Alas, poor fools, must you be first shall feel
The sworn destruction of Damascus?
They know my custom ; could they not as well
Have sent ye out when first my milk-white
    flags,
Through which sweet Mercy threw her gentle
    beams,
Reflexing them on your disdainful eyes,
As now, when fury and incensed hate
Flings slaughtering terror from my coal-black
    tents,   9
And tells for truth submissions comes too late?
    1 VIRG. Most happy King and Emperor of
    the earth,
Image of honor and nobility,
For whom the powers divine have made the
    world,
And on whose throne the holy Graces sit ;
In whose sweet person is compris'd the sum
Of Nature's skill and heavenly majesty ;
Pity our plights ! O pity poor Damascus !
Pity old age, within whose silver hairs
Honor and reverence evermore have reign'd !
Pity the marriage bed, where many a lord, [20
In prime and glory of his loving joy,
Embraceth now with tears of ruth and blood
The jealous body of his fearful wife,
Whose cheeks and hearts, so punish'd with con-
    ceit
To think thy puissant, never-stayed arm
Will part their bodies, and prevent their souls
From heavens of comfort yet their age might
    bear,
Now wax all pale and withered to the death,
As well for grief our ruthless governor
[Hath] [11] thus refus'd the mercy of thy hand [30
(Whose sceptre angels kiss and Furies dread)

---

[3] Pity.   [6] Merciful conclusions.
[4] Prayers.   [7] *I.e.*, the laurel.
[5] Moderate.

[8] Though the Virgins remain on stage, the scene
changes to the camp.   After l. 343 it changes again,
to the battlefield.
[9] Turtledoves.
[10] Frightened.
[11] Oo 3, 4 ; Oo 1, 2, *haue.*

As for their liberties, their loves, or lives !
O then for these, and such as we ourselves,
For us, for infants, and for all our bloods,
That never nourish'd thought against thy rule,
Pity, O pity, sacred Emperor,
The prostrate service of this wretched town,
And take in sign thereof this gilded wreath,
Whereto each man of rule hath given his hand,
And wish'd, as worthy subjects, happy means
To be investers of thy royal brows   41
Even with the true Egyptian diadem.

TAMB. Virgins, in vain ye labor to prevent
That which mine honor swears shall be per-
    form'd.
Behold my sword ! what see you at the point ?
  [1] VIRG. Nothing but fear and fatal steel,
    my Lord.
TAMB. Your fearful minds are thick and
    misty then ;
For there sits Death, there sits imperious
    Death,
Keeping his circuit [12] by the slicing edge.
But I am pleas'd you shall not see him there ;
He now is seated on my horsemen's spears, [51
And on their points his fleshless body feeds. —
Techelles, straight go charge a few of them
To charge these dames, and show my servant,
    Death,
Sitting in scarlet on their armed spears.
  OMNES. O pity us !
  TAMB. Away with them, I say, and show
    them Death. — *They take them away.*
I will not spare these proud Egyptians,
Nor change my martial observations
For all the wealth of Gihon's golden waves, [60
Or for the love of Venus, would she leave
The angry god of arms and lie with me.
They have refus'd the offer of their lives ;
And know my customs are as peremptory
As wrathful planets, death, or destiny.

        Re enter TECHELLES.

What, have your horsemen shown the virgins
    Death ?
  TECH. They have, my Lord, and on Damas-
    cus' walls
Have hoisted up their slaughtered carcases.
  TAMB. A sight as baneful to their souls, I
    think,
As are Thessalian drugs or mithridate.   70
But go, my Lords ; put the rest to the sword. —
    Exeunt [all except TAMBURLAINE].
Ah, fair Zenocrate ! divine Zenocrate !
Fair is too foul an epithet for thee,

[12] Court.

That in thy passion,[13] for thy country's love,
And fear to see thy kingly father's harm,
With hair dishevell'd wip'st thy watery
    cheeks ;
And, like to Flora in her morning's pride
Shaking her silver tresses in the air,
Rain'st on the earth resolved [14] pearl in show-
    ers,
And sprinklest sapphires on thy shining face,
Where Beauty, mother to the Muses, sits   81
And comments volumes with her ivory pen,
Taking instructions from thy flowing eyes,
Eyes when that Ebena [15] steps to Heaven,
In silence of thy solemn evening's walk,
Making the mantle of the richest night,
The moon, the planets, and the meteors, light ;
There angels in their crystal armors fight
A doubtful battle with my tempted thoughts
For Egypt's freedom, and the Soldan's life, [90
His life that so consumes Zenocrate ;
Whose sorrows lay more siege unto my soul,
Than all my army to Damascus' walls,
And neither [Persia's] [16] sovereign nor the
    Turk
Troubled my senses with conceit of foil [17]
So much by much as doth Zenocrate.
What is beauty, saith my sufferings, then ?
If all the pens that ever poets held
Had fed the feeling of their masters' thoughts,
And every sweetness that inspir'd their hearts,
Their minds, and muses on admired themes ;
If all the heavenly quintessence they still [18]
From their immortal flowers of poesy,   103
Wherein, as in a mirror, we perceive
The highest reaches of a human wit ;
If these had made one poem's period,
And all combin'd in beauty's worthiness,
Yet should there hover in their restless heads
One thought, one grace, one wonder, at the
    least,
Which into words no virtue [19] can digest.   110
But how unseemly is it for my sex,
My discipline of arms and chivalry,
My nature, and the terror of my name,
To harbor thoughts effeminate and faint !
Save only that in beauty's just applause,
With whose instinct the soul of man is
    touch'd —
And every warrior that is rapt with love

[13] *I.e.*, sorrow.
[14] Dissolved.
[15] Unidentified ; the line is doubtless corrupt.
[16] Emend. Robinson ; old eds. *Perseans.*
[17] Idea of defeat.
[18] Distill.
[19] Power.

Of fame, of valor, and of victory,
Must needs have beauty beat on his conceits, —
I thus conceiving and subduing both   120
That which hath [stoop'd the temper] [20] of the
      gods,
Even from the fiery-spangled veil of Heaven,
To feel the [lowly] [21] warmth of shepherds'
      flames,
And [watch] [22] in cottages of strowed [reeds], [23]
Shall give the world to note, for all my birth,
That virtue solely is the sum of glory,
And fashions men with true nobility. —
Who's within there?

Enter two or three.

Hath Bajazeth been fed to-day?
    AN [ATTENDANT]. Ay, my Lord.   130
    TAMB. Bring him forth ; and let us know if
the town be ransack'd.   [*Exeunt* Attendants.]

Enter TECHELLES, THERIDAMAS, USUMCA-
        SANE, *and others.*

    TECH. The town is ours, my Lord, and fresh
        supply
Of conquest and of spoil is offered us.
    TAMB. That's well, Techelles ; what's the
        news?
    TECH. The Soldan and the Arabian King
        together
March on us with such eager violence
As if there were no way but one with us.
    TAMB. No more there is not, I warrant thee,
        Techelles.
        They bring in the Turk [*and* ZABINA].
    THER. We know the victory is ours, my
        Lord ;   140
But let us save the reverend Soldan's life,
For fair Zenocrate that so laments his state.
    TAMB. That will we chiefly see unto, Theri-
        damas,
For sweet Zenocrate, whose worthiness
Deserves a conquest over every heart.
And now, my footstool, if I lose the field,
You hope of liberty and restitution ! —
Here let him stay, my masters, from the tents,
Till we have made us ready for the field. —
Pray for us, Bajazeth ; we are going.   150
        Exeunt [*all but* BAJAZETH *and* ZABINA].
    BAJ. Go, never to return with victory !
Millions of men encompass thee about,

And gore thy body with as many wounds !
Sharp, forked arrows light upon thy horse !
Furies from the black Cocytus lake
Break up the earth, and with their firebrands
Enforce thee run upon the baneful pikes !
Volleys of shot pierce through thy charmed
      skin,
And every bullet dipp'd in poisoned drugs,
Or roaring cannons sever all thy joints,   160
Making thee mount as high as eagles soar !
    ZAB. Let all the swords and lances in the
        field
Stick in his breast as in their proper rooms !
At every pore let blood come dropping forth,
That ling'ring pains may massacre his heart
And madness send his damned soul to hell !
    BAJ. Ah, fair Zabina, we may curse his
        power,
The heavens may frown, the earth for anger
      quake,
But such a star hath influence in his sword [16.
As rules the skies and countermands the gods,
More than Cimmerian Styx or Destiny ;
And then shall we in this detested guise,
With shame, with hunger, and with horror
      aye
Griping our bowels with retorqued [24] thoughts,
And have no hope to end our ecstasies?
    ZAB. Then is there left no Mahomet, no
        God,
No Fiend, no Fortune, nor no hope of end
To our infamous, [25] monstrous slaveries !
Gape, earth, and let the fiends infernal view
[A] [26] hell as hopeless and as full of fear   180
As are the blasted banks of Erebus,
Where shaking ghosts with ever-howling
      groans
Hover about the ugly ferryman,
To get a passage to Elysium. [27]
Why should we live? O, wretches, beggars,
      slaves !
Why live we, Bajazeth, and build up nests
So high within the region of the air
By living long in this oppression,
That all the world will see and laugh to scorn
The former triumphs of our mightiness   190
In this obscure, infernal servitude?
    BAJ. O life, more loathsome to my vexed
        thoughts
Than noisome parbreak [28] of the Stygian
      snakes,

---

[20] Old eds. *stopt the tempest,* certainly corrupt ;
the reading of this ed. combines guesses of Dyce and
Collier.
  [21] Conj. Collier ; old eds. *louely.*
  [22] Emend. present Ed. Old eds. *martch.*
  [23] Emend. Dyce ; old eds. *weeds.*

[24] *I.e.,* retrospective.
  [25] Accented on second syllable.
  [26] Cor. Robinson ; old eds. *As.*
  [27] Old eds. *Elisian.*
  [28] Vomit.

Which fills the nooks of hell with standing
   air,
Infecting all the ghosts with cureless griefs !
O dreary engines [29] of my loathed sight,
That sees my crown, my honor, and my name
Thrust under yoke and thraldom of a thief,
Why feed ye still on day's accursed beams
And sink not quite into my tortur'd soul? [200
You see my wife, my queen, and emperess,
Brought up and propped by the hand of Fame,
Queen of fifteen contributory queens,
Now thrown to rooms of black abjection,
Smear'd with blots of basest drudgery,
And villeiness [30] to shame, disdain, and misery.
Accursed Bajazeth, whose words of ruth,
(That would with pity cheer Zabina's heart,
And make our souls resolve in ceaseless tears ;)
Sharp hunger bites upon, and gripes the root
From whence the issues of my thoughts do
   break.   211
O poor Zabina, O my queen, my queen,
Fetch me some water for my burning breast,
To cool and comfort me with longer date ;
That in the short'ned sequel of my life
I may pour forth my soul into thine arms
With words of love, whose moaning intercourse
Hath hitherto been stay'd with wrath and hate
Of our expressless bann'd inflictions.
  ZAB. Sweet Bajazeth, I will prolong thy life,
As long as any blood or spark of breath   221
Can quench or cool the torments of my grief.
                        She goes out.
  BAJ. Now, Bajazeth, abridge thy baneful
   days,
And beat thy brains out of thy conquer'd head,
Since other means are all forbidden me
That may be ministers of my decay.
O highest lamp of ever-living Jove,
Accursed day, infected with my griefs,
Hide now thy stained face in endless night,
And shut the windows of the lightsome
   heavens !   230
Let ugly Darkness with her rusty coach,
Engirt with tempests, wrapp'd in pitchy
   clouds,
Smother the earth with never-fading mists,
And let her horses from their nostrils breathe
Rebellious winds and dreadful thunderclaps,
That in this terror Tamburlaine may live,
And my pin'd soul, resolv'd in liquid [air],[31]
May still excruciate his tormented thoughts !
Then let the stony dart of senseless cold

[29] Instruments.
[30] Serf.
[31] Cor. O 3 ; Oo 1, 2, *ay.*

Pierce through the centre of my withered
   heart,   240
And make a passage for my loathed life !
            He brains himself against the cage.

              Re-enter ZABINA.

  ZAB. What do mine eyes behold, my husband dead?
His skull all riven in twain, his brains dash'd
   out?
The brains of Bajazeth, my lord and sovereign !
O Bajazeth, my husband and my lord,
O Bajazeth, O Turk, O Emperor !
Give him his liquor? Not I. Bring milk and
fire, and my blood I bring him again. — Tear
me in pieces ! Give me the sword with a ball
of wildfire upon it. — Down with him ! Down
with him ! — Go to, my child ! Away ! [251
away ! away ! Ah, save that infant ! save him,
save him ! — I, even I, speak to her. — The
sun was down. Streamers white, red, black,
here, here, here ! — Fling the meat in his face
— Tamburlaine, Tamburlaine ! — Let the soldiers be buried. — Hell ! Death ! Tamburlaine ! Hell ! — Make ready my coach, my
chair, my jewels ; I come, I come, I come !
   She runs against the cage and brains herself.

    [*Enter*] ZENOCRATE *with* ANIPPE.

  [ZENO.] Wretched Zenocrate ! that livest to
   see   260
Damascus' walls dy'd with Egyptian blood,
Thy father's subjects and thy countrymen ;
Thy streets strowed with dissevered joints of
   men
And wounded bodies gasping yet for life.
But most accurs'd, to see the sun-bright troop
Of heavenly virgins and unspotted maids,
Whose looks might make the angry god of
   arms
To break his sword and mildly treat of love,
On horsemen's lances to be hoisted up
And guiltlessly endure a cruel death ;   270
For every fell and stout Tartarian steed,
That stamp'd on others with their thund'ring
   hoofs
When all their riders charg'd their quivering
   spears,
Began to check the ground and rein them-
   selves,
Gazing upon the beauty of their looks.
Ah, Tamburlaine, wert thou the cause of this
That term'st Zenocrate thy dearest love?
Whose lives were dearer to Zenocrate

Than her own life, or aught save thine own
　　love. —
But see, another bloody spectacle!　　　　280
Ah, wretched eyes, the enemies of my heart,
How are ye glutted with these grievous objects,
And tell my soul more tales of bleeding ruth!
See, see, Anippe, if they breathe or no.
　　ANIPPE.　No breath, nor sense, nor motion
　　　　in them both;
Ah, madam, this their slavery hath enforc'd,
And ruthless cruelty of Tamburlaine.
　　ZENO.　Earth, cast up fountains from thy
　　　　entrails,[32]
And wet thy cheeks for their untimely deaths!
Shake with their weight in sign of fear and
　　grief!　　　　　　　　　　　　290
Blush, Heaven, that gave them honor at their
　　birth
And let them die a death so barbarous.
Those that are proud of fickle empery
And place their chiefest good in earthly pomp,
Behold the Turk and his great Emperess!
Ah, Tamburlaine, my love, sweet Tambur-
　　laine,
That fights for sceptres and for slippery
　　crowns,
Behold the Turk and his great Emperess!
Thou, that in conduct of thy happy stars
Sleep'st every night with conquest on thy
　　brows,　　　　　　　　　　　　300
And yet wouldst shun the wavering turns of
　　war,
In fear and feeling of the like distress,
Behold the Turk and his great Emperess!
Ah, mighty Jove and holy Mahomet,
Pardon my love!　O, pardon his contempt
Of earthly fortune and respect of pity,
And let not conquest, ruthlessly pursu'd,
Be equally against his life incens'd
In this great Turk and hapless Emperess!
And pardon me that was not mov'd with ruth
To see them live so long in misery!　　311
Ah, what may chance to thee, Zenocrate?
　　ANIPPE.　Madam, content yourself, and be
　　　　resolv'd [33]
Your love hath Fortune so at his command,
That she shall stay and turn her wheel no
　　more,
As long as life maintains his mighty arm
That fights for honor to adorn your head.

　　　　Enter [PHILEMUS,] *a* Messenger.

　　ZENO.　What other heavy news now brings
　　　　Philemus?

[32] Trisyllabic.　　　　[33] Assured.

　　PHIL.　Madam, your father, and th' Arabian
　　　　King,
The first affecter [34] of your excellence,　320
Comes now, as Turnus 'gainst Æneas did,
Armed with lance into the Egyptian fields,
Ready for battle 'gainst my Lord, the King.
　　ZENO.　Now shame and duty, love and fear,
　　　　presents
A thousand sorrows to my martyred soul.
Whom should I wish the fatal victory,
When my poor pleasures are divided thus
And rack'd by duty from my cursed heart?
My father and my first-betrothed love　329
Must fight against my life and present love;
Wherein the change I use condemns my faith,
And makes my deeds infamous through the
　　world.
But as the gods, to end the Troyans' toil,
Prevented Turnus of Lavinia
And fatally enrich'd Æneas' love,
So, for a final issue to my griefs,
To pacify my country and my love
Must Tamburlaine by their resistless powers
With virtue of a gentle victory
Conclude a league of honor to my hope;　340
Then, as the Powers divine have preordain'd,
With happy safety of my father's life
Send like defence of fair Arabia.
　　　　They sound to the battle: and TAM-
　　　　BURLAINE *enjoys the victory. After,*
　　　　[*the* KING OF] ARABIA *enters*
　　　　wounded.
　　K. of ARAB.　What cursed power guides the
　　　　murdering hands
Of this infamous tyrant's soldiers;
That no escape may save their enemies,
Nor fortune keep themselves from victory?
Lie down, Arabia, wounded to the death,
And let Zenocrate's fair eyes behold
That, as for her thou bear'st these wretched
　　arms,　　　　　　　　　　　　350
Even so for her thou diest in these arms,
Leaving thy blood for witness of thy love.
　　ZENO.　Too dear a witness for such love, my
　　　　Lord.
Behold Zenocrate, the cursed object,
Whose fortunes never mastered her griefs;
Behold her wounded, in conceit, for thee,
As much as thy fair body is for me.
　　K. of ARAB.　Then shall I die with full con-
　　　　tented heart,
Having beheld divine Zenocrate,　　　359
Whose sight with joy would take away my life
As now it bringeth sweetness to my wound,

[34] Lover.

If I had not been wounded as I am.
Ah, that the deadly pangs I suffer now
Would lend an hour's license to my tongue,
To make discourse of some sweet accidents
Have chanc'd thy merits in this worthless
    bondage;
And that I might be privy to the state
Of thy deserv'd contentment, and thy love;
But, making now a virtue of thy sight
To drive all sorrow from my fainting soul, 370
Since death denies me further cause of joy,
Depriv'd of care, my heart with comfort dies,
Since thy desired hand shall close mine eyes.
                    [*He dies.*]

Re-enter TAMBURLAINE *leading the* SOLDAN,
TECHELLES, THERIDAMAS, USUMCASANE, *with
others.*

  TAMB. Come, happy father of Zenocrate,
A title higher than thy Soldan's name;
Though my right hand have thus enthralled
    thee,
Thy princely daughter here shall set thee free;
She that hath calm'd the fury of my sword,
Which had ere this been bath'd in streams of
    blood
As vast and deep as Euphrates [35] or Nile. 380
  ZENO. O sight thrice welcome to my joyful
    soul,
To see the King, my father, issue safe
From dangerous battle of my conquering love!
  SOLD. Well met, my only dear Zenocrate,
Though with the loss of Egypt and my crown.
  TAMB. 'T was I, my Lord, that gat the vic-
    tory,
And therefore grieve not at your overthrow,
Since I shall render all into your hands,
And add more strength to your dominions
Than ever yet confirm'd th' Egyptian crown.
The god of war resigns his room to me, 391
Meaning to make me general of the world.
Jove, viewing me in arms, looks pale and wan,
Fearing my power should pull him from his
    throne.
Where'er I come the Fatal Sisters sweat,
And grisly Death, by running to and fro,
To do their ceaseless homage to my sword;
And here in Afric, where it seldom rains,
Since I arriv'd with my triumphant host,
Have swelling clouds, drawn from wide-gasp-
    ing wounds, 400
Been oft resolv'd in bloody purple showers,
A meteor that might terrify the earth
And make it quake at every drop it drinks.

[35] Accented on first syllable here.

Millions of souls sit on the banks of Styx,
Waiting the back return of Charon's boat;
Hell and Elysium [36] swarm with ghosts of men
That I have sent from sundry foughten fields,
To spread my fame through hell and up to
    Heaven.
And see, my Lord, a sight of strange import,
Emperors and kings lie breathless at my feet:
The Turk and his great Emperess, as it seems,
Left to themselves while we were at the fight,
Have desperately despatch'd their slavish
    lives; 413
With them Arabia, too, hath left his life —
All sights of power to grace my victory!
And such are objects fit for Tamburlaine;
Wherein, as in a mirror, may be seen
His honor, that consists in shedding blood,
When men presume to manage arms with him.
  SOLD. Mighty hath God and Mahomet
    made thy hand, 420
Renowmed Tamburlaine, to whom all kings
Of force must yield their crowns and emperies;
And I am pleas'd with this my overthrow,
If, as beseems a person of thy state,
Thou hast with honor us'd Zenocrate.
  TAMB. Her state and person wants no
    pomp, you see;
And for all blot of foul inchastity
I record Heaven her heavenly self is clear.
Then let me find no further time to grace 429
Her princely temples with the Persian crown.
But here these kings that on my fortunes wait,
And have been crown'd for proved worthiness,
Even by this hand that shall establish them,
Shall now, adjoining all their hands with mine,
Invest her here my Queen of Persia.
What saith the noble Soldan and Zenocrate?
  SOLD. I yield with thanks and protestations
Of endless honor to thee for her love.
  TAMB. Then doubt I not but fair Zenocrate
Will soon consent to satisfy us both. 440
  ZENO. Else should I much forget myself, my
    Lord.
  THER. Then let us set the crown upon her
    head,
That long hath ling'red for so high a seat.
  TECH. My hand is ready to perform the
    deed,
For now her marriage time shall work us rest.
  USUM. And here 's the crown, my Lord;
    help set it on.
  TAMB. Then sit thou down, divine Zeno-
    crate;
And here we crown thee Queen of Persia

[36] Old eds. *Elisian.*

And all the kingdoms and dominions
That late the power of Tamburlaine subdu'd.
As Juno, when the giants were suppress'd, [451
That darted mountains at her brother Jove,
So looks my love, shadowing in her brows
Triumphs and trophies for my victories ;
Or as Latona's daughter,[37] bent to arms,
Adding more courage to my conquering
    mind.
To gratify the sweet Zenocrate,
Egyptians, Moors, and men of Asia,
From Barbary unto the western Indie,
Shall pay a yearly tribute to thy sire ;   460
And from the bounds of Afric to the banks
Of Ganges shall his mighty arm extend. —
And now, my Lords and loving followers,

[37] Diana.

That purchas'd kingdoms by your martial
    deeds,
Cast off your armor, put on scarlet robes,
Mount up your royal places of estate,
Environed with troop of noblemen,
And there make laws to rule your provinces.
Hang up your weapons on Alcides' post,[38]
For Tamburlaine takes truce with all the
    world. —   470
Thy first-betrothed love, Arabia,
Shall we with honor, as beseems, entomb,
With this great Turk and his fair Emperess.
Then, after all these solemn exequies,
We will our [39] rites of marriage solemnize.

                            [*Exeunt.*]

[38] *I.e.*, at the temple door. See Horace, *Epistles*, **I,**
i, 4, 5. (Ellis-Fermor.)
[39] Old eds. add *celebrated.*

THE TRAGICALL

History of D. Faustus.

As it hath bene Acted by the Right
Honorable the Earle of Nottingham his seruants.

Written by Ch. Marl.

LONDON
Printed by V. S. for Thomas Bushell. 1604.

INTRODUCTORY NOTE

As Tamburlaine aspired to the world's mastery by force of arms, Faustus sought it through knowledge; thus Marlowe exhibits in this play another aspect of the Renaissance will to freedom. In its original form *Doctor Faustus* must have been a sublime poem, and it still retains what *Tamburlaine* lacks, scenes of primarily dramatic power. Unfortunately, though the play was probably produced about 1589 (Boas inclines to 1592 but minimizes the significance of a ballad on Faustus licensed in 1589 and presumably inspired by the play), the first edition appeared only in 1604. By that time, eleven years after the author's death, the piece had been mangled by stage alterations.

In 1602 Henslowe, whose company, the Admiral's (or Nottingham's) Men, acted it, paid £4 to William Bird and Samuel Rowley for additions. And doubtless, both before and after their work, there was fairly constant tampering. The Quarto of 1616 gives us a version widely different from the first edition, and the Quarto of 1663 contains grotesque additions partly adapted from *The Jew of Malta*. The tendency of the early stage was to treat the Devil as a comic character; and as new material was successively introduced for the low comedians, the original was repeatedly pared down to make room for it. *Doctor Faustus*, then, is to be approached like a temple of the antique world; we are the losers if we allow partial collapse, inartistic restoration, and unauthentic and impudent addition to obscure the surviving traces of its beauty. (For a sketch of the probable process of corruption see Percy Simpson's article in *Essays and Studies by Members of the English Association*, VII, 143–155.) Aside from interpolation and excision, the most notable changes are the mangling of metre and the substitution of prose paraphrases for the original verse.

Marlowe's source was evidently not the German *Historia Von D. Johann Fausten* (Frankfurt am Main, 1587), but the not very faithful English translation of it, the *Historie of Doctor Iohn Faustus* (London, 1592), which Marlowe (unless we are to date the play after its appearance) must have read in MS or in an earlier edition. The moral application of the story is a prominent feature of the source, which also shows an anti-Papal bias. The play closely follows selected materials of the English Faust Book; but, as Boas remarks, "it is the questing spirit of the youthful Marlowe that transfigures it." The core of the legend is the compact with the Devil and the consequent retribution. The interval of twenty years is replete in the Faust Book with a great variety of experiences, including the episodes with the Pope, the horse-courser, and the clowns. It is generally believed that Marlowe's soaring pen was incapable of the comic scenes and that a collaborator furnished them. Marlowe was clearly more interested in the aspiration of Faustus, and with that fact in mind the reader must attempt as best he may to hold in his mind's eye the noble outlines of the original structure. "How greatly," said Goethe, "is it all planned."

Whatever the date of the original production, Henslowe records performances of *Doctor Faustus* by the Admiral's Men, with Edward Alleyn in the title rôle, in 1594–97. It continued to be acted, in more and more degraded versions, till well into the eighteenth century. The Case edition of this play is the work of F. S. Boas (1932).[1] Among other editions are Hermann Breymann's parallel texts of Qq 1604 and 1616 (vol. II of the *Historisch-Kritische Ausgabe* of Marlowe's Works, 1889); modernized editions by A. W. Ward (fourth edition, 1901), and I. Gollancz (1897); and a facsimile of Q 1604 by J. S. Farmer (1920). Professor Brooke (*Philological Quarterly*, January, 1933) has supplemented these editions with several valuable bibliographical and exegetical notes.

---

[1] The present edition has profited, during correction of proofs, by T. M. Parrott's review of Boas (*Modern Language Notes*, June, 1933).

Faustus was first printed, in quarto, in 1604 (reprinted 1609, 1611). In 1616 (reprinted 1619, 1620, 1624, 1628, 1631) a new version added about 550 lines and rewrote much of the play. Since Q 1616 evidently rests in part, not on an earlier quarto, but on independent MS authority, an extremely difficult textual problem is presented. Boas thinks Q 1616 more authentic; but the present edition is based on Breymann's and Brooke's reprints of Q 1604, though with indicated restorations and rearrangements from Q 1616 as given by them; for Q 1604 presents a badly cut and garbled stage version. Q 1616, on the contrary, constantly betrays, in the opinion of the present editor, the hand of an "improver", who smooths out difficult expressions; and it contains a number of new passages that are certainly not Marlovian.

As for the authorship of the version of 1604, Boas's conclusions seem reasonable and may be applied as follows. Marlowe probably wrote the first two acts, through II, ii (the episode of the Seven Deadly Sins is a possible exception); the chorus and the next fifty-three lines of Act III; Act IV, chorus, i, ii (1–9), iii; and Act V. The prose comic scenes may be a collaborator's. subsequently modified, in any case, by the steady pressure of theatrical conditions.

THE TRAGICAL HISTORY OF DOCTOR FAUSTUS

BY

CHRISTOPHER MARLOWE

[DRAMATIS PERSONAE

THE POPE.
CARDINAL OF LORRAINE.
CHARLES V, EMPEROR OF GERMANY.
DUKE OF VANHOLT.[1]
FAUSTUS.
VALDES, } friends to FAUSTUS.
CORNELIUS,
WAGNER, servant to FAUSTUS.
Clown.
ROBIN.
RALPH.
Vintner.
Horse-Courser.[2]
Knight.
Old Man.

Scholars, Friars, and Attendants.

DUCHESS OF VANHOLT.

LUCIFER.
BELZEBUB.
MEPHISTOPHILIS.
Good Angel.
Evil Angel.
The Seven Deadly Sins.
Devils.
Spirits in the shapes of ALEXANDER THE GREAT, of his Paramour, and of HELEN of TROY.
Chorus.]

[ACT I]

Enter Chorus.

[CHORUS.] Not marching now in fields of
   Thrasimene,
Where Mars did mate[3] the Carthaginians;
Nor sporting in the dalliance of love,
In courts of kings where state is overturn'd;
Nor in the pomp of proud, audacious deeds,
Intends our Muse to [vaunt][4] his[5] heavenly
   verse: —
Only this, gentlemen: we must perform
The form of Faustus' fortunes, good or bad.
To patient judgments we appeal our plaud,[6]
And speak for Faustus in his infancy.   10
Now is he born, his parents base of stock,
In Germany, within a town call'd Rhodes;[7]

Of riper years to Wittenberg he went,
Whereas his kinsmen chiefly brought him up.
So soon he profits in divinity,
The fruitful plot of scholarism grac'd,[8]
That shortly he was grac'd[9] with doctor's
   name,
Excelling all whose sweet delight disputes
In heavenly matters of theology;   19
Till, swoln with cunning,[10] of a self-conceit,
His waxen[11] wings did mount above his reach,
And melting Heavens conspir'd his overthrow;
For, falling to a devilish exercise,
And glutted more[12] with learning's golden
   gifts,
He surfeits upon cursed necromancy.
Nothing so sweet as magic is to him,
Which he prefers before his chiefest bliss.
And this[13] the man that in his study sits.
        Exit.

---

[1] Anholt.   [2] Horse trader.
[3] Defeat. But Hannibal won this battle. The author may be confused; and the whole speech may be non-Marlovian.
[4] Proudly display; so Q 1616; earlier eds. *daunt.*
[5] Cf. Shakespeare, *Sonnets*, XXI, 1, 2.
[6] For our applause. Q 1616: *And now to patient iudgements we appeale,* typical of that ed.'s efforts to smooth the original version.
[7] Roda, in the Duchy of Saxe-Altenburg.

[8] Full of graces. (Cf. *Macbeth*, III, iv, 41.)
[9] Punning on the official "grace" (at Cambridge) by virtue of which a candidate took his degree.
[10] Puffed up with knowledge.
[11] *I.e.*, insecure, like the wings of Icarus.
[12] Q 1616 *now.*
[13] This is.

[SCENE I] [14]

Enter FAUSTUS *in his study.*

FAUST. Settle thy studies, Faustus, and
    begin
To sound the depth of that thou wilt profess.
Having commenc'd,[15] be a divine in show ;
Yet level [16] at the end of every art,
And live and die in Aristotle's works.
Sweet Analytics,[17] 't is thou hast ravish'd me,
Bene disserere est finis logices.
Is to dispute well logic's chiefest end ?
Affords this art no greater miracle ?
Then read no more ; thou hast attain'd the
    end —   10
A greater subject fitteth Faustus' wit.
Bid [ὃν καὶ μὴ ὄν] [18] farewell, Galen come :
Seeing *Ubi desinit philosophus, ibi incipit
    medicus ;* [19]
Be a physician, Faustus, heap up gold,
And be eterniz'd for some wondrous cure.
Summum bonum medicinæ sanitas :
The end of physic is our body's health.
Why, Faustus, hast thou not attain'd that
    end ?
Is not thy common talk sound Aphorisms ? [20]
Are not thy bills [21] hung up as monuments,   20
Whereby whole cities have escap'd the plague,
And thousand desp'rate maladies been eas'd ?
Yet art thou still but Faustus and a man.
Wouldst thou make man [22] to live eternally,
Or, being dead, raise them to life again ?
Then this profession were to be esteem'd.
Physic, farewell. Where is Justinian ?
                   [*Reads.*]
*Si una eademque res legatur duobus,
Alter rem, alter valorem rei, &c.*[23]
A pretty [24] case of paltry legacies ! [*Reads.*]   30
Exhæreditare filium non potest pater nisi. . . .[25]

[14] Wittenberg. Faustus is "discovered" on the inner stage.
[15] Taken a degree.
[16] Aim.
[17] Aristotelian logic.
[18] Aristotle's "being and not being"; emend. Bullen ; Q₁ *Oncaymaeon ;* later eds. *Oeconomy.*
[19] Where the philosopher leaves off, there the physician begins. (Adapted from Aristotle, as is l. 16.)
[20] Medical memoranda, so called from the Aphorisms of Hippocrates. (Ward.)
[21] Prescriptions. (Wheeler.)
[22] Qq₁,₂ ; later eds. *men.*
[23] If one and the same thing is bequeathed to two persons, one shall take the thing and the other its value. (An incorrect version of a rule in the *Institutes.*) (Boas.)
[24] Q 1616 *petty.*
[25] A father cannot disinherit his son, except . . . (Adapted from the *Institutes* of Justinian, codifier of the Roman law.)

Such is the subject of the Institute
And universal body of the [law].[26]
His [27] study fits a mercenary drudge,
Who aims at nothing but external trash ; [28]
[Too servile] [29] and illiberal for me.
When all is done, divinity is best ;
Jerome's Bible,[30] Faustus, view it well.
                   [*Reads.*]
Stipendium peccati mors est. Ha ! *Stipendium,
    &c. :*
The reward of sin is death. — That 's hard.   40
                   [*Reads.*]
*Si peccasse negamus, fallimur, et nulla est in
    nobis veritas :*
If we say that we have no sin we deceive ourselves, and there 's no truth in us. — Why then,
belike we must sin and so consequently die.
Ay, we must die an everlasting death.
What doctrine call you this, *Che sera, sera :*
" What will be shall be ? " — Divinity, adieu !
These metaphysics of magicians
And necromantic books are heavenly ;
Lines, circles, scenes,[31] letters, and characters,
Ay, these are those that Faustus most desires.
O what a world of profit and delight,   52
Of power, of honor, of omnipotence
Is promis'd to the studious artisan !
All things that move between the quiet [32] poles
Shall be at my command. Emperors and kings
Are but obey'd in their several provinces,
Nor can they raise the wind or rend the clouds ;
But his dominion that exceeds [33] in this
Stretcheth as far as doth the mind of man.   60
A sound magician is a mighty god :
Here, Faustus, try thy [34] brains to gain [35] a
    deity.

Enter WAGNER.

Wagner ! commend me to my dearest friends,
The German Valdes and Cornelius ; [36]
Request them earnestly to visit me.
WAG. I will, sir.   *Exit.*

[26] Q 1616 ; earlier eds. *Church.*
[27] Its.
[28] *I.e.,* money.
[29] Q 1616 ; earlier eds. *The deuill.*
[30] The Vulgate.
[31] Logeman conj. *schemes.*
[32] *I.e.,* fixed.
[33] Excels.
[34] Q 1616 *tire my.*
[35] Q 1616 *get.*
[36] Marlowe takes this name from Henry Cornelius Agrippa von Nettesheim, a friend of Faustus and a magician ; but this character is not Agrippa (see ll. 116, 117). Brooke suggests that " the German Valdes " is a complimentary title for a mythical character, in allusion to the sixteenth-century Spanish humanist, Juan de Valdes.

FAUST. Their conference [37] will be a greater help to me
Than all my labors, plod I ne'er so fast.

Enter the Good Angel *and the* Evil Angel.

G. ANG. O Faustus, lay that damned book aside,
And gaze not on it lest it tempt thy soul   70
And heap God's heavy wrath upon thy head.
Read, read the Scriptures; that is blasphemy.
E. ANG. Go forward, Faustus, in that famous art,
Wherein all Nature's treasury is contain'd;
Be thou on earth as Jove is in the sky,
Lord and commander of these elements.
                              Exeunt [Angels.]
FAUST. How am I glutted with conceit of this! [38]
Shall I make spirits fetch me what I please,
Resolve me of all ambiguities,
Perform what desperate enterprise I will?   80
I'll have them fly to India [39] for gold,
Ransack the ocean for orient [40] pearl,
And search all corners of the new-found world
For pleasant fruits and princely delicates.
I'll have them read me strange philosophy
And tell the secrets of all foreign kings;
I'll have them wall all Germany with brass,
And make swift Rhine circle fair [Wittenberg]; [41]
I'll have them fill the public schools [42] with [silk], [43]
Wherewith the students shall be bravely clad;
I'll levy soldiers with the coin they bring,   91
And chase the Prince of Parma [44] from our land,
And reign sole king of all our provinces;
Yea, stranger engines for the brunt of war
Than was the fiery keel [45] at Antwerp's bridge,
I'll make my servile spirits to invent.
Come, German Valdes and Cornelius,
And make me blest with your sage conference.

Enter VALDES *and* CORNELIUS.

Valdes, sweet Valdes, and Cornelius,
Know that your words have won me at the last   100
To practise magic and concealed arts;
Yet not your words only, but mine own fantasy,
That will receive no object; [46] for my head
But ruminates on necromantic skill.
Philosophy is odious and obscure;
Both law and physic are for petty wits;
Divinity is basest of the three,
Unpleasant, harsh, contemptible, and vild; [47]
'T is magic, magic, that hath ravish'd me.
Then, gentle friends, aid me in this attempt;
And I that have with concise syllogisms   111
Gravell'd the pastors of the German church,
And made the flow'ring pride of Wittenberg
Swarm to my problems, [48] as the infernal spirits
On sweet Musæus, when he came to hell,
Will be as cunning as Agrippa was,
Whose shadows [49] made all Europe honor him.
VALD. Faustus, these books, thy wit, and our experience
Shall make all nations to canonize us.
As Indian Moors [50] obey their Spanish lords,
So shall the subjects [51] of every element   121
Be always serviceable to us three;
Like lions shall they guard us when we please;
Like Almain rutters [52] with their horsemen's staves,
Or Lapland giants, trotting by our sides;
Sometimes like women or unwedded maids,
Shadowing [53] more beauty in their airy [54] brows
Than in [the] [55] white breasts of the Queen of Love:
[From] [56] Venice shall they drag huge argosies, [57]
And from America the golden fleece   130

[37] Conversation.
[38] How am I filled with this notion.
[39] Probably, the West Indies, America.
[40] Lustrous.
[41] For the *Wittenberge* of Q 1616, Q₁ has *Wertenberge*. Brooke suggests that Marlowe thought of the university town as the capital of Würtemberg.
[42] University lecture-halls.
[43] Emend. Dyce; old eds. *skill*. Brooke cites Cambridge regulations which forbade the wearing of silk by the students.
[44] The Spanish governor-general (1579–1592) of the Netherlands, nominally a part of the Empire.
[45] A Dutch "devil-ship" (filled with explosives) which damaged Parma's bridge at the siege of Antwerp.

[46] *I.e.*, my own fancy, which will entertain no regular academic subject — nor anything else but necromancy. Brooke differs from mod. eds., who insert the semicolon and omit the old texts' comma after "head"; but the antithesis is between "words" and "fantasy."
[47] Vile.
[48] Mathematical and logical lectures. (Ward.)
[49] Shades raised from the dead.
[50] American Indians.
[51] Q 1616 *spirits*.
[52] German troopers.
[53] Shadowing forth, portraying.
[54] Because insubstantial.
[55] Q 1616; Q₁ *their*. Q 1616 reads *has* for *in*.
[56] Cor. Q 1609; Q₁ *For*.
[57] Large merchantmen.

That yearly stuffs [58] old Philip's treasury ;
If learned Faustus will be resolute.
  FAUST. Valdes, as resolute am I in this
As thou to live ; therefore object it not.
  CORN. The miracles that magic will per-
    form
Will make thee vow to study nothing else.
He that is grounded in astrology,
Enrich'd with tongues, well seen [59] [in] [60] min-
    erals,
Hath all the principles magic doth require.
Then doubt not, Faustus, but to be renowm'd,
And more frequented for this mystery   141
Than heretofore the Delphian oracle.
The spirits tell me they can dry the sea
And fetch the treasure of all foreign wracks,
Ay, all the wealth that our forefathers hid
Within the massy entrails of the earth ;
Then tell me, Faustus, what shall we three
    want ?
  FAUST. Nothing, Cornelius. O, this cheers
    my soul !
Come, show me some demonstrations magical,
That I may conjure in some lusty [61] grove,
And have these joys in full possession.   151
  VALD. Then haste thee to some solitary
    grove,
And bear wise Bacon's [62] and Albanus' [63]
    works,
The Hebrew Psalter and New Testament ;
And whatsoever else is requisite
We will inform thee ere our conference
    cease.
  CORN. Valdes, first let him know the words
    of art ;
And then, all other ceremonies learn'd,
Faustus may try his cunning by himself.
  VALD. First I'll instruct thee in the rudi-
    ments,   160
And then wilt thou be perfecter than I.
  FAUST. Then come and dine with me, and
    after meat
We'll canvass every quiddity [64] thereof ;
For ere I sleep I'll try what I can do :
This night I'll conjure though I die therefore.
                         Exeunt.

[58] Q 1616 *stuff'd*, altered after the death of
Philip II. Note inconsistency with the appearance
of Charles V in this play.
  [59] Versed.
  [60] Add. Q 2.
  [61] Pleasant. Qq 2, 3, *little* ; Q 1616 *bushy.*
  [62] Roger Bacon's.
  [63] Possibly Pietro d'Albano, a thirteenth-century
alchemist ; or, misprinted, Albertus Magnus, the
German Dominican of the same century, supposed
to be a magician.
  [64] Essential point.

[SCENE II] [65]

Enter two Scholars.

  1 SCHOL. I wonder what's become of Faustus, that was wont to make our schools ring
with *sic probo ?* [66]
  2 SCHOL. That shall we know, for see here
comes his boy.

Enter WAGNER.

  1 SCHOL. How now, sirrah ! Where's thy
master?
  WAG. God in Heaven knows.
  2 SCHOL. Why, dost not thou know?
  WAG. Yes, I know ; but that follows not. 10
  1 SCHOL. Go to, sirrah ; leave your jesting, and tell us where he is.
  WAG. That follows not necessary by force
of argument, that you, being licentiate, [67]
should stand upon 't ; therefore acknowledge
your error and be attentive.
  2 SCHOL. Why, didst thou not say thou
knew'st?
  WAG. Have you any witness on 't ?
  1 SCHOL. Yes, sirrah, I heard you.   20
  WAG. Ask my fellow if I be a thief.
  2 SCHOL. Well, you will not tell us?
  WAG. Yes, sir, I will tell you ; yet if you
were not dunces, you would never ask me such
a question ; for is not he *corpus naturale ?* [68]
and is not that *mobile ?* Then wherefore
should you ask me such a question? But that
I am by nature phlegmatic, slow to wrath, and
prone to lechery — to love, I would say, — it
were not for you to come within forty foot [30
of the place of execution, [69] although I do not
doubt to see you both hang'd the next sessions.
Thus having triumph'd over you, I will set my
countenance like a precisian, [70] and begin to
speak thus : — Truly, my dear brethren, my
master is within at dinner, with Valdes and
Cornelius, as this wine, if it could speak, it
would inform your Worships ; and so the Lord
bless you, preserve you, and keep you, my dear
brethren, my dear brethren.   *Exit.* 40
  1 SCHOL. Nay, then, I fear he has fall'n into

  [65] Before Faustus's house.
  [66] Thus I prove (a scholastic formula).
  [67] Licensed to ascend to a Master's or Doctor's
degree. (Boas.)
  [68] "'Corpus naturale seu mobile' is the current
scholastic expression for the subject-matter of
physics." (Ward.)
  [69] *I.e.*, the dining-room. (Wagner.)
  [70] Puritan.

that damned art, for which they two are infamous through the world.

2 SCHOL. Were he a stranger, and not allied
to me, yet should I grieve for him. But come,
let us go and inform the Rector,[71] and see if
he by his grave counsel can reclaim him.

1 SCHOL. O, but I fear me nothing can reclaim him.

2 SCHOL. Yet let us try what we can do. 50

Exeunt.

[SCENE III] [72]

Enter FAUSTUS *to conjure.*

FAUST. Now that the gloomy shadow of the
earth,[73]
Longing to view Orion's drizzling look,
Leaps from th' antar[c]tic world unto the
sky
And dims the welkin with her pitchy breath,
Faustus, begin thine incantations,
And try if devils will obey thy hest,
Seeing thou hast pray'd and sacrific'd to
them.
Within this circle is Jehovah's name,
Forward and backward anagrammatiz'd,
The breviated names of holy saints,   10
Figures of every adjunct to [74] the Heavens,
And characters of signs and erring stars,[75]
By which the spirits are enforc'd to rise.
Then fear not, Faustus, but be resolute,
And try the uttermost magic can perform.
*Sint mihi Dei Acherontis propitii! Valeat
numen triplex Iehovae! Ignei, aerii, aquatani* [76]
*spiritus, salvete! Orientis Princeps Belzebub,
inferni ardentis monarcha, et Demogorgon, pro-
pitiamus vos, ut appareat et surgat Mephis-* [20
tophilis. [Quid tu moraris?] [77] *Per Iehovam,
Gehennam, et consecratam aquam quam nunc
spargo, signumque crucis quod nunc facio, et per*

vota nostra, ipse nunc surgat nobis dicatus [78]
Mephistophilis! [79]

Enter [MEPHISTOPHILIS,] [80] *a* Devil.

I charge thee to return and change thy shape;
Thou art too ugly to attend on me.
Go, and return an old Franciscan friar;
That holy shape becomes a devil best.

Exit Devil.

I see there's virtue in my heavenly words;
Who would not be proficient in this art? 31
How pliant is this Mephistophilis,
Full of obedience and humility!
Such is the force of magic and my spells.
[Now,] [81] Faustus, thou art conjuror laureate;
Thou canst command great Mephistophilis: ·
Quin regis Mephistophilis fratris imagine. [82]

Re-enter MEPHISTOPHILIS [*like a Franciscan
Friar*].

MEPH. Now, Faustus, what wouldst thou
have me do?

FAUST. I charge thee wait upon me whilst I
live,
To do whatever Faustus shall command, 40
Be it to make the moon drop from her sphere
Or the ocean to overwhelm the world.

MEPH. I am a servant to great Lucifer,
And may not follow thee without his leave;
No more than he commands must we perform.

FAUST. Did he not charge thee to appear to
me?

MEPH. No, I came now hither of mine own
accord.

FAUST. Did not my conjuring speeches
raise thee? Speak!

MEPH. That was the cause, but yet per accident;

For when we hear one rack [83] the name of
God, 50

[71] The head of the university.
[72] A grove.
[73] Q 1616 *night.* But, as Brooke notes, Orion is a
winter constellation (hence " drizzling "), and when
it is visible the sun is below the equator; thus the
earth's shadow " can be said to be projected from
the southern hemisphere . . . unto the sky."
[74] Every star joined to.
[75] Planets.
[76] So old eds. Emend. Brooke *aquatici.*
[77] Conj. Schröer; old eds. *quod tumeraris.* For
Mephastophilis of the earlier eds., Qq 1616 *et seq.*
have *Mephostophilis Dragon.* Boas conj. *Enter
Dragon above.* This is unlikely, but there may have
been a note anticipatory of some feature of the entrance of " a Devil " immediately after this speech.
The whole question is discussed by Root, *Englische
Studien,* XLIII, 144–149.
[78] Cor. Q 1620; earlier eds. *dicatis.*
[79] Unto me be the gods of Acheron propitious.
May the triple name of Jehovah prevail. Spirits
of fire, air, and water, hail! Belzebub, Prince of
the East, Sovereign of burning Hell, and Demogorgon, we propitiate you, that Mephistophilis may
appear and rise. Why delayest thou? By Jehovah, Gehenna, and the holy water which now I
sprinkle, and the sign of the cross which now I make,
and by our prayer, may Mephistophilis, by us
summoned, now arise.
[80] But not the actor who played Mephistophilis.
Cf. on l. 21. In the Faust Book " a mighty Dragon "
appears at this point.
[81] Emend. Albers; old eds. *No.*
[82] Indeed thou rulest Mephistophilis in his likeness of a friar. (Boas, who adopts, however, Taylor's
emendation, *redis* for *regis.*)
[83] Torture into anagrams.

Abjure the Scriptures and his Savior Christ,
We fly, in hope to get his glorious soul ;
Nor will we come, unless he use such means
Whereby he is in danger to be damn'd.
Therefore the shortest cut for conjuring
Is stoutly to abjure the Trinity,
And pray devoutly to the Prince of Hell.
    FAUST. So Faustus hath
Already done, and holds this principle :
There is no chief but only Belzebub,   60
To whom Faustus doth dedicate himself.
This word " damnation " terrifies not him,
For he confounds hell in [84] Elysium ;
His ghost be with the old philosophers !
But, leaving these vain trifles of men's souls,
Tell me what is that Lucifer, thy lord?
    MEPH. Arch-regent and commander of all
        spirits.
    FAUST. Was not that Lucifer an angel once?
    MEPH. Yes, Faustus, and most dearly lov'd
        of God.
    FAUST. How comes it then that he is prince
        of devils?   70
    MEPH. Oh, by aspiring pride and insolence,
For which God threw him from the face of
        Heaven.
    FAUST. And what are you that live with
        Lucifer?
    MEPH. Unhappy spirits that fell with Lu-
        cifer,
Conspir'd against our God with Lucifer,
And are for ever damn'd with Lucifer.
    FAUST. Where are you damn'd?
    MEPH. In hell.
    FAUST. How comes it then that thou art
        out of hell?   79
    MEPH. Why this is hell, nor am I out of it !
Think'st thou that I, who saw the face of God,
And tasted the eternal joys of Heaven,
Am not tormented with ten thousand hells
In being depriv'd of everlasting bliss?
O Faustus, leave these frivolous demands,
Which strike a terror to my fainting soul.
    FAUST. What, is great Mephistophilis so
        passionate [85]
For being depriv'd of the joys of Heaven?
Learn thou of Faustus manly fortitude,
And scorn those joys thou never shalt possess.
Go bear [these] [86] tidings to great Lucifer :   91
Seeing Faustus hath incurr'd eternal death
By desp'rate thoughts against Jove's [87] deity,

Say he surrenders up to him his soul,
So [88] he will spare him four-and-twenty years,
Letting him live in all voluptuousness,
Having thee ever to attend on me,
To give me whatsoever I shall ask,
To tell me whatsoever I demand,
To slay mine enemies, and aid my friends,   100
And always be obedient to my will.
Go, and return to mighty Lucifer,
And meet me in my study at midnight,
And then resolve [89] me of thy master's mind.
    MEPH. I will, Faustus.   *Exit.*
    FAUST. Had I as many souls as there be
        stars,
I'd give them all for Mephistophilis.
By him I'll be great emp'ror of the world,
And make a bridge through [90] the moving air,
To pass the ocean with a band of men ;   110
I'll join the hills that bind the Afric shore,
And make that [country] [91] continent to [92] Spain,
And both contributory to my crown.
The Emperor shall not live but by my leave,
Nor any potentate of Germany.
Now that I have obtain'd what I desire,
I'll live in speculation [93] of this art
Till Mephistophilis return again.   *Exit.*

[SCENE IV] [94]

Enter WAGNER *and the* Clown.

    WAG. Sirrah boy, come hither.
    CLOWN. How, " boy " ! Swowns,[95] " boy " !
I hope you have seen many boys with such
pickadevaunts [96] as I have. " Boy," quotha !
    WAG. Tell me, sirrah, hast thou any com-
ings in?
    CLOWN. Ay, and goings out too. You
may see else.
    WAG. Alas, poor slave ! See how poverty
jesteth in his nakedness ! The villain is [10
bare and out of service, and so hungry that I
know he would give his soul to the Devil for a
shoulder of mutton, though it were blood-raw.
    CLOWN. How? My soul to the Devil for a
shoulder of mutton, though 't were blood-raw !
Not so, good friend. By 'r Lady, I had need

[84] Makes no distinction between hell and.
[85] Emotionally disturbed, grieved.
[86] Cor. Q 1616 ; earlier eds. *those.*
[87] Common in Elizabethan literature for the
Christian God.
[88] Provided that.
[89] Inform.
[90] Dissyllabic.
[91] Q 1616 ; earlier eds. *land.*
[92] Adjoining.
[93] Contemplative study.
[94] Unlocated ; perhaps a field or wood near Wittenberg.
[95] Zounds, God's wounds.
[96] Pointed beards.

have it well roasted and good sauce to it, if I pay so dear.

WAG. Well, wilt thou serve me, and I 'll make thee go like *Qui mihi discipulus?* [97] 20

CLOWN. How, in verse?

WAG. No, sirrah; in beaten silk [98] and stavesacre. [99]

CLOWN. How, how, Knave's acre! [100] Ay, I thought that was all the land his father left him. Do ye hear? I would be sorry to rob you of your living.

WAG. Sirrah, I say in stavesacre.

CLOWN. Oho! Oho! Stavesacre! Why, then, belike, if I were your man I should be full of vermin. 31

WAG. So thou shalt, whether thou beest with me or no. But, sirrah, leave your jesting, and bind yourself presently unto me for seven years, or I 'll turn all the lice about thee into familiars, and they shall tear thee in pieces.

CLOWN. Do you hear, sir? You may save that labor; they are too familiar with me already. Swowns! they are as bold with my flesh as if they had paid for my meat and [40 drink.

WAG. Well, do you hear, sirrah? Hold, take these guilders.

CLOWN. Gridirons! what be they?

WAG. Why, French crowns.

CLOWN. Mass, but for the name of French crowns, a man were as good have as many English counters. And what should I do with these?

WAG. Why, now, sirrah, thou art at an [50 hour's warning, whensoever or wheresoever the Devil shall fetch thee.

CLOWN. No, no. Here, take your gridirons again.

WAG. Truly, I 'll none of them.

CLOWN. Truly, but you shall.

WAG.[101] Bear witness I gave them him.

CLOWN. Bear witness I give them you again.

WAG. Well, I will cause two devils presently to fetch thee away — Baliol [102] and Belcher. 61

CLOWN. Let your Baliol and your Belcher come here, and I 'll knock them, they were never so knock'd since they were devils. Say I should kill one of them, what would folks

say? " Do ye see yonder tall [103] fellow in the round slop? [104] — he has kill'd the Devil." So I should be call'd Kill-devil all the parish over.

WAG. Baliol and Belcher! (*Enter two* Devils *and the* Clown *runs up and down crying.*) Spirits, away! *Exeunt* [Devils]. [70

CLOWN. What, are they gone? A vengeance on them; they have vild long nails! There was a he-devil, and a she-devil; I 'll tell you how you shall know them: all he-devils has horns, and all she-devils has clifts and cloven feet.

WAG. Well, sirrah, follow me.

CLOWN. But, do you hear — if I should serve you, would you teach me to raise up Banios and Belcheos? 80

WAG. I will teach thee to turn thyself to anything; to a dog, or a cat, or a mouse, or a rat, or anything.

CLOWN. How? a Christian fellow to a dog or a cat, a mouse, or a rat? No, no, sir; if you turn me into anything, let it be in the likeness of a little pretty frisking flea, that I may be here and there and everywhere. O, I 'll tickle the pretty wenches' plackets [105]; I 'll be amongst them, i' faith. 90

WAG. Well, sirrah, come.

CLOWN. But, do you hear, Wagner?

WAG. How! — Baliol and Belcher!

CLOWN. O Lord! I pray, sir, let Banio and Belcher go sleep.

WAG. Villain, call me Master Wagner, and let thy left eye be diametarily fix'd upon my right heel, with *quasi vestigias nostras insistere.*[106] *Exit.*

CLOWN. God forgive me, he speaks [100 Dutch fustian! [107] Well, I 'll follow him; I 'll serve him; that's flat. *Exit.*

[ACT II — SCENE I]

Enter FAUSTUS *in his study.*

FAUST. Now, Faustus, must
Thou needs be damn'd,[1] and canst thou not be
    saved!
What boots it then to think of God or Heaven?
Away with such vain fancies, and despair
Despair in God, and trust in Belzebub.

---

[97] The first words of W. Lily's *Ad discipulos carmen de moribus.* (Dyce.)
[98] Silk with metal embroidery hammered into it.
[99] A kind of larkspur, used to kill lice.
[100] Poultney Street, Soho, where junk-dealers were established.
[101] To the audience.
[102] Belial.

[103] Valiant.
[104] Loose breeches.
[105] Slits in skirts and petticoats.
[106] As if to tread my tracks.
[107] Highfalutin.
[1] Dyce's line division; in old eds. l. 1 ends here.

Now go not backward; no, Faustus, be resolute.
Why waverest thou?   O, something soundeth
    in mine ears,
" Abjure this magic ; turn to God again."
Ay, and Faustus will turn to God again.
To God? — He loves thee not ;   10
The God thou servest is thine own appetite,
Wherein is fix'd the love of Belzebub ;
To him I 'll build an altar and a church,
And offer lukewarm blood of newborn babes.

    Enter Good Angel *and* Evil [Angel].

  G. Ang. Sweet Faustus, leave that execrable
    art.
  [E. Ang. Go forward, Faustus, in that fa-
    mous art.[2]]
  Faust. Contrition,   prayer,   repentance !
    What of them?
  G. Ang. O, they are means to bring thee
    unto Heaven.
  E. Ang. Rather illusions, fruits of lunacy,
That makes men foolish that do trust them
    most.   20
  G. Ang. Sweet Faustus, think of Heaven,
    and heavenly things.
  E. Ang. No, Faustus, think of honor and[3]
    wealth.   *Exeunt* [Angels].
  Faust.   Of wealth !
Why, the signiory of Emden[4] shall be mine.
When Mephistophilis shall stand by me,
What God can hurt thee, Faustus?   Thou art
    safe ;
Cast[5] no more doubts. Come, Mephistoph-
    ilis,
And bring glad tidings from great Lucifer ! —
Is 't not midnight? — Come, Mephistophilis :
Veni, veni, Mephistophile!

    Enter Mephistophilis.

Now tell [me],[6] what says Lucifer, thy lord? 30
  Meph. That I shall wait on Faustus while
    [he lives],[7]
So[8] he will buy my service with his soul.
  Faust. Already Faustus hath hazarded
    that for thee.
  Meph. But, Faustus, thou must bequeath
    it solemnly
And write a deed of gift with thine own blood,
For that security craves great Lucifer.
If thou deny it, I will back to hell.

  [2] Add. Q 1616, before l. 15.
  [3] Q₂ adds *of.*
  [4] Then a great port.
  [5] Reckon up.
  [6] Add. Q 1616.
  [7] Q 1616 ; earlier eds. *I liue.*
  [8] Provided that.

  Faust. Stay, Mephistophilis ! and tell me
    what good
Will my soul do thy lord.
  Meph.   Enlarge his kingdom.
  Faust. Is that the reason [why][9] he tempts
    us thus?   40
  Meph. *Solamen miseris socios habuisse dolo-
    ris.*[10]
  Faust. [Why],[11] have you any pain, that
    tortures others?
  Meph. As great as have the human souls of
    men.
But tell me, Faustus, shall I have thy soul?
And I will be thy slave, and wait on thee,
And give thee more than thou hast wit to ask.
  Faust. Ay, Mephistophilis, I give it thee.
  Meph. Then, [Faustus],[12] stab thine arm
    courageously,
And bind thy soul that at some certain day
Great Lucifer may claim it as his own ;   50
And then be thou as great as Lucifer.
  Faust. Lo, Mephistophilis, for love of thee
I cut mine arm, and with my proper blood
Assure my soul to be great Lucifer's,
Chief lord and regent of perpetual night.
View here the blood that trickles from mine
    arm,
And let it be propitious for my wish.
  Meph. But, Faustus, thou must
Write it in manner of a deed of gift.
  Faust. Ay, so I will. [*Writes.*] But, Meph-
    istophilis,   60
My blood congeals, and I can write no more.
  Meph. I 'll fetch thee fire to dissolve it
    straight.   *Exit.*
  Faust. What might the staying of my
    blood portend?
Is it unwilling I should write this bill?
Why streams it not that I may write afresh?
" Faustus gives to thee his soul." Ah, there it
    stay'd.
Why shouldst thou not? Is not thy soul
    thine own?
Then write again, " Faustus gives to thee his
    soul."

    Re-enter Mephistophilis *with a chafer of coals.*

  Meph. Here 's fire. Come, Faustus, set
    it[13] on.
  Faust. So ; now the blood begins to clear
    again ;   70

  [9] Add. Q 1616.
  [10] *I.e.,* misery loves company.
  [11] Add. Q 1616.
  [12] Add. Q 1616.
  [13] The dish of blood.

Now will I make an end immediately. [*Writes.*]

MEPH. [*aside*] O, what will no**t** I do to obtain his soul?

FAUST. *Consummatum est:* this bill is ended,
And Faustus hath bequeath'd his soul to Lucifer.
But what is this inscription on mine arm?
Homo, fuge! Whither should I fly?
If unto God, he 'll throw thee down to hell.
My senses are deceiv'd; here 's nothing writ! —
I see it plain; here in this place is writ
Homo, fuge! Yet shall not Faustus fly.   80

MEPH. [*aside*] I 'll fetch him somewhat to delight his mind.   *Exit.*

Re-enter [MEPHISTOPHILIS] *with* Devils, *giving crowns and rich apparel to* FAUSTUS, *and dance, and then depart.*

FAUST. Speak, Mephistophilis; what means this show?

MEPH. Nothing, Faustus, but to delight thy mind withal,
And to show thee what magic can perform.

FAUST. But may I raise up spirits when I please?

MEPH. Ay, Faustus, and do greater things than these.

FAUST. Then there 's enough for a thousand souls.
Here, Mephistophilis, receive this scroll,
A deed of gift of body and of soul;
But yet conditionally that thou perform   90
All articles prescrib'd between us both.

MEPH. Faustus, I swear by hell and Lucifer
To effect all promises between us made.

FAUST. Then hear me read them: " On these conditions following. First, that Faustus may be a spirit in form and substance. Secondly, that Mephistophilis shall be his servant, and at his command. Thirdly, that Mephistophilis shall do for him and bring him whatsoever. Fourthly, that he shall be in [100 his chamber or house invisible. Lastly, that he shall appear to the said John Faustus, at all times, in what form or shape soever he please. I, John Faustus, of Wittenberg, Doctor, by these presents do give both body and soul to Lucifer, Prince of the East, and his minister, Mephistophilis; and furthermore grant unto them, that four-and-twenty years being expired, the articles above written inviolate, full power to fetch or carry the said John [110 Faustus, body and soul, flesh, blood, or goods,
into their habitation wheresoever. By me, John Faustus."

MEPH. Speak, Faustus: do you deliver this as your deed?

FAUST. Ay, take it, and the Devil give thee good on 't.

MEPH. Now, Faustus, ask what thou wilt.

FAUST. First will I question with thee about hell.
Tell me, where is the place that men call hell?

MEPH. Under the Heavens.

FAUST. Ay, [so are all things else ;] [14] but whereabout?   120

MEPH. Within the bowels of these elements,
Where we are tortur'd and remain for ever;
Hell has no limits, nor is circumscrib'd
In one self place; for where we are is hell,
And where hell is [there] [14] must we ever be;
And, to conclude, when all the world dissolves,
And every creature shall be purified,
All places shall be hell that is not Heaven.

FAUST. Come, I think hell 's a fable.

MEPH. Ay, think so still, till experience change thy mind.   130

FAUST. Why, think'st thou then that Faustus shall be damn'd?

MEPH. Ay, of necessity; for here 's the scroll Wherein thou hast given thy soul to Lucifer.

FAUST. Ay, and body too; but what of that?
Think'st thou that Faustus is so fond [15] to imagine
That after this life there is any pain?
Tush! these are trifles, and mere old wives' tales!

MEPH. But, Faustus, I am an instance to prove the contrary,
For I am damn'd, and am now in hell.

FAUST. How! now in hell!   140
Nay, an this be hell, I 'll willingly be damn'd here;
What, [16] walking, disputing, etc?
But, leaving off this, let me have a wife,
The fairest maid in Germany;
For I am wanton and lascivious,
And cannot live without a wife.

MEPH. How! a wife?
I prithee, Faustus, talk not of a wife.

FAUST. Nay, sweet Mephistophilis, fetch me one, for I will have one.

MEPH. Well, thou wilt have one. Sit there till I come;   150
I 'll fetch thee a wife in the Devil's name.
[*Exit.*]

[14] Add. Q 1616.   [15] Foolish.
[16] Q 1616 adds *sleeping, eating.*

Re-enter [MEPHISTOPHILIS] *with a* Devil *dress'd*
like a woman, with fireworks.

MEPH. Tell, Faustus, how dost thou like
thy wife?

FAUST. A plague on her for a hot whore !

MEPH. Tut, Faustus,
Marriage is but a ceremonial toy ;
If thou lovest me, think [no] [17] more of it.
I 'll cull thee out the fairest courtesans
And bring them ev'ry morning to thy bed ;
She whom thine eye shall like, thy heart shall
have,
Be she as chaste as was Penelope,   160
As wise as Saba,[18] or as beautiful
As was bright Lucifer before his fall.
Hold, take this book ; peruse it thoroughly :
The iterating of these lines brings gold ;
The framing of this circle on the ground
Brings whirlwinds, tempests, thunder and
lightning ;
Pronounce this thrice devoutly to thyself,
And men in armor shall appear to thee,
Ready to execute what thou desir'st.

FAUST. Thanks, Mephistophilis ; yet [170
fain would I have a book wherein I might behold all spells and incantations, that I might
raise up spirits when I please.

MEPH. Here they are, in this book.
                    There turn to them.

FAUST. Now would I have a book where I
might see all characters and planets of the
Heavens, that I might know their motions and
dispositions.

MEPH. Here they are too.   *Turn to them.*

FAUST. Nay, let me have one book [180
more — and then I have done — wherein I
might see all plants, herbs, and trees that grow
upon the earth.

MEPH. Here they be.

FAUST. O, thou art deceived.

MEPH. Tut, I warrant thee.   *Turn to them.*
                    [*Exeunt.*]

[SCENE II] [19]

[*Enter* FAUSTUS *in his study, and* MEPHIS-
TOPHILIS.] [20]

FAUST. When I behold the Heavens, then I
repent,

17 Add. Q2.   18 The Queen of Sheba.
19 The same.
20 Add. Q 1616, which prefaces the entrance with
a short version of Wagner's speech at the opening of
Act III. Q1 has no break. Evidently the end of Sc. i
was tampered with before 1604 ; it may originally
have been followed by a comic scene.

And curse thee, wicked Mephistophilis,
Because thou hast depriv'd me of those joys.

MEPH. Why, Faustus,
Think'st thou Heaven is such a glorious thing ?
I tell thee 't is not half so fair as thou,
Or any man that breathes on earth.

FAUST. How provest thou that ?

MEPH. It was made for man ;   therefore is
man more excellent.

FAUST. If it were made for man, 't was
made for me !   10
I will renounce this magic and repent.

Enter Good Angel *and* Evil Angel.

G. ANG. Faustus, repent ; yet God will pity
thee.

E. ANG. Thou art a spirit ; God cannot pity
thee.

FAUST. Who buzzeth in mine ears I am a
spirit ?
Be I a devil, yet God may pity me ;
Ay, God will pity me if I repent.

E. ANG. Ay, but Faustus never shall repent.
                    Exeunt [Angels].

FAUST. My heart 's so hard'ned I cannot
repent.
Scarce can I name salvation, faith, or Heaven,
But fearful echoes thunder in mine ears   20
" Faustus, thou art damn'd ! "   Then swords
and knives,
Poison, guns, halters, and envenom'd steel
Are laid before me to despatch myself ;
And long ere this I should have slain myself,
Had not sweet pleasure conquer'd deep despair.
Have I not made blind Homer sing to me
Of Alexander's [21] love and Œnon's death ?
And hath not he that built the walls of Thebes
With ravishing sound of his melodious harp
Made music with my Mephistophilis ?   30
Why should I die then, or basely despair ?
I am resolv'd ; Faustus shall ne'er repent.
Come, Mephistophilis, let us dispute again,
And argue of divine astrology.
Tell me, are there many heavens above the
moon ?
Are all celestial bodies but one globe,
As is the substance of this centric earth ?

MEPH. As are the elements, such are the
spheres
Mutually folded in each other's orb,
And, Faustus,   40
All jointly move upon one axletree,
Whose terminine is term'd the world's wide
pole ;

21 Paris's.

Nor are the names of Saturn, Mars, or Jupiter
Feign'd, but are erring stars.

FAUST. But tell me, have they all one motion, both *situ et tempore?* [22]

MEPH. All jointly move from east to west in
four-and-twenty hours upon the poles of the
world, but differ in their motion upon the poles
of the zodiac.   50

FAUST. Tush! These slender trifles Wagner can decide.

Hath Mephistophilis no greater skill?

Who knows not the double motion of the
planets?

The first is finish'd in a natural day;

The second thus: as Saturn in thirty years;
Jupiter in twelve; Mars in four; the Sun,
Venus, and Mercury in a year; the moon in
twenty-eight days. Tush, these are fresh-
men's suppositions. But tell me, hath every
sphere a dominion or *intelligenti*[a]?   60

MEPH. Ay.

FAUST. How many heavens, or spheres, are
there?

MEPH. Nine: the seven planets, the firmament, and the empyreal heaven.

FAUST. Well, resolve me in this question:
Why have we not conjunctions, oppositions,
aspects, eclipses, all at one time, but in some
years we have more, in some less?

MEPH. *Per inæqualem motum respectu to-
tius.*[23]   70

FAUST. Well, I am answered. Tell me who
made the world.

MEPH. I will not.

FAUST. Sweet Mephistophilis, tell me.

MEPH. Move me not, for I will not tell
thee.

FAUST. Villain, have I not bound thee to
tell me anything?

MEPH. Ay, that is not against our kingdom; but this is.

Think thou on hell, Faustus, for thou art
damn'd.

FAUST. Think, Faustus, upon God that
made the world.

MEPH. Remember this.   *Exit.* 80

FAUST. Ay, go, accursed spirit, to ugly hell;
'T is thou hast damn'd distressed Faustus' soul.
Is 't not too late?

---

[22] In both the direction and the duration of their
revolutions.
[23] On account of their unequal motion in relation
to the whole. — After l. 65 Q 1616 adds:
   Faust. But is there not *Cœlum igneum, & Crista-
    linum?*
   Meph. No Faustus they be but Fables.

Re-enter Good Angel *and* Evil [Angel].

E. ANG.   Too late.

G. ANG. Never too late, if Faustus can
repent.

E. ANG. If thou repent, devils shall tear
thee in pieces.

G. ANG. Repent, and they shall never raze
thy skin.

                      Exeunt [Angels].

FAUST. Ah, Christ, my Savior,
Seek to save distressed Faustus' soul.

Enter LUCIFER, BELZEBUB, *and* MEPHIS-
TOPHILIS.

LUC. Christ cannot save thy soul, for he is
just;   90
There's none but I have int'rest in the same.

FAUST. O, who art thou that look'st so
terrible?

LUC. I am Lucifer,
And this is my companion prince in hell.

FAUST. O Faustus, they are come to fetch
away thy soul!

LUC. We come to tell thee thou dost injure
us;
Thou talk'st of Christ, contrary to thy prom-
ise;
Thou shouldst not think of God: think of the
Devil,
And of his dam, too.[24]

FAUST. Nor will I henceforth; pardon me
in this,   100
And Faustus vows never to look to Heaven,
Never to name God, or to pray to Him,
To burn his Scriptures, slay his ministers,
And make my spirits pull his churches down.

LUC. Do so, and we will highly gratify thee.
Faustus, we are come from hell to show thee
some pastime. Sit down, and thou shalt see
all the Seven Deadly Sins appear in their
proper shapes.

FAUST. That sight will be pleasing unto me
As Paradise was to Adam the first day   [111
Of his creation.

LUC. Talk not of Paradise nor creation, but
mark this show; talk of the Devil, and nothing
else. — Come away!

Enter the Seven Deadly Sins.

Now, Faustus, examine them of their several
names and dispositions.

FAUST. What art thou — the first?

PRIDE. I am Pride. I disdain to have any

---

[24] Evidently an actor's gag.

parents. I am like to Ovid's flea[25] : I can [120 creep into every corner of a wench ; sometimes, like a periwig, I sit upon her brow ; [26] or like a fan of feathers, I kiss her lips ; [27] indeed I do — what do I not? But, fie, what a scent is here ! I 'll not speak another word, except the ground were perfum'd, and covered with cloth of arras.

FAUST. What art thou — the second?

COVET. I am Covetousness, begotten of an old churl in an old leathern bag ; and might I have my wish, I would desire that this [130 house and all the people in it were turn'd to gold, that I might lock you up in my good chest. O, my sweet gold !

FAUST. What art thou — the third?

WRATH. I am Wrath. I had neither father nor mother : I leap'd out of a lion's mouth when I was scarce half an hour old ; and ever since I have run up and down the world with this case [28] of rapiers, wounding myself when I had nobody to fight withal. I was born in [140 hell ; and look to it, for some of you shall be [29] my father.

FAUST. What art thou — the fourth?

ENVY. I am Envy, begotten of a chimney sweeper and an oyster-wife. I cannot read, and therefore wish all books were burnt. I am lean with seeing others eat. O, that there would come a famine through all the world, that all might die, and I live alone ! Then thou shouldst see how fat I would be. But [150 must thou sit and I stand? Come down with a vengeance !

FAUST. Away, envious rascal ! — What art thou — the fifth?

GLUT. Who, I, sir? I am Gluttony. My parents are all dead, and the devil a penny they have left me, but a bare pension, and that is thirty meals a day and ten bevers [30] — a small trifle to suffice nature. O, I come of a royal parentage ! My grandfather was a [160 gammon of bacon, my grandmother a hogshead of claret wine ; my godfathers were these : Peter Pickleherring and Martin Martlemas-beef.[31] O, but my godmother, she

was a jolly gentlewoman, and well beloved in every good town and city ; her name was Mistress Margery March-beer. Now, Faustus, thou hast heard all my progeny,[32] wilt thou bid me to supper?

FAUST. No, I 'll see thee hanged ; thou [170 wilt eat up all my victuals.

GLUT. Then the Devil choke thee !

FAUST. Choke thyself, glutton ! — Who art thou — the sixth?

SLOTH. I am Sloth. I was begotten on a sunny bank, where I have lain ever since ; and you have done me great injury to bring me from thence. Let me be carried thither again by Gluttony and Lechery. I 'll not speak another word for a king's ransom.   180

FAUST. What are you, Mistress Minx, — the seventh and last?

LECH. Who, I, sir? I am one that loves an inch of raw mutton [33] better than an ell of fried stockfish ; [34] and the first letter of my name begins with Lechery.

LUC. Away ! to hell, to hell !
                            Exeunt the Sins.

— Now, Faustus, how dost thou like this?

FAUST. O, this feeds my soul !

LUC. Tut, Faustus, in hell is all manner of
     delight.   189

FAUST. O might I see hell, and return again,
How happy were I then !

LUC. Thou shalt ; I will send for thee at
     midnight.

In meantime take this book ; peruse it
     throughly,
And thou shalt turn thyself into what shape
     thou wilt.

FAUST. Great thanks, mighty Lucifer !
This will I keep as chary as my life.

LUC. Farewell, Faustus, and think on the
     Devil.

FAUST. Farewell, great Lucifer ! — Come,
     Mephistophilis.
                            Exeunt omnes.

[SCENE III] [35]

Enter ROBIN *the Ostler with a book in his hand.*

ROBIN. O, this is admirable ! Here I ha' stol'n one of Dr. Faustus' conjuring books,

---

[25] The *Carmen de Pulice*, probably of medieval origin, was attributed to Ovid. (Boas.)
[26] Q 1616 adds *next, like a Necke-lace I hang about her Necke.*
[27] In place of the next seven words Q 1616 reads *And then turning my selfe to a wrought Smocke do what I list.*
[28] Pair.
[29] One of you devils is doubtless.
[30] Between-meal refreshments.
[31] The feast of St. Martin (Nov. 11) "was the customary time for hanging up [salted] provisions." (Nares.)

[32] Lineage.
[33] Punning on "mutton" = wench, harlot.
[34] Salted or dried fish.
[35] An inn-yard. Q₁ places this scene, erroneously, after the chorus which opens Act IV, and immediately before the comic scene, III. ii. Q 1616

and i' faith I mean to search some circles [36] for my own use ! Now will I make all the maidens in our parish dance at my pleasure, stark naked before me ; and so by that means I shall see more than e'er I felt or saw yet.

Enter RALPH [37] *calling* ROBIN.

RALPH. Robin, prithee come away ; there's a gentleman tarries to have his horse, and he would have his things rubb'd and made [10 clean. He keeps such a chafing with my mistress about it ; and she has sent me to look thee out. Prithee come away.

ROBIN. Keep out, keep out, or else you are blown up, you are dismemb'red, Ralph ; keep out, for I am about a roaring piece of work.

RALPH. Come, what doest thou with that same book ? Thou canst not read.

ROBIN. Yes, my master and mistress shall find that I can read, he for his forehead,[38] she [20 for her private study ; she's born to bear with me, or else my art fails.

RALPH. Why, Robin, what book is that ?

ROBIN. What book ! Why, the most intolerable book for conjuring that e'er was invented by any brimstone devil.

RALPH. Canst thou conjure with it ?

ROBIN. I can do all these things easily with it : first, I can make thee drunk with ippocras [39] at any ta[v]ern in Europe for noth- [30 ing , that's one of my conjuring works.

RALPH. Our Master Parson says that's nothing.

ROBIN. True, Ralph ; and more, Ralph, if thou hast any mind to Nan Spit, our kitchenmaid, then turn her and wind her to thy own use, as often as thou wilt, and at midnight.

RALPH. O brave, Robin, shall I have Nan Spit, and to mine own use? On that condition I'll feed thy devil with horsebread as [40 long as he lives, of free cost.

ROBIN. No more, sweet Ralph ; let's go and make clean our boots, which lie foul upon our hands, and then to our conjuring in the Devil's name. *Exeunt.*

---

correctly places II, iii, though in an altered version ; Ralph becomes Dick, a hostler, and Robin seems to be the clown of I, iv. Brooke suggests that the appearance of II, iii, and III, iii, consecutively in Q₁ " is presumably due to the fact that they were not in the original MS, but formed a supplement on separate sheets.''

[36] Common with a double meaning in these plays.

[37] Old eds. *Rafe*, throughout.

[38] Innumerable jests in these plays allude to the horns which were supposed to grow in the brows of a deceived husband.

[39] A drink made of wine, sugared and spiced.

[ACT III]

Enter WAGNER, *solus* [*as* Chorus].[1]

WAGNER. Learned Faustus, to know the secrets of astronomy
Graven in the book of Jove's high firmament,
Did mount himself to scale Olympus' top,
Being seated in a chariot burning bright,
Drawn by the strength of yoky dragons' [2] necks.
[He views the clouds, the planets, and the stars,
The tropic zones, and quarters of the sky,
From the bright circle of the horned moon
Even to the height of *Primum Mobile ;* [3]
And, whirling round with this circumference,   11
Within the concave compass of the pole,
From east to west his dragons swiftly glide
And in eight days did bring him home again.
Not long he stayed within his quiet house,
To rest his bones after his weary toil ;
But new exploits do hale him out again,
And, mounted then upon a dragon's back,
That with his wings did part the subtle air,]
He now is gone to prove cosmography,
[That measures coasts and kingdoms of the earth :]   20
And, as I guess, will first arrive at Rome,
To see the Pope and manner of his court,
And take some part of holy Peter's feast,
That to this day is highly solemniz'd.

Exit WAGNER

[SCENE I] [4]

Enter FAUSTUS *and* MEPHISTOPHILIS.

FAUST. Having now, my good Mephistophilis,
Pass'd with delight the stately town of Trier,[5]
Environ'd round with airy mountain-tops,
With walls of flint, and deep entrenched lakes,
Not to be won by any conquering prince ;
From Paris next, coasting the realm of France,
We saw the river Maine fall into Rhine,

---

[1] In Q₁ this speech, assigned to Wagner, and cut for the stage, comes between II, ii, and III, i. In Q 1616 it appears, incorrectly, between II, i and ii, and again (assigned to Chorus) to open Act III, with the addition of the bracketed lines.

[2] Among properties for this play Henslowe lists a dragon. Wagner suggests that Faustus may have alighted from it at the opening of III, i. But see, also, on S. D. following I, iii, 25.

[3] "The axle of the heavens, that moveth the whole firmament." (English Faust Book.)

[4] Rome. The Pope's privy-chamber.

[5] Treves.

Whose banks are set with groves of fruitful
    vines ;
Then up to Naples, rich Campania,[6]
Whose buildings fair and gorgeous to the eye,
The streets straight forth, and pav'd with
    finest brick,   11
Quarters the town in four equivalents.
There saw we learned Maro's [7] golden tomb,
The way he cut, an English mile in length,
Thorough a rock of stone in one night's space ;
From thence to Venice, Padua, and the rest,
In midst of which a sumptuous temple stands ; [8]
That threats the stars with her aspiring top,
[Whose frame is paved with sundry-colored
    stones
And roof'd aloft with curious work in gold.]
Thus hitherto hath Faustus spent his time :   21
But tell me, now, what resting-place is this?
Hast thou, as erst I did command,
Conducted me within the walls of Rome?

    MEPH. [I have, my Faustus ; and, for
        proof thereof,
This is the goodly palace of the Pope ;
And 'cause we are no common guests,
I choose his privy-chamber for our use.] [9]

    FAUST. I hope his Holiness will bid us wel-
        come.

    MEPH. [All 's one, for we 'll be bold with his
        ven'son.]   30
And now, my Faustus, that thou mayst per-
    ceive
What Rome containeth to delight thee with,
Know that this city stands upon seven hills
That underprops the groundwork of the same.
[Just through the midst runs flowing Tiber's
    stream,
With winding banks that cut it in two parts,] [10]
Over the which four stately bridges lean,

That makes safe passage to each part of Rome.
Upon the bridge call'd Ponto Angelo
Erected is a castle passing strong,   40
Within whose walls such store of ordnance are,
And double cannons, fram'd of carved brass,
As match the days within one complete year ;
Besides the gates and high pyramides,
Which Julius Cæsar brought from Africa.

    FAUST. Now by the kingdoms of infernal
        rule,
Of Styx, Acheron, and the fiery lake
Of ever-burning Phlegethon, I swear
That I do long to see the monuments
And situation of bright-splendent Rome :   50
Come, therefore ; let 's away.

    MEPH. Nay, Faustus, stay ; I know you 'd
        fain see the Pope,
And take some part of holy Peter's feast,
[11] Where thou shalt see a troop of bald-pate
    friars,
Whose *summum bonum* is in belly-cheer.

    FAUST. Well, I am content to compass,
        then, some sport,
And by their folly make us merriment.
Then charm me, that I may be invisible, to
    do what I please,
Unseen of any whilst I stay in Rome.
                [MEPHISTOPHILIS *charms him.*]

    MEPH. So, Faustus ; now   60
Do what thou wilt, thou shalt not be discerned.

Sound a sennet.[12]   *Enter the* POPE *and the* CAR-
DINAL *of* LORRAINE *to the banquet, with* Friars
attending.

    POPE. My Lord of Lorraine, wilt please you
        draw near?

    FAUST. Fall to, and the Devil choke you
        an [13] you spare !

    POPE. How now ! Who 's that which
        spake? — Friars, look about.

    [1] FRIAR. Here 's nobody, if it like your
Holiness.

    POPE. My Lord, here is a dainty dish was
sent me from the Bishop of Milan.

    FAUST. I thank you, sir.   *Snatch it.*

    POPE. How now ! Who 's that which [70
snatch'd the meat from me? Will no man
look? — My Lord, this dish was sent me from
the Cardinal of Florence.

---

[6] The English Faust Book reads " to Campania
[*i.e.*, the province] in the Kingdom of Naples."
Brooke observes that Marlowe evidently took
" Campania " as another name for the *city* of Naples.
    [7] Virgil's. A tunnel near it was supposed to be
the work of his magic.
    [8] St. Mark's, at Venice : not, as Brooke suggests,
a " composite structure in a nameless city." Though
in the Faust Book Padua is visited and St. Anthony's
there is admired, " sumptuous " occurs in the E. F.
B.'s description of St. Mark's, and any great church
may be said to be lofty. For " and the rest ", Q 1616
misunderstandingly reads " and the East ", and for
" in *midst* of which " it despairingly reads " in *one* of
which," another indication of its inferiority. Padua
is here taken as a Venetian possession ; " the rest "
are the other territories of Venice. Ll. 19, 20, un-
questionably genuine, are added (*i.e.*, preserved) by
Q 1616.
    [9] This speech, and the next line of Mephistophilis,
are from Q 1616 ; earlier eds. replace them by actors'
marbled prose.
    [10] Add. Q 1616.

[11] The next seven lines are replaced in Q 1616 by
an addition of 205 ll., probably by Rowley, in which
Faust and Mephistophilis, disguised as cardinals,
play a part in the Pope's disposition of a rival, the
" Saxon Bruno."
    [12] Fanfare of trumpets.
    [13] If.

FAUST. You say true ; I 'll ha 't.
[*Snatches it.*]
POPE. What, again ? — My Lord, I 'll drink to your Grace.
FAUST. I 'll pledge your Grace.
[*Snatches the cup.*]
C. of LOR. My Lord, it may be some ghost newly crept out of purgatory, come to beg a pardon of your Holiness. 80
POPE. It may be so. — Friars, prepare a dirge to lay the fury of this ghost. — Once again, my Lord, fall to.
The POPE *crosseth himself.*
FAUST. What, are you crossing of yourself ? Well, use that trick no more, I would advise you. — (*Cross again.*) Well, there 's the second time. Aware the third, I give you fair warning.
Cross again, and FAUSTUS *hits him a box of the ear ; and they all run away.*
Come on, Mephistophilis, what shall we do ?
MEPH. Nay, I know not. We shall be curs'd with bell, book, and candle. 91
FAUST. How ! bell, book, and candle, — candle, book, and bell,
Forward and backward to curse Faustus to hell !
Anon you shall hear a hog grunt, a calf bleat, and an ass bray,
Because it is Saint Peter's holiday.

Re-enter all the Friars *to sing the dirge.*

[1] FRIAR. Come, brethren, let 's about our business with good devotion.

Sing this :

Cursed be he that stole away his Holiness' meat from the table ! *Maledicat Dominus !* [14]
Cursed be he that struck his Holiness a 100 blow on the face ! *Maledicat Dominus !*
Cursed be he that took Friar Sandelo a blow on the pate ! *Maledicat Dominus !*
Cursed be he that disturbeth our holy dirge ! *Maledicat Dominus !*
Cursed be he that took away his Holiness' wine ! *Maledicat Dominus ! Et omnes sancti !* [15] *Amen !*
[MEPHISTOPHILIS *and* FAUSTUS] *beat the* Friars, *and fling fireworks among them. and so exeunt.*

[14] May the Lord curse him.
[15] And all the Saints.

[SCENE II] [16]
Enter ROBIN *and* RALPH [17] *with a silver goblet.*

ROBIN. Come, Ralph, did not I tell thee we were for ever made by this Doctor Faustus book ? *Ecce signum,* here 's a simple purchase [18] for horsekeepers ; our horses shall eat no hay as long as this lasts.

Enter the Vintner.

RALPH. But, Robin, here comes the vintner.
ROBIN. Hush ! I 'll gull him supernaturally. — Drawer, I hope all is paid ; God be with you. — Come, Ralph.
VINT. Soft, sir ; a word with you. I [10 must yet have a goblet paid from you, ere you go.
ROBIN. I, a goblet, Ralph ; I, a goblet ! I scorn you, and you are but a &c. [19] I, a goblet ! Search me.
VINT. I mean so, sir, with your favor.
[*Searches him.*]
ROBIN. How say you now ?
VINT. I must say somewhat to your fellow. You, sir ! [19
RALPH. Me, sir ! me, sir ! Search your fill. [Vintner *searches him.*] Now, sir, you may be ashamed to burden honest men with a matter of truth. [20]
VINT. Well, t' one of you hath this goblet about you.
ROBIN. [*aside*] You lie, drawer ; 't is afore me. — Sirrah you, I 'll teach ye to impeach honest men ; stand by ; I 'll scour you for a goblet ! Stand aside you had best, I charge you in the name of Belzebub.—[*aside to* RALPH] Look to the goblet, Ralph. 31
VINT. What mean you, sirrah ?
ROBIN. I 'll tell you what I mean. (*He reads* [*from the book.*]) *Sanctobulorum, Periphrasticon* — Nay, I 'll tickle you, vintner. — [*aside to* RALPH] Look to the goblet, Ralph. — [*Reads.*] *Polypragmos Belseborams framanto pacostiphos tostu, Mephistophilis, etc.*

Enter MEPHISTOPHILIS, *sets squibs at their backs,* [*and then exit*]. [21] *They run about.*

[16] An inn. In Q 1616 this scene, as here, follows III, i. In Q₁ the order is III, i ; chorus to IV ; II, iii ; III, ii. The scene in Q 1616 differs widely.
[17] Old eds. *Rafe* throughout.
[18] Piece of loot.
[19] The low comedian was expected to supply a string of racy invectives.
[20] A question of honesty.
[21] Add. Dyce, in view of Mephistophilis's re-entry. The double entrance indicates textual corruption. The squibs were "an afterthought." (Simpson.)

VINT. *O nomine Domine!* [22] what mean'st thou, Robin? Thou hast no goblet. 40

RALPH. *Peccatum peccatorum!* [23] Here's thy goblet, good vintner.

ROBIN. *Misericordia pro nobis!* [24] What shall I do? Good Devil, forgive me now, and I'll never rob thy library more.

Re-enter to them MEPHISTOPHILIS.

MEPH. Vanish, villains!
Th' one like an ape, another like a bear, the third an ass, for doing this enterprise. — [25]

[*Exit* Vintner.]
Monarch of hell, under whose black survey
Great potentates do kneel with awful fear, 50
Upon whose altars thousand souls do lie,
How am I vexed with these villains' charms!
From Constantinople am I hither come
Only for pleasure of these damned slaves.

ROBIN. How? from Constantinople? You have had a great journey. Will you take sixpence in your purse to pay for your supper, and be gone?

MEPH. Well, villains, for your presumption, I transform thee into an ape, and thee into [60 a dog; and so, begone! *Exit.*

ROBIN. How, into an ape? That's brave! I'll have fine sport with the boys. I'll get nuts and apples enow.

RALPH. And I must be a dog.

ROBIN. I' faith thy head will never be out of the pottage pot. *Exeunt.*

[ACT IV]

Enter Chorus.[26]

CHORUS. When Faustus had with pleasure ta'en the view
Of rarest things and royal courts of kings,
He stay'd his course and so returned home;
Where such as bear his absence but with grief,
I mean his friends and near'st companions,
Did gratulate his safety with kind words,
And in their conference of what befell,
Touching his journey through the world and air,

[22] The Vintner's imperfect Latin for "in the name of the Lord."
[23] Sin of sins.
[24] Mercy on us.
[25] Mod. eds. omit this speech; it may be an alternative ending for the scene. The double transformation indicates corruption.
[26] Q 1616 om. this speech; in Q₁ it appears, misplaced, after III, i.

They put forth questions of astrology,
Which Faustus answer'd with such learned skill 10
As they admir'd and wond'red at his wit.
Now is his fame spread forth in every land;
Amongst the rest the Emperor is one;
Carolus the Fifth, at whose palace now
Faustus is feasted 'mongst his noblemen.
What there he did in trial of his art,
I leave untold — your eyes shall see perform'd.
Exit.

[SCENE I] [27]

Enter EMPEROR, FAUSTUS, [MEPHISTOPHILIS,]
and a Knight, *with attendants.*

EMP. Master Doctor Faustus, I have heard strange report of thy knowledge in the black art, how that none in my empire nor in the whole world can compare with thee for the rare effects of magic; they say thou hast a familiar spirit, by whom thou canst accomplish what thou list. This, therefore, is my request, that thou let me see some proof of thy skill, that mine eyes may be witnesses to confirm what mine ears have heard reported; and here I [10 swear to thee, by the honor of mine imperial crown, that, whatever thou doest, thou shalt be no ways prejudiced or endamaged.

KNIGHT. (*aside*) I' faith he looks much like a conjuror.

FAUST. My gracious Sovereign, though I must confess myself far inferior to the report men have published, and nothing answerable [28] to the honor of your imperial Majesty, yet for that love and duty binds me thereunto, I [20 am content to do whatsoever your Majesty shall command me.

EMP. Then, Doctor Faustus, mark what I shall say.
As I was sometime solitary set
Within my closet, sundry thoughts arose
About the honor of mine ancestors,
How they had won by prowess such exploits,
Got such riches, subdued so many kingdoms,
As we that do succeed, or they that shall
Hereafter possess our throne, shall 30
(I fear me) ne'er attain to that degree
Of high renown and great authority;
Amongst which kings is Alexander the Great,
Chief spectacle of the world's preëminence,

[27] A room in the imperial palace (at Innsbruck). Q 1616 rewrites and expands this scene, which it prefaces with another at the Emperor's court.
[28] In no respect adequate.

The bright shining of whose glorious acts
Lightens the world with his [29] reflecting beams,
As, when I heard but motion [30] made of him,
It grieves my soul I never saw the man.
If, therefore, thou by cunning of thine art
Canst raise this man from hollow vaults below,
Where lies entomb'd this famous conqueror, [41
And bring with him his beauteous paramour,
Both in their right shapes, gesture, and attire
They us'd to wear during their time of life,
Thou shalt both satisfy my just desire
And give me cause to praise thee whilst I live.

FAUST. My gracious Lord, I am ready to
accomplish your request so far forth as by art,
and power of my spirit, I am able to perform.

KNIGHT. (*aside*) I' faith that's just nothing
at all.   51

FAUST. But, if it like your Grace, it is not
in my ability to present before your eyes the
true substantial bodies of those two deceased
princes, which long since are consumed to dust.

KNIGHT. (*aside*) Ay, marry, Master Doctor,
now there's a sign of grace in you, when you
will confess the truth.

FAUST. But such spirits as can lively resemble Alexander and his paramour shall [60
appear before your Grace in that manner that
they best liv'd in, in their most flourishing
estate; which I doubt not shall sufficiently
content your imperial Majesty.

EMP. Go to, Master Doctor; let me see
them presently.[31]

KNIGHT. Do you hear, Master Doctor?
You bring Alexander and his paramour before
the Emperor!

FAUST. How then, sir?   70

KNIGHT. I' faith that's as true as Diana
turn'd me to a stag!

FAUST. No, sir, but when Actæon died, he
left the horns for you. Mephistophilis, begone.   *Exit* MEPHISTOPHILIS.

KNIGHT. Nay, an you go to conjuring, I'll
be gone.   *Exit* Knight.

FAUST. I'll meet with you anon for interrupting me so. — Here they are, my gracious
Lord.   80

Re-enter MEPHISTOPHILIS *with* [Spirits *in the
shapes of*] ALEXANDER *and his* Paramour.

EMP. Master Doctor, I heard this lady
while she liv'd had a wart or mole in her neck.
How shall I know whether it be so or no?

FAUST. Your Highness may boldly go and
see.   [*Exeunt* Spirits.]

[29] Its.   [30] Mention.   [31] At once.

EMP. Sure these are no spirits, but the true
substantial bodies of those two deceased
princes.

FAUST. Will't please your Highness now to
send for the knight that was so pleasant with
me here of late?   91

EMP. One of you call him forth.
                              [*Exit* Attendant.]

Re-enter the Knight *with a pair of horns on
his head.*

How now, Sir Knight! Why I had thought
thou hadst been a bachelor; but now I see thou
hast a wife, that not only gives thee horns, but
makes thee wear them. Feel on thy head.

KNIGHT. Thou damned wretch and exe-
crable dog,
Bred in the concave of some monstrous rock,
How dar'st thou thus abuse a gentleman?
Villain, I say, undo what thou hast done! [100

FAUST. O, not so fast, sir; there's no haste;
but, good, are you rememb'red how you crossed
me in my conference with the Emperor? I
think I have met with you for it.

EMP. Good Master Doctor, at my entreaty
release him; he hath done penance sufficient.

FAUST. My gracious Lord, not so much for
the injury he off'red me here in your presence,
as to delight you with some mirth, hath [110
Faustus worthily requited this injurious
knight; which being all I desire, I am content
to release him of his horns; and, Sir Knight,
hereafter speak well of scholars. — Mephistophilis, transform him straight. [MEPHIS-
TOPHILIS *removes the horns.*] Now, my good
Lord, having done my duty I humbly take
my leave.

EMP. Farewell, Master Doctor; yet, ere
you go,
Expect from me a bounteous reward. [*Exeunt.*]

[SCENE II] [32]

[*Enter* FAUSTUS *and* MEPHISTOPHILIS.]

FAUST. Now, Mephistophilis, the restless
course
That Time doth run with calm and silent foot,
Short'ning my days and thread of vital life,
Calls for the payment of my latest years;

[32] A green; afterwards Faustus's house. The
wreckage of several scenes probably confronts us
here; most of this is rubbish, but note the Marlovian
column still standing in ll. 45–50. Two additional
scenes precede this in Q 1616, which reduces our
Sc. ii.

Therefore, sweet Mephistophilis, let us
Make haste to Wittenberg.

MEPH. What, will you go on horseback or
    on foot?

FAUST. Nay, till I am past this fair and
    pleasant green,
I 'll walk on foot.

Enter a Horse-Courser.

HORSE-C. I have been all this day seek- [10
ing one Master Fustian ; mass, see where he
is ! — God save you, Master Doctor !

FAUST. What, horse-courser ! You are
well met.

HORSE-C. Do you hear, sir? I have
brought you forty dollars for your horse.

FAUST. I cannot sell him so ; if thou lik'st
him for fifty, take him.

HORSE-C. Alas, sir, I have no more. — I
pray you speak for me.	20

MEPH. I pray you let him have him ; he is
an honest fellow, and he has a great charge,
neither wife nor child.

FAUST. Well, come, give me your money.
[Horse-Courser *gives* FAUSTUS *the money.*]
My boy will deliver him to you. But I must
tell you one thing before you have him : ride
him not into the water at any hand.

HORSE-C. Why, sir, will he not drink of all
waters?	29

FAUST. O yes, he will drink of all waters,
but ride him not into the water ; ride him over
hedge or ditch, or where thou wilt, but not
into the water.

HORSE-C. Well, sir. — [*aside*] Now am I
made man for ever. I 'll not leave my horse
for forty.[33] If he had but the quality of hey
ding ding, hey ding ding, I 'd make a brave
living on him ; he has a buttock as slick as an
eel. — Well, God buy, sir ; your boy will [39
deliver him me. But hark ye, sir ; if my
horse be sick or ill at ease, if I bring his water
to you, you 'll tell me what it is?

Exit Horse-Courser.

FAUST. Away, you villain ; what, dost
think I am a horse-doctor? —
What art thou, Faustus, but a man con-
    demn'd to die?
Thy fatal time doth draw to final end ;
Despair doth drive distrust unto my thoughts.
Confound these passions with a quiet sleep.
Tush, Christ did call the thief upon the cross ;
Then rest thee, Faustus, quiet in conceit.	50
Sleep in his chair.

[33] *I.e.*, any number of others. (Boas.)

Re-enter Horse-Courser, *all wet, crying.*

HORSE-C. Alas, alas ! Doctor Fustian,
quotha? Mass, Doctor Lopus [34] was never
such a doctor. Has given me a purgation has
purg'd me of forty dollars ; I shall never see
them more. But yet, like an ass as I was, I
would not be ruled by him, for he bade me I
should ride him into no water. Now I, thinking my horse had had some rare quality that he
would not have had me known of, I, like a [59
vent'rous youth, rid him into the deep pond at
the town's end. I was no sooner in the middle
of the pond, but my horse vanish'd away, and
I sat upon a bottle [35] of hay, never so near
drowning in my life. But I 'll seek out my
Doctor, and have my forty dollars again, or I 'll
make it the dearest horse — O, yonder is his
snipper-snapper.[36] — Do you hear? You hey-
pass,[37] where 's your master?

MEPH. Why, sir, what would you? You
cannot speak with him.	70

HORSE-C. But I will speak with him.

MEPH. Why, he 's fast asleep. Come some
other time.

HORSE-C. I 'll speak with him now, or I 'll
break his glass windows about his ears.

MEPH. I tell thee he has not slept this
eight nights.

HORSE-C. An he have not slept this eight
weeks, I 'll speak with him.

MEPH. See where he is, fast asleep.	80

HORSE-C. Ay, this is he. — God save ye,
Master Doctor ! Master Doctor, Master
Doctor Fustian ! — Forty dollars, forty dollars
for a bottle of hay !

MEPH. Why, thou seest he hears thee not.

HORSE-C. So ho, ho ! — so ho, ho ! (*Holla in
his ear.*) No, will you not wake? I 'll make
you wake ere I go. (*Pull him by the leg, and
pull it away.*) Alas, I am undone ! What
shall I do?	90

FAUST. O my leg, my leg ! Help, Mephistophilis ! Call the officers. My leg, my leg !

MEPH. Come, villain, to the constable.

HORSE-C. O Lord, sir, let me go, and I 'll
give you forty dollars more.

MEPH. Where be they?

HORSE-C. I have none about me. Come to
my ostry [38] and I 'll give them you.

[34] Queen Elizabeth's physician, Roderigo Lopez, a
Spanish Jew, charged with conspiring to poison her
and executed in 1594 — nearly a year after Marlowe's
death !
[35] Truss.
[36] Whippersnapper.
[37] Juggler, since this was his cry. (Dyce, Ward.)
[38] Hostelry, inn.

MEPH. Begone quickly.

Horse-Courser runs away.

FAUST. What, is he gone? Farewell he! [100
Faustus has his leg again, and the horse-courser, I take it, a bottle of hay for his labor. Well, this trick shall cost him forty dollars more.

Enter WAGNER.

How now, Wagner, what's the news with thee?

WAG. Sir, the Duke of Vanholt doth earnestly entreat your company.

FAUST. The Duke of Vanholt! an honorable gentleman, to whom I must be no niggard [110 of my cunning. Come, Mephistophilis, let's away to him.   *Exeunt.*

[SCENE III] 39

Enter 40 *the* DUKE [*of* VANHOLT], *the* DUCHESS, [FAUSTUS, *and* MEPHISTOPHILIS.]

DUKE. Believe me, Master Doctor, this merriment hath much pleased me.

FAUST. My gracious Lord, I am glad it contents you so well. — But it may be, madam, you take no delight in this. I have heard that great-bellied women do long for some dainties or other. What is it, madam? Tell me, and you shall have it.

DUCHESS. Thanks, good Master Doctor; and for I see your courteous intent to pleas- [10 ure me, I will not hide from you the thing my heart desires; and were it now summer, as it is January and the dead time of the winter, I would desire no better meat than a dish of ripe grapes.

FAUST. Alas, madam, that's nothing. Mephistophilis, begone. (*Exit* MEPHISTOPHILIS.) Were it a greater thing than this, so it would content you, you should have it.

Re-enter MEPHISTOPHILIS *with the grapes.*

Here they be, madam; wilt please you taste on them?   21

DUKE. Believe me, Master Doctor, this makes me wonder above the rest, that being in the dead time of winter and in the month of January, how you should come by these grapes.

FAUST. If it like your Grace, the year is divided into two circles over the whole world,

that, when it is here winter with us, in the contrary circle it is summer with them, as in India, Saba,41 and farther countries in the East; [30 and by means of a swift spirit that I have, I had them brought hither, as ye see. — How do you like them, madam; be they good?

DUCHESS. Believe me, Master Doctor, they be the best grapes that e'er I tasted in my life before.

FAUST. I am glad they content you so, madam.

DUKE. Come, madam, let us in, where you must well reward this learned man for the great kindness he hath show'd to you.   41

DUCHESS. And so I will, my Lord; and, whilst I live, rest beholding for this courtesy.

FAUST. I humbly thank your Grace.

DUKE. Come, Master Doctor, follow us and receive your reward.   *Exeunt.*

[ACT V — SCENE I] 1

Enter WAGNER, *solus.*

WAG. I think my master means to die
        shortly,
For he hath given to me all his goods;
And yet, methinks if that death were near,
He would not banquet and carouse and swill
Amongst the students, as even now he doth,
Who are at supper with such belly-cheer
As Wagner ne'er beheld in all his life.
See where they come! Belike the feast is
        ended.   [*Exit.*]

Enter FAUSTUS, *with two or three* Scholars [*and* MEPHISTOPHILIS].

1 SCHOL. Master Doctor Faustus, since our conference about fair ladies, which was the [10 beautiful'st in all the world,2 we have determined with ourselves that Helen of Greece was the admirablest lady that ever lived. Therefore, Master Doctor, if you will do us that favor, as to let us see that peerless dame of Greece, whom all the world admires for majesty, we should think ourselves much beholding unto you.

FAUST. Gentlemen,
For that I know your friendship is unfeigned,
And Faustus' custom is not to deny   21

---

39 A residence of the Duke of "Vanholt." In Q 1616 another comic scene, with the horse-courser, precedes this. Sc. iii is expanded in Q 1616.
40 Q₁ adds *to them,* indicating corruption, since Faustus and Mephistophilis have just left the stage.

41 Sheba.
1 Wittenberg. A room in Faustus's house.
2 Simpson notes the survival of a Marlovian line, beginning "which", indicating that this prose is an adapter's work.

The just requests of those that wish him well,
You shall behold that peerless dame of Greece,
No otherways for pomp and majesty
Than when Sir Paris cross'd the seas with her
And brought the spoils to rich Dardania.
Be silent, then ; for danger is in words.
>   *Music sounds, and* HELEN *passeth over*
>   *the stage.*
2 SCHOL. Too simple is my wit to tell her
>   praise,
Whom all the world admires for majesty.
3 SCHOL. No marvel though the angry
>   Greeks pursu'd   30
With ten years' war the rape [3] of such a queen,
Whose heavenly beauty passeth all compare.
1 SCHOL. Since we have seen the pride of
>   Nature's works
And only paragon of excellence,
Let us depart ; and for this glorious deed
Happy and blest be Faustus evermore.
FAUSTUS. Gentlemen, farewell ; the same I
>   wish to you.
>   *Exeunt* Scholars.

Enter an Old Man.

OLD MAN. Ah, Doctor Faustus, that I
>   might prevail
To guide thy steps unto the way of life,
By which sweet path thou mayst attain the
>   goal   40
That shall conduct thee to celestial rest !
Break heart, drop blood, and mingle it with
>   tears,
Tears falling from repentant heaviness
Of thy most vild and loathsome filthiness,
The stench whereof corrupts the inward soul
With such flagitious crimes of heinous sins
As no commiseration may expel,
But mercy, Faustus, of thy Savior sweet,
Whose blood alone must wash away thy guilt.
FAUST. Where art thou, Faustus? Wretch,
>   what hast thou done?   50
Damn'd art thou, Faustus, damn'd ; despair
>   and die !
Hell calls for right, and with a roaring voice
Says " Faustus, come ; thine hour is [almost] [4]
>   come ! "
And Faustus [now] [4] will come to do thee
>   right.
>   MEPHISTOPHILIS *gives him a dagger.*
OLD MAN. Ah, stay, good Faustus, stay
>   thy desperate steps !
I see an angel hovers o'er thy head,

And, with a vial full of precious grace,
Offers to pour the same into thy soul ;
Then call for mercy, and avoid despair.
FAUST. Ah, my sweet friend, I feel   60
Thy words do comfort my distressed soul.
Leave me awhile to ponder on my sins.
OLD MAN. I go, sweet Faustus, but with
>   heavy cheer,
Fearing the ruin of thy hopeless soul.   [*Exit.*]
FAUST. Accursed Faustus, where is mercy
>   now?
I do repent, and yet I do despair ;
Hell strives with grace for conquest in my
>   breast.
What shall I do to shun the snares of death?
MEPH. Thou traitor, Faustus, I arrest thy
>   soul
For disobedience to my sovereign lord ;   70
Revolt, or I 'll in piecemeal tear thy flesh.
FAUST. [I do repent I e'er offended him ;] [5]
Sweet Mephistophilis, entreat thy lord
To pardon my unjust presumption,
And with my blood again I will confirm
My former vow I made to Lucifer.
MEPH. Do it now then quickly, with un-
>   feigned heart,
Lest danger do attend thy drift.
FAUST. Torment, sweet friend, that base
>   and crooked age [6]
That durst dissuade me from my Lucifer,   80
With greatest torments that our hell affords.
MEPH. His faith is great ; I cannot touch
>   his soul ;
But what I may afflict his body with
I will attempt, which is but little worth.
FAUST. One thing, good servant, let me
>   crave of thee,
To glut the longing of my heart's desire,
That I might have unto my paramour
That heavenly Helen, which I saw of late,
Whose sweet embracings may extinguish
>   clean
These thoughts that do dissuade me from my
>   vow,   90
And keep mine oath I made to Lucifer.
MEPH. Faustus, this or what else thou shalt
>   desire
Shall be perform'd in twinkling of an eye.

>   *Re-enter* HELEN.

FAUST. Was this the face that launch'd a
>   thousand ships,
And burnt the topless [7] towers of Ilium?

---

[3] Capture.   [4] Add. Q 1616.

[5] Add. Q 1616.
[6] Old man.   [7] Incomparably lofty.

Sweet Helen, make me immortal with a kiss. —
Her lips sucks forth my soul ; see where it
    flies ! —
Come, Helen, come, give me my soul again.
Here will I dwell, for Heaven be in these lips,
And all is dross that is not Helena.   100
I will be Paris, and for love of thee,
Instead of Troy shall Wittenberg be sack'd ;
And I will combat with weak Menelaus,
And wear thy colors on my plumed crest ;
Yea, I will wound Achilles in the heel,
And then return to Helen for a kiss.
O, thou art fairer than the evening air
Clad in the beauty of a thousand stars ;
Brighter art thou than flaming Jupiter
When he appear'd to hapless Semele ;   110
More lovely than the monarch of the sky
In wanton Arethusa's azur'd arms ; [8]
And none but thou shalt be my paramour.

Re-enter Old Man.[9]   *Exeunt [the others].*

OLD MAN. Accursed Faustus, miserable
    man,
That from thy soul exclud'st the grace of
    Heaven,
And fliest the throne of his tribunal seat !

Enter the Devils.

Satan begins to sift [10] me with his pride.[11]
As in this furnace God shall try my faith,
My faith, vile hell, shall triumph over thee.
Ambitious fiends, see how the Heavens smiles
At your repulse, and laughs your state to
    scorn !   121
Hence, hell ! for hence I fly unto my God.
                    Exeunt.

[SCENE II] [12]

Enter FAUSTUS *with the* Scholars.

FAUST. Ah, gentlemen !
1 SCHOL. What ails Faustus?
FAUST. Ah, my sweet chamber-fellow, had
I lived with thee, then had I lived still ! but
now I die eternally. Look, comes he not?
comes he not?
2 SCHOL. What means Faustus?

3 SCHOL. Belike he is grown into some sickness by being oversolitary.
1 SCHOL. If it be so, we'll have physi- [10
cians to cure him. — 'T is but a surfeit ; never
fear, man.
FAUST. A surfeit of deadly sin that hath
damn'd both body and soul.
2 SCHOL. Yet, Faustus, look up to Heaven ;
remember God's mercies are infinite.
FAUST. But Faustus' offence can ne'er be
pardoned ; the serpent that tempted Eve may
be sav'd, but not Faustus. Ah, gentlemen,
hear me with patience, and tremble not at [20
my speeches. Though my heart pants and
quivers to remember that I have been a student here these thirty years, oh, would I had
never seen Wittenberg, never read book ! And
what wonders I have done, all Germany
can witness, yea, all the world ; for which
Faustus hath lost both Germany and the
world, yea, Heaven itself, Heaven, the seat of
God, the throne of the blessed, the kingdom of
joy ; and must remain in hell for ever, hell, [30
ah, hell, for ever ! Sweet friends, what shall
become of Faustus, being in hell for ever?
3 SCHOL. Yet, Faustus, call on God.
FAUST. On God, whom Faustus hath ab-
jur'd ! on God, whom Faustus hath blas-
phemed ! Ah, my God, I would weep, but the
Devil draws in my tears. Gush forth blood
instead of tears ! Yea, life and soul — Oh, he
stays my tongue ! I would lift up my hands,
but see, they hold them, they hold them ! [40
ALL. Who, Faustus?
FAUST. Lucifer and Mephistophilis.[13] Ah,
gentlemen ! I gave them my soul for my cunning.[14]
ALL. God forbid !
FAUST. God forbade it indeed ; but Faustus hath done it. For vain pleasure of four-
and-twenty years hath Faustus lost eternal
joy and felicity. I writ them a bill with mine
own blood ; the date is expired, the time [50
will come, and he will fetch me.
1 SCHOL. Why did not Faustus tell us of
this before, that divines might have prayed for
thee?
FAUST. Oft have I thought to have done
so ; but the Devil threat'ned to tear me in
pieces if I nam'd God ; to fetch both body
and soul if I once gave ear to divinity ; and

---

[8] No such episode is known to classical mythology.
(Boas.) Brooke suggests that *Arethusa* may be a
slip (or possibly an intentional alteration) for Leu-
cothoe, beloved by Apollo. (See Ovid's *Metamorphoses*, IV, 230, ff.)
[9] Om. Q 1616 ; in Q₁ placed before l. 101.
[10] Cf. *Luke*, xxii, 31.
[11] Display (of power).
[12] The same.

[13] In Q 1616 Lucifer, Belzebub, and Mephistophilis open the scene, and the last speaks twice in
an interpolation of 48 ll., which comes after l. 77.
[14] Knowledge.

now 't is too late. Gentlemen, away ! lest you
perish with me.   60
    2 Schol. Oh, what shall we do to [save] [15]
Faustus?
    Faust. Talk not of me, but save yourselves,
and depart.
    3 Schol. God will strengthen me. I will
stay with Faustus.
    1 Schol. Tempt not God, sweet friend ; but
let us into the next room, and there pray for him.
    Faust. Ay, pray for me, pray for me ! and
what noise soever ye hear come not unto me,
for nothing can rescue me.   71
    2 Schol. Pray thou, and we will pray that
God may have mercy upon thee.
    Faust. Gentlemen, farewell. If I live till
morning I 'll visit you ; if not, Faustus is gone
to hell.
    All. Faustus, farewell !
    Exeunt Scholars. The clock strikes eleven.
    Faust. Ah, Faustus,
Now hast thou but one bare hour to live,   79
And then thou must be damn'd perpetually !
Stand still, you ever-moving spheres of Heaven,
That time may cease, and midnight never come;
Fair Nature's eye, rise, rise again and make
Perpetual day ; or let this hour be but
A year, a month, a week, a natural day,
That Faustus may repent and save his soul !
O lente, lente, currite noctis equi ! [16]
The stars move still, [17] time runs, the clock will
    strike,
The Devil will come, and Faustus must be
    damn'd.
O, I 'll leap up to my God ! Who pulls me
    down?   90
See, see where Christ's blood streams in the
    firmament !
One drop would save my soul — half a drop !
    ah, my Christ ! —
Ah, rend not my heart for naming of my
    Christ ! —
Yet will I call on him ! — O, spare me, Luci-
    fer ! —
Where is it now? 'T is gone ; and see where
    God
Stretcheth out his arm, and bends his ireful
    brows ! —
Mountain and hills, come, come and fall
    on me,
And hide me from the heavy wrath of God !

No ! no ! —   99
Then will I headlong run into the earth ! —
Earth, gape ! — O no, it will not harbor
    me ! —
You stars that reign'd at my nativity,
Whose influence hath allotted death and
    hell,
Now draw up Faustus like a foggy mist
Into the entrails of yon lab'ring cloud,
That when you vomit forth into the air,
My limbs may issue from their smoky
    mouths, [18]
So [19] that my soul may but ascend to Heaven.
                              The watch strikes.
Ah, half the hour is past ! 'T will all be past
    anon !
O God,   110
If thou wilt not have mercy on my soul,
Yet for Christ's sake, whose blood hath ran-
    som'd me,
Impose some end to my incessant pain ;
Let Faustus live in hell a thousand years,
A hundred thousand, and at last be sav'd ! —
O, no end is limited to damned souls !
Why wert thou not a creature wanting
    soul?
Or why is this immortal that thou hast?
Ah, Pythagoras' metempsychosis ! were that
    true,
This soul should fly from me, and I be
    chang'd   120
Unto some brutish beast ! All beasts are
    happy,
For, when they die,
Their souls are soon dissolv'd in elements ;
But mine must live, still to be plagu'd in
    hell.
Curs'd be the parents that engend'red me !
No, Faustus, curse thyself, curse Lucifer,
That hath depriv'd thee of the joys of Heaven.
                              The clock striketh twelve.
O, it strikes, it strikes ! Now, body, turn to
    air,
Or Lucifer will bear thee quick to hell !
                              Thunder and lightning.
O soul, be chang'd into little water-drops,   130
And fall into the ocean — ne'er be found ! —
My God, my God, look not so fierce on me !

---

[15] Add. Q 1616.
[16] Run slowly, slowly, steeds of the night. (Ovid,
Amores, I, xiii, 40.)
[17] Unceasingly.

[18] Brooke, calling attention to the censor's mutila-
tion of this soliloquy in Q 1616, and to the actors'
unmetrical insertions in Q 1, suggests that ll. 106, 107,
may have stood in place of the "doubtless histrionic"
l. 99. "Their dislocation may have been occasioned
by the fact that originally each movement of the invocation ended [with l. 108]."
[19] Provided that.

Enter Devils.

Adders and serpents, let me breathe awhile ! —
Ugly hell, gape not ! — Come not, Lucifer ! —
I 'll burn my books ! — Ah, Mephistophilis ! [20]
　　　Exeunt [Devils] *with him.*

Enter Chorus.

Cho. Cut is the branch that might have
　　grown full straight,
And burned is Apollo's laurel bough,

That sometime [21] grew within this learned
　　man.
Faustus is gone ; regard his hellish fall,
Whose fiendful fortune may exhort the wise
Only to wonder at unlawful things,　　　141
Whose deepness doth entice such forward wits
To practise more than heavenly power permits.
　　　　　　　　　　　　　　　　[*Exit.*]

Terminat hora diem ; terminat author opus.[22]

[20] Q 1616 adds 18 lines, in which the scholars dis-cover Faustus's dismembered body.

[21] Formerly.
[22] The hour ends the day ; the author ends his work.

The Famous
TRAGEDY
OF
THE RICH IEVV
OF *MALTA*.

AS IT WAS PLAYD
BEFORE THE KING AND
QVEENE, IN HIS MAJESTIES
Theatre at *White-Hall*, by her Majesties
Servants at the *Cock-pit*.

Written by CHRISTOPHER MARLO.

LONDON;
Printed by *I. B.* for *Nicholas Vavasour*, and are to be sold
at his Shop in the Inner-Temple, neere the
Church. 1 6 3 3.

INTRODUCTORY NOTE

As in the case of *Faustus*, so long a period intervened between the production of *The Jew of Malta* (c. 1590) and the appearance of the first (known) edition (1633) that our text is very corrupt. Again we must try to reconstruct a splendid edifice which has fallen into partial ruin and been put to base uses. Yet here the initial collapse seems due to the author, who evidently began a tragedy and failed to sustain it. Barabas, like Faustus and Tamburlaine, is a child of the Renaissance; though he is not like them a hero, but a hero-villain. The play is a melodrama rather than a tragedy, or, as has been seriously suggested, a farce. Barabas is the crafty (to the Elizabethans, Machiavellian) scoundrel who, clever as he is, finally overreaches himself. The audience doubtless laughed derisively at his villainous asides and hugely enjoyed his fall. The conclusion is irresistible that, whatever his original intention, Marlowe turned his efforts into capitalizing anti-Semitic prejudice.

He certainly succeeded. The great puzzle is the flagging, toward the end of Act II, of the undeniable power and grandeur of the opening. Various theories have been proposed to account for it; but, unless indeed the second half of the play is largely a reconstruction, Professor Brooke's seems most reasonable. The thread of the plot is throughout probably Marlowe's, but in the first two acts the central character is humanized. In the rest of the play we have the bare plot, possibly with interpolations and alterations, but certainly stripped of the humanizing touches with which Shakespeare manages to keep Shylock invested even after the game goes against him. In both cases the Elizabethans gloated over the villain's ruin. But Shakespeare's Jew, execrated though he be, is always a fellow-creature. Shakespeare's original conception was less bold than Marlowe's. Perhaps it was easier to sustain.

No source for the play has been found. Eminent sixteenth-century Jews resident in Constantinople and powerful politically and commercially have been suggested as possible inspirations by Professors Kellner and Brooke (see introduction to Bennett's edition for references and summaries). Marlowe may have learned about them through his diplomatic connections (he was for a time an agent of the Privy Council), or from London Jews.

Henslowe records that Lord Strange's company was acting *The Jew of Malta* in 1592–93, and that it was not then a new play. It was apparently the most popular of Marlowe's dramas. In 1594 several companies performed it; but it finally rested in the possession of the Admiral's Men, who acted it at least till 1596, with Edward Alleyn in the title rôle. There was a revival in 1601, and another probably not long prior to the publication of Q 1633. On the latter occasion it was acted at the Cockpit and also at court, with prologues and epilogues by Thomas Heywood, who may have revised it. And there may have been an earlier revision in 1601.

The Jew of Malta was edited for the Case Marlowe by H. S. Bennett (1931). Though an entry was made in the Stationers' Register in 1594, the first surviving edition is that of 1633, in quarto, on which the present text is based.

THE JEW OF MALTA

BY

CHRISTOPHER MARLOWE

[DRAMATIS PERSONAE

FERNEZE, Governor of Malta.
LODOWICK, his son.
SELIM CALYMATH, son to the Grand Seignior.
MARTIN DEL BOSCO, Vice-Admiral of Spain.
MATHIAS, a gentleman.
BARABAS, a wealthy Jew.
ITHAMORE, his slave.
JACOMO, } friars.
BARNARDINE, } friars.
PILIA-BORZA, a bully.
Two Merchants.

Three Jews.
Knights, Bassoes, Officers, Reader, Guard, Messenger, Slaves, and Carpenters.

KATHERINE, mother to Mathias.
ABIGAIL, daughter to Barabas.
BELLAMIRA, a courtesan.
Abbess.
A Nun.

MACHIAVEL, speaker of the prologue.

THE SCENE — *Malta.*]

[THE PROLOGUE]

[*Enter*] MACHIAVEL.

ALBEIT the world think Machiavel is dead,
Yet was his soul but flown beyond the Alps,
And, now the Guise [1] is dead, is come from France
To view this land and frolic with his friends.
To some, perhaps, my name is odious,
But such as love me guard me from their tongues;
And let them know that I am Machiavel,
And weigh not men, and therefore not men's words.
Admir'd I am of those that hate me most.
Though some speak openly against my books, [2]   10
Yet will they read me, and thereby attain
To Peter's chair; and when they cast me off,
Are poison'd by my climbing followers.
I count religion but a childish toy,
And hold there is no sin but ignorance.

Birds of the air will tell of murders past —
I am asham'd to hear such fooleries.
Many will talk of title to a crown:
What right had Cæsar to the empery? [3]
Might first made kings, and laws were then most sure   20
When, like the Draco's, [4] they were writ in blood.
Hence comes it that a strong-built citadel
Commands much more than letters can import;
Which maxim had Phalaris observ'd,
H' had never bellowed, in a brazen bull,
Of great ones' envy. O' the poor petty wits [5]
Let me be envi'd and not pitied!
But whither am I bound? I come not, I,
To read a lecture here in Britainy, [6]
But to present the tragedy of a Jew,   30
Who smiles to see how full his bags are cramm'd,
Which money was not got without my means.
I crave but this: grace him as he deserves,
And let him not be entertain'd the worse
Because he favors me.   [*Exit.*]

---

[1] Assassinated in 1588; he organized the Massacre of St. Bartholomew in 1572. See Marlowe's play on that subject.
[2] *The Prince*, and others.
[3] Q *Empire.*
[4] Q *Drancus.*
[5] So Brereton; mod. eds. *wights;* Q *wites.*
[6] So Bullen; Q *Britaine.*

[ACT I — SCENE I]

Enter[7] BARABAS *in his countinghouse, with heaps of gold before him.*

BAR. So that of thus much that return was
    made ;
And of the third part of the Persian ships,
There was the venture summ'd and satisfied.
As for those [Scaenites],[8] and the men of Uz,
That bought my Spanish oils and wines of
    Greece,
Here have I purs'd their paltry silver[l]ings.[9]
Fie, what a trouble 't is to count this trash !
Well fare the Arabians, who so richly pay
The things they traffic for with wedge of gold,
Whereof a man may easily in a day   10
Tell[10] that which may maintain him all his life.
The needy groom, that never fing'red groat,
Would make a miracle of thus much coin ;
But he whose steel-barr'd coffers are cramm'd
    full,
And all his lifetime hath been tired,[11]
Wearying his fingers' ends with telling it,
Would in his age be loath to labor so,
And for a pound to sweat himself to death.
Give me the merchants of the Indian mines,
That trade in metal of the purest mold ;   20
The wealthy Moor, that in the eastern rocks
Without control can pick his riches up,
And in his house heap pearl like pebble-
    stones,
Receive them free, and sell them by the weight ;
Bags of fiery opals, sapphires, amethysts,
Jacinths, hard topaz, grass-green emeralds,
Beauteous rubies, sparkling diamonds,
And seld-seen costly stones of so great price
As one of them, indifferently rated,[12]
And of a carat of this quantity,   30
May serve in peril of calamity
To ransome great kings from captivity.
This is the ware wherein consists my wealth ；
And thus methinks should men of judgment
    frame
Their means of traffic from[13] the vulgar trade,
And as their wealth increaseth, so inclose
Infinite riches in a little room.
But now how stands the wind?

Into what corner peers my halcyon's bill?[14]
Ha ! to the east? Yes. See, how stands the
    vanes?   40
East and by south ; why, then, I hope my
    ships
I sent for Egypt and the bordering isles
Are gotten up by Nilus' winding banks ;
Mine argosy[15] from Alexandria,
Loaden with spice and silks, now under sail,
Are smoothly gliding down by Candy[16] shore
To Malta, through our Mediterranean sea.
But who comes here? How now?

Enter a Merchant.

MERCH.   Barabas, thy ships are safe,
Riding in Malta road, and all the merchants
With other merchandise are safe arriv'd,   50
And have sent me to know whether yourself
Will come and custom[17] them.
BAR. The ships are safe thou say'st, and
    richly fraught?
MERCH. They are.
BAR.   Why then go bid them come
    ashore,
And bring with them their bills of entry.[11]
I hope our credit in the customhouse
Will serve as well as I were present there.
Go send 'em threescore camels, thirty mules,
And twenty wagons to bring up the ware.
But art thou master in a ship of mine,   60
And is thy credit not enough for that?
MERCH. The very custom barely comes to
    more
Than many merchants of the town are worth,
And therefore far exceeds my credit, sir.
BAR. Go tell 'em the Jew of Malta sent thee,
    man :
Tush ! who amongst 'em knows not Barabas?
MERCH. I go.
BAR.   So, then ; there 's somewhat
    come.
Sirrah, which of my ships art thou master of ?
MERCH. Of the Speranza, sir.
BAR.   And saw'st thou not
Mine argosy at Alexandria?   70
Thou couldst not come from Egypt, or by
    Caire,
But at the entry there into the sea,
Where Nilus pays his tribute to the main,
Thou needs must sail by Alexandria.

---

[7] He was actually "discovered" in the inner stage.
[8] Arab nomads mentioned by the cosmographers. Conj. Miss Seaton (*Review of English Studies*, V, 398). Q *Samintes*.
[9] Shekels.
[10] Count.
[11] Trisyllabic.
[12] Impartially valued.
[13] Away from.

[14] One of the "vulgar errors" mentioned by Sir Thomas Browne is "that a kingfisher, hanged by the bill, showeth in what quarter the wind is."
[15] Large merchantmen.
[16] Cretan.
[17] Pay the customs.

MERCH. I neither saw them, nor inquir'd of
    them ;
But this we heard some of our seamen say,
They wond'red how you durst with so much
    wealth
Trust such a crazed vessel, and so far.
    BAR. Tush, they are wise ! I know her and
    her strength.
[But] [18] go, go thou thy ways, discharge thy
    ship,   80
And bid my factor bring his loading in.
                                    [*Exit* Merchant.]
And yet I wonder at this argosy.

Enter a second Merchant.

2 MERCH. Thine argosy from Alexandria,
Know, Barabas, doth ride in Malta road,
Laden with riches and exceeding store
Of Persian silks, of gold, and orient [19] pearl.
    BAR. How chance you came not with those
    other ships
That sail'd by Egypt?
    2 MERCH.   Sir, we saw 'em not.
    BAR. Belike they coasted round by Candy
    shore
About their oils, or other businesses.   90
But 't was ill done of you to come so far
Without the aid or conduct of their ships.
    2 MERCH. Sir, we were wafted by a Spanish
    fleet,
That never left us till within a league,
That had the galleys of the Turk in chase.
    BAR. O ! they were going up to Sicily.
Well, go,
And bid the merchants and my men despatch
And come ashore, and see the fraught dis-
    charg'd.
    2 MERCH. I go.   *Exit.*   100
    BAR. Thus trolls our fortune in by land
    and sea,
And thus are we on every side enrich'd.
These are blessings promis'd to the Jews,
And herein was old Abram's happiness.
What more may Heaven do for earthly man
Than thus to pour out plenty in their laps,
Ripping the bowels of the earth for them,
Making the sea their servants, and the winds
To drive their substance with successful
    blasts?
Who hateth me but for my happiness?   110
Or who is honor'd now but for his wealth?
Rather had I, a Jew, be hated thus,
Than pitied in a Christian poverty ;

[18] Emend. Dyce ; Q *By.*
[19] Lustrous.

For I can see no fruits in all their faith,
But malice, falsehood, and excessive pride,
Which, methinks, fits not their profession.
Haply some hapless man hath conscience,
And for his conscience lives in beggary.
They say we are a scatter'd nation ;
I cannot tell, but we have scambled [20] up   120
More wealth by far than those that brag of
    faith.
There's Kirriah Jairim, the great Jew of
    Greece,
Obed in Bairseth, Nones in Portugal,
Myself in Malta, some in Italy,
Many in France, and wealthy every one ;
Ay, wealthier far than any Christian.
I must confess we come not to be kings ;
That's not our fault : alas, our number's
    few,
And crowns come either by succession,
Or urg'd by force ; and nothing violent,   130
Oft have I heard tell, can be permanent.
Give us a peaceful rule, make Christians kings,
That thirst so much for principality.
I have no charge, nor many children,
But one sole daughter, whom I hold as dear
As Agamemnon did his Iphigen ;
And all I have is hers. But who comes here?

Enter three Jews. [21]

    1 JEW. Tush, tell not me ; 't was done of
    policy.
    2 JEW. Come, therefore, let us go to Bara-
    bas,
For he can counsel best in these affairs ;   140
And here he comes.
    BAR.   Why, how now, countrymen !
Why flock you thus to me in multitudes? [22]
What accident's betided to the Jews?
    1 JEW. A fleet of warlike galleys, Barabas,
Are come from Turkey, and lie in our road ;
And they this day sit in the council-house
To entertain them and their embassy.
    BAR. Why, let 'em come, so they come not
    to war ;
Or let 'em war, so we be conquerors : —
(*aside*) Nay, let 'em combat, conquer, and kill
    all,   150
So they spare me, my daughter, and my
    wealth.

[20] Scrambled.
[21] The outer stage now being the street before
Barabas's house.
[22] Here and in Scene ii, the three Jews stand for a
multitude ; like the "three or four most vile and
ragged foils" Shakespeare asks us to consider an
army in *Henry V.*

1 JEW. Were it for confirmation of a league,
They would not come in warlike manner thus.
2 JEW. I fear their coming will afflict us
all.
BAR. Fond [23] men! what dream you of
their multitudes?
What need they treat of peace that are in
league?
The Turks and those of Malta are in league.
Tut, tut, there is some other matter in 't.
1 JEW. Why, Barabas, they come for peace
or war.
BAR. Happily for neither, but to pass along
Towards Venice by the Adriatic Sea;   161
With [24] whom they have attempted many
times,
But never could effect their stratagem.
3 JEW. And very wisely said. It may be
so.
2 JEW. But there's a meeting in the senate-
house,
And all the Jews in Malta must be there.
BAR. Hum; all the Jews in Malta must be
there?
Ay, like enough. Why, then, let every man
Provide him, and be there for fashion sake.[25]
If anything shall there concern our state,   170
Assure yourselves I'll look — (*aside*) unto my-
self.
1 JEW. I know you will. Well, brethren,
let us go.
2 JEW. Let's take our leaves. Farewell,
good Barabas.
BAR. Do so. Farewell, Zaareth; farewell,
Temainte.   [*Exeunt the three* Jews.]
And, Barabas, now search this secret out;
Summon thy senses, call thy wits together;
These silly men mistake the matter clean.
Long to the Turk did Malta contribute;
Which tribute, all in policy, I fear,
The Turks have let increase to such a sum   180
As all the wealth of Malta cannot pay;
And now by that advantage thinks, belike,
To seize upon the town; ay, that he seeks.
Howe'er the world go, I'll make sure for one,
And seek in time to intercept the worst,
Warily guarding that which I ha' got.
Ego mihimet sum semper proximus.[26]
Why, let 'em enter, let 'em take the town.
    [*Exit.*]

[23] Foolish.
[24] Against.
[25] As a formality.
[26] Misquoted from Terence, *Andria,* IV, i, 12:
Proximus sum egomet mihi: i.e., number one comes
first.

[SCENE II] [27]

Enter [FERNEZE, *governor*] [28] *of Malta,* Knights,
[*and* Officers;] *met by* CALYMATH [*and*] Bassoes *of the Turk.*

FERN. Now, Bassoes, what demand you at
our hands?
[1] BAS. Know, Knights of Malta, that we
came from Rhodes,
From Cyprus, Candy, and those other isles
That lie betwixt the Mediterranean seas.
FERN. What's Cyprus, Candy, and those
other isles
To us or Malta? What at our hands demand
ye?
CAL. The ten years' tribute that remains
unpaid.
FERN. Alas! my Lord, the sum is over-
great;
I hope your Highness will consider us.
CAL. I wish, grave [Governor,] [29] 't were in
my power   10
To favor you; but 't is my father's cause,
Wherein I may not, nay, I dare not dally.
FERN. Then give us leave, great Selim Caly-
math.
CAL. Stand all aside, and let the Knights
determine,
And send to keep our galleys under sail,
For happily [30] we shall not tarry here. —
Now, Governor, how are you resolv'd?
FERN. Thus: since your hard conditions
are such
That you will needs have ten years' tribute
past,
We may have time to make collection   20
Amongst the inhabitants of Malta for 't.
[1] BAS. That's more than is in our com-
mission.
CAL. What, Callapine! a little courtesy.
Let's know their time, perhaps it is not long;
And 't is more kingly to obtain by peace
Than to enforce conditions by constraint.
What respite ask you, Governor?
FERN.   But a month.
CAL. We grant a month, but see you keep
your promise.
Now launch our galleys back again to sea,
Where we'll attend the respite you have
ta'en,   30

[27] The Senate-house; afterwards, a street between
it and Barabas's house.
[28] Q *Gouernors.* Ferneze's first speech is tagged
Gouer. and thereafter *Gov.* throughout.
[29] Q *Gouernor;* also in ll. 17, 27, 32, 129.
[30] Haply.

And for the money send our messenger.
Farewell, great Governor and brave Knights
     of Malta.
               Exeunt [CALYMATH *and* Bassoes].
   FERN. And all good fortune wait on Caly-
     math!
Go one and call those Jews of Malta hither.
Were they not summon'd to appear to-day?
   OFF. They were, my Lord, and here they
     come.

     Enter BARABAS *and three* Jews.

   1 KNIGHT. Have you determined what to
     say to them?
   FERN. Yes, give me leave; — and, He-
     brews, now come near.
From the Emperor of Turkey is arriv'd
Great Selim Calymath, his Highness' son,   40
To levy of us ten years' tribute past;
Now then, here know that it concerneth us —
   BAR. Then, good my Lord, to keep your
     quiet still,
Your Lordship shall do well to let them have it.
   FERN. Soft, Barabas, there's more 'longs to
     't than so.
To what this ten years' tribute will amount,
That we have cast,[31] but cannot compass it
By reason of the wars that robb'd our store;
And therefore are we to request your aid.
   BAR. Alas, my Lord, we are no soldiers;   50
And what's our aid against so great a prince?
   1 KNIGHT. Tut, Jew, we know thou art no
     soldier;
Thou art a merchant and a moneyed man,
And 't is thy money, Barabas, we seek.
   BAR. How, my Lord! my money?
   FERN.   Thine and the rest.
For, to be short, amongst you 't must be
     had.
   1 JEW. Alas, my Lord, the most of us are
     poor.
   FERN. Then let the rich increase your por-
     tions.
   BAR. Are strangers[32] with your tribute to
     be tax'd?
   2 KNIGHT. Have strangers leave with us to
     get their wealth?   60
Then let them with us contribute.
   BAR. How? equally?
   FERN.   No, Jew, like infidels.
For through our sufferance of your hateful
     lives,
Who stand accursed in the sight of Heaven,
These taxes and afflictions are befall'n,

[31] Computed.   [32] Foreigners.

And therefore thus we are determined. —
Read there the articles of our decrees.
   READER. "First, the tribute-money of the
Turks shall all be levied amongst the Jews, and
each of them to pay one-half of his estate." [70
   BAR. [*aside*] How, half his estate? I hope
     you mean not mine.
   FERN. Read on.
   READER. "Secondly, he that denies to pay
shall straight become a Christian."
   BAR. [*aside*] How, a Christian? Hum,
     what's here to do?
   READER. "Lastly, he that denies this shall
absolutely lose all he has."
   ALL THREE JEWS. O my Lord, we will give
     half.
   BAR. O [33] earth-mettl'd villains, and no
     Hebrews born!
And will you basely thus submit yourselves [80
To leave your goods to their arbitrament?
   FERN. Why, Barabas, wilt thou be chris-
     t'ned?
   BAR. No, Governor, I will be no convertite.[34]
   FERN. Then pay thy half.
   BAR. Why, know you what you did by this
     device?
Half of my substance is a city's wealth.
Governor, it was not got so easily;
Nor will I part so slightly therewithal.
   FERN. Sir, half is the penalty of our decree,
Either pay that, or we will seize on all.   90
   BAR. *Corpo di Dio!* stay! you shall have
     half;
Let me be us'd but as my brethren are.
   FERN. No, Jew; thou hast denied the
     articles,
And now it cannot be recall'd.
           [*Exeunt* Officers, *on a sign from*
           FERNEZE.]
   BAR. Will you then steal my goods?
Is theft the ground of your religion?
   FERN. No, Jew; we take particularly thine
To save the ruin of a multitude;
And better one want for a common good
Than many perish for a private man.   100
Yet, Barabas, we will not banish thee;
But here in Malta, where thou gott'st thy
     wealth,
Live still, and, if thou canst, get more.
   BAR. Christians, what or how can I multi-
     ply?
Of naught is nothing made.

[33] A hypermetrical monosyllable often begins a
line of Elizabethan blank verse.
[34] Convert.

1 KNIGHT. From naught at first thou cam'st
    to little wealth,
From little unto more, from more to most.
If your first curse fall heavy on thy head,
And make thee poor and scorn'd of all the
    world,
'T is not our fault, but thy inherent sin.   110
    BAR. What, bring you Scripture to confirm
    your wrongs?
Preach me not out of my possessions.
Some Jews are wicked, as all Christians are ;
But say the tribe that I descended of
Were all in general cast away for sin,
Shall I be tried by their transgression?
The man that dealeth righteously shall live ;
And which of you can charge me otherwise?
    FERN. Out, wretched Barabas !
Sham'st thou not thus to justify thyself,   120
As if we knew not thy profession?
If thou rely upon thy righteousness,
Be patient and thy riches will increase.
Excess of wealth is cause of covetousness ;
And covetousness, O, 't is a monstrous sin.
    BAR. Ay, but theft is worse. Tush ! take
    not from me then,
For that is theft ; and if you rob me thus,
I must be forc'd to steal and compass more.
    1 KNIGHT. Grave Governor, list not to his
    exclaims.
Convert his mansion to a nunnery ;   130

Re-enter Officers.

His house will harbor many holy nuns.
    FERN. It shall be so. Now, officers, have
    you done?
    OFF. Ay, my Lord, we have seiz'd upon the
    goods
And wares of Barabas, which being valued,
Amount to more than all the wealth in
    Malta.
And of the other we have seized half.
    [FERN.] [35] Then we 'll take order for the
    residue.[36]
    BAR. Well then, my Lord, say, are you sat-
    isfied?
You have my goods, my money, and my
    wealth,
My ships, my store, and all that I enjoy'd ; [140
And, having all, you can request no more,
Unless your unrelenting, flinty hearts
Suppress all pity in your stony breasts,
And now shall move you to bereave my life.

FERN. No, Barabas, to stain our hands with
    blood
Is far from us and our profession.
    BAR. Why, I esteem the injury far less
To take the lives of miserable men
Than be the causers of their misery.
You have my wealth, the labor of my life, [150
The comfort of mine age, my children's hope,
And therefore ne'er distinguish of the wrong.[37]
    FERN. Content thee, Barabas, thou hast
    naught but right.
    BAR. Your extreme right does me exceeding
    wrong ;
But take it to you, i' the Devil's name.
    FERN. Come, let us in, and gather of these
    goods
The money for this tribute of the Turk.
    1 KNIGHT. 'T is necessary that be look'd
    unto ;
For if we break our day, we break the league,
And that will prove but simple policy.   160
        Exeunt [all but BARABAS *and the*
        Jews].[38]
    BAR. Ay, policy ! that's their profession,
And not simplicity, as they suggest.
The plagues of Egypt, and the curse of Heaven,
Earth's barrenness, and all men's hatred [39]
Inflict upon them, thou great *Primus Motor !* [40]
And here upon my knees, striking the earth,
I ban their souls to everlasting pains
And extreme tortures of the fiery deep,
That thus have dealt with me in my distress.
    1 JEW. O yet be patient, gentle Barabas. [170
    BAR. O silly brethren, born to see this day,
Why stand you thus unmov'd with my la-
    ments?
Why weep you not to think upon my wrongs?
Why pine not I, and die in this distress?
    1 JEW. Why, Barabas, as hardly can we
    brook
The cruel handling of ourselves in this ;
Thou seest they have taken half our goods.
    BAR. Why did you yield to their extortion?
You were a multitude, and I but one ;
And of me only have they taken all.   180
    1 JEW. Yet, Brother Barabas, remember
    Job.
    BAR. What tell you me of Job? I wot his
    wealth
Was written thus : he had seven thousand
    sheep,

[35] Om. Q. Sup. Robinson.
[36] We 'll make arrangements for the rest of this business.
[37] *I.e.*, make a distinction between the two injuries.
[38] The outer stage now represents the street.
[39] Trisyllabic.
[40] God, First Cause of motion.

Three thousand camels, and two hundred yoke
Of laboring oxen, and five hundred
She-asses ; but for every one of those,
Had they been valued at indifferent rate,
I had at home, and in mine argosy,
And other ships that came from Egypt last,
As much as would have bought his beasts and
    him,   190
And yet have kept enough to live upon ;
So that not he, but I, may curse the day,
Thy fatal birthday, forlorn Barabas,
And henceforth wish for an eternal night,
That clouds of darkness may inclose my flesh,
And hide these extreme sorrows from mine
    eyes :
For only I have toil'd to inherit here
The months of vanity and loss of time,
And painful nights, have been appointed me.[41]
    2 JEW. Good Barabas, be patient.[42]
    BAR.   Ay, ay ; [200
Pray, leave me in my patience. You that
Were ne'er possess'd of wealth, are pleas'd
    with want ;
But give him liberty at least to mourn,
That in a field amidst his enemies
Doth see his soldiers slain, himself disarm'd,
And knows no means of his recovery.
Ay, let me sorrow for this sudden chance ;
'T is in the trouble of my spirit I speak ;
Great injuries are not so soon forgot.
    1 JEW. Come, let us leave him ; in his ireful
    mood   210
Our words will but increase his ecstasy.[43]
    2 JEW. On, then ; but trust me 't is a
    misery
To see a man in such affliction. —
Farewell, Barabas !   *Exeunt [the three* Jews].
    BAR.   Ay, fare you well.
See the simplicity of these base slaves,
Who, for the villains have no wit themselves,
Think me to be a senseless lump of clay
That will with every water wash to dirt.
No, Barabas is born to better chance,   219
And fram'd of finer mold than common men,
That measure naught but by the present time.
A reaching thought will search his deepest wits,
And cast [44] with cunning for the time to come ;
For evils are apt to happen every day. —
But whither wends my beauteous Abigail ?

    Enter ABIGAIL, *the Jew's daughter.*

O, what has made my lovely daughter sad ?

[41] Cf. *Job*, iii, 1, ff. "Which" is understood before
"have."
[42] Trisyllabic.   [43] Fit of emotion.   [44] Plan.

What, woman ! moan not for a little loss ;
Thy father has enough in store for thee.
    ABIG. Not for myself, but aged Barabas ;
Father, for thee lamenteth Abigail.   230
But I will learn to leave these fruitless tears,
And, urg'd thereto with my afflictions,
With fierce exclaims run to the senate-house,
And in the senate reprehend them all,
And rent [45] their hearts with tearing of my
    hair,
Till they reduce [46] the wrongs done to my
    father.
    BAR. No, Abigail, things past recovery
Are hardly cur'd with exclamations.
Be silent, Daughter ; sufferance breeds ease,
And time may yield us an occasion   240
Which on the sudden cannot serve the turn.
Besides, my girl, think me not all so fond
As negligently to forego so much
Without provision for thyself and me.
Ten thousand portagues,[47] besides great pearls,
Rich costly jewels, and stones infinite,
Fearing the worst of this before it fell,
I closely hid.
    ABIG.   Where, father ?
    BAR.   In my house, my girl.
    ABIG. Then shall they ne'er be seen of
    Barabas,
For they have seiz'd upon thy house and
    wares.   250
    BAR. But they will give me leave once more,
    I trow,
To go into my house.
    ABIG.   That may they not ;
For there I left the Governor placing nuns,
Displacing me ; and of thy house they mean
To make a nunnery, where none but their own
    sect [48]
Must enter in, men generally barr'd.
    BAR. My gold, my gold, and all my wealth
    is gone !
You partial heavens, have I deserv'd this
    plague ?
What, will you thus oppose me, luckless stars,
To make me desperate in my poverty ?   260
And knowing me impatient in distress,
Think me so mad as I will hang myself,
That I may vanish o'er the earth in air,
And leave no memory that e'er I was ?
No, I will live ; nor loathe I this my life ;
And, since you leave me in the ocean thus

To sink or swim, and put me to my shifts,
I 'll rouse my senses and awake myself. —
Daughter, I have it ! Thou perceiv'st the plight
Wherein these Christians have oppressed me.
Be rul'd by me, for in extremity   271
We ought to make bar of no policy.
    ABIG. Father, whate'er it be to injure them
That have so manifestly wronged us,
What will not Abigail attempt?
    BAR.   Why, so ;
Then thus : thou told'st me they have turn'd
    my house
Into a nunnery, and some nuns are there.
    ABIG. I did.
    BAR.   Then, Abigail, there must my girl
Entreat the abbess to be entertain'd.   279
    ABIG. How, as a nun?
    BAR.   Ay, Daughter, for religion
Hides many mischiefs from suspicion.
    ABIG. Ay, but, Father, they will suspect me
    there.
    BAR. Let 'em suspect ; but be thou so pre-
    cise [49]
As they may think it done of holiness.
Entreat 'em fair, and give them friendly
    speech,
And seem to them as if thy sins were great,
Till thou has gotten to be entertain'd.
    ABIG. Thus, Father, shall I much dissemble.
    BAR.   Tush !
As good dissemble that thou never mean'st,
As first mean truth and then dissemble it.   290
A counterfeit profession is better
Than unseen hypocrisy.
    ABIG. Well, Father, say I be entertain'd,
What then shall follow?
    BAR.   This shall follow then :
There have I hid, close underneath the plank
That runs along the upper-chamber floor,
The gold and jewels which I kept for thee.
But here they come ; be cunning, Abigail.
    ABIG. Then, Father, go with me.
    BAR.   No, Abigail, in this
It is not necessary I be seen ;   300
For I will seem offended with thee for't.
Be close, [50] my girl, for this must fetch my gold.
                         [*They retire.*]

Enter Friars [JACOMO *and* BARNARDINE, *an*
    Abbess, *and a* Nun.] [51]

    [F. JAC.] Sisters,
We now are almost at the new-made nunnery.

[ABB.] [52] The better ; for we love not to be
    seen.
'T is thirty winters long since some of us
Did stray so far amongst the multitude.
    F. JAC. But, madam, this house
And waters of this new-made nunnery [53]
Will much delight you.   310
    [ABB.] It may be so ; but who comes here?
                   [ABIGAIL *comes forward.*]
    ABIG. Grave abbess, and you, happy vir-
    gins' guide,
Pity the state of a distressed maid.
    ABB. What art thou, daughter?
    ABIG. The hopeless daughter of a hapless
    Jew,
The Jew of Malta, wretched Barabas ;
Sometimes [54] the owner of a goodly house,
Which they have now turn'd to a nunnery.
    ABB. Well, daughter, say, what is thy suit
    with us?
    ABIG. Fearing the afflictions which my
    father feels   320
Proceed from sin, or want of faith in us,
I 'd pass away my life in penitence,
And be a novice in your nunnery,
To make atonement for my laboring soul.
    F. JAC. No doubt, brother, but this pro-
    ceedeth of the spirit.
    F. BARN. Ay, and a moving spirit too,
    brother ; but come,
Let us entreat she may be entertain'd.
    ABB. Well, daughter, we admit you for a
    nun.
    ABIG. First let me as a novice learn to
    frame
My solitary life to your strait laws,   330
And let me lodge where I was wont to lie.
I do not doubt, by your divine precepts
And mine own industry, but to profit much.
    BAR. [*aside*] As much, I hope, as all I hid is
    worth.
    ABB. Come, daughter, follow us.
    BAR. [*coming forward*] Why, how now, Abi-
    gail, what mak'st [55] thou
Amongst these hateful Christians?
    F. JAC. Hinder her not, thou man of little
    faith,
For she has mortified herself. [56]
    BAR.   How ! mortified?
    F. JAC. And is admitted to the sisterhood.

---

[49] Pious, puritanical.   [50] Secret.
[51] Q *Enter three Fryars and two Nuns.* They are
not named in speech tags, throughout.

[52] Q *1Nun,* and for her next speech *Nun.*
[53] This repetition, and the metrical irregularities
of the passage, indicate corruption, probably due to
the omission of part of the original text.
[54] Formerly.   [55] Dost.
[56] Rendered herself dead to the world.

Bar. Child of perdition, and thy father's
    shame,   341
What wilt thou do among these hateful fiends?
I charge thee on my blessing that thou leave
These devils, and their damned heresy.

    Abig. Father, give [57] me —

    Bar. (*whispers to her.*)   Nay, back,
    Abigail,
And think upon the jewels and the gold ;
The board is marked thus that covers it. —
Away, accursed, from thy father's sight.

    F. Jac. Barabas, although thou art in mis-
    belief,
And wilt not see thine own afflictions,   350
Yet let thy daughter be no longer blind.

    Bar. Blind friar, I reck not thy persua-
    sions, —   [*aside to* Abigail]
The board is marked thus + that covers it. —
For I had rather die than see her thus.
Wilt thou forsake me too in my distress,
Seduced daughter? — (*aside to her*) Go ; for-
    get n[o]t ! —
Becomes it Jews to be so credulous? —
(*aside to her*) To-morrow early I 'll be at the
    door. —
No, come not at me ; if thou wilt be damn'd,
Forget me, see me not, and so begone. — 360
(*aside to her*) Farewell, remember to-morrow
    morning. —
Out, out, thou wretch !
[*Exeunt, on one side* Barabas, *on the other side*
    Friars, Abbess, Nun, *and* Abigail.]

Enter Mathias.

    Math. Who's this? Fair Abigail, the rich
    Jew's daughter,
Become a nun? Her father's sudden fall
Has humbled her and brought her down to
    this.
Tut, she were fitter for a tale of love,
Than to be tired out with orisons ;
And better would she far become a bed,
Embraced in a friendly lover's arms,
Than rise at midnight to a solemn mass. 370

Enter Lodowick.

    Lod. Why, how now, Don Mathias, in a
    dump?

    Math. Believe me, noble Lodowick, I have
    seen
The strangest sight, in my opinion,
That ever I beheld.

    Lod.   What was 't, I prithee?

    Math. A fair young maid, scarce **fourteen**
    years of age,
The sweetest flower in Cytherea's field,
Cropp'd from the pleasures of the **fruitful**
    earth,
And strangely metamorph[o]s'd nun

    Lod. But say, what was she?

    Math.   Why, the rich Jew's **daughter.**

    Lod. What, Barabas, whose goods **were**
    lately seiz'd?   380
Is she so fair?

    Math.   And matchless beautiful,
As, had you seen her, 't would have mov'd
    your heart,
Though [countermur'd] [58] with walls of brass,
    to love,
Or at the least to pity.

    Lod. An if she be so fair as you report,
'T were time well spent to go and visit her.
How say you, shall we?

    Math. I must and will, sir ; there's no
    remedy.

    Lod. And so will I, too, or it shall go hard.
Farewell, Mathias.

    Math.   Farewell, Lodowick. 390
                    Exeunt.

ACT II — [Scene I] [1]

Enter Barabas *with a light.*

    Bar. Thus, like the sad presaging raven,
    that tolls
The sick man's passport in her hollow beak,
And in the shadow of the silent night
Doth shake contagion from her sable wings,
Vex'd and tormented runs poor Barabas
With fatal curses towards these Christians.
The incertain pleasures of swift-footed Time
Have ta'en their flight, and left me in despair ;
And of my former riches rests no more
But bare remembrance, like a soldier's scar,
That has no further comfort for his maim. 11
O Thou that with a fiery pillar ledd'st
The sons of Israel through the dismal shades,
Light Abraham's offspring, and direct the
    hand
Of Abigail this night ; or let the day
Turn to eternal darkness after this !
No sleep can fasten on my watchful eyes,
Nor quiet enter my distemper'd thoughts,
Till I have answer of my Abigail.

[57] Emend. Dyce, *forgive.* But probably Abigail is
about to request a paternal blessing.

[58] Conj. Deighton ; Q *countermin'd.* Cf. *Spanish
Tragedy*, III, vii, 16.
[1] Before Barabas's house.

Enter ABIGAIL *above.*

ABIG. Now have I happily espi'd a time   20
To search the plank my father did appoint ;
And here behold, unseen, where I have found
The gold, the pearls, and jewels, which he hid.

BAR. Now I remember those old women's
   words,
Who in my wealth would tell me winter's tales,
And speak of spirits and ghosts that glide by
   night
About the place where treasure hath been hid ;
And now methinks that I am one of those,
For whilst I live here lives my soul's sole hope,
And, when I die, here shall my spirit walk.   30

ABIG. Now that my father's fortune were
   so good
As but to be about this happy place.
'T is not so happy ; yet, when we parted last,
He said he would attend me in the morn.
Then, gentle sleep, where'er his body rests,
Give charge to Morpheus that he may dream
A golden dream, and of the sudden walk,
Come, and receive the treasure I have found.

BAR. *Bueno para todos mi ganado no era.*[2]
As good go on as sit so sadly thus.   40
But stay, what star shines yonder in the east?
The loadstar of my life, if Abigail.
Who 's there?

ABIG.   Who 's that?

BAR.   Peace, Abigail, 't is I.

ABIG. Then, Father, here receive thy happiness.

BAR.   Hast thou 't?

               [She] throws down bags.

ABIG. Here, hast thou 't? There 's more,
   and more, and more.

BAR. O my girl, my gold, my fortune, my
   felicity !
Strength to my soul, death to mine enemy,
Welcome, the first beginner of my bliss !
O A[b]igail, Abigail, that I had thee here too ;
Then my desires were fully satisfied.   50
But I will practise [3] thy enlargement thence.
O girl, O gold, O beauty, O my bliss !

               Hugs his bags.

ABIG. Father, it draweth towards midnight
   now,
And 'bout this time the nuns begin to wake ;
To shun suspicion, therefore, let us part.

BAR. Farewell, my joy, and by my fingers
   take

---

[2] My flock was not good for all. Emend. Dyce ; Q
(garbling the Spanish) : *Birn para todos, my ganada
no er. I.e.,* my wealth does not avail me in every
emergency.   [3] Plot.

A kiss from him that sends it from his soul.
Now Phœbus ope the eyelids of the day,
And, for the raven, wake the morning lark,
That I may hover with her in the air,   60
Singing o'er these, as she does o'er her young,
Hermoso [placer de los dineros.] [4]   *Exeunt.*

[SCENE II] [5]

Enter Governor [FERNEZE], MARTIN DEL
   Bosco, [and] the Knights.

FERN. Now, captain, tell us whither thou
   art bound?
Whence is thy ship that anchors in our road?
And why thou cam'st ashore without our
   leave?

BOSC. Governor of Malta, hither am I
   bound ;
My ship, the Flying Dragon, is of Spain,
And so am I ; Del Bosco is my name,
Vice-admiral unto the Catholic King.

1 KNIGHT. 'T is true, my Lord ; therefore
   entreat [6] him well.

BOSC. Our fraught is Grecians, Turks, and
   Afric Moors.
For late upon the coast of Corsica,   10
Because we vail'd [7] not to the [Turkish] [8] fleet,
Their creeping galleys had us in the chase.
But suddenly the wind began to rise,
And then we [luff'd and tack'd] [9] and fought at
   ease.
Some have we fir'd, and many have we sunk ;
But one amongst the rest became our prize.
The captain 's slain ; the rest remain our slaves,
Of whom we would make sale in Malta here.

FERN. Martin del Bosco, I have heard of
   thee ;
Welcome to Malta, and to all of us.   20
But to admit a sale of these thy Turks
We may not, nay, we dare not give consent,
By reason of a tributary league.

1 KNIGHT. Del Bosco, as thou lovest and
   honor'st us,
Persuade our governor against the Turk ;
This truce we have is but in hope of gold,
And with that sum he craves might we wage
   war.

BOSC. Will Knights of Malta be in league
   with Turks,
And buy it basely, too, for sums of gold?   29

---

[4] Beautiful pleasure of money. Emend. Dyce;
Q *Hermoso Piarer, de les Dinirch.*
[5] Unlocated ; presumably the senate-house.
[6] Treat.
[7] Struck topsails or dipped flags in deference.
[8] Emend. Gilchrist ; Q *Spanish.*
[9] Emend. Dyce ; Q *left and tooke.*

My Lord, remember that, to Europe's shame,
The Christian Isle of Rhodes, from whence you
    came,
Was lately lost, and you were stated [10] here
To be at deadly enmity with Turks.

FERN. Captain, we know it; but our force
    is small.

BOSC. What is the sum that Calymath re-
    quires?

FERN. A hundred thousand crowns.

BOSC. My lord and king hath title to this
    isle,
And he means quickly to expel you hence;
Therefore be rul'd by me, and keep the gold.
I'll write unto his Majesty for aid,   40
And not depart until I see you free.

FERN. On this condition shall thy Turks
    be sold.
Go, officers, and set them straight in show.
                   [*Exeunt* Officers.]
Bosco, thou shalt be Malta's general;
We and our warlike knights will follow thee
Against these barbarous, misbelieving Turks.

BOSC. So shall you imitate those you suc-
    ceed;
For when their hideous force environ'd Rhodes,
Small though the number was that kept the
    town,
They fought it out, and not a man surviv'd [50
To bring the hapless news to Christendom.[11]

FERN. So will we fight it out. Come, let's
    away!
Proud, daring Calymath, instead of gold,
We'll send the[e] bullets wrapp'd in smoke
    and fire.
Claim tribute where thou wilt, we are resolv'd;
Honor is bought with blood and not with
    gold.   *Exeunt.*

[SCENE III] [12]

Enter Officers *with* [ITHAMORE *and other*] Slaves.

1 OFF. This is the market-place, here let 'em
    stand;
Fear not their sale, for they'll be quickly
    bought.

2 OFF. Every one's price is written on his
    back,
And so much must they yield or not be sold.

---

[10] Stationed. The Knights of St. John of Jerusalem were expelled from Rhodes by the Turks in
1522; Charles V granted Malta to them in 1529.
[11] On the contrary, the Knights made excellent
terms.
[12] The market-place, ll. 1-6, 98-168; a street,
ll. 7-98; the street before Barabas's new house,
l. 169 to end.

1 OFF. Here comes the Jew; had not his
    goods been seiz'd,
He'd **give** us present money for them all.

Enter BARABAS.

BAR. In spite of these swine-eating Chris-
    tians, —
Unchosen nation, never circumcis'd,
Such as, poor villains, were ne'er thought
    upon
Till Titus and Vespasian conquer'd us —   10
Am I become as wealthy as I was.
They hop'd my daughter would ha' been a
    nun;
But she's at home, and I have bought a house
As great and fair as is the Governor's.
And there in spite of Malta will I dwell,
Having Ferneze's hand, [13] whose heart I'll
    have;
Ay, and his son's too, or it shall go hard.
I am not of the tribe of Levi, I,
That can so soon forget an injury.
We Jews can fawn like spaniels when we
    please;   20
And when we grin we bite, yet are our looks
As innocent and harmless as a lamb's.
I learn'd in Florence [14] how to kiss my hand,
Heave up my shoulders when they call me
    dog,
And duck as low as any barefoot friar;
Hoping to see them starve upon a stall,[15]
Or else be gather'd for in our synagogue,
That, when the offering-basin comes to me,
Even for charity I may spit into 't.
Here comes Don Lodowick, the Governor's
    son,   30
One that I love for his good father's sake.

Enter LODOWICK.

LOD. I hear the wealthy Jew walked this
    way.
I'll seek him out, and so insinuate
That I may have a sight of Abigail;
For Don Mathias tells me she is fair.

BAR. [*aside*] Now will I show myself
To have more of the serpent than the dove;
That is, more knave than fool.

LOD. Yond' walks the Jew; now for fair
    Abigail.

BAR. [*aside*] Ay, ay, no doubt but she's at
    your command.   40

---

[13] Probably a promise of safety, in writing.
[14] The home of Machiavelli; the reiteration of *policy* in this play is also referable to the Elizabethan notion of his theories.
[15] Assigned quarters (in an almshouse). (*N.E.D.*)

Lod. Barabas, thou know'st I am the Governor's son.

Bar. I would you were his father, too, sir; That's all the harm I wish you. — [*aside*] The slave [16] looks
Like a hog's cheek new sing'd.

Lod.   Whither walk'st thou, Barabas?

Bar. No further; 't is a custom held with us,
That when we speak with Gentiles like to you,
We turn into the air to purge ourselves;
For unto us the promise doth belong.

Lod. Well, Barabas, canst help me to a diamond?   49

Bar. O, sir, your father had my diamonds.
Yet I have one left that will serve your turn. —
[*aside*] I mean my daughter; but ere he shall have her
I 'll sacrifice her on a pile of wood.
I ha' the poison of the city [17] for him,
And the white leprosy.

Lod. What sparkle does it give without a foil? [18]

Bar. The diamond that I talk of ne'er was foil'd. —
[*aside*] But when he touches it, it will be foil'd. [19] —
Lord Lodowick, it sparkles bright and fair.

Lod. Is it square or pointed, pray let me know.   60

Bar. Pointed [20] it is, good sir — (*aside*) but not for you.

Lod. I like it much the better.

Bar.   So do I too.

Lod. How shows it by night?

Bar.   Outshines Cynthia's rays:
— (*aside*) You 'll like it better far a-nights than days.

Lod. And what 's the price?

Bar. [*aside*]   Your life an if you have it. —
O my Lord,
We will not jar about the price; come to my house
And I will give 't your Honor — (*aside*) with a vengeance.

Lod. No, Barabas, I will deserve it first.

Bar. Good sir,   70
Your father has deserv'd it at my hands,
Who, of mere charity and Christian ruth,
To bring me to religious purity,

And as it were in catechising sort,
To make me mindful of my mortal sins,
Against my will, and whether I would or no,
Seiz'd all I had, and thrust me out a' doors,
And made my house a place for nuns most chaste.

Lod. No doubt your soul shall reap the fruit of it.

Bar. Ay, but, my Lord, the harvest is far off.   80
And yet I know the prayers of those nuns
And holy friars, having money for their pains,
Are wondrous; — (*aside*) and indeed do no man good —
And seeing they are not idle, but still doing,
'T is likely they in time may reap some fruit —
I mean in fullness of perfection.

Lod. Good Barabas, glance not at [21] our holy nuns.

Bar. No, but I do it through a burning zeal, —
(*aside*) Hoping ere long to set the house afire;
For though they do a while increase and multiply,   90
I 'll have a saying [22] to that nunnery. —
As for the diamond, sir, I told you of,
Come home and there 's no price shall make us part,
Even for your honorable father's sake. —
(*aside*) It shall go hard but I will see your death. —
But now I must be gone to buy a slave.

Lod. And, Barabas, I 'll bear thee company.

Bar. Come, then; — here 's the marketplace.
What 's the price of this slave? Two hundred crowns!
Do the Turk[s] weigh so much?

1 Off.   Sir, that 's his price. [100

Bar. What, can he steal, that you demand so much?
Belike he has some new trick for a purse;
And if he has, he is worth three hundred plates, [23]
So that, being bought, the town seal might be got
To keep him for his lifetime from the gallows.
The sessions day is critical to thieves,
And few or none 'scape but by being purg'd.

Lod. Ratest thou this Moor but at two hundred plates?

1 Off. No more, my Lord.

---

[16] His neatly shaved face.
[17] Possibly a misprint. (Dyce.)
[18] Metal leaf placed under a gem to increase its brilliance.   [19] Defiled.
[20] Punning on "pointed" and "appointed."

[21] Cast no reflections on.   [23] Silver coins.
[22] Something to say.

BAR. Why should this Turk be dearer than
    that Moor?   110
1 OFF. Because he is young and has more
    qualities.
BAR. What, hast thou the philosopher's
stone?[24] An thou hast, break my head with
it; I'll forgive thee.
[SLAVE.][25] No, sir; I can cut and shave.
BAR. Let me see, sirrah, are you not an old
shaver?
[SLAVE.] Alas, sir! I am a very youth.
BAR. A youth? I'll buy you, and marry
you to Lady Vanity,[26] if you do well.   120
[SLAVE.] I will serve you, sir.
BAR. Some wicked trick or other. It may
be, under color of shaving, thou'lt cut my
throat for my goods. Tell me, hast thou thy
health well?
[SLAVE.] Ay, passing well.
BAR. So much the worse; I must have one
that's sickly, [an't][27] be but for sparing vict-
uals. 'T is not a stone of beef a day will
maintain you in these chops;[28] let me see one
that's somewhat leaner.   131
1 OFF. Here's a leaner; how like you him?
BAR.   Where was thou born?
ITHA. In Thrace; brought up in Arabia.
BAR. So much the better; thou art for my
    turn.
An hundred crowns? I'll have him; there's
    the coin.
1 OFF. Then mark him, sir, and take him
    hence.
BAR. [aside] Ay, mark him, you were best;
    for this is he
That by my help shall do much villainy. —
My Lord, farewell. — Come, sirrah, you are
    mine. —
As for the diamond, it shall be yours;   140
I pray, sir, be no stranger at my house;
All that I have shall be at your command.

Enter MATHIAS [*and his* Mother, KATHERINE].

MATH. [aside] What makes the Jew and
    Lodowick so private?
I fear me 't is about fair Abigail.
BAR. Yonder comes Don Mathias; let us
    stay;[29]
He loves my daughter, and she holds him dear:

[24] Sought by alchemists, to turn other metals into
gold.
[25] Q assigns to Ithamore, throughout.
[26] A character in the Morality plays.
[27] Q *and*.
[28] Jaws; *i.e.,* your fat face.   [29] Stop talking.

But I have sworn to frustrate both their hopes,
And be reveng'd upon the — [*aside*] Governor!
                         [*Exit* LODOWICK.]
    [KATH.][30] This Moor is comeliest, is he not?
    Speak, Son.
MATH. No, this is the better, Mother; view
    this well.   150
BAR. [*aside to* MATHIAS] Seem not to know
    me here before your mother,
Lest she mistrust the match that is in hand.
When you have brought her home, come to my
    house;
Think of me as thy father; Son, farewell.
MATH. [*aside to* BARABAS] But wherefore
    talk'd Don Lodowick with you?
BAR. [*aside to* MATHIAS] Tush, man! we
    talk'd of diamonds, not of Abigail.
KATH. Tell me, Mathias, is not that the
    Jew?
BAR. As for the comment on the Macca-
    bees,
I have it, sir, and 't is at your command.
MATH. Yes, madam, and my talk with him
    was   160
About the borrowing of a book or two.
KATH. Converse not with him; he is cast
    off from Heaven. —
Thou hast thy crowns, fellow. — Come, let's
    away.
MATH. Sirrah, Jew, remember the book.
BAR. Marry will I, sir.
            Exeunt [MATHIAS *and his* Mother].
OFF.   Come, I have made
A reasonable market; let's away.
            [*Exeunt* Officers *with* Slaves.]
BAR. Now let me know thy name, and
    therewithal
Thy birth, condition, and profession.
ITHA. Faith, sir, my birth is but mean; my
name's Ithamore; my profession what you
please.   171
BAR. Hast thou no trade? Then listen to
    my words,
And I will teach [thee][31] that shall stick by
    thee.
First be thou void of these affections:
Compassion, love, vain hope, and heartless
    fear;
Be mov'd at nothing, see thou pity none,
But to thyself smile when the Christians
    moan.
ITHA. O, brave! Master, I worship your
    nose[32] for this.

[30] Q *Mater*, throughout.   [31] Add. Reed.
[32] Barabas was played with a false nose.

BAR. As for myself, I walk abroad a-nights
And kill sick people groaning under walls ;
Sometimes I go about and poison wells ; 181
And now and then, to cherish Christian thieves,
I am content to lose some of my crowns,
That I may, walking in my gallery,[33]
See 'em go pinion'd along by my door.
Being young, I studied physic, and began
To practise first upon the Italian ;
There I enrich'd the priests with burials,
And always kept the sextons' arms in ure [34]
With digging graves and ringing dead men's
    knells. 190
And after that was I an engineer,
And in the wars 'twixt France and Germany,
Under pretence of helping Charles the Fifth,
Slew friend and enemy with my stratagems.
Then after that was I an usurer,
And with extorting, cozening,[35] forfeiting,
And tricks belonging unto brokery,
I fill'd the jails with bankrouts in a year,
And with young orphans planted hospitals,
And every moon made some or other mad, [200
And now and then one hang himself for grief,
Pinning upon his breast a long great scroll
How I with interest tormented him.
But mark how I am blest for plaguing them :
I have as much coin as will buy the town.
But tell me now, how hast thou spent thy
    time?
    ITHA. Faith, master,
In setting Christian villages on fire,
Chaining of eunuchs, binding galley-slaves.
One time I was an ostler in an inn, 210
And in the nighttime secretly would I steal
To travellers' chambers, and there cut their
    throats.
Once at Jerusalem, where the pilgrims kneel'd,
I strowed powder on the marble stones,
And therewithal their knees would rankle so,
That I have laugh'd a-good [36] to see the
    cripples
Go limping home to Christendom on stilts.[37]
    BAR. Why this is something. Make ac-
    count of me
As of thy fellow ; we are villains both, 219
Both circumcised, we hate Christians both.
Be true and secret, thou shalt want no gold.
But stand aside ; here comes Don Lodowick.

Re-enter LODOWICK.

    LOD. O, Barabas, well met ;
Where is the diamond you told me of?

[33] Balcony.
[34] Use, practice.
[35] Cheating, befooling.
[36] Heartily, in earnest.
[37] Crutches.

    BAR. I have it for you, sir ; please you walk
    in with me.
What ho, Abigail ! open the door, I say.

Enter ABIGAIL

    ABIG. In good time, father ; here are letters
    come
From Ormus, and the post [38] stays here within.
    BAR. Give me the letters. — (*aside*) Daugh-
    ter, do you hear,
Entertain Lodowick, the Governor's son, 230
With all the courtesy you can afford,
Provided that you keep your maidenhead.
Use him as if he were a Philistine ;
Dissemble, swear, protest, vow to love him ;
He is not of the seed of Abraham. —
I am a little busy, sir, pray pardon me.
Abigail, bid him welcome for my sake.
    ABIG. For your sake and his own he's wel-
    come hither.
    BAR. Daughter, a word more ; — [*aside*]
    kiss him, speak him fair,
And like a cunning Jew so cast about 240
That ye be both made sure [39] ere you come out.
    ABIG. [*aside*] O father ! Don Mathias is my
    love.
    BAR. [*aside*] I know it ; yet I say, make love
    to him ;
Do, it is requisite it should be so. —
Nay, on my life, it is my factor's hand ;
But go you in, I'll think upon the account.
    [*Exeunt* ABIGAIL *and* LODOWICK
    into the house.]
The account is made, for Lodowick dies.
My factor sends me word a merchant's fled
That owes me for a hundred tun of wine.
I weigh it thus much [*snapping his fingers*] ; I
    have wealth enough. 250
For now by this has he kiss'd Abigail ;
And she vows love to him, and he to her.
As sure as Heaven rain'd manna for the Jews,
So sure shall he and Don Mathias die :
His father was [40] my chiefest enemy.

Re-enter MATHIAS.

Whither goes Don Mathias? Stay awhile.
    MATH. Whither but to my fair love,
    Abigail?
    BAR. Thou know'st, and Heaven can wit-
    ness it is true,
That I intend my daughter shall be thine.
    MATH. Ay, Barabas, or else thou wrong'st
    me much. 260

[38] Messenger.
[39] Betrothed.
[40] *I.e.*, in the late proceedings.

BAR. O, Heaven forbid I should have such a thought.

Pardon me though I weep ; the Governor's son
Will, whether I will or no, have Abigail :
He sends her letters, bracelets, jewels, rings.

MATH. Does she receive them?

BAR. She? No, Mathias, no, but sends them back ;
And when he comes, she locks herself up fast ;
Yet through the keyhole will he talk to her,
While she runs to the window looking out
When you should come and hale him from the door.   270

MATH. O treacherous Lodowick !

BAR. Even now, as I came home, he slipp'd me in ;
And I am sure he is with Abigail.

MATH. I 'll rouse him thence.

BAR. Not for all Malta ; therefore sheathe your sword.
If you love me, no quarrels in my house ;
But steal you in, and seem to see him not.
I 'll give him such a warning ere he goes
As he shall have small hopes of Abigail.
Away, for here they come.   280

Re-enter LODOWICK [*and*] ABIGAIL.

MATH. What, hand in hand ! I cannot suffer this.

BAR. Mathias, as thou lov'st me, not a word.

MATH. Well, let it pass ; another time shall serve.   *Exit.*

LOD. Barabas, is not that the widow's son?

BAR. Ay, and take heed, for he hath sworn your death.

LOD. My death? What, is the baseborn peasant mad?

BAR. No, no ; but happily [41] he stands in fear
Of that which you, I think, ne'er dream upon,
My daughter here, a paltry silly girl.

LOD. Why, loves she Don Mathias?   290

BAR. Doth she not with her smiling answer you?

ABIG. [*aside*] He has my heart ; I smile against my will.

LOD. Barabas, thou know'st I have lov'd thy daughter long.

BAR. And so has she done you, even from a child.

LOD. And now I can no longer hold my mind.

BAR. Nor I the affection that I bear to you.

[41] Haply.

LOD. This is thy diamond ; tell me shall I have it?

BAR. Win it, and wear it ; it is yet [unfoil'd].[42]
O, but I know your Lordship would disdain
To marry with the daughter of a Jew ;   300
And yet I 'll give her many a golden cross,[43]
With Christian posies [44] round about the ring.

LOD. 'T is not thy wealth, but her that I esteem.
Yet crave I thy consent.

BAR. And mine you have, yet let me talk to her. —
(*Aside*) This offspring of Cain, this Jebusite,
That never tasted of the Passover
Nor e'er shall see the land of Canaan
Nor our Messias that is yet to come,
This gentle [45] maggot, Lodowick, I mean, [310
Must be deluded. Let him have thy hand,
But keep thy heart till Don Mathias comes.

ABIG. [*aside*] What, shall I be betroth'd to Lodowick?

BAR. [*aside*] It 's no sin to deceive a Christian,
For they themselves hold it a principle
Faith is not to be held with heretics ;
But all are heretics that are not Jews ;
This follows well, and therefore, Daughter, fear not. —
I have entreated her, and she will grant.

LOD. Then, gentle Abigail, plight thy faith to me.   320

ABIG. I cannot choose, seeing my father bids.
Nothing but death shall part my love and me.

LOD. Now have I that for which my soul hath long'd.

BAR. (*aside.*) So have not I, but yet I hope I shall.

ABIG. [*aside*] O wretched Abigail, what hast [thou] [46] done?

LOD. Why on the sudden is your color chang'd?

ABIG. I know not, but farewell ; I must be gone.

BAR. Stay her, but let her not speak one word more.

LOD. Mute a' the sudden ! Here 's a sudden change.

BAR. O, muse not at it, 't is the Hebrews' guise,   330

[42] Emend. Collier ; Q *vnsoyl'd.*
[43] Coin with a cross on one side.
[44] Mottoes ; *i.e.*, the inscriptions.
[45] Punning on "gentile."
[46] Q *thee.*

That maidens new betroth'd should weep
  awhile.
Trouble her not ; sweet Lodowick, depart ;
She is thy wife, and thou shalt be mine heir.
    Lod. O, is 't the custom? Then I am re-
    solv'd ; [47]
But rathe[r] let the brightsome heavens be
  dim
And nature's beauty choke with stifling
  clouds,
Than my fair Abigail should frown on me. —
There comes the villain ; now I 'll be reveng'd.

    Re-enter Mathias.

    Bar. Be quiet, Lodowick ; it is enough
That I have made thee sure to Abigail.   340
    Lod. Well, let him go.   *Exit.*
    Bar. Well, but for me, as you went in at
    doors
You had been stabb'd ; but not a word on 't
  now ;
Here must no speeches pass nor swords be
  drawn.
    Math. Suffer me, Barabas, but to follow
    him.
    Bar. No ; so shall I, if any hurt be done,
Be made an accessary of your deeds.
Revenge it on him when you meet him next.
    Math. For this I 'll have his heart.   349
    Bar. Do so ; lo, here I give thee Abigail.
    Math. What greater gift can poor Mathias
    have?
Shall Lodowick rob me of so fair a love?
My life is not so dear as Abigail.
    Bar. My heart misgives me that, to cross
    your love,
He 's with your mother ; therefore after
  him.
    Math. What, is he gone unto my mother?
    Bar. Nay, if you will, stay till she comes
    herself.
    Math. I cannot stay ; for if my mother
    come,
She 'll die with grief.   *Exit.*
    Abig. I cannot take my leave of him for
    tears. —   360
Father, why have you thus incens'd them
  both?
    Bar. What 's that to thee?
    Abig.   I 'll make 'em friends again.
    Bar. You 'll make 'em friends ! Are there
    not Jews enow
In Malta, but thou must dote upon a Christian?

[47] Satisfied.

    Abig. I will have Don Mathias ; he is my
    love.
    Bar. Yes, you shall have him. — Go, put
    her in.
    Itha. Ay, I 'll put her in.
                   [Puts Abigail *in.]*
    Bar. Now tell me, Ithamore, how lik'st
    thou this?
    Itha. Faith, master, I think by this   369
You purchase both their lives ; is it not so?
    Bar. True ; and it shall be cunningly per-
    form'd.
    Itha. O master, that I might have a hand
    in this.
    Bar. Ay, so thou shalt ; 't is thou must do
    the deed.
Take this, and bear it to Mathias straight,
                   [Gives a letter.]
And tell him that it comes from Lodowick.
    Itha. 'T is poison'd, is it not?
    Bar. No, no ; and yet it might be done that
    way.
It is a challenge feign'd from Lodowick.
    Itha. Fear not ; I 'll so set his heart afire
That he shall verily think it comes from him.
    Bar. I cannot choose but like thy readi-
    ness ;   381
Yet be not rash, but do it cunningly.
    Itha. As I behave myself in this, employ
    me hereafter.
    Bar. Away then.   *Exit* [Ithamore].
So ; now will I go in to Lodowick
And, like a cunning spirit, feign some lie,
Till I have set 'em both at enmity.   *Exit.*

      ACT III — [Scene I] [1]

    Enter [Bellamira,] *a courtesan.*

    Bell. Since this town was besieg'd, my gain
    grows cold.
The time has been that, but for one bare
  night,
A hundred ducats have been freely given ;
But now against my will I must be chaste,
And yet I know my beauty doth not fail.
From Venice merchants and from Padua
Were wont to come rare-witted gentlemen,
Scholars, I mean, learned and liberal ;
And now, save Pilia-Borza, comes there
  none,
And he is very seldom from my house ;   10
And here he comes.

[1] A street near Bellamira's house.

Enter PILIA-BORZA.

PILIA. Hold thee, wench; there's something for thee to spend. [*Shows a bag of silver.*]

BELL. 'T is silver; I disdain it.

PILIA. Ay, but the Jew has gold,
And I will have it, or it shall go hard.

COURT. Tell me, how cam'st thou by this?

PILIA. Faith, walking the back lanes, through the gardens, I chanc'd to cast mine eye up to the Jew's countinghouse, where [20 I saw some bags of money, and in the night I clamber'd up with my hooks, and, as I was taking my choice, I heard a rumbling in the house; so I took only this, and run my way. But here's the Jew's man.

Enter ITHAMORE.

BELL. Hide the bag.

PILIA. Look not towards him; let's away. Zoons, what a looking thou keep'st; thou 'lt betray 's anon.

[*Exeunt* BELLAMIRA *and* PILIA-BORZA.]

ITHA. O the sweetest face that ever I [30 beheld! I know she is a courtesan by her attire. Now would I give a hundred of the Jew's crowns that I had such a concubine.
Well, I have deliver'd the challenge in such sort
As meet they will, and fighting die — brave sport!   *Exit.*

[SCENE II] [2]

Enter MATHIAS.

MATH. This is the place; now Abigail shall see
Whether Mathias holds her dear or no.

Enter LODOWICK, *reading.* [3]

MATH. What, dares the villain write in such base terms?

LOD. I did it; and revenge it if thou dar'st.
    [*They*] *fight.*

Enter BARABAS, *above.*

BAR. O, bravely fought; and yet they thrust not home.
Now, Lodowick! now, Mathias! — So!
    [*Both fall.*]
So now they have show'd themselves to be tall [4] fellows.

[2] Before the house of Barabas.
[3] Cf. III, iii, 20–22.
[4] Valiant.

[*Cries*] *within.* Part 'em, part 'em

BAR. Ay, part 'em now they are dead.
Farewell, farewell.   *Exit.*

Enter FERNEZE, KATHERINE [*and* Attendants].

FERN. What sight is this? — my Lodowick slain!   10
These arms of mine shall be thy sepulchre.

KATH. Who is this? My son Mathias slain!

FERN. O Lodowick! hadst thou perish'd by the Turk,
Wretched Ferneze might have veng'd thy death.

KATH. Thy son slew mine, and I 'll revenge his death.

FERN. Look, Katherine, look; thy son gave mine these wounds.

KATH. O, leave to grieve me; I am griev'd enough.

FERN. O, that my sighs could turn to lively breath,
And these my tears to blood, that he might live.

KATH. Who made them enemies? 20

FERN. I know not, and that grieves me most of all.

KATH. My son lov'd thine.

FERN.   And so did Lodowick him.

KATH. Lend me that weapon that did kill my son,
And it shall murder me.

FERN. Nay, madam, stay; that weapon was my son's,
And on that rather should Ferneze die.

KATH. Hold; let's inquire the causers of their deaths,
That we may venge their blood upon their heads.

FERN. Then take them up, and let them be interr'd
Within one sacred monument of stone; 30
Upon which altar I will offer up
My daily sacrifice of sighs and tears,
And with my prayers pierce impartial Heavens,
Till they [reveal] [5] the causers of our smarts,
Which forc'd their hands divide united hearts.
Come, Katherina, our losses equal are;
Then of true grief let us take equal share.
    Exeunt [*with the bodies*].

[5] Conj. Dyce; om. Q.

[SCENE III] [6]

Enter ITHAMORE.

ITHA. Why, was there ever seen such vil-
    lainy,
So neatly plotted, and so well perform'd?
Both held in hand,[7] and flatly both beguil'd?

Enter ABIGAIL.

ABIG. Why, how now, Ithamore, why
    laugh'st thou so?
ITHA. O mistress, ha! ha! ha!
ABIG. Why, what ail'st thou?
ITHA. O my master!
ABIG. Ha!
ITHA. O mistress! I have the bravest,[8]
gravest, secret, subtle, bottle-nos'd knave to
my master, that ever gentleman had.   11
ABIG. Say, knave, why rail'st upon my
    father thus?
ITHA. O, my master has the bravest policy.
ABIG. Wherein?
ITHA. Why, know you not?
ABIG. Why, no.
ITHA. Know you not of Mathias' and Don
Lodowick's disaster?
ABIG. No; what was it?   19
ITHA. Why, the Devil invented a challenge,
my master writ it, and I carried it, first to
Lodowick, and *imprimis* to Mathias.
And then they met, [and,][9] as the story says,
In doleful wise they ended both their days.
ABIG. And was my father furtherer of their
    deaths?
ITHA. Am I Ithamore?
ABIG. Yes.
ITHA. So sure did your father write, and I
carry the challenge.
ABIG. Well, Ithamore, let me request thee
    this: 30
Go to the new-made nunnery, and inquire
For any of the friars of Saint [Jacques,][10]
And say I pray them come and speak with me.
ITHA. I pray, mistress, will you answer me
to one question?[11]
ABIG. Well, sirrah, what is 't?
ITHA. A very feeling one: have not the
nuns fine sport with the friars now and then?

---

[6] Unlocated; presumably a room in Barabas's
house.
[7] Led on and deluded.
[8] Finest.
[9] Add. Robinson.
[10] "Jacobins," *i.e.*, Dominicans. Cor. Collier;
Q *Iaynes*.
[11] An interpolated piece of clowning? (Bennett,
on ll. 34–41.)

ABIG. Go to, sirrah sauce; is this your
question? Get ye gone.   40
ITHA. I will, forsooth, mistress.   *Exit.*
ABIG. Hard-hearted father, unkind Bara-
    bas!
Was this the pursuit of thy policy?
To make me show them favor severally,
That by my favor they should both be slain?
Admit thou lov'dst not Lodowick for his
    [sire],[12]
Yet Don Mathias ne'er offended thee;
But thou wert set upon extreme revenge,
Because the [sire][13] dispossess'd thee once,
And couldst not venge it, but upon his son,
Nor on his son, but by Mathias' means,   51
Nor on Mathias, but by murdering me.
But I perceive there is no love on earth,
Pity in Jews, nor piety in Turks.
But here comes cursed Ithamore, with the friar.

Enter ITHAMORE *[and]* Friar *[*JACOMO].

F. JAC. *Virgo, salve.*
ITHA. When! duck you?[14]
ABIG. Welcome, grave friar; Ithamore, be-
    gone. —   *Exit* [ITHAMORE].
Know, holy sir, I am bold to solicit thee.
F. JAC. Wherein?   60
ABIG. To get me be admitted for a nun.
F. JAC. Why, Abigail, it is not yet long since
That I did labor thy admission,
And then thou didst not like that holy life.
ABIG. Then were my thoughts so frail and
    unconfirm'd,
And I was chain'd to follies of the world;
But now experience, purchased with grief,
Has made me see the difference of things.
My sinful soul, alas, hath pac'd too long
The fatal labyrinth of misbelief,   70
Far from the Son[15] that gives eternal life.
F. JAC. Who taught thee this?
ABIG.   The abbess of the house,
Whose zealous admonition I embrace.
Oh, therefore, Jacom[o], let me be one,
Although unworthy, of that sisterhood.
F. JAC. Abigail, I will; but see thou change
    no more.
For that will be most heavy to thy soul.
ABIG. That was my father's fault.
F. JAC.   Thy father's! how?
ABIG. Nay, you shall pardon me. — [*aside*]
    O Barabas,

---

[12] Emend. Dyce; Q *sinne*.
[13] Conj. Brooke; Q *Pryor*.
[14] The Friars were given to bobs and curtsies.
"When" is an exclamation of impatience.
[15] With a pun on *sun*.

Though thou deservest hardly at my hands, 80
Yet never shall these lips bewray thy life.
    F. JAC. Come, shall we go?
    ABIG.   My duty waits on you.
                         Exeunt.

[SCENE IV] [16]

Enter BARABAS, *reading a letter.*

    BAR. What, Abigail become a nun again !
False and unkind ; [17] what, hast thou lost thy
    father?
And all unknown, and unconstrain'd of me,
Art thou again got to the nunnery?
Now here she writes, and wills me to repent.
Repentance ! *Spurca!* [18] what pretendeth [19]
    this?
I fear she knows — 't is so — of my device
In Don Mathias' and Lodovico's deaths.
If so, 't is time that it be seen into ;
For she that varies from me in belief   10
Gives great presumption that she loves me
    not ;
Or, loving, doth dislike of something done.
But who comes here?

[*Enter* ITHAMORE.]

                 O Ithamore, come near ;
Come near, my love ; come near, thy master's
    life ;
My trusty servant, nay, my second [self] : [20]
For I have now no hope but even in thee,
And on that hope my happiness is built.
When saw'st thou Abigail?
    ITHA.   To-day.
    BAR.   With whom?
    ITHA.   A friar.
    BAR. A friar ! false villain, he hath done
    the deed.   19
    ITHA. How, sir?
    BAR.   Why, made mine Abigail a nun.
    ITHA. That 's no lie, for she sent me for him.
    BAR.   O unhappy day !
False, credulous, inconstant Abigail !
But let 'em go ; and, Ithamore, from hence
Ne'er shall she grieve me more with her dis-
    grace ;
Ne'er shall she live to inherit aught of mine,
Be bless'd of me, nor come within my gates,
But perish underneath my bitter curse,
Like Cain by Adam for his brother's death.

    ITHA. O master !
    BAR. Ithamore, entreat not for her, I am
    mov'd,   30
And she is hateful to my soul and me ;
And ['less] [21] thou yield to this that I entreat,
I cannot think but that thou hat'st my life.
    ITHA. Who, I, master? Why, I 'll run to
    some rock
And throw myself headlong into the sea ;
Why, I 'll do anything for your sweet sake.
    BAR. O trusty Ithamore, no servant, but
    my friend,
I here adopt thee for mine only heir ;
All that I have is thine when I am dead,   39
And whilst I live use half ; spend as myself.
Here take my keys, — I 'll give 'em thee anon.
Go buy thee garments ; but thou shalt not
    want.
Only know this, that thus thou art to do ;
But first go fetch me in the pot of rice
That for our supper stands upon the fire.
    ITHA. [*aside*] I hold [22] my head my master's
    hungry. — I go, sir.   *Exit.*
    BAR. Thus every villain ambles after wealth,
Although he ne'er be richer than in hope.
But, hush 't !

Re-enter ITHAMORE *with the pot.*

    ITHA.   Here 't is, master.
    BAR.   Well said,[23] Ithamore.
What, hast thou brought the ladle with thee
    too?   50
    ITHA. Yes, sir ; the proverb says he that
eats with the Devil had need of a long spoon.
I have brought you a ladle.
    BAR. Very well, Ithamore ; then now be
    secret ;
And for thy sake, whom I so dearly love,
Now shalt thou see the death of Abigail,
That thou mayst freely live to be my heir.
    ITHA. Why, master, will you poison her with
a mess of rice porridge? That will preserve
life, make her round and plump, and batten
more than you are aware.   61
    BAR. Ay, but, Ithamore, seest thou this?
It is a precious powder that I bought
Of an Italian in Ancona once,
Whose operation is to bind, infect,
And poison deeply, yet not appear
In forty hours after it is ta'en.
    ITHA. How, master?
    BAR. Thus, Ithamore.
This even they use in Malta here — 't is called

[16] A room in Barabas's house.
[17] Unnatural.
[18] An opprobrious exclamation. (Lat. *spurcus.*)
[19] Portendeth.
[20] Conj. Dyce ; Q *life.*

[21] Conj. Collier ; Q *least.*
[22] Bet.   [23] Well done.

Saint Jacques' Even, — and then, I say, they
use   71
To send their alms unto the nunneries.
Among the rest bear this, and set it there ;
There's a dark entry where they take it in,
Where they must neither see the messenger,
Nor make inquiry who hath sent it them.

ITHA. How so?

BAR. Belike there is some ceremony in 't.
There, Ithamore, must thou go place this
[pot] ! [24]
Stay, let me spice it first.   80

ITHA. Pray do, and let me help you, master.
Pray let me taste first.

BAR. Prithee do. — What say'st thou now?

ITHA. Troth, master, I'm loath such a pot
of pottage should be spoil'd.

BAR. Peace, Ithamore ; 't is better so than
spar'd.
Assure thyself thou shalt have broth by the
eye : [25]
My purse, my coffer, and myself is thine.

ITHA. Well, master, I go.

BAR. Stay, first let me stir it, Ithamore. [90
As fatal be it to her as the draught
Of which great Alexander drunk and died ;
And with her let it work like Borgia's wine,
Whereof his sire, the Pope, was poisoned.
In few,[26] the blood of Hydra, Lerna's bane,
The juice of hebon,[27] and Cocytus' breath,
And all the poisons of the Stygian pool
Break from the fiery kingdom, and in this
Vomit your venom and envenom her
That like a fiend hath left her father thus. [100

ITHA. [aside] What a blessing has he giv'n 't !
Was ever pot of rice porridge so sauc'd? —
What shall I do with it?

BAR. O, my sweet Ithamore, go set it down,
And come again so soon as thou hast done,
For I have other business for thee.

ITHA. Here's a drench to poison a whole
stable of Flanders mares. I'll carry 't to the
nuns with a powder.[28]

BAR. And the horse pestilence to boot ;
away !

ITHA. I am gone.   111
Pay me my wages, for my work is done. *Exit.*

BAR. I'll pay thee with a vengeance, Itha-
more.   *Exit.*

[24] Cor. Reed ; Q *plot.*   [25] In abundance.
[26] In short.
[27] A poison ; perhaps henbane, perhaps yew. —
Lerna, a marshy district near Argos, was the place
where Hercules killed the Hydra. The river Cocytus, a tributary of the Acheron, was one of the rivers
of Hades. So was the Styx.
[28] In haste. With an obvious pun.

[SCENE V] [29]

Enter FERNEZE, DEL BOSCO, Knights, [*and a*]
Bashaw.

FERN. Welcome, great [Bashaw] [30] ; how
fares Calymath?
What wind drives you thus into Malta road?

BAS. The wind that bloweth all the world
besides —
Desire of gold.

FERN.   Desire of gold, great sir?
That 's to be gotten in the Western Ind ;
In Malta are no golden minerals.

BAS. To you of Malta thus saith Calymath :
The time you took for respite is at hand,
For the performance of your promise pass'd ;
And for the tribute money I am sent.   10

FERN. Bashaw, in brief, shalt have no trib-
ute here,
Nor shall the heathens live upon our spoil.
First will we raze the city walls ourselves,
Lay waste the island, hew the temples down,
And, shipping off [31] our goods to Sicily,
Open an entrance for the wasteful sea,
Whose billows, beating the resistless banks,
Shall overflow it with their refluence.

BAS. Well, Governor, since thou hast broke
the league
By flat denial of the promis'd tribute,   20
Talk not of razing down your city walls.
You shall not need trouble yourselves so far,
For Selim Calymath shall come himself,
And with brass bullets batter down your towers
And turn proud Malta to a wilderness
For these intolerable wrongs of yours ;
And so, farewell.

FERN. Farewell. —   [*Exit* Basso.]
And now, you men of Malta, look about,
And let 's provide to welcome Calymath.   30
Close your portcullis, charge your basilisks,[32]
And as you profitably take up arms,
So now courageously encounter them ;
For by this answer, broken is the league,
And naught is to be look'd for now but wars ;
And naught to us more welcome is than wars.
                                                        Exeunt.

[SCENE VI] [33]

Enter [*the*] *two* Friars [JACOMO *and*
BARNARDINE].

F. JAC. O, brother, brother, all the nuns are
sick,

[29] Unlocated ; perhaps the senate-house.
[30] Q *Bashaws.*   [31] Q *of.*   [32] Large cannon.
[33] The courtyard of the nunnery.

And physic will not help them ; they must
   die.
   F. Barn. The Abbess sent for me to be con-
   fess'd ;
O, what a sad confession will there be !
   F. Jac. And so did fair Maria send for me.
I 'll to her lodging ; hereabouts she lies. *Exit.*

         Enter Abigail.

   F. Barn. What, all dead, save only Abi-
   gail?
   Abig. And I shall die too, for I feel death
   coming.
Where is the friar that convers'd with me?   9
   F. Barn. O, he is gone to see the other nuns.
   Abig. I sent for him, but seeing you are
   come,
Be you my ghostly father ; and first know
That in this house I liv'd religiously,
Chaste, and devout, much sorrowing for my
   sins ;
But ere I came ——
   F. Barn. What then?
   Abig. I did offend high Heaven so griev-
   ously
As I am almost desperate for my sins ;
And one offence torments me more than all.
You knew Mathias and Don Lodowick?   20
   F. Barn. Yes, what of them?
   Abig. My father did contract me to 'em
   both :
First to Don Lodowick ; him I never lov'd ;
Mathias was the man that I held dear ;
And for his sake did I become a nun.
   F. Barn. So, say how was their end?
   Abig. Both jealous of my love, envied [34]
   each other,
And by my father's practice,[35] which is there
Set down at large, the gallants were both slain.
                    [Gives a paper.]
   F. Barn. O monstrous villainy !   30
   Abig. To work my peace, this I confess to
   thee ;
Reveal it not, for then my father dies.
   F. Barn. Know that confession must not be
   reveal'd ;
The canon law forbids it, and the priest
That makes it known, being degraded first,
Shall be condemn'd and then sent to the fire.
   Abig. So I have heard ; pray, therefore,
   keep it close.[36]
Death seizeth on my heart ; ah, gentle friar,

---

[34] Entertained a grudge against.
[35] Plot.
[36] Secret.

Convert my father, that he may be sav'd,
And witness that I die a Christian. *[Dies.]* 40
   F. Barn. Ay, and a virgin too ; that grieves
   me most.
But I must to the Jew and exclaim on [37] him,
And make him stand in fear of me.

       Re-enter Friar [Jacomo].

   F. Jac. O brother, all the nuns are dead ;
   let's bury them.
   F. Barn. First help to bury this ; then go
   with me
And help me to exclaim against the Jew.
   F. Jac. Why, what has he done?
   F. Barn. A thing that makes me tremble to
   unfold.
   F. Jac. What, has he crucified a child?
   F. Barn. No, but a worse thing ; 't was
   told me in shrift ;   50
Thou know'st 't is death an if it be reveal'd.
Come, let 's away.   *Exeunt.*

      ACT IV — [Scene I] [1]

Enter Barabas [*and*] Ithamore. *Bells within.*

   Bar. There is no music to [2] a Christian's
   knell :
How sweet the bells ring now the nuns are
   dead,
That sound at other times like tinkers' pans !
I was afraid the poison had not wrought ;
Or, though it wrought, it would have done no
   good,
For every year they swell, and yet they live.
Now all are dead ; not one remains alive.
   Itha. That 's brave, master ; but think you
   it will not be known?
   Bar. How can it, if we two be secret?
   Itha. For my part fear you not.   10
   Bar. I 'd cut thy throat if I did.
   Itha.   And reason too.
But here 's a royal monastery hard by ;
Good master, let me poison all the monks.
   Bar. Thou shalt not need, for now the nuns
   are dead
They 'll die with grief.
   Itha. Do you not sorrow for your
   daughter's death?
   Bar. No, but I grieve because she liv'd so
   long.

---

[37] Accuse.
[1] The street before Barabas's house.
[2] Comparable to.

An Hebrew born, and would become a Christian !
[Catso],[3] *diabol*[o] !

Enter the two Friars [JACOMO *and* BARNARDINE].

ITHA. Look, look, master ; here come two
religious caterpillars.   21
   BAR. I smelt 'em ere they came.
   ITHA. God-a-mercy, nose ! Come, let 's
     be gone.
   F. BARN. Stay, wicked Jew ; repent, I say,
     and stay.
   F. JAC. Thou hast offended, therefore must
     be damn'd.
   BAR. [*aside to* ITHAMORE] I fear they know
     we sent the poison'd broth.
   ITHA. [*aside*] And so do I, master ; there-
     fore speak 'em fair.
   F. BARN. Barabas, thou hast ——
   F. JAC. Ay, that thou hast ——
   BAR. True, I have money, what though I
     have?   30
   F. BARN. Thou art a ——
   F. JAC. Ay, that thou art, a —
   BAR. What needs all this? I know I am a
     Jew.
   F. BARN. Thy daughter ——
   F. JAC. Ay, thy daughter ——
   BAR. O speak not of her ! then I die with
     grief.
   F. BARN. Remember that ——
   F. JAC. Ay, remember that ——
   BAR. I must needs say that I have been a
     great usurer.
   F. BARN. Thou hast committed ——   40
   BAR. Fornication — but that was in
another country ; and besides, the wench is
dead.
   F. BARN. Ay, but, Barabas,
Remember Mathias and Don Lodowick.
   BAR. Why, what of them?
   F. BARN. I will not say that by a forged
     challenge they met.
   BAR. (*aside*) She has confess'd, and we are
     both undone —
My bosom inmates [4] ! but I must dissemble. —
O holy friars, the burden of my sins   50
Lie heavy on my soul ; then pray you tell me,
Is 't not too late now to turn Christian?
I have been zealous in the Jewish faith,
Hard-hearted to the poor, a covetous wretch,

That would for lucre's sake have sold my soul.
A hundred for a hundred I have ta'en ;
And now for store of wealth may I compare
With all the Jews of Malta ; but what is
   wealth?
I am a Jew, and therefore am I lost.
Would penance serve for this my sin,   60
I could afford to whip myself to death, —
   ITHA. And so could I ; but penance will
     not serve.
   BAR. To fast, to pray, and wear a shirt of
     hair,
And on my knees creep to Jerusalem.
Cellars of wine, and sollars [5] full of wheat,
Warehouses stuff'd with spices and with drugs,
Whole chests of gold, in bullion and in coin,
Besides I know not how much weight in pearl,
Orient [6] and round, have I within my house ;
At Alexandria, merchandise unsold.   70
But yesterday two ships went from this town ;
Their voyage will be worth ten thousand
   crowns.
In Florence, Venice, Antwerp, London, Seville,
Frankfort, Lübeck, Moscow, and where not,
Have I debts owing ; and, in most of these,
Great sums of money lying in the banco ;
All this I 'll give to some religious house
So [7] I may be baptiz'd and live therein.
   F. JAC. O good Barabas, come to our house.
   F. BARN. O no, good Barabas, come to our
     house ;   80
And, Barabas, you know ——
   BAR. I know that I have highly sinn'd.
You shall convert me, you shall have all my
   wealth.
   F. JAC. O Barabas, their laws are strict.
   BAR. I know they are, and I will be with
     you.
   F. BARN. They wear no shirts, and they go
     barefoot too.
   BAR. Then 't is not for me ; and I am re-
     solv'd
You shall confess me, and have all my goods.
   F. JAC. Good Barabas, come to me.
   BAR. [*aside to* F. JAC.] You see I answer
     him, and yet he stays ;   90
Rid him away, and go you home with me.
   F. JAC. I 'll be with you to-night.
   BAR. Come to my house at one a'clock this
     night.
   F. JAC. You hear your answer, and you may
     be gone.
   F. BARN. Why, go ; get you away.
   F. JAC. I will not go for thee.

---

[3] Cor. Dyce ; Q *Catho*, for *cazzo*, an obscene
(Italian) exclamation.
[4] *I.e.*, the friars are now in my secrets ; though
possibly the plural is erroneous and the reference is
to Abigail.

[5] Lofts.   [6] Lustrous.   [7] Provided that.

F. Barn. Not? then I'll make thee go!

F. Jac. How, dost call me rogue?[8] *Fight.*

Itha. Part 'em, master, part 'em.

Bar. This is mere frailty, brethren; be content.   100

Friar Barnadine, go you with Ithamore. —
[*aside*] You know my mind; let me alone with
him.[9]

[F. Jac.] Why does he go to thy house?
Let him be gone.

Bar. I'll give him something and so stop
his mouth.

    Exit [Ithamore *with* Friar Barnardine].

I never heard of any man but he
Malign'd the order of the Jacobins.
But do you think that I believe his words?
Why, brother, you converted Abigail;
And I am bound in charity to requite it, 109
And so I will. O Jacom[o], fail not, but come.

F. Jac. But, Barabas, who shall be your
godfathers?

For presently you shall be shriv'd.

Bar. Marry, the Turk[10] shall be one of my
godfathers;

But not a word to any of your covent.[11]

F. Jac. I warrant thee, Barabas. *Exit.*

Bar. So; now the fear is past, and I am
safe;

For he that shriv'd her is within my house.
What if I murder'd him ere Jacom[o] comes?
Now I have such a plot for both their lives
As never Jew nor Christian knew the like. [120
One turn'd my daughter, therefore he shall die;
The other knows enough to have my life,
Therefore 't is not requisite he should live.
But are not both these wise men to suppose
That I will leave my house, my goods, and all,
To fast and be well whipp'd? I'll none of that.
Now, Friar Barnardine, I come to you;
I'll feast you, lodge you, give you fair words,
And after that, I and my trusty Turk — 129
No more, but so; it must and shall be done.

[Scene II][12]

Enter Ithamore [*to* Barabas].

Bar. Ithamore, tell me, is the friar asleep?

Itha. Yes; and I know not what the reason
is,

[8] Misunderstanding "go."
[9] Leave me to deal with him. (Q assigns this line and the next to Ithamore.)
[10] Ithamore.   [11] Convent.
[12] The stage now represents a room in Barabas's house; Friar Barnardine is asleep behind the curtains of the inner stage. After l. 24 the outer stage represents the street before the house.

Do what I can he will not strip himself,
Nor go to bed, but sleeps in his own clothes.
I fear me he mistrusts what we intend.

Bar. No, 't is an order which the friars use.
Yet, if he knew our meanings, could he scape?

Itha. No, none can hear him, cry he ne'er
so loud.

Bar. Why, true; therefore did I place him
there.   9

The other chambers open towards the street.

Itha. You loiter, master; wherefore stay
we thus?

O how I long to see him shake his heels.

Bar. Come on, sirrah.

Off with your girdle; make a handsome
noose. —

Friar, awake!

    [*They put the noose round the* Friar's
    neck.]

F. Barn.   What, do you mean to
strangle me?

Itha. Yes, 'cause you use to confess.

Bar. Blame not us but the proverb, "Confess and be hang'd." Pull hard!

F. Barn. What, will you [have][13] my life?

Bar. Pull hard, I say. — You would have
had my goods.   20

Itha. Ay, and our lives too; therefore pull
amain. —   [*They strangle him.*]

'T is neatly done, sir; here's no print at all.

Bar. Then is it as it should be; take him
up.

Itha. Nay, master; be rul'd by me a little.
[*Stands the body against the wall with a staff in
its hand.*] So; let him lean upon his staff.
Excellent! he stands as if he were begging of
bacon.

Bar. Who would not think but that this
friar liv'd?

What time o' night is 't now, sweet Ithamore?

Itha. Towards one.   30

Bar. Then will not Jacom[o] be long from
hence.   [*Exeunt.*]

[Scene III][14]

Enter [Friar] Jacom[o].

F. Jac. This is the hour wherein I shall proceed;[15]

O happy hour, wherein I shall convert
An infidel and bring his gold into our treasury!
But soft, is not this Barnardine? It is;
And, understanding I should come this way,

[13] Emend. Reed; Q *saue.*
[14] The same.   [15] Get on, succeed.

Stands here a'purpose, meaning me some
 wrong
And intercept my going to the Jew. —
Barnardine!
Wilt thou not speak? Thou think'st I see
 thee not;
Away, I'd wish thee, and let me go by.   10
No, wilt thou not? Nay, then, I'll force my
 way;
And see, a staff stands ready for the purpose.
As thou lik'st that, stop me another time.
                              Strike him; he falls.

Enter BARABAS [*and* ITHAMORE].

BAR. Why, how now, Jacom[o]; what hast
 thou done?
F. JAC. Why, stricken him that would have
 struck at me.
BAR. Who is it? Barnardine! Now out,
alas, he is slain!
ITHA. Ay, master, he's slain; look how his
brains drop out on's nose.
F. JAC. Good sirs, I have done 't; but [20
nobody knows it but you two; I may escape.
BAR. So might my man and I hang with
you for company.
ITHA. No, let us bear him to the magis-
trates.
F. JAC. Good Barabas, let me go.
BAR. No, pardon me; the law must have
 its course.
I must be forc'd to give in evidence
That, being importun'd by this Barnardine
To be a Christian, I shut him out
And there he sat. Now I, to keep my word,
And give my goods and substance to your
 house,   31
Was up thus early, with intent to go
Unto your friary, because you stay'd.
ITHA. Fie upon 'em, master; will you turn
Christian when holy friars turn devils and
murder one another?
BAR. No, for this example I'll remain a Jew.
Heaven bless me! What, a friar a murderer!
When shall you see a Jew commit the like?
ITHA. Why, a Turk could ha' done no more.
BAR. To-morrow is the sessions; you shall
 to it.   41
Come, Ithamore, let's help to take him
 hence.
F. JAC. Villains, I am a sacred person;
 touch me not.
BAR. The law shall touch you; we'll but
 lead you, we.
'Las, I could weep at your calamity!

Take in the staff, too, for that must be shown;
Law wills that each particular be known.
                              Exeunt.

[SCENE IV] [16]

Enter Courtesan [BELLAMIRA] *and* PILIA-
BORZA.

[BELL.] [17] Pilia-Borza, didst thou meet with
Ithamore?
PILIA. I did.
BELL. And didst thou deliver my letter?
PILIA. I did.
BELL. And what think'st thou? Will he
come?
PILIA. I think so, and yet I cannot tell; for
at the reading of the letter he look'd like a man
of another world.   10
BELL. Why so?
PILIA. That such a base slave as he should
be saluted by such a tall [18] man as I am, from
such a beautiful dame as you.
BELL. And what said he?
PILIA. Not a wise word; only gave me a
nod, as who should say, "Is it even so?" and
so I left him, being driven to a non-plus at the
critical aspect of my terrible countenance.
BELL. And where didst meet him?   20
PILIA. Upon mine own freehold, within
forty foot of the gallows, conning his neck-
verse, I take it, looking of a friar's execution,
whom I saluted with an old hempen proverb,
Hodie tibi, cras mihi, and so I left him to the
mercy of the hangman; but, the exercise [19]
being done, see where he comes.

Enter ITHAMORE.

ITHA. I never knew a man take his death so
patiently as this friar. He was ready to leap
off ere the halter was about his neck; and [30
when the hangman had put on his hempen
tippet, he made such haste to his prayers as
if he had had another cure to serve. Well, go
whither he will, I'll be none of his followers
in haste; and, now I think on 't, going to the
execution, a fellow met me with a muschatoes [20]
like a raven's wing, and a dagger with a hilt like
a warming pan, and he gave me a letter from
one Madam Bellamira, saluting me in such sort
as if he had meant to make clean my boots [40
with his lips; the effect was that I should come

[16] The street before Bellamira's house; after l. 100,
the curtains of the inner stage doubtless being
opened, a room in the house.
[17] Q. *Curt.*, throughout.   [19] Ceremony, service.
[18] Valiant.   [20] Moustache.

to her house. I wonder what the reason is ; it may be she sees more in me than I can find in myself, for she writes further that she loves me ever since she saw me ; and who would not requite such love? Here's her house, and here she comes, and now would I were gone ; I am not worthy to look upon her.

PILIA. This is the gentleman you writ to.

ITHA. [*aside*] Gentleman! he flouts me ; [50 what gentry can be in a poor Turk of tenpence? I'll be gone.

BELL. Is't not a sweet-fac'd youth, Pilia?

ITHA. [*aside*] Again, "sweet youth!"— Did not you, sir, bring the sweet youth a letter?

PILIA. I did, sir, and from this gentlewoman, who, as myself, and the rest of the family, stand or fall at your service.

BELL. Though woman's modesty should
    hale me back, 60
I can withhold no longer ; welcome, sweet love.

ITHA. [*aside*] Now am I clean, or rather foully, out of the way.

BELL. Whither so soon?

ITHA. [*aside*] I'll go steal some money from my master to make me handsome. — Pray pardon me, I must go and see a ship discharg'd.

BELL. Canst thou be so unkind to leave me thus?

PILIA. An ye did but know how she loves you, sir. 70

ITHA. Nay, I care not how much she loves me. — Sweet Bellamira, would I had my master's wealth for thy sake.

PILIA. And you can have it, sir, an if you please.

ITHA. If 't were above ground, I could and would have it ; but he hides and buries it up, as partridges do their eggs, under the earth.

PILIA. And is 't not possible to find it out?

ITHA. By no means possible.

BELL. [*aside to* PILIA-BORZA] What shall we do with this base villain then? 80

PILIA. [*aside to her*] Let me alone ; do but you speak him fair. —
But you know some secrets of the Jew,
Which if they were reveal'd would do him harm.

ITHA. Ay, and such as — go to, no more! I'll make him send me half he has, and glad he scapes so, too. Pen and ink! I'll write unto him ; we'll have money straight.

PILIA. Send for a hundred crowns at least.
        [ITHAMORE] *writes.*

ITHA. Ten hundred thousand crowns. "Master Barabas."

PILIA. Write not so submissively, but threat'ning him. 90

ITHA. [*writing*] "Sirrah Barabas, send me a hundred crowns."

PILIA. Put in two hundred at least.

ITHA. [*writing*] "I charge thee send me three hundred by this bearer, and this shall be your warrant : if you do not — no more, but so."

PILIA. Tell him you will confess.

ITHA. [*writing*] "Otherwise I'll confess all." — Vanish, and return in a twinkle.

PILIA. Let me alone ; I'll use him in his kind.[21] 100
        [*Exit* PILIA-BORZA.]

ITHA. Hang him, Jew!

BELL. Now, gentle Ithamore, lie in my lap. —
Where are my maids? Provide a running[22] banquet.
Send to the merchant ; bid him bring me silks.
Shall Ithamore, my love, go in such rags?

ITHA. And bid the jeweller come hither, too.

BELL. I have no husband, sweet ; I'll marry thee.

ITHA. Content ; but we will leave this paltry land,
And sail from hence to Greece, to lovely Greece.
I'll be thy Jason, thou my golden fleece ; 110
Where painted carpets o'er the meads are hurl'd,
And Bacchus' vineyards o'erspread the world,
Where woods and forests go in goodly green,
I'll be Adonis, thou shalt be Love's Queen.
The meads, the orchards, and the primrose lanes,
Instead of sedge and reed, bear sugar canes ;
Thou in those groves, by Dis above,
Shalt live with me and be my love.

BELL. Whither will I not go with gentle Ithamore?

Re-enter PILIA-BORZA.

ITHA. How now! hast thou the gold? [120

PILIA. Yes.

ITHA. But came it freely? Did the cow give down her milk freely?

PILIA. At reading of the letter, he star'd and stamp'd and turn'd aside. I took him by the [beard],[23] and look'd upon him thus ;

---

[21] According to his nature.
[22] Hasty.   [23] Cor. Reed ; Q *sterd.*

told him he were best to send it; then he hugg'd and embrac'd me.

ITHA. Rather for fear than love.   129

PILIA. Then, like a Jew, he laugh'd and jeer'd, and told me he lov'd me for your sake, and said what a faithful servant you had been.

ITHA. The more villain he to keep me thus. Here's goodly 'parel, is there not?

PILIA. To conclude, he gave me ten crowns.[24]

ITHA. But ten? I'll not leave him worth a gray groat. Give me a ream [25] of paper; we'll have a kingdom of gold for 't.

PILIA. Write for five hundred crowns.   139

ITHA. [*writing*] "Sirrah Jew, as you love your life send me five hundred crowns, and give the bearer one hundred." Tell him I must have 't.

PILIA. I warrant your Worship shall have 't.

ITHA. And if he ask why I demand so much, tell him I scorn to write a line under a hundred crowns.

PILIA. You'd make a rich poet, sir. I am gone.   *Exit.*

ITHA. Take thou the money; spend it for my sake.

BELL. 'T is not thy money, but thyself I weigh;   150
Thus Bellamira esteems of gold. [*Throws it aside.*] But thus of thee. *Kiss him.*

ITHA. That kiss again! she runs division [26] of my lips.
What an eye she casts on me! It twinkles like a star.

BELL. Come, my dear love, let's in and sleep together.

ITHA. O, that ten thousand nights were put in one,
That we might sleep seven years together afore we wake!

BELL. Come, amorous wag, first banquet and then sleep.   *Exeunt.*

[SCENE V] [27]

Enter BARABAS, *reading a letter.*

BAR. "Barabas, send me three hundred crowns." —
Plain Barabas! O, that wicked courtesan!
He was not wont to call me Barabas.
"Or else I will confess;" ay, there it goes;

But, if I get him, *coupe de gorge* for that.
He sent a shaggy totter'd,[28] staring slave,
That when he speaks draws out his grisly beard,
And winds it twice or thrice about his ear;
Whose face has been a grindstone for men's swords;
His hands are hack'd, some fingers cut quite off;   10
Who, when he speaks, grunts like a hog, and looks
Like one that is employ'd in catzerie [29]
And crossbiting,[30] — such a rogue
As is the husband to a hundred whores;
And I by him must send three hundred crowns!
Well, my hope is he will not stay there still;
And when he comes — O, that he were but here!

Enter PILIA-BORZA.

PILIA. Jew, I must ha' more gold.

BAR. Why, want'st thou any of thy tale? [31]

PILIA. No; but three hundred will not serve his turn.   21

BAR. Not serve his turn, sir?

PILIA. No, sir; and therefore I must have five hundred more.

BAR. I'll rather ——

PILIA. O good words, sir, and send it you were best! See, there's his letter.

BAR. Might he not as well come as send? Pray bid him come and fetch it; what he writes for you, ye shall have straight.   30

PILIA. Ay, and the rest too, or else ——

BAR. (*aside*) I must make this villain away.
— Please you dine with me, sir; — and you shall be most heartily poison'd.

PILIA. No, God-a-mercy. Shall I have these crowns?

BAR. I cannot do it; I have lost my keys.

PILIA. O, if that be all, I can pick ope your locks.

BAR. Or climb up to my countinghouse window — you know my meaning.   39

PILIA. I know enough, and therefore talk not to me of your countinghouse. The gold! or know, Jew, it is in my power to hang thee.

BAR. [*aside*] I am betray'd. —
'T is not five hundred crowns that I esteem;

---

[24] *I.e.*, as a tip, besides the three hundred.
[25] Punning on *realm*, often spelled without the "l."
[26] Executes "a rapid melodic passage." (*N. E. D.*) A musical term.
[27] Unlocated; presumably a room in Barabas's house, despite l. 59.
[28] Tattered.
[29] Nares derives from *catso* (see on IV, i, 19). It evidently means rascality of some sort.
[30] Swindling. The next line alludes to the practice of blackmailing a man by decoying him into a compromising situation with a prostitute and then confronting him with a confederate who poses as her husband.
[31] Reckoning.

I am not mov'd at that : this angers me,
That he, who knows I love him as myself,
Should write in this imperious vein. Why, sir,
You know I have no child, and unto whom
Should I leave all but unto Ithamore?
    PILIA. Here's many words, but no crowns.
      The crowns!   50
    BAR. Commend me to him, sir, most hum-
      bly,[32]
And unto your good mistress, as unknown.[33]
    PILIA. Speak, shall I have 'em, sir?
    BAR.   Sir, here they are. —
O, that I should part with so much gold! —
Here, take 'em, fellow, with as good a will ——
[aside] As I would see thee hang'd. — O, love
    stops my breath ;
Never lov'd man servant as I do Ithamore.
    PILIA. I know it, sir.
    BAR. Pray, when, sir, shall I see you at my
      house?
    PILIA. Soon enough, to your cost, sir. Fare
      you well.   *Exit.* [60
    BAR. Nay, to thine own cost, villain, if
      thou com'st. —
Was ever Jew tormented as I am?
To have a shag-rag knave to come [34] —
Three hundred crowns — and then five hun-
    dred crowns !
Well, I must seek a means to rid 'em all,
And presently [35] ; for in his villainy
He will tell all he knows, and I shall die for 't.—
I have it !
I will in some disguise go see the slave,   69
And how the villain revels with my gold. *Exit.*

[SCENE VI] [36]

Enter Courtesan [BELLAMIRA,] ITHAMORE,
    [*and*] PILIA-BORZA.

    BELL. I'll pledge thee, love, and therefore
      drink it off.
    ITHA. Say'st thou me so ? Have at it ; and
      do you hear?   [*Whispers.*]
    BELL. Go to, it shall be so.
    ITHA. Of that condition I will drink it up.
Here's to thee !
    [BELL.]   Nay, I'll have all or none.
    ITHA. There, if thou lov'st me, do not leave
      a drop.
    BELL. Love thee ! Fill me three glasses.

    ITHA. Three-and-fifty dozen, I'll pledge
      thee.
    PILIA. Knavely spoke, and like a knight at
      arms.
    ITHA. Hey, *Rivo Castiliano!* [37] A man's a
      man !   10
    BELL. Now to the Jew.
    ITHA. Ha ! to the Jew, and send me money
      you [38] were best.
    PILIA. What wouldst thou do if he should
      send thee none?
    ITHA. Do nothing ; but I know what I
know ; he's a murderer.
    BELL. I had not thought he had been so
      brave a man.
    ITHA. You knew Mathias and the Gov-
    ernor's son ; he and I kill'd 'em both, and yet
never touch'd 'em.
    PILIA. O, bravely done.   20
    ITHA. I carried the broth that poison'd the
nuns ; and he and I — snickle! hand to!
fast ! [39] — strangled a friar.
    BELL. You two alone?
    ITHA. We two ; and 't was never known,
nor never shall be for me.
    PILIA. [*aside to* BELLAMIRA] This shall with
      me unto the Governor.
    BELL. [*aside to* PILIA-BORZA] And fit it
      should ; but first let's ha' more gold. —
Come, gentle Ithamore, lie in my lap.
    ITHA. Love me little, love me long. Let
      music rumble   30
Whilst I in thy incony [40] lap do tumble.

Enter BARABAS, *with a lute, disguis'd.*

    BELL. A French musician ! Come, let's
      hear your skill.
    BAR. Must tuna my lute for sound, twang,
twang, first.
    ITHA. Wilt drink, Frenchman ? Here's to
thee with a —— pox on this drunken hiccup !
    BAR. *Gramercy, mounsier.*
    BELL. Prithee, Pilia-Borza, bid the fiddler
give me the posy in his hat there.

---

[32] Trisyllabic.
[33] As yet unknown to me.
[34] A word has perhaps been omitted.
[35] At once.
[36] Inside Bellamira's house, and also, apparently,
the street before it.
[37] A bacchanalian exclamation of uncertain origin.
"Rivo" may = "stream" (Ital.). On "Castiliano"
see [London] *Times Lit. Sup.*, May 4, 1933, p. 312·
It may = *Castiglione*, which seems to have been a
name for the Italian wine usually called *Lacrimae
Christi.*
[38] There is no need to emend *he*. It is more dramatic for the drunken Turk to shake his fist at the
absent Jew.
[39] Q *snicle hand too fast.* Punctuated and explained by Kittredge, = Snare him ! lay your hand
to it ! firmly now ! (With appropriate gestures.)
[40] Dainty. Cor. Reed ; Q *incoomy.*

PILIA. Sirrah, you must give my mistress
your posy.   41

BAR. *A voustre commandement, madam.*

BELL. How sweet, my Ithamore, the flowers
smell.

ITHA. Like thy breath, sweetheart; no violet like 'em.

PILIA. Foh! methinks they stink like a
hollyhock.

BAR. [*aside*] So, now I am reveng'd upon
'em all.

The scent thereof was death; I poison'd it.

ITHA. Play, fiddler, or I 'll cut your cat's
guts into chitterlings.   51

BAR. *Pardona moy;* be no in tune yet; so
now, now all be in.

ITHA. Give him a crown, and fill me out
more wine.

PILIA. There 's two crowns for thee; play.

BAR. (*aside*) How liberally the villain gives
me mine own gold!   [*Plays.*]

PILIA. Methinks he fingers very well.

BAR. (*aside*) So did you when you stole my
gold.   60

PILIA. How swift he runs!

BAR. (*aside*) You run swifter when you
threw my gold out of my window.

BELL. Musician, hast been in Malta long?

BAR. Two, three, four month, madam.

ITHA. Dost not know a Jew, one Barabas?

BAR. Very mush; mounsier, you no be his
man?

PILIA. His man?

ITHA. I scorn the peasant; tell him so. [70

BAR. [*aside.*] He knows it already.

ITHA. 'T is a strange thing of that Jew; he
lives upon pickled grasshoppers and sauc'd
mushrooms.

BAR. (*aside*) What a slave 's this! The
Governor feeds not as I do.

ITHA. He never put on clean shirt since he
was circumcis'd.

BAR. (*aside*) O rascal! I change myself
twice a day.   80

ITHA. The hat he wears Judas left under
the elder when he hang'd himself.

BAR. (*aside*) 'T was sent me for a present
from the great Cham.

PILIA. A masty [41] slave he is. — Whither
now, fiddler?

BAR. *Pardona moy, mounsier,* [me] [42] be no
well.   *Exit.*

[41] Burly. Some eds., perhaps rightly, emend *nasty*
or *musty.*
[42] Cor. Reed; Q *we.*

PILIA. Farewell, fiddler! — One letter more
to the Jew.   90

BELL. Prithee, sweet love, one more, and
write it sharp.

ITHA. No, I 'll send by word of mouth now.
— Bid him deliver thee a thousand crowns, by
the same token that the nuns lov'd rice,
that Friar Barnardine slept in his own clothes;
any of 'em will do it.

PILIA. Let me alone to urge it, now I know
the meaning.

ITHA. The meaning has a meaning. — Come
let 's in.   99
To undo a Jew is charity, and not sin.   *Exeunt.*

ACT V — [SCENE I] [1]

Enter Governor [FERNEZE], Knights, MARTIN
DEL BOSCO, [*and*] Officers].

FERN. Now, gentlemen, betake you to your
arms,
And see that Malta be well fortifi'd;
And it behoves you to be resolute;
For Calymath, having hover'd here so long,
Will win the town or die before the walls.

[1] KNIGHT. And die he shall, for we will
never yield.

Enter Courtesan [BELLAMIRA *and*] PILIA-
BORZA.

BELL. O, bring us to the Governor.

FERN. Away with her! She is a courtesan.

BELL. Whate'er I am, yet, Governor, hear
me speak;   9
I bring thee news by whom thy son was slain:
Mathias did it not; it was the Jew.

PILIA. Who, besides the slaughter of these
gentlemen,
Poison'd his own daughter and the nuns,
Strangled a friar and I know not what
Mischief beside.

FERN.   Had we but proof of this ——

BELL. Strong proof, my Lord; his man 's
now at my lodging,
That was his agent; he 'll confess it all.

FERN. Go fetch him straight. —
                            [*Exeunt* Officers.]
              I always fear'd that Jew.

Enter [Officers *with* BARABAS *the*] Jew [*and*]
ITHAMORE.

BAR. I 'll go alone; dogs, do not hale me
thus.

[1] The senate-house.

ITHA. Nor me neither; I cannot outrun you, constable. — O my belly! 21

BAR. [*aside*] One dram of powder more had made all sure.

What a damn'd slave was I !

FERN. Make fires, heat irons, let the rack be fetch'd.

[1] KNIGHT. Nay, stay, my Lord; 't may be he will confess.

BAR. Confess! what mean you, Lords? Who should confess?

FERN. Thou and thy Turk; 't was you that slew my son.

ITHA. Guilty, my Lord, I confess. Your son and Mathias were both contracted unto Abigail; [he] [2] forg'd a counterfeit challenge.

BAR. Who carried that challenge? 31

ITHA. I carried it, I confess; but who writ it? Marry, even he that strangled Barnardine, poison'd the nuns and his own daughter.

FERN. Away with him! his sight is death to me.

BAR. For what, you men of Malta? Hear me speak:

She is a courtesan, and he a thief,
And he my bondman. Let me have law,
For none of this can prejudice my life.

FERN. Once more, away with him; you shall have law. 40

BAR. [*aside*] Devils, do your worst! I live in spite of you. —

As these have spoke, so be it to their souls! —
[*aside*] I hope the poison'd flowers will work anon.

> [*Exeunt* Officers *with* BARABAS *and* ITHAMORE, BELLAMIRA, *and* PILIA-BORZA.]

Enter [KATHERINE].

KATH. Was my Mathias murder'd by the Jew?

Ferneze, 't was thy son that murder'd him.

FERN. Be patient, gentle madam; it was he; He forged the daring challenge made them fight.

KATH. Where is the Jew? Where is that murderer?

FERN. In prison till the law has pass'd on him.

Re-enter [*an*] Officer.

OFF. My Lord, the courtesan and her man are dead; 50
So is the Turk and Barabas the Jew.

[2] Add. Reed.

FERN. Dead!

OFF. Dead, my Lord; and here they bring his body.[3]

BOSCO. This sudden death of his is very strange.

FERN. Wonder not at it, sir: the Heavens are just;

Their deaths were like their lives; then think not of 'em.

Since they are dead, let them be buried;
For the Jew's body, throw that o'er the walls,
To be a prey for vultures and wild beasts. —
So now away, and fortify the town. *Exeunt.* [60

[SCENE II] [4]

BAR. What, all alone? Well fare, sleepy drink.

I 'll be reveng'd on this accursed town;
For by my means Calymath shall enter in.
I 'll help to slay their children and their wives,
To fire the churches, pull their houses down,
Take my goods, too, and seize upon my lands.
I hope to see the Governor a slave,
And, rowing in a galley, whipp'd to death.

Enter CALYMATH, Bashaws, [*and*] Turks.

CALY. Whom have we there, a spy?

BAR. Yes, my good Lord, one that can spy a place 10
Where you may enter, and surprise the town;
My name is Barabas; I am a Jew.

CALY. Art thou that Jew whose goods we heard were sold
For tribute money?

BAR.   The very same, my Lord;
And since that time they have hir'd a slave, my man,
To accuse me of a thousand villainies.
I was imprison'd, but 'scap'd their hands.

CALY. Didst break prison?

BAR. No, no;
I drank of poppy and cold mandrake juice; 20
And being asleep, belike they thought me dead,
And threw me o'er the walls; so, or how else,
The Jew is here, and rests at your command.

CALY. 'T was bravely done; but tell me, Barabas,
Canst thou, as thou reportest, make Malta ours?

[3] Barabas may have been carried on at this point; if so he was probably borne out at the end of this scene.

[4] Outside the city walls. Probably Barabas was "discovered," coming back to consciousness, on the inner stage.

Bar. Fear not, my Lord, for here against
the [sluice] ⁵
The rock is hollow, and of purpose digg'd
To make a passage for the running streams
And common channels ⁶ of the city.
Now, whilst you give assault unto the walls, [30
I 'll lead five hundred soldiers through the
vault
And rise with them i' th' middle of the town,
Open the gates for you to enter in ;
And by this means the city is your own.
  Caly. If this be true, I 'll make thee gov-
ernor.
  Bar. And if it be not true, then let me die.
  Caly. Thou 'st doom'd thyself.   Assault it
presently.   *Exeunt.*

[Scene III] ⁷

Alarums. Enter [Calymath, Bassoes,] *Turks,
[and]* Barabas, [with Ferneze] *and* Knights,
prisoners.

  Caly. Now vail ⁸ your pride, you captive
Christians,
And kneel for mercy to your conquering foe.
Now where 's the hope you had of haughty
Spain?
Ferneze, speak ; had it not been much better
To kept thy promise than be thus surpris'd?
  Fern. What should I say?   We are cap-
tives and must yield.
  Caly. Ay, villains, you must yield, and
under Turkish yokes
Shall groaning bear the burden of our ire ;
And, Barabas, as erst we promis'd thee,
For thy desert we make thee governor ;   10
Use them at thy discretion.
  Bar.   Thanks, my Lord.
  Fern. O fatal day, to fall into the hands
Of such a traitor and unhallowed Jew !
What greater misery could Heaven inflict?
  Caly. 'T is our command ; and, Barabas,
we give
To guard thy person these our Janizaries ;
Entreat ⁹ them well, as we have used thee.
And now, brave bashaws, come, we 'll walk
about
The ruin'd town, and see the wrack we
made. —   19
Farewell, brave Jew ; farewell, great Barabas.
             Exeunt [Calymath *and* Bassoes].

⁵ Emend. Collier ; Q *Truce.*
⁶ Gutters.
⁷ Unlocated, but evidently a place within the city.
⁸ Lower.
⁹ Treat.

  Bar. May all good fortune follow Caly-
math. —
And now, as entrance to our safety,
To prison with the Governor and these
Captains, his consorts and confederates.
  Fern. O villain !   Heaven will be reveng'd
on thee.
  Bar. Away ! no more ; let him not trouble
me.
             Exeunt [Turks, *with* Ferneze
                              and Knights].
Thus hast thou gotten, by thy policy,
No simple place, no small authority.
I now am governor of Malta ; true,
But Malta hates me ; and, in hating me,   30
My life 's in danger, and what boots it thee,
Poor Barabas, to be the governor,
Whenas thy life shall be at their command?
No, Barabas, this must be look'd into ;
And since by wrong thou gott'st authority,
Maintain it bravely by firm policy ;
At least unprofitably lose it not :
For he that liveth in authority,
And neither gets him friends, nor fills his bags,
Lives like the ass, that Aesop speaketh of,   40
That labors with a load of bread and wine,
And leaves it off to snap on thistle-tops ;
But Barabas will be more circumspect.
Begin betimes ; occasion's bald behind ;
Slip not thine opportunity, for fear too late
Thou seek'st for much, but canst not compass
it. —
Within here !

          Enter [Ferneze] *with a* Guard.

  Fern.   My Lord?
  Bar.   Ay, " lord ; " thus slaves
will learn.
Now, Governor ; — stand by there ; wait with-
in.   [*Exeunt* Guard.]
This is the reason that I sent for thee :
Thou seest thy life and Malta's happiness   50
Are at my arbitrament ; and Barabas
At his discretion may dispose of both.
Now tell me, Governor, and plainly too,
What think'st thou shall become of it and thee?
  Fern. This, Barabas ; since things are in
thy power,
I see no reason but of Malta's wrack,
Nor hope of thee but extreme cruelty ;
Nor fear I death, nor will I flatter thee.
  Bar. Governor, good words ; be not so
furious.
'T is not thy life which can avail me aught ; [60
Yet you do live, and live for me you shall ;

And, as for Malta's ruin, think you not
'T were slender policy for Barabas
To dispossess himself of such a place?
For sith,[10] as once you said, within this isle,
In Malta here, that I have got my goods,
And in this city still have had success,
And now at length am grown your governor,
Yourselves shall see it shall not be forgot;
For, as a friend not known but in distress, 70
I 'll rear up Malta, now remediless.

FERN. Will Barabas recover Malta's loss?
Will Barabas be good to Christians?

BAR. What wilt thou give me, Governor, to
procure
A dissolution of the slavish bands
Wherein the Turk hath yok'd your land and
you?
What will you give me if I render you
The life of Calymath, surprise his men,
And in an outhouse of the city shut
His soldiers, till I have consum'd 'em all with
fire? 80
What will you give him that procureth this?

FERN. Do but bring this to pass which thou
pretendest,[11]
Deal truly with us as thou intimatest,
And I will send amongst the citizens,
And by my letters privately procure
Great sums of money for thy recompense;
Nay more, do this, and live thou governor still.

BAR. Nay, do thou this, Ferneze, and be
free;
Governor, I enlarge thee; live with me,
Go walk about the city, see thy friends; 90
Tush, send not letters to 'em, go thyself,
And let me see what money thou canst make.
Here is my hand that I 'll set Malta free;
And thus we cast it: to a solemn feast
I will invite young Selim Calymath,
Where be thou present only to perform
One stratagem that I 'll impart to thee,
Wherein no danger shall betide thy life,
And I will warrant Malta free for ever.

FERN. Here is my hand; believe me, Bara-
bas, 100
I will be there and do as thou desirest.
When is the time?

BAR. Governor, presently;
For Calymath, when he hath view'd the town,
Will take his leave and sail toward Ottoman.

FERN. Then will I, Barabas, about this coin,
And bring it with me to thee in the evening.

BAR. Do so, but fail not; now farewell,
Ferneze! — [*Exit* FERNEZE.]

---

10 Since. 11 Extendest, settest forth.

And thus far roundly goes the business.
Thus, loving neither, will I live with both,
Making a profit of my policy; 110
And he from whom my most advantage comes
Shall be my friend.
This is the life we Jews are us'd to lead;
And reason too, for Christians do the like.
Well, now about effecting this device;
First to surprise great Selim's soldiers,[12]
And then to make provision for the feast,
That at one instant all things may be done.
My policy detests prevention;
To what event my secret purpose drives, 120
I know, and they shall witness with their lives.
Exit.

[SCENE IV] [13]

Enter CALYMATH *and* Bashaws.

CALY. Thus have we view'd the city, seen
the sack,
And caus'd the ruins to be new-repair'd,
Which with our bombards' [14] shot and basilisk
We rent in sunder at our entry; [15]
And now I see the situation,
And how secure this conquer'd island stands
Environ'd with the Mediterranean Sea,
Strong [countermur'd] [16] with other petty isles,
And, toward Calabria, back'd by Sicily,
[Where] [17] Syracusian Dionysius reign'd, 10
Two lofty turrets that command the town.
I wonder how it could be conquer'd thus.

Enter a Messenger.

MESS. From Barabas, Malta's governor, I
bring
A message unto mighty Calymath;
Hearing his sovereign was bound for sea,
To sail to Turkey, to great Ottoman,
He humbly would entreat your Majesty
To come and see his homely citadel,
And banquet with him ere thou leav'st the isle.

CALY. To banquet with him in his citadel?
I fear me, messenger, to feast my train 21
Within a town of war so lately pillag'd
Will be too costly and too troublesome;
Yet would I gladly visit Barabas,
For well has Barabas deserv'd of us.

---

12 Trisyllabic.
13 Unlocated, but evidently another spot within
the city.
14 Large cannons'.
15 Trisyllabic.
16 Conj. Deighton; Q *contermin'd.* Cf. on I, ii,
383.
17 Q *When;* cor. Robinson, who also corrects this
line and the next, transposed in Q.

MESS. Selim, for that, thus saith the Governor:
That he hath in store a pearl so big,
So precious, and withal so orient,
As, be it valued but indifferently,
The price thereof will serve to entertain   30
Selim and all his soldiers for a month ;
Therefore he humbly would entreat your Highness
Not to depart till he has feasted you.
   CALY. I cannot feast my men in Malta walls,
Except he place his tables in the streets.
   MESS. Know, Selim, that there is a monastery
Which standeth as an outhouse to the town ;
There will he banquet them, but thee at home,
With all thy bashaws and brave followers.
   CALY. Well, tell the Governor we grant his suit ;   40
We'll in this summer evening feast with him.
   MESS. I shall, my Lord.   *Exit.*
   CALY. And now, bold bashaws, let us to our tents,
And meditate how we may grace us best
To solemnize our governor's great feast.
                                        Exeunt.

[SCENE V] [18]

Enter Governor [FERNEZE], Knights, [*and*] DEL BOSCO.

   FERN. In this, my countrymen, be rul'd by me ;
Have special care that no man sally forth
Till you shall hear a culverin discharg'd
By him that bears the linstock, kindled thus ;
Then issue out and come to rescue me,
For happily I shall be in distress,
Or you released of this servitude.
   1 KNIGHT. Rather than thus to live as Turkish thralls,
What will we not adventure?
   FERN. On then ; begone.
   KNIGHTS. Farewell, grave Governor ! [10
                                        [*Exeunt.*]

[SCENE VI] [19]

Enter [BARABAS,] *with a hammer, above, very busy ;* [*Carpenters also discovered*].

   BAR. How stand the cords ? How hang these hinges ? Fast?
Are all the cranes and pulleys sure?

---

[18] Unlocated ; presumably the same as Sc. iv.
[19] A hall in the citadel. Barabas appears on the upper stage ; the caldron is on the inner stage, concealed by its curtains till s. D. after l. 62.

[CARP.] [20]   All fast.
   BAR. Leave nothing loose, all levell'd to my mind.
Why now I see that you have art indeed.
There, carpenters, divide that gold amongst you ;
Go swill in bowls of sack and muscadine !
Down to the cellar, taste of all my wines.
   CARP. We shall, my Lord, and thank you.
                                Exeunt [Carpenters].
   BAR. And, if you like them, drink your fill and die ;
For, so I live, perish may all the world !   10
Now, Selim Calymath, return me word
That thou wilt come, and I am satisfied.

Enter Messenger.

Now, sirrah, what, will he come?
   MESS. He will ; and has commanded all his men
To come ashore and march through Malta streets,
That thou mayst feast them in thy citadel.
   BAR. Then now are all things as my wish would have 'em ;
There wanteth nothing but the governor's pelf,
And see, he brings it.

Enter Governor [FERNEZE].

                        Now, Governor, the sum.
   FERN. With free consent, a hundred thousand pounds.   20
   BAR. Pounds, say'st thou, Governor ? Well, since it is no more,
I'll satisfy myself with that ; nay, keep it still,
For if I keep not promise, trust not me.
And, Governor, now partake my policy :
First, for his army, they are sent before,
Enter'd the monastery, and underneath
In several places are fieldpieces pitch'd,
Bombards, whole barrels full of gunpowder,
That on the sudden shall dissever it,
And batter all the stones about their ears,   30
Whence none can possibly escape alive ;
Now as for Calymath and his consorts,
Here have I made a dainty gallery,
The floor whereof, this cable being cut,
Doth fall asunder, so that it doth sink
Into a deep pit past recovery.
Here, hold that knife, and when thou seest he comes,
And with his bashaws shall be blithely set,
A warning piece shall be shot off from the tower,

---

[20] Q *Serv.*

To give thee knowledge when to cut the
cord   40
And fire the house. Say, will not this be brave?
FERN. O, excellent! here, hold thee, Barabas,
I trust thy word; take what I promis'd thee.
BAR. No, Governor, I'll satisfy thee first;
Thou shalt not live in doubt of anything.
Stand close, for here they come. [FERNEZE re-
tires.] — Why, is not this
A kingly kind of trade, to purchase towns
By treachery and sell 'em by deceit?
Now tell me, worldlings, underneath the [sun] 21
If greater falsehood ever has been done.   50

Enter CALYMATH *and* Bashaws.

CALY. Come, my companion bashaws; see,
I pray,
How busy Barabas is there above
To entertain us in his gallery.
Let us salute him. — Save thee, Barabas!
BAR. Welcome, great Calymath!
FERN. [*aside*] How the slave jeers at him.
BAR. Will't please thee, mighty Selim Caly-
math,
To ascend our homely stairs?
CALY.   Ay, Barabas. —
Come, bashaws, attend.
FERN. [*coming forward*]   Stay, Calymath!
For I will show thee greater courtesy   60
Than Barabas would have afforded thee.
KNIGHT [*within*] Sound a charge there!
A charge [*sounded within.* FERNEZE *cuts*] *the
cable:* [*the floor of the gallery gives way*]; *a
caldron discovered,* [*into which* BARABAS *has
fallen.*]

[*Enter* DEL BOSCO *and* Knights.]

CALY. How now! what means this?
BAR.   Help, help me. Christians, help!
FERN. See, Calymath; this was devis'd for
thee!
CALY. Treason! treason! Bashaws, fly!
FERN. No, Selim, do not fly;
See his end first, and fly then if thou canst.
BAR. O help me, Selim! help me, Christians!
Governor, why stand you all so pitiless?
FERN. Should I in pity of thy plaints or thee,
Accursed Barabas, base Jew, relent?   71
No, thus I'll see thy treachery repaid,
But wish thou hadst behav'd thee otherwise.
BAR. You will not help me, then?
FERN.   No, villain, no.
BAR. And, villains, know you cannot help
me now. —

Then, Barabas, breathe forth thy latest fate,22
And in the fury of thy torments strive
To end thy life with resolution. —
Know, Governor, 't was I that slew thy son;
I fram'd the challenge that did make them
meet.   80
Know, Calymath, I aim'd thy overthrow,
And, had I but escap'd this stratagem,
I would have brought confusion on you all,
Damn'd Christians, dogs, and Turkish infidels!
But now begins the extremity of heat
To pinch me with intolerable pangs.
Die, life! fly, soul! tongue, curse thy fill, and
die!   [*Dies.*]
CALY. Tell me, you Christians, what doth
this portend?
FERN. This train he laid to have entrapp'd
thy life.
Now, Selim, note the unhallowed deeds of
Jews;   90
Thus he determin'd to have handled thee,
But I have rather chose to save thy life.
CALY. Was this the banquet he prepar'd
for us?
Let's hence, lest further mischief be pre-
tended.23
FERN. Nay, Selim, stay; for since we have
thee here,
We will not let thee part so suddenly;
Besides, if we should let thee go, all's one,24
For with thy galleys couldst thou not get
hence,
Without fresh men to rig and furnish them.
CALY. Tush, Governor, take thou no care
for that;   100
My men are all aboard,
And do attend 25 my coming there by this.
FERN. Why, heard'st thou not the trumpet
sound a charge?
CALY. Yes, what of that?
FERN.   Why, then the house was fir'd,
Blown up, and all thy soldiers massacred.
CALY. O monstrous treason!
FERN.   A Jew's courtesy;
For he that did by treason work our fall,
By treason hath delivered thee to us.
Know, therefore, till thy father hath made
good
The ruins done to Malta and to us,   110
Thou canst not part; for Malta shall be
freed,
Or Selim ne'er return to Ottoman.

---

21 Cor. Reed; Q *Summe.*

22 Cunningham emends *hate.*
23 Intended.
24 It's all the same.   25 Await.

CALY. Nay, rather, Christians, let me go to Turkey,
In person there to [mediate] [26] your peace ;
To keep me here will naught advantage you.
    FERN. Content thee, Calymath ; here thou must stay,
And live in Malta prisoner ; for come [all] [27] the world
To rescue thee, so will we guard us now,
As sooner shall they drink the ocean dry
Than conquer Malta, or endanger us. —   120
So march away, and let due praise be given
Neither to Fate nor Fortune, but to Heaven.

                          [*Exeunt.*]

[26] Conj. Collier; Q *meditate.*

[27] Emend. Reed; Q *call.*

The troublesome

raigne and lamentable death of
Edward *the second*, *King of*
England: with the tragicall
fall of proud Mortimer:

As it was sundrie times publiquely acted
in the honourable citie of London, *by the*
right honourable the Earle of Pem-
brooke his feruants.

Written by Chri. Marlow *Gent.*

Imprinted at London for. *William Iones,*
dwelling neere Holbourne conduit at the
signe of the Gunne, 1594

INTRODUCTORY NOTE

WITH *Edward II*, probably produced in 1591–92, Marlowe carries the chronicle play to its highest level prior to Shakespeare's best "histories." Technically, though not imaginatively, it marks the culmination of Marlowe's dramatic powers. Characterization is now extended beyond one or two central figures, difficult problems of selection and condensation are surmounted with ease, and a masterly transfer of sympathy is accomplished. Whatever the King's faults, his death is affecting; to enlist the emotions of the audience for a monarch so weakly bad as Edward is a feat which does not suffer in comparison with Shakespeare's similar treatment of Richard II. On the greater dramatist's technical development Marlowe's most mature play may have exerted considerable influence. On the other hand, there are fewer lyrical outbursts than in the earlier works; it is curious that Marlowe's best play seems less Marlovian than the others.

The chief source of *Edward II* was Holinshed's *Chronicles*, though Fabyan's and Stowe's were also used for a few details. How popular the play was on the stage, and how long it remained in the repertory are unknown; but the number of early editions indicates considerable success. The title pages of the old editions state that it was acted by the Earl of Pembroke's company. It was revived, according to the Fourth Quarto, by Queen Anne's Men at the Red Bull.

Edward II was edited for the Malone Society by W. W. Greg (1925); for the Case Marlowe the editors are to be H. B. Charlton and R. A. Waller. Among other editions are those of A. W. Verity (1896) and W. D. Briggs (1914). The present text is based on the first edition, the best of the early texts of Marlowe, the octavo of 1594 (reprinted in quarto 1598, 1612, 1622), as reproduced by Greg and Brooke.

The latter was the first to observe that the Dyce copy of Q 1598 contains a transcript (supplying the absence of the first two leaves of that Quarto) dated, on the title page, 1593. This MS is given in facsimile by Greg. Since the text of the MS is closer to the first than to the second of the surviving editions, it rather looks as though an edition, now quite lost, had preceded them. Of the first surviving edition, but two copies are known; they are in the Landesbibliothek of Cassel and the Zentralbibliothek of Zurich.

THE TROUBLESOME REIGN AND LAMENTABLE DEATH OF EDWARD THE SECOND

BY

CHRISTOPHER MARLOWE

[DRAMATIS PERSONAE

KING EDWARD THE SECOND.
PRINCE EDWARD, his son, afterwards King Edward the Third.
EDMUND, EARL OF KENT, half-brother to King Edward the Second.
PIERCE DE GAVESTON, a Gascon courtier, afterwards Earl of Cornwall.
ARCHBISHOP OF CANTERBURY.
BISHOP OF COVENTRY.
BISHOP OF WINCHESTER.
GUY, EARL OF WARWICK.
THOMAS, EARL OF LANCASTER.
AYMER, EARL OF PEMBROKE.
EARL OF ARUNDEL.
EARL OF LEICESTER.
THOMAS, LORD BERKELEY.[1]
LORD MORTIMER, the elder, of Chirke.
LORD ROGER MORTIMER, the younger, of Wigmore, his nephew.
HUGH SPENCER, the elder, afterwards Earl of Winchester.

HUGH SPENCER, the younger, his son, afterwards Earl of Gloucester and Wiltshire.
ROBERT BALDOCK, a scholar.
HENRY DE BEAUMONT.
SIR WILLIAM TRUSSEL.
SIR THOMAS GURNEY.
JOHN, LORD MATREVIS.
LIGHTBORN.
SIR JOHN OF HAINAULT.
LEVUNE.
RICE AP HOWELL.
JAMES.
Abbot, Monks, Herald, Lords, Poor Men, Mower, Champion, Messengers, Soldiers, and Attendants.

QUEEN ISABELLA, wife to King Edward the Second.
Niece to King Edward the Second, daughter to the late Earl of Gloucester.
Ladies.]

[ACT I — SCENE I] [2]

Enter GAVESTON, *reading on a letter that was brought him from the King.*

[GAV.] " My father is deceas'd ; come, Gaveston,
And share the kingdom with thy dearest friend."
Ah, words that make me surfeit with delight !
What greater bliss can hap to Gaveston
Than live and be the favorite of a king?
Sweet prince, I come ; these, these thy amorous lines
Might have enforc'd me to have swum from France,
And, like Leander, gasp'd upon the sand,

So [3] thou wouldst smile and take me in thy arms.
The sight of London to my exiled eyes   10
Is as Elysium to a new-come soul ;
Not that I love the city or the men,
But that it harbors him I hold so dear,
The King, upon whose bosom let me die,[4]
And with the world be still at enmity.
What need the arctic people love starlight,
To whom the sun shines both by day and night ?
Farewell base stooping to the lordly peers ;
My knee shall bow to none but to the King.
As for the multitude, that are but sparks   20
Rak'd up in embers of their poverty,
Tanti! [5]   I 'll [fawn] [6] first on the wind
That glanceth at my lips, and flyeth away.

---

[1] Old eds. *Bartley.*
[2] Unlocated ; presumably a street in Westminster.
[3] Provided that.   [4] *I.e.,* swoon.
[5] So much for them.
[6] Cor. Robinson ; old eds. *fanne.*

Enter three Poor Men.

But how now, what are these?

POOR MEN. Such as desire your Worship's
service.

GAV. What canst thou do?

1 P. MAN. I can ride.

GAV. But I have no horses. — What art
thou?

2 P. MAN. A traveller.

GAV. Let me see ; thou wouldst do well   30
To wait at my trencher and tell me lies at
dinner time ;
And as I like your discoursing, I'll have you. —
And what art thou?

3 P. MAN. A soldier that hath serv'd
against the Scot.

GAV. Why, there are hospitals [7] for such as
you.
I have no war, and therefore, sir, begone.

3 P. MAN. Farewell, and perish by a soldier's hand,
That wouldst reward them with an hospital.

GAV. [*aside*] Ay, ay, these words of his move
me as much
As if a goose should play the porpentine,[8]   40
And dart her plumes, thinking to pierce my
breast.
But yet it is no pain to speak men fair ;
I'll flatter these, and make them live in
hope. —
You know that I came lately out of France,
And yet I have not view'd my Lord the
King ;
If I speed well, I'll entertain you all.

OMNES. We thank your Worship.

GAV. I have some business ; leave me to
myself.

OMNES. We will wait here about the court.
Exeunt [*the* Poor Men].

GAV. Do. — These are not men for me ; [50
I must have wanton poets, pleasant wits,
Musicians, that with touching of a string
May draw the pliant King which way I please.
Music and poetry is his delight ;
Therefore I'll have Italian masques by night,
Sweet speeches, comedies, and pleasing shows ;
And in the day, when he shall walk abroad,
Like sylvan [9] nymphs my pages shall be clad ;
My men, like satyrs grazing on the lawns,
Shall with their goat-feet dance an antic hay.[10]
Sometime a lovely boy in Dian's shape,   61
With hair that gilds the water as it glides,

Crownets [11] of pearl about his naked arms,
And in his sportful hands an olive tree,
To hide those parts which men delight to see,
Shall bathe him in a spring ; and there, hard by,
One like Actaeon peeping through the grove
Shall by the angry goddess be transform'd,
And running in the likeness of an hart
By yelping hounds pull'd down, and seem to
die ;   70
Such things as these best please his Majesty,
My lord. — Here comes the King and the
nobles
From the parliament ; I'll stand aside.
[*Retires.*]

Enter the KING [EDWARD II], LANCASTER,
MORTIMER SENIOR, MORTIMER JUNIOR,
EDMUND EARL *of* KENT, GUY EARL *of* WAR-
WICK, *etc.*

K. EDW. Lancaster.

LAN. My Lord.

GAV. [*aside*] That Earl of Lancaster do I
abhor.

K. EDW. Will you not grant me this? —
[*aside*] In spite of them
I'll have my will ; and these two Mortimers,
That cross me thus, shall know I am displeas'd.

ELDER MOR. [12] If you love us, my Lord,
hate Gaveston.   80

GAV. [*aside*] That villain Mortimer ! I'll be
his death.

YOUNG MOR. Mine uncle here, this earl,
and I myself
Were sworn to your father at his death,
That he should ne'er return into the realm ;
And know, my Lord, ere I will break my oath,
This sword of mine, that should offend your
foes,
Shall sleep within the scabbard at thy need ;
And underneath thy banners march who will,
For Mortimer will hang his armor up.

GAV. [*aside*] *Mort Dieu!*   90

K. EDW. Well, Mortimer, I'll make thee
rue these words.
Beseems it thee to contradict thy king?
Frown'st thou thereat, aspiring Lancaster?
The sword shall plane the furrows of thy brows,
And hew these knees that now are grown so
stiff.
I will have Gaveston, and you shall know
What danger 't is to stand against your king.

GAV. [*aside*] Well done, Ned !

---

[7] Almshouses.   [8] Porcupine.
[9] So MS (?1593) ; old eds. *Siluian.*
[10] Grotesque country-dance.
[11] Coronets ; *i.e.*, bracelets.
[12] Speech-tags of old eds. *Mor. se.* and *Mor. iu.*,
throughout.

LAN. My Lord, why do you thus incense
your peers,
That naturally would love and honor you   100
But for that base and obscure Gaveston?
Four earldoms have I, besides Lancaster —
Derby, Salisbury, Lincoln, Leicester. —
These will I sell, to give my soldiers pay,
Ere Gaveston shall stay within the realm ;
Therefore, if he be come, expel him straight.

KENT. Barons and earls, your pride hath
made me mute ;
But now I 'll speak, and to the proof, I hope.
I do remember in my father's days
Lord Percy of the north, being highly mov'd,
Brav'd Mowbray [13] in presence of the King ;   111
For which, had not his Highness lov'd him well,
He should have lost his head ; but with his look
The undaunted spirit of Percy was appeas'd,
And Mowbray and he were reconcil'd ;
Yet dare you brave the King unto his face ? —
Brother, revenge it ; and let these their heads
Preach upon poles, for trespass of their tongues.

WAR. O, our heads !

K. EDW. Ay, yours ; and therefore I would
wish you grant.   120

WAR. Bridle thy anger, gentle Mortimer.

Y. MOR. I cannot, nor I will not ; I must
speak.
Cousin, our hands I hope shall fence our heads,
And strike off his that makes you threaten us.
Come, Uncle, let us leave the brainsick king,
And henceforth parle[y] with our naked swords.

E. MOR. Wiltshire hath men enough to save
our heads.

WAR. All Warwickshire will love him for
my sake.

LAN. And northward Gaveston hath many
friends. —
Adieu, my Lord ; and either change your
mind,   130
Or look to see the throne, where you should sit,
To float in blood, and at thy wanton head
The glozing [14] head of thy base minion thrown.
Exeunt [all but KING EDWARD, KENT,
GAVESTON, *and* Attendants].

K. EDW. I cannot brook these haughty
menaces.
Am I a king, and must be overrul'd ? —
Brother, display my ensigns in the field ;
I 'll bandy [15] with the barons and the earls,
And either die or live with Gaveston.

GAV. [*coming forward*] I can no longer keep
me from my lord.

[13] Trisyllabic ; old eds. *Mowberie.*
[14] Flattering.   [15] Contend.

K. EDW. What, Gaveston, welcome ! —
Kiss not my hand !   140
Embrace me, Gaveston, as I do thee !
Why shouldst thou kneel? Knowest thou
not who I am?
Thy friend, thyself, another Gaveston !
Not Hylas was more mourned of Hercules,
Than thou hast been of me since thy exile.

GAV. And since I went from hence, no soul
in hell
Hath felt more torment than poor Gaveston.

K. EDW. I know it. — Brother, welcome
home my friend.
Now let the treacherous Mortimers conspire,
And that high-minded Earl of Lancaster ;   150
I have my wish, in that I joy thy sight ;
And sooner shall the sea o'erwhelm my land,
Than bear the ship that shall transport thee
hence.
I here create thee Lord High Chamberlain,
Chief Secretary to the state and me,
Earl of Cornwall, King and Lord of Man.

GAV. My Lord, these titles far exceed my
worth.

KENT. Brother, the least of these may well
suffice
For one of greater birth than Gaveston.

K. EDW. Cease, Brother, for I cannot brook
these words. —   160
Thy worth, sweet friend, is far above my gifts ;
Therefore, to equal it, receive my heart.
If for these dignities thou be envied,[16]
I 'll give thee more ; for but to honor thee
Is Edward pleas'd with kingly regiment.[17]
Fear'st thou [18] thy person? Thou shalt have
a guard.
Wants thou gold? Go to my treasury.
Wouldst thou be lov'd and fear'd? Receive
my seal :
Save or condemn, and in our name command
Whatso thy mind affects, or fancy likes.   170

GAV. It shall suffice me to enjoy your love,
Which whiles I have, I think myself as great
As Caesar riding in the Roman street,
With captive kings at his triumphant car.

Enter the BISHOP OF COVENTRY.

K. EDW. Whither goes my Lord of Coventry so fast?

B. OF COV. To celebrate your father's exequies.
But is that wicked Gaveston return'd?

[16] Accented on second syllable.
[17] Rule.   [18] Fearest thou for.

K. Edw. Ay, priest, and lives to be reveng'd
　　on thee,
That wert the only cause of his exile.
　　Gav. 'T is true ; and but for reverence of
　　　these robes,　　　　　　　　　　　180
Thou shouldst not plod one foot beyond this
　　place.
　　B. of Cov. I did no more than I was bound
　　　to do ;
And, Gaveston, unless thou be reclaim'd,
As then I did incense the parliament,
So will I now, and thou shalt back to France.
　　Gav. Saving your reverence, you must par-
　　　don me.
　　K. Edw. Throw off his golden mitre, rend
　　　his stole,
And in the channel[19] christen him anew.
　　Kent. Ah, Brother, lay not violent hands
　　　on him,
For he 'll complain unto the see of Rome. 190
　　Gav. Let him complain unto the see of hell ;
I 'll be reveng'd on him for my exile.
　　K. Edw. No, spare his life, but seize upon
　　　his goods.
Be thou Lord Bishop and receive his rents,
And make him serve thee as thy chaplain :
I give him thee — here, use him as thou wilt.
　　Gav. He shall to prison, and there die in
　　　bolts.
　　K. Edw. Ay, to the Tower, the Fleet, or
　　　where thou wilt.
　　B. of Cov. For this offence, be thou ac-
　　　curs'd of God.
　　K. Edw. Who 's there? Convey this priest
　　　to the Tower.　　　[*Enter* Guards.] 200
　　B. of Cov.　　　　　　True, true.[20]
　　K. Edw. But in the meantime, Gaveston,
　　　away
And take possession of his house and goods.
Come, follow me, and thou shalt have my guard
To see it done, and bring thee safe again.
　　Gav. What should a priest do with so fair a
　　　house?
A prison may best beseem his holiness.
　　　　　　　　　　　　　　　[*Exeunt.*]

[Scene II][21]

Enter both the Mortimers, Warwick, *and*
Lancaster.

War. 'T is true, the Bishop is in the Tower,
And goods and body given to Gaveston.

---

[19] Gutter.
[20] *I.e.,* you well may say "convey" (= steal).
[21] The same.

Lan. What ! will they tyrannize upon the
　　Church?
Ah, wicked King ! accursed Gaveston !
This ground, which is corrupted with their
　　steps,
Shall be their timeless[22] sepulchre or mine.
　　Y. Mor. Well, let that peevish Frenchman
　　　guard him sure ;
Unless his breast be sword-proof, he shall die.
　　E. Mor. How now ! why droops the Earl of
　　　Lancaster?
　　Y. Mor. Wherefore is Guy of Warwick dis-
　　　content?　　　　　　　　　　　　10
　　Lan. That villain Gaveston is made an earl.
　　E. Mor. An earl !
　　War. Ay, and besides Lord Chamberlain of
　　　the realm,
And Secretary too, and Lord of Man.
　　E. Mor. We may not, nor we will not suffer
　　　this.
　　Y. Mor. Why post we not from hence to
　　　levy men?
　　Lan. " My Lord of Cornwall " now at
　　　every word !
And happy is the man whom he vouchsafes,
For vailing[23] of his bonnet, one good look. [19
Thus, arm in arm, the King and he doth march ;
Nay more, the guard upon his Lordship waits,
And all the court begins to flatter him.
　　War. Thus leaning on the shoulder of the
　　　King,
He nods and scorns and smiles at those that
　　pass.
　　E. Mor. Doth no man take exceptions at
　　　the slave?
　　Lan. All stomach[24] him, but none dare
　　　speak a word.
　　Y. Mor. Ah, that bewrays[25] their baseness,
　　　Lancaster ;
Were all the earls and barons of my mind,
We 'll hale him from the bosom of the King,
And at the court gate hang the peasant up,　30
Who, swoln with venom of ambitious pride,
Will be the ruin of the realm and us.

Enter the [Arch]bishop of Canterbury [*and
an* Attendant].

War. Here comes my Lord of Canterbury's
　　Grace.
　　Lan. His countenance bewrays he is dis-
　　　pleas'd.
　　A. of Cant. First were his sacred garments
　　　rent and torn ;

---

[22] Untimely.　　　　　[23] Doffing.
[24] Resent.　　　　　　[25] Discloses.

Then laid they violent hands upon him ; next
Himself imprisoned, and his goods asseiz'd.
This certify the Pope.   Away, take horse.
                    [*Exit* Attendant.]
  Lan. My Lord, will you take arms against
    the King?
  A. of Cant. What need I?   God himself is
    up in arms,   40
When violence is offered to the Church.
  Y. Mor. Then will you join with us, that
    be his peers,
To banish or behead that Gaveston?
  A. of Cant. What else, my Lords? for it
    concerns me near ;
The bishopric of Coventry is his.

Enter the Queen [Isabella].

  Y. Mor. Madam, whither walks your
    Majesty so fast?
  Q. Isab. Unto the forest,[26] gentle Mortimer,
To live in grief and baleful discontent ;
For now my Lord the King regards me not,
But dotes upon the love of Gaveston.   50
He claps his cheeks, and hangs about his neck,
Smiles in his face, and whispers in his ears ;
And when I come he frowns, as who should say,
" Go whither thou wilt, seeing I have
    Gaveston."
  E. Mor. Is it not strange that he is thus
    bewitch'd?
  Y. Mor. Madam, return unto the court
    again.
That sly inveigling Frenchman we 'll exile,
Or lose our lives ; and yet, ere that day come,
The King shall lose his crown ; for we have
    power,
And courage too, to be reveng'd at full.   60
  A. of Cant. But yet lift not your swords
    against the King.
  Lan. No ; but we 'll lift Gaveston from
    hence.
  War. And war must be the means, or he 'll
    stay still.
  Q. Isab. Then let him stay ; for rather than
    my lord
Shall be oppress'd by civil mutinies,
I will endure a melancholy life
And let him frolic with his minion.
  A. of Cant. My Lords, to ease all this, but
    hear me speak.
We and the rest, that are his counsellors,
Will meet and with a general consent   70

Confirm him banishment with our hands and
    seals.
  Lan. What we confirm the King will frus-
    trate.
  Y. Mor. Then may we lawfully revolt from
    him.
  War. But say, my Lord, where shall this
    meeting be?
  A. of Cant. At the New Temple.
  Y. Mor. Content.
  A. of Cant. And, in the meantime, I 'll en-
    treat you all
To cross to Lambeth,[27] and there stay with me.
  Lan. Come, then ; let 's away.
  Y. Mor. Madam, farewell.   80
  Q. Isab. Farewell, sweet Mortimer ; and
    for my sake,
Forbear to levy arms against the King.
  Y. Mor. Ay, if words will serve ; if not, I
    must.   [*Exeunt.*]

[Scene III] [28]

Enter Gaveston *and the* Earl of Kent.

  Gav. Edmund, the mighty Prince of Lan-
    caster,
That hath more earldoms than an ass can bear,
And both the Mortimers, two goodly men,
With Guy of Warwick, that redoubted knight,
Are gone towards Lambeth ; there let them
    remain !   *Exeunt.*

[Scene IV] [29]

Enter Nobles [Lancaster, Warwick, Pembroke, *the* Elder Mortimer, Young Mortimer, *the* Archbishop of Canterbury, *and*
Attendants].

  Lan. Here is the form of Gaveston's exile.
May it please your Lordship to subscribe your
    name.
  A. of Cant. Give me the paper.
    [*He subscribes, as the others do after him.*]
  Lan. Quick, quick, my Lord ; I long to
    write my name.
  War. But I long more to see him banish'd
    hence.
  Y. Mor. The name of Mortimer shall fright
    the King,
Unless he be declin'd from that base peasant.

---

[26] A metaphor, = "into seclusion," as Bullen
notes.

[27] The archepiscopal palace, across the Thames.
[28] Unlocated ; presumably at Westminster.
[29] London. The New Temple. It stood between
Fleet Street and the Thames. Upon the fall of the
Knights Templars Edward II had given it to Pembroke.

Enter the KING, GAVESTON, [*and* KENT].

K. EDW. What! are you mov'd that Gaveston sits here?
It is our pleasure ; we will have it so.
LAN. Your Grace doth well to place him by your side,   10
For nowhere else the new earl is so safe.
E. MOR. What man of noble birth can brook this sight?
Quam male conveniunt! [30]
See what a scornful look the peasant casts !
PEM. Can kingly lions fawn on creeping ants?
WAR. Ignoble vassal, that like Phaëthon
Aspir'st unto the guidance of the sun !
Y. MOR. Their downfall is at hand, their forces down ;
We will not thus be fac'd and over-peer'd.
K. EDW. Lay hands on that traitor Mortimer !   20
E. MOR. Lay hands on that traitor Gaveston !   [*They seize* GAVESTON.]
KENT. Is this the duty that you owe your king?
WAR. We know our duties ; let him know his peers.
K. EDW. Whither will you bear him? Stay, or ye shall die.
E. MOR. We are no traitors ; therefore threaten not.
GAV. No, threaten not, my Lord, but pay them home.
Were I a king——
Y. MOR. Thou villain, wherefore talks thou of a king,
That hardly art a gentleman by birth?
K. EDW. Were he a peasant, being my minion,   30
I 'll make the proudest of you stoop to him.
LAN. My Lord, you may not thus disparage us. ——
Away, I say, with hateful Gaveston.
E. MOR. And with the Earl of Kent that favors him.
[*Attendants* remove KENT *and* GAVESTON.]
K. EDW. Nay, then, lay violent hands upon your king.
Here, Mortimer, sit thou in Edward's throne ;
Warwick and Lancaster, wear you my crown.
Was ever king thus overrul'd as I?
LAN. Learn then to rule us better, and the realm.

Y. MOR. What we have done our heart-blood shall maintain.   40
WAR. Think you that we can brook this upstart pride?
K. EDW. Anger and wrathful fury stops my speech.
A. OF CANT. Why are you mov'd? Be patient,[31] my Lord,
And see what we your counsellors have done.
Y. MOR. My Lords, now let us all be resolute,
And either have our wills or lose our lives.
K. EDW. Meet you for this, proud overdaring peers?
Ere my sweet Gaveston shall part from me,
This isle shall fleet [32] upon the ocean,
And wander to the unfrequented Inde.   50
A. OF CANT. You know that I am legate to the Pope.
On your allegiance to the see of Rome,
Subscribe, as we have done, to his exile.
Y. MOR. Curse him, if he refuse ; and then may we
Depose him and elect another king.
K. EDW. Ay, there it goes ! but yet I will not yield,
Curse me, depose me, do the worst you can.
LAN. Then linger not, my Lord, but do it straight.
A. OF CANT. Remember how the Bishop was abus'd ;   59
Either banish him that was the cause thereof,
Or I will presently discharge these lords
Of duty and allegiance due to thee.
K. EDW. [*aside*] It boots me not to threat ; I must speak fair. ——
The legate of the Pope will be obey'd.
My Lord, you shall be Chancellor of the realm ;
Thou, Lancaster, High Admiral of our fleet ;
Young Mortimer and his uncle shall be earls ;
And you, Lord Warwick, President of the North ;
And [*to* PEMBROKE] thou, of Wales. If this content you not,
Make several kingdoms of this monarchy,   70
And share it equally amongst you all,
So I may have some nook or corner left,
To frolic with my dearest Gaveston.
A. OF CANT. Nothing shall alter us ; we are resolv'd.
LAN. Come, come, subscribe.
Y. MOR. Why should you love him whom the world hates so?

---

[30] How ill they agree !   [31] Trisyllabic.   [32] Float.

K. Edw. Because he loves me more than all the world.

Ah, none but rude and savage-minded men
Would seek the ruin of my Gaveston ;
You that be noble born should pity him.   80
 War. You that are princely born should shake him off ;
For shame subscribe, and let the lown [33] depart.
 E. Mor. Urge him, my Lord.
 A. of Cant. Are you content to banish him the realm?
 K. Edw. I see I must, and therefore am content.
Instead of ink, I 'll write it with my tears.
                          [*Subscribes.*]
 Y. Mor. The king is lovesick for his minion.
 K. Edw. 'T is done ; and now, accursed hand, fall off.
 Lan. Give it me ; I 'll have it published in the streets.
 Y. Mor. I 'll see him presently [34] despatched away.   90
 A. of Cant. Now is my heart at ease.
 War.   And so is mine.
 Pem. This will be good news to the common sort.
 E. Mor. Be it or no, he shall not linger here.
                 Exeunt [*all but* King Edward].
 K. Edw. How fast they run to banish him I love.
They would not stir, were it to do me good.
Why should a king be subject to a priest?
Proud Rome, that hatchest such imperial grooms,
For these thy superstitious taper-lights,
Wherewith thy antichristian churches blaze,
I 'll fire thy crazed buildings, and enforce   100
The papal towers to kiss the lowly ground,
With slaughtered priests [make] [35] Tiber's channel swell,
And banks rais'd higher with their sepulchres !
As for the peers, that back the clergy thus,
If I be king, not one of them shall live.

Re-enter Gaveston.

 Gav. My Lord, I hear it whispered everywhere,
That I am banish'd, and must fly the land.
 K. Edw. 'T is true, sweet Gaveston — O, were it false !
The legate of the Pope will have it so,
And thou must hence, or I shall be depos'd. [110
But I will reign to be reveng'd of them ;

And therefore, sweet friend, take it patiently.
Live where thou wilt, I 'll send thee gold enough ;
And long thou shalt not stay, or, if thou dost,
I 'll come to thee ; my love shall ne'er decline.
 Gav. Is all my hope turn'd to this hell of grief ?
 K. Edw. Rend not my heart with thy too piercing words.
Thou from this land, I from myself am banish'd.
 Gav. To go from hence grieves not poor Gaveston ;
But to forsake you, in whose gracious looks [120
The blessedness of Gaveston remains,
For nowhere else seeks he felicity.
 K. Edw. And only this torments my wretched soul,
That, whether I will or no, thou must depart.
Be governor of Ireland in my stead,
And there abide till fortune call thee home.
Here, take my picture, and let me wear thine ;
O, might I keep thee here as I do this,
Happy were I ! but now most miserable !   129
 Gav. 'T is something to be pitied of a king.
 K. Edw. Thou shalt not hence — I 'll hide thee, Gaveston.
 Gav. I shall be found, and then 't will grieve me more.
 K. Edw. Kind words and mutual talk makes our grief greater ;
Therefore with dumb embracement let us part. —
Stay, Gaveston, I cannot leave thee thus.
 Gav. For every look, my Lord drops down a tear.
Seeing I must go, do not renew my sorrow.
 K. Edw. The time is little that thou hast to stay,
And, therefore, give me leave to look my fill.
But come, sweet friend, I 'll bear thee on thy way.   140
 Gav. The peers will frown.
 K. Edw. I pass [36] not for their anger. Come, let 's go ;
O that we might as well return as go.

Enter Edmund *and* Queen Isabell[a].

 Q. Isab. Whither goes my Lord?
 K. Edw. Fawn not on me, French strumpet ! Get thee gone !
 Q. Isab. On whom but on my husband should I fawn ?

---

[33] Lout.   [34] At once.
[35] Emend. Dodsley ; old eds. *may.*   [36] Care, am moved.

GAV. On Mortimer, with whom, ungentle
Queen —
I say no more. Judge you the rest, my
Lord.
Q. ISAB. In saying this, thou wrong'st me,
Gaveston.   149
Is 't not enough that thou corrupts my lord,
And art a bawd to his affections,
But thou must call mine honor thus in ques-
tion?
GAV. I mean not so ; your Grace must par-
don me.
K. EDW. Thou art too familiar with that
Mortimer,
And by thy means is Gaveston exil'd ;
But I would wish thee reconcile the lords,
Or thou shalt ne'er be reconcil'd to me.
Q. ISAB. Your Highness knows it lies not in
my power.
K. EDW. Away then ! touch me not ! —
Come, Gaveston.
Q. ISAB. Villain, 't is thou that robb'st me
of my lord.   160
GAV. Madam, 't is you that rob me of my
lord.
K. EDW. Speak not unto her ; let her droop
and pine.
Q. ISAB. Wherein, my Lord, have I deserv'd
these words?
Witness the tears that Isabella sheds,
Witness this heart, that, sighing for thee,
breaks,
How dear my lord is to poor Isabel.
K. EDW. And witness Heaven how dear
thou art to me !
There weep ; for till my Gaveston be repeal'd,
Assure thyself thou com'st not in my sight.
                    Exeunt EDWARD *and* GAVESTON.
Q. ISAB. O miserable and distressed queen !
Would, when I left sweet France and was em-
bark'd,   171
That charming [37] Circes, walking on the waves,
Had chang'd my shape, or at the marriage day
The cup of Hymen had been full of poison,
Or with those arms that twin'd about my neck
I had been stifled, and not lived to see
The King, my lord, thus to abandon me !
Like frantic Juno will I fill the earth
With ghastly murmur of my sighs and cries ;
For never doted Jove on Ganymede   180
So much as he on cursed Gaveston.
But, that will more exasperate his wrath,
I must entreat him, I must speak him fair,
And be a means to call home Gaveston.

[37] Able to enchant.

And yet he 'll ever dote on Gaveston ;
And so am I for ever miserable.

Re-enter the Nobles [LANCASTER, WARWICK,
PEMBROKE, *the* Elder MORTIMER, *and* Young
MORTIMER] *to the* Queen.

LAN. Look where the sister of the King of
France
Sits wringing of her hands, and beats her
breast.
WAR. The King, I fear, hath ill entreated
her.
PEM. Hard is the heart that injures such a
saint.   190
Y. MOR. I know 't is 'long of Gaveston she
weeps.
E. MOR. Why? He is gone.
Y. MOR.   Madam, how fares your Grace?
Q. ISAB. Ah, Mortimer ! now breaks the
King's hate forth,
And he confesseth that he loves me not.
Y. MOR. Cry quittance, madam, then ; and
love not him.
Q. ISAB. No, rather will I die a thousand
deaths !
And yet I love in vain ; he 'll ne'er love me.
LAN. Fear ye not, madam ; now his
minion 's gone,
His wanton humor will be quickly left.   199
Q. ISAB. O never, Lancaster ! I am enjoin'd
To sue upon you all for his repeal ;
This wills my Lord, and this must I perform,
Or else be banish'd from his Highness' presence.
LAN. For his repeal? Madam, he comes
not back,
Unless the sea cast up his shipwrack['d] body.
WAR. And to behold so sweet a sight as that,
There 's none here but would run his horse to
death.
Y. MOR. But, madam, would you have us
call him home?
Q. ISAB. Ay, Mortimer, for till he be re-
stor'd,   209
The angry King hath banished me the court ;
And, therefore, as thou lovest and tend'rest me,
Be thou my advocate unto these peers.
Y. MOR. What, would ye have me plead
for Gaveston?
E. MOR. Plead for him he that will, I am
resolv'd.
LAN. And so am I, my Lord. Dissuade
the Queen.
Q. ISAB. O Lancaster, let him dissuade the
King ;
For 't is against my will he should return.

WAR. Then speak not for him; let the peasant go.

Q. ISAB. 'T is for myself I speak, and not for him.

PEM. No speaking will prevail, and therefore cease.   220

Y. MOR. Fair Queen, forbear to angle for the fish

Which, being caught, strikes him that takes it dead;

I mean that vile torpedo,[38] Gaveston,

That now, I hope, floats on the Irish seas.

Q. ISAB. Sweet Mortimer, sit down by me awhile,

And I will tell thee reasons of such weight

As thou wilt soon subscribe to his repeal.

Y. MOR. It is impossible; but speak your mind.

Q. ISAB. Then thus; — but none shall hear it but ourselves.

        [*Talks to* Young MORTIMER *apart.*]

LAN. My Lords, albeit the Queen win Mortimer,   230

Will you be resolute, and hold with me?

E. MOR. Not I, against my nephew.

PEM. Fear not, the Queen's words cannot alter him.

WAR. No? Do but mark how earnestly she pleads.

LAN. And see how coldly his looks make denial.

WAR. She smiles; now, for my life, his mind is chang'd.

LAN. I 'll rather lose his friendship, I, than grant.

Y. MOR. Well, of necessity it must be so. —

My Lords, that I abhor base Gaveston,

I hope your Honors make no question;   240

And therefore, though I plead for his repeal,

'T is not for his sake, but for our avail;

Nay for the realm's behoof, and for the King's.

LAN. Fie, Mortimer, dishonor not thyself.

Can this be true, 't was good to banish him?

And is this true, to call him home again?

Such reasons make white black, and dark night day.

Y. MOR. My Lord of Lancaster, mark the respect.[39]

LAN. In no respect can contraries be true.

Q. ISAB. Yet, good my Lord, hear what he can allege.   250

WAR. All that he speaks is nothing; we are resolv'd.

Y. MOR. Do you not wish that Gaveston were dead?

PEM. I would he were.

Y. MOR. Why, then, my Lord, give me but leave to speak.

E. MOR. But, Nephew, do not play the sophister.

Y. MOR. This which I urge is of a burning zeal

To mend the King, and do our country good.

Know you not Gaveston hath store of gold,

Which may in Ireland purchase him such friends

As he will front the mightiest of us all?   260

And whereas [40] he shall live and be belov'd,

'T is hard for us to work his overthrow.

WAR. Mark you but that, my Lord of Lancaster.

Y. MOR. But were he here, detested as he is,

How easily might some base slave be suborn'd

To greet his Lordship with a poniard,

And none so much as blame the murderer,

But rather praise him for that brave attempt,

And in the chronicle enroll his name

For purging of the realm of such a plague.   270

PEM. He saith true.

LAN. Ay, but how chance this was not done before?

Y. MOR. Because, my Lords, it was not thought upon.

Nay, more, when he shall know it lies in us

To banish him, and then to call him home,

'T will make him vail [41] the top-flag of his pride,

And fear to offend the meanest nobleman.

E. MOR. But how if he do not, Nephew?

Y. MOR. Then may we with some color [42] rise in arms;

For howsoever we have borne it out,   280

'T is treason to be up against the King.

So we shall have the people of our side,

Which for his father's sake lean to the King,

But cannot brook a night-grown mushroom,

Such a one as my Lord of Cornwall is,

Should bear us down of the nobility.

And when the commons and the nobles join,

'T is not the King can buckler Gaveston;

We 'll pull him from the strongest hold he hath.

My Lords, if to perform this I be slack,   290

Think me as base a groom as Gaveston.

LAN. On that condition, Lancaster will grant.

WAR. And so will Pembroke and I.

---

[38] Electric ray.   [39] Consideration.
[40] Where.   [41] Lower.
[42] Excuse, show of reason.

E. MOR.   And I.

Y. MOR. In this I count me highly gratified,
And Mortimer will rest at your command.

Q. ISAB. And when this favor Isabel for-
gets,
Then let her live abandon'd and forlorn. —
But see, in happy time, my Lord the King,
Having brought the Earl of Cornwall on his
way,
Is new return'd. This news will glad him much,
Yet not so much as me. I love him more [301
Than he can Gaveston; would he lov'd me
But half so much: then were I treble-blest.
                              [*They retire.*]

Re-enter KING EDWARD, *mourning,* [*with*
BEAUMONT *and other* Attendants].

K. EDW. He's gone, and for his absence
thus I mourn.
Did never sorrow go so near my heart
As doth the want of my sweet Gaveston;
And could my crown's revenue [43] bring him
back,
I would freely give it to his enemies,
And think I gain'd, having bought so dear a
friend.

Q. ISAB. [*aside to the* Nobles] Hark how he
harps upon his minion.   310

K. EDW. My heart is as an anvil unto sor-
row,
Which beats upon it like the Cyclops' ham-
mers,
And with the noise turns up my giddy brain,
And makes me frantic for my Gaveston.
Ah, had some bloodless Fury rose from hell,
And with my kingly sceptre struck me dead,
When I was forc'd to leave my Gaveston!

LAN. [*aside to the* Nobles] *Diablo!* What
passions call you these?

Q. ISAB. [*advancing*] My gracious Lord, I
come to bring you news.

K. EDW. That you have parle[y]'d with
your Mortimer!   320

Q. ISAB. That Gaveston, my Lord, shall be
repeal'd.

K. EDW. Repeal'd! The news is too sweet
to be true.

Q. ISAB. But will you love me, if you find it
so?

K. EDW. If it be so, what will not Edward
do?

Q. ISAB. For Gaveston, but not for Isabel.

K. EDW. For thee, fair Queen, if thou lovest
Gaveston.

[43] Accented on second syllable.

I'll hang a golden tongue about thy neck,
Seeing thou hast pleaded with so good success.

Q. ISAB. No other jewels hang about my
neck
Than these, my Lord; nor let me have more
wealth   330
Than I may fetch from this rich treasury.
O how a kiss revives poor Isabel.

K. EDW. Once more receive my hand; and
let this be
A second marriage 'twixt thyself and me.

Q. ISAB. And may it prove more happy
than the first.
My gentle Lord, bespeak these nobles fair,
That wait attendance for a gracious look,
And on their knees salute your Majesty.

K. EDW. Courageous Lancaster, embrace
thy King!
And, as gross vapors perish by the sun,   340
Even so let hatred with thy sovereign['s] [44]
smile.
Live thou with me as my companion.

LAN. This salutation overjoys my heart.

K. EDW. Warwick shall be my chiefest
counsellor;
These silver hairs will more adorn my court
Than gaudy silks, or rich embroidery.
Chide me, sweet Warwick, if I go astray.

WAR. Slay me, my Lord, when I offend
your Grace.

K. EDW. In solemn triumphs, and in public
shows,
Pembroke shall bear the sword before the
King.   350

PEM. And with this sword Pembroke will
fight for you.

K. EDW. But wherefore walks young Morti-
mer aside?
Be thou commander of our royal fleet;
Or, if that lofty office like thee not,
I make thee here Lord Marshal of the realm.

Y. MOR. My Lord, I'll marshal so your
enemies,
As England shall be quiet, and you safe.

K. EDW. And as for you, Lord Mortimer of
Chirke,
Whose great achievements in our foreign
war
Deserves no common place nor mean reward,
Be you the general of the levied troops,   361
That now are ready to assail the Scots.

E. MOR. In this your Grace hath highly
honored me,
For with my nature war doth best agree.

[44] Add. Q 1612; om. earlier eds.

Q. Isab. Now is the King of England rich
and strong,
Having the love of his renowned peers.
K. Edw. Ay, Isabel, ne'er was my heart so
light.
Clerk of the crown, direct our warrant forth
For Gaveston to Ireland. Bea[u]mont, fly
As fast as Iris or Jove's Mercury.   370
Beau. It shall be done, my gracious Lord.
                                      [*Exit.*]
K. Edw. Lord Mortimer, we leave you to
your charge. —
Now let us in, and feast it royally.
Against our friend the Earl of Cornwall comes,
We'll have a general tilt and tournament;
And then his marriage shall be solemnized.
For wot you not that I have made him sure [45]
Unto our cousin,[46] the Earl of Gloucester's
heir?
Lan. Such news we hear, my Lord.
K. Edw. That day, if not for him, yet for
my sake,   380
Who in the triumph will be challenger,
Spare for no cost; we will requite your love.
War. In this, or aught, your Highness shall
command us.
K. Edw. Thanks, gentle Warwick; come,
let's in and revel.
        Exeunt [all except the] Mortimers.
E. Mor. Nephew, I must to Scotland; thou
stayest here.
Leave now to oppose thyself against the King.
Thou seest by nature he is mild and calm,
And, seeing his mind so dotes on Gaveston,
Let him without controlment have his will.
The mightiest kings have had their minions:
Great Alexander loved Hephaestion;   391
The conquering [Hercules] [47] for Hylas wept;
And for Patroclus stern Achilles droop'd;
And not kings only, but the wisest men:
The Roman Tully [48] lov'd Octavi[u]s;
Grave Socrates, wild Alcibiades.
Then let his Grace, whose youth is flexible,
And promiseth as much as we can wish,
Freely enjoy that vain, light-headed earl;
For riper years will wean him from such toys.
Y. Mor. Uncle, his wanton humor grieves
not me;   401
But this I scorn, that one so basely born
Should by his sovereign's favor grow so pert,
And riot it with the treasure of the realm.
While soldiers mutiny for want of pay,

He wears a lord's revenue on his back;
And Midas-like, he jets [49] it in the court,
With base outlandish cullions [50] at his heels,
Whose proud fantastic liveries make such show
As if that Proteus, god of shapes, appear'd.
I have not seen a dapper Jack so brisk;   411
He wears a short Italian hooded cloak,
Larded with pearl, and, in his Tuscan cap,
A jewel of more value than the crown.
Whiles other walk below, the King and he
From out a window laugh at such as we,
And flout our train, and jest at our attire.
Uncle, 't is this that makes me impatient.
E. Mor. But, Nephew, now you see the
King is chang'd.
Y. Mor. Then so am I, and live to do him
service;   420
But whiles I have a sword, a hand, a heart,
I will not yield to any such upstart.
You know my mind; come, Uncle, let's away.
                                    Exeunt.

[ACT II — Scene I] [1]

Enter [Young] Spencer *and* Baldock.

Bald. Spencer, seeing that our lord th'
Earl of Gloucester's dead,
Which of the nobles dost thou mean to serve?
Y. Spen. Not Mortimer, nor any of his side,
Because the king and he are enemies.
Baldock, learn this of me: a factious lord
Shall hardly do himself good, much less us;
But he that hath the favor of a king,
May with one word advance us while we live.
The liberal Earl of Cornwall is the man
On whose good fortune Spencer's hope de-
pends.   10
Bald. What, mean you then to be his fol-
lower?
Y. Spen. No, his companion; for he loves
me well,
And would have once preferr'd me to the
King.
Bald. But he is banish'd; there's small
hope of him.
Y. Spen. Ay, for a while; but, Baldock,
mark the end.
A friend of mine told me in secrecy
That he's repeal'd, and sent for back again;

[45] Betrothed him.   [46] *I.e.*, niece.
[47] Old eds. *Hector*. But note metre.
[48] Cicero; this allegation is pure invention.

[49] Struts.   [50] Low fellows.
[1] A room in the late Earl's residence at Gloucester.
The historical Lady of Gloucester's brother, the Earl,
was killed at Bannockburn.

And even now a post came from the court
With letters to our lady from the King ;
And as she read she smil'd, which makes me
    think   20
It is about her lover Gaveston.
    BALD. 'T is like enough ; for since he was
        exil'd
She neither walks abroad, nor comes in sight.
But I had thought the match had been broke
    off,
And that his banishment had chang'd her
    mind.
    Y. SPEN. Our lady's first love is not waver-
        ing ;
My life for thine, she will have Gaveston.
    BALD. Then hope I by her means to be pre-
        ferr'd,
Having read unto her since she was a child.
    Y. SPEN. Then, Baldock, you must cast the
        scholar off,   30
And learn to court it like a gentleman.
'T is not a black coat and a little band,
A velvet-cap'd cloak, fac'd before with serge,
And smelling to a nosegay all the day,
Or holding of a napkin in your hand,
Or saying a long grace at a table's end,
Or making low legs [2] to a nobleman,
Or looking downward with your eyelids close,
And saying, " Truly, an't may please your
    Honor,"
Can get you any favor with great men.   40
You must be proud, bold, pleasant, resolute,
And now and then stab, as occasion serves.
    BALD. Spencer, thou knowest I hate such
        formal toys,
And use them but of mere hypocrisy.
Mine old lord whiles he liv'd was so precise,[3]
That he would take exceptions at my buttons,
And being like pin's heads, blame me for the
    bigness ;
Which made me curate-like in mine attire,
Though inwardly licentious enough
And apt for any kind of villainy.   50
I am none of these common [pedants] [4] I,
That cannot speak without *propterea quod*.[5]
    Y. SPEN. But one of those that saith *quan-
        doquidem*,[6]
And hath a special gift to form a verb.
    BALD. Leave off this jesting ; here my
        Lady comes.   [*They retire.*]

Enter the Lady [*of Gloucester, King Edward's*
    Niece.]

    [NIECE.] [7] The grief for his exile was not so
        much
As is the joy of his returning home.
This letter came from my sweet Gaveston.
What need'st thou, love, thus to excuse thyself ?
I know thou couldst not come and visit me. 60
" I will not long be from thee, though I die."
This argues the entire love of my lord.
" When I forsake thee, death seize on my
    heart." —
But rest thee here where Gaveston shall sleep.
        [*Puts the letter into her bosom.*]
Now to the letter of my Lord the King. —
He wills me to repair unto the court
And meet my Gaveston. Why do I stay,
Seeing that he talks thus of my marriage
    day ? —
Who 's there ? Baldock !
See that my coach be ready ; I must hence. 70
    BALD. It shall be done, madam.   *Exit.*
    NIECE. And meet me at the park pale
        presently. —
Spencer, stay you and bear me company,
For I have joyful news to tell thee of.
My Lord of Cornwall is a-coming over,
And will be at the court as soon as we.
    Y. SPEN. I knew the King would have him
        home again.
    NIECE. If all things sort out [8] as I hope
        they will,
Thy service, Spencer, shall be thought upon.
    Y. SPEN. I humbly thank your Ladyship.[80
    NIECE. Come, lead the way ; I long till I
        am there.   [*Exeunt.*]

            [SCENE II] [9]

Enter [KING] EDWARD, *the* QUEEN [ISABELLA],
    LANCASTER, [Young] MORTIMER, WARWICK,
    PEMBROKE, KENT, [*and*] Attendants.

    K. EDW. The wind is good ; I wonder why
        he stays.
I fear me he is wrack'd upon the sea.
    Q. ISAB. [*aside*] Look, Lancaster, how pas-
        sionate [10] he is,
And still his mind runs on his minion.
    LAN. My Lord.
    K. EDW. How now ! what news ? Is Gaves-
        ton arriv'd ?

---

[2] Bows.
[3] Puritanical.
[4] Cor. Q 1598 ; O[1] *pendants.*
[5] Because.
[6] Since. "In spite of his disclaimer, he *is* apt
(Spencer hints) to give his reasons." (Verity.)

[7] Speech-tags in old eds. *Lady,* or *Lad.,* throughout.
[8] Happen, befall.
[9] Tynemouth ; presumably a hall in the castle.
[10] Sorrowful.

Y. Mor. Nothing but Gaveston! What means your Grace?
You have matters of more weight to think upon.
The King of France sets foot in Normandy.
K. Edw. A trifle! we 'll expel him when we please!   10
But tell me, Mortimer, what 's thy device [11]
Against the stately triumph we decreed?
Y. Mor. A homely one, my Lord, not worth the telling.
K. Edw. Prithee let me know it.
Y. Mor. But, seeing you are so desirous, thus it is :
A lofty cedar tree, fair flourishing,
On whose top branches kingly eagles perch ;
And by the bark a canker [12] creeps me up,
And gets unto the highest bough of all ;
The motto, *Aeque tandem*.[13]   20
K. Edw. And what is yours, my Lord of Lancaster?
Lan. My Lord, mine 's more obscure than Mortimer's.
Pliny reports there is a flying fish
Which all the other fishes deadly hate ;
And therefore, being pursued, it takes the air.
No sooner is it up, but there 's a fowl
That seizeth it. This fish, my Lord, I bear ;
The motto this, *Undique mors est*.[14]
K. Edw. Proud Mortimer, ungentle Lancaster,
Is this the love you bear your sovereign?   30
Is this the fruit your reconcilement bears?
Can you in words make show of amity,
And in your shields display your rancorous minds?
What call you this but private libelling
Against the Earl of Cornwall and my brother?
Q. Isab. Sweet Husband, be content ; they all love you.
K. Edw. They love me not that hate my Gaveston.
I am that cedar — shake me not too much ;
And you the eagles — soar ye ne'er so high,
I have the [jesses] [15] that will pull you down; [40
And *Aeque tandem* shall that canker cry
Unto the proudest peer of Britainy.
Though thou compar'st him to a flying fish,
And threatenest death whether he rise or fall,
'T is not the hugest monster of the sea,
Nor foulest harpy, that shall swallow him.

Y. Mor. [*aside to the* Nobles] If in his absence thus he favors him,
What will he do whenas he shall be present?
Lan. [*aside*] That shall we see ; look where his Lordship comes.

Enter GAVESTON.

K. Edw. My Gaveston!   50
Welcome to Tynemouth! Welcome to thy friend!
Thy absence made me droop and pine away ;
For, as the lovers of fair Danaë,
When she was lock'd up in a brazen tower,
Desir'd her more and wax'd outrageous,
So did it, sure,[16] with me ; and now thy sight
Is sweeter far than was thy parting hence
Bitter and irksome to my sobbing heart.
Gav. Sweet Lord and King, your speech preventeth [17] mine ;
Yet have I words left to express my joy.   60
The shepherd nipp'd with biting winter's rage
Frolics not more to see the painted spring
Than I do to behold your Majesty.
K. Edw. Will none of you salute my Gaveston?
Lan. Salute him? yes. Welcome, Lord Chamberlain!
Y. Mor. Welcome is the good Earl of Cornwall!
War. Welcome, Lord Governor of the Isle of Man!
Pem. Welcome, Master Secretary!
Kent.   Brother, do you hear them?
K. Edw. Still will these earls and barons use me thus?
Gav. My Lord, I cannot brook these injuries.   70
Q. Isab. [*aside*] Aye me, poor soul, when these begin to jar.
K. Edw. Return it to their throats ; I 'll be thy warrant.
Gav. Base, leaden earls, that glory in your birth,
Go sit at home and eat your tenants' beef ;
And come not here to scoff at Gaveston,
Whose mounting thoughts did never creep so low
As to bestow a look on such as you.
Lan. Yet I disdain not to do this for you.
[*Draws his sword and offers to stab* GAVESTON.]

---

[11] Painting on shield.   [12] Cankerworm.
[13] Justly at length.   [14] On all sides is death.
[15] The straps on a hawk's legs, to which the leash was attached. Old eds. *gresses*.

[16] Q 1622 and most mod. eds. *fare*.
[17] Anticipateth.

K. Edw. Treason! treason; where's the traitor?

Pem.   Here! here!

K. Edw. Convey hence Gaveston; they'll murder him.   80

Gav. The life of thee shall salve this foul disgrace.

Y. Mor. Villain, thy life, unless I miss mine aim.   [*Wounds* Gaveston.]

Q. Isab. Ah, furious Mortimer, what hast thou done?

Y. Mor. No more than I would answer, were he slain.

    [*Exit* Gaveston *with* Attendants.]

K. Edw. Yes, more than thou canst answer, though he live.

Dear shall you both abye[18] this riotous deed.

Out of my presence! Come not near the court.

Y. Mor. I'll not be barr'd the court for Gaveston.

Lan. We'll hale him by the ears unto the block.

K. Edw. Look to your own heads; his is sure enough.   90

War. Look to your own crown, if you back him thus.

Kent. Warwick, these words do ill beseem thy years.

K. Edw. Nay, all of them conspire to cross me thus;

But if I live, I'll tread upon their heads

That think with high looks thus to tread me down.

Come, Edmund, let's away and levy men;

'T is war that must abate these barons' pride.

   Exit the King [*with* Queen Isabella *and* Kent].

War. Let's to our castles, for the King is mov'd.

Y. Mor. Mov'd may he be, and perish in his wrath!   99

Lan. Cousin, it is no dealing with him now;

He means to make us stoop by force of arms.

And therefore let us jointly here protest,

To prosecute that Gaveston to the death.

Y. Mor. By Heaven, the abject villain shall not live!

War. I'll have his blood, or die in seeking it.

Pem. The like oath Pembroke takes.

Lan.   And so doth Lancaster.

Now send our heralds to defy the King;

And make the people swear to put him down.

Enter a Post.

Y. Mor. Letters, from whence?

Mess.   From Scotland, my Lord.

    [*Gives letters to* Mortimer.]

Lan. Why, how now, cousin, how fares all our friends?   110

Y. Mor. My uncle's taken prisoner by the Scots.

Lan. We'll have him ransom'd, man; be of good cheer.

Y. Mor. They rate his ransom at five thousand pound.

Who should defray the money but the King,

Seeing he is taken prisoner in his wars?

I'll to the King.

Lan. Do, cousin, and I'll bear thee company.

War. Meantime, my Lord of Pembroke and myself

Will to Newcastle here, and gather head.[19]

Y. Mor. About it, then, and we will follow you.   120

Lan. Be resolute and full of secrecy.

War. I warrant you. [*Exit with* Pembroke.]

Y. Mor. Cousin, an if he will not ransom him,

I'll thunder such a peal into his ears,

As never subject did unto his king.

Lan. Content; I'll beár my part — Holla! who's there?

    [*Enter* Guard.]

Y. Mor. Ay, marry, such a guard as this doth well.

Lan. Lead on the way.

Guard. Whither will your Lordships?

Y. Mor. Whither else but to the King? [130

Guard. His Highness is dispos'd to be alone.

Lan. Why, so he may, but we will speak to him.

Guard. You may not in, my Lord.

Y. Mor. May we not?

    [*Enter* King Edward *and* Kent.]

K. Edw. How now!

What noise is this? Who have we there?

  Is 't you?   [*He starts to leave.*]

Y. Mor. Nay, stay, my Lord; I come to bring you news;

Mine uncle's taken prisoner by the Scots.

K. Edw. Then ransom him.

Lan. 'T was in your wars; you should ransom him.   140

[18] Pay for. O₁ *abie;* other old eds. *abide.*

[19] Raise troops.

Y. Mor. And you shall ransom him, or
    else ——

Kent. What, Mortimer, you will not
    threaten him?

K. Edw. Quiet yourself; you shall have the
    broad seal

To gather [20] for him thoroughout the realm.

Lan. Your minion Gaveston hath taught
    you this.

Y. Mor. My Lord, the family of the Mor-
    timers

Are not so poor but, would they sell their land,

Would [21] levy men enough to anger you.

We never beg, but use such prayers as these.

K. Edw. Shall I still be haunted thus? 150

Y. Mor. Nay, now you are here alone, I 'll
    speak my mind.

Lan. And so will I, and then, my Lord,
    farewell.

Y. Mor. The idle triumphs, masques, las-
    civious shows,

And prodigal gifts bestowed on Gaveston,

Have drawn thy treasure dry and made thee
    weak,

The murmuring commons overstretched
    hath.[22]

Lan. Look for rebellion; look to be depos'd.

Thy garrisons are beaten out of France,

And, lame and poor, lie groaning at the gates.

The wild O'Neill, with swarms of Irish kerns,[23]

Lives uncontroll'd within the English pale.[161]

Unto the walls of York the Scots made road,

And unresisted drave away rich spoils.

Y. Mor. The haughty Dane commands the
    narrow seas,

While in the harbor ride thy ships unrigg'd.

Lan. What foreign prince sends thee am-
    bassadors?

Y. Mor. Who loves thee, but a sort [24] of
    flatterers?

Lan. Thy gentle Queen, sole sister to
    Valois,[25]

Complains that thou hast left her all forlorn.

Y. Mor. Thy court is naked, being bereft of
    those   170

That make a king seem glorious to the world;

I mean the peers, whom thou shouldst dearly
    love.

Libels are cast again [26] thee in the street;

Ballads and rhymes made of thy overthrow.

Lan. The   Northern   borderers,   seeing
    [their] [27] houses burnt,

Their wives and children slain, run up and
    down,

Cursing the name of thee and Gaveston.

Y. Mor. When wert thou in the field with
    banner spread?

But once! and then thy soldiers march'd like
    players,   179

With garish robes, not armor; and thyself,

Bedaub'd with gold, rode laughing at the rest,

Nodding and shaking of thy spangled crest,

Where women's favors hung like labels [28] down.

Lan. And thereof came it, that the fleer-
    ing Scots,

To England's high disgrace, have made this
    jig:

Maids of England, sore may you mourn,
For your lemans [29] you have lost at Bannocks-
    bourn; [30]
    With a heave and a ho!
What weeneth the King of England,
So soon to have won Scotland?   190
    With a rombelow!

Y. Mor. Wigmore shall fly,[31] to set my
    uncle free.

Lan. And when 't is gone, our swords shall
    purchase more.

If ye be mov'd, revenge it as you can;

Look next to see us with our ensigns spread.

                              Exeunt Nobles.

K. Edw. My swelling heart for very anger
    breaks.

How oft have I been baited by these peers,

And dare not be reveng'd, for their power is
    great!

Yet, shall the crowing of these cockerels

Affright   a   lion?   Edward,   unfold   thy
    paws,   200

And let their lives' blood slake thy fury's hun-
    ger.

If I be cruel and grow tyrannous,

Now let them thank themselves, and rue too
    late.

Kent. My Lord, I see your love to Gaves-
    ton

Will be the ruin of the realm and you;

---

[20] *I.e.*, a patent to collect money.
[21] Qq 1612, 1622, *twoul'd*.
[22] Emend. Dodsley *break*.
[23] Foot soldiers.
[24] Set.
[25] Isabella was sister to the last of the Capet kings, Charles IV, and his two predecessors. Philip VI, first king of the house of Valois, did not ascend the throne till after the death of Edward II.

[26] Against.   [27] Cor. Q 1598; O₁ *the*.
[28] Narrow strips dangling from legal documents; they carried the seals. — "Fleering" (l. 184) = jeering.
[29] Lovers.
[30] This battle, and the raid of l. 162, came two years after Gaveston's death. The jig is from Fabyan.
[31] *I.e.*, I 'll sell my estate.

For now the wrathful nobles threaten wars,
And therefore, Brother, banish him for ever.
  K. Edw. Art thou an enemy to my Gaveston?
  Kent. Ay, and it grieves me that I favored
    him.
  K. Edw. Traitor, begone! whine thou with
    Mortimer.   210
  Kent. So will I, rather than with Gaveston.
  K. Edw. Out of my sight, and trouble me
    no more!
  Kent. No marvel though thou scorn thy
    noble peers,
When I, thy brother, am rejected thus.
  K. Edw. Away!   *Exit* [Kent].
Poor Gaveston, that has no friend but me!
Do what they can, we'll live in Tynemouth
  here;
And, so I walk with him about the walls,
What care I though the earls begirt us round?—
Here comes she that's cause of all these jars.

Enter the Queen [Isabella] *with* [*King
Edward's* Niece, *two*] Ladies, [Gaveston,]
Baldock, *and* [Young] Spencer.

  Q. Isab. My Lord, 't is thought the earls
    are up in arms.   221
  K. Edw. Ay, and 't is likewise thought you
    favor him.[32]
  Q. Isab. Thus do you still suspect me with-
    out cause.
  Niece. Sweet Uncle, speak more kindly to
    the Queen.
  Gav. [*aside to* King Edward] My Lord,
    dissemble with her; speak her fair.
  K. Edw. Pardon me, sweet; I forgot my-
    self.
  Q. Isab. Your pardon is quickly got of
    Isabel.
  K. Edw. The younger Mortimer is grown
    so brave
That to my face he threatens civil wars.
  Gav. Why do you not commit him to the
    Tower?   230
  K. Edw. I dare not, for the people love him
    well.
  Gav. Why, then, we'll have him privily
    made away.
  K. Edw. Would Lancaster and he had both
    carous'd
A bowl of poison to each other's health!
But let them go,[33] and tell me what are these.

  Niece. Two of my father's servants whilst
    he liv'd;
May 't please your Grace to entertain them
    now.
  K. Edw. Tell me, where wast thou born?
    What is thine arms?
  Bald. My name is Baldock, and my gentry
I fetch'd from Oxford, not from heraldry. [240
  K. Edw. The fitter art thou, Baldock, for
    my turn.
Wait on me, and I'll see thou shalt not
    want.
  Bald. I humbly thank your Majesty.
  K. Edw. Knowest thou him, Gaveston?
  Gav.   Ay, my Lord.
His name is Spencer; he is well allied.[34]
For my sake, let him wait upon your Grace;
Scarce shall you find a man of more desert.
  K. Edw. Then, Spencer, wait upon me; for
    his sake
I'll grace thee with a higher style [35] ere long.
  Y. Spen. No greater titles happen unto
    me   250
Than to be favored of your Majesty.
  K. Edw. Cousin, this day shall be your
    marriage feast. —
And, Gaveston, think that I love thee well
To wed thee to our niece, the only heir
Unto the Earl of Gloucester late deceas'd.
  Gav. I know, my Lord, many will stomach [36]
    me;
But I respect [37] neither their love nor hate.
  K. Edw. The headstrong barons shall not
    limit me:
He that I list to favor shall be great.
Come, let's away; and, when the marriage
    ends,   260
Have at the rebels, and their 'complices!
                          Exeunt omnes.

                [Scene III] [38]

Enter Lancaster, [Young] Mortimer, Warwick, Pembroke, Kent, [*and others*].

  Kent. My Lords, of love to this our native
    land,
I come to join with you and leave the King;
And in your quarrel and the realm's behoof
Will be the first that shall adventure life.
  Lan. I fear me, you are sent of policy,
To undermine us with a show of love.

---

[32] Young Mortimer. Dyce emends *'em.*
[33] Never mind them.
[34] Of good family.   [35] Title.
[36] Feel resentment toward.   [37] Heed.
[38] Near Tynemouth Castle.

WAR. He is your brother, therefore have we
    cause
To cast [39] the worst, and doubt of your revolt.
    KENT. Mine honor shall be hostage of my
    truth ;   9
If that will not suffice, farewell, my Lords.
          [*Speaks aside with* LANCASTER.]
    Y. MOR. Stay, Edmund ; never was Plan-
    tagenet
False of his word, and therefore trust we thee.
    PEM. But what's the reason you should
    leave him now?
    KENT. I have inform'd the Earl of Lan-
    caster.
    LAN. And it sufficeth. Now, my Lords,
    know this,
That Gaveston is secretly arriv'd,
And here in Tynemouth frolics with the King.
Let us with these our followers scale the walls,
And suddenly surprise them unawares.
    Y. MOR. I'll give the onset.
    WAR.   And I'll follow thee. 20
    Y. MOR. This tottered [40] ensign of my
    ancestors,
Which swept the desert shore of that Dead Sea
Whereof we got the name of Mortimer, [41]
Will I advance upon this castle walls.
Drums, strike alarum, raise them from their
    sport,
And ring aloud the knell of Gaveston !
    LAN. None be so hardy as to touch the
    King ;
But neither spare you Gaveston nor his friends.
                    Exeunt.

            [SCENE IV] [42]

Enter the KING *and* [Young] SPENCER.

    K. EDW. O tell me, Spencer, where is Gaves-
    ton?
    SPEN. I fear he is slain, my gracious Lord.
    K. EDW. No, here he comes ; now let them
    spoil and kill !

To them [*enter*] GAVESTON, [QUEEN ISABELLA,
    King Edward's Niece,] *etc.*

Fly, fly, my Lords : the earls have got the
    hold ; [43]
Take shipping and away to Scarborough ;
Spencer and I will post away by land.
    GAV. O stay, my Lord ; they will not injure
    you.

    K. EDW. I will not trust them ; Gaveston,
    away !
    GAV. Farewell, my Lord.
    K. EDW. Lady, farewell.   10
    NIECE. Farewell, sweet Uncle, till we meet
    again.
    K. EDW. Farewell, sweet Gaveston ; and
    farewell, Niece.
    Q. ISAB. No farewell to poor Isabel, thy
    queen?
    K. EDW. Yes, yes, for Mortimer, your
    lover's sake.
        Exeunt omnes [*but* QUEEN] ISABELLA.
    Q. ISAB. Heavens can witness I love none
    but you ! —
From my embracements thus he breaks away.
O that mine arms could close this isle about,
That I might pull him to me where I would !
Or that these tears that drizzle from mine eyes
Had power to mollify his stony heart,   20
That when I had him we might never part.

Enter the Barons, [LANCASTER, WARWICK,
    Young MORTIMER, *and others*]. *Alarums.*

    LAN. I wonder how he scap'd.
    Y. MOR.   Who's this? The Queen?
    Q. ISAB. Ay, Mortimer, the miserable
    Queen,
Whose pining heart her inward sighs have
    blasted,
And body with continual mourning wasted.
These hands are tir'd with haling of my Lord
From Gaveston, from wicked Gaveston,
And all in vain ; for, when I speak him fair,
He turns away and smiles upon his minion.
    Y. MOR. Cease to lament, and tell us
    where's the King?   30
    Q. ISAB. What would you with the King?
    Is't him you seek?
    LAN. No, madam, but that cursed Gaves-
    ton.
Far be it from the thought of Lancaster
To offer violence to his sovereign.
We would but rid the realm of Gaveston.
Tell us where he remains, and he shall die.
    Q. ISAB. He's gone by water unto Scarbor-
    ough ;
Pursue him quickly, and he cannot scape ;
The King hath left him, and his train is small.
    WAR. Foreslow [44] no time, sweet Lancaster ;
    let's march.   40
    Y. MOR. How comes it that the King and
    he is parted?

[39] Surmise.
[40] Tattered.
[41] A fanciful derivation.
[42] The same.
[43] Fortress.
[44] Delay.

Q. Isab. That this [45] your army, going several ways,
Might be of lesser force ; and, with the power [46]
That he intendeth presently to raise,
Be easily suppress'd ; and therefore be gone.
　　Y. Mor. Here in the river rides a Flemish hoy ; [47]
Let's all aboard, and follow him amain.
　　Lan. The wind that bears him hence will fill our sails.
Come, come aboard ; 't is but an hour's [48] sailing.
　　Y. Mor. [drawing the Queen aside] Madam, stay you within this castle here. 　　50
　　Q. Isab. No, Mortimer, I 'll to my Lord the King.
　　Y. Mor. Nay, rather sail with us to Scarborough.
　　Q. Isab. You know the King is so suspicious [49]
As, if he hear I have but talk'd with you,
Mine honor will be call'd in question ;
And therefore, gentle Mortimer, begone.
　　Y. Mor. Madam, I cannot stay to answer you ;
But think of Mortimer as he deserves.
　　Q. Isab. So well hast thou deserv'd, sweet Mortimer,
As Isabel could live with thee for ever. — 　　60
In vain I look for love at Edward's hand,
Whose eyes are fix'd on none but Gaveston ;
Yet once more I 'll importune him with prayers ;
If he be strange [50] and not regard my words,
My son and I will over into France,
And to the King, my brother, there complain
How Gaveston hath robb'd me of his love :
But yet I hope my sorrows will have end,
And Gaveston this blessed day be slain.
　　　　　　　　　　　　　　　　　Exeunt.

[Scene V] [51]

Enter Gaveston, *pursued.*

　　Gav. Yet, lusty lords, I have escap'd your hands,
Your threats, your 'larums, and your hot pursuits ;
And though divorced from King Edward's eyes,

Yet liveth Pierce of Gaveston unsurpris'd, [52]
Breathing, in hope (*malgrado* [53] all your beards,
That muster rebels thus against your king),
To see his royal sovereign once again.

Enter the Nobles, [Warwick, Lancaster, Pembroke, Young Mortimer ; Soldiers, James, *and other* Attendants of Pembroke].

　　War. Upon him, soldiers ; take away his weapons.
　　Y. Mor. Thou proud disturber of thy country's peace,
Corrupter of thy king, cause of these broils, 　10
Base flatterer, yield ! and were it not for shame,
Shame and dishonor to a soldier's name,
Upon my weapon's point here shouldst thou fall,
And welter in thy gore.
　　Lan. 　　　　　　　Monster of men,
That, like the Greekish strumpet, [54] train'd [55] to arms
And bloody wars so many valiant knights,
Look for no other fortune, wretch, than death !
Kind Edward is not here to buckler thee.
　　War. Lancaster, why talk'st thou to the slave ?
Go, soldiers, take him hence ; for, by my sword, 　　20
His head shall off. Gaveston, short warning
Shall serve thy turn ; it is our country's cause
That here severely we will execute
Upon thy person. Hang him at a bough.
　　Gav. My Lord !
　　War. 　　　　　Soldiers, have him away ! —
But for thou wert the favorite of a king,
Thou shalt have so much honor [56] at our hands.
　　Gav. I thank you all, my Lords ; then I perceive
That heading is one, and hanging is the other,
And death is all.

Enter Earl of Arundel.

　　Lan. How now, my Lord of Arundel ? [30
　　Arun. My Lords, King Edward greets you all by me.
　　War. Arundel, say your message.
　　Arun. 　　　　　　　　　His Majesty,
Hearing that you had taken Gaveston,
Entreateth you by me, yet but he may
See him before he dies ; forwhy, [57] he says,

---

[45] Dodsley emends *thus*.　　[46] Army.
[47] Small coasting vessel.　　[48] Dissyllabic.
[49] Quadrisyllabic.　　[50] Unresponsive.
[51] Country near Scarborough.

[52] Uncaptured.　　[53] In spite of.
[54] Helen of Troy.　　[55] Enticed.
[56] Of being beheaded like a gentleman instead of hanged like a churl.
[57] Because.

And sends you word, he knows that die he
    shall ;
And if you gratify his Grace so far,
He will be mindful of the courtesy.
    WAR.   How now?
    GAV.   Renowmed Edward, how thy name
Revives poor Gaveston.
    WAR.   No, it needeth not ; [40
Arundel, we will gratify the King
In other matters ; he must pardon us in this. —
Soldiers, away with him !
    GAV.   Why, my Lord of Warwick,
Will not these delays beget my hopes?
I know it, Lords, it is this life you aim at ;
Yet grant King Edward this.
    Y. MOR.   Shalt thou appoint
What we shall grant? — Soldiers, away with
    him ! —
Thus we 'll gratify the King :
We 'll send his head by thee ; let him bestow
His tears on that, for that is all he gets   50
Of Gaveston, or else his senseless trunk.
    LAN.   Not so, my Lords, lest he bestow more
    cost
In burying him than he hath ever earn'd.
    ARUN.   My Lords, it is his Majesty's re-
    quest ;
And in the honor of a king he swears
He will but talk with him and send him back.
    WAR.   When, can you tell? — Arundel, no ;
We wot he that the care of realm remits,
And drives his nobles to these exigents,[58]
For Gaveston, will, if he seize [59] him once, 60
Violate any promises to possess him.
    ARUN.   Then if you will not trust his Grace
    in keep,
My Lords, I will be pledge for his return.
    Y. MOR.   It is honorable in thee to offer
    this ;
But, for we know thou art a noble gentleman,
We will not wrong thee so, to make away
A true man for a thief.
    GAV.   How mean'st thou, Mortimer? That
    is overbase.
    Y. MOR.   Away, base groom, robber of
    kings' renowm !   69
Question with thy companions and thy mates.
    PEM.   My Lord Mortimer, and you, my
    Lords, each one,
To gratify the King's request therein,
Touching the sending of this Gaveston,
Because his Majesty so earnestly

Desires to see the man before his death,
I will upon mine honor undertake
To carry him, and bring him back again ;
Provided this, that you, my Lord of Arundel,
Will join with me.
    WAR.   Pembroke, what wilt thou do? [79
Cause yet more bloodshed?   Is it not enough
That we have taken him, but must we now
Leave him on " had I wist ",[60] and let him go?
    PEM.   My Lords, I will not overwoo your
    Honors ;
But if you dare trust Pembroke with the pris-
    oner,
Upon mine oath, I will return him back.
    ARUN.   My Lord of Lancaster, what say
    you in this?
    LAN.   Why, I say, let him go on Pembroke's
    word.
    PEM.   And you, Lord Mortimer?
    Y. MOR.   How say you, my Lord
    of Warwick?
    WAR.   Nay, do your pleasures ; I know how
    't will prove.
    PEM.   Then give him me.
    GAV.   Sweet sovereign, yet I come [90
To see thee ere I die.
    WAR.   *[aside]*   Yet not, perhaps,
If Warwick's wit and policy prevail.
    Y. MOR.   My Lord of Pembroke, we deliver
    him you ;
Return him on your honor. — Sound ; away !
        Exeunt [all but] PEMBROKE, [ARUN-
        DEL] [61] GAVESTON, [JAMES, *and*]
        Pembroke's men, four Soldiers.
    PEM.   My Lord, you shall go with me.
My house is not far hence ; out of the way
A little, but our men shall go along.
We that have pretty wenches to our wives,
Sir, must not come so near and balk their lips.
    [ARUN.]   'T is very kindly spoke, my Lord of
    Pembroke.   100
Your Honor hath an adamant of power,[62]
To draw a prince.
    PEM.   So, my Lord. — Come hither, James.
I do commit this Gaveston to thee ;
Be thou this night his keeper ; in the morning
We will discharge thee of thy charge. Begone.
    GAV.   Unhappy Gaveston, whither goest
    thou now?
        Exit [with JAMES *and the rest of Pem-
        broke's* Men].

---

[58] Extreme measures.
[59] O₁ *zease ;* other old eds. *seaze ;* emend. Cunningham *sees.*

[60] " *I.e.*, had I known, — the exclamation of those
who repent of what they have rashly done." (Dyce.)
[61] Old eds. *Mat.[revis* for *Arundel* from this point
on ; doubtless because the same actor played both
parts.   [62] Powerful magnet.

HORSE-BOY. My Lord, we'll quickly be at Cobham.   *Exeunt.*[63]

[ACT III — SCENE I][1]

Enter GAVESTON *mourning and* [JAMES *and*] *the Earl of Pembroke's* Men.

GAV. O treacherous Warwick, thus to wrong thy friend!

JAMES. I see it is your life these arms pursue.

GAV. Weaponless must I fall, and die in bands?[2]

O! must this day be period of my life?
Centre[3] of all my bliss? An ye be men,
Speed to the King.

Enter WARWICK *and his* Company.

WAR.   My Lord of Pembroke's men,
Strive you no longer; I will have that Gaveston.

JAMES. Your Lordship does dishonor to yourself,
And wrong our lord, your honorable friend.

WAR. No, James; it is my country's cause
I follow. —   10
Go, take the villain; soldiers, come away.
We'll make quick work. — Commend me to your master,
My friend, and tell him that I watch'd it well. —
Come, let thy shadow[4] parley with King Edward.

GAV. Treacherous Earl, shall I not see the King?

WAR. The King of Heaven, perhaps; no other king. —
Away!   *Exeunt* WARWICK *and his men, with* GAVESTON.

JAMES. Come, fellows, it booted not for us to strive;
We will in haste go certify our lord.   *Exeunt.*

[SCENE II][5]

Enter KING EDWARD *and* [Young] SPENCER, [BALDOCK, *and* Nobles *of the King's side, and* Soldiers] *with drums and fifes.*

K. EDW. I long to hear an answer from the barons

Touching my friend, my dearest Gaveston.
Ah, Spencer, not the riches of my realm
Can ransom him! Ah, he is mark'd to die!
I know the malice of the younger Mortimer;
Warwick I know is rough, and Lancaster
Inexorable, and I shall never see
My lovely Pierce, my Gaveston again;
The barons overbear me with their pride.

Y. SPEN. Were I King Edward, England's sovereign,   10
Son to the lovely Eleanor of Spain,
Great Edward Longshanks' issue, would I bear
These braves, this rage, and suffer uncontroll'd
These barons thus to beard me in my land,
In mine own realm? My Lord, pardon my speech.
Did you retain your father's magnanimity,[6]
Did you regard the honor of your name,
You would not suffer thus your majesty
Be counterbuff'd of your nobility![7]
Strike off their heads, and let them preach on poles!   20
No doubt such lessons they will teach the rest
As by their preachments they will profit much
And learn obedience to their lawful king.

K. EDW. Yea, gentle Spencer, we have been too mild,
Too kind to them, but now have drawn our sword;
And if they send me not my Gaveston,
We'll steel it[8] on their crest and poll their tops.[9]

BALD. This haught resolve becomes your Majesty,
Not to be tied to their affection,[10]
As though your Highness were a schoolboy still,   30
And must be aw'd and govern'd like a child.

Enter HUGH SPENCER, *an old man, father to the* Young SPENCER, *with his truncheon and* Soldiers.

E. SPEN. Long live my sovereign, the noble Edward,
In peace triumphant, fortunate in wars!

K. EDW. Welcome, old man, com'st thou in Edward's aid?
Then tell thy prince of whence, and what thou art.

E. SPEN. Lo, with a band of bowmen and of pikes,

[63] Old eds. *Exeunt ambo.*   [1] The open country.
[2] Bonds.   [3] Lowest point.
[4] Ghost.
[5] Unlocated, but presumably near Boroughbridge in Yorkshire, since the barons were defeated there.

[6] Greatness of spirit.
[7] Rebuffed by your nobles.
[8] Lay on our steel.
[9] *I.e.*, shorten their stature by beheading, as a tree is "polled."   [10] Caprice.

Brown bills and targeteers,[11] four hundred
    strong,
Sworn to defend King Edward's royal right,
I come in person to your Majesty,
Spencer, the father of Hugh Spencer there,   40
Bound to your Highness everlastingly,
For favors done, in him, unto us all.
    K. EDW. Thy father, Spencer?
    Y. SPEN.   True, an it like your Grace,
That pours, in lieu of all your goodness shown,
His life, my Lord, before your princely feet.
    K. EDW. Welcome ten thousand times, old
        man, again. —
Spencer,[12] this love, this kindness to thy king,
Argues thy noble mind and disposition.
Spencer, I here create thee Earl of Wil[t]shire,
And daily will enrich thee with our favor,   50
That, as the sunshine, shall reflect o'er thee.
Beside, the more to manifest our love,
Because we hear Lord Bruce doth sell his land,
And that the Mortimers are in hand withal,[13]
Thou shalt have crowns of us t' outbid the
    barons ;
And, Spencer, spare them not, but lay it on. —
Soldiers, a largess, and thrice welcome all !
    Y. SPEN. My Lord, here comes the Queen.

Enter the QUEEN [ISABELLA,] *and her son*
[PRINCE EDWARD,] *and* LEVUNE,[14] *a Frenchman.*

    K. EDW.   Madam, what news?
    Q. ISAB. News of dishonor, Lord, and dis-
        content.   59
Our friend Levune, faithful and full of trust,
Informeth us, by letters and by words,
That Lord Valois our brother, King of France,
Because your Highness hath been slack in
    homage,
Hath seized Normandy [15] into his hands.
These be the letters, this the messenger.
    K. EDW. Welcome, Levune. — Tush, Sib,[16]
        if this be all,

---

[11] Men armed with bill (a kind of halberd) and
shield.
[12] Addressed to the younger. Although Holinshed
mentions the manor of Fasterne in Wiltshire as belonging to the elder Spencer, this nobleman was
Earl of Winchester. Briggs suggests that since the
earldom of Wiltshire provided a courtesy title for
the eldest son of the Marquess of Winchester,
Marlowe here confers it, though unhistorically, on
the younger Spencer. Holinshed refers to Edward's
bestowal on the *younger* Spencer of money for the
purchase mentioned in ll. 53-56.
[13] In negotiation for it.
[14] Cor. Dyce ; old eds. *Lewne,* throughout. He is
not mentioned by Holinshed.
[15] Actually Ponthieu and Guienne. (Briggs.)
[16] " Short " for *Isabel.* (Kittredge.)

Valois and I will soon be friends again. —
But to my Gaveston ; shall I never see,
Never behold thee now? — Madam, in this
    matter,
We will employ you and your little son ;   70
You shall go parley with the King of France. —
Boy, see you bear you bravely to the King,
And do your message with a majesty.
    P. EDW. Commit not to my youth things of
        more weight
Than fits a prince so young as I to bear ;
And fear not, Lord and Father : Heaven's
    great beams
On Atlas' shoulder shall not lie more safe,
Than shall your charge committed to my trust.
    Q. ISAB. Ah, boy, this towardness makes
        thy mother fear   79
Thou art not mark'd to many days on earth.
    K. EDW. Madam, we will that you with
        speed be shipp'd,
And this our son ; Levune shall follow you
With all the haste we can despatch him hence.
Choose of our lords to bear you company,
And go in peace ; leave us in wars at home
    Q. ISAB. Unnatural wars, where subjects
        brave their king ;
God end them once ! My Lord, I take my
    leave,
To make my preparation for France.
                   [*Exit with* PRINCE EDWARD.]

Enter LORD [ARUNDEL].

    K. EDW. What, Lord [Arundel,] dost thou
        come alone?
    [ARUN.] Yea, my good Lord, for Gaveston
        is dead.   90
    K. EDW. Ah, traitors ! have they put my
        friend to death?
Tell me, Arundel, died he ere thou cam'st,
Or didst thou see my friend to take his death?
    ARUN. Neither, my Lord ; for as he was
        surpris'd,[17]
Begirt with weapons and with enemies round,
I did your Highness' message to them all,
Demanding him of them, entreating rather,
And said, upon the honor of my name,
That I would undertake to carry him   99
Unto your Highness, and to bring him back.
    K. EDW. And tell me, would the rebels deny
        me that?
    [Y.] SPEN. Proud recreants !
    K. EDW.   Yea, Spencer, traitors all.
    ARUN. I found them at the first inexorable ;

---

[17] Captured.

The Earl of Warwick would not bide the hear-
   ing,
Mortimer hardly ; Pembroke and Lancaster
Spake least ; and when they flatly had denied,
Refusing to receive me pledge for him,
The Earl of Pembroke mildly thus bespake :
" My Lords, because our sovereign sends for
   him,
And promiseth he shall be safe return'd,   110
I will this undertake, to have him hence,
And see him redelivered to your hands."
   K. Edw. Well, and how fortunes that he
   came not?
   [Y.] Spen. Some treason, or some villainy,
   was cause.
   Arun. The Earl of Warwick seiz'd him on
   his way ;
For, being delivered unto Pembroke's men,
Their lord rode home thinking his prisoner
   safe ;
But ere he came, Warwick in ambush lay,
And bare him to his death ; and in a trench
Strake off his head, and march'd unto the
   camp.   120
   [Y.] Spen. A bloody part, flatly against law
   of arms !
   K. Edw. O shall I speak, or shall I sigh and
   die?
   [Y.] Spen. My Lord, refer your vengeance
   to the sword
Upon these barons ; hearten up your men ;
Let them not unreveng'd murder your friends !
Advance your standard, Edward, in the field,
And march to fire them from their starting
   holes.[18]
   K. Edw. (*kneels and saith.*) By earth, the
   common mother of us all,
By Heaven, and all the moving orbs thereof,
By this right hand, and by my father's sword,
And all the honors 'longing to my crown,   131
I will have heads and lives for him as many
As I have manors, castles, towns, and tow-
   ers ! —   [*Rises.*]
Treacherous Warwick ! traitorous Mortimer !
If I be England's king, in lakes of gore
Your headless trunks, your bodies, will I trail,
That you may drink your fill, and quaff in
   blood,
And stain my royal standard with the same,
That so my bloody colors may suggest
Remembrance of revenge immortally   140
On your accursed traitorous progeny,
You villains, that have slain my Gaveston !

And in this place of honor and of trust,
Spencer, sweet Spencer, I adopt thee here ;
And merely of our love we do create thee
Earl of Gloucester, and Lord Chamberlain,
Despite of times, despite of enemies.
   [Y.] Spen. My Lord, [here is][19] a messenger
   from the barons
Desires access unto your Majesty.
   K. Edw. Admit him near.   150

Enter the Herald *from the barons, with his coat
of arms.*

   Her. Long live King Edward, England's
   lawful lord !
   K. Edw. So wish not they, I wis,[20] that
   sent thee hither.
Thou com'st from Mortimer and his 'com-
   plices ;
A ranker rout of rebels never was.
Well, say thy message.
   Her. The barons up in arms by me salute
Your Highness with long life and happiness,
And bid me say, as plainer [21] to your Grace,
That if without effusion of blood
You will this grief have ease and remedy, 160
That from your princely person you remove
This Spencer, as a putrifying branch,
That deads the royal vine, whose golden leaves
Empale your princely head, your diadem,
Whose brightness such pernicious upstarts
   dim,
Say they, and lovingly advise your Grace
To cherish virtue and nobility,
And have old servitors in high esteem,
And shake off smooth dissembling flatterers.
This granted, they, their honors, and their
   lives,   170
Are to your Highness vow'd and consecrate.
   [Y.] Spen. Ah, traitors ! will they still
   display their pride?
   K. Edw. Away ! tarry no answer, but be-
   gone !
Rebels, will they appoint their sovereign
His sports, his pleasures, and his company?
Yet, ere thou go, see how I do divorce
                  Embrace Spencer.
Spencer from me. — Now get thee to thy
   lords,
And tell them I will come to chastise them
For murdering Gaveston ; hie thee ! get thee
   gone !

[18] As hunted animals are driven from their holes
by fire.

[19] Cor. Dodsley ; O₁, according to Greg, *heres is;*
according to Brooke, *heres in.*
[20] I know ; a popular misunderstanding of M. E.
ywis = certainly.
[21] Complainer, plaintiff.

Edward with fire and sword follows at thy
    heels. —   [*Exit* Herald.] 180
My Lord, perceive you how these rebels
    swell? —
Soldiers, good hearts, defend your sovereign's
    right ;
For now, even now, we march to make them
    stoop.
Away !   *Exeunt.*

[SCENE III] [22]

*Alarums, excursions, a great fight, and a retreat
[sounded, within].   Enter the* KING, SPENCER
the father, SPENCER *the son, and the* Noblemen *of the King's side.*

K. EDW. Why do we sound retreat? Upon
    them, Lords !
This day I shall pour vengeance with my sword
On those proud rebels that are up in arms
And do confront and countermand their king.
    Y. SPEN. I doubt it not, my Lord, right will
        prevail.
    E. SPEN. 'T is not amiss, my Liege, for
        either part
To breathe awhile ; our men, with sweat and
    dust
All chok'd well near, begin to faint for heat ;
And this retire refresheth horse and man.
    Y. SPEN. Here come the rebels.

Enter the Barons, [Young] MORTIMER, LANCAS-
TER, WARWICK, [*and*] PEMBROKE, *cum cæteris.*

Y. MOR.   Look, Lancaster ;
    yonder is Edward   10
Among his flatterers.
    LAN.   And there let him be
Till he pay dearly for their company.
    WAR. And shall, or Warwick's sword shall
        smite in vain.
    K. EDW. What, rebels, do you shrink and
        sound retreat?
    Y. MOR. No, Edward, no ; thy flatterers
        faint and fly.
    LAN. Th 'ad best betimes forsake [them] [23]
        and their trains,[24]
For they 'll betray thee, traitors as they are.
    Y. SPEN. Traitor on thy face, rebellious
        Lancaster !
    PEM. Away, base upstart ; brav'st thou
        nobles thus?

[22] Unlocated ; doubtless the battlefield at Boroughbridge.
[23] Emend. Brooke ; old eds. *thee.*
[24] Enticements, plots.

    E. SPEN. A noble attempt and honorable
        deed,   20
Is it not, trow ye, to assemble aid
And levy arms against your lawful king?
    K. EDW. For which ere long their heads
        shall satisfy,
T' appease the wrath of their offended king.
    Y. MOR. Then, Edward, thou wilt fight it
        to the last,
And rather bathe thy sword in subjects' blood,
Than banish that pernicious company?
    K. EDW. Ay, traitors all, rather than thus
        be brav'd,
Make England's civil towns huge heaps of
    stones,
And ploughs to go about our palace gates. 30
    WAR. A desperate and unnatural resolu-
        tion !
Alarum to the fight ! [25]
St. George for England and the barons' right !
    K. EDW. Saint George for England, and
        King Edward's right !
             [*Exeunt the two parties severally.*]

[SCENE IV] [26]

[*Alarums.*]   *Enter* [KING] EDWARD [*and his followers,*] *with the* Barons [*and* KENT], *captives.*

    K. EDW. Now, lusty lords, now, not by
        chance of war,
But justice of the quarrel and the cause,
Vail'd is your pride ; methinks you hang the
    heads ;
But we 'll advance [27] them, traitors. Now 't is
    time
To be aveng'd on you for all your braves,
And for the murder of my dearest friend,
To whom right well you knew our soul was
    knit,
Good Pierce of Gaveston, my sweet favorite.
Ah, rebels, recreants, you made him away.
    KENT. Brother, in regard of thee and of thy
        land,   10
Did they remove that flatterer from thy
    throne.
    K. EDW. So, sir, you have spoke ; away,
        avoid our presence !   [*Exit* KENT.]
Accursed wretches, was 't in regard of us,
When we had sent our messenger to request
He might be spar'd to come to speak with us,
And Pembroke undertook for his return,
That thou, proud Warwick, watch'd the pris-
    oner,

[25] Possibly a stage direction ; but note the **rhyme.**
[26] The same.   [27] Raise.

Poor Pierce, and headed him against law of
    arms?
For which thy head shall overlook the rest,
As much as thou in rage outwent'st the rest!
    WAR. Tyrant, I scorn thy threats and men-
    aces;   21
It is but temporal that thou canst inflict.
    LAN. The worst is death, and better die to
    live
Than live in infamy under such a king.
    K. EDW. Away with them, my Lord of
    Winchester![28]
These lusty leaders, Warwick and Lancaster,
I charge you roundly off with both their heads!
Away!
    WAR. Farewell, vain world!
    LAN.   Sweet Mortimer, farewell.
    Y. MOR. England, unkind to thy nobility, [30
Groan for this grief; behold how thou art
    maimed.
    K. EDW. Go take that haughty Mortimer
to the Tower;
There see him safe bestowed; and, for the rest,
Do speedy execution on them all.
Begone!
    Y. MOR. What, Mortimer, can ragged stony
    walls
Immure thy virtue, that aspires to Heaven?
No, Edward, England's scourge, it may not be;
Mortimer's hope surmounts his fortune far.
                  [The captive Barons are led off.]
    K. EDW. Sound drums and trumpets!
    March with me, my friends;   40
Edward this day hath crown'd him king anew.
        [Exeunt all but] SPENCER *filius*, LE-
        VUNE, *and* BALDOCK.
    Y. SPEN. Levune, the trust that we repose
    in thee
Begets the quiet of King Edward's land.
Therefore begone in haste, and with advice
Bestow that treasure on the lords of France,
That, therewith all[29] enchanted, like the guard
That suffered Jove to pass in showers of gold
To Danaë, all aid may be denied
To Isabel, the Queen, that now in France
Makes friends, to cross the seas with her young
    son,   50
And step into his father's regiment.
    LEVUNE. That's it these barons and the
    subtle Queen
Long [levell'd][30] at.

BAL.   Yea; but, Levune, thou seest
These barons lay their heads on blocks to-
    gether;
What they intend the hangman frustrates clean.
    LEVUNE. Have you no doubts, my Lords,
I 'll clap s[o][31] close
Among the lords of France with England's gold
That Isabel shall make her plaints in vain,
And France shall be obdurate with her tears.
    Y. SPEN. Then make for France amain;
    Levune, away!   60
Proclaim King Edward's wars and victories.
                            Exeunt omnes.

[ACT IV — SCENE I][1]

Enter EDMUND, [EARL OF KENT].

    KENT. Fair blows the wind for France;
    blow, gentle gale,
Till Edmund be arriv'd for England's good!
Nature, yield to my country's cause in this.
A brother? No, a butcher of thy friends!
Proud Edward, dost thou banish me thy pres-
    ence?
But I 'll to France, and cheer the wronged
    Queen,
And certify what Edward's looseness is.
Unnatural king! to slaughter noblemen
And cherish flatterers! Mortimer, I stay
Thy sweet escape; stand gracious, gloomy
    night,   10
To his device.

Enter [Young] MORTIMER, *disguised.*

    Y. MOR.   Holla! who walketh there?
Is 't you, my Lord?
    KENT.   Mortimer, 't is I;
But hath thy potion wrought so happily?
    Y. MOR. It hath, my Lord; the warders,
    all asleep,
I thank them, gave me leave to pass in peace.
But hath your Grace got shipping unto France?
    KENT. Fear it not.   *Exeunt.*

[SCENE II][2]

Enter the QUEEN [ISABELLA] *and her son*
[PRINCE EDWARD].

    Q. ISAB. Ah, boy, our friends do fail us all
    in France.

---

[28] Spencer Senior. Not, as has been asserted, a
slip; Holinshed mentions the elder Spencer's promotion to this earldom. See on III, ii, 47.
[29] Very likely for *therewithal.*
[30] Aimed. Conj. Dodsley; old eds. *leuied.*

[31] Emend. Dodsley; old eds. *claps.*
[1] Unlocated; presumably London, near the
Thames and not far from the Tower.
[2] Paris; presumably a room in Queen Isabella's
lodging.

The lords are cruel, and the King unkind ;
What shall we do?
    P. Edw.   Madam, return to England,
And please my father well ; and then a fig
For all my uncle's friendship here in France.
I warrant you, I 'll win his Highness quickly ;
'A loves me better than a thousand Spencers.
    Q. Isab. Ah, boy, thou art deceiv'd, at
    least in this,
To think that we can yet be tun'd together ;
No, no, we jar too far. Unkind Valois !   10
Unhappy Isabel ! when France rejects,
Whither, oh, whither dost thou bend thy
    steps?

    Enter Sir John of Hainault.

Sir J. Madam, what cheer?
    Q. Isab.   Ah ! good Sir John of Hainault,
Never so cheerless, nor so far distress'd.
    Sir J. I hear, sweet lady, of the King's un-
    kindness ;
But droop not, madam ; noble minds contemn
Despair. Will your Grace with me to Hain-
    ault,
And there stay time's advantage with your
    son?
How say you, my Lord, will you go with your
    friends,
And [share of] [3] all our fortunes equally?   20
    P. Edw. So pleaseth the Queen, my mother,
    me it likes.
The King of England, nor the court of France,
Shall have me from my gracious mother's side,
Till I be strong enough to break a staff [4] ;
And then have at the proudest Spencer's head.
    Sir J. Well said, my Lord.
    Q. Isab. O, my sweetheart, how do I moan
    thy wrongs,
Yet triumph in the hope of thee, my joy !
Ah, sweet Sir John, even to the utmost verge
Of Europe, or the shore of Tanais,[5]   30
Will we with thee to Hainault, so we will ;
The Marquis is a noble gentleman ;
His Grace, I dare presume, will welcome me.
But who are these?

    Enter Edmund [Earl of Kent] *and* [Young]
        Mortimer.

    Kent.   Madam, long may you live,
Much happier than your friends in England
    do !
    Q. Isab. Lord Edmund and Lord Morti-
    mer alive !

Welcome to France ! The news was here, my
    Lord,
That you were dead, or very near your death.
    Y. Mor. Lady, the last was truest of the
    twain ;
But Mortimer, reserv'd for better hap,   40
Hath shaken off the thraldom of the Tower,
And lives t' advance your standard, good my
    Lord.
    P. Edw. How mean you, an the King,
    my father, lives?
No, my Lord Mortimer, not I, I trow.
    Q. Isab. Not, son ! why not? I would it
    were no worse.
But, gentle lords, friendless we are in France.
    Y. Mor. Monsieur le Grand, a noble friend
    of yours,
Told us, at our arrival, all the news :
How hard the nobles, how unkind the King
Hath show'd himself ; but, madam, right
    makes room   50
Where weapons want ; and, though a many
    friends
Are made away, as Warwick, Lancaster,
And others of our party and faction,
Yet have we friends, assure your Grace, in
    England
Would cast up caps, and clap their hands for
    joy,
To see us there, appointed [6] for our foes.
    Kent. Would all were well, and Edward
    well reclaim'd,
For England's honor, peace, and quietness.
    Y. Mor. But by the sword, my Lord, it
    must be deserv'd ;
The King will ne'er forsake his flatterers.   60
    Sir J. My Lords of England, sith [7] the un-
    gentle King
Of France refuseth to give aid of arms
To this distressed queen, his sister, here,
Go you with her to Hainault. Doubt ye
    not,
We will find comfort, money, men, and friends
Ere long, to bid the English king a base.[8]
How say, young Prince? What think you of
    the match?
    P. Edw. I think King Edward will outrun
    us all.
    Q. Isab. Nay, son, not so ; and you must
    not discourage   69
Your friends, that are so forward in your aid.
    Kent. Sir John of Hainault, pardon us, I
    pray ;

---

[3] Emend. Brooke ; old eds. *shake off*.
[4] *I.e.*, lance.   [5] The Don.
[6] Equipped.   [7] Since.
[8] Challenge (from the game of prisoner's base).

These comforts that you give our woful queen
Bind us in kindness all at your command.
    Q. Isab. Yea, gentle Brother; and the God of Heaven
Prosper your happy motion,[9] good Sir John.
    Y. Mor. This noble gentleman, forward in arms,
Was born, I see, to be our anchor-hold. —
Sir John of Hainault, be it thy renown,
That England's Queen and nobles in distress
Have been by thee restored and comforted. 80
    Sir J. Madam, along, and you, my Lord, with me,
That England's peers may Hainault's welcome see.   [*Exeunt.*]

[SCENE III][10]

Enter the King, [Arundel, *and*] *the two*
Spencers, *with others.*

    K. Edw. Thus after many threats of wrathful war,
Triumpheth England's Edward with his friends;
And triumph, Edward, with his friends[11] uncontroll'd!
My Lord of Gloucester, do you hear the news?
    Y. Spen. What news, my Lord?
    K. Edw.   Why, man, they say there is
Great execution done through the realm;
My Lord of Arundel, you have the note, have you not?
    Arun. From the Lieutenant of the Tower, my Lord.
    K. Edw. I pray let us see it. [*Takes the note.*]
What have we there?
Read it, Spencer.   10
    [Young] Spencer *reads their names.*[12]
Why, so; they bark'd apace a month ago;
Now, on my life, they'll neither bark nor bite.
Now, sirs, the news from France. Gloucester, I trow
The Lords of France love England's gold so well
As Isabel gets no aid from thence.
What now remains? Have you proclaim'd, my Lord,
Reward for them can bring in Mortimer?

    Y. Spen. My Lord, we have; and if he be in England,
'A will be had ere long, I doubt it not.
    K. Edw. If, dost thou say? Spencer, as true as death,   20
He is in England's ground; our port-masters
Are not so careless of their King's command.

Enter a Post.

How now, what news with thee? From whence come these?
    Post. Letters, my Lord, and tidings forth of France,
To you, my Lord of Gloucester, from Levune.
    K. Edw. Read.
    [Y.] Spen. (*reads the letter.*) " My duty to your Honor [premised],[13] &c., I have, according to instructions in that behalf, dealt with the King of France his lords, and effected that [30 the Queen, all discontented and discomforted, is gone; whither if you ask, with Sir John of Hainault, brother to the Marquis, into Flanders. With them are gone Lord Edmund, and the Lord Mortimer, having in their company divers of your nation, and others; and, as constant report goeth, they intend to give King Edward battle in England, sooner than he can look for them. This is all the news of import.   40
    Your Honor's in all service, Levune."
    K. Edw. Ah, villains! hath that Mortimer escap'd?
With him is Edmund gone associate?
And will Sir John of Hainault lead the round?[14]
Welcome, a' God's name, madam, and your son;
England shall welcome you and all your rout.
Gallop apace, bright Phoebus, through the sky,
And dusky night, in rusty iron car,
Between you both, shorten the time, I pray,
That I may see that most desired day   50
When we may meet these traitors in the field.
Ah, nothing grieves me but my little boy
Is thus misled to countenance their ills.
Come, friends, to Bristow,[15] there to make us strong;
And, winds, as equal be to bring them in,
As you injurious were to bear them forth.
    [*Exeunt.*]

    [9] Proposal.
    [10] Unlocated; perhaps a room in the royal palace at Westminster.
    [11] Almost certainly corrupt. Broughton suggests *henceforth.*
    [12] They were doubtless taken from Holinshed's list (ed. 1807, II, 569) of executions at various places.

    [13] O₁ *promised:* Q 1598 *praemised.*
    [14] Dance.   [15] Bristol.

[SCENE IV] [16]

Enter the QUEEN [ISABELLA], *her son* [PRINCE
EDWARD,] EDMUND [EARL OF KENT, Young]
MORTIMER, *and* SIR JOHN [OF HAINAULT].

Q. ISAB. Now, Lords, our loving friends
    and countrymen,
Welcome to England all, with prosperous
    winds !
Our kindest friends in Belgia have we left,
To cope with friends at home ; a heavy case
When force to force is knit, and sword and
    glaive
In civil broils makes kin and countrymen
Slaughter themselves in others, and their sides
With their own weapons gor'd ! But what's
    the help?
Misgoverned kings are cause of all this wrack ;
And, Edward, thou art one among them all, [10
Whose looseness hath betrayed thy land to
    spoil,
Who made the channels [17] overflow with blood.
Of thine own people patron shouldst thou be,
But thou ——
    Y. MOR.   Nay, madam, if you be a
        warrior,
Ye must not grow so passionate in speeches. —
Lords, sith that we are by sufferance of Heaven
Arrived and armed in this prince's right,
Here for our country's cause swear we to him
All homage, fealty, and forwardness ;
And for the open wrongs and injuries   20
Edward hath done to us, his Queen, and land,
We come in arms to wreak [18] it with the
    [sword] ; [19]
That England's Queen in peace may repossess
Her dignities and honors ; and withal
We may remove these flatterers from the King,
That havocs England's wealth and treasury.
    SIR. J. Sound trumpets, my Lord, and for-
        ward let us march ;
Edward will think we come to flatter him.
    KENT. I would he never had been flattered
        more.   [*Exeunt.*]

[SCENE V] [20]

Enter the KING, BALDOCK, *and* SPENCER *the
son, flying about the stage.*

    [Y.] SPEN. Fly, fly, my Lord ! the Queen is
        overstrong ;

Her friends do multiply, and yours do fail.
Shape we our course to Ireland, there to
    breathe.
    K. EDW. What ! was I born to fly and run
        away,
And leave the Mortimers conquerors behind?
Give me my horse, and let's r'enforce our
    troops,
And in this bed of honor [21] die with fame.
    BALD. O no, my Lord ; this princely resolu-
        tion
Fits not the time ; away ! we are pursu'd.
                            [*Exeunt.*]

[*Enter*] EDMUND [EARL *of* KENT], *alone, with
a sword and target.*

    KENT. This way he fled, but I am come too
        late.   10
Edward, alas, my heart relents for thee.
Proud traitor, Mortimer, why dost thou chase
Thy lawful king, thy sovereign, with thy
    sword?
Vild wretch ! and why hast thou, of all un-
    kind,[22]
Borne arms against thy brother and thy king?
Rain showers of vengeance on my cursed head,
Thou God, to whom in justice it belongs
To punish this unnatural revolt !
Edward, this Mortimer aims at thy life !
O fly him, then ! But, Edmund, calm this
    rage ;   20
Dissemble, or thou diest ; for Mortimer
And Isabel do kiss, while they conspire ;
And yet she bears a face of love, forsooth.
Fie on that love that hatcheth death and hate !
Edmund, away ! Bristow to Longshanks'
    blood
Is false. Be not found single for suspect : [23]
Proud Mortimer pries near into thy walks.

Enter the QUEEN [ISABELLA, Young] MORTI-
MER, *the young* PRINCE [EDWARD,] *and* SIR
JOHN OF HAINAULT.

    Q. ISAB. Successful battles gives the God of
        kings
To them that fight in right and fear his wrath !
Since, then, successfully we have prevailed, [30
Thanks [24] be Heaven's great Architect, and
    you.
Ere farther we proceed, my noble Lords,
We here create our well-beloved son,
Of love and care unto his royal person,

---

[16] Unlocated, but presumably in the vicinity of
Harwich, near which this expedition landed.
    [17] Streams.   [18] Old eds. *wrecke.*
    [19] Cor. Q 1598 ; O₁ *swords.*   [20] Near Bristol.

[21] Zurich copy of O₁ ; Cassel copy *honors.*
[22] Unnatural.
[23] On account of suspicion.
[24] Q 1598 *et seq., thankt.*

Lord Warden of the realm; and sith the fates
Have made his father so infortunate,
Deal you, my Lords, in this, my loving Lords,
As to your wisdoms fittest seems in all.

KENT. Madam, without offence, if I may
ask,
How will you deal with Edward in his fall?   40
P. EDW. Tell me, good Uncle, what Edward
do you mean?
KENT. Nephew, your father; I dare not
call him king.
[Y.] MOR. My Lord of Kent, what needs
these questions?
'T is not in her controlment, nor in ours,
But as the realm and parliament shall please,
So shall your brother be disposed of. —
[*aside to the* QUEEN] I like not this relenting
mood in Edmund.
Madam, 't is good to look to him betimes.
Q. ISAB. My Lord, the Mayor of Bristow
knows our mind.
[Y.] MOR. Yea, madam, and they scape
not easily   50
That fled the field.
Q. ISAB.   Baldock is with the King,
A goodly chancellor, is he not, my Lord?
SIR J. So are the Spencers, the father and
the son.
KENT. This Edward is the ruin of the realm.

Enter RICE AP HOWELL *and the* Mayor *of*
Bristow, *with* SPENCER *the father* [*prisoner,
and* Attendants].

RICE. God save Queen Isabel, and her
princely son!
Madam, the Mayor and citizens of Bristow,
In sign of love and duty to this presence,
Present by me this traitor to the state,
Spencer, the father to that wanton Spencer,
That, like the lawless Catiline of Rome,   60
Revell'd in England's wealth and treasury.
Q. ISAB. We thank you all.
Y. MOR.   Your loving care in this
Deserveth princely favors and rewards.
But where's the King and the other Spencer
fled?
RICE. Spencer the son, created Earl of
Gloucester,
Is with that smooth-tongu'd scholar Baldock
gone
And shipp'd but late for Ireland with the King.
Y. MOR. [*aside*] Some whirlwind fetch them
back or sink them all! —
They shall be started [25] thence, I doubt it not.

[25] *I.e.*, like hunted animals.

P. EDW. Shall I not see the King, my
father, yet?   70
KENT. [*aside*] Unhappy's Edward, chas'd
from England's bounds.
SIR J. Madam, what resteth? [26] why stand
ye in a muse?
Q. ISAB. I rue my lord's ill fortune; but
alas!
Care of my country call'd me to this war.
Y. MOR. Madam, have done with care and
sad complaint;
Your King hath wrong'd your country and
himself,
And we must seek to right it as we may.
Meanwhile, have hence this rebel to the block.
Your lordship cannot privilege your head.
E. SPEN. Rebel is he that fights against his
prince;   80
So fought not they that fought in Edward's
right.
[Y.] MOR. Take him away; he prates. —
[*Exeunt* Attendants *with the* Elder
SPENCER.]
                    You, Rice ap Howell,
Shall do good service to her Majesty,
Being of countenance [27] in your country here,
To follow these rebellious runagates. [28]
We in meanwhile, madam, must take advice
How Baldock, Spencer, and their 'complices
May in their fall be followed to their end.
                              Exeunt omnes.

[SCENE VI] [29]

Enter the Abbot, Monks, [KING] EDWARD,
[Young] SPENCER, *and* BALDOCK, [*the three
latter disguised*].

ABBOT. Have you no doubt, my Lord;
have you no fear;
As silent and as careful will we be
To keep your royal person safe with us,
Free from suspect and fell invasion
Of such as have your Majesty in chase,
Yourself, and those your chosen company,
As danger of this stormy time requires.
K. EDW. Father, thy face should harbor no
deceit.
O, hadst thou ever been a king, thy heart,
Pierced deeply with sense of my distress,   10
Could not but take compassion of my state.

[26] Remaineth to be done.
[27] Influence.
[28] Runaways.
[29] A room in an abbey (of Neath, in Glamor-
ganshire).

Stately and proud, in riches and in train,
Whilom I was powerful and full of pomp ;
But what is he whom rule and empery
Have not in life or death made miserable?
Come, Spencer ; come, Baldock ; come, sit
    down by me ;
Make trial now of that philosophy,
That in our famous nurseries of arts
Thou sucked'st from Plato and from Aristotle.
Father, this life contemplative is Heaven. 20
O that I might this life in quiet lead !
But we, alas, are chas'd ; and you, my friends,
Your lives and my dishonor they pursue.
Yet, gentle monks, for treasure, gold, nor fee,
Do you betray us and our company.
    MONKS. Your Grace may sit secure, if none
    but we
Do wot of your abode.
    [Y.] SPEN. Not one alive ; but shrewdly I
    suspect
A gloomy fellow in a mead below.
'A gave a long look after us, my Lord ; 30
And all the land I know is up in arms,
Arms that pursue our lives with deadly hate.
    BALD. We were embark'd for Ireland,
    wretched we,
With awkward winds and sore [30] tempests
    driven
To fall on shore, and here to pine in fear
Of Mortimer and his confederates.
    K. EDW. Mortimer, who talks of Mortimer?
Who wounds me with the name of Mortimer,
That bloody man? Good father, on thy lap
Lay I this head, laden with mickle [31] care. 40
O might I never open these eyes again,
Never again lift up this drooping head,
O nevermore lift up this dying heart !
    Y. SPEN. Look up, my Lord. — Baldock,
    this drowsiness
Betides no good ; here even we are betray'd.

Enter, with Welsh hooks, RICE AP HOWELL, *a*
    Mower, *and the* EARL OF LEICESTER.

    MOW. Upon my life, these be the men ye
    seek.
    RICE. Fellow, enough. — My Lord, I pray
    be short ;
A fair commission warrants what we do.
    LEICES. The Queen's commission, urg'd by
    Mortimer ;
What cannot gallant Mortimer with the
    Queen? 50
Alas, see where he sits, and hopes unseen
T' escape their hands that seek to reave his life.

Too true it is, *Quem dies vidit veniens*
Superbum, hunc dies vidit fugiens iacentem.[32]
But, Leicester, leave to grow so passionate.
Spencer and Baldock, by no other names,
I [33] arrest you of high treason here.
Stand not on titles, but obey th' arrest ;
'T is in the name of Isabel, the Queen. —
My Lord, why droop you thus? 60
    K. EDW. O day, the last of all my bliss on
    earth,
Centre of all misfortune ! O my stars !
Why do you lour unkindly on a king?
Comes Leicester, then, in Isabella's name
To take my life, my company from me?
Here, man, rip up this panting breast of mine,
And take my heart in rescue of my friends !
    RICE. Away with them !
    Y. SPEN.   It may become thee yet
To let us take our farewell of his Grace.
    ABBOT. [*aside*] My heart with pity earns [34]
    to see this sight — 70
A king to bear these words and proud com-
    mands.
    K. EDW. Spencer, ah, sweet Spencer, thus
    then must we part?
    Y. SPEN. We must, my Lord ; so will the
    angry Heavens.
    K. EDW. Nay, so will hell and cruel Morti-
    mer ;
The gentle Heavens have not to do in this.
    BALD. My Lord, it is in vain to grieve or
    storm.
Here humbly of your Grace we take our leaves ;
Our lots are cast ; I fear me, so is thine.
    K. EDW. In Heaven we may, in earth never
    shall we meet ;
And, Leicester, say, what shall become of us?
    LEICES. Your Majesty must go to Killing-
    worth.[35] 81
    K. EDW. Must ! it is somewhat hard, when
    kings " must " go.
    LEICES. Here is a litter ready for your
    Grace,
That waits your pleasure ; and the day grows
    old.
    RICE. As good be gone, as stay and be be-
    nighted.
    K. EDW. A litter hast thou? Lay me in a
    hearse,
And to the gates of hell convey me hence ;
Let Pluto's bells ring out my fatal knell,
And hags howl for my death at Charon's shore ;

---

[32] Whom dawn sees proud, evening sees prostrate.
(Seneca, *Thyestes*, ll. 613, 614.)
[33] Robinson conj. *I do.*
[34] Yearns, grieves.   [35] Kenilworth.

[30] Dissyllabic.   [31] Much.

For friends hath Edward none but these and
these,   90
And these must die under a tyrant's sword.

RICE. My Lord, be going; care not for
these,
For we shall see them shorter by the heads.

K. EDW. Well, that shall be, shall be; part
we must;
Sweet Spencer, gentle Baldock, part we must.
Hence feigned weeds! unfeigned are my
woes. —
                    [*Throws off his disguise.*]
Father, farewell! — Leicester, thou stay'st for
me,
And go I must. Life, farewell, with my
friends.
            Exeunt EDWARD *and* LEICESTER.

Y. SPEN. O, is he gone? Is noble Edward
gone?
Parted from hence, never to see us more?   100
Rent, sphere of Heaven! and, fire, forsake thy
orb!
Earth, melt to air! gone is my sovereign,
Gone, gone, alas! never to make return.

BALD. Spencer, I see our souls are fleeted [36]
hence;
We are depriv'd the sunshine of our life;
Make for a new life, man; throw up thy eyes,
And heart, and hand to Heaven's immortal
throne;
Pay nature's debt with cheerful countenance;
Reduce we all our lessons unto this:
To die, sweet Spencer, therefore live we all;
Spencer, all live to die, and rise to fall.   111

RICE. Come, come, keep these preachments
till you come to the place appointed. You,
and such as you are, have made wise work in
England. Will your Lordships away?

MOW. Your Worship, I trust, will remember me?

RICE. Remember thee, fellow! what else?
Follow me to the town.   [*Exeunt.*]

            [ACT V — SCENE I] [1]

Enter the KING [*and*] LEICESTER, *with* [*the*]
BISHOP [OF WINCHESTER] *for the crown,* [*and*
TRUSSEL].

LEICES. Be patient, good my Lord; cease
to lament;
Imagine Killingworth Castle were your court,

And that you lay for pleasure here a space,
Not of compulsion or necessity.

K. EDW. Leicester, if gentle words might
comfort me,
Thy speeches long ago had eas'd my sorrows;
For kind and loving hast thou always been.
The griefs of private men are soon allay'd,
But not of kings. The forest deer, being
struck,   9
Runs to an herb [2] that closeth up the wounds;
But when the imperial lion's flesh is gor'd,
He rends and tears it with his wrathful paw,
Highly scorning that the lowly earth
Should drink his blood, mounts up into the air.
And so it fares with me, whose dauntless mind
The ambitious Mortimer would seek to curb,
And that unnatural queen, false Isabel,
That thus hath pent and mew'd me in a prison;
For such outrageous passions cloy my soul,
As with the wings of rancor and disdain   20
Full often am I soaring up to Heaven,
To plain me to the gods against them both.
But when I call to mind I am a king,
Methinks I should revenge me of the wrongs
That Mortimer and Isabel have done.
But what are kings, when regiment is gone,
But perfect shadows in a sunshine day?
My nobles rule, I bear the name of king;
I wear the crown, but am controll'd by them,
By Mortimer, and my unconstant Queen,   30
Who spots my nuptial bed with infamy,
Whilst I am lodg'd within this cave of care,
Where sorrow at my elbow still attends,
To company my heart with sad laments,
That bleeds within me for this strange ex-
change.
But tell me, must I now resign my crown,
To make usurping Mortimer a king?

B. OF WIN. Your Grace mistakes; it is for
England's good,
And princely Edward's right, we crave the
crown.

K. EDW. No, 't is for Mortimer, not
Edward's head;   40
For he 's a lamb, encompassed by wolves,
Which in a moment will abridge his life.
But if proud Mortimer do wear this crown,
Heavens turn it to a blaze of quenchless fire!
Or like the snaky wreath of Tisiphon, [3]
Engirt the temples of his hateful head;
So shall not England's vines be perished,
But Edward's name survives, though Edward
dies.

[36] Vanished, fled.
[1] A room in Kenilworth Castle.

[2] Dittany.
[3] Tisiphone, one of the Furies.

LEICES. My Lord, why waste you thus the time away?

They stay your answer; will you yield your crown?   50

    K. EDW. Ah, Leicester, weigh how hardly I can brook

To lose my crown and kingdom without cause;
To give ambitious Mortimer my right,
That like a mountain overwhelms my bliss,
In which extreme my mind here murdered is.
But what the Heavens appoint, I must obey.
Here, take my crown, the life of Edward too;
                    [*He takes off the crown.*]
Two kings in England cannot reign at once.
But stay awhile, let me be king till night,
That I may gaze upon this glittering crown;
So shall my eyes receive their last content,   61
My head, the latest honor due to it,
And jointly both yield up their wished right.
Continue ever, thou celestial sun;
Let never silent night possess this clime;
Stand still you watches of the element; [4]
All times and seasons, rest you at a stay,
That Edward may be still fair England's king!
But day's bright beams doth vanish fast away,
And needs I must resign my wished crown.   70
Inhuman creatures, nurs'd with tiger's milk,
Why gape you for your sovereign's overthrow?
My diadem I mean, and guiltless life.
See, monsters, see, I'll wear my crown again!
                    [*He puts on the crown.*]
What, fear you not the fury of your king?
But, hapless Edward, thou art fondly [5] led;
They pass not for thy frowns as late they did,
But seeks to make a new-elected king;
Which fills my mind with strange despairing thoughts,
Which thoughts are martyred with endless torments,   80
And in this torment comfort find I none,
But that I feel the crown upon my head;
And therefore let me wear it yet awhile.

    TRUS. My Lord, the parliament must have present news,
And therefore say, will you resign or no?
                    The KING *rageth.*

    K. EDW. I'll not resign; but whilst I live —
Traitors, be gone and join you with Mortimer!
Elect, conspire, install, do what you will;
Their blood and yours shall seal these treacheries!

    B. of WIN. This answer we'll return, and so farewell.   90

LEICES. Call them again, my Lord, and speak them fair;
For if they go, the Prince shall [6] lose his right.

    K. EDW. Call thou them back; I have no power to speak.

    LEICES. My Lord, the King is willing to resign.

    B. OF WIN. If he be not, let him choose.

    K. EDW. O would I might; but Heavens and earth conspire
To make me miserable! Here receive my crown;
Receive it? No, these innocent hands of mine
Shall not be guilty of so foul a crime.
He of you all that most desires my blood,   100
And will be called the murderer of a king,
Take it. — What, are you mov'd? Pity you me?
Then send for unrelenting Mortimer,
And Isabel, whose eyes, [being] [7] turn'd to steel,
Will sooner sparkle fire than shed a tear.
Yet stay; for, rather than I'll look on them,
Here, here! —   [*Gives the crown.*]
             Now, sweet God of Heaven,
Make me despise this transitory pomp,
And sit for aye enthronized in Heaven!
Come, death, and with thy fingers close my eyes,   110
Or if I live, let me forget myself.

    [B. OF WIN.] [8] My Lord —

    K. EDW. Call me not lord; away! out of my sight!
Ah, pardon me; grief makes me lunatic.
Let not that Mortimer protect my son [9];
More safety is there in a tiger's jaws,
Than his embracements. Bear this to the Queen,
Wet with my tears, and dried again with sighs;
          [*Gives a handkerchief.*]
If with the sight thereof she be not mov'd,
Return it back and dip it in my blood.   120
Commend me to my son, and bid him rule
Better than I. Yet how have I transgress'd,
Unless it be with too much clemency?

    TRUS. And thus most humbly do we take our leave.

    K. EDW. Farewell. — [*Exeunt the* BISHOP OF WINCHESTER *and* TRUSSEL.]
I know the next news that they bring
Will be my death; and welcome shall it be;
To wretched men, death is felicity.

---

[4] Sky.
[5] Foolishly.
[6] Will be certain to.
[7] Cor. Q 1598; O₁ *beene*.
[8] Old eds. *Bartley*, whose entrance they indicate (too early) at this point.
[9] *I.e.*, be Lord Protector during my son's minority.

Enter Berkeley,[10] [*who gives a paper to* Leicester].

Leices. Another post! what news brings
    he?
K. Edw. Such news as I expect — come,
    Berkeley, come,
And tell thy message to my naked breast. 130
  Berk. My Lord, think not a thought so vil-
    lainous
Can harbor in a man of noble birth.
To do your Highness service and devoir,
And save you from your foes, Berkeley would
    die.
  Leices. My Lord, the Council of the Queen
    commands
That I resign my charge.
  K. Edw. And who must keep me now?
    Must you, my Lord?
  Berk. Ay, my most gracious Lord; so 't is
    decreed.
  K. Edw. [*taking the paper*] By Mortimer,
    whose name is written here!
Well may I rent his name that rends my
    heart! — 140
This poor revenge has something eas'd my
    mind.
So may his limbs be torn, as is this paper!
Hear me, immortal Jove, and grant it too!
  Berk. Your Grace must hence with me to
    Berkeley straight.
  K. Edw. Whither you will; all places are
    alike,
And every earth is fit for burial.
  Leices. Favor him, my Lord, as much as
    lieth in you.
  Berk. Even so betide my soul as I use him.
  K. Edw. Mine enemy hath pitied my estate,
And that's the cause that I am now remov'd.
  Berk. And thinks your Grace that Berk-
    eley will be cruel? 151
  K. Edw. I know not; but of this am I as-
    sured,
That death ends all, and I can die but once. —
Leicester, farewell.
  Leices. Not yet, my Lord; I 'll bear you on
    your way.   *Exeunt omnes.*

[Scene II][11]

Enter [Young] Mortimer *and* Queen Isabell[a].

[10] Old eds. *Bartley*, throughout.
[11] Unlocated; probably a room in the Palace at Westminster.

  Y. Mor. Fair Isabel, now have we our de-
    sire;
The proud corrupters of the light-brain'd King
Have done their homage to the lofty gallows,
And he himself lies in captivity.
Be rul'd by me, and we will rule the realm.
In any case take heed of childish fear;
For now we hold an old wolf [12] by the ears,
That, if he slip, will seize upon us both,
And grip the sorer, being gripp'd himself.
Think therefore, madam, that imports as [13]
    much   10
To erect your son with all the speed we may,
And that I be Protector over him;
For our behoof will bear the greater sway
Whenas a king's name shall be underwrit.
  Q. Isab. Sweet Mortimer, the life of Isabel,
Be thou persuaded that I love thee well,
And therefore, so [14] the Prince, my son, be safe,
Whom I esteem as dear as these mine eyes,
Conclude against his father what thou wilt,
And I myself will willingly subscribe.   20
  Y. Mor. First would I hear news that he
    were depos'd,
And then let me alone [15] to handle him.

Enter Messenger.

Letters! from whence?
  Mess.   From Killingworth, my Lord.
  Q. Isab. How fares my Lord, the King?
  Mess. In health, madam, but full of pen-
    siveness.
  Q. Isab. Alas, poor soul, would I could ease
    his grief!

[*Enter the* Bishop *of* Winchester, *with the crown.*]

Thanks, gentle Winchester. — [*to the* Messen-
    ger] Sirrah, be gone. [*Exit* Messenger.]
  B. of Win. The King hath willingly
    resign'd his crown.
  Q. Isab. O happy news! Send for the
    Prince, my son.
  B. of Win. Further, or [16] this letter was
    sealed Lord Berkeley came;   30
So that he now is gone from Killingworth;
And we have heard that Edmund laid a plot
To set his brother free; no more but so.
The Lord of Berkeley is so pitiful
As Leicester that had charge of him before.
  Q. Isab. Then let some other be his
    guardian.

[12] *I.e.*, England.   [13] Qq 1612, 1622, *us.*
[14] Provided that.   [15] Leave it to me.
[16] Before.

Y. Mor. Let me alone; here is the privy seal.

[*Exit the* Bishop *of* Winchester.]

Who 's there? [*to* Attendants *within*] Call hither Gurney and Matrevis. —

To dash the heavy-headed Edmund's drift,[17] [39 Berkeley shall be discharg'd, the King remov'd, And none but we shall know where he lieth.

Q. Isab. But, Mortimer, as long as he survives,

What safety rests for us, or for my son?

Y. Mor. Speak, shall he presently be despatch'd and die?

Q. Isab. I would he were, so 't were not by my means.

Enter Matrevis *and* Gurney.

Y. Mor. Enough. — Matrevis, write a letter presently

Unto the Lord of Berkeley from ourself

That he resign the King to thee and Gurney;

And when 't is done, we will subscribe our name. 49

Mat. It shall be done, my Lord.

Y. Mor.   Gurney.

Gur.   My Lord.

Y. Mor. As thou intendest to rise by Mortimer,

Who now makes Fortune's wheel turn as he please,

Seek all the means thou canst to make him droop,

And neither give him kind word nor good look.

Gur. I warrant you, my Lord.

Y. Mor. And this above the rest: because we hear

That Edmund casts [18] to work his liberty,

Remove him still [19] from place to place by night,

[Till] [20] at the last he come to Killingworth, 59

And then from thence to Berkeley back again;

And by the way, to make him fret the more,

Speak curstly [21] to him, and in any case

Let no man comfort him; if he chance to weep,

But amplify his grief with bitter words.

Mat. Fear not, my Lord; we 'll do as you command.

Y. Mor. So now away; post thitherwards amain.

Q. Isab. Whither goes this letter? To my Lord the King?

Commend me humbly to his Majesty,

And tell him that I labor all in vain

To ease his grief and work his liberty; 70

And bear him this as witness of my love.

[*Gives a ring.*]

Mat. I will, madam.

Exeunt Matrevis *and* Gurney.

Enter the young Prince [Edward,] *and the* Earl of Kent *talking with him.*

Y. Mor. Finely dissembled. Do so still, sweet Queen.

Here comes the young Prince with the Earl of Kent.

Q. Isab. Something he whispers in his childish ears.

Y. Mor. If he have such access unto the Prince,

Our plots and stratagems will soon be dash'd.

Q. Isab. Use Edmund friendly, as if all were well.

Y. Mor. How fares my honorable Lord of Kent?

Kent. In health, sweet Mortimer. — How fares your Grace? 80

Q. Isab. Well, if my Lord, your brother, were enlarg'd.

Kent. I hear of late he hath depos'd himself.

Q. Isab. The more my grief.

Y. Mor.   And mine.

Kent. [*aside*]   Ah, they do dissemble.

Q. Isab. Sweet son, come hither; I must talk with thee.

Y. Mor. Thou being his uncle, and the next of blood,

Do look to be Protector over the Prince.

Kent. Not I, my Lord; who should protect the son,

But she that gave him life? I mean the Queen.

P. Edw. Mother, persuade me not to wear the crown; 89

Let him be king; I am too young to reign.

Q. Isab. But be content, seeing it his Highness' pleasure.

P. Edw. Let me but see him first, and then I will.

Kent. Ay, do, sweet Nephew.

Q. Isab. Brother, you know it is impossible.

P. Edw. Why, is he dead?

Q. Isab. No, God forbid.

Kent. I would those words proceeded from your heart.

Y. Mor. Inconstant Edmund, dost thou favor him,

That wast a cause of his imprisonment?

---

[17] Plot.   [18] Plans.   [19] Continually.
[20] Cor. Q 1598; O₁ *And.*   [21] Crossly.

KENT. The more cause have I now to make amends.   100

Y. MOR. [*to* QUEEN] I tell thee, 't is not meet that one so false

Should come about the person of a prince. —

My Lord, he hath betrayed the King, his brother,

And therefore trust him not.

P. EDW. But he repents, and sorrows for it now.

Q. ISAB. Come, Son, and go with this gentle lord and me.

P. EDW. With you I will, but not with Mortimer.

Y. MOR. Why, youngling, 'sdain'st thou so of Mortimer?

Then I will carry thee by force away.

P. EDW. Help, Uncle Kent! Mortimer will wrong me.   110

Q. ISAB. Brother Edmund, strive not; we are his friends;

Isabel is nearer than the Earl of Kent.

KENT. Sister, Edward is my charge; redeem him.

Q. ISAB. Edward is my son, and I will keep him.

KENT. Mortimer shall know that he hath wrong'd me! —

[*aside*] Hence will I haste to Killingworth Castle,

And rescue aged Edward from his foes,

To be reveng'd on Mortimer and thee.

                                           Exeunt omnes.

[SCENE III] [22]

Enter MATREVIS *and* GURNEY [*and* Soldiers,] *with the* KING.

MAT. My Lord, be not pensive; we are your friends;

Men are ordain'd to live in misery;

Therefore come; dalliance dangereth our lives.

K. EDW. Friends, whither must unhappy Edward go?

Will hateful Mortimer appoint no rest?

Must I be vexed like the nightly bird,

Whose sight is loathsome to all winged fowls?

When will the fury of his mind assuage?

When will his heart be satisfied with blood?

If mine will serve, unbowel straight this breast,

And give my heart to Isabel and him;   11

It is the chiefest mark they level [23] at.

GUR. Not so, my Liege; the Queen hath given this charge

To keep your Grace in safety;

Your passions make your dolors to increase.

K. EDW. This usage makes my misery increase.

But can my air of life [24] continue long

When all my senses are annoy'd with stench?

Within a dungeon England's King is kept,

Where I am starv'd for want of sustenance. [20

My daily diet is heartbreaking sobs,

That almost rents the closet of my heart.

Thus lives old Edward not reliev'd by any,

And so must die, though pitied by many.

O, water, gentle friends, to cool my thirst,

And clear my body from foul excrements!

MAT. Here's channel water, as our charge is given.

Sit down, for we'll be barbers to your Grace.

K. EDW. Traitors, away! What, will you murder me,

Or choke your sovereign with puddle water?[30

GUR. No; but wash your face, and shave away your beard,

Lest you be known and so be rescued.

MAT. Why strive you thus? Your labor is in vain!

K. EDW. The wren may strive against the lion's strength,

But all in vain; so vainly do I strive

To seek for mercy at a tyrant's hand.

                They wash him with puddle water,
                and shave his beard away.

Immortal powers, that knows the painful cares

That waits upon my poor distressed soul,

O level all your looks upon these daring men,[25]

That wrongs their liege and sovereign, England's king!   40

O Gaveston, it is for thee I am wrong'd;

For me, both thou and both the Spencers died!

And for your sakes a thousand wrongs I 'll take.

The Spencers' ghosts, wherever they remain,

Wish well to mine; then tush, for them I 'll die.

MAT. 'Twixt theirs and yours shall be no enmity.

Come, come, away. — Now put the torches out;

We 'll enter in by darkness to Killingworth.

Enter EDMUND [EARL OF KENT].

GUR. How now, who comes there?

MAT. Guard the King sure; it is the Earl of Kent.   50

---

[22] Near Kenilworth.   [23] Aim.

[24] "A Latinism — *aura vitae*." (Dyce.)

[25] Not an Alexandrine. "O" is hypermetrical, and "level all" forms a trisyllabic foot.

K. Edw. O gentle Brother, help to rescue
me!

Mat. Keep them asunder; thrust in the
King.

Kent. Soldiers, let me but talk to him one
word.

Gur. Lay hands upon the Earl for this
assault.

Kent. Lay down your weapons! Traitors,
yield the King!

Mat. Edmund, yield thou thyself, or thou
shalt die.

Kent. Base villains, wherefore do you gripe
me thus?

Gur. Bind him and so convey him to the
court.

Kent. Where is the court but here?   Here
is the King;

And I will visit him; why stay you me?   60

Mat. The court is where Lord Mortimer
remains;

Thither shall your Honor go; and so farewell.
                    Exeunt Matrevis *and* Gurney,
                              with the King.

Kent. O miserable is that commonweal

Where lords keep courts, and kings are lock'd
in prison!

Sol. Wherefore stay we?   On, sirs, to the
court!

Kent. Ay, lead me whither you will, even
to my death,

Seeing that my brother cannot be releas'd.
                    Exeunt omnes.

[Scene IV] [26]

Enter [Young] Mortimer, *alone.*

Y. Mor. The King must die, or Mortimer
goes down;

The commons now begin to pity him.

Yet he that is the cause of Edward's death

Is sure to pay for it when his son is of age;

And therefore will I do it cunningly.

This letter, written by a friend [27] of ours,

Contains his death, yet bids them save his life.
                              [*Reads.*]

" *Edwardum occidere nolite timere, bonum est:*

Fear not to kill the King; 't is good he die."

But read it thus, and that 's another sense: 10

" *Edwardum occidere nolite, timere bonum est:*

Kill not the King; 't is good to fear the worst."

Unpointed as it is, thus shall it go,

That, being dead, if it chance to be found,

Matrevis and the rest may bear the blame,

And we be quit that caus'd it to be done.

Within this room is lock'd the messenger

That shall convey it, and perform the rest;

And by a secret token that he bears,

Shall he be murdered when the deed is done. —

Lightborn, come forth!   21

[*Enter* Lightborn.]

Art thou as resolute as thou wast?

Light. What else, my Lord? and far more
resolute.

Y. Mor. And hast thou cast how to accomplish it?

Light. Ay, ay; and none shall know which
way he died.

Y. Mor. But at his looks, Lightborn, thou
wilt relent.

Light. Relent! ha, ha!   I use much to
relent.

Y. Mor. Well, do it bravely, and be secret.

Light. You shall not need to give instructions;

'T is not the first time I have killed a man.   30

I learn'd in Naples how to poison flowers;

To strangle with a lawn [28] thrust through the
throat;

To pierce the windpipe with a needle's point;

Or whilst one is asleep, to take a quill

And blow a little powder in his ears,

Or open his mouth and pour quicksilver down.

And yet I have a braver [29] way than these.

Y. Mor. What's that?

Light. Nay, you shall pardon me; none
shall know my tricks.

Y. Mor. I care not how it is, so it be not
spy'd.   40

Deliver this to Gurney and Matrevis.
                              [*Gives letter.*]

At every ten miles' end thou hast a horse.

[*Giving money*] Take this; away! and never
see me more.

Light. No?

Y. Mor. No;

Unless thou bring me news of Edward's death.

Light. That will I quickly do.   Farewell,
my Lord.   [*Exit.*]

Y. Mor. The Prince I rule; the Queen do
I command;

And, with a lowly congee to the ground,

The proudest lords salute me as I pass;   50

I seal, I cancel, I do what I will.

Fear'd am I more than lov'd — let me be fear'd,

---

[26] A hall in the Palace at Westminster.
[27] According to Holinshed, the Bishop of Hereford.
[28] A piece of fine linen.   [29] Finer.

And, when I frown, make all the court look
   pale.
I view the Prince with Aristarchus' [30] eyes,
Whose looks were as a breeching to a boy.
They thrust upon me the Protectorship,
And sue to me for that that I desire.
While at the council table, grave enough,
And not unlike a bashful p[u]ritan,
First I complain of imbecility,[31]   60
Saying it is *onus quam gravissimum*,[32]
Till, being interrupted by my friends,
Suscepi that *provinciam*,[33] as they term it ;
And to conclude, I am Protector now.
Now is all sure : the Queen and Mortimer
Shall rule the realm, the King ; and none rule
   us.
Mine enemies will I plague, my friends ad-
   vance ;
And what I list command who dare control?
Maior sum quam cui possit fortuna nocere.[34]
And that this be the coronation day,   70
It pleaseth me, and Isabel the Queen.
           [*Trumpets within.*]
The trumpets sound ; I must go take my place.

Enter the young KING, [*the* ARCH]BISHOP [*OF*
   CANTERBURY,] Champion, Nobles, [*and*]
   QUEEN.

  [A. *of* CANT.] [35] Long live King Edward,
   by the grace of God
King of England and Lord of Ireland !
  CHAM. If any Christian, Heathen, Turk, or
   Jew,
Dares but affirm that Edward's not true king,
And will avouch his saying with the sword,
I am the champion that will combat him !
  Y. MOR. None comes ; sound trumpets.
           [*Trumpets sound.*]
  K. [EDW. THIRD.]   Champion, here's
   to thee.[36]
  Q. ISAB. Lord Mortimer, now take him to
   your charge.   80

Enter Soldiers, *with the* EARL OF KENT
   prisoner.

  Y. MOR. What traitor have we there with
   blades and bills?
  SOL. Edmund, the Earl of Kent.

[30] The Alexandrian critic, d. 143 B.C.
[31] *I.e.*, my incapacity.
[32] A very heavy burden.
[33] I have assumed that office.
[34] I am too great for fortune to injure. (Ovid,
Metamorphoses, vi, 195.)
[35] Old eds. *Bish.*
[36] The champion regularly appeared at the coronation banquet ; the sovereign drank to him and
gave him the cup as a fee.

  K. EDW. THIRD.   What hath he done?
  SOL. 'A would have taken the King away
   perforce,
As we were bringing him to Killingworth.
  Y. MOR. Did you attempt his rescue,
   Edmund? Speak !
  KENT. Mortimer, I did ; he is our king,
And thou compell'st this prince to wear the
   crown.
  Y. MOR. Strike off his head ! he shall have
   martial law.
  KENT. Strike off my head ! Base traitor, I
   defy thee !
  K. EDW. THIRD. My Lord, he is my uncle,
   and shall live.   90
  Y. MOR. My Lord, he is your enemy, and
   shall die.
  KENT. Stay, villains !
  K. EDW. THIRD. Sweet Mother, if I cannot
   pardon him,
Entreat my Lord Protector for his life.
  Q. ISAB. Son, be content ; I dare not speak
   a word.
  K. EDW. THIRD. Nor I ; and yet methinks
   I should command ;
But, seeing I cannot, I 'll entreat for him. —
My Lord, if you will let my uncle live,
I will requite it when I come to age.
  Y. MOR. 'T is for your Highness' good, and
   for the realm's. —   100
How often shall I bid you bear him hence?
  KENT. Art thou king? Must I die at thy
   command?
  Y. MOR. At our command. — Once more
   away with him.
  KENT. Let me but stay and speak ; I will
   not go.
Either my brother or his son is king,
And none of both [them] [37] thirst for Edmund's
   blood ;
And therefore, soldiers, whither will you hale
   me?
       They hale EDMUND *away, and carry*
         him to be beheaded.
  K. EDW. THIRD. What safety may I look
   for at his hands,
If that my uncle shall be murdered thus?
  Q. ISAB. Fear not, sweet boy ; I 'll guard
   thee from thy foes ;   110
Had Edmund liv'd, he would have sought thy
   death.
Come, Son, we 'll ride a-hunting in the park.
  K. EDW. THIRD. And shall my uncle Ed-
   mund ride with us?

[37] Cor. Q 1598 ; O₁ *then.*

Q. Isab. He is a traitor ; think not on him ;
come.   *Exeunt omnes.*

[Scene V] [38]

Enter Matrevis *and* Gurney.

Mat. Gurney, I wonder the King dies not,
Being in a vault up to the knees in water,
To which the channels [39] of the castle run,
From whence a damp continually ariseth,
That were enough to poison any man,
Much more a king brought up so tenderly.

Gur. And so do I, Matrevis ; yesternight
I opened but the door to throw him meat,
And I was almost stifled with the savor.

Mat. He hath a body able to endure   10
More than we can inflict ; and therefore now
Let us assail his mind another while.

Gur. Send for him out thence, and I will
anger him.

Mat. But stay ; who 's this?

Enter Lightborn.

Light.   My Lord Protector greets you.
                              [*Gives letter.*]

Gur. What 's here? I know not how to
conster [40] it.

Mat. Gurney, it was left unpointed for the
nonce : [41]

" *Edwardum occidere nolite timere:* "
That 's his meaning.

Light. Know you this token? I must
have the King.   [*Gives token.*]

Mat. Ay, stay awhile ; thou shalt have
answer straight. —   20

[*aside to* Gurney] This villain's sent to
make away the King.

Gur. [*aside*] I thought as much.

Mat. [*aside*]   And when the murder 's
done,
See how he must be handled for his labor.
Pereat iste! [42] Let him have the King.
What else? Here is the keys ; this is the lake ; [43]
Do as you are commanded by my Lord.

Light. I know what I must do. Get you
away.
Yet be not far off ; I shall need your help ;
See that in the next room I have a fire,
And get me a spit, and let it be red-hot. [44] 30

Mat. Very well.

Gur.   Need you anything besides?

Light. What else? A table and a feather-
bed.

Gur. That 's all?

Light. Ay, ay ; so ; when I call you, bring
it in.

Mat. Fear not you that.

Gur. Here 's a light, to go into the dungeon.
            [*Gives a light, and then exit with*
            Matrevis.]

Light. So now
Must I about this gear ; [45] ne'er was there any
So finely handled as this king shall be.   39
Foh ! here 's a place indeed, with all my heart !
            [*Discovers* King Edward II.] [46]

K. Edw. Who 's there? What light is
that? Wherefore comes thou?

Light. To comfort you, and bring you joyful news.

K. Edw. Small comfort finds poor Edward
in thy looks ;
Villain, I know thou com'st to murder me.

Light. To murder you, my most gracious
Lord !
Far is it from my heart to do you harm.
The Queen sent me to see how you were used,
For she relents at this your misery.
And what eyes can refrain from shedding tears,
To see a king in this most piteous state?   50

K. Edw. Weep'st thou already?   List
awhile to me,
And then thy heart, were it as Gurney's is,
Or as Matrevis', hewn from the Caucasus,
Yet will it melt, ere I have done my tale.
This dungeon where they keep me is the sink
Wherein the filth of all the castle falls.

Light. O villains !

K. Edw. And there in mire and puddle
have I stood
This ten days' space ; and, lest that I should
sleep,
One plays continually upon a drum.   60
They give me bread and water, being a king ;
So that, for want of sleep and sustenance,
My mind 's distempered, and my body 's
numb'd,
And whether I have limbs or no I know not.
O, would my blood dropp'd out from every
vein,
As doth this water from my tattered robes !
Tell Isabel, the Queen, I look'd not thus

[38] A room in Berkeley Castle.   [39] Drains.
[40] Construe, interpret.   [41] Purposely.
[42] Let him perish.
[43] Dungeon. (*N. E. D.*)
[44] According to Holinshed, the hot spit was
"thrust up into his body" while Edward was held
down with "heavy featherbeds or a table, as some
write."

[45] Affair.
[46] Edward is probably behind one of the down-
stage doors, since the bed would be on the inner
stage.

When for her sake I ran at tilt in France,
And there unhors'd the Duke of Clere-
　mont.
　　Light. O speak no more, my Lord! This
　　breaks my heart.　　　　　　　　　70
Lie on this bed, and rest yourself awhile.
　　K. Edw. These looks of thine can harbor
　　naught but death.
I see my tragedy written in thy brows.
Yet stay awhile; forbear thy bloody hand,
And let me see the stroke before it comes,
That [47] even then when I shall lose my life,
My mind may be more steadfast on my God.
　　Light. What means your Highness to mis-
　　trust me thus?
　　K. Edw. What means thou to dissemble
　　with me thus?
　　Light. These hands were never stain'd with
　　innocent blood,　　　　　　　　　80
Nor shall they now be tainted with a king's.
　　K. Edw. Forgive my thought for having
　　such a thought.
One jewel have I left; receive thou this. —
Still fear I, and I know not what's the cause,
But every joint shakes as I give it thee.
O, if thou harbor'st murder in thy heart,
Let this gift change thy mind, and save thy
　soul.
Know that I am a king; O, at that name
I feel a hell of grief.　Where is my crown?
Gone, gone! and do I remain alive?　　90
　　Light. You're overwatch'd,[48] my Lord;
　　lie down and rest.
　　K. Edw. But that grief keeps me waking,
　　I should sleep;
For not these ten days have these eyelids
　clos'd.
Now as I speak they fall, and yet with fear
Open again.　O wherefore sits thou here?
　　Light. If you mistrust me, I'll be gone, my
　　Lord.
　　K. Edw. No, no; for if thou mean'st to
　　murder me,
Thou wilt return again; and therefore stay.
　　Light. He sleeps.
　　K. Edw. [*waking*] O let me not die yet!
　　Stay, O stay awhile!　　　　　　100
　　Light. How now, my Lord?
　　K. Edw. Something still buzzeth in mine
　　ears,
And tells me if I sleep I never wake;
This fear is that which makes me tremble thus.
And therefore tell me, wherefore art thou
　come?

　　Light. To rid thee of thy life. — Matrevis,
　　come!

[*Enter* Matrevis *and* Gurney.]

　　K. Edw. I am too weak and feeble to resist.
Assist me, sweet God, and receive my soul.
　　Light. Run for the table.
　　K. Edw. O spare me, or despatch me in a
　　trice. [Matrevis *brings in a table.*] 110
　　Light. So; lay the table down, and stamp
　　on it,
But not too hard, lest that you bruise his body.
　　[King Edward *is murdered, shrieking.*]
　　Mat. I fear me that this cry will raise the
　　town;
And therefore let us take horse and away.
　　Light. Tell me, sirs, was it not bravely [49]
　　done?
　　Gur. Excellent well; take this for thy
　　reward.
　　Then Gurney *stabs* Lightborn, [*who dies*].
Come, let us cast the body in the moat,
And bear the King's to Mortimer, our Lord;
Away!　　　　　　　　*Exeunt omnes.*

[Scene VI] [50]

Enter [Young] Mortimer *and* Matrevis.

　　Y. Mor. Is't done, Matrevis, and the mur-
　　derer dead?
　　Mat. Ay, my good Lord; I would it were
　　undone!
　　Y. Mor. Matrevis, if thou now growest
　　penitent
I'll be thy ghostly father; therefore choose
Whether thou wilt be secret in this
Or else die by the hand of Mortimer.
　　Mat. Gurney, my Lord, is fled, and will, I
　　fear,
Betray us both; therefore let me fly.
　　Y. Mor. Fly to the savages!
　　Mat.　　　　I humbly thank your Honor.
　　　　　　　　　　　　[*Exit.*]
　　Y. Mor. As for myself, I stand as Jove's
　　huge tree,[51]　　　　　　　　　　10
And others are but shrubs compar'd to me.
All tremble at my name, and I fear none;
Let's see who dare impeach me for his death!

Enter the Queen.

　　Q. Isab. Ah, Mortimer, the King, my son,
　　hath news
His father's dead, and we have murdered him!

---

[47] Old eds. *that and.*　　　[48] Wearied by waking.
[49] Finely.
[50] Unlocated; presumably a room in the Palace at
Westminster.　　　　　　　　　[51] The oak.

Y. Mor. What if he have? The King is yet a child.

Q. Isab. Ay, ay, but he tears his hair, and wrings his hands,

And vows to be reveng'd upon us both.
Into the council chamber he is gone,
To crave the aid and succor of his peers.   20
Ay, me! see here he comes, and they with him;
Now, Mortimer, begins our tragedy.

Enter the King [Edward the Third], *with the* Lords [*and* Attendants].

[1 *Lord*].[52] Fear not, my Lord; know that you are a king.

K. Edw. Third. Villain!

Y. Mor. How now, my Lord!

K. Edw. Third. Think not that I am frighted with thy words!

My father's murdered through thy treachery;
And thou shalt die, and on his mournful hearse [53]
Thy hateful and accursed head shall lie,
To witness to the world that by thy means
His kingly body was too soon interr'd.   31

Q. Isab. Weep not, sweet Son!

K. Edw. Third. Forbid me not to weep; he was my father;

And, had you lov'd him half so well as I,
You could not bear his death thus patiently.
But you, I fear, conspir'd with Mortimer.

1 Lord. Why speak you not unto my Lord the King?

Y. Mor. Because I think scorn to be accus'd.

Who is the man dare say I murdered him?

K. Edw. Third. Traitor! in me my loving father speaks,   40

And plainly saith 't was thou that murd'redst him.

Y. Mor. But has your Grace no other proof than this?

K. Edw. Third. Yes, if this be the hand of Mortimer.   [*Showing letter.*]

Y. Mor. [*aside to the* Queen] False Gurney hath betray'd me and himself.

Q. Isab. [*aside*] I fear'd as much; murder cannot be hid.

Y. Mor. 'T is my hand; what gather you by this?

K. Edw. Third. That thither thou didst send a murderer.

Y. Mor. What murderer? Bring forth the man I sent.

K. Edw. Third. Ah, Mortimer, thou knowest that he is slain;

And so shalt thou be too. — Why stays he here?   50

Bring him unto a hurdle, drag him forth;
Hang him, I say, and set his quarters up;
But bring his head back presently to me.

Q. Isab. For my sake, sweet son, pity Mortimer.

Y. Mor. Madam, entreat not; I will rather die

Than sue for life unto a paltry boy.

K. Edw. Third. Hence with the traitor, with the murderer!

Y. Mor. Base Fortune, now I see that in thy wheel

There is a point, to which when men aspire,
They tumble headlong down; that point I touch'd,   60
And, seeing there was no place to mount up higher,
Why should I grieve at my declining fall? —
Farewell, fair Queen; weep not for Mortimer,
That scorns the world, and, as a traveller,
Goes to discover countries yet unknown.

K. Edw. Third. What! suffer you the traitor to delay?

[*Young* Mortimer *is taken away by* 1 Lord *and* Attendants.]

Q. Isab. As thou received'st thy life from me,

Spill not the blood of gentle Mortimer!

K. Edw. Third. This argues that you spilt my father's blood;

Else would you not entreat for Mortimer.   70

Q. Isab. I spill his blood? No!

K. Edw. Third. Ay, madam, you; for so the rumor runs.

Q. Isab. That rumor is untrue; for loving thee,

Is this report rais'd on poor Isabel.

K. Edw. Third. I do not think her so unnatural.

[2 Lord.] [54] My Lord, I fear me it will prove too true.

K. Edw. Third. Mother, you are suspected for his death,

And therefore we commit you to the Tower
Till further trial may be made thereof;
If you be guilty, though I be your son,   80
Think not to find me slack or pitiful.

Q. Isab. Nay, to my death, for too long have I liv'd

Whenas my son thinks to abridge my days.

[52] Old eds. *Lords*, throughout. Speech-tags for Edward III *King*, throughout.   [53] Coffin.

[54] See on l. 23.

K. Edw. Third. Away with her ; her words enforce these tears,
And I shall pity her if she speak again.

Q. Isab. Shall I not mourn for my beloved Lord,
And with the rest accompany him to his grave?

2 Lord. Thus, madam, 't is the King's will you shall hence.

Q. Isab. He hath forgotten me ; stay, I am his mother.

2 Lord. That boots not ; therefore, gentle madam, go. 90

Q. Isab. Then come, sweet death, and rid me of this grief. [*Exit, guarded.*]

[*Re-enter* 1 Lord, *with the head of* Young Mortimer.]

1 Lord. My Lord, here is the head of Mortimer.

K. Edw. Third. Go fetch my father's hearse, where it shall lie ;
And bring my funeral robes. —

[*Exeunt* Attendants.]
Accursed head,
Could I have rul'd thee then, as I do now,
Thou hadst not hatch'd this monstrous treachery ! —
Here comes the hearse ; help me to mourn, my Lords. —

[*Re-enter* Attendants *with the hearse and funeral robes.*]

Sweet father, here unto thy murdered ghost
I offer up this wicked traitor's head ;
And let these tears, distilling from mine eyes, 100
Be witness of my grief and innocency.
[*Exeunt.*]

ENDIMION,

The Man in the
Moone.

Playd before the Queenes Maieſtie at Greenewich on Candlemas day
at night, by the Chyldren of
Paules.

AT LONDON,
Printed by I. Charlewood, for
the widdowe Broome.
1591.

INTRODUCTORY NOTE

ACCORDING to the title page of the earliest edition (1591), *Endymion* was "Playd before the Queenes Maiestie at Greenewich on Candlemas day at night, by the Chyldren of Paules." Nothing further is known of its stage history, if it had any; and speculation regarding the date of its composition and first performance has ranged from 1579 to 1588. Sir Edmund Chambers (*Elizabethan Stage*, III, 415) follows Fleay in favoring 1588, on the ground that only in that year have we any records that point to a Candlemas performance at Greenwich by the Paul's boys. Bond thinks the play was written about the middle of Lyly's dramatic career.

Nothing could be more sharply in contrast with the robust drama of Marlowe than this bloodless and overliterary play. Had the Jacobean masters followed the lead of the early court playwrights instead of cultivating the coarser but livelier entertainments of the popular theatres, the greatest triumphs of the greatest age of English drama would never have been achieved. None the less, Lyly exercised a salutary and civilizing influence on Shakespeare and his colleagues. It was not instruction in the human heart they needed so much as the example of a considered style. The drama of passion might be powerful, but it was too often crude and flamboyant. If Lyly's writing is precious in its euphuism and anaemic in its avoidance of strong emotion, it is a virtuoso prose, and the delicacy of its flavor is not without a certain charm. Prattled by little boys it was probably more amusing to a fastidious audience, unused to grace in the theatre, than it seems to us, who expect it.

Aside from the classical myth of Endymion's sleep and the kiss of Cynthia, no source is known for Lyly's play; but elaborate attempts have been made to read an allegory into it. The Queen's relations with Robert Dudley, Earl of Leicester, and her rivalry with Mary Stuart (Tellus), have been suggested; James VI of Scotland has been proposed for Endymion instead of Leicester; and even minor characters have been variously identified as the Earl of Shrewsbury (Geron) and his Countess (Dipsas), Sir Philip Sidney or the Earl of Sussex (Eumenides), Stephen Gosson or Gabriel Harvey (Sir Tophas), and Penelope Devereux or Frances Sidney (Semele), to mention only a few. A contrast between heavenly and earthly love has also been offered as the key to the play. But recent opinion, while not challenging the obvious references to Elizabeth, nor denying the presence of topical allusions, is sceptical of the proposed allegories. (See P. W. Long's articles, *Publications of the Modern Language Association of America*, XXIV, 164–184, and *Modern Philology*, VIII, 599–605.)

It seems probable that the play was produced at court with a multiple stage setting; whether or not they were physically represented, the vicinity of the palace, the lunary bank, the fountain, and the castle in the desert are all supposed to occupy various parts of the stage simultaneously and continuously.

The standard edition of Lyly's Works is that of R. W. Bond (1902). *Endymion* was separately edited by G. P. Baker (1894). It originally appeared, without Lyly's name, in quarto, in 1591. In 1632 it was republished as the first of *Sixe Court Comedies. Often Presented and Acted before Queene Elizabeth, by the Children of her Maiesties Chapell, and the Children of Paules. Written By the only Rare Poet of that Time The Wittie, Comicall, Facetiously-Quicke and vnparalelled: Iohn Lilly, Master of Arts.* The publisher was Edward Blount. The second edition corrects some errors and introduces others. It also supplies the texts of the songs, the ascription of which to Lyly has been questioned, and has been defended by Bond. (For bibliography of the controversy see his articles, *Review of English Studies*, VI, 295–299; VII, 442–447.) The present text is based on the Quarto, with the additions, and a few corrections, from the Blount edition.

ENDYMION,

THE MAN IN THE MOON

BY

JOHN LYLY

[DRAMATIS PERSONAE

ENDYMION, in love with Cynthia.
EUMENIDES, his friend, in love with Semele.
CORSITES, a captain, in love with Tellus.
PANELION, }
ZONTES, } lords of Cynthia's court.
PYTHAGORAS, a Greek philosopher.
GYPTES, an Egyptian soothsayer.
GERON, an old man, husband to Dipsas.
SIR TOPHAS, a braggart.
DARES, page to Endymion.
SAMIAS, page to Eumenides.
EPITON, page to Sir Tophas.

Master Constable.
First Watchman.
Second Watchman.

CYNTHIA, the Queen.
TELLUS, in love with Endymion.
FLOSCULA, her friend.
SEMELE, loved by Eumenides.
SCINTILLA, }
FAVILLA, } maids in waiting at court.
DIPSAS, an old enchantress.
BAGOA, her servant.

Fairies; Three Ladies and an Old Man in the Dumb Show.]

THE PROLOGUE

MOST high and happy Princess, we must tell you a tale of the Man in the Moon, which, if it seem ridiculous for the method, or superfluous for the matter, or for the means incredible, for three faults we can make but one excuse: it is a tale of the Man in the Moon.[1]

It was forbidden in old time to dispute of Chimæra because it was a fiction; we hope in our times none will apply pastimes,[2] because they are fancies; for there liveth none under the sun that knows what to make of the Man in the Moon. We present neither comedy, nor tragedy, nor story, nor anything but that whosoever heareth may say this: Why, here is a tale of the Man in the Moon.

ACT I — SCENE I[3]

[Enter] ENDYMION *[and]* EUMENIDES.

ENDYMION. I find, Eumenides, in all things both variety to content, and satiety to glut, saving only in my affections, which are so staid, and withal so stately, that I can neither satisfy my heart with love, nor mine eyes with wonder. My thoughts, Eumenides, are stitched to the stars, which being as high as I can see, thou mayst imagine how much higher they are than I can reach.

EUM. If you be enamored of anything [10 above the moon, your thoughts are ridiculous, for that things immortal are not subject to affections; if allured or enchanted with these transitory things under the moon, you show yourself senseless to attribute such lofty titles to such [low][4] trifles.

END. My love is placed neither under the moon nor above.

EUM. I hope you be not sotted[5] upon the Man in the Moon. 20

END. No; but settled either to die or possess the moon herself.

EUM. Is Endymion mad, or do I mistake? Do you love the moon, Endymion?

[1] *I.e.*, a fantasy.
[2] Make (political, topical, or personal) applications of this (our play, which is merely) sport.
[3] Unlocated. Bond: "Gardens of Cynthia's palace."
[4] Emend. Bond; old eds. *loue*.
[5] Besotted, infatuated.

145

END. Eumenides, the moon.

EUM. There was never any so peevish [6] to imagine the moon either capable of affection or shape of a mistress; for as impossible it is to make love fit to her humor, which no man knoweth, as a coat to her form, which [30] continueth not in one bigness whilst she is measuring. Cease off, Endymion, to feed so much upon fancies. That melancholy blood must be purged which draweth you to a dotage no less miserable than monstrous.

END. My thoughts have no veins, and yet unless they be let blood, I shall perish.

EUM. But they have vanities, which being reformed, you may be restored.

END. O fair Cynthia, why do others [40] term thee unconstant whom I have ever found unmovable? Injurious time, corrupt manners, unkind men, who, finding a constancy not to be matched in my sweet mistress, have christ-'ned her with the name of wavering, waxing, and waning! Is she inconstant that keepeth a settled course; which, since her first crea-tion, altereth not one minute in her moving? There is nothing thought more admirable or commendable in the sea than the ebbing [50] and flowing; and shall the moon, from whom the sea taketh this virtue, be accounted fickle for increasing and decreasing? Flowers in their buds are nothing worth till they be blown, nor blossoms accounted till they be ripe fruit; and shall we then say they be changeable for that they grow from seeds to leaves, from leaves to buds, from buds to their perfection? Then, why be not twigs that become trees, children that become men, and mornings [60] that grow to evenings, termed wavering, for that they continue not at one stay? Ay, but Cynthia, being in her fullness, decayeth, as not delighting in her greatest beauty, or with-ering when she should be most honored. When malice cannot object anything, folly will, making that a vice which is the greatest virtue. What thing (my mistress excepted), being in the pride of her beauty and latter minute of her age, that waxeth young [70] again? Tell me, Eumenides, what is he that having a mistress of ripe years and infinite vir-tues, great honors and unspeakable beauty, but would wish that she might grow tender again, getting youth by years, and never-decaying beauty by time; whose fair face neither the summer's blaze can scorch, nor winter's blast chap, nor the numb'ring of

[6] Silly.

years breed altering of colors? Such is my sweet Cynthia, whom time cannot touch [80] because she is divine, nor will offend because she is delicate. O Cynthia, if thou shouldest always continue at thy fullness, both gods and men would conspire to ravish thee. But thou, to abate the pride of our affections, dost detract from thy perfections, thinking it suf-ficient if once in a month we enjoy a glimpse of thy majesty; and then, to increase our griefs, thou dost decrease thy gleams, coming out of thy royal robes, wherewith thou daz- [90] zlest our eyes, down into thy swathe clouts [7] beguiling our eyes; and then —

EUM. Stay there, Endymion; thou that committest idolatry wilt straight blaspheme, if thou be suffered. Sleep would do thee more good than speech; the moon heareth thee not, or, if she do, regardeth thee not.

END. Vain Eumenides, whose thoughts never grow higher than the crown of thy head! Why troublest thou me, having neither [100] head to conceive the cause of my love or a heart to receive the impressions? Follow thou thine own fortunes, which creep on the earth, and suffer me to fly to mine, whose fall, though it be desperate, yet shall it come by daring. Farewell.   *[Exit.]*

EUM. Without doubt Endymion is be-witched; otherwise in a man of such rare vir-tues there could not harbor a mind of such extreme madness. I will follow him, lest [110] in this fancy of the moon he deprive himself of the sight of the sun.   *Exit.*

SCENE II [8]

[Enter] TELLUS [9] *[and]* FLOSCULA.

TELLUS. Treacherous and most perjur'd Endymion, is Cynthia the sweetness of thy life and the bitterness of my death? What revenge may be devised so full of shame as my thoughts are replenished with [10] malice? Tell me, Floscula, if falseness in love can possibly be punished with extremity of hate? As long as sword, fire, or poison may be hired, no trai-tor to my love shall live unrevenged. Were thy oaths without number, thy kisses [10] without measure, thy sighs without end, forged to deceive a poor credulous virgin, whose sim-plicity had been worth thy favor and better

[7] *I.e.*, back to thy infancy.
[8] Unlocated; presumably the same.
[9] Goddess of the Earth in the Roman mythology.
[10] Full of.

fortune? If the gods sit unequal [11] beholders of injuries, or laughers at lovers' deceits, then let mischief be as well forgiven in women as perjury winked at in men.

FLOSC. Madam, if you would compare the state [12] of Cynthia with your own, and the height of Endymion his thoughts with the [20 meanness of your fortune, you would rather yield than contend, being between you and her no comparison; and rather wonder than rage at the greatness of his mind, being affected with a thing more than mortal.

TELLUS. No comparison, Floscula? And why so? Is not my beauty divine, whose body is decked with fair flowers, and veins are vines, yielding sweet liquor to the dullest sp[i]rits; whose ears are corn, to bring strength; and [30 whose hairs are grass, to bring abundance? Doth not frankincense and myrrh breathe out of my nostrils, and all the sacrifice of the gods breed in my bowels? Infinite are my creatures, without which neither thou, nor Endymion, nor any, could love or live.

FLOSC. But know you not, fair lady, that Cynthia governeth all things? Your grapes would be but dry husks, your corn but chaff, and all your virtues vain, were it not Cyn- [40 thia that preserveth the one in the bud and nourisheth the other in the blade, and by her influence both comforteth all things, and by her authority commandeth all creatures. Suffer, then, Endymion to follow his affections, though to obtain her be impossible; and let him flatter himself in his own imaginations, because they are immortal.

TELLUS. Loath I am, Endymion, thou shouldest die, because I love thee well; [50 and that thou shouldest live, it grieveth me, because thou lovest Cynthia too well. In these extremities, what shall I do? Floscula, no more words; I am resolved. He shall neither live nor die.

FLOSC. A strange practice,[13] if it be possible.

TELLUS. Yes. I will entangle him in such a sweet net that he shall neither find the means to come out, nor desire it. All allurements of pleasure will I cast before his eyes, inso- [60 much that he shall slake that love which he now voweth to Cynthia, and burn in mine, of which he seemeth careless. In this languishing, between my amorous devices and his own loose desires, there shall such dissolute thoughts take root in his head, and over his

heart grow so thick a skin, that neither hope of preferment, nor fear of punishment, nor counsel of the wisest, nor company of the worthiest, shall alter his humor, nor make [70 him once to think of his honor.

FLOSC. A revenge incredible, and, if it may be, unnatural.

TELLUS. He shall know the malice of a woman to have neither mean nor end; and of a woman deluded in love to have neither rule nor reason. I can do it; I must; I will! All his virtues will I shadow with vices; his person (ah, sweet person!) shall he deck with such rich robes as he shall forget it is [80 his own person; his sharp wit (ah, wit too sharp that hath cut off all my joys!) shall he use in flattering of my face and devising sonnets in my favor. The prime of his youth and pride of his time shall be spent in melancholy passions, careless behavior, untamed thoughts, and unbridled affections.

FLOSC. When this is done, what then? Shall it continue till his death, or shall he dote forever in this delight? 90

TELLUS. Ah, Floscula, thou rendest my heart in sunder in putting me in remembrance of the end.

FLOSC. Why, if this be not the end, all the rest is to no end.

TELLUS. Yet suffer me to imitate Juno, who would turn Jupiter's lovers to beasts on the earth, though she knew afterwards they should be stars in heaven.

FLOSC. Affection that is bred by en- [100 chantment is like a flower that is wrought in silk: in color and form most like, but nothing at all in substance or savor.

TELLUS. It shall suffice me if the world talk that I am favored of Endymion.

FLOSC. Well, use your own will; but you shall find that love gotten with witchcraft is as unpleasant as fish taken with medicines [14] unwholesome.

TELLUS. Floscula, they that be so poor [110 that they have neither net nor hook will rather poison dough than pine with hunger; and she that is so oppress'd with love that she is neither able with beauty nor wit to obtain her friend,[15] will rather use unlawful means than try [16] untolerable pains. I will do it. *Exit.*

FLOSC. Then about it. Poor Endymion, what traps are laid for thee because thou honorest one that all the world wond'reth at!

[11] Partial, inequitable.
[12] Rank.   [13] Plot.

[14] Drugs; *i.e.*, poisoned dough.
[15] Lover.   [16] Undergo.

And what plots are cast to make thee [120 unfortunate that studiest of all men to be the faithfulest !   *Exit.*

SCENE III [17]

[Enter] DARES *[and]* SAMIAS.

DARES. Now our masters are in love up to the ears, what have we to do but to be in knavery up to the crowns?

SAMIAS. Oh, that we had Sir Tophas, that brave squire, in the midst of our mirth — *et ecce autem*, " Will you see the Devil? "

Enter SIR TOPHAS *[and* EPITON*].*

TOP. Epi !

EPI. Here, sir.

TOP. I brook not this idle humor of love ; it tickleth not my liver, from whence the [10 lovemongers in former age seemed to infer they should proceed.

EPI. Love, sir, may lie in your lungs ; and I think it doth, and that is the cause you blow and are so pursy.

TOP. Tush, boy, I think it [18] but some device of the poet to get money.

EPI. A poet? What's that?

TOP. Dost thou not know what a poet is?

EPI. No.   20

TOP. Why, fool, a poet is as much as one should say — a poet. But soft, yonder be two wrens ; shall I shoot at them?

EPI. They are two lads.

TOP. Larks or wrens, I will kill them.

EPI. Larks ! Are you blind? They are two little boys.

TOP. Birds or boys, they are both but a pittance for my breakfast ; therefore have at them, for their brains must as it were em- [30 broider my bolts.[19]

SAM. Stay your courage, valiant knight, for your wisdom is so weary that it stayeth itself.

DAR. Why, Sir Tophas, have you forgotten your old friends?

TOP. Friends? *Nego argumentum.*

SAM. And why not friends?

TOP. Because *amicitia* (as in old [annals] [20] we find) is *inter pares*. Now, my pretty companions, you shall see how unequal you be [40 to me ; but I will not cut you quite off, you shall be my half-friends for reaching to my middle ; so far as from the ground to the waist I will be your friend.

DAR. Learnedly. But what shall become of the rest of your body, from the waist to the crown?

TOP. My children, *quod supra vos nihil ad vos ;* you must think the rest immortal, because you cannot reach it.   50

EPI. Nay, I tell ye my master is more than a man.

DAR. And thou less than a mouse.

TOP. But what be you two?

SAM. I am Samias, page to [Eumenides].[21]

DAR. And I Dares, page to [Endymion].

TOP. Of what occupation [22] are your masters?

DAR. Occupation, you clown ! Why, they are honorable and warriors.   60

TOP. Then are they my prentices.

DAR. Thine ! And why so?

TOP. I was the first that ever devised war, and therefore by Mars himself given me for my arms a whole armory ; and thus I go, as you see, clothed with artillery. It is not silks — milksops — nor tissues, nor the fine wool of [Seres],[23] but iron, steel, swords, flame, shot, terror, clamor, blood, and ruin, that rocks asleep my thoughts, which never had any [70 other cradle but cruelty. Let me see, do you not bleed?

DAR. Why so?

TOP. Commonly my words wound.

SAM. What then do your blows?

TOP. Not only [wound],[24] but also confound.

SAM. How dar'st thou come so near thy master, Epi? Sir Tophas, spare us.

TOP. You shall live : you, Samias, because you are little ; you, Dares, because you are [80 no bigger ; and both of you, because you are but two ; for commonly I kill by the dozen, and have for every particular adversary a peculiar weapon.

SAM. May we know the use, for our better skill in war?

TOP. You shall. Here is a bird-bolt [25] for the ugly beast the blackbird.

DAR. A cruel sight.

TOP. Here is the musket for the un- [90 tamed or, as the vulgar sort term it, the wild mallard.

SAM. O desperate attempt !

EPI. Nay, my master will match them.

---

[17] Unlocated ; presumably the same.
[18] Love.
[19] Blunt arrows.   [20] So Blount ; Q *Annuals.*

[21] Cor. Bond ; old eds. transpose the names.   See IV, ii, 1, 2.   [22] Trade, craft.
[23] Emend. Bond ; old eds. *Ceres.*   See Virgil, *Georgics,* II, 121.
[24] Cor. Fairholt ; old eds. *confound.*
[25] So Blount ; Q *burbolt.*

DAR. [*aside*] Ay, if he catch them.

TOP. Here is a spear and shield, and both necessary, the one to conquer, the other to subdue or overcome the terrible trout, which although he be under the water, yet tying a string to the top of my spear and an engine [100 of iron to the end of my line, I overthrow him, and then herein I put him.

SAM. O wonderful war! — [*aside*] Dares, didst thou ever hear such a dolt?

DAR. [*aside*] All the better; we shall have good sport hereafter, if we can get leisure.

SAM. [*aside*] Leisure! I will rather lose my master's service than his company! Look how he strouts.[26] — But what is this? Call you it your sword? 110

TOP. No, it is my scimitar; which I, by construction often studying to be compendious, call my smiter.

DAR. What, are you also learned, sir?

TOP. Learned? I am all Mars and Ars.

SAM. Nay, you are all mass and ass.

TOP. Mock you me? You shall both suffer, yet with such weapons as you shall make choice of the weapon wherewith you shall perish. Am I all a mass or lump; is there [120 no proportion in me? Am I all ass; is there no wit in me? Epi, prepare them to the slaughter.

SAM. I pray, sir, hear us speak! We call you mass, which your learning doth well understand is all man, for *mas, maris* is a man. Then *as* (as you know) is a weight, and we for your virtues account you a weight.

TOP. The Latin hath saved your lives, the which a world of silver could not have [130 ransom'd. I understand you, and pardon you.

DAR. Well, Sir Tophas, we bid you farewell, and at our next meeting we will be ready to do you service.

TOP. Samias, I thank you; Dares, I thank you; but especially I thank you both.

SAM. [*aside*] Wisely. Come, next time we'll have some pretty gentlewomen with us to walk, for without doubt with them he will be very dainty. 140

DAR. Come, let us see what our masters do; it is high time. *Exeunt* [SAMIAS *and* DARES].

TOP. Now will I march into the field, where, if I cannot encounter with my foul enemies, I will withdraw myself to the river, and there fortify for fish, for there resteth no minute free from fight.

Exit [Sir TOPHAS *with* EPITON].

[26] Swells, puffs up.

SCENE IV [27]

[*Enter at one side*] TELLUS [*and*] FLOSCULA, [*at the other*] DIPSAS.

TELLUS. Behold, Floscula, we have met with the woman by chance that we sought for by travail. I will break my mind to her without ceremony or circumstance, lest we lose that time in advice that should be spent in execution.

FLOSC. Use your discretion; I will in this case neither give counsel nor consent, for there cannot be a thing more monstrous than to force affection by sorcery, neither do I [10 imagine anything more impossible.

TELLUS. Tush, Floscula, in obtaining of love, what impossibilities will I not try? And for the winning of Endymion, what impieties will I not practise? — Dipsas, whom as many honor for age as wonder at for cunning, listen in few words to my tale, and answer in one word to the purpose, for that neither my burning desire can afford long speech, nor the short time I have to stay many delays. Is [20 it possible by herbs, stones, spells, incantation, enchantment, exorcisms, fire, metals, planets, or any practice, to plant affection where it is not, and to supplant it where it is?

DIPSAS. Fair lady, you may imagine that these hoary hairs are not void of experience, nor the great name that goeth of my cunning to be without cause. I can darken the sun by my skill and remove the moon out of her course; I can restore youth to the aged [30 and make hills without bottoms. There is nothing that I cannot do but that only which you would have me do; and therein I differ from the gods, that I am not able to rule hearts; for were it in my power to place affection by appointment, I would make such evil appetites, such inordinate lusts, such cursed desires, as all the world should be filled both with superstitious heats and extreme love.

TELLUS. Unhappy Tellus, whose de- [40 sires are so desperate that they are neither to be conceived of any creature, nor to be cured by any art!

DIPSAS. This I can: breed slackness in love, though never root it out. What is he whom you love, and what she that he honoreth?

TELLUS. Endymion, sweet Endymion is he that hath my heart; and Cynthia, too, too fair Cynthia, the miracle of nature, of time, of fortune, is the lady that he delights in, [50

[27] Unlocated.

and dotes on every day, and dies for ten thousand times a day.

DIPSAS. Would you have his love either by absence or sickness aslaked? [28] Would you that Cynthia should mistrust him, or be jealous of him without color? [29]

TELLUS. It is the only thing I crave, that, seeing my love to Endymion, unspotted, cannot be accepted, his truth to Cynthia, though it be unspeakable, may be suspected.   60

DIPSAS. I will undertake it, and overtake [30] him, that [31] all his love shall be doubted of, and therefore become desperate ; but this will wear out with time, that treadeth all things down but truth.

TELLUS. Let us go.

DIPSAS. I follow.   *Exeunt.*

ACT II — SCENE I [1]

[Enter] ENDYMION.

END. O fair Cynthia ! O unfortunate Endymion ! Why was not thy birth as high as thy thoughts, or her beauty less than heavenly ; or why are not thine honors as rare as her beauty or thy fortunes as great as thy deserts? Sweet Cynthia, how wouldst thou be pleased, how possessed? Will labors, patient of all extremities, obtain thy love? There is no mountain so steep that I will not climb, no monster so cruel that I will not tame, no [10 action so desperate that I will not attempt. Desirest thou the passions of love, the sad and melancholy moods of perplexed minds, the not-to-be-expressed torments of racked thoughts? Behold my sad tears, my deep sighs, my hollow eyes, my broken sleeps, my heavy countenance. Wouldst thou have me vow'd only to thy beauty and consume every minute of time in thy service? Remember my solitary life almost these seven years. [20 Whom have I entertained but mine own thoughts and thy virtues? What company have I used but contemplation? Whom have I wond'red at but thee? Nay, whom have I not contemned for thee? Have I not crept to those on whom I might have trodden, only because thou didst shine upon them? Have not injuries been sweet to me, if thou vouchsafest I should bear them? Have I not spent my

golden years in hopes, waxing old with [30 wishing, yet wishing nothing but thy love? With Tellus, fair Tellus, have I dissembled, using her but as a cloak for mine affections ; that others, seeing my mangled and disordered mind, might think it were for one that loveth me, not for Cynthia, whose perfection alloweth no companion nor comparison. In the midst of these distemp'red thoughts of mine thou art not only jealous of my truth, but careless, suspicious, and secure ; which strange [40 humor maketh my mind as desperate as thy conceits are doubtful. I am none of those wolves that bark most when thou shinest brightest, but that fish (thy fish, Cynthia, in the flood [Araris])[2] which at thy waxing is as white as the driven snow, and at thy waning as black as deepest darkness. I am that Endymion, sweet Cynthia, that have carried my thoughts in equal balance with my actions, being always as free from imagining ill as [50 enterprising ; [3] that Endymion whose eyes never esteemed anything fair but thy face, whose tongue termed nothing rare but thy virtues, and whose heart imagined nothing miraculous but thy government ; yea, that Endymion who, divorcing himself from the amiableness of all ladies, the bravery [4] of all courts, the company of all men, hath chosen in a solitary cell to live only by feeding on thy favor, accounting in the world — but thyself — [60 nothing excellent, nothing immortal : thus mayst thou see every vein, sinew, muscle, and artery of my love, in which there is no flattery, nor deceit, error, nor art. But soft, here cometh Tellus. I must turn my other face to her, like Janus, lest she be as suspicious as Juno.

Enter TELLUS, [FLOSCULA, *and* DIPSAS].

TELLUS. Yonder I espy Endymion. I will seem to suspect nothing, but soothe him, that, seeing I cannot obtain the depth of his [70 love, I may learn the height of his dissembling. Floscula and Dipsas, withdraw yourselves out of our sight, yet be within the hearing of our saluting. — How now, Endymion, always solitary? No company but your own thoughts, no friend but melancholy fancies?

END. You know, fair Tellus, that the sweet remembrance of your love is the only com-

---

[28] Abated.   [30] Overcome.
[29] Excuse.   [31] So that.
[1] Unlocated ; presumably the same as I, i.

[2] Old eds. *Aranis:* cor. Baker, who cites " the fish Scolopidus in the floud Araris." (*Euphues,* ed. Bond, I, 232.) See *i Tamburlaine,* II, i, 63, and note.
[3] From undertaking [evil].
[4] Splendor.

panion of my life, and thy presence, my paradise ; so that I am not alone when nobody [80 is with me, and in Heaven itself when thou art with me.

TELLUS. Then you love me, Endymion?

END. Or else I live not, Tellus.

TELLUS. Is it not possible for you, Endymion to dissemble?

END. Not, Tellus, unless I could make me a woman.

TELLUS. Why, is dissembling joined to their sex inseparable, as heat to fire, heaviness [90 to earth, moisture to water, thinness to air?

END. No, but found in their sex as common as spots upon doves, moles upon faces, caterpillars upon sweet apples, cobwebs upon fair windows.

TELLUS. Do they all dissemble?

END. All but one.

TELLUS. Who is that?

END. I dare not tell ; for if I should say you, then would you imagine my flattery [100 to be extreme ; if another, then would you think my love to be but indifferent.

TELLUS. You will be sure I shall take no vantage of your words. But, in sooth, Endymion, without more ceremonies, is it not Cynthia?

END. You know, Tellus, that of the gods we are forbidden to dispute, because their deities come not within the compass of our reasons ; and of Cynthia we are allowed [110 not to talk but to wonder, because her virtues are not within the reach of our capacities.

TELLUS. Why, she is but a woman.

END. No more was Venus.

TELLUS. She is but a virgin.

END. No more was Vesta.

TELLUS. She shall have an end.

END. So shall the world.

TELLUS. Is not her beauty subject to time?

END. No more than time is to standing still.

TELLUS. Wilt thou make her immortal?

END. No, but incomparable.   122

TELLUS. Take heed, Endymion, lest like the wrastler in Olympia, that striving to lift an impossible weight catch'd an incurable strain, thou, by fixing thy thoughts above thy reach, fall into a disease without all recure ! But I see thou art now in love with Cynthia.

END. No, Tellus ; thou knowest that the stately cedar, whose top reacheth unto [130 the clouds, never boweth his head to the shrubs that grow in the valley ; nor ivy, that climbeth up by the elm, can ever get hold of

the beams of the sun. Cynthia I honor in all humility, whom none ought or dare adventure to love, whose affections are immortal, and virtues infinite. Suffer me, therefore, to gaze on the moon, at whom, were it not for thyself, I would die with wondering.   *Exeunt.*

SCENE II [5]

[Enter] DARES, SAMIAS, SCINTILLA, *[and]* FAVILLA.

DAR. Come, Samias, diddest thou ever hear such a sighing, the one for Cynthia, the other for Semele, and both for moonshine in the water?

SAM. Let them sigh, and let us sing. How say you, gentlewomen ; are not our masters too far in love?

SCINT. Their tongues, happily,[6] are dipp'd to the root in amorous words and sweet discourses, but I think their hearts are scarce [10 tipp'd on the side [7] with constant desires.

DAR. How say you, Favilla, is not love a lurcher,[8] that taketh men's stomachs [9] away that [10] they cannot eat, their spleen that they cannot laugh, their hearts that they cannot fight, their eyes that they cannot sleep, and leaveth nothing but livers to make nothing but lovers?

FAVIL. Away, peevish boy ; a rod were better under thy girdle than love in thy [20 mouth ! It will be a forward cock that croweth in the shell.

DAR. Alas, good old gentlewoman, how it becometh you to be grave !

SCINT. Favilla, though she be but a spark, yet is she fire.

FAVIL. And you, Scintilla, be not much more than a spark, though you would be esteemed a flame.

SAM. *[aside to* DARES] It were good sport [30 to see the fight between two sparks.

DAR. *[aside to* SAMIAS] Let them to it, and we will warm us by their words.

SCINT. You are not angry, Favilla?

FAVIL. That is, Scintilla, as you list to take it.

SAM. That, that ! [11]

SCINT. This it is to be matched with girls, who coming but yesterday from making of

---

[5] Unlocated ; presumably the same.
[6] Haply.
[7] *I.e.*, even slightly touched.
[8] Lurker, thief.   [9] Appetites.
[10] So that.   [11] A cry of encouragement

babies,[12] would before to-morrow be ac- [40 counted matrons.

FAVIL. I cry your Matronship mercy. Because your pantables [13] be higher with cork, therefore your feet must needs be higher in the insteps. You will be mine elder because you stand upon a stool and I on the floor.

SAM. Good, good!

DAR. [*aside to* SAMIAS] Let them alone, and see with what countenance they will become friends. 50

SCINT. Nay, you think to be the wiser, because you mean to have the last word.

SAM. [*aside to* DARES] Step between them lest they scratch. — In faith, gentlewomen, seeing we came out to be merry, let not your jarring mar our jests; be friends. How say you?

SCINT. I am not angry, but it spited me to see how short [14] she was.

FAVIL. I meant nothing till she would [60 needs cross me.

DAR. Then, so let it rest.

SCINT. I am agreed.

FAVIL. And I. Yet I never took anything so unkindly in my life. [*Weeps.*]

SCINT. 'T is I have the cause, that never offered the occasion. [*Weeps.*]

DAR. Excellent, and right like a woman.

SAM. A strange sight to see water come out of fire. 70

DAR. It is their property to carry in their eyes fire and water, tears and torches, and in their mouths honey and gall.

SCINT. You will be a good one if you live. But what is yonder formal fellow?

Enter Sir TOPHAS [*and* EPITON].

DAR. Sir Tophas, Sir Tophas, of whom we told you. If you be good wenches, make as though you love him, and wonder at him.

FAVIL. We will do our parts.

DAR. But first let us stand aside, and [80 let him use his garb,[15] for all consisteth in his gracing. [*The four retire.*]

TOP. Epi!

EPI. At hand, sir.

TOP. How likest thou this martial life, where nothing but blood besprinkleth our bosoms? Let me see, be our enemies [16] fat?

EPI. Passing fat; and I would not change this life to be a lord; and yourself passeth all comparison, for other captains kill and [90 beat, and there is nothing you kill but you also eat.

TOP. I will draw out their guts out of their bellies, and tear the flesh with my teeth, so mortal is my hate and so eager my unstaunched stomach.

EPI. [*aside*] My master thinks himself the valiantest man in the world if he kill a wren; so warlike a thing he accounteth to take away life, though it be from a lark. [100

TOP. Epi, I find my thoughts to swell and my spirit to take wings, insomuch that I cannot continue within the compass of so slender combats.

FAVIL. [*aside*] This passeth! [17]

SCINT. [*aside*] Why, is he not mad?

SAM. [*aside*] No, but a little vainglorious.

TOP. Epi!

EPI. Sir.

TOP. I will encounter that black and [110 cruel enemy that beareth rough and untewed [18] locks upon his body, whose sire throweth down the strongest walls, whose legs are as many as both ours, on whose head are placed most horrible horns by nature as a defence from all harms.

EPI. What mean you, master, to be so desperate?

TOP. Honor inciteth me, and very hunger compelleth me. 120

EPI. What is that monster?

TOP. The monster *Ovis*. I have said, — let thy wits work.

EPI. I cannot imagine it. Yet let me see — a black enemy with rough locks. It may be a sheep, and *Ovis* is a sheep. His sire so strong — a ram is a sheep's sire, that being also an engine of war. Horns he hath, and four legs — so hath a sheep. Without doubt, this monster is a black sheep. Is it not a [130 sheep that you mean?

TOP. Thou hast hit it; that monster will I kill and sup with.

SAM. [*aside*] Come let us take him off. [SAMIAS, DARES, FAVILLA, *and* SCINTILLA *come forward.*] Sir Tophas, all hail!

TOP. Welcome, children; I seldom cast mine eyes so low as to the crowns of your heads, and therefore pardon me that I spake not all this while. 139

---

[12] Dolls.
[13] Pantofles, slippers, embroidered shoes.
[14] Punning on the meanings "cross" and "short of stature."			[15] Show his style.
[16] Presumably the trout Epiton is carrying in the shield.

[17] Surpasses.
[18] Uncombed. (Webster.)

DAR. No harm done. Here be fair ladies come to wonder at your person, your valor, your wit, the report whereof hath made them careless of their own honors, to glut their eyes and hearts upon yours.

TOP. Report cannot but injure me, for that not knowing fully what I am, I fear she hath been a niggard in her praises.

SCINT. No, gentle knight, report hath been prodigal, for she hath left you no equal, nor herself credit, so much hath she told, yet [150 no more than we now see.

DAR. [*aside*] A good wench.

FAVIL. If there remain as much pity toward women as there is in you courage against your enemies, then shall we be happy, who, hearing of your person, came to see it, and seeing it are now in love with it.

TOP. Love me, ladies? I easily believe it, but my tough heart receiveth no impression with sweet words. Mars may pierce it ; [160 Venus shall not paint on it.

FAVIL. A cruel saying.

SAM. [*aside*] There's a girl.

DAR. Will you cast these ladies away, and all for a little love? Do but speak kindly.

TOP. There cometh no soft syllable within my lips ; custom hath made my words bloody and my heart barbarous. That pelting [19] word love, how wat'rish it is in my mouth ; it carrieth no sound. Hate, horror, [170 death, are speeches that nourish my spirits. I like honey, but I care not for the bees ; I delight in music, but I love not to play on the bagpipes ; I can vouchsafe to hear the voice of women, but to touch their bodies I disdain it as a thing childish and fit for such men as can digest nothing but milk.

SCINT. A hard heart! Shall we die for your love and find no remedy?

TOP. I have already taken a surfeit. 180

EPI. Good master, pity them.

TOP. Pity them, Epi? No, I do not think that this breast shall be pest'red with such a foolish passion. What is that the gentlewoman carrieth in a chain?

EPI. Why, it is a squirrel.

TOP. A squirrel? O gods, what things are made for money !

DAR. [*aside*] Is not this gentleman overwise? 190

FAVIL. [*aside*] I could stay all day with him, if I feared not to be shent.[20]

[19] Paltry.
[20] Disgraced (by laughing at him).

SCINT. [*aside*] Is it not possible to meet again?

DAR. [*aside*] Yes, at any time.

FAVIL. [*aside*] Then let us hasten home.

SCINT. Sir Tophas, the god of war deal better with you than you do with the god of love. 199

FAVIL. Our love we may dissemble, digest we cannot ; but I doubt not but time will hamper you and help us.

TOP. I defy time, who hath no interest in my heart. Come, Epi, let me to the battle with that hideous beast. Love is pap, and hath no relish in my taste because it is not terrible.

DAR. [*aside*] Indeed a black sheep is a perilous beast ; but let us in till another time.

FAVIL. [*aside*] I shall long for that time.

Exeunt.

SCENE III [21]

[*Enter*] ENDYMION ; DIPSAS [*and*] BAGOA [*in the background.*]

END. No rest, Endymion! Still uncertain how to settle thy steps by day or thy thoughts by night ! Thy truth is measured by thy fortune, and thou art judged unfaithful because thou art unhappy. I will see if I can beguile myself with sleep, and if no slumber will take hold in my eyes, yet will I embrace the golden thoughts in my head, and wish to melt by musing ; that as ebony, which no fire can scorch, is yet consumed with sweet savors, [10 so my heart, which cannot be bent by the hardness of fortune, may be bruised by amorous desires. On yonder bank never grew anything but lunary,[22] and hereafter I will never have any bed but that bank. O Endymion, Tellus was fair. But what availeth beauty without wisdom? Nay, Endymion, she was wise. But what availeth wisdom without honor? She was honorable, Endymion ; belie her not. Ay, but how obscure is honor [20 without fortune. Was she not fortunate whom so many followed? Yes, yes, but base is fortune without majesty ; thy majesty, Cynthia, all the world knoweth and wondereth at, but not one in the world that can imitate it or comprehend it. No more, Endymion. Sleep or die. Nay, die ; for to sleep, it is impossible — and yet I know not how it

[21] A grove. The lunary bank was probably a curtained recess. Baker (followed by Neilson) brings Dipsas and Bagoa in after Endymion's speech. [22] Moonwort.

cometh to pass, I feel such a heaviness both in mine eyes and heart that I am sud- [30 denly benumbed, yea, in every joint. It may be weariness, for when did I rest? It may be deep melancholy, for when did I not sigh? Cynthia! Ay, so. — I say, Cynthia!

He falls asleep.

Dipsas [*advancing*] Little dost thou know, Endymion, when thou shalt wake; for hadst thou placed thy heart as low in love as thy head lieth now in sleep, thou mightest have commanded Tellus, whom now, instead of a mistress, thou shalt find a tomb. These [40 eyes must I seal up by art, not nature, which are to be opened neither by art nor nature. Thou that lay'st down with golden locks shalt not awake until they be turned to silver hairs; and that chin on which scarcely appeareth soft down shall be filled with bristles as hard as broom. Thou shalt sleep out thy youth and flow'ring time, and become dry hay before thou knewest thyself green grass; and ready by age to step into the grave when thou [50 wakest, that was youthful in the court when thou laid'st thee down to sleep. The malice of Tellus hath brought this to pass, which if she could not have entreated of me by fair means, she would have commanded by menacing, for from her gather we all our simples to maintain our sorceries. — [*to* Bagoa] Fan with this hemlock over his face, and sing the enchantment for sleep, whilst I go in and finish those ceremonies that are required in our [60 art. Take heed ye touch not his face, for the fan is so seasoned that whoso it toucheth with a leaf shall presently die, and over whom the wind of it breatheth, he shall sleep forever.

Bagoa. Let me alone; [23] I will be careful. [*Exit* Dipsas.] — What hap hadst thou, Endymion, to come under the hands of Dipsas? O fair Endymion, how it grieveth me that that fair face must be turned to a withered skin and taste the pains of death before it feel the [70 reward of love! I fear Tellus will repent that which the Heavens themselves seemed to rue. But I hear Dipsas coming! I dare not repine, lest she make me pine, and rock me into such a deep sleep that I shall not awake to my marriage.

Re-enter Dipsas.

Dipsas. How now, have you finished?

Bagoa. Yea.

Dipsas. Well then, let us in; and see that you do not so much as whisper that I did [80 this, for if you do, I will turn thy hairs to adders and all thy teeth in thy head to tongues. Come away, come away.

Exeunt [Dipsas *and* Bagoa].

A DUMB SHOW [24]

Music sounds. Three ladies enter: one with a knife and a looking-glass, who, by the procurement of one of the other two, offers to stab Endymion as he sleeps; but the third wrings her hands, lamenteth, offering still to prevent it, but dares not. At last, the first lady, looking in the glass, casts down the knife. Exeunt.

Enters an ancient man with books with three leaves; offers the same twice. Endymion refuseth. He rendeth [25] two, and offers the third, where he stands awhile; and then Endymion offers to take it. Exit [*the Old Man*].

ACT III — Scene I [26]

[*Enter*] Cynthia, Tellus, [Semele, Eumenides, Corsites, Panelion, *and* Zontes].

Cynthia. Is the report true, that Endymion is stricken into such a dead sleep that nothing can either wake him or move him?

Eum. Too true, madam, and as much to be pitied as wondered at.

Tellus. As good sleep and do no harm as wake and do no good.

Cynth. What maketh you, Tellus, to be so short? The time was Endymion only was.

Eum. It is an old saying, madam, that [10 a waking dog doth afar off bark at a sleeping lion.

Sem. It were good, Eumenides, that you took a nap with your friend, for your speech beginneth to be heavy.

Eum. Contrary to your nature, Semele, which hath been always accounted light.

Cynth. What, have we here before my face these unseemly and malapert overthwarts? [27] I will tame your tongues and your [20 thoughts, and make your speeches answerable

---

[23] Leave it to me. The song (see l. 58) has been lost.

[24] Om. Q, but appears in Blount. It represents Endymion's dream.

[25] Cor. Dilke; Blount *readeth*. This feature of the dumb show is "adapted from the fable of Tarquin and the Sibyl, related by Aulus Gellius (*Noctes Atticae*, I, xix)." (Bond.)

[26] Unlocated; presumably the same as I, i. Instead of the entrance direction Q has *Cynthia, three lordes, Tellus.*

[27] Impertinent wranglings. (Fairholt.)

to your duties, and your conceits fit for my dignity, else will I banish you both my person and the world.

EUM. Pardon, I humbly ask; but such is my unspotted faith to Endymion that whatsoever seemeth a needle to prick his finger is a dagger to wound my heart.

CYNTH. If you be so dear to him, how happeneth it you neither go to see him, nor [30 search for remedy for him?

EUM. I have seen him to my grief, and sought recure with despair, for that I cannot imagine who should restore him that is the wonder to all men. Your Highness, on whose hands the compass of the earth is at command, though not in possession, may show yourself both worthy your sex, your nature, and your favor, if you redeem that honorable Endymion, whose ripe years foretell rare [40 virtues, and whose unmellowed conceits promise ripe counsel.

CYNTH. I have had trial of Endymion, and conceive greater assurance of his age than I could hope of his youth.

TELLUS. But timely, madam, crooks that tree that will be a cammock,[28] and young it pricks that will be a thorn; and therefore he that began without care to settle his life, it is a sign without amendment he will end it. [50

CYNTH. Presumptuous girl, I will make thy tongue an example of unrecoverable displeasure. — Corsites, carry her to the castle in the desert, there to remain and weave.

CORS. Shall she work stories or poetries?

CYNTH. It skilleth[29] not which. Go to, in both; for she shall find examples infinite in either what punishment long tongues have. Eumenides, if either the soothsayers in Egypt, or the enchanters in Thessaly, or the phi- [60 losophers in Greece, or all the sages of the world can find remedy, I will procure it; therefore, dispatch with all speed: you, Eumenides, into Thessaly; you, Zontes, into Greece, because you are acquainted in Athens; you, Pan[e]llion, to Egypt; saying that Cynthia sendeth, and, if you will, commandeth.

EUM. On bowed knee I give thanks, and with wings on my legs, I fly for remedy.

ZON. We are ready at your Highness' [70 command, and hope to return to your full content.

CYNTH. It shall never be said that Cynthia, whose mercy and goodness filleth the Heavens with joys and the world with

marvels, will suffer either Endymion or any to perish, if he may be protected.

EUM. Your Majesty's words have been always deeds, and your deeds virtues. *Exeunt.*

SCENE II [30]

[Enter] CORSITES *[and]* TELLUS.

CORS. Here is the castle, fair Tellus, in which you must weave, till either time end your days, or Cynthia her displeasure. I am sorry so fair a face should be subject to so hard a fortune, and that the flower of beauty, which is honored in courts, should here wither in prison.

TELLUS. Corsites, Cynthia may restrain the liberty of my body, of my thoughts she cannot; and therefore do I esteem myself [10 most free, though I am in greatest bondage.

CORS. Can you then feed on fancy, and subdue the malice of envy by the sweetness of imagination?

TELLUS. Corsites, there is no sweeter music to the miserable than despair; and therefore the more bitterness I feel, the more sweetness I find; for so vain were liberty, and so unwelcome the following of higher fortune, that I choose rather to pine in this castle than to [20 be a prince in any other court.

CORS. A humor contrary to your years and nothing agreeable to your sex; the one commonly allured with delights, the other always with sovereignty.

TELLUS. I marvel, Corsites, that you being a captain, who should sound nothing but terror and suck nothing but blood, can find in your heart to talk such smooth words, for that it agreeth not with your calling to use words [30 so soft as that of love.

CORS. Lady, it were unfit of wars to discourse with women, into whose minds nothing can sink but smoothness; besides, you must not think that soldiers be so rough-hewn, or of such knotty mettle, that beauty cannot allure, and you, being beyond perfection, enchant.

TELLUS. Good Corsites, talk not of love, but let me to my labor. The little beauty I have shall be bestowed on my loom, which [40 I now mean to make my lover.

CORS. Let us in; and what favor Corsites can show, Tellus shall command.

TELLUS. The only favor I desire is now and then to walk. *Exeunt.*

---

[28] A crooked one.   [29] Matters.

[30] Before a castle.

SCENE III [31]

[*Enter*] Sir TOPHAS *and* EPITON.

TOPHAS. Epi!

EPI. Here, sir.

TOPHAS. Unrig me. Heigho!

EPI. What's that?

TOPHAS. An interjection, whereof some are of mourning; as, *eho, vah.*[32]

EPI. I understand you not.

TOPHAS. Thou seest me.

EPI. Ay.

TOPHAS. Thou hear'st me.   10

EPI. Ay.

TOPHAS. Thou feelest me.

EPI. Ay.

TOPHAS. And not understand'st me?

EPI. No.

TOPHAS. Then am I but three-quarters of a noun substantive. But alas, Epi, to tell thee the troth, I am a noun adjective.

EPI. Why?

TOPHAS. Because I cannot stand with- [20 out another.

EPI. Who is that?

TOPHAS. Dipsas.

EPI. Are you in love?

TOPHAS. No; but love hath, as it were, milk'd my thoughts and drained from my heart the very substance of my accustomed courage; it worketh in my head like new wine, so as I must hoop my sconce with iron, lest my head break, and so I bewray [33] my [30 brains. But, I pray thee, first discover [34] me in all parts, that I may be like a lover, and then will I sigh and die. Take my gun and give me a gown: *C[e]dant arma togæ.*[35]

EPI. Here.

TOPHAS. Take my sword and shield and give me beard-brush and scissors: *Bella gerant alii, tu Pari semper ama.*[36]

EPI. Will you be trimm'd, sir?

TOPHAS. Not yet; for I feel a conten- [40 tion within me whether I shall frame the bodkin beard or the bush. But take my pike and give me pen: *Dicere quæ puduit, scribere jussit amor.*[37]

EPI. I will furnish you, sir.

TOPHAS. Now, for my bow and bolts give me ink and paper, for my smiter a pen-knife; for

Scalpellum, calami, atramentum, charta, libelli,
Sint semper studiis arma parata meis.[38]   50

EPI. Sir, will you give over wars and play with that bauble called love?

TOPHAS. Give over wars? No, Epi, *Militat omnis amans, et habet sua cast[r]a Cupido.*[39]

EPI. Love hath made you very eloquent, but your face is nothing fair.

TOPHAS. *Non formosus erat, sed erat facundus Ulysses.*[40]

EPI. Nay, I must seek a new master if [60 you can speak nothing but verses.

TOPHAS. *Quicquid conabar dicere, versus erat.*[41] Epi, I feel all Ovid *De Arte Amandi* lie as heavy at my heart as a load of logs. Oh, what a fine, thin hair hath Dipsas! What a pretty low forehead! What a tall [42] and stately nose! What little hollow eyes! What great and goodly lips! How harmless she is, being toothless; her fingers fat and short, adorned with long nails like a bitter[n]! [70 In how sweet a proportion her cheeks hang down to her breasts like dugs and her paps to her waist like bags! What a low stature she is, and yet what a great foot she carrieth! How thrifty must she be in whom there is no waist! How virtuous is she like to be, over whom no man can be jealous!

EPI. Stay, master, you forget yourself.

TOPHAS. O Epi, even as a dish melteth by the fire, so doth my wit increase by love. [80

EPI. Pithily, and to the purpose! But what, begin you to nod?

TOPHAS. Good Epi, let me take a nap; for as some man may better steal a horse than another look over the hedge, so divers shall be sleepy when they would fainest take rest.

He sleeps.

EPI. Who ever saw such a woodcock? [43] Love Dipsas! Without doubt all the world

---

[31] Unlocated; presumably the same as I, i.

[32] These and the following allusions are to the Latin Grammar of William Lilly.

[33] Expose.

[34] Uncover, undress; *i.e.*, disarrange my apparel.

[35] Let arms give way to the toga (the garb of peace). (Cicero, *De Officiis,* I, xxii, 76.)

[36] Let others war; thou, Paris, ever love. (Adapted from Ovid, *Heroides,* xvii, 254. Cf. xiii, 84.)

[37] Love bade me write those things I shamed to speak. (Ovid, *Heroides,* iv, 10.)

[38] These two lines seem to be of Lyly's composition. (Bond.) They may be translated:

May knife, reeds, ink, books, paper, ever be
A ready armament for studious me.

[39] Every lover's in the army, and Cupid has his camp. (Ovid, *Amores,* I, ix, 1.)

[40] Not handsome, but eloquent was Ulysses. (Ovid, *Ars Amatoria,* ii, 123.)

[41] Whatever I tried to say, it was verse. (Adapted from Ovid, *Tristia,* IV, x, 26.)

[42] Cor. Blount; Q *tale.*

[43] Simpleton.

will now account him valiant, that ventureth
on her whom none durst undertake. But [90
here cometh two wags.

Enter DARES *and* SAMIAS.

SAM. Thy master hath slept his share.

DAR. I think he doth it because he would
not pay me my board-wages.

SAM. It is a thing most strange; and I
think mine will never return, so that we must
both seek new masters, for we shall never live
by our manners.

EPI. If you want masters, join with me and
serve Sir Tophas, who must needs keep [100
more men, because he is toward marriage.

SAM. What, Epi, where's thy master?

EPI. Yonder, sleeping in love.

DAR. Is it possible?

EPI. He hath taken his thoughts a hole
lower,[44] and saith, seeing it is the fashion of
the world, he will vail [45] bonnet to beauty.

SAM. How is he attired?

EPI. Lovely.[46]

DAR. Whom loveth this amorous knight?

EPI. Dipsas.   111

SAM. That ugly creature? Why, she is
a fool, a scold, fat, without fashion, and
quite without favor.[47]

EPI. Tush, you be simple; my master hath
a good marriage.

DAR. Good! As how?

EPI. Why, in marrying Dipsas he shall have
every day twelve dishes of meat to his dinner,
though there be none but Dipsas with [120
him: four of flesh, four of fish, four of fruit.

SAM. As how, Epi?

EPI. For flesh these: woodcock, goose,
bitter[n], and rail.

DAR. Indeed, he shall not miss, if Dipsas be
there.

EPI. For fish these: crab, carp, lump, and
pouting.

SAM. Excellent, for of my word she is both
crabbish, lumpish, and carping.   130

EPI. For fruit these: fretters,[48] medlars,[49]

[44] Come down a peg.
[45] Doff.   [46] As a lover.   [47] Good looks.
[48] Blount *fritters*. *N. E. D.* conj. "a species of apple."
[49] Fruit resembling small apples; it rots prematurely. As Professor Kittredge observes, all these are puns, the viands being selected because their names are capable of meaning various kinds of annoyances. At every dinner Dipsas will be fretful and meddlesome, will choke his heart (make him heartsick), and will trouble him with her ladylike longings (with an illusion to the extravagant longings of pregnant women.)

hartichokes, and lady-longings. Thus you
see he shall fare like a king, though he be
but a beggar.

DAR. Well, Epi, dine thou with him, for I
had rather fast than see her face. But see,
thy master is asleep; let us have a song to
wake this amorous knight.

EPI. Agreed.

SAM. Content.   140

THE FIRST SONG [50]

EPI. Here snores Tophas,
That amorous ass,
Who loves Dipsas,
With face so sweet
Nose and chin meet.

ALL THREE. { At sight of her each Fury skips
{ And flings into her lap their whips.

DAR. Holla, holla in his ear.   148

SAM. The witch, sure, thrust her fingers there.

EPI. Cramp him, or wring the fool by th' nose;

DAR. Or clap some burning flax to his toes.

SAM. What music's best to wake him?

EPI. Baw-wow, let bandogs shake him!

DAR. Let adders hiss in's ear;

SAM. Else earwigs wriggle there.

EPI. No, let him batten; when his tongue
Once goes, a cat is not worse strung.

ALL THREE. { But if he ope nor mouth nor eyes,
{ He may in time sleep himself wise.

TOP. Sleep is a binding of the senses, love a
loosing.   161

EPI. [*aside*] Let us hear him awhile.

TOP. There appeared in my sleep a goodly
owl, who, sitting upon my shoulder, cried
" Twit, twit "; and before mine eyes presented herself the express image of Dipsas. I
marvelled what the owl said, till at the last
I perceived " Twit, twit," " To it, to it," only
by contraction admonished by this vision to
make account of my sweet Venus.   170

SAM. Sir Tophas, you have overslept yourself.

TOP. No, youth, I have but slept over
my love.

DAR. Love? Why, it is impossible that
into so noble and unconquered a courage love
should creep, having first a head as hard to
pierce as steel, then to pass to a heart arm'd
with a shirt of mail.   179

EPI. Ay, but my master yawning one day in
the sun, Love crept into his mouth before he
could close it, and there kept such a tumbling
in his body that he was glad to untruss the
points [51] of his heart and entertain Love as
a stranger.

TOP. If there remain any pity in you, plead
for me to Dipsas.

[50] Q merely notes *Song*. The text is added by Blount.
[51] Untie the lacings.

Dar. Plead! Nay, we will press her to it. — [*aside to* Samias] Let us go with him to [189 Dipsas, and there shall we have good sport. — But, Sir Tophas, when shall we go? For I find my tongue voluble, and my heart venturous, and all myself like myself.

Sam. [*aside to* Dares] Come, Dares, let us not lose him until we find our masters, for as long as he liveth, we shall lack neither mirth nor meat.

Epi. We will [traverse].[52] Will you go, sir?

Top. *I præ; sequar.*[53]   *Exeunt.* [200

Scene IV [54]

[*Enter*] Eumenides [*and*] Geron.

Eum. Father, your sad music [55] being tuned on the same key that my hard fortune is, hath so melted my mind that I wish to hang at your mouth's end till my life end.

Ger. These tunes, gentleman, have I been accustomed with these fifty winters, having no other house to shroud myself but the broad heavens; and so familiar with me hath use made misery that I esteem sorrow my chiefest solace, and welcomest is that guest to me [10 that can rehearse the saddest tale or the bloodiest tragedy.

Eum. A strange humor.[56] Might I inquire the cause?

Ger. You must pardon me if I deny to tell it, for knowing that the revealing of griefs is, as it were, a renewing of sorrow, I have vowed therefore to conceal them, that I might not only feel the depth of everlasting discontentment, but despair of remedy. But whence [20 are you? What fortune hath thrust you to this distress?

Eum. I am going to Thessaly, to seek remedy for Endymion, my dearest friend, who hath been cast into a dead sleep almost these twenty years, waxing old and ready for the grave, being almost but newly come forth of the cradle.

Ger. You need not for recure travel far, for whoso can clearly see the bottom of this [30 fountain shall have remedy for anything.

52 March. Emend. Baker; old eds. *trauice.*
53 Go ahead; I 'll follow. (Terence, *Andria*, I, i, 144.)
54 At a fountain. According to l. 258 it is at some distance from Cynthia's court; but according to IV, ii, 90, it is "hard by" the lunary bank, which is not far from the court.
55 Evidently another song has been lost.
56 Disposition, whim.

Eum. That methinketh is unpossible. Why, what virtue can there be in water?

Ger. Yes, whosoever can shed the tears of a faithful lover shall obtain anything he would. Read these words engraven about the brim.

Eum. Have you known this by experience, or is it placed here of purpose to delude men?

Ger. I only would have experience of it, and then should there be an end of my [40 misery; and then would I tell the strangest discourse that ever yet was heard.

Eum. Ah, Eumenides!

Ger. What lack you, gentleman; are you not well?

Eum. Yes, father, but a qualm that often cometh over my heart doth now take hold of me. But did never any lovers come hither?

Ger. Lusters, but not lovers; for often have I seen them weep, but never could I [50 hear they saw the bottom.

Eum. Came there women also?

Ger. Some.

Eum. What did they see?

Ger. They all wept, that the fountain overflowed with tears; but so thick became the water with their tears that I could scarce discern the brim, much less behold the bottom.

Eum. Be faithful lovers so scant?

Ger. It seemeth so, for yet heard I [60 never of any.

Eum. Ah, Eumenides, how art thou perplexed! Call to mind the beauty of thy sweet mistress and the depth of thy never-dying affections. How oft hast thou honored her, not only without spot, but suspicion of falsehood! And how hardly hath she rewarded thee without cause or color [57] of despite. How secret hast thou been these seven years, that hast not, nor once darest not to name her, [70 for discontenting her. How faithful, that hast offered to die for her, to please her! Unhappy Eumenides!

Ger. Why, gentleman, did you once love?

Eum. Once! Ay, father, and ever shall.

Ger. Was she unkind and you faithful?

Eum. She of all women the most froward, and I of all creatures the most fond.

Ger. You doted then, not loved; for affection is grounded on virtue, and virtue is [80 never peevish; or on beauty, and beauty loveth to be praised.

Eum. Ay, but if all virtuous ladies should yield to all that be loving, or all amiable gentlewomen entertain all that be amorous, their

57 Pretext.

virtues would be accounted vices and their beauties deformities; for that love can be but between two, and that not proceeding of him that is most faithful but most fortunate.

GER. I would you were so faithful that [90 your tears might make you fortunate.

EUM. Yea, father, if that my tears clear not this fountain, then may you swear it is but a mere mockery.

GER. So saith every one yet that wept.

EUM. Ah, I faint, I die! Ah, sweet Semele, let me alone, and dissolve,[58] by weeping, into water.   [*He gazes into the fountain.*]

GER. This affection seemeth strange; if he see nothing, without doubt this dissem- [100 bling passeth,[59] for nothing shall draw me from the belief.

EUM. Father, I plainly see the bottom, and there in white marble engraven these words: "Ask one for all, and but one thing at all."

GER. O fortunate Eumenides (for so have I heard thee call thyself), let me see. I cannot discern any such thing. I think thou dream-est.

EUM. Ah, father, thou art not a faithful [110 lover, and therefore canst not behold it.

GER. Then ask, that I may be satisfied by the event, and thyself blessed.

EUM. Ask? So I will. And what shall I do but ask, and whom should I ask but Semele, the possessing of whose person is a pleasure that cannot come within the compass of comparison; whose golden locks seem most curious when they seem most careless; whose sweet looks seem most alluring when they [120 are most chaste; and whose words the more virtuous they are, the more amorous they be accounted? I pray thee, Fortune, when I shall first meet with fair Semele, dash my delight with some light disgrace, lest embracing sweetness beyond measure, I take a surfeit without recure. Let her practise her accustomed coyness, that I may diet myself upon my desires; otherwise, the fulness of my joys will diminish the sweetness, and I shall [130 perish by them before I possess them.

Why do I trifle the time in words? The least minute being spent in the getting of Semele is more worth than the whole world; therefore let me ask. — What now, Eumenides! Whither art thou drawn? Hast thou forgotten both friendship and duty, care of Endymion, and the commandment of Cynthia? Shall he die in a leaden sleep be-

cause thou sleepest in a golden dream? — [140 Ay, let him sleep ever, so I slumber but one minute with Semele. Love knoweth neither friendship nor kindred. Shall I not hazard the loss of a friend for the obtaining of her for whom I would often lose myself? — Fond [60] Eumenides, shall the enticing beauty of a most disdainful lady be of more force than the rare fidelity of a tried friend? The love of men to women is a thing common and of course; the friendship of man to man in- [150 finite and immortal. — Tush! Semele doth possess my love. — Ay, but Endymion hath deserved it. I will help Endymion. I found Endymion unspotted in his truth. — Ay, but I shall find Semele constant in her love. I will have Semele. — What shall I do? Father, thy gray hairs are ambassadors of experience. Which shall I ask?

GER. Eumenides, release Endymion, for all things, friendship excepted, are subject [160 to fortune: love is but an eye-worm, which only tickleth the head with hopes and wishes; friendship the image of eternity, in which there is nothing movable, nothing mischievous. As much difference as there is between beauty and virtue, bodies and shadows, colors and life, so great odds is there between love and friendship.

Love is a chameleon, which draweth nothing into the mouth but air, and nourisheth [170 nothing in the body but lungs. Believe me, Eumenides, desire dies in the same moment that beauty sickens, and beauty fadeth in the same instant that it flourisheth. When adversities flow, then love ebbs; but friendship standeth stiffly in storms. Time draweth wrinkles in a fair face, but addeth fresh colors to a fast friend, which neither heat, nor cold, nor misery, nor place, nor destiny, can alter or diminish. O friendship! of all things [180 the most rare, and therefore most rare because most excellent, whose comforts in misery is always sweet, and whose counsels in prosperity are ever fortunate! Vain love, that, only coming near to friendship in name, would seem to be the same or better in nature!

EUM. Father, I allow your reasons, and will therefore conquer mine own. Virtue shall subdue affections, wisdom lust, friendship beauty. Mistresses are in every place, [190 and as common as hares in Atho[s], bees in Hybla, fowls in the air; but friends to be found are like the phœnix in Arabia, but one;

---

[58] Let me dissolve.   [59] Surpasses.   [60] Foolish.

or the philadelphi in Arays,[61] never above two. I will have Endymion. Sacred fountain, in whose bowels are hidden divine secrets, I have increased your waters with the tears of unspotted thoughts, and therefore let me receive the reward you promise. Endymion, the truest friend to me, and faithfullest [200 lover to Cynthia, is in such a dead sleep that nothing can wake or move him.

GER. Dost thou see anything?

EUM. I see in the same pillar these words : "When she whose figure of all is the perfectest, and never to be measured; always one, yet never the same; still inconstant, yet never wavering; shall come and kiss Endymion in his sleep, he shall then rise; else never." This is strange.   210

GER. What see you else?

EUM. There cometh over mine eyes either a dark mist, or upon the fountain a deep thickness, for I can perceive nothing. But how am I deluded, or what difficult, nay impossible, thing is this?

GER. Methinketh it easy.

EUM. Good father, and how?

GER. Is not a circle of all figures the perfectest?   220

EUM. Yes.

GER. And is not Cynthia of all circles the most absolute?

EUM. Yes.

GER. Is it not impossible to measure her, who still worketh by her influence, never standing at one stay?

EUM. Yes.

GER. Is she not always Cynthia, yet seldom in the same bigness ; always wavering in [230 her waxing or waning, that our bodies might the better be governed, our seasons the dailier give their increase ; yet never to be removed from her course, as long as the heavens continue theirs?

EUM. Yes.

GER. Then who can it be but Cynthia, whose virtues being all divine must needs bring things to pass that be miraculous? Go, humble thyself to Cynthia ; tell her the [240 success,[62] of which myself shall be a witness. And this assure thyself, that she that sent to find means for his safety will now work her cunning.

---

[61] Possibly, as Peck suggests (cited by Baker), for the Spanish *Aranjuez*, famous for its gardens; and the plant may be the mock-orange (*philadelphus hirsutus*), the flowers of which grow usually in pairs.

[62] Sequel, outcome.

EUM. How fortunate am I, if Cynthia be she that may do it !

GER. How fond art thou, if thou do not believe it !

EUM. I will hasten thither that I may entreat on my knees for succor, and embrace in mine arms my friend.   251

GER. I will go with thee, for unto Cynthia must I discover all my sorrows, who also must work in me a contentment.

EUM. May I now know the cause?

GER. That shall be as we walk, and I doubt not but the strangeness of my tale will take away the tediousness of our journey.

EUM. Let us go.   259

GER. I follow.   *Exeunt.*

ACT IV — SCENE I [1]

[Enter] TELLUS.

TELLUS. I marvel Corsites giveth me so much liberty — all the world knowing his charge to be so high and his nature to be most strange, — who hath so ill entreated ladies of great honor that he hath not suffered them to look out of windows, much less to walk abroad. It may be he is in love with me, for, Endymion, hardhearted Endymion, excepted, what is he that is not enamor'd of my beauty? But what respectest thou the love of all the world? [10 Endymion hates thee. Alas, poor Endymion, my malice hath exceeded my love, and thy faith to Cynthia quenched my affections. Quenched, Tellus? Nay, kindled them afresh ; insomuch that I find scorching flames for dead embers, and cruel encounters of war in my thoughts instead of sweet parleys. Ah, that I might once again see Endymion ! Accursed girl, what hope hast thou to see Endymion, on whose head already are grown gray [20 hairs, and whose life must yield to nature, before Cynthia end her displeasure? Wicked Dipsas, and most devilish Tellus, the one for cunning too exquisite, the other for hate too intolerable ! Thou wast commanded to weave the stories and poetries wherein were showed both examples and punishments of tattling tongues, and thou hast only embroidered the sweet face of Endymion, devices of love, melancholy imaginations, and what not, out [30 of thy work, that thou shouldst study to pick out of thy mind. But here cometh Corsites.

---

[1] Before Corsites's castle.

I must seem yielding, and stout ; full of mildness, yet tempered with a majesty ; for if I be too flexible, I shall give him more hope than I mean ; if too froward, enjoy less liberty than I would. Love him I cannot, and therefore will practise that which is most contrary [2] to our sex, to dissemble.

Enter CORSITES.

COR. Fair Tellus, I perceive you rise [40 with the lark, and to yourself sing with the nightingale.

TELLUS. My Lord, I have no playfellow but fancy ; being barred of all company, I must question [3] with myself, and make my thoughts my friends.

COR. I would you would account my thoughts also your friends, for they be such as are only busied in wondering at your beauty and wisdom ; and some such as [50 have esteemed your fortune too hard ; and divers of that kind that offer to set you free, if you will set them free.

TELLUS. There are no colors so contrary as white and black, nor elements so disagreeing as fire and water, nor anything so opposite as men's thoughts and their words.

COR. He [4] that gave Cassandra the gift of prophesying, with the curse that, spake she never so true, she should never be believed, [60 hath I think poisoned the fortune of men, that, uttering the extremities of their inward passions, are always suspected of outward perjuries.

TELLUS. Well, Corsites, I will flatter myself and believe you. What would you do to enjoy my love?

COR. Set all the ladies of the castle free, and make you the pleasure of my life ; more I cannot do, less I will not.   70

TELLUS. These be great words, and fit your calling ; for captains must promise things impossible. But will you do one thing for all?

COR. Anything, sweet Tellus, that am ready for all.

TELLUS. You know that on the lunary bank sleepeth Endymion.

COR. I know it.

TELLUS. If you will remove him from that place by force, and convey him into some [80 obscure cave by policy, I give you here the faith of an unspotted virgin that you only shall possess me as a lover, and in spite of malice have me for a wife.

COR. Remove him, Tellus? Yes, Tellus, he shall be removed, and that so soon as [5] thou shalt as much commend my diligence as my force. I go.

TELLUS. Stay ; will yourself attempt it?

COR. Ay, Tellus ; as I would have none [90 partaker of my sweet love, so shall none be partners of my labors. But I pray thee go at your best leisure, for Cynthia beginneth to rise, and if she discover our love, we both perish ; for nothing pleaseth her but the fairness of virginity. All things must be not only without lust but without suspicion of lightness.

TELLUS. I will depart, and go you to Endymion.

COR. I fly, Tellus, being of all men the [100 most fortunate.   *Exit.*

TELLUS. Simple Corsites, I have set thee about a task, being but a man, that the gods themselves cannot perform ; for little dost thou know how heavy his head lies, how hard his fortune ; but such shifts must women have to deceive men, and under color of things easy entreat that which is impossible ; otherwise we should be cumb'red with importunities, oaths, sighs, letters, and all implements of love, [110 which to one resolved to the contrary are most loathsome. I will in, and laugh with the other ladies at Corsites' sweating.   *Exit.*

SCENE II [6]

[Enter] SAMIAS *and* DARES.

SAM. Will thy master never awake?

DAR. No ; I think he sleeps for a wager. But how shall we spend the time? Sir Tophas is so far in love that he pineth in his bed and cometh not abroad.

SAM. But here cometh Epi in a pelting chafe.[7]

[Enter EPITON.]

EPI. A pox of all false proverbs, and were a proverb a page, I would have him by the ears !

SAM. Why art thou angry?   10

EPI. Why? You know it is said, " The tide tarrieth no man."

---

[2] Bond unnecessarily emends to *customary*, which spoils the joke.
[3] Converse.
[4] The Thymbraean Apollo ; the curse was added in consequence of her resistance to his desires. (Bond.)

[5] That.
[6] Near the lunary bank.
[7] Petty rage ; *i.e.*, the anger of a diminutive person.

Sam. True.

Epi. A monstrous lie; for I was tied two hours, and tarried for one to unloose me.

Dar. Alas, poor Epi!

Epi. Poor! No, no, you base-conceited [8] slaves; I am a most complete gentleman, although I be in disgrace with Sir Tophas.

Dar. Art thou out with him? 20

Epi. Ay, because I cannot get him a lodging with Endymion. He would fain take a nap for forty or fifty years.

Dar. A short sleep, considering our long life.

Sam. Is he still in love?

Epi. In love? Why he doth nothing but make sonnets.

Sam. Canst thou remember any one of his poems? 30

Epi. Ay, this is one: —

> The beggar, Love, that knows not where to lodge,
> At last within my heart, when I slept,
> He crept,
> I wak'd, and so my fancies began to fodge.[9]

Sam. That's a very long verse.

Epi. Why, the other was short. The first is called from the thumb to the little finger; the second from the little finger to the elbow; and some he hath made to reach to the [40] crown of his head, and down again to the sole of his foot. It is set to the tune of the black Saunce;[10] *ratio est*, because Dipsas is a black saint.

Dar. Very wisely. But pray thee, Epi, how art thou complete; and being from thy master, what occupation wilt thou take?

Epi. [Know],[11] my hearts, I am an absolute *microcosmus*, a petty world of myself: my library is my head, for I have no other [50] books but my brains; my wardrobe on my back, for I have no more apparel than is on my body; my armory at my fingers' ends, for I use no other artillery than my nails;[12] my treasure in my purse. *Sic omnia mea mecum porto.*[13]

Dar. Good!

Epi. [Know],[14] sirs, my palace is pav'd with grass, and tiled with stars; for *C[œ]lo tegitur*

qui non habet urnam,[15] — he that hath no [60] house must lie in the yard.

Sam. A brave resolution! But how wilt thou spend thy time?

Epi. Not in any melancholy sort; for mine exercise I will walk horses.

Dar. Too bad!

Epi. Why, is it not said, "It is good walking when one hath his horse in his hand"?

Sam. Worse and worse! But how wilt thou live? 70

Epi. By angling. Oh, 't is a stately occupation to stand four hours in a cold morning, and to have his nose bitten with frost before his bait be mumbled with a fish.

Dar. A rare attempt! But wilt thou never travel?

Epi. Yes, in a western barge,[16] when with a good wind and lusty pugs,[17] one may go ten miles in two days.

Sam. Thou art excellent at thy choice. [80] But what pastime wilt thou use? None?

Epi. Yes, the quickest of all.

Sam. What, dice?

Epi. No, when I am in haste, one-and-twenty[18] games at chess, to pass a few minutes.

Dar. A life for a little lord, and full of quickness.

Epi. Tush, let me alone! But I must needs see if I can find where Endymion lieth, and then go to a certain fountain hard by, [90] where they say faithful lovers shall have all things they will ask. If I can find out any of these, *Ego et magister meus erimus in tuto:* I and my master shall be friends. He is resolved to weep some three or four pailfuls to avoid the rheum of love that wambleth [19] in his stomach.

Enter [Master Constable *and two of*] *the Watch.*

Sam. Shall we never see thy master, Dares?

Dar. Yes; let us go now, for to-morrow Cynthia will be there. 100

Epi. I will go with you. But how shall we see for the Watch?

Sam. Tush, let me alone! I'll begin to them. — Masters, God speed you.

1 Watch. Sir boy, we are all sped already.

Epi. [*aside*] So, methinks; for they smell all of drink, like a beggar's beard.

---

[8] Low-minded.
[9] Fadge, thrive.
[10] Black Sanctus, a burlesque hymn to St. Satan.
[11] Emend. Baker; old eds. *No.*
[12] "Perhaps alluding to the boys' trick of flipping small objects." (Bond.)
[13] Thus all that's mine I carry round with me. (Adapted from a quotation ascribed to Bias by Cicero, *Paradoxa Stoicorum*, I, i.) (Baker.)
[14] Emend. Baker; old eds. *Now.*

[15] Prince, if your noble ashes lack an urn,
The sheltering sky will have to serve your turn. (Lucan, vii, 819.)
[16] On the Thames.   [17] Bargemen.
[18] So Blount; Q xxj.   [19] Rumbles.

DAR. But I pray, sirs, may we see Endymion?

2 WATCH. No, we are commanded in [110 Cynthia's name, that no man shall see him.

SAM. No man! Why, we are but boys.

1 WATCH. Mass, neighbors, he says true; for if I swear I will never drink my liquor by the quart, and yet call for two pints, I think with a safe conscience I may carouse both.

DAR. Pithily, and to the purpose.

2 WATCH. Tush, tush, neighbors; take me with you.[20]

SAM. [*aside*] This will grow hot.   120

DAR. [*aside*] Let them alone.

2 WATCH. If I say to my wife, " Wife, I will have no raisins in my pudding," she puts in currants; small raisins are raisins, and boys are men; even as my wife should have put no raisins in my pudding, so shall there no boys see Endymion.

DAR. Learnedly.

EPI. Let Master Constable speak; I think he is the wisest among you.   130

MAST. CONST. You know, neighbors, 't is an old said saw, " Children and fools speak true."

ALL *say*. True.

MAST. CONST. Well, there you see the men be the fools, because it is provided from the children.[21]

DAR. Good.

MAST. CONST. Then, say I, neighbors, that children must not see Endymion, because children and fools speak true.   140

EPI. O wicked application!

SAM. Scurvily brought about!

1 WATCH. Nay, he says true, and therefore till Cynthia have been here, he shall not be uncovered. Therefore, away!

DAR. [*aside to* SAMIAS *and* EPITON] A watch, quoth you! A man may watch seven years for a wise word, and yet go without it. Their wits are all as rusty as their bills.[22] — But come on, Master Constable, shall we have [150 a song before we go?

MAST. CONST. With all my heart.

THE SECOND SONG [23]

WATCH. Stand![24] Who goes there?
We charge you appear

'Fore our constable here,
In the name of the Man in the Moon.
To us billmen relate
Why you stagger so late,
And how you come drunk so soon.
    PAGES. What are ye, scabs? [25]
    WATCH.   The Watch;   160
This the Constable.
    PAGES.   A patch.[26]
    CONST. Knock 'em down unless they all stand;
If any run away,
'T is the old watchman's play,
To reach him a bill of his hand.
    PAGES. O gentlemen, hold,
Your gowns freeze [27] with cold,
And your rotten teeth dance in your head;
    EPI. Wine nothing shall cost ye;
    SAM. Nor huge fires to roast ye;   170
    DARES. Then soberly let us be led.
    CONST. Come, my brown bills,[28] we 'll roar,[29]
Bounce loud at tavern door,
    OMNES. And i' th' morning steal all to bed.
                             Exeunt.

SCENE III [30]

CORSITES *solus*, [ENDYMION *asleep.*]

CORSITES. I am come in sight of the lunary bank. Without doubt Tellus doteth upon me; and cunningly, that I might not perceive her love, she hath set me to a task that is done before it is begun. Endymion, you must change your pillow; and if you be not weary of sleep, I will carry you where at ease you shall sleep your fill. It were good that without more ceremonies I took him, lest being espied, I be entrapp'd, and so incur the displeasure of [10 Cynthia, who commonly setteth watch that Endymion have no wrong. (*He lifts.*) What now, is your Mastership so heavy, or are you nail'd to the ground? Not stir one whit? Then use all thy force, though he feel it and wake. What, stone-still? Turn'd, I think, to earth with lying so long on the earth. Didst not thou, Corsites, before Cynthia, pull up a tree that forty years was fast'ned with roots and wreathed in knots to the ground? [20 Didst not thou, with main force, pull open the iron gates which no ram or engine could move? Have my weak thoughts made brawn-fallen [31] my strong arms, or is it the nature of love, or the quintessence of the mind, to breed numbness or litherness,[32] or I know not what lan-

[20] Let me understand you.
[21] *I.e.*, having said " true," they all come under the provisions of the saw, and the men are fools; but, since the conclusion that the boys are also fools is explicitly provided against (*from*) by the terms of the saw, their saying "true" does not make them fools.
[22] A kind of halbert.
[23] Q *Song;* the text first appears in Blount.
[24] Halt!

[25] Rascals.
[26] Fool.
[27] With a play on frieze, the material. (Schelling.)
[28] Billmen; their weapons were brown "either from rust, or because painted to keep them from it." (Bond.)
[29] Swagger, revel.
[30] At the lunary bank, till l. 54; then at Cynthia's court till l. 72; then *en route* till l. 95; then at the lunary bank, again.
[31] Unmuscular.   [32] Languor.

guishing in my joints and sinews, being but the base strings of my body? Or doth the remembrance of Tellus so refine my spirits into a matter so subtle and divine that the other [30 fleshy parts cannot work whilst they muse? Rest thyself, rest thyself; nay, rent thyself in pieces, Corsites, and strive, in spite of love, fortune, and nature, to lift up this dulled body, heavier than dead and more senseless than death.

Enter Fairies.

But what are these so fair fiends that cause my hairs to stand upright and spirits to fall down? Hags, — out alas, nymphs, I crave pardon. Ay me, out! what do I hear?   40
> *The* Fairies *dance, and with a song
> pinch him, and he falleth asleep.
> They kiss* Endymion *and depart.*

The Third Song, by Fairies [33]

Omnes. Pinch him, pinch him, black and blue,
Saucy mortals must not view
What the Queen of Stars is doing,
Nor pry into our fairy wooing.
1 Fairy. Pinch him blue.
2 Fairy. And pinch him black;
3 Fairy. Let him not lack
Sharp nails to pinch him blue and red,
Till sleep has rock'd his addle head.
4 Fairy. For the trespass he hath done,   50
Spots o'er all his flesh shall run.
Kiss Endymion, kiss his eyes;
Then to our midnight heidegyes.[34]

[*Enter*] Cynthia, Floscula, Semele, Panelion, Zontes, Pythagoras, *and* Gyptes.

Cynth. You see, Pythagoras, what ridiculous opinions you hold, and I doubt not but you are now of another mind.

Pythag. Madam, I plainly perceive that the perfection of your brightness hath pierced through the thickness that covered my mind; insomuch that I am no less glad to be re- [60 formed than ashamed to remember my grossness.

Gyptes. They are thrice fortunate that live in your palace, where truth is not in colors but life, virtues not in imagination but execution.

Cynth. I have always studied to have rather living virtues than painted gods, the body of truth than the tomb. But let us walk to Endymion; it may be it lieth in your arts to deliver him; as for Eumenides, I fear he [70 he is dead.

Pythag. I have alleged all the natural reasons I can for such a long sleep.

Gyptes. I can do nothing till I see him.

Cynth. Come, Floscula; I am sure you are glad that you shall behold Endymion.

Flosc. I were blessed, if I might have him recovered.

Cynth. Are you in love with his person?

Flosc. No, but with his virtue.   [80

Cynth. What say you, Semele?

Sem. Madam, I dare say nothing for fear I offend.

Cynth. Belike you cannot speak except you be spiteful; but as good be silent as saucy. Panelion, what punishment were fit for Semele, in whose speech and thoughts is only contempt and sourness?

Panel. I love not, madam, to give any judgment; yet, sith your Highness com- [90 mandeth, I think to commit her tongue close prisoner to her mouth.

Cynth. Agreed. Semele, if thou speak this twelvemonth, thou shalt forfeit thy tongue. — Behold Endymion! Alas, poor gentleman, hast thou spent thy youth in sleep, that once vowed all to my service? Hollow eyes, gray hairs, wrinkled cheeks, and decayed limbs! Is it destiny or deceit that hath brought this to pass? If the first, who could prevent thy [100 wretched stars? If the latter, I would I might know thy cruel enemy. I favored thee, Endymion, for thy honor, thy virtues, thy affections; but to bring thy thoughts within the compass of thy fortunes, I have seemed strange,[35] that I might have thee staid; and now are thy days ended before my favor begin. But whom have we here? Is it not Corsites?

Zon. It is, but more like a leopard [36] than a man.   110

Cynth. Awake him. — How now, Corsites, what make you here? How came you deformed? Look on thy hands, and then thou seest the picture of thy face.

Cors. Miserable wretch, and accursed! How am I deluded! Madam, I ask pardon for my offence, and you see my fortune deserveth pity.

Cynth. Speak on; thy offence cannot deserve greater punishment; but see thou [120 rehearse the truth, else shalt thou not find me as thou wishest me.

Cors. Madam, as it is no offence to be in love, being a man mortal, so I hope can it be no shame to tell with whom, my lady being heavenly. Your Majesty committed to my charge

---

[33] Heading and text first appear in Blount.
[34] Hays, dances.

[35] Distant, cold.
[36] See the fairies' song.

fair Tellus, whose beauty in the same moment took my heart captive that I undertook to carry her body prisoner. Since that time have I found such combats in my thoughts be- [130 tween love and duty, reverence and affection, that I could neither endure the conflict, nor hope for the conquest.

CYNTH. In love? A thing far unfitting the name of a captain, and (as I thought) the tough and unsmoothed nature of Corsites. But forth!

CORS. Feeling this continual war, I thought rather by parley to yield than by certain danger to perish. I unfolded to Tellus the [140 depth of my affections, and framed my tongue to utter a sweet tale of love, that was wont to sound nothing but threats of war. She, too fair to be true and too false for one so fair, after a nice [37] denial, practised a notable deceit, commanding me to remove Endymion from this cabin,[38] and carry him to some dark cave; which I, seeking to accomplish, found impossible; and so by fairies or fiends have been thus handled.   150

CYNTH. How say you, my Lords, is not Tellus always practising of some deceits? In sooth, Corsites, thy face is now too foul for a lover, and thine heart too fond for a soldier. You may see when warriors become wantons how their manners alter with their faces. Is it not a shame, Corsites, that having lived so long in Mars his camp, thou shouldest now be rock'd in Venus' cradle? Dost thou wear Cupid's quiver at thy girdle and make [160 lances of looks? Well, Corsites, rouse thyself and be as thou hast been; and let Tellus, who is made all of love, melt herself in her own looseness.

CORS. Madam, I doubt not but to recover my former state, for Tellus' beauty never wrought such love in my mind as now her deceit hath despite; and yet to be revenged of a woman were a thing than love itself more womanish.   170

GYPTES. These spots, gentleman, are to be worn out, if you rub them over with this lunary; so that in place where you received this maim [39] you shall find a medicine.

CORS. I thank you for that. The gods bless me from love and these pretty ladies that haunt this green.

FLOSC. Corsites, I would Tellus saw your amiable face.

ZONT. How spitefully Semele laugheth, [180 that dare not speak.

CYNTH. Could you not stir Endymion with that doubled strength of yours?

CORS. Not so much as his finger with all my force.

CYNTH. Pythagoras and Gyptes, what think you of Endymion? What reason is to be given, what remedy?

PYTH. Madam, it is impossible to yield reason for things that happen not in compass [190 of nature. It is most certain that some strange enchantment hath bound all his senses.

CYNTH. What say you, Gyptes?

GYPTES. With Pythagoras, that it is enchantment, and that so strange that no art can undo it; for that heaviness argueth a malice unremovable in the enchantress, and that no power can end it, till she die that did it, or the heavens show some means more than [200 miraculous.

FLOSC. O Endymion, could spite itself devise a mischief so monstrous as to make thee dead with life, and living, being altogether dead? Where others number their years, their hours, their minutes, and step to age by stairs, thou only hast thy years and times in a cluster, being old before you rememb'rest thou wast young.

CYNTH. No more, Floscula; pity doth [210 him no good. I would anything else might; and I vow by the unspotted honor of a lady he should not miss it. But is this all, Gyptes, that is to be done?

GYPTES. All as yet. It may be that either the enchantress shall die or else be discovered; if either happen, I will then practise the utmost of my art. In the mean season, about this grove would I have a watch, and the first living thing that toucheth Endymion to be [220 taken.

CYNTH. Corsites, what say you, will you undertake this?

CORS. Good madam, pardon me! I was overtaken too late.[40] I should rather break into the midst of a main battle than again fall into the hands of those fair babies.[41]

CYNTH. Well, I will provide others. Pythagoras and Gyptes, you shall yet remain in my

---

[37] Coy, finical.
[38] The scene of the lunary bank, evidently corresponding to the inner stage of the public theatres.
[39] Q *maine*.

[40] Too recently overcome.
[41] Dolls, for the fairies were supposed to be diminutive.

court, till I hear what may be done in this [230 matter.

PYTH. We attend.

CYNTH. Let us go in.   *Exeunt.*

ACT V — SCENE I [1]

[*Enter*] SAMIAS [*and*] DARES.

SAMIAS. Eumenides hath told such strange tales as I may well wonder at them, but never believe them.

DAR. The other old man, what a sad speech used he, that caused us almost all to weep. Cynthia is so desirous to know the experiment of her own virtue, and so willing to ease Endymion's hard fortune, that she no sooner heard the discourse but she made herself in a readiness to try the event.[2]   10

SAM. We will also see the event. But whist! here cometh Cynthia with all her train. Let us sneak in amongst them.

Enter CYNTHIA, FLOSCULA, SEMELE, [EUMENI-DES,] PANELION, *etc.*

CYNTH. Eumenides, it cannot sink into my head that I should be signified by that sacred fountain, for many things are there in the world to which those words may be applied.

EUM. Good madam, vouchsafe but to try; else shall I think myself most unhappy that I asked not my sweet mistress.[3]   20

CYNTH. Will you not yet tell me her name?

EUM. Pardon me, good madam, for if Endymion awake, he shall; myself have sworn never to reveal it.

CYNTH. Well, let us to Endymion. — I will not be so stately, good Endymion, not to stoop to do thee good; and if thy liberty consist in a kiss from me, thou shalt have it; and although my mouth hath been heretofore as untouched as my thoughts, yet now to recover thy life, [30 though to restore thy youth it be impossible, I will do that to Endymion which yet never mortal man could boast of heretofore, nor shall ever hope for hereafter.   *She kisseth him.*

EUM. Madam, he beginneth to stir.

CYNTH. Soft, Eumenides; stand still.

EUM. Ah, I see his eyes almost open.

CYNTH. I command thee once again, stir not. I will stand behind him.

[1] The same. Endymion still sleeps.
[2] Issue, outcome.
[3] *I.e.,* for Semele.

PAN. What do I see? Endymion al- [40 most awake?

EUM. Endymion, Endymion, art thou deaf or dumb, or hath this long sleep taken away thy memory? Ah, my sweet Endymion, seest thou not Eumenides, thy faithful friend, thy faithful Eumenides, who for thy safety hath been careless of his own content? Speak, Endymion! Endymion! Endymion!

END. Endymion? I call to mind such a name.   50

EUM. Hast thou forgotten thyself, Endymion? Then do I not marvel thou remember'st not thy friend. I tell thee thou art Endymion, and I Eumenides. Behold also Cynthia, by whose favor thou art awaked, and by whose virtue thou shalt continue thy natural course.

CYNTH. Endymion, speak, sweet Endymion! Knowest thou not Cynthia?

END. O Heavens, whom do I behold? [60 Fair Cynthia, divine Cynthia?

CYNTH. I am Cynthia, and thou Endymion.

END. Endymion! What do I here? What, a gray beard, hollow eyes, withered body, decayed limbs, — and all in one night?

EUM. One night! Thou hast here slept forty years, by what enchantress as yet it is not known; and behold, the twig to which thou layed'st thy head is now become a tree. Callest thou not Eumenides to remembrance? [70

END. Thy name I do remember by the sound, but thy favor [4] I do not yet call to mind; only divine Cynthia, to whom time, fortune, destiny, and death are subject, I see and remember, and in all humility I regard and reverence.

CYNTH. You have good cause to remember Eumenides, who hath for thy safety forsaken his own solace.

END. Am I that Endymion who was [80 wont in court to lead my life, and in justs, tourneys, and arms, to exercise my youth? Am I that Endymion?

EUM. Thou art that Endymion, and I Eumenides. Wilt thou not yet call me to remembrance?

END. Ah, sweet Eumenides, I now perceive thou art he, and that myself have the name of Endymion; but that this should be my body I doubt, for how could my curled locks be [90 turned to gray hairs and my strong body to a dying weakness, having waxed old, and not knowing it?

[4] Features.

CYNTH. Well, Endymion, arise. Awhile sit down, for that thy limbs are stiff and not able to stay [5] thee, and tell what hast thou seen in thy sleep all this while, what dreams, visions, thoughts, and fortunes; for it is impossible but in so long time thou shouldest see things strange. 100

END. Fair Cynthia, I will rehearse what I have seen, humbly desiring that when I exceed in length, you give me warning, that I may end; for to utter all I have to speak would be troublesome, although happily the strangeness may somewhat abate the tediousness.

CYNTH. Well, Endymion, begin.

END. Methought I saw a lady passing fair, but very mischievous, who in the one hand carried a knife with which she offered to cut [110 my throat, and in the other a looking-glass, wherein seeing how ill anger became ladies, she refrained from intended violence. She was accompanied with other damsels, one of which, with a stern countenance, and as it were with a settled malice engraven in her eyes, provoked her to execute mischief; another, with visage sad, and constant only in sorrow, with her arms crossed, and watery eyes, seemed to lament my fortune, but durst not offer to prevent the [120 force. I started in my sleep, feeling my very veins to swell and my sinews to stretch with fear; and such a cold sweat bedewed all my body that death itself could not be so terrible as the vision.

CYNTH. A strange sight! Gyptes, at our better leisure, shall expound it.

END. After long debating with herself, mercy overcame anger, and there appeared in her heavenly face such a divine majesty [130 mingled with a sweet mildness that I was ravished with the sight above measure, and wished that I might have enjoyed the sight without end; and so she departed with the other ladies, of which the one retained still an unmovable cruelty, the other a constant pity.

CYNTH. Poor Endymion, how wast thou affrighted! What else?

END. After her, immediately appeared an aged man with a beard as white as snow, [140 carrying in his hand a book with three leaves, and speaking, as I remember, these words: "Endymion, receive this book with three leaves, in which are contained counsels, policies, and pictures," and with that he offered me the book, which I rejected; wherewith, moved with a disdainful pity, he rent the first leaf in

a thousand shivers. The second time he offered it, which I refused also; at which, bending his brows, and pitching his eyes fast to the [150 ground, as though they were fixed to the earth and not again to be removed, then suddenly casting them up to the heavens, he tore in a rage the second leaf, and offered the book only with one leaf. I know not whether fear to offend or desire to know some strange thing moved me; I took the book, and so the old man vanished.

CYNTH. What diddest thou imagine was in the last leaf? 160

END. There [6] portray'd to life, with a cold quaking in every joint, I beheld many wolves barking at thee, Cynthia, who, having ground their teeth to bite, did with striving bleed themselves to death. There might I see Ingratitude with an hundred eyes gazing for benefits, and with a thousand teeth gnawing on the bowels wherein she was bred; Treachery stood all clothed in white, with a smiling countenance, but both her hands bathed [170 in blood; Envy with a pale and meager face (whose body was so lean that one might tell all her bones, and whose garment was so totter'd that it was easy to number every thread) stood shooting at stars, whose darts fell down again on her own face. There might I behold drones or beetles — I know not how to term them — creeping under the wings of a princely eagle, who, being carried into her nest, sought there to suck that vein that would have [180 killed the eagle. I mused that things so base should attempt a fact [7] so barbarous, or durst imagine a thing so bloody. And many other things, madam, the repetition whereof may at your better leisure seem more pleasing; for bees surfeit sometimes with honey, and the gods are glutted with harmony, and your Highness may be dulled with delight.

CYNTH. I am content to be dieted; therefore, let us in. Eumenides, see that En- [190 dymion be well tended, lest either eating immoderately or sleeping again too long, he fall into a deadly surfeit or into his former sleep. See this also be proclaimed: that whosoever will discover this practice [8] shall have of Cynthia infinite thanks and no small rewards.

[*Exeunt all except* ENDYMION, EU-
MENIDES, FLOSCULA, *and* SEMELE.]

FLOSC. Ah, Endymion, none so joyful as Floscula of thy restoring.

[6] Old eds. *There I.*
[7] Deed.   [8] Expose this plot.

[5] Support.

Eum. Yes, Floscula, let Eumenides be some-what gladder, and do not that wrong to [200 the settled friendship of a man as to compare it with the light affection of a woman. Ah, my dear friend Endymion, suffer me to die with gazing at thee.

End. Eumenides, thy friendship is immortal and not to be conceived ; and thy good will, Floscula, better than I have deserved ; but let us all wait on Cynthia. I marvel Semele speaketh not a word.

Eum. Because if she do, she loseth her [210 tongue.

End. But how prospereth your love ?

Eum. I never yet spake word since your sleep.

End. I doubt not but your affection is old and your appetite cold.

Eum. No, Endymion ; thine hath made it stronger, and now are my sparks grown to flames and my fancies almost to frenzies. But let us follow, and within we will debate all [220 this matter at large. *Exeunt.*

Scene II [9]

[*Enter*] Sir Tophas [*and*] Epiton.

Top. Epi, Love hath justled my liberty from the wall,[10] and taken the upper hand of my reason.

Epi. Let me then trip up the heels of your affection and thrust your good will into the gutter.

Top. No, Epi ; Love is a Lord of Misrule [11] and keepeth Christmas in my corpse.

Epi. No doubt there is good cheer. What dishes of delight doth his Lordship feast [10 you withal?

Top. First, with a great platter of plum porridge of pleasure, wherein is stewed the mutton of distrust.

Epi. Excellent love-lap.[12]

Top. Then cometh a pie of patience, a hen of honey, a goose of gall, a capon of care, and many other viands, some sweet and some sour, which proveth love to be, as it was said of in old years, *Dulce venenum.*[13] 20

Epi. A brave banquet !

Top. But, Epi, I pray thee feel on my chin ; something pricketh me. What dost thou feel or see?

Epi. There are three or four little hairs.

Top. I pray thee call it my beard. How shall I be troubled when this young spring [14] shall grow to a great wood !

Epi. Oh, sir, your chin is but a quiller [15] yet ; you will be most majestical when it is [30 full fledge. But I marvel that you love Dipsas, that old crone.

Top. *Agnosco veteris vestigia flammæ* [16]: I love the smoke of an old fire.

Epi. Why she is so cold that no fire can thaw her thoughts.

Top. It is an old goose, Epi, that will eat no oats ; old kine will kick, old rats gnaw cheese, and old sacks will have much patching. I prefer an old cony [17] before a rabbit-sucker,[18] [40 and an ancient hen before a young chicken-peeper.

Epi. [*aside*] *Argumentum ab antiquitate ;* my master loveth antique work.

Top. Give me a pippin that is withered like an old wife !

Epi. Good, sir.

Top. Then — *a contrario sequitur argumentum* — give me a wife that looks like an old pippin. 50

Epi. [*aside*] Nothing hath made my master a fool but flat scholarship.

Top. Knowest thou not that old wine is best?

Epi. Yes.

Top. And thou knowest that like will to like?

Epi. Ay.

Top. And thou knowest that Venus loved the best wine? 60

Epi. So.

Top. Then I conclude that Venus was an old woman in an old cup of wine, for *est Venus in vinis, ignis in igne fuit.*[19]

Epi. *O lepidum caput,*[20] O madcap master ! You were worthy to win Dipsas, were she as old again ; for in your love you have worn the nap of your wit quite off and made it thread-bare. But soft, who comes here?

---

[9] Unlocated ; presumably the same as I, i.
[10] *I.e.,* love has proved superior to my freedom, as one man, meeting another on the street jostles him from the most desirable place, that next the wall.
[11] Chairman of Christmas revels.
[12] Baker emends to *pap.*
[13] Delightful poison.

[14] Grove of young trees.   [15] Unfledged bird.
[16] The signs of former blazes well I know. (Virgil, *Aeneid,* iv, 23.)
[17] Rabbit (Lat. *cuniculus*).   [18] Sucking rabbit.
[19] Where grapes are crushed doth Venus live and move :
   Within the fire of wine, the fire of love !
(Ovid, *Ars Amatoria,* i, 244.)
[20] Terence, *Adelphi,* V, ix, 9.

[*Enter* SAMIAS *and* DARES.]

TOP. My solicitors.   70

SAM. All hail, Sir Tophas; how feel you
yourself?

TOP. Stately in every joint, which the common people term stiffness. Doth Dipsas
stoop? Will she yield? Will she bend?

DAR. Oh, sir, as much as you would wish,
for her chin almost toucheth her knees.

EPI. Master, she is bent, I warrant you.

TOP. What conditions doth she ask?

SAM. She hath vowed she will never love [80
any that hath not a tooth in his head less than
she.

TOP. How many hath she?

DAR. One.

EPI. That goeth hard, master, for then you
must have none.

TOP. A small request, and agreeable to the
gravity of her years. What should a wise man
do with his mouth full of bones like a charnel
house? [21] The turtle [22] true hath ne'er a [90
tooth.

SAM [*aside*] Thy master is in a notable vein,
that will lose his teeth to be like a turtle.

EPI. [*aside*] Let him lose his tongue, too;
I care not.

DAR. Nay, you must also have no nails, for
she long since hath cast hers.

TOP. That I yield to. What a quiet life
shall Dipsas and I lead when we can neither
bite nor scratch! You may see, youths, [100
how age provides for peace.

SAM [*aside*] How shall we do to make him
leave his love? For we never spake to her.

DAR. [*aside*] Let me alone. — [*to* Sir
TOPHAS] She is a notable witch, and hath
turn'd her maid Bagoa to an aspen tree, for
bewraying her secrets.

TOP. I honor her for her cunning; for now,
when I am weary of walking on two legs, what
a pleasure may she do me to turn me to [110
some goodly ass, and help me to four.

DAR. Nay, then I must tell you the truth.
Her husband, Geron, is come home, who this
fifty years hath had her to wife.

TOP. What do I hear? Hath she an husband? Go to the sexton [23] and tell him Desire
is dead, and will him to dig his grave. O
Heavens, an husband! What death is agreeable to [24] my fortune?

---

[21] Q *channel house.*
[22] Dove.
[23] Q *Sexteene.*
[24] Suits, is in keeping with.

SAM. Be not desperate, and we will [120
help you to find a young lady.

TOP. I love no grissels [25]; they are so brittle
they will crack like glass, or so dainty that
if they be touched they are straight of the
fashion of wax; *animus majoribus instat* [26]:
I desire old matrons. What a sight would it
be to embrace one whose hair were as orient as
the pearl, whose teeth shall be so pure a
watchet [27] that they shall stain the truest
turquoise, whose nose shall throw more [130
beams from it than the fiery carbuncle, whose
eyes shall be environ'd about with redness
exceeding the deepest coral, and whose lips
might compare with silver for the paleness!
Such a one if you can help me to, I will by
piecemeal curtail [28] my affections towards
Dipsas, and walk my swelling thoughts till
they be cold.

EPI. Wisely provided. How say you, my
friends; will you angle for my master's [140
cause?

SAM. Most willingly.

DAR. If we speed him [29] not shortly, I will
burn my cap. We will serve him of the spades,
and dig an old wife out of the grave that shall
be answerable to his gravity.

TOP. Youths, adieu; he that bringeth me
first news shall possess mine inheritance.

[*Exit.*]

DAR. What, is thy master landed?

EPI. Know you not that my master is [150
liber tenens?

SAM. What 's that?

EPI. A freeholder. But I will after him.

SAM. And we to hear what news of Endymion for the conclusion.   *Exeunt.*

SCENE III [30]

[*Enter*] PANELION [*and*] ZONTES.

PAN. Who would have thought that Tellus,
being so fair by nature, so honorable by birth,
so wise by education, would have ent'red into
a mischief to the gods so odious, to men so
detestable, and to her friend [31] so malicious.

---

[25] Immature girls.
[26] Ovid, *Ars Amatoria*, ii, 535.
[27] Pale blue.
[28] Baker suggests a play on curtal, a bobtailed
horse; and Bond adds that *walke . . . cold* may
bear out the idea, referring to exercising a fiery
horse. The allusion is rather to walking a horse to
cool him down gradually *after* exercise.
[29] Make him successful.
[30] Unlocated; presumably the same.
[31] Lover.

Zon. If Bagoa had not bewrayed it, how then should it have come to light? But we see that gold and fair words are of force to corrupt the strongest men, and therefore able to work silly women like wax. 10

Pan. I marvel what Cynthia will determine in this cause.

Zon. I fear, as in all causes : hear of it in justice, and then judge of it in mercy ; for how can it be that she that is unwilling to punish her deadliest foes with disgrace, will revenge injuries of her train with death?

Pan. That old witch, Dipsas, in a rage, having understood her practice to be discovered, turned poor Bagoa to an aspen tree. But [20 let us make haste and bring Tellus before Cynthia, for she was coming out after us.

Zon. Let us go.   *Exeunt.*

[*Enter*] Cynthia, Semele, Floscula, Dipsas, Endymion, Eumenides, [Geron, Pythagoras, Gyptes, *and* Sir Tophas].

Cynth. Dipsas, thy years are not so many as thy vices, yet more in number than commonly nature doth afford or justice should permit. Hast thou almost these fifty years practised that detested wickedness of witchcraft? Wast thou, so simple as for to know the nature of simples, of all creatures to be [30 most sinful? Thou hast threat'ned to turn my course awry and alter by thy damnable art the government that I now possess by the eternal gods ; but know thou, Dipsas, and let all the enchanters know, that Cynthia, being placed for light on earth, is also protected by the powers of Heaven. Breathe out thou mayst words ; gather thou mayst herbs ; find out thou mayst stones agreeable to thine art ; yet of no force to appal my heart, in [40 which courage is so rooted, and constant persuasion of the mercy of the gods so grounded, that all thy witchcraft I esteem as weak as the world doth thy case wretched.

This noble gentleman, Geron, once thy husband but now thy mortal hate, didst thou procure to live in a desert, almost desperate ; Endymion, the flower of my court and the hope of succeeding time, hast thou bewitched by art, before thou wouldest suffer him to flourish [50 by nature.

Dipsas. Madam, things past may be repented, not recalled ; there is nothing so wicked that I have not done, nor anything so wished for as death ; yet among all the things that I committed, there is nothing so much tor-

menteth my rented [32] and ransack'd thoughts as that in the prime of my husband's youth I divorced him by my devilish art ; for which if to die might be amends, I would not live [60 till to-morrow ; if to live and still be more miserable would better content him, I would wish of all creatures to be oldest and ugliest.

Geron. Dipsas, thou hast made this difference between me and Endymion, that being both young, thou hast caused me to wake in melancholy, losing the joys of my youth, and him to sleep, not rememb'ring youth.

Cynth. Stay, here cometh Tellus ; we shall now know all. 70

[*Re-enter*] Panelion [*and* Zontes *with*] Corsites [*and*] Tellus.

Cors. I would to Cynthia thou couldest make as good an excuse in truth as to me thou hast done by wit.

Tellus. Truth shall be mine answer, and therefore I will not study for an excuse.

Cynth. Is it possible, Tellus, that so few years should harbor so many mischiefs? Thy swelling pride have I borne, because it is a thing that beauty maketh blameless, which the more it exceedeth fairness in measure, the [80 more it stretcheth itself in disdain. Thy devices against Corsites I smile at, for that wits, the sharper they are, the shrewder [33] they are ; but this unacquainted [34] and most unnatural practice with a vile enchantress against so noble a gentleman as Endymion I abhor as a thing most malicious, and will revenge as a deed most monstrous.

And as for you, Dipsas, I will send you into the desert amongst wild beasts, and try [90 whether you can cast lions, tigers, boars, and bears into as dead a sleep as you did Endymion, or turn them to trees, as you have done Bagoa. — But tell me, Tellus, what was the cause of this cruel part, far unfitting thy sex, in which nothing should be but simpleness, and much disagreeing from thy face, in which nothing seemed to be but softness?

Tellus. Divine Cynthia, by whom I receive my life and am content to end it, I [100 can neither excuse my fault without lying, nor confess it without shame ; yet were it possible that in so heavenly thoughts as yours there could fall such earthly motions as mine, I would then hope, if not to be pardoned with-

[32] Torn.
[33] More mischievous.
[34] *I.e.*, unheard of.

out extreme punishment, yet to be heard without great marvel.

CYNTH. Say on, Tellus; I cannot imagine anything that can color [35] such a cruelty.

TELLUS. Endymion, that Endymion, in [110 the prime of his youth so ravish'd my heart with love that to obtain my desires I could not find means, nor to resi[s]t [36] them reason. What was she that favored not Endymion, being young, wise, honorable, and virtuous; besides, what metal was she made of (be she mortal) that is not affected with the spice, nay, infected with the poison of that not-to-be-expressed yet always-to-be-felt love, which breaketh the brains and never bruiseth the [120 brow, consumeth the heart and never toucheth the skin, and maketh a deep wound to be felt before any scar at all be seen? [37] My heart, too tender to withstand such a divine fury, yielded to love. Madam, I not without blushing confess, yielded to love.

CYNTH. A strange effect of love, to work such an extreme hate. How say you, Endymion? All this was for love!

END. I say, madam, then the gods send [130 me a woman's hate.

CYNTH. That were as bad, for then by contrary you should never sleep. But on, Tellus; let us hear the end.

TELLUS. Feeling a continual burning in all my bowels, and a bursting almost in every vein, I could not smother the inward fire, but it must needs be perceived by the outward smoke; and, by the flying abroad of divers sparks, divers judged of my scalding [140 flames. Endymion, as full of art as wit, marking mine eyes, (in which he might see almost his own,) my sighs, (by which he might ever hear his name sounded,) aimed at my heart, in which he was assured his person was imprinted, and by questions wrung out that which was ready to burst out. When he saw the depth of my affections, he sware that mine in respect of his were as fumes to Ætna, valleys to Alps, ants to eagles, and nothing could [150 be compared to my beauty but his love and eternity. Thus drawing a smooth shoe upon a crooked foot,[38] he made me believe that (which all of our sex willingly acknowledge) I was beautiful, and to wonder (which indeed

is a thing miraculous) that any of his sex should be faithful.

CYNTH. Endymion, how will you clear yourself?

END. Madam, by mine own accuser.   160

CYNTH. Well, Tellus, proceed; but briefly, lest taking delight in uttering thy love, thou offend us with the length of it.

TELLUS. I will, madam, quickly make an end of my love and my tale. Finding continual increase of my tormenting thoughts, and that the enjoying of my love made deeper wounds than the entering into it, I could find no means to ease my grief but to follow Endymion, and continually to have him in [170 the object of mine eyes who had me slave and subject to his love. But in the moment that I feared his falsehood and fried myself most in mine affections, I found — ah, grief, even then I lost myself! — I found him in most melancholy and desperate terms cursing his stars, his state, the earth, the heavens, the world, and all for the love of —

CYNTH. Of whom? Tellus, speak boldly.

TELLUS. Madam, I dare not utter, for [180 fear to offend.

CYNTH. Speak, I say; who dare take offence, if thou be commanded by Cynthia?

TELLUS. For the love of Cynthia.

CYNTH. For my love, Tellus? That were strange. — Endymion, is it true?

END. In all things, madam, Tellus doth not speak false.

CYNTH. What will this breed to in the end? Well, Endymion, we shall hear all.   190

TELLUS. I, seeing my hopes turn'd to mishaps, and a settled dissembling towards me, and an unmovable desire to Cynthia, forgetting both myself and my sex, fell unto this unnatural hate; for knowing your virtues, Cynthia, to be immortal, I could not have an imagination to withdraw him; and finding mine own affections unquenchable, I could not carry the mind that any else should possess what I had pursued. For though in maj- [200 esty, beauty, virtue, and dignity, I always humbled and yielded myself to Cynthia, yet in affections I esteemed myself equal with the goddesses, and all other creatures, according to their states, with myself; for stars to their bigness have their lights, and the sun hath no more, and little pitchers, when they can hold no more, are as full as great vessels that run over. Thus, madam, in all truth have I uttered the unhappiness of my love and [210

---

[35] Make plausible, excuse.
[36] Q *resite;* Blount *recite.*
[37] So Bond, transposing (on Daniel's suggestion) old eds. *scar . . . seen . . . wound . . . felt.*
[38] Referring to the story of the cripple, Demonidis; Plutarch, *De Audiendis Poetis,* iii. (Bond.)

the cause of my hate, yielding wholly to that divine judgment which never erred for want of wisdom or envied [39] for too much partiality.

CYNTH. How say you, my Lords, to this matter? — But what say you, Endymion; hath Tellus told truth?

END. Madam, in all things but in that she said I loved her and swore to honor her.

CYNTH. Was there such a time whenas for my love thou didst vow thyself to death, [220 and in respect of it loath'd thy life? Speak, Endymion; I will not revenge it with hate.

END. The time was, madam, and is, and ever shall be, that I honored your Highness above all the world; but to stretch it so far as to call it love I never durst. There hath none pleased mine eye but Cynthia, none delighted mine ears but Cynthia, none possessed my heart but Cynthia. I have forsaken all other fortunes to follow Cynthia, and here I [230 stand ready to die, if it please Cynthia. Such a difference hath the gods set between our states that all must be duty, loyalty, and reverence; nothing (without it vouchsafe your Highness) be termed love. My unspotted thoughts, my languishing body, my discontented life, let them obtain by princely favor that which to challenge they must not presume, only wishing of impossibilities; with imagination of which I will spend my spirits, and to my- [240 self, that no creature may hear, softly call it love; and if any urge to utter what I whisper, then will I name it honor. From this sweet contemplation if I be not driven, I shall live of all men the most content, taking more pleasure in mine aged thoughts than ever I did in my youthful actions.

CYNTH. Endymion, this honorable respect of thine shall be christ'ned love in thee, and my reward for it, favor. Persevere, Endy- [250 mion, in loving me, and I account more strength in a true heart than in a walled city. I have labored to win all, and study to keep such as I have won; but those that neither my favor can move to continue constant, nor my offered benefits get to be faithful, the gods shall either reduce to truth, or revenge their treacheries with justice. Endymion, continue as thou hast begun, and thou shalt find that Cynthia shineth not on thee in vain. [260

END. Your Highness hath blessed me, and your words have again restored my youth; methinks I feel my joints strong and these mouldy hairs to moult, and all by your virtue,

[39] Harbored malevolence.

Cynthia, into whose hands the balance that weigheth time and fortune are committed.

CYNTH. What, young again? Then it is pity to punish Tellus.

TELLUS. Ah, Endymion, now I know thee and ask pardon of thee; suffer me still to [270 wish thee well.

END. Tellus, Cynthia must command what she will.

FLOSC. Endymion, I rejoice to see thee in thy former estate.

END. Good Floscula, to thee also am I in my former affections.

EUM. Endymion, the comfort of my life, how am I ravished with a joy matchless, saving only the enjoying of my mistress.   280

CYNTH. Endymion, you must now tell who Eumenides shrineth for his saint.

END. Semele, madam.

CYNTH. Semele, Eumenides? Is it Semele, the very wasp of all women, whose tongue stingeth as much as an adder's tooth?

EUM. It is Semele, Cynthia, the possessing of whose love must only prolong my life.

CYNTH. Nay, sith Endymion is restored, we will have all parties pleased. Semele, [290 are you content after so long trial of his faith, such rare secrecy, such unspotted love, to take Eumenides? Why speak you not? Not a word?

END. Silence, madam, consents; that is most true.

CYNTH. It is true, Endymion. Eumenides, take Semele; take her, I say.

EUM. Humble thanks, madam; now only do I begin to live.   300

SEM. A hard choice, madam, either to be married if I say nothing, or to lose my tongue if I speak a word. Yet do I rather choose to have my tongue cut out than my heart distempered; I will not have him.

CYNTH. Speaks the parrot? She shall nod hereafter with signs. Cut off her tongue, nay her head, that having a servant of honorable birth, honest manners, and true love, will not be persuaded.   310

SEM. He is no faithful lover, madam; for then would he have asked [40] his mistress.

GER. Had he not been faithful, he had never seen into the fountain, and so lost [41] his friend and mistress.

EUM. Thine own thoughts, sweet Semele, witness against thy words; for what hast thou

[40] Asked for (at the fountain).
[41] Would have lost.

found in my life but love? And as yet what have I found in my love but bitterness? Madam, pardon Semele, and let my [320 tongue ransom hers.

CYNTH. Thy tongue, Eumenides? What, shouldst thou live wanting a tongue to blaze the beauty of Semele? Well, Semele, I will not command love, for it cannot be enforced; let me entreat it.

SEM. I am content your Highness shall command, for now only do I think Eumenides faithful, that is willing to lose his tongue for my sake; yet loath, because it should [330 do me better service. Madam, I accept of Eumenides.

CYNTH. I thank you, Semele.

EUM. Ah, happy Eumenides, that hast a friend so faithful and a mistress so fair! With what sudden mischief will the gods daunt this excess of joy? Sweet Semele, I live or die as thou wilt.

CYNTH. What shall become of Tellus? Tellus, you know Endymion is vowed to [340 a service from which death cannot remove him. Corsites casteth still a lovely [42] [look] [43] towards you. How say you, will [you] [44] have your Corsites, and so receive pardon for all that is past?

TELLUS. Madam, most willingly.

CYNTH. But I cannot tell whether Corsites be agreed.

CORS. Ay, madam, more happy to enjoy Tellus than the monarchy of the world.   350

EUM. Why, she caused you to be pinch'd with fairies.

CORS. Ay, but her fairness hath pinched my heart more deeply.

CYNTH. Well, enjoy thy love. — But what have you wrought in the castle, Tellus?

TELLUS. Only the picture of Endymion.

CYNTH. Then so much of Endymion as his picture cometh to, possess and play withal.

CORS. Ah, my sweet Tellus, my love shall be as thy beauty is, matchless.   361

CYNTH. Now it resteth,[45] Dipsas, that if thou wilt forswear that vile art of enchanting, Geron hath promised again to receive thee; otherwise, if thou be wedded to that wickedness, I must and will see it punished to the uttermost.

DIPSAS. Madam, I renounce both substance and shadow of that most horrible and hateful trade, vowing to the gods contin- [370 ual penance, and to your Highness obedience.

CYNTH. How say you, Geron; will you admit her to your wife?

GER. Ay, with more joy than I did the first day, for nothing could happen to make me happy but only her forsaking that lewd [46] and detestable course. — Dipsas, I embrace thee.

DIPSAS. And I thee, Geron, to whom I will hereafter recite the cause of these my first follies.   380

CYNTH. Well, Endymion, nothing resteth now but that we depart. Thou hast my favor, Tellus her friend, Eumenides in Paradise with his Semele, Geron contented with Dipsas.

SIR TOP. Nay, soft; I cannot handsomely go to bed without Bagoa.

CYNTH. Well, Sir Tophas, it may be there are more virtues in me than myself knoweth of, for Endymion I awaked, and at my words [390 he waxed young. I will try whether I can turn this tree again to thy true love.

TOP. Turn her to a true love òr false, so she be a wench I care not.

CYNTH. Bagoa, Cynthia putteth an end to thy hard fortunes; for, being turn'd to a tree for revealing a truth, I will recover thee again, if in my power be the effect of truth.

[BAGOA *recovers human shape.*]

TOP. Bagoa, a bots [47] upon thee!

CYNTH. Come, my Lords, let us in. [400 You, Gyptes and Pythagoras, if you [can] [48] content yourselves in our court, to fall from vain follies of philosophers to such virtues as are here practised, you shall be entertained according to your deserts, for Cynthia is no stepmother to strangers.

PYTHAG. I had rather in Cynthia's court spend [one hour] [49] than in Greece [ten years].[49]

GYPTES. And I choose rather to live by the sight of Cynthia than by the possessing [410 of all Egypt.

CYNTH. Then follow.

EUM. We all attend.   *Exeunt.*

[42] Loving.   [43] Q *lookes.*   [44] Om. Q.   [45] Remains.

[46] Wicked.
[47] Larvae of the botfly. Here equivalent to "Plague take you."
[48] Emend. Bond; old eds. *cannot.*
[49] Old (and mod.) eds. transpose.

THE EPILOGUE

A MAN walking abroad, the Wind and Sun strove for sovereignty, the one with his blast, the other with his beams. The Wind blew hard; the man wrapped his garment about him harder. It blust'red more strongly; he then girt it fast to him. "I cannot prevail," said the Wind. The Sun, casting her crystal beams, began to warm the man; he unloosed his gown. Yet it shined brighter; he then put it off. "I yield," said the Wind, "for if thou continue shining, he will also put off his coat."

Dread Sovereign, the malicious that seek to overthrow us with threats, do but stiffen our thoughts, and make them sturdier in storms; but if your Highness vouchsafe with your favorable beams to glance upon us, we shall not only stoop, but with all humility lay both our hands and hearts at your Majesty's feet.

THE
HONORABLE HISTORIE
of frier Bacon, and frier Bongay.

As it was plaid by her Maiesties seruants.

Made by *Robert Greene* Maister of Arts.

LONDON,
Printed for Edward White, and are to be sold at his shop, at
the little North dore of Poules, at the signe of
the Gun. 1594.

INTRODUCTORY NOTE

IN this charming comedy a great thirteenth-century scientist, long reputed a magician, is extolled because he practises for England's glory an art less devilish but no less astounding than that of Faustus. Though the dates of composition and production are uncertain, 1589 or just after seems most likely; and there can be little doubt that it was Marlowe's play which prompted Greene to glorify Roger Bacon. His source for that part of his theme is *The Famous History of Friar Bacon*, probably written late in the sixteenth century, though the earliest extant edition was in 1627. From it Greene also took the feud of the two neighbors and their sons.

The love story, however, seems to be original. The historical background is almost entirely fictitious; there is no warrant in fact for the Prince's relations with either Bacon or Margaret. But the latter has a higher claim to our regard: she is the first thoroughly admirable heroine of the Elizabethan theatre. Whatever delight the spectator may have taken in the conjuring tricks of Bacon and in his triumph over his German rival, the most delightful part of the play for the modern reader is the dewy story of the Fair Maid of Fressingfield. This is sheer romance; we are not to ask embarrassing questions about historicity, nor apply to the cruel test imposed by Lacy the criteria of realism. Here is fairy-tale material, gracefully woven into a play otherwise compounded of patriotic fervor and somewhat clumsy burlesque.

Henslowe's "Diary" furnishes several clues which indicate the play's survival on the stage. It was being acted in 1592 and 1593 by Lord Strange's Men, by the Queen's and Sussex's Men jointly in 1594, and by the Admiral's Men in 1602, when Thomas Middleton wrote for it a prologue and an epilogue which have not been preserved. The Quarto of 1630 states that the company of the Prince Palatine (successors of the Admiral's) has "lately" played it.

The standard edition of Greene's *Plays and Poems* is that of J. C. Collins (1905). *Friar Bacon and Friar Bungay* was edited by A. W. Ward with *Faustus* (Fourth Edition, 1901), by C. M. Gayley (*Representative English Comedies*, 1903), by J. S. Farmer (1914), and by W. W. Greg (1926). It first appeared, in quarto, in 1594 (reprinted 1630, 1655). The present text is based on the Harvard copy of the first edition, of which but two other copies seem to have survived. The text has also been collated with Greg's reprint of the British Museum copy. Since the Harvard copy lacks leaves A 4, I 1, 2, the present edition rests at those points on photographs of the Huntington Library copy.

THE HONORABLE HISTORY OF FRIAR BACON AND FRIAR BUNGAY

BY

ROBERT GREENE

[DRAMATIS PERSONAE

KING HENRY THE THIRD.
EDWARD, Prince of Wales, his son.
FREDERICK II, EMPEROR OF GERMANY.[1]
FERDINAND III, KING OF CASTILE.
DUKE OF SAXONY.
LACY, Earl of Lincoln.[2]
JOHN WARREN, Earl of Sussex.[3]
ERMSBY, a gentleman.
RALPH SIMNELL, the King's Fool.
FRIAR BACON.
MILES,[4] his poor scholar.
FRIAR BUNGAY.[5]
JACQUES VANDERMAST,[6] a German.
BURDEN, }
MASON, } doctors of Oxford.
CLEMENT, }
LAMBERT, } gentlemen.
SERLSBY, }

Two Scholars, their sons.
The Keeper of Fressingfield.
THOMAS, } rustics.
RICHARD, }
Constable.
A Post.
A Friend to the Keeper and Margaret.
Lords, Country Clowns, &c.

ELINOR, daughter to the King of Castile.
MARGARET, daughter to the Keeper.
JOAN, a country wench.
Hostess of the Bell at Henley.

A Devil.
Spirit in the shape of HERCULES.]

[ACT I — SCENE I] [7]

Enter [PRINCE] EDWARD [8] *malcontented; with*
LACY, EARL OF LINCOLN; JOHN WARREN,
EARL OF SUSSEX; ERMSBY, *gentleman;*
and RALPH [9] SIMNELL, *the King's Fool.*

LACY. [*aside to* WARREN *and* ERMSBY] Why
    looks my Lord like to a troubled sky
When heaven's bright shine is shadowed with a
    fog?

Alate [10] we ran the deer, and through the
    lawnds
Stripp'd [11] with our nags the lofty frolic bucks,
That scudded 'fore the teasers [12] like the wind.
Ne'er was the deer of merry Fressingfield
So lustily pull'd down by jolly mates,
Nor shar'd the farmers such fat venison,
So frankly [13] dealt, this hundred years before;
Nor have I seen my Lord more frolic in the
    chase,   10
And now — chang'd to a melancholy dump.
    WAR. After the Prince got to the Keeper's
        lodge,
And had been jocund in the house awhile,
Tossing off ale and milk in country cans,
Whether it was the country's sweet content,
Or else the bonny damsel fill'd us drink,
That seem'd so stately in her stammel [14] red,

[1] He was brother-in-law to Henry III.
[2] Henry de Lacy, afterwards one of the counsellors of Edward I.
[3] Historically, of Surrey.
[4] Probably a corruption of *Michael*. (Ward.)
[5] A distinguished 13th-century Franciscan; he lectured at both Oxford and Cambridge.
[6] No original is known for this character, whose name is Dutch; the Netherlands still were part of the Empire.
[7] Unlocated. Presumably the Prince's lodgings at Framlingham (see II, i, 33).
[8] Old eds. *Edward the first*.
[9] Old eds. *Raphe* or *Raph*, throughout.

[10] Of late.   [11] Outstripped.
[12] Hounds that roused the game.
[13] Liberally.
[14] A kind of coarse woolen.

Or that a qualm did cross his stomach then —
But straight he fell into his passions.[15]

ERMS. Sirrah Ralph, what say you to your
    master? 20
Shall he thus all amort [16] live malcontent?

RALPH. Hearest thou, Ned? — Nay, look
if he will speak to me!

EDW. What say'st thou to me, fool?

RALPH. I prithee, tell me, Ned, art thou in
love with the Keeper's daughter?

EDW. How if I be? what then?

RALPH. Why, then, sirrah, I'll teach thee
how to deceive Love.

EDW. How, Ralph? 30

RALPH. Marry, Sirrah Ned, thou shalt put
on my cap and my coat and my dagger, and I
will put on thy clothes and thy sword; and so
thou shalt be my fool.

EDW. And what of this?

RALPH. Why, so thou shalt beguile Love;
for Love is such a proud scab,[17] that he will
never meddle with fools nor children. Is not
Ralph's counsel good, Ned?

EDW. Tell me, Ned Lacy, didst thou mark
    the maid, 40
How lively in her country weeds she look'd?
A bonnier wench all Suffolk cannot yield —
All Suffolk! nay, all England holds none such.

RALPH. Sirrah Will Ermsby, Ned is deceived.

ERMS. Why, Ralph?

RALPH. He says all England hath no such,
and I say, and I'll stand to it, there is one better in Warwickshire.

WAR. How provest thou that, Ralph? 50

RALPH. Why, is not the abbot a learned
man, and hath read many books, and thinkest
thou he hath not more learning than thou to
choose a bonny wench? Yes, I warrant thee,
by his whole grammar.

ERMS. A good reason, Ralph.

EDW. I tell thee, Lacy, that her sparkling
    eyes
Do lighten forth sweet love's alluring fire;
And in her tresses she doth fold the looks
Of such as gaze upon her golden hair; 60
Her bashful white, mix'd with the morning's
    red,
Luna doth boast upon her lovely cheeks;
Her front [18] is Beauty's table, where she paints
The glories of her gorgeous excellence;
Her teeth are shelves of precious marguerites,[19]
Richly enclosed with ruddy coral cliffs.[20]

Tush, Lacy, she is Beauty's overmatch,
If thou survey'st her curious imagery.[21]

LACY. I grant, my Lord, the damsel is as
    fair
As simple Suffolk's homely towns can yield; [70
But in the court be quainter [22] dames than she,
Whose faces are enrich'd with honor's taint,[23]
Whose beauties stand upon the stage of Fame,
And vaunt their trophies in the courts of love.

EDW. Ah, Ned, but hadst thou watch'd her
    as myself,
And seen the secret beauties of the maid,
Their courtly coyness were but foolery.

ERMS. Why, how watch'd you her, my
    Lord?

EDW. Whenas she swept like Venus through
    the house,
And in her shape fast folded up my thoughts,
Into the milkhouse went I with the maid, [81
And there amongst the cream bowls she did
    shine
As Pallas 'mongst her princely huswifery.
She turn'd her smock over her lily arms,
And dived them into milk to run her cheese;
But, whiter than the milk, her crystal skin,
Checked with lines of azure, made her blush [24]
That art or nature durst bring for compare.
Ermsby, if thou hadst seen, as I did note it
    well,
How Beauty play'd the huswife, how this girl,
Like Lucrece, laid her fingers to the work, [91
Thou wouldest, with Tarquin, hazard Rome
    and all
To win the lovely maid of Fressingfield.

RALPH. Sirrah Ned, wouldst fain have her?

EDW. Ay, Ralph.

RALPH. Why, Ned, I have laid the plot in
my head; thou shalt have her already.

EDW. I'll give thee a new coat, an learn [25]
me that.

RALPH. Why, Sirrah Ned, we'll ride to [100
Oxford to Friar Bacon. O, he is a brave
scholar, sirrah; they say he is a brave necromancer, that he can make women of devils, and
he can juggle cats into costermongers.

EDW. And how then, Ralph?

RALPH. Marry, sirrah, thou shalt go to him;
and because thy father Harry shall not miss
thee, he shall turn me into thee; and I'll to the
court, and I'll prince it out; and he shall make

[15] *I.e.*, moodiness.   [16] Dejected.   [17] Rascal.
[18] Forehead.   [19] Pearls.   [20] Old eds. *cleues*.

[21] Her exquisitely beautiful appearance.
[22] More elegant.
[23] Tincture.
[24] Would have made that woman blush whom art,
    etc.
[25] If thou teachest.

thee either a silken purse full of gold, or [110 else a fine wrought smock.

EDW. But how shall I have the maid?

RALPH. Marry, sirrah, if thou beest a silken purse full of gold, then on Sundays she 'll hang thee by her side, and you must not say a word. Now, sir, when she comes into a great press of people, for fear of the cutpurse on a sudden she 'll swap [26] thee into her plackerd; [27] then, sirrah, being there, you may plead for yourself. 120

ERMS. Excellent policy!

EDW. But how if I be a wrought smock?

RALPH. Then she 'll put thee into her chest and lay thee into lavender, and upon some good day she 'll put thee on; and at night when you go to bed, then being turn'd from a smock to a man, you may make up the match.

LACY. Wonderfully wisely counselled, Ralph.

EDW. Ralph shall have a new coat.

RALPH. God thank you when I have [130 it on my back, Ned.

EDW. Lacy, the fool hath laid a perfect plot;

Forwhy [28] our country Margaret is so coy,
And stands so much upon her honest points,[29]
That marriage or no market with the maid.
Ermsby, it must be necromantic spells
And charms of art that must enchain her love,
Or else shall Edward never win the girl.
Therefore, my wags, we 'll horse us in the morn,
And post to Oxford to this jolly friar; 140
Bacon shall by his magic do this deed.

WAR. Content, my Lord; and that 's a speedy way
To wean these headstrong puppies from the teat.

EDW. I am unknown, not taken for the prince;
They only deem us frolic courtiers,
That revel thus among our liege's game;
Therefore I have devised a policy.
Lacy, thou know'st next Friday is Saint James',[30]
And then the country flocks to Harleston Fair;
Then will the Keeper's daughter frolic there,
And overshine the troop of all the maids 151
That come to see and to be seen that day.
Haunt thee disguis'd among the country swains;

Feign th' art a farmer's son, not far from thence;
Espy her loves, and who she liketh best;
Cote [31] him, and court her, to control the clown;
Say that the courtier tired all in green,
That help'd her handsomely to run her cheese,
And fill'd her father's lodge with venison,
Commends him, and sends fairings to herself.
Buy something worthy of her parentage, 161
Not worth her beauty; for, Lacy, then the fair
Affords no jewel fitting for the maid.
And when thou talkest of me, note if she blush:
O, then she loves; but if her cheeks wax pale,
Disdain it is. Lacy, send how she fares,
And spare no time nor cost to win her loves.

LACY. I will, my Lord, so execute this charge
As if that Lacy were in love with her.

P. EDW. Send letters speedily to Oxford of the news. 170

RALPH. And, Sirrah Lacy, buy me a thousand thousand million of fine bells.

LACY. What wilt thou do with them, Ralph?

RALPH. Marry, every time that Ned sighs for the Keeper's daughter, I 'll tie a bell about him; and so within three or four days I will send word to his father Harry that his son and my master Ned is become love's morris dance.

P. EDW. Well, Lacy, look with care unto thy charge,
And I will haste to Oxford to the friar, 180
That he by art and thou by secret gifts
Mayst make me lord of merry Fressingfield.

LACY. God send your Honor your heart's desire.

Exeunt.

[SCENE II] [32]

Enter FRIAR BACON, *with* MILES, *his poor scholar, with books under his arm; with them* BURDEN, MASON, [and] CLEMENT, *three doctors.*

BACON. Miles, where are you?

MILES. *Hic sum, do[c]tissime et reverendissime doctor.*

BACON. [*Attulistin'*] [33] *libros meos de necromantia?*

MILES. *Ecce quam bonum et quam jucundum habitare* [34] *libros in unum!* [35]

---

[26] Clap.
[27] Placket, slit in skirt or petticoat.
[28] Because.
[29] Insists to such an extent on considerations of chastity. [30] July 25.
[31] Outstrip, surpass.
[32] Oxford. Friar Bacon's cell.
[33] Old eds. *Attulisti nos.*
[34] Q1 *iocundum, habitares.*
[35] A parody of Psalm cxxxiii, 1.

Bacon. Now, masters of our academic state,
That rule in Oxford, viceroys in your place, [9
Whose heads contain maps of the liberal arts,
Spending your time in depth of learned skill,
Why flock you thus to Bacon's secret cell,
A friar newly stall'd in Brazen-nose? [36]
Say what's your mind, that I may make reply.

Burd. Bacon, we hear that [37] long we have
　　suspect,
That thou art read in magic's mystery;
In pyromancy, to divine by flames;
To tell, by [hydromantic],[38] ebbs and tides;
By aeromancy to discover doubts,
To plain out [39] questions, as Apollo did. 20

Bacon. Well, Master Burden, what of all
　　this?

Miles. Marry, sir, he doth but fulfil, by re-
hearsing of these names, the fable of the Fox
and the Grapes; that which is above us pertains nothing to us.

Burd. I tell thee, Bacon, Oxford makes re-
　　port,
Nay, England and the court of Henry says,
Th'art making of a brazen head by art,
Which shall unfold strange doubts and apho-
　　risms,
And read a lecture in philosophy; 30
And, by the help of devils and ghastly fiends,
Thou mean'st, ere many years or days be past,
To compass England with a wall of brass.

Bacon. And what of this?

Miles. What of this, master! Why, he
doth speak mystically; for he knows, if your
skill fail to make a brazen head, yet Mother
Waters' strong ale will fit his turn to make him
have a copper nose.

Clem. Bacon, we come not grieving at thy
　　skill, 40
But joying that our academy [40] yields
A man suppos'd the wonder of the world;
For if thy cunning work these miracles,
England and Europe shall admire thy fame,
And Oxford shall in characters of brass,
And statues, such as were built up in Rome,
Eternize [41] Friar Bacon for his art.

Mason. Then, gentle friar, tell us thy in-
　　tent.

Bacon. Seeing you come as friends unto the
　　friar, 49

Resolve you,[42] Doctors, Bacon can by books
Make storming Boreas thunder from his cave,
And dim fair Luna to a dark eclipse.
The great archruler, potentate of hell,
Trembles when Bacon bids him or his fiends
Bow to the force of his [pentagonon].[43]
What art can work, the frolic friar knows;
And therefore will I turn my magic books,
And strain out necromancy to the deep.
I have contriv'd and fram'd a head of brass
(I made Belcephon hammer out the stuff), [60
And that by art shall read philosophy;
And I will strengthen England by my skill,
That if ten Cæsars liv'd and reign'd in Rome,
With all the legions Europe doth contain,
They should not touch a grass of English
　　ground.
The work that Ninus rear'd at Babylon,
The brazen walls fram'd by Semiramis,
Carved out like to the portal of the sun,
Shall not be such as rings the English strand
From Dover to the marketplace of Rye. 70

Burd. Is this possible?

Miles. I'll bring ye two or three witnesses.

Burd. What be those?

Miles. Marry, sir, three or four as honest
devils and good companions as any be in hell.

Mason. No doubt but magic may do much
　　in this;
For he that reads but mathematic rules
Shall find conclusions that avail to work
Wonders that pass the common sense of
　　men.

Burd. But Bacon roves a bow beyond his
　　reach,[44] 80
And tells of more than magic can perform,
Thinking to get a fame by fooleries.
Have I not pass'd as far in state [45] of schools,
And read of many secrets? Yet to think
That heads of brass can utter any voice,
Or more, to tell of deep philosophy,
This is a fable Æsop had forgot.

Bacon. Burden, thou wrong'st me in de-
　　tracting thus;
Bacon loves not to stuff himself with lies.
But tell me 'fore these doctors, if thou dare, 90
Of certain questions I shall move to thee.

[36] Brasenose College was not founded till 1509,
but one of its buildings, "Brazen Nose Hall," was
very old.
[37] That which.
[38] Old eds. *Hadromaticke.*
[39] Explain.
[40] Accented on third syllable.
[41] Accented on second syllable.

[42] Be assured.
[43] Old eds. *Pentageron*, but cf. IV, iii, 92. Pentacle or pentagram, the five-rayed star, made by
projecting the sides of a regular pentagon, and from
ancient times a mystic symbol.
[44] *I.e.*, is shooting (that is, trying to shoot) beyond
the extent of his power. "To rove" = to shoot, not
at a fixed target, but for distance. "Bow" = bow-
length, or (possibly) bow-shot. The stone markers
set up for distance-shooting were called "rovers."
[45] Rank; *i.e.*, degrees, "honors."

BURD. I will ; ask what thou can.

MILES. Marry, sir, he 'll straight be on your pick-pack,[46] to know whether the feminine or the masculine gender be most worthy.

BACON. Were you not yesterday, Master Burden, at Henley upon the Thames?

BURD. I was ; what then?

BACON. What book studied you there on all night?   100

BURD. I? none at all ; I read not there a line.

BACON. Then, Doctors, Friar Bacon's art knows naught.

CLEM. What say you to this, Master Burden? Doth he not touch you?

BURD. I pass not of [47] his frivolous speeches.

MILES. Nay, Master Burden, my master, ere he hath done with you, will turn you from a doctor to a dunce, and shake you so small that he will leave no more learning in you than is in Balaam's ass.   110

BACON. Masters, for that learned Burden's skill is deep,

And sore he doubts of Bacon's cabalism,

I 'll show you why he haunts to Henley oft :

Not, Doctors, for to taste the fragrant air,

But there to spend the night in alchemy,

To multiply with secret spells of art ;

Thus private steals he learning from us all.

To prove my saying's true, I 'll show you straight

The book he keeps at Henley for himself.

MILES. Nay, now my master goes to conjuration, take heed.   121

BACON. Masters, stand still ; fear not ; I 'll show you but his book.   *Here he conjures.*

Per omnes deos infernales, Belcephon!

Enter a Woman *with a shoulder of mutton on a spit, and a* Devil.

MILES. O master, cease your conjuration, or you spoil all ; for here 's a she-devil come with a shoulder of mutton on a spit. You have marr'd the Devil's supper ; but no doubt he thinks our college fare is slender, and so hath sent you his cook with a shoulder of mut- [130 ton, to make it exceed.

HOSTESS. O, where am I, or what 's become of me?

BACON. What art thou?

HOSTESS. Hostess at Henley, mistress of the Bell.

BACON. How camest thou here?

HOSTESS. As I was in the kitchen 'mongst the maids,

Spitting the meat against supper for my [guests],[48]

A motion moved me to look forth of door.

No sooner had I pried into the yard,

But straight a whirlwind hoisted me from thence,   140

And mounted me aloft unto the clouds.

As in a trance, I thought nor feared naught,

Nor know I where or whither I was ta'en,

Nor where I am nor what these persons be.

BACON. No? Know you not Master Burden?

HOSTESS. O, yes, good sir ; he is my daily guest. —

What, Master Burden ! 't was but yesternight

That you and I at Henley play'd at cards.

BURD. I know not what we did. — A pox of all conjuring friars !   150

CLEM. Now, jolly friar, tell us, is this the book

That Burden is so careful to look on?

BACON. It is. — But, Burden, tell me now,

Thinkest thou that Bacon's necromantic skill

Cannot perform his head and wall of brass,

When he can fetch thine hostess in such post?

MILES. I 'll warrant you, master, if Master Burden could conjure as well as you, he would have his book every night from Henley to study on at Oxford.   160

MASON. Burden,

What, are you mated [49] by this frolic friar? —

Look how he droops ; his guilty conscience

Drives him to bash,[50] and makes his hostess blush.

BACON. Well, mistress, for I will not have you miss'd,

You shall to Henley to cheer up your guests

'Fore supper 'gin. — Burden, bid her adieu ;

Say farewell to your hostess 'fore she goes. —

Sirrah, away, and set her safe at home.

HOSTESS. Master Burden, when shall [170 we see you at Henley?

Exeunt Hostess *and the* Devil.

BURD. The Devil take thee and Henley too.

MILES. Master, shall I make a good motion?

BACON. What 's that?

MILES. Marry, sir, now that my hostess is gone to provide supper, conjure up another spirit, and send Doctor Burden flying after.

[46] Pick-a-back, on your shoulders, at you.

[47] Am unmoved by, care not for.

[48] Old eds. *guesse;* cf. "the Americanism 'less' for 'let us.' " (Ward.)

[49] Confounded.   [50] Be abashed.

BACON. Thus, rulers of our academic state,
You have seen the friar frame his art by proof ;
And as the college called Brazen-nose   180
Is under him, and he the master there,
So surely shall this head of brass be fram'd,
And yield forth strange and uncouth [51] apho-
      risms ;
And hell and Hecate [52] shall fail the friar,
But I will circle England round with brass.
  Miles. So be it *et nunc et semper*, amen.
                                    Exeunt omnes.

[SCENE III] [53]

Enter MARGARET, *the fair maid of Fressingfield,*
  with JOAN, THOMAS, [RICHARD,] *and other*
  Clowns ; [*and*] LACY *disguised in country*
  apparel.

  THOM. By my troth, Margaret,[54] here's a
weather is able to make a man call his father
whoreson ; if this weather hold, we shall have
hay good cheap,[55] and butter and cheese at
Harleston will bear no price.
  MAR. Thomas, maids when they come to
      see the fair
Count not to make a cope [56] for dearth of hay ;
When we have turn'd our butter to the salt,
And set our cheese safely upon the racks,
Then let our fathers price it as they please. 10
We country sluts of merry Fressingfield
Come to buy needless naughts to make us fine,
And look that young men should be frank [57]
      this day,
And court us with such fairings as they can.
Phœbus [58] is blithe, and frolic looks from
      Heaven,
As when he courted lovely Semele,
Swearing the pedlars shall have empty packs,
If that fair weather may make chapmen buy.
  LACY. But, lovely Peggy, Semele is dead,
And therefore Phœbus from his palace pries,
And, seeing such a sweet and seemly saint,   21
Shows all his glories for to court yourself.
  MAR. This is a fairing, gentle sir, indeed,
To soothe me up with such smooth flattery ;
But learn of me, your scoff 's too broad be-
      fore. — [59]
Well, Joan, our beauties must abide their jests ;
We serve the turn in jolly Fressingfield.

  JOAN. Margaret, a farmer's daughter for a
      farmer's son !
I warrant you, the meanest of us both
Shall have a mate to lead us from the church.—
But, Thomas, what's the news? What, in a
      dump?   31
Give me your hand, we are near a pedlar's
      shop ;
Out with your purse : we must have fairings
      now.
  THOM. Faith, Joan, and shall. I'll bestow
a fairing on you, and then we will to the tavern,
and snap off a pint of wine or two.
      All this while LACY *whispers* MAR-
        GARET *in the ear.*
  MAR. Whence are you, sir? Of Suffolk?
      For your terms
Are finer than the common sort of men.
  LACY. Faith, lovely girl, I am of Beccles by,
Your neighbor, not above six miles from
      hence,   40
A farmer's son, that never was so quaint [60]
But that he could do courtesy to such dames.
But trust me, Margaret, I am sent in charge
From him that revell'd in your father's house,
And fill'd his lodge with cheer and venison,
Tired in green. He sent you this rich purse,
His token that he help'd you run your cheese,
And in the milkhouse chatted with yourself.
  MAR. To me? You forget yourself.[61]   49
  LACY. Women are often weak in memory.
  MAR. O, pardon, sir, I call to mind the man.
'T were little manners to refuse his gift,
And yet I hope he sends it not for love ;
For we have little leisure to debate of that.
  JOAN. What, Margaret ! blush not ; maids
      must have their loves.
  THOM. Nay, by the mass, she looks pale as
if she were angry.
  RICH. Sirrah, are you of Beccles? I pray,
how doth Goodman Cob? My father bought
a horse of him. — I'll tell you, Margaret, [60
'a were good to be a gentleman's jade, for of all
things the foul hilding [62] could not abide a
doongcart.
  MAR. [*aside*] How different is this farmer
      from the rest
That erst [63] as yet hath pleas'd my wand'ring
      sight !
His words are witty, quickened with a smile,

---

[51] Uncanny.   [52] Trisyllabic.
[53] Harleston Fair.
[54] Old eds. *Margret* here and usually throughout,
even when trisyllabic.   [55] At a low price.
[56] Transaction, bargain.
[57] Liberal.
[58] It was Zeus who courted Semele.
[59] On the face of it. (Gayley.)

[60] Fastidious.
[61] *I.e.*, you are mistaken. Dyce, Ward, and Neilson give these three words to Lacy. Probably
something has dropped out.
[62] Wretch.
[63] In the time just past. (Webster.)

His courtesy gentle, smelling of the court ;
Facile and debonair in all his deeds,
Proportion'd as was Paris, when, in gray,[64]
He courted Œnon in the vale by Troy.   70
Great lords have come and pleaded for my
love —
Who but the Keeper's lass of Fressingfield?
And yet methinks this farmer's jolly son
Passeth the proudest that hath pleas'd mine
eye.
But, Peg, disclose not that thou art in love,
And show as yet no sign of love to him,
Although thou well wouldst wish him for thy
love ;
Keep that to thee till time doth serve thy turn,
To show the grief wherein thy heart doth
burn. —
Come, Joan and Thomas, shall we to the
fair ? —   80
You, Beccles man, will not forsake us now.
    LACY. Not whilst I may have such quaint [65]
     girls as you.
    MAR. Well, if you chance to come by Fres-
     singfield,
Make but a step into the Keeper's lodge,
And such poor fare as woodmen can afford,
Butter and cheese, cream, and fat venison,
You shall have store, and welcome therewithal.
    LACY. Gramercies, Peggy ; look for me ere
     long.   *Exeunt omnes.*

        [ACT II — SCENE I][1]

Enter [KING] HENRY THE THIRD, *the* EMPEROR,
  the KING OF CASTILE, ELINOR *his daughter,*
  [*and*] JACQUES VANDERMAST *a German.*

    HEN. Great men of Europe, monarchs of
     the West,
Ring'd with the walls of old Oceanus,
Whose lofty [surge is][2] like the battlements
That compass'd high-built Babel in with
towers,
Welcome, my Lords, welcome, brave western
kings,
To England's shore, whose promontory cliffs
Shows Albion is another little world ;
Welcome says English Henry to you all ;
Chiefly unto the lovely Elinor,
Who dar'd for Edward's sake cut through the
seas,   10

And venture as Agenor's [3] damsel through the
deep,
To get the love of Henry's wanton [4] son.
    CAST. England's rich monarch, brave Plan-
     tagenet,
The Pyren Mounts swelling above the clouds,
That ward the wealthy Castile in with walls,
Could not detain the beauteous Elinor ;
But, hearing of the fame of Edward's youth,
She dar'd to brook Neptunus' haughty pride,
And bide the brunt of froward Æolus :   19
Then may fair England welcome her the more.
    ELIN. After that English Henry by his lords
Had sent Prince Edward's lovely counterfeit,
A present to the Castile Elinor,
The comely portrait of so brave a man,
The virtuous fame discoursed of his deeds,
Edward's courageous resolution,
Done at the Holy Land 'fore Damas' [5] walls,
Led both mine eye and thoughts in equal links
To like so of the English monarch's son
That I attempted perils for his sake.   30
    EMP. Where is the Prince, my Lord?
    HEN. He posted down, not long since, from
     the court,
To Suffolk side, to merry Framlingham,[6]
To sport himself amongst my fallow deer ;
From thence, by packets sent to Hampton
House,[7]
We hear the Prince is ridden with his lords
To Oxford, in the academy there
To hear dispute amongst the learned men.
But we will send forth letters for my son,
To will him come from Oxford to the court. 40
    EMP. Nay, rather, Henry, let us, as we be,
Ride for to visit Oxford with our train.
Fain would I see your universities,
And what learned men your academy yields.
From Ha[p]sburg [8] have I brought a learned
clerk
To hold dispute with English orators.
This doctor, surnam'd Jacques Vandermast,
A German born, pass'd into Padua,
To Florence and to fair Bologna,[9]

---

[64] The conventional garb of literary shepherds.
[65] Dainty.
[1] A hall in Hampton Court (see l. 35 and note).
[2] Cor. Dyce ; old eds. *surges.*

[3] Improperly accented here on the first syllable.
[4] Amorous.
[5] Damascus'. Edward never fought there. He
had been married to Eleanor for sixteen years when
he went on this crusade.
[6] Old eds. *Fremingham*, indicating the pronunciation.
[7] This palace was built by Cardinal Wolsey ; perhaps its association with Henry VIII, its first royal
owner, is responsible for its assignment here to
another "English Henry."
[8] Frederick was actually of the Suabian house of
Hohenstaufen. (Ward.)
[9] Old eds. *Bolonia*, indicating pronunciation.

To Paris, Rheims, and stately Orleans,   50
And, talking there with men of art, put down
The chiefest of them all in aphorisms,[10]
In magic, and the mathematic rules ;
Now let us, Henry, try him in your schools.
    HEN. He shall, my Lord ; this motion [11]
        likes me well.
We 'll progress straight to Oxford with our
        trains,
And see what men our academy brings. —
And, wonder Vandermast, welcome to me.
In Oxford shalt thou find a jolly friar
Call'd Friar Bacon, England's only flower : [60
Set him but nonplus in his magic spells,
And make him yield in mathematic rules,
And for thy glory I will bind thy brows,
Not with a poet's garland made of bays,
But with a coronet of choicest gold.
Whilst,[12] then, we set [13] to Oxford with our
        troops,
Let 's in and banquet in our English court.
                                    [*Exeunt.*]

[SCENE II] [14]

Enter RALPH SIMNELL *in* [PRINCE] EDWARD'S
apparel ; and [PRINCE] EDWARD, WARREN,
[*and*] ERMSBY, *disguised.*

    RALPH. Where be these vagabond knaves,
that they attend no better on their master?
    EDW. If it please your Honor, we are all
ready at an inch.[15]
    RALPH. Sirrah Ned, I 'll have no more post-
horse to ride on ; I 'll have another fetch.[16]
    ERMS. I pray you, how is that, my Lord?
    RALPH. Marry, sir, I 'll send to the Isle of
Ely for four or five dozen of geese, and I 'll have
them ti'd six and six together with whip- [10
cord.   Now upon their backs will I have a fair
field-bed with a canopy ; and so, when it is my
pleasure, I 'll flee into what place I please.
This will be easy.
    WAR. Your Honor hath said well ; but
shall we to Brazen-nose College before we pull
off our boots?
    ERMS. Warren, well motion'd ; we will to
        the friar
Before we revel it within the town. —
Ralph, see you keep your countenance like a
        prince.   20

    RALPH. Wherefore have I such a company
of cutting [17] knaves to wait upon me, but to
keep and defend my countenance against all
mine enemies?   Have you not good swords
and bucklers?

Enter [FRIAR] BACON *and* MILES.

    ERMS. Stay, who comes here?
    WAR. Some scholar ; and we 'll ask him
where Friar Bacon is.
    BACON. Why, thou arrant dunce, shall I
never make thee good scholar?   Doth not [30
all the town cry out and say, Friar Bacon's
subsizar [18] is the greatest blockhead in all Oxford?   Why, thou canst not speak one word of
true Latin.
    MILES. No, sir — yes, what is this else?
Ego sum tuus homo : I am your man — I warrant you, sir, as good Tully's phrase [19] as any
is in Oxford.
    BACON. Come on, sirrah ; what part of
speech is *Ego ?*   40
    MILES. *Ego,* that is " I " ; marry, *nomen
substantivo.*
    BACON. How prove you that?
    MILES. Why, sir, let him prove himself an
'a will ; I can be heard, felt, and understood.[20]
    BACON. O gross dunce !   *Here beat him.*
    EDW. Come, let us break off this dispute
between these two. — Sirrah, where is Brazen-
nose College?
    MILES. Not far from Coppersmith's Hall.
    EDW. What, doest thou mock me?   51
    MILES. Not I, sir ; but what would you at
Brazen-nose?
    ERMS. Marry, we would speak with Friar
Bacon.
    MILES. Whose men be you?
    ERMS. Marry, scholar, here 's our master.
    RALPH. Sirrah, I am the master of these
good fellows ; mayst thou not know me to be
a lord by my reparrel?   60
    MILES. Then here 's good game for the
hawk ; for here 's the master-fool and a covey
of coxcombs.   One wise man, I think, would
spring you [21] all.
    EDW. Gog's wounds !   Warren, kill him.
    WAR. Why, Ned, I think the Devil be in
my sheath ; I cannot get out my dagger.

---

[10] Statements of scientific principles.
[11] Proposal.
[12] Till.
[13] Emend. Dyce. Q 1 *fit ;* Qq 2, 3, *sit.* Greg conj. *flit.*
[14] Oxford. A street.
[15] Close at hand, in immediate readiness.(*N.E.D.*)
[16] Trick, device.

[17] Swaggering.
[18] Student who received aid in the form of a
scholarship or free board, and of whom menial
services were required.
[19] Ciceronian Latin.
[20] " A humorous condensation of the definition of
a noun substantive." (Ward.)
[21] Make you fly off.

ERMS. Nor I mine. 'Swones, Ned, I think I am bewitch'd.

MILES. A company of scabs! The [70 proudest of you all draw your weapon, if he can. — [*to the audience*] See how boldly I speak, now my master is by.

EDW. I strive in vain; but, if my sword be shut
And conjured fast by magic in my sheath,
Villain, here is my fist.

     Strike him a box on the ear.

MILES. O, I beseech you conjure his hands too, that he may not lift his arms to his head, for he is light-fingered!   79

RALPH. Ned, strike him; I'll warrant thee, by mine honor.

BACON. What means the English Prince to wrong my man?

EDW. To whom speakest thou?

BACON. To thee.

EDW. Who art thou?

BACON. Could you not judge when all your swords grew fast,
That Friar Bacon was not far from hence?
Edward, King Henry's son and Prince of Wales,
Thy fool disguis'd cannot conceal thyself.
I know both Ermsby and the Sussex Earl, 90
Else Friar Bacon had but little skill.
Thou comest in post from merry Fressingfield,
Fast-fancied to [22] the Keeper's bonny lass,
To crave some succor of the jolly friar;
And Lacy, Earl of Lincoln, hast thou left
To treat fair Margaret to allow thy loves;
But friends are men, and love can baffle lords;
The Earl both woos and courts her for himself.

WAR. Ned, this is strange; the friar knoweth all.

ERMS. Apollo could not utter more than this.   100

EDW. I stand amazed to hear this jolly friar Tell even the very secrets of my thoughts. — But, learned Bacon, since thou knowest the cause
Why I did post so fast from Fressingfield,
Help, friar, at a pinch, that I may have
The love of lovely Margaret to myself,
And, as I am true Prince of Wales, I'll give
Living and lands to strength thy college state. [23]

WAR. Good friar, help the Prince in this. [109

RALPH. Why, servant Ned, will not the friar do it? Were not my sword glued to my

[22] Fast in love with.
[23] The estate of thy college.

scabbard by conjuration, I would cut off his head, and make him do it by force.

MILES. In faith, my Lord, your manhood and your sword is all alike; they are so fast conjured that we shall never see them.

ERMS. What, Doctor, in a dump? Tush, help the Prince,
And thou shalt see how liberal he will prove.

BACON. Crave not such actions greater dumps than these?   119
I will, my Lord, strain out my magic spells;
For this day comes the Earl to Fressingfield,
And 'fore that night shuts in the day with dark,
They'll be betrothed each to other fast.
But come with me; we'll to my study straight,
And in a glass prospective I will show
What's done this day in merry Fressingfield.

EDW. Gramercies, Bacon; I will quit thy pain.

BACON. But send your train, my Lord, into the town;
My scholar shall go bring them to their inn.
Meanwhile we'll see the knavery of the Earl.

EDW. Warren, leave me; and, Ermsby, take the Fool;   131
Let him be master, and go revel it,
Till I and Friar Bacon talk awhile.

WAR. We will, my Lord.

RALPH. Faith, Ned, and I'll lord it out till that comest. I'll be Prince of Wales over all the blackpots [24] in Oxford.   *Exeunt.*

[SCENE III] [25]

[FRIAR] BACON *and* [PRINCE] EDWARD *goes into the study.*

BACON. Now, frolic Edward, welcome to my cell;
Here tempers Friar Bacon many toys, [26]
And holds this place his consistory court,
Wherein the devils pleads homage to his words.
Within this glass prospective thou shalt see
This day what's done in merry Fressingfield
'Twixt lovely Peggy and the Lincoln Earl.

EDW. Friar, thou gladd'st me. Now shall Edward try
How Lacy meaneth to his sovereign lord.

BACON. Stand there and look directly in the glass.   10

[24] Topers. (*N. E. D.*)
[25] Friar Bacon's cell. This is represented by the inner stage ("study"), while on the outer stage appear the figures the Prince is supposed to see (but not hear) in the magic glass.
[26] Here Bacon fashions many trifles.

Enter MARGARET *and* FRIAR BUNGAY.

What sees my Lord?

EDW. I see the Keeper's lovely lass appear,
As [brightsome] [27] as the paramour of Mars,
Only attended by a jolly friar.

BACON. Sit still, and keep the crystal in
your eye.

MAR. But tell me, Friar Bungay, is it true
That this fair,[28] courteous country swain,
Who says his father is a farmer nigh,
Can be Lord Lacy, Earl of Lincolnshire?

BUN. Peggy, 't is true, 't is Lacy for my
life,   20
Or else mine art and cunning both doth fail,
Left by Prince Edward to procure his loves ;
For he in green, that holp you run your cheese,
Is son to Henry and the Prince of Wales.

MAR. Be what he will, his lure is but for
lust.
But did Lord Lacy like poor Margaret,
Or would he deign to wed a country lass,
Friar, I would his humble handmaid be,
And for great wealth quit him with courtesy.

BUN. Why, Margaret, doest thou love him?

Mar. His personage, like the pride of vaunt-
ing Troy,   31
Might   well   avouch   to   shadow [29] Helen's
[scape] ; [30]
His wit is quick and ready in conceit,
As Greece afforded in her chiefest prime ;
Courteous, ah, friar, full of pleasing smiles !
Trust me, I love too much to tell thee more ;
Suffice, to me he 's England's paramour.

BUN. Hath not each eye that view'd thy
pleasing face
Surnamed thee Fair Maid of Fressingfield?

MAR. Yes, Bungay ; and would God the
lovely Earl   40
Had that in *esse* that so many sought.

BUN. Fear not, the friar will not be behind
To show his cunning to entangle love.

EDW. I think the friar courts the bonny
wench ;
Bacon, methinks he is a lusty churl.

BACON. Now look, my Lord.

Enter LACY [*disguised as before*].

EDW. Gog's wounds, Bacon, here comes
Lacy !

BACON. Sit still, my Lord, and mark the
comedy.

BUN. Here 's Lacy, Margaret ; step aside
awhile.

LACY. Daphne, the damsel that caught
Phœbus fast,   50
And lock'd him in the brightness of her looks,
Was not so beauteous in Apollo's eyes
As is fair Margaret to the Lincoln Earl.
Recant thee, Lacy ; thou art put in trust :
Edward, thy sovereign's son, hath chosen thee,
A secret friend, to court her for himself ;
And darest thou wrong thy prince with treach-
ery?
Lacy, love makes no exception of a friend,
Nor deems it of a prince but as a man.
Honor bids thee control him in his lust ;   60
His wooing is not for to wed the girl,
But to entrap her and beguile the lass.
Lacy, thou lovest ; then brook not such abuse,
But wed her, and abide thy prince's frown ;
For better die than see her live disgrac'd.

MAR. Come, friar, I will shake him from his
dumps. —
[*coming forward*] How cheer you, sir? A
penny for your thought !
You 're early up ; pray God it be the near.[31]
What, come from Beccles in a morn so soon?

LACY. Thus watchful are such men as live in
love,   70
Whose eyes brook broken slumbers for their
sleep.
I tell thee, Peggy, since last Harleston Fair
My mind hath felt a heap of passions.

MAR. A trusty man, that court it for your
friend.
Woo you still for the courtier all in green?
I marvel that he sues not for himself.

LACY. Peggy,
I pleaded first to get your grace for him ;
But when mine eyes survey'd your beauteous
looks,
Love, like a wag, straight dived into my heart,
And there did shrine the idea [32] of yourself. 81
Pity me, though I be a farmer's son,
And measure not my riches, but my love.

MAR. You are very hasty ; for, to garden
well,
Seeds must have time to sprout before they
spring.
Love ought to creep as doth the dial's shade,
For timely [33] ripe is rotten too, too soon.

---

[27] Cor. Dyce ; old eds. *bright-sunne.*
[28] Dissyllabic ; the line is regular, save that the
initial unstressed syllable is lacking.
[29] Excuse.
[30] Sin. (*N. E. D.*) (Cf. II, iv, 145). Emend. Gayley ; old eds. *cape.*

[31] Nearer ; alluding to the proverb, "Early up and
never the nearer."
[32] Image.   [33] Early.

Bun. [*coming forward*] *Deus hic ;* room for a merry friar !

What, youth of Beccles, with the Keeper's lass?

'T is well ; but tell me, hear you any news?   90

Mar. No, friar. What news?

Bun. Hear you not how the pursuivants [34] do post

With proclamations through each country town?

Lacy. For what, gentle friar? Tell the news.

Bun. Dwell'st thou in Beccles, and hear'st not of these news?

Lacy, the Earl of Lincoln, is late fled

From Windsor court, disguised like a swain,

And lurks about the country here unknown.

Henry suspects him of some treachery,

And therefore doth proclaim in every way, [100

That who can take the Lincoln Earl shall have,

Paid in the Exchequer, twenty thousand crowns.

Lacy. The Earl of Lincoln! Friar, thou art mad.

It was some other ; thou mistakest the man.

The Earl of Lincoln! Why, it cannot be.

Mar. Yes, very well, my Lord, for you are he :

The Keeper's daughter took you prisoner.

Lord Lacy, yield ; I 'll be your jailer once.

Edw. How familiar they be, Bacon !

Bacon. Sit still, and mark the sequel of their loves.   110

Lacy. Then am I double prisoner to thyself.

Peggy, I yield. But are these news in jest?

Mar. In jest with you, but earnest unto me ;

Forwhy [35] these wrongs do wring me at the heart.

Ah, how these earls and noble men of birth

Flatter and feign to forge poor women's ill !

Lacy. Believe me, lass, I am the Lincoln Earl ;

I not deny but, tired thus in rags,

I liv'd disguis'd to win fair Peggy's love.

Mar. What love is there where wedding ends not love?   120

Lacy. I meant, fair girl, to make thee Lacy's wife.

Mar. I little think that earls will stoop so low.

Lacy. Say, shall I make thee countess ere I sleep?

Mar. Handmaid unto the Earl, so please himself ;

A wife in name, but servant in obedience.

Lacy. The Lincoln Countess, for it shall be so ;

I 'll plight the bands,[36] and seal it with a kiss.

Edw. Gog's wounds, Bacon, they kiss ! I 'll stab them.

Bacon. O, hold your hands, my Lord ; it is the glass !

Edw. Choler to see the traitors gree so well   130

Made me think the shadows substances.

Bacon. 'T were a long poniard, my Lord, to reach between

Oxford and Fressingfield ; but sit still and see more.

Bun. Well, Lord of Lincoln, if your loves be knit,

And that [37] your tongues and thoughts do both agree,

To avoid ensuing jars, I 'll hamper [38] up the match.

I 'll take my portace [39] forth and wed you here.

Then go to bed and seal up your desires.

Lacy. Friar, content. — Peggy, how like you this?

Mar. What likes my Lord is pleasing unto me.   140

Bun. Then handfast [40] hand, and I will to my book.

Bacon. What sees my Lord now?

Edw. Bacon, I see the lovers hand in hand,

The friar ready with his portace there

To wed them both ; then am I quite undone.

Bacon, help now, if e'er thy magic serv'd ;

Help, Bacon ! Stop the marriage now,

If devils or necromancy may suffice,

And I will give thee forty thousand crowns.

Bacon. Fear not, my Lord, I 'll stop the jolly friar   150

For [41] mumbling up his orisons this day.

Lacy. Why speak'st not, Bungay? Friar, to thy book.

Bungay is mute, crying, " Hud, hud."

Mar. How lookest thou, friar, as a man distraught !

Reft of thy senses, Bungay? Show by signs,

If thou be dumb, what passions [42] holdeth thee.

Lacy. He's dumb indeed. Bacon hath with his devils

[34] Royal warrant-officers.
[35] Because.
[36] Matrimonial bonds.   [37] If.   [38] Bind.
[39] Portable breviary.
[40] Clasp.
[41] With regard to, from.
[42] Qq 2, 3, *passion.*

Enchanted him, or else some strange disease
Or apoplexy hath possess'd his lungs.
But, Peggy, what he cannot with his book,
We 'll 'twixt us both unite it up in heart.   160
   Mar. Else let me die, my Lord, a miscreant.[43]
   Edw. Why stands Friar [Bungay][44] so amaz'd?
   Bacon. I have struck him dumb, my Lord; and, if your Honor please,
I 'll fetch this Bungay straightway from Fressingfield
And he shall dine with us in Oxford here.
   Edw. Bacon, do that, and thou contentest me.
   Lacy. Of courtesy, Margaret, let us lead the friar
Unto thy father's lodge, to comfort him
With broths, to bring him from this hapless trance.
   Mar. Or else, my Lord, we were passing unkind   170
To leave the friar so in his distress.

Enter a Devil, *and carry [out]* Bungay *on his back.*

O, help, my Lord! a devil, a devil, my Lord!
Look how he carries Bungay on his back!
Let 's hence, for Bacon's spirits be abroad.
             Exeunt [Margaret *and* Lacy].
   Edw. Bacon, I laugh to see the jolly friar
Mounted upon the devil, and how the Earl
Flees with his bonny lass for fear.
As soon as Bungay is at Brazen-nose,
And I have chatted with the merry friar,
I will in post hie me to Fressingfield,   180
And quit these wrongs on Lacy ere it be long.
   Bacon. So be it, my Lord; but let us to our dinner;
For ere we have taken our repast awhile,
We shall have Bungay brought to Brazen-nose.
                    Exeunt.

[Scene IV][45]

Enter three Doctors, Burden, Mason, [*and*] Clement.

   Mason. Now that we are gathered in the Regent House,
It fits us talk about the King's repair;
For he, troop'd with all the western kings,
That lie alongst the Danzig seas by east,
North by the clime of frosty Germany,

The Almain monarch, and the [Saxon][46] duke,
Castile and lovely Elinor with him,
Have in their [gests][47] resolv'd for Oxford town.
   Burd. We must lay plots of stately tragedies,
Strange comic shows, such as proud Roscius [10
Vaunted before the Roman emperors,
To welcome all the western potentates.[48]
   Clem. But more; the King by letters hath foretold
That Frederick, the Almain Emperor,
Hath brought with him a German of esteem,
Whose surname is Don Jaques Vandermast,
Skilful in magic and those secret arts.
   Mason. Then must we all make suit unto the friar,
To Friar Bacon, that he vouch[49] this task,
And undertake to countervail[50] in skill   20
The German; else there 's none in Oxford can
Match and dispute with learned Vandermast.
   Burd. Bacon, if he will hold the German play,
[Will][51] teach him what an English friar can do.
The Devil, I think, dare not dispute with him.
   Clem. Indeed, Mas' Doctor, he pleasured you,
In that he brought your hostess with her spit
From Henley, posting unto Brazen-nose.
   Burd. A vengeance on the friar for his pains!
But leaving that, let 's hie to Bacon straight,
To see if he will take this task in hand.   31
   Clem. Stay, what rumor[52] is this? The town is up in a mutiny. What hurly-burly is this?

Enter a Constable, *with* Ralph [Simnell], Warren, Ermsby, [*all three disguised as before*], *and* Miles.

   Cons. Nay, masters, if you were ne'er so good, you shall before the doctors to answer your misdemeanor.
   Burd. What 's the matter, fellow?
   Cons. Marry, sir, here 's a company of rufflers,[53] that, drinking in the tavern, have [40
made a great brawl, and almost kill'd the vintner.

---

[43] *I.e.,* destitute of conscience. (Webster.)
[44] Old eds. *Bacon.*
[45] The Regent House.
[46] Emend. Dyce; old eds. *Scocon.*
[47] Stages of royal journeys. Emend. Editor; old
    eds. *iests.*
[48] Old eds. give this line to Clement.
[49] Answer for.
[50] Neutralize, match.
[51] Cor. Dyce; old eds. *Weele, We'le.*
[52] Noise.
[53] Bullies.

MILES. *Salve*, Doctor Burden!
This lubberly lurden,[54]
Ill-shap'd and ill-faced,
Disdain'd and disgraced,
What he tells unto *vobis*
Mentitur de nobis.

BURD. Who is the master and chief of this crew?   50

MILES. *Ecce asinum mundi*
F[i]gura rotundi,
Neat, [feat],[55] and fine,
As brisk as a cup of wine.

BURD. What are you?

RALPH. I am, Father Doctor, as a man would say, the bellwether of this company; these are my lords, and I the Prince of Wales.

CLEM. Are you Edward, the King's son?

RALPH. Sirrah Miles, bring hither the tap-ster that drew the wine, and, I warrant, [61 when they see how soundly I have broke his head, they 'll say 't was done by no less man than a prince.

MASON. I cannot believe that this is the Prince of Wales.

WAR. And why so, sir?

MASON. For they say the Prince is a brave and a wise gentleman.

WAR. Why, and thinkest thou, Doctor, that he is not so?   70
Dar'st thou detract and derogate from him,
Being so lovely and so brave a youth?

ERMS. Whose face, shining with many a sug'red smile,
Bewrays that he is bred of princely race.

MILES. And yet, Master Doctor,
To speak like a proctor,
And tell unto you
What is veriment and true;
To cease of this quarrel,
Look but on his apparel;   80
Then mark but my talis,
He is great Prince of Walis,
The chief of our *gregis,*
And *filius regis:*
Then 'ware what is done,
For he is Henry's white [56] son.

RALPH. Doctors, whose doting nightcaps are not capable of my ingenious dignity, know that I am Edward Plantagenet, whom if you displease will make a ship that shall hold all your colleges, and so carry away the nini- [91 versity with a fair wind to the Bankside in Southwark. — How say'st thou, Ned Warren, shall I not do it?

WAR. Yes, my good Lord; and, if it please your Lordship, I will gather up all your old pantofles,[57] and with the cork [58] make you a pinnace of five hundred ton, that shall serve the turn marvellous well, my Lord.

ERMS. And I, my Lord, will have pioners to undermine the town, that the very gar- [101 dens and orchards be carried away for your summer-walks.

MILES. And I, with *scientia*
And great *diligentia,*
Will conjure and charm,
To keep you from harm;
That *utrum horum mavis,*
Your very great *navis,*
Like Bartlet's [59] ship,   110
From Oxford do skip
With colleges and schools,
Full loaden with fools.
Quid dic[i]s ad hoc,
Worshipful *Domine* Dawcock?

CLEM. Why, hare-brain'd courtiers, are you drunk or mad,
To taunt us up with such scurrility?
Deem you us men of base and light esteem,
To bring us such a fop for Henry's son? —
Call out the beadles and convey them hence
Straight to Bocardo; [60] let the roisters lie   121
Close clapp'd in bolts, until their wits be tame.

ERMS. Why, shall we to prison, my Lord?

RALPH. What say'st, Miles; shall I honor the prison with my presence?

MILES. No, no; out with your blades,
And hamper these jades;
Have a flurt and a crash,
Now play revel-dash,
And teach these *sacerdos*   130
That the Bocardos,
Like peasants and elves,
Are meet for themselves.

MASON. To the prison with them, con-stable.

WAR. Well, Doctors, seeing I have sported me
With laughing at these mad and merry wags,
Know that Prince Edward is at Brazen-nose,
And this, attired like the Prince of Wales,
Is Ralph, King Henry's only loved fool;

[54] Lout. Miles's verses parody the metre and some of the mannerisms of Skelton.
[55] Emend. Kittredge. Q *sheat.*   [56] **Darling.**
[57] Embroidered shoes.
[58] It was used for heels and inner soles.
[59] Either the compositor's or Miles's blunder for *Barclay,* translator of *The Ship of Fools.*
[60] The old north gate of Oxford, used as a prison.

I, Earl of [Sussex],[61] and this Ermsby,[62]   140
One of the privy chamber to the King;
Who, while the Prince with Friar Bacon stays,
Have revell'd it in Oxford as you see.

MASON. My Lord, pardon us; we knew not
what you were;
But courtiers may make greater scapes [63] than
these.
Wilt please your Honor dine with me to-day?

WAR. I will, Master Doctor, and satisfy the
vintner for his hurt; only, I must desire you
to imagine him all this forenoon the Prince of
Wales.   150

MASON. I will, sir.

RALPH. And upon that I will lead the way;
only, I will have Miles go before me, because
I have heard Henry say that wisdom must go
before majesty.   *Exeunt omnes.*

[ACT III — SCENE I][1]

Enter PRINCE EDWARD *with his poniard in his
hand,* LACY, *and* MARGARET.

EDW. Lacy, thou canst not shroud thy
traitorous thoughts,
Nor cover, as did Cassius all his wiles;
For Edward hath an eye that looks as far
As Lynceus[2] from the shores of Græcia.
Did not I sit in Oxford by the friar,
And see thee court the maid of Fressingfield,
Sealing thy flattering fancies with a kiss?
Did not proud Bungay draw his portace forth,
And, joining hand in hand, had married you,
If Friar Bacon had not struck him dumb,   10
And mounted him upon a spirit's back,
That we might chat at Oxford with the friar?
Traitor, what answer'st? Is not all this true?

LACY. Truth all, my Lord; and thus I
make reply:
At Harleston Fair, there courting for your
Grace,
Whenas mine eye survey'd her curious shape,
And drew the beauteous glory of her looks
To dive into the centre of my heart,
Love taught me that your Honor did but
jest,
That princes were in fancy[3] but as men;   20
How that the lovely maid of Fressingfield

Was fitter to be Lacy's wedded wife
Than concubine unto the Prince of Wales.

EDW. Injurious Lacy, did I love thee more
Than Alexander his Hephæstion?
Did I unfold the [passions][4] of my love,
And lock them in the closet of thy thoughts?
Wert thou to Edward second to himself,
Sole friend, and partner of his secret loves?
And could a glance of fading beauty break [30
The enchained fetters of such private friends?
Base coward, false, and too effeminate
To be corrival[5] with a prince in thoughts!
From Oxford have I posted since I din'd,
To quit[6] a traitor 'fore that Edward sleep.

MAR. 'T was I, my Lord, not Lacy stepp'd
awry:
For oft he sued and courted for yourself,
And still woo'd for the courtier all in green;
But I, whom fancy made but overfond,
Pleaded myself with looks as if I lov'd;   40
I fed mine eye with gazing on his face,
And still bewitch'd lov'd Lacy with my looks;
My heart with sighs, mine eyes pleaded with
tears,
My face held pity and content at once,
And more I could not cipher out by signs
But that I lov'd Lord Lacy with my heart.
Then, worthy Edward, measure with thy mind
If women's favors will not force men fall,
If beauty, and if darts of piercing love,
Is not of force to bury thoughts of friends.   50

EDW. I tell thee, Peggy, I will have thy
loves;
Edward or none shall conquer Margaret.
In frigates bottom'd with rich Sethin[7] planks,
Topp'd with the lofty firs of Lebanon,
Stemm'd and incas'd with burnish'd ivory,
And overlaid with plates of Persian wealth,
Like Thetis shalt thou wanton on the waves,
And draw the dolphins to thy lovely eyes,
To dance lavoltas in the purple streams;
Sirens, with harps and silver psalteries,   60
Shall wait with music at thy frigate's stem,
And entertain fair Margaret with [their][8] lays.
England and England's wealth shall wait on
thee;
Britain shall bend unto her prince's love,
And do due homage to thine excellence,
If thou wilt be but Edward's Margaret.

MAR. Pardon, my Lord: if Jove's great
royalty
Sent me such presents as to Danaë;

---

[61] Old eds. *Essex*.   [62] Trisyllabic.
[63] Escapades, scrapes.
[1] Fressingfield. Before the Keeper's lodge.
[2] One of the Argonauts, celebrated for his keen
eyesight.
[3] Love.

[4] So Qq 2, 3; Q 1 *passion*.
[5] Sharer.   [6] Requite.   [7] Shittim.
[8] Cor. Dyce; old eds. *her*.

If Phœbus, [tired] [9] in Latona's webs,
Come courting from the beauty of his lodge ;
The dulcet tunes of frolic Mercury,   71
[Nor] [10] all the wealth Heaven's treasury af-
    fords,
Should make me leave Lord Lacy or his love.
   Edw. I have learn'd at Oxford, then, this
    point of schools :
Ab[l]ata causa, tollitur effectus.[11]
Lacy, the cause that Margaret cannot love
Nor fix her liking on the English prince,
Take him away, and then th' effects will fail.
Villain, prepare thyself ; for I will bathe
My poniard in the bosom of an earl.   80
   Lacy. Rather than live, and miss fair Mar-
    garet's love,
Prince Edward, stop not at the fatal doom,
But stab it home ; end both my loves and life.
   Mar. Brave Prince of Wales, honored for
    royal deeds,
'T were sin to stain fair Venus' courts with
    blood ;
Love's conquests ends, my Lord, in courtesy.
Spare Lacy, gentle Edward ; let me die,
For so both you and he do cease your loves.
   Edw. Lacy shall die as traitor to his lord.
   Lacy. I have deserved it, Edward ; act it
    well.   90
   Mar. What hopes the Prince to gain by
    Lacy's death?
   Edw. To end the loves 'twixt him and
    Margaret.
   Mar. Why, thinks King Henry's son that
    Margaret's love
Hangs in the uncertain balance of proud time?
That death shall make a discord of our
    thoughts?
No, stab the Earl, and, 'fore the morning sun
Shall vaunt him [12] thrice over the lofty east,
Margaret will meet her Lacy in the Heavens.
   Lacy. If aught betides to lovely Margaret
That wrongs or wrings her honor from con-
    tent,   100
Europe's rich wealth nor England's monarchy
Should not allure Lacy to overlive.[13]
Then, Edward, short my life, and end her
    loves.
   Mar. Rid me, and keep a friend worth
    many loves.
   Lacy. Nay, Edward, keep a love worth
    many friends.

   Mar. An if thy mind be such as fame hath
    blaz'd,
Then, princely Edward, let us both abide
The fatal resolution of thy rage.
Banish thou fancy [14] and embrace revenge,
And in one tomb knit both our carcasses, 110
Whose hearts were linked in one perfect love.
   Edw. [*aside*] Edward, art thou that famous
    Prince of Wales,
Who at Damasco beat the Saracens,
And brought'st home triumph on thy lance's
    point?
And shall thy plumes be pull'd by Venus
    down?
Is it princely to dissever lovers' leagues,
To part such friends as glory in their loves?
Leave, Ned, and make a virtue of this fault,
And further Peg and Lacy in their loves ;
So, in subduing fancy's passion,   120
Conquering thyself, thou gett'st the richest
    spoil. ——
Lacy, rise up. — Fair Peggy, here's my hand.
The Prince of Wales hath conquered all his
    thoughts,
And all his loves he yields unto the Earl. —
Lacy, enjoy the maid of Fressingfield ;
Make her thy Lincoln Countess at the church,
And Ned, as he is true Plantagenet,
Will give her to thee frankly for thy wife.
   Lacy. Humbly I take her of my sovereign,
As if that Edward gave me England's right,
And rich'd me with the Albion diadem.   131
   Mar. And doth the English Prince mean
    true?
Will he vouchsafe to cease his former loves,
And yield the title of a country maid
Unto Lord Lacy?
   Edw. I will, fair Peggy, as I am true lord.
   Mar. Then, lordly sir, whose conquest is as
    great,
In conquering love, as Cæsar's victories,
Margaret, as mild and humble in her thoughts
As was Aspasia [15] unto Cyrus' self,   140
Yields thanks, and, next Lord Lacy, doth en-
    shrine
Edward the second secret in her heart.
   Edw. Gramercy, Peggy. — Now that vows
    are past,
And that your loves are not [to] [16] be revolt,[17]
Once, Lacy, friends again ; come, we will post
To Oxford ; for this day the King is there,

---

[9] Emend. Dyce ; Q 1 *tied;* Q 2 *tyed;* Q 3 *try.*
[10] Conj. Dyce ; old eds. *Not.*
[11] If the cause be removed, the effect disappears.
[12] Proudly display himself.
[13] Survive.

[14] Love.
[15] Milto of Phocaea, favorite concubine of Cyrus
the Younger, was called Aspasia by him.
[16] So Qq 2, 3 ; om. Q 1.
[17] Overthrown.

And brings for Edward Castile Elinor. —
Peggy, I must go see and view my wife :
I pray God I like her as I loved thee. —
Beside, Lord Lincoln, we shall hear dispute [150
'Twixt Friar Bacon and learned Vander-
    mast. —
Peggy, we 'll leave you for a week or two.
    MAR. As it please Lord Lacy ; but love's
    foolish looks
Think footsteps miles and minutes to be hours.
    LACY. I 'll hasten, Peggy, to make short re-
    turn. ——
But please your Honor go unto the lodge,
We shall have butter, cheese, and venison ;
And yesterday I brought for Margaret
A lusty bottle of neat claret wine :
Thus can we feast and entertain your Grace.
    EDW. 'T is cheer, Lord Lacy, for an em-
    peror,   161
If he respect the person and the place.
Come, let us in ; for I will all this night
Ride post until I come to Bacon's cell.
                          Exeunt.

[SCENE II] [18]

Enter [KING] HENRY, [*the*] EMPEROR, [*the*
    KING OF] CASTILE, [*the* DUKE OF SAXONY,]
    ELINOR, VANDERMAST, [*and*] BUNGAY.

    EMP. Trust me, Plantagenet, these Oxford
    schools
Are richly seated near the riverside ;
The mountains full of fat and fallow deer,
The battling [19] pastures lade with kine and
    flocks,
The town gorgeous with high-built colleges,
And scholars seemly in their grave attire,
Learned in searching principles of art. —
What is thy judgment, Jaques Vandermast?
    VAN. That lordly are the buildings of the
    town,   9
Spacious the rooms, and full of pleasant walks ;
But for the doctors, how that they be learned,
It may be meanly, for aught I can hear.
    BUN. I tell thee, German, Hapsburg holds
    none such,
None read so deep as Oxenford contains.
There are within our academic state
Men that may lecture it in Germany
To all the doctors of your Belgic schools.
    HEN. Stand to him, Bungay ; charm this
    Vandermast,
And I will use thee as a royal king.

[18] Oxford ; a hall in Brasenose College.
[19] Battening, fattening.

    VAN. Wherein darest thou dispute with
    me?   20
    BUN. In what a doctor and a friar can.
    VAN. Before rich Europe's worthies put
    thou forth
The doubtful question unto Vandermast.
    BUN. Let it be this, — Whether the spirits
of pyromancy or geomancy be most predomi-
nant in magic?
    VAN. I say, of pyromancy.
    BUN. And I, of geomancy.
    VAN. The cabalists that write of magic
    spells,
As Hermes,[20] Melchie,[21] and Pythagoras,   30
Affirm that, 'mongst the quadruplicity
Of elemental essence,[22] *terra* is but thought
To be a *punctum* squared to the rest ; [23]
And that the compass [24] of ascending ele-
    ments
Exceed in bigness as they do in height ;
Judging the concave circle of the sun
To hold the rest in his circumference.
If, then, as Hermes says, the fire be great'st,
Purest, and only giveth shape to spirits,
Then must these demons that haunt that place
Be every way superior to the rest.   41
    BUN. I reason not of elemental shapes,
Nor tell I of the concave latitudes,
Noting their essence nor their quality,
But of the spirits that pyromancy calls,
And of the vigor of the geomantic fiends.
I tell thee, German, magic haunts the
    [ground] ; [25]
And those strange necromantic spells,
That work such shows and wondering in the
    world,
Are acted by those geomantic spirits   50
That Hermes calleth *terræ filii.*
The fiery spirits are but transparent shades,
That lightly pass as heralds to bear news ;
But earthly fiends, clos'd in the lowest deep,
Dissever mountains, if they be but charg'd,
Being more gross and massy in their power.
    VAN. Rather these earthly geomantic spirits
Are dull and like the place where they remain ;
For when proud Lucifer fell from the Heavens,
The spirits and angels that did sin with him
Retain'd their local essence as their faults, 61
All subject under Luna's continent.
They which offended less hang in the fire,

[20] Trismegistus.
[21] Porphyry (Malchus), the disciple of Plotinus.
(Dyce.)
[22] The four elements.
[23] Merely a point, in comparison with the others.
[24] Sizes.   [25] Old eds. *grounds.*

And second [26] faults did rest within the air ;
But Lucifer and his proud-hearted fiends
Were thrown into the centre of the earth,
Having less understanding than the rest,
As having greater sin and lesser grace.
Therefore such gross and earthly spirits do
    serve
For jugglers, witches, and vild sorcerers ;   70
Whereas the pyromantic ge[n]ii
Are mighty, swift, and of far-reaching power.
But grant that geomancy hath most force ;
Bungay, to please these mighty potentates,
Prove by some instance what thy art can do.
    BUN. I will.
    EMP. Now, English Harry, here begins the
        game ;
We shall see sport between these learned men.
    VAN. What wilt thou do?
    BUN. Show thee the tree, leav'd with re-
        fined gold,   80
Whereon the fearful dragon held his seat,
That watch'd the garden call'd Hesperides,
Subdu'd and won by conquering Hercules.
    VAN. Well done!

Here BUNGAY *conjures, and the tree appears*
    with the dragon shooting fire.

    HEN. What say you, royal Lordings, to my
        friar?
Hath he not done a point of cunning skill?
    VAN. Each scholar in the necromantic spells
Can do as much as Bungay hath perform'd.
But as Alcmena's bastard raz'd this tree,
So will I raise him up as when he lived,   90
And cause him pull the dragon from his seat,
And tear the branches piecemeal from the
    root. —
Hercules ! [*Prodi*],[27] *prodi*, Hercules !

HERCULES *appears in his lion's skin.*

    HER. *Quis me vult?*
    VAN. Jove's bastard son, thou Libyan Her-
        cules,
Pull off the sprigs from off the Hesperian
    tree,
As once thou didst to win the golden fruit.
    HER. *Fiat.*
        Here he begins to break the branches.
    VAN. Now, Bungay, if thou canst by magic
       charm
The fiend, appearing like great Hercules,   100
From pulling down the branches of the tree,
Then art thou worthy to be counted learned.

    BUN. I cannot.
    VAN. Cease, Hercules, until I give thee
       charge. —
Mighty commander of this English isle,
Henry, come from the stout Plantagenets,
Bungay is learned enough to be a friar ;
But to compare with Jaques Vandermast,
Oxford and Cambridge must go seek their cells
To find a man to match him in his art.   110
I have given nonplus to the Paduans,
To them of Sien, Florence, and Bologna,
Rheims, Louvain, and fair Rotterdam,
Frankfort,[28] [Lutetia],[29] and Orleans ;
And now must Henry, if he do me right,
Crown me with laurel, as they all have done.

Enter BACON.

    BACON. All hail to this royal company,
That sit to hear and see this strange dis-
       pute ! —
Bungay, how stand'st thou as a man amaz'd !
What, hath the German acted more than
       thou?   120
    VAN. What art thou that questions thus?
    BACON. Men call me Bacon.
    VAN. Lordly thou lookest, as if that thou
       wert learn'd ;
Thy countenance as if science held her seat
Between the circled arches of thy brows.
    HEN. Now, monarchs, hath the German
       found his match.
    EMP. Bestir thee, Jaques, take not now the
       foil,
Lest thou doest lose what foretime thou didst
       gain.
    VAN. Bacon, wilt thou dispute?
    BACON. No, unless he were more learn'd
       than Vandermast ;   130
For yet, tell me, what hast thou done?
    VAN. Rais'd Hercules to ruinate that tree
That Bungay mounted by his magic spells.
    BACON. Set Hercules to work.
    VAN. Now, Hercules, I charge thee to thy
       task ;
Pull off the golden branches from the root.
    HER. I dare not. Seest thou not great
       Bacon here,
Whose frown doth act more than thy magic
       can?
    VAN. By all the thrones, and dominations,
Virtues, powers, and mighty hierarchies,   140
I charge thee to obey to Vandermast.

[26] Secondary, lesser.
[27] Old eds, *Prodie.*

[28] Frankfurt an der Oder. — *Sien* = Siena.
[29] Paris. Conj. Fleay ; old eds. *Lutrech.* Utrecht
was not a university until 1636. (Ward.)

HER. Bacon, that bridles headstrong Bel-
cephon,
And rules Asmenoth, guider of the north,
Binds me from yielding unto Vandermast.
HEN. How now, Vandermast? Have you
met with your match?
VAN. Never before was 't known to Vander-
mast
That men held devils in such obedient awe.
Bacon doth more than art, or else I fail.[30]
EMP. Why, Vandermast, art thou over-
come? —
Bacon, dispute with him, and try his skill. [150
BACON. I come not, monarchs, for to hold
dispute
With such a novice as is Vandermast;
I come to have your royalties to dine
With Friar Bacon here in Brazen-nose;
And, for[31] this German troubles but the place,
And holds this audience with a long suspense,
I'll send him to his academy hence. —
Thou Hercules, whom Vandermast did raise,
Transport the German unto Hapsburg straight,
That he may learn by travail, 'gainst[32] the
[spring],[33]   160
More secret dooms and aphorisms of art.
Vanish the tree, and thou away with him!
          Exit the spirit [of HERCULES] *with*
               VANDERMAST *and the tree.*
EMP. Why, Bacon, whither dost thou send
him?
BACON. To Hapsburg; there your High-
ness at return
Shall find the German in his study safe.
HEN. Bacon, thou hast honored England
with thy skill,
And made fair Oxford famous by thine art;
I will be English Henry to thyself.
But tell me, shall we dine with thee to-day?
BACON. With me, my Lord; and while I
[f]it my cheer,   170
See where Prince Edward comes to welcome
you,
Gracious[34] as the morning star of Heaven.
                                        Exit.

Enter [PRINCE] EDWARD, LACY, WARREN,
               [*and*] ERMSBY.

EMP. Is this Prince Edward, Henry's royal
son?
How martial is the figure of his face!
Yet lovely and beset with amorets.[35]

HEN. Ned, where hast thou been?
EDW. At Framlingham, my Lord, to try
your bucks
If they could scape [the][36] teasers or the toil.
But hearing of these lordly potentates   179
Landed, and progress'd[37] up to Oxford town,
I posted to give entertain to them:
Chief, to the Almain monarch; next to him,
And joint with him, Castile and Saxony
Are welcome as they may be to the English
court.
Thus for the men; but see, Venus appears,
Or one that overmatcheth Venus in her shape!
Sweet Elinor, beauty's high-swelling pride,
Rich nature's glory and her wealth at once,
Fair of all fairs, welcome to Albion;   189
Welcome to me, and welcome to thine own,
If that thou deign'st the welcome from myself.
ELIN. Martial Plantagenet, Henry's high-
minded son,
The mark that Elinor did count her aim,
I lik'd thee 'fore I saw thee; now I love,
And so as in so short a time I may,
Yet so as time shall never break that so,
And therefore so accept of Elinor.
CAST. Fear not, my Lord, this couple will
agree,
If love may creep into their wanton eyes: —
And therefore, Edward, I accept thee here, [200
Without suspense, as my adopted son.
HEN. Let me that joy in these consorting
greets,
And glory in these honors done to Ned,
Yield thanks for all these favors to my son,
And rest a true Plantagenet to all.

Enter MILES *with a cloth and trenchers and
salt.*

MILES. *Salvete, omnes reges,*
That govern your *greges*
In Saxony and Spain,
In England and in Almain!
For all this frolic rabble   210
Must I cover [the][38] table
With trenchers, salt, and cloth;
And then look for your broth.
EMP. What pleasant fellow is this?
HEN. 'T is, my Lord, Doctor Bacon's poor
scholar.
MILES. [*aside*] My master hath made me
sewer[39] of these great lords; and, God knows,
I am as serviceable at a table as a sow is

---

[30] Am mistaken.   [31] Since.   [32] By.
[33] Old eds. *springs.*
[34] Trisyllabic.   [35] Love-kindling looks.

[36] Cor. Q₂; Q₁ *they.*
[37] Engaged in a royal "progress."
[38] Cor. Q₂; Q₁ *thee.*   [39] Waiter.

under an apple tree. 'T is no matter ; [220
their cheer shall not be great, and therefore
what skills [40] where the salt stand, before or
behind?   [*Exit.*]

    CAST. These scholars knows more skill in
      axioms,
How to use quips and sleights of sophistry,
Than for to cover courtly for a king.

Re-enter MILES *with a mess of pottage and broth ;
and, after him,* BACON.

    MILES. Spill, sir? why, do you think I never
carried twopenny chop [41] before in my life?
By your leave, *nobile decus,*
For here comes Doctor Bacon's *pecus,*   230
Being in his full age
To carry a mess of pottage.

    BACON. Lordings, admire [42] not if your
      cheer be this,
For we must keep our academic fare ;
No riot where philosophy doth reign.
And therefore, Henry, place these potentates,
And bid them fall unto their frugal cates.

    EMP. Presumptuous friar ! What, scoff'st
      thou at a king?
What, doest thou taunt us with thy peasants'
      fare,   239
And give us cates [43] fit for country swains? —
Henry, proceeds this jest of thy consent,
To twit us with such a pittance of such price?
Tell me, and Frederick will not grieve thee
      long.

    HEN. By Henry's honor, and the royal faith
The English monarch beareth to his friend,
I knew not of the friar's feeble fare,
Nor am I pleas'd he entertains you thus.

    BACON. Content thee, Frederick ; for I
      show'd the cates,
To let thee see how scholars use to feed,   249
How little meat refines our English wits. —
Miles, take away, and let it be thy dinner.

    MILES. Marry, sir, I will.
This day shall be a festival day with me ;
For I shall exceed in the highest degree.
                     Exit MILES.

    BACON. I tell thee, monarch, all the Ger-
      man peers
Could not afford thy entertainment such,
So royal and so full of majesty,
As Bacon will present to Frederick.
The basest waiter that attends thy cups

[40] What matters it.
[41] ? Chopped meat in broth. (*N. E. D.*)
[42] Wonder.
[43] "The Emperor supplied a gulp of rage."
(Gayley.)

Shall be in honors [44] greater than thyself ;   260
And for thy cates, rich Alexandria drugs, [45]
Fetch'd by carvels from Egypt's richest straits,
Found in the wealthy strand of Africa,
Shall royalize the table of my king ;
Wines richer than the 'Gyptian courtesan
Quaff'd to Augustus' kingly countermatch [46]
Shall be carous'd in English Henry's feast ;
Candy shall yield the richest of her canes ;
Persia, down her Volga by canoes,
Send down the secrets of her spicery ;   270
The Afric dates, myrobalans [47] of Spain,
Conserves and suckets [48] from Tiberias,
Cates from Judæa, choicer than the lamp [49]
That fired Rome with sparks of gluttony,
Shall beautify the board for Frederick :
And therefore grudge not at a friar's feast.
                     [*Exeunt.*]

[SCENE III] [50]

Enter two gentlemen, LAMBERT *and* SERLSBY,
with the Keeper.

    LAM. Come, frolic Keeper of our liege's
      game,
Whose table spread hath ever venison
And jacks [51] of wine to welcome passengers,
Know I am in love with jolly Margaret,
That overshines our damsels as the moon
Dark'neth the brightest sparkles of the night.
In Laxfield here my land and living [52] lies ;
I 'll make thy daughter jointer [53] of it all,
So [54] thou consent to give her to my wife ;
And I can spend five hundred marks a year. [10

    SER. I am the landslord, Keeper, of thy
      holds ;
By copy all thy living lies in me ; [55]
Laxfield did never see me raise my due.
I will enfeoff fair Margaret in all,
So she will take her to a lusty squire.

    KEEP. Now, courteous gentles, if the Keep-
      er's girl

[44] *I.e.,* outward show. (Ward.)
[45] Spices.
[46] Rival ; *i.e.,* Antonius.
[47] Span. *mirabolaños* = plum-like fruits. Old eds.
mirabiles.
[48] Sweetmeats.
[49] Torch. *I.e.,* the viands mentioned are choicer
than the delicacies which in ancient times gave fire
to (incited) Roman gluttony.
[50] Fressingfield. Near the Keeper's lodge.
[51] (Leathern) jugs or tankards.
[52] Income.
[53] Jointress.
[54] Provided that.
[55] All your income is derived from land of mine
which you occupy by copyhold tenure. (A tenant
by copyhold had only a copy of the record of the
manorial court to show for his right of occupancy.)

Hath pleased the liking fancy of you both,
And with her beauty hath subdued your
　　thoughts,
'T is doubtful to decide the question.
It joys me that such men of great esteem　20
Should lay their liking on this base estate,
And that her state should grow so fortunate
To be a wife to meaner men than you.[56]
But sith such squires will stoop to keeper's
　　fee,[57]
I will, to avoid displeasure of you both,
Call Margaret forth, and she shall make her
　　choice.　　　　　　　　　　　　　*Exit.*
LAM. Content, Keeper; send her unto us.
Why, Serlsby, is thy wife so lately dead,
Are all thy loves so lightly passed over,
As thou canst wed before the year be out?　30
　　SER. I live not, Lambert, to content the
　　　　dead,
Nor was I wedded but for life to her;
The [grave][58] ends and begins a married state.

Enter MARGARET.

LAM. Peggy, the lovely flower of all towns,
Suffolk's fair Helen, and rich England's star,
Whose beauty, tempered with her huswifery,
Makes England talk of merry Fressingfield!
　　SER. I cannot trick it up with poesies,
Nor paint my passions with comparisons,[59]
Nor tell a tal[e] of Phœbus and his loves;　40
But this believe me: Laxfield here is mine,
Of ancient rent seven hundred pounds a year;
And if thou canst but love a country squire,
I will enfeoff thee, Margaret, in all.
I cannot flatter; try me, if thou please.
　　MAR. Brave neighboring squires, the stay
　　　　of Suffolk's clime,
A keeper's [daughter][60] is too base in gree [61]
To match with men accounted of such worth;
But might I not displease, I would reply.
　　LAM. Say, Peggy; naught shall make us
　　　　discontent.　　　　　　　　　　　　50
　　MAR. Then, gentles, note that love hath
　　　　little stay,[62]
Nor can the flames that Venus sets on fire
Be kindled but by fancy's motion; [63]
Then pardon, gentles, if a maid's reply
Be doubtful, while [64] I have debated with my-
　　self,
Who, or of whom, love shall constrain me like.

SER. Let it be me; and trust me, Margaret,
The meads environed with the silver streams,
Whose battling pastures fatt'neth all my
　　flocks,
Yielding forth fleeces stapled with such wool [65]
As Leominster [66] cannot yield more finer
　　stuff,　　　　　　　　　　　　　　　61
And forty kine with fair and burnish'd heads,
With strouting [67] dugs that paggle [68] to the
　　ground,
Shall serve thy dairy, if thou wed with me.
　　LAM. Let pass the country wealth, as flocks
　　　　and kine,
And lands that wave with Ceres' golden
　　sheaves,
Filling my barns with plenty of the fields;
But, Peggy, if thou wed thyself to me,
Thou shalt have garments of embroid'red silk,
Lawns, and rich networks for thy head-
　　attire;　　　　　　　　　　　　　　70
Costly shall be thy fair [h]abiliments,
If thou wilt be but Lambert's loving wife.
　　MAR. Content you, gentles; you have
　　　　proffer'd fair,
And more than fits a country maid's degree.
But give me leave to counsel me a time,
For fancy blooms not at the first assault;
Give me but ten days' respite, and I will reply,
Which or to whom myself affectionates.
　　SER. Lambert, I tell thee, thou art impor-
　　　　tunate;
Such beauty fits not such a base esquire;　80
It is for Serlsby to have Margaret.
　　LAM. Think'st thou with wealth to over-
　　　　reach me?
Serlsby, I scorn to brook thy country braves.[69]
I dare thee, coward, to maintain this wrong,
At dint of rapier, single in the field.
　　SER. I 'll answer, Lambert, what I have
　　　　avouch'd. —
Margaret, farewell; another time shall serve.
　　　　　　　　　　　　　Exit SERLSBY.
　　LAM. I 'll follow. — Peggy, farewell to thy-
　　　　self;
Listen how well I 'll answer for thy love.
　　　　　　　　　　　　　Exit LAMBERT.
　　MAR. How Fortune tempers lucky haps
　　　　with frowns,　　　　　　　　　　　90
And wrongs me with the sweets of my delight!
Love is my bliss, and love is now my bale.

---

[56] *I.e.*, it would please me if she should be so
fortunate as to marry even a man of less wealth
than you, much more one as wealthy as you.
[57] Estate.　[58] Cor. Q₂; Q₁ *graues.*　[59] Similes.
[60] Cor. Q₂; Q₁ *daughters.*　[61] Degree.
[62] Steadiness.　[63] Love's impulse.　[64] Till.

[65] Consisting of wool of so fine a staple (*i.e.*, length
and quality). (Collins.)
[66] Old eds. *Lempster*, indicating dissyllabic pronunciation.　[67] Swelling.
[68] Hang loosely [like a bag]. (*N. E. D.*)
[69] Defiances.

Shall I be Helen in my forward fates,
As I am Helen in my matchless hue,
And set rich Suffolk with my face afire?
If lovely Lacy were but with his Peggy,
The cloudy darkness of his bitter frown
Would check the pride of these aspiring squires.
Before the term of ten days be expired,
Whenas they look for answer of their loves, 100
My lord will come to merry Fressingfield,
And end their fancies and their follies both :
Till when, Peggy, be blithe and of good cheer.

Enter a Post *with a letter and a bag of gold.*

POST. Fair lovely damsel, which way leads
    this path?
How might I post me unto Fressingfield?
Which footpath leadeth to the Keeper's lodge?
    MAR. Your way is ready, and this path is
    right ;
Myself do dwell hereby in Fressingfield,
And if the Keeper be the man you seek,
I am his daughter ; may I know the cause? 110
    POST. Lovely, and once beloved of my
    lord, —
No marvel if his eye was lodg'd so low,
When brighter beauty is not in the heavens, —
The Lincoln Earl hath sent you letters here,
And, with them, just an hundred pounds in
    gold.
Sweet, bonny wench, read them, and make
    reply.
    MAR. The scrolls that Jove sent Danaë,
Wrapp'd in rich closures of fine burnish'd gold,
Were not more welcome than these lines to me.
Tell me, whilst that I do unrip the seals,   120
Lives Lacy well? How fares my lovely lord?
    POST. Well, if that wealth may make men
    to live well.

The letter, and MARGARET *reads it.*

    MAR. "The blooms of the almond tree grow
in a night, and vanish in a morn ; the flies
hæmeræ,[70] fair Peggy, take life with the
sun, and die with the dew ; fancy, that slippeth
in with a gaze, goeth out with a wink ; and
too timely [71] loves have ever the shortest
length. I write this as thy grief, and my folly,
who at Fressingfield lov'd that which [130
time hath taught me to be but mean dainties.
Eyes are dissemblers, and fancy is but queasy ;
therefore know, Margaret, I have chosen a
Spanish lady to be my wife, chief waiting

woman to the Princess Elinor ; a lady fair,
and no less fair than thyself, honorable and
wealthy. In that I forsake thee, I leave thee
to thine own liking ; and for thy dowry I have
sent thee an hundred pounds ; and ever assure
thee of my favor, which shall avail thee [140
and thine much. Farewell.
            Not thine, nor his own,
                EDWARD LACY."

Fond Ate, doomer of bad-boding fates,
That wraps proud Fortune in thy snaky locks,
Didst thou enchant my birthday with such
    stars
As light'ned mischief from their infancy?
If Heavens had vow'd, if stars had made
    decree,
To show on me their froward influence,
If Lacy had but lov'd, Heavens, hell, and all
Could not have wrong'd the patience of my
    mind.   151
    POST. It grieves me, damsel ; but the Earl
    is forc'd
To love the lady by the King's command.
    MAR. The wealth combin'd within the
    English shelves,[72]
Europe's commander, nor the English King,
Should not have mov'd the love of Peggy from
    her lord.
    POST. What answer shall I return to my
    Lord?
    MAR. First, for thou cam'st from Lacy,
    whom I lov'd, —
Ah, give me leave to sigh at every thought ! —
Take thou, my friend, the hundred pound he
    sent,   160
For Margaret's resolution craves no dower.
The world shall be to her as vanity ;
Wealth, trash ; love, hate ; pleasure, despair :
For I will straight to stately Framlingham,
And in the abbey there be shorn a nun,
And yield my loves and liberty to God.
Fellow, I give thee this, not for the news,
For those be hateful unto Margaret,
But for th'art Lacy's man, once Margaret's
    love.
    POST. What I have heard, what passions I
    have seen,   170
I'll make report of them unto the Earl.
                        Exit Post.
    MAR. Say that she joys his fancies be at
    rest,
And prays that his misfortune may be hers.
                            Exit.

[70] Ephemerae. Old eds. *Hæmere.*
[71] Premature.

[72] Coasts.

[ACT IV — SCENE I] [1]

Enter FRIAR BACON *drawing the curtains with a white stick, a book in his hand, and a lamp lighted by him; and the Brazen Head, and* MILES *with weapons by him.*

BACON. Miles, where are you?

MILES. Here, sir.

BACON. How chance you tarry so long?

MILES. Think you that the watching of the Brazen Head craves no furniture? [2] I warrant you, sir, I have so armed myself that if all your devils come, I will not fear them an inch.

BACON. Miles, thou knowest that I have dived into hell,

And sought the darkest palaces of fiends; [10

That with my magic spells great Belcephon

Hath left his lodge and kneeled at my cell;

The rafters of the earth rent from the poles,

And three-form'd [3] Luna hid her silver looks,

Trembling upon her concave continent,

When Bacon read upon his magic book.

With seven years' tossing [4] necromantic charms,

Poring upon dark Hecate's principles,

I have fram'd out a monstrous head of brass, 19

That, by the enchanting forces of the Devil,

Shall tell out strange and uncouth aphorisms,

And girt fair England with a wall of brass.

Bungay and I have watch'd these threescore days,

And now our vital spirits crave some rest.

If Argus liv'd, and had his hundred eyes,

They could not overwatch Phobetor's [5] night.

Now, Miles, in thee rests Friar Bacon's weal:

The honor and renown of all his life

Hangs in the watching of this Brazen Head; 29

Therefore I charge thee by the immortal God,

That holds the souls of men within his fist,

This night thou watch; for ere the morning star

Sends out his glorious glister on the north,

The Head will speak: then, Miles, upon thy life,

Wake me; for then by magic art I'll work

To end my seven years' task with excellence.

---

[1] Oxford. Friar Bacon's cell.
[2] Weapons.
[3] As Diana, Luna, and Hecate.
[4] Turning over.
[5] Son of Morpheus. (Ovid, *Metamorphoses*, xi, 640)

If that a wink but shut thy watchful eye,

Then farewell Bacon's glory and his fame!

Draw close the curtains, Miles; now, for thy life, 39

Be watchful, and — *Here he falleth asleep.*

MILES. So; I thought you would talk yourself asleep anon; and 't is no marvel, for Bungay on the days, and he on the nights, have watch'd just these ten and fifty days: now this is the night, and 't is my task, and no more. Now, Jesus bless me, what a goodly head it is! and a nose! you talk of *nos autem glorificare;* [6] but here's a nose that I warrant may be call'd *nos autem pop[u]lare* for the [49 people of the parish. Well, I am furnished with weapons: now, sir, I will set me down by a post, and make it as good as a watchman to wake me, if I chance to slumber. I thought, Goodman Head, I would call you out of your *memento* . . . (*Sit down and knock your head.*) [7] — Passion o' God, I have almost broke my pate! Up, Miles, to your task; take your brown bill in your hand; here's some of your master's hobgoblins abroad.

With this a great noise. The Head speaks.

THE BRAZEN HEAD. Time is! 60

MILES. Time is! Why, Master Brazen Head, have you such a capital nose, and answer you with syllables, " Time is "? Is this all my master's cunning, to spend seven years' study about " Time is "? Well, sir, it may be we shall have some better orations of it anon. Well, I'll watch you as narrowly as ever you were watch'd, and I'll play with you as the nightingale with the slowworm; I'll set a prick against my breast. [8] Now rest there, [70 Miles. . . . [*He falls.*] — Lord have mercy upon me, I have almost kill'd myself! [*A great noise.*] Up, Miles; list how they rumble.

THE BRAZEN HEAD. Time was!

MILES. Well, Friar Bacon, you spent your seven years' study well, that can make your Head speak but two words at once, " Time was." Yea, marry, time was when my master was a wise man, but that was before he began to make the Brazen Head. You [80 shall lie while [9] your arse ache, an your head speak no better. Well, I will watch, and walk up and down, and be a peripatetian and a phi-

---

[6] *Nos autem gloriari opportet* are the opening words of an introit.
[7] Greg gives this marginal note, which has been partly cut away in the Harvard copy of Q₁.
[8] As the nightingale was supposed to use a thorn ‧ Miles props up his brown bill.
[9] Till.

losopher of Aristotle's stamp. [*A great noise.*] — What, a fresh noise? Take thy pistols in hand, Miles.

Here the Head speaks, and a lightning flasheth forth, and a hand appears that breaketh down the Head with a hammer.

THE BRAZEN HEAD. Time is past!

MILES. Master, master, up! Hell's broken loose! Your Head speaks; and there's such a thunder and lightning that I [90 warrant all Oxford is up in arms. Out of your bed, and take a brown bill in your hand; the Latter Day is come.

BACON. Miles, I come. O, passing warily watch'd!

Bacon will make thee next himself in love. When spake the Head?

MILES. When spake the Head! Did not you say that he should tell strange principles of philosophy? Why, sir, it speaks but two words at a time.   100

BACON. Why, villain, hath it spoken oft?

MILES. Oft! ay, marry, hath it, thrice; but in all those three times it hath uttered but seven words.

BACON. As how?

MILES. Marry, sir, the first time he said "Time is," as if Fabius Cumentator[10] should have pronounc'd a sentence; [the second time][11] he said, "Time was"; and the third time, with thunder and lightning, as in [110 great choler, he said, "Time is past."

BACON. 'T is past indeed. Ah, villain! time is past;

My life, my fame, my glory, all are past. — Bacon, the turrets of thy hope are ruin'd down, Thy seven years' study lieth in the dust! Thy Brazen Head lies broken through a slave That watch'd, and would not when the Head did will. —

What said the Head first?

MILES. Even, sir, "Time is."

BACON. Villain, if thou hadst call'd to Bacon then,   120

If thou hadst watch'd, and wak'd the sleepy friar,

The Brazen Head had uttered aphorisms, And England had been circled round with brass;

But proud [Asmenoth],[12] ruler of the north,

And Demogorgon, master of the fates, Grudge that a mortal man should work so much.

Hell trembled at my deep, commanding spells; Fiends frown'd to see a man their overmatch; Bacon might boast more than a man might boast.   129

But now the braves of Bacon hath an end; Europe's conceit of Bacon hath an end; His seven years' practice sorteth to ill end; And, villain, sith[13] my glory hath an end, I will appoint thee to some fatal[14] end. Villain, avoid! Get thee from Bacon's sight! Vagrant, go roam and range about the world, And perish as a vagabond on earth!

MILES. Why, then, sir, you forbid me your service?

BACON. My service, villain! with a fatal curse,   139

That direful plagues and mischief fall on thee.

MILES. 'T is no matter; I am against you with the old proverb: The more the fox is curs'd,[15] the better he fares. God be with you, sir. I'll take but a book in my hand, a wide-sleeved gown on my back, and a crowned[16] cap on my head, and see if I can want promotion.

BACON. Some fiend or ghost haunt on thy weary steps,

Until they do transport thee quick to hell; For Bacon shall have never merry day, To lose the fame and honor of his Head.   150

[*Exeunt.*]

[SCENE II][17]

Enter [the] EMPEROR, [the KING OF] CASTILE, [KING] HENRY, ELINOR, [PRINCE] EDWARD, LACY, [and] RALPH [SIMNELL].

EMP. Now, lovely Prince, the prince[18] of Albion's wealth,

How fares the Lady Elinor and you? What, have you courted and found Castile fit To answer England in equivalence? Will 't be a match 'twixt bonny Nell and thee?

EDW. Should Paris enter in the courts of Greece,

And not lie fettered in fair Helen's looks? Or Phœbus scape those piercing amorets That Daphne glanced at his deity?

---

[10] Miles's (or the compositor's) blunder for *Cuncta-tor.* Qq 2, 3, *Commentator.*
[11] Add. Dodsley.
[12] Cf. III, ii, 143; old eds. *Astmeroth.*
[13] Since.
[14] Old eds. *fatall to some.*
[15] With a pun on *coursed*, and *fares* = goes. (Neilson).
[16] *I.e.*, collegiate.
[17] Unlocated; perhaps at Hampton Court again.
[18] Dyce emends to *prime.*

Can Edward, then, sit by a flame and freeze, [10
Whose heat puts Helen and fair Daphne
    down?
Now, monarchs, ask the lady if we gree.

HEN. What, madam, hath my son found
    grace or no?

ELIN. Seeing, my Lord, his lovely counter-
    feit,[19]
And hearing how his mind and shape agreed,
I come not, troop'd with all this warlike train,
Doubting of love, but so affectionate
As Edward hath in England what he won in
    Spain.[20]

CAST. A match, my Lord; these wantons
    needs must love;
Men must have wives, and women will be
    wed.   20
Let's haste the day to honor up the rites.

RALPH. Sirrah Harry, shall Ned marry
Nell?

HEN. Ay, Ralph: how then?

RALPH. Marry, Harry, follow my counsel:
send for Friar Bacon to marry them, for he'll
so conjure him and her with his necromancy,
that they shall love together like pig and
lamb whilst they live.

CAST. But hear'st thou, Ralph, art thou
content to have Elinor to thy lady?   31

RALPH. Ay, so she will promise me two
things.

CAST. What's that, Ralph?

RALPH. That she will never scold with Ned,
nor fight with me. — Sirrah Harry, I have put
her down with a thing unpossible.

HEN. What's that, Ralph?

RALPH. Why, Harry, didst thou ever see
that a woman could both hold her tongue [40
and her hands? No; but when egg-pies
grows on apple trees, then will thy grey mare
prove a bagpiper.

EMP. What says the Lord of Castile and
the Earl of Lincoln, that they are in such
earnest and secret talk?

CAST. I stand, my Lord, amazed at his talk,
How he discourseth of the constancy
Of one surnam'd, for beauty's excellence,
The Fair [21] Maid of merry Fressingfield.   50

HEN. 'T is true, my Lord, 't is wondrous
    for to hear;
Her beauty passing Mars's paramour,
Her virgin's right as rich as Vesta's was.[22]
Lacy and Ned hath told me miracles.

CAST. What says Lord Lacy? Shall she
    be his wife?

LACY. Or else Lord Lacy is unfit to live. —
May it please your Highness give me leave to
    post
To Fressingfield, I'll fetch the bonny girl,
And prove, in true appearance at the court, 59
What I have vouched often with my tongue.

HEN. Lacy, go to the 'querry of my stable,
And take such coursers as shall fit thy turn;
Hie thee to Fressingfield, and bring home the
    lass;
And, for her fame flies through the English
    coast,
If it may please the Lady Elinor,
One day shall match your excellence and her.

ELIN. We Castile ladies are not very coy;
Your Highness may command a greater boon;
And glad were I to grace the Lincoln Earl
With being partner of his marriage day.   70

EDW. Gramercy, Nell, for I do love the
    lord,
As he that's second to myself in love.

RALPH. You love her! — Madam Nell,
never believe him you, though he swears he
loves you.

ELIN. Why, Ralph?

RALPH. Why, his love is like unto a tapster's glass, that is broken with every touch;
for he loved the fair maid of Fressingfield
once out of all ho.[23] — Nay, Ned, never [80
wink upon me; I care not, I.

HEN. Ralph tells all; you shall have a
good secretary of him. —
But, Lacy, haste thee post [24] to Fressingfield;
For ere thou hast fitted all things for her state,
The solemn marriage day will be at hand.

LACY. I go, my Lord.   *Exit* LACY.

EMP. How shall we pass this day, my
    Lord?

HEN. To horse, my Lord; the day is pass-
    ing fair;
We'll fly the partridge, or go rouse the
    deer.   90
Follow, my Lords; you shall not want for
    sport.

                                        Exeunt.

[SCENE III] [25]

Enter FRIAR BACON *with* FRIAR BUNGAY *to his
    cell.*

BUN. What means the friar that frolick'd
    it of late,

---

[19] Picture.   [20] An Alexandrine.   [21] Dissyllabic.
[22] Her right to the name of virgin equal in worth
to that of Vesta.

[23] Immeasurably.   [24] Quickly.
[25] Oxford. Friar Bacon's cell.

To sit as melancholy in his cell
As if he had neither lost nor won to-day?
   Bacon. Ah, Bungay, my Brazen Head is
     spoil'd,
My glory gone, my seven years' study lost!
The fame of Bacon, bruited through the world,
Shall end and perish with this deep disgrace.
   Bun. Bacon hath built foundation [of] [26]
     his fame
So surely on the wings of true report,
With [27] acting strange and uncouth miracles,
As this cannot infringe what he deserves.   11
   Bacon. Bungay, sit down, for by prospec-
     tive skill
I find this day shall fall out ominous.
Some deadly act shall 'tide me ere I sleep,
But what and wherein little can I guess.
   Bun. My mind is heavy, whatsoe'er shall
     hap.[28]

Enter two Scholars, *sons to Lambert and Serlsby.*
Knock.

   Bacon. Who's that knocks?
   Bun. Two scholars that desires to speak
     with you.
   Bacon. Bid them come in. —
Now, my youths, what would you have?   20
   First Schol. Sir, we are Suffolk men and
     neighboring friends;
Our fathers in their countries lusty squires;
Their lands adjoin: in Cratfield [29] mine doth
     dwell,
And his in Laxfield. We are college mates,
Sworn brothers, as our fathers lives as friends.
   Bacon. To what end is all this?
   Second Schol. Hearing your Worship kept
     within your cell
A glass prospective, wherein men might see
Whatso their thoughts or hearts' desire could
     wish,
We come to know how that our fathers fare. 30
   Bacon. My glass is free for every honest
     man.
Sit down, and you shall see ere long,
How or in what state your friendly [fathers
     live].[30]
Meanwhile, tell me your names.
   First Schol. Mine Lambert.
   Second Schol. And mine Serlsby.
   Bacon. Bungay, I smell there will be a
     tragedy.

Enter Lambert *and* Serlsby *with rapiers and*
daggers.

   Lam. Serlsby, thou hast kept thine hour
     like a man;
Th'art worthy of the title of a squire,
That durst, for proof of thy affection   40
And for thy mistress' favor, prize [31] thy blood.
Thou know'st what words did pass at Fres-
     singfield,
Such shameless braves as manhood cannot
     brook:
Ay, for I scorn to bear such piercing taunts,
Prepare thee, Serlsby; one of us will die.
   Ser. Thou seest I single [meet] [32] thee [in] [32]
     the field,
And what I spake, I'll maintain with my
     sword.
Stand on thy guard: I cannot scold it out.
An if thou kill me, think I have a son,   49
That lives in Oxford in the Broadgates Hall,[33]
Who will revenge his father's blood with blood.
   Lam. And, Serlsby, I have there a lusty
     boy,
That dares at weapon buckle with thy son,
And lives in Broadgates too, as well as thine.
But draw thy rapier, for we'll have a bout.
   Bacon. Now, lusty younkers, look within
     the glass,
And tell me if you can discern your sires.
   First Schol. Serlsby, 'tis hard; thy father
     offers wrong,
To combat with my father in the field.
   Second Schol. Lambert, thou liest; my
     father's is th' abuse; [34]   60
And thou shalt find it, if my father harm.
   Bun. How goes it, sirs?
   First Schol. Our fathers are in combat
     hard by Fressingfield.
   Bacon. Sit still, my friends, and see the
     event.
   Lam. Why stand'st thou, Serlsby?
     Doubt'st thou of thy life?
A veney,[35] man! Fair Margaret craves so
     much.
   Ser. Then this for her.
   First Schol. Ah, well thrust!
   Second Schol. But mark the ward.

[Lambert *and* Serlsby] *fight and kill each*
other.

   Lam. O, I am slain!   70
   Ser. And I, Lord have mercy on me!

---

[26] Old eds. *on*, which may be right.   [27] By.
[28] Grosart gives this line to Bacon. Another possibility is that the line is an Alexandrine and that
Bungay is a vocative in it.   [29] Old eds. *Crackfield*.
[30] Cor.(?) Q₃; earlier eds. *father liues*.

[31] Stake, risk.   [32] Add. Dyce.
[33] Afterwards absorbed by Pembroke College.
[34] Injury.   [35] Bout.

FIRST SCHOL. My father slain! — Serlsby,
ward that.

The two Scholars *stab one another [and die].*

SECOND SCHOL. And so is mine! — Lambert, I'll quit thee well.

BUN. O strange stratagem!

BACON. See, friar, where the fathers both
lie dead! —

Bacon, thy magic doth effect this massacre;
This glass prospective worketh many woes.
And therefore, seeing these brave, lusty
Brutes,[36]
These friendly youths, did perish by thine art,
End all thy magic and thine art at once.   80
The poniard that did end the fatal [37] lives,
Shall break the cause [efficient] [38] of their woes.
So fade the glass, and end with it the shows
That necromancy did infuse the crystal with.

He breaks the glass.

BUN. What means learned Bacon thus to
break his glass?

BACON. I tell thee, Bungay, it repents me
sore
That ever Bacon meddled in this art.
The hours I have spent in pyromantic spells,
The fearful tossing [39] in the latest night
Of papers full of necromantic charms,   90
Conjuring and adjuring devils and fiends,
With stole and alb and strange pentag[o]non,[40]
The wresting of the holy name of God,
As Soter, Elohim [41] and Adonai,
Alpha, [Sabaoth] and Tetragrammaton,
With praying to the fivefold powers of [hell] [42]
Are instances that Bacon must be damn'd
For using devils to countervail [43] his God. —
Yet, Bacon, cheer thee; drown not in despair:
Sins have their salves, repentance can do
much;   100
Think Mercy sits where Justice holds her seat,
And from those wounds those bloody Jews did
pierce,
Which by thy magic oft did bleed afresh,

---

[36] Britons. Old eds. *brutes.*
[37] Ill-fated, doomed.
[38] Old eds. *efficiat.*   [39] Turning over.
[40] See on I, ii, 55.
[41] Q₁ *Sother, Elaim.* Σωτήρ = Savior. *Elohim, Adonai,* and *Alpha* are names of God; *Tetragrammaton* (Q₁ *Tetragramiton*) is the four-lettered unpronounceable Hebrew name, translated in the English Bible as *Jehovah.* As for *Sabaoth* (old eds. *Manoth*), Kittredge cites (Harleian MS 2267, fol. 28vᵒ) a list of ten names from directions for making pentacles. *Elohim, Adonay, Tetragramaton,* and *Sabaoth* are among them. Hence Kittredge conjectures that *Manoth* is an error for *Sabaoth.*
[42] Emend. Kittredge; old eds. *heaven.* "Fivefold" alludes to the pentacle, in which Bacon has "wrested" the holy names, in order to call up devils.
[43] Equal in strength.

From thence for thee the dew of mercy drops,
To wash the wrath of high Jehovah's ire,
And make thee as a newborn babe from sin. —
Bungay, I'll spend the remnant of my life
In pure devotion, praying to my God
That he would save what Bacon vainly lost.

[*Exeunt.*]

[ACT V — SCENE I][1]

Enter MARGARET *in nun's apparel,* [the]
Keeper *her father, and their* Friend.

KEEPER. Margaret, be not so headstrong in
these vows;
O, bury not such beauty in a cell,
That England hath held famous for the hue!
Thy father's hair, like to the silver blooms
That beautify the shrubs of Africa,
Shall fall before the dated time of death,
Thus to forgo his lovely Margaret.

MAR. Ah, Father, when the harmony of
Heaven
Soundeth the measures of a lively faith,
The vain illusions of this flattering world   10
Seems odious to the thoughts of Margaret.
I loved once — Lord Lacy was my love;
And now I hate myself for that I lov'd,
And doted more on him than on my God;
For this I scourge myself with sharp repents.
But now the touch of such aspiring sins
Tells me all love is lust but love of [Heaven];[2]
That beauty us'd for love is vanity;
The world contains naught but alluring baits:
Pride, flattery, and inconstant thoughts.   20
To shun the pricks of death, I leave the world,
And vow to meditate on heavenly bliss,
To live in Framlingham [3] a holy nun,
Holy and pure in conscience and in deed;
And for to wish all maids to learn of me
To seek Heaven's joy before earth's vanity.

FRIEND. And will you, then, Margaret, be
shorn a nun, and so leave us all?

MAR. Now farewell world, the engine of all
woe!
Farewell to friends and father; welcome
Christ!   30
Adieu to dainty robes; this base attire
Better befits an humble mind to God
Than all the show of rich [h]abiliments.
[Farewell,] [4] O love! and, with fond love, farewell

---

[1] Fressingfield. Near the Keeper's lodge.
[2] Old eds. *heauens.*   [3] Q₁ *Framingham.*
[4] Emend. Dyce; old eds. *Loue.*

Sweet Lacy, whom I loved once so dear!
Ever be well, but never in my thoughts,
Lest I offend to think on Lacy's love;
But even to that, as to the rest, farewell!

Enter LACY, WARREN, [*and*] ERMSBY, *booted
and spurr'd.*

LACY. Come on, my wags, we're near the
    Keeper's lodge.
Here have I oft walk'd in the wat'ry meads,   40
And chatted with my lovely Margaret.
WAR. Sirrah Ned, is not this the Keeper?
LACY. 'T is the same.
ERM. The old lecher hath gotten holy mut-
ton [5] to him: a nun, my Lord.
LACY. Keeper, how farest thou? Holla,
    man, what cheer?
How doth Peggy, thy daughter and my love?
KEEPER. Ah, good my Lord! O, woe is
    me for Pegg[y]!
See where she stands clad in her nun's attire,
Ready for to be shorn in Framlingham;   50
She leaves the world because she left your love.
O, good my Lord, persuade her if you can!
LACY. Why, how now, Margaret! What,
    a malcontent?
A nun? What holy father taught you this,
To task yourself to such a tedious life
As die a maid? 'T were injury to me,
To smother up such beauty in a cell.
MAR. Lord Lacy, thinking of thy former
    miss,[6]
How fond [7] the prime of wanton years were
    spent
In love (oh, fie upon that fond conceit,   60
Whose hap and essence hangeth in the eye!),
I leave both love and love's content at once,
Betaking me to Him that is true love,
And leaving all the world for love of Him.
LACY. Whence, Peggy, comes this meta-
    morphosis?
What, shorn a nun? and I have from the court
Posted with coursers to convey thee hence
To Windsor, where our marriage shall be kept!
Thy wedding robes are in the tailor's hands.
Come, Peggy, leave these peremptory vows. 70
MAR. Did not my Lord resign his interest,
And make divorce 'twixt Margaret and him?
LACY. 'T was but to try sweet Peggy's con-
    stancy.
But will fair Margaret leave her love and lord?

MAR. Is not Heaven's joy before earth's
    fading bliss,
And life above sweeter than life in love?
LACY. Why, then, Margaret will be shorn a
    nun?
MAR. Margaret hath made a vow which
    may not be revok'd.
WAR. We cannot stay, my Lord; an if she
    be so strict,
Our leisure grants us not to woo afresh.   80
ERMS. Choose you, fair damsel; yet the
    choice is yours,
Either a solemn nunnery or the court,
God or Lord Lacy. Which contents you best,
To be a nun or else Lord Lacy's wife?
LACY. A good motion. — Peggy, your an-
    swer must be short.
MAR. The flesh is frail; my Lord doth
    know it well,
That when he comes with his enchanting face,
Whatsoe'er betide, I cannot say him nay.
Off goes the habit [8] of a maiden's heart,   89
And, seeing fortune will, fair Framlingham,
And all the show of holy nuns, farewell!
Lacy for me, if he will be my lord.
LACY. Peggy, thy lord, thy love, thy hus-
    band.
Trust me, by truth of knighthood, that the
    King
Stays for to marry matchless Elinor,
Until I bring thee richly to the court,
That one day may both marry her and thee. —
How say'st thou, Keeper? Art thou glad of
    this?
KEEP. As if the English King had given
The park and deer of Fressingfield to me. 100
ERM. I pray thee, my Lord of Sussex, why
art thou in a brown study?
WAR. To see the nature of women; that
be they never so near God, yet they love to
die in a man's arms.
LACY. What have you fit for breakfast?
    We have hied
And posted all this night to Fressingfield.
MAR. Butter and cheese, and umbles [9] of a
    deer,
Such as poor keepers have within their lodge.
LACY. And not a bottle of wine?   110
MAR. We'll find one for my lord.
LACY. Come, Sussex, let's in; we shall
    have more,
For she speaks least, to hold her promise sure.
                                        Exeunt.

---

[5] *Mutton* was a cant word for an unchaste woman.
[6] Fault; *i.e.*, your former mistaken love for me.
But possibly we should read *my* for *thy.*
[7] Foolishly.

[8] Garb.
[9] Numbles, pluck. Q 1 *humbls.*

[SCENE II] [10]

Enter a Devil *to seek* MILES.

DEVIL. How restless are the ghosts of
    hellish spirits,
When every charmer with his magic spells
Calls us from ninefold-trenched [Phle-
    gethon],[11]
To scud and overscour the earth in post
Upon the speedy wings of swiftest winds!
Now Bacon hath rais'd me from the darkest
    deep,
To search about the world for Miles, his man,
For Miles, and to torment his lazy bones
For careless watching of his Brazen Head.
See where he comes. Oh, he is mine!   10

Enter MILES *with a gown and a corner-cap.*

MILES. A scholar, quoth you! Marry, sir,
I would I had been made a bottlemaker when
I was made a scholar ; for I can get neither to
be a deacon, reader,[12] nor schoolmaster, no, not
the clerk of a parish. Some call me dunce;
another saith my head is as full of Latin as an
egg's full of oatmeal. Thus I am tormented,
that the Devil and Friar Bacon haunts me.
— Good Lord, here's one of my master's
devils! I'll go speak to him. — What, [20
Master Plutus,[13] how cheer you?
DEV. Dost thou know me?
MILES. Know you, sir! Why, are not you
one of my master's devils, that were wont to
come to my master, Doctor Bacon, at Brazen-
nose?
DEV. Yes, marry, am I.
MILES. Good Lord, Master Plutus, I have
seen you a thousand times at my master's, and
yet I had never the manners to make you [30
drink. But, sir, I am glad to see how con-
formable you are to the statute.[14] — I warrant
you, he's as yeomanly a man as you shall see ;
mark you, masters,[15] here's a plain honest
man, without welt or guard.[16] But I pray
you, sir, do you come lately from hell?
DEV. Ay, marry ; how then?
MILES. Faith, 't is a place I have desired
long to see. Have you not good tippling-

houses there? May not a man have a [40
lusty fire there, a pot of good ale, a pair [17]
of cards, a swinging [18] piece of chalk, and a
brown toast that will clap a white waistcoat
on a cup of good drink?
DEV. All this you may have there.
MILES. You are for me, friend, and I am
for you. But I pray you, may I not have an
office there?
DEV. Yes, a thousand. What wouldst
thou be?   50
MILES. By my troth, sir, in a place where I
may profit myself. I know hell is a hot place,
and men are marvellous dry, and much drink
is spent there ; I would be a tapster.
DEV. Thou shalt.
MILES. There's nothing lets [19] me from
going with you but that 't is a long journey
and I have never a horse.
DEV. Thou shalt ride on my back.
MILES. Now surely here's a courteous [60
devil, that, for to pleasure his friend, will not
stick to make a jade of himself. — But I pray
you, goodman friend, let me move a question
to you.
DEV. What's that?
MILES. I pray you, whether is your pace a
trot or an amble?
DEV. An amble.
MILES. 'T is well, but take heed it be not a
trot ; but 't is no matter — I'll prevent it. [70
DEV. What dost?
MILES. Marry, friend, I put on my spurs ;
for if I find your pace either a trot or else uneasy, I'll put you to a false gallop ; [20] I'll make
you feel the benefit of my spurs.
DEV. Get up upon my back.
MILES. O Lord, here's even a goodly marvel, when a man rides to hell on the Devil's
back!

                        Exeunt, roaring.

[SCENE III] [21]

Enter the EMPEROR *with a pointless sword;* [22]
    next the KING OF CASTILE *carrying a sword*
    with a point; [23] LACY *carrying the globe;*
    [PRINCE] EDWARD ; WARREN *carrying a rod*
    of gold with a dove on it; [24] ERMSBY *with a*

---

[10] Unlocated.
[11] Not this fiery river of hell, but the Styx, is
described as winding nine times. Q 1 *Blegiton.*
[12] A minor order of the church.
[13] *I.e.,* Pluto.
[14] Which prohibited the wearing of finery above
one's station.
[15] Gentlemen. (Addressed to the audience.)
[16] Both words mean border or facing, usually of
lace.

[17] Pack.
[18] Mighty. The chalk is to score up the bill, in
lieu of cash.
[19] Prevents.   [20] Canter.
[21] Unlocated ; presumably the same as in IV, ii.
[22] The sword of mercy, or *curtana.*
[23] The sword of justice.
[24] The "rod of equity."

crown and sceptre; the [PRINCESS ELINOR][25]
with the Fair Maid of Fressingfield *on her left
hand;* [KING] HENRY; [*and*] BACON; *with
other* Lords *attending.*

EDW. Great potentates, earth's miracles
 for state,
Think that Prince Edward humbles at your
 feet,
And, for these favors, on his martial sword
He vows perpetual homage to yourselves,
Yielding these honors unto Elinor.
 HEN. Gramercies, Lordlings; old Planta-
 genet,
That rules and sways the Albion diadem,
With tears discovers those conceived joys,
And vows requital, if his men at arms,
The wealth of England, or due honors done 10
To Elinor, may quit his favorites.
But all this while what say you to the dames,
That shine like to the crystal lamps of heaven?
 EMP. If but a third were added to these two,
They did surpass those gorgeous images
That gloried Ida with rich beauty's wealth.
 MAR. 'T is I, my Lords, who humbly on
 my knee
Must yield her orisons to mighty Jove
For lifting up his handmaid to this state, 19
Brought from her homely cottage to the court,
And grac'd with [26] kings, princes, and emper-
 ors;
To whom, next to the noble Lincoln Earl,
I vow obedience and such humble love
As may a handmaid to such mighty men.
 ELIN. Thou martial man that wears the
 Almain crown,
And you, the western potentates of might,
The Albion Princess, English Edward's wife,
Proud that the lovely star of Fressingfield,
Fair Margaret, Countess to the Lincoln Earl,
Attends on Elinor, — gramercies, Lord, for
 her, — 30
'T is I give thanks for Margaret to you all,
And rest for her due bounden to yourselves.
 HEN. Seeing the marriage is solemnized,
Let's march in triumph to the royal feast. —
But why stands Friar Bacon here so mute?
 BACON. Repentant for the follies of my
 youth,
That magic's secret mysteries misled,
And joyful that this royal marriage
Portends such bliss unto this matchless realm.
 HEN. Why, Bacon, 40

[25] Old eds. *Queen.* [26] Honored by.

What strange event shall happen to this
 land?
Or what shall grow from Edward and his
 Queen?
  BACON. I find by deep prescience of mine
 art,
Which once I temp'red in my secret cell,
That here where Brute did build his Troyno-
 vant,
From forth the royal garden of a king
Shall flourish out so rich and fair a bud [27]
Whose brightness shall deface proud Phœbus'
 flow'r,
And overshadow Albion with her leaves.
Till then Mars shall be master of the field; 50
But then the stormy threats of wars shall
 cease,
The horse shall stamp as careless of the pike,
Drums shall be turn'd to timbrels of delight;
With wealthy favors plenty shall enrich
The strond that gladded wand'ring Brute to
 see,
And peace from Heaven shall harbor in these
 leaves
That gorgeous beautifies this matchless flower.
Apollo's heliotropion then shall stoop,
And Venus' hyacinth shall vail her top;
Juno shall shut her gilliflowers up, 60
And Pallas' bay shall 'bash her brightest
 green;
Ceres' carnation, in consort with those,
Shall stoop and wonder at Diana's rose.
 HEN. This prophecy is mystical. —
But, glorious commanders of Europa's love,
That makes fair England like that wealthy
 isle
Circled with Gihon [28] and [swift] [29] Euphrates,
In royalizing Henry's Albion
With presence of your princely mightiness,
Let's march; the tables all are spread, 70
And viands, such as England's wealth affords,
Are ready set to furnish out the boards.
You shall have welcome, mighty potentates;
It rests to furnish up this royal feast;
Only your hearts be frolic, for the time
Craves that we taste of naught but jouissance.
Thus glories England over all the west.
          Exeunt omnes.

Omne tulit punctum qui miscuit utile dulci.[30]

[27] Queen Elizabeth.
[28] The Amu-Darya, the Oxus.
[29] Cor. Dyce; old eds. *first.*
[30] He wins every suffrage who mingles the useful
with the agreeable.

The Spanish Tragedie

OR,

Hieronimo is mad againe.

Containing the lamentable end of *Don Horatio*, and
Belimperia; with the pittifull death of *Hieronimo*.

Newly corrected, amended, and enlarged with new
Additions of the *Painters* part, and others, as
it hath of late been diuers times acted.

LONDON,
Printed by W. White, for I. White and T. Langley,
and are to be sold at their Shop ouer-againſt the
Sarazens head without New-gate. 1615.

INTRODUCTORY NOTE

FEW if any of the Elizabethan plays equalled *The Spanish Tragedy* in popularity or influence. Playgoers and play readers alike devoured it, and many of its features may be traced in subsequent tragedies. To be sure, there are bombast and rawness and clumsiness in *The Spanish Tragedy;* to be sure, it lacks the winged imagination and superb rhetoric that redeem Marlowe's bombast. But a lively melodrama is always preferable to a dead tragedy, and Kyd's play is no ordinary melodrama. Its great merit, as a piece of the 1580's, resides in the author's sincerity and his absorption in the human passions which his story involves. Of all the immediate predecessors of Shakespeare, Kyd is the one with the real flair for the stage. As an example of construction, this play is open to much objection, especially for its labored beginning; and Kyd is stylistically quite inferior to his colleagues. But he surpasses them all in building his scenes around the emotional responses of his characters to the pressure of circumstances, in effective preparation for scenes of rapid action, and in employing a more definitely theatrical technique to move the hearts of his audience. All of which is only saying that Kyd's genius was a more dramatic genius than that of the others.

No source for the plot has been found; yet it is not unlikely that Kyd took it from some romantic tale which has not survived. The political and military background of the play is unhistorical, though there was war between Spain and Portugal in 1580. The influence of Seneca (translated in 1581) is obvious in the frequent stichomythia, the messenger, the ghost, and the revenge theme with its attendant horrors. It is highly significant that the Senecan machinery appears here in, not an academic, but a popular play. Elizabethan tragedy was to continue to be molded more or less of the Senecan clay; it was Kyd who breathed life into it. Besides Seneca, Garnier (translated in 1585) and Vergil are drawn upon for some details.

As the London drama developed, and taste and craft were more refined, *The Spanish Tragedy,* though still a great popular success, became an object of scorn to the sophisticated. From a derisive reference by Jonson in the induction to *Bartholemew Fair,* it seems likely that the play was produced between 1584 and 1589. The absence of any allusion to the Armada suggests an earlier date than 1588; c. 1586 cannot be far out of the way. Apparently the play was often called simply *Jeronimo.* Of its long theatrical career there can be no doubt, but records of actual performances are scanty. It was played sixteen times at the Rose by Lord Strange's Men between March 14, 1592, and January 22, 1593, sometimes in conjunction with *The Spanish Comedy of Don Horatio.* Neither that play, nor *The Comedy of Jeronimo* (their texts have not survived, and they may be alternative titles for the same piece), nor the (probably) later *First Part of Jeronimo* (printed in 1605) had, as far as is known, any connection with Kyd himself. Another substantial run of *The Spanish Tragedy* is recorded, this time by the Admiral's Men, who acted it thirteen times between January 7 and October 11, 1597.

The standard edition of Kyd's works is that of F. S. Boas (1901). *The Spanish Tragedy* has been separately edited by Josef Schick (1898) and by W. W. Greg (1925). No copy of the original edition of the play is known to have survived and but one of the second, an undated octavo in the British Museum, conjecturally assigned by Greg to 1592. The second surviving edition appeared in 1594, and the third in 1599. The next was the Quarto of 1602, "newly corrected, amended, and enlarged." It was reprinted in 1603, 1611, 1615, 1618, 1623, and 1633, the last four quartos carrying on their title pages a woodcut which depicts the discovery of Horatio's body. This second version (1602, *et seq.*) contains the added passages printed in smaller type in the present edition. They have been ascribed to Ben Jonson because Henslowe twice during the season of 1601–1602 records advancing him considerable sums for additions to this play. It is argued, without much cogency, that these cannot be the additions of Quarto

1602, because their romantic fervor is unlike the bulk of Jonson's work.   More impressive are Dr. Greg's suggestions that Jonson appears to have received as large a fee as was ordinarily paid for a new play, that the surviving additions are not sufficiently extensive to warrant it, and that it seems unlikely that the company would have permitted the publication of a version so newly made.   The additions of Quarto 1602 may, therefore, represent a still earlier revision.   There must have been at least one such, for in 1597 Henslowe entered the play in his "Diary" as "new", and in *Cynthia's Revels* (1600) Jonson refers to it "as it was first acted."

As for Kyd's authorship of the original, our chief reliance is on the quotation and ascription to him of V, i, 83–85, by Thomas Heywood in his *Apology for Actors* (1612).   The present text is based on Boas's reprint of the first surviving edition and on his and Greg's reprints of the additions of 1602.   It has also been collated throughout with Greg's text of Q 1602 and with his list of the variants between that edition and the earliest.

THE SPANISH TRAGEDY

OR

HIERONIMO IS MAD AGAIN

BY

THOMAS KYD

[DRAMATIS PERSONAE

GHOST OF ANDREA, a Spanish courtier, ⎫
REVENGE, ⎬ Chorus.
KING OF SPAIN. ⎭
DON CYPRIAN, DUKE OF CASTILE, his brother.
LORENZO, the Duke's son.
VICEROY OF PORTUGAL.
BALTHAZAR, his son.
DON PEDRO, brother to the Viceroy.
HIERONIMO, Marshal of Spain.
HORATIO, his son.
Spanish General.
Deputy.
DON BAZULTO, an old man.
Three Citizens.
Portuguese Ambassador.
ALEXANDRO, ⎫ Portuguese Noblemen.
VILLUPPO,[1] ⎭
Two Portuguese.
PEDRINGANO, servant to Bel-imperia.
CHRISTOPHIL, custodian of Bel-imperia.
Page to Lorenzo.

SERBERINE, servant to Balthazar.
Messenger.
Hangman.
BAZARDO, a painter, ⎫
PEDRO and JAQUES, Hiero- ⎬ in the additions.
nimo's servants, ⎭
Army, Royal Suites, Nobles, Halberdiers, Officers, Three Watchmen, Servants, etc.

BEL-IMPERIA, daughter to Don Cyprian.
ISABELLA, wife to Hieronimo.
Maid to Isabella.

SOLIMAN, Sultan of Turkey (Balthazar), ⎫
ERASTUS, Knight of Rhodes (Lorenzo), ⎬ in Hieronimo's play.
BASHAW (Hieronimo), ⎪
PERSEDA (Bel-imperia), ⎭

Three Kings and three Knights, in the first dumb show.
HYMEN and two torchbearers, in the second.]

ACT I

[CHORUS]

Enter the GHOST OF ANDREA, *and with him* REVENGE.

GHOST. When this eternal substance of my soul
Did live imprison'd in my wanton flesh,
Each in their function serving other's need,
I was a courtier in the Spanish court.
My name was Don Andrea ; my descent,
Though not ignoble, yet inferior far
To gracious fortunes of my tender youth.

For there in prime and pride of all my years,
By duteous service and deserving love,
In secret I possess'd a worthy dame, 10
Which hight sweet Bel-imperia by name.
But in the harvest of my summer joys
Death's winter nipp'd the blossoms of my bliss,
Forcing divorce betwixt my love and me.
For in the late conflict with Portingale
My valor drew me into danger's mouth
Till life to death made passage through my wounds.
When I was slain, my soul descended straight [2]

[1] An Italian word. = confusion.

[2] The rest of the speech is adapted from Vergil's *Aeneid*, Book VI. The opening lines imitate the appearance of the ghost of Tantalus, with which Seneca's *Thyestes* begins.

211

To pass the flowing stream of Acheron ;
But churlish Charon, only boatman there, 20
Said that, my rites of burial not perform'd,
I might not sit amongst his passengers.
Ere Sol had slept three nights in Thetis' lap,
And slak'd his smoking chariot in her flood,
By Don Horatio, our knight marshal's son,
My funerals and obsequies were done.
Then was the ferryman of Hell content
To pass me over to the slimy strond
That leads to fell Avernus' ugly waves.
There, pleasing Cerberus with honey'd
    speech, 30
I pass'd the perils of the foremost porch.
Not far from hence, amidst ten thousand
    souls,
Sat Minos, Aeacus, and Rhadamanth ;
To whom no sooner 'gan I make approach,
To crave a passport for my wand'ring ghost,
But Minos, in graven leaves of lottery,
Drew forth the manner of my life and death.
" This knight," quoth he, " both liv'd and
    died in love,
And for his love tried fortune of the wars,
And by war's fortune lost both love and
    life." 40
" Why then," said Aeacus, " convey him
    hence,
To walk with lovers in our fields of love,
And spend the course of everlasting time
Under green myrtle trees and cypress shades."
" No, no," said Rhadamanth, " it were not
    well
With loving souls to place a martialist.
He died in war and must to martial fields,
Where wounded Hector lives in lasting pain,
And Achilles' Myrmidons do scour the plain."
Then Minos, mildest censor of the three, 50
Made this device to end the difference :
" Send him," quoth he, " to our infernal King,
To doom him as best seems his Majesty."
To this effect my passport straight was drawn.
In keeping on my way to Pluto's court,
Through dreadful shades of ever-glooming
    night,
I saw more sights than thousand tongues can
    tell,
Or pens can write, or mortal hearts can think.
Three ways there were : that on the right-
    hand side
Was ready way unto the 'foresaid fields, 60
Where lovers live and bloody martialists,
But either sort contain'd within his bounds.
The left-hand path, declining fearfully,
Was ready downfall to the deepest hell,

Where bloody Furies shakes their whips of
    steel,
And poor Ixion turns an endless wheel ;
Where usurers are chok'd with melting gold,
And wantons are embrac'd with ugly snakes,
And murderers groan with never-killing
    wounds,
And perjur'd wights scalded in boiling lead, [70
And all foul sins with torments overwhelm'd.
'Twixt these two ways I trod the middle path,
Which brought me to the fair Elysian green,[3]
In midst whereof there stands a stately tower,
The walls of brass, the gates of adamant.
Here finding Pluto with his Proserpine,
I show'd my passport, humbled on my knee ;
Whereat fair Proserpine began to smile,
And begg'd that only she might give my doom.
Pluto was pleas'd, and seal'd it with a kiss. 80
Forthwith, Revenge, she rounded[4] thee in th'
    ear,
And bade thee lead me through the gates of
    hor[n],
Where dreams have passage in the silent night.
No sooner had she spoke but we were here
(I wot not how) in twinkling of an eye.
   REVENGE. Then know, Andrea, that thou
    art arriv'd
Where thou shalt see the author of thy death,
Don Balthazar, the Prince of Portingale,
Depriv'd of life by Bel-imperia.
Here sit we down to see the mystery, 90
And serve for Chorus in this tragedy.

[SCENE I][5]

Enter SPANISH KING, General, CASTILE,
    [*and*] HIERONIMO.

   KING. Now say, Lord General, how fares
    our camp?
   GEN. All well, my sovereign Liege, except
    some few
That are deceas'd by fortune of the war.
   KING. But what portends thy cheerful
    countenance,
And posting to our presence thus in haste?
Speak, man, hath fortune given us victory?
   GEN. Victory, my Liege, and that with
    little loss.
   KING. Our Portingals will pay us tribute
    then?

---

[3] In the prefatory epistle to *Menaphon,* Nash sneers
at "those that thrust Elysium into hell."
[4] Whispered.
[5] Before a castle of the Spanish King.

GEN. Tribute and wonted homage therewithal.

KING. Then bless'd be Heaven and Guider
of the Heavens, 10
From whose fair influence such justice flows.

CAST. *O multum dilecte Deo, tibi militat*
aether,
Et conjuratae curvato poplit[e] gentes
Succumbunt: recti soror est victoria juris.[6]

KING. Thanks to my loving brother of
Castile. —
But, General, unfold in brief discourse
Your form of battle and your war's success,
That, adding all the pleasure of thy news
Unto the height of former happiness,
With deeper wage and greater dignity 20
We may reward thy blissful chivalry.

GEN. Where Spain and Portingale do
jointly knit
Their frontiers, leaning on each other's bound,
There met our armies in their proud array ;
Both furnish'd well, both full of hope and fear,
Both menacing alike with daring shows,
Both vaunting sundry colors of device,[7]
Both cheerly sounding trumpets, drums, and
fifes,
Both raising dreadful clamors to the sky,
That[8] valleys, hills, and rivers made re-
bound, 30
And heaven itself was frighted with the sound.
Our battles[9] both were pitch'd in squadron
form,
Each corner strongly fenc'd with wings of
shot ;
But ere we join'd and came to push of pike,
I brought a squadron of our readiest shot
From out our rearward to begin the fight.
They brought another wing to encounter us.
Meanwhile, our ordnance play'd on either side,
And captains strove to have their valors
tried.
Don Pedro, their chief horsemen's colonel, 40
Did with his cornet[10] bravely make attempt
To break the order of our battle ranks ;
But Don Rogero, worthy man of war,
March'd forth against him with our musket-
eers,

And stopp'd the malice of his fell approach.
While they maintain hot skirmish to and fro,
Both battles join and fall to handy-blows,
Their violent shot resembling th' ocean's rage,
When, roaring loud, and with a swelling tide,
It beats upon the rampires[11] of huge rocks [50
And gapes to swallow neighbor-bounding
lands.
Now, while Bellona rageth here and there,
Thick storms of bullets [rain][12] like winter's
hail,
And shivered lances dark[13] the troubled air.
Pede pes et cuspide cuspis ;
[Arma] sonant [armis],[14] *vir petiturque viro.*
On every side drop captains to the ground,
And soldiers, some ill-maim'd, some slain out-
right ;
Here falls a body s[u]nd'red from his head,
There legs and arms lie bleeding on the
grass, 60
Mingled with weapons and unbowell'd steeds,
That scattering overspread the purple plain.
In all this turmoil, three long hours and more,
The victory to neither part inclin'd ;
Till Don Andrea, with his brave lanciers,
In their main battle made so great a breach,
That, half dismay'd, the multitude retir'd ;
But Balthazar, the Portingals' young Prince,
Brought rescue and encourag'd them to stay.
Here-hence the fight was eagerly renew'd, 70
And in that conflict was Andrea slain,
Brave man at arms, but weak to Balthazar.
Yet while the Prince, insulting[15] over him,
Breath'd out proud vaunts, sounding to our
reproach,
Friendship and hardy valor, join'd in one,
Prick'd forth Horatio, our knight marshal's
son,
To challenge forth that Prince in single fight.
Not long between these twain the fight en-
dur'd,
But straight the Prince was beaten from his
horse,
And forc'd to yield him prisoner to his foe. 80
When he was taken, all the rest they fled,
And our carbines pursued them to the death,
Till, Phoebus waving[16] to the western deep,
Our trumpeters were charg'd to sound retreat.

[6] O much loved of God, Heaven wars for thee, and
on bended knee fall the conspiring nations: victory
is the sister of just equity. (Adapted from Clau-
dian's *De Tertio Consulatu Honorii*, ll. 96–98.)
[7] Proudly displaying their heraldic bearings,
painted in various colors.
[8] So that.
[9] Armies. "Battle" could also mean a subdivision of an army, as in l. 66. "Squadron" here =
square.
[10] Troop.

[11] Ramparts.
[12] Emend. Editor ; old eds. *ran.*
[13] Q 1594 *et seq., darkt* or *dark'd.*
[14] Cor. Q 1633 ; earlier eds. *Anni . . . annis.*
"Foot against foot and point against point ; arms
clash on arms, and man rushes on man." These lines
are adapted from Statius's *Thebais*, viii, 399, and
Curtius's *De Gestis Alexandri Magni*, iii, 2.
[15] Exulting. [16] Declining. (*N. E. D.*)

KING. Thanks, good Lord General, for
　　these good news ;
And for some argument [17] of more to come,
Take this and wear it for thy sovereign's sake.
　　　　　　　　Give him his chain.
But tell me now, hast thou confirm'd a peace?
　GEN. No peace, my Liege, but peace con-
　　ditional,
That if with homage tribute be well paid,　90
The fury of your forces will be stay'd ;
And to this peace their viceroy hath sub-
　　scrib'd,
　　　　　　　Give the KING *a paper.*
And made a solemn vow that, during life,
His tribute shall be truly paid to Spain.
　KING. These words, these deeds, become
　　thy person well.
But now, Knight Marshal, frolic with thy
　　king,
For 't is thy son that wins this battle's prize.
　HIER. Long may he live to serve my sov-
　　ereign Liege,
And soon decay, unless he serve my Liege.
　KING. Nor thou nor he shall die without
　　reward. 　　　　*A tucket afar off.* [100
What means this warning of this trumpet's
　　sound?
　GEN. This tells me that your Grace's men
　　of war,
Such as war's fortune hath reserv'd from
　　death,
Come marching on towards your royal seat,
To show themselves before your Majesty ;
For so I gave in charge at my depart.
Whereby by demonstration shall appear
That all, except three hundred or few more,
Are safe return'd, and by their foes enrich'd.

The Army *enters;* BALTHAZAR, *between* LO-
RENZO *and* HORATIO, *captive.*

　KING. A gladsome sight ! I long to see
　　them here. 　*They enter and pass by.*　110
Was that the warlike Prince of Portingale,
That by our nephew was in triumph led?
　GEN. It was, my Liege, the Prince of Por-
　　tingale.
　KING. But what was he that on the other
　　side
Held him by th' arm, as partner of the prize?
　HIER. That was my son, my gracious Sov-
　　ereign ;
Of whom though from his tender infancy
My loving thoughts did never hope but well,
He never pleas'd his father's eyes till now,

Nor fill'd my heart with overcloying joys.　120
　KING. Go, let them march once more about
　　these walls.
That, staying them, we may confer and talk
With our brave prisoner and his double guard.
　　　　　　　[*Exit a* Messenger.]
Hieronimo, it greatly pleaseth us
That in our victory thou have a share,
By virtue of thy worthy son's exploit.

Enter again.

Bring hither the young Prince of Portingale.
The rest march on ; but, ere they be dismiss'd,
We will bestow on every soldier
Two ducats and on every leader ten,　130
That they may know our largess welcomes
　　them.
　　　Exeunt all [the Army] *but* BALTHAZAR,
　　　　　LORENZO, [*and*] HORATIO.
Welcome, Don Balthazar ! welcome, Nephew !
And thou, Horatio, thou art welcome too.
Young Prince, although thy father's hard mis-
　　deeds,
In keeping back the tribute that he owes,
Deserve but evil measure at our hands,
Yet shalt thou know that Spain is honorable.
　BAL. The trespass that my father made in
　　peace
Is now controll'd [18] by fortune of the wars ;
And cards once dealt, it boots not ask why
　　so. 　　　　　　　　　　140
His men are slain, a weakening to his realm ;
His colors seiz'd, a blot unto his name ;
His son distress'd, a corsive [19] to his heart :
These punishments may clear his late offence.
　KING. Ay, Balthazar, if he observe this
　　truce,
Our peace will grow the stronger for these wars.
Meanwhile live thou, though not in liberty,
Yet free from bearing any servile yoke ;
For in our hearing thy deserts were great,
And in our sight thyself art gracious,　150
　BAL. And I shall study to deserve this
　　grace.
　KING. But tell me — for their holding
　　makes me doubt —
To which of these twain art thou prisoner?
　LOR. To me, my Liege.
　HOR. 　　　　　　To me, my Sovereign.
　LOR. This hand first took his courser by
　　the reins.
　HOR. But first my lance did put him from
　　his horse.

---

[18] Checked. 　　　　　　[19] Corrosive.

LOR. I seiz'd his weapon, and enjoy'd it first.

HOR. But first I forc'd him lay his weapons down.

KING. Let go his arm, upon our privilege.[20]

Let him go.

Say, worthy Prince, to whether [21] didst thou yield?   160

BAL. To him in courtesy, to this perforce.
He spake me fair, this other gave me strokes;
He promis'd life, this other threat'ned death;
He won my love, this other conquered me,
And, truth to say, I yield myself to both.

HIER. But that I know your Grace for just and wise,
And might seem partial in this difference,
Enforc'd by nature and by law of arms
My tongue should plead for young Horatio's right.
He hunted well that was a lion's death,   170
Not he that in a garment wore his skin;
So hares may pull dead lions by the beard.

KING. Content thee, Marshal, thou shalt have no wrong;
And, for thy sake, thy son shall want no right.
Will both abide the censure of my doom?

LOR. I crave no better than your Grace awards.

HOR. Nor I, although I sit beside my right.

KING. Then, by my judgment, thus your strife shall end:
You both deserve, and both shall have reward. —
Nephew, thou took'st his weapon and his horse;   180
His weapons and his horse are thy reward. —
Horatio, thou didst force him first to yield;
His ransom therefore is thy valor's fee:
Appoint the sum, as you shall both agree. —
But, Nephew, thou shalt have the Prince in guard,
For thine estate best fitteth such a guest;
Horatio's house were small for all his train.
Yet, in regard thy substance passeth his,
And that just guerdon may befall desert,
To him we yield the armor of the Prince. —
How likes Don Balthazar of this device? 191

BAL. Right well, my Liege, if this proviso were,
That Don Horatio bear us company,
Whom I admire and love for chivalry.

KING. Horatio, leave him not that loves thee so. —
Now let us hence to see our soldiers paid,
And feast our prisoner as our friendly guest.

Exeunt.

[SCENE II] [22]

Enter VICEROY, ALEXANDRO, VILLUPPO, [*and* Attendants.]

VIC. Is our ambassador despatch'd for Spain?

ALEX. Two days, my Liege, are past since his depart.

VIC. And tribute payment gone along with him?

ALEX. Ay, my good Lord.

VIC. Then rest we here awhile in our unrest,
And feed our sorrows with some inward sighs,
For deepest cares break never into tears.
But wherefore sit I in a regal throne?
This better fits a wretch's endless moan. —
Yet this is higher than my fortunes reach, 10
And therefore better than my state deserves. —

Falls to the ground.

Ay, ay, this earth, image of melancholy,
Seeks him whom fates adjudge to misery.
Here let me lie; now am I at the lowest.
Qui jacet in terra, non habet unde cadat.
In me consumpsit vires fortuna nocendo;
Nil superest ut jam possit obesse magis.[23]
Yes, Fortune may bereave me of my crown:
Here, take it now; let Fortune do her worst,
She will not rob me of this sable weed.   20
O no, she envies none but pleasant things.
Such is the folly of despiteful chance.
Fortune is blind, and sees not my deserts;
So is she deaf, and hears not my laments;
And could she hear, yet is she wilful-mad,
And therefore will not pity my distress.
Suppose that she could pity me, what then?
What help can be expected at her hands
Whose foot [is] [24] standing on a rolling stone,
And mind more mutable than fickle winds? [30]
Why wail I, then, where 's hope of no redress?
O yes, complaining makes my grief seem less.
My late ambition hath distain'd my faith;

---

[20] Royal right. A king's presence was supposed to be immune from witnessing a brawl.
[21] Which of the two.

[22] The throne-room in the palace of the Portuguese Viceroy.
[23] Who lies on the ground can fall no further. Fortune has used up all her power to harm me. Nothing is left now that can hurt me any more. (The source of these lines has not been found.)
[24] Add. Dodsley.

My breach of faith occasion'd bloody wars ;
Those bloody wars have spent my treasure ; 25
And with my treasure 25 my people's blood ;
And with their blood, my joy and best beloved,
My best beloved, my sweet and only son.
O, wherefore went I not to war myself?
The cause was mine ; I might have died for
 both.   40
My years were mellow, his but young and
 green ;
My death were natural, but his was forced.
 ALEX. No doubt, my Liege, but still the
  Prince survives.
 VIC. Survives ! Ay, where?
 ALEX. In Spain, a prisoner by mischance of
  war.
 VIC. Then they have slain him for his
  father's fault.
 ALEX. That were a breach to common law
  of arms.
 VIC. They reck no laws that meditate re-
  venge.
 ALEX. His ransom's worth will stay from
  foul revenge.
 VIC. No ; if he lived, the news would soon
  be here.   50
 ALEX. Nay, evil news fly faster still 26 than
  good.
 VIC. Tell me no more of news, for he is dead.
 VIL. My Sovereign, pardon the author of
  ill news,
And I 'll bewray 27 the fortune of thy son.
 VIC. Speak on ; I 'll guerdon thee, whate'er
  it be.
Mine ear is ready to receive ill news,
My heart grown hard 'gainst mischief's bat-
 tery.
Stand up, I say, and tell thy tale at large.
 VIL. Then hear that truth which these mine
  eyes have seen.
When both the armies were in battle join'd, 60
Don Balthazar, amidst the thickest troops,
To win renown did wondrous feats of arms.
Amongst the rest, I saw him, hand to hand,
In single fight with their lord general ;
Till Alexandro, that here counterfeits
Under the color of a duteous friend,
Discharged his pistol at the Prince's back
As though he would have slain their general ;
But therewithal Don Balthazar fell down ;
And when he fell, then we began to fly ; 70
But, had he lived, the day had sure been ours.
 ALEX. O wicked forgery ! O traitorous
  miscreant !
---
25 Trisyllabic. 26 Always. 27 Reveal.

 VIC. Hold thou thy peace ! — But now,
  Villuppo, say,
Where then became 28 the carcass of my son?
 VIL. I saw them drag it to the Spanish
  tents.
 VIC. Ay, ay, my nightly dreams have told
  me this. —
Thou false, unkind, unthankful, traitorous
 beast,
Wherein had Balthazar offended thee,
That thou shouldst thus betray him to our
 foes?
Was 't Spanish gold that bleared so thine
 eyes   80
That thou couldst see no part of our deserts?
Perchance, because thou art Terceira's 29 lord,
Thou hadst some hope to wear this diadem,
If first my son and then myself were slain ;
But thy ambitious thought shall break thy
 neck.
Ay, this was it that made thee spill his blood ;
   Take the crown and put it on again.
But I 'll now wear it till thy blood be spilt.
 ALEX. Vouchsafe, dread Sovereign, to hear
  me speak.
 VIC. Away with him ! His sight is second
  hell.
Keep him till we determine of his death. — 90
If Balthazar be dead, he shall not live.
Villuppo, follow us for thy reward.
  Exit VICEROY, [*with* ALEXANDRO, *guarded.*]
 VIL. Thus have I with an envious,30 forged
  tale
Deceived the King, betray'd mine enemy,
And hope for guerdon of my villainy. *Exit.*

[SCENE III] 31

Enter HORATIO *and* BEL-IMPERIA.

 BEL. Signior Horatio, this is the place and
  hour
Wherein I must entreat thee to relate
The circumstance of Don Andrea's death,
Who, living, was my garland's sweetest flower,
And in his death hath buried my delights.
 HOR. For love of him and service to yourself,
I nill 32 refuse this heavy doleful charge ;
Yet tears and sighs, I fear, will hinder me.
---
28 What then became of.
29 Terceira is one of the Azores.
30 Malicious.
31 A banqueting hall at the Spanish court, though
it does not become localized as such till l. 110.
32 Will not.

When both our armies were enjoin'd in fight,
Your worthy chevalier amidst the thick'st,   10
For glorious cause still aiming at the fairest,
Was at the last by young Don Balthazar
Encount'red hand to hand. Their fight was
      long,
Their hearts were great, their clamors menac-
      ing,
Their strength alike, their strokes both dan-
      gerous.
But wrathful Nemesis, that wicked power,
Envying [33] at Andrea's praise and worth,
Cut short his life, to end his praise and worth.
She, she herself, disguis'd in armor's mask,
As Pallas was before proud Pergamus,[34]   20
Brought in a fresh supply of halberdiers,
Which paunch'd [35] his horse and ding'd [36] him
      to the ground.
Then young Don Balthazar with ruthless rage,
Taking advantage of his foe's distress,
Did finish what his halberdiers begun,
And left not till Andrea's life was done.
Then, though too late, incens'd with just re-
      morse,[37]
I with my band [38] set forth against the Prince,
And brought him prisoner from his halber-
      diers.
      BEL. Would thou hadst slain him that so
            slew my love!   30
But then was Don Andrea's carcass lost?
      HOR. No, that was it for which I chiefly
            strove ;
Nor stepp'd I back till I recover'd him.
I took him up and wound him in mine arms,
And wielding him unto my private tent
There laid him down and dew'd him with my
      tears,
And sighed and sorrowed as became a friend.
But neither friendly sorrow, sighs, nor tears
Could win pale Death from his usurped right.
Yet this I did, and less I could not do :   40
I saw him honored with due funeral.
This scarf I pluck'd from off his lifeless arm,
And wear it in remembrance of my friend.
      BEL. I know the scarf ; would he had kept
            it still !
For had he lived, he would have kept it still,
And worn it for his Bel-imperia's sake ;
For 't was my favor at his last depart.
But now wear thou it both for him and me ;
For after him thou hast deserved it best.
But, for thy kindness in his life and death,   50

---

[33] Accented on the second syllable.
[34] Cf. Vergil's *Aeneid*, ii, 615, 616.
[35] Stabbed in the belly.   [36] Knocked.
[37] Pity, regret.   [38] So Greg ; Boas *hand*.

Be sure, while Bel-imperia's life endures,
She will be Don Horatio's thankful friend.
      HOR. And, madam, Don Horatio will not
            slack
Humbly to serve fair Bel-imperia.
But now, if your good liking stand thereto,
I 'll crave your pardon to go seek the Prince ;
For so the Duke, your father, gave me charge.
                                          Exit.
      BEL. Ay, go, Horatio ; leave me here alone ;
For solitude best fits my cheerless mood. —
Yet what avails to wail Andrea's death,   60
From whence Horatio proves my second
      love?
Had he not loved Andrea as he did,
He could not sit in Bel-imperia's thoughts.
But how can love find harbor in my breast
Till I revenge the death of my beloved?
Yes, second love shall further my revenge :
I 'll love Horatio, my Andrea's friend,
The more to spite the Prince, that wrought his
      end.
And where [39] Don Balthazar, that slew my
      love,
Himself now pleads for favor at my hands,   70
He shall, in rigor of my just disdain,
Reap long repentance for his murderous
      deed !
For what was 't else but murderous cowardice,
So many to oppress one valiant knight,
Without respect of honor in the fight?
And here he comes that murd'red my delight.

            Enter LORENZO *and* BALTHAZAR.

      LOR. Sister, what means this melancholy
            walk?
      BEL. That for a while I wish no company.
      LOR. But here the Prince is come to visit
            you.
      BEL. That argues that he lives in lib-
            erty.   80
      BAL. No, madam, but in pleasing servi-
            tude.
      BEL. Your prison then, belike, is your
            conceit.[40]
      BAL. Ay, by conceit my freedom is en-
            thrall'd.
      BEL. Then with conceit enlarge yourself
            again.
      BAL. What, if conceit have laid my heart
            to gage?
      BEL. Pay that you borrowed, and recover
            it.
      BAL. I die, if it return from whence it lies.

---

[39] Whereas.   [40] Imagination.

BEL. A heartless man, and live? A miracle!

BAL. Ay, lady, love can work such miracles.

LOR. Tush, tush, my Lord! let go these ambages,[41]   90
And in plain terms acquaint her with your love.

BEL. What boots complaint, when there's no remedy?

BAL. Yes, to your gracious self must I complain,
In whose fair answer lies my remedy,
On whose perfection all my thoughts attend,
On whose aspect mine eyes find beauty's bower,
In whose translucent breast my heart is lodg'd.

BEL. Alas, my Lord, these are but words of course,[42]
And but [devis'd][43] to drive me from this place.

She, in going in, lets fall her glove, which HORATIO, *coming out, takes up.*

HOR. Madam, your glove.   100

BEL. Thanks, good Horatio; take it for thy pains.

BAL. Signior Horatio stoop'd in happy time.

HOR. I reap'd more grace than I deserv'd or hop'd.

LOR. My Lord, be not dismay'd for what is past;
You know that women oft are humorous.[44]
These clouds will overblow with little wind;
Let me alone;[45] I'll scatter them myself.
Meanwhile, let us devise to spend the time
In some delightful sports and revelling.

HOR. The King, my Lords, is coming hither straight,   110
To feast the Portingal ambassador;
Things were in readiness before I came.

BAL. Then here it fits us to attend the King,
To welcome hither our ambassador,
And learn my father and my country's health.

Enter[46] *the banquet,* Trumpets, *the* KING, [DON CYPRIAN, Lords, Ladies,] *and* Ambassador.

KING. See, Lord Ambassador, how Spain entreats

Their prisoner Balthazar, thy viceroy's son.
We pleasure more in kindness than in wars.

AMB. Sad is our king, and Portingale laments,
Supposing that Don Balthazar is slain.   120

BAL. [*aside to* BEL-IMPERIA]. So am I slain, by beauty's tyranny! —
You see, my Lord, how Balthazar is slain:
I frolic with the Duke of Castile's son,
Wrapp'd every hour in pleasures of the court,
And grac'd with favors of his Majesty.

KING. Put off your greetings, till our feast be done;
Now come and sit with us, and taste our cheer.
          Sit to the banquet.
Sit down, young Prince; you are our second guest.
Brother, sit down; and, Nephew, take your place.
Signior Horatio, wait thou upon our cup;   130
For well thou hast deserved to be honored.
Now, Lordings, fall to; Spain is Portugal,
And Portugal is Spain; we both are friends;
Tribute is paid, and we enjoy our right.
But where is old Hieronimo, our marshal?
He promis'd us, in honor of our guest,
To grace our banquet with some pompous[47] jest. —

Enter HIERONIMO, *with a drum, three* Knights, *each his scutcheon; then he fetches three* Kings; *they take their crowns and them captive.*

Hieronimo, this masque contents mine eye,
Although I sound not well the mystery.

HIER. The first arm'd knight, that hung his scutcheon up,   140
          He takes the scutcheon and gives it to the KING.
Was English Robert, Earl of Gloucester,
Who, when King Stephen bore sway in Albion,
Arrived with five-and-twenty thousand men
In Portingale, and by success of war
Enforc'd the king, then but a Saracen,
To bear the yoke of the English monarchy.[48]

KING. My Lord of Portingale, by this you see
That which may comfort both your king and you,
And make your late discomfort seem the less. —
But say, Hieronimo, what was the next?   150

41 Circumlocutions.   42 Conventional phrases.
43 Cor. ed. 1599; earlier eds. *deuise.*
44 Capricious.
45 Leave it to me.
46 Mod. eds. begin a new scene here.

47 Stately.
48 Moorish Lisbon was taken in 1147 with the help of an English fleet, but Robert of Gloucester was not present.

HIER. The second knight, that hung his
    scutcheon up, (*He doth as he did before.*)
Was Edmund, Earl of Kent in Albion,
When English Richard wore the diadem.
He came likewise, and razed Lisbon walls,
And took the King of Portingale in fight ;
For which and other such like service done,
He after was created Duke of York.[49]

KING. This is another special argument,
That Portingale may deign to bear our yoke,
When it by little England hath been yok'd. —
But now, Hieronimo, what were the last? 161

HIER. The third and last, not least, in our
    account,   *Doing as before.*
Was, as the rest, a valiant Englishman,
Brave John of Gaunt, the Duke of Lancaster,
As by his scutcheon plainly may appear.
He with a puissant army came to Spain
And took our King of Castile prisoner.[50]

AMB. This is an argument for our viceroy
That Spain may not insult for her success,
Since English warriors likewise conquered
    Spain,   170
And made them bow their knees to Albion.

KING. Hieronimo, I drink to thee for this
    device,
Which hath pleas'd both the ambassador and
    me.
Pledge me, Hieronimo, if thou love the
    King. —   *Takes the cup of* HORATIO.
My Lord, I fear we sit but overlong,
Unless our dainties were more delicate ;
But welcome are you to the best we have.
Now let us in, that you may be despatch'd ;
I think our council is already set.
                  Exeunt omnes.

[CHORUS]

ANDREA. Come we for this from depth of
    underground,   180
To see him feast that gave me my death's
    wound?
These pleasant sights are sorrow to my soul !
Nothing but league, and love, and banquet-
    ing?

REVENGE. Be still, Andrea ; ere we go from
    hence,
I 'll turn their friendship into fell despite,
Their love to mortal hate, their day to night,

Their hope into despair, their peace to war,
Their joys to pain, their bliss to misery.

ACT II — [SCENE I] [1]

Enter LORENZO *and* BALTHAZAR.

LOR. My Lord, though Bel-imperia seem
    thus coy,
Let reason hold you in your wonted joy.
In time the savage bull sustains the yoke,[2]
In time all haggard [3] hawks will stoop to lure,
In time small wedges cleave the hardest oak,
In time the flint is pierc'd with softest shower,
And she in time will fall from her disdain
And rue the sufferance of your friendly pain.

BAL. No, she is wilder, and more hard
    withal,
Than beast, or bird, or tree, or stony wall. 10
But wherefore blot I Bel-imperia's name?
It is my fault, not she, that merits blame.
My feature is not to content her sight ;
My words are rude and work her no delight.
The lines I send her are but harsh and ill,
Such as do drop from Pan and Marsyas' quill.
My presents are not of sufficient cost,
And being worthless, all my labor 's lost.
Yet might she love me for my valiancy —
Ay, but that 's sland'red by captivity.   20
Yet might she love me to content her sire —
Ay, but her reason masters his desire.
Yet might she love me as her brother's
    friend —
Ay, but her hopes aim at some other end.
Yet might she love me to uprear her state —
Ay, but perhaps she hopes some nobler mate.
Yet might she love me as her [beauty's] [4]
    thrall —
Ay, but I fear she cannot love at all.

LOR. My Lord, for my sake leave [this
    ecstasy,] [5]
And doubt not but we 'll find some remedy. 30
Some cause there is that lets you not be loved ;
First that must needs be known, and then re-
    moved.
What if my sister love some other knight?

BAL. My summer's day will turn to winter's
    night.

[49] Edmund Langley, fifth son of Edward III, made
an expedition to Portugal in 1381, but it came to
nothing. His dukedom was awarded later, for service against the Scots.

[50] On the contrary he had to retreat from Spain,
though he afterwards married one of his daughters to
the heir of Castile.

[1] A room in the palace of Don Cyprian.

[2] Ll. 3–6 and 9, 10 are adapted from Thomas
Watson's *Hecatompathia*, Sonnet 47, which in
turn adapts ll. 1–4 of Sonnet 103 of Serafino
d'Acquila.

[3] Wayward, fractious. — " Lure " = bait, a device
to entice the hawk to return.

[4] Cor. Q 1615 ; earlier eds. *beauteous.*

[5] Emend. Schick ; old eds. *these extasies*

Lor. I have already found a stratagem
To sound the bottom of this doubtful theme.
My Lord, for once you shall be rul'd by me ;
Hinder me not, whate'er you hear or see.
By force or fair means will I cast about
To find the truth of all this question out. — 40
Ho, Pedringano !
    Ped. [*within*]   *Signior!*
    Lor.   *Vien qui presto.*[6]

        Enter Pedringano.

    Ped. Hath your Lordship any service to
      command me?
    Lor. Ay, Pedringano, service of import ;
And, not to spend the time in trifling words,
Thus stands the case : it is not long, thou
      know'st,
Since I did shield thee from my father's wrath,
For thy conveyance [7] in Andrea's love,
For which thou wert adjudg'd to punishment.
I stood betwixt thee and thy punishment ;
And since, thou knowest how I have favored
      thee.   50
Now to these favors will I add reward,
Not with fair words, but store of golden coin,
And lands and living join'd with dignities,
If thou but satisfy my just demand.
Tell truth, and have me for thy lasting friend.
    Ped. Whate'er it be your Lordship shall
      demand,
My bounden duty bids me tell the truth,
If case it lie in me to tell the truth.
    Lor. Then, Pedringano, this is my demand :
Whom loves my sister Bel-imperia?   60
For she reposeth all her trust in thee.
Speak, man, and gain both friendship and re-
    ward.
I mean, whom loves she in Andrea's place?
    Ped. Alas, my Lord, since Don Andrea's
    death
I have no credit with her as before,
And therefore know not if she love or no.
    Lor. Nay, if thou dally, then I am thy foe ;
                  [*Draw his sword.*] [8]
And fear shall force what friendship cannot
    win.
Thy death shall bury what thy life conceals ;
Thou diest for more esteeming her than me. 70
    Ped. O, stay, my Lord.
    Lor. Yet speak the truth, and I will guer-
    don thee,
And shield thee from whatever can ensue,

And will conceal whate'er proceeds from thee.
But if thou dally once again, thou diest.
    Ped. If madam Bel-imperia be in love —
    Lor. What, villain, — if's and and's? [9]
                  [*Offer to kill him.*] [8]
    Ped. O, stay, my Lord : she loves Horatio.
              Balthazar *starts back.*
    Lor. What, Don Horatio, our knight mar-
    shal's son?
    Ped. Even him, my Lord.   80
    Lor. Now say but how knowest thou he is
    her love,
And thou shalt find me kind and liberal.
Stand up, I say, and fearless tell the truth.
    Ped. She sent him letters, which myself
    perus'd,
Full-fraught with lines and arguments of love,
Preferring him before Prince Balthazar.
    Lor. Swear on this cross [10] that what thou
    sayest is true,
And that thou wilt conceal what thou hast
    told.
    Ped. I swear to both, by Him that made
    us all.
    Lor. In hope thine oath is true, here's thy
    reward ;   90
But if I prove thee perjur'd and unjust,
This very sword whereon thou took'st thine
    oath
Shall be the worker of thy tragedy.
    Ped. What I have said is true, and shall,
    for me,[11]
Be still conceal'd from Bel-imperia.
Besides, your Honor's liberality
Deserves my duteous service, even till death.
    Lor. Let this be all that thou shalt do for
    me :
Be watchful when and where these lovers meet,
And give me notice in some secret sort.   100
    Ped. I will, my Lord.
    Lor. Then shalt thou find that I am liberal.
Thou know'st that I can more advance thy
    state
Than she ; be therefore wise, and fail me not.
Go and attend her, as thy custom is,
Lest absence make her think thou dost amiss.
                    Exit Pedringano.
Why so !   *Tam armis quam ingenio :*
Where words prevail not, violence prevails ;
But gold doth more than either of them both.
How likes Prince Balthazar this stratagem?

---

[6] Come here quickly.
[7] Acting as a medium of communication.
[8] Add. Q 1602.
[9] In his jeering allusions to Kyd in the prefatory
epistle to *Menaphon*, Nash accuses him of "bodging
up a blank verse with 'if's and 'and's.'"
[10] Probably the hilt of his sword.
[11] As far as I am concerned.

BAL. Both well and ill; it makes me glad
and sad :   111
Glad that I know the hinderer of my love,
Sad that I fear she hates me whom I love;
Glad that I know on whom to be reveng'd,
Sad that she 'll fly me if I take revenge.
Yet must I take revenge, or die myself,
For love resisted grows impatient.
I think Horatio be my destin'd plague !
First, in his hand he brandished a sword,   119
And with that sword he fiercely waged war,
And in that war he gave me dangerous wounds,
And by those wounds he forced me to yield,
And by my yielding I became his slave ;
Now in his mouth he carries pleasing words,
Which pleasing words do harbor sweet con-
ceits,
Which sweet conceits are lim'd with sly deceits,
Which sly deceits smooth Bel-imperia's ears,
And through her ears dive down into her heart,
And in her heart set him where I should stand.
Thus hath he ta'en my body by his force,   130
And now by sleight would captivate my soul ;
But in his fall I 'll tempt the Destinies,
And either lose my life or win my love.
LOR. Let 's go, my Lord ; your staying
stays revenge.
Do you but follow me, and gain your love ;
Her favor must be won by his remove. *Exeunt.*

[SCENE II] [12]

Enter HORATIO *and* BEL-IMPERIA.

HOR. Now, madam, since by favor of your
love
Our hidden smoke is turned to open flame,
And that [13] with looks and words we feed our
thoughts
(Two chief contents, where more cannot be
had) ;
Thus, in the midst of love's fair blandishments,
Why show you sign of inward languishments?
PEDRINGANO *showeth all to the* PRINCE
and LORENZO, *placing them in
secret.*
BEL. My heart, sweet friend, is like a ship
at sea :
She wisheth port, where, riding all at ease,
She [may] [14] repair what stormy times have
worn,

[12] Another room. The eavesdroppers doubtless appear either on the balcony above the inner stage or
at a window.
[13] Since.
[14] Cor. Q 1602; earlier eds. *mad, made.*

And, leaning on the shore, may sing with joy
That pleasure follows pain, and bliss annoy.   11
Possession of thy love is th' only port
Wherein my heart, with fears and hopes long
toss'd,
Each hour doth wish and long to make resort,
There to repair the joys that it hath lost,
And, sitting safe, to sing in Cupid's choir
That sweetest bliss is crown of love's desire.
BALTHAZAR [*and* LORENZO *speak*]
above.
BAL. O sleep, mine eyes : see not my love
profan'd ;
Be deaf, my ears : hear not my discontent ;
Die, heart : another joys what thou deservest.
LOR. Watch still, mine eyes, to see this love
disjoin'd ;   21
Hear still, mine ears, to hear them both
lament ;
Live, heart, to joy at fond Horatio's fall.
BEL. Why stands Horatio speechless all this
while?
HOR. The less I speak, the more I meditate.
BEL. But whereon dost thou chiefly medi-
tate?
HOR. On dangers past, and pleasures to
ensue.
BAL. On pleasures past, and dangers to
ensue.
BEL. What dangers and what pleasures
dost thou mean?
HOR. Dangers of war, and pleasures of our
love.   30
LOR. Dangers of death, but pleasures none
at all.
BEL. Let dangers go ; thy war shall be with
me,
But such a warring as breaks no bond of peace.
Speak thou fair words, I 'll cross them with
fair words ;
Send thou sweet looks, I 'll meet them with
sweet looks ;
Write loving lines, I 'll answer loving lines ;
Give me a kiss, I 'll countercheck thy kiss :
Be this our warring peace, or peaceful war.
HOR. But, gracious madam, then appoint
the field
Where trial of this war shall first be made. [40
BAL. Ambitious villain, how his boldness
grows !
BEL. Then be thy father's pleasant bower
the field,
Where first we vow'd a mutual amity.
The court were dangerous ; that place is safe.
Our hour shall be when Vesper 'gins to rise,

That summons home distressful travaillers.[15]
There none shall hear us but the harmless birds ;
Happily the gentle nightingale
Shall carol us asleep, ere we be 'ware,
And, singing with the prickle [16] at her breast,
Tell our delight and mirthful dalliance.   51
Till then each hour will seem a year and more.
    HOR. But, honey-sweet and honorable love,
Return we now into your father's sight ;
Dangerous suspicion waits on our delight.
    LOR. Ay, danger mix'd with jealous [17] despite
Shall send thy soul into eternal night.
                                                Exeunt.

[SCENE III] [18]

Enter KING OF SPAIN, Portingale Ambassador, DON CYPRIAN, *etc.*

    KING. Brother of Castile, to the Prince's love
What says your daughter, Bel-imperia?
    CYP. Although she coy it, as becomes her kind,
And yet dissemble that she loves the Prince,
I doubt not, I, but she will stoop in time.
And were she froward, which she will not be,
Yet herein shall she follow my advice,
Which is to love him, or forgo my love.
    KING. Then, Lord Ambassador of Portingale,
Advise thy King to make this marriage up, 10
For strengthening of our late-confirmed league ;
I know no better means to make us friends.
Her dowry shall be large and liberal ;
Besides that she is daughter and half heir
Unto our brother here, Don Cyprian,
And shall enjoy the moiety of his land,
I'll grace her marriage with an uncle's gift ;
And this it is, in case the match go forward :
The tribute which you pay shall be releas'd ;
And if by Balthazar she have a son,   20
He shall enjoy the kingdom after us.
    AMB. I'll make the motion to my sovereign liege,
And work it, if my counsel may prevail.
    KING. Do so, my Lord ; and, if he give consent,

I hope his presence here will honor us,
In celebration of the nuptial day ;
And let himself determine of the time.
    AMB. Will't please your Grace command me aught beside?
    KING. Commend me to the King, and so farewell.
But where's Prince Balthazar to take his leave?   30
    AMB. That is perform'd already, my good Lord.
    KING. Amongst the rest of what you have in charge,
The Prince's ransom must not be forgot.
That's none of mine, but his that took him prisoner ;
And well his forwardness deserves reward.
It was Horatio, our knight marshal's son.
    AMB. Between us there's a price already pitch'd,
And shall be sent with all convenient speed.
    KING. Then once again farewell, my Lord.
    AMB. Farewell, my Lord of Castile, and the rest.   *Exit.* [40
    KING. Now, Brother, you must take some little pains
To win fair Bel-imperia from her will.
Young virgins must be ruled by their friends.
The Prince is amiable, and loves her well ;
If she neglect him and forgo his love,
She both will wrong her own estate and ours.
Therefore, whiles I do entertain the Prince
With greatest pleasure that our court affords,
Endeavor you to win your daughter's [thought] : [19]   49
If she give back, all this will come to naught.
                                                Exeunt.

[SCENE IV] [20]

Enter HORATIO, BEL-IMPERIA, *and* PEDRINGANO.

    HOR. Now that the night begins with sable wings
To overcloud the brightness of the sun,
And that in darkness pleasures may be done,
Come, Bel-imperia, let us to the bower,
And there in safety pass a pleasant hour.
    BEL. I follow thee, my love, and will not back,
Although my fainting heart controls my soul.

---

[15] Toilers. Qq 1623, 1633, *travailers;* earlier eds. *trauellers.*
[16] Thorn. Cf. *Friar Bacon and Friar Bungay,* IV, i, 70, and note.
[17] Trisyllabic : jealious. (Kittredge, cited by Manly.)   [18] A room in the royal palace.

[19] Cor. Q 1615 ; earlier eds. *thoughts.*
[20] Hieronimo's garden, the inner stage representing the arbor.

HOR. Why, make you doubt of Pedringano's faith?

BEL. No, he is as trusty as my second
self. —

Go, Pedringano, watch without the gate,   10
And let us know if any make approach.

PED. [*aside*] Instead of watching, I 'll deserve more gold

By fetching Don Lorenzo to this match.

Exit PEDRINGANO.

HOR. What means my love?

BEL.   I know not what myself;

And yet my heart foretells me some mischance.

HOR. Sweet, say not so; fair fortune is our
friend,

And heavens have shut up day to pleasure us.

The stars, thou seest, hold back their twinkling shine,

And Luna hides herself to pleasure us.

BEL. Thou hast prevail'd; I 'll conquer my
misdoubt,   20

And in thy love and counsel drown my fear.

I fear no more; love now is all my thoughts.

Why sit we not? for pleasure asketh ease.

HOR. The more thou sitt'st within these
leafy bowers,

The more will Flora deck it with her flowers.

BEL. Ay, but if Flora spy Horatio here,

Her jealous eye will think I sit too near.

HOR. Hark, madam, how the birds record [21]
by night,

For joy that Bel-imperia sits in sight.

BEL. No, Cupid counterfeits the nightingale,   30

To frame sweet music to Horatio's tale.

HOR. If Cupid sing, then Venus is not far;

Ay, thou art Venus, or some fairer star.

BEL. If I be Venus, thou must needs be
Mars;

And where Mars reigneth, there must needs be
[wars].[22]

HOR. Then thus begin our wars: put forth
thy hand,

That it may combat with my ruder hand.

BEL. Set forth thy foot to try the push of
mine.

HOR. But first my looks shall combat
against thine.

BEL. Then ward thyself: I dart this kiss at
thee.   40

HOR. Thus I retort the dart thou threw'st
at me.

BEL. Nay, then, to gain the glory of the
field,

My twining arms shall yoke and make thee
yield.

HOR. Nay, then, my arms are large and
strong withal:

Thus elms by vines are compass'd, till they fall.

BEL. O, let me go, for in my troubled eyes

Now mayst thou read that life in passion dies.

HOR. O, stay awhile, and I will die with
thee;

So shalt thou yield, and yet have conquer'd me.

BEL. Who 's there, Pedringano? We are
betray'd!   50

Enter LORENZO, BALTHAZAR, SERBERINE, [*and*]
PEDRINGANO, *disguised.*

LOR. My Lord, away with her; take her
aside. —

O, sir, forbear; your valor is already tri'd.

Quickly dispatch, my masters.

They hang him in the arbor.

HOR.   What, will you murder me?

LOR. Ay, thus, and thus! these are the
fruits of love.   *They stab him.*

BEL. O, save his life, and let me die for
him!

O, save him, Brother; save him, Balthazar!

I loved Horatio but he loved not me.

BAL. But Balthazar loves Bel-imperia.

LOR. Although his life were still ambitious-
proud,

Yet is he at the highest now he is dead.   60

BEL. Murder! murder! Help, Hieronimo,
help!

LOR. Come, stop her mouth; away with
her.   *Exeunt.*

Enter HIERONIMO *in his shirt, etc.*

HIER. What outcries pluck me from my
naked bed,

And chill my throbbing heart with trembling
fear,

Which never danger yet could daunt before?

Who calls Hieronimo? Speak, here I am. —

I did not slumber; therefore 't was no dream.

No, no, it was some woman cri'd for help,

And here within this garden did she cry,

And in this garden must I rescue her. —   70

But stay, what murd'rous spectacle is this?

A man hang'd up and all the murderers gone!

And in my bower, to lay the guilt on me!

This place was made for pleasure, not for
death.

He cuts him down.

Those garments that he wears I oft have
seen —

Alas, it is Horatio, my sweet son!
O no, but he that whilom was my son!
O, was it thou that call'dst me from my bed?
O speak, if any spark of life remain!
I am thy father. Who hath slain my son? 80
What savage monster, not of human kind,
Hath here been glutted with thy harmless blood,
And left thy bloody corpse dishonored here,
For me, amidst [these] [23] dark and deathful shades,
To drown thee with an ocean of my tears?
O Heavens, why made you night to cover sin?
By day this deed of darkness had not been.
O earth, why didst thou not in time devour
The vild profaner of this sacred bower?
O poor Horatio, what hadst thou misdone, 90
To leese [24] thy life, ere life was new begun?
O wicked butcher, whatsoe'er thou wert,
How could thou strangle virtue and desert?
Ay me most wretched, that have lost my joy,
In leesing my Horatio, my sweet boy!

Enter ISABELL[A].

ISAB. My husband's absence makes my heart to throb! —
Hieronimo!
HIER. Here, Isabella, help me to lament;
For sighs are stopp'd, and all my tears are spent.
ISAB. What world of grief! my son, Horatio! 100
Oh, where's the author of this endless woe?
HIER. To know the author were some ease of grief,
For in revenge my heart would find relief.
ISAB. Then is he gone? and is my son gone too?
O, gush out, tears, fountains and floods of tears;
Blow, sighs, and raise an everlasting storm;
For outrage fits our cursed wretchedness.

[25] [Ay me, Hieronimo, sweet husband, speak!
HIER. He supp'd with us to-night, frolic and merry,
And said he would go visit Balthazar 110
At the Duke's palace; there the Prince doth lodge.
He had no custom to stay out so late;
He may be in his chamber; some go see.
Roderigo, ho!

Enter PEDRO *and* JAQUES.

ISAB. Ay me, he raves! — Sweet Hieronimo!
HIER. True, all Spain takes note of it.
Besides, he is so generally beloved;
His Majesty the other day did grace him

With waiting on his cup: these be favors
Which do assure me he cannot be short-lived. 120
ISAB. Sweet Hieronimo!
HIER. I wonder how this fellow got his clothes! —
Sirrah, sirrah, I'll know the truth of all! —
Jaques, run to the Duke of Castile's presently,
And bid my son Horatio to come home.
I and his mother have had strange dreams to-night.
Do ye hear me, sir?
JAQUES.　　　　　　Ay, sir.
HIER.　　　　　　　　　Well, sir, begone. —
Pedro, come hither; knowest thou who this is?
PED. Too well, sir.
HIER. Too well! Who, who is it? — Peace, Isabella! — 130
Nay, blush not, man.
PED.　　　　　　It is my Lord Horatio.
HIER. Ha, ha, St. James! but this doth make me laugh,
That there are more deluded than myself.
PED. Deluded?
HIER. Ay! I would have sworn, myself, within this hour,
That this had been my son Horatio —
His garments are so like.
Ha! are they not great persuasions?
ISAB. O, would to God it were not so!
HIER. Were not, Isabella? Doest thou dream it is? 140
Can thy soft bosom entertain a thought
That such a black deed of mischief should be done
On one so [pure] [26] and spotless as our son?
Away, I am ashamed.
ISAB.　　　　　　Dear Hieronimo,
Cast a more serious eye upon thy grief;
Weak apprehension gives but weak belief.
HIER. It was a man, sure, that was hanged up here;
A youth, as I remember. I cut him down.
If it should prove my son now after all!
Say you? say you? — Light! lend me a taper; 150
Let me look again. — O God!
Confusion, mischief, torment, death, and hell,
Drop all your stings at once in my cold bosom,
That now is stiff with horror; kill me quickly!
Be gracious to me, thou inflective [27] night,
And drop this deed of murder down on me;
Gird in my waste of grief with thy large darkness,
And let me not survive to see the light
May put me in the mind I had a son.
ISAB. O sweet Horatio! O my dearest son! 160
HIER. How strangely had I lost my way to grief!]

Sweet, lovely rose, ill-pluck'd before thy time,
Fair, worthy son, not conquer'd, but betray'd,
I'll kiss thee now, for words with tears are [stay'd]. [28]
ISAB. And I'll close up the glasses of his sight,
For once these eyes were only my delight.
HIER. Seest thou this handkercher besmear'd with blood?
It shall not from me till I take revenge.
Seest thou those wounds that yet are bleeding fresh?
I'll not entomb them till I have reveng'd. 170
Then will I joy amidst my discontent;
Till then my sorrow never shall be spent.

---

[23] Old eds. *this.*
[24] Qq 1623, 1633, *lose.*
[25] First passage of additions begins here.

[26] Cor. Q 1615; earlier eds. *poore.*
[27] Infectious.
[28] Cor. Q 1603; earlier eds. *stainde.*

Isab. The Heavens are just ; murder can-
not be hid ;
Time is the author both of truth and right,
And time will bring this treachery to light.
Hier. Meanwhile, good Isabella, cease thy
plaints,
Or, at the least, dissemble them awhile ;
So shall we sooner find the practice [29] out,
And learn by whom all this was brought about.
Come, Isabel, now let us take him up,   180
They take him up.
And bear him in from out this cursed place.
I 'll say his dirge ; singing fits not this case.

[30] *O   aliquis mihi quas pulchrum v[e]r educ[a]t*
herbas,
(Hieronimo *sets his breast unto his sword.*)
Misceat, et nostro detur medicina dolori ;
Aut, si qui faciunt ann[or]um obli[v]ia, succos
Pr[ae]beat ; ipse met[a]m magn[u]m quaecunque
per orbem
Gramina Sol pulchras [effert] [31] *in luminis oras ;*
Ipse bibam quicquid meditatur saga vene[n]i,
Quicquid et [herbarum vi caeca nenia] [32] *nectit :*
Omnia perpetiar, lethum quoque, dum semel
omnis   190
Noster in extincto moriatur pector[e] sensus. —
Ergo tuos oculos nunquam, mea vita, videbo,
Et tua perpetuus sepelivit lumina somnus ?
Emoriar tecum : sic, juvat ire sub umbras. —
At tamen absistam properato cedere letho,
Ne mortem vindicta tuam tam nulla sequatur.
(*Here he throws it from him and bears*
the body away.)

[Chorus]

Andrea. Brought'st thou me hither to increase my pain ?
I look'd that Balthazar should have been slain ;

But 'tis my friend Horatio that is slain,
And they abuse fair Bel-imperia,   200
O[n] whom I doted more than all the world,
Because she lov'd me more than all the world.
Revenge. Thou talkest of harvest, when
the corn is green ;
The end is crown of every work well done ;
The sickle comes not till the corn be ripe.
Be still ; and ere I lead thee from this place,
I 'll show thee Balthazar in heavy case.

ACT III — [Scene I] [1]

Enter Viceroy of Portingale, Nobles, [*and*]
Villuppo.

Vic. Infortunate condition of kings,
Seated amidst so many helpless doubts !
First we are plac'd upon extremest height,
And oft supplanted with exceeding [hate],[2]
But ever subject to the wheel of chance ;
And at our highest never joy we so
As we both doubt and dread our overthrow.
So striveth not the waves with sundry winds
As Fortune toileth in the affairs of kings,
That would be fear'd, yet fear to be be-
loved,   10
Sith fear or love to kings is flattery.[3]
For instance, Lordings, look upon your king,
By hate deprived of his dearest son,
The only hope of our successive line.
[1] Nob. I had not thought that Alexandro's
heart
Had been envenom'd with such extreme
hate ;
But now I see that words have several works,
And there 's no credit in the countenance.
Vil. No ; for, my Lord, had you beheld
the train [4]
That feigned love had colored in his looks, [20
When he in camp consorted [5] Balthazar,
Far more inconstant had you thought the
sun,
That hourly coasts [6] the centre of the earth,
Than Alexandro's purpose to the Prince.
Vic. No more, Villuppo ; thou hast said
enough ;
And with thy words thou slayest our wounded
thoughts.
Nor shall I longer dally with the world,

---

[29] Plot.
[30] This passage is a hodgepodge of tags from classical poetry and lines of Kyd's own composition. (Boas.) " Oh, may someone blend me the herbs that beauteous Spring doth bear, and let our anguish be medicined ; or let him proffer potions, if such there be that cause forgetfulness of the years. May I my-self reap throughout the wide world whatever plants the sun's warmth brings forth to earthly realms of light. May I drink any poison the wise woman may prepare, and whatever herbs her incantation unites in occult power. Let me endure all, nay death also, if once for all may die all feeling in a heart that is dead. Nevermore, then, shall I see thy eyes, my life ? And has an everlasting slumber buried thy light ? With thee may I perish : so would I go into the shadows. But nevertheless I shall hold off from yielding speedily to death, lest then no vengeance follow thy death."
[31] Conj. Traube (quoted by Schick) ; old eds. *effecit.*
[32] So Schick ; old eds. *irraui euecaeca menia.*

[1] The Portuguese court. A place of execution.
[2] Cor. Q 1599 ; earlier eds. *heat.*
[3] Adapted from Seneca's *Agamemnon,* ll. 57–73.
[4] Guile.
[5] Accompanied.   [6] Moves around.

Procrastinating Alexandro's death. — ˙
Go some of you, and fetch the traitor forth,
[*Exit a* Nobleman.]
That, as he is condemned, he may die.   30

Enter ALEXANDRO *with a* Nobleman *and* Halberds.

[1] NOB. In such extremes will nought but
patience serve.
ALEX. But in extremes what patience shall
I use?
Nor discontents it me to leave the world,
With whom there nothing can prevail but
wrong.
NOB. Yet hope the best.
ALEX.   'T is Heaven is my hope.
As for the earth, it is too much infect
To yield me hope of any of her mold.
VIC. Why linger ye? Bring forth that
daring fiend,
And let him die for his accursed deed.
ALEX. Not that I fear the extremity of
death   40
(For nobles cannot stoop to servile fear)
Do I, O King, thus discontented live.
But this, O this, torments my laboring soul,
That thus I die suspected of a sin
Whereof, as Heavens have known my secret
thoughts,
So am I free from this suggestion.[7]
VIC. No more, I say! to the tortures!
When![8]
Bind him, and burn his body in those flames
They bind him to the stake.
That shall prefigure those unquenched fires
Of Phlegethon,[9] prepared for his soul.   50
ALEX. My guiltless death will be aveng'd
on thee,
On thee, Villuppo, that hath malic'd[10] thus,
Or for thy meed hast falsely me accus'd.
VIL. Nay, Alexandro, if thou menace me,
I 'll lend a hand to send thee to the lake
Where those thy words shall perish with thy
works,
Injurious traitor! monstrous homicide!

Enter Ambassador [*and* Attendants].

AMB. Stay, hold a while;
And here, with pardon of his Majesty,
Lay hands upon Villuppo.
VIC.   Ambassador,   60
What news hath urg'd this sudden entrance?

[7] Temptation, incitement to evil.
[8] An exclamation of impatience.
[9] The fiery river of Hades.
[10] Desired to injure.

AMB. Know, Sovereign Lord, that Baltha-
zar doth live.
VIC. What sayest thou? Liveth Baltha-
zar, our son?
AMB. Your Highness' son, Lord Balthazar,
doth live;
And, well entreated in the court of Spain,
Humbly commends him to your Majesty.
These eyes beheld, and these my followers;
With these, the letters of the King's com-
mends,   *Gives him letters.*
Are happy witnesses of his Highness' health.
*The King looks on the letters, and
proceeds.*
VIC. " Thy son doth live; your tribute is
receiv'd;   70
Thy peace is made, and we are satisfied.
The rest resolve upon as things propos'd
For both our honors and thy benefit."
AMB. These are his Highness' farther
articles.   *He gives him more letters.*
VIC. Accursed wretch, to intimate these
ills
Against the life and reputation
Of noble Alexandro! — Come, my Lord, un-
bind him. —
Let him unbind thee, that is bound to death,
To make a quital[11] for thy discontent.
They unbind him.
ALEX. Dread Lord, in kindness[12] you could
do no less   80
Upon report of such a damned fact;[13]
But thus we see our innocence hath sav'd
The hopeless life which thou, Villuppo, sought
By thy suggestions to have massacred.
VIC. Say, false Villuppo, wherefore didst
thou thus
Falsely betray Lord Alexandro's life?
Him whom thou knowest that no unkindness
else
But even the slaughter of our dearest son
Could once have moved us to have miscon-
ceived.
ALEX. Say, treacherous Villuppo, tell the
King: 90
Or wherein hath Alexandro used thee ill?
VIL. Rent with remembrance of so foul a
deed,
My guilty soul submits me to thy doom;
For not for Alexandro's injuries,
But for reward and hope to be preferr'd,
Thus have I shamelessly hazarded his life.
VIC. Which, villain, shall be ransomed with
thy death;

[11] Requital.   [12] Nature.   [13] Deed.

And not so mean [14] a torment as we here
Devis'd for him who, thou said'st, slew our
  son,
But with the bitterest torments and ex-
  tremes   100
That may be yet invented for thine end.

ALEXANDRO seems to entreat.

Entreat me not. — Go, take the traitor
  hence. —

Exit VILLUPPO [guarded].

And, Alexandro, let us honor thee
With public notice of thy loyalty. —
To end those things articulated here
By our great lord, the mighty King of Spain,
We with our council will deliberate.
Come, Alexandro, keep us company.

Exeunt.

[SCENE II] [15]

Enter HIERONIMO.

HIER. O eyes! no eyes, but fountains
  fraught with tears; [16]
O life! no life, but lively form of death;
O world! no world, but mass of public wrongs,
Confus'd and fill'd with murder and misdeeds.
O sacred Heav'ns! if this unhallowed deed,
If this inhuman and barbarous attempt,
If this incomparable murder thus
Of mine, but now no more my son,
Shall unreveal'd and unrevenged pass,
How should we term your dealings to be
  just,   10
If you unjustly deal with those that in your
  justice trust? [17]
The night, sad secretary [18] to my moans,
With direful visions wake my vexed soul,
And with the wounds of my distressful son
Solicit me for notice of his death.
The ugly fiends do sally forth of hell,
And frame my steps to unfrequented paths,
And fear my heart with fierce inflamed
  thoughts.
The cloudy day my discontents records,
Early begins to register my dreams,   20
And drive me forth to seek the murderer.
Eyes, life, world, Heav'ns, hell, night, and
  day,
See, search, show, send some man, some mean,
  that may —   *A letter falleth.*

What's here? a letter? Tush! it is not
  so! —
A letter written to Hieronimo! —   *Red ink.*
" For want of ink, receive this bloody writ.
Me hath my hapless brother hid from thee;
Revenge thyself on Balthazar and him:
For these were they that murd'red thy son.
Hieronimo, revenge Horatio's death,   30
And better fare than Bel-imperia doth." —
What means this unexpected miracle?
My son slain by Lorenzo and the Prince!
What cause had they Horatio to malign? [19]
Or what might move thee, Bel-imperia,
To accuse thy brother, had he been the mean?
Hieronimo, beware! — thou art betray'd,
And to entrap thy life this train [20] is laid.
Advise thee, therefore; be not credulous:
This is devised to endanger thee,   40
That thou, by this, Lorenzo shouldst accuse;
And he, for thy dishonor done, should draw
Thy life in question and thy name in hate.
Dear was the life of my beloved son,
And of his death behoves me be reveng'd.
Then hazard not thine own, Hieronimo,
But live t' effect thy resolution.
I therefore will by circumstances [21] try,
What I can gather to confirm this writ;
And, hearkening near the Duke of Castile's
  house,   50
Close, if I can, with Bel-imperia,
To listen more, but nothing to bewray.

Enter PEDRINGANO.

Now, Pedringano.
PED.   Now, Hieronimo.
HIER. Where's thy lady?
PED.   I know not; here's my lord.

Enter LORENZO.

LOR. How now, who's this? Hieronimo?
HIER.   My Lord.
PED. He asketh for my Lady Bel-imperia.
LOR. What to do, Hieronimo? The Duke,
  my father, hath
Upon some disgrace awhile remov'd her hence;
But, if it be aught I may inform her of,
Tell me, Hieronimo, and I'll let her know
  it.
HIER. Nay, nay, my Lord, I thank you;
  it shall not need.   61
I had a suit unto her, but too late;
And her disgrace makes me unfortunate.
LOR. Why so, Hieronimo; use me.

---

[14] Moderate.
[15] Spain. Before the palace of Don Cyprian.
[16] The opening lines of this speech were much
parodied.
[17] A fourteener.   [18] *I.e.*, confidant.

[19] Plot against.   [20] Snare.
[21] Indirect methods.

HIER. O no, my Lord, I dare not ; it must not be.
I humbly thank your Lordship.

[22] [HIER. Who? you, my Lord?
I reserve your favor for a greater honor ;
This is a very toy,[23] my Lord, a toy.
    LOR. All 's one,[24] Hieronimo ; acquaint me with it.
    HIER. I' faith, my Lord, it is an idle thing ;   70
I must confess I ha' been too slack, too tardy,
Too remiss unto your Honor.
    LOR. How now, Hieronimo?
    HIER. In troth, my Lord, it is a thing of nothing :
The murder of a son, or so ——
A thing of nothing, my Lord !]

    LOR. Why then, farewell.
    HIER. [*aside*] My grief no heart, my thoughts no tongue can tell.   *Exit.*
    LOR. Come hither, Pedringano ; seest thou this?
    PED. My Lord, I see it, and suspect it too.
    LOR. This is that damned villain, Serberine,
That hath, I fear, reveal'd Horatio's death.   80
    PED. My Lord, he could not, 't was so lately done ;
And since, he hath not left my company.
    LOR. Admit he have not, his condition[25]'s such
As fear or flattering words may make him false.
I know his humor,[25] and therewith repent
That e'er I us'd him in this enterprise.
But, Pedringano, to prevent the worst,
And 'cause I know thee secret as my soul,
Here, for thy further satisfaction, take thou this,   *Gives him more gold.*
And hearken to me : thus it is devis'd.   90
This night thou must (and, prithee, so resolve),
Meet Serberine at Saint Luigi's Park ——
Thou knowest 't is here hard by behind the house ; ——
There take thy stand, and see thou strike him sure,
For die he must, if we do mean to live.
    PED. But how shall Serberine be there, my Lord?
    LOR. Let me alone ; I 'll send to him to meet
The Prince and me, where thou must do this deed.
    PED. It shall be done, my Lord ; it shall be done ;
And I 'll go arm myself to meet him there.   100

    LOR. When things shall alter, as I hope they will,
Then shalt thou mount for this ; thou knowest my mind.   *Exit* PEDRINGANO.
Che le Ieron! [26]

Enter Page.

    PAGE. My Lord?
    LOR. Go, sirrah,
To Serberine, and bid him forthwith meet
The Prince and me at Saint Luigi's Park,
Behind the house, this evening, boy.
    PAGE. I go, my Lord.
    LOR. But, sirrah, let the hour be eight a'clock :
Bid him not fail.
    PAGE. I fly, my Lord.   *Exit.*
    LOR. Now to confirm the complot thou hast cast [27]   109
Of all these practices,[28] I 'll spread the watch,
Upon precise commandment from the King,
Strongly to guard the place where Pedringano
This night shall murder hapless Serberine.
Thus must we work that will avoid distrust ;
Thus must we practise to prevent mishap,
And thus one ill another must expulse.
This sly enquiry of Hieronimo
For Bel-imperia breeds suspicion,
And this suspicion bodes a further ill.
As for myself, I know my secret fault,   120
And so do they ; but I have dealt for them.
They that for coin their souls endangered,
To save my life for coin shall venture theirs ;
And better it 's that base companions [29] die
Than by their life to hazard our good haps.
Nor shall they live, for me to fear their faith :
I 'll trust myself, myself shall be my friend ;
For die they shall : slaves are ordain[e]d to no other end.[30]   *Exit.*

[SCENE III] [31]

Enter PEDRINGANO, *with a pistol.*

    PED. Now, Pedringano, bid thy pistol hold ;
And hold on, Fortune ! once more favor me ;
Give but success to mine attempting spirit,
And let me shift [32] for taking of mine aim.
Here is the gold : this is the gold propos'd ;
It is no dream that I adventure for,
But Pedringano is possess'd thereof.

---

[22] Second passage of additions begins here, replacing ll. 65, 66.
    [23] Trifle.
        [4] It 's all the same, just the same, no matter.
        [5] Disposition.

[26] Apparently a corruption of the summons, or perhaps of the page's name.
    [27] Planned.   [28] Schemes.
    [29] Fellows.   [30] A fourteener.
    [31] Saint Luigi's Park.   [32] Leave it to me.

And he that would not strain his conscience
For him that thus his liberal purse hath
    stretch'd,
Unworthy such a favor, may he fail,   10
And, wishing, want when such as I prevail.
As for the fear of apprehension,
I know, if need should be, my noble lord
Will stand between me and ensuing harms;
Besides, this place is free from all suspect.
Here therefore will I stay and take my stand.

Enter the Watch [*unobserved by* PEDRINGANO].

    1 [WATCH]. I wonder much to what intent
      it is
That we are thus expressly charg'd to watch.
    2 [WATCH]. 'T is by commandment in the
      King's own name.
    3 [WATCH]. But we were never wont to
      watch and ward   20
So near the Duke his brother's house before.
    2 [WATCH]. Content yourself; stand close;
      there 's somewhat in 't.

Enter SERBERINE.

    SER. Here, Serberine, attend and stay thy
      pace;
For here did Don Lorenzo's page appoint
That thou by his command shouldst meet
    with him.
How fit a place, if one were so dispos'd,
Methinks this corner is to close with one.[33]
    PED. [*aside*] Here comes the bird that I
      must seize upon.
Now, Pedringano, or never, play the man!
    SER. I wonder that his Lordship stays so
      long,   30
Or wherefore should he send for me so late.
    PED. For this, Serberine; and thou shalt
      ha 't.   *Shoots the dag.*[34]
So, there he lies; my promise is perform'd.

The Watch [*advances*].

    1 [WATCH]. Hark, gentlemen, this is a pis-
      tol shot.
    2 [WATCH]. And here 's one slain. Stay the
      murderer.[35]
    PED. Now by the sorrows of the souls in
      hell,   *He strives with the* Watch.
Who first lays hand on me, I 'll be his priest.[36]
    3 [WATCH]. Sirrah, confess, and therein
      play the priest;

Why hast thou thus unkindly[37] kill'd the
    man?
    PED. Why? Because he walk'd abroad so
      late.   40
    3 [WATCH]. Come, sir, you had been better
      kept your bed,
Than have committed this misdeed so late.
    2 [WATCH]. Come, to the Marshal's with
      the murderer.
    1 [WATCH]. On to Hieronimo's! Help me
      here
To bring the murd'red body with us too.
    PED. Hieronimo? Carry me before whom
      you will.
Whate'er he be, I 'll answer him and you;
And do your worst, for I defy you all.
                    Exeunt.

[SCENE IV][38]

Enter LORENZO *and* BALTHAZAR.

    BAL. How now, my Lord, what makes you
      rise so soon?
    LOR. Fear of preventing our mishaps too
      late.
    BAL. What mischief is it that we not mis-
      trust?
    LOR. Our greatest ills we least mistrust, my
      Lord,
And inexpected harms do hurt us most.
    BAL. Why, tell me, Don Lorenzo, tell me,
      man,
If aught concerns our honor and your own.
    LOR. Nor you, nor me, my Lord, but both
      in one;
For I suspect, and the presumption 's great,
That by those base confederates in our fault
Touching the death of Don Horatio,   11
We are betray'd to old Hieronimo.
    BAL. Betray'd, Lorenzo? Tush, it cannot
      be.
    LOR. A guilty conscience, urged with the
      thought
Of former evils, easily cannot err.
I am persuaded, and dissuade me not,
That all 's revealed to Hieronimo.
And therefore know that I have cast it thus —

[*Enter* Page.][39]

But here 's the page. How now? what news
    with thee?

[33] To meet a person secretly.
[34] Pistol.
[35] Note the metrical value of the pause.
[36] Be in attendance at his death; *i.e.*, kill him.

[37] Unnaturally.
[38] Unlocated; presumably a room in the palace of Don Cyprian.
[39] Add. Q 1615.

PAGE. My Lord, Serberine is slain.
BAL.   Who? Serberine, my man? 20
PAGE. Your Highness' man, my Lord.
LOR.   Speak, page, who murdered him?
PAGE. He that is apprehended for the fact.[40]
LOR. Who?
PAGE. Pedringano.
BAL. Is Serberine slain, that lov'd his lord
    so well?
Injurious villain, murderer of his friend!
    LOR. Hath Pedringano murdered Serber-
    ine?
My Lord, let me entreat you to take the pains
To exasperate and hasten his revenge
With your complaints unto my Lord the King.
This their dissension breeds a greater doubt. 31
    BAL. Assure thee, Don Lorenzo, he shall
    die,
Or else his Highness hardly shall deny.[41]
Meanwhile I'll haste the marshal sessions,
For die he shall for this his damned deed.
                    Exit BALTHAZAR.
    LOR. [*aside*] Why, so; this fits our former
    policy,
And thus experience bids the wise to deal.
I lay the plot; he prosecutes the point.
I set the trap; he breaks the worthless twigs,
And sees not that wherewith the bird was
    lim'd.[42]   40
Thus hopeful men, that mean to hold their
    own,
Must look like fowlers to their dearest friends.
He runs to kill whom I have holp[43] to catch,
And no man knows it was my reaching f[e]tch.[44]
'T is hard to trust unto a multitude,
Or any one, in mine opinion,
When men themselves their secrets will
    reveal. —

    Enter a Messenger *with a letter.*

Boy!
    PAGE. My Lord.
    LOR. What's he?
    MES. I have a letter to your Lordship. [50
    LOR. From whence?
    MES.   From Pedringano, that's
    imprisoned.
    LOR. So he is in prison, then?
    MES.   Ay, my good Lord.

LOR. What would he with us? — He writes
    us here,
To stand good lord, and help him in distress. —
Tell him I have his letters, know his mind;
And what we may, let him assure him of.
Fellow, begone; my boy shall follow thee. —
                    Exit Messenger.
[*aside*] This works like wax; yet once more
    try thy wits. —
Boy, go, convey this purse to Pedringano;
Thou knowest the prison; closely[45] give it
    him,   60
And be advis'd that none be thereabout.
Bid him be merry still, but secret;
And though the marshal sessions be to-day,
Bid him not doubt of his delivery.
Tell him his pardon is already sign'd,
And thereon bid him boldly be resolved;
For, were he ready to be turned off[46] —
As 't is my will the uttermost be tri'd —
Thou with his pardon shalt attend him still.
Show him this box, tell him his pardon's
    in 't;   70
But open 't not, an if thou lovest thy life;
But let him wisely keep his hopes unknown.
He shall not want while Don Lorenzo lives.
Away!
    PAGE. I go, my Lord, I run.
    LOR. But, sirrah, see that this be cleanly[47]
    done. —   *Exit* Page.
Now stands our fortune on a tickle[48] point,
And now or never ends Lorenzo's doubts.
One only thing is uneffected yet,
And that's to see the executioner.   80
But to what end? I list not trust the air
With utterance of our pretence[49] therein,
For fear the privy whisp'ring of the wind
Convey our words amongst unfriendly ears,
That lie too open to advantages.
[*E*][50] *quel che voglio i[o], nessun lo sa;*
Intendo io: quel mi [basterà].[51]   *Exit.*

    [SCENE V][52]

    Enter Boy *with the box.*

[BOY.] My master hath forbidden me to look
in this box; and, by my troth, 't is likely, if
he had not warned me, I should not have had
so much idle time; for we men's-kind in our

---

[40] Deed.
[41] *I.e.*, I will make it hard for him to deny my request.
[42] Caught. Small birds were caught by smearing twigs with sticky lime.
[43] Helped.
[44] Far-reaching stratagem.

[45] Secretly.   [46] Hanged.
[47] Without bungling. [48] Insecure, critical.
[49] Intention.   [50] Old eds. *Et.*
[51] So Schick; old eds. *bassara.* "And what I desire none knows; I know: which is enough for me."
[52] Unlocated; presumably a street.

minority are like women in their uncertainty : that they are most forbidden, they will soonest attempt. So I now. — By my bare honesty, here's nothing but the bare empty box ! Were it not sin against secrecy, I would say it were a piece of gentlemanlike knavery. [10 I must go to Pedringano, and tell him his pardon is in this box ; nay, I would have sworn it, had I not seen the contrary. I cannot choose but smile to think how the villain will flout the gallows, scorn the audience, and descant on the hangman, and all presuming of his pardon from hence. Will 't not be an odd jest for me to stand and grace every jest he makes, pointing my finger at this box, as who would say, " Mock on ; here's thy war- [20 rant." Is 't not a scurvy jest that a man should jest himself to death? Alas ! poor Pedringano, I am in a sort sorry for thee ; but if I should be hanged with thee, I cannot weep. *Exit.*

[SCENE VI] [53]

Enter HIERONIMO *and the* Deputy.

HIER. Thus must we toil in other men's extremes,
That know not how to remedy our own,
And do them justice, when unjustly we,
For all our wrongs, can compass no redress.
But shall I never live to see the day
That I may come, by justice of the Heavens,
To know the cause that may my cares allay?
This toils my body, this consumeth age,
That only I to all men just must be,
And neither gods nor men be just to me.   10
DEP. Worthy Hieronimo, your office asks
A care to punish such as do transgress.
HIER. So is 't my duty to regard his death
Who, when he lived, deserved my dearest blood.
But come, for that we came for. Let's begin,
For here lies that [54] which bids me to be gone.

Enter Officers, Boy, *and* PEDRINGANO, *with a letter in his hand,* bound.

DEP. Bring forth the prisoner, for the court is set.
PED. Gramercy, boy, but it was time to come ;
For I had written to my Lord anew
A nearer matter that concerneth him,   20

For fear his Lordship had forgotten me.
But sith [55] he hath rememb'red me so well,
Come, come, come on, when shall we to this gear? [56]
HIER. Stand forth, thou monster, murderer of men,
And here, for satisfaction of the world,
Confess thy folly, and repent thy fault ;
For there's thy place of execution.
PED. This is short work. Well, to your Marshalship
First I confess, nor fear I death therefore,
I am the man, 't was I slew Serberine.   30
But, sir, then you think this shall be the place
Where we shall satisfy you for this gear?
DEP. Ay, Pedringano.
PED.   Now I think not so.
HIER. Peace, impudent ; for thou shalt find it so ;
For blood with blood shall, while I sit as judge,
Be satisfied, and the law discharg'd.
And though myself cannot receive the like,
Yet will I see that others have their right.
Despatch ; the fault's approved [57] and confess'd,
And by our law he is condemn'd to die.   40

[*Enter* Hangman.] [58]

HANGM. Come on, sir ; are you ready?
PED. To do what, my fine, officious knave?
HANGM. To go to this gear.
PED. O sir, you are too forward : thou wouldst fain furnish me with a halter, to disfurnish me of my habit. [59] So I should go out of this gear, my raiment, into that gear, the rope. But, hangman, now I spy your knavery, I 'll not change without boot, [60] that's flat.
HANGM. Come, sir.   50
PED. So, then, I must up?
HANGM. No remedy.
PED. Yes, but there shall be for my coming down.
HANGM. Indeed, here's a remedy for that.
PED. How? be turn'd off?
HANGM. Ay, truly. Come, are you ready? I pray, sir, dispatch ; the day goes away.
PED. What, do you hang by the hour? If you do, I may chance to break your old custom.   61

---

[55] Since.   [56] Affair.   [57] Proved.
[58] Add. Q 1615, though the hangman might well enter with the other officers.
[59] The hangman got the clothes of those he executed.
[60] Additional compensation.
[53] A place of justice, with a gallows.
[54] The handkerchief besmeared with Horatio's blood.

HANGM. Faith, you have reason ; for I am like to break your young neck.

PED. Dost thou mock me, hangman? Pray God, I be not preserved to break your knave's pate for this.

HANGM. Alas, sir, you are a foot too low to reach it, and I hope you will never grow so high while I am in the office.

PED. Sirrah, dost see yonder boy with the box in his hand? 71

HANGM. What, he that points to it with his finger?

PED. Ay, that companion.

HANGM. I know him not ; but what of him?

PED. Dost thou think to live till his old doublet will make thee a new truss? [61]

HANGM. Ay, and many a fair year after, to truss up many an honester man than either thou or he. 81

PED. What hath he in his box, as thou think'st?

HANGM. Faith, I cannot tell, nor I care not greatly. Methinks you should rather hearken to your soul's health.

PED. Why, sirrah hangman, I take it that that is good for the body is likewise good for the soul ; and it may be in that box is balm for both. 90

HANGM. Well, thou art even the merriest piece of man's flesh that e'er groan'd at my office door.

PED. Is your roguery become an office with a knave's name?

HANGM. Ay, and that shall all they witness that see you seal it with a thief's name.

PED. I prithee, request this good company to pray with me. 99

HANGM. Ay, marry, sir, this is a good motion.[62] My masters, you see here's a good fellow.

PED. Nay, nay, now I remember me, let them alone till some other time ; for now I have no great need.

HIER. I have not seen a wretch so impudent.

O monstrous times, where murder's set so light,

And where the soul, that should be shrin'd in Heaven,

Solely delights in interdicted things,

Still wand'ring in the thorny passages 110

That intercepts itself of [63] happiness.

Murder ! O bloody monster ! God forbid

[61] Jacket. [62] Proposal. [63] Bar it from.

A fault so foul should scape unpunished.

Dispatch, and see this execution done ! —

This makes me to remember thee, my son.

Exit HIERONIMO.

PED. Nay, soft, no haste.

DEP. Why, wherefore stay you? Have you hope of life?

PED. Why, ay.

HANGM. As how?

PED. Why, rascal, by my pardon from the King. 120

HANGM. Stand you on that? Then you shall off with this.

He turns him off.

DEP. So, executioner ; convey him hence ;

But let his body be unburied :

Let not the earth be choked or infect

With that which Heavens contemns, and men neglect. *Exeunt.*

[SCENE VII] [64]

Enter HIERONIMO.

HIER. Where shall I run to breathe abroad my woes,

My woes, whose weight hath wearied the earth?

Or mine exclaims, that have surcharg'd the air

With ceaseless plaints for my deceased son?

The blust'ring winds, conspiring with my words,

At my lament have moved the leafless trees,

Disrob'd the meadows of their flow'red green,

Made mountains marsh with spring tides of my tears,

And broken through the brazen gates of hell.

Yet still tormented is my tortured soul 10

With broken sighs and restless passions,

That, winged, mount and, hovering in the air,

Beat at the windows of the brightest Heavens,

Soliciting for justice and revenge.

But they are plac'd in those empyreal [65] heights,

Where, countermur'd [66] with walls of diamond,

I find the place impregnable ; and they

Resist my woes, and give my words no way.

Enter Hangman *with a letter.*

HANGM. O Lord, sir ! God bless you, sir ! the man, sir, Petergade, sir, he that was so full of merry conceits — 21

[64] Unlocated ; presumably a room in Hieronimo's house.
[65] Cor. Schick ; old eds. *imperiall.*
[66] Defended by a wall within a wall ; *i.e.*, doubly walled.

HIER. Well, what of him?

HANGM. O Lord, sir, he went the wrong way ; the fellow had a fair commission to the contrary. Sir, here is his passport ; I pray you, sir, we have done him wrong.

HIER. I warrant thee ; give it me.

HANGM. You will stand between the gallows and me?

HIER. Ay, ay.

HANGM. I thank your Lord Worship.　　30
　　　　　　　　　Exit Hangman.

HIER. And yet, though somewhat nearer me concerns,
I will, to ease the grief that I sustain,
Take truce with sorrow while I read on this.
" My lord, I [writ] [67] as mine extremes re-
　　quir'd,
That you would labor my delivery ;
If you neglect, my life is desperate,
And in my death I shall reveal the troth.
You know, my Lord, I slew him for your sake,
And was confederate with the Prince and
　　you ;
Won by rewards and hopeful promises,　　40
I holp to murder Don Horatio too." —
Holp he to murder mine Horatio?
And actors in th' accursed tragedy
Wast thou, Lorenzo, Balthazar and thou,
Of whom my son, my son, deserved so well?
What have I heard, what have mine eyes
　　beheld?
O sacred Heavens, may it come to pass
That such a monstrous and detested deed,
So closely smother'd, and so long conceal'd,
Shall thus by this be venged or reveal'd?　　50
Now see I what I durst not then suspect,
That Bel-imperia's letter was not feign'd.
Nor feigned she, though falsely they have
　　wrong'd
Both her, myself, Horatio, and themselves.
Now may I make compare 'twixt hers and
　　this,
Of every accident I ne'er could find
Till now, and now I feelingly perceive
They did what Heav'n unpunish'd would not
　　leave.
O false Lorenzo, are these thy flattering looks?
Is this the honor that thou didst my son?　　60
And Balthazar — bane to thy soul and me —
Was this the ransom he reserv'd thee for?
Woe to the cause of these constrained wars !
Woe to thy baseness and captivity !
Woe to thy birth, thy body, and thy soul,
Thy cursed father, and thy conquered self !

[67] Emend. Manly ; old eds. *write*. (Cf. IV, ii, 7.)

And bann'd with bitter execrations be
The day and place where he did pity thee !
But wherefore waste I mine unfruitful words,
When naught but blood will satisfy my woes?
I will go plain me to my Lord the King,　　71
And cry aloud for justice through the court,
Wearing the flints with these my withered feet,
And either purchase justice by entreats,
Or tire them all with my revenging threats.
　　　　　　　　　　　　　　Exit.

[ACT IV — SCENE I] [1]

Enter ISABELL[A] *and her* Maid.

ISAB. So that you say this herb will purge
　　the eye,
And this, the head?
Ah, but none of them will purge the heart.
No, there's no medicine left for my disease,
Nor any physic to recure [2] the dead.
　　　　　　　　　　　　She runs lunatic.
Horatio ! O, where's Horatio?

MAID. Good madam, affright not thus
　　yourself
With outrage [3] for your son Horatio.
He sleeps in quiet in the Elysian fields.

ISAB. Why, did I not give you gowns and
　　goodly things,　　10
Bought you a whistle and a whipstalk too,
To be revenged on their villainies?

MAID. Madam, these humors [4] do torment
　　my soul.

ISAB. " My soul " — poor soul, thou talks
　　of things
Thou know'st not what — my soul hath silver
　　wings,
That mounts me up unto the highest Heavens.
To Heaven ! Ay, there sits my Horatio,
Back'd with a troop of fiery cherubins,
Dancing about his newly healed wounds,
Singing sweet hymns and chanting heavenly
　　notes,　　20
Rare harmony to greet his innocence,
That died, ay died, a mirror in our days.
But say, where shall I find the men, the mur-
　　derers,

[1] Unlocated ; presumably the same. According to the old eds. the play is in four acts, separated by the Chorus. If this division is correct, Act III constitutes nearly half the play. There may have been no Chorus to introduce Act IV, or it may have been omitted, as Greg suggests, accidentally. The present edition follows Hawkins in beginning Act IV here.
[2] Recover.　　　[3] Outcry.　　　[4] Whims.

That slew Horatio? Whither shall I run
To find them out that murdered my son?
Exeunt.

[SCENE II] [5]

BEL-IMPERIA, *at a window.*

BEL. What means this outrage that is
offered me?
Why am I thus sequest'red from the court?
No notice! Shall I not know the cause
Of this [6] my secret and suspicious ills?
Accursed brother, unkind murderer,
Why bends thou thus thy mind to martyr me?
Hieronimo, why writ I of thy wrongs,
Or why art thou so slack in thy revenge?
Andrea, O Andrea! that thou sawest
Me for thy friend Horatio handled thus, 10
And him for me thus causeless murdered! —
Well, force perforce, I must constrain myself
To patience, and apply me [7] to the time,
Till Heaven, as I have hoped, shall set me free.

Enter CHRISTOPHIL.

CHRIS. Come, Madam Bel-imperia, this
may not be. *Exeunt.*

[SCENE III] [8]

Enter LORENZO, BALTHAZAR, *and the* Page.

LOR. Boy, talk no further; thus far things
go well.
Thou art assur'd that thou sawest him dead?
PAGE. Or else, my Lord, I live not.
LOR. That 's enough.
As for his resolution in his end,
Leave that to him with whom he sojourns now.
Here, take my ring and give it Christophil,
And bid him let my sister be enlarg'd,
And bring her hither straight. — *Exit* Page.
This that I did was for a policy,
To smooth and keep the murder secret, 10
Which, as a nine-days' wonder, being o'er-
blown,
My gentle sister will I now enlarge.
BAL. And time, Lorenzo; for my Lord the
Duke,
You heard, inquired for her yesternight.
LOR. Why, and, my Lord, I hope you heard
me say

Sufficient reason why she kept away;
But that 's all one. [9] My Lord, you love her?
BAL. Ay.
LOR. Then in your love beware; deal cun-
ningly;
Salve all suspicions; only soothe me up; [10]
And if she hap to stand on terms [11] with us, 20
As for her sweetheart and concealment so,
Jest with her gently: under feigned jest
Are things conceal'd that else would breed un-
rest.
But here she comes.

Enter BEL-IMPERIA.

Now, Sister —
BEL. Sister? No!
Thou art no brother, but an enemy;
Else wouldst thou not have used thy sister so:
First, to affright me with thy weapons drawn,
And with extremes abuse my company; [12]
And then to hurry me, like whirlwind's rage,
Amidst a crew of thy confederates, 30
And clap me up where none might come at me,
Nor I at any to reveal my wrongs.
What madding fury did possess thy wits?
Or wherein is 't that I offended thee?
LOR. Advise you better, Bel-imperia,
For I have done you no disparagement;
Unless, by more discretion than deserv'd,
I sought to save your honor and mine own.
BEL. Mine honor? Why, Lorenzo, wherein
is 't
That I neglect my reputation so, 40
As you, or any, need to rescue it?
LOR. His Highness and my father were
resolv'd
To come confer with old Hieronimo
Concerning certain matters of estate
That by the Viceroy was determined.
BEL. And wherein was mine honor touch'd
in that?
BAL. Have patience, Bel-imperia; hear the
rest.
LOR. Me, next in sight, as messenger they
sent
To give him notice that they were so nigh.
Now, when I came, consorted with the Prince,
And unexpected in an arbor there 51
Found Bel-imperia with Horatio —
BEL. How then?
LOR. Why, then, rememb'ring that old
disgrace,

Which you for Don Andrea had endur'd,
And now were likely longer to sustain,
By being found so meanly accompanied,
Thought rather, for I knew no readier mean,
To thrust Horatio forth my father's way.

BAL. And carry you obscurely somewhere
    else,   60
Lest that his Highness should have found you
    there.

BEL. Ev'n so, my Lord? And you are
    witness
That this is true which he entreateth of?
You, gentle Brother, forged this for my sake,
And you, my Lord, were made his instrument!
A work of worth, worthy the noting too!
But what's the cause that you conceal'd me
    since?

LOR. Your melancholy, Sister, since the
    news
Of your first favorite Don Andrea's death,
My father's old wrath hath exasperate.   70

BAL. And better was't for you, being in
    disgrace,
To absent yourself, and give his fury place.

BEL. But why had I no notice of his ire?

LOR. That were to add more fuel to your
    fire,
Who burnt like Aetna for Andrea's loss.

BEL. Hath not my father then inquir'd
    for me?

LOR. Sister, he hath; and thus excus'd I
    thee: *He whispereth in her ear.*
But Bel-imperia, see the gentle Prince;
Look on thy love, behold young Balthazar,
Whose passions by thy presence are increas'd;
And in whose melancholy thou mayest see   81
Thy hate, his love; thy flight, his following
    thee.

BEL. Brother, you are become an orator —
I know not, I, by what experience —
Too politic for me, past all compare,
Since last I saw you; but content yourself:
The Prince is meditating higher things.

BAL. 'T is of thy beauty, then, that con-
    quers kings;
Of those thy tresses, Ariadne's twines,
Wherewith my liberty thou hast surpris'd;   90
Of that thine ivory front,[13] my sorrow's map,
Wherein I see no haven to rest my hope.

BEL. To love and fear, and both at once,
    my Lord,
In my conceit, are things of more import
Than women's wits are to be busied with.

BAL. 'T is I that love.

         [13] Face.

BEL.   Whom?

BAL.   Bel-imperia.

BEL. But I that fear.

BAL.   Whom?

BEL.   Bel-imperia.

LOR. Fear yourself?

BEL.   Ay, Brother.

LOR.   How?

BEL.   As those
That what they love are loth and fear to lose.

BAL. Then, fair, let Balthazar your keeper
    be.   100

BEL. No, Balthazar doth fear as well as we:
Et [14] *tremulo metui pavidum iunxere timorem —*
Est vanum stolidae proditionis opus.[15]

LOR. Nay, and you argue things so cun-
    ningly,
We'll go continue this discourse at court.

BAL. Led by the loadstar of her heavenly
    looks,
Wends poor oppressed Balthazar,
As o'er the mountains walks the wanderer,
Incertain to effect his pilgrimage.   *Exeunt.*

[SCENE IV] [16]

Enter two Portingales, *and* HIERONIMO *meets
them.*

1 [PORT]. By your leave, sir.

HIER. [17] ['T is neither as you think, nor as you
    think,
Nor as you think; [18] you're wide all:
These slippers are not mine; they were my son Ho-
    ratio's.
My son — and what's a son? A thing begot
Within a pair of minutes, thereabout;
A lump bred up in darkness, and doth serve
To ballace [19] these light creatures we call women;
And, at nine months' end, creeps forth to light.
What is there yet in a son,   10
To make a father dote, rave, or run mad?
Being born, it pouts, cries, and breeds teeth.
What is there yet in a son? He must be fed,
Be taught to go,[20] and speak. Ay, or yet
Why might not a man love a calf as well?
Or melt in passion o'er a frisking kid,
As for a son? Methinks, a young bacon,[21]
Or a fine little smooth horse colt,
Should move a man as much as doth a son.
For one of these, in very little time,   20
Will grow to some good use; whereas a son,
The more he grows in stature and in years,
The more unsquar'd, unbevelled,[22] he appears,
Reckons his parents among the rank of fools,

    [14] Transposed with *Est* in old eds.
    [15] Another patchwork. "And I feared to add dread-
ful alarm to a trembling man — vain is the work of
senseless treachery."
    [16] A street near Don Cyprian's palace.
    [17] Third passage of additions begins here.
    [18] Perhaps addressed to the audience.
    [19] Ballast.   [20] Walk.
    [21] Pig.   [22] *I.e.,* uneven [and] unsmoothed.

Strikes care upon their heads with his mad riots,
Makes them look old before they meet with age.
This is a son! And what a loss were this,
Consider'd truly? —— O, but my Horatio
Grew out of reach of these insatiate humors:
He loved his loving parents;   30
He was my comfort, and his mother's joy,
The very arm that did hold up our house:
Our hopes were stored up in him.
None but a damned murderer could hate him.
He had not seen the back of nineteen year,
When his strong arm unhors'd
The proud Prince Balthazar, and his great mind,
Too full of honor, took him [unto] [23] mercy,
That valiant but ignoble Portingale.
Well, Heaven is Heaven still;   40
And there is Nemesis, and Furies,
And things call'd whips,
And they sometimes do meet with murderers;
They do not always scape; that's some comfort.
Ay, ay, ay; and then time steals on,
And steals, and steals, till violence leaps forth
Like thunder wrapp'd in a ball of fire,
And so doth bring confusion to them all.]

Good leave have you; nay, I pray you go,
For I'll leave you, if you can leave me so. 50
    2 [PORT]. Pray you, which is the next way
        to my Lord the Duke's?
    HIER. The next way from me.
    1 [PORT].   To his house, we mean.
    HIER. O, hard by; 'tis yon house that you
        see.
    2 [PORT]. You could not tell us if his son
        were there?
    HIER. Who, my Lord Lorenzo?
    1 [PORT].   Ay, sir.
        He goeth in at one door and comes
            out at another.
    HIER.   O, forbear!
For other talk for us far fitter were.
But if you be importunate to know
The way to him, and where to find him out,
Then list to me, and I'll resolve your doubt.
There is a path upon your left-hand side   60
That leadeth from a guilty conscience
Unto a forest of distrust and fear,
A darksome place, and dangerous to pass.
There shall you meet with melancholy
        thoughts,
Whose baleful humors if you but uphold,[24]
It will conduct you to despair and death;
Whose rocky cliffs when you have once beheld,
Within a hugy dale of lasting night,
That, kindled with the world's iniquities,
Doth cast up filthy and detested fumes, — 70
Not far from thence, where murderers have
        built
A habitation for their cursed souls,
There, in a brazen caldron, fix'd by Jove,

[23] Cor. Boas; old eds. *vs to.*
[24] Preserve, maintain.

In his fell wrath, upon a sulphur flame,
Yourselves shall find Lorenzo bathing him
In boiling lead and blood of innocents.
    1 [PORT]. Ha, ha, ha!
    HIER. Ha, ha, ha! Why, ha, ha, ha! Fare-
        well, good ha, ha, ha!   *Exit.*
    2 [PORT]. Doubtless this man is passing
        lunatic,
Or imperfection of his age doth make him dote.
Come, let's away to seek my Lord the Duke.[81
                            Exeunt.

[SCENE V] [25]

Enter HIERONIMO, *with a poniard in one hand*
        and a rope in the other.

    HIER. Now, sir, perhaps I come and see
        the King;
The King sees me, and fain would hear my
        suit.
Why, is not this a strange and seld-seen thing,
That standers-by with toys should strike me
        mute?
Go to; I see their shifts, and say no more.
Hieronimo, 'tis time for thee to trudge.
Down by the dale that flows with purple gore
Standeth a fiery tower; there sits a judge
Upon a seat of steel and molten brass,
And 'twixt his teeth he holds a firebrand, 10
That leads unto the lake where hell doth stand.
Away, Hieronimo! to him be gone.
He'll do thee justice for Horatio's death.
Turn down this path; thou shalt be with him
        straight;
Or this, and then thou need'st not take thy
        breath.
This way or that way? — Soft and fair, not
        so!
For if I hang or kill myself, let's know
Who will revenge Horatio's murder then?
No, no! fie, no! pardon me, I'll none of that.
        He flings away the dagger and halter.
This way I'll take, and this way comes the
        King: 20
                    He takes them up again.
And here I'll have a fling at him; that's flat.
And, Balthazar, I'll be with thee to bring,[26]
And thee, Lorenzo! Here's the King — nay,
        stay;
And here, ay here — there goes the hare
        away.[27]

[25] Unlocated, but presumably a hall in the royal
palace.
[26] Bring thee to reason, chastise thee. (Boas.)
[27] That's the upshot.

Enter KING, Ambassador, CASTILE, *and*
LORENZO.

KING. Now show, ambassador, what our
    viceroy saith.
Hath he receiv'd the articles we sent?
    HIER. Justice, oh, justice to Hieronimo.
    LOR. Back! seest thou not the King is
    busy?
    HIER.   Oh, is he so?
    KING. Who is he that interrupts our busi-
    ness?
    HIER. Not I. — [*aside*] Hieronimo, beware!
    go by, go by! [28]   30
    AMB. Renowned King, he hath received and
    read
Thy kingly proffers, and thy promis'd league;
And, as a man extremely overjoy'd
To hear his son so princely entertain'd,
Whose death he had so solemnly bewail'd,
This for thy further satisfaction
And kingly love he kindly lets thee know:
First, for the marriage of his princely son
With Bel-imperia, thy beloved niece,
The news are more delightful to his soul   40
Than myrrh or incense to the offended Heav-
    ens.
In person, therefore, will he come himself,
To see the marriage rites solemnized,
And, in the presence of the court of Spain,
To knit a sure [inexplicable] [29] band
Of kingly love and everlasting league
Betwixt the crowns of Spain and Portingal.
There will he give his crown to Balthazar,
And make a queen of Bel-imperia.
    KING. Brother, how like you this our vice-
    roy's love?   50
    CAST. No doubt, my Lord, it is an argument
Of honorable care to keep his friend,
And wondrous zeal to Balthazar his son;
Nor am I least indebted to his Grace,
That bends his liking to my daughter thus.
    AMB. Now last, dread Lord, here hath his
    Highness sent
(Although he send not that his son return)
His ransom due to Don Horatio.
    HIER. Horatio! who calls Horatio?
    KING. And well rememb'red; thank his
    Majesty.   60
Here, see it given to Horatio.
    HIER. Justice, oh, justice, justice, gentle
    King!
    KING. Who is that? Hieronimo?

    HIER. Justice, oh, justice! oh, my son, my
    son,
My son, whom naught can ransom or redeem!
    LOR. Hieronimo, you are not well-advis'd.
    HIER. Away, Lorenzo, hinder me no more;
For thou hast made me bankrupt of my
    bliss.
Give me my son! you shall not ransom him!
Away! I'll rip the bowels of the earth,   70
        He diggeth with his dagger.
And ferry over to th' Elysian plains,
And bring my son to show his deadly wounds.
Stand from about me!
I'll make a pickaxe of my poniard,
And here surrender up my marshalship;
For I'll go marshal up the fiends in hell,
To be avenged on you all for this.
    KING. What means this outrage? [30]
Will none of you restrain his fury?
    HIER. Nay, soft and fair! you shall not
    need to strive.   80
Needs must he go that the devils drive.
                    Exit.
    KING. What accident hath happ'd Hiero-
    nimo?
I have not seen him to demean him so.
    LOR. My gracious Lord, he is with extreme
    pride,
Conceiv'd of young Horatio, his son,
And covetous of having to himself
The ransom of the young Prince Balthazar,
Distract, and in a manner lunatic.
    KING. Believe me, Nephew, we are sorry
    for't;
This is the love that fathers bear their
    sons. —   90
But, gentle Brother, go give to him this gold,
The Prince's ransom; let him have his due.
For what he hath, Horatio shall not want;
Haply Hieronimo hath need thereof.
    LOR. But if he be thus helplessly distract,
'T is requisite his office be resign'd,
And given to one of more discretion.
    KING. We shall increase his melancholy so.
'T is best that we see further in it first,
Till when, ourself will exempt [31] the place. 100
And, Brother, now bring in the ambassador,
That he may be a witness of the match
'Twixt Balthazar and Bel-imperia,
And that we may prefix a certain time,
Wherein the marriage shall be solemnized,
That we may have thy lord, the Viceroy, here.

[28] This sentence became a stock expression.
[29] Inextricable. So old eds. except the first, which
reads *inexecrable.*

[30] Outburst.
[31] *I.e*, we will hold it immune from the necessity
of being filled (by someone else). (But there may
be a corruption here.)

AMB. Therein your Highness highly shall content
His Majesty, that longs to hear from hence.
KING. On, then, and hear you, Lord Ambassador —   *Exeunt.*

[SCENE VI] [32]

[33] [Enter JAQUES and PEDRO.

JAQ. I wonder, Pedro, why our master thus
At midnight sends us with our torches light,
When man and bird and beast are all at rest,
Save those that watch for rape and bloody murder.
PED. O Jaques, know thou that our master's mind
Is much distraught, since his Horatio died,
And — now his aged years should sleep in rest,
His heart in quiet — like a desperate man,
Grows lunatic and childish for his son.
Sometimes, as he doth at his table sit,   10
He speaks as if Horatio stood by him;
Then starting in a rage, falls on the earth,
Cries out, "Horatio, where is my Horatio?"
So that with extreme grief and cutting sorrow
There is not left in him one inch of man.
See, where he comes.

Enter HIERONIMO.

HIER. I pry through every crevice of each wall,
Look on each tree, and search through every brake,
Beat at the bushes, stamp our grandam earth,
Dive in the water, and stare up to Heaven, 20
Yet cannot I behold my son Horatio. —
How now, who's there? sprites, sprites?
PED. We are your servants, that attend you, sir.
HIER. What make you with your torches in the dark?
PED. You bid us light them, and attend you here.
HIER. No, no, you are deceiv'd! — not I; you are deceiv'd!
Was I so mad to bid you light your torches now?
Light me your torches at the mid of noon,
Whenas the sun god rides in all his glory;
Light me your torches then.
PED.   Then we burn [34] daylight. 30
HIER. Let it be burnt; Night is a murderous slut,
That would not have her treasons to be seen;
And yonder pale-fac'd Hecate there, the moon,
Doth give consent to that is done in darkness;
And all those stars that gaze upon her face,
Are ag[le]ts [35] on her sleeve, pins on her train;
And those that should be powerful and divine
Do sleep in darkness when they most should shine.
PED. Provoke them not, fair sir, with tempting words;   40
The Heavens are gracious, and your miseries
And sorrow makes you speak you know not what.
HIER. Villain, thou liest! and thou doest naught
But tell me I am mad! Thou liest! I am not mad!
I know thee to be Pedro, and he Jaques.
I'll prove it to thee; and were I mad, how could I?
Where was she that same night when my Horatio
Was murd'red? She should have shone; search thou the book.
Had the moon shone, in my boy's face there was a kind of grace,

[32] Hieronimo's garden.
[33] Fourth passage of additions begins here.
[34] *I.e.*, waste.
[35] Ornamental tags or laces of metal. (Cor. Q 1611; Q 1602 *aggots.*)

That I know — nay, I do know — had the murderer seen him,
His weapon would have fall'n and cut the earth, 50
Had he been framed of naught but blood and death.
Alack, when mischief doth it knows not what,
What shall we say to mischief?

Enter ISABELLA.

ISAB. Dear Hieronimo, come in a'doors;
O, seek not means so to increase thy sorrow.
HIER. Indeed, Isabella, we do nothing here;
I do not cry — ask Pedro, and ask Jaques;
Not I, indeed; we are very merry, very merry.
ISAB. How? be merry here, be merry here?
Is not this the place, and this the very tree, 60
Where my Horatio [d]ied, where he was murdered?
HIER. Was — do not say what; let her weep it out.
This was the tree; I set it of a kernel;
And when our hot Spain could not let it grow,
But that the infant and the human sap
Began to wither, duly twice a morning
Would I be sprinkling it with fountain water.
At last it grew and grew, and bore and bore,
Till at the length
It grew a gallows and did bear our son; 70
It bore thy fruit and mine — O wicked, wicked plant!

     One knocks within at the door.
See who knocks there.
PED.   It is a painter, sir.
HIER. Bid him come in, and paint some comfort;
For surely there's none lives but painted comfort.
Let him come in! — One knows not what may chance:
God's will that I should set this tree! — But even so
Masters ungrateful servants rear from naught,
And then they hate them that did bring them up.

     Enter the Painter.

PAINT. God bless you, sir.
HIER.   Wherefore? Why, thou scornful villain? 79
How, where, or by what means should I be bless'd?
ISAB. What wouldst thou have, good fellow?
PAINT.   Justice, madam.
HIER. O ambitious beggar,
Wouldest thou have that that lives not in the world?
Why, all the undelved mines cannot buy
An ounce of justice, 't is a jewel so inestimable.
I tell thee, God hath engrossed all justice in his hands,
And there is none but what comes from him.
PAINT.   O, then I see
That God must right me for my murd'red son.
HIER. How, was thy son murdered?
PAINT. Ay, sir; no man did hold a son so dear.
HIER. What, not as thine? That's a lie, 91
As massy as the earth. I had a son
Whose least unvalued hair did weigh
A thousand of thy sons; and he was murdered.
PAINT. Alas, sir, I had no more but he.
HIER. Nor I, nor I; but this same one of mine
Was worth a legion. But all is one.
Pedro, Jaques, go in a'doors; Isabella, go;
And this good fellow here and I
Will range this hideous orchard [36] up and down, [100
Like to two lions reaved [37] of their young.
Go in a'doors, I say.
     Exeunt. The Painter *and he sits down.*
     Come, let's talk wisely now.
Was thy son murdered?
PAINT.   Ay, sir.
HIER.   So was mine.
How dost take it? Art thou not sometimes mad?
Is there no tricks [38] that comes before thine eyes?

[36] Garden.   [37] Robbed.   [38] Illusions.

PAINT. O Lord, yes, sir.

HIER. Art a painter? Canst paint me a tear, or a wound, a groan, or a sigh? Canst paint me such a tree [39] as this?

PAINT. Sir, I am sure you have heard of [110 my painting; my name's Bazardo.

HIER. Bazardo! Afore God, an excellent fellow. Look you, sir, do you see? I'd have you paint me my gallery, in your oil-colors matted,[40] and draw me five years younger than I am — do ye see, sir, let five years go, let them go — like the marshal of Spain; my wife Isabella standing by me, with a speaking look to my son Horatio, which should intend to this or some such like purpose: "God bless thee, my sweet son"; and my hand leaning upon [120 his head, thus, sir, do you see? May it be done?

PAINT. Very well, sir.

HIER. Nay, I pray mark me, sir. Then, sir, would I have you paint me this tree, this very tree. Canst paint a doleful cry?

PAINT. Seemingly, sir.

HIER. Nay, it should cry; but all is one. Well, sir, paint me a youth run thorough and thorough with villains' swords, hanging upon this tree. Canst thou draw a murderer?   130

PAINT. I'll warrant you, sir; I have the pattern of the most notorious villains that ever lived in all Spain.

HIER. O, let them be worse, worse; stretch thine art, and let their beards be of Judas his own color;[41] and let their eyebrows jutty over — in any case observe that. Then, sir, after some violent noise, bring me forth in my shirt, and my gown under mine arm, with my torch in my hand, and my sword reared up, thus — and with these words: 140 "What noise is this? Who calls Hieronimo?" May it be done?

PAINT. Yea, sir.

HIER. Well, sir; then bring me forth, bring me thorough alley and alley, still with a distracted countenance going along, and let my hair heave up my nightcap. Let the clouds scowl, make the moon dark, the stars extinct, the winds blowing, the bells tolling, the owl shrieking, the toads croaking, the minutes j[a]rring,[42] and the clock striking twelve. [150 And then at last, sir, starting, behold a man hanging, and tottering and tottering, as you know the wind will wave a man, and I with a trice to cut him down. And looking upon him by the advantage of my torch, find it to be my son Horatio. There you may [show][43] a passion, there you may show a passion! Draw me like old Priam of Troy, crying, "The house is afire, the house is afire, as the torch over my head!" Make me curse, make me rave, make me cry, make me mad, make me well again, make me curse [160 hell, invocate Heaven, and in the end leave me in a trance — and so forth.

PAINT. And is this the end?

HIER. O no, there is no end; the end is death and madness. As I am never better than when I am mad; then methinks I am a brave fellow; then I do wonders; but reason abuseth [44] me, and there's the torment, there's the hell. At the last, sir, bring me to one of the murderers; were he as strong as Hector, thus would I tear and drag him up and [170 down.

He beats the Painter *in, then comes out again, with a book in his hand.*]

Enter HIERONIMO, *with a book in his hand.*

Vindicta mihi !

Ay, Heaven will be revenged of every ill;

Nor will they suffer murder unrepaid.

Then stay, Hieronimo, attend their will;

For mortal men may not appoint their time.

Per scelus semper tutum est sceleribus iter: [45]

Strike, and strike home, where wrong is off'red thee;

For evils unto ills conductors be,

And death's the worst of resolution.[46]   180

For he that thinks with patience to contend

To quiet life, his life shall easily end.[47] —

Fata si miseros juvant, habes salutem;

Fata si vitam negant, habes sepulchrum: [48]

If destiny thy miseries do ease,

Then hast thou health, and happy shalt thou be.

If destiny deny thee life, Hieronimo,

Yet shalt thou be assured of a tomb;

If neither, yet let this thy comfort be:

Heaven covereth him that hath no burial. 190

And to conclude, I will revenge his death.

But how? Not as the vulgar wits of men,

With open, but inevitable ills,[49]

As by a secret, yet a certain mean,

Which under kindship [50] will be cloaked best.

Wise men will take their opportunity,

Closely and safely fitting things to time.

But in extremes advantage hath no time;

And therefore all times fit not for revenge.

Thus therefore will I rest me in unrest,   [200

Dissembling quiet in unquietness,

Not seeming that I know their villainies,

That my simplicity [51] may make them think

That ignorantly I will let all slip;

For ignorance, I wot, and well they know,

Remedium malorum iners est.[52]

Nor aught avails it me to menace them,

Who, as a wintry storm upon a plain,

Will bear me down with their nobility.

No, no, Hieronimo, thou must enjoin   210

Thine eyes to observation, and thy tongue

To milder speeches than thy spirit affords,

Thy heart to patience, and thy hands to rest,

[45] Crime's safest course leads ever through more crime. (Adapted from Seneca's *Agamemnon*, l. 115.)

[46] *I.e.*, the worst that can happen as a consequence of a bold course is only death. (Or, since "resolution" sometimes = "dissolution", "death", perhaps: the worst thing that can happen is only death.)

[47] *I.e.*, the man who thinks he can win a quiet life by the exercise of patient endurance may lose his life [as] easily [as a bold man may].

[48] Seneca, *Troades*, ll. 511, 512.

[49] Not with open but with inevitable injuries. (Neilson.)

[50] Kindness.

[51] Stupidity, ignorance.

[52] Is an idle remedy for ills. (Adapted from Seneca's *Oedipus*, l. 515.)

[39] Boas notes *teare* as the reading of at least one copy of Q 1602.

[40] Like a mat; *i.e.*, laid on thick.

[41] Red.   [42] Ticking.

[43] Add. Schick.   [44] Deceives.

Thy cap to courtesy, and thy knee to bow,
Till to revenge thou know when, where, and
     how.   *A noise within.*
How now, what noise? What coil[53] is that
     you keep?

Enter a Servant.

SERV. Here are a sort[54] of poor petitioners
That are importunate, an it shall please you,
     sir,
That you should plead their cases to the King.
     HIER. That I should plead their several
     actions?   220
Why, let them enter, and let me see them.

Enter three Citizens *and an* Old Man.

1 [CIT].[55] So ; I tell you this : for learning
     and for law,
There is not any advocate in Spain
That can prevail, or will take half the pain
That he will, in pursuit of equity.
     HIER. Come near, you men, that thus
importune me. —
[*aside*] Now must I bear a face of gravity ;
For thus I us'd, before my marshalship,
To plead in causes as corregidor. —[56]
Come on, sirs, what's the matter?
     2 CIT.   Sir, an action.   230
     HIER. Of battery?
     1 CIT.   Mine of debt.
     HIER.   Give place.
     2 CIT. No, sir, mine is an action of the case.[57]
     3 CIT. Mine an *ejectione firma*[e][58] by a
     lease.
     HIER. Content you, sirs ; are you deter-
     mined
That I should plead your several actions?
     1 CIT. Ay, sir, and here's my declaration.
     2 CIT. And here is my band.[59]
     3 CIT.   And here is my lease.
                They give him papers.
     HIER. But wherefore stands yon silly[60]
     man so mute,
With mournful eyes and hands to Heaven up-
     rear'd?   239
Come hither, father, let me know thy cause.

SENEX. O worthy sir, my cause, but slightly
     known,
May move the hearts of warlike Myrmidons,
And melt the Corsic rocks[61] with ruthful tears.
     HIER. Say, father, tell me, what's thy suit?
     SENEX.   No, sir ; could my woes
Give way unto my most distressful words,
Then should I not in paper, as you see,
With ink bewray what blood began in me.
     HIER. What's here? " The humble sup-
     plication
Of Don Bazulto for his murd'red son."   249
     SENEX. Ay, sir.
     HIER.   No, sir ; it was my murd'red son !
O my son, my son, O my son Horatio !
But mine, or thine, Bazulto, be content.
Here, take my handkercher and wipe thine
     eyes,
Whiles wretched I in thy mishaps may see
The lively portrait of my dying self.
            He draweth out a bloody napkin.
O no, not this ; Horatio, this was thine ;
And when I dy'd it in thy dearest blood,
This was a token 'twixt thy soul and me
That of thy death revenged I should be.
But here, take this, and this — what, my
     purse? —   260
Ay, this, and that, and all of them are thine ;
For all as one are our extremities,
     1 CIT. O, see the kindness of Hieronimo !
     2 CIT. This gentleness shows him a gentle-
     man.
     HIER. See, see ; oh, see thy shame, Hiero-
     nimo !
See here a loving father to his son !
Behold the sorrows and the sad laments,
That he delivereth for his son's decease !
If love's effects so strives in lesser things,
If love enforce such moods in meaner wits, [270
If love express such power in poor estates,
Hieronimo, [as when][62] a raging sea,
Toss'd with the wind and tide, [o'erturneth][63]
     then
The upper billows, course of waves to keep,
Whilst lesser waters labor in the deep,

---

[53] Disturbance.   [54] Group, set.
[55] Om. throughout these speech-tags, in old eds.
[56] Properly, "magistrate" ; but evidently taken by
Kyd as "advocate."
[57] "An universal remedy . . . so called because
the plaintiff's whole . . . cause of complaint is set
forth at length in the original writ." (Blackstone,
cited by *N. E. D.*)
[58] Writ of ejection against a tenant.
[59] Bond.
[60] Humble, simple.

[61] Mentioned in Seneca's *Octavia*, l. 382.
[62] Emend. Kittredge (in Manly) ; old eds. *when as*.
[63] Emend. Hawkins ; old eds. *oreturnest, ore-
turned*. The sense of this clumsy, if not corrupt,
passage seems to be : "If the force of love is so
mighty in those of low estate, just as when a raging
sea is agitated in its upper waters, only to continue
its course in its depths ; then art not thou, Hieronimo, ashamed to neglect [being a man of high
estate] the pursuit of thy vengeance?" The in-
felicity of the marine simile arises from the lack
of harmony between its indirect reference to the
high rank of Hieronimo and its direct applicability
to the humble station of Bazulto.

Then shamest thou not, Hieronimo, to neglect
The sweet revenge of thy Horatio?
Though on this earth justice will not be found,
I'll down to hell, and in this passion
Knock at the dismal gates of Pluto's court, [280
Getting by force, as once Alcides did,
A troop of Furies and tormenting hags
To torture Don Lorenzo and the rest.
Yet, lest the triple-headed porter should
Deny my passage to the slimy strond,
The Thracian poet thou shalt counterfeit.
Come on, old father, be my Orpheus,
And if thou canst [64] no notes upon the harp,
Then sound the burden of thy sore heart's
    grief,
Till we do gain that Proserpine may grant   290
Revenge on them that murd'red my son.
Then will I rent and tear them, thus, and thus,
Shivering their limbs in pieces with my teeth.
                              Tear the papers.
    1 CIT. O sir, my declaration!
                Exit HIERONIMO, *and they after.*
    2. CIT.   Save my bond!

Re-enter HIERONIMO.

    2 CIT. Save my bond!
    3 CIT. Alas, my lease! it cost me ten pound,
And you, my Lord, have torn the same.
    HIER. That cannot be; I gave it never a
        wound.
Show me one drop of blood fall from the same!
How is it possible I should slay it, then?   300
Tush, no; run after, catch me if you can.
        Exeunt all but the Old Man. BA-
        ZULTO *remains till* HIERONIMO
        *enters again, who, staring him in
        the face, speaks.*
    HIER. And art thou come, Horatio, from
        the depth,
To ask for justice in this upper earth,
To tell thy father thou art unreveng'd,
To wring more tears from Isabella's eyes,
Whose lights are dimm'd with overlong la-
    ments?
Go back, my son; complain to Aeacus,
For here's no justice; gentle boy, begone,
For justice is exiled from the earth;
Hieronimo will bear thee company.   310
Thy mother cries on righteous Rhadamanth
For just revenge against the murderers.
    SENEX. Alas, my Lord, whence springs this
        troubled speech?
    HIER. But let me look on my Horatio.

[64] Knowest; *i.e.*, canst play.

Sweet boy, how art thou chang'd in death's
    black shade!
Had Proserpine no pity on thy youth,
But suffered thy fair crimson-colored spring
With withered winter to be blasted thus?
Horatio, thou art older than thy father.
Ah, ruthless [fate],[65] that favor[66] thus trans-
    forms!   320
    BAZ. Ah, my good Lord, I am not your
        young son.
    HIER. What, not my son? Thou then a
        Fury art,
Sent from the empty kingdom of black night
To summon me to make appearance
Before grim Minos and just Rhadamanth,
To plague Hieronimo that is remiss,
And seeks not vengeance for Horatio's death.
    BAZ. I am a grieved man, and not a ghost,
That came for justice for my murdered son.
    HIER. Ay, now I know thee, now thou
        namest thy son.   330
Thou art the lively image of my grief;
Within thy face my sorrows I may see.
Thy eyes are gumm'd with tears, thy cheeks
    are wan,
Thy forehead troubled, and thy mutt'ring lips
Murmur sad words abruptly broken off
By force of windy sighs thy spirit breathes;
And all this sorrow riseth for thy son,
And selfsame sorrow feel I for my son.
Come in, old man, thou shalt to Isabel.
Lean on my arm; I thee, thou me, shalt stay;
And thou, and I, and she will sing a song, [341
Three parts in one, but all of discords fram'd.—
Talk not of cords, but let us now be gone;
For with a cord Horatio was slain.   *Exeunt.*

[SCENE VII] [67]

Enter [on one side] KING OF SPAIN, *the* DUKE,
    LORENZO, BALTHAZAR, BEL-IMPERIA, [*and*
    Attendants; *and, on the other,*] VICEROY,
    DON PEDRO, [*and* Attendants].

    KING. Go, Brother, it is the Duke of Cas-
        tile's cause;
Salute the Viceroy in our name.
    CAST.   I go.
    VIC. Go forth, Don Pedro, for thy nephew's
        sake,
And greet the Duke of Castile.

[65] Emend. Dodsley; old eds. *Father.*
[66] Face, appearance.
[67] Unlocated; presumably at or near the royal
palace.

PED. It shall be so.

KING. And now to meet these Portuguese ;
For as we now are, so sometimes were these,
Kings and commanders of the western Indies.
Welcome, brave Viceroy, to the court of Spain,
And welcome all his honorable train !
'T is not unknown to us for why you come, 10
Or have so kingly cross'd the seas.
Sufficeth it, in this we note the troth
And more than common love you lend to us.
So is it that mine honorable niece
(For it beseems us now that it be known)
Already is betroth'd to Balthazar ;
And by appointment and our condescent [68]
To-morrow are they to be married.
To this intent we entertain thyself,
Thy followers, their pleasure, and our peace.
Speak, men of Portingal, shall it be so ? [21
If ay, say so ; if not, say flatly no.
  VIC. Renowmed King, I come not, as thou
    think'st,
With doubtful followers, unresolved men,
But such as have upon thine articles
Confirmed thy motion, and contented me.
Know, Sovereign, I come to solemnize
The marriage [69] of thy beloved niece,
Fair Bel-imperia, with my Balthazar,
With thee, my son ; whom sith I live to see, 30
Here take my crown ; I give it her and thee ;
And let me live a solitary life,
In ceaseless prayers,
To think how strangely Heaven hath thee pre-
    served.
  KING. See, Brother, see, how nature strives
    in him !
Come, worthy Viceroy, and accompany
Thy friend with thine extremities ; [70]
A place more private fits this princely mood.
  VIC. Or here, or where your Highness thinks
    it good.
        Exeunt all but CASTILE *and* LORENZO.
  CAST. Nay, stay, Lorenzo ; let me talk
    with you. 40
Seest thou this entertainment of these kings?
  LOR. I do, my Lord, and joy to see the
    same.
  CAST. And knowest thou why this meeting
    is?
  LOR. For her, my Lord, whom Balthazar
    doth love,
And to confirm their promised marriage.
  CAST. She is thy sister?

[68] Consent.   [69] Trisyllabic.
[70] Unrestrained manifestations of emotion. L. 33
is presumably pieced out by them.

  LOR. Who, Bel-imperia? Ay,
My gracious Lord, and this is the day
That I have long'd so happily to see.
  CAST. Thou wouldst be loth that any fault
    of thine
Should intercept her in her happiness? 50
  LOR. Heavens will not let Lorenzo err so
    much.
  CAST. Why then, Lorenzo, listen to my
    words :
It is suspected, and reported too,
That thou, Lorenzo, wrong'st Hieronimo,
And in his suits towards his Majesty
Still keep'st him back, and seeks to cross his
    suit.
  LOR. That I, my Lord?
  CAST. I tell thee, Son, myself have heard it
    said,
When, to my sorrow, I have been ashamed
To answer for thee, though thou art my son. 60
Lorenzo, knowest thou not the common love
And kindness that Hieronimo hath won
By his deserts within the court of Spain?
Or seest thou not the King my brother's care
In his behalf, and to procure his health?
Lorenzo, shouldst thou thwart his passions,
And he exclaim against thee to the King,
What honor were 't in this assembly,
Or what a scandal were 't among the kings
To hear Hieronimo exclaim on thee? 70
Tell me — and look thou tell me truly too —
Whence grows the ground of this report in
    court?
  LOR. My Lord, it lies not in Lorenzo's
    power
To stop the vulgar, liberal of their tongues.
A small advantage makes a water-breach,
And no man lives that long contenteth all.
  CAST. Myself have seen thee busy to keep
    back
Him and his supplications from the King.
  LOR. Yourself, my Lord, hath seen his pas-
    sions,
That ill beseem'd the presence of a king ; 80
And, for I pitied him in his distress,
I held him thence with kind and courteous
    words
As free from malice to Hieronimo
As to my soul, my Lord.
  CAST. Hieronimo, my son, mistakes thee
    then.
  LOR. My gracious father, believe me, so he
    doth.
But what 's a silly man, distract in mind
To think upon the murder of his son?

Alas, how easy is it for him to err!
But for his satisfaction and the world's,   90
'T were good, my Lord, that Hieronimo and I
Were reconcil'd, if he misconster me.

CAST. Lorenzo, thou hast said ; it shall be
    so. —
Go one of you, and call Hieronimo.[71]

Re-enter BALTHAZAR *and* BEL-IMPERIA.

BAL. Come, Bel-imperia, Balthazar's con-
    tent,
My sorrow's ease and sovereign of my bliss,
Sith Heaven hath ordain'd thee to be mine ;
Disperse those clouds and melancholy looks,
And clear them up with those thy sun-bright
    eyes,
Wherein my hope and Heaven's fair beauty
    lies.   100
BEL. My looks, my Lord, are fitting for my
    love,
Which, new-begun, can show [no][72] brighter
    yet.
BAL. New-kindled flames should burn as
    morning sun.
BEL. But not too fast, lest heat and all be
    done.
I see my Lord my father.
BAL.   Truce, my love ;
I will go salute him.
CAST.   Welcome, Balthazar,
Welcome, brave Prince, the pledge of Castile's
    peace ;
And welcome, Bel-imperia. — How now, girl?
Why comest thou sadly to salute us thus?
Content thyself, for I am satisfied.   110
It is not now as when Andrea liv'd ;
We have forgotten and forgiven that,
And thou art graced with a happier love. —
But, Balthazar, here comes Hieronimo ;
I 'll have a word with him.

Enter HIERONIMO *and a* Servant.

HIER. And where 's the Duke?
SERV.   Yonder.
HIER.   Even so. —
[*aside*] What new device have they devised,
    trow ?[73]
Pocas palabras! [74] mild as the lamb !
Is 't I will be reveng'd? No, I am not the
    man.
CAST. Welcome, Hieronimo.   120
LOR. Welcome, Hieronimo.

[71] Castile evidently calls off stage.
[72] Add. ed. 1594.
[73] I wonder, do you suppose?   [74] Few words.

BAL. Welcome, Hieronimo.
HIER. My Lords, I thank you for Horatio.
CAST. Hieronimo, the reason that I sent
To speak with you, is this.
HIER.   What, so short?
Then I 'll be gone; I thank you for 't.
CAST. Nay, stay, Hieronimo ! — Go, call
    him, Son.
LOR. Hieronimo, my father craves a word
    with you.
HIER. With me, sir? — Why, my Lord, I
    thought you had done.
LOR. No. — [*aside*] Would he had !
CAST.   Hieronimo, I hear
You find yourself aggrieved at my son,   131
Because you have not access unto the King ;
And say 't is he that intercepts your suits.
HIER. Why, is not this a miserable thing,
    my Lord?
CAST. Hieronimo, I hope you have no cause,
And would be loth that one of your deserts
Should once have reason to suspect my son,
Considering how I think of you myself.
HIER. Your son Lorenzo ! Whom, my noble
    Lord?
The hope of Spain, mine honorable friend?   140
Grant me the combat of them, if they dare !
            Draws out his sword.
I 'll meet him face to face, to tell me so !
These be the scandalous reports of such
As love not me, and hate my Lord too much.
Should I suspect Lorenzo would prevent
Or cross my suit, that lov'd my son so well?
My Lord, I am ashamed it should be said.
LOR. Hieronimo, I never gave you cause.
HIER. My good Lord, I know you did not.
CAST.   There then pause ;
And for the satisfaction of the world,   150
Hieronimo, frequent my homely house,
The Duke of Castile, Cyprian's ancient seat ;
And when thou wilt, use me, my son, and it ;
But here, before Prince Balthazar and me,
Embrace each other, and be perfect friends.
HIER. Ay, marry, my Lord, and shall.
Friends, quoth he? See, I 'll be friends with
    you all !
Especially with you, my lovely Lord ;
For divers causes it is fit for us
That we be friends : the world is suspicious,
And men may think what we imagine not.   161
BAL. Why, this is friendly done, Hieronimo.
LOR. And that, I hope, old grudges are for-
    got.
HIER. What else? It were a shame it
    should not be so.

Cast. Come on, Hieronimo, at my request ;
Let us entreat your company to-day.
                    Exeunt [all but Hieronimo].
Hier. Your Lordship's to command. —
    Pah ! keep your way :
[*Chi mi fa più carezze che non suole,*
Tradito mi ha, o tradir mi vuole.] [75]   *Exit.*

[Chorus] [76]

Ghost. Awake, Ericht[ho] ! Cerberus,
    awake !
Solicit Pluto, gentle Proserpine !
To combat, Ach[er]on and Er[eb]us !
For ne'er, by Styx and Phlegethon in hell, [77]
[O'er] [78] ferried Charon to the fiery lakes
Such fearful sights as poor Andrea see[s]. [79]
Revenge, awake !
    Revenge.   Awake ? For why ?
Ghost. Awake, Revenge ! for thou art
    ill-advis'd
T[o] sleep away what thou art warn'd to watch.
    Revenge. Content thyself, and do not
        trouble me.   10
    Ghost. Awake, Revenge ! if love -— as love
        hath had —
Have yet the power or prevalence in hell !
Hieronimo with Lorenzo is join'd in league,
And intercepts our passage to revenge.
Awake, Revenge, or we are woebegone !
    Revenge. Thus worldlings ground what
        they have dream'd upon. [80]
Content thyself, Andrea ; though I sleep,
Yet is my mood soliciting their souls.
Sufficeth thee that poor Hieronimo
Cannot forget his son Horatio.   20
Nor dies Revenge, although he sleep awhile ;
For in unquiet, quietness is feign'd,
And slumb'ring is a common worldly wile.
Behold, Andrea, for an instance, how
Revenge hath slept, and then imagine thou,
What 't is to be subject to destiny.

Enter a Dumb Show.

Ghost. Awake, Revenge ; reveal this mys-
    tery.
Revenge. The two first the nuptial torches
    bore
As brightly burning as the midday's sun ;
But after them doth Hymen hie as fast,   30

Clothed in sable and a saffron robe,
And blows them out, and quencheth them with
    blood,
As discontent that things continue so.
    Ghost. Sufficeth me ;   thy meaning's
        understood ;
And thanks to thee and those infernal powers
That will not tolerate a lover's woe.
Rest thee, for I will sit to see the rest.
    Revenge. Then argue not, for thou hast
        thy request. [81]

ACT [V — Scene I] [1]

Enter Bel-imperia *and* Hieronimo.

Bel. Is this the love thou bear'st Horatio ?
Is this the kindness that thou counterfeits ?
Are these the fruits of thine incessant tears ?
Hieronimo, are these thy passions,
Thy protestations and thy deep laments,
That thou wert wont to weary men withal ?
O unkind father ! O deceitful world !
With what excuses canst thou show thyself [2]
From this dishonor and the hate of men,
Thus to neglect the loss and life of him   10
Whom both my letters and thine own belief
Assures thee to be causeless slaughtered ?
Hieronimo, for shame, Hieronimo,
Be not a history to aftertimes
Of such ingratitude unto thy son !
Unhappy mothers of such children then !
But monstrous fathers to forget so soon
The death of those whom they with care and
    cost
Have tend'red so, thus careless should be lost !
Myself, a stranger in respect of thee,   20
So loved his life, as still I wish their deaths.
Nor shall his death be unreveng'd by me,
Although I bear it out for fashion's sake.
For here I swear, in sight of Heaven and earth,
Shouldst thou neglect the love thou shouldst
    retain,
And give it over and devise no more,
Myself should send their hateful souls to hell
That wrought his downfall with extremest
    death.
    Hier. But may it be that Bel-imperia   29
Vows such revenge as she hath deign'd to say ?

---

[75] So Schick, correcting the corrupt text of the
old eds. " Who me caresses more than was his way
Has me betrayed — or wishes to betray."
[76] Old eds. *Enter Ghost and Revenge.*
[77] Old eds. attach *in hell* to l. 3.
[78] Emend. Schick ; old eds. *Nor.*
[79] Cor. Q 1602 ; earlier eds. *see.*
[80] Rely on what they have dreamed.

[81] Old eds. add *Exeunt.*
[1] Unlocated ; perhaps a room in the palace of
Don Cyprian. Old eds. *Actus Quartus.*
[2] Old eds. perpetuate the compositor's blunder
by inserting between ll. 8 and 9 *With what dishonour
and the hate of men.*

Why, then I see that Heaven applies our
    drift,[3]
And all the saints do sit soliciting
For vengeance on those cursed murderers.
Madam, 't is true, and now I find it so,
I found a letter, written in your name,
And in that letter, how Horatio died.
Pardon, O pardon, Bel-imperia,
My fear and care in not believing it ;
Nor think I thoughtless think upon a mean
To let his death be unreveng'd at full.   40
And here I vow — so[4] you but give consent,
And will conceal my resolution —
I will ere long determine of their deaths
That causeless thus have murdered my son.
    BEL. Hieronimo, I will consent, conceal,
And aught that may effect for thine avail
Join with thee to revenge Horatio's death.
    HIER. On, then ; whatsoever I devise,
Let me entreat you, grace my practices ;
Forwhy[5] the plot 's already in mine head.   50
Here they are.

Enter BALTHAZAR *and* LORENZO.

    BAL.   How now, Hieronimo?
What, courting Bel-imperia?
    HIER.   Ay, my Lord ;
Such courting as, I promise you,
She hath my heart ;[6] but you, my Lord, have
    hers.
    LOR. But now, Hieronimo, or never, we
Are to entreat your help.
    HIER.   My help?
Why, my good Lords, assure yourselves of me ;
For you have giv'n me cause — ay, by my
    faith have you !
    BAL. It pleas'd you, at the entertainment
    of the ambassador,
To grace the King so much as with a show.   60
Now, were your study so well furnished,
As, for the passing of the first night's sport,
To entertain my father with the like,
Or any such like pleasing motion,[7]
Assure yourself, it would content them well.
    HIER. Is this all?
    BAL.   Ay, this is all.
    HIER.   Why then, I 'll fit you ;
    say no more.
When I was young, I gave my mind
And pli'd myself to fruitless poetry ;

Which though it profit the professor naught,
Yet is it passing pleasing to the world.   70
    LOR. And how for that?
    HIER.   Marry, my good Lord, thus : —
And yet methinks, you are too quick with us —
When in Toledo there I studied,
It was my chance to write a tragedy —
See here, my Lords —   *He shows them a book.*
Which, long forgot, I found this other day.
Now would your Lordships favor me so much
As but to grace me with your acting it —
I mean each one of you to play a part —   79
Assure you it will prove most passing strange,
And wondrous plausible[8] to that assembly.
    BAL. What ! would you have us play a
    tragedy?
    HIER. Why, Nero thought it no disparage-
    ment,
And kings and emperors have ta'en delight
To make experience of their wits in plays.
    LOR. Nay, be not angry, good Hieronimo ;
The Prince but ask'd a question.
    BAL.   In faith, Hieronimo,
An you be in earnest, I 'll make one.
    LOR.   And I another.
    HIER. Now, my good Lord, could you en-
    treat
Your sister, Bel-imperia, to make one?   90
For what 's a play without a woman in it?
    BEL. Little entreaty shall serve me, Hier-
    onimo ;
For I must needs be employed in your play.
    HIER. Why, this is well. I tell you, Lord-
    ings,
It was determined to have been acted
By gentlemen and scholars too,
Such as could tell what to speak.
    BAL.   And now
It shall be play'd by princes and courtiers,
Such as can tell how to speak —
If, as it is our country manner,   100
You will but let us know the argument.
    HIER. That shall I roundly. The chron-
    icles of Spain
Record this written of a knight of Rhodes :
He was betrothed, and wedded at the length,
To one Perseda, an Italian dame,
Whose beauty ravished all that her beheld,
Especially the soul of Soliman,[9]
Who at the marriage was the chiefest guest.

---

[3] Allies itself to our plan.
[4] Provided that.
[5] Because.
[6] Playing on "heart" = secrets.
[7] Show. (Usually puppet show ; but Nash, cited
by *N. E. D.*, links "pomps, pageants, motions,
masks.")

[8] Pleasing.
[9] The anonymous *Tragedy of Soliman and Perseda*
(entered in the Stationers' Register in 1592) has been
ascribed by some to Kyd. It is based on Henry
Wotton's *Courtly Controversy of Cupid's Cautels*
(1578), a translation of Jaques Yver's *Printemps
d'Iver* (1572).

By sundry means sought Soliman to win   109
Perseda's love, and could not gain the same.
Then 'gan he break his passions to a friend,
One of his bashaws,[10] whom he held full dear.
Her had this bashaw long solicited,
And saw she was not otherwise to be won
But by her husband's death, this knight of Rhodes,
Whom presently by treachery he slew.
She, stirr'd with an exceeding hate therefore,
As cause of this slew Soliman,
And, to escape the bashaw's tyranny,
Did stab herself ; and this the tragedy.   120
    LOR. Oh, excellent !
    BEL.   But say, Hieronimo,
What then became of him that was the bashaw?
    HIER. Marry, thus : moved with remorse of his misdeeds,
Ran to a mountain top, and hung himself.
    BAL. But which of us is to perform that part?
    HIER. Oh, that will I, my Lords ; make no doubt of it :
I'll play the murderer, I warrant you ;
For I already have conceited that.
    BAL. And what shall I?   129
    HIER. Great Soliman, the Turkish emperor.
    LOR. And I?
    HIER.   Erast[o], the knight of Rhodes.
    BEL. And I?
    HIER.   Perseda, chaste and resolute.
And here, my Lords, are several abstracts drawn,
For each of you to note your parts,
And act it, as occasion's off'red you.
You must provide a Turkish cap,
A black mustachio, and a falchion ;
                Gives a paper to BALTHAZAR.
You, with a cross, like to a knight of Rhodes ;
                Gives another to LORENZO.
And, madam, you must attire yourself
                He giveth BEL-IMPERIA *another.*
Like Phoebe, Flora, or the Huntress,[11]   140
Which to your discretion shall seem best.
And as for me, my Lords, I'll look to one,[12]
And, with the ransom that the Viceroy sent,
So furnish and perform this tragedy
As all the world shall say Hieronimo
Was liberal in gracing of it so.
    BAL. Hieronimo, methinks a comedy were better.
    HIER. A comedy?

Fie ! comedies are fit for common wits ,
But to present a kingly troop withal,   150
Give me a stately-written tragedy ;
Tragoedia cothurnata, fitting kings,
Containing matter, and not common things.
My Lords, all this must be performed,
As fitting for the first night's revelling.
The Italian tragedians were so sharp of wit,
That in one hour's meditation
They would perform anything in action.
    LOR. And well it may ; for I have seen the like
In Paris 'mongst the French tragedians.   160
    HIER. In Paris? mass, and well remem-b'red !
There's one thing more that rests for us to do.
    BAL. What's that, Hieronimo? Forget not anything.
    HIER. Each one of us
Must act his part in unknown languages,
That it may breed the more variety :
As you, my Lord, in Latin, I in Greek,
You in Italian ; and, for because I know
That Bel-imperia hath practised the French,
In courtly French shall all her phrases be. [170
    BEL. You mean to try my cunning then, Hieronimo?
    BAL. But this will be a mere confusion
And hardly shall we all be understood.
    HIER. It must be so ; for the conclusion
Shall prove the invention[13] and all was good.
And I myself in an oration,
And with a strange and wondrous show be-sides,[14]
That I will have there behind a curtain,
Assure yourself, shall make the matter known ;
And all shall be concluded in one scene,   180
For there's no pleasure ta'en in tediousness.
    BAL. How like you this?
    LOR. [*aside to* BALTHAZAR]   Why, thus, my Lord,
We must resolve to soothe his humors up.
    BAL. On then, Hieronimo ; farewell till soon.
    HIER. You'll ply this gear?
    LOR.   I warrant you.
                Exeunt all but HIERONIMO.
    HIER.   Why so !
Now shall I see the fall of Babylon,
Wrought by the Heavens in this confusion.
And if the world like not this tragedy,
Hard is the hap of old Hieronimo.   *Exit.*

---

[10] Pashas.   [11] Diana. *Huntress* is trisyllabic.
[12] Get a costume.
[13] So Greg and Schick ; Boas *intention.*
[14] Transposed with preceding line in first three editions.

[SCENE II] [15]

Enter ISABELLA *with a weapon.*

ISAB. Tell me no more! — Oh, monstrous
   homicides!
Since neither piety or pity moves
The King to justice or compassion,
I will revenge myself upon this place,
Where thus they murdered my beloved son.
           She cuts down the arbor.
Down with these branches and these loath-
   some boughs
Of this unfortunate and fatal pine!
Down with them, Isabella; rent them up,
And burn the roots from whence the rest is
   sprung!
I will not leave a root, a stalk, a tree,   10
A bough, a branch, a blossom, nor a leaf,
No, not an herb within this garden plot,
Accursed complot [16] of my misery!
Fruitless for ever may this garden be,
Barren the earth, and blissless whosoever
Imagines not to keep it unmanur'd! [17]
An eastern wind, commix'd with noisome
   airs,
Shall blast the plants and the young saplings;
The earth with serpents shall be pestered,
And passengers, for fear to be infect,   20
Shall stand aloof, and, looking at it, tell:
" There, murd'red, died the son of Isabel."
Ay, here he di'd, and here I him embrace!
See, where his ghost solicits with his wounds
Revenge on her that should revenge his
   death.
Hieronimo, make haste to see thy son;
For sorrow and despair hath cited me
To hear Horatio plead with Rhadamanth.
Make haste, Hieronimo, to hold excus'd
Thy negligence in pursuit [18] of their deaths [30
Whose hateful wrath bereav'd him of his
   breath.
Ah, nay, thou doest delay their deaths,
Forgives the murderers of thy noble son,
And none but I bestir me — to no end!
And as I curse this tree from further fruit,
So shall my womb be cursed for his sake;
And with this weapon will I wound the
   breast,
The hapless breast, that gave Horatio suck.
           She stabs herself.

[15] Hieronimo's garden.
[16] Co-plotter, accomplice. Properly, "conspiracy."
Note the pun.
[17] Uncultivated.
[18] Accented on first syllable.

[SCENE III] [19]

Enter HIERONIMO; *he knocks up the curtain.*[20]
   Enter the DUKE OF CASTILE.

CAST. How now, Hieronimo, where's your
   fellows,
That you take all this pain?
  HIER.   O sir, it is for the author's
Credit, to look that all things may go well.
But, good my Lord, let me entreat your Grace
To give the King the copy of the play:
This is the argument of what we show.
  CAST. I will, Hieronimo.
  HIER.   One thing more, my good Lord.
  CAST. What's that?
  HIER.   Let me entreat your Grace
That, when the train are pass'd into the gal-
   lery,
You would vouchsafe to throw me down the
   key.   10
  CAST. I will, Hieronimo.   *Exit* CASTILE.
  HIER.   What, are you ready, Balthazar?
Bring a chair and a cushion for the King.

   Enter BALTHAZAR, *with a chair.*

              Well done, Balthazar;
Hang up the title: our scene is Rhodes. What,
  is your beard on?
  BAL. Half on; the other is in my hand.
  HIER.   Dispatch for shame;
Are you so long? —   *Exit* BALTHAZAR.
         Bethink thyself, Hieronimo,
Recall thy wits, recount thy former wrongs
Thou hast received by murder of thy son,
And lastly, not least, how Isabel,
Once his mother and thy dearest wife,
All woebegone for him, hath slain herself. 20
Behoves thee then, Hieronimo, to be reveng'd.
The plot is laid of dire revenge!
On, then, Hieronimo, pursue revenge;
For nothing wants but acting of revenge.

Enter SPANISH KING, VICEROY, DUKE OF
  CASTILE, [DON PEDRO], *and their train* [*to
  the gallery*].[21] *Exit Hieronimo.*

  KING. Now, Viceroy, shall we see the
   tragedy

[19] A hall in Don Cyprian's palace. Presumably
Isabella's suicide has taken place on the inner stage,
the curtains of which are then closed.
[20] See V, i, 177, 178; and V, iii, 111.
[21] Add. Manly. The gallery (see ll. 9, 10) was
doubtless the balcony over the inner stage. Castile
locks the doors to it and throws the key down to
Hieronimo. In the old eds. the latter's exit is given
before the entrance of the royal party.

Of Soliman, the Turkish emperor,
Perform'd of pleasure by your son the Prince,
My nephew Don Lorenzo, and my niece.
Vic. Who? Bel-imperia?
King.   Ay, and Hieronimo, our marshal,
At whose request they deign to do 't them-
    selves.   30
These be our pastimes in the court of Spain.
Here, Brother, you shall be the bookkeeper:
This is the argument of that they show.

                     He giveth him a book.

(Gentlemen, this play of Hieronimo, *in sundry*
languages, was thought good to be set down in
English, more largely for the easier understand-
ing to every public reader.)

Enter Balthazar, Bel-imperia, *and*
                Hieronimo.

Bal. *Bashaw, that Rhodes is ours, yield*
    Heavens the honor,
And holy Mahomet, our sacred prophet!
And be thou grac'd with every excellence
That Soliman can give, or thou desire.
But thy desert in conquering Rhodes is less
Than in reserving this fair Christian nymph,
Perseda, blissful lamp of excellence,   40
Whose eyes compel, like pow'rful adamant,
The warlike heart of Soliman to wait.

King. See, Viceroy, that is Balthazar, your
    son,
That represents the emperor Soliman:
How well he acts his amorous passion!
Vic. Ay, Bel-imperia hath taught him that.
Cast. That 's because his mind runs all on
    Bel-imperia.

Hier. *Whatever joy earth yields betide your*
    Majesty.
Bal. *Earth yields no joy without Perseda's*
    love.   49
Hier. *Let then Perseda on your Grace attend.*
Bal. *She shall not wait on me, but I on her:*
Drawn by the influence of her lights,[22] *I yield.*
But let my friend, the Rhodian knight, come
    forth,
Erasto, dearer than my life to me,
That he may see Perseda, my beloved.

             Enter Erasto.

King. Here comes Lorenzo: look upon the
    plot,
And tell me, Brother, what part plays he?

[22] Eyes.

Bel. *Ah, my Erasto, welcome to Perseda.*
Lor. *Thrice happy is Erasto that thou livest;*
Rhodes' loss is nothing to Erasto's joy;   60
Sith his Perseda lives, his life survives.
Bal. *Ah, bashaw, here is love betwixt Erasto*
And fair Perseda, sovereign of my soul.
Hier. *Remove Erasto, mighty Soliman,*
And then Perseda will be quickly won.
Bal. *Erasto is my friend; and while he lives,*
Perseda never will remove her love.
Hier. *Let not Erasto live to grieve great*
    Soliman.
Bal. *Dear is Erasto in our princely eye.*
Hier. *But if he be your rival, let him die.* [70
Bal. *Why, let him die — so love commandeth*
    me;
Yet grieve I that Erasto should so die.
Hier. *Erasto, Soliman saluteth thee,*
And lets thee wit by me his Highness' will,
Which is, thou shouldst be thus employ'd.
                              Stab him.
Bel.   *Ay me,*
Erasto! See, Soliman; Erasto's slain!
Bal. *Yet liveth Soliman to comfort thee.*
Fair queen of beauty, let not favor die,
But with a gracious eye behold his grief,
That with Perseda's beauty is increas'd,   80
If by Perseda [his][23] *grief be not releas'd.*
Bel. *Tyrant, desist soliciting vain suits;*
Relentless are mine ears to thy laments,
As thy butcher is pitiless and base,
Which seiz'd on my Erasto, harmless knight.
Yet by thy power thou thinkest to command,
And to thy power Perseda doth obey;
But, were she able, thus she would revenge
Thy treacheries on thee, ignoble Prince:
                              Stab him.
And on herself she would be thus reveng'd.   90
                              Stab herself.

King. Well said![24] — Old Marshal, this
    was bravely done!
Hier. But Bel-imperia plays Perseda well!
Vic. Were this in earnest, Bel-imperia,
You would be better to my son than so.
King. But now what follows for Hiero-
    nimo?
Hier. Marry, this follows for Hieronimo;—
Here break we off our sundry languages,
And thus conclude I in our vulgar tongue.
Haply you think — but bootless are your
    thoughts —
That this is fabulously counterfeit,   100
And that we do as all tragedians do:

[23] So Schick; old eds. *s.*   [24] Good, well done.

To die to-day, for fashioning our scene —
The death of Ajax or some Roman peer —
And in a minute, starting up again,
Revive to please to-morrow's audience.
No, Princes; know I am Hieronimo,
The hopeless father of a hapless son,
Whose tongue is tun'd to tell his latest tale,
Not to excuse gross errors in the play.
I see your looks urge instance of these words;
Behold the reason urging me to this!   111
Shows his dead son.
See here my show; look on this spectacle!
Here lay my hope, and here my hope hath
     end!
Here lay my heart, and here my heart was
     slain!
Here lay my treasure, here my treasure lost!
Here lay my bliss, and here my bliss bereft!
But hope, heart, treasure, joy, and bliss,
All fled, fail'd, died, yea, all decay'd, with
     this.
From forth these wounds came breath that
     gave me life;
They murd'red me that made these fatal
     marks.   120
The cause was love, whence grew this mortal
     hate;
The hate, Lorenzo and young Balthazar;
The love, my son to Bel-imperia.
But night, the coverer of accursed crimes,
With pitchy silence hush'd these traitors'
     harms,
And lent them leave, for they had sorted [25]
     leisure
To take advantage in my garden plot
Upon my son, my dear Horatio.
There merciless they butcher'd up my boy,
In black, dark night, to pale, dim, cruel death.
He shrieks; I heard — and yet, methinks, I
     hear —   131
His dismal outcry echo in the air.
With soonest speed I hasted to the noise,
Where hanging on a tree I found my son,
Through-girt [26] with wounds, and slaught'red
     as you see.
And grieved I, think you, at this spectacle?
Speak, Portuguese, whose loss resembles mine:
If thou canst weep upon thy Balthazar,
'T is like I wail'd for my Horatio. —
And you, my Lord, whose reconciled son   140
March'd in a net, and thought himself un-
     seen,
And rated me for brainsick lunacy,
With " God amend that mad Hieronimo ! " —

How can you brook our play's catastrophe? —
And here behold this bloody handkercher,
Which at Horatio's death I weeping dipp'd
Within the river of his bleeding wounds:
It, as propitious, see, I have reserved,
And never hath it left my bloody heart,
Soliciting remembrance of my vow   150
With these, oh, these accursed murderers!
Which now perform'd, my heart is satisfied.
And to this end the bashaw I became,
That might revenge me on Lorenzo's life,
Who therefore was appointed to the part,
And was to represent the knight of Rhodes,
That I might kill him more conveniently.
So, Viceroy, was this Balthazar, thy son,
That Soliman which Bel-imperia,
In person of Perseda, murdered,   160
Solely appointed to that tragic part
That she might slay him that offended her.
Poor Bel-imperia miss'd her part in this;
For though the story saith she should have
     died,
Yet I of kindness, and of care to her,
Did otherwise determine of her end;
But love of him whom they did hate too much
Did urge her resolution [27] to be such.
And, Princes, now behold Hieronimo,
Author and actor in this tragedy,   170
Bearing his latest fortune in his fist;
And will as resolute conclude his part
As any of the actors gone before.
And, gentles, thus I end my play;
Urge no more words — I have no more to say.
He runs to hang himself.
   KING. O hearken, Viceroy! — Hold, Hiero-
     nimo!
Brother, my nephew and thy son are slain!
   VIC. We are betray'd; my Balthazar is
     slain!
Break ope the doors; run, save Hieronimo.
[They break in and hold HIERONIMO.] [28]
Hieronimo, do but inform the King of these
     events;   180
Upon mine honor, thou shalt have no harm.
   HIER. Viceroy, I will not trust thee with
     my life,
Which I this day have offered to my son. —
Accursed wretch,
Why stayest thou him that was resolv'd to die?
   KING. Speak, traitor! damned, bloody
     murderer, speak!
For now I have thee, I will make thee speak.
Why hast thou done this undeserving deed?

---

[25] Chosen.   [26] Pierced, smitten through.

[27] Either "death" or "determination."
[28] Add. Q 1602.

Vic. Why hast thou murdered my Balthazar?

Cast. Why hast thou butchered both my
children thus?   190

Hier. O, good words! [29]
As dear to me was my Horatio
As yours, or yours, or yours, my Lord, to you.
My guiltless son was by Lorenzo slain,
And by Lorenzo and that Balthazar
Am I at last revenged thoroughly,
Upon whose souls may Heavens be yet
avenged
With greater far than these afflictions.

Cast. But who were thy confederates in
this?   199

Vic. That was thy daughter, Bel-imperia;
For by her hand my Balthazar was slain :
I saw her stab him.

King.   Why speakest thou not?

Hier. What lesser liberty can kings afford
Than harmless silence? Then afford it me.
Sufficeth, I may not, nor I will not tell thee.

King. Fetch forth the tortures! Traitor as
thou art,
I'll make thee tell.

Hier. Indeed,
Thou mayest torment me as his wretched son
Hath done in murd'ring my Horatio;   210
But never shalt thou force me to reveal
The thing which I have vow'd inviolate.
And therefore, in despite of all thy threats,
Pleas'd with their deaths, and eas'd with their
revenge,
First take my tongue, and afterwards my
heart.

[30] [Hier. But are you sure they are dead?
Cast.   Ay, slave,[31] too sure.
Hier. What, and yours too?
Vic. Ay, all are dead; not one of them survive.
Hier. Nay, then I care not; come, and we shall
be friends;
Let us lay our heads together: 220
See, here's a goodly noose will hold them all.
Vic. O damned devil, how secure[32] he is!
Hier. Secure? Why, doest thou wonder at it?
I tell thee, Viceroy, this day I have seen [revenge],
And in that sight am grown a prouder monarch
Than ever sat under the crown of Spain.
Had I as many lives as there be stars,
As many Heavens to go to, as those lives,
I'd give them all, ay, and my soul to boot,
But I would see thee ride in this red pool.   230
Cast. Speak! who were thy confederates in
this?
Vic. That was thy daughter Bel-imperia;
For by her hand my Balthazar was slain :
I saw her stab him.

[29] Ll. 191–215 were replaced by the added passage,
ll. 216–265.
[30] Fifth passage of additions begins here. See on
l. 191.
[31] Some copies read *slaine*.   [32] Sure of himself.

Hier. O, good words!
As dear to me was my Horatio,
As yours, or yours, or yours, my Lord, to you.
My guiltless son was by Lorenzo slain,
And by Lorenzo and that Balthazar
Am I at last revenged thoroughly;   240
Upon whose souls may Heavens be yet revenged
With greater far than these afflictions.
Methinks, since I grew inward[33] with revenge,
I cannot look with scorn enough on death.
King. What, doest thou mock us, slave? — Bring
tortures forth!
Hier. Do, do, do; and meantime I'll torture
you.
You had a son, as I take it; and your son
Should ha' been married to your daughter.
Ha, was 't not so? — You had a son, too;
He was my Liege's nephew. He was proud 250
And politic; had he lived, he might 'a' come
To wear the crown of Spain. I think 't was so —
'T was I that killed him; look you, this same hand,
'T was it that stabb'd his heart — do you see? this
hand —
For one Horatio, if you ever knew him: a youth,
One that they hanged up in his father's garden;
One that did force your valiant son to yield,
While your more valiant son did take him prisoner.
Vic. Be deaf, my senses; I can hear no more.
King. Fall, Heaven, and cover us with thy sad
ruins.   260
Cast. Roll all the world within thy pitchy cloud.
Hier. Now do I applaud what I have acted.
Nunc [iners cadat][34] manus!
Now to express the rupture of my part —
First take my tongue, and afterward my heart.
                    [*He bites out his tongue.*]

King. O monstrous resolution of a wretch!
See, Viceroy, he hath bitten forth his tongue,
Rather than to reveal what we requir'd.

Cast. Yet can he write.

King. And if in this he satisfy us not, 270
We will devise th' extremest kind of death
That ever was invented for a wretch.
          *Then he makes signs for a knife to
          mend his pen.*

Cast. Oh, he would have a knife to mend
his pen.

Vic. Here, and advise thee that thou write
the troth.

King. Look to my brother! save Hieronimo! [35]
          He with a knife stabs the Duke *and
          himself.*

What age hath ever heard such monstrous
deeds?

My brother, and the whole succeeding hope
That Spain expected after my decease!

Go, bear his body hence, that we may mourn
The loss of our beloved brother's death, 280
That he may be entomb'd, whate'er befall.
I am the next, the nearest, last of all.

[33] Got on intimate terms.
[34] Emend. Schick; old eds. *mors caede, mers
cadae.* "Now let the hand fall idle."
[35] Old eds. give this line to Viceroy; cor. Boas.

VIC. And thou, Don Pedro, do the like for
    us ;
Take up our hapless son, untimely slain ;
Set me with him, and he with woeful me,
Upon the mainmast of a ship unmann'd,
And let the wind and tide [hale] [36] me along
To Scylla's barking and untamed [gulf,] [37]
Or to the loathsome pool of Acheron,   289
To weep my want for my sweet Balthazar ;
Spain hath no refuge for a Portingale.

The trumpets sound a dead march;
[exeunt omnes,] the KING OF SPAIN
mourning after his brother's body,
and the KING OF PORTINGAL *bear-*
ing the body of his son.

[CHORUS] [38]

GHOST. Ay, now my hopes have end in
    their effects,
When blood and sorrow finish my desires :
Horatio murdered in his father's bower,
Vild Serberine by Pedringano slain,
False Pedringano hang'd by quaint device,
Fair Isabella by herself misdone,
Prince Balthazar by Bel-imperia stabb'd,
The Duke of Castile and his wicked son
Both done to death by old Hieronimo,
My Bel-imperia fall'n as Dido fell,   10
And good Hieronimo slain by himself :
Ay, these were spectacles to please my soul.
Now will I beg at lovely Proserpine
That, by the virtue of her princely doom,
I may consort my friends in pleasing sort,
And on my foes work just and sharp revenge.
I 'll lead my friend Horatio through those fields

[36] Cor. ed. 1599 ; earlier eds. *hall.*
[37] Cor. Q 1623 ; earlier eds. *greefe.*
[38] Old eds. *Enter Ghost and Revenge.*

Where never-dying wars are still inur'd ; [39]
I 'll lead fair Isabella to that train
Where pity weeps, but never feeleth pain ;   20
I 'll lead my Bel-imperia to those joys
That vestal virgins and fair queens possess ;
I 'll lead Hieronimo where Orpheus plays,
Adding sweet pleasure to eternal days. —
But say, Revenge, for thou must help, or none,
Against the rest how shall my hate be shown?
    REV. This hand shall hale them down to
        deepest hell,
Where none but Furies, bugs,[40] and tortures
    dwell.
    GHOST. Then, sweet Revenge, do this at
        my request :
Let me be judge, and doom them to unrest.   30
Let loose poor Tityus from the vulture's gripe,
And let Don Cyprian supply his room ;
Place Don Lorenzo on Ixion's wheel,
And let the lover's endless pains surcease
(Juno forgets old wrath, and grants him ease) ;
Hang Balthazar about Chimaera's neck,
And let him there bewail his bloody love,
Repining at our joys that are above ;
Let Serberine go roll the fatal stone,
And take from Sisyphus his endless moan ; 40
False Pedringano, for his treachery,
Let him be dragg'd through boiling Acheron,
And there live, dying still in endless flames,
Blaspheming gods and all their holy names.
    REV. Then haste we down to meet thy
        friends and foes :
To place thy friends in ease, the rest in woes ;
For here though death hath end their misery
I 'll there begin their endless tragedy.
                     Exeunt.

[39] Waged.
[40] Bugbears, terrors.

Euery

MAN IN

HIS

HVMOVR.

A Comœdie.

Acted in the yeere 15 9 8. By the then
Lord Chamberlaine his
Seruants.

The Author B. I.

I u v e n.

Haud tamen inuideas vati, quem pulpita pascunt.

LONDON,

Printed by WILLIAM STANSBY.

M. D C. XVI.

INTRODUCTORY NOTE

In 1616 Jonson personally saw through the press the First Folio of his collected works (Second Folio, 1631–1640; Third Folio, 1692). From it we learn that *Every Man in His Humor* was first performed in 1598, and that Shakespeare (perhaps as Lorenzo Senior, the Elder Knowell of the Italian version) was one of the actors. The play was an immediate success. It was also destined to a long career on the London stage: Kitely was one of Garrick's famous rôles; in 1845 Charles Dickens, a gifted amateur actor, played Bobadill with great gusto.

Jonson wrote on a neoclassical theory: comedy in his opinion ought to be realistic, and it ought to "sport with human follies, not with crimes." While the prologue as we have it may have been written after the original production, in offering "one such to-day as other plays should be", he challenged the prevailing romantic comedy with his "humors." Unlike Shakespeare, who ordinarily starts with a plot, Jonson begins with ideas or "manners", creates characters to exemplify them, and uses plot chiefly as a means of displaying them. To Shakespeare comedy was usually a vehicle for putting a romantic tale on the stage; to Jonson it was an opportunity for wielding the lash of the satirist. Hence the latter's addiction to his "humors", since caricature is an obvious means of ridicule. Zealous to avoid romanticizing and prettifying, Jonson exaggerates the various weaknesses of most of his persons, denying them common sense and complexity, till in many cases his depiction of the dominating trait, the "humor", of each subject of his portraiture crowds everything else off the canvas.

Plautus was his principal source. From the Roman comedy he took the deceived father and the sporting son, the clever slave, the boastful captain, and the gull — all stock characters; as the manipulation of events by the servant in behalf of his young master, the marriage *sub rosa*, and the disguisings and mistaken identity were all stock situations. Despite the Latin origin of his patterns, and his original Italian coloring, Jonson weaves a racy tapestry of contemporary London life. This is a play bound to disappoint the reader for whom narrative is the prime requisite of fiction. This is for the man who delights in the sights and sounds and smells of a great city, the sort of person who finds the top of a bus a vantage point.

In his turn Jonson became the inspiration of the best English comic writers for two centuries. The historical importance, therefore, of *Every Man in His Humor* can hardly be overstated, even though its intrinsic merit is considerably below that of the three masterpieces which follow it in the present edition. For several years Shakespeare was powerfully influenced by these humors, Middleton and Fletcher followed Jonson's lead, and the comic dramatists of the Restoration were profoundly indebted to him.

The standard editions of Jonson's Works are those of William Gifford (re-edited by Francis Cunningham, 1875), and of C. H. Herford and Percy Simpson (1925–). The most useful separate editions of *Every Man in His Humor* are by Percy Simpson (1919) and H. H. Carter (1921; date of editor's preface, 1914). The play originally appeared, in quarto, in 1601, with Italian characters and scene. Jonson afterwards, perhaps about 1612, made a careful revision, transferring both to London. This version appears in the Folios. There is a good deal of stylistic overhauling, especially in the verse passages, as well as excision of oaths (in accordance with the act against profanity in plays — 3 *Jac.* I, ch. 21), a slight rearrangement of acts and scenes, a more concise handling of the closing scenes, a general tightening up of theatrical effectiveness, and a few additional strokes of characterization. The present text is based on the First Folio, with some corrections and additions, especially in stage directions, from the Quarto and the later Folios.

EVERY MAN IN HIS HUMOR

BY

BEN JONSON

THE PERSONS OF THE PLAY

KNOWELL, an old gentleman.
EDWARD KNOWELL, his son.
BRAINWORM, the father's man.
MASTER STEPHEN, a country gull.[1]
[GEORGE] DOWNRIGHT, a plain squire.
WELLBRED, his half-brother.
JUSTICE CLEMENT, an old, merry magistrate.
ROGER FORMAL, his clerk.
[THOMAS] KITELY, a merchant.
MASTER MATTHEW, the town gull.

[THOMAS] CASH, Kitely's man.
[OLIVER] COB, a water-bearer.
CAPTAIN BOBADILL, a Paul's man.[2]
[A Servant to Wellbred.]
[Other Servants.]

DAME KITELY, [Kitely's] wife.
MISTRESS BRIDGET, his sister.
TIB, [Cob's] wife.

THE SCENE — *London.*

PROLOGUE

THOUGH need make many poets, and some such
As art and nature have not better'd much,
Yet ours for want hath not so lov'd the stage
As he dare serve th'ill customs of the age,
Or purchase your delight at such a rate
As, for it, he himself must justly hate :
To make a child, now swaddled, to proceed
Man, and then shoot up, in one beard and
    weed,
Past threescore years[3] ; or, with three rusty
    swords,
And help of some few foot-and-half-foot
    words,   10
Fight over York and Lancaster's long jars,[4]
And in the tiring-house[5] bring wounds to scars.
He rather prays you will be pleas'd to see
One such to-day, as other plays should be ;
Where neither chorus wafts you o'er the seas,[6]
Nor creaking throne comes down the boys to
    please,[7]
Nor nimble squib is seen to make afeard
The gentlewomen, nor roll'd bullet[8] heard
To say it thunders, nor tempestuous drum
Rumbles to tell you when the storm doth
    come ;[9]   20
But deeds and language such as men do use,
And persons such as comedy would choose
When she would show an image of the times,
And sport with human follies, not with crimes ;
Except we make 'em such, by loving still
Our popular errors, when we know th'are ill.
I mean such errors as you 'll all confess,
By laughing at them, they deserve no less :
Which when you heartily do, there 's hope left,
    then,
You, that have so grac'd monsters, may like
    men.   30

[1] Fool, dupe.
[2] *I.e.*, loafer. The centre aisle of the cathedral was a lounging-place, as well as the scene of business appointments.
[3] In the present play Jonson observes the unity of time. "The clock ticks audibly in every act." (Simpson.) Steevens mentions *Endymion* as an offender. This prologue is heavily indebted to Sidney's *Defence of Poesie.*
[4] A direct hit at Shakespeare's *King Henry VI.*
[5] Dressing-room.
[6] *E.g.*, as in Shakespeare's *King Henry V* and Heywood's *The Four Prentices of London.*
[7] *E.g.*, as in Greene's *Alphonsus.*
[8] Cannon ball.
[9] Malone suggests an allusion to Shakespeare's *The Tempest.* Cf. l. 30.

ACT I — SCENE I [10]

[*Enter*] KNOWELL [*and* BRAINWORM]. [11]

KNOW. A goodly day toward ! and a fresh
     morning ! —
Brainworm, call up your young master : bid
     him rise, sir.
Tell him I have some business to employ
     him.
     BRAI. I will, sir, presently. [12]
     KNOW.   But hear you, sirrah,
If he be at [13] his book, disturb him not.
     BRAI.   Well, sir. [*Exit.*] [14]
     KNOW. How happy yet should I esteem my-
     self,
Could I, by any practice, [15] wean the boy
From one vain course of study he affects.
He is a scholar, if a man may trust
The liberal voice of fame ; in her report   10
Of good account in both our universities,
Either of which hath favor'd him with graces :
But their indulgence must not spring in me
A fond [16] opinion that he cannot err.
Myself was once a student, and indeed
Fed with the selfsame humor he is now,
Dreaming on naught but idle poetry,
That fruitless and unprofitable art,
Good unto none, but least to the professors ;
Which then I thought the mistress of all knowl-
     edge ;   20
But since, time and the truth have wak'd my
     judgment,
And reason taught me better to distinguish
The vain from th' useful learnings.

[*Enter* MASTER STEPHEN.]

     Cousin Stephen !
What news with you, that you are here so
     early?
     STEP. Nothing, but e'en come to see how
you do, Uncle.
     KNOW. That 's kindly done ; you are wel-
come, Coz.
     STEP. Ay, I know that, sir ; I would not ha'

---

[10] Before Knowell's house in Hoxton, a London
suburb.
[11] So Q. Mod. eds., properly following F textually,
have failed to observe the importance of stage
directions in Q. F follows the classical method of
listing the characters at the head of the scene.
[12] Immediately.
[13] F *be 'at*, to indicate rapid pronunciation.
[14] So Q. Om. F. Similar cases are not cited, except
occasionally, in these notes. It should be added that
the names of the characters are not the same in Q.
[15] Device, trick.
[16] Foolish.

---

come else. How [doth] [17] my cousin Edward,
Uncle?   31
     KNOW. O, well, Coz ; go in and see ; I
doubt he be scarce stirring yet.
     STEP. Uncle, afore I go in, can you tell me
an he have e'er a book of the sciences of hawking and hunting? I would fain borrow it.
     KNOW. Why, I hope you will not a-hawking
now, will you?
     STEP. No, wusse ; [18] but I 'll practise against
next year, Uncle. I have bought me a [40
hawk, and a hood, and bells, and all ; I lack
nothing but a book to keep it by.
     KNOW. Oh, most ridiculous !
     STEP. Nay, look you now, you are angry,
Uncle. — Why, you know an a man have not
skill in the hawking and hunting languages
nowadays, I 'll not give a rush for him.
They are more studied than the Greek, or the
Latin. He is for no gallant's company without
'em ; and by gadslid [19] I scorn it, I, so I do, [50
to be a consort for every humdrum : hang 'em,
scroyles ! [20] there 's nothing in 'em i' the world.
What do you talk on it? Because I dwell at
Hogsden, [21] I shall keep company with none
but the archers of Finsbury, or the citizens that
come a-ducking [22] to Islington ponds? A fine
jest, i' faith ! 'Slid, a gentleman mun [23] show
himself like a gentleman. Uncle, I pray you
be not angry ; I know what I have to do, I
trow ; I am no novice.   60
     KNOW. You are a prodigal, absurd cox-
     comb, go to !
Nay, never look at me — 't is I that speak ;
Take 't as you will, sir — I 'll not flatter you.
Ha' you not yet found means enow to waste
That which your friends have left you, but you
     must
Go cast away your money on a kite,
And know not how to keep it, when you ha'
     done?
O, it 's comely ! This will make you a gentle-
     man !
Well, Cousin, well ! I see you are e'en past
     hope
Of all reclaim. — Ay, so, now you are told on
     it,   70
You look another way.
     STEP.   What would you ha' me do?

---

[17] F[1] *doe*, which Simpson retains. Q *doeth;* Ff [2, 3],
does.
[18] Certainly, iwis.
[19] By God's (*i.e.*, Christ's) eyelid ; usually, as in
l. 57, *'slid.*
[20] Scurvy fellows.
[21] Hoxton.
[22] Duck shooting.   [23] Must.

KNOW. What would I have you do? I'll
   tell you, kinsman :
Learn to be wise, and practise how to thrive ;
That would I have you do ; and not to spend
Your coin on every bauble that you fancy,
Or every foolish brain that humors you.
I would not have you to invade each place,
Nor thrust yourself on all societies,
Till men's affections, or your own desert,
Should worthily invite you to your rank.   80
He that is so respectless in his courses
Oft sells his reputation at cheap market.
Nor would I you should melt away yourself
In flashing bravery,[24] lest,-while you affect
To make a blaze of gentry to the world,
A little puff of scorn extinguish it ;
And you be left like an unsavory snuff,
Whose property is only to offend.
I'd ha' you sober, and contain yourself,
Not that your sail be bigger than your boat ;
But moderate your expenses now, at first,   91
As you may keep the same proportion still ;
Nor stand so much on your gentility,
Which is an airy and mere borrow'd thing,
From dead men's dust and bones ; and none of
     yours,
Except you make, or hold it. Who comes
   here?

SCENE II [25]

[To] KNOWELL *[and]* STEPHEN *[enter a]*
Servant.

SERV. Save you, gentlemen !
STEP. Nay, we do not stand much on our
gentility, friend ; yet you are welcome, and I
assure you mine uncle here is a man of a thousand a year, Middlesex land. He has but one
son in all the world, I am his next heir, at the
common law, Master Stephen, as simple as I
stand here, if my cousin die, as there's hope
he will. I have a pretty living o' mine own
too, beside, hard by here.   10
SERV. In good time,[26] sir.
STEP. In good time, sir ! Why, and in very
good time, sir ! You do not flout, friend, do
you?
SERV. Not I, sir.
STEP. Not you, sir ! You were not best,
sir ; an you should, here be them can perceive
it, and that quickly too ; go to. And they can
give it again soundly too, an need be.

SERV. Why, sir, let this satisfy you ; good
faith, I had no such intent.   21
STEP. Sir, an I thought you had, I would
talk with you, and that presently.
SERV. Good Master Stephen, so you may,
sir, at your pleasure.
STEP. And so I would, sir, good my saucy
companion ![27] An you were out o' mine
uncle's ground, I can tell you ; though I do not
stand upon my gentility neither, in 't.
KNOW. Cousin ! Cousin ! Will this ne'er
be left?   31
STEP. Whoreson, base fellow ! a mechanical
serving man ! By this cudgel, an 't were not
for shame, I would ——
KNOW. What would you do, you peremp-
   tory[28] gull?
If you cannot be quiet, get you hence.
You see the honest man demeans himself
Modestly to'ards you, giving no reply
To your unseason'd, quarrelling, rude fashion ;
And still you huff it,[29] with a kind of carriage
As void of wit as of humanity.   41
Go, get you in ; 'fore Heaven, I am asham'd
Thou hast a kinsman's interest in me.
    [Exit MASTER STEPHEN.]
SERV. I pray you, sir, is this Master Know-
ell's house?
KNOW. Yes, marry is it, sir.
SERV. I should inquire for a gentleman here,
one Master Edward Knowell ; do you know
any such, sir, I pray you?
KNOW. I should forget myself else, sir.   50
SERV. Are you the gentleman? Cry you
mercy, sir. I was requir'd by a gentleman i'
the city, as I rode out at this end o' the town,
to deliver you this letter, sir.
KNOW. To me, sir ! What do you mean?
Pray you remember your court'sy.[30] — *[read-*
ing] " To his most selected friend, Master Edward Knowell." What might the gentleman's
name be, sir, that sent it? Nay, pray you be
cover'd.   60
SERV. One Master Wellbred, sir.
KNOW. Master Wellbred ! A young gentleman, is he not?
SERV. The same, sir ; Master Kitely married his sister — the rich merchant i' the Old
Jewry.
KNOW. You say very true. — Brainworm !

[Enter BRAINWORM.]

BRAI. Sir.

---

[24] Waste your substance on flashy finery.
[25] The same.
[26] "A formula of polite acquiescence . . . but it
could be ironical or incredulous." (Simpson.) Cf.
à la bonne heure.

[27] Fellow.
[28] Absolute, utter.
[29] Bluster.
[30] Put on your hat.

KNOW. Make this honest friend drink here.
Pray you, go in. 70

[*Exeunt* BRAINWORM *and* Servant.]

This letter is directed to my son ;
Yet I am Edward Knowell too, and may,
With the safe conscience of good manners, use
The fellow's error to my satisfaction.
Well, I will break it ope (old men are curious),
Be it but for the style's sake and the phrase,
To see if both do answer my son's praises,
Who is almost grown the idolater
Of this young Wellbred. — What have we
  here? What's this?

(*The letter.*)   "Why, Ned, I beseech [80
thee, hast thou forsworn all thy friends i' the
Old Jewry? or dost thou think us all Jews
that inhabit there yet? If thou dost, come
over and but see our frippery ; [31] change an old
shirt for a whole smock with us. Do not conceive that antipathy between us and Hogsden
as was between Jews and hogs' flesh. Leave
thy vigilant father alone, to number over his
green apricots, evening and morning, o' the
northwest wall. An I had been his son, I [90
had sav'd him the labor long since, if taking in
all the young wenches that pass by at the back
door, and coddling every kernel of the fruit for
'em, would ha' serv'd. But prithee, come over
to me quickly this morning. I have such a
present for thee ! — our Turkey Company
never sent the like to the Grand Signior. One
is a rhymer, sir, o' your own batch, your own
leaven ; but doth think himself poet-major o'
the town, willing to be shown, and worthy [100
to be seen. The other — I will not venture
his description with you, till you come, because
I would ha' you make hither with an appetite.
If the worst of 'em be not worth your journey,
draw your bill of charges, as unconscionable as
any Guildhall verdict will give it you, and you
shall be allow'd your viaticum.

From the *Windmill*.[32] "

From the Bordello,[33] it might come as well —
The Spittle,[34] or Pict-hatch.[35] Is this the
  man 110
My son hath sung so, for the happiest wit,
The choicest brain, the times have sent us
  forth?
I know not what he may be in the arts,

---

[31] Old clothes shop.
[32] Described in Stowe's *Survey of London* (1598)
as a wine tavern, which had once been a Jewish
synagogue.
[33] Brothel.
[34] Hospital, especially for the treatment of venereal diseases.
[35] A well-known resort of prostitutes.

Nor what in schools ; but, surely, for his man-
  ners,
I judge him a profane and dissolute wretch ;
Worse by possession of such great good gifts,
Being the master of so loose a spirit.
Why, what unhallow'd ruffian would have
  writ
In such a scurrilous manner to a friend?
Why should he think I tell my apricots? [120
Or play th' Hesperian dragon with my fruit,
To watch it? Well, my son, I had thought
Y' had had more judgment t' have made elec-
  tion
Of your companions, than t' have ta'en on
  trust
Such petulant, jeering gamesters, that can
  spare
No argument or subject from their jest.
But I perceive affection makes a fool
Of any man too much the father. — Brain-
  worm !

[*Re-enter* BRAINWORM.]

BRAI. Sir.
KNOW.   Is the fellow gone that brought
  this letter?
BRAI. Yes, sir, a pretty while since.
KNOW.   And where 's your young
  master? 130
BRAI. In his chamber, sir.
KNOW.   He spake not with the fellow,
  did he?
BRAI. No, sir, he saw him not.
KNOW. Take you this letter, and deliver it
  my son ;
But with no notice that I have open'd it, on
  your life.
BRAI. O Lord, sir ! that were a jest indeed.
  [*Exit.*]
KNOW. I am resolv'd I will not stop his
  journey,
Nor practise any violent mean to stay
The unbridled course of youth in him ; for
  that
Restrain'd grows more impatient ; and in
  kind
Like to the eager but the generous [36] grey-
  hound, 140
Who, ne'er so little from his game withheld,
Turns head and leaps up at his holder's throat.
There is a way of winning more by love
And urging of the modesty, than fear :
Force works on servile natures, not the free.
He that 's compell'd to goodness may be good,

---

[36] High-spirited.

But 't is but for that fit ; where others, drawn
By softness and example, get a habit.
Then, if they stray, but warn 'em, and the
  same   149
They should for virtue have [37] done, they 'll do
  for shame.   [*Exit.*]

SCENE [III] [38]

[*Enter*] EDWARD KNOWELL [*with a letter, followed by*] BRAINWORM.

E. KNOW. Did he open it, sayest thou?

BRAI. Yes, o' my word, sir, and read the
contents.

E. KNOW. That scarce contents me. What
countenance, prithee, made he i' the reading of
it? Was he angry or pleas'd?

BRAI. Nay, sir, I saw him not read it, nor
open it, I assure your Worship.

E. KNOW. No? How know'st thou then
that he did either?   10

BRAI. Marry, sir, because he charg'd me,
on my life, to tell nobody that he open'd it ;
which, unless he had done, he would never fear
to have it reveal'd.

E. KNOW. That 's true. Well, I thank thee,
Brainworm.   [*Reads the letter.*]

[*Enter* STEPHEN.]

STEP. O, Brainworm, didst thou not see a
fellow here in a what-sha'-call-him doublet?
He brought mine uncle a letter e'en now.   19

BRAI. Yes, Master Stephen ; what of him?

STEP. O, I ha' such a mind to beat him ——
where is he, canst thou tell?

BRAI. Faith, he is not of that mind : he is
gone, Master Stephen.

STEP. Gone ! which way? When went he?
How long since?

BRAI. He is rid hence ; he took horse at the
street door.

STEP. And I stay'd i' the fields ! Whoreson
Scanderbag [39] rogue ! O that I had but a [30
horse to fetch him back again !

BRAI. Why, you may ha' my master's gelding, to save your longing, sir.

STEP. But I ha' no boots, that 's the spite
on 't.

BRAI. Why, a fine wisp of hay, roll'd hard,
Master Stephen.

STEP. No, faith, it 's no boot to follow him
now ; let him e'en go and hang. Pray thee,
help to truss [40] me a little. He does so vex [40
me ——

BRAI. You 'll be worse vex'd when you are
truss'd, Master Stephen. Best keep unbrac'd,
and walk yourself till you be cold ; your
choler may founder you else.

STEP. By my faith, and so I will, now thou
tell'st me on 't. How dost thou like my leg,
Brainworm?

BRAI. A very good leg, Master Stephen !
but the woolen stocking does not commend [50
it so well.

STEP. Foh ! the stockings be good enough,
now summer is coming on, for the dust. I 'll
have a pair of silk again' [41] winter, that I go to
dwell i' the town. I think my leg would show
in a silk hose.

BRAI. Believe me, Master Stephen, rarely
well.

STEP. In sadness,[42] I think it would ; I have
a reasonable good leg.   60

BRAI. You have an excellent good leg,
Master Stephen ; but I cannot stay to praise
it longer now, and I am very sorry for it.

STEP. Another time will serve, Brainworm.
Gramercy for this.   [*Exit* BRAINWORM.]

E. KNOW. (*laughs, having read the letter.*)
Ha, ha, ha !

STEP. 'Slid, I hope he laughs not at me ; an
he do ——

E. KNOW. Here was a letter indeed, to be intercepted by a man's father, and do him [70
good with him ! He cannot but think most virtuously, both of me and the sender, sure, that
make the careful costermonger of him in our
"Familiar Epistles." Well, if he read this with
patience I 'll be gelt, and troll ballads for Master John Trundle [43] yonder, the rest of my mortality. It is true, and likely, my father may
have as much patience as another man, for he
takes much physic ; and oft taking physic
makes a man very patient. But would [80
your packet, Master Wellbred, had arriv'd at
him in such a minute of his patience. Then
we had known the end of it, which now is
doubtful, and threatens —— [*seeing* STEPHEN]
What ! my wise cousin ! Nay, then I 'll furnish our feast with one gull more to'ard the

---

[37] Old eds. frequently indicate rapid pronunciation, as here : *vertu' have.*

[38] Unlocated ; probably the same as the preceding
scene. F₁ misnumbers *Scene II.*

[39] A common corruption of Iskander Bey, Prince
Alexander, the Turkish name of the Albanian
patriot, George Castriot (1414–1467).

[40] Tie the "points", the tagged laces that held
up the breeches or hose. Brainworm plays on
"truss" = beat.

[41] Against, in readiness for.

[42] Seriously.

[43] A well-known publisher and bookseller.

mess.[44] He writes to me of a brace, and here's one, that's three. Oh, for a fourth! Fortune, if ever thou 'lt use thine eyes, I entreat thee —

STEP. Oh, now I see who he laugh'd at : [90 he laugh'd at somebody in that letter. By this good light, an he had laugh'd at me —

E. KNOW. How now, Cousin Stephen, melancholy?

STEP. Yes, a little : I thought you had laugh'd at me, Cousin.

E. KNOW. Why, what an I had, Coz? What would you ha' done?

STEP. By this light, I would ha' told mine uncle. 100

E. KNOW. Nay, if you would ha' told your uncle, I did laugh at you, Coz.

STEP. Did you, indeed?

E. KNOW. Yes, indeed.

STEP. Why, then —

E. KNOW. What then?

STEP. I am satisfied ; it is sufficient.

E. KNOW. Why, be so, gentle Coz. And, I pray you, let me entreat a courtesy of you. I am sent for this morning by a friend i' [110 the Old Jewry, to come to him ; it 's but crossing over the fields to Moorgate. Will you bear me company? I protest it is not to draw you into bond or any plot against the state, Coz.

STEP. Sir, that 's all one, an 't were ; you shall command me twice so far as Moorgate, to do you good in such a matter. Do you think I would leave you? I protest —

E. KNOW. No, no, you shall not protest, Coz. 121

STEP. By my fackins,[45] but I will, by your leave : — I 'll protest more to my friend than I 'll speak of at this time.

E. KNOW. You speak very well, Coz.

STEP. Nay, not so neither, you shall pardon me ; but I speak to serve my turn.

E. KNOW. Your turn, Coz ! Do you know what you say? A gentleman of your sort,[46] parts, carriage, and estimation, to talk o' [130 your turn[47] i' this company, and to me alone, like a tankard-bearer at a conduit ! Fie ! A wight that, hitherto, his every step hath left the stamp of a great foot behind him, as every word the savor of a strong spirit ! and he ! this man ! so grac'd, gilded, or, to use a more fit metaphor, so tin-foil'd, by nature, as not ten

housewives' pewter, again' a good time,[48] shows more bright to the world than he ! and he ! (as I said last, so I say again, and [140 still shall say it) this man ! to conceal such real ornaments as these, and shadow their glory, as a milliner's wife does her wrought stomacher, with a smoky lawn, or a black cypress ![49] O, Coz ! it cannot be answer'd ; go not about it. Drake's old ship[50] at De[p]tford may sooner circle the world again. Come, wrong not the quality of your desert, with looking downward, Coz ; but hold up your head, so ; and let the idea[51] of what you are be [150 portray'd i' your face, that men may read i' your physnomy, "Here, within this place, is to be seen the true, rare, and accomplish'd monster, or miracle of nature," which is all one. What think you of this, Coz?

STEP. Why, I do think of it ; and I will be more proud, and melancholy, and gentlemanlike, than I have been, I 'll insure you.

E. KNOW. Why, that 's resolute, Master Stephen ! — [aside] Now, if I can but hold [160 him up to his height, as it is happily begun, it will do well for a suburb humor : we may hap have a match with the City, and play him for forty pound. — Come, Coz.

STEP. I 'll follow you.

E. KNOW. Follow me ! You must go before.

STEP. Nay, an I must, I will. Pray you show me, good Cousin. [Exeunt.]

SCENE IV [52]

[Enter] MASTER MATTHEW.

MAT. I think this be the house. What, ho !

[Enter COB.]

COB. Who 's there? Oh, Master Matthew ! Gi' your Worship good morrow.

MAT. What, Cob ! How dost thou, good Cob? Dost thou inhabit here, Cob?

COB. Ay, sir, I and my lineage ha' kept a poor house here, in our days.

MAT. Thy lineage, Monsieur Cob ! What lineage, what lineage?

COB. Why, sir, an ancient lineage, and a [10 princely. Mine ance'try came from a king's belly, no worse man ; and yet no man either — by your Worship's leave, I did lie in that —

[44] Set of four.
[45] Faith.   [46] Rank.
[47] Water-bearers carried wooden "tankards" holding about three gallons each. A trip from a conduit and back again was called a turn.
[48] In readiness for a festival.
[49] Thin crêpe.
[50] The Golden Hind.
[51] Image.
[52] Before Cob's house.

but herring, the king of fish [53] (from his belly I proceed), one o' the monarchs o' the world, I assure you. The first red herring that was broil'd in Adam and Eve's kitchen do I fetch my pedigree from, by the harrots' [54] books. His cob [55] was my great-great-mighty-great-grandfather. 20

MAT. Why mighty, why mighty, I pray thee?

COB. O, it was a mighty while ago, sir, and a mighty great cob.

MAT. How know'st thou that?

COB. How know I! Why, I smell his ghost ever and anon.

MAT. Smell a ghost! O unsavory jest! and the ghost of a herring cob!

COB. Ay, sir. With favor of your Wor- [30 ship's nose, Master Matthew, why not the ghost of a herring cob, as well as the ghost of Rasher Bacon?

MAT. Roger Bacon, thou wouldst say!

COB. I say Rasher Bacon. They were both broil'd o' the coals! and a man may smell broil'd meat, I hope! You are a scholar; upsolve me that now.

MAT. O raw ignorance! — Cob, canst thou show me of a gentleman, one Captain [40 Bobadill, where his lodging is?

COB. O, my guest, sir, you mean!

MAT. Thy guest! alas, ha, ha!

COB. Why do you laugh, sir? Do you not mean Captain Bobadill?

MAT. Cob, pray thee advise thyself well; do not wrong the gentleman, and thyself too. I dare be sworn he scorns thy house, he! He lodge in such a base obscure place as thy house! Tut, I know his disposition so [50 well, he would not lie in thy bed if thou'dst gi' it him.

COB. I will not give it him though, sir. Mass, I thought somewhat was in 't, we could not get him to bed all night! Well, sir, though he lie not o' my bed, he lies o' my bench; an 't please you to go up, sir, you shall find him with two cushions under his head, and his cloak wrapp'd about him, as though he had neither won nor lost; and yet, I [60 warrant, he ne'er cast [56] better in his life, than he has done to-night. [57]

MAT. Why, was he drunk?

COB. Drunk, sir? You hear not me say so.

Perhaps he swallow'd a tavern token, [58] or some such device, sir; I have nothing to do withal. I deal with water and not with wine. — Gi' me my tankard there, ho! — God b' w' you, sir. It's six a'clock: I should ha' carried two turns by this. What ho! my stopple! come. [70

[Enter TIB *with a water-tankard.]*

MAT. Lie in a water-bearer's house! A gentleman of his havings! Well, I'll tell him my mind.

COB. What, Tib; show this gentleman up to the Captain. *[Exeunt* TIB *and* MATTHEW.] Oh, an my house were the Brazen Head [59] now! Faith, it would e'en speak *Mo* [60] *fools yet.* You should ha' some now would take this Master Matthew to be a gentleman, at the least. His father's an honest man, a [80 worshipful fishmonger, [61] and so forth; and now does he creep and wriggle into acquaintance with all the brave gallants about the town, such as my guest is (oh, my guest is a fine man), and they flout him invincibly. He useth every day to a merchant's house where I serve water, one Master Kitely's, i' the Old Jewry; and here's the jest: he is in love with my master's sister, Mistress Bridget, and calls her "Mistress"; and there [90 he will sit you a whole afternoon, sometimes, reading o' these same abominable, vile (a pox on 'em, I cannot abide them), rascally verses, poyetrie, poyetrie, and speaking of interludes; 't will make a man burst to hear him. And the wenches, they do so jeer, and ti-he at him. — Well, should they do so much to me, I'd forswear them all, by the foot of Pharaoh! — There's an oath! How many water-bearers shall you hear swear such an oath? [100 O, I have a guest — he teaches me — he does swear the legiblest of any man christ'ned: "By St. George!" "The foot of Pharaoh!" "The body of me!" "As I am [a] [62] gentleman and a soldier!" Such dainty oaths! And withal he does take this same filthy roguish tobacco, the finest and cleanliest! It would do a man good to see the fume come forth at 's tonnels. [63] — Well, he owes me forty shillings, my wife lent him out of her [110 purse, by sixpence a time, besides his lodging; I would I had it! I shall ha' it, he says, the

[53] For the herring as king see *Nashes Lenten Stuff.* Nash's Works, ed. McKerrow, III, 201-204.
[54] Heralds'.   [55] Herring-head.
[56] Punning on *cast* = diced, and = vomited.
[57] Last night.

[58] A small coin issued by a tradesman. "To swallow a tavern token" = to get drunk.
[59] See *Friar Bacon and Friar Bungay.*
[60] More.
[61] A member of the Fishmongers' Company.
[62] Add. F 2.   [63] Tunnels; *i.e.*, nostrils.

next action.[64] Helter skelter, hang sorrow, care'll kill a cat, up-tails all, and a louse for the hangman! [*Exit.*]

SCENE V [65]

BOBADILL *is discovered lying on his bench.*

BOB. Hostess, hostess!

[*Enter* TIB.]

TIB. What say you, sir?

BOB. A cup o' thy small beer, sweet hostess.

TIB. Sir, there's a gentleman below would speak with you.

BOB. A gentleman! 'odso, I am not within.

TIB. My husband told him you were, sir.

BOB. What a plague — what meant he?

MAT. [*within*] [66] Captain Bobadill!

BOB. Who's there! — Take away the basin, good hostess. — Come up, sir. 11

TIB. He would desire you to come up, sir. You come into a cleanly house, here!

[*Enter* MATTHEW.]

MAT. 'Save you, sir; 'save you, Captain!

BOB. Gentle Master Matthew! Is it you, sir? Please you sit down.

MAT. Thank you, good Captain; you may see I am somewhat audacious.

BOB. Not so, sir. I was requested to supper last night by a sort [67] of gallants, where [20 you were wish'd for, and drunk to, I assure you.

MAT. Vouchsafe me by whom, good Captain.

BOB. Marry, by young Wellbred, and others. — Why, hostess, a stool here for this gentleman.

MAT. No haste, sir, 't is very well.

BOB. Body of me! It was so late ere we parted last night, I can scarce open my [30 eyes yet; I was but new risen, as you came. How passes the day abroad, sir? you can tell.

MAT. Faith, some half hour to seven. Now, trust me, you have an exceeding fine lodging here, very neat, and private!

BOB. Ay, sir; sit down, I pray you. Master Matthew, in any case possess no gentlemen of our acquaintance with notice of my lodging.

MAT. Who? I, sir? No. 40

BOB. Not that I need to care who know it, for the cabin [68] is convenient; but in regard I would not be too popular, and generally visited, as some are.

MAT. True, Captain, I conceive you.

BOB. For, do you see, sir, by the heart of valor in me, except it be to some peculiar and choice spirits, to whom I am extraordinarily engag'd, as yourself, or so, I could not extend thus far. 50

MAT. O Lord, sir! I resolve so.

BOB. I confess I love a cleanly and quiet privacy, above all the tumult and roar of fortune. What new book ha' you there? What! "Go by, Hieronymo!" [69]

MAT. Ay: did you ever see it acted? Is't not well penn'd?

BOB. Well penn'd! I would fain see all the poets of these times pen such another play as that was! They'll prate and swagger, [60 and keep a stir of art and devices, when, as I am a gentleman, read 'em, they are the most shallow, pitiful, barren fellows that live upon the face of the earth again!

MAT. Indeed here are a number of fine speeches in this book.[70] "O eyes, no eyes, but fountains fraught with tears!" There's a conceit! "Fountains fraught with tears!" "O life, no life, but lively form of death!" — another! "O world, no world, but mass [70 of public wrongs!" — a third! "Confus'd and fill'd with murder and misdeeds!" — a fourth! Oh, the muses! Is't not excellent? Is't not simply the best that ever you heard, Captain? Ha! how do you like it?

BOB. 'T is good.

MAT. "To thee, the purest object to my sense,
The most refined essence Heaven covers,
Send I these lines, wherein I do commence
The happy state of turtle-billing lovers. 80
If they prove rough, unpolish'd, harsh, and rude,
Haste made the waste. Thus, mildly, I conclude." [71]

BOB. Nay, proceed, proceed. Where's this?
BOBADILL *is making him ready all this while.*

MAT. This, sir? A toy [72] o' mine own, in my nonage, the infancy of my muses! But when will you come and see my study?

---

[64] Campaign.
[65] A room in Cob's house. Bobadill is "discovered" on the inner stage.
[66] So Q.
[67] Set, company.
[68] Cf. III, vii, 83.
[69] See *The Spanish Tragedy*, IV, v, 30.
[70] *Ibid.*, III, ii, 1–4.
[71] Matthew's originality is suspect, but no source for these lines has been found. [72] Trifle.

Good faith, I can show you some very good things I have done of late. — That boot becomes your leg passing well, Captain, methinks.   90

BOB. So, so; it's the fashion gentlemen now use.

MAT. Troth, Captain, and now you speak o' the fashion, Master Wellbred's elder brother and I are fall'n out exceedingly. This other day, I happ'ned to enter into some discourse of a hanger,[73] which, I assure you, both for fashion and workmanship, was most peremptory [74] beautiful and gentlemanlike; yet he condemn'd, and cri'd it down for the most pied [75] and ridiculous that he ever saw.   101

BOB. Squire Downright, the half-brother, was't not?

MAT. Ay, sir, he.

BOB. Hang him, rook![76] He! why he has no more judgment than a malt-horse. By St. George, I wonder you'd lose a thought upon such an animal; the most peremptory absurd clown of Christendom, this day, he is holden. I protest to you, as I am a [110 gentleman and a soldier, I ne'er chang'd words with his like. By his discourse, he should eat nothing but hay. He was born for the manger, pannier, or packsaddle! He has not so much as a good phrase in his belly, but all old iron and rusty proverbs! a good commodity for some smith to make hobnails of.

MAT. Ay, and he thinks to carry it away [77] with his manhood still, where he comes. He brags he will gi' me the bastinado, as I hear.   121

BOB. How! He the bastinado! How came he by that word, trow? [78]

MAT. Nay, indeed, he said cudgel me; I term'd it so, for my more grace.

BOB. That may be; for I was sure it was none of his word. But when, when said he so?

MAT. Faith, yesterday, they say; a young gallant, a friend of mine, told me so.

BOB. By the foot of Pharaoh, an 't were [130 my case now, I should send him a cartel presently. The bastinado! A most proper and sufficient dependence,[79] warranted by the great Carranza.[80] Come hither. You shall

cartel him. I'll show you a trick or two you shall kill him with at pleasure; the first stoccata,[81] if you will, by this air.

MAT. Indeed, you have absolute knowledge i' the mystery, I have heard, sir.

BOB. Of whom, of whom, ha' you heard it, I beseech you?   141

MAT. Troth, I have heard it spoken of divers, that you have very rare and un-in-one-breath-utterable skill, sir.

BOB. By Heaven, no, not I; no skill i' the earth — some small rudiments i' the science, as to know my time, distance, or so. I have profess'd it more for noblemen and gentlemen's use, than mine own practice, I assure you. — Hostess, accommodate us with another [150 bedstaff [82] here quickly. [*Re-enter* TIB.] Lend us another bedstaff. — The woman does not understand the words of action. — Look you, sir: exalt not your point above this state, at any hand, and let your poniard maintain your defence, thus. — Give it the gentleman, and leave us. [*Exit* TIB.] So, sir. Come on. Oh, twine your body more about, that you may fall to a more sweet, comely, gentlemanlike guard. So! indifferent.[83] [160 Hollow your body more, sir, thus. Now, stand fast o' your left leg, note your distance, keep your due proportion of time — oh, you disorder your point most irregularly!

MAT. How is the bearing of it now, sir?

BOB. Oh, out of measure ill. A well-experienc'd hand would pass upon you at pleasure.

MAT. How mean you, sir, pass upon me?

BOB. Why, thus, sir — make a thrust at me — come in upon the answer, control [170 your point, and make a full career [84] at the body. The best-practis'd gallants of the time name it the passada; [85] a most desperate thrust, believe it!

MAT. Well, come, sir.

BOB. Why, you do not manage your weapon with any facility or grace to invite me. I have no spirit to play with you. Your dearth of judgment renders you tedious.

MAT. But one venue,[86] sir.   180

BOB. "Venue!" Fie. Most gross denomination as ever I heard. Oh, the "stoccata," while you live, sir; note that. — Come

---

[73] Straps on which the sword hung from the belt.
[74] Absolutely, utterly.
[75] Variegated; *i.e.*, overornate.
[76] Fool, simpleton.
[77] Carry it off.
[78] Do you suppose?
[79] Ground of quarrel.
[80] Jeronimo de Carranza's *De la filosofia de las armas* was a well-known sixteenth-century treatise.
[81] Thrust.
[82] Used for smoothing the bed when making it up, and also (according to Dr. Johnson) to hold the bedding in place. See on *The White Devil*, V, i, 213.
[83] Fair.
[84] Thrust.
[85] A lunge with one foot advanced.
[86] Bout.

put on your cloak, and we 'll go to some private place where you are acquainted, some tavern, or so — and have a bit. I 'll send for one of these fencers, and he shall breathe [87] you, by my direction ; and then I will teach you your trick. You shall kill him with it at the first, if you please. Why, I will learn you, by the [190 true judgment of the eye, hand, and foot, to control any enemy's point i' the world. Should your adversary confront you with a pistol, 't were nothing, by this hand, you should, by the same rule, control his bullet, in a line, except it were hail-shot, and spread. What money ha' you about you, Master Matthew?

MAT. Faith, I ha' not past a two shillings or so. 200

BOB. 'T is somewhat with the least [88] ; but come, we will have a bunch of radish and salt to taste our wine, and a pipe of tobacco to close the orifice of the stomach ; and then we 'll call upon young Wellbred. Perhaps we shall meet the Corydon [89] his brother there, and put him to the question. [*Exeunt.*]

ACT II — SCENE I [1]

[*Enter*] KITELY, CASH, *and* DOWNRIGHT.

KIT. Thomas, come hither.
There lies a note within upon my desk ;
Here, take my key — it is no matter neither. —
Where is the boy?
CASH.   Within, sir, i' the warehouse.
KIT. Let him tell over straight that Spanish gold,
And weigh it, with th' pieces of eight.[2] Do you
See the delivery of those silver stuffs
To Master Lucar. Tell him, if he will,
He shall ha' the grograns [3] at the rate I told him,
And I will meet him on the Exchange anon. 10
CASH. Good, sir.   [*Exit.*]
KIT.   Do you see that fellow, Brother Downright?
Dow. Ay, what of him?

---

[87] Exercise.   [88] *I.e.*, 't is very little.
[89] Clown, rustic.
[1] A room in Kitely's house in the Old Jewry. This street ran from the north side of the Poultry (which connected Cheapside and Cornhill), and derived its name from its medieval occupancy as a Jewish quarter.
[2] Spanish *pesos*, worth eight *reales* each.
[3] Grograns, coarse cloth of silk or silk and mohair.

KIT.   He is a jewel, Brother.
I took him of a child up at my door,
And christ'ned him, gave him mine own name, Thomas ;
Since bred him at the Hospital ; [4] where proving
A toward imp,[5] I call'd him home, and taught him
So much, as I have made him my cashier,
And giv'n him, who had none, a surname, Cash ;
And find him in his place so full of faith
That I durst trust my life into his hands. 20
Dow. So would not I in any bastard's, Brother,
As it is like he is, although I knew
Myself his father. But you said y' had somewhat
To tell me, gentle Brother. What is 't, what is 't?
KIT. Faith, I am very loth to utter it,
As fearing it may hurt your patience ;
But that I know your judgment is of strength
Against the nearness of affection ——
Dow. What need this circumstance? [6]
Pray you, be direct. 29
KIT. I will not say how much I do ascribe
Unto your friendship, nor in what regard
I hold your love ; but let my past behavior,
And usage of your sister, but confirm
How well I 'ave been affected to your —
Dow. You are too tedious ; come to the matter, the matter.
KIT. Then, without further ceremony, thus.
My brother Wellbred, sir, I know not how,
Of late is much declin'd in what he was,
And greatly alter'd in his disposition. 39
When he came first to lodge here in my house,
Ne'er trust me if I were not proud of him ;
Methought he bare himself in such a fashion,
So full of man, and sweetness in his carriage,
And, what was chief, it show'd not borrowed in him,
But all he did became him as his own,
And seem'd as perfect, proper, and possess'd,
As breath with life, or color with the blood.
But now, his course is so irregular,
So loose, affected, and depriv'd of grace,
And he himself withal so far fall'n off 50
From that first place, as scarce no note remains,
To tell men's judgments where he lately stood.

He 's grown a stranger to all due respect,
Forgetful of his friends ; and, not content
To stale himself [7] in all societies,
He makes my house here common as a mart,
A theatre, a public receptacle
For giddy humor, and diseased riot ;
And here, as in a tavern or a stews,   59
He and his wild associates spend their hours,
In repetition of lascivious jests,
Swear, leap, drink, dance, and revel night by
          night,
Control my servants ; and, indeed, what not?

Dow. 'Sdeynes,[8] I know not what I should
say to him, i' the whole world ! He values me
at a crack'd three-farthings, for aught I see.
It will never out o' the flesh that 's bred i' the
bone. I have told him enough, one would
think, if that would serve ; but counsel to him
is as good as a shoulder of mutton to a sick [70
horse.[9] Well ! he knows what to trust to, 'fore
George ! Let him spend, and spend, and domineer, till his heart ache ; an he think to be
reliev'd by me, when he is got into one o' your
city pounds, the Counters,[10] he has the wrong
sow by the ear, i' faith ; and claps his dish [11]
at the wrong man's door. I 'll lay my hand o'
my halfpenny, ere I part with 't to fetch him
out, I 'll assure him.

Kit. Nay, good Brother, let it not trouble
you thus.   80

Dow. 'Sdeath, he mads me ; I could eat my
very spur-leathers for anger ! But, why are
you so tame? Why do not you speak to him,
and tell him how he disquiets your house?

Kit. O, there are divers reasons to dissuade,
Brother.[12]
But, would yourself vouchsafe to travail in it
(Though but with plain and easy circum-
          stance),[13]
It would both come much better to his sense,
And savor less of stomach,[14] or of passion.
You are his elder brother, and that title   90
Both gives and warrants you authority,
Which, by your presence seconded, must breed
A kind of duty in him, and regard ;
Whereas, if I should intimate the least,
It would but add contempt to his neglect,
Heap worse on ill, make up a pile of hatred,
That in the rearing would come tott'ring down,

[7] Make himself cheap.
[8] By God's dines ; *i.e.*, by God's dignity or honor.
(*N.E.D.*)
[9] A stock expression.   [10] The City jails.
[11] Beggars clapped the covers of their wooden
dishes to attract attention.
[12] An " apparent " Alexandrine.
[13] *I.e.*, tactfully.   [14] Resentment.

And in the ruin bury all our love.
Nay, more than this, Brother ; if I should
          speak,   99
He would be ready, from his heat of humor,[15]
And overflowing of the vapor in him,
To blow the ears of his familiars
With the false breath of telling what disgraces
And low disparagements I had put upon him ;
Whilst they, sir, to relieve him in the fable,[16]
Make their loose comments upon every word,
Gesture, or look, I use ; mock me all over,
From my flat cap [17] unto my shining [18] shoes ;
And, out of their impetuous rioting phant'sies,
Beget some slander that shall dwell with
          me.   110
And what would that be, think you? Marry,
          this :
They would give out, because my wife is fair,
Myself but lately married, and my sister
Here sojourning a virgin in my house,
That I were jealous ! — nay, as sure as death,
That they would say ; and how that I had
          quarrell'd
My brother purposely, thereby to find
An apt pretext to banish them my house.

Dow. Mass, perhaps so ; they are like
          enough to do it.

Kit. Brother, they would, believe it ; so
          should I,   120
Like one of these penurious quacksalvers,
But set the bills [19] up to mine own disgrace,
And try experiments upon myself ;
Lend scorn and envy opportunity
To stab my reputation and good name —

Scene II [20]

[*To*] Kitely [*and*] Downright [*enter*] Mat-
          thew [*struggling with*] Bobadill.

Mat. I will speak to him —

Bob. Speak to him ! away ! By the foot of
Pharaoh, you shall not ! you shall not do him
that grace. — The time of day to you, gentleman o' the house. Is Master Wellbred
stirring?

Dow. How then? What should he do?

Bob. Gentleman of the house, it is to you.
Is he within, sir?

Kit. He came not to his lodging to-night,
sir, I assure you.   11

[15] Hot temper.
[16] During the narrative.
[17] It was one of the marks of the citizen.
[18] *I.e.*, blacked.
[19] Advertising posters.
[20] The same.

Dow. Why, do you hear, you?

Bob. The gentleman citizen hath satisfied me; I'll talk to no scavenger.

         [*Exeunt* Bobadill *and* Matthew.]

Dow. How! scavenger? Stay, sir, stay!

Kit. Nay, Brother Downright.

Dow. 'Heart! stand you away, an you love me.

Kit. You shall not follow him now, I pray you, Brother;
Good faith you shall not; I will overrule
you.   20

Dow. Ha! scavenger? Well, go to, I say little; but, by this good day (God forgive me I should swear), if I put it up [21] so, say I am the rankest cow that ever piss'd. 'Sdeins, an I swallow this, I'll ne'er draw my sword in the sight of Fleet Street again while I live; I'll sit in a barn with madge-howlet, and catch mice first. Scavenger! Heart! and I'll go near to fill that huge tumbrel-slop [22] of yours with somewhat, an I have good luck: your Garagantua breech cannot carry it away so. [31]

Kit. Oh, do not fret yourself thus; never think on't.

Dow. These are my brother's consorts, these! These are his cam'rades, his walking mates! He's a gallant, a cavaliero too, right hangman cut! [23] Let me not live, an I could not find in my heart to swinge the whole ging [24] of 'em, one after another, and begin with him first. I am griev'd it should be said he is my brother, and take these courses. Well, as [40 he brews, so he shall drink, 'fore George, again. Yet he shall hear on't, and that tightly too, an I live, i' faith.

Kit. But, Brother, let your reprehension, then,
Run in an easy current, not o'erhigh
Carried with rashness, or devouring choler;
But rather use the soft persuading way,
Whose powers will work more gently, and compose
Th' imperfect thoughts you labor to reclaim;
More winning than enforcing the consent.   50

Dow. Ay, ay, let me alone for that, I warrant you. —   *Bell rings.*

Kit. How now! Oh, the bell rings to breakfast.
Brother, I pray you go in, and bear my wife Company till I come. I'll but give order

For some dispatch of business to my servants.   [*Exit* Downright.]

Scene III [25]

To Kitely, [*enter*] Cob.

Kit. What, Cob! our maids will have you by the back, i' faith, for coming so late this morning.

Cob. Perhaps so, sir; take heed somebody have not them by the belly, for walking so late in the evening. (*He passes by with his tankard.*)

Kit. Well; yet my troubled spirit's somewhat eas'd,
Though not repos'd in that security
As I could wish. But I must be content,
Howe'er I set a face on't to the world.   10
Would I had lost this finger, at a venture,
So Wellbred had ne'er lodg'd within my house.
Why't cannot be, where there is such resort
Of wanton gallants and young revellers,
That any woman should be honest [26] long.
Is't like that factious beauty will preserve
The public weal of chastity unshaken,
When such strong motives muster and make head [27]
Against her single peace? No, no! Beware
When mutual appetite doth meet to treat,   20
And spirits of one kind and quality
Come once to parley in the pride of blood [28] —
It is no slow conspiracy that follows.
Well, to be plain, if I but thought the time
Had answer'd their affections,[29] all the world
Should not persuade me but I were a cuckold.
Marry, I hope they ha' not got that start;
For opportunity hath balk'd 'em yet,
And shall do still, while I have eyes and ears
To attend the impositions of my heart.   30
My presence shall be as an iron bar
'Twixt the conspiring motions of desire;
Yea, every look or glance mine eye ejects
Shall check occasion, as one doth his slave,
When he forgets the limits of prescription.

[*Enter* Dame Kitely.]

Dame K. Sister Bridget, pray you fetch down the rose-water,[30] above in the closet. — Sweetheart, will you come in to breakfast?

Kit. [*aside*] An she have overheard me now!

Dame Kit. I pray thee, good muss,[31] we [40 stay for you.

---

[21] Pocket it, submit to it.
[22] An extravagant fashion in breeches made them absurdly large by stuffing them.
[23] Regular hangman's style.
[24] Beat the whole gang.

[25] The same.   [26] Chaste.
[27] Gather forces, rebel.   [28] Passion.
[29] *I.e.*, had given them a suitable opportunity to indulge their desires.
[30] Served with fruit.   [31] Mouse.

KIT. [aside] By Heaven, I would not for a thousand angels.[32]

DAME K. What ail you, sweetheart? are you not well? Speak, good muss.

KIT. Troth my head aches extremely on a sudden.[33]

DAME K. Oh, the Lord!

KIT. How now! What?

DAME K. Alas, how it burns! Muss, keep you warm; good truth it is this new disease![34] There's a number are troubled withal! [50 For love's sake, sweetheart, come in out of the air.

KIT. How simple, and how subtle, are her answers!
A new disease, and many troubled with it!
Why true; she heard me, all the world to nothing.

DAME K. I pray thee, good sweetheart, come in; the air will do you harm, in troth.

KIT. The air! she has me i' the wind![35] — Sweetheart!
I'll come to you presently; 't will away, I hope.   59

DAME K. Pray Heaven it do.   [Exit.]

KIT. A new disease! I know not, new or old,
But it may well be call'd poor mortals' plague;
For, like a pestilence, it doth infect
The houses[36] of the brain. First it begins
Solely to work upon the phantasy,
Filling her seat with such pestiferous air
As soon corrupts the judgment; and from thence
Sends like contagion to the memory,
Still each to other giving the infection,
Which, as a subtle vapor, spreads itself   70
Confusedly through every sensive part,
Till not a thought or motion in the mind
Be free from the black poison of suspect.[37]
Ah, but what misery[38] is it to know this!
Or, knowing it, to want the mind's erection

In such extremes? Well, I will once more strive,
In spite of this black cloud, myself to be,
And shake the fever off that thus shakes me.   [Exit.]

SCENE IV [39]

[Enter] BRAINWORM [disguised as a soldier].

BRAI. 'Slid, I cannot choose but laugh to see myself translated thus, from a poor creature to a creator; for now must I create an intolerable sort[40] of lies, or my present profession loses the grace. And yet the lie, to a man of my coat, is as ominous a fruit as the fico.[41] O, sir, it holds for good polity ever, to have that outwardly in vilest estimation, that inwardly is most dear to us. So much for my borrowed shape.[42] Well, the troth is, my old master intends to fol- [10 low my young, dry-foot,[43] over Moorfields to London, this morning. Now, I, knowing of this hunting-match, or rather conspiracy, and to insinuate with my young master (for so must we that are blue waiters,[44] and men of hope and service do, or perhaps we may wear motley at the year's end, and who wears motley,[45] — you know), have got me afore, in this disguise, de-termining here to lie in ambuscado, and inter-cept him in the midway. If I can but get [20 his cloak, his purse, his hat, nay, anything to cut him off, that is, to stay his journey, *Veni, vidi, vici,* I may say with Captain Caesar: I am made for ever, i' faith. Well, now must I practise to get the true garb[46] of one of these lance-knights,[47] my arm here, and my[48] —— young Master! and his cousin, Master Ste-phen, as I am true counterfeit man of war, and no soldier!   [He retires.]

[Enter EDWARD KNOWELL and STEPHEN.]

E. KNOW. So, sir! and how then, Coz? [30

STEP. 'Sfoot! I have lost my purse, I think.

E. KNOW. How! lost your purse? Where? When had you it?

STEP. I cannot tell; stay.

BRAI. [aside] 'Slid, I am afeard they will know me; would I could get by them!

E. KNOW. What, ha' you it?

STEP. No; I think I was bewitch'd, I ——

---

[32] Gold coins worth about ten shillings each.
[33] The inevitable jest on the horns which were supposed to grow on the cuckold's forehead.
[34] This term appears to have been used for various fevers which the medical science of the time was unable to cope with. Prince Henry died of a fever called "the new disease."
[35] She scents (my suspicions).
[36] The three ventricles of the current anatomy; they housed imagination, reason, and memory.
[37] Suspicion.
[38] F₁ *miserie 'is,* indicating elision or rapid pro-nunciation. Since in speaking blank verse the latter method of coping with metrical excess is usually preferable, the present edition does not give as elided such expressions as *I 'have,* which most modern editors print *I 've.*

[39] Moorfields.   [40] Set, lot.
[41] To make the fig was an obscene gesture.
[42] Costume.
[43] By the scent, without the track. Carter sug-gests a humorous allusion to the marshy character of Moorfields.
[44] Blue was the ordinary livery of serving men.
[45] Fools.   [46] Bearing.   [47] Pikemen.
[48] Q *my: Gods so, young master.*

E. Know. Nay, do not weep the loss ; hang it, let it go. 41

Step. Oh, it 's here. No, an it had been lost, I had not car'd, but for a jet ring Mistress Mary sent me.

E. Know. A jet ring ! Oh, the posy, the posy ?

Step. Fine, i' faith !

"Though Fancy sleep,
　My love is deep."

Meaning that, though I did not fancy her, [50 yet she loved me dearly.

E. Know. Most excellent !

Step. And then I sent her another, and my posy was,

"The deeper the sweeter,
　I 'll be judg'd by St. Peter."

E. Know. How, by St. Peter? I do not conceive that !

Step. Marry, St. Peter, to make up the metre. 60

E. Know. Well, there the saint was your good patron : he help'd you at your need ; thank him, thank him.

Brai. [*aside*] I cannot take leave on 'em so ; I will venture, come what will. — (*He is come back.*) Gentlemen, please you change a few crowns for a very excellent good blade here? I am a poor gentleman, a soldier, one that in the better state of my fortunes scorn'd so mean a refuge ; but now it is the humor of neces- [70 sity to have it so. You seem to be gentlemen well affected to martial men, else I should rather die with silence, than live with [49] shame. However, vouchsafe to remember it is my want speaks, not myself. This condition agrees not with my spirit ——

E. Know. Where hast thou serv'd?

Brai. May it please you, sir, in all the late wars of Bohemia, Hungaria, Dalmatia, Po- land,[50] — where not, sir? I have been a [80 poor servitor by sea and land any time this four- teen years, and follow'd the fortunes of the best commanders in Christendom. I was twice shot at the taking of Aleppo,[51] once at the relief of Vienna ;[52] I have been at Marseilles, Naples, and the Adriatic gulf ;[53] a gentleman-

slave in the galleys, thrice, where I was most dangerously shot in the head, through both the thighs ; and yet, being thus maim'd, I am void of maintenance, nothing left me but my scars, the noted marks of my resolution. 91

Step. How will you sell this rapier, friend?

Brai. Generous sir, I refer it to your own judgment ; you are a gentleman ; give me what you please.

Step. True, I am a gentleman, I know that, friend ; but what though? I pray you say, what would you ask !

Brai. I assure you, the blade may become the side or thigh of the best prince in Europe.

E. Know. Ay, with a velvet scabbard, [101 I think.

Step. Nay, an 't be mine, it shall have a velvet scabbard, Coz, that 's flat. I 'd not wear it, as 't is, and you would give me an angel.

Brai. At your Worship's pleasure, sir ; nay, 't is a most pure Toledo.

Step. I had rather it were a Spaniard ! But tell me, what shall I give you for it? [110 An it had a silver hilt ——

E. Know. Come, come, you shall not buy it. Hold, there 's a shilling, fellow ; take thy rapier.

Step. Why, but I will buy it now, because you say so ; and there 's another shilling, fel- low. I scorn to be outbidden. What, shall I walk with a cudgel, like Higginbottom,[54] and may have a rapier for money? 119

E. Know. You may buy one in the City.

Step. Tut ! I 'll buy this i' the field, so I will ; I have a mind to 't, because 't is a field rapier. — Tell me your lowest price.

E. Know. You shall not buy it, I say.

Step. By this money, but I will, though I give more than 't is worth.

E. Know. Come away, you are a fool.

Step. Friend, I am a fool, that 's granted ; but I 'll have it, for that word's sake. Follow me for your money. 130

Brai. At your service, sir. [*Exeunt.*]

Scene V [55]

[Enter] Knowell.

Know. I cannot lose the thought, yet, of this letter

Sent to my son ; nor leave t' admire [56] the change

---

[49] By.

[50] All these countries were involved during the sixteenth century in the attempt of the Turks to extend their empire westward.

[51] By the Turks in 1516.

[52] Unsuccessfully besieged by the Turks in 1529. Marseilles and Naples had endured sieges not long before.

[53] Perhaps at the battle of Lepanto in 1571. (Nicholson, cited by Carter.)

[54] Evidently a topical allusion, but unidentified as yet.　　　[55] The same.　　　[56] Wonder at.

Of manners, and the breeding of our youth
Within the kingdom, since myself was one.
When I was young, he liv'd not in the stews
Durst have conceiv'd a scorn, and utter'd it,
On a gray head ; age was authority
Against a buffoon, and a man had then
A certain reverence paid unto his years,
That had none due unto his life. So much [10
The sanctity of some prevail'd for others.
But now we all are fall'n ; youth, from their
     fear,
And age, from that which bred it, good ex-
     ample.
Nay, would ourselves were not the first, even
     parents,[57]
That did destroy the hopes in our own chil-
     dren ;
Or they not learn'd our vices in their cradles,
And suck'd in our ill customs with their milk !
Ere all their teeth be born, or they can speak,
We make their palates cunning ! The first
     words
We form their tongues with are licentious
     jests !   20
Can it call " whore "? cry " bastard "? Oh,
     then kiss it !
A witty child ! — Can't swear? The father's
     darling !
Give it two plums. Nay, rather than 't shall
     learn
No bawdy song, the mother herself will teach
     it !
But this is in the infancy, the days
Of the long coat ; when it puts on the breeches,
It will put off all this. Ay, it is like,
When it is gone into the bone already.
No, no ; this dye goes deeper than the coat,
Or shirt, or skin ; it stains unto the liver   30
And heart, in some ; and, rather than it should
     not,
Note what we fathers do ! Look how we live !
What mistresses we keep ! at what expense,
In our sons' eyes ! where they may handle our
     gifts,
Hear our lascivious courtships, see our dal-
     liance,
Taste of the same provoking meats with us,
To ruin of our states ! Nay, when our own
Portion is fled, to prey on their remainder
We call them into fellowship of vice !
Bait 'em with the young chambermaid, to
     seal ! [58]   40

And teach 'em all bad ways to buy affliction !
This is one path ! but there are millions more,
In which we spoil our own, with leading them.
Well, I thank Heaven, I never yet was he
That travell'd with my son, before sixteen,
To show him the Venetian courtesans ;
Nor read the grammar of cheating I had made,
To my sharp boy, at twelve, repeating still
The rule, " Get money ; " still, " Get money,
     boy ;
No matter by what means ; money will do [50
More, boy, than my Lord's letter." [59]   Neither
     have I
Dress'd snails or mushrooms curiously before
     him,
Perfum'd my sauces, and taught him how to
     make 'em ;
Preceding still, with my gray gluttony,
At all the ordinaries, and only fear'd
His palate should degenerate, not his manners.
These are the trade of fathers, now ! However,
My son, I hope, hath met within my threshold
None of these household precedents, which are
     strong
And swift to rape youth to their precipice.   60
But let the house at home be ne'er so clean
Swept, or kept sweet from filth, nay dust and
     cobwebs,
If he will live abroad with his companions,
In dung and leystals,[60] it is worth a fear ;
Nor is the danger of conversing less
Than all that I have mention'd of example.

          [*Enter* BRAINWORM, *disguised.*]

  BRAI. [*aside*] My master ! nay, faith, have
at you ; I am flesh'd [61] now, I have sped [62] so
well. — Worshipful sir, I beseech you, respect[63]
the estate of a poor soldier ; I am asham'd [70
of this base course of life, — God's my comfort
— but extremity provokes me to 't : what
remedy?
  KNOW. I have not for you, now.
  BRAI. By the faith I bear unto truth, gentleman, it is no ordinary custom in me, but
only to preserve manhood. I protest to you, a
man I have been ; a man I may be, by your
sweet bounty.
  KNOW. 'Pray thee, good friend, be satisfied.   80
  BRAI. Good sir, by that hand, you may do
the part of a kind gentleman, in lending a poor

---

[57] This tirade is based on Quintilian's *Institutio Oratoria*, I, ii, 6–8, combined with Juvenal, xiv, 1–83.
[58] To sign away their rights in property.
[59] Based on Horace's first epistle. The rest of the speech is indebted to the fourteenth satire of Juvenal.
[60] Dunghills.
[61] Initiated.   [62] Fared, done.   [63] Heed.

soldier the price of two cans of beer, a matter of small value. The King of Heaven shall pay you, and I shall rest thankful. Sweet Worship ——

KNOW. Nay, an you be so importunate ——

BRAI. Oh, tender sir, need will have its course ; I was not made to this vile use. Well, the edge of the enemy could not have [90 abated me so much ; it's hard when a man hath serv'd in his prince's cause, and be thus — (*He weeps.*) Honorable Worship, let me derive a small piece of silver from you ; it shall not be given in the course of time.[64] By this good ground, I was fain to pawn my rapier last night for a poor supper ; I had suck'd the hilts long before, I am a pagan else. Sweet Honor ——

KNOW. Believe me, I am taken with some wonder,
To think a fellow of thy outward presence [100
Should, in the frame and fashion of his mind,
Be so degenerate, and sordid-base !
Art thou a man, and sham'st thou not to beg?
To practise such a servile kind of life?
Why, were thy education ne'er so mean,
Having thy limbs, a thousand fairer courses
Offer themselves to thy election.
Either the wars might still supply thy wants,
Or service of some virtuous gentleman,
Or honest labor ; nay, what can I name, 110
But would become thee better than to beg?
But men of thy condition feed on sloth,
As doth the beetle on the dung she breeds in ;
Nor caring how the mettle of your minds
Is eaten with the rust of idleness.
Now, afore me,[65] whate'er he be, that should
Relieve a person of thy quality,
While thou insists [66] in this loose desperate course,
I would esteem the sin not thine, but his.

BRAI. Faith, sir, I would gladly find [120 some other course, if so ——

KNOW. Ay, you'd gladly find it, but you will not seek it.

BRAI. Alas, sir, where should a man seek? In the wars, there's no ascent by desert in these days ; but —— and for service, would it were as soon purchas'd,[67] as wish'd for ! — The air's my comfort. — I know what I would say —

KNOW. What's thy name?

BRAI. Please you, Fitz-Sword, sir.

KNOW. Fitz-Sword? — 130
Say that a man should entertain thee now,
Wouldst thou be honest, humble, just, and true?

BRAI. Sir, by the place and honor of a soldier ——

KNOW. Nay, nay, I like not those affected oaths.
Speak plainly, man, what think'st thou of my words?

BRAI. Nothing, sir, but wish my fortunes were as happy as my service should be honest.

KNOW. Well, follow me ; I'll prove thee, if thy deeds
Will carry a proportion to thy words. [*Exit.*]

BRAI. Yes, sir, straight ; I'll but garter [140 my hose. — Oh, that my belly were hoop'd now, for I am ready to burst with laughing ! Never was bottle or bagpipe fuller. 'Slid, was there ever seen a fox in years to betray himself thus? Now shall I be possess'd of all his counsels ; and, by that conduit, my young master. Well, he is resolv'd to prove [68] my honesty ; faith, and I am resolv'd to prove his patience ; oh, I shall abuse [69] him intolerably. This small piece of service will bring him clean [150 out of love with the soldier for ever. He will never come within the sign of it, the sight of a cassock,[70] or a musket-rest again. He will hate the musters at Mile End [71] for it, to his dying day. It's no matter ; let the world think me a bad counterfeit, if I cannot give him the slip [72] at an instant. Why, this is better than to have stay'd his journey ! Well, I'll follow him. Oh, how I long to be employed ! [*Exit.*]

ACT III — SCENE I [1]

[Enter] MATTHEW, WELLBRED, *[and]* BOBADILL.

MAT. Yes, faith, sir, we were at your lodging to seek you too.

WEL. Oh, I came not there to-night.

BOB. Your brother delivered us as much.

WEL. Who, my brother Downright?

BOB. He. Master Wellbred, I know not in what kind you hold me ; but let me say to you this : as sure as honor, I esteem it so much out

---

[64] *I.e.*, it shall be given with a time-limit, as a loan. (Perhaps with the further implication that it will make the same return as bread cast upon the waters.)
[65] A mild oath.   [66] Persistest.
[67] Got, acquired.

[68] Test.   [69] Deceive.
[70] Soldier's cloak.
[71] Where the London militia drilled.
[72] Punning on "slip" = counterfeit coin.
[1] The old Jewry. A room in the Windmill tavern

of the sunshine of reputation to throw the least
beam of regard upon such a —— 10

WEL. Sir, I must hear no ill words of my
brother.

BOB. I protest to you, as I have a thing to
be sav'd about me, I never saw any gentlemanlike part ——

WEL. Good Captain, faces about to some
other discourse.

BOB. With your leave, sir, an there were no
more men living upon the face of the earth, I
should not fancy him, by St. George ! 20

MAT. Troth, nor I ; he is of a rustical cut, I
know not how ; he doth not carry himself like
a gentleman of fashion —

WEL. Oh, Master Matthew, that's a grace
peculiar but to a few, *quos aequus amavit
Jupiter.*[2]

MAT. I understand you, sir.

WEL. No question, you do — [*aside*] or you
do not, sir. —

YOUNG KNOWELL *enters* [*with* STEPHEN].

Ned Knowell ! by my soul, welcome. How [30
doest thou, sweet spirit, my genius? 'Slid, I
shall love Apollo and the mad Thespian girls[3]
the better, while I live, for this, my dear Fury ;
now I see there's some love in thee ! Sirrah,
these be the two I writ to thee of : nay, what a
drowsy humor is this now? Why doest thou
not speak?

E. KNOW. Oh, you are a fine gallant ; you
sent me a rare letter !

WEL. Why, was't not rare? 40

E. KNOW. Yes, I'll be sworn, I was ne'er
guilty of reading the like ; match it in all
Pliny, or Symmachus'[4] epistles, and I'll have
my judgment burn'd in the ear for a rogue :
make much of thy vein, for it is inimitable.
But I mar'l[5] what camel it was that had the
carriage of it ; for doubtless he was no ordinary
beast that brought it !

WEL. Why?

E. KNOW. " Why? " sayest thou? [50
Why, doest thou think that any reasonable
creature, especially in the morning, the sober
time of the day, too, could have mista'en my
father for me?

WEL. 'Slid, you jest, I hope !

[2] Whom the just Jove has loved. (Vergil, *Aeneid*,
vi, 129, 130.)
[3] The Muses.
[4] A famous Roman statesman and letter-writer of
the fourth century.
[5] Marvel.

E. KNOW. Indeed, the best use we can turn
it to, is to make a jest on 't, now ; but I'll assure you, my father had the full view o' your
flourishing style some hour before I saw it.

WEL. What a dull slave was this ! But, [60
sirrah, what said he to it, i' faith?

E. KNOW. Nay, I know not what he said ;
but I have a shrewd guess what he thought.

WEL. What, what?

E. KNOW. Marry, that thou art some
strange, dissolute young fellow, and I a grain
or two better, for keeping thee company.

WEL. Tut ! that thought is like the moon in
her last quarter ; 't will change shortly. But,
sirrah, I pray thee be acquainted with my [70
two hang-bys here ; thou wilt take exceeding
pleasure in 'em if thou hear'st 'em once go —
my wind instruments. I'll wind 'em up —
but what strange piece of silence is this? The
sign of the Dumb Man?

E. KNOW. Oh, sir, a kinsman of mine, one
that may make your music the fuller, an he
please ; he has his humor, sir.

WEL. Oh, what is 't, what is 't?

E. KNOW. Nay, I'll neither do your [80
judgment nor his folly that wrong as to prepare your apprehension ; I'll leave him to the
mercy o' your search ; if you can take him, so !

WEL. Well, Captain Bobadill, Master Matthew, pray you know this gentleman here ; he
is a friend of mine, and one that will deserve
your affection. — (*to* MASTER STEPHEN) I
know not your name, sir, but I shall be glad of
any occasion to render me more familiar to you.

STEP. My name is Master Stephen, sir ; [90
I am this gentleman's own cousin, sir ; his
father is mine uncle, sir. I am somewhat melancholy ; but you shall command me, sir, in
whatsoever is incident to a gentleman.

BOB. (*to* KNOWELL) Sir, I must tell you
this, I am no general man ; but for Master
Wellbred's sake (you may embrace it at what
height of favor you please), I do communicate
with you, and conceive you to be a gentleman
of some parts ; I love few words. 100

E. KNOW. And I fewer, sir ; I have scarce
enough to thank you.

MAT. (*to* MASTER STEPHEN) But are you,
indeed, sir, so given to it?

STEP. Ay, truly, sir, I am mightily given to
melancholy.

MAT. Oh, it's your only fine humor, sir :
your true melancholy breeds your perfect fine
wit, sir. I am melancholy myself, divers times,
sir, and then do I no more but take pen [110

and paper presently, and overflow you half a score or a dozen of sonnets at a sitting.

E. KNOW. [*aside*] [6] Sure he utters them [7] then by the gross.

STEP. Truly, sir, and I love such things out of measure. [8]

E. KNOW. [*aside*] Ay, faith, better than in measure, [9] I 'll undertake.

MAT. Why, I pray you, sir, make use of my study; it 's at your service.   120

STEP. I thank you, sir; I shall be bold, I warrant you. Have you a stool there to be melancholy upon?

MAT. That I have, sir, and some papers there of mine own doing, at idle hours, that you 'll say there 's some sparks of wit in 'em, when you see them.

WEL. [*aside*] Would the sparks would kindle once, and become a fire amongst 'em! I might see self-love burnt for her heresy.   130

STEP. Cousin, is it well? Am I melancholy enough?

E. KNOW. Oh, ay, excellent.

WEL. Captain Bobadill, why muse you so?

E. KNOW. He is melancholy too.

BOB. Faith, sir, I was thinking of a most honorable piece of service, was perform'd tomorrow, being St. Mark's day, shall be some ten years now!

E. KNOW. In what place, Captain?   140

BOB. Why, at the beleag'ring of Strigonium, [10] where, in less than two hours, seven hundred resolute gentlemen, as any were in Europe, lost their lives upon the breach. I 'll tell you, gentlemen, it was the first, but the best leaguer that ever I beheld with these eyes, except the taking in [11] of — what do you call it? [12] last year, by the Genoways; [13] but that, of all other, was the most fatal and dangerous exploit that ever I was rang'd in, [150 since I first bore arms before the face of the enemy, as I am a gentleman and [14] soldier!

STEP. So! I had as lief as an angel I could swear as well as that gentleman!

E. KNOW. Then, you were a servitor at both, it seems; at Strigonium, and what do you call 't?

BOB. O Lord, sir! By St. George, I was

the first man that ent'red the breach; and had I not effected it with resolution, I had [160 been slain if I had had a million of lives.

E. KNOW. [*aside*] 'T was pity you had not ten; a cat's and your own, i' faith. — But, was it possible?

MAT. Pray you mark this discourse, sir.

STEP. So I do.

BOB. I assure you, upon my reputation, 't is true, and yourself shall confess.

E. KNOW. [*aside*] You must bring me to the rack, first.   170

BOB. Observe me judicially, sweet sir. They had planted me three demi-culverins [15] just in the mouth of the breach; now, sir, as we were to give on, [16] their master-gunner (a man of no mean skill and mark, you must think), confronts me with his linstock, [17] ready to give fire; I, spying his intendment, discharg'd my petronel [18] in his bosom, and with these single arms, my poor rapier, ran violently upon the Moors that guarded the ordnance, and [180 put 'em pellmell to the sword.

WEL. To the sword! To the rapier, Captain!

E. KNOW. Oh, it was a good figure observ'd, sir! — But did you all this, Captain, without hurting your blade?

BOB. Without any impeach o' the earth: you shall perceive, sir. — It is the most fortunate weapon that ever rid on poor gentleman's thigh. Shall I tell you, sir? You talk [190 of Morglay, Excalibur, Durindana, [19] or so? Tut! I lend no credit to that is fabled of 'em. I know the virtue of mine own, and therefore I dare the boldlier maintain it.

STEP. I mar'l whether it be a Toledo or no.

BOB. A most perfect Toledo, I assure you, sir.

STEP. I have a countryman of his here.

MAT. Pray you, let 's see, sir; yes, faith, it is.   200

BOB. This a Toledo? Pish!

STEP. Why do you pish, Captain?

BOB. A Fleming, by Heaven! I 'll buy them for a guilder apiece, an I would have a thousand of them.

E. KNOW. How say you, Cousin? I told you thus much!

WEL. Where bought you it, Master Stephen?

[6] Indicated in F[1] by parentheses around the speech.
[7] Puts them into circulation.
[8] Exceedingly.
[9] *I.e.*, metrically correct.
[10] Gran in Hungary, recaptured from the Turks in 1595.
[11] Capture.   [12] Q *Tortosa*.   [13] Genoese.
[14] F[3] adds *a*.

[15] A kind of cannon.
[16] Charge.
[17] The staff that held the lighted match.
[18] Carbine.
[19] The swords of Bevis, Arthur, and Orlando.

STEP. Of a scurvy rogue soldier, — a [210 hundred of lice go with him! He swore it was a Toledo.

BOB. A poor provant [20] rapier, no better.

MAT. Mass, I think it be indeed, now I look on 't better !

E. KNOW. Nay, the longer you look on 't, the worse. Put it up, put it up.

STEP. Well, I will put it up ; but by — I ha' forgot the Captain's oath ; I thought to ha' sworn by it — an e'er I meet him —— 220

WEL. O, it is past help now, sir ; you must have patience.

STEP. Whoreson, cony-catching [21] rascal ! I could eat the very hilts for anger.

E. KNOW. A sign of good digestion ! You have an ostrich stomach, Cousin.

STEP. A stomach ! Would I had him here, you should see an I had a stomach.[22]

WEL. It 's better as 't is. — Come, gentlemen, shall we go? 230

SCENE II [23]

[To them enter] BRAINWORM.

E. KNOW. A miracle, Cousin ; look here, look here !

STEP. Oh ! God's lid. By your leave, do you know me, sir?

BRAI. Ay, sir, I know you by sight.

STEP. You sold me a rapier, did you not?

BRAI. Yes, marry, did I, sir.

STEP. You said it was a Toledo, ha?

BRAI. True, I did so.

STEP. But it is none? 10

BRAI. No, sir, I confess it ; it is none.

STEP. Do you confess it? Gentlemen, bear witness, he has confess'd it. By God's will, an you had not confess'd it ——

E. KNOW. Oh, Cousin, forbear, forbear.

STEP. Nay, I have done, Cousin.

WEL. Why, you have done like a gentleman ; he has confess'd it : what would you more?

STEP. Yet, by his leave, he is a rascal, [20 under his favor, do you see?

E. KNOW. Ay, by his leave, he is, and under favor — a pretty piece of civility ! — *[aside to* WELLBORN] Sirrah, how doest thou like him?

WEL. *[aside]* Oh, it 's a most precious fool ; make much on him. I can compare him to

nothing more happily than a drum ; for every one may play upon him.

E. KNOW. *[aside]* No, no, a child's whistle were far the fitter. 30

BRAI. Shall I entreat a word with you?

E. KNOW. With me, sir? You have not another Toledo to sell, ha' you?

BRAI. You are conceited,[24] sir. Your name is Master Knowell, as I take it?

E. KNOW. You are i' the right ! You mean not to proceed in the catechism, do you?

BRAI. No, sir ; I am none of that coat.[25]

E. KNOW. Of as bare a coat, though ! Well, say, sir. 40

BRAI. *[taking him aside]* Faith, sir, I am but servant to the drum extraordinary ; [26] and indeed, this smoky varnish being wash'd off, and three or four patches remov'd, I appear your Worship's in reversion, after the decease of your good father, Brainworm.

E. KNOW. Brainworm ! 'Slight, what breath of a conjurer hath blown thee hither in this shape?

BRAI. The breath o' your letter, sir, this [50 morning ; the same that blew you to the Windmill, and your father after you.

E. KNOW. My father !

BRAI. Nay, never start ; 't is true ; he has follow'd you over the fields by the foot, as you would do a hare i' the snow.

E. KNOW. Sirrah Wellbred, what shall we do, sirrah? My father is come over after me.

WEL. *[joining them]* Thy father ! Where is he? 60

BRAI. At Justice Clement's house, here [27] in Coleman Street, where he but stays my return ; and then ——

WEL. Who 's this? Brainworm?

BRAI. The same, sir.

WEL. Why how, i' the name of wit, com'st thou transmuted thus?

BRAI. Faith, a device, a device ; nay, for the love of reason, gentlemen, and avoiding the danger, stand not here ; withdraw ; and [70 I 'll tell you all.

WEL. But art thou sure he will stay thy return?

BRAI. Do I live, sir? What a question is that !

WEL. We 'll prorogue his expectation, then, a little. Brainworm, thou shalt go with us. —

---

[20] *I.e.,* of the sort regularly issued by the government.
[21] Swindling.
[22] Punning on "stomach" = resentment.
[23] The same.

[24] Witty.
[25] *I.e.,* I am not a cleric.
[26] *I.e.,* I am not a regular follower of the drum, not a genuine soldier. (Kittredge.)
[27] F [2, 3], om. *here.*

Come on, gentlemen. — Nay, I pray thee,
sweet Ned, droop not. 'Heart, an our wits be
so wretchedly dull that one old plodding [80
brain can outstrip us all, would we were e'en
press'd to make porters of, and serve out the
remnant of our days in Thames Street, or at
Customhouse Quay, in a civil war against the
carmen !

BRAI. Amen, amen, amen, say I. [*Exeunt.*]

SCENE III [28]

[*Enter*] KITELY [*and*] CASH.

KIT. What says he, Thomas? Did you
    speak with him?
CASH. He will expect you, sir, within this
    half hour.
KIT. Has he the money ready, can you tell?
CASH. Yes, sir, the money was brought in
    last night.
KIT. O, that is well ; fetch me my cloak,
    my cloak ! —   [*Exit* CASH.]
Stay, let me see ; an hour to go and come ;
Ay, that will be the least ; and then 't will be
An hour before I can dispatch with him,
Or very near ; well, I will say two hours.
Two hours ! ha ! things never dreamt of yet,
May be contriv'd, ay, and effected too,   11
In two hours' absence — well, I will not go.
Two hours ! No, fleering Opportunity,
I will not give your subtilty that scope.
Who will not judge him worthy to be robb'd,
That sets his doors wide open to a thief,
And shows the felon where his treasure lies?
Again, what earthly spirit but will attempt
To taste the fruit of beauty's golden tree,
When leaden sleep seals up the dragon's eyes?
I will not go. Business, go by, for once. 21
No, beauty, no ; you are of too good caract [29]
To be left so, without a guard, or open !
Your lustre, too, 'll inflame at any distance,
Draw courtship to you, as a jet doth straws ;
Put motion in a stone, strike fire from ice,
Nay, make a porter leap you, with his burden.
You must be then kept up, close, and well
    watch'd,
For, give you opportunity, no quicksand
Devours or swallows swifter ! He that lends
His wife, if she be fair, or time or place   31
Compels her to be false. I will not go.
The dangers are too many. — And then the
    dressing
Is a most main attractive ! Our great heads

Within the City never were in safety
Since our wives wore these little caps. I 'll
    change 'em ;
I 'll change 'em straight in mine. Mine shall
    no more
Wear three-pil'd [30] acorns, to make my horns
    ache.
Nor will I go. I am resolv'd for that.

[*Re-enter* CASH *with a cloak.*]

Carry in my cloak again. — Yet stay. — Yet
    do, too :   40
I will defer going, on all occasions.
    CASH. Sir, Snare, your scrivener, will be
    there with th' bonds.
    KIT. That 's true ! Fool on me ! I had
    clean forgot it ;
I must go. What 's a'clock?
    CASH.   Exchange time,[31] sir.
    KIT. 'Heart, then will Wellbred presently
    be here too,
With one or other of his loose consorts.
I am a knave if I know what to say,
What course to take, or which way to resolve.
My brain, methinks, is like an hourglass,
Wherein my imaginations run like sands, 50
Filling up time ; but then are turn'd and
    turn'd.
So that I know not what to stay upon,
And less, to put in act. — It shall be so.
Nay, I dare build upon his secrecy ;
He knows not to deceive me. — Thomas !
    CASH.   Sir.
    KIT. Yet now I have bethought me, too, I
    will not. —
Thomas, is Cob within?
    CASH.   I think he be, sir.
    KIT. But he 'll prate, too ; there's no
    speech of him.
No, there were no man o' the earth to [32]
    Thomas,
If I durst trust him ; there is all the doubt. 60
But should he have a chink in him, I were gone.
Lost i' my fame for ever, talk for th' Ex-
    change !
The manner he hath stood with, till this pres-
    ent,
Doth promise no such change ! What should
    I fear then?
Well, come what will, I 'll tempt my fortune
    once.

[28] Kitely's warehouse.
[29] *I.e.*, carat, value.

[30] *I.e.*, rich velvet.
[31] Q *Past ten.* Note that the whole action occupies
but a single day.
[32] Comparable to.

Thomas — you may deceive me, but I hope —
Your love to me is more —
　CASH.　　　　　　　　Sir, if a servant's
Duty, with faith, may be call'd love, you are
More than in hope, you are possess'd of it.
　KIT. I thank you heartily, Thomas ; gi' me
　　your hand ;　　　　　　　　　　　70
With all my heart, good Thomas. I have,
　Thomas,
A secret to impart unto you — but,
When once you have it, I must seal your lips
　up —
So far I tell you, Thomas.
　CASH.　　　　　　　　Sir, for that ——
　KIT. Nay, hear me out. Think I esteem
　　you, Thomas,
When I will let you in thus to my private.
It is a thing sits nearer to my crest,[33]
Than thou art 'ware of, Thomas ; if thou
　shouldst
Reveal it, but ——
　CASH.　　　　How, I reveal it ?
　KIT.　　　　　　　　　　　　Nay,
I do not think thou wouldst ; but if thou
　shouldst,　　　　　　　　　　　80
'T were a great weakness.
　CASH.　　　　　A great treachery ;
Give it no other name.
　KIT.　　　　　Thou wilt not do 't, then ?
　CASH. Sir, if I do, mankind disclaim me
　　ever.
　KIT. [aside] He will not swear ; he has some
　　reservation,
Some conceal'd purpose, and close[34] meaning
　sure ;
Else, being urg'd so much, how should he
　choose
But lend an oath to all this protestation ?
He 's no precisian,[35] that I am certain of,
Nor rigid Roman Catholic. He 'll play
At fayles, and tick-tack ;[36] I have heard him
　swear.　　　　　　　　　　　90
What should I think of it ? Urge him again,
And by some other way ? I will do so. ——
Well, Thomas, thou hast sworn not to disclose ;
Yes, you did swear !
　CASH.　　　　Not yet, sir ; but I will,
Please you ——
　KIT. No, Thomas, I dare take thy word ;
But, if thou wilt swear, do as thou think'st
　good ;

I am resolv'd[37] without it ; at thy pleas-
　ure.[38]
　CASH. By my soul's safety then, sir, I pro-
　　test,
My tongue shall ne'er take knowledge of a
　word
Deliver'd me in nature of your trust.　　100
　KIT. It is too much ; these ceremonies need
　　not ;
I know thy faith to be as firm as rock.
Thomas, come hither, near ; we cannot be
Too private in this business. So it is. —
[aside] Now he has sworn, I dare the safelier
　venture. —
I have of late, by divers observations ——
[aside] But whether his oath can bind him, yea,
　or no,
Being not taken lawfully ![39] Ha ! say you ?
I will ask counsel ere I do proceed. —
Thomas, it will be now too long to stay ;　110
I 'll spy some fitter time soon, or to-morrow.
　CASH. Sir, at your pleasure !
　KIT. [aside] I will think. — And, Thomas,
I pray you search the books 'gainst my return,
For the receipts 'twixt me and Traps.
　CASH.　　　　　　　　I will, sir.
　KIT. And hear you, if your mistress'
　　brother, Wellbred,
Chance to bring hither any gentlemen
Ere I come back, let one straight bring me
　word.
　CASH. Very well, sir.
　KIT.　　　　To the Exchange, do you hear ?
Or here in Coleman Street, to Justice Clem-
　ent's.
Forget it not, nor be not out of the way.　120
　CASH. I will not, sir.
　KIT.　　　　I pray you have a care on 't,
Or, whether he come or no, if any other,
Stranger, or else, fail not to send me word.
　CASH. I shall not, sir.
　KIT.　　　　　Be 't your special business
Now to remember it.
　CASH.　　　　　Sir, I warrant you.
　KIT. But, Thomas, this is not the secret,
　　Thomas,
I told you of.
　CASH.　　　No, sir ; I do suppose it.
　KIT. Believe me, it is not.
　CASH.　　　　　　Sir, I do believe you.
　KIT. By Heaven it is not ; that 's enough.
　　But, Thomas,

[33] Head, top (with an allusion to the horns of the cuckold).
[34] Secret.
[35] Puritan.
[36] Varieties of backgammon.

[37] Convinced.
[38] *I.e.*, swear or not, as you choose.
[39] Before a magistrate.

I would not you should utter it, do you see,
To any creature living ; yet, I care not.　131
Well, I must hence.　Thomas, conceive thus
　　much :
It was a trial : [40] of you, when I meant
So deep a secret to you ; I mean not this,
But that I have to tell you ; this is nothing,
　　this.
But, Thomas, keep this from my wife, I charge
　　you.
Lock'd up in silence, midnight, buried here. —
[*aside*] No greater hell than to be slave to fear.
　　　　　　　　　　　　　　　　[*Exit.*]
　　CASH. " Lock'd up in silence, midnight,
　　buried here."
Whence should this flood of passion, trow, take
　　head ? ha ?　　　　　　　　　　　　140
Best dream no longer of this running humor,
For fear I sink ! The violence of the stream
Already hath transported me so far,
That I can feel no ground at all.　But soft —
Oh, 't is our water-bearer : somewhat has
　　cross'd him now.

SCENE IV [41]

[*To*] CASH [*enter*] COB.

COB. Fasting days ! what tell you me of
fasting days ? 'Slid, would they were all on
a lit fire for me ! [42] They say the whole world
shall be consum'd with fire one day, but would
I had these Ember weeks and villanous Fridays [43] burnt in the mean time, and then ——

CASH. Why, how now, Cob, what moves
thee to this choler, ha ?

COB. Collar, Master Thomas ! I scorn
your collar, I, sir ; I am none o' your cart- [10
horse, though I carry and draw water.　An
you offer to ride me with your collar or halter
either, I may hap show you a jade's trick, sir.

CASH. O, you'll slip your head out of the
collar ? Why, Goodman Cob, you mistake me.

COB. Nay, I have my rheum, and I can be
angry as well as another, sir.

CASH. Thy rheum, Cob ? Thy humor, thy
humor ! Thou mistak'st. [44]

COB. Humor ! mack ! [45] I think it be [20

---

[40] Dissyllabic.
[41] The same.
[42] On fire for all of me, on fire as far as I'm concerned.
[43] Reflecting the popular grievance against
statutes forbidding the eating of meat on these
(and other) days.　Their object was to foster the
fisheries.
[44] Since "humor", not "rheum" was now the
fashionable word for whim, mood, disposition.
[45] Mass.

so indeed.　What is that humor ? Some rare
thing, I warrant.

CASH. Marry, I'll tell thee, Cob : it is a
gentlemanlike monster, bred in the special
gallantry of our time by affectation, and fed
by folly.

COB. How ! must it be fed ?

CASH. Oh, ay, humor is nothing if it be not
fed.　Didst thou never hear that ? It's a
common phrase, " Feed my humor."　　30

COB. I'll none on it : humor, avaunt ! I
know you not ; begone ! Let who will make
hungry meals for your Monstership, it shall
not be I.　Feed you, quoth he ! 'Slid, I ha'
much ado to feed myself, especially on these
lean rascally days too ; an't had been any
other day but a fasting day — a plague on
them all for me ! By this light, one might
have done the commonwealth good service,
and have drown'd them all i' the flood, two [40
or three hundred thousand years ago.　O, I
do stomach [46] them hugely ! I have a maw [47]
now an't were for Sir Bevis his horse, [48] against
'em.

CASH. I pray thee, good Cob, what makes
thee so out of love with fasting days ?

COB. Marry, that which will make any man
out of love with 'em, I think : their bad conditions, an you will needs know.　First, they
are of a Flemish breed, I am sure on't, for [50
they raven up more butter than all the days
of the week beside ; next, they stink of fish
and leek porridge miserably ; thirdly, they'll
keep a man devoutly hungry all day, and at
night send him supperless to bed.

CASH. Indeed, these are faults, Cob.

COB. Nay, an this were all, 't were something ; but they are the only known enemies
to my generation.　A fasting day no sooner
comes, but my lineage goes to [w]rack ; poor [60
cobs, they smoke for it, they are made martyrs
o' the gridiron, they melt in passion ; and your
maids too know this, and yet would have me
turn Hannibal, [49] and eat my own fish [50] and
blood.　My princely Coz (*he pulls out a red
herring*), fear nothing ; I have not the heart
to devour you, an I might be made as rich as
King Cophetua.　Oh, that I had room for my
tears.　I could weep salt water enough now
to preserve the lives of ten thousand of [70

---

[46] Resent.
[47] Stomach ; *i.e.*, resentment.
[48] *I.e.*, comparable to that of Sir Bevis's horse.
[49] Cob's blunder for "cannibal."
[50] Altered to *flesh* by F [3] and subsequent editors,
who miss the joke.

my kin! But I may curse none but these filthy almanacs; for an 't were not for them, these days of persecution would ne'er be known. I 'll be hang'd an some fishmonger's son do not make of 'em, and puts in more fasting days than he should do, because he would utter [51] his father's dried stockfish and stinking conger.

CASH. 'Slight, peace! Thou 'lt be beaten like a stockfish [52] else. Here is Master [80 Matthew. Now must I look out for a messenger to my master.   [*Exeunt.*]

SCENE V [53]

[*Enter*] WELLBRED, EDWARD KNOWELL, BRAINWORM, BOBADILL, MATTHEW, [*and*] STEPHEN.

WEL. Beshrew me, but it was an absolute good jest, and exceedingly well carried!

E. KNOW. Ay, and our ignorance maintain'd it as well, did it not?

WEL. Yes, faith; but was it possible thou shouldst not know him? — [*aside to* EDWARD] I forgive Master Stephen, for he is stupidity itself!

E. KNOW. 'Fore God, not I, an I might have been join'd patten [54] with one of the [10 seven wise masters for knowing him. He had so writhen [55] himself into the habit of one of your poor infantry, your decay'd, ruinous, worm-eaten gentlemen of the round; [56] such as have vowed to sit on the skirts of the city, let your provost and his half-dozen of halberdiers do what they can; and have translated begging out of the old hackney pace to a fine easy amble, and made it run as smooth off the tongue as a shove-groat shilling. [57] Into [20 the likeness of one of these reformados [58] had he molded himself so perfectly, observing every trick of their action, as, varying the accent, swearing with an emphasis, indeed, all with so special and exquisite a grace, that, hadst thou seen him, thou wouldst have sworn he might have been sergeant-major, [59] if not lieutenant-colonel to the regiment.

[51] Vend.   [52] Dried codfish, beaten before cooking.
[53] The same.
[54] Made a sharer, by letters patent, in a privilege or office. (Simpson.)
[55] Twisted.
[56] Officers of the guard (who make the rounds, inspecting the sentries).
[57] *I.e.*, a smooth shilling used in the game of shovel-board.
[58] Officers of disbanded companies.
[59] Equivalent to the present major in rank and charged with the duties of adjutant.

WEL. Why, Brainworm, who would have thought thou hadst been such an artificer? [30

E. KNOW. An artificer! an architect! Except a man had studied begging all his lifetime, and been a weaver of language from his infancy for the clothing of it, I never saw his rival!

WEL. Where gott'st thou this coat, I mar'l?

BRAI. Of a Houndsditch man, sir; one of the Devil's near kinsmen, a broker.

WEL. That cannot be, if the proverb hold; for "A crafty knave needs no broker."   40

BRAI. True, sir; but I did need a broker; *ergo* ——

WEL. Well put off: "no crafty knave," you 'll say.

E. KNOW. Tut, he has more of these shifts.

BRAI. And yet, where I have one the broker has ten, [60] sir.

[*Re-enter* CASH.]

CASH. Francis! Martin! Ne'er a one to be found now? What a spite 's this!

WEL. How now, Thomas? Is my [50 brother Kitely within?

CASH. No, sir, my master went forth e'en now; but Master Downright is within. — Cob! what, Cob! Is he gone too?

WEL. Whither went your master, Thomas, canst thou tell?

CASH. I know not; to Justice Clement's, I think, sir. — Cob!

E. KNOW. Justice Clement! what 's he?

WEL. Why, doest thou not know him? [60 He is a city magistrate, a justice here, an excellent good lawyer, and a great scholar; but the only mad, merry old fellow in Europe! I show'd him you the other day.

E. KNOW. Oh, is that he? I remember him now. Good faith, and he has a very strange presence methinks; it shows as if he stood out of the rank from other men. I have heard many of his jests i' [the] [61] University. They say he will commit a man for taking the [70 wall of his horse.

WEL. Ay, or wearing his cloak of one shoulder, or serving of God — anything indeed, if it come in the way of his humor.

CASH *goes in and out calling.*

CASH. Gasper! Martin! Cob! 'Heart, where should they be, trow?

BOB. Master Kitely's man, pray thee vouchsafe us the lighting of this match.

[60] Punning on "shifts" = tricks, and = changes of clothing.
[61] Add. F₂.

Cash. Fire on your match! No time but now to " vouchsafe "? — Francis! Cob! [80
[*Exit.*]

Bob. Body o' me! Here's the remainder of seven pound since yesterday was seven-night. 'T is your right Trinidado! Did you never take any, Master Stephen?

Step. No, truly, sir! but I'll learn to take it now, since you commend it so.

Bob. Sir, believe me, upon my relation; for what I tell you, the world shall not re-prove.[62] I have been in the Indies, where this herb grows; where neither myself, nor [90 a dozen gentlemen more, of my knowledge, have received the taste of any other nutriment in the world for the space of one-and-twenty weeks but the fume of this simple[63] only. Therefore it cannot be but 't is most divine! Further, take it in the nature, in the true kind; so, it makes an antidote, that, had you taken the most deadly poisonous plant in all Italy, it should expel it and clarify you, with as much ease as I speak. And, for your [100 green wound, your balsamum and your St. John's wort are all mere gulleries and trash to it — especially your Trinidado; your Nico-tian[64] is good too. I could say what I know of the virtue of it, for the expulsion of rheums, raw humors, crudities, obstructions, with a thousand of this kind; but I profess myself no quacksalver. Only thus much: by Hercules, I do hold it, and will affirm it before any prince in Europe, to be the most sovereign and [110 precious weed that ever the earth tend'red to the use of man.

E. Know. This speech would ha' done de-cently in a tobacco trader's mouth.

[*Re-enter* Cash *with* Cob.]

Cash. At Justice Clement's he is, in the middle of Coleman Street.

Cob. Oh, oh!

Bob. Where's the match I gave thee, Master Kitely's man?

Cash. Would his match and he, and [120 pipe and all, were at Sancto Domingo! I had forgot it. [*Exit.*]

Cob. By God's me, I mar'l what pleasure or felicity they have in taking this roguish to-bacco! It's good for nothing[65] but to choke a man, and fill him full of smoke and embers. There were four died out of one house last week with taking of it, and two more the bell went for yesternight; one of them, they say, will ne'er scape it; he voided a bushel of [130 soot yesterday, upward and downward. By the stocks, an there were no wiser men than I, I'd have it present whipping, man or woman, that should but deal with a tobacco pipe. Why, it will stifle them all in the end, as many as use it; it's little better than ratsbane or rosaker.[66]

Bobadill *beats him with a cudgel.*

All. Oh, good Captain, hold, hold!

Bob. You base cullion,[67] you!

Re-enter Cash.

Cash. Sir, here's your match. — Come, [140 thou must needs be talking too; th'art well enough serv'd.

Cob. Nay, he will not meddle with his match, I warrant you. Well, it shall be a dear beating, an I live.

Bob. Do you prate? Do you murmur?

E. Know. Nay, good Captain, will you regard the humor of a fool? — Away, knave.

Wel. Thomas, get him away.
[*Exeunt* Cash *and* Cob.]

Bob. A whoreson filthy slave, a dung- [150 worm, an excrement! Body o' Caesar, but that I scorn to let forth so mean a spirit, I'd ha' stabb'd him to the earth.

Wel. Marry, the law forbid, sir!

Bob. By Pharaoh's foot, I would have done it.

Step. [*aside*] Oh, he swears admirably! " By Pharaoh's foot!" " Body of Caesar!" I shall never do it, sure. — Upon mine honor, and by St. George! — No, I ha' not the [160 right grace.

Mat. Master Stephen, will you any? By this air, the most divine tobacco that ever I drunk![68]

Step. None, I thank you, sir. — [*aside*] Oh, this gentleman does it rarely too! but nothing like the other. By this air! As I am a gentleman! By ——
[*Exeunt* Bobadill *and* Matthew.]

---

[62] Disprove.
[63] Herb.
[64] Tobacco was so called from Nicot, who intro-duced it into France. Bobadill may be blundering, or he may be gulling Stephen, or Jonson may be confused, or there may have been a special variety so named.
[65] Similar accusations were made by writers against the weed.
[66] Both are preparations of arsenic.
[67] Low fellow, wretch.
[68] Smoked.

BRAI. Master, glance, glance! Master
Wellbred!   170

       MASTER STEPHEN *is practising, to the*
                 post.

STEP. [*aside*] As I have somewhat to be
saved, I protest ——

WEL. [*aside*] You are a fool; it needs no
affidavit.

E. KNOW. Cousin, will you any tobacco?

STEP. Ay, sir! Upon my reputation ——

E. KNOW. How now, Cousin!

STEP. I protest, as I am a gentleman, but
no soldier, indeed ——

WEL. No, Master Stephen? As I re- [180
member, your name is ent'red in the Artillery
Garden! [69]

STEP. Ay, sir, that's true. Cousin, may I
swear as I am a soldier, by that?

E. KNOW. O yes, that you may. It is all
you have for your money.

STEP. Then, as I am a gentleman and a
soldier, it is divine tobacco!

WEL. But soft, where's Master Matthew?
gone?   190

BRAI. No, sir; they went in here.

WEL. Oh, let's follow them. Master Matthew is gone to salute his mistress in verse.
We shall ha' the happiness to hear some of his
poetry now; he never comes unfurnish'd. —
Brainworm!

STEP. Brainworm! Where? Is this Brainworm?

E. KNOW. Ay, Cousin; no words of it, upon
your gentility.   200

STEP. Not I, body o' me! By this air!
St. George! and the foot of Pharaoh!

WEL. Rare! Your cousin's discourse is
simply drawn out with oaths.

E. KNOW. 'T is larded with 'em; a kind of
French dressing, [70] if you love it.   [*Exeunt.*]

SCENE VI [71]

[*Enter*] KITELY [*and*] COB.

KIT. Ha! how many are there, sayest
thou?

COB. Marry, sir, your brother, Master
Wellbred ——

KIT. Tut, beside him: what strangers are
there, man?

COB. Strangers? let me see, one, two;
mass, I know not well, there are so many.

KIT. How! so many?

COB. Ay, there's some five or six of them
at the most.

KIT. [*aside*] A swarm, a swarm!   10
Spite of the devil! how they sting my head
With forked stings, thus wide and large! [72]
      But, Cob,
How long hast thou been coming hither, Cob?

COB. A little while, sir.

KIT.   Didst thou come running?

COB.   No, sir.

KIT. Nay, then I am familiar with thy
      haste! —

[*aside*] Bane to my fortunes! what meant I to
      marry?
I, that before was rank'd in such content,
My mind at rest too, in so soft a peace,
Being free master of mine own free thoughts,
And now become a slave? What! never a
      sigh;   20
Be of good cheer, man; for thou art a cuckold:
'T is done, 't is done! Nay, when such flowing
      store,
Plenty itself, falls in my wife's lap,
The cornucopiae will be mine, I know. — But,
      Cob,
What entertainment had they? I am sure
My sister and my wife would bid them wel-
      come, ha?

COB. Like enough, sir; yet I heard not a
word of it.

KIT. No, — [*aside*] their lips were seal'd
      with kisses, and the voice,
Drown'd in a flood of joy at their arrival,   30
Had lost her motion, state, and faculty. —
Cob, which of them was 't that first kiss'd my
      wife?
My sister, I should say. My wife, alas,
I fear not her. Ha! who was it, say'st
      thou?

COB. By my troth, sir, will you have the
truth of it?

KIT. Oh, ay, good Cob, I pray thee heartily.

COB. Then I am a vagabond, and fitter for
Bridewell [73] than your Worship's company, if I
saw anybody to be kiss'd, unless they [40
would have kiss'd the post in the middle of the
warehouse; for there I left them all at their
tobacco, with a pox! [74]

---

[69] The training ground of the Honorable Artillery
Company. "Artillery" does not here indicate cannon; its use also embraced small arms and even the
bow.
[70] The French being proverbial swearers.
[71] Coleman Street. A room in Justice Clement's
house.

[72] With a gesture representing the horns of the
cuckold, also alluded to in l. 24.
[73] The famous house of correction, or "workhouse."
[74] Plague take them.

KIT. How ! were they not gone in then ere thou cam'st !

COB. Oh, no, sir.

KIT. Spite of the devil ! What [75] do I stay here then ? Cob, follow me.   ]*Exit.*]

COB. Nay, soft and fair ; I have eggs on the spit ; [76] I cannot go yet, sir. Now am I, for some five-and-fifty reasons, hammering, hammering revenge. Oh, for three or four [50 gallons of vinegar, to sharpen my wits. Revenge, vinegar, revenge ; vinegar and mustard, revenge ! Nay, an he had not lien in my house, 't would never have griev'd me ; but being my guest, one that, I 'll be sworn, my wife has lent him her smock off her back, while his one [77] shirt has been at washing ; pawn'd her neckerchers for clean bands [78] for him ; sold almost all my platters, to buy him tobacco ; and he to turn mon- [60 ster of ingratitude, and strike his lawful host ! Well, I hope to raise up an host of fury for 't : here comes Justice Clement.

SCENE VII [79]

[*To*] COB, [*enter* JUSTICE] CLEMENT, KNOWELL, [*and*] FORMAL.

CLEM. What, 's Master Kitely gone, Roger ?

FORM. Ay, sir.

CLEM. 'Heart o' me ! what made him leave us so abruptly ? — How now, sirrah ! what make you here ? What would you have, ha ?

COB. An 't please your Worship, I am a poor neighbor of your Worship's ——

CLEM. A poor neighbor of mine ! Why, speak, poor neighbor.

COB. I dwell, sir, at the sign of the [10 Water-tankard, hard by the Green Lattice ; [80] I have paid scot and lot [81] there any time this eighteen years.

CLEM. To the Green Lattice ?

COB. No, sir, to the parish. Marry, I have seldom scap'd scot-free at the Lattice.

CLEM. Oh, well ! What business has my poor neighbor with me ?

COB. An 't like your Worship, I am come to crave the peace [82] of your Worship.   20

CLEM. Of me, knave ? Peace of me,

[75] Why.   [76] I 'm busy.
[77] Q *owne.*
[78] Neckbands, collars.
[79] The same.
[80] A tavern. Cob lives by the city wall, at the foot of Coleman Street.
[81] Parish assessments.
[82] *I.e.,* to petition you to require a surety of the peace from one who has injured or threatened me.

knave ? Did I e'er hurt thee, or threaten thee, or wrong thee, ha ?

COB. No, sir ; but your Worship's warrant for one that has wrong'd me, sir. His arms are at too much liberty ; I would fain have them bound to a treaty of peace, an my credit could compass it with your Worship.

CLEM. Thou goest far enough about for 't, I am sure.   30

KNOW. Why, doest thou go in danger of thy life for him, friend ?

COB. No, sir ; but I go in danger of my death every hour, by his means ; an I die within a twelvemonth and a day, [83] I may swear by the law of the land that he kill'd me.

CLEM. How, how, knave, swear he kill'd thee, and by the law ? What pretence, what color, hast thou for that ?

COB. Marry, an 't please your Worship, [40 both black and blue ; color enough, I warrant you. I have it here to show your Worship.

CLEM. What is he that gave you this, sirrah ?

COB. A gentleman and a soldier, he says he is, of the city here.

CLEM. A soldier o' the city ! What call you him ?

COB. Captain Bobadill.

CLEM. Bobadill ! and why did he bob [84] [50 and beat you, sirrah ? How began the quarrel betwixt you ? Ha ! Speak truly, knave, I advise you.

COB. Marry, indeed, an['t] please your Worship, only because I spake against their vagrant tobacco, as I came by 'em when they were taking on 't ; for nothing else.

CLEM. Ha ? you speak against tobacco ? Formal, his name.

FORM. What 's your name, sirrah ?   60

COB. Oliver, sir, Oliver Cob, sir.

CLEM. Tell Oliver Cob he shall go to the jail, Formal.

FORM. Oliver Cob, my master, Justice Clement, says you shall go to the jail.

COB. O, I beseech your Worship, for God's sake, dear Master Justice !

CLEM. Nay, God's precious ! an such drunkards and tankards as you are, come to dispute of tobacco once, I have done ! [70 Away with him !

COB. O, good Master Justice ! — [*to* KNOWELL] Sweet old gentleman !

[83] The legal period for determining the cause of a death from wounds.
[84] Strike.

KNOW. Sweet Oliver, would I could do thee any good! — Justice Clement, let me entreat you, sir.

CLEM. What! a threadbare rascal, a beggar, a slave that never drunk out of better than pisspot metal [85] in his life! and he to deprave and abuse the virtue of an herb [80 so generally receiv'd in the courts of princes, the chambers of nobles, the bowers of sweet ladies, the cabins of soldiers! — Roger, away with him, by God's precious! I say, go to.

COB. Dear Master Justice, let me be beaten again — I have deserv'd it; but not the prison, I beseech you.

KNOW. Alas, poor Oliver!

CLEM. Roger, make him a warrant. — He shall not go; I but fear [86] the knave.   90

FORM. Do not stink, sweet Oliver: [87] you shall not go; my master will give you a warrant.

COB. O, the Lord maintain his Worship, his worthy Worship!

CLEM. Away, dispatch him.

            [*Exeunt* FORMAL *and* COB.]
— How now, Master Knowell! in dumps, in dumps? Come, this becomes not.

KNOW. Sir, would I could not feel my cares.

CLEM. Your cares are nothing! They [100 are like my cap, soon put on, and as soon put off. What! your son is old enough to govern himself. Let him run his course; it's the only way to make him a staid man. If he were an unthrift, a ruffian, a drunkard, or a licentious liver, then you had reason; you had reason to take care. But, being none of these, mirth's my witness, an I had twice so many cares as you have, I'd drown them all in a cup of sack. [88] Come, come, let's try [110 it; I muse [89] your parcel [90] of a soldier returns not all this while.   [*Exeunt.*]

ACT IV — SCENE I [1]

[*Enter*] DOWNRIGHT [*and*] DAME KITELY.

Dow. Well, Sister, I tell you true; and you'll find it so in the end.

---

[85] Pewter.   [86] Frighten.
[87] Simpson notes that this is "a stock epithet for the rival of 'mad' Orlando in Ariosto's epic"; and also that there was a favorite ballad, beginning, "O sweet Oliver."
[88] Dry Spanish and Portuguese wines, especially sherry.
[89] Marvel.   [90] Piece, fragment.
[1] A room in Kitely's house.

DAME K. Alas, Brother, what would you have me to do? I cannot help it; you see my brother brings 'em in here; they are his friends.

Dow. His friends? his fiends! 'Slud! [2] they do nothing but haunt him up and down like a sort of unlucky sprites, and tempt him to all manner of villainy that can be thought of. Well, by this light, a little thing would [10 make me play the devil with some of 'em; an't were not more for your husband's sake than anything else, I'd make the house too hot for the best on 'em; they should say, and swear, hell were broken loose, ere they went hence. But, by God's will, 't is nobody's fault but yours; for an you had done as you might have done, they should have been parboil'd, [3] and bak'd too, every mother's son, ere they should ha' come in, e'er a one of 'em.   20

DAME K. God's my life! did you ever hear the like? What a strange man is this! Could I keep out all them, think you? I should put myself against half a dozen men, should I? Good faith, you'd mad the patient'st body in the world, to hear you talk so, without any sense or reason!

SCENE II [4]

[*To them enter*] MISTRESS BRIDGET, MASTER MATTHEW, *and* BOBADILL; [*followed at a distance by*] WELLBRED, EDWARD KNOWELL, STEPHEN, *and* BRAINWORM.

BRID. Servant, [5] in troth you are too prodigal
Of your wit's treasure, thus to pour it forth
Upon so mean a subject as my worth!

MAT. You say well, mistress, and I mean as well.

Dow. [*aside*] Hoy-day, here is stuff!

WEL. [*aside*] Oh, now stand close; pray Heaven, she can get him to read. He should do it of his own natural impudency.

            [*They listen, unobserved.*]

BRID. Servant, what is this same, I pray you?   10

MAT. Marry, an elegy, an elegy, an odd toy ——

Dow. [*aside*] To mock an ape withal! [6] Oh, I could sew up his mouth, now.

DAME K. Sister, I pray you let's hear it.

Dow. [*aside*] Are you rhyme-given too?

---

[2] A corruption of *'slid*. See on I, i, 50.
[3] Thoroughly boiled.
[4] The same.
[5] Lover, cavalier, admirer.
[6] To dupe a fool with.

MAT. Mistress, I'll read it, if you please.

BRID. Pray you do, servant.

Dow. [*aside*] Oh, here's no foppery! Death! I can endure the stocks better.   20

[*Exit.*]

E. KNOW. What ails thy brother? Can he not hold his water at reading of a ballad?

WEL. Oh, no; a rhyme to him is worse than cheese, or a bagpipe. But, mark, you lose the protestation.

MAT. Faith, I did it in a humor; I know not how it is; but please you come near, sir. This gentleman has judgment, he knows how to censure of a —— [7] pray you, sir, you can judge?   30

STEP. Not I, sir; upon my reputation, and by the foot of Pharaoh!

WEL. O, chide your cousin for swearing.

E. KNOW. Not I, so long as he does not forswear himself.

BOB. Master Matthew, you abuse the expectation of your dear mistress, and her fair sister. Fie! while you live, avoid this prolixity.

MAT. I shall, sir; well, *incipere dulce.* [8]   40

E. KNOW. [*aside*] How! *insipere dulce?* "A sweet thing to be a fool," indeed.

WEL. [*aside*] What, do you take *in[c]ipere* in that sense?

E. KNOW. [*aside*] You do not, you? This was your villainy, to gull him with a mot.

WEL. [*aside*] O, the benchers' [9] phrase: *pauca verba, pauca verba.*

MAT. [*reading*] "Rare creature, let me speak without offence;   49
Would God my rude words had the influence
To rule thy thoughts, as thy fair looks do mine,
Then shouldst thou be his prisoner, who is thine."

E. KNOW. [*aside*] This is in "Hero and Leander!"

WEL. [*aside*] Oh, ay! peace, we shall have more of this.

MAT. "Be not unkind and fair: misshapen stuff
Is of behavior boisterous and rough."

WEL. How like you that, sir?   59

MASTER STEPHEN *answers with shaking his head.*

E. KNOW. [*aside*] 'Slight, he shakes his head like a bottle, to feel an there be any brain in it!

MAT. But observe the catastrophe, now:
"And I in duty will exceed all other,
As you in beauty do excel Love's mother."

E. KNOW. [*aside*] Well, I'll have him free of the wit-brokers [10] for he utters nothing but stol'n remnants.

WEL. [*aside*] Oh, forgive it him.

E. KNOW. [*aside*] A filching rogue! hang him! — and from the dead! It's worse [70 than sacrilege.

[WELLBRED, EDWARD KNOWELL, *and* STEPHEN *come forward.*]

WEL. Sister, what ha' you here? verses? Pray you, let's see. Who made these verses? They are excellent good.

MAT. O, Master Wellbred, 't is your disposition to say so, sir. They were good i' the morning; I made 'em *extempore* this morning.

WEL. How! *extempore?*

MAT. Ay, would I might be hang'd else; ask Captain Bobadill; he saw me write them, [80 at the —— pox on it! — the Star, yonder.

BRAI. Can he find in his heart to curse the stars so?

E. KNOW. Faith, his are even with him; they ha' curs'd him enough already.

STEP. [*aside to* EDWARD KNOWELL] Cousin, how do you like this gentleman's verses?

E. KNOW. [*aside*] Oh, admirable! the best that ever I heard, Coz!   89

STEP. Body o' Caesar! they are admirable! the best that I ever heard, as I am a soldier.

[*Re-enter* DOWNRIGHT.]

Dow. I am vext; I can hold ne'er a bone of me still! Heart, I think they mean to build and breed here!

WEL. Sister, you have a simple servant here, that crowns your beauty with such encomiums and devices; you may see what it is to be the mistress of a wit that can make your perfections so transparent that every blear eye may look through them, and see him [100 drown'd over head and ears in the deep well of desire. — Sister Kitely, I marvel you get you not a servant that can rhyme, and do tricks too.

Dow. O monster! impudence itself! tricks? [11]

DAME K. Tricks, Brother? what tricks?

BRID. Nay, speak, I pray you, what tricks?

---

[7] "The aposiopesis is here a sign of vacuity." (Simpson.)

[8] It is sweet to begin. The *c*'s were pronounced like *s*'s.

[9] Benchers were tavern loafers.

[10] As one was said to be free of, say, the Fishmongers; *i.e.*, a member of that City Company.

[11] From punning on "merry tricks" and Lat. *meretrix*, "the word acquired an equivocal meaning." (Simpson.)

DAME K. Ay, never spare anybody here; but say what tricks?   110

BRID. Passion of my heart! do tricks?

WEL. 'Slight, here's a trick vied and revied![12] Why, you monkeys, you, what a caterwauling do you keep! Has he not given you rhymes and verses and tricks?

Dow. O, the fiend!

WEL. Nay, you — lamp of virginity, that take it in snuff[13] so! come, and cherish this tame poetical fury in your servant; you'll [119 be begg'd else shortly for a concealment:[14] go to, reward his muse. You cannot give him less than a shilling in conscience, for the book he had it out of cost him a teston[15] at least. — How now, gallants! Master Matthew! Captain! what, all sons of silence? No spirit?

Dow. Come, you might practise your ruffian tricks somewhere else, and not here, I wuss;[16] this is no tavern nor drinking-school, to vent your exploits in.   129

WEL. How now! whose cow has calv'd?

Dow. Marry, that has mine, sir. Nay, boy, never look askance at me for the matter; I'll tell you of it, ay, sir, you and your companions; mend yourselves when I ha' done!

WEL. My companions!

Dow. Yes, sir, you[17] companions, so I say; I am not afraid of you, nor them neither; your hang-bys here. You must have your poets and your potlings,[18] your soldados and foolados to follow you up and down the city; [140 and here they must come to domineer and swagger. — Sirrah, you ballad singer, and Slops[19] your fellow there, get you out, get you home; or by this steel, I'll cut off your ears, and that presently.

WEL. 'Slight, stay; let's see what he dare do; cut off his ears! cut a whetstone. You are an ass, do you see? Touch any man here, and by this hand I'll run my rapier to the hilts in you.   150

[12] "Vie" = risk a sum of money on a hand of cards; "revie" = "raise" the stake by covering the original hazard with a larger sum.

[13] Take offence.

[14] Queen Elizabeth had granted commissions for searching concealments; *i.e.*, properties privately retained though lawfully belonging to the crown, such as land owned by the monasteries at the time of their dissolution. Such commissions, begged by courtiers, sometimes became a means of vexation and even oppression; they were revoked in 1572 and 1579.

[15] Tester, sixpence.

[16] Iwis, to be sure.

[17] Ff $_{2,3}$, *your*; but F$_1$ may well be right, since "companions" = low fellows.

[18] Tipplers (a nonce-word — *N.E.D.*)

[19] Big Breeches.

Dow. Yea, that would I fain see, boy.

They all draw, and [CASH and others] of the house make out to part them.

DAME K. O Jesu! murder! Thomas! Gasper!

BRID. Help, help! Thomas!

E. KNOW. Gentlemen, forbear, I pray you.

BOB. Well, sirrah, you Holofernes; by my hand, I will pink your flesh full of holes with my rapier for this; I will, by this good Heaven! Nay, let him come, let him come, gentlemen; by the body of St. George, I'll not kill him.   161

They offer to fight again, and are parted.

CASH. Hold, hold, good gentlemen.

Dow. You whoreson, bragging coystril![20]

SCENE III [21]

To them [enter] KITELY.

KIT. Why, how now! what's the matter, what's the stir here?

Whence springs the quarrel? Thomas! where is he?

Put up your weapons, and put off this rage. —

[*aside*] My wife and sister, they are cause of this. —

What, Thomas! where is this knave?

CASH. Here, sir.

WEL. Come, let's go; this is one of my brother's ancient humors, this.

STEP. I am glad nobody was hurt by his ancient humor.   10

[*Exeunt* WELLBRED, STEPHEN, MATTHEW, EDWARD KNOWELL, BOBADILL, *and* BRAINWORM.]

KIT. Why, how now, Brother, who enforc'd this brawl?

Dow. A sort of lewd rakehells, that care neither for God nor the Devil! And they must come here to read ballads, and roguery, and trash! I'll mar the knot of 'em ere I sleep, perhaps; especially Bob there, he that's all manner of shapes; and Songs and Sonnets, his fellow!

BRID. Brother, indeed you are too violent, Too sudden in your humor; and you know [20 My brother Wellbred's temper will not bear Any reproof, chiefly in such a presence, Where every slight disgrace he should receive Might wound him in opinion and respect.

Dow. Respect! what talk you of respect 'mong such as ha' nor spark of manhood nor

[20] Knave.   [21] The same.

good manners? 'Sdeins, I am asham'd to
hear you! respect!   [*Exit.*]

BRID. Yes, there was one, a civil gentleman,
And very worthily demean'd himself!   30

KIT. O, that was some love of yours, Sister.

BRID. A love of mine! I would it were no
        worse, Brother!
You'd pay my portion sooner than you think
        for.

DAME K. Indeed he seem'd to be a gentleman of an exceeding fair disposition, and of
very excellent good parts!

        [*Exeunt* DAME KITELY *and* BRIDGET.]

KIT. Her love, by Heaven! my wife's
        minion!
" Fair disposition! excellent good parts! "
Death! these phrases are intolerable!
Good parts! how should she know his
        parts?   40
His parts! Well, well, well, well, well, well!
It is too plain, too clear. — Thomas, come
        hither.
What, are they gone?

CASH.   Ay, sir, they went in.
My mistress and your sister ——

KIT. Are any of the gallants within?

CASH. No, sir; they are all gone.

KIT. Art thou sure of it?

CASH. I can assure you, sir.

KIT. What gentleman was that they prais'd
        so, Thomas?

CASH. One, they call him Master Knowell,
a handsome young gentleman, sir.   51

KIT. Ay, I thought so; my mind gave me
        as much.
I'll die, but they have hid him i' the house
Somewhere; I'll go and search; go with me,
        Thomas.
Be true to me, and thou shalt find me a
        master.²²   [*Exeunt.*]

SCENE IV ²³

[*Enter*] COB.

COB. What, Tib! Tib, I say.

TIB. [*within*] How now, what cuckold is
that knocks so hard?

[*Enter* TIB.]

O, husband, is 't you? What's the news?

COB. Nay, you have stunn'd me, i' faith;
you ha' giv'n me a knock o' the forehead will
stick by me! Cuckold! 'Slid, cuckold!

TIB. Away, you fool! did I know it was

you that knock'd? Come, come, you may call
me as bad when you list.   10

COB. May I? Tib, you are a whore.

TIB. You lie in your throat, husband.

COB. How, the lie? and in my throat too?
Do you long to be stabb'd, ha?

TIB. Why, you are no soldier,²⁴ I hope.

COB. O, must you be stabb'd by a soldier?
Mass, that's true! When was Bobadill here,
your captain? that rogue, that foist,²⁵ that
fencing Burgullian? ²⁶ I'll tickle him, i' faith.

TIB. Why, what's the matter, trow?   20

COB. O, he has basted me rarely, sumptuously! but I have it here in black and white
[*showing the warrant*], for his black and blue
shall pay him. O, the Justice, the honestest
old brave Trojan in London! I do honor the
very flea of his dog. A plague on him, though;
he put me once in a villainous filthy fear;
marry, it vanish'd away like the smoke of tobacco; but I was smok'd ²⁷ soundly first. I
thank the Devil, and his good angel, my [30
guest. Well, wife, or Tib, which you will, get
you in, and lock the door; I charge you let
nobody in to you, wife; nobody in to you;
those are my words: not Captain Bob himself, nor the fiend in his likeness. You are a
woman; you have flesh and blood enough in
you to be tempted; therefore keep the door
shut upon all comers.

TIB. I warrant you, there shall nobody
enter here without my consent.   40

COB. Nor with your consent, sweet Tib;
and so I leave you.

TIB. It's more than you know, whether
you leave me so.

COB. How?

TIB. Why, " sweet."

COB. Tut, sweet or sour, thou art a flower.
Keep close thy door; I ask no more. [*Exeunt.*]

SCENE V ²⁸

[*Enter*] EDWARD KNOWELL, WELLBRED,
        STEPHEN, [*and*] BRAINWORM.

E. KNOW. Well, Brainworm, perform this
business happily, and thou makest a purchase
of my love for ever.

WEL. I' faith, now let thy spirits use their
best faculties; but, at any hand, remember

---

²² Q *finde me bountiful.*   ²³ Before Cob's house.
²⁴ Stabbing was almost proverbially the soldier's
response to the accusation of lying.
²⁵ Rogue.
²⁶ Bully (a nonce-word — *N.E.D.*).
²⁷ Ridiculed.
²⁸ Unlocated. Perhaps a room at the Windmill.

the message to my brother ; for there's no other means to start him.

BRAI. I warrant you, sir ; fear nothing ; I have a nimble soul has wak'd all forces of my phant'sie by this time, and put 'em in true [10 motion. What you have possess'd[29] me withal, I'll discharge it amply, sir ; make it no question.   [*Exit.*]

WEL. Forth, and prosper, Brainworm. — Faith, Ned, how dost thou approve of my abilities in this device?

E. KNOW. Troth, well, howsoever ; but it will come excellent if it take.

WEL. Take, man ! why it cannot choose but take, if the circumstances miscarry not. [20 But, tell me ingenuously, dost thou affect my sister Bridget as thou pretend'st?

E. KNOW. Friend, am I worth belief?

WEL. Come, do not protest. In faith, she is a maid of good ornament, and much modesty ; and, except I conceiv'd very worthily of her, thou shouldest not have her.

E. KNOW. Nay, that, I am afraid, will be a question yet, whether I shall have her, or no.

WEL. 'Slid, thou shait have her ; by [30 this light thou shalt.

E. KNOW. Nay, do not swear.

WEL. By this hand thou shalt have her ; I'll go fetch her, presently. 'Point but where to meet, and as I am an honest man I'll bring her.

E. KNOW. Hold, hold ; be temperate.

WEL. Why, by —— what shall I swear by? Thou shalt have her, as I am ——

E. KNOW. 'Pray thee, be at peace ; I [40 am satisfied, and do believe thou wilt omit no offered occasion to make my desires complete.

WEL. Thou shalt see, and know, I will not.   [*Exeunt.*]

SCENE VI [30]

[Enter] FORMAL *[and]* KNOWELL.

FORM. Was your man a soldier, sir?

KNOW.   Ay, a knave ; I took him begging o' the way, this morning, As I came over Moorfields !

[Enter BRAINWORM.]

O, here he is ! — y'have made fair speed, believe me !

Where, i' the name of sloth, could you be thus —

BRAI. Marry, peace be my comfort, where I thought I should have had little comfort of your Worship's service.

KNOW. How so?

BRAI. O, sir, your coming to the city, [10 your entertainment of me, and your sending me to watch —— indeed all the circumstances either of your charge, or my employment, are as open to your son as to yourself !

KNOW. How should that be? unless that villain, Brainworm,

Have told him of the letter, and discover'd All that I strictly charg'd him to conceal? 'T is so.

BRAI. I am partly o' the faith, 't is so, indeed.

KNOW. But, how should he know thee to be my man?   20

BRAI. Nay, sir, I cannot tell ; unless it be by the black art ! Is not your son a scholar, sir?

KNOW. Yes, but I hope his soul is not allied Unto such hellish practice ; if it were, I had just cause to weep my part in him, And curse the time of his creation. But, where didst thou find them, Fitz-Sword?

BRAI. You should rather ask where they found me, sir ; for I'll be sworn, I was going along in the street, thinking nothing, when, [31 of a sudden, a voice calls, "Master Knowell's man !" another cries, "Soldier !" and thus half a dozen of 'em, till they had call'd me within a house, where I no sooner came, but th[e]y seem'd men,[31] and out flew all their rapiers at my bosom, with some three or four score oaths to accompany 'em, and all to tell me I was but a dead man, if I did not confess where you were, and how I was employed, [40 and about what ; which when they could not get out of me (as, I protest, they must ha' dissected, and made an anatomy [32] o' me first, and so I told 'em), they lock'd me up into a room i' the top of a high house, whence by great miracle, having a light heart, I slid down by a bottom [33] of packthread into the street, and so scap'd. But, sir, thus much I can assure you, for I heard it while I was lock'd up, there were a great many rich merchants [50 and brave citizens' wives with 'em at a feast ; and your son, Master Edward, withdrew with one of 'em, and has 'pointed to meet her anon at one Cob's house, a water-bearer that dwells by the Wall. Now, there your Worship shall

---

[29] Instructed.   [30] A street.

[31] *I.e.*, displayed their manly valor.
[32] Subject of dissection, lifeless form.   [33] Ball.

be sure to take him, for there he preys, and
fail he will not.

KNOW. Nor will I fail to break his match,
    I doubt not.
Go thou along with Justice Clement's man,
And stay there for me. At one Cob's house,
    say'st thou?   60
BRAI. Ay, sir, there you shall have
him. — [*Exit* KNOWELL.] Yes! invisible!
Much wench, or much son! 'Slight, when he
has stay'd there three or four hours, travailing
with the expectation of wonders, and at length
be deliver'd of air! Oh, the sport that I
should then take to look on him, if I durst!
But now, I mean to appear no more afore him
in this shape. I have another trick to act yet.
O that I were so happy as to light on a [70
nupson [34] now of this justice's novice! — Sir,
I make you stay somewhat long.

FORM. Not a whit, sir. Pray you what do
you mean, sir?

BRAI. I was putting up some papers.

FORM. You ha' been lately in the wars, sir,
it seems.

BRAI. Marry have I, sir, to my loss, and
expense of all, almost.

FORM. Troth, sir, I would be glad to [80
bestow a bottle of wine o' you, if it please you
to accept it ——

BRAI. Oh, sir ——

FORM. But to hear the manner of your
services, and your devices in the wars; they
say they be very strange, and not like those
a man reads in the Roman histories, or sees at
Mile End.[35]

BRAI. No, I assure you, sir; why at any
time when it please you, I shall be ready [90
to discourse to you all I know — [*aside*] and
more, too, somewhat.

FORM. No better time than now, sir; we'll
go to the Windmill; there we shall have a
cup of neat grist,[36] we call it. I pray you, sir,
let me request you to the Windmill.

BRAI. I'll follow you, sir; — [*aside*] and
make grist o' you, if I have good luck.

                               [*Exeunt.*]

SCENE VII [37]

[*Enter*] MATTHEW, EDWARD KNOWELL, BOBA-
         DILL, [*and*] STEPHEN.

MAT. Sir, did your eyes ever taste the like
clown of him where we were to-day, Master

Wellbred's half-brother? I think the whole
earth cannot show his parallel, by this daylight.

E. KNOW. We were now speaking of him;
Captain Bobadill tells me he is fall'n foul o'
you, too.

MAT. O, ay, sir, he threat'ned me with the
bastinado.

BOB. Ay, but I think I taught you pre- [10
vention this morning, for that. You shall kill
him beyond question, if you be so generously
minded.

MAT. Indeed, it is a most excellent trick.

                   He practices at a post.

BOB. O, you do not give spirit enough to
your motion; you are too tardy, too heavy!
O, it must be done like lightning — hay! [38]

MAT. Rare, Captain!

BOB. Tut! 't is nothing, an 't be not done
in a —— punto! [39]   20

E. KNOW. Captain, did you ever prove
yourself upon any of our masters of defence
here?

MAT. O good sir! yes, I hope he has.

BOB. I will tell you, sir. Upon my first
coming to the city, after my long travel [40] for
knowledge in that mystery only, there came
three or four of 'em to me, at a gentleman's
house where it was my chance to be resident
at that time, to entreat my presence at [30
their schools, and withal so much importun'd
me that, I protest to you as I am a gentleman,
I was asham'd of their rude demeanor, out of
all measure. Well, I told 'em that to come to
a public school, they should pardon me; it
was opposite, in diameter, to my humor; but
if so [41] they would give their attendance at my
lodging, I protested to do them what right or
favor I could, as I was a gentleman, and so
forth.   40

E. KNOW. So, sir, then you tried their skill?

BOB. Alas, soon tried! You shall hear, sir.
Within two or three days after, they came;
and, by honesty, fair sir, believe me, I grac'd
them exceedingly, show'd them some two or
three tricks of prevention have purchas'd 'em,
since, a credit to admiration! They cannot
deny this; and yet now they hate me; and
why? because I am excellent, and for no other
vile reason on the earth.   50

---

[34] Simpleton.   [35] Where the city trainbands drilled.
[36] *I.e.*, the grist of the Windmill, malt liquor.
Q *wine*, since the tavern in that version is the Mermaid.   [37] Unlocated.

[38] Italian *hai*, you have it; an exclamation accom-
panying a successful lunge.
[39] Instant; with a pun on the meaning (see l. 99)
"thrust."
[40] *Travel* and *travail* were not distinguished in
spelling; here the meaning includes both senses.
[41] Ff $_{2, 3}$, *so be.*

E. Know. This is strange and barbarous, as ever I heard !

Bob. Nay, for a more instance of their preposterous natures, but note, sir. They have assaulted me some three, four, five, six of them together, as I have walk'd alone in divers skirts i' the town, as Turnbull, Whitechapel, Shoreditch,[42] which were then my quarters ; and since, upon the Exchange, at my lodging, and at my ordinary :[43] where I have driven [60 them afore me the whole length of a street, in the open view of all our gallants, pitying to hurt them, believe me. Yet all this lenity will not o'ercome their spleen ; they will be doing with the pismire,[44] raising a hill a man may spurn abroad with his foot at pleasure. By myself, I could have slain them all, but I delight not in murder. I am loth to bear any other than this bastinado for 'em ; yet I hold it good polity not to go disarm'd ; for, [70 though I be skilful, I may be oppress'd with multitudes.

E. Know. Ay, believe me, may you, sir ; and in my conceit, our whole nation should sustain the loss by it, if it were so.

Bob. Alas, no. What's a peculiar [45] man to a nation? Not seen.

E. Know. O, but your skill, sir !

Bob. Indeed, that might be some loss ; but who respects it? I will tell you, sir, by the [80 way of private, and under seal ; I am a gentleman, and live here obscure, and to myself ; but were I known to her Majesty and the Lords — observe me — I would undertake, upon this poor head and life, for the public benefit of the state, not only to spare the entire lives of her subjects in general ; but to save the one-half, nay, three parts of her yearly charge in holding war, and against what enemy soever. And how would I do it, think you?   90

E. Know. Nay, I know not, nor can I conceive.

Bob. Why thus, sir. I would select nineteen more, to myself, throughout the land ; gentlemen they should be of good spirit, strong, and able constitution ; I would choose them by an instinct, a character that I have. And I would teach these nineteen the special rules, as your punto, your reverso, your stoccata, your imbroccata, your passada, your [100 montanto ;[46] till they could all play very

near, or altogether, as well as myself. This done, say the enemy were forty thousand strong, we twenty would come into the field the tenth of March, or thereabouts ; and we would challenge twenty of the enemy ; they could not in their honor refuse us. Well, we would kill them ; challenge twenty more, kill them ; twenty more, kill them ; twenty more, kill them too ; and thus would we kill [110 every man his twenty a day, that's twenty score ; twenty score, that's two hundred ;[47] two hundred a day, five days a thousand : forty thousand ; forty times five, five times forty, two hundred days kills them all up by computation. And this will I venture my poor gentlemanlike carcass to perform, provided there be no treason practis'd upon us, by fair and discreet manhood ; that is, civilly by the sword.   120

E. Know. Why, are you so sure of your hand, Captain, at all times?

Bob. Tut ! never miss thrust, upon my reputation with you.

E. Know. I would not stand in Downright's state then, an you meet him, for the wealth of any one street in London.

Bob. Why, sir, you mistake me ! If he were here now, by this welkin, I would not draw my weapon on him ! Let this [130 gentleman do his mind ; but I will bastinado him, by the bright sun, wherever I meet him.

Mat. Faith, and I 'll have a fling at him, at my distance.

E. Know. God's so, look where he is, yonder he goes.

           Downright *walks over the stage.*[48]

Dow. What peevish luck have I, I cannot meet with these bragging rascals !

Bob. It is not he, is it?

E. Know. Yes, faith, it is he !   140

Mat. I 'll be hang'd, then, if that were he.

E. Know. Sir, keep your hanging good for some greater matter, for I assure you that was he.

Step. Upon my reputation, it was he.

Bob. Had I thought it had been he, he must not have gone so ; but I can hardly be induc'd to believe it was he yet.

E. Know. That I think, sir.

           [*Re-enter* Downright.]

But see, he is come again.   150

---

42 All disreputable districts.
43 Tavern, public dining-place.
44 Ant.
45 Private, individual.
46 Various thrusts.

47 "Bobadill is too much of a borrower to be an accurate reckoner." (Gifford.)
48 Probably the inner stage.

Dow. Oh, Pharaoh's foot, have I found you? Come, draw, to your tools; draw, gipsy,[49] or I'll thresh you.

Bob. Gentleman of valor, I do believe in thee; hear me ——

Dow. Draw your weapon then.

Bob. Tall [50] man, I never thought on it till now, body of me: I had a warrant of the peace served on me, even now as I came along, by a water-bearer; this gentleman saw it, [160 Master Matthew.

Dow. 'S death! you will not draw then?
He beats him and disarms him. Mat-
THEW *runs away.*

Bob. Hold, hold! under thy favor, forbear!

Dow. Prate again, as you like this, you whoreson foist you! You'll "control the point," you! Your consort is gone? Had he stay'd he had shar'd with you, sir. [*Exit.*]

Bob. Well, gentlemen, bear witness, I was bound to the peace, by this good day.

E. Know. No, faith, it's an ill day, [170 Captain; never reckon it other. But, say you were bound to the peace, the law allows you to defend yourself; that'll prove but a poor excuse.

Bob. I cannot tell, sir. I desire good con-struction in fair sort. I never sustain'd the like disgrace, by Heaven! Sure I was struck with [51] a planet thence, for I had no power to touch my weapon.

E. Know. Ay, like enough; I have [180 heard of many that have been beaten under a planet. Go, get you to a surgeon. 'Slid! an these be your tricks, your passadas, and your mountantos, I'll none of them. [*Exit* Bobadill.] Oh, manners! that this age should bring forth such creatures! that nature should be at leisure to make them! Come, Coz.

Step. Mass, I'll ha' this cloak.

E. Know. God's will, 'tis Downright's. [190

Step. Nay, it's mine now; another might have ta'en ['t] [52] up as well as I. I'll wear it, so I will.

E. Know. How an he see it? He'll chal-lenge it, assure yourself.

Step. Ay, but he shall not ha' it; I'll say I bought it.

E. Know. Take heed you buy it not too dear, Coz.
[*Exeunt.*]

[49] Rogue.
[50] Bold.
[51] By (the malign influence of).
[52] So F 2; Q *tane it*; F 1 *tane*.

Scene VIII [53]

[*Enter*] KITELY, WELLBRED, DAME KITELY, [*and*] BRIDGET.

Kit. Now, trust me, Brother, you were much to blame
T' incense his anger and disturb the peace
Of my poor house, where there are sentinels
That every minute watch to give alarms
Of civil war, without adjection [54]
Of your assistance or occasion.

Wel. No harm done, Brother, I warrant you: since there is no harm done. Anger costs a man nothing; and a tall man is never his own man till he be angry. To keep his [10 valor in obscurity, is to keep himself as it were in a cloakbag. What's a musician, unless he play? What's a tall man unless he fight? For, indeed, all this my wise brother stands upon absolutely; and that made me fall in with him so resolutely.

Dame K. Ay, but what harm might have come of it, Brother!

Wel. Might, Sister? So might the good warm clothes your husband wears be [20 poison'd, for anything he knows, or the whole-some wine he drunk even now at the table.

Kit. [*aside*] Now, God forbid! O me! now I remember
My wife drunk to me last, and chang'd the cup,
And bade me wear this cursed suit to-day.
See, if Heaven suffer murder undiscover'd! —
I feel me ill; give me some mithridate,[55]
Some mithridate and oil, good Sister, fetch me;
O, I am sick at heart! I burn, I burn.
If you will save my life, go fetch it me. 30

Wel. O strange humor! my very breath has poison'd him.

Brid. Good Brother, be content; what do you mean?
The strength of these extreme conceits [56] will kill you.

Dame K. Beshrew your heart-blood, Brother Wellbred, now,
For putting such a toy into his head!

Wel. Is a fit simile a toy? Will he be poison'd with a simile? Brother Kitely, what a strange and idle imagination is this! For shame, be wiser. O' my soul, there's no such matter. 40

[53] A room in Kitely's house.
[54] Addition.
[55] An antidote.
[56] Notions, fancies.

KIT. Am I not sick? How am I, then, not
     poison'd?
Am I not poison'd? How am I, then, so sick?
     DAME K. If you be sick, your own thoughts
     make you sick.
     WEL. His jealousy is the poison he has taken.

[BRAINWORM] *comes, disguis'd like Justice*
                 Clement's man.

BRAI. Master Kitely, my master, Justice
Clement, salutes you, and desires to speak with
you with all possible speed.
     KIT. No time but now, when I think I am
sick? very sick! Well, I will wait upon his
Worship. — Thomas! Cob! I must seek [50
them out, and set 'em sentinels till I return. —
Thomas! Cob! Thomas!   [*Exit.*]
     WEL. [*aside*] This is perfectly rare, Brain-
worm! But how gott'st thou this apparel of
the Justice's man?
     BRAI. [*aside*] Marry, sir, my proper fine
penman would needs bestow the grist o' me,
at the Windmill, to hear some martial discourse; where I so marshall'd him that I
made him drunk with admiration! and, [60
because too much heat was the cause of his
distemper, I stripp'd him stark naked as he
lay along asleep, and borrowed his suit to
deliver this counterfeit message in, leaving a
rusty armor, and an old brown bill to watch
him till my return; which shall be when I
ha' pawn'd his apparel and spent the better
part o' the money, perhaps.
     WEL. [*aside*] Well, thou art a successful
merry knave Brainworm; his absence will [70
be a good subject for more mirth. I pray thee
return to thy young master, and will him to
meet me and my sister Bridget at the Tower [57]
instantly; for here, tell him, the house is so
stor'd with jealousy there is no room for love
to stand upright in. We must get our fortunes committed to some larger prison, say;
and than the Tower I know no better air, nor
where the liberty of the house may do us more
present service. Away!   80
                 [*Exit* BRAINWORM.]

[*Re-enter* KITELY, *talking aside to* CASH.]

KIT. Come hither, Thomas. Now my
     secret's ripe,
And thou shalt have it: lay to both thine ears.
Hark what I say to thee. I must go forth,
     Thomas;

Be careful of thy promise, keep good watch,
Note every gallant, and observe him well,
That enters in my absence to thy mistress.
If she would show him rooms, the jest is stale;
Follow 'em, Thomas, or else hang on him,
And let him not go after; mark their looks;
Note if she offer but to see his band,   90
Or any other amorous toy about him —
But praise his leg, or foot; or if she say
The day is hot, and bid him feel her hand,
How hot it is; oh, that's a monstrous thing!
Note me all this, good Thomas; mark their
     sighs,
And if they do but whisper, break 'em off.
I'll bear thee out in it. Wilt thou do this?
Wilt thou be true, my Thomas?
     CASH.   As truth's self, sir.
     KIT. Why, I believe thee. — Where is Cob,
     now? Cob!   [*Exit.*]
     DAME K. He's ever calling for Cob! [100
I wonder how he employs Cob so!
     WEL. Indeed, Sister, to ask how he em-
ploys Cob, is a necessary question for you that
are his wife, and a thing not very easy for you
to be satisfied in; but this I'll assure you,
Cob's wife is an excellent bawd, Sister, and
oftentimes your husband haunts her house;
marry, to what end I cannot altogether accuse
him; imagine you what you think convenient. But I have known fair hides have [110
foul hearts ere now, Sister.
     DAME K. Never said you truer than that,
Brother; so much I can tell you for your
learning. Thomas, fetch your cloak and go
                 [*Exit* CASH.]
with me. I'll after him presently. I would
to fortune I could take him there, i'faith. I'd
return him his own, I warrant him.   [*Exit.*]
     WEL. So, let 'em go; this may make sport
anon. Now, my fair sister-in-law, that you
knew but how happy a thing it were to be [120
fair and beautiful!
     BRID. That touches not me, Brother.
     WEL. That's true; that's even the fault of
it; for indeed, beauty stands a woman in no
stead, unless it procure her touching. But,
Sister, whether it touch you or no, it touches
your beauties; and I am sure they will abide
the touch; an they do not, a plague of all
ceruse [58] say I! And it touches me, too, in part,
though not in the —— [59] Well, there's [130
a dear and respected friend of mine, Sister,
stands very strongly and worthily affected

---

[57] Since the Tower was extraparochial, a hasty
marriage could be performed there.

[58] A cosmetic of white lead.
[59] Probably an obscene innuendo is intended.

toward you, and hath vow'd to inflame whole bonfires of zeal at his heart, in honor of your perfections. I have already engag'd my promise to bring you where you shall hear him confirm much more. Ned Knowell is the man, Sister. There's no exception against the party. You are ripe for a husband; and a minute's loss to such an occasion is a [140 great trespass in a wise beauty. What say you, Sister? On my soul he loves you. Will you give him the meeting?

BRID. Faith, I had very little confidence in mine own constancy, Brother, if I durst not meet a man; but this motion of yours savors of an old knight adventurer's servant a little too much, methinks.

WEL. What's that, Sister?

BRID. Marry, of the squire.[60]   150

WEL. No matter if it did; I would be such an one for my friend. But see, who is re-turn'd to hinder us?

[Re-enter KITELY.]

KIT. What villainy is this? Call'd out on a false message!
This was some plot! I was not sent for. — Bridget,
Where is your sister?

BRID.   I think she be gone forth, sir.

KIT. How! is my wife gone forth? Whither, for God's sake?

BRID. She's gone abroad with Thomas.

KIT. Abroad with Thomas! oh, that villain dors[61] me.
He hath discover'd all unto my wife!   160
Beast that I was, to trust him. Whither, I pray you
Went she?

BRID. I know not, sir.

WEL.   I'll tell you, Brother,
Whither I suspect she's gone.

KIT.   Whither, good Brother?

WEL. To Cob's house, I believe; but keep my counsel.

KIT. I will, I will. To Cob's house! Doth she haunt Cob's?
She's gone a' purpose now to cuckold me
With that lewd rascal, who, to win her favor,
Hath told her all.   *[Exit.]*

WEL.   Come, he's once more gone;
Sister, let's lose no time; th' affair is worth it.   *[Exeunt.]*

---

[60] Pander.
[61] Makes a fool of.

SCENE IX [62]

[Enter] MATTHEW *[and]* BOBADILL.

MAT. I wonder, Captain, what they will say of my going away, ha?

BOB. Why, what should they say, but as of a discreet gentleman, quick, wary, respectful of nature's fair lineaments? and that's all.

MAT. Why so! but what can they say of your beating?

BOB. A rude part, a touch with soft wood, a kind of gross battery us'd, laid on strongly, borne most patiently; and that's all.   10

MAT. Ay, but would any man have offered it in Venice, as you say?

BOB. Tut, I assure you, no. You shall have there your *nobilis*, your *gentilezza*, come in bravely upon your reverse, stand you close, stand you firm, stand you fair, save your retri-cato[63] with his left leg, come to the assalto with the right, thrust with brave steel, defy your base wood! But wherefore do I awake this remembrance? I was fascinated, by [20 Jupiter, fascinated; but I will be unwitch'd and reveng'd by law.

MAT. Do you hear? Is't not best to get a warrant, and have him arrested and brought before Justice Clement?

BOB. It were not amiss. Would we had it.

[Enter BRAINWORM, *disguised as* FORMAL.]

MAT. Why, here comes his man; let's speak to him.

BOB. Agreed; do you speak.

MAT. Save you, sir.   30

BRAI. With all my heart, sir!

MAT. Sir, there is one Downright hath abus'd this gentleman and myself, and we determine to make our amends by law. Now, if you would do us the favor to procure a war-rant to bring him afore your master, you shall be well considered, I assure you, sir.

BRAI. Sir, you know my service is my liv-ing; such favors as these gotten of my master is his only preferment,[64] and therefore you [40 must consider me as I may make benefit of my place.

MAT. How is that, sir?

BRAI. Faith, sir, the thing is extraordinary, and the gentleman may be of great account; yet, be he what he will, if you will lay me

---

[62] A street.
[63] This word has not been satisfactorily explained. Onions (cited by Simpson) suggests confusion with *rintricato* = entangled.
[64] The only advancement he gives me.

down a brace of angels in my hand you shall have it; otherwise not.

MAT. How shall we do, Captain? He asks a brace of angels. You have no [50 money?

BOB. Not a cross,[65] by fortune.

MAT. Nor I, as I am a gentleman; but two-pence left of my two shillings in the morning for wine and radish; let's find him some pawn.

BOB. Pawn! we have none to the value of his demand.

MAT. O, yes. I'll pawn this jewel in my ear, and you may pawn your silk stockings, [60 and pull up your boots; they will ne'er be miss'd. It must be done now.

BOB. Well, an there be no remedy, I'll step aside and pull 'em off.

MAT. Do you hear, sir? We have no store of money at this time, but you shall have good pawns; look you, sir, this jewel, and that gentleman's silk stockings; because we would have it dispatch'd ere we went to our chambers.   70

BRAI. I am content, sir; I will get you the warrant presently. What's his name, say you? Downright?

MAT. Ay, ay, George Downright.

BRAI. What manner of man is he?

MAT. A tall, big man, sir; he goes in a cloak most commonly of silk russet, laid about with russet lace.

BRAI. 'T is very good, sir.

MAT. Here, sir, here's my jewel!   80

BOB. And here are stockings!

BRAI. Well, gentlemen, I'll procure you this warrant presently; but who will you have to serve it?

MAT. That's true, Captain; that must be consider'd.

BOB. Body o' me, I know not; 't is service of danger!

BRAI. Why, you were best get one o' the varlets o' the city, a serjeant. I'll ap- [90 point you one, if you please.

MAT. Will you, sir? Why, we can wish no better.

BOB. We'll leave it to you, sir.

           [*Exeunt* BOBADILL *and* MATTHEW.]

BRAI. This is rare! Now will I go and pawn this cloak of the justice's man's at the broker's for a varlet's suit, and be the varlet myself; and get either more pawns, or more money of Downright, for the arrest.   [*Exit.*]

[65] Certain small coins bore it.

SCENE X [66]

         [*Enter*] KNOWELL.

KNOW. Oh, here it is; I am glad I have found it now.
Ho! who is within here?

TIB. [*within*] I am within, sir. What's your pleasure?

KNOW. To know who is within besides yourself.

TIB. Why, sir, you are no constable, I hope?

KNOW. O, fear you the constable? Then I doubt not
You have some guests within deserve that fear.
I'll fetch him straight.

           [*Enter* TIB.]

TIB.   O' God's name, sir!

KNOW. Go to. Come tell me, is not young Knowell here?

TIB. Young Knowell! I know none such, sir, o' mine honesty!   10

KNOW. Your honesty! Dame, it flies too lightly from you.
There is no way but fetch the constable.

TIB. The constable! The man is mad, I think.   [*Exit.*]

     [*Enter* DAME KITELY *and* CASH.]

CASH. Ho, who keeps house here?

KNOW. [*aside*] O, this is the female copes-mate[67] of my son!
Now shall I meet him straight.

DAME K.   Knock, Thomas, hard.

CASH. Ho, goodwife!

         [*Re-enter* TIB.]

TIB.   Why, what's the matter with you?

DAME K. Why, woman, grieves it you to ope your door?
Belike you get something to keep it shut.

TIB. What mean these questions, pray ye?

DAME K. So strange you make it! Is not my husband here?   21

KNOW. [*aside*] Her husband!

DAME K.   My tried husband, Master Kitely.

TIB. I hope he needs not to be tried here.

DAME K. No, dame, he does it not for need, but pleasure.

[66] Before Cob's house.
[67] Companion; *i.e.*, paramour.

TIB. Neither for need nor pleasure is he here.

KNOW. [*aside*] This is but a device to balk me withal.

[*Enter* KITELY, *muffled in his cloak.*]

Soft, who is this? 'T is not my son, disguis'd?

DAME K. (*spies her husband come, and runs to him.*) O, sir, have I forestall'd your honest market?

Found your close [68] walks? You stand amaz'd now, do you?

I' faith, I am glad I have smok'd [69] you yet at last. 30

What is your jewel, trow? In, come, let's see her;

Fetch forth your huswife,[70] dame; if she be fairer,

In any honest judgment, than myself,

I'll be content with it; but she is change,

She feeds you fat, she soothes your appetite,

And you are well! Your wife, an honest woman,

Is meat twice sod [71] to you, sir! O, you treachour! [72]

KNOW. [*aside*] She cannot counterfeit thus palpably.

KIT. Out on thy more than strumpet's impudence!

Steal'st thou thus to thy haunts? and have I taken 40

Thy bawd and thee, and thy companion,

(*pointing to old* KNOWELL)

This hoary-headed lecher, this old goat,

Close at your villainy, and wouldst thou 'scuse it

With this stale harlot's jest, accusing me?

O, old incontinent (*to him*), dost thou not shame,

When all thy powers in chastity is spent,

To have a mind so hot, and to entice,

And feed th' enticements of a lustful woman?

DAME K. Out, I defy thee, I, dissembling wretch!

KIT. Defy me, strumpet! Ask thy pander [73] here, 50

Can he deny it, or that wicked elder?

KNOW. Why, hear you, sir.

KIT.　　　　　Tut, tut, tut; never speak.

Thy guilty conscience will discover thee.

KNOW. What lunacy is this, that haunts this man?

KIT. Well, goodwife B-A-'D,[74] Cob's wife, and you,

That make your husband such a hoddy-doddy; [75]

And you, young apple-squire,[76] and old cuckold-maker;

I'll ha' you every one before a justice:

Nay, you shall answer it; I charge you go.

KNOW. Marry, with all my heart, sir; I go willingly; 60

Though I do taste this as a trick put on me,

To punish my impertinent search, and justly;

And half forgive my son for the device.

KIT. Come, will you go?

DAME K.　　　　Go! to thy shame, believe it.

[*Enter* COB.]

COB. Why, what's the matter here? What's here to do?

KIT. O, Cob, art thou come? I have been abus'd,

And i' thy house. Never was man so wrong'd!

COB. 'Slid, in my house? my master Kitely? Who wrongs you in my house?

KIT. Marry, young lust in old, and old in young here; 70

Thy wife's their bawd; here have I taken 'em.

COB. How! bawd! is my house come to that? Am I preferr'd thither? Did I not charge you to keep your doors shut, Is'bel? and do you let 'em lie open for all comers?

He falls upon his wife and beats her.

KNOW. Friend, know some cause, before thou beat'st thy wife.

This's madness in thee.

COB.　　　　　Why, is there no cause?

KIT. Yes, I'll show cause before the Justice, Cob;

Come, let her go with me.

COB.　　　　　Nay, she shall go.

TIB. Nay, I will go. I'll see an you [80 may be allow'd to make a bundle o' hemp [77] o' your right and lawful wife thus, at every cuckoldy knave's pleasure. Why do you not go?

KIT. A bitter quean.[78] Come, we will ha' you tam'd. [*Exeunt.*]

[68] Secret.　　　[69] Observed.
[70] Hussy.　　　[71] Boiled.
[72] Traitor.
[73] Ff, in margin, *By Thomas; i.e.*, with reference to Thomas.
[74] Spelling the word, and making a BAD pun on "bawd."
[75] *I.e.*, cuckold; lit., snail-shell.
[76] Pander, pimp.
[77] Prepared by beating.
[78] Hussy.

Scene XI [79]

[*Enter*] Brainworm, [*disguised as a City serjeant.*]

Brai. Well, of all my disguises yet, now am
I most like myself, being in this serjeant's
gown. A man of my present profession never
counterfeits, till he lays hold upon a debtor
and says he 'rests him ; for then he brings him
to all manner of unrest. A kind of little kings
we are, bearing the diminutive of a mace,
made like a young artichoke, that always carries pepper and salt in itself. [80]   Well, I know
not what danger I undergo by this exploit ; [10
pray Heaven I come well off !

[*Enter* Matthew *and* Bobadill.]

Mat. See, I think, yonder is the varlet, by
his gown.
Bob. Let 's go in quest of him.
Mat. 'Save you, friend ! Are not you here
by appointment of Justice Clement's man ?
Brai. Yes, an't please you, sir ; he told me
two gentlemen had will'd him to procure a
warrant from his master, which I have about
me, to be serv'd on one Downright.
Mat. It is honestly done of you both ; [20
and see where the party comes you must
arrest ; serve it upon him quickly, afore he be
aware —
Bob. Bear back, Master Matthew.

[*Enter* Stephen *in Downright's cloak.*]

Brai. Master Downright, I arrest you i'
the Queen's name, and must carry you afore a
justice by virtue of this warrant.
Step. Me, friend ! I am no Downright, I ;
I am Master Stephen. You do not well to
arrest me, I tell you, truly ; I am in nobody's
bonds nor books, I would you should [31
know it. A plague on you heartily, for making me thus afraid afore my time.
Brai. Why, now are you deceived, gentlemen ?
Bob. He wears such a cloak, and that deceived us. But see, here 'a comes indeed !
This is he, officer.

[*Enter* Downright.]

Dow. Why how now, Signior Gull ! Are
you turn'd filcher of late ? Come, deliver [40
my cloak.

80 A street.
81 A quibble on "mace", the spice. (Simpson.)

Step. Your cloak, sir ! I bought it even
now, in open market.
Brai. Master Downright, I have a war-
rant I must serve upon you, procur'd by these
two gentlemen.
Dow. These gentlemen ? These rascals !
Brai. Keep the peace, I charge you in her
Majesty's name.
Dow. I obey thee. What must I do, [50
officer ?
Brai. Go before Master Justice Clement,
to answer what they can object against you,
sir. I will use you kindly, sir.
Mat. Come, let 's before, and make [81] the
justice, Captain —
Bob. The varlet 's a tall man, afore
Heaven !

[*Exeunt* Bobadill *and* Matthew.]

Dow. Gull, you 'll gi' me my cloak ?
Step. Sir, I bought it, and I 'll keep it.   60
Dow. You will ?
Step. Ay, that I will.
Dow. Officer, there 's thy fee, arrest him.
Brai. Master Stephen, I must arrest you.
Step. Arrest me ! I scorn it. There, take
your cloak, I 'll none on 't.
Dow. Nay, that shall not serve your turn
now, sir. Officer, I 'll go with thee to the
justice's ; bring him along.
Step. Why, is not here your cloak ? What
would you have ?   71
Dow. I 'll ha' you answer it, sir.
Brai. Sir, I 'll take your word, and this
gentleman's too, for his appearance.
Dow. I 'll ha' no words taken. Bring him
along.
Brai. Sir, I may choose to do that ; I may
take bail.
Dow. 'T is true, you may take bail, and
choose, at another time ; but you shall not [80
now, varlet. Bring him along, or I 'll swinge [82]
you.
Brai. Sir, I pity the gentleman's case.
Here 's your money again.
Dow. 'Sdeins, tell not me of my money ;
bring him away, I say.
Brai. I warrant you he will go with you of
himself, sir.
Dow. Yet more ado ?
Brai. [*aside*] I have made a fair mash on 't.
Step. Must I go ?   91
Brai. I know no remedy, Master Stephen.
Dow. Come along afore me here ; I do not
love your hanging look behind.

81 Prepare.   82 Beat.

STEP. Why, sir, I hope you cannot hang me for it. Can he, fellow?

BRAI. I think not, sir; it is but a whipping matter, sure!

STEP. Why, then, let him do his worst;   99 I am resolute.   [*Exeunt.*]

ACT V — SCENE I [1]

[*Enter*] CLEMENT, KNOWELL, KITELY, DAME KITELY, TIB, CASH, COB, [*and*] Servants.

CLEM. Nay, but stay, stay; give me leave. — My chair, sirrah. — You, Master Knowell, say you went thither to meet your son.

KNOW. Ay, sir.

CLEM. But who directed you thither?

KNOW. That did mine own man, sir.

CLEM. Where is he?

KNOW. Nay, I know not now; I left him with your clerk, and appointed him to stay here for me.   10

CLEM. My clerk! About what time was this?

KNOW. Marry, between one and two, as I take it.

CLEM. And what time came my man with the false message to you, Master Kitely?

KIT. After two, sir.

CLEM. Very good; but, Mistress Kitely, how [chance] [2] that you were at Cob's, ha?

DAME K. An['t] please you, sir, I'll tell [20 you. My brother Wellbred told me that Cob's house was a suspected place ——

CLEM. So it appears, methinks; but on.

DAME K. And that my husband us'd thither daily.

CLEM. No matter, so he us'd himself well, mistress.

DAME K. True, sir; but you know what grows by such haunts oftentimes.

CLEM. I see rank fruits of a jealous [30 brain, Mistress Kitely. But did you find your husband there, in that case, as you suspected?

KIT. I found her there, sir.

CLEM. Did you so? That alters the case. Who gave you knowledge of your wife's being there?

KIT. Marry, that did my brother Wellbred.

CLEM. How? Wellbred first tell her; then tell you after? Where is Wellbred?

KIT. Gone with my sister, sir, I know [40 not whither.

CLEM. Why this is a mere trick, a device; you are gull'd in this most grossly all! Alas, poor wench, wert thou beaten for this?

TIB. Yes, most pitifully, an't please you.

COB. And worthily, I hope, if it shall prove so.

CLEM. Ay, that's like, and a piece of a sentence. —

[*Enter a* Servant.]

How now, sir! what's the matter?   50

SERV. Sir, there's a gentleman i' the court without, desires to speak with your Worship.

CLEM. A gentleman? what's he?

SERV. A soldier, sir, he says.

CLEM. A soldier! Take down my armor; my sword, quickly. A soldier speak with me! Why, when, knaves! Come on, come on: (*He arms himself.*) hold my cap there, so; give me my gorget, [3] my sword. — Stand by, I will end your matters anon. —— Let [60 the soldier enter.   [*Exit Servant.*]

SCENE II [4]

[*To them enter*] BOBADILL [*and*] MATTHEW.

Now, sir, what ha' you to say to me?

[MAT.] By your Worship's favor ——

CLEM. Nay, keep out, sir; I know not your pretence. — You send me word, sir, you are a soldier; why, sir, you shall be answer'd here; here be them have been amongst soldiers. Sir, your pleasure.

BOB. Faith, sir, so it is, this gentleman and myself have been most uncivilly wrong'd and beaten by one Downright, a coarse fellow [10 about the town here; and for mine own part, I protest, being a man in no sort given to this filthy humor of quarrelling, he hath assaulted me in the way of my peace, despoil'd me of mine honor, disarm'd me of my weapons, and rudely laid me along, [5] in the open streets, when I not so much as once offer'd to resist him.

CLEM. O, God's precious! is this the soldier? Here, take my armor off quickly; [20 't will make him swoon, I fear; he is not fit to look on 't, that will put up a blow.

MAT. An't please your Worship, he was bound to the peace.

---

[1] Coleman Street. A room in Justice Clement's house.
[2] Add. F₂.
[3] Armor for the throat.
[4] The same. Old eds. print the first line at the end of Sc. i.
[5] Knocked me down.

CLEM. Why, an he were, sir, his hands were not bound, were they?

[*Re-enter* Servant.]

SERV. There's one of the varlets of the City, sir, has brought two gentlemen here; one, upon your Worship's warrant.

CLEM. My warrant!   30

SERV. Yes, sir. The officer says, procur'd by these two.

CLEM. Bid him come in. [*Exit* Servant.] Set by this picture.[6]

SCENE III [7]

[*To them enter*] DOWNRIGHT, STEPHEN, [*and*] BRAINWORM.

What, Master Downright! Are you brought in at Master Freshwater's [8] suit here? [9]

Dow. I' faith, sir; and here's another brought at my suit.

CLEM. What are you, sir?

STEP. A gentleman, sir; O, Uncle!

CLEM. Uncle! Who? Master Knowell?

KNOW. Ay, sir! This is a wise kinsman of mine.

STEP. God's my witness, Uncle, I am [10] wrong'd here monstrously; he charges me with stealing of his cloak, and would I might never stir, if I did not find it in the street by chance.

Dow. O, did you find it now? You said you bought it erewhile.

STEP. And you said I stole it. Nay, now my uncle is here, I'll do well enough with you.

CLEM. Well, let this breathe awhile. You that have cause to complain there, stand [20] forth. — [*They all step forward.*] Had you my warrant for this gentleman's apprehension?

BOB. Ay, an't please your Worship.

CLEM. Nay, do not speak in passion [10] so. Where had you it?

BOB. Of your clerk, sir!

CLEM. That's well! an my clerk can make warrants, and my hand not at 'em! Where is the warrant? Officer, have you it?

BRAI. No, sir. Your Worship's man, [30] Master Formal, bid me do it for these gentlemen, and he would be my discharge.

6 *I.e.*, mere picture, without substance.
7 The same.
8 A freshwater soldier was one who had never seen overseas service.
9 Old eds. print at end of Sc. ii.
10 Emotionally, sorrowfully.

CLEM. Why, Master Downright, are you such a novice, to be serv'd and never see the warrant?

Dow. Sir, he did not serve it on me.

CLEM. No? how then?

Dow. Marry, sir, he came to me, and said he must serve it, and he would use me kindly, and so —   40

CLEM. O, God's pity, was it so, sir? "He must serve it!" — Give me my long-sword there, and help me off — so; come on, sir varlet, I must cut off your legs, sirrah. [BRAINWORM *kneels.*] Nay, stand up; I'll use you kindly; I must cut off your legs, I say.

He flourishes over him with his long-sword.

BRAI. O, good sir, I beseech you; nay, good Master Justice!

CLEM. I must do it; there is no remedy. I must cut off your legs, sirrah; I must cut [50] off your ears, you rascal; I must do it: I must cut off your nose; I must cut off your head.

BRAI. O, good your Worship.

CLEM. Well, rise; how doest thou do now? Doest thou feel thyself well? Hast thou no harm?

BRAI. No, I thank your good Worship, sir.

CLEM. Why, so! I said I must cut off thy legs, and I must cut off thy arms, and I must cut off thy head; but I did not do it. So, [60] you said you must serve this gentleman with my warrant, but you did not serve him. You knave, you slave, you rogue, do you say you must, sirrah? Away with him to the jail; I'll teach you a trick for your "must," sir.

BRAI. Good sir, I beseech you, be good to me.

CLEM. Tell him he shall to the jail; away with him, I say.

BRAI. Nay, sir, if you will commit me, [70] it shall be for committing more than this. I will not lose by my travail any grain of my fame, certain.

[*Throws off his serjeant's gown.*]

CLEM. How is this?

KNOW. My man, Brainworm!

STEP. O, yes, Uncle; Brainworm has been with my cousin Edward and I all this day.

CLEM. I told you all there was some device!

BRAI. Nay, excellent Justice, since I have laid myself thus open to you, now stand [80] strong for me, both with your sword and your balance.

CLEM. Body o' me, a merry knave! Give me a bowl of sack. If he belong to you, Master Knowell, I bespeak your patience.

BRAI. That is it I have most need of. Sir, if you 'll pardon me only, I 'll glory in all the rest of my exploits.

KNOW. Sir, you know I love not to have my favors come hard from me. — You [90 have your pardon, though I suspect you shrewdly for being of counsel with my son against me.

BRAI. Yes, faith, I have, sir, though you retain'd me doubly this morning for yourself: first, as Brainworm; after, as Fitz-Sword. I was your reform'd soldier, sir. 'T was I sent you to Cob's upon the errand without end.

KNOW. Is it possible? or that thou [100 shouldst disguise thy language so as I should not know thee?

BRAI. O, sir, this has been the day of my metamorphosis! It is not that shape alone that I have run through to-day. I brought this gentleman, Master Kitely, a message too, in the form of Master Justice's man here, to draw him out o' the way, as well as your Worship, while Master Wellbred might make a conveyance of Mistress Bridget to my young master. 111

KIT. How! my sister stol'n away?

KNOW. My son is not married, I hope!

BRAI. Faith, sir, they are both as sure [11] as love, a priest, and three thousand pound, which is her portion, can make 'em; and by this time are ready to bespeak their wedding supper at the Windmill, except some friend here prevent [12] 'em, and invite 'em home.

CLEM. Marry, that will I; I thank thee [120 for putting me in mind on 't. — Sirrah, go you and fetch them hither upon my warrant. [*Exit* Servant.] — Neither's friends have cause to be sorry, if I know the young couple aright. Here, I drink to thee for thy good news. But I pray thee, what hast thou done with my man, Formal?

BRAI. Faith, sir, after some ceremony past, as making him drunk, first with story, and then with wine, (but all in kindness,) [130 and stripping him to his shirt, I left him in that cool vein, departed, sold your Worship's warrant to these two, pawn'd his livery for that varlet's gown, to serve it in, and thus have brought myself by my activity to your Worship's consideration.

CLEM. And I will consider thee, in another cup of sack. Here 's to thee, which having drunk off, this my sentence: Pledge me.

Thou hast done, or assisted to nothing, in [140 my judgment, but deserves to be pardon'd for the wit o' the offence. If thy master, or any man here, be angry with thee, I shall suspect his ingine,[13] while I know him, for 't. How now! what noise is that?

[*Enter* Servant.]

SERV. Sir, it is Roger is come home.

CLEM. Bring him in, bring him in.

SCENE IV [14]

To them [*enter*] FORMAL [*in a suit of armor.*]

What! drunk? In arms against me? Your reason, your reason for this.[15]

FORM. I beseech your Worship to pardon me; I happen'd into ill company by chance, that cast me into a sleep, and stripp'd me of all my clothes.

CLEM. Well, tell him I am Justice Clement, and do pardon him. But what is this to your armor? What may that signify?

FORM. An 't please you, sir, it hung up i' [10 the room where I was stripp'd; and I borrow'd it of one of the drawers [16] to come home in, because I was loth to do penance through the street i' my shirt.

CLEM. Well, stand by a while.

SCENE V [17]

To them [*enter*] EDWARD KNOWELL, WELLBRED, [*and*] BRIDGET.

Who be these? Oh, the young company; welcome, welcome. Gi' you joy. Nay, Mistress Bridget, blush not; you are not so fresh a bride but the news of it is come hither afore you. Master Bridegroom, I ha' made your peace; give me your hand. So will I for all the rest ere you forsake my roof.[18]

E. KNOW. We are the more bound to your humanity, sir.

CLEM. Only these two have so little of [10 man in 'em, they are no part of my care.

WEL. Yes, sir, let me pray you for this gentleman; he belongs to my sister the bride.

CLEM. In what place, sir?

WEL. Of her delight, sir, below the stairs, and in public: her poet, sir.

CLEM. A poet! I will challenge him my-self presently at extempore:

---

[11] Fast contracted.   [12] Anticipate.

[13] Wit.   [14] The same.
[15] Ff print this speech at the end of Sc. iii.
[16] Tapsters, waiters.   [17] The same.
[18] Ff print this speech at the end of Sc. iv.

Mount up thy Phlegon,[19] Muse, and testify

How Saturn, sitting in an ebon cloud,   20
Disrob'd his podex, white as ivory,

And through the welkin thund'red all aloud.

WEL. He is not for extempore, sir. He is all for the pocket muse ; please you command a sight of it.

CLEM. Yes, yes ; search him for a taste of his vein.   [*They search* MATTHEW'S *pockets.*]

WEL. You must not deny the Queen's justice, sir, under a writ o' rebellion.

CLEM. What ! all this verse ? Body o' [30 me, he carries a whole realm,[20] a commonwealth of paper, in 's hose ! Let 's see some of his subjects !

[*Reads.*] "Unto the boundless ocean of thy face,
Runs this poor river, charg'd with streams of
     eyes." [21]

How ! this is stol'n !

E. KNOW. A parody ! a parody ! with a kind of miraculous gift, to make it absurder than it was.

CLEM. Is all the rest of this batch ? [40 Bring me a torch ; lay it together, and give fire. Cleanse the air. [*Sets the papers on fire.*] Here was enough to have infected the whole city, if it had not been taken in time ! See, see, how our poet's glory shines ! brighter and brighter ! Still it increases ! Oh, now it's at the highest ; and now it declines as fast. You may see, *sic transit gloria mundi.*

KNOW. There 's an emblem [22] for you, son, and your studies !   50

CLEM. Nay, no speech or act of mine be drawn against such as profess it worthily. They are not born every year, as an alderman.

There goes more to the making of a good poet than a sheriff, Master Kitely. You look upon me ! Though I live i' the city here, amongst you, I will do more reverence to him, when I meet him, than I will to the mayor, out of his year. But these paper-peddlers ! these ink-dabblers ! They cannot expect [60 reprehension or reproach. They have it with the fact.

E. KNOW. Sir, you have sav'd me the labor of a defence.[23]

CLEM. It shall be discourse for supper between your father and me, if he dare undertake me. But to dispatch away these : you sign o' the soldier, and picture o' the poet, (but both so false, I will not ha' you hang'd out at my door till midnight,) while we are at [70 supper you two shall penitently fast it out in my court without ; and, if you will, you may pray there that we may be so merry within as to forgive or forget you when we come out. Here 's a third, because we tender your safety, shall watch you ; he is provided [24] for the purpose. — Look to your charge, sir.

STEP. And what shall I do ?

CLEM. Oh ! I had lost a sheep an he had not bleated ! — Why, sir, you shall give [80 Master Downright his cloak ; and I will entreat him to take it. A trencher and a napkin you shall have i' the butt'ry, and keep Cob and his wife company here ; whom I will entreat first to be reconcil'd ; and you to endeavor with your wit to keep 'em so.

STEP. I 'll do my best.

COB. Why, now I see thou art honest, Tib,

---

[19] One of the horses of the Sun.
[20] Punning on "ream."
[21] A burlesque of part of the opening sonnet of Samuel Daniel's *Delia.*
[22] "A picture and short posie expressing some particular conceit." (Cotgrave, cited by Simpson.)
[23] In Q this part of the scene is protracted by more of Matthew's efforts, and derisive comment on them, and by the following defence ; Lorenzo Junior = Edward Knowell.

GIU. Call you this poetry ?
LO. JU. Poetry ! Nay, then call blasphemy religion,
Call devils angels, and sin piety ;
Let all things be preposterously transchang'd.
LO. SE. Why, how now, son ? What, are you startled now ?
Hath the brize prick'd you, ha ? Go to ! You see
How abjectly your poetry is rank'd
In general opinion.
LO. JU. Opinion ! O God, let gross opinion
Sink and be damn'd as deep as Barathrum.
If it may stand with your most wish'd content,
I can refell opinion and approve
The state of poesy, such as it is,
Blessed, eternal, and most true divine.

Indeed, if you will look on Poesie
As she appears in many, poor and lame,
Patch'd up in remnants and old, worn rags,
Half starv'd for want of her peculiar food,
Sacred invention, — then I must confirm
Both your conceit and censure of her merit.
But view her in her glorious ornaments,
Attired in the majesty of art,
Set high in spirit with the precious taste
Of sweet philosophy, and, which is most,
Crown'd with the rich traditions of a soul
That hates to have her dignity profan'd
With any relish of an earthly thought,
Oh, then how proud a presence doth she bear.
Then is she like herself, fit to be seen
Of none but grave and consecrated eyes.
Nor is it any blemish to her fame
That such lean, ignorant, and blasted wits,
Such brainless gulls, should utter their stol'n wares
With such applauses in our vulgar ears ;
Or that their slubber'd lines have current pass
From the fat judgments of the multitude ;
But that this barren and infected age
Should set no difference 'twixt these empty spirits,
And a true poet, than which reverend name
Nothing can more adorn humanity !

[24] Equipped (with his armor).

I receive thee as my dear and mortal wife
again.   90

TIB. And I you, as my loving and obedient
husband.

CLEM. Good compliment! It will be their
bridal night too. They are married anew.
Come, I conjure the rest to put off all discon-
tent. You, Master Downright, your anger;
you, Master Knowell, your cares; Master
Kitely and his wife, their jealousy.
For, I must tell you both, while that is fed,
Horns i' the mind are worse than o' the
     head.[25]   100

KIT. Sir, thus they go from me; kiss me,
sweetheart. —
" See what a drove of horns fly in the air,
Wing'd with my cleansed and my credulous
     breath!

---

[25] The Q version of this couplet is part of the
following passage quoted by Kitely.

Watch 'em, suspicious eyes, watch where they
     fall.
See, see! on heads that think th' have none
     at all!
Oh, what a plenteous world of this will come!
When air rains horns, all may be sure of
     [some]. [26]
— I ha' learn'd so much verse out of a jealous
man's part in a play.   110

CLEM. 'T is well, 't is well! This night
we 'll dedicate to friendship, love, and laughter. Master Bridegroom, take your bride
and lead; every one, a fellow. Here is my
mistress — Brainworm! to whom all my
addresses of courtship shall have their reference; whose adventures this day, when our
grandchildren shall hear to be made a fable,
I doubt not but it shall find both spectators
and applause.   [*Exeunt.*] 120

---

[26] Cor. F₂; F₁ *fame.* Q *some.*

VOLPONE,

OR

THE FOXE.

A Comædie.

Acted in the yeere 1605. By
the K. MAIESTIES
SERVANTS.

The Author B. I.

HORAT.
Simul & iucunda, & idonea dicere vitæ.

LONDON,
Printed by WILLIAM STANSBY.

M. DC. XVI.

INTRODUCTORY NOTE

THE earliest of Jonson's masterpieces stands among the very greatest of English plays. According to the Folio, it was originally acted in 1605; early in 1606, New Style, seems probable, since the year began on March 25, and the whale of II, i, 46, appeared, as Fleay notes, subsequently to January 19, 1605/6. *Volpone* was performed at the Globe by the King's Men, Shakespeare's company, and also at both the universities. It remained active in the London repertory throughout the seventeenth and eighteenth centuries, and in a debased and perverted adaptation had much success in Germany, France, and the United States about a decade after the World War.

The plot is original, though it is based on the ancient practice of legacy-hunting (*captatio*), which is repeatedly satirized by Lucian, Horace, and Juvenal, forms the subject of an episode in the *Satyricon* of Petronius Arbiter, and is mentioned by Erasmus in his *Moriae Encomium.* The subplot involving Sir Politic and his Lady is wholly Jonson's invention. Professor Rea has argued that the Knight was intended as a caricature of Sir Henry Wotton, the English ambassador to Venice, who was full of "observations" and "projects." But though the scene is transferred to contemporary Venice, since Italy was the natural home of villainy on the Elizabethan stage, and though the direct inspiration of some apparently classical details is to be found, as Professor Rea has shown, in the works of Renaissance humanists, the fabric of the text itself is woven from the poet's reading in classical literature. The idea of Mosca and of the bird and animal characters comes from Erasmus and Horace (*Satires*, II, v). (See introduction to Rea's edition for references and summaries.) In the notes of Lambinus's edition of Horace there is a suggestion for the story of Celia. Lady Would-be is founded on the twenty-sixth declamation of Libanius, in which Morosus accuses his garrulous wife.

That such are the poet's materials does not, however, warrant the conclusion that Volpone is essentially a work of the scissors. Broadly based on the author's wide reading, the edifice owes its structural vigor and its beauty to his union of commanding literary powers with first-rate dramatic genius. In *Volpone* Jonson abandons his earlier profession of sporting with human follies and dedicates himself to a savage attack on the baseness of human nature. He plies a terrible scourge; but the hideous darkness of the play is relieved by the pure and radiant character of Celia, and by the almost Marlovian brilliance, the inexhaustible enthusiasm, the sheer virtuosity, of Volpone himself. The fantastic humors of the Would-bes, though, like the tedious entertainment of Nano and his associates, they are architecturally inharmonious with the masterly treatment of the major subject,[1] nevertheless help keep the play a comedy. But it is the terrific energy of the main plot and its characters, and the far from neoclassical color and exuberance of Jonson's style, that keep it in the main current of the English Renaissance.

The play was first published, in quarto, in 1608 (title page, 1607). The present text is based on the Folio of 1616, the most authoritative of the old editions of Jonson. *Volpone* was separately edited in 1919 by J. D. Rea.

[1] See Rea's edition, p. xxvii, for an ingenious defence. If Jonson's purpose was simply the castigation of folly in a variety of forms, the professional fools quite properly introduce the subject, and the Would-bes serve admirably to illustrate other aspects of it than the greed and credulity of the suitors. But whatever the author's original intention, he found himself composing a passionate drama. The Nano and Would-be scenes clash with the mood induced by it, and they are too long to be taken merely as comic relief from the grim humor of the main plot.

VOLPONE; OR, THE FOX

BY

BEN JONSON

TO THE MOST NOBLE AND MOST EQUAL SISTERS, THE TWO FAMOUS UNIVERSITIES, FOR THEIR LOVE AND ACCEPTANCE SHOWN TO HIS POEM IN THE PRESENTATION, BEN JONSON, THE GRATEFUL ACKNOWLEDGER, DEDICATES BOTH IT AND HIMSELF.[1]

THE PERSONS OF THE PLAY

VOLPONE,[2] a magnifico.
MOSCA,[3] his parasite.
VOLTORE,[4] an advocate.
CORBACCIO,[5] an old gentleman.
CORVINO,[6] a merchant.
BONARIO,[7] a young gentleman, [son to Corbaccio.]
[SIR] POLITIC WOULD-BE, a knight.
PEREGRINE, a gentleman traveller.
NANO, a dwarf.
CASTRONE, an eunuch.
ANDROGYNO, a hermaphrodite.

Grege [or Mob].
Commandadori, officers.
Mercatori, three merchants.
Avocatori, four magistrates.
Notario, the register.
[Workmen.]
Servitore, a servant.

Fine MADAM WOULD-BE, the knight's wife.
CELIA, [Corvino] the merchant's wife.
Women.

THE SCENE — *Venice.*

THE ARGUMENT [8]

V olpone, childless, rich, feigns sick, despairs,
O ffers his state to hopes of several heirs,
L ies languishing; his parasite receives
P resents of all, assures, deludes; then weaves
O ther cross plots, which ope themselves, are told.
N ew tricks for safety are sought; they thrive: when, bold,
E ach tempts th' other again, and all are sold.

PROLOGUE

Now, luck yet [9] send us, and a little wit
  Will serve to make our play hit;
According to the palates of the season,
  Here is rhyme, not empty of reason.
This we were bid to credit from our poet,
  Whose true scope, if you would know it,

In all his poems still hath been this measure,
  To mix profit with your pleasure;
And not as some, whose throats their envy failing,
  Cry hoarsely, " All he writes is railing," [10

[1] Old eds. also print an epistle dedicatory, in which Jonson airs his critical opinions, attacks certain current literary tendencies, and disclaims personal satire in his play. Q also gives ten commendatory poems contributed by various admirers of the author.
[2] "An old fox . . . an old crafty, sly, subtle companion." (These and the following quoted descriptions are cited by Rea from Florio's *World of Words,* 1598.)
[3] "Any kind of fly." (Lat. *musca,* a common name for a parasite.)
[4] "A ravenous bird, called a vulture." (Erasmus says that legacy-hunters were called *vultures.*)
[5] "A filthy great raven." [6] Crow, raven.
[7] "Debonair, honest, good, uncorrupt."
[8] Imitated, both in its acrostic form and in its rough style, from the lines prefixed by some later writer to the various comedies of Plautus.
[9] Q *God.*

And when his plays come forth, think they
    can flout them,
    With saying he was a year about them.
To this there needs no lie, but this his creature,
    Which was two months since no feature ;
And, though he dares give them five lives to
    mend it,
    'T is known, five weeks fully penn'd it,
From his own hand, without a coadjutor,
    Novice, journeyman, or tutor.
Yet thus much I can give you as a token
    Of his play's worth : no eggs are broken, [20
Nor quaking custards with fierce teeth
    affrighted,[10]
Wherewith your rout are so delighted ;
Nor hales he in a gull, old ends reciting,
    To stop gaps in his loose writing ;
With such a deal of monstrous and forc'd
    action,
    As might make Bet'lem a faction : [11]
Nor made he his play for jests stol'n from each
    table,
    But makes jests to fit his fable ;
And so presents quick comedy refined,
    As best critics have designed ;   30
The laws of time, place, persons he observeth,
    From no needful rule he swerveth.
All gall and copperas [12] from his ink he
    draineth ;
    Only, a little salt remaineth ;
Wherewith he 'll rub your cheeks, till, red with
    laughter,
    They shall look fresh a week after.

ACT I — SCENE I [13]

[Enter] VOLPONE *[and]* MOSCA.

VOLP. Good morning to the day ; and next,
    my gold.
Open the shrine, that I may see my saint. —
Hail the world's soul,[14] and mine.   More glad
    than is
The teeming earth to see the long'd-for sun
Peep through the horns of the celestial Ram,

Am I, to view thy splendor darkening his ;
That, lying here, amongst my other hoards,
Show'st like a flame by night, or like the day
Struck out of chaos, when all darkness fled
Unto the center.[15]   O thou son of Sol,[16]   10
But brighter than thy father, let me kiss,
With adoration, thee, and every relic
Of sacred treasure in this blessed room.
Well did wise poets, by thy glorious name,
Title that age which they would have the best ;
Thou being the best of things, and far tran-
    scending
All style of joy, in children, parents, friends,
Or any other waking dream on earth.
Thy looks when they to Venus did ascribe,
They should have giv'n her twenty thousand
    Cupids ;   20
Such are thy beauties and our loves ! Dear
    saint,
Riches, the dumb god,[17] that giv'st all men
    tongues,
That canst do nought, and yet mak'st men do
    all things ;
The price of souls ; even hell, with thee to
    boot,
Is made worth Heaven.   Thou art virtue,
    fame,
Honor, and all things else ! Who can get thee,
He shall be noble, valiant, honest, wise — [18]
    Mos. And what he will, sir.   Riches are in
        fortune
A greater good than wisdom is in nature.
    VOLP. True, my beloved Mosca.   Yet I
        glory   30
More in the cunning purchase [19] of my wealth
Than in the glad possession, since I gain
No common way ; I use no trade, no venture ;
I wound no earth with ploughshares, fat no
    beasts
To feed the shambles ; have no mills for iron,
Oil, corn, or men, to grind 'em into powder ;
I blow no subtle glass, expose no ships
To threat'nings of the furrow-faced sea ;
I turn no monies in the public bank,
No usure private —
    Mos.   No, sir, nor devour 40
Soft prodigals.   You shall ha' some will swal-
    low
A melting heir as glibly as your Dutch
Will pills of butter, and ne'er purge for 't ;

---

[10] Alluding to "a burlesque representation of a
city feast . . . of which an immense custard always
made a conspicuous part." (Gifford.)
[11] *I.e.*, might provide Bedlam (Bethlehem, the
hospital for the insane) with a [still more] disorderly
party.
[12] Green vitriol : used, like "gall", in making ink.
Here they stand for bitterness and malignity, as
"salt" does for wit.
[13] A room in Volpone's house.
[14] Punning on "Sol."

[15] Of the earth.
[16] As gold was considered by the alchemists.
[17] Since silence is golden.
[18] This speech is indebted to Euripides, Horace,
and Erasmus.
[19] Acquisition.

Tear forth the fathers of poor families
Out of their beds, and coffin them alive
In some kind clasping prison, where their bones
May be forthcoming, when the flesh is rotten.
But your sweet nature doth abhor these
    courses ;
You loathe the widow's or the orphan's tears
Should wash your pavements, or their piteous
    cries   50
Ring in your roofs, and beat the air for ven-
    geance.
    VOLP.   Right, Mosca ; I do loathe it. —
    MOS.   And, besides, sir,
You are not like the thresher that doth stand [20]
With a huge flail, watching a heap of corn,[21]
And, hungry, dares not taste the smallest
    grain,
But feeds on mallows, and such bitter herbs ;
Nor like the merchant, who hath fill'd his
    vaults
With Romagnía,[22] rich and Candian [23] wines,
Yet drinks the lees of Lombard's vinegar.
You will not lie in straw, whilst moths and
    worms   60
Feed on your sumptuous hangings and soft
    beds.
You know the use of riches, and dare give now
From that bright heap, to me, your poor ob-
    server,[24]
Or to your dwarf, or your hermaphrodite,
Your eunuch, or what other household trifle
Your pleasure allows maintenance. —
    VOLP.   Hold thee, Mosca ;
Take of my hand ; thou strik'st on truth in all,
And they are envious term thee parasite.
Call forth my dwarf, my eunuch, and my fool,
And let 'em make me sport.   [*Exit* MOSCA.]
               What should I do, [70
But cocker up my genius, and live free
To all delights my fortune calls me to?
I have no wife, no parent, child, ally,
To give my substance to ; but whom I make
Must be my heir ; and this makes men ob-
    serve [25] me.
This draws new clients daily to my house,
Women and men of every sex and age,
That bring me presents, send me plate, coin,
    jewels,
With hope that when I die (which they expect

Each greedy minute) it shall then return   80
Tenfold upon them ; whilst some, covetous
Above the rest, seek to engross me, whole,
And counter work the one unto the other,
Contend in gifts, as they would seem in love ;
All which I suffer, playing with their hopes,
And am content to coin 'em into profit,
And look upon their kindness, and take more,
And look on that ; still bearing them in hand,[26]
Letting the cherry knock against their lips,
And draw it by their mouths, and back
    again. —   90
How now !

SCENE II [27]

[*To him re-enter*] MOSCA, [*with*] NANO, AN-
    DROGYNO, [*and*] CASTRONE.

    NAN.   Now, room for fresh gamesters, who do will
        you to know
They do bring you neither play nor university
    show,
And therefore do entreat you that whatsoever they
    rehearse
May not fare a whit the worse for the false pace of
    the verse.
If you wonder at this, you will wonder more ere we
    pass ;
For know, here [28] is enclos'd the soul of Pythagoras,
That juggler divine,[29] as hereafter shall follow,
Which soul, fast and loose, sir, came first from
    Apollo,
And was breath'd into Aethalides,[30] Mercurius his
    son,
Where it had the gift to remember all that ever was
    done.   10
From thence it fled forth, and made quick transmi-
    gration
To goldy-lock'd Euphorbus, who was kill'd, in good
    fashion,
At the siege of old Troy, by the cuckold of Sparta.[31]
Hermotimus [32] was next (I find it in my charta) ;
To whom it did pass, where no sooner it was missing,
But with one Pyrrhus of Delos [32] it learn'd to go
    a-fishing ;
And thence did it enter the sophist [33] of Greece.
From Pythagore, she went into a beautiful piece,
Hight Aspasia, the meretrix ; and the next toss of
    her
Was again of a whore — she became a philosopher,
Crates [34] the cynic, as itself [35] doth relate it.   21
Since, kings, knights, and beggars, knaves, lords,
    and fools gat it,
Besides ox and ass, camel, mule, goat, and brock,[36]

---

[20] The speech is adapted from Horace, *Satires*,
II, iii, 111–121.
[21] Grain.
[22] From Romania ; *i.e.*, Greek. Note accent of
Folio.
[23] Cretan.
[24] Obsequious follower.
[25] Be obsequious to me.

[26] Deluding them by holding out false hopes.
[27] The same. The interlude which follows is
chiefly based on Lucian's dialogue of the Cock ;
with the addition of some details from Diogenes
Laertius.
[28] In Androgyno.
[29] He is so called by Lucian.
[30] Herald of the Argonauts.
[31] Menelaus.
[32] Mentioned by Diogenes Laertius, VIII, i, 5.
[33] Pythagoras.
[34] Crates of Thebes, a pupil of Diogenes.
[35] Probably Androgyno ; possibly the soul ; possibly an allusion to the cock which tells the story
in Lucian.
[36] Badger.

In all which it hath spoke, as in the cobbler's cock.
But I come not here to discourse of that matter,
Or his one, two, or three, or his great oath, " By
    QUATER ! [37] "
His musics, his trigon,[38] his golden thigh,[39]
Or his telling how elements shift ; but I
Would ask, how of late thou hast suffered transla-
    tion,
And shifted thy coat in these days of reforma-
    tion.   30
   AND.   Like one of the reformed,[40] a fool, as you
    see,
Counting all old doctrine heresy.
   NAN.   But not on thine own forbid meats hast
    thou ventur'd ?
   AND.   On fish, when first a Carthusian I enter'd.[41]
   NAN.   Why, then thy dogmatical silence [42] hath
    left thee?
   AND.   Of that an obstreperous lawyer bereft me.
   NAN.   O wonderful change !   When sir lawyer
    forsook thee,
For Pythagore's sake, what body then took thee?
   AND.   A good dull mule.
   NAN.   And how ! by that means
Thou wert brought to allow of the eating of beans?
   AND.   Yes.
   NAN.   But from the mule into whom didst
    thou pass?   41
   AND.   Into a very strange beast, by some writers
    call'd an ass ;
By others a precise,[43] pure, illuminate brother
Of those devour flesh — and sometimes one another ;
And will drop you forth a libel, or a sanctifi'd lie,
Betwixt every spoonful of a nativity-pie.[44]
   NAN.   Now quit thee, fore Heaven, of that pro-
    fane nation ;
And gently report thy next transmigration.
   AND.   To the same that I am.
   NAN.   A creature of delight,
And, what is more than a fool, an hermaphro-
    dite !   50
Now, pray thee, sweet soul, in all thy variation,
Which body wouldst thou choose to take up thy
    station?
   AND.   Troth, this I am in ; even here would I
    tarry.
   NAN.   'Cause here the delight of each sex thou
    canst vary?
   AND.   Alas, those pleasures be stale and forsaken ;
No, 't is your fool wherewith I am so taken,
The only one creature that I can call blessed ;
For all other forms I have prov'd most distressed.
   NAN.   Spoke true, as thou wert in Pythagoras
    still.
This learned opinion we celebrate will,   60
Fellow eunuch, as behoves us, with all our wit and
    art,
To dignify that whereof ourselves are so great and
    special a part.

   VOLP.   Now, very, very pretty.   Mosca,
    this
Was thy invention?

---

[37] The *quaternio* or "tetraktys of the dekad",
which graphically represented the number ten as
the triangle of four.
  [38] Triangle.
  [39] Mentioned by Lucian and also by Diogenes
Laertius.
  [40] The Puritans.
  [41] *I.e.*, and not till then, the Pythagorean rule
being even stricter.
  [42] *I.e.*, the five years' silence of the Pythagorean
rule.
  [43] Puritanical.
  [44] Christmas-pie.

   MOS.   If it please my patron,
Not else.
   VOLP.   It doth, good Mosca.
   MOS.   Then it was, sir.

            SONG

Fools they are the only nation
Worth men's envy or admiration ;
Free from care or sorrow taking,
Selves and others merry making :
All they speak or do is sterling.   70
Your fool he is your great man's dearling,
And your ladies' sport and pleasure ;
Tongue and bauble [45] are his treasure.
E'en his face begetteth laughter,
And he speaks truth free from slaughter ; [46]
He 's the grace of every feast,
And sometimes the chiefest guest ;
Hath his trencher and his stool,
When wit waits upon the fool.
    O, who would not be   80
    He, he, he?

             One knocks without.
   VOLP.   Who 's that?   Away !   Look, Mosca.
   MOS.   Fool, begone !

    [*Exeunt* NANO, CASTRONE, *and* AN-
    DROGYNO.]

'T is Signior Voltore, the advocate ;
I know him by his knock.
   VOLP.   Fetch me my gown,
My furs, and nightcaps ; say my couch is
    changing,
And let him entertain himself awhile
Without, i' th' gallery.   [*Exit* MOSCA.]   Now,
    now my clients
Begin their visitation !   Vulture, kite,[47]
Raven, and gorcrow,[48] all my birds of prey,
That think me turning carcase, now they
    come :   90
I am not for 'em yet.

    [*Re-enter* MOSCA, *with the gown, etc.*]
             How now ! the news?
   MOS.   A piece of plate, sir.
   VOLP.   Of what bigness?
   MOS.   Huge,
Massy, and antique, with your name inscrib'd,
And arms engraven.
   VOLP.   Good ! and not a fox
Stretch'd on the earth, with fine delusive
    sleights,
Mocking a gaping crow? ha, Mosca?
   MOS.   Sharp, sir.
   VOLP.   Give me my furs. — Why dost thou
    laugh so, man?

---

  [45] Old eds. *bable.*
  [46] *I.e.*, with impunity.
  [47] Not one of the three suitors ; possibly Lady
Would-be, though she is later termed a she-wolf.
  [48] Carrion crow.

Mos. I cannot choose, sir, when I appre-
    hend
What thoughts he has without [49] now, as he
    walks :   99
That this might be the last gift he should give,
That this would fetch you ; if you died to-day,
And gave him all, what he should be to-mor-
    row ;
What large return would come of all his ven-
    tures ;
How he should worshipp'd be, and reverenc'd ;
Ride with his furs and footcloths, waited on
By herds of fools and clients ; have clear way
Made for his mule, as letter'd as himself ;
Be call'd the great and learned advocate !
And then concludes there's nought impos-
    sible.
    Volp. Yes, to be learned, Mosca.
    Mos.   O, no ! rich
Implies it. Hood an ass with reverend
    purple,   111
So you can hide his two ambitious ears, [50]
And he shall pass for a cathedral doctor. [51]
    Volp. My caps, my caps, good Mosca.
    Fetch him in.
    Mos. Stay, sir ; your ointment for your
    eyes.
    Volp.   That's true ;
Dispatch, dispatch ; I long to have possession
Of my new present.
    Mos.   That, and thousands more,
I hope to see you lord of.
    Volp.   Thanks, kind Mosca.
    Mos. And that, when I am lost in blended
    dust,   119
And hundreds such as I am, in succession —
    Volp. Nay, that were too much, Mosca.
    Mos.   You shall live
Still to delude these harpies.
    Volp.   Loving Mosca !
'T is well ; my pillow now, and let him enter.
                       [*Exit* Mosca.]
Now, my feign'd cough, my phthisic, [52] and my
    gout,
My apoplexy, palsy, and catarrhs,
Help, with your forced functions this my pos-
    ture,
Wherein, this three year, I have milk'd their
    hopes.
He comes ; I hear him — Uh, uh, uh, uh ! —
    Oh !

[49] Q *within.*
[50] Which, because of their size, will not be content
to stay under the hood.
[51] *I.e.*, a doctor who holds a professorial chair.
[52] Phthisis, consumption.

SCENE III [53]

[*To*] Volpone ; [*re-enter* Mosca,] [*with*] Vol-
    TORE.

    Mos. You still are what you were, sir.
    Only you,
Of all the rest, are he commands his love,
And you do wisely to preserve it thus,
With early visitation and kind notes
Of your good meaning to him, which, I know,
Cannot but come most grateful. Patron ! sir !
Here 's Signior Voltore is come ——
    Volp.   What say you?
    Mos. Sir, Signior Voltore is come this
    morning
To visit you.
    Volp.   I thank him.
    Mos.   And hath brought
A piece of antique plate, bought of St. Mark, [54]
With which he here presents you.
    Volp.   He is welcome. [11
Pray him to come more often.
    Mos.   Yes.
    Volt.   What says he?
    Mos. He thanks you, and desires you see
    him often.
    Volp. Mosca.
    Mos.   My patron !
    Volp.   Bring him near. Where is he?
I long to feel his hand.
    Mos.   The plate is here, sir.
    Volt. How fare you, sir?
    Volp.   I thank you, Signior Voltore.
Where is the plate? mine eyes are bad.
    Volt.   I 'm sorry
To see you still thus weak.
    Mos. [*aside*]   That he is not weaker.
    Volp. You are too munificent.
    Volt.   No, sir; would to Heaven
I could as well give health to you, as that
    plate.   20
    Volp. You give, sir, what you can. I
    thank you. Your love
Hath taste in this, and shall not be unanswer'd.
I pray you see me often.
    Volt.   Yes, I shall, sir.
    Volp. Be not far from me.
    Mos.   Do you observe that, sir?
    Volt. You are a happy man, sir ; know
    your good.
    Volp. I cannot now last long ——

[53] The same. Volpone lies in the inner stage.
[54] *I.e.*, at a goldsmith's shop near the church.

Mos. [*aside*]   You are his heir, sir.

Volt. [*aside*] Am I?

Volp.   I feel me going — uh, uh, uh, uh! —
I 'm sailing to my port — uh, uh, uh, uh! —
And I am glad I am so near my haven.   30

    Mos. Alas, kind gentleman ; well, we must
       all go ——

    Volt. But, Mosca ——

    Mos.   Age will conquer.

    Volt.   'Pray thee, hear me.
Am I inscrib'd his heir, for certain?

    Mos.   Are you !
I do beseech you, sir, you will vouchsafe
To write me i' your family.[55]   All my hopes
Depend upon your Worship.   I am lost
Except the rising sun do shine on me.

    Volt. It shall both shine, and warm thee,
       Mosca.

    Mos.   Sir,
I am a man that hath not done your love
All the worst offices : here I wear your keys,
See all your coffers and your caskets lock'd, [41
Keep the poor inventory of your jewels,
Your plate, and monies ; am your steward, sir,
Husband your goods here.

    Volt.   But am I sole heir?

    Mos. Without a partner, sir : confirm'd
       this morning :
The wax is warm yet, and the ink scarce dry
Upon the parchment.

    Volt.   Happy, happy me !
By what good chance, sweet Mosca?

    Mos.   Your desert, sir ;
I know no second cause.

    Volt.   Thy modesty
Is loth to know it ; well, we shall requite it. [50

    Mos. He ever lik'd your course, sir ; that
       first took him.
I oft have heard him say how he admir'd [56]
Men of your large profession, that could speak
To every cause, and things mere contraries,
Till they were hoarse again, yet all be law ;
That, with most quick agility, could turn,
And return ; make knots, and undo them ; [57]
Give forked counsel ; take provoking gold
On either hand, and put it up [58] ; these men,
He knew, would thrive with their humility. [60
And, for his part, he thought he should be
     blest
To have his heir of such a suffering spirit,

So wise, so grave, of so perplex'd a tongue,
And loud withal, that would not wag, nor
     scarce
Lie still, without a fee ; when every word
Your Worship but lets fall, is a *cecchine* ! [59]

                Another knocks.
Who 's that?   One knocks ; I would not have
     you seen, sir.
And yet — pretend you came and went in
     haste ;
I 'll fashion an excuse.   And, gentle sir,
When you do come to swim in golden lard,   70
Up to the arms in honey, that [60] your chin
Is borne up stiff with fatness of the flood,[61]
Think on your vassal ; but remember me :
I ha' not been your worst of clients.

    Volt.   Mosca ——

    Mos. When will you have your inventory
       brought, sir?
Or see a copy of the will? — Anon. —
I 'll bring 'em to you, sir.   Away, begone,
Put business i' your face.   [*Exit* Voltore.]

    Volp.   Excellent,[62] Mosca !
Come hither, let me kiss thee.

    Mos.   Keep you still, sir.
Here is Corbaccio.

    Volp.   Set the plate away :   80
The vulture 's gone, and the old raven 's come.

Scene IV [63]

Mosca [*and*] Volpone [*remain.*]

    Mos. Betake you to your silence, and your
       sleep. —
[*To the plate*] Stand there and multiply. —
     [*aside*] Now shall we see
A wretch who is indeed more impotent
Than this [64] can feign to be ; yet hopes to hop
Over his grave. —

       [*He admits* Corbaccio.]

           Signior Corbaccio !
Yo' are very welcome, sir.

    Corb.   How does your patron?

    Mos. Troth, as he did, sir ; no amends.

    Corb.   What? mends he?

    Mos. No, sir : he is rather worse.

    Corb.   That 's well.   Where is he?

    Mos. Upon his couch, sir, newly fall'n
       asleep.

---

[55] Enroll me as one of your servants.
[56] Based on chapter 93 of Cornelius Agrippa of
Nettesheim's *De Incertitudine et Vanitate Scien-
tiarum atque Artium.* (Rea.)
[57] A nine-syllable line.
[58] Pocket it.

[59] Sequin, an obsolete gold coin of Italy and
Turkey, worth about $2.25. (Webster.) Trisyllabic.
[60] So that.
[61] Cf. Chaloner's translation (1549) of a note on a
clause in Erasmus's *Moriae Encomium:* "as if they
swam up to the chins in a sea of honey." (Rea.)
[62] Q omits comma.   [63] The same.   [64] Volpone.

Corb. Does he sleep well?

Mos.   No wink, sir, all this night, 10
Nor yesterday ; but slumbers.[65]

Corb.   Good ! he should take
Some counsel of physicians. I have brought
      him
An opiate here, from mine own doctor —

Mos. He will not hear of drugs.

Corb.   Why? I myself
Stood by while 't was made, saw all th' ingre-
      dients ;
And know it cannot but most gently work.
My life for his, 't is but to make him sleep.

Volp. [aside] Ay, his last sleep, if he would
      take it.

Mos.   Sir,
He has no faith in physic.

Corb.   Say you? say you?

Mos. He has no faith in physic ; [66] he does
      think   20
Most of your doctors are the greater danger,
And worse disease, t' escape. I often have
Heard him protest that your physician
Should never be his heir.

Corb.   Not I his heir?

Mos. Not your physician, sir.

Corb.   O, no, no, no ;
I do not mean it.

Mos.   No, sir, nor their fees
He cannot brook : he says they flay a man
Before they kill him.

Corb.   Right, I do conceive you.

Mos. And then they do it by experiment ;
For which the law not only doth absolve 'em,
But gives them great reward ; and he is loth
To hire his death so.

Corb.   It is true, they kill 32
With as much licence as a judge.

Mos.   Nay, more ;
For he but kills, sir, where the law condemns,
And these can kill him too.

Corb.   Ay, or me,
Or any man. How does his apoplex?
Is that strong on him still?

Mos.   Most violent.
His speech is broken, and his eyes are set,
His face drawn longer than 't was wont ——

Corb.   How? how?
Stronger than he was wont?

Mos.   No, sir ; his face [40
Drawn longer than 't was wont.

Corb.   O, good.

Mos.   His mouth
Is ever gaping, and his eyelids hang.

Corb.   Good.

Mos. A freezing numbness stiffens all his
      joints,
And makes the color of his flesh like lead.

Corb.   'T is good.

Mos. His pulse beats slow, and dull.

Corb.   Good symptoms still.

Mos. And from his brain ——

Corb.   Ha? How? Not from his brain?

Mos. Yes, sir, and from his brain —

Corb.   I conceive you ; good.

Mos. Flows a cold sweat, with a continual
      rheum,
Forth the resolved [67] corners of his eyes.   49

Corb. Is 't possible? Yet I am better, ha !
How does he with the swimming of his head?

Mos. O, sir, 't is past the scotomy ; [68] he
      now
Hath lost his feeling, and hath left to snort : [69]
You hardly can perceive him, that he breathes.

Corb. Excellent, excellent ; sure I shall
      outlast him ;
This makes me young again, a score of years.

Mos. I was a-coming for you, sir.

Corb.   Has he made his will?
What has he giv'n me?

Mos.   No, sir.

Corb.   Nothing? ha?

Mos. He has not made his will, sir.

Corb.   Oh, oh, oh.
What then did Voltore, the lawyer, here? 60

Mos. He smelt a carcass, sir, when he but
      heard
My master was about his testament ;
As I did urge him to it for your good ——

Corb. He came unto him, did he? I
      thought so.

Mos. Yes, and presented him this piece of
      plate.

Corb. To be his heir?

Mos.   I do not know, sir.

Corb.   True ;
I know it too.

Mos. [aside] By your own scale, sir.

Corb.   Well,
I shall prevent [70] him yet. See, Mosca, look,
Here I have brought a bag of bright *cecchines*,
Will quite weigh down his plate.

Mos.   Yea, marry, sir. 70

---

[65] Dozes.
[66] These comments on physicians are also taken
from Cornelius Agrippa. (Rea.)

[67] Dissolving.
[68] Giddiness.
[69] Stopped snoring. (A bad symptom.)
[70] Get ahead of.

This is true physic, this your sacred medicine ;
No talk of opiates to this great elixir !
    CORB. 'T is *aurum palpabile*, if not *pota-
       bile.*[71]
    MOS. It shall be minister'd to him in his
       bowl !
    CORB. Ay, do, do, do.
    MOS.   Most blessed cordial !
This will recover him.
    CORB.   Yes, do, do, do.
    MOS. I think it were not best, sir.
    CORB.   What ?
    MOS.   To recover him.
    CORB. O, no, no, no ; by no means.
    MOS.   Why, sir, this
Will work some strange effect, if he but feel it.
    CORB. 'T is true ; therefore forbear. I 'll
       take my venture ;   80
Give me 't again.
    MOS.   At no hand ;[72] pardon me :
You shall not do yourself that wrong, sir. I
Will so advise you, you shall have it all.
    CORB. How ?
    MOS.   All, sir ; 't is your right, your
       own ; no man
Can claim a part : 't is yours without a rival,
Decreed by destiny.
    CORB.   How, how, good Mosca ?
    MOS. I 'll tell you, sir. This fit he shall re-
       cover —
    CORB. I do conceive you.
    MOS.   And, on first advantage
Of his gain'd sense, will I re-importune him
Unto the making of his testament :   90
And show him this.   [*Points to the money.*]
    CORB.   Good, good.
    MOS.   'T is better yet,
If you will hear, sir.
    CORB.   Yes, with all my heart.
    MOS. Now would I counsel you, make home
       with speed ;
There, frame a will ; whereto you shall in-
       scribe
My master your sole heir.
    CORB.   And disinherit
My son ?
    MOS.   O, sir, the better ; for that color[73]
Shall make it much more taking.
    CORB.   O, but[74] color ?
    MOS. This will, sir, you shall send it unto
       me.
Now, when I come to enforce, as I will do,

Your cares, your watchings, and your many
    prayers,   100
Your more than many gifts, your this day's
    present,
And last, produce your will ; where (without
    thought
Or least regard unto your proper[75] issue,
A son so brave, and highly meriting)
The stream of your diverted love hath thrown
    you
Upon my master, and made him your heir ;
He cannot be so stupid or stone-dead,
But, out of conscience and mere gratitude ——
    CORB. He must pronounce me his ?
    MOS.   'T is true.
    CORB.   This plot
Did I think on before.
    MOS.   I do believe it.   110
    CORB. Do you not believe it ?
    MOS.   Yes, sir.
    CORB.   Mine own project.
    MOS. Which, when he hath done, sir ——
    CORB.   Publish'd me his heir ?
    MOS. And you so certain to survive him —
    CORB.   Ay.
    MOS. Being so lusty a man ——
    CORB.   'T is true.
    MOS.   Yes, sir ——
    CORB. I thought on that too. See, how he
       should be
The very organ to express my thoughts !
    MOS. You have not only done yourself a
       good ——
    CORB. But multiplied it on my son !
    MOS.   'T is right, sir.
    CORB. Still, my invention.
    MOS.   'Las, sir ! Heaven knows,
It hath been all my study, all my care,   120
(I e'en grow gray withal) how to work things —
    CORB. I do conceive, sweet Mosca.
    MOS.   You are he
For whom I labor here.
    CORB.   Ay, do, do, do.
I 'll straight about it.
    MOS. [*aside*]   Rook go with you,[76] raven.
    CORB. I know thee honest.
    MOS.   You do lie, sir —
    CORB.   And ——
    MOS. Your knowledge is no better than
       your ears, sir.
    CORB. I do not doubt to be a father to thee.
    MOS. Nor I to gull my brother of his bless-
       ing.

[71] Gold in solution was a sovereign remedy.
[72] By no means.
[73] Pretence.   [74] Merely.
[75] Own.
[76] May you be rooked (= cheated), you raven.

CORB. I may ha' my youth restor'd to me,
    why not?

MOS. Your Worship is a precious ass —

CORB.   What say'st thou?

MOS. I do desire your Worship to make
    haste, sir.   131

CORB. 'T is done, 't is done ; I go. [*Exit.*]

VOLP. [*leaping from his couch*] [77] Oh, I
    shall burst !
Let out my sides, let out my sides ——

MOS.   Contain
Your flux of laughter, sir ; you know this hope
Is such a bait, it covers any hook.

VOLP. O, but thy working, and thy placing
    it !
I cannot hold ; good rascal, let me kiss thee :
I never knew thee in so rare a humor.

MOS. Alas, sir, I but do as I am taught ;
Follow your grave instructions, give 'em
    words,   140
Pour oil into their ears, and send them hence.

VOLP. 'T is true, 't is true. What a rare
    punishment
Is avarice to itself !

MOS.   Ay, with our help, sir.

VOLP. So many cares, so many maladies [78]
So many fears attending on old age.
Yea, death so often call'd on, as no wish
Can be more frequent with 'em, their limbs
    faint,
Their senses dull, their seeing, hearing, going,[79]
All dead before them ; yea, their very teeth,
Their instruments of eating, failing them : [150
Yet this is reckon'd life ! Nay, here was one,
Is now gone home, that wishes to live longer !
Feels not his gout, nor palsy ; feigns himself
Younger by scores of years, flatters his age
With confident belying it, hopes he may
With charms like Aeson [80] have his youth re-
    stor'd ;
And with these thoughts so battens, as if fate
Would be as easily cheated on as he ;
And all turns air ! Who's that there, now? a
    third?   *Another knocks.*

MOS. Close ; to your couch again ; I hear
    his voice.   160
It is Corvino, our spruce merchant.

VOLP. [*lying down*]   Dead.

MOS. Another bout, sir, with your eyes.
    [*anointing them*] — Who's there?

SCENE V [81]

[*To them enter*] CORVINO.

Signior Corvino ! come most wish'd for ! Oh,
How happy were you, if you knew it, now !

CORV. Why? what? wherein?

MOS.   The tardy hour is come, sir.

CORV. He is not dead?

MOS.   Not dead, sir, but as good ;
He knows no man.

CORV.   How shall I do then?

MOS.   Why, sir?

CORV. I have brought him here a pearl.

MOS.   Perhaps he has
So much remembrance left as to know you,
    sir :
He still calls on you ; nothing but your name
Is in his mouth. Is your pearl orient,[82] sir?

CORV. Venice was never owner of the like. [10

VOLP. Signior Corvino !

MOS.   Hark !

VOLP.   Signior Corvino.

MOS. He calls you ; step and give it him. —
    H' is here, sir.
And he has brought you a rich pearl.

CORV.   How do you, sir? —
Tell him it doubles the twelfth [83] carat.

MOS.   Sir,
He cannot understand : his hearing's gone ;
And yet it comforts him to see you ——

CORV.   Say
I have a diamond for him, too.

MOS.   Best show 't, sir ;
Put it into his hand ; 't is only there
He apprehends ; he has his feeling yet.
See, how he grasps it !

CORV.   'Las, good gentleman ! [20
How pitiful the sight is !

MOS.   Tut, forget, sir.
The weeping of an heir should still be laugh-
    ter [84]
Under a visor.[85]

CORV.   Why, am I his heir?

MOS. Sir, I am sworn, I may not show the
    will
Till he be dead. But here has been Corbaccio,
Here has been Voltore, here were others too —
I cannot number 'em, they were so many ——
All gaping here for legacies ; but I,
Taking the vantage of his naming you,

---

[77] Add. Gifford.
[78] This speech is taken from the *Moriae Encomium*. (Rea.)
[79] Ability to walk.
[80] Whom, according to Ovid, Medea restored to
youth.

[81] The same.   [82] *I.e.*, especially lustrous, a fine one.
[83] So Gifford ; old eds. *twelfe.*
[84] Quoted by Aulus Gellius from a mime of Publius
Syrus, and also in a note by Lambinus on Horace,
Satires, II, v, 103, 104. (Rea.) Line 37 is from
the same satire, ll. 68, 69.   [85] Mask.

" Signior Corvino, Signior Corvino," took [30
Paper, and pen, and ink, and there I ask'd him
Whom he would have his heir! " Corvino."
      Who
Should be executor? " Corvino." And
To any question he was silent to,
I still interpreted the nods he made,
Through weakness, for consent; and sent
      home th' others,
Nothing bequeath'd them, but to cry and
      curse.
    Corv. Oh, my dear Mosca. (*They em-
    brace.*) Does he not perceive us?
    Mos. No more than a blind harper. He
    knows no man,
No face of friend, nor name of any servant, 40
Who 't was that fed him last, or gave him
      drink;
Not those he hath begotten, or brought up,
Can he remember.
    Corv.   Has he children?
    Mos.   Bastards,
Some dozen, or more, that he begot on beggars,
Gypsies, and Jews, and black-moors, when he
      was drunk.
Knew you not that, sir? 'T is the common
      fable.
The dwarf, the fool, the eunuch, are all his;
H' is the true father of his family,[86]
In all save me. But he has giv'n 'em nothing.
    Corv. That 's well, that 's well. Art sure
    he does not hear us?   50
    Mos. Sure, sir! Why, look you, credit
    your own sense.
                    [*Shouts in* Volpone's *ear.*]
The pox approach, and add to your diseases,
If it would send you hence the sooner, sir;
For your incontinence it hath deserv'd it
Throughly and throughly, and the plague to
      boot!—
You may come near, sir.—Would you would
      once close
Those filthy eyes of yours, that flow with
      slime
Like two frog-pits; and those same hanging
      cheeks,
Cover'd with hide instead of skin—Nay, help,
      sir[87]——
That look like frozen dishclouts set on end. 60
    Corv. Or like an old smok'd wall, on which
    the rain
Ran down in streaks.

    Mos.   Excellent, sir! speak out;
You may be louder yet; a culverin[88]
Discharged in his ear would hardly bore it.
    Corv. His nose is like a common sewer, still
    running.
    Mos. 'T is good! And what his mouth?
    Corv.   A very draught.
    Mos. O, stop it up——
    Corv.   By no means.
    Mos.   Pray you, let me;
Faith, I could stifle him rarely with a pillow
As well as any woman that should keep[89] him.
    Corv. Do as you will; but I 'll be gone.
    Mos.   Be so; [70
It is your presence makes him last so long.
    Corv. I pray you use no violence.
    Mos.   No, sir? why?
Why should you be thus scrupulous, 'pray
      you, sir?
    Corv. Nay, at your discretion.
    Mos.   Well, good sir, begone.
    Corv. I will not trouble him now to take[90]
    my pearl?
    Mos. Pooh, nor your diamond. What a
    needless care
Is this afflicts you? Is not all here yours?
Am not I here, whom you have made, your
      creature,
That owe my being to you?
    Corv.   Grateful Mosca! [79
Thou art my friend, my fellow, my companion,
My partner, and shalt share in all my for-
      tunes.
    Mos. Excepting one.
    Corv.   What 's that?
    Mos.   Your gallant wife, sir.
                            [*Exit* Corvino.]
Now is he gone; we had no other means
To shoot him hence but this.
    Volp.   My divine Mosca!
Thou hast to-day outgone thyself. Who 's
      there?
                        Another knocks.
I will be troubled with no more. Prepare
Me music, dances, banquets, all delights;
The Turk is not more sensual in his pleasures
Than will Volpone. [*Exit* Mosca.] Let me
      see; a pearl!
A diamond! plate! *cecchines!* Good morn-
      ing's purchase.[91]   90
Why, this is better than rob churches, yet;

---

[86] A Latinism = household of servants. The line
is from Martial, I, 84.
[87] *I.e.*, to abuse Volpone.

[88] Musket or small cannon.
[89] Take care, watch over.
[90] *I.e.*, to get from his hand.
[91] Loot, booty.

Or fat,[92] by eating, once a month, a man ——

[*Re-enter* MOSCA.]

Who is 't?

Mos.   The beauteous Lady Would-be, sir,
Wife to the English knight, Sir Politic Would-
    be ——
This is the style, sir, is directed me ——
Hath sent to know how you have slept to-
    night,
And if you would be visited.

VOLP.   Not now.
Some three hours hence ——

Mos.   I told the squire [93] so much.

VOLP. When I am high with mirth and
    wine ; then, then.   99
'Fore Heaven, I wonder at the desperate valor
Of the bold English, that they dare let loose
Their wives to all encounters !

Mos.   Sir, this knight
Had not his name for nothing : he is politic,
And knows, howe'er his wife affect strange
    airs,
She hath not yet the face to be dishonest.[94]
But had she Signior Corvino's wife's face ——

VOLP. Hath she so rare a face?

Mos.   O, sir, the wonder,
The blazing star of Italy ! a wench
Of the first year ![95] a beauty ripe as harvest !
Whose skin is whiter than a swan, all over !
Than silver, snow, or lilies ! a soft lip,   111
Would tempt you to eternity of kissing !
And flesh that melteth in the touch to blood ! [96]
Bright as your gold ! and lovely as your gold !

VOLP. Why had not I known this before?

Mos.   Alas, sir,
Myself but yesterday discover'd it.

VOLP. How might I see her?

Mos.   Oh, not possible ;
She 's kept as warily as is your gold ;
Never does come abroad, never takes air   119
But at a windore.[97] All her looks are sweet,
As the first grapes or cherries, and are watch'd
As near as they are.

VOLP.   I must see her ——

Mos.   Sir,
There is a guard of ten spies thick upon her,
All his whole household ; each of which is set
Upon his fellow, and have all their charge,
When he goes out, when he comes in, examin'd.

VOLP. I will go see her, though but at her
    windore.

Mos. In some disguise then.

VOLP.   That is true ; I must
Maintain mine own shape still the same ; we 'll
    think.   [*Exeunt.*]

ACT II — SCENE I [1]

[*Enter* SIR] POLITIC WOULD-BE, [*and*] PERE-
    GRINE.

POL. Sir, to a wise man, all the world 's his
    soil :
It is not Italy, nor France, nor Europe,
That must bound me, if my fates call me forth.
Yet I protest, it is no salt desire
Of seeing countries, shifting a religion,
Nor any disaffection to the state
Where I was bred, and unto which I owe
My dearest plots, hath brought me out ; much
    less
That idle, antic, stale, grey-headed project
Of knowing men's minds and manners, with
    Ulysses !   10
But a peculiar humor of my wife's
Laid for this height of Venice,[2] to observe,
To quote,[3] to learn the language, and so
    forth ——
I hope you travel, sir, with license? [4]

PER.   Yes.

POL. I dare the safelier converse. —— How
    long, sir,
Since you left England?

PER.   Seven weeks.

POL.   So lately !
You ha' not been with my Lord Ambassador?

PER.   Not yet, sir.

POL. Pray you, what news, sir, vents our
    climate?
I heard last night a most strange thing reported
By some of my Lord's followers, and I long [20
To hear how 't will be seconded !

PER.   What was 't, sir?

POL. Marry, sir, of a raven that should
    build
In a ship royal of the king's.

PER. [*aside*]   This fellow,
Does he gull me, trow? or is gull'd? — Your
    name, sir?

POL. My name is Politic Would-be.

---

[92] Grow fat.
[93] Follower. Probably with a glance at the meaning " pander."
[94] Unchaste.
[95] Cf. *Leviticus*, xiv, 10: "ewe-lamb a year old
without blemish."
[96] Passion.   [97] Window.

[1] Before Corvino's house in St. Mark's Square.
[2] *I.e.*, Venice at the height (of the season).
[3] Make notes.
[4] Permission (of the British government).

PER. [*aside*]   O, that speaks him. —
A knight, sir?

POL.   A poor knight, sir.

PER.   Your lady
Lies [5] here in Venice, for intelligence
Of tires and fashions and behavior,
Among the courtesans? [6] The fine Lady
     Would-be?

POL. Yes, sir; the spider and the bee [7] oft-
     times   30
Suck from one flower.

PER.   Good Sir Politic!
I cry you mercy; I have heard much of you:
'T is true, sir, of your raven.

POL.   On your knowledge?

PER. Yes, and your lion's whelping in the
     Tower.

POL. Another whelp! [8]

PER.   Another, sir.

POL.   Now Heaven!
What prodigies be these? The fires [9] at
     Berwick!
And the new star! These things concurring,
     strange!
And full of omen! Saw you those meteors?

PER. I did, sir.

POL.   Fearful! Pray you, sir, confirm
     me,
Were there three porpoises seen, above the
     Bridge, [10]   40
As they give out?

PER.   Six, and a sturgeon, sir.

POL. I am astonish'd!

PER.   Nay, sir, be not so;
I 'll tell you a greater prodigy then these —

POL. What should these things portend?

PER.   The very day,
Let me be sure, that I put forth from Lon-
     don,
There was a whale discover'd in the river,
As high as Woolwich, that had waited there,
Few know how many months, for the subver-
     sion
Of the Stode [11] fleet.

POL.   Is 't possible? Believe it,
'T was either sent from Spain, or the Arch-
     duke's!   50

Spinola's [12] whale, upon my life, my credit!
Will they not leave these projects? Worthy
     sir,
Some other news.

PER.   Faith, Stone, the fool, is dead,
And they do lack a tavern fool extremely.

POL. Is Mas' Stone dead?

PER.   He 's dead, sir; why, I hope
You thought him not immortal? — [*aside*] Oh,
     this knight,
Were he well known, would be a precious thing
To fit our English stage. He that should write
But such a fellow, should be thought to feign
Extremely, if not maliciously.

POL.   Stone dead!   60

PER. Dead. — Lord! how deeply, sir, you
     apprehend it!
He was no kinsman to you?

POL.   That [13] I know of.
Well! that same fellow was an unknown [14]
     fool.

PER. And yet you knew him, it seems?

POL.   I did so. Sir,
I knew him one of the most dangerous heads
Living within the state, and so I held him.

PER. Indeed, sir?

POL.   While he liv'd, in action,
He has receiv'd weekly intelligence,
Upon my knowledge, out of the Low Coun-
     tries,
For all parts of the world, in cabbages;   70
And those dispens'd again to ambassadors,
In oranges, muskmelons, apricots,
Lemons, pome-citrons, and such like; some-
     times
In Colchester oysters, and your Selsey cockles.

PER. You make me wonder!

POL.   Sir, upon my knowledge.
Nay, I have observ'd him, at your public
     ordinary,
Take his advertisement [15] from a traveller
(A conceal'd statesman) in a trencher of meat;
And instantly, before the meal was done,
Convey an answer in a toothpick.

PER.   Strange!   80
How could this be, sir?

POL.   Why, the meat was cut
So like his character, and so laid as he
Must easily read the cipher.

PER.   I have heard
He could not read, sir.

---

[5] Sojourns.
[6] The most famous in Europe.
[7] *I.e.*, courtesans and chaste women.
[8] According to Stowe's *Survey of London*, cubs were born to a lioness in the Tower several times during 1604 and 1605.
[9] A meteor. This and the new star were observed in 1604.
[10] Stowe mentions the appearance of a porpoise at West Ham on January 19, 1606.
[11] A port near Hamburg.

[12] The Marquis of Spinola commanded the Spanish army that reduced Ostend in 1604.
[13] *I.e.*, not that.
[14] Inexpressible.
[15] Information.

Pol.   So 't was given out,
In polity, by those that did employ him ;
But he could read, and had your languages,
And to 't, as sound a noddle ——
    Per.   I have heard, sir,
That your baboons were spies, and that they
    were
A kind of subtle nation near to China.
    Pol. Ay, ay, your Mam[a]luchi.[16] Faith,
    they had   90
Their hand in a French plot or two ; but they
Were so extremely given to women, as [17]
They made discovery of all : yet I
Had my advices here, on Wednesday last,
From one of their own coat, they were return'd,
Made their relations, as the fashion is,
And now stand fair for fresh employment.
    Per. [aside]   Heart !
This Sir Pol will be ignorant of nothing. ——
It seems, sir, you know all.
    Pol.   Not all, sir. But
I have some general notions. I do love   100
To note and to observe. Though I live out,
Free from the active torrent, yet I 'd mark
The currents and the passages of things
For mine own private use ; and know the
    ebbs
And flows of state.
    Per.   Believe it, sir, I hold
Myself in no small tie [18] unto my fortunes,
For casting me thus luckily upon you,
Whose knowledge, if your bounty equal it,
May do me great assistance, in instruction
For my behavior, and my bearing, which [110
Is yet so rude and raw ——
    Pol.   Why? came you forth
Empty of rules for travel?
    Per.   Faith, I had
Some common ones, from out that vulgar
    grammar,
Which he that cri'd Italian to me, taught me.
    Pol. Why, this it is that spoils all our
    brave bloods,
Trusting our hopeful gentry unto pedants,
Fellows of outside, and mere bark. You seem
To be a gentleman of ingenuous race. ——
I not profess it, but my fate hath been
To be where I have been consulted with, [120
In this high kind,[19] touching some great men's
    sons,
Persons of blood and honor. ——
    Per.   Who be these, sir?

[*To them enter*] Mosca [*and*] Nano [*disguised,
    with* Workmen *who erect a stage.*]

    Mos. Under that windore, there 't must be.
        The same.
    Pol. Fellows to mount a bank ! Did your
        instructor
In the dear tongues never discourse to you
Of the Italian mountebanks?
    Per.   Yes, sir.
    Pol.   Why,
Here shall you see one.
    Per.   They are quacksalvers,
Fellows that live by venting oils and drugs !
    Pol. Was that the character he gave you
        of them?
    Per. As I remember.
    Pol.   Pity his ignorance.
They are the only knowing men of Europe !
Great general scholars, excellent physi-
    cians,   10
Most admir'd statesmen, profess'd favorites
And cabinet counsellors to the greatest
    princes !
The only languag'd men of all the world !
    Per. And, I have heard, they are most
        lewd [21] impostors ;
Made all of terms and shreds ; no less beliers
Of great men's favors, than their own vile
    med'cines ;
Which they will utter [22] upon monstrous oaths ;
Selling that drug for twopence, ere they part,
Which they have valu'd at twelve crowns be-
    fore.
    Pol. Sir, calumnies are answer'd best with
        silence.   20
Yourself shall judge. — Who is it mounts, my
    friends?
    Mos. Scoto of Mantua,[23] sir.
    Pol.   Is 't he? Nay, then
I 'll proudly promise, sir, you shall behold
Another man than has been phant'sied [24] to
    you.
I wonder yet, that he should mount his bank
Here in this nook, that has been wont t' appear
In face of the Piazza ! Here he comes.

[*Enter* Volpone, *disguised as a mountebank
    doctor, and followed by a crowd of people.*]

    Volp. [*to* Nano] Mount, zany.
    Gre. Follow, follow, follow, follow, follow.

---

[16] Mamelukes.   [17] That.
[18] Obligation.
[19] In matters of this important sort.
[20] The same.   [21] Ignorant.   [22] Vend.
[23] The name of an Italian juggler who was in England about this time. (Gifford.)
[24] Falsely pictured.

Pol. See how the people follow him! h' is
 a man   30
May write ten thousand crowns in bank here.
 Note,
Mark but his gesture — I do use to observe
The state he keeps in getting up!

Per.   'T is worth it, sir.

Volp. Most noble gentlemen, and my
worthy patrons, it may seem strange that I,
your Scoto Mantuano, who was ever wont to
fix my bank in the face of the public Piazza,
near the shelter of the portico to the Pro-
curatia,[25] should now, after eight months'
absence from this illustrious city of Venice, [40
humbly retire myself into an obscure nook of
the Piazza.

Pol. Did not I now object the same?

Per.   Peace, sir.

Volp. Let me tell you: I am not, as your
Lombard proverb saith, cold on my feet; or
content to part with my commodities at a
cheaper rate than I accustomed — look not for
it. Nor that the calumnious reports of that
impudent detractor, and shame to our profession (Alessandro Buttone,[26] I mean), who [50
gave out, in public, I was condemn'd *a' sfor-
zato*[27] to the galleys, for poisoning the Cardinal
Bembo's — [28] cook, hath at all attached, much
less dejected me. No, no, worthy gentlemen;
to tell you true, I cannot endure to see the
rabble of these ground *ciarlitani*[29] that spread
their cloaks on the pavement, as if they meant
to do feats of activity, and then come in
lamely, with their mouldy tales out of Boc-
cacio, like stale Tabarin,[30] the fabulist; [60
some of them discoursing their travels, and of
their tedious captivity in the Turk's galleys,
when, indeed, were the truth known, they were
the Christian's galleys, where very temperately
they ate bread, and drunk water, as a wholesome penance, enjoin'd them by their con-
fessors, for base pilferies.

Pol. Note but his bearing, and contempt
 of these.

Volp. These turdy-facy-nasty-paty-lousy-
fartical rogues, with one poor groat's-worth [70
of unprepar'd antimony, finely wrapp'd up in

several *scartoccios*,[31] are able, very well, to kill
their twenty a week, and play; yet these
meagre, starv'd spirits, who have half stopp'd
the organs of their minds with earthy oppila-
tions,[32] want not their favorers among your
shrivell'd salad-eating artisans, who are overjoy'd that they may have their half-pe'rth of
physic; though it purge 'em into another
world, 't makes no matter.   80

Pol. Excellent! ha' you heard better language, sir?

Volp. Well, let 'em go. And, gentlemen,
honorable gentlemen, know that for this time
our bank, being thus remov'd from the
clamours of the *canaglia*,[33] shall be the scene of
pleasure and delight; for I have nothing to
sell, little or nothing to sell.

Pol. I told you, sir, his end.

Per.   You did so, sir.

Volp. I protest I and my six servants are
not able to make of this precious liquor so [90
fast as it is fetch'd away from my lodging by
gentlemen of your city, strangers of the Terra-
firma,[34] worshipful merchants, ay, and senators,
too: who, ever since my arrival, have detained
me to their uses, by their splendidous liberali-
ties. And worthily. For what avails your
rich man to have his magazines stuff'd with
moscadelli, or of the purest grape, when his
physicians prescribe him, on pain of death, to
drink nothing but water cocted[35] with [100
aniseeds? O health! health! the blessing of
the rich! the riches of the poor! who can buy
thee at too dear a rate, since there is no enjoying this world without thee? Be not then so
sparing of your purses, honorable gentlemen,
as to abridge the natural course of life —

Per. You see his end.

Pol.   Ay, is 't not good?

Volp. For, when a humid flux, or catarrh,
by the mutability of air, falls from your head
into an arm or shoulder, or any other part, [110
take you a ducat, or your *cecchine* of gold, and
apply to the place affected; see what good
effect it can work. No, no; 't is this blessed
unguento,[36] this rare extraction, that hath only
power to disperse all malignant humors that
proceed either of hot, cold, moist, or windy
causes —

Per. I would he had put in dry too.

Pol.   'Pray you, observe.

---

[25] Residence of the procurator in charge of St.
Mark's.

[26] Unidentified. [27] At forced labor.

[28] The dash has not been explained. Possibly it
is intended to delude the audience into expecting
something spicy, for Bembo's life was notoriously
sumptuous and voluptuous.

[29] Petty impostors.

[30] A traditional name, though there was a Tabarin
who was buffoon of a French charlatan's troupe
at Paris early in the seventeenth century.

[31] Folded papers. [32] Obstructions.

[33] Mob, *canaille*.

[34] Venetian territory on the mainland.

[35] Boiled. *Moscadelli* = muscatel wine.

[36] Ointment.

VOLP. To fortify the most indigest and crude stomach, ay, were it of one that, through [120 extreme weakness, vomited blood, applying only a warm napkin to the place, after the unction and fricace ; [37] — for the *vertigine* [38] in the head, putting but a drop into your nostrils, likewise behind the ears, a most sovereign and approv'd remedy ; the *mal caduco*,[39] cramps, convulsions, paralyses, epilepsies, *tremor cordia*, retir'd [40] nerves, ill vapors of the spleen, stoppings of the liver, the stone, the strangury, *hernia ventosa, iliaca passio;* [41] stops a [130 *dysenteria* immediately ; easeth the torsion of the small guts ; and cures *melancholia hypocondriaca*, being taken and applied according to my printed receipt. (*Pointing to his bill and his glass*) For this is the physician, this the medicine ; this counsels, this cures ; this gives direction, this works the effect ; and, in sum, both together may be term'd an abstract of the theoric and practic in the Aesculapian art. 'T will cost you eight crowns. — And, [140 Zan Fritada,[42] pray thee sing a verse, extempore, in honor of it.

POL. How do you like him, sir?

PER. Most strangely, I !

POL. Is not his language rare?

PER. But [43] alchemy, I never heard the like, or Broughton's [44] books.

SONG

Had old Hippocrates, or Galen,
That to their books put med'cines all in,
But known this secret, they had never
(Of which they will be guilty ever)
Been murderers of so much paper,   150
Or wasted many a hurtless taper;
No Indian drug had e'er been famed,
Tobacco, sassafras, not named ;
Ne yet of guacum [45] one small stick, sir,
Nor Raymund Lully's [46] great elixir.
Ne had been known the Danish Gonswart,[47]
Or Paracelsus, with his long-sword.[48]

PER. All this, yet, will not do ; eight crowns is high.

---

[37] Chafing.   [38] Vertigo.
[39] Epilepsy.
[40] Contracted, shrunk. (*N.E.D.*)
[41] Colic.
[42] Nano's name in this masquerade.
[43] Except for.
[44] Hugh Broughton was an eccentric contemporary divine of Puritan leanings.
[45] A drug obtained from trees of the genus *guaiacum*.
[46] Ramon Lull, the great Majorcan mystic and (reputed) alchemist (d. 1315).
[47] Johannes Wessel, a fifteenth-century physician. (Holt.)
[48] He carried his familiar there. Much of the material for these speeches so taken from the writings of Paracelsus. (See Rea's notes.)

VOLP. No more. — Gentlemen, if I had but time to discourse to you the miraculous [160 effects of this my oil, surnamed *oglio del Scoto*, with the countless catalogue of those I have cured of th' aforesaid, and many more diseases ; the patents and privileges of all the princes and commonwealths of Christendom ; or but the depositions of those that appear'd on my part, before the signiory of the Sanità [49] and most learned College of Physicians ; where I was authorized, upon notice taken of the admirable virtues of my medicaments, and mine [170 own excellency in matter of rare and unknown secrets, not only to disperse them publicly in this famous city, but in all the territories that happily joy under the government of the most pious and magnificent states of Italy. But may some other gallant fellow say, " Oh, there be divers that make profession to have as good, and as experimented receipts as yours." Indeed, very many have assay'd,[50] like apes, in imitation of that which is really and [180 essentially in me, to make of this oil ; bestow'd great cost in furnaces, stills, alembics, continual fires, and preparation of the ingredients (as indeed there goes to it six hundred several simples, besides some quantity of human fat, for the conglutination, which we buy of the anatomists) ; but when these practitioners come to the last decoction — blow, blow, puff, puff, and all flies in fumo.[51] Ha, ha, ha ! Poor wretches ! I rather pity their folly [190 and indiscretion, than their loss of time and money ; for those may be recovered by industry ; but to be a fool born, is a disease incurable. For myself, I always from my youth have endeavor'd to get the rarest secrets, and book them, either in exchange or for money ; I spared nor cost nor labor where anything was worthy to be learned. And, gentlemen, honorable gentlemen, I will undertake, by virtue of chemical art, out of the honorable [200 hat that covers your head, to extract the four elements ; that is to say, the fire, air, water, and earth, and return you your felt without burn or stain. For, whilst others have been at the *balloo* [52] I have been at my book ; and am now past the craggy paths of study, and come to the flow'ry plains of honor and reputation.

POL. I do assure you, sir, that is his aim.

---

[49] *I.e.*, the directors of the hospital.
[50] Essayed.   [51] Smoke.
[52] Probably a game of ball, called "balloon."

VOLP. But, to our price.

PER.   And that withal,[53] Sir Pol. [210

VOLP. You all know, honorable gentlemen, I never valu'd this *ampulla*, or vial, at less than eight crowns ; but for this time, I am content to be depriv'd of it for six ; six crowns is the price, and less in courtesy I know you cannot offer me ; take it or leave it, howsoever, both it and I am at your service. I ask you not as the value of the thing, for then I should demand of you a thousand crowns ; so the Cardinals Montalto, Fernese, the great Duke [220 of Tuscany, my gossip,[54] with divers other princes, have given me ; but I despise money. Only to show my affection to you, honorable gentlemen, and your illustrious state here, I have neglected the messages of these princes, mine own offices,[55] fram'd my journey hither, only to present you with the fruits of my travels. — Tune your voices once more to the touch of your instruments, and give the [229 honorable assembly some delightful recreation.

PER. What monstrous and most painful circumstance
Is here, to get some three or four gazets,[56]
Some threepence i' the whole ! for that 't will
      come to.

SONG

You that would last long, list to my song;
Make no more coil, but buy of this oil.
Would you be ever fair, and young?
Stout of teeth, and strong of tongue?
Tart of palate? quick of ear?
Sharp of sight? of nostril clear?   240
Moist of hand? and light of foot?
Or (I will come nearer to 't)
Would you live free from all diseases?
Do the act your mistress pleases,
Yet fright all aches[57] from your bones?
Here's a med'cine for the nones.[58]

VOLP. Well, I am in a humor, at this time, to make a present of the small quantity my coffer contains ; to the rich in courtesy, and to the poor for God's sake. [250 Wherefore now mark : I ask'd you six crowns ; and six crowns, at other times, you have paid me ; you shall not give me six crowns, nor five, nor four, nor three, nor two, nor one ; nor half a ducat ; no, nor a *m[o]ccinigo*.[59] Six— pence it will cost you, or six hundred pound — expect no lower price, for, by the banner of my front, I will not bate a bagatine,[60] — that I will have, only, a pledge of your loves, to carry something from amongst you, to show I am [260 not contemn'd by you. Therefore, now, toss your handkerchiefs, cheerfully, cheerfully ; and be advertised, that the first heroic spirit that deigns to grace me with a handkerchief, will give it a little remembrance of something beside, shall please it better than if I had presented it with a double pistolet.[61]

PER. Will you be that heroic spark, Sir Pol?

    CELIA, *at the windo[w], throws down her handkerchief.*

O, see ! the windore has prevented[62] you.

VOLP. Lady, I kiss your bounty ; and, [270 for this timely grace you have done your poor Scoto of Mantua, I will return you, over and above my oil, a secret of that high and inestimable nature, shall make you for ever enamor'd on that minute wherein your eye first descended on so mean, yet not altogether to be despis'd, an object. Here is a powder conceal'd in this paper, of which, if I should speak to the worth, nine thousand volumes were but as one page, that page as a [280 line, that line as a word ; so short is this pilgrimage of man, which some call life, to the expressing of it. Would I reflect on the price? Why, the whole world is but as an empire, that empire as a province, that province as a bank, that bank as a private purse, to the purchase of it. I will only tell you : it is the powder that made Venus a goddess, given her by Apollo, that kept her perpetually young, clear'd her wrinkles, firm'd her gums, fill'd [290 her skin, color'd her hair ; from her deriv'd to Helen, and at the sack of Troy unfortunately lost ; till now, in this our age, it was as happily recover'd, by a studious antiquary, out of some ruins of Asia, who sent a moiety of it to the court of France (but much sophisticated), wherewith the ladies there now color their hair. The rest, at this present, remains with me, extracted to a quintessence ; so that, wherever it but touches, in youth it per- [300 petually preserves, in age restores the complexion ; seats your teeth, did they dance like virginal jacks,[63] firm as a wall ; makes them white as ivory, that were black as —

---

[53] In addition.   [54] Crony.
[55] Duties.
[56] Trivial Venetian coins.
[57] Pronounced *aitches.*
[58] For the purpose.
[59] A Venetian coin worth about eighteen cents.

[60] An Italian coin worth about one-sixth of a cent.
[61] A Spanish goldpiece. A pistolet was worth about $1.50.
[62] Anticipated.
[63] Intermediate pieces of wood to which were attached the quills that plucked the strings of the virginals. Also used, loosely, for the keys.

SCENE III [64]

[*To them enter*] CORVINO.

COR. Spite o' the devil, and my shame!
    Come down here;
Come down! — No house but mine to make
    your scene?
Signior Flaminio,[65] will you down, sir? down?
What, is my wife your Franciscina,[66] sir?
No windores on the whole piazza, here,
To make your properties, but mine? but
    mine?
        He beats away the mountebank, etc.
Heart! ere to-morrow I shall be new christen'd,
And called the *Pantalone di B[i]sognosi;* [67]
About the town.
    PER.   What should this mean, Sir Pol?
    POL. Some trick of state, believe it; I will
        home.   10
    PER. It may be some design on you.
    POL.   I know not.
I'll stand upon my guard.
    PER.   It is your best, sir.
    POL. This three weeks, all my advices, all
        my letters,
They have been intercepted.
    PER.   Indeed, sir?
Best have a care.
    POL.   Nay, so I will.
    PER. [*aside*]   This knight,
I may not lose him, for my mirth, till night.
                        [*Exeunt.*]

SCENE IV [68]

[*Enter*] VOLPONE, [*and*] MOSCA.

VOLP. O, I am wounded.
MOS.   Where, sir?
VOLP.   Not without;
Those blows were nothing; I could bear them
    ever.
But angry Cupid, bolting [69] from her eyes,
Hath shot himself into me like a flame;
Where now he flings about his burning heat,
As in a furnace some [70] ambitious fire
Whose vent is stopp'd. The fight is all within
    me.
I cannot live, except thou help me, Mosca;
My liver melts, and I, without the hope

  [64] The same.
  [65] Alluding, apparently, to Flaminio Scala, leader
of a troupe of Italian actors. (Holt.)
  [66] *I.e.,* the Columbine of the troupe.
  [67] The old gull of the commedia dell'arte. Lit.,
Fool of the Needy.
  [68] A room in Volpone's house.
  [69] Shooting.
  [70] So Ff, Q; some copies of F1 *an.*

Of some soft air from her refreshing breath, 10
Am but a heap of cinders.
    MOS.   'Las, good sir,
Would you had never seen her.
    VOLP.   Nay, would thou
Hadst never told me of her.
    MOS.   Sir, 't is true;
I do confess I was unfortunate,
And you unhappy; but I am bound in con-
    science,
No less than duty, to effect my best
To your release of torment, and I will, sir.
    VOLP. Dear Mosca, shall I hope?
    MOS.   Sir, more than **dear,**
I will not bid you to despair of aught
Within a human compass.
    VOLP.   O, there spoke [20
My better angel. Mosca, take my keys,
Gold, plate, and jewels, all's at thy devotion;
Employ them how thou wilt: nay, coin me
    too:
So thou in this but crown my longings, Mosca!
    MOS. Use but your patience.
    VOLP.   So I have.
    MOS.   I doubt not
To bring success to your desires.
    VOLP.   Nay, then,
I not repent me of my late disguise.
    MOS. If you can horn [71] him, sir, you need
    not.
    VOLP.   True.
Besides, I never meant him for my heir.
Is not the color o' my beard and eyebrows [30
To make me known?
    MOS.   No jot.
    VOLP.   I did it well.
    MOS. So well, would I could follow you in
    mine,
With half the happiness; and yet I would
Escape your epilogue.[72]
    VOLP.   But were they gull'd
With a belief that I was Scoto?
    MOS.   Sir,
Scoto himself could hardly have distinguish'd!
I have not time to flatter you now; we'll part:
And as I prosper, so applaud my art. [*Exeunt.*]

SCENE V [73]

[*Enter*] CORVINO, [*with his sword in his hand,*
dragging in] CELIA.

CORV. Death of mine honor, with the city's
    fool!

  [71] Cuckold.   [72] *I.e.,* the beating.
  [73] A room in Corvino's house.

A juggling, tooth-drawing, prating mounte-
    bank !
And at a public windore ! where, whilst he,
With his strain'd action, and his dole of faces,[74]
To his drug-lecture draws your itching ears,
A crew of old, unmarried, noted lechers,
Stood leering up like satyrs ; and you smile
Most graciously ! and fan your favors forth,
To give your hot spectators satisfaction !
What, was your mountbank their call ? their
    whistle ?   10
Or were you enamor'd on his copper rings,
His saffron jewel, with the toad-stone [75] in 't,
Or his embroid'red suit, with the cope-stitch,[76]
Made of a hearse cloth, or his old tilt-feather,
Or his starch'd beard ?   Well ! you shall have
    him, yes.
He shall come home, and minister unto you
The fricace[77] for the mother.[78]   Or, let me see,
I think you 'd rather mount ! [79]   Would you
    not mount ?
Why, if you 'll mount, you may ; yes, truly,
    you may.
And so you may be seen, down to th' foot. [20
Get you a cittern, Lady Vanity,
And be a dealer with the virtuous man ;
Make one.   I 'll but protest myself a cuckold,
And save your dowry.   I am a Dutchman, I !
For if you thought me an Italian,
You would be damn'd ere you did this, you
    whore.
Thou 'dst tremble to imagine that the murder
Of father, mother, brother, all thy race,
Should follow, as the subject of my justice !
    CEL. Good sir, have patience !
    CORV.   What couldst thou propose [30
Less to thyself, than in this heat of wrath,
And stung with my dishonor, I should strike
This steel into thee, with as many stabs
As thou wert gaz'd upon with goatish eyes ?
    CEL. Alas, sir, be appeas'd !   I could not
    think
My being at the windore should more now
Move your impatience than at other times.
    CORV. No ? not to seek and entertain a
    parley
With a known knave ? before a multitude ?
You were an actor with your handkerchief ! [40

Which he most sweetly kiss'd in the receipt,
And might, no doubt, return it with a letter
And 'point the place where you might meet ;
    your sister's,
Your mother's, or your aunt's might serve the
    turn.
    CEL. Why, dear sir, when do I make these
    excuses,
Or ever stir abroad, but to the church ?
And that so seldom ——
    CORV.   Well, it shall be less ;
And thy restraint before was liberty,
To what I now decree ; and therefore mark
    me.
First, I will have this bawdy light [80] damm'd
    up ;   50
And till 't be done, some two or three yards
    off
I 'll chalk a line ; o'er which if thou but chance
To set thy desp'rate foot, more hell, more
    horror,
More wild remorseless rage shall seize on thee
Than on a conjuror that had heedless left
His circle's safety ere his devil was laid.
Then here 's a lock [81] which I will hang upon
    thee,
And, now I think on 't, I will keep thee back-
    wards ;
Thy lodging shall be backwards, thy walks
    backwards,
Thy prospect — all be backwards, and no
    pleasure,   60
That thou shalt know but backwards.   Nay,
    since you force
My honest nature, know it is your own
Being too open, makes me use you thus.
Since you will not contain your subtle nostrils
In a sweet room, but they must snuff the air
Of rank and sweaty passengers [82] — (*knock
    within*) one knocks.
Away, and be not seen, pain of thy life ;
Nor look toward the windore ; if thou dost ——
Nay, stay, hear this —— let me not prosper,
    whore,
But I will make thee an anatomy,[83]   70
Dissect thee mine own self, and read a lecture
Upon thee to the city, and in public.
Away ! ——   [*Exit* CELIA.]

[*Enter* Servitore.]

            Who 's there ?
    SER.   'T is Signior Mosca, sir.

---

[74] Grimaces.
[75] The fabulous jewel in the toad's head ; set in
a ring it defended the wearer from "pains of the
belly and small guts."
[76] Embroidery.   [77] Massage.
[78] The rising of the mother (*matrix*), hysteria.
[79] *I.e.*, jump up on Volpone's stage and join his
troupe, playing the part of Vanity in the old interludes.
[80] The window.
[81] Probably a girdle of chastity.
[82] Passers-by.   [83] Cadaver.

Scene VI [84]

Corvino [*and* Servitore *remain.*]

Corv. Let him come in. [*Exit* Servitore.]
— His master's dead! There's yet
Some good to help the bad. —— [*Enter*
Mosca.] My Mosca, welcome;
I guess your news.
    Mos.   I fear you cannot, sir.
    Corv. Is 't not his death?
    Mos.   Rather the contrary.
    Corv. Not his recovery?
    Mos.   Yes, sir.
    Corv.   I am curs'd;
I am bewitch'd; my crosses meet to vex me.
How? how? how? how?
    Mos.   Why, sir, with Scoto's oil!
Corbaccio and Voltore brought of it,
Whilst I was busy in an inner room ——
    Corv. Death! that damn'd mountebank!
      but for the law,   10
Now, I could kill the rascal. 'T cannot be
His oil should have that virtue. Ha' not I
Known him a common rogue, come fiddling in
To th' osteria,[85] with a tumbling whore,[86]
And, when he has done all his forc'd tricks,
been glad
Of a poor spoonful of dead wine, with flies in 't?
It cannot be. All his ingredients
Are a sheep's gall, a roasted bitch's marrow,
Some few sod [87] earwigs, pounded caterpillars,
A little capon's grease, and fasting spittle: [20
I know 'em to a dram.
    Mos.   I know not, sir;
But some on 't, there, they pour'd into his ears,
Some in his nostrils, and recover'd him;
Applying but the fricace.
    Corv.   Pox o' that fricace.
    Mos. And, since, to seem the more officious
And flatt'ring of his health, there, they have
had,
At extreme fees, the college of physicians
Consulting on him, how they might restore
him;
Where one would have a cataplasm [88] of spices,
Another a flay'd ape clapp'd to his breast, 30
A third would ha' it a dog, a fourth an oil,
With wildcats' skins. At last, they all resolv'd
That, to preserve him, was no other means
But some young woman must be straight
sought out,
Lusty, and full of juice, to sleep by him;

And to this service most unhappily,
And most unwillingly, am I now employ'd,
Which here I thought to pre-acquaint you
with,
For your advice, since it concerns you most;
Because I would not do that thing might cross
Your ends, on whom I have my whole de-
pendence, sir.   41
Yet, if I do not they may delate [89]
My slackness to my patron, work me out
Of his opinion; and there all your hopes,
Ventures, or whatsoever, are all frustrate.
I do but tell you, sir. Besides, they are all
Now striving who shall first present him.
      Therefore ——
I could entreat you, briefly, conclude some-
    what:
Prevent 'em if you can.
    Corv.   Death to my hopes!
This is my villainous fortune! Best to hire [50
Some common courtesan!
    Mos.   Ay, I thought on that, sir;
But they are all so subtle, full of art —
And age again doting and flexible,
So as — I cannot tell — we may, perchance,
Light on a quean may cheat us all.
    Corv.   'T is true.
    Mos. No, no; it must be one that has no
    tricks, sir,
Some simple thing, a creature made unto [90] it;
Some wench you may command. Ha' you no
    kinswoman?
Gods so — Think, think, think, think, think,
    think, think, sir.   59
One o' the doctors offer'd there his daughter.
    Corv. How!
    Mos.   Yes, Signior Lupo, the physician.
    Corv. His daughter!
    Mos.   And a virgin, sir. Why, alas,
He knows the state of 's body, what it is:
That naught can warm his blood, sir, but a
    fever,
Nor any incantation raise his spirit;
A long forgetfulness hath seiz'd that part.
Besides, sir, who shall know it? Some one or
    two —
    Corv. I pray thee give me leave. — [*step-
    ping aside*] If any man
But I had had this luck — The thing in 't
    self,
I know, is nothing. — Wherefore should not I
As well command my blood and my affec-
    tions [91]   71

[84] The same.   [85] Hostelry, tavern. Q *Osteria.*
[86] *I.e.*, a female acrobat.
[87] Sodden, boiled.   [88] Poultice.

[89] Denounce.   [90] Prepared for, put up to.
[91] My fleshly nature and my feelings.

As this dull doctor? In the point of honor,
The cases are all one of wife and daughter.
   Mos. [*aside*] I hear him coming.[92]
   Corv. [*aside*]   She shall do 't ; 't is done.
'Slight ! [93] if this doctor, who is not engag'd,
Unless 't be for his counsel, which is nothing,
Offer his daughter, what should I, that am
So deeply in? I will prevent him. Wretch !
Covetous wretch ! — Mosca, I have deter-
    min'd.
   Mos. How, sir?
   Corv.   We 'll make all sure. The
    party you wot of   80
Shall be mine own wife, Mosca.
   Mos.   Sir, the thing,
But that I would not seem to counsel you,
I should have motion'd [94] to you, at the first ;
And make your count,[95] you have cut all their
    throats.
Why ! 't is directly taking a possession !
And in his next fit, we may let him go.
'T is but to pull the pillow from his head,
And he is thr[o]ttled ; it had been done before
But for your scrupulous doubts.
   Corv.   Ay, a plague on 't ;
My conscience fools my wit ! Well, I 'll be
    brief,   90
And so be thou, lest they should be before us.
Go home ; prepare him ; tell him with what
    zeal
And willingness I do it. Swear it was
On the first hearing, as thou mayst do, truly,
Mine own free motion.
   Mos.   Sir, I warrant you,
I 'll so possess him with it, that the rest
Of his starv'd clients shall be banish'd all ;
And only you receiv'd. But come not, sir,
Until I send, for I have something else
To ripen for your good — you must not
    know 't.   100
   Corv. But do not you forget to send, now.
   Mos.   Fear not. [*Exit.*]

Scene VII [96]

Corvino [*remains.*]

   Corv. Where are you, Wife? My Celia !
    Wife !

[*Enter* Celia.]

                — What, blubbering?
Come, dry those tears. I think thou thought'st
    me in earnest ;

---

[92] Into my trap.   [93] God's light.   [94] Proposed.
[95] Count on it.   [96] The same.

Ha? By this light I talk'd so but to try thee.
Methinks, the lightness of the occasion
Should ha' confirm'd thee. Come, I am not
    jealous.
   Cel. No?
   Corv.   Faith I am not, I, nor never was ;
It is a poor, unprofitable humor.
Do not I know, if women have a will,
They 'll do 'gainst all the watches o' the
    world,
And that the fiercest spies are tam'd with
    gold?   10
Tut, I am confident in thee, thou shalt see 't ;
And see I 'll give thee cause, too, to believe it.
Come, kiss me. — Go, and make thee ready
    straight,
In all thy best attire, thy choicest jewels,
Put 'em all on, and, with 'em, thy best looks :
We are invited to a solemn feast,
At old Volpone's, where it shall appear
How far I am free from jealousy or fear.
                       [*Exeunt.*]

ACT III — Scene I [1]

[*Enter*] Mosca.

   Mos. I fear I shall begin to grow in love
With my dear self and my most prosp'rous
    parts ;
They do so spring and burgeon. I can feel
A whimsy i' my blood — I know not how —
Success hath made me wanton. I could skip
Out of my skin now, like a subtle snake,
I am so limber. Oh ! your parasite
Is a most precious thing, dropp'd from above,
Not bred 'mongst clods and clotpolls, here on
    earth.
I muse the mystery [2] was not made a science,
It is so liberally profess'd ! Almost   11
All the wise world is little else, in nature,
But parasites or sub-parasites. And yet
I mean not those that have your bare town-art,
To know who 's fit to feed 'em ; have no house,
No family, no care, and therefore mold
Tales for men's ears, to bait that sense [3] ; or
    get
Kitchen-invention, and some stale receipts
To please the belly, and the groin ; nor those,
With their court dog-tricks, that can fawn
    and fleer,   20

---

[1] A street.
[2] Profession.
[3] To feed the sense of hearing ; *i.e.*, love of gossip.

Make their revenue [4] out of legs and faces, [5]
Echo my Lord, and lick away a mote :
But your fine, elegant rascal, that can rise
And stoop, almost together, like an arrow ;
Shoot through the air as nimbly as a star ;
Turn short as doth a swallow ; and be here,
And there, and here, and yonder, all at once ;
Present to any humor, all occasion ;
And change a visor swifter than a thought !   29
This is the creature had the art born with him ;
Toils not to learn it, but doth practise it
Out of most excellent nature ; [6] and such
     sparks
Are the true parasites, others but their zanies.

Scene II [7]

[*To*] Mosca [*enter*] Bonario.

Mos. Who's this? Bonario, old Corbac-
     cio's son?
The person I was bound to seek.   Fair sir,
You are happ'ly met.
     Bon.   That cannot be by thee.
Mos. Why, sir?
     Bon.   Nay, 'pray thee know thy way,
     and leave me.
I would be loth to interchange discourse
With such a mate [8] as thou art.
     Mos.   Courteous sir,
Scorn not my poverty.
     Bon.   Not I, by Heaven ;
But thou shalt give me leave to hate thy base-
     ness.
     Mos. Baseness !
     Bon.   Ay ; answer me, is not thy sloth
Sufficient argument? thy flattery?   10
Thy means of feeding?
     Mos.   Heaven be good to me.
These imputations are too common, sir,
And eas'ly stuck on virtue, when she's poor.
You are unequal [9] to me, and howe'er
Your sentence may be righteous, yet you are
     not,
That, ere you know me, thus proceed in cen-
     sure.
St. Mark bear witness 'gainst you, 't is in-
     human.   [*Weeps.*]
     Bon. [*aside*] What ! does he weep? the
     sign is soft and good !
I do repent me that I was so harsh.
     Mos. 'T is true, that, sway'd by strong
     necessity,   20

I am enforc'd to eat my careful bread
With too much obsequy ; [10] 't is true, beside,
That I am fain to spin mine own poor raiment
Out of my mere observance, [11] being not born
To a free fortune ; but that I have done
Base offices, in rending friends asunder,
Dividing families, betraying counsels,
Whispering false lies, or mining men with
     praises,
Train'd [12] their credulity with perjuries,
Corrupted chastity, or am in love   30
With mine own tender ease, but would not
     rather
Prove the most rugged and laborious course,
That might redeem my present estimation,
Let me here perish, in all hope of goodness.
     Bon. [*aside*] This cannot be a personated
     passion ! —
I was to blame, so to mistake thy nature ;
'Pray thee forgive me ; and speak out thy
     bus'ness.
     Mos. Sir, it concerns you ; and though I
     may seem
At first to make a main offence in manners,
And in my gratitude unto my master,   40
Yet for the pure love which I bear all right,
And hatred of the wrong, I must reveal it.
This very hour your father is in purpose
To disinherit you —
     Bon.   How !
     Mos.   And thrust you forth,
As a mere stranger to his blood ; 't is true, sir.
The work no way engageth me, but as
I claim an interest in the general state
Of goodness and true virtue, which I hear
T' abound in you ; and for which mere re-
     spect, [13]
Without a second aim, sir, I have done it.   50
     Bon. This tale hath lost thee much of the
     late trust
Thou hadst with me ; it is impossible.
I know not how to lend it any thought
My father should be so unnatural.
     Mos. It is a confidence that well becomes
Your piety ; [14] and form'd, no doubt, it is
From your own simple innocence ; which
     makes
Your wrong [15] more monstrous and abhorr'd.
     But, sir,
I now will tell you more.   This very minute,
It is, or will be doing ; and if you   60

4 Accented on second syllable.
5 Bows and smirks.
6 *I.e.*, the art is innate in him.
7 The same.   8 Fellow.   9 Unjust.
10 Obsequiousness.
11 Service, attendance.
12 Led on, decoyed.
13 On which consideration alone.
14 Filial duty.   15 The injury to you.

Shall be but pleas'd to go with me, I'll bring
you,
I dare not say where you shall see, but where
Your ear shall be a witness of the deed ;
Hear yourself written bastard, and profess'd
The common issue of the earth.
    Bon.   I'm maz'd !
    Mos. Sir, if I do it not, draw your just
      sword,
And score your vengeance on my front and
    face ;
Mark me your villain. You have too much
    wrong,
And I do suffer for you, sir. My heart   69
Weeps blood in anguish —
    Bon.   Lead. I follow thee. [*Exeunt.*]

SCENE III [16]

[*Enter*] VOLPONE, NANO, ANDROGYNO, [*and*]
CASTRONE.

    VOLP. Mosca stays long, methinks. — Bring
forth your sports,
And help to make the wretched time more
    sweet.

NAN. Dwarf, fool, and eunuch, well met here
    we be.
A question it were now, whether of us three,
Being all the known delicates [17] of a rich man,
In pleasing him, claim the precedency can?
    CAS. I claim for myself.
    AND.   And so doth the fool.
    NAN. 'Tis foolish indeed ; let me set you both
    to school.
First for your dwarf, he's little and witty,
And everything, as it is little, is pretty ;   10
Else why do men say to a creature of my shape,
So soon as they see him, "It's a pretty little ape"?
And why a pretty ape, but for pleasing imitation
Of greater men's action, in a ridiculous fashion?
Beside, this feat [18] body of mine doth not crave
Half the meat, drink, and cloth, one of your bulks
    will have.
Admit your fool's face be the mother of laughter,
Yet, for his brain, it must always come after ;
And though that do feed him, it's a pitiful case,
His body is beholding to such a bad face.   20
                    One knocks.
    VOLP. Who's there? My couch ; away !
    Look, Nano, see. —
      [*Exeunt* ANDROGYNO *and* CASTRONE.]
Give me my caps first — go, inquire. [*Exit*
    NANO.] Now, Cupid
Send it be Mosca, and with fair return.

[*Re-enter* NANO.]

NAN. It is the beauteous Madam —
VOLP.   Would-be — is it?

[16] A room in Volpone's house.
[17] All of us being, as is well known, the delights.
[18] Graceful, dainty.

NAN. The same.
VOLP. Now torment on me ! Squire her in ;
For she will enter, or dwell here for ever.
Nay, quickly. [*Exit* NANO ; VOLPONE *retires
    to his couch.*] — That my fit were past !
    I fear
A second hell too, that my loathing this
Will quite expel my appetite to the other.
Would she were taking now her tedious leave.
Lord, how it threats me what I am to suffer ! [31

SCENE IV [19]

[*To him enter*] NANO [*and*] LADY [POLITIC
WOULD-BE].

    LADY. I thank you, good sir. Pray you
    signify
Unto your patron I am here. — This band
Shows not my neck enough. — I trouble you,
    sir ;
Let me request you bid one of my women
Come hither to me. [*Exit* NANO] — In good
    faith, I am dress'd
Most favorably to-day ; it is no matter ;
'T is well enough.

[*Re-enter* NANO *with a* Waiting Woman.]

           Look, see, these petulant things !
How they have done this !
    VOLP.   [*aside*] I do feel the fever
Ent'ring in at mine ears ; oh, for a charm
To fright it hence.
    LADY.   Come nearer. Is this curl [10
In his [20] right place? or this? Why is this
    higher
Than all the rest? You ha' not wash'd your
    eyes yet?
Or do they not stand even i' your head?
Where 's your fellow? call her. [*Exit* Woman.]
    NAN [*aside*]   Now, St. Mark
Deliver us ! anon she'll beat her women,
Because her nose is red.

[*Re-enter* Woman *with another*.]

    LADY.   I pray you view
This tire,[21] forsooth. Are all things apt, or no?
    WOM. One hair a little here sticks out, for-
    sooth.
    LADY. Does't so, forsooth ! and where was
    your dear [22] sight,
When it did so, forsooth? What now ! bird-
    ey'd? [23]   20

[19] The same. [20] Its. [21] Headdress. [22] Precious.
[23] *I.e.*, just glancing and then looking away ; not
giving proper attention. (Kittredge.)

And you, too? 'Pray you, both approach and
  mend it.
Now, by that light I muse yo' are not asham'd!
I, that have preach'd these things so oft unto
  you,
Read you the principles, argu'd all the grounds,
Disputed every fitness, every grace,
Call'd you to counsel of so frequent dressings—
    NAN. [*aside*] More carefully than of your
      fame or honor.
    LADY. Made you acquainted what an ample
      dowry
The knowledge of these things would be unto
  you,
Able alone to get you noble husbands   30
At your return ; and you thus to neglect it!
Besides, you seeing what a curious [24] nation
Th' Italians are, what will they say of me?
" The English lady cannot dress herself."
Here 's a fine imputation to our country!
Well, go your ways, and stay i' the next room.
This fucus [25] was too coarse too ; it 's no mat-
      ter. —
Good sir, you 'll give 'em entertainment?
            [*Exeunt* NANO *and* Waiting Women.]
    VOLP. [*aside*] The storm comes toward me.
    LADY [*going to the couch*]   How does
      my Volp[one]?
    VOLP. Troubled with noise ; I cannot sleep.
      I dreamt   40
That a strange Fury ent'red now my house,
And, with the dreadful tempest of her breath,
Did cleave my roof asunder.
    LADY.   Believe me, and I
Had the most fearful dream, could I remem-
      ber 't —
    VOLP. [*aside*] Out on my fate! I ha' giv'n
      her the occasion
How to torment me : she will tell me hers.
    LADY. Methought the golden mediocrity,
Polite, and delicate —
    VOLP.   O, if you do love me,
No more ; I sweat, and suffer, at the mention
Of any dream. Feel how I tremble yet.   50
    LADY. Alas, good soul! the passion of the
      heart. [26]
Seed-pearl were good now, boil'd with syrup of
  apples,
Tincture of gold, and coral, citron-pills,
Your elecampane root, myrobalans [27] —
    VOLP. Ay me, I have ta'en a grasshopper
      by the wing! [28]

LADY. Burnt silk and amber. You have
  muscadel
Good i' the house —
    VOLP.   You will not drink, and part? [29]
    LADY. No, fear not that. I doubt we shall
      not get
Some English saffron — half a dram would
  serve ;   59
Your sixteen cloves, a little musk, dried mints,
Bugloss, and barley meal —
    VOLP.   [*aside*] She 's in again ;
Before I feign'd diseases — now I have one.
    LADY. And these appli'd with a right scar-
      let cloth —
    VOLP. [*aside*] Another flood of words! a
      very torrent!
    LADY. Shall I, sir, make you a poultice?
    VOLP.   No, no, no.
I am very well ; you need prescribe no more.
    LADY. I have a little studied physic ; but
      now
I 'm all for music, save, i' the forenoons,
An hour or two for painting. I would have
A lady, indeed, t' have all letters and arts, [70
Be able to discourse, to write, to paint ;
But principal, as Plato holds, your music
(And so does wise Pythagoras, I take it)
Is your true rapture, when there is concent [30]
In face, in voice, and clothes, and is, in-
  deed,
Our sex's chiefest ornament.
    VOLP.   The poet
As old in time as Plato, and as knowing,
Says that your highest female grace is silence.
    LADY. Which o' your poets? Petrarch, or
      Tasso, or Dante?
Guarini? Ariosto? Aretine?   80
Cieco [31] di Hadria? I have read them all.
    VOLP. [*aside*] Is everything a cause to my
      destruction?
    LADY. I think I ha' two or three of 'em
      about me.
    VOLP. [*aside*] The sun, the sea, will sooner
      both stand still
Than her eternal tongue! Nothing can scape
  it.
    LADY. Here 's *Pastor Fido* [32] ——
    VOLP.   [*aside*] Profess obstinate silence ;
That 's now my safest.
    LADY.   All our English writers,
I mean such as are happy in th' Italian,
Will deign to steal out of this author, mainly ;

---

[24] Particular, fastidious.   [25] Cosmetic.
[26] Heartburn.   [27] Plum-like fruits.
[28] *I.e.*, a cicada ; when so held it makes still more
noise.

[29] Go.   [30] Harmony.
[31] The blind man ; Luigi Groto (d. 1585).
[32] The famous pastoral drama of Guarini.

Almost as much as from Montagnié [33] : 90
He has so modern and facile a vein,
Fitting the time, and catching the court-ear.
Your Petrarch is more passionate, yet he,
In days of sonnetting, trusted 'em with much.[34]
Dante is hard, and few can understand him.
But for a desperate wit, there 's Aretine !
Only, his pictures are a little obscene ——
You mark me not !

VOLP.　　　　　Alas, my mind 's perturb'd.

LADY. Why, in such cases, we must cure
　　ourselves,
Make use of our philosophy ——

VOLP.　　　　　Oh, [a]y me ! 100

LADY. And as we find our passions do rebel,
Encounter 'em with reason, or divert 'em,
By giving scope unto some other humor
Of lesse[r] danger : as, in politic bodies,
There 's nothing more doth overwhelm the
　　judgment,
And clouds the understanding, than too much
Settling and fixing, and, as 't were, subsiding
Upon one object. For the incorporating
Of these same outward things into that part
Which we call mental, leaves some certain
　　faeces　　　　　　　110
That stop the organs, and, as Plato says,
Assassinates our knowledge.

VOLP.　　　　　[*aside*] Now, the spirit
Of patience help me.

LADY.　　　　　Come, in faith, I must
Visit you more, a'days, and make you well ——
Laugh and be lusty.

VOLP. [*aside*]　　My good angel save me !

LADY. There was but one sole man in all
　　the world
With whom I e'er could sympathise ; and he
Would lie you, often, three, four hours to-
　　gether
To hear me speak ; and be sometime so rapt,
As he would answer me quite from the pur-
　　pose,　　　　　　　120
Like you, and you are like him, just. I 'll dis-
　　course,
An 't be but only, sir, to bring you asleep,
How we did spend our time and loves together,
For some six years.

VOLP.　　　　　Oh, oh, oh, oh, oh, oh !

LADY. For　we　were　coaetanei,[35]　and
　　brought up ——

VOLP. [*aside*] Some power, some fate, some
　　fortune rescue me !

---

[33] So Q. Ff omit accent.
[34] Lent the English poets much ; *i.e.*, was plun-
dered by them.
[35] Of equal age.

[*To them enter*] MOSCA.

Mos. God save you, madam.

LADY.　　　　　Good sir.

VOLP.　　　　　Mosca ! welcome ——
[*aside*] Welcome to my redemption.

Mos. [*aside*]　　　　　Why, sir?

VOLP. [*aside*]　　　　　Oh,
Rid me of this my torture, quickly, there ;
My madam with the everlasting voice.
The bells, in time of pestilence, ne'er made
Like noise, or were in that perpetual motion ——
The cockpit comes not near it. All my
　　house,
But now, [steam'd] [37] like a bath with her
　　thick breath,
A lawyer could not have been heard ; nor
　　scarce
Another woman, such a hail of words　　10
She has let fall. For hell's sake, rid her hence.

Mos. Has she presented? [38]

VOLP.　　　　　Oh, I do not care ;
I 'll take her absence upon any price,
With any loss.

Mos.　　　　　Madam ——

LADY.　　　　　I ha' brought your patron
A toy, a cap here, of mine own work ——

Mos.　　　　　'T is well.
I had forgot to tell you I saw your knight
Where you 'd little think it ——

LADY.　　　　　Where?

Mos.　　　　　Marry,
Where yet, if you make haste, you may appre-
　　hend him,
Rowing upon the water in a gondola,
With the most cunning courtesan of Venice. [20

LADY. Is 't true?

Mos.　　Pursue 'em, and believe your eyes ;
Leave me to make your gift.

　　　　　　　[*Exit* LADY.]
　　　　　—— I knew 't would take ;
For, lightly, they that use themselves most
　　licence,
Are still most jealous.

VOLP.　　　　　Mosca, hearty thanks
For thy quick fiction, and delivery of me.
Now to my hopes, what say'st thou?

[*Re-enter* LADY.]

LADY.　　　　　But do you hear, sir? ——

VOLP. [*aside*] Again ! I fear a paroxysm.

---

[36] The same.
[37] So Q, F₂ ; F₁ *stream'd.*
[38] Made a present.

LADY.   Which way
Row'd they together?
Mos.   Toward the Rialto.
LADY. I pray you lend me your dwarf.
Mos.   I pray you take him. [*Exit* LADY.]
Your hopes, sir, are like happy blossoms, fair,
And promise timely fruit, if you will stay   31
But the maturing. Keep you at your couch ;
Corbaccio will arrive straight, with the will ;
When he is gone, I 'll tell you more.   [*Exit.*]
VOLP.   My blood,
My spirits are return'd ; I am alive ;
And, like your wanton gamester at primero,[39]
Whose thought had whisper'd to him, not go [40]
    less,
Methinks I lie, and draw ―― for an encoun-
    ter.[41]

SCENE VI [42]

[*Enter*] MOSCA [*and*] BONARIO.

Mos. Sir, here conceal'd [*opening a door*] [43]
    you may hear all. But, pray you,
Have patience, sir ; [*One knocks.*] the same 's
    your father knocks.
I am compell'd to leave you.   [*Exit.*]
BON.   Do so. ― Yet
Cannot my thought imagine this a truth.
                                    [*Goes in.*]

SCENE VII [44]

[*Enter*] MOSCA, CORVINO, [*and*] CELIA.

Mos. Death on me ! You are come too
    soon. What meant you?
Did not I say I would send?
CORV.   Yes, but I fear'd
You might forget it, and then they prevent us.
Mos. Prevent ! ― [*aside.*] Did e'er man
    haste so for his horns?
A courtier would not ply it so for a place. ―
Well, now there is no helping it, stay here ;
I 'll presently return.   [*Exit.*]
CORV.   Where are you, Celia?
You know not wherefore I have brought you
    hither?
CEL. Not well, except you told [45] me.
CORV.   Now I will.
Hark hither.   [*They retire to one side.*] [46]

[39] A card game.   [40] Bid, bet.
[41] These are terms of primero, on which Volpone
puns with reference to his immediate situation.
As he ends his speech he closes the curtains of the
inner stage.
[42] The same.   [43] So Neilson.
[44] The same.
[45] Unless you tell.
[46] So Neilson ; Gifford begins a new scene.

[*Re-enter* MOSCA.]

Mos. (*to* BONARIO)   Sir, your father
    hath sent word   10
It will be half an hour ere he come ;
And therefore, if you please to walk the while
Into that gallery ― at the upper end,
There are some books to entertain the time ;
And I 'll take care no man shall come unto you,
    sir,
BON. Yes, I will stay there. ― [*aside*] I do
    doubt this fellow.   [*Exit.*]
Mos. [*looking after him*] There ; he is far
    enough ; he can hear nothing.
And for his father, I can keep him off.[47]
CORV. [*advancing with Celia*] Nay, now,
    there is no starting back, and there-
    fore,
Resolve upon it : I have so decreed.   20
It must be done. Nor would I move 't [48] afore,
Because I would avoid all shifts and tricks,
That might deny me.
CEL.   Sir, let me beseech you,
Affect not these strange trials; if you doubt
My chastity, why, lock me up for ever ;
Make me the heir of darkness. Let me live
Where I may please your fears, if not your
    trust.
CORV. Believe it, I have no such humor, I.
All that I speak I mean ; yet I am not mad ;
Not horn-mad,[49] see you? Go to, show your-
    self   30
Obedient, and a wife.
CEL.   O Heaven !
CORV.   I say it,
Do so.
CEL. Was this the train?
CORV.   I have told you reasons ;
What the physicians have set down ; how
    much
It may concern me ; what my engagements
    are ;
My means, and the necessity of those means
For my recovery. Wherefore, if you be
Loyal, and mine, be won : respect my venture.
CEL. Before your honor?
CORV.   Honor ! tut, a breath.
There 's no such thing in nature ; a mere term
Invented to awe fools. What is my gold   40
The worse for touching, clothes for being
    look'd on?

[47] At this point Mosca goes back and opens the
curtains, discovering Volpone on his couch.
(Neilson.)
[48] Propose it.
[49] Stark mad (like an enraged horned beast), with
the usual pun on the horns of the cuckold.

Why, this 's no more. An old decrepit wretch,
That has no sense, no sinew ; takes his meat
With others' fingers ; only knows to gape
When you do scald his gums ; a voice, a
    shadow ;
And what can this man hurt you ?

    CEL.   [*aside*] Lord ! what spirit
Is this hath ent'red him ?

    CORV.   And for your fame,
That 's such a jig [50] ; as if I would go tell it,
Cry it on the Piazza ! Who shall know it
But he that cannot speak it, and this fellow, [50
Whose lips are i' my pocket ? Save yourself —
If you 'll proclaim 't, you may, — I know no
    other
Should come to know it.

    CEL.   Are Heaven and saints then
    nothing?
Will they be blind or stupid ?

    CORV.   How ?

    CEL.   Good sir,
Be jealous still, emulate them ; and think
What hate they burn with toward every sin.

    CORV. I grant you ; if I thought it were a
    sin
I would not urge you. Should I offer this
To some young Frenchman, or hot Tuscan
    blood
That had read Aretine, conn'd all his prints, [60
Knew every quirk within lust's labyrinth,
And were profess'd critic in lechery ;
And I would look upon him, and applaud
    him ;
This were a sin : but here, 't is contrary,
A pious work, mere charity, for physic,
And honest polity, to assure mine own.

    CEL. O Heaven ! canst thou suffer such a
    change?

    VOLP. [*aside*] Thou art mine honor, Mosca,
    and my pride,
My joy, my tickling, my delight ! Go bring
    'em.

    MOS. Please you draw near, sir.

    CORV.   Come on, what —
You will not be rebellious? By that light —

    MOS. Sir, Signior Corvino, here, is come to
    see you.   72

    VOLP. Oh.

    MOS.   And hearing of the consultation
    had,
So lately, for your health, is come to offer,
Or rather, sir, to prostitute —

    CORV.   Thanks, sweet Mosca.

    MOS. Freely, unask'd, or unentreated —

[50] Joke.

    CORV.   Well.

    MOS. As the true fervent instance of his
    love,
His own most fair and proper [51] wife, the
    beauty
Only of price [52] in Venice ——

    CORV.   'T is well urg'd.

    MOS. To be your comfortress, and to pre-
    serve you.   80

    VOLP. Alas, I am past, already ! 'Pray you,
    thank him
For his good care and promptness ; but for
    that,
'T is a vain labor e'en to fight 'gainst Heaven ;
Applying fire to a stone — uh, uh, uh, uh ! ——
Making a dead leaf grow again. I take
His wishes gently, though ; and you may tell
    him
What I have done for him ; marry, my state is
    hopeless !
Will him to pray for me ; and t' use his for-
    tune
With reverence when he comes to 't.

    MOS.   Do you hear, sir?
Go to him with your wife.

    CORV.   Heart of my father ! 90
Wilt thou persist thus? Come, I pray thee,
    come.
Thou seest 't is nothing, Celia. By this hand,
I shall grow violent. Come, do 't, I say.

    CEL. Sir, kill me, rather. I will take down
    poison,
Eat burning coals, do anything ——

    CORV.   Be damn'd !
Heart, I will drag thee hence home by the hair ;
Cry thee a strumpet through the streets ; rip
    up
Thy mouth unto thine ears ; and slit thy nose,
Like a raw rochet [53] — Do not tempt me,
    come ;
Yield ; I am loth — Death ! I will buy some
    slave   100
Whom I will kill, and bind thee to him alive,
And at my windore hang you forth, devising
Some monstrous crime, which I, in capital
    letters,
Will eat into thy flesh with aqua fortis,
And burning cor'sives, [54] on this stubborn
    breast.
Now, by the blood thou hast incens'd, I 'll do
    it !

[51] Very own.
[52] The most precious beauty.
[53] The red gurnard, which has a disproportion-
ately large head.
[54] Corrosives.

CEL. Sir, what you please, you may ; I am
   your martyr.
CORV. Be not thus obstinate ; I ha' not
   deserv'd it.
Think who it is entreats you. 'Pray thee,
   sweet ;
Good faith, thou shalt have jewels, gowns,
   attires,   110
What thou wilt think, and ask. Do but go
   kiss him.
Or touch him but. For my sake. At my
   suit.
This once. No? not? I shall remember this.
Will you disgrace me thus? Do you thirst
   my undoing?
   Mos. Nay, gentle lady, be advis'd.
   CORV.   No, no.
She has watch'd her time. God's precious,
   this is scurvy,
'T is very scurvy ; and you are ——
   Mos.   Nay, good sir.
   CORV. An errant [55] locust — by Heaven, a
   locust ! — Whore,
Crocodile, that hast thy tears prepar'd,
Expecting how thou 'lt bid 'em flow.
   Mos.   Nay, 'pray you, sir ! [120
She will consider.
   CEL.   Would my life would serve
To satisfy ——
   CORV. 'Sdeath ! if she would but speak to
   him,
And save my reputation, 't were somewhat ;
But spitefully to affect my utter ruin !
   Mos. [*aside to* CORVINO] Ay, now you have
   put your fortune in her hands.
Why, i' faith, it is her modesty, I must quit [56]
   her.
If you were absent, she would be more coming ;
I know it, and dare undertake for her.
What woman can before her husband? 'Pray
   you,
Let us depart and leave her here.
   CORV.   Sweet Celia, 130
Thou mayst redeem all yet ; I 'll say no more.
If not, esteem yourself as lost. — Nay, stay
   there.
              [*Exit with* MOSCA.]
   CEL. O God, and his good angels ! whither,
   whither,
Is shame fled human breasts? that with such
   ease,
Men dare put off your honors, and their own?
Is that which ever was a cause of life [57]

[55] Arrant.   [56] Acquit.
[57] The marriage bond.

Now plac'd beneath the basest circumstance,
And modesty an exile made, for money?
   VOLP. Ay, in Corvino, and such earth-fed
   minds,   *He leaps off from his couch.*
That never tasted the true heav'n of love. [140
Assure thee, Celia, he that would sell thee,
Only for hope of gain, and that uncertain,
He would have sold his part of Paradise
For ready money, had he met a copeman.[58]
Why art thou maz'd to see me thus reviv'd?
Rather applaud thy beauty's miracle ;
'T is thy great work, that hath, not now alone,
But sundry times, rais'd me, in several shapes,
And, but this morning, like a mountebank,
To see thee at thy windore ; ay, before   150
I would have left my practice [59] for thy love,
In varying figures I would have contended
With the blue Proteus, or the horned flood.[60]
Now art thou welcome.
   CEL.   Sir !
   VOLP.   Nay, fly me not,
Nor let thy false imagination
That I was bedrid, make thee think I am so —
Thou shalt not find it. I am now as fresh,
As hot, as high, and in as jovial plight
As when, in that so celebrated scene,
At recitation of our comedy,   160
For entertainment of the great Valois,[61]
I acted young Antinous, and attracted
The eyes and ears of all the ladies present,
T' admire each graceful gesture, note, and
   footing.

SONG [62]

Come, my Celia, let us prove,
While we can, the sports of love.
Time will not be ours for ever,
He, at length, our good will sever.
Spend not then his gifts in vain.
Suns that set may rise again ;   170
But if once we lose this light,
'T is with us perpetual night.
Why should we defer our joys?
Fame and rumor are but toys.
Cannot we delude the eyes
Of a few poor household spies?
Or his easier ears beguile,
Thus removed by our wile?
'T is no sin love's fruits to steal,
But the sweet thefts to reveal ;   180
To be taken, to be seen,
These have crimes accounted been.

   CEL. Some serene [63] blast me, or dire lightning strike
This my offending face.

[58] Dealer.   [59] Plot.   [60] Oceanus.
[61] Henry III of France was entertained in Venice
in 1574.
[62] Adapted in part from the fifth ode of Catullus.
[63] The (supposedly noxious) dew or mist after
sunset.

VOLP.   Why droops my Celia?
Thou hast, in place of a base husband, found
A worthy lover : use thy fortune well,
With secrecy and pleasure. See, behold,
What thou art queen of ; not in expectation,
As I feed others, but possess'd and crown'd.
See, here, a rope of pearl ; and each more
     orient   190
Than that the brave Egyptian queen carous'd :
Dissolve and drink 'em. See, a carbuncle,
May put out both the eyes of our St. Mark ;
A diamond would have bought Lollia
     Paulina,[64]
When she came in like starlight, hid with
     jewels
That were the spoils of provinces ; take these,
And wear and lose 'em ; yet remains an ear-
     ring
To purchase them again, and this whole state.
A gem but [65] worth a private patrimony
Is nothing ; we will eat such at a meal.   200
The heads of parrots, tongues of nightingales,
The brains of peacocks and of estriches,
Shall be our food ; and, could we get the phœ-
     nix,
Though nature lost her kind,[66] she were our
     dish.
     CEL. Good sir, these things might move a
         mind affected
With such delights ; but I, whose innocence
Is all I can think wealthy, or worth th' enjoy-
     ing,
And which, once lost, I have naught to lose
     beyond it,
Cannot be taken with these sensual baits.
If you have conscience —
     VOLP.   'T is the beggar's virtue ;
If thou hast wisdom, hear me, Celia.   211
Thy baths shall be the juice of July flowers,
Spirit of roses and of violets,
The milk of unicorns, and panthers' breath [67]
Gather'd in bags and mix'd with Cretan wines.
Our drink shall be prepared gold and amber,
Which we will take until my roof whirl round
With the vertigo ; and my dwarf shall dance,
My eunuch sing, my fool make up the antic,
Whilst we, in changed shapes,[68] act Ovid's
     tales :   220
Thou like Europa now, and I like Jove ;

Then I like Mars, and thou like Erycine ; [69]
So of the rest, till we have quite run through
And wearied all the fables of the gods.
Then will I have thee in more modern forms,
Attired like some sprightly dame of France,
Brave Tuscan lady, or proud Spanish beauty ;
Sometimes unto the Persian sophy's wife,
Or the Grand Signior's mistress ; and, for
     change,
To one of our most artful courtesans,   230
Or some quick Negro, or cold Russian ;
And I will meet thee in as many shapes,
Where we may so transfuse our wand'ring souls
Out at our lips, and score up sums of pleasures,

> That the curious shall not know
> How to tell them as they flow ;
> And the envious, when they find
> What their number is, be pin'd.

     CEL. If you have ears that will be pierc'd
         — or eyes
That can be open'd — a heart, may be
     touch'd —   240
Or any part that yet sounds man about you —
If you have touch of holy saints, or Heaven,
Do me the grace to let me 'scape. If not,
Be bountiful and kill me. You do know
I am a creature hither ill betray'd
By one whose shame I would forget it were ;
If you will deign me neither of these graces,
Yet feed your wrath, sir, rather than your lust,
(It is a vice comes nearer manliness,)
And punish that unhappy crime of nature, [250
Which you miscall my beauty ; flay my face,
Or poison it with ointments for seducing
Your blood [70] to this rebellion. Rub these
     hands
With what may cause an eating leprosy,
E'en to my bones and marrow, anything
That may disfavor me, save in my honor.
And I will kneel to you, pray for you, pay down
A thousand hourly vows, sir, for your health ;
Report, and think you virtuous ——
     VOLP.   Think me cold,
Frozen, and impotent, and so report me ! [260
That I had Nestor's hernia, thou wouldst
     think.
I do degenerate, and abuse my nation,
To play with opportunity thus long ;
I should have done the act, and then have
     parley'd.
Yield, or I 'll force thee.
     CEL.   O ! just God !
     VOLP.   In vain ——

---

[64] Wife of the Emperor Caligula. Pliny the Elder
tells about the jewels.
[65] Merely.
[66] Species, for the bird was unique.
[67] From the time of Aristotle credited with sweetness.
[68] Costumes.

[69] Venus, from Mt. Eryx in Sicily, where she was
worshipped.
[70] Passion.

Bon. (*leaps out from where* Mosca *had plac'd him.*) Forbear, foul ravisher, libidinous swine ;
Free the forc'd lady, or thou di'st, impostor.
But that I am loth to snatch thy punishment
Out of the hand of justice, thou shouldst yet
Be made the timely sacrifice of vengeance, [270
Before this altar and this dross, thy idol. —
Lady, let's quit the place ; it is the den
Of villainy ; fear naught : you have a guard ;
And he ere long shall meet his just reward.

               [*Exeunt* Bonario *and* Celia.]

Volp. Fall on me, roof, and bury me in ruin ;
Become my grave, that wert my shelter.   Oh !
I am unmask'd, unspirited, undone,
Betray'd to beggary, to infamy ———

Scene VIII [71]

[*To*] Volpone [*enter*] Mosca.

Mos. Where shall I run, most wretched shame of men,
To beat out my unlucky brains?
Volp.   Here, here.
What ! dost thou bleed?
Mos.   O, that his well-driv'n sword
Had been so courteous to have cleft me down
Unto the navel, ere I liv'd to see
My life, my hopes, my spirits, my patron, all
Thus desperately engaged, by my error.
Volp. Woe on thy fortune.
Mos.   And my follies, sir.
Volp. Th' hast made me miserable.
Mos.   And myself, sir.
Who would have thought he would have hearken'd so?   10
Volp. What shall we do?
Mos.   I know not ; if my heart
Could expiate the mischance, I'd pluck it out.
Will you be pleas'd to hang me, or cut my throat?
And I'll requite you, sir. Let's die like Romans,[72]
Since we have liv'd like Grecians.[73]

                They knock without.

Volp.   Hark ! who's there?
I hear some footing ; officers, the saffi,[74]
Come to apprehend us ! I do feel the brand
Hissing already at my forehead ; now
Mine ears are boring.
Mos.   To your couch, sir, you ;

Make that place good, however.[75] [Volpone *lies down as before.*] — [*aside*] Guilty men   20
Suspect what they deserve still.[76] — Signior Corbaccio !

Scene IX [77]

[*To them enter*] Corbaccio.

Corb. Why, how now, Mosca?
Mos.   O, undone, amaz'd, sir.
Your son, I know not by what accident,
Acquainted with your purpose to my patron,
Touching your will and making him your heir,
Ent'red our house with violence, his sword drawn,
Sought for you, call'd you wretch, unnatural,
Vow'd he would kill you.
Corb.   Me?
Mos.   Yes, and my patron.
Corb. This act shall disinherit him indeed.
Here is the will.
Mos.   'T is well, sir.
Corb.   Right and well :
Be you as careful now for me.

           [*Enter* Voltore *behind.*]

Mos.   My life, sir, 10
Is not more tender'd [78] ; I am only yours.
Corb. How does he? Will he die shortly, think'st thou?
Mos.   I fear
He'll outlast May.
Corb.   To-day?
Mos.   No, last out May, sir.
Corb. Couldst thou not gi' him a dram?
Mos.   Oh, by no means, sir.
Corb. Nay, I'll not bid you.
Volt. [*coming forward*] This is a knave, I see.
Mos. [*aside*] How ! Signior Voltore ! did he hear me?
Volt.   Parasite !
Mos. Who's that? — Oh, sir, most timely welcome —
Volt.   Scarce,
To the discovery of your tricks, I fear.
You are his, only? and mine also, are you not?
Mos. Who? I, sir !
Volt.   You, sir. What device is this [20
About a will?
Mos.   A plot for you, sir.
Volt.   Come,

---

[71] The same.
[72] *I.e.*, by suicide.
[73] *I.e.*, merrily.
[74] Bailiffs.
[75] In any case.
[76] Always.
[77] The same.
[78] Cared for.

Put not your foists [79] upon me ; I shall scent
   'em.
  Mos. Did you not hear it ?
  Volt.   Yes, I hear Corbaccio
Hath made your patron there his heir.
  Mos.   'T is true,
By my device, drawn to it by my plot,
With hope ——
  Volt.   Your patron should reciprocate ?
And you have promis'd ?
  Mos.   For your good I did, sir.
Nay, more, I told his son, brought, hid him
   here,
Where he might hear his father pass the deed ;
Being persuaded to it by this thought, sir,   30
That the unnaturalness, first, of the act,
And then his father's oft disclaiming in him
(Which I did mean t' help on), would sure en-
   rage him
To do some violence upon his parent,
On which the law should take sufficient hold,
And you be stated in a double hope.
Truth be my comfort, and my conscience,
My only aim was to dig you a fortune
Out of these two rotten sepulchres ——
  Volt. I cry thee mercy, Mosca.
  Mos.   Worth your patience, 40
And your great merit, sir. And see the
   change !
  Volt. Why, what success ?
  Mos.   Most hapless ! You must help, sir.
Whilst we expected th' old raven, in comes
Corvino's wife, sent hither by her husband——
  Volt. What, with a present ?
  Mos.   No, sir, on visitation
(I 'll tell you how anon) ; and, staying long,
The youth he grows impatient, rushes forth,
Seizeth the lady, wounds me, makes her swear
(Or he would murder her — that was his vow)
T' affirm my patron to [80] have done her rape ;
Which how unlike it is, you see ! and hence, [51
With that pretext he 's gone, t' accuse his
   father,
Defame my patron, defeat you ——
  Volt.   Where 's her husband ?
Let him be sent for straight.
  Mos.   Sir, I 'll go fetch him.
  Volt. Bring him to the Scrutineo. [81]
  Mos.   Sir, I will.
  Volt. This must be stopp'd.
  Mos.   Oh, you do nobly, sir.
Alas, 't was labor'd all, sir, for your good ;
Nor was there want of counsel in the plot.

---

[79] Tricks.   [80] Q *would.*
[81] Senate-house.

But Fortune can, at any time, o'erthrow   59
The projects of a hundred learned clerks, sir.
  Corb. [*listening*] What 's that ?
  Volt.   Wilt please you, sir, to go along ?
      [*Exit* Corbaccio, *followed by* Vol-
      tore.]
  Mos. Patron, go in, and pray for our suc-
   cess.
  Volp. Need makes devotion ; Heaven your
   labor bless !   [*Exeunt.*]

ACT IV — Scene I [1]

[*Enter* Sir] Politic [Would-be *and*] Pere-
        grine.

  Pol. I told you, sir, it was a plot [2] ; you
   see
What observation is. You mention'd [3] me
For some instructions ; I will tell you, sir,
(Since we are met here in this height of Venice,)
Some few particulars I have set down,
Only for this meridian, fit to be known
Of your crude traveller ; and they are these.
I will not touch, sir, at your phrase, or clothes,
For they are old.
  Per.   Sir, I have better.
  Pol.   Pardon,
I meant, as they are themes. [4]
  Per.   Oh, sir, proceed ; 10
I 'll slander you no more of wit, good sir.
  Pol. First, for your garb, [5] it must be grave
   and serious,
Very reserv'd and lock'd ; not tell a secret
On any terms, not to your father ; scarce
A fable, but with caution ; make sure choice
Both of your company and discourse ; beware
You never [speak] [6] a truth ——
  Per.   How !
  Pol.   Not to strangers,
For those be they you must converse with
   most ;
Others I would not know, sir, but at distance
So as I still might be a saver in 'em —   20
You shall have tricks else pass'd upon you,
   hourly.
And then, for your religion, profess none,
But wonder at the diversity of all ;
And, for your part, protest, were there no other

---

[1] A street.
[2] Evidently referring to II, iii.
[3] Referred to.
[4] *I.e.*, we have already discussed those subjects.
[5] Personal bearing, conduct.
[6] So Q and F₂ ; F₁ *spake.*

But simply the laws o' th' land, you could content you.

Nic. Machiavel and Monsieur Bodin,[7] both
Were of this mind. Then must you learn the use
And handling of your silver fork at meals,
The metal of your glass (these are main mat-
ters
With your Italian) ; and to know the hour [30
When you must eat your melons and your figs.

PER. Is that a point of state too?

POL.   Here, it is ;
For your Venetian, if he see a man
Preposterous in the least, he has him straight ;
He has ; he strips him. I 'll acquaint you, sir,
I now have liv'd here, 't is some fourteen
months.
Within the first week of my landing here,
All took me for a citizen of Venice,
I knew the forms so well ——

PER. [*aside*]   And nothing else.

POL. I had read Contarene,[8] took me a
house,   40
Dealt with my Jews to furnish it with movables [9] ——
Well, if I could but find one man, one man,
To mine own heart, whom I durst trust, I
would ——

PER. What? what, sir?

POL.   Make him rich ; make him a
fortune :
He should not think again. I would command
it.

PER. As how?

POL.   With certain projects that I have,
Which I may not discover.

PER. [*aside*]   If I had
But one to wager with, I would lay odds now,
He tells me instantly.

POL.   One is, (and that
I care not greatly who knows), to serve the
state   50
Of Venice with red herrings for three years,
And at a certain rate, from Rotterdam,
Where I have correspondence. There 's a let-
ter,
Sent me from one o' th' states,[10] and to that
purpose ;
He cannot write his name, but that 's his mark.

PER. He is a chandler?[11]

POL.   No, a cheesemonger.
There are some other too with whom I treat
About the same negotiation ;
And I will undertake it ; for 't is thus :
I 'll do 't with ease ; I have cast [12] it all. Your
hoy [13]   60
Carries but three men in her, and a boy ;
And she shall make me three returns a year :
So if there come but one of three, I save ;
If two, I can defalk.[14] But this is now,
If my main project fail.

PER.   Then you have others?

POL. I should be loth to draw the subtle
air
Of such a place without my thousand aims.
I 'll not dissemble, sir : where'er I come,
I love to be considerative ; and 't is true,
I have at my free hours thought upon   70
Some certain goods unto the state of Venice,
Which I do call my cautions ; and, sir, which
I mean, in hope of pension, to propound
To the Great Council, then unto the Forty.
So to the Ten. My means are made already—

PER. By whom?

POL.   Sir, one that though his
place b' obscure,
Yet he can sway, and they will hear him.
H' is
A *commandadore*.

PER.   What, a common serjeant?

POL. Sir, such as they are, put it in their
mouths,
What they should say, sometimes ; as well as
greater.   80
I think I have my notes to show you ——
             [*Searching his pockets.*]

PER.   Good sir.

POL. But you shall swear unto me, on your
gentry,
Not to anticipate ——

PER.   I, sir?

POL.   Nor reveal
A circumstance —— my paper is not with me.

PER. O, but you can remember, sir.

POL.   My first is
Concerning tinder boxes. You must know,
No family is here without its box.
Now, sir, it being so portable a thing,
Put case [15] that you or I were ill affected
Unto the state, sir ; with it in our pockets, [90

---

[7] Jean Bodin (d. 1596), a French advocate and
political philosopher.
[8] Cardinal Gasparo Contarini ; his *Commonwealth
and Government of Venice* appeared in London in
1599.
[9] Furniture.
[10] Nobles, persons of high rank or authority.

[11] Observing a greasy spot on the letter.
[12] Calculated.
[13] A coasting sloop.
[14] Defalcate (in the old sense of make a reduction.)
[15] Suppose, assume.

Might not I go into the Arsenal,
Or you come out again, and none the wiser?

PER. Except yourself, sir.

POL.   Go to, then. I therefore
Advertise to the state, how fit it were
That none but such as were known patriots,
Sound lovers of their country, should be suf-
    fer'd
T' enjoy them in their houses ; and even those
Seal'd at some office, and at such a bigness
As might not lurk in pockets.

PER.   Admirable !

POL. My next is, how t' inquire, and be re-
    solv'd   100
By present demonstration, whether a ship,
Newly arriv'd from Soria,[16] or from
Any suspected part of all the Levant,
Be guilty of the plague ; and where [17] they use
To lie out forty, fifty days, sometimes,
About the Lazaretto,[18] for their trial,
I 'll save that charge and loss unto the mer-
    chant,
And in an hour clear the doubt.

PER.   Indeed, sir?

POL. Or —— I will lose my labor.

PER.   'My faith, that 's much.

POL. Nay, sir, conceive me. 'T will cost
    me in onions,   110
Some thirty livres ——

PER.   Which is one pound sterling.

POL. Beside my waterworks. For this I
    do, sir :
First, I bring in your ship 'twixt two brick
    walls —
But those the state shall venture. On the one
I strain me a fair tarpaulin, and in that
I stick my onions, cut in halves ; the other
Is full of loopholes, out at which I thrust
The noses of my bellows ; and those bellows
I keep, with waterworks, in perpetual motion,
(Which is the easi'st matter of a hundred).   120
Now, sir, your onion, which doth naturally
Attract th' infection, and your bellows blowing
The air upon him, will show, instantly,
By his chang'd color, if there be contagion ;
Or else remain as fair as at the first.
Now 't is known, 't is nothing.

PER.   You are right, sir.

POL. I would I had my note.

PER.   'Faith, so would I ;
But you ha' done well for once, sir.

POL.   Were I false,
Or would be made so, I could show you reasons

How I could sell this state now to the Turk,
Spite of their galleys, or their ——
              [*Examining his papers.*]

PER.   Pray you, Sir Pol.[19]   [131

POL. I have 'em not about me.

PER.   That I fear'd.
They are there, sir?

POL.   No, this is my diary,
Wherein I note my actions of the day.

PER. Pray you let 's see, sir. — What is
    here? " *Notandum,*
A rat had gnawn my spur-leathers ; notwith-
    standing,
I put on new, and did go forth ; but first
I threw three beans over the threshold.   *Item,*
I went and bought two toothpicks, whereof
    one
I burst immediately, in a discourse   140
With a Dutch merchant, 'bout *ragion' del
    stato.*[20]
From him I went and paid a *moccinigo*
For piecing my silk stockings ; by the way
I cheapen'd [21] sprats ; and at St. Mark's I
    urin'd." —
'Faith these are politic notes !

POL.   Sir, I do slip
No action of my life, thus but I quote [22] it.

PER. Believe me, it is wise !

POL.   Nay, sir, read forth.

SCENE II [23]

[*Enter, at a distance,*] LADY [POLITIC WOULD-
BE], NANO, [*and the two* Waiting] Women.

LADY. Where should this loose knight be,
    trow? Sure h' is hous'd.

NAN. Why, then he 's fast.

LADY.   Ay, he plays both [24] with me.
I pray you stay. This heat will do more harm
To my complexion than his heart is worth.
(I do not care to hinder, but to take him.)
How it comes off !   [*Rubs her cheeks.*]

WOM.   My master 's yonder.

LADY.   Where?

WOM. With a young gentleman.

LADY P.   That same 's the party !
In man's apparel. — Pray you, sir, jog my
    knight.
I will be tender to his reputation,
However he demerit.

POL.   My lady !

---

[16] Syria.   [17] Whereas.
[18] Pesthouse.

[19] *I.e.,* be careful what you say.
[20] Politics.
[21] Priced, bargained for.
[22] Make a note on.
[23] The same.   [24] Fast and loose.

PER. Where? [10
POL. 'T is she indeed, sir; you shall know
her. She is,
Were she not mine, a lady of that merit,
For fashion and behavior, and for beauty,
I durst compare ——
PER. It seems you are not jealous,
That dare commend her.
POL. Nay, and for discourse ——
PER. Being your wife, she cannot miss that.
POL. Madam,
Here is a gentleman, 'pray you use him fairly;
He seems a youth, but he is ——
LADY. None?
POL. Yes, one
Has put his face as soon into the world ——
LADY. You mean, as early? But to-day?
POL. How's this! [20
LADY. Why, in this habit, sir; you appre-
hend me.
Well, Master Would-be, this doth not become
you;
I had thought the odor, sir, of your good name
Had been more precious to you; that you
would not
Have done this dire massacre on your honor;
One of your gravity, and rank besides!
But knights, I see, care little for the oath
They make to ladies — chiefly their own ladies.
POL. Now, by my spurs, the symbol of my
knighthood ——
PER. [aside] Lord, how his brain is humbled
for an oath.[25] 30
POL. I reach[26] you not.
LADY. Right, sir: your polity
May bear it through thus. — [to PEREGRINE]
Sir, a word with you.
I would be loth to contest publicly
With any gentlewoman, or to seem
Froward, or violent, as the courtier says;
It comes too near rusticity in a lady,
Which I would shun by all means; and how-
ever
I may deserve from Master Would-be, yet
T' have one fair gentlewoman thus be made
Th' unkind instrument to wrong another, 40
And one she knows not, ay, and to persever,[27]
In my poor judgment, is not warranted
From being a solecism in[28] our sex,
If not in manners.
PER. How is this!

POL. Sweet madam,
Come nearer to your aim.
LADY. Marry, and will, sir.
Since you provoke me with your impudence,
And laughter of your light land-siren here,
Your Sporus,[29] your hermaphrodite ——
PER. What's here?
Poetic fury and historic storms! 49
POL. The gentleman, believe it, is of worth
And of our nation.
LADY. Ay, your Whitefriars[30] nation?
Come, I blush for you, Master Would-be, I;
And am asham'd you should ha' no more fore-
head[31]
Than thus to be the patron, or St. George,
To a lewd harlot, a base fricatrice,[32]
A female devil, in a male outside.
POL. Nay,
An you be such a one! I must bid adieu
To your delights. The case appears too
liquid.[33]
[Exit.]
LADY. Ay, you may carry 't clear, with
your state-face! —
But for your carnival concupiscence,[34] 60
Who here is fled for liberty of conscience,
From furious persecution of the marshal,
Her will I disc'ple.[35]
PER. This is fine, i' faith!
And do you use this often? Is this part
Of your wit's exercise, 'gainst you have occa-
sion?
Madam ——
LADY. Go to, sir.
PER. Do you hear me, lady?
Why, if your knight have set you to beg shirts,
Or to invite me home, you might have done it
A nearer way by far.
LADY. This cannot work you
Out of my snare.
PER. Why, am I in it, then? 70
Indeed your husband told me you were fair,
And so you are; only your nose inclines,
That side that's next the sun, to the queen-
apple.[36]

[25] A derisive allusion to the cheapening of the order by King James's creation of many new knights.
[26] Understand.
[27] Accented on the second syllable.
[28] With respect to

[29] The eunuch Nero married.
[30] Or Alsatia, a district of London where, because of the privilege of sanctuary formerly enjoyed by the Carmelites' church and extended under James I, fraudulent debtors, gamblers, and prostitutes re-sided with little molestation from the law.
[31] Sense of shame.   [32] Prostitute.
[33] Clear. Sir Politic, credulous as ever, believes his wife's charge.
[34] Object of carnival lust. "Carnival" refers to that time as one of indulgence.   [35] Discipline.
[36] A variety of cider-apple. (Webster.) *I.e.*, your nose is as red as an apple.

LADY. This cannot be endur'd by any patience.

SCENE III [37]

[To them enter] MOSCA.

Mos. What's the matter, madam?

LADY.   If the Senate
Right not my quest in this, I will protest 'em
To all the world no aristocracy.

Mos. What is the injury, lady?

LADY.   Why, the callet [38]
You told me of, here I have ta'en disguis'd.

Mos. Who? this? what means your Ladyship? The creature
I mention'd to you is apprehended now,
Before the Senate; you shall see her ——

LADY.   Where?

Mos. I'll bring you to her. This young gentleman,
I saw him land this morning at the port.   10

LADY. Is't possible? How has my judgment wander'd!
Sir, I must, blushing, say to you, I have err'd;
And plead your pardon.

PER.   What! more changes yet?

LADY. I hope yo' ha' not the malice to remember
A gentlewoman's passion. If you stay
In Venice here, please you to use me, sir ——

Mos. Will you go, madam?

LADY.   'Pray you, sir, use me; in faith,
The more you see [39] me the more I shall conceive
You have forgot our quarrel.

       [Exeunt LADY WOULD-BE, MOSCA,
         NANO, *and* Waiting Women.]

PER.   This is rare!
Sir Politic Would-be? No, Sir Politic Bawd!
To bring me thus acquainted with his wife! [21
Well, wise Sir Pol, since you have practis'd thus
Upon my freshmanship, I'll try your salthead, [40]
What proof it is against a counterplot.

               [Exit.]

SCENE IV [41]

[Enter] VOLTORE, CORBACCIO, CORVINO,
[and] MOSCA.

VOLT. Well, now you know the carriage of the business, [42]

Your constancy is all that is requir'd
Unto the safety of it.   *[He stands aside.]*

Mos.   Is the lie
Safely convey'd [43] amongst us? Is that sure?
Knows every man his burden?

CORV.   Yes.

Mos.   Then shrink not.

CORV. But knows the advocate the truth?

Mos.   Oh, sir.
By no means; I devis'd a formal tale,
That salv'd your reputation. But [44] be valiant, sir.

CORV. I fear no one but him, that this his pleading
Should make him stand for a co-heir ——

Mos.   Co-halter! 10
Hang him; we will but use his tongue, his noise,
As we do croaker's [45] here.

CORV.   Ay, what shall he do?

Mos. When we ha' done, you mean?

CORV.   Yes.

Mos.   Why, we'll think;
Sell him for mummia: [46] he's half dust already. ——
(To VOLTORE) Do you not smile, to see this buffalo, [47]
How he doth sport it with his head? — *[aside]* I should,
If all were well and past. — *(To* CORBACCIO) Sir, only you
Are he that shall enjoy the crop of all,
And these not know for whom they toil.

CORB.   Ay, peace.

Mos. *(to* CORVINO) But you shall eat it.
— *[aside]* Much! — *(Then to* VOLTORE *again)* Worshipful sir,   20
Mercury sit upon your thund'ring tongue,
Or the French Hercules, [48] and make your language
As conquering as his club, to beat along,
As with a tempest, flat, our adversaries;
But much more yours, sir.

VOLT.   Here they come; ha' done.

Mos. I have another witness, if you need, sir,
I can produce.

VOLT.   Who is it?

Mos.   Sir, I have her.

---

[37] The same.   [38] Prostitute.   [39] Q *use.*
[40] *I.e.,* your seniorship.
[41] The Scrutineo, or Senate-house.
[42] The way to conduct this case.

[43] Arranged.   [44] Only.   [45] Corbaccio's.
[46] Used medicinally.
[47] *I.e.,* horned animal, cuckold.
[48] The Gallic or Celtic Hercules was a symbol of eloquence. Lucian wrote a treatise on him. (Upton.) — As herald of the gods, Mercury was god of eloquence.

SCENE V [49]

[*To them enter*] 4 Avocatori, BONARIO, CELIA, Notario, Commandadori, [Saffi, *and other* Officers of Justice.]

1 Avoc. The like of this the Senate never heard of.

2 Avoc. 'T will come most strange to them when we report it.

4 Avoc. The gentlewoman has been ever held
Of unreproved name.

3 Avoc.   So, the young man.[50]

4 Avoc. The more unnatural part that of his father.

2 Avoc. More of the husband.

1 Avoc.   I not know to give
His act a name, it is so monstrous!

4 Avoc. But the impostor, he is a thing created
T' exceed example!

[1] Avoc.   And all after-times!

2 Avoc. I never heard a true voluptuary [10
Describ'd but him.

3 Avoc.   Appear yet those were cited?

NOT. All but the old magnifico, Volpone.

1 Avoc. Why is not he here?

MOS.   Please your Fatherhoods,
Here is his advocate. Himself 's so weak,
So feeble ——

4 Avoc.   What are you?

BON.   His parasite,
His knave, his pander. I beseech the court
He may be forc'd to come, that your grave eyes
May bear strong witness of his strange impostures.

VOLT. Upon my faith and credit with your Virtues,
He is not able to endure the air.   20

2 Avoc. Bring him, however.

3 Avoc.   We will see him.

4 Avoc.   Fetch him.

VOLT. Your Fatherhoods' fit pleasures be obey'd;   [*Exeunt* Officers.]
But sure, the sight will rather move your pities
Than indignation. May it please the court,
In the mean time, he may be heard in me.
I know this place most void of prejudice,
And therefore crave it, since we have no reason
To fear our truth should hurt our cause.

3 Avoc.   Speak free.

VOLT. Then know, most honor'd fathers, I must now
Discover to your strangely abused [51] ears, [30

The most prodigious and most frontless [52] piece
Of solid impudence and treachery
That ever vicious nature yet brought forth
To shame the state of Venice. This lewd woman,
That wants no artificial looks or tears
To help the visor she has now put on,
Hath long been known a close [53] adulteress
To that lascivious youth there; not suspected,
I say, but known, and taken in the act   39
With him; and by this man, the easy husband,
Pardon'd; whose timeless [54] bounty makes him now
Stand here, the most unhappy, innocent person
That ever man's own goodness made accus'd.
For these, not knowing how to owe [55] a gift
Of that dear grace, but with their shame, being plac'd
So above all powers of their gratitude,
Began to hate the benefit, and, in place
Of thanks, devise t' extirp the memory
Of such an act: wherein I pray your Fatherhoods
To observe the malice, yea, the rage of creatures   50
Discover'd in their evils; and what heart
Such take, ev'n from their crimes. But that anon
Will more appear. This gentleman, the father,
Hearing of this foul fact,[56] with many others,
Which daily struck at his too tender ears,
And griev'd in nothing more than that he could not
Preserve himself a parent (his son's ills
Growing to that strange flood), at last decreed
To disinherit him.

1 Avoc.   These be strange turns!

2 Avoc. The young man's fame was ever fair and honest.   60

VOLT. So much more full of danger is his vice,
That can beguile so, under shade of virtue.
But, as I said, my honor'd sires, his father
Having this settled purpose, by what means
To him betray'd, we know not, and this day
Appointed for the deed; that parricide,
I cannot style him better, by confederacy
Preparing this his paramour to be there,
Ent'red Volpone's house (who was the man, [69
Your Fatherhoods must understand, design'd
For the inheritance), there sought his father :—

---

[52] Shameless.   [53] Secret.   [54] Untimely.
[55] Own.   [56] Deed.

[49] The same.   [50] Q *So has the youth.*   [51] Deceived.

But with what purpose sought he him, my
    Lords?
I tremble to pronounce it, that a son
Unto a father, and to such a father,
Should have so foul, felonious intent —
It was to murder him ; when, being prevented
By his more happy absence, what then did he?
Not check his wicked thoughts ; no, now new
    deeds
(Mischief doth ever [57] end where it begins) —
An act of horror, fathers ! He dragg'd forth
The aged gentleman that had there lien bed-
    rid   81
Three years and more, out off his innocent
    couch,
Naked upon the floor ; there left him ;
    wounded
His servant in the face ; and with this strum-
    pet,
The stale [58] to his forg'd practice,[59] who was
    glad
To be so active, — I shall here desire
Your Fatherhoods to note but my collections,[60]
As most remarkable, — thought at once to
    stop
His father's ends, discredit his free choice
In the old gentleman, redeem themselves,   90
By laying infamy upon this man,
To whom, with blushing, they should owe
    their lives.
    1 Avoc. What proofs have you of this?
    Bon.   Most honor'd fathers,
I humbly crave there be no credit given
To this man's mercenary tongue.
    2 Avoc.   Forbear.
    Bon. His soul moves in his fee.
    3 Avoc.   O, sir.
    Bon.   This fellow,
For six sols [61] more would plead against his
    Maker.
    1 Avoc. You do forget yourself.
    Volt.   Nay, nay, grave fathers,
Let him have scope ! Can any man imagine
That he will spare his accuser, that would not
Have spar'd his parent?
    1 Avoc.   Well, produce your proofs. [101
    Cel. I would I could forget I were a crea-
    ture.
    Volt. Signior Corbaccio.

    4 Avoc.   What is he?
    Volt.   The father.
    2 Avoc. Has he had an oath?
    Not.   Yes.
    Corb.   What must I do now?
    Not. Your testimony's crav'd.
    Corb.   Speak to the knave?
I'll ha' my mouth first stopp'd with earth ; my
    heart
Abhors his knowledge : I disclaim in [62] him.
    1 Avoc. But for what cause?
    Corb.   The mere portent of nature.
He is an utter stranger to my loins.   109
    Bon. Have they made you to [63] this !
    Corb.   I will not hear thee,
Monster of men, swine, goat, wolf, parricide,
Speak not, thou viper.
    Bon.   Sir, I will sit down,
And rather wish my innocence should suffer
Than I resist the authority of a father.
    Volt. Signior Corvino.
    2 Avoc.   This is strange !
    1 Avoc.   Who's this?
    Not. The husband.
    4 Avoc.   Is he sworn?
    Not.   He is.
    3 Avoc.   Speak then.
    Corv. This woman, please your Father-
    hoods, is a whore,
Of most hot exercise, more than a partridge,
Upon record ——
    1 Avoc.   No more.
    Corv.   Neighs like a jennet.
    Not. Preserve the honor of the court.
    Corv.   I shall, [120
And modesty of your most reverend ears.
And yet I hope that I may say these eyes
Have seen her glu'd unto that piece of cedar,
That fine well-timber'd gallant ; and that
    here
The letters may be read, thorough the horn,[64]
That make the story perfect.
    Mos. [*aside to* Corvino]   Excellent, sir !
    Corv. [*aside to* Mosca] There is no shame [65]
    in this now, is there ?
    Mos. [*aside to* Corvino]   None.
    Corv. Or if I said, I hop'd that she were on-
    ward
To her damnation, if there be a hell

---

[57] Emend. Whalley *never;* but the line may mean,
"Mischief begins in evil thoughts and ends in evil
deeds."
[58] Stalking-horse, prostitute used by thieves as a
decoy.
[59] Fabricated plot.
[60] Deductions.
[61] Trivial coins of different value in various places.

[62] Disown.
[63] Wrought you to, prepared you to say.
[64] As easily as the alphabet on the "hornbook"
(so called because the card was covered with transparent horn). At "here" Corvino doubtless makes
the sign of the horn; *i.e.,* Celia's guilt is attested
by his being branded cuckold.
[65] Q *harme.*

Greater than whore and woman, a good Catho-
　　lic [66]　　　　　　　　　　　　　　130
May make the doubt.
　3 Avoc.　　His grief hath made him frantic.
　1 Avoc.　Remove him hence.
　2 Avoc.　　　　　　Look to the woman.
　　　　　　　　　　　　　　She swoons.
　　Corv.　　　　　　　　　　　　Rare!
Prettily feign'd! again!
　4 Avoc.　　　　　Stand from about her.
　1 Avoc.　Give her the air.
　3 Avoc. [*to* Mosca]　What can you say?
　Mos.　　　　　　　　　　My wound,
May 't please your Wisdoms, speaks for me,
　　receiv'd
In aid of my good patron, when he miss'd
His sought-for father, when that well-taught
　　dame
Had her cue giv'n her to cry out, " A rape! "
　Bon.　O most laid [67] impudence! Fathers —
　3 Avoc.　　　　　Sir, be silent; [139
You had your hearing free, so must they theirs.
　2 Avoc.　I do begin to doubt th' imposture
　　here.
　4 Avoc.　This woman has too many moods.
　Volt.　　　　　　　　Grave fathers,
She is a creature of a most profess'd
And prostituted lewdness.
　Corv.　　　　　　Most impetuous!
Unsatisfied, grave fathers!
　Volt.　　　　　　May her feignings
Not take your wisdoms.　But this day [68] she
　　baited
A stranger, a grave knight, with her loose eyes
And more lascivious kisses.　This man saw 'em
Together on the water, in a gondola.
　Mos.　Here is the lady herself, that saw 'em
　　too,　　　　　　　　　　　　　150
Without; who then had in the open streets
Pursu'd them, but for saving her knight's
　　honor.
　1 Avoc.　Produce that lady.
　2 Avoc.　　Let her come.　[*Exit* Mosca.]
　4 Avoc.　　　　　　　These things,
They strike with wonder!
　3 Avoc.　　　　　I am turn'd a stone!

Scene VI [69]

[To them re-enter] Mosca [*with*] Lady
　　　　　　[Would-Be.]

Mos.　Be resolute, madam.
Lady.　　　　　Ay, this same is she. —

Out, thou chameleon harlot! now thine eyes
Vie tears with the hyena.　Dar'st thou look
Upon my wronged face? — I cry your par-
　　dons.
I fear I have forgettingly transgress'd
Against the dignity of the court ——
　2 Avoc.　　　　　　　　No, madam.
　Lady.　And been exorbitant ——
　[2] Avoc.　　　　　You have not, lady.
　4 Avoc.　These proofs are strong.
　Lady.　　　　　Surely, I had no purpose
To scandalize your honors, or my sex's.
　3 Avoc.　We do believe it.
　Lady.　　　　Surely you may believe it.　10
　2 Avoc.　Madam, we do.
　Lady.　　　　Indeed you may; my breeding
Is not so coarse ——
　4 Avoc.　　　　　We know it.
　Lady.　　　　　　　To offend
With pertinacy ——
　3 Avoc.　　　　Lady ——
　Lady.　　　　　　Such a presence;
No, surely.
　1 Avoc.　We will think it.
　Lady.　　　　You may think it.
　1 Avoc.　Let her o'ercome. — What wit-
　　nesses have you,
To make good your report?
　Bon.　　　　　Our consciences.
　Cel.　And Heaven, that never fails the inno-
　　cent.
　1 Avoc.　These are no testimonies.
　Bon.　　　　Not in your courts,
Where multitude and clamor overcomes.
　1 Avoc.　Nay, then you do wax insolent.

　　Volpone *is brought in, as impotent.*

Volt.　　　　　　　Here, here, [20
The testimony comes that will convince,
And put to utter dumbness their bold tongues.
See here, grave fathers, here 's the ravisher,
The rider on men's wives, the great impostor,
The grand voluptuary!　Do you not think
These limbs should affect venery? or these
　　eyes
Covet a concubine?　Pray you mark these
　　hands.
Are they not fit to stroke a lady's breasts?
Perhaps he doth dissemble!
　Bon.　　　　　　So he does.
　Volt.　Would you ha' him tortur'd?
　Bon.　　　　I would have him prov'd. [30
　Volt.　Best try him then with goads, or
　　burning irons;
Put him to the strappado; I have heard

---

[66] Q *Christian.*　　　[67] Well-laid, carefully planned.
[68] Only to-day.　　　[69] The same.

The rack hath cur'd the gout ; faith, give it
him,
And help him of a malady ; be courteous.
I 'll undertake, before these honor'd fathers,
He shall have yet as many left diseases,
As she has known adulterers, or thou strum-
pets.
O, my most equal [70] hearers, if these deeds,
Acts of this bold and most exorbitant strain,
May pass with sufferance, what one citizen [40
But owes the forfeit of his life, yea, fame,
To him that dares traduce him? Which of
you
Are safe, my honor'd fathers? I would ask,
With leave of your grave Fatherhoods, if their
plot
Have any face or color like to truth?
Or if, unto the dullest nostril here,
It smell not rank, and most abhorred slander?
I crave your care of this good gentleman,
Whose life is much endanger'd by their fable ;
And as for them, I will conclude with this :   50
That vicious persons, when they are hot, and
flesh'd
In impious acts, their constancy [71] abounds :
Damn'd deeds are done with greatest confi-
dence.
    1 Avoc. Take 'em to custody, and sever
them.
    2 Avoc. 'T is pity two such prodigies should
live.
    1 Avoc. Let the old gentleman be return'd
with care.
           [*Exeunt* Officers *with* VOLPONE.]
I am sorry our credulity wrong'd him.
    4 Avoc. These are two creatures !
    3 Avoc.   I have an earthquake in me !
    2 Avoc. Their shame, even in their cradles,
fled their faces.
    4 Avoc. You have done a worthy service to
the state, sir,   60
In their discovery.
    1 Avoc.   You shall hear, ere night,
What punishment the court decrees upon 'em.
          [*Exeunt* Avocatori, Notario, *and*
          Officers *with* BONARIO *and* CELIA.]
    VOLT. We thank your Fatherhoods. — How
like you it?
    Mos.   Rare.
I 'd ha' your tongue, sir, tipp'd with gold for
this ;
I 'd ha' you be the heir to the whole city ;
The earth I 'd have want men ere you want
living :

[70] Just.   [71] Persistence, resolution.

They are bound to erect your statue in St.
Mark's. —
Signior Corvino, I would have you go
And show yourself that you have conquer'd.
    CORV.   Yes.
    Mos. It was much better that you should
profess   70
Yourself a cuckold thus, than that the other
Should have been prov'd.
    CORV.   Nay, I consider'd that ;
Now it is her fault.
    Mos.   Then, it had been yours.
    CORV. True. — [*aside to* MOSCA] I do doubt
this advocate still.
    Mos. [*aside*]   I' faith,
You need not ; I dare ease you of that care.
    CORV. [*aside*] I trust thee, Mosca.
    Mos. [*aside*]   As your own soul, sir.
                 [*Exit* CORVINO.]
    CORB.   Mosca !
    Mos. Now for your business, sir.
    CORB.   How? ha' you business?
    Mos. Yes, yours, sir.
    CORB.   O, none else?
    Mos.   None else, not I.
    CORB. Be careful then.
    Mos.   Rest you with both
your eyes, sir.[72]
    CORB. Dispatch it.
    Mos.   Instantly.
    CORB.   And look that all,   80
Whatever, be put in, jewels, plate, monies,
Household stuff, bedding, curtains.
    Mos.   Curtain-rings, sir ;
Only, the advocate's fee must be deducted.
    CORB. I 'll pay him now ; you 'll be too
prodigal.
    Mos. Sir, I must tender it.
    CORB.   Two *cecchines* is well.
    Mos. No, six, sir.
    CORB.   'T is too much.
    Mos.   He talk'd a great while ;
You must consider that, sir.
    CORB.   Well, there 's three ——
    Mos. I 'll give it him.
    CORB. Do so, and there 's for thee. [*Exit.*]
    Mos. [*aside*] Bountiful bones ! What hor-
rid strange offence
Did he commit 'gainst nature, in his youth, [90
Worthy this age? — [*aside to* VOLTORE] You
see, sir, how I work
Unto your ends ; take you no notice.
    VOLT.   No,
I 'll leave you.

[72] *I.e.*, leave everything to me.

Mos. [*aside*]   All is yours, the devil and all,
Good advocate. — Madam, I'll bring you home.
Lady. No, I'll go see your patron.
Mos.   That you shall not ;
I'll tell you why. My purpose is to urge
My patron to reform his will, and for
The zeal you have shown to-day, whereas before
You were but third or fourth, you shall be now   99
Put in the first ; which would appear as begg'd
If you were present. Therefore ——
Lady.   You shall sway me. [*Exeunt.*]

ACT V — Scene I [1]

[*Enter*] Volpone.

Volp. Well, I am here, and all this brunt is past.
I ne'er was in dislike with my disguise
Till this fled moment : here 't was good, in private ;
But in your public, — *cave*,[2] whilst I breathe.
'Fore God, my left leg 'gan to have the cramp.
And I apprehended straight some power had struck me
With a dead palsy. Well, I must be merry,
And shake it off. A many of these fears
Would put me into some villainous disease,
Should they come thick upon me. I'll prevent 'em.   10
Give me a bowl of lusty wine, to fright
This humor from my heart. — (*He drinks.*)
     Hum, hum, hum ! —
'T is almost gone already ; I shall conquer.
Any device now of rare ingenious knavery,
That would possess me with a violent laughter,
Would make me up again ! — (*Drinks again.*)
     So, so, so, so ! —
This heat is life ; 't is blood by this time. —
     Mosca !

Scene II [3]

[*To*] Volpone [*enter*] Mosca.

Mos. How now, sir ? Does the day look clear again ?
Are we recover'd, and wrought out of error,

[1] A room in Volpone's house.
[2] Beware, look out.
[3] The same.

Into our way, to see our path before us ?
Is our trade free once more ?
Volp.   Exquisite Mosca !
Mos. Was it not carri'd learnedly ?
Volp.   And stoutly :
Good wits are greatest in extremities.
Mos. It were folly beyond thought to trust
Any grand act unto a cowardly spirit.
You are not taken with it enough, methinks.
Volp. Oh, more than if I had enjoy'd the wench ;   10
The pleasure of all womankind 's not like it.
Mos. Why, now you speak, sir. We must here be fix'd ;
Here we must rest ; this is our masterpiece ;
We cannot think to go beyond this.
Volp.   True,
Thou hast play'd thy prize, my precious Mosca.
Mos.   Nay, sir,
To gull the court ——
Volp.   And quite divert the torrent
Upon the innocent.
Mos.   Yes, and to make
So rare a music out of discords ——
Volp.   Right.
That yet to me 's the strangest ! how th' hast borne it !
That these, being so divided 'mongst themselves,   20
Should not scent somewhat, or in me or thee,
Or doubt their own side.
Mos.   True, they will not see 't.
Too much light blinds 'em, I think. Each of 'em
Is so possess'd and stuff'd with his own hopes
That anything unto the contrary,
Never so true, or never so apparent,
Never so palpable, they will resist it —
Volp. Like a temptation of the Devil.
Mos.   Right, sir.
Merchants may talk of trade, and your great signiors
Of land that yields well ; but if Italy   30
Have any glebe more fruitful than these fellows,
I am deceiv'd. Did not your advocate rare ?
Volp. Oh — " My most honor'd fathers, my grave fathers,
Under correction of your Fatherhoods,
What face of truth is here ? If these strange deeds
May pass, most honor'd fathers " — I had much ado
To forbear laughing.

Mos.   'T seem'd to me you sweat, sir.
VOLP. In troth, I did a little.
Mos.   But confess, sir,
Were you not daunted?
VOLP.   In good faith, I was
A little in a mist, but not dejected ;   40
Never, but still myself.
Mos.   I think it, sir.
Now, so truth help me, I must needs say this,
        sir,
And out of conscience for your advocate,
He has taken pains, in faith, sir, and deserv'd,
In my poor judgment, I speak it under favor,
Not to contrary you, sir, very richly —
Well — to be cozen'd.[4]
VOLP.   Troth, and I think so too,
By that I heard him in the latter end.

Mos. O, but before, sir : had you heard him
        first
Draw it to certain heads, then aggravate,[5] [50
Then use his vehement figures — I look'd still
When he would shift [6] a shirt ; and doing this
Out of pure love, no hope of gain ——
VOLP.   'T is right.
I cannot answer him, Mosca, as I would,
Not yet ; but for thy sake, at thy entreaty,
I will begin, ev'n now — to vex 'em all,
This very instant.
Mos.   Good sir.
VOLP.   Call the dwarf
And eunuch forth.
Mos.   Castrone, Nano !

[*Enter* CASTRONE *and* NANO.]

NANO.   Here.
VOLP. Shall we have a jig [7] now?
Mos.   What you please, sir.
VOLP.   Go,
Straight give out about the streets, you two, [60
That I am dead ; do it with constancy,
Sadly,[8] do you hear? Impute it to the grief
Of this late slander.
                [*Exeunt* CASTRONE *and* NANO.]
Mos.   What do you mean, sir?
VOLP.   Oh,
I shall have instantly my Vulture, Crow,
Raven, come flying hither, on the news,
To peck for carrion, my she-wolf, and all,
Greedy, and full of expectation ——
Mos. And then to have it ravish'd from
        their mouths?

---

[4] Deceived, cheated.
[5] Add weight, bring charges.
[6] I was constantly expecting that he would have
to change.
[7] Farcical entertainment.   [8] Seriously.

VOLP. 'T is true. I will ha' thee put on a
        gown,
And take upon thee, as thou wert mine
        heir ;   70
Show 'em a will. Open that chest, and reach
Forth one of those that has the blanks. I 'll
        straight
Put in thy name.
Mos.   It will be rare, sir.
VOLP.   Ay,
When they e'en gape, and find themselves
        deluded ——
Mos. Yes.
VOLP.   And thou use them scurvily.
        Dispatch ;
Get on thy gown.
Mos.   But what, sir, if they ask
After the body?
VOLP.   Say, it was corrupted.
Mos. I 'll say it stunk, sir ; and was fain t'
        have it
Coffin'd up instantly, and sent away.
VOLP. Anything ; what thou wilt. — Hold,
        here 's my will.   80
Get thee a cap, a count-book, pen and ink,
Papers afore thee ; sit as thou wert taking
An inventory of parcels. I 'll get up
Behind the curtain, on a stool, and hearken ;
Sometime peep over, see how they do look,
With what degrees their blood doth leave their
        faces !
O, 't will afford me a rare meal of laughter.
Mos. Your advocate will turn stark dull
        upon it.
VOLP. It will take off his oratory's edge.
Mos. But your clarissimo, old roundback,
        he   90
Will crump you [9] like a hog-louse, with the
        touch.
VOLP. And what Corvino?
Mos.   O, sir, look for him,
To-morrow morning, with a rope and a dagger,
To visit all the streets ; he must run mad.
My Lady too, that came into the court,
To bear false witness for your Worship —
VOLP.   Yes,
And kiss'd me 'fore the fathers, when my face
Flow'd all with oils ——
Mos.   And sweat, sir. Why, your gold
Is such another med'cine, it dries up
All those offensive savors. It transforms [100
The most deformed, and restores 'em lovely,
As 't were the strange poetical girdle.[10] Jove

---

[9] Curl up. "You" is an ethical dative.
[10] The cestus of Venus.

Could not invent t' himself a shroud more
    subtle
To pass Acrisius' [11] guards. It is the thing
Makes all the world her grace, her youth, her
    beauty.
VOLP. I think she loves me.
MOS.   Who? the lady, sir?
She 's jealous of you.
VOLP.   Dost thou say so?
                    [*Knocking within.*]
MOS.   Hark.
There 's some already.
VOLP.   Look.
MOS.   It is the Vulture ;
He has the quickest scent.
VOLP.   I 'll to my place,
Thou to thy posture.
           [*Goes behind the curtain.*[12]]
MOS.   I am set.
VOLP.   But, Mosca, [110
Play the artificer now : torture 'em rarely.

SCENE III [13]

[*To*] MOSCA [*enter*] VOLTORE.

VOLT. How now, my Mosca?
MOS. [*writing*] Turkey carpets, nine ——
VOLT. Taking an inventory ! that is well.
MOS. Two suits of bedding, tissue ——
VOLT.   Where 's the will?
Let me read that the while.

[*Enter* Servants *with* CORBACCIO *in a chair*.]

CORB.   So, set me down,
And get you home.   [*Exeunt* Servants.]
VOLT.   Is he come now, to trouble us?
MOS. Of cloth of gold, two more ——
CORB.   Is it done, Mosca?
MOS. Of several velvets, eight ——
VOLT.   I like his care.
CORB. Dost thou not hear?

[*Enter* CORVINO.]

CORV.   Ha ! is the hour come, Mosca?
VOLP. [*aside*] Ay, now they muster.
          Peeps from behind a traverse.[14]
CORV.   What does the advocate here?
Or this Corbaccio?
CORB.   What do these here?

[11] He was Danaë's father.
[12] Of the inner stage.
[13] The same.
[14] One of the curtains that closed off the inner
stage.

[*Enter* LADY WOULD-BE.]
LADY.   Mosca ! [10
Is his thread spun?
MOS.   Eight chests of linen ——
VOLP. [*aside*]   Oh,
My fine Dame Would-be, too !
CORB.   Mosca, the will,
That I may show it these, and rid 'em hence.
MOS. Six chests of diaper, four of damask —
    there.
                [*Gives the will.*]
CORB. Is that the will?
MOS. [*writing*]   Down-beds, and bol-
    sters ——
VOLP. [*aside*]   Rare !
Be busy still. Now they begin to flutter ;
They never think of me. Look, see, see, see !
How their swift eyes run over the long deed,
Unto the name, and to the legacies,
What is bequeath'd them there ——
MOS.   Ten suits of hangings —— [20
VOLP. [*aside*] Ay, in their garters, Mosca.
    Now their hopes
Are at the gasp.
VOLT.   Mosca the heir !
CORB.   What 's that?
VOLP. [*aside*] My advocate is dumb ; look
    to my merchant —
He has heard of some strange storm ; a ship
    is lost —
He faints. My Lady will swoon. Old
    glazen-eyes,
He hath not reach'd his despair yet.
CORB.   All these
Are out of hope ; I am, sure, the man.
             [*Takes the will.*]
CORV.   But, Mosca ——
MOS. Two cabinets ——
CORV.   Is this in earnest?
MOS.   One
Of ebony ——
CORV.   Or do you but delude me?
MOS. The other, mother-of-pearl — I am
    very busy.   30
Good faith, it is a fortune thrown upon me —
Item, one salt [15] of agate — not my seeking.
LADY. Do you hear, sir?
MOS.   A perfum'd box — 'pray you for-
    bear ;
You see I am troubled — made of an onyx ——
LADY.   How !
MOS. To-morrow or next day, I shall be at
    leisure
To talk with you all.
[15] Saltcellar.

Corv.   Is this my large hope's issue?

Lady. Sir, I must have a fairer answer.

Mos.   Madam!

Marry, and shall : 'pray you, fairly quit my house.

Nay, raise no tempest with your looks ; but hark you,

Remember what your Ladyship off'red me [40

To put you in an heir ; go to ; think on it.

And what you said e'en your best madams did

For maintenance, and why not you? Enough.

Go home, and use the poor Sir Pol, your knight, well,

For fear I tell some riddles ; go, be melancholic.   [*Exit* Lady Would-be.]

Volp. [*aside*] Oh, my fine devil!

Corv.   Mosca, pray you a word.

Mos. Lord! will not you take your dispatch hence yet?

Methinks, of all, you should have been th' example.

Why should you stay here? with what thought, what promise?

Hear you ; do not you know, I know you an ass,   50

And that you would most fain have been a wittol [16]

If fortune would have let you? that you are

A declar'd cuckold, on good terms? This pearl,

You'll say, was yours? right ; this diamond?

I'll not deny't, but thank you. Much here else?

It may be so. Why, think that these good works

May help to hide you[r] bad. I'll not betray you ;

Although you be but extraordinary,

And have it [17] only in title, it sufficeth :

Go home ; be melancholic too, or mad.   60
                       [*Exit* Corvino.]

Volp. [*aside*] Rare Mosca! how his villainy becomes him!

Volt. [*aside*] Certain he doth delude all these for me.

Corb. Mosca the heir?

Volp. [*aside*]   O, his four eyes have found it!

Corb. I am cozen'd, cheated, by a parasite-slave ;

Harlot,[18] t' hast gull'd me.

Mos.   Yes, sir. Stop your mouth,

Or I shall draw the only tooth is left.

Are not you he, that filthy covetous wretch,

With the three legs, that here, in hope of prey,

Have, any time this three year, snuff'd about,

With your most grov'ling nose, and would have hir'd   70

Me to the pois'ning of my patron, sir?

Are not you he that have to-day in court

Profess'd the disinheriting of your son?

Perjur'd yourself? Go home, and die, and stink ;

If you but croak a syllable, all comes out :

Away, and call your porters! [19] [*Exit* Corbaccio.] Go, go, stink.

Volp. [*aside*] Excellent varlet!

Volt.   Now, my faithful Mosca,

I find thy constancy——

Mos.   Sir!

Volt.   Sincere.

Mos. [*writing*]   A table

Of porphyry — I mar'l you'll be thus troublesome.

Volt. Nay, leave off now, they are gone.

Mos.   Why, who are you? [80

What! who did send for you? Oh, cry you mercy,

Reverend sir! Good faith, I am griev'd for you,

That any chance of mine should thus defeat

Your (I must needs say) most deserving travails ;

But I protest, sir, it was cast upon me,

And I could almost wish to be without it,

But that the will o' th' dead must be observ'd.

Marry, my joy is that you need it not ;

You have a gift, sir, (thank your education),

Will never let you want, while there are men,   90

And malice, to breed causes.[20] Would I had

But half the like, for all my fortune, sir.

If I have any suits, as I do hope,

Things being so easy and direct, I shall not,

I will make bold with your obstreperous [21] aid ;

Conceive me — for your fee, sir. In meantime,

You that have so much law, I know ha' the conscience

Not to be covetous of what is mine.

Good sir, I thank you for my plate ; 't will help

To set up a young man. Good faith, you look   100

---

[16] Acquiescent cuckold.   [17] Cuckoldry.
[18] Scoundrel (originally applied to males).

[19] To remove the sedan chair. Presumably they do so shortly after Corbaccio's exit.
[20] Lawsuits.   [21] Vociferous.

As you were costive ; best go home and purge,
sir. [*Exit* VOLTORE.]
VOLP. [*coming from behind the curtain*] Bid
him eat lettuce [22] well. My witty
mischief,
Let me embrace thee. O that I could now
Transform thee to a Venus ! — Mosca, go,
Straight take my habit of clarissimo,[23]
And walk the streets ; be seen, torment 'em
more :
We must pursue, as well as plot. Who would
Have lost this feast ?
MOS. I doubt it will lose them.
VOLP. O, my recovery shall recover all.
That I could now but think on some dis-
guise 110
To meet 'em in, and ask 'em questions.
How I would vex 'em still at every turn !
Mos. Sir, I can fit you.
VOLP. Canst thou?
Mos. Yes, I know
One o' the commandadori, sir ; so like you,[24]
Him will I straight make drunk, and bring
you his habit.
VOLP. A rare disguise, and answering thy
brain !
O, I will be a sharp disease unto 'em.
Mos. Sir, you must look for curses ——
VOLP. Till they burst ;
The Fox fares ever best when he is curs'd.[25]
[*Exeunt.*]

SCENE IV [26]

[*Enter*] PEREGRINE [*disguised and*] *three* Mercatori.

PER. Am I enough disguis'd?
1 MER. I warrant you.
PER. All my ambition is to fright him only.
2 MER. If you could ship him away, 't were
excellent.
3 MER. To Zant,[27] or to Aleppo !
PER. Yes, and ha' his
Adventures put i' th' Book of Voyages,[28]
And his gull'd story regist'red for truth !
Well, gentlemen, when I am in awhile,
And that you think us warm in our discourse,
Know your approaches.
1 MER. Trust it to our care.
[*Exeunt* Merchants.]

[22] As a laxative. (Cf. Martial, III, 89.)
[23] Grandee.
[24] If it please you. [25] Proverbial.
[26] A hall in Sir Politic's house.
[27] Zante, one of the Ionian islands : also its port.
[28] Doubtless Hakluyt's *Principal Navigations.*

[*Enter* Waiting Woman.]
PER. Save you, fair lady ! Is Sir Pol
within? 10
WOM. I do not know, sir.
PER. 'Pray you say unto him
Here is a merchant, upon earnest business,
Desires to speak with him.
WOM. I will see, sir. [*Exit.*]
PER. 'Pray you.
I see the family is all female here.

[*Re-enter* Waiting Woman.]
WOM. He says, sir, he has weighty affairs of
state,
That now require him whole ; some other time
You may possess him.
PER. 'Pray you say again,
If those require him whole, these will exact
him.
Whereof I bring him tidings. [*Exit* Woman.]
What might be
His grave affair of state now ! How to
make 20
Bolognian sausages here in Venice, sparing
One o' th' ingredients?

[*Re-enter* Waiting Woman.]
WOM. Sir, he says he knows
By your word " tidings," [29] that you are no
statesman,
And therefore wills you stay.
PER. Sweet, 'pray you return him
I have not read so many proclamations,
And studied them for words, as he has
done ——
But — here he deigns to come.
[*Exit* Woman.]

[*Enter* SIR POLITIC.]
POL. Sir, I must crave
Your courteous pardon. There hath chanc'd
to-day
Unkind disaster 'twixt my lady and me ;
And I was penning my apology, 30
To give her satisfaction, as you came now.
PER. Sir, I am griev'd I bring you worse
disaster.
The gentleman you met at th' port to-day,
That told you he was newly arriv'd ——
POL. Ay, was
A fugitive punk [30]?
PER. No, sir, a spy set on you ;
And he has made relation to the Senate,

[29] Instead of "intelligence." (Gifford.)
[30] Prostitute.

That you profess'd to him to have a plot
To sell the state of Venice to the Turk.

Pol.　O me!

Per.　For which warrants are sign'd by this time,
To apprehend you, and to search your study　　40
For papers ——

Pol.　Alas, sir, I have none, but notes
Drawn out of play-books ——

Per.　　　　　　　　All the better, sir.

Pol.　And some essays.　What shall I do?

Per.　　　　　　　　　　Sir, best
Convey yourself into a sugar-chest;
Or, if you could lie round, a frail [31] were rare; [32]
And I could send you aboard.

Pol.　　　　　　Sir, I but talk'd so.
For discourse sake merely.

　　　　　　　　　　　They knock without.

Per.　　　　　　Hark! they are there.

Pol.　I am a wretch, a wretch!

Per.　　　　　　What will you do, sir?
Have you ne'er a curran[t]-butt to leap into?
They'll put you to the rack; you must be sudden.　　50

Pol.　Sir, I have an engine [33] ——

3 Mer.　[*within*]　　Sir Politic Would-be!

2 Mer.　[*within*] Where is he?

Pol.　　　　That I've thought upon, before time.

Per.　What is it?

Pol.　　　I shall ne'er endure the torture. —
Marry, it is, sir, of a tortoise shell,
Fitted [34] for these extremities; 'pray you, sir, help me.
Here I have a place, sir, to put back my legs,
Please you to lay it on, sir, [*Lies down while* Peregrine *places the shell upon him.*] with this cap,
And my black gloves. I'll lie, sir, like a tortoise,
Till they are gone.

Per.　　　　　　And call you this an engine?

Pol.　Mine own device. —— Good sir, bid my wife's women　　60
To burn my papers.　　　[*Exit* Peregrine.]

[*The three* Merchants] *rush in.*

1 Mer.　　　　　Where's he hid?

3 Mer.　　　　　　　We must,
And will, sure, find him.

2 Mer.　　　　Which is his study?

[*Re-enter* Peregrine.]

1 Mer.　　　　　　　　　What
Are you, sir?

Per.　　I am a merchant, that came here
To look upon this tortoise.

3 Mer.　　　　　　　How?

1 Mer.　　　　　　　St. Mark!
What beast is this?

Per.　　　　　　It is a fish.

2 Mer.　　　　　　Come out here!

Per.　Nay, you may strike him, sir, and tread upon him;
He'll bear a cart.

1 Mer.　　　What, to run over him?

Per.　　　　　　　　Yes, sir.

3 Mer.　Let's jump upon him.

2 Mer.　　　　　Can he not go?

Per.　　　　　　　He creeps, sir.

1 Mer.　Let's see him creep.

Per.　　No, good sir, you will hurt him.

2 Mer.　Heart, I'll see him creep, or prick his guts.　　70

3 Mer.　Come out here.

Per.　　　　　Pray you, sir! — [*aside to* Sir Politic] Creep a little.

1 Mer.　　　　　　　　Forth.

2 Mer.　Yet further.

Per.　　Good sir! — [*aside*] Creep!

2 Mer.　　　　　　We'll see his legs.
　　　　　They pull off the shell and discover him.

3 Mer.　Gods so, he has garters!

1 Mer.　　　　　　Ay, and gloves!

2 Mer.　　　　　　　Is this
Your fearful tortoise?

Per.　[*discovering himself*]　　Now, Sir Pol, we are even;
For your next project I shall be prepar'd;
I am sorry for the funeral of your notes, sir.

1 Mer.　'T were a rare motion [35] to be seen in Fleet Street.

2 Mer.　Ay, i' the term. [36]

1 Mer.　　　Or Smithfield, in the fair. [37]

3 Mer.　Methinks 't is but a melancholic sight!

Per.　Farewell, most politic tortoise.
　　　　[*Exeunt* Peregrine *and* Merchants.]

[*Re-enter* Waiting Woman.]

Pol.　　　　　Where's my Lady?　80
Knows she of this?

Wom.　　　　I know not, sir.

---

[31] Basket.
[32] Would be just the thing.
[33] Contrivance.　　　　[34] Q *apted*.

[35] Side-show.
[36] When the courts were sitting; cf. "the season."
[37] Bartholomew Fair.

Pol. Inquire. —
Oh, I shall be the fable of all feasts,
The freight of the gazetti,[38] ship-boys' tale ;
And, which is worst, even talk for ordinaries.[39]
  Wom. My Lady's come most melancholic
    home,
And says, sir, she will straight to sea, for
    physic.
  Pol. And I, to shun this place and clime
    for ever,
Creeping with house on back, and think it well
To shrink my poor head in my politic shell.
                          [*Exeunt.*]

Scene V [40]

[*Enter*] Volpone [*and*] Mosca, *the first in the habit of a commandadore, the other of a clarissimo.*

  Volp. Am I then like him?
  Mos.   O, sir, you are he ;
No man can sever [41] you.
  Volp.   Good.
  Mos.   But what am I?
  Volp. 'Fore Heav'n, a brave clarissimo ;
    thou becom'st it !
Pity thou wert not born one.
  Mos.   If I hold
My made one,[42] 't will be well.
  Volp.   I 'll go and see
What news first at the court.   [*Exit.*]
  Mos.   Do so. — My Fox
Is out on his hole, and ere he shall re-enter,
I 'll make him languish in his borrow'd case,[43]
Except he come to composition [44] with me. —
Androgyno, Castrone, Nano !

[*Enter* Androgyno, Castrone, *and* Nano.]

  All.   Here.   10
  Mos. Go, recreate yourselves abroad ; go,
    sport. —   [*Exeunt all but* Mosca.]
So, now I have the keys, and am possess'd.
Since he will needs be dead afore his time,
I 'll bury him, or gain by him. I am his heir,
And so will keep me, till he share, at least.
To cozen him of all, were but a cheat
Well plac'd ; no man would construe it a sin :
Let his sport pay for 't. This is call'd the Fox-
    trap.   [*Exit.*]

[38] *I.e.*, the subject of the newspapers.
[39] Taverns.
[40] A room in Volpone's house.
[41] *I.e.*, distinguish.
[42] *I.e.*, if I can keep up my assumed rank. Probably not an aside.
[43] Costume, skin.
[44] Terms, agreement.

Scene VI [45]

[*Enter*] Corbaccio [*and*] Corvino.

  Corb. They say the court is set.
  Corv.   We must maintain
Our first tale good, for both our reputations.
  Corb. Why, mine 's no tale ; my son would
    there have kill'd me.
  Corv. That 's true ; I had forgot ; — [*aside*]
    mine is, I am sure. —
But for your will, sir.
  Corb.   Ay, I 'll come upon him
For that hereafter, now his patron 's dead.

[*Enter* Volpone *disguised.*]

  Volp. Signior Corvino ! and Corbaccio !
    sir,
Much joy unto you.
  Corv.   Of what?
  Volp.   The sudden good
Dropp'd down upon you ——
  Corb.   Where?
  Volp.   And none knows how —
From old Volpone, sir.
  Corb.   Out, errant knave ! 10
  Volp. Let not your too much wealth, sir,
    make you furious.
  Corb. Away, thou varlet.
  Volp.   Why, sir?
  Corb.   Dost thou mock me?
  Volp. You mock the world, sir ; did you
    not change wills?
  Corb. Out, harlot.
  Volp.   O ! belike you are the man,
Signior Corvino? Faith, you carry it well ;
You grow not mad withal ; I love your spirit.
You are not overleaven'd [46] with your fortune.
You should ha' some would swell now like a
    wine-fat,[47]
With such an autumn. — Did he gi' you all,
    sir?
  Corb. Avoid,[48] you rascal.
  Volp.   Troth, your wife has shown [20
Herself a very woman ; but you are well,
You need not care, you have a good estate,
To bear it out, sir, better by this chance —
Except Corbaccio have a share.
  Corb.   Hence, varlet.
  Volp. You will not be acknown,[49] sir ; why,
    't is wise.
Thus do all gamesters, at all games, dissemble :

[45] A street.
[46] *I.e.*, puffed up.
[47] Cask.   [48] Begone.   [49] Recognized.

No man will seem [50] to win. [*Exeunt* Corvino
    and Corbaccio.] Here comes my
    vulture,
Heaving his beak up i' the air, and snuffing.

Scene VII [51]

[*To*] Volpone [*enter*] Voltore.

Volt. Outstripp'd thus, by a parasite ! a
    slave !
Would run on errands, and make legs for
    crumbs !
Well, what I 'll do ——
    Volp.   The court stays for you[r]
        Worship.
I e'en rejoice, sir, at your Worship's happiness,
And that it fell into so learned hands,
That understand the fingering ——
    Volt.   What do you mean ?
    Volp. I mean to be a suitor to your Wor-
        ship,
For the small tenement, out of reparations, [52]
That at the end of your long row of houses,
By the Piscaria ; it was, in Volpone's time, [10
Your predecessor, ere he grew diseas'd,
A handsome, pretty, custom'd [53] bawdyhouse
As any was in Venice, none disprais'd ;
But fell with him : his body and that house
Decay'd together.
    Volt.   Come, sir, leave your prating.
    Volp. Why, if your Worship give me but
        your hand
That I may ha' the refusal, I have done.
'T is a mere toy to you, sir, candle-rents ; [54]
As your learn'd Worship knows ——
    Volt.   What do I know ?
    Volp. Marry, no end of your wealth, sir ;
        God decrease it !   20
    Volt. Mistaking knave ! what, mock'st
        thou my misfortune ?   [*Exit.*]
    Volp. His blessing on your heart, sir ;
        would 't were more ! ——
Now to my first again, at the next corner.
                                [*Exit.*]

Scene VIII [55]

[*Enter*] Corbaccio *and* Corvino, (Mosca
            passant.)

Corb. See, in our habit ! [56] see the impu-
    dent varlet !

Corv. That I could shoot mine eyes at him,
    like gun-stones. [57]

        [*Enter* Volpone.]

Volp. But is this true, sir, of the parasite ?
Corb. Again, t' afflict us ? monster !
Volp.   In good faith, sir,
I am heartily griev'd, a beard of your grave
    length
Should be so overreach'd. I never brook'd [58]
That parasite's hair ; methought his nose
    should cozen :
There still was somewhat in his look, did prom-
    ise
The bane of a clarissimo.
    Corb.   Knave ——
    Volp.   Methinks
Yet you, that are so traded i' the world,   10
A witty merchant, the fine bird, Corvino,
That have such moral emblems on your
    name, [59]
Should not have sung you[r] shame, and
    dropp'd your cheese,
To let the Fox laugh at you[r] emptiness.
    Corv. Sirrah, you think the privilege of the
        place,
And your red saucy cap, that seems to me
Nail'd to your jolt-head [60] with those two
    cecchines, [61]
Can warrant your abuses ; come you hither :
You shall perceive, sir, I dare beat you ;
    approach.
    Volp. No haste, sir, I do not know your
        valor well,   20
Since you durst publish what you are, sir.
    Corv.   Tarry,
I 'd speak with you.
    Volp.   Sir, sir, another time ——
    Corv. Nay, now.
    Volp.   O God, sir ! I were a wise man,
Would stand the fury of a distracted cuckold.
                    Mosca *walks by 'em.*
    Corb. What, come again !
    Volp.   Upon 'em, Mosca ; save me.
    Corb. The air 's infected where he breathes
    Corv.   Let 's fly him.
            [*Exeunt* Corvino *and* Corbaccio.]
    Volp. Excellent basilisk ! [62] turn upon the
        Vulture.

---

[50] Is willing to appear.   [51] The same.
[52] Repair. — "Piscaria" =fish market.
[53] Well-patronized.
[54] Income derived from deteriorating property.
[55] Another corner of the street.
[56] Dressed as a clarissimo.
[57] Cannon balls.
[58] Could endure.
[59] Of crow.
[60] Blockhead.
[61] *I.e.*, gilt buttons.
[62] The fabulous serpent, hatched from a cock's
egg, which killed by "the beams of its eyes."

Scene IX [63]

[*To them enter*] Voltore.

Volt. Well, flesh-fly, it is summer with you
    now ;
Your winter will come on.
    Mos.   Good advocate,
'Pray thee not rail, nor threaten out of place
    thus ;
Thou 'lt make a solecism, as Madam says.
Get you a biggin [64] more ; your brain breaks
    loose.   [*Exit.*]
    Volt. Well sir.
    Volp.   Would you ha' me beat the
    insolent slave ?
Throw dirt upon his first good clothes ?
    Volt.   This same
Is doubtless some familiar ! [65]
    Volp.   Sir, the court,
In troth, stays for you. I am mad, a mule
That never read Justinian should get up   10
And ride an advocate. Had you no quirk
To avoid gullage, sir, by such a creature ?
I hope you do but jest ; he has not done't :
This 's but confederacy to blind the rest.
You are the heir ?
    Volt.   A strange, officious,
Troublesome knave ! Thou dost torment me.
    Volp.   I know ——
It cannot be, sir, that you should be cozen'd ;
'T is not within the wit of man to do it ;
You are so wise, so prudent ; and 't is fit
That wealth and wisdom still should go to-
    gether.   [*Exeunt.*]   20

Scene X [66]

[*Enter*] 4 Avocatori, Notario, Bonario, Celia,
    Corbaccio, Corvino, Commandadori,
    [Saffi, *etc.*]

1 Avoc. Are all the parties here ?
Not.   All but the advocate.
2 Avoc. And here he comes.

[*Enter* Voltore *and* Volpone.]

[1] Avoc.   Then bring 'em forth to
    sentence.
Volt. O, my most honor'd fathers, let your
    mercy
Once win upon your justice, to forgive —
I am distracted ——

Volp. [*aside*] [67]   What will he do now ?
Volt.   Oh,
I know not which t' address myself to first ;
Whether your Fatherhoods, or these inno-
    cents —
    Corv. [*aside*] Will he betray himself ?
    Volt.   Whom equally
[I have abus'd, out of most covetous ends ——
    Corv. The man is mad !
    Corb.   What 's that ?
    Corv.   He is possess'd.] [68] [10
    Volt. For which, now struck in conscience,
    here I prostrate
Myself at your offended feet, for pardon.
    1, 2 Avoc. Arise.
    Cel.   O Heav'n, how just thou art !
    Volp.   I am caught
I' mine own noose ——
    Corv. [*to* Corbaccio]   Be constant,
    sir ; naught now
Can help but impudence.
    1 Avoc.   Speak forward.
    Com.   Silence !
    Volt. It is not passion in me, reverend
    fathers,
But only conscience, conscience, my good sires,
That makes me now tell truth. That parasite,
That knave, hath been the instrument of all.
    1 Avoc. Where is that knave? Fetch
    him.
    Volp.   I go.   [*Exit.*]
    Corv.   Grave fathers,   20
This man 's distracted ; he confess'd it now :
For, hoping to be old Volpone's heir,
Who now is dead ——
    3 Avoc.   How ?
    2 Avoc.   Is Volpone dead ?
    Corv. Dead since,[69] grave fathers.
    Bon.   O sure vengeance !
    1 Avoc.   Stay ;
Then he was no deceiver ?
    Volt.   Oh, no, none.
This parasite, grave fathers —
    Corv.   He does speak
Out of mere envy, 'cause the servant's made
The thing he gap'd for. Please your Father-
    hoods,
This is the truth, though I 'll not justify
The other, but he may be somedeal [70]
    faulty.   30

---

[63] The same.
[64] The coif of a serjeant-at-law.
[65] Spirit.   [66] The Scrutineo.

[67] The aside is indicated, as often, by parentheses.
These sometimes, however, enclose speeches which
are not asides.
[68] So Q. These lines have dropped out of F₁.
F₂ *By my false accusation.*
[69] Since the trial.   [70] Q *somewhere.*

VOLT. Ay, to your hopes, as well as mine,
    Corvino ;
But I'll use modesty.[71] Pleaseth your
    Wisdoms
To view these certain notes, and but confer [72]
    them ;
As I hope favor, they shall speak clear truth.
  CORV. The Devil has ent'red him !
  BON.   Or bides in you.
  4 Avoc. We have done ill, by a public officer
To send for him, if he be heir.
  2 Avoc.   For whom?
  4 Avoc. Him that they call the parasite.
  3 Avoc.   'T is true,
He is a man of great estate, now left.
  4 Avoc. Go you, and learn his name, and
    say the court   40
Entreats his presence here, but to the clearing
Of some few doubts.   [*Exit* Notary.]
  2 Avoc.   This same's a labyrinth !
  1 Avoc. Stand you unto your first report?
  CORV.   My state,
My life, my fame ——
  BON.   Where is't?
  CORV.   Are at the stake.
  1 Avoc. Is yours so too?
  CORB.   The advocate's a knave,
And has a forked tongue ——
  2 Avoc.   Speak to the point.
  CORB. So is the parasite too.
  1 Avoc.   This is confusion.
  VOLT. I do beseech your Fatherhoods, read
    but those —   [*Giving them papers.*]
  CORV. And credit nothing the false spirit
    hath writ :   49
It cannot be but he's possess'd, grave fathers.
              [*The scene closes.*] [73]

SCENE XI [74]

[*Enter*] VOLPONE.

VOLP. To make a snare for mine own neck,
    and run
My head into it, wilfully ! with laughter !
When I had newly 'scap'd, was free and
    clear !
Out of mere wantonness ! Oh, the dull devil
Was in this brain of mine when I devis'd it,
And Mosca gave it second ; he must now
Help to sear up this vein, or we bleed dead.

[71] Moderation.
[72] Compare.
[73] So Gifford ; all the characters being grouped on
the inner stage, the curtains were drawn.
[74] A street.

[*Enter* NANO, ANDROGYNO, *and* CASTRONE.]

How now ! Who let you loose? Whither go
    you now?
What, to buy gingerbread, or to drown kit-
    lings?
  NAN. Sir, Master Mosca call'd us out of
    doors,   10
And bid us all go play, and took the keys.
  AND. Yes.
  VOLP.   Did Master Mosca take the
    keys? Why, so !
I'm farther in. These are my fine conceits !
I must be merry, with a mischief to me !
What a vile wretch was I, that could not bear
My fortune soberly? I must ha' my crochets,
And my conundrums ! — Well, go you, and
    seek him ;
His meaning may be truer than my fear.
Bid him he straight come to me to the court ;
Thither will I, and, if 't be possible,   20
Unscrew my advocate, upon new hopes.
When I provok'd him, then I lost myself.
              [*Exeunt.*]

SCENE XII [75]

Avocatori, *etc.* [*are discovered, as before.*]

  1 Avoc. These things can ne'er be recon-
    cil'd. He here   [*Shows the papers.*]
Professeth that the gentleman was wrong'd,
And that the gentlewoman was brought
    thither,
Forc'd by her husband, and there left.
  VOLT.   Most true.
  CEL. How ready is Heav'n to those that
    pray !
  1 Avoc.   But that
Volpone would have ravish'd her, he holds
Utterly false, knowing his impotence.
  CORV. Grave fathers, he is possess'd ; again,
    I say,
Possess'd ; nay, if there be possession,
And obsession, he has both.
  3 Avoc.   Here comes our officer. 10

[*Enter* VOLPONE.]

  VOLP. The parasite will straight be here,
    grave fathers.
  4 Avoc. You might invent some other
    name, Sir Varlet.
  3 Avoc. Did not the notary meet him?
  VOLP.   Not that I know.
  4 Avoc. His coming will clear all.
  2 Avoc.   Yet it is misty.

[75] The Scrutineo.

VOLT. May 't please your Fatherhoods ——
VOLP. (*whispers the* Advocate.)   Sir,
    the parasite
Will'd me to tell you that his master lives;
That you are still the man; your hopes the
    same;
And this was only a jest —
    VOLT.   How?
    VOLP.   Sir, to try
If you were firm, and how you stood affected.
    VOLT. Art sure he lives?
    VOLP.   Do I live, sir?
    VOLT.   O me! [20
I was too violent.
    VOLP.   Sir, you may redeem it.
They said you were possess'd; fall down, and
    seem so:
I 'll help to make it good. (VOLTORE *falls.*)
    God bless the man! ——
[*aside to* VOLTORE] Stop your wind hard, and
    swell. — See, see, see, see!
He vomits crooked pins! [76] His eyes are set,
Like a dead hare's hung in a poulter's shop!
His mouth's running away! Do you see,
    signior?
Now it is in his belly.
    CORV.   Ay, the devil!
    VOLP. Now in his throat.
    CORV.   Ay, I perceive it plain.
    VOLP. 'T will out, 't will out! stand clear.
    See where it flies!   30
In shape of a blue toad, with a bat's wings!
Do not you see it, sir?
    CORB.   What? I think I do.
    CORV. 'T is too manifest.
    VOLP.   Look! he comes t' himself!
    VOLT. Where am I?
    VOLP.   Take good heart, the worst is
    past, sir.
You 're dispossess'd.
    1 AVOC.   What accident is this?
    2 AVOC. Sudden and full of wonder!
    3 AVOC.   If he were
Possess'd, as it appears, all this is nothing.
    CORV. He has been often subject to these
    fits.
    1 AVOC. Show him that writing: — do you
    know it, sir?
    VOLP. [*aside to* VOLTORE] Deny it, sir,
    forswear it; know it not.   40
    VOLT. Yes, I do know it well: it is my hand;
But all that it contains is false.
    BON.   O practice!
    2 AVOC. What maze is this!

[76] As bewitched persons were said to **do.**

    1 AVOC.   Is he not guilty then,
Whom you there name the parasite?
    VOLT.   Grave fathers,
No more than his good patron, old Volpone.
    4 AVOC. Why, he is dead.
    VOLT.   O no, my honor'd fathers.
He lives ——
    1 AVOC.   How! lives?
    VOLT.   Lives.
    2 AVOC.   This is subtler yet!
    3 AVOC. You said he was dead!
    VOLT.   Never.
    3 AVOC.   You said so!
    CORV.   I heard so.
    4 AVOC. Here comes the gentleman; make
    him way.

          [*Enter* MOSCA.]

    3 AVOC.   A stool,
    4 AVOC. [*aside*] A proper [77] man! and, were
    Volpone dead,   50
A fit match for my daughter.
    3 AVOC.   Give him way.
    VOLP. [*aside to* MOSCA] Mosca, I was a'most
    lost: the advocate
Had betray'd all; but now it is recover'd;
All 's on the hinge again —— say I am living.
    MOS. What busy knave is this? — Most
    reverend fathers,
I sooner had attended your grave pleasures,
But that my order for the funeral
Of my dear patron did require me ——
    VOLP. [*aside*]   Mosca!
    MOS. Whom I intend to bury like a gentle-
    man.
    VOLP. [*aside*] Ay, quick,[78] and cozen me
    of all.
    2 AVOC.   Still stranger!   60
More intricate!
    1 AVOC.   And come about again!
    4 AVOC. [*aside*] It is a match; my daughter
    is bestow'd.
    MOS. [*aside to* VOLPONE] Will you gi' me
    half?
    VOLP. [*aside*]   First I 'll be hang'd.
    MOS. [*aside*]   I know
Your voice is good; cry not so loud.
    1 AVOC.   Demand
The advocate. — Sir, did not you affirm
Volpone was alive?
    VOLP.   Yes, and he is;
This gent'man told me so. — [*aside to* MOSCA]
    Thou shalt have half.

[77] Handsome.
[78] Alive.

Mos. Whose drunkard is this same?
  Speak, some that know him ;
I never saw his face. — [*aside to* VOLPONE] I
  cannot now
Afford it you so cheap.
  VOLP. [*aside*]   No?
  1 AVOC.   What say you? [70
  VOLT. The officer told me.
  VOLP.   I did, grave fathers,
And will maintain he lives, with mine own life,
And that this creature [*pointing to* MOSCA] told
  me. — [*aside*] I was born
With all good stars my enemies.
  Mos.   Most grave fathers,
If such an insolence as this must pass
Upon me, I am silent ; 't was not this
For which you sent, I hope.
  2 AVOC.   Take him away.
  VOLP. Mosca !
  3 AVOC.   Let him be whipp'd.
  VOLP. [*aside to* MOSCA] Wilt thou betray me?
Cozen me?
  3 AVOC.   And taught to bear himself
Toward a person of his rank.
  4 AVOC.   Away.   80
  Mos. I humbly thank your Fatherhoods.
  VOLP.   Soft, soft ; — [*aside*] whipp'd !
And lose all that I have ! If I confess,
It cannot be much more.
  4 AVOC.   Sir, are you married?
  VOLP. They 'll be alli'd anon ; I must be
  resolute ;
The Fox shall here uncase.
                    He puts off his disguise.
  Mos. [*aside*]   Patron !
  VOLP.   Nay, now
My ruins shall not come alone ; your match
I 'll hinder sure ; my substance shall not glue
  you,
Nor screw you into a family.
  Mos. [*aside*]   Why, patron !
  VOLP. I am Volpone, and this [*pointing to*
  MOSCA] is my knave ;
This [*to* VOLTORE], his own knave ; this [*to*
  CORBACCIO], avarice's fool ;   90
This [*to* CORVINO], a chimaera of wittol, fool,
  and knave :
And, reverend fathers, since we all can hope
Naught but a sentence, let 's not now despair it.
You hear me brief.
  CORV.   May it please your Fatherhoods —
  COM.   Silence.
  1 AVOC. The knot is now undone, by
  miracle !
  2 AVOC. Nothing can be more clear.

  3 AVOC.   Or can more prove
These innocent.
  1 AVOC.   Give 'em their liberty.
  BON. Heaven could not long let such gross
  crimes be hid.
  2 AVOC. If this be held the highway to get
  riches,
May I be poor.
  3 AVOC.   This 's not the gain, but torment.
  1 AVOC. These possess wealth, as sick men
  possess fevers,   101
Which trulier may be said to possess them.
  2 AVOC. Disrobe that parasite.
  CORV. [and] MOS.   Most honor'd
  fathers ——
  1 AVOC. Can you plead aught to stay the
  course of justice?
If you can, speak.
  CORV. [and] VOLT.   We beg favor.
  CEL.   And mercy.
  1 AVOC. You hurt your innocence, suing for
  the guilty.
Stand forth ; and, first, the parasite. You
  appear
T' have been the chiefest minister, if not plot-
  ter,
In all these lewd impostures, and now, lastly,
Have with your impudence abus'd the court,
And habit of a gentleman of Venice,   111
Being a fellow of no birth or blood ;
For which our sentence is, first, thou be
  whipp'd ;
Then live perpetual prisoner in our galleys.
  VOLP. I thank you for him.
  MOS.   Bane to thy wolfish nature !
  1 AVOC. Deliver him to the saffi.[79] —
  Thou, Volpone,
By blood and rank a gentleman, canst not fall
Under like censure ; but our judgment on thee
Is that thy substance all be straight confiscate
To the hospital of the Incurabili.   120
And since the most was gotten by imposture,
By feigning lame, gout, palsy, and such dis-
  eases,
Thou art to lie in prison, cramp'd with irons,
Till thou be'st sick and lame indeed. — Re-
  move him.
  VOLP. This is called mortifying of a Fox.
  1 AVOC. Thou, Voltore, to take away the
  scandal
Thou hast giv'n all worthy men of thy profes-
  sion,
Art banish'd from their fellowship, and our
  state. —

  [79] Bailiffs.

Corbaccio ! — Bring him near. — We here possess
Thy son of all thy state,[80] and confine thee [130
To the monastery of San' Spirito ;
Where, since thou knew'st not how to live well here,
Thou shalt be learn'd to die well.

CORB.   Ha ! what said he?

COM. You shall know anon, sir.

1 Avoc.   Thou, Corvino, shalt
Be straight embark'd from thine own house, and row'd
Round about Venice, through the Grand Canal,
Wearing a cap, with fair long ass's ears,
Instead of horns ; and so to mount, a paper
Pinn'd on thy breast, to the Berlin[a].[81]

CORV.   Yes,
And have mine eyes beat out with stinking fish,   140
Bruis'd fruit, and rotten eggs — 't is well. I am glad
I shall not see my shame yet.

1 Avoc.   And to expiate

Thy wrongs done to thy wife, thou art to send her
Home to her father, with her dowry trebled :
And these are all your judgments.

ALL.   Honor'd fathers ——

1 Avoc. Which may not be revok'd.   Now you begin,
When crimes are done and past, and to be punish'd,
To think what your crimes are. — Away with them !
Let all that see these vices thus rewarded,
Take heart, and love to study 'em.   Mischiefs feed   150
Like beasts, till they be fat, and then they bleed.   [*Exeunt.*]

VOLPONE

The seasoning of a play is the applause.
Now, though the Fox be punish'd by the laws,
He yet doth hope, there is no suff'ring due,
For any fact which he hath done 'gainst you ;
If there be, censure him ; here he doubtful stands.
If not, fare jovially, and clap your hands.
                    [*Exit.*]

---

[80] Q *estate.*   [81] Pillory.

THE
ALCHEMIST.

A Comœdie.

Acted in the yeere 1 6 1 o. By the
Kings MAIESTIES
Seruants.

The Author B. I.

LVCRET

———*petere inde coronam,*
Vnde priùs nulli velarint tempora Musæ.

L ONDON,
Printed by VVILLIAM STANSBY

M. D C. XVI.

INTRODUCTORY NOTE

IN this play Jonson gives us the most nearly perfect example of his peculiar comedy, and one of the great plays of the London stage. Rarely has any writer brought so diverse and so brilliant a group of characters within the compass of a single drama. With scarcely an exception, each is etched meticulously; yet the play is never slowed down. In *Bartholomew Fair* the thread sometimes disappears amidst the profusion of sheer physical detail; in *The Alchemist* the author, occupied with a single situation but inexhaustibly fertile in displaying every aspect of it, maintains with consummate skill a breathless pace. Once more the atmosphere is wholly comic; yet this is serious comedy; and, if we no longer cringe under the knout of *Volpone*, Jonson's lighter lash has plenty of sting. It is now applied, not as in *The Fox* to the fundamental defects of human character, but more specifically to a notorious current abuse, and to the gullibility of those who hope to substitute short cuts and supernaturalism for hard work and common sense. Here Jonson seems more like a playwright of the second great renascence of the British drama; for this is throughout a socially-minded play.

It was written, and produced by the King's Men, in 1610, a severe plague year, and the time of the action of the play. Between *Volpone* and the composition of *The Alchemist*, Jonson had written the fourth in excellence of his major comedies, the brilliant but farcical trifle, *Epicoene*. Now he turns again to the high yet racy comedy of manners that was his gift to the English theatre, turns to the dramatic materials that lay readiest to his hand, and to the most pretentious quackery known to his age. He played indeed a manly part in driving this particular relic of obscurantism from the light of scientific respectability.

There was, however, a well-established literary tradition against, as well as in glorification of, the alchemists. Yet Jonson's sources are only indirectly Ariosto, Lyly, or the *Candelaio* of Bruno. While the setting owes something to Plautus, and Face plays the same part as Tranio, the clever slave of the *Mostellaria*, and while Erasmus's *De Alcumista* provides some details, Jonson, who was one of the most thoroughgoing Londoners that ever lived, had no need of leaving his native city for the materials of his realism. Simon Forman, the notorious charlatan, was cutting a great figure there when the play was written. Even Face is, after all, not Tranio, nor Mosca, but Jeremy Butler.

Few English comedies have been more successful on the stage. Popular under the Restoration, *The Alchemist* was revived by Garrick, who first acted Face and later Abel Drugger. It was published, in quarto, in 1612. The present text is based on the Folio of 1616, with some corrections from the Quarto and the later Folios. The play has been separately edited by C. M. Hathaway (1903) and (with *Eastward Ho*) by F. E. Schelling (1905).

THE ALCHEMIST

BY

BEN JONSON

THE PERSONS OF THE PLAY

SUBTLE, the alchemist.
FACE, the housekeeper.
DOL COMMON, their colleague.
DAPPER, a clerk.
DRUGGER, a tobacco man.
LOVEWIT, master of the house.
[SIR] EPICURE MAMMON, a knight.

[PERTINAX] SURLY, a gamester.
TRIBULATION [WHOLESOME], a pastor of Amsterdam.
ANANIAS, a deacon there.
KASTRILL, the angry boy.
DAME PLIANT, his sister, a widow.
Neighbors, Officers, Mutes.

THE SCENE — London.

THE ARGUMENT

T HE sickness hot,[1] a master quit, for fear,
H is house in town, and left one servant there.
E ase him corrupted, and gave means to know
A cheater and his punk,[2] who, now brought low,
L eaving their narrow practice, were become
C oz'ners [3] at large, and only wanting some
H ouse to set up; and with him they here contract,
E ach for a share, and all begin to act.
M uch company they draw, and much abuse,[4]
I n casting figures,[5] telling fortunes, news,   10
S elling of flies,[6] flat bawdry, with [7] the stone,[8]
T ill it, and they, and all, in fume [9] are gone.

PROLOGUE

FORTUNE, that favors fools,[10] these two short hours
We wish away, both for your sakes and ours,
Judging spectators; and desire, in place,
To th' author justice, to ourselves but grace.
Our scene is London, 'cause we would make known
No country's mirth is better than our own.
No clime breeds better matter for your whore,
Bawd, squire,[11] impostor, many persons more
Whose manners, now call'd humors,[12] feed the stage;
And which have still [13] been subject for the rage   10
Or spleen of comic writers. Though this pen

---

1 The plague being violent.
2 Wench, strumpet.
3 Swindlers.   4 Deceive.
5 Calculating astrological tables showing the disposition of the heavenly bodies at given times.
6 Familiar spirits.   7 I.e., and.
8 The philosopher's stone, the elixir (or powder) which was the object of the alchemists' search.
9 Smoke.   10 Proverbially.
11 Pander.
12 By a "humor" Jonson meant not a merely superficial eccentricity, but an ingrained and dominating characteristic of the temperament.
13 Always.

Did never aim to grieve, but better, men,
Howe'er, the age he lives in both endure
The vices that she breeds, above their cure.
But when the wholesome remedies are sweet,
And in their working gain and profit meet,
He hopes to find no spirit so much diseas'd,
But will with such fair correctives[14] be
pleas'd.
For here he doth not fear who can apply.[15]
If there be any that will sit so nigh   20
Unto the stream, to look what it doth run,
They shall find things, they'd think, or
wish, were done;
They are so natural follies, but so shown,
As even the doers may see, and yet not own.

ACT I — SCENE I[1]

[*Enter*] FACE [*in a captain's uniform, and*]
SUBTLE [*with a vial, quarrelling, and followed by*] DOL COMMON.

FACE. Believe 't, I will.
SUB.   Thy worst. I fart at thee.
DOL. Ha' you your wits? Why, gentle-
men! for love ——
FACE. Sirrah, I 'll strip you ——
SUB.   What to do? Lick figs[2]
Out at my ——
FACE.   Rogue, rogue! — out of all your
sleights.[3]
DOL. Nay, look ye! Sovereign, General,
are you madmen?
SUB. Oh, let the wild sheep[4] loose. I 'll
gum your silks
With good strong water,[5] an you come.
DOL.   Will you have
The neighbors hear you? Will you betray
all?
Hark! I hear somebody.
FACE.   Sirrah ——
SUB.   I shall mar
All that the tailor has made, if you approach.

FACE. You most notorious whelp, you in-
solent slave,   11
Dare you do this?
SUB.   Yes, faith; yes, faith.
FACE.   Why! who
Am I, my mongrel? Who am I?
SUB.   I 'll tell you,
Since you know not yourself.
FACE.   Speak lower, rogue.
SUB. Yes. You were once (time 's not long
past) the good,
Honest, plain, livery-three-pound-thrum,[6] that
kept
Your master's Worship's house here in the
Friars,[7]
For the vacations[8] ——
FACE.   Will you be so loud?
SUB. Since, by my means, translated sub-
urb-captain.[9]
FACE. By your means, Doctor Dog!
SUB.   Within man's memory,   20
All this I speak of.
FACE.   Why, I pray you, have I
Been countenanc'd[10] by you, or you by me?
Do but collect, sir, where I met you first.
SUB. I do not hear well.
FACE.   Not of this, I think it.
But I shall put you in mind, sir: at Pie Cor-
ner,
Taking your meal of steam in, from cooks'
stalls,
Where, like the father of hunger,[11] you did
walk
Piteously costive,[12] with your pinch'd-horn-
nose,
And your complexion of the Roman wash,[13]
Stuck full of black and melancholic worms,   30
Like powder-corns[14] shot at th' Artillery Yard.
SUB. I wish you could advance your voice
a little.
FACE. When you went pinn'd up in the
several rags
Yo' had rak'd and pick'd from dunghills, be-
fore day;
Your feet in mouldy slippers, for your kibes;[15]

[14] Accented on first syllable.
[15] Make a personal application.
[1] A room in Lovewit's house.
[2] See Rabelais, iv, 45.
[3] Away with your tricks.
[4] Presumably Dol, since "mutton" meant a loose
woman. Apparently Dol is clinging to Face in order
to keep him from rushing on Subtle.
[5] Subtle keeps Face off by threatening to ruin
his clothes with the chemical, presumably an acid,
in his vial. "Gum" is used metaphorically, since
silks were treated with gum to perfume them or to
stiffen them.

[6] Evidently = mere servant. It appears from
Jonson's *The Devil Is an Ass* that a servant usually
received £4 a year besides his keep. "Thrums" are
the waste ends of the weaver's warp.
[7] The precinct of Blackfriars.
[8] Intervals between the terms of court.
[9] Transformed into a captain — of the suburbs
(which were notorious districts).
[10] Sanctioned.
[11] An allusion to the *Aureli, pater esuritionem,* of
Catullus, xxi, 1. (Gifford.)
[12] From hunger.   [13] *I.e.*, swarthy.
[14] Grains of powder.   [15] Chilblains.

A felt of rug,[16] and a thin threaden cloak,
That scarce would cover your no-buttocks —
 SUB.   So, sir !
 FACE. When all your alchemy, and your
    algebra,
Your minerals, vegetals, and animals,
Your conjuring, coz'ning, and your dozen of
    trades,   40
Could not relieve your corpse with so much
    linen
Would make you tinder, but to see a fire ; [17]
I ga' you count'nance, credit for your coals,
Your stills, your glasses, your materials ;
Built you a furnace, drew you customers,
Advanc'd all your black arts, lent you, beside,
A house to practise in ——
 SUB.   Your master's house !
 FACE. Where you have studied the more
    thriving skill
Of bawdry, since.
 SUB.   Yes, in your master's house.
You and the rats here kept possession.   50
Make it not strange.[18] I know yo' were one
    could keep
The butt'ry-hatch still lock'd, and save the
    chippings,
Sell the dole beer to aqua vitae men,[19]
The which, together with your Christmas
    vails,[20]
At post-and-pair your letting out of coun-
    ters,[21]
Made you a pretty stock, some twenty marks,
And gave you credit to converse with cob-
    webs,
Here, since your mistress' death hath broke
    up house.
 FACE. You might talk softlier, rascal.
 SUB.   No, you scarab,[22]
I 'll thunder you in pieces. I will teach you [60
How to beware to tempt a Fury again
That carries tempest in his hand and voice.
 FACE. The place has made you valiant.
 SUB.   No, your clothes.
Thou vermin, have I ta'en thee, out of dung,
So poor, so wretched, when no living thing

Would keep thee company, but a spider or
    worse?
Rais'd thee from brooms, and dust, and wat'r-
    ing pots,
Sublim'd thee, and exalted thee, and fix'd thee
In the third region, call'd [23] our state of grace?
Wrought thee to spirit, to quintessence,[24] with
    pains   70
Would twice have won me the philosophers'
    work? [25]
Put thee in words and fashion? made thee fit
For more than ordinary fellowships?
Giv'n thee thy oaths, thy quarrelling dimen-
    sions? [26]
Thy rules to cheat at horse race, cockpit, cards,
Dice, or whatever gallant tincture [27] else?
Made thee a second in mine own great art?
And have I this for thank? Do you rebel?
Do you fly out i' the projection? [28]   79
Would you be gone now?
 DOL.   Gentlemen, what mean you?
Will you mar all?
 SUB.   Slave, thou hadst had no name —
 DOL. Will you undo yourselves with civil
    war?
 SUB. Never been known, past *equi
    clibanum* [29]
The heat of horse-dung, under ground, in cel-
    lars,
Or an alehouse darker than deaf John's,[30] been
    lost
To all mankind, but laundresses and tapsters,
Had not I been.
 DOL.   Do you know who hears you,
    Sovereign?
 FACE. Sirrah ——
 DOL.   Nay, General, I thought
    you were civil.
 FACE. I shall turn desperate, if you grow
    thus loud.
 SUB. And hang thyself, I care not.
 FACE.   Hang thee, collier,[31] [90
And all thy pots and pans, in picture [32] I will,
Since thou hast mov'd me ——

---

[16] Hat of coarse material.
[17] Could not get you clothes enough to have made
tinder even for a fire so tiny as to give no warmth
but only be visible.
[18] Don't pretend to forget.
[19] Liquor dealers ; thus the poor were defrauded
of their dole of beer and broken bread ("chippings").
[20] Tips.
[21] Chips, to the card players, for which servants
were tipped. In this game bets were *posted* on hands
of three cards, the highest hand being a *pair* royal,
i.e., three of a kind.
[22] Which lives and breeds in dung.

[23] In the alchemists' jargon.
[24] Accented on first syllable.
[25] The philosophers' stone.
[26] Due proportions for conducting a quarrel.
[27] Tinge of gallantry.
[28] Explode at the moment of success (continuing
the alchemical metaphor).
[29] Horse-oven ; *i.e.,* a furnace heated as described,
used by alchemists. Subtle continues to describe
Face as a subject of his art.
[30] Unidentified.
[31] A term of abuse, the collier being black, like
the Devil ; it is especially applicable to Subtle since
coals were one of the prime requisites of his art.
[32] Figuratively speaking.

Dol. [*aside*]   Oh, this 'll o'erthrow all.

Face. Write thee up bawd in Paul's[33] ;
    have all thy tricks

Of coz'ning with a hollow coal, dust, scrap-
    ings,[34]

Searching for things lost, with a sieve and
    shears,

Erecting figures[35] in your rows of houses,[36]

And taking in of shadows with a glass,[37]

Told in red letters[38] ; and a face cut for thee,[39]

Worse than Gamaliel Ratsey's.[40]

Dol.   Are you sound?[41]

Ha' you your senses, masters?

Face.   I will have   100

A book, but rarely reckoning thy impostures,

Shall prove a true philosopher's stone to
    printers.

Sub. Away, you trencher-rascal.

Face.   Out, you dog-leech,

The vomit of all prisons ——

Dol.   Will you be

Your own destructions, gentlemen?

Face.   Still spew'd out

For lying too heavy o' the basket.[42]

Sub.   Cheater!

Face. Bawd!

Sub.   Cowherd!

Face.   Conjurer!

Sub.   Cutpurse!

Face.   Witch!

Dol.   O me!

We are ruin'd! lost! Ha' you no more regard

To your reputations? Where 's your judg-
    ment? 'Slight,[43]   109

Have yet some care of me, o' your republic —

Face. Away, this brach.[44] I 'll bring thee,
    rogue, within

The statute of sorcery, tricesimo tertio

Of Harry the Eight ;[45] ay, and perhaps thy
    neck

Within a noose, for laund'ring gold and barb-
    ing it.[46]

Dol. You 'll bring your head within a
    cockscomb, will you?[47]

        She catcheth out Face *his sword, and
            breaks* Subtle's *glass.*

And you, sir, with your menstrue![48] — Gather
it up.

'Sdeath, you abominable pair of stinkards,

Leave off your barking, and grow one[49] again,

Or, by the light that shines, I 'll cut your
    throats.

I 'll not be made a prey unto the marshal [120

For ne'er a snarling dog-bolt[50] o' you both.

Ha' you together cozen'd all this while,

And all the world, and shall it now be said

Yo' have made most courteous shift to cozen
    yourselves? —

[*to* Face] You will accuse him? You will
    bring him in

Within the statute? Who shall take your
    word?

A whoreson, upstart, apocryphal captain,

Whom not a Puritan in Blackfriars[51] will trust

So much as for a feather! — [*to* Subtle] and
    you, too,

Will give the cause, forsooth? You will insult,

And claim a primacy in the divisions?   131

You must be chief? As if you, only, had

The powder to project[52] with, and the work

Were not begun out of equality!

The venture tripartite! All things in common!

Without priority! 'Sdeath! you perpetual
    curs,

Fall to your couples again, and cozen kindly,

And heartily, and lovingly, as you should,

And lose not the beginning of a term,[53]

Or, by this hand, I shall grow factious too, 140

And take my part, and quit you.

Face.   'T is his fault ;

He ever murmurs, and objects his pains,

And says the weight of all lies upon him.

Sub. Why, so it does.

Dol.   How does it? Do not we

Sustain our parts?

Sub.   Yes, but they are not equal.

---

[33] Notices were posted at the cathedral.

[34] See Chaucer's *Canterbury Tales*, "The Canon's
Yeoman's Tale", where this swindle is described,
silver filings being placed in the coal which the
swindler professed to be able to turn into silver.

[35] Making charts showing the relative positions of
planets and constellations.

[36] Divisions of the zodiac, used in astrology.

[37] Crystal-gazing.

[38] *I.e.*, on his poster at St. Paul's.

[39] For an illustration.

[40] A notorious highwayman, hanged in 1605. The
allusion may be his own villainous face, to his hideous mask, or to a portrait which may have adorned
his *Life and Death*.

[41] Sane.

[42] Eating more than your share of the provisions
collected for the prisoners.

[43] By God's light.   [44] Bitch.

[45] 33 Henry VIII, chap. 8; it provided the death
penalty for various forms of sorcery.

[46] Washing gold coins in an acid bath and clipping
them.

[47] Fool's cap.

[48] Solvent.   [49] Agree.

[50] Blunt-headed arrow ; *i.e.*, a mean fellow.

[51] Center of the trade in feathers and other appur-
tenances of fashion, and also noted as the residence
of Puritans.

[52] The philosopher's stone to transmute metals
with.

[53] One of the four terms of court, and hence seasons
of metropolitan activity.

Dol. Why, if your part exceed to-day, I hope

Ours may to-morrow match it.

Sub. Ay, they may.

Dol. May, murmuring mastiff! Ay, and do. Death on me![54]

Help me to thr[o]ttle him.

Sub. Dorothy! Mistress Dorothy! 'Ods precious, I'll do anything. What do you mean? 150

Dol. Because o' your fermentation and cibation?[55]

Sub. Not I, by Heaven——

Dol. Your Sol and Luna[56] — [to Face] help me.

Sub. Would I were hang'd then. I'll conform myself.

Dol. Will you, sir? Do so, then, and quickly: swear.

Sub. What should I swear?

Dol. To leave your faction,[57] sir, And labor kindly in the common work.

Sub. Let me not breathe if I meant aught beside.

I only us'd those speeches as a spur To him.

Dol. I hope we need no spurs, sir. — Do we?

Face. 'Slid, prove to-day who shall shark best.

Sub. Agreed. 160

Dol. Yes, and work close and friendly.

Sub. 'Slight, the knot Shall grow the stronger for this breach, with me.

Dol. Why, so, my good baboons! Shall we go make

A sort[58] of sober, scurvy, precise[59] neighbors, That scarce have smil'd twice sin' the King came in,[60]

A feast of laughter at our follies? rascals, Would run themselves from breath, to see me ride,[61]

Or you t' have but a hole to thrust your heads in,[62]

For which you should pay ear-rent?[63] No, agree.

And may Don Provost[64] ride a-feasting long,

In his old velvet jerkin and stain'd scarfs, 171 My noble Sovereign, and worthy General, Ere we contribute a new crewel[65] garter To his most worsted Worship.

Sub. Royal Dol! Spoken like Claridiana,[66] and thyself!

Face. For which at supper, thou shalt sit in triumph, And not be styl'd Dol Common, but Dol Proper, Dol Singular: the longest cut, at night, Shall draw thee for his Dol Particular.

[*Bell rings without.*]

Sub. Who's that? One rings. To the window.[67]

Dol. Pray Heav'n, 180 The master do not trouble us this quarter.

Face. O, fear not him. While there dies one a week O' the plague, he's safe from thinking toward London.

Beside, he's busy at his hop-yards now; I had a letter from him. If he do, He'll send such word, for airing o' the house, As you shall have sufficient time to quit it; Though we break up a fortnight,[68] 't is no matter.

Sub. Who is it, Dol?

Dol. A fine young quodling.[69]

Face. Oh, My lawyer's clerk, I lighted on last night, 190 In Holborn, at the Dagger.[70] He would have (I told you of him) a familiar,[71] To rifle[72] with at horses,[73] and win cups.

Dol. Oh, let him in.

Sub. Stay. Who shall do't?

Face. Get you Your robes on. I will meet him, as going out.

Dol. And what shall I do?

Face. Not be seen; away! [*Exit* Dol.] — Seem you very reserv'd.

Sub. Enough. [*Exit.*]

Face. [*aloud*] God b' w' you, sir. I pray you let him know that I was here. His name is Dapper. I would gladly have stay'd, but——

[54] Q *God's will.*
[55] Alchemical processes.
[56] Gold and silver.
[57] Stop rebelling.
[58] Set.
[59] Puritanical.
[60] Since the accession of James I in 1603.
[61] Carted as a whore.
[62] In the pillory.
[63] Have your ears cropped.
[64] *I.e.*, the hangman, to whom fell the clothes of the executed criminal.
[65] So much as a yarn garter; with puns on *cruel* and perhaps "worsted" = baffled.
[66] The heroine of the famous romance, *The Mirror of Knighthood.*
[67] Old eds. *windo'*.
[68] Hence.
[69] Codling, immature apple, raw youth.
[70] A low tavern, notorious as a gambling-house.
[71] Attendant spirit.
[72] Raffle.
[73] Lottery tickets.

Scene II [74]

Face [*remains.*]

Dap. [*within*] Captain, I am here.
Face.   Who 's that? — He 's come, I
think, Doctor.

[*He admits* Dapper.]

Good faith, sir, I was going away.
Dap.   In truth,
I am very sorry, Captain.
Face.   But I thought
Sure I should meet you.
Dap.   Ay, I am very glad.
I had a scurvy writ or two to make,
And I had lent my watch last night to one
That dines to-day at the sheriff's, and so was
    robb'd
Of my pass-time.[75]

[*Re-enter* Subtle *in his velvet cap and gown.*]
                    Is this the cunning man?
Face. This is his Worship.
Dap.   Is he a doctor?
Face.   Yes.
Dap. And ha' you broke [76] with him, Cap-
    tain?
Face.   Ay.
Dap.   And how?   10
Face. Faith, he does make the matter, sir,
    so dainty,[77]
I know not what to say. —
Dap.   Not so, good Captain.
Face. Would I were fairly rid on 't, believe
    me.
Dap. Nay, now you grieve me, sir. Why
    should you wish so?
I dare assure you, I 'll not be ungrateful.
Face. I cannot think you will, sir. But the
    law
Is such a thing —— and then he says, Read's [78]
    matter
Falling so lately ——
Dap.   Read! he was an ass,
And dealt, sir, with a fool.
Face.   It was a clerk,[79] sir.
Dap. A clerk?

Face.   Nay, hear me, sir. You know
    the law   20
Better, I think ——
Dap.   I should, sir, and the danger:
You know I show'd the statute to you.
Face.   You did so.
Dap. And will I tell then? By this hand of
    flesh,
Would it might never write good court-hand
    more,
If I discover. What do you think of me,
That I am a chiaus? [80]
Face.   What 's that?
Dap.   The Turk was here:
As one would say, do you think I am a
    Turk?
Face. I 'll tell the Doctor so.
Dap.   Do, good sweet Captain.
Face. Come, noble Doctor, 'pray thee let 's
    prevail;
This is the gentleman, and he is no chiaus.   30
Sub. Captain, I have return'd you all my
    answer.
I would do much, sir, for your love —— but
    this
I neither may nor can.
Face.   Tut, do not say so.
You deal now with a noble fellow, Doctor,
One that will thank you richly; and h' is no
    chiaus:
Let that, sir, move you.
Sub.   Pray you, forbear ——
Face.   He has
Four angels here.
Sub.   You do me wrong, good sir.
Face. Doctor, wherein? To tempt you
    with these spirits? [81]
Sub. To tempt my art and love, sir, to my
    peril.
'Fore Heav'n, I scarce can think you are my
    friend,   40
That so would draw me to apparent danger.
Face. I draw you! A horse draw you,[82]
    and a halter,
You and your flies [83] together ——
Dap.   Nay, good Captain.
Face. That know no difference of men.
Sub.   Good words, sir.
Face. Good deeds, sir, Doctor Dogs'-meat.
    'Slight, I bring you

[74] The same.
[75] *I.e.*, timepiece. They were scarce, and Dapper's reference is a little vain.
[76] Broached the subject.
[77] Has such scruples on the subject.
[78] Pardoned in 1608, having been indicted for conjuring.
[79] Tobias Matthews, for whom Read endeavored by occult means to learn the identity of one who had robbed him.

[80] Turkish messenger. According to Gifford's unsubstantiated account, a chiaus "choused" some oriental merchants in London in 1609.
[81] *I.e.*, the coins, the angels.
[82] *I.e.*, to the gallows.
[83] Familiar spirits.

No cheating Clim o' the Cloughs [84] or Claribels,
That look as big as five-and-fifty, and flush ; [85]
And spit out secrets like hot custard ——
  DAP.   Captain !
  FACE. Nor any melancholic underscribe,
Shall tell the vicar ; but a special gentle,   50
That is the heir to forty marks a year,
Consorts with the small poets of the time,
Is the sole hope of his old grandmother ;
That knows the law, and writes you six fair
   hands,
Is a fine clerk, and has his ciph'ring perfect.
Will take his oath o' the Greek Xenophon, [86]
If need be, in his pocket ; and can court
His mistress out of Ovid.
  DAP.   Nay, dear Captain —
  FACE. Did you not tell me so ?
  DAP.   Yes ; but I'd ha' you
Use Master Doctor with some more respect. 60
  FACE. Hang him, proud stag, with his
   broad velvet head ! [87] —
But for your sake, I'd choke ere I would
  change
An article of breath with such a puck-fist — [88]
Come, let's be gone.
  SUB.   Pray you, le' me speak with you.
  DAP. His Worship calls you, Captain.
  FACE.   I am sorry
I e'er embark'd myself in such a business.
  DAP. Nay, good sir.   He did call you.
  FACE.   Will he take, then ?
  SUB. First, hear me ——
  FACE.   Not a syllable, 'less you take.
  SUB. Pray ye, sir ——
  FACE.   Upon no terms but an *assumpsit*. [89]
  SUB. Your humor must be law.
        He takes the money.
  FACE.   Why now, sir, talk. 70
Now I dare hear you with mine honor.   Speak.
So may this gentleman, too.
  SUB.   Why, sir ——
  FACE.   No whisp'ring.
  SUB. 'Fore Heav'n, you do not apprehend
   the loss
You do yourself in this.

[84] Ravines. Clim was a famous archer in the tales
of Robin Hood. Claribel was presumably a character of popular romance. There is a Claribell in
Spenser's *Faerie Queene* (IV, ix), but he hardly fits
the context here. Face means that Dapper is no
pompous, domineering romantic hero.
[85] The best hand in primero. (Gifford.)
[86] Q *Testament;* F changes in accordance with the
statute against profanity.
[87] *I.e.,* his astrologer's cap, which Face compares
to velvety antlers.
[88] Puff-ball, blow-hard.
[89] *I.e.,* a promise to undertake for a consideration.

  FACE.   Wherein ? for what ?
  SUB. Marry, to be so importunate for one
That, when he has it, will undo [90] you all :
He'll win up all the money i' the town.
  FACE. How !
  SUB.   Yes, and blow up gamester after
   gamester,
As they do crackers in a puppet-play.
If I do give him a familiar,   80
Give you him all you play for ; never set [91]
   him :
For he will have it.
  FACE.   Y'are mistaken, Doctor.
Why, he does ask one but for cups and horses,
A rifling fly ; none o' your great familiars.
  DAP. Yes, Captain, I would have it for all
   games.
  SUB. I told you so.
  FACE. [*taking* DAPPER *aside*]   'Slight,
   that's a new business !
I understood you, a tame bird, to fly
Twice in a term, or so ; on Friday nights,
When you had left the office, for a nag
Of forty or fifty shillings.
  DAP.   Ay, 't is true, sir ;   90
But I do think, now, I shall leave the law,
And therefore ——
  FACE.   Why, this changes quite the case !
Do you think that I dare move him ?
  DAP.   If you please, sir ;
All's one to him, I see.
  FACE.   What ! for that money ?
I cannot with my conscience.   Nor should you
Make the request, methinks.
  DAP.   No, sir, I mean
To add consideration.
  FACE.   Why, then, sir,
I'll try. — [*Goes to* SUBTLE.] Say that it were
   for all games, Doctor ?
  SUB. I say then, not a mouth shall eat for [92]
   him
At any ordinary, but o' the score : [93]   100
That is a gaming mouth, conceive me.
  FACE.   Indeed !
  SUB. He'll draw you all the treasure of the
   realm,
If it be set him.
  FACE.   Speak you this from art ?
  SUB. Ay, sir, and reason too, the ground o'
   art.
H' is o' the only best complexion,
The Queen of Faërie loves.

[90] Ruin.
[91] Challenge ; *i.e.,* bet against.
[92] Because of.   [93] Except on credit.

FACE.   What! Is he?
SUB.   Peace.
He'll overhear you. Sir, should she but see
    him —
    FACE. What?
SUB.   Do not you tell him.
FACE.   Will he win at cards, too?
SUB. The spirits of dead Holland, living
    Isaac,[94]
You'd swear, were in him; such a vigorous
    luck   110
As cannot be resisted. 'Slight, he'll put
Six o' your gallants to a cloak,[95] indeed.
    FACE. A strange success, that some man
      shall be born to!
    SUB. He hears you, man ——
    DAP.   Sir, I'll not be ingrateful.
    FACE. Faith, I have a confidence in his
      good nature.
You hear, he says he will not be ingrateful.
    SUB. Why, as you please; my venture
      follows yours.
    FACE. Troth, do it, Doctor; think him
      trusty, and make him.
He may make us both happy[96] in an hour,
Win some five thousand pound, and send us
    two on 't.   120
    DAP. Believe it, and I will, sir.
    FACE.   And you shall, sir.
You have heard all?   FACE *takes him aside.*
    DAP.   No; what was 't? Nothing, I, sir.
    FACE. Nothing?
    DAP.   A little, sir.
    FACE.   Well, a rare star
Reign'd at your birth.
    DAP.   At mine, sir! No.
    FACE.   The Doctor
Swears that you are —
    SUB.   Nay, Captain, you'll tell all now.
    FACE. Allied to the Queen of Faërie.
    DAP.   Who? that I am?
Believe it, no such matter —
    FACE.   Yes, and that
Yo' were born with a caul o' your head.
    DAP.   Who says so?
    FACE.   Come,
You know it well enough, though you dis-
    semble it.

DAP. I' fac,[97] I do not. You are mistaken.
FACE.   How!   130
Swear by your fac, and in a thing so known
Unto the Doctor? How shall we, sir, trust you
I' the other matter? Can we ever think,
When you have won five or six thousand
    pound,
You'll send us shares in 't, by this rate?
    DAP.   By Jove,[98] sir,
I'll win ten thousand pound, and send you
    half.
I' fac 's no oath.
    SUB.   No, no, he did but jest.
    FACE. Go to. Go, thank the Doctor. He's
      your friend,
To take it so.
    DAP.   I thank his Worship.
    FACE.   So!
Another angel.
    DAP.   Must I?
    FACE.   Must you! 'Slight, 140
What else is thanks? Will you be trivial? —
    Doctor, [DAPPER *gives him the money.*]
When must he come for his familiar?
    DAP. Shall I not ha' it with me?
    SUB.   Oh, good sir!
There must a world of ceremonies pass —
You must be bath'd and fumigated first;
Besides, the Queen of Faërie does not rise
Till it be noon.
    FACE.   Not if she danc'd to-night.[99]
    SUB. And she must bless it.
    FACE.   Did you never see
Her Royal Grace yet?
    DAP.   Whom?
    FACE.   Your aunt of Faërie?
    SUB. Not since she kiss'd him in the cradle,
      Captain;   150
I can resolve you that.
    FACE.   Well, see her Grace,
Whate'er it cost you, for a thing that I know!
It will be somewhat hard to compass; but,
However, see her. You are made, believe it,
If you can see her. Her Grace is a lone
    woman,
And very rich; and if she take a fancy,
She will do strange things. See her, at any
    hand.
'Slid, she may hap to leave you all she has!
It is the Doctor's fear.
    DAP.   How will 't be done, then?
    FACE. Let me alone;[100] take you no
      thought. Do you   160

[94] There were two early sixteenth-century alchemists named Isaac and John Isaac Holland.
Since the context calls for an allusion to notorious
gamblers, and since the Hollands were both dead,
Jonson seems to be doubly inaccurate.
[95] *I.e.*, strip them, reduce each to the point where
all his clothes are gambled away save a cloak to
cover his nakedness with.
[96] *I.e.*, rich.

[97] Faith.   [98] Q *Gad.*   [99] Last night.
[100] Leave it to me.

But say to me, " Captain, I 'll see her
     Grace."
    DAP.   " Captain, I 'll see her Grace."
    FACE.   Enough.   *One knocks without.*
    SUB.   Who 's there?
Anon. — [*aside to* FACE] Conduct him forth
     by the back way. —
Sir, against one a'clock prepare yourself.
Till when, you must be fasting ; only take
Three drops of vinegar in at your nose,
Two at your mouth, and one at either ear ;
Then bathe your fingers' ends and wash your
     eyes,
To sharpen your five senses, and cry *hum*   169
Thrice, and then *buz* as often ; and then, come.
                              [*Exit.*]
    FACE. Can you remember this?
    DAP.   I warrant you.
    FACE. Well then, away. It is but your
     bestowing
Some twenty nobles 'mong her Grace's serv-
     ants ;
And put on a clean shirt.[101] You do not know
What grace her Grace may do you in clean
     linen.
            [*Exeunt* FACE *and* DAPPER.]

SCENE III [102]

    SUB. [*within*] Come in ! — Good wives, I
     pray you forbear me [103] now.
Troth, I can do you no good till afternoon. —

    [*Enter* SUBTLE, *followed by* DRUGGER.]

    SUB. What is your name, say you? Abel
     Drugger?
    DRUG.   Yes, sir.
    SUB. A seller of tobacco?
    DRUG.   Yes, sir.
    SUB.   'Umh.
Free of the Grocers? [104]
    DRUG.   Ay, an 't please you.
    SUB.   Well ——
Your business, Abel?
    DRUG.   This, an 't please your Worship ;
I am a young beginner, and am building
Of a new shop, an 't like your Worship, just
At corner of a street : — Here 's the plot [105]
     on 't.   9
And I would know by art, sir, of your Worship,

Which way I should make my door, by necro-
     mancy,
And where my shelves ; and which should be
     for boxes,
And which for pots. I would be glad to thrive
     sir ;
And I was wish'd [106] to your Worship by a
     gentleman,
One Captain Face, that says you know men's
     planets,[107]
And their good angels, and their bad.
    SUB.   I do,
If I do see 'em [108] ——

         [*Enter* FACE.]

    FACE.   What ! my honest Abel?
Thou art well met here !
    DRUG.   Troth, sir, I was speaking,
Just as your Worship came here, of your Wor-
     ship.
I pray you speak for me to Master Doctor.   20
    FACE. He shall do anything. Doctor, do
     you hear?
This is my friend, Abel, an honest fellow ;
He lets me have good tobacco, and he does not
Sophisticate it with sack-lees or oil,
Nor washes it in muscadel and grains,
Nor buries it in gravel, under ground,
Wrapp'd up in greasy leather, or piss'd clouts ;
But keeps it in fine lily pots, that, open'd,
Smell like conserve of roses, or French beans.
He has his maple block,[109] his silver tongs,   30
Winchester pipes, and fire of juniper :
A neat, spruce, honest fellow, and no gold-
     smith.[110]
    SUB. H' is a fortunate fellow, that I am
     sure on.
    FACE. Already, sir, ha' you found it? Lo
     thee, Abel !
    SUB. And in right way toward riches ——
    FACE.   Sir.
    SUB.   This summer,
He will be of the clothing of his company,[111]
And, next spring, call'd to the scarlet ; [112] spend
     what he can.
    FACE. What, and so little beard?

[106] Recommended.
[107] *I.e.*, the stars which, according to the astrolo-
gists, control men's fortunes.
[108] Punning on "angels", the coins.
[109] For shredding the tobacco. The tongs were to
hold the coal which lighted the pipe ; the coal was
of juniper, which holds fire for a long time.
[110] *I.e.*, usurer (as many goldsmiths were).
[111] Wear the livery, which was a mark of belonging
to the upper class within the company, many of
whose members were not "of the livery."
[112] Be chosen sheriff.

---

[101] Hatred of uncleanliness was one of the fundamental traits of fairy character.
[102] The same.
[103] Let me go, excuse me.
[104] A member of that company.
[105] Plat.

SUB. Sir, you must think,
He may have a receipt to make hair come :
But he 'll be wise, preserve his youth, and
fine [113] for 't ; 40
His fortune looks for him another way.

FACE. 'Slid, Doctor, how canst thou know
this so soon?
I am amus'd [114] at that !

SUB. By a rule, Captain,
In met[o]poscopy,[115] which I do work by ;
A certain star i' the forehead, which you see
not.
Your chestnut or your olive-color'd face
Does never fail ; and your long ear doth
promise.
I knew 't, by certain spots, too, in his teeth,
And on the nail of his mercurial finger.

FACE. Which finger 's that?

SUB. His little finger. Look. 50
Yo' were born upon a Wednesday?

DRUG. Yes, indeed, sir.

SUB. The thumb, in chiromancy, we give
Venus ;
The forefinger, to Jove ; the midst, to Saturn ;
The ring, to Sol ; the least, to Mercury,
Who was the lord, sir, of his horoscope,
His house of life being Libra ; which for-
show'd
He should be a merchant, and should trade
with balance.

FACE. Why, this is strange ! Is 't not,
honest Nab?

SUB. There is a ship now coming from
Ormuz,
That shall yield him such a commodity 60
Of drugs —— This is the west, and this the
south? [*Pointing to the plat.*]

DRUG. Yes, sir.

SUB. And those are your two sides?

DRUG. Ay, sir.

SUB. Make me your door then, south ; your
broad side, west :
And on the east side of your shop, aloft,
Write Mathlai, Tarmiel, and Baraborat ;
Upon the north part, Rael, Velel, Thiel.
They are the names of those Mercurial spirits
That do fright flies from boxes.

DRUG. Yes, sir.

SUB. And
Beneath your threshold, bury me a loadstone

To draw in gallants that wear spurs ; the
rest, 70
They 'll seem [116] to follow.

FACE. That 's a secret, Nab !

SUB. And, on your stall, a puppet, with a
vice [117]
And a court-fucus,[118] to call city dames :
You shall deal much with minerals.

DRUG. Sir, I have,
At home, already ——

SUB. Ay, I know, you 've arsenic,
Vitriol, sal-tartar, argaile,[119] alkali,
Cinoper : [120] I know all. — This fellow, Cap-
tain,
Will come, in time, to be a great distiller,
And give a say [121] — I will not say directly,
But very fair — at the philosophers' stone. 80

FACE. Why, how now, Abel ! Is this true?

DRUG. [*aside to* FACE] Good Captain,
What must I give?

FACE. Nay, I 'll not counsel thee.
Thou hear'st what wealth (he says spend what
thou canst),
Th' art like to come to.

DRUG. I would gi' him a crown.

FACE. A crown ! 'nd toward such a fortune?
Heart,
Thou shalt rather gi' him thy shop. No gold
about thee?

DRUG. Yes, I have a portague,[122] I ha' kept
this half-year.

FACE. Out on thee, Nab ! 'Slight, there was
such an offer —
'Shalt keep 't no longer, I 'll gi' it him for
thee ! Doctor,
Nab prays your Worship to drink this, and
swears 90
He will appear more grateful, as your skill
Does raise him in the world.

DRUG. I would entreat
Another favor of his Worship.

FACE. What is 't, Nab?

DRUG. But to look over, sir, my almanac,
And cross out my ill days,[123] that I may neither
Bargain, nor trust upon them.

FACE. That he shall, Nab.
Leave it, it shall be done, 'gainst [124] afternoon.

SUB. And a direction for his shelves.

---

[113] Pay a fine for declining the office of sheriff.
[114] Bemused, amazed.
[115] The art of character reading or fortune telling
from the face or forehead.
[116] Think fit. (*N.E.D.*)
[117] Device, mechanism.
[118] Cosmetic.
[119] Argol, crude tartar.
[120] Cinnabar, red mercuric sulphide.
[121] Have a try.
[122] A gold coin worth about $18.
[123] Unlucky days.
[124] By.

FACE.   Now, Nab!
Art thou well pleas'd, Nab?
  DRUG.   'Thank, sir, both your Worships.
  FACE.   Away. [*Exit* DRUGGER.]
Why, now, you smoky persecutor of
     nature !   100
Now do you see that something's to be done
Beside your beech-coal, and your cor'sive [125]
     waters,
Your crosslets,[126] crucibles, and cucurbites? [127]
You must have stuff brought home to you, to
     work on !
And yet you think I am at no expense
In searching out these veins, then following
     'em,
Then trying 'em out. 'Fore God, my intelli-
     gence [128]
Costs me more money than my share oft comes
     to,
In these rare works.
  SUB.   You are pleasant, sir. — How now !

SCENE IV [129]

[*To*] FACE [*and*] SUBTLE [*enter*] DOL.

  SUB. What says my dainty Dolkin?
  DOL.   Yonder fishwife
Will not away. And there's your giantess,
The bawd of Lambeth.
  SUB.   Heart, I cannot speak with 'em.
  DOL. Not afore night, I have told 'em in a
     voice,
Thorough the trunk [130] like one of your fa-
     miliars.
But I have spied Sir Epicure Mammon ——
  SUB.   Where?
  DOL. Coming along, at far end of the lane,
Slow of his feet, but earnest of his tongue
To one that's with him.
  SUB.   Face, go you and shift.[131]
Dol, you must presently make ready too —   10
                      [*Exit* FACE.]
  DOL. Why, what's the matter?
  SUB.   Oh, I did look for him
With the sun's rising. Marvel he could sleep !
This is the day I am to perfect for him
The magisterium, our great work, the stone ;
And yield it, made, into his hands ; of which
He has, this month, talk'd as he were possess'd.
And now he's dealing pieces on 't away.
Methinks I see him ent'ring ordinaries,

Dispensing for the pox, and plaguy houses,
Reaching his dose ; walking Moorfields for
     lepers ;   20
And off'ring citizens' wives pomander [132] brace-
     lets,
As his preservative, made of the elixir ;
Searching the 'spital to make old bawds young,
And the highways, for beggars to make rich.
I see no end of his labors. He will make
Nature asham'd of her long sleep, when art,
Who's but a step-dame, shall do more than
     she,
In her best love to mankind, ever could.
If his dream last, he'll turn the age to gold.
                       [*Exeunt.*]

ACT II — SCENE I [1]

[*Enter* Sir EPICURE] MAMMON [*and*] SURLY.

  MAM. Come on, sir. Now you set your
     foot on shore
In *Novo Orbe;* here's the rich Peru ;
And there within, sir, are the golden mines,
Great Solomon's Ophir ! He was sailing to 't
Three years, but we have reach'd it in ten
     months.
This is the day wherein, to all my friends,
I will pronounce the happy word, " Be rich ;
This day you shall be spectatissimi." [2]
You shall no more deal with the hollow [3] die,
Or the frail card ; no more be at charge of
     keeping   10
The livery-punk [4] for the young heir, that must
Seal,[5] at all hours, in his shirt ; no more,
If he deny, ha' him beaten to 't, as he is
That brings him the commodity ; [6] no more
Shall thirst of satin, or the covetous hunger
Of velvet entrails [7] for a rude-spun cloak,
To be display'd at Madam Augusta's,[8] make
The sons of Sword and Hazard [9] fall before
The golden calf, and on their knees,[10] whole
     nights,
Commit idolatry with wine and trumpets ;
Or go a-feasting, after drum and ensign.   21

[132] A case, or ball, of perfumes carried against
infection.
  [1] The same.   [2] Cynosures.   [3] And loaded.
  [4] Hired prostitute.
  [5] See on *Every Man in His Humor,* II, v, 40.
  [6] See on III, iv, 90.
  [7] Lining. Fashion prescribed that this should be
even richer than the outside.
  [8] Evidently the madam of a brothel (or of a tavern,
which was often much the same thing).
  [9] Of whom Surly is one.
  [10] In drinking toasts to their luck.

---

[125] Corrosive.   [126] Crucibles.
[127] Gourd-shaped vessels used in distillation.
[128] Information.   [129] The same.
[130] Speaking-tube.
[131] Change your costume.

No more of this. You shall start up young
    viceroys,
And have your punks and punkettees,[11] my
    Surly.
And unto thee I speak it first, " Be rich."
Where is my Subtle there? Within, ho!
  [FACE.] (*within*)   Sir,
He'll come to you by and by.[12]
  MAM.   That's his fire-drake,[13]
His Lungs, his Zephyrus, he that puffs his
    coals,
Till he firk [14] nature up, in her own centre.
You are not faithful,[15] sir. This night I'll
    change
All that is metal in thy [16] house to gold;   30
And, early in the morning, will I send
To all the plumbers and the pewterers,
And buy their tin and lead up; and to Loth-
    bury [17]
For all the copper.
  SUR.   What, and turn that, too?
  MAM. Yes, and I'll purchase Devonshire
    and Cornwall,
And make them perfect Indies! [18] You ad-
    mire now?
  SUR. No, faith.
  MAM.   But when you see th' effects
    of the great med'cine,
Of which one part projected on a hundred
Of Mercury, or Venus, or the Moon,
Shall turn it to as many of the Sun,[19]   40
Nay, to a thousand, so *ad infinitum*,
You will believe me.
  SUR.   Yes, when I see 't, I will.
But if my eyes do cozen me so, and I
Giving 'em no occasion, sure I'll have
A whore, shall piss 'em out [20] next day.
  MAM.   Ha! why?
Do you think I fable with you? I assure you,
He that has once the flower of the sun,
The perfect ruby, which we call elixir,
Not only can do that, but by its virtue
Can confer honor, love, respect, long life; 50
Give safety, valor, yea, and victory,
To whom he will. In eight-and-twenty days,
I'll make an old man of fourscore, a child.
  SUR. No doubt; he's that already.

  MAM.   Nay, I mean,
Restore his years, renew him, like an eagle,
To the fifth age; make him get sons and
    daughters,
Young giants; as our philosophers have done,
The ancient patriarchs, afore the flood,
But taking, once a week, on a knife's point,
The quantity of a grain of mustard of it: 60
Become stout Marses, and beget young Cu-
    pids.
  SUR. The decay'd vestals of Pickt-hatch [21]
    would thank you,
That keep the fire alive there.
  MAM.   'T is the secret
Of nature naturiz'd [22] 'gainst all infections,
Cures all diseases coming of all causes:
A month's grief in a day, a year's in twelve,
And of what age soever in a month —
Past all the doses of your drugging doctors.
I'll undertake, withal, to fright the plague
Out o' the kingdom in three months.
  SUR.   And I'll
Be bound, the players shall sing your praises
    then,   71
Without their poets.[23]
  MAM.   Sir, I'll do 't. Meantime,
I'll give away so much unto my man,
Shall serve th' whole city with preservative
Weekly; each house his dose, and at the
    rate ——
  SUR. As he that built the Waterwork [24] does
    with water?
  MAM. You are incredulous.
  SUR.   Faith, I have a humor:
I would not willingly be gull'd. Your stone
Cannot transmute me.
  MAM.   Pertinax Surly,
Will you believe antiquity? records? 80
I'll show you a book where Moses, and his
    sister,[25]
And Solomon have written of the art;
Ay, and a treatise penn'd by Adam ——
  SUR.   How!

[11] A diminutive, probably with no special meaning.
[12] At once.
[13] Dragon.
[14] Rouse, make frisky.
[15] Full of faith, disposed to believe.
[16] Q *my*.
[17] The street of the copper-founders.
[18] Turn their tin to gold.
[19] Turn mercury, copper, and silver to gold.
[20] Urine was applied to the eyes as a remedy.
[21] A notorious haunt of prostitutes and sharpers.
[22] *Natura naturata* (theologically distinguished from *natura naturans* = God as creator); *i.e.*, the created universe, the properties of which are derivative rather than original. In this case, the stone is endowed with immunization, etc. These claims are by no means Jonson's invention.
[23] *I.e.*, since the theatres had to close when the plague was severe, expression of the actors' gratitude will not require the intermediary of the dramatists, who normally provide them with their utterances.
[24] Not Sir Hugh Myddleton's "New River", but Bevis Bulmer's, on the Thames, built in 1595.
[25] Miriam. All these names were cited by alchemists.

MAM. O' the philosopher's stone, and in High Dutch.

SUR. Did Adam write, sir, in High Dutch?[26]

MAM. He did;

Which proves it was the primitive tongue.

SUR. What paper?

MAM. On cedar board.

SUR. O that, indeed, they say,

Will last 'gainst worms.

MAM. 'T is like your Irish wood

'Gainst cobwebs. I have a piece of Jason's fleece,[27] too, 89

Which was no other than a book of alchemy,

Writ in large sheepskin, a good fat ram-vellum.

Such was Pythagoras' thigh, Pandora's tub,

And all that fable of Medea's charms,

The manner of our work; the bulls, our furnace,

Still breathing fire; our argent-vive,[28] the dragon;

The dragon's teeth, mercury sublimate,

That keeps the whiteness, hardness, and the biting;

And they are gather'd into Jason's helm,

Th' alembic,[29] and then sow'd in Mars his field, 99

And thence sublim'd so often, till they are fix'd.

Both this, th' Hesperian garden, Cadmus' story,

Jove's shower, the boon of Midas, Argus' eyes,

Boccace his Demogorgon,[30] thousands more,

All abstract riddles of our stone. — How now?

SCENE II [31]

[*To*] MAMMON [*and*] SURLY [*enter*] FACE, [*as a servant.*]

MAM. Do we succeed? Is our day come? and holds it?

FACE. The evening will set red upon you, sir;

You have color for it, crimson; the red ferment

Has done his office. Three hours hence prepare you

To see projection.[32]

MAM. Pertinax, my Surly,

Again I say to thee, aloud, " Be rich."

[26] This had been seriously asserted.
[27] Such attempts to rationalize mythology were common.
[28] Quicksilver.   [29] The cap of a still.
[30] A mighty demon; Boccaccio mentions him.
[31] The same.
[32] The final alchemical process; the substance then turned red, and was ready for use in transmutation.

This day thou shalt have ingots; and to-morrow

Give lords th' affront. — Is it, my Zephyrus, right?

Blushes the bolt's-head? [33]

FACE. Like a wench with child, sir,

That were but now discover'd to her master.

MAM. Excellent witty Lungs! — My only care is 11

Where to get stuff enough now, to project on;

This town will not half serve me.

FACE. No, sir? Buy

The covering off o' churches.

MAM. That 's true.

FACE. Yes.

Let 'em stand bare, as do their auditory; [34]

Or cap 'em new with shingles.

MAM. No, good thatch;

Thatch will lie light upo' the rafters, Lungs.

Lungs, I will manumit thee from the furnace;

I will restore thee thy complexion, Puff,

Lost in the embers; and repair this brain, 20

Hurt wi' the fume o' the metals.

FACE. I have blown, sir,

Hard, for your Worship; thrown by many a coal,

When 't was not beech; weigh'd those I put in, just,

To keep your heat still even. These blear'd eyes

Have wak'd to read your several colors, sir,

Of the pale citron, the green lion, the crow,

The peacock's tail, the plumed swan.[35]

MAM. And, lastly,

Thou hast descried the flower, the *sanguis agni*?

FACE. Yes, sir.

MAM. Where 's master?

FACE. At 's prayers, sir; he,

Good man, he 's doing his devotions 30

For the success.

MAM. Lungs, I will set a period

To all thy labors; thou shalt be the master

Of my seragli[o].

FACE. Good, sir.

MAM. But do you hear?

I 'll geld you, Lungs.

FACE. Yes, sir.

MAM. For I do mean

To have a list of wives and concubines

Equal with Solomon, who had the stone

Alike with me; and I will make me a back

[33] A long, straight-necked retort.
[34] Congregation.
[35] Colors at various stages of the process.

With the elixir, that shall be as tough
As Hercules, to encounter fifty a night. —
Th' art sure thou saw'st it blood?
    FACE.   Both blood and spirit, sir. 40
    MAM. I will have all my beds blown up, not
        stuff'd ;
Down is too hard. And then, mine oval room
Fill'd with such pictures as Tiberius took
From Elephantis, and dull Aretine
But coldly imitated. Then, my glasses
Cut in more subtle angles, to disperse
And multiply the figures, as I walk
Naked between my succubae.[36] My mists
I 'll have of perfume, vapor'd 'bout the room,
To lose ourselves in ; and my baths, like pits
To fall into ; from whence we will come forth
And roll us dry in gossamer and roses. — 52
Is it arrived at ruby? —— Where I spy
A wealthy citizen or rich lawyer
Have a sublim'd pure wife, unto that fellow
I 'll send a thousand pound to be my cuckold.
    FACE. And I shall carry it?
    MAM.   No. I 'll ha' no bawds
But fathers and mothers. They will do it best,
Best of all others. And my flatterers
Shall be the pure [37] and gravest of divines 60
That I can get for money. My mere fools,
Eloquent burgesses ; [38] and then my poets
The same that writ so subtly of the fart,[39]
Whom I will entertain still for that subject.
The few that would give out themselves to be
Court and town stallions, and, eachwhere, bely
Ladies who are known most innocent, for
    them,[40] —
Those will I beg, to make me eunuchs of ;
And they shall fan me with ten estrich tails
Apiece, made in a plume to gather wind. 70
We will be brave, Puff, now we ha' the med'-
    cine.
My meat shall all come in, in Indian shells,
Dishes of agate set in gold, and studded
With emeralds, sapphires, hyacinths, and ru-
    bies.
The tongues of carps, dormice, and camels'
    heels,
Boil'd i' the spirit of Sol, and dissolv'd pearl
(Apicius' [41] diet, 'gainst the epilepsy) ;

And I will eat these broths with spoons of am-
    ber,
Headed with diamond and carbuncle.
My footboy shall eat pheasants, calver'd [42]
    salmons,   80
Knots,[43] godwits, lampreys. I myself will
    have
The beards of barbels serv'd instead of salads,
Oil'd mushrooms, and the swelling unctuous
    paps
Of a fat pregnant sow, newly cut off,
Dress'd with an exquisite and poignant sauce,
For which I 'll say unto my cook, " There 's
    gold ;
Go forth, and be a knight." [44]
    FACE.   Sir, I 'll go look
A little, how it heightens.   [*Exit.*]
    MAM.   Do. — My shirts
I 'll have of taffeta-sars'net, soft and light
As cobwebs ; and for all my other raiment, 90
It shall be such as might provoke the Persian,
Were he to teach the world riot anew.
My gloves of fishes and birds' skins, perfum'd
With gums of paradise, and Eastern air ——
    SUR. And do you think to have the stone
        with this?
    MAM. No, I do think t' have all this with
        the stone.
    SUR. Why, I have heard he must be *homo
        frugi*,
A pious, holy, and religious man,
One free from mortal sin, a very virgin.
    MAM. That makes it, sir ; he is so. But I
        buy it ;   100
My venture brings it me. He, honest wretch,
A notable, superstitious, good soul,
Has worn his knees bare, and his slippers bald,
With prayer and fasting for it ; and, sir, let
    him
Do it alone, for me, still. Here he comes.
Not a profane word afore him ; 't is poison. —

SCENE III [45]

[*To*] MAMMON [*and*] SURLY [*enter*] SUBTLE.

    MAM. Good morrow, father.
    SUB.   Gentle son, good morrow,
And to your friend there. What is he is with
    you?
    MAM. An heretic, that I did bring along,
In hope, sir, to convert him.

---

[36] *I.e.*, concubines. All these voluptuous ideas Jonson found in his classical reading. On Tiberius see Suetonius's *Life*, chap. 43.
[37] Purest. Q *best*.   [38] Members of Parliament.
[39] See, for example, *Musarum Deliciae* (1656).
[40] For all of them, as far as they are concerned.
[41] The famous gourmand. He is mentioned in chapter 18 of Lampridius's *Vita Heliogabali*, in the *Scriptores Historiae Augustae*, from which Jonson takes most of these delicacies.

[42] Specially dressed, but just how is uncertain.
[43] Red-breasted sandpipers.
[44] A hit at the cheapening of knighthood which resulted from James's lavish creations.
[45] The same.

SUB.   Son, I doubt
Yo' are covetous, that thus you meet your time
I' the just [46] point ; prevent [47] your day at
    morning.
This argues something worthy of a fear
Of importune and carnal appetite.
Take heed you do not cause the blessing leave
    you,
With your ungovern'd haste.   I should be
    sorry
To see my labors, now e'en at perfection,   11
Got by long watching and large patience,
Not prosper where my love and zeal hath
    plac'd 'em.
Which (Heaven I call to witness, with yourself,
To whom I have pour'd my thoughts) in all
    my ends,
Have look'd no way, but unto public good,
To pious uses, and dear charity,
[Now][48] grown a prodigy with men.   Wherein
If you, my son, should now prevaricate,
And to your own particular lusts employ   20
So great and catholic a bliss, be sure
A curse will follow, yea, and overtake
Your subtle and most secret ways.
   MAM.   I know, sir ;
You shall not need to fear me.   I but come
To ha' you confute this gentleman.
   SUR.   Who is,
Indeed, sir, somewhat costive of belief
Toward your stone ; would not be gull'd.
   SUB.   Well, son,
All that I can convince him in, is this :
The work is done ; bright Sol is in his robe.
We have a med'cine of the triple soul,[49]   30
The glorified spirit.   Thanks be to Heaven,
And make us worthy of it ! — Ulen ©piegel ! [50]
   FACE. [*within*] Anon, sir.
   SUB.   Look well to the register.[51]
And let your heat still lessen by degrees,
To the aludels.[52]
   FACE. [*within*] Yes, sir.
   SUB.   Did you look
O' the bolt's-head yet ?
   FACE. [*within*]   Which ?   On D, sir ?
   SUB.   Ay ;
What 's the complexion ?
   FACE. [*within*]   Whitish.

SUB.   Infuse vinegar,
To draw his volatile substance and his tinc-
    ture ;
And let the water in glass E be filt'red,
And put into the gripe's egg.[53]   Lute [54] him
    well ;   40
And leave him clos'd *in balneo*.[55]
   FACE. [*within*]   I will, sir.
   SUR. [*aside*] What a brave language here is !
    next to canting ! [56]
   SUB. I have another work you never saw,
    son,
That three days since pass'd the philosopher's
    wheel,[57]
In the lent heat of Athanor ; [58] and 's become
Sulphur o' Nature.[59]
   MAM.   But 't is for me ?
   SUB.   What need you ?
You have enough, in that [60] is perfect.
   MAM.   O, but ——
   SUB. Why, this is covetise ! [61]
   MAM.   No, I assure you,
I shall employ it all in pious uses,
Founding of colleges and grammar schools, [50
Marrying [62] young virgins, building hospitals,
And, now and then, a church.

           [*Re-enter* FACE]

SUB.   How now !
FACE.   Sir, please you,
Shall I not change the filter ?
   SUB.   Marry, yes ;
And bring me the complexion of glass B.
                   [*Exit* FACE.]
   MAM. Ha' you another ?
   SUB.   Yes, son ; were I assur'd
Your piety were firm, we would not want
The means to glorify it.   But I hope the best.
I mean to tinct C in sand-heat to-morrow,
And give him imbibition.[63]
   MAM.   Of white oil ?
   SUB. No, sir, of red.   F is come over the
    helm[64] too,   60

---

[46] Exact.   [47] Anticipate.
[48] Cor. F₂ ; Q, F₁, *No*.
[49] A triple spirit ("vital", "natural", and
"animal") was supposed to knit man's soul to his
body.
[50] Owlglass, the knavish hero of an early German
jest-book.
[51] Which regulated the draft.
[52] Pear-shaped vessels, open at both ends.
[53] Griffin's egg : a vessel so shaped.
[54] Seal (especially with clay).
[55] In a bath ; *i.e.*, in warm water or sand.
[56] The jargon of the underworld, of rogues, vagabonds, and beggars.
[57] A series of alchemical operations.   (Hathaway.)
[58] A self-feeding furnace which maintained an
even and mild ("lent") temperature.
[59] Sulphur vive, or red sulphur.   In this state
(never reached) sulphur was perfect for the further
stages of the alchemical process.
[60] *I.e.*, in having that which.
[61] Covetousness.
[62] *I.e.*, providing dowries for.
[63] Saturation.
[64] The cap of the still.

I thank my Maker, in Saint Mary's bath.[65]
And shows *lac virginis*.[66] Blessed be Heaven.
I sent you of his faeces [67] there calcin'd :
Out of that calx, I ha' won the salt of mercury.

MAM. By pouring on your rectified [68]
     water?

SUB. Yes, and reverberating [69] in Athanor.

[*Re-enter* FACE.]

How now? what color says it?

FACE.   The ground black, sir.

MAM. That's your crow's head?

SUB. [*aside*]   Your cock's comb's, is 't
     not?

SUB. No, 't is not perfect ; would it were
     the crow.   69
That work wants something.

SUR. [*aside*]   Oh, I look'd for this.
The hay [70] is a-pitching.

SUB.   Are you sure you loos'd 'em
In their own menstrue? [71]

FACE.   Yes, sir, and then married 'em,
And put 'em in a bolt's-head nipp'd [72] to diges-
     tion,[73]
Accord as you bade me, when I set
The liquor of Mars [74] to circulation
In the same heat.

SUB.   The process then was right.

FACE. Yes, by the token, sir, the retort
     brake,
And what was sav'd was put into the pelican,[75]
And sign'd with Hermes seal.[76]

SUB.   I think 't was so.
We should have a new amalgama.

SUR. [*aside*]   O, this ferret [77]   80
Is rank [78] as any polecat.

SUB.   But I care not ;
Let him e'en die ; we have enough beside,
In embryon.[79] He has his white shirt on?

FACE.   Yes, sir,
He 's ripe for inceration : [80] he stands warm,

In his ash-fire. I would not you should let
Any die now, if I might counsel, sir,
For luck's sake to the rest ; it is not good.

MAM. He says right.

SUR. [*aside*]   Ay, are you bolted? [81]

FACE.   Nay, I know 't, sir ;
I have seen th' ill fortune. What is some
     three ounces
Of fresh materials?

MAM.   Is 't no more?

FACE.   No more, sir ;   90
Of gold, t' amalgam with some six of mercury.

MAM. Away ; here 's money. What will
     serve?

FACE.   Ask him, sir.

MAM. How much?

SUB.   Give him nine pound ;
     you may gi' him ten.

SUR. [*aside*] Yes, twenty, and be cozen'd,
     do.

MAM.   There 't is.

SUB. This needs not ; but that you will
     have it so,
To see conclusions of all. For two
Of our inferior works are at fixation ; [82]
A third is in ascension.[83] Go your ways.
Ha' you set the oil of Luna in kemia ? [84]

FACE. Yes, sir.

SUB.   And the philosophers' vinegar?

FACE.   Ay. [*Exit.*]   100

SUR. [*aside*] We shall have a salad.

MAM.   When do you make projection?

SUB. Son, be not hasty ; I exalt our med'-
     cine,
By hanging him *in balneo vaporoso*,
And giving him solution ; then congeal him ;
And then dissolve him ; then again congeal
     him ;
For look, how oft I iterate the work,
So many times I add unto his virtue.
As, if at first one ounce convert a hundred,
After his second loose, he 'll turn a thousand ;
His third solution, ten ; his fourth, a hundred ;
After his fifth, a thousand thousand ounces [110
Of any imperfect metal, into pure
Silver or gold, in all examinations
As good as any of the natural mine.
Get you your stuff here against afternoon,
Your brass, your pewter, and your andirons.

MAM. Not those of iron?

SUB.   Yes, you may bring them too ;
We 'll change all metals.

---

[65] In this process one vessel is heated by being placed in another which holds water to which the fire is applied.
[66] Water of mercury.
[67] Dregs.   [68] Purified.
[69] Heating indirectly.
[70] Net for catching rabbits.
[71] Solvent.
[72] *I.e.*, pinched up, sealed.
[73] To undergo the resolving process.
[74] Iron.
[75] An alembic made with tubes that allowed free circulation.
[76] Hermetically sealed, by heating the vessel's neck and twisting it.
[77] *I.e.*, rabbit-catcher.
[78] *I.e.*, his intentions are as obvious.
[79] In embryo, unseparated.
[80] Softening.

[81] Like a rabbit into the net.
[82] In process of reduction to a solid.
[83] Distillation.   [84] In a cucurbit.

Sur.   I believe you in that.
Mam. Then I may send my spits?
Sub.   Yes, and your racks.
Sur. And dripping pans, and pot hangers,
    and hooks?   120
Shall he not?
Sub.   If he please.
Sur.   — To be an ass.
Sub. How sir!
Mam.   This gent'man you must
    bear withal.
I told you he had no faith.
Sur.   And little hope, sir;
But much less charity, should I gull myself.
Sub. Why, what have you observ'd, sir, in
    our art,
Seems so impossible?
Sur.   But your whole work, no more.
That you should hatch gold in a furnace, sir,
As they do eggs in Egypt!
Sub.   Sir, do you
Believe that eggs are hatch'd so?
Sur.   If I should?
Sub. Why, I think that the greater miracle.
No egg but differs from a chicken more   131
Than metals in themselves.
Sur.   That cannot be.
The egg's ordain'd by nature to that end,
And is a chicken *in potentia*.
Sub. The same we say of lead and other
    metals.
Which would be gold if they had time.
Mam.   And that
Our art doth further.
Sub.   Ay, for 't were absurd
To think that nature in the earth bred gold
Perfect i' the instant; something went before.
There must be remote matter.
Sur.   Ay, what is that? [140
Sub. Marry, we say ——
Mam.   Ay, now it heats; stand, father;
Pound him to dust.
Sub.   It is, of the one part,
A humid exhalation, which we call
Materia liquida, or the unctuous water;
On th' other part, a certain crass and viscous
Portion of earth; both which, concorporate,
Do make the elementary matter of gold;
Which is not yet *propria materia*,
But common to all metals and all stones.
For, where it is forsaken of that moisture, 150
And hath more dryness, it becomes a stone;
Where it retains more of the humid fatness,
It turns to sulphur, or to quicksilver,
Who are the parents of all other metals.

Nor can this remote matter suddenly
Progress so from extreme unto extreme,
As to grow gold, and leap o'er all the means.
Nature doth first beget th' imperfect; then
Proceeds she to the perfect. Of that airy
And oily water, mercury is engend'red;   160
Sulphur o' the fat and earthy part; the one,
Which is the last, supplying the place of male,
The other of the female, in all metals.
Some do believe hermaphrodeity,
That both do act and suffer. But these two
Make the rest ductile, malleable, extensive.
And even in gold they are; for we do find
Seeds of them by our fire, and gold in them;
And can produce the species of each metal
More perfect thence than nature doth in
    earth.   170
Beside, who doth not see in daily practice
Art can beget bees, hornets, beetles, wasps,
Out of the carcases and dung of creatures; [85]
Yea, scorpions of an herb, being rightly plac'd?
And these are living creatures, far more per-
    fect
And excellent than metals.
Mam.   Well said, father! —
Nay, if he take you in hand, sir, with an argu-
    ment,
He'll bray you in a mortar.
Sur.   Pray you, sir, stay.
Rather than I'll be bray'd, sir, I'll believe
That alchemy is a pretty kind of game,   180
Somewhat like tricks o' the cards, to cheat a
    man
With charming.
Sub.   Sir?
Sur.   What else are all your terms,
Whereon no one o' your writers 'grees with
    other?
Of your elixir, your *lac virginis*,
Your stone, your med'cine, and your chryso-
    sperm,[86]
Your sal, your sulphur, and your mercury,
Your oil of height,[87] your tree of life, your
    blood,
Your marcasite, your tutty, your magnesia,
Your toad,[88] your crow, your dragon,[89] and
    your panther,[90]
Your sun, your moon, your firmament, your
    adrop,[91]   190

[85] All these were stock arguments.
[86] Gold-seed.
[87] Highly refined oil.
[88] The "green lion."
[89] Mercury.
[90] The color of another stage.
[91] Apparently = either the stone itself, or the matter from which it is to be extracted.

Your lato, azoch, zernich, chibrit,[92] heautarit,
And then your red man, and your white
   woman,[93]
With all your broths, your menstrues, and ma-
   terials
Of piss and eggshells, women's terms, man's
   blood,
Hair o' the head, burnt clouts, chalk, merds,[94]
   and clay,
Powder of bones, scalings of iron, glass,
And worlds of other strange ingredients,
Would burst a man to name?

SUB.   And all these, nam'd,
Intending but one thing; which art our writers
Us'd to obscure their art.

MAM.   Sir, so I told him; 200
Because [95] the simple idiot should not learn it,
And make it vulgar.

SUB.   Was not all the knowledge
Of the Egyptians writ in mystic symbols?
Speak not the scriptures oft in parables?
Are not the choicest fables of the poets,
That were the fountains and first springs of
   wisdom,
Wrapp'd in perplexed allegories?

MAM.   I urg'd that,
And clear'd to him that Sisyphus was damn'd
To roll the ceaseless stone, only because
He would have made ours common. (DOL *is*
   seen) [*at the door*.] — Who is this? 210

SUB. God's precious! — What do you
   mean? Go in, good lady,
Let me entreat you. [DOL *retires*.] — Where's
   this varlet?

[*Re-enter* FACE.]

FACE.   Sir?

SUB. You very knave! do you use me thus?

FACE.   Wherein, sir?

SUB. Go in and see, you traitor. Go!
                    [*Exit* FACE.]

MAM.   Who is it, sir?

SUB. Nothing, sir; nothing.

MAM.   What's the matter, good sir?
I have not seen you thus distemp'red. Who
   is 't?

SUB. All arts have still had, sir, their adversaries;
But ours the most ignorant. —

FACE *returns.*

                     What now?

FACE. 'T was not my fault, sir; she would
   speak with you.

SUB. Would she, sir! Follow me. [*Exit.*]

MAM.   Stay, Lungs.

FACE.   I dare not, sir. 220

MAM. Stay, man; what is she?

FACE.   A lord's sister, sir.[96]

MAM. How! 'pray thee, stay!

FACE.   She's mad, sir, and sent hither —
He'll be mad too. —

MAM.   I warrant thee.[97] — Why sent
   hither?

FACE. Sir, to be cur'd.

SUB. [*within*] Why, rascal!

FACE.   Lo you! — Here, sir!
                      He goes out.

MAM. 'Fore God, a Bradamante,[98] a brave
   piece.

SUR. Heart, this is a bawdyhouse! I'll be
   burnt else.

MAM. O, by this light, no. Do not wrong
   him. H' is
Too scrupulous that way: it is his vice.
No, h' is a rare physician, do him right,
An excellent Paracelsian, and has done 230
Strange cures with mineral physic.[99] He deals
   all
With spirits, he. He will not hear a word
Of Galen, or his tedious recipes. —

FACE *again.*

                How now, Lungs!

FACE. Softly, sir; speak softly. I meant
To ha' told your Worship all. This must not
   hear.

MAM. No, he will not be gull'd; let him
   alone.

FACE. Y' are very right; sir, she is a most
   rare scholar,
And is gone mad with studying Br[o]ugh-
   ton's [100] works.
If you but name a word touching the Hebrew,
She falls into her fit, and will discourse 240
So learnedly of genealogies,
As you would run mad, too, to hear her, sir.

MAM. How might one do t' have conference
   with her, Lungs?

---

[92] Red; purified mercury; arsenic trisulphide; sulphur. "Heautarit" remains unexplained, and many other of these words can only be approximated in modern terms.

[93] The alchemists were fond of the biological analogy.

[94] Excrement.

[95] In order that.

[96] So Q and Gifford. This and the following line are transposed in Ff.

[97] Against the effects of Subtle's anger.

[98] She appears in Ariosto's *Orlando Furioso.*

[99] Instead of using the vegetable remedies of the orthodox physicians, who followed Galen.

[100] See on *Volpone*, II, ii, 145.

FACE. O, divers have run mad upon the conference.

I do not know, sir; I am sent in haste
To fetch a vial.

SUR. Be not gull'd, Sir Mammon.

MAM. Wherein? 'Pray ye, be patient.

SUR. Yes, as you are;
And trust confederate knaves and bawds and whores.

MAM. You are too foul, believe it. — Come here, Ulen;

One word.

FACE. I dare not, in good faith.

MAM. Stay, knave. 250

FACE. H' is extreme angry that you saw her, sir.

MAM. Drink that. [*Gives him money.*] What is she when she's out of her fit?

FACE. O, the most affablest creature, sir! so merry!

So pleasant! She'll mount you up, like quicksilver,

Over the helm; and circulate, like oil;

A very vegetal:[101] discourse of state,

Of mathematics, bawdry, anything ——

MAM. Is she no way accessible? no means,

No trick to give a man a taste of her — wit —
Or so? — Ulen.[102]

FACE. I'll come to you again, sir. 260
[*Exit.*]

MAM. Surly, I did not think one o' your breeding

Would traduce personages of worth.

SUR. Sir Epicure,
Your friend to use; yet still loth to be gull'd.

I do not like your philosophical bawds.

Their stone is lechery enough to pay for,

Without this bait.

MAM. 'Heart, you abuse yourself.

I know the lady, and her friends, and means,

The original of this disaster. Her brother

Has told me all.

SUR. And yet you ne'er saw her till now!

MAM. Oh yes, but I forgot. I have, believe it, 270

One o' the treacherou'st memories, I do think,

Of all mankind.

SUR. What call you her brother?

MAM. My Lord ——

He wi' not have his name known, now I think on't.

SUR. A very treacherous memory!

MAM. O' my faith ——

SUR. Tut, if you ha' it not about you, pass it

Till we meet next.

MAM. Nay, by this hand, 't is true.

He's one I honor, and my noble friend;

And I respect his house.

SUR. Heart! can it be

That a grave sir, a rich, that has no need,

A wise sir, too, at other times, should thus, 280

With his own oaths, and arguments, make hard means

To gull himself? An this be your elixir,

Your *lapis mineralis*, and your lunary,[103]

Give me your honest trick yet at primero,

Or gleek,[104] and take your *lutum sapientis*,[105]

Your *menstruum* [106] *simplex!* I'll have gold before you,

And with less danger of the quicksilver,

Or the hot sulphur.[107]

[*Re-enter* FACE.]

FACE. (*to* SURLY) Here's one from Captain Face, sir.

Desires you meet him i' the Temple Church,

Some half-hour hence, and upon earnest business. — 290

(*Whispers* MAMMON.) Sir, if you please to quit us now, and come

Again within two hours, you shall have

My master busy examining o' the works;

And I will steal you in unto the party,

That you may see her converse.[108] — Sir, shall I say

You'll meet the Captain's worship?

SUR. Sir, I will. — [*aside*]

But, by attorney,[109] and to a second purpose.

Now, I am sure it is a bawdyhouse;

I'll swear it, were the marshal here to thank me: 299

The naming this commander doth confirm it.

Don Face! why, he's the most authentic dealer

I' these commodities! the superintendent

To all the quainter traffickers in town.

He is their visitor, and does appoint

Who lies with whom, and at what hour, what price,

---

101 Animated person. (Lat. *vegetus*)
102 Om. Q. Gifford assigns to Subtle.
103 Moonwort.
104 A three-handed card game.
105 Philosopher's lute, the clay for sealing vessels.
106 Menstrue, solvent.
107 *I.e.*, with less risk of contracting either syphilis or the itch, for which favorite remedies were, respectively, mercury and sulphur.
108 With a pun on sexual "conversation."
109 With reference to his subsequent disguise

Which gown, and in what smock, what fall,[110]
what tire.[111]
Him will I prove, by a third person, to find
The subtleties of this dark labyrinth ;
Which if I do discover, dear Sir Mammon,
You 'll give your poor friend leave, though no
    philosopher,   310
To laugh ; for you that are, 't is thought, shall
    weep.
    FACE. Sir, he does pray you 'll not forget.
    SUR.   I will not, sir. —
Sir Epicure, I shall leave you.   [*Exit.*]
    MAM.   I follow you straight.
    FACE. But do so, good sir, to avoid suspi-
        cion.
This gent'man has a parlous head.
    MAM.   But wilt thou, Ulen,
Be constant to thy promise ?
    FACE.   As my life, sir.
    MAM. And wilt thou insinuate what I am,
        and praise me,
And say I am a noble fellow ?
    FACE.   Oh, what else, sir ?
And that you 'll make her royal with the
    stone,   319
An empress ; and yourself King of Bantam.[112]
    MAM. Wilt thou do this ?
    FACE.   Will I, sir !
    MAM.   Lungs, my Lungs !
I love thee.
    FACE. Send your stuff, sir, that my master
May busy himself about projection.
    MAM. Th' hast witch'd me, rogue ; take,
        go.   [*Gives him money.*]
    FACE.   Your jack,[113] and all, sir.
    MAM. Thou art a villain — I will send my
        jack,
And the weights too. Slave, I could bite thine
    ear.
Away, thou dost not care for me.
    FACE.   Not I, sir ?
    MAM. Come, I was born to make thee, my
        good weasel,
Set thee on a bench, and ha' thee twirl a
    chain
With the best lord's vermin of 'em all.
    FACE.   Away, sir. [330
    MAM. A count, nay, a count palatine ——
    FACE.   Good sir, go.
    MAM. Shall not advance thee better ; no,
        nor faster.   [*Exit.*]

[110] Sometimes = collar ; here probably = veil.
[111] Headdress.
[112] In Java.
[113] For turning the spit.

SCENE IV [114]

[*To*] FACE [*enter*] SUBTLE [*and*] DOL.

    SUB. Has he bit? has he bit?
    FACE.   And swallow'd, too, my
        Subtle.
I ha' giv'n him line, and now he plays, i' faith.
    SUB. And shall we twitch him ?
    FACE.   Thorough both the gills.
A wench is a rare bait, with which a man
No sooner 's taken but he straight firks
    mad.[115]
    SUB. Dol, my Lord What's-hum's [116] sister,
        you must now
Bear yourself Statlich.[117]
    DOL.   Oh, let me alone ;
I 'll not forget my race, I warrant you.
I 'll keep my distance, laugh, and talk aloud ;
Have all the tricks of a proud scurvy lady,   10
And be as rude as her woman.
    FACE.   Well said, sanguine.[118]
    SUB. But will he send his andirons ?
    FACE.   His jack, too,
And 's iron shoeing-horn ; I ha' spoke to him.
    Well,
I must not lose my wary gamester yonder.
    SUB. Oh, Monsieur Caution, that will not
        be gull'd ?
    FACE. Ay, if I can strike a fine hook into
        him, now ! —
The Temple Church, there I have cast mine
    angle.
Well, pray for me. I 'll about it.
                            (*One knocks.*)
    SUB.   What, more gudgeons ! [119]
Dol, scout, scout ! [DOL *goes to the window.*]
    — Stay, Face, you must go to the door ;
'Pray God it be my Anabaptist. — Who is 't,
    Dol ?   20
    DOL. I know him not. He looks like a
        gold-end-man.[120]
    SUB. Gods so ! 't is he ; he said he would
        send — what call you him ?
The sanctified elder, that should deal
For Mammon's jack and andirons ! Let him
    in.
Stay ; help me off, first, with my gown. —
    Away,

[114] The same.
[115] Is stirred up to the point of madness.
[116] Q *Whachums.*
[117] Old eds. *statelich.* Ff print this word and *Ulen*
in black letter.
[118] Perhaps with reference to Dol's hair, nose, or
blonde complexion in general.
[119] *I.e.,* fools, that will bite at anything.
[120] One who buys broken bits of gold and silver.

Madam, to your withdrawing chamber. Now,

                      [*Exit* DOL.]

In a new tune, new gesture, but old lan-

     guage. —   [*Exit* FACE.]

This fellow is sent from one negotiates with me

About the stone too ; for the holy brethren

Of Amsterdam, the exil'd saints, that hope   30

To raise their discipline [121] by it. I must use

     him

In some strange fashion now, to make him ad-

     mire me.

SCENE V [122]

[*To*] SUBTLE [*enter*] ANANIAS.

SUB. Where is my drudge?

             [*Enter*] FACE.

FACE.   Sir.

SUB.   Take away the recipient,[123]

And rectify [124] your menstrue from the phleg-

ma.[125]

Then pour it o' the Sol, in the cucurbit,

And let 'em macerate together.

FACE.   Yes, sir.

And save the ground? [126]

SUB.   No : *terra damnata* [126]

Must not have entrance in the work. — Who

     are you?

ANA. A faithful brother,[127] if it please you.

SUB.   What 's that?

A Lullianist? a Ripley? [128]   *Filius artis?*

Can you sublime and dulcify? [129]   calcine?

Know you the sapor pontic? sapor stiptic? [130]

Or what is homogene, or heterogene?   11

ANA. I understand no heathen language,

     truly.

SUB. Heathen ! You Knipperdoling ! [131]   Is

     Ars sacra,

Or chrysopoeia, or spagyrica,[132]

Or the pamphysic, or panarchic [133] knowledge,

A heathen language?

ANA.   Heathen Greek, I take it.

SUB. How ! Heathen Greek?

ANA.   All 's heathen but the Hebrew.

SUB. Sirrah my varlet, stand you forth and

     speak to him

Like a philosopher ; answer i' the language.

Name the vexations and the martyrizations [134]

Of metals in the work.

FACE.   Sir, putrefaction,   21

Solution, ablution, sublimation,

Cohobation, calcination, ceration,[135] and

Fixation.

SUB.   This is heathen Greek, to you,

     now? —

And when comes vivification? [136]

FACE.   After mortification.[137]

SUB. What 's cohobation?

FACE.   'T is the pouring on

Your *aqua regis*, and then drawing him off,

To the trine circle of the seven spheres.

SUB. What 's the proper passion [138] of met-

     als.

FACE.   Malleation.

SUB. What 's your *ultimum supplicium*

     auri? [139]

FACE.   Antimonium.[140]   30

SUB. This 's heathen Greek to you? — and

     what 's your mercury?

FACE. A very fugitive ; he will be gone, sir.

SUB. How know you him?

FACE.   By his viscosity,

His oleosity, and his suscitability.[141]

SUB. How do you sublime him?

FACE.   With the calce [142] of eggshells,

White marble, talc.

SUB.   Your magisterium [143] now?

What 's that?

FACE.   Shifting, sir, your elements,

Dry into cold, cold into moist, moist into hot,

Hot into dry.

SUB.   This 's heathen Greek to you

     still? —

Your *lapis philosophicus?*

FACE.   'T is a stone,   40

And not a stone : a spirit, a soul, and a body ;

---

[121] Ecclesiastical polity.   [122] The same.

[123] Vessel that receives the distillation.

[124] Purify.

[125] Moisture distilled from vegetable matter.

[126] Grounds, residue.

[127] *I.e.*, a Puritan, but Subtle pretends to misunderstand.

[128] A follower of Ramon Lull, the famous (reputed)
alchemist of Majorca (d. 1315), or of George Ripley,
author of *The Compound of Alchemy* (1471).

[129] Refine, and neutralize acidity.

[130] Degrees of sourness to the taste (sapor).

[131] An Anabaptist leader associated with John of
Leyden in the revolt at Münster in 1534.

[132] All synonyms of *alchemy*.

[133] Both these words are presumably coined by
Subtle for the occasion ; they appear to signify
(1) the (knowledge) of all nature and (2) sovereign
(knowledge).

[134] Terms figuratively applied to the processes
undergone by the metals. (Hathaway.)

[135] Softening.

[136] Restoration to the natural state.

[137] *I.e.*, the reaction.

[138] Susceptibility to external agents.

[139] Final punishment of gold ; *i.e.*, when its im-
purities are being expelled.

[140] Since gold loses its malleability when alloyed
with antimony. (Hathaway.)

[141] Oiliness and excitability.   [142] Calx.

[143] Mastery ; a synonym for the philosophers' stone
though here the use seems a little hazy.

Which if you do dissolve, it is dissolv'd ;
If you coagulate, it is coagulated ;
If you make it to fly, it flieth.
    Sub.   Enough. [*Exit* Face.]
This 's heathen Greek to you? What are you,
    sir?
    Ana. Please you, a servant of the exil'd
    brethren,
That deal with widows' and with orphans'
    goods,
And make a just account unto the saints :
A deacon.
    Sub.   O, you are sent from Master
    Wholesome,
Your teacher?
    Ana.   From Tribulation Wholesome, 50
Our very zealous pastor.
    Sub.   Good. I have
Some orphans' goods to come here.
    Ana.   Of what kind, sir?
    Sub. Pewter and brass, andirons and kitch-
    enware.
Metals, that we must use our med'cine on ;
Wherein the brethren may have a penn'orth
For ready money.
    Ana.   Were the orphans' parents
Sincere professors?
    Sub.   Why do you ask?
    Ana.   Because
We then are to deal justly, and give, in truth,
Their utmost value.
    Sub.   'Slid, you 'd cozen else, 59
An if their parents were not of the faithful? —
I will not trust you, now I think on it,
Till I ha' talk'd with your pastor. Ha' you
    brought money
To buy more coals?
    Ana.   No, surely.
    Sub.   No? How so?
    Ana. The brethren bid me say unto you,
    sir,
Surely, they will not venture any more
Till they may see projection.
    Sub.   How!
    Ana.   Yo' have had
For the instruments, as bricks, and loam, and
    glasses,
Already thirty pound ; and for materials,
They say, some ninety more. And they have
    heard, since,
That one, at Heidelberg, made it of an egg, 70
And a small paper of pin-dust.
    Sub.   What 's your name?
    Ana. My name is Ananias.
    Sub.   Out, the varlet

That cozen'd the apostles ! Hence, away,
Flee mischief. Had your holy consistory
No name to send me of another sound
Than wicked Ananias? Send your elders
Hither, to make atonement for you, quickly,
And gi' me satisfaction ; or out goes
The fire ; and down th' alembics, and the fur-
    nace,   79
Piger Henricus,[144] or what not. Thou wretch,
Both *sericon* and *bufo* [145] shall be lost,
Tell 'em. All hope of rooting out the bishops
Or th' antichristian hierarchy shall perish,
If they stay threescore minutes : the aqueity,
Terreity, and sulphureity
Shall run together again, and all be annull'd,
Thou wicked Ananias. [*Exit* Ananias.] —
    This will fetch 'em,
And make 'em haste towards their gulling
    more.
A man must deal like a rough nurse, and fright
Those that are froward, to an appetite.   90

Scene VI [146]

[*To*] Subtle [*enter*] Face [*in his uniform, with*]
    Drugger.

    Face. He 's busy with his spirits, but we 'll
    upon him.
    Sub. How now ! What mates, what Bay-
    ards [147] ha' we here?
    Face. I told you he would be furious. —
    Sir, here 's Nab
Has brought yo' another piece of gold to look
    on ;
— We must appease him. Give it me : — and
    prays you
You would devise — what is it, Nab?
    Drug.   A sign, sir.
    Face. Ay, a good lucky one, a thriving sign,
    Doctor.
    Sub. I was devising now.
    Face. [*aside to* Subtle]   'Slight, do not
    say so ;
He will repent he ga' you any more. —
What say you to his constellation, Doctor, 10
The Balance?
    Sub.   No, that way is stale and common.
A townsman born in Taurus gives the bull
Or the bull's head ; in Aries, the ram —

---

[144] A slow furnace.
[145] Not satisfactorily explained; according to Gifford = black and red tincture.
[146] The same.
[147] *I.e.*, bold ones, Bayard being the magic horse
in (*e.g.*) Ariosto's *Orlando Furioso*, and the occasion
of the proverb "As bold as blind Bayard." "Mates"
= fellows (contemptuously).

A poor device! No, I will have his name
Form'd in some mystic character, whose *radii*,
Striking the senses of the passers-by,
Shall, by a virtual influence,[148] breed affections
That may result upon the party owns it;
As thus —— 19
   FACE.   Nab!
   SUB.   He first shall have *a bell,*
     that's *Abel;*
And by it standing one whose name is *Dee,*[149]
In a *rug*[150] gown, there's D, and *Rug,* that's
    drug;
And right anenst him a dog snarling *er:*
There's Drugger, Abel Drugger. That's his
    sign. ——
[*aside*] And here's now mystery and hiero-
    glyphic!
   FACE. Abel, thou art made.
   DRUG.   Sir, I do thank his Worship.
   FACE. Six o' thy legs[151] more will not do it,
    Nab.
He has brought you a pipe of tobacco, Doctor.
   DRUG.   Yes, sir;
I have another thing I would impart —— 29
   FACE. Out with it, Nab.
   DRUG.   Sir, there is lodg'd, hard by me,
A rich young widow ——
   FACE.   Good! a bona roba?[152]
   DRUG. But nineteen at the most.
   FACE.   Very good, Abel.
   DRUG. Marry, sh' is not in fashion yet;
    she wears
A hood, but 't stands a-cop.[153]
   FACE.   No matter, Abel.
   DRUG. And I do now and then give her a
    fucus[154] ——
   FACE. What! dost thou deal, Nab?
   SUB.   I did tell you, Captain.
   DRUG. And physic too, sometime, sir; for
    which she trusts me
With all her mind. She's come up here of pur-
    pose
To learn the fashion.
   FACE.   Good! — [*aside*] His match
    too! — On, Nab.
   DRUG. And she does strangely long to know
    her fortune.   40
   FACE. God's lid, Nab; send her to the
    Doctor, hither.
   DRUG. Yes, I have spoke to her of his Wor-
    ship already;

But she's afraid it will be blown abroad,
And hurt her marriage.
   FACE.   Hurt it! 't is the way
To heal it, if 't were hurt; to make it more
Follow'd and sought. Nab, thou shalt tell her
    this.
She'll be more known, more talk'd of; and
    your widows
Are ne'er of any price till they be famous;
Their honor is their multitude of suitors.   49
Send her; it may be thy good fortune. What!
Thou dost not know.
   DRUG.   No, sir, she'll never marry
Under a knight; her brother has made a vow.
   FACE. What! and dost thou despair, my
    little Nab,
Knowing what the Doctor has set down for
    thee,
And seeing so many o' the city dubb'd?[155]
One glass o' thy water, with a madam, I know,
Will have it done, Nab. What's her brother?
    a knight?
   DRUG. No, sir, a gentleman newly warm in
    's land, sir,
Scarce cold in his one-and-twenty, that does
    govern
His sister here; and is a man himself   60
Of some three thousand a year, and is come up
To learn to quarrel, and to live by his wits,
And will go down again, and die i' the country.
   FACE. How! to quarrel?
   DRUG.   Yes, sir, to carry quarrels,
As gallants do, and manage 'em by line.
   FACE. 'Slid, Nab! The Doctor is the only
    man
In Christendom for him. He has made a
    table,
With mathematical demonstrations,
Touching the art of quarrels. He will give him
An instrument to quarrel by. Go, bring 'em
    both,   70
Him and his sister. And, for thee, with her
The Doctor happ'ly may persuade. Go to.
'Shalt give his Worship a new damask suit
Upon the premises.
   SUB.   Oh, good Captain!
   FACE.   He shall;
He is the honestest fellow, Doctor. Stay not,
No offers; bring the damask, and the parties.
   DRUG. I'll try my power, sir.
   FACE.   And thy will too, Nab.
   SUB. 'T is good tobacco, this! What is 't
    an ounce?
   FACE. He'll send you a pound, Doctor.

[148] By the operation of its power.
[149] Alluding to John Dee, the astrologer (d. 1608).
[150] Of coarse stuff.
[151] Bows.   [152] Pretty girl.
[153] Probably = on top.   [154] Cosmetic.
[155] Knighted.

SUB.   Oh, no.
FACE.   He will do 't.
It is the goodest soul ! — Abel, about it.   80
Thou shalt know more anon.   Away, begone.
                                        [*Exit* ABEL.]
A miserable rogue, and lives with cheese,
And has the worms.   That was the cause, indeed,
Why he came now : he dealt with me in private,
To get a med'cine for 'em.
SUB.   And shall, sir.   This works.
FACE.   A wife, a wife for one on us, my dear
    Subtle.
We 'll e'en draw lots, and he that fails shall
    have
The more in goods, the other has in tail.
SUB.   Rather the less ; for she may be so
    light
She may want grains.[156]
FACE.   Ay ; or be such a burden,   90
A man would scarce endure her for the whole.
SUB.   Faith, best let 's see her first, and then
    determine.
FACE.   Content.   But Dol must ha' no
    breath on 't.
SUB.   Mum.
Away you, to your Surly yonder ; catch him.
FACE.   'Pray God I ha' not stay'd too long.
SUB.   I fear it. [*Exeunt.*]

ACT III — SCENE I [1]

[*Enter*] TRIBULATION [WHOLESOME *and*] ANA-
                        NIAS.

TRI.   These chastisements are common to
    the saints,
And such rebukes [2] we of the Separation
Must bear with willing shoulders, as the trials
Sent forth to tempt our frailties.
ANA.   In pure zeal,
I do not like the man ; he is a heathen,
And speaks the language of Canaan, truly.
TRI.   I think him a profane person indeed.
ANA.   He bears
The visible mark of the Beast in his forehead.
And for his stone, it is a work of darkness,
And with philosophy blinds the eyes of man.   10

---

[156] *I.e.,* she may be under the due weight.
[1] Before Lovewit's house.
[2] Q continues: *th' Elect must beare, with patience;*
They are the exercises of the Spirit,
And sent to tempt, etc.

TRI.   Good brother, we must bend unto all
    means
That may give furtherance to the holy cause.
ANA.   Which his cannot ; the sanctified
    cause
Should have a sanctified course.
TRI.   Not always necessary.
The children of perdition are ofttimes
Made instruments even of the greatest works.
Beside, we should give somewhat to man's
    nature,
The place he lives in, still about the fire,
The fume of metals, that intoxicate
The brain of man and make him prone to
    passion.   20
Where have you greater atheists than your
    cooks?
Or more profane, or choleric, than your glass-
    men?
More antichristian than your bell founders?
What makes the Devil so devilish, I would ask
    you,
Sathan, our common enemy, but his being
Perpetually about the fire, and boiling
Brimstone and ars'nic ? We must give, I say,
Unto the motives, and the stirrers up
Of humors in the blood.   It may be so,
Whenas the work is done, the stone is made,
This heat of his may turn into a zeal,   31
And stand up for the beauteous discipline
Against the menstruous cloth and rag of Rome.
We must await his calling, and the coming
Of the good spirit.   You did fault, t' upbraid
    him
With the brethren's blessing of Heidelberg,
    weighing
What need we have to hasten on the work,
For the restoring of the silenc'd saints,[3]
Which ne'er will be but by the philosopher's
    stone.
And so a learned elder, one of Scotland,   40
Assur'd me ; *aurum potabile* [4] being
The only med'cine for the civil magistrate,
T' incline him to a feeling of the cause ;
And must be daily us'd in the disease.
ANA.   I have not edified more, truly, by
    man ;
Not since the beautiful light first shone on me ;
And I am sad my zeal hath so offended.
TRI.   Let us call on him then.
ANA.   The motion 's good.
And of the spirit ; I will knock first. —
    [*Knocks.*] Peace be within !

---

[3] The dissenting clergy, who were prohibited from
preaching.   [4] *I.e.,* bribery.

SCENE II [5]

[*To them enter*] SUBTLE.

SUB. Oh, are you come? 'T was time.
    Your threescore minutes
Were at the last thread, you see; and down
    had gone
Furnus acediae, turris circulatorius: [6]
Limbec, bolt's-head, retort, and pelican
Had all been cinders. Wicked Ananias!
Art thou return'd? Nay, then it goes down
    yet.
    TRI. Sir, be appeased; he is come to
    humble
Himself in spirit, and to ask your patience,
If too much zeal hath carried him aside
From the due path.
    SUB.   Why, this doth qualify! [7] 10
    TRI. The brethren had no purpose, verily,
To give you the least grievance, but are ready
To lend their willing hands to any project
The spirit and you direct.
    SUB.   This qualifies more!
    TRI. And for the orphans' goods, let them
    be valu'd,
Or what is needful else to the holy work,
It shall be numb'red; here, by me, the saints
Throw down their purse before you.
    SUB.   This qualifies most!
Why, thus it should be; now you understand.
Have I discours'd so unto you of our stone, 20
And of the good that it shall bring your cause?
Show'd you (beside the main of hiring forces
Abroad, drawing the Hollanders, your friends,
From th' Indies, to serve you, with all their
    fleet)
That even the med'cinal use shall make you a
    faction
And party in the realm? As, put the case
That some great man in state, he have the
    gout,
Why, you but send three drops of your elixir,
You help him straight; there you have made a
    friend.
Another has the palsy or the dropsy: 30
He takes of your incombustible stuff —
He's young again; there you have made a
    friend.
A lady that is past the feat of body,
Though not of mind, and hath her face decay'd
Beyond all cure of paintings, you restore

With the oil of talc; [8] there you have made a
    friend —
And all her friends. [9] A lord that is a leper,
A knight that has the bone-ache, or a squire
That hath both these, you make 'em smooth
    and sound   39
With a bare fricace [10] of your med'cine; still
You increase your friends.
    TRI.   Ay, 't is very pregnant.
    SUB. And then the turning of this lawyer's
    pewter
To plate at Christmas ——
    ANA.   Christ-tide, I pray you.
    SUB. Yet, Ananias?
    ANA.   I have done.
    SUB.   Or changing
His parcel [11] gilt to massy gold. You cannot
But raise you friends. Withal, to be of power
To pay an army in the field, to buy
The King of France out of his realms, or Spain
Out of his Indies. What can you not do
Against lords spiritual or temporal,   50
That shall oppone [12] you?
    TRI.   Verily, 't is true.
We may be temporal lords ourselves, I take it.
    SUB. You may be anything, and leave off to
    make
Long-winded exercises; or suck up
Your *ha!* and *hum!* in a tune. I not deny
But such as are not graced in a state,
May, for their ends, be adverse in religion,
And get a tune to call the flock together;
For, to say sooth, a tune does much with
    women
And other phlegmatic people; it is your bell.
    ANA. Bells are profane; a tune may be
    religious.   61
    SUB. No warning with you? Then fare-
    well my patience.
'Slight, it shall down; I will not be thus tor-
    tur'd.
    TRI. I pray you, sir.
    SUB.   All shall perish. I have spoke it.
    TRI. Let me find grace, sir, in your eyes;
    the man,
He stands corrected: neither did his zeal,
But as yourself, allow a tune somewhere,
Which now, being to'ard [13] the stone, we shall
    not need.
    SUB. No, nor your holy vizard, [14] to win
    widows

---

[5] The Puritans remain on stage, but the scene is now a room in Lovewit's house.
[6] A slow furnace; a circulatory alembic.
[7] Modifies the situation.
[8] The elixir in a particular form and color. Q *Talck;* Ff *Talek.*
[9] Lovers.   [10] Rubbing.   [11] Partly.
[12] Oppose.   [13] On the point of attaining to.
[14] Mask of holiness.

To give you legacies, or make zealous wives   70
To rob their husbands for the common cause ;
Nor take the start of bonds broke but one day,
And say they were forfeited by providence.
Nor shall you need o'er night to eat huge
    meals,
To celebrate your next day's fast the better ;
The whilst the brethren and the sisters, hum-
    bled,
Abate the stiffness of the flesh.   Nor cast
Before your hungry hearers scrupulous
    bones ; [15]
As whether a Christian may hawk or hunt,
Or whether matrons of the holy assembly   80
May lay their hair out, or wear doublets,
Or have that idol, starch, about their linen.
    ANA. It is indeed an idol.
    TRI.   Mind him not, sir. —
I do command thee, spirit (of zeal, but trouble),
To peace within him. — Pray you, sir, go on.
    SUB. Nor shall you need to libel 'gainst the
    prelates,
And shorten so your ears [16] against the hearing
Of the next wire-drawn grace.   Nor of neces-
    sity
Rail against plays, to please the alderman
Whose daily custard you devour ; nor lie   90
With zealous rage till you are hoarse.   Not one
Of these so singular arts.   Nor call yourselves
By names of Tribulation, Persecution,
Restraint, Long-patience, and such like,
    affected
By the whole family or wood [17] of you,
Only for glory, and to catch the ear
Of the disciple.
    TRI.   Truly, sir, they are
Ways that the godly brethren have invented
For propagation of the glorious [18] cause,
As very notable means, and whereby also   100
Themselves grow soon, and profitably, famous.
    SUB. O, but the stone, all's idle to it ! [19]
    nothing !
The art of angels, nature's miracle,
The divine secret that doth fly in clouds
From east to west ; and whose tradition
Is not from men, but spirits.
    ANA.   I hate traditions ; [20]
I do not trust them ——
    TRI.   Peace !
    ANA.   They are popish all.
I will not peace.   I will not ——

---

[15] Bones of contention concerning scruples.
[16] Have them cropped in punishment.
[17] Collection, miscellaneous lot.   [18] Q *holy*.
[19] In comparison with it.
[20] Ananias considers the Bible sufficient.

    TRI.   Ananias !
    ANA. Please the profane, to grieve the
    godly ; I may not.
    SUB. Well, Ananias, thou shalt overcome.
    TRI. It is an ignorant zeal that haunts
    him, sir ;   111
But truly else a very faithful brother,
A botcher, [21] and a man by revelation
That hath a competent knowledge of the
    truth.
    SUB. Has he a competent sum there i' the
    bag
To buy the goods within ? I am made guardian,
And must, for charity and conscience' sake,
Now see the most be made for my poor orphan ;
Though I desire the brethren, too, good
    gainers.
There they are within. When you have
    view'd and bought 'em,   120
And ta'en the inventory of what they are,
They are ready for projection ; there's no
    more
To do : cast on the med'cine, so much silver
As there is tin there, so much gold as brass,
I'll gi' it you in by weight.
    TRI.   But how long time,
Sir, must the saints expect [22] yet ?
    SUB.   Let me see,
How's the moon now ? Eight, nine, ten days
    hence,
He will be silver potate ; [23] then three days
Before he citronize. [24]   Some fifteen days,
The magisterium will be perfected.   130
    ANA. About the second day of the third
    week,
In the ninth month ?
    SUB.   Yes, my good Ananias.
    TRI. What will the orphans' goods arise to,
    think you ?
    SUB. Some hundred marks, as much as
    fill'd three cars,
Unladed now ; you'll make six millions of
    'em ——
But I must ha' more coals laid in.
    TRI.   How !
    SUB.   Another load,
And then we ha' finish'd. We must now in-
    crease
Our fire to *ignis ardens*; [25] we are past
Fimus equinus, balnei, cineris,[26]

---

[21] A tailor whose work is limited to repairs.
[22] Wait.
[23] The elixir will be liquefied silver.
[24] Turn the color of citron.
[25] A hot fire.
[26] Heat of horse-dung, warm bath, (and) ashes.

And all those lenter [27] heats. If the holy
purse   140
Should with this draught fall low, and that [28]
the saints
Do need a present sum, I have [a] [29] trick
To melt the pewter you shall buy now in-
stantly,
And with a tincture make you as good Dutch
dollars
As any are in Holland.

TRI.   Can you so?

SUB. Ay, and shall bide the third examination.

ANA. It will be joyful tidings to the brethren.

SUB. But you must carry it secret.

TRI.   Ay ; but stay :
This act of coining, is it lawful?

ANA.   Lawful!
We know no magistrate ; or, if we did,   150
This 's foreign coin.

SUB.   It is no coining, sir.
It is but casting.

TRI.   Ha ! you distinguish well ;
Casting of money may be lawful.

ANA.   'T is, sir.

TRI. Truly, I take it so.

SUB.   There is no scruple,
Sir, to be made of it ; believe Ananias :
This case of conscience he is studied in.

TRI. I 'll make a question of it to the
brethren.

ANA. The brethren shall approve it lawful,
doubt not.
Where shall 't be done?

SUB.   For that we 'll talk anon.
                              Knock without.
There 's some to speak with me. Go in, I
pray you,   160
And view the parcels. That 's the inventory.
I 'll come to you straight. [*Exeunt* TRIBULA-
    TION *and* ANANIAS.] Who is it? —
Face ! appear.

SCENE III [30]

[*To*] SUBTLE [*enter*] FACE [*in his uniform*].

SUB. How now? good prize?

FACE.   Good pox ! Yond' costive cheater
Never came on.

SUB.   How then?

FACE.   I ha' walk'd the round
Till now, and no such thing.

SUB.   And ha' you quit him?

27 Gentler.   28 If.   29 Add. F 2.   30 The same.

FACE. Quit him ! An hell would quit him
too, he were happy.
'Slight ! would you have me stalk like a mill-
jade,
All day, for one that will not yield us grains?
I know him of old.

SUB.   Oh, but to ha' gull'd him
Had been a mast'ry.

FACE.   Let him go, black [31] boy,
And turn thee, that some fresh news may pos-
sess thee.
A noble count, a don of Spain, my dear   10
Delicious compeer, and my party [32]-bawd,
Who is come hither private for his conscience
And brought munition with him, six great
slops,[33]
Bigger than three Dutch hoys,[34] beside round
trunks,[35]
Furnish'd with pistolets,[36] and pieces of eight,[37]
Will straight be here, my rogue, to have thy
bath,
(That is the color,[38]) and to make his batt'ry
Upon our Dol, our castle, our cinque-port,[39]
Our Dover pier, our what thou wilt. Where is
she?
She must prepare perfumes, delicate linen, 20
The bath in chief, a banquet, and her wit,
For she must milk [40] his epididymis.
Where is the doxy? [41]

SUB.   I 'll send her to thee,
And but dispatch my brace of little John Ley-
dens [42]
And come again myself.

FACE.   Are they within then?

SUB. Numb'ring the sum.

FACE.   How much?

SUB.   A hundred marks, boy. [*Exit.*]

FACE. Why, this 's a lucky day. Ten
pounds of Mammon !
Three o' my clerk ! A portague o' my grocer !
This o' the brethren ! Beside reversions
And states to come, i' the widow, and my
count !   30
My share to-day will not be bought for forty —

[*Enter* DOL.]

DOL.   What?

31 Foul, malignant.   32 Partner.
33 Big breeches.   34 Small coasting vessels.
35 Trunk hose.
36 Gold coins worth about $1.50 each.
37 Spanish dollars (*pesos*), worth eight reals each.
38 Pretext.
39 One of the five fortified and specially privileged
ports of southeastern England ; *i.e.*, (cf. "Dover
pier") our port of entry for the goods of the don.
40 Q *feele.*   41 Harlot, wench.
42 See on II, v, 13.

FACE. Pounds, dainty Dorothy! Art thou so near?

DOL. Yes; say, Lord General, how fares our camp? [43]

FACE. As with the few that had entrench'd themselves
Safe, by their discipline, against a world, Dol,
And laugh'd within those trenches, and grew fat
With thinking on the booties, Dol, brought in
Daily by their small parties. This dear hour,
A doughty don is taken with my Dol;
And thou mayst make his ransom what thou wilt,   40
My Dousabel.[44] He shall be brought here, fetter'd
With thy fair looks, before he sees thee; and thrown
In a down-bed, as dark as any dungeon;
Where thou shalt keep him waking with thy drum;
Thy drum, my Dol, thy drum; till he be tame
As the poor blackbirds were i' the great frost,[45]
Or bees are with a basin;[46] and so hive him
I' the swan-skin coverlid and cambric sheets,
Till he work honey and wax, my little God's-gift.[47]

DOL. What is he, General?

FACE.   An ad[e]lantado,[48]   50
A grandee, girl. Was not my Dapper here yet?

DOL. No.

FACE.   Nor my Drugger?

DOL.   Neither.

FACE.   A pox on 'em,
They are so long a-furnishing! Such stinkards
Would not be seen upon these festival days. —

[*Re-enter* SUBTLE.]

How now! ha' you done?

SUB.   Done. They are gone; the sum
Is here in bank, my Face. I would we knew
Another chapman now would buy 'em out-right.

FACE. 'Slid, Nab shall do 't against he ha' the widow,
To furnish household.

SUB.   Excellent, well thought on;
Pray God he come.

FACE.   I pray he keep away   60
Till our new business be o'erpast.

SUB.   But, Face,
How cam'st thou by this secret don?

[FACE.]   A spirit
Brought me th' intelligence in a paper here,
As I was conjuring yonder in my circle [49]
For Surly; I ha' my flies [50] abroad. Your bath
Is famous, Subtle, by my means. Sweet Dol,
You must go tune your virginal, no losing
O' the least time. And — do you hear? good action!
Firk [51] like a flounder; kiss like a scallop, close;
And tickle him with thy mother tongue. His great   70
Verdugoship [52] has not a jot of language;
So much the easier to be cozen'd, my Dolly.
He will come here in a hir'd coach, obscure,
And our own coachman, whom I have sent as guide,
No creature else. (*One knocks.*) Who's that?
                    [DOL *goes to the window.*]

SUB.   It i' not he?

FACE. Oh, no, not yet this hour.

SUB.   Who is 't?

DOL.   Dapper,
Your clerk.

FACE.   God's will then, Queen of Faërie,
On with your tire; [53] [*Exit* DOL.] and, Doctor, with your robes.
Let's despatch him, for God's sake.

SUB.   'T will be long.

FACE. I warrant you, take but the cues I give you,   80
It shall be brief enough. [*Goes to the window.*]
    'Slight, here are more!
Abel, and I think the angry boy, the heir,
That fain would quarrel.

SUB.   And the widow?

FACE.   No,
Not that I see. Away! — O sir, you are welcome.   [*Exit* SUBTLE.]

SCENE IV [54]

[*To*] FACE [*enter*] DAPPER.

FACE. The Doctor is within a-moving for you. —
I have had the most ado to win him to it.—
He swears you 'll be the darling o' the dice:

---

[43] *Spanish Tragedy*, I, i, 1.
[44] *Douce et belle.*   [45] Of 1608.
[46] By beating on a basin.
[47] The Greek meaning of *Dorothea.*
[48] Governor (Span.).

[49] *I.e.*, as he "walk'd the round" at the Temple Church.
[50] Familiar spirits.   [51] Be frisky.
[52] Verdugo = hangman. Possibly an allusion to Surly's extensive wardrobe.
[53] Attire, costume.
[54] The same.

He never heard her Highness dote till now,
  he says.[55]
Your aunt has giv'n you the most gracious
  words
That can be thought on.
  DAP.   Shall I see her Grace?
  FACE. See her, and kiss her too. —

  [*Enter* ABEL *and* KASTRIL.]

                          What, honest Nab!
Hast brought the damask?
  NAB.   No, sir; here's tobacco.
  FACE. 'T is well done, Nab. Thou'lt bring
    the damask too?
  DRUG. Yes. Here's the gentleman, Cap-
    tain, Master Kastril,   10
I have brought to see the Doctor.
  FACE.   Where's the widow?
  DRUG. Sir, as he likes,[56] his sister, he says,
    shall come.
  FACE. O, is it so? 'Good time. Is your
    name Kastril, sir?
  KAS. Ay, and the best o' the Kastrils, I'd
    be sorry else,
By fifteen hundred a year.[57] Where is this
    doctor?
My mad tobacco boy here tells me of one
That can do things. Has he any skill?
  FACE.   Wherein, sir?
  KAS. To carry a business, manage a quarrel
    fairly,
Upon fit terms.
  FACE.   It seems, sir, you are but young
About the town, that can make that a ques-
    tion!
  KAS. Sir, not so young but I have heard
    some speech   21
Of the angry boys,[58] and seen 'em take
    tobacco,
And in his shop; and I can take it too.
And I would fain be one of 'em, and go down
And practise i' the country.
  FACE.   Sir, for the duello,
The Doctor, I assure you, shall inform you,
To the least shadow of a hair; and show you
An instrument he has, of his own making,
Wherewith, no sooner shall you make report
Of any quarrel, but he will take the height
    on 't
Most instantly, and tell in what degree   31
Of safety it lies in, or mortality.

And how it may be borne, whether in a right
    line,
Or a half circle; or may else be cast
Into an angle blunt, if not acute;
And this he will demonstrate. And then,
    rules
To give and take the lie by.
  KAS.   How! to take it?
  FACE. Yes, in oblique he'll show you, or
    in circle;[59]
But never in diameter.[60] The whole town
Study his theorems, and dispute them ordi-
    narily   40
At the eating academies.
  KAS.   But does he teach
Living by the wits too?
  FACE.   Anything whatever.
You cannot think that subtlety but he reads it.
He made me a captain. I was a stark pimp,
Just o' your standing, 'fore I met with him;
It i' not two months since. I'll tell you his
    method:
First, he will enter you at some ordinary.
  KAS. No, I'll not come there; you shall
    pardon me.
  FACE.   For why, sir?
  KAS. There's gaming there, and tricks.
  FACE.   Why, would you be
A gallant, and not game?
  KAS.   Ay, 't will spend a man.   50
  FACE. Spend you! It will repair you when
    you are spent.
How do they live by their wits there, that have
    vented
Six times your fortunes?
  KAS.   What, three thousand a year?
  FACE. Ay, forty thousand.
  KAS.   Are there such?
  FACE.   Ay, sir,
And gallants yet. Here's a young gentleman
Is born to nothing — [*pointing to* DAPPER]
    forty marks a year,
Which I count nothing. H' is to be initiated,
And have a fly o' the Doctor. He will win you
By unresistible luck, within this fortnight, 59
Enough to buy a barony. They will set him
Upmost, at the groom porter's,[61] all the Christ-
    mas;
And for the whole year through at every place
Where there is play, present him with the
    chair,

55 Q om. *he says.*
56 According as he likes (the doctor).
57 *I.e.,* I am richer by £1500 a year than the
others.
58 "Roaring boys", young bucks, "sports."

59 Forms of the lie circumstantial.
60 The lie direct.
61 This officer of the royal household had charge
of gaming at court.

The best attendance, the best drink, some-
    times
Two glasses of Canary, and pay nothing ;
The purest linen and the sharpest knife,
The partridge next his trencher ; and some-
    where
The dainty bed, in private, with the dainty.
You shall ha' your ordinaries bid for him,
As playhouses for a poet ; and the master 70
Pray him aloud to name what dish he affects,
Which must be butter'd shrimps ; and those
    that drink
To no mouth else, will drink to his, as being
The goodly president mouth of all the board.
    KAS. Do you not gull one?
    FACE.   'Ods my life ! Do you think it?
You shall have a cast commander, (can but get
In credit with a glover, or a spurrier,
For some two pair of either's ware aforehand,)
Will, by most swift posts, dealing with him,
Arrive at competent means to keep himself, 80
His punk, and naked boy, in excellent fashion,
And be admir'd for 't.
    KAS.   Will the Doctor teach this?
    FACE. He will do more, sir ; when your
    land is gone,
(As men of spirit hate to keep earth long),
In a vacation, when small money is stirring,
And ordinaries suspended till the term,
He 'll show a perspective,[62] where on one side
You shall behold the faces and the persons
Of all sufficient young heirs in town,
Whose bonds are current for commodity ; [63]
On th' other side, the merchants' forms, and
    others,   91
That without help of any second broker,
Who would expect a share, will trust such
    parcels ;
In the third square, the very street and sign
Where the commodity dwells, and does but wait
To be deliver'd, be it pepper, soap,
Hops, or tobacco, oatmeal, woad,[64] or cheeses.
All which you may so handle, to enjoy
To your own use, and never stand oblig'd. 99
    KAS. I' faith ! is he such a fellow?
    FACE.   Why, Nab here knows him.

[62] A multiple picture, which showed two or more
separate subjects, according to the angle from which
one looked at it.
[63] Alluding to the commodity swindle. The borrower had to take part or all of the loan in kind ; this
was likely to be inferior in quality or to consist of
highly specialized goods for which there was little or
no demand. Through an agent the swindler would
then buy them back at a fraction of their value
as computed in the loan, and retaining a handsome
profit return them to the merchant who had lent
them to him.   [64] A dyestuff.

And then for making matches for rich widows,
Young gentlewomen, heirs, the fortunat'st
    man !
He 's sent to, far and near, all over England,
To have his counsel, and to know their for-
    tunes.
    KAS. God's will, my suster shall see him.
    FACE.   I 'll tell you, sir,
What he did tell me of Nab. It 's a strange
    thing ! —
By the way, you must eat no cheese, Nab ; it
    breeds melancholy,
And that same melancholy breeds worms, —
    but pass it —
He told me honest Nab here was ne'er at
    tavern   109
But once in 's life !
    DRUG.   Truth, and no more I was not.
    FACE. And then he was so sick ——
    DRUG.   Could he tell you that too?
    FACE. How should I know it?
    DRUG.   In troth, we had been a-shooting,
And had a piece of fat ram-mutton to supper,
That lay so heavy o' my stomach ——
    FACE.   And he has no head
To bear any wine ; for what with the noise o'
    the fiddlers,
And care of his shop, for he dares keep no
    servants ——
    DRUG. My head did so ache ——
    FACE.   As he was fain to be brought
    home.
The Doctor told me ; and then a good old
    woman ——
    DRUG. Yes, faith, she dwells in Seacoal
    Lane, — did cure me,   119
With sodden ale, and pellitory [65] o' the wall,
Cost me but twopence. I had another sickness
Was worse than that.
    FACE.   Ay, that was with the grief
Thou took'st for being 'sess'd [66] at eighteen-
    pence,
For the waterwork.
    DRUG.   In truth, and it was like
T' have cost me almost my life.
    FACE.   Thy hair went off?
    DRUG. Yes, sir ; 't was done for spite.
    FACE.   Nay, so says the Doctor.
    KAS. Pray thee, tobacco boy, go fetch my
    suster ;
I 'll see this learned boy before I go ;
And so shall she.
    FACE.   Sir, he is busy now ;
But if you have a sister to fetch hither,   130

[65] A medicinal root.   [66] Assessed.

Perhaps your own pains may command her
  sooner ;
And he by that time will be free.
  Kas.   I go. [*Exit.*]
  Face. Drugger, she 's thine : the damask !
    [*Exit* Drugger.] — [*aside*] Subtle and I
Must wrastle for her. — Come on, Master
  Dapper.
You see how I turn clients here away,
To give your cause dispatch. Ha' you per-
  form'd
The ceremonies were enjoin'd you ?
  Dap.   Yes, o' the vinegar,
And the clean shirt.
  Face.   'T is well ; that shirt may do you
More worship than you think.   Your aunt 's
  afire,
But that she will not show it, t' have a sight
  on you.   140
Ha' you provided for her Grace's servants ?
  Dap. Yes, here are sixscore Edward shil-
    lings.
  Face.   Good.
  Dap. And an old Harry's sovereign.[67]
  Face.   Very good.
  Dap. And three James shillings, and an
    Elizabeth groat :
Just twenty nobles.[68]
  Face.   Oh, you are too just.
I would you had had the other noble in
  Maries.[69]
  Dap. I have some Philip and Maries.
  Face.   Ay, those same
Are best of all.   Where are they ?   Hark, the
  doctor.

Scene V [70]

[*To*] Face [*and*] Dapper [*enter*] Subtle, *disguis'd like a priest of Faërie.*

  Sub. Is yet her Grace's cousin come ?
  Face.   He is come.
  Sub. And is he fasting ?
  Face.   Yes.
  Sub.   And hath cried " hum " ?
  Face. Thrice, you must answer.
  Dap.   Thrice.
  Sub.   And as oft " buz " ?
  Face. If you have, say.
  Dap.   I have.
  Sub.   Then, to her coz,
Hoping that he hath vinegar'd his senses,

As he was bid, the Fairy Queen dispenses,
By me, this robe, the petticoat of Fortune ;
Which that he straight put on, she doth impor-
  tune.
And though to Fortune near be her petticoat,
Yet nearer is her smock, the Queen doth
  note ;   10
And therefore, even of that a piece she hath
  sent,
Which, being a child, to wrap him in was rent ;
And prays him for a scarf he now will wear it,
With as much love as then her Grace did tear
  it,
About his eyes, to show he is fortunate.
            They blind him with a rag.
And, trusting unto her to make his state,
He 'll throw away all worldly pelf about him ;
Which that he will perform, she doth not doubt
  him.
  Face. She need not doubt him, sir.   Alas,
    he has nothing
But what he will part withal as willingly,   20
Upon her Grace's word — throw away your
  purse —
As she would ask it : — handkerchiefs and
  all —
She cannot bid that thing but he 'll obey. —
If you have a ring about you, cast it off,
Or a silver seal at your wrist ; her Grace will
  send (*He throws away, as they bid him.*)
Her fairies here to search you ; therefore deal
Directly [71] with her Highness.   If they find
That you conceal a mite, you are undone.
  Dap. Truly, there 's all.
  Face.   All what ?
  Dap.   My money ; truly.
  Face. Keep nothing that is transitory
    about you.   30
— [*aside to* Subtle] Bid Dol play music. —
    Look, the elves are come
            Dol *enters with a cittern.*
To pinch you, if you tell not truth. (*They
    pinch him.*) Advise you.
  Dap. Oh, I have a paper with a spur-ryal [72]
    in 't.
  Face.   *Ti, ti.* —
They knew 't, they say.
  Sub.   *Ti, ti, ti, ti ;* — he has more yet.
  Face. *Ti, ti-ti-ti.*   I' the tother pocket ?
  Sub.   *Titi, titi, titi, titi.* —
They must pinch him or he will never confess,
    they say.   [*They pinch him again.*]

[67] Valued, says Whalley, at only ten shillings.
[68] Worth 6*s*. 8*d*. each.
[69] Since all the other reigns since Henry VIII are
represented.
[70] The same.
[71] Straightforwardly.
[72] Spur-royal, a gold coin of Edward IV, worth
15*s*. ; so-called because the sun on it looked like the
rowel of a spur.

DAP. Oh, oh!

FACE. Nay, pray you, hold; he is her Grace's nephew —

Ti, ti, ti! — What care you! Good faith, you shall care. — 39
Deal plainly, sir, and shame the fairies. Show
You are an innocent.

DAP. By this good light, I ha' nothing.

SUB. *Ti ti, ti ti to, ta.* — He does equivocate she says.

Ti, ti do ti, ti ti do, ti da, — and swears by the light when he is blinded.

DAP. By this good dark, I ha' nothing but a half-crown
Of gold about my wrist, that my love gave me;
And a leaden heart I wore sin' she forsook me.

FACE. I thought 't was something. And would you incur
Your aunt's displeasure for these trifles? Come,
I had rather you had thrown away twenty half-crowns. [*Takes it off.*]
You may wear your leaden heart still. — [*aside*] How now! 50
[DOL *comes from the window.*]

SUB. [*aside*] What news, Dol?

DOL. [*aside*] Yonder 's your knight, Sir Mammon.

FACE. [*aside*] God's lid, we never thought of him till now.
Where is he?

DOL. [*aside*] Here hard by. H' is at the door.

SUB. [*aside*] And you are not ready, now! Dol, get his suit. [*Exit* DOL.]
He must not be sent back.

FACE. [*aside*] O, by no means.
What shall we do with this same puffin here, Now he 's o' the spit?

SUB. [*aside*] Why, lay him back awhile, With some device.

[*Re-enter* DOL *with* FACE's *clothes.*]

— *Ti, ti ti, ti ti ti.* Would her Grace speak with me?
I come. — [*aside*] Help, Dol![73]

FACE. (*speaks* [*aside*] *through the keyhole, the other knocking*) Who 's there?
Sir Epicure;
My master 's i' the way. Please you to walk
Three or four turns, but till his back be turn'd, 61
And I am for you. — [*aside*] Quickly, Dol!

[73] Help Face out of his uniform and into his servant's clothes.

SUB. Her Grace
Commends her kindly to you, Master Dapper.

DAP. I long to see her Grace.

SUB. She now is set
At dinner in her bed, and she has sent you
From her own private trencher, a dead mouse,
And a piece of gingerbread, to be merry withal,
And stay your stomach, lest you faint with fasting.
Yet if you could hold out till she saw you, she says,
It would be better for you.

FACE. Sir, he shall 70
Hold out, an 't were this two hours, for her Highness;
I can assure you that. We will not lose
All we ha' done. ——

SUB. He must not see, nor speak
To anybody, till then.

FACE. For that we 'll put, sir,
A stay in 'is mouth.

SUB. Of what?

FACE. Of gingerbread.
Make you it fit. He that hath pleas'd her Grace
Thus far, shall not now crinkle,[74] for a little —
Gape, sir, and let him fit you.
[*They thrust a gag of gingerbread into his mouth.*]

SUB. [*aside*] Where shall we now Bestow him?

DOL. [*aside*] I' the privy. —

SUB. Come along, sir,
I must now show you Fortune's privy lodgings. 80

FACE. Are they perfum'd, and his bath ready?

SUB. All;
Only, the fumigation 's somewhat strong.

FACE. [*speaking through the keyhole*] Sir Epicure, I am yours, sir, by and by.[75]
[*Exeunt all but* FACE.]

ACT IV — SCENE I[1]

[*To*] FACE [*enter*] MAMMON.

FACE. Oh, sir, yo' are come i' the only finest time ——

MAM. Where 's master?

FACE. Now preparing for projection, sir.
Your stuff will b' all chang'd shortly.

MAM. Into gold?

[74] Turn aside.   [75] At once.   [1] The same.

FACE. To gold and silver, sir.

MAM.   Silver I care not for.

FACE. Yes, sir, a little to give beggars.

MAM.   Where 's the lady?

FACE. At hand here. I ha' told her such
brave things o' you,

Touching your bounty and your noble spirit —

MAM.   Hast thou?

FACE. As she is almost in her fit to see you.
But, good sir, no divinity ² i' your conference,
For fear of putting her in rage ——

MAM.   I warrant thee. 10

FACE. Six men will not hold her down.
And then,

If the old man should hear or see you ——

MAM.   Fear not.

FACE. The very house, sir, would run mad.
You know it,

How scrupulous he is, and violent,

'Gainst the least act of sin. Physic or mathematics,

Poetry, state,³ or bawdry, as I told you,

She will endure, and never startle ; but

No word of controversy.

MAM.   I am school'd, good Ulen.

FACE. And you must praise her house, remember that,

And her nobility.

MAM.   Let me alone :   20

No herald, no, nor antiquary, Lungs,

Shall do it better. Go.

FACE. [aside]   Why, this is yet

A kind of modern happiness,⁴ to have

Dol Common for a great lady.   [Exit.]

MAM.   Now, Epicure,

Heighten thyself ; talk to her all in gold ;

Rain her as many showers as Jove did drops

Unto his Danaë ; show the god a miser,

Compar'd with Mammon. What ! the stone
will do 't.

She shall feel gold, taste gold, hear gold, sleep
gold ;

Nay, we will *concumbere* gold. I will be
puissant,   30

And mighty in my talk to her ! —

[*Re-enter* FACE *with* DOL *richly dressed.*]

               Here she comes.

FACE. [aside] To him, Dol ; suckle him. —
This is the noble knight

I told your Ladyship ——

MAM.   Madam, with your pardon,

I kiss your vesture.

---

² Theology.   ³ Politics.
⁴ Felicity, appropriateness.

DOL.   Sir, I were uncivil

If I would suffer that ; my lip to you, sir.

MAM. I hope my Lord your brother be in
health, lady?

DOL. My Lord my brother is, though I no
lady, sir.

FACE. [aside] Well said, my Guinea bird.⁵

MAM.   Right noble madam ——

FACE [aside] Oh, we shall have most fierce
idolatry !

MAM. 'T is your prerogative.

DOL.   Rather your courtesy. 40

MAM. Were there naught else t' enlarge
your virtues to me,

These answers speak your breeding and your
blood.

DOL. Blood we boast none, sir ; a poor
baron's daughter.

MAM. Poor ! and gat you? Profane not.
Had your father

Slept all the happy remnant of his life

After that act, lien but there still, and panted,

H' had done enough to make himself, his issue,

And his posterity noble.

DOL.   Sir, although

We may be said to want the gilt and trappings,

The dress of honor, yet we strive to keep   50

The seeds and the materials.

MAM.   I do see

The old ingredient, virtue, was not lost,

Nor the drug, money, us'd to make your compound.

There is a strange nobility i' your eye,

This lip, that chin ! Methinks you do resemble

One o' the Austriack princes.

FACE. [aside]   Very like !

Her father was an Irish costermonger.

MAM. The house of Valois just had such a
nose,

And such a forehead yet the Medici

Of Florence boast.

DOL.   Troth, and I have been lik'ned 60

To all these princes.

FACE. [aside]   I 'll be sworn, I heard it.

MAM. I know not how ! it is not any one,

But e'en the very choice of all their features.

FACE. [aside] I 'll in, and laugh.   [Exit.]

MAM.   A certain touch, or air,

That sparkles a divinity beyond

An earthly beauty !

DOL.   Oh, you play the courtier.

MAM. Good lady, gi' me leave ——

DOL.   In faith, I may not,

To mock me, sir.

---

⁵ "Guinea-hen" = prostitute.

MAM.　　　　To burn i' this sweet flame ;
The phoenix never knew a nobler death.

　　DOL. Nay, now you court the courtier, and
　　　　destroy　　　　　　　　　　　　　　70
What you would build.　This art, sir, i' your
　　words,
Calls your whole faith in question.

　　MAM.　　　　　　　By my soul ——

　　DOL. Nay, oaths are made o' the same air,
　　　　sir.

　　MAM.　　　　Nature
Never bestow'd upon mortality
A more unblam'd, a more harmonious feature ;
She play'd the stepdame in all faces else :
Sweet madam, le' me be particular ——

　　DOL. Particular,[6] sir !　I pray you, know
　　　　your distance.

　　MAM. In no ill sense, sweet lady : but to ask
How your fair graces pass the hours?　I see　80
Yo' are lodg'd here, i' the house of a rare man,
An excellent artist ; but what's that to you?

　　DOL. Yes, sir.　I study here the mathe-
　　　　matics,
And distillation.[7]

　　MAM.　　　　O, I cry your pardon.
H' is a divine instructor !　can extract
The souls of all things by his art ; call all
The virtues, and the miracles of the sun,
Into a temperate furnace ; teach dull nature
What her own forces are.　A man, the emp'ror
Has courted above Kelley ; [8] sent his medals
And chains, t' invite him.

　　DOL.　　　Ay, and for his physic, sir ——

　　MAM. Above the art of Aesculapius,　　92
That drew the envy of the thunderer ! [9]
I know all this, and more.

　　DOL.　　　　Troth, I am taken, sir,
Whole with these studies that contemplate na-
　　ture.

　　MAM. It is a noble humor.　But this form
Was not intended to so dark a use !
Had you been crooked, foul, of some coarse
　　mold,
A cloister had done well ; but such a feature,
That might stand up the glory of a kingdom,
To live recluse is a mere solecism,　　101
Though in a nunnery !　It must not be.
I muse my Lord your brother will permit it !
You should spend half my land first, were I he.
Does not this diamond better on my finger
Than i' the quarry?

　　DOL.　　　　Yes.

　　MAM.　　　　　Why, you are like it.
You were created, lady, for the light !
Here, you shall wear it ; take it, the first
　　pledge
Of what I speak, to bind you to believe me.

　　DOL. In chains of adamant? [10]

　　MAM.　　　Yes, the strongest bands.　110
And take a secret too. — Here, by your side,
Doth stand this hour the happiest man in
　　Europe.

　　DOL. You are contented, sir?

　　MAM.　　　　　Nay, in true being,
The envy of princes and the fear of states.

　　DOL. Say you so, Sir Epicure !

　　MAM.　　　Yes, and thou shalt prove it,
Daughter of honor.　I have cast mine eye
Upon thy form, and I will rear this beauty
Above all styles.

　　DOL.　　　　You mean no treason, sir !

　　MAM. No, I will take away that jealousy.
I am the lord of the philosopher's stone,　　120
And thou the lady.

　　DOL.　　　　How, sir !　ha' you that?

　　MAM. I am the master of the mast'ry [11]
This day the good old wretch here o' the house
Has made it for us.　Now he's at projec-
　　tion.
Think therefore thy first wish now, let me hear
　　it,
And it shall rain into thy lap, no shower,
But floods of gold, whole cataracts, a deluge,
To get a nation on thee !

　　DOL.　　　　You are pleas'd, sir,
To work on the ambition of our sex.

　　MAM. I am pleas'd the glory of her sex
　　　　should know　　　　　　　　　　130
This nook here of the Friars [12] is no climate
For her to live obscurely in, to learn
Physic and surgery, for the constable's wife
Of some odd hundred in Essex ; but come
　　forth,
And taste the air of palaces ; eat, drink
The toils of emp'rics,[13] and their boasted prac-
　　tice,
Tincture of pearl, and coral, gold, and amber ;
Be seen at feasts and triumphs ; have it ask'd
What miracle she is ; set all the eyes
Of court afire, like a burning glass,　　140
And work 'em into cinders, when the jewels
Of twenty states adorn thee, and the light

---

[6] Familiar.
[7] *I.e.*, astrology and alchemy.
[8] John Dee's partner ; Rudolph II, whom he visited at Prague in 1584, was one of his dupes.
[9] Zeus, who killed him with a thunderbolt.

[10] Punning on *diamond*, spelled *diamant* in the old eds.
[11] Magisterium, the "stone." (Trisyllabic.)
[12] Blackfriars.
[13] Experimenters, laboratory scientists.

Strikes out the stars; that, when thy name
    is mention'd,
Queens may look pale; and, we but showing
    our love,
Nero's Poppaea may be lost in story!
Thus will we have it.
    Dol.   I could well consent, sir.
But in a monarchy, how will this be?
The prince will soon take notice, and both
    seize
You and your stone, it being a wealth unfit
For any private subject.
    Mam.   If he knew it.   150
    Dol. Yourself do boast it, sir.
    Mam.   To thee, my life.
    Dol. Oh, but beware, sir! You may come
    to end
The remnant of your days in a loath'd prison,
By speaking of it.
    Mam.   'T is no idle fear!
We'll therefore go with all, my girl, and live
In a free state; where we will eat our mullets
Sous'd in high-country wines, sup pheasants'
    eggs,
And have our cockles boil'd in silver shells,
Our shrimps to swim again, as when they
    liv'd,
In a rare butter made of dolphins' milk,   160
Whose cream does look like opals; and with
    these
Delicate meats set ourselves high for pleas-
    ure,
And take us down again, and then renew
Our youth and strength with drinking the
    elixir,
And so enjoy a perpetuity
Of life and lust. And thou shalt ha' thy ward-
    robe
Richer than Nature's, still to change thyself,
And vary oft'ner, for thy pride, than she,
Or Art, her wise and almost equal servant.

              [Re-enter Face.]

    Face. Sir, you are too loud. I hear you
    every word   170
Into the laboratory. Some fitter place;
The garden, or great chamber above. —
    [aside] How like you her?
    Mam. Excellent, Lungs! There's for thee.
                      [Gives him money.]
    Face. *[aside]*   But do you hear?
Good sir, beware, no mention of the rabbins.
    Mam. We think not on 'em.
         [Exeunt Mammon and Dol.]
    Face.   O, it is well, sir. — Subtle!

SCENE II [14]

[To] Face *[enter]* Subtle.

    Face. Dost thou not laugh?
    Sub.   Yes. Are they gone?
    Face.   All's clear.
    Sub. The widow is come.
    Face.   And your quarreling disciple?
    Sub. Ay.
    Face.   I must to my captainship again
    then.
    Sub. Stay, bring 'em in first.
    Face.   So I meant. What is she?
A bonnibel? [15]
    Sub.   I know not.
    Face.   We'll draw lots.
You'll stand to that?
    Sub.   What else?
    Face.   Oh, for a suit,
To fall now like a curtain, flap! [16]
    Sub.   To th' door, man.
    Face. You'll ha' the first kiss, 'cause I am
    not ready.   *[Exit.]*
    Sub. Yes, and perhaps hit you through both
    the nostrils. [17]
    Face. *[within]* Who would you speak with?
    Kas. *[within]*   Where's the captain?
    Face. *[within]*   Gone, sir,   10
About some business.
    Kas. *[within]*   Gone!
    Face. *[within]*   He'll return straight.
But, Master Doctor, his lieutenant, is here.

    [Enter Kastril, and Dame Pliant.]

    Sub. Come near, my worshipful boy, my
    terrae fili,
That is, my boy of land [18]; make thy ap-
    proaches.
Welcome; I know thy lusts and thy desires,
And I will serve and satisfy 'em. Begin,
Charge me from thence, or thence, or in this
    line;
Here is my centre: ground thy quarrel.
    Kas.   You lie.
    Sub. How, child of wrath and anger! the
    loud lie?
For what, my sudden boy?
    Kas.   Nay, that look you to,   20
I am aforehand.
    Sub.   O, this 's no true grammar,

---

[14] The same.
[15] *Bonne et belle.*
[16] And so relieve him of the necessity of leaving
Subtle with the lady.
[17] Put your nose out of joint. (Neilson.)
[18] But it also means a person of obscure parentage.

And as ill logic![19] You must render causes,
　child,
Your first and second intentions, know your
　canons
And your divisions, moods, degrees, and differ-
　ences,
Your prædicaments, substance, and accident,
Series extern and intern, with their causes,
Efficient, material, formal, final,
And ha' your elements perfect —
KAS.　　　　　　　　　　What is this!
The angry [20] tongue he talks in?
SUB.　　　　　　　That false precept,
Of being aforehand, has deceiv'd a number,
And made 'em enter quarrels oftentimes　31
Before they were aware ; and afterward,
Against their wills.
KAS.　　　　　How must I do then, sir?
SUB. I cry this lady mercy ; she should first
Have been saluted. I do call you lady,
Because you are to be one ere 't be long,
My soft and buxom widow. (*He kisses her.*)
KAS.　　　　　　　Is she, i' faith?
SUB. Yes, or my art is an egregious liar.
KAS. How know you?
SUB.　　　　By inspection on her forehead,
And subtlety of her lip, which must be tasted
Often to make a judgment. (*He kisses her
　again.*) 'Slight, she melts　　　41
Like a myrobalan. Here is yet a line,
In *rivo frontis* [21] tells me he is no knight.
DAME P. What is he then, sir?
SUB.　　　　　　Let me see your hand.
O, your *linea fortunae* makes it plain ;
And *stella* here *in monte Veneris*,
But, most of all, *junctura annularis.* [22]
He is a soldier, or a man of art, lady,
But shall have some great honor shortly.
DAME P.　　　　　　　　Brother,
He 's a rare man, believe me!

[*Re enter* FACE, *in his uniform.*]

KAS.　　　　　Hold your peace.　50
Here comes the tother rare man. — 'Save you,
　Captain.
FACE. Good Master Kastril. Is this your
　sister?
KAS.　　　Ay, sir.
Please you to kuss her, and be proud to know
　her!

[19] The terms which follow are from the jargon of
scholastic philosophy. For the refinements of giving
and resenting the lie see such treatises as *The Book
of Honor and Arms* (1590) or Vincentio Saviola, *His
Practise* (1595).
　[20] Swaggering.　　　　[21] Frontal vein.
　[22] Stock phrases of palmistry.

FACE. I shall be proud to know you, lady.
　　　　　　　　　　　　[*Kisses her.*]
DAME P.　　　　　　　Brother,
He calls me lady, too.
KAS.　　　　　　Ay, peace. I heard it.
　　　　　　　　　　　[*Takes her aside.*]
FACE. The Count is come.
SUB.　　　　　　　Where is he?
FACE.　　　　　　　At the door.
SUB. Why, you must entertain him.
FACE.　　　　　　What 'll you do
With these the while?
SUB.　　　Why, have 'em up, and show 'em
Some fustian book,[23] or the dark [24] glass.
FACE.　　　　　　'Fore God,
She is a delicate dabchick! I must have her.
　　　　　　　　　　　　[*Exit.*]
SUB. Must you? Ay, if your fortune will,
　you must. —　　　　　　　61
Come, sir, the Captain will come to us pres-
　ently.
I 'll ha' you to my chamber of demonstrations,
Where I 'll show you both the grammar and
　logic
And rhetoric of quarreling, my whole method
Drawn out in tables, and my instrument,
That hath the several scale upon 't, shall make
　you
Able to quarrel at a straw's breadth by moon-
　light.
And, lady, I 'll have you look in a glass,　69
Some half an hour, but to clear your eyesight,
Against you see [25] your fortune ; which is
　greater
Than I may judge upon the sudden, trust me.
　　　　　　　　　　　　[*Exeunt.*]

SCENE III [26]

[*Enter*] FACE.

FACE. Where are you, Doctor?
SUB. [*within*]　I 'll come to you presently.
FACE. I will ha' this same widow, now I ha'
　seen her,
On any composition.[27]

[*Enter* SUBTLE]

SUB.　　　　　　What do you say?
FACE. Ha' you dispos'd of them?
SUB.　　　　　　I ha' sent 'em up.
FACE. Subtle, in troth, I needs must have
　this widow.
SUB. Is that the matter?

[23] Some book full of highfalutin.
[24] Secret.　　　[25] In preparation for seeing.
[26] The same.　　　[27] Terms.

FACE.   Nay, but hear me.
SUB.   Go to.
If you rebel once, Dol shall know it all ;
Therefore be quiet, and obey your chance.
    FACE. Nay, thou art so violent now — Do
      but conceive,
Thou art old, and canst not serve ——
    SUB.   Who cannot? I? 10
'Slight, I will serve her with thee, for a ——
    FACE.   Nay,
But understand ; I 'll gi' you composition.
    SUB. I will not treat with thee. What, sell
      my fortune?
'T is better than my birthright. Do not mur-
    mur.
Win her, and carry her. If you grumble, Dol
Knows it directly.
    FACE.   Well, sir, I am silent.
Will you go help to fetch in Don in state?
                              [Exit.]
    SUB. I follow you, sir. — We must keep
      Face in awe,
Or he will overlook us like a tyran[t]. —

[Re-enter FACE, *with]* SURLY *like a Spaniard.*

Brain of a tailor ! who comes here? Don
    John ! [28]   20
    SUR. *Señores, beso las manos à vuestras*
      mercedes.[29]
    SUB. Would you had stoop'd a little, and
      kiss'd our *anos.*
    FACE. Peace, Subtle !
    SUB.   Stab me ; I shall never hold, man.
He looks in that deep ruff like a head in a plat-
    ter,
Serv'd in by a short cloak upon two trestles ! [30]
    FACE. Or what do you say to a collar of
      brawn,[31] cut down
Beneath the souse,[32] and wriggled [33] with a
    knife?
    SUB. 'Slud, he does look too fat to be a
      Spaniard.
    FACE. Perhaps some Fleming or some Hol-
      lander got him
In d'Alva's [34] time ; Count Egmont's [35] bas-
    tard.
    SUB.   Don,   30
Your scurvy, yellow, Madrid face is welcome.

[28] Don John of Austria, the famous Spaniard who commanded at Lepanto.
[29] Gentlemen, I kiss hands to your Honors.
[30] Instead of like a human being.
[31] Neck (or rolled piece) of pork.
[32] Ear.   [33] Slashed.
[34] The Spanish Duke of Alva governed the Low Countries 1567–73.
[35] Egmont (d. 1568) was a famous Flemish patriot.

SUR. *Gratia.*
    SUB.   He speaks out of a fortification.
'Pray God he ha' no squibs in those deep sets.[36]
    SUR. *Por dios, señores, muy linda casa!* [37]
    SUB. What says he?
    FACE.   Praises the house, I think ;
I know no more but 's action.
    SUB.   Yes, the *casa,*
My precious Diego, will prove fair enough
To cozen you in. Do you mark? You shall
Be cozened, Diego.[38]
    FACE.   Cozened, do you see,
My worthy Donzel,[39] cozened.
    SUR.   *Entiendo.*[40] 40
    SUB. Do you intend it? So do we, dear
    Don.
Have you brought pistolets or portagues,
My solemn Don? — [*To* FACE] Dost thou feel
    any?
    FACE. *(feels his pockets.)*   Full.
    SUB. You shall be emptied, Don, pumped
      and drawn
Dry, as they say.
    FACE.   Milked, in troth, sweet Don.
    SUB. See all the monsters ; the great lion of
    all,[41] Don.
    SUR. *Con licencia, se puede ver à esta se-*
      ñora ? [42]
    SUB. What talks he now?
    FACE.   O' the señora.
    SUB.   Oh, Don,
This is the lioness, which you shall see
Also, my Don.
    FACE. 'Slid, Subtle, how shall we do? 50
    SUB. For what?
    FACE.   Why, Dol's employ'd, you know.
    SUB.   That 's true !
'Fore Heav'n I know not ; he must stay, that 's
    all.
    FACE. Stay ! that he must not, by no
    means.
    SUB.   No? why?
    FACE. Unless you 'll mar all. 'Slight, he 'll
    suspect it ;
And then he will not pay, not half so well.
This is a travell'd punk-master, and does know
All the delays ; a notable hot rascal,
And looks already rampant.
    SUB.   'Sdeath ! and Mammon
Must not be troubled.

[36] The plaits of his huge ruff.
[37] By God, gentlemen, a very handsome house.
[38] A name for a Spaniard.
[39] Diminutive of "Don."   [40] I understand.
[41] "Showing the lions" = showing the sights.
[42] If you please, may I see the lady?

FACE.   Mammon! in no case!

SUB. What shall we do then?

FACE.   Think: you must be sudden. 60

SUR. *Entiendo que la señora es tan hermosa, que codìcio tan à verla como la bien aventuránça de mi vida.*[43]

FACE. *Mi vida!* 'Slid, Subtle, he puts me in mind o' the widow.

What dost thou say to draw her to 't, ha?

And tell her it is her fortune? All our venture

Now lies upon it. It is but one man more,

Which on 's[44] chance to have her; and beside,

There is no maidenhead to be fear'd or lost.

What dost thou think on 't, Subtle?

SUB.   Who, I? why —— 70

FACE. The credit of our house too is en-gag'd.

SUB. You made me an offer for my share erewhile.

What wilt thou gi' me, i' faith?

FACE.   Oh, by that light,

I 'll not buy now. You know your doom[45] to me.

E'en take your lot, obey your chance, sir; win her,

And wear her — out, for me.[46]

SUB.   'Slight, I 'll not work her then.

FACE. It is the common cause; therefore bethink you.

Dol else must know it, as you said.

SUB.   I care not.

SUR. *Señores, porque se tarda tant[o]?*[47]

SUB. Faith, I am not fit; I am old.

FACE.   That 's now no reason, sir.

SUR. *Puede ser de hazer burla de mi amor?*[48]   81

FACE. You hear the don too? By this air I call,

And loose the hinges. Dol!

SUB.   A plague of hell ——

FACE. Will you then do?

SUB.   Yo' are a terrible rogue;

I 'll think of this. Will you, sir, call the widow?

FACE. Yes, and I 'll take her too with all her faults,

Now I do think on 't better.

SUB.   With all my heart, sir;

Am I discharg'd o' the lot?

FACE.   As you please.

SUB.   Hands. [*They shake hands.*]

FACE. Remember now, that upon any change   89

You never claim her.

SUB.   Much good joy and health to you, sir.

Marry a whore! Fate, let me wed a witch first.

SUR. *Por estas honradas barbas*[49] ——

SUB.   He swears by his beard.

Dispatch, and call the brother, too.

[*Exit* FACE.]

SUR. [*Tengo duda,*][50] *señores, que no me hágan alguna traycion.*[51]

SUB. How, issue on? Yes, *praesto, señor.* Please you

Enthratha the *chambratha*, worthy don;

Where if it please the fates, in your *bathada,*

You shall be soak'd, and strok'd, and tubb'd, and rubb'd,

And scrubb'd, and fubb'd,[52] dear don, before you go.   100

You shall in faith, my scurvy baboon don,

Be curried, claw'd, and flaw'd,[53] and taw'd,[54] indeed.

I will the heartilier go about it now,

And make the widow a punk so much the sooner,

To be reveng'd on this impetuous Face:

The quickly doing of it is the grace.

[*Exeunt* SUBTLE *and* SURLY.]

SCENE IV [55]

[*Enter*] FACE, KASTRIL, [*and*] DAME PLIANT.

FACE. Come, lady. — I knew the Doctor would not leave

Till he had found the very nick of her fortune.

KAS. To be a countess, say you?

[FACE.][56]   A Spanish countess, sir.

DAME P. Why, is that better than an English countess?

FACE. Better! 'Slight, make you that a question, lady?

KAS. Nay, she is a fool, Captain; you must pardon her.

FACE. Ask from your courtier to your inns-of-court man,

To your mere milliner; they will tell you all,

---

[43] I understand that the lady is so handsome that I long to see her as the most fortunate event of my life.

[44] Whichever of us.

[45] Decree.

[46] As far as I am concerned.

[47] Gentlemen, why such delay?

[48] Is it possible you make sport of my love?

[49] By this honored beard.

[50] Old eds. *Tiengo dùda.*

[51] I fear, gentlemen, that you play me some trick. (In this scene Jonson seems to have had the *Poenulus* of Plautus in view. — Gifford.)

[52] Cheated.   [53] Cracked.

[54] Soaked (like a hide in the tannery).

[55] The same.   [56] So Q; Ff omit.

Your Spanish jennet is the best horse ; your Spanish   9
Stoop is the best garb ; [57] your Spanish beard
Is the best cut ; your Spanish ruffs are the best
Wear ; your Spanish pavin the best dance ;
Your Spanish titillation in a glove
The best perfume. And for your Spanish pike,
And Spanish blade, let your poor Captain
    speak. —
Here comes the Doctor.

[*Enter* SUBTLE *with a paper.*]

SUB.   My most honor'd lady,
For so I am now to style you, having found
By this my scheme,[58] you are to undergo
An honorable fortune very shortly,   19
What will you say now, if some ——
    FACE.   I ha' told her all, sir,
And her right worshipful brother here, that
    she shall be
A countess ; do not delay 'em, sir ; a Spanish
    countess.
    SUB. Still, my scarce-worshipful Captain,
    you can keep
No secret ! Well, since he has told you,
    madam,
Do you forgive him, and I do.
    KAS.   She shall do that, sir ;
I 'll look to 't ; 't is my charge.
    SUB.   Well then. Naught rests
But that she fit her love now to her fortune.
    DAME P. Truly I shall never brook a Span-
    iard.
    SUB.   No?
    DAME P. Never sin' eighty-eight [59] could I
    abide 'em,
And that was some three year afore I was
    born, in truth.   30
    SUB. Come, you must love him, or be miser-
    able ;
Choose which you will.
    FACE.   By this good rush,[60] persuade her ;
She will cry [61] strawberries else within this
    twelvemonth.
    SUB. Nay, shads and mack'rel, which is
    worse.
    FACE.   Indeed, sir !
    KAS. God's lid, you shall love him, or I 'll
    kick you.
    DAME P.   Why,
I 'll do as you will ha' me, Brother.

[57] The Spanish bow is the best attitude or posture.
[58] Horoscope.
[59] The year of the Armada.
[60] Floors (and the stage) were strewn with rushes.
[61] As a hawker.

    KAS.   Do,
Or, by this hand, I 'll maul you.
    FACE.   Nay, good sir,
Be not so fierce.
    SUB.   No, my enraged child ;
She will be rul'd. What, when she comes to
    taste   39
The pleasures of a countess ! to be courted ——
    FACE. And kiss'd and ruffled !
    SUB.   Ay, behind the hangings.
    FACE. And then come forth in pomp !
    SUB.   And know her state !
    FACE. Of keeping all th' idolaters o' the
    chamber
Barer to her than at their prayers !
    SUB.   Is serv'd
Upon the knee !
    FACE.   And has her pages, [ushers],[62]
Footmen, and coaches ——
    SUB.   Her six mares ——
    FACE.   Nay, eight !
    SUB. To hurry her through London, to th'
    Exchange,[63]
Bet'lem,[64] the China-houses [65] ——
    FACE.   Yes, and have
The citizens gape at her, and praise her tires,
And my Lord's goose-turd [66] bands,[67] that
    rides with her !   50
    KAS. Most brave ! By this hand, you are
    not my suster
If you refuse.
    DAME P.   I will not refuse, Brother.

[*Enter* SURLY.]

    SUR. *Que es esto, señores, que non se venga?*
Esta tardanza me mata! [68]
    FACE.   It is the count come !
The Doctor knew he would be here, by his art.
    SUB. *En gallanta, madama, Don! gallantis-*
    sima!
    SUR. *Por todos los dioses, la mas acabada*
Hermosura, que he visto en mi vida! [69]
    FACE. Is 't not a gallant language that they
    speak?
    KAS. An admirable language ! Is 't not
    French?   60
    FACE. No, Spanish, sir.

[62] So F2 ; Q, F1, *huishers.*
[63] The Royal Exchange ; there were shops in it.
[64] A visit to Bethlehem Hospital, the London madhouse, was an Elizabethan amusement.
[65] Oriental shops.
[66] A shade of green.   [67] Collar.
[68] Why doesn't she come, gentlemen? This delay
is killing me.
[69] By all the gods, the most perfect beauty I have
seen in all my life.

KAS.   It goes like law French,
And that, they say, is the courtliest [70] lan-
    guage.

FACE.   List, sir.

SUR. *El sol ha perdido su lumbre, con el*
Resplandor que tràe esta dama! Valgame dios! [71]

FACE. He admires your sister.

KAS.   Must not she make curt'sy?

SUB. 'Ods will, she must go to him, man,
    and kiss him!
It is the Spanish fashion, for the women
To make first court.

FACE.   'T is true he tells you, sir:
His art knows all.

SUR.   *Porque no se acùde?* [72]

KAS. He speaks to her, I think?

FACE.   That he does, sir. 70

SUR. *Por el amor de dios, que es esto que se*
    tàrda? [73]

KAS. Nay, see; she will not understand
    him! Gull! Noddy!

DAME P. What say you, Brother?

KAS.   Ass, my suster!
Go kuss him, as the cunning man would ha'
    you;
I'll thrust a pin i' your buttocks else.

FACE.   Oh, no, sir.

SUR. *Señora mia, mi persona muy indigna*
est[à]
A llegar à tanta hermosura. [74]

FACE. Does he not use her bravely?

KAS.   Bravely, i' faith!

FACE. Nay, he will use her better.

KAS.   Do you think so?

SUR. *Señora, si sera servida, entrem[o]s.* [75] 80
         [*Exit with* DAME PLIANT.]

KAS. Where does he carry her?

FACE.   Into the garden, sir;
Take you no thought; I must interpret for
    her.

SUB. [*aside to* FACE, *who goes out*] Give Dol
    the word.
      — Come, my fierce child, advance;
We'll to our quarreling lesson again.

KAS.   Agreed.
I love a Spanish boy with all my heart.

SUB. Nay, and by this means, sir, you shall
    be brother
To a great count.

KAS.   Ay, I knew that at first.
This match will advance the house of the Kas-
    trils.

SUB. 'Pray God your sister prove but pliant.

KAS.   Why,
Her name is so, by her other husband.

SUB.   How! 90

KAS. The Widow Pliant. Knew you not
    that?

SUB.   No, faith, sir;
Yet, by the erection of her figure, [76] I guess'd
    it.
Come, let's go practise.

KAS.   Yes, but do you think, Doctor,
I e'er shall quarrel well?

SUB.   I warrant you. [*Exeunt.*]

SCENE V [77]

[*Enter*] DOL [*and*] MAMMON.

DOL. [78] (*in her fit of talking*) For after
    Alexander's death ——

MAM.   Good lady ——.

DOL. That Perdiccas and Antigonus were
    slain;
The two that stood, Seleuc' and Ptolemy ——

MAM.   Madam.

DOL. Made up the two legs, and the fourth
    beast,
That was Gog-north and Egypt-south: which
    after
Was called Gog-iron-leg and South-iron-leg ——

MAM.   Lady ——

Dol. And then Gog-horned. So was
    Egypt, too:
Then Egypt-clay-leg, and Gog-clay-leg ——

MAM.   Sweet madam ——

DOL. And last Gog-dust, and Egypt-dust,
    which fall   9
In the last link of the fourth chain. And these
Be stars in story, which none see, or look at ——

MAM. What shall I do?

DOL.   For, as he [79] says, except
We call the rabbins, and the heathen Greeks ——

MAM. Dear lady —.

DOL.   To come from Salem, [80] and from
    Athens,
And teach the people of Great Britain ——

---

[70] Since it was used in *court.*
[71] The sun has lost his light with the splendor
this lady brings, so help me God.
[72] Why don't you approach?
[73] For the love of God, why this delay?
[74] My Lady, my person is very unworthy of
approaching such beauty.
[75] Madam, if you please, let's go in.

[76] Calculation of her horoscope, with a pun on
another meaning of the phrase: her bearing.
[77] The same.
[78] Doll's ravings are chiefly unrelated phrases
from Hugh Broughton's *Concent of Scripture.*
[79] Broughton.
[80] Jerusalem.

[*Enter* FACE, *in his servant's dress.*]

FACE.   What's the matter, sir?

DOL. To speak the tongue of Eber and Javan [81] ——

MAM.   Oh,
Sh' is in her fit.

DOL.   We shall know nothing——

FACE.   Death, sir,
We are undone.

DOL.   Where then a learned linguist
Shall see the ancient us'd communion
Of vowels and consonants ——

FACE.   My master will hear! 20

DOL. A wisdom, which Pythagoras held
     most high ——

MAM. Sweet honorable lady.

DOL.   To comprise
All sounds of voices, in few marks of letters —

FACE. Nay, you must never hope to lay her
     now.   *They speak together.*

[82] DOL. And so we may arrive by Talmud
     skill,
And profane Greek, to raise the building up
Of Helen's house against the Ismaelite,
King of Thogarma, and his habergions
Brimstony, blue, and fiery; and the force
Of King Abaddon, and the beast of Cittim [83]:
Which Rabbi David Kimchi, Onkelos,   31
And Aben Ezra do interpret Rome.

FACE. How did you put her into 't?

MAM.   Alas, I talk'd
Of a fifth monarchy I would erect
With the philosopher's stone, by chance, and
     she
Falls on the other four straight.

FACE.   Out of Broughton!
I told you so. 'Slid, stop her mouth.

MAM.   Is 't best?

FACE. She'll never leave else. If the old
     man hear her,
We are but faeces, ashes.

SUB. [*within*]   What's to do there?

FACE. Oh, we are lost! Now she hears
     him, she is quiet.   40

Upon SUBTLE'S *entry they disperse.*

MAM. Where shall I hide me?

SUB.   How! What sight is here?
Close deeds of darkness, and that shun the
     light!

Bring him again. Who is he? What, my son!
Oh, I have liv'd too long.

MAM.   Nay, good, dear father,
There was no unchaste purpose.

SUB.   Not? and flee me
When I come in?

MAM.   That was my error.

SUB.   Error?
Guilt, guilt, my son; give it the right name.
     No marvel
If I found check in our great work within,
When such affairs as these were managing! 49

MAM. Why, have you so?

SUB.   It has stood still this half hour:
And all the rest of our less works gone back.
Where is the instrument of wickedness,
My lewd, false drudge?

MAM.   Nay, good sir, blame not him;
Believe me, 't was against his will or knowl-
     edge.
I saw her by chance.

SUB.   Will you commit more sin,
T' excuse a varlet?

MAM.   By my hope, 't is true, sir.

SUB. Nay, then I wonder less, if you, for
     whom
The blessing was prepar'd, would so tempt
     Heaven,
And lose your fortunes.

MAM.   Why, sir?

SUB.   This will retard
The work a month at least.

MAM.   Why, if it do, 60
What remedy? But think it not, good
     father;
Our purposes were honest.[84]

SUB.   As they were,
So the reward will prove. (*A great crack and
     noise within.*) — How now! ay me!
God and all saints be good to us. ——

[*Re-enter* FACE.]

         What's that?

FACE. Oh, sir, we are defeated! All the
     works
Are flown *in fumo*, every glass is burst;
Furnace and all rent down! as if a bolt
Of thunder had been driven through the house.
Retorts, receivers, pelicans, bolt-heads,   69
All struck in shivers!

         SUBTLE *falls down as in a swoon*
         Help, good sir! Alas,
Coldness and death invades him. Nay, Sir
     Mammon,

[81] Respectively the great-grandson of Shem and
the son of Japheth; the "tongues" are Hebrew and
Greek.

[82] In Q and F_1 this and following speeches of Face
and Mammon are printed in parallel columns.

[83] Italy, according to Broughton. (Hathaway.)

[84] Chaste.

Do the fair offices of a man ! You stand
As you were readier to depart than he.
                                One knocks.
Who 's there? My Lord her brother is come.
MAM.   Ha, Lungs !
FACE. His coach is at the door. Avoid his
    sight,
For he 's as furious as his sister is mad.
  MAM. Alas !
FACE   My brain is quite undone with
    the fume, sir ;
I ne'er must hope to be mine own man again.
  MAM. Is all lost, Lungs? Will nothing be
    preserv'd
Of all our cost?
  FACE.   Faith, very little, sir ;   80
A peck of coals or so, which is cold comfort,
    sir.
  MAM. Oh, my voluptuous mind! I am
    justly punish'd.
  FACE. And so am I, sir.
  MAM.   Cast from all my hopes —
  FACE. Nay, certainties, sir.
  MAM.   By mine own base affections.
  SUB. (*seems to come to himself.*) Oh, the
    curs'd fruits of vice and lust !
  MAM.   Good father,
It was my sin. Forgive it.
  SUB.   Hangs my roof
Over us still, and will not fall, O Justice,
Upon us, for this wicked man !
  FACE.   Nay, look, sir,
You grieve him now with staying in his
    sight.
Good sir, the nobleman will come too, and
    take you,   90
And that may breed a tragedy.
  MAM.   I 'll go.
  FACE. Ay, and repent at home, sir. It may
    be,
For some good penance you may ha' it yet ;
A hundred pound to the box at Bet'lem ——
  MAM.   Yes.
  FACE. For the restoring such as ha' their
    wits.
  MAM. I 'll do 't.
  FACE. I 'll send one to you to receive it.
  MAM.   Do.
Is no projection left?
  FACE.   All flown, or stinks, sir.
  MAM. Will nought be sav'd that 's good for
    med'cine, think'st thou?
  FACE. I cannot tell, sir. There will be per-
    haps
Something about the scraping of the shards,

Will cure the itch ; though not your itch of
    mind, sir.   101
It shall be sav'd for you, and sent home.
    Good sir,
This way, for fear the lord shall meet you.
                        [*Exit* MAMMON.]
  SUB.   Face.
  FACE. Ay.
  SUB.   Is he gone?
  FACE.   Yes, and as heavily
As all the gold he hop'd for were in his blood.
Let us be light though.
  SUB.   Ay, as balls, and bound
And hit our heads against the roof for joy.
There 's so much of our care now cast away.
  FACE. Now to our don.
  SUB.   Yes, your young widow by this time
Is made a countess, Face. Sh' has been in
    travail   110
Of a young heir for you.
  FACE.   Good, sir.
  SUB.   Off with your case,
And greet her kindly, as a bridegroom should,
After these common hazards.
  FACE.   Very well, sir.
Will you go fetch Don Diego off the while?
  SUB. And fetch him over too, if you 'll be
    pleas'd, sir.
Would Dol were in her place, to pick his pock-
    ets now !
  FACE. Why, you can do it as well, if you
    would set to 't.
I pray you prove your virtue.[85]
  SUB.   For your sake, sir. [*Exeunt.*]

SCENE VI [86]

[*Enter*] SURLY [*and*] DAME PLIANT.

  SUR. Lady, you see into what hands you
    are fall'n ;
'Mongst what a nest of villains ! and how near
Your honor was t' have catch'd a certain clap,
Through your credulity, had I but been
So punctually forward, as place, time,
And other circumstance would ha' made a
    man.
For yo' are a handsome woman ; would yo'
    were wise, too !
I am a gentleman come here disguis'd
Only to find the knaveries of this citadel ;
And where I might have wrong'd your honor,
    and have not,   10
I claim some interest in your love. You are,
They say, a widow, rich ; and I 'm a bachelor.

[85] Powers.   [86] The same.

Worth naught.　Your fortunes may make me
　　a man,
As mine ha' preserv'd you a woman.　Think
　　upon it,
And whether I have deserv'd you or no.
　DAME P.　　　　　　　　　　　I will, sir.
　SUR. And for these household rogues, let
　　me alone
To treat with them.

[*Enter* SUBTLE.]

　SUB.　　　　　　How doth my noble Diego,
And my dear madam Countess?　Hath the
　　Count
Been courteous, lady? liberal and open?
Donzel, methinks you look melancholic,　20
After your *coitum*, and scurvy!　Truly,
I do not like the dulness of your eye;
It hath a heavy cast, 't is upsy [87] Dutch,
And says you are a lumpish whoremaster.
Be lighter: I will make your pockets so.
　　　　　　　He falls to picking of them.
　SUR. Will you, Don Bawd and Pick-purse?
　　[*Knocks him down.*] How now!　Reel
　　you?
Stand up, sir; you shall find, since I am so
　　heavy,
I 'll gi' you equal weight.
　SUB.　　　　　　　　Help! murder.
　SUR.　　　　　　　　　　　　　No, sir,
There 's no such thing intended.　A good cart
And a clean whip shall ease you of that fear.
I am the Spanish don that should be cozened,
Do you see? cozened?　Where 's your Cap-
　　tain Face,　　　　　　　　　　　31
That parcel broker, and whole bawd, all ras-
　　cal?

[*Enter* FACE *in his uniform.*]

　FACE. How, Surly!
　SUR.　　　　　　Oh, make your approach,
　　good Captain.
I have found from whence your copper rings
　　and spoons
Come now, wherewith you cheat abroad in tav-
　　erns.
'T was here you learn'd t' anoint your boot
　　with brimstone,
Then rub men's gold on 't for a kind of touch,
And say 't was naught, when you had chang'd
　　the color,
That you might ha 't for nothing!　And this
　　doctor,
Your sooty, smoky bearded compere, he　40

[87] Thoroughly. Old eds. *upsee.*

Will close you so much gold, in a bolt's-head,
And, on a turn, convey, i' the stead, another
With sublim'd mercury, that shall burst i' the
　　heat,
And fly out all *in fumo!*　Then weeps Mam-
　　mon;
Then swoons his Worship.　Or, [*Exit* FACE.]
　　he is the Faustus,
That casteth figures and can conjure, cures
Plagues, piles, and pox, by the ephemerides; [88]
And holds intelligence with all the bawds
And midwives of three shires: while you send
　　in ——
Captain! — What, is he gone? — damsels
　　with child,　　　　　　　　　　　50
Wives that are barren, or the waiting maid
With the greensickness.[89] — [*Seizes* SUBTLE.]
　　Nay, sir, you must tarry,
Though he be scap'd; and answer by the ears,
　　sir.

SCENE VII [90]

[*To them re-enter*] FACE [*with*] KASTRIL.

　FACE. Why, now 's the time, if ever you
　　will quarrel
Well, as they say, and be a true-born child.
The Doctor and your sister both are abus'd.
　KAS. Where is he?　Which is he?　He is a
　　slave.
Whate'er he is, and the son of a whore. — Are
　　you
The man, sir, I would know?
　SUR.　　　　　　I should be loth, sir,
To confess so much.
　KAS.　　　　　Then you lie i' your throat.
　SUR.　　　　　　　　　　　　　How?
　FACE. [*to* KASTRIL] A very errant rogue, sir,
　　and a cheater,
Employ'd here by another conjurer
That does not love the doctor, and would cross
　　him　　　　　　　　　　　　　　10
If he knew how ——
　SUR.　　　　Sir, you are abus'd.
　KAS.　　　　　　　　　　　You lie;
And 't is no matter.
　FACE.　　　　　　Well said, sir!　He is
The impudent'st rascal ——
　SUR.　　　　You are indeed. — Will you hear
　　me, sir?
　FACE. By no means.　Bid him be gone.
　KAS.　　　　　　Begone, sir, quickly.
　SUR. This 's strange! — Lady, do you in-
　　form your brother.

[88] Astrological almanac.
[89] Chlorosis.　　　　　　[90] The same.

398 *The Alchemist* IV. vii.

FACE. There is not such a foist [91] in all the
town.
The Doctor had him presently ; and finds yet
The Spanish count will come here. — [*aside*]
Bear up, Subtle.
SUB. Yes, sir, he must appear within this
hour.
FACE. And yet this rogue would come in a
disguise, 20
By the temptation of another spirit,[92]
To trouble our art, though he could not hurt
it !
KAS. Ay,
I know — [*to his sister*] Away, you talk like a
foolish mauther.[93]
SUR. Sir, all is truth she says.
FACE. Do not believe him, sir.
He is the lying'st swabber ! Come your ways,
sir.
SUR. You are valiant, out of company.
KAS. Yes, how then, sir?

[*Enter* DRUGGER *with a piece of damask.*]

FACE. Nay, here's an honest fellow too that
knows him,
And all his tricks. — [*aside to* DRUGGER] Make
good what I say, Abel.
This cheater would ha' cozen'd thee o' the
widow. —
He owes this honest Drugger, here, seven
pound, 30
He has had on him in twopenny'orths of to-
bacco.
DRUG. Yes, sir. And h' has damn'd him-
self three terms to pay me.
FACE. And what does he owe for lotium? [94]
DRUG. Thirty shillings, sir ;
And for six syringes.
SUR. Hydra of villainy !
FACE. Nay, sir, you must quarrel him out o'
the house.
KAS. I will.
— Sir, if you get not out o' doors, you lie ;
And you are a pimp.
SUR. Why, this is madness, sir,
Not valor in you ; I must laugh at this.
KAS. It is my humor ; you are a pimp and
a trig.[95]
And an Amadis de Gaul, or a Don Quixote. 40
DRUG. Or a knight o' the curious coxcomb,
do you see ?

[*Enter* ANANIAS.]

ANA. Peace to the household.
KAS. I'll keep peace for no man.
ANA. Casting of dollars is concluded lawful.
KAS. Is he the constable?
SUB. Peace, Ananias.
FACE. No, sir.
KAS. Then you are an otter, and a shad, a
whit,[96]
A very tim.
SUR. You'll hear me, sir?
KAS. I will not.
ANA. What is the motive?
SUB. Zeal in the young gentleman,
Against his Spanish slops.
ANA. They are profane,
Lewd, superstitious, and idolatrous breeches.
SUR. New rascals !
KAS. Will you be gone, sir?
ANA. Avoid, Sathan ; 50
Thou art not of the light. That ruff of pride
About thy neck betrays thee ; and is the same
With that which the unclean birds, in seventy-
seven,[97]
Were seen to prank it with on divers coasts.
Thou look'st like Antichrist, in that lewd hat.
SUR. I must give way.
KAS. Begone, sir.
SUR. But I'll take
A course with you. ——
ANA. Depart, proud Spanish fiend.
SUR. Captain and Doctor —
ANA. Child of perdition.
KAS. Hence, sir ! [*Exit* SURLY.]
— Did I not quarrel bravely?
FACE. Yes, indeed, sir.
KAS. Nay, an I give my mind to 't, I shall
do 't. 60
FACE. O, you must follow, sir, and threaten
him tame.
He'll turn again else.
KAS. I'll re-turn him then. [*Exit.*]
FACE. Drugger, this rogue prevented us, for
thee ;
We had determin'd that thou should'st ha'
come
In a Spanish suit, and ha' carried her so ; and
he,
A brokerly slave, goes, puts it on himself.

[91] Rogue.
[92] *I.e.*, incited by a rival.
[93] Wench. (Eastern dialect.)
[94] A lotion.
[95] Dandy, cockscomb.
[96] Particle. — For "tim" (from "Timothy"), cf.
Fletcher, *The Mad Lover* (II, ii) : a boy is addressed
as "small Tim Treble." (Kittredge.)
[97] This allusion remains unexplained ; perhaps
there was a migration of birds, notable for ruffled
necks, which came in such numbers that they constituted a foul nuisance.

Hast brought the damask?
    DRUG. Yes, sir.
    FACE. Thou must borrow
A Spanish suit. Hast thou no credit with the
    players?
    DRUG. Yes, sir; did you never see me play
    the Fool? [98]
    FACE. I know not, Nab; [*aside*] thou shalt,
    if I can help it. —   70
Hieronimo's old cloak, ruff, and hat will serve;
I'll tell thee more when thou bring'st 'em.
    [*Exit* DRUGGER.] SUBTLE *hath whis-*
    per'd with [ANANIAS] *this while.*
    ANA. Sir, I know
The Spaniard hates the brethren, and hath
    spies
Upon their actions; and that this was one
I make no scruple. — But the holy synod
Have been in prayer and meditation for it;
And 't is reveal'd no less to them than me,
That casting of money is most lawful.
    SUB. True.
But here I cannot do it; if the house
Should chance to be suspected, all would out,
And we be lock'd up in the Tower for ever, 81
To make gold there for th' state, never come
    out;
And then are you defeated.
    ANA. I will tell
This to the elders and the weaker brethren,
That the whole company of the separation
May join in humble prayer again.
    SUB. And fasting.
    ANA. Yea, for some fitter place. The peace
    of mind
Rest with these walls!   [*Exit.*]
    SUB. Thanks, courteous Ananias.
    FACE. What did he come for?
    SUB. About casting dollars,
Presently, out of hand. And so I told him 90
A Spanish minister came here to spy,
Against the faithful ——
    FACE. I conceive. Come, Subtle,
Thou art so down upon the least disaster!
How wouldst thou ha' done, if I had not help'd
    thee out?
    SUB. I thank thee, Face, for the angry boy,
    i' faith.
    FACE. Who would ha' look'd it should ha'
    been that rascal
Surly? He had dy'd his beard and all. Well,
    sir;
Here's damask come to make you a suit.

    SUB. Where's Drugger?
    FACE. He is gone to borrow me a Spanish
    habit;
I'll be the count now.
    SUB. But where's the widow?
    FACE. Within, with my Lord's sister;
    Madam Dol   101
Is entertaining her.
    SUB. By your favor, Face,
Now she is honest, I will stand again.
    FACE. You will not offer it?
    SUB. Why?
    FACE. Stand to your word,
Or — here comes Dol. She knows ——
    SUB. You are tyrannous still.

    [*Enter* DOL.]

    FACE. Strict for my right. — How now,
    Dol! Hast told her
The Spanish count will come?
    DOL. Yes; but another is come,
You little look'd for!
    FACE. Who's that?
    DOL. Your master —
The master of the house.
    SUB. How, Dol!
    FACE. She lies;
This is some trick. Come, leave your quib-
    lins,[99] Dorothy.   110
    DOL. Look out and see.
    [FACE *goes to the window.*]
    SUB. Art thou in earnest?
    DOL. 'Slight,
Forty o' the neighbors are about him, talking.
    FACE. 'T is he, by this good day.
    DOL. 'T will prove ill day
For some on us.
    FACE. We are undone, and taken.
    DOL. Lost, I'm afraid.
    SUB. You said he would not come,
While there died one a week within the liber-
    ties.[100]
    FACE. No; 't was within the walls.
    SUB. Was't so? Cry you mercy.
I thought the liberties. What shall we do
    now, Face?
    FACE. Be silent: not a word, if he call or
    knock.   119
I'll into mine old shape again and meet him,
Of Jeremy, the butler. I' the meantime,
Do you two pack up all the goods and pur-
    chase [101]

---

[98] Evidently the actor who played **Drugger** was accustomed to appear as the Fool.
[99] Quibbles.
[100] Districts outside the boundaries, but subject to the control of the city.   [101] Loot.

That we can carry i' the two trunks.   I 'll keep him

Off for to-day, if I cannot longer ; and then
At night, I 'll ship you both away to Ratcliff,¹⁰²
Where we 'll meet to-morrow, and there we 'll share.
Let Mammon's brass and pewter keep the cel-
lar ;
We 'll have another time for that.   But, Dol,
Prithee go heat a little water quickly ;
Subtle must shave me.   All my captain's
beard   130
Must off, to make me appear smooth Jeremy.
You 'll do 't?
    Sub.   Yes, I 'll shave you as well as I can.
    Face.   And not cut my throat, but trim me?
    Sub.   You shall see, sir.   [*Exeunt.*]

ACT V — Scene I ¹

[*Enter*] Lovewit [*and*] Neighbors.

    Love.   Has there been such resort, say you?
    1 Nei.   Daily, sir.
    2 Nei.   And nightly, too.
    3 Nei.   Ay, some as brave as lords.
    4 Nei.   Ladies and gentlewomen.
    5 Nei.   Citizens' wives.
    1 Nei.   And knights.
    6 Nei.   In coaches.
    2 Nei.   Yes, and oyster-women.
    1 Nei.   Beside other gallants.
    3 Nei.   Sailors' wives.
    4 Nei.   Tobacco men.
    5 Nei.   Another Pimlico.²
    Love.   What should my knave advance,
To draw this company?   He hung out no banners
Of a strange calf with five legs to be seen,
Or a huge lobster with six claws?
    6 Nei.   No, sir.
    3 Nei.   We had gone in then, sir.
    Love.   He has no gift   10
Of teaching i' the nose ³ that e'er I knew of !
You saw no bills set up that promis'd cure
Of agues or the toothache?
    2 Nei.   No such thing, sir !
    Love.   Nor heard a drum struck for baboons
or puppets?
    5 Nei.   Neither, sir.

¹⁰² A hamlet in Stepney.
¹ Before the house.
² A summer resort.
³ *I.e.*, like a Puritan preacher.

    Love.   What device should he bring forth now?
I love a teeming wit as I love my nourishment.
'Pray God he ha' not kept such open house
That he hath sold my hangings, and my bed-
ding —
I left him nothing else.   If he have eat 'em,
A plague o' the moth, say I.   Sure he has got   20
Some bawdy pictures to call all this ging : ⁴
The Friar and the Nun ; or the new motion ⁵
Of the knight's courser covering the parson's mare ;
The boy of six year old, with the great thing ;
Or 't may be, he has the fleas that run at tilt
Upon a table, or some dog to dance !
When saw you him?
    1 Nei.   Who, sir, Jeremy?
    2 Nei.   Jeremy butler?
We saw him not this month.
    Love.   How !
    [3] Nei.   Not these five weeks, sir.
    [4] Nei.   These six weeks, at the least.
    Love.   Yo' amaze me, neighbors !
    5 Nei.   Sure, if your Worship know not
where he is,   30
He 's slipp'd away.
    6 Nei.   Pray God he be not made away !
    Love.   Ha?   It 's no time to question, then.
        He knocks.
    6 Nei.   About
Some three weeks since I heard a doleful cry,
As I sat up a-mending my wife's stockings.
    Love.   This 's strange that none will an-
swer !   Didst thou hear
A cry, say'st thou?
    6 Nei.   Yes, sir, like unto a man
That had been strangled an hour, and could not speak.
    2 Nei.   I heard it, too, just this day three
weeks, at two a'clock
Next morning.
    Love.   These be miracles, or you make
'em so !
A man an hour strangled, and could not speak,
And both you heard him cry?
    3 Nei.   Yes, downward, sir.   41
    Love.   Thou art a wise fellow.   Give me
thy hand, I pray thee.
What trade art thou on?
    3 Nei.   A smith, an 't please your Wor-
ship.
    Love.   A smith !   Then lend me thy help to
get this door open.

⁴ Gang.   ⁵ Puppet-show.

3 NEI. That I will presently, sir ; but fetch
my tools — [*Exit.*]

1 NEI. Sir, best to knock again afore you
break it.

SCENE II [6]

LOVEWIT [*and*] Neighbors [*remain.*]

LOVE. I will.

[*Enter* FACE *in his butler's livery.*]

FACE. What mean you, sir?

1, 2, 4 NEI. Oh, here's Jeremy!

FACE. Good sir, come from the door.

LOVE. Why, what's the matter?

FACE. Yet farther, you are too near yet.

LOVE. I' the name of wonder!
What means the fellow?

FACE. The house, sir, has been visited.

LOVE. What, with the plague? Stand thou
then farther.

FACE. No, sir,
I had it not.

LOVE. Who had it then? I left
None else but thee 'i the house!

FACE. Yes, sir; my fellow,
The cat that kept the butt'ry, had it on her
A week before I spied it ; but I got her
Convey'd away i' the night. And so I shut 10
The house up for a month ——

LOVE. How!

FACE. Purposing then, sir,
T' have burnt rose-vinegar, treacle, and tar,
And ha' made it sweet, that you should ne'er
ha' known it ;
Because I knew the news would but afflict you,
sir.

LOVE. Breathe less, and farther off. Why
this is stranger!
The neighbors tell me all here that the doors
Have still been open ——

FACE. How, sir!

LOVE. Gallants, men and women,
And of all sorts, tag-rag, been seen to flock here
In threaves,[7] these ten weeks, as to a second
Hogsden,[8]
In days of Pimlico and Eye-bright.[9]

FACE. Sir, 20
Their wisdoms will not say so!

LOVE. To-day they speak
Of coaches and gallants ; one in a French hood
Went in, they tell me ; and another was seen

In a velvet gown at the windore! divers more
Pass in and out!

FACE. They did pass through the
doors, then,
Or walls, I assure their eyesights, and their
spectacles ;
For here, sir, are the keys, and here have been,
In this my pocket, now above twenty days!
And for before, I kept the fort alone there.
But that 't is yet not deep i' the afternoon, 30
I should believe my neighbors had seen double
Through the black pot,[10] and made these ap-
paritions!
For, on my faith to your Worship, for these
three weeks
And upwards, the door has not been open'd.

LOVE. Strange!

1 NEI. Good faith, I think I saw a coach!

2 NEI. And I too,
I'd ha' been sworn!

LOVE. Do you but think it now?
And but one coach?

4 NEI. We cannot tell, sir ; Jeremy
Is a very honest fellow.

FACE. Did you see me at all?

1 NEI. No ; that we are sure on.

2 NEI. I'll be sworn o' that.

LOVE. Fine rogues to have your testimonies
built on! 40

[*Re-enter* Third Neighbor, *with his tools.*]

3 NEI. Is Jeremy come?

1 NEI. Oh, yes ; you may leave your
tools ;
We were deceiv'd, he says.

2 NEI. He has had the keys ;
And the door has been shut these three weeks.

3 NEI. Like enough.

LOVE. Peace, and get hence, you change-
lings.

FACE. [*aside*] Surly come!
And Mammon made acquainted! They'll tell
all.
How shall I beat them off? What shall I do?
Nothing's more wretched than a guilty con-
science.[11]

SCENE III [12]

[*To them enter*] SURLY [*and*] MAMMON.

SUR. No, sir, he was a great physician.
This,

---

[6] The same.
[7] *I.e.*, in droves (lit. = two dozens of sheaves).
  Hoxton, then a resort of the citizens.
[9] Possibly a malt or vinous beverage ; possibly the
name of a tavern or its keeper.

[10] *I.e.*, as a result of drinking too much.
[11] The inspiration of this line, and of the scene, is
in the *Mostellaria* (III, i) of Plautus.
[12] The same.

It was no bawdyhouse, but a mere [13] chancel.
You knew the lord and his sister.

MAM.   Nay, good Surly ——

SUR. The happy word, " Be rich " ——

MAM.   Play not the tyran[t] —

SUR. Should be to-day pronounc'd to all
  your friends.
And where be your andirons now? and your
  brass pots,
That should ha' been golden flagons, and great
  wedges?

MAM. Let me but breathe. What! They
  ha' shut their doors,
Methinks !   MAMMON *and* SURLY *knock.*

SUR.   Ay, now 't is holiday with them.

MAM.   Rogues,
Cozeners, impostors, bawds !

FACE.   What mean you, sir? 10

MAM. To enter if we can.

FACE.   Another man's house?
Here is the owner, sir ; turn you to him,
And speak your business.

MAM.   Are you, sir, the owner?

LOVE. Yes, sir.

MAM.   And are those knaves within,
  your cheaters?

LOVE. What knaves? what cheaters?

MAM.   Subtle and his Lungs.

FACE. The gentleman is distracted, sir !
No lungs
Nor lights ha' been seen here these three weeks,
  sir,
Within these doors upon my word !

SUR.   Your word,
Groom arrogant !

FACE.   Yes, sir, I am the housekeeper,
And know the keys ha' not been out o' my
  hands.   20

SUR. This 's a new Face !

FACE.   You do mistake the house, sir !
What sign was 't at?

SUR.   You rascal ! This is one
O' the confederacy. Come, let 's get officers,
And force the door.

LOVE.   'Pray you stay, gentlemen.

SUR. No, sir, we 'll come with warrant.

MAM.   Ay, and then
We shall ha' your doors open.

          [*Exeunt* MAMMON *and* SURLY.]

LOVE.   What means this?

FACE. I cannot tell, sir !

1 NEI.   These are two o' the gallants
That we do think we saw.

FACE.   Two o' the fools !

[13] Absolute, actual.

You talk as idly as they. Good faith, sir,
I think the moon has craz'd 'em all. — [*aside*]
  Oh me,   30
The angry boy come too? He 'll make a noise,
And ne'er away till he have betray'd us all.

          KASTRIL [*enters and*] *knocks.*

KAS. What, rogues, bawds, slaves, you 'll
  open the door anon !
Punk, cockatrice, my suster ! By this light
I 'll fetch the marshal to you. You are a
  whore
To keep your castle ——

FACE.   Who would you speak with, sir?

KAS. The bawdy doctor, and the cozening
  captain,
And puss my suster.

LOVE.   This is something, sure !

FACE. Upon my trust, the doors were never
  open, sir.

KAS. I have heard all their tricks told me
  twice over,   40
By the fat knight and the lean gentleman.

LOVE. Here comes another.

          [*Enter* ANANIAS *and* TRIBULATION.]

FACE. [*aside*]   Ananias too !
And his pastor !

TRI.   The doors are shut against us.
                    They beat, too, at the door.

ANA. Come forth, you seed of sulphur, sons
  of fire ;
Your stench it is broke forth ; abomination
Is in the house.

KAS.   Ay, my suster 's there.

ANA.   The place,
It is become a cage of unclean birds.

KAS. Yes, I will fetch the scavenger, and
  the constable.

TRI. You shall do well.

ANA.   We 'll join to weed them out.

KAS. You will not come then? punk-
  devise,[14] my suster !   50

ANA. Call her not sister ; she is a harlot
  verily.

KAS. I 'll raise the street.

LOVE.   Good gentlemen, a word.

ANA. Sathan avoid, and hinder not our zeal.

          [*Exeunt* ANANIAS, TRIBULATION, *and*
                    KASTRIL.]

LOVE. The world 's turn'd Bet'lem.

FACE.   These are all broke loose,
Out of St. Kather'ne's, where they use to keep
The better sort of mad-folks.

[14] Perfect.

1 NEI.   All these persons
We saw go in and out here.
2 NEI.   Yes, indeed, sir.
3 NEI. These were the parties.
FACE.   Peace, you drunkards. — Sir,
I wonder at it! Please you to give me leave
To touch the door; I'll try an the lock be
    chang'd.   60
    LOVE. It mazes me!
FACE. [*going to the door.*]   Good faith, sir,
    I believe
There's no such thing. 'T is all *deceptio
    visus.* —
[*aside*] Would I could get him away.
    DAP. (*cries out within.*)   Master
        Captain! Master Doctor!
    LOVE. Who's that?
FACE. [*aside*]   Our clerk within, that
    I forgot! — I know not, sir.
    DAP. [*within*] For God's sake, when will
        her Grace be at leisure?
FACE.   Ha!
Illusions, some spirit o' the air! — [*aside*] His
    gag is melted,
And now he sets out the throat.
    DAP. [*within*]   I am almost stifled ——
FACE. [*aside*] Would you were altogether.
    LOVE.   'T is i' the house.
Ha! list.
    FACE.   Believe it, sir, i' the air!
    LOVE.   Peace, you —
    DAP. [*within*] Mine aunt's Grace does not
        use me well.
    SUB. [*within*]   You fool,   70
Peace; you'll mar all.
    FACE. [*speaks through the keyhole, while
        LOVEWIT advances to the door unob-
        served.*]   Or you will else, you rogue.
    LOVE. Oh, is it so? Then you converse
        with spirits!
Come, sir. No more o' your tricks, good
    Jeremy.
The truth, the shortest way.
    FACE.   Dismiss this rabble, sir. —
[*aside*] What shall I do? I am catch'd,
    LOVE.   Good neighbors,
I thank you all. You may depart. [*Exeunt
    Neighbors.*] — Come, sir,
You know that I am an indulgent master;
And therefore conceal nothing. What's your
    med'cine,
To draw so many several sorts of wild fowl?
    FACE. Sir, you were wont to affect mirth
        and wit —   80
But here's no place to talk on 't i' the street.

Give me but leave to make the best of my for-
    tune,
And only pardon me th' abuse of your house:
It's all I beg. I'll help you to a widow,
In recompense, that you shall gi' me thanks
    for,
Will make you seven years younger, and a rich
    one.
'T is but your putting on a Spanish cloak;
I have her within. You need not fear the
    house;
It was not visited.
    LOVE.   But by me, who came
Sooner than you expected.
    FACE.   It is true, sir.   90
'Pray you forgive me.
    LOVE.   Well, let's see your widow.
                                        [*Exeunt.*]

SCENE IV [15]

[*Enter*] SUBTLE [*leading in*] DAPPER, [*with his
    eyes bound as before*].

    SUB. How! ha' you eaten your gag?
    DAP.   Yes, faith, it crumbled
Away i' my mouth.
    SUB.   You ha' spoil'd all then.
    DAP.   No;
I hope my aunt of Faërie will forgive me.
    SUB. Your aunt's a gracious lady; but in
        troth
You were to blame.
    DAP.   The fume did overcome me,
And I did do 't to stay my stomach. 'Pray
    you
So satisfy her Grace.

[*Enter* FACE.]

                        Here comes the Captain.
    FACE. How now! Is his mouth down?
    SUB.   Ay, he has spoken!
    FACE. [*aside to* SUBTLE] A pox, I heard him,
        and you too. — He's undone then. —
[*aside*] I have been fain to say the house is
        haunted   10
With spirits, to keep churl back.
    SUB. [*aside*]   And hast thou done it?
    FACE. [*aside*] Sure, for this night.
    SUB. [*aside*]   Why, then triumph and
        sing
Of Face so famous, the precious king
Of present wits.
    FACE. [*aside*]   Did you not hear the coil
About the door?

_____
[15] A room inside the house.

SUB. [*aside*]   Yes, and I dwindled with it.
FACE. Show him his aunt, and let him be
dispatch'd ;
I 'll send her to you.   [*Exit* FACE.]
SUB.   Well, sir, your aunt, her Grace,
Will give you audience presently, on my suit, —
And the Captain's word that you did not eat
your gag
In any contempt of her Highness.
                        [*Unbinds his eyes.*]
DAP.   Not I, in troth, sir. 20

[*Enter*] DOL *like the Queen of Faërie.*

SUB. Here she is come.   Down o' your
knees and wriggle ;
She has a stately presence. — Good.   Yet
nearer,
And bid, God save you.
DAP.   Madam !
SUB.   And your aunt.
DAP. And my most Gracious aunt, God
save your Grace.
DOL. Nephew, we thought to have been
angry with you ;
But that sweet face of yours hath turn'd the
tide,
And made it flow with joy, that ebb'd of
love.
Arise, and touch our velvet gown.
SUB.   The skirts,
And kiss 'em.   So !
DOL.   Let me now stroke that head.
Much, Nephew, shalt thou win, much shalt thou
spend ;   30
Much shalt thou give away, much shalt thou lend.
SUB. [*aside*] Ay, much ! indeed. — Why do
you not thank her Grace ?
DAP. I cannot speak for joy.
SUB.   See, the kind wretch !
Your Grace's kinsman right.
DOL.   Give me the bird.[16] ——
Here is your fly [16] in a purse, about your neck,
Cousin ;
Wear it, and feed it about this day sev'n-night,
On your right wrist ——
SUB.   Open a vein with a pin
And let it suck but once a week ; till then,
You must not look on 't.
DOL.   No ; and, kinsman,
Bear yourself worthy of the blood you come
on.
SUB. Her Grace would ha' you eat no
more Woolsack [17] pies,   41

Nor Dagger [17] frume'ty.
DOL.   Nor break his fast
In Heaven [17] and Hell.[17]
SUB.   She 's with you everywhere !
Nor play with costermongers, at mumchance,[18]
traytrip,[18]
God-make-you-rich [18] (whenas your aunt has
done it) ; but keep
The   gallant'st   company,   and   the   best
games ——
DAP.   Yes, sir.
SUB. Gleek [18] and primero ; [18] and what
you get, be true to us.
DAP. By this hand, I will.
SUB.   You may bring 's a thousand pound
Before to-morrow night, if but three thousand
Be stirring, an you will.
DAP.   I swear I will then. 50
SUB. Your fly will learn you all games.
FACE. [*within*]   Ha' you done there ?
SUB. Your Grace will command him no
more duties ?
DOL.   No ;
But come and see me often.   I may chance
To leave him three or four hundred chests of
treasure,
And some twelve thousand acres of faërie land,
If he game well and comely with good game-
sters.
SUB. There 's a kind aunt.   Kiss her de-
parting part. —
But you must sell you[r] forty mark a year
now.
DAP. Ay, sir, I mean.
SUB.   Or, gi 't away ; pox on 't !
[DAP.] I 'll gi' 't mine aunt.   I 'll go and
fetch the writings.   [*Exit.*] 60
SUB. 'T is well ; away.

[*Re-enter* FACE.]

FACE.   Where 's Subtle ?
SUB.   Here ; what news ?
FACE. Drugger is at the door ; go take his
suit,
And bid him fetch a parson presently.
Say he shall marry the widow.   Thou shalt
spend
A hundred pound by the service !
                        [*Exit* SUBTLE.]
                    Now, Queen Dol,
Ha' you pack'd up all ?
DOL.   Yes.

[16] Familiar spirit.
[17] Taverns.   The last two were in Westminster ;
[18] Games of chance.

FACE.   And how do you like
The Lady Pliant?

DOL.   A good dull innocent.

[*Re-enter* SUBTLE.]

SUB. Here's your Hieronimo's cloak and
hat.

FACE.   Give me 'em.

SUB. And the ruff too?

FACE.   Yes; I'll come to you presently.
                                        [*Exit.*]

SUB. Now he is gone about his project,
    Dol,   70
I told you of, for the widow.

DOL.   'T is direct
Against our articles.

SUB.   Well, we'll fit him, wench.
Hast thou gull'd her of her jewels or her brace-
    lets?

DOL. No, but I will do 't.

SUB.   Soon at night, my Dolly,
When we are shipp'd, and all our goods aboard,
Eastward for Ratcliff, we will turn our course
To Brainford,[19] westward, if thou say'st the
    word,
And take our leaves of this o'erweening rascal,
This peremptory Face.

DOL.   Content; I am weary of him.

SUB. Tho' hast cause, when the slave will
    run a-wiving, Dol,   80
Against the instrument that was drawn be-
    tween us.

DOL. I'll pluck his bird as bare as I can.

SUB.   Yes, tell her
She must by any means address some present
To th' cunning man; make him amends for
    wronging
His art with her suspicion; send a ring,
Or chain of pearl; she will be tortur'd else
Extremely in her sleep, say, and ha' strange
    things
Come to her. Wilt thou?

DOL.   Yes.

SUB.   My fine flittermouse,[20]
My bird o' the night; we'll tickle it at the
    Pigeons,[21]   89
When we have all, and may unlock the trunks,
And say, this's mine, and thine, and thine,
    and mine.   *They kiss.*

Re-enter FACE.

FACE. What now! a-billing?

SUB.   Yes, a little exalted
In the good passage of our stock-affairs.

---

[19] Brentford.   [20] Bat.   [21] An inn at Brentford.

FACE. Drugger has brought his parson;
    take him in, Subtle,
And send Nab back again to wash his face.

SUB. I will; and shave himself?   [*Exit.*]

FACE.   If you can get him.

DOL. You are hot upon it, Face, whate'er
    it is!

FACE. A trick that Dol shall spend ten
    pound a month by.

[*Re-enter* SUBTLE.]

Is he gone?

SUB.   The chaplain waits you i' the
    hall, sir.

FACE. I'll go bestow him.   [*Exit.*]

DOL.   He'll now marry her instantly.

SUB. He cannot yet; he is not ready.
    Dear Dol,   101
Cozen her of all thou canst. To deceive him
Is no deceit, but justice, that would break
Such an inextricable tie as ours was.

DOL. Let me alone to fit him.

[*Re-enter* FACE.]

FACE.   Come, my venturers,
You ha' pack'd up all? Where be the trunks?
    Bring forth.

SUB. Here.

FACE.   Let's see 'em. Where's the
    money?

SUB.   Here,
In this.

FACE.   Mammon's ten pound; eight-
    score before.
The brethren's money this. Drugger's and
    Dapper's.
What paper's that?

DOL.   The jewel of the waiting maid's,
That stole it from her lady, to know cer-
    tain ——   111

FACE. If she should have precedence of her
    mistress?

DOL.   Yes.

FACE. What box is that?

SUB.   The fishwife's rings, I think,
And th' alewife's single money.[22] Is 't not,
    Dol?

DOL. Yes; and the whistle that the sailor's
    wife
Brought you, to know an her husband were
    with Ward.[23]

FACE. We'll wet it to-morrow; and our
    silver beakers

---

[22] Small change.
[23] A famous pirate.

And tavern cups.　Where be the French petti-
　　coats
And girdles and hangers?
SUB.　　　　　　　　　　　Here, i' the trunk,
And the bolts of lawn.
FACE.　　　　　Is Drugger's damask there,
And the tobacco?
SUB.　　　　Yes.
FACE.　　　　　　　Give me the keys.　121
DOL.　Why you the keys?
SUB.　　　　　　　No matter, Dol; because
We shall not open 'em before he comes.
FACE.　'T is true, you shall not open them,
　　indeed ;
Nor have 'em forth.　Do you see?　Not
　　forth, Dol.
DOL.　　　　　　No !
FACE.　No, my smock rampant.　The right
　　is, my master
Knows all, has pardon'd me, and he will keep
　　'em.
Doctor, 't is true — you look — for all your
　　figures ;
I sent for him, indeed.　Wherefore, good part-
　　ners,
Both he and she, be satisfied ; for here　130
Determines [24] the indenture tripartite
'Twixt Subtle, Dol, and Face.　All I can do
Is to help you over the wall, o' the back
　　side,
Or lend you a sheet to save your velvet gown,
　　Dol.
Here will be officers presently ; bethink you
Of some course suddenly to scape the dock,
For thither you 'll come else.　(*Some knock.*)
　　Hark you, thunder.
SUB.　You are a precious fiend !
OFFICERS.　[*without*]　　　　Open the door.
FACE.　Dol, I am sorry for thee i' faith.
But hear'st thou?
It shall go hard but I will place thee some-
　　where ;　　　　　　　　　　　　　140
Thou shalt ha' my letter to Mistress Amo ——
DOL.　　　　　　　　　　Hang you —
FACE.　Or Madam Caesarean.
DOL.　　　　　　Pox upon you, rogue ;
Would I had but time to beat thee.
FACE.　　　　　　　　　　Subtle,
Let's know where you set up next ; I 'll send
　　you
A customer now and then, for old acquaint-
　　ance.
What new course ha' you?
SUB.　　　　　　Rogue, I 'll hang myself ;

[24] Ends.

That I may walk a greater devil than thou,
And haunt thee i' the flock-bed [25] and the but-
　　tery.　　　　　　　　　　[*Exeunt.*]

SCENE V [26]

[*Enter*] LOVEWIT [*in the Spanish dress, with the
　　Parson.　Loud knocking at the door.*]

LOVE.　What do you mean, my masters?
MAM.　[*without*]　　　　Open your door,
Cheaters, bawds, conjurers.
OFFI.　[*without*]　　　Or we 'll break it open.
LOVE.　What warrant have you?
OFFI.　[*without*]　　　Warrant enough, sir,
　　doubt not,
If you 'll not open it.
LOVE.　　　　　Is there an officer there?
OFFI.　[*without*] Yes, two or three for [27]
　　failing.
LOVE.　　　　　　　Have but patience,
And I will open it straight.

[*Enter* FACE.]

FACE.　　　　　　　Sir, ha' you done?
Is it a marriage? perfect?
LOVE.　　　　　　　Yes, my brain.
FACE.　Off with your ruff and cloak then ;
　　be yourself, sir.
SUR.　[*without*] Down with the door.
KAS.　[*without*]　　　'Slight, ding [28] it open.
LOVE.　[*opening the door*]　　　Hold,
Hold, gentlemen ; what means this vio-
　　lence?　　　　　　　　　　10

[*Enter* MAMMON, SURLY, KASTRIL, ANANIAS,
　　TRIBULATION, *and* Officers.]

MAM.　Where is this collier?
SUR.　　　　　　And my Captain Face ?
MAM.　These day-owls.
SUR.　　　That are birding [29] in men's purses.
MAM.　Madam Suppository.
KAS.　　　　　　　Doxy, my suster.
ANA.　　　　　　　　Locusts
Of the foul pit.
TRI.　　　Profane as Bel and the Dragon.
ANA.　Worse than the grasshoppers, or the
　　lice of Egypt.
LOVE.　Good gentlemen, hear me.　Are you
　　officers,
And cannot stay this violence?
[1] OFFI.　　　　　Keep the peace.

[25] Mattress.
[26] The outer room of the same.
[27] Against, for fear of.
[28] Smash.　　[29] Pilfering.

LOVE. Gentlemen, what is the matter?
    Whom do you seek?
MAM. The chemical cozener.
SUR.   And the captain pander.
KAS. The nun my suster.
MAM.   Madam Rabbi.
ANA.   Scorpions, 20
And caterpillars.
LOVE.   Fewer at once, I pray you.
[1] OFFI. One after another, gentlemen, I
    charge you,
By virtue of my staff ——
ANA.   They are the vessels
Of pride, lust, and the cart.
LOVE.   Good zeal, lie still
A little while.
TRI.   Peace, Deacon Ananias.
LOVE. The house is mine here, and the
    doors are open ;
If there be any such persons as you seek for,
Use your authority, search on o' God's name.
I am but newly come to town, and finding
This tumult 'bout my door, to tell you true, 30
It somewhat maz'd me ; till my man here,
    fearing
My more displeasure, told me [he] [30] had done
Somewhat an insolent part : let out my house
(Belike presuming on my known aversion
From any air o' the town while there was sick-
    ness),
To a doctor and a captain ; who, what they are
Or where they be, he knows not.
MAM.   Are they gone?
LOVE. You may go in and search, sir.
    (*They enter.*) Here, I find
The empty walls worse than I left 'em, smok'd,
A few crack'd pots, and glasses, and a furnace ;
The ceiling fill'd with poesies of the candle,[31] 41
And " Madam with a dildo " [32] writ o' the
    walls.
Only one gentlewoman I met here
That is within, that said she was a widow ——
KAS. Ay, that's my suster ; I'll go thump
    her. Where is she?   [*Exit.*]
LOVE. And should ha' married a Spanish
    count, but he,
When he came to 't, neglected her so grossly,
That I, a widower, am gone through with her.
SUR. How ! have I lost her then?
LOVE.   Were you the don, sir?
Good faith, now she does blame yo' extremely,
    and says   50

You swore, and told her you had ta'en the
    pains
To dye your beard, and umber o'er your face,
Borrowed a suit and ruff, all for her love ;
And then did nothing. What an oversight
And want of putting forward, sir, was this !
Well fare an old harquebusier [33] yet,
Could prime his powder, and give fire, and hit,
All in a twinkling !   MAMMON *comes forth.*
MAM.   The whole nest are fled !
LOVE. What sort of birds were they?
MAM.   A kind of choughs,
Or thievish daws, sir, that have pick'd my
    purse,   60
Of eightscore and ten pounds within these
    five weeks,
Beside my first materials ; and my goods,
That lie i' the cellar, which I am glad they ha'
    left ;
I may have home yet.
LOVE.   Think you so, sir?
MAM.   Ay.
LOVE. By order of law, sir, but not other-
    wise.
MAM. Not mine own stuff?
LOVE.   Sir, I can take no knowledge
That they are yours, but by public means.
If you can bring certificate that you were
    gull'd of 'em,
Or any formal writ out of a court,
That you did cozen yourself, I will not hold
    them.   70
MAM. I'll rather lose 'em.
LOVE.   That you shall not, sir,
By me, in troth ; upon these terms, they are
    yours.
What, should they ha' been, sir, turn'd into
    gold, all?
MAM.   No.
I cannot tell. — It may be they should. —
    What then?
LOVE. What a great loss in hope have you
    sustain'd !
MAM. Not I ; the commonwealth has.
FACE.   Ay, he would ha' built
The city new ; and made a ditch about it
Of silver, should have run with cream from
    Hogsden ;
That every Sunday in Moorfields the younk-
    ers,
And tits [34] and tomboys should have fed on,
    gratis.   80
MAM. I will go mount a turnip-cart, and
    preach

---

[30] Add. F₂.
[31] *I.e.*, marks of soot.
[32] Probably a line from an obscene song.

[33] Musketeer.   [34] Wenches.

The end o' the world within these two months. Surly,

What! in a dream?

SUR.   Must I needs cheat myself
With that same foolish vice of honesty!
Come, let us go and hearken out the rogues.
That Face I'll mark for mine, if e'er I meet him.

FACE. If I can hear of him, sir, I'll bring you word
Unto your lodging; for in troth, they were strangers
To me; I thought 'em honest as myself, sir.
[ANANIAS *and* TRIBULATION] *come forth.*

TRI. 'T is well; the saints shall not lose all yet. Go   90
And get some carts ——

LOVE.   For what, my zealous friends?

ANA. To bear away the portion of the righteous
Out of this den of thieves.

LOVE.   What is that portion?

ANA. The goods, sometimes [35] the orphans', that the brethren
Bought with their silver pence.

LOVE.   What, those i' the cellar,
The knight Sir Mammon claims?

ANA.   I do defy
The wicked Mammon, so do all the brethren,
Thou profane man! I ask thee with what conscience
Thou canst advance that idol against us,
That have the seal? [36] Were not the shillings numb'red   100
That made the pounds; were not the pounds told out
Upon the second day of the fourth week,
In the eighth month, upon the table dormant,
The year of the last patience of the saints,
Six hundred and ten?

LOVE.   Mine earnest vehement botcher,
And deacon also, I cannot dispute with you:
But if you get you not away the sooner,
I shall confute you with a cudgel.

ANA.   Sir.

TRI. Be patient, Ananias.

ANA.   I am strong,   109
And will stand up, well girt, against an host
That threaten Gad in exile.

LOVE.   I shall send you
To Amsterdam, to your cellar.

ANA.   I will pray there,
Against thy house. May dogs defile thy walls,

And wasps and hornets breed beneath thy roof,
This seat of falsehood, and this cave of coz'-nage!
[*Exeunt* ANANIAS *and* TRIBULATION.]

DRUGGER *enters, and* [LOVEWIT] *beats him away.*

LOVE. Another too?

DRUG.   Not I, sir; I am no brother.

LOVE. Away, you Harry Nicholas! [37] do you talk?   [*Exit* DRUGGER.]

FACE. (*to the* Parson) No, this was Abel Drugger. Good sir, go,
And satisfy him; tell him all is done;
He stay'd too long a-washing of his face.   120
The Doctor, he shall hear of him at Westchester; [38]
And of the Captain, tell him, at Yarmouth, or
Some good port town else, lying for a wind.
[*Exit* Parson.]
If you can get off the angry child now, sir —

[*Enter* KASTRIL *and* DAME PLIANT.]

KAS. (*to his sister*) Come on, you ewe, you have match'd most sweetly, ha' you not?
Did not I say I would never ha' you tupp'd
But by a dubb'd boy,[39] to make you a lady-tom?
'Slight, you are a mammet![40] O, I could touse you now.
Death, mun[41] you marry, with a pox!

LOVE.   You lie, boy;
As sound as you; and I am aforehand with you.

KAS.   Anan?[42]   130

LOVE. Come, will you quarrel? I will feeze[43] you, sirrah;
Why do you not buckle to your tools?

KAS.   God's light,
This is a fine old boy as e'er I saw!

LOVE. What, do you change your copy now? Proceed;
Here stands my dove: stoop[44] at her if you dare.

KAS. 'Slight, I must love him! I cannot choose, i' faith!

[35] Formerly.
[36] *I.e.*, are sealed as God's people.
[37] *I.e.*, fanatic. Nicholas, a Westphalian, founded the sect called "The Family of Love."
[38] *I.e.*, nowhere.
[39] Knight.   [40] Puppet.
[41] Must.   [42] Eh?
[43] Rout, do for, beat.
[44] Pounce (with punning allusion to "Kastril" = hawk).

An I should be hang'd for 't. Suster, I protest,
I honor thee for this match.

    Love.   Oh, do you so, sir?
    Kas. Yes, an thou canst take tobacco and
    drink, old boy,
I 'll give her five hundred pound more to her
    marriage,   140
Than her own state.

    Love.   Fill a pipeful, Jeremy.
    Face. Yes ; but go in and take it, sir.
    Love.   We will.
I will be rul'd by thee in anything, Jeremy.

    Kas. 'Slight, thou art not hidebound !
    thou art a jovy [45] boy !
Come, let 's in, I pray thee, and take our
whiffs.

    Love. Whiff in with your sister, brother
    boy.
        [*Exeunt* Kastril *and* Dame Pliant.]
                — That master
That had receiv'd such happiness by a serv-
ant,
In such a widow, and with so much wealth,
Were very ungrateful, if he would not be

[45] Jovial.

A little indulgent to that servant's wit,   150
And help his fortune, though were some small
    strain
Of his own candor.[46] — [*advancing*] Therefore,
    gentlemen,
And kind spectators, if I have outstripp'd
An old man's gravity, or strict canon, think
What a young wife and a good brain may do ·
Stretch age's truth sometimes, and crack it
    too. —
Speak for thyself, knave.

    Face.   So I will, sir. — Gentlemen,
My part a little fell in this last scene,
Yet 't was decorum.[47] And though I am clean
Got off from Subtle, Surly, Mammon, Dol, 160
Hot Ananias, Dapper, Drugger, all
With whom I traded, yet I put myself
On you, that are my country ;[48] and this
    pelf
Which I have got, if you do quit [49] me, rests,
To feast you often, and invite new guests.
                  [*Exeunt.*]

[46] Integrity.
[47] *I.e.*, the author has preserved the dramatic
propriety of my character.
[48] The jury that is to render a verdict in my case.
[49] Acquit.

BARTHOLMEW FAYRE:

A COMEDIE,

ACTED IN THE YEARE, 1614.

By the Lady *ELIZABETHS* SERVANTS.

And then dedicated to King IAMES, of most *Blessed Memorie*;

By the Author, BENIAMIN IOHNSON.

Si foret in terris, rideret Democritus : *nam*
Spectaret populum ludis attentius ipsis,
Vt sibi præbentem, mimo spectacula plura.
Scriptores autem narrare putaret asello
Fabellam surdo. Hor.lib.2.Epist. I.

LONDON,
Printed by *I.B.* for ROBERT ALLOT, and are
to be sold at the signe of the *Beare*, in *Pauls*
Church-yard. 1631.

INTRODUCTORY NOTE

THIS gaudiest of Elizabethan plays, and most unctuously comic of Jonson's masterpieces, was produced in 1614 but was not included in the Folio of 1616, perhaps because the Lady Elizabeth's Men, who acted it, were unwilling to release a still successful piece. It was separately printed, in folio, in 1631, and reissued in 1640 in the Second Folio, which was edited by Sir Kenelm Digby. According to Aubrey, Jonson wrote it at King James's suggestion. Whether or not the tradition is authentic, the play was given at court the day after its opening performance at the Hope on October 31, 1614. The monarch who wished to harry the whole Puritan sect out of his kingdom must have enjoyed with the keenest relish this attempt at laughing them out of it.

Yet so wide is the net of his satire, and so carefully does he refrain from mounting the rostrum *in propria persona*, that Jonson almost succeeds in giving the impression that we are not listening to the prejudices of a court dramatist but are actually watching his victims as, against the multi-colored background of the best fair in English literature, they expose themselves. Comparison with the other great dramatic indictment of religious hypocrisy is inevitable, and not wholly to Jonson's discredit. For if, excepting its conclusion, Molière's is the better drama, Tartuffe himself is but a pale abstraction beside the immortal pig-eater, Rabbi Busy. And the latter is surrounded by a gallery of Hogarthian portraits unsurpassed, if indeed equalled, in dramatic literature. Rogues, hypocrites, and fools are the satirist's staples, and here they are — in droves. Though the action takes place on a single day, plot sometimes sinks temporarily out of sight beneath the glittering surface of the Fair itself; but character, never. Jonson is everything in this play that the dramatist of manners ought to be : fascinated by the human circus, but sceptical of its fiery hoops and tinsel; full himself of fantastic clowneries, but steadily dominated by an idea; amused by all excesses, even of wickedness, but morally unshaken by his amusement; and, above all, omniscient. How he gained his knowledge, how he gained even his several vocabularies, we had perhaps better not inquire. But gain them he did, and not from books.

Attempts have been made to identify various contemporaries as the objects of personal satire. The most plausible suggestion is that Lantern Leatherhead is in part intended to ridicule the great architect Inigo Jones, Jonson's collaborator in staging his court masques, and afterwards his detested enemy.

Unlike *Catiline*, its immediate predecessor on the pubic stage, *Bartholomew Fair* was a great success. Jonson had made up his mind to give his public not, as before, what he considered best for it, but what he knew it wanted. The Induction still betrays a Shavian complex of superiority to the drama's patrons, who are supposed to promulgate its laws; but now the tone is genial, and the author's tolerance is even extended to his characters : this time the rascals get off scot-free. This relaxation of Jonson's habitual severity is not unwelcome, for if all the rogues and simpletons of the Fair came by their deserts we should have a conclusion far too dismal and depressing to be subject to the comic spirit that presides over this play.

The success of *Bartholomew Fair* continued under the Restoration, when, as might be expected, its revival captivated the Merry Monarch and his courtiers, whose long exile had been enforced by the triumph of the party it derides. The play has been separately edited by C. S. Alden (1904). The present text is based on the Folio of 1631, with a few corrections from the Folio of 1692.

BARTHOLOMEW[1] FAIR

BEN JONSON

THE PERSONS OF THE PLAY

John Littlewit, a proctor.[2]

Zeal-of-the-land Busy, suitor [to Dame Purecraft], a Banbury [3] man.

Winwife, his rival, a gentleman.

[Tom] Quarlous, his companion, a gamester.

Bartholemew Cokes [4], an esquire of Harrow.

Humphrey Wasp, his man.

Adam Overdo, a justice of the peace.

Lant[ern] Leatherhead, a hobbyhorse [5] seller.

[Solomon, Littlewit's man.]

Ezekiel Edgeworth, a cutpurse.

Nightingale, a ballad singer.

Mooncalf, tapster [to Ursula].

" Jordan " Knockhum,[6] a hourse-courser [7] and ranger o' Turnbull.[8]

Val. Cutting, a roarer.[9]

Captain Whit, a bawd.

Troubleall, a madman.

[Bristle,] [Haggis,] } watchmen.

[Pocher, a beadle.]

[Filcher,] [Sharkwell,] } doorkeepers [to the puppet-show.]

[A] Clothier, [a Northern man].

[Puppy, a] Wrestler, [a Western man].

A Costardmonger.[10]

[A Corn-cutter.]

A Mousetrap Man [also called a Tinderbox Man].

Win [-the-fight] Littlewit, wife [to John Littlewit].

Dame Purecraft, her mother and a widow.

Dame [Alice] Overdo, [the Justice's] wife.

Grace Wellborn, ward [to Justice Overdo].

Joan Trash, a gingerbread woman.

Urs[u]la, a pig woman.

Punk [11] Alice, mistress o' the game.

Watchmen, Porters, Puppets, [Officers, Boys, and Passengers.]

[The Scene — *London*.]

THE PROLOGUE

TO THE KING'S MAJESTY

Your Majesty is welcome to a fair :
Such place, such men, such language, and such ware
You must expect ; with these, the zealous noise
Of your land's faction,[12] scandaliz'd at toys,
As [13] babies,[14] hobbyhorses, puppet-plays,
And such like, rage, whereof the petulant ways

---

[1] Almost invariably spelled *Bartholmew*. Founded in the twelfth century, and so called because it was held in the precinct of St. Bartholomew's Priory in Smithfield, and at Bartholomew tide, the Fair, which with few exceptions was held annually till 1855, became a great cloth mart, but by the seventeenth century had to a considerable extent lost that dignified character and become a sort of carnival. At the time of our play the Fair lasted three days (August 23–25), beginning the afternoon before St. Bartholomew's Day.

[2] Procurator ; one who conducts cases before ecclesiastical courts.

[3] A Puritan centre.

[4] Cokes = simpleton.

[5] " Toy."

[6] Cunningham suggests that this word is equivalent to "knacker"; *i.e.*, one who kills old horses and sells the flesh for dog's meat.

[7] Horse trader.

[8] A disreputable street in Clerkenwell.

[9] Bully.

[10] Fruit-seller.

[11] Prostitute.

[12] The Puritans, noisy zealots in Jonson's opinion.

[13] Such as.   [14] Dolls.

413

Yourself have known, and have been vex'd with long.
These for your sport, without particular wrong,
Or just complain of [15] any private man
Who of himself or shall think well or can,
The maker doth present, and hopes to-night
To give you for a fairing [16] true delight.

THE INDUCTION

On the Stage

[*Enter the*] Stage-keeper.[17]

STAGE. Gentlemen, have a little patience; they are e'en upon [18] coming, instantly. He that should begin the play, Master Littlewit, the proctor, has a stitch new fall'n in his black silk stocking; 'twill be drawn up ere you can tell [19] twenty. He plays one o' the Arches [20] that dwells about the Hospital,[21] and he has a very pretty part. But for the whole play, will you ha' the truth on 't? — I am looking, lest the poet hear me, or his man, Master [10] Brome,[22] behind the arras [23] — it is like to be a very conceited,[24] scurvy one, in plain English. When 't comes to the Fair once, you were e'en as good go to Virginia, for anything there is of Smithfield. He has not hit the humors; he does not know 'em; he has not convers'd with the Bartholomew birds, as they say; he has ne'er a sword and buckler man in his Fair; nor a little Davy,[25] to take toll o' the bawds there, as in my time; nor a Kindheart,[26] [20] if anybody's teeth should chance to ache, in his play; nor a juggler with a well-educated ape, to come over the chain for the King of England and back again for the Prince,[27] and sit still on his arse for the Pope and the King of Spain! None o' these fine sights!

Nor has he the canvas cut i' the night, for a hobbyhorse man to creep into his she-neighbor, and take his leap there! Nothing! No! an some writer that I know had had but [30] the penning o' this matter, he would ha' made you such a jig-a-jog i' the booths, you should ha' thought an earthquake had been i' the Fair! But these master-poets, they will ha' their own absurd courses; they will be inform'd of nothing. He has (sir reverence) [28] kick'd me three or four times about the tiring-house, I thank him, for but offering to put in with my experience. I'll be judg'd by you, gentlemen, now, but for one conceit [29] of [40 mine! Would not a fine pump upon the stage ha' done well for a property now? and a punk set under upon her head, with her stern upward, and ha' been sous'd by my witty young masters [30] o' the Inns o' Court? [31] What think you o' this for a show, now? he will not hear o' this! I am an ass! I! and yet I kept the stage in Master Tarleton's [32] time, I thank my stars. Ho! an that man had liv'd to have play'd in *Bartholomew Fair*, you [50 should ha' seen him ha' come in, and ha' been cozened i' the cloth-quarter [33] so finely! and Adams,[34] the rogue, ha' leap'd and caper'd upon him, and ha' dealt his vermin about, as though they had cost him nothing! and then a substantial watch to ha' stol'n in upon 'em, and taken 'em away, with mistaking words,[35] as the fashion is in the stage practice.

---

[15] Specific accusation against.
[16] A present purchased at a fair.
[17] A menial employee.
[18] On the point of.   [19] Count.
[20] *I.e.*, a proctor of the Court of Arches, the highest court of the Archbishop of Canterbury. It was then held in St. Mary-le-Bow Church in Cheapside, the first church in London, according to Stowe, to be built on arches, from which both it and the court got their names.
[21] St. Bartholomew's hospital in Smithfield; Littlefield lives near it and, therefore, near the Fair.
[22] Richard Brome, in Jonson's service, and afterwards a dramatist on his account.
[23] The curtain that concealed the inner stage.
[24] Fantastic.
[25] Alden cites *Tarleton's Jests* (1611) in which there is an account of a prostitute's bully (*i.e.*, hired protector), named Black Davie. Apparently Davy became a generic name.
[26] A generic name for itinerant toothpullers.
[27] Charles.

[28] Saving your reverence; *i.e.*, if I may be allowed to employ vulgar language.
[29] Notion.
[30] Gentlemen.
[31] *I.e.*, the law students.
[32] Richard Tarleton, the famous comedian. He died in 1588.
[33] A separate section of the Fair. Alden notes a possible allusion to a story of how Tarleton's clothing was stolen while he was drinking, in his dressing gown, with some musicians who had serenaded him at his tavern.
[34] John Adams, an associate of Tarleton's, in the old Queen's Company.
[35] As in Shakespeare's *Much Ado about Nothing*, III, iii, 178 ff.

[*Enter the*] Bookholder [36] [*and*] a Scrivener
to him.

Book. How now! what rare discourse
are you fall'n upon, ha? Ha' you found [60
any familiars here, that you are so free?
What's the business?

Stage. Nothing, but the understanding
gentlemen o' the ground [37] here ask'd my
judgment.

Book. Your judgment, rascal! for what?
sweeping the stage, or gathering up the broken
apples for the bears within? [38] Away, rogue;
it's come to a fine degree in these spectacles,
when such a youth [39] as you pretend to [70
a judgment. [*Exit* Stage-keeper] — And yet
he may, i' the most o' this matter, i' faith;
for the author has writ it just to his meridian,
and the scale of the grounded judgments here,
his playfellows in wit. — Gentlemen, not for
want of a prologue, but by way of a new one,
I am sent out to you here, with a scrivener,
and certain articles drawn out in haste between our author and you; which if you
please to hear, and, as they appear reason- [80
able, to approve of, the play will follow presently. Read, scribe; gi' me the counter-
pane.[40]

Scriv. " Articles of agreement, indented,[41]
between the spectators or hearers at the
Hope [42] on the Bankside [43] in the county of
Surrey on the one party; and the author of
Bartholomew Fair, in the said place and county,
on the other party: the one-and-thirtieth day
of October, 1614, and in the twelfth year of [90
the reign of our sovereign lord, James, by
the grace of God King of England, France,
and Ireland, Defender of the Faith; and of
Scotland the seven-and-fortieth.

" *Imprimis:* It is covenanted and agreed,
by and between the parties abovesaid, and
the said spectators and hearers, as well the

curious [44] and envious [45] as the favoring and
judicious, as also the grounded judgments
and understandings, do for themselves [100
severally covenant and agree to remain in
the places their money or friends have put
them in, with patience, for the space of two
hours and an half, and somewhat more. In
which time the author promiseth to present
them, by us, with a new, sufficient play, called
Bartholomew Fair, merry, and as full of noise
as sport, made to delight all and to offend
none, provided they have either the wit or the
honesty to think well of themselves. 110

" It is further agreed that every person
here have his or their free will of censure,[46]
to like or dislike at their own charge, the
author having now departed with [47] his right.
It shall be lawful for any man to judge his six
pen'orth, his twelve pen'orth, so to his eigh-
teenpence, two shillings, half a crown,[48] to
the value of his place; provided always his
place get not above his wit.[49] And if he pay
for half a dozen, he may censure for all [120
them too, so [50] that he will undertake that
they shall be silent. He shall put in for censures here, as they do for lots at the lottery;
marry, if he drop but sixpence at the door
and will censure a crown's-worth, it is thought
there is no conscience or justice in that.

" It is also agreed that every man here
exercise his own judgment, and not censure
by contagion, or upon trust, from another's
voice or face, that sits by him, be he never [130
so first in the commission of wit; as also,
that he be fix'd and settled in his censure,
that [51] what he approves or not approves to-
day he will do the same to-morrow; and, if
to-morrow, the next day; and so the next
week, if need be; and not to be brought
about by any that sits on the bench [52] with
him, though they indict and arraign plays
daily. He that will swear *Jeronimo* [53] or
Andronicus [54] are the best plays yet shall [140
pass unexcepted at here, as a man whose judgment shows it is constant and hath stood still

[36] Prompter.
[37] The groundlings, who were admitted for a
trifling fee to stand in the yard. Their tastes were
less refined than those of the occupants of the
galleries.
[38] The Hope theatre was also used for bear-bait-
ing.
[39] The Stage-keeper is evidently represented
as an ancient.
[40] One half of the pair of indentures.
[41] Indentures were duplicate copies of an agreement, written on the same sheet, which was then
irregularly cut in two. Each party to the agreement
held one half.
[42] Erected on the Bankside the year previous to
the production of this play.
[43] The chief theatrical district, on the southern
bank of the Thames, west of London Bridge.

[44] Over-fastidious.   [45] Malicious.
[46] Judgment.   [47] Abandoned.
[48] This scale of prices is higher than appears to
have been usual, probably because it was raised
for the opening performance.
[49] Jonson's thinly-veiled contempt for his audience, though characteristic of him, was on the
present occasion partly inspired by the failure of
his latest play, *Catiline.*
[50] Provided.   [51] So that.
[52] The judicial bench.   [53] *The Spanish Tragedy.*
[54] Shakespeare's *Titus Andronicus,* c. 1593. But
it was probably a revision of a still older play.

these five-and-twenty or thirty years. Though it be an ignorance, it is a virtuous and staid ignorance ; and, next to truth, a confirm'd error does well ; such a one the author knows where to find him.

" It is further covenanted, concluded, and agreed that how great soever the expectation be, no person here is to expect more than [150 he knows, or better ware than a fair will afford ; neither to look back to the sword and buckler age of Smithfield, but content himself with the present.   Instead of a little Davy, to take toll o' the bawds, the author doth promise a strutting horse-courser, with a leer [55] drunkard, two or three to attend him, in as good equipage as you would wish.   And then, for Kindheart the toothdrawer, a fine, oily pig woman, with her tapster, to bid [160 you welcome, and a consort of roarers,[56] for music ; a wise Justice of Peace meditant,[57] instead of a juggler with an ape ; a civil cut-purse searchant ; a sweet singer of new ballads allurant ; and as fresh an hypocrite as ever was broach'd, rampant.   If there be never a servant monster [58] i' the Fair, who can help it, he says? nor a nest of antics : [59] he is loth to make Nature afraid in his plays, like those that beget ' Tales ', ' Tempests ',[60] and [170 such like drolleries,[61] to mix his head with other men's heels.   Let the concupiscence of jigs [62] and dances reign as strong as it will amongst you ; yet if the puppets will please anybody they shall be entreated to come in.

" In consideration of which, it is finally agreed, by the foresaid hearers and spectators, that they neither in themselves conceal, nor suffer by them to be concealed, any state-decipherer, or politic picklock of the [180 scene, so solemnly ridiculous as to search out who was meant by the gingerbread woman, who by the hobbyhorse man, who by the cos-tardmonger, nay, who by their wares ; or that will pretend to affirm, on his own inspired ignorance, what Mirror of Magistrates [63] is meant by the Justice, what great lady by the pig woman, what conceal'd statesman by the seller of mousetraps, and so of the rest ; but that such person, or persons, so [190 found, be left discovered to the mercy of the author, as a forfeiture to the stage, and your laughter aforesaid.   As also such as shall so desperately, or ambitiously, play the fool by his place aforesaid, to challenge the author of scurrility, because the language somewhere savors of Smithfield, the booth, and the pig-broth, or of profaneness because a madman cries, ' God quit [64] you,' or ' bless you ! ' "   In witness whereof, as you have preposter- [200 ously [65] put to your seals already, which is your money, you will now add the other part of suffrage, your hands. — The play shall presently begin.   And, though the Fair be not kept in the same region that some here perhaps would have it, yet think that therein the author hath observ'd a special decorum,[66] the place being as dirty as Smithfield, and as stinking every whit.

Howsoever, he prays you to believe [210 his ware is still the same ; else you will make him justly suspect that he that is so loth to look on a baby or an hobbyhorse here, would be glad to take up a commodity [67] of them, at any laughter or loss, in another place.   [*Exeunt.*]

ACT I — Scene I [1]

[Enter] Littlewit, *[with a paper.]*

Lit. A pretty conceit, and worth the finding !   I ha' such luck to spin out these fine things still, and, like a silkworm, out of myself.   Here's Master Bartholomew Cokes, of Harrow o' th' Hill, i' th' county of Middlesex, Esquire, takes forth his license to marry Mistress Grace Wellborn, of the said place and county.   And when does he take it forth? to-day !   the four-and-twentieth of August !   Bartholomew Day !   Bartholomew upon [10 Bartholomew !   there's the device !   Who would have mark'd such a leapfrog chance,

---

[55] Sly.   [56] Gang of bullies.

[57] This and the following adjectives in *-ant* are used jocosely after the manner of heraldic terminology.

[58] Probably an allusion to Caliban in *The Tempest.*

[59] Buffoons.

[60] An unmistakable allusion to two of Shakespeare's last plays.

[61] Puppet-shows.

[62] Light entertainments.

[63] *I.e.*, what distinguished magistrate ; the phrase is the title of the famous collection of poems on the fall of princes and magistrates.

[64] Requite.

[65] *I.e.*, reversing the usual order, which was sign and seal.

[66] An allusion to the neoclassical doctrine.

[67] An allusion to a current swindle.   A borrower was required to take a part of the loan in some unsaleable commodity, which an agent of the lender would then buy back at a greatly reduced figure.

[1] A room in Littlewit's house.

now? A very [2] less than ames-ace,[3] on two dice! Well, go thy ways, John Littlewit, Proctor John Littlewit: one of the pretty wits o' Paul's,[4] the Littlewit of London, so thou art call'd, and something beside. When a quirk [5] or a quiblin [6] does scape thee, and thou dost not watch and apprehend it, and bring it afore the constable of conceit [20 (there now, I speak quib too), let 'em carry thee out o' the Archdeacon's court [7] into his kitchen, and make a Jack [8] of thee, instead of a John. — There I am again, la! —

[Enter Mrs. Littlewit.]

Win, good morrow, Win. Ay, marry, Win, now you look finely indeed, Win! this cap does convince.[9] You'd not ha' worn it, Win, nor ha' had it velvet, but a rough country beaver, with a copper band, like the coney-skin woman of Budge Row! [10] Sweet Win, [30 let me kiss it. And her fine high shoes, like the Spanish lady! Good Win, go [11] a little; I would fain see thee pace, pretty Win. By this fine cap, I could never leave kissing on 't.

Mrs. Lit. Come, indeed, la; you are such a fool still!

Lit. No, but half a one, Win; you are the tother half: man and wife make one fool, Win. (Good!) Is there the proctor, or doctor indeed, i' the diocese, that ever [40 had the fortune to win him such a Win? (There I am again!) I do feel conceits coming upon me, more than I am able to turn tongue to. A pox o' these pretenders to wit! your Three Cranes, Mitre, and Mermaid men! [12] not a corn [13] of true salt, nor a grain of right mustard, amongst them all. They may stand for places, or so, again [14] the next wit-fall, and pay twopence in a quart more for their canary than other men. But gi' me the man [50 can start up a justice of wit out of six-shillings beer, and give the law to all the poets and poet-suckers i' town; because they are the players'

gossips! [15] 'Slid! other men have wives as fine as the players, and as well dress'd. Come hither, Win. *[Kisses her.]*

Scene II [16]

[Enter] Winwife, *[to]* Littlewit *[and* Mistress Littlewit.]

Winw. Why, how now, Master Littlewit! measuring of lips, or molding of kisses? which is it?

Lit. Troth, I am a little taken with my Win's dressing here! Does 't not fine, Master Winwife? How do you apprehend,[17] sir? she would not ha' worn this habit. I challenge all Cheapside to show such another: Moorfields,[18] Pimlico [19] path, or the Exchange,[20] in a summer evening — with [10 a lace to boot, as this has. Dear Win, let Master Winwife kiss you. He comes a-wooing to our mother, Win, and may be our father perhaps, Win. There 's no harm in him, Win.

Winw. None i' the earth, Master Littlewit. *[Kisses her.]*

Lit. I envy no man my delicates, sir.

Winw. Alas, you ha' the garden where they grow still! [21] A wife here with a [20 strawberry breath, cherry lips, apricot cheeks, and a soft velvet head,[22] like a melocoton.[23]

Lit. Good, i' faith! — *[aside]* Now dullness upon me, that I had not that before him, that I should not light on 't as well as he! velvet head!

Winw. But my taste, Master Littlewit, tends to fruit of a later kind — the sober matron, your wife's mother.

Lit. Ay, we know you are a suitor, [30 sir; Win and I both wish you well. By this license here, would you had her, that your two names were as fast in it as here are a couple. Win would fain have a fine young father-i'-law, with a feather: [24] that her mother might hood it and chain it with Mistress Overdo. But you do not take the right course, Master Winwife.

---

[2] Gifford adds *little*.
[3] Ambs ace, double aces.
[4] The cathedral was used as a lounge and for business appointments.
[5] Quibble.   [6] Pun.
[7] The court of Arches was the highest court of the Archbishop of Canterbury; the judge was called the Dean of Arches. Archdeacons, suggests Alden, may have presided over routine cases.
[8] Turnspit.   [9] Conquers.
[10] The east end of Watling street; the skinners lived there.
[11] Walk.
[12] Jonson's own circle, and other frequenters of these well-known taverns.
[13] Grain.   [14] Against, in preparation for.

[15] Cronies.
[16] The same. Old eds. *Win.* for Mrs. Littlewit in entrance directions and speech-tags, throughout.
[17] What do you think.
[18] Outside the northern walls.
[19] A summer resort near Hoxton.
[20] The Royal Exchange, an arcaded quadrangle of shops.
[21] Ever.   [22] Headdress.
[23] A peach grafted on a quince.
[24] The mark of a gallant.

WINW. No, Master Littlewit? Why?

LIT. You are not mad enough.   40

WINW. How! Is madness a right course?

LIT. I say nothing, but I wink upon Win. You have a friend, one Master Quarlous, comes here sometimes.

WINW. Why, he makes no love to her, does he?

LIT. Not a tokenworth [25] that ever I saw, I assure you; but —

WINW. What?

LIT. He is the more madcap o' the [50 two. You do not apprehend me.

MRS. LIT. You have a hot coal i' your mouth now, you cannot hold.

LIT. Let me out with it, dear Win.

MRS. LIT. I 'll tell him myself.

LIT. Do, and take all the thanks; and much do good thy pretty heart, Win!

MRS. LIT. Sir, my mother has had her nativity-water [26] cast [27] lately by the cunning men in Cow Lane; and they ha' told [60 her her fortune, and do ensure her she shall never have happy hour unless she marry within this se'nnight; and, when it is, it must be a madman, they say.

LIT. Ay, but it must be a gentleman madman.

MRS. LIT. Yes, so the tother man of Moorfields says.

WINW. But does she believe 'em?

LIT. Yes, and has been at Bedlam twice [70 since every day, to inquire if any gentleman be there or to come there mad.

WINW. Why, this is a confederacy,[28] a mere piece of practice [29] upon her by these impostors!

LIT. I tell her so; or else say I that they mean some young madcap gentleman (for the Devil can equivocate as well as a shopkeeper); and therefore would I advise you to be a little madder than Master Quarlous hereafter.   80

WINW. Where is she? stirring yet?

LIT. Stirring! yes; and studying an old elder come from Banbury, a suitor that puts in here at mealtide, to praise the painful [30] brethren, or pray that the sweet singers may be restor'd; [31] says a grace as long as his

breath lasts him! Sometime the spirit is so strong with him, it gets quite out of him; and then my mother, or Win, are fain to fetch it again with malmsey or aqua cœlestis.[32]   90

MRS. LIT. Yes, indeed, we have such a tedious life with him for [33] his diet, and his clothes too! He breaks his buttons and cracks seams at every saying he sobs out.

LIT. He cannot abide my vocation, he says.

MRS. LIT. No; he told my mother a proctor was a claw of the Beast,[34] and that she had little less than committed abomination in marrying me so as she has done.   100

LIT. Every line, he says, that a proctor writes, when it comes to be read in the Bishop's court, is a long black hair kemb'd out of the tail of Antichrist.

WINW. When came this proselyte?

LIT. Some three days since.

SCENE III [35]

[*Enter*] QUARLOUS [*to*] LITTLEWIT, MRS. LITTLEWIT, [*and*] WINWIFE.

QUAR. Oh, sir, ha' you ta'en soil [36] here? It 's well a man may reach you after three hours' running yet! What an unmerciful companion [37] art thou, to quit thy lodging at such ungentlemanly hours! None but a scatter'd covey of fiddlers, or one of these rag-rakers in dunghills, or some marrowbone man [38] at most, would have been up when thou wert gone abroad, by all description. I pray thee what ailest thou, thou canst not [10 sleep? Hast thou thorns i' thy eyelids, or thistles i' thy bed?

WINW. I cannot tell; it seems you had neither i' your feet, that took this pain to find me.

QUAR. No; an I had, all the lime- [39] hounds o' the city should have drawn after you by the scent rather. — Master John Littlewit! God save you, sir. 'T was a hot night with some of us, last night, John. Shall we [20

---

[25] Tokens were issued by tradesmen in lieu of small change.

[26] Urine used to cast a horoscope.

[27] Figured.

[28] Conspiracy. It was, indeed, a not unknown cheat.

[29] Trickery.   [30] Careful.

[31] *I.e.*, that the silenced Puritan ministers may be permitted to preach again.

[32] Spirits. (Gifford.)

[33] On account of.

[34] Antichrist.

[35] The same.

[36] Taken refuge. A deer "took soil" when it sought refuge in a stretch of water.

[37] Fellow.

[38] Zealous man, eager to be at his morning prayers "Marrowbones" = knees. (Alden.)

[39] From "liam" = leash. (*N. E. D.*)

pluck a hair o' the same wolf to-day,[40] Proctor John?

LIT. Do you remember, Master Quarlous, what we discours'd on last night?

QUAR. Not I, John, nothing that I either discourse or do; at those times I forfeit all to forgetfulness.

LIT. No? not concerning Win? Look you, there she is, and dress'd as I told you she should [41] be. Hark you, sir, [*whis-* [30 *pering*]. — Had you forgot?

QUAR. By this head, I'll beware how I keep you company, John, when I [drink],[42] an you have this dangerous memory, that's certain!

LIT. Why, sir?

QUAR. Why? we were all a little stain'd last night, sprinkled with a cup or two, and I agreed with Proctor John here, to come and do somewhat with Win (I know not [40 what 't was) to-day; and he puts me in mind on 't now; he says he was coming to fetch me. Before truth, if you have that fearful quality, John, to remember when you are sober, John, what you promise drunk, John, I shall take heed of you, John. For this once I am content to wink at [43] you. Where's your wife? — Come hither, Win.

He kisseth her.

MRS. LIT. Why, John! Do you see this, John? Look you! help me, John.   50

LIT. O Win, fie, what do you mean, Win? Be womanly, Win; make an outcry to your mother, Win! Master Quarlous is an honest gentleman, and our worshipful good friend, Win; and he is Master Winwife's friend too; and Master Winwife comes a suitor to your mother, Win, as I told you before, Win, and may perhaps be our father, Win: they'll do you no harm, Win; they are both our worshipful good friends. Master Quarlous! you [60 must know Master Quarlous, Win; you must not quarrel with Master Quarlous, Win.

QUAR. No, we'll kiss again, and fall in.[44]

[Kisses her again.]

LIT. Yes, do, good Win.

MRS. LIT. I' faith, you are a fool, John.

LIT. A fool-John, she calls me; do you mark that, gentlemen? Pretty Littlewit of velvet! a fool-John!

QUAR. [*aside*] She may call you an apple-John,[45] if you use [46] this.   70

[Kisses her again.]

WINW. Pray thee, forbear, for my respect, somewhat.

QUAR. Hoy-day! how respective you are become o' the sudden! I fear this family will turn you reformed [47] too; pray you come about again.[48] Because she is in possibility to be your daughter-in-law, and may ask you blessing hereafter, when she courts it to Totnam,[49] to eat cream! Well, I will forbear, sir; but, i' faith, would thou wouldst [80 leave thy exercise of widow-hunting once, this drawing after an old reverend smock by the splay-foot! [50] There cannot be an ancient tripe or trillibub i' the town, but thou art straight nosing it; and 't is a fine occupation thou 'lt confine thyself to when thou hast got one: scrubbing a piece of buff,[51] as if thou hadst the perpetuity of Pannier Alley [52] to stink in; or, perhaps, worse, currying a carcass that thou hast bound thyself to alive. [90 I'll be sworn, some of them that thou art or hast been a suitor to are so old as no chaste or married pleasure can ever become 'em; the honest instrument of procreation has forty years since left to belong to 'em; thou must visit 'em as thou wouldst do a tomb, with a torch or three handfuls of link,[53] flaming hot, and so thou mayst hap to make 'em feel thee, and after come to inherit [54] according to thy inches.[55] A sweet course for [100 a man to waste the brand of life for, to be still raking himself a fortune in an old woman's embers! We shall ha' thee, after thou hast been but a month married to one of 'em, look like the quartan ague [56] and the black jaundice met in a [57] face, and walk as if thou hadst borrow'd legs of a spinner [58] and voice of a cricket. I would endure to hear fifteen sermons a week for [59] her, and such coarse and loud ones as some of 'em must be! I [110

[40] "A proverbial phrase for getting intoxicated again with the same liquor." (Gifford.)
[41] Was certain to.
[42] Conj. Cunningham. F₁ *drunk;* F₃ *am drunk.*
[43] Close my eyes to, condone.
[44] Agree, be reconciled.
[45] John-apple; it was said to keep for two years and be at its best when shrivelled. It is here intentionally confused with "apple-squire" = pimp.
[46] Make a practice of.
[47] Make a Puritan out of you.
[48] Change your course.   [49] Tottenham.
[50] Tracking down an old woman by following her flat feet.
[51] Tough leather; it was used for jerkins.
[52] Off Newgate Street. Tripe-sellers lived there.
[53] Stuff for torches.   [54] Take possession.
[55] Juvenal, *Satires,* I, i, 41.
[56] A malarial fever, so called because of the recurrence of its paroxysms every fourth day.
[57] One.   [58] Spider.   [59] Instead of.

would e'en desire of fate I might dwell in a drum and take in my sustenance with an old broken tobacco pipe and a straw. Dost thou ever think to bring thine ears or stomach to the patience of a dry grace as long as thy tablecloth ; and dron'd out by thy son here (that might be thy father), till all the meat o' thy board has forgot it was that day i' the kitchen ? [60] or to brook the noise made in a question of predestination by the good labor- [120] ers and painful [61] eaters assembled together, put to 'em by the matron, your spouse, who moderates with a cup of wine ever and anon, and a sentence out of Knox between? or the perpetual spitting before and after a sober-drawn exhortation of six hours, whose better part was the hum-ha-hum? or to hear prayers groan'd out over thy iron chests, as if they were charms to break 'em? And all this, for the hope of two apostlespoons, [62] to [130] suffer! and a cup to eat a caudle in! For that will be thy legacy. She 'll ha' convey'd her state [63] safe enough from thee, an she be a right widow.

WINW. Alas, I am quite off that scent now.

QUAR. How so?

WINW. Put off by a brother of Banbury, one that, they say, is come here, and governs all already.   140

QUAR. What do you call him? I knew divers of those Banburians when I was in Oxford.

WINW. Master Littlewit can tell us.

LIT. Sir! — Good Win, go in, and if Master Bartholomew Cokes his man come for the license (the little old fellow), let him speak with me. [*Exit* MRS. LITTLEWIT.] — What say you, gentlemen?

WINW. What call you the reverend [150] elder you told me of, your Banbury man?

LIT. Rabbi Busy, sir ; he is more than an elder : he is a prophet, sir.

QUAR. Oh, I know him! a baker, is he not?

LIT. He was a baker, sir, but he does dream now and see visions ; he has given over his trade.

QUAR. I remember that too — out of a scruple he took that, in spic'd conscience, those cakes he made were serv'd to bridals, [160] maypoles, morrises, and such profane feasts

and meetings. His Christian name is Zeal-of-the-land.

LIT. Yes, sir ; Zeal-of-the-land Busy.

WINW. How! what a name's there!

LIT. Oh, they have all such names, sir. He was witness for Win here — they will not be called godfathers — and nam'd her Win-the-fight ; you thought her name had been Winifred, did you not?   170

WINW. I did indeed.

LIT. He would ha' thought himself a stark reprobate if it had.

QUAR. Ay, for there was a blue-starch woman o' the name at the same time. [64] A notable hypocritical vermin it is. I know him : one that stands upon his face [65] more than his faith at all times ; ever in seditious motion and reproving for vainglory ; of a most lunatic conscience and spleen, and [180] affects the violence of singularity in all he does. He has undone a grocer here in New-gate Market that broke with him, trusted him with curran[t]s ; as errant a zeal as he (that's by the way). By his profession he will ever be i' the state of innocence, though, and childhood ; derides all antiquity, defies any other learning than inspiration ; and what discretion soever years should afford him, it is all prevented in his original igno- [190] rance. Ha' not to do with him, for he is a fellow of a most arrogant and invincible dull-ness, I assure you. — Who is this?

SCENE IV [66]

[*Re-enter* MRS. LITTLEWIT *with*] WASP [*to*] LITTLEWIT, WINWIFE, [*and*] QUARLOUS.

WASP. By your leave, gentlemen, with all my heart to you ; and God you good morrow. — Master Littlewit, my business is to you. Is this license ready?

LIT. Here, I ha' it for you in my hand, Master Humphrey.

WASP. That's well ; nay, never open or read it to me ; it's labor in vain, you know. I am no clerk ; I scorn to be sav'd by my book ; [67] i' faith, I'll hang first. Fold it up [10] o' your word, and gi' it me. What must you ha' for 't?

[60] *I.e.*, has grown cold.
[61] Painstaking.
[62] Spoons ornamented with the figure of an apostle.
[63] Estate.

[64] Starch was denounced by the Puritans.
[65] Relies upon his (sanctimonious) appearance.
[66] The same.
[67] By benefit of clergy ; Jonson himself by demonstrating his ability to read, was exempted from paying (though he was branded) a more serious penalty for killing the actor, Gabriel Spencer, in a duel.

LIT. We'll talk of that anon, Master Humphrey.

WASP. Now, or not at all, good Master Proctor; I am for no anons, I assure you.

LIT. Sweet Win, bid Solomon send me the little black box within in my study.

WASP. Ay, quickly, good mistress, I pray you; for I have both eggs o' the spit [20 and iron i' the fire. [*Exit* MRS. LITTLEWIT.] — Say what you must have, good Master Little-wit.

LIT. Why, you know the price, Master Numps.[68]

WASP. I know! I know nothing, I! what tell you me of knowing? Now I am in haste, sir, I do not know, and I will not know, and I scorn to know; and yet, now I think on't, I will, and do know as well [30 as another; you must have a mark [69] for your thing here, and eightpence for the box; I could ha' sav'd twopence i' that, an I had bought it myself; but here's fourteen shillings for you. Good Lord, how long your little wife stays! Pray God, Solomon, your clerk, be not looking i' the wrong box, Master Proctor.

LIT. Good i' faith! No, I warrant you; Solomon is wiser than so, sir. 40

WASP. Fie, fie, fie, by your leave, Master Littlewit, this is scurvy, idle, foolish, and abominable, with all my heart; I do not like it. [*Walks aside.*]

WINW. Do you hear, Jack Littlewit? What business does thy pretty head think this fellow may have, that he keeps such a coil [70] with?

QUAR. More than buying of gingerbread i' the cloister [71] here, for that we allow him, [50 or a gilt pouch in the Fair?

LIT. Master Quarlous, do not mistake him; he is his master's both-hands, I assure you.

QUAR. What? to pull on his boots a-mornings, or his stockings, does he?

LIT. Sir, if you have a mind to mock him, mock him softly, and look tother way; for if he apprehend you flout him once, he will fly at you presently. A terrible testy old [60 fellow, and his name is Wasp too.

QUAR. Pretty insect! Make much on him.

[68] Humphrey.
[69] 13 *s.* 4 *d; i.e.*, one-third of £1 sterling.
[70] Bustle, commotion.
[71] "One of the most corrupt places in the Fair." (Alden.)

WASP. [*returning*] A plague o' this box, and the pox [72] too, and on him that made it, and her that went for't, and all that should ha' sought it, sent it, or brought it! do you see, sir?

LIT. Nay, good Master Wasp.

WASP. Good Master Hornet, turd i' [70 your teeth; hold you your tongue. Do not I know you? Your father was a pothecary, and sold glysters, more than he gave, I wusse.[73] And turd i' your little wife's teeth too — here she comes —

[*Re-enter* MRS. LITTLEWIT, *with the box.*]

'twill make her spit, as fine as she is, for all her velvet custard on her head, sir.

LIT. Oh! be civil, Master Numps.

WASP. Why, say I have a humor not to be civil; how then? who shall compel me? [80 you?

LIT. Here is the box now.

WASP. Why, a pox o' your box, once again! Let your little wife stale [74] in it, an she will. Sir, I would have you to understand, and these gentlemen too, if they please —

WINW. With all our hearts, sir.

WASP. That I have a charge, gentlemen.

LIT. They do apprehend, sir.

WASP. Pardon me, sir, neither they [90 nor you can apprehend me yet. You are an ass. I have a young master; he is now upon his making and marring; the whole care of his well-doing is now mine. His foolish schoolmasters have done nothing but run up and down the country with him to beg puddings and cake-bread of his tenants, and almost spoiled him; he has learn'd nothing but to sing catches and repeat, "Rattle, bladder, rattle!" and "O Madge!" I dare [100 not let him walk alone for fear of learning of vile tunes, which he will sing at supper and in the sermon-times! If he meet but a carman i' the street, and I find him not talk to keep him off on him, he will whistle him and all his tunes over at night in his sleep! He has a head full of bees. I am fain now, for this little time I am absent, to leave him in charge with a gentlewoman. 'Tis true, she is a justice of peace his wife, and a gentle- [110 woman o' the hood, and his natural sister; but what may happen under a woman's gov-

[72] Syphilis.
[73] Iwis, assuredly.
[74] Urinate.

ernment, there's the doubt. Gentlemen, you do not know him; he is another manner of piece than you think for! but nineteen year old, and yet he is taller than either of you by the head, God bless him!

QUAR. [*aside*] Well, methinks this is a fine fellow!   119

WINW. [*aside*] He has made his master a finer by this description, I should think.

QUAR. [*aside*] 'Faith, much about one; it's cross and pile [75] whether for a new farthing.

WASP. I'll tell you, gentlemen —

LIT. Will't please you drink, Master Wasp?

WASP. Why, I ha' not talk'd so long to be dry, sir. You see no dust or cobwebs come out o' my mouth, do you? You'd ha' me gone, would you?

LIT. No; but you were in haste e'en [130 now, Master Numps.

WASP. What an I were? So I am still, and yet I will stay too; meddle you with your match, your Win there; she has as little wit as her husband, it seems. I have others to talk to.

LIT. She's my match indeed, and as *littlewit* as I. Good!

WASP. We ha' been but a day and a half in town, gentlemen, 'tis true; and yes- [140 terday i' the afternoon we walk'd London, to show the city to the gentlewoman he shall marry, Mistress Grace; but afore I will endure such another half day with him, I'll be drawn with a good gib-cat [76] through the great pond at home, as his uncle Hodge was! Why, we could not meet that heathen thing all day but stay'd him: he would name you all the signs over, as he went, aloud; and where he spied a parrot or a monkey, [150 there he was pitch'd, with all the little long coats [77] about him, male and female; no getting him away! I thought he would ha' run mad o' the black boy in Bucklersbury [78] that takes the scurvy, roguy tobacco there.

LIT. You say true, Master Numps; there's such a one indeed.

WASP. It's no matter whether there be or no; what's that to you?

QUAR. [*aside*] He will not allow of [160 John's reading [79] at any hand. [80]

[75] Heads or tails.
[76] Gilbert-cat, tomcat.
[77] The children.
[78] Noted for grocers and apothecaries. Tobacco was sold by the latter.
[79] Interpretation, comment.
[80] On any consideration.

SCENE V

[*Enter*] COKES, MISTRESS OVERDO, [*and*] GRACE, [*to*] WASP, QUARLOUS, WINWIFE, LITTLEWIT, [*and*] MRS. LITTLEWIT.

COKES. Oh, Numps! are you here, Numps? Look where I am, Numps! and Mistress Grace too! Nay, do not look angerly, Numps; my sister is here and all; [81] I do not come without her.

WASP. What the mischief [82] do you come with her? or she with you?

COKES. We came all to seek you, Numps.

WASP. To seek me! Why, did you all think I was lost, or run away with your [10 fourteen shillings' worth of small ware here? or that I had chang'd it in the Fair for hobby-horses? 'Sprecious [83] — to seek me!

MRS. OVER. Nay, good Master Numps, do you show discretion, though he be exorbitant, as Master Overdo says, an 't be but for conservation of the peace.

WASP. Marry gip, [84] Goody She-justice, Mistress French-hood! Turd 'n your teeth, and turd in your French-hood's teeth, [20 too, to do you service, do you see? Must you quote your Adam to me? You think you are Madam Regent still, Mistress Overdo, when I am in place! No such matter, I assure you; your reign is out when I am in, dame.

MRS. OVER. I am content to be in abeyance, sir, and be govern'd by you; so should he too, if he did well; but 't will be expected you should also govern your passions. [30

WASP. Will 't so, forsooth! Good Lord, how sharp you are, with being at Bedlam yesterday! Whetstone [85] has set an edge upon you, has he?

MRS. OVER. Nay, if you know not what belongs to your dignity, I do yet to mine.

[81] Also.
[82] Why the devil.
[83] By God's precious [body, etc.]
[84] An exclamation of surprise or derision. *N. E. D.* derives it from "by Mary Gipcy"; *i.e.* "by St. Mary of Egypt."
[85] Cf. Chaucer, *Troilus*, i, 630–632:

> "A fool may eek a wyse man ofte gyde.
> A whetston is no kerving instrument,
> And yet it maketh sharpe kerving-tolis."

Cf. also Ascham, *Toxophilus* (Whole Works, ed. Giles, 1864, II, 9): "Yet some man will marvel why that I being an imperfect shooter, should take in hand to write of making a perfect archer: the same man, perchance, will marvel how a whetstone, which is blunt, can make the edge of a knife sharp." Similarly, the senseless patients at Bedlam have served to set an edge on Mrs. Overdo. (Kittredge.)

WASP. Very well then.

COKES. Is this the license, Numps? For love's sake let me see 't; I never saw a license.   40

WASP. Did you not so? Why, you shall not see 't then.

COKES. An you love me, good Numps.

WASP. Sir, I love you, and yet I do not love you i' these fooleries. Set your heart at rest; there's nothing in 't but hard words; and what would you see 't for?

COKES. I would see the length and the breadth on 't, that's all; and I will see 't now, so I will.   50

WASP. You sha' not see it here.

COKES. Then I 'll see 't at home, and I 'll look upo' the case here.

WASP. Why, do so. — A man must give way to him a little in trifles, gentlemen. These are errors, diseases of youth, which he will mend when he comes to judgment and knowledge of matters. I pray you conceive so, and I thank you. And I pray you pardon him, and I thank you again. [*Walks aside* [60
with COKES, MRS. OVERDO, *and* GRACE.]

QUAR. Well, this dry nurse, I say still, is a delicate man.

WINW. And I am for the cosset,[86] his charge. Did you ever see a fellow's face more accuse him for an ass?

QUAR. Accuse him! It confesses him one without accusing. What pity 't is yonder wench should marry such a Cokes![87]

WINW. 'T is true.

QUAR. She seems to be discreet, and [70 as sober as she is handsome.

WINW. Ay, and, if you mark her, what a restrain'd scorn she casts upon all his behavior and speeches!

COKES. Well, Numps, I am now for another piece of business more — the Fair, Numps, and then —

WASP. Bless me! deliver me! help, hold me! the Fair!   79

COKES. Nay, never fidge up and down, Numps, and vex itself.[88] I am resolute Bartholomew in this; I 'll make no suit on 't to you; 't was all the end of my journey indeed, to show Mistress Grace my Fair. I call 't my Fair, because of Bartholomew: you know my name is Bartholomew, and Bartholomew Fair.

LIT. That was mine afore, gentlemen; this morning. I had that, i' faith, upon his license; believe me, there he comes after me. [90

QUAR. Come, John, this ambitious wit of yours, I am afraid, will do you no good i' the end.

LIT. No? why, sir?

QUAR. You grow so insolent with it, and overdoing, John, that if you look not to it, and tie it up, it will bring you to some obscure place in time, and there 't will leave you.

WINW. Do not trust it too much, John; be more sparing, and use it but now and [100 then; a wit is a dangerous thing in this age: do not overbuy it.

LIT. Think you so, gentlemen? I 'll take heed on 't hereafter.

MRS. LIT. Yes, do, John.

COKES. A pretty little soul, this same Mistress Littlewit; would I might marry her.

GRACE. [*aside*] So would I, or anybody else,[89] so[90] I might scape you.   109

COKES. Numps, I will see it, Numps; 't is decreed; never be melancholy for the matter.

WASP. Why, see it, sir, see it, do see it! Who hinders you? Why do you not go see it? 'Slid, see it!

COKES. The Fair, Numps, the Fair!

WASP. Would the Fair and all the drums and rattles in 't were i' your belly for me.[91] They are already i' your brain! He that had the means to travel your head now, should meet finer sights than any are i' the Fair, [120 and make a finer voyage on 't; to see it all hung with cockleshells, pebbles, fine wheat straws, and here and there a chicken's feather, and a cobweb.

QUAR. [*aside*] Good faith, he looks, methinks, an you mark him, like one that were made to catch flies, with his Sir Cranion legs.[92]

WINW. [*aside*] And his Numps,[93] to flap 'em away.   129

WASP. God be w' you, sir! There 's your bee in a box, and much good do 't you!
                        [*Gives* COKES *the box.*]

COKES. Why, your friend, and Bartholomew, an you be so contumacious.

QUAR. What mean you, Numps?
              [*Takes* WASP *aside as he is going out.*]

---

[86] A pet lamb, especially one brought up by hand.
[87] See on *Dramatis Personae.*
[88] Yourself.

[89] So do I wish that you would marry her or anyone else.
[90] Provided that.
[91] For all of me, as far as I am concerned.
[92] Thin legs, like an insect's; here a spider's are thought of, though in Drayton's *Nimphidia* we have Fly Cranion.
[93] Numps = a stupid person.

WASP. I 'll not be guilty, I, gentlemen.

MRS. OVER. You will not let him go, Brother, and lose him?

COKES. Who can hold that will away? [94] I had rather lose him than the Fair, I wusse.   140

WASP. You do not know the inconvenience, gentlemen, you persuade to, nor what trouble I have with him in these humors.   If he go to the Fair, he will buy of everything to a baby there, and household stuff for that [95] too.   If a leg or an arm on him did not grow on, he would lose it i' the press.   Pray Heaven I bring him off with but one stone! [96]   And then he is such a ravener after fruit!   You will not believe what a coil I had tother day [150 to compound a business between a Cat'er'ne-pear [97] woman and him, about snatching! 'T is intolerable, gentlemen.

WINW. Oh! but you must not leave him now to these hazards, Numps.

WASP. Nay, he knows too well I will not leave him; and that makes him presume. — Well, sir, will you go now?   If you have such an itch i' your feet, to foot it to the Fair, why do you stop?   Am I your tarriers?   Go, [160 will you go, sir?   why do you not go?

COKES. Oh, Numps!   Have I brought you about? — Come, Mistress Grace, and Sister; I am resolute Bat, [98] i' faith, still.

GRA. Truly, I have no such fancy to the Fair, nor ambition to see it; there 's none goes thither of any quality [99] or fashion.

COKES. O Lord, sir!   You shall pardon me, Mistress Grace; we are enow of our-selves to make it a fashion; and, for qualities, let Numps alone — he 'll find qualities.   171

[*Exeunt* COKES, MISTRESS OVERDO, GRACE, *and* WASP.]

QUAR. What a rogue in apprehension is this, to understand her language no better!

WINW. Ay, and offer to marry to her! Well, I will leave the chase of my widow for to-day, and directly to the Fair.   These flies cannot, this hot season, but engender us excellent creeping sport.

QUAR. A man that has but a spoonful of brain would think so. — Farewell, John.   180

[*Exeunt* QUARLOUS *and* WINWIFE.]

LIT. Win, you see 't is in fashion to go to the Fair, Win; we must to the Fair too,

you and I, Win.   I have an affair i' the Fair, Win, a puppet-play of mine own making (say nothing), that I writ for the motion [100] man, which you must see, Win.

MRS. LIT. I would I might, John; but my mother will never consent to such a profane motion, [101] she will call it.   189

LIT. Tut! we 'll have a device, a dainty one. — Now, Wit, help at a pinch, good Wit, come, come, good Wit, an 't be thy will! — I have it, Win; I have it, i' faith, and 't is a fine one. Win, long [102] to eat of a pig, sweet Win, i' the Fair, do you see?   i' the heart o' the Fair, not at Pie Corner. [103]   Your mother will do anything, Win, to satisfy your longing, you know; pray thee long presently; and be sick o' the sudden, good Win.   I 'll go in and tell her; cut thy lace i' the meantime, and [200 play the hypocrite, sweet Win.

MRS. LIT. No, I 'll not make me un-ready [104] for it.   I can be hypocrite enough, though I were never so straight-lac'd.

LIT. You say true, you have been bred i' the family, and brought up to 't.   Our mother is a most elect hypocrite, and has maintain'd us all this seven year with it like gentlefolks.   209

MRS. LIT. Ay, let her alone, John; she is not a wise, wilful widow for nothing, nor a sanctified sister for a song.   And let me alone too; I ha' somewhat o' the mother in me, you shall see; fetch her, fetch her.   [*Exit* LIT-TLEWIT.] — Ah! ah!

SCENE VI [105]

[*Re-enter*] LITTLEWIT [*with* DAME] PURECRAFT, [*to*] MRS. LITTLEWIT.

PURE. Now the blaze of the beauteous discipline [106] fright away this evil from our house! — How now, Win-the-fight, child! How do you?   Sweet child, speak to me.

MRS. LIT. Yes, forsooth.

PURE. Look up, sweet Win-the-fight, and suffer not the enemy to enter you at this door.   Remember that your education has been with the purest.   What polluted one was it that nam'd first the unclean beast, [10 pig, to you, child?

---

[94] Hold him who wants to go.
[95] The doll.   [96] Testicle.
[97] Catherine pear; a small, early variety.
[98] Bartholomew.
[99] Social standing.

[100] Puppet-show.
[101] A play on the meanings (1) proposal, (2) puppet-show.
[102] Win's pregnancy was doubtless indicated by her costume.
[103] At the entrance to the Fair.
[104] I'll not undress.   [105] The same.
[106] Ecclesiastical system; *i.e.*, of the reformers.

MRS. LIT. Uh, uh!

LIT. Not I, o' my sincerity, Mother. She long'd above three hours ere she would let me know it. — Who was it, Win?

MRS. LIT. A profane black thing with a beard, John.

PURE. Oh, resist it, Win-the-fight : it is the tempter, the wicked tempter ; you may know it by the fleshly motion of pig. Be [20 strong against it and its foul temptations in these assaults, whereby it broacheth flesh and blood, as it were on the weaker side ; and pray against its carnal provocations ; good child, sweet child, pray.

LIT. Good Mother, I pray you that she may eat some pig, and her bellyful too ; and do not you cast away your own child, and perhaps one of mine, with your tale of the tempter. How do you, Win? Are you [30 not sick?

MRS. LIT. Yes, a great deal, John. — Uh, uh!

PURE. What shall we do? Call our zealous brother Busy hither, for his faithful fortification in this charge of the Adversary. [*Exit* LITTLEWIT.] — Child, my dear child, you shall eat pig ; be comforted, my sweet child.

MRS. LIT. Ay, but i' the Fair, Mother. [40

PURE. I mean i' the Fair, if it can be any way made or found lawful.

[Re-enter LITTLEWIT.]

Where is our brother Busy? Will he not come? — Look up, child.

LIT. Presently, Mother, as soon as he has cleans'd his beard. I found him fast by the teeth i' the cold turkey pie i' the cupboard, with a great white loaf on his left hand, and a glass of malmsey on his right. 49

PURE. Slander not the brethren, wicked one.

LIT. Here he is now, purified, Mother.

[Enter ZEAL-OF-THE-LAND BUSY.]

PURE. O brother Busy! your help here, to edify and raise us up in a scruple. My daughter Win-the-fight is visited with a natural disease [107] of women, call'd a longing to eat pig.

LIT. Ay, sir, a Bartholomew pig ; and in the Fair. 59

PURE. And I would be satisfied from you, religiously-wise, whether a widow of the

[107] Discomfort.

sanctified assembly, or a widow's daughter, may commit the act without offence to the weaker sisters.

BUSY. Verily, for the disease of longing, it is a disease, a carnal disease or appetite, incident to women ; and, as it is carnal and incident, it is natural, very natural. Now pig, it is a meat, and a meat that is nourishing and may be long'd for, and so consequently [70 eaten ; it may be eaten, very exceeding well eaten. But in the Fair, and as a Bartholomew pig, it cannot be eaten ; for the very calling it a Bartholomew pig, and to eat it so, is a spice of idolatry, and you make the Fair no better than one of the high places.[108] This, I take it, is the state of the question : a high place.

LIT. Ay, but in state of necessity, place should give place, Master Busy. (I have a conceit left yet.) 81

PURE. Good Brother Zeal-of-the-land, think to make it as lawful as you can.

LIT. Yes, sir, and as soon as you can ; for it must be, sir. You see the danger my little wife is in, sir.

PURE. Truly, I do love my child dearly, and I would not have her miscarry, or hazard her first fruits, if it might be otherwise. 89

BUS. Surely, it may be otherwise ; but it is subject to construction — subject ; and hath a face of offence,[109] with the weak ; a great face, a foul face. But that face may have a veil put over it, and be shadowed, as it were : it may be eaten, and in the Fair, I take it, in a booth — the tents of the wicked : the place is not much, not very much ; we may be religious in midst of the profane — so it be eaten with a reformed mouth, with sobriety and humbleness ; not [100 gorg'd in with gluttony or greediness — there's the fear. For, should she go there as taking pride in the place, or delight in the unclean dressing, to feed the vanity of the eye or the lust of the palate, it were not well, it were not fit, it were abominable, and not good.

LIT. Nay, I knew that afore, and told her on 't. — But courage, Win ; we'll be humble enough : we'll seek out the homeliest booth i' the Fair, that's certain ; rather than fail, we'll eat it o' the ground. 112

PURE. Ay, and I'll go with you myself,

[108] Where the Jews were sometimes seduced into the worship of the heathen gods.
[109] Appearance of sinfulness.

Win-the-fight, and my brother Zeal-of-the-land shall go with us too, for our better consolation.

MRS. LIT. Uh, uh!

LIT. Ay, and Solomon too, Win; the more the merrier. — [*aside*] Win, we'll leave Rabbi Busy in a booth. — Solomon, my cloak. 120

[*Enter* SOLOMON *with the cloak.*]

SOL. Here, sir.

BUS. In the way of comfort to the weak, I will go and eat. I will eat exceedingly, and prophesy; there may be a good use made of it too, now I think on 't: by the public eating of swine's flesh, to profess our hate and loathing of Judaism, whereof the brethren stand taxed. I will therefore eat; yea, I will eat exceedingly. 129

LIT. Good, i' faith; I will eat heartily too, because I will be no Jew; I could never away with [110] that stiff-necked generation. And truly, I hope my little one will be like me, that cries for pig so i' the mother's belly.

BUS. Very likely, exceeding likely, very exceeding likely.

[*Exeunt.*]

ACT II — SCENE I [1]

[*A number of booths, stalls, etc., set out.* LANTERN LEATHERHEAD, JOAN TRASH, *and others, sitting by their wares. Enter*] JUSTICE OVERDO, [*disguised; he stands aside.*]

OVER. Well, in Justice' name, and the King's, and for the Commonwealth! Defy all the world, Adam Overdo, for a disguise, and all story; for thou hast fitted thyself, I swear. Fain would I meet the Lynceus [2] now, that eagle's eye, that piercing Epidaurian serpent (as my Quintus Horace [3] calls him), that could discover a justice of peace (and lately of the Quorum),[4] under this covering. They may have seen many a fool in the [10] habit of a justice; but never till now, a justice in the habit of a fool. Thus must we do though, that wake for the public good; and thus hath the wise magistrate done in all ages. There is a doing of right out of wrong,

if the way be found. Never shall I enough commend a worthy worshipful man,[5] sometime a capital member of this city, for his high wisdom in this point, who would take you now the habit of a porter, now of a car- [20] man, now of the dog-killer, in this month of August;[6] and in the winter, of a seller of tinderboxes. And what would he do in all these shapes? Marry, go you into every alehouse, and down into every cellar; measure the length of puddings,[7] take the gauge of black pots and cans, ay, and custards, with a stick; and their circumference, with a thread; weigh the loaves of bread on his middle finger; then would he send for 'em [30] home; give the puddings to the poor, the bread to the hungry, the custards to his children; break the pots, and burn the cans, himself: he would not trust his corrupt officers; he would do 't himself. Would all men in authority would follow this worthy precedent![8] for, alas, as we are public persons, what do we know? nay, what can we know? We hear with other men's ears, we see with other men's eyes! A foolish constable or [40] a sleepy watchman is all our information. He slanders a gentleman by the virtue of his place, as he calls it, and we, by the vice of ours, must believe him. As, awhile agone, they made me, yea, me, to mistake an honest zealous pursuivant [9] for a seminary; [10] and a proper [11] young bachelor of music, for a bawd. This we are subject to that live in high place; all our intelligence is idle, and most of our intelligencers,[12] knaves; and, by your [50] leave, ourselves thought little better, if not errant fools, for believing 'em. I, Adam Overdo, am resolv'd therefore to spare spy-money hereafter, and make mine own discoveries. Many are the yearly enormities of this Fair, in whose courts of Pie-powders [13] I have had the honor, during the three days, sometimes to sit as judge. But this is the special day for detection of those foresaid enormities. Here is my black book for [60] the purpose; this the cloud that hides me;

[110] Endure.
[1] The Fair. Before Ursula's booth.
[2] One of the Argonauts, famous for his keen sight.
[3] *Satires*, I, iii, 26.
[4] Select justices of the peace, without whose presence a bench could not be constituted.
[5] Sir Thomas Hayes, Lord Mayor of London in 1614. (Alden.)
[6] When rabies was especially feared.
[7] Sausages.
[8] Old eds. *president*.
[9] A royal warrant-officer.
[10] Seminarist; an Englishman educated as a Roman Catholic priest in a seminary on the continent; they were banished from England.
[11] Handsome. [12] Spies.
[13] The courts of the fairs. From Fr. *pieds poudreux*, dusty feet. Old eds. *Pye-pouldres*.

under this covert I shall see and not be seen. On, Junius Brutus![14] And, as I began, so I'll end; in Justice' name, and the King's, and for the Commonwealth!

SCENE II [15]

[OVERDO *overhears*] LEATHERHEAD [*and*] TRASH.

LEATH. The Fair's pestilence [16] dead methinks; people come not abroad to-day, whatever the matter is. — Do you hear, Sister Trash, Lady o' the Basket? Sit farther with your gingerbread progeny there, and hinder not the prospect of my shop, or I'll ha' it proclaim'd i' the Fair, what stuff they are made on.

TRASH. Why, what stuff are they made on, Brother Leatherhead? Nothing but [10 what's wholesome, I assure you.

LEATH. Yes, stale bread, rotten eggs, musty ginger, and dead honey, you know.

OVER. Ay! have I met with enormity so soon? [*Makes a note in his black book.*]

LEATH. I shall mar your market, old Joan.

TRASH. Mar my market, thou too-proud peddler? Do thy worst; I defy thee, ay, and thy stable of hobbyhorses. I pay for my ground as well as thou dost. An thou [20 wrong'st me, for all thou art parcel-poet [17] and an inginer,[18] I'll find a friend shall right me and make a ballad of thee and thy cattle all over. Are you puff'd up with the pride of your wares, your arsedine? [19]

LEATH. Go to, old Joan, I'll talk with you anon; and take you down, too, afore Justice Overdo. He is the man must charm [20] you; I'll have you in the Pie-powders.

TRASH. Charm me? I'll meet thee [30 face to face, afore his Worship, when thou dar'st: and, though I be a little crooked o' my body, I'll be found as upright in my dealing as any woman in Smithfield, I. Charm me!

OVER. [*aside*] I am glad to hear my name is their terror yet; this is doing of justice!

[14] Overdo thinks of himself as no less zealous for the state.
[15] The same.
[16] Plaguy. As a matter of fact the Fair had been suspended in 1603 on account of the plague.
[17] Partly poet; *i.e.* a poetaster.
[18] Engineer, designer. Inigo Jones may be referred to.
[19] A gilt alloy of zinc and copper used to ornament toys.
[20] Subdue.

[*Enter* Passengers; *they cross the stage and exeunt.*]

LEATH. What do you lack? what is 't you buy? what do you lack? rattles, drums, halberts, horses, babies o' the best, fiddles [40 o' th' finest!

Enter Costermonger.

COST. Buy any pears, pears, fine, very fine pears? [*Exit* Costardmonger.]

TRASH. Buy any gingerbread, gilt gingerbread?

[*Enter* NIGHTINGALE.]

NIGHT. Hey, [*Sings.*]
> Now the Fair's a-filling!
> Oh, for a tune to startle
> The birds o' the booths here billing,
> Yearly with old Saint Bartle!   50
> The drunkards they are wading,
> The punks and chapmen [21] trading;
> Who'd see the Fair without his lading?

Buy any ballads, new ballads?

[*Enter* URSULA *from inside her booth.*]

URS. Fie upon't! who would wear out their youth and prime thus in roasting of pigs that had any cooler vocation? Hell's a kind of cold cellar to't, a very fine vault, o' my conscience! — What, Mooncalf!

MOON. [*within*] Here, Mistress.   60

NIGHT. How now, Urs'la? in a heat, in a heat?

URS. [*to* MOONCALF] My chair, you false faucet, you; and my morning's draught, quickly: a bottle of ale, to quench me, rascal. — I am all fire and fat, Nightingale; I shall e'en melt away to the first woman, a rib again, I am afraid. I do water the ground in knots, as I go, like a great garden pot; you may follow me by the esses [22] I make.   70

NIGHT. Alas, good Urs. Was Zekiel here this morning?

URS. Zekiel? what Zekiel?

NIGHT. Zekiel Edgeworth, the civil cutpurse — you know him well enough: he that talks bawdy to you still; I call him my secretary.

URS. He promis'd to be here this morning, I remember.

NIGHT. When he comes, bid him stay; I'll be back again presently.   81

URS. Best take your morning's dew in your belly, Nightingale. —

[21] Merchants.
[22] F 1631 *S.S.S.*

MOONCALF *brings in the chair.*

Come, sir, set it here ; did not I bid you should
get this chair let out o' the sides for me, that
my hips might play? You'll never think of
anything till your dame be rump-gall'd.
'T is well, changeling ; [23] because it can take
in your grasshopper's thighs, you care for no
more. Now you look as you had been i' [90
the corner o' the booth, fleaing your breech
with a candle's end, and set fire o' the Fair.
Fill, stoat,[24] fill.

OVER. [*aside*] This pig woman do I know
and I will put her in, for my second enormity ;
[*making a note*] she hath been before me, punk,
pinnace,[25] and bawd, any time these two-and-
twenty years upon record i' the Pie-powders.

URS. Fill again, you unlucky vermin !

MOON. Pray you be not angry, Mistress ;
I'll ha' it widen'd anon.   101

URS. No, no, I shall e'en dwindle away
to 't ere the Fair be done, you think, now you
ha' heated me ! A poor vex'd thing I am ;
I feel myself dropping already as fast as I can ;
two stone a' suet a day is my proportion.
I can but hold life and soul together with
this (here's to you, Nightingale), — and a
whiff of tobacco at most. — Where's my pipe
now? not fill'd? thou arrant incubee.[26]   [110

NIGHT. Nay, Urs'la, thou'lt gall between the tongue and the teeth, with fretting,
now.

URS. How can I hope that ever he'll discharge his place of trust, tapster, a man of
reckoning under me, that remembers nothing
I say to him? [*Exit* NIGHTINGALE.] — But
look to 't, sirrah, you were best. Threepence a pipeful I will ha' made of all my whole
half pound of tobacco, and a quarter [120
of a pound of coltsfoot mix'd with it too, to
[eke] [27] it out. I, that have dealt so long in the
fire, will not be to seek in [28] smoke now. Then
six-and-twenty shillings a barrel I will advance
o' my beer, and fifty shillings a hundred o'
my bottle-ale ; I ha' told you the ways how
to raise it. Froth your cans well i' the filling,
at length, rogue, and jog your bottles o'
the buttock, sirrah ; then skink out [29] the
first glass ever, and drink with all companies,
though you be sure to be drunk — [131
you'll misreckon the better, and be less

asham'd on 't. But your true trick, rascal,
must be to be ever busy, and mistake away
the bottles and cans, in haste, before they be
half drunk off, and never hear anybody call
(if they should chance to mark you), till you
ha' brought fresh, and be able to forswear
'em. Give me a drink of ale.

OVER. [*aside*] This is the very womb [140
and bed of enormity ! gross as herself ! This
must all down for enormity, all, every whit
on 't.   [*Makes another note.*] — *One knocks.*

URS. Look who's there, sirrah ; five shillings a pig is my price, at least ; if it be a sow
pig, sixpence more. If she be a great-bellied
wife and long for 't, sixpence more for that.
                                    [*Exit* MOONCALF.]

OVER. [*aside*] *O tempora! O mores!* I would
not ha' lost my discovery of this one grievance,
for my place and worship o' the bench. [150
How is the poor subject abus'd here ! Well,
I will fall in with her and with her Mooncalf,
and win out wonders of enormity. —

[*Re-enter* MOONCALF.]

By thy leave, goodly woman, and the fatness
of the Fair, oily as the King's constable's
lamp, and shining as his shoeing-horn ! Hath
thy ale virtue,[30] or thy beer strength, that
the tongue of man may be tickled, and his
palate pleas'd in the morning? Let thy
pretty nephew [31] here go search and see. [160

URS. What new roarer [32] is this?

MOON. O Lord, do you not know him,
Mistress? 't is mad Arthur of Bradley,[33]
that makes the orations. — Brave master, old
Arthur of Bradley, how do you? Welcome
to the Fair ! When shall we hear you again,
to handle your matters,[34] with your back
again' a booth, ha? I ha' been one o' your
little disciples i' my days !

OVER. Let me drink, boy, with my [170
love, thy aunt here, that I may be eloquent :
but of thy best, lest it be bitter in my mouth,
and my words fall foul on the Fair.

URS. Why dost thou not fetch him drink,
and offer him to sit?

---

[23] Idiot.   [24] Weasel, lean one.
[25] Go-between, procuress.
[26] For "incubus"; *i.e.*, nuisance.
[27] F 1631 *itch;* F 1692 *eech.*
[28] Will not be at a loss as regards.
[29] Pour, draw.

[30] Potency.
[31] Thus indirectly terming Ursula "aunt", as he
does directly a moment later. "Aunt" is here a
term of respect.
[32] Bully, big-talker.
[33] There was a whimsical popular character of
this name, about whom ballads were composed.
But, though "mad" may be equivalent to "eccentric", Overdo has told us that he is in the garb of
a fool. There may be a topical allusion here.
[34] Discuss your topics.

Moon. Is it ale or beer, Master Arthur?

Over. Thy best, pretty stripling, thy best; the same thy dove drinketh and thou drawest on holidays.

Urs. [*aside to* Mooncalf] Bring him [180 a sixpenny bottle of ale; they say a fool's handsel [35] is lucky.

Over. Bring both, child. Ale for Arthur, and beer for Bradley. Ale for thine aunt, boy. [*Exit* Mooncalf.] — [*aside*] My disguise takes to the very wish and reach of it. I shall, by the benefit of this, discover enough and more, and yet get off with the reputation of what I would be — a certain middling thing, between a fool and a madman. 190

Scene III [36]

[*Enter*] Knockhum *to them.*

Knock. What, my little lean Urs'la! my she-bear! [37] art thou alive yet, with thy litter of pigs to grunt out another Bartholomew Fair? ha?

Urs. Yes, and to amble afoot, when the Fair is done, to hear you groan out of a car, up the heavy hill.[38]

Knock. Of Holborn,[39] Urs'la; mean'st thou so? For what, for what, pretty Urs?

Urs. For cutting halfpenny purses, or [10 stealing little penny dogs out o' the Fair.

Knock. Oh! good words, good words, Urs!

Over. [*aside*] Another special enormity. A cutpurse of the sword, the boot, and the feather! those are his marks. [*Makes another note.*]

[*Re-enter* Mooncalf *with the ale, etc.*]

Urs. You are one of those horseleeches that gave out I was dead, in Turnbull Street, of a surfeit of bottle-ale and tripes!

Knock. No, 't was better meat, Urs: cows' udders, cows' udders! 21

Urs. Well, I shall be meet [40] with your mumbling mouth one day.

Knock. What! thou 'lt poison me with a newt in a bottle of ale, wilt thou? or a spider in a tobacco pipe, Urs? Come, there 's no malice in these fat folks! I never fear thee,

an I can scape thy lean Mooncalf here. Let 's drink it out, good Urs, and no vapors! [41] 29
[*Exit* Ursula.]

Over. Dost thou hear, boy? There 's for thy ale, and the remnant for thee. — [*aside to* Mooncalf] Speak in thy faith of a faucet now; is this goodly person before us here, this vapors, a knight of the knife?

Moon. [*aside to* Overdo] What mean you by that, Master Arthur?

Over. [*aside to* Mooncalf] I mean a child of the horn-thumb,[42] a babe of booty, boy, a cutpurse. 39

Moon. [*aside to* Overdo] O Lord, sir! far from it. This is Master Dan Knockhum: Jordan,[43] the ranger of Turnbull.[44] He is a horse-courser, sir.

Over. [*aside to* Mooncalf] Thy dainty dame, though, call'd him cutpurse.

Moon. [*aside to* Overdo] Like enough, sir; she 'll do forty such things in an hour, an you listen to her, for her recreation, if the toy take her i' the greasy kerchief: [45] it makes her fat, you see; she battens with it. 50

Over. [*aside*] Here might I ha' been deceiv'd now, and ha' put a fool's blot upon myself, if I had not play'd an after game [46] o' discretion!

Urs'la *comes in again, dropping.*[47]

Knock. Alas, poor Urs! this 's an ill season for thee.

Urs. Hang yourself, hackneyman!

Knock. How, how, Urs! vapors? motion breed vapors? 59

Urs. Vapors! Never tusk,[48] nor twirl your dibble,[49] good Jordan; I know what you 'll take to a very drop. Though you be captain o' the roarers, and fight well at the case of pisspots,[50] you shall not fright me with your lion-chap,[51] sir, nor your tusks.

[35] "The first money taken by a trader in the morning." (*N.E.D.*)
[36] The same.
[37] *Ursula* means "she-bear."
[38] On the way to the gallows at Tyburn.
[39] It was on the route to Tyburn.
[40] Even.

[41] This word occurs frequently in this play. It sometimes means humor, whim, conceit; sometimes bad humor; sometimes a contradictory or hectoring style in conversation; sometimes, as here, quarrelling, either real or feigned as a sort of conversational game.
[42] Cutpurses wore on the thumb a horn thimble, against which to draw the edge of the knife.
[43] Evidently Knockhum's nickname. It means chamber pot.
[44] See on *Persons of the Play*, Knockhum.
[45] If the whim comes into her greasy head.
[46] A second game, undertaken to retrieve one's fortune.
[47] Sweating.   [48] Probably = gnash your teeth.
[49] "Play with your dagger." (Cunningham.) Better: "twist your pointed beard." (Gifford.) Best: "twirl your moustache." (*N.E.D.*)
[50] Instead of pistols.   [51] Jaw.

You angry? You are hungry. Come, a pig's head will stop your mouth, and stay your stomach at all times.

KNOCK. Thou art such another mad, [69 merry Urs, still! Troth, I do make conscience of vexing thee now i' the dog days, this hot weather, for fear of found'ring thee i' the body, and melting down a pillar of the Fair. Pray thee, take thy chair again, and keep state, and let's have a fresh bottle of ale and a pipe of tobacco, and no vapors. I'll ha' this belly o' thine taken up, and thy grass [52] scour'd, wench. — Look, here's Ezekiel Edgeworth; a fine boy of his inches, as any is i' the Fair! has still money in his purse, [80 and will pay all, with a kind heart and good vapors.

SCENE IV [53]

[*Enter*] EDGEWORTH *to them.*

EDG. That I will indeed, willingly, Master Knockhum. — Fetch some ale and tobacco.

[*Exit* MOONCALF. *Passengers* cross *the stage.*]

LEATH. What do you lack, gentlemen? — Maid, see a fine hobbyhorse for your young master; cost you but a token a week his provender.

[*Enter* Corn-cutter *and* Tinderbox Man.]

CORN. Ha' you any corns i' your feet and toes?

TIN. Buy a mousetrap, a mousetrap, or a tormentor [54] for a flea? 10

TRASH. Buy some gingerbread?

[*Enter* NIGHTINGALE.]

NIGHT. Ballads, ballads! fine new ballads! Hear for your love, and buy for your money, A delicate ballad o' " The Ferret and the Coney "; [55] A preservative again' the punk's evil; Another of goose-green starch [56] and the Devil; " A Dozen of Divine Points "; [57] and " The Godly Garters ";

[52] Grasso, a contemporary horse-doctor's term for fat. It was to be scoured by "natural and gentle purging medicines." (Alden.)
[53] The same.
[54] "Some device for catching fleas." (*N.E.D.*)
[55] Pronounced, and often spelled, cunny. Here it means the dupe of the ferret, the seller in the commodity swindle, already explained more than once. See on *The Alchemist*, III, iv, 90.
[56] Colored ruffs were an extravagance of the time.
[57] Tagged laces which held various portions of the clothing together.

" The Fairing of Good Counsel," of an ell and three-quarters.
(What is 't you buy?)
The windmill blown down by the witch's fart, 20
Or " Saint George," that, oh! did break the dragon's heart?

[*Re-enter* MOONCALF.]

EDG. Master Nightingale, come hither; leave your mart a little.

NIGHT. Oh, my secretary! what says my secretary? [*They step aside.*]

OVER. Child o' the bottles, what's he? what [58] he? [*Points to* EDGEWORTH.]

MOON. A civil young gentleman, Master Arthur, that keeps company with the roarers, and disburses all still. He has ever money [30 in his purse; he pays for them, and they roar for him; one does good offices for another. They call him the secretary, but he serves nobody. A great friend of the ballad man's; they are never asunder.

OVER. What pity 't is, so civil a young man should haunt this debauch'd company! Here's the bane of the youth of our time apparent. A proper penman, I see 't in his countenance; he has a good clerk's look [40 with him, and, I warrant him, a quick hand.

MOON. A very quick hand, sir! [*Exit.*]

EDG. All the purses and purchase [59] I give you to-day by conveyance, bring hither to Urs'la's presently. Here we will meet at night in her lodge, and share. Look you choose good places for your standing i' the Fair, when you sing, Nightingale. (*This they whisper, that* OVERDO *hears it not.*)

URS. Ay, near the fullest passages; and shift 'em often. 50

EDG. And i' your singing you must use your hawk's eye nimbly, and fly the purse to a mark [60] still, where 't is worn, and o' which side; that you may gi' me the sign with your beak, or hang your head that way i' the tune.

URS. Enough, talk no more on 't: your friendship, masters, is not now to begin. Drink your draught of indenture, [61] your sup of covenant, and away. The Fair fills apace, company begins to come in, and I have [60 ne'er a pig ready yet.

[58] F 3 *what's.*
[59] Booty.
[60] A term from falconry. The hawk was supposed to stand and mark the spot where a covey had disappeared.
[61] Contract.

KNOCK. Well said! Fill the cups, and light the tobacco : let's give fire i' th' works, and noble vapors.

EDG. And shall we ha' smocks,[62] Urs'la, and good whimsies,[62] ha?

URS. Come, you are i' your bawdy vein! The best the Fair will afford, Zekiel, if bawd Whit keep his word. —

[Re-enter MOONCALF.]

How do the pigs, Mooncalf?   70

MOON. Very passionate, Mistress ; one on 'em has wept out an eye.[63] Master Arthur o' Bradley is melancholy here : nobody talks to him. — Will you any tobacco, Master Arthur?

OVER. No, boy ; let my meditations alone.

MOON. He's studying for an oration now.

OVER. *[aside]* If I can with this day's travail, and all my policy, but rescue this youth here out of the hands of the lewd man and [80 the strange woman,[64] I will sit down at night, and say with my friend Ovid, " *Jamque opus exegi, quod nec Jovis ira, nec ignis,*" etc.[65]

KNOCK. Here, Zekiel, here's a health to Urs'la, and a kind vapor ; thou hast money i' thy purse still, and store! How dost thou come by it? Pray thee, vapor thy friends some in a courteous vapor.

EDG. Half I have, Master Dan Knockhum, is always at your service.   90

OVER. *[aside]* Ha, sweet nature! what goshawk would prey upon such a lamb?

KNOCK. Let's see what 't is, Zekiel ; count it. Come, fill him to pledge me.

SCENE V [66]

[Enter] WINWIFE *[and]* QUARLOUS *to them.*

WINW. We are here before 'em, methinks.

QUAR. All the better ; we shall see 'em come in now.

LEATH. What do you lack, gentlemen, what is 't you lack? a fine horse? a lion? a bull? a bear? a dog or a cat? an excellent fine Bartholomew bird? or an instrument? What is 't you lack?

QUAR. 'Slid! here's Orpheus among the beasts, with his fiddle and all!   10

[62] Wenches.
[63] A sign it is nearly done.
[64] Bawd.
[65] And now I have completed the work, which neither the wrath of Jove, nor fire. . . . (Ovid, *Metamorphoses*, xv, 871.)
[66] The same.

TRASH. Will you buy any comfortable bread,[67] gentlemen?

QUAR. And Ceres selling her daughter's [68] picture, in ginger-work!

WINW. That these people should be so ignorant to think us chapmen[69] for 'em! Do we look as if we would buy gingerbread, or hobbyhorses?

QUAR. Why, they know no better ware than they have, nor better customers than [20 come. And our very being here makes us fit to be demanded, as well as others. Would Cokes would come! there were a true customer for 'em!

KNOCK. *[to EDGEWORTH]* How much is 't? thirty shillings? Who's yonder? Ned Winwife and Tom Quarlous, I think! Yes. Gi' me it all, gi' me it all.[70] — Master Winwife! Master Quarlous! will you take a pipe of tobacco with us? — Do not discredit me now, [30 Zekiel.   *[EDGEWORTH gives him his purse.]*

WINW. *[aside to QUARLOUS]* Do not see him ; he is the roaring horse-courser ; pray thee, let's avoid him : turn down this way.

QUAR. *[aside]* 'Slud, I'll see him, and roar with him, too, an he roar'd as loud as Neptune ; pray thee, go with me.

WINW. *[aside]* You may draw me to as likely an inconvenience,[71] when you please, as this.   40

QUAR. *[aside]* Go to, then ; come along ; we ha' nothing to do, man, but to see sights now.

[They advance to URSULA's booth.]

KNOCK. Welcome, Master Quarlous, and Master Winwife! Will you take any froth and smoke with us?

QUAR. Yes, sir ; but you'll pardon us if we knew not of so much familiarity between us afore.

KNOCK. As what, sir?   50

QUAR. To be so lightly invited to smoke and froth.

KNOCK. A good vapor! Will you sit down, sir? This is old Urs'la's mansion — how like you her bower? Here you may ha' your punk and your pig in state, sir, both piping hot.

QUAR. I had rather ha' my punk cold,[72] sir.

[67] Spiced gingerbread.
[68] Persephone's.
[69] Customers.
[70] Alden suggests that as his instructor in purse-cutting Knockhum was entitled to share in Edgeworth's gains.
[71] As promising a piece of mischief.
[72] *I.e.*, not at all.

OVER. [*aside*] There's for me : punk ! and pig !   60

[*Makes another note.*]

URS. (*calls within.*) What Mooncalf, you rogue !

MOON. By and by ;[73] the bottle is almost off,[74] Mistress. — Here, Master Arthur.

URS. [*within*] I'll part you and your play-fellow there i' the guarded[75] coat, an you sunder not the sooner.

KNOCK. Master Winwife, you are proud, methinks ; you do not talk, nor drink ; are you proud?   70

WINW. Not of the company I am in, sir, nor the place, I assure you.

KNOCK. You do not except at the company, do you? are you in vapors, sir?

MOON. Nay, good Master Dan Knockhum, respect my mistress' bower, as you call it ; for the honor of our booth, none o' your vapors here.

[URSULA] *comes out with a firebrand.*

URS. [*aside to* MOONCALF] Why, you thin, lean polecat you, an they have a mind [80 to be i' their vapors, must you hinder 'em? What did you know, vermin, if they would ha' lost a cloak, or such a trifle? Must you be drawing the air of pacification here, while I am tormented within i' the fire, you weasel?

MOON. [*aside to* URSULA] Good Mistress, 't was in the behalf of your booth's credit[76] that I spoke.

URS. [*aside to* MOONCALF] Why ! would my booth ha' broke[77] if they had fall'n out [90 in 't, sir? or would their heat ha' fir'd it? — In, you rogue, and wipe the pigs, and mend the fire, that they fall not, or I'll both baste and roast you till your eyes drop out, like 'em. Leave the bottle behind you, and be curs'd[78] awhile !   [*Exit* MOONCALF.]

QUAR. Body o' the Fair ![79] what 's this? mother o' the bawds?

KNOCK. No, she's mother o' the pigs, sir, mother o' the pigs.   100

WINW. Mother o' the Furies, I think, by her firebrand.

QUAR. Nay, she is too fat to be a Fury ; sure, some walking sow of tallow !

WINW. An inspir'd[80] vessel of kitchen stuff !

QUAR. She'll make excellent gear for the coachmakers here in Smithfield to anoint wheels and axletrees with.

She drinks this while.

URS. Ay, ay, gamesters ; mock a plain, [110 plump, soft wench o' the suburbs,[81] do, be-cause she's juicy and wholesome. You must ha' your thin pinch'd ware, pent up i' the compass of a dog-collar, or 't will not do — that looks like a long-lac'd conger set upright, and a green feather, like fennel, i' the jowl[82] on 't.

KNOCK. Well said, Urs, my good Urs. To 'em, Urs.

QUAR. Is she your quagmire,[83] Dan [120 Knockhum? Is this your bog?

NIGHT. We shall have a quarrel presently.

KNOCK. How ! bog? quagmire? foul va-pors ! hum'h !

QUAR. Yes, he that would venture for 't, I assure him, might sink into her and be drown'd a week ere any friend he had could find where he were.

WINW. And then he would be a fortnight weighing up again.   130

QUAR. 'T were like falling into a whole shire of butter ; they had need be a team of Dutchmen should draw him out.

KNOCK. Answer 'em, Urs ! Where's thy Bartholomew wit now, Urs, thy Bartholomew wit?

URS. Hang 'em, rotten, roguy cheaters ! I hope to see 'em plagu'd one day (pox'd they are already, I am sure) with lean playhouse poultry,[84] that has the bony rump sticking [140 out like the ace of spades or the point of a partisan,[85] that every rib of 'em is like the tooth of a saw, and will so grate 'em with their hips and shoulders as, take 'em alto-gether, they were as good lie with a hurdle.[86]

QUAR. Out upon her, how she drips ! She's able to give a man the sweating sick-ness[87] with looking on her.

URS. Marry look off, with a patch o' your

---

[73] At once.
[74] Gone, finished.
[75] Faced, trimmed, ornamented.
[76] Reputation.
[77] Gone bankrupt ; punning on *credit.*
[78] *I.e.*, the devil take you.
[79] Cf. "Body of Christ !", "Body o' me !", etc.

[80] Inflated.
[81] Where the brothels were established.
[82] Head. Fennel was used to garnish fish.
[83] As a horse-dealer Knockhum might be expected to have a patch of soft ground for lame horses to stand in.
[84] Prostitutes who picked up customers at the theatres.
[85] Halberd.
[86] The bars or wattles of which would make it an extremely uncomfortable bedfellow.
[87] It was frequently epidemic and rapidly fatal.

face and a dozen i' your breech,[88] though [150 they [89] be o' scarlet, sir! I ha' seen as fine outsides as either o' yours bring lousy linings to the brokers, ere now, twice a week!

QUAR. Do you think there may be a fine new cucking-stool i' the Fair, to be purchas'd — one large enough, I mean. I know there is a pond [90] of capacity for her.

URS. For your mother, you rascal! Out, you rogue, you hedge-bird,[91] you pimp, you pannier-man's [92] bastard, you!   160

QUAR. Ha, ha, ha!

URS. Do you sneer, you dog's-head, you trendle-tail! [93] You look as you were begotten atop of a cart in harvest time, when the whelp was hot and eager. Go, snuff after your brother's bitch, Mistress Commodity; [94] that 's the livery you wear : 't will be out at the elbows shortly. It 's time you went to 't for the tother remnant.

KNOCK. Peace, Urs; peace, Urs. — [170 [aside] They 'll kill the poor whale and make oil of her. — Pray thee, go in.

URS. I 'll see 'em pox'd first, and pil'd,[95] and double pil'd.

WINW. Let 's away. Her language grows greasier than her pigs.

URS. Does 't so, snotty-nose? Good Lord! are you snivelling? You were engend'red on a she-beggar in a barn, when the bald thrasher, your sire, was scarce warm.   180

WINW. Pray thee, let 's go.

QUAR. No, faith; I 'll stay the end of her now; I know she cannot last long : I find by her similes she wanes apace.

URS. Does she so? I 'll set you gone. — Gi' me my pig-pan hither a little. — I 'll scald you hence, an you will not go.

                            [*Exit* URSULA.]

KNOCK. Gentlemen, these are very strange vapors, and very idle vapors, I assure you!

QUAR. You are a very serious ass, we [190 assure you.

KNOCK. Humh! "Ass"? and "serious"? Nay, then pardon me my vapor. I have a foolish vapor, gentlemen. Any man that does vapor me the "ass", Master Quarlous —

QUAR. What then, Master Jordan?

KNOCK. I do vapor him the lie.

<hr>

88 As a result of syphilis.   89 Your breeches.
90 Stowe calls it Smithfield Pond.
91 Vagrant.   92 Fish or meat peddler's.
93 Curly-tailed dog.
94 Another allusion to the commodity swindle.
95 Stripped of hair by the pox.

QUAR. Faith, and to any man that vapors me the lie, I do vapor that.   200

                            [*Strikes him.*]

KNOCK. Nay then, vapors upon vapors.

                            They fight.

URS'LA *comes in with the scalding-pan.*

EDG. [AND] NIGHT. 'Ware the pan, the pan, the pan — she comes with the pan, gentlemen! — (*She falls with it.*) God bless the woman.

URS. Oh!

               [*Exeunt* QUARLOUS *and* WINWIFE.]

TRASH. [*running to the booth, as does* LEATHERHEAD, *also*]. — What 's the matter?

OVER. Goodly woman!

MOON. Mistress!

URS. Curse of hell, that ever I saw [210 these fiends! Oh! I ha' scalded my leg, my leg, my leg, my leg! I ha' lost a limb in the service! Run for some cream and salad oil, quickly. Are you underpeering, you baboon? Rip off my hose, an you be men, men, men.

MOON. Run you for some cream, good Mother Joan. I 'll look to your basket.

                            [*Exit* TRASH.]

LEATH. Best sit up i' your chair, Urs'la. Help, gentlemen.

KNOCK. Be of good cheer, Urs; thou [220 hast hind'red me the currying of a couple of stallions here, that abus'd the good racebawd [96] o' Smithfield ; 't was time for 'em to go.

NIGHT. I' faith, when the pan came; they had made you run else. — [*aside to* EDGEWORTH.] This had been a fine time for purchase, if you had ventur'd.

EDG. [*aside to* NIGHTINGALE] Not a whit; these fellows were too fine to carry money.

KNOCK. Nightingale, get some help to [230 carry her leg out o' the air; take off her shoes. Body o' me! she has the mallanders, the scratches, the crown scab, and the quittorbone [97] i' the tother leg.

URS. Oh, the pox! why do you put me in mind o' my leg thus, to make it prick and shoot? Would you ha' me i' the hospital afore my time?

KNOCK. Patience, Urs; take a good heart; 't is but a blister as big as a windgall. I 'll [240 take it away with the white of an egg, a little honey and hog's grease, ha' thy pasterns well roll'd,[98] and thou shalt pace again by to-

<hr>

96 Jocosely analogous to race horse.
97 All diseases of the legs or feet of horses.
98 Bandaged.

morrow. I'll tend thy booth, and look to thy affairs the while; thou shalt sit i' thy chair, and give directions, and shine Ursa Major.

[*Exeunt* KNOCKHUM *and* MOONCALF *with* URSULA *in her chair.*]

SCENE VI [99]

OVER. These are the fruits of bottle-ale and tobacco! the foam of the one, and the fumes of the other! — Stay, young man, and despise not the wisdom of these few hairs that are grown grey in care of thee.

EDG. [*aside to* NIGHTINGALE] Nightingale, stay a little. Indeed I'll hear some o' this!

[*Enter* COKES, *with his box*, WASP, MISTRESS OVERDO, *and* GRACE.]

COKES. Come, Numps, come, where are you? Welcome into the Fair, Mistress Grace. 10

EDG. [*aside to* NIGHTINGALE] 'Slight,[100] he will call company, you shall see, and put us into doings presently.

OVER. Thirst not after that frothy liquor, ale; for who knows, when he openeth the stopple, what may be in the bottle? Hath not a snail, a spider, yea, a newt been found there? Thirst not after it, youth; thirst not after it.

COKES. This is a brave [101] fellow, [20 Numps; let's hear him.

WASP. 'Sblood! how brave [102] is he? in a guarded coat! You were best truck [103] with him; e'en strip, and truck presently; it will become you. Why will you hear him? because he is an ass, and may be akin to the Cokeses? [104]

COKES. Oh, good Numps!

OVER. Neither do thou lust after that tawny weed, tobacco. 30

COKES. Brave words!

OVER. Whose complexion is like the Indian's that vents it.

COKES. Are they not brave words, Sister?

OVER. And who can tell, if before the gathering and making up thereof, the alligarta hath not piss'd thereon?

WASP. 'Heart! let 'em be brave words, as brave as they will! An they were all the brave words in a country, how then? [40 Will you away yet? Ha' you enough on him? — Mistress Grace, come you away; I

pray you be not you accessory. — If you do lose your licence, or somewhat else, sir, with list'ning to his fables, say Numps is a witch, with all my heart; do, say so.

COKES. Avoid, i' your satin doublet, Numps!

OVER. The creeping venom of which subtle serpent, as some late writers affirm, [50 neither the cutting of the perilous plant, nor the drying of it, nor the lighting or burning, can any way persway [105] or assuage.

COKES. Good, i' faith! is't not, Sister?

OVER. Hence it is that the lungs of the tobacconist are rotted, the liver spotted, the brain smok'd like the backside of the pig woman's booth here, and the whole body within, black as her pan you saw e'en now without. 60

COKES. [*to* EDGEWORTH] A fine similitude that, sir! Did you see the pan?

EDG. Yes, sir.

OVER. Nay, the hole in the nose here of some tobacco-takers, or the third nostril, if I may so call it, which makes that they can vent the tobacco out, like the ace of clubs, or rather the flower-de-l[u]ce,[106] is caused from the tobacco, the mere tobacco! when the poor innocent pox, having nothing to do [70 there, is miserably and most unconscionably slander'd.

COKES. Who would ha' miss'd this, Sister?

MRS. OVER. Not anybody but Numps.

COKES. He does not understand.

EDG. [*aside*] Nor you feel!

He picketh his purse.

COKES. What would you have, Sister, of a fellow that knows nothing but a baskethilt, and an old fox [107] in't? The best music i' the Fair will not move a log. 80

EDG. [*aside, passing the purse to* NIGHTINGALE.] In, to Urs'la, Nightingale, and carry her comfort. See it told.[108] This fellow was sent to us by Fortune, for our first fairing.

[*Exit* NIGHTINGALE.]

OVER. But what [109] speak I of the diseases of the body, children of the Fair?

COKES. That's to us, Sister. Brave, i' faith!

OVER. Hark, O you sons and daughters of Smithfield! and hear what malady it doth the mind: it causeth swearing, it causeth [90

[99] The same.   [100] By God's light.   [101] Fine.
[102] Finely dressed.   [103] Barter.
[104] See on *Persons of the Play.*

[105] Alleviate.
[106] *I.e.*, in threefold forms. The "third nostril" would be caused, of course, by syphilis, which often attacks the nose.
    [107] Broadsword.   [108] Counted.   [109] Why.

swaggering, it causeth snuffling and snarling, and now and then a hurt.[110]

MRS. OVER. He hath something of Master Overdo, methinks, Brother.

COKES. So methought, Sister, very much of my brother Overdo ; and 't is when he speaks.

OVER. Look into any angle o' the town, the Straits, or the Bermudas,[111] where the [99 quarrelling lesson is read, and how do they entertain the time, but with bottle-ale and tobacco? The lecturer is o' one side, and his pupils o' the other ; but the seconds are still bottle-ale and tobacco, for which the lecturer reads, and the novices pay. Thirty pound a week in bottle-ale ! forty in tobacco ! and ten more in ale again ! Then, for a suit to drink in, so much ; and, that being slaver'd, so much for another suit ; and then a third suit, and a fourth suit ! and still the bottle- [110 ale slavereth, and the tobacco stinketh !

WASP. [*to* COKES] Heart of a madman ! are you rooted here? w[i]ll you never away? What can any man find out in this bawling fellow to grow here for? — He is a full handful higher sin' he heard him. — Will you fix here, and set up a booth, sir?

OVER. I will conclude briefly —

WASP. Hold your peace, you roaring rascal, I 'll run my head i' your chaps else. — [120 You were best build a booth, and entertain him ; make your will, an you say the word, and him your heir ! — Heart, I never knew one taken with a mouth of a peck [112] afore. — By this light, I 'll carry you away o' my back, an you will not come.

He gets him up on pick-pack.

COKES. Stay, Numps, stay ; set me down. I ha' lost my purse, Numps. Oh, my purse ! One o' my fine purses is gone !

MRS. OVER. Is 't indeed, Brother?   130

COKES. Ay, as I am an honest man. Would I were an errant rogue else ! A plague of all roguy damn'd cutpurses for me.

WASP. Bless 'em with all my heart, with all my heart, do you see? Now, as I am no infidel, that I know of, I am glad on 't. Ay, I am (here 's my witness !), do you see, sir? I did not tell you of his fables, I ! No, no, I am a dull malthorse,[113] I ; I know nothing.

[110] Wound.
[111] Names of a disreputable district within the city walls.
[112] As big as a peck measure. (Murray, cited by Alden.)
[113] The brewer's horse, frequently used as a symbol of drudgery.

Are you not justly serv'd, i' your con- [140 science now? speak i' your conscience ! Much good do you with all my heart, and his good heart that has it, with all my heart again.

EDG. [*aside*] This fellow is very charitable : would he had a purse too ! But I must not be too bold all at a time.

COKES. Nay, Numps, it is not my best purse.

WASP. Not your best ! Death ! why should it be your worst? Why should it be any, indeed, at all? Answer me to that : gi' me a reason from you, why it should be any.   152

COKES. Nor my gold, Numps ; I ha' that yet. — Look here else, Sister.

                [*Shows the other purse.*]

WASP. Why, so ; there 's all the feeling he has !

MRS. OVER. I pray you have a better care of that, Brother.

COKES. Nay, so I will, I warrant you ; let him catch this that catch can. I would fain see him get this, look you here.   161

WASP. So, so, so, so, so, so, so, so ! Very good !

COKES. I would ha' him come again now, and but offer at it. Sister, will you take notice of a good jest? I will put it just where th' other was, and, if we ha' good luck, you shall see a delicate fine trap to catch the cutpurse nibbling.

EDG. [*aside*] Faith, and he 'll try ere you be out o' the Fair.   171

COKES. Come, Mistress Grace, pri'thee be not melancholy for my mischance ; sorrow wi' not keep it,[114] sweetheart.

GRACE. I do not think on 't, sir.

COKES. 'T was but a little scurvy white money, hang it ! It may hang the cutpurse one day. I ha' gold left to gi' thee a fairing yet, as hard as the world goes. Nothing angers me but that nobody here [180 look'd like a cutpurse, unless 't were Numps.

WASP. How ! I? I look like a cutpurse? Death ! your sister 's a cutpurse ! and your mother and father, and all your kin, were cutpurses ! And here is a rogue is the bawd o' the cutpurses, whom I will beat to begin with.

        They speak all together, and WASP
                   beats the JUSTICE.

COKES. Numps, Numps.

MRS. OVER. Good Master Humphrey. [189

[114] *I.e.*, restore the purse.

OVER. Hold thy hand, child of wrath, and heir of anger ; make it not Childermas Day [115] in thy fury, or the feast of the French Bartholomew, parent of the massacre.

WASP. You are the patrico,[116] are you? the patriarch of the cutpurses? You share, sir, they say ; let them share this with you. Are you i' your hot fit of preaching again? I'll cool you!

OVER. Murder, murder, murder!

[Exeunt.]

ACT III — SCENE I [1]

LEATHERHEAD [*and*] TRASH [*are seated by their wares*]. [*Enter*] WHIT, HAGGIS, [*and*] BRISTLE.

WHIT.[2] Nay, 'tish [3] all gone, now! Dish [4] tish, phen tou vilt not be phitin call, Master Offisher ; phat ish a man te better to lishen out noyshes [5] for tee, and tou art in an oder 'orld, being very shuffishient noyshes, and gallantsh, too? One o' their brabblesh would have fed ush all dish fortnight, but tou art so bushy about beggersh still, tou hast no leshure to intend [6] shentlemen, an 't be.

HAG. Why, I told you, Davy Bristle.   10

BRI. Come, come, you told me a pudding, Toby Haggis ; a matter of nothing ; I am sure it came to nothing. You said, let's go to Urs'la's, indeed ; but then you met the man with the monsters, and I could not get you from him. An old fool! not leave seeing yet?

HAG. Why, who would ha' thought anybody would ha' quarrell'd so early ; or that the ale o' the fair would ha' been up so soon? [20

WHIT. Phy, phat a' clock toest tou [7] tink it ish, man?

HAG. I cannot tell.

WHIT. Tou art a vishe [8] vatchman, i' te mean teem.[9]

HAG. Why, should the watch go by the clock, or the clock by the watch, I pray?

BRI. One should go by another, if they did well.

WHIT. Tou art right now! Phen didst [30 tou ever know or hear of a shuffishient vatch-

man, but he did tell the clock, phat bushiness soever he had?

BRI. Nay, that's most true, a sufficient watchman knows what a'clock it is.

WHIT. Shleeping or vaking! Ash well as te clock himshelf, or te Jack dat shtrikes him! [10

BRI. Let's inquire of Master Leatherhead, or Joan Trash here. — Master Leather- [40 head, do you hear, Master Leatherhead?

WHIT. If it be a Ledderhead, tish a very tick Ledderhead, tat sho mush noish vill not piersh him.

LEATH. I have a little business now, good friends ; do not trouble me.

WHIT. Phat, because o' ty wrought neetcap,[11] and ty phelvet sherkin, man? Phy! I have sheen tee in ty ledder sherkin, ere now, mashter o' de hobbyhorses, as bushy and [50 as stately as tou sheem'st to be.

TRASH. Why, what an you have, Captain Whit? He has his choice of jerkins, you may see by that, and his caps too, I assure you, when he pleases to be either sick or employ'd.

LEATH. God-a-mercy, Joan, answer for me.

WHIT. Away, be not sheen i' my company ; here be shentlemen, and men of vorship.

[Exeunt HAGGIS *and* BRISTLE.]

SCENE II [12]

Enter QUARLOUS *and* WINWIFE [*to them*].

QUAR. We had wonderful ill luck, to miss this prologue o' the purse ; but the best is, we shall have five acts of him ere night : he'll be spectacle enough! I'll answer for 't.

WHIT. O Creesh! [13] Duke Quarlous, how dosht tou? Tou dosht not know me, I fear! I am te vishesht man, but Justish Overdo, in all Bartholomew Fair now. Gi' me twelvepence from tee, I vill help tee to a vife vorth forty marks for 't, an 't be.   10

QUAR. Away, rogue ; pimp, away.

WHIT. And she shall shew tee as fine cut'ork [14] for 't in her shmock too as tou cansht vish, i' faith. — Vilt tou have her, vorshipful Vinvife? I vill help tee to her here, be an 't be,[15] in te pig-quarter ; gi' me ty [16] twel'pence from tee.

---

[115] *I.e.*, another Slaughter of the Innocents.
[116] The orator and chaplain of strolling beggars and gipsies.
[1] The same.
[2] Whit's brogue is supposed to be Irish.
[3] 'Tis.   [4] This.   [5] Noises, disturbances.
[6] Attend to.   [7] Dost thou.   [8] Wise.
[9] In the meantime.

[10] It.
[11] Thy embroidered nightcap.
[12] The same.   [13] Christ!   [14] Cut-work.
[15] By and by, at once.
[16] Thy.

WINW. Why, there's twel'pence; pray thee, wilt thou be gone?

WHIT. Tou art a vorthy man, and a [20 vorshipful man still.

QUAR. Get you gone, rascal.

WHIT. I do mean it, man. — Prinsh Quarlous, if tou hasht need on me, tou shalt find me here at Urs'la's. I vill see phat ale and punk ish i' te pigshty for tee, bless ty good Vorship.   [*Exit.*]

QUAR. Look, who comes here! John Littlewit!

WINW. And his wife, and my widow, [30 her mother : the whole family.

QUAR. 'Slight, you must gi' 'em all fairings now!

WINW. Not I, I 'll not see 'em.

QUAR. They are going a-feasting. What schoolmaster's that is with 'em?

WINW. That's my rival, I believe, the baker!

[*Enter* BUSY, DAME PURECRAFT, LITTLEWIT, *and* MRS. LITTLEWIT.]

BUSY. So; walk on in the middle way, fore-right;[17] turn neither to the right [40 hand nor to the left; let not your eyes be drawn aside with vanity, nor your ear with noises.

QUAR. [*aside*] Oh, I know him by that start!

LEATH. What do you lack, what do you buy, pretty mistress? a fine hobbyhorse, to make your son a tilter? a drum, to make him a soldier? a fiddle, to make him a reveler? What is 't you lack? little dogs for your [50 daughters? or babies, male or female?

BUSY. Look not toward them; hearken not; the place is Smithfield, or the field of smiths,[18] the grove of hobbyhorses and trinkets; the wares are the wares of devils, and the whole Fair is the shop of Satan! They are hooks and baits, very baits, that are hung out on every side, to catch you, and to hold you, as it were, by the gills, and by the nostrils, as the fisher doth; therefore you [60 must not look nor turn toward them. The heathen man could stop his ears with wax against the harlot o' the sea.[19] Do you the like with your fingers against the bells of the Beast.

[17] Directly forward.
[18] The name is actually derived from "smooth field."
[19] Alluding to Ulysses and the Sirens, though it was the crew, not the commander, whose ears were stopped up.

WINW. [*aside*] What flashes comes from him!

QUAR. [*aside*] Oh, he has those of his oven! A notable hot baker 't was when he plied the peel.[20] He is leading his flock into the [70 Fair now.

WINW. [*aside*] Rather driving 'em to the pens; for he will let 'em look upon nothing.

[*Enter* KNOCKHUM *and* WHIT *from* URSULA'S *booth.*] LITTLEWIT *is gazing at the sign, which is the pig's head, with a large writing under it.*

KNOCK. Gentlewomen, the weather's hot. Whither walk you? Have a care o' your fine velvet caps; the Fair is dusty. Take a sweet delicate booth, with boughs, here i' the way, and cool yourselves i' the shade, you and your friends. The best pig and bottle-ale i' the Fair, sir. Old Urs'la is cook, there [80 you may read : the pig's head speaks it. Poor soul, she has had a s[t]ringhalt, the maryhinchco;[21] but she's prettily amended.

WHIT. A delicate show-pig, little mistress, with shweet sauce, and crackling, like de bay leaf i' de fire, la! Tou shalt ha' de clean side o' de tablecloct, and di glass vash'd with phatersh of Dame Annesh Clear.[22]

LIT. This's fine, verily : here be the best pigs, and she does roast 'em as well as [90 ever she did, the pig's head says.

KNOCK. Excellent, excellent, mistress, with fire o' juniper and rosemary branches! — The oracle of the pig's head, that, sir.

PURE. Son, were you not warn'd of the vanity of the eye? Have you forgot the wholesome admonition so soon?

LIT. Good Mother, how shall we find a pig, if we do not look about for 't? Will it run off o' the spit, into our mouths, think [100 you, as in Lubberland,[23] and cry " wee, wee "?

BUSY. No, but your mother, religiously wise, conceiveth it may offer itself by other means to the sense, as by way of steam, which I think it doth, here in this place — huh, huh — (BUSY *scents after it like a hound*) yes, it doth. And it were a sin of obstinacy, great obstinacy, high and horrible obstinacy,

[20] The shovel with which bakers handle their bread in the oven.
[21] Both are names for a disease which causes certain muscles of a horse's hind legs to contract spasmodically.
[22] Thy glass washed with waters from a well in Hoxton called Dame Annis the clear (originally *Agnes le clair*).
[23] An imaginary land of plenty and ease.

to decline or resist the good titillation of the famelic [24] sense, which is the smell. [110 Therefore be bold — huh, huh, huh — follow the scent. Enter the tents of the unclean, for once, and satisfy your wife's frailty. Let your frail wife be satisfied; your zealous mother and my suffering self will also be satisfied.

LIT. Come, Win, as good winny [25] here as go farther and see nothing.

BUSY. We scape so much of the other vanities by our early ent'ring.   120

PURE. It is an edifying consideration.

MRS. LIT. This is scurvy, that we must come into the Fair, and not look on 't.

LIT. Win, have patience, Win; I 'll tell you more anon. [*Exeunt, into the booth,* LITTLEWIT, MRS. LITTLEWIT, BUSY, *and* DAME PURECRAFT.]

KNOCK. Mooncalf, entertain within there the best pig i' the booth, a porklike pig. — These are Banbury bloods, o' the sincere stud,[26] come a-pig-hunting. — Whit, wait, Whit; look to your charge.   130
      [*Exit* WHIT.]

BUSY [*within*] A pig prepare presently; let a pig be prepared to us.

      [*Enter, from the booth,* MOONCALF *and* URSULA.]

MOON. 'Slight, who be these?

URS. Is this the good service, Jordan, you 'd do me?

KNOCK. Why, Urs! why, Urs! thou 'lt ha' vapors i' thy leg again presently. Pray thee go in; 't may turn to the scratches [27] else.

URS. Hang your vapors; they are stale, [140 and stink like you! Are these the guests o' the game you promis'd to fill my pit withal to-day?

KNOCK. Ay; what ail they, Urs?

URS. Ail they! they are all sippers, sippers o' the city; they look as they would not drink off two penn'orth of bottle-ale amongst 'em.

MOON. A body may read that i' their small printed ruffs.

KNOCK. Away! thou art a fool, Urs, [150 and thy Mooncalf too! I' your ignorant vapors now? Hence! Good guests, I say, right hypocrites, good gluttons. — In, and set a couple o' pigs o' the board, and half a dozen

of the biggest bottles afore 'em, and call Whit. [*Exit* MOONCALF.] — I do not love to hear innocents abus'd: fine ambling hypocrites! and a stone-puritan [28] with a sorrel head and beard; good mouth'd gluttons; two to a pig. Away!   160

URS. Are you sure they are such?

KNOCK. O' the right breed; thou shalt try 'em by the teeth, Urs. — Where 's this Whit?

      [*Re-enter* WHIT.]

WHIT.

> Behold, man, and see,
> What a worthy man am ee!
> With the fury of my sword,
> And the shaking of my beard,
> I will make ten thousand men afeard.

KNOCK. Well said, brave Whit! — In, [170 and fear the ale out o' the bottles into the bellies of the brethren, and the sisters.[29] Drink to the cause, and pure vapors.

      [*Exeunt* KNOCKHUM, WHIT, *and* URSULA.]

QUAR. My roarer is turn'd tapster, methinks. Now were a fine time for thee, Winwife, to lay aboard [30] thy widow; thou 'lt never be master of a better season or place. She that will venture herself into the Fair and a pig-box will admit any assault, be assur'd of that.   180

WINW. I love not enterprises of that suddenness, though.

QUAR. I 'll warrant thee, then, no wife out o' the widow's hundred.[31] If I had but as much title to her as to have breath'd once on that straight stomacher of hers, I would now assure myself to carry her yet, ere she went out of Smithfield; or she should carry me, which were the fitter sight, I confess. But you are a modest undertaker — by [190 circumstances and degrees. Come, 't is disease in thee, not judgment; I should offer at all together. — Look, here 's the poor fool again, that was stung by the Wasp erewhile.

SCENE III [32]

      [*Enter* OVERDO; *they stand aside.*]

OVER. I will make no more orations shall draw on these tragical conclusions. And I begin now to think that, by a spice [33] of collateral justice, Adam Overdo deserv'd this beating; for I, the said Adam, was one cause (a

---

[24] Appetizing, hunger-arousing.
[25] Wone, dwell, remain.
[26] Puritan breed.   [27] See on II, v, 234.

[28] He-Puritan; on the analogy of stone-horse.
[29] Ff lack punctuation after *sisters*.
[30] Run [thy ship] alongside.
[31] Subdivision, category.
[32] The same.   [33] Species.

by-cause) why the purse was lost; and my wife's brother's purse too, which they know not of yet. But I shall make very good mirth with it at supper — that will be the sport — and put my little friend Master Hum- [10 phrey Wasp's choler quite out of countenance, when, sitting at the upper end o' my table, as I use, and drinking to my brother Cokes, and Mistress Alice Overdo, as I will, my wife, for their good affection to old Bradley, I deliver to 'em it was I that was cudgel'd, and show 'em the marks. To see what bad events may peep out o' the tail of good purposes! The care I had of that civil young man I took fancy to this morning (and have not left [20 it yet) drew me to that exhortation; which drew the company indeed; which drew the cutpurse; which drew the money; which drew my brother Cokes his loss; which drew on Wasp's anger; which drew on my beating: a pretty gradation! And they shall ha' it i' their dish, i' faith, at night for fruit; [34] I love to be merry at my table. I had thought once, at one special blow he ga' me, to have revealed myself! But then (I thank thee, forti- [30 tude) I rememb'red that a wise man, and who is ever so great a part o' the commonwealth in himself, for no particular disaster ought to abandon a public good design. The husbandman ought not, for one unthankful year, to forsake the plough; the shepherd ought not, for one scabb'd sheep, to throw by his tar-box; [35] the pilot ought not, for one leak i' the poop, to quit the helm; nor the alderman ought not, for one custard more at [40 a meal, to give up his cloak; the constable ought not to break his staff, and forswear the watch, for one roaring night; nor the piper o' the parish, *ut* [36] *parvis componere magna solebam*, to put up his pipes for one rainy Sunday. These are certain knocking conclusions; out of which, I am resolv'd, come what come can, come beating, come imprisonment, come infamy, come banishment, nay, come the rack, come the hurdle (welcome [50 all), I will not discover who I am, till my due time; and yet still all shall be, as I said ever, in Justice' name, and the King's, and for the Commonwealth. [*Exit.*]

WINW. What does he talk to himself, and act so seriously? poor fool!

QUAR. No matter what. Here's fresher argument: intend [37] that. [*They stand aside.*]

SCENE IV [38]

[*Enter to them* COKES, MISTRESS OVERDO, *and* GRACE WELLBORN, *followed by* WASP, *loaded with toys.*]

COKES. Come, Mistress Grace, come, Sister, here's more fine sights yet, i' faith. God'slid! where's Numps?

LEATH. What do you lack, gentlemen? what is 't you buy? fine rattles, drums, babies, little dogs, and birds for ladies? What do you lack?

COKES. Good honest Numps, keep afore; I am so afraid thou'lt lose somewhat. My heart was at my mouth when I miss'd thee. [10

WASP. You were best buy a whip i' your hand to drive me.

COKES. Nay, do not mistake, Numps; thou art so apt to mistake. I would but watch the goods. Look you now, the treble fiddle was e'en almost like to be lost.

WASP. Pray you take heed you lose not yourself; your best way were e'en get up and ride for more surety. Buy a token's worth of great pins, to fasten yourself to my [20 shoulder.

LEATH. What do you lack, gentlemen? fine purses, pouches, pin-cases, pipes? What is 't you lack? a pair o' smiths [39] to wake you i' the morning? or a fine whistling bird?

COKES. Numps, here be finer things than any we ha' bought, by odds! and more delicate horses, a great deal. Good Numps, stay, and come hither.

WASP. Will you scourse [40] with him? [30 You are in Smithfield; you may fit yourself with a fine easy-going street-nag, for your saddle, again' Michaelmas term; do! Has he ne'er a little odd cart for you to make a caroche on i' the country, with four pied hobbyhorses? Why the measles should you stand here, with your train, cheaping of dogs, birds, and babies? You ha' no children to bestow 'em on, ha' you?

COKES. No, but again' [41] I ha' chil- [40 dren, Numps, that's all one. [42]

[34] The final course.
[35] For healing the sores.
[36] Virgil *sic*. "Thus was I accustomed to compare great things to small." (*Eclogues*, I, 23.)

[37] Give attention to.
[38] The same.
[39] Evidently a clock with "Jacks" like smiths to strike the hours.
[40] Trade.
[41] In preparation for the time when.
[42] It's all the same.

WASP. Do, do, do, do! How many shall you have, think you? An I were as you, I'd buy for all my tenants too. They are a kind o' civil savages that will part with their children for rattles, pipes, and knives. You were best buy a hatchet or two, and truck with 'em.

COKES. Good Numps, hold that little tongue o' thine, and save it a labor. I [50 am resolute Bat, thou know'st.

WASP. A resolute fool you are, I know, and a very sufficient coxcomb,[43] with all my heart! Nay, you have it, sir, an you be angry: turd i' your teeth, twice, if I said it not once afore, and much good do you!

WINW. [aside] Was there ever such a self-affliction, and so impertinent?

QUAR. [aside] Alas, his care will go near to crack him; let's in and comfort him.   60
[*They come forward.*]

WASP. Would I had been set i' the ground, all but the head on me, and had my brains bowl'd at or thresh'd out when first I underwent this plague of a charge!

QUAR. How now, Numps! almost tir'd i' your protectorship? overparted?[44] overparted?

WASP. Why, I cannot tell, sir; it may be I am; does 't grieve you?

QUAR. No, I swear does 't not, Numps; [70 to satisfy you.

WASP. Numps! 'Sblood, you are fine and familiar! How long ha' we been acquainted, I pray you?

QUAR. I think it may be rememb'red, Numps, that! 't was since morning, sure.

WASP. Why, I hope I know 't well enough, sir; I did not ask to be told.

QUAR. No? why, then?

WASP. It's no matter why; you see [80 with your eyes now what I said to you to-day! You'll believe me another time!

QUAR. Are you removing the Fair, Numps?

WASP. A pretty question, and a very civil one! Yes, faith, I ha' my lading, you see, or shall have anon; you may know whose beast I am by my burden. If the pannier-man's jack were ever better known by his loins of mutton, I'll be flay'd, and feed dogs for him when his time comes.   90

WINW. How [melancholic][45] Mistress Grace is yonder! Pray thee, let's go enter ourselves in grace with her.

COKES. Those six horses, friend, I'll have —

WASP. How!

COKES. And the three Jew's-trumps; and half a dozen o' birds; and that drum (I have one drum already); and your smiths: I like that device o' your smiths, very pretty well; and four halberts — and, le' me see, that [100 fine painted great lady and her three women for state, I'll have.

WASP. No, the shop; buy the whole shop, it will be best; the shop, the shop!

LEATH. If his Worship please.

WASP. Yes, and keep it during the Fair, Bobchin.[46]

COKES. Peace, Numps. — Friend, do not meddle with him, an' you be wise, and would show your head aboveboard;[47] he will [110 sting thorough your wrought nightcap, believe me. A set of these violins I would buy too, for a delicate young noise[48] I have i' the country, that are every one a size less than another, just like your fiddles. I would fain have a fine young masque at my marriage, now I think on 't; but I do want such a number o' things! And Numps will not help me now, and I dare not speak to him.

TRASH. Will your Worship buy any [120 gingerbread, very good bread, comfortable bread?

COKES. Gingerbread! yes, let's see!
[*He runs to her shop.*]

WASP. There's the tother springe![49]

LEATH. Is this well, goody Joan, to interrupt my market in the midst, and call away my customers? Can you answer this at the pie-powders?

TRASH. Why, if his Mastership have a mind to buy, I hope my ware lies as [130 open as another's; I may show my ware as well as you yours.

COKES. Hold your peace; I'll content you both. I'll buy up his shop, and thy basket.

WASP. Will you, i' faith?

LEATH. Why should you put him from it, friend?

WASP. Cry you mercy! You'd be sold too, would you? What's the price on [140 you, jerkin and all, as you stand? Ha' you any qualities?

---

[43] Fool.   [44] Burdened with too difficult a part.
[45] So F 1692; F 1631 *melancholi'*.

[46] One who bobs his chin (*N.E.D.*); *i.e.*, one who keeps his jaw wagging, a silly chatterer. (Kittredge.)
[47] In plain sight.
[48] A fine band of young musicians. Cf. V, iii, 71.
[49] Snare.

TRASH. Yes, Goodman Angry-man, you shall find he has qualities, if you cheapen him.

WASP. Gods-so! you ha' the selling of him! What are they? Will they be bought for love or money?

TRASH. No, indeed, sir.

WASP. For what then, victuals?

TRASH. He scorns victuals, sir; he has [150 bread and butter at home, thanks be to God! And yet he will do more for a good meal, if the toy take [50] him, i' the belly — marry, then they must not set him at lower end; if they do, he'll go away, though he fast. But put him a-top o' the table, where his place is, and he'll do you forty fine things. He has not been sent for and sought out for nothing, at your great city suppers, to put down Coryat [51] and Cokely, [52] and been laugh'd at for his [160 labor; he'll play you all the puppets i' the town over, and the players, every company, and his own company too; he spares nobody!

COKES. I' faith?

TRASH. He was the first, sir, that ever baited the fellow i' the bear's skin, [53] an't like your Worship; no dog ever came near him since. And for fine motions!

COKES. Is he good at those too? Can he set out a masque, trow?   170

TRASH. O Lord, master! sought to far and near for his inventions; and he engrosses all; he makes all the puppets i' the Fair.

COKES. Dost thou, in troth, old velvet jerkin? Give me thy hand.

TRASH. Nay, sir, you shall see him in his velvet jerkin, and a scarf too at night, when you hear him interpret Master Littlewit's motion.

COKES. Speak no more, but shut up [180 shop presently, friend. I'll buy both it and thee too, to carry down with me; and her hamper beside. Thy shop shall furnish out the masque, and hers the banquet. I cannot go less, to set out anything with credit. What's the price, at a word, o' thy whole shop, case, and all as it stands?

LEATH. Sir, it stands me in six-and-twenty shillings, sevenpence, halfpenny; besides three shillings for my ground.   190

COKES. Well, thirty shillings will do all then! — And what comes yours to?

TRASH. Four shillings and elevenpence, sir, ground and all, an't like your Worship.

COKES. Yes, it does like my Worship very well, poor woman; that's five shillings more. What a masque shall I furnish out, for forty shillings (twenty pound Scotch) and a banquet of gingerbread! There's a stately thing! Numps! Sister! And my wedding [200 gloves too! — that I never thought on afore! All my wedding gloves, gingerbread! [54] O me! what a device will there be, to make 'em eat their fingers' ends! And delicate brooches for the bridemen! and all! And then I'll ha' this poesie [55] put to 'em, " For the best grace," meaning Mistress Grace, my wedding poesie.

GRACE. I am beholden to you, sir, and to your Bartholomew wit.

WASP. You do not mean this, do you? [210 Is this your first purchase?

COKES. Yes, faith; and I do not think, Numps, but thou'lt say it was the wisest act that ever I did in my wardship.

WASP. Like enough! I shall say anything, I!

SCENE V [56]

[Enter] EDGEWORTH *[and]* NIGHTINGALE, *[followed by]* JUSTICE *[OVERDO]*.

OVER. *[aside]* I cannot beget a project, with all my political brain, yet. My project is how to fetch off this proper young man from his debauch'd company. I have followed him all the Fair over, and still I find him with this songster; and I begin shrewdly to suspect their familiarity, and the young man of a terrible taint, poetry! with which idle disease if he be infected, there's no hope of him in a state-course. *Actum est* of him [10 for a commonwealth's-man, [57] if he go to 't in rhyme once.

EDG. *[aside to* NIGHTINGALE*]* Yonder he is, buying o' gingerbread; set in quickly, before he part with too much on his money.

NIGHT *[advancing and singing]*

"My masters and friends, and good people, draw
    near", etc. —

COKES. Ballads! hark, hark! Pray thee, fellow, stay a little. — Good Numps, look to the goods. — What ballads hast thou? Let me see; let me see myself. [20

He runs to the Ballad Man.

WASP. Why so! he's flown to another lime-bush.[58] There he will flutter as long more; till he ha' ne'er a feather left. Is there a vexation like this, gentlemen? Will you believe me now hereafter? shall I have credit with you?

QUAR. Yes, faith, shalt thou, Numps; and thou art worthy on 't, for thou sweatest for 't. — [*aside to the rest*] I never saw a [29 young pimp-errant and his squire better match'd.

WINW. Faith, the sister comes after 'em well too.

GRACE. Nay, if you saw the justice her husband, my guardian, you were fitted for the mess;[59] he is such a wise one his way —

WINW. I wonder we see him not here.

GRACE. Oh, he is too serious for this place, and yet better sport then than the other [40 three, I assure you, gentlemen, where'er he is, though 't be o' the bench.

COKES. How dost thou call it? "A Caveat against Cutpurses"! a good jest, i' faith! I would fain see that demon, your cutpurse you talk of, that delicate-handed devil. They say he walks hereabout; I would see him walk, now. Look you, Sister, here, here (*He shows his purse boastingly*). Let him come, Sister, and welcome. [50 Ballad man, does any cutpurses haunt hereabout? Pray thee raise me one or two; begin, and show me one.

NIGHT. Sir, this is a spell against 'em, spick and span new; and 't is made as 't were in mine own person, and I sing it in mine own defence. But 't will cost a penny alone, if you buy it.

COKES. No matter for the price; thou dost not know me, I see; I am an odd [60 Bartholomew.

MRS. OVER. Has 't a fine picture, Brother?

COKES. O, Sister, do you remember the ballads over the nursery chimney at home o' my own pasting up? There be brave pictures, other manner of pictures than these, friend.

WASP. Yet these will serve to pick the pictures[60] out o' your pockets, you shall see.

[58] A bush smeared with bird-lime; *i.e.*, a snare.
[59] Set of four.
[60] The coins, with the sovereigns' portraits or other devices.

COKES. So I heard 'em say. — Pray [70 thee mind him not, fellow; he'll have an oar in everything.

NIGHT. It was intended, sir, as if a purse should chance to be cut in my presence now; I may be blameless though, as by the sequel will more plainly appear.

COKES. We shall find that i' the matter. Pray thee begin.

NIGHT. To the tune of "Paggington's Pound,"[61] sir. 80

COKES. [*singing*] Fa, la la la, la la la, fa la la la! — Nay, I'll put thee in tune and all! Mine own country-dance! Pray thee begin.

NIGHT. It is a gentle admonition, you must know, sir, both to the purse-cutter and the purse-bearer.

COKES. Not a word more out o' the tune, an thou lov'st me! — Fa, la la la, la la la, fa la la la. — Come, when?

NIGHT.

My masters, and friends, and good people, draw near, 90
And look to your purses; for that I do say;

COKES. Ha, ha, this chimes! Good counsel at first dash.

NIGHT.

And, though little money in them you do bear,
It cost more to get than to lose in a day.

COKES. Good!

NIGHT.

    You oft have been told,
    Both the young and the old,
And bidden beware of the cutpurse so bold; 99
Then, if you take heed not, free me from the curse,
Who both give you warning for and[62] the cutpurse.

COKES. Well said! He were to blame that would not, i' faith.

NIGHT.

Youth, youth, thou hadst better been starv'd by thy nurse,
Than live to be hanged for cutting a purse.

COKES. Good, i' faith. How say you, Numps? is there any harm i' this?

NIGHT.

It hath been upbraided to men of my trade,
That oftentimes we are the cause of this crime;

COKES. The more coxcombs they that [110 did it, I wusse.

NIGHT.

Alack and for pity, why should it be said?
As if they regarded or places or time.
    Examples have been
    Of some that were seen

[61] A country-dance tune; it survives.
[62] And moreover.

In Westminster Hall,[63] yea, the pleaders between;
Then why should the judges be free from this curse,
More than my poor self, for cutting the purse?

COKES. God 'a mercy for that! Why
should they be more free indeed?   120

NIGHT.

Youth, youth, thou hadst better been starv'd by
      thy nurse,
Than live to be hanged for cutting a purse.

COKES. That again, good ballad man, that
again. (*He sings the burden with him.*) Oh,
rare! — I would fain rub mine elbow now,
but I dare not pull out my hand. — On, I
pray thee; he that made this ballad shall be
poet to my masque.

NIGHT.

At Worcester 'tis known well, and even i' the jail,
A knight of good worship did there show his face,
Against the foul sinners in zeal for to rail,   131
And lost *ipso facto* his purse in the place.

COKES. Is it possible?

NIGHT.

      Nay, once from the seat
        Of judgment so great,
A judge there did lose a fair pouch of velvéte.

COKES. I' faith?

NIGHT.

O Lord for thy mercy, how wicked or worse
Are those that so venture their necks for a purse!
Youth, youth, etc.   140

COKES. [*singing with him*] " Youth, youth,"
etc. — Pray thee, stay a little, friend. — Yet,
o' thy conscience, Numps, speak, is there any
harm i' this?

WASP. To tell you true, 't is too good for
you, 'less you had grace to follow it.

OVER. [*aside*] It doth discover enormity;
I'll mark it more. I ha' not lik'd a paltry
piece of poetry so well a good while.

COKES. " Youth, youth," etc. —   [150
Where's this youth, now? A man must call
upon him for his own good, and yet he will
not appear. Look here, here's for him:
(*He shows his purse.*) Handy dandy,[64] which
hand will he have? On, I pray thee with
the rest; I do hear of him, but I cannot see
him, this Master Youth, the cutpurse.

NIGHT.

At plays, and at sermons, and at the sessions,
'Tis daily their practice such booty to make;
Yea, under the gallows at executions,   160
They stick not the stare-abouts' purses to take
      Nay, one without grace,
        At a better place,
At court, and in Christmas, before the King's face!

[63] The law courts were held there.
[64] An allusion to the children's game of handy
dandy, or which hand will you have?

COKES. That was a fine fellow! I would
have him, now.

NIGHT.

Alack then for pity must I bear the curse,
That only belongs to the cunning cutpurse?

COKES. But where's their cunning now,
when they should use it? They are all [170
chain'd now, I warrant you. — " Youth,
youth, thou hadst better," etc. — The rat-
catchers' charm[s] are all fools and asses to
this! A pox on 'em, that they will not come!
that a man should have such a desire to a
thing, and want it.

QUAR. 'Fore God I'd give half the Fair, an
't were mine, for a cutpurse for him, to save
his longing.   179

COKES. (*shows his purse again.*) Look you,
sister: here, here, where is 't now? Which
pocket is 't in, for a wager?

WASP. I beseech you leave your wagers,
and let him end his matter, an't may be.

COKES. Oh, are you edified, Numps?

OVER. [*aside*] Indeed he does interrupt him
too much; there Numps spoke to purpose.

COKES. (*again*) Sister, I am an ass, I cannot keep my purse! — On, on, I pray thee,
friend. (EDGEWORTH *gets up to him and* [190
*tickles him in the ear with a straw twice to
draw his hand out of his pocket.*)

NIGHT.

But O you vile nation of cutpurses all,
Relent and repent, and amend and be sound,
And know that you ought not, by honest men's fall,
Advance your own fortunes, to die above ground; [65]
      And, though you go gay
        In silks, as you may,—

WINW.[66] [*aside to* QUARLOUS] Will you see
sport? Look, there's a fellow gathers up to
him; mark.

QUAR. [*aside*] Good, i' faith! Oh, he [200
has lighted on the wrong pocket.[67]

WINW. [*aside*] He has it! 'Fore God, he
is a brave fellow. Pity he should be detected.

NIGHT.

It is not the highway to Heaven, as they say.
Repent then, repent you, for better, for worse,
And kiss not the gallows for cutting a purse.
Youth, youth, thou hadst better been starv'd by
      thy nurse
Than live to be hanged for cutting a purse.

ALL. An excellent ballad! an excellent
ballad!   210

[65] Be hanged.
[66] This group of speeches, as well as most of those
of Cokes preceding, are printed in the Folios at
the right of the text of the song, indicating simul-
taneous delivery.
[67] Actually, however, Edgeworth is stealing the
handkerchief.

EDG. Friend, let me ha' the first, let me ha'
the first, I pray you. [*As* NIGHTINGALE *reaches
out the ballad,* EDGEWORTH *slips the purse into
his hand.*]

COKES. Pardon me, sir. First come first
serv'd; and I 'll buy the whole bundle too.

WINW. [*aside*] That conveyance was better
than all. Did you see 't? He has given
the purse to the ballad singer.

QUAR. [*aside*] Has he?

EDG. Sir, I cry you mercy.[68] I 'll not hinder
the poor man's profit; pray you, mistake me
not.　　　　　　　　　　　　　　　　221

COKES. Sir, I take you for an honest gentleman, if that be mistaking; I met you to-day
afore — ha! humh! O God! my purse
is gone, my purse, my purse! etc.[69]

WASP. Come, do not make a stir, and cry
yourself an ass thorough the Fair afore your
time.[70]

COKES. Why, hast thou it, Numps? Good
Numps, how came you by it? I mar'l![71] [230

WASP. I pray you seek some other gamester to play the fool with; you may lose it time
enough, for all your Fair wit.

COKES. By this good hand, glove and all,
I ha' lost it already, if thou hast it not; feel
else, and Mistress Grace's handkercher too,
out o' the tother pocket.

WASP. Why, 't is well, very well, exceeding pretty, and well.

EDG. Are you sure you ha' lost it, sir? [240

COKES. O God! yes; as I am an honest
man, I had it but e'en now, at "Youth,
youth."

NIGHT. I hope you suspect not me,
sir?

EDG. Thee! that were a jest indeed!
Dost thou think the gentleman is foolish?
Where hadst thou hands, I pray thee? —
[*aside*] Away, ass, away!

[*Exit* NIGHTINGALE.]

OVER. [*aside*] I shall be beaten again if I
be spi'd.　　　　　　　　　　　　　　251

EDG. Sir, I suspect an odd fellow, yonder,
is stealing away.

MRS. OVER. Brother, it is the preaching
fellow! You shall suspect him. He was at
your tother purse, you know! —— [*seizing*
OVERDO] Nay, stay, sir, and view the work you

ha' done; an you be benefic'd at the gallows,[72]
and preach there, thank your own handiwork.

COKES. Sir, you shall take no pride in your
preferment; you shall be silenc'd quickly.
[*They seize* OVERDO.]

OVER. What do you mean, sweet buds[73]
of gentility?　　　　　　　　　　　263

COKES. To ha' my pennyworths out on
you, bud. No less than two purses a day
serve you? I thought you a simple fellow,
when my man Numps beat you i' the morning, and pitied you —

MRS. OVER. So did I, I 'll be sworn,
Brother; but now I see he is a lewd and pernicious enormity, as Master Overdo calls him.

OVER. [*aside*] Mine own words turn'd [272
upon me like swords!

COKES. Cannot a man's purse be at quiet
for you i' the master's pocket, but you must
entice it forth, and debauch it?
[OVERDO *is carried off.*]

WASP. Sir, sir, keep your debauch, and
your fine Bartholomew terms to yourself, and
make as much on 'em as you please. But gi'
me this from you i' the meantime, I beseech
you; see if I can look to this.　　　281

COKES. Why, Numps?

WASP. Why! because you are an ass, sir;
there 's a reason the shortest way, an you will
needs ha' it. Now you ha' got the trick
of losing, you 'd lose your breech, an 't were
loose. I know you, sir, come, deliver. (WASP
takes [*the box with*] *the license from him.*) You 'll
go and crack the vermin you breed now,[74] will
you? 'T is very fine. Will you ha' the truth
on 't? They are such reckless flies as [291
you are that blow[75] cutpurses abroad in every
corner; your foolish having of money makes
'em. An there were no wiser than I, sir, the
trade should lie open for you, sir;[76] it
should, i' faith, sir. I would teach your wit
to come to your head, sir, as well as your land
to come into your hand, I assure you, sir.

WINW. Alack, good Numps!　　　299

WASP. Nay, gentlemen, never pity me; I
am not worth it. — Lord send me at home

[68] Beg your pardon.
[69] *I.e., ad lib.* The actor is to supply his own
exclamation.
[70] *I.e.,* before the date when inevitably you will
be exposed an ass.
[71] Marvel.

[72] If you, who aspire to preaching, receive the
rope as your ecclesiastical living.
[73] A term of endearment.
[74] *I.e.,* now you 'll go and have the cutpurse
hanged, though his existence is due to your own
inviting carelessness.
[75] Cause to blossom.
[76] *I.e.,* if it weren't that wiser heads than mine
would not permit it, I would turn you loose to ply
your trade of creating cutpurses.

once to Harrow o' the Hill again! If I travel any more, call me Coryat,[77] with all my heart.

[*Exeunt* WASP, COKES, *and* MRS. OVERDO.]

QUAR. [*stopping* EDGEWORTH] Stay, sir, I must have a word with you in private. Do you hear?

EDG. With me, sir? What's your pleasure, good sir? 308

QUAR. Do not deny it: you are a cutpurse, sir; this gentleman here and I saw you; nor do we mean to detect you, though we can sufficiently inform ourselves toward the danger of concealing you; but you must do us a piece of service.

EDG. Good gentlemen, do not undo me; I am a civil young man, and but a beginner indeed.

QUAR. Sir, your beginning shall bring on your ending for us;[78] we are no catchpoles nor constables. That you are to undertake is this: you saw the old fellow with the black box here? 322

EDG. The little old governor, sir?

QUAR. That same. I see you have flown him to a mark[79] already. I would ha' you get away that box from him, and bring it us.

EDG. Would you ha' the box and all, sir, or only that that is in 't? I'll get you that, and leave him the box to play with still, which will be the harder o' the two, because I would gain your Worship's good opinion of me. 332

WINW. He says well; 't is the greater mast'ry, and 't will make the more sport when 't is miss'd.

EDG. Ay, and 't will be the longer a-missing, to draw on the sport.

QUAR. But look you do it, now, sirrah, and keep your word; or —

EDG. Sir, if ever I break my word with a gentleman, may I never read word at my need.[80] Where shall I find you? 342

QUAR. Somewhere i' the Fair hereabouts. Dispatch it quickly. — [*Exit* EDGEWORTH.] — I would fain see the careful fool deluded! Of all beasts, I love the serious ass: he that takes pains to be one, and plays the fool with the greatest diligence that can be.

GRACE. Then you would not choose, sir, but love my guardian, Justice Overdo, who is answerable to that description in every hair of him. 352

QUAR. So I have heard. But how came you, Mistress Wellborn, to be his ward, or have relation to him at first?

GRACE. Faith, through a common calamity; he bought me,[81] sir; and now he will marry me to his wife's brother, this wise gentleman that you see; or else I must pay value o' my land. 360

QUAR. 'Slid! Is there no device of disparagement[82] or so? Talk with some crafty fellow, some picklock o' the law. Would I had studied a year longer i' the Inns of Court, an't had been but i' your case.

WINW. [*aside*] Ay, Master Quarlous, are you proffering?

GRACE. You'd bring but little aid, sir.

WINW. [*aside*] I'll look to you, i' faith, gamester. — An unfortunate foolish tribe you are fall'n into, lady; I wonder you can endure 'em. 372

GRACE. Sir, they that cannot work their fetters off must wear 'em.

WINW. You see what care they have on you, to leave you thus.

GRACE. Faith, the same they have of themselves, sir. I cannot greatly complain if this were all the plea I had against 'em. [379

WINW. 'T is true! But will you please to withdraw with us a little, and make them think they have lost you? I hope our manners ha' been such hitherto, and our language, as will give you no cause to doubt yourself in our company.

GRACE. Sir, I will give myself no cause; I am so secure of mine own manners as I suspect not yours.

QUAR. Look where John Littlewit comes.

WINW. Away; I'll not be seen by him.

QUAR. No, you were not best; he'd [391 tell his mother, the widow.

WINW. Heart! what do you mean?

QUAR. Cry you mercy, is the wind there?[83] Must not the widow be named?

[*Exeunt all but* LEATHERHEAD *and* TRASH.]

[77] See on III, iv, 159.
[78] For all of us, for aught we care.
[79] See on II, iv, 53.   [80] See on I, iv, 10.

[81] Certain classes of landholders were during nonage the king's wards, and he could sell or bestow the right of guardianship.
[82] The guardian could offer the ward a match, provided it was "without disparagement or inequality." If the ward refused it, the guardian was entitled, out of the ward's property, to a recompense equal in value to what a suitor would have paid him for the ward's hand. Quarlous proposes Grace's asking redress on the ground that marriage to Cokes would be a "disparagement," *i.e.*, beneath her.
[83] So that's the state of the case, is it?

SCENE VI [84]

[*Enter to them*] LITTLEWIT [*and*] MRS. LITTLE-
WIT, [*from* URSULA'S *booth*.]

LIT. Do you hear, Win, Win?

MRS. LIT. What say you, John?

LIT. While they are paying the reckoning,
Win, I 'll tell you a thing, Win : we shall never
see any sights i' the Fair, Win, except you
long still, Win. Good Win, sweet Win, long
to see some hobbyhorses, and some drums,
and rattles, and dogs, and fine devices, Win.
The bull with the five legs, Win ; and the
great hog. Now you ha' begun with pig, [10
you may long for anything, Win, and so for
my motion,[85] Win.

MRS. LIT. But we sha' not eat o' the bull
and the hog, John. How shall I long, then?

LIT. O yes, Win. You may long to see as
well as to taste, Win. How did the pothecary's wife, Win, that long'd to see the anatomy,[86] Win? or the lady, Win, that desir'd
to spit i' the great lawyer's mouth, after an
eloquent pleading? I assure you, they [20
long'd, Win. Good Win, go in and long.

[*Exeunt* LITTLEWIT *and* MRS.
LITTLEWIT *into the booth*.]

TRASH. I think we are rid of our new customer, Brother Leatherhead ; we shall hear
no more of him. *They plot to be gone.*

LEATH. All the better ; let 's pack up all
and be gone, before he find us.

TRASH. Stay a little ; yonder comes a
company. It may be we may take some
more money. 29

[*Enter* KNOCKHUM *and* BUSY *from the booth*.]

KNOCK. Sir, I will take your counsel, and
cut my hair,[87] and leave vapors. I see that
tobacco and bottle-ale and pig and Whit and
very Urs'la herself — is all vanity.

BUSY. Only pig was not comprehended in
my admonition ; the rest were. For [88] long
hair, it is an ensign of pride, a banner ; and
the world is full of those banners, very full of
banners. And bottle-ale is a drink of Satan's,
a diet-drink of Satan's, devised to puff us
up, and make us swell in this latter age [40
of vanity, as the smoke of tobacco, to keep
us in mist and error. But the fleshly woman,
which you call Urs'la, is above all to be
avoided, having the marks upon her of the
three enemies of man : the World, as being in

the Fair ; the Devil, as being in the fire ; and
the Flesh, as being herself.

[*Enter* DAME PURECRAFT *from the booth*.]

PURE. Brother Zeal-of-the-land ! what shall
we do? My daughter Win-the-fight is fall'n
into her fit of longing again. 50

BUSY. For more pig? There is no more,
is there?

PURE. To see some sights i' the Fair.

BUSY. Sister, let her fly the impurity of the
place swiftly, lest she partake of the pitch
thereof. — Thou art the seat of the Beast, O
Smithfield, and I will leave thee. Idolatry
peepeth out on every side of thee. 58

KNOCK. [*aside*] An excellent right hypocrite ! Now his belly is full, he falls a-railing
and kicking, the jade. A very good vapor !
I 'll in, and joy Urs'la, with telling how her
pig works ; two and a half he ate to his share.
And he has drunk a pailful. He eats with
his eyes, as well as his teeth. [*Exit*.]

LEATH. What do you lack, gentlemen?
What is 't you buy? rattles, drums,
babies — 68

BUSY. Peace, with thy apocryphal wares,
thou profane publican : thy bells, thy dragons,
and thy Tobie's dogs.[89] Thy hobbyhorse is
an idol, a very idol, a fierce and rank idol ; and
thou the Nebuchadnezzar, the proud Nebuchadnezzar of the Fair, that sett'st it up, for
children to fall down to, and worship.

LEATH. Cry you mercy, sir ; will you buy
a fiddle to fill up your noise? [90]

[*Re-enter* LITTLEWIT *and his wife*.]

LIT. Look, Win, do, look, a' God's
name, and save your longing. Here be fine
sights. 80

PURE. Ay, child, so you hate 'em, as our
brother Zeal does, you may look on 'em.

LEATH. Or what do you say to a drum,
sir?

BUSY. It is the broken belly of the Beast,
and thy bellows there are his lungs, and these
pipes are his throat, those feathers are of his
tail, and thy rattles the gnashing of his
teeth. 89

TRASH. And what 's my gingerbread, I
pray you?

BUSY. The provender that pricks him up.
Hence with thy basket of popery, thy nest of
images, and whole legend of ginger-work.

---

[84] The same. [85] Puppet-show. [86] Skeleton.
[87] Like a Puritan. [88] As for.
[89] See *Tobit* v, 16, and *Bel and the Dragon*, in the
Apocrypha.
[90] Band of musicians.

LEATH. Sir, if you be not quiet the quick-lier, I 'll ha' you clapp'd fairly by the heels,[91] for disturbing the Fair.

BUSY. The sin of the Fair provokes me; I cannot be silent.

PURE. Good Brother Zeal!   100

LEATH. Sir, I 'll make you silent, believe it.

LIT. [*aside to* LEATHERHEAD] I 'd give a shilling you could, i' faith, friend.

LEATH. [*aside*] Sir, give me your shilling. I 'll give you my shop, if I do not; and I 'll leave it in pawn with you i' the meantime.

LIT. [*aside*] A match, i' faith; but do it quickly then.   [*Exit* LEATHERHEAD.] [108

BUSY. (*speaks to the* Widow.) Hinder me not, woman. I was mov'd in spirit, to be here this day, in this Fair, this wicked and foul Fair (and fitter may it be called a foul than a fair); to protest against the abuses of it, the foul abuses of it, in regard of the afflicted saints, that are troubled, very much troubled, exceedingly troubled, with the opening of the merchandise of Babylon again, and the peeping of popery upon the stalls here, here, in the high places. See you not Goldylocks, the purple strumpet there, in her yellow [120 gown and green sleeves? the profane pipes, the tinkling timbrels? A shop of relics!

       [*Attempts to seize the toys.*]

LIT. Pray you forbear; I am put in trust with 'em.

BUSY. And this idolatrous grove of images, this flasket [92] of idols, which I will pull down —

       Overthrows the gingerbread.

TRASH. Oh, my ware, my ware! God bless it!

BUSY. In my zeal, and glory to be thus exercis'd.   130

LEATHERHEAD *re-enters, with* Officers, [BRISTLE *and* HAGGIS].

LEATH. Here he is. Pray you lay hold on his zeal; we cannot sell a whistle for him in tune. Stop his noise first.

BUSY. Thou canst not; 't is a sanctified noise. I will make a loud and most strong noise, till I have daunted the profane enemy. And for this cause —

LEATH. Sir, here 's no man afraid of you, or your cause. You shall swear it i' the stocks, sir.   140

BUSY. I will thrust myself into the stocks, upon the pikes of the land.

LEATH. Carry him away.

[91] Set in the stocks.   [92] Shallow basket.

PURE. What do you mean, wicked men?

BUSY. Let them alone; I fear them not.

    [*Exeunt* Officers *with* BUSY, *followed by* DAME PURECRAFT.]

LIT. Was not this shilling well ventur'd, Win, tor our liberty? Now we may go play, and see over the Fair, where we list ourselves. My mother is gone after him, and let her e'en go, and loose us.[93]   150

MRS. LIT. Yes, John; but I know not what to do.

LIT. For what, Win?

MRS. LIT. For a thing I am asham'd to tell you, i' faith; and 't is too far to go home.

LIT. I pray thee be not asham'd, Win. Come, i' faith, thou shall not be asham'd. Is it anything about the hobbyhorse man? An't be, speak freely.   159

MRS. LIT. Hang him, base Bobchin, I scorn him. No, I have very great what sha' call 'um, John.

LIT. Oh! is that all, Win? We 'll go back to Captain Jordan, to the pig woman's, Win. He 'll help us, or she, with a dripping-pan, or an old kettle, or something. The poor greasy soul loves you, Win; and after we 'll visit the Fair all over, Win, and see my puppet-play, Win; you know it 's a fine matter, Win.   [*Exeunt into* URSULA's *booth.*] 170

LEATH. Let 's away; I counsell'd you to pack up afore, Joan.

TRASH. A pox of his Bedlam purity! He has spoil'd half my ware. But the best is, we lose nothing if we miss our first merchant.

LEATH. It shall be hard for him to find or know us, when we are translated, Joan.

                        [*Exeunt.*]

ACT IV — SCENE I [1]

[*The stocks. Enter* BRISTLE *and* HAGGIS, *and* Officers *with* OVERDO *in custody; followed by* COKES *and* TROUBLEALL.]

TRO. My masters, I do make no doubt but you are officers.

BRI. What then, sir?

TRO. And the King's loving and obedient subjects.

BRI. Obedient, friend! Take heed what

[93] F 1692 *lose.*
[1] Another part of the Fair. The stocks are on the inner stage.

you speak, I advise you. Oliver [2] Bristle advises you. His loving subjects, we grant you; but not his obedient, at this time, by your leave; we know ourselves a little [10 better than so; we are to command, sir, and such as you are to be obedient. Here's one of his obedient subjects going to the stocks; and we'll make you such another, if you talk.

TRO. You are all wise enough i' your places, I know.

BRI. If you know it, sir, why do you bring it in question?

TRO. I question nothing, pardon me. I do only hope you have warrant for what [20 you do, and so quit you,[3] and so multiply [4] you.   *He goes away again.*

HAG. What's he? — Bring him up to the stocks there. Why bring you him not up?

TRO. (*comes again.*) If you have Justice Overdo's warrant, 't is well; you are safe: that is the warrant of warrants. I'll not give this button for any man's warrant else.

BRI. Like enough, sir; but let me tell you, an you play away your buttons thus, you [30 will want 'em ere night, for any store I see about you. You might keep 'em, and save pins, I wuss.   [TROUBLEALL] *goes away.*

OVER. [*aside*] What should he be, that doth so esteem and advance my warrant? He seems a sober and discreet person! It is a comfort to a good conscience to be follow'd with a good fame in his sufferings. The world will have a pretty taste by this, how I can bear adversity; and it will beget a kind of [40 reverence toward me hereafter, even from mine enemies, when they shall see I carry my calamity nobly, and that it doth neither break me nor bend me.

HAG. Come, sir, here's a place for you to preach in. Will you put in your leg?

OVER. That I will, cheerfully.
    They put him in the stocks.

BRI. O' my conscience, a seminary! [5] He kisses the stocks.   49

COKES. Well, my masters, I'll leave him with you; now I see him bestow'd, I'll go look for my goods and Numps. [*Exit* COKES.]

HAG. You may, sir, I warrant you. — Where's the tother bawler? Fetch him too. You shall find 'em both fast enough.
    [*Exeunt* Officers.]

OVER. [*aside*] In the midst of this tumult, I will yet be the author of mine own rest, and, not minding their fury, sit in the stocks in that calm as shall be able to trouble a triumph.   59

TRO. (*comes again.*) Do you assure me upon your words? May I undertake for you, if I be ask'd the question, that you have this warrant?

HAG. What's this fellow, for God's sake?

TRO. Do but show me Adam Overdo, and I am satisfied.   *Goes out.*

BRI. He is a fellow that is distracted, they say; one Troubleall: he was an officer in the court of pie-powders here last year, and put out on his place by Justice Overdo.   70

OVER. [*aside*] Ha!

BRI. Upon which he took an idle conceit,[6] and 's run mad upon 't. So that ever since he will do nothing but by Justice Overdo's warrant; he will not eat a crust, nor drink a little, nor make him in his apparel ready. His wife (sir reverence) [7] cannot get him make his water, or shift his shirt, without his warrant.   79

OVER. [*aside*] If this be true, this is my greatest disaster. How am I bound to satisfy this poor man, that is of so good a nature to me, out of his wits, where there is no room left for dissembling!

TROUBLEALL *comes in.*

TRO. If you cannot show me Adam Overdo, I am in doubt of you; I am afraid you cannot answer it.   *Goes again.*

HAG. Before me, neighbor Bristle — and now I think on 't better — Justice Overdo is a very parantory [8] person.   90

BRI. Oh, are you advis'd of that? and a severe justicer, by your leave.

OVER. [*aside*] Do I hear ill o' that side too?

BRI. He will sit as upright o' the bench, and you mark him, as a candle i' the socket, and give light to the whole court in every business.

HAG. But he will burn blue, and swell like a bile,[9] God bless us, an he be angry.   99

BRI. Ay, and he will be angry too, when [him] [10] list: that's more; and, when he is angry, be it right or wrong, he has the law on 's side ever. Ay, mark that too.

OVER. [*aside*] I will be more tender hereafter. I see compassion may become a jus-

---

[2] He is called *Davy* in III, i, 10.
[3] May God requite you. (Kittredge, cited by Alden.)
[4] May God increase you, may your tribe increase.
[5] See on II, i, 46.

[6] Groundless notion.
[7] See on Induction, l. 36.
[8] Peremptory.   [9] Boil.   [10] Ff *his.*

tice, though it be a weakness, I confess, and nearer a vice than a virtue.

HAG. Well, take him out o' the stocks again ; we'll go a sure way to work ; we'll ha' the ace of hearts of our side, if we can. [110
They take the JUSTICE *out.*

[*Enter* POCHER, *and* Officers *with* BUSY, *followed by* DAME PURECRAFT.]

POCH. Come, bring him away to his fellow there. — Master Busy, we shall rule your legs, I hope, though we cannot rule your tongue.

BUSY. No, minister of darkness, no ; thou canst not rule my tongue. My tongue it is mine own, and with it I will both knock and mock down your Bartholomew abominations, till you be made a hissing to the neighbor parishes round about. 120

HAG. Let him alone ; we have devis'd better upon 't.

PURE. And shall he not into the stocks, then?

BRI. No, mistress, we'll have 'em both to Justice Overdo, and let him do over 'em as is fitting. Then I, and my gossip Haggis, and my beadle Pocher, are discharg'd.[11]

PURE. Oh, I thank you, blessed honest men ! 130

BRI. Nay, never thank us ; but thank this madman that comes here ; he put it in our heads.

[TROUBLEALL] *comes again.*

PURE. Is he mad? now Heaven increase his madness, and bless it, and thank it ! — Sir, your poor handmaid thanks you.

TRO. Have you a warrant? An you have a warrant, show it.

PURE. Yes, I have a warrant out of the Word,[12] to give thanks for removing any [140 scorn intended to the brethren.

TRO. It is Justice Overdo's warrant that I look for ; if you have not that, keep your word, I'll keep mine. Quit ye, and multiply ye. [*Exeunt all but* TROUBLEALL.]

SCENE II [13]

[*Enter, to*] TROUBLEALL, EDGEWORTH [*and*] NIGHTINGALE.

EDG. Come away, Nightingale, I pray thee.

TRO. Whither go you? Where's your warrant?

EDG. Warrant ! for what, sir?

TRO. For what you go about. You know how fit it is ; an you have no warrant, bless you, I'll pray for you ; that's all I can do.
Goes out.

EDG. What means he?

NIGHT. A madman that haunts the [10 Fair. Do you not know him? It's marvel he has not more followers after his ragged heels.

EDG. Beshrew him, he startled me. I thought he had known of our plot. Guilt's a terrible thing. Ha' you prepar'd the costardmonger?

NIGHT. Yes, and agreed for his basket of pears ; he is at the corner here, ready. And your prize, he comes down sailing [20 that way all alone, without his protector ; he is rid of him, it seems.

EDG. Ay, I know ; I should ha' followed his Protectorship, for a feat I am to do upon him. But this offer'd itself so i' the way, I could not let it scape. Here he comes. Whistle ; be this sport call'd Dorring the Dottrel.[14]

[*Enter* COKES.]

NIGHT. (*whistles.*) Wh, wh, wh, wh, etc.

COKES. By this light, I cannot find my [30 gingerbread wife,[15] nor my hobbyhorse man, in all the Fair now, to ha' my money again.[16] And I do not know the way out on 't, to go home for more. — Do you hear, friend, you that whistle? What tune is that you whistle?

NIGHT. A new tune I am practising, sir.

COKES. Dost thou know where I dwell, I pray thee? Nay, on with thy tune ; I ha' no such haste for an answer. I'll practise with thee. 40

[*Enter* Passengers *and* Costardmonger.]

COS. Buy any pears, very fine pears, pears fine. NIGHTINGALE *sets his foot afore him, and he falls with his basket.*

COKES. Gods-so ! a muss,[17] a muss, a muss, a muss !

COS. Good gentlemen, my ware, my ware ; I am a poor man. Good sir, my ware.

COKES *falls a-scrambling whilst they run away with his things.*

NIGHT. Let me hold your sword, sir ; it troubles you.

---

[11] *I.e.,* freed of responsibility.
[12] Scripture.   [13] The same.
[14] Hoaxing the simpleton.
[15] Woman.   [16] Back.   [17] Scramble.

COKES. Do, and my cloak, an thou wilt, and my hat too.   50

EDG. [*aside*] A delicate great boy! Methinks he out-scrambles 'em all. I cannot persuade myself but he goes to grammar school yet, and plays the truant to-day.

NIGHT. [*aside*] Would he had another purse to cut, Zekiel.

EDG. [*aside*] Purse! a man might cut out his kidneys, I think, and he never feel 'em, he is so earnest at the sport.

NIGHT. [*aside*] His soul is halfway out on 's body at the game.   61

EDG. [*aside*] Away, Nightingale—that way.

[*Exit* NIGHTINGALE.]

COKES. I think I am furnish'd for Cather'ne pears, for one undermeal.[18] Gi' me my cloak.

Cos. Good gentleman, give me my ware.

COKES. Where 's the fellow I ga' my cloak to? my cloak! and my hat! Ha! God's lid, is he gone? Thieves! thieves! Help me to cry, gentlemen.   *He runs out.*   [69

EDG. Away, costermonger; come to us to Urs'la's. [*Exit* Costardmonger.] — Talk of him to have a soul! 'Heart, if he have any more than a thing given him instead of salt, only to keep him from stinking, I 'll be hang'd afore my time, presently. Where should it be, trow? in his blood? He has not so much toward it in his whole body as will maintain a good flea! An if he take this course, he will not ha' so much land left as to rear a calf, within this twelvemonth. Was there ever green [80 plover[19] so pull'd![20] That his little overseer had been here now, and been but tall enough to see him steal pears, in exchange for his beaver hat and his cloak thus! I must go find him out next, for his black box, and his patent, it seems, he has of his place;[21] which I think the gentleman would have a reversion[22] of, that spoke to me for it so earnestly. [*Exit.*] [88

[COKES] *comes again.*

COKES. Would I might lose my doublet, and hose, too, as I am an honest man, and never stir, if I think there be anything but thieving and coz'ning i' this whole Fair. Bartholomew Fair, quoth he![23] An ever any

Bartholomew had that luck in 't that I have had, I 'll be martyr'd for him, and in Smithfield,[24] too. I ha' paid for my pears, a rot on 'em! I 'll keep 'em no longer. (*Throws away his pears.*) You were choke-pears to me. I had been better ha' gone to mumchance[25] for you, I-wuss. Methinks the Fair should [100 not have us'd me thus, an 't were but for my name's sake. I would not ha' us'd a dog o' the name so. Oh, Numps will triumph now!—

TROUBLEALL *comes again.*

Friend, do you know who I am, or where I lie?[26] I do not myself, I 'll be sworn. Do but carry me home, and I 'll please thee; I ha' money enough there. I ha' lost myself, and my cloak, and my hat, and my fine sword, and my sister, and Numps, and Mistress Grace, a gentlewoman that I should ha' [110 married, and a cut-work handkercher she ga' me, and two purses, to-day. And my bargain o' hobbyhorses and gingerbread, which grieves me worst of all.

TRO. By whose warrant, sir, have you done all this?

COKES. Warrant! thou art a wise fellow indeed; as if a man need a warrant to lose anything with.

TRO. Yes, Justice Overdo's warrant, [120 a man may get and lose with, I 'll stand to 't.

COKES. Justice Overdo! dost thou know him? I lie there; he is my brother-in-law; he married my sister. Pray thee, show me the way; dost thou know the house?

TRO. Sir, show me your warrant; I know nothing without a warrant, pardon me.

COKES. Why, I warrant thee; come along. Thou shalt see I have wrought pillows there, and cambric sheets,[27] and sweet bags[28] too. Pray thee, guide me to the house.   131

TRO. Sir, I 'll tell you; go you thither yourself first alone, tell your worshipful brother your mind, and but bring me three lines of his hand, or his clerk's, with Adam Overdo underneath (here I 'll stay[29] you), I 'll obey you, and I 'll guide you presently.

COKES. 'Slid! this is an ass; I ha' found him, pox upon me; what do I talking to such a dull fool? Farewell! you are a very coxcomb, do you hear?   [*Exit.*] [141

18 Afternoon luncheon.
19 Inexperienced prostitute.
20 Plucked; *i.e.*, cheated.
21 A patent of place was the document conferring an appointment or privilege. Wasp's custody of the license is a symbol of his governorship.
22 The reversion of an office was the promise of possessing it upon the incumbent's death or surrender of it.
23 They call it.

24 Many heretics had been burned there.
25 A game at dice or cards. (Skeat-Mayhew.)
26 Lodge.   27 Luxuries then.
28 Perfumed or filled with odoriferous herbs; they were used in chambers.
29 Wait for.

TRO. I think I am; if Justice Overdo sign to it, I am, and so we are all. He'll quit [30] us all, multiply us all.

SCENE III [31]

[To him] enter GRACE, *[and]* QUARLOUS *[and]* WINWIFE *with their swords drawn.*

GRACE. Gentlemen, this is no way that you take; you do but breed one another trouble and offence, and give me no contentment at all. I am no she that affects to be quarrell'd for or have my name or fortune made the question of men's swords.

QUAR. 'Sblood, we love you!

GRACE. If you both love me, as you pretend, your own reason will tell you but one can enjoy me; and to that point there [10] leads a directer line than by my infamy, which must follow if you fight. 'T is true, I have profess'd it to you ingenuously, that, rather than to be yok'd with this bridegroom is appointed me, I would take up any husband almost upon any trust; though subtlety would say to me, I know, he is a fool, and has an estate, and I might govern him, and enjoy a friend [32] beside. But these are not my aims; I must have a husband I must [33] love, or [20] I cannot live with him. I shall ill make one of these politic wives!

WINW. Why, if you can like either of us, lady, say which is he, and the other shall swear instantly to desist.

QUAR. Content; I accord to that willingly.

GRACE. Sure you think me a woman of an extreme levity, gentlemen, or a strange fancy, that, meeting you by chance in such a [30] place as this, both at one instant, and not yet of two hours' acquaintance, neither of you deserving afore the other of me, I should so forsake my modesty, though I might affect one more particularly, as to say, "This is he," and name him.

QUAR. Why, wherefore should you not? What should hinder you?

GRACE. If you would not give it to my modesty, allow it yet to my wit. Give me [40] so much of woman and cunning as not to betray myself impertinently. How can I judge of you, so far as to a choice, without knowing you more? You are both equal, and alike to me yet, and so indifferently affected [34] by me, as each of you might be the man, if the other were away. For you are reasonable creatures, you have understanding and discourse; and, if fate send me an understanding husband, I have no fear at all but mine [50] own manners shall make him a good one.

QUAR. Would I were put forth to making for you then.

GRACE. It may be you are; you know not what's toward you. Will you consent to a motion [35] of mine, gentlemen?

WINW. Whatever it be, we'll presume reasonableness, coming from you.

QUAR. And fitness, too.

GRACE. I saw one of you buy a pair of [60] tables [36] e'en now.

WINW. Yes, here they be, and maiden ones too, unwritten in.

GRACE. The fitter for what they may be employed in. You shall write either of you here a word or a name, what you like [37] best, but of two or three syllables at most; and the next person that comes this way, because destiny has a high hand in business of this nature,[38] I'll demand which of the two [70] words he or she doth approve, and according to that sentence fix my resolution and affection without change.

QUAR. Agreed; my word is conceived already.

WINW. And mine shall not be long creating after.

GRACE. But you shall promise, gentlemen, not to be curious to know which of you it is, taken; but give me leave to conceal [80] that till you have brought me either home or where I may safely tender myself.

WINW. Why, that's but equal.[39]

QUAR. We are pleas'd.

GRACE. Because I will bind both your endeavors to work together friendly and jointly, each to the other's fortune, and have myself fitted with some means to make him that is forsaken a part of amends.

---

[30] Requite.
[31] The scene is unchanged, and Troubleall remains on stage, but the last speech shows that we are again in the vicinity of Ursula's booth.
[32] Lover.
[33] The repetition of this word may be a compositor's error.

[34] Impartially regarded.
[35] Proposal, suggestion.
[36] A memorandum book.
[37] What is agreeable to you, what you choose.
[38] Alluding to the proverb, "Hanging and wiving goes by destiny."
[39] Impartial, fair.

QUAR. These conditions are very courte- [90
ous. Well, my word is out of the " Arcadia,"
then : *Argalus*.[40]

WINW. And mine out of the play : *Palemon*.[41]

TROUBLEALL *comes again.*

TRO. Have you any warrant for this,
gentlemen?

QUAR. [AND] WINW. Ha?

TRO. There must be a warrant had, believe it.

WINW. For what?　　　　　　　　　　　100

TRO. For whatsoever it is, anything indeed, no matter what.

QUAR. 'Slight! here's a fine ragged prophet
dropp'd down i' the nick!

TRO. Heaven quit you, gentlemen!

QUAR. Nay, stay a little. Good lady, put
him to the question.

GRACE. You are content then?

WINW. [AND] QUAR. Yes, yes.
　　　　　　　　　　　　[*They step aside.*]

GRACE. Sir, here are two names written —
TRO. Is [Justice] [42] Overdo one?　　111

GRACE. How, sir? I pray you read 'em
to yourself ; it is for a wager between these
gentlemen ; and with a stroke or any difference
mark which you approve best.

TRO. They may be both worshipful names
for aught I know, mistress ; but *Adam Overdo*
had been worth three of 'em, I assure you, in
this place ; that's in plain English.

GRACE. This man amazes me! I pray [120
you like one of 'em, sir.

TRO. I do like him there, that has the best
warrant, mistress, to save your longing, and
(multiply him) it may be this. But I am still
for Justice Overdo — that's my conscience ;
and quit you.

WINW. Is 't done, lady?

GRACE. Ay, and strangely as ever I saw!
What fellow is this, trow?　　　　　　129

QUAR. No matter what ; a fortune teller
we ha' made him. Which is 't, which is 't?

GRACE. Nay, did you not promise not to
inquire?

[*Enter* EDGEWORTH.]

QUAR. 'Slid, I forgot that! pray you pardon me. — Look, here's our Mercury come.
The license arrives i' the finest time too! 't is

but scraping out Cokes his name, and 't is
done.

WINW. How now, lime-twig,[43] hast thou
touch'd?　　　　　　　　　　　　　　140

EDG. Not yet, sir ; except you would go
with me and see 't, it's not worth speaking on.
The act is nothing without a witness. Yonder he is, your man with the box, fall'n into
the finest company, and so transported with
vapors. They ha' got in a northern clothier ; [44]
and one Puppy, a western man, that's come to
wrestle before my Lord Mayor [45] anon ; and
Captain Whit ; and one Val Cutting, that helps
Captain Jordan to roar, a circling boy ; [46] [150
with whom your Numps is so taken that you
may strip him of his clothes, if you will. I'll
undertake to geld him for you, if you had but
a surgeon ready to sear him. And Mistress
Justice there is the goodest woman! She
does so love 'em all over in terms of justice
and the style of authority, with her hood upright, that I beseech you come away, gentlemen, and see 't.

QUAR. 'Slight, I would not lose it for [160
the Fair. What'll you do, Ned?

WINW. Why, stay hereabout for you ;
Mistress Wellborn must not be seen.

QUAR. Do so, and find out a priest i' the
meantime. I'll bring the license. — Lead ;
which way is 't?

EDG. Here, sir, you are o' the backside o'
the booth already ; you may hear the noise.

　　　　　　　　　　　　　[*Exeunt.*]

SCENE IV [47]

KNOCKHUM, NORDERN, PUPPY, CUTTING,
　WHIT, WASP, *and* [MRS.] OVERDO [*are dis-
　covered*].[48]

KNOCK. [*aside*] Whit, bid Val Cutting continue the vapors for a lift,[49] Whit, for a lift.

NOR. I'll ne mare, I'll ne mare ; the eale's
too meeghty.[50]

KNOCK. How now! my Galloway nag, the
staggers? Ha! Whit, gi' him a slit i' the forehead. Cheer up, man ; a needle and thread
to stitch his ears. I'd cure him now, an I had
it, with a little butter and garlic, long pepper
and grains. Where's my horn? I'll gi' [10

[40] The hero of a love-story in Sidney's romance.
[41] As Gifford notes, a prominent character in
Daniel's *The Queen's Arcadia* (acted 1605).
[42] So F 1692 ; F 1631 *Iudice*.
[43] For things stick to Edgeworth's fingers.
[44] Come to traffic in the cloth market which was
still a section of the Fair.
[45] Who annually visited the Fair on St. Bartholomew's Day and watched the wrestling.
[46] See IV, iv, 170 ff.
[47] Inside Ursula's booth.
[48] On the inner stage.　　　　　[49] Theft.
[50] No more ; the ale's too mighty.

him a mash presently, shall take away this dizziness.

Pup. Why, where are you, zurs? Do you vlinch,[51] and leave us i' the zuds now?

Nor. I 'll ne mare; I is e'en as vull as a paiper's bag,[52] by my troth, I.

Pup. Do my northern cloth zhrink i' the wetting, ha?

Knock. Why, well said, old flea-bitten; thou 'lt never tire, I see.[53]   20

They fall to their vapors again.

Cut. No, sir, but he may tire if it please him.

Whit. Who told dee sho, that he vuld never teer, man?

Cut. No matter who told him so, so long as he knows.

Knock. Nay, I know nothing, sir; pardon me there.

[*Enter* Edgeworth *and* Quarlous.][54]

Edg. [*aside to* Quarlous] They are at it still, sir; this they call vapors.   30

Whit. He shall not pardon dee, captain; dou shalt not be pardon'd. Pre'dee, shweetheart, do not pardon him.

Cut. 'Slight, I 'll pardon him, an I list, whosoever says nay to 't.

Quar. [*aside*] Where's Numps? I miss him.

Here they continue their game of "vapors," which is nonsense; every man to oppose the last man that spoke, whether it concern'd him or no.

Wasp. Why, I say nay to 't.

Quar. Oh, there he is.

Knock. To what do you say nay, sir? [40

Wasp. To anything, whatsoever it is, so long as I do not like it.

Whit. Pardon me, little man, dou musht like it a little.

Cut. No, he must not like it at all, sir; there you are i' the wrong.

Whit. I tink I be: he musht not like it, indeed.

Cut. Nay, then he both must and will like it, sir, for all you.   50

Knock. If he have reason, he may like it, sir.

Whit. By no meensh, captain, upon reason; he may like nothing upon reason.

[51] Flinch, weaken in drinking your share.
[52] Piper's bagpipe.
[53] An allusion to the saying, "A flea-bitten horse never tires." (Gifford.)
[54] Probably by one of the side doors, down stage.

Wasp. I have no reason, nor I will hear of no reason, nor I will look for no reason, and he is an ass that either knows any, or looks for 't from me.

Cut. Yes, in some sense you may have reason, sir.   60

Wasp. Ay, in some sense, I care not if I grant you.

Whit. Pardon me, thou ougsht to grant him nothing in no shensh, if dou do love dyshelf, angry man.

Wasp. Why then, I do grant him nothing, and I have no sense.

Cut. 'T is true, thou hast no sense indeed.   69

Wasp. 'Slid, but I have sense, now I think on 't better; and I will grant him anything, do you see?

Knock. He is i' the right, and does utter a sufficient vapor.

Cut. Nay, it is no sufficient vapor neither. I deny that.

Knock. Then it is a sweet vapor.

Cut. It may be a sweet vapor.

Wasp. Nay, it is no sweet vapor neither, sir; it stinks, and I 'll stand to 't.   80

Whit. Yes, I tink it dosh shtink, captain. All vapor dosh shtink.

Wasp. Nay, then it does not stink, sir, and it shall not stink.

Cut. By your leave, it may, sir.

Wasp. Ay, by my leave it may stink, I know that.

Whit. Pardon me, thou knowesht nothing; it cannot by thy leave, angry man.

Wasp. How can it not?   90

Knock. Nay, never question him, for he is i' the right.

Whit. Yesh, I am i' de right, I confesh it; so ish de little man too.

Wasp. I 'll have nothing confess'd that concerns me. I am not i' the right, nor never was i' the right, nor never will be i' the right, while I am in my right mind.

Cut. Mind! Why, here's no man minds you, sir, nor anything else.   100

They drink again.

Pup. [*offering* Nordern *the cup*] Vriend, will you mind this that we do?

Quar. [*aside to* Edgeworth] Call you this vapors? This is such belching of quarrel as I never heard. Will you mind your business,[55] sir?

[55] *I.e.*, try to steal the license.

EDG. [*aside to* QUARLOUS] You shall see, sir. —   [*Goes to* WASP.]

NOR. I 'll ne maire, my waimb warkes too mickle [56] with this auready.   110

EDG. Will you take that, Master Wasp, that nobody should mind you?

WASP. Why! what ha' you to do? Is 't any matter to you?

EDG. No, but methinks you should not be unminded, though.

WASP. Nor I wu' [57] not be, now I think on 't. — Do you hear, new acquaintance? Does no man mind me, say you?

CUT. Yes, sir, every man here minds you — but how?   121

WASP. Nay, I care as little how as you do; that was not my question.

WHIT. No, noting was ty question; tou art a learned man, and I am a valiant man, i' faith la; tou shalt speak for me, and I vill fight for tee.

KNOCK. Fight for him, Whit? a gross vapor! He can fight for himself.

WASP. It may be I can, but it may [130 be I wu' not. How then?

CUT. Why, then you may choose.

WASP. Why, and I 'll choose whether I 'll choose or no.

KNOCK. I think you may, and 't is true; and I allow it for a resolute vapor.

WASP. Nay then, I do think you do not think, and it is no resolute vapor.   138

CUT. Yes, in some sort he may allow you.

KNOCK. In no sort, sir, pardon me; I can allow him nothing. You mistake the vapor.

WASP. He mistakes nothing, sir, in no sort.

WHIT. Yes, I pre dee now, let him mistake.

WASP. A turd i' your teeth! Never pre dee me, for I will have nothing mistaken.

KNOCK. Turd, ha, turd? a noisome vapor! strike, Whit!   [WHIT *and* WASP] *fall by the ears,* [*while* EDGEWORTH *steals the license out of the box, and exit.*]

MRS. OVER. Why, gentlemen, why, gentlemen, I charge you upon my authority, conserve the peace. In the King's name, and my husband's, put up your weapons; I shall be driven to commit you myself else.   152

QUAR. Ha, ha, ha.

WASP. Why do you laugh, sir?

QUAR. Sir, you 'll allow me my Christian liberty: I may laugh, I hope.

CUT. In some sort you may, and in some sort you may not, sir.

KNOCK. Nay, in some sort, sir, he may neither laugh nor hope in this company.   160

WASP. Yes, then he may both laugh and hope in any sort, an 't please him.

QUAR. Faith, and I will then, for it doth please me exceedingly.

WASP. No exceeding [58] neither, sir.

KNOCK. No, that vapor is too lofty.

QUAR. Gentlemen, I do not play well at your game of vapors; I am not very good at it; but —   169

CUT. Do you hear, sir? I would speak with you in circle!

                    He draws a circle on the ground.

QUAR. In circle, sir? What would you with me in circle?

CUT. Can you lend me a piece, a Jacobus, in circle? [59]

QUAR. 'Slid! your circle will prove more costly than your vapors, then. Sir, no; I lend you none.

CUT. Your beard 's not well turn'd up, sir.

QUAR. How, rascal! Are you playing with my beard? I 'll break circle with you.   181

                    They draw all and fight.

PUP. [AND] NOR. Gentlemen, gentlemen!

KNOCK. [*aside*] Gather up, Whit, gather up, Whit; good vapors!   [*Exit, while* WHIT *takes up the cloaks and hides them.*]

MRS. OVER. What mean you? are you rebels, gentlemen? Shall I send out a sergeant at arms, or a writ o' rebellion against you? I 'll commit you, upon my womanhood, for a riot; upon my justicehood, if you persist. [*Exeunt* QUARLOUS *and* CUTTING.] [190

WASP. Upon your justicehood! Marry shit o' your hood. You 'll commit! Spoke like a true justice of peace's wife, indeed, and a fine female lawyer! Turd i' your teeth for a fee, now.

MRS. OVER. Why, Numps, in Master Overdo's name, I charge you.

WASP. Good Mistress Underdo, hold your tongue.

MRS. OVER. Alas, poor Numps!   200

WASP. Alas! and why alas from you, I beseech you? or why poor Numps, Goody Rich? Am I come to be pitied by your tuft-

---

[58] Overstepping the limits of propriety.

[59] A Jacobus was a gold coin, the sovereign, originally worth $4.85. — By drawing the circle Cutting is daring Quarlous to invade it and fight. Quarlous asks, "What do you want me to enter that circle for?" "Merely," replies Cutting, "to ask you for a loan." Quarlous still fails to take the procedure as a challenge, whereupon Cutting directly insults him. Quarlous then accepts the challenge. (Kittredge.)

---

[56] My belly works too much.   [57] Will.

taffeta [60] now? Why, mistress, I knew Adam the clerk, your husband, when he was Adam Scrivener, [61] and writ for twopence a sheet, as high as he bears his head now, or you your hood, dame —

The Watch *comes in,* [*led by* BRISTLE].

What are you, sir?

BRI. We be men, and no infidels; [210 what is the matter here, and the noises, can you tell?

WASP. Heart, what ha' you to do? Cannot a man quarrel in quietness, but he must be put out on 't by you? What are you?

BRI. Why, we be his Majesty's watch, sir.

WASP. Watch! 'Sblood, you are a sweet watch indeed. A body would think, an you watch'd well a-nights, you should be contented to sleep at this time a' day. Get you to your fleas and your flock-beds, you rogues, your kennels, and lie down close.   222

BRI. Down? yes, we will down, I warrant you. — Down with him, in his Majesty's name; down, down with him, and carry him away, to the pigeon-holes. [62] [*Some of the* Watch *seize* WASP, *and carry him off.*]

MRS. OVER. I thank you, honest friends, in the behalf o' the Crown, and the peace, and in Master Overdo's name, for suppressing enormities.   230

WHIT. Stay, Bristle, here ish anoder brashe [63] o' drunkards, but very quiet, special drunkards, will pay dee five shillings very well. [*Points to* NORDERN *and* PUPPY, *drunk and asleep on the bench.*] Take 'em to dee, in de graish o' God; one of 'em does change cloth for ale in the Fair here; te toder ish a strong man, a mighty man, my Lord Mayor's man, and a wrastler. He has wrashled so long with the bottle here, that [240 the man with the beard [64] hash almosht streek up his heelsh.

BRI. 'Slid, the clerk o' the market has been to cry him all the Fair over here, for my Lord's service.

WHIT. Tere he ish; pre dee taik him hensh, and make ty best on him. [*Exeunt* BRISTLE *and the rest of the* Watch *with* NORDERN *and* PUPPY.] — How now, woman o' shilk, vat ailsh ty shweet faish? Art tou melancholy?

MRS. OVER. A little distemper'd [250 with these enormities. Shall I entreat a courtesy of you, captain?

WHIT. Entreat a hundred, velvet voman, I vill do it; shpeak out.

MRS. OVER. I cannot with modesty speak it out; but — [*Whispers to him.*]

WHIT. I vill do it, and more and more, for dee. — What, Urs'la, an 't be bitch, an 't be bawd, an 't be!

[*Enter* URSULA.]

URS. How now, rascal; What roar [260 you for, old pimp?

WHIT. [*aside*] Here, put up de cloaks, Ursh, de purchase. — Pre dee now, shweet Ursh, help dis good, brave voman, to a jordan, an 't be.

URS. 'Slid, call your Captain Jordan to her, can you not?

WHIT. Nay, pre dee leave dy consheits, and bring the velvet woman to de —

URS. I bring her, hang her. Heart, must I find a common pot for every punk i' [271 your purlieus?

WHIT. O, good voordsh, Ursh; it ish a guest o' velvet, i' fait, la.

URS. Let her sell her hood, and buy a sponge, with a pox to her. My vessel [is] [65] employed, sir. I have but one, and 't is the bottom of an old bottle. An honest proctor and his wife are at it within; if she 'll stay her time, so.   [*Exit.*]

WHIT. As soon ash tou cansht, shwe[e]t [281 Ursh. — Of a valiant man I tink I am te patientsh man i' the world, or in all Smithfield.

[*Re-enter* KNOCKHUM.]

KNOCK. How now, Whit! Close vapors! Stealing your leaps? Covering [66] in corners, ha?

WHIT. No, fait, captain, dough tou beesht a vishe man, dy vit is a mile hence, now. I vas procuring a shmall courtesie for a woman of fashion here.   291

MRS. OVER. Yes, captain, though I am justice of peace's wife, I do love men of war and the sons of the sword, when they come before my husband.

KNOCK. Say'st thou so, filly? Thou shalt have a leap presently; I 'll horse thee myself else.

[60] A kind of silk.
[61] An allusion to Chaucer's verses addressed to Adam, his own scrivener.
[62] Stocks.
[63] Brace.
[64] A common decoration on tavern jugs.
[65] Supplied by F 1692.
[66] Copulating. Knockhum's terminology is consistently horsy.

Urs. [*within*] Come, will you bring her in now, and let her [take] [67] her turn? 300

Whit. Grammercy, good Ursh, I tank dee.

Mrs. Over. Master Overdo shall thank her. [*Exit.*]

Scene V [68]

[*Enter*] Urs'la, Littlewit, *and* Mrs. Little-wit, [*to*] Whit, [*and*] Knockhum.

Lit. Good gammer Urs, Win and I are exceedingly beholden to you, and to Captain Jordan and Captain Whit. — Win, I 'll be bold to leave you i' this good company, Win, for half an hour or so, Win, while I go and see how my matter goes forward, and if the puppets be perfect; [69] and then I 'll come and fetch you, Win.

Mrs. Lit. [*aside*] Will you leave me alone with two men, John? 10

Lit. [*aside to* Win] Ay, they are honest gentlemen, Win, Captain Jordan and Captain Whit; they 'll use you very civilly, Win. God b' w' you, Win. [*Exit.*]

Urs. [*aside to* Knockhum] What, 's her husband gone?

Knock. [*aside*] On his false gallop, [70] Urs, away.

Urs. [*aside*] An you be right Bartholomew birds, now show yourselves so. We are [20 undone for want of fowl [71] i' the Fair here. Here will be Zekiel Edgeworth, and three or four gallants with him at night, and I ha' neither plover [71] nor quail [71] for 'em. Persuade this between you two, to become a bird o' the game, while I work the velvet woman within, as you call her.

Knock. [*aside*] I conceive thee, Urs! go thy ways. [*Exit* Ursula.] — Doest thou hear, Whit? Is 't not pity my delicate dark [30 chestnut here, with the fine lean head, large forehead, round eyes, even mouth, sharp ears, long neck, thin crest, close withers, plain back, deep sides, short fillets, and full flanks; with a round belly, a plump buttock, large thighs, knit knees, straight legs, short pasterns, smooth hoofs, and short heels, should lead a dull honest woman's life, that might live the life of a lady?

Whit. Yes, by my fait and trot it is, [40 captain; de honesht woman's life is a scurvy dull life, indeed, la.

Mrs. Lit. How, sir? Is an honest woman's life a scurvy life?

Whit. Yes, fait, shweetheart, believe him, de leef of a bondwoman! But if dou vilt hearken to me, I vill make tee a free woman and a lady: dou shalt live like a lady, as te captain saysh.

Knock. Ay, and be honest [72] too some- [50 times; have her wires [73] and her tires, [74] her green gowns and velvet petticoats.

Whit. Ay, and ride to Ware and Romford i' dy coash, shee de players, be in love vit 'em, sup vit gallantsh, be drunk, and cost dee noting.

Knock. Brave vapors!

Whit. And lie by twenty on 'em, if dou pleash, shweetheart.

Mrs. Lit. What, and be honest still? [60 That were fine sport.

Whit. 'T ish common, shweetheart; tou mayst do it, by my hand. It shall be justified to ty husband's faish now. Tou shalt be as honesht as the skin between his hornsh, [75] la!

Knock. Yes, and wear a dressing, top and topgallant, to compare with e'er a husband on 'em all, for a foretop. [76] It is the vapor of spirit in the wife to cuckold nowadays, as it is the vapor of fashion in the hus- [70 band not to suspect. Your prying cat-eyed citizen is an abominable vapor.

Mrs. Lit. Lord, what a fool have I been!

Whit. Mend then, and do everyting like a lady hereafter; never know ty husband from another man.

Knock. Nor any one man from another, but i' the dark.

Whit. Ay, and then it ish no disgrash to know any man. 80

Urs. [*within*] Help, help here!

Knock. How now! What vapor's there?

[*Re-enter* Ursula.]

Urs. Oh, you are a sweet ranger, and look well to your walks! Yonder is your punk of Turnbull, ramping Alice, has fall'n upon the poor gentlewoman within, and pull'd her hood over her ears, and her hair through it.

[67] Cor. ed. 1716. F 1631 *talke;* F 1692 *talk.*
[68] The same.
[69] Have their parts memorized (!).
[70] Canter, with a play on "false." [71] Wenches.
[72] Chaste.
[73] For ruffs and for supporting the dressing of the hair.
[74] Headdresses.
[75] The horns of the cuckold, substituted here for the "brows" of the proverb.
[76] Her husband's foretop is to be his horns.

ALICE *enters, beating the* Justice's Wife.

MRS. OVER. Help, help, i' the King's name !   90

ALICE. A mischief on you ; they are such as you are, that undo [77] us and take our trade from us, with your tuft-taffeta haunches.

KNOCK. How now, Alice !

ALICE. The poor common whores can ha' no traffic for [78] the privy rich ones. Your caps and hoods of velvet call away our customers, and lick the fat from us.

URS. Peace, you foul, ramping jade, you —

ALICE. Od's foot, you bawd in grease, [100 are you talking?

KNOCK. Why, Alice, I say !

ALICE. Thou sow of Smithfield, thou !

URS. Thou tripe of Turnbull !

KNOCK. Catamountain vapors ! Ha !

URS. You know where you were taw'd [79] lately ; both lash'd and slash'd you were in Bridewell.[80]

ALICE. Ay, by the same token, you rid [81] that week, and broke out the bottom o' [110 the cart, night-tub.[82]

KNOCK. Why, lion face, ha ! Do you know who I am ? Shall I tear ruff, slit waistcoat, make rags of petticoat ? Ha ! go to, vanish, for fear of vapors. Whit, a kick, Whit, in the parting vapor. [*They kick* ALICE *out.*] — Come, brave woman, take a good heart, thou shalt be a lady, too.

WHIT. Yes, fait, dey shall all both be ladies, and write madam. I vill do 't my- [120 self for dem. *Do* is the vord, and *D* is the middle letter of *madam ; DD,* put 'em together, and make deeds, without which all words are alike, la !

KNOCK. 'T is true : Urs'la, take 'em in, open thy wardrope, and fit 'em to their calling. Green gowns, crimson petticoats, green [83] women ! my Lord Mayor's green women ! guests o' the game, true bred. I 'll provide you a coach to take the air in.   130

MRS. LIT. But do you think you can get one ?

KNOCK. Oh, they are as common as wheelbarrows where there are great dunghills. Every pettifogger's wife has 'em ; for first he buys a coach that he may marry, and then he marries that he may be made

cuckold in 't. For, if their wives ride not to their cuckolding, they do 'em no credit. " Hide and be hidden, ride and be rid- [140 den," says the vapor of experience.

> [*Exeunt* URSULA, MRS. LITTLEWIT, *and* MRS. OVERDO.]

SCENE VI [84]

[*Enter*] TROUBLEALL [*to*] KNOCKHUM [*and*] WHIT.

TRO. By what warrant does it say so ?

KNOCK. Ha, mad child o' the pie-powders ! art thou there ? Fill us a fresh can, Urs ; we may drink together.

TRO. I may not drink without a warrant, captain.

KNOCK. 'Slood,[85] thou 'll not stale [86] without a warrant, shortly. — Whit, give me pen, ink, and paper. I 'll draw him a warrant presently.   10

TRO. It must be Justice Overdo's !

KNOCK. I know, man. Fetch the drink, Whit.

WHIT. I pre dee now, be very brief, captain ; for de new ladies stay for dee.

> [*Exit, and re-enter with a can.*]

KNOCK. Oh, as brief as can be ; here 't is, already : " Adam Overdo."

> [*Gives* TROUBLEALL *a paper.*]

TRO. Why, now I 'll pledge you, captain.

> [*Drinks.*]

KNOCK. Drink it off ; I 'll come to thee anon, again.   [*Exeunt.*] [20

[*Enter*] QUARLOUS [*and* EDGEWORTH] *the* Cutpurse.

QUAR. Well, sir. You are now discharg'd. Beware of being spi'd hereafter.

EDG. Sir, will it please you enter in here at Urs'la's, and take part of a silken gown, a velvet petticoat, or a wrought smock ? I am promis'd such, and I can spare any gentleman a moiety.[87]

QUAR. Keep it for your companions in beastliness ; I am none of 'em, sir. If I had not already forgiven you a greater trespass, [30 or thought you yet worth my beating, I would instruct your manners to whom you made your offers. But go your ways ; talk not to me : the hangman is only fit to discourse

---

[77] Ruin.   [78] Because of.   [79] Beaten.
[80] The famous workhouse and house of correction.
[81] Were carted as a bawd.
[82] A tub containing the excrementitious matter removed by night from cesspools.
[83] Unchaste.

[84] The same ; but, as in IV, iii, the scene varies. At l. 21 the curtains of the inner stage were probably closed ; the outer stage thereafter represents the ground in front of Ursula's booth, till l. 60 ; after which we are back at the stocks.
[85] By God's blood.   [86] Urinate.   [87] Share.

with you ; the hand of beadle [88] is too merciful a punishment for your trade of life.

[*Exit* EDGEWORTH.]

I am sorry I employ'd this fellow, for he thinks me such ; *facinus quos inquinat æquat.*[89] But, it was for sport. And, would I make it serious, the getting of this license is [40 nothing to me, without other circumstances concur. I do think how impertinently I labor, if the word be not mine that the ragged fellow mark'd. And what advantage I have given Ned Winwife in this time now of working her, though it be mine. He 'll go near to form to her what a debauch'd rascal I am, and fright her out of all good conceit of me. I should do so by him, I am sure, if I had the opportunity. But my hope is in her [50 temper yet ; and it must needs be next to despair, that is grounded on any part of a woman's discretion. I would give, by my troth now, all I could spare, to my clothes and my sword, to meet my tatter'd soothsayer again, who was my judge i' the question, to know certainly whose word he has damn'd or sav'd. For, till then, I live but under a reprieve. I must seek him. Who be these?

Enter WASP *with the* Officers, [*led by* BRISTLE].

WASP. Sir, you are a Welsh cuckold, [60 and a prating runt, and no constable.

BRI. You say very well. — Come, put in his leg in the middle roundel, and let him hole there.

WASP. You stink of leeks, metheglin, and cheese. You rogue !

BRI. Why, what is that to you, if you sit sweetly in the stocks in the meantime? If you have a mind to stink too, your breeches sit close enough to your bum. Sit you [70 merry, sir.

QUAR. How now, Numps?

WASP. It is no matter how ; pray you look off.

QUAR. Nay, I 'll not offend you, Numps ; I thought you had sat there to be seen.

WASP. And to be sold, did you not? Pray you mind your business, an you have any.

QUAR. Cry you mercy, Numps. Does your leg lie high enough?   80

[Enter HAGGIS.]

BRI. How now, neighbor Haggis. What

[88] *I.e.,* flogging.
[89] Crime puts those it stains on the same level. (Lucan, *Pharsalia,* V, 290.)

says Justice Overdo's Worship to the other offenders?

HAG. Why, he says just nothing. What should he say? Or where should he say? He is not to be found, man. He ha' not been seen i' the Fair here all this livelong day, never since seven a'clock i' the morning. His clerks know not what to think on 't. There is no court of pie-powders yet. Here [90 they be return'd.

[*Enter* Officers *with* BUSY *and* OVERDO.]

BRI. What shall be done with 'em then, in your discretion? [90]

HAG. I think we were best put 'em in the stocks in discretion [91] (there they will be safe in discretion) [92] for the valure [93] of an hour, or such a thing, till his Worship come.

BRI. It is but a hole matter if we do, neighbor Haggis. — [*to* WASP] Come, sir, here is company for you. — Heave up the [100 stocks.

WASP. I shall put a trick upon your Welsh diligence perhaps.

As they open the stocks, WASP puts
his shoe on his hand, and slips it
in for his leg.

BRI. [*to* BUSY] Put in your leg, sir.

They bring BUSY and put him in,
[and then stand aside.]

QUAR. What, Rabbi Busy ! Is he come?

BUSY. I do obey thee. The lion may roar, but he cannot bite. I am glad to be thus separated from the heathen of the land, and put apart in the stocks, for the holy cause.

WASP. What are you, sir?   110

BUSY. One that rejoiceth in his affliction, and sitteth here to prophesy the destruction of fairs and May-games, wakes, and Whitsunales,[94] and doth sigh and groan for the reformation of these abuses.

WASP. [*to* OVERDO] And do you sigh and groan, too, or rejoice in your affliction?

OVER. I do not feel it ; I do not think of it ; it is a thing without me. Adam, thou art above these batteries, these contume- [120 lies. *In te manca ruit fortuna,* as thy friend Horace [95] says. Thou art one, *Quem*

[90] Opinion, judgment.   [91] As a matter of prudence.
[92] Disjunction, separation.   [93] Value, worth.
[94] Festivals at Whitsuntide.
[95] " 'Gainst thee, when Fortune runs, she's sure
          to trip . . .
      Whom neither poverty, nor dungeon drear,
      Nor death itself can ever put to fear."

(Satires, II, vii, 84–88.)

neque pauperies, neque mors, neque vincula terrent. And therefore, as another friend of thine says, I think it be thy friend Persius, *Non te quæsiveris extra.*[96]

QUAR. What's here! a stoic i' the stocks? The fool is turn'd philosopher.   128

BUSY. Friend, I will leave to communicate my spirit with you, if I hear any more of those superstitious relics, those lists[97] of Latin, the very rags of Rome, and patches of popery.

WASP. Nay, an you begin to quarrel, gentlemen, I'll leave you. I ha' paid for quarrelling too lately. Look you, a device, but shifting in a hand for a foot. God b' w' you.
                                    He gets out.

BUSY. Wilt thou then leave thy brethren in tribulation?

WASP. For this once, sir.   [*Exit.*]

BUSY. Thou art a halting[98] neutral. — Stay him there; stop him that will not endure the heat of persecution.   142

BRI. How now, what's the matter?

BUSY. He is fled, he is fled, and dares not sit it out.

BRI. What, has he made an escape? which way? — Follow, neighbor Haggis.
        [*Exeunt* HAGGIS *and the other* Officers.]

[*Enter* DAME PURECRAFT.]

PURE. O me! in the stocks! Have the wicked prevail'd?

BUSY. Peace, religious sister; it is my [150 calling; comfort yourself; an extraordinary calling, and done for my better standing, my surer standing, hereafter.

[TROUBLEALL] *the* Madman *enters,* [*with a can*].

TRO. By whose warrant, by whose warrant, this?

QUAR. [*aside*] Oh, here's my man dropp'd in I look'd for.

OVER. Ha!

PURE. Oh, good sir, they have set the faithful here to be wonder'd at, and provided holes for the holy of the land.   161

TRO. Had they warrant for it? Show'd they Justice Overdo's hand? If they had no warrant, they shall answer it.

[*Re-enter* HAGGIS.]

BRI. Sure, you did not lock the stocks sufficiently, neighbor Toby!

HAG. No! See if you can lock 'em better.

BRI. They are very sufficiently lock'd, and truly; yet something is the matter.

TRO. True; your warrant is the matter that is in question; by what warrant?   171

BRI. Madman, hold your peace; I will put you in his room else, in the very same hole, do you see?

QUAR. How? is he a madman?

TRO. Show me Justice Overdo's warrant. I obey you.

HAG. You are a mad fool; hold your tongue.   [*Exeunt* HAGGIS *and* BRISTLE.]

TRO. In Justice Overdo's name, I drink to you, and here's my warrant.   181
                            Shows his can.

OVER. Alas, poor wretch! How it earns[99] my heart for him.

QUAR. [*aside*] If he be mad, it is in vain to question him. I'll try him, though. — Friend, there was a gentlewoman show'd you two names some hour since, *Argalus* and *Palemon*, to mark in a book. Which of 'em was it you mark'd?

TRO. I mark no name but Adam Overdo: that is the name of names. He only is [191 the sufficient magistrate; and that name I reverence; show it me.

QUAR. [*aside*] This fellow's mad indeed: I am further off now than afore.

OVER. [*aside*] I shall not breathe in peace till I have made him some amends.

QUAR. [*aside*] Well, I will make another use of him is come in my head: I have a nest of beards in my trunk,[100] one something like his.   201

The Watchmen, [HAGGIS *and* BRISTLE,] *come back again.*

BRI. This mad fool has made me that I know not whether I have lock'd the stocks or no; I think I lock'd 'em. [*Tries the lock.*]

TRO. Take Adam Overdo in your mind, and fear nothing.

BRI. 'Slid, madness itself! Hold thy peace, and take that.   [*Strikes him.*]

TRO. Strikest thou without a warrant? Take thou that.   210
            The Madman *fights with 'em, and they leave open the stocks.*

BUSY. We are delivered by miracle; fellow in fetters, let us not refuse the means:

[96] *I.e.*, seek no opinion but your own. (*Satires,* I, 7.)
[97] *I.e.*, scraps.   [98] Lame.

[99] Yearns, grieves.
[100] For trunk-hose were often stuffed with hair.

this madness was of the spirit : the malice of the enemy hath mock'd itself.

[*Exeunt* BUSY *and* OVERDO.]

PURE. Mad do they call him ! The world is mad in error, but he is mad in truth. I love him o' the sudden (the cunning man said all true) and shall love him more and more. How well it becomes a man to be mad in [219 truth ! Oh, that I might be his yokefellow, and be mad with him ! What a many should we draw to madness in truth with us ! [*Exit.*]

The Watch, *missing them, are affrighted.*

BRI. How now ! all scaped ? Where 's the woman ? It is witchcraft ! Her velvet hat is a witch, o' my conscience, or my key ! t' one. [101] — The madman was a devil, and I am an ass ; so bless me, my place, and mine office. [*Exeunt.*]

ACT V — SCENE I [1]

[*Enter*] LANTERN [LEATHERHEAD, *as a showman*], FILCHER, *and* SHARKWELL.

LEATH. Well, luck and Saint Bartholomew ! Out with the sign of our invention, in the name of wit, and do you beat the drum the while. All the foul i' the Fair ; I mean, all the dirt in Smithfield — that 's one of Master Littlewit's carwhitchets [2] now — will be thrown at our banner to-day, if the matter does not please the people. Oh, the motions that I, Lantern Leatherhead, have given light to, i' my time, since my Master [10 Pod died ! [3] "Jerusalem" was a stately thing, and so was "Nineveh," and "The City of Norwich," and "Sodom and Gomorrah, with the rising of the prentices, and pulling down the bawdyhouses there upon Shrove Tuesday" [4]; but "The Gunpowder Plot," there was a get-penny ! I have presented that to an eighteen or twentypence audience, nine times in an afternoon. Your home-born projects prove ever the best ; they are so easy [20 and familiar. They put too much learning i' their things now o' days ; and that, I fear, will be the spoil of this. Littlewit ? I say,

Micklewit ! if not too mickle ! Look to your gathering there, Goodman Filcher.

FILCH. I warrant you, sir.

LEATH. An there come any gentlefolks, take twopence apiece, Sharkwell.

SHARK. I warrant you, sir ; threepence, an we can. [*Exeunt.*] [30

SCENE II [5]

The JUSTICE *comes in like a porter.*

OVER. This later disguise I have borrow'd of a porter ; shall carry me out to all my great and good ends, which, however interrupted, were never destroyed in me ; neither is the hour of my severity yet come, to reveal myself ; wherein, cloud-like, I will break out in rain and hail, lightning and thunder, upon the head of enormity. Two main works I have to prosecute : first, one is to invent some satisfaction for the poor [10 kind wretch who is out of his wits for my sake, and yonder I see him coming ; I will walk aside and project for it.

[*Enter* WINWIFE *and* GRACE, *and stand aside.*]

WINW. I wonder where Tom Quarlous is, that he returns not ; it may be he is struck in here to seek us.

GRACE. See, here 's our madman again.

QUARLOUS, [*entering*] *in the habit of the* Madman, *is mistaken by* MRS. PURECRAFT.

QUAR. [*aside*] I have made myself as like him as his gown and cap will give me leave.

PURE. Sir, I love you, and would be glad [20 to be mad with you, in truth.

WINW. [*aside*] How ! My widow in love with a madman ?

PURE. Verily, I can be as mad in spirit as you.

QUAR. By whose warrant ? Leave your canting. [6] — [*aside*] Gentlewoman, have I found you ? — [*to* GRACE] Save ye, quit ye, and multiply ye ! Where 's your book ? 'T was a sufficient name I mark'd ; let me see 't ; be [30 not afraid to show 't me. [7]

GRACE. What would you with it, sir ?

QUAR. Mark it again and again, at your service.

GRACE. Here it is, sir ; this was it you mark'd.

---

[101] One or the other of them.
[1] Another part of the Fair. Before the booth of a puppet-show.
[2] Puns.
[3] Old eds. note marginally : "Pod was a Master of motions before him."
[4] An old London custom.

[5] The same.
[6] Stop speaking in your sectarian idiom.
[7] Old eds. note marginally "He desires to see the book of Mistress Grace,"

QUAR. *Palemon!* Fare you well, fare you well.

WINW. How, *Palemon?*

GRACE. Yes, faith, he has discover'd it [40 to you now, and therefore 'twere vain to disguise it longer ; I am yours, sir, by the benefit of your fortune.

WINW. And you have him, mistress, believe it, that shall never give you cause to repent her benefit, but make you rather to think that in this choice she had both her eyes.

GRACE. I desire to put it to no danger of protestation. [*Exeunt* GRACE *and* WINWIFE.]

QUAR. [*aside*] *Palemon* the word, and [50 Winwife the man !

PURE. Good sir, vouchsafe a yokefellow in your madness ; shun not one of the sanctified sisters, that would draw with you in truth.

QUAR. Away ! You are a herd of hypocritical proud ignorants, rather wild than mad ; fitter for woods and the society of beasts than houses and the congregation of men. You are the second part of the so- [60 ciety of canters,⁸ outlaws to order and discipline, and the only privileg'd church-robbers of Christendom. Let me alone ! — [*aside*] *Palemon* the word, and Winwife the man !

PURE. [*aside*] I must uncover myself unto him, or I shall never enjoy him, for all the cunning men's promises. — Good sir, hear me ; I am worth six thousand pound ; my love to you is become my rack ; I 'll tell you all and the truth, since you hate the hypoc- [70 risy of the parti-colored⁹ brotherhood. These seven years I have been a wilful holy widow, only to draw feasts and gifts from my entangled suitors. I am also by office an assisting sister of the deacons, and a devourer, instead of a distributor, of the alms. I am a special maker of marriages for our decayed brethren with our rich widows, for a third part of their wealth, when they are married, for the relief of the poor elect ; as also [80 our poor handsome young virgins, with our wealthy bachelors or widowers ; to make them steal from their husbands, when I have confirmed them in the faith, and got all put into their custodies. And, if I ha' not my bargain, they may sooner turn a scolding drab into a silent minister than make me leave pronouncing " reprobation " and " damna-

tion " unto them. Our elder, Zeal-of-the-land, would have had me ; but I know him [90 to be the capital knave of the land, making himself rich by being made feoff in trust ¹⁰ to deceased brethren, and coz'ning their heirs by swearing the absolute gift ¹¹ of their inheritance. And thus, having eas'd my conscience and utter'd my heart with the tongue of my love, enjoy all my deceits together. I beseech you. I should not have revealed this to you, but that in time I think you are mad, and I hope you 'll think me so too, sir ! [100

QUAR. Stand aside ; I 'll answer you presently. — (*He consider*[*s*] *with himself of it.*) Why should not I marry this six thousand pound, now I think on 't, and a good trade too that she has beside, ha? The tother wench Winwife is sure of ; there 's no expectation for me there ! Here I may make myself some saver ; yet, if she continue mad, there 's the question. It is money that I want ; why should I not marry the money when [110 't is offer'd me? I have a license and all ; it is but razing out one name, and putting in another. There 's no playing with a man 's fortune ! I am resolv'd : I were truly mad an I would not ! — Well, come your ways, follow me ; an you will be mad, I 'll show you a warrant !

PURE. Most zealously ; it is that I zealously desire.   *He takes her along with him.*
                     The JUSTICE *calls him.*

OVER. Sir, let me speak with you.   120

QUAR. By whose warrant?

OVER. The warrant that you tender ¹² and respect so, Justice Overdo's ! I am the man, friend Troubleall, though thus disguis'd, as the careful magistrate ought, for the good of the republic in the Fair, and the weeding out of enormity. Do you want a house, or meat, or drink, or clothes? Speak whatsoever it is, it shall be supplied you. What want you?

QUAR. Nothing but your warrant.   130

OVER. My warrant ! for what?

QUAR. To be gone, sir.

OVER. Nay, I pray thee stay ; I am serious, and have not many words nor much time to exchange with thee. Think what may do thee good.

QUAR. Your hand and seal will do me a great deal of good ; nothing else in the whole Fair that I know.

---

⁸ *I.e.*, of those who speak a jargon ; the first part of that society consists of thieves, vagabonds, etc.
⁹ "Checkered" ; *i.e.*, inconsistent.

¹⁰ "A trustee invested with a freehold estate in land." (*N.E.D.*)
¹¹ *I.e.*, that the land was possessed as a gift of the deceased, rather than as a trust.   ¹² Esteem.

OVER. If it were to any end, thou [140 shouldst have it willingly.

QUAR. Why, it will satisfy me, that's end enough, to look on ; an you will not gi' it me, let me go.

OVER. Alas, thou shalt ha' it presently ; I'll but step into the scrivener's hereby, and bring it. Do not go away.

The JUSTICE *goes out.*

QUAR. [*aside*] Why, this madman's shape [13] will prove a very fortunate one, I think ! Can a ragged robe produce these effects? [150 If this be the wise justice, and he bring me his hand, I shall go near to make some use on't.

[OVERDO] *returns.*

He is come already !

OVER. Look thee ! Here is my hand and seal : *Adam Overdo.* If there be anything to be written above in the paper that thou want'st now, or at any time hereafter, think on't : it is my deed ; I deliver it so. Can your friend write?

QUAR. Her hand for a witness, and all [160 is well.

OVER. With all my heart.

He urgeth MISTRESS PURECRAFT.

QUAR. [*aside*] Why should not I ha' the conscience to make this a bond of a thousand pound now, or what I would else?

OVER. Look you, there it is, and I deliver it as my deed again.

QUAR. Let us now proceed in madness.

He takes her in with him.

OVER. Well, my conscience is much eas'd ; I ha' done my part ; though it doth him [170 no good, yet Adam hath offer'd satisfaction ! The sting is removed from hence. Poor man, he is much alter'd with his affliction, it has brought him low ! Now for my other work, reducing [14] the young man I have follow'd so long in love, from the brink of his bane [15] to the center of safety. Here, or in some such like vain place, I shall be sure to find him. I will wait the good time. [*He steps aside.*]

SCENE III [16]

[*Enter*] SHARKWELL [*and*] FILCHER, [*with bills, and*] COKES. *The Boys o' the Fair follow him.*

COKES. How now ! What's here to do? friend, art thou the master of the monuments? [17]

SHARK. 'T is a motion, an't please your Worship.

OVER. [*aside*] My fantastical brother-in-law, Master Bartholomew Cokes !

COKES. A motion? what's that? (*He reads the bill.*) " The ancient modern history of Hero and Leander, otherwise called [10 The Touchstone of True Love, with as true a trial of friendship between Damon and Pythias, two faithful friends o' the Bank-side." [18] — Pretty, i' faith ! What's the meaning on't? Is't an interlude? or what is't?

FILCH. Yes, sir, please you come near, we'll take your money within.

COKES. Back with these children ; they do so follow me up and down.

[*Enter* LITTLEWIT.]

LIT. By your leave, friend.   20

FILCH. You must pay, sir, an you go in.

LIT. Who? I? I perceive thou know'st not me. Call the master of the motion.

SHARK. What, do you not know the author, fellow Filcher? You must take no money of him ; he must come in gratis. Master Little-wit is a voluntary ; [19] he is the author.

LIT. Peace, speak not too loud. I would not have any notice taken that I am the author, till we see how it passes.   30

COKES. Master Littlewit, how dost thou?

LIT. Master Cokes ! You are exceeding well met. What, in your doublet and hose, without a cloak or a hat?

COKES. I would I might never stir, as I am an honest man, and by that fire ; [20] I have lost all i' the Fair, and all my acquaintance too. Didst thou meet anybody that I know, Master Littlewit? My man Numps, or my sister Overdo, or Mistress Grace? [40 Pray thee, Master Littlewit, lend me some money to see the interlude here ; I'll pay thee again, as I am a gentleman. If thou'lt but carry me home, I have money enough there.

LIT. Oh, sir, you shall command it. What, will a crown serve you?

COKES. I think it w[i]ll. What do we pay for coming in, fellows?

FILCH. Twopence, sir.

COKES. Twopence ! There's twelve- [50 pence, friend. Nay, I am a gallant, as simple as I look now, if you see me with my man about me and my artillery [21] again.

---

[13] Costume, disguise.   [14] Bringing back.
[15] Destruction.   [16] The same.   [17] Effigies.

[18] See on Induction, l. 86.
[19] Volunteer.   [20] Of hell. (Alden.)
[21] Implements of war ; *i.e.*, his sword and dagger.

LIT. Your man was i' the stocks e'en now, sir.

COKES. Who, Numps?

LIT. Yes, faith.

COKES. For what, i' faith? I am glad o' that; remember to tell me on 't anon; I have enough now! What manner of mat- [60 ter is this, Master Littlewit? What kind of actors ha' you? Are they good actors?

LIT. Pretty youths, sir, all children both old and young; here 's the master of 'em —

[*Enter* LEATHERHEAD.]

LEATH. (*whispers to* LITTLEWIT.) Call me not Leatherhead, but Lantern.

LIT. Master Lantern, that gives light to the business.

COKES. In good time, sir! [22] I would fain see 'em. I would be glad drink with the [70 young company. Which is the tiring-house?

LEATH. Troth, sir, our tiring-house is somewhat little; we are but beginners yet; pray, pardon us: you cannot go upright in 't.

COKES. No? not now my hat is off? What would you have done with me, if you had had me feather and all, as I was once to-day? Ha' you none of your pretty impudent boys now, to bring stools, fill tobacco, fetch ale, and beg money, as they have at other [80 houses? Let me see some o' your actors.

LIT. Show him 'em, show him 'em. Master Lantern, this is a gentleman that is a favorer of the quality. [23] [*Exit* LEATHERHEAD.]

OVER. [*aside*] Ay, the favoring of this licentious quality is the consumption of many a young gentleman; a pernicious enormity.

[LEATHERHEAD] *brings them out in a basket.*

COKES. What! do they live in baskets?

LEATH. They do lie in a basket, sir; they are o' the small players.   90

COKES. These be players minors indeed. Do you call these players?

LEATH. They are actors, sir, and as good as any, none disprais'd — for dumb shows: indeed, I am the mouth of 'em all.

COKES. Thy mouth will hold 'em all. I think one tailor [24] would go near to beat all this company with a hand bound behind him.

LIT. Ay, and eat 'em all too, an they were in cake-bread.   100

COKES. I thank you for that, Master Littlewit; a good jest! Which is your Burbage [25] now?

LEATH. What mean you by that, sir?

COKES. Your best actor, your Field? [26]

LIT. Good, i' faith! You are even with me, [27] sir.

LEATH. This is he, that acts young Leander, sir. He is extremely belov'd of the womenkind; they do so affect his action, [28] [110 the green gamesters [29] that come here! And this is lovely Hero; this with the beard, Damon; and this, pretty Pythias. This is the ghost of King Dionysius in the habit of a scrivener; as you shall see anon at large.

COKES. Well, they are a civil company; I like 'em for that; they offer not to fleer, nor jeer, nor break jests, as the great [30] players do. And then, there goes not so much charge to the feasting of 'em, or making 'em [120 drunk, as to the other, by reason of their littleness. Do they use to play perfect? Are they never fluster'd?

LEATH. No, sir, I thank my industry and policy for it; they are as well govern'd a company, though I say it — and here is young Leander is as proper an actor of his inches, and shakes his head like an hostler.

COKES. But do you play it according to the printed book? I have read that.   130

LEATH. By no means, sir.

COKES. No? how then?

LEATH. A better way, sir; that is too learned and poetical for our audience: what do they know what Hellespont is, " guilty of true love's blood "? or what Abydos is? or " the other, Sestos hight "? [31]

COKES. Th' art i' the right; I do not know myself.

LEATH. No, I have entreated Master [140 Littlewit to take a little pains to reduce it to a more familiar strain for our people.

COKES. How, I pray thee, good Master Littlewit?

LIT. It pleases him to make a matter of it, sir. But there is no such matter, I assure you: I have only made it a little easy and modern for the times, sir, that 's all. As, for the Hellespont, I imagine our Thames here;

[25] Richard Burbage, the principal actor of the King's Men, Shakespeare's company.
[26] Nathan Field, star of the Lady Elizabeth's Men.
[27] *I.e.*, in jesting.
[28] Like his acting.
[29] Strumpets.   [30] Full-grown.
[31] Quotations from the opening lines of Marlowe's *Hero and Leander.*

[22] *I.e.*, well met.
[23] The profession of acting.
[24] Symbol of pusillanimity.

and then Leander I make a dyer's son [150 about Puddle Wharf ; [32] and Hero a wench o' the Bankside, who, going over one morning to Old Fish Street,[33] Leander spies her land at Trig Stairs, and falls in love with her. Now do I introduce Cupid, having metamorphos'd himself into a drawer,[34] and he strikes Hero in love with a pint of sherry. And other pretty passages there are o' the friendship that will delight you, sir, and please you of judgment. 160

COKES. I 'll be sworn they shall ! I am in love with the actors already, and I 'll be allied to them presently. They respect gentlemen, these fellows. Hero shall be my fairing : but which of my fairings ? — le' me see — i' faith, my fiddle, and Leander my fiddlestick ; then Damon my drum, and Pythias my pipe, and the ghost of Dionysius my hobbyhorse. All fitted !

SCENE IV [35]

[Enter] to them WINWIFE *[and]* GRACE.

WINW. Look, yonder 's your Cokes gotten in among his playfellows ; I thought we could not miss him at such a spectacle.

GRACE. Let him alone ; [36] he is so busy he will never spy us.

COKES *is handling the puppets.*

LEATH. Nay, good sir !

COKES. I warrant thee, I will not hurt her, fellow. What, dost think me uncivil ? I pray thee be not jealous ; I am toward a wife.[37] 10

LIT. Well, good Master Lantern, make ready to begin, that I may fetch my wife ; and look you be perfect ; you undo me else i' my reputation.

LEATH. I warrant you, sir. Do not you breed too great an expectation of it among your friends ; that 's the only hurter of these things.

LIT. No, no, no. [*Exit.*]

COKES. I 'll stay here and see ; pray [20 thee, let me see.

WINW. How diligent and troublesome he is !

GRACE. The place becomes him, methinks.

OVER. [*aside*] My ward, Mistress Grace, in

the company of a stranger ! I doubt [38] I shall be compell'd to discover myself before my time !

[*Enter* KNOCKHUM, EDGEWORTH, *and* MRS. LITTLEWIT, *followed by* WHIT *supporting* MRS. OVERDO, *both women masked.*]

FILCH.[39] Twopence apiece, gentlemen ; an excellent motion. 30

KNOCK. Shall we have fine fireworks and good vapors ?

SHARK. Yes, captain, and waterworks too.

WHIT. I pre dee take a care o' dy shmall lady there, Edgeworth ; I will look to dish tall lady myself.

LEATH. Welcome, gentlemen ! welcome, gentlemen ! [40]

WHIT. Pre dee, mashter o' de monshtersh, help a very sick lady here to a chair to [40 shit in.

LEATH. Presently, sir.

WHIT. Good fait now, Urs'la's ale and aqua vitæ ish to blame for 't. (*They bring* MISTRESS OVERDO *a chair.*) — Shit down shweetheart, shit down, and shleep a little.

EDG. [*to* MRS. LITTLEWIT] Madam, you are very welcome hither.

KNOCK. Yes, and you shall see very good vapors. 50

OVER. [*aside*] Here is my care [41] come ! I like to see him in so good company, and yet I wonder that persons of such fashion should resort hither !

EDG. This is a very private house,[42] madam.

The Cutpurse *courts* MISTRESS LITTLEWIT.

LEATH. Will it please your Ladyship sit, madam ?

MRS. LIT. Yes, good man. — [*aside to* EDGEWORTH] They do so all-to-be-madam me, I think they think me a very lady ! 60

EDG. [*aside*] What else, madam ?

MRS. LIT. [*aside*] Must I put off my mask to him ?

EDG. [*aside*] Oh, by no means.

MRS. LIT. [*aside*] How should my husband know me then ?

---

[32] In Blackfriars.
[33] A centre of the fish trade and also noted for its taverns.
[34] Tapster.   [35] The same.
[36] Don't mind him.
[37] About to marry.

[38] Fear.
[39] Old eds. note : "The doorkeepers speak."
[40] The inner stage now represents the interior of the booth, and by the time the audience is fully assembled the outer stage is probably supposed to be indistinguishable from the inner.
[41] Old eds. annotate : "By Edgeworth."
[42] In contradistinction to the public theatre, which was large, only partly roofed, and patronized by a more heterogeneous audience.

KNOCK. [*aside*] Husband! an idle vapor; he must not know you, nor you him : there's the true vapor.

OVER. [*aside*] Yea! I will observe more [70 of this. — Is this a lady, friend?

WHIT. Ay, and dat is anoder lady, shweet-heart; if dou hasht a mind to 'em, give me twelvepence from tee, and dou shalt have eder-oder on 'em.

OVER. [*aside*] Ay! this will prove my chiefest enormity. I will follow this.

EDG. [*aside to* MRS. LITTLEWIT] Is not this a finer life, lady, than to be clogg'd with a husband?   80

MRS. LIT. [*aside*] Yes, a great deal. When will they begin, trow,[43] in the name o' the motion?

EDG. [*aside*] By and by, madam; they stay but for company.

KNOCK. Do you hear, puppet-master? These are tedious vapors. When begin you?

LEATH. We stay but for Master Littlewit, the author, who is gone for his wife; and we begin presently.   90

MRS. LIT. [*aside to* EDGEWORTH] That's I, that's I.

EDG. [*aside*] That was you, lady; but now you are no such poor thing.

KNOCK. Hang the author's wife, a running vapor! Here be ladies will stay for ne'er a Delia o' 'em all.

WHIT. But hear me now, here ish one o' de ladiesh ashleep; stay till she but vake, man.   100

[*Enter* WASP.]

WASP. How now, friends! what's here to do?

FILCH.[44] Twopence apiece, sir, the best motion in the Fair.

WASP. I believe you lie; if you do, I'll have my money again, and beat you.

MRS. LIT. [*aside*] Numps is come!

WASP. Did you see a master of mine come in here, a tall young squire of Harrow o' the Hill, Master Bartholomew Cokes?   110

FILCH. I think there be such a one within.

WASP. Look he be, you were best; but it is very likely. I wonder I found him not at all the rest. I ha' been at the eagle, and the black wolf, and the bull with the five legs and two pizzles — he was a calf at Uxbridge Fair two years agone — and at the dogs that

dance the morris, and the hare o' the tabor; and miss'd him at all these! Sure this must needs be some fine sight that holds him [120 so, if it have him.

COKES. Come, come, are you ready now?

LEATH. Presently, sir.

WASP. Hoyday, he's at work in his doublet and hose. — Do you hear, sir? Are you employ'd, that you are bareheaded and so busy?

COKES. Hold your peace, Numps; you ha' been i' the stocks, I hear.

WASP. Does he know that? Nay, [130 then the date of my authority is out; I must think no longer to reign; my government is at an end. He that will correct another must want fault in himself.

WINW. Sententious Numps! I never heard so much from him before.

LEATH. Sure Master Littlewit will not come. — Please you take your place, sir, we'll begin.

COKES. I pray thee do, mine ears long [140 to be at it, and mine eyes too. — Oh, Numps, i' the stocks, Numps? Where's your sword, Numps?

WASP. I pray you intend [45] your game, sir; let me alone.

COKES. Well then, we are quit for all. Come, sit down, Numps; I'll interpret to thee. Did you see Mistress Grace? It's no matter neither now I think on't; tell me anon.   150

WINW. [*aside to* GRACE] A great deal of love and care he expresses.

GRACE. [*aside*] Alas, would you have him to express more than he has? That were tyranny!

COKES. Peace, ho! now, now!

LEATH. Gentles, that no longer your expectations may wander,
Behold our chief actor, amorous Leander,[46]
With a great deal of cloth, lapp'd about him like a scarf,   159
For he yet serves his father, a dyer at Puddle Wharf,
Which place we'll make bold with, to call it our Abydus,
As the Bankside is our Sestos; and let it not be deni'd us.
Now, as he is beating to make the dye take the fuller,
Who chances to come by, but fair Hero in a sculler;[47]
And, seeing Leander's naked leg and goodly calf,
Cast at him from the boat a sheep's eye and a half

---

[43] Do you suppose?
[44] Old eds. note: "The doorkeepers again."
[45] Attend to.
[46] " Amorous Leander, beautiful and young,
      Whose tragedy divine Musaeus sung."
                                        (Marlowe.)
[47] Rowboat.

Now she is landed, and the sculler come back.
By and by you shall see what Leander doth lack.
  LEAN. Cole, Cole, old Cole!
  LEATH. That is the sculler's [48] name, without
    control.   170
  LEAN. Cole, Cole, I say, Cole!
  LEATH.   We do hear you.
  LEAN.   Old Cole!
  LEATH. Old Cole! Is the dyer turned collier?
    How do you sell?
  LEAN. A pox o' your manners, kiss my hole
    here, and smell.
  LEATH. Kiss your hole and smell! there's
    manners indeed.
  LEAN. Why, Cole, I say, Cole!
  LEATH. It's the sculler you need!
  LEAN. Ay, and be hang'd.
  LEATH. Be hang'd! look you yonder.
Old Cole, you must go hang with Master Leander.
  COLE. Where is he?   180
  LEAN. Here, Cole; what fairest of fairs
Was that fare that thou lande[d]st but now a[t] Trig
    Stairs?

COKES. What was that, fellow? Pray thee
tell me; I scarce understand 'em.

  LEATH. Leander does ask, sir, what fairest of
    fairs
Was the fare [that] he landed but now at Trig Stairs!
  COLE. It is lovely Hero.
  LEAN.   Nero?
  COLE. No, Hero.
  LEATH.   It is Hero
Of the Bankside, he saith, to tell you truth without
    erring,
Is come over into Fish Street to eat some fresh
    herring.   190
Leander says no more, but as fast as he can,
Gets on all his best clothes, and will after to the
    Swan.[49]

COKES. Most admirable good, is't not?

  LEATH. Stay, sculler.
  COLE.   What say you?
  LEATH.   You must stay for Leander,
And carry him to the wench.
  COLE.   You rogue, I am no pander.

COKES. He says he is no pander. 'T is a
fine language; I understand it now.

  LEATH. Are you no pander, Goodman Cole?
    here's no man says you are;
You'll grow a hot coal, it seems; pray you, stay
    for your fare.
  COLE. Will he come away?
  LEATH.   What do you say?
  COLE.   I'd ha' him come away.
  LEATH. Would you ha' Leander come away?
    why, pray, sir, stay.   201
You are angry, Goodman Cole; I believe the fair
    maid
Came over w' you a' trust: tell us, sculler, are you
    paid?
  COLE. Yes, Goodman Hog-rubber [50] o' Pickt-
    hatch.[51]
  LEATH. How, Hog-rubber o' Pickt-hatch!
  COLE. Ay, Hog-rubber of Pickt-hatch. Take you
    that.   *The puppet strikes him over the pate.*
  LEATH.   Oh, my head!
  COLE. Harm watch, harm catch.

---

 [48] Waterman's.
 [49] A tavern in Old Fish Street.
 [50] Clown.
 [51] A notorious hang-out of thieves and prostitutes.

COKES. "Harm watch, harm catch," he
says; very good, i' faith. — The sculler had
like to ha' knock'd you, sirrah.   210

LEATH. Yes, but that his fare call'd him
away.

  LEAN. Row apace, row apace, row, row, row,
    row, row.
  LEATH. You are knavishly loaden, sculler, take
    heed where you go.
  COLE. Knave i' your face, Goodman Rogue.
  LEAN. Row, row, row, row, row, row.

COKES. He said, "knave i' your face,"
friend.

LEATH. Ay, sir, I heard him. But there's
no talking to these watermen; they will [220
ha' the last word.

COKES. God's my life! I am not allied
to the sculler yet; he shall be *Dauphin, my
boy*.[52] But my fiddlestick [53] does fiddle in and
out too much. I pray thee speak to him on't;
tell him I would have him tarry in my sight
more.

LEATH. I pray you be content; you'll
have enough on him, sir.

Now, gentles, I take it, here is none of you so stupid,
But that you have heard of a little god of love call'd
    Cupid;   231
Who out of kindness to Leander, hearing he but
    saw her,
This present day and hour doth turn himself to a
    drawer.
And because he would have their first meeting to
    be merry,
He strikes Hero in love to him with a pint of sherry,
Which he tells her from amorous Leander is sent
    her,
Who after him into the room of Hero doth venter.
    PUPPET LEANDER *goes into Mistress Hero's
        room.*
  PUPPET JONAS. A pint of sack, score a pint of
    sack i' the Cony.[54]

COKES. Sack! you said but e'en now it
should be sherry.   240

  JONAS. Why, so it is; sherry, sherry, sherry!

COKES. "Sherry, sherry, sherry!" By my
troth, he makes me merry. I must have
a name for Cupid too. Let me see, thou
might'st help me now, an thou wouldest,
Numps, at a dead lift; [55] but thou art dreaming o' the stocks still! Do not think on't,
I have forgot it; 't is but a nine days' wonder,
man; let it not trouble thee.

WASP. I would the stocks were about [250
your neck, sir; condition I hung by the heels in

---

 [52] Alluding to the ballad with this refrain; presumably Cokes has bought it in the Fair. Cf.
Shakespeare's *King Lear*, III, iv, 104.
 [53] Leander. See V, iii, 166.
 [54] Tavern rooms were named, not numbered.
 [55] *I.e.*, at a pinch.

them till the wonder were off from you, with all my heart.

COKES. Well said, resolute Numps! — But, hark you, friend, where 's the friendship all this while between my drum, Damon, and my pipe, Pythias?

LEATH. You shall see by and by, sir.

COKES. You think my hobbyhorse is forgotten, too. No, I 'll see 'em all enact before [260 I go ; I shall not know which to love best else.

KNOCK. This gallant has interrupting vapors, troublesome vapors. Whit, puff [56] with him.

WHIT. No, I pre dee, captain, let him alone. He is a child, i' faith, la.

LEATH. Now, gentles, to the friends, who in number are two,
And lodg'd in that alehouse in which fair Hero does do.
Damon, for some kindness done him the last week,
Is come, fair Hero in Fish Street this morning to seek. 270
Pythias does smell the knavery of the meeting,
And now you shall see their true friendly greeting.
PYTHIAS. You whoremasterly slave, you.

COKES. " Whoremasterly slave, you ! " very friendly and familiar that !

DAMON. Whoremaster i' thy face.
Thou hast lien with her thyself ; I 'll prove 't i' this place.

COKES. Damon says Pythias has lien with her himself ; he 'll prove 't in this place.

LEATH. They are whoremasters both, sir ; that 's a plain case. 280
PYTHIAS. You lie like a rogue.
LEATH. Do I lie like a rogue?
PYTHIAS. A pimp and a scab.
LEATH. A pimp and a scab !
I say, between you, you have both but one drab.
DAMON. You lie again.
LEATH. Do I lie again?
DAMON. Like a rogue again.
LEATH. Like a rogue again !
PYTHIAS. And you are a pimp again.

COKES. And you are a pimp again, he says.

DAMON. And a scab again. 290

COKES. And a scab again, he says.

LEATH. And I say again, you are both whoremasters again, and you have both but one drab again.
DAMON [and] PYTHIAS. Dost thou, dost thou, dost thou? *They fight* [LEATHERHEAD.]
LEATH. What, both at once?
PYTHIAS. Down with him, Damon.
DAMON. Pink his guts, Pythias.
LEATH. What, so malicious? Will ye murder me, masters both, i' mine own house?

COKES. Ho ! well acted, my drum, well acted, my pipe, well acted still !

WASP. Well acted, with all my heart. 300

LEATH. Hold, hold your hands.

[56] "Vapor", bully him. (Alden.)

COKES. Ay, both your hands, for my sake ! for you ha' both done well.

DAMON. Gramercy, pure Pythias.
PYTHIAS. Gramercy, dear Damon.

COKES. Gramercy to you both, my pipe and my drum.

PYTHIAS [and] DAMON. Come, now we 'll together to breakfast to Hero.
LEATH. 'Tis well you can now go to breakfast to Hero.
You have given [me] my breakfast, with a hone [57] and honero ! 310

COKES. How is 't, friend, ha' they hurt thee?

LEATH. Oh, no !
Between you and I, sir, we do but make show. —

Thus, gentles, you perceive, without any denial,
'Twixt Damon and Pythias here, friendship's true trial.
Though hourly they quarrel thus, and roar each with other,
They fight you no more than does brother with brother ;
But friendly together, at the next man they meet,
They let fly their anger, as here you might see 't.

COKES. Well, we have seen 't, and [321 thou hast felt it, whatsoever thou sayest. What 's next, what 's next?

LEATH. This while young Leander with fair Hero is drinking,
And Hero grown drunk, to any man's thinking !
Yet was it not three pints of sherry could flaw her, [58]
Till Cupid, distinguish'd like Jonas the drawer,
From under his apron, where his lechery lurks,
Put love in her sack. Now mark how it works.
HERO. O Leander, Leander, my dear, my dear Leander, 330
I 'll for ever be thy goose, so thou 'lt be my gander.

COKES. Excellently well said, Fiddle. — She 'll ever be his goose, so he 'll be her gander ; was 't not so?

LEATH. Yes, sir, but mark his answer now.

LEAN. And, sweetest of geese, before I go to bed,
I 'll swim o'er the Thames, my goose, thee to tread.

COKES. Brave ! He will swim o'er the Thames, and tread his goose to-night, he says.

LEATH. Ay, peace, sir, they 'll be angry if they hear you eavesdropping, now they are setting their match. [59] 342

LEAN. But, lest the Thames should be dark, my goose, my dear friend,
Let thy window be provided of a candle's end.
HERO. Fear not, my gander, I protest I should handle
My matters very ill, if I had not a whole candle.
LEAN. Well then, look to 't, and kiss me to boot.
LEATH. Now here come the friends again, Pythias and Damon,
And under their cloaks they have of bacon a gammon. [60]

[57] Ochone, alas.
[58] Make her drunk. [59] Appointment.
[60] Old eds. add. "Damon and Pythias enter."

PYTHIAS. Drawer, fill some wine here.
LEATH.   How, some wine there!
There's company already, sir, pray forbear!   351
DAMON. 'T is Hero.
LEATH.   Yes, but she will not be taken,
After sack and fresh herring, with your Dunmow [61]
    bacon.
PYTHIAS. You lie; it's Westfabian.
LEATH.   Westphalian, [62] you should say.
DAMON. If you hold not your peace, you are a
    coxcomb, I would say.
                    LEANDER *and* HERO *are kissing.*
PYTHIAS. [63] What's here, what's here? kiss, kiss
    upon kiss.
LEATH. Ay, wherefore should they not? What
    harm is in this?
'Tis Mistress Hero.
DAMON.   Mistress Hero's a whore.
LEATH. Is she a whore? Keep you quiet, or,
    sir knave, out of door.
DAMON. Knave out of door?   360
HERO. Yes, knave out of door.
DAMON. Whore out of door.   *Here the*
    puppets quarrel and fall together by the ears.
HERO. I say, knave out of door.
DAMON. I say, whore out of door.
PYTHIAS. Yea, so say I too.
HERO. Kiss the whore o' the arse.
LEATH. Now you ha' something to do: you
must kiss her o' the arse, she says.
DAMON [and] PYTHIAS. So we will, so we will.
                    [*They kick her.*]
HERO. Oh, my haunches, oh, my haunches,
    hold, hold.
LEATH.   Stand'st thou still?
Leander, where art thou? Stand'st thou still like
    a sot,   371
And not offer'st to break both their heads with a
    pot?
See who's at thine elbow there! Puppet Jonas-
    and-Cupid.
JONAS. Upon 'em, Leander; be not so stupid.
                    They fight.
LEAN. You goat-bearded slave!
DAMON. You whoremaster knave.
LEAN. Thou art a whoremaster.
JONAS.   Whoremasters all.
LEATH. See, Cupid with a word has ta'en up the
    brawl.

KNOCK. These be fine vapors!

COKES. By this good day, they fight
bravely! do they not, Numps?   381

WASP. Yes, they lack'd but you to be their
second all this while.

LEATH. This tragical encounter falling out thus
    to busy us,
It raises up the ghost of their friend Dionysius;
Not like a monarch, but the master of a school,
In a scrivener's furr'd gown, which shows he is no
    fool;
For therein he hath wit enough to keep himself
    warm.
"O Damon," he cries, "and Pythias, what harm
Hath poor Dionysius done you in his grave,   390
That after his death you should fall out thus and
    rave,
And call amorous Leander whoremaster knave?"

---

[61] This village in Essex is famous for an ancient
custom of awarding a flitch of bacon to the couple
able to satisfy a jury that they had not once quar-
reled during the first year of their marriage.
    [62] Westphalia is famous for its hams and bacons.
    [63] Old eds. *Pup.* Speech-tags for the puppets
are regularly *Pup. L., Pup. H.,* etc.

DAMON. I cannot, I will not, I promise you,
endure it.

SCENE V [64]

To them [enter] BUSY.

BUSY. Down with Dagon! [65] down with
Dagon! 't is I will no longer endure your prof-
anations.

LEATH. What mean you, sir?

BUSY. I will remove Dagon there, I say,
that idol, that heathenish idol, that remains,
as I may say, a beam, a very beam — not a
beam of the sun, nor a beam of the moon, nor
a beam of a balance, neither a house-beam, nor
a weaver's beam, but a beam in the eye, [10
in the eye of the brethren, a very great beam,
an exceeding great beam; such as are your
stage-players, rhymers, and morris dancers,
who have walked hand in hand, in contempt
of the brethren and the cause, and been borne
out by instruments of no mean countenance.

LEATH. Sir, I present nothing but what
is licens'd by authority.

BUSY. Thou art all license, even licen-
tiousness itself, Shimei! [66]   20

LEATH. I have the Master of the Revels' [67] hand for 't, sir.

BUSY. The master of rebels' hand thou
hast — Satan's! Hold thy peace, thy scurrility; [68] shut up thy mouth; thy profession
is damnable; and in pleading for it thou dost
plead for Baal. I have long opened my mouth
wide, and gaped. I have gaped, as the oyster
for the tide, after thy destruction, but cannot
compass it by suit or dispute; so that I [30
look for a bickering ere long, and then a battle.

KNOCK. Good Banbury vapors!

COKES. Friend, you'd have an ill match
on 't, if you bicker with him here; though
he be no man o' the fist, he has friends that
will go to cuffs for him. — Numps, will not
you take our side?

EDG. Sir, it shall not need; in my mind
he offers him a fairer course, to end it by
disputation! — Hast thou nothing to say [40
for thyself, in defence of thy quality? [69]

LEATH. Faith, sir, I am not well-studied
in these controversies between the hypocrites
and us. But here's one of my motion, Puppet

---

[64] The same.   [65] See *i Samuel,* v, 2–5.
[66] See *ii Samuel,* xvi, 5 ff.
[67] This official licensed the performance of plays.
[68] F 1631 lacks punctuation here; F 1692 supplies
a comma. It is possible that the second *thy* is a
misprint for *thou.*
[69] Profession.

Dionysius, shall undertake him; and I'll
venture the cause on 't.

COKES. Who? my hobbyhorse? Will he
dispute with him?

LEATH. Yes, sir, and make a hobby-ass of
him, I hope.   50

COKES. That's excellent! Indeed he looks
like the best scholar of 'em all. Come, sir,
you must be as good as your word now.

BUSY. I will not fear to make my spirit
and gifts known! Assist me, zeal, fill me,
fill me, that is, make me full!

WINW. [*aside to* GRACE] What a desperate,
profane wretch is this! Is there any ignorance
or impudence like his, to call his zeal to fill
him against a puppet?   60

[GRACE] [70] [*aside*] I know no fitter match
than a puppet to commit with an hypocrite!

BUSY. First, I say unto thee, idol, thou
hast no calling.

DION. You lie: I am call'd Dionysius.

LEATH. The motion says you lie; he is
call'd Dionysius i' the matter,[71] and to that
calling he answers.

BUSY. I mean no vocation, idol, no present
lawful calling.   70

DION. Is yours a lawful calling?

LEATH. The motion asketh if yours be
a lawful calling?

BUSY. Yes, mine is of the spirit.

DION. Then idol is a lawful calling.

LEATH. He says, then idol is a lawful
calling! For you call'd him idol, and your
calling is of the spirit.

COKES. Well disputed, hobbyhorse!

BUSY. Take not part with the wicked, [80
young gallant; he neigheth and hinnieth: all
is but hinnying sophistry. I call him idol
again. Yet, I say, his calling, his profession
is profane. — It is profane, idol.

DION. It is not profane.

LEATH. It is not profane, he says.

BUSY. It is profane.

DION. It is not profane.

BUSY. It is profane.

DION. It is not profane.   90

LEATH. Well said, confute him with *not*
still. — You cannot bear him down with your
bass noise, sir.

BUSY. Nor he me, with his treble creaking,
though he creak like the chariot wheels of
Satan; I am zealous for the cause —

LEATH. As a dog for a bone.

BUSY. And I say it is profane, as being the

page of Pride, and the waiting woman of
Vanity.   100

DION. Yea? What say you to your tire-
women then?

LEATH. Good.

DION. Or feather-makers i' the Friars,[72]
that are o' your faction of faith? Are not
they, with their perukes, and their puffs,
their fans, and their huffs,[73] as much pages of
Pride, and waiters upon Vanity? What say
you, what say you, what say you?

BUSY. I will not answer for them.   110

DION. Because you cannot, because you
cannot. Is a bugle-maker a lawful calling?
or the confect-maker's? — such you have
there — or your French fashioner? You'd
have all the sin within yourselves, would you
not, would you not?

BUSY. No, Dagon.

DION. What then, Dagonet?[74] Is a puppet worse than these?

BUSY. Yes, and my main argument [120
against you is, that you are an abomination;
for the male among you putteth on the apparel
of the female, and the female of the male.

DION. You lie, you lie, you lie abominably.

COKES. Good, by my troth! He has given
him the lie thrice.

DION. It is your old stale argument against
the players, but it will not hold against the
puppets; for we have neither male nor female
amongst us; and that thou mayst see, if [130
thou wilt, like a malicious purblind zeal as thou
art!   *The* Puppet *takes up his garment.*

EDG. By my faith, there he has answer'd
you, friend, by plain demonstration.

DION. Nay, I'll prove, against e'er a
Rabbin of 'em all, that my standing is as
lawful as his; that I speak by inspiration, as
well as he; that I have as little to do with
learning as he; and do scorn her helps as much
as he.   140

BUSY. I am confuted; the cause hath
failed me.

DION. Then be converted, be converted.

LEATH. Be converted, I pray you, and let
the play go on!

BUSY. Let it go on; for I am chang'd, and
will become a beholder with you!

[70] Old eds. *Qua.*   [71] Text.

[72] The feather-makers of Blackfriars were great
Puritans.
[73] Italian huffs, huff-shoulders; *i.e.,* shoulders arti-
ficially puffed or elevated.
[74] Possibly an allusion to King Arthur's fool, but
whether or not a jocose diminutive of *Dagon* in the
preceding line.

COKES. That's brave, i' faith. — Thou hast carried it away,[75] hobbyhorse. On with the play.   150

OVER. (*discovers himself.*) Stay, now do I forbid, I,[76] Adam Overdo! Sit still, I charge you.

COKES. What, my brother-i'-law!

GRACE. My wise guardian!

EDG. Justice Overdo!

OVER. It is time to take enormity by the forehead, and brand it; for I have discover'd enough.

SCENE VI [77]

To them [enter] QUARLOUS, *like the* Madman, *[and* DAME*]* PURECRAFT.

QUAR. Nay, come, Mistress Bride; you must do as I do, now. You must be mad with me, in truth. I have here Justice Overdo for it.

OVER. Peace, good Troubleall; come hither, and you shall trouble none. I will take the charge of you, and your friend, too. — (*to the* Cutpurse *and* MISTRESS LITTLEWIT) You also, young man, shall be my care; stand there.

EDG. [*aside*] Now, mercy upon me!   10

KNOCK. [*aside*] Would we were away, Whit; these are dangerous vapors; best fall off with our birds, for fear o' the cage.

           The rest are stealing away.

OVER. Stay, is not my name your terror?

WHIT. Yesh, faith, man, and it ish for tat we would be gone, man.

[*Enter* LITTLEWIT.]

LIT. Oh, gentlemen! did you not see a wife of mine? I ha' lost my little wife, as I shall be trusted; my little, pretty Win. [19 I left her at the great woman's house in trust yonder, the pig woman's, with Captain Jordan and Captain Whit, very good men, and I cannot hear of her. Poor fool, I fear she's stepp'd aside. — Mother, did you not see Win?

OVER. If this grave matron be your mother, sir, stand by her, *et digito compesce labellum:* [78] I may perhaps spring [79] a wife for you anon. — Brother Bartholomew, I am sadly sorry to see you so lightly given, and such a disciple of enormity, with your [30

grave governor Humphrey. But stand you both there, in the middle place; I will reprehend you in your course. — Mistress Grace, let me rescue you out of the hands of the stranger.

WINW. Pardon me, sir, I am a kinsman of hers.

OVER. Are you so? of what name, sir?

WINW. Winwife, sir.   39

OVER. Master Winwife? I hope you have won no wife of her, sir. If you have, I will examine the possibility of it at fit leisure. — Now, to my enormities: look upon me, O London! and see me, O Smithfield! the example of justice, and Mirror of Magistrates; the true top of formality [80] and scourge of enormity. Hearken unto my labors, and but observe my discoveries; and compare Hercules with me, if thou dar'st, of old; or [49 Columbus, Magellan, or our countryman Drake, of later times. Stand forth, you weeds of enormity, and spread. — (*to* BUSY) First Rabbi Busy, thou superlunatical hypocrite. — (*to* LANTERN) Next thou other extremity, thou profane professor of puppetry, little better than poetry. — (*to the* Horse-Courser) Then thou strong debaucher and seducer of youth; ([*pointing to the*] Cutpurse) witness this easy and honest young man. — (*Then* [*to*] [59 CAPT. WHIT) Now, thou esquire of dames, madams, and twelvepenny ladies. — [*to*] MISTRESS LITTLEWIT) Now, my green madam herself of the price; let me unmask your Ladyship.

LIT. Oh, my wife, my wife, my wife!

OVER. Is she your wife? *Redde te Harpocratem.* [81]

Enter TROUBLEALL, [*with a dripping-pan, followed by* URSULA *and* NIGHTINGALE.]

TRO. By your leave, stand by, my masters, be uncover'd.

URS. Oh, stay him, stay him; help to [70 cry, Nightingale; my pan, my pan!

OVER. What's the matter?

NIGHT. He has stolen gammer Urs'la's pan.

TRO. Yes; and I fear no man but Justice Overdo.

OVER. Urs'la! Where is she? — Oh, the sow of enormity, this! — (*to* URS'LA *and* NIGHTINGALE) Welcome, stand you there; — you, songster, there.   79

---

[75] Won.
[76] F 1692 adds *am.*
[77] The same.
[78] *I.e.,* be silent. Juvenal, *Satires,* I, 160. (Alden.)
[79] Produce, disclose.

[80] Propriety.
[81] *I.e.,* commit yourself to secrecy. "Harpocrates" = the Egyptian god Horus, born with his finger on his lips.

URS. An't please your Worship, I am in no fault : a gentleman stripp'd him in my booth, and borrow'd his gown, and his hat ; and he ran away with my goods here, for it.

OVER. (*to* QUARLOUS) Then this is the true madman, and you are the enormity !

QUAR. You are i' the right ; I am mad but from the gown outward.

OVER. Stand you there.

QUAR. Where you please, sir.

MISTRESS OVERDO *is sick, and her husband is silenc'd.*

MRS. OVER. Oh, lend me a basin, I [90 am sick, I am sick ! Where's Master Overdo ? Bridget, call hither my Adam.

OVER. How ?

WHIT. Dy very own wife, i' fait, worshipful Adam.

MRS. OVER. Will not my Adam come at me ? Shall I see him no more, then ?

QUAR. Sir, why do you not go on with the enormity ? are you oppress'd with it ? I'll help you ; hark you, sir, i' your [100 ear : — [*whispering*] Your innocent young man you have ta'en such care of all this day, is a cutpurse that hath got all your brother Cokes his things, and help'd you to your beating and the stocks. If you have a mind to hang him now, and show him your magistrate's wit, you may ; but I should think it were better recovering the goods, and to save your estimation in him. — I thank you, sir, for the gift of your ward, Mistress Grace. Look you, [110 here is your hand and seal, by the way. — Master Winwife, give you joy ; you are *Palemon ;* you are possess'd o' th' gentlewoman ; but she must pay me value ; here's warrant for it. — And, honest madman, there's thy gown and cap again ; I thank thee for my wife. — (*to the* Widow) Nay, I can be mad, sweetheart, when I please still ; never fear me.[82] — And careful Numps, where's he ? I thank him for my license. [120

WASP. How !

QUAR. 'T is true, Numps.

WASP. I'll be hang'd then.

QUAR. Look i' your box, Numps. (WASP *misseth the license.*) — Nay, sir, [*to* OVERDO]

[82] Concerning me.

stand not you fix'd here, like a stake in Finsbury,[83] to be shot at, or the whipping-post i' the Fair, but get your wife out o' the air — it will make her worse else ; and remember you are but Adam, flesh and blood ! [130 you have your frailty ; forget your other name of Overdo, and invite us all to supper. There you and I will compare our discoveries, and drown the memory of all enormity in your bigg'st bowl at home.

COKES. How now, Numps, ha' you lost it ? I warrant 'twas when thou wert i' the stocks. Why dost not speak ?

WASP. I will never speak while I live again, for aught I know. 140

OVER. Nay, Humphrey, if I be patient, you must be so too. This pleasant conceited gentleman hath wrought upon my judgment, and prevail'd. I pray you take care of your sick friend, Mistress Alice, and my good friends all —

QUAR. And no enormities.

OVER. I invite you home with me to my house to supper : I will have none fear to go along, for my intents are *Ad correctionem,* [150 *non ad destructionem ; ad ædificandum, non ad diruendum.* So lead on.

COKES. Yes, and bring the actors along ; we'll ha' the rest o' the play at home.

[*Exeunt.*]

THE EPILOGUE

Your Majesty hath seen the play, and you
Can best allow it from your ear and view.
You know the scope of writers, and what store
Of leave is given them, if they take not more,
And turn it into license ; you can tell
If we have us'd that leave you gave us well,
Or whether we to rage or license break,
Or be profane, or make profane men speak !
This is your power to judge, great Sir, and not
The envy of a few ; which if we have got, [10
We value less what their dislike can bring,
If it so happy be t' have pleas'd the King.

[83] To Finsbury Fields the citizens resorted for archery.

EASTVVARD
HOE.

As

It was playd in the
Black-friers.

By

The Children of her Maiesties Reuels.

Made by

GEO: CHAPMAN. BEN: IONSON. IOH: MARSTON.

AT LONDON
Printed for *William Aspley.*
1605,

INTRODUCTORY NOTE

In this diverting comedy the authors elect to show a more attractive side of the London cit than the cuckoldy skinflint so often presented by Their Majesties' Servants. This time, though the usurer and the lawyer are roughly handled, too, it is the new gentry and their apes who are the principal objects of genial derision. The hero is the mildly eccentric but sterling businessman, and the youthful winners of love and cash the good apprentice and the obedient daughter. The play is a bid for the favor of the Jacobean Babbitts, and as such is an interesting forerunner of the bourgeois drama of the eighteenth century and after. The shopkeepers and their code are buttered as assiduously as ever in a court play the flattery of the monarch was trowelled on. But if Golding and Mildred are prigs, they are neither hypocrites nor social climbers; and their almost nauseating consciousness of rectitude does not keep us from relishing the discomfiture of those who are.

As realistic as Middleton's amoral comedies of intrigue, *Eastward Ho* seems partly intended for a sage and serious preachment. The immediate occasion of its composition was pretty clearly the success of the Paul's Boys with one of the earliest of the new comedies of cynical realism, *Westward Ho*, by Dekker and Webster. In *Eastward Ho* three staunch moralists wheel their batteries into line. But the play is none the less a good-humored one, and gentle sentiment is not barred. The eleventh-hour repentances and the forgiving of the erring are not handled perfunctorily, but with a humorous joyfulness that has its affecting moments.

No source is known for the main plot, though it belongs to the repentant prodigal type. The Petronel-Winifred story comes from the fortieth *novella* of Masuccio. It is generally believed that the play was published not long after its composition. It was entered in the Stationers' Register on September 4, 1605. Three quarto editions appeared in that year, the first being twice issued. Of the first issue of the First Quarto but one surviving copy is known. Its importance is due to its preservation of an offensive passage in III, iii; this was omitted from the second issue, in which new matter has been substituted on leaves E3 and E4. The deleted passage is also preserved in a copy of the second issue in the Dyce collection, the original leaves having been bound up along with the cancels which were supposed to replace them. With the exception of this passage (which is here reprinted from photographs of the first issue kindly supplied by Dr. J. Q. Adams) the present text is based on the second issue of the first edition. It has also been collated with the text of Herford and Simpson, which is based on the first issue. The First Quarto was twice reprinted in 1605; *i.e.*, the type for Qq 2 and 3 was almost entirely reset in each case, while the two issues of Q 1 are from the same type-setting except for the resetting on leaves E3 and E4 required by the omission of the suppressed text. The standard edition of Chapman's plays is that of T. M. Parrott (1914), and of Marston's that of A. H. Bullen (1887). The most recent edition of *Eastward Ho* appears in vol. IV of the Oxford Jonson, edited by Herford and Simpson. Separate editions have been published by J. W. Cunliffe (in Gayley's *Representative English Comedies*, vol. II) in 1913, by F. E. Schelling (with Jonson's *Poetaster*) in 1905, and by Miss J. H. Harris in 1926.

It is not known to what extent *Eastward Ho* was acted before the closing of the theatres in 1642. Either the production, by the Children of the Queen's Revels at the Blackfriars, or the appearance of the First Quarto in its original state, created a scandal. King James was naturally offended by the gibes at the Scots in III, iii, and the rendition of the royal accent in IV, i; and Chapman and Marston were imprisoned, Jonson joining them voluntarily, according to the account of the affair he gave Drummond of Hawthornden. Letters to James and to a number of powerful patrons soon secured their release, with their ears uncropped. That Marston was actually in duress vile is not certain. Drummond's recollection of what Jonson told him may have been faulty, and Ben himself may have drawn the long bow. At any rate his letters and Chapman's, fortunately preserved, mention only their own incarceration, and agree in denying their authorship of the objectionable clauses. Jonson, a firm friend of Chapman, had been at odds with Marston and had pilloried him in his *Poetaster* (1601). The hatchet had evidently been buried, as witness their collaboration and also Marston's dedication of *The Malcontent* in 1604.   In 1606, however, there is evidence that Marston had dug it up; perhaps *Eastward Ho* and its aftermath were the cause.

Dr. Adams (*Studies in Philology*, XXVIII, 689–701) argues that it was the performance of the play that led to the authors' imprisonment and to its early publication, as well as to the suspension of the Blackfriars company.   He demonstrates, by analyzing the bibliographical peculiarities of the first edition, that even the first *issue* must have deleted a good deal of the original text, subsequently to the arrangement of the type in pages.   The cancellation of leaves E3 and E4 came still later.

The play continued on the boards, but the last pre-Wars reference is to a performance before the King in 1614.   Like many of Shakespeare's plays, *Eastward Ho* was subjected after the Restoration to degrading adaptation; this was at the hands of Nahum Tate, under the title of *Cuckold's Haven*.   Garrick ventured to revive the original play in 1751; undiscouraged by its failure, he successfully produced in 1775 a new version by Mrs. Charlotte Lennox, entitled *Old City Manners*.

The precise share of the original collaborators cannot be determined.   Professor Parrott's conclusions are widely accepted.   He gives to Chapman II, iii; III, i, ii, iii(the offensive passage, however, being touched up by Marston), iv (or to Marston); IV, i (with a Jonsonian interpolation, Quicksilver's chemical proposals); to Marston I, i, ii; II, i, ii (perhaps revised by Jonson); IV, ii; V, i (both revised by Jonson); to Jonson the revisions already mentioned, the prologue, and V, ii, iii, iv, and v.   In other words, the general conception of the plot is probably Marston's, and the dramatization of Masuccio's tale largely Chapman's; while Jonson's contribution was general supervision and the composition of the ending.   But though stylistic tricks of all the authors may be detected, it is evident that they worked in close coöperation; doubtless there was much discussion, and perhaps revision, all the way along.   And, adds Professor Parrott, Chapman's influence is " diffused throughout. Less bitter than Marston, less severe than Jonson, Chapman has a larger portion than either of the laughing spirit of true comedy."

EASTWARD HO[1]

BY

GEORGE CHAPMAN, BEN JONSON, AND JOHN MARSTON

[DRAMATIS PERSONAE

TOUCHSTONE,[2] a goldsmith.
QUICKSILVER, } his apprentices.
GOLDING,
SIR PETRONEL FLASH.
SECURITY, an old usurer.
BRAMBLE, a lawyer.
SEAGULL, a sea captain.
SCAPETHRIFT, } adventurers bound for Virginia.
SPENDALL,
SLITGUT, a butcher's apprentice.
POLDAVY, a tailor.
HOLDFAST, } officers of the Counter.[3]
WOLF,
HAMLET, a footman.

POTKIN, a tankard-bearer.
TOBY, a prisoner.

MISTRESS TOUCHSTONE.
GERTRUDE, } her daughters.
MILDRED,
WINIFRED, wife to Security.
SINDEFY, mistress to Quicksilver.
BETTRICE, a waiting woman.
MISTRESS FOND.
MISTRESS GAZER.

Drawer, Coachman, Scrivener, Page, Constable, Officers, Messenger, Two Prisoners and their Friend, Gentlemen.

THE SCENE — *London and Thames-side.*]

PROLOGUS

Not out of envy, for there's no effect
Where there's no cause ; nor out of imitation,
For we have evermore been imitated ;
Nor out of our contention to do better
Than that which is oppos'd to ours in title,[4]
For that was good ; and better cannot be :
And, for the title, if it seem affected,
We might as well have call'd it, " God you
   good even : "[5]
Only that eastward westwards still exceeds —
Honor the sun's fair rising, not his setting. 10
Nor is our title utterly enforc'd,
As by the points we touch at you shall see.
Bear with our willing pains, if dull or witty ;
We only dedicate it to the City.

[1] Like "Westward Ho," a cry of the watermen who plied the Thames.
[2] This stone was used to determine the quality of gold by comparing the mark it made with similar marks on gold of known standards.
[3] There were two debtors' prisons so called. The one in our play was in Southwark.
[4] *Westward Ho.* See introductory note above.
[5] Good evening.

ACT I — SCENE I [6]

Enter MASTER TOUCHSTONE *and* QUICKSILVER
at several doors, QUICKSILVER *with his hat,
pumps, short sword and dagger, and a racket
trussed up under his cloak. At the middle
door, enter* GOLDING, *discovering*[7] *a goldsmith's shop and walking short turns before it.*

TOUCH. And whither with you now? what loose action are you bound for? Come, what comrades are you to meet withal? where's the supper? where's the rendezvous?

QUICK. Indeed, and in very good sober truth, sir ——

TOUCH. " Indeed, and in very good sober truth, sir ! " Behind my back thou wilt swear faster than a French footboy, and talk more bawdily than a common midwife ; [10 and now " indeed, and in very good sober truth, sir ! " But, if a privy search should be made, with what furniture are you rigg'd now? Sirrah, I tell thee, I am thy master,

[6] Goldsmith's Row.
[7] *I.e.,* in the inner stage.

477

William Touchstone, goldsmith; and thou my prentice, Francis Quicksilver; and I will see whither you are running. Work upon that now![8]

QUICK. Why, sir, I hope a man may use his recreation with his master's profit. 20

TOUCH. Prentices' recreations are seldom with their masters' profit. Work upon that now! You shall give up your cloak, though you be no alderman.[9] — (TOUCHSTONE *uncloaks* QUICKSILVER.) Heyday! Ruffi[a]ns Hall![10] Sword, pumps, here 's a racket indeed!

QUICK. Work upon that now!

TOUCH. Thou shameless varlet! dost thou jest at thy lawful master, contrary to thy indentures?[11] 30

QUICK. Why, 'zblood, sir! my mother 's a gentlewoman, and my father a justice of peace and of quorum;[12] and, though I am a younger brother and a prentice, yet I hope I am my father's son; and by God's lid, 't is for your worship and for your commodity[13] that I keep company. I am entertain'd among gallants, true; they call me cousin Frank, right; I lend them moneys, good; they spend it, well. But, when they are [40 spent, must not they strive to get more? Must not their land fly? — and to whom? Shall not your Worship ha' the refusal? Well, I am a good member of the City, if I were well considered. How would merchants thrive, if gentlemen would not be unthrifts? How could gentlemen be unthrifts if their humors were not fed? How should their humors be fed but by whitemeat[14] and cunning seconding? Well, the City might consider us. [50 I am going to an ordinary[15] now: the gallants fall to play; I carry light gold[16] with me. The gallants call, " Cousin Frank, some gold for silver; " I change, gain by it; the gallants lose the gold, and then call, " Cousin Frank, lend me some silver." Why ——

TOUCH. Why? I cannot tell. Seven score pound art thou out in the cash; but

look to it, I will not be gallanted out of my moneys. And, as for my rising by other [60 men's fall, God shield me! Did I gain my wealth by ordinaries? no! by exchanging of gold? no! by keeping of gallants' company? no! I hired me a little shop, fought low, took small gain, kept no debt book, garnished my shop, for want of plate, with good wholesome thrifty sentences: as, " Touchstone, keep thy shop, and thy shop will keep thee "; " Light gains makes heavy purses; " " 'T is good to be merry and wise." And, when [70 I was wiv'd, having something to stick to, I had the horn of suretyship ever before my eyes. — [*to the audience*] You all know the device of the horn, where the young fellow slips in at the butt end, and comes squeez'd out at the buccal.[17] — And I grew up, and, I praise Providence, I bear my brows now as high[18] as the best of my neighbors: but thou — well, look to the accounts; your father's bond lies for you: seven score pound [80 is yet in the rear.[19]

QUICK. Why, 'slid, sir, I have as good, as proper[20] gallants' words for it as any are in London — gentlemen of good phrase, perfect language, passingly[21] behav'd; gallants that wear socks and clean linen, and call me " kind cousin Frank," " good cousin Frank," for they know my father: and, by God's lid, shall not I trust 'em? — not trust?

Enter a Page, *as inquiring for Touchstone's shop.*

GOLD. What do ye lack, sir? what [90 is 't you 'll buy, sir?

TOUCH. Ay, marry sir; there 's a youth of another piece. There 's thy fellow-prentice, as good a gentleman born as thou art: nay, and better mean'd. But does he pump it, or racket it? Well, if he thrive not, if he outlast not a hundred such crackling bavins[22] as thou art, God and men neglect industry.

GOLD. (*to the* Page) It is his shop, and here my master walks. 100

[8] This expression is usually italicized in the old eds.

[9] The City prescribed the materials and color of an alderman's cloak, as well as the garb of an apprentice.

[10] A name for West Smithfield; there was much brawling there.

[11] Articles of apprenticeship.

[12] A specially designated justice of the peace, whose presence was necessary to constitute a bench.

[13] Profit.

[14] Food made of milk, eggs, bread, and the like.

[15] Tavern.

[16] Gold coins below standard weight.

[17] Mouthpiece. Schelling refers to a description (*Notes and Queries*, ser. VII, vol. iv, p. 323) of an old picture showing "of suretyship [*i.e.*, legal responsibility for another person] what harm doth grow; " the victim comes out at the small end of the horn in a sorry plight.

[18] The inevitable joke on the horns of the cuckold, though without the slightest application in Touchstone's case.

[19] In arrears.

[20] Handsome, fine.

[21] Surpassingly well.

[22] Bundles of brushwood for kindling.

TOUCH. With me, boy?

PAGE. My master, Sir Petronel Flash, recommends his love to you, and will instantly visit you.

TOUCH. To make up the match with my eldest daughter, my wife's dilling,[23] whom she longs to call madam. — He shall find me unwillingly ready, boy. (*Exit* Page.) — [*to the audience*] There's another affliction too. As I have two prentices, the one of a bound- [110 less prodigality, the other of a most hopeful industry, so have I only two daughters : the eldest, of a proud ambition and nice wantonness ;[24] the other, of a modest humility and comely soberness. The one must be ladyfied, forsooth, and be attir'd just to the court cut and long tail.[25] So far is she ill-natur'd to the place and means of my preferment and fortune that she throws all the contempt and despite hatred itself can cast upon it. Well, [120 a piece of land she has ; 't was her grandmother's gift ; let her and her Sir Petronel flash out that ; but, as for my substance, she that scorns me, as I am a citizen and tradesman, shall never pamper her pride with my industry, shall never use me as men do foxes — keep themselves warm in the skin, and throw the body that bare it to the dunghill. I must go entertain this Sir Petronel. — Golding, my utmost care's for thee, and only [130 trust in thee ; look to the shop. — As for you, Master Quicksilver, think of husks, for thy course is running directly to the prodigal's hogs' trough ; husks, sirrah ![26] Work upon that now !

Exit TOUCHSTONE

QUICK. Marry faugh, Goodman Flat-cap ![27] 'Sfoot ! though I am a prentice, I can give arms ;[28] and my father's a justice a' peace by descent, and, 'zblood ! —

GOLD. Fie, how you swear !   140

QUICK. 'Sfoot, man, I am a gentleman, and may swear by my pedigree, God's my life ! Sirrah Golding, wilt be ruled by a fool? Turn good fellow, turn swaggering gallant, and " let the welkin roar, and Erebus also." Look not westward to the fall of Don Phœbus, but to the east — Eastward Ho !

---

[23] Darling, favorite.
[24] Affected wilfulness, wilful affectation.
[25] *I.e.*, precisely in accordance with the court fashion in all respects (with particular reference to the length of dresses. "Cut" [= docked] and long tail means "one and all.").
[26] Old eds. *S*ʳ*a*.
[27] One of the marks of a citizen.
[28] Have a right to armorial bearings.

Where radiant beams of lusty Sol appear,
And bright Eous [29] makes the welkin clear.   149

We are both gentlemen, and therefore should be no coxcombs ; let's be no longer fools to this flat-cap, Touchstone, — Eastward, bully ! — this satin belly and canvas-back'd Touchstone. 'S life, man ! his father was a malt man, and his mother sold gingerbread in Christ Church.[30]

GOLD. What would ye ha' me do?

QUICK. Why, do nothing ; be like a gentleman, be idle ; the curse of man is labor. Wipe thy bum with testones,[31] and make [160 ducks and drakes with shillings. What, Eastward Ho ! Wilt thou cry, " What is 't ye lack? " — stand with a bare pate and a dropping nose, under a wooden penthouse,[32] and art a gentleman? Wilt thou bear tankards,[33] and mayst bear arms? Be rul'd ; turn gallant. Eastward Ho ! — Ta ly re, ly re ro ! " Who calls Jeronimo? Speak, here I am." — Gods-so ! how like a sheep thou [169 look'st ; a' my conscience, some cowherd begot thee, thou Golding of Golding Hall ! Ha, boy?

GOLD. Go ; ye are a prodigal coxcomb ! I a cowherd's son, because I turn not a drunken, whore-hunting rakehell like thyself?

QUICK. Rakehell? rakehell?

Offers to draw, and GOLDING *trips
up his heels and holds him.*

GOLD. Pish, in soft terms, ye are a cowardly, bragging boy. I'll ha' you whipp'd.

QUICK. Whipp'd? — that's good, i' faith ! Untruss [34] me !   180

GOLD. No, thou wilt undo [35] thyself. Alas ! I behold thee with pity, not with anger ; thou common shot-clog,[36] gull of all companies ; methinks I see thee already walking in Moorfields [37] without a cloak, with half a hat, without a band, a doublet with three buttons, without a girdle, a hose with one point, and no garter, with a cudgel under thine arm, borrowing and begging threepence.

[Takes his sword, and releases him.]

---

[29] Eos, goddess of the dawn.
[30] A London parish ; the church is in Newgate Street.
[31] Sixpences (though it was also a name for the depreciated Henry VII shilling).
[32] *I.e.*, in the shop.
[33] Carrying water was one of the apprentice's duties.
[34] Let me go ; but it could also mean undo the laces that held up the breeches.
[35] Ruin, with an obvious pun.
[36] A dupe tolerated because he pays the bill (shot).   [37] A resort of beggars.

QUICK. Nay, 'slife! take this and [38] [190 take all. As I am a gentleman born, I 'll be drunk, grow valiant, and beat thee. *Exit.*

GOLD. Go, thou most madly vain, whom nothing can recover but that which reclaims atheists, and makes great persons sometimes religious — calamity. As for my place and life, thus I have read :

Whate'er some vainer youth may term disgrace,
The gain of honest pains is never base ; 199
From trades, from arts, from valor, honor springs ;
These three are founts of gentry, yea, of kings.

[*Exit.*]

SCENE II [39]

Enter GERTRUDE,[40] MILDRED, BETTRICE, *and* POLDAVY [41] *a tailor;* POLDAVY *with a fair gown, Scotch farthingale, and French fall [42] in his arms;* GERTRUDE *in a French head attire and citizen's gown;* MILDRED *sewing; and* BETTRICE *leading a monkey after her.*

GER. For the passion of patience, look if Sir Petronel approach — that sweet, that fine, that delicate, that — for love's sake, tell me if he come. Oh, sister Mil, though my father be a low-capp'd tradesman, yet I must be a lady ; and I praise God my mother must call me Madam. Does he come? — Off with this gown, for shame's sake ; off with this gown : let not my knight take me in the city cut in any hand : [43] tear 't, pax [44] on 't ! — [10 Does he come? tear 't off. — [*singing*] " Thus, whilst she sleeps, I sorrow for her sake," [45] etc.

MIL. Lord, Sister, with what an immodest impatiency and disgraceful scorn do you put off your city tire. I am sorry to think you imagine to right yourself in wronging that which hath made both you and us.

GER. I tell you I cannot endure it ; I must be a lady. Do you wear your quoif [46] with a London licket,[47] your stammel [48] petticoat [20 with two guards,[49] the buffin [50] gown with the tuf[t]-taffety [51] cape and the velvet lace. I must be a lady, and I will be a lady. I like

[38] If you take my sword you may as well.
[39] A room in Touchstone's house.
[40] Old eds. *Girtred* throughout.
[41] A coarse canvas.
[42] A falling-band, a flat collar.
[43] Under any circumstances.
[44] Her affected pronunciation of *pox.*
[45] From John Dowland's *First Book of Songs or Airs.* (Bullen.)
[46] Coif, cap.
[47] Uncertain : perhaps, "flap"; perhaps, "rag."
[48] A coarse woollen cloth, usually red.
[49] Ornamental borders.
[50] A coarse cloth.
[51] A kind of silk.

some humors of the city dames well : to eat cherries only at an angel [52] a pound, good ; to dye rich scarlet black, pretty ; to line a grogram gown clean [53] thorough with velvet, tolerable ; their pure linen, their smocks of three pounds a smock, are to be borne withal. But your mincing niceries, taffeta [30 pipkins,[54] durance [55] petticoats, and silver bodkins — God 's my life, as I shall be a lady, I cannot endure it ! — Is he come yet? Lord, what a long knight 't is ! — [*singing*] " And ever she cried, ' Sho[o]t [56] home' ! " — And yet I knew one longer. — " And ever she cried, ' Sho[o]t home,' fa, la, ly, re, lo, la ! "

MIL. Well, Sister, those that scorn their nest, oft fly with a sick wing.

GER. Bow-bell ! [57] 40

MIL. Where titles presume to thrust before fit means to second them, wealth and respect often grow sullen, and will not follow. For sure in this I would for your sake I spake not truth : where ambition of place goes before fitness of birth, contempt and disgrace follow. I heard a scholar once say that Ulysses, when he counterfeited himself mad, yok'd cats and foxes and dogs [58] together to draw his plough, whilst he followed and sowed [50 salt ; but, sure, I judge them truly mad, that yoke citizens and courtiers, tradesmen and soldiers, a goldsmith's daughter and a knight. Well, Sister, pray God my father sow not salt too.

GER. Alas ! poor Mil, when I am a lady, I 'll pray for thee yet, i' faith : nay, and I 'll vouchsafe to call thee Sister Mil still ; for, though thou art not like to be a lady as I am, yet sure thou art a creature of [60 God's making ; and mayest peradventure to be sav'd as soon as I. — Does he come? — [*singing.*] " And ever and anon she doubled in her song." Now, Lady's [59] my comfort ! what a profane ape 's here ! Tailor, Poldavy,[60]

[52] A gold coin worth about $2.50.
[53] A4 *verso* of Q1 begins here, and runs through "my steel in-", l. 72. This page was reset by the printer, as witness blank spaces left between speeches and the arrangement of part of Gertrude's last speech in short lines. Evidently there was originally an incriminating passage ; the Oxford editors suggest that the monkey may have been used to ridicule the Scots. Cf. l. 65.
[54] Doubtless = hats. (Parrott.)
[55] A stout woollen material.
[56] Emend. Collier ; old eds. *shoute.*
[57] Cockney ! You were one if you were born within hearing of the bells of St. Mary le Bow in Cheapside.
[58] A variation of Hyginus's *Fable XCV.*
[59] Virgin Mary's.   [60] Old eds. *Poldauis.*

prithee, fit it, fit it : is this a right Scot? [61]
Does it clip close, [62] and bear up round?

POLD. Fine and stiffly, i' faith ; 't will keep
your thighs so cool, and make your waist so
small ; here was a fault in your body, but [70
I have supplied the defect, with the effect
of my steel instrument, which, though it have
but one eye, can see to rectify the imperfection of the proportion.

GER. Most edifying tailor ! I protest you
tailors are most sanctified members, [63] and
make many crooked thing go upright. How
must I bear my hands? light? light?

POLD. Oh, ay ; now you are in the lady-
fashion, you must do all things light. Tread
light, light. Ay, and fall so ; that's the [81
court amble. [64]

She trips about the stage.

GER. Has the court ne'er a trot?

POLD. No, but a false gallop, [65] lady.

GER. [*singing*] "And if she will not go to
bed — "

BET. The knight's come, forsooth.

GER. Is my knight come? O the Lord,
my band ! [66] Sister, do my cheeks look well?
Give me a little box a' the ear, that I may
seem to blush ; now, now! So, there, there,
there !   91

Enter SIR PETRONEL, MASTER TOUCHSTONE,
and MISTRESS TOUCHSTONE.

Here he is ! O my dearest delight ! Lord,
Lord ! and how does my knight?

TOUCH. Fie ! with more modesty.

GER. Modesty ! Why, I am no citizen
now. Modesty? Am I not to be married?
Y' are best to keep me modest, now I am to
be a lady !

PET. Boldness is good fashion and court-
like.   100

GER. Ay, in a country lady I hope it is,
as I shall be. And how chance ye came no
sooner, knight?

PET. Faith, I was so entertain'd in the
progress with one Count Epernoum, a Welsh
knight; we had a match at balloon, [67] too,
with my Lord Whachum, for four crowns.

GER. At baboon? Jesu ! you and I will
play at baboon in the country, knight !

PET. Oh, sweet lady : 't is a strong [110
play with the arm.

GER. With arm or leg, or any other member, if it be a court sport. And when shall's
be married, my knight?

PET. I come now to consummate it ; and
your father may call a poor knight son-in-law.

TOUCH. Sir, ye are come. What is not
mine to keep I must not be sorry to
forgo. A hundred pound land [68] her grandmother left her ; 't is yours. Herself, as [120
her mother's gift, is yours. But, if you expect aught from me, know my hand and mine
eyes open together : I do not give blindly.
Work upon that now !

PET. Sir, you mistrust not my means? I
am a knight.

TOUCH. Sir, sir, what I know not, you will
give me leave to say I am ignorant of.

MIST. T. Yes, that he is a knight ! I know
where he had money to pay the gentle- [130
men ushers and heralds their fees. [69] Ay, that
he is a knight ! And so might you have been
too, if you had been aught else than an ass, as
well as some of your neighbors. An I thought
you would not ha' been knighted, as I am an
honest woman, I would ha' dubb'd you myself.
I praise God I have wherewithal. But, as
for you, Daughter ——

GER. Ay, Mother, I must be a lady to-
morrow ; and, by your leave, Mother [140
(I speak it not without my duty, but only in
the right of my husband), I must take place
of you, Mother.

MIST. T. That you shall, Lady-Daughter,
and have a coach as well as I, too.

GER. Yes, Mother. But by your leave,
Mother (I speak it not without my duty, but
only in my husband's right), my coach horses
must take the wall of your coach horses.

TOUCH. Come, come, the day grows low. [150
'T is supper time : use my house ; the wedding solemnity is at my wife's cost ; thank
me for nothing but my willing blessing ; for —
I cannot feign — my hopes are faint. And,
sir, respect my daughter ; she has refus'd for
you wealthy and honest matches, known good
men, well moneyed, better traded, best
reputed.

GER. Body a' truth ! chitizens, chitizens !

---

[61] *I.e.*, a true Scotch farthingale.
[62] A surviving joke on the Scots.
[63] Members of the sanctified (Puritan) sect.
[64] Artificial gait.
[65] Canter.
[66] The French fall.
[67] A strenuous game in which a large inflated
ball was batted with wooden pieces attached to
the players' arms.

[68] Land bringing in £100 a year. (Cunliffe.)
[69] A gibe at James's indiscriminate creating of
knights, for cash down.

Sweet knight, as soon as ever we are mar- [160 ried, take me to thy mercy out of this miserable chity ; presently carry me out of the scent of Newcastle coal and the hearing of Bowbell ; I beseech thee, down with me,[70] for God sake !

Touch. Well, Daughter, I have read that old wit sings :

The greatest rivers flow from little springs: Though thou art full, scorn not thy means at first; He that's most drunk may soonest be athirst.

Work upon that now ! 171

All but Touchstone, Mildred,
and Golding *depart.*

No, no ! yond' stand my hopes. — Mildred, come hither, Daughter. And how approve you your sister's fashion? how do you fancy[71] her choice? what dost thou think?

Mil. I hope, as a sister, well.

Touch. Nay, but, nay, but how dost thou like her behavior and humor? Speak freely.

Mil. I am loath to speak ill ; and yet — I am sorry of this — I cannot speak well. [180

Touch. Well ; very good, as I would wish ; a modest answer. — Golding, come hither ; hither, Golding. How dost thou like the knight, Sir Flash? Does he not look big? How lik'st thou the elephant? He says he has a castle in the country.

Gold. Pray Heaven, the elephant carry not his castle on his back.[72]

Touch. 'Fore Heaven, very well ! But, seriously, how dost repute him? 190

Gold. The best I can say of him is, I know him not !

Touch. Ha, Golding ! I commend thee, I approve thee, and will make it appear my affection is strong to thee. My wife has her humor, and I will ha' mine. Dost thou see my daughter here? She is not fair, well-favored or so, indifferent,[73] which modest measure of beauty shall not make it thy only work to watch her, nor sufficient mischance [200 to suspect her. Thou art towardly, she is modest ; thou art provident, she is careful. She's now mine. Give me thy hand ; she's now thine. Work upon that now !

Gold. Sir, as your son, I honor you ; and, as your servant, obey you.

Touch. Sayest thou so? — Come hither,

Mildred. Do you see yond' fellow? He is a gentleman, though my prentice, and has somewhat to take[74] too : a youth of [210 good hope ; well friended, well parted.[75] Are you mine? You are his. Work, you, upon that now !

Mil. Sir, I am all yours ; your body gave me life ; your care and love, happiness of life ; let your virtue still direct it, for to your wisdom I wholly dispose myself.

Touch. Say'st thou so? Be you two better acquainted. — Lip her, lip her, knave. So, shut up shop ; in. We must make [220 holiday. *Exeunt* Golding *and* Mildred. This match shall on, for I intend to prove Which thrives the best, the mean or lofty love :
Whether fit wedlock vow'd 'twixt like and like,
Or prouder hopes, which daringly o'erstrike
Their place and means. 'T is honest time's expense,[76]
When seeming lightness[77] bears a moral sense.

Work upon that now. *Exit.*

ACT II — Scene I[1]

Touchstone, Golding, *and* Mildred [*are discovered*] *sitting on either side of the stall.*

Touch. Quicksilver ! — Master Francis Quicksilver ! — Master Quicksilver !

Enter Quicksilver.

Quick. Here, sir ; (ump !)

Touch. So, sir ; nothing but flat " Master Quicksilver," without any familiar addition[2] will fetch you. Will you truss my points,[3] sir?

Quick. Ay, forsooth ; (ump !)

Touch. How now, sir ! the drunken hiccup so soon this morning?

Quick. 'Tis but the coldness of my [10 stomach, forsooth.

Touch. What ! have you the cause natural for it? Y' are a very learned drunkard : I

---

[70] Into the country.
[71] Old eds. *phantsie.*
[72] In pictures the elephant frequently carried a castle or howdah. The suggestion is that Sir Petronel may have sold his estate to purchase his fine clothes.
[73] Moderately.
[74] Receive as heir.
[75] Gifted.
[76] Expenditure of time.
[77] *I.e.,* the apparent frivolity of matchmaking.
[1] Goldsmith's Row. The inner stage represents Touchstone's stall.
[2] Title, style of address.
[3] Tie the tagged laces which were freely used by the Elizabethans instead of buttons.

believe I shall miss some of my silver spoons with your learning. The nuptial night will not moisten your throat sufficiently, but the morning likewise must rain her dews into your gluttonous weasand.

QUICK. An't please you, sir, we did but drink (ump!) to the coming off of the [20 knightly bridegroom.

TOUCH. To the coming off an [4] him?

QUICK. Ay, forsooth, we drunk to his coming on (ump!), when we went to bed ; and, now we are up, we must drink to his coming off : for that's the chief honor of a soldier, sir ; and therefore we must drink so much the more to it, forsooth (ump!)

TOUCH. A very capital reason! So that you go to bed late, and rise early to com- [30 mit drunkenness! You fulfil the scripture [5] very sufficient wickedly, forsooth.

QUICK. The knight's men, forsooth, be still a' their knees at it [6] (ump!) and because 'tis for your credit, sir, I would be loath to flinch.

TOUCH. I pray, sir, e'en to 'em again, then ; y'are one of the separated crew,[7] one of my wife's faction, and my young lady's, with whom, and with their great match, I will have nothing to do. 40

QUICK. So, sir ; now I will go keep my (ump!) credit with 'em, an't please you, sir.

TOUCH. In any case, sir, lay one cup of sack more a' your cold stomach, I beseech you.

QUICK. Yes, forsooth.

Exit QUICKSILVER.

TOUCH. This is for my credit! Servants ever maintain drunkenness in their master's house for their master's credit — a good idle serving man's reason. I thank Time the night is past ; I ne'er wak'd to such cost ; [50 I think we have stow'd more sorts of flesh in our bellies than ever Noah's ark received ; and, for wine, why my house turns giddy with it, and more noise in it than at a conduit. Ay, me, even beasts condemn our gluttony. Well, 'tis our city's fault, which, because we commit seldom, we commit the more sinfully ; we lose no time in our sensuality, but we make amends for it. Oh, that we would do so in virtue and religious negligences ! But see, here are all [60 the sober parcels my house can show. I'll eavesdrop — hear what thoughts they utter this morning.

[GOLDING *and* MILDRED *come forward.*]

GOLD. But is it possible that you, seeing your sister preferr'd to the bed of a knight, should contain your affections in the arms of a prentice?

MIL. I had rather make up the garment of my affections in some of the same piece than, like a Fool, wear gowns of two colors, or mix [70 sackcloth with satin.

GOLD. And do the costly garments, the title and fame of a lady, the fashion, observation, and reverence proper to such preferment, no more inflame you than such convenience as my poor means and industry can offer to your virtues?

MIL. I have observ'd that the bridle given to those violent flatteries of fortune is seldom recover'd ; they bear one headlong in desire [80 from one novelty to another ; and where those ranging appetites reign, there is ever more passion than reason : no stay, and so no happiness. These hasty advancements are not natural. Nature hath given us legs to go [8] to our objects ; not wings to fly to them.

GOLD. How dear an object you are to my desires I cannot express ; whose fruition would my master's absolute consent and yours vouchsafe me, I should be absolutely happy. [90 And, though it were a grace so far beyond my merit that I should blush with unworthiness to receive it, yet thus far both my love and my means shall assure your requital : you shall want nothing fit for your birth and education ; what increase of wealth and advancement the honest and orderly industry and skill of our trade will afford in any, I doubt not will be aspir'd by me ; I will ever make your contentment the end of my endeavors ; I will love [100 you above all ; and only your grief shall be my misery, and your delight my felicity.

TOUCH. [*aside*] Work upon that now! By my hopes, he woos honestly and orderly ; he shall be anchor of my hopes. Look, see the ill-yok'd monster, his fellow !

Re-enter QUICKSILVER, *unlac'd, a towel about his neck, in his flat cap, drunk.*

QUICK. Eastward Ho ! "Holla, ye pampered jades of Asia !" [9]

TOUCH. [*aside*] Drunk now downright, a' my fidelity ! 110

---

[4] On, of.
[5] *Isaiah*, v, 11.
[6] Drinking healths on their knees.
[7] Puritans.

[8] Walk.
[9] *ii Tamburlaine*, IV, iv, 1. Quoted by Pistol in Shakespeare's *ii Henry IV*, II, iv, 178.

QUICK. (Ump!) Pulldo, pulldo![10] showse,[11] quoth the caliver.[12]

GOLD. Fie, fellow Quicksilver, what a pickle are you in!

QUICK. Pickle? Pickle in thy throat;[13] 'zouns, pickle! — Wa, ha, ho![14] — Good morrow, knight Petronel. — Morrow, lady Goldsmith. — Come off, knight, with a counterbuff,[15] for the honor of knighthood.

GOLD. Why, how now, sir? Do ye [120 know where you are?

QUICK. Where I am? Why, 'sblood, you jolt-head,[16] — where I am!

GOLD. Go to, go to, for shame go to bed, and sleep out this immodesty; thou sham'st both my master and his house.

QUICK. Shame? what shame? I thought thou wouldst show thy bringing up; an thou wert a gentleman as I am, thou wouldst think it no shame to be drunk. Lend me some [130 money; save my credit; I must dine with the serving men and their wives — and their wives, sirrah!

GOLD. E'en who you will; I'll not lend thee threepence.

QUICK. 'Sfoot; lend me some money; " hast thou not Hyren here? "[17]

TOUCH. Why, how now, sirrah? what vein's this, ha?

QUICK. " Who cries on murther? [140 Lady, was it you? "[18] How does our master? Pray thee, cry " Eastward Ho! "

TOUCH. Sirrah, sirrah, y' are past your hiccup now; I see y' are drunk —

QUICK. 'Tis for your credit, Master.

TOUCH. And hear you keep a whore in town.

QUICK. 'Tis for your credit, Master.

TOUCH. And what you are out in cash I know.   150

QUICK. So do I. My father's a gentleman. Work upon that now! Eastward Ho!

TOUCH. Sir, " Eastward Ho " will make you go Westward Ho![19] I will no longer dis-

honest my house, nor endanger my stock with your license. There, sir: there's your indenture; all your apparel (that I must know) is on your back; and from this time my door is shut to you: from me be free; but, for other freedom and the moneys you have wasted, [160 " Eastward Ho " shall not serve you.

QUICK. Am I free a' my fetters? Rent, fly with a duck in thy mouth;[20] and now I tell thee, Touchstone —

TOUCH. Good sir ——

QUICK. " When this eternal substance of my soul — "

TOUCH. Well said; change your gold ends for your play ends.

QUICK. " Did live imprison'd in my wanton flesh —"

TOUCH. What then, sir?   170

QUICK. " I was a courtier in the Spanish court,

And Don Andrea was my name. "[21]

TOUCH. Good Master Don Andrea, will you march?

QUICK. Sweet Touchstone, will you lend me two shillings?

TOUCH. Not a penny.

QUICK. Not a penny? I have friends, and I have acquaintance; I will piss at thy shop posts, and throw rotten eggs at thy sign. [180 Work upon that now!

Exit, staggering.

TOUCH. Now, sirrah, you! hear you? You shall serve me no more neither — not an hour longer.

GOLD. What mean you, sir?

TOUCH. I mean to give thee thy freedom, and with thy freedom my daughter, and with my daughter a father's love; and, with all these, such a portion as shall make knight Petronel himself envy thee! Y' are both [190 agreed, are ye not?

AMBO. With all submission, both of thanks and duty.

TOUCH. Well then, the great power of Heaven bless and confirm you. And, Golding, that my love to thee may not show less than my wife's love to my eldest daughter, thy marriage feast shall equal the knight's and hers.   199

[10] So some copies of Q1; other old eds., *Am pum pull eo, Pullo.* Perhaps from a cry of the watermen. (Collier.)

[11] Bang.

[12] Matchlock.

[13] *I.e.,* you lie.

[14] A falconer's cry to his hawk.

[15] Return buffet or stroke in boxing or fencing.

[16] Blockhead.

[17] Another of Pistol's quotations, probably from the lost *Mahomet and Hiren the Fair Greek* by George Peele.

[18] From sc. ix of Chapman's *The Blind Beggar of Alexandria.*

[19] To be hanged at Tyburn.

[20] *I.e.,* good-bye to my financial resources — I renounce them cheerfully with all that they imply or amount to. (Cf. Middleton, *The Family of Love,* V, iii, 112, 113: " matter that shall carry meat i' th' mouth.") (Kittredge.)

[21] From the opening speech of *The Spanish Tragedy.*

GOLD. Let me beseech you, no, sir; the superfluity and cold meat left at their nuptials will, with bounty, furnish ours. The grossest prodigality is superfluous cost of the belly; nor would I wish any invitement of states [22] or friends; only your reverend presence and witness shall sufficiently grace and confirm us.

TOUCH. Son to mine own bosom, take her and my blessing. The nice fondling,[23] my Lady Sir-reverence,[24] that I must not now presume to call daughter, is so ravish'd with [210 desire to hansel[25] her new coach and see her knight's Eastward Castle, that the next morning will sweat with her busy setting forth. Away will she and her mother; and, while their preparation is making, ourselves, with some two or three other friends, will consummate the humble match we have in God's name concluded.
'Tis to my wish; for I have often read,
Fit birth, fit age, keeps long a quiet bed. 220
'Tis to my wish; for tradesmen, well 'tis known,
Get with more ease than gentry keeps his own.
[*Exeunt.*]

SCENE II [26]

[*Enter*] SECURITY, *solus.*

SEC. My privy guest, lusty Quicksilver, has drunk too deep of the bride-bowl; but, with a little sleep, he is much recovered; and, I think, is making himself ready to be drunk in a gallanter likeness. My house is as 't were the cave where the young outlaw hoards the stolen vails [27] of his occupation; and here, when he will revel it in his prodigal similitude, he retires to his trunks, and (I may say softly) his punks: he dares trust me with [10 the keeping of both; for I am security itself; my name is Security, the famous usurer.

Enter QUICKSILVER *in his prentice's coat and cap, his gallant breeches and stockings, gartering himself.*[28]

QUICK. Come, old Security, thou father of destruction! th' indented sheepskin [29] is

burn'd wherein I was wrapp'd; and I am now loose, to get more children of perdition into [thy] [30] usurous bonds. Thou feed'st my lechery, and I thy covetousness; thou art pander to me for my wench, and I to thee for thy cozenages. K. me, K. thee [31] runs [20 through court and country.

SEC. Well said, my subtle Quicksilver! These K's ope the doors to all this world's felicity; the dullest forehead sees it. Let not Master Courtier think he carries all the knavery on his shoulders; I have known poor Hob in the country, that has worn hobnails on 's shoes, have as much villainy in 's head as he that wears gold buttons in 's cap.

QUICK. Why, man, 't is the London [30 highway to thrift; if virtue be us'd, 't is but as a scrap to [32] the net of villainy. They that use it simply, thrive simply,[33] I warrant. Weight and fashion makes goldsmiths cuckolds.

Enter SINDEFY, *with* QUICKSILVER'S *doublet, cloak, rapier, and dagger.*

SIN. Here, sir, put of[f] the other half of your prenticeship.

QUICK. Well said, sweet Sin. Bring forth my bravery.
Now let my trunks [34] shoot forth their silks conceal'd;
I now am free, and now will justify 40
My trunks and punks. Avaunt, dull flat cap, then!
Via, the curtain that shadowed Borgia![35]
There lie, thou husk of my envassall'd state;
I, Samson, now have burst the Philistines' bands,
And in thy lap, my lovely Dali[l]a,
I 'll lie and snore out my enfranchis'd state.
[*Singing*]

When Samson was a tall young man,
His power and strength increased than; [36]
He sold no more nor cup nor can;
But did them all despise. 50
Old Touchstone, now write to thy friends
For one to sell thy base gold ends;
Quicksilver now no more attends
Thee, Touchstone.

[22] Persons of rank.
[23] This word meant both "pet" and "silly one."
[24] A contraction of "saving your reverence" = "with an apology for the vulgarity of my language." It finally came to mean, as a noun, a piece of excrement.
[25] Use for the first time. [26] Before Security's house.
[27] Profits, perquisites.
[28] Old eds. add *Securitie following.* This may indicate that a new scene originally began here, the former having been shortened.
[29] Articles of apprenticeship.

[30] Old eds. *my.*
[31] Ka me, ka thee; one good turn deserves another. *Ka, K,* and *key* were pronounced alike.
[32] Bait for (Parrott); nothing in comparison with (Schelling). Q2 *scap*; Q3 *scape.*
[33] *I.e.,* like simpletons.
[34] Also = "pea-shooters."
[35] An unidentified allusion.
[36] Then. The first two lines are from an old ballad, which Quicksilver proceeds to parody.

But, dad, hast thou seen my running gelding dress'd to-day?

SEC. That I have, Frank. The ostler a' th' Cock dressed him for a breakfast.

QUICK. What, did he eat him?

SEC. No, but he ate his breakfast for [60 dressing him ; and so dress'd him for breakfast.

QUICK. O witty age ! where age is young in wit,

And all youths' words have graybeards full of it !

SIN. But alas, Frank ! how will all this be maintain'd now? [37] Your place maintain'd it before.

QUICK. Why, and I maintain'd my place. I 'll to the court : another manner of place for maintenance, I hope, than the silly city. I heard my father say, I heard my mother [70 sing an old song and a true : " Thou art a she fool, and know'st not what belongs to our male wisdom." I shall be a merchant, forsooth ! trust my estate in a wooden trough as he does? What are these ships but tennis balls for the winds to play withal? — toss'd from one wave to another ; now under-line,[38] now over the house ; sometimes brick-wall'd against a rock, so that the guts fly out again ; sometimes struck under the wide hazard,[39] [80 and farewell, Master Merchant.

SIN. Well, Frank, well : the seas, you say, are uncertain : but he that sails in your court seas shall find 'em ten times fuller of hazard ; wherein to see what is to be seen is torment more than a free spirit can endure ; but, when you come to suffer, how many injuries swallow you ! What care and devotion must you use to humor an imperious lord, proportion your looks to his looks, smiles to [90 his smiles ; fit your sails to the winds of his breath !

QUICK. Tush ! he 's no journeyman in his craft that cannot do that.

SIN. But he 's worse then a prentice that does it, not only humoring the lord, but every trencher-bearer, every groom that by indulgence and intelligence crept into his favor, and by panderism into his chamber. He rules the roast ; and, when my honorable [100 Lord says it shall be thus, my worshipful rascal, the groom of his close-stool, says it shall

not be thus, claps the door after him, and who dares enter? A prentice, quoth you? [40] 'T is but to learn to live ; and does that disgrace a man? He that rises hardly, stands firmly ; but he that rises with ease, alas, falls as easily.

QUICK. A pox on you ! who taught you this morality? 110

[41] SEC. 'T is 'long of this witty age, Master Francis. But, indeed, Mistress Sindefy, all trades complain of inconvenience, and therefore 't is best to have none. The merchant, he complains and says, " Traffic is subject to much uncertainty and loss." Let 'em keep their goods on dry land, with a vengeance, and not expose other men's substances to the mercy of the winds, under protection of a wooden wall, as Master [120 Francis says ; and all for greedy desire to enrich themselves with unconscionable gain, two for one, or so ; where I, and such other honest men as live by lending money, are content with moderate profit, thirty or forty i' th' hundred, so we may have it with quietness, and out of peril of wind and weather, rather than run those dangerous courses of trading, as they do.

QUICK. Ay, dad, thou mayst well be [130 called Security, for thou takest the safest course.

SEC. Faith, the quieter, and the more contented, and, out of doubt, the more godly ; for merchants, in their courses, are never pleas'd, but ever repining against Heaven : one prays for a westerly wind, to carry his ship forth ; another for an easterly, to bring his ship home ; and, at every shaking of a leaf, he falls into an agony, to think what dan- [140 ger his ship is in on such a coast, and so forth. The farmer, he is ever at odds with the weather : sometimes the clouds have been too barren ; sometimes the heavens forget themselves.[42] Their harvests answer not their hopes : sometimes the season falls out too fruitful, corn will bear no price, and so forth. Th' artificer, he 's all for a stirring world : if his trade be too [dull],[43] and fall short of his expectation, then falls he out of joint. [150 Where [44] we that trade nothing but money are

---

[37] At this point in Q1, C *verso* begins; it runs through "morality", l. 110. It was reset by the printer. Cf. on I, ii, 27.

[38] Instead of over it, as the tennis player should.

[39] Into one of the recesses in the walls of the tennis court.

[40] *I.e.*, you scorn being an apprentice, do you?

[41] At this point C 2 *recto* of Q 1 begins; it runs through " in good part," l. 155. There has been minor deletion and resetting. Cf. on I, ii, 27.

[42] *I.e.*, urinate at unpropitious times.

[43] Emend. Simpson ; old eds. *full*.

[44] Whereas.

free from all this; we are pleas'd with all weathers. Let it rain or hold up, be calm or windy, let the season be whatsoever, let trade go how it will, we take all in good part, e'en what please the Heavens to send us, so [45] the sun stand not still and the moon keep her usual returns, and make up days, months, and years.

QUICK. And you have good security! [160]

SEC. Ay, marry, Frank, that's the special point.

QUICK. And yet, forsooth, we must have trades to live withal; for we cannot stand without legs, nor fly without wings, and a number of such scurvy phrases. No, I say still, he that has wit, let him live by his wit; he that has none, let him be a tradesman.

SEC. Witty Master Francis! 'T is pity any trade should dull that quick brain of [170] yours. Do but bring knight Petronel into my parchment toils once, and you shall never need to toil in any trade, a' my credit. You know his wife's land?

QUICK. Even to a foot, sir; I have been often there: a pretty fine seat, good land, all entire within itself.

SEC. Well wooded?

QUICK. Two hundred pounds' worth of wood ready to fell. And a fine sweet [180] house, that stands just in the midst an 't, like a prick[46] in the midst of a circle; would I were your farmer, for a hundred pound a year!

SEC. Excellent Master Francis! how I do long to do thee good! How I do hunger and thirst to have the honor to enrich thee! Ay, even to die, that thou mightest inherit my living: even hunger and thirst! For, a' my religion, Master Francis — and so [190] tell knight Petronel — I do it to do him a pleasure.

QUICK. Marry, dad, his horses are now coming up to bear down his lady; wilt thou lend him thy stable to set 'em in?

SEC. Faith, Master Francis, I would be loth to lend my stable out of doors; in a greater matter I will pleasure him, but not in this.

QUICK. A pox of your hunger and [200] thirst! Well, dad, let him have money; all he could anyway get is bestowed on a ship now bound for Virginia; the frame of which voyage is so closely convey'd[47] that his

new lady nor any of her friends know it. Notwithstanding, as soon as his lady's hand is gotten to the sale of her inheritance, and you have furnish'd him with money, he will instantly hoist sail and away.

SEC. Now a frank gale of wind go with [210] him, Master Frank! we have too few such knight adventurers! Who would not sell away competent certainties to purchase, with any danger, excellent uncertainties? Your true knight venturer ever does it. Let his wife seal to-day; he shall have his money to-day.

QUICK. To-morrow she shall, dad, before she goes into the country; to work her to which action with the more engines, I pur- [220] pose presently to prefer my sweet Sin here to the place of her gentlewoman; whom you, for the more credit, shall present as your friend's daughter, a gentlewoman of the country, new come up with a will for awhile to learn fashions forsooth, and be toward some lady; and she shall buzz pretty devices into her lady's ear; feeding her humors so serviceably, as the manner of such as she is, you know —   230

SEC. True, good Master Francis.[48]

QUICK. That she shall keep her port open to anything she commends to her.

SEC. A' my religion, a most fashionable project; as good she spoil the lady, as the lady spoil her; for 't is three to one of one side. — Sweet Mistress Sin, how are you bound to Master Francis! I do not doubt to see you shortly wed one of the head men of our city.   240

SIN. But, sweet Frank, when shall my father Security present me?

QUICK. With all festination; I have broken the ice to it already; and will presently to the knight's house, whither, my good old dad, let me pray thee, with all formality to man her.

SEC. Command me, Master Francis; I do hunger and thirst to do thee service! — Come, sweet Mistress Sin, take leave of my Winifred, and we will instantly meet [250] frank Master Francis at your lady's.

Enter WINIFRED *above.*

WIN. Where is my Cu there? Cu!

SEC. Ay, Winnie.

WIN. Wilt thou come in, sweet Cu?

SEC. Ay, Winnie, presently.

Exeunt [all but QUICKSILVER].

---

[45] Provided that, as long as.
[46] Dot.   [47] Secretly conducted.
[48] Qq add *Enter Sindefie*, perhaps (as Simpson suggests) a sign of compression.

Quick. "Ay, Winnie," quod he. That's all he can do, poor man ; he may well cut off her name at "Winnie." [49] Oh, 't is an egregious pander ! What will not an usurous knave be, so he may be rich? Oh, 't is a no- [260 table Jews' trump ! I hope to live to see dogs' meat made of the old usurer's flesh, dice of his bones, and indentures of his skin ; and yet his skin is too thick to make parchment ; 't would make good boots for a peterman [50] to catch salmon in. Your only smooth skin to make fine vellum is your Puritan's skin ; they be the smoothest and slickest knaves in a country.

Enter SIR PETRONEL, *in boots, with a riding-wan*[d].

Pet. I 'll out of this wicked town as [270 fast as my horse can trot ! Here's now no good action for a man to spend his time in. Taverns grow dead ; ordinaries are blown up ; plays are at a stand ; houses of hospitality at a fall ; not a feather waving, nor a spur jingling anywhere. I 'll away instantly.

Quick. Y' ad best take some crowns in your purse, knight, or else your Eastward Castle will smoke but miserably.

Pet. Oh, Frank ! my castle? Alas ! [280 all the castles I have are built with air, thou know'st.

Quick. I know it, knight, and therefore wonder whither your lady is going.

Pet. Faith, to seek her fortune, I think. I said I had a castle and land eastward, and eastward she will, without contradiction ; her coach and the coach of the sun must meet full butt. And, the sun being outshined with her Ladyship's glory, she fears he goes [290 westward to hang himself.[51]

Quick. And I fear, when her enchanted castle becomes invisible, her Ladyship will return and follow his example.

Pet. Oh, that she would have the grace ! for I shall never be able to pacify her, when she sees herself deceived so.

Quick. As easily as can be. Tell her she mistook your directions, and that shortly your-self will down with her to approve it ; [300 and then clothe but her crupper in a new gown, and you may drive her any way you list. For these women, sir, are like Essex [52]

[49] With a pun on "whinny" (?).
[50] Fisherman.
[51] See on II, i, 154.
[52] Supposed to produce the finest calves in England.

calves : you must wriggle 'em on by the tail still, or they will never drive orderly.

Pet. But, alas, sweet Frank ! thou know'st my ability will not furnish her blood with those costly humors.

Quick. Cast that cost on me, sir. I have spoken to my old pander, Security, for [310 money or commodity ; [53] if you will, I know he will procure you.

Pet. Commodity ! Alas ! what commodity ?

Quick. Why, sir, what say you to figs and raisins ?

Pet. A plague of figs and raisins, and all such frail [54] commodities ! We shall make nothing of 'em.

Quick. Why then, sir, what say you [320 to forty pound in roasted beef ?

Pet. Out upon 't. I have less stomach to [55] that than to the figs and raisins. I 'll out of town, though I sojourn with a friend of mine ; for stay here I must not : my credit-tors have laid to arrest me, and I have no friend under heaven but my sword to bail me.

Quick. God's me, knight, put 'em in sufficient sureties, rather than let your sword bail you ! Let 'em take their choice, [330 either the King's Bench [56] or the Fleet,[57] or which of the two Counters [58] they like best, for, by the Lord, I like none of 'em.

Pet. Well, Frank, there is no jesting with my earnest necessity ; thou know'st if I make not present money to further my voyage begun, all 's lost, and all I have laid out about it.

Quick. Why, then, sir, in earnest ; if you can get your wise lady to set her hand to [340 the sale of her inheritance, the bloodhound, Security, will smell out ready money for you instantly.

Pet. There spake an angel : to bring her to which conformity, I must fain myself extremely amorous ; and, alleging urgent excuses for my stay behind, part with her as passionately as she would from her foisting [59] hound.

Quick. You have the sow by the right [350

[53] In this swindle, the borrower was obliged to take part of the loan in unsalable goods, which the lender's agent bought back at a great reduction.
[54] Punning on "frail" = rush basket.
[55] Appetite for.
[56] The prison, at Westminster, for those convicted by the court so named.
[57] The famous prison on Fleet Ditch.
[58] See on *Dramatis Personae*.
[59] *I.e.*, stinking.

ear, sir. I warrant there was never child long'd more to ride a cockhorse or wear his new coat than she longs to ride in her new coach. She would long for everything when she was a maid, and now she will run mad for 'em. I lay my life, she will have every year four children; and what charge and change of humor you must endure while she is with child, and how she will tie you to your tackling [60] till she be with child, a dog [360 would not endure. Nay, there is no turnspit dog bound to his wheel more servilely than you shall be to her wheel; for, as that dog can never climb the top of his wheel but when the top comes under him, so shall you never climb the top of her contentment but when she is under you.

PET. 'Slight, how thou terrifiest me!

QUICK. Nay, hark you, sir; what nurses, what midwives, what fools, what physi- [370 cians, what cunning women must be sought for (fearing sometimes she is bewitch'd, sometimes in a consumption), to tell her tales, to talk bawdy to her, to make her laugh, to give her glisters,[61] to let her blood under the tongue and betwixt the toes; how she will revile and kiss you, spit in your face, and lick it off again; how she will vaunt you are her creature; she made you of nothing; how she could have had thousand-mark [62] join- [380 tures; she could have been made a lady by a Scotch knight, and never ha' married him;[63] she could have had panadas [64] in her bed every morning; how she set you up, and how she will pull you down — you'll never be able to stand of your legs to endure it.

PET. Out of my fortune! what a death is my life bound face to face to! The best is, a large time-fitted [65] conscience is bound to nothing: marriage is but a form in the [390 school of policy, to which scholars sit fast'ned only with painted chains. Old Security's young wife is ne'er the further of[f] with me.

QUICK. Thereby lies a tale, sir. The old usurer will be here instantly, with my punk Sindefy, whom you know your lady has promis'd me to entertain for her gentlewoman; and he, with a purpose to feed on you, invites you most solemnly by me to supper.

PET. It falls out excellently fitly; I [400 see desire of gain makes jealousy venturous.

Enter GERTRUDE.

See, Frank, here comes my lady. Lord, how she views thee! She knows thee not, I think, in this bravery.[66]

GER. How now? who be you, I pray?

QUICK. One Master Francis Quicksilver, an't please your Ladyship.

GER. [*aside*] God's my dignity! as I am a lady, if he did not make me blush so that mine eyes stood a-water. Would I were un- [410 married again! —

Enter SECURITY *and* SINDEFY.

Where's my woman, I pray?

QUICK. See, madam, she now comes to attend you.

SEC. God save my honorable knight and his worshipful lady!

GER. Y' are very welcome; you must not put on your hat yet.

SEC. No, madam; till I know your Lady- ship's further pleasure, I will not presume. [420

GER. And is this a gentleman's daugh- ter new come out of the country?

SEC. She is, madam; and one that her father hath a special care to bestow in some honorable lady's service, to put her out of her honest humors,[67] forsooth; for she had a great desire to be a nun, an't please you.

GER. A nun? what nun? a nun sub- stantive? or a nun adjective?

SEC. A nun substantive, madam, I [430 hope if a nun be a noun. But, I mean, lady, a vow'd maid of that order.

GER. I'll teach her to be a maid of the order, I warrant you. And can you do any work belongs to a lady's chamber?

SIN. What I cannot do, madam, I would be glad to learn.

GER. Well said! Hold up, then; hold up your head, I say; come h[i]ther a little.

SIN. I thank your Ladyship.   440

GER. And hark you — good man, you may put on your hat now; I do not look on you — I must have you of my faction now; not of my knight's, maid.

SIN. No, forsooth, Madam, of yours.

GER. And draw all my servants in my bow,[68] and keep my counsel, and tell me tales, and

---

[60] Gear, business.
[61] Clysters, enemas.
[62] A mark was worth about $3.33.
[63] "Perhaps a reflection on the laxness of Scotch marriage laws." (Parrott.)
[64] Bread boiled to a pulp, and flavored with cur- rants, sugar, etc. (Skeat.) Old eds. *poynados*.
[65] *I.e.*, elastic.
[66] These fine clothes.
[67] *I.e.*, whimsical inclination to chastity.
[68] *I.e.*, bring them all under my control.

put me riddles, and read on a book sometimes when I am busy, and laugh at country gentle-women, and command anything in the [450 house for my retainers ; and care not what you spend, for it is all mine ; and, in any case, be still a maid, whatsoever you do, or what-soever any man can do unto you.

SEC. I warrant your Ladyship for that.

GER. Very well ; you shall ride in my coach with me into the country, to-morrow morning. — Come, knight, pray thee let 's make a short supper, and to bed presently.[69]

SEC. Nay, good madam, this night I [460 have a short supper at home waits on his Wor-ship's acceptation.

GER. By my faith, but he shall not go, sir ; I shall swoon an he sup from me.

PET. Pray thee, forbear ; shall he lose his provision ?

GER. Ay, by[r] Lady, sir, rather than I lose my longing. Come in, I say ; as I am a lady, you shall not go.

QUICK. [*aside*] I told him what a burr [470 he had gotten.

SEC. If you will not sup from your knight, madam, let me entreat your Ladyship to sup at my house with him.

GER. No, by my faith, sir ; then we can-not be abed soon enough after supper.

PET. [*aside*] What a med'cine is this ! — Well, Master Security, you are new married as well as I ; I hope you are bound as well. We must honor our young wives, you know.

QUICK. [*aside to* SECURITY] In policy, [481 dad, till to-morrow she has seal'd.

SEC. I hope in the morning yet your Knighthood will breakfast with me.

PET. As early as you will, sir.

SEC. Thank your good Worship ; I do hunger and thirst to do you good, sir !

GER. Come, sweet knight, come ; I do hunger and thirst to be abed with thee !

Exeunt.

ACT III — SCENE I[1]

Enter PETRONEL, QUICKSILVER, SECURITY, BRAMBLE, *and* WINIFRED.

PET. Thanks for our[2] feastlike breakfast, good Master Security ; I am sorry, by reason

---

69 Immediately.
1 The same, or possibly inside the house.
2 Qq 2, 3, *your.*

---

of my instant haste to so long a voyage as Virginia, I am without means by any kind amends to show how affectionately I take your kindness, and to confirm by some worthy ceremony a perpetual league of friendship betwixt us.

SEC. Excellent knight ! let this be a token betwixt us of inviolable friendship. I am [10 new married to this fair gentlewoman, you know ; and, by my hope to make her fruitful, though I be something in years, I vow faith-fully unto you to make you godfather, though in your absence, to the first child I am blest withal ; and henceforth call me gossip,[3] I beseech you, if you please to accept it.

PET. In the highest degree of gratitude, my most worthy gossip ; for confirmation of which friendly title, let me entreat my fair [20 gossip, your wife here, to accept this diamond, and keep it as my gift to her first child, where-soever my fortune, in event of my voyage, shall bestow me.

SEC. How now, my coy wedlock ![4] Make you strange of[5] so noble a favor? Take it, I charge you, with all affection, and, by way of taking your leave, present boldly your lips to our honorable gossip.

QUICK. [*aside*] How vent'rous he is to [30 him, and how jealous to others !

PET. Long may this kind touch of our lips print in our hearts all the forms of affection. — And now, my good gossip, if the writings be ready to which my wife should seal, let them be brought this morning before she takes coach into the country, and my kindness shall work her to dispatch it.

SEC. The writings are ready, sir. My learned counsel here, Master Bramble the [40 lawyer, hath perus'd them ; and within this hour I will bring the scrivener with them to your worshipful lady.

PET. Good Master Bramble, I will here take my leave of you, then. God send you fortunate pleas, sir, and contentious clients !

BRAM. And you foreright[6] winds, sir, and a fortunate voyage.   *Exit.*

Enter a Messenger.

MESS. Sir Petronel, here are three or four gentlemen desire to speak with you.   50

PET. What are they?

QUICK. They are your followers in this voyage, knight : Captain Seagull and his

---

3 Friend, crony.   4 Wife.
5 Are you surprised at.   6 Directly favorable.

associates ; I met them this morning, and told them you would be here.

PET. Let them enter, I pray you ; I know they long to be gone, for their stay is dangerous.

Enter SEAGULL, SCAPETHRIFT, *and*
SPENDALL.

SEA. God save my honorable colonel !

PET. Welcome, good Captain Seagull [60 and worthy gentlemen. If you will meet my friend Frank here and me at the Blue Anchor Tavern by Billin[g]sgate this evening, we will there drink to our happy voyage, be merry, and take boat to our ship with all expedition.[7]

[SPEND]. Defer it no longer, I beseech you, sir ; but, as your voyage is h[i]therto carried closely,[8] and in another knight's name, so for your own safety and ours, let it be continued ; our meeting and speedy purpose of depart- [70 ing known to as few as is possible, lest your ship and goods be attach'd.

QUICK. Well advis'd, captain ; our colonel shall have money this morning, to dispatch all our departures. Bring those gentlemen at night to the place appointed, and, with our skins full of vintage, we'll take occasion by the vantage, and away.

SPEND. We will not fail but be there, sir.

PET. Good morrow, good Captain, and [80 my worthy associates. — Health and all sovereignty to my beautiful gossip ! — For you, sir, we shall see you presently with the writings.

SEC. With writings and crowns to my honorable gossip. I do hunger and thirst to do you good, sir.

Exeunt.

SCENE II [9]

Enter a Coachman *in haste, in's frock, feeding.*

COACH. Here's a stir when citizens ride out of town, indeed, as if all the house were afire ! 'Slight ! they will not give a man leave to eat's breakfast afore he rises.

Enter HAMLET, *a footman, in haste.*

HAM. What, coachman ! My Lady's coach, for shame ! Her Ladyship's ready to come down.

[7] Haste.
[8] See on, II, ii, 204.
[9] An innyard.

Enter POTKIN, *a tankard-bearer.*

POT. 'Sfoot, Hamlet, are you mad? Whither run you now? You should brush up my old mistress !   10
                                    [*Exit* HAMLET.]

Enter SINDEFY.

SIN. What, Potkin ! You must put off your tankard and put on your blue coat,[10] and wait upon Mistress Touchstone into the country.   *Exit.*

POT. I will, forsooth, presently.   *Exit.*

Enter MISTRESS FOND *and* MISTRESS
GAZER.

FOND. Come, sweet Mistress Gazer, let's watch here, and see my Lady Flash take coach.

GAZ. A' my word, here's a most fine place to stand in ; did you see the new ship [20 launch'd last day,[11] Mistress Fond ?

FOND. O God ! an we citizens should lose such a sight !

GAZ. I warrant here will be double as many people to see her take coach as there were to see it take water.

FOND. Oh, she's married to a most fine castle i' th' country, they say !

GAZ. But there are no giants in the castle, are there?   30

FOND. Oh, no ; they say her knight kill'd 'em all ; and therefore he was knighted.

GAZ. Would to God her Ladyship would come away !

Enter GERTRUDE, MISTRESS TOUCHSTONE,
SINDEFY, HAMLET, [*and*] POTKIN.

FOND. She comes, she comes, she comes !

GAZ. [AND] FOND. Pray Heaven bless your Ladyship !

GER. Thank you, good people ! — My coach, for the love of Heaven, my coach ! In good truth I shall swoon else.   40

HAM. Coach, coach, my Lady's coach !
                                        Exit.

GER. As I am a lady, I think I am with child already, I long for a coach so. May one be with child afore they are married, Mother?

MIST. T. Ay, by'r Lady, madam ; a little thing does that : I have seen a little prick no bigger then a pin's head swell bigger and

[10] The usual garb of a serving man.
[11] Yesterday.

bigger, till it has come to an ancome ; [12] and e'en so 't is in these cases.

Re-enter HAMLET.

HAM. Your coach is coming, madam. 50

GER. That's well said. — Now, Heaven! methinks I am e'en up to the knees in preferment.

[*singing*]

But a little higher, but a little higher, but a little higher,
There, there, there lies Cupid's fire ! [13]

MIST. T. But must this young man, an't please you, madam, run by your coach all the way afoot?

GER. Ay, by my faith, I warrant him ; he gives no other milk,[14] as I have another [60 servant does.

MIST. T. Alas ! 't is e'en pity, methinks ; for God's sake, madam, buy him but a hobby-horse ; let the poor youth have something betwixt his legs to ease 'em. Alas ! we must do as we would be done to.

GER. Go to, hold your peace, dame ; you talk like an old fool, I tell you !

Enter PETRONEL *and* QUICKSILVER.

PET. Wilt thou be gone, sweet honey-suckle, before I can go with thee ? 70

GER. I pray thee, sweet knight, let me ; I do so long to dress up thy castle afore thou com'st. But I mar'l how my modest sister occupies herself this morning, that she cannot wait on me to my coach, as well as her mother.

QUICK. Marry, madam, she's married by this time to prentice Golding. Your father, and someone more, stole to church with 'em in all the haste, that the cold meat left at your wedding might serve to furnish their [80 nuptial table.

GER. There's no base fellow, my father, now ; but he's e'en fit to father such a daughter. He must call me " daughter " no more now : but " madam," and " please you, madam " ; and " please your Worship, madam," indeed. Out upon him ! marry his daughter to a base prentice ?

MIST. T. What should one do ? Is there no law for one that marries a woman's [90 daughter against her will ? How shall we punish him, madam ?

GER. As I am a lady, an't would snow,

we'd so pebble 'em with snowballs as they come from church ; but, sirrah Frank Quick-silver —

QUICK. Ay, madam.

GER. Dost remember since thou and I clapp'd what-d'ye-call'ts in the garret ?

QUICK. I know not what you mean, [100 madam.

GER. [*singing*]

His head as white as milk,
All flaxen was his hair ;
But now he is dead,
And laid in his bed,
And never will come again.[15]

God be at your labor !

Enter TOUCHSTONE, GOLDING, [*and*] MILDRED *with rosemary.*[16]

PET. [*aside*] Was there ever such a lady ?

QUICK. See, madam, the bride and bride-groom ! 110

GER. God's my precious ! God give you joy, Mistress What-lack-you ! Now out upon thee, baggage ! My sister married in a taffeta hat ! Marry, hang you ! Westward with a wanion [17] t' ye ! Nay, I have done wi' ye, minion, then, i' faith ; never look to have my countenance any more, nor anything I can do for thee. Thou ride in my coach, or come down to my castle ? fie upon thee ! I charge thee in my Ladyship's name, call me " sister " no more. 121

TOUCH. An't please your Worship, this is not your sister : this is my daughter, and she call[s] me " Father," and so does not your Ladyship, an't please your Worship, madam.

MIST. T. No, nor she must not call thee father by heraldry, because thou mak'st thy prentice thy son as well as she. Ah, thou misproud prentice ! dar'st thou presume to marry a lady's sister ? 130

GOLD. It pleas'd my master, forsooth, to embolden me with his favor ; and, though I confess myself far unworthy so worthy a wife, being in part her servant, as I am your prentice, yet, since (I may say it without boasting) I am born a gentleman, and, by the trade I have learn'd of my master, which I trust taints not my blood, able, with mine own industry and portion, to maintain your daughter, my hope is Heaven will so bless our [140

---

[12] Boil, felon.
[13] The refrain of a song in Campion's *Book of Airs*.
[14] *I.e.*, has no other function.

[15] One of the numerous allusions to *Hamlet* in this scene.
[16] Used at weddings, as a symbol of constancy.
[17] With bad luck.

humble beginning that in the end I shall be no disgrace to the grace with which my master hath bound me his double prentice.

TOUCH. Master me no more, son, if thou think'st me worthy to be thy father.

GER. " Sun " ? Now, good Lord, how he shines, an you mark him ! He 's a gentleman !

GOLD. Ay, indeed, madam, a gentleman born.   149

PET. Never stand a' your gentry, Master Bridegroom ; if your legs be no better than your arms, you 'll be able to stand upon neither shortly.

TOUCH. An 't please your good Worship, sir, there are two sorts of gentlemen.

PET. What mean you, sir ?

TOUCH. Bold to put off my hat to your Worship——

PET. Nay, pray forbear, sir, and then forth with your two sorts of gentlemen.   160

TOUCH. If your Worship will have it so ! — I say there are two sorts of gentlemen. There is a gentleman artificial, and a gentleman natural. Now, though your Worship be a gentleman natural [18] — work upon that now !

QUICK. Well said, old Touchstone ; I am proud to hear thee enter a set speech, i' faith ; forth, I beseech thee.

TOUCH. Cry you mercy, sir, your Worship 's a gentleman I do not know. If you be [170 one of my acquaintance, y' are very much disguis'd, sir.

QUICK. Go to, old quipper ; forth with thy speech, I say.

TOUCH. What, sir, my speeches were ever in vain to your gracious Worship ; and therefore, till I speak to you gallantry [19] indeed I will save my breath for my broth anon. Come, my poor son and daughter, let us hide ourselves in our poor humility, and live [180 safe. Ambition consumes itself with the very show. Work upon that now !

[*Exeunt* TOUCHSTONE, GOLDING *and* MILDRED.]

GER. Let him go, let him go, for God's sake ! let him make his prentice his son, for God's sake ! give away his daughter, for God's sake ! and when they come a-begging to us, for God's sake, let 's laugh at their good husbandry for God's sake. Farewell, sweet knight, pray thee make haste after.

PET. What shall I say ? I would not [190 have thee go.

[18] Fool.
[19] *I.e.*, speak in fashionable terms.

QUICK. [*singing*]

Now, oh, now, I must depart ;
Parting, though it absence move — [20]

This ditty, knight, do I see in thy looks in capital letters. —
[*singing*]

What a grief 'tis to depart, and leave the flower that has my heart !
My sweet lady, and, alack for woe, why should we part so?

Tell truth, knight, and shame all dissembling lovers ; does not your pain lie on that side?

PET. If it do, canst thou tell me how I [200 may cure it?

QUICK. Excellent easily. Divide yourself in two halves, just by the girdlestead ; [21] send one half with your lady, and keep the tother yourself ; or else do as all true lovers do, part with your heart and leave your body behind. I have seen 't done a hundred times : 't is as easy a matter for a lover to part without a heart from his sweetheart, and he ne'er the worse, as for a mouse to get from a trap [210 and leave her tail behind [her].[22] See, here comes the writings.

Enter SECURITY, *with a* Scrivener.

SEC. Good morrow to my worshipful Lady. I present your Ladyship with this writing, to which, if you please to set your hand with your knight's, a velvet gown shall attend your journey, a' my credit.

GER. What writing is it, knight?

PET. The sale, sweetheart, of the poor tenement I told thee of, only to make a little [220 money to send thee down furniture for my castle, to which my hand shall lead thee.

GER. Very well. Now give me your pen, I pray.

QUICK. [*aside*] It goes down without chewing, i' faith.

SCRIV. Your Worships deliver this as your deed?

AMBO. We do.

GER. So now, knight, farewell till I [230 see thee !

PET. All farewell to my sweetheart.

MIST. T. Good-bye,[23] son knight.

PET. Farewell, my good mother !

GER. Farewell, Frank ! I would fain take thee down if I could.

[20] Misquoted from Dowland's *First Book of Airs*.
[21] Waist.
[22] Old eds. *him*.
[23] Old eds. *God-boye*.

QUICK. I thank your good Ladyship. — Farewell, Mistress Sindefy!

Exeunt [GERTRUDE *and her party.*]

PET. O tedious voyage, whereof there is no end!
What will they think of me? 240

QUICK. Think what they list. They long'd for a vagary into the country; and now they are fitted. So a woman marry to ride in a coach, she cares not if she ride to her ruin. 'T is the great end of many of their marriages. This is not first time a lady has rid a false journey in her coach, I hope.

PET. Nay, 't is no matter, I care little what they think; he that weighs men's [249 thoughts has his hands full of nothing. A man, in the course of this world, should be like a surgeon's instrument, work in the wounds of others, and feel nothing himself. The sharper and subtler, the better.

QUICK. As it falls out now, knight, you shall not need to devise excuses, or endure her outcries, when she returns; we shall now be gone before, where they can not reach us.

PET. Well, my kind compere,[24] you have now th' assurance we both can make you; [260 let me now entreat you the money we agreed on may be brought to the Blue Anchor, near to Billingsgate, by six a'clock; where I and my chief friends, bound for this voyage, will with feasts attend you.

SEC. The money, my most honorable compere, shall without fail observe your appointed hour.

PET. Thanks, my dear gossip. I must now impart
To your approved love a loving secret, 270
As one on whom my life doth more rely
In friendly trust than any man alive.
Nor shall you be the chosen secretary
Of my affections for affection only;
For I protest, if God bless my return,
To make you partner in my action's gain
As deeply as if you had ventur'd with me 277
Half my expenses. Know then, honest gossip,
I have enjoyed with such divine content-
ment
A gentlewoman's bed whom you well know,
That I shall ne'er enjoy this tedious voyage,
Nor live the least part of the time it asketh,
Without her presence; so "I thirst and
hunger"[25]
To taste the dear feast of her company.

And, if the "hunger" and "the thirst" you vow
As my sworn gossip, to my wished good
Be, as I know it is, unfeign'd and firm,
Do me an easy favor in your power. 288

SEC. Be sure, brave gossip, all that I can do,
To my best nerve,[26] is wholly at your service.
Who is the woman, first, that is your friend?

PET. The woman is your learned counsel's wife,
The lawyer, Master Bramble; whom would you
Bring out this even in honest neighbor-
hood,[27]
To take his leave, with you, of me your gossip,
I, in the mean time, will send this my friend
Home to his house, to bring his wife, dis-
guis'd,
Before his face, into our company;
For love hath made her look for such a wile,
To free her from his tyrannous jealousy; [300
And I would take this course before another,
In stealing her away, to make us sport,
And gull his circumspection the more grossly;
And I am sure that no man like yourself
Hath credit with him to entice his jealousy
To so long stay abroad as may give time
To her enlargement in such safe disguise.

SEC. A pretty, pithy, and most pleasant project!
Who would not strain a point of neighbor-
hood
For such a point-device?[28] — that, as the ship
Of famous Draco[29] went about the world, [311
Will wind about the lawyer, compassing
The world, himself; he hath it in his arms,
And that's enough for him, without his wife.
A lawyer is ambitious, and his head
Cannot be prais'd nor rais'd too high,
With any fork[30] of highest knavery.
I'll go fetch [him][31] straight.

Exit SECURITY.

PET. So, so! Now, Frank, go thou home to his house, 319
'Stead of his lawyer's, and bring his wife hither,
Who, just like to the lawyer's wife, is prison'd
With his stern usurous jealousy, which could never
Be overreach'd thus but with overreaching.

[24] Friend, "gossip."
[25] Words quoted are italized in old eds.
[26] To the best of my powers.
[27] Neighborliness.
[28] Piece of perfection.
[29] Sir Francis Drake's *Golden Hind*, laid up as a memorial at Deptford.
[30] Alluding to the horns of the cuckold.
[31] Conj. R. H. Case; old eds. *her*.

Re-enter SECURITY.

SEC. And, Master Francis, watch you th'
  instant time
To enter with his exit : 't will be rare,
Two fine [32] horn'd beasts, a camel [33] and a
  lawyer !   [*Exit.*]
  QUICK. How the old villain joys in villainy !

Re-enter SECURITY.

SEC. And hark you, gossip, when you have
  her here,
Have your boat ready, ship her to your ship
With utmost haste, lest Master Bramble stay
  you.   330
To o'erreach that head that outreacheth all
  heads !
'T is a trick rampant ! — 't is a very quib-
  lin ! [34]
I hope this harvest to pitch cart with law-
  yers,
Their heads will be so forked. This sly
  touch
Will get apes [35] to invent a number such.
                                              Exit.
  QUICK. Was ever rascal honeyed so with
    poison ?
" He that delights in slavish avarice,
Is apt to joy in every sort of vice."
Well, I 'll go fetch his wife, whilst he the
  [lawyer].[36]
  PET. But stay, Frank, let 's think how we
    may disguise her.   340
Upon this sudden.
  QUICK.   God's me, there 's the mischief !
But hark you, here 's an excellent device —
'Fore God, a rare one ! I will carry her
A sailor's gown and cap, and cover her,
And a player's beard.
  PET.   And what upon her head ?
  QUICK. I tell you, a sailor's cap ! 'Slight,
    God forgive me !
What kind of figent [37] memory have you ?
  PET. Nay, then, what kind of figent wit
    hast thou ?
A sailor's cap ? — how shall she put it off
When thou present'st her to our company ?
  QUICK. Tush, man, for that, make her a
    saucy sailor !   351

PET. Tush, tush ! 't is no fit sauce for such
  sweet mutton.[38]
I know not what t' advise.

Enter SECURITY *with his wife's gown.*

SEC.   Knight, knight, a rare device !
PET. Sownes,[39] yet again ?
QUICK.   What stratagem have you now ?
SEC. The best that ever — you talk'd of
  disguising ?
PET. Ay, marry, gossip, that 's our present
  care.
SEC. Cast care away then ; here 's the
  best device
For plain Security (for I am no better),
I think, that ever liv'd ; here 's my wife's
  gown,
Which you may put upon the lawyer's wife,
And which I brought you, sir, for two great
  reasons :   361
One is, that Master Bramble may take hold
Of some suspicion that it is my wife,
And gird me so perhaps with his law wit ;
The other, which is policy indeed,
Is that my wife may now be tied at home,
Having no more but her old gown abroad,
And not show me a quirk,[40] while I firk [41]
  others.
Is not this rare ?
  AMBO.   The best that ever was. [369
  SEC. Am I not born to furnish gentlemen ?
  PET. O my dear gossip !
  SEC.   Well, hold, Master Francis ;
Watch, when the lawyer 's out, and put it in.
And now — I will go fetch him.   *Exit.*
  QUICK.   O my dad !
He goes as 't were the Devil to fetch the law-
  yer ;
And devil shall he be, if horns will make him.

Re-enter SECURITY.

PET. Why, how now, gossip ? why stay
  you there musing ?
SEC. A toy, a toy runs in my head, i' faith.
QUICK. A pox of that head ! is there more
  toys yet ?
PET. What is it, pray thee, gossip ?
SEC.   Why, sir, what if you
Should slip away now with my wife's best
  gown,
I having no security for it ?   381

---

[32] So some copies of Q₁; the rest, and Qq₂,₃, *to
finde.*
[33] Chapman has many references to camels with
horns. (Parrott.)
[34] Trick.
[35] Imitators.
[36] Conj. Case; old eds. *Lawyers.*
[37] Fidgety.
[38] A "mutton" was slang for a light woman.
[39] Zounds, 'swounds, by God's wounds.
[40] Trick.
[41] Cheat.

QUICK. For that, I hope, dad, you will take our words.

SEC. Ay, by th' mass, your word; that's a proper staff
For wise Security to lean upon!
But 't is no matter; once I 'll trust my name
On your crack'd credits; let it take no shame.
Fetch the wench, Frank. *Exit.*

QUICK. I 'll wait upon you, sir. —
And fetch you over, you were ne'er so fetch'd.[42]
Go to the tavern, knight; your followers
Dare not be drunk, I think, before their captain. *Exit.* 390

PET. Would I might lead them to no hotter service
Till our Virginian gold were in our purses!
Exit.

[SCENE III][43]

Enter SEAGULL, SPENDALL, *and* SCAPETHRIFT, *in the tavern, with a* Drawer.

SEAGULL. Come, drawer, pierce your neatest[44] hogsheads, and let 's have cheer, not fit for your Billingsgate tavern, but for our Virginian colonel; he will be here instantly.

DRAW. You shall have all things fit, sir; please you have any more wine?

SPEND. More wine, slave! Whether we drink it or no, spill it, and draw more.

SCAPE. Fill all the pots in your house with all sorts of liquor, and let 'em wait [10 on us here like soldiers in their pewter coats; and, though we do not employ them now, yet we will maintain 'em till we do.

DRAW. Said like an honorable captain; you shall have all you can command, sir.
Exit Drawer.

SEA. Come, boys, Virginia longs till we share the rest of her maidenhead.

SPEND. Why, is she inhabited already with any English?

SEA. A whole country of English is [20 there, man, bred of those that were left there in '79; [45] they have married with the Indians, and make 'em bring forth as beautiful faces as any we have in England; and therefore the Indians are so in love with 'em that all the treasure they have they lay at their feet.

SCAPE. But is there such treasure there, Captain, as I have heard?

SEA. I tell thee, gold is more plentiful there than copper is with us; and for as [30 much red copper as I can bring, I 'll have thrice the weight in gold. Why, man, all their dripping-pans and their chamber pots are pure gold;[46] and all the chains with which they chain up their streets are massy gold; all the prisoners they take are fetter'd in gold; and, for[47] rubies and diamonds, they go forth on holidays and gather 'em by the seashore, to hang on their children's coats, and stick in their caps, as commonly as our [40 children wear saffron gilt[48] brooches and groats with holes in 'em.

SCAPE. And is it a pleasant country withal?

SEA. As ever the sun shin'd on; temperate, and full of all sorts of excellent viands: wild boar is as common there as our tamest bacon is here; venison, as mutton. And then you shall live freely there, without sergeants,[49] or courtiers, or lawyers, or intelligencers,[50] [51] only a few industrious Scots, [50 perhaps, who indeed are dispers'd over the face of the whole earth. But, as for them, there are no greater friends to Englishmen and England, when they are out [o]n 't, in the world, than they are. And, for my part, I would a hundred thousand of 'em were there, for we are all one countrymen now, ye know; and we should find ten times more comfort of them there than we do here.[52] Then, for your means to advancement there, it is [60 simple, and not preposterously mix'd. You may be an alderman there, and never be scavenger; you may be [a nobleman],[53] and never be a slave. You may come to preferment enough, and never be a pander; to riches and fortune enough, and have never the more villainy nor the less wit.[54]

[46] This touch, like others in this speech, is from More's *Utopia*, as Schelling notes.
[47] As for.
[48] A cheap imitation of gold.
[49] Court officers charged with arresting and summoning.
[50] Spies, informers.
[51] Here begins the passage which appears only in the first issue of Q 1.
[52] Here the expunged passage ends.
[53] So only in the first issue of Q 1; second issue, and Qq 2, 3, *any other officer.*
[54] At this point the second issue of Q 1, followed by Qq 2, 3, adds the following, to fill out the page shortened in the original state: *Besides, there we shall haue no more Law then Conscience, and not too much of either; serue God inough, eate and drinke inough; and* inough is as good as a Feast.

[42] Tricked.
[43] A room in the Blue Anchor Tavern in Billingsgate.
[44] Purest.
[45] Probably alluding to the "lost colony" of 1587. The first recorded attempt to settle was in 1585.

SPEND. Gods me! and how far is it thither?

SEA. Some six weeks' sail, no more, with [70 any indifferent good wind. And, if I get to any part of the coast of Africa, I'll sail thither with any wind; or, when I come to Cape Finisterre, there's a foreright wind continually wafts us till we come at Virginia. — See, our colonel's come.

Enter SIR PETRONEL.

PET. Well met, good Captain Seagull and my noble gentlemen! Now the sweet hour of our freedom is at hand. — Come, drawer! Fill us some carouses, and prepare [80 us for the mirth that will be occasioned presently. Here will be a pretty wench, gentlemen, that will bear us company all our voyage.

SEA. Whatsoever she be, here's to her health, noble colonel, both with cap and knee.

PET. Thanks, kind Captain Seagull; she's one I love dearly and must not be known, till we be free from all that know us. And so, gentlemen, here's to her health. 90

AMBO.[55] Let it come, worthy Colonel; we do hunger and thirst for it!

PET. Afore Heaven, you have hit the phrase of one that her presence will touch from the foot to the forehead,[56] if ye knew it.

SPEND. Why, then, we will join his forehead with her health, sir; and, Captain Scapethrift, here's to 'em both.

Enter SECURITY *and* BRAMBLE.

SEC. See, see, Master Bramble, 'fore Heaven, their voyage cannot but prosper! [100 they are o' their knees for success to it!

BRAM. And they pray to god Bacchus.

SEC. God save my brave colonel, with all his tall captains and corporals.[57] See, sir, my worshipful learned counsel, Master Bramble, is come to take his leave of you.

PET. Worshipful Master Bramble, how far do you draw us into the sweet briar of your kindness! — Come, Captain Seagull, another health to this rare Bramble, that [110 hath never a prick about him.

SEA. I pledge his most smooth disposition, sir. — Come, Master Security, bend your sup-

porters,[58] and pledge this notorious [59] health here.

SEC. Bend you yours likewise, Master Bramble; for it is you shall pledge me.

SEA. Not so, Master Security; he must not pledge his own health.

SEC. No, Master Captain? 120

Enter QUICKSILVER, *with* WINNIE, *disguis'd.*

Why, then, here's one is fitly come to do him that honor.

QUICK. Here's the gentlewoman your cousin, sir, whom, with much entreaty, I have brought to take her leave of you in a tavern; asham'd whereof, you must pardon her if she put not off her mask.

PET. Pardon me, sweet Cousin; my kind desire to see you before I went made me so importunate to entreat your presence [130 here.

SEC. How now, Master Francis, have you honor'd this presence with a fair gentlewoman?

QUICK. Pray, sir, take you no notice of her, for she will not be known to you.

SEC. But my learned counsel, Master Bramble here, I hope may know her.

QUICK. No more than you, sir, at this time; his learning must pardon her. 140

SEC. Well, God pardon her, for my part; and I do, I'll be sworn. And so, Master Francis, here's to all that are going eastward to-night towards Cuckold's Haven; [60] and so to the health of Master Bramble.

QUICK. I pledge it, sir. [*kneeling*] Hath it gone round, captains?

SEA. It has, sweet Frank; and the round closes with thee.

QUICK. Well, sir, here's to all eastward [150 and toward [61] cuckolds, and so to famous Cuckold's Haven, so fatally rememb'red.

Surgit.

PET. [*to* WINIFRED] Nay, pray thee, coz, weep not. — Gossip Security.

SEC. Ay, my brave gossip.

PET. A word, I beseech you, sir. — [*aside*] Our friend, Mistress Bramble here, is so dissolv'd in tears, that she drowns the whole mirth of our meeting. Sweet gossip, take her aside and comfort her. 160

SEC. [*aside to* WINIFRED] Pity of all true love, Mistress Bramble; what, weep you

---

[55] Spendall and Scapethrift.
[56] Alluding to the horns of Security.
[57] There were petty officers so termed.

[58] Kneel.   [59] Very notable, remarkable.
[60] On the Surrey side a mile or so below London Bridge.   [61] Promising.

to enjoy your love? What's the cause, lady?
Is't because your husband is so near, and
your heart earns [62] to have a little abus'd [63]
him? Alas, alas! the offence is too common
to be respected.[64] So great a grace hath seldom chanc'd to so unthankful a woman;
to be rid of an old jealous dotard, to enjoy
the arms of a loving young knight, that, [170
when your prickless Bramble is withered with
grief of your loss, will make you flourish
afresh in the bed of a lady.

Re-enter Drawer.

DRAW. Sir Petronel, here's one of your
watermen come to tell you it will be flood
these three hours; and that 't will be dangerous going against the tide; for the sky is
overcast, and there was a porpoise even now
seen at London Bridge, which is always the
messenger of tempests, he says. 180
PET. A porpoise! — what's that to th'
purpose? [65] Charge him, if he love his life,
to attend [66] us. Can we not reach Blackwall,
where my ship lies, against the tide, and in
spite of tempests? Captains and gentlemen,
we'll begin a new ceremony at the beginning
of our voyage, which I believe will be follow'd
of all future adventurers.
SEA. What's that, good Colonel?
PET. This, Captain Seagull. We'll [190
have our provided supper brought aboard Sir
Francis Drake's ship,[67] that hath compass'd
the world; where, with full cups and banquets, we will do sacrifice for a prosperous
voyage. My mind gives me that some good
spirits of the waters should haunt the desert
ribs of her, and be auspicious to all that honor
her memory, and will with like orgies enter
their voyages.
SEA. Rarely conceited! [68] One health [200
more to this motion, and aboard to perform
it. He that will not this night be drunk, may
he never be sober.

They compass in WINIFRED, *dance
the drunken round, and drink
carouses.*

BRAM. Sir Petronel and his honorable
captains, in these young services we old
servitors may be spar'd. We only came to take

[62] Yearns, grieves.
[63] Deceived.
[64] Considered.
[65] Note the pun.
[66] Wait for.
[67] At Deptford.
[68] *I.e.*, an excellent idea.

our leaves, and, with one health to you all, I'll
be bold to do so. Here, neighbor Security,
to the health of Sir Petronel and all his
captains. 210
SEC. You must bend, then, Master Bramble. [*They kneel.*] So, now I am for you.
I have one corner of my brain, I hope, fit
to bear one carouse more. Here, lady, to
you that are encompass'd there, and are
asham'd of our company. [*They drink, and
rise.*] Ha, ha, ha! by my troth, my learn'd
counsel, Master Bramble, my mind runs so
of Cuckold's Haven to-night that my head
runs over with admiration.[69] 220
BRAM. [*aside to* SECURITY] But is not that
your wife, neighbor?
SEC. [*aside to* BRAMBLE.] No, by my troth,
Master Bramble. Ha, ha, ha! A pox of all
Cuckold's Havens, I say!
BRAM. [*aside to* SECURITY] A' my faith, her
garments are exceeding like your wife's.
SEC. *Cucullus non facit monachum*,[70] my
learned counsel; all are not cuckolds that
seem so; nor all seem not that are so. [230
Give me your hand, my learn'd counsel;
you and I will sup somewhere else than at
Sir Francis Drake's ship to-night. — Adieu,
my noble gossip!
BRAM. Good fortune, brave captains; fair
skies God send ye!
OMNES. Farewell, my hearts, farewell!
PET. Gossip, laugh no more at Cuckold's
Haven, gossip.
SEC. I have done, I have done, sir. — [240
Will you lead, Master Bramble? Ha, ha, ha!
PET. Captain Seagull, charge a boat.
OMNES. A boat, a boat, a boat!

Exeunt [*all except* Drawer.]

DRAW. Y' are in a proper taking indeed,
to take a boat, especially at this time of night,
and against tide and tempest. They say
yet, "Drunken men never take harm." This
night will try the truth of that proverb. *Exit.*

[SCENE IV] [71]

Enter SECURITY.

SEC. What, Winnie! — Wife, I say! —
Outdoors at this time! Where should I
seek the gadfly? — Billingsgate, Billingsgate,
Billingsgate! She's gone with the knight,
she's gone with the knight! woe be to thee,

[69] Wonder.
[70] The cowl does not make the monk.
[71] Security's house.

Billingsgate! — A boat! a boat! a boat! a full hundred marks for a boat!   *Exit.*

ACT IV — SCENE I[1]

Enter SLITGUT *with a pair of ox-horns, discovering Cuckold's Haven above.*[2]

SLIT. All hail, fair haven of married men only! for there are none but married men cuckolds. For my part, I presume not to arrive here but in my master's behalf, a poor butcher[3] of Eastcheap, who sends me to set up, in honor of Saint Luke,[4] these necessary ensigns of his homage. And up I got this morning, thus early, to get up to the top of this famous tree, that is all fruit and no leaves, to advance this crest of my master's occu- [10 pation. Up then! — Heaven and Saint Luke bless me, that I be not blown into the Thames as I climb, with this furious tempest. 'Slight! I think the Devil be abroad, in likeness of a storm, to rob me of my horns! Hark how he roars! Lord! what a coil the Thames keeps! She bears some unjust burthen, I believe, that she kicks and curvets thus to cast it. Heaven bless all honest passengers that are upon her back now; for the bit is out of her mouth, [20 I see, and she will run away with 'em! — So, so! I think I have made it look the right way. — It runs against London Bridge, as it were, even full butt. And now let me discover from this lofty prospect, what pranks the rude Thames plays in her desperate lunacy. O me! here's a boat has been cast away hard by. Alas, alas, see one of her passengers laboring for his life to land at this haven here! Pray Heaven he may recover it! His [30 next land is even just under me. — Hold out yet a little; whatsoever thou art, pray, and take a good heart to thee. — 'T is a man;

— take a man's heart to thee; yet a little further, get up a' thy legs, man; now 't is shallow enough. So, so, so! Alas! he's down again. Hold thy wind, father. — 'T is a man in a nightcap. So! now he's got up again; now he's past the worst: yet, thanks be to Heaven, he comes toward me pretty and [40 strongly.

Enter SECURITY, *without his hat, in a nightcap, wet band, etc.*

SEC. Heaven, I beseech thee, how have I offended thee! where am I cast ashore now, that I may go a righter way home by land? Let me see; Oh, I am scarce able to look about me. Where is there any sea-mark that I am acquainted withal?

SLIT. Look up, father; are you acquainted with this mark?

SEC. What! landed at Cuckold's [50 Haven? Hell and damnation! I will run back and drown myself.   *He falls down.*

SLIT. Poor man, how weak he is! the weak water has wash'd away his strength.

SEC. Landed at Cuckold's Haven! If it had not been to die twenty times alive, I should never have 'scap'd death! I will never arise more; I will grovel here and eat dirt till I be chok'd; I will make the gentle earth do that which the cruel water has denied me. 60

SLIT. Alas, good father, be not so desperate! Rise man; if you will, I'll come presently and lead you home.

SEC. Home! shall I make any know my home that has known me thus abroad? How low shall I crouch away, that no eye may see me? I will creep on the earth while I live, and never look heaven in the face more.

Exit, creep[ing].

SLIT. What young planet reigns now, trow, that old men are so foolish? What des- [70 perate young swaggerer would have been abroad such a weather as this, upon the water? — Ay me, see another remnant of this unfortunate shipwrack! — or some other. A woman, i' faith, a woman; though it be almost at Saint Kath'rine's,[5] I discern it to be a woman, for all her body is above the water, and her clothes swim about her most handsomely. Oh, they bear her up most bravely! Has not a woman reason to love the tak- [80 ing up of her clothes the better while she lives, for this? Alas, how busy the rude Thames

---

[1] Cuckold's Haven; the scene shifts, however, temporarily (as hereafter noted) to other points along Thames-side.

[2] Evidently he opens the curtains of the balcony above the inner stage, disclosing a representation of the pole that stood at Cuckold's Haven with a pair of horns on it.

[3] The London butchers kept the pole repaired and supplied with horns.

[4] A fair, called "Horn Fair", was held annually on St. Luke's Day (October 18) at Charlton, near Greenwich. Both Cuckold's Haven and the Fair were supposed to be connected with an amour of King John's; caught by the husband, the King gave him an estate, with the stipulation that on every St. Luke's Day he must perambulate it with a pair of horns on his head.

[5] A women's reformatory, on the north bank, near the Tower.

is about her ! A pox a' that wave ! It will drown her, i' faith, 't will drown her ! Cry God mercy, she has scap'd it ! I thank Heaven she has scap'd it ! Oh, how she swims, like a mermaid ! Some vigilant body look out and save her. That 's well said ; [6] just where the priest fell in,[7] there 's one sets down a ladder, and goes to take her up. God's blessing [90 a' thy heart, boy ! Now take her up in thy arms and to bed with her. She 's up, she 's up ! She 's a beautiful woman, I warrant her ; the billows durst not devour her.

Enter the Drawer *in the tavern before, with* WINIFRED.[8]

DRAW. How fare you now, lady?

WIN. Much better, my good friend, than I wish : as one desperate of her fame, now my life is preserv'd.

DRAW. Comfort yourself. That Power that preserved you from death can like- [100 wise defend you from infamy, howsoever you deserve it. Were not you one that took boat late this night, with a knight and other gentle-men at Billingsgate?

WIN. Unhappy that I am, I was.

DRAW. I am glad it was my good hap to come down thus far after you, to a house of my friends here in Saint Kath'rine's, since I am now happily made a mean to your rescue from the ruthless tempest, which, when [110 you took boat, was so extreme, and the gentle-man that brought you forth so desperate and unsober, that I fear'd long ere this I should hear of your shipwrack, and therefore, with little other reason, made thus far this way. And this I must tell you, since perhaps you may make use of it, there was left behind you at our tavern, brought by a porter hir'd by the young gentleman that brought you, a gentlewoman's gown, hat, stockings, and [120 shoes ; which, if they be yours, and you please to shift you, taking a hard bed here in this house of my friend, I will presently go fetch you.

WIN. Thanks, my good friend, for your more than good news. The gown with all things bound with it are mine ; which if you please to fetch as you have promis'd, I

will boldly receive the kind favor you have offered till your return ; entreating you, [130 by all the good you have done in preserving me hitherto, to let none take knowledge of what favor you do me, or where such a one as I am bestowed, lest you incur me much more damage in my fame than you have done me pleasure in preserving my life.

DRAW. Come in, lady, and shift yourself ; resolve that nothing but your own pleasure shall be us'd in your discovery.

WIN. Thank you, good friend ; the [140 time may come, I shall requite you.

Exeunt [Drawer *and* WINIFRED].

SLIT.[9] See, see, see ! I hold my life, there 's some other a-taking up at Wapping [10] now ! Look, what a sort [11] of people cluster about the gallows there ! in good troth, it is so. O me ! a fine young gentleman ! What, and taken up at the gallows? Heaven grant he be not one day taken down there ! A' my life, it is ominous. Well, he is delivered for the time. I see the people have all left [150 him ; yet will I keep my prospect awhile, to see if any more have been shipwrack'd.

Enter QUICKSILVER, *bareheade[d].*[12]

QUICK. Accurs'd that ever I was sav'd or
  born !
How fatal is my sad arrival here !
As if the stars and Providence spake to me,
And said, " The drift of all unlawful courses,
Whatever end they dare propose themselves,
In frame of their licentious policies,
In the firm order of just destiny,
They are the ready highways to our ruins." [160
I know not what to do ; my wicked hopes
Are, with this tempest, torn up by the roots.
Oh, which way shall I bend my desperate
  steps,
In which unsufferable shame and misery
Will not attend them? I will walk this bank,
And see if I can meet the other relics
Of our poor shipwrack'd crew, or hear of them.
The knight, alas, was so far gone with wine,
And th' other three, that I refus'd their boat,
And took the hapless woman in another, 170
Who cannot but be sunk, whatever Fortune
Hath wrought upon the others' desperate
  lives. [*Exit.*]

[6] Done.
[7] No more is known of this event, though it is also mentioned by Taylor, the Water Poet. (Harris.)
[8] The scene is now near St. Katherine's, though Slitgut, whose presence we are supposed to ignore, remains on his perch. Perhaps the curtains of the upper stage were closed at this point.

[9] The scene is again Cuckold's Haven.
[10] On the north bank, a little below the city. Pirates were hanged there, at the water's edge.
[11] Group.
[12] The scene is now Wapping.

Enter PETRONEL *and* SEAGULL, *bareheaded.*[13]

PET. Zounds, Captain, I tell thee we are cast up o' the coast of France. 'Sfoot! I am not drunk still, I hope! Dost remember where we were last night?

SEA. No, by my troth, knight, not I; but methinks we have been a horrible while upon the water and in the water.

PET. Ay me, we are undone forever. [180 Hast any money about thee?

SEA. Not a penny, by Heaven!

PET. Not a penny betwixt us, and cast ashore in France!

SEA. Faith, I cannot tell that; my brains nor mine eyes are not mine own yet.

Enter two Gentlemen.

PET. 'Sfoot! wilt not believe me? I know 't by th' elevation of the pole, and by the altitude and latitude of the climate. See! Here comes a couple of French gentlemen; [190 I knew we were in France; dost thou think our Englishmen are so Frenchified that a man knows not whether he be in France or in England, when he sees 'em? What shall we do? We must e'en to 'em, and entreat some relief of 'em. Life is sweet, and we have no other means to relieve our lives now but their charities.

SEA. Pray you, do you beg on 'em then; you can speak French. 200

PET. *Monsieur, plaist il d'avoir pitie de nostre grande infortunes? Je suis un povre chevalier d'Angleterre qui a souffri l'infortune de naufrage.*

1 GENT. *Un povre chevalier d'Angleterre?*

PET. *Oui, monsieur, il est trop vraye; mais vous scaves bien nous sommes toutes subject a fortune.*

2 GENT. A poor knight of England? — a poor knight of Windsor,[14] are you not? [210 Why speak you this broken French, when y' are a whole Englishman? On what coast are you, think you?

PET. On the coast of France, sir.

1 GENT. On the coast of Dogs, sir; y' are i' th' Isle a' Dogs, I tell you. I see y' ave been wash'd in the Thames here, and I believe ye were drown'd in a tavern before, or else you would never have took boat in such a dawning as this was. Farewell, farewell; [220 we will not know you, for shaming of you. — I ken the man weel; he 's one of my thirty pound knights.[15]

2 GENT. No, no, this is he that stole his knighthood o' the grand day for four pound, giving to a page all the money in 's purse, I wot well. *Exeunt* [Gentlemen].

SEA. Death! Colonel, I knew you were overshot.

PET. Sure I think now, indeed, Captain Seagull, we were something overshot. 231

Enter QUICKSILVER.

What! my sweet Frank Quicksilver! dost thou survive, to rejoice me? But what! nobody at thy heels, Frank? Ay me! what is become of poor Mistress Security?

QUICK. Faith, gone quite from her name, as she is from her fame, I think; I left her to the mercy of the water.

SEA. Let her go, let her go! Let us go to our ship at Blackwall, and shift us. 240

PET. Nay, by my troth, let our clothes rot upon us, and let us rot in them; twenty to one our ship is attach'd by this time! If we set her not under sail this last tide, I never look'd for any other. Woe, woe is me! what shall become of us? The last money we could make [16] the greedy Thames has devour'd; and, if our ship be attach'd, there is no hope can relieve us.

QUICK. 'Sfoot, knight! what an un- [250 knightly faintness transports thee! Let our ship sink, and all the world that 's without us be taken from us, I hope I have some tricks in this brain of mine shall not let us perish.

SEA. Well said, Frank, i' faith. O my nimble-spirited Quicksilver! 'Fore God, would thou hadst been our colonel!

PET. I like his spirit rarely; but I see no means he has to support that spirit.

QUICK. Go to, knight! I have more [260 means than thou art aware of. I have not liv'd amongst goldsmiths and goldmakers all this while but I have learned something worthy of my time with 'em. And, not to let thee stink where thou stand'st, knight, I 'll let thee know some of my skill presently.

SEA. Do, good Frank, I beseech thee.

QUICK. I will blanch copper so cunningly that it shall endure all proofs but the test:

---

[13] The scene is now the Isle of Dogs, a marshy peninsula nearly opposite Greenwich.
[14] Pensioners of the king, who gave them quarters in Windsor Castle.
[15] A gibe at James' indiscriminate creation of knights. The Scotch brogue here can only be meant to mimic the King's accent. It is strange that this passage was not expunged. [16] Raise, get together.

it shall endure malleation,[17] it shall have [270
the ponderosity of Luna,[18] and the tenacity
of Luna, by no means friable.

PET. 'Slight! where learn'st thou these
terms, trow?

QUICK. Tush, knight! the terms of this
art every ignorant quacksalver is perfect in;
but I'll tell you how yourself shall blanch
copper thus cunningly. Take ars'nic, otherwise called realga (which indeed is plain
ratsbane); sublime [him][19] three or [280
four times; then take the sublimate of this
realga and put [him][19] into a glass, into
chymia,[20] and let [him][19] have a convenient decoction natural, four-and-twenty
hours, and he will become perfectly fix'd;
then take this fixed powder, and project
him upon well-purg'd copper, *et habebis
magisterium*.[21]

AMBO. Excellent Frank, let us hug thee!

QUICK. Nay, this I will do besides: [290
I'll take you off twelvepence from every
angel, with a kind of *aqua fortis*, and never
deface any part of the image.

PET. But then it will want weight!

QUICK. You shall restore that thus: take
your *sal achyme*[22] prepar'd, and your distill'd urine, and let your angels lie in it but
four-and-twenty hours, and they shall have
their perfect weight again. Come on, now;
I hope this is enough to put some spirit [300
into the livers of you; I'll infuse more another
time. We have saluted the proud air long
enough with our bare sconces. Now will I
have you to a wench's house of mine at London, there make shift to shift us,[23] and, after,
take such fortunes as the stars shall assign us.

AMBO. Notable Frank, we will ever adore
thee!   *Exeunt* [*all but* SLITGUT].

Enter Drawer *with* WINIFRED *new attir'd*.[24]

WIN. Now, sweet friend, you have brought
me near enough your tavern, which I [310
desired that I might with some color be seen
near, inquiring for my husband, who, I must
tell you, stale[25] thither last night with my
wet gown we have left at your friend's, which,

to continue your former honest kindness, let
me pray you to keep close[26] from the knowledge of any; and so, with all vow of your
requital, let me now entreat you to leave me
to my woman's wit, and fortune.

DRAW. All shall be done you desire; [320
and so all the fortune you can wish for attend
you.   *Exit* Drawer.

Enter SECURITY.

SEC. I will once more to this unhappy
tavern before I shift one rag of me more; that
I may there know what is left behind, and
what news of their passengers. I have bought
me a hat and band with the little money I
had about me, and made the streets a little
leave staring at my nightcap.

WIN. Oh, my dear husband! where [330
have you been to-night?[27] All night abroad at
taverns? Rob me of my garments, and fare
as one run away from me? Alas! is this
seemly for a man of your credit, of your age,
and affection to your wife?

SEC. What should I say? how miraculously sorts this! Was not I at home, and
call'd thee last night?

WIN. Yes, sir, the harmless sleep you
broke; and my answer to you would [340
have witness'd it, if you had had the patience
to have stay'd and answered me; but your
so sudden retreat made me imagine you were
gone to Master Bramble's, and so rested
patient and hopeful of your coming again,
till this your unbelieved[28] absence brought
me abroad with no less than wonder, to seek
you where the false knight had carried you.

SEC. Villain and monster that I was! How
have I abus'd thee! I was suddenly [350
gone indeed, for my sudden jealousy transferred me! I will say no more but this, dear
wife: I suspected thee.

WIN. Did you suspect me?

SEC. Talk not of it, I beseech thee; I am
ashamed to imagine it. I will home, I will
home; and every morning on my knees ask
thee heartily forgiveness.

       Exeunt [SECURITY *and* WINIFRED].

SLIT.[29] Now will I descend my honorable
prospect, the farthest-seeing sea-mark of [360
the world: no marvel, then, if I could see
two miles about me. I hope the red tempest's
anger be now overblown, which sure I think
Heaven sent as a punishment for profaning

---

[17] Hammering.
[18] Silver.
[19] Conj. Simpson; old eds. *'hem*.
[20] Chemical process or reaction (?).
[21] Thou wilt have the philosopher's stone.
[22] Unexplained.
[23] Change our clothes.
[24] The scene is now in the city, near the Blue
Anchor, at Billingsgate.
[25] Q₃ *stole*.

[26] Secret.   [27] Last night.   [28] Incredible.
[29] The scene is again Cuckold's Haven.

holy Saint Luke's memory with so ridiculous a custom. Thou dishonest satire! Farewell to honest married men! farewell to all sorts and degrees of thee![30] Farewell, thou horn of hunger,[31] that call'st th' inns a' court [32] to their manger! Farewell, thou horn [370 of abundance,[33] that adornest [34] the headsmen of the commonwealth! Farewell, thou horn of direction, that is the city lanthorn![35] Farewell, thou horn of pleasure, the ensign of the huntsman! Farewell, thou horn of destiny, th' ensign of the married man! Farewell, thou horn tree, that bearest nothing but stone [36] fruit!   *Exit.*

[SCENE II] [37]

TOUCH. Ha, sirrah! thinks my knight adventurer we can [38] no point of our compass? Do we not know north-north-east, north-east and by east, east and by north, nor plain eastward? Ha! have we never heard of Virginia, nor the *Cavallaria*, nor the *Colonoria?* [39] Can we discover no discoveries? Well, mine errant Sir Flash, and my runagate Quicksilver, you may drink drunk, crack cans, hurl away a brown [40] dozen of [10 Monmouth caps [41] or so, in sea-ceremony to your *bon voyage;* but, for reaching any coast, save the coast of Kent or Essex, with this tide, or with this fleet, I'll be your warrant for a Gravesend [42] toast. There's that gone afore will stay your admiral [43] and vice-admiral and rear-admiral, were they all (as they are) but one pinnace, and under sail, as well as a remora,[44] doubt it not; and from this sconce,[45]

---

[30] *I.e.,* O thou unchaste satire! I will now say farewell to chaste married men, and (what is the same thing, since cuckoldom is universal), farewell to all the varieties of thee, O satirical horned pole; for all cuckolds, since like thee they bear horns, may be termed varieties of thee.
[31] Dinner horn.
[32] Where the law students lived.
[33] Cornucopia.
[34] *I.e.,* ad-hornest.
[35] With another pun on *horn;* it was used in lanterns.
[36] With a pun on the meaning "testicle."
[37] A room in Touchstone's house.
[38] Know.
[39] "Latin law terms signifying the landholding of a knight and of an ordinary colonist." (Schelling.)
[40] Round.
[41] Sailors' caps.
[42] *I.e.,* since this port was far down the river, "final", "farewell", with an obvious pun.
[43] Flagship.
[44] "The sucking-fish which was supposed to fasten upon the bottom of ships and arrest their progress." (Parrott.)
[45] (1) head, (2) fort.

without either powder or shot. Work [20 upon that now! Nay, an you'll show tricks, we'll vie with you a little. My daughter, his lady, was sent eastward by land to a castle of his i' the air, in what region [46] I know not, and, as I hear, was glad to take up her lodging in her coach, she and her two waiting women (her maid, and her mother), like three snails in a shell, and the coachman a-top on [47] 'em, I think. Since, they have all found the way back again by Weeping Cross; [48] but I'll [30 not see 'em. And, for two on 'em, madam and her malkin,[49] they are like to bite o' the bridle for William,[50] as the poor horses have done all this while that hurried 'em, or else go graze o' the common. So should my Dame Touchstone too; but she has been my cross these thirty years, and I'll now keep her to fright away sprites, i' faith. I wonder I hear no news of my son Golding! He was sent for to the Guildhall this morning [40 betimes,[51] and I marvel at the matter; if I had not laid up comfort and hope in him, I should grow desperate of all. See, he is come i' my thought!—

Enter GOLDING.

How now, son? What news at the Court of Aldermen?

GOLD. Troth, sir, an accident somewhat strange; else, it hath little in it worth the reporting.

TOUCH. What? It is not borrowing [50 of money, then?

GOLD. No, sir; it hath pleas'd the worshipful Commoners [52] of the city to take me one i' their number at presentation of the inquest [53]——

TOUCH. Ha!

GOLD. And the alderman of the ward wherein I dwell to appoint me his deputy ——

TOUCH. How?

GOLD. In which place I have had an [60 oath minist'red me, since I went.

TOUCH. Now, my dear and happy son, let me kiss thy new Worship, and a little boast mine own happiness in thee. — What a fortune was it (or rather my judgment,

---

[46] Division of the atmosphere according to height.
[47] Of.
[48] *I.e.,* have repented.
[49] Maid.
[50] *I.e.,* chew the bit (instead of food) for all of me.
[51] Early.
[52] Common Councilors.
[53] Committee of inquiry; *i.e.,* on report of the nominating committee.

indeed) for me first to see that in his disposition which a whole city so conspires to second! Ta'en into the livery of his company [54] the first day of his freedom! Now, not a week married, chosen Commoner and alderman's [70 deputy in a day! Note but the reward of a thrifty course. The wonder of his time! Well, I will honor Master Alderman for this act, as becomes me, and shall think the better of the Common Council's wisdom and worship, while I live, for thus meeting, or but coming after me, in the opinion of his desert. Forward, my sufficient [55] son! and, as this is the first, so esteem it the least step to that high and prime honor that expects thee.   80

GOLD. Sir, as I was not ambitious of this, so I covet no higher place; it hath dignity enough, if it will but save me from contempt; and I had rather my bearing in this or any other office should add worth to it than the place give the least opinion to me.

TOUCH. Excellently spoken! This modest answer of thine blushes, as if it said, "I will wear scarlet [56] shortly." Worshipful son! I cannot contain myself; I must tell thee, [90 I hope to see thee one o' the monuments of our city, and reckon'd among her worthies, to be rememb'red the same day with the Lady Ramsey [57] and grave Gresham,[58] when the famous fable of Whittington and his puss shall be forgotten, and thou and thy acts become the posies [59] for hospitals; when thy name shall be written upon conduits, and thy deeds play'd i' thy lifetime by the best companies of actors, and be call'd their get-penny. This I divine; this I prophesy.   101

GOLD. Sir, engage not your expectation farder than my abilities will answer; I, that know mine own strengths, fear 'em; and there is so seldom a loss in promising the least that commonly it brings with it a welcome deceit. I have other news for you, sir.

TOUCH. None more welcome, I am sure.

GOLD. They have their degree of welcome, I dare affirm. The colonel and all his [110 company, this morning putting forth drunk from Billingsgate, had like to have been cast away o' this side Greenwich; and, as I have

intelligence by a false brother,[60] are come dropping to town like so many masterless men, i' their doublets and hose, without hat or cloak or any other ——

TOUCH. A miracle! the justice of Heaven! Where are they? Let's go presently and lay for 'em.   120

GOLD. I have done that already, sir, both by constables and other officers, who shall take 'em at their old Anchor, and with less tumult or suspicion than if yourself were seen in 't, under color of a great press [61] that is now abroad; and they shall here be brought afore me.

TOUCH. Prudent and politic son! Disgrace 'em all that ever thou canst; their ship I have already arrested. How to my wish [130 it falls out that thou hast the place of a justicer upon 'em! I am partly glad of the injury done to me, that thou mayst punish it. Be severe i' thy place, like a new officer o' the first quarter, unreflected.[62] You hear how our lady is come back with her train from the invisible castle?

GOLD. No; where is she?

TOUCH. Within; but I ha' not seen her yet, nor her mother, who now begins to [140 wish her daughter undubb'd, they say, and that she had walk'd a foot-pace with her sister. Here they come; stand back.

[*Enter*] MISTRESS TOUCHSTONE, GERTRUDE, MILDRED, [*and*] SINDEFY.

God save your Ladyship; 'save your good Ladyship! Your Ladyship is welcome from your enchanted castle; so are your beauteous retinue. I hear your knight errant is travell'd on strange adventures. Surely, in my mind, your Ladyship hath "fish'd fair, and caught a frog," [63] as the saying is.   150

MIST. TOUCH. Speak to your father, madam, and kneel down.

GER. Kneel? I hope I am not brought so low yet; though my knight be run away, and has sold my land, I am a lady still.

TOUCH. Your Ladyship says true, madam; and it is fitter and a greater decorum that I should curtsy to you that are a knight's wife and a lady than you be brought a' your knees to me, who am a poor cullion [64] and your [160 father.

---

[54] Not all the members of the companies had the privilege of wearing the livery.
[55] Able, competent.
[56] Become an alderman.
[57] Wife of the Lord Mayor of 1577, and benefactress of Christ's Hospital.
[58] The great Elizabethan financier and philanthropist.
[59] Inscriptions.

[60] Informer.   [61] Impressment.
[62] Incapable of being deflected.
[63] This and most of the following sayings, not all of which are italicized in the old eds., may be found in John Heywood's *Proverbs*.   [64] Base fellow.

GER. Law! my father knows his duty.

MIST. T. Oh, child!

TOUCH. And therefore I do desire your Ladyship, my good Lady Flash, in all humility, to depart my obscure cottage, and return in quest of your bright and most transparent castle, "how ever presently conceal'd to mortal eyes." And, as for one poor woman of your train here, I will take that order [170 she shall no longer be a charge unto you, nor help to spend your Ladyship; she shall stay at home with me, and not go abroad, not put you to the pawning of an odd coach horse or three wheels, but take part with the Touchstone. If we lack, we will not complain to your Ladyship. And so, good madam, with your damosel here, please you to let us see your straight backs in equipage; [65] for truly here is no roost for such chickens as you are, or birds o' [180 your feather, if it like your Ladyship.

GER. Marry, fyste [66] o' [67] your kindness! I thought as much. Come away, Sin; we shall " as soon get a fart from a dead man as a farthing " of court'sy here.

MIL. Oh, good Sister!

GER. Sister, Sir Reverence! Come away, I say; hunger drops out at his nose.

GOLD. Oh, madam, " Fair words never hurt the tongue."   190

GER. How say you by that? You come out with your gold-ends now!

MIST. T. Stay, Lady-daughter. Good husband —

TOUCH. Wife, " no man loves his fetters, be they made of gold." I list not " ha' my head fast'ned under my child's girdle ; " " as she has brew'd, so let her drink," a' God's name. She " went witless to wedding," now she may " go wisely a-begging." It's [200 but honeymoon yet with her Ladyship; she has coach horses, apparel, jewels yet left; she needs care for no friends, nor take knowledge of father, mother, brother, sister, or anybody. When those are pawn'd or spent, perhaps we shall return into the list of her acquaintance.

GER. I scorn it, i' faith. — Come, Sin.

MIST. T. Oh, madam, why do you provoke your father thus?

Exit GERTRUDE [*with* SINDEFY].

TOUCH. Nay, nay, e'en " let pride go [210 afore; shame will follow after," I warrant you. Come, why dost thou weep now?

Thou art not " the first good cow " hast " had an ill calf," I trust. — [*Exit* MISTRESS TOUCHSTONE.] What 's the news with that fellow?

Enter Constable.

GOLD. Sir, the knight and your man Quicksilver are without; will you ha' 'em brought in?

TOUCH. Oh, by any means.[68] [*Exit* Constable.] And, son, here 's a chair; ap- [220 pear terrible unto 'em on the first interview. Let them behold the melancholy [69] of a magistrate, and taste the fury of a citizen in office.

GOLD. Why, sir, I can do nothing to 'em, except you charge 'em with somewhat.

TOUCH. I will charge 'em and recharge 'em, rather than authority should want foil to set it off.   [*Offers* GOLDING *a chair.*]

GOLD. No, good sir, I will not.

TOUCH. Son, it is your place; by any [230 means —

GOLD. Believe it, I will not, sir.

Enter KNIGHT PETRONEL, QUICKSILVER, Constable, [*and*] Officers.

PET. How misfortune pursues us still in our misery!

QUICK. Would it had been my fortune to have been truss'd up [70] at Wapping rather than ever ha' come here!

PET. Or mine to have famish'd in the Island!

QUICK. Must Golding sit upon us?   240

CON. You might carry [a *Master*] [71] under your girdle to Master Deputy's Worship.

GOLD. What are those, Master Constable?

CON. An't please your Worship, a couple of masterless men I press'd for the Low Countries, sir.

GOLD. Why do you not carry 'em to Bridewell,[72] according to your order, they may be shipp'd away?

CON. An't please your Worship, one [250 of 'em says he is a knight; and we thought good to show him to your Worship, for our discharge.[73]

GOLD. Which is he?

CON. This, sir.

---

[65] In marching order.
[66] Break wind.
[67] On.

[68] Certainly, by all means.
[69] Anger.
[70] *I.e.*, hanged like a pirate.
[71] *I.e.*, you might say *Master* in referring to the Deputy. Old eds. *an M.*
[72] The London workhouse; vagabonds were detained there.
[73] To clear ourselves of responsibility.

GOLD. And what's the other?

CON. A knight's fellow, sir, an't please you.

GOLD. What! a knight and his fellow thus accout'red? Where are their hats and [260 feathers, their rapiers and their cloaks?

QUICK. [aside] Oh, they mock us.

CON. Nay, truly, sir, they had cast both their feathers and hats, too, before we see 'em. Here's all their furniture,[74] an't please you, that we found. They say knights are now to be known without feathers, like cock'rels by their spurs, sir.

GOLD. What are their names, say they?

TOUCH. [aside] Very well, this. He [270 should not take knowledge of 'em in his place, indeed.

CON. This is Sir Petronel Flash.

TOUCH. How!

CON. And this, Francis Quicksilver.

TOUCH. Is't possible? I thought your Worship had been gone for Virginia, sir; you are welcome home, sir. Your Worship has made a quick return, it seems, and no doubt a good voyage. Nay, pray you be cov- [280 er'd, sir. How did your biscuit hold out, sir? — Methought I had seen this gentleman afore. Good Master Quicksilver, how a degree to the southward has chang'd you!

GOLD. Do you know 'em, Father? — Forbear your offers [75] a little, you shall be heard anon.

TOUCH. Yes, Master Deputy; I had a small venture with them in the voyage — a thing call'd a son-in-law, or so. — Offi- [290 cers, you may let 'em stand alone: they will not run away; I'll give my word for them, a couple of very honest gentlemen. One of 'em was my prentice, Master Quicksilver here; and when he had two year to serve, kept his whore and his hunting nag, would play his hundred pound at gresco or primero [76] as familiarly (and all a' my purse) as any bright piece of crimson on 'em all; had his change-able trunks of apparel standing at livery, [300 with his mare, his chest of perfum'd linen, and his bathing-tubs, which, when I told him of, why he — he was a gentleman, and I a poor Cheapside groom! The remedy was, we must part. Since when he hath had the gift of gathering up some small parcels of mine, to the value of five hundred pound, dispers'd

among my customers, to furnish this his Vir-ginian venture; wherein this knight was the chief, Sir Flash — one that married a [310 daughter of mine, ladified her, turned two thousand pounds' worth of good land of hers into cash within the first week, bought her a new gown and a coach; sent her to seek her fortune by land, whilst himself prepared for his fortune by sea; took in fresh flesh at Billingsgate, for his own diet, to serve him the whole voyage — the wife of a certain usurer call'd Security, who hath been the broker for 'em in all this business. Please, [320 Master Deputy, work upon that now!

GOLD. If my worshipful father have ended —

TOUCH. I have, it shall please Master Deputy.

GOLD. Well then, under correction ——

TOUCH. [aside] Now, son, come over 'em with some fine gird, as thus, "Knight, you shall be encount'red," that is, had to the Counter; or, "Quicksilver, I will put [330 you in a crucible," or so.

GOLD. Sir Petronel Flash, I am sorry to see such flashes as these proceed from a gentle-man of your quality and rank; for mine own part, I could wish I could say I could not see them; but such is the misery of magistrates and men in place, that they must not wink [77] at offenders. — Take him aside. — I will hear you anon, sir.

TOUCH. [aside] I like this well, yet; [340 there's some grace i' the knight left: he cries.

GOLD. Francis Quicksilver, would God thou hadst turn'd quacksalver, rather than run into these dissolute and lewd courses! It is great pity; thou art a proper [78] young man, of an honest and clean face, somewhat near a good one; God hath done his part in thee; but thou hast made too much, and been too proud, of that face, with the rest of thy body; for maintenance of which in [350 neat and garish attire, only to be look'd upon by some light housewives,[79] thou hast prodi-gally consumed much of thy master's estate; and, being by him gently admonish'd at sev-eral times, hast return'd thyself haughty and rebellious in thine answers, thund'ring out uncivil comparisons, requiting all his kind-ness with a coarse and harsh behavior; never returning thanks for any one benefit, but

---

[74] Equipment.
[75] Attempts (to speak).
[76] Card games.

[77] Shut their eyes.
[78] Handsome.
[79] Hussies.

receiving all as if they had been debts to [360 thee, and no courtesies. I must tell thee, Francis, these are manifest signs of an ill nature; and God doth often punish such pride and *outrecuidance* [80] with scorn and infamy, which is the worst of misfortune. — My worshipful father, what do you please to charge them withal? — From the press I will free 'em, Master Constable.

CON. Then I'll leave your Worship, sir.

GOLD. No, you may stay; there will [370 be other matters against 'em.

TOUCH. Sir, I do charge this gallant, Master Quicksilver, on suspicion of felony; and the knight, as being accessary in the receipt of my goods.

QUICK. O God, sir!

TOUCH. Hold thy peace, impudent varlet, hold thy peace! With what forehead or face dost thou offer to chop logic with me, having run such a race of riot as thou hast done? [380 Does not the sight of this worshipful man's fortune and temper confound thee, that was thy younger fellow in household, and now come to have the place of a judge upon thee? Dost not observe this? Which of all thy gallants and gamesters, thy swearers and thy swaggerers, will come now to moan thy misfortune, or pity thy penury? They'll look out at a window, as thou rid'st in triumph to Tyburn, and cry, "Yonder goes honest [390 Frank, mad Quicksilver!" "He was a free boon companion, when he had money," says one. "Hang him, fool;" says another; "he could not keep it when he had it!" "A pox o' the cullion, his master," says a third; "he has brought him to this;" when their pox of pleasure, and their piles of perdition, would have been better bestowed upon thee, that hast vent'red for 'em with the best, and by the clue of thy knavery brought thyself [400 weeping to the cart of calamity.

QUICK. Worshipful Master!

TOUCH. Offer not to speak, crocodile; I will not hear a sound come from thee. Thou hast learn'd to whine at the play yonder. — Master Deputy, pray you commit 'em both to safe custody, till I be able farther to charge 'em.

QUICK. O me! what an infortunate thing am I!   410

PET. Will you not take security,[81] sir?

TOUCH. Yes, marry, will I, Sir Flash, if

I can find him, and charge him as deep as the best on you. He has been the plotter of all this; he is your enginer,[82] I hear. Master Deputy, you'll dispose of these? In the mean time, I'll to my Lord Mayor, and get his warrant to seize that serpent, Security, into my hands, and seal up both house and goods to the King's use or my satisfaction.   420

GOLD. Officers, take 'em to the Counter.

QUICK. [AND] PET. O God!

TOUCH. Nay, on, on; you see the issue of your sloth. Of sloth cometh pleasure, of pleasure cometh riot, of riot comes whoring, of whoring comes spending, of spending comes want, of want comes theft, of theft comes hanging; and there is my Quicksilver fix'd.

Exeunt.

ACT V — SCENE I [1]

[Enter] GERTRUDE *[and]* SINDEFY.

GER. Ah, Sin! hast thou ever read i' the chronicle of any lady and her waiting woman driven to that extremity that we are, Sin?

SIN. Not I, truly, madam; and, if I had, it were but cold comfort should come out of books, now.

GER. Why, good faith, Sin, I could dine with a lamentable story, now. *O hone, hone, o no nera! etc.* Canst thou tell ne'er a one, Sin?   10

SIN. None but mine own, madam, which is lamentable enough: first to be stol'n from my friends, which were worshipful and of good account, by a prentice in the habit and disguise of a gentleman, and here brought up to London, and promis'd marriage, and now likely to be forsaken, for he is in possibility to be hang'd!

GER. Nay, weep not, good Sin; my Petronel is in as good possibility as he. [20 Thy miseries are nothing to mine, Sin; I was more than promis'd marriage, Sin; I had it, Sin; and was made a lady; and by a knight, Sin; which is now as good as no knight, Sin. And I was born in London, which is more then brought up, Sin; and already forsaken, which is past likelihood, Sin; and, instead of land i' the country, all my knight's living lies i' the Counter, Sin; there's his castle, now!   30

---

[80] Arrogance.   [81] *I.e.*, accept bail.

[82] Planner.
[1] An alehouse.

Sin. Which he cannot be forc'd out of, madam.

Ger. Yes, if he would live hungry a week or two. " Hunger," they say, " breaks stone walls." But he is e'en well enough serv'd, Sin, that, so soon as ever he had got my hand to the sale of my inheritance, run away from me, [as] [2] I had been his punk, God bless us! Would the Knight o' the Sun or Palmerin of England,[3] have us'd their ladies so, Sin? [40 or Sir Lancelot or Sir Tristram?

Sin. I do not know, madam.

Ger. Then thou know'st nothing, Sin. Thou art a fool, Sin. The knighthood nowadays are nothing like the knighthood of old time. They rid a-horseback; ours go afoot. They were attended by their squires, ours by their lackeys. They went buckled in their armor, ours muffled in their cloaks. They travell'd wildernesses and deserts; ours [50 dare scarce walk the streets. They were still press'd [4] to engage their honor, ours still ready to pawn their clothes. They would gallop on at sight of a monster; ours run away at sight of a sergeant. They would help poor ladies; ours make poor ladies.

Sin. Ay, madam, they were knights of the Round Table at Winchester, that sought adventures; but these, of the Square Table at ordinaries, that sit at hazard.[5]   60

Ger. True, Sin; let him vanish. And tell me, what shall we pawn next?

Sin. Ay, marry, madam, a timely consideration; for our hostess, profane woman, has sworn by bread and salt she will not trust us another meal.

Ger. Let it stink in her hand then. I'll not be beholding to her. Let me see; my jewels be gone, and my gowns, and my red velvet petticoat that I was married in, [70 and my wedding silk stockings, and all thy best apparel, poor Sin! Good faith, rather than thou shouldest pawn a rag more I'd lay my ladyship in lavender [6] — if I knew where.

Sin. Alas, madam, your ladyship?

Ger. Ay. Why? You do not scorn my ladyship, though it is in a waistcoat? God's my life! you are a peat [7] indeed! Do I

offer to mortgage my ladyship for you and for your avail, and do you turn the [80 lip and the " alas! " to my ladyship?

Sin. No, madam; but I make question who will lend anything upon it.

Ger. Who? marry, enow, I warrant you, if you'll seek 'em out. I'm sure I remember the time when I would ha' given a thousand pound, if I had it, to have been a lady; and I hope I was not bred and born with that appetite alone; some other gentleborn o' the city have the same longing, [90 I trust. And, for my part, I would afford 'em a penny'rth; [8] my ladyship is little the worse for the wearing, and yet I would bate a good deal of the sum. I would lend it, let me see, for forty pounds in hand, Sin; that would apparel us; and ten pound a year: that would keep me and you, Sin, with our needles; and we should never need to be beholding to our scurvy parents! Good Lord! that there are no fairies [100 nowadays, Sin.

Sin. Why, madam?

Ger. To do miracles, and bring ladies money. Sure, if we lay in a cleanly house, they would haunt it, Sin! I'll try. I'll sweep the chamber soon at night, and set a dish of water o' the hearth. A fairy may come and bring a pearl, or a diamond. We do not know, Sin. Or there may be a pot of gold hid o' the back-side, if we had tools [110 to dig for't! Why may not we two rise early i' the morning, Sin, afore anybody is up, and find a jewel i' the streets worth a hundred pound? May not some great court-lady, as she comes from revels at midnight, look out of her coach as 't is running, and lose such a jewel, and we find it? Ha?

Sin. They are pretty waking dreams, these.

Ger. Or may not some old usurer be [120 drunk overnight, with a bag of money, and leave it behind him on a stall? For God-sake, Sin, let's rise to-morrow by break of day and see. I protest, law, if I had as much money as an alderman, I would scatter some on't i' th' streets for poor ladies to find, when their knights were laid up. And, now I remember my song o' the " Golden Show'r ": why may not I have such fortune? I'll sing it, and try what luck I shall have after it.   130

> Fond fables tell of old
>   How Jove in Danaë's lap

---

[2] Emend. Dodsley; old eds. *me, and;* Simpson *me. And.*

[3] Heroes of Spanish romances, translated and popular in England as *The Mirror of Knighthood* and *Palmerin of England.*

[4] Always ready.

[5] A dicing game.

[6] *I.e.,* pawn my rank.

[7] Pet, spoiled child.

[8] A bargain.

 Fell in a shower of gold,
  By which she caught a clap;
 Oh, had it been my hap,
 (Howe'er the blow doth threaten)
 So well I like the play,
  That I could wish all day
And night to be so beaten.

Enter MISTRESS TOUCHSTONE.

Oh, here's my mother! Good luck, I [140 hope. — Ha' you brought any money, Mother? Pray you, Mother, your blessing. Nay, sweet Mother, do not weep.

MIST. TOUCH. God bless you! I would I were in my grave!

GER. Nay, dear Mother, can you steal no more money from my father? Dry your eyes, and comfort me. Alas! it is my knight's fault, and not mine, that I am in a waistcoat, and attired thus simply. 150

MIST. T. Simply? 'T is better than thou deserv'st. Never whimper for the matter. "Thou should'st have look'd before thou hadst leap'd." Thou wert afire to be a lady, and now your ladyship and you may both "blow at the coal,"[9] for aught I know. "Self do, self have." "The hasty person never wants woe," they say.

GER. Nay then, Mother, you should ha' look'd to it. A body would think you [160 were[10] the older! I did but my kind,[11] I. He was a knight, and I was fit to be a lady. 'T is not lack of liking, but lack of living, that severs us. And you talk like yourself and a citiner[12] in this, i' faith. You show what husband you come on, iwis. You smell the Touchstone — he that will do more for his daughter that he has married [to][13] a scurvy gold-end man and his prentice, than he will for his tother daughter, that has [170 wedded a knight and his customer. By this light, I think he is not my legitimate father.

SIN. Oh, good madam, do not take up your mother so!

MIST. T. Nay, nay, let her e'en alone. Let her Ladyship grieve me still, with her bitter taunts and terms. I have not dole enough to see her in this miserable case, ay, without her velvet gowns, without ribands, without jewels, without French wires,[14] [180 or cheat bread,[15] or quails, or a little dog, or

a gentleman usher, or anything, indeed, that's fit for a lady —

SIN. [*aside*] Except her tongue.

MIST. T. And I not able to relieve her, neither, being kept so short by my husband. Well, God knows my heart. I did little think that ever she should have need of her sister Golding!

GER. Why Mother, I ha' not yet. [190 Alas! good Mother, be not intoxicate[16] for me; I am well enough; I would not change husbands with my sister, I. "The leg of a lark is better than the body of a kite."

MIST. T. I know that; but —

GER. What, sweet Mother, what?

MIST. T. It's but ill food, when nothing's left but the claw.

GER. That's true, Mother. Ay me!

MIST. T. Nay, sweet ladybird, sigh [200 not. Child, madam; why do you weep thus? Be of good cheer; I shall die if you cry, and mar your complexion thus.

GER. Alas, Mother, what should I do?

MIST. T. Go to thy sister's, child; she'll be proud thy Ladyship will come under her roof. She'll win thy father to release thy knight, and redeem thy gowns and thy coach and thy horses, and set thee up again.

GER. But will she get him to set my [210 knight up too?

MIST. T. That she will, or anything else thou 'lt ask her.

GER. I will begin to love her, if I thought she would do this.

MIST. T. Try her, good chuck[17]; I warrant thee.

GER. Dost thou think she'll do 't?

SIN. Ay, madam, and be glad you will receive it. 220

MIST. T. That's a good maiden; she tells you true. Come, I'll take order[18] for your debts i' the alehouse.

GER. Go, Sin, and pray for thy Frank, as I will for my Pet. [*Exeunt.*]

SCENE II[19]

Enter TOUCHSTONE, GOLDING, [*and*] WOLF.

TOUCH. I will receive no letters, Master Wolf; you shall pardon me.

GOLD. Good Father, let me entreat you.

---

[9] "Let them that be a-cold blow at the coal." (Heywood's *Proverbs*.)
[10] *I.e.*, anyone can see you are.
[11] According to my nature.
[12] Citizen.
[13] Om. old eds.
[14] To support the hair and the ruff.
[15] Wheat bread made of branless flour.
[16] Upset, excited.
[17] Chick, dear one.
[18] Make arrangements.
[19] Unlocated; presumably Goldsmith's Row.

Touch. Son Golding, I will not be tempted ; I find mine own easy nature, and I know not what a well-penn'd, subtle letter may work upon it ; there may be tricks, packing,[20] do you see? Return with your packet, sir.

Wolf. Believe it, sir, you need fear no packing here ; these are but letters of sub- [10 mission, all.

Touch. Sir, I do look for no submission. I will bear myself in this like blind Justice. Work upon that now ! When the sessions come, they shall hear from me.

Gold. From whom come your letters, Master Wolf?

Wolf. An't please you, sir, one from Sir Petronel, another from Francis Quicksilver, and a third from old Security, who is [20 almost mad in prison. There are two to your Worship : one from Master Francis, sir; another from the knight.

Touch. I do wonder, Master Wolf, why you should travail thus, in a business so contrary to kind or the nature o' your place ; that you, being the keeper of a prison, should labor the release of your prisoners ; whereas, methinks, it were far more natural and kindly [21] in you to be ranging about for [30 more, and not let these scape you have already under the tooth. But they say you wolves, when you ha' suck'd the blood, once that they are dry, you ha' done.

Wolf. Sir, your Worship may descant [22] as you please o' my name ; but I protest I was never so mortified with [23] any men's discourse or behavior in prison ; yet I have had of all sorts of men i' the kingdom under my keys ; and almost of all religions i' the [40 land, as Papist, Protestant, Puritan, Brownist,[24] Anabaptist, Millenary,[25] Family o' Love,[26] Jew, Turk, Infidel, Atheist, Good Fellow,[27] etc.

Gold. And which of all these, thinks Master Wolf, was the best religion?

Wolf. Troth, Master Deputy, they that pay fees best ; we never examine their consciences farder.

Gold. I believe you, Master Wolf. — [50 Good faith, sir, here's a great deal of humility i' these letters !

Wolf. Humility, sir? Ay. Were your Worship an eyewitness of it, you would say so. The knight will i' the Knights' Ward,[28] do what we can, sir ; and Master Quicksilver would be i' the Hole,[29] if we would let him. I never knew or saw prisoners more penitent or more devout. They will sit you up all night singing of psalms, and edifying the [60 whole prison ; only Security sings a note too high sometimes, because he lies i' the Twopenny Ward, far off, and cannot take his tune.[30] The neighbors can not rest for him, but come every morning to ask what godly prisoners we have.

Touch. Which on 'em is 't is so devout, the knight or the tother?

Wolf. Both, sir ; but the young man especially. I never heard his like. He has [70 cut his hair too.[31] He is so well given, and has such good gifts. He can tell you almost all the stories of the *Book of Martyrs*,[32] and speak you all the *Sick Man's Salve*[33] without book.

Touch. Ay, if he had had grace, he was brought up where it grew, iwis. — On, Master Wolf.

Wolf. And he has converted one Fangs, a sergeant, a fellow could neither write nor [80 read ; he was called the Bandog[34] o' the Counter ; and he has brought him already to pare his nails and say his prayers ; and 't is hop'd, he will sell his place shortly, and become an intelligencer.[35]

Touch. No more ; I am coming already. If I should give any farther ear, I were taken. Adieu, good Master Wolf. — Son, I do feel mine own weaknesses ; do not importune me. Pity is a rheum that I am subject to ; [90 but I will resist it. Master Wolf, " Fish is cast away that is cast in dry pools." Tell Hypocrisy it will not do ; I have touch'd and tried too often ; I am yet proof, and I will remain so. When the sessions come, they shall hear from me. In the meantime, to all suits, to all entreaties, to all letters, to all tricks, I will be deaf as an adder and blind as a beetle, lay mine ear to the ground, and lock mine eyes i' my hand against all temptations. *Exit.*

[20] Plotting, fraud.
[21] According to your nature.
[22] Expatiate, ring the changes on.
[23] Rendered dead to sin by.
[24] A Puritan sect.
[25] Adventist, believer in the **millennium**.
[26] A fanatical sect.
[27] Thief.

[28] A less desirable part of the prison than the Master's side. (Cunliffe.)
[29] The worst part of the prison.
[30] *I.e.*, get the pitch.
[31] In the citizen's style.
[32] John Fox's *Acts and Monuments* (1563).
[33] A devotional work by Thomas Becon (1561).
[34] A fierce dog, originally one tied up as a watchdog.   [35] Spy, informer.

GOLD. You see, Master Wolf, how in- [101 exorable he is. There is no hope to recover him. Pray you commend me to my brother knight, and to my fellow Francis [*giving money*] ; present 'em with this small token of my love ; tell 'em, I wish I could do 'em any worthier office ; but, in this, 't is desperate : yet I will not fail to try the uttermost of my power for 'em. And, sir, as far as I have any credit with you, pray you let 'em want [110 nothing ; though I am not ambitious they should know so much.

WOLF. Sir, both your actions and words speak you to be a true gentleman. They shall know only what is fit, and no more.

Exeunt.

SCENE III [36]

[*Enter*] HOLDFAST [*and*] BRAMBLE.

HOLD. Who would you speak with, sir?

BRAM. I would speak with one Security, that is prisoner here.

HOLD. You are welcome, sir. Stay there, I 'll call him to you. — Master Security !

[SECURITY *appears at a grating.*]

SEC. Who calls?

HOLD. Here 's a gentleman would speak with you.

SEC. What is he? Is 't one that grafts my forehead now I am in prison, and comes [10 to see how the horns shoot up and prosper?

HOLD. You must pardon him, sir ; the old man is a little craz'd with his imprisonment. [*Exit.*]

SEC. What say you to me, sir? Look you here, my learned counsel, Master Bramble ! Cry you mercy, sir ! When saw you my wife?

BRAM. She is now at my house, sir ; and desir'd me that I would come to visit you, [20 and inquire of you your case, that we might work some means to get you forth.

SEC. My case, Master Bramble, is stone walls and iron grates ; you see it ; this is the weakest part on 't. And, for getting me forth, no means but hang myself, and so to be carried forth, from which they have here bound me in intolerable bands.

BRAM. Why, but what is 't you are in for, sir? 30

SEC. For my sins, for my sins, sir, whereof marriage is the greatest. Oh, had I never married, I had never known this purgatory, to which hell is a kind of cool bath in respect [37] ; my wife's confederacy, sir, with old Touchstone, that she might keep her jubilee and the feast of her new moon.[38] Do you understand me, sir?

Enter QUICKSILVER.

QUICK. Good sir, go in and talk with him. The light does him harm, and his ex- [40 ample will be hurtful to the weak prisoners. — Fie, Father Security, that you 'll be still so profane ! Will nothing humble you?

[*Exeunt* SECURITY, BRAMBLE, *and* QUICKSILVER.]

Enter two Prisoners, *with a* Friend.

FRIEND. What 's he?

1 PRIS. Oh, he is a rare young man ! Do you not know him?

FRIEND. Not I. I never saw him I can remember.

2 PRIS. Why, it is he that was the gallant prentice of London — Master Touch- [50 stone's man.

FRIEND. Who? Quicksilver?

1 PRIS. Ay, this is he.

FRIEND. Is this he? They say he has been a gallant indeed.

[2] PRIS. Oh, the royallest fellow that ever was bred up i' the city. He would play you his thousand pound a night at dice ; keep knights and lords company ; go with them to bawdyhouses ; had his six men in [60 a livery ; kept a stable of hunting horses, and his wench in her velvet gown and her cloth of silver. Here 's one knight with him here in prison.

FRIEND. And how miserably he is chang'd !

1 PRIS. Oh, that 's voluntary in him ; he gave away all his rich clothes, as soon as ever he came in here, among the prisoners ; and will eat o' the basket,[39] for humility.

FRIEND. Why will he do so? 70

1 PRIS. Alas, he has no hope of life ! He mortifies himself. He does but linger on till the sessions.

2 PRIS. O, he has penn'd the best thing, that he calls his " Repentance " or his " Last Farewell," that ever you heard. He is a pretty poet ; and, for prose — you would wonder how many prisoners he has help'd out,

[36] A room in the Counter.

[37] Comparison.

[38] Alluding to its horns, another reminder of cuckoldom.

[39] Of broken victuals upon which the poorest prisoners lived.

with penning petitions for 'em, and not take a penny. Look! this is the knight, in the [80 rug-gown.[40] Stand by.

Enter PETRONEL, BRAMBLE, [*and*] QUICK-
SILVER.

BRAM. Sir, for Security's case, I have told him: say he should be condemned to be carted or whipp'd for a bawd, or so, why, I'll lay an execution on him o' two hundred pound; let him acknowledge a judgment, he shall do it in half an hour; they shall not all fetch him out without paying the execution, o' my word.

PET. But can we not be bail'd, Master [90 Bramble?

BRAM. Hardly; there are none of the judges in town, else you should remove yourself, in spite of him, with a *habeas corpus.* But, if you have a friend to deliver your tale sensibly to some justice o' the town, that he may have feeling of it, do you see, you may be bail'd; for, as I understand the case, 't is only done *in terrorem*; [41] and you shall have an action of false imprisonment against him [100 when you come out, and perhaps a thousand pound costs.

Enter MASTER WOLF.

QUICK. How now, Master Wolf? what news? what return?

WOLF. Faith, bad all: yonder will be no letters received. He says the sessions shall determine it. Only Master Deputy Golding commends him to you, and, with this token, wishes he could do you other good.
[*Gives money.*]

QUICK. I thank him. — Good Master [110 Bramble, trouble our quiet no more; do not molest us in prison thus with your winding devices; pray you depart. [*Exit* BRAM-BLE.] — For my part, I commit my cause to Him that can succor me; let God work his will. Master Wolf, I pray you let this be distributed among the prisoners, and desire 'em to pray for us.

WOLF. It shall be done, Master Francis.
[*Exit* QUICKSILVER.]

1 PRIS. An excellent temper!   120

2 PRIS. Now God send him good luck.
Exeunt [*two* Prisoners *and* Friend].

PET. But what said my father-in-law, Master Wolf?

40 A gown of coarse frieze.
41 By way of a threat.

Re-enter HOLDFAST.

HOLD. Here's one would speak with you, sir.

WOLF. I'll tell you anon, Sir Petronel. [*Exit* PETRONEL.] — Who is 't?

HOLD. A gentleman, sir, that will not be seen.

WOLF. Where is he?   130

Enter GOLDING.

Master Deputy! your Worship is welcome —

GOLD. Peace!

WOLF. Away, sirrah![42] [*Exit* HOLDFAST.]

GOLD. Good faith, Master Wolf, the estate of these gentlemen, for whom you were so late and willing a suitor, doth much affect me; and, because I am desirous to do them some fair office, and find there is no means to make my father relent so likely as to bring him to be a spectator of their miser- [140 ies, I have ventur'd on a device; which is to make myself your prisoner, entreating you will presently go report it to my father, and feigning an action, at suit of some third person, pray him, by this token, [*giving a ring*] that he will presently, and with all secrecy, come hither for my bail; which train, if any, I know will bring him abroad; and then, having him here, I doubt not but we shall be all fortunate in the event.   150

WOLF. Sir, I will put on my best speed to effect it. Please you come in.

GOLD. Yes; and let me rest conceal'd, I pray you.

WOLF. See here a benefit truly done, when it is done timely, freely, and to no ambition.   [*Exeunt.*]

SCENE IV [43]

Enter TOUCHSTONE, Wife, Daughters, SIN-
DEFY, [*and*] WINIFRED.

TOUCH. I will sail by you, and not hear you, like the wise Ulysses.

MIL. Dear Father!

MIST. T. Husband!

GER. Father!

WIN. AND SIN. Master Touchstone!

TOUCH. Away, sirens, I will inmure myself against your cries, and lock myself up to your lamentations.

MIST. T. Gentle husband, hear me!   10

42 Old eds. *S^rah.*
43 A room in Touchstone's house.

GER. Father, it is I, Father, my Lady Flash. My sister and I am friends.

MIL. Good Father!

WIN. Be not hard'ned, good Master Touchstone!

SIN. I pray you, sir, be merciful!

TOUCH. I am deaf; I do not hear you; I have stopp'd mine ears with shoemakers' wax, and drunk Lethe and mandragora, to forget you. All you speak to me I commit [20 to the air.   [*He retires.*] [44]

Enter WOLF.

MIL. How now, Master Wolf?

WOLF. Where's Master Touchstone? I must speak with him presently; I have lost my breath for haste.

MIL. What's the matter, sir? Pray all be well.

WOLF. Master Deputy Golding is arrested upon an execution, and desires him presently to come to him forthwith.   30

MIL. Ay me! do you hear, Father?

TOUCH. [*within*] Tricks, tricks, confederacy, tricks! I have 'em in my nose — I scent 'em!

WOLF. Who's that? Master Touchstone?

MIST. T. Why, it is Master Wolf himself, husband.

MIL. Father!

TOUCH. [*within*] I am deaf still, I say. I will neither yield to the song of the siren [40 nor the voice of the hyena,[45] the tears of the crocodile nor the howling o' the Wolf : avoid my habitation, monsters!

WOLF. Why, you are not mad, sir? I pray you look forth and see the token I have brought you, sir.

TOUCH. [*coming forward*] Ha! what token is it?

WOLF. [*aside to* TOUCHSTONE] Do you know it, sir?   50

TOUCH. [*aside*] My son Golding's ring! Are you in earnest, Master Wolf?

WOLF. [*aside*] Ay, by my faith, sir. He is in prison, and requir'd me to use all speed and secrecy to you.

TOUCH. My cloak there (pray you be patient). — I am plagu'd for my austerity. — My cloak! — At whose suit, Master Wolf?

WOLF. I'll tell you as we go, sir.

Exeunt.

[SCENE V] [46]

Enter Friend [*and the two*] Prisoners.

FRIEND. Why, but is his offence such as he cannot hope of life?

1 PRIS. Troth, it should seem so; and 't is a great pity, for he is exceeding penitent.

FRIEND. They say he is charg'd but on suspicion of felony yet.

2 PRIS. Ay, but his master is a shrewd [47] fellow; he'll prove great matter against him.

FRIEND. I'd as lief as anything I could see his "Farewell."   10

1 PRIS. Oh, 't is rarely written; why, Toby may get him to sing it to you; he's not curious [48] to anybody.

2 PRIS. Oh, no! He would that all the world should take knowledge of his repentance, and thinks he merits in 't, the more shame he suffers.

1 PRIS. Pray thee, try what thou canst do.

2 PRIS. I warrant you he will not deny it, if he be not hoarse with the often repeating [20 of it.   *Exit.*

1 PRIS. You never saw a more courteous creature than he is; and the knight too : the poorest prisoner of the house may command 'em. You shall hear a thing admirably penn'd.

FRIEND. Is the knight any scholar too?

1 PRIS. No, but he will speak very well, and discourse admirably of running horses and Whitefriars,[49] and against bawds, and [30 of cocks; and talk as loud as a hunter, but is none.

Enter WOLF *and* TOUCHSTONE.

WOLF. Please you stay here, sir; I'll call his Worship down to you.

[*Exit* WOLF; TOUCHSTONE *stands aside.*]

1 PRIS. See, he has brought him, and the knight too. Salute him.

Re-enter [Second Prisoner *with*] QUICKSILVER [*and*] PETRONEL; [*re-enter* WOLF *with* GOLDING, *and they stand aside.*]

1 PRIS. I pray, sir, this gentleman, upon our report, is very desirous to hear some piece of your "Repentance."

[44] Probably to the inner stage.
[45] Supposed to be able to imitate the human voice and entice dogs out to their destruction.

[46] A room or yard in the Counter.
[47] Ill-natured.
[48] Fastidious, particular.
[49] A notoriously tough district, in which debtors, as well as criminals, often hid from the law.

QUICK. Sir, with all my heart ; and, [40 as I told Master Toby, I shall be glad to have any man a witness of it ; and, the more openly I profess it, I hope it will appear the heartier, and the more unfeigned.

TOUCH. [*aside*] Who is this? my man Francis and my son-in-law?

QUICK. Sir, it is all the testimony I shall leave behind me to the world and my master that I have so offended.

FRIEND. Good sir ! 50

QUICK. I writ it when my spirits were oppress'd.

PET. Ay, I 'll be sworn for you, Francis.

QUICK. It is in imitation of Mannington's, he that was hang'd at Cambridge,[50] that cut off the horse's head at a blow.

FRIEND. So, sir !

QUICK. To the tune of " I wail in woe, I plunge in pain." [51]

PET. An excellent ditty it is, and worthy [60 of a new tune.

QUICK.

> In Cheapside, famous for gold and plate,
> Quicksilver, I did dwell of late ;
> I had a master good and kind,
> That would have wrought me to his mind.
> He bade me still, "Work upon that";
> But, alas ! I wrought I knew not what.
> He was a Touchstone, black, but true,
> And told me still what would ensue ;
> Yet woe is me ! I would not learn ; 70
> I saw, alas ! but could not discern !

FRIEND. Excellent, excellent well !

GOLD. [*aside*] O, let him alone.[52] He [53] is taken already.

QUICK.

> I cast my coat and cap away ;
> I went in silks and satins gay ;
> False metal of good manners I
> Did daily coin unlawfully ;
> I scorn'd my master, being drunk ;
> I kept my gelding and my punk ; 80
> And with a knight, Sir Flash by name,
> Who now is sorry for the same —

PET. I thank you, Francis.

QUICK.

> I thought by sea to run away,
> But Thames and tempest did me stay.

TOUCH. [*aside*] This cannot be feigned sure. Heaven pardon my severity ! " The ragged colt may prove a good horse."

---

[50] In 1576.
[51] The tune, that is, of Mannington's ballad, which thus begins; its old name was Lablandashot. The ballad may be found in Clement Robinson's *Handful of Pleasant Delights* (ed. H. E. Rollins, pp. 65–68).
[52] Leave it to Quicksilver.
[53] Touchstone.

GOLD. [*aside*] How he listens ! and is trans- ported ! He has forgot me. 90

QUICK.

> Still "Eastward Ho" was all my word ;
> But westward I had no regard,
> Nor never thought what would come after,
> As did, alas ! his youngest daughter.
> At last the black ox trod o' my foot,[54]
> And I saw then what 'long'd unto 't ;
> Now cry I, "Touchstone, touch me still,
> And make me current by thy skill."

TOUCH. [*aside*] And I will do it, Francis.

WOLF. [*aside to* GOLDING] Stay him, [100 Master Deputy ; now is the time : we shall lose the song else.

FRIEND. I protest it is the best that ever I heard.

QUICK. How like you it, gentlemen?

ALL. Oh, admirable, sir !

QUICK. This stanza now following alludes to the story of Mannington, from whence I took my project for my invention.

FRIEND. Pray you go on, sir. 110

QUICK.

> O Mannington, thy stories show,
> Thou cutt'st a horse-head off at a blow.
> But I confess I have not the force
> For to cut off the head of a horse ;
> Yet I desire this grace to win,
> That I may cut off the horse-head of Sin,
> And leave his body in the dust
> Of sin's highway and bogs of lust,
> Whereby I may take Virtue's purse,
> And live with her for better, for worse. 120

FRIEND. Admirable, sir, and excellently conceited !

QUICK. Alas, sir !

TOUCH. [*aside*] Son Golding and Master Wolf, I thank you : the deceit is welcome, especially from thee, whose charitable soul in this hath shown a high point of wisdom and honesty. Listen, I am ravished with his repentance, and could stand here a whole prenticeship to hear him. 130

FRIEND. Forth, good sir.

QUICK. This is the last, and the " Fare- well."

> Farewell, Cheapside ; farewell, sweet trade
> Of goldsmiths all, that never shall fade ;
> Farewell, dear fellow prentices all,
> And be you warned by my fall :
> Shun usurers, bawds, and dice, and drabs ;
> Avoid them as you would French scabs.[55]
> Seek not to go beyond your tether, 140
> But cut your thongs unto your leather ;
> So shall you thrive by little and little,
> Scape Tyburn, Counters, and the Spital.[56]

TOUCH. [*coming forward*] And scape them shalt thou, my penitent and dear Francis !

---

[54] Proverbial for "trouble came upon me."
[55] Syphilis.
[56] Hospital (for the treatment of venereal disease).

QUICK. Master!

PET. Father!

TOUCH. I can no longer forbear to do your humility right. Arise, and let me honor your repentance with the hearty and [150 joyful embraces of a father and friend's love. Quicksilver, thou hast ate into my breast, Quicksilver, with the drops of thy sorrow, and kill'd the desperate opinion I had of thy reclaim.

QUICK. Oh, sir, I am not worthy to see your worshipful face!

PET. Forgive me, Father.

TOUCH. Speak no more; all former passages are forgotten; and here my word [160 shall release you. — Thank this worthy brother, and kind friend, Francis. — Master Wolf, I am their bail.

A shout in the prison, [and SECURITY *appears at the grating].*

SEC. Master Touchstone! Master Touchstone!

TOUCH. Who's that?

WOLF. Security, sir.

SEC. Pray you, sir, if you'll be won with a song, hear my lamentable tune too:

SONG

O Master Touchstone,   170
    My heart is full of woe;
Alas, I am a cuckold!
    And why should it be so?
Because I was a usurer
    And bawd, as all you know;
For which, again I tell you,
    My heart is full of woe.

TOUCH. Bring him forth, Master Wolf, and release his bands. This day shall be sacred to mercy, and the mirth of this [180 encounter in the Counter. — See, we are encount'red with more suitors.

Enter MISTRESS TOUCHSTONE, GERTRUDE, MILDRED, SINDEFY, [*and*] WINIFRED; [*and* WOLF *with* SECURITY].

Save your breath, save your breath! All things have succeeded to your wishes; and we are heartily satisfied in their events.

GER. Ah, runaway, runaway! have I caught you? And how has my poor knight done all this while?

PET. Dear Lady-wife, forgive me!

GER. As heartily as I would be for- [190 given, knight. Dear Father, give me your blessing, and forgive me too; I ha' been proud and lascivious, Father; and a fool,

Father; and, being rais'd to the state of a wanton coy thing, call'd a lady, Father, have scorn'd you, Father, and my sister, and my sister's velvet cap, too, and would make a mouth at the city as I rid through it, and stop mine ears at Bow-bell. I have said your beard was a base one, Father; and that [200 you looked like Twierpipe, the taborer; [57] and that my mother was but my midwife.

MIST. T. Now, God forgi' you, child madam!

TOUCH. No more repetitions. What is else wanting to make our harmony full?

GOLD. Only this, sir, that my fellow Francis make amends to Mistress Sindefy with marriage.

QUICK. With all my heart.   210

GOLD. And Security give her a dower, which shall be all the restitution he shall make of that huge mass he hath so unlawfully gotten.

TOUCH. Excellently devis'd! a good motion! What says Master Security?

SEC. I say anything, sir, what you'll ha' me say. Would I were no cuckold!

WIN. Cuckold, husband? Why, I think this wearing of yellow [58] has infected you.

TOUCH. Why, Master Security, that [220 should rather be a comfort to you than a corrosive. If you be a cuckold, it's an argument you have a beautiful woman to your wife; then you shall be much made of; you shall have store of friends, never want money; you shall be eas'd of much o' your wedlock pain; others will take it for you. Besides, you being a usurer, and likely to go to hell, the devils will never torment you: they'll take you for one o' their own race.[59] Again, if you [230 be a cuckold, and know it not, you are an innocent; [60] if you know it and endure it, a true martyr.

SEC. I am resolv'd, sir. Come hither, Winny.

TOUCH. Well, then, all are pleas'd; or shall be anon. Master Wolf, you look hungry, methinks. Have you no apparel to lend Francis, to shift him?

QUICK. No, sir, nor I desire none; but [240 here make it my suit that I may go home, through the streets in these, as a spectacle, or rather an example, to the children of Cheapside.

[57] Drummer.
[58] The color of his prison garb, and of jealousy.
[59] Because of your horns.
[60] With a pun on the meaning, "idiot."

Touch. Thou hast thy wish. Now, Lon-
  don, look about,
And in this moral see thy glass run out :
Behold the careful father, thrifty son,
The solemn deeds, which each of us have
  done ;
The usurer punish'd, and from fall so steep
The prodigal child reclaim'd, and the lost
  sheep.   250

EPILOGUS

[Quick.] Stay, sir, I perceive the multitude are gather'd together to view our coming
out at the Counter. See, if the streets and
the fronts of the houses be not stuck with
people, and the windows fill'd with ladies, as
on the solemn day of the pageant ! [61] —
Oh, may you find in this our pageant
  here,
The same contentment which you came to
  seek ;
And, as that show but draws you once a
  year,
May this attract you hither once a week.   10
                                    [*Exeunt.*]

[61] The Lord Mayor's Show.

Buſſy D'Ambois:

A TRAGEDIE:

As it hath been often Acted with
great Applauſe.

*Being much corrected and amended
by the Author before his death.*

LONDON:
Printed by *A. N.* for *Robert Lunne.*
1 6 4 1.

INTRODUCTORY NOTE

CHAPMAN'S most famous play was acted, according to the title page of the first edition, by the Boys of St. Paul's. Since that company disappears in 1606, since a leap year is indicated by I, ii, 85, and since allusions to Elizabeth and to the new knights are evidently subsequent to the accession of James, 1604 seems probable for the date of composition. The play is one of a group which Chapman founded on recent French history. Here, as elsewhere, the inspiration of Marlowe is apparent, for some of the same characters appear in *The Massacre at Paris.* Nor is Bussy, with his reckless individualism and romantic extravagance, far removed from Marlowe's aspiring heroes.

Extant accounts of this intrepid chevalier and his spectacular end appeared only after the play had been published; the precise sources of Chapman's information remain unknown. Louis de Clermont d'Amboise, Seigneur de Bussy, was born in 1549 of a noble house. At a tender age he won military distinction, during the massacre of St. Bartholomew murdered a Huguenot cousin with whom he had a lawsuit, in the civil wars was repeatedly wounded, and became withal a brilliant figure at court, the lover of Marguerite de Valois, and a colonel in the service of the Duc d'Anjou, who stood next to Henry III in the succession. This prince, the Machiavellian Monsieur of our play, finally broke with Bussy, whom he had made governor of Anjou, and told the King of his intrigue with Françoise de Maridort. Henry at once betrayed him to her husband, Charles de Chambes, Comte de Montsoreau, who forced her to make an assignation with Bussy on the night of August 15, 1579, when with an overwhelming party the Count attacked and killed him. Though their agreement may be fortuitous, it is possible that Chapman and Dumas Père (in his *La Dame de Montsoreau*) derived from some common source their departure from the historical facts as we know them. Both make Monsieur the direct informant of the Count, and motivate the former's treachery by ascribing to him an unsuccessful passion for the Countess.

Though this is his earliest surviving tragedy, Chapman surpasses in his structural treatment of these materials the epic method of all save the last of Marlowe's important plays. Characterization, except for the hero, is inadequate; but the plot is dramatically conceived, and the play abounds in effective situations. Chapman had not observed in vain the technical advances made by Shakespeare. He was also influenced, like all the Elizabethan tragic writers, by the plays of Seneca, most notably in the employment of the Messenger and the Ghost, and (by his *Hercules Oetaeus*) in the handling of Bussy's death. It is, of course, Bussy as an acting rôle that makes the play. His Titanic energy, though not expressed in poetry equal to Marlowe's, is reminiscent of the heroes of the earlier dramatist, but is more thoroughly worked up in terms of action. And his end is genuinely moving, because he is more than a mere swordsman. The sceptical and stoical temper of Chapman gives Bussy a philosophy of self-reliance : once again we look on while Fate grinds the individual into less than dust.

The play may well have been written, as Professor Parrott thinks, for the Children at the Blackfriars, and been carried to the Paul's Boys when Kirkham went over to them in 1605. From the prologue in the Quarto of 1641 we learn that the famous Nat Field had played the title rôle, very likely for the Queen's Revels at Whitefriars in 1609–1612. It was afterwards revived by the King's Men, evidently in competition with a rival company ; it was acted by them at least as late as 1634, when there was a performance at court. The surviving prologue was presumably written for it. The eminent Restoration tragedian, Charles Hart, had much success as Bussy ; and in 1691 the play was again revived in an adaptation by Tom Durfey.

The standard edition of Chapman's plays is that of T. M. Parrott (1910). This tragedy has also been edited, along with its inferior sequel, *The Revenge of Bussy d'Ambois*, by F. S. Boas (1905). With a number of additions and corrections from the first edition, the Quarto of 1607 (reissued 1608), the present text is based on that of the Quarto of 1641 (reissued 1646 and 1657), which was " much corrected and amended by the author before his death."

BUSSY D'AMBOIS

BY

GEORGE CHAPMAN

[DRAMATIS PERSONAE

HENRY III, King of France.
MONSIEUR,[1] his brother.
DUKE OF GUISE.[2]
COUNT OF MONTSURRY.
BUSSY D'AMBOIS.
BARRISOR,
L'ANOU, } courtiers ; enemies to D'Ambois.
PYRHOT,
BRISAC, } courtiers ; friends to D'Ambois.
MELYNELL,
BEAUMOND, an attendant on King Henry.
FRIAR COMOLET.
MAFFÉ, steward to Monsieur.
NUNTIUS.

Murderers.
BEHEMOTH, } spirits.
CARTOPHYLAX,
UMBRA OF FRIAR.

ELENOR, Duchess of Guise.
TAMYRA, Countess of Montsurry.
BEAUPRÉ, niece to Elenor.
ANNABELLE, maid to Elenor.
PERO, maid to Tamyra.
CHARLOTTE, maid to Beaupré.
PYRA, a court lady.

Courtiers, Ladies, Pages, Servants, Spirits, etc.

THE SCENE — *Paris*.]

PROLOGUE [3]

NOT out of confidence that none but we [4]
Are able to present this tragedy,
Not out of envy at the grace of late
It did receive, nor yet to derogate
From their deserts who [5] give out boldly that
They move with equal feet on the same flat ;
Neither for all nor any of such ends
We offer it, gracious and noble friends,
To your review ; we, far from emulation
And (charitably judge) from imitation,   10
With this work entertain you, a piece known
And still believ'd in Court to be our own.
To quit our claim, doubting our right or merit,

Would argue in us poverty of spirit
Which we must not subscribe to.   Field [6] is gone,
Whose action first did give it name, and one [7]
Who came the nearest to him is deni'd
By his gray beard to show the height and pride
Of D'Ambois' youth and bravery ; yet to hold
Our title still afoot, and not grow cold   20
By giving it o'er, a third man [8] with his best
Of care and pains defends our interest ;
As Richard [9] he was lik'd, nor do we fear
In personating D'Ambois he 'll appear
To faint, or go less, so [10] your free consent,
As heretofore, give him encouragement.

---

[1] A title given to the next younger brother of the King of France. This Duke of Anjou is the same prince as the Duke of Alençon who courted Queen Elizabeth.
[2] The great Catholic leader in the civil wars.
[3] Probably not by Chapman. It first appears in Q 1641.
[4] The King's Men.   [5] Some rival company.

[6] Formerly one of the King's Men.
[7] Perhaps Taylor. (Chambers.)
[8] Probably Eliard Swanston.
[9] Probably Shakespeare's Richard III, not Ricardo in Massenger's *The Picture*.
[10] Provided that.

519

ACT I — SCENE I [11]

Enter BUSSY D'AMBOIS, *poor.*

BUS. Fortune, not Reason, rules the state of things ;
Reward goes backwards, Honor on his head ;
Who is not poor, is monstrous ; only need
Gives form and worth to every human seed.
As cedars beaten with continual storms,
So great men flourish ; and do imitate
Unskilful statuaries, who suppose,
In forming a Colossus, if they make him
Straddle enough, strut, and look big, and gape,
Their work is goodly : so men merely great [12]
In their affected gravity of voice, 11
Sourness of countenance, manners' cruelty,
Authority, wealth, and all the spawn of fortune,
Think they bear all the kingdom's worth before them ;
Yet differ not from those colossic statues,
Which, with heroic forms without o'erspread,
Within are nought but mortar, flint, and lead.
Man is a torch borne in the wind ; a dream
But of a shadow, summ'd with all his substance ; 19
And as great seamen, using all their wealth [13]
And skills in Neptune's deep invisible paths,
In tall ships richly built and ribb'd with brass,
To put a girdle round about the world,
When they have done it (coming near their haven)
Are glad to give a warning-piece,[14] and call
A poor, staid fisherman, that never pass'd
His country's sight, to waft and guide them in :
So when we wander furthest through the waves
Of glassy glory, and the gulfs of state, 29
Topp'd with all titles, spreading all our reaches,
As if each private arm would sphere the earth,
We must to Virtue for her guide resort,
Or we shall shipwrack in our safest port.
Procumbit.

[*Enter*] MONSIEUR, *with two Pages.*

MONS. [*aside*] There is no second place in numerous state [15]
That holds more than a cipher ; in a king
All places are contain'd. His word and looks
Are like the flashes and the bolts of Jove ;
His deeds inimitable, like the sea
That shuts still as it opes, and leaves no tracts [16]
Nor prints of precedent for mean men's facts.[17] 40
There's but a thread betwixt me and a crown ;
I would not wish it cut, unless by nature.
Yet, to prepare me for that possible fortune,
'T is good to get resolved [18] spirits about me.
I follow'd D'Ambois to this green retreat —
A man of spirit beyond the reach of fear,
Who, discontent with his neglected worth,
Neglects the light and loves obscure abodes ;
But he is young and haughty, apt to take
Fire at advancement, to bear state,[19] and flourish ; 50
In his rise therefore shall my bounties shine.
None loathes the world so much, nor loves to scoff it,
But gold and grace will make him surfeit of it.
What, D'Ambois?
BUS. He, sir.
MONS. Turn'd to earth, alive?
Up, man ; the sun shines on thee.
BUS. Let it shine ;
I am no mote to play in 't, as great men are.
MONS. Callest thou men great in state, motes in the sun? [20]
They say so that would have thee freeze in shades,
That, like the gross Sicilian gourmandist,
Empty their noses in the cates [21] they love, 60
That none may eat but they. Do thou but bring
Light to the banquet Fortune sets before thee,
And thou wilt loathe lean darkness like thy death.
Who would believe thy mettle could let sloth
Rust and consume it? If Themistocles
Had liv'd obscur'd thus in th' Athenian state,
Xerxes had made both him and it his slaves.
If brave Camillus had lurk'd so in Rome,
He had not five times been Dictator there, 69
Nor four times triumph'd. If Epaminondas,
Who liv'd twice twenty years obscur'd in Thebes,
Had liv'd so still, he had been still unnam'd,
And paid his country nor himself their right ;
But, putting forth his strength, he rescu'd both
From imminent ruin, and, like burnish'd steel,
After long use he shin'd ; for, as the light
Not only serves to show, but render us

---

[11] Unlocated ; but evidently near the court, and out of doors.
[12] Q 1 *our tympanouse statists.*
[13] Q 1 *powers.*
[14] Fire a signal gun.
[15] Punning on (1) the series of numbers, (2) a populous kingdom. (Boas.)
[16] Tracks. [17] Deeds. [18] Resolute.
[19] To bear himself proudly.
[20] This speech is a mosaic from Plutarch's *De Latenter Vivendo.* (Parrott.)
[21] Delicacies.

Mutually profitable, so our lives
In acts exemplary, not only win
Ourselves good names, but do to others give 80
Matter for virtuous deeds, by which we live.
  Bus. What would you wish me?
  Mons.   Leave the troubled streams,
And live, where thrivers do, at the well-head.
  Bus. At the well-head? Alas, what should
    I do
With that enchanted glass? See devils there?
Or, like a strumpet, learn to set my looks
In an eternal brake,[22] or practise juggling,
To keep my face still fast, my heart still loose ;
Or bear, like dame's schoolmistresses their rid-
    dles,   89
Two tongues, and be good only for a shift ;[23]
Flatter great lords, to put them still in mind
Why they were made lords ; or please humor-
    ous[24] ladies
With a good carriage, tell them idle tales
To make their physic work ; spend a man's life
In sights and visitations, that will make
His eyes as hollow as his mistress' heart ;
To do none good, but those that have no need ;
To gain being forward, though you break for
    haste
All the commandments ere you break your
    fast ;
But believe backwards, make your period 100
And creed's last article, " I believe in God " ;
And, hearing villainies preach'd, t' unfold their
    art
Learn to commit them?[25] 'T is a great man's
    part.
Shall I learn this there?
  Mons.   No, thou need'st not learn,
Thou hast the theory ; now go there and
    practise.
  Bus. Ay, in a threadbare suit ; when men
    come there,
They must have high naps,[26] and go from
    thence bare.
A man may drown the parts[27] of ten rich
    men
In one poor suit ; brave barks[28] and outward
    gloss   109
Attract Court loves, be in parts ne'er so gross.
  Mons. Thou shalt have gloss enough, and
    all things fit

---

[22] Vise ; *i.e.*, assume a mask.
[23] Piece of trickery.
[24] Capricious. Q 1 *portly.*
[25] Hearing villainies preached against, study to commit them, in order to exemplify their ingenuity.
[26] *I.e.*, good clothes.
[27] Accomplishments, abilities.
[28] Fine coverings.

T' enchase in all show thy long-smothered
    spirit.
Be rul'd by me, then. The old Scythians
Painted blind Fortune's powerful hands with
    wings,
To show her gifts come swift and suddenly,
Which, if her favorite be not swift to take,
He loses them for ever. Then be wise :
Stay but awhile here, and I 'll send to thee.
          Exit Monsieur [*with* Pages].
  Bus. What will he send? some crowns?
    It is to sow them   119
Upon my spirit, and make them spring a crown
Worth millions of the seed-crowns he will send.
Like to disparking[29] noble husbandmen,
He 'll put his plow into me, plow me up.
But his unsweating thrift is policy,
And learning-hating policy is ignorant
To fit his seed-land soil[30] ; a smooth, plain
    ground
Will never nourish any politic seed.
I am for honest actions, not for great ;
If I may bring up a new fashion,   129
And rise in court for virtue, speed his plow !
The King hath known me long as well as he,
Yet could my fortune never fit the length
Of both their understandings till this hour.
There is a deep nick in Time's restless wheel
For each man's good, when which nick comes,
    it strikes ;
As rhetoric yet works not persuasion,
But only is a mean to make it work,
So no man riseth by his real merit,
But when it cries " clink " in his raiser's spirit.
Many will say, that cannot rise at all,   140
Man's first hour's rise is first step to his fall.
I 'll venture that ; men that fall low must die,
As well as men cast headlong from the sky.

           Enter Maffé.

  Maf. Humor of princes ! Is this wretch
    endu'd
With any merit worth a thousand crowns?
Will my Lord have me be so ill a steward
Of his revenue,[31] to dispose a sum
So great with so small cause as shows in him?
I must examine this. Is your name D'Ambois?
  Bus. Sir?
  Maf.   Is your name D'Ambois?
  Bus.   Who have we here?   150
Serve you the Monsieur?

---

[29] Putting parks into cultivation.
[30] Q 1 reads (for *To . . . soil*). *But he 's no husband heere*, and omits ll. 122–125.
[31] Accented on second syllable.

MAF.   How?

BUS.   Serve you the Monsieur?

MAF. Sir, y'are very hot. I do serve the
Monsieur;

But in such place as gives me the command

Of all his other servants. And because

His Grace's pleasure is to give your good

His pass [32] through my command, methinks
you might

Use me with more respect.

BUS.   Cry you mercy! [33]

Now you have opened my dull eyes, I see you,

And would be glad to see the good you speak
of.

What might I call your name?

MAF.   Monsieur Maffé.

BUS. Monsieur Maffé? Then, good Monsieur Maffé,   161

Pray let me know you better.

MAF.   Pray do so,

That you may use me better. For yourself,

By your no better outside, I would judge you

To be some poet; have you given my Lord

Some pamphlet?

BUS.   Pamphlet?

MAF.   Pamphlet, sir, I say.

BUS. Did your great master's goodness
leave the good

That is to pass your charge to my poor use,

To your discretion?

MAF.   Though he did not, sir,

I hope 't is no rude office to ask reason   170

How that his Grace gives me in charge, goes
from me?

BUS. That's very perfect, sir.

MAF.   Why, very good, sir.

I pray then give me leave; if for no pamphlet,

May I not know what other merit in you

Makes his compunction willing to relieve
you?

BUS. No merit in the world, sir.

MAF.   That is strange.

Y' are a poor soldier, are you?

BUS.   That I am, sir.

MAF. And have commanded?

BUS.   Ay, and gone without, sir.

MAF. [*aside*] I see the man; a hundred
crowns will make him

Swagger and drink healths to his Grace's
bounty,   180

And swear he could not be more bountiful;

So there's nine hundred crowns sav'd.— Here,
tall [34] soldier.

His Grace hath sent you a whole hundred
crowns.

BUS. A hundred, sir! Nay, do his Highness right;

I know his hand is larger, and perhaps

I may deserve more than my outside shows.

I am a scholar, as I am a soldier,

And I can poetize [35] and, being well encourag'd,

May sing his fame for giving, yours for delivering,   189

Like a most faithful steward, what he gives.

MAF. What shall your subject be?

BUS.   I care not much

If to his bounteous Grace I sing the praise

Of fair great noses, [36] and to you of long ones.

What qualities have you, sir, beside your
chain

And velvet jacket? [37] Can your Worship
dance?

MAF. [*aside*] A pleasant fellow, faith;
it seems my Lord

Will have him for his jester; and, by 'r lady,

Such men are now no fools; 't is a knight's
place.

If I, to save his Grace some crowns, should
urge him   199

T'abate his bounty, I should not be heard;

I would to Heaven I were an errant ass,

For then I should be sure to have the ears

Of these great men, where now their jesters
have them.

'T is good to please him, yet I 'll take no notice

Of his preferment, [38] but in policy

Will still be grave and serious, lest he think

I fear his wooden dagger. [39] Here, Sir Ambo!

BUS. How, Ambo, sir?

MAF.   Ay, is not your name Ambo?

BUS. You call'd me lately D'Ambois; has
your Worship

So short a head?

MAF.   I cry thee mercy, D'Ambois.

A thousand crowns I bring you from my Lord.

[Serve God;] [40] play the good husband, you
may make   212

This a good standing living: 't is a bounty

His Highness might perhaps have bestow'd
better.

BUS. Go, y' are a rascal; hence, away, you
rogue!

[32] Its passage.

[33] I beg your pardon.   [34] Bold.

[35] The historical Bussy could, and did.

[36] Monsieur's nose was a mark for the satirists of
the time. (Parrott.)

[37] The symbols of his office.

[38] Advancement.

[39] Carried by Fools.

[40] So Q₁; Q 1641 *If you be thriftie, and,* in deference to the statute against profanity.

MAF. What mean you, sir?

BUS.   Hence! prate no more!
Or, by thy villain's blood, thou prat'st thy
    last!
A barbarous groom grudge at his master's
    bounty!
But since I know he would as much abhor   219
His hind should argue what he gives his
    friend,
Take that, sir, for your aptness to dispute.
              [*Strikes him.*]   *Exit.*

MAF. These crowns are set in blood; blood
    be their fruit.   *Exit.*

[SCENE II] [41]

HENRY [*and*] GUISE [*are discovered at chess;
also enter*] MONTSURRY, ELENOR, TAMYRA,
BEAUPRÉ,   PERO,   CHARLOTTE,   PYRA,[42]
[*and*] ANNABELLE.[43]

HEN. Duchess of Guise, your Grace is much
    enrich'd
In the attendance of that English virgin,[44]
That will initiate her prime of youth,
Dispos'd to court conditions, under the hand
Of your preferr'd instructions and command,
Rather than any in the English court,
Whose ladies are not match'd in Christendom
For graceful and confirm'd behaviors,
More than the court where they are bred is
    equall'd.

GUISE. I like not their court fashion; it is
    too crestfall'n   10
In all observance, making demigods
Of their great nobles, and of their old queen
An ever-young and most immortal goddess.

MONS. No question she's the rarest queen
    in Europe.

GUISE. But what's that to [45] her immortal-
    ity? [46]

HEN. Assure you, cousin Guise, so great a
    courtier,
So full of majesty and royal parts,
No queen in Christendom may vaunt herself.
Her court approves it, that 's a court indeed,

Not mix'd with clowneries us'd in common
    houses,   20
But, as courts should be, th' abstracts of their
    kingdoms,
In all the beauty, state, and worth they hold;
So is hers, amply, and by her inform'd.
The world is not contracted in a man
With more proportion and expression,
Than in her court, her kingdom.   Our French
    court
Is a mere mirror of confusion to it:
The king and subject, lord and every slave,
Dance a continual hay; [47] our rooms of state
Kept like our stables; no place more observ'd
Than a rude market-place: and though our
    custom   31
Keep this assur'd confusion from our eyes,
'T is ne'er the less essentially unsightly,
Which they would soon see, would they change
    their form
To this of ours, and then compare them both ·
Which we must not affect,[48] because in king-
    doms
Where the king's change doth breed the sub-
    ject's terror,
Pure innovation is more gross than error.

MONS. No question we shall see them im-
    itate,
Though afar off, the fashions of our courts,   40
As they have ever ap'd us in attire.
Never were men so weary of their skins,
And apt to leap out of themselves as they;
Who, when they travail [49] to bring forth rare
    men,
Come home, delivered of a fine French suit.
Their brains lie with their tailors, and get
    babies
For their most complete issue; he 's sole heir
To all the moral virtues that first greets
The light with a new fashion, which becomes
    them   49
Like apes, disfigur'd with the attires of men.

HEN. No question they much wrong their
    real worth
In affectation of outlandish scum;
But they have faults, and we more; they
    foolish-proud
To jet [50] in others' plumes so haughtily;
We proud, they that are proud of foolery,
Holding our worths more complete for their
    vaunts.

---

41 A room in the royal palace. That the source
of Q 1641 was the prompt-copy (or a transcription
of it) is indicated by the following notation, which
it prints after I, i, 153: *Table, Chesbord & Tapers
behind the Arras.* "Arras" = the curtains of the
inner stage.
42 No speeches are assigned to this character,
which suggests that the original version of the play
may have been longer.
43 Old eds. *Annable,* throughout.
44 Annabelle.
45 What has that to do with.
46 Ll. 14, 15, om. Q₁.

47 A winding rustic dance.   48 Desire.
49 Old eds. *travell,* punning on both meanings,
which were not distinguished in spelling.
50 Strut. Q₁ *To be the pictures of our vanitie,*
omitting the following line.

Enter MONSIEUR [*and*] D'AMBOIS.

MONS. Come, mine own sweetheart, I will
    enter thee. —
Sir, I have brought a gentleman to court,
And pray you would vouchsafe to do him grace.
    HEN. D'Ambois, I think?
    BUS. That's still my name, my Lord,   60
Though I be something altered in attire.
    HEN. We like your alteration, and must tell
    you
We have expected [51] th' offer of your service;
For we, in fear to make mild virtue proud,
Use not to seek her out in any man.
    BUS. Nor doth she use to seek out any man:
He that will win must woo her; [she's not
    shameless.] [52]
    MONS. I urg'd her modesty in him, my Lord,
And gave her those rites that he says she
    merits.
    HEN. If you have woo'd and won, then,
    Brother, wear him.   70
    MONS. Th' art mine, sweetheart. See,
    here's the Guise's Duchess,
The Countess of Montsurreau, Beaupré.
Come, I'll enseam [53] thee. Ladies, y' are too
    many
To be in council; I have here a friend
That I would gladly enter in your graces.
    BUS. Save you, ladies.
    DUCH. If you enter him in our graces, my
Lord, methinks by his blunt behavior he
should come out of himself.
    TAM. Has he never been courtier, my [80
Lord?
    MONS. Never, my Lady.
    BEAU. And why did the toy [54] take him in
th' head now?
    BUS. 'T is leap year, lady, and therefore
very good to enter a courtier.
    HEN. Mark, Duchess of Guise, there is one
is not bashful.
    DUCH. No, my Lord, he is much guilty of
the bold extremity.   90
    TAM. The man's a courtier at first sight.
    BUS. I can sing pricksong, [55] lady, at first
sight; and why not be a courtier as suddenly?
    BEAU. Here's a courtier rotten before he
be ripe.
    BUS. Think me not impudent, lady; I am
yet no courtier; I desire to be one, and would
gladly take entrance, madam, under your
princely colors.

---

[51] Been waiting for.   [52] So Q₁; om. Q 1641.
[53] Introduce.   [54] Whim.
[55] Vocal music written down with points.

Enter BARRISOR, L'ANOU, [*and*] PYRHOT.

    DUCH. Soft, sir, you must rise by de- 100
grees, first being the servant [56] of some common lady, or knight's wife; then a little higher
to a lord's wife; next a little higher to a countess; yet a little higher to a duchess, and
then turn the ladder. [57]
    BUS. Do you allow a man, then, four mis-
tresses when the greatest mistress is allowed
but three servants?
    DUCH. Where find you that statute, sir?
    BUS. Why, be judged by the groom- [110
porters. [58]
    DUCH. The groom-porters?
    BUS. Ay, madam; must not they judge of
all gamings i' th' court?
    DUCH. You talk like a gamester.
    GUISE. Sir, know you me?
    BUS. My Lord?
    GUISE. I know not you. Whom do you
serve?
    BUS. Serve, my Lord?   120
    GUISE. Go to, companion, [59] your court-
ship's too saucy.
    BUS. [*aside*] Saucy! Companion! 'T is
the Guise, but yet those terms might have been
spared of the Guisard. [60] Companion! He's
jealous, by this light. Are you blind [61] of that
side, Duke? I'll to her again for that. —
Forth, princely mistress, for the honor of
courtship. Another riddle!
    GUISE. Cease your courtship, or by [130
Heaven I'll cut your throat.
    BUS. Cut my throat? Cut a whetstone,
young Accius Naevius. [62] Do as much with
your tongue, as he did with a razor. Cut my
throat!
    BAR. What new-come gallant have we here,
that dares mate [63] the Guise thus?
    L'AN. 'Sfoot, 't is D'Ambois. The Duke
mistakes him, on my life, for some knight of
the new edition. [64]   140
    BUS. Cut my throat! I would the King
fear'd thy cutting of his throat no more than
I fear thy cutting of mine.

---

[56] Cavalier, professed admirer.
[57] Probably = turn off the ladder, be hanged to
you. (Parrott.)
[58] Who at the English court had charge of gaming
and the implements for it.   [59] Fellow.
[60] Adherent of the Guise; probably with a pun
on "gizzard", *i.e.*, throat.
[61] Unguarded, assailable.
[62] Attus Navius, the Roman augur who performed
the feat before Tarquin.
[63] Claim equality with.
[64] Alluding to the cheapening of the order by
James's numerous creations.

GUISE. I 'll do 't, by this hand.

BUS. That hand dares not do 't. Y' ave cut too many throats already, Guise; and robb'd the realm of many thousand souls, more precious than thine own.[65] — Come madam, talk on. 'Sfoot, can you not talk? Talk on, I say; another riddle. 150

PYR. Here 's some strange distemper.

BAR. Here 's a sudden transmigration with D'Ambois — out of the knight's ward [66] into the Duchess' bed.

L'AN. See what a metamorphosis a brave suit can work.

PYR. 'Slight, step to the Guise and discover him.

BAR. By no means; let the new suit work; we 'll see the issue. 160

GUISE. Leave your courting.

BUS. I will not. — I say, mistress, and I will stand unto it, that if a woman may have three servants, a man may have threescore mistresses.

GUISE. Sirrah, I 'll have you whipp'd out of the court for this insolence.

BUS. Whipp'd? Such another syllable out a' th' presence, if thou dar'st, for thy dukedom. 170

GUISE. Remember, poltroon.

MONS. Pray thee, forbear.

BUS. Passion of death! Were not the king here, he should strow [67] the chamber like a rush.

MONS. But leave courting his wife, then.

BUS. I will not. I 'll court her in despite of him. Not court her! — Come, madam, talk on; fear me nothing. — [*to* GUISE] Well mayst thou drive thy master from the court, but never D'Ambois. 181

MONS. His great heart will not down; 't is like the sea,
That partly by his own internal heat,
Partly the stars' daily and nightly motion,
Their heat and light, and partly of the place
The divers frames,[68] but chiefly by the moon,
Bristled with surges, never will be won
(No, not when th' hearts of all those powers are burst)
To make retreat into his settled home, 189
Till he be crown'd with his own quiet foam.

HEN. You have the mate.[69] Another.

GUISE. No more. *Flourish short.*
Exit GUISE, *after him the* KING,
MONSIEUR *whispering.*

BAR. Why, here 's the lion, scar'd with the throat of a dunghill cock, a fellow that has new shak'd off his shackles; now does he crow for that victory.

L'AN. 'T is one of the best jigs [70] that ever was acted.

PYR. Whom does the Guise suppose him to be, trow? [71] 200

L'AN. Out of doubt, some new denizen'd lord,[72] and thinks that suit newly drawn out a' th' mercer's books.

BAR. I have heard of a fellow, that by a fix'd imagination looking upon a bull-baiting, had a visible pair of horns grew out of his forehead; and I believe this gallant, overjoyed with the conceit of Monsieur's cast [73] suit, imagines himself to be the Monsieur.

L'AN. And why not; as well as the ass, [210 stalking in the lion's case,[74] bare himself like a lion, braying all the huger beasts out of the forest?

PYR. Peace, he looks this way.

BAR. Marry, let him look, sir. What will you say now if the Guise be gone to fetch a blanket [75] for him?

L'AN. Faith, I believe it for his honor sake. 219

PYR. But, if D'Ambois carry it clean? [76]
Exeunt Ladies.

BAR. True, when he curvets in the blanket.

PYR. Ay, marry, sir.

L'AN. 'Sfoot, see how he stares on 's.

BAR. Lord bless us, let 's away.

BUS. Now, sir, take your full view; how does the object please ye?

BAR. If you ask my opinion, sir, I think your suit sits as well as if 't had been made for you.

BUS. So, sir; and was that the subject [230 of your ridiculous jollity?

L'AN. What 's that to you, sir?

BUS. Sir, I have observ'd all your fleerings; [77] and resolve yourselves ye shall give a strict account for 't.

Enter BRISAC [*and*] MELYNELL.

BAR. Oh, miraculous jealousy! [78] Do you think yourself such a singular subject for

---

[65] Alluding to the Massacre of St. Bartholomew.
[66] A part of the Counter, a prison for poor debtors.
[67] Strew.
[68] Nature or structure of "the place", the ocean's bed.
[69] Checkmate, in the game of chess.

[70] Farcical entertainments. [71] Do you suppose?
[72] Alluding to the Scots who swarmed to London upon the accession of James. [73] Discarded.
[74] Covering, skin. [75] To toss him in.
[76] Come off superior. [77] Scoffs. [78] Suspicion.

laughter that none can fall into the matter of our merriment but you?

L'AN. This jealousy of yours, sir, con- [240 fesses some close defect in yourself, that we never dream'd of.

PYR. We held discourse of a perfum'd ass that, being disguis'd in a lion's case, imagin'd himself a lion. I hope that touch'd not you.

BUS. So, sir; your descants [79] do marvellous well fit this ground.[80] We shall meet where your buffoonly laughters will cost ye the best blood in your bodies.

BAR. For life's sake let's be gone; he'll [250 kill's outright else.

BUS. Go, at your pleasures; I'll be your ghost to haunt you; an ye sleep on't, hang me.

L'AN. Go, go, sir; court your mistress.

PYR. And be advis'd; we shall have odds against you.

BUS. Tush! valor stands not in number; I'll maintain it, that one man may beat three boys. 260

BRIS. Nay, you shall have no odds of him in number, sir; he's a gentleman as good as the proudest of you, and ye shall not wrong him.

BAR. Not, sir?

MEL. Not, sir; though he be not so rich, he's a better man than the best of you; and I will not endure it.

L'AN. Not you, sir?

BRIS. No, sir, nor I. 270

BUS. I should thank you for this kindness, if I thought these perfum'd musk cats, being out of this privilege,[81] durst but once mew at us.

BAR. Does your confident spirit doubt that, sir? Follow us and try.

L'AN. Come, sir, we'll lead you a dance.
Exeunt.

ACT II — SCENE I [1]

[*Enter*] HENRY, GUISE, [BEAUMOND,] [2] *and* Attendants.

HEN. This desperate quarrel sprung out of their envies

To D'Ambois' sudden bravery,[3] and great spirit.

GUISE. Neither is worth their envy.

HEN. Less than either Will make the gall of envy overflow.
She feeds on outcast entrails like a kite;
In which foul heap, if any ill lies hid,
She sticks her beak into it, shakes it up,
And hurls it all abroad, that all may view it.
Corruption is her nutriment; but touch her
With any precious ointment, and you kill her.
Where she finds any filth in men, she feasts, 11
And with her black throat bruits it through the world,
(Being [4] sound and healthful). But if she but taste
The slenderest pittance of commended virtue,
She surfeits [5] of it, and is like a fly
That passes all the body's soundest parts,
And dwells upon the sores; or if her squint eye
Have power to find none there, she forges some.
She makes that crooked ever which is straight;
Calls valor giddiness, justice tyranny; 20
A wise man may shun her, she not herself;
Whithersoever she flies from her harms,
She bears her foe still clasp'd in her own arms:
And therefore, Cousin Guise, let us avoid her.

Enter NUNTIUS.

NUN. What Atlas or Olympus lifts his head
So far past covert, that with air enough
My words may be inform'd, and from their height
I may be seen and heard through all the world?
A tale so worthy, and so fraught with wonder,
Sticks in my jaws and labors with event. 30

HEN. Com'st thou from D'Ambois?

NUN. From him, and the rest,
His friends and enemies; whose stern fight I saw,
And heard their words before and in the fray.

HEN. Relate at large what thou hast seen and heard.

NUN. I saw fierce D'Ambois and his two brave friends
Enter the field, and at their heels their foes;
Which were the famous soldiers, Barrisor,
L'Anou, and Pyrhot, great in deeds of arms;
All which arriv'd at the evenest piece of earth
The field afforded, the three challengers 40
Turn'd head, drew all their rapiers, and stood rank'd;

---

[79] Punning on the two meanings: "comments" and "musical embellishment." Descant was the earliest form of counterpoint.
[80] Punning on the two meanings: "place" (where there can be no fighting) and "musical theme."
[81] *I.e.*, the court, where any fighting was an affront to the sovereign.
[2] So Q1; Q 1641 *Montsurry*, economizing in personnel, though in the next scene Montsurry is informed by Guise of the pardon. Ll. 1–50, however, of II, ii, are omitted in Q 1641.
[1] The same.

[3] Finery. [4] She being.
[5] Sickens from over-feeding, is disgusted by.

When face to face the three defendants met
    them,
Alike prepar'd, and resolute alike.
Like bonfires of contributory wood
Every man's look show'd, fed with either's
    spirit ;
As one had been a mirror to another,
Like forms of life and death, each took from
    other ;
And so were life and death mix'd at their
    heights,
That you could see no fear of death, for life,
Nor love of life, for death ; but in their brows
Pyrrho's [6] opinion in great letters shone :   51
That life and death in all respects are one.
    Hen. Pass'd there no sort of words at their
      encounter?
    Nun. As Hector, 'twixt the hosts of Greece
      and Troy,
When Paris and the Spartan king should end
The nine years' war, held up his brazen lance
For signal that both hosts should cease from
    arms,
And hear him speak : so Barrisor, advis'd,[7]
Advanc'd his naked rapier 'twixt both sides,
Ripp'd up [8] the quarrel, and compar'd six
    lives   60
Then laid in balance with six idle words ;
Offer'd remission and contrition too ;
Or else that he and D'Ambois might conclude
The others' dangers. D'Ambois lik'd the last ;
But Barrisor's friends, being equally engag'd
In the main quarrel, never would expose
His life alone to that they all deserv'd.
And, for the other offer of remission,
D'Ambois, that like a laurel put in fire   69
Sparkl'd and spit, did much more than scorn
That his wrong should incense him so like chaff
To go so soon out, and like lighted paper
Approve his spirit at once both fire and ashes.
So drew they lots and in them fates appointed
That Barrisor should fight with fiery D'Am-
    bois ;
Pyrhot with Melynell ; with Brisac, L'Anou :
A̓nd then like flame and powder they com-
    mix'd,
So spritely, that I wish'd they had been spirits,
That the ne'er-shutting wounds they needs
    must open
Might, as they open'd, shut, and never kill.   80
But D'Ambois' sword, that light'ned as it flew,
Shot like a pointed comet at the face
Of manly Barrisor ; and there it stuck.

Thrice pluck'd he [9] at it, and thrice drew on
    thrusts,
From him [10] that of himself [10] was free as fire ;
Who [10] thrust still as he [9] pluck'd, yet (past
    belief)
He [9] with his subtle eye, hand, body, scap'd.
At last, the deadly bitten point tugg'd off,
On fell his yet undaunted foe so fiercely
That, only made [11] more horrid with his
    wound,   90
Great D'Ambois shrunk, and gave a little
    ground ;
But soon return'd, redoubled [12] in his danger,
And at the heart of Barrisor seal'd his anger.
Then, as in Arden [13] I have seen an oak
Long shook with tempests, and his lofty top
Bent to his root, which being at length made
    loose
Even groaning with his weight, he 'gan to nod
This way and that, as loth his curled brows,
Which he had oft wrapp'd in the sky with
    storms,
Should stoop ; and yet, his radical fibres
    burst,   100
Storm-like he fell, and hid the fear-cold earth :
So fell stout Barrisor, that had stood the shocks
Of ten set battles in your Highness' war,
'Gainst the sole soldier of the world, Navarre.
    Guise. Oh, piteous and horrid murder !
    Beaum.   Such a life
Methinks had metal [14] in it to survive
An age of men.
    Hen.   Such often soonest end.
Thy felt report calls on [15] : we long to know
On what events the other have arriv'd.
    Nun. Sorrow and fury, like two opposite
      fumes   110
Met in the upper region of a cloud,
At the report made by this worthy's fall,
Brake from the earth, and with them rose
    Revenge,
Ent'ring with fresh powers his two noble
    friends ;
And under that odds fell surcharg'd [16] Brisac,
The friend of D'Ambois, before fierce L'Anou ;
Which D'Ambois seeing, as I once did see,
In my young travels through Armenia,
An angry unicorn in his full career

---

[6] Pyrrhon, the sceptic, of Elis.
[7] *I.e.*, with deliberation.   [8] Analyzed.

[9] Bussy.   [10] Barrisor.
[11] Barrisor only being made.
[12] Thrusting himself into danger for the second
time.
[13] The Ardennes.
[14] Undistinguished in spelling from "mettle."
[15] Thy report, heard by us with emotion, incites
us.
[16] Overborne, vanquished.

Charge with too swift a foot a jeweller   120
That watch'd him for the treasure of his brow,[17]
And, ere he could get shelter of a tree,
Nail him with his rich antler to the earth :
So D'Ambois ran upon reveng'd L'Anou,
Who eying th' eager point borne in his face,
And giving back, fell back ; and in his fall
His foe's uncurbed sword stopp'd in his heart ;
By which time all the life-strings of th' tw'
     other
Were cut, and both fell as their [spirits] [18]
     flew   129
Upwards ; and still hunt honor at the view : [19]
And now, of all the six, sole D'Ambois stood
Untouch'd save only with the others' blood.
     Hen. All slain outright?
     Nun.   All slain outright but he,
Who kneeling in the warm life of his friends,
All freckled with the blood his rapier rain'd,
He kiss'd their pale lips, and bade both
     farewell :
And see the bravest man the French earth
     bears !

     Enter Monsieur [*and*] D'Ambois *bare.* [20]

     Bus. Now is the time ; y' are princely
     vow'd my friend ;
Perform it princely, and obtain my pardon.
     Mons. Else Heaven forgive not me ! Come
     on, brave friend ! —   140
If ever nature [21] held herself her own,
When the great trial of a king and subject
Met in one blood, both from one belly spring-
     ing ;
Now prove her virtue [22] and her greatness one,
Or make the tone the greater with the tother,
As true kings should, and for your brother's
     love,
Which is a special species of true virtue,
Do that you could not do, not being a king.
     Hen. Brother, I know your suit ; these
     wilful murders
Are ever past our pardon.
     Mons.   Manly slaughter [150
Should never bear th' account of wilful murder ;
It being a spice [23] of justice, where with life
Offending past [24] law, equal life is laid
In equal balance, to scourge that offence
By law of reputation, which to men

Exceeds all positive law, and what that [25]
     leaves
To true men's valors (not prefixing [26] rights
Of satisfaction, suited to their wrongs)
A free man's eminence may supply and take.
     Hen. This would make every man that
     thinks him wrong'd   160
Or is offended, or in wrong or right,
Lay on this violence, and all vaunt them-
     selves
Law-menders and suppliers, though mere
     butchers ;
Should this fact [27] (though of justice) be
     forgiven?
     Mons. Oh, no, my Lord ; it would make
     cowards fear
To touch the reputations of true men
When only they are left to imp [28] the law.
Justice will soon distinguish murderous minds
From just revengers. Had my friend been
     slain,
His enemy surviving, he [29] should die,   170
Since he had added to a murder'd fame,
Which was in his intent, a murdered man,
And this had worthily been wilful murder ;
But my friend only sav'd his fame's dear life,
Which is above life, taking th' under value,
Which in the wrong it did, was forfeit to him ;
And in this fact only preserves a man
In his uprightness, worthy to survive
Millions of such as murder men alive.
     Hen. Well, Brother, rise, and raise your
     friend withal   180
From death to life ; and D'Ambois, let your
     life,
Refin'd, by passing through this merited death,
Be purg'd from more such foul pollution ;
Nor on your scape nor valor more presuming
To be again so daring.[30]
     Bus.   My Lord,
I loathe as much a deed of unjust death
As law itself doth, and to tyrannize,
Because I have a little spirit to dare
And power to do, as to be tyranniz'd.
This is a grace that, on my knees redoubled,[31]
I crave, to double this, my short life's gift ; 191
And shall your royal bounty centuple :
That I may so make good what [God] [32] and
     nature

---

[17] His horn, supposed to have medicinal **prop-**
erties.
[18] So Q 1 ; Q 1641 *spirit.*
[19] *I.e.*, like hounds in sight of the quarry.
[20] Bareheaded.
[21] *I.e.*, the natural bond between brothers.
[22] Power.
[23] Kind.   [24] Beyond, outside.

[25] *I.e.*, positive law.
[26] Settling beforehand.
[27] Deed.
[28] Graft onto, piece out.
[29] The enemy.
[30] Q 1 *violent.*
[31] Kneeling a second time.
[32] So Q 1 ; Q 1641 *Law.*

Have given me for my good ; since I am free,
Offending no just law, let no law make
By any wrong it does, my life her slave ;
When I am wrong'd, and that law fails to right
  me,
Let me be king myself (as man was made),
And do a justice that exceeds the law ;   199
If my wrong pass the power of single valor
To right and expiate, then be you my king,
And do a right, exceeding law and nature.
Who to himself is law, no law doth need,
Offends no law, and is a king indeed.

     HEN. Enjoy what thou entreat'st ; we give
       but ours.
     BUS. What you have given, my Lord, is
       ever yours.
           Exit REX *cum* BEAUMOND.
     GUISE. [*Mort dieu!*] [33] who would have
       pardon'd such a murder?   *Exit.*
     MONS. Now vanish horrors into court
       attractions,
For which let this balm make thee fresh and
  fair.
And now forth with thy service to the
  Duchess,   210
As my long love will to Montsurry's Countess.
                         Exit.
     BUS. To whom my love hath long been
       vow'd in heart,
Although in hand for show I held [34] the
  Duchess.
And now, through blood and vengeance, deeds
  of height
And hard to be achiev'd, 't is fit I make
Attempt of her perfection. I need fear
No check in his rivality, since her virtues
Are so renown'd, and he of all dames hated.[35]
                         Exit.

[SCENE II] [36]

[*Enter* MONTSURRY, TAMYRA, BEAUPRÉ,
  PERO, CHARLOTTE, [*and*] PYRA.

     MONT. He will have pardon, sure.
     TAM.   'T were pity, else :
For though his great spirit something over-
  flow,
All faults are still borne that from greatness
  grow ;
But such a sudden courtier saw I never.

[33] So Q₁; om. Q 1641.
[34] *I.e.*, Although for the sake of appearances I deceived.
[35] Ll. 210–218 om. Q₁.
[36] A room in Montsurry's house. The first part
of this scene, through l. 50, is omitted in Q 1641.

     BEAU. He was too sudden, which indeed
       was rudeness.
     TAM. True, for it argued his no due con-
       ceit [37]
Both of the place and greatness of the persons,
Nor of our sex : all which (we all being
  strangers
To his encounter) should have made more
  manners
Deserve more welcome.
     MONT.   All this fault is found
Because he lov'd the Duchess and left you. [11
     TAM. Alas, love give her joy ; I am so far
From envy of her honor, that I swear,
Had he encounter'd me with such proud slight,
I would have put that project [38] face of his
To a more test than did her Duchessship.
     BEAU. Why, by your leave, my Lord, I'll
       speak it here,
Although she be my aunt, she scarce was
  modest,
When she perceived the Duke, her husband,
  take
Those late exceptions to her servant's court-
  ship,   20
To entertain him.
     TAM.   Ay, and stand him still,
Letting her husband give her servant place.
Though he did manly, she should be a woman.

           Enter GUISE.

     GUISE. D'Ambois is pardon'd ! Where's a
       king? where law?
See how it runs, much like a turbulent sea,
Here high and glorious as it did contend
To wash the heavens and make the stars more
  pure,
And here so low it leaves the mud of hell
To every common view ; come, Count Mont-
  surry,   29
We must consult of this.
     TAM.   Stay not, sweet lord.
     MONT. Be pleased, I'll straight return.
                 Exit cum GUISE.
     TAM. [*aside*]   Would that would
       please me !
     BEAU. I'll leave you, madam, to your pas-
       sions ;
I see there's change of weather in your looks.
Exit cum suis. [TAMYRA *and* PERO *remain.*]
     TAM. I cannot cloak it ; but, as when a
       fume,
Hot, dry, and gross, within the womb of earth

[37] Understanding.
[38] Base. (*N.E.D.*)

Or in her superficies begot,
When extreme cold hath struck it to her
    heart,
The more it is compress'd, the more it rageth,
Exceeds his prison's strength that should con-
    tain it ;
And then it tosseth temples in the air,   40
All bars made engines to his insolent fury ;
So, of a sudden, my licentious fancy
Riots within me : not my name and house
Nor my religion, to this hour observ'd,
Can stand above it. I must utter that
That will in parting break more strings in me
Than death when life parts ; and that holy
    man
That, from my cradle, counsell'd for my soul,
I now must make an agent for my blood.[39]]   49

Enter Monsieur.[40]

[Mons. Yet, is my mistress gracious?
Tam.   Yet unanswered?]
Mons. Pray thee regard thine own good,
    if not mine,
And cheer my love for that ; you do not know
What you may be by me. nor what without
    me ;
I may have power t' advance and pull down
    any.
Tam. That's not my study. One way I
    am sure
You shall not pull down me ; my husband's
    height
Is crown to all my hopes ; and his retiring
To any mean state, shall be my aspiring ;
My honor's in mine own hands, spite of kings.
Mons. Honor, what's that? Your second
    maidenhead !   60
And what is that? A word. The word is
    gone,
The thing remains : the rose is pluck'd, the
    stalk
Abides ; an easy loss where no lack's found.
Believe it, there's as small lack in the loss
As there is pain i' th' losing ; archers ever
Have two strings to a bow ; and shall great
    Cupid
Archer of archers both in men and women,
Be worse provided than a common archer?
A husband and a friend [41] all wise wives have.
Tam. Wise wives they are that on such
    strings depend,   70
With a firm husband joining a loose friend !

Mons. Still you stand on your husband ;
    so do all
The common sex of you, when y' are en-
    counter'd
With one ye cannot fancy. All men know
You live in court, here, by your own election,
Frequenting all our common sports and tri-
    umphs,
All the most youthful company of men.
And wherefore do you this? To please your
    husband?
'T is gross and fulsome ! if your husband's
    pleasure
Be all your object, and you aim at honor   80
In living close to him, get you from court —
You may have him at home ; these common
    put-offs
For common women serve : " My honor !
    husband ! "
Dames maritorious [42] ne'er were meritorious.
Speak plain, and say, " I do not like you, sir ;
Y' are an ill-favor'd [43] fellow in my eye ; "
And I am answer'd.
Tam.   Then, I pray, be answer'd :
For in good faith, my Lord, I do not like you
In that sort [44] you like.
Mons.   Then have at you, here !
Take, with a politic hand, this rope of
    pearl ;   90
And though you be not amorous, yet be wise :
Take me for wisdom ; he that you can love
Is ne'er the further from you.
Tam.   Now it comes
So ill-prepar'd, that I may take a poison,
Under a medicine as good cheap [45] as it ;
I will not have it were it worth the world.
Mons. Horror of death ! could I but please
    your eye,
You would give me the like, ere you would lose
    me.
" Honor and husband ! "
Tam.   By this light, my Lord,
Y' are a vile fellow, and I 'll tell the King   100
Your occupation of dishonoring ladies
And of his court. A lady cannot live
As she was born, and with that sort of pleasure
That fits her state, but she must be defam'd
With an infamous lord's detraction.
Who would endure the court if these attempts
Of open and profess'd lust must be borne? —
Who's there? Come on, dame ; you are at
    your book

---

[39] Passion.
[40] Q 1641 adds *Tamyra and Pero with a book.*
[41] Lover.

[42] Overfond of their husbands.   [43] Ugly.
[44] Way.
[45] At as good a bargain; *i.e.*, as readily as.

When men are at your mistress ; have I taught
    you
Any such waiting woman's quality?   110
    Mons. Farewell, good " husband."
                       Exit Monsieur.
    Tam.   Farewell, wicked lord.

         Enter Montsurry

    Mont. Was not the Monsieur here?
    Tam.   Yes, to good purpose ;
And your cause is as good to seek him, too,
And haunt his company.
    Mont.   Why, what 's the matter?
    Tam. Matter of death, were I some hus-
    bands' wife.
I cannot live at quiet in my chamber,
For opportunities [46] almost to rapes
Offer'd me by him.
    Mont.   Pray thee bear with him.
Thou know'st he is a bachelor and a courtier,
Ay, and a prince ; and their prerogatives [120
Are to their laws, as to their pardons are
Their reservations, after parliaments [47] —
One quits another ; form gives all their essence.
That prince doth high in virtue's reckoning
    stand
That will entreat a vice, and not command.
So far bear with him ; should another man
Trust to his privilege, he should trust to death.
Take comfort, then, my comfort ; nay,
    triumph
And crown thyself, thou part'st [48] with victory ;
My presence is so only dear to thee   130
That other men's appear worse than they be.
For this night yet, bear with my forced
    absence ;
Thou know'st my business ; and with how
    much weight.
My vow hath charg'd it.
    Tam.   True, my Lord, and never
My fruitless love shall let [49] your serious
    honor : [50]
Yet, sweet lord, do no[t] stay ; you know my
    soul
Is so long time without me, and I dead,
As you are absent.
    Mont.   By this kiss, receive
My soul for hostage, till I see my love.   139
    Tam. The morn shall let me see you?

    Mont.   With the sun
I 'll visit thy more comfortable [51] beauties.
    Tam. This is my comfort, that the sun hath
    left
The whole world's beauty ere my sun leaves
    me.
    Mont. 'T is late night now indeed ; fare-
    well, my light.   *Exit.*
    Tam. Farewell, my light and life — but not
    in him :
In mine own dark love and light bent to
    another.
Alas that in the [wane] [52] of our affections
We should supply it with a full dissembling,
In which each youngest maid is grown a
    mother ;
Frailty is fruitful, one sin gets another.   150
Our loves like sparkles are that brightest shine
When they go out ; most vice shows most
    divine. —
Go, maid, to bed ; lend me your book, I pray ;
Not like yourself for form ; I 'll this night
    trouble
None of your services. Make sure the doors,
And call your other fellows to their rest.
    Pero. I will. — [*aside*] Yet I will watch [53]
    to know why you watch.   *Exit.*
    Tam. Now all ye peaceful regents of the
    night,
Silently gliding exhalations,
Languishing winds, and murmuring falls of
    waters,   160
Sadness of heart and ominous secureness,
Enchantments, dead sleeps, all the friends of
    rest,
That ever wrought upon the life of man,
Extend your utmost strengths, and this
    charm'd hour
Fix like the centre ; [54] make the violent wheels
Of Time and Fortune stand ; and great Ex-
    istence,
The Maker's treasury, now not seem to be,
To all but my approaching friends and me.
They come ; alas, they come ! Fear, fear and
    hope
Of one thing, at one instant fight in me ;   170
I love what most I loathe, and cannot live
Unless I compass that which holds my death ;
For life 's mere death, loving one that loathes
    me,
And he I love will loathe me, when he sees

---

[46] Importunities.
[47] *I.e.*, the royal prerogative bears the same relation to the laws as a monarch's exceptions (from
pardons) made after Parliament is prorogued do
to the original pardons.
[48] Leavest (the field).
[49] Hinder.   [50] Q₁ *profit.*

[51] Comforting.
[52] Emend. Dilke ; old eds. *wave.*
[53] Stay up.
[54] Of the earth.

I fly my sex, my virtue, my renown,
To run so madly on a man unknown.

The vault opens.

See, see, a vault is opening that was never
Known to my lord and husband, nor to any
But him that brings the man I love, and me.
How shall I look on him? How shall I live,
And not consume in blushes? I will in,   181
And cast myself off, as I ne'er had been.[55]

Exit.

Ascendit Friar *and* D'Ambois.

Friar. Come, worthiest son, I am past
     measure glad,
That you, whose worth I have approv'd so
     long,
Should be the object of her fearful love ;
Since both your wit and spirit can adapt
Their full force to supply her utmost weakness.
You know her worths and virtues, for report
Of all that know is to a man a knowledge ; [189
You know besides, that our affections' storm,
Rais'd in our blood, no reason can reform.
Though she seek then their satisfaction
(Which she must needs, or rest unsatisfied),
Your judgment will esteem her peace, thus
     wrought,
Nothing less dear than if yourself had sought ;
And (with another color,[56] which my art
Shall teach you to lay on) yourself must seem
The only agent, and the first orb move [57]
In this our set and cunning world of love.

Bus. Give me the color, my most honor'd
     father,   200
And trust my cunning then to lay it on.

Friar. 'T is this, good son : Lord Barrisor,
     whom you slew,
Did love her dearly, and with all fit means
Hath urg'd his acceptation, of all which
She keeps one letter written in his blood.
You must say thus, then, that you heard from
     me
How much herself was touch'd in conscience
With a report, which is in truth dispers'd
That your main quarrel grew about her love,
Lord Barrisor imagining your courtship   210
Of the great Guise's Duchess in the presence,
Was by you made to his elected mistress
And so made me your mean now to resolve her,

---

[55] Undress as if I had never been watching here. (Boas.)

[56] Pretence.

[57] *I.e.*, must move initially yourself, thus setting her passion in action ; just as, in the Ptolemaic system, the Primum Mobile, the tenth and outer sphere, impelled the motion of all the inner spheres.

Choosing, by my direction, this night's depth
For the more clear avoiding of all note
Of your presumed presence ; and with this,
To clear her hands of such a lover's blood,
She will so kindly thank and entertain you —
Methinks I see how — ay, and ten to one,
Show you the confirmation in his blood,   220
Lest you should think report and she did feign,
That you shall so have circumstantial means
To come to the direct, which must be used :
For the direct is crooked ; love comes flying ;
The height of love is still won with denying.

Bus. Thanks, honor'd father.

Friar.   She must never know
That you know anything of any love
Sustain'd on her part : for, learn this of me,
In anything a woman does alone,
If she dissemble, she thinks 't is not done ; [230
If not dissemble, nor a little chide,
Give her her wish, she is not satisfi'd ;
To have a man think that she never seeks,
Does her more good than to have all she likes :
This frailty sticks in them beyond their sex,
Which to reform, reason is too perplex.
Urge reason to them, it will do no good ;
Humor, that is the chariot of our food
In everybody, must in them be fed,
To carry their affections by it bred.   240
Stand close.

Re-enter Tamyra *with a book.*

Tam. Alas, I fear my strangeness [58] will
     retire him.
If he go back, I die ; I must prevent it,
And cheer his onset with my sight at least,
And that 's the most ; though every step he
     takes
Goes to my heart. I 'll rather die than seem
Not to be strange to that I most esteem.

Friar. Madam.

Tam.   Ah !

Friar.   You will pardon me, I hope,
That so beyond your expectation,
And at a time for visitants so unfit,   250
I, with my noble friend here, visit you.
You know that my access at any time
Hath ever been admitted ; and that friend
That my care will presume to bring with me
Shall have all circumstance of worth in him
To merit as free welcome as myself.

Tam. Oh, father ! but at this suspicious
     hour
You know how apt best men are to suspect us,
In any cause that makes suspicious shadow

---

[58] Coyness.

No greater than the shadow of a hair ;   260
And y' are to blame. What though my lord
  and husband
Lie forth to-night, and, since I cannot sleep
When he is absent, I sit up to-night?
Though all the doors are sure, and all our
  servants
As sure bound with their sleeps, yet there is
  One
That wakes above, whose eye no sleep can
  bind.
He sees through doors and darkness and our
  thoughts ;
And therefore as we should avoid with fear
To think amiss ourselves before his search,
So should we be as curious to shun   270
All cause that other think not ill of us.
  Bus. Madam, 't is far from that ; I only
  heard,
By this my honor'd father, that your con-
  science
Made some deep scruple with a false report
That Barrisor's blood should something touch
  your honor,
Since he imagin'd I was courting you,
When I was bold to change words with the
  Duchess,
And therefore made his quarrel ; his long love
And service, as I hear, being deeply vowed
To your perfections, which my ready pres-
  ence,   280
Presum'd on with my father at this season
For the more care of your so curious [59] honor,
Can well resolve [60] your conscience, is most
  false.
  Tam. And is it therefore that you come,
  good sir?
Then crave I now your pardon and my father's,
And swear your presence does me so much
  good,
That all I have it binds to your requital.
Indeed, sir, 't is most true that a report
Is spread, alleging that his love to me
Was reason of your quarrel, and because 290
You shall not think I feign it for my glory
That he importun'd me for his court service,[61]
I 'll show you his own hand, set down in blood
To that vain purpose. Good sir, then come
  in.
Father, I thank you now a thousand fold.
       Exit Tamyra *and* D'Ambois.

[59] Scrupulous.
[60] Assure.
[61] *I.e.*, to be my "servant", according to the terminology of courtly love.

Friar. May it be worth it to you, honor'd
  daughter.   *Descendit* Friar.

ACT III — Scene I [1]

Enter D'Ambois, [*and*] Tamyra *with a chain
of pearl.*

  Bus. Sweet mistress, cease ! Your con-
  science is too nice,[2]
And bites too hotly of the Puritan spice.
  Tam. Oh, my dear servant, in thy close
  embraces,
I have set open all the doors of danger
To my encompass'd honor, and my life.
Before I was secure against death and hell,
But now am subject to the heartless fear
Of every shadow and of every breath,
And would change firmness with an aspen leaf ;
So confident a spotless conscience is,   10
So weak a guilty. Oh, the dangerous siege
Sin lays about us, and the tyranny
He exercises when he hath expugn'd ! [3]
Like to the horror of a winter's thunder,
Mix'd with a gushing storm, that suffer noth-
  ing
To stir abroad on earth but their own rages,
Is sin, when it hath gathered head above us ;
No roof, no shelter can secure us so,
But he will drown our cheeks in fear or woe.
  Bus. Sin is a coward, madam, and insults
But on our weakness, in his truest valor ; [4] 21
And so our ignorance tames us, that we let
His shadows fright us ; and like empty clouds,
In which our faulty apprehensions forge
The forms of dragons, lions, elephants,
When they hold no proportion, the sly charms
Of the witch, Policy, makes him like a mon-
  ster
Kept only to show men for servile money.
That false hag often paints him in her cloth
Ten times more monstrous than he is in troth.
In three of us, the secret of our meeting 31
Is only guarded, and three friends as one
Have ever been esteem'd, as our three powers [5]
That in [our] [6] one soul are as one united.
Why should we fear then? For myself I
  swear

[1] The same.
[2] Scrupulous.
[3] Taken by storm.
[4] Only triumphs over our weakness, if its valor
be accurately estimated.
[5] The vegetative, sensitive, and reasoning faculties. (Boas.)
[6] So Q₁ ; om. Q 1641.

Sooner shall torture be the sire to pleasure,
And health be grievous to one long time sick,
Than the dear jewel of your fame in me
Be made an outcast to your infamy ;
Nor shall my value, sacred to your virtues,   40
Only give free course to it, from myself,
But make it fly out of the mouths of kings
In golden vapors and with awful wings.

TAM.   It rests as [7] all kings' seals were set in thee.

Now let us call my father, whom I swear
I could extremely chide, but that I fear
To make him so suspicious of my love
Of which, sweet servant, do not let him know
For all the world.

BUS.   Alas ! he will not think it. [49

TAM. Come, then. — Ho !   Father, ope, and take your friend.   *Ascendit* FRIAR.

FRIAR. Now, honor'd daughter, is your doubt resolv'd.

TAM. Ay, father, but you went away too soon.

FRIAR. Too soon ?

TAM.   Indeed you did ; you should have stayed ;
Had not your worthy friend been of your bringing,
And that contains all laws to temper me,
Not all the fearful danger that besieged us,
Had aw'd my throat from exclamation.

FRIAR. I know your serious disposition well. —
Come, son, the morn comes on.

BUS.   Now, honor'd mistress,
Till farther service call, all bliss supply you. [60

TAM. And you this chain of pearl, and my love only.

Descendit FRIAR *and* D'AMBOIS.

It is not I, but urgent destiny,
That, as great statesmen for their general end
In politic justice make poor men offend,
Enforceth my offence to make it just.
What shall weak dames do, when th' whole work of nature
Hath a strong finger in each one of us ?
Needs must that sweep away the silly cobweb
Of our still-undone labors ; that lays still
Our powers to it,[8] as to the line, the stone, [70
Not to the stone, the line should be oppos'd ;
We cannot keep our constant course in virtue.
What is alike at all parts ?   Every day

Differs from other : every hour and minute ;
Ay, every thought in our false clock of life,
Ofttimes inverts the whole circumference :
We must be sometimes one, sometimes another.
Our bodies are but thick clouds to our souls,
Through which they cannot shine when they desire.
When all the stars, and even the sun himself, [80
Must stay the vapors' times that he exhales
Before he can make good his beams to us,
Oh, how can we, that are but motes to him,
Wand'ring at random in his ordered rays,
Disperse our passions' fumes with our weak labors,
That are more thick and black than all earth's vapors?

Enter MONTSURRY.

MONT. Good day, my love ; what, up and ready [9] too !

TAM. Both, my dear Lord ; not all this night made I
Myself unready, or could sleep a wink.

MONT. Alas ! what troubled my true love, my peace,   90
From being at peace within her better self ?
Or how could sleep forbear to seize thine eyes
When he might challenge them as his just prize ?

TAM. I am in no pow'r earthly, but in yours ;
To what end should I go to bed, my Lord,
That wholly miss'd the comfort of my bed?
Or how should sleep possess my faculties,
Wanting the proper closer of mine eyes?

MONT. Then will I nevermore sleep night from thee.
All mine own business, all the King's affairs, [100
Shall take the day to serve them ; every night
I 'll ever dedicate to thy delight.

TAM. Nay, good my Lord, esteem not my desires
Such doters on their humors that my judgment
Cannot subdue them to your worthier pleasure ;
A wife's pleas'd husband must her object be
In all her acts, not her sooth'd fantasy.[10]

MONT. Then come, my love, now pay those rites to sleep
Thy fair eyes owe him.   Shall we now to bed?

TAM. Oh, no, my Lord ; your holy friar says   110

---

[7] Remains (as inviolable) as if.
[8] Nature ever brings our powers into line with itself, just as the builder brings the stone into line with his plan.

[9] Dressed.
[10] Caprice, whim.

All couplings in the day that touch the bed
Adulterous are, even in the married ;
Whose grave and worthy doctrine, well I
    know,
Your faith in him will liberally allow.
    MONT. He's a most learned and religious
    man.
Come to the presence, then, and see great
    D'Ambois,
Fortune's proud mushroom shot up in a night,
Stand like an Atlas under our King's arm ;
Which greatness [11] with him Monsieur now
    envies [12]
As bitterly and deadly as the Guise.   120
    TAM. What, he that was but yesterday his
    maker,
His raiser and preserver?
    MONT.   Even the same.
Each natural agent works but to this end,
To render that it works on like itself ;
Which since the Monsieur in his act on D'Am-
    bois
Cannot to his ambitious end effect,
But that, quite opposite, the King hath power
In his love borne to D'Ambois, to convert
The point of Monsieur's aim on his own
    breast,
He turns his outward love to inward hate.   130
A prince's love is like the lightning's fume,
Which no man can embrace, but must con-
    sume.   *Exeunt.*

[SCENE II] [13]

Enter HENRY, D'AMBOIS, MONSIEUR, GUISE,
DUCHESS, ANNABELLE, CHARLOTTE, [*and*]
Attendants.

    HEN. Speak home, Bussy ; [14] thy impartial
    words
Are like brave falcons that dare truss [15] a fowl
Much greater than themselves ; flatterers are
    kites
That check at [16] sparrows ; thou shalt be my
    eagle,
And bear my thunder underneath thy wings ;
Truth's words like jewels hang in th' ears of
    kings.
    BUS. Would I might live to see no Jews
    hang there

---

[11] *I.e.*, favor.
[12] Accented on second syllable.
[13] Unlocated. Presumably within the royal palace ;
certainly, after Maffé's entrance, the apartments of
Monsieur.
[14] Q₁ *my Bussy.*
[15] Seize.
[16] Turn from the game, to pursue.

Instead of jewels ; sycophants, I mean,
Who use truth like the Devil, his true foe,
Cast by the angel to the pit of fears,   10
And bound in chains ; truth seldom decks
    kings' ears.
Slave Flattery (like a rippier's [17] legs roll'd up
In boots of hay ropes) with kings' soothed guts
Swaddled and strappl'd, [18] now lives only free.
Oh, 't is a subtle knave ; how like the plague
Unfelt he strikes into the brain of man,
And rageth in his entrails, when he can,
Worse than the poison of a red-hair'd man ! [19]
    HEN. Fly at him and his brood ; I cast
    thee off, [20]
And once more give thee surname of mine
    eagle.   20
    BUS. I'll make you sport enough, then ;
    let me have
My lucerns [21] too, or dogs inur'd to hunt
Beasts of most rapine, but to put them up, [22]
And if I truss not, let me not be trusted.
Show me a great man (by the people's voice,
Which is the voice of God) that by his great-
    ness
Bombasts [23] his private roofs with public
    riches ;
That affects royalty, rising from a clapdish ; [24]
That rules so much more by his suffering
    king, [25]
That he makes kings of his subordinate slaves :
Himself and them graduate [26] like wood-
    mongers,   31
Piling a stack of billets from the earth,
Raising each other into steeples' heights ;
Let him convey this on the turning props
Of Protean [27] law, and, his own counsel keep-
    ing, [28]
Keep all upright ; let me but hawk at him,
I'll play the vulture, and so thump his liver,
That, like a huge unlading argosy,
He shall confess all, and you then may hang
    him.

---

[17] *Rippier* = "one who carries fish inland to
sell." (*N.E.D.*)
[18] Strapped, bound.
[19] *I.e.*, from his body ; the common representation
of Judas as red-headed seems to have given rise
to this superstition.
[20] Loose thee at the game.
[21] Here = "hounds", though properly " lynxes."
[22] Start them up.
[23] Stuffs.
[24] The wooden dish of the beggar, who clapped
the cover against it to attract attention.
[25] By his king's sufferance.   Q₁ *than.*
[26] Rise by steps.
[27] *I.e.*, assuming various forms to suit various
exigencies.
[28] *I.e.*, retaining a lawyer especially for his affairs.

Show me a clergyman, that is in voice   40
A lark of heaven, in heart a mole of earth ;
That hath good living, and a wicked life ;
A temperate look, and a luxurious gut ;
Turning the rents of his superfluous cures [29]
Into your pheasants and your partridges ;
Venting their quintessence as men read He-
    brew ; [30]
Let me but hawk at him, and, like the other,
He shall confess all, and you then may hang
    him.
Show me a lawyer that turns sacred law
(The equal rend'rer of each man his own,   50
The scourge of rapine and extortion,
The sanctuary and impregnable defence
Of retir'd learning and besieged virtue)
Into a harpy, that eats all but 's own,
Into the damned sins it punisheth ;
Into the synagogue of thieves and atheists,
Blood into gold, and justice into lust ;
Let me but hawk at him, as at the rest,
He shall confess all, and you then may hang
    him.

    Enter MONTSURRY, TAMYRA, *and* PERO.

GUISE. Where will you find such game as
    you would hawk at?   60
BUS. I 'll hawk about your house for one of
    them.
GUISE. Come, y' are a glorious [31] ruffian,
    and run proud
Of the King's headlong graces. Hold your
    breath,
Or, by that poison'd vapor, not the King
Shall back your murderous valor against me.
BUS. I would the King would make his
    presence free
But for one bout betwixt us : by the rever-
    ence
Due to the sacred space 'twixt kings and sub-
    jects,
Here would I make thee cast that popular [32]
    purple,[33]
In which thy proud soul sits and braves thy
    sovereign.   70
MONS. Peace, peace, I pray thee peace.
BUS.   Let him peace first
That made the first war.
MONS.   He 's the better man.
BUS. And therefore may do worst?

MONS.   He has more titles.
BUS. So Hydra had more heads.
MONS.   He 's greater known.
BUS. His greatness is the people's ; mine 's
    mine own.
MONS. He 's [nobler] [34] born.
BUS.   He is not, I am noble ;
And noblesse in his [35] blood hath no gradation,
But in his merit.
GUISE.   Th' art not nobly born,
But bastard to the Cardinal of Ambois.[36]
BUS. Thou liest, proud Guiserd. — Let me
    fly, my Lord.   80
HEN. Not in my face, my eagle ; violence
    flies
The sanctuaries of a prince's eyes.
BUS. Still shall we chide and foam upon
    this bit?
Is the Guise only great in faction? [37]
Stands he not by himself? Proves he th'
    opinion
That men's souls are without them? Be a
    duke,[38]
And lead me to the field.
GUISE.   Come, follow me.
HEN. Stay them ! — Stay, D'Ambois. —
    Cousin Guise, I wonder
Your honor'd disposition brooks so ill
A man so good, that only would uphold   90
Man in his native noblesse, from whose fall
All our dimensions rise ; that in himself,
Without the outward patches of our frailty,
Riches and honor, knows he comprehends
Worth with the greatest. Kings had never
    borne
Such boundless empire over other men,
Had all maintain'd the spirit and state of
    D'Ambois ;
Nor had the full impartial hand of nature
That all things gave in her original [39]   99
Without these definite terms of mine and thine,
Been turn'd unjustly to the hand of Fortune,
Had all preserv'd her in her prime, like D'Am-
    bois.
No envy, no disjunction had dissolv'd,
Or pluck'd one stick out of the golden faggot
In which the world of Saturn [40] bound our
    lives,
Had all been held together with the nerves,

---

[29] As a pluralist.
[30] Backwards.
[31] Vainglorious, bragging.
[32] Alluding to the fact that Guise was more popular than Henry with the Parisians.
[33] *I.e.*, the garment betokening your royal blood.

[34] Emend. Neilson ; old eds. *nobly.*
[35] Its.
[36] He was actually Bussy's great-uncle, and died long before the latter's birth.
[37] As a fomenter of political faction.
[38] Since *dux* = leader.
[39] Beginning.   [40] The Golden Age.

The genius, and th' ingenuous [41] soul of D'Am-
  bois.
Let my hand therefore be the Hermean rod [42]
To part and reconcile, and so conserve you,
As my combin'd embracers and supporters.
  BUS. 'T is our King's motion, and we shall
    not seem   111
To worst eyes womanish, though we change
    thus soon
Never so great grudge for his greater pleasure.
  GUISE. I seal to that; and, so the manly
    freedom
That you so much profess, hereafter prove
    not
A bold and glorious license to deprave,[43]
To me his hand shall hold the Hermean vir-
    tue
His Grace affects, in which submissive sign
On this his sacred right hand I lay mine.
  BUS. 'T is well, my Lord, and, so your
    worthy greatness   120
Decline not to the greater insolence,
Nor make you think it a prerogative
To rack men's freedoms with the ruder wrongs,
My hand, stuck full of laurel, in true sign
'T is wholly dedicate to righteous peace,
In all submission kisseth th' other side.
  HEN. Thanks to ye both; and kindly I
    invite ye
Both to a banquet, where we 'll sacrifice
Full cups to confirmation of your loves;   129
At which, fair ladies, I entreat your presence;
And hope you, madam, will take one carouse
For reconcilement of your lord and servant.
  DUCH. If I should fail, my Lord, some other
    lady
Would be found there to do that for my serv-
    ant.
  MONS. Any of these here?
  DUCH.   Nay, I know not that.
  BUS. Think your thoughts like my mis-
    tress', honor'd lady?
  TAM. I think not on you, sir; y' are one I
    know not.
  BUS. Cry you mercy, madam.
  MONT.   Oh, sir, has she met you?

Exeunt HENRY, D'AMBOIS, [*and*] Ladies.

  MONS. What had my bounty drunk when
    it rais'd him?

  GUISE. Y' ave stuck us up a very worthy
    flag,   140
That takes more wind than we with all our
    sails.
  MONS. Oh, so he spreads and flourishes.
  GUISE.   He must down;
Upstarts should never perch too near a crown.
  MONS. 'T is true, my Lord; and as this
    doting hand,
Even out of earth, like Juno, struck this
    giant,[44]
So Jove's great ordnance shall be here impli'd
To strike him under th' Ætna of his pride;
To which work lend your hands, and let us
    cast [45]
Where we may set snares for his ranging [46]
    greatness.   149
I think it best, amongst our greatest women;
For there is no such trap to catch an upstart
As a loose downfall; for you know their falls
Are th' ends of all men's rising. If great men
And wise make scapes to please advantage,[47]
'T is with a woman: women that worst may
Still hold men's candles; [48] they direct and
    know
All things amiss in all men; and their women [49]
All things amiss in them; through whose
    charm'd mouths,
We may see all the close scapes of the court.
When the most royal beast of chase, the hart,
Being old and cunning in his lairs and haunts,
Can never be discovered to the bow,   162
The piece,[50] or hound; yet where, behind some
    quitch,[51]
He breaks his gall, and rutteth with his hind,
The place is mark'd, and by his venery
He still is taken. Shall we then attempt
The chiefest mean to that discovery here,
And court our greatest ladies' chiefest women
With shows of love and liberal promises?
'T is but our breath. If something given in
    hand   170
Sharpen their hopes of more, 't will be well
    ventur'd.
  GUISE. No doubt of that; and 't is the
    cunning'st point
Of your devis'd investigation.

[41] So Q₁; Q 1641 *ingenious*. The words were not
distinguished in spelling.
[42] The caduceus. Its twining serpents had been
fighting when Hermes separated them with his rod.
[43] Malign.
[44] An allusion to the myth of Typhon.
[45] Plan.
[46] Q ₁ *gadding*.
[47] Indulge in escapades which give (their enemies)
opportunity. Parrott emends *advantages*.
[48] Women that can actually do least, nevertheless
see all that is going on.
[49] Waiting women.
[50] Gun.
[51] Grass.

MONS.   I have broken
The ice to it already with the woman
Of your chaste lady, and conceive good hope
I shall wade thorough to some wished shore
At our next meeting.
MONT.   Nay, there's small hope there.
GUISE. Take say [52] of her, my Lord, she
    comes most fitly.
MONS. Starting back?

Enter CHARLOTTE, ANNABELLE, [*and*] PERO.

GUISE. Y' are engag'd, indeed.   180
ANNA. Nay, pray, my Lord, forbear.
MONT. [*drawing* ANNABELLE *aside*] What,
skittish, servant?
ANNA. No, my Lord, I am not so fit for your
service.
CHAR. Pray pardon me now, my Lord;
my Lady expects me.
GUISE. [*drawing* CHARLOTTE *aside*] I'll satisfy her expectation, as far as an uncle may.
MONS. Well said; a spirit of court- [190
ship of all hands. — [*drawing* PERO *aside*] Now
mine own Pero, hast thou rememb'red me for
the discovery I entreated thee make of thy
mistress? Speak boldly, and be sure of all
things I have sworn to thee.
PERO. Building on that assurance, my
Lord, I may speak; and much the rather,
because my Lady hath not trusted me with
that I can tell you; for now I cannot be said
to betray her.   200
MONS. That's all one, so we reach our
objects. Forth, I beseech thee.
PERO. To tell you truth, my Lord, I have
made a strange discovery.
MONS. Excellent! Pero, thou reviv'st me.
May I sink quick to perdition if my tongue
discover [53] it.
PERO. 'T is thus, then: this last night, my
Lord lay forth; and I, watching my lady's
sitting up, stole up at midnight from my [210
pallet; and (having before made a hole both
through the wall and arras to her inmost
chamber) I saw D'Ambois and herself read-
ing a letter.[54]
MONS. D'Ambois?
PERO. Even he, my Lord.
MONS. Dost thou not dream, wench?
PERO. I swear he is the man.
MONS. The Devil he is, and thy lady his
dam! — [*aside*] Why, this was the hap- [220

piest shot that ever flew! The just plague
of hypocrisy levell'd [55] it. Oh, the infinite
regions betwixt a woman's tongue and her
heart! Is this our goddess of chastity? I
thought I could not be so slighted if she had
not her fraught besides, and therefore plotted
this with her woman, never dreaming of
D'Ambois. — Dear Pero, I will advance thee
for ever; but tell me now — God's precious,
it transforms me with admiration [56] — [230
sweet Pero, whom should she trust with this
conveyance? Or, all the doors being made
sure, how should his conveyance be made?
PERO. Nay, my Lord, that amazes me; I
cannot by any study so much as guess at it.
MONS. Well, let's favor our apprehensions
with forbearing that a little; for if my heart
were not hoop'd with adamant, the conceit [57]
of this would have burst it. But hark thee.
                                    Whispers.
[CHAR. I swear to your Grace, all that [240
I can conjecture touching my Lady your
niece, is a strong affection she bears to the
English Milor'.
GUISE. All, quod you? 'T is enough, I
assure you; but tell me —] [58]
MONT. I pray thee, resolve me; the Duke
will never imagine that I am busy about 's
wife. Hath D'Ambois any privy access to
her?
ANNA. No, my Lord; D'Ambois neg- [250
lects her, as she takes it, and is therefore suspicious that either your lady, or the Lady
Beaupré hath closely [59] entertain'd him.
MONT. By 'r lady, a likely suspicion, and
very near the life,[60] especially of my wife.
MONS. Come, we'll disguise all with seeming only to have courted. — Away, dry palm: [61]
sh'as a liver [62] as dry as a biscuit; a man may
go a whole voyage with her, and get nothing
but tempests from her windpipe.   260
GUISE. Here's one, I think, has swallowed
a porcupine, she casts pricks from her tongue
so.
MONT. And here's a peacock seems to have
devour'd one of the Alps, she has so swelling a
spirit, and is so cold of her kindness.
CHAR. We are no windfalls, my Lord; ye
must gather us with the ladder of matrimony,
or we'll hang till we be rotten.

---

[52] Make trial.   [53] Reveal.
[54] For "herself . . . letter" Q₁ reads *she set close
at a banquet.*

[55] Aimed.   [56] Wonder.
[57] Thought.   [58] So Q₁; om. Q 1641.
[59] Secretly.
[60] Q₁ inserts *if she marks it.*
[61] Supposed to be a sign of chastity.
[62] Supposed to be the seat of love.

MONS. Indeed, that's the way to make [270
ye right openarses.[63] But, alas! ye have no
portions fit for such husbands as we wish you.

PERO. Portions, my Lord? Yes, and such
portions as your principality cannot purchase.

MONS. What, woman? what are those portions?

PERO. Riddle my riddle, my Lord.

MONS. Ay, marry, wench, I think thy portion is a right riddle : a man shall never find
it out. But let's hear it.   280

PERO. You shall, my Lord.
" What's that, that being most rare's most
     cheap?
That when you sow, you never reap?
That when it grows most, most you in [64] it?
And still you lose it when you win it ;
That when 't is commonest, 't is dearest,
And when 't is farthest off, 't is nearest?"

MONS. Is this your great portion?

PERO. Even this, my Lord.

MONS. Believe me, I cannot riddle it.   290

PERO. No, my Lord : 't is my chastity,
which you shall neither riddle nor fiddle.

MONS. Your chastity? Let me begin with
the end of it ; how is a woman's chastity nearest a man when 't is furthest off?

PERO. Why, my Lord, when you cannot
get it, it goes to th' heart on you ; and that,
I think, comes most near you ; and I am sure
it shall be far enough off. And so we leave
you to our mercies.   300

                Exeunt Women.

MONS. Farewell, riddle.

GUISE. Farewell, medlar.

MONT. Farewell, winter plum.

MONS. Now, my Lords, what fruit of our
inquisition? Feel you nothing budding yet?
Speak, good my Lord Montsurry.

MONT. Nothing but this : D'Ambois is
thought negligent in observing the Duchess,
and therefore she is suspicious that your
niece or my wife closely entertains him.   310

MONS. Your wife, my Lord? Think you
that possible?

MONT. Alas, I know she flies him like her
last hour.

MONS. Her last hour? Why, that comes
upon her the more she flies it. Does
D'Ambois so, think you?

MONT. That's not worth the answering.
'T is miraculous to think with what monsters

women's imaginations engross them when [320
they are once enamor'd, and what wonders
they will work for their satisfaction. They
will make sheep valiant, a lion fearful.

MONS. [*aside*] And an ass confident. —
Well, my Lord, more will come forth shortly ;
get you to the banquet.

GUISE. Come, my Lord ; I have the blind
side of one of them.

         Exit GUISE *cum* MONTSURRY.

MONS. Oh, the unsounded sea of women's
     bloods,   329
That when 't is calmest, is most dangerous ;
Not any wrinkle creaming [65] in their faces
When in their hearts are Scylla and Charybdis,
Which still are hid in dark and standing fogs,
Where never day shines, nothing never grows
But weeds and poisons, that no statesman
     knows ;
Not Cerberus ever saw the damned nooks
Hid with the veils of women's virtuous looks.
[66] But what a cloud of sulphur have I drawn
Up to my bosom in this dangerous secret !   339
Which if my haste with any spark should light,
Ere D'Ambois were engag'd [67] in some sure plot,
I were blown up ; he would be, sure, my death.
Would I had never known it, for before
I shall persuade th' importance to Montsurry,
And make him with some studied stratagem
Train D'Ambois to his wreak,[68] his maid may
     tell it,
Or I, out of my fiery thirst to play
With the fell tiger, up in darkness tied,
And give it some light, make it quite break
     loose.
I fear it, afore Heaven, and will not see   350
D'Ambois again, till I have told Montsurry
And set a snare with him to free my fears. —
Who's there?

         Enter MAFFÉ.

MAF.   My Lord?

MONS.   Go call the Count Montsurry,
And make the doors fast ; I will speak with
     none
Till he come to me.

---

[63] Medlars, so called with reference to the large
open disk between the persistent calyx-lobes.
(*N.E.D.*)   [64] Boas emends *thin*.

[65] *I.e.*, wrinkling.   [67] *I.e.*, caught.
[66] Instead of ll. 338–407, Q₁ reads :
    I will conceale all yet, and give more time
    To D'Ambois' triall, now upon my hooke ;
    He awes my throat ; else, like Sybillas cave,
    It should breathe oracles ; I feare him strangely,
    And may resemble his advanced valour
    Unto a spirit rais'd without a circle,
    Endangering him that ignorantly rais'd him,
    And for whose furie he hath learn'd no limit.
[68] Lure D'Ambois to the vengeance of Montsurry.

MAF.   Well, my Lord.   *Exiturus.*
MONS.   Or else
Send you some other, and see all the doors
Made safe yourself, I pray ; haste, fly about it.
    MAF. You 'll speak with none but with the
        Count Montsurry?
    MONS. With none but he, except it be the
        Guise.
    MAF. See even by this, there 's one excep-
        tion more !   360
Your Grace must be more firm in the com-
    mand,
Or else shall I as weakly execute.
The Guise shall speak with you?
    MONS.   He shall, I say.
    MAF. And Count Montsurry?
    MONS.   Ay, and Count Montsurry.
    MAF. Your Grace must pardon me, that I
        am bold
To urge the clear and full sense of your pleas-
    ure ;
Which, whensoever I have known, I hope
Your Grace will say I hit it to a hair.
    MONS. You have.
    MAF.   I hope so, or I would be glad —
    MONS. I pray thee get thee gone ; thou art
        so tedious   370
In the strict form of all thy services
That I had better have one negligent.
You hit my pleasure well when D'Ambois hit
    you,
Did you not, think you?
    MAF.   D'Ambois? Why, my Lord —
    MONS. I pray thee talk no more, but shut
        the doors :
Do what I charge thee.
    MAF.   I will, my Lord, and yet
I would be glad the wrong I had of D'Am-
    bois —
    MONS. Precious ! then it is a fate that
        plagues me   378
In this man's foolery ; I may be murdered
While he stands on protection of his folly. —
Avaunt ; about thy charge.
    MAF.   I go, my Lord. —
[*aside*] I had my head broke in his faithful
    service ;
I had no suit the more, nor any thanks,
And yet my teeth must still be hit with
    D'Ambois —
D'Ambois, my Lord, shall know —
    MONS.   The Devil and D'Ambois !
                      Exit MAFFÉ.
How am I tortur'd with this trusty fool !
Never was any curious in his place

To do things justly, but he was an ass ;
We cannot find one trusty that is witty,[69]
And therefore bear their disproportion.   390
Grant thou, great star and angel [70] of my life,
A sure lease of it but for some few days,
That I may clear my bosom of the snake
I cherish'd there, and I will then defy
All check to it but Nature's, and her altars
Shall crack with vessels crown'd with every
    liquor
Drawn from her highest and most bloody hu-
    mors.
I fear him strangely ; his advanced valor
Is like a spirit rais'd without a circle,[71]   399
Endangering him   that   ignorantly   rais'd
    him,
And for whose fury he hath learnt no limit.

Re-enter MAFFÉ *hastily.*

    MAF. I cannot help it — what should I do
        more ?
As I was gathering a fit guard to make
My passage to the doors, and the doors sure,
The man of blood is enter'd.   [*Exit* MAFFÉ.]
    MONS.   Rage of death !
If I had told the secret, and he knew it,
Thus had I been endanger'd.

Enter D'AMBOIS.

                         My sweetheart !
How now, what leap'st thou at?
    BUS.   O royal object !
    MONS. Thou dream'st, awake ; object in
        th' empty air?
    BUS. Worthy the brows of Titan, worth
        his chair.   410
    MONS. Pray thee, what mean'st thou?
    BUS.   See you not a crown
Impale [72] the forehead of the great King
    Monsieur?
    MONS. Oh, fie upon thee !
    BUS.   Prince, that is the subject
Of all these your retir'd and sole discourses.
    MONS. Wilt thou not leave that wrongful
        supposition?
    BUS. Why wrongful, to suppose the doubt-
        less right
To the succession worth the thinking on?
    MONS. Well, leave these jests. How I
        am overjoyed

[69] Intelligent.
[70] Tutelary genius.
[71] The magic circle drawn by a conjurer ; as long as it intervened he was safe from the spirits he raised.
[72] Surround.

With thy wish'd presence, and how fit thou
    com'st!
For, of mine honor, I was sending for thee. [420
    Bus. To what end?
    Mons.   Only for thy company,
Which I have still in thought; but that's
    no payment
On thy part made with personal appearance.
Thy absence so long suffered, oftentimes
Put me in some little doubt thou dost not love
    me.
Wilt thou do one thing therefore now sin-
    cerely?
    Bus. Ay, anything, but killing of the King.
    Mons. Still in that discord, and ill-taken
    note?
How most unseasonable thou playest the
    cuckoo,
In this thy fall of friendship!
    Bus.   Then do not doubt, [430
That there is any act within my nerves,
But killing of the King, that is not yours.
    Mons. I will not, then; to prove which
    by my love
Shown to thy virtues, and by all fruits else
Already sprung from that still-flourishing tree,
With whatsoever may hereafter spring,
I charge thee utter, even with all the freedom
Both of thy noble nature and thy friendship,
The full and plain state of me in thy thoughts.
    Bus. What, utter plainly what I think of
    you?   440
    Mons. Plain as truth.
    Bus. Why, this swims quite against the
    stream of greatness;
Great men would rather hear their flatteries,
And if they be not made fools, are not wise.[73]
    Mons. I am no such great fool, and there-
    fore charge thee,
Even from the root of thy free heart, display
    me.
    Bus. Since you affect [74] it in such serious
    terms,
If yourself first will tell me what you think
As freely and as heartily of me,
I'll be as open in my thoughts of you.   450
    Mons. A bargain, of mine honor; and
    make this,
That prove we in our full dissection
Never so foul, live still the sounder friends.
    Bus. What else, sir? Come, pay me
    home; I'll bide it bravely.

    Mons. I will, I swear. I think thee then
    a man
That dares as much as a wild horse or tiger;
As headstrong and as bloody; and, to feed
The ravenous wolf of thy most cannibal valor,
Rather than not employ it thou wouldst turn
Hackster [75] to any whore, slave to a Jew   460
Or English usurer, to force possessions
(And cut men's throats) of mortgaged estates;
Or thou wouldst 'tire thee like a tinker's
    strumpet,
And murder market-folks, quarrel with sheep,
And run as mad as Ajax; [76] serve a butcher;
Do anything but killing of the King:
That in thy valor th' art like other naturals [77]
That have strange gifts in nature, but no soul
Diffus'd quite through, to make them of a
    piece,
But stop at humors that are more absurd, [470
Childish, and villainous than that hackster,
    whore,
Slave, cutthroat, tinker's bitch, compar'd
    before;
And in those humors wouldst envy, betray,
Slander, blaspheme, change each hour a reli-
    gion,
Do anything but killing of the King:
That in thy valor (which is still the dunghill,
To which hath reference [78] all filth in thy
    house)
Th' art more ridiculous and vainglorious
Than any mountebank, and impudent   479
Than any painted bawd; which, not to soothe
And glorify thee like a Jupiter Hammon,
Thou eat'st thy heart in vinegar; and thy gall
Turns all thy blood to poison, which is cause
Of that toad-pool that stands in thy com-
    plexion,
And makes thee with a cold and earthy mois-
    ture,
Which is the dam of putrefaction,
As plague to thy damn'd pride, rot as thou
    liv'st,
To study calumnies and treacheries,
To thy friends' slaughters like a screech-owl
    sing,   489
And do all mischiefs — but to kill the King.
    Bus. So! have you said?
    Mons.   How think'st thou? Do I flatter?
Speak I not like a trusty friend to thee?
    Bus. That ever any man was blest withal.
So here's for me. I think you are, at worst,

---

[73] Do not consider themselves wise unless they
are being made fools of by their flatterers.
[74] Desire.

[75] Bully, hired protector.
[76] See the *Ajax* of Sophocles.
[77] Idiots.   [78] Is carried.

No devil, since y' are like to be no king;
Of which, with any friend of yours, I'll lay
This poor stillado [79] here, 'gainst all the stars,
Ay, and 'gainst all your treacheries, which are
    more,
That you did never good, but to do ill;
But ill of all sorts, free and for itself :   500
That, like a murdering-piece,[80] making lanes
    in armies,
The first man of a rank,[81] the whole rank
    falling,
If you have wrong'd one man, you are so far
From making him amends that all his race,
Friends, and associates, fall into your chase :
That y' are for perjuries the very prince
Of all intelligencers ; [82] and your voice
Is like an eastern wind, that where it flies
Knits nets of caterpillars, with which you
    catch   509
The prime of all the fruits the kingdom yields.
That your political head is the curs'd fount
Of all the violence, rapine, cruelty,
Tyranny, and atheism flowing through the
    realm :
That y' ave a tongue so scandalous, 't will cut
The purest crystal ; [83] and a breath that will
Kill to [84] that wall a spider : you will jest
With God, and your soul to the Devil tender ; [85]
For lust kiss horror, and with death engender :
That your foul body is a Lernean fen [86]
Of all the maladies breeding in all men :   520
That you are utterly without a soul ;
And, for your life, the thread of that was
    spun
When Clotho slept, and let her breathing rock [87]
Fall in the dirt ; and Lachesis still draws it,
Dipping her twisting fingers in a bowl
Defil'd, and crown'd [88] with virtue's forced
    soul :
And lastly (which I must for gratitude
Ever remember) that of all my height
And dearest life, you are the only spring,
Only in royal hope to kill the King.   530
    Mons. Why, now I see thou lov'st me.
    Come to the banquet.   *Exeunt.*

[79] Stiletto.
[80] A small cannon for short ranges.
[81] File.
[82] Spies.
[83] *I.e.*, the diamond. (Parrott.)
[84] At the distance of.
[85] Parrott's punctuation; old eds. have none
after *tender*, and a semicolon after *lust*.
[86] The lair of the Hydra.
[87] Her life-giving distaff.
[88] Brimming. The thread of Monsieur's life is
stained by Lachesis with evil from a bowl filled with
filth and injury to the innocent.

ACT IV — Scene I [1]

[*Enter*] Henry, Monsieur *with a letter*, Guise,
    Montsurry, Bussy, Elenor, Tamyra,
    Beaupré, Pero, Charlotte, Annabelle,
    [*and*] Pyra, *with four* Pages.

    Hen. Ladies, ye have not done our banquet
    right,
Nor look'd upon it with those cheerful rays
That lately turn'd your breaths to floods of
    gold ;
Your looks, methinks, are not drawn out with
    thoughts
So clear and free as heretofore, but foul,
As if the thick complexions of men
Govern'd within them.
    Bus.   'T is not like, my Lord,
That men in women rule, but contrary ;
For as the moon, of all things God created,
Not only is the most appropriate image   10
Or glass to show them how they wax and wane,
But in her height and motion likewise
    bears
Imperial influences that command
In all their powers, and make them wax and
    wane ;
So women, that, of all things made of nothing,
Are the most perfect idols [2] of the moon,
Or still-unwean'd sweet moon-calves with
    white faces,
Not only are patterns of change to men,
But, as the tender moonshine of their beauties
Clears or is cloudy, make men glad or sad ;   20
So then they rule in men, not men in them.
    Mons. But here the moons are chang'd, as
    the King notes,
And either men rule in them, or some power
Beyond their voluntary faculty,[3]
For nothing can recover their lost faces.
    Mont.[4] None can be always one; our
    griefs and joys
Hold several sceptres in us, and have times
For their divided empires ; which [5] grief now,
    in them
Doth prove as proper to his diadem.
    Bus. And grief 's a natural sickness of the
    blood,   30
That time to part asks, as his coming had ;
Only slight fools griev'd suddenly are glad.
A man may say t' a dead man, " Be reviv'd,"
As well as to one sorrowful, " Be not griev'd ; "

[1] A room in the palace.
[2] Q 1 *images.*
[3] Q 1 *motions.*
[4] Q 1 gives this speech to Bussy.
[5] *I.e.*, "times."

And therefore, princely mistress,[6] in all wars
Against these base foes that insult on weak-
    ness,
And still fight hous'd behind the shield of Na-
    ture,
Of privilege, law, treachery, or beastly need,
Your servant cannot help ; authority here
Goes with corruption : something like some
    states,   40
That back worst men ; valor to them must
    creep
That, to themselves left, would fear him asleep.
 DUCH. Ye all take that for granted that
    doth rest
Yet to be prov'd ; we all are as we were,
As merry and as free in thought as ever.
 GUISE. And why then can ye not disclose
    your thoughts?
 TAM. Methinks the man hath answer'd for
    us well.
 MONS. The man? Why, madam, d' ye not
    know his name?
 TAM. Man is a name of honor for a king ;
Additions[7] take away from each chief thing ;
The school of modesty not to learn learns
    dames :   51
They sit in high forms[8] there, that know men's
    names.
 MONS. [*to* BUSSY] Hark ! sweetheart, here's
    a bar set to your valor ;
It cannot enter here ; no, not to notice
Of what your name is. Your great eagle's
    beak,
Should you fly at her, had as good encounter
An Albion cliff, as her more craggy liver.[9]
 BUS. I'll not attempt her, sir ; her sight
    and name,
By which I only know her, doth deter me. 59
 HEN. So do they all men else.
 MONS.   You would say so[10]
If you knew all.
 TAM.   Knew all, my Lord? What mean
    you?
 MONS. All that I know, madam.
 TAM.   That you know? Speak it.
 MONS. No, 't is enough I feel it.
 HEN.   But, methinks
Her courtship is more pure than heretofore ;
True courtiers should be modest, and not
    nice ;[11]

Bold, but not impudent ; pleasure love, not
    vice.
 MONS. [*aside to* BUSSY] Sweetheart ! come
    hither, what if one should make
Horns at Montsurry? Would it not strike
    him jealous
Through all the proofs of his chaste lady's vir-
    tues?
 BUS. [*aside to* MONSIEUR] If he be wise,
    not.   70
 MONS. [*aside to* BUSSY] What? Not if I
    should name the gardener
That I would have him think hath grafted
    him?
 BUS. [*aside to* MONSIEUR] So the large
    licence that your greatness uses
To jest at all men may be taught indeed
To make a difference of the grounds you play
    on,
Both in the men you scandal, and the matter.
 MONS. [*aside to* BUSSY] As how? as how?
 BUS. [*aside to* MONSIEUR]   Perhaps led
    with a train[12]
Where you may have your nose made less and
    slit,
Your eyes thrust out.
 MONS. [*aside to* BUSSY]   Peace, peace, I
    pray thee peace.   79
Who dares do that? The brother of his king?
 BUS. [*aside to* MONSIEUR] Were your king-
    brother in you ; all your powers
(Stretch'd in the arms of great men and their
    bawds),
Set close down by you ; all your stormy laws
Spouted with lawyers' mouths, and gushing
    blood
Like to so many torrents ; all your glories
Making you terrible, like enchanted flames
Fed with bare cockscombs and with crooked
    hams ;
All your prerogatives, your shames, and tor-
    tures ;
All daring Heaven, and opening hell about
    you :
Were I the man ye wrong'd so and provok'd,
Though ne'er so much beneath you, like a box
    tree[13]   91
I would out of the [toughness][14] of my root
Ram hardness, in my lowness, and like death
Mounted on earthquakes, I would trot through
    all
Honors and horrors, thorough foul and fair,

---

[6] The Duchess.
[7] Titles.
[8] On stools of disgrace. (Boas.)
[9] The seat of love. There is also an allusion to the myth of Prometheus.
[10] *I.e.*, all men except Bussy. [11] Overfastidious.

[12] By a trick.
[13] Symbol of lowliness.
[14] So Q[1]; Q 1641 *roughness*.

And from your whole strength toss you into
    the air.
Mons. [*aside to* Bussy] Go, th' art a devil;
    such another spirit
Could not be still'd from all th' Armenian
    dragons.
O my love's glory! Heir to all I have,
(That's all I can say, and that all I swear) 100
If thou outlive me, as I know thou must,
Or else hath nature no proportion'd end
To her great labors; she hath breath'd a mind
Into thy entrails, of desert to swell
Into another great Augustus Cæsar,
Organs and faculties fitted to her greatness;
And should that perish like a common spirit,
Nature's a courtier and regards no merit.
  Hen. Here's naught but whispering with
    us; like a calm
Before a tempest, when the silent air   110
Lays her soft ear close to the earth to hearken
For that she fears steals on to ravish her;
Some fate doth join our ears to hear it coming.
Come, my brave eagle, let's to covert fly;
I see almighty Aether in the smoke
Of all his clouds descending; and the sky
Hid in the dim ostents [15] of tragedy.
      Exit Henry *with* D'Ambois *and* Ladies.
  Guise. Now stir the humor, and begin the
    brawl.
  Mont. The King and D'Ambois now are
    grown all one.
  Mons. Nay, they are two,[16] my Lord.
  Mont.   How's that?
  Mons.   No more. 120
  Mont. I must have more, my Lord.
  Mons.   What, more than two?
  Mont. How monstrous is this!
  Mons.   Why?
  Mont.   You make me horns.
  Mons. Not I; it is a work without my
    power;
Married men's ensigns are not made with
    fingers;
Of divine fabric they are, not men's hands.
Your wife, you know, is a mere [17] Cynthia,[18]
And she must fashion horns out of her nature.
  Mont. But doth she — dare you charge
    her? Speak, false prince.
  Mons. I must not speak, my Lord; but if
    you'll use

The learning of a nobleman, and read,   130
Here's something to those points; soft, you
    must pawn [19]
Your honor having read it to return it.

      Enter Tamyra [*and*] Pero.

  Mont. Not I. I pawn mine honor for a
    paper!
  Mons. You must not buy it under.
            Exeunt Guise *and* Monsieur.
  Mont.   Keep it then,
And keep fire in your bosom.
  Tam.   What says he?
  Mont. You must make good the rest.
  Tam.   How fares my Lord?
Takes my love anything to heart he says?
  Mont. Come y' are a ——
  Tam.   What, my Lord?
  Mont.   The plague of Herod [20]
Feast in his rotten entrails.
  Tam.   Will you wreak
Your anger's just cause given by him, on
    me?   140
  Mont. By him?
  Tam.   By him, my Lord. I have admir'd [21]
You could all this time be at concord with him,
That still hath play'd such discords on your
    honor.
  Mont. Perhaps 't is with some proud [22]
    string of my wife's.
  Tam. How's that, my Lord?
  Mont.   Your tongue will still admire,
Till my head be the miracle of the world.
  Tam. Oh, woe is me!
              She seems to swound.
  Pero. What does your Lordship mean? —
Madam, be comforted; my Lord but tries you.
Madam! — Help, good my Lord, are you not
    mov'd?
Do your set looks print in your words your
    thoughts?   150
Sweet Lord, clear up those eyes, [for shame
    of noblesse,] [23]
Unbend that masking forehead; whence is it
You rush upon her with these Irish wars,[24]

---

[15] Manifestations.
[16] Here Monsieur makes the sign of the cuckold at Montsurry.
[17] Absolute.
[18] A double allusion to Diana as goddess of chastity and as the horned moon.
[19] Pledge. The historical Bussy was betrayed by a letter to Monsieur in which he boasted of his conquest of the Countess.
[20] See *Acts*, xii, 23.
[21] Wondered.
[22] Lascivious.
[23] So Q₁; om. Q 1641.
[24] They are not mentioned in Q₁. Parrott dates the revision of the play shortly after the Irish troubles of 1607 and 1608, since thereafter Ireland was at peace till after Chapman's death. Q₁ (for ll. 152–154), *Mercilesse creature; but it is enough.*

More full of sound than hurt? But it is
enough;
You have shot home; your words are in her
heart;
She has not liv'd to bear a trial now.
    MONT. Look up, my love, and by this kiss
receive
My soul amongst thy spirits for supply
To thine, chas'd with my fury.
    TAM.   Oh, my Lord,
I have too long liv'd to hear this from you. 160
    MONT. 'T was from my troubled blood, and
not from me. —
[*aside*] I know not how I fare; a sudden night
Flows through my entrails, and a headlong
chaos
Murmurs within me, which I must digest,
And not drown her in my confusions,
That was my life's joy, being best inform'd.[25]—
Sweet, you must needs forgive me, that my
love,
Like to a fire disdaining his suppression,
Rag'd being discourag'd; my whole heart is
wounded   169
When any least thought in you is but touch'd,
And shall be till I know your former merits,
Your name and memory, altogether crave
In just oblivion their eternal grave;
And then, you must hear from me, there's no
mean
In any passion I shall feel for you.
Love is a razor, cleansing being well us'd,
But fetcheth blood still being the least abus'd.
To tell you briefly all: the man that left
me
When you appear'd, did turn me worse than
woman,
And stabb'd me to the heart thus, with his
fingers.   180
    TAM. Oh, happy woman! Comes my
stain from him?
It [26] is my beauty, and that innocence proves
That slew Chimaera, rescued Peleus
From all the savage beasts in Pelion,
And rais'd the chaste Athenian prince [27] from
hell;
All suffering with me, they for women's lusts,
I for a man's, that the Augean stable
Of his foul sin would empty in my lap.
How his guilt shunn'd me, sacred innocence

That where thou fear'st, art dreadful! [28] and
his face   190
Turn'd in flight from thee, that had thee in
chase!
Come, bring me to him; I will tell the serpent
Even to his venom'd teeth, from whose curs'd
seed
A pitch'd field starts up 'twixt my lord and
me,[29]
That his throat lies, and he shall curse his
fingers,
For being so govern'd by his filthy soul.
    MONT. I know not if himself, will vaunt
t' have been
The princely author of the slavish sin,
Or any other; he would have resolv'd [30] me
Had you not come; not by his word, but
writing,   200
Would I have sworn to give it him again,
And pawn'd mine honor to him for a paper.
    TAM. See how he flies me still; 't is a foul
heart
That fears his own hand.[31] Good my Lord,
make haste
To see the dangerous paper; papers hold
Ofttimes the forms and copies of our souls,
And, though the world despise them, are the
prizes
Of all our honors; make your honor then
A hostage for it, and with it confer
My nearest woman here, in all she knows; 210
Who, if the sun or Cerberus could have seen
Any stain in me, might as well as they;
And, Pero, here I charge thee by my love,
And all proofs of it, which I might call bounties,
By all that thou hast seen seem good in me,
And all the ill which thou shouldst spit from
thee,
By pity of the wound this touch hath given me,
Not as thy mistress now, but a poor woman
To death given over, rid me of my pains, 219
Pour on thy powder, clear thy breast of me.
My Lord is only here; here speak thy worst:
Thy best will do me mischief. If thou spar'st
me,
Never shine good thought on thy memory!
Resolve my Lord, and leave me desperate.
    PERO. My Lord! My Lord hath play'd a
prodigal's part,
To break his stock for nothing; and an inso-
lent,

---

[25] When I am not reduced to chaos by suspicion.
(Parrott.)
[26] My stain.
[27] Bellerophon (who slew the Chimaera), Peleus,
and Hippolytus (whom Aesculapius restored to
earth) all rejected adulterous advances by women.

[28] Inspirest terror even in those of whom thou
art afraid. (Boas.)
[29] Alluding to Cadmus and the dragon's teeth.
[30] Informed.
[31] Implying that Monsieur had forged the paper.

To cut a gordian when he could not loose it.
What violence is this, to put true fire
To a false train? to blow up long-crown'd peace
With sudden outrage, and believe a man   230
Sworn to the shame of women, 'gainst a woman,
Born to their honors? But I will to him.

TAM. No, I will write (for I shall never more
Meet with the fugitive) where I will defy him,
Were he ten times the brother of my king.
To him, my Lord, and I 'll to cursing him.
Exeunt.

[SCENE II] [32]

Enter D'AMBOIS *and* FRIAR.

BUS. I am suspicious, my most honor'd father,
By some of Monsieur's cunning passages,
That his still ranging and contentious nostrils,
To scent the haunts of Mischief, have so us'd
The vicious virtue of his busy sense,
That he trails hotly of him,[33] and will rouse him,
Driving him all enrag'd and foaming on us;
And therefore have entreated your deep skill
In the command of good aërial spirits,
To assume these magic rites, and call up one
To know if any have reveal'd unto him   11
Anything touching my dear love and me.

FR. Good son, you have amaz'd me but to make
The least doubt of it, it concerns so nearly
The faith and reverence of my name and order.
Yet will I justify, upon my soul,
All I have done. If any spirit i' th' earth or air
Can give you the resolve,[34] do not despair.
[*They retire.*]

Music: and TAMYRA *enters with* PERO, *her maid, bearing a letter.*

TAM. Away, deliver it.   *Exit* PERO.
    — Oh, may my lines,
Fill'd with the poison of a woman's hate,   20
When he shall open them shrink up his curs'd eyes
With torturous darkness, such as stands in hell,
Stuck full of inward horrors, never lighted,
With which are all things to be fear'd, affrighted. — [35]

BUS. [*advancing*] [36] How is it with my honor'd mistress?

TAM. Oh, servant, help, and save me from the gripes
Of shame and infamy. Our love is known;
Your Monsieur hath a paper where is writ
Some secret tokens that decipher it.

BUS. What cold, dull northern brain, what fool but he   30
Durst take into his Epimethean [37] breast
A box of such plagues as the danger yields
Incurr'd in this discovery? He had better
Ventur'd his breast in the consuming reach
Of the hot surfeits cast out of the clouds,
Or stood the bullets that, to wreak the sky,[38]
The Cyclops ram in Jove's artillery.[39]

FRIAR. We soon will take the darkness from his face
That did that deed of darkness; we will know
What now the Monsieur and your husband do,   40
What is contain'd within the secret paper
Offer'd by Monsieur, and your love's events:
To which ends, honor'd daughter, at your motion,
I have put on these exorcising rites,
And, by my power of learned holiness
Vouchsaf'd me from above, I will command
Our resolution of [40] a raised spirit.

TAM. Good father, raise him in some beauteous form
That with least terror I may brook his sight.

FRIAR. Stand sure together, then, whate'er you see;   50
And stir not, as ye tender all our lives.
He puts on his robes.

Occidentalium legionum spiritualium imperator (magnus ille Behemoth) veni, veni, comitatus cum Asaroth locotenente invicto. Adjuro te per Stygis inscrutabilia arcana, per ipsos irremeabiles anfractus Averni: adesto o Behemoth, tu cui pervia sunt Magnatum scrinia; veni, per Noctis & tenebrarum abdita profundissima; per labentia sydera; per ipsos motus horarum furtivos, Hecatesq[ue] altum silentium! Appare in [60

---

[32] Unlocated; presumably a room in Montsurry's house. Ll. 1–18, and s. D., are added by Q 1641.
[33] Is hot on the trail of Mischief.   [34] Information.
[35] By which (even) all fear-inspiring things are themselves frightened.

[36] Q₁ Continues Tamyra's speech: *Father;* a s. D. follows: *Ascendit Bussy with Comolet.* This was cut in the version of Q 1641 because of the new lines at the beginning of the scene.
[37] It was Epimetheus who opened Pandora's box.
[38] To avenge Uranus, deposed by Saturn and the Titans. (Parrott.)
[39] In Jove's war against the Titans.
[40] Information from.

forma spiritali, lucente, splendida, & amabili.[41]
> *Thunder. Ascendit* [BEHEMOTH *with*
> CARTOPHYLAX [42] *and other spirits*].

BEH. What would the holy Friar?

FRIAR.   I would see
What now the Monsieur and Montsurry do,
And see the secret paper that the Monsieur
Offer'd to Count Montsurry, longing much
To know on what events the secret loves
Of these two honor'd persons shall arrive.

BEH. Why call'dst thou me to this accursed
> light
To these light purposes? I am emperor
Of that inscrutable darkness where are hid   70
All deepest truths and secrets never seen,
All which I know ; and command legions
Of knowing spirits that can do more than these.
Any of this my guard that circle me
In these blue fires, and out of whose dim fumes
Vast murmurs use to break, and from their
> sounds
Articulate voices, can do ten parts more
Than open such slight truths as you require.

FRIAR. From the last night's black depth I
> call'd up one
Of the inferior ablest ministers,   80
And he could not resolve me. Send one then
Out of thine own command, to fetch the paper
That Monsieur hath to show to Count Mont-
> surry.

BEH. I will. — Cartophylax, thou that
> properly
Hast in thy power all papers so inscrib'd,
Glide through all bars to it and fetch that
> paper.

CAR. I will.   *A* Torch *removes.*

FRIAR.   Till he returns, great Prince
> of darkness,
Tell me if Monsieur and the Count Montsurry
Are yet encounter'd?

BEH.   Both them and the Guise
Are now together.

FRIAR.   Show us all their persons, [90
And represent the place, with all their actions.

BEH. The spirit will straight return, and
> then I 'll show thee. [*A* Torch *returns.*]

[41] Emperor of the legions of the western spirits,
great Behemoth, come, come, attended by [Ash-
toreth], thy unconquered lieutenant. I adjure thee
by the Styx's inscrutable secrets, by the windings of
Avernus, whence there is no return, appear, O
Behemoth, thou unto whom are accessible the
letter-files of the great. Come! — by the hidden
deeps of Night and of the infernal regions, by the
wandering stars, by the stealthy motion of the hours,
and the deep silence of Hecate! Appear in the
form of a spirit, bright, resplendent, and amiable.
[42] Guardian of papers.

See, he is come. — Why brought'st thou not
> the paper?

CAR. He hath prevented me, and got a
> spirit
Rais'd by another, great in our command,[43]
To take the guard of it before I came.

BEH. This is your slackness, not t' invoke
> our powers
When first your acts set forth to their effects ;
Yet shall you see it and themselves.   Behold
They come here, and the Earl now holds the
> paper.   100

Enter MONSIEUR, GUISE, [*and*] MONTSURRY
> *with a paper.*

BUS. May we not hear them?

[FRIAR.] [44]   No, be still and see.

BUS. I will go fetch the paper.

FRIAR.   Do not stir ;
There 's too much distance and too many locks
'Twixt you and them, how near soe'er they
> seem,
For any man to interrupt their secrets.

TAM. O honor'd spirit, fly into the fancy
Of my offended lord, and do not let him
Believe what there the wicked man hath
> written.

BEH. Persuasion hath already enter'd him
Beyond reflection ; peace till their departure !

MONS. There is a glass of ink [45] where you
> may see   111
How to make ready black-fac'd tragedy.
You now discern, I hope, through all her paint-
> ings,
Her gasping wrinkles and fame's sepulchres.[46]

GUISE. Think you he feigns, my Lord?
> What hold you now?
Do we malign your wife, or honor you?

MONS. What, stricken dumb ! Nay fie,
> Lord, be not daunted ;
Your case is common ; were it ne'er so rare,
Bear it as rarely.   Now to laugh were manly.
A worthy man should imitate the weather, [120
That sings in tempests, and being clear is
> silent.

GUISE. Go home, my Lord, and force your
> wife to write
Such loving lines to D'Ambois as she us'd
When she desir'd his presence.

MONS.   Do, my Lord,

[43] Legion.
[44] Cor. Boas ; old eds. *Monsieur.*
[45] *I.e.*, this paper is a mirror.
[46] The tomb of her reputation.

And make her name her conceal'd messenger,
That close and most inenarrable [47] pander,
That passeth all our studies to exquire ; [48]
By whom convey the letter to her love.
And so you shall be sure to have him come
Within the thirsty reach of your revenge ;   130
Before which, lodge an ambush in her chamber,
Behind the arras, of your stoutest men
All close and soundly arm'd ; and let them
    share
A spirit amongst them that would serve a
    thousand.

Enter PERO *with a letter.*

GUISE. Yet stay a little ; see, she sends for
    you.
MONS. Poor, loving lady ; she'll make all
    good yet,
Think you not so, my Lord?
                Exit MONTSURRY *and stabs* PERO.
GUISE.   Alas, poor soul !
MONS. That was cruelly done, i' faith.
PERO.   'T was nobly done.
And I forgive his Lordship from my soul.
    MONS. Then much good do't thee, Pero !
    Hast a letter?   140
PERO. I hope it rather be a bitter volume
Of worthy curses for your perjury.
GUISE. To you, my Lord.
MONS.   To me? Now, out upon her.
GUISE. Let me see, my Lord.
MONS. You shall presently. How fares
    my Pero?

Enter Servant.

Who's there? Take in this maid — sh'as
    caught a clap ;
And fetch my surgeon to her. Come, my
    Lord,
We'll now peruse our letter.
                Exeunt MONSIEUR [*and*] GUISE.
                Lead her out.
PERO.   Furies rise
Out of the black lines, and torment his soul.

TAM. Hath my Lord slain my woman?
BEH.   No, she lives.   [150
FRIAR. What shall become of us?
BEH.   All I can say,
Being call'd thus late, is brief, and darkly this :
If D'Ambois' mistress dye not [her] [49] white
    hand

In her forc'd blood, he shall remain untouch'd ;
So, father, shall yourself, but by yourself.
To make this augury plainer : when the voice
Of D'Ambois shall invoke me, I will rise,
Shining in greater light, and show him all
That will betide ye all.   Meantime be wise,
And curb his valor with your policies.   160
                Descendit cum suis.
    BUS. Will he appear to me when I invoke
    him?
FRIAR. He will, be sure.
BUS.   It must be shortly then ;
For his dark words have tied my thoughts on
    knots,
Till he dissolve and free them.
TAM.   In meantime,
Dear servant, till your powerful voice revoke
    him, [50]
Be sure to use the policy he advis'd ;
Lest fury in your too quick knowledge taken
Of our abuse, and your defence of me,
Accuse me more than any enemy.
And, father, you must on my Lord impose [170
Your holiest charges, and the Church's power,
To temper his hot spirit and disperse
The cruelty and the blood I know his hand
Will shower upon our heads, if you put not
Your finger to the storm, and hold it up,
As my dear servant here must do with Mon-
    sieur.
    BUS. I'll soothe his plots, and strow my
    hate with smiles,
Till all at once the close mines of my heart
Rise at full date, and rush into his blood.
I'll bind his arm in silk, and rub his flesh,
To make the vein swell, that his soul may gush
Into some kennel, [51] where it longs [52] to lie, [181
And policy shall be flank'd [53] with policy.
Yet shall the feeling [54] center [55] where we meet
Groan with the weight of my approaching
    feet ;
I'll make th' inspired thresholds of his court
Sweat with the weather of my horrid steps,
Before I enter ; yet will I appear
Like calm security before a ruin.
A politician must, like lightning, melt
The very marrow, and not taint the skin ; [190
His ways must not be seen ; the superficies
Of the green center must not taste his feet,

---

[47] Indescribable.
[48] That is beyond all our efforts to find out.
[49] Emend. Dilke. Qq *his.*
[50] Call him back.
[51] Gutter.
[52] Belongs, is fitting.
[53] Outflanked.
[54] With a proleptic sense : Bussy's feet will make
it feel.
[55] Earth, the centre of the Ptolemaic system.

When hell is plow'd up with his wounding
    tracts ;
And all his harvest reap'd by hellish facts.
                   Exeunt.

ACT V — SCENE I [56]

[*Enter*] MONTSURRY *bare, unbrac'd, pulling*
TAMYRA *in by the hair;* FRIAR ; [*and*] One
bearing light, a standish,[57] *and paper, which
sets a table* [*and exit.*]

TAM. Oh, help me, father.
FRIAR.   Impious Earl, forbear.
Take violent hand from her, or by mine order
The King shall force thee.
MONT.   'T is not violent ;
Come you not willingly?
TAM.   Yes, good my Lord.
FRIAR. My Lord, remember that your soul
    must seek
Her peace, as well as your revengeful blood.[58]
You ever to this hour have prov'd yourself
A noble, zealous, and obedient son,
T' our Holy Mother ; be not an apostate.
Your wife's offence serves not, were it the
    worst   10
You can imagine, without greater proofs,
To sever your eternal bonds and hearts,
Much less to touch her with a bloody hand ;
Nor is it manly, much less husbandly,
To expiate any frailty in your wife
With churlish strokes or beastly odds of
    strength.
The stony birth of clouds [59] will touch no
    laurel,
Nor any sleeper ; your wife is your laurel,
And sweetest sleeper ; do not touch her then ;
Be not more rude than the wild seed of vapor,
To her that is more gentle than that [60] rude ; [21
In whom kind nature suffer'd one offence
But to set off her other excellence.
    MONT. Good father, leave us ; interrupt no
        more
The course I must run for mine honor sake.
Rely on my love to her, which her fault
Cannot extinguish. Will she but disclose
Who was the secret minister of her love,
And through what maze he serv'd it, we are
    friends.

[56] A room in Montsurry's house.
[57] Stand for ink and pens.
[58] As well as the indulgence of your passion for
revenge.
[59] Thunderstone, thunderbolt.
[60] That is.

FRIAR. It is a damn'd work to pursue those
    secrets   30
That would ope more sin, and prove springs
    of slaughter ;
Nor is 't a path for Christian feet to tread,
But out of all way to the health of souls ;
A sin impossible to be forgiven,
Which he that dares commit ——
    MONT.   Good father, cease your terrors ;
Tempt not a man distracted ; I am apt
To outrages that I shall ever rue ;
I will not pass the verge that bounds a Chris-
    tian,
Nor break the limits of a man nor husband.
    FRIAR. Then [God] [61] inspire you both with
        thoughts and deeds   40
Worthy his high respect, and your own souls.
TAM. Father !
FRIAR.   I warrant thee, my dearest
    daughter,
He will not touch thee ; think'st thou him a
    pagan?
His honor and his soul lies for thy safety.
                         Exit.
    MONT. Who shall remove the mountain
        from my breast?
Stand the opening [62] furnace of my thoughts,
And set fit outcries for a soul in hell?
                MONTSURRY *turns a key.*
For now it nothing fits my woes to speak
But thunder, or to take into my throat
The trump of Heaven, with whose determi-
    nate [63] blasts   50
The winds shall burst and the devouring seas
Be drunk up in his sounds ; that my hot woes,
Vented enough, I might convert to vapor,
Ascending from my infamy unseen ;
Shorten the world, preventing the last breath [64]
That kills the living and regenerates death.[65]
    TAM. My Lord, my fault, as you may cen-
        sure [66] it
With too strong arguments, is past your par-
    don ;
But how the circumstances may excuse me
[God] knows, and your more temperate mind
    hereafter   60
May let my penitent miseries make you know.
    MONT. Hereafter? 'T is a suppos'd in-
    finite,
That from this point will rise eternally.
Fame grows in going ; in the scapes [67] of virtue

[61] So Q₁ ; Q 1641 *Heaven.* So also in l. 60.
[62] Q₁ *Ope the seven-times heat*[ed].
[63] Final.
[64] *I.e.,* anticipating the Last Trump.
[65] The dead.   [66] Judge.   [67] Escapades.

Excuses damn her : they be fires in cities
Enrag'd with those winds that less lights ex-
    tinguish.
Come, siren, sing, and dash against my rocks
Thy ruffian galley,[68] rigg'd with quench for [69]
    lust ;
Sing, and put all the nets into thy voice
With which thou drew'st into thy strumpet's
    lap   70
The spawn of Venus ; and in which ye
    danc'd [70] ;
That, in thy lap's stead, I may dig his tomb,
And quit his manhood with a woman's sleight,
Who never is deceiv'd in her deceit.
Sing — that is, write, — and then take from
    mine eyes
The mists that hide the most inscrutable
    pander
That ever lapp'd up an adulterous vomit,
That I may see the devil, and survive
To be a devil, and then learn to wive ;
That I may hang him, and then cut him down,
Then cut him up, and with my soul's beams
    search   81
The cranks and caverns of his brain, and study
The errant wilderness of a woman's face ;
Where men cannot get out, for [71] all the
    comets [72]
That have been lighted at it ; though they
    know
That adders lie a-sunning in their [73] smiles,
That basilisks drink their poison from their
    eyes,
And no way there to coast out to their hearts ;
Yet still they [74] wander there,[75] and are not
    stay'd
Till they be fetter'd, nor secure before   90
All cares devour them, nor in human consort,[76]
Till they embrace within their wife's two
    breasts
All Pelion and Cythaeron with their beasts.
Why write you not?
    TAM.   O good my Lord, forbear
In wreak of great faults, to engender greater,
And make my love's corruption generate
    murder.
    MONT. It follows needfully as child and
    parent ;

The chain-shot of thy lust is yet aloft,
And it must murder ; 't is thine own dear
    twin :
No man can add height to a woman's sin.   100
Vice never doth her just hate so provoke
As when she rageth under virtue's cloak.
Write ! for it must be — by this ruthless steel,
By this impartial torture, and the death
Thy tyrannies have invented in my entrails,
To quicken life in dying, and hold up
The spirits in fainting, teaching to preserve
Torments in ashes, that will ever last.
Speak ! Will you write?
    TAM.   Sweet Lord, enjoin my sin
Some other penance than what makes it
    worse ;   11
Hide in some gloomy dungeon my loath'd face,
And let condemned murderers let me down,
Stopping their noses, my abhorred food ;
Hang me in chains, and let me eat these arms
That have offended ; bind me face to face
To some dead woman, taken from the cart
Of execution, till death and time
In grains of dust dissolve me : I 'll endure ;
Or any torture that your wrath's invention
Can fright all pity from the world withal.   120
But to betray a friend with show of friendship,
That is too common for the rare revenge
Your rage affecteth. Here then are my
    breasts,
Last night your pillows ; here my wretched
    arms,
As late the wished confines of your life ;
Now break them as you please, and all the
    bounds
Of manhood, noblesse, and religion.
    MONT. Where all these have been broken,
    they are kept
In doing their justice there with any show
Of the like [77] cruelty ; thine arms have lost
Their privilege in lust, and in their torture [131
Thus they must pay it.   _Stabs her._
    TAM.   O Lord !
    MONT.   Till thou writ'st,
I 'll write in wounds, my wrong 's fit characters,
Thy right of sufferance. Write.
    TAM.   Oh, kill me, kill me ;
Dear husband, be not crueller than death.
You have beheld some Gorgon ; feel, oh, feel
How you are turn'd to stone. With my heart-
    blood
Dissolve yourself again, or you will grow

---

[68] _I.e._, Bussy.   [69] Q₁ _laden for thy._
[70] _I.e._, acted under the delusion that you were
unobserved.
[71] In spite of.
[72] Which were portents of disaster.
[73] Women's.
[74] Men.
[75] In the wilderness of a woman's face.
[76] Lacking human fellowship.

[77] Q 1641 inserts _cruel_, probably through the compositor's blunder, as Parrott observes. Q₁ omits
with . . . crueltu.

Into the image of all tyranny.

MONT. As thou art of adultery! I will
     ever   140
Prove thee my parallel, being most a monster;
Thus I express thee [78] yet.   *Stabs her again.*
     TAM.   And yet I live.
     MONT. Ay, for thy monstrous idol is not
          done yet; [79]
This tool hath wrought enough; now, torture,
     use

Enter Servants [*and put her on the rack*].

This other engine on th' habituate powers
Of her thrice-damn'd and whorish fortitude.
Use the most madding pains in her that ever
Thy venoms soak'd through, making most of
     death;
That she may weigh her wrongs with them,
     and then
Stand, Vengeance, on thy steepest rock, a
     victor.
     TAM. Oh, who is turn'd into my lord and
          husband?   151
Husband! My lord! None but my lord
     and husband!
Heaven, I ask thee remission of my sins,
Not of my pains; husband, oh, help me, hus-
     band!

Ascendit FRIAR *with a sword drawn.*

     FRIAR. What rape of honor and religion —
Oh, wrack of nature!   *Falls and dies.*
     TAM.   Poor man; oh, my father.
Father, look up; oh, let me down, my Lord,
And I will write.
     MONT.   Author of prodigies!
What new flame breaks out of the firmament,
That turns up counsels never known before?
Now is it true earth moves and Heaven stands
     still;   161
Even Heaven itself must see and suffer ill.
The too huge bias [80] of the world hath sway'd
Her back part upwards, and with that she
     braves
This hemisphere, that long her mouth hath
     mock'd; [81]
The gravity of her religious face,

Now grown too weighty with her sacrilege
And here discern'd sophisticate enough,
Turns to th' antipodes; and all the forms
That her illusions have impress'd in her,   170
Have eaten through her back; and now all
     see
How she is riveted with [82] hypocrisy. —
Was this the way? Was he the mean betwixt
     you?
     TAM. He was, he was; kind, worthy man,
          he was.
     MONT. Write, write a word or two.
     TAM.   I will, I will —
[*aside*] I 'll write, but with my blood, that he [83]
     may see
These lines come from my wounds, and not
     from me.   *Writes.*
     MONT. Well might he [84] die for thought;
          methinks the frame
And shaken joints of the whole world should
     crack
To see her parts so disproportionate;   180
And that his [85] general beauty cannot stand
Without these stains in the particular man.
Why wander I so far? [86] Here, here was she
That was a whole world without spot to me,
Though now a world of spots. Oh, what a
     lightning
Is man's delight in women! What a bubble
He builds his state, fame, life on, when he
     marries!
Since all earth's pleasures are so short and
     small,
The way t' enjoy it is t' abjure it all.
Enough! I must be messenger myself,   190
Disguis'd like this strange creature. — In, [87]
     I 'll after,
To see what guilty light gives this cave eyes,
And to the world sing new impieties.
        He puts the FRIAR *in the vault and*
        follows. She wraps herself in the
        arras. [88]   *Exeunt* [Servants].

[SCENE II] [89]

Enter MONSIEUR *and* GUISE.

     MONS. Now shall we see that Nature hath
          no end

---

[78] *I.e.*, by being monstrous, and so continuing to be a parallel to you.
[79] *I.e.*, I have not yet completed my image of you.
[80] Tendency (toward wickedness).
[81] The world has reversed itself, so Montsurry concludes upon learning that the pander was the Friar; it has turned upside down; its back part now shows itself arrogantly to our side of the universe, which formerly the world's mouth had mocked (by pretending virtue).

[82] *I.e.*, that her real structure is.   [83] Bussy.
[84] The Friar.   [85] Referring to *man*, in the next line.
[86] For an example.
[87] To the Friar's body.
[88] The curtains of the inner stage.
[89] Another room in Montsurry's house. This scene appears in Q₁ at the beginning of V, iv, with the omission of ll. 54–59 and the s. D. for Montsurry's entrance.

In her great works responsive [90] to their
  worths;
That she, that makes so many eyes and souls
To see and foresee, is stark blind herself;
And as illiterate men say Latin prayers
By rote of heart and daily iteration,
Not knowing what they say, [91] so Nature lays
A deal of stuff together, and by use,
Or by the mere necessity of matter,
Ends such a work, fills it, or leaves it empty   10
Of strength or virtue, error or clear truth,
Not knowing what she does; but usually
Gives that which [we call] [92] merit to a man,
And [believe should] [93] arrive him on [94] huge
  riches,
Honor, and happiness, that effects his ruin;
Even as in ships of war, whose lasts [95] of pow-
  der
Are laid, men think, [96] to make them last, and
  guard [them], [97]
When a disorder'd spark, that powder taking,
Blows up with sudden violence and horror
Ships that kept empty had [98] sail'd long, with
  terror. [99]   20
  GUISE. He that observes, but like a worldly
    man,
That which doth oft succeed, and by th' events
Values the worth of things, will think it true
That Nature works at random, just with you;
But with as much proportion she may make
A thing that from the feet up to the throat
Hath all the wondrous fabric man should have,
And leave it headless, for a perfect man,
As give a full man valor, virtue, learning,
Without an end more excellent than those   30
On whom she no such worthy part bestows.
  MONS. Yet shall you see it here [100]; here
    will be one
Young, learned, valiant, virtuous, and full
  mann'd;

One on whom Nature spent so rich a hand
That with an ominous eye she wept to see
So much consum'd her virtuous treasury. [1]
Yet, as the winds sing through a hollow tree,
And, since it lets them pass through, lets it
  stand;
But a tree solid, since it gives no way
To their wild rage, they rend up by the root;
So this whole man,   41
That will not wind with every crooked way,
Trod by the servile world, shall reel and fall
Before the frantic puffs of blind-born chance,
That pipes through empty men, and makes
  them dance.
Not so the sea raves on the Lybian sands, [2]
Tumbling her billows in each other's neck;
Not so the surges of the Euxine sea
Near to the frosty pole, where free Boötes
From those dark deep waves turns his radiant
  team,   50
Swell, being enrag'd even from their inmost
  drop,
As Fortune swings about the restless state
Of virtue, now thrown into all men's hate.

  Enter MONTSURRY *disguis'd, with the*
    Murderers.

Away, my Lord, you are perfectly disguis'd;
Leave us to lodge your ambush.
  MONT.   Speed me, vengeance. *Exit.*
  MONS. Resolve, my masters, you shall meet
    with one
Will try what proofs your privy coats [3] are
  made on;
When he is ent'red, and you hear us stamp,
Approach, and make all sure.
  MURD.   We will, my Lord. *Exeunt.*

[SCENE III] [4]

[*Enter*] D'AMBOIS, *with two* Pages *with tapers.*

  BUS. Sit up to-night, and watch; I 'll speak
    with none
But the old Friar, who bring to me.
  PAGES.   We will, sir. *Exeunt.*
  BUS. What violent heat is this? Me-
    thinks the fire
Of twenty lives doth on a sudden flash
Through all my faculties; the air goes high
In this close chamber, and the frighted earth
                                          Thunder.

[90] Answerable, corresponding.
[91] For *Not . . . say* Q₁ reads:
In whose hot zeale a man would thinke they knew
What they ranne so away with, and were sure
To have rewards proportion'd to their labours;
Yet may implore their owne confusions
For anything they know, which oftentimes
It fals out they incurre.
[92] So Q₁; Q 1641 *she calls.* As Parrott notes,
Chapman corrected this speech but was misread
by the printer; the version of Q 1641 is unintelli-
gible.
[93] So Q₁; Q 1641 *beliefe must.*
[94] Bring him to.
[95] A last of powder = 24 barrels.
[96] Boas and Parrott emend *methinks.*
[97] So Q₁; om. Q 1641.
[98] Would have.
[99] *I.e.,* to their enemies.
[100] In the case of Bussy.

[1] Stock of virtues.
[2] Ll. 46–53 are adapted from Seneca's *Agamemnon,*
ll. 64–72. (Boas.)
[3] Hidden shirts of mail.
[4] A room in Bussy's house.

Trembles, and shrinks beneath me ; the whole house
Nods with his [5] shaken burthen. —

Enter UMBRA FRIAR.

                   Bless me, Heaven !
UMB. Note what I want, dear son, and be forewarn'd ;
Oh, there are bloody deeds past and to come.
I cannot stay ; a fate doth ravish me ;   11
I 'll meet thee in the chamber of thy love.
                          Exit.
   BUS. What dismal change is here ; the good old Friar
Is murder'd, being made known to serve my love ;
And now his restless spirit would forewarn me
Of some plot dangerous and imminent.
Note what he wants? He wants his upper weed,[6]
He wants his life and body ; which of these
Should be the want he means, and may supply me
With any fit forewarning? This strange vision,   20
Together with the dark prediction
Us'd by the Prince of Darkness that was rais'd
By this embodied shadow,[7] stir my thoughts
With reminiscion of the spirit's promise,
Who told me that by any invocation
I should have power to raise him, though it wanted
The powerful words and decent rites of art.
Never had my set [8] brain such need of spirit
T' instruct and cheer it ; now, then, I will claim
Performance of his free and gentle vow   30
T' appear in greater light, and make more plain
His rugged oracle. I long to know
How my dear mistress fares, and be inform'd
What hand she now holds on the troubled blood [9]
Of her incensed lord. Methought the spirit,
When he had utter'd his perplex'd presage
Threw his chang'd countenance headlong into clouds ;
His forehead bent, as it would hide his face,
He knock'd his chin against his dark'ned breast,

And struck a churlish silence through his powers.   40
Terror of darkness ! O thou king of flames ! [10]
That with thy music-footed horse dost strike
The clear light out of crystal on dark earth,
And hurl'st instructive fire about the world,
Wake, wake the drowsy and enchanted night,
That sleeps with dead eyes in this heavy riddle !
Or thou great prince of shades, where never sun
Sticks his far-darted beams, whose eyes are made
To shine in darkness, and see ever best
Where men are blindest, open now the heart   50
Of thy abashed oracle, that, for fear
Of some ill it includes, would fain lie hid,
And rise thou with it in thy greater light.
         Thunders. Surgit Spiritus cum suis.
   [BEH.] [11] Thus to observe my vow of apparition
In greater light, and explicate thy fate,
I come ; and tell thee that if thou obey
The summons that thy mistress next will send thee,
Her hand shall be thy death.
   BUS.   When will she send?
   BEH. Soon as I set again, where late I rose.
   BUS. Is the old Friar slain?
   BEH.   No, and yet lives not. [60
   BUS. Died he a natural death?
   BEH.   He did.
   BUS.   Who then
Will my dear mistress send?
   BEH.   I must not tell thee.
   BUS. Who lets [12] thee?
   BEH.   Fate.
   BUS.   Who are Fate's ministers?
   BEH. The Guise and Monsieur.
   BUS.   A fit pair of shears
To cut the threads of kings and kingly spirits,
And consorts fit to sound forth harmony,
Set to the falls of kingdoms. Shall the hand
Of my kind mistress kill me?
   BEH.   If thou yield
To her next summons. Y' are fair-warn'd ; farewell !
         Thunders. Exit [cum suis].
   BUS. I must fare well, however, though I die,
My death consenting [13] with his augury.   71

[5] Its.
[6] His outer garment, his gown (which Montsurry has donned.)
[7] This ghost when it was still alive.
[8] Determined.
[9] Passion (of anger).

[10] The sun-god.
[11] Old eds. *Sp.*, throughout.
[12] Stops.
[13] If my death agrees.

Should not my powers obey when she commands,
My motion must be rebel to my will,
My will to life ; if, when I have obey'd,
Her hand should so reward me, they must
    arm it,
Bind me or force it ; or, I lay my life,
She rather would convert it many times
On her own bosom, even to many deaths.
But were there danger of such violence,
I know 't is far from her intent to send ;   80
And who she should send is as far from
    thought,
Since he is dead, whose only mean she us'd. —
                  Knocks.
Who 's there ? Look to the door, and let him
    in,
Though politic Monsieur or the violent Guise.

Enter MONTSURRY, *like the Friar, with a letter
            written in blood.*

MONT. Hail to my worthy son.
BUS.   Oh, lying spirit,
To say the Friar was dead ! I 'll now believe
Nothing of all his forg'd predictions. —
My kind and honor'd father, well reviv'd ;
I have been frighted with your death and mine,
And told my mistress' hand should be my
    death
If I obey'd this summons.
MONT.   I believ'd   91
Your love had been much clearer than to give
Any such doubt a thought, for she is clear ;
And having freed her husband's jealousy,
Of which her much abus'd hand here is witness,
She prays, for urgent cause, your instant pres-
    ence.
BUS. Why, then your prince of spirits may
    be call'd
The prince of liars.
MONT.   Holy Writ so calls him.
BUS. What, writ in blood?
MONT.   Ay, 't is the ink of lovers.
BUS. Oh 't is a sacred witness of her love.
So much elixir of her blood as this   101
Dropp'd in the lightest dame, would make her
    firm
As heat to fire ; and, like to all the signs,[14]
Commands the life confin'd in all my veins.
Oh, how it multiplies my blood with spirit,
And makes me apt t' encounter death and
    hell. —
But come, kind father, you fetch me to
    Heaven,

[14] Of the heavenly bodies.

And to that end your holy weed was given.
                     Exeunt.

[SCENE IV] [15]

Thunder. Intrat UMBRA FRIAR, *and discovers*
              TAMYRA.[16]

UMB. Up with these stupid thoughts, still
    loved daughter,
And strike away this heartless trance of
    anguish.
Be like the sun, and labor in eclipses ;
Look to the end of woes : oh, can you sit
Mustering the horrors of your servant's
    slaughter
Before your contemplation, and not study
How to prevent it ? Watch when he shall rise,
And with a sudden outcry of his murder,
Blow [17] his retreat before he be revenged.
TAM. O father, have my dumb woes wak'd
    your death ?   10
When will our human griefs be at their height ?
Man is a tree that hath no top in cares,
No root in comforts ; all his power to live
Is given to no end, but ['t] [18] have power to
    grieve.
UMB. It is the misery of our creation. Your
    true friend,[19]
Led by your husband, shadowed in my weed,
Now enters the dark vault.
TAM.   But, my dearest father,
Why will not you appear to him yourself,
And see that none of these deceits annoy him ?
UMB. My power is limited ; alas ! I cannot.
All that I can do — see, the cave opens.   21
           Exit. D'AMBOIS *at the gulf.*
TAM. Away, my love, away ; thou wilt be
    murder'd !

Enter MONSIEUR *and* GUISE *above.*

BUS. Murder'd ? I know not what that
    Hebrew means :
That word had ne'er been nam'd had all been
    D'Ambois.

[15] A room in Montsurry's house.
[16] By opening the curtains of the inner stage, in which she wrapped herself at the close of V, i. Q₁: *Intrat umbra Comolet to the Countesse, wrapt in a canapie.*
[17] Sound a call for.
[18] So Q₁ ; om. Q 1641.
[19] For ll. 15–21 Q₁ reads:

Tis the just curse of our abus'd creation,
Which wee must suffer heere, and scape heereafter:
He hath the great mind that submits to all
He sees inevitable ; he the small
That carps at earth, and her foundation shaker,
And rather than himselfe, will mend his maker.

Murder'd? By Heaven he is my murderer

That shows me not a murderer; what such bug [20]

Abhorreth not the very sleep of D'Ambois?

Murder'd? Who dares give all the room I see

To D'Ambois' reach? or look with any odds

His fight i' th' face, upon whose hand sits death, 30

Whose sword hath wings, and every feather pierceth?

If I scape Monsieur's 'pothecary shops,

Foutre [21] for Guise's shambles! 'T was ill plotted;

They should have maul'd me here,

When I was rising. I am up and ready.

Let in my politic visitants, let them in,

Though ent'ring like so many moving armors,

Fate is more strong than arms and sly than treason,

And I at all parts buckl'd in my fate.

MONS. ⎫
GUISE. ⎭ [aside] Why enter not the coward villains? 40

BUS. Dare they not come?

Enter Murderers, *with* [UMBRA] FRIAR *at the other door.*

TAM.   They come.

1 MUR.   Come all at once.

UMB. Back, coward murderers, back.

OMN.   Defend us, Heaven.

             Exeunt all but the First.

1 MUR. Come ye not on?

BUS.   No, slave, nor goest thou off. —
             [*Thrusts at him.*]

Stand you so firm? Will it not enter here? [22]

You have a face yet. — So! [*Kills him.*] — In thy life's flame,

I burn the first rites to my mistress' fame.

UMB. Breathe thee, brave son, against the other charge.

BUS. Oh, is it true then that my sense first told me?

Is my kind father dead?

TAM.   He is, my love.

'T was the Earl, my husband, in his weed that brought thee. 50

BUS. That was a speeding sleight,[23] and well resembled.

Where is that angry Earl? — My Lord, come forth

And show your own face in your own affair;

Take not into your noble veins the blood

Of these base villains, nor the light reports

Of blister'd tongues for clear and weighty truth:

But me against the world, in pure defence

Of your rare lady, to whose spotless name

I stand here as a bulwark, and project

A life to her renown, that ever yet 60

Hath been untainted, even in envy's eye,

And, where it would protect, a sanctuary.

Brave Earl, come forth, and keep your scandal in;

'T is not our fault if you enforce the spot,[24]

Nor the wreak yours if you perform it not.

Enter MONTSURRY, *with all the* Murderers.[25]

MONT. Cowards, a fiend or spirit beat ye off!

They are your own faint spirits that have forg'd

The fearful shadows that your eyes deluded.

The fiend was in you; cast him out then, thus.

             D'AMBOIS *hath* MONTSURRY *down.*

TAM. Favor my Lord, my love, oh, favor him! 70

BUS. I will not touch him. — Take your life, my Lord,

And be appeas'd. —   *Pistols shot within.*

             Oh, then the coward Fates

Have maim'd themselves, and ever lost their honor.

UMB. What have ye done, slaves? — Irreligious lord!

BUS. Forbear them, father; 't is enough for me

That Guise and Monsieur, death and destiny,

Come behind D'Ambois. — Is my body, then,

But penetrable flesh? And must my mind

Follow my blood? Can my divine part add

No aid to th' earthly in extremity? 80

Then these divines are but for form, not fact.[26]

Man is of two sweet courtly friends compact,

A mistress and a servant; [27] let my death

Define life nothing but a courtier's breath.

Nothing is made of nought, of all things made,

Their abstract being a dream but of a shade.

I 'll not complain to earth yet, but to Heaven,

And, like a man, look upwards even in death.

And if Vespasian thought in majesty

[20] Bugbear; *i.e.*, threat of murder.
[21] An obscene expression of contempt.
[22] An account of a "privy coat."
[23] Successful trick.

[24] Emphasize the stain on your honor. (Boas.)
[25] Q 1 *with others.*
[26] *I.e.*, theologians are unrealistic.
[27] *I.e.*, body and soul are like mistress and lover, the second of each pair being dependent on the first.

An emperor might die standing, why not I ? [90

She offers to help him.

Nay, without help, in which I will exceed him ;
For he died splinted with his chamber grooms.
Prop me, true sword, as thou hast ever done ;
The equal thought I bear of life and death
Shall make me faint on no side ; I am up.
Here like a Roman statue I will stand
Till death hath made me marble.   O my fame,
Live in despite of murder ; take thy wings
And haste thee where the grey-ey'd morn per-
fumes
Her rosy chariot with Sabaean spices ;   100
Fly where the evening from th' Iberian vales
Takes on her swarthy shoulders Hecate,
Crown'd with a grove of oaks ; fly where men
feel
The burning axletree ; and those that suffer
Beneath the chariot of the snowy Bear ;
And tell them all that D'Ambois now is hast-
ing
To the eternal dwellers, that a thunder
Of all their sighs together (for their frailties
Beheld in me) may quit my worthless [28] fall
With a fit volley for my funeral.   110
UMB.   Forgive thy murderers.
BUS.   I forgive them all ;
And you, my Lord, their fautor ; [29] for true
sign
Of which unfeign'd remission, take my
sword ;
Take it, and only give it motion,
And it shall find the way to victory
By his own brightness, and th' inherent valor
My fight hath still'd into 't, with charms of
spirit.
Now let me pray you that my weighty blood
Laid in one scale of your impartial spleen,
May sway the forfeit of my worthy love   120
Weigh'd in the other ; [30] and be reconcil'd
With all forgiveness to your matchless wife.
TAM.   Forgive thou me, dear servant, and
this hand
That led thy life to this unworthy end ;
Forgive it, for the blood with which 't is
stain'd,
In which I writ the summons of thy death —
The forced summons, by this bleeding wound,
By this here is my bosom, and by this
That makes me hold up both my hands im-
bru'd

[28] Unworthy.   [29] Protector.
[30] *I.e.*, may my blood, balanced impartially in the scale of your anger, outweigh the claim (to vengeance) you have as a result of my worthy love to the Countess.

For thy dear pardon.
BUS.   Oh, my heart is broken ! [130
Fate, nor these murderers, Monsieur nor the
Guise,
Have any glory in my death, but this,
This killing spectacle, this prodigy.
My sun is turn'd to blood, in whose red beams
Pindus and Ossa, hid in drifts of snow
Laid on my heart and liver, from their veins
Melt like two hungry torrents, eating rocks
Into the ocean of all human life,
And make it bitter, only with my blood.[31]
O frail condition of strength, valor, virtue,
In me (like warning fire upon the top   141
Of some steep beacon on a steeper hill)
Made to express it : like a falling star
Silently glanc'd, that like a thunderbolt
Look'd to have stuck [32] and shook the firma-
ment.

Moritur.

UMB.   [My terrors are struck inward, and
no more
My penance will allow they shall enforce
Earthly afflictions but upon myself.] [33] —
Farewell, brave relics of a complete man !
Look up and see thy spirit made a star ;   150
[Join] flames with [Hercules,][34] and when thou
sett'st
Thy radiant forehead in the firmament,
Make the vast crystal [35] crack with thy
receipt ;
Spread to a world of fire ; and the aged sky
Cheer with new sparks of old humanity. —
[*To* MONT.] Son of the earth, whom my un-
rested soul,
Rues t' have begotten in the faith of Heaven,
[Since thy revengeful spirit hath rejected
The charity it commands, and the remission
To serve and worship the blind rage of blood,][36]
Assay to gratulate [37] and pacify   161
The soul fled from this worthy by performing
The Christian reconcilement he besought

[31] *I.e.*, Tamyra, the light of my life, is bleeding ; the sight of those bloody rays sweeps away my life into the ocean of eternity and embitters it with my blood (which has itself been embittered by the sight) — sweeps away my life as when on Pindus and Ossa the sun melts the snow and the ensuing torrents sweep even rocks away.
[32] Pierced. Boas emends *struck.*
[33] Q 1641 omits the first three lines of this speech ; the first ten, in Q₁, form the closing speech of the play.
[34] So Q₁ ; Q 1641 garbles : *Jove flames with her rules.*
[35] The highest, or crystalline, sphere, in which Bussy is to be set as a star.
[36] So Q₁ ; om. Q 1641.
[37] Gratify.

Betwixt thee and thy lady. Let her wounds,
Manlessly [38] digg'd in her, be eas'd and cur'd
With balm of thine own tears ; or be assur'd
Never to rest free from my haunt and horror.

MONT. See how she merits this, still kneel-
    ing by,
And mourning his fall more than her own fault.

UMB. Remove, dear daughter, and content
    thy husband ;   170
So piety wills thee, and thy servant's peace.
                             [*Exit.*] [39]

TAM. O wretched piety, that are so distract
In thine own constancy, and in thy right
Must be unrighteous. If I right my friend,
I wrong my husband ; if his wrong I shun,
The duty of my friend I leave undone.
Ill plays on both sides ; here and there it
    riseth ;
No place, no good, so good but ill compriseth.
[My soul more scruple breeds, than my blood,
    sin.
Virtue imposeth more than any stepdame.] [40]
O had I never married but for form,   181
Never vow'd faith but purpos'd to deceive,
Never made conscience of any sin,
But cloak'd it privately and made it com-
    mon,
Nor never honor'd been in blood or mind,
Happy had I been then, as others are
Of the like licence ; I had then been honor'd ;
Liv'd without envy ; custom had benumb'd
All sense of scruple, and all note of frailty ;
My fame had been untouch'd, my heart un-
    broken :   190
But, shunning all, I strike on all offence.
O husband ! Dear friend ! O my conscience !

MONS. Come, let's away ; my senses are
    not proof
Against those plaints.
        Exeunt GUISE [*and*] MONSIEUR ;
        D'AMBOIS *is borne off.*

MONT. I must not yield to pity, nor to
    love.
So servile and so traitorous. Cease, my
    blood, [41]
To wrastle with my honor, fame, and judg-
    ment. —
Away ! Forsake my house ; forbear com-
    plaints
Where thou hast bred them : here all things
    [are] [42] full

Of their own shame and sorrow. Leave my
    house.   200

TAM. Sweet lord, forgive me, and I will be
    gone ;
And till these wounds, that never balm shall
    close
Till death hath enter'd at them, so I love them,
Being opened by your hands, by death be cur'd,
I never more will grieve you with my sight,
Never endure that any roof shall part
Mine eyes and Heaven, but to the open deserts,
Like to a hunted tigress, I will fly,
Eating my heart, shunning the steps of men,
And look on no side till I be arriv'd.   210

MONT. I do forgive thee, and upon my
    knees,
With hands held up to Heaven, wish that
    mine honor
Would suffer reconcilement to my love ;
But since it will not, honor never serve
My love with flourishing object till it starve ; [43]
And as this taper, though it upwards look,
Downwards must needs consume, so let our
    love ;
As having lost his honey, the sweet taste
Runs into savor, and will needs retain
A spice of his first parents, [44] till, like life,   220
It sees and dies ; so let our love ; and lastly,
As when the flame is suffer'd to look up,
It keeps his lustre, but, being thus turn'd
    down,
His natural course of useful light inverted,
His own stuff [45] puts it out ; so let our love.
Now turn from me, as here I turn from thee,
And may both points of Heaven's straight
    axletree
Conjoin in one, before thyself and me.
                    Exeunt severally.

EPILOGUE [46]

WITH many hands you have seen D'Ambois
    slain,
Yet by your grace he may revive again,
And every day grow stronger in his skill
To please, as we presume he is in will.
The best deserving actors of the time
Had their ascents, and by degrees did climb
To their full height, a place to study due.
To make him tread in their path lies in you ;
He'll not forget his makers, but still prove
His thankfulness as you increase your love.   10

[38] Unmanfully.
[39] Add. Parrott.
[40] So Q₁ ; om. Q 1641.
[41] Emotions (of love and pity).
[42] Add. Dilke.
[43] Perish.
[44] The bees.
[45] The melting wax.
[46] First appears in Q 1641.

THE

MALCONTENT.

Augmented by *Marston*.

With the Additions played by the Kings
Maiesties seruants.

Written by *Ihon Webster*.

1 6 0 4.

AT LONDON
Printed by V.S. for William Aspley, and
are to be sold at his shop in Paules
Church-yard.

INTRODUCTORY NOTE

DEDICATED to Ben Jonson, with whom the author had recently broken a lance in the "Wars of the Theatres", Marston's masterpiece was first published in 1604. The source of its plot is unknown. Three editions appeared in 1604, the last being "Augmented by Marston" and containing "the Additions played by the King's Majesty's Servants. Written by John Webster." Professor E. E. Stoll has argued conclusively that, except for the induction, the additions are the work of Marston. To some extent they may be, as he believes, parts of the original text which had previously been cut for the stage; on the other hand, the Third Quarto, as Lucas points out, seems to represent a careful revision by Marston, who may well have had a hand in the expropriation of the play by the King's Men. They performed it, we may infer from Burbage's remarks in the induction, as a species of retaliation for the acting of one of their plays, probably *The First Part of Jeronimo*, by the Children of the Queen's Revels, at the Blackfriars, to whom *The Malcontent* had belonged.

When the latter play was written and originally produced it is impossible to say. Current opinion inclines to 1604; but Stoll argues for 1600 (*John Webster*, pp. 55-60), and (*Modern Philology*, III, 281-303) for the influence of Malevole upon Shakespeare's Hamlet and Jacques. This seems somewhat dubious, especially since Stoll points to Feliche in Marston's *i Antonio and Mellida* (1599) as exhibiting all the main features of Malevole. But that Marston was much influenced by Jonson there can be little question, though the splenetic moroseness of Malevole is less comic than Jonson's humors prior to 1604. Nor has it much in common with the genial crustiness of Jacques or the fantastic impudence of Hamlet's pretended madness. It may, however, as Stoll suggests, owe something to the Hamlet of Kyd.

The Malcontent is tragi-comedy, and stands halfway between Jonson's satiric comedy and the corrosive tragedy of Webster. As a play, it is full of effective situations, and exhibits in the Jonsonian fashion a gorgeous gallery of character portraits. Mendoza is one of the best examples of the Machiavellian villain; the weakness and amiability of the successful Pietro are skilfully contrasted with the force and scepticism of the deposed Altofronto; while in Bilioso and Maquerelle the courtiers of James I were treated to a scathing indictment which, bitter as it is, yet remains truly comic.

The standard edition of Marston's works is that of A. H. Bullen (1887). *The Malcontent* has been included in some editions of John Webster; it may be found entire in Dyce's, and Lucas reprints the induction in his. The present text is based on the Third Quarto, with a few restorations and corrections from the First.

THE MALCONTENT

JOHN MARSTON

BENIAMINI IONSONIO, POETAE ELEGANTISSIMO, GRAVISSIMO, AMICO SVO, CANDIDO ET CORDATO, IOHANNES MARSTON, MVSARVM ALVMNVS, ASPERAM HANC SVAM THALIAM D.D.

DRAMATIS PERSONAE

GIOVANNI ALTOFRONTO, disguised [as] MALE-VOLE, sometime Duke of Genoa.
PIETRO JACOMO, Duke of Genoa.
MENDOZ[A], a minion to the Duchess of Pietro Jacomo.
[COUNT] CELSO, a friend to Altofronto.
BILIOSO, an old choleric marshal.
PREPASSO, a gentleman usher.
FERNEZE, a young courtier, and enamored on the Duchess.
FERRARDO, a minion to Duke Pietro Jacomo.

[COUNT] EQUATO,
GUERRINO, } two courtiers.
PASSARELLO, fool to Bilioso.

AURELIA, Duchess to Duke Pietro Jacomo.
MARIA, Duchess to Duke Altofronto.
EMILIA, } two ladies attend-
BIANCA, [wife to Bilioso,] } ing on Aurelia.
MAQUERELLE, an old pand'ress.

[Suitors, a Perfumer, a Captain, Halberdiers, Pages; Actors of the King's Men for the Induction, and Mercury for the Masque.]

[THE SCENE — *Genoa*.]

TO THE READER

I AM an ill orator; and, in truth, use to indite more honestly than eloquently; for it is my custom to speak as I think, and write as I speak.

In plainness, therefore, understand that in some things I have willingly erred, as in supposing a Duke of Genoa, and in taking names different from that city's families; for which some may wittily accuse me, but my defence shall be as honest as many reproofs unto me have been most malicious; since, I heartily protest, it was my care to write so far from reasonable offence that even strangers, in whose state I laid my scene, should not from thence draw any disgrace to any, dead or living. Yet, in despite of my endeavors, I understand some have been most unadvisedly overcunning in misinterpreting me, and with subtlety as deep as hell have maliciously spread ill rumors, which, springing from themselves, might to themselves have heavily returned. Surely [10 I desire to satisfy every firm spirit, who, in all his actions, proposeth to himself no more ends than God and virtue do, whose intentions are always simple; to such I protest that, with my free understanding, I have not glanced at disgrace of any but of those whose unquiet studies labor innovation, contempt of holy policy, reverend comely superiority, and establish'd unity: for the rest of my supposed tartness, I fear not but unto every worthy mind it will be approved so general and honest as may modestly pass with the freedom of a satire. I would fain leave the paper; only one thing afflicts me, to think that scenes, invented merely to be spoken, should be enforcively published to be read, and that the least hurt I can receive is to do myself the wrong. But, since others otherwise would do me more, the least inconvenience is to be accepted. I have myself, therefore, set forth this comedy; but so, that my enforced absence must much rely upon [20 the printer's discretion: but I shall entreat slight errors in orthography may be as slightly overpassed, and that the unhandsome shape which this trifle in reading presents may be pardoned for the pleasure it once afforded you when it was presented with the soul of lively action.

Sine aliqua dementia nullus Phoebus.   I. M.

< THE INDUCTION [1]

TO

THE MALCONTENT, AND THE ADDITIONS[2] ACTED BY THE KING'S MAJESTY'S SERVANTS

WRITTEN BY JOHN WEBSTER

Enter W. SLY,[3] *a* Tire-man *following him with a stool.*

TIRE-MAN. Sir, the gentlemen will be angry if you sit here.

SLY. Why, we may sit upon the stage at the private house.[4] Thou doest not take me for a country gentleman, doest? Doest think I fear hissing? I'll hold my life thou took'st me for one of the players.

TIRE-MAN. No, sir.

SLY. By God's slid, if you had, I would have given you but sixpence [5] for your [10 stool. Let them that have stale suits sit in the galleries. Hiss at me! He that will be laugh'd out of a tavern or an ordinary,[6] shall seldom feed well, or be drunk in good company. — Where's Harry Condell, Dick [7] Burb[a]dge, and Will [8] Sly? Let me speak with some of them.

TIRE-MAN. An't please you to go in, sir, you may.

SLY. I tell you, no ; I am one that hath [20 seen this play often, and can give them intelligence for their action. I have most of the jests here in my table-book.[9]

Enter SINKLO.

SINKLO. Save you, coz!

SLY. Oh, cousin, come, you shall sit between my legs here.[10]

SINKLO. No, indeed, cousin : the audience then will take me for a viol-de-gamb[a], and think that you play upon me.

SLY. Nay, rather that I work upon you, [30 coz.

SINKLO. We stayed for you at supper last night at my cousin Honeymoon's, the woollendraper. After supper we drew cuts for a score of apricocks, the longest cut still [11] to draw an apricock ; by this light, 't was Mistress Frank Honeymoon's fortune still to have the longest cut — I did measure for the women. — What be these, coz?

Enter D. BURBADGE, H. CONDELL, *and* J. LOWIN.

SLY. The players. — God save you!   40

BURBADGE. You are very welcome.

SLY. I pray you, know this gentleman, my cousin ; 't is Master Doomsday's son, the usurer.

CONDELL. I beseech you, sir, be cover'd.

SLY. No, in good faith, for mine ease. Look you, my hat's the handle to this fan.[12] God's so,[13] what a beast was I, I did not leave my feather at home! — Well, but I'll take an order with you.   50

Puts his feather in his pocket.

BURBADGE. Why do you conceal your feather, sir?

SLY. Why, do you think I'll have jests broken upon me in the play, to be laugh'd at? This play hath beaten all your gallants out of the feathers. Blackfriars hath almost spoil'd Blackfriars for feathers.[14]

SINKLO. God's so, I thought 't was for somewhat our gentlewomen at home coun-

[1] First appears in Q 3.
[2] The additions are indicated in the present edition by pointed brackets.
[3] All the persons of the Induction were King's Men.
[4] The Blackfriars, where the play had previously been acted. The King's Men played at the Globe.
[5] The minimum fee.   [6] Eating-house.
[7] Q *D:.*   [8] Q *W:.*   [9] Notebook.
[10] Sinklo (or Sincler) seems to have been notoriously thin. (Lucas.)

[11] Always, each time.
[12] An enormous feather.
[13] Gadso, Catso (from It. *cazzo*). See on *Jew of Malta*, IV, i, 19.
[14] *I.e.*, this play (see V, iii, 46), as acted at the Blackfriars theatre, has almost ruined the feathertrade of Blackfriars (that district being the center of it).

sell'd me to wear my feather to the play; [60 yet I am loth to spoil it.[15]

SLY. Why, coz?

SINKLO. Because I got it in the tilt-yard — there was a herald broke my pate for taking it up; but I have worn it up and down the Strand, and met him forty times since, and yet he dares not challenge it.

SLY. Do you hear, sir? this play is a bitter play.

CONDELL. Why, sir, 't is neither satire [70 nor moral, but the mean passage of a history; yet there are a sort of discontented creatures that bear a stingless envy to great ones, and these will wrest the doings of any man to their base, malicious applyment;[16] but should their interpretation come to the test, like your marmoset, they presently turn their teeth to their tail and eat it.

SLY. I will not go so far with you; but I say, any man that hath wit may censure,[17] [80 if he sit in the twelve-penny room;[18] and I say again, the play is bitter.

BURBADGE. Sir, you are like a patron that, presenting a poor scholar to a benefice, enjoins him not to rail against anything that stands within compass of his patron's folly. Why should not we enjoy the ancient freedom of poesy? Shall we protest to the ladies that their painting makes them angels? or to my young gallant that his expense in the [90 brothel shall gain him reputation? No, sir, such vices as stand not accountable to law should be cured as men heal tetters, by casting ink upon them. Would you be satisfied in anything else, sir?

SLY. Ay, marry, would I! I would know how you came by this play.

CONDELL. Faith, sir, the book was lost; and because 't was pity so good a play should be lost, we found it, and play it. 100

SLY. I wonder you would play it, another company having interest in it.

CONDELL. Why not Malevole in folio[19] with us, as Jeronimo in decimo-sexto[20] with them? They taught us a name for our play; we call it *One For Another.*

SLY. What are your additions?

BURBADGE. Sooth, not greatly needful; only as your sallet[21] to your great feast, to entertain a little more time, and to abridge [110

[15] By pocketing it.
[16] Application.
[17] Judge.   [18] Box.
[19] *I.e.,* acted by adults.
[20] *I.e.,* acted by boys.   [21] Salad.

the not-received custom of music in our theatre.[22] I must leave you, sir.

Exit BURBADGE.

SINKLO. Doth he play the Malcontent?

CONDELL. Yes, sir.

SINKLO. I durst lay four of mine ears the play is not so well acted as it hath been.

CONDELL. Oh, no, sir, nothing *ad Parm[e]nonis suem.*[23]

LOWIN. Have you lost your ears,[24] sir, that you are so prodigal of laying them? 120

SINKLO. Why did you ask that, friend?

LOWIN. Marry, sir, because I have heard of a fellow would offer to lay a hundred-pound wager, that was not worth five baubees;[25] and in this kind you might venture four of your elbows; yet God defend[26] your coat should have so many!

SINKLO. Nay, truly, I am no great censurer;[27] and yet I might have been one of the college of critics once. My cousin here [130 hath an excellent memory, indeed, sir.

SLY. Who? I? I 'll tell you a strange thing of myself; and I can tell you, for one that never studied the art of memory, 't is very strange too.

CONDELL. What 's that, sir?

SLY. Why, I 'll lay a hundred pound, I 'll walk but once down by the Goldsmith's Row in Cheap, take notice of the signs, and tell you them with a breath instantly. 140

LOWIN. 'T is very strange.

SLY. They begin as the world did, with Adam and Eve. There 's in all just five-and-fifty.[28] I do use to meditate much when I come to plays too. What do you think might come into a man's head now, seeing all this company?

CONDELL. I know not, sir.

SLY. I have an excellent thought. If some fifty of the Grecians that were cramm'd in [150 the horse' belly had eaten garlic, do you not think the Trojans might have smelt out their knavery?[29]

CONDELL. Very likely.

[22] Shorten the musical interludes customary at the children's performances but not usual here.
[23] Not comparable to Parmeno's pig. Plutarch (*Symposium* V, i) tells how some prejudiced persons, certain that Parmeno's imitation of grunting was unequalled, declared it superior to the efforts of a real pig, which a joker had concealed.
[24] As a punishment.
[25] Scotch halfpennies.
[26] Forbid.
[27] Judge.
[28] An exaggeration.
[29] A hit at the groundlings. (Lucas.)

SLY. By God, I would [they] [30] had, for I love Hector horribly.

SINKLO. O, but, coz, coz!

" Great Alexander, when he came to the tomb of Achilles,

Spake with a big loud voice, O thou thrice blessed and happy ! " [31]

SLY. Alexander was an ass to speak so [160 well of a filthy cullion.[32]

LOWIN. Good sir, will you leave the stage? I 'll help you to a private room.

SLY. Come, coz, let 's take some tobacco. — Have you never a prologue?

LOWIN. Not any, sir.

SLY. Let me see, I will make one extempore. —

> *Come to them, and fencing of a con-*
> *gee* [33] *with arms and legs, be round* [34]
> *with them.*[35]

Gentlemen, I could wish for the women's sakes you had all soft cushions; and [170 gentlewomen, I could wish that for the men's sakes you had all more easy standings.

What would they wish more but the play now? and that they shall have instantly.

[*Exeunt.*] >

ACT I [1] — SCENE I [2]

The vilest out-of-tune music being heard, enter BILIOSO *and* PREPASSO.

BIL. Why, how now! Are ye mad, or drunk, or both, or what?

PRE. Are ye building Babylon there?

BIL. Here 's a noise in court! You think you are in a tavern, do you not?

PRE. You think you are in a brothel-house, do you not? — This room is ill-scented.

Enter One *with a perfume.*

So ; perfume, perfume ; some upon me, I pray thee.

The Duke is upon instant entrance ; so, make place there !

Enter the DUKE PIETRO, FERRARDO, COUNT EQUATO, COUNT CELSO *before, and* GUERRINO.

PIETRO. Where breathes that music?

BIL. The discord rather than the music is heard from the malcontent Malevole's chamber.

FER. [*calling*] Malevole !

MAL. (*out of his chamber*) [4] Yaugh, god-a-man, what dost thou there? Duke's Ganymede, Juno 's jealous of thy long stockings. Shadow of a woman, what wouldst, weasel? Thou lamb o' court, what dost thou bleat [10 for? Ah, you smooth-chinn'd catamite ! [5]

PIETRO. Come down, thou [rugged] [6] cur, and snarl here ; I give thy dogged sullenness free liberty ; trot about and bespurtle [7] whom thou pleasest.

MAL. I 'll come among you, you goatish-blooded toderers,[8] as gum into taffeta, to fret, to fret.[9] I 'll fall like a sponge into water, to suck up, to suck up. — (*Howl again.*) [10] I 'll go to church [11] and come to you.   20

[*Exit above.*]

PIETRO. This Malevole is one of the most prodigious affections [12] that ever convers'd with nature : a man, or rather a monster, more discontent than Lucifer when he was thrust out of the presence. His appetite is unsatiable as the grave ; as far from any content as from Heaven. His highest delight is to procure others' vexation, and therein he thinks he truly serves Heaven ; for 't is his position, whosoever in this earth can be [30 contented is a slave and damn'd ; therefore does he afflict all in that to which they are most affected.[13] Th' elements struggle within him ; his own soul is at variance <within herself> ; his speech is halter-worthy at all hours. I like him, faith : he gives good intelligence to my spirit, makes me understand those weaknesses which others' flattery palliates. Hark ! they sing.

---

[30] Emend. Dyce ; Q *he.*
[31] From the 153rd Sonnet of Petrarch, translated by John Harvey.
[32] Rogue.
[33] Making an extravagant bow.
[34] Be peremptory.
[35] Printed as part of Sly's speech in Q, and by Lucas.
[1] Old eds. have in margin *Vexat censura columbas.* (Juvenal, *Satires*, ii, 63.)
[2] A room in the ducal palace.

[3] The same.
[4] The balcony above the stage.
[5] Male prostitute.
[6] So Q [1] ; Q [3] *ragged.*
[7] Befoul.
[8] " Goatish-blooded " = lascivious. " Toderers " has not been satisfactorily explained.
[9] Playing on the meanings "fray" and "annoy."
[10] Printed in old eds. as part of the speech.
[11] Q [1] *Ile pray.*
[12] Extraordinary dispositions.
[13] Inclined.

Scene III [14]

Enter Malevole *after the song.*

[Pietro.] See, he comes. Now shall you hear the extremity of a malcontent; he is as free as air: he blows over every man. — And, sir, whence come you now?

Mal. From the public place of much dissimulation, <the church.>

Pietro. What didst there?

Mal. Talk with a usurer; take up at interest.

Pietro. I wonder what religion thou [10 art <of>?

Mal. Of a soldier's religion.

Pietro. And what dost thou think makes most infidels now?

Mal. Sects, sects. I have seen seeming Piety change her robe so oft, that sure none but some arch-devil can shape her a [new] [15] petticoat.

Pietro. Oh, a religious policy.

Mal. But damnation on a politic [20 religion! <I am weary: would I were one of the Duke's hounds now!>

Pietro. But what's the common news abroad, Malevole? Thou dogg'st rumor still.

Mal. Common news? Why, common words are, "God save ye," "Fare ye well;" common actions, flattery and cozenage; common things, women and cuckolds. — And how does my little Ferrard? Ah, ye lecherous animal! my little ferret! He goes [30 sucking up and down the palace into every hen's nest, like a weasel. — And to what dost thou addict thy time to now more than to those antique painted drabs that are still affected of [16] young courtiers, Flattery, Pride, and Venery?

Fer. I study languages. Who dost think to be the best linguist of our age?

Mal. Phew! the Devil! Let him possess thee: he'll teach thee to speak all lan- [40 guages most readily and strangely; and great reason, marry: he's travel'd greatly i' the world, and is everywhere.

Fer. Save i' th' court.

Mal. Ay, save i' th' court. — (*to* Bilioso) And how does my old muckhill, overspread with fresh snow? Thou half a man, half a goat, all a beast! How does thy young wife, old huddle? [17]

Bil. Out, you improvident rascal!   50

Mal. Do, kick, thou hugely-horn'd Old Duke's ox, good Master Make-pleas.

Pietro. How dost thou live nowadays, Malevole?

Mal. Why, like the knight, Sir Patrick Penlolians,[18] with killing o' spiders for my lady's monkey.

Pietro. How dost spend the night? I hear thou never sleep'st.

Mal. Oh, no; but dream the most [60 fantastical! O Heaven! O fubbery,[19] fubbery!

Pietro. Dream! What dream'st?

Mal. Why, methinks I see that signior pawn his footcloth,[20] that metreza [21] her plate; this madam takes physic that tother monsieur may minister to her; here is a pander jewel'd; there <is> a fellow in shift of satin this day, that could not shift a shirt tother night; here a Paris supports that Helen; [70 there's a Lady Guinever bears up that Sir Lancelot. Dreams, dreams, visions, fantasies, chimaeras, imaginations, tricks, conceits! — (*to* Prepasso) Sir Tristram Trimtram, come aloft, Jackanapes, with a whimwham; [22] here's a knight of the land of Catito shall play at trap [23] with any page in Europe; do the sword dance with any morris dancer in Christendom; ride at the ring [24] till the fin [25] of his eyes look as blue as the welkin; [80 and run the wild-goose chase even with Pompey the Huge.

Pietro. You run!

Mal. To the Devil. — Now, Sign[i]or Guerrino, that thou from a most pitied prisoner shouldst grow a most loath'd flatterer! — Alas, poor Celso, thy star's oppress'd; thou art an honest lord: 'tis pity.

Equato. Is't pity?

Mal. Ay, marry is't, philosophical [90 Equato; and 'tis pity that thou, being so excellent a scholar by art, shouldst be so ridic-

---

[14] The same.
[15] So Q₁; om. Q₃. — For *Oh* (l. 19) Q₁ reads *Of*.
[16] Desired by.   [17] Hunks, miserly old fellow.
[18] Q₁ *Penlobrans*. This knight remains unidentified.
[19] Deception.
[20] A richly ornamented cloth laid over the back of a horse and reaching nearly to the ground. It was considered a mark of dignity.
[21] Ital., mistress.
[22] The cry of the apeward as he orders his monkey to perform its tricks.
[23] Trap-ball. — "Catito" is a coinage from "cat", which (like "trap") is the name of a boyish game. "Catito" = sport-land, boys' play-land. (Kittredge.)
[24] The rider tried to thrust his lance through a suspended ring.
[25] Lid.

ulous a fool by nature. — I have a thing to tell you, Duke; bid 'em avaunt, bid 'em avaunt.

PIETRO. Leave us, leave us.

Exeunt all saving PIETRO *and*
MALEVOLE.

Now, sir, what is 't?

MAL. Duke, thou art a becco,[26] a cornuto.[27]

PIETRO. How?

MAL. Thou art a cuckold. 100

PIETRO. Speak, unshale [28] him quick.

MAL. With most tumbler-like nimbleness.

PIETRO. Who? By whom? I burst with desire.

MAL. Mendoza is the man makes thee a horn'd beast; Duke, 't is Mendoza cornutes thee.

PIETRO. What conformance? [29] Relate; short, short.

MAL. As a lawyer's beard. 110
There is an old crone in the court, her name is
　Maquerelle;
She is my mistress, sooth to say, and she doth
　ever tell me.
Blirt [30] a' rhyme, blirt a' rhyme! Maquerelle is a cunning bawd; I am an honest villain; thy wife is a close drab; [31] and thou art a notorious cuckold. Farewell, Duke.

PIETRO. Stay, stay.

MAL. Dull, dull Duke, can lazy patience make lame revenge? O God, for a woman to make a man that which God never [120 created, never made!

PIETRO. What did God never make?

MAL. A cuckold! To be made a thing that's hoodwink'd with kindness, whilst every rascal fillips his brows; to have a coxcomb with egregious horns pinn'd to a lord's back, every page sporting himself with delightful laughter, whilst he must be the last must know it. Pistols and poniards! pistols and poniards! 130

PIETRO. Death and damnation!

MAL. Lightning and thunder!

PIETRO. Vengeance and torture!

MAL. Catso! [32]

PIETRO. O, revenge!

[33] MAL. <Nay, to select among ten thousand fairs

---

[26] Ital., cuckold.　　　[27] Horned one.
[28] Reveal.
[29] *I.e.*, what facts have you that agree with your statement?
[30] Blurt. "An eruptive emission of breath . . . expressive of contempt." (*N.E.D.*)
[31] Secret strumpet.　　　[32] See on Ind., l. 48.
[33] Ll. 136–181 add. Q₃.

A lady far inferior to the most
In fair proportion both of limb and soul;
To take her from austerer check of parents,
To make her his by most devoutful rites, 140
Make her commandress of a better essence
Than is the gorgeous world, even of a man;
To hug her with as rais'd an appetite
As usurers do their delv'd-up treasury,
Thinking none tells [34] it but his private self;
To meet her spirit in a nimble kiss,
Distilling panting ardor to her heart;
True to her sheets, nay, diets strong his blood,
To give her height of hymeneal sweets, —

PIETRO. O God! 150

MAL. Whilst she lisps, and gives him some
　court-*quelquechose*,[35]
Made only to provoke, not satiate:
And yet, even then, the thaw of her delight
Flows from lewd heat of apprehension,[36]
Only from strange imagination's rankness,
That forms the adulterer's presence in her
　soul
And makes her think she clips [37] the foul
　knave's loins.

PIETRO. Affliction to my blood's root!

MAL. Nay, think, but think what may
　proceed of this;
Adultery is often the mother of incest. 160

PIETRO. Incest!

MAL. Yes, incest; mark: — Mendoza of his wife begets perchance a daughter; Mendoza dies, his son marries this daughter. Say you? Nay, 't is frequent; not only probable, but no question often acted; whilst ignorance, fearless ignorance, clasps his own seed.

PIETRO. Hideous imagination! 169

MAL. Adultery! Why, next to the sin of simony, 't is the most horrid transgression under the cope of salvation.[38]

PIETRO. Next to simony!

MAL. Ay, next to simony, in which our men in next age shall not sin.

PIETRO. Not sin? why?

MAL. Because, thanks to some churchmen, our age will leave them nothing to sin with. But adultery, O dulness! [should show] [39] [179 exemplary punishment, that intemperate bloods may freeze but to think it.> I would damn him and all his generation: my own hands should do it; ha, I would not trust Heaven with my vengeance anything.

---

[34] Counts.　　　[35] Kickshaws, fancy dishes.
[36] Anticipation.　　　[37] Embraces.
[38] *I.e.*, under the heavens.　　　[39] Q *shue, should.*

PIETRO. Anything, anything, Malevole! Thou shalt see instantly what temper my spirit holds. Farewell; remember I forget thee not; farewell. *Exit* PIETRO.

<40 MAL. Farewell.
Lean thoughtfulness, a sallow meditation, [190
Suck thy veins dry! Distemperance rob thy sleep!
The heart's disquiet is revenge most deep:
He that gets blood, the life of flesh but spills,
But he that breaks heart's peace, the dear soul kills. —
Well, this disguise doth yet afford me that
Which kings do seldom hear, or great men use —
Free speech; and though my state's usurp'd,
Yet this affected strain gives me a tongue
As fetterless as is an emperor's.
I may speak foolishly, ay, knavishly,   200
Always carelessly, yet no one thinks it fashion
To poise ⁴¹ my breath; for he that laughs and strikes
Is lightly felt, or seldom struck again.
Duke, I'll torment thee now: my just revenge
From thee than crown a richer gem shall part:
Beneath God, naught's so dear as a calm heart.>

SCENE IV ⁴²

Enter CELSO.

CELSO. My honor'd Lord, —
MAL. Peace, speak low, peace! O Celso, constant lord,
Thou to whose faith I only rest discovered,
Thou, one of full ten millions of men,
That lovest virtue only for itself;
Thou in whose hands old Ops may put her soul,
Behold forever-banish'd Altofront,
This Genoa's last year's duke. O truly noble!
I wanted those old instruments of state,⁴³
Dissemblance and suspect: I could not time it, Celso;   10
My throne stood like a point in middest of a circle,
To all of equal nearness; bore with none;
Rein'd all alike; so slept in fearless virtue,
Suspectless, too suspectless; till the crowd,
Still likerous of ⁴⁴ untried novelties,
Impatient with severer government,
Made strong with Florence, banish'd Altofront.

⁴⁰ This speech add. Q₃.
⁴¹ Weigh; *i.e.*, take seriously.   ⁴² The same.
⁴³ I lacked those old political tools.
⁴⁴ Craving.

CELSO. Strong with Florence! ay, thence your mischief rose;
For when the daughter of the Florentine
Was matched once with this Pietro, now duke,
No stratagem of state untri'd was left,   21
Till you of all —
MAL.   Of all was quite bereft.
Alas, Maria too, close prisoned,
My true faith'd duchess, i' the citadel!
CELSO. I'll still adhere; let's mutiny and die.
MAL. Oh, <no,> climb not a falling tower, Celso;
'T is well held desperation, no zeal,
Hopeless to strive with fate. Peace! Temporize!
Hope, hope, that never forsak'st the wretched'st man,   29
Yet bidd'st me live, and lurk in this disguise!
What, play I well the free-breath'd discontent?
Why,⁴⁵ man, we are all philosophical monarchs
Or natural fools. Celso, the court's afire;
The Duchess' sheets will smoke for't ere it be long:
Impure Mendoza, that sharp-nos'd lord, that made
The cursed match link'd Genoa with Florence,
Now broad-horns the Duke, which he now knows.
Discord to malcontents is very manna;
When the ranks are burst, then scuffle, Altofront.
CELSO. Ay, but durst, —   40
MAL. 'T is gone; 't is swallowed like a mineral;
Some way 't will work; phewt, I'll not shrink:
He's resolute who can no lower sink. —

⁴⁶ <BILIOSO *entering,* MALEVOLE *shifteth his speech.*

O the father of Maypoles! Did you never see a fellow whose strength consisted in his breath, respect in his office, religion on his lord, and love in himself, why, then, behold!
BIL. Signior, —
MAL. My right worshipful Lord, your court nightcap makes you have a passing high [50 forehead.
BIL. I can tell you strange news, but I am sure you know them already: the Duke speaks much good of you.

⁴⁵ Old eds. print rest of speech as prose.
⁴⁶ The colloquy with Bilioso is added by Q₃.

Mal. Go to, then; and shall you and I now enter into a strict friendship?

Bil. Second one another?

Mal. Yes.

Bil. Do one another good offices?

Mal. Just! What though I call'd [60 thee old ox, egregious wittol, broken-bellied coward, rotten mummy? Yet, since I am in favor —

Bil. Words of course, terms of disport. His Grace presents you by me a chain, as his grateful remembrance for — I am ignorant for what; marry, ye may impart: yet howsoever — come — dear friend, dost know my son?

Mal. Your son!　　　　　　　　　　70

Bil. He shall eat woodcocks, dance jigs, make possets, and play at shuttlecock with any young lord about the court: he has as sweet a lady, too. Dost know her little bitch?

Mal. 'T is a dog, man.

Bil. Believe me, a she-bitch. Oh, 't is a good creature! Thou shalt be her servant.[47] I 'll make thee acquainted with my young wife too: what! I keep her not at court for nothing. 'T is grown to supper-time; come [80 to my table: that, anything I have, stands open to thee.

Mal. ([*aside*] *to* Celso) How smooth to him that is in state of grace,

How servile is the rugged'st courtier's face!

What profit, nay, what nature would keep down,

Are heav'd to them are minions to a crown.

Envious ambition never sates his thirst,

Till, sucking all, he swells and swells, and bursts.

Bil. I shall now leave you with my always-best wishes; only let 's hold betwixt us a [90 firm correspondence, a mutual friendly-reciprocal kind of a steady-unanimous-heartily-leagued ——

Mal. Did your Signiorship ne'er see a pigeon-house that was smooth, round, and white without, and full of holes and stink within? Ha' ye not, old courtier?

Bil. O, yes, 't is the form, the fashion of them all.

Mal. Adieu, my true court-friend;　100 farewell, my dear Castilio.[48]

Exit Bilioso.>

Celso. Yonder 's Mendoza.

Mal. (*descries* Mendoza.) True, the privy key.

Celso. I take my leave, sweet lord.

Mal. 　　'T is fit; away! *Exit* Celso.

SCENE V [49]

Enter Mendoza *with three or four* Suitors.

Men. Leave your suits with me; I can and will. Attend my secretary; leave me.

[*Exeunt* Suitors.]

Mal. Mendoza, hark ye, hark ye. You are a treacherous villain — God b' wi' ye!

Men. Out, you baseborn rascal!

Mal. We are all the sons of Heaven, though a tripe-wife were our mother. Ah, you whoreson, hot-rein'd he-marmoset! Aegisthus! [50] didst ever hear of one Aegisthus?

Men. Gisthus?　　　　　　　　　10

Mal. Ay, Aegisthus: he was a filthy incontinent fleshmonger, such a one as thou art.

Men. Out, grumbling rogue!

Mal. Orestes,[51] beware Orestes!

Men. Out, beggar!

Mal. I once shall rise!

Men. Thou rise!

Mal. Ay, at the resurrection.

No vulgar seed but once may rise and shall;

No king so huge but 'fore he die may fall. [20

Exit.

Men. Now, good Elysium! what a delicious heaven is it for a man to be in a prince's favor! O sweet God! O pleasure! O fortune! O all thou best of life! What should I think, what say, what do? To be a favorite, a minion! To have a general timorous respect observe[52] a man, a stateful silence in his presence, solitariness in his absence, a confused hum and busy murmur of obsequious suitors training [53] him; the cloth held up, and way proclaim'd [30 before him; petitionary vassels licking the pavement with their slavish knees, whilst some odd palace-lampreels [54] that engender with snakes, and are full of eyes on both sides, with a kind of insinuated humbleness, fix all their delights [55] upon his brow. O blessed state! what a ravishing prospect doth the Olympus of

[47] Cavalier, lover according to the code of courtly love.

[48] *I.e.*, courtier, that being the title of Castiglione's famous book.

[49] The same.

[50] Paramour of Clytemnestra, wife of Agamemnon, whom they murdered.

[51] The avenging son of Agamemnon, who killed his mother and her lover.

[52] Be obsequious to.

[53] Following in a train.

[54] Some eel-like fish resembling the lamprey; perhaps, young lampreys.　　[55] Q₁ *lights*.

favor yield! Death! I cornute the Duke! Sweet women! most sweet ladies! nay, angels! by Heaven, he is more accursed than [40 a devil that hates you, or is hated by you; and happier than a god that loves you, or is beloved by you. You preservers of mankind, lifeblood of society, who would live, nay, who can live, without you? O paradise! how majestical is your austerer presence! how imperiously chaste is your more modest face! but, oh, how full of ravishing attraction is your pretty, petulant, languishing, lasciviously-composed countenance! these amorous smiles, those [50 soul-warming sparkling glances, ardent as those flames that singed the world by heedless Phaëthon! in body how delicate, in soul how witty, in discourse how pregnant, in life, how wary, in favors how judicious, in day how sociable, and in night how — O pleasure unutterable! indeed, it is most certain, one man cannot deserve only to enjoy a beauteous woman — but a duchess! In despite of Phoebus, I'll write a sonnet instantly in praise of her.   *Exit.* [60

Scene VI [56]

Enter Ferneze *ushering* Aurelia, Emilia *and* Maquerelle *bearing up her train,* Bianca *attending; all go out but* Aurelia, Maquerelle, *and* Ferneze.

Aurel. And is 't possible? Mendoza slight me! Possible?

Fer. Possible!
What can be strange in him that's drunk with favor,
Grows insolent with grace? — Speak, Maquerelle, speak.

Maq. To speak feelingly, more, more richly in solid sense than worthless words, give me those jewels of your ears to receive my enforced duty. As for my part, 't is well known I can put [up] [57] anything (Ferneze *privately* [10 *feeds* Maquerelle's *hands with jewels during this speech*), can bear patiently with any man; but when I heard he wronged your precious sweetness, I was enforced to take deep offence. 'T is most certain he loves Emilia with high appetite; and, as she told me (as you know we women impart our secrets one to another), when she repulsed his suit, in that he was possessed with your endeared grace, Mendoza most ingratefully renounced all faith to you.

Fer. Nay, call'd you — Speak, Maquerelle, speak.   20

Maq. By Heaven, witch, dri'd biscuit; and contested blushlessly he lov'd you but for a spurt or so.

Fer. For maintenance.

Maq. Advancement and regard.

Aurel. O villain! O impudent Mendoza!

Maq. Nay, he is the rustiest[-jaw'd], [58] the foulest mouth'd knave in railing against our sex; he will rail against women —

Aurel. How? how?   30

Maq. I am asham'd to speak 't, I.

Aurel. I love to hate him: speak.

Maq. Why, when Emilia scorn'd his base unsteadiness, the black-throated rascal scolded, and said —

Aurel. What?

Maq. Troth, 't is too shameless.

Aurel. What said he?

Maq. Why, that, at four, women were fools; at fourteen, drabs; at forty, bawds; [40 at fourscore, witches; and a hundred, cats.

Aurel. O unlimitable impudency!

Fer. But as for poor Ferneze's fixed heart,
Was never shadeless meadow drier parch'd
Under the scorching heat of heaven's dog,
Than is my heart with your enforcing eyes.

Maq. A hot simile.

Fer. Your smiles have been my Heaven, your frowns my hell.
Oh, pity, then! grace should with beauty dwell.

Maq. Reasonable perfect, by 'r lady.   50

Aurel. I will love thee, be it but in despite Of that Mendoza: — witch! Ferneze, witch! — Ferneze, thou art the Duchess' favorite: Be faithful, private — but 't is dangerous.

Fer. His love is lifeless that for love fears breath:
The worst that's due to sin, oh, would 't were death!

Aurel. Enjoy my favor. I will be sick instantly and take physic; therefore in depth of night visit.   59

Maq. Visit her chamber, but conditionally you shall not offend her bed—by this diamond!

Fer. By this diamond.   *Gives it to* Maquerelle.

Maq. Nor tarry longer than you please — by this ruby!

Fer. By this ruby.   *Gives again.*

Maq. And that the door shall not creak.

Fer. And that the door shall not creak.

Maq. Nay, but swear.

Fer. By this purse.   *Gives her his purse.*

---

[56] The same.   [57] Om. Q3.   [58] Q3 *jade.*

Maq. Go to ; I 'll keep your oaths for [70
you : remember, visit.

Enter Mendoza, *reading a sonnet.*

Aurel. Dri'd biscuit ! — Look where the
base wretch comes.

Men. " Beauty's life, Heaven's model,
love's queen," —

Maq. That 's his Emilia.

Men. " Nature's triumph, best on [59]
earth," —

Maq. Meaning Emilia.

Men. " Thou only wonder that the world
hath seen," —

Maq. That 's Emilia.

Aurel. Must I, then, hear her prais'd ? —
Mendoza !　　　　　　　　　　80

Men. Madam, your Excellency is graciously encount'red : I have been writing passionate flashes in honor of —　*Exit* Ferneze.

Aurel. Out, villain, villain !
O judgment, where have been my eyes ? —
What
Bewitched election made me dote on thee ?
What sorcery made me love thee ? But be-
gone ;
Bury thy head.　O, that I could do more
Than loathe thee ! — hence, worst of ill !
No reason ask ; our reason is our will.[60]　90

Exit with Marquerelle.

Men. Women ! nay, Furies ; nay, worse ;
for they torment only the bad, but women
good and bad.　Damnation of mankind !
Breath, hast thou prais'd them for this ? and
is 't you, Ferneze, are wriggled into smock-
grace ?　Sit sure.　Oh that I could rail against
these monsters in nature, models of hell, curse
of the earth, women ! that dare attempt anything, and what they attempt they care not
how they accomplish ; without all premed- [100
itation or prevention ; rash in asking, desperate in working, impatient in suffering, extreme
in desiring, slaves unto appetite, mistresses in
dissembling, only constant in unconstancy,
only perfect in counterfeiting ; their words are
feigned, their eyes forged, their sights [61] dissembled, their looks counterfeit, their hair
false, their given hopes deceitful, their very
breath artificial ; their blood [62] is their only
god ; bad clothes and old age are only [110
the devils they tremble at.　That I could rail
now !

[59] Q : *of.*
[60] Q 1 *No reason else, my reason is my will.* Qq
print this speech as prose.
[61] Sighs.　　　　　　[62] Passions.

Scene VII [63]

Enter Pietro, *his sword drawn.*

Pietro. A mischief fill thy throat, thou
foul-jaw'd slave !
Say thy prayers.

Men.　　　　　I ha' forgot 'em.

Pietro.　　　　　　　　Thou shalt die.

Men. So shalt thou.　I am heart-mad.

Pietro.　　　　　　　　I am horn-mad.

Men. Extreme mad.

Pietro.　　　　Monstrously mad.

Men.　　　　　　　　　　Why ?

Pietro. Why ! thou, thou hast dishonored
my bed.

Men. I ! Come, come, [sir] [64] ; here 's my
bare heart to thee,
As steady as is this centre to the glorious
world. —
And yet, hark, thou art a cornuto — but by
me ?

Pietro. Yes, slave, by thee.

Men. Do not, do not with tart and spleen-
ful breath　　　　　　　　　10
Lose him can lose thee.　I offend my duke !
Bear record, O ye dumb and raw-air'd nights,
How vigilant my sleepless eyes have been
To watch the traitor !　Record, thou spirit of
truth,
With what debasement I ha' thrown myself
To under offices, only to learn
The truth, the party, time, the means, the
place,
By whom, and when, and where thou wert dis-
grac'd !
And am I paid with " slave " ?　Hath my in-
trusion
To places private and prohibited,　　　20
Only to observe the closer passages,
Heaven knows with vows of revelation,
Made me suspected, made me deem'd a vil-
lain ?
What rogue hath wronged us ?

Pietro.　　　　　　Mendoza, I may err.

Men. Err ! 't is too mild a name ; but err
and err,
Run giddy with suspect, 'fore through me thou
know
That which most creatures, save thyself, do
know.
Nay, since my service hath so loath'd reject,
'Fore I 'll reveal, shalt find them clipp'd together.　　　　　　　　　29

[63] The same.
[64] Old eds. *sit.* (Dyce's suggestion.)

PIETRO. Mendoza, thou know'st I am a most plain-breasted man.

MEN. The fitter to make a cuckold; would your brows were most plain too!

PIETRO. Tell me — indeed, I heard thee rail —

MEN. At women, true. Why, what cold phlegm could choose,
Knowing a lord so honest, virtuous,
So boundless loving, bounteous, fair-shap'd, sweet,
To be contemn'd, abus'd, defam'd, made cuckold?
Heart! I hate all women for 't — sweet sheets,
wax lights, antique bedposts, cambric [40
smocks, villainous curtains, arras pictures, oil'd
hinges, and all the tongue-ti'd lascivious witnesses of great creatures' wantonness — what
salvation can you expect?

PIETRO. Wilt thou tell me?

MEN. Why, you may find it yourself; observe, observe.

PIETRO. I ha' not the patience. Wilt thou deserve me, tell, give it.

MEN. Take 't : why, Ferneze is the man, [50
Ferneze. I 'll prove 't; this night you shall take him in your sheets. Will 't serve?

PIETRO. It will; my bosom 's in some peace; till night —

MEN. What?

PIETRO. Farewell.

MEN. God! how weak a lord are you!
Why, do you think there is no more but so?

PIETRO. Why?

MEN. Nay, then, will I presume to counsel you:
It should be thus. You with some guard upon the sudden
Break into the Princess' chamber. I stay behind,
Without the door, through which he needs must pass. 60
Ferneze flies: let him. To me he comes; he 's kill'd
By me, observe, by me. You follow; I rail,
And seem to save the body. Duchess comes,
On whom, respecting her advanced birth,
And your fair nature, I know, nay, I do know,
No violence must be used; she comes. I storm,
I praise, excuse Ferneze, and still maintain
The Duchess' honor; she for this loves me.
I honor you; shall know her soul, you mine:
Then naught shall she contrive in vengeance
(As women are most thoughtful in revenge) [71

Of her Ferneze, but you shall sooner know 't
Than she can think 't. Thus shall his death come sure,
Your duchess brain-caught: so your life secure.

PIETRO. It is too well; my bosom and my heart
When nothing helps, cut off the rotten part.
Exit.

MEN. Who cannot feign friendship can ne'er produce the effects of hatred. Honest fool Duke! subtle lascivious Duchess! silly novice Ferneze! I do laugh at ye. My [80 brain is in labor till it produce mischief, and I feel sudden throes, proofs sensible the issue is at hand.
As bears shape young, so I 'll form my device,
Which grown proves horrid; vengeance makes men wise. *[Exit.]*

<[SCENE VIII] [65]

Enter MALEVOLE *and* PASSARELLO.

MAL. Fool, most happily encount'red. Canst sing, fool?

PASS. Yes, I can sing, fool, if you 'll bear the burden; and I can play upon instruments, scurvily, as gentlemen do. Oh, that I had been gelded! I should then have been a fat fool for a chamber, a squeaking fool for a tavern, and a private fool for all the ladies.

MAL. You are in good case since you came to court, fool: what, guarded,[66] guarded! [10

PASS. Yes, faith, even as footmen and bawds wear velvet, not for an ornament of honor, but for a badge of drudgery; for, now the Duke is discontented, I am fain to fool him asleep every night.

MAL. What are his griefs?

PASS. He hath sore eyes.

MAL. I never observed so much.

PASS. Horrible sore eyes; and so hath every cuckold, for the roots of the horns spring in [20 the eyeballs, and that 's the reason the horn of a cuckold is as tender as his eye, or as that growing in the woman's forehead, twelve years since, that could not endure to be touch'd.[67] The Duke hangs down his head like a columbine.

MAL. Passarello, why do great men beg fools? [68]

---

[65] The same. This scene is added by Q₃.
[66] Adorned, trimmed with facings.
[67] A pamphlet describing it appeared in 1588.
[68] Apply to the king for the guardianship of idiots (in order to have the use of their property).

PASS. As the Welshman stole rushes when there was nothing else to filch ; only to [30 keep begging in fashion.

MAL. Pooh, thou givest no good reason ; thou speakest like a fool.

PASS. Faith, I utter small fragments, as your knight courts your city widow with jingling of his gilt spurs, advancing his bush-colored beard, and taking tobacco ; this is all the mirror of their knightly complements.[69] Nay, I shall talk when my tongue is a-going once ; 't is like a citizen on horseback, evermore in [40 a false gallop.

MAL. And how doth Maquerelle fare nowadays?

PASS. Faith, I was wont to salute her as our English women are at their first landing in Flushing :[70] I would call her whore. But now that antiquity leaves her as an old piece of plastic t' work by,[71] I only ask her how her rotten teeth fare every morning, and so leave her. She was the first that ever invented [50 perfum'd smocks for the gentlewomen, and woolen shoes, for fear of creaking, for the visitant. She were an excellent lady, but that her face peeleth like Muscovy glass.[72]

MAL. And how doth thy old lord, that hath wit enough to be a flatterer, and conscience enough to be a knave?

PASS. Oh, excellent ; he keeps beside me fifteen jesters, to instruct him in the art of fooling, and utters their jests in private to the [60 Duke and Duchess. He 'll lie like to your Switzer or lawyer ; he 'll be of any side for most money.

MAL. I am in haste : be brief.

PASS. As your fiddler when he is paid. — He 'll thrive, I warrant you, while your young courtier stands like Good Friday in Lent : men long to see it, because more fatting days come after it ; else he 's the leanest and pitifull'st actor in the whole pageant. Adieu, Malevole. 71

MAL. O world most vile, when thy loose vanities,
Taught by this fool, do make the fool seem wise !

PASS. You 'll know me again, Malevole.

[69] Accomplishments. Of the four copies of Q₃ collated for the present ed., two give ll. 35, 36, as here ; the others read *with something of his guilt: some aduancing his high colored.*

[70] Temporarily held by the English as security for a loan to the Dutch.

[71] Like an old model, merely to serve as an example.

[72] Mica, talc, isin-glass.

MAL. O, ay, by that velvet.

PASS. Ay, as a pettifogger by his buckram bag. I am as common in the court as an hostess's lips in the country ; knights, and clowns, and knaves, and all share me ; the court cannot possibly be without me. Adieu, Malevole.
[*Exeunt.*]>

ACT II — SCENE I[1]

Enter MENDOZA, *with a sconce,*[2] *to observe* FERNEZE'S *entrance, who, whilst the act is playing, enter unbraced, two* Pages *before him with lights ; is met by* MAQUERELLE *and conveyed in. The* Pages *are sent away.*

MEN. He 's caught, the woodcock's head is i' th' noose.
Now treads Ferneze in dangerous path of lust,
Swearing his sense is merely [3] deified :
The fool grasps clouds, and shall beget Centaurs ;
And now, in strength of panting faint delight,
The goat bids Heaven envy him. — Good goose,
I can afford thee nothing
But the poor comfort of calamity, pity.
Lust 's like the plummets hanging on clock-lines —
Will ne'er ha' done till all is quite undone ;   10
Such is the course salt, sallow lust doth run,
Which thou shalt try. I 'll be reveng'd.
      Duke, thy suspect ;
Duchess, thy disgrace ; Ferneze, thy rivalship ;
Shall have swift vengeance. Nothing so holy,
No band of nature so strong,
No law of friendship so sacred,
But I 'll profane, burst, violate, 'fore I 'll
Endure disgrace, contempt, and poverty.
Shall I, whose very " hum " struck all heads bare,
Whose face made silence, creaking of whose shoe   20
Forc'd the most private passages fly ope,
Scrape like a servile dog at some latch'd door?
Learn now to make a leg, and cry " Beseech ye,
Pray ye, is such a lord within? " be aw'd
At some odd usher's scoff'd formality?
First sear my brains ! *Unde cadis non quo, refert ;* [4]

[1] An antechamber in the Duchess's apartments.
[2] Lantern.
[3] Absolutely.
[4] Adapted from Seneca's *Thyestes,* l. 926 : Whence you fall, not whither, is what counts.

My heart cries, " Perish all ! " How ! how ! what fate
Can once avoid revenge, that 's desperate?
I 'll to the Duke ; if all should ope — If ? tush !
Fortune still dotes on those who cannot blush. [*Exit.*] [30

Enter MALEVOLE *at one door ;* BIANCA, EMILIA, *and* MAQUERELLE *at the other door.*

MAL. Bless ye, cast [6] a' ladies ! — Ha, Dipsas ! [7] how dost thou, old coal?

MAQ. Old coal !

MAL. Ay, old coal ; methinks thou liest like a brand under [these] [8] billets of green wood. He that will inflame a young wench's heart, let him lay close to her an old coal that hath first been fir'd, a pand'ress, my half-burnt lint, who though thou canst not flame thyself, yet art able to set a thousand virgins' ta- [10 pers afire. — And how doth Janivere thy husband, my little periwinkle? Is he troubled with the cough of the lungs still? Does he hawk a-nights still? He will not bite.

BIAN. No, by my troth, I took him with his mouth empty of old teeth.

MAL. And he took thee with thy belly full of young bones ; marry, he took his maim by the stroke of his enemy.

BIAN. And I mine by the stroke of my [20 friend.

MAL. The close stock ! [9] O mortal wench ! Lady, ha' ye now no restoratives for your decayed Jasons? Look ye, crab's guts bak'd, distill'd ox-pith, the pulverized hairs of a lion's upper lip, jelly of cock-sparrows, he-monkey's marrow, or powder of fox stones? — And whither are [all] [10] you ambling now?

BIAN. [Why,] [10] to bed, to bed.

MAL. Do your husbands lie with ye? 30

BIAN. That were country fashion, i' faith.

MAL. Ha' ye no foregoers about you? Come, whither in good deed, la now?

[MAQ.] [11] In good indeed, law, now, to eat the most miraculously, admirably, astonishable-compos'd posset with three curds, without any drink. Will ye help me with a he-fox? — Here 's the Duke. *The* Ladies *go out.*

<MAL. (*to* BIANCA) Fri'd frogs are very good, and Frenchlike too.> 40

[5] The same. [6] Set, suit.
[7] *I.e.,* old enchantress. See *Endymion.*
[8] So Q 1 ; om. Q 3.
[9] *Stoccata,* thrust. [10] So Q 1 ; om. Q 3.
[11] So Q 1 ; Q 3 gives speech to Bianca.

Enter DUKE PIETRO, COUNT CELSO, COUNT EQUATO, BILIOSO, FERRARDO, *and* MENDOZA.

PIETRO. The night grows deep and foul ; what hour is 't?

CELSO. Upon the stroke of twelve.

MAL. Save ye, Duke !

PIETRO. From thee ! Begone ! I do not love thee ! Let me see thee no more ; we are displeas'd.

MAL. Why, God be with thee ! Heaven hear my curse : may thy wife and thee live long together ! 10

PIETRO. Begone, sirrah !

MAL. " When Arthur first in court began " — Agamemnon — Menelaus [13] — was ever any duke a cornuto?

PIETRO. Begone ! hence !

MAL. What religion wilt thou be of next?

MEN. Out with him !

MAL. With most servile patience. — Time will come
When wonder of thy error will strike dumb
Thy bezzl'd [14] senses. — 20
Slaves ! ay, favor ! [15] ay, marry, shall he rise !
Good God ! how subtle hell doth flatter vice !
Mounts him aloft, and makes him seem to fly,
As fowl the tortoise mock'd, who to the sky
The ambitious shellfish rais'd ! Th' end of all
Is only, that from height he might dead fall.

[16] <Bil. Why, when ! [17] Out, ye rogue ! begone, ye rascal !

MAL. I shall now leave ye with all my best wishes. 30

BIL. Out, ye cur !

MAL. Only let 's hold together a firm correspondence.

BIL. Out !

MAL. A mutual-friendly-reciprocal-perpetual kind of steady-unanimous-heartily-leagued —

BIL. Hence, ye gross-jaw'd, peasantly — out, go !

MAL. Adieu, pigeon-house ; thou burr, [40 that only stickest to nappy fortunes. The serpigo, [18] the strangury, an eternal uneffectual priapism seize thee !

[12] The same.
[13] Three famous cuckolds.
[14] Drunken.
[15] Emend. Dyce : *The slave's in favour.*
[16] This passage between Malevole and Bilioso is added by Q 3.
[17] An exclamation of impatience.
[18] Ringworm.

BIL. Out, rogue!

MAL. Mayest thou be a notorious wittolly pander to thine own wife, and yet get no office, but live to be the utmost misery of mankind, a beggarly cuckold!> *Exit.*

PIETRO. It shall be so.

MEN. It must be so, for where great states revenge, 50
'T is requisite the parts [which] [19] piety
And [soft] [20] respect forbears, be closely dogg'd:
Lay one into his breast shall sleep with him,
Feed in the same dish, run in self [21] faction,
Who may discover any shape of danger;
For once disgrac'd, displayed in offence,
It makes man blushless, and man is, all confess,
More prone to vengeance than to gratefulness.
Favors are writ in dust; but stripes we feel
Depraved nature stamps in lasting steel. 60

PIETRO. You shall be leagu'd with the Duchess.

EQUATO. The plot is very good.

[PIETRO.] [22] You shall both kill, and seem the corse to save.

FER. A most fine brain-trick.

CELSO. [*aside*] Of a most cunning knave.

PIETRO. My Lords, the heavy action we intend
Is death and shame, two of the ugliest shapes
That can confound a soul; think, think of it.
I strike, but yet, like him that 'gainst stone walls
Directs, his shafts rebounds in his own face; [69]
My lady's shame is mine, O God, 't is mine!
Therefore I do conjure all secrecy;
Let it be as very little as may be,
Pray ye, as may be;
Make frightless entrance, salute her with soft eyes,
Stain naught with blood; only Ferneze dies,
But not before her brows. O gentlemen,
God knows I love her! Nothing else, but this:—
I am not well; if grief, that sucks veins dry,
Rivels [23] the skin, casts ashes in men's faces, [79]
Be-dulls the eye, unstrengthens all the blood,
Chance to remove me to another world,
As sure I once must die, let him succeed:
I have no child; all that my youth begot
Hath been your loves, which shall inherit me;

Which as it ever shall, I do conjure it,
Mendoza may succeed; he's noble born;
With me of much desert.

CELSO. [*aside*] Much!

PIETRO. Your silence answers, " Ay."
I thank you. Come on now. Oh, that I might die 90
Before her shame's display'd! Would I were forc'd
To burn my father's tomb, [unhill] [24] his bones
And dash them in the dirt, rather than this!
This both the living and the dead offends:
Sharp surgery where naught but death amends.
Exit with the others.

SCENE IV [25]

Enter MAQUERELLE, EMILIA, *and* BIANCA, *with a posset.*

MAQ. Even here it is, three curds in three regions individually distinct, most methodical according to art compos'd, without any drink.

BIAN. Without any drink!

MAQ. Upon my honor. Will ye sit and eat?

EMIL. Good; the composure, the receipt, how is 't?

MAQ. 'T is a pretty pearl; by this pearl (how does 't with me? [26]) thus it is: seven-and-thirty yolks of Barbary hens' eggs; eight- [10 een spoonfuls and a half of the juice of cocksparrow bones; one ounce, three drams, four scruples and one-quarter of the syrup of Ethiopian dates; sweet'ned with three-quarters of a pound of pure candied Indian eryngoes; strewed over with the powder of pearl of America, amber of Cataia, [27] and lamb stones of Muscovia.

BIAN. Trust me, the ingredients are very cordial, and, no question, good, and most [20 powerful in restoration.

MAQ. I know not what you mean by restoration; but this it doth: it purifieth the blood, smootheth the skin, enliveneth the eye, strengtheneth the veins, mundifieth [28] the teeth, comforteth the stomach, fortifieth the back, and quickeneth the wit; that's all.

EMIL. By my troth, I have eaten but two spoonfuls, and methinks I could discourse most swiftly and wittily already. 30

MAQ. Have you the art to seem honest? [29]

BIAN. I thank advice and practice.

---

[19] Old eds. *with.*
[20] So both copies of Q1 collated for the present ed.; other old eds. *loft.*
[21] The same. [22] Old eds. *Mend.*
[23] Wrinkles.

[24] So Q1; Q3 *vnheale.*
[25] The same. [26] How does it become me?
[27] Cathay, China. — "Eryngoes" = candied seaholly root, valued as an aphrodisiac.
[28] Cleanseth. [29] Chaste.

MAQ. Why, then, eat me o' this posset, quicken your blood, and preserve your beauty. Do you know Doctor Plaster-face? By this curd, he is the most exquisite in forging of veins, spright'ning of eyes, dyeing of hair, sleeking of skins, blushing of cheeks, surphling [30] of breasts, blanching and bleaching of teeth, that ever made an old lady gracious [40 by torchlight; by this curd, law.

BIAN. Well, we are resolved, what God has given us we'll cherish.

MAQ. Cherish anything saving your husband; keep him not too high, lest he leap the pale. But, for your beauty, let it be your saint: bequeath two hours to it every morning in your closet. I ha' been young, and yet, in my conscience, I am not above five-and-twenty; but, believe me, preserve and use [50 your beauty; for youth and beauty once gone, we are like beehives without honey, out-a'-fashion apparel that no man will wear; therefore use me your beauty.

EMIL. Ay, but men say —

MAQ. Men say! let men say what they will! Life a' woman! they are ignorant of your wants. The more in years, the more in perfection they grow: if they lose youth and beauty, they gain wisdom and discretion; [60 but when our beauty fades, good night with us. There cannot be an uglier thing to see than an old woman; from which, O pruning, pinching, and painting, deliver all sweet beauties!

BIAN. Hark! music!

MAQ. Peace, 't is i' the Duchess' bed-chamber. Good rest, most prosperously-grac'd ladies.

EMIL. Good night, sentinel.

BIAN. Night, dear Maquerelle. 70
Exeunt all but MAQUERELLE.

MAQ. May my posset's operation send you my wit and honesty; and me, your youth and beauty; the pleasing'st rest! *Exit.*

SCENE V [31]

A Song [within].

Whilst the song is singing, enter MENDOZA *with his sword drawn, standing ready to murder* FERNEZE *as he flies from the Duchess' chamber.*

ALL. [*within*] Strike, strike!

AUR. [*within*] Save my Ferneze! Oh, save my Ferneze!

[30] Beautifying with cosmetics. [31] The same.

Enter FERNEZE *in his shirt, and is receiv'd upon Mendoza's sword.*

ALL. [*within*] Follow, pursue .

AUR. [*within*] Oh, save Ferneze!

MEN. Pierce, pierce! — Thou shallow fool, drop there!
He that attempts a princess' lawless love
Must have broad hands, close heart, with Argus' eyes,
And back of Hercules, or else he dies.
Thrusts his rapier in FERNEZE.

Enter AURELIA, DUKE PIETRO, FERRARDO, BILIOSO, CELSO, *and* EQUATO.

ALL. Follow, follow!

MEN. Stand off, forbear, ye most uncivil lords!

PIETRO. Strike!

MEN. Do not; tempt not a man resolv'd.
Would you, inhuman murderers, more than death? 10

AUR. O poor Ferneze!

MEN. Alas, now all defence too late!

AUR. He 's dead.

PIETRO. I am sorry for our shame. — Go to your bed;
Weep not too much, but leave some tears to shed
When I am dead.

AUR. What, weep for thee! my soul no tears shall find.

PIETRO. Alas, alas, that women's souls are blind!

MEN. Betray such beauty!
Murder such youth! Contemn civility!
He loves him not that rails not at him. 20

PIETRO. Thou canst not move us; we have blood enough. —
And please you, lady, we have quite forgot
All your defects; if not, why, then —

AUR. Not.

PIETRO. Not! The best of rest; good-night.
Exit PIETRO, *with other* Courtiers.

AUR. Despite go with thee!

MEN. Madam, you ha' done me foul disgrace; you have wrong'd him much loves you too much. Go to; your soul knows you have.

AUR. I think I have.

MEN. Do you but think so?

AUR. Nay, sure, I have; my eyes have [30 witnessed thy love; thou hast stood too firm for me.

Men. Why, tell me, fair-cheek'd lady, who even in tears art powerfully beauteous, what unadvised passion struck ye into such a violent heat against me? Speak, what mischief wrong'd us? What devil injur'd us? Speak.

Aur. The thing ne'er worthy of the name of man, Ferneze.

Ferneze swore thou lov'st Emilia;
Which to advance, with most reproachful breath   40
Thou both didst blemish and denounce my love.

Men. Ignoble villain! did I for this bestride
Thy wounded limbs? [for this, rank opposite
Even to my sovereign?] [32] for this, O God, for this,
Sunk all my hopes, and with my hopes my life?
Ripp'd bare my throat unto the hangman's axe? —
Thou most dishonor'd trunk! — Emilia!
By life, I know her not. — Emilia! —
Did you believe him?

Aur.   Pardon me, I did.

Men. Did   you?   And   thereupon   you graced him?   50

Aur. I did.

Men.   Took him to favor, nay even clasp'd
With him?

Aur.   Alas, I did!

Men.   This night?

Aur.   This night.

Men. And in your lustful twines the Duke took you?

Aur. A most sad truth.

Men. O God, O God! how we dull honest souls,
Heavy-brain'd men, are swallowed in the bogs
Of a deceitful ground, whilst nimble bloods,
Light-jointed spirits, [speed], [33] cut good men's throats,
And scape! Alas, I am too honest for this age,
Too full of phlegm and heavy steadiness; 60
Stood still whilst this slave cast a noose about me;
Nay, then to stand in honor of him and her,
Who had even slic'd my heart!

Aur.   Come, I did err,
And am most sorry I did err.

Men. Why, we are both but dead: the Duke hates us;

And those whom princes do once groundly [34] hate,
Let them provide to die, as sure as fate.
Prevention [35] is the heart of policy.

Aur. Shall we murder him?

Men. Instantly?   70

Aur. Instantly; before he casts a plot,
Or further blaze my honor's much-known blot,
Let's murder him.

Men.   I would do much for you. Will ye marry me?

Aur. I'll make thee duke. We are of Medicis;
Florence our friend; in court my faction
Not meanly strengthful; the Duke then dead,
We well prepar'd for change, the multitude
Irresolutely reeling, we in force,
Our party seconded, the kingdom maz'd,
No doubt of [36] swift success all shall be grac'd.   80

Men. You do confirm me; we are resolute;
To-morrow look for change; rest confident.
'T is now about the immodest waste of night:
The mother of moist dew with pallid light
Spreads gloomy shades about the numbed earth.
Sleep, sleep, whilst we contrive our mischief's birth.
This man I'll get inhum'd. Farewell; to bed.
Ay, kiss the pillow; dream the Duke is dead.
So, so; good night.   *Exit* Aurelia.
          — How fortune dotes on impudence!
I am in private the adopted son   90
Of yon good prince.
I must be duke; why, if I must, I must.
Most silly lord, name me! O Heaven! I see
God made honest fools to maintain crafty knaves.
The Duchess is wholly mine too, must kill her husband
To quit her shame. Much! then marry her! Ay.
Oh, I grow proud in prosperous treachery!
As wrestlers clip, so I'll embrace you all,
Not to support, but to procure your fall.

Enter Malevole.

Mal. God arrest thee!   100

Men. At whose suit?

Mal. At the Devil's. Ah, you treacherous, damnable monster, how dost? how dost, thou treacherous rogue? Ah, ye rascal! I am banish'd the court, sirrah.

---

[32] So Q1; om. Q3.
[33] Emend. Dodsley; Q1 *pent;* Q3 *spent.*
[34] Profoundly.   [35] Forestalling.
[36] With.

MEN. Prithee, let's be acquainted; I do love thee, faith.

MAL. At your service, by the Lord, law: shall's go to supper? Let's be once drunk together and so unite a most virtuously- [110 strength'ned friendship: shall's, Huguenot? [37] shall's?

MEN. Wilt fall upon my chamber to-morrow morn?

MAL. As a raven to a dunghill. They say there's one dead here, prick'd for the pride of the flesh.

MEN. Ferneze: there he is; prithee, bury him.

MAL. O, most willingly; I mean to turn pure Rochelle churchman, I.[38] 120

MEN. Thou churchman! Why, why?

MAL. Because I'll live lazily, rail upon authority, deny kings' supremacy in things indifferent, and be a pope in mine own parish.

MEN. Wherefore dost thou think churches were made?

MAL. To scour ploughshares: I ha' seen oxen plough up altars; *et nunc seges ubi Sion* [39] *fuit.*

MEN. Strange! 130

MAL. Nay, monstrous! I ha' seen a sumptuous steeple turned to a stinking privy; more beastly, the sacredest place made a dogs' kennel; nay, most inhuman, the stoned coffins of long-dead Christians burst up, and made hogs' troughs: *hic finis Priami.*[40] Shall I ha' some sack and cheese at thy chamber? Good night, good mischievous incarnate devil; good night, Mendoza; ah, you inhuman villain, good night! night, fub.[41] 140

MEN. Good night: to-morrow morn?
Exit.

MAL. Ay, I will come, friendly damnation, I will come. — I do descry cross-points; honesty and courtship [42] straddle as far asunder as a true Frenchman's legs.

FER. Oh!

MAL. Proclamations! more proclamations!

FER. Oh! a surgeon!

MAL. Hark! lust cries for a surgeon. — What news from Limbo? How doeth the [150 grand cuckold, Lucifer?

FER. Oh help, help! conceal and save me.
FERNEZE *stirs, and* MALEVOLE *helps him up and conveys him away.*

MAL. Thy shame more than thy wounds do grieve me far:

Thy wounds but leave upon thy flesh some scar;

But fame [43] ne'er heals, still rankles worse and worse;

Such is of uncontrolled lust the curse.

Think what it is in lawless sheets to lie;

But, oh Ferneze, what in lust to die!

Then thou that shame respects, oh, fly converse 159

With women's eyes and lisping wantonness!

Stick candles 'gainst a virgin wall's white back,

If they not burn, yet at the least they'll black.

Come, I'll convey thee to a private port,

Where thou shalt live (O happy man!) from court.

The beauty of the day begins to rise,

From whose bright form night's heavy shadow flies.

Now 'gins close plots to work; the scene grows full,

And craves his eyes who hath a solid skull.
Exeunt.

ACT III — SCENE I [1]

Enter PIETRO THE DUKE, MENDOZA, COUNT EQUATO, *and* BILIOSO.

PIETRO. 'T is grown to youth of day. How shall we waste this light?

My heart's more heavy than a tyrant's crown.

Shall we go hunt? Prepare for field.
Exit EQUATO.

MEN. Would ye could be merry!

PIETRO. Would God I could! Mendoza, bid 'em haste. *Exit* MENDOZA.

I would fain shift place; O vain relief!

Sad souls may well change place, but not change grief;

As deer, being struck, fly thorough many soils,[2]

Yet still the shaft sticks fast, so ——

BIL. A good old simile, my honest Lord. 10

PIETRO. I am not much unlike to some sick man

That long desired hurtful drink: at last

Swills in and drinks his last, ending at once

Both life and thirst. Oh, would I ne'er had known

[37] *I.e.*, rebel, traitor.
[38] Rochelle was held by the Huguenots.
[39] For the *Troia* of Ovid, *Heroides*, I, 53.
[40] Quoted inaccurately from Vergil's *Aeneid*, II, 554.   [41] Cheat.   [42] Courtiership.

[43] Evil repute.   [1] A room in the palace.
[2] Stretches of water in which the deer's scent may be lost.

My own dishonor !   Good God, that men
should desire
To search out that, which, being found, kills
all
Their joy of life ! to taste the tree of knowledge,
And then be driven from out paradise ! ——
Canst give me some comfort ?

BIL.   My Lord, I have some books which [20
have been dedicated to my honor, and I ne'er
read 'em, and yet they had very fine names,
*Physic for Fortune, Lozenges of Sanctified Sin-
cerity :* very pretty works of curates, scriveners,
and schoolmasters.   Marry, I remember one
Seneca, Lucius Annaeus Seneca ——

PIETRO.   Out upon him ! he writ of temper-
ance and fortitude, yet lived like a voluptuous
epicure, and died like an effeminate coward. —
Haste thee to Florence.   30
Here, take our letters ; see 'em seal'd ; away !
Report in private to the honor'd Duke
His daughter's forc'd disgrace ; tell him at
length
We know too much ; due compliments ad-
vance.
There's naught that's safe and sweet but
ignorance.   *Exit.*

[3]< *Enter* BIANCA.

BIL.   Madam, I am going ambassador for
Florence ;   't will be great charges to me.

BIAN.   No matter, my Lord, you have the
lease of two manors come out [4] next Christmas ;
you may lay your tenants on the greater [40
rack for it ; and when you come home again,
I 'll teach you how you shall get two hundred
pounds a year by your teeth.

BIL.   How, madam ?

BIAN.   Cut off so much from housekeeping :
that which is saved by the teeth, you know, is
got by the teeth.

BIL.   'Fore God, and so I may ; I am in
wondrous credit, lady.

BIAN.   See the use of flattery ; I did [50
ever counsel you to flatter greatness, and you
have profited well.   Any man that will do so
shall be sure to be like your Scotch barnacle,
now a block,[5] instantly a worm, and presently
a great goose : [6] this it is to rot and putrefy in
the bosom of greatness.

BIL.   Thou art ever my politician.   Oh,
how happy is that old lord that hath a politician to his young lady !   I 'll have fifty
gentlemen shall attend upon me ; marry, [60
the most of them shall be farmers' sons, because
they shall bear their own charges ; and they
shall go apparell'd thus : — in sea-water-green
suits, ash-color cloaks, watchet [7] stockings,
and popinjay-green feathers.   Will not the
colors do excellent ?

BIAN.   Out upon 't ! they 'll look like citizens riding to their friends at Whitsuntide ;
their apparel just so many several parishes.

BIL.   I 'll have it so ; and Passarello, my [70
fool, shall go along with me ; marry, he shall
be in velvet.

BIAN.   A fool in velvet !

BIL.   Ay, 't is common for your fool to wear
satin ; I 'll have mine in velvet.

BIAN.   What will you wear, then, my Lord ?

BIL.   Velvet too ; marry, it shall be embroidered, because I 'll differ from the fool
somewhat.   I am horribly troubled with the
gout ; nothing grieves me, but that my [80
doctor hath forbidden me wine, and you know
your ambassador must drink.   Didst thou ask
thy doctor what was good for the gout ?

BIAN.   Yes ; he said ease, wine, and women
were good for it.

BIL.   Nay, thou hast such a wit !   What
was good to cure it, said he ?

BIAN.   Why, the rack.   All your empirics
could never do the like cure upon the gout the
rack did in England, or your Scotch boot.[8] [90
The French harlequin will instruct you.

BIL.   Surely, I do wonder how thou, having
for the most part of thy lifetime been a
country body, shouldest have so good a wit.

BIAN.   Who, I ?   Why, I have been a
courtier thrice two months.

BIL.   So have I this twenty year, and yet
there was a gentleman usher called me coxcomb tother day, and to my face too.   Was 't
not a backbiting rascal ?   I would I were [100
better travell'd, that I might have been better
acquainted with the fashions of several
countrymen ; but my secretary, I think, he
hath sufficiently instructed me.

BIAN.   How, my Lord ?

BIL.   " Marry, my good Lord," quoth he,
" your Lordship shall ever find amongst
a hundred Frenchmen forty hot-shots ; [9]

---

[3] The rest of this scene is added by Q 3.
[4] Expire.
[5] Part of a tree.
[6] A common superstition. The *anser scoticus* was
first an excrescence on a tree ; it fell into the water
and eventually became a goose.

[7] Light blue.
[8] An instrument of torture used in Scotland and
France.   The rest of the speech = " Any empiric's
zany can tell you."
[9] Hot-heads.

amongst a hundred Spaniards, threescore braggarts ; amongst a hundred Dutchmen [110 fourscore drunkards ; amongst an hundred Englishmen, fourscore and ten madmen ; and amongst an hundred Welshmen " ——

BIAN. What, my Lord?

BIL. " Fourscore and nineteen gentlemen." [10]

BIAN. But since you go about a sad embassy, I would have you go in black, my Lord.

BIL. Why, dost think I cannot mourn [120 unless I wear my hat in cypress, [11] like an alderman's heir? That's vile, very old, in faith.

BIAN. I'll learn of you shortly. Oh, we should have a fine gallant of you, should not I instruct you! How will you bear yourself when you come into the Duke of Florence' court?

BIL. Proud enough, and 't will do well enough. As I walk up and down the [130 chamber, I'll spit frowns about me, have a strong perfume in my jerkin, let my beard grow to make me look terrible, salute no man beneath the fourth button ; and 't will do excellent.

BIAN. But there is a very beautiful lady there ; how will you entertain her?

BIL. I'll tell you that, when the lady hath entertain'd me ; but to satisfy thee, here comes the fool.   140

Enter PASSARELLO.

Fool, thou shalt stand for the fair lady.

PASS. Your fool will stand for your lady most willingly and most uprightly.

BIL. I'll salute her in Latin.

PASS. Oh, your fool can understand no Latin.

BIL. Ay, but your lady can.

PASS. Why, then, if your lady take down your fool, your fool will stand no longer for your lady.   150

BIL. A pestilent fool! 'fore God, I think the world be turn'd upside down too.

PASS. Oh, no, sir ; for then your lady and all the ladies in the palace should go with their heels upward, and that were a strange sight, you know.

BIL. There be many will repine at my preferment.

---

[10] A gibe at the Welshman's notorious pride in his ancestors.
[11] Crape.

PASS. Oh, ay, like the envy of an elder sister, that hath her younger made a lady [160 before her.

BIL. The Duke is wondrous discontented.

PASS. Ay, and more melancholic than a usurer having all his money out at the death of a prince.

BIL. Didst thou see Madam Floria to-day?

PASS. Yes, I found her repairing her face to-day ; the red upon the white showed as if her cheeks should have been served in for two dishes of barberries in stewed broth, and [170 the flesh to them a woodcock.

BIL. A bitter fool! [12] Come, madam, this night thou shalt enjoy me freely, and tomorrow for Florence.

Exit [with BIANCA].

PASS. What a natural fool is he that would be a pair of bodies [13] to a woman's petticoat, to be truss'd and pointed to them! Well, I'll dog my Lord ; and the word is proper : for when I fawn upon him, he feeds me ; when I snap him by the fingers, he spits in my [180 mouth. If a dog's death were not strangling, I had rather be one than a serving man ; for the corruption of coin is either the generation of a usurer or a lousy beggar.

[Exit PASSARELLO.] >

SCENE II. [14]

Enter MALEVOLE *in some frieze gown, whilst* BILIOSO *[who also enters]* [15] *reads his patent.*

MAL. I cannot sleep ; my eyes' ill-neigh-
    boring lids
Will hold no fellowship. O thou pale sober
    night,
Thou that in sluggish fumes all sense dost
    steep ;
Thou that gives all the world full leave to
    play,
Unbend'st the feebled veins of sweaty labor!
The galley-slave, that all the toilsome day
Tugs at his oar against the stubborn wave,
Straining his rugged veins, snores fast ;
The stooping scythe-man, that doth barb [16]
    the field,
Thou mak'st wink [17] sure ; in night all crea-
    tures sleep ;   10
Only the malcontent, that 'gainst his fate

---

[12] Q *fowle;* possibly a pun.
[13] Pair of stays, bodice.
[14] The same.
[15] In the unaugmented version he has not left the stage.
[16] Mow.   [17] Slumber.

Repines and quarrels — alas he 's Goodman
  Tell-clock !
His sallow jaw-bones sink with wasting moan ;
Whilst others' beds are down, his pillow's
  stone.

BIL. Malevole !

MAL. Elder of Israel, thou honest defect of
wicked nature and obstinate ignorance, when
did thy wife let thee lie with her?

BIL. I am going ambassador to Florence.

MAL. Ambassador ! Now, for thy [20
country's honor, prithee, do not put up mutton
and porridge i' thy cloak-bag. Thy young
lady wife goes to Florence with thee too, does
she not?

BIL. No ; I leave her at the palace.

MAL. At the palace ! Now, discretion
shield, man ! For God's love, let 's ha' no
more cuckolds ! Hymen begins to put off his
saffron robe : keep thy wife i' the state of
grace. Heart a' truth, I would sooner [30
leave my lady singled in a bordello than in
the Genoa palace :

Sin there appearing in her sluttish shape,
Would soon grow loathsome, even to blushes'
  sense ;
Surfeit would [choke] [18] intemperate appetite,
Make the soul scent the rotten breath of lust.
When in an Italian lascivious palace,
A lady guardianless,
Left to the push of all allurement,
The strongest incitements to immodesty, 40
To have her bound, incensed with wanton
  sweets,
Her veins fill'd high with heating delicates,
Soft rest, sweet music, amorous masquerers,
Lascivious banquets, sin itself gilt o'er,
Strong fantasy tricking up strange delights,
Presenting it dressed pleasingly to sense,
Sense leading it unto the soul, confirm'd
With potent example, impudent custom,
Entic'd by that great bawd, Opportunity —
Thus being prepar'd, clap to her easy ear 50
Youth in good clothes, well-shap'd, rich,
Fair-spoken, promising, noble, ardent, blood-
  full,
Witty, flattering, — Ulysses absent,
O Ithacan, can chastest Penelope hold out?

BIL. Mass, I 'll think on 't. Farewell.

MAL. Farewell. Take thy wife with thee.
  Farewell. — *Exit* BILIOSO

To Florence ; um ! it may prove good, it
  may !
And we may once unmask our brows.

[18] So Dyce ; old eds. *cloake, cloke.*

Enter COUNT CELSO.

CELSO. My honor'd Lord —,

MAL. Celso, peace ! How is 't? Speak
  low : pale fears
Suspect that hedges, walls, and trees have
  ears.
Speak ; how runs all?

CELSO. I' faith, my Lord, that beast with
  many heads,
The staggering multitude, recoils apace :
Though thorough great men's envy, most
  men's malice,
Their much-intemperate heat hath banish'd
  you,
Yet now they find envy and malice ne'er
Produce faint reformation.   10
The Duke, the too soft Duke, lies as a block,
For which two tugging factions seem to saw ;
But still the iron through the ribs they draw.

MAL. I tell thee, Celso, I have ever found
Thy breast most far from shifting cowardice
And fearful baseness ; therefore I 'll tell thee,
  Celso,
I find the wind begins to come about ;
I 'll shift my suit of fortune.
I know the Florentine, whose only force, [20]
By marrying his proud daughter to this
  prince,   20
Both banish'd me and made this weak lord
  duke,
Will now forsake them all ; be sure he will.
I 'll lie in ambush for conveniency,
Upon their severance to confirm myself.

CELSO. Is Ferneze interr'd?

MAL. Of that at leisure — he lives.

CELSO. But how stands Mendoza? How
is 't with him?

MAL. Faith, like a pair of snuffers, snibs [21]
filth in other men, and retains it in itself. [30

CELSO. He does fly from public notice, methinks, as a hare does from hounds ; the feet
whereon he flies betray him.

MAL. I can track him, Celso.
O, my disguise fools him most powerfully !
For that I seem a desperate malcontent,
He fain would clasp with me ; he is the true
  slave
That will put on the most affected grace
For some vild second cause.

[19] The same.
[20] Whose power alone.
[21] Rebukes.

Enter MENDOZA.

CELSO.   He's here.

MAL.   Give place. [39
                                   Exit CELSO.
Ill, ho, ho, ho! art there, old truepenny?
Where hast thou spent thyself this morning?
I see flattery in thine eyes, and damnation in
thy soul. Ha, thou huge rascal!

MEN. Thou are very merry.

MAL. As a scholar, *futuens gratis*. How
doth the devil go with thee now?

MEN. Malevole, thou art an arrant knave.

MAL. Who, I? I have been a sergeant,
man.

MEN. Thou art very poor.   50

MAL. As Job, an alchemist, or a poet.

MEN. The Duke hates thee.

MAL. As Irishmen do bum-cracks.

MEN. Thou has lost his amity.

MAL. As pleasing as maids lose their virginity.

MEN. Would thou wert of a lusty spirit!
Would thou wert noble!

MAL. Why, sure my blood gives me I am
noble, sure I am of noble kind; for I find [60
myself possessed with all their qualities: love
dogs, dice, and drabs, scorn wit in stuff-
clothes; have beat my shoemaker, knock'd
my seamstress, cuckold' my 'pothecary, and
undone my tailor. Noble! why not? since
the stoic [22] said, *Neminem servum non ex
regibus, neminem regem non ex servis esse
oriundum;* only busy Fortune touses, and the
provident Chances [23] blends them together.
I'll give you a simile. Did you e'er see a [70
well with two buckets: whilst one comes up
full to be emptied, another goes down empty
to be filled? Such is the state of all humanity.
Why, look you, I may be the son of some duke;
for, believe me, intemperate lascivious bastardy
makes nobility doubtful; I have a lusty daring
heart, Mendoza.

MEN. Let's grasp; I do like thee infinitely.
Wilt enact one thing for me?

MAL. Shall I get by it? — ([MENDOZA] [80
gives him his purse.) Command me; I am
thy slave, beyond death and hell.

MEN. Murder the Duke.

MAL. My heart's wish, my soul's desire,
my fantasy's dream, my blood's longing, the
only height of my hopes! How, O God, how!
Oh, how my united spirits throng together,
[to] [24] strengthen my resolve!

[22] Cited from Plato by Seneca, *Epistolae*, xliv.
[23] Luck.   [24] Old eds. *So.*

MEN. The Duke is now a-hunting.

MAL. Excellent, admirable, as the Devil [90
would have it! Lend me, lend me, rapier,
pistol, crossbow; so, so, I'll do it.

MEN. Then we agree.

MAL. As Lent and fishmongers. Come,
a-cap-a-pe, how? Inform.

MEN. Know that this weak-brained Duke,
                    who only stands
On Florence' stilts, hath out of witless zeal
Made me his heir, and secretly confirmed
The wreath to me after his life's full point.

MAL. Upon what merit?

MEN.   Merit! by Heaven, I horn him.
Only Ferneze's death gave me state's life. [101
Tut, we are politic; he must not live now.

MAL. No reason, marry; but how must he
die now?

MEN. My utmost project is to murder the
Duke, that I might have his state, because he
makes me his heir; to banish the Duchess,
that I might be rid of a cunning Lacedaemonian, because I know Florence will forsake her;
and then to marry Maria, the banished [110
Duke Altofront's wife, that her friends might
strengthen me and my faction: that is all,
law.

MAL. Do you love Maria?

MEN. Faith, no great affection, but as wise
men do love great women, to ennoble their
blood and augment their revenue. To accomplish this now, thus now. The Duke is in the
forest, next the sea; single him, kill him,
hurl him i' the main, and proclaim thou [120
sawest wolves eat him.

MAL. Um! Not so good. Methinks,
                    when he is slain,
To get some hypocrite, some dangerous
                    wretch
That's muffled [o'er] [25] with feigned holiness,
To swear he heard the Duke on some steep cliff
Lament his wife's dishonor, and, in an agony
Of his heart's torture, hurled his groaning sides
Into the swoln sea, — this circumstance
Well made sounds probable; and hereupon
The Duchess ——

MEN.   May well be banished.   130
O unpeerable invention! rare!
Thou god of policy! it honeys me.

MAL. Then fear not for the wife of Alto-
                    front;
I'll close [26] to her.

MEN. Thou shalt, thou shalt. Our Excellency is pleas'd:

[25] Old eds. *or.*   [26] Conclude matters.

Why wert not thou an emperor? When we
Are duke, I'll make thee some great man,
 sure.
  MAL. Nay. Make me some rich knave,
   and I'll make myself
Some great man.
  MEN. In thee be all my spirit;
Retain ten souls, unite thy virtual powers; 140
Resolve; ha, remember greatness! Heart,
 farewell;
The fate of all my hopes in thee doth dwell.
                          [*Exit.*]
               Re-enter CELSO.

  MAL. Celso, didst hear? — O Heaven, didst
   hear
Such devilish mischief? Sufferest thou the
   world
Carouse damnation even with greedy swallow,
And still dost wink, still does thy vengeance
   slumber?
If now thy brows are clear, when will they
   thunder?   [*Exeunt.*]

               SCENE IV [27]

Enter PIETRO, FERRARDO, PREPASSO, *and*
         three Pages.

  FER. The dogs are at a fault.
                    Cornets like horns.
  PIETRO. Would God nothing but the dogs
were at it! Let the deer pursue [28] safely, the
dogs follow the game, and do you follow the
dogs; as for me, 't is unfit one beast [29] should
hunt another; I ha' one chaseth me; an 't
please you, I would be rid of you a little.
  FER. Would your grief would as soon leave
you as we, to quietness!
  PIETRO. I thank you. —   10
     Exeunt [FERRARDO *and* PREPASSO].
Boy, what dost thou dream of now?
  1 PAGE. Of a dry summer, my Lord; for
here 's a hot world towards. But, my Lord,
I had a strange dream last night.
  PIETRO. What strange dream?
  1 PAGE. Why, methought I pleased you
with singing, and then I dreamt that you gave
me that short sword.
  PIETRO. Prettily begg'd: hold thee, I'll
prove thy dream true; take 't.   20
                    [*Giving sword.*]
  1 PAGE. My duty. But still I dreamt on,
my Lord; and methought, an 't shall please

[27] A forest near the sea.   [28] Continue, run on.
[29] Alluding to his cuckoldom, which makes him
a horned beast.

your Excellency, you would needs out of your
royal bounty give me that jewel in your hat.
  PIETRO. Oh, thou didst but dream, boy; do
not believe it: dreams prove not always true;
they may hold in a short sword, but not in a
jewel. But now, sir, you dreamt you had
pleased me with singing. Make that true, as
I ha' made the other.   30
  1 PAGE. Faith, my Lord, I did but dream;
and dreams, you say, prove not always true;
they may hold in a good sword, but not in a
good song. The truth is, I ha' lost my voice.
  PIETRO. Lost thy voice! How?
  1 PAGE. With dreaming, faith; but here 's
a couple of sirenical rascals shall enchant ye.
What shall they sing, my good Lord?
  PIETRO. Sing of the nature of women; and
then the song shall be surely full of variety, [40
old crotchets, and most sweet closes [30]; it shall
be humorous, grave, fantastic, amorous, melancholy, sprightly, one in all, and all in one.
  1 PAGE. All in one!
  PIETRO. By 'r lady, too many. Sing! my
speech grows culpable of unthrifty idleness
— sing!

       Song [*by* 2 *and* 3 Pages].

               SCENE V [31]

Enter MALEVOLE, *with crossbow and pistol.*

  [PIETRO.] Ah, so; so; sing. — I am heavy.[32]
Walk off; I shall talk in my sleep; walk off.
                       Exeunt Pages.
  MAL. Brief, brief! Who? The Duke! Good
   Heaven, that fools
Should stumble upon greatness! — Do not
   sleep, Duke;
Give ye good morrow. You [33] must be brief,
   Duke:
I am fee'd to murder thee. — Start not. — Men-
   doza,
Mendoza hired me; here 's his gold, his pistol,
Crossbow, sword: 't is all as firm as earth.
O fool, fool, chok'd with the common maze
Of easy idiots, credulity!   10
Make him thine heir! What, thy sworn mur-
   derer!
  PIETRO. O, can it be?
  MAL. Can!
  PIETRO. Discovered he not Ferneze?
  MAL. Yes, but why? but why? For love to
   thee?
Much, much! To be reveng'd upon his rival,

[30] Cadences.   [31] The same.   [32] Drowsy.
[33] So Q₃; om. Q₁.

Who had thrust his jaws awry ;
Who being slain, supposed by thine own hands,
Defended by his sword, made thee most loath-
      some,
Him most gracious with thy loose Princess :
Thou, closely yielding egress and regress to her,
Madest him heir ; whose hot unquiet lust [20
Straight tous'd [34] thy sheets, and now would
      seize thy state.
Politician ! Wise man ! Death ! to be
Led to the stake like a bull by the horns ;
To make even kindness cut a gentle throat !
Life, why art thou numb'd ? Thou foggy dul-
      ness, speak :
Lives not more faith in a home-thrusting
      tongue
Than in those fencing tip-tap courtiers ?

Enter CELSO, *with a hermit's gown and beard.*

[PIETRO.] [35] Lord Malevole, if this be true—
   MAL. If ! Come, shade thee with this disguise. If ! Thou shalt handle it ; he shall [30
thank thee for killing thyself. Come, follow
my directions, and thou shalt see strange
sleights.
   PIETRO. World, whither wilt thou ?
   MAL. Why, to the Devil. Come, the morn
      grows late ;
A steady quickness is the soul of state.[36]
                                   Exeunt.

ACT IV — SCENE I [37]

Enter MAQUERELLE, *knocking at the ladies'
      door.*

   MAQ. Medam,[38] medam, are you stirring,
medam ? If you be stirring, medam, — if I
thought I should disturb ye —

                [*Enter* Page.]

   PAGE. My lady is up, forsooth.
   MAQ. A pretty boy, faith. How old art
thou ?
   PAGE. I think fourteen.
   MAQ. Nay, an ye be in the teens — are ye a
gentleman born ? Do you know me ? My
name is Medam Maquerelle ; I lie in the [10
old cunny court.

[34] Tousled.
[35] Old eds. *Cel.*
[36] Statecraft.
[37] The palace. An antechamber to the apartments
of the ladies in waiting.
[38] Evidently an affected pronunciation.

Enter BIANCA *and* EMILIA.

   [PAGE.] See, here the ladies.
   BIAN. A fair day to ye, Maquerelle.
   EMIL. Is the Duchess up yet, sentinel ?
   MAQ. O ladies, the most abominable mischance ! O dear ladies the most piteous disaster ! Ferneze was taken last night in the
Duchess' chamber. Alas, the Duke catch'd
him and kill'd him !
   BIAN. Was he found in bed ?   20
   MAQ. Oh, no ; but the villainous certainty
is the door was not bolted, the tongue-tied
hatch held his peace ; so the naked troth is, he
was found in his shirt, whilst I, like an arrant
beast, lay in the outward chamber, heard
nothing ; and yet they came by me in the dark,
and yet I felt them not, like a senseless creature as I was. O beauties, look to your busk-
points ; [39] if not chastely, yet charily : be sure
the door be bolted. — Is your lord gone to
Florence ?   31
   BIAN. Yes, Maquerelle.
   MAQ. I hope you 'll find the discretion to
purchase a fresh gown for his return. — Now,
by my troth, beauties, I would ha' ye once
wise. He loves ye ; pish ! He is witty ;
bubble ! Fair-proportioned ; mew ! Nobly-
born ; wind ! Let this be still your fix'd
position : esteem me every man according to
his good gifts, and so ye shall ever remain [40
most dear and most worthy to be most dear
ladies.
   EMIL. Is the Duke return'd from hunting
      yet ?
   MAQ. They say not yet.
   BIAN.   'T is now in midst of day.
   EMIL. How bears the Duchess with this
      blemish now ?
   MAQ. Faith, boldly ; strongly defies defame, as one that has a duke to her father.
And there 's a note to you : be sure of a stout
friend in a corner, that may always awe
your husband. Mark the havior of the [50
Duchess now : she dares defame ; cries,
" Duke, do what thou canst, I 'll quit [40] mine
honor ; " nay, as one confirmed in her own
virtue against ten thousand mouths that
mutter her disgrace, she 's presently for dances.

Enter FERRARDO.

   BIAN. For dances !
   MAQ. Most true.

[39] The tagged laces by which the busk (the upright piece of whalebone in the front of the stays)
was fastened.   [40] Acquit.

EMIL. Most strange.

[BIAN.] [41] See, here's my servant, young Ferrardo. How many servants think'st [60 thou I have, Maquerelle?

MAQ. The more, the merrier. 'T was well said, use your servants as you do your smocks : have many, use one, and change often ; for that's most sweet and courtlike.

FER. Save ye, fair ladies ! Is the Duke return'd?

BIAN. Sweet sir, no voice of him as yet in court.

FER. 'T is very strange.

BIAN. And how like you my servant, Maquerelle?

MAQ. I think he could hardly draw [70 Ulysses' bow ; but, by my fidelity, were his nose narrower, his eyes broader, his hands thinner, his lips thicker, his legs bigger, his feet lesser, his hair blacker, and his teeth whiter, he were a tolerable sweet youth, i' faith. An he will come to my chamber, I will read him the fortune of his beard.

Cornets sound.

FER. Not yet, return'd ! I fear — but the Duchess approacheth.

SCENE II [42]

Enter MENDOZA *supporting the* DUCHESS, [and] GUERRINO : *the* Ladies *that are on the stage rise :* FERRARDO *ushers in the* DUCHESS, *and then takes a* Lady *to tread a measure.*[43]

AUR. We will dance. Music ! — we will dance.

GUER. *Les quanto,*[44] lady, *Pensez bien, Passa regis,* or *Bianca's brawl?*

AUR. We have forgot the brawl.

FER. [*aside*] So soon? 'T is wonder.

GUER. Why, 't is but two singles on the left, two on the right, three doubles forward, a traverse of six round ; do this twice, three singles side, galliard trick-of-twenty, coranto-pace ; [10 a figure of eight, three singles broken down, come up, meet, two doubles, fall back, and then honor.

AUR. O Daedalus, thy maze ! I have quite forgot it.

MAQ. Trust me, so have I, saving the falling back, and then honor.

Enter PREPASSO.

AUR. Music, music !

PREP. Who saw the Duke? the Duke?

Enter EQUATO.

AUR. Music !   20

EQUATO. The Duke? is the Duke returned?

AUR. Music !

Enter CELSO.

CELSO. The Duke is either quite invisible, or else is not.

AUR. We are not pleased with your intrusion upon our private retirement ; we are not pleased ; you have forgot yourselves.

Enter a Page.

CELSO. Boy, thy master? Where's the Duke?   [29

PAGE. Alas, I left him burying the earth with his spread joyless limbs ; he told me he was heavy, would sleep ; bid me walk off, for that the strength of fantasy oft made him talk in his dreams. I straight obeyed, nor ever saw him since ; but whereso'er he is, he's sad.

AUR. Music, sound high, as is our heart ! Sound high !

SCENE III [45]

Enter MALEVOLE, *and* PIETRO *disguised like an hermit.*

MAL. The Duke — peace ! — the Duke is dead.

AUR. Music !

MAL. Is 't music?

MEN. Give proof.

FER. How?

CELSO. Where?

PREP. When?

MAL. Rest in peace, as the Duke does ; quietly sit ; for my own part, I beheld him [10 but dead ; that's all. Marry, here's one can give you a more particular account of him.

MEN. Speak holy father, nor let any brow Within this presence fright thee from the truth ; Speak confidently and freely.

AUR.   We attend,

---

[41] Old eds. give this speech to Emilia, but erroneously, as Neilson notes.
[42] Though the persons of the preceding scene remain on stage, the scene is now a hall in the palace.
[43] A slow and stately dance.
[44] There is a reference (cited by Dyce) in Munday's *Banquet of Dainty Conceits* to "a courtlie daunce, called *Les Quanto*."
[45] The same.

PIETRO. Now had the mounting sun's all-
ripening wings
Swept the cold sweat of night from earth's
dank breast,
When I, whom men call Hermit of the Rock,
Forsook my cell, and clamber'd up a cliff, 19
Against whose base the heady Neptune dash'd
His high-curl'd brows; there 't was I eas'd my
limbs.
When, lo! my entrails melted with the moan
Some one, who far 'bove me was climb'd, did
make —
I shall offend.
MEN. Not.
AUR. On.
PIETRO. Methinks I hear him yet: " O fe-
male faith!
Go sow the ingrateful sand, and love a woman!
And do I live to be the scoff of men?
To be the wittol-cuckold, even to hug 30
My poison? Thou knowest, O truth!
Sooner hard steel will melt with southern wind,
A seaman's whistle calm the ocean,
A town on fire [46] be extinct with tears,
Than women, vow'd to blushless impudence,
With sweet behavior and soft minioning [47]
Will turn from that where appetite is fix'd.
O powerful blood! how thou dost slave their
soul!
I wash'd an Ethiop, who, for recompense, 39
Sulli'd my name; and must I, then, be forc'd
To walk, to live thus black? Must! must! fie!
He that can bear with ' must,' he cannot die."
With that he sigh'd [so] [48] passionately deep,
That the dull air even groan'd; at last he cries,
" Sink shame in seas, sink deep enough!" so
dies;
For then I viewed his body fall and souse
Into the foamy main. Oh, then I saw,
That which methinks I see, it was the Duke;
Whom straight the nicer-stomach'd sea belch'd
up;
But then —— 50
MAL. Then came I in; but, 'las, all was too
late!
For even straight he sunk.
PIETRO. Such was the Duke's sad fate.
CELSO. A better fortune to our Duke Men-
doza!
OMNES. Mendoza! *Cornets flourish.*
MEN. A guard, a guard!

Enter a Guard.

We, full of hearty tears,
For our good father's loss,
(For so we well may call him
Who did beseech your loves for our succes-
sion),
Cannot so lightly over-jump his death
As leave his woes revengeless. — (*to* AURELIA)
Woman of shame, 60
We banish thee for ever to the place
From whence this good man comes; nor per-
mit,
On death, unto [thy] [49] body any ornament;
But, base as was thy life, depart away.
AUR. Ungrateful!
MEN. Away!
AUR. Villain, hear me!
PREPASSO *and* GUERRINO *lead away
the* DUCHESS.
MEN. Begone! — My Lords,
Address to [50] public council; 't is most fit:
The train of fortune is borne up by wit.
Away! our presence shall be sudden; haste.
All depart saving MENDOZA, MAL-
EVOLE, *and* PIETRO.
MAL. Now, you egregious devil! Ha, [70
ye murdering politician! How dost, Duke?
How dost look now? Brave Duke, i' faith.
MEN. How did you kill him?
MAL. Slatted his brains out; then sous'd
him in the briny sea.
MEN. Brain'd him, and drown'd him too?
MAL. Oh, 't was best, sure work; for he
that strikes a great man, let him strike
home, or else 'ware, he 'll prove no man.
Shoulder not a huge fellow, unless you may [80
be sure to lay him in the kennel.
MEN. A most sound brain-pan! I 'll make
you both emperors.
MAL. Make us Christians, make us Chris-
tians.
MEN. I 'll hoist ye, ye shall mount.
MAL. To the gallows, say ye? Come:
praemium incertum petit, certum scelus. [51] How
stands the progress?
MEN. Here, take my ring unto the cit-
adel; 90
Have entrance to Maria, the grave duchess
Of banish'd Altofront. Tell her we love her;
Omit no circumstance to grace our person:
do 't.

---

[46] Dissyllabic.
[47] *I.e.*, being treated as a minion or darling.
(Dyce.)
[48] So Q1; Q3 *too.*
[49] Old eds. *the.*
[50] Make ready for.
[51] Uncertain the reward he seeks, certain the
guilt. (Seneca, *Phoenissae,* l. 632.)

MAL. I 'll make an excellent pander. Duke, farewell : 'dieu, adieu, Duke.

MEN. Take Maquerelle with thee ; for 't is found

None cuts a diamond but a diamond.

Exit MALEVOLE.

Hermit,

Thou art a man for me, my confessor !
O thou selected spirit, born for my good,
Sure thou wouldst make　　　　　　　　100
An excellent elder in a deformed [52] church.
Come, we must be inward,[53] thou and I all one.

PIETRO. I am glad I was ordained for ye.

MEN. Go to, then ; thou must know that Malevole is a strange villain ; dangerous, very dangerous. You see how broad 'a speaks — a gross-jawed rogue. I would have thee poison him. He 's like a corn upon my great toe — I cannot go for him ; [54] he must be cored out, he must. Wilt do 't, ha?　　　110

PIETRO. Anything, anything.

MEN. Heart of my life ! Thus, then — to the citadel ;

Thou shalt consort with this Malevole ;
There being at supper, poison him. It shall be laid
Upon Maria, who yields love or dies.
Scud quick.

PIETRO. [Like lightning] : [55] good deeds crawl, but mischief flies. *Exit* PIETRO.

Re-enter MALEVOLE.

MAL. Your Devilship's ring has no virtue : the buff-captain, the sallow Westphalian gammon-faced zaza [56] cries, "Stand out !" [120 Must have a stiffer warrant, or no pass into the castle of comfort.

MEN. Command our sudden letter. — Not enter ! sha't ; [57] what place is there in Genoa but thou shalt? into my heart, into my very heart : come, let 's love ; we must love, we two, soul and body.

MAL. How didst like the hermit? A strange hermit, sirrah.

MEN. A dangerous fellow, very peril- [130 ous. He must die.

MAL. Ay, he must die.

MEN. Thou 'st [58] kill him. We are wise ; we must be wise.

MAL. And provident.

MEN. Yea, provident : beware an hypo-
crite ;
A churchman once corrupted, oh, avoid !
A fellow that makes religion his stalking-
horse.[59]
He breeds a plague.

Thou shalt poison him.

MAL. Ho, 't is wondrous necessary : how?

MEN. You both go jointly to the citadel ;
There sup, there poison him ; and Maria, [141
Because she is our opposite,[60] shall bear
The sad suspect ; [61] on which she dies or loves us.

MAL. I run.　　　　　　　*Exit* MALEVOLE.

MEN. We that are great, our sole self-good still moves us.

They shall die both, for their deserts crave more

Than we can recompense : their presence still

Imbraids [62] our fortunes with beholdingness,

Which we abhor ; like deed, not doer. Then conclude,

They live not to cry out "Ingratitude !" [150
One stick burns tother ; steel cuts steel alone :
'T is good trust few ; but, oh, 't is best trust none !　　　　　　　　　*Exit.*

SCENE IV [63]

Enter MALEVOLE *and* PIETRO, *still disguised, at several doors.*

MAL. How do you? How dost, Duke?

PIETRO.　　　　　　　　　　Oh, let
The last day fall ! drop, drop on our cursed heads !

Let Heaven unclasp itself, vomit forth flames.

MAL. Oh, do not [rant],[64] do not turn player ; there 's more of them than can well live one by another already. What, art an infidel still?

PIETRO. I am amaz'd, struck in a swoon with wonder : I am commanded to poison thee —　　　　　　　　　　　　　[10

MAL. I am commanded to poison thee at supper —

PIETRO. At supper !

MAL. In the citadel —

PIETRO. In the citadel !

MAL. Cross-capers ! tricks ! Truth a' Heaven ! <he> would discharge us as boys

[52] Irregular ; *i.e.*, Puritan.
[53] Intimate.
[54] I cannot walk on account of him.
[55] So Q 1 ; Q 3 adds to Mendoza's speech.
[56] ? Low German *Sasse* = Saxon. (Conj. Prof. William Kurrelmeyer.)
[57] Shalt.
[58] Thou must.

[59] Q 3 glosses marginally *shootes vnder his belly.*
[60] Adversary.
[61] The weighty suspicion.　　　[62] Upbraids.
[63] A room or courtyard in the palace.
[64] Q 3 *rand :* Q 1 *raue.*

do eldern guns, one pellet to strike out another. Of what faith art now?

PIETRO. All is damnation ; wickedness extreme : [20
There is no faith in man.

MAL. In none but usurers and brokers ; they deceive no man : men take 'em for bloodsuckers, and so they are. Now, God deliver me from my friends !

PIETRO. Thy friends !

MAL. Yes, from my friends ; for from mine enemies I'll deliver myself. Oh, cutthroat friendship is the rankest villainy ! Mark this Mendoza ; mark him for a villain : but [30 Heaven will send a plague upon him for a rogue.

PIETRO. O world !

MAL. World ! 't is the only region of death, the greatest shop of the Devil ; the cruelest prison of men, out of the which none pass without paying their dearest breath for a fee ; there's nothing perfect in it but extreme, extreme calamity, such as comes yonder.

SCENE V [65]

Enter AURELIA, *two* Halberts *before and two after, supported by* CELSO *and* FERRARDO ; AURELIA *in base mourning attire.*

AUR. To banishment ! led on to banishment !

PIETRO. Lady, the blessedness of repentance to you !

AUR. Why? why? I can desire nothing but death,
Nor deserve anything but hell. If Heaven
Should give sufficiency of grace to clear
My soul, it would make Heaven graceless :
My sins would make the stock of mercy poor ;
Oh, they would tire Heaven's goodness to reclaim them !
Judgment is just, yet from [66] that vast villain ;
But, sure, he shall not miss sad punishment [10
'Fore he shall rule. — On to my cell of shame !

PIETRO. My cell 't is, lady ; where, instead of masks,
Music, tilts, tourneys, and such court-like shows,
The hollow murmur of the checkless winds
Shall groan again ; whilst the unquiet sea
Shakes the whole rock with foamy battery.
There usherless the air comes in and out :
The rheumy vault will force your eyes to weep,

Whilst you behold true desolation.
A rocky barrenness shall pierce [67] your eyes, [20
Where all at once one reaches, where he stands.
With brows the roof, both walls with both his hands.

AUR. It is too good. — Blessed spirit of my lord,
Oh, in what orb so'er thy soul is thron'd,
Behold me worthily most miserable !
Oh, let the anguish of my contrite spirit
Entreat some reconciliation !
If not, oh, joy, triumph in my just grief !
Death is the end of woes and tears' relief.

PIETRO. Belike your lord not lov'd you, was unkind. 30

AUR. O heaven ! As the soul [loves] [68] the body, so lov'd he :
'T was death to him to part my presence ; Heaven
To see me pleased. Yet I, like a wretch given o'er
To hell, brake all the sacred rites of marriage,
To clip a base, ungentle, faithless villain ;
O God ! a very pagan reprobate —
What should I say ? — ungrateful, throws me out,
For whom I lost soul, body, fame, and honor.
But 't is most fit : why should a better fate
Attend on any who forsake chaste sheets, [40
Fly the embrace of a devoted heart,
Join'd by a solemn vow 'fore God and man,
To taste the brackish [69] [flood] [70] of beastly lust
In an adulterous touch? — O ravenous immodesty !
Insatiate impudence of appetite !
Look, here's your end ; for mark, what sap in dust,
What sin in good, even so much love in lust.
Joy to thy ghost, sweet Lord ! pardon to me !

CELSO. 'T is the Duke's pleasure this night you rest in court.

AUR. Soul, lurk in shades ; run, shame, from brightsome skies ; 50
In night the blind man misseth not his eyes.

Exit [with CELSO, FERRARDO, *and* Halberts].

MAL. Do not weep, kind cuckold ; take comfort, man ; thy betters have been beccos : [71]
Agamemnon, emperor of all the merry Greeks, that tickled all the true Trojans,was a cornuto ; Prince Arthur, that cut off twelve kings' beards, was a cornuto ; Hercules, whose back

---

[65] The same.   [66] Distant from.

[67] Q₁ *pain.*   [68] Old eds. *lou'd.*
[69] Salty, lustful.   [70] Old eds. *bloud.*
[71] Cuckolds.

bore up heaven, and got forty wenches with child in one night, —

PIETRO. Nay, 't was fifty.　　　　　　60

MAL. Faith, forty 's enow, a' conscience, — yet was a cornuto. Patience ; mischief grows proud. Be wise.

PIETRO. Thou pinchest too deep ; art too keen upon me.

MAL. Tut, a pitiful surgeon makes a dangerous sore ; I 'll tent [72] thee to the ground. Thinkest I 'll sustain myself by flattering thee, because thou art a prince? I had rather follow a drunkard, and live by licking up his [70 vomit, than by servile flattery.

PIETRO. Yet great men ha' done 't.

MAL. Great slaves fear better than love, born naturally for a coal-basket ; [73] though the common usher of princes' presence, Fortune, hath blindly given them better place. I am vowed to be thy affliction.

PIETRO. Prithee, be ;

I love much misery, and be thou son to me. [79

MAL. Because you are an usurping duke. —

Enter BILIOSO.

Your Lordship 's well return'd from Florence.

BIL. Well return'd, I praise my horse.

MAL. What news from the Florentines?

BIL. I will conceal the Great Duke's pleasure ; only this was his charge : his pleasure is that his daughter die, Duke Pietro be banished for [publishing] [74] his blood's dishonor, and that Duke Altofront be reaccepted. This is all ; but I hear Duke Pietro is dead.

MAL. Ay, and Mendoza is duke. What [90 will you do?

BIL. Is Mendoza strongest?

MAL. Yet he is.

BIL. Then yet I 'll hold with him.

MAL. But if that Altofront should turn straight again?

BIL. Why, then, I would turn straight again.

'T is good run still with him that has most might :

I had rather stand with wrong, than fall with right.

MAL. What religion will you be of now? [100

BIL. Of the Duke's religion, when I know what it is.

MAL. O Hercules !

BIL. Hercules ! Hercules was the son of Jupiter and Alcmena.

MAL. Your Lordship is a very wit-all.

BIL. Wittol !

MAL. Aye, all-wit.

BIL. Amphitryo[n] was a cuckold.

MAL. Your Lordship sweats ; your [110 young lady will get you a cloth for your old Worship's brows. (*Exit* BILIOSO.) Here 's a fellow to be damned ; this is his inviolable maxim : flatter the greatest and oppress the least — a whoreson flesh-fly, that still gnaws upon the lean gall'd backs.

PIETRO. Why dost, then, salute him?

MAL. I' faith, as bawds go to church — for fashion sake. Come, be not confounded ; thou art but in danger to lose a dukedom. [120 Think this : this earth is the only grave and Golgotha wherein all things that live must rot ; 't is but the draught wherein the heavenly bodies discharge their corruption ; the very muck-hill on which the sublunary orbs cast their excrements. Man is the slime of this dung pit, and princes are the governors of these men ; for, for our souls, they are as free as emperors, all of one piece ; there goes but a pair of shears betwixt [75] an emperor and [130 the son of a bagpiper : only the dyeing, dressing, pressing, glossing, makes the difference. Now, what art thou like to lose?

A gaoler's office to keep men in bonds,

Whilst toil and treason all life's good confounds.

PIETRO. I here renounce for ever regency !

O Altofront, I wrong thee to supplant thy right,

To trip thy heels up with a devilish sleight !

For which I now from throne am thrown : world-tricks abjure ;

For vengeance, though 't comes slow, yet it comes sure.　　　　　　140

Oh, I am chang'd ! for here, 'fore the dread Power,

In true contrition, I do dedicate

My breath to solitary holiness,

My lips to prayer, and my breast's care shall be

Restoring Altofront to regency.

MAL. Thy vows are heard, and we accept thy faith.　　　　*Undisguiseth himself.*

Re-enter FERNEZE *and* CELSO.

Banish amazement. Come, we four must stand

---

[72] Probe.

[73] To carry coals ; *i.e.*, to be menials, and to submit to affronts.

[74] Emend. Deighton ; old eds. *banishing.*

[75] *I.e.*, from the same cloth are cut.

Full shock of fortune. Be not so wonder-
    stricken.

PIETRO. Doth Ferneze live?

FER. For your pardon.   150

PIETRO. Pardon and love. Give leave to
    recollect
My thoughts dispers'd in wild astonishment.
My vows stand fix'd in Heaven, and from
    hence
I crave all love and pardon.

MAL. Who doubts of Providence,
That sees this change? A hearty faith to all!
He needs must rise [who] [76] can no lower fall.
For still impetuous vicissitude
Touseth the world; then let no maze intrude
Upon your spirits: wonder not I rise;   160
For who can sink that close can temporize?
The time grows ripe for action: I'll detect
My privat'st plot, lest ignorance fear suspect.
Let's close to counsel, leave the rest to fate:
Mature discretion is the life of state. *Exeunt.*

ACT V — < SCENE I [1]

Enter BILIOSO *and* PASSARELLO.

BIL. Fool, how dost thou like my calf in a
long stocking?

PASS. An excellent calf, my Lord.

BIL. This calf hath been a reveller this
twenty year. When Monsieur Gundi lay
here ambassador, I could have carried a lady
up and down at arm's end in a platter; and
I can tell you, there were those at that time
who, to try the strength of a man's back and
his arm, would be coister'd.[2] I have meas- [10
ured calves with most of the palace, and they
come nothing near me; besides, I think there
be not many armors in the arsenal will fit me,
especially for the headpiece. I'll tell thee —

PASS. What, my Lord?

BIL. I can eat stew'd broth as it comes
seething off the fire, or a custard as it comes
reeking out of the oven; and I think there
are not many lords can do it. A good pomander,[3] a little decayed in the scent: but six [20
grains of musk, ground with rose-water and
temper'd with a little civet, shall fetch her [4]
again presently.

[76] So Q1; om. Q3.
[1] A room in the palace. This scene is added by Q3.
[2] Not satisfactorily explained.
[3] A ball of perfumes. Bilioso is showing his to
Passarello.
[4] *I.e.*, restore the efficacy of the pomander.

PASS. Oh, ay, as a bawd with aqua-vitae.

BIL. And, what, dost thou rail upon the
ladies as thou wert wont?

PASS. I were better roast a live cat, and
might do it with more safety. I am as secret
to [them] [5] as their painting. There's Maquerelle, oldest bawd and a perpetual beggar — [30
did you never hear of her trick to be known in
the city?

BIL. Never.

PASS. Why, she gets all the picture-makers
to draw her picture; when they have done,
she most courtly finds fault with them one
after another, and never fetcheth them.
They, in revenge of this, execute her in pictures as they do in Germany, and hang her in
their shops. By this means is she better [40
known to the stinkards [6] than if she had been
five times carted.[7]

BIL. 'Fore God, an excellent policy.

PASS. Are there any revels to-night, my
Lord?

BIL. Yes.

PASS. Good my Lord, give me leave to
break a fellow's pate that hath abused me.

BIL. Whose pate?

PASS. Young Ferrardo, my Lord.   50

BIL. Take heed: he's very valiant; I have
known him fight eight quarrels in five days,
believe it.

PASS. Oh, is he so great a quarreller?
Why, then, he's an arrant coward.

BIL. How prove you that?

PASS. Why, thus: he that quarrels seeks
to fight; and he that seeks to fight seeks to
die; and he that seeks to die seeks never
to fight more; and he that will quarrel, [60
and seeks means never to answer a man more,
I think he's a coward.

BIL. Thou canst prove anything.

PASS. Anything but a rich knave; for I
can flatter no man.

BILL. Well, be not drunk, good fool. I
shall see you anon in the presence.

                              [Exeunt.]>

SCENE [II] [8]

Enter MALEVOLE *and* MAQUERELLE, *at several*
doors opposite, singing.

MAL. " The Dutchman for a drunkard,"—

MAQ. " The Dane for golden locks," —

[5] Emend. Dyce; Q3 *thieues*: Bullen *the thieves.*
[6] The mob.
[7] As a prostitute or bawd.
[8] Before the citadel.

MAL. " The Irishman for usquebaugh," —
MAQ. " The Frenchman for the ( )." [9]
MAL. Oh, thou art a blessed creature! Had I a modest woman to conceal, I would put her to thy custody; for no reasonable creature would ever suspect her to be in thy company. Ha, thou art a melodious Maquerelle — thou picture of a woman, and sub- [10 stance of a beast!

[10] < *Enter* PASSARELLO [*with wine*].

MAQ. O fool, will ye be ready anon to go with me to the revels? The hall will be so pest'red [11] anon.
PASS. Ay, as the country is with attorneys.
MAL. What hast thou there, fool?
PASS. Wine; I have learned to drink since I went with my Lord Ambassador; I 'll drink to the health of Madam Maquerelle.
MAL. Why, thou wast wont to rail [20 upon her.
PASS. Ay; but since I borrow'd money of her, I 'll drink to her health now, as gentlemen visit brokers, or as knights send venison to the City, either to take up more money, or to procure longer forbearance.
MAL. Give me the bowl. I drink a health to Altofront, our deposed Duke.
PASS. I 'll take it [*drinks*] : — so! Now I 'll begin a health to Madam Maquerelle. [30
[*Drinks.*]
MAL. Pew! I will not pledge her.
PASS. Why, I pledg'd your lord.
MAL. I care not.
PASS. Not pledge Madam Maquerelle! Why, then, will I spew up your lord again with this fool's finger.
MAL. Hold; I 'll take it. [*Drinks.*]
MAQ. Now thou hast drunk my health, fool, I am friends with thee.
PASS. Art? art?   40
" When Griffon [12] saw the reconciled quean Offering about his neck her arms to cast,
He threw off sword and heart's malignant [spleen],[13]
And lovely her below the loins embrac'd." — Adieu, Madam Maquerelle.   *Exit.* >
MAL. And how dost thou think a' this transformation of state now?

[9] So in old eds. The missing word is, of course, "pox."
[10] Passarello's entrance and the ensuing dialogue are added by Q₃.
[11] Crowded.
[12] One of the heroes in *Orlando Furioso.* (Reed.)
[13] Emend. Bullen; Q₃ *stream.*

MAQ. Verily, very well; for we women always note the falling of the one is the rising of the other; some must be fat, some must [50 be lean; some must be fools, and some must be lords; some must be knaves, and some must be officers; some must be beggars, some must be knights; some must be cuckolds, and some must be citizens. As for example, I have two court-dogs, the most fawning curs, the one called Watch, th' other Catch. Now I, like Lady Fortune, sometimes love this dog, sometimes raise that dog, sometimes favor Watch, most commonly fancy Catch. [60 Now, that dog which I favor I feed; and he 's so ravenous that what I give he never chaws it, gulps it down whole, without any relish of what he has, but with a greedy expectation of what he shall have. The other dog now —
MAL. No more dog, sweet Maquerelle, no more dog. And what hope hast thou of the Duchess Maria? Will she stoop to the Duke's lure? [14] Will she come, think'st?
MAQ. Let me see, where 's the sign now? [70 Ha' ye e'er a calendar? Where 's the sign, trow you?
MAL. Sign! why is there any moment in that?
MAQ. O, believe me, a most secret power: look ye, a Chaldean or an Assyrian, I am sure 't was a most sweet Jew, told me, court any woman in the right sign, you shall not miss. But you must take her in the right vein then; as, when the sign is in Pisces, a [80 fishmonger's wife is very sociable; in Cancer, a precisian's [15] wife is very flexible; in Capricorn, a merchant's wife hardly holds out; in Libra, a lawyer's wife is very tractable, especially if her husband be at the term; only in Scorpio 't is very dangerous meddling. Has the Duke sent any jewel, any rich stones?

Enter Captain.

MAL. Ay, I think those are the best signs to take a lady in.[16] By your favor, signior, I must discourse with the Lady [90 Maria, Altofront's Duchess; I must enter for the Duke.
CAPT. She here shall give you interview. I received the guardship of this citadel from the good Altofront, and for his use I 'll keep 't, till I am of no use.
MAL. Wilt thou? O Heavens, that a Christian should be found in a buff-jerkin!

[14] Bait; the language of falconry.
[15] Puritan's.   [16] Capture a lady.

Captain Conscience, I love thee, captain. We attend. (*Exit* Captain.) And what [100 hope hast thou of this Duchess' easiness?

MAQ. 'T will go hard ; she was a cold creature ever. She hated monkeys, fools, jesters, and gentlemen ushers extremely ; she had the vild trick on 't, not only to be truly modestly honorable in her own conscience, but she would avoid the least wanton carriage that might incur suspect ; as, God bless me, she had almost brought bed-pressing out of fashion. I could scarce get a fine [17] [110 for the lease of a lady's favor once in a fort-night.

MAL. Now, in the name of immodesty, how many maidenheads hast thou brought to the block?

MAQ. Let me see — Heaven forgive us our misdeeds ! — Here 's the Duchess.

SCENE [III] [18]

Enter MARIA *and* Captain.

MAL. God bless thee, lady !

MARIA. Out of thy company !

MAL. We have brought thee tender of a husband.

MARIA. I hope I have one already.

MAQ. Nay, by mine honor, madam, as good ha' ne'er a husband as a banish'd husband ; he 's in another world now. I 'll tell ye, lady, I have heard of a sect that main-tained when the husband was asleep the [10 wife might lawfully entertain another man, for then her husband was as dead ; much more when he is banished.

MARIA. Unhonest creature !

MAQ. Pish, honesty is but an art to seem so. Pray ye, what 's honesty, what 's constancy, But fables feigned, odd old fools' chat, devis'd By jealous fools to wrong our liberty?

MAL. Molly, he that loves thee is a duke, Mendoza ; he will maintain thee royally, [20 love thee ardently, defend thee powerfully, marry thee sumptuously, and keep thee in despite of Rosicleer or Donzel del Phoebo.[19] There 's jewels : if thou wilt, so ; if not, so.

MARIA. Captain, for God's sake, save poor wretchedness From tyranny of lustful insolence ! Enforce me in the deepest dungeon dwell, Rather than here ; here round about is hell. — O my dear'st Altofront ! where'er thou breathe,

Let my soul sink into the shades beneath, [30 Before I stain thine honor ! This thou hast, And long as I can die, I will live chaste.

MAL. 'Gainst him that can enforce how vain is strife !

MARIA. She that can be enforc'd has ne'er a knife ! She that through force her limbs with lust en-rolls, Wants Cleopatra's asps and Portia's coals. God amend you ! *Exit with* Captain.

MAL. Now, the fear of the Devil for ever go with thee ! — Maquerelle, I tell thee, I have found an honest woman ! Faith, I per- [40 ceive, when all is done, there is of women, as of all other things, some good, most bad ; some saints, some sinners. For as nowadays no courtier but has his mistress, no captain but has his cockatrice,[20] no cuckold but has his horns, and no fool but has his feather ; even so, no woman but has her weakness and feather too, no sex but has his — I can hunt the letter no farder. — [*aside*] O God, how loathsome this toying is to me ! That a [50 duke should be forc'd to fool it ! Well, *stulto-rum plena sunt omnia:* [21] better play the fool lord than be the fool lord. — Now, where 's your sleights, Madam Maquerelle?

MAQ. Why, ye ignorant that 't is said a squeamish, affected niceness is natural to women, and that the excuse of their yield-ing is only, forsooth, the difficult obtaining? You must put her to 't ; women are flax, and will fire in a moment. 60

MAL. Why, was the flax put into thy mouth, and yet thou — Thou set fire, thou inflame her !

MAQ. Marry, but I 'll tell ye now, you were too hot.

MAL. The fitter to have inflamed the flax, woman.

MAQ. You were too boisterous, spleeny, for indeed —

MAL. Go, go, thou art a weak pand'ress ; now I see, Sooner earth's fire Heaven itself shall waste, Than all with heat can melt a mind that 's chaste. Go ; thou the Duke's lime-twig ! [22] I 'll make the Duke turn thee out of thine office. [70 What, not get one touch of hope, and had her at such advantage !

---

[17] Fee.   [18] The same.
[19] Heroes in *The Mirror of Knighthood*.
[20] Prostitute.
[21] Cicero, *Epistolae ad Familiares*, ix, 22.
[22] Snare.

MAQ. Now, a' my conscience, now I think in my discretion, we did not take her in the right sign ; the blood was not in the true vein, sure.　　　　　　　　　　　*Exit.*

[SCENE] IV [23]

< *Enter* BILIOSO.

BIL. Make way there ! The Duke returns from the enthronement. — Malevole —

MAL. Out, rogue !

BIL. Malevole, —

MAL. " Hence, ye gross-jaw'd, peasantly — out, go ! "

BIL. Nay, sweet Malevole, since my return I hear you are become the thing I always prophesied would be — an advanced virtue, a worthily-employed faithfulness, a man a' [10 grace, dear friend. Come ; what ! *Si quoties peccant homines* [24] — if as often as courtiers play the knaves, honest men should be angry — why, look ye, we must collogue [25] sometimes, forswear sometimes.

MAL. Be damn'd sometimes.

BIL. Right : *nemo omnibus horis sapit :* " no man can be honest at all hours ; " necessity often depraves virtue.

MAL. I will commend thee to the Duke. [20

BIL. Do : let us be friends, man.

MAL. And knaves, man.

BIL. Right : let us prosper and purchase ; [26] our lordships shall live, and our knavery be forgotten.

MAL. He that by any ways gets riches, his means never shames him.

BIL. True.

MAL. For impudency and faithlessness are the mainstays to greatness.　　　　　　30

BIL. By the Lord, thou art a profound lad.

MAL. By the Lord, thou art a perfect knave : out, ye ancient damnation !

BIL. Peace, peace ! an thou wilt not be a friend to me as I am a knave, be not a knave to me as I am thy friend, and disclose me. Peace ! cornets ! >

Enter PREPASSO *and* FERRARDO, *two Pages with lights,* CELSO *and* EQUATO, MENDOZA *in duke's robes, and* GUERRINO.

MEN. On, on ; leave us, leave us.

　　　Exeunt all saving MALEVOLE [*and* MENDOZA].

Stay, where is the hermit ?　　　　　　40

[23] The same. The first 38 lines are added by Q3.
[24] Ovid, *Tristia*, ii, 33.　　[25] Flatter.　　[26] Acquire.

MAL. With Duke Pietro, with Duke Pietro.

MEN. Is he dead ? Is he poisoned ?

MAL. Dead — as the Duke is.

MEN. Good, excellent ; he will not blab : secureness lives in secrecy. Come hither, come hither.

MAL. Thou hast a certain strong villainous scent about thee my nature cannot endure.

MEN. Scent, man ! What returns Maria, what answer to our suit ?　　　　　　50

MAL. Cold, frosty ; she is obstinate.

MEN. Then she 's but dead ; 't is resolute, she dies :

Black deed only through black deed safely flies.

MAL. Pew ! *per scelera semper sceleribus tutum est iter.* [27]

MEN. What, art a scholar ? Art a politician ? Sure, thou art an arrant knave.

MAL. Who, I ? I ha' been twice an under-sheriff, man. [28]

< Well, I will go rail upon some great man, [60 that I may purchase the bastinado, or else go marry some rich Genoan lady, and instantly go travel.

MEN. Travel, when thou art married ?

MAL. Ay, 't is your young lord's fashion to do so, though he was so lazy, being a bachelor, that he would never travel so far as the university : yet, when he married her, tale's off, [29] and, Catso, for England !

MEN. And why for England ?　　　　　　70

MAL. Because there is no brothel-houses there.

MEN. Nor courtesans ?

MAL. Neither ; your whore went down with the stews, and your punk came up with your Puritan. >

MEN. Canst thou empoison ? Canst thou empoison ?

MAL. Excellently ; no Jew, 'pothecary, or politician better. Look ye, here 's a [80 box. Whom wouldst thou empoison ? Here 's a box [*giving it*], which, opened and the fume taken up in conduits thorough which

[27] For crime the safe road ever lies through crime. (Seneca, *Agamemnon*, l. 115.)
[28] Q3 inserts here : *Enter Malevole and Mendoza. Mend. Hast bin with Maria? Mal. As your scriuener to your vsurer I have delt about taking of this commoditie, but shes could-frosty. Well, I will go raile, &c.* These lines are probably a stage condensation, perhaps written on the margin of the prompt copy and erroneously incorporated by the scribe or compositor. Ll. 60–76 are added by Q3.
[29] The account is closed ; the business is finished. (Kittredge.)

the brain purges itself, doth instantly for twelve hours' space bind up all show of life in a deep senseless sleep. Here's another [*giving it*], which, being opened under the sleeper's nose, chokes all the [pores] [30] of life, kills him suddenly.

MEN. I'll try experiments; 't is good [90 not to be deceived. — So, so; catso!

   Seems to poison MALEVOLE, [*who falls*].

" Who would fear that may destroy?
Death hath no teeth or tongue;
And he that's great, to him are slaves,
Shame, murder, fame, and wrong." —
Celso!

    Enter CELSO.

CELSO. My honored Lord?

MEN. The good Malevole, that plain-
  tongu'd man,
Alas, is dead on sudden, wondrous strangely!
He held in our esteem good place. Celso, [100
See him buried, see him buried.

CELSO.   I shall observe ye.

MEN. And, Celso, prithee, let it be thy
  care to-night
To have some pretty show, to solemnize
Our high instalment — some music, mas-
  query.
We'll give fair entertain unto Maria,
The duchess to the banish'd Altofront:
Thou shalt conduct her from the Citadel
Unto the Palace. Think on some masquery.

CELSO. Of what shape, sweet Lord?

MEN. [What] [31] shape! Why, any quick-
  done fiction;   110
As some brave spirits of the Genoan dukes,
To come out of Elysium, forsooth,
Led in by Mercury, to gratulate
Our happy fortune; some such anything,
Some far-fet trick good for ladies, some stale
  toy
Or other, no matter, so 't be of our devising.
Do thou prepare 't; 't is but for a fashion
  sake.
Fear not, it shall be grac'd, man, it shall
  take.

CELSO. All service.

MEN. All thanks; our hand shall not be
  close [32] to thee; farewell. — 120
[*aside*] Now is my treachery secure, nor can
  we fall;
Mischief that prospers, men do virtue call.

[30] So Q₁; Q₃ *power*.
[31] Old eds. *Why*.
[32] Tight, niggardly.

I'll trust no man; he that by tricks gets
  wreaths
Keeps them with steel; no man securely
  breathes
Out of deserved ranks; the crowd will mutter
  " fool!"
Who cannot bear with spite, he cannot rule.
The chiefest secret for a man of state
Is to live senseless of a strengthless hate.
           [*Exit.*]

MAL. (*starts up and speaks.*) Death of the
damn'd thief! I'll make one i' the [130
masque; thou shalt ha' some brave spirits of
the antique dukes.

CELSO. My Lord, what strange delusion?

MAL. Most happy, dear Celso, poison'd
with an empty box. I'll give thee all, anon.
My lady comes to court; there is a whirl of
fate comes tumbling on; the castle's captain
stands for me, the people pray for me, and
the great Leader of the just stands for me:
then courage, Celso;   140
For no disastrous chance can ever move him
That leaveth nothing but a God above him.
          Exeunt.

    [SCENE V] [33]

Enter PREPASSO *and* BILIOSO, *two Pages
before them;* MAQUERELLE, BIANCA, *and*
EMILIA.

BIL. Make room there, room for the ladies!
Why, gentlemen, will not ye suffer the ladies to
be ent'red in the great chamber? Why, gallants! and you, sir, to drop your torch where
the beauties must sit too?

PRE. And there's a great fellow plays the
knave; why dost not strike him?

BIL. Let him play the knave, a' God's
name; think'st thou I have no more wit than
to strike a great fellow? — The music! [10
more lights! revelling-scaffolds! do you
hear? Let there be oaths enow ready at the
door, swear out the Devil himself. Let's
leave the ladies, and go see if the lords be
ready for them.

    All save the Ladies *depart.*

MAQ. And, by my troth, beauties, why do
you not put you into the fashion? This is a
stale cut; you must come in fashion: look
ye, you must be all felt, felt and feather, a
felt upon your bare hair. Look ye, these [20
tiring things are justly out of request now;
and, do ye hear? you must wear falling-

[33] The Presence-chamber.

bands,[34] you must come into the falling fashion; there is such a deal a' pinning these ruffs, when the fine clean fall is worth all; and again, if you should chance to take a nap in the afternoon, your falling-band requires no poting-stick[35] to recover his form — believe me, no fashion to[36] the falling, I say.

BIAN. And is not Signior St. Andrew a [30 gallant fellow now?

MAQ. By my maidenhead, la, honor and he agrees as well together as a satin suit and woolen stockings.

EMILIA. But is not Marshal Make-room, my servant in reversion, a proper gentleman?

MAQ. Yes, in reversion, as he had his office; as, in truth, he hath all things in reversion: he has his mistress in reversion, his clothes in reversion, his wit in reversion; [40 and, indeed, is a suitor to me for my dog in reversion. But, in good verity, la, he is as proper a gentleman in reversion as — and, indeed, as fine a man as may be, having a red beard and a pair of warp'd legs.

BIAN. But, i' faith, I am most monstrously in love with Count Quidlibet-in-quodlibet: is he not a pretty, dapper, unidle gallant?

MAQ. He is even one of the most busy-fingered lords; he will put the beauties [50 to the squeak most hideously.

[*Re-enter* BILIOSO.]

BIL. Room! make a lane there! the Duke is ent'ring: stand handsomely for beauty's sake: take up the ladies there! So, cornets, cornets!

SCENE [VI] [37]

Enter PREPASSO, *joins to* BILIOSO; [*enter*] *two* Pages *and lights*, FERRARDO, [*and*] MENDOZA; *at the other door, two* Pages *with lights, and the* Captain *leading in* MARIA; *the* DUKE *meets* MARIA *and closeth with her; the rest fall back.*

MEN. Madam, with gentle ear receive my suit;
A kingdom's safety should o'erpeise[38] slight rites;
Marriage is merely nature's policy.
Then, since unless our royal beds be join'd
Danger and civil tumults frights the state,
Be wise as you are fair: give way to fate.

MARIA. What wouldst thou, thou affliction to our house?
Thou ever-devil, 't was thou that banished'st
My truly noble lord!
MEN. I! 10
MARIA. Ay, by thy plots, by thy black stratagems:
Twelve moons have suff'red change since I beheld
The loved presence of my dearest lord.
O thou far worse than Death! He parts but soul
From a weak body; but thou soul from soul
Disseverest that which God's own hand did knit;
Thou scant of honor, full of devilish wit!
MEN. We'll check your too intemperate lavishness!
I can and will.
MARIA. What canst? 20
MEN. Go to; in banishment thy husband dies.
MARIA. He ever is at home that's ever wise.
MEN. You 'st[39] ne'er meet more; reason should love control.
MARIA. Not meet!
She that dear loves, her love's still in her soul.
MEN. You are but a woman, lady, you must yield.
MARIA. Oh, save me, thou innated bashfulness,
Thou only ornament of woman's modesty!
MEN. Modesty! Death, I'll torment[40] thee.
MARIA. Do, urge all torments, all afflictions try; 30
I'll die my lord's as long as I can die.
MEN. Thou obstinate, thou shalt die. — Captain, that lady's life
Is forfeited to justice; we have examined her,
And we do find she hath empoisoned
The reverend hermit; therefore we command
Severest custody. — [*to* MARIA] Nay, if you'll do's no good,
You 'st do's no harm; a tyrant's peace is blood.
MARIA. Oh, thou art merciful; O gracious devil,
Rather by much let me condemned be
For seeming murder than be damn'd for thee!
I'll mourn no more; come, girt my brows with flowers; 41

---

[34] Flat collars (instead of ruffs).
[35] Poking-stick (used to set the pleats of the ruff).
[36] Comparable to.
[37] The same.   [38] Outweigh.
[39] You must.   [40] Torture.

Revel and dance, soul, now thy wish thou
    hast ;
Die like a bride, poor heart, thou shalt die
    chaste.

Enter AURELIA *in mourning habit.*

AUR. " Life is a frost of cold felicity,
And death the thaw of all our vanity : " [41]
Was 't not an honest priest that wrote so?
    MEN. Who let her in?
    BIL. Forbear !
    PRE. Forbear !
    AUR. Alas, calamity is everywhere ;   50
Sad misery, despite your double doors,
Will enter even in court.
    BIL. Peace !
    AUR. I ha' done. One word, —
    [PRE.] [42] Take heed !
    AUR. I ha' done.

Enter MERCURY *with loud music.*

    MER. Cyllenian Mercury, the god of
        ghosts
From gloomy shades that spread the lower
    coasts,[43]
Calls four high-famed Genoan dukes to come,
And make this presence their Elysium,   60
To pass away this high triumphal night
With song and dances, court's more soft
    delight.
    AUR. Are you god of ghosts? I have a
suit pending in hell betwixt me and my con-
science ; I would fain have thee help me to
an advocate.
    BIL. Mercury shall be your lawyer, lady.
    AUR. Nay, faith, Mercury has too good a
face to be a right lawyer.
    PRE. Peace, forbear ! Mercury presents
    the masque.   70

Cornets : the song to the cornets, which play-
    ing, the masque enters ; MALEVOLE, PIETRO,
    FERNEZE, *and* CELSO, *in white robes, with*
    duke's crowns upon laurel wreaths, pistolets
    and short swords under their robes.

    MEN. Celso, Celso, [court] [44] Maria for
        our love. —
Lady, be gracious, yet grace.
    MARIA. With me, sir?
                MALEVOLE *takes his* Wife *to dance.*
    MAL.   Yes, more loved than my breath,
With you I 'll dance.

----
[41] Thomas Bastard's *Chrestoleros* (1598), iv, 32.
[42] Old eds. assign to Aurelia.
[43] Regions.   [44] So Q₁ ; Q₃ *count.*

    MARIA. Why, then, you dance with death.
But, come, sir, I was ne'er more apt to mirth.
Death gives eternity a glorious breath ;
Oh, to die honor'd, who would fear to die?
    MAL. They die in fear who live in vil-
        lainy.
    MEN. Yes, believe him, lady, and be rul'd
        by him.   80
    PIETRO. Madam, with me?
            PIETRO *takes his wife,* AURELIA, *to*
                dance.
    AUR. Wouldst, then, be miserable?
    PIETRO. I need not wish.
    AUR. Oh, yet forbear my hand ! away !
        fly ! fly !
Oh, seek not her that only seeks to die !
    PIETRO. Poor loved soul !
    AUR.   What, wouldst court misery?
    PIETRO.   Yes.
    AUR. She 'll come too soon. — Oh, my
        griev'd heart !
    PIETRO. Lady, ha' done, ha' done ;
Come, let 's dance : be once from sorrow free.
    AUR. Art a sad man?
    PIETRO.   Yes, sweet.
    AUR.   Then we 'll agree.
        FERNEZE *takes* MAQUERELLE ; *and*
            CELSO, BIANCA : *then the cornets*
            sound the measure, one change and
            rest.

    FER. (*to* BIANCA) Believe it, lady ; shall I [90
swear? Let me enjoy you in private, and I 'll
marry you, by my soul.
    BIAN. I had rather you would swear by
your body ; I think that would prove the
more regarded oath with you.
    FER. I 'll swear by them both, to please
you.
    BIAN. Oh, damn them not both to please
me, for God's sake !
    FER. Faith, sweet creature, let me en- [100
joy you to-night, and I 'll marry you to-morrow fortnight, by my troth, la.
    MAQ. On his troth, la ! believe him not :
that kind of cony-catching [45] is as stale as Sir
Oliver Anchovy's perfum'd jerkin : promise
of matrimony by a young gallant, to bring a
virgin lady into a fool's paradise, make her
a great woman, and then cast her off — 't is
as common [and] [46] natural to a courtier, as
jealousy to a citizen, gluttony to a Puritan, [110
wisdom to an alderman, pride to a tailor, or
an empty handbasket to one of these six-

----
[45] Cheating.
[46] Old eds. *as.*

penny [47] damnations.[48] Of his troth, la ! Believe him not : traps to catch polecats.[49]

MAL. (*to* MARIA) Keep your face constant ;
    let no sudden passion
Speak in your eyes.

MARIA. O my Altofront !

PIETRO. [*to* AURELIA] A tyrant's jealousies
Are very nimble ; you receive it all?

AUR. (*to* PIETRO) My heart, though not
    my knees, doth 'umbly fall   120
Low as the earth, to thee.

[MAL.] [50]   Peace ! next change ; no words.

MARIA. Speech to such, ay, oh, what will
    affords !
      Cornets sound the measure over again ;
        which danced, they unmask.

MEN. Malevole !
      They environ MENDOZA, *bending their*
        pistols on him.

MAL. No.

MEN. Altofront ! Duke Pietro ! Ferneze !
ha !

ALL. Duke Altofront ! Duke Altofront !
      Cornets, a flourish. — They seize upon
      MENDOZA.

MEN. Are we surpris'd? What strange
    delusions mock
Our senses? Do I dream? or have I dreamt
This two days' space? Where am I?

MAL.   Where an arch-villain is.

MEN. Oh, lend me breath till I am fit to
    die !   131
For peace with Heaven, for your own souls'
    sake,
Vouchsafe me life !

PIETRO. Ignoble villain ! whom neither
    Heaven nor hell,
Goodness of God or man, could once make
    good !

MAL. Base, treacherous wretch ! what
    grace canst thou expect,
That hast grown impudent in graceless-
    ness?

MEN. Oh, life !

MAL. Slave, take thy life.
Wert thou defenced, through blood and
    wounds,   140
The sternest horror of a civil fight,
Would I achieve thee ; but prostrate at my
    feet,
I scorn to hurt thee : 't is the heart of slaves

That deigns to triumph over peasants' graves ;
For such thou art, since birth doth ne'er
    enroll
A man 'mong monarchs, but a glorious soul.
[51] <Oh, I have seen strange accidents of state !
The flatterer, like the ivy, clip the oak,
And waste it to the heart ; lust so confirm'd
That the black act of sin itself not sham'd [150
To be term'd courtship.
Oh, they that are as great as be their sins,
Let them remember that th' inconstant people
Love many princes merely for their faces
And outward shows ; and they do covet
    more
To have a sight of these than of their
    virtues.
Yet thus much let the great ones still [con-
    ceive] : [52]
When they observe not Heaven's impos'd
    conditions,
They are no kings, but forfeit their commis-
    sions.   159

MAQ. O good my Lord, I have lived in the
court this twenty year ; they that have been
old courtiers, and come to live in the city, they
are spited at, and thrust to the walls like apricocks, good my Lord.

BIL. My Lord, I did know your Lordship
in this disguise ; you heard me ever say, if
Altofront did return I would stand for him ;
besides, 't was your Lordship's pleasure to call
me wittol and cuckold : you must not [169
think, but that I knew you, I would have put
it up so patiently.>

MAL. (*to* PIETRO *and* AURELIA) You o'er-
    joy'd spirits, wipe your long-wet eyes.
Hence with this man (*kicks out* MENDOZA) : an
    eagle takes not flies. —
(*to* PIETRO *and* AURELIA) You to your vows.
    — (*to* MAQUERELLE) And thou into the
    suburbs.[53] —
(*to* BILIOSO) You to my worst friend I would
    hardly give :
Thou art a perfect old knave. — (*to* CELSO
    and the Captain) All-pleased live
You two unto my breast. — (*to* MARIA) Thou
    to my heart.
The rest of idle actors idly part ;
And as for me, I here assume my right,
To which I hope all 's pleas'd : to all, good
    night.   180
      Cornets, a flourish.   *Exeunt omnes.*

---

[47] That may be hired for sixpence.
[48] *I.e.*, the lowest class of prostitutes.
[49] Prostitutes.
[50] Old eds. *Pietro.*

[51] Ll. 147–171 are added by Q₃.
[52] Emend. Dyce ; Q₃ *conceale.*
[53] Where the brothels flourished.

AN IMPERFECT ODE, BEING BUT ONE STAFF

SPOKEN BY THE PROLOGUE

To wrest each hurtless thought to private
    sense
Is the foul use of ill-bred impudence :
    Immodest censure now grows wild,
        All overrunning.
    Let innocence be ne'er so chaste,
        Yet at the last
        She is defil'd
    With too nice-brained cunning.
        O you of fairer soul,
          Control   10
    With an Herculean arm
        This harm ;
And once teach all old freedom of a pen,
Which still must write of fools, whiles 't writes
    of men !

EPILOGUS

YOUR modest silence, full of heedy stillness,
Makes me thus speak : a voluntary illness

Is merely [54] senseless ; but unwilling error,
Such as proceeds from too rash youthful fer-
    vor,
May well be call'd a fault, but not a sin :
Rivers take names from founts where they
    begin.
Then let not too severe an eye peruse
The slighter bracks [55] of our reformed Muse,
Who could herself herself of faults detect,
But that she knows 't is easy to correct,   10
Though some men's labor : troth, to err is
    fit,
As long as wisdom's not profess'd, but wit.
Then till another's [56] happier Muse appears,
Till his Thalia feast your learned ears,
To whose desertful lamps pleas'd Fates im-
    part
Art above nature, judgment above art,
Receive this piece, which hope nor fear yet
    daunteth :
He that knows most knows most how much he
    wanteth.

[54] Utterly.   [55] Defects, flaws.
[56] Jonson's.

A
WOMAN
KILDE
with Kindneſſe.

Written by Tho: Heywood.

PRV
DEN
TIA

LONDON
Printed by William Iaggard dwelling in Barbican, and
are to be ſold in Paules Church-yard.
by Iohn Hodgets. 1607.

INTRODUCTORY NOTE

THE proverbial phrase which forms the title of Heywood's masterpiece emphasizes its most extraordinary feature; for here is an Elizabethan tragedy which reaches its pathetic end without shedding the blood of any important character. The prose Shakespeare, as Charles Lamb called him, was not a great poet; but neither was he, despite his enormous productivity, merely a hack. Only Shakespeare surpasses him in tenderness; both men must have been great lovers of human nature.

In the play before us we have a domestic tragedy, the main plot of which is thoroughly sentimental in the best sense of that maligned adjective, while the subplot is equally sentimental, in the worst of all possible senses. For Heywood is deeply interested in the sentiments of his characters: affection, delicacy, sensitiveness, consideration, high-mindedness — these are no empty terms to him, nor is their expression anything but noble. We may justly cavil at the fantastic honor of Sir Charles Mountford and at the bungling portrait of Wendoll as villain. The latter would seem less preposterous on the stage, where until recent times rascality has been taken for granted without elaborate motivation; the former, in all likelihood, would be even less plausible in the theatre than it is to the reader. And the sudden reversal of Sir Francis Acton is almost as absurd as the resolution of *The Two Gentlemen of Verona*. These are serious flaws, and there are others; yet, given the current conceptions of marriage and the technical conventions of the Elizabethan stage, the play is a masterpiece, and the author far ahead of his time in perceiving that vital human relationships do not need the panoply of war and politics and high estate to be poignantly affecting in the theatre.

Heywood received his fee for this play in February and March, 1603. It was performed by the Earl of Worcester's Men, who soon afterwards came under the patronage of Queen Anne. Though literary sources have been suggested, there is no reason to suppose that the simple structure of the main plot is not Heywood's own. As for the subplot, it is ultimately derived from an early sixteenth-century Sienese *novella*, which appears in Bandello and in Belleforest, and in English translation was available to Heywood in both William Painter's *Palace of Pleasure* (II, 30) and Sir Geoffrey Fenton's *Tragicall Discourses* (where it stands first).

The play was thrice printed in quarto, but only the first and last of these editions are extant, those of 1607 and 1617. The standard modern edition of Heywood is still the unsatisfactory Pearson reprint (1874). The best separate edition of *A Woman Killed with Kindness* is that of Katharine Lee Bates (1917), in the Belles-Lettres Series (with *The Fair Maid of the West*). Like the present text, it is based on the Second (extant) Quarto, instead of on the badly printed *editio princeps*. A number of the readings of the First Quarto have, nevertheless, been adopted by the present Editor. For these, though the text has been collated throughout with the Pearson reprint of Q1, the Editor has found Miss Bates's textual notes more useful.

A WOMAN KILLED WITH KINDNESS

BY

THOMAS HEYWOOD

[DRAMATIS PERSONAE

SIR FRANCIS ACTON, brother to Mistress Frankford.
SIR CHARLES MOUNTFORD.
JOHN FRANKFORD.
MALBY, friend to Sir Francis.
WENDOLL, friend to Frankford.
CRANWELL, an old gentleman.
SHAFTON, false friend to Sir Charles.
OLD MOUNTFORD, uncle to Sir Charles.
SANDY, former friend to Sir Charles.
RODER, former tenant to Sir Charles.
TIDY, cousin to Sir Charles.
NICHOLAS,
JENKIN, } household servants to
SPIGOT, the butler, } Frankford.

ROGER BRICKBAT, } country fellows.
JACK SLIME, }
Sheriff.
Keeper of Prison.

ANNE FRANKFORD.
SUSAN, sister to Sir Charles Mountford.
CICELY MILKPAIL, maid to Mistress Frankford.

Sheriff's Officers, Sergeant, Huntsmen, Falconers, Coachman, Carters, Servants, Musicians, Children, Serving Women and Country Wenches.

THE SCENE — *Yorkshire.*]

THE PROLOGUE

I COME but as a harbinger, being sent
To tell you what these preparations mean.
Look for no glorious state : our Muse is bent
Upon a barren subject, a bare scene.
We could afford this twig a timber-tree,
Whose strength might boldly on your favors
    build ;
Our russet, tissue ; drone, a honey-bee ;
Our barren plot, a large and spacious field ;
Our coarse fare, banquets ; our thin water,
    wine ;
Our brook, a sea ; our bat's eyes, eagle's
    sight ;   10
Our poet's dull and earthy Muse, divine ;
Our ravens, doves ; our crows' black feathers,
    white.
  But gentle thoughts, when they may give
    the foil,[1]
  Save them that yield, and spare where they
    may spoil.

[1] Can defeat.

[ACT I — SCENE I] [2]

Enter MASTER JOHN FRANKFORD, MISTRESS [FRANKFORD],[3] SIR FRANCIS ACTON, SIR CHARLES MOUNTFORD, MASTER MALBY, MASTER WENDOLL, *and* MASTER CRANWELL.

SIR F. Some music, there ! None lead the
    bride a dance?
SIR C. Yes, would she dance *The Shaking of
    the Sheets !* [4]
But that's the dance her husband means to
    lead her !
WEN. That's not the dance that every man
    must dance,
According to the ballad.[5]

[2] A room in Frankford's house.
[3] Q1 *Acton;* Q2 *Anne.* She is *Anne* throughout the speech-tags of the old eds.
[4] A popular Elizabethan tune and ballad.
[5] "Make ready then your winding-sheet
  And see how you can bestir your feet,
  For death is the man that all must meet."

SIR F.   Music, ho !
By your leave, Sister, — by your husband's
    leave,
I should have said, — the hand that but this
    day
Was given you in the church I 'll borrow. —
    Sound !
This marriage music hoists me from the
    ground.
FRANK. Ay, you may caper ; you are light
    and free.   10
Marriage hath yok'd my heels ; pray, par-
    don me.
SIR F. I 'll have you dance too, Brother !
SIR C.   Master Frankford,
Y' are a happy man, sir, and much joy
Succeed your marriage mirth ; you have a wife
So qualified, and with such ornaments
Both of the mind and body. First, her birth
Is noble, and her education such
As might become the daughter of a prince ;
Her own tongue speaks all tongues, and her
    own hand
Can teach all strings to speak in their best
    grace,   20
From the shrill'st [6] treble to the hoarsest bass.
To end her many praises in one word,
She 's Beauty and Perfection's eldest daughter,
Only found by yours, though many a heart
    hath sought her.
FRANK. But that I know your virtues and
    chaste thoughts,
I should be jealous of your praise, Sir Charles.
CRAN. He speaks no more than you ap-
    prove.
MAL. Nor flatters he that gives to her her
    due.
MRS. F. I would your praise could find a
    fitter theme
Than my imperfect beauty [7] to speak on ! 30
Such as they be, if they my husband please,
They suffice me now I am married.
His sweet content is like a flatt'ring glass,
To make my face seem fairer to mine eye ;
But the least wrinkle from his stormy brow
Will blast the roses in my cheeks that grow.
SIR F. A perfect wife already, meek and
    patient.
How strangely the word " husband " fits your
    mouth,
Not married three hours since. Sister, 't is
    good ;   39
You that begin betimes thus must needs prove

Pliant and duteous in your husband's love. —
Gramercies,[8] Brother ! Wrought her to 't
    already :
" Sweet husband," and a curtsy, the first day?
Mark this, mark this, you that are bachelors,
And never took the grace of honest man ; [9]
Mark this, against [10] you marry, this one
    phrase :
In a good time that man both wins and woos
That takes his wife down in her wedding
    shoes.[11]
FRANK. Your sister takes not after you,
    Sir Francis ;
All his wild blood your father spent on you : 50
He got her in his age, when he grew civil.
All his mad tricks were to his land entail'd,
And you are heir to all ; your sister, she
Hath to her dow'r her mother's modesty.
SIR C. Lord, sir, in what a happy state live
    you :
This morning, which to many seems a burden,
Too heavy to bear, is unto you a pleasure.
This lady is no clog, as many are ;
She doth become you like a well-made suit,
In which the tailor hath us'd all his art ; 60
Not like a thick coat of unseason'd frieze,
Forc'd on your back in summer. She 's no
    chain
To tie your neck, and curb ye to the yoke ;
But she 's a chain of gold to adorn your neck :
You both [adore] [12] each other, and your hands,
Methinks, are matches.[13] There 's equality
In this fair combination ; y' are both
Scholars, both young, both being descended
    nobly.
There 's music in this sympathy ; it carries
Consort and expectation of much joy,   70
Which God bestow on you from this first day
Until your dissolution, that 's for aye !
SIR F. We keep you here too long, good
    Brother Frankford.
Into the hall ; away, go cheer your guests.
What, bride and bridegroom both withdrawn
    at once?
If you be miss'd, the guests will doubt their
    welcome,
And charge you with unkindness.
FRANK.   To prevent it,
I 'll leave you here, to see the dance within.

[6] Q[1] *shrill.*
[7] Emend. Collier *beauties.*
[8] Q[1] *Godamercies.*
[9] Assumed the honorable estate of husband.
(Bates.)
[10] In preparation for the time when.
[11] Gets the upper hand of his wife immediately.
[12] So Q[1] ; Q[2] *adorne.*
[13] *I.e.,* you are excellent matches for each other.

MRS. F. And so will I.

[*Exeunt* MASTER AND MISTRESS
FRANKFORD.]

SIR F.　　　　　To part you it were sin. —
Now, gallants, while the town musicians　　80
Finger their frets [14] within, and the mad lads
And country lasses, every mother's child,
With nosegays and bride-laces [15] in their
　　hats,
Dance all their country measures, rounds, and
　　jigs,
What shall we do? Hark! They are all on
　　the hoigh; [16]
They toil like mill-horses, and turn as round, —
Marry, not on the toe! Ay, and they caper,
But [17] without cutting; you shall see, to-
　　morrow,
The hall-floor peck'd and dinted like a mill-
　　stone,
Made with their high shoes. Though their
　　skill be small,　　　　　　　　　90
Yet they tread heavy where their hobnails
　　fall.

SIR C. Well, leave them to their sports! —
Sir Francis Acton,
I'll make a match with you. Meet me to-
　　morrow
At Chevy Chase; I'll fly my hawk with
　　yours.

SIR F. For what? For what?

SIR C.　　　　　Why, for a hundred pound.

SIR F. Pawn me some gold of that.

SIR C.　　　　　Here are ten angels; [18]
I'll make them good a hundred pound to-mor-
　　row
Upon my hawk's wing.

SIR F.　　　　　'T is a match; 't is done.
Another hundred pound upon your dogs —
Dare ye, Sir Charles?

SIR C.　　I dare! Were I sure to lose, [100
I durst do more than that; here's my
　　hand,
The first course [19] for a hundred pound.

SIR F.　　　　　　　A match.

WEN. Ten angels on Sir Francis Acton's
　　hawk,
As much upon his dogs.

CRAN. I am for Sir Charles Mountford; I
　　have seen

His hawk and dog both tri'd. What, clap
　　ye hands, [20]
Or is't no bargain?

WEN.　　　Yes, and stake them down.
Were they five hundred, they were all my
　　own.

SIR F. Be stirring early with the lark to-
　　morrow;
I'll rise into my saddle ere the sun　　110
Rise from his bed.

SIR C.　　　　If there you miss me, say
I am no gentleman. I'll hold my day.

SIR F. It holds on all sides. — Come, to-
　　night let's dance;
Early to-morrow let's prepare to ride —
We had need be three hours up before the
　　bride.　　　　　　　　　[*Exeunt.*]

[SCENE II] [21]

Enter NICK *and* JENKIN, JACK SLIME, ROGER
BRICKBAT, *with* Country Wenches, *and two
or three* Musicians.

JEN. Come, Nick, take you Joan Miniver,
to trace withal; Jack Slime, traverse you with
Cicely Milkpail; I will take Jane Trubkin,
and Roger Brickbat shall have Is'bel Motley.
And now that they are busy in the parlor,
come, strike up; we'll have a crash [22] here in
the yard.

NICK. My humor is not compendious:
dancing I possess not, though I can foot it;
yet, since I am fall'n into the hands of [10
Cicely Milkpail, [23] I consent.

SLIME. Truly, Nick, though we were never
brought up like serving courtiers, yet we have
been brought up with serving creatures — ay,
and God's creatures, too; for we have been
brought up to serve sheep, oxen, horses,
hogs, and such like; and, though we be but
country fellows, it may be in the way of dancing we can do the horse-trick as well as the
serving men.　　　　　　　　　20

BRICK. Ay, and the cross-point [23a] too.

JEN. O Slime, O Brickbat, do not you know
that comparisons are odious? Now we are
odious ourselves, too; therefore there are no
comparisons to be made betwixt us.

NICK. I am sudden, and not superfluous;

[14] The ridges across the finger board for stopping
the strings.
[15] Streamers.
[16] Excited.
[17] So Pearson and both copies of Q 2 collated for the
present ed. Miss Bates *Not*.
[18] Gold coins worth about $2.50 each.
[19] Run.

[20] Are you going to shake hands?
[21] The yard of Frankford's house.
[22] A bout of revelry.
[23] Since Jenkin had assigned her to Slime, we must
suppose that during Nick's speech she has indicated
a preference for him.
[23a] A dance step.

I am quarrelsome, and not seditious;
I am peaceable, and not contentious;
I am brief, and not compendious.

SLIME. Foot it quickly. If the music [30
overcome not my melancholy, I shall quarrel;
and if they suddenly do not strike up, I shall
presently strike thee down.

JEN. No quarrelling, for God's sake!
Truly, if you do, I shall set a knave between
ye.

SLIME. I come to dance, not to quarrel.
Come, what shall it be? *Rogero?* [24]

JEN. *Rogero?* no; we will dance *The Be-*
ginning of the World. [24]   40

CICELY. I love no dance so well as *John*
Come Kiss Me Now. [24]

NICK. I that have ere now deserv'd a cushion, call for the *Cushion-dance.* [25]

BRICK. For my part, I like nothing so well
as *Tom Tyler.* [24]

JEN. No; we'll have *The Hunting of the*
Fox. [26]

SLIME. *The Hay,* [27] *The Hay!* There's
nothing like *The Hay.*   50

NICK. I have said, I do say, and I will say
again ——

JEN. Every man agree to have it as Nick
says.

ALL. Content.

NICK. It hath been, it now is, and it shall
be ——

CICELY. What, Master Nicholas? What?

NICK. *Put on your Smock a' Monday.* [24]

JEN. So the dance will come cleanly off. [60
Come, for God's sake, agree of something; if
you like not that, put it to the musicians; or
let me speak for all, and we'll have *Sellenger's*
Round. [28]

ALL. That, that, that.

NICK. No, I am resolv'd thus it shall be;
First take hands, then take you to your heels.

JEN. Why, would ye have us run away?

NICK. No; but I would have you shake
your heels. — Music, strike up.   70

> *They dance;* NICK, *dancing, speaks*
> *stately and scurvily;* [29] *the rest after*
> *the country fashion.*

JEN. Hey! Lively, my lasses! Here's a
turn for thee!   [*Exeunt.*]

[24] The name of a well-known tune.
[25] In which the chosen partner knelt on a cushion
and was kissed.
[26] This tune has not been identified.
[27] A boisterous rustic dance.
[28] One of the oldest country dances.
[29] Sourly.

[SCENE III] [30]

Wind horns. Enter SIR CHARLES [MOUNT-
FORD], SIR FRANCIS [ACTON], MALBY, CRAN-
WELL, WENDOLL, Falconers, *and* Huntsmen.

SIR C. So; well cast off! Aloft, aloft!
Well flown!
Oh, now she takes her at the souse, [31] and
strikes her
Down to th' earth, like a swift thunderclap.

WEN. She hath struck ten angels out of my
way.

SIR F. A hundred pound from me.

SIR C.   What, falconer!

FALC.   At hand, sir.

SIR C. Now she hath seiz'd the fowl and
'gins to plume [32] her,
[Rebuke] her not; rather stand still and
[cherk] her. [33]
So, seize her gets, [34] her jesses, [35] and her bells!
Away!

SIR F.   My hawk kill'd, too.

SIR C.   Ay, but 't was at the querre, [36]
Not at the mount like mine.

SIR F.   Judgment, my masters! [10

CRAN. Yours miss'd her at the ferre. [37]

WEN. Ay, but our merlin first hath plum'd
the fowl,
And twice renew'd her [38] from the river too.
Her bells, Sir Francis, had not both one weight,
Nor was one semi-tune above the other.
Methinks, these Milan bells do sound too full,
And spoil the mounting of your hawk.

SIR C.   'T is lost.

SIR F. I grant it not. Mine likewise seiz'd
a fowl
Within her talons, and you saw her paws
Full of the feathers; both her petty singles [20
And her long singles [39] grip'd her more than
other;

[30] Chevy Chase.   [31] In a swoop.   [32] Pluck.
[33] Emend. Bates; old eds. *Rebecke . . . checke*
her. Heywood, as Miss Bates shows, is following the
instructions of treatises on hawking, which advise
the falconer, in order to avoid the hawk's flying up
into a tree with the quarry, not to "rebuke" her
but, when she begins "pluming", to advance toward
her "cherking", *i.e.*, chirping, or whistling to her
when she seems alarmed.
[34] Not precisely identified, but evidently something attached to the jesses.
[35] Leg-straps.
[36] Defined in the *Boke of St. Albans* (1486, *et seq.*)
as = before the quarry rose from the ground.
(Bates.)
[37] Uncertain; perhaps = higher or further point.
[38] Driven her by a fresh attack.
[39] The "uttermost" claws and the claws "that
are upon the middle stretchers." (*Boke of St. Albans,*
cited by Bates.)

The terrials [40] of her legs were stain'd with
    blood :
Not of the fowl only she did discomfit
Some of her feathers, but she brake away.
Come, come ; your hawk is but a rifler.[41]
    SIR C.   How?
    SIR F. Ay, and your dogs are trindle-tails [42]
      and curs.
    SIR C. You stir my blood.
You keep not a good hound in all your kennel,
Nor one good hawk upon your perch.
    SIR F.   How, knight !
    SIR C. So, knight. You will not swagger,[43]
      sir ?   30
    SIR F. Why, say I did?
    SIR C.   Why, sir,
I say you would gain as much by swagg'ring
As you have got by wagers on your dogs.
You will come short in all things.
    SIR F.   Not in this !
Now I 'll strike home. [*Strikes* SIR CHARLES.]
    SIR C.   Thou shalt to thy long home,
Or I will want my will.
    SIR F. All they that love Sir Francis, follow
      me.
    SIR C. All that affect SIR CHARLES, draw on
      my part.
    CRAN. On this side heaves my hand.
    WEN.   Here goes my heart.
    They divide themselves. SIR CHARLES,
      CRANWELL, *Falconer, and* Hunts-
      man *fight against* SIR FRANCIS,
      WENDOLL, *his* Falconer, *and*
      Huntsman ; *and* SIR CHARLES
      hath the better, and beats them
      away, killing both [44] *of* SIR FRAN-
      CIS *his men.*[45] [*Exeunt all but*
      SIR CHARLES MOUNTFORD.]
    SIR C. My God, what have I done? What
      have I done?   40
My rage hath plung'd into a sea of blood,
In which my soul lies drown'd. Poor inno-
    cents,[46]
For whom we are to answer. Well, 't is done,

[40] Not certainly identified. Perhaps the talons
that tore the quarry ; perhaps, misprinted, the
"terriets", the loops that tied the bells to the hawk's
legs. (Bates.)
[41] "Oftentimes . . . a Hawke . . . seaseth but
the feathers ; . . . such Hawkes be called Riflers."
(*Boke of St. Albans*, cited by Bates.)
[42] Curly-tailed.
[43] Behave like a bully. Hawking was notorious as
an "extreame stirrer up of passions." See *Mod. Lang.
Notes*, XLV, 514, 515, for W. L. Ustick's citation from
King James's *Instructions* to Prince Henry.
[44] So Q 2 ; Q 1 *one.*
[45] So Q 2 ; Q 1 *huntsmen.*
[46] So Q 2 ; Q 1 *innocent.*

And I remain the victor. A great conquest,
When I would give this right hand, nay, this
    head,
To breathe in them new life whom I have
    slain. —
Forgive me, God. 'T was in the heat of
    blood,
And anger quite removes me from myself.
It was not I, but rage, did this vile murder ;
Yet I, and not my rage, must answer it.   50
Sir Francis Acton, he is fled the field ;
With him all those that did partake his quar-
    rel ;
And I am left alone with sorrow dumb,
And in my height of conquest overcome.

        Enter SUSAN.[47]

    SUSAN. O God ! My brother wounded
      'mong the dead :
Unhappy jests, that in such earnest ends ! —
The rumor of this fear stretch'd to my ears,
And I am come to know if you be wounded.
    SIR C. O Sister, Sister, wounded at the
      heart.
    SUSAN. My God forbid !   60
    SIR C. In doing that thing which he for-
      bade,
I am wounded, Sister.
    SUSAN.   I hope, not at the heart.
    SIR C. Yes, at the heart.
    SUSAN.   O God ! A surgeon, there.
    SIR C. Call me a surgeon, Sister, for my
      soul ;
The sin of murder, it hath pierc'd my heart
And made a wide wound there ; but for these
    scratches,
They are nothing, nothing.
    SUSAN.   Charles, what have you done?
Sir Francis hath great friends, and will pursue
    you
Unto the utmost danger [48] of the law.
    SIR C. My conscience is become mine en-
      emy,   70
And will pursue me more than Acton can.
    SUSAN. Oh, fly, sweet Brother.
    SIR C.   Shall I fly from thee?
Why, Sue, [49] art weary of my company?
    SUSAN. Fly from your foe.
    SIR C.   You, Sister, are my friend,
And flying you, I shall pursue my end.
    SUSAN. Your company is as my eyeball
      dear ;
Being far from you, no comfort can be near.

[47] Q 1 *Jane*, throughout this scene.
[48] Penalty.   [49] Q 1 *What Jane.*

Yet fly to save your life ; what would I care
To spend my future age in black despair,
So you were safe? And yet to live one week
Without my brother Charles, through every
    cheek   81
My streaming tears would downwards run so
    rank,[50]
Till they could set on either side a bank,
And in the midst a channel ; so my face
For two salt-water brooks shall still find place.
    SIR C. Thou shall not weep so much ; for I
        will stay,
In spite of danger's teeth. I 'll live with thee,
Or I 'll not live at all. I will not sell
My country and my father's patrimony,
No[r] thy sweet sight, for a vain hope of life. [90

Enter Sheriff, *with* Officers.

    SHER. Sir Charles, I am made the unwilling
        instrument
Of your attach [51] and apprehension.
I 'm sorry that the blood of innocent men
Should be of you exacted. It was told me
That you were guarded with a troop of friends,
And therefore came arm'd.
    SIR C.   Oh, Master Sheriff,
I came into the field with many friends,
But see, they all have left me ; only one
Clings to my sad misfortune, my dear sister.
I know you for an honest gentleman ;   100
I yield my weapons, and submit to you.
Convey me where you please.
    SHER.   To prison, then,
To answer for the lives of these dead men.
    SUSAN. O God ! O God !
    SIR C.   Sweet Sister, every strain
Of sorrow from your heart augments my pain ;
Your grief abounds,[52] and hits against my
    breast.
    SHER. Sir, will you go?
    SIR C.   Even where it likes you best.
                          [*Exeunt.*]

[ACT II — SCENE I] [1]

Enter MASTER FRANKFORD *in a study.*

FRANK. How happy am I amongst other
    men,
That in my mean [2] estate embrace content.
I am a gentleman, and by my birth
Companion with a king ; a king's no more.

[50] Profusely.   [51] Arrest.   [52] Rebounds.
[1] A room in Frankford's house.   [2] Moderate.

I am possess'd of many fair revenues,[3]
Sufficient to maintain a gentleman.
Touching my mind, I am studied in all arts ;
The riches of my thoughts and of my time
Have been a good proficient ; [4] but, the chief
Of all the sweet felicities on earth,   10
I have a fair, a chaste, and loving wife :
Perfection all, all truth, all ornament.
If man on earth may truly happy be,
Of these at once possess'd, sure, I am he.

Enter NICHOLAS.

    NICH. Sir, there 's a gentleman attends
        without
To speak with you.
    FRANK.   On horseback?
    NICH.   Ay, on horseback.
    FRANK. Entreat him to alight ; and I 'll
        attend him.
Know'st thou him, Nick?
    NICH. Know him? Yes his name 's Wendoll.
It seems he comes in haste : his horse is booted
Up to the flank in mire, himself all spotted [20
And stain'd with plashing. Sure, he rid in
    fear,
Or for a wager. Horse and man both sweat ;
I ne'er saw two in such a smoking heat.
    FRANK. Entreat him in ; about it instantly !
                    [*Exit* NICHOLAS.]
This Wendoll I have noted, and his carriage
Hath pleas'd me much ; by observation
I have noted many good deserts in him :
He 's affable, and seen [5] in many things,
Discourses well, a good companion,
And though of small means yet a gentleman [30
Of a good house, somewhat press'd by want,
I have preferr'd him to a second place
In my opinion and my best regard.

Enter WENDOLL, MISTRESS FRANKFORD, *and*
NICK.

    MRS. F. O, Master Frankford, Master
        Wendoll here
Brings you the strangest news that e'er you
    heard.
    FRANK. What news, sweet Wife? — What
        news, good Master Wendoll?
    WEN. You knew the match made 'twixt
        Sir Francis Acton
And Sir Charles Mountford.
    FRANK.   True ; with their hounds and
        hawks.

[3] Accented on second syllable.
[4] *I.e.*, I have improved my time intellectually.
[5] Well-versed.

WEN. The matches were both play'd.

FRANK.   Ha! and which won?

WEN. Sir Francis, your wife's brother, had
the worst,   40
And lost the wager.

FRANK.   Why, the worse his chance;
Perhaps the fortune of some other day
Will change his luck.

MRS. F.   Oh, but you hear not all.
Sir Francis lost, and yet was loth to yield.
In brief, the two knights grew to difference,
From words to blows, and so to banding sides;[6]
Where valorous Sir Charles slew, in his spleen,
Two of your brother's men, — his falc'ner
And his good huntsman, whom he lov'd so
well.
More men were wounded, no more slain out-
right.   50

FRANK. Now, trust me, I am sorry for the
knight.
But is my brother safe?

WEN.   All whole and sound,
His body not being blemish'd with one wound.
But poor Sir Charles is to the prison led,
To answer at th' assize for them that's dead.

FRANK. I thank your pains, sir. Had the
news been better,
Your will was to have brought it, Master Wen-
doll. —
Sir Charles will find hard friends; his case is
heinous
And will be most severely censur'd on.[7]
I'm sorry for him. — Sir, a word with you. 60
I know you, sir, to be a gentleman
In all things, your possibility[8] but mean;
Please you to use my table and my purse;
They are yours.

WEN. O Lord, sir! I shall never deserve it.

FRANK. O sir, disparage not your worth too
much;
You are full of quality[9] and fair desert.
Choose of my men which shall attend you, sir,
And he is yours. I will allow you, sir,
Your man, your gelding, and your table, all
At my own charge; be my companion.   70

WEN. Master Frankford, I have oft been
bound to you
By many favors; this exceeds them all,
That I shall never merit your least favor.
But when your last remembrance I forget,
Heaven at my soul exact that weighty debt.

FRANK. There needs no protestation; for I
know you
Virtuous, and therefore grateful. — Prithee,
Nan,
Use him with all thy loving'st courtesy.

MRS. F. As far as modesty may well extend,
It is my duty to receive your friend.   80

FRANK. To dinner! Come, sir, from this
present day,
Welcome to me for ever! Come, away!

        Exit [FRANKFORD *with* MISTRESS
              FRANKFORD *and* WENDOLL].

NICH. I do not like this fellow by no means;
I never see him but my heart still earns.[10]
Zounds, I could fight with him, yet know not
why;
The Devil and he are all one in my eye.

        Enter JENKIN.

JEN. O Nick, what gentleman is that comes
to lie at our house? My master allows him
one to wait on him, and I believe it will fall to
thy lot.   90

NICH. I love my master; by these hilts,[11] I
do;
But rather than I'll ever come to serve him,
I'll turn away my master.

        Enter CICELY.

CIC. Nich'las! where are you, Nich'las?
You must come in, Nich'las, and help the
gentleman[12] off with his boots.

NICH. If I pluck off his boots, I'll eat the
spurs,
And they shall stick fast in my throat like
burrs.

CIC. Then, Jenkin, come you.

JEN. Nay, 't is no boot for me to deny it. [100
My master hath given me a coat here, but he
takes pains himself to brush it once or twice a
day with a holly wand.

CIC. Come, come, make haste, that you
may wash your hands again, and help to serve
in dinner.

JEN. [*to the audience*] You may see, my
masters, though it be afternoon with you, 't is
but early days with us, for we have not din'd
yet. Stay a little; I'll but go in and [110
help to bear up the first course, and come to
you again presently.   [*Exeunt.*]

---

[6] Forming parties.
[7] Judged.
[8] Resources.
[9] Accomplishments.

[10] Grieves.
[11] Evidently Nick wears a sword or dagger;
cf. II, iii, 174–177.
[12] Q₁ *young gentleman.*

[SCENE II] [13]

Enter MALBY *and* CRANWELL.

MAL. This is the sessions day; pray can you tell me
How young Sir Charles hath sped? Is he acquit,
Or must he try the law's strict penalty?
  CRAN. He's clear'd of all, spite of his enemies,
Whose earnest labor was to take his life.
But in this suit of pardon he hath spent [14]
All the revenues that his father left him;
And he is now turn'd a plain countryman,
Reform'd [15] in all things. See, sir, here he comes.

Enter SIR [CHARLES] *and his* Keeper.

KEEP. Discharge your fees, and you are then at freedom.   10
  SIR C. Here, Master Keeper, take the poor remainder
Of all the wealth I have. My heavy foes
Have made my purse light; but, alas, to me
'T is wealth enough that you have set me free.
  MAL. God give you joy of your delivery.
I am glad to see you abroad, Sir Charles.
  SIR C. The poorest knight in England, Master Malby.
My life hath cost me all the patrimony
My father left his son. Well, God forgive them
That are the authors of my penury.   20

Enter SHAFTON.

SHAFT. Sir Charles! A hand, a hand! At liberty?
Now, by the faith I owe, I am glad to see it.
What want you? Wherein may I pleasure you?
  SIR C. O me! O most unhappy gentleman!
I am not worthy to have friends stirr'd up,
Whose hands may help me in this plunge of want.
I would I were in Heaven, to inherit there
Th' immortal birthright which my Savior keeps,
And by no unthrift can be bought and sold;
For here on earth what pleasures should we trust?   30

SHAFT. To rid you from these contemplations,
Three hundred pounds you shall receive of me;
Nay, five for fail. [16] Come, sir, the sight of gold
Is the most sweet receipt for melancholy,
And will revive your spirits. You shall hold law
With your proud adversaries. Tush! let Frank Acton
Wage, [with] [17] his knighthood, like expense with me,
And 'a will sink, he will. Nay, good Sir Charles,
Applaud your fortune and your fair escape
From all these perils.
  SIR C.   O sir, they have undone me. [40
Two thousand and five hundred pound a year
My father at his death possess'd me of;
All which the envious [18] Acton made me spend;
And, notwithstanding all this large expense,
I had much ado to gain my liberty;
And I have only now a house of pleasure,
With some five hundred pounds reserved,
Both to maintain me and my loving sister.
  SHAFT. [*aside*] That must I have; it lies convenient for me.
If I can fasten but one finger on him,   50
With my full hand I'll gripe him to the heart.
'T is not for love I proffer'd him this coin,
But for my gain and pleasure. — Come, Sir Charles,
I know you have need of money; take my offer.
  SIR C. Sir, I accept it, and remain indebted
Even to the best of my unable [19] power.
Come, gentlemen, and see it tend'red down! [20]
          [*Exeunt.*]

[SCENE III] [21]

Enter WENDOLL, *melancholy.*

WEN. I am a villain, if I apprehend [22]
But such a thought; then, to attempt the deed,
Slave, thou art damn'd without redemption. —
I'll drive away this passion with a song.
A song! Ha, ha! A song! as if, fond [23] man,
Thy eyes could swim in laughter, when thy soul
Lies drench'd and drowned in red tears of blood.

---

13 Unlocated; perhaps before the jail.
14 In gifts to influential persons.
15 Transformed.
16 If necessary (to avoid failure).
17 So Q1; Q2: *Wage his Knight-hood-like.*
18 Malicious.   19 Feeble.   20 Paid.
21 A room in Frankford's house.
22 Conceive.   23 Foolish.

I 'll pray, and see if God within my heart
Plant better thoughts. — Why, prayers are
    meditations,
And when I meditate (oh, God forgive me) [10
It is on her divine perfections.
I will forget her ; I will arm myself
Not t' entertain a thought of love to her ;
And, when I come by chance into her presence,
I 'll hale [24] these balls, until my eye-strings
    crack,
From being pull'd and drawn to look that
    way.

Enter, over the stage, FRANKFORD, *his* Wife,
    and NICK [*and exeunt*].

O God, O God ! with what a violence
I 'm hurried to my own destruction.
There goest thou, the most perfect's[t] man
That ever England bred a gentleman ;   20
And shall I wrong his bed? — Thou God of
    thunder,
Stay, in thy thoughts of vengeance and of
    wrath,
Thy great, almighty, and all-judging hand
From speedy execution on a villain,
A villain and a traitor to his friend.

Enter JENKIN.

JEN. Did your Worship call?
WEN. He doth maintain me ; he allows me
    largely
Money to spend.
JEN. [*aside*] By my faith, so do not you me ;
I cannot get a cross [25] of you.
WEN.   My gelding, and my man.   30
JEN. [*to the audience*] That 's Sorrel and I.
WEN. This kindness grows of no alliance [26]
    'twixt us.
JEN. [*aside*] Nor is my service of any great
    acquaintance.
WEN. I never bound him to me by desert.
Of a mere stranger, a poor gentleman,
A man by whom in no kind he could gain,
And he hath plac'd me in his highest thoughts,
Made me companion with the best and chiefest
In Yorkshire. He cannot eat without me,
Nor laugh without me ; I am to his body   40
As necessary as his digestion,
And equally do make him whole or sick.
And shall I wrong this man? Base man !
    Ingrate !

[24] Constrain.
[25] Originally a coin stamped with a cross, and
then any coin.
[26] Relationship.

Hast thou the power, straight with thy gory
    hands,
To rip thy image from his bleeding heart,
To scratch thy name from out the holy book
Of his remembrance, and to wound his name
That holds thy name so dear? Or rend his
    heart
To whom thy heart was knit and join'd to-
    gether?   49
And yet I must. Then, Wendoll, be content ;
Thus villains, when they would, cannot repent.
JEN. [*aside*] What a strange humor is my
new master in. Pray God he be not mad ;
if he should be so, I should never have any
mind to serve him in Bedlam. It may be
he is mad for missing of me.
WEN. What, Jenkin ; where 's your mis-
tress?
JEN. Is your Worship married?
WEN. Why dost thou ask?   60
JEN. Because you are my master ; and if I
have a mistress, I would be glad, like a good
servant, to do my duty to her.
WEN. I mean Mistress Frankford.
JEN. Marry, sir, her husband is riding out
of town, and she went very lovingly to bring
him on his way to horse. Do you see, sir?
Here she comes, and here I go.
WEN. Vanish.   [*Exit* JENKIN.]

Enter MISTRESS FRANKFORD.

MRS. F. Y' are well met, sir ; now, in troth,
    my husband,   70
Before he took horse, had a great desire
To speak with you ; we sought about the
    house,
Halloo'd into the fields, sent every way,
But could not meet you. Therefore, he en-
    join'd me
To do unto you his most kind commends.
Nay, more, he wills you, as you prize his
    love,
Or hold in estimation his kind friendship,
To make bold in his absence, and command
Even as himself were present in the house ; [79
For you must keep his table, use his servants,
And be a present Frankford in his absence.
WEN. I thank him for his love. —
[*aside*] Give me a name, you, whose infectious
    tongues
Are tipp'd with gall and poison : as you would
Think on a man that had your father slain,
Murd'red your [27] children, made your wives
    base strumpets,

[27] So Q ○ : Q₁ *thy*.

So call me, call me so; print in my face
The most stigmatic [28] title of a villain,
For hatching treason to so true a friend.

MRS. F. Sir, you are much beholding [29] to
    my husband;   90
You are a man most dear in his regard.

WEN. I am bound unto your husband, and
    you too.
[*aside*] I will not speak to wrong a gentleman
Of that good estimation, my kind friend.
I will not; zounds, I will not. I may choose,
And I will choose. Shall I be so misled?
Or shall I purchase to [30] my father's crest
The motto of a villain? If I say
I will not do it, what thing can enforce me?
What can compel me? What sad destiny
Hath such command upon my yielding
    thoughts?   101
I will not. Ha! some Fury pricks me on;
The swift Fates drag me at their chariot
    wheel,
And hurry me to mischief. Speak I must;
Injure myself, wrong her, deceive his trust.

MRS. F. Are you not well, sir, that you
    seem thus troubled?
There is sedition in your countenance!

WEN. And in my heart, fair angel, chaste
    and wise!
I love you! Start not, speak not, answer not;
I love you! Nay, let me speak the rest; [110
Bid me to swear, and I will call to record
The host of Heaven.

MRS. F.   The host of Heaven forbid
Wendoll should hatch such a disloyal thought!

WEN. Such is my fate; to this suit [31] was I
    born,
To wear rich pleasure's crown, or fortune's
    scorn.

MRS. F. My husband loves you.

WEN.   I know it.

MRS. F.   He esteems you,
Even as his brain, his eyeball, or his heart.

WEN. I have tried it.

MRS. F. His purse is your exchequer, and
    his table   119
Doth freely serve you.

WEN.   So I have found it.

MRS. F. Oh, with what face of brass, what
    brow of steel,
Can you, unblushing, speak this to the face
Of the espous'd wife of so dear a friend?
It is my husband that maintains your state.
Will you dishonor him? I am his wife

That in your power hath left his whole affairs:
It is to me you speak!

WEN.   Oh, speak no more;
For more than this I know, and have recorded
Within the red-leav'd table [32] of my heart.
Fair, and of all belov'd, I was not fearful [130
Bluntly to give my life into your hand,
And at one hazard all my earthly means.
Go, tell your husband; he will turn me off,
And I am then undone. I care not, I:
'T was for your sake. Perchance in rage he'll
    kill me;
I care not: 't was for you. Say I incur
The general name of villain through the
    world,
Of traitor to my friend; I care not, I.
Beggary, shame, death, scandal, and re-
    proach,   139
For you I'll hazard all. Why,[33] what care I?
For you I'll live, and in your love I'll die.

MRS. F. You move me, sir, to passion and
    to pity.[34]
The love I bear my husband is as precious
As my soul's health.

WEN.   I love your husband, too,
And for his love I will engage my life.
Mistake me not; the augmentation
Of my sincere affection borne to you
Doth no whit lessen my regard to him.
I will be secret, lady, close as night;   149
And not the light of one small glorious star
Shall shine here in my forehead, to bewray [35]
That act of night.

MRS. F. [*aside*] What shall I say?
My soul is wand'ring, and hath lost her way. —
Oh, Master Wendoll! Oh!

WEN.   Sigh not, sweet saint;
For every sigh you breathe draws from my
    heart
A drop of blood.[36]

MRS. F.   I ne'er offended yet!
My fault, I fear, will in my [37] brow be writ.
Women that fall, not quite bereft of grace,
Have their offences noted in their face.   160
I blush, and am asham'd. Oh, Master Wen-
    doll,
Pray God I be not born to curse your tongue,
That hath enchanted me. This maze I am
    in
I fear will prove the labyrinth of sin.

---

[28] Stigmatizing.   [29] Beholden, obligated.
[30] Acquire as an addition to.   [31] Endeavor.

[32] Notebook, tablet.   [33] Om. Q 1.
[34] To a strong feeling of pity.   [35] Divulge.
[36] It was supposed that every sigh cost the sigher's
heart a drop of blood. Wendoll is gracefully asserting
that his heart is hers.
[37] Om. Q 1.

Enter NICK [*behind*].

WEN. The path of pleasure and the gate to
　　bliss,
Which on your lips I knock at with a kiss.
NICH. I 'll kill the rogue.
WEN. Your husband is from home ; your
　　bed's no blab.
Nay, look not down and blush.
　　　　[*Exeunt* WENDOLL *and* MISTRESS
　　　　　FRANKFORD.]
NICH.　　　　　　　Zounds, I 'll stab.
Ay, Nick, was it thy chance to come just in the
　　nick?　　　　　　　　　　　　　　170
I love my master, and I hate that slave ;
I love my mistress, but these tricks I like not.
My master shall not pocket up this wrong ;
I 'll eat my fingers first. What say'st thou,
　　metal?
Does not the rascal Wendoll go on legs
That thou must cut off? Hath he not ham-
　　strings
That thou must hock? Nay, metal, thou
　　shalt stand
To all I say. I 'll henceforth turn a spy,
And watch them in their close conveyances.[38]
I never look'd for better of that rascal,　　180
Since he came miching [39] first into our house.
It is that Satan hath corrupted her,
For she was fair and chaste. I 'll have an
　　eye
In all their gestures. Thus I think of them,
If they proceed as they have done before :
Wendoll 's a knave, my mistress is a ——
　　　　　　　　　　　　　　　Exit.

[ACT III — SCENE I][1]

Enter [SIR] CHARLES [MOUNTFORD] *and* SUSAN
　　　　[*in rustic attire*].

SIR C. Sister, you see we are driven to hard
　　shift,
To keep this poor house we have left unsold.
I 'm now enforc'd to follow husbandry,
And you to milk ; and do we not live well?
Well, I thank God.
SUSAN.　　　　Oh, Brother, here 's a change,
Since old Sir Charles died in our father's house.
SIR C. All things on earth thus change,
　　some up, some down ;
Content 's a kingdom, and I wear that crown.

Enter SHAFTON, *with a* Sergeant.

SHAFT. God morrow, morrow, Sir Charles.
　　What, with your sister,
Plying your husbandry? — Sergeant, stand
　　off. —　　　　　　　　　　　　　　10
You have a pretty house here, and a garden,
And goodly ground about it. Since it lies
So near a lordship that I lately bought,
I would fain buy it of you. I will give you——
　　SIR C. Oh, pardon me ; this house succes-
　　　sively
Hath long'd [2] to me and my progenitors
Three hundred years. My great-great-grand-
　　father,
He in whom first our gentle style [3] began,
Dwelt here, and in this ground increas'd this
　　mole-hill
Unto that mountain which my father left me.
Where he, the first of all our house, begun [21
I now, the last, will end, and keep this house,
This virgin title, never yet deflow'r'd
By any unthrift of the Mountfords' line.
In brief, I will not sell it for more gold
Than you could hide or pave the ground withal.
　　SHAFT. Ha, ha ! a proud mind and a beg-
　　　gar's purse !
Where 's my three hundred pounds, beside the
　　use? [4]
I have brought it to an execution　　　29
By course of law. What, is my monies ready?
　　SIR C. An execution, sir, and never tell me
You put my bond in suit? You deal ex-
　　tremely.[5]
　　SHAFT. Sell me the land, and I 'll acquit you
　　straight.
　　SIR C. Alas, alas ! 'T is all trouble hath
　　left me
To cherish me and my poor sister's life.
If this were sold, our [names] [6] should [7] then be
　　quite
Raz'd from the beadroll [8] of gentility.
You see what hard shift we have made to keep
　　it
Allied still to our own name. This palm you see,
Labor hath glow'd within ; her silver brow, [40
That never tasted a rough winter's blast
Without a mask or fan, doth with a grace
Defy cold winter, and his storms outface.
　　SUSAN. Sir, we feed sparing, and we labor
　　hard ;
We lie uneasy, to reserve to us
And our succession this small spot of ground.

---

[38] Secret dealings.
[39] Sneaking.
[1] Before Sir Charles Mountford's house.

[2] Belonged.　　[3] Title to gentility.　　[4] Interest.
[5] With great severity.　　[6] Old eds. *meanes.*
[7] Would inevitably.　　[8] List.

SIR C. I have so bent my thoughts to husbandry
That I protest I scarcely can remember
What a new fashion is, how silk or satin   49
Feels in my hand. Why, pride is grown to us
A mere, mere stranger. I have quite forgot
The names of all that ever waited on me.
I cannot name ye any of my hounds,
Once from whose echoing mouths I heard all music
That e'er my heart desired. What should I say?
To keep this place, I have chang'd myself away.

SHAFT. Arrest him at my suit. — Actions and actions
Shall keep thee in continual bondage fast ;
Nay, more, I'll sue thee by a late appeal,[9]
And call thy former life in question.[10]   60
The keeper is my friend ; thou shalt have irons,
And usage such as I'll deny to dogs!
Away with him.

SIR C. Ye are too timorous ;[11] but trouble is my master,
And I will serve him truly. — My kind Sister,
Thy tears are of no use to mollify
This flinty man. Go to my father's brother,
My kinsmen, and allies ; entreat them for me
To ransom me from this injurious man
That seeks my ruin.

SHAFT.   Come, irons, irons! Come away!   70
I'll see thee lodg'd far from the sight of day.
                              Exeunt [all but SUSAN].

SUSAN. My heart's so hard'ned with the frost of grief,
Death cannot pierce it through. Tyrant too fell!
So lead the fiends condemned souls to hell.

Enter [SIR FRANCIS] ACTON *and* MALBY.

SIR F. Again to prison! Malby, hast thou seen
A poor slave better tortur'd? Shall we hear
The music of his voice cry from the grate,[12]
" Meat, for the Lord sake?" No, no, yet I am not

Throughly reveng'd. They say, he hath a pretty wench
To his sister ; shall I, in my mercy sake   80
To him and to his kindred, bribe the fool
To shame herself by lewd, dishonest lust?
I'll proffer largely ; but, the deed being done,
I'll smile to see her base confusion.

MAL. Methinks, Sir Francis, you are full reveng'd
For greater wrongs than he can proffer you.
See where the poor sad gentlewoman stands.

SIR. F. Ha, ha! Now will I flout her poverty,
Deride her fortunes, scoff her base estate ; [89
My very soul the name of Mountford hate.
But stay, my heart! [Oh,][13] what a look did fly
To strike my soul through with thy piercing eye.
I am enchanted ; all my spirits are fled ;
And with one glance my envious spleen[14] struck dead.

SUSAN. Acton, that seeks our blood!
                              Runs away.

SIR F.   O chaste and fair!

MAL. Sir Francis. Why, Sir Francis, in a trance?
Sir Francis, what cheer, man? Come, come, how is 't?

SIR F. Was she not fair? Or else this judging eye
Cannot distinguish beauty.

MAL.   She was fair. 99

SIR F. She was an angel in a mortal's shape,
And ne'er descended from old Mountford's line.
But soft, soft, let me call my wits together.
A poor, poor wench, to my great adversary
Sister, whose very souls denounce stern war
One against other! How now, Frank, turn'd fool
Or madman, whether? But no! Master of
My perfect senses and directest wits.
Then why should I be in this violent humor
Of passion and of love? And with a person
So different every way, and so oppos'd   110
In all contractions[15] and still-warring actions?
Fie, fie! How I dispute against my soul!
Come, come ; I'll gain her, or in her fair quest
Purchase my soul free and immortal rest.
                              [*Exeunt.*]

[9] Charge.
[10] *I.e.*, put in jeopardy the life which you formerly saved.
[11] Terrible, dreadful.
[12] Of the debtor's prison.
[13] Old eds. *or.*   [14] Malicious rage.
[15] Dealings.

[SCENE II] [16]

Enter three or four Serving Men, [*among them*
SPIGOT *the butler, and* NICHOLAS] ; *one with a
voider* [17] *and a wooden knife, to take away;
another the salt and bread ; another the tablecloth and napkins; another the carpet;* [18]
JENKIN *with two lights after them.*

JEN. So ; march in order, and retire in
battle array. My master and the guests have
supp'd already ; all 's taken away. Here, now
spread for the serving men in the hall ! — Butler, it belongs to your office.

BUT. I know it, Jenkin. What d' ye call
the gentleman that supp'd there to-night?

JEN. Who? my master?

BUT. No, no ; Master Wendoll, he 's a
daily guest. I mean the gentleman that [10
came but this afternoon.

JEN. His name is Master Cranwell. God's
light ! Hark, within there ; my master calls to
lay more billets [19] upon the fire. Come, come !
Lord, how we that are in office [20] here in the
house are troubled ! One spread the carpet in
the parlor, and stand ready to snuff the lights ;
the rest be ready to prepare their stomachs. [21]
More lights in the hall, there ! Come, Nich'las.
　　　　　　　Exeunt [*all but* NICHOLAS].

NICH. I cannot eat ; but had I Wendoll's
heart,　　　　　　　　　　　　　20
I would eat that. The rogue grows impudent ;
Oh, I have seen such vild, notorious tricks,
Ready to make my eyes dart from my head.
I 'll tell my master ; by this air, I will ;
Fall what may fall, I 'll tell him. Here he
　　comes.

Enter MASTER FRANKFORD, *as it were brushing
the crumbs from his clothes with a napkin, as
newly risen from supper.*

FRANK. Nich'las, what make you here?
　　Why are not you
At supper in the hall among your fellows?

NICH. Master, I stay'd your rising from the
　　board,
To speak with you.

FRANK. Be brief then, gentle Nich'las ; [29
My wife and guests attend [22] me in the parlor.
Why dost thou pause? Now, Nich'las, you
　　want money,
And, unthrift-like, would eat into your wages

Ere you have earn'd it. Here, sir, 's half a
　　crown ;
Play the good husband, [23] and away to supper.

NICH. [*aside*] By this hand, an honorable
　　gentleman. I will not see him
　　wrong'd. —
Sir, I have serv'd you long ; you entertain'd
　　me [24]
Seven years before your beard. You knew
　　me, sir,
Before you knew my mistress.

FRANK. What of this, good Nich'las?

NICH. I never was a make-bate [25] or a
　　knave ;　　　　　　　　　　　40
I have no fault but one : I 'm given to
　　quarrel —
But not with women. I will tell you, Master,
That which will make your heart leap from
　　your breast,
Your hair to startle from your head, your ears
　　to tingle.

FRANK. What preparation 's this to dismal
　　news?

NICH. 'Sblood, sir, I love you better than
　　your wife.
I 'll make it good.

FRANK. Y' are a knave, and I have much
　　ado
With wonted patience to contain my rage, [49
And not to break thy pate. Th' art a knave.
I 'll turn you, with your base comparisons,
Out of my doors.

NICH.　　　　Do, do ; there is not room
For Wendoll and me too both in one house.
O Master, Master, that Wendoll is a villain.

FRANK. Ay, saucy?

NICH. Strike, strike, do strike ; yet hear me.
　　I am no fool ;
I know a villain, when I see him act
Deeds of a villain. Master, Master, that base
　　slave
Enjoys my mistress, and dishonors you.

FRANK. Thou hast kill'd me with a weapon
　　whose sharp point　　　　　　60
Hath prick'd quite through and through my
　　shiv'ring heart.
Drops of cold sweat sit dangling on my
　　hairs,
Like morning's dew upon the golden flowers,
And I am plung'd into strange agonies.
What didst thou say? If any word that
　　touch'd
His credit, or her reputation,

---

[16] A room in Frankford's house.
[17] Tray or basket for clearing the table.
[18] Table-cover.　　[19] Sticks.　　[20] Service.
[21] Appetites.　　　　[22] Are waiting for.

[23] Be thrifty.　　[24] Took me into service.
[25] Trouble-maker.

It is as hard to enter my belief,
As Dives into Heaven.

NICH.   I can gain nothing ;
They are two that never wrong'd me. I knew
    before
'T was but a thankless office, and perhaps [70
As much as my service, or my life
Is worth. All this I know ; but this, and
    more,
More by a thousand dangers, could not hire me
To smother such a heinous wrong from you.
I saw, and I have said.

FRANK. [*aside*] 'T is probable. Though
    blunt, yet he is honest.
Though I durst pawn my life, and on their
    faith
Hazard the dear salvation of my soul,
Yet in my trust I may be too secure.   79
May this be true? Oh, may it? Can it be?
Is it by any wonder possible?
Man, woman, what thing mortal can we trust,
When friends and bosom wives prove so un-
    just? —
What instance [26] hast thou of this strange re-
    port?

NICH. Eyes, master, eyes.[27]

FRANK. Thy eyes may be deceiv'd, I tell
    thee ;
For should an angel from the Heavens drop
    down,
And preach this to me that thyself hast told,
He should have much ado to win belief,
In both their loves I am so confident.   90

NICH. Shall I discourse the same by circum-
    stance? [28]

FRANK. No more ! To supper, and com-
    mand your fellows
To attend us and the strangers. Not a word,
I charge thee, on thy life ! Be secret then ;
For I know nothing.

NICH. I am dumb ; and, now that I have
    eas'd my stomach,[29]
I will go fill my stomach.   *Exit.*

FRANK.   Away ; begone ! —
She is well born, descended nobly ;
Virtuous her education ; her repute
Is in the general voice of all the country [100
Honest and fair ; her carriage, her demeanor,
In all her actions that concern the love
To me her husband, modest, chaste, and godly.
Is all this seeming gold plain copper?
But he, that Judas that hath borne my purse,
And sold me for a sin ! O God ! O God !

Shall I put up [30] these wrongs? No ! Shall I
    trust
The bare report of this suspicious groom,
Before the double-gilt, the well-hatch['d][31] ore[32]
Of their two hearts? No, I will loose these
    thoughts ;   110
Distraction I will banish from my brow,
And from my looks exile sad discontent.
Their wonted favors in my tongue shall
    flow ;
Till I know all, I'll nothing seem to know. —
Lights and a table there ! Wife, Master
    Wendoll,
And gentle Master Cranwell !

Enter MISTRESS FRANKFORD, MASTER WEN-
    DOLL, MASTER CRANWELL, NICK, *and*
    JENKIN, *with cards, carpets, stools, and other
    necessaries.*

FRANK. Oh, Master Cranwell, you are a
    stranger here,
And often balk [33] my house ; faith, y' are a
    churl ! —
Now we have supp'd, a table, and to cards.

JEN. A pair [34] of cards, Nich'las, and a [120
carpet to cover the table ! Where's Cicely,
with her counters and her box? Candles and
candlesticks, there ! Fie ! We have such a
household of serving creatures ! Unless it be
Nick and I, there's not one amongst them all
that can say bo to a goose. — Well said,[35]
Nick !

            *They spread a carpet, set down
                lights and cards.*

MRS. F. Come, Master Frankford, who
shall take my part? [36]

FRANK. Marry, that will I, sweet wife.

WEN. No, by my faith, sir, when you [130
are together, I sit out. It must be Mistress
Frankford and I, or else it is no match.

FRANK. I do not like that match.

NICH. [*aside*] You have no reason, marry,
    knowing all.

FRANK. 'T is no great matter, neither. —
Come, Master Cranwell, shall you and I take
them up? [37]

CRAN. At your pleasure, sir.

FRANK. I must look to you, Master Wendoll, for you'll be playing false. Nay, [140
so will my wife, too.

NICH. [*aside*] Ay, I will be sworn she will.

---

[26] Evidence.   [27] Q₁, *Eyes, eyes.*
[28] Circumstantially.   [29] Anger.

[30] Put up with.   [31] Add. Verity.
[32] *I.e.*, the gold of noble origin. Cf. "hatchment."
[33] Shun.   [34] Pack.   [35] Well done.
[36] Be my partner.
[37] Take them on, play against them.

MRS. F. Let them that are taken false,
forfeit the set.

FRANK. Content; it shall go hard but I'll
take you.

CRAN. Gentlemen, what shall our game be?

WEN. Master Frankford, you play best at
noddy.[38]

FRANK. You shall not find it so; indeed,
you shall not.

MRS. F. I can play at nothing so well as
double-ruff.[39]

FRANK. If Master Wendoll and my wife be
together, there's no playing against them [150
at double-hand.

NICH. I can tell you, sir, the game that
Master Wendoll is best at.

WEN. What game is that, Nick?

NICH. Marry, sir, knave out of doors.

WEN. She and I will take you at lodam.[40]

MRS. F. Husband, shall we play at saint?[41]

FRANK. [aside] My saint's turn'd devil. —
No, we'll none of saint.
You're best at new-cut,[40] wife, you'll play at
that.

WEN. If you play at new-cut, I'm [160
soonest hitter of any here, for a wager.

FRANK. [aside] 'T is me they play on. —
Well, you may draw out,
For all your cunning; 't will be to your shame;
I'll teach you, at your new-cut, a new game.
Come, come.

CRAN. If you cannot agree upon the game,
To post and pair![42]

WEN. We shall be soonest pairs; and my
good host,
When he comes late home, he must kiss the
post.[43]

FRANK. Whoever wins, it shall be to thy
cost.   170

CRAN. Faith, let it be vide-ruff,[39] and let's
make honors.

FRANK. If you make honors, one thing let
me crave:
Honor the king and queen; except the knave.

WEN. Well, as you please for that. — Lift,[44]
who shall deal.

MRS. F. The least in sight. What are you,
Master Wendoll?

WEN. I am a knave.

NICH. [aside]   I'll swear it.

MRS. F.   I a queen.

FRANK. [aside] A quean,[45] thou shouldst
say. — Well, the cards are mine;
They are the grossest pair[46] that e'er I felt.

MRS. F. Shuffle; I'll cut; would I had
never dealt!

FRANK. I have lost my dealing.

WEN.   Sir, the fault's in me; 180
This queen I have more than mine own, you
see.
Give me the stock![46]

FRANK.   My mind's not on my game.
Many a deal I have lost; the more's your
shame.
You have serv'd me a bad trick, Master Wendoll.

WEN. Sir, you must take your lot. To end
this strife,
I know I have dealt better with your wife.

FRANK. Thou hast dealt falsely, then.

MRS. F. What's trumps?

WEN. Hearts. Partner, I rub.[47]

FRANK. [aside] Thou robb'st me of my soul,
of her chaste love;   190
In thy false dealing thou hast robb'd my
heart. —
Booty you play;[48] I like a loser stand,
Having no heart, or here or in my hand.
I will give o'er the set; I am not well.
Come, who will hold my cards?

MRS. F. Not well, sweet Master Frankford?
Alas, what ail you? 'T is some sudden
qualm.

WEN. How long have you been so, Master
Frankford?

FRANK. Sir, I was lusty, and I had my
health,
But I grew ill when you began to deal. — 200
Take hence this table! — Gentle Master Cran-
well,
You are welcome; see your chamber at your
pleasure.
I am sorry that this megrim takes me so,
I cannot sit and bear you company. —
Jenkin, some lights, and show him to his
chamber!

[*Exeunt* CRANWELL *and* JENKIN.]

---

[38] A game similar to cribbage. Frankford plays
on *noddy* = fool.
[39] An early variety of whist.   [40] An old card game.
[41] How *cent* was played is unknown; the winning
sum of points was one hundred.
[42] Apparently a relatively simple game, though how
it was played is not known.
[43] Be shut out.
[44] Cut (to determine).
[45] Hussy.   [46] Pack.
[47] Probably = "ruff", *i.e..*, take the four cards
not distributed by the dealer; they went to the
holder of the ace of trumps. (Ward.)
[48] You are playing in league with a confederate
to victimize another player.

MRS. F. A nightgown [49] for my husband,
  quickly there.
It is some rheum or cold.
WEN.   Now, in good faith,
This illness you have got by sitting late
Without your gown.
FRANK.   I know it, Master Wendoll.
Go, go to bed, lest you complain like me. —
Wife, prithee, Wife, into my bedchamber. [211
The night is raw and cold, and rheumatic.[50]
Leave me my gown and light ; I 'll walk away
  my fit.
WEN. Sweet sir, good night.
FRANK. My self, good night.
                    [*Exit* WENDOLL.]
MRS. F.   Shall I attend you, Husband ?
FRANK. No, gentle Wife, thou 't catch cold
  in thy head.
Prithee, begone, sweet ; I 'll make haste to
  bed.
MRS. F. No sleep will fasten on mine eyes,
  you know,
Until you come.   *Exit.*
FRANK.   Sweet Nan, I prithee, go ! —
I have bethought me : get me by degrees [220
The keys of all my doors, which I will mold
In wax, and take their fair impression,
To have by them new keys. This being com-
  pass'd,
At a set hour a letter shall be brought me,
And when they think they may securely
  play,
They nearest are to danger. — Nick, I must
  rely
Upon thy trust and faithful secrecy.
NICH. Build on my faith.
FRANK.   To bed, then, not to rest ;
Care lodges in my brain, grief in my breast.
                    [*Exeunt.*]

[SCENE III] [51]

Enter Sir Charles his sister [SUSAN], OLD
  MOUNTFORD, SANDY, RODER, *and* TIDY.

OLD MOUNT. You say my nephew is in great
  distress :
Who brought it to him but his own lewd
  life?
I cannot spare a cross. I must confess,
He was my brother's son ; why, Niece, what
  then ?
This is no world in which to pity men.

SUSAN. I was not born a beggar, though his
  extremes [52]
Enforce this language from me, I protest
No fortune of mine own [53] could lead my tongue
To this base key. I do beseech you, Uncle,
For the name's sake, for Christianity, —   10
Nay, for God's sake, to pity his distress.
He is deni'd the freedom of the prison,
And in the hole [54] is laid with men condemn'd ;
Plenty he hath of nothing but of irons,
And it remains in you to free him thence.
OLD MOUNT. Money I cannot spare ; men
  should take heed.
He lost my kindred when he fell to need. [*Exit.*]
SUSAN. Gold is but earth ; thou earth
  enough shalt have,
When thou hast once took measure of thy
  grave. —
You know me, Master Sandy, and my suit. [20
SANDY. I knew you, lady, when the old
  man liv'd ;
I knew you ere your brother sold his land.
Then you were Mistress Sue, trick'd up in
  jewels ;
Then you sung well, play'd sweetly on the
  lute ; [55]
But now I neither know you nor your suit.
                    [*Exit.*]
SUSAN. You, Master Roder, was my
  brother's tenant ;
Rent-free he plac'd you in that wealthy farm,
Of which you are possess'd.
RODER.   True, he did ;
And have I not there dwelt still for his sake?
I have some business now ; but, without
  doubt,   30
They that have hurl'd him in will help him
  out.   *Exit.*
SUSAN. Cold comfort still. What say you,
  cousin Tidy?
TIDY. I say this comes of roisting,[56] swag-
  g'ring.
Call not me cousin ; each man for himself !
Some men are born to mirth, and some to sor-
  row :
I am no cousin unto them that borrow. *Exit.*
SUSAN. O Charity, why art thou fled to
  Heaven,
And left all things on this earth uneven?
Their scoffing answers I will ne'er return,
But to myself his grief in silence mourn.   40

[49] Dressing-gown.
[50] Accented on the first syllable.
[51] Unlocated ; perhaps before old Mountford's house.
[52] Extremities.   [53] Q₁ omits *own*.
[54] One of the worst apartments in the Counter ; hence = worst sort of prison-cell.
[55] So Q₂ ; Q₁ *flute.*   [56] Bullying.

Enter SIR FRANCIS *and* MALBY.

SIR F. She is poor ; I'll therefore tempt her
    with this gold. —
Go, Malby, in my name deliver it,
And I will stay thy answer.
    [MAL.] Fair mistress, as I understand your
      grief
Doth grow from want, so I have here in
    store
A means to furnish you, a bag of gold,
Which to your hands I freely tender you.
    SUSAN. I thank you, Heavens. I thank
      you, gentle sir.
God make me able to requite this favor.
    MAL. This gold Sir Francis Acton sends by
      me,   50
And prays you ——
    SUSAN. Acton? O God! That name I'm
      born to curse.
Hence, bawd ; hence, broker! See, I spurn
    his gold.
My honor never shall for gain be sold.
    SIR F. Stay, lady, stay!
    SUSAN.   From you I'll posting hie,
Even as the doves from feather'd eagles fly.
                                  Exit.
    SIR F. She hates my name, my face ; how
      should I woo?
I am disgrac'd in every thing I do.
The more she hates me, and disdains my
    love,
The more I am rapt ⁵⁷ in admiration   60
Of her divine and chaste perfections.
Woo her with gifts I cannot, for all gifts
Sent in my name she spurns ; with looks I can
    not,
For she abhors my sight ; nor yet with let-
    ters,
For none she will receive. How then? how
    then?
Well, I will fasten such a kindness on her
As shall o'ercome her hate and conquer it.
Sir Charles, her brother, lies in execution ⁵⁸
For a great sum of money ; and, besides,
The appeal is sued still for my huntsmen's ⁵⁹
    death,   70
Which only I have power to reverse.
In her I'll bury all my hate of him. —
Go seek the keeper, Malby ; bring me to
    him.
To save his body, I his debts will pay ;
To save his life, I his appeal will stay. [*Exeunt.*]

⁵⁷ Old eds. *wrapt.*
⁵⁸ Legal punishment.
⁵⁹ So Q₂ ; Q₁ *huntsmans.*

[ACT IV — SCENE I] [1]

Enter SIR CHARLES [MOUNTFORD] *in prison,
with irons, his feet bare, his garments all
ragged and torn.*

SIR C. Of all on the earth's face most miser-
    able,
Breathe in this hellish dungeon thy laments !
Thus like a slave ragg'd, like a felon gyv'd.
O unkind uncle ! O my friends ingrate ! [2]
That hurls thee headlong to this base estate. —
Unthankful kinsmen ! Mountfords all too
    base,
To let thy name lie fetter'd in disgrace.
A thousand deaths here in this grave I die ;
Fear, hunger, sorrow, cold, all threat my death,
And join together to deprive my breath.   10
But that which most torments me, my dear
    sister
Hath left [3] to visit me, and from my friends
Hath brought no hopeful answer ; therefore I
Divine they will not help my misery.
If it be so, shame, scandal, and contempt
Attend their covetous thoughts ; need make
    their graves.
Usurers they live, and may they die like slaves !

Enter Keeper.

    KEEP. Knight, be of comfort, for I bring
      thee freedom
From all thy troubles.
    SIR C.   Then I am doom'd to die ;
Death is the end of all calamity.   20
    KEEP. Live ! Your appeal is stay'd ; the
      execution
Of all your debts discharg'd ; your creditors
Even to the utmost penny satisfied.
In sign whereof your shackles I knock off.
You are not left so much indebted to us
As for your fees ; all is discharg'd ; all paid.
Go freely to your house, or where you please ;
After long miseries, embrace your ease.
    SIR C. Thou grumblest out the sweetest
      music to me
That ever organ play'd. — Is this a dream? 30
Or do my waking senses apprehend
The pleasing taste of these applausive [4] news?
Slave that I was, to wrong such honest friends,
My loving kinsmen, and my near allies.
Tongue, I will bite thee for the scandal breath
Against such faithful kinsmen ; they are all

¹ York Castle.
² Emend. Editor ; this and the following line are
transposed in old eds.
³ Ceased.   ⁴ Agreeable.

Compos'd of pity and compassion,
Of melting charity and of moving ruth.
That which I spake before was in my rage ;
They are my friends, the mirrors of this
    age,   40
Bounteous and free.   The noble Mountfords'
    race
Ne'er bred a covetous thought or humor base.

Enter SUSAN.

SUSAN. [*aside*] I cannot longer stay from
    visiting
My woful brother.   While I could, I kept
My hapless tidings from his hopeful ear.
SIR C. Sister, how much am I indebted to
    thee
And to thy travail !
SUSAN.   What, at liberty?
SIR C. Thou seest I am, thanks to thy in-
    dustry.
Oh, unto which of all my courteous friends
Am I thus bound?   My uncle Mountford, he
Even of an infant lov'd me ; was it he?   51
So did my cousin Tidy ; was it he?
So Master Roder, Master Sandy, too.
Which of all these did this high kindness do?
SUSAN. Charles, can you mock me in your
    poverty,
Knowing your friends deride your misery?
Now, I protest I stand so much amaz'd,
To see your bonds free, and your irons knock'd
    off,
That I am rapt [5] into a maze of wonder ;
The rather for I know not by what means [60
This happiness hath chanc'd.
SIR C.   Why, by my uncle,
My cousins, and my friends ; who else, I pray,
Would take upon them all my debts to pay?
SUSAN. Oh, Brother ! they are men all of
    flint,
Pictures of marble,[6] and as void of pity
As [chafed] [7] bears.   I begg'd, I sued, I kneel'd,
Laid open all your griefs and miseries,
Which they derided ; more than that, deni'd us
A part in their alliance ; but, in pride,
Said that our kindred with our plenty di'd. [70
SIR C. Drudges too much,[8] what did they?
    Oh, known evil !
Rich fly the poor, as good men shun the Devil.
Whence should my freedom come?   Of whom
    alive,
Saving of those, have I deserved so well?

Guess, Sister, call to mind, remember [9] me.
These I have rais'd, they follow the world's
    guise :
Whom rich in [10] honor, they in woe despise.
SUSAN. My wits have lost themselves ; let 's
    ask the keeper.
SIR C. Jailer.
KEEP. At hand, sir.   80
SIR C. Of courtesy resolve me one demand.
What was he took the burthen of my debts,
From off my back, stay'd my appeal to death,
Discharg'd my fees, and brought me liberty?
KEEP. A courteous knight, one call'd Sir
    Francis Acton.
SIR C. Ha ! Acton ! O me, more dis-
    tress'd in this
Than all my troubles.   Hale me back,
Double my irons, and my sparing meals
Put into halves, and lodge me in a dungeon
More deep, more dark, more cold, more com-
    fortless.   90
By Acton freed !   Not all thy manacles
Could fetter so my heels, as this one word
Hath thrall'd my heart ; and it must now lie
    bound
In more strict prison than thy stony gaol.
I am not free, I go but under bail.
KEEP. My charge is done, sir, now I have
    my fees.
As we get little, we will nothing leese.[11] [*Exit.*]
SIR C. By Acton freed, my dangerous oppo-
    site ! [12]
Why, to what end?   On what occasion?   Ha !
Let me forget the name of enemy,   100
And with indifference balance [13] this high
    favor !
Ha !
SUSAN. [*aside*] His love to me ; upon my
    soul, 't is so !
That is the root from whence these strange
    things grow.
SIR C. Had this proceeded from my father,
    he
That by the law of Nature is most bound
In offices of love, it had deserv'd
My best employment to requite that grace.
Had it proceeded from my friends, or him,
From them this action had deserv'd my
    life —   110
And from a stranger more, because from such
There is less execution [14] of good deeds.
But he, nor father, nor ally, nor friend,

---

[5] Old eds. *wrap'd.*   [6] Statues.
[7] Conj. Miss Bates ; Q₁ *chased;* Q₂ *chaced.*
[8] Too base in their conduct.   (Ward.)

[9] Remind.   [10] Neilson emends *they.*
[11] Lose.   [12] Enemy.   [13] Impartially weigh.
[14] Collier unnecessarily proposes *expectation.*

More than a stranger, both remote in blood,
And in his heart oppos'd my enemy,
That this high bounty should proceed from
 him —
Oh, there I lose myself. What should I say,
What think, what do, his bounty to repay?
 SUSAN. You wonder, I am sure, whence this
  strange kindness   119
Proceeds in Acton. I will tell you, Brother.
He dotes on me, and oft hath sent me gifts,
Letters, and tokens ; I refus'd them all.
 SIR C. I have enough, though poor ; my
  heart is set,
In one rich gift to pay back all my debt.
            Exeunt.

[SCENE II] [15]

Enter FRANKFORD *and* NICK, *with keys and a
 letter in his hand.*

 FRANK. This is the night that I must play
  my part,[16]
To try two seeming angels. — Where's my
 keys?
 NICH. They are made according to your
  mold in wax.
I bade the smith be secret, gave him money,
And here they are. The letter, sir.
 FRANK. True, take it, there it is ;
And when thou seest me in my pleasant's[t]
 vein,
Ready to sit to supper, bring it me.
 NICH. I'll do't ; make no more question
  but I'll do't.   *Exit.*

Enter MISTRESS FRANKFORD, CRANWELL,
 WENDOLL, *and* JENKIN.

MRS. F. Sirrah, 't is six a'clock already
 struck ;   10
Go bid them spread the cloth, and serve in
 supper.
 JEN. It shall be done, forsooth. Mistress,
where's Spigot, the butler, to give us our [17]
salt and trenchers?
 WEN. We that have been a-hunting all the
  day
Come with prepared stomachs. — Master
 Frankford,
We wish'd you at our sport.
 FRANK. My heart was with you, and my
  mind was on you. —
Fie, Master Cranwell ; you are still thus
 sad. —

A stool, a stool ! Where's Jenkin, and where's
 Nick?   20
'T is supper time at least an hour ago. —
What's the best news abroad?
 WEN. I know none good.
 FRANK. [*aside*] But I know too much
  bad.

Enter [SPIGOT *the*] *butler and* JENKIN, *with a
 tablecloth, bread, trenchers, and salt;* [*then
 exeunt*].

 CRAN. Methinks, sir, you might have that
  interest
In [18] your wife's brother, to be more remiss [19]
In this hard dealing against poor Sir Charles,
Who, as I hear, lies in York Castle, needy
And in great want.
 FRANK. Did not more weighty business of
  mine own
Hold me away, I would have labor'd peace [30
Betwixt them with all care ; indeed I would,
 sir.
 MRS. F. I'll write unto my brother ear-
  nestly
In that behalf.
 WEN.   A charitable deed,
And will beget the good opinion
Of all your friends that love you, Mistress [20]
 Frankford.
 FRANK. That's you, for one ; I know you
  love Sir Charles,
And my wife, too, well.
 WEN.   He deserves the love
Of all true gentlemen ; be yourselves judge.
 FRANK. But supper, ho ! — Now, as thou
  lov'st me, Wendoll,   39
Which I am sure thou doest, be merry, pleasant,
And frolic it to-night. — Sweet Master Cran-
 well,
Do you the like. — Wife, I protest, my heart
Was ne'er more bent on sweet alacrity.[21]
Where be those lazy knaves to serve in supper?

Enter NICK.

 NICH. Sir, here's a letter.
 FRANK.   Whence comes it, and who
  brought it?
 NICH. A stripling that below attends your
  answer,
And, as he tells me, it is sent from York.
 FRANK. Have him into the cellar ; let him
  taste
A cup of our March beer ; go, make him drink.

---

[15] A room in Frankford's house.
[16] Q₁ *and I must play the trick.*
[17] Q₁ *out.*

NICH. I'll make him drunk, if he be a
Trojan.[22]   50
FRANK. My boots and spurs! Where's
Jenkin? God forgive me,
How I neglect my business! — Wife, look
here;
I have a matter to be tri'd to-morrow
By eight a'clock; and my attorney writes me
I must be there betimes with evidence,
Or it will go against me. Where's my boots?

Enter JENKIN, *with boots and spurs.*

MRS. F. I hope your business craves no
such dispatch,
That you must ride to-night.
WEN. [*aside*]   I hope it doth.
FRANK. God's me! No such dispatch? —
Jenkin, my boots! Where's Nick? Saddle
my roan,   60
And the grey dapple for himself. — Content
ye;
It much concerns me. — Gentle Master Cran-
well,
And Master Wendoll, in my absence use
The very ripest pleasures of my house.
WEN. Lord, Master Frankford, will you
ride to-night?
The ways are dangerous.
FRANK.   Therefore will I ride
Appointed[23] well; and so shall Nick, my
man.
MRS. F. I'll call you up by five a'clock to-
morrow.
FRANK. No, by my faith, wife, I'll not trust
to that;
'T is not such easy rising in a morning   70
From one I love so dearly. No, by my faith,
I shall not leave so sweet a bedfellow,
But with much pain. You have made me a
sluggard
Since I first knew you.
MRS. F.   Then, if you needs will go
This dangerous evening, Master Wendoll,
Let me entreat you bear him company.
WEN. With all my heart, sweet mistress. —
My boots, there!
FRANK. Fie, fie, that for my private bus-
iness
I should disease[24] my friend, and be a trouble
To the whole house. — Nick!
NICH.   Anon,[25] sir. [80
FRANK. Bring forth my gelding. — As you
love me, sir,

Use no more words. — A hand, good Master
Cranwell.
CRAN. Sir, God be your good speed.
FRANK. Good night, sweet Nan; nay, nay,
a kiss, and part. —
[*aside*] Dissembling lips, you suit not with my
heart.
                              Exit [*with* NICHOLAS].
WEN. [*aside*] How business, time, and hours
all gracious prove,
And are the furtherers to my newborn love! —
I am husband now in Master Frankford's place,
And must command the house. My pleas-
ure is
We will not sup abroad so publicly,   90
But in your private chamber, Mistress Frank-
ford.
MRS. F. [*aside to* WENDOLL] Oh, sir! you
are too public in your love,
And Master Frankford's wife ——
CRAN.   Might I crave favor,
I would entreat you I might see my chamber.
I am on the sudden grown exceeding ill,
And would be spar'd from supper.
WEN.   Light there, ho! —
See you want nothing, sir, for if you do,
You injure that good man, and wrong me too.
CRAN. I will make bold; good night.
                                        Exit.
WEN.   How all conspire
To make our bosom[26] sweet, and full entire.
Come, Nan, I prythee, let us sup within. [101
MRS. F. Oh! what a clog unto the soul is
sin!
We pale offenders are still full of fear;
Every suspicious eye brings danger near;
When they whose clear heart from offence
are free
Despise report, base scandals do[27] outface,
And stand at mere defiance with disgrace.
WEN. Fie, fie! You talk too like a Puritan.
MRS. F. You have tempted me to mischief,
Master Wendoll;
I have done I know not what. Well, you
plead custom;   110
That which for want of wit I granted erst,
I now must yield through fear. Come, come,
let's in;
Once o'er shoes, we are straight o'er head in
sin.
WEN. My jocund soul is joyful beyond
measure;
I'll be profuse in Frankford's richest treas-
ure.   *Exeunt*

---

[22] A regular toper. [23] Armed.
[24] Incommode. [25] At once.
[26] Intimacy. [27] So Q 2; Q 1 to.

[SCENE III] [28]

Enter CICELY, JENKIN, [SPIGOT *the*] *butler,*
and other Serving Men.

JEN. My mistress and Master Wendoll, my
master, sup in her chamber to-night. Cicely,
you are preferr'd,[29] from being the cook, to be
chambermaid. Of all the loves betwixt thee
and me, tell me what thou think'st of this?

CIC. Mum; there's an old proverb: when
the cat's away, the mouse may play.

JEN. Now you talk of a cat, Cicely, I smell
a rat.

CIC. Good words, Jenkin, lest you be [10
call'd to answer them.

JEN. Why, God make my mistress an
honest[30] woman! Are not these good words?
Pray God my new master play not the knave
with my old master! Is there any hurt in
this? God send no villainy intended; and if
they do sup together, pray God they do not lie
together! God make my mistress chaste, and
make us all His servants! What harm is there
in all this? Nay, more; here is my hand, [20
thou shalt never have my heart, unless thou
say, Amen.

CIC. Amen, I pray God, I say.

Enter Serving Man.

SERVING MAN. My mistress sends that you
should make less noise, to lock up the doors,
and see the household all got to bed. You,
Jenkin, for this night are made the porter, to
see the gates shut in.

JEN. Thus by little and little I creep into
office. Come, to kennel, my masters, to
kennel; 't is eleven a'clock already.   31

SERVING MAN. When you have lock'd the
gates in, you must send up the keys to my
mistress.

CIC. Quickly, for God's sake, Jenkin; for I
must carry them. I am neither pillow nor
bolster, but I know more than both.

JEN. To bed, good Spigot; to bed, good
honest serving creatures; and let us sleep as
snug as pigs in pease-straw!   40

Exeunt.

[SCENE IV] [31]

Enter FRANKFORD *and* NICK.

FRANK. Soft, soft. We have tied our
geldings to a tree,

Two flight-shoot [32] off, lest by their thundering
hoofs

They blab our coming. Hear'st thou no noise?

NICH. Hear? I hear nothing but the owl
and you.

FRANK. So; now my watch's hand points
upon twelve,

And it is just midnight. Where are my keys?

NICH. Here, sir.

FRANK. This is the key that opes my outward gate;

This is the hall door; this, my withdrawing-
chamber;

But this, that door that's bawd unto my
shame,   10

Fountain and spring of all my bleeding
thoughts,

Where the most hallowed order and true knot

Of nuptial sanctity hath been profan'd:

It leads to my polluted bedchamber,

Once my terrestrial Heaven, now my earth's
hell,

The place where sins in all their ripeness
dwell.—

But I forget myself; now to my gate!

NICH. It must ope with far less noise than

Cripplegate, or your plot's dash'd.

FRANK. So; reach me my dark lantern to
the rest.[33]   20

Tread softly, softly.

NICH.   I will walk on eggs this pace.

FRANK. A general silence hath surpris'd
the house,

And this is the last door. Astonishment,

Fear, and amazement beat upon [34] my heart,

Even as a madman beats upon a drum.

Oh, keep my eyes, you Heavens, before I enter,

From any sight that may transfix my soul;

Or, if there be so black a spectacle,

Oh, strike mine eyes stark blind; or, if not so,

Lend me such patience to digest my grief, [30

That I may keep this white and virgin hand

From any violent outrage, or red murder.

And with that prayer I enter.

[Exit.]

NICH.   Here's a circumstance,[35] indeed!

A man may be made a cuckold in the time

He's about it. An the case were mine,

As 't is my master's, 'sblood! (that he makes
me swear!),

I would have plac'd his action,[36] enter'd there;

I would, I would!

[*Enter* FRANKFORD.]

FRANK.   Oh! oh!

NICH.   Master! 'Sblood! Master,
     Master!

FRANK. O me unhappy! I have found
     them lying
Close in each other's arms, and fast asleep. [40
But that I would not damn two precious souls,
Bought with my Savior's blood, and send
     them, laden
With all their scarlet sins upon their backs,
Unto a fearful judgment, their two lives
Had met upon my rapier.

NICH. Master, what, have you left them
     sleeping still?
Let me go wake 'em.

FRANK.   Stay, let me pause awhile. —
O God, O God, that it were possible
To undo things done; to call back yesterday;
That Time could turn up his swift sandy glass,
To untell [37] the days, and to redeem these
     hours.   51
Or that the sun
Could, rising from the west, draw his coach
     backward,
Take from th' account of time so many min-
     utes,
Till he had all these seasons call'd again,
Those minutes, and those actions done in them,
Even from her first offence; that I might take
     her
As spotless as an angel in my arms.
But, oh! I talk of things impossible,
And cast beyond the moon. God give me
     patience;   60
For I will in, and wake them.
                                              Exit.

NICH.   Here's patience perforce.
He needs must trot afoot that tires his horse.

Enter WENDOLL, *running over the stage in a
     night-gown,*[38] [FRANKFORD] *after him with his
     sword drawn; the maid*[39] *in her smock stays
     his hand, and clasps hold on him.   He pauses
     for awhile.*

FRANK. I thank thee, maid; thou, like an
     angel's hand,
Hast stay'd me from a bloody sacrifice.[40] —
Go, villain; and my wrongs sit on thy soul
As heavy as this grief doth upon mine.
When thou record'st my many courtesies,

[37] Un-number.   [38] Dressing-gown.
[39] Presumably Cicely.
[40] Alluding to the purposed sacrifice of Isaac by
Abraham.

And shalt compare them with thy treacherous
     heart,
Lay them together, weigh them equally —
'T will be revenge enough.   Go, to thy friend
A Judas; pray, pray, lest I live to see   71
Thee, Judas-like, hang'd on an elder tree.

Enter MISTRESS FRANKFORD *in her smock,
     night-gown, and night-attire.*

MRS. F. Oh, by what word, what title, or
     what name,
Shall I entreat your pardon?   Pardon! oh,
I am as far from hoping such sweet grace,
As Lucifer from Heaven.   To call you hus-
     band, —
O me, most wretched, I have lost that name;
I am no more your wife.

NICH.   'Sblood, sir, she swoons.[41]

FRANK. Spare thou thy tears, for I will weep
     for thee;
And keep thy count'nance, for I'll blush for
     thee.   80
Now I protest I think 't is I am tainted,
For I am most asham'd; and 't is more hard
For me to look upon thy guilty face
Than on the sun's clear brow.   What, would'st
     thou speak?

MRS. F. I would I had no tongue, no ears,
     no eyes,
No apprehension, no capacity.
When do you spurn me like a dog? when tread
     me
Under feet? when drag me by the hair?
Though I deserve a thousand thousand-fold
More than you can inflict — yet, once my
     husband,   90
For womanhood, to which I am [a shame],[42]
Though once an ornament — even for His
     sake,
That hath redeem'd our souls, mark not my
     face,
Nor hack me with your sword; but let me go
Perfect and undeformed to my tomb.
I am not worthy that I should prevail
In the least suit; no, not to speak to you,
Nor look on you, nor to be in your presence;
Yet, as an abject,[43] this one suit I crave;
This granted, I am ready for my grave.   100

FRANK. My God, with patience arm me. —
     Rise, nay, rise,
And I'll debate with thee.   Was it for want
Thou play'dst the strumpet?   Wast thou not
     suppli'd

[41] Old eds. *sounds.*   [42] Old eds. *asham'd.*
[43] Outcast.

With every pleasure, fashion, and new toy,
Nay, even beyond my calling? [44]
    Mrs. F.   I was.
    Frank. Was it, then, disability in me ;
Or in thine eye seem'd he a properer [45] man?
    Mrs. F. Oh, no.
    Frank.   Did not I lodge thee in my
        bosom?
Wear thee in my heart?
    Mrs. F.   You did.
    Frank. I did, indeed ; witness my tears, I
    did. —   110
Go, bring my infants hither. —
           [Two Children *are brought in.]*
                 O Nan, O Nan,
If neither [46] fear of shame, regard of honor,
The blemish of my house, nor my dear love,
Could have withheld thee from so lewd a
    fact ; [47]
Yet for these infants, these young, harmless
    souls,
On whose white brows thy shame is character'd,
And grows in greatness as they wax in years —
Look but on them, and melt away in tears ! —
Away with them ; lest, as her spotted body
Hath stain'd their names with stripe of bas-
    tardy,   120
So her adulterous breath may blast their
    spirits
With her infectious thoughts. Away with
    them.   *[The* Children *are taken out.]*
    Mrs. F. In this one life, I die ten thousand
    deaths.
    Frank. Stand up, stand up ; I will do
    nothing rashly.
I will retire awhile into my study,
And thou shalt hear thy sentence presently.
                        Exit.
    Mrs. F. 'T is welcome, be it death. O me,
    base strumpet,
That, having such a husband, such sweet chil-
    dren,
Must enjoy neither ! Oh, to redeem my
    honor,
I would have this hand cut off, these my
    breasts sear'd ;   130
Be rack'd, strappado'd, put to any torment.
Nay, to whip but this scandal out, I would
    hazard
The rich and dear redemption of my soul.
He cannot be so base as to forgive me,
Nor I so shameless to accept his pardon.
O, women, women, you that yet have kept

Your holy matrimonial vow unstain'd,
Make me your instance ; [48] when you tread
    awry,
Your sins, like mine, will on your conscience
    lie.

Enter Cicely, Spigot, *all the* Serving Men, *and*
    Jenkin, *as newly come out of bed.*

    All. O, Mistress, Mistress ! What have
    you done, Mistress?   140
    Nich. What a caterwauling keep you here.
    Jen. O Lord, Mistress, how comes this to
pass? My master is run away in his shirt,
and never so much as call'd me to bring his
clothes after him.
    Mrs. F. See what guilt is ! Here stand I
    in this place,
Asham'd to look my servants in the face.

Enter Master Frankford *and* Cranwell ;
    whom seeing, she falls on her knees.

    Frank. My words are regist'red in Heaven
    already.
With patience hear me. I 'll not martyr thee,
Nor mark thee for a strumpet ; but with usage
Of more humility torment thy soul,   151
And kill thee even with kindness.
    Cran. Master Frankford ——
    Frank. Good Master Cranwell. — Woman,
    hear thy judgment.
Go make thee ready in thy best attire ;
Take with thee all thy gowns, all thy apparel ;
Leave nothing that did ever call thee mistress,
Or by whose sight, being left here in the house,
I may remember such a woman by.
Choose thee a bed and hangings for thy
    chamber ;
Take with thee every thing which hath thy
    mark,   161
And get thee to my manor seven mile off,
Where live ; 't is thine ; I freely give it thee.
My tenants by [49] shall furnish thee with wains
To carry all thy stuff within two hours ;
No longer will I limit [50] thee my sight.
Choose which of all my servants thou lik'st
    best,
And they are thine to attend thee.
    Mrs. F.   A mild sentence.
    Frank. But, as thou hop'st for Heaven, as
    thou believ'st
Thy name's recorded in the book of life,   170
I charge thee never after this sad day
To see me, or to meet me ; or to send,

By word or writing, gift or otherwise,
To move me, by thyself, or by thy friends ;
Nor challenge [51] any part in my two children.
So farewell, Nan ; for we will henceforth be
As we had never seen, ne'er more shall see.

 Mrs. F. How full my heart is, in my eyes
  appears ;
What wants in words, I will supply in tears.

 Frank. Come, take your coach, your stuff ;
  all must along.   180
Servants and all make ready ; all begone. —
It was thy hand cut two hearts out of one.

          [Exeunt.]

   [ACT V — Scene I] [1]

Enter Sir Charles [Mountford], *gentlemanlike, and* [Susan] *his sister, gentlewoman-like.*

 Susan. Brother, why have you trick'd [2]
  me like a bride,
Bought me this gay attire, these ornaments?
Forget you our estate, our poverty?

 Sir C. Call me not brother, but imagine
  me
Some barbarous outlaw, or uncivil kern ; [3]
For if thou shutt'st thy eye, and only hear'st
The words that I shall utter, thou shalt judge
  me
Some staring [4] ruffian, not thy brother Charles.
Oh, Sister —

 Susan. Oh, Brother, what doth this strange
  language mean?   10

 Sir C. Dost love me, Sister? Wouldst
  thou see me live
A bankrupt beggar in the world's disgrace,
And die indebted to my enemies?
Wouldst thou behold me stand like a huge beam
In the world's eye, a byword and a scorn?
It lies in thee of these to acquit me free,
And all my debt I may outstrip by thee.

 Susan. By me ! Why, I have nothing,
  nothing left ;
I owe even for the clothes upon my back ;
I am not worth——

 Sir C.   O Sister, say not so ; 20
It lies in you my downcast state to raise,
To make me stand on even points with the
  world.
Come, Sister, you are rich ; indeed you are !
And in your pow'r you have, without delay
Acton's five hundred pound back to repay.

 Susan. Till now I had thought y' had lov'd
  me. By my honor,
Which I have [5] kept as spotless as the moon,
I ne'er was mistress of that single doit [6]
Which I reserv'd not to supply your wants !
And d' ye think that I would hoard from
  you?   30
Now, by my hopes in Heaven, knew I the
  means
To buy you from the slavery of your debts,
Especially from Acton, whom I hate,
I would redeem it with my life or blood.

 Sir C. I challenge it, and, kindred set
  apart,
Thus, ruffian-like, I lay siege to your heart.
What do I owe to Acton?

 Susan. Why, some five hundred pounds ;
  towards which, I swear,
In all the world I have not one denier. [7]

 Sir C. It will not prove so. Sister, now
  resolve [8] me :   40
What do you think (and speak your conscience)
Would Acton give, might he enjoy your bed?

 Susan. He would not shrink to spend a
  thousand pound
To give the Mountfords' name so deep a
  wound.

 Sir C. A thousand pound ! I but five hundred owe :
Grant him your bed, he's paid with int'rest
  so.

 Susan. Oh, Brother !

 Sir C.   Oh, Sister, only this one way,
With that rich jewel you my debts may
  pay.
In speaking this my cold heart shakes with
  shame ;
Nor do I woo you in a brother's name, 50
But in a stranger's. Shall I die in debt
To Acton, my grand foe, and you still wear
The precious jewel that he holds so dear?

 Susan. My honor I esteem as dear and precious
As my redemption. [9]

 Sir C.   I esteem you, Sister,
As dear, for so dear prizing it.

 Susan.   Will Charles
Have me cut off my hands, and send them
  Acton?
Rip up my breast, and with my bleeding heart
Present him as a token?

---

[51] Claim.
[1] Before the house of Sir Francis Acton.
[2] Decked. [3] Peasant. [4] Wild.

[5] So Q [2] ; Q [1] *had.*
[6] A trifling Dutch coin, worth about one cent.
[7] Penny. [8] Tell, assure. [9] Salvation.

SIR C.   Neither, Sister ; [10]
But hear me in my strange assertion.   60
Thy honor and my soul are equal in my re-
    gard ;
Nor will thy brother Charles survive thy
    shame.
His kindness, like a burden, hath surcharged
    me,
And under his good deeds I stooping go,
Not with an upright soul. Had I remain'd
In prison still, there doubtless I had died.
Then unto him that freed me from that prison
Still do I owe that life. What mov'd my foe
To enfranchise me? 'T was, Sister, for your
    love ;
With full five hundred pounds he bought your
    love ;   70
And shall he not enjoy it? Shall the weight
Of all this heavy burden lean on me,
And will not you bear part? You did par-
    take
The joy of my release ; will you not stand
In joint-bond bound to satisfy the debt?
Shall I be only charg'd?
    SUSAN.   But that I know
These arguments come from an honor'd mind,
As in your most extremity of need
Scorning to stand in debt to one you hate, —
Nay, rather would engage your unstain'd
    honor,   80
Than to be held ingrate, — I should condemn
    you.
I see your resolution, and assent ;
So Charles will have me, and I am content.
    SIR C. For this I trick'd you up.
    SUSAN.   But here 's a knife,
To save mine honor, shall slice out my life.
    SIR C. I know thou pleasest me a thousand
    times
More in that resolution than thy grant. —
Observe her love ; to soothe [them in] [11] my suit,
Her honor she will hazard, though not lose ;
To bring me out of debt, her rigorous hand [90
Will pierce her heart. O wonder ! that will
    choose,
Rather than stain her blood, her life to lose.
Come, you sad sister to a woful brother,
This is the gate. I 'll bear him such a present,
Such an acquittance for the knight to seal,
As will amaze his senses, and surprise
With admiration [12] all his fantasies. [13]

[10] So Q 2 ; Q 1 *Jane.*
[11] So Q 1 ; Q 2 *to soorh it to.*
[12] Wonder.
[13] All his powers of apprehension.

Enter [SIR FRANCIS] ACTON *and* MALBY.

    SUSAN. Before his unchaste thoughts shall
    seize on me,
'T is here shall my imprison'd soul set free.
    SIR F. How ! Mountford with his sister,
    hand in hand.   100
What miracle 's afoot?
    MAL.   It is a sight
Begets in me much admiration.
    SIR C. Stand not amaz'd to see me thus
    attended.
Acton, I owe thee money, and, being unable
To bring thee the full sum in ready coin,
Lo ! for thy more assurance, here 's a pawn —
My sister, my dear sister, whose chaste honor
I prize above a million. Here ! nay, take her ;
She 's worth your money, man ; do not for-
    sake her.
    SIR F. I would he were in earnest.   110
    SUSAN. Impute it not to my immodesty.
My brother, being rich in nothing else
But in his interest that he hath in me,
According to his poverty hath brought you
Me, all his store ; whom, howsoe'er you prize,
As forfeit to your hand, he values highly,
And would not sell, but to acquit your debt,
For any emperor's ransom.
    SIR F.   Stern heart, relent ;
Thy former cruelty at length repent.
Was ever known, in any former age,   120
Such honorable wrested [14] courtesy?
Lands, honors, life, [15] and all the world forego,
Rather than stand engag'd to such a foe.
    SIR C. Acton, she is too poor to be thy
    bride,
And I too much oppos'd to be thy brother.
There, take her to thee ; if thou hast the
    heart
To seize her as a rape or lustful prey,
To blur our house, that never yet was stain'd,
To murder her that never meant thee harm,
To kill me now, whom once thou sav'dst from
    death,   130
Do them at once ; on her all these rely,
And perish with her spotted chastity.
    SIR F. You overcome me in your love, Sir
    Charles.
I cannot be so cruel to a lady
I love so dearly. Since you have not spar'd
To engage your reputation to the world,
Your sister's honor, which you prize so dear,
Nay, all the comfort which you hold on earth,
To grow out of my debt, being your foe, —

[14] Forced (*i.e.,* motivated) by honor.
[15] So Q 2 ; Q 1 *lives.*

Your honor'd thoughts, lo, thus I recompense.
Your metamorph[o]s'd foe receives your gift
In satisfaction of all former wrongs.   142
This jewel I will wear here in my heart ;
And where [16] before I thought her, for her wants,
Too base to be my bride ; to end all strife,
I seal you my dear brother, her my wife.
  SUSAN. You still exceed us. I will yield to fate,
And learn to love, where I till now did hate.
  SIR C. With that enchantment you have charm'd my soul
And made me rich even in those very words.
I pay no debt, but am indebted more ;   151
Rich in your love, I never can be poor.
  SIR F. All 's [17] mine is yours ; we are alike in state ;
Let 's knit in love what was oppos'd in hate.
Come, for our nuptials we will straight provide,
Blest only in our brother and fair bride.
                                                    [*Exeunt.*]

[SCENE II] [18]

Enter CRANWELL, FRANKFORD, *and* NICK.

  CRAN. Why do you search each room about your house,
Now that you have dispatch'd your wife away?
  FRANK. Oh, sir, to see that nothing may be left
That ever was my wife's. I lov'd her dearly ;
And when I do but think of her unkindness,
My thoughts are all in hell ; to avoid which torment,
I would not have a bodkin or a cuff,
A bracelet, necklace, or rabato [19] wire,
Nor anything that ever was call'd hers
Left me, by which I might remember her. — [10
Seek round about.
  NICH. 'Sblood! Master, here 's her lute flung in a corner.
  FRANK. Her lute! O God, upon this instrument
Her fingers have ran [20] quick division,[21]
Sweeter than that which now divides our hearts.
These frets have made me pleasant,[22] that have now
Frets of my heart-strings made. Oh, Master Cranwell,

Oft hath she made this melancholy wood,
Now mute and dumb for her disastrous chance,
Speak sweetly many a note, sound many a strain   20
To her own ravishing voice ; which being well strung,
What pleasant strange airs have they jointly rung ! [23] —
Post with it after her. — Now nothing 's left ;
Of her and hers I am at once bereft.
  NICH. I 'll ride and overtake her ; do my message,
And come back again.   [*Exit.*]
  CRAN.   Meantime, sir, if you please,
I 'll to Sir Francis Acton, and inform him
Of what hath pass'd betwixt you and his sister.
  FRANK. Do as you please. — How ill am I bestead,
To be a widower ere my wife be dead.   30
                                                    [*Exeunt.*]

[SCENE III] [24]

Enter MISTRESS FRANKFORD, *with* JENKIN, *her maid* CICELY, *her* Coachman, *and three* Carters.

  MRS. F. Bid my coach stay. Why should I ride in state,
Being hurl'd so low down by the hand of fate?
A seat like to my fortunes let me have :
Earth for my chair, and for my bed a grave !
  JEN. Comfort, good Mistress ; you have watered your coach with tears already. You have but two mile now to go to your manor. A man cannot say by my old master Frankford as he may say by me, that he wants manors ; for he hath three or four, of [10 which this is one that we are going to now.
  CIC. Good mistress, be of good cheer. Sorrow, you see, hurts you, but helps you not ; we all mourn to see you so sad.
  CARTER. Mistress, I see one of my landlord's men
Come riding post ; [25] 't is like he brings some news.
  MRS. F. Comes he from Master Frankford, he is welcome ;
So is his news, because they come from him.

Enter NICK.

  NICH. There.
  MRS. F. I know the lute. Oft have I sung to thee ;   20
We both are out of tune, both out of time.

---

[16] Whereas.   [17] So Q 2 ; Q 1 *Alas.*
[18] A room in Frankford's house.
[19] A kind of ruff. The wire supported it.
[20] Q 1 *run.*   [21] Variation.   [22] Merry.
[23] Q 1 *sung.*   [24] A read   [25] At full speed.

NICH. Would that had been the worst instrument that e'er you played on. My master commends him unto ye; [26] there's all he can find that was ever yours; he hath nothing left that ever you could lay claim to [27] but his own heart — an he could afford you that! All that I have to deliver you is this: he prays you to forget him; and so he bids [you] [28] farewell.   30

MRS. F. I thank him; he is kind, and ever was.

All you that have true feeling of my grief,
That know my loss, and have relenting hearts,
Gird me about, and help me with your tears
To wash my spotted sins! My lute shall
    groan;
It cannot weep, but shall lament my moan.
                                    [*She plays.*]

Enter WENDOLL [*behind*].

WEN. Pursu'd with horror of a guilty soul,
And with the sharp scourge of repentance
    lash'd,
I fly from mine own shadow. O my stars!
What have my parents in their lives de-
    serv'd,   40
That you should lay this penance on [their] [29]
    son?
When I but think of Master Frankford's love,
And lay it to my treason, or compare
My murdering him for his relieving me,
It strikes a terror like a lightning's flash,
To scorch my blood up. Thus I, like the owl,
Asham'd of day, live in these shadowy woods,
Afraid of every leaf or murmuring blast,
Yet longing to receive some perfect knowledge
How he hath dealt with her. — [*seeing* MIS-
    TRESS FRANKFORD] O my sad fate! [50
Here, and so far from home, and thus attended.
O God, I have divorc'd the truest turtles [30]
That ever liv'd together, and, being divided,
In several places make their several moan;
She in the fields laments, and he at home.
So poets write that Orpheus made the trees
And stones to dance to his melodious harp,
Meaning the rustic and the barbarous hinds,
That had no understanding part in them;
So from these rude carters tears extracts, [61
Making their flinty hearts with grief to rise,
And draw down [31] rivers from their rocky
    eyes.

MRS. F. [*to* NICHOLAS] If you return unto
    [your] [32] master, say
(Though not from me, for I am all unworthy
To blast his name so [33] with a strumpet's
    tongue)
That you have seen me weep, wish myself
    dead.
Nay, you may say, too, for my vow is pass'd,[34]
Last night you saw me eat and drink my last.
This to your master you may say and swear;
For it is writ in Heaven, and decreed here. [70

NICH. I'll say you wept; I'll swear you
    made me sad.

Why, how now, eyes? what now? what's
    here to do?
I'm gone, or I shall straight turn baby too.

WEN. I cannot weep; my heart is all on
    fire.

Curs'd be the fruits of my unchaste desire.

MRS. F. Go break this lute upon [35] my
    coach's wheel,
As the last music that I e'er shall make;
Not as my husband's gift, but my farewell
To all earth's joy; and so your master tell.

NICH. If I can for crying.

WEN.   Grief, have done; [80
Or, like a madman, I shall frantic run.

MRS. F. You have beheld the woful'st
    wretch on earth,
A woman made of tears; would you had
    words
To express but what you see. My inward
    grief
No tongue can utter; yet unto your power [36]
You may describe my sorrow, and disclose
To thy sad master my abundant woes.

NICH. I'll do your commendations.[37]

MRS. F.   Oh, no.
I dare not so presume; nor to my children.
I am disclaim'd in both; alas, I am.   90
Oh, never teach them, when they come to
    speak,
To name the name of mother; chide their
    tongue,
If they by chance light on that hated word;
Tell them 't is naught; [38] for when that word
    they name,
Poor, pretty souls, they harp on their own
    shame.

WEN. To recompense her wrongs, what
    canst thou do?

---

[26] Sends you his compliments.
[27] Q₁ *claim to lay*.   [28] Q₁ *your*; Q₂ *yon*.
[29] So Pearson and Miss Bates. Both copies of Q₂ collated by the present Editor, *your*.
[30] Turtledoves.   [31] Q₁ omits *down*.

[32] So Q₁; Q₂ *my*.   [33] Q₁ omits *so*.   [34] Made.
[35] Q₁ omits *upon*.   [36] As far as you can.
[37] Present your compliments, deliver your greetings.
[38] Wicked.

Thou hast made her husbandless, and child-
less too.
Mrs. F. I have no more to say. — Speak
not for me ;
Yet you may tell your master what you see.
Nich. I 'll do 't.   *Exit.* [100
Wen. I 'll speak to her, and comfort her in
grief.
Oh, but her wound cannot be cur'd with words.
No matter, though ; I 'll do my best good will
To work a cure on her whom I did kill.
Mrs. F. So, now unto my coach, then to
my home,
So to my deathbed ; for from this sad hour,
I never will nor eat, nor drink, nor taste
Of any cates [39] that may preserve my life.
I never will nor smile, nor sleep, nor rest ;
But when my tears have wash'd my black soul
white,   110
Sweet Savior, to thy hands I yield my sprite.
Wen. [*advancing*] Oh, Mistress Frankford !
Mrs. F.   Oh, for God's sake, fly !
The Devil doth come to tempt me, ere I die. —
My coach ! — This sin, that with an angel's
face
Conjur'd [40] mine honor, till he sought my
wrack,
In my repentant eye seems ugly, black.
        Exeunt all [except Wendoll *and*
        Jenkin], *the* Carters *whistling.*[41]
Jen. What, my young master, that fled
in his shirt ! How come you by your clothes
again ? You have made our house in a sweet
pickle, ha' ye not, think you? What, [120
shall I serve you still, or cleave to the old
house?
Wen. Hence, slave ; away, with thy unseason'd [42] mirth !
Unless thou canst shed tears, and sigh, and
howl,
Curse thy sad fortunes, and exclaim on fate,
Thou art not for my turn.
Jen. Marry, an you will not, another will ;
farewell, and be hang'd. Would you had
never come to have kept this coil [43] within our
doors. We shall ha' you run away like [130
a sprite again.   [*Exit.*]
Wen. She 's gone to death ; I live to want
and woe,
Her life, her sins, and all upon my head.
And I must now go wander, like a Cain,
In foreign countries and remoted climes,

Where the report of my ingratitude
Cannot be heard. I 'll over first to France,
And so to Germany and Italy ;
Where, when I have recovered, and by travel
Gotten those perfect tongues,[44] and that [45]
these rumors   140
May in their height abate, I will return.
And I divine, however now dejected,
My worth and parts being by some great man
prais'd,
At my return I may in court be rais'd.
                                Exit.

[Scene IV] [46]

Enter Sir Francis [Acton], Sir Charles
[Mountford], Cranwell, *and* Susan.

Sir F. Brother, and now my wife, I think
these troubles
Fall on my head by justice of the Heavens,
For being so strict to you in your extremities ;
But we are now aton'd.[47] I would my sister
Could with like happiness o'ercome her griefs
As we have ours.
Susan. You tell us, Master Cranwell, won-
drous things
Touching the patience of that gentleman,
With what strange virtue he demeans [48] his
grief.
Cran. I told you what I was witness of ; [10
It was my fortune to lodge there that night.
Sir F. Oh, that same villain, Wendoll !
'T was his tongue
That did corrupt her ; she was of herself
Chaste and devoted well.[49] Is this the house?
Cran. Yes, sir ; I take it, here your sister
lies.[50]
Sir F. My brother Frankford show'd too
mild a spirit
In the revenge of such a loathed crime.
Less than he did, no man of spirit could do.
I am so far from blaming his revenge,
That I commend it. Had it been my case, [20
Their souls at once had from their breasts been
freed ;
Death to such deeds of shame is the due meed.

Enter Jenkin [*and* Cicely].

Jen. Oh, my mistress, mistress, my poor
mistress !
Cicely. Alas ! that ever I was born ; what
shall I do for my poor mistress?

---

[39] Food.   [40] Q₁ *Courted.*
[41] For which they were famous.
[42] Unseasonable.   [43] Made this trouble.
[44] Perfectly acquired the languages of those countries.
[45] When.   [46] Before Mrs. Frankford's house
[47] Reconciled.   [48] Manages.   [49] Pious.
[50] Lives.

SIR C. Why, what of her?

JEN. Oh, Lord, sir, she no sooner heard that her brother and his friends were come to see how she did, but she, for very shame of her [30 guilty conscience, fell into such a swoon, that we had much ado to get life in her.

SUSAN. Alas, that she should bear so hard a fate ;

Pity it is repentance comes too late.

SIR F. Is she so weak in body?

JEN. Oh, sir, I can assure you there's no hope of life in her, for she will take no sust'-nance ; she hath plainly starv'd herself, and now she's as lean as a lath. She ever looks for the good hour. Many gentlemen and gen- [40 tlewomen of the country are come to comfort her.

[SCENE V] [51]

[*To* SIR CHARLES MOUNTFORD, SIR FRANCIS ACTON, CRANWELL, SUSAN, JENKIN, *and* CICELY,] *enter* MISTRESS FRANKFORD *in her bed* [*with* MALBY *at the bedside*].

MAL. How fare you, Mistress Frankford?

MRS. F. Sick, sick, oh, sick. Give me some air, I pray [you].[52]

Tell me, oh, tell me, where's Master Frank-ford?

Will not [he] [52] deign to see me ere I die?

MAL. Yes, Mistress Frankford ; divers gentlemen,

Your loving neighbors, with that just request Have mov'd, and told him of your weak estate Who, though with much ado to get belief, Examining of the general circumstance, Seeing your sorrow and your penitence,   10 And hearing therewithal the great desire You have to see him ere you left the world, He gave to us his faith to follow us, And sure he will be here immediately.

MRS. F. You have half reviv'd me with the pleasing news ;

Raise me a little higher in my bed. —

Blush I not, Brother Acton? [53] Blush I not, Sir Charles?

Can you not read my fault writ in my cheek?

Is not my crime there, tell me, gentlemen?

SIR C. Alas, good mistress, sickness hath not left you   20

Blood in your face enough to make you blush.

MRS. F. Then, sickness, like a friend, my fault would hide. —

Is my husband come? My soul but tarries His arrive, then I am fit for Heaven.

SIR F. I came to chide you, but my words of hate

Are turn'd to pity and compassionate grief.

I came to rate you, but my brawls,[54] you see, Melt into tears, and I must weep by thee.

SIR C. Here's Master Frankford now.

Enter FRANKFORD.

FRANK. Good morrow, Brother ; morrow, gentlemen.   30

God, that hath laid this cross upon our heads, Might, had He pleas'd, have made our cause of meeting

On a more fair and more contented ground ; But He that made us made us to this woe.

MRS. F. And is he come? Methinks, that voice I know.

FRANK. How do you, woman?

MRS. F. Well, Master Frankford, well ; but shall be better,

I hope within this hour. Will you vouchsafe, Out of your grace and your humanity, To take a spotted strumpet by the hand? [40

FRANK. That hand once held my heart in faster bonds

Than now 't is gripp'd by me. God pardon them

That made us first break hold.

MRS. F.   Amen, amen.

Out of my zeal to Heaven, whither I'm now bound,

I was so impudent to wish you here ;

And once more beg your pardon. O good man,

And father to my children, pardon me.

Pardon, oh, pardon me. My fault so heinous is,

That if you in this world forgive it not,

Heaven will not clear it in the world to come.

Faintness hath so usurp'd upon my knees [51

That kneel I cannot ; but on my heart's knees

My prostrate soul lies thrown down at your feet,

To beg your gracious pardon. Pardon, oh, pardon me.

FRANK. As freely, from the low depth of my soul,

As my Redeemer hath forgiven His death,

I pardon thee. I will shed tears for thee ; pray with thee ;

And, in mere pity of thy weak estate,
I 'll wish to die with thee.
 ALL.   So do we all.
 NICH. [*aside*] So will not I ;   60
I 'll sigh and sob, but, by my faith, not die.
 SIR F. Oh, Master Frankford, all the near
  alliance
I lose by her, shall be suppli'd in thee.
You are my brother by the nearest way ;
Her kindred hath fallen off, but yours doth
  stay.
 FRANK. Even as I hope for pardon, at that
  day
When the great Judge of Heaven in scarlet
  sits,
So be thou pardon'd. Though thy rash of-
  fence
Divorc'd our bodies, thy repentant tears
Unite our souls.
 SIR C. Then comfort, Mistress Frankford ;
You see your husband hath forgiven your
  fall ;   71
Then rouse your spirits, and cheer your faint-
  ing soul !
 SUSAN. How is it with you?
 SIR F.   How d' ye feel yourself ?
 MRS. F. Not of this world.
 FRANK. I see you are not, and I weep to see
  it.
My wife, the mother to my pretty babes —
Both those lost names I do restore thee
  back,
And with this kiss I wed thee once again.
Though thou art wounded in thy honor'd
  name,
And with that grief upon thy deathbed liest,
Honest in heart, upon my soul, thou diest. [81
 MRS. F. Pardon'd on earth, soul, thou in
  Heaven art free ;
Once more thy wife,[55] dies thus embracing
  thee.   [*Dies.*]
 FRANK. New-married, and new-widow'd ;
  oh, she 's dead,
And a cold grave must be her nuptial bed.
 SIR C. Sir, be of good comfort, and your
  heavy sorrow
Part equally amongst us ; storms divided
Abate their force, and with less rage are
  guided.

[55] A squinting construction : (1) once more (I am)
thy wife ; (2) thy wife dies.

 CRAN. Do, Master Frankford ; he that
  hath least part,
Will find enough to drown one troubled heart.
 SIR F. Peace with thee, Nan. — Brothers
  and gentlemen,   91
All we that can plead interest in her grief,
Bestow upon her body funeral tears,
Brother, had you with threats and usage bad
Punish'd her sin, the grief of her offence
Had not with such true sorrow touch'd her
  heart.
 FRANK. I see it had not ; therefore, on her
  grave
Will I bestow this funeral epitaph,
Which on her marble tomb shall be engrav'd,
In golden letters shall these words be fill'd :[56]
Here lies she whom her husband's kindness
  kill'd.   101

THE EPILOGUE

AN honest crew, disposed to be merry,
 Came to a tavern by,[57] and call'd for wine.
The drawer brought it, smiling like a cherry,
 And told them it was pleasant, neat,[58] and
  fine.
" Taste it," quoth one. He did so. " Fie ! "
  quoth he,
" This wine was good ; now 't runs too near
  the lee."

Another sipp'd, to give the wine his due,
 And said unto the rest it drunk too flat ;
The third said, it was old ; the fourth, too new ;
 " Nay," quoth the fifth, " the sharpness likes
  me not."   10
Thus, gentlemen, you see how, in one hour,
The wine was new, old, flat, sharp, sweet, and
  sour.

Unto this wine we do allude [59] our play,
 Which some will judge too trivial, some too
  grave.
You as our guests we entertain this day,
 And bid you welcome to the best we have.
Excuse us, then ; good wine may be disgrac'd,
When every several mouth hath sundry taste.

[56] *I.e.*, the engraved letters shall be filled in with
gold.
 [57] Near-by.   [58] Unadulterated.   [59] Compare.

THE
SHOMAKERS
Holiday.
OR
The Gentle Craft.

With the humorous life of Simon
Eyre, shoomaker, and Lord Maior
of London.

As it was acted before the Queenes most excellent Ma-
ieste on New-yeares day at night last, by the right
honourable the Earle of Notingham, Lord high Ad-
mirall of England, his seruants.

Printed by Valentine Sims dwelling at the foote of Adling
hill, neere Bainards Castle, at the signe of the White
Swanne, and are there to be sold.
1 6 0 0.

INTRODUCTORY NOTE

ORIGINALLY produced by the Admiral's Men in 1599, this favorite comedy is based on several tales about shoemakers in Thomas Deloney's prose tract, *The Gentle Craft*, published in 1598. Here may be found, with unhistorical embellishments, the story though not the character of that early fifteenth-century worthy Sir Simon Eyre, from the hiring of the new foreign workman to the feasting of the apprentices. Here also are the Enoch Arden return, in this case of a wife supposed to be dead; and the legend of St. Crispin, who, in his adoption of the gentle craft and his clandestine marriage, is emulated by Lacy.

These materials are deftly interwoven by Dekker, and highly colored from his own intimate and ardent acquaintance with London life. True, the rise of Eyre is pretty rapid, even for a romantic comedy. Nor is the dramatist critical, like Jonson, as he surveys the contemporary scene. This is a play of romantic plot curiously allied with realistic manners, the first so charming and the second depicted with a gusto so nearly Chaucerian that the combination is irresistible. Simon Eyre wins every reader's heart as easily as he wins the King's. And it is the heart, not the mind, that Dekker, on the threshold of his career, addresses in this play.

The first edition appeared, in quarto, in 1600 (reprinted 1610, 1618, 1624, 1631, 1657). Dekker's authorship is indicated by a note in Henslowe's " Diary." The standard edition of his plays is still the inadequate Pearson reprint (1873). Among separate editions of *The Shoemakers' Holiday* are those of Karl Warnke and Ludwig Proescholdt (1886), and A. F. Lange in Gayley's *Representative English Comedies*, vol. III (1914). The present text is based on the Quarto of 1600, with occasional corrections from the subsequent Quartos.

THE SHOEMAKERS' HOLIDAY: A PLEASANT COMEDY OF THE GENTLE CRAFT

BY

THOMAS DEKKER

[DRAMATIS PERSONAE

KING HENRY V.
THE EARL OF CORNWALL.
SIR HUGH LACY, Earl of Lincoln.
ROWLAND LACY,
   for a time disguised as } his nephews.
   HANS,
ASKEW,
SIR ROGER OATELEY, Lord Mayor of London.
HAMMON,
WARNER, } citizens of London.
SCOTT,
SIMON EYRE, a shoemaker.

ROGER,
FIRK, } Eyre's journeymen.
RALPH,
LOVELL.
DODGER, a servant to the Earl of Lincoln.
A Dutch Skipper.
A Boy.

ROSE, daughter to Sir Roger.
SYBIL, her maid.
MARGERY, wife to Simon Eyre.
JANE, wife to Ralph.

Courtiers, Attendants, Officers, Soldiers, Hunters, Shoemakers, Apprentices, and Servants.

THE SCENE — *London and Old Ford.*]

THE PROLOGUE

As it was pronounced before the Queen's Majesty

As wretches in a storm, expecting day,
With trembling hands and eyes cast up to Heaven,
Make prayers the anchor of their conquer'd hopes,
So we, dear Goddess, wonder of all eyes,
Your meanest vassals, through mistrust and fear
To sink into the bottom of disgrace
By our imperfect pastimes, prostrate thus
On bended knees, our sails of hope do strike,
Dreading the bitter storms of your dislike.
Since then, unhappy men, our hap is such   10
That to ourselves ourselves no help can bring,
But needs must perish, if your saint-like ears,
Locking the temple where all mercy sits,
Refuse the tribute of our begging tongues;
Oh, grant, bright mirror of true chastity,
From those life-breathing stars, your sun-like eyes,
One gracious smile; for your celestial breath
Must send us life, or sentence us to death.

[ACT I] [1]

Enter LORD MAYOR [*and the* EARL OF] LINCOLN.

LINC. My Lord Mayor, you have sundry
    times
Feasted myself and many courtiers more ;
Seldom or never can we be so kind
To make requital of your courtesy.
But leaving this, I hear my cousin [2] Lacy
Is much affected to [3] your daughter Rose.
    L. MAYOR. True, my good Lord, and she
    loves him so well
That I mislike her boldness in the chase.
    LINC. Why, my Lord Mayor, think you it
    then a shame,
To join a Lacy with an Oateley's name?   10
    L. MAYOR. Too mean is my poor girl for his
    high birth ;
Poor citizens must not with courtiers wed,
Who will in silks and gay apparel spend
More in one year than I am worth, by far ;
Therefore your Honor need not doubt [4] my
    girl.
    LINC. Take heed, my Lord, advise you what
    you do !
A verier unthrift lives not in the world,
Than is my cousin ; for I 'll tell you what :
'T is now almost a year since he requested
To travel countries for experience.   20
I furnish'd him with coin, bills of exchange,
Letters of credit, men to wait on him,
Solicited my friends in Italy
Well to respect him. But, to see the end,
Scant had he journeyed through half Germany,
But all his coin was spent, his men cast off,
His bills embezzl'd, [5] and my jolly coz, [6]
Asham'd to show his bankrupt presence here,
Became a shoemaker in Wittenberg,
A goodly science for a gentleman   30
Of such descent ! Now judge the rest by this :
Suppose your daughter have a thousand
    pound,
He did consume me more in one half year ;
And make him heir to all the wealth you have,
One twelvemonth's rioting will waste it all.
Then seek, my Lord, some honest citizen
To wed your daughter to.
    L. MAYOR.   I thank your Lordship. —
[*aside*] Well, fox, I understand your sub-
    tlety. —

As for your nephew, let your Lordship's eye
But watch his actions, and you need not fear,
For I have [sent] [7] my daughter far enough. [41
And yet your cousin Rowland might do well,
Now he hath learn'd an occupation. —
[*aside*] And yet I scorn to call him son-in-law.
    LINC. Ay, but I have a better trade for him.
I thank his Grace, [8] he hath appointed him
Chief colonel of all those companies
Must'red in London and the shires about,
To serve his Highness in those wars of France.
See where he comes ! —

Enter LOVELL, LACY, *and* ASKEW.

                Lovell, what news with you?
    LOVELL. My Lord of Lincoln, 't is his
    Highness' will,   51
That presently [9] your cousin ship for France
With all his powers ; [10] he would not for a
    million
But they should land at Dieppe within four
    days.
    LINC. Go certify his Grace it shall be done.
                     Exit LOVELL.
Now, Cousin Lacy, in what forwardness
Are all your companies?
    LACY.   All well prepar'd.
The men of Hertfordshire lie at Mile End ;
Suffolk and Essex train in Tothill Fields ;
The Londoners and those of Middlesex,   60
All gallantly prepar'd in Finsbury,
With frolic spirits long for their parting hour.
    L. MAYOR. They have their imprest, [11]
    coats, and furniture ; [12]
And, if it please your cousin Lacy come
To the Guildhall, he shall receive his pay ;
And twenty pounds besides my brethren [13]
Will freely give him, to approve our loves
We bear unto my Lord, your uncle here.
    LACY. I thank your Honor.
    LINC.   Thanks, my good Lord Mayor.
    L. MAYOR. At the Guildhall we will expect [14]
    your coming.   *Exit.* [70
    LINC. To approve your loves to me? No,
    subtlety !
Nephew, that twenty pound he doth bestow
For joy to rid you from his daughter Rose.
But, Cousins both, now here are none but
    friends,
I would not have you cast an amorous eye
Upon so mean a project as the love
Of a gay, wanton, painted citizen.

---

[1] A street in London.
[2] Nephew. (Used of anyone collaterally related,
except a brother or sister.)
[3] Fond of.   [4] Be apprehensive concerning.
[5] Squandered.   [6] Cousin, nephew.

[7] Om. Q 1.   [8] The King.   [9] At once.
[10] Troops.   [11] Advance pay.
[12] Equipment.   [13] Trisyllabic.   [14] Await.

I know this churl even in the height of scorn
Doth hate the mixture of his blood with thine.
I pray thee, do thou so !   Remember, Coz, [80
What honorable fortunes wait on thee.
Increase the King's love, which so brightly
    shines,
And gilds thy hopes.   I have no heir but
    thee —
And yet not thee, if with a wayward spirit
Thou start from the true bias [15] of my love.
    LACY. My Lord, I will for honor, not desire
Of land or livings, or to be your heir,
So guide my actions in pursuit of France,
As shall add glory to the Lacys' name.
    LINC. Coz, for those words here's thirty
    Portuguese,[16]   90
And, Nephew Askew, there's a few for you.
Fair Honor, in her loftiest eminence,
Stays in France for you, till you fetch her
    thence.
Then, Nephews, clap swift wings on your de-
    signs.
Begone, begone ; make haste to the Guildhall ;
There presently I'll meet you.   Do not stay ;
Where honor [beckons] [17] shame attends delay.
                             Exit.
    ASKEW. How gladly would your uncle have
        you gone !
    LACY. True, Coz, but I'll o'erreach his pol-
        icies.   99
I have some serious business for three days,
Which nothing but my presence can dispatch.
You, therefore, Cousin, with the companies,
Shall haste to Dover ; there I'll meet with
    you.
Or, if I stay past my prefixed time,
Away for France ; we'll meet in Normandy.
The twenty pounds my Lord Mayor gives to
    me
You shall receive, and these ten Portuguese,
Part of mine uncle's thirty.   Gentle Coz,
Have care to our great charge ; I know your
    wisdom
Hath tri'd itself in higher consequence.   110
    ASKEW. Coz, all myself am yours ; yet
        have this care,
To lodge in London with all secrecy.
Our uncle Lincoln hath, besides his own,
Many a jealous eye, that in your face
Stares only to watch means for your dis-
    grace.
    LACY. Stay, Cousin, who be these?

Enter SIMON EYRE, *his wife* [MARGERY],
   HODGE, FIRK, JANE, *and* RALPH [18] *with a
   piece.*[19]

    EYRE. Leave whining, leave whining !
Away with this whimp'ring, this puling, these
blubb'ring tears, and these wet eyes !   I'll get
thy husband discharg'd, I warrant thee, sweet
Jane ; go to !   121
    HODGE. Master, here be the captains.
    EYRE. Peace, Hodge ; husht, ye knave,
husht !
    FIRK. Here be the cavaliers and the colo-
nels, Master.
    EYRE. Peace, Firk ; peace, my fine Firk !
Stand by with your pishery-pashery,[20] away !
I am a man of the best presence ; I'll speak to
them, an they were popes. — Gentlemen, [130
captains, colonels, commanders !   Brave men,
brave leaders, may it please you to give me
audience.   I am Simon Eyre, the mad shoemaker of Tower Street ; this wench with the
mealy mouth [21] that will never tire, is my wife,
I can tell you ; here's Hodge, my man and my
foreman ; here's Firk, my fine firking [22] journeyman, and this is blubbered Jane.   All we
come to be suitors for this honest Ralph.
Keep him at home, and as I am a true [140
shoemaker and a gentleman of the gentle craft,
buy spurs yourself, and I'll find ye boots these
seven years.
    MARG. Seven years, husband?
    EYRE. Peace, midriff,[23] peace !   I know
what I do.   Peace !
    FIRK. Truly, master cormorant,[24] you shall
do God good service to let Ralph and his
wife stay together.   She's a young new-married woman ; if you take her husband [150
away from her a-night, you undo her ; she may
beg in the daytime ; for he's as good a workman at a prick and an awl as any is in our
trade.
    JANE. O let him stay, else I shall be undone.
    FIRK. Ay, truly, she shall be laid at one side
like a pair of old shoes else, and be occupied [25]
for no use.
    LACY. Truly, my friends it lies not in my
    power ;

[18] Old eds. *Rafe* or *Raph*, throughout.
[19] Probably = musket ; possibly, as Lange thinks,
= piece of work ; *i.e.*, the shoes for Jane.
[20] Trifling talk.
[21] *I.e.*, Margery is soft-spoken, given to mince
matters. (*N.E.D.*)   [22] Frisking.
[23] Diaphragm ; probably a slighting allusion to
Margery's corpulence.
[24] For colonel, often spelled coronel.
[25] With a play on an indecent meaning.

[15] Propensity.
[16] Gold coins worth about $20 each.
[17] Emend. Malone ; old eds. *become, becomes.*

The Londoners are press'd,[26] paid, and set
forth 160
By the Lord Mayor ; I cannot change a man.

HODGE. Why, then you were as good be
a corporal as a colonel, if you cannot discharge one good fellow ; and I tell you true,
I think you do more than you can answer, to
press a man within a year and a day of his
marriage.[27]

EYRE. Well said, melancholy Hodge ; gramercy, my fine foreman.

MARG. Truly, gentlemen, it were ill [170
done for such as you, to stand so stiffly against
a poor young wife, considering her case, she
is new-married ; but let that pass. I pray,
deal not roughly with her ; her husband is a
young man, and but newly ent'red ; [28] but let
that pass.

EYRE. Away with your pishery-pashery,
your pols and your edipols ! [29] Peace, midriff ; silence, Cicely Bumtrinket ! [30] Let your
head [31] speak. 180

FIRK. Yea, and the horns [32] too, Master.

EYRE. Too soon,[33] my fine Firk, too soon !
Peace, scoundrels ! — See you this man? Captains, you will not release him ? Well, let him
go ; he's a proper shot ; let him vanish !
Peace, Jane, dry up thy tears ; they'll make his
powder dankish. Take him, brave men ; Hector of Troy was an hackney to him, Hercules
and Termagant [34] scoundrels, Prince Arthur's
Round Table — by the Lord of Ludgate [35] [190
— ne'er fed such a tall,[36] such a dapper swordman ; by the life of Pharaoh, a brave resolute
swordman ! Peace, Jane ! I say no more,
mad knaves.

FIRK. See, see, Hodge, how my master
raves in commendation of Ralph !

HODGE. Ralph, th'art a gull,[37] by this
hand, an thou goest.[38]

[26] Into the army.
[27] See *Deuteronomy*, xxiv, 5.
[28] Recently entered upon his profession. The chief comic effect of Margery's speech resides in her unintentional double-entendres.
[29] Both words = asseverations, from Lat. *pol*, a contraction of *Pollux*, and *edepol* = by Pollux.
[30] Probably only an epithet for Margery ; cf. II, iii, 48, where it is applied to one of her maids.
[31] Eyre.
[32] The familiar jocose allusion to the constant imminence of cuckoldom.
[33] Eyre admits the possibility.
[34] A blustering character in the moralities and interludes ; he was supposed to be a Mohammedan deity.
[35] Not certainly explained ; the expression may well be a coinage of Eyre's.
[36] Valiant. [37] Fool, ass.
[38] Q 1631 and mod. eds. add *not;* but a humorous reversal may be intended in ll. 208, ff.

ASKEW. I am glad, good Master Eyre, it is
my hap
To meet so resolute a soldier. 200
Trust me, for your report and love to him,
A common slight regard shall not respect [39]
him.

LACY. Is thy name Ralph?

RALPH. Yes, sir.

LACY. Give me thy hand ;
Thou shalt not want, as I am a gentleman.
Woman, be patient ; God, no doubt, will send
Thy husband safe again ; but he must go :
His country's quarrel says it shall be so.

HODGE. Th'art a gull, by my stirrup,[40] if
thou dost not go. I will not have thee strike
thy gimlet into these weak vessels ; prick thine
enemies, Ralph. 211

Enter DODGER.

DODGER. My Lord, your uncle on the
Tower Hill
Stays with the Lord Mayor and the aldermen,
And doth request you, with all speed you may,
To hasten thither.

ASKEW. Cousin, let's go.

LACY. Dodger, run you before ; tell them
we come. — *Exit* DODGER.
[*aside to* ASKEW] This Dodger is mine uncle's
parasite,
The arrant'st varlet that e'er breath'd on
earth ;
He sets more discord in a noble house 219
By one day's broaching of his pickthank
tales,[41]
Than can be salv'd [42] again in twenty years ;
And he, I fear, shall go with us to France,
To pry into our actions.

ASKEW. Therefore, Coz,
It shall behove you to be circumspect.

LACY. Fear not, good Cousin. — Ralph,
hie to your colors.
[*Exeunt* LACY *and* ASKEW.]

RALPH. I must, because there's no remedy ;
But, gentle Master and my loving dame,
As you have always been a friend to me,
So in mine absence think upon my wife.

JANE. Alas, my Ralph.

MARG. She cannot speak for weeping.

EYRE. Peace, you crack'd groats,[43] you [231

[39] Regard ; give heed to.
[40] The shoemaker's strap, by which he keeps his last on his knee.
[41] Sycophantic tattling.
[42] Cured.
[43] *I.e.*, worthless ones ; a sound groat was only worth about fourpence.

mustard tokens; [44] disquiet not the brave soldier. — Go thy ways, Ralph!

JANE. Ay, ay, you bid him go; what shall I do
When he is gone?

FIRK. Why, be doing with me or my fellow Hodge; be not idle.

EYRE. Let me see thy hand, Jane. This fine hand, this white hand, these pretty fingers must spin, must card, must work; work, [240 you bombast cotton-candle [45] quean; [46] work for your living, with a pox to you. — Hold thee, Ralph, here's five sixpences for thee; fight for the honor of the gentle craft, for the gentlemen shoemakers, the courageous cordwainers, the flower of St. Martin's, [47] the mad knaves of Bedlam, Fleet Street, Tower Street, and Whitechapel; crack me the crowns of the French knaves, a pox on them, crack them; fight, by the Lord of Ludgate; fight, my [250 fine boy!

FIRK. Here, Ralph, here's three twopences: two carry into France; the third shall wash our souls at parting, for sorrow is dry. For my sake, firk [48] the *Basa-mon-cues.* [49]

HODGE. Ralph, I am heavy [50] at parting; but here's a shilling for thee. God send [51] thee to cram thy slops [52] with French crowns, and thy enemies' bellies with bullets.

RALPH. I thank you, Master, and I thank you all. — 260
Now, gentle Wife, my loving lovely Jane,
Rich men, at parting, give their wives rich gifts,
Jewels and rings, to grace their lily hands.
Thou know'st our trade makes rings for women's heels:
Here take this pair of shoes, cut out by Hodge,
Stitch'd by my fellow Firk, seam'd by myself,
Made up and pink'd [53] with letters for thy name.
Wear them, my dear Jane, for thy husband's sake,
And every morning when thou pull'st them on,

[44] *I.e.*, worthless ones; originally = a token given to a purchaser of mustard, entitling him to a small repayment when a certain number had been accumulated. (*N.E.D.*)
[45] Candle with a cotton wick; *bombast* = (1) cotton; (2) padded, perhaps with an allusion to Jane's plumpness.
[46] Hussy.
[47] The parish of St. Martin's Le Grand, a centre of the craft.
[48] Trounce.
[49] The kiss-my-tails.
[50] Sad.   [51] Grant.
[52] Breeches.
[53] Decorated (by piercing them with small holes).

Remember me, and pray for my return. 270
Make much of them; for I have made them so
That I can know them from a thousand mo.

Sound drum. Enter LORD MAYOR, [*the* EARL OF] LINCOLN, LACY, ASKEW, DODGER, *and* Soldiers. *They pass over the stage;* RALPH *falls in amongst them;* FIRK *and the rest cry " Farewell," etc., and so exeunt.*

[ACT II — SCENE I] [1]

Enter ROSE, *alone, making a garland.*

ROSE. Here sit thou down upon this flow'ry bank
And make a garland for thy Lacy's head.
These pinks, these roses, and these violets,
These blushing gilliflowers, these marigolds,
The fair embroidery of his coronet,
Carry not half such beauty in their cheeks,
As the sweet count'nance of my Lacy doth.
O my most unkind father! O my stars,
Why low'r'd you so at my nativity,
To make me love, yet live robb'd of my love?
Here as a thief am I imprisoned 11
For my dear Lacy's sake within those walls,
Which by my father's cost were builded up
For better purposes. Here must I languish
For him that doth as much lament, I know,
Mine absence, as for him I pine in woe.

Enter SYBIL.

SYBIL. Good morrow, young Mistress. I am sure you make that garland for me, against I shall be Lady of the Harvest.

ROSE. Sybil, what news at London? 20

SYBIL. None but good; my Lord Mayor, your father, and Master Philpot, your uncle, and Master Scott, your cousin, and Mistress Frigbottom by Doctors' Commons, [2] do all, by my troth, send you most hearty commendations. [3]

ROSE. Did Lacy send kind greetings to his love?

SYBIL. Oh yes, out of cry, [4] by my troth. I scant knew him; here 'a wore [a] scarf, and here a scarf, here a bunch of feathers, and [30

[1] The garden of Oatley's house at Old Ford (northeast of the City).
[2] The buildings of the College of Doctors of Civil Law, south of St. Paul's.
[3] Regards.   [4] Beyond measure.

here precious stones and jewels, and a pair of garters — oh, monstrous! like one of our yellow silk curtains at home here in Old Ford House here, in Master Bellymount's chamber. I stood at our door in Cornhill, look'd at him, he at me indeed, spake to him, but he not to me, not a word; marry gup [5] thought I, with a wanion! [6] He pass'd by me as proud — Marry, foh! are you grown humorous? [7] thought I; and so shut the door, and in I [40 came.

ROSE. Oh, Sybil, how dost thou my Lacy wrong!
My Rowland is as gentle as a lamb,
No dove was ever half so mild as he.

SYBIL. Mild? yea, as a bushel of stamp'd crabs.[8] He look'd upon me as sour as verjuice.[9] Go thy ways, thought I; thou mayst be much in my gaskins,[10] but nothing in my netherstocks.[11] This is your fault, Mistress, to love him that loves not you; he thinks [50 scorn to do as he's done to; but if I were as you, I'd cry, "Go by, Jeronimo, go by!"[12] I'd set mine old debts against my new driblets, And the hare's foot against the goose giblets;[13] For if ever I sigh, when sleep I should take, Pray God I may lose my maidenhead when I wake.

ROSE. Will my love leave me then, and go to France?

SYBIL. I know not that, but I am sure I see him stalk before the soldiers. By my troth, he is a proper [14] man; but he is proper that [60 proper doth. Let him go snick up,[15] young Mistress.

ROSE. Get thee to London, and learn perfectly
Whether my Lacy go to France, or no.
Do this, and I will give thee for thy pains
My cambric apron and my Romish gloves,
My purple stockings and a stomacher.
Say, wilt thou do this, Sybil, for my sake?

SYBIL. Will I, quoth 'a? At whose suit? By my troth, yes, I'll go. A cambric apron, [70 gloves, a pair of purple stockings, and a

stomacher! I'll sweat in purple, Mistress, for you; I'll take anything that comes a' God's name. Oh, rich! a cambric apron! Faith, then have at 'up tails all.'[16] I'll go jiggy-joggy to London, and be here in a trice, young Mistress. *Exit.*

ROSE. Do so, good Sybil. — Meantime wretched I
Will sit and sigh for his lost company. *Exit.*

[SCENE II][17]

Enter ROWLAND LACY, *like a Dutch shoemaker.*

LACY. How many shapes have gods and kings devis'd,
Thereby to compass their desired loves!
It is no shame for Rowland Lacy, then,
To clothe his cunning with the gentle craft,
That, thus disguis'd, I may unknown possess
The only happy presence of my Rose.
For her have I forsook my charge in France,
Incurr'd the King's displeasure, and stirr'd up
Rough hatred in mine uncle Lincoln's breast.
O love, how powerful art thou, that canst change   10
High birth to [baseness,][18] and a noble mind
To the mean semblance of a shoemaker!
But thus it must be; for her cruel father,
Hating the single union of our souls,
Has secretly convey'd my Rose from London,
To bar me of her presence; but I trust
Fortune and this disguise will furder me
Once more to view her beauty, gain her sight.
Here in Tower Street with Eyre the shoemaker
Mean I awhile to work; I know the trade: [20
I learnt it when I was in Wittenberg.
Then cheer thy hoping spirits, be not dismay'd;
Thou canst not want: do Fortune what she can,
The gentle craft is living for a man.   *Exit.*

[SCENE III][19]

Enter EYRE, *making himself ready.*

EYRE. Where be these boys, these girls, these drabs, these scoundrels? They wallow in the fat brewis [20] of my bounty, and lick up the crumbs of my table, yet will not rise to see my walks cleansed. — Come out, you powder-beef [21] queans! What, Nan! what, Madge Mumble-crust! Come out, you fat

---

[5] Go up. Cf. "come up."
[6] With a vengeance.
[7] Capricious.   [8] Crushed crabapples.
[9] The sour juice of green fruits.
[10] Breeches.
[11] Stockings. The meaning seems to be that though we may be acquainted, we are not intimate friends. (Neilson.)
[12] *Spanish Tragedy*, IV, v, 30.
[13] A proverbial saying. Sybil's application is "Off with the old love, on with the new; an even exchange." (Lange.)
[14] Handsome.   [15] Go hang.
[16] A card game; also a tune.
[17] A London street.
[18] Cor. Q 1631; earlier eds. *barenesse.*
[19] Before Eyre's house.
[20] Broth.   [21] Corned beef.

midriff, swag-belly whores, and sweep me these kennels, that the noisome stench offend not the nose [22] of my neighbors. — What, Firk, I [10 say ; what, Hodge ! Open my shop windows ! What, Firk, I say !

Enter FIRK.

FIRK. O Master, is 't you that speak bandog [23] and Bedlam this morning ? I was in a dream, and mused what madman was got into the street so early. Have you drunk this morning that your throat is so clear ?

EYRE. Ah, well said, Firk ; well said, Firk. To work, my fine knave, to work ! Wash thy face, and thou 't be more blest.   20

FIRK. Let them wash my face that will eat it. Good master, send for a souse-wife,[24] if you'll have my face cleaner.

Enter HODGE.

EYRE. Away, sloven ! avaunt, scoundrel ! — Good morrow, Hodge ; good morrow, my fine foreman.

HODGE. O Master, good morrow ; y' are an early stirrer. Here 's a fair morning. — Good morrow, Firk. I could have slept this hour. Here 's a brave day towards.[25]   30

EYRE. Oh, haste to work, my fine foreman, haste to work.

FIRK. Master, I am dry as dust to hear my fellow Roger talk of fair weather ; let us pray for good leather, and let clowns [26] and plough-boys and those that work in the fields pray for brave days. We work in a dry shop ; what care I if it rain ?

Enter Eyre's wife [MARGERY].

EYRE. How now, Dame Margery, can you see to rise ? Trip and go ; call up the [40 drabs, your maids.

MARG. See to rise ? I hope 't is time enough ; 't is early enough for any woman to be seen abroad. I marvel how many wives in Tower Street are up so soon. Gods me, 't is not noon, — here 's a yawling ! [27]

EYRE. Peace, Margery, peace ! Where 's Cicely Bumtrinket, your maid ? She has a privy fault : she farts in her sleep. Call the quean up ; if my men want shoe-thread, [50 I 'll swinge [28] her in a stirrup.

FIRK. Yet, that 's but a dry beating ; here 's still a sign of drought.

Enter LACY [*disguised*], *singing.*

LACY. *Der was een bore van Gelderland,*
    Frolick si[e] *byen ;*
He was als dronck he cold nyet stand,
    Upsolce s[i]*e byen.*
Tap eens de canneken,
    Drincke, scho[n]*e mannekin.*[29]

FIRK. Master, for my life, yonder 's a [60 brother of the gentle craft ; if he bear not Saint Hugh's bones,[30] I 'll forfeit my bones ; he 's some uplandish [31] workman. Hire him, good Master, that I may learn some gibble-gabble ; 't will make us work the faster.

EYRE. Peace, Firk ! A hard world ! Let him pass, let him vanish ; we have journey-men enow. Peace, my fine Firk !

MARG. Nay, nay, y' are best follow your man's counsel ; you shall see what will [70 come on 't. We have not men enow, but we must entertain every butter-box ; [32] but let that pass.

HODGE. Dame, 'fore God, if my master follow your counsel, he 'll consume little beef. He shall be glad of men an he can catch them.

FIRK. Ay, that he shall.

HODGE. 'Fore God, a proper man, and I warrant, a fine workman. — Master, farewell ; Dame, adieu ; if such a man as he cannot [80 find work, Hodge is not for you.   *Offer to go.*

EYRE. Stay, my fine Hodge.

FIRK. Faith, an your foreman go, Dame, you must take a journey to seek a new journey-man ; if Roger remove, Firk follows. If Saint Hugh's bones shall not be set a-work, I may prick mine awl in the walls, and go play. Fare ye well, Master ; God buy, Dame.

EYRE. Tarry, my fine Hodge, my brisk foreman ! Stay, Firk ! — [*to* MARGERY] [90 Peace, pudding-broth ! — By the Lord of Ludgate, I love my men as my life. Peace, you gallimaufry ! [33] Hodge, if he want work,

[29] There was a boor from Gelderland,
    Merry they be ;
He was so drunk he could not stand,
    [Dead drunk] they be.
Draw once the cannikin,
    Drink, pretty mannikin.
(For *upsolce*, Lange conj. *upsee al* = thoroughly drunk all.)
[30] According to Deloney, St. Hugh was befriended by journeymen shoemakers, "in requital of which kindness he called them Gentlemen of the Gentle Craft" and bequeathed them his bones. After his martyrdom they secretly secured his skeleton, which they made into the tools of their trade. "which ever since have been called S. Hugh's bones."
[31] Rustic.   [32] Dutchman.
[33] Hash, hodge-podge.

[22] Q 1618 *noses.*
[23] A chained dog ; *i.e.*, speak so ferociously.
[24] Pickled-pork woman.   [25] Impending.
[26] Rustics.   [27] Bawling.   [28] Beat.

I 'll hire him. One of you to him ; stay — he comes to us.

LACY. *Goeden dach, meester, ende u vro oak.*[34]

FIRK. Nails,[35] if I should speak after him without drinking, I should choke. — And you, friend Oak, are you of the gentle craft?

LACY. *Yaw, yaw, ik bin den skomawker.* [100

FIRK. *Den skomaker,* quoth 'a ! And hark you, *skomaker,* have you all your tools, a good rubbing-pin, a good stopper, a good dresser, your four sorts of awls, and your two balls of wax, your paring knife, your hand and thumb leathers, and good St. Hugh's bones to smooth up your work?

LACY. *Yaw, yaw ; be niet vorveard.*[36] *Ik hab all de dingen voour mack skoes groot and cleane.*[37] 110

FIRK. Ha, ha ! Good master, hire him ; he 'll make me laugh so that I shall work more in mirth than I can in earnest.

EYRE. Hear ye, friend, have ye any skill in the mystery [38] of cordwainers?

LACY. *Ik weet niet wat yow seg ; ich ve[r]staw you niet.*[39]

FIRK. Why, thus, man ! [*imitating by gesture a shoemaker at work*] — *Ich verste u niet,* quoth 'a. 120

LACY. *Yaw, yaw, yaw ; ick can dat wel doen.*

FIRK. *Yaw, yaw !* He speaks yawing like a jackdaw that gapes to be fed with cheese-curds. Oh, he 'll give a villainous pull at a can of double-beer ; but Hodge and I have the vantage : we must drink first, because we are the eldest journeymen.

EYRE. What is thy name?

LACY. Hans — Hans Meulter.

EYRE. Give me thy hand ; th'art wel- [130 come. — Hodge, entertain him ; Firk, bid him welcome ; come, Hans. Run, wife, bid your maids, your trullibubs,[40] make ready my fine men's breakfasts. To him, Hodge !

HODGE. Hans, th'art welcome ; use thyself friendly, for we are good fellows ; if not, thou shalt be fought with, wert thou bigger than a giant.

FIRK. Yea, and drunk with, wert thou Gargantua. My master keeps no cowards, I [140 tell thee. — Ho, boy, bring him an heel-block ;[41] here 's a new journeyman.

Enter Boy.

LACY. O, *ich wersto you ; ich moet een halve dossen cans betaelen ; here, boy, nempt dis skilling, tap eens freelicke.*[42] *Exit* Boy.

EYRE. Quick, snipper-snapper, away ! Firk, scour thy throat ; thou shalt wash it with Castilian liquor.

Enter Boy.

Come, my last of the fives,[43] give me a can. Have to thee, Hans ; here, Hodge ; here, [150 Firk ; drink, you mad Greeks, and work like true Trojans, and pray for Simon Eyre, the shoemaker. — Here, Hans, and th'art welcome.

FIRK. Lo, Dame, you would have lost a good fellow that will teach us to laugh. This beer came hopping in well.

MARG. Simon, it is almost seven.

EYRE. Is 't so, Dame Clapper-dudgeon?[44] is 't seven a'clock, and my men's breakfast not ready? Trip and go, you sous'd conger,[45] [160 away ! Come, you mad Hyperboreans ;[46] follow me, Hodge ; follow me, Hans ; come after, my fine Firk ; to work, to work awhile, and then to breakfast. *Exit.*

FIRK. Soft ! *Yaw, yaw,* good Hans, though my master have no more wit but to call you afore me, I am not so foolish to go behind you, I being the elder journeyman. *Exeunt.*

[SCENE IV] [47]

Hollowing [48] *within. Enter* WARNER *and* HAMMON, *like hunters.*

HAM. Cousin, beat every brake; the game 's not far ;
This way with winged feet he fled from death,
Whilst the pursuing hounds, scenting his steps,
Find out his highway to destruction.
Besides, the miller's boy told me even now,
He saw him take soil,[49] and he halloaed him,
Affirming him [to have been] [50] so emboss'd [51]
That long he could not hold.

---

[34] Good-day, master, and you, goodwife, also.
[35] By God's nails.   [36] Don't be afraid.
[37] Large and small.   [38] Craft.
[39] I don't know what you say ; I don't understand you.
[40] Trillibubs, the (edible) entrails of animals; *i.e.* trifles.
[41] Used in fastening a lift to a shoe.
[42] Oh, I understand you ; I must pay for half a dozen cans ; here boy, take this shilling ; draw once freely.
[43] Alluding to the diminutive stature of the boy, since number five is a small last.
[44] Because her tongue is as noisy as the wooden cover of a beggar's clap-dish.
[45] Pickled conger-eel.
[46] The fabulous people, in the Greek mythology, who lived far to the north in a state of perpetual happiness.
[47] A field near Old Ford.
[48] Hallooing. — "Like" = costumed as.
[49] Take refuge in a stretch of water.
[50] Add. Warnke and Proescholdt.
[51] Exhausted.

WARN. 　　　　　If it be so,
'T is best we trace these meadows by Old Ford.

A noise of Hunters *within.　Enter a* Boy.

HAM. How now, boy? Where's the deer?
　　speak! saw'st thou him?　　　　　　10

BOY. Oh yea; I saw him leap through a
hedge, and then over a ditch, then at my Lord
Mayor's pale; over he skipp'd me, and in he
went me, and "holla" the hunters cri'd, and
"there, boy; there, boy!" But there he is,
a' mine honesty.

HAM. Boy, God-a-mercy.[52] Cousin, let's
　　away;
I hope we shall find better sport to-day.
　　　　　　　　　　　　　　　　Exeunt.

[SCENE V] [53]

Hunting within.　Enter ROSE *and* SYBIL.

ROSE. Why, Sybil, wilt thou prove a for-
　　ester?

SYBIL. Upon some,[54] no. Forester? Go
by; no, faith, Mistress. The deer came running into the barn through the orchard and
over the pale; I wot well I look'd as pale as a
new cheese to see him. But whip, says Goodman Pinclose, up with his flail, and our Nick
with a prong, and down he fell, and they upon
him, and I upon them. By my troth, we had
such sport; and in the end we ended him; [10
his throat we cut, flay'd him, unhorn'd him,
and my Lord Mayor shall eat of him anon,
when he comes.　　　*Horns sound within.*

ROSE. Hark, hark, the hunters come; y'
　　are best take heed:
They 'll have a saying to you for this deed.

Enter HAMMON, WARNER, Huntsmen, *and*
Boy.

HAM. God save you, fair ladies.

SYBIL. 　　　　　Ladies! Oh, gross![55]

WARN. Came not a buck this way?

ROSE. 　　　　　No, but[56] two does.

HAM. And which way went they? Faith,
　　we 'll hunt at those.

SYBIL. At those? Upon some, no. When,
　　can you tell?

WARN. Upon some, ay.

SYBIL. 　Good Lord!

52 Thanks.
53 Not precisely located; perhaps the garden at
Old Ford.
54 Apparently a modish expression of assertion,
formed after "upon my honor." (Warnke-
Proescholdt.)
55 How dull.
56 Merely.

WARN. 　Wounds![57] Then farewell! [20

HAM. Boy, which way went he?

BOY. 　　　　　This way, sir, he ran.

HAM. This way he ran indeed, fair Mistress
　　Rose;
Our game was lately in your orchard seen.

WARN. Can you advise which way he took
　　his flight?

SYBIL. Follow your nose; his horns will
　　guide you right.

WARN. Th'art a mad wench.

SYBIL. 　　　　　Oh, rich!

ROSE. 　　　　　Trust me, not I
It is not like [that][58] the wild forest deer
Would come so near to places of resort;
You are deceiv'd; he fled some other way.

WARN. Which way, my sugar-candy, can
　　you show?　　　　　　30

SYBIL. Come up, good honeysops, upon
　　some, no.

ROSE. Why do you stay, and not pursue
　　your game?

SYBIL. I 'll hold my life, their hunting nags
　　be lame.

HAM. A deer more dear is found within this
　　place.

ROSE. But not the deer, sir, which you had
　　in chase.

HAM. I chas'd the deer, but this dear
　　chaseth me.

ROSE. The strangest hunting that ever I see.
But where's your park? (*She offers to go away.*)

HAM. 　　　'T is here. Oh, stay!

ROSE. Impale[59] me, and then I will not
　　stray.

WARN. They wrangle, wench; we are more
　　kind than they.　　　　40

SYBIL. What kind of hart is that dear heart
　　you seek?

WARN. A hart, dear heart.

SYBIL. 　　　　Who ever saw the like?

ROSE. To lose your heart, is 't possible you
　　can?

HAM. My heart is lost.

ROSE. 　　　　Alack, good gentleman!

HAM. This poor lost heart would I wish you
　　might find.

ROSE. You, by such luck, might prove your
　　hart a hind.[60]

HAM. Why Luck had horns, so have I heard
　　some say.

ROSE. Now, God, an 't be his will, send
　　Luck into your way.

57 By God's wounds.
58 Add. Q 2.　　　59 Fence.　　　60 A doe.

Enter LORD MAYOR *and* Servants.

L. MAYOR. What, Master Hammon? Welcome to Old Ford!

SYBIL. Gods pittikins,[61] hands off, sir! Here's my Lord.   50

L. MAYOR. I hear you had ill luck, and lost your game.

HAM. 'T is true, my Lord.

L. MAYOR.   I am sorry for the same. What gentleman is this?

HAM.   My brother-in-law.

L. MAYOR. Y' are welcome both; sith [62] Fortune offers you

Into my hands, you shall not part from hence,

Until you have refresh'd your wearied limbs.

Go, Sybil, cover the board! You shall be guest

To no good cheer, but even a hunter's feast.

HAM. I thank your Lordship. — Cousin, on my life,

For our lost venison I shall find a wife.   60

         Exeunt [*all but* MAYOR].

L. MAYOR. In gentlemen; I 'll not be absent long. —

This Hammon is a proper gentleman,

A citizen by birth, fairly allied;

How fit an husband were he for my girl!

Well, I will in, and do the best I can

To match my daughter to this gentleman.

         Exit.

[ACT III — SCENE I][1]

Enter LACY [*as* HANS], Skipper, HODGE, *and* FIRK.

Skip. *Ick sal yow wat seggen,*[2] *Hans; dis skip dat comen from Candy, is all wol* [3] *by Got's sacrament, van sugar, civet, almonds, cambrick, end alle dingen, towsand towsand ding. Nempt* [4] *it, Hans, nempt it vor u meester. Daer be de bils van laden. Your meester Simon Eyre sal hae good copen.*[5] *Wat seggen yow, Hans?*

FIRK. *Wat seggen de reggen de copen, slopen* — laugh, Hodge, laugh!

LACY. *Mine liever* [6] *broder Firk, bringt* [10 *Meester Eyre* [tot] [7] *den signe un Swannekin;* [8] *daer sal yow finde dis skipper end me. Wat*

---

[61] By God's pity.   [62] Since.
[1] A room in Eyre's house.
[2] I 'll tell you what.   [3] Full.   [4] Take.
[5] A good bargain.
[6] Dear.
[7] Old eds. *lot.*
[8] *I.e.,* to the sign of the Swan.

---

seggen yow, broder Firk? Doot [9] *it, Hodge. —* *Come, skipper.*   *Exeunt* [LACY *and* Skipper].

FIRK. Bring him, quod you? Here's no knavery, to bring my master to buy a ship worth the lading of two or three hundred thousand pounds. Alas, that's nothing; a trifle, a bauble, Hodge.

HODGE. The truth is, Firk, that the [20 merchant owner of the ship dares not show his head, and therefore this skipper that deals for him, for the love he bears to Hans, offers my master Eyre a bargain in the commodities. He shall have a reasonable day of payment; he may sell the wares by that time, and be an huge gainer himself.

FIRK. Yea, but can my fellow Hans lend my master twenty porpentines as an earnest penny?   [30

HODGE. Portuguese, thou wouldst say; here they be, Firk; hark, they jingle in my pocket like St. Mary Overy's [10] bells.

Enter EYRE *and his wife* [MARGERY].

FIRK. Mum, here comes my dame and my master. She 'll scold, on my life, for loitering this Monday; but all 's one: let them all say what they can, Monday 's our holiday.

MARG. You sing, Sir Sauce, but I beshrew your heart:

I fear for this your singing we shall smart. [39

FIRK. Smart for me, dame; why, dame, why?

HODGE. Master, I hope you 'll not suffer my dame to take down your journeymen.

FIRK. If she take me down, I 'll take her up; yea, and take her down too, a buttonhole lower.

EYRE. Peace, Firk; not I, Hodge; by the life of Pharaoh, by the Lord of Ludgate, by this beard, every hair whereof I value at a king's ransom, she shall not meddle with [50 you. — Peace, you bombast cotton-candle quean; away, queen of clubs; [11] quarrel not with me and my men, with me and my fine Firk; I 'll firk [12] you, if you do.

MARG. Yea, yea, man, you may use me as you please; but let that pass.

EYRE. Let it pass, let it vanish away; peace! Am I not Simon Eyre? Are not these my brave men, brave shoemakers, all gentlemen of the gentle craft? Prince am [60

---

[9] Do.
[10] Cor. Q₅; earlier eds. *Queries.* This church, also called St. Saviour's, stands on the Bankside.
[11] *I.e.,* of the prentices; or possibly in allusion to her complexion.   [12] Beat.

I none, yet am I nobly born, as being the sole son of a shoemaker.[13] Away, rubbish! vanish, melt; melt, like kitchen-stuff.[14]

MARG. Yea, yea, 't is well; I must be call'd rubbish, kitchen-stuff, for a sort[15] of knaves.

FIRK. Nay, Dame, you shall not weep and wail in woe for me. Master, I'll stay no longer; here's an [i]nventory of my shop tools. Adieu, Master; Hodge, farewell.   70

HODGE. Nay, stay, Firk; thou shalt not go alone.

MARG. I pray, let them go; there be mo maids than Mawkin, more men than Hodge, and more fools than Firk.

FIRK. Fools? Nails! if I tarry now, I would my guts might be turn'd to shoe-thread.

HODGE. And if I stay, I pray God I may be turn'd to a Turk, and set in Finsbury[16] for boys to shoot at. — Come, Firk.   80

EYRE. Stay, my fine knaves, you arms of my trade, you pillars of my profession. What, shall a tittle-tattle's words make you forsake Simon Eyre? — Avaunt, kitchen-stuff! Rip,[17] you brown-bread[18] Tannikin;[19] out of my sight! Move me not! Have not I ta'en you from selling tripes in Eastcheap, and set you in my shop, and made you hail-fellow with Simon Eyre, the shoemaker? And now do you deal thus with my journeymen? [90 Look, you powder-beef quean, on the face of Hodge, here's a face for a lord.

FIRK. And here's a face for any lady in Christendom.

EYRE. Rip, you chitterling,[20] avaunt! Boy! [*Enter* Boy.] Bid the tapster of the Boar's Head fill me a dozen cans of beer for my journeymen.

FIRK. A dozen cans? O, brave! Hodge, now I'll stay.   100

EYRE. [*aside to the* Boy] An the knave fills any more than two, he pays for them. [*Exit* Boy.] — A dozen cans of beer for my journeymen. [*Re-enter* Boy.] Here,[21] you mad Mesopotamians, wash your livers with this liquor. Where be the odd ten? — No more, Madge, no more. — Well said.[22] Drink and to work! — What work dost thou, Hodge? What work?   109

HODGE. I am a making a pair of shoes for my Lord Mayor's daughter, Mistress Rose.

FIRK. And I a pair of shoes for Sybil, my Lord's maid. I deal with her.

EYRE. Sybil? Fie, defile not thy fine workmanly fingers with the feet of kitchen-stuff and basting-ladles. Ladies of the court, fine ladies, my lads, commit their feet to our apparelling; put gross work to Hans. Yark[23] and seam, yark and seam!

FIRK. For yarking and seaming let me [120 alone, an I come to 't.

HODGE. Well, master, all this is from the bias.[24] Do you remember the ship my fellow Hans told you of? The skipper and he are both drinking at the Swan. Here be the Portuguese to give earnest. If you go through with it, you cannot choose but be a lord at least.

FIRK. Nay, dame, if my master prove not a lord, and you a lady, hang me.   130

MARG. Yea, like enough, if you may loiter and tipple thus.

FIRK. Tipple, dame? No, we have been bargaining with Skellum[25] Skanderbag[26] Can-you-Dutch-speaken[27] for a ship of silk cypress, laden with sugar-candy.

Re-enter the Boy *with a velvet coat and an alderman's gown.* EYRE *puts it on.*

EYRE. Peace, Firk; silence, Tittle-tattle! Hodge, I'll go through with it. Here's a seal-ring, and I have sent for a guarded[28] gown and a damask cassock. See where [140 it comes; look here, Maggy; help me, Firk; apparel me, Hodge; silk and satin, you mad Philistines, silk and satin.

FIRK. Ha, ha, my master will be as proud as a dog in a doublet, all in beaten[29] damask and velvet.

EYRE. Softly, Firk, for rearing[30] of the nap, and wearing threadbare my garments. How

[13] An allusion to the vaunt of Crispianus that "a shoemaker's son is a prince born"; his brother Crispin's son by the Princess Ursula made good the boast.
[14] *I.e.*, the greasy refuse of the kitchen.
[15] Set.
[16] A field to the north of the City, where archery was practiced.
[17] Move on.   [18] Homely, unrefined.
[19] Dutchwoman.
[20] Small intestine, for eating.
[21] Harvard and Folger copies of Q₁ *Heare*, though Lange reads Qq ₁, ₂, *heave.*

[22] Well done, good for you.
[23] Twitch (the stitch tight).
[24] Out of the way.
[25] Rogue. Du. *Schelm.*
[26] John Castriota, the Albanian patriot, called by the Turks Iskanderbey = Prince Alexander.
[27] Old eds. have no punctuation between *we* and *spreaken* but the last phrase is evidently part of the name Firk gives the skipper.
[28] Ornamented.
[29] Wrought with metal trimmings.
[30] Ruffling up.

dost thou like me, Firk? How do I look, my fine Hodge? 150

HODGE. Why, now you look like yourself, Master. I warrant you, there's few in the city but will give you the wall,[31] and come upon you with [32] the Right Worshipful.

FIRK. Nails, my master looks like a threadbare cloak new turn'd and dress'd. Lord, Lord, to see what good raiment doth! Dame, dame, are you not enamored?

EYRE. How say'st thou, Maggy, am I not brisk? Am I not fine? 160

MARG. Fine? By my troth, sweetheart, very fine! By my troth, I never lik'd thee so well in my life, sweetheart; but let that pass. I warrant there be many women in the city have not such handsome husbands, but only for their apparel; but let that pass too.

Re-enter [LACY *as*] HANS, *and* Skipper.

HANS. *Godden day, mester. Dis be de skipper dat heb de skip van marchandice; de commodity ben good; nempt it, master, nempt it.* 170

EYRE. God-a-mercy, Hans; welcome, skipper. Where lies this ship of merchandise?

SKIP. *De skip ben in rovere;* [33] *dor be van sugar, civet, almonds, cambricke, and a towsand, towsand tings, Gotz sacrament; nempt it, mester: yo sal het good copen.*

FIRK. To him, Master! O sweet Master! O sweet wares! Prunes, almonds, sugar-candy, carrot-roots, turnips, O brave fatting meat! Let not a man buy a nutmeg [180 but yourself.

EYRE. Peace, Firk! Come, skipper, I'll go [aboard] [34] with you. — Hans, have you made him drink?

SKIP. *Yaw, yaw, ic heb veale gedrunck.*[35]

EYRE. Come, Hans, follow me. Skipper, thou shalt have my countenance in the city.

Exeunt [EYRE, LACY, *and* Skipper.]

FIRK. *Yaw heb veale gedrunck*, quoth 'a. They may well be called butter-boxes, when they drink fat veal and thick beer too. [190 But come, Dame, I hope you'll chide us no more.

MARG. No, faith, Firk; no, perdy,[36] Hodge. I do feel honor creep upon me, and which is

more, a certain rising in my flesh; but let that pass.

FIRK. Rising in your flesh do you feel, say you? Ay, you may be with child; but why should not my master feel a rising in his flesh, having a gown and a gold ring on? But [200 you are such a shrew, you'll soon pull him down.

MARG. Ha, ha! prithee, peace! Thou mak'st my Worship laugh; but let that pass. Come, I'll go in; Hodge, prithee, go before me; Firk, follow me.

FIRK. Firk doth follow: Hodge, pass out in state. *Exeunt.*

[SCENE II] [37]

Enter [*the* EARL OF] LINCOLN *and* DODGER.

LINC. How now, good Dodger; what's the news in France?

DODGER. My Lord, upon the eighteen day of May

The French and English were prepar'd to fight;

Each side with eager fury gave the sign

Of a most hot encounter. Five long hours

Both armies fought together; at the length

The lot of victory fell on our sides.

Twelve thousand of the Frenchmen that day di'd,

Four thousand English, and no man of name

But Captain Hyam and young Ardington, [10

Two gallant gentlemen, I knew them well.

LINC. But Dodger, prithee, tell me, in this fight

How did my cousin Lacy bear himself?

DODGER. My Lord, your cousin Lacy was not there.

LINC. Not there?

DODGER. No, my good Lord.

LINC. Sure, thou mistakest.

I saw him shipp'd, and a thousand eyes beside

Were witnesses [38] of the farewells which he gave,

When I, with weeping eyes, bid him adieu.

Dodger, take heed.

DODGER. My Lord, I am advis'd [39]

That what I spake is true; to prove it so, [20

His cousin Askew, that suppli'd his place,

Sent me for him from France, that secretly

He might convey himself hither.[40]

LINC. Is't even so?

Dares he so carelessly venture his life

---

[31] *I.e.*, show you deference.
[32] Approach you with the title of. — Eyre is disguising himself as a magnate in order to induce the skipper to sell him the cargo. In Deloney much more is made of this trick.
[33] River. [34] Cor. Q 3; Qq 1, 2, *abroade.*
[35] Drunk much. [36] *Par Dieu.*

[37] Unlocated; perhaps a room in the Earl's house.
[38] Q 3 *et seq.*, *witnesse.*
[39] Informed. [40] *I.e.*, thither.

Upon the indignation of a king?
Hath he despis'd my love, and spurn'd those
    favors
Which I with prodigal hand pour'd on his
    head?
He shall repent his rashness with his soul ;
Since of my love he makes no estimate,
I 'll make him wish he had not known my
    hate.   30
Thou hast no other news?
    DODGER.   None else, my Lord.
    LINC. None worse I know thou hast. —
      Procure the King
To crown his giddy brows with ample honors,
Send him chief colonel,[41] and all my hope
Thus to be dash'd! But 't is in vain to
    grieve ;
One evil cannot a worse relieve.
Upon my life, I have found out his plot ;
That old dog, Love, that fawn'd upon him so,
Love to that puling girl, his fair-cheek'd Rose,
The Lord Mayor's daughter, hath distracted
    him ;   40
And in the fire of that love's lunacy
Hath he burnt up himself, consum'd his credit,
Lost the King's love, yea, and I fear, his life,
Only to get a wanton to his wife ;
Dodger, it is so.
    DODGER.   I fear so, my good Lord.
    LINC. It is so — nay, sure it cannot be !
I am at my wits' end, Dodger !
    DODGER.   Yea, my Lord.
    LINC. Thou art acquainted with my neph-
      ew's haunts ;   48
Spend this gold for thy pains : go seek him out.
Watch at my Lord Mayor's — there if he live,
Dodger, thou shalt be sure to meet with him.
Prithee, be diligent. — Lacy, thy name
Liv'd once in honor ; now ['t is] [42] dead in
    shame. —
Be circumspect.   *Exit.*
    DODGER.   I warrant you, my Lord. *Exit.*

[SCENE III] [43]

Enter LORD MAYOR *and* MASTER SCOTT.

    L. MAYOR. Good Master Scott, I have
      been bold with you
To be a witness to a wedding knot
Betwixt young Master Hammon and my
    daughter.
Oh, stand aside ; see where the lovers come.

---

41 Trisyllabic.
42 Add. Lange. Om. old eds.
43 A room in the Lord Mayor's house in London.

Enter HAMMON *and* ROSE.

    ROSE. Can it be possible you love me so ?
No, no ; within those eyeballs I espy
Apparent likelihoods of flattery.
Pray now, let go my hand.
    HAM.   Sweet Mistress Rose,
Misconstrue not my words, nor misconceive
Of my affection, whose devoted soul   10
Swears that I love thee dearer than my
    heart.
    ROSE. As dear as your own heart? I judge
    it right,
Men love their hearts best when th 'are out of
    sight.
    HAM. I love you, by this hand.
    ROSE.   Yet hands off now !
If flesh be frail, how weak and frail 's your
    vow !
    HAM. Then by my life I swear.
    ROSE.   Then do not brawl ;
One quarrel loseth wife and life and all.
Is not your meaning thus?
    HAM.   In faith, you jest.
    ROSE. Love loves to sport ; therefore leave
    love, y 'are best.
    L. MAYOR. [*aside to* SCOTT] What? square [44]
    they, Master Scott?
    SCOTT. [*aside to* MAYOR]   Sir, never
    doubt,   20
Lovers are quickly in, and quickly out.
    HAM. Sweet Rose, be not so strange in
    fancying me.
Nay, never turn aside, shun not my sight ;
I am not grown so fond, to fond [45] my love
On any that shall quit [46] it with disdain ;
If you will love me, so ; — if not, farewell.
    L. MAYOR. [*advancing*] Why, how now,
    lovers, are you both agreed?
    HAM. Yes, faith, my Lord.
    L. MAYOR. 'T is well, give me your hand ;
Give me yours, Daughter. — How now, both
    pull back !
What means this, girl?
    ROSE.   I mean to live a maid. [30
    HAM. (*aside*) But not to die one ; pause, ere
    that be said.
    L. MAYOR. Will you still cross me, still be
    obstinate?
    HAM. Nay, chide her not, my Lord, for do-
    ing well ;
If she can live an happy virgin's life,
'T is far more blessed than to be a wife.

---

44 Quarrel.
45 Found, punning on fond. (Neilson.)
46 Requite.

Rose. Say, sir, I cannot; I have made a
    vow,
Whoever be my husband, 't is not you.
    L. Mayor. Your tongue is quick; but
        Master Hammon, know
I bade you welcome to another end.
    Ham. What, would you have me pule and
        pine and pray,   40
With " lovely lady," " mistress of my heart,"
" Pardon your servant; " and the rhymer
    play,
Railing on Cupid and his tyrant's-dart;
Or shall I undertake some martial spoil,
Wearing your glove at tourney and at tilt,
And tell how many gallants I unhors'd —
Sweet, will this pleasure you?
    Rose.   Yea, when wilt begin?
What, love rhymes, man? Fie on that deadly
    sin!
    L. Mayor. If you will have her, I'll make
        her agree.
    Ham. Enforced love is worse than hate to
        me. —   50
[*aside*] There is a wench keeps shop in the Old
    Change,
To her will I (it is not wealth I seek;
I have enough) and will prefer her love
Before the world. — My good Lord Mayor,
    adieu;
Old love for me: I have no luck with new.
                                            Exit.
    L. Mayor. Now, mammet,[47] you have well
        behav'd yourself;
But you shall curse your coyness if I live. —
Who's within there? See you convey your
    mistress
Straight to th' Old Ford! — I'll keep you
    straight[48] enough. —   59
'Fore God, I would have sworn the puling girl
Would willingly accepted Hammon's love;
But banish him, my thoughts! — Go, minion,
    in! —   *Exit* Rose.
Now tell me, Master Scott, would you have
    thought
That Master Simon Eyre, the shoemaker,
Had been of wealth to buy such merchandise?
    Scott. 'T was well, my Lord, your Honor
        and myself
Grew partners with him; for your bills of
    lading
Show that Eyre's gains in one commodity
Rise at the least to full three thousand pound,
Besides like gain in other merchandise.   70

⁴⁷ Maumet, puppet.
⁴⁸ In order.

L. Mayor. Well, he shall spend some of his
    thousands now,
For I have sent for him to the Guildhall.

                Enter Eyre.

See, where he comes. — Good morrow, Master
    Eyre.
    Eyre. Poor Simon Eyre, my Lord, your
        shoemaker.
    L. Mayor. Well, well, it likes [49] yourself to
        term you so. —

                Enter Dodger.

Now Master Dodger, what's the news with
    you?
    Dodger. I'd gladly speak in private to
        your Honor.
    L. Mayor. You shall, you shall. — Master
        Eyre and Master Scott,
I have some business with this gentleman;
I pray, let me entreat you to walk before   80
To the Guildhall; I'll follow presently.
Master Eyre, I hope ere noon to call you
    sheriff.
    Eyre. I would not care, my Lord, if you
        might call me
King of Spain. — Come, Master Scott.
                [*Exeunt* Eyre *and* Scott.]
    L. Mayor. Now, Master Dodger, what's
        the news you bring?
    Dodger. The Earl of Lincoln by me greets
        your Lordship,
And earnestly requests you if you can
Inform him where his nephew Lacy keeps.
    L. Mayor. Is not his nephew Lacy now in
        France?
    Dodger. No, I assure your Lordship, but
        disguis'd   90
Lurks here in London.
    L. Mayor.   London? Is't even so?
It may be; but upon my faith and soul,
I know not where he lives, or whether he lives.
So tell my Lord of Lincoln. Lurk in London?
Well, Master Dodger, you perhaps may start
    him;
Be but the means to rid him into France,
I'll give you a dozen angels [50] for your pains;
So much I love his Honor, hate his nephew.
And, prithee, so inform thy lord from me.
    Dodger. I take my leave. *Exit* Dodger.
    L. Mayor.   Farewell, good Master
        Dodger. —   100
Lacy in London? I dare pawn my life,

⁴⁹ Is pleasing to.
⁵⁰ Gold coins worth about $2.50 each.

My daughter knows thereof, and for that cause
Deni'd young Master Hammon in his love.
Well, I am glad I sent her to Old Ford.
Gods Lord, 't is late ! to Guildhall I must hie ;
I know my brethren stay [51] my company. *Exit.*

[SCENE IV] [52]

Enter FIRK, *Eyre's wife* [MARGERY, LACY *as*]
HANS, *and* ROGER.

MARG. Thou goest too fast for me, Roger.
— Oh, Firk.

FIRK. Ay, forsooth.

MARG. I pray thee, run — do you hear? —
run to Guildhall, and learn if my husband,
Master Eyre, will take that worshipful vocation of Master Sheriff upon him. Hie thee,
good Firk.

FIRK. Take it? Well, I go ; an he should
not take it, Firk swears to forswear him. [10
Yes, forsooth, I go to Guildhall.

MARG. Nay, when? [53] Thou art too compendious and tedious.

FIRK. O rare ! your excellence is full of eloquence ; how like a new cart-wheel my dame
speaks, and she looks like an old musty ale-
bottle [54] going to scalding.

MARG. Nay, when? Thou wilt make me
melancholy.

FIRK. God forbid your Worship should [20
fall into that humor — I run.   *Exit.*

MARG. Let me see now, Roger and Hans.

HODGE. Ay, forsooth, Dame — Mistress, I
should say, but the old term so sticks to the
roof of my mouth, I can hardly lick it off.

MARG. Even what thou wilt, good Roger ;
dame is a fair name for any honest Christian ;
but let that pass. How dost thou, Hans?

HANS. *Mee tanck you, vro.* [55]

MARG. Well, Hans and Roger, you see [30
God hath bless'd your master ; and, perdy, if
ever he comes to be Master Sheriff of London
— as we are all mortal — you shall see, I will
have some odd thing or other in a corner for
you : I will not be your backfriend ; [56] but let
that pass. — Hans, pray thee, tie my shoe.

HANS. *Yaw, ic sal, vro.*

MARG. Roger, thou know'st the length of
my foot : as it is none of the biggest, so I thank
God, it is handsome enough ; prithee, let [40

me have a pair of shoes made, cork,[57] good
Roger, wooden heel too.

HODGE. You shall.

MARG. Art thou acquainted with never a
farthingale-maker, nor a French-hood-maker?
I must enlarge my bum, ha, ha ! How shall
I look in a hood, I wonder ! Perdy, oddly I
think.

HODGE. [*aside*] As a cat out of [58] a pillory. —
Very well, I warrant you, Mistress.   50

MARG. Indeed, all flesh is grass ; and,
Roger, canst thou tell where I may buy a good
hair?

HODGE. Yes, forsooth, at the poulterer's in
Gracious [59] Street.

MARG. Thou art an ungracious wag ; perdy,
I mean a false hair for my periwig.

HODGE. Why, Mistress, the next time I cut
my beard, you shall have the shavings of it ;
but they are all true hairs.   60

MARG. It is very hot ; I must get me a fan
or else a mask.

HODGE. [*aside*] So you had need, to hide
your wicked face.

MARG. Fie upon it, how costly this world's
calling is ; perdy, but that it is one of the wonderful works of God, I would not deal with it.
— Is not Firk come yet? — Hans, be not so
sad, let it pass and vanish, as my husband's
Worship says.   70

HANS. *Ick bin vrolicke ; lot see yow soo.* [60]

HODGE. Mistress, will you drink [61] a pipe of
tobacco?

MARG. Oh, fie upon it, Roger, perdy !
These filthy tobacco pipes are the most idle
slavering baubles that ever I felt. Out upon
it ! God bless us, men look not like men that
use them.

Enter RALPH [*with a crutch*] *being lame.*

HODGE. What, fellow Ralph? — Mistress,
look here, Jane's husband ! — Why, how [80
now,[62] lame? Hans, make much of him ; he's
a brother of our trade, a good workman, and a
tall [63] soldier.

HANS. You be welcome, broder.

MARG. Perdy, I knew him not. — How dost
thou, good Ralph? I am glad to see thee
well.

[51] Await.
[52] Before Eyre's house.
[53] An exclamation of impatience.
[54] *I.e.*, a leathern one.
[55] Mistress.
[56] False friend.

[57] *I.e.*, with a raised sole, to add height.
[58] *I.e.*, in ; for the French hood framed the
wearer's face with a large fold.
[59] Or Grass Street.
[60] I 'm merry ; let 's see you so.   [61] Smoke.
[62] So Folger copy of Q₁ ; Harvard copy om. *now.*
[63] Brave.

RALPH. I would [to] [64] God you saw me,
　　dame, as well
As when I went from London into France. [89

MARG. Trust me, I am sorry, Ralph, to
see thee impotent. Lord, how the wars have
made him sunburnt! The left leg is not well;
't was a fair gift of God the infirmity took not
hold a little higher, considering thou camest
from France; [65] but let that pass.

RALPH. I am glad to see you well, and I
　　rejoice
To hear that God hath bless'd my master so
Since my departure.

MARG. Yea, truly, Ralph, I thank my
Maker; but let that pass.　　　　　　　　100

HODGE. And, sirrah Ralph, what news,
what news in France?

RALPH. Tell me, good Roger, first, what
　　news in England?
How does my Jane? When didst thou see my
　　wife?
Where lives my poor heart? She'll be poor
　　indeed,
Now I want limbs to get whereon to feed.

HODGE. Limbs? Hast thou not hands,
man? Thou shalt never see a shoemaker
want bread, though he have but three fingers
on a hand.　　　　　　　　　　　　　　110

RALPH. Yet all this while I hear not of my
　　Jane.

MARG. Oh, Ralph, your wife — perdy, we
know not what 's become of her. She was
here a while, and because she was married,
grew more stately than became her; I check'd
her, and so forth; away she flung, never returned, nor said bye nor bah; and, Ralph,
you know, " ka me, ka thee." [66] And, so as
I tell ye — Roger, is not Firk come yet?

HODGE. No, forsooth.　　　　　　　　120

MARG. And so, indeed, we heard not of
her; but I hear she lives in London; but let
that pass. If she had wanted, she might have
opened her case to me or my husband, or to
any of my men; I am sure, there 's not any of
them, perdy, but would have done her good to
his power. — Hans, look if Firk be come.

HANS. *Yaw, [ik]* [67] *sal, vro.*　　　*Exit* HANS.

MARG. And so, as I said — but, Ralph, why
dost thou weep? Thou knowest that naked
we came out of our mother's womb, and [131

naked we must return; and, therefore, thank
God for all things.

HODGE. No, faith, Jane is a stranger here;
but, Ralph, pull up a good heart; I know thou
hast one. Thy wife, man, is in London; one
told me, he saw her awhile ago very brave [68]
and neat; we 'll ferret her out, an London hold
her.

MARG. Alas, poor soul, he 's overcome [140
with sorrow; he does but as I do, weep for the
loss of any good thing. — But, Ralph, get
thee in, call for some meat and drink; thou
shalt find me worshipful towards thee.

RALPH. I thank you, dame; since I want
　　limbs and lands,
I 'll [trust] [69] to God, my good friends, and
　　to these my hands.　　　　　　　　*Exit.*

Enter [LACY *as*] HANS *and* FIRK, *running.*

FIRK. Run, good Hans! O Hodge, O
Mistress! Hodge, heave up thine ears;
Mistress, smug up [70] your looks; on with your
best apparel; my master is chosen, my [150
master is called, nay, condemn'd by the cry of
the country, to be sheriff of the city for this
famous year now to come. And, time now
being, a great many men in black gowns were
ask'd for their voices [71] and their hands, and
my master had all their fists about his ears
presently, and they cried " Ay, ay, ay, ay,"—
and so I came away —
　　Wherefore without all other grieve
　　I do salute you, Mistress Shrieve. [72] [160

HANS. *Yaw, my mester is de groot man, de
shrieve.*

HODGE. Did not I tell you, Mistress? Now
I may boldly say, " Good morrow to your
Worship."

MARG. Good morrow, good Roger. — I
thank you, my good people all. — Firk, hold
up thy hand: here 's a threepenny piece for
thy tidings.

FIRK. 'T is but three halfpence, I think.
Yes, 't is threepence, I smell the rose. [73]　171

HODGE. But, Mistress, be rul'd by me, and
do not speak so pulingly.

FIRK. 'T is her Worship speaks so, and not
she. No, faith, Mistress, speak me in the old
key: " To it, Firk;" " there, good Firk;"
" ply your business, Hodge;" " Hodge, with a

---

[64] Om. old eds.
[65] Alluding to syphilis, "the French disease."
[66] If you "ka" me, I 'll "ka" thee; "ka" is found
only in this expression, implying mutual help, service,
or flattery. (*N.E.D.*)　　　[67] I; old eds. *it.*

[68] Well dressed.　[69] Om. Qq 1, 2; later Qq om. *these.*
[70] Smarten up.　　[71] Votes.　　[72] Sheriff.
[73] The silver threepence of Elizabeth had the
Queen's head and a rose on the obverse side. It
was not in general circulation, but was used for
maundy money. Margery is acting the rôle of a
sovereign dispensing alms.

full mouth ; " " I'll fill your bellies with good
cheer, till they cry twang."

Enter Simon Eyre *wearing a gold chain.*

Hans. See, myn liever broder, heer compt [180
my meester.

Marg. Welcome home, Master Shrieve ;
I pray God continue you in health and
wealth.

Eyre. See here, my Maggy, a chain, a gold
chain for Simon Eyre. I shall make thee a
lady ; here 's a French hood for thee ; on with
it, on with it ! dress thy brows with this flap of
a shoulder of mutton, to make thee look
lovely. — Where be my fine men ? — [190
Roger, I 'll make over my shop and tools to
thee ; Firk, thou shalt be the foreman ; Hans
thou shalt have an hundred for twenty.[74] Be
as mad knaves as your master Sim Eyre hath
been, and you shall live to be sheriffs of London. — How dost thou like me, Margery ? —
Prince am I none, yet am I princely born. —
Firk, Hodge, and Hans !

All Three. Ay, forsooth, what says your
Worship, Mistress [75] Sheriff ?   200

Eyre. Worship and honor, you Babylonian
knaves, for the gentle craft. But I forgot
myself ; I am bidden by my Lord Mayor to
dinner to Old Ford : he 's gone before ; I must
after. — Come, Madge, on with your trinkets !
— Now, my true Trojans, my fine Firk, my
dapper Hodge, my honest Hans, some device,
some odd crotchets, some morris, or such like,
for the honor of the gentle [76] shoemakers.
Meet me at Old Ford ; you know my mind. —
Come, Madge, away. Shut up the shop,
knaves, and make holiday.   212

      Exeunt [Eyre *and* Margery].

Firk. O rare ! O brave ! Come, Hodge ;
follow me, Hans ;
We 'll be with them for a morris dance.

      Exeunt.

[Scene V] [77]

Enter Lord Mayor, [Rose,] Eyre, *his wife*
[Margery] *in a French hood,*[78] Sybil, *and
other* Servants.

L. Mayor. Trust me, you are as welcome to
Old Ford
As I myself.

[74] In return for his loan of the "Portuguese."

[75] Q₆ and mod. eds. *Master ;* but this speech may
well be taken as a response to Margery's donning
the French hood.

[76] So Qq 1, 2 ; later Qq *gentleman, gentlemen.*

[77] A room in the Lord Mayor's house at Old Ford.

[78] Qq 1, 2, erroneously bestow the French hood on
Sybil.

Marg.   Truly, I thank your Lordship.

L. Mayor. Would our bad cheer were
worth the thanks you give.

Eyre. Good cheer, my Lord Mayor, fine
cheer !
A fine house, fine walls, all fine and neat.

L. Mayor. Now, by my troth, I 'll tell
thee, Master Eyre,
It does me good, and all my brethren,
That such a madcap fellow as thyself
Is ent'red into our society.

Marg. Ay, but, my Lord, he must learn
now to put on gravity.   10

Eyre. Peace, Maggy ; a fig for gravity !
When I go to Guildhall in my scarlet gown,
I 'll look as demurely as a saint, and speak as
gravely as a justice of peace ; but now I am
here at Old Ford, at my good Lord Mayor's
house, let it go by, vanish, Maggy ; I 'll be
merry ; away with flip-flap, these fooleries,
these gulleries. What, honey ? Prince am
I none, yet am I princely born. What says
my Lord Mayor ?   20

L. Mayor. Ha, ha, ha ! I had rather than
a thousand pound, I had an heart but half so
light as yours.

Eyre. Why, what should I do, my Lord?
A pound of care pays not a dram of debt.
Hum, let 's be merry, whiles we are young ; old
age, sack and sugar will steal upon us, ere we
be aware.

The First Three-Man's Song [79]

Oh, the month of May, the merry month of May,
   So frolic, so gay, and so green, so green, so
     green !   30
Oh, and then did I unto my true love say,
   " Sweet Peg, thou shalt be my summer's queen

" Now the nightingale, the pretty nightingale,
   The sweetest singer in all the forest's choir,
Entreats thee, sweet Peggy, to hear thy true love's
     tale ;
   Lo, yonder she sitteth, her breast against a brier.

" But oh, I spy the cuckoo, the cuckoo, the cuckoo ;
   See where she sitteth — come away, my joy ;
Come away, I prithee ! I do not like the cuckoo
   Should sing where my Peggy and I kiss and
     toy."   40

Oh, the month of May, the merry month of May,
   So frolic, so gay, and so green, so green, so green !
And then did I unto my true love say,
   " Sweet Peg, thou shalt be my summer's queen ! "

L. Mayor. It 's well done. — Mistress
Eyre, pray, give good counsel to my daughter.

Marg. I hope Mistress Rose will have the
grace to take nothing that 's bad.

[79] Both songs are printed before the play in the
old eds., which fail to indicate when they were
sung.

L. Mayor. Pray God she do ; for i' faith, Mistress Eyre,
I would bestow upon that peevish [80] girl   50
A thousand marks more than I mean to give her,
Upon condition she 'd be rul'd by me.
The ape still crosseth me.   There came of late
A proper gentleman of fair revenues,
Whom gladly I would call son-in-law :
But my fine cockney would have none of him. —
You 'll prove a coxcomb for it, ere you die ;
A courtier, or no man, must please your eye.

Eyre. Be rul'd, sweet Rose ; th 'art ripe for a man.   Marry not with a boy that [60 has no more hair on his face than thou hast on thy cheeks.   A courtier, wash,[81] go by ; stand not upon pishery-pashery [82] : those silken fellows are but painted images, outsides, outsides, Rose ; their inner linings are torn.   No, my fine mouse, marry me with a gentleman grocer like my Lord Mayor, your father ; a grocer is a sweet trade — plums, plums.   Had I a son or daughter should marry out of the generation and blood of the shoemakers, [70 he should pack.   What, the gentle trade is a living for a man through Europe, through the world.

A noise within of a tabor and a pipe.
L. Mayor. What noise is this ?
Eyre. O my Lord Mayor, a crew of good fellows that for love to your Honor are come hither with a morris dance. — Come in, my Mesopotamians,[83] cheerily.

Enter Hodge, [Lacy *as*] Hans, Ralph, Firk, *and other* Shoemakers, *in a morris ; after a little dancing, the* Lord Mayor *speaks.*

L. Mayor. Master Eyre, are all these shoemakers ?   80
Eyre. All cordwainers, my good Lord Mayor.
Rose. [*aside*] How like my Lacy looks yond shoemaker !
Hans. [*aside*] Oh, that I durst but speak unto my love !
L. Mayor. Sybil, go fetch some wine to make these drink. — You are all welcome.
All. We thank your Lordship.
    Rose *takes a cup of wine and goes to* Hans.

Rose. For his sake whose fair shape thou represent'st,
Good friend, I drink to thee.
Hans. *Ic bedancke, good frister.*[84]   90
Marg. I see, Mistress Rose, you do not want judgment ; you have drunk to the properest [85] man I keep.
Firk. Here be some have done their parts to be as proper as he.
L. Mayor. Well, urgent business calls me back to London.
Good fellows, first go in and taste our cheer ;
And to make merry as you homeward go,
Spend these two angels in beer at Stratford-Bow.
Eyre. To these two, my mad lads, [100 Sim Eyre adds another ; then cheerily, Firk ; tickle it, Hans, and all for the honor of shoemakers.

    All [*the* Shoemakers] *go dancing out.*
L. Mayor. Come, Master Eyre, let 's have your company.
    Exeunt [Mayor, Eyre, *and* Margery.]
Rose. Sybil, what shall I do ?
Sybil.   Why, what 's the matter ?
Rose. That Hans the shoemaker is my love Lacy,
Disguis'd in that attire to find me out.
How should I find the means to speak with him ?
Sybil. What, Mistress, never fear ; I dare venture my maidenhead to nothing, and [110 that 's great odds, that Hans the Dutchman, when we come to London, shall not only see and speak with you, but in spite of all your father's policies steal you away and marry you. Will not this please you ?
Rose. Do this, and ever be assured of my love.
Sybil. Away, then, and follow your father to London, lest your absence cause him to suspect something :
To-morrow, if my counsel be obey'd,   120
I 'll bind you prentice to the gentle trade.
    [*Exeunt.*]

[ACT IV — Scene I] [1]

Enter Jane *in a seamster's shop, working ; and* Hammon, *muffled, at another door ; he stands aloof.*

Ham. Yonder 's the shop,[2] and there my fair love sits.

---

[80] Silly.   [81] Swill (?).
[82] Fal-lals. (Skeat.) But perhaps = trifling talk, as in I, i, 128.
[83] Presumably Eyre uses this and other names from the geography of the Near East because he likes the sound of them.
[84] Miss.   [85] Handsomest.
[1] A street in London.   [2] Within the inner stage.

She's fair and lovely, but she is not mine.
Oh, would she were! Thrice have I courted her,
Thrice hath my hand been moist'ned with her hand,
Whilst my poor famish'd eyes do feed on that
Which made them famish. I am infortunate :
I still love one, yet nobody loves me.
I muse in other men what women see
That I so want! Fine Mistress Rose was coy,
And this too curious!³ Oh, no, she is chaste ; [11
And for ⁴ she thinks me wanton, she denies [11
To cheer my cold heart with her sunny eyes.
How prettily she works! O pretty hand!
O happy work! It doth me good to stand
Unseen to see her. Thus I oft have stood
In frosty evenings, a light burning by her,
Enduring biting cold, only to eye her.
One only look hath seem'd as rich to me
As a king's crown ; such is love's lunacy.
Muffled I'll pass along, and by that try   20
Whether she know me.
     JANE.   Sir, what is't you buy?
What is't you lack, sir, calico, or lawn,
Fine cambric shirts, or bands, what will you buy?
     HAM. [*aside*] That which thou wilt not sell.
     Faith, yet I'll try. —
How do you sell this handkerchief?
     JANE.   Good cheap.⁵
     HAM. And how these ruffs?
     JANE.   Cheap too.
     HAM.   And how this band?
     JANE. Cheap too.
     HAM.   All cheap ; how sell you then this hand?
     JANE. My hands are not to be sold.
     HAM.   To be given then !
Nay, faith, I come to buy.
     JANE.   But none knows when.
     HAM. Good sweet, leave work a little while ;
     let's play.   30
     JANE. I cannot live by keeping holiday.
     HAM. I'll pay you for the time which shall be lost.
     JANE. With me you shall not be at so much cost.
     HAM. Look, how you wound this cloth, so you wound me.
     JANE. It may be so.
     HAM.   'T is so.
     JANE.   What remedy?
     HAM. Nay, faith, you are too coy.
     JANE.   Let go my hand.

³ Fastidious.   ⁴ Because.   ⁵ At a bargain.

     HAM. I will do any task at your command ;
I would let go this beauty, were I not
In mind to disobey you by a power
That controls kings : I love you !
     JANE.   So ; now part. [40
     HAM. With hands I may, but never with my heart.
In faith, I love you.
     JANE.   I believe you do.
     HAM. Shall a true love in me breed hate in you?
     JANE. I hate you not.
     HAM.   Then you must love?
     JANE.   I do.
What are you better now? I love not you.
     HAM. All this, I hope, is but a woman's fray,
That means, " Come to me," when she cries, " Away ! "
In earnest, mistress, I do not jest,
A true chaste love hath ent'red in my breast.
I love you dearly, as I love my life ;   50
I love you as a husband loves a wife ;
That, and no other love, my love requires.
Thy wealth, I know, is little ; my desires
Thirst not for gold. Sweet, beauteous Jane, what's mine
Shall, if thou make myself thine, all be thine.
Say, judge, what is thy sentence, life or death ?
Mercy or cruelty lies in thy breath.
     JANE. Good sir, I do believe you love me well ;
For 't is a silly conquest, silly pride
For one like you — I mean a gentleman — [60
To boast that by his love-tricks he hath brought
Such and such women to his amorous lure.
I think you do not so ; yet many do,
And make it even a very trade to woo.
I could be coy, as many women be,
Feed you with sunshine smiles and wanton looks,
But I detest witchcraft ; say that I
Do constantly believe you, constant have ——
     HAM. Why dost thou not believe me?
     JANE.   I believe you ; [69
But yet, good sir, because I will not grieve you
With hopes to taste fruit which will never fall,
In simple truth this is the sum of all :
My husband lives, at least, I hope he lives.
Press'd was he to these bitter wars in France ;
Bitter they are to me by wanting him.
I have but one heart, and that heart's his due.
How can I then bestow the same on you?
Whilst he lives, his I live, be it ne'er so poor,
And rather be his wife than a king's whore.

HAM. Chaste and dear woman, I will not
 abuse thee,   80
Although it cost my life, if thou refuse me.
Thy husband, press'd for France, what was his
 name?
JANE. Ralph Damport.
HAM.   Damport? — Here's a letter sent
From France to me, from a dear friend of
 mine,
A gentleman of place ; here he doth write
Their names that have been slain in every
 fight.
JANE. I hope death's scroll contains not my
 love's name.
HAM. Cannot you read?
JANE.   I can.
HAM.   Peruse the same.
To my remembrance such a name I read
Amongst the rest. — See here.
JANE.   Ay me, he's dead ! [90
He's dead ! If this be true, my dear heart's
 slain !
HAM. Have patience, dear love.
JANE.   Hence, hence !
HAM.   Nay, sweet Jane,
Make not poor sorrow proud with these rich
 tears.
I mourn thy husband's death, because thou
 mourn'st.
JANE. That bill is forg'd ; 't is sign'd by
 forgery.
HAM. I'll bring thee letters sent besides to
 many,
Carrying the like report ; Jane, 't is too true.
Come, weep not ; mourning, though it rise
 from love,
Helps not the mourned, yet hurts them that
 mourn.
JANE. For God's sake, leave me.
HAM.   Whither dost thou turn? [100
Forget the de[a]d, love them that are alive ;
His love is faded, try how mine will thrive.
JANE. 'T is now no time for me to think on
 love.
HAM. 'T is now best time for you to think
 on love,
Because your love lives not.
JANE.   Though he be dead,
My love to him shall not be buried ;
For God's sake, leave me to myself alone.
HAM. 'T would kill my soul, to leave thee
 drown'd in moan.
Answer me to my suit, and I am gone ;
Say to me yea or no.
JANE.   No.

HAM.   Then farewell ! — [110
One farewell will not serve ; I come again.
Come dry these wet cheeks ; tell me, faith,
 sweet Jane,
Yea or no, once more.
JANE   Once more I say no ;
Once more begone, I pray ; else will I go.
 HAM. Nay, then I will grow rude, by this
  white hand,
Until you change that cold " no " ; here I'll
 stand
Till by your hard heart ——
 JANE.   Nay, for God's love, peace !
My sorrows by your presence more increase.
Not that you thus are present, but all grief
Desires to be alone ; therefore in brief 120
Thus much I say, and saying bid adieu :
If ever I wed man, it shall be you.
 HAM. O blessed voice ! Dear Jane, I'll
  urge no more ;
Thy breath hath made me rich.
 JANE.   Death makes me poor.
         Exeunt.

[SCENE II] [6]

Enter HODGE, *at his shop-board,* RALPH, FIRK,
[LACY *as*] HANS, *and a Boy, at work.*

 ALL. Hey, down a down, down derry.
 HODGE. Well said, my hearts ; ply your
work to-day ; we loit'red yesterday ; to it pell-
mell, that we may live to be lord mayors, or
aldermen at least.
 FIRK. Hey, down a down, derry.
 HODGE. Well said, i' faith ! How say'st
thou, Hans, doth not Firk tickle it ?
 HANS. *Yaw, mester.*
 FIRK. Not so neither, my organ-pipe [10
squeaks this morning for want of liquoring.
Hey, down a down, derry !
 HANS. *Forwar*[e], *Firk, tow best un jolly
youngster. Hort* [7] *'ee, mester ; ic bid yo cut me
un pair vampres* [8] *vor Mester Jeffre's boots.*
 HODGE. Thou shalt, Hans.
 FIRK. Master !
 HODGE. How now, boy?
 FIRK. Pray, now you are in the cutting vein,
cut me out a pair of counterfeits,[9] or else [20
my work will not pass current ; hey, down a
down !

---

[6] Hodge's shop.
[7] Hark. For *'ee* old eds. read *I.* — For *Forware*
(= indeed), old eds. read *Forward.*
[8] Vamps, uppers.
[9] *I.e.,* patterns ; " counterfeits " is used for the
sake of the pun. (Kittredge.)

HODGE. Tell me, sirs, are my cousin Mistress Priscilla's shoes done?

FIRK. Your cousin? No, master; one of your aunts,[10] hang her; let them alone.

RALPH. I am in hand with them; she gave charge that none but I should do them for her.

FIRK. Thou do for her? Then't will be a lame doing, and that she loves not. Ralph, [30 thou might'st have sent her to me; in faith, I would have yark'd and firk'd your Priscilla. Hey, down a down, derry. This gear will not hold.

HODGE. How say'st thou, Firk, were we not merry at Old Ford?

FIRK. How, merry! Why, our buttocks went jiggy-joggy like a quagmire. Well, Sir Roger Oatmeal, if I thought all meal of that nature, I would eat nothing but bag- [40 puddings.

RALPH. Of all good fortunes my fellow Hans had the best.

FIRK. 'T is true, because Mistress Rose drank to him.

HODGE. Well, well, work apace. They say seven of the aldermen be dead, or very sick.

FIRK. I care not; I'll be none.

RALPH. No, nor I; but then my Master Eyre will come quickly to be lord mayor. 50

Enter SYBIL.

FIRK. Whoop, yonder comes Sybil.

HODGE. Sybil, welcome, i' faith; and how dost thou, mad wench?

FIRK. Syb, whore, welcome to London.

SYBIL. Godamercy, sweet Firk; good Lord, Hodge, what a delicious shop you have got! You tickle it, i' faith.

RALPH. Godamercy, Sybil, for our good cheer at Old Ford.

SYBIL. That you shall have, Ralph. 60

FIRK. Nay, by the mass, we had tickling cheer, Sybil; and how the plague dost thou and Mistress Rose and my Lord Mayor? — I put the women in first.

SYBIL. Well, Godamercy; but God's me, I forget myself, where's Hans the Fleming?

FIRK. Hark, butter-box, now you must yelp out some *spreken.*

HANS. *Wat begaie [y]ou? Vat vod [y]ou, Frister?* [11] 70

SYBIL. Marry, you must come to my young mistress, to pull on her shoes you made last.

HANS. *Vare ben your [edle][12] fro, vare ben your mistris?*

SYBIL. Marry, here at our London house in [Cornhill.] [13]

FIRK. Will nobody serve her turn but Hans?

SYBIL. No, sir. — Come, Hans, I stand upon needles. 80

HODGE. Why then, Sybil, take heed of pricking.

SYBIL. For that let me alone. I have a trick in my budget. Come, Hans.

HANS. *Yaw, yaw, ic sall meete yo gane.* [14]

Exeunt HANS and SYBIL.

HODGE. Go, Hans, make haste again. — Come, who lacks work?

FIRK. I, Master, for I lack my breakfast; 't is munching-time, and past.

HODGE. Is 't so? — Why, then leave [90 work, Ralph. — To breakfast! — Boy, look to the tools. — Come, Ralph; come, Firk.

Exeunt.

[SCENE III] [15]

Enter a Serving Man.

SERV. Let me see now, the sign of the Last in Tower Street. Mass, yonder's the house. What, haw! Who's within?

Enter RALPH

RALPH. Who calls there? What want you, sir?

SERV. Marry, I would have a pair of shoes made for a gentlewoman against to-morrow morning. What, can you do them?

RALPH. Yes, sir, you shall have them. But what length's her foot? 10

SERV. Why you must make them in all parts like this shoe; but, at any hand, fail not to do them, for the gentlewoman is to be married very early in the morning.

RALPH. How? by this shoe must it be made? By this? Are you sure, sir, by this?

SERV. How, by this? am I sure, by this? — Art thou in thy wits? I tell thee, I must have a pair of shoes — dost thou mark me? A pair of shoes, two shoes, made by this very shoe, [20 this same shoe, against to-morrow morning by four a'clock. Dost understand me? Canst thou do't?

RALPH. Yes, sir, yes — I — I — I can do't. By this shoe, you say? I should know this

10 Mistresses.
11 What do you want? What would you, Miss?
12 Noble. Old eds. *egle.*
13 So Q5; earlier eds. *Cornewaile, Cornwall.*
14 With you go.
15 Before the shop.

shoe. Yes, sir yes, by this shoe, I can do 't.
Four a'clock. Well! Whither shall I bring
them?

SERV. To the sign of the Golden Ball in
Watling Street ; inquire for one Master [30
Hammon, a gentleman, my master.

RALPH. Yea, sir ; by this shoe, you say?

SERV. I say, Master Hammon at the Gold-
en Ball ; he 's the bridegroom, and those shoes
are for his bride.

RALPH. They shall be done by this shoe.
Well, well, Master Hammon at the Golden
Shoe — I would say, the Golden Ball ; very
well, very well. But I pray you, sir, where
must Master Hammon be married?   40

SERV. At Saint Faith's Church, under
Paul's.[16] But what 's that to thee? Prithee,
dispatch those shoes, and so farewell.   *Exit.*

RALPH. By this shoe, said he. How am I
amaz'd
At this strange accident ! Upon my life,
This was the very shoe I gave my wife,
When I was press'd for France ; since when,
alas !
I never could hear of her. It is the same,
And Hammon's bride no other but my Jane.

Enter FIRK.

FIRK. 'Snails,[17] Ralph, thou hast lost [50
thy part of three pots a countryman of mine
gave me to breakfast.

RALPH. I care not ; I have found a better
thing.

FIRK. A thing? Away! Is it a man's
thing, or a woman's thing?

RALPH. Firk, dost thou know this shoe?

FIRK. No, by my troth ; neither doth that
know me ! I have no acquaintance with it,
't is a mere stranger to me.   60

RALPH. Why, then I do ; this shoe, I durst
be sworn,
Once covered the instep of my Jane.
This is her size, her breadth, thus trod my
love ;
These true-love knots I prick'd. I hold my
life,
By this old shoe I shall find out my wife.

FIRK. Ha, ha ! Old shoe, that wert new !
How a murrain came this ague-fit of foolishness upon thee?

RALPH. Thus, Firk : even now here came a
serving man ;
By this shoe would he have a new pair made [70

Against to-morrow morning for his mistress,
That 's to be married to a gentleman.
And why may not this be my sweet Jane?

FIRK. And why mayst not thou be my
sweet ass? Ha, ha !

RALPH. Well, laugh and spare not ! But
the truth is this :
Against to-morrow morning I 'll provide
A lusty crew of honest shoemakers,
To watch the going of the bride to church.
If she prove Jane, I 'll take her in despite
From Hammon and the Devil, were he by. 80
If it be not my Jane, what remedy?
Hereof am I sure, I shall live till I die
Although I never with a woman lie.
                            Exit [RALPH].

FIRK. Thou lie with a woman to build
nothing but Cripplegates ! Well, God sends
fools fortune, and it may be, he may light upon
his matrimony by such a device ; for wedding
and hanging goes by destiny.   *Exit.*

[SCENE IV] [18]

Enter [LACY *as*] HANS *and* ROSE, *arm in arm.*

HANS. How happy am I by embracing
thee !
Oh, I did fear such cross mishaps did reign
That I should never see my Rose again.

ROSE. Sweet Lacy, since fair opportunity
Offers herself to furder our escape,
Let not too over-fond esteem of me
Hinder that happy hour. Invent the means,
And Rose will follow thee through all the
world.

HANS. Oh, how I surfeit with excess of joy,
Made happy by thy rich perfection !   10
But since thou pay'st sweet interest to my
hopes,
Redoubling love on love, let me once more
Like to a bold-fac'd debtor crave of thee
This night to steal abroad, and at Eyre's house,
Who now by death of certain aldermen
Is mayor of London, and my master once,
Meet thou thy Lacy, where in spite of change,
Your father's anger, and mine uncle's hate,
Our happy nuptials will we consummate.

Enter SYBIL.

SYBIL. O God, what will you do, mis- [20
tress? Shift for yourself, your father is at
hand ! He 's coming, he 's coming ! Master
Lacy, hide yourself in my mistress ! For
God's sake, shift for yourselves !

HANS. Your father come! Sweet Rose, what shall I do?
Where shall I hide me? How shall I escape?
ROSE. A man, and want wit in extremity?
Come, come, be Hans still; play the shoe-maker;
Pull on my shoe.

Enter LORD MAYOR.

HANS. Mass, and that's well rememb'red.
SYBIL. Here comes your father.   30
HANS. *Forware,*[19] *metresse, 't is un good skow; it sal vel dute,*[20] *or ye sal neit betallen.*[21]
ROSE. O God, it pincheth me; what will you do?
HANS. [*aside*] Your father's presence pinch-eth, not the shoe.
LORD MAYOR. Well done; fit my daughter well, and she shall please thee well.
HANS. *Yaw, yaw, ick weit*[22] *dat well; for-ware, 't is un good skoo, 't is gimait van neits leither: se ever, mine here.*[23]

Enter a Prentice.

L. MAYOR. I do believe it. — What's the news with you?   40
PRENTICE. Please you, the Earl of Lincoln at the gate
Is newly lighted,[24] and would speak with you.
L. MAYOR. The Earl of Lincoln come speak with me?
Well, well, I know his errand. — Daughter Rose,
Send hence your shoemaker; dispatch, have done!
Syb, make things handsome! Sir Boy, follow me.   *Exit* [*with the* Prentice].
HANS. Mine uncle come! Oh, what may this portend?
Sweet Rose, this of our love threatens an end.
ROSE. Be not dismay'd at this; whate'er befall,   49
Rose is thine own. To witness I speak truth,
Where thou appoints the place, I'll meet with thee.
I will not fix a day to follow thee,
But presently[25] steal hence. Do not reply;
Love, which gave strength to bear my father's hate,
Shall now add wings to further our escape.
            Exeunt.

[19] Indeed.
[20] Do it, serve.
[21] Pay.   [22] Know.
[23] 'T is made of neat's leather; just look, sir.
[24] Dismounted.   [25] Immediately.

[SCENE V][26]

Enter LORD MAYOR *and* [*the* EARL OF] LIN-COLN.

L. MAYOR. Believe me, on my credit, I speak truth :
Since first your nephew Lacy went to France
I have not seen him. It seem'd strange to me,
When Dodger told me that he stay'd behind,
Neglecting the high charge the King imposed.
LINCOLN. Trust me, Sir Roger Oateley, I did think
Your counsel had given head to this attempt,
Drawn to it by the love he bears your child.
Here I did hope to find him in your house;
But now I see mine error, and confess   10
My judgment wrong'd you by conceiving so.
L. MAYOR. Lodge in my house, say you? Trust me, my Lord,
I love your nephew Lacy too too dearly,
So much to wrong his honor; and he hath done so,
That first gave him advice to stay from France.
To witness I speak truth, I let you know
How careful I have been to keep my daughter
Free from all conference or speech of him;
Not that I scorn your nephew, but in love
I bear your Honor, lest your noble blood   20
Should by my mean worth be dishonored.
LINCOLN. [*aside*] How far the churl's tongue wanders from his heart! —
Well, well, Sir Roger Oateley, I believe you,
With more than many thanks for the kind love
So much you seem to bear me. But, my Lord,
Let me request your help to seek my nephew,
Whom if I find, I'll straight embark for France.
So shall [your][27] Rose be free, [my] thoughts at rest,
And much care die which now [lies][28] in my breast.

Enter SYBIL.

SYBIL. Oh Lord! Help, for God's sake! [30
My mistress; oh, my young mistress!
L. MAYOR. Where is thy mistress? What's become of her?
SYBIL. She's gone; she's fled!
L. MAYOR. Gone! Whither is she fled?
SYBIL. I know not, forsooth; she's fled out of doors with Hans the shoemaker; I saw them scud, scud, scud, apace, apace!

[26] The same.
[27] Transposed with my in Qq 1, 2.
[28] Cor. Q 2; Q 1 *dies.*

L. Mayor. Which way? — What, John!
Where be my men? — Which way?   40
Sybil. I know not, an it please your Wor-
ship.
L. Mayor. Fled with a shoemaker? Can
this be true?
Sybil. Oh Lord, sir, as true as God's in
Heaven.
Lincoln. Her love turn'd shoemaker? —
[*aside*] I am glad of this.
L. Mayor. A Fleming butter-box, a shoe-
maker!
Will she forget her birth, requite my care
With such ingratitude? Scorn'd she young
Hammon
To love a honniken,[29] a needy knave?
Well, let her fly; I 'll not fly after her: 50
Let her starve, if she will — she 's none of
mine.
Lincoln. Be not so cruel, sir.

Enter Firk *with shoes.*

Sybil. [*aside*]   I am glad she 's scap'd.
L. Mayor. I 'll not account of her as of my
child.
Was there no better object for her eyes,
But a foul drunken lubber, swill-belly,
A shoemaker? That 's brave!
Firk. Yea, forsooth; 't is a very brave
shoe, and as fit as a pudding.
L. Mayor. How now, what knave is this?
From whence comest thou?   60
Firk. No knave, sir. I am Firk the shoe-
maker, lusty Roger's chief lusty journeyman,
and I have come hither to take up the pretty
leg of sweet Mistress Rose, and thus hoping
your Worship is in as good health as I was at
the making hereof, I bid you farewell, yours —
Firk.
L. Mayor. Stay, stay, Sir Knave!
Lincoln.   Come hither, shoemaker!
Firk. 'T is happy the knave is put before
the shoemaker, or else I would not have [70
vouchsafed to come back to you. I am
moved, for I stir.
L. Mayor. My Lord, this villain calls us
knaves by craft.
Firk. Then 't is by the gentle craft, and
to call one knave gently, is no harm. Sit your
Worship merry! Syb, your young mistress —
[*aside*] I 'll so bob[30] the[m], now my master,
Master Eyre, is Lord Mayor of London.
L. Mayor. Tell me, sirrah, whose man are
you?   80

Firk. I am glad to see your Worship so
merry. I have no maw to this gear,[31] no stomach as yet to a red petticoat.
          Pointing to Sybil.
Lincoln. He means not, sir, to woo you to
his maid,
But only doth demand whose man you are.
Firk. I sing now to the tune of Rogero.[32]
Roger, my fellow, is now my master.
Lincoln. Sirrah, know'st thou one Hans,
a shoemaker?
Firk. Hans, shoemaker? Oh, yes, stay,
yes, I have him. I tell you what, I speak [90
it in secret: Mistress Rose and he are by this
time — no, not so, but shortly are to come
over one another with,[33] "Can you dance the
shaking of the sheets?"[34] It is that Hans —
[*aside*] I 'll so gull these diggers![35]
L. Mayor. Know'st thou, then, where he
is?
Firk. Yes, forsooth; yea, marry!
Lincoln. Canst thou, in sadness[36] ——
Firk. No, forsooth, no, marry!   100
L. Mayor. Tell me, good honest fellow,
where he is,
And thou shalt see what I 'll bestow of thee.
Firk. Honest fellow? No, sir; not so,
sir; my profession is the gentle craft. I care
not for seeing; I love feeling: let me feel it
here; *aurium tenus*, ten pieces of gold; *genuum
tenus*, ten pieces of silver;[37] and then Firk
is your man — [*aside*] in a new pair of stretchers.[38]
L. Mayor. Here is an angel, part of thy reward,   110
Which I will give thee; tell me where he is.
Firk. No point. Shall I betray my
brother? No! Shall I prove Judas to Hans?
No! Shall I cry treason to my corporation?
No, I shall be firk'd and yerk'd[39] then. But
give me your angel; your angel shall tell you.

---

[29] A low fellow. (Skeat.)   [30] Cheat.

[31] Appetite for this affair.
[32] A well-known tune.
[33] Cf. III, i, 153, 154.
[34] See *A Woman Killed with Kindness*, I, i, 2–5,
and notes.
[35] Delvers (into secrets).   [36] Seriously.
[37] *Aurium tenus* = up to the ears; *genuum tenus* =
up to the knees. Firk pretends (punningly) that
tenus means "ten" and *aurium*, "pieces of gold."
He also alludes to the supposed fondness of shoemakers for *feeling* the legs of their female customers
— they are not satisfied with merely *seeing*. (Cf. l.
105.) With that in mind, he says *genuum tenus* (of
which he and his interlocutor know the real meaning),
and then pretends to translate it as "ten pieces of
silver." (Kittredge.)
[38] Punning on the meanings (1) shoe-stretchers,
(2) lies.
[39] Synonyms, = drubbed.

Lincoln. Do so, good fellow ; 't is no hurt to thee.

Firk. Send simpering Syb away.

L. Mayor.   Huswife,[40] get you in.

Exit Sybil.

Firk. Pitchers have ears, and maids have wide mouths ; but for Hans Prans,[41] upon [120 my word, to-morrow morning he and young Mistress Rose go to this gear : they shall be married together, by this rush, or else turn Firk to a firkin of butter, to tan leather withal.

L. Mayor. But art thou sure of this?

Firk. Am I sure that Paul's steeple is a handful higher than London Stone,[42] or that the Pissing Conduit [43] leaks nothing but pure Mother Bunch? [44] Am I sure I am lusty Firk? God's nails, do you think I am so base to [130 gull you?

Lincoln. Where are they married? Dost thou know the church?

Firk. I never go to church, but I know the name of it ; it is a swearing church — stay awhile, 't is — ay, by the mass ; no, no, — 't is, ay, by my troth ; no, nor that ; 't is — ay, by my faith : that, that, 't is, ay, By My Faith's Church under Paul's Cross. There they shall be knit like a pair of stockings in matrimony ; there they 'll be inconie.[45]   140

Lincoln. Upon my life, my nephew Lacy walks

In the disguise of this Dutch shoemaker.

Firk. Yes, forsooth.

Lincoln. Doth he not, honest fellow?

Firk. No, forsooth ; I think Hans is no-body but Hans, no spirit.

L. Mayor. My mind misgives me now, 't is so, indeed.

Lincoln. My cousin speaks the language, knows the trade.

L. Mayor. Let me request your company, my Lord ;

Your honorable presence may, no doubt,   150
Refrain their headstrong rashness, when my-self

Going alone perchance may be o'erborne.
Shall I request this favor?

Lincoln.   This, or what else.

Firk. Then you must rise betimes,[46] for they mean to fall to their hey-pass and repass,[47] pindy-pandy,[48] which hand will you have, very early.

L. Mayor. My care shall every way equal their haste.

This night accept your lodging in my house ;
The earlier shall we stir, and at Saint Faith's
Prevent this giddy hare-brain'd nuptial.   161
This traffic of hot love shall yield cold gains :
They ban [49] our loves, and we 'll forbid their banns.   [*Exit.*]

Lincoln. At Saint Faith's Church thou say'st?

Firk.   Yes, by their troth.

Lincoln. Be secret, on thy life.   *Exit.*

Firk.   Yes, when I kiss your wife !

Ha, ha, here 's no craft in the gentle craft. I came hither of purpose with shoes to Sir Roger's Worship, whilst Rose, his daughter, be cony-catch'd [50] by Hans. Soft now ; these two gulls will be at Saint Faith's Church to-morrow [170 morning, to take Master Bridegroom and Mistress Bride napping, and they, in the mean-time, shall chop up the matter at the Savoy.[51] But the best sport is, Sir Roger Oateley will find my fellow lame Ralph's wife going to marry a gentleman, and then he 'll stop her in-stead of his daughter. Oh brave ! there will be fine tickling sport. Soft now, what have I to do? Oh, I know ; now a mess of shoemakers meet at the Woolsack [52] in Ivy Lane, to [180 cozen [53] my gentleman of lame Ralph's wife, that 's true.

Alack, alack !
Girls, hold out tack ! [54]
For now smocks for this jumbling
Shall go to wrack.

Exit.

[40] Hussy, wench.
[41] Old eds. *Hauns Prauns.*
[42] It was supposed to mark the centre from which the Romans' military roads radiated.
[43] A small but famous conduit, also mentioned in Shakespeare's *ii Henry VI*, IV, vi, 4.
[44] *I.e.*, water. Mother Bunch's ale was famous, but Nashe (ed. McKerrow, I, 173, 174) calls it "slimie." By the date of our play she was probably dead (see Nashe's Works, ed. McK., IV, 103, 104, and *The Weakest Goeth to the Wall*, Farmer's facs., and Malone Soc. reprint, sig. B₂r°) ; certainly her name had become a byword. Apparently her ale had lost its reputation, and "Mother Bunch" had come to mean "very thin drink", and hence (as here) "water." (Kittredge.)
[45] A pretty sight.
[46] Early.
[47] Jugglers' terms.
[48] Alluding to the children's game of handy-dandy, or which hand will you have?
[49] Curse. — For "banns" old eds. read *baines.*
[50] Beguiled.
[51] A hospital ; its chapel served as a parish church.
[52] A well-known tavern.
[53] Cheat.
[54] Hold out, endure. (Skeat.)

[ACT V — SCENE I][1]

Enter EYRE, *his wife* [MARGERY], [LACY *as*] HANS, *and* ROSE.

EYRE. This is the morning, then ; stay, my bully, my honest Hans, is it not?

HANS. This is the morning that must make us two

Happy or miserable ; therefore, if you ——

EYRE. Away with these ifs and ands, Hans, and these et caeteras ! By mine honor, Rowland Lacy, none but the King shall wrong thee. Come, fear nothing, am not I Sim Eyre? Is not Sim Eyre Lord Mayor of London? — Fear nothing, Rose : let them [10 all say what they can ; dainty, come thou to me — laughest thou?

MARG. Good my Lord, stand her friend in what thing you may.

EYRE. Why, my sweet Lady Madgy, think you Simon Eyre can forget his fine Dutch journeyman? No, vah ! Fie, I scorn it ; it shall never be cast in my teeth, that I was unthankful. Lady Madgy, thou hadst never cover'd thy Saracen's head [2] with this [20 French flap, nor loaden thy bum with this farthingale, ('t is trash, trumpery, vanity) ; Simon Eyre had never walk'd in a red petticoat, nor wore a chain of gold ; but for my fine journeyman's Portuguese. — And shall I leave him? No ! Prince am I none, yet bear a princely mind.

HANS. My Lord, 't is time for us to part from hence.

EYRE. Lady Madgy, Lady Madgy, take two or three of my pie-crust eaters, [30 my buff-jerkin [3] varlets, that do walk in black gowns at Simon Eyre's heels ; take them, good Lady Madgy ; trip and go, my brown queen of periwigs,[4] with my delicate Rose and my jolly Rowland to the Savoy ; see them link'd, countenance the marriage ; and when it is done, cling, cling together, you Hamborow [5] turtledoves. I'll bear you out : come to Simon Eyre ; come, dwell with me, Hans, thou shalt eat minc'd-pies and march- [40 pane.[6] — Rose, away, cricket ; trip and go, my Lady Madgy, to the Savoy. — Hans, wed, and to bed ; kiss, and away ! Go, vanish !

MARG. Farewell, my Lord.

ROSE. Make haste, sweet love.

MARG. She'd fain the deed were done.

HANS. Come, my sweet Rose ; faster than deer we'll run. *They go out.*

EYRE. Go, vanish, vanish ! Avaunt, I say ! By the Lord of Ludgate, it's a mad life to be a lord mayor ; it's a stirring life, a fine life, a velvet life, a careful life. Well, Simon [50 Eyre, yet set a good face on it, in the honor of Saint Hugh. Soft, the King this day comes to dine with me, to see my new buildings ; his Majesty is welcome : he shall have good cheer, delicate cheer, princely cheer. This day, my fellow prentices of London come to dine with me too ; they shall have fine cheer, gentlemanlike cheer. I promised the mad Cappadocians,[7] when we all served at the Conduit together,[8] that if ever I came to be [60 mayor of London, I would feast them all, and I'll do 't, I'll do 't, by the life of Pharaoh ; by this beard, Sim Eyre will be no flincher. Besides, I have procur'd that upon every Shrove-Tuesday, at the sound of the pancake bell, my fine dapper Assyrian lads shall clap up their shop windows, and away. This is the day, and this day they shall do 't, they shall do 't. 69

Boys, that day are you free ; let masters care ; And prentices shall pray for Simon Eyre. (*Exit.*)

[SCENE II][9]

Enter HODGE, FIRK, RALPH, *and five or six* Shoemakers, *all with cudgels or such weapons.*

HODGE. Come, Ralph ; stand to it, Firk. My masters, as we are the brave bloods of the shoemakers, heirs apparent to Saint Hugh, and perpetual benefactors to all good fellows, thou shalt have no wrong : were Hammon a king of spades, he should not delve in thy close without thy sufferance. But tell me, Ralph, art thou sure 't is thy wife?

RALPH. Am I sure this is Firk? This morning, when I strok'd on her shoes, [10 I look'd upon her, and she upon me, and she sigh'd, ask'd me if ever I knew one Ralph. Yes, said I. For his sake, said she — tears standing in her eyes — and for thou art somewhat like him, spend this piece of gold. I

[1] A room in Eyre's house.
[2] Alluding to the numerous signs which bore a ferocious face so called.
[3] Military jacket of leather.
[4] Since she now has wigged flunkies to attend her.
[5] Hamburg.
[5] A sweatmeat of almond paste.

[7] Possibly, as Skeat thinks, in allusion to the caps of the citizens ; but cf. *Assyrians*, l. 66, and *Mesopotamians*, III, v, 78.
[8] The prentices had to serve as water-carriers for their masters.
[9] A street near St. Paul's.

took it ; my lame leg and my travel beyond
sea made me unknown. All is one for that ;
I know she 's mine.

FIRK. Did she give thee this gold? O
glorious, glittering gold ! She 's thine own, [20
't is thy wife, and she loves thee ; for I 'll
stand to 't, there 's no woman will give gold
to any man, but she thinks better of him than
she thinks of them she gives silver to. And
for Hammon, neither Hammon nor hangman
shall wrong thee in London ! Is not our old
master Eyre, lord mayor? Speak, my hearts.

ALL. Yes, and Hammon shall know it to
his cost.

Enter HAMMON, *his* Man, JANE, *and* Others.

HODGE. Peace, my bullies ; yonder [30
they come.

RALPH. Stand to 't, my hearts. Firk, let
me speak first.

HODGE. No, Ralph, let me. — Hammon,
whither away so early?

HAM. Unmannerly, rude slave, what 's
that to thee?

FIRK. To him, sir? Yes, sir, and to me,
and others. — Good morrow, Jane, how dost
thou? Good Lord, how the world is changed
with you ! God be thanked !   40

HAM. Villains, hands off ! How dare you
touch my love?

ALL. Villains? Down with them ! Cry
clubs [10] for prentices !

HODGE. Hold, my hearts ! — Touch her,
Hammon? Yea, and more than that : we 'll
carry her away with us. — My masters and
gentlemen, never draw your bird-spits ; shoemakers are steel to the back, men every inch
of them, all spirit.

ALL OF HAMMON'S SIDE. Well, and [50
what of all this?

HODGE. I 'll show you. — Jane, dost thou
know this man? 'T is Ralph, I can tell thee ;
nay, 't is he in faith, though he be lam'd by
the wars. Yet look not strange, but run to
him, fold him about the neck and kiss him.

JANE. Lives then my husband? O God,
let me go ;
Let me embrace my Ralph.

HAM.   What means my Jane?

JANE. Nay, what meant you, to tell me he
was slain?

HAM. Pardon me, dear love, for being
misled. —   60

[*To* RALPH] 'T was rumor'd here in London
thou wert dead.

FIRK. Thou seest he lives. — Lass, go,
pack home with him. —

Now, Master Hammon, where 's your mistress, your wife?

SERV. 'Swounds, Master, fight for her !
Will you thus lose her?

ALL. Down with that creature ! Clubs !
Down with him !

HODGE. Hold, hold !

HAM. Hold, fool ! — Sirs, he shall do no
wrong. —

Will my Jane leave me thus, and break her
faith?   70

FIRK. Yea, sir ! She must, sir ! She shall,
sir ! What then? Mend it !

HODGE. Hark, fellow Ralph, follow my
counsel : set the wench in the midst, and let
her choose her man, and let her be his woman.

JANE. Whom shall I choose? Whom
should my thoughts affect
But him whom Heaven hath made to be my
love?
Thou art my husband, and these humble
weeds
Makes thee more beautiful than all his wealth.
Therefore, I will but put off his attire,   80
Returning it into the owner's hand,
And after ever be thy constant wife.

HODGE. Not a rag, Jane ! The law 's on our
side : he that sows in another man's ground
forfeits his harvest. Get thee home, Ralph ;
follow him, Jane ; he shall not have so much
as a busk-point [11] from thee.

FIRK. Stand to that, Ralph ; the appurte-
nances are thine own. — Hammon, look not
at her !   90

SERV. Oh, swounds, no !

FIRK. Blue coat,[12] be quiet ; we 'll give you
a new livery else ; we 'll make Shrove Tuesday Saint George's Day for you. — Look not,
Hammon, leer not ! I 'll firk you ! For thy
head now, one glance, one sheep's eye, anything, at her ! Touch not a rag, lest I and my
brethren beat you to clouts.

SERV. Come, Master Hammon, there 's no
striving here.

[10] The apprentices' call for help from their fellows
and their rallying cry.

[11] The tagged lace that fastened the busk, the
wooden strip which reënforced the front of the
stays.

[12] Servant ; blue was the usual wear for servants.
This one, however, is evidently not in blue, or there
would be no point to what follows : "We 'll give
you a new livery of blue ;" that was the appropriate color for St. George's Day, and Firk apparently means, "We 'll beat you (black and) blue."

HAM. Good fellows, hear me speak ; and,
      honest Ralph,   100
Whom I have injured most by loving Jane,
Mark what I offer thee : here in fair gold
Is twenty pound ; I 'll give it for thy Jane.
If this content thee not, thou shalt have more.
      HODGE. Sell not thy wife, Ralph ; make
      her not a whore.
      HAM. Say, wilt thou freely cease thy claim
      in her,
And let her be my wife?
      ALL.   No, do not, Ralph.
      RALPH. Sirrah Hammon, Hammon, dost
thou think a shoemaker is so base to be a
bawd to his own wife for commodity? [110
Take thy gold; choke with it ! Were I not
lame, I would make thee eat thy words.
      FIRK. A shoemaker sell his flesh and blood?
O, indignity !
      HODGE. Sirrah, take up your pelf, and be
packing.
      HAM. I will not touch one penny, but in
      lieu
Of that great wrong I offered thy Jane,
To Jane and thee I give that twenty pound.
Since I have fail'd of her, during my life, [120
I vow, no woman else shall be my wife.
Farewell, good fellows of the gentle trade :
Your morning's mirth my mourning day hath
      made.
                  Exeunt [HAMMON *and his party*].
      FIRK. [*to the* Serving Man] Touch the gold,
creature, if you dare ! Y' are best be trudging.
— Here, Jane, take thou it. — Now let 's
home, my hearts.
      HODGE. Stay ! Who comes here? Jane,
on again with thy mask !

Enter [*the* EARL OF] LINCOLN, LORD MAYOR,
      and Servants.

      LINCOLN. Yonder 's the lying varlet mock'd
      us so.   130
      L. MAYOR. Come hither, sirrah !
      FIRK. I, sir? I am sirrah? You mean me,
do you not?
      LINCOLN. Where is my nephew married?
      FIRK. Is he married? God give him joy ;
I am glad of it. They have a fair day, and the
sign is in a good planet, Mars in Venus.
      L. MAYOR. Villain, thou told'st me that
      my daughter Rose
This morning should be married at Saint
      Faith's ;
We have watch'd there these three hours at
      the least,   140

Yet see we no such thing.
      FIRK. Truly, I am sorry for 't ; a bride 's a
pretty thing.
      HODGE. Come to the purpose. Yonder 's
the bride and bridegroom you look for, I hope.
Though you be lords, you are not to bar by
your authority men from women, are you?
      L. MAYOR. See, see, my daughter 's mask'd.
      LINCOLN.   True, and my nephew,
To hide his guilt, counterfeits him lame.
      FIRK. Yea, truly ; God help the poor [150
couple, they are lame and blind.
      L. MAYOR. I 'll ease her blindness.
      LINCOLN.   I 'll his lameness cure.
      FIRK. [*aside to the* Shoemakers] Lie down,
sirs, and laugh ! My fellow Ralph is taken
for Rowland Lacy, and Jane for Mistress
Damask Rose. This is all my knavery.
      L. MAYOR. What, have I found you,
      minion?
      LINCOLN.   O base wretch !
Nay, hide thy face : the horror of thy guilt
Can hardly be wash'd off. Where are thy
      powers? [13]   159
What battles have you made? Oh, yes, I see,
Thou fought'st with shame, and shame hath
      conquer'd thee.
This lameness will not serve.
      L. MAYOR.   Unmask yourself.
      LINCOLN. Lead home your daughter.
      L. MAYOR.   Take your nephew hence.
      RALPH. Hence ! Swounds, what mean
you? Are you mad? I hope you cannot
enforce my wife from me. Where 's Hammon?
      L. MAYOR. Your wife?
      LINCOLN. What Hammon?
      RALPH. Yea, my wife ; and, therefore, [170
the proudest of you that lay hands on her
first, I 'll lay my crutch 'cross his pate.
      FIRK. To him, lame Ralph ! Here 's brave
sport !
      RALPH. Rose call you her? Why, her
name is Jane. Look here else ; do you know
her now?
                              [JANE *unmasks.*]
      LINCOLN. Is this your daughter?
      L. MAYOR.   No, nor this your nephew.
My Lord of Lincoln, we are both abus'd [14]
By this base, crafty varlet.   180
      FIRK. Yea, forsooth, no varlet ; forsooth,
no base ; forsooth, I am but mean ; no crafty
neither, but of the gentle craft.

[13] Troops.
[14] Deceived.

L. MAYOR. Where is my daughter Rose?
Where is my child?

LINCOLN. Where is my nephew Lacy married?

FIRK. Why, here is good lac'd mutton,[15] as
I promis'd you.

LINCOLN. Villain, I'll have thee punish'd
for this wrong.

FIRK. Punish the journeyman villain, but
not the journeyman shoemaker.   190

Enter DODGER.

DODGER. My Lord, I come to bring unwel-
come news.
Your nephew Lacy and your daughter Rose
Early this morning wedded at the Savoy,
None being present but the Lady Mayoress.
Besides, I learnt among the officers,
The Lord Mayor vows to stand in their de-
fence
'Gainst any that shall seek to cross the
match.

LINCOLN. Dares Eyre the shoemaker uphold the deed?

FIRK. Yes, sir, shoemakers dare stand in a
woman's quarrel, I warrant you, as deep [200
as another, and deeper too.

DODGER. Besides, His Grace to-day dines
with the Mayor;
Who on his knees humbly intends to fall
And beg a pardon for your nephew's fault.

LINCOLN. But I'll prevent him! Come, Sir
Roger Oateley;
The King will do us justice in this cause.
Howe'er their hands have made them man and
wife,
I will disjoin the match, or lose my life.

Exeunt [LINCOLN, MAYOR, DODGER,
and Servants.]

FIRK. Adieu, Monsieur Dodger! Farewell, fools! — Ha, ha! Oh, if they had [210
stay'd, I would have so lamb'd[16] them with
flouts! O heart, my codpiece-point[17] is ready
to fly in pieces every time I think upon Mistress Rose. But let that pass, as my Lady
Mayoress says.

HODGE. This matter is answer'd. Come,
Ralph; home with thy wife. Come, my fine
shoemakers, let's to our master's the new
Lord Mayor, and there swagger this Shrove

Tuesday.[18] I'll promise you wine enough, [220
for Madge keeps the cellar.

ALL. O rare! Madge is a good wench.

FIRK. And I'll promise you meat enough,
for simp'ring Susan keeps the larder. I'll
lead you to victuals, my brave soldiers; follow your captain. Oh, brave! Hark, hark!

Bell rings.

ALL. The pancake bell[19] rings, the pancake bell! Trilill, my hearts!

FIRK. Oh, brave! O sweet bell! O [229
delicate pancakes! Open the doors, my
hearts, and shut up the windows! keep in the
house, let out the pancakes! Oh, rare, my
hearts! Let's march together for the honor
of Saint Hugh to the great new hall[20] in
Gracious Street corner, which our master,
the new Lord Mayor, hath built.

RALPH. O the crew of good fellows that will
dine at my Lord Mayor's cost to-day!

HODGE. By the Lord, my Lord Mayor [239
is a most brave man. How shall prentices
be bound to pray for him and the honor of
the gentlemen shoemakers! Let's feed and
be fat with my Lord's bounty.

FIRK. O musical bell, still! O Hodge, O
my brethren! There's cheer for the heavens:
venison-pasties[21] walk up and down piping
hot, like serjeants; beef and brewis[22] comes
marching in dry-vats,[23] fritters and pancakes
comes trolling[24] in in wheelbarrows; hens
and oranges hopping in porters' baskets, [250
collops and eggs in scuttles;[25] and tarts and
custards comes quavering in in malt-shovels.

Enter more Prentices.

ALL. Whoop, look here, look here!

HODGE. How now, mad lads, whither away
so fast?

1 PRENTICE. Whither? Why, to the great
new hall, know you not why? The Lord
Mayor hath bidden all the prentices in London to breakfast this morning.   259

ALL. O brave shoemaker, O brave lord of
incomprehensible good-fellowship! Whoo!
Hark you! The pancake bell rings.

Cast up caps.

---

[15] Slang for a strumpet; but the point is the pun
with "Lacied", and no reflection on Jane's character is intended.
[16] Lammed, lambasted, beaten.
[17] The lace of the bagged appendage worn at the
front of tight hose or breeches.

[18] The great holiday of the apprentices.
[19] In every parish the bell was rung early on
Shrove Tuesday as a reminder of shriving. Pancakes being popular as a substitute for meat, it
came to be called the pancake bell, and was the
signal for the beginning of the holiday merriment.
[20] Leadenhall.
[21] Q₁ *pastimes.*
[22] Beef broth.   [23] Casks.   [24] Rolling.
[25] Vegetable or fruit baskets.

FIRK. Nay, more, my hearts! Every Shrove Tuesday is our year of jubilee; and when the pancake bell rings, we are as free as my Lord Mayor; we may shut up our shops, and make holiday; I 'll have it call'd Saint Hugh's Holiday.

ALL. Agreed, agreed! Saint Hugh's Holiday. 270

HODGE. And this shall continue for ever.

ALL. Oh, brave! Come, come, my hearts! Away, away!

FIRK. Oh, eternal credit to us of the gentle craft! March fair, my hearts! Oh, rare!

Exeunt.

[SCENE III] [26]

Enter [the] KING *and his* Train *over the stage.*

KING. Is our Lord Mayor of London such a gallant?

NOBLEMAN. One of the merriest madcaps in your land.
Your Grace will think, when you behold the man,
He 's rather a wild ruffian than a mayor.
Yet thus much I 'll ensure your Majesty,
In all his actions that concern his state [27]
He is as serious, provident, and wise,
As full of gravity amongst the grave,
As any mayor hath been these many years.

KING. I am with child [28] till I behold this huffcap.[29] 10
But all my doubt is, when we come in presence,
His madness will be dash'd clean out of countenance.

NOBLEMAN. It may be so, my Liege.

KING. Which to prevent,
Let someone give him notice 't is our pleasure
That he put on his wonted merriment. —
Set forward!

ALL. On afore! *Exeunt.*

[SCENE IV] [30]

Enter EYRE, HODGE, FIRK, RALPH, *and other* Shoemakers, *all with napkins on their shoulders.*

EYRE. Come, my fine Hodge, my jolly gentlemen shoemakers; soft, where be these cannibals, these varlets, my officers? Let them all walk and wait upon my brethren; for my meaning is that none but shoemakers, none but the livery of my company, shall in their satin hoods wait upon the trencher of my sovereign.

FIRK. O my Lord, it will be rare!

EYRE. No more. Firk; come, lively! [10 Let your fellow prentices want no cheer; let wine be plentiful as beer, and beer as water. Hang these penny-pinching fathers, that cram wealth in innocent lamb-skins.[31] Rip, knaves, avaunt! Look to my guests!

HODGE. My Lord, we are at our wits' end for room; those hundred tables will not feast the fourth part of them.

EYRE. Then cover me those hundred tables again, and again, till all my jolly pren- [20 tices be feasted. Avoid, Hodge! Run, Ralph! Frisk about my nimble Firk! Carouse me fathom-healths to the honor of the shoemakers. Do they drink lively, Hodge? Do they tickle it, Firk?

FIRK. Tickle it? Some of them have taken their liquor standing so long that they can stand no longer; but for meat, they would eat it an they had it.

EYRE. Want they meat? Where's [30 this swag-belly, this greasy kitchen-stuff cook? Call the varlet to me! Want meat? Firk, Hodge, lame Ralph, run, my tall men, beleaguer the shambles,[32] beggar all Eastcheap, serve me whole oxen in chargers,[33] and let sheep whine upon the tables like pigs for want of good fellows to eat them. Want meat? Vanish, Firk! Avaunt, Hodge!

HODGE. Your Lordship mistakes my man Firk; he means their bellies want meat, [40 not the boards, for they have drunk so much they can eat nothing.

THE SECOND THREE-MAN'S SONG [34]

(This is to be sung at the latter end.)

Cold 's the wind, and wet 's the rain;
  Saint Hugh be our good speed;
Ill is the weather that bringeth no gain,
  Nor helps good hearts in need.

Troll [35] the bowl, the jolly nut-brown bowl,
  And here, kind mate, to thee;
Let 's sing a dirge for Saint Hugh's soul,
  And down it [36] merrily. 50

[26] A street. [27] Government.
[28] Impatiently expectant.
[29] Swaggerer. [30] A great hall.

[31] Probably alluding to their use as parchment for recording deeds, transfers, etc.
[32] The butchers' shops.
[33] Great platters.
[34] Mod. eds. plausibly introduce the second song here, but without warrant in the old eds.
[35] Circulate.
[36] Sing the burden, "down-a-down", etc. (Warnke-Proescholdt.)

Down a down, hey down a down,
  Hey derry derry, down a down!
            (*Close with the tenor boy:*)
Ho, well done; to me let come!
Ring compass, gentle joy.[37]

Troll the bowl, the nut-brown bowl,
  And here, kind, etc. [*Repeat*] *as often as there be
  men to drink; at last, when all have drunk, this
  verse:*

Cold 's the wind, and wet 's the rain;
  Saint Hugh be our good speed;
Ill is the weather that bringeth no gain,
  Nor helps good hearts in need.   60

  Enter [LACY *as*] HANS, ROSE, *and wife*
            [MARGERY.]

MARG. Where is my Lord?

EYRE. How now, Lady Madgy?

MARG. The King's most excellent Majesty
is new come; he sends me for thy Honor;
one of his most worshipful peers bade me tell
thou must be merry, and so forth; but let
that pass.

EYRE. Is my sovereign come? Vanish,
my tall shoemakers, my nimble brethren;
look to my guests, the prentices. Yet stay [70
a little! How now, Hans? How looks my
little Rose?

HANS. Let me request you to remember me.
I know your Honor easily may obtain
Free pardon of the King for me and Rose,
And reconcile me to my uncle's grace.

EYRE. Have done, my good Hans, my
honest journeyman; look cheerily! I 'll fall
upon both my knees, till they be as hard as
horn, but I 'll get thy pardon.   80

MARG. Good my Lord, have a care what
you speak to his Grace.

EYRE. Away, you Islington whitepot![38]
hence, you h[o]pper[39]-arse! hence, you barley-
pudding, full of maggots! you broiled car-
bonado![40] avaunt, avaunt, avoid, Mephis-
tophilus! Shall Sim Eyre [learn][41] to speak
of you, Lady Madgy? Vanish, Mother
Miniver[42]-cap; vanish, go, trip and go;
meddle with your partlets[43] and your pish- [90
ery-pashery, your flews[44] and your whirligigs;
go, rub,[45] out of mine alley! Sim Eyre knows

how to speak to a pope, to Sultan Soliman,[46]
to Tamburlaine, an he were here; and shall I
melt, shall I droop before my sovereign?
No, come, my Lady Madgy! Follow me,
Hans! About your business, my frolic free-
booters! Firk, frisk about, and about, and
about, for the honor of mad Simon Eyre, Lord
Mayor of London.   100

FIRK. Hey, for the honor of the shoemakers!   *Exeunt.*

          [SCENE V] [47]

A long flourish or two. Enter [*the*] KING, *Nobles,* EYRE, *his wife* [MARGERY], LACY,
[*and*] ROSE. LACY *and* ROSE *kneel.*

KING. Well, Lacy, though the fact was
            very foul
Of your revolting from our kingly love
And your own duty, yet we pardon you.
Rise both, and, Mistress Lacy, thank my Lord
            Mayor
For your young bridegroom here.

EYRE. So, my dear Liege, Sim Eyre and
my brethren, the gentlemen shoemakers, shall
set your sweet Majesty's image cheek by jowl
by Saint Hugh for this honor you have done
poor Simon Eyre. I beseech your Grace, [10
pardon my rude behavior; I am a handicrafts-
man, yet my heart is without craft; I would
be sorry at my soul, that my boldness should
offend my King.

KING. Nay, I pray thee, good Lord Mayor,
            be even as merry
As if thou wert among thy shoemakers;
It does me good to see thee in this humor.

EYRE. Say'st thou me so, my sweet Diocle-
sian?[48] Then, hump![49] Prince am I none,
yet am I princely born. By the Lord of [20
Ludgate, my liege, I 'll be as merry as a pie.[50]

KING. Tell me, in faith, mad Eyre, how old
            thou art.

EYRE. My Liege, a very boy, a stripling, a
younker; you see not a white hair on my head,
not a gray in this beard. Every hair, I assure
thy Majesty, that sticks in this beard, Sim
Eyre values at the King of Babylon's ransom;
Tama[r] Cham's[51] beard was a rubbing-brush

---

[37] Complete the circle, my dear love; *i.e.*, let the
drinks go round. (Kittredge.)

[38] A dish made of milk, eggs, sugar, etc., boiled
in a pot. (Skeat.)

[39] Presumably with reference to the shape.

[40] Steak.

[41] Cor. Q₃: earlier eds. *leaue.*

[42] *I.e.*, trimmed or lined with that fur.

[43] Neckerchiefs.

[44] Flapping skirts. (Skeat.) More probably the
flaps of the French hood.

[45] Obstacle (in bowling).

[46] Evidently an allusion to the anonymous play,
Soliman and Perseda, attributed by some to Kyd.

[47] The same.

[48] Diocletian, *i.e.*, Emperor. St. Hugh's martyrdom occurred in his time, which may account for
Dekker's mention of him here.

[49] Humph! Merely used as an interjection of
jollity. (Kittredge.)

[50] Magpie.

[51] *I.e.*, the Khan Timur, Tamburlaine.

to 't : yet I 'll shave it off, and stuff tennis-balls with it, to please my bully King.   30

KING. But all this while I do not know your age.

EYRE. My Liege, I am six-and-fifty year old, yet I can cry hump ! with a sound heart for the honor of Saint Hugh. Mark this old wench, my King : I danc'd the shaking of the sheets with her six-and-thirty years ago, and yet I hope to get two or three young lord mayors, ere I die. I am lusty still, Sim Eyre still. Care and cold lodging brings white hairs. My sweet Majesty, let care van- [40 ish ; cast it upon thy nobles ; it will make thee look always young like Apollo, and cry hump ! Prince am I none, yet am I princely born.

KING. Ha, ha ! Say, Cornwall, didst thou ever see his like?

NOBLEMAN. Not I, my Lord.

Enter [the EARL OF] LINCOLN *and [the former]* LORD MAYOR.

KING.   Lincoln, what news with you?

LINCOLN. My gracious Lord, have care unto yourself,

For there are traitors here.

ALL.   Traitors? Where? Who?

EYRE. Traitors in my house? God forbid ! Where be my officers? I 'll spend my soul, ere my King feel harm.   51

KING. Where is the traitor, Lincoln?

LINCOLN.   Here he stands.

KING. Cornwall, lay hold on Lacy ! — Lincoln, speak,

What canst thou lay unto thy nephew's charge?

LINCOLN. This, my dear Liege : your Grace, to do me honor,

Heap'd on the head of this degenerous [52] boy Desertless [53] favors ; you made choice of him To be commander over powers in France. But he ——

KING.   Good Lincoln, prithee, pause awhile !

Even in thine eyes I read what thou wouldst speak.   60

I know how Lacy did neglect our love,

Ran himself deeply, in the highest degree,

Into vile treason.

LINCOLN.   Is he not a traitor?

KING. Lincoln, he was ; now have we pard'ned   him.

[52] Degenerate.
[53] Undeserved.

'T was not a base want of true valor's fire,

That held him out of France, but love's desire.

LINCOLN. I will not bear his shame upon my back.

KING. Nor shalt thou, Lincoln ; I forgive you both.

LINCOLN. Then, good my Liege, forbid the boy to wed

One whose mean birth will much disgrace his bed.   70

KING. Are they not married?

LINCOLN.   No, my Liege.

BOTH.   We are.

KING. Shall I divorce them then? Oh, be it far

That any hand on earth should dare untie

The sacred knot, knit by God's Majesty ;

I would not for my crown disjoin their hands

That are conjoin'd in holy nuptial bands.

How say'st thou, Lacy, wouldst thou lose thy Rose?

LACY. Not for all [India's] [54] wealth, my Sovereign.

KING. But Rose, I am sure, her Lacy would forego.

ROSE. If Rose were ask'd that question, she'd say no.   80

KING. You hear them, Lincoln.

LINCOLN.   Yea, my Liege, I do.

KING. Yet canst thou find i' th' heart to part these two?

Who seeks, besides you, to divorce these lovers?

L. MAYOR. I do, my gracious Lord ; I am her father.

KING. Sir Roger Oateley, our last mayor, I think?

NOBLEMAN. The same, my Liege.

KING.   Would you offend Love's laws?

Well, you shall have your wills ; you sue to me,

To prohibit the match. Soft, let me see —

You both are married, Lacy, art thou not?

LACY. I am, dread Sovereign.

KING.   Then, upon thy life, [90

I charge thee, not to call this woman wife.

L. MAYOR. I thank your Grace.

ROSE.   O my most gracious Lord !

                              Kneel.

KING. Nay, Rose, never woo me ; I tell you true,

Although as yet I am a bachelor,

Yet I believe I shall not marry you.

[54] Old eds. *Indians.*

Rose. Can you divide the body from the soul,
Yet make the body live?
King.   Yea, so profound?
I cannot, Rose ; but you I must divide. —
This [55] fair maid, bridegroom, cannot be your bride. —
Are you pleas'd, Lincoln? — Oateley. are you pleas'd?   100
Both. Yes, my Lord.
King.   Then must my heart be eas'd ;
For, credit me, my conscience lives in pain,
Till these whom I divorc'd, be join'd again.
Lacy, give me thy hand ; Rose, lend me thine !
Be what you would be ! Kiss now ! So, that 's fine.
At night, lovers, to bed ! — Now, let me see,
Which of you all mislikes this harmony.
  L. Mayor. Will you then take from me my child perforce?
  King. Why tell me, Oateley : shines not Lacy's name   109
As bright in the world's eye as the gay beams
Of any citizen?
  Lincoln.   Yea, but, my gracious Lord,
I do mislike the match far more than he ;
Her blood is too too base.
  King.   Lincoln, no more.
Dost thou not know that love respects no blood,
Cares not for difference of birth or state?
The maid is young, well born, fair, virtuous,
A worthy bride for any gentleman.
Besides, your nephew for her sake did stoop
To bare necessity, and, as I hear,   119
Forgetting honors and all courtly pleasures,
To gain her love, became a shoemaker.
As for the honor which he lost in France,
Thus I redeem it : Lacy, kneel thee down ! —
Arise, Sir Rowland Lacy ! Tell me now,
Tell me in earnest, Oateley, canst thou chide,
Seeing thy Rose a lady and a bride?
  L. Mayor. I am content with what your Grace hath done.
  Lincoln. And I, my Liege, since there 's no remedy.
  King. Come on, then, all shake hands : I 'll have you friends ;
Where there is much love, all discord ends. [130
What says my mad Lord Mayor to all this love?
  Eyre. O my Liege, this honor you have done to my fine journeyman here, Rowland

Lacy, and all these favors which you have shown to me this day in my poor house, will make Simon Eyre live longer by one dozen of warm summers more than he should.
  King. Nay, my mad Lord Mayor, (that shall be thy name ;)
If any grace of mine can length thy life,
One honor more I 'll do thee : that new building,   140
Which at thy cost in Cornhill is erected,
Shall take a name from us ; we 'll have it call'd
The Leadenhall, because in digging it
You found the lead that covereth the same.[56]
  Eyre. I thank your Majesty.
  Marg.   God bless your Grace !
  King. Lincoln, a word with you !

Enter Hodge, Firk, Ralph, *and more* Shoemakers.

  Eyre. How now, my mad knaves ? Peace, speak softly, yonder is the King.
  King. With the old troop which there we keep in pay,
We will incorporate a new supply.   150
Before one summer more pass o'er my head,
France shall repent England was injured. —
What are all those?
  Lacy.   All shoemakers, my Liege,
Sometimes [57] my fellows ; in their companies
I liv'd as merry as an emperor.
  King. My mad Lord Mayor, are all these shoemakers?
  Eyre. All shoemakers, my Liege ; all gentlemen of the gentle craft, true Trojans, courageous cordwainers ; they all kneel to the shrine of holy Saint Hugh.   160
  All. God save your Majesty ! all shoemaker[s] ! [58]
  King. Mad Simon, would they anything with us?
  Eyre. Mum, mad knaves ! Not a word ! I 'll do 't ; I warrant you. — They are all beggars, my Liege ; all for themselves, and I for them all on both my knees do entreat that for the honor of poor Simon Eyre and the good of his brethren, these mad knaves, your Grace would vouchsafe some privilege to [170 my new Leadenhall, that it may be lawful

---

[55] In old eds. *this* is transposed to follow "maid." (Cor. Fritsche.)

[56] The name actually long antedates the historical Eyre's erection of a public granary in 1419.
[57] Formerly.
[58] Qq₃ *et seq.* omit the last two words, which some mod. eds. take for a stage direction or speech-tag.

for us to buy and sell leather [59] there two days a week.

    KING. Mad Sim, I grant your suit; you shall have patent
To hold two market days in Leadenhall,
Mondays and Fridays, those shall be the times.
Will this content you?

    ALL.   Jesus bless your Grace!

    EYRE. In the name of these my poor brethren shoemakers, I most humbly thank your Grace. But before I rise, seeing [180 you are in the giving vein and we in the begging, grant Sim Eyre one boon more.

    KING. What is it, my Lord Mayor?

    EYRE. Vouchsafe to taste of a poor banquet that stands sweetly waiting for your sweet presence.

    KING. I shall undo [60] thee, Eyre, only with feasts;
Already have I been too troublesome;
Say, have I not?

    EYRE. O my dear King, Sim Eyre was [190 taken unawares upon a day of shroving,[61]

[59] Leadenhall as a leather market was an Elizabethan institution; the historical Eyre was in fact not a shoemaker at all, but (according to Stowe's *Survey*) a draper.
[60] Ruin.   [61] Carnival.

which I promis'd long ago to the prentices of London. For, an't please your Highness, in time past, I bare the water-tankard, and my coat sits not a whit the worse upon my back; and then, upon a morning, some mad boys — it was Shrove Tuesday, even as 't is now — gave me my breakfast, and I swore then by the stopple of my tankard, if ever I came to be Lord Mayor of London, I would feast all [200 the prentices. This day, my Liege, I did it, and the slaves had an hundred tables five times covered; they are gone home and vanish'd.

Yet add more honor to the gentle trade:
Taste of Eyre's banquet, Simon's happy made.

    KING. Eyre, I will taste of thy banquet, and will say
I have not met more pleasure on a day. —
Friends of the gentle craft, thanks to you all;
Thanks, my kind Lady May'ress, for our cheer. —   210
Come, lords, awhile let's revel it at home!
When all our sports and banquetings are done,
Wars must right wrongs which Frenchmen have begun.

                             Exeunt.

THE

Honeſt Whore,

With,

The Humours of the Patient Man,
and the Longing Wife.

Tho: Dekker.

LONDON
Printed by V. S. for Iohn Hodgets, and are to
be folde at his ſhop in Paules
church-yard 1604.

INTRODUCTORY NOTE

THE second part of this play is Dekker's masterpiece. A payment recorded by Henslowe in behalf of Prince Henry's Men early in 1604 fixes the date of *Part I* and also indicates that Thomas Middleton was co-author, though his share is generally believed to be slight. *Part II* was doubtless written fairly soon after by Dekker alone.

No source for the plot is known; it belongs to the realistic intrigue type of which Middleton is a brilliant exponent. His influence, however, hardly went deeper. It is in response to the dictates of his own maturing genius, and possibly in conscious harmony with the changing temper of the Jacobean era, that Dekker strikes a deeper chord in *The Honest Whore*. The subplot of humors is perhaps not entirely a concession to the groundlings. The patience of Candido affords a comic parallel to the fortitude of Bellafront; and it is likely that Dekker, thoroughly middle-class in his loyalties, saw this sturdy citizen not only as a figure of fun but also as a bright exemplar of homely virtue.

It is, of course, the main plot that dignifies the play for us. In the five years since *The Shoemakers' Holiday* the dramatist's experience with life has deepened his art; now he comes more closely to grips with both. This is a soberer, less romantic Dekker, still the virtuoso of the City, still capable of Dickensian humor; but wiser, more critical, a half-disillusioned idealist, a thoughtful observer conscious of his power to penetrate far below the surface of life, an artist sure of every mordant stroke, but still too tender-hearted to be, like Jonson, austerely just to his characters at the end, or, like Middleton, to rest merely amused by the spectacle of simpering folly or of vice triumphant. Pity is strangely mixed with irony in this play. The portrait, so terrible and so comic, of Matheo might have been done by either of the great Jacobean masters of realistic comedy; but the portrait of Orlando Friscobaldo, with its whimsy and its heartache, could have been painted by no other than Thomas Dekker. For at his best moments he is one of the greatest of them all; no failure, not even Marlowe's, is sadder than his. The great moments are all too few; and Dekker, though he lived for a quarter of a century after he wrote *The Honest Whore*, led the miserable existence of a hack, always dogged by debt and sometimes imprisoned for it, and lending his genius out in collaboration with a dozen dramatists who were no such poets at heart as he.

Part I of *The Honest Whore* was published in 1604 (reprinted n.d., 1605, 1615, 1616, and 1635); *Part II* was apparently not printed till 1630, though it was entered in the Stationers' Register in 1608. The most useful annotated edition appears in volume III of Dyce's Middleton. The present text is based on the first edition of each part, with, in the case of *Part I*, a number of corrections from Q 1605 (as cited by Dyce and the Pearson editor) and the undated Quarto. (The Editor has not seen copies of Qq 1605 and 1615.) Q n.d. was printed in part from the same setting of types as Q_1 (1604), but only in part. Its variant readings agree with Dyce's and the Pearson citations from Q 1605. While inferior at many points to Q_1, it makes a number of further corrections (see, *e.g.*, on I, v, 264, and on II, i, 154), not mentioned in the Pearson notes nor reproduced in the Pearson text, which is based on Q 1605. The Editor became aware of the importance of Q n.d. in time to incorporate the corrections of the Folger copy in proofs of the present text, but not in time to secure photographs of Q 1605 and determine its precise relation to that edition. The Folger copy of Q n.d. lacks leaves A 1 (with title page), I 3, and K 1–4. Its running title, which varies in spelling and typography, is *The Converted Courtesan*. In the footnotes to the present text " Q_1 " = Q 1604, and " Q_2 " = Q 1605.

THE HONEST [1] WHORE

PART I

BY

THOMAS DEKKER

[DRAMATIS PERSONAE

GASPARO TREBATZI, Duke of Milan.
HIPPOLITO, a count.
CASTRUCHIO, ⎫
SINEZI, ⎪
PIORATTO, ⎬ courtiers.
FLUELLO, ⎭
MATHEO, a friend to Hippolito.
BENEDICT, a doctor.
ANSELMO, a friar.
FUSTIGO, brother to Viola.
CANDIDO, a linen-draper.
GEORGE, his apprentice.

CRAMBO, ⎫
POH,[2] ⎬ bravos.
ROGER, servant to Bellafront.
Porter.
Sweeper.
Apprentices, Madmen, Servants, etc.

INFELICHE, daughter to the Duke.
BELLAFRONT, a harlot.
VIOLA, wife to Candido.
MISTRESS FINGERLOCK, a bawd.

THE SCENE — *Milan and Vicinity*.]

ACT I — SCENE I [3]

Enter at one door a funeral, a coronet lying on the hearse, scutcheons and garlands hanging on the sides, attended by GASPARO TREBATZI *Duke of Milan,* CASTRUCHIO, SINEZI, PIORATTO, FLUELLO, *and others. At another door enter* HIPPOLITO, *in discontented appearance,* [and] MATHEO, *a gentleman, his friend, laboring to hold him back.*

DUKE. Behold, yon comet shows his head
   again!
Twice hath he thus at cross-turns thrown on
   us
Prodigious looks; twice hath he troubled
The waters of our eyes. See, he's turn'd wild.
Go on, in God's name.
  ALL.   On afore there, ho!
  DUKE. Kinsmen and friends, take from
   your manly sides
Your weapons to keep back the desp'rate boy
From doing violence to the innocent dead.
  HIP. I prithee, dear Matheo ——

MAT.   Come, y' are mad!
  HIP. I do arrest thee, murderer! Set
   down,   10
Villains, set down that sorrow; 't is all mine.
  DUKE. I do beseech you all, for my blood's
   sake
Send hence your milder spirits, and let wrath
Join in confederacy with your weapons' points;
If he proceed to vex us, let your swords
Seek out his bowels: funeral grief loathes
   words.
  ALL. Set on.
  HIP.   Set down the body!
  MAT.   O my Lord!
Y' are wrong! I' th' open street? You see
   she 's dead.
  HIP. I know she is not dead.
  DUKE.   Frantic young man,
Wilt thou believe these gentlemen? — Pray
   speak. —   20
Thou dost abuse my child, and mock'st the
   tears
That here are shed for her. If to behold
Those roses withered that set out [4] her cheeks,
That pair of stars that gave her body light
Dark'ned and dim for ever, all those rivers

[1] Chaste.
[2] So Q n.d., throughout. The other old eds. seen by the Editor, and Pearson, usually *Poli*, but occasionally *Poh*.
[3] A street in Milan.
[4] Set off, adorned.

That fed her veins with warm and crimson streams
Frozen and dried up : if these be signs of death,
Then is she dead.   Thou unreligious youth,
Art not asham'd to empty all these eyes
Of funeral tears, a debt due to the dead,   30
As mirth is to the living?   Sham'st thou not
To have them stare on thee?   Hark, thou art curs'd
Even to thy face, by those that scarce can speak.
Hip.   My Lord ——
Duke.   What wouldst thou have?   Is she not dead?
Hip.   Oh, you ha' kill'd her by your cruelty.
Duke.   Admit I had, thou kill'st her now again,
And art more savage than a barbarous Moor.
Hip.   Let me but kiss her pale and bloodless lip.
Duke.   O fie, fie, fie!
Hip.   Or if not touch her, let me look on her.
Mat.   As you regard your honor ——
Hip.   Honor?   smoke! [41
Mat.   Or if you lov'd her living, spare her now.
Duke.   Ay, well done, sir ; you play the gentleman. —
[*to the* Attendants] Steal hence ; — [*to* Matheo] 't is nobly done ; — [*to the* Attendants] away ; — [*to* Matheo] I 'll join
My force to yours, to stop this violent torment.[5] —
[*to the* Attendants] Pass on.
                Exeunt, with funeral, [*all except the* Duke, Hippolito, *and* Matheo].
Hip.   Matheo, thou dost wound me more.
Mat.   I give you physic,[6] noble friend, not wounds.
Duke.   Oh, well said, well done, a true gentleman!
Alack, I know the sea of lovers' rage
Comes rushing with so strong a tide, it beats [50
And bears down all respects [7] of life, of honor,
Of friends, of foes.   Forget her, gallant youth.
Hip.   Forget her?
Duke.   Nay, nay, be but patient ;
Forwhy [8] death's hand hath sued a strict divorce
'Twixt her and thee.   What 's beauty but a corse?

What but fair sand-dust are earth's purest forms?
Queen's bodies are but trunks to put in worms.
Mat.   Speak no more sentences,[9] my good Lord, but slip hence ; you see they are but fits ;
I 'll rule him, I warrant ye.   Ay, so ; tread [60
gingerly ; your Grace is here somewhat too long already.   [*Exit* Duke.] — 'Sblood, the jest were now, if, having ta'en some knocks o' th' pate already, he should get loose again, and like a mad ox, toss my new black cloaks [10] into the kennel.[11]   I must humour his Lordship. — My Lord Hippolito, is it in your stomach [12] to go to dinner?
Hip.   Where is the body?
Mat.   The body, as the Duke spake very [70 wisely, is gone to be worm'd.
Hip.   I cannot rest ; I 'll meet it at next turn.
I 'll see how my love looks.
                Matheo *holds him in 's arms.*
Mat.   How your love looks? worse than a scarecrow.   Wrastle not with me ; the great fellow gives the fall for a ducat.
Hip.   I shall forget myself.
Mat.   Pray, do so ; leave yourself behind yourself, and go whither you will.   'Sfoot, do you long to have base rogues, that maintain [80 a Saint Anthony's fire [13] in their noses by nothing but twopenny ale, make ballads of you?
If the Duke had but so much mettle in him as is in a cobbler's awl, he would ha' been a vex'd thing ; he and his train had blown you up, but that their powder has taken the wet of cowards.   You 'll bleed three pottles of Ali-[c]ant,[14] by this light, if you follow 'em ; and then we shall have a hole made in a wrong place, to have surgeons roll thee up like a [90 baby in swaddling clouts.
Hip.   What day is to-day, Matheo?
Mat.   Yea, marry, this is an easy question ; why to-day is — let me see — Thursday.
Hip.   Oh, Thursday.
Mat.   Here 's a coil [15] for a dead commodity. — 'Sfoot, women when they are alive are but dead commodities, for you shall have one woman lie upon many men's hands.
Hip.   She died on Monday then.   100
Mat.   And that 's the most villainous day of all the week to die in ; and she was well, and ate a mess of water-gruel on Monday morning.

---

[5] Dyce emends *torrent.*
[6] Medicine.
[7] Considerations.
[8] Because.

[9] Maxims.
[10] *I.e.,* the mourners.
[11] Gutter.
[12] Inclination.   [13] Erysipelas.
[14] A red wine.   [15] Commotion.

HIP.   Ay ; it cannot be
Such a bright taper should burn out so soon.

MAT. O yes, my Lord. So soon? Why, I
ha' known them that at dinner have been as
well, and had so much health that they were
glad to pledge it, yet before three a'clock have
been found dead — drunk.   110

HIP. On Thursday buried ! and on Mon-
day died !
Quick haste, byrlady.[16] Sure her winding
sheet
Was laid out 'fore her body ; and the worms
That now must feast with her were even be-
spoke,
And solemnly invited like strange guests.

MAT. Strange feeders they are indeed, my
Lord, and, like your jester, or young courtier,
will enter upon any man's trencher without
bidding.

HIP. Curs'd be that day for ever that
robb'd her   120
Of breath, and me of bliss ! Henceforth let it
stand
Within the wizard's book, the calendar,
Mark'd with a marginal finger,[17] to be chosen
By thieves, by villains, and black murderers,
As the best day for them to labor in.
If henceforth this adulterous, bawdy world
Be got with child with treason, sacrilege,
Atheism, rapes, treacherous friendship, per-
jury,
Slander (the beggar's sin), lies (sin of fools),
Or any other damn'd impieties,   130
On Monday let 'em be delivered.
I swear to thee, Matheo, by my soul,
Hereafter weekly on that day I 'll glue
Mine eyelids down, because they shall not
gaze
On any female cheek. And being lock'd up
In my close [18] chamber, there I 'll meditate
On nothing but my Infeliche's end,
Or on a dead man's skull draw out mine own.

MAT. You 'll do all these good works now
every Monday, because it is so bad ; but [140
I hope upon Tuesday morning I shall take
you with a wench.

HIP. If ever, whilst frail [19] blood through
my veins run,
On woman's beams [20] I throw affection,

Save her that 's dead ; or that [21] I loosely fly
To th' shore of any other wafting eye,
Let me not prosper, Heaven ! I will be true,
Even to her dust and ashes. Could her tomb
Stand whilst I liv'd, so long that it might rot,
That should fall down, but she be ne'er forgot.

MAT. If you have this strange monster,
honesty,[22] in your belly, why so jig-makers [23]
and chroniclers shall pick something out of [153
you ; but an I smell not you and a bawdyhouse out within these ten days, let my nose
be as big as an English bag-pudding.[24] I 'll
follow your Lordship, though it be to the place
aforenamed.   *Exeunt.*

[SCENE II] [25]

Enter FUSTIGO *in some fantastic sea-suit at one
door ; a* Porter *meets him at another.*

FUS. How now, porter, will she come?

POR. If I may trust a woman, sir, she will
come.

FUS. [*giving money*] There 's for thy pains.
Godamercy, if I ever stand in need of a wench
that will come with a wet finger,[26] porter, thou
shalt earn my money before any clarissimo [27]
in Milan ; yet, so God sa' [28] me, she 's mine
own sister, body and soul, as I am a Christian
gentleman. Farewell ; I 'll ponder till she [10
come. Thou hast been no bawd in fetching
this woman. I assure thee.

POR. No matter if I had, sir ; better men
than porters are bawds.

FUS. O God, sir, many that have borne offices. But, porter, art sure thou went'st into
a true [29] house?

POR. I think so, for I met with no thieves.

FUS. Nay, but art sure it was my sister
Viola?   20

POR. I am sure, by all superscriptions, it
was the party you ciphered.

FUS. Not very tall?

POR. Nor very low ; a middling woman.

FUS. 'T was she, 'faith 't was she. A pretty
plump cheek, like mine?

POR. At a blush,[30] a little very much like
you.

---

[16] By Our Lady.
[17] The pointing hand "on the margins of old
books to direct the reader's attention to particular
passages." (Dyce.)
[18] Private.
[19] Liable to sin.
[20] Glances.

[21] If.
[22] Chastity.
[23] Ballad-makers.
[24] Pudding boiled in a bag.
[25] Another street.
[26] Readily.
[27] Grandee.
[28] Save.
[29] *I.e.*, the right one ; the porter, however, takes
true in the sense of honest.
[30] Glance.

Fus. Godso, I would not for a ducat she had kick'd up her heels,[31] for I ha' spent an [30 abomination [32] this voyage ; marry, I did it amongst sailors and gentlemen. There's a little modicum more, porter, for making thee stay ; farewell, honest porter.

Por. I am in your debt, sir ; God preserve you. *Exit.*

Enter VIOLA.

Fus. Not so, neither, good porter. — God's lid, yonder she comes. — Sister Viola, I am glad to see you stirring. It's news to have me here, is't not, Sister? 40

Vio. Yes, trust me. I wond'red who should be so bold to send for me. You are welcome to Milan, Brother.

Fus. Troth, Sister, I heard you were married to a very rich chuff,[33] and I was very sorry for it, that I had no better clothes, and that made me send ; for you know we Milaners love to strut upon Spanish leather. And how does all our friends?

Vio. Very well. You ha' travelled enough now, I trow, to sow your wild oats. 51

Fus. A pox on 'em ! Wild oats? I ha' not an oat to throw at a horse. Troth, Sister, I ha' sow'd my oats, and reap'd two hundred ducats, if I had 'em here. Marry, I must entreat you to lend me some thirty or forty till the ship come. By this hand, I'll discharge [34] at my day, by this hand.

Vio. These are your old oaths.

Fus. Why, Sister, do you think I'll [60 forswear my hand?

Vio. Well, well, you shall have them. Put yourself into better fashion, because I must employ you in a serious matter.

Fus. I'll sweat like a horse if I like the matter.

Vio. You ha' cast off all your old swaggering humors?

Fus. I had not sail'd a league in that great fishpond, the sea, but I cast up my very gall.

Vio. I am the more sorry, for I must em- [71 ploy a true swaggerer.

Fus. Nay by this iron, Sister, they shall find I am powder and touch-box,[35] if they put fire once into me.

Vio. Then lend me your ears.

Fus. Mine ears are yours, dear Sister.

Vio. I am married to a man that has wealth enough, and wit enough.

Fus. A linen-draper, I was told, Sister. [80

Vio. Very true, a grave citizen ; I want nothing that a wife can wish from a husband. But here's the spite : he has not all things belonging to a man.

Fus. God's my life, he's a very mandrake,[36] or else (God bless us) one a' these whiblins,[37] and that's worse ; and then all the children that he gets lawfully of your body, Sister, are bastards by a statute.

Vio. O, you run over me too fast, Brother ; I have heard it often said, that he who can- [91 not be angry is no man. I am sure my husband is a man in print,[38] for all things else save only in this : no tempest can move him.

Fus. 'Slid, would he had been at sea with us. He should ha' been mov'd, and mov'd again, for I'll be sworn, la, our drunken ship reel'd like a Dutchman.

Vio. No loss of goods can increase in him a wrinkle, no crabbed language make his [100 countenance sour, the stubbornness of no servant shake him ; he has no more gall in him than a dove, no more sting than an ant ; musician will he never be (yet I find much music in him), but he loves no frets,[39] and is so free from anger that many times I am ready to bite off my tongue, because it wants that virtue which all women's tongues have — to anger their husbands. Brother, mine can by no thunder turn him into a sharpness. 110

Fus. Belike his blood, Sister, is well brew'd then.

Vio. I protest to thee, Fustigo, I love him most affectionately ; but I know not — I ha' such a tickling within me — such a strange longing ; nay verily I do long.

Fus. Then y' are with child, Sister, by all signs and tokens ; nay, I am partly a physician, and partly something else. I ha' read Albertus Magnus [40] and Aristotle's Emblems.[41]

Vio. Y' are wide a' th' bow hand [42] still, [121

---

[36] The root of which was supposed to look like the human body ; *i.e.*, then he's no man at all.
[37] The meaning is uncertain and perhaps vague. *N.E.D.* suggests "thingumbobs."
[38] A perfect man.
[39] Punning on the meanings (1) ridges on the fingerboards of plucked instruments, (2) irritations.
[40] The famous German scholastic (d. 1280). He wrote on medicine.
[41] No such work is known. Dodsley emends to *Problems*, since a book thus entitled and ascribed to Aristotle "with other philosophers and physicians" appeared in 1595, as Dyce notes.
[42] Wide of the mark.

---

[31] Died.   [32] Disgusting amount.
[33] Miserly churl.
[34] Discharge the obligation, pay.
[35] Box for touch (priming) powder, carried by musketeers.

Brother; my longings are not wanton, but wayward. I long to have my patient husband eat up a whole porcupine, to the intent the bristling quills may stick about his lips like a Flemish mustachio, and be shot at me. I shall be leaner than the new moon, unless I can make him horn-mad.[43]

Fus. 'Sfoot, half a quarter of an hour does that: make him a cuckold. 130

Vio. Pooh, he would count such a cut no unkindness.

Fus. The honester citizen he; then make him drunk and cut off his beard.

Vio. Fie, fie; idle, idle! He's no Frenchman, to fret at the loss of a little scald [44] hair. No, Brother, thus it shall be — you must be secret.

Fus. As your midwife, I protest, Sister, or a barber-surgeon. 140

Vio. Repair to the Tortoise here in St. Christopher's Street; I will send you money; turn yourself into a brave [45] man: instead of the arms of your mistress, let your sword and your military scarf hang about your neck.

Fus. I must have a great horseman's French feather too, Sister.

Vio. Oh, by any means, to show your light head, else your hat will sit like a coxcomb. To be brief, you must be in all points a [150 most terrible wide-mouth'd swaggerer.

Fus. Nay, for swaggering points let me alone.[46]

Vio. Resort then to our shop, and, in my husband's presence, kiss me, snatch rings, jewels, or anything — so you give it back again, Brother, in secret.

Fus. By this hand, Sister.

Vio. Swear as if you came but new from knighting. 160

Fus. Nay, I'll swear after [47] four hundred a year.

Vio. Swagger worse than a lieutenant among freshwater soldiers,[48] call me your love, your ingle,[49] your cousin, or so; but Sister at no hand.

Fus. No, no, it shall be cousin, or rather coz; that's the gulling word between the citizens' wives and their [madcaps] [50] that

man [51] 'em to the garden; to call you one a' mine aunts,[52] Sister, were as good as call [171 you arrant whore; no, no, let me alone to cousin [53] you rarely.

Vio. H'as heard I have a brother, but never saw him; therefore put on a good face.

Fus. The best in Milan, I warrant.

Vio. Take up wares, but pay nothing, rifle my bosom, my pocket, my purse, the boxes, for money to dice withal; but, Brother, you must give all back again in secret. 180

Fus. By this welkin [54] that here roars I will, or else let me never know what a secret is: why, Sister, do you think I'll cony-catch [55] you, when you are my cousin? God's my life, then I were a stark ass. If I fret not his guts, beg me for a fool.[56]

Vio. Be circumspect, and do so then. Farewell.

Fus. The Tortoise, Sister! I'll stay there; forty ducats. *Exit.*

Vio. Thither I'll send. — This law can none deny: 190
Women must have their longings, or they die.
Exit.

[SCENE III] [57]

[*Enter*] GASPARO *the Duke*, DOCTOR BENEDICT, [*and*] *two* Servants.

DUKE. Give charge that none do enter; lock the doors;
And fellows, what your eyes and ears receive,
Upon your lives trust not the gadding air
To carry the least part of it. The glass, the hourglass!

DOCT. Here, my Lord.

DUKE. Ah, 't is [near] [58] spent.
But, Doctor Benedict, does your art speak truth?
Art sure the soporiferous stream will ebb,
And leave the crystal banks of her white body
Pure as they were at first, just at the hour?

---

[43] Raving mad. Fustigo makes the inevitable punning allusion to the horns of the cuckold.
[44] Scurfy.   [45] Handsomely dressed.
[46] Leave it to me.
[47] After the manner of.
[48] Whose service had not taken them overseas to real fighting.
[49] Bosom friend.
[50] So Qq 2 and n.d.; other old eds. *olde dames.*

[51] Escort. Summer houses in suburban *gardens* were notorious places of assignation.
[52] *Aunt* was also a canting word for mistress. Q n.d. *a my naunts.*
[53] With a pun on "cozen" = cheat.
[54] The vault of the heavens; it "roars", presumably, with the echoes of Fustigo's laughter.
[55] Cheat.
[56] *I.e.* call me a fool; in origin an allusion to the practice of obtaining from the sovereign the profitable guardianship of a wealthy idiot.
[57] A chamber in the Duke's palace. — Qq 2 and n.d. spell the doctor's name *Benedict;* other old eds. *Benedick.*
[58] Conj. Dyce; old eds. *meere,* but see l. 18.

Doct. Just at the hour, my Lord.

Duke.   Uncurtain her [10

> [Infeliche *is discovered lying on a couch.*]

Softly ; [see,][59] doctor, what a coldish heat
Spreads over all her body.

Doct.   Now it works.
The vital spirits that by a sleepy charm
Were bound up fast, and threw an icy rust [60]
On her exterior parts, now 'gin to break ;
Trouble her not, my Lord.

Duke.   Some stools ! — You call'd
For music, did you not? — Oh ho, it speaks.

> [*Music.*]

It speaks ! — Watch, sirs, her waking ; note
    those sands. —
Doctor, sit down.   A dukedom that should
    weigh
Mine own down twice, being put into one scale,
And that fond [61] desperate boy, Hippolito, [21
Making the weight up, should not at my hands
Buy her i' th' tother, were her state more light
Than hers who makes a dowry up with alms.
Doctor, I 'll starve her on the Apennine
Ere he shall marry her.   I must confess
Hippolito is nobly born ; a man —
Did not mine enemies' blood boil in his veins —
Whom I would court to be my son-in-law.
But princes, whose high spleens [62] for empery
    swell,   30
Are not with easy art made parallel.[63]

Servants.[64] She wakes, my Lord.

Duke.   Look, Doctor Benedict. —
I charge you on your lives, maintain for truth
What e'er the doctor or myself aver ;
For you shall bear her hence to [Bergamo.] [65]

Inf. O God, what fearful dreams !

Doct.   Lady.

Inf.   Ha !

Duke.   Girl.
Why, Infeliche, how is 't now, ha?   Speak !

Inf. I 'm well — what makes [66] this doctor
    here? — I 'm well.

Duke. Thou wert not so even now, sick-
    ness' pale hand
Laid hold on thee even in the [mid'st] [67] of
    feasting ;   40

[59] So Qq 2 and n.d. Other old eds. *sweete.*
[60] Dyce conjectures *crust.*
[61] Foolish.
[62] Resolute minds.
[63] Made to conform.
[64] Old eds. *2 Ser.*
[65] So Q n.d. and Pearson (and, presumably, Q 2).
Q 1, etc., *Bergaine.*
[66] Does.
[67] So Qq 2 and n.d. ; other old eds. *deadst.*

And when a cup crown'd with thy lover's
    health
Had touch'd thy lips, a sensible [68] cold dew
Stood on thy cheeks, as if that death had wept
To see such beauty [alter].[69]

Inf.   I remember
I sat at banquet, but felt no such change.

Duke. Thou hast forgot, then, how a mes-
    senger
Came wildly in, with this unsavory news :
That he was dead?

Inf.   What messenger?   Who 's dead?

Duke. Hippolito.   Alack, wring not thy
    hands.

Inf. I saw no messenger, heard no such
    news.   50

Doct. Trust me you did, sweet lady.

Duke.   La, you now ! [70

Ser. Yes, indeed, madam.

Duke.   La, you now. — 'T is well, [good
    knaves].[71]

Inf. You ha' slain him, and now you 'll
    murder me.

Duke. Good Infeliche, vex not thus thyself.
Of this the bad report before did strike
So coldly to the heart that the swift currents
Of life were all frozen up.

Inf.   It is untrue,
'T is most untrue ; O most unnatural father !

Duke. And we had much to do by art's best
    cunning,
To fetch life back again.

Doct.   Most certain, lady. [60

Duke. Why, la, you now, you 'll not believe
    me. — Friends,
Sweat we not all?   Had we not much to do?

Ser. Yes, indeed, my Lord, much.

Duke. Death drew such fearful pictures in
    thy face
That were Hippolito alive again,
I 'd kneel and woo the noble gentleman
To be thy husband.   Now I sore repent
My sharpness to him, and his family.
Nay, do not weep for him ; we all must die. —
Doctor, this place where she so oft hath seen [70
His lively presence, [hurts] [72] her, does it not?

Doct. Doubtless, my Lord, it does.

Duke.   It does, it does.
Therefore, sweet girl, thou shalt to Bergamo.

Inf. Even where you will ; in any place
    there 's woe.

[68] Perceptible.
[69] So Qq 2 and n.d. Other old eds. *alterd, altered.*
[70] There, you see !
[71] So Qq 2 and n.d. Other old eds. *God knowes.*|
[72] Qq 2 and n.d. *hnrts;* other old eds. *haunts.*

DUKE. A coach is ready; Bergamo doth stand

In a most wholesome air; sweet walks, there's deer —

Ay, thou shalt hunt and send us venison,

Which, like some [goddess in the Cyprian] [73] groves,

Thine own fair hand shall strike. — Sirs, you shall teach her

To stand, and how to shoot; ay, she shall hunt. — 80

Cast off this sorrow. In, girl, and prepare

This night to ride away to Bergamo.

INF. O most unhappy maid! *Exit.*

DUKE. Follow [her] [74] close.

No words that she was buried, on your lives!

Or that her ghost walks now after she's dead;

I'll hang you if you name a funeral.

1 SER. I'll speak Greek, my Lord, ere I speak that deadly word.

2 SER. And I'll speak Welsh, which is harder than Greek. *Exeunt* [Servants]. [90

DUKE. Away, look to her. — Doctor Benedict,

Did you observe how her complexion alt'red

Upon his name and death? Oh, would 't were true.

DOCT. It may, my Lord.

DUKE. May! How? I wish his death.

DOCT. And you may have your wish; say but the word,

And 't is a strong spell to rip up [75] his grave.

I have good knowledge [76] with Hippolito;

He calls me friend; I'll creep into his bosom, [77]

And sting him there to death; poison can do 't.

DUKE. Perform it, I'll create thee half mine heir. 100

DOCT. It shall be done, although the fact [78] be foul.

DUKE. Greatness hides sin; the guilt upon my soul! *Exeunt.*

[SCENE IV] [79]

Enter CASTRUCHIO, PIORATTO, *and* FLUELLO.

CAS. Signior Pioratto, Signior Fluello, shall's be merry? Shall's play the wags now?

FLU. Ay, anything that may beget the child of laughter.

CAS. Truth, I have a pretty sportive conceit new crept into my brain, will move excellent mirth.

PIO. Let's ha 't, let's ha 't; and where shall the scene of mirth lie?

CAS. At Signior Candido's house, the [10 patient man, nay, the monstrous patient man. They say his blood [80] is immoveable, that he has taken all patience from a man, and all constancy from a woman.

FLU. That [81] makes so many whores nowadays.

CAS. Ay, and so many knaves too.

PIO. Well, sir.

CAS. To conclude, the report goes he's so mild, so affable, so suffering, that nothing [20 indeed can move him. Now do but think what sport it will be to make this fellow, the mirror of patience, as angry, as vex'd, and as mad as an English cuckold.

FLU. Oh, 't were admirable mirth, that; but how will 't be done, signior?

CAS. Let me alone; I have a trick, a conceit, a thing, a device, will sting him, i' faith, if he have but a thimbleful of blood in 's belly, or a spleen [82] not so big as a tavern token. [83] [30

PIO. Thou stir him? thou move him? thou anger him? Alas, I know his approved temper. [84] Thou vex him? Why he has a patience above man's injuries; thou mayst sooner raise a spleen in an angel, than rough humor in him. Why, I'll give you instance for it. This wonderfully temper'd Signior Candido upon a time invited home to his house certain Neapolitan lords, of curious [85] taste and no mean palates, conjuring his [40 wife, of all loves, [86] to prepare cheer fitting for such honorable trenchermen. She, just of a woman's nature, covetous to try the uttermost of vexation and thinking at last to get the start of his humor, willingly [87] neglected the preparation, and became unfurnish'd, not only of dainty, but of ordinary dishes. He, according to the mildness of his breast, entertained the lords, and with courtly discourse beguiled the time, as much as a [50 citizen might do. To conclude, they were

---

[73] So Qq 2 and n.d.; other old eds. *gods . . . Coprian.*
[74] So Qq 2 and n.d.; other old eds. *it.*
[75] Dig.
[76] Considerable intimacy.
[77] Confidence.
[78] Deed.
[79] A street.

[80] Temper.
[81] *I.e.*, the loss of that.
[82] Supposed to be the seat of anger.
[83] A small piece of brass or copper issued by tradesmen, especially tavern keepers, for use as small change.
[84] Tested disposition.
[85] Fastidious.
[86] For love's sake.
[87] Willfully.

hungry lords, for there came no meat in ; their stomachs were plainly gull'd, and their teeth deluded, and if anger could have seiz'd a man, there was matter enough i' faith to vex any citizen in the world, if he were not too much made a fool by his wife.

FLU. Ay, I 'll swear for 't. 'Sfoot, had it been my case, I should ha' play'd mad tricks with my wife and family. First, I would [60 ha' spitted the men, stew'd the maids, and bak'd the mistress, and so served them in.

PIO. Why 't would ha' temp[t]ed any blood but his ;
And thou to vex him? thou to anger him
With some poor shallow jest?

CAS. 'Sblood, Signior Pioratto, you that disparage my conceit,[88] I 'll wage a hundred ducats upon the head on 't, that it moves him, frets him, and galls him.

PIO. Done, 't is a lay ; [89] join golls [90] [70 on 't. — Witness, Signior Fluello.

CAS. Witness ; 't is done.
Come, follow me ; the house is not far off.
I 'll thrust him from his humor, vex his breast,
And win a hundred ducats by one jest.

Exeunt.

[SCENE V] [91]

Enter [VIOLA] *Candido's wife,* GEORGE, *and two* Prentices *in the shop.*

VIO. Come, you put up your wares in good order here, do you not, think you? One piece cast this way, another that way ! You had need have a patient master indeed.

GEO. [*aside*] Ay, I 'll be sworn, for we have a curst [92] mistress.

VIO. You mumble? do you mumble? I would your master or I could be a note more angry, for two patient folks in a house spoil all the servants that ever shall come under [10 them.

1 PREN. [*aside*] You patient ! Ay, so is the Devil when he is horn-mad.

Enter CASTRUCHIO, FLUELLO, *and* PIORATTO.

ALL THREE.[93] Gentlemen, what do you lack ? [94] What is 't you buy? See fine hollands, fine cambrics, fine lawns.

GEO. What is 't you lack?
2 PREN. What is 't you buy?
CAS. Where 's Signior Candido, thy master ?
GEO. Faith, signior, he 's a little nego- [20 tiated ; [95] he 'll appear presently.

CAS. Fellow, let 's see a lawn, a choice one, sirrah.

GEO. The best in all Milan, gentlemen, and this is the piece. I can fit you gentlemen with fine calicoes, too, for doublets, the only sweet fashion now, most delicate and courtly, a meek, gentle calico, cut upon two double affable taffetas — ah, most neat, feat,[96] and unmatchable.   30

FLU. A notable voluble-tongu'd villain.

PIO. I warrant this fellow was never begot without much prating.

CAS. What, and is this she, say'st thou?

GEO. Ay, and the purest she that ever you finger'd since you were a gentleman. Look how even she is, look how clean she is, ha ! as even as the brow of Cynthia, and as clean as your sons and heirs when they ha' spent all.

CAS. Pooh, thou talk'st ; pox on 't, [40 't is rough.

GEO. How? Is she rough? But if you bid [97] pox on 't, sir, 't will take away the roughness presently.

FLU. Ha, signior ; has he fitted your French [98] curse?

GEO. Look you, gentlemen, here 's another. Compare them I pray, *compara Virgilium cum Homero :* compare virgins with harlots.

CAS. Pooh, I ha' seen better, and as [50 you term them, evener and cleaner.

GEO. You may see further for your mind, but trust me, you shall not find better for your body.

Enter CANDIDO.

CAS. O here he comes ; let 's make as though we pass. —
Come, come, we 'll try in some other shop.
CAND. How now? What 's the matter?
GEO. The gentlemen find fault with this lawn, fall out with it, and without a cause too.
CAND. Without a cause?   60
And that makes you to let 'em pass away ! —
Ah, may I crave a word with you, gentlemen?
FLU. He calls us.
CAS.   Makes the better for the jest.

---

[88] Idea.   [89] Bet.   [90] Hands.
[91] Candido's shop, represented by the inner stage. Viola, George, and the prentices are discovered there ; the outer stage represents the street. The shops in Elizabethan London were open during the day, much like the booths of a fair, though shutters protected them at night.
[92] Cross.   [93] *I.e.,* George and the prentices.
[94] The characteristic cry of the shopkeeper.
[95] Busy.
[96] Becoming, elegant.
[97] Pray, invoke.
[98] Since syphilis, or the pox, was known as the French disease.

CAND. I pray come near; y' are very welcome, gallants.
Pray pardon my man's rudeness, for I fear me
H'as talk'd above a prentice with you. — Lawns!
Look you, kind gentlemen; this — no — ay, this —
Take this upon my honest-dealing faith,
To be a true weave, not too hard nor slack,
But e'en as far from falsehood as from black.

    CAS. Well, how do you rate it?   71
    CAND. Very conscionably, eighteen shillings a yard.
    CAS. That's too dear. How many yards
does the whole piece contain, think you?
    CAND. Why, some seventeen yards, I think, or thereabouts.
How much would serve your turn, I pray?
    CAS. Why, let me see — would it were better too.
    CAND. Truth, 't is the best in Milan, at few words.
    CAS. Well, let me have then a whole pennyworth.
    CAND. Ha, ha! y' are a merry gentleman.
    CAS. A penn'orth, I say.   81
    CAND. Of lawn!
    CAS. Of lawn? Ay, of lawn, a penn'orth.
'Sblood, dost not hear? A whole penn'orth, are you deaf?
    CAND. Deaf? no, sir; but I must tell you,
Our wares do seldom meet such customers.
    CAS. Nay, an you and your lawns be so squeamish, fare you well.
    CAND. Pray stay; a word, pray, signior.
For what purpose is it, I beseech you?   91
    CAS. 'Sblood, what's that to you? I'll
have a pennyworth.
    CAND. A pennyworth! Why you shall:
I'll serve you presently.[99]
    2 PREN. 'S foot, a pennyworth, mistress!
    VIO. A pennyworth! Call you these gentlemen?
    CAS. No, no; not there.
    CAND. What then, kind gentleman? what, at this corner here?   101
    CAS. No, nor there neither;
I'll have it just in the middle, or else not.
    CAND. Just in the middle! ha! you shall too. What,
Have you a single penny?
    CAS.   Yes, here's one.
    CAND. Lend it me, I pray.[100]

[99] Immediately.
[100] To cut a piece of cloth the size of a penny.

    FLU. An exc'llent followed jest.
    VIO. What, will he spoil the lawn now?
    CAND. Patience, good Wife.
    VIO. Ay, that patience makes a fool [110
of you. — Gentlemen, you might ha' found
some other citizen to have made a kind gull
on,[101] besides my husband.
    CAND. Pray, gentlemen, take her to be a woman;
Do not regard her language. — Oh, kind soul,
Such words will drive away my customers.
    VIO. Customers, with a murrain![102] Call
you these customers?
    CAND. Patience, good Wife.
    VIO. Pax a' your patience.   120
    GEO. 'Sfoot, Mistress, I warrant these are
some cheating companions.[103]
    CAND. Look you, gentleman, there's your
ware. I thank you; I have your money
here. Pray know my shop; pray let me have
your custom.
    VIO. Custom, quoth'a!
    CAND. Let me take more of your money.
    VIO. You had need so.
    PIO. [*aside to* CASTRUCHIO] Hark in [130
thine ear: th'ast lost an hundred ducats.
    CAS. [*aside to* PIORATTO] Well, well, I
know 't. Is 't possible that *homo*
Should be nor man nor woman? Not once mov'd?
No not at such an injury, not at all!
Sure he's a pigeon, for he has no gall.
    FLU. Come, come, y' are angry though you smother it:
Y' are vex'd i' faith; confess.
    CAND.   Why, gentlemen,
Should you conceit[104] me to be vex'd or mov'd?
He has my ware, I have his money for 't,
And that's no argument I am angry; no, [140
The best logician cannot prove me so.
    FLU. Oh, but the hateful name of a penny worth of lawn,
And then cut out i' th' middle of the piece.
Pah, I guess it by myself, ['t] would move a lamb,
Were he a linen-draper, 't would, i' faith.
    CAND. Well, give me leave to answer you for that.
We [a]re set here to please all customers,
Their humors and their fancies, offend none;
We get by many, if we leese[105] by one.   149

[101] An obliging dupe of.   [102] Plague.   [103] Fellows
[104] Imagine.
[105] Lose.

Maybe his mind stood to no more than that ;
A penn'orth serves him ; and 'mongst trades
  't is found,
Deny a penn'orth, it may cross a pound.
Oh, he that means to thrive, with patient eye
Must please the Devil, if he come to buy.
  FLU. O wondrous man, patient 'bove wrong
    or woe ;
How blest were men, if women could be so.
  CAND. And to express how well my breast
    is pleas'd,
And satisfied in all, — George, fill a beaker.
                        Exit GEORGE.
I 'll drink unto that gentleman, who lately [159
Bestowed his money with me.
  VIO.   God 's my life,
We shall have all our gains drunk out in
    beakers,
To make amends for pennyworths of lawn.

                Re-enter GEORGE.

  CAND. Here, Wife, begin you to the gentie-
    man.
  VIO. I begin to him !   [*Spills the wine.*]
  CAND.   George, fill 't up again. —
'T was my fault ; my hand shook.
                        Exit GEORGE.
  PIO.   How strangely this doth show !
A patient man link'd with a waspish shrew.
  FLU. [*aside*] A silver and gilt beaker ; I
    have a trick
To work upon that beaker ; sure 't will fret
    him ;
It cannot choose but vex him. — [*aside to*
    CASTRUCHIO] Signior Castruchio,
In pity to thee I have a conceit,   170
Will save thy hundred ducats yet ; 't will do 't,
And work him to impatience.
  CAS. [*aside*]   Sweet Fluello,
I should be bountiful to that conceit.[106]
  FLU. Well, 't is enough.

                Re-enter GEORGE.

  CAND.   Here, gentleman, to you ;
I wish your custom ; y' are exceeding welcome.
  CAS. I pledge you, Signior Candido —
Here, [to][107] you that must receive a hundred
    ducats.
  PIO. I 'll pledge them deep, i' faith, Cas-
    truchio. —
Signior Fluello.
  FLU.   Come, play 't off ; to me —
I am your last man.

  CAND.   George, supply the cup.
  FLU. So, so, good honest George —   181
Here Signior Candido, all this to you.
  CAND. O, you must pardon me ; I use it
    not.[108]
  FLU. Will you not pledge me then ?
  CAND.   Yes, but not that ;
Great love is shown in little.
  FLU.   Blurt [109] on your sentences !
'Sfoot, you shall pledge me all.
  CAND.   Indeed I shall not.
  FLU. Not pledge me ? 'Sblood, I 'll carry
    away the beaker then.
  CAND. The beaker ? Oh ! that at your
    pleasure, sir.
  FLU. Now by this drink I will.
  CAS.   Pledge him ; he 'll do 't else.
  FLU. So ; I ha' done you right on my
    thumb-nail.[110]   190
What, will you pledge me now ?
  CAND.   You know me, sir ;
I am not of that sin.
  FLU.   Why, then, farewell ;
I 'll bear away the beaker, by this light.
  CAND. That 's as you please ; 't is very
    good.
  FLU. Nay, it doth please me, and as you
    say,
'T is a very good one. Farewell, Signior
    Candido.
  PIO. Farewell, Candido.
  CAND. Y' are welcome, gentlemen.
  CAS.   Heart ! not mov'd yet ?
I think his patience is above our wit.
      Exeunt [CASTRUCHIO, FLUELLO
        carrying off the beaker, and PIO-
        RATTO].

  GEO. I told you before, Mistress, they [200
were all cheaters.
  VIO. Why, fool, why, Husband ; why,
madman ; I hope you will not let 'em sneak
away so with a silver and gilt beaker, the best
in the house too. — Go, fellows ; make hue
and cry after them.
  CAND. Pray let your tongue lie still ; all
    will be well. —
Come hither, George ; hie to the constable,

---

[106] *I.e.*, if your notion succeeds, I 'll reward you.
[107] Apparently only Q n.d.

[108] I am not accustomed to such drinking;
Candido has already drunk to them, and is unwilling to "pledge" Fluello by drinking the amount
he insists on.
[109] An eruptive emission of breath, expressive of
contempt. (*N.E.D.*)
[110] Fluello inverts the vessel and allows the remaining liquor to form a drop on his thumb-nail;
since there is only a drop, which does not run, he
has "done him right."

And in calm order wish him to attach them.
Make no great stir, because they're gentle-
men,   210
And a thing partly done in merriment.
'T is but a size above a jest thou know'st;
Therefore pursue it mildly. Go, begone;
The constable's hard by; bring him along;
Make haste again.   *Exit* GEORGE.

VIO. O y' are a goodly patient woodcock,[111]
are you not now? See what your patience
comes to: every one saddles you and rides
you; you'll be shortly the common stone-
horse [112] of Milan; a woman's well holp'd [220
up with such a meacock.[113] I had rather
have a husband that would swaddle [114] me
thrice a day, than such a one, that will be
gull'd twice in half an hour. Oh, I could burn
all the wares in my shop for anger.

CAND. Pray wear a peaceful temper; be
    my wife,
That is, be patient; for a wife and husband
Share but one soul between them: this being
    known,
Why should not one soul then agree in one?

VIO. Hang your agreements! but if my
beaker be gone —   *Exit.* [231

Re-enter CASTRUCHIO, FLUELLO, PIORATTO,
    and GEORGE.

CAND. Oh, here they come.

GEO. The constable, sir, let 'em come along
with me, because [115] there should be no wond'-
ring; he stays at door.

CAS. Constable, Goodman Abram.[116]

FLU. Now Signior Candido; 'sblood, why
do you attach us?

CAS. 'Sheart! attach us!

CAND.   Nay swear not, gallants;
Your oaths may move your souls, but not
    move me;   240
You have a silver beaker of my wife's.

FLU. You say not true: 't is gilt.

CAND.   Then you say true;
And being gilt, the guilt lies more on you.

CAS. I hope y' are not angry, sir.

CAND. Then you hope right; for I am not
    angry.

FLU. No, but a little mov'd.

111 Fool.
112 Stallion; *i.e.*, in general demand.
113 Coward, effeminate person.
114 Beat.
115 So that.
116 A wandering beggar. Doubtless many such
feigned idiocy.

CAND. I mov'd! 'T was you were mov'd;
    you were brought hither.

CAS. But you, out of your anger and impa-
    tience,
Caus'd us to be attach'd.

CAND.   Nay, you misplace it;
Out of my quiet sufferance I did that,   250
And not of any wrath. Had I shown anger,
I should have then pursu'd you with the
    law,
And hunted you to shame, as many world-
    lings
Do build their anger upon feebler grounds,
The more's the pity: many lose their lives
For scarce so much coin as will hide their
    palm,
Which is most cruel; those have vexed spirits
That pursue lives. In this opinion rest:
The loss of millions could not move my breast.

FLU. Thou art a blest man, and with peace
    dost deal;   260
Such a meek spirit can bless a commonweal.

CAND. Gentlemen, now 't is upon eating-
    time;
Pray part not hence, but dine with me to-day.

CAS. I never heard a [courtier] [117] yet say nay
To such a motion. I 'll not be the first.

PIO. Nor I.

FLU. Nor I.

CAND. The constable shall bear you com-
    pany.
George, call him in; let the world say what it
    can,
Nothing can drive me from a patient man. 270
          Exeunt.

[ACT II — SCENE I] [1]

Enter ROGER *with a stool, cushion, looking-glass,
    and chafing-dish* [2]; *those being set down, he
    pulls out of his pocket a vial with white color
    in it, and two boxes, one with white, another
    red, painting; he places all things in order,
    and a candle by them, singing with the ends of
    old ballads as he does it. At last* BELLA-
FRONT, *as he rubs his cheek with the colors,
    whistles within.*

ROG. Anon, forsooth.

BELL. [*within*] What are you playing the
rogue about?

117 Apparently only Q n.d. Other old eds. *carter.*
1 A room in Bellafront's house.
2 For heating the curling-bodkin and the poking
stick.

Rog. About you, forsooth; I'm drawing up a hole in your white silk stocking.

Bell. Is my glass there? and my boxes of complexion?

Rog. Yes, forsooth, your boxes of complexion are here, I think; yes, 't is here. Here's your two complexions — [*aside*] and if I had [10 all the four complexions,³ I should ne'er set a good face upon 't. Some men, I see, are born under hard-favor'd ⁴ planets as well as women. Zounds, I look worse now than I did before; and it makes her face glister most damnably. There's knavery in daubing, I hold my life; or else this is only female pomatum.

Enter Bellafront *not full ready, without a gown; she sits down; with her bodkin ⁵ curls her hair, colors her lips.*

Bell. Where's my ruff and poker,⁶ you blockhead?

Rog. Your ruff [and] ⁷ your poker are en- [20 gend'ring together upon the cupboard of the court, or the court cupboard.⁸

Bell. Fetch 'em. — Is the pox in your hams, you can go no faster?

Rog. Would the pox were in your fingers, unless you could leave flinging! Catch! ⁹
Exit.

Bell. I'll catch you, you dog, by and by. Do you grumble? *She sings.*

Cupid is a God, as naked as my nail; 29
I'll whip him with a rod, if he my true love fail.

[*Re-enter* Roger *with ruff and poker.*]

Rog. There's your ruff. Shall I poke it?

Bell. Yes, honest Roger — no, stay; prithee, good boy, hold here.

[*Sings.* Roger *holds the glass and candle.*]

Down, down, down, down, I fall down and arise — down —
I never shall arise.

Rog. Troth, Mistress, then leave the trade, if you shall never rise.

Bell. What trade, Goodman Abram?

Rog. Why that [o]f down and arise, or the falling trade. 40

Bell. I'll fall ¹⁰ with you by and by.

Rog. If you do I know who shall smart ¹¹ for 't.

Troth, Mistress, what do I look like now?

Bell. Like as you are; a panderly sixpenny rascal.

Rog. I may thank you for that; in faith, I look like an old proverb, "Hold the candle before the Devil."

Bell. Ud's life, I'll stick my knife in your guts an you prate to me so! — What? 50
She sings.

Well met, pug,¹² the pearl of beauty; umh, umh.
How now, Sir Knave? you forget your duty; umh, umh.
Marry, muff,¹³ sir, are you grown so dainty? fa, la, la, etc.
Is it you, sir? the worst of twenty; fa, la, la, leera, la.

Pox on you; how doest thou hold my glass?

Rog. Why, as I hold your door: with my fingers.

Bell. Nay, pray thee, sweet honey Roger, hold up handsomely.

Sing,¹⁴ pretty wantons, warble, etc. 60

We shall ha' guests to-day, I lay ¹⁵ my little maidenhead, my nose itches so.

Rog. I said so too last night, when our fleas twing'd me.

Bell. So; poke my ruff now; my gown, my gown! Have I my fall? ¹⁶ Where's my fall, Roger?

Rog. Your fall, forsooth, is behind.
One knocks.

Bell. God's my pittikins! some fool or other knocks. 70

Rog. Shall I open to the fool, mistress?

Bell. And all these baubles lying thus? Away with it quickly. — Ay, ay, knock, and be damn'd, whosoever you be! — So; give the fresh salmon line now; let him come ashore. He shall serve for my breakfast, though he go against my stomach.

Roger *fetch in* Fluello, Castruchio, *and* Pioratto.

Flu. Morrow, coz.

Cas. How does my sweet acquaintance?

---

³ Temperaments (sanguine, phlegmatic, choleric, melancholy).
⁴ Ill-featured.   ⁵ Curling-iron.
⁶ Poking stick, for pleating ruffs.
⁷ Apparently only in Q n.d.
⁸ Sideboard, china cabinet.
⁹ Apparently she throws something at him, and he catches it.
¹⁰ Meet; *i.e.*, settle.

¹¹ As the result of the beating you'll give me; perhaps with a double entente on "smart" = suffer from venereal disease.
¹² Monkey — as a term of endearment.
¹³ A term of contempt, originally applied to Germans.
¹⁴ Perhaps, as the Pearson ed. suggests, a stage direction.
¹⁵ Bet.
¹⁶ A collar which fell flat around the neck.

PIO. Save thee, little marmoset; [17] how [80 doest thou, good pretty rogue?

BELL. Well, God-a-mercy, good pretty rascal.

FLU. Roger, some light, I prithee.

ROG. You shall, signior; for we that live here in this vale of misery are as dark as hell.
Exit for a candle.

CAS. Good tobacco, Fluello?

FLU. Smell.

PIO. It may be tickling gear,[18] for it plays with my nose already.   90

Re-enter ROGER [with candle].

ROG. Here's another light angel,[19] signior.

BELL. What, you pied curtal; [20] what's that you are neighing?

ROG. I say God send us the light of Heaven, or some more angels.

BELL. Go fetch some wine, and drink half of it.

ROG. I must fetch some wine, gentlemen, and drink half of it.

FLU. Here, Roger.

CAS. No, let me send, prithee.

FLU. Hold, you cankerworm.

ROG. You shall send both, if you [100 please, signiors.

PIO. Stay, what's best to drink a' mornings?

ROG. Hippocras,[21] sir, for my mistress, if I fetch it, is most dear to her.

FLU. Hippocras! There, then; here's a teston [22] for you, you snake.

ROG. Right sir; here's three shillings sixpence for a pottle [23] and a manchet.[24]   *Exit.*

CAS. Here's most [Herculian] [25] to- [110 bacco; ha' some, acquaintance?

BELL. Fah, not I; makes your breath stink like the piss of a fox. Acquaintance, where supp'd you last night?

CAS. At a place, sweet acquaintance, where your health danc'd the canaries,[26] i' faith; you shou'd ha' been there.

BELL. I there among your punks! [27] Marry, fah, hang 'em; [I] scorn 't. Will

you never leave sucking of eggs in other [120 folk's hens' nests?

CAS. Why, in good troth, if you'll trust me, acquaintance, there was not one hen at the board; ask Fluello.

FLU. No, faith, coz, none but cocks. Signior Malavella drunk to thee.

BELL. O, a pure beagle; that horse-leech there?

FLU. And the knight, Sir Oliver Lollio, swore he would bestow a taffeta petticoat [130 on thee, but to break his fast with thee.

BELL. With me! I'll choke him then, hang him, molecatcher! [28] It's the dreaming'st snotty-nose.

PIO. Well, many took that Lollio for a fool; but he's a subtle fool.

BELL. Ay, and he has fellows; of all filthy, dry-fisted [29] knights, I cannot abide that he should touch me.

CAS. Why, wench? Is he scabbed? [30] [140

BELL. Hang him, he'll not live to be so honest, nor to the credit to have scabs about him; his betters have 'em. But I hate to wear out any of his coarse knighthood, because he's made like an alderman's nightgown,[31] fac'd all with cony [32] before, and within nothing but fox. This sweet Oliver will eat mutton [33] till he be ready to burst, but the lean-jaw'd slave will not pay for the scraping of his trencher.   150

PIO. Plague him; set him beneath the salt, and let him not touch a bit, till every one has had his full cut.

FLU. [Sordello,] [34] the gentleman usher, came in to us too; marry 't was in our cheese,[35] for he had been to borrow money for his lord, of a citizen.

CAS. What an ass is that lord, to borrow money of a citizen!

BELL. Nay, God's my pity, what an [160 ass is that citizen to lend money [to] a lord!

Enter MATHEO, and HIPPOLITO who, saluting the company as a stranger, walks off.[36] ROGER comes in sadly behind them, with a pottle pot, and stands aloof off.

[17] Monkey.
[18] Gratifying stuff.
[19] Punning on *angel* = "coin."
[20] Docked horse.
[21] A spiced wine.
[22] Sixpence.
[23] Two quarts.
[24] Small loaf of white bread.
[25] Powerful. So Qq 2 and n.d. Q 1 *Herculanian.*
[26] A lively Spanish dance, with a punning allusion to Canary wine.
[27] Strumpets.

[28] A vague term of abuse.
[29] "A moist hand is vulgarly accounted a sign of an amorous constitution." (Reed.)
[30] Syphilitic.
[31] Dressing gown; punning with *knight-hood.*
[32] Rabbit fur.   [33] Slang for prostitute.
[34] So Q n.d.; other old eds. seen by present Ed., and Pearson, *Lord Ello.*
[35] At the end of our meal.
[36] Withdraws to one side or to the rear of the stage.

Mat. Save you, gallants. Signior Fluello, exceedingly well met, as I may say.

Flu. Signior Matheo, exceedingly well met too, as I may say.

Mat. And how fares my little pretty mistress?

Bell. E'en as my little pretty servant; [37] sees three court dishes before her, and not one good bit in them : — How now? Why [170 the devil stand'st thou so? Art in a trance?

Rog. Yes, forsooth.

Bell. Why dost not fill out their wine?

Rog. Forsooth, 't is fill'd out already : all the wine that the signior has bestow'd upon you is cast away ; a porter ran a little [38] at me, and so fac'd me down that I had not a drop.

Bell. I 'm accurs'd to let such a withered artichoke-faced rascal grow under my nose. Now you look like an old he-cat, going to [180 the gallows. I 'll be hang'd if he ha' not put up [39] the money to cony-catch [40] us all.

Rog. No, truly, forsooth ; 't is not put up yet.

Bell. How many gentlemen hast thou served thus?

Rog. None but five hundred, besides prentices and serving men.

Bell. Doest think I 'll pocket it up [41] at thy hands?   190

Rog. Yes, forsooth, I fear you will pocket it up.[42]

Bell. Fie, fie, cut my lace, good servant ; I shall ha' the mother [43] presently, I 'm so vex'd at this horse-plum.[44]

Flu. Plague, not for a scald [45] pottle of wine.

Mat. Nay, sweet Bellafront, for a little pig's wash ! [46]

Cas. Here Roger, fetch more. [*Gives* [200 *money.*] A mischance, i' faith, acquaintance.

Bell. Out of my sight, thou ungodly puritanical creature.

Rog. For the tother pottle? Yes, forsooth.

Bell. Spill that too. [*Exit* Roger.] — What gentleman is that, servant? your friend?

---

[37] Lover.
[38] Dyce conj. *tilt.*
[39] Pocketed.
[40] Cheat.
[41] Put up with it.
[42] Alluding to the swindle. Roger had, of course, to hand Bellafront the money later.
[43] Hysterics.
[44] A small red plum.
[45] Scurvy, paltry.
[46] Swill.

Mat. Gods so ; a stool, a stool. If you love me, mistress, entertain this gentleman respectively,[47] and bid him welcome. 210

Bell. He 's very welcome. — Pray, sir, sit.

Hip. Thanks, lady.

Flu. Count Hippolito, is 't not? — Cry you mercy, signior ; you walk here all this while, and we not heard you? Let me bestow a stool upon you, beseech you ; you are a stranger here ; we know the fashions a' th' house.

Cas. Please you be here, my Lord?

         [*Offers*] *tobacco.*

Hip. No, good Castruchio.   220

Flu. You have abandoned the court, I see, my Lord, since the death of your mistress. Well, she was a delicate piece. — Beseech you, sweet, come, let us serve under the colors of your acquaintance still for all that. — Please you to meet here at [the] [48] lodging of my coz, I shall bestow a banquet upon you.

Hip. I never can deserve this kindness, sir. What may this lady be, whom you call coz?

Flu. Faith, sir, a poor gentlewoman, [230 of passing good carriage ; [49] one that has some suits in law, and lies here in an attorney's house.

Hip. Is she married?

Flu. Ha, as all your punks are, a captain's wife, or so. Never saw her before, my Lord?

Hip. Never, trust me ; a goodly creature.

Flu. By gad, when you know her as we do, you 'll swear she is the prettiest, kindest, sweetest, most bewitching honest ape [240 under the pole. A skin, your satin is not more soft, nor lawn whiter.

Hip. Belike, then, she 's some sale [50] courtesan.

Flu. Troth, as all your best faces are ; a good wench.

Hip. Great pity that she 's a good wench.[51]

Mat. Thou shalt [have, it] [52] i' faith, mistress. — How now, signiors? What, whispering? Did not I lay a wager I should take [250 you, within seven days, in a house of vanity?

Hip. You did ; and, I beshrew your heart, you have won.

Mat. How do you like my mistress?

Hip. Well, for such a mistress ; better, if

---

[47] With respect.
[48] So Q n.d. Other old eds. seen by present Ed., and Pearson, *my.*
[49] Demeanor.
[50] For sale.
[51] Strumpet.
[52] So Q n.d. Other old eds. seen by present Ed., and Pearson, *ha.*

your mistress be not your master. — I must break manners, gentlemen ; fare you well.

MAT. 'Sfoot, you shall not leave us.

BELL. The gentleman likes not the taste of our company. 260

OMN[ES]. Beseech you stay.

HIP. Trust me, my affairs beckon for me ; pardon me,

MAT. Will you call for me half an hour hence here?

HIP. Perhaps I shall.

MAT. Perhaps? fah! I know you can! swear to me you will.

HIP. Since you will press me, on my word, I will. *Exit.* [270

BELL. What sullen picture is this, servant?

MAT. It 's Count Hippolito, the brave count.

PIO. As gallant a spirit as any in Milan, you sweet Jew.

FLU. Oh, he 's a most essential gentleman, coz.

CAS. Did you never hear of Count Hippolito, acquaintance?

BELL. Marry, muff a' your counts, an [280 be no more life in 'em.

MAT. He 's so malcontent! Sirrah [53] Bellafront, — an you be honest gallants, let 's sup together, and have the Count with us ; — thou shalt sit at the upper end, punk.

BELL. Punk, you sous'd [54] gurnet? [55]

MAT. King's truce! [56] Come, I 'll bestow the supper to have him but laugh.

CAS. He betrays his youth too grossly to that tyrant melancholy. 290

MAT. All this is for a woman.

BELL. A woman! some whore! What sweet jewel is 't?

PIO. Would she heard you.

FLU. Troth, so would I.

CAS. And I, by Heaven.

BELL. Nay, good servant, what woman?

MAT. Pah.

BELL. Prithee, tell me ; a buss and tell me. I warrant he 's an honest fellow, if [300 he take on thus for a wench. Good rogue, who?

MAT. By th' Lord I will not, must not, faith, mistress.—Is 't a match, sirs? this night, at th' Antelope ; ay, for there 's best wine, and good boys.

OMNES. It 's done ; at th' Antelope.

BELL. I cannot be there to-night.

MAT. Cannot? By th' Lord, you shall.

BELL. By the Lady, I will not. Shall! [310

FLU. Why, then, put it off till Friday ; wu't [57] come then, coz?

BELL. Well.

Re-enter ROGER.

MAT. Y'are the waspishest ape. — Roger, put your mistress in mind [58] to sup with us on Friday next. Y' are best come like a madwoman, without a band, in your waistcoat,[59] and the linings of your kirtle outward, like every common hackney [60] that steals out at the back gate of her sweet knight's lodging.

BELL. Go, go, hang yourself! 321

CAS. It 's dinner-time, Matheo ; shall's hence?

OMNES. Yes, yes. — Farewell, wench.

Exeunt.

BELL. Farewell, boys. — Roger, what wine sent they for?

ROG. Bastard wine ; [61] for if it had been truly begotten, it would not ha' been asham'd to come in. Here 's six shillings, to pay for nursing the bastard.

BELL. A company of rooks! [62] O good [330 sweet Roger, run to the poulter's, and buy me some fine larks.

ROG. No woodcocks?

BELL. Yes, faith, a couple, if they be not dear.

ROG. I 'll buy but one ; there 's one [63] already here. *Exit.*

Enter HIPPOLITO.

HIP. Is the gentleman, my friend, departed, mistress?

BELL. His back is but new turn'd, sir.

HIP. Fare you well.

BELL. I can direct you to him.

HIP. Can you? pray.

BELL. If you please stay, he 'll not be absent long. 340

HIP. I care not much.

BELL. Pray sit, forsooth.

[53] Applied to both sexes.
[54] Pickled.
[55] The name of this fish was a term of opprobrium.
[56] A cry (like "Time out!") for the discontinuance of a game.
[57] Wilt.
[58] Q n.d. adds *your scur[v]y mistress here.*
[59] A sleeveless garment worn by women under the over-dress. The omission of the latter was a mark of the prostitute.
[60] Hired harlot.
[61] A sweet Spanish wine.
[62] Simpletons.
[63] "Woodcock" was synonymous with "fool."

HIP.   I'm hot.
If [I] may use your room, I'll rather walk.
      BELL. At your best pleasure. — Whew!
         some rubbers [64] there.
      HIP. Indeed, I'll none — indeed I will not,
         thanks.
Pretty fine lodging.   I perceive my friend
Is old in your acquaintance.
      BELL.   Troth, sir, he comes
As other gentlemen, to spend spare hours.
If yourself like our roof, such as it is,
Your own acquaintance may be as old as his.
      HIP. Say I did like ; what welcome should I
         find ?   350
      BELL. Such as my present fortunes can
         afford.
      HIP. But would you let me play Matheo's
         part ?
      BELL. What part ?
      HIP.   Why, embrace you, dally with you,
         kiss.
Faith, tell me, will you leave him and love me ?
      BELL. I am in bonds to no man, sir.
      HIP.   Why then,
Y' are free for any man ; if any, me.
But I must tell you, lady, were you mine,
You should be all mine ; I could brook no
         sharers ;
I should be covetous, and sweep up all.   359
I should be pleasure's usurer ; faith, I should.
      BELL. O fate !
      HIP. Why sigh you, lady ?   May I know ?
      BELL. 'T has never been my fortune yet to
         single
Out that one man whose love could fellow
         mine,
As I have ever wish'd it.   O my stars !
Had I but met with one kind gentleman,
That would have purchas'd sin alone to him-
         self,
For his own private use, although scarce
         proper, [65]
Indifferent handsome, meetly legg'd and
         thighed,
And my allowance reasonable, i' faith,
According to my body, by my troth,   370
I would have been as true unto his pleasures,
Yea, and as loyal to his afternoons,
As ever a poor gentlewoman could be.
      HIP. This were well now to one but newly
         fledg'd,
And scarce a day old in this subtle world ;
'T were pretty art, good bird-lime, cunning net ;

But come, come, faith, confess : how many
         men
Have drunk this selfsame protestation,
From that red 'ticing lip ?
      BELL.   Indeed, not any.
      HIP. " Indeed ! " and blush not !
      BELL.   No, in truth, not any.
      HIP. " Indeed ! " " In truth ! " — how wa-
         rily you swear.   381
'T is well, if ill it be not ; yet had I
The ruffian in me, and were drawn before you
But in light colors, I do know indeed,
You could not swear " indeed," but thunder
         oaths
That should shake Heaven, drown the harmo-
         nious spheres,
And pierce a soul that lov'd her Maker's
         honor
With horror and amazement.
      BELL.   Shall I swear ? —
Will you believe me then ?
      HIP.   Worst then of all ;
Our sins by custom seem, at last, but
         small.   390
Were I but o'er your threshold, a next man,
And after him a next, and then a fourth,
Should have this golden hook and lascivious
         bait
Thrown out to the full length.   Why, let me
         tell you,
I ha' seen letters sent from that white hand,
Tuning such music to Matheo's ear.
      BELL. Matheo ! that's true ; but believe
         it, I
No sooner had laid hold upon your presence,
But straight mine eye convey'd you to my
         heart. [66]
      HIP. Oh, you cannot feign with me.   Why
         I know, lady,   400
This is the common [fashion] [67] of you all,
To hook in a kind gentleman, and then
Abuse his coin, conveying it to your lover ;
And in the end you show him a French trick, [68]
And so you leave him, that a coach may run
Between his legs for breadth.
      BELL.   Oh, by my soul !
Not I ! therein I'll prove an honest whore,
In being true to one, and to no more.
      HIP. If any be dispos'd to trust your oath,
Let him ; I'll not be he.   I know you feign

      [66] Q n.d. :
         "Matheo ! thats true, but if youle beleeue
         My honest tongue, my eyes no sooner met you,
         But they conueid and lead you to my heart."
      [67] Apparently only Q n.d. Other old eds. *passion.*
      [68] Infect him with venereal disease.

      [64] Towels.
      [65] Hardly good-looking.

All that you speak ; ay, for a mingled [69] harlot
Is true in nothing but in being false.   412
What ! shall I teach you how to loathe your-
    self ?
And mildly, too, not without sense or reason ?
    BELL. I am content ; I would feign loathe
      myself,
If you not love me.
    HIP.   Then if your gracious blood
Be not all wasted, I shall assay to do 't.
Lend me your silence, and attention. —
You have no soul : that makes you weigh so
    light ;
Heaven's treasure bought it. —   420
And half a crown hath sold it ; for your body
Is like the common shore,[70] that still [71] receives
All the town's filth. The sin of many men
Is within you ; and thus much I suppose :
That if all your committers [72] stood in rank,
They'd make a lane, in which your shame
    might dwell,
And with their spaces reach from hence to hell.
Nay, shall I urge it more ? There has been
    known
As many by one harlot maim'd and dismem-
    b'red
As would ha' stuff'd an hospital. This I
    might   430
Apply to you, and perhaps do you right.
O y' are as base as any beast that bears :
Your body is e'en hir'd, and so are theirs.
For gold and sparkling jewels, if he can,
You 'll let a Jew get you with Christian ;
Be he a Moor, a Tartar, though his face
Look uglier [73] than a dead man's skull ;
Could the Devil put on a human shape,
If his purse shake out crowns, up then he gets :
Whores will be rid to hell with golden bits. [440
So that y' are crueller than Turks, for they
Sell Christians only ; you sell yourselves away.
Why, those that love you, hate you, and will
    term you
Liquorish [74] damnation ; with themselves half
    sunk
After the sin is laid out, and e'en curse
Their fruitless riot ; for what one begets
Another poisons ; lust and murder hit : [75]
A tree being often shook, what fruit can knit ?
    BELL. O me unhappy !

[69] Cf. *mixtures*, l. 529.
[70] Sewer.
[71] Constantly.
[72] All those who have committed sin with you.
[73] Quadrisyllabic.
[74] Lustful.
[75] Agree.

HIP.   I can vex you more. —
A harlot is like Dunkirk,[76] true to none,   450
Swallows both English, Spanish, fulsome
    Dutch,
[Back] [77]-door'd Italian, last of all the French ;
And he sticks to you — faith, gives you your
    diet,
Brings you acquainted first with Monsieur
    Doctor,
And then you know what follows.
    BELL.   Misery.
Rank, stinking, and most loathsome misery.
    HIP. Methinks a toad is happier than a
      whore ;
That with one poison swells, with thousands
    more
The other stocks her veins. Harlot ? fie, fie !
You are the miserablest creatures breathing,
The very slaves of nature. Mark me else :
You put on rich attires, others' eyes wear
    them ;   462
You eat, but to supply your blood with sin ;
And this strange curse e'en haunts you to your
    graves :
From fools you get, and spend it upon slaves.
Like bears and apes, y' are baited and show
    tricks
For money ; but your bawd the sweetness
    licks.
Indeed, you are their journeywomen, and do
All base and damn'd works they list set you
    to ;
So that you ne'er are rich ; for do but show
    me,   470
In present memory or in ages past,
The fairest and most famous courtesan,
Whose flesh was dear'st, that rais'd the price
    of sin
And held it up, to whose intemperate bosom
Princes, earls, lords — the worst has been a
    knight,
The mean'st a gentleman — have off'red up
Whole hecatombs of sighs, and rain'd in
    showers
Handfuls of gold ; yet, for all this, at last
Diseases suck'd her marrow, then grew so poor
That she has begg'd e'en at a beggar's door.
And, wherein Heav'n has a finger, when this
    idol,   481
From coast to coast, has leap'd on foreign
    shores,

[76] This important town on the Straits of Dover
was long an object of attack and intrigue by various
powers.
[77] Emend. Dyce ; old eds. *black.* "Back-door'd"
probably = subtle, sly.

And had more worship than th' outlandish [78]
    whores,
When several nations have gone over her,
When for each several city she has seen
Her maidenhead has been new, and been sold
    dear,
Did live well there, and might have di'd un-
    known
And undefam'd, back comes she to her own,
And there both miserably lives and dies,
Scorn'd even of those that once ador'd her
    eyes;   490
As if her fatal-circled life thus ran,
Her pride should end there where it first be-
    gan. —
What, do you weep to hear your story read?
Nay, if you spoil your cheeks, I'll read no
    more.
    BELL. O yes, I pray, proceed;
Indeed, 't will do me good to weep, indeed.
    HIP. To give those tears a relish, this I add:
Y' are like the Jews, scatter'd, in no place
    certain;
Your days are tedious, your hours burden-
    some;
And were 't not for full suppers, midnight
    revels,   500
Dancing, wine, riotous meetings, which do
    drown
And bury quite in you all virtuous thoughts,
And on your eyelids hang so heavily
They have no power to look so high as Heaven,
You'd sit and muse on nothing but despair,
Curse that devil lust, that so burns up your
    blood,
And in ten thousand shivers break your glass
For his temptation. Say you taste delight,
To have a golden gull from rise to set, [79]
To mete [80] you in his hot luxurious [81] arms;
Yet your nights pay for all: I know you
    dream   511
Of warrants, whips, and beadles, and then
    start
At a door's windy creak; think every weasel
To be a constable, and every rat
A long-tail'd officer. Are you now not slaves?
Oh, you have damnation without pleasure for
    it!
Such is the state of harlots. To conclude,
When you are old and can well paint no more,
You turn bawd and are then worse than before.
Make use of this; farewell.

[78] Foreign.
[79] To have a rich dupe from sunrise to sunset.
[80] Measure; *i.e.*, embrace.
[81] Lustful.

BELL.   Oh, I pray, stay.
HIP. [I] [82] see Matheo comes not; time
    hath barr'd me.   521
Would all the harlots in the town had heard
    me.   *Exit.*
BELL. Stay yet a little longer. — No! quite
    gone!
Curs'd be that minute — for it was no more,
So soon a maid is chang'd into a whore —
Wherein I first fell; be it for ever black.
Yet why should sweet Hippolito shun mine
    eyes,
For whose true love I would become pure-
    honest,
Hate the world's mixtures, [83] and the smiles of
    gold?   529
Am I not fair? Why should he fly me then?
Fair creatures are desir'd, not scorn'd of men.
How many gallants have drunk healths to
    me,
Out of their dagger'd arms, [84] and thought them
    blest
Enjoying but mine eyes at prodigal feasts!
And does Hippolito detest my love?
Oh, sure their heedless lusts but flatt'red me;
I am not pleasing, beautiful, nor young.
Hippolito hath spied some ugly blemish,
Eclipsing all my beauties; I am foul.
"Harlot!" Ay, that's the spot that taints
    my soul.   540
What! has he left his weapon here behind him
And gone forgetful? O fit instrument [85]
To let forth all the poison of my flesh!
Thy master hates me, 'cause my blood [86] hath
    rang'd; [87]
But when 't is forth, then he'll believe I'm
    chang'd.

    [*As she is about to stab herself*] re-enter
                HIPPOLITO.

HIP. Mad woman, what art doing?
BELL.   Either love me,
Or split my heart upon [88] thy rapier's point;
Yet do not, neither; for thou then destroy'st
That which I love thee for, thy virtues. Here,
    here;
             [*Gives sword to* HIPPOLITO.]

[82] So Q n.d., and Q2 (according to Pearson); other
old eds. om.
[83] Promiscuous sexual intercourse.
[84] The gallant stabbed his arm, let it bleed into
a glass of wine, and drank his mistress's health.
[85] Qq2 and n.d., for these two lines: *his weapon
left heere? O fit instrument.*
[86] Sexual passion.
[87] Roved.
[88] Qq2 and n.d. *Or cleaue my bosome on.*

Th' art crueller, and kill'st me with dis-
dain ;   550
To die so sheds no blood, yet 't is worse pain.
                                    Exit HIPPOLITO.
Not speak to me ! Not bid farewell ? A
scorn ! [89]
Hated ! this must not be ; some means I 'll
try.
Would all whores were as honest now as I !
                                              [*Exit.*]

[ACT III] — SCENE [I] [1]

Enter CANDIDO, *his wife* [VIOLA], GEORGE, *and
two* Prentices *in the shop;* FUSTIGO *enters,
walking by.*

GEO. See, gentlemen, what you lack ; a fine
holland, a fine cambric ; see what you buy.

1 PREN. Holland for shirts, cambric for
bands ; what is 't you lack?

FUS. [*aside*] 'Sfoot, I lack 'em all ; nay,
more, I lack money to buy 'em. Let me see,
let me look again ; mass, this is the shop. —
What, Coz ! sweet Coz ! how dost, i' faith,
since last night after candlelight? We had
good sport, i' faith, had we not? And [10
when shall 's laugh again?

VIO. When you will, Cousin.

FUS. Spoke like a kind Lacedemonian.[2] I
see yonder 's thy husband.

VIO. Ay, there 's the sweet youth, God
bless him.

FUS. And how is 't, Cousin? and how, how
is 't, thou squall? [3]

VIO. Well, Cousin, how fare you?

FUS. How fare I? Troth, for sixpence [20
a meal, wench, as well as heart can wish, with
calves' chawdrons,[4] and chitterlings ; besides,
I have a punk after supper, as good as a roasted
apple.

CAND. Are you my wife's cousin?

FUS. [I] am, sir ; what hast thou to do with
that?

CAND. Oh, nothing, but y' are welcome.

FUS. The Devil's dung in thy teeth ! I 'll
be welcome whether thou wilt or no, I. [30
— What ring 's this, Coz? Very pretty and
fantastical, i' faith ; let 's see it.

VIO. Pooh ! nay, you wrench my finger.

FUS. I ha' sworn I 'll ha 't, and I hope you
will not let my oaths be crack'd in the ring,[5]
will you? — I hope, sir, you are not mali-
cholly [6] at this, for all your great looks. Are
you angry?

CAND. Angry? Not I, sir ; nay, if she can
part
So easily with her ring, 't is with my heart. [40

GEO. Suffer this, sir, and suffer all. A
whoreson gull, to —

CAND. Peace, George ; when she has reap'd
what I have sown,
She 'll say one grain tastes better of her own
Than whole sheaves gather'd from another's
land :
Wit 's never good, till bought at a dear hand.

GEO. But in the meantime she makes an
ass of somebody.

2 PREN. See, see, see, sir ; as you turn
your back they do nothing but kiss.   50

CAND. No matter, let 'em ; when I touch
her lip,
I shall not feel his kisses, no, nor miss
Any of her lip ; no harm in kissing is.
Look to your business, pray ; make up your
wares.

FUS. Troth, Coz, and well rememb'red. I
would thou wouldst give me five yards of
lawn, to make my punk some falling bands a'
the fashion : three falling one upon another,
for that 's the new edition now. She 's out of
linen horribly, too ; troth, sh 'as never [60
a good smock to her back neither, but one
that has a great many patches in 't, and that
I 'm fain to wear myself for want of shift, too.
Prithee, put me into wholesome napery,[7] and
bestow some clean commodities upon us.

VIO. Reach me those cambrics and the
lawns hither.

CAND. What to do, wife? to lavish out my
goods upon a fool?

FUS. Fool ! 'Snails,[8] eat [9] the " fool ", [70
or I 'll so batter your crown that it shall scarce
go for five shillings.[10]

2 PREN. Do you hear, sir? Y' are best be
quiet, and say a fool tells you so.

FUS. 'Nails, I think so for [11] thou tell'st me.

---

[89] Qq 2 and n.d. *Not speake to me! not looke!
not bid farewell!*
[1] Candido's shop. (See note on I, v.) Old eds.,
Scena 7.
[2] Cf. on *The Shoemakers' Holiday*, III, v, 78.
[3] Wench.   [4] Entrails.

[5] Since coins were not perfectly circular the ring
which formed part of the design assumed great
importance ; a defect which extended inside it rendered the coin uncurrent.
[6] An obsolete form of *melancholy.*
[7] Linen.
[8] By God's nails.
[9] Swallow, retract.
[10] The value of one crown.   [11] Because.

CAND. Are you angry, sir, because I nam'd thee fool?

Trust me, you are not wise in my own house
And to my face to play the antic [12] thus.
If you 'll needs play the madman, choose a stage
Of lesser compass, where few eyes may note [80
Your action's error ; but if still you miss,
As here you do, for one clap, ten will hiss.

FUS. 'Zwounds, Cousin, he talks to me as if I were a scurvy tragedian.

2 PREN. [*aside*] Sirrah George, I ha' thought upon a device, how to break his pate, beat him soundly, and ship him away.

GEO. [*aside*] Do 't.

2 PREN. [*aside*] I 'll go in, pass thorough the house, give some of our fellow prentices [90 the watchword when they shall enter, then come and fetch my master in by a wile, and place one in the hall to hold him in conference, whilst we cudgel the gull out of his coxcomb.

GEO. [*aside*] Do 't ; away, do 't.

[*Exit* 2 Prentice.]

VIO. Must I call twice for these cambrics and lawns?

CAND. Nay, see, you anger her, George ; prithee despatch.

[1] PREN. Two of the choicest pieces [100 are in the warehouse, sir.

CAND. Go fetch them presently.

Exit 1 Prentice.

FUS. Ay, do, make haste, sirrah.

CAND. Why were you such a stranger all this while, being my wife's cousin?

FUS. Stranger? [13] No sir, I 'm a natural Milaner born.

CAND. I perceive still it is your natural guise to mistake [14] me ; but you are welcome, sir ; I much wish your acquaintance. 110

FUS. My acquaintance? I scorn that, i' faith ; I hope my acquaintance goes in chains of gold three-and-fifty times double ; you know who I mean, Coz ; the posts of his gate are a-painting, too.[15]

Re-enter the 2 Prentice.

2 PREN. Signior Pandulfo the merchant desires conference with you.

CAND. Signior Pandulfo? I 'll be with him straight ;

Attend your mistress and the gentleman.

Exit.

VIO. When do you show those pieces? [120

FUS. Ay, when do you show those pieces?

OMNES. [*within*] Presently, sir, presently ; we are but charging [16] them.

FUS. Come, sirrah, you flat-cap,[17] where be these whites?

[*Re-enter* 1 Prentice *with pieces.*]

GEO. Flat-cap ! [*aside to* FUSTIGO] Hark in your ear, sir, y' are a flat fool, an ass, a gull, and I 'll thrum [18] you. — Do you see this cambric, sir?

FUS. 'Sfoot, Coz, a good jest ! did you [130 hear him? He told me in my ear I was a flat fool, an ass, a gull, and I 'll thrum you. — Do you see this cambric, sir? [19]

VIO. What, not my men, I hope?

FUS. No, not your men, but one of your men, i' faith.

1 PREN. I pray, sir, come hither ; what say you to this? [Here 's] [20] an excellent good one.

FUS. Ay, marry, this likes [21] me well ; cut me off some half-score yards. 140

2 PREN. [*aside to* FUSTIGO] Let your whores cut ; y' are an impudent coxcomb ; you get none, and yet I 'll thrum you. — A very good cambric, sir.

FUS. Again, again, as God judge me ! — 'Sfoot, Coz, they stand thrumming here with me all day, and yet I get nothing.

1 PREN. [*aside to* FUSTIGO] A word, I pray, sir ; you must not be angry. Prentices have hot bloods, — young fellows. [150 — What say you to this piece? Look you, 't is so delicate, so soft, so even, so fine a thread, that a lady may wear it.

FUS. 'Sfoot, I think so ; if a knight marry my punk, a lady shall wear it. Cut me off twenty yards ; th' art an honest lad.

1 PREN. [*aside to* FUSTIGO] Not without money, gull ; and I 'll thrum you too.

OMNES. [*within*] Gull, we 'll thrum you.

FUS. O Lord, Sister, did you not hear [160 something cry thrum? Zounds, your men here make a plain ass of me.

VIO. What, to my face so impudent?

---

[12] Buffoon.
[13] Foreigner.
[14] Misunderstand.
[15] *I.e.*, he will soon be sheriff. At the door of that office large posts, on which it was customary to stick proclamations, were always set up. (Steevens.)
[16] Loading.
[17] "The citizens . . . continued to wear flat round caps long after they had ceased to be fashionable." (Dyce.)
[18] Beat.
[19] The last sentence may have been repeated erroneously by the compositor.
[20] So Qq 2 and n.d. ; other old eds. *here.*
[21] Is pleasing to.

GEO. Ay, in a cause so honest, we'll not suffer
Our master's goods to vanish moneyless.

VIO. You will not suffer them!

2 PREN.   No, and you may blush,
In going about to vex so mild a breast
As is our master's.

VIO.   Take away those pieces;
Cousin, I give them freely.

FUS. Mass, and I'll take 'em as freely. [170

OMNES. We'll make you lay 'em down again more freely.

[Enter other Prentices *and attack* FUSTIGO *with their clubs.]*

VIO. Help, help! my brother will be murdered.

Re-enter CANDIDO.

CAND. How now, what coil[22] is here? Forbear I say.

     [Exeunt all the Prentices *except* GEORGE *and the* 1 *and* 2.]

GEO. He calls us flat-caps, and abuses us.

CAND. Why, sirs, do such examples flow from me?

VIO. They are of your keeping, sir. — Alas, poor Brother.

FUS. I 'faith they ha' pepper'd me, Sister; look, does 't[23] not spin? Call you these prentices? I'll ne'er play at cards more when clubs is trump. I have a goodly coxcomb,[24] Sister, have I not?   181

CAND. Sister and brother? brother to my wife?

FUS. If you have any skill in heraldry, you may soon know that; break but her pate, and you shall see her blood and mine is all one.

CAND. A surgeon! run, a surgeon! *[Exit* 1 Prentice.] — Why then wore you that forged name of cousin?

FUS. Because it's a common thing to call coz and ningle[25] nowadays all the world over. 190

CAND. Cousin! A name of much deceit, folly, and sin;
For under that common abused word,
Many an honest-temp'red citizen
Is made a monster,[26] and his wife train'd out[27]
To foul adulterous action, full of fraud.
I may well call that word a city's bawd.

[22] Tumult.
[23] His head.
[24] Head, fool's cap, cock's comb.
[25] Mine ingle; my intimate, crony, or darling.
[26] Cuckolded.   [27] Enticed.

FUS. Troth, Brother, my sister would needs ha' me take upon me to gull your patience a little; but it has made double gules[28] on my coxcomb.   200

VIO. What, playing the woman? blabbing now, you fool?

CAND. Oh, my wife did but exercise a jest upon your wit.

FUS. 'Sfoot, my wit bleeds for 't, methinks.

CAND. Then let this warning more of sense afford;
The name of cousin is a bloody word.

FUS. I'll ne'er call coz again whilst I live, to have such a coil about it. This should be a coronation day; for my head runs claret[29] [210 lustily.   *Exit.*

Enter an Officer.

CAND. Go, wish[30] the surgeon to have great respect.[31] —   *[Exit* 2 Prentice.]
How now, my friend? What, do they sit to-day?

OFFI. Yes, sir; they expect you at the senate-house.

CAND. I thank your pains; I'll not be last man there. —   *Exit* Officer.
My gown, George; go, my gown. *[Exit* GEORGE.] A happy land,
Where grave men meet, each cause to understand;
Whose consciences are not cut out in bribes
To gull the poor man's right, but in even scales,
Peize[32] rich and poor, without corruption's vails.[33]   220

[Re-enter GEORGE.]

Come, where's the gown?

GEO.   I cannot find the key, sir.

CAND. Request it of your mistress.

VIO. Come not to me for any key;
I'll not be troubled to deliver it.

CAND. Good Wife, kind Wife, it is a needful trouble,
But for my gown.

VIO.   Moths swallow down your gown!
You set my teeth an[34] edge with talking on 't.

CAND. Nay, prithee, sweet; I cannot meet without it;
I should have a great fine set on my head.

[28] The heraldic term for red.
[29] As certain conduits did on great occasions.
[30] Desire, request.
[31] Take great care.
[32] Weigh.
[33] Perquisites.   [34] **On.**

VIO. Set on your coxcomb! tush, fine me
no fines! 230

CAND. Believe me, sweet, none greets the
senate-house

Without his robe of reverence; that's his gown.

VIO. Well, then, y' are like to cross that
custom once;

You get nor key nor gown; and so depart. —

[aside] This trick will vex him sure, and fret
his heart. *Exit.*

CAND. Stay, let me see; I must have some
device.

My cloak's too short; fie, fie, no cloak will
do 't;

It must be something fashioned like a gown,

With my arms out. O George, come hither,
George;

I prithee, lend me thine advice. 240

GEO. Troth, sir, were it any but you, they
would break open chest.

CAND. Oh, no! break open chest! that 's
a thief's office.

Therein you counsel me against my blood;

'Twould show impatience, that; any meek
means

I would be glad to embrace. Mass, I have
got it.

Go, step up, fetch me down one of the carpets,³⁵

The saddest ³⁶-color'd carpet, honest George;

Cut thou a hole i' th' middle for my neck,

Two for mine arms. Nay, prithee, look not
strange. 250

GEO. I hope you do not think, sir, as you
mean.

CAND. Prithee, about it quickly; the hour
chides me;

Warily, George, softly; take heed of eyes.
Exit GEORGE.

Out of two evils he 's accounted wise,

That can pick out the least; the fine impos'd

For an ungowned senator is about

Forty crusadoes,³⁷ the carpet not 'bove four.

Thus have I chosen the lesser evil yet,

Preserv'd my patience, foil'd her desperate wit.

Re-enter GEORGE.

GEO. Here, sir, here 's the carpet. 260

CAND. Oh, well done, George; we 'll cut
it just i' th' midst. —

[*They cut the carpet.*]

'T is very well; I thank thee; help it on.

GEO. It must come over your head, sir,
like a wench's petticoat.

CAND. Th' art in the right, good George;
it must indeed.

Fetch me a nightcap; for I 'll gird it close,

As if my health were queasy. 'T will show
well

For a rude, careless nightgown,³⁸ will 't not,
think'st?

GEO. Indifferent ³⁹ well, sir, for a nightgown, being girt and pleated. 270

CAND. Ay, and a nightcap on my head.

GEO. That 's true, sir; I 'll run and fetch
one, and a staff. *Exit* GEORGE.

CAND. For thus they cannot choose but
conster ⁴⁰ it:

One that is out of health, takes no delight,

Wears his apparel without appetite,

And puts on heedless raiment without form. —

Re-enter GEORGE.

So, so, kind George; [*putting on nightcap
and taking staff*] — be secret now; and,
prithee, do not laugh at me till I 'm out of
sight. 280

GEO. I laugh? Not I, sir.

CAND. Now to the senate-house.

Methinks, I 'd rather wear, without a frown,

A patient carpet than an angry gown. *Exit.*

GEO. Now looks my master just like one
of our carpet knights,⁴¹ only he 's somewhat
the honester of the two.

Re-enter [VIOLA,] *Candido's wife.*

VIO. What, is your master gone?

GEO. Yes, forsooth; his back is but new
turn'd.

VIO. And in his cloak? Did he not vex
and swear?

GEO. [*aside*] No, but he 'll make you swear
anon. — 290

No indeed, he went away like a lamb.

VIO. Key, sink to hell! Still patient, patient
still!

I am with child ⁴² to vex him. Prithee,
George,

If e'er thou look'st for favor at my hands,

Uphold one jest for me.

GEO. Against my master?

VIO. 'T is a mere jest, in faith. Say, wilt
thou do 't?

---

³⁵ Table-covers.   ³⁶ Soberest.
³⁷ Crusados, Portuguese coins worth about $.75
each.

³⁸ Dressing gown.   ³⁹ Moderately.
⁴⁰ Construe.
⁴¹ Not dubbed on the battlefield; another hit at
the too numerous creations of James.
⁴² I long inordinately.

GEO. Well, what is 't?

VIO. Here, take this key; thou know'st where all things lie.

Put on thy master's best apparel, gown,   299
Chain, cap, ruff, everything; be like himself;
And, 'gainst [43] his coming home, walk in the shop;
Feign the same carriage, and his patient look;
'T will breed but a jest, thou know'st; speak, wilt thou?

GEO. 'T will wrong my master's patience.

VIO.   Prithee, George.

GEO. Well, if you 'll save me harmless, and put me under covert barn,[44] I am content to please you, provided it may breed no wrong against him.

VIO. No wrong at all. Here take the key; begone.

If any vex him, this; if not this, none.   310
          Exeunt.

SCENE [II] [45]

Enter a Bawd [MISTRESS FINGERLOCK] *and* ROGER.

MRS. F. O Roger, Roger, where 's your mistress, where 's your mistress? There 's the finest, neatest gentleman at my house, but newly come over. Oh, where is she, where is she, where is she?

ROG. My mistress is abroad, but not amongst 'em. My mistress is not the whore now that you take her for.

MRS. F. How? Is she not a whore? Do you go about to take away her good name, [10 Roger? You are a fine pander indeed.

ROG. I tell you, Madonna Fingerlock, I am not sad for nothing; I ha' not eaten one good meal this three-and-thirty days. I had used to get sixteen pence by fetching a pottle of hippocras; but now those days are past. We had as good things, Madonna Fingerlock, she within doors, and I without, as any poor young couple in Milan.

MRS. F. God 's my life, and is she [20 chang'd now?

ROG. I ha' lost by her squeamishness more than would have builded twelve bawdyhouses.

MRS. F. And had she no time to turn hon-

est but now? What a vile woman is this! Twenty pound a night, I 'll be sworn, Roger, in good gold and no silver. Why here was a time! If she should ha' pick'd out a time, it could not be better! gold enough stirring; choice of men, choice of hair, choice of [30 beards, choice of legs, and choice of every, every, everything. It cannot sink into my head, that she should be such an ass. Roger, I never believe it.

ROG. Here she comes now.

Enter BELLAFRONT.

MRS. F. O sweet madonna, on with your loose gown,[46] your felt [47] and your feather; there 's the sweetest, prop'rest,[48] gallantest gentleman at my house; he smells all of musk and ambergris, his pocket full of crowns, [40 flame-colored doublet, red satin hose,[49] carnation silk stockings, and a leg and a body, oh!

BELL. Hence thou, our sex's monster, poisonous bawd,
Lust's factor,[50] and damnation's orator,
Gossip [51] of hell! Were all the harlots' sins
Which the whole world contains numb'red together,
Thine far exceeds them all; of all the creatures
That ever were created, thou art basest.
What serpent would beguile thee of thy office?
It is detestable; for thou liv'st   50
Upon the dregs of harlots, guard'st the door,
Whilst couples go to dancing. O coarse devil!
Thou art the bastard's curse — thou brand'st his birth;
The lecher's French disease, for thou dry-suck'st him;
The harlot's poison, and thine own confusion.

MRS. F. Marry come up, with a pox! Have you nobody to rail against but your bawd now?

BELL. And you, knave pander, kinsman to a bawd.

ROG. [*to* MISTRESS FINGERLOCK] You and I, madonna, are cousins.   60

BELL. Of the same blood and making, near allied;
Thou, that slave to sixpence, base-metall'd villain!

ROG. Sixpence? Nay, that 's not so;
I never took under two shillings fourpence;
I hope I know my fee.

[43] In readiness for.
[44] That he may rob with impunity. "Barn" is a corruption of "baron," and in law a wife is said to be under covert baron, being sheltered by marriage under her husband. (Dyce.)
[45] An outer room in Bellafront's house. Old eds. *Scena 8.*

[46] The common dress of courtesans. (Dyce.)
[47] Hat.   [48] Handsomest.   [49] Breeches.
[50] Agent, representative.
[51] Companion, crony.

BELL. I know not against which most to inveigh ;
For both of you are damn'd so equally.
Thou never spar'st for oaths, swear'st anything,
As if thy soul were made of shoe-leather :　69
" God damn me, gentlemen, if she be within ! "
When in the next room she 's found dallying.

ROG. If it be my vocation to swear, every man in his vocation. I hope my betters swear and damn themselves, and why should not I ?

BELL. Roger, you cheat kind gentlemen.

ROG. The more gulls they.

BELL. Slave, I cashier thee.

MRS. F. An you do cashier him, he shall be entertain'd.　80

ROG. Shall I ? Then blurt a' your service.

BELL. As hell would have it, entertain'd by you !
I dare the Devil himself to match those two.　　　　　　　　　　*Exit.*

MRS. F. Marry, gup,[52] are you grown so holy, so pure, so honest, with a pox ?

ROG. Scurvy honest punk ! But stay, madonna, how must our agreement be now ? For, you know, I am to have all the comings-in at the hall-door, and you at the chamber-door.　90

MRS. F. True, Roger, except my vails.[53]

ROG. Vails ? What vails ?

MRS. F. Why as thus : if a couple come in a coach, and light to lie down a little, then, Roger, that 's my fee, and you may walk abroad ; for the coachman himself is their pander.

ROG. Is 'a[54] so ? In truth I have almost forgot, for want of exercise. But how if I fetch this citizen's wife to that gull, and that madonna to that gallant, how then ?　101

MRS. F. Why then, Roger, you are to have sixpence a lane ;[55] so many lanes, so many sixpences.

ROG. Is 't so ? Then I see we two shall agree, and live together.

MRS. F. Ay, Roger, so long as there be any taverns and bawdyhouses in Milan.
　　　　　　　　　　Exeunt.

SCENE [III] [56]

Enter BELLAFRONT *with lute, pen, ink, and paper being plac'd before her.*

SONG

The courtier's flatt'ring jewels,
Temptation's only fuels ;
The lawyer's ill-got moneys,
That suck up poor bees' honeys ;
The citizen's son's riot,
The gallant['s] costly diet :
Silks and velvets, pearls and ambers,
Shall not draw me to their chambers.
　　Silks and velvets, &c.

　　　　　　　　　　She writes.

Oh, 't is in vain to write ! it will not please ; [10
Ink on this paper would ha' but presented
The foul black spots that stick upon my soul,
And rather make me loathsomer, than wrought
My love's impression in Hippolito's thought.
No, I must turn the chaste leaves of my breast,
And pick out some sweet means to breed my rest.
Hippolito, believe me, I will be
As true unto thy heart, as thy heart to thee,
And hate all men, their gifts, and company. [19

Enter MATHEO, CASTRUCHIO, FLUELLO, [*and*] PIORATTO.

MAT. You, goody punk, *subaudi* [57] cockatrice,[58] oh, y' are a sweet whore of your promise, are you not, think you ? How well you came to supper to us last night ! Mew, a whore, and break her word ! Nay, you may blush, and hold down your head at it well enough. 'Sfoot, ask these gallants if we stay'd not till we were as hungry as sergeants.

FLU. Ay, and their yeom[e]n too.

CAS. Nay, faith, acquaintance, let me tell you, you forgat yourself too much. We [30 had excellent cheer, rare vintage, and were drunk after supper.

PIO. And when we were in our woodcocks,[59] sweet rogue, a brace of gulls, dwelling here in the city, came in, and paid all the shot.

MAT. Pox on her ! let her alone.

BELL. Oh, I pray do, if you be gentlemen ;
I pray, depart the house. Beshrew[60] the door
For being so easily entreated ! Faith,
I lent but little ear unto your talk ;　40
My mind was busied otherwise, in troth,

---

[52] Go up, get along.
[53] Perquisites.
[54] He.
[55] *I.e.*, for each lane you pass through in conducting them. (Kittredge.)

[56] Another room in Bellafront's house. Old eds. *Scena 9.* Probably the inner stage.
[57] Understand, supply.　　[58] Harlot.
[59] When we were eating our woodcocks ; with a pun on "woodcocks" = "fools."　[60] Confound.

And so your words did unregarded pass.
Let this suffice : I am not as I was.

FLU. I am not what I was ! No, I 'll be
sworn thou art not ; for thou wert honest at
five, and now th' art a punk at fifteen.   Thou
wert yesterday a simple whore, and now
th' art a cunning, cony-catching [61] baggage
to-day.

BELL. I 'll say I 'm worse ; I pray, forsake
me then ;   50
I do desire you leave me, gentlemen,
And leave yourselves.   Oh, be not what you
    are,
Spendthrifts of soul and body ;
Let me persuade you to forsake all harlots,
Worse than the deadliest poisons, they are
    worse,
For o'er their souls hangs an eternal curse.
In being slaves to slaves, their labors perish ;
Th' are seldom blest with fruit ; for, ere it
    blossoms,
Many a worm confounds it.
They have no issue but four ugly ones,   60
That run along with them, e'en to their graves ;
For, 'stead of children, they breed rank dis-
    eases,
And all you gallants can bestow on them
Is that French infant, which ne'er acts, but
    speaks.
What shallow son and heir, then, foolish gal-
    lant,
Would waste all his inheritance, to purchase
A filthy, loath'd disease, and pawn his body
To a dry evil?   That usury's worst of all,
When th' interest will eat out the principal.

MAT. [*aside*] 'Sfoot, she gulls 'em the [70
best !   This is always her fashion, when she
would be rid of any company that she cares
not for, to enjoy mine alone.

FLU. What's here? instructions, admoni-
tions, and caveats?   Come out, you scabbard of vengeance.

MAT. Fluello, spurn your hounds when
they foist ; [62] you shall not spurn my punk ;
I can tell you my blood is vex'd.

FLU. Pox a' your blood !   make it a [80
quarrel.

MAT. Y' are a slave !   Will that serve turn?

OMNES. 'Sblood, hold, hold !

CAS. Matheo, Fluello, for shame, put up.[63]

MAT. Spurn my sweet varlet ! [64]

[61] Cheating.
[62] Break wind silently. Old eds. *fyste.*
[63] Sheathe your swords.
[64] This line is omitted by Pearson, and by all qtos.
seen by present Ed. except Qq₁ and n.d.

BELL.   Oh, how many thus,
Mov'd with a little folly, have let out
Their souls in brothel-houses, fell down and
    died
Just at their harlot's foot, as 't were in pride.

FLU. Matheo, we shall meet.

MAT. Ay,   ay,   anywhere,   saving   at
    church ;   90
Pray take heed we meet not there.

FLU. Adieu, damnation.

CAS.   Cockatrice, farewell.

PIO. There's more deceit in women than
    in hell.

    Exeunt [CASTRUCHIO, FLUELLO, *and*
        PIORATTO].

MAT. Ha, ha, thou doest gull 'em so rarely,
so naturally !   If I did not think thou hadst
been in earnest !   Thou art a sweet rogue for 't,
i' faith.

BELL. Why are not you gone too, Signior
    Matheo?
I pray depart my house ; you may believe
    me ;
In troth, I have no part of harlot in me. [100

MAT. How 's this?

BELL. Indeed, I love you not, but hate
    you worse
Than any man, because you were the first
Gave money for my soul.   You brake the ice,
Which after turn'd a puddle ; I was led
By your temptation, to be miserable.
I pray seek out some other that will fall,
Or rather, I pray, seek out none at all.

MAT. Is 't possible to be impossible?   An
honest whore !   I have heard many hon- [110
est wenches turn strumpets with a wet finger,[65]
but for a harlot to turn honest is one of Hercules' labors.   It was more easy for him in
one night to make fifty queans, than to make
one of them honest again in fifty years.
Come, I hope thou dost but jest.

BELL. 'T is time to leave off jesting ;   I
    had almost
Jested away salvation.   I shall love you,
If you will soon forsake me.

MAT.   God buy thee.[66]

BELL. Oh, tempt no more women !   Shun
    their weighty curse !   120
Women, at best, are bad ; make them not
    worse.
You gladly seek our sex's overthrow,
But not to raise our states.   For all your
    wrongs,

[65] Readily, easily.
[66] Goodbye.

Will you vouchsafe me but due recompense,
To marry with me?

MAT. How! marry with a punk, a cockatrice, a harlot? Marry, fogh, I'll be burnt
thorough the nose first.

BELL. Why, la! these are your oaths! You
love to undo [67] us,
To put Heaven from us, whilst our best hours
waste ; 130
You love to make us lewd, but never chaste.

MAT. I'll hear no more of this; this
ground upon,
Th' art damn'd for alt'ring thy religion.
Exit.

BELL. Thy lust and sin speak so much.
Go thou, my ruin,
The first fall my soul took. By my example
I hope few maidens now will put their heads
Under men's girdles ; who least trusts is most
wise :
Men's oaths do cast a mist before our eyes.
My best of wit, be ready ; now I go,
By some device to greet Hippolito. 140

[ACT IV] — SCENE [I] [1]

Enter a Servant *setting out a table, on which he
places a skull, a picture, a book, and a taper.*

SER. So ; this is Monday morning, and
now must I to my huswif'ry. Would I had
been created a shoemaker, for all the gentle
craft are gentlemen every Monday by their
copy,[2] and scorn then to work one true stitch.
My master means sure to turn me into a student, for here's my book, here my desk, here
my light, this my close chamber, and here my
punk ; so that this dull, drowsy first day of
the week makes me half a priest, half a [10
chandler, half a painter, half a sexton, ay, and
half a bawd ; for all this day my office is to
do nothing but keep the door. To prove it,
look you, this good face and yonder gentleman, so soon as ever my back's turn'd, will
be naught [3] together.

Enter HIPPOLITO.

HIP. Are all the windows shut?

SER. Close, sir, as the fist of a courtier that
hath stood in three reigns.

HIP. Thou art a faithful servant, and observ'st 20

The calendar both of my solemn vows
And ceremonious sorrow. Get thee gone ;
I charge thee on thy life, let not the sound
Of any woman's voice pierce through that
door.

SER. If they do, my Lord, I'll pierce some
of them.

What will your Lordship have to breakfast?

HIP. Sighs.

SER. What to dinner?

HIP. Tears.

SER. The one of them, my Lord, will fill
you too full of wind, the other wet you [30
too much. What to supper?

HIP. That which now thou canst not get
me, the constancy of a woman.

SER. Indeed that's harder to come by than
ever was Ostend.[4]

HIP. Prithee, away.

SER. I'll make away myself presently,
which few servants will do for their lords, but
rather help to make them away. Now to my
door-keeping ; I hope to pick something [40
out of it. *Exit.*

HIP. [*taking the picture*] My Infeliche's
face, her brow, her eye,
The dimple on her cheek ; and such sweet
skill
Hath from the cunning workman's pencil
flown,
These lips look fresh and lively as her own,
Seeming to move and speak. 'Las ! now I see
The reason why fond [5] women love to buy
Adulterate complexion ! Here, 't is read,
False colors last after the true be dead.
Of all the roses grafted on her cheeks, 50
Of all the graces dancing in her eyes,
Of all the music set upon her tongue,
Of all that was past woman's excellence
In her white bosom — look ! a painted board
Circumscribes all. Earth can no bliss afford.
Nothing of her but this? This cannot speak ;
It has no lap for me to rest upon,
No lip worth tasting ; here the worms will
feed,
As in her coffin. Hence, then, idle art ;
True love's best pictur'd in a true-love's
heart. 60
Here art thou drawn, sweet maid, till this be
dead ;
So that thou liv'st twice, twice art buried.

---

[67] Ruin.
[1] A room in Hippolito's house. Old eds. *Scena 10.*
[2] Indentures. See *N.E.D.* "copy", 5, quotation of 1550.
[3] Wicked.

[4] After a siege of three years and ten weeks Ostend was captured by the Marquis of Spinola on September 8, 1604.
[5] Foolish.

Thou figure of my friend, lie there. — What's
here?   [*Takes the skull.*]
Perhaps this shrewd pate was mine enemy's.
'Las! say it were; I need not fear him now!
For all his braves, his contumelious breath,
His frowns, though dagger-pointed, all his
plot,
Though ne'er so mischievous, his Italian pills,
His quarrels, and that common fence, his law,
See, see, they're all eaten out; here's not
left one;   70
How clean they're pick'd away! to the bare
bone!
How mad are mortals, then, to rear great
names
On tops of swelling houses! or to wear out
Their fingers' ends in dirt, to scrape up gold!
Not caring, so [6] that sumpter-horse,[7] the back,
Be hung with gaudy trappings, with what
coarse,
Yea, rags most beggarly, they clothe the soul;
Yet, after all, their gayness looks thus foul.
What fools are men to build a garish tomb,
Only to save the carcass whilst it rots,   80
To maintain't long in stinking, make good
carrion,
But leave no good deeds to preserve them
sound;
For good deeds keep men sweet, long above
ground.
And must all come to this? fools, wise, all
hither?
Must all heads thus at last be laid together?
Draw me my picture then, thou grave, neat
workman,
After this fashion, not like this; [8] these colors
In time, kissing but air, will be kiss'd off.
But here's a fellow; that which he lays on
Till doomsday alters not complexion.   90
Death's the best painter then; they that
draw shapes,
And live by wicked faces, are but God's apes.
They come but near the life, and there they
stay.
This fellow draws life too; his art is fuller;
The pictures which he makes are without
color.[9]

Re-enter his Servant.

SER. Here's a person would speak with
you, sir.

---

[6] Provided that, so long as.
[7] Pack-horse.
[8] Like the skull, not like Infeliche's picture.
[9] With a pun on "color" = false appearance.

HIP. Ha!
SER. A parson,[10] sir, would speak with you.
HIP. Vicar?   100
SER. Vicar! No, sir; has too good a face
to be a vicar yet; a youth, a very youth.
HIP. What youth? Of man or woman?
Lock the doors.
SER. If it be a woman, marrow-bones [11]
and potato pies [11] keep me for meddling with
her, for the thing has got the breeches; 't is
a male-varlet sure, my Lord, for a woman's
tailor ne'er measur'd him.
HIP. Let him give thee his message and be
gone.
SER. He says he's Signior Matheo's [110
man, but I know he lies.
HIP. How doest thou know it?
SER. 'Cause has ne'er a beard. 'T is his
boy, I think, sir, whosoe'er paid for his nurs-
ing.
HIP. Send him and keep the door.
           [*Exit* Servant.]
(*Reads.*) *Fata si liceat mihi.*
Fingere arbitrio meo,
Temperem zephyro levi
Vela: [12]   120
I'd sail, were I to choose, not in the ocean;
Cedars are shaken, when shrubs do feel no
bruise.

Enter BELLAFRONT, *like a page,* [*with a letter*].

How? from Matheo?
    BELL.   Yes, my Lord.
    HIP.   Art sick?
    BELL. Not all in health, my Lord.
    HIP.   Keep off.
    BELL.   I do. —
[*aside*] Hard fate when women are compell'd
to woo.
    HIP. This paper does speak nothing.
    BELL.   Yes, my Lord,
Matter of life it speaks, and therefore writ
In hidden character; to me instruction
My master gives, and, 'less you please to
stay
Till you both meet, I can the text display. [130
    HIP. Do do; read out.
    BELL.   I am already out! [13]
Look on my face, and read the strangest story!
    HIP. What, villain, ho!

---

[10] So spelled in the old eds. to indicate the servant's pronunciation of "person."
[11] Used as aphrodisiacs.
[12] Seneca, *Oedipus*, ll. 882 ff.
[13] At a loss for words.

Re-enter his Servant.

SER. Call you, my Lord?

HIP. Thou slave, thou hast let in the Devil.

SER. Lord bless us, where? He 's not cloven, my Lord, that I can see! Besides, the Devil goes more like a gentleman than a page. Good my Lord, *buon coraggio*.[14]

HIP. Thou hast let in a woman in man's shape;   140
And thou art damn'd for 't.

SER.   Not damn'd, I hope,
For putting in a woman to a lord,

HIP. Fetch me my rapier — do not; I shall kill thee.
Purge this infected chamber of that plague,
That runs upon me thus! Slave, thrust her hence.

SER. Alas, my Lord, I shall never be able to thrust her hence without help! — Come, mermaid, you must to sea again.

BELL. Hear me but speak; my words shall be all music;
Hear me but speak.   [*Knocking within.*]

HIP.   Another beats the door, [150
Tother she-devil; look.

SER.   Why, then, hell 's broke loose.

HIP. Hence; guard the chamber; let no more come on;   *Exit* [Servant].
One woman serves for man's damnation. —
Beshrew thee, thou dost make me violate
The chastest and most sanctimonious [15] vow,
That e'er was ent'red in the court of Heaven.
I was, on meditation's spotless wings,
Upon my journey thither; like a storm
Thou beat's[t] my ripened cogitations,
Flat to the ground, and like a thief dost stand,   160
To steal devotion from the holy land.

BELL. If woman were thy mother; if thy heart
Be not all marble, — or, if 't marble be,
Let my tears soften it, to pity me; —
I do beseech thee, do not thus with scorn
Destroy a woman.

HIP.   Woman, I beseech thee,
Get thee some other suit; this fits thee not.
I would not grant it to a kneeling queen;
I cannot love thee, nor I must not. See
                        [*Points to the picture.*]
The copy of that obligation   170
Where my soul's bound in heavy penalties.

BELL. She 's dead, you told me; she 'll let fall her suit.

[14] Good courage. (Ital.) Old eds. *Boon couragio*.
[15] Sacred.

HIP. My vows to her fled after her to Heaven;
Were thine eyes clear as mine, thou might'st behold her
Watching upon yon battlements of stars
How I observe them. Should I break my bond,
This board would rive in twain, these wooden lips
Call me most perjur'd villain. Let it suffice,
I ha' set thee in the path; is 't not a sign
I love thee, when with one so most, most dear,   180
I 'll have thee fellows? All are fellows there.

BELL. Be greater than a king; save not a body,
But from eternal shipwrack keep a soul.
If not, and that [16] again sin's path I tread,
The grief be mine, the guilt fall on thy head.

HIP. Stay, and take physic for it: read this book;
Ask counsel of this head, what 's to be done.[17]
He 'll strike it dead, that 't is damnation
If you turn Turk again.[18] Oh, do it not;
[Though] [19] Heaven cannot allure you to do well,   190
From doing ill let hell fright you; and learn this:
The soul whose bosom lust did never touch
Is God's fair bride, and maidens' souls are such;
The soul that, leaving chastity's white shore,
Swims in hot sensual streams, is the Devil's whore. —

Re-enter his Servant.

How now, who comes?

SER. No more knaves, my Lord, that wear smocks. Here 's a letter from Doctor Benedict. I would not enter his man, though he had hairs at his mouth, for fear he should [200 be a woman, for some women have beards; marry, they are half witches. 'Slid, you are a sweet youth to wear a codpiece, and have no pins to stick upon 't.[20]

HIP. I 'll meet the doctor, tell him; yet tonight

[16] If.
[17] Take physic for it — to cure you of sinning. Read this book — learn a lesson from this skull: that will be your cure. Ask it what you ought to do.
[18] The skull will strike your sin dead, so that, if you turn Turk again (return to whoredom), you will deservedly be damned. (Kittredge.)
[19] Qq[1] and n.d. *The.* Other qtos. seen by Ed., and Pearson, *Tho.*
[20] "The custom of sticking pins in this [indelicate] part of the male dress is often mentioned by our early writers." (Dyce.)

I cannot ; but at morrow rising sun
I will not fail. — Go, woman ; fare thee well.
                    Exeunt [HIPPOLITO *and* Servant].

BELL. The lowest fall can be but into
hell.
It does not move him ; I must therefore
fly
From this undoing [21] city, and with tears   [210
Wash off all anger from my father's brow.
He cannot, sure, but joy, seeing me new
born.
A woman honest first, and then turn
whore,
Is, as with me, common to thousands more ;
But from a strumpet to turn chaste, that
sound
Has oft been heard, that woman hardly found.
                    Exit.

SCENE [II] [22]

Enter FUSTIGO, CRAMBO, *and* POH.[23]

FUS. Hold up your hands, gentlemen ;
here's one, two, three [*giving money*] — nay,
I warrant they are sound pistoles, and without flaws ; I had them of my sister and I know
she uses to put [up] [24] nothing that's crack'd —
three, four, five, six, seven, eight, and nine ; by
this hand, bring me but a piece of his blood, and
you shall have nine more. I'll lurk in a tavern not far off, and provide supper to close
up the end of the tragedy. The linen- [10
draper's, remember. Stand to't, I beseech
you, and play your parts perfectly.

CRAM. Look you, signior, 't is not your gold
that we weigh —

FUS. Nay, nay, weigh it and spare not ; if
it lack one grain of corn, I'll give you a bushel
of wheat to make it up.

CRAM. But by your favor, signior, which of
the servants is it ? because we'll punish justly.

FUS. Marry, 't is the head man ; you [20
shall taste him by his tongue ; a pretty, tall,
prating fellow, with a Tuscalonian [25] beard.

POH. Tuscalonian ! very good.

FUS. Cod's life, I was ne'er so thrumm'd
since I was a gentleman. My coxcomb was
dry-beaten,[26] as if my hair had been hemp.

CRAM. We'll dry-beat some of them.

FUS. Nay, it grew so high, that my sister
cried murder out, very manfully. I have

her consent, in a manner, to have him [30
pepper'd ; else I'll not do 't, to win more than
ten cheaters do at a rifling.[27] Break but his
pate, or so, only his mazer,[28] because I'll have
his head in a cloth as well as mine ; he's a
linen-draper, and may take enough. I could
enter mine action of battery against him, but
we may [perhaps] [29] be both dead and rotten
before the lawyers would end it.

CRAM. No more to do, but ensconce yourself i' th' tavern ; provide no great cheer : [40
[a] couple of capons, some pheasants, plovers,
an orangeado [30] pie, or so. But, how bloody
so-e'er the day be, sally you not forth.

FUS. No, no ; nay, if I stir, somebody shall
stink. I'll not budge ; I'll lie like a dog in
a manger.

CRAM. Well, well, to the tavern ; let not
our supper be raw, for you shall have blood
enough, your bellyful.

FUS. That's all, so God sa' me, I thirst [50
after ; blood for blood, bump for bump, nose
for nose, head for head, plaster for plaster ;
and so farewell. What shall I call your
names ? because I'll leave word, if any such
come to the bar.

CRAM. My name is Corporal Crambo.

POH. And mine, Lieutenant Poh.

CRAM. Poh is as tall a man as ever
opened oyster ; I would not be the Devil to
meet Poh. Farewell.   60

FUS. Nor I, by this light, if Poh be such
a Poh.   *Exeunt.*

[SCENE III] [31]

Enter Candido's wife [VIOLA] *in her shop, and
the two* Prentices.

VIO. What's a'clock now?
2 PREN.   'T is almost twelve.
VIO.   That's well :
The Senate will leave wording presently.
But is George ready?
2 PREN.   Yes, forsooth, he's furbish'd.
VIO. Now, as you ever hope to win my
                              favor,
Throw both your duties and respects on him
With the like awe as if he were your master ;
Let not your looks betray it with a smile
Or jeering glance to any customer ;

---

[21] Ruinous.
[22] A street. Old eds. *11 Sce.*
[23] See on *Dramatis Personae.*
[24] Supplied by Q n.d.
[25] Tuscan, straw-colored.
[26] Soundly beaten.
[27] Gambling game.
[28] Mazzard, head.
[29] So Pearson and Qq 1616, 1635 ; Qq₁ and n.d.
haps.
[30] Candied orange peel.
[31] Candido's shop. The new scene is unmarked
in the old eds.

Keep a true settled countenance, and beware
You laugh not, whatsoever you hear or see. [10

2 PREN. I warrant you, mistress ; let us
alone for keeping our countenance ; for, if I
list, there's never a fool in all Milan shall
make me laugh, let him play the fool never
so like an ass, whether it be the fat court fool,
or the lean city fool.

VIO. Enough, then ; call down George.

2 PREN.   I hear him coming.

Enter GEORGE [*in Candido's apparel*].

VIO. Be ready with your legs,[32] then ; let
    me see
How court'sy would become him.—Gallantly !
Beshrew my blood, a proper seemly man. [20
Of a choice carriage, walks with a good port.

GEO. I thank you, Mistress ; my back's
broad enough, now my master's gown's on.

VIO. Sure, I should think 't were the least
    of sin,
To mistake the master, and to let him in.

GEO. 'T were a good comedy of errors
that, i' faith.

2 PREN. Whist, whist, my master !

Enter CANDIDO, [*dressed as before in the carpet ;
he stares at* GEORGE,] *and exit presently*.

VIO. You all know your tasks. — God's my
life, what's that he has got upon's back ? [30
Who can tell ?

GEO. [*aside*] That can I, but I will not.

VIO. Girt about him like a madman.
What, has he lost his cloak, too ? This is the
maddest fashion that e'er I saw. What said
he, George, when he pass'd by thee ?

GEO. Troth, mistress, nothing ; not so
much as a bee, he did not hum ; not so much
as a bawd, he did not hem ; not so much as
a cuckold, he did not ha ; neither hum, [40
hem, nor ha ; only star'd me in the face,
pass'd along, and made haste in, as if my looks
had work'd with him, to give him a stool.[33]

VIO. Sure he's vex'd now ; this trick has
    mov'd his spleen ;
He's ang'red now, because he utt'red noth-
    ing ;
And wordless wrath breaks out more violent.
Maybe he'll strive for place, when he comes
    down ;
But if thou lov'st me, George, afford him none.

GEO. Nay, let me alone to play my master's

prize,[34] as long as my mistress warrants [50
me. I'm sure I have his best clothes on, and
I scorn to give place to any that is inferior in
apparel to me ; that's an axiom, a principle,
and is observ'd as much as the fashion. Let
that persuade you, then, that I'll shoulder
with him for the upper hand in the shop, as
long as this chain will maintain it.

VIO. Spoke with the spirit of a master,
though with the tongue of a prentice.

Re-enter CANDIDO *like*[35] *a prentice*.

Why how now, madman ? What, in your
    tricksy[36] coats ?   60

CAND. O peace, good Mistress.

Enter CRAMBO *and* POH.

See what you lack ! What is't you buy ?
Pure calicos, fine hollands, choice cambrics,
neat lawns ! See what you buy ! Pray come
near ; my master will use you well ; he can
afford you a pennyworth.

VIO. Ay, that he can, out of a whole piece
of lawn, i' faith.

CAND. Pray see your choice here, gentle-
men.   70

VIO. O fine fool ! what, a madman ! a
patient madman ! Who ever heard of the
like ? Well, sir, I'll fit you and your humor
presently. What, cross-points ?[37] I'll untie
'em all in a trice ;
I'll vex you i' faith. Boy, take your cloak,
    quick, come.   *Exit* [*with* 1 Prentice].

CAND. Be covered,[38] George ; this chain
    and welted[39] gown
Bare to this coat ? Then the world's upside
    down.

GEO. Umh, umh, hum.

CRAM. That's the shop, and there's the
fellow.   80

POH. Ay, but the master is walking in there.

CRAM. No matter, we'll in.

POH. 'Sblood, doest long to lie in limbo ?[40]

CRAM. An[41] limbo be in hell, I care not.

[32] Bows.
[33] *I.e.*, as if my looks had had a cathartic effect
on him.
[34] "A quibble. In the art of fencing there were
three degrees, — a Master's, a Provost's, and a
Scholar's, for each of which a prize was played
publicly." (Dyce.)
[35] Dressed like.
[36] Spruce, trim.
[37] The pun on points, (1) = arguments, and
(2) = tagged laces, was common.
[38] Put on your cap.
[39] Trimmed, fringed.
[40] Jail ; but the word also means a region on the
borders of hell.
[41] If.

CAND. Look you, gentlemen, your choice. Cambrics?

CRAM. No, sir, some shirting.

CAND. You shall.

CRAM. Have you none of this strip'd canvas for doublets?   90

CAND. None strip'd, sir; but [42] plain.

2 PREN. I think there be one piece strip'd within.

GEO. Step, sirrah, and fetch it; hum, hum, hum.

> [*Exit* CANDIDO [43] *and returns with the piece.*]

CAND. Look you, gentlemen, I'll make but one spreading; here's a piece of cloth, fine, yet shall wear like iron. 'T is without fault; take this upon my word, 't is without fault.

CRAM. Then 't is better than you, [100 sirrah.

CAND. Ay, and a number more. Oh, that each soul
Were but as spotless as this innocent white,
And had as few breaks in it.

CRAM.   'T would have some then;
There was a fray here last day in this shop.

CAND. There was, indeed, a little flea-biting.

POH. A gentleman had his pate broke; call you that but a flea-biting?

CAND. He had so.

CRAM. Zouns, do you stand in 't?   110

> *He strikes him.*

GEO. 'Sfoot! clubs, clubs! Prentices, down with 'em!

[*Enter several* Prentices *with clubs, who disarm* CRAMBO *and* POH.]

Ah, you rogues; strike a citizen in 's shop?

CAND. None of you stir, I pray; forbear, good George.

CRAM. I beseech you, sir, we mistook our marks; deliver us our weapons.

GEO. Your head bleeds, sir; cry clubs.

CAND. I say you shall not; pray be patient;
Give them their weapons. Sirs, you 're best be gone;
I tell you here are boys more tough than bears.
Hence, lest more fists do walk about your ears.   120

BOTH. We thank you, sir.   *Exeunt.*

CAND.   You shall not follow them;

Let them alone, pray; this did me no harm.
Troth, I was cold, and the blow made me warm;
I thank 'em for 't. Besides, I had decreed [44]
To have a vein prick'd; I did mean to bleed;
So that there 's money sav'd. They are honest men;
Pray use 'em well when they appear again.

GEO. Yes, sir, we 'll use 'em like honest men.

CAND. Ay, well said, George, like honest men, though they be arrant knaves, for [13c that 's the phrase of the city. Help to lay up these wares.

Re-enter his Wife *with* Officers.

VIO. Yonder he stands.

[1] OFF.   What in a prentice-coat?

VIO. Ay, ay; mad, mad; pray take heed.

CAND. How now! what news with them? What make they [45] with my wife?
Officers, is she attach'd? — Look to your wares.

VIO. He talks to himself; oh, he 's much gone indeed.

[1] OFF. Pray, pluck up a good heart; be not so fearful. —
Sirs, hark; we 'll gather to him by degrees.   140

VIO. Ay, ay, by degrees, I pray. O me! What makes he with the lawn in his hand?
He 'll tear all the ware in my shop.

[1] OFF. Fear not; we 'll catch him on a sudden.

VIO. You had need do so; pray take heed of your warrant.

[1] OFF. I warrant, mistress. Now, Signior Candido.

CAND. Now, sir, what news with you, sir?

VIO. What news with you? he says; oh, he 's far gone!   150

[1] OFF. I pray, fear nothing; let 's alone with him. —
Signior, you look not like yourself, methinks;—
Steal you a' tother side; — y' are chang'd, y' are alt'red.

CAND. Chang'd, sir? why true, sir. Is change strange? 'T is not
The fashion unless it alter. Monarchs turn
To beggars, beggars creep into the nests
Of princes, masters serve their prentices,
Ladies their serving men, men turn to women.

---

[42] Only.
[43] Mod. eds. *2 Prentice*, but Dyce's suggestion of Candido is certainly right.
[44] Decided.
[45] Are they doing.

[1] OFF. And women turn [46] to men.

CAND. Ay, and women turn to men, [160 you say true. Ha, ha, a mad world, a mad world.   [*Officers seize* CANDIDO.]

[1] OFF. Have we caught you, sir?

CAND. Caught me! Well, well, you have caught me.

VIO.   He laughs in your faces.

GEO. A rescue, prentices! my master's catch-poll'd.[47]

[1] OFF. I charge you, keep the peace, or have your legs

Gartered with irons! We have from the Duke
A warrant strong enough for what we do.

CAND. I pray, rest quiet; I desire no rescue.

VIO. La, he desires no rescue; 'las, poor heart,   170
He talks against himself.

CAND.   Well, what's the matter?

[1] OFF. Look to that arm. Pray, make sure work; double the cord.
            [*Officers bind* CANDIDO.]

CAND. Why, why?

VIO. Look how his head goes. Should he get but loose,
Oh, 't were as much as all our lives were worth.

[1] OFF. Fear not; we'll make all sure, for our own safety.

CAND. Are you at leisure now? Well, what's the matter?
Why do I enter into bonds thus, ha?

[1] OFF. Because y' are mad, put fear upon your wife.   180

VIO. Oh, ay; I went in danger of my life every minute.

CAND. What, am I mad, say you, and I not know it?

[1] OFF. That proves you mad, because you know it not.

VIO. Pray talk to him as little as you can;
You see he's too far spent.

CAND.   Bound with strong cord —
A sister's thread,[48] i' faith, had been enough
To lead me anywhere. — Wife, do you long?
You are mad too, or else you do me wrong.

GEO. But are you mad indeed, Master?

CAND.   My wife says so; [190
And what she says, George, is all truth, you know. —

And whither now, to Bethlem Monastery,[49]
Ha? whither?

1 OFF.   Faith, e'en to the madmen's pound.

CAND. A' God's name! Still I feel my patience sound.   [*Exit with* Officers.]

GEO. Come, we'll see whither he goes. If the master be mad, we are his servants, and must follow his steps; we'll be madcaps too. Farewell, Mistress; you shall have us all in Bedlam.   *Exeunt* [GEORGE *and* Prentices].

VIO. I think I ha' fitted you now, you and your clothes.   200
If this move not his patience, nothing can;
I'll swear then I have a saint, and not a man.
            Exit.

SCENE [IV] [50]

Enter DUKE, DOCTOR [BENEDICT], FLUELLO, CASTRUCHIO, [*and*] PIORATTO.

DUKE. Give us a little leave. —
            [*Exeunt* FLUELLO, CASTRUCHIO, *and* PIORATTO.]
            Doctor, your news.

DOCT. I sent for him, my Lord; at last he came,
And did receive all speech that went from me,
As gilded pills made to prolong his health.
My credit with him wrought it; for some men
Swallow even empty hooks, like fools that fear
No drowning where 't is deepest, 'cause 't is clear.
In th' end we sat and ate; a health I drank
To Infeliche's sweet departed soul.
This train [51] I knew would take.

DUKE.   'T was excellent. [10

DOCT. He fell with such devotion on his knees,
To pledge the same —

DUKE.   Fond, superstitious fool!

DOCT. That had been inflam'd with zeal of prayer,
He could not pour 't out with more reverence.
About my neck he hung, wept on my cheek,
Kiss'd it, and swore he would adore my lips,
Because they brought forth Infeliche's name.

DUKE. Ha, ha; alack, alack.

---

[46] Incline.
[47] Arrested, especially for debt.
[48] There was such a thread; perhaps it got its name from "sister" = nun. Q₁ *Cisters*.
[49] London's lunatic asylum.
[50] Not precisely located; presumably the grounds of the Duke's palace; for the scene is continuous, although the Doctor's summoning of the supposedly deceased Hippolito to the very spot where the Duke heard the report of his death would be absurd on a picture-stage. Old eds. *Scena 13.*
[51] Stratagem.

DOCT. The cup he lifts up high, and thus
  he said :
" Here, noble maid ! " — drinks, and was
  poisoned.   20
  DUKE. And died?
  DOCT.   And died, my Lord.
  DUKE.   Thou in that word
Hast piec'd mine aged hours out with more
  years
Than thou hast taken from Hippolito.
A noble youth he was, but lesser branches,
Hind'ring the greater's growth, must be
  lopp'd off
And feed the fire. Doctor, w' are now all
  thine,
And use us so ; be bold.
  DOCT.   Thanks, gracious Lord ;
My honored Lord, —
  DUKE. Hmh.
  DOCT. I do beseech your Grace to bury
  deep,   30
This bloody act of mine.
  DUKE.   Nay, nay, for [52] that,
Doctor, look you to 't , me it shall not move ;
They 're curs'd that ill do, not that ill do love.
  DOCT. You throw an angry forehead on my
  face ;
But be you pleas'd backward thus far to look,
That for your good this evil I undertook —
  DUKE. Ay, ay, we conster [53] so.
  DOCT. And only for your love.
  DUKE.   Confess'd ; 't is true.
  DOCT. Nor let it stand against me as a bar
To thrust me from your presence ; nor believe,
As [54] princes have quick thoughts, that now
  my finger   41
Being dipp'd in blood, I will not spare the
  hand,
But that for gold — as what can gold not do ? —
I may be hir'd to work the like on you.
  DUKE. Which to prevent —
  DOCT.   'T is from my heart as far.
  DUKE. No matter, doctor ; 'cause I 'll fear-
  less sleep,
And that you shall stand clear of that sus-
  picion,
I banish thee for ever from my court.
This principle is old, but true as fate :
Kings may love treason, but the traitor hate.
                                             Exit.
  DOCT. Is 't so? Nay then, Duke, your
  stale principle,   51

With one as stale, the doctor thus shall quit :
He falls himself that digs another's pit.

Enter the Doctor's Man.

How now ! Where is he? will he meet me?
  MAN. Meet you, sir? He might have
met with three fencers in this time, and have
received less hurt than by meeting one doctor
of physic. Why, sir, has walk'd under the
old abbey wall yonder this hour, till he 's more
cold than a citizen's country house in [60
January.[55] You may smell him behind, sir ;
la you, yonder he comes.

Enter HIPPOLITO.

  DOCT. Leave me.
  MAN. I' th' lurch, if you will.   *Exit.*
  DOCT. O my most noble friend !
  HIP.   Few but yourself
Could have entic'd me thus to trust the
  air
With my close sighs. You [sent] [56] for me ;
  what news?
  DOCT. Come, you must doff this black,
  dye that pale cheek
Into his [57] own color, go attire yourself
Fresh as a bridegroom when he meets his
  bride.   70
The Duke has done much treason to thy love ;
'T is now revealed ; 't is now to be reveng'd.
Be merry, honor'd friend : thy lady lives.
  HIP. What lady?
  DOCT.   Infeliche ; she 's reviv'd.
Reviv'd? Alack ! death never had the heart
To take breath from her.
  HIP.   Umh ; I thank you, sir ;
Physic prolongs life, when it cannot save :
This helps not my hopes ; mine are in their
  grave ;
You do some wrong to mock me.
  DOCT.   By that love
Which I have ever borne you, what I speak [80
Is truth ; the maiden lives ; that funeral,
Duke's tears, the mourning, was all counter-
  feit.
A sleepy draught cozen'd the world and you ;
I was his minister, and then chamb'red up,
To stop discovery.
  HIP.   O treacherous Duke !
  DOCT. He cannot hope so certainly for
  bliss,
As he believes that I have poison'd you.

[52] As for.
[53] Construe.
[54] As well you may believe, since.

[55] Old eds. *Ianiuere.*
[56] Qq 1 and n.d. *send.*
[57] Its.

He woo'd me to 't ; I yielded, and confirm'd
   him
In his most bloody thoughts.
  HIP.   A very devil !
  DOCT. Her did he closely coach to Ber-
    gamo,   90
And thither —
  HIP.   Will I ride ; stood Bergamo
In the low countries of black hell, I 'll to her.
  DOCT. You shall to her, but not to Ber-
    gamo.
How passion makes you fly beyond yourself !
Much of that weary journey I ha' cut off ;
For she by letters hath intelligence
Of your supposed death, her own interment,
And all those plots which that false Duke,
  her father,
Has wrought against you ; and she 'll meet
  you —
  HIP. Oh, when?   100
  DOCT. Nay, see ; how covetous are your
    desires.
Early to-morrow morn.
  HIP.   Oh, where, good father?
  DOCT. At Bethlem Monastery ; are you
    pleas'd now?
  HIP. At Bethlem Monastery ! The place
    well fits ;
It is the school where those that lose their
  wits
Practise again to get them. I am sick
Of that disease ; all love is lunatic.
  DOCT. We 'll steal away this night in some
    disguise.
Father Anselmo, a most reverend friar,
Expects our coming ; before whom we 'll lay
Reasons so strong that he shall yield [58] in
  bonds [59]   111
Of holy wedlock to tie both your hands.
  HIP. This is such happiness
That to believe it, 't is impossible.
  DOCT. Let all your joys then die in misbe-
    lief ;
I will reveal no more.
  HIP.   Oh, yes, good father,
I am so well acquainted with despair,
I know not how to hope. I believe all.
  DOCT. We 'll hence this night. Much
    must be done, much said ;
But if the doctor fail not in his charms,   120
Your lady shall ere morning fill these arms.
  HIP. Heavenly physician ! far thy fame
    shall spread,

[58] Consent.
[59] Qq 2 and n.d. *bands.*

That mak'st two lovers speak when they be
  dead.   *Exeunt.*

[ACT V — SCENE I] [1]

Enter Candido's wife, [VIOLA, *with a petition,*]
  and GEORGE. PIORATTO *meets them.*

  VIO. Oh, watch, good George, watch which
way the Duke comes.
  GEO. Here comes one of the butterflies ;
ask him.
  VIO. Pray, sir, comes the Duke this way?
  PIO. He 's upon [2] coming, mistress.   *Exit.*
  VIO. I thank you, sir. — George, are there
many mad folks where thy master lies?
  GEO. Oh, yes, of all countries some ; but especially mad Greeks,[3] they swarm. Troth, [10
Mistress, the world is altered with you ; you
had not wont to stand thus with a paper humbly complaining. But you 're well enough
serv'd ; provender prick'd [4] you, as it does
many of our city wives besides.
  VIO. Doest think, George, we shall get him
forth?
  GEO. Truly, Mistress, I cannot tell ; I think
you 'll hardly get him forth. Why, 't is
strange ! 'Sfoot, I have known many [20
women that have had mad rascals to their husbands, whom they would belabor by all means
possible to keep 'em in their right wits ; but of
a woman to long to turn a tame man into a
madman, why the Devil himself was never us'd
so by his dam.
  VIO. How does he talk, George? Ha !
good George, tell me.
  GEO. Why, you 're best go see.
  VIO. Alas, I am afraid !   30
  GEO. Afraid ! you had more need be
asham'd. He may rather be afraid of you.
  VIO. But, George, he 's not stark mad, is
he? He does not rave, he 's not horn-mad,[5]
George, is he?
  GEO. Nay I know not that ; but he talks
like a justice of peace, of a thousand matters,
and to no purpose.
  VIO. I 'll to the monastery. I shall be mad
till I enjoy him [6] ; I shall be sick till I see [40

[1] A hall in the Duke's palace.   [2] On the point of.
  [3] Jovial fellows, boon companions. It also meant
sharpers.
  [4] Good food spurred ; *i.e.,* your whim was the
result of high feeding.
  [5] Raving mad. George's reply glances at the
customary pun on the horns of the cuckold.
  [6] Have his company.

him ; yet when I do see him, I shall weep out mine eyes.

GEO. Ay, I'd fain see a woman weep out her eyes ! That's as true as to say, a man's cloak burns when it hangs in the water. I know you'll weep, mistress ; but what says the painted cloth?[7]

> Trust not a woman when she cries,
> For she'll pump water from her eyes
> With a wet finger,[8] and in faster showers   50
> Than April when he rains down flowers.

VIO. Ay, but George, that painted cloth is worthy to be hang'd up [9] for lying. All women have not tears at will, unless they have good cause.

GEO. Ay, but Mistress, how easily will they find a cause ; and as one of our cheese-trench-ers [10] says very learnedly :

> As out of wormwood bees suck honey,
> As from poor clients lawyers firk [11] money,   60
> As parsley from a roasted cony ; [12]
> So, though the day be ne'er so sunny,
> If wives will have it rain, down then it drives, —
> The calmest husbands make the storm[i]est wives.

VIO. [True],[13] George ; but I ha' done storming now.

GEO. Why that's well done. Good Mis-tress, throw aside this fashion of your humor ; be not so fantastical in wearing it ; storm no more, long no more. This longing has [70 made you come short of many a good thing that you might have had from my master. Here comes the Duke.

Enter DUKE, FLUELLO, PIORATTO, [*and*] SINEZI.

VIO. Oh, I beseech you, pardon my offence, In that I durst abuse your Grace's warrant ; Deliver forth my husband, good my Lord.

DUKE. Who is her husband?

FLU.   Candido, my Lord.

DUKE. Where is he?

VIO.   He's among the lunatics. He was a man made up without a gall ; Nothing could move him, nothing could con-vert   80

His meek blood into fury ; yet like a monster, I often beat at the most constant rock Of his unshaken patience, and did long To vex him.

DUKE.   Did you so?

VIO.   And for that purpose Had warrant from your Grace to carry him To Bethlem Monastery, whence they will not free him Without your Grace's hand [14] that sent him in.

DUKE. You have long'd fair ; 't is you are mad, I fear ; It's fit to fetch him thence, and keep you there. If he be mad, why would you have him forth?   90

GEO. An please your Grace, he's not stark mad, but only talks like a young gentleman, somewhat fantastically, that's all. There's a thousand about your court, city, and country madder than he.

DUKE. Provide a warrant ; you shall have our hand.

GEO. Here's a warrant ready drawn, my Lord.

[DUKE.] [15] Get pen and ink, get pen and ink.   [*Exit* GEORGE.]

Enter CASTRUCHIO.

CAS. Where is my Lord the Duke?

DUKE.   How now ! more madmen?

CAS. I have strange news, my Lord.

DUKE.   Of what? of whom?   100

CAS. Of Infeliche, and a marriage.

DUKE. Ha ! where? with whom?

CAS.   Hippolito.

[*Re-enter* GEORGE, *with pen and ink.*]

GEO. Here, my Lord.

DUKE. Hence with that woman. — Void the room.

FLU. Away ; the Duke's vex'd.

GEO. Whoop, come, Mistress ; the Duke's mad, too.   *Exeunt* [VIOLA *and* GEORGE].

DUKE. Who told me that Hippolito was dead?

CAS. He that can make any man dead, the doctor. But, my Lord, he's as full of life [110 as wildfire, and as quick. Hippolito, the doc-tor, and one more rid hence this evening ; the inn at which they light is Bethlem Monastery ; Infeliche comes from Bergamo and meets them

---

[7] A cheap substitute for tapestry ; it often had mottoes, as well as figures, painted on it.
[8] Easily, readily.
[9] It was, of course, a wall hanging.
[10] They used to be inscribed with proverbial say-ings.
[11] Rob, cheat.
[12] Rabbit.
[13] Conj. Dyce. Old eds. *Tame.*

[14] *I.e.*, authorization in writing.
[15] Qq 1 and n.d. *Cast.*

there.   Hippolito is mad, for he means this day to be married ; the afternoon is the hour, and Friar Anselmo is the knitter.

DUKE. From Bergamo? is 't possible? it cannot be.

It cannot be.

CAS.   I will not swear, my Lord ;
But this intelligence I took from one   120
Whose brains works in the plot.

DUKE.   What 's he?

CAS.   Matheo.

FLU. Matheo knows all.

PIOR.   He 's Hippolito's bosom.[16]

DUKE. How far stands Bethlem hence?

OMNES.   Six or seven miles.

DUKE. Is 't even so? not married till the afternoon, you say? [17]

Stay, stay ; let 's work out some prevention. How !

This is most strange ; can none but madmen serve

To dress their wedding dinner?   All of you Get presently to horse ; disguise yourselves Like country gentlemen,

Or riding citizens, or so ; and take   130
Each man a several [18] path, but let us meet At Bethlem Monastery, some space of time Being spent between the arrival each of other, As if we came to see the lunatics.

To horse, away ; be secret on your lives.
Love must be punish'd that unjustly thrives.
                    Exeunt [all but FLUELLO].

FLU. Be secret on your lives !   Castruchio, Y' are but a scurvy spaniel.   Honest lord, Good lady !   Zounds, their love is just, 't is good,

And I 'll prevent you, though I swim in blood.   *Exit.*   140

[SCENE II] [19]

Enter FRIAR ANSELMO, HIPPOLITO, MATHEO, [*and*] INFELICHE.

HIP. Nay, nay, resolve,[20] good father, or deny.

ANS. You press me to an act both full of danger

And full of happiness ; for I behold

Your father's frowns, his threats, nay, perhaps death

---

[16] Confidant.
[17] So Qq 1 and n.d. Later qtos. om. *even* and *you say*, which may be actor's interpolations.
[18] Separate, different.
[19] An apartment at Bethlehem.
[20] Make up your mind (to it).

To him that dare do this.   Yet, noble Lord, Such comfortable beams break through these clouds

By this blest marriage, that your honor'd word Being pawn'd in my defence, I will tie fast The holy wedding knot.

HIP.   Tush, fear not the Duke.

ANS. O son ! wisely to fear is to be free from fear.   10

HIP. You have our words, and you shall have our lives,

To guard you safe from all ensuing danger.

MAT. Ay, ay, chop [21] 'em up, and away.

ANS. Stay ; when is 't fit for me, safest for you,

To entertain this business?

HIP.   Not till the evening.

ANS. Be 't so ; there is a chapel stands hard by,

Upon the west end of the abbey wall ;
Thither convey yourselves, and when the sun Hath turn'd his back upon this upper world, I 'll marry you ; that done, no thund'ring voice Can break the sacred bond ; yet, lady, here [21
You are most safe.

INF.   Father, your love 's most dear.

MAT. Ay, well said ; lock us into some little room by ourselves, that we may be mad for an hour or two.

HIP. O, good Matheo, no, let 's make no noise.

MAT. How? no noise ! Do you know where you are? 'Sfoot, amongst all the madcaps in Milan ; so that to throw the house out at window will be the better, and no man [30 will suspect that we lurk here to steal mutton.[22] The more sober we are, the more scurvy [23] 't is. And though the friar tell us that here we are safest, I'm not of his mind ; for if those lay here that had lost their money, none would ever look after them ; but here are none but those that have lost their wits ; so that if hue and cry be made, hither they 'll come ; and my reason is, because none goes to be married till he be stark mad.   40

HIP. Muffle yourselves ; yonder 's Fluello.

Enter FLUELLO.

MAT.   Zounds !

FLU. O my Lord, these cloaks are not for this rain.   The tempest is too great.   I come sweating to tell you of it, that you may get out of it.

---

[21] Settle their bargain.   [22] To steal a wench.
[23] *I.e.,* suspicious. (Neilson.)

MAT. Why, what's the matter?

FLU. What's the matter? You have matter'd [24] it fair; the Duke's at hand.

OMNES. The Duke?

FLU.   The very Duke.

HIP.   Then all our plots
Are turn'd upon our heads, and we are blown
     up   50
With our own underminings. 'Sfoot, how
     comes he?
What villain durst betray our being here?

FLU. Castruchio; Castruchio told the
Duke, and Matheo here told Castruchio.

HIP. Would you betray me to Castruchio?

MAT. 'Sfoot, he damn'd himself to the pit
of hell, if he spake on't again.

HIP. So did you swear to me; so were you
     damn'd.

MAT. Pox on 'em; and there be no faith in
men, if a man shall not believe oaths. He [60
took bread and salt,[25] by this light, that he
would never open his lips.

HIP. O God, O God!

ANS.   Son, be not desperate;
Have patience; you shall trip your enemy
Down by his own sleights.[26] — How far is the
Duke hence?

FLU. He's but new set out; Castruchio,
Pioratto, and Sinezi come along with him.
You have time enough yet to prevent [27] them,
if you have but courage.

ANS. Ye shall steal secretly into the
     chapel,   70
And presently [28] be married. If the Duke
Abide here still, spite of ten thousand eyes,
You shall scape hence like friars.

HIP. O blest [disguise]! [29] O happy man!

ANS. Talk not of Happiness till your clos'd
     hand
Have her by th' forehead, like the lock of
     Time.
Be nor too slow nor hasty, now you climb
Up to the tow'r of bliss; only be wary
And patient, that's all. If you like my plot,
Build and dispatch; if not, farewell, then not.

HIP. Oh, yes, we do applaud it. We'll dis-
     pute [30]   81
No longer, but will hence and execute.
Fluello, you'll stay here; let us be gone.

[24] Have made a fine matter of it!
[25] *I.e.*, ate it, to confirm his oath.
[26] Subtle schemes.
[27] Anticipate, get ahead of.
[28] Immediately.
[29] Q₁ *disguisde*.
[30] Discuss.

The ground that frighted lovers tread upon
Is stuck with thorns.

ANS.   Come, then, away; 't is meet,
To escape those thorns, to put on winged feet.
       Exeunt [ANSELMO, HIPPOLITO, *and*
         INFELICHE].

MAT. No words, I pray, Fluello, for't
stands us upon.[31]

FLU. Oh, sir, let that be your lesson! —
                        [*Exit* MATHEO.]
Alas, poor lovers! On what hopes and
     fears   90
Men toss themselves for women! When she's
     got,
The best has in her that which pleaseth not.

Enter to FLUELLO, *the* DUKE, CASTRUCHIO, PIO-
RATTO, *and* SINEZI *from several doors, muffled.*

DUKE. Who's there?

CAS.   My Lord.

DUKE.   Peace; send that "Lord" away.
A lordship will spoil all; let's be all fellows.
What's he?

CAS. Fluello, or else Sinezi, by his little
     legs.

OMNES. All friends, all friends.

DUKE. What, met upon the very point of
     time!
Is this the place?

PIO.   This is the place, my Lord.

DUKE. Dream you on lordships? Come no
     more "Lords," pray.   100
You have not seen these lovers yet?

OMNES.   Not yet.

DUKE. Castruchio, art thou sure this wed-
     ding feat
Is not till afternoon?

CAS.   So 't is given out, my Lord.

DUKE. Nay, nay, 't is like; thieves must
     observe their hours;
Lovers watch minutes like astronomers.
How shall the interim hours by us be spent?

FLU. Let's all go see the madmen.[32]

OMNES.   Mass, content.

Enter a Sweeper.[33]

DUKE. Oh, here comes one; question him,
question him.

[31] It is necessary for us (to avoid suspicion).
Matheo urges Fluello not to reveal his participation.
Fluello retorts that Matheo (judging by the past)
is the one who needs to study silence.
[32] A common form of amusement in Dekker's
London.
[33] Old. eds. *Enter Towne like a sweeper*, and his
speeches are tagged *Towne*. This is Thomas
Towne, one of the principal members of Prince
Henry's Men.

FLU. How now, honest fellow, dost thou [110 belong to the house?

SWEEP. Yes, forsooth, I am one of the implements ; I sweep the madmen's rooms, and fetch straw for 'em, and buy chains to tie 'em, and rods to whip 'em.[34] I was a mad wag myself here, once ; but I thank Father Anselm, he lash'd me into my right mind again.

DUKE. Anselmo is the friar must marry them ;

Question him where he is.   119

CAS. And where is Father Anselmo now?

SWEEP. Marry, he 's gone but e'en now.

DUKE. Ay, well done. — Tell me, whither is he gone?

SWEEP. Why, to God a'mighty.

FLU. Ha, ha! this fellow 's a fool, talks idly.

PIO. Sirrah, are all the mad folks in Milan brought hither?

SWEEP. How, all! There 's a wise question indeed! Why if all the mad folks in Milan should come hither, there would not be [130 left ten men in the city.

DUKE. Few gentlemen or courtiers here, ha?

SWEEP. Oh, yes, abundance, abundance! Lands no sooner fall into their hands but straight they run out a' their wits. Citizens' sons and heirs are free of the house by their fathers' copy.[35] Farmers' sons come hither like geese, in flocks ; and when they ha' sold all their cornfields, here they sit and pick the straws.   140

SIN. Methinks you should have women here as well as men.

SWEEP. Oh, ay, a plague on 'em ; there 's no ho[36] with them ; they are madder than March hares.

FLU. Are there no lawyers here amongst you?

SWEEP. Oh, no, not one ; never any lawyer. We dare not let a lawyer come in, for he 'll make 'em mad faster than we can recover 'em.   150

DUKE. And how long is 't ere you recover any of these?

SWEEP. Why, according to the quantity of the moon that 's got into 'em. An alderman's son will be mad a great while, a very great while, especially if his friends left him well. A whore will hardly come to her wits again. A Puritan, there 's no hope of him, unless he may

pull down the steeple, and hang himself i' th' bell-ropes.   160

FLU. I perceive all sorts of fish come to your net.

SWEEP. Yes, in truth, we have blocks [37] for all heads ; we have good store of wild oats here ; for the courtier is mad at the citizen, the citizen is mad at the countrym[a]n ; the shoemaker is mad at the cobbler, the cobbler at the carman ;[38] the punk is mad that the merchant's wife is no whore ; the merchant's wife is mad that the punk is so common a [170 whore. Gods so, here 's Father Anselmo ; pray say nothing that I tell tales out of the school.   *Exit.*

Re-enter ANSELMO [*and* Servants].

OMNES. God bless you, father.

ANS.   Thank you, gentlemen.

CAS. Pray, may we see some of those wretched souls

That here are in your keeping?

ANS.   Yes, you shall ; But gentlemen, I must disarm you then.

There are of mad men, as there are of tame,

All humor'd not alike. We have here some,

So apish and fantastic, play with a feather, [180

And, though 't would grieve a soul to see God's image

So blemish'd and defac'd, yet do they act

Such antic [39] and such pretty lunacies,

That spite of sorrow they will make you smile.

Others again we have like hungry lions,

Fierce as wild bulls, untamable as flies,

And these have oftentimes from strangers' sides

Snatch'd rapiers suddenly, and done much harm ;

Whom if you 'll see, you must be weaponless.

OMNES. With all our hearts.

         [ANSELMO *takes their weapons.*]

ANS.   Here, take these weapons in. — 190

         [*Exit* Servant *with weapons.*]

Stand off a little, pray ; so, so ; 't is well.

I 'll show you here a man that was sometimes [40]

A very grave and wealthy citizen ;

Has serv'd a prenticeship to this misfortune,

Been here seven years,[41] and dwelt in Bergamo.

DUKE. How fell he from his wits?

---

[34] As a part of the cure.
[35] Abundance. (Lat. *cōpia.*) With a pun.
[36] Cessation, intermission, limit. "Ho" = "whoa", the cry to stop.
[37] Hats ; properly, molds for hats.
[38] Carter.
[39] Fantastic.
[40] Formerly.
[41] The term of apprenticeship.

ANS.   By loss at sea.
I'll stand aside ; question him you alone,
For if he spy me he'll not speak a word,
Unless he's throughly vex'd.
> *Discovers* [42] *an* Old Man, *wrapp'd in a net.*

FLU.   Alas, poor soul !
CAS. A very old man.   200
DUKE. God speed, father.
1 MAD. God speed the plow ; [43] thou shalt
not speed me.
PIO. We see you, old man, for all you dance
in a net.[44]
1 MAD. True, but thou wilt dance in a
halter, and I shall not see thee.
ANS. Oh, do not vex him, pray.
CAS. Are you a fisherman, father?
1 MAD. No, I'm neither fish nor flesh. [210
FLU. What do you with that net, then?
1 MAD. Doest not see, fool? There's a
fresh salmon in 't ; if you step one foot furder,
you'll be over shoes, for you see I'm over head
and ear [45] in the salt water ; and if you fall into
this whirlpool where I am, y' are drown'd,
y' are a drown'd rat. I am fishing here for five
ships, but I cannot have a good draught, for
my net breaks still, and breaks ; but I'll break
some of your necks an I catch you in my [220
clutches. Stay, stay, stay, stay, stay ; where's
the wind? where's the wind? where's the
wind? where's the wind? Out, you gulls, you
goose-caps,[46] you gudgeon-eaters ! [47] Do you
look for the wind in the heavens? Ha, ha, ha,
ha ! no, no ! Look there, look there, look
there ! the wind is always at that door ; hark
how it blows, pooff, pooff, pooff !
OMNES. Ha, ha, ha !
1 MAD. Do you laugh at God's crea- [230
tures? Do you mock old age, you rogues?
Is this gray beard and head counterfeit, that
you cry ha, ha, ha? Sirrah, art not thou my
eldest son?
PIO. Yes, indeed, father.
1 MAD. Then th' art a fool ; for my eldest
son had a polt-foot,[48] crooked legs, a verjuice [49]
face, and a pear-color'd [50] beard. I made

[42] Probably by opening the curtains of the inner stage. Doubtless the old man advances to the outer stage toward the end of his first long speech.
[43] A proverbial saying.
[44] A common expression, = to proceed under observation while supposing oneself unobserved.
[45] Q 1635 *ears.*
[46] Numskulls.
[47] Boobies.
[48] Club-foot.
[49] Sour, crabbed.
[50] *I.e.,* russet.

him a scholar, and he made himself a fool.
— Sirrah, thou there, hold out thy hand. [240
DUKE. My hand? Well, here 't is.
1 MAD. Look, look, look, look ! Has he
not long nails, and short hair?
FLU. Yes, monstrous short hair, and abominable long nails.
1 MAD. Tenpenny nails, are they not?
FLU. Yes, tenpenny nails.
1 MAD. Such nails had my second boy.
Kneel down, thou varlet, and ask thy father
blessing. Such nails had my middle- [250
most son, and I made him a promoter ; [51] and
he scrap'd, and scrap'd, and scrap'd, till he
got the devil and all ; but he scrap'd thus, and
thus, and thus, and it went under his legs,
till at length a company of kites, taking him
for carrion, swept up all, all, all, all, all, all, all.
If you love your lives, look to yourselves ; see,
see, see, see, the Turks' galleys are fighting
with my ships. Bounce,[52] goes the guns !
Oooh ! cry the men ! Rumble, rumble, go [260
the waters ! Alas, there ; 't is sunk, 't is sunk !
I am undone, I am undone ; you are the
damn'd pirates have undone me ; you are, by
the Lord, you are, you are ! — Stop 'em ! —
you are !
ANS. Why, how now, sirrah ! Must I fall
    to tame you?
1 MAD. Tame me ! No, I'll be madder
than a roasted cat. See, see, I am burnt with
gunpowder — these are our close fights !
ANS. I'll whip you, if you grow unruly [270
    thus.
1 MAD. Whip me? Out you toad ! Whip
me ! What justice is this, to whip me because
I'm a beggar? Alas ! I am a poor man, a
very poor man ! I am starv'd, and have had
no meat, by this light, ever since the great
flood ; I am a poor man.
ANS. Well, well, be quiet, and you shall
    have meat.
1 MAD. Ay, ay, pray do ; for, look you, here
be my guts : these are my ribs — you may look
through my ribs — see how my guts come [280
out ! These are my red guts, my very guts,
oh, oh !
ANS. Take him in there.
> [*Servants* remove 1 Madman.]
OMNES.   A very piteous sight.
CAS. Father, I see you have a busy charge.
ANS. They must be us'd like children,
    pleas'd with toys,

[51] Informer.
[52] Bang.

And anon whipp'd for their unruliness.
I'll show you now a pair quite different
From him that's gone. He was all words;
    and these,
Unless you urge 'em, seldom spend their
    speech,   289
But [save][53] their tongues.
        [*Opens a door, from which enter 2 and*
          3 *Madmen.*]
                  La, you ; this hithermost
Fell from the happy quietness of mind
About a maiden that he lov'd, and died.
He followed her to church, being full of tears,
And as her body went into the ground,
He fell stark mad. This is a married man,
Was jealous of a fair, but, as some say,
A very virtuous, wife ; and that spoil'd
    him.
    3 MAD.[54] All these are whoremongers, and
lay with my wife ; whore, whore, whore,
whore, whore!   300
    FLU. Observe him.
    3 MAD. Gaffer shoemaker, you pull'd on my
wife's pumps, and then crept into her pantofles ;[55] lie there, lie there! — This was her
tailor. You cut out her loose-bodied gown,
and put in a yard more than I allowed her ; lie
there by the shoemaker. — O master doctor!
are you here? You gave me a purgation, and
then crept into my wife's chamber to feel her
pulses, and you said, and she said, and her [310
maid said, that they went pit-a-pat, pit-a-pat,
pit-a-pat. Doctor, I'll put you anon into my
wife's urinal. — Heigh, come aloft, Jack![56]
This was her schoolmaster, and taught her to
play upon the virginals ; and still his jacks[57]
leap'd up, up. You prick'd her out[58] nothing
but bawdy lessons ; but I'll prick you all,
fiddler, doctor, tailor, shoemaker ; shoemaker,
fiddler, doctor, tailor! So! lie with my wife
again, now!   320
    CAS. See how he notes the other, now he
       feeds.
    3 MAD. Give me some porridge.
    2 MAD. I'll give thee none.
    3 MAD. Give me some porridge.
    2 MAD. I'll not give thee a bit.

[53] So Pearson ; old eds. seen by present Ed., *haue.*
[54] Old eds. transpose speech-tags for 2 and 3
Madmen.
[55] Slippers.
[56] The cry of its master to a trained ape.
[57] The double ententes in this speech are obvious.
"Jacks" were part of the wooden mechanism of the
virginal, a small spinet. When the key was struck
the jack was raised.
[58] Wrote down in musical notation.

    3 MAD. Give me that flapdragon.[59]
    2 MAD. I'll not give thee a spoonful. Thou
liest, it's no dragon ; 't is a parrot that I
bought for my sweetheart, and I'll keep it.
    3 MAD. Here's an almond for parrot.[60] [330
    2 MAD. Hang thyself!
    3 MAD. Here's a rope for parrot.[60]
    2 MAD. Eat it, for I'll eat this.
    3 MAD. I'll shoot at thee, an thou't give
me none.
    2 MAD. Wu't thou?
    3 MAD. I'll run a tilt at thee, an thou't give
me none.
    2 MAD. Wu't thou? Do an thou dar'st.
    3 MAD. Bounce![61]   340
    2 MAD. Oh, oh! I am slain! Murder,
murder, murder! I am slain ; my brains
are beaten out!
    ANS. How now, you villains! Bring me
       whips ; I'll whip you.
    2 MAD. I am dead! I am slain! ring out
the bell, for I am dead!
    DUKE. How will you do now, sirrah? You
       ha' kill'd him.
    3 MAD. I'll answer't at sessions ; he was
eating of almond-butter, and I long'd for't.
The child had never been delivered out [350
of my belly, if I had not kill'd him. I'll answer't at sessions, so my wife may be burnt i'
th' hand, too.
    ANS. Take 'em in both ; bury him, for he's
       dead.
    2 MAD. Ay, indeed, I am dead ; put me, I
pray, into a good pit-hole.
    3 MAD. I'll answer't at sessions.
        [*Servants* remove 2 *and* 3 *Madmen.*]

        Enter BELLAFRONT *mad.*

    ANS. How now, huswife,[62] whither gad you?
    BELL. A-nutting, forsooth. How do you,
gaffer? How do you, gaffer? There's [360
a French cur[t]sey for you, too.
    FLU. 'T is Bellafront.
    PIO. 'T is the punk, by th' Lord.
    DUKE. Father, what's she, I pray?
    ANS.   As yet I know not ;
She came but in this day, talks little idly,
And therefore has the freedom of the house.
    BELL. Do not you know me? — nor you? —
nor you? — nor you?

[59] A burning raisin floating on a cup of liquor
and swallowed flaming. Needless to say, it exists
here only in the lunatic's imagination.
[60] A common expression.
[61] Bang! Mod. eds. unnecessarily add "Strikes
him."   [62] Hussy, wench.

OMNES. No, indeed.

BELL. Then you are an ass, — and you [370 an ass, — and you are an ass, — for I know you.

ANS. Why, what are they? Come, tell me, what are they?

BELL. They're fish-wives; will you buy any gudgeons? [63]

God's santy! [64] yonder come friars; I know them, too. —

Enter HIPPOLITO, MATHEO, *and* INFELICHE, *disguis'd in the habits of friars.*

How do you, friar?

ANS. Nay, nay, away; you must not trouble friars. —

[*aside to* HIPPOLITO *and his companions*] The Duke is here; speak nothing.

BELL. Nay, indeed, you shall not go; we'll run at barley-break [65] first, and you shall [380 be in hell.

MAT. [*aside*] My punk turn'd mad whore, as all her fellows are!

HIP. [*aside to* INFELICHE *and* MATHEO] Say nothing; but steal hence, when you spy time.

ANS. I'll lock you up, if y'are unruly; fie!

BELL. Fie! Marry, so; they shall not go indeed, till I ha' told 'em their fortunes.

DUKE. Good father, give her leave.

BELL. Ay, pray, good father, and I'll give you my blessing.

ANS. Well then, be brief; but if you are thus unruly,   390

I'll have you lock'd up fast.

PIO.   Come, to their fortunes.

BELL. Let me see; one, two, three, and four. I'll begin with the little friar [66] first. Here's a fine hand, indeed; I never saw friar have such a dainty hand; here's a hand for a lady. Here's your fortune:

You love a friar better than a nun;

Yet long you'll love no friar, nor no friar's son.

Bow a little, the line of life is out, yet I'm afraid,

For all you're holy, you'll not die a maid. [400

God give you joy! — Now to you, Friar Tuck.[67]

MAT. God send me good luck.

BELL. You love one, and one loves you;

You are a false knave, and she's a Jew; [68]

Here is a dial that false ever goes —

MAT. Oh, your wit drops!

BELL.   Troth, so does your nose! —

Nay, let's shake hands with you, too; pray open, here's a fine hand!

Ho friar, ho! God be here!

So He had need. You'll keep good cheer; [410

Here's a free table,[69] but a frozen breast;

For you'll starve those that love you best.[70]

Yet you have good fortune, for if I am no liar,

Then you are no friar; nor you, nor you no friar!

Ha, ha, ha, ha!   *Discovers them.*

DUKE. Are holy habits cloaks for villany? Draw all your weapons.

HIP. Do, draw all your weapons.

DUKE. Where are your weapons? Draw.

OMNES. The friar has gull'd us of 'em.

MAT.   O rare trick! [420

You ha' learn'd one mad point of arithmetic.

HIP. Why swells your spleen [71] so high? Against what bosom

Would you your weapons draw? Her's? 'T is your daughter's.

Mine? 'T is your son's.

DUKE.   Son?

MA[T].   Son, by yonder sun.

HIP. You cannot shed blood here but 't is your own;

To spill your own blood were damnation.

Lay smooth that wrinkled brow, and I will throw

Myself beneath your feet;

Let it [72] be rugged still and flinted o'er,[73]

What can come forth but sparkles, that will burn   430

Yourself and us? She's mine; my claim's most good;

She's mine by marriage, though she's yours by blood.

[ANS., *kneeling*] [74] I have a hand, dear Lord, deep in this act,

For I foresaw this storm, yet willingly

Put forth to meet it. Oft have I seen a father

Washing the wounds of his dear son in tears,

---

[63] Since this small fish was used for bait to catch larger fish, one who takes a gudgeon is a fool.

[64] Probably from "sanctity."

[65] A country game, played by couples, one of which was in "hell" and was obliged to catch the other players.

[66] Infeliche.

[67] For, like Matheo in this disguise, Robin Hood's chaplain was not all his gown indicated.

[68] *I.e.*, a wicked person.

[69] With a play on "table" = palm.

[70] Bellafront alludes to Hippolito's rejection of her love.

[71] Anger.

[72] Your brow.

[73] Mod. eds. *ore.* Q₁ *o're.*

[74] Old eds. print this speech as a continuation of Hippolito's.

A son to curse the sword that struck his father,
Both slain i' th' quarrel of your families.
Those scars are now ta'en off ; and I beseech
   you
To seal our pardon ! All was to this end : [440
To turn the ancient hates of your two houses
To fresh green friendship, that your loves
   might look
Like the spring's forehead, comfortably sweet,
And your vex'd souls in peaceful union meet.
Their blood will now be yours, yours will be
   theirs,
And happiness shall crown your silver hairs.

   FLU. You see, my Lord, there's now no
   remedy.

   OMNES. Beseech your Lordship !

   DUKE. You beseech fair ; you have me in
   in place fit
To bridle me. — Rise, friar ; you may be glad
You can make madmen tame, and tame men
   mad.   451
Since Fate hath conquered, I must rest con-
   tent ;
To strive now would but add new punishment.
I yield unto your happiness ; be blest ;
Our families shall henceforth breathe in rest.

   OMNES. O happy change !

   DUKE.   Yours now is my con[t]ent ;
I throw upon your joys my full consent.

   BELL. Am not I a good girl, for finding
" The Friar in the Well ? "[75] Gods so, you
are a brave man ! Will not you buy [460
me some sugarplums, because I am so good
a fortune-teller ?

   DUKE. Would thou hadst wit, thou pretty
   soul, to ask,
As I have will to give.

   BELL. Pretty soul ? A pretty soul is better
than a pretty body. Do not you know my
pretty soul ? I know you. Is not your name
Matheo ?

   MAT. Yes, lamb.

   BELL. Baa, lamb ! there you lie, for [470
I am mutton. — Look, fine man ! he was
mad for me once, and I was mad for him once,
and he was mad for her once, and were you
never mad ? Yes, I warrant ; I had a fine
jewel once, a very fine jewel, and that naughty
man stole it away from me, a very fine [and a
rich] [76] jewel.

   DUKE. What jewel, pretty maid ?

   BELL. Maid ? Nay, that's a lie. Oh,
't was a very rich jewel, call'd a maidenhead :
and had not you it, leerer ?   481

   MAT. Out, you mad ass ! away !

   DUKE.   Had he thy maidenhead ?
He shall make thee amends, and marry thee.

   BELL. Shall he ? O brave Arthur of Bradley,[77] then !

   DUKE. An if he bear the mind of a gentleman, I know he will.

   MAT. I think I rifled her of some such paltry jewel.

   DUKE. Did you ? Then marry her ; you
   see the wrong   490
Has led her spirits into a lunacy.

   MAT. How ? marry her, my Lord ? 'Sfoot,
marry a madwoman ? Let a man get the tamest wife he can come by, she 'll be mad enough
afterward, do what he can.

   DUKE. Nay then, Father Anselmo here
   shall do his best
To bring her to her wits ; and will you then ?

   MAT. I cannot tell ; I may choose.

   DUKE. Nay, then, law shall compel. I tell
   you, sir,
So much her hard fate moves me, you should
   not breathe   500
Under this air, unless you married her.

   MAT. Well, then, when her wits stand in
   their right place,
I 'll marry her.

   BELL. I thank your Grace. — Matheo, thou
   art mine !
I am not mad, but put on this disguise
Only for you, my Lord ; for you can tell
Much wonder of me. But you are gone ; fare-
   well. —
Matheo, thou didst first turn my soul black ;
Now make it white again. I do protest,
I 'm pure as fire now, chaste as Cynthia's
   breast.   510

   HIP. I durst be sworn, Matheo, she 's indeed.

   MAT. Cony-catch'd, gull'd ! Must I sail in
   your fly-boat,[78]
Because I help'd to rear your mainmast first ?
Plague 'found [79] you for 't ; 't is well.
The cuckold's stamp goes current in all na-
   tions ;
Some men have horns given them at their crea-
   tions.
If I be one of those, why so ; 't is better

---

[75] The title of a popular tale and ballad, in which
a virtuous maid plays a trick on a would-be seducer.

[76] Om. Q1.

[77] The ballads about this popular character deal
largely with his marriage.

[78] A fast sailing vessel.

[79] Confound.

To take a common wench, and make her good,
Than one that simpers, and at first will scarce
Be tempted forth over the threshold door, [520
Yet in one se'nnight, zounds, turns arrant
      whore.
Come wench, thou shalt be mine ; give me thy
      golls,[80]
We 'll talk of legs [81] hereafter. — See, my Lord,
God give us joy !
      OMNES. God give you joy !

Enter Candido's wife [VIOLA] *and* GEORGE.

      GEO. Come Mistress, we are in Bedlam
now ; mass, and see, we come in pudding-
time,[82] for here 's the Duke.
      VIO. My husband, good my Lord !
      DUKE. Have I thy husband?   530
      CAST. It 's Candido, my Lord ; he 's here
among the lunatics. Father Anselmo, pray
fetch him forth. [*Exit* ANSELMO.] This
mad woman is his wife ; and though she were
not with child, yet did she long most spitefully
to have her husband mad ; and because she
would be sure he should turn Jew, she plac'd
him here in Bethlem. Yonder he comes.

Enter CANDIDO *with* ANSELMO.

      DUKE. Come hither, signior ; are you mad?
      CAND. You are not mad.   540
      DUKE. Why, I know that.
      CAND. Then may you know I am not mad,
      that know
You are not mad, and that you are the Duke.
None is mad here but one. — How do you,
      Wife?
What do you long for now? — Pardon, my
      Lord :
She had lost her child's nose else. I did cut
      out
Pennyworths of lawn ; the lawn was yet mine
      own.
A carpet was [83] my gown ; yet 't was mine own.
I wore my man's coat, yet the cloth mine own.
Had a crack'd crown — the crown was yet
      mine own.   550
She says for this I 'm mad ; were her words
      true,
I should be mad indeed. O foolish skill ! [84]
Is patience madness? I 'll be a madman still.

80 Hands.
81 Bows. Evidently Bellafront has started to
kneel or to curtsey in gratitude.
82 In good time. Dinner often began with pudding. (Skeat.)
83 Q₁ *was yet.*
84 Reason.

      VIO. [*kneeling*] Forgive me, and I 'll vex
      your spirit no more.
      DUKE. Come, come ; we 'll have you
      friends ; join hearts, join hands.
      CAND. See, my Lord, we are even. —
[*to* VIOLA] Nay, rise ; for ill deeds kneel unto
      none but Heaven.
      DUKE. Signior, methinks patience has laid
      on you
Such heavy weight that you should loathe it.
      CAND.   Loathe it !
      DUKE. For he whose breast is tender, blood
      so cool,   560
That no wrongs heat it, is a patient fool.
What comfort do you find in being so calm?
      CAND. That which green wounds receive
      from sovereign balm.
Patience, my Lord ! why, 't is the soul of
      peace ;
Of all the virtues, 't is near'st kin to Heaven.
It makes men look like gods. The best of men
That e'er wore earth about him was a sufferer,
A soft, meek, patient, humble, tranquil spirit,
The first true gentleman that ever breath'd.
The stock of patience, then, cannot be
      poor ;   570
All it desires, it has ; what monarch more?
It is the greatest enemy to law
That can be ; for it doth embrace all wrongs,
And so chains up lawyers' and women's
      tongues.
'T is the perpetual prisoner's liberty,
His walks and orchards. 'T is the bond slave's
      freedom,
And makes him seem proud of each iron chain,
As though he wore it more for state than pain.
It is the beggars' music, and thus sings,   [579
Although their bodies beg, their souls are kings.
O my dread Liege ! it is the sap of bliss,
Rears us aloft, makes men and angels kiss.
And last of all, to end a household strife,
It is the honey 'gainst a waspish wife.
      DUKE. Thou giv'st it lively colors ; who
      dare say
He 's mad, whose words march in so good array?
'T were sin all women should such husbands
      have,
For every man must then be his wife's slave.
Come, therefore ; you shall teach our court to
      shine ;
So calm a spirit is worth a golden mine.   [590
Wives with meek husbands that to vex them
      long,
In Bedlam must they dwell, else dwell they
      wrong.   *Exeunt.*

THE
SECOND
PART OF THE
HONEST VVHORE,

VVITH THE HVMORS
of the Patient Man, the Impatient
Wife : the Honeſt Whore, perſwaded by
ſtrong Arguments to turne Curtizan
againe: her braue refuting thoſe
Arguments.

And laſtly, the Comicall Paſſages of an Italian
Bridewell, where the Sцæne ends.

Written by TH O M A S DE K K E R.

LONDON,
Printed by *Elizabeth All-de,* for *Nathaniel Butter.*
An. Dcm. 1 6 3 0.

THE HONEST WHORE

PART II

BY

THOMAS DEKKER

[DRAMATIS PERSONÆ

GASPARO TREBATZI, Duke of Milan.
HIPPOLITO, a count, husband to Infeliche.
ORLANDO FRISCOBALDO, father to Bellafront.
MATHEO, husband to Bellafront.
CANDIDO, a linen-draper.
LODOVICO SFORSA, a courtier.
BERALDO,
CAROLO, } gentlemen in Hippolito's
FONTINELL, } service.
ASTOLFO,
ANTONIO GEORGIO, a poor scholar.
LUKE, a prentice to Candido.

BRYAN, an Irish footman.
BOTS, a pander.
Masters of Bridewell, Apprentices, Servants,
Constable, Billmen, etc.

INFELICHE, wife to Hippolito.
BELLAFRONT, wife to Matheo.
Candido's Bride.
MISTRESS HORSELEECH, a bawd.
DOROTHEA TARGET,
PENELOPE WHOREHOUND, } harlots.
CATHARINA BOUNTINALL,

THE SCENE — *Milan.*]

ACT I — SCENE I [1]

Enter, at one door, BERALDO, CAROLO, FONTI-
NELL, [*and*] ASTOLFO, *with* Serving Men, *or*
Pages, *attending on them; at another door,
enter* LODOVICO, *meeting them.*

LOD. Good day, gallants.

OMNES. Good morrow, sweet Lodovico.

LOD. How doest thou, Carolo?

CAR. Faith, as physicians do in a plague :
see the world sick, and am well myself.

FON. Here 's a sweet morning, gentlemen.

LOD. Oh, a morning to tempt Jove from his
ningle,[2] Ganymede ; which is but to give dairy-
wenches green gowns [3] as they are going
a-milking. What, is thy lord stirring yet? [10

AST. Yes, he will not be hors'd this hour,
sure.

BER. My lady swears he shall, for she longs
to be at court.

CAR. Oh, we shall ride switch and spur ;
would we were there once.

Enter BRYAN, *the footman.*

LOD. How now, is thy lord ready?

BRY. No, so crees sa' [4] me ; my lady will
have some little ting in her pelly first.

CAR. Oh, then they 'll to breakfast. 20

LOD. Footman, does my Lord ride i' th'
coach with my Lady, or on horseback?

BRY. No, foot,[5] la ; my Lady will have me
Lord sheet wid her, my Lord will sheet in de
one side, and my Lady sheet in de toder side.
[*Exit.*]

LOD. My Lady sheet in de toder side ! Did
you ever hear a rascal talk so like a pagan?
Is 't not strange that a fellow of his star
should be seen here so long in Italy, yet
speak so from [6] a Christian? 30

Enter ANTONIO GEORGIO, *a poor scholar.*

AST. An Irishman in Italy ! that so strange ?
Why, the nation have running heads !
Exchange walk.[7]

LOD. Nay, Carolo, this is more strange ; I
ha' been in France — there 's few of them.
Marry, England they count a warm chimney
corner, and there they swarm like crickets to
the crevice of a brew-house ; but sir, in England I have noted one thing.

---

[1] A hall in Hippolito's house.   [2] Darling.
[3] From lying on the grass with their lovers.
[4] Christ save.   [5] By God's foot.
[6] Different from, unlike.
[7] Promenade, as on the Exchange. (Neilson.)

OMNES. What's that, what's that of England?   40

LOD. Marry this, sir — what's he yonder?

BER. A poor fellow would speak with my Lord.

LOD. In England, sir — troth, I ever laugh when I think on't : to see a whole nation should be mark'd i' th' forehead, as a man may say, with one iron — why, sir, there all coster-mongers [8] are Irishmen.

CAR. Oh, that's to show their antiquity, as coming from Eve, who was an apple-wife ; [50 and they take after the mother.

OMNES. Good, good ! ha, ha !

LOD. Why, then, should all your chimney-sweepers likewise be Irishmen? Answer that now ; come, your wit.

CAR. Faith, that's soon answered ; for St. Patrick, you know, keeps purgatory : he makes the fire, and his countrymen could do nothing, if they cannot sweep the chimneys.

OMNES. Good again.   60

LOD. Then, sir, have you many of them, like this fellow, especially those of his hair,[9] footmen to noblemen and others, and the knaves are very faithful where they love. By my faith, very proper [10] men, many of them, and as active as the clouds, — whirr, hah !

OMNES. Are they so?

LOD. And stout ! [11] exceeding stout ; why, I warrant, this precious wild villain, if he were put to 't, would fight more desperately [70 than sixteen Dunkirks.[12]

AST. The women, they say, are very fair.

LOD. No, no, our country [13] *bona-robas*,[14] oh ! are the sug'rest, delicious rogues !

AST. Oh, look, he has a feeling of them !

LOD. Not I, I protest. There's a saying when they commend nations. It goes, the Irishman for his hand, [the] Welshman for a leg, the Englishman for a face, the Dutch-man for a beard.   80

FON. I' faith, they may make swabbers [15] of them.

LOD. The Spaniard, — let me see, — for a little foot, I take it ; the Frenchman, — what a pox hath he? [16] And so of the rest. Are they at breakfast yet? Come walk.

AST. This Lodovico is a notable tongued fellow.

FON. Discourses well.

BER. And a very honest gentleman.   90

AST. Oh ! he's well valued by my Lord.

Enter BELLAFRONT, *with a petition.*

FON. How now, how now, what's she?

BER. Let's make towards her.

BELL. Will it be long, sir, ere my Lord come forth?

AST. Would you speak with my Lord?

LOD. How now, what's this, a nurse's bill? Hath any here got thee with child and now will not keep it?   99

BELL. No, sir, my business is unto my Lord.

LOD. He's about his own wife['s] now ; he'll hardly dispatch two causes in a morning.

AST. No matter what he says, fair lady ; he's a knight — there's no hold to be taken at his words.

FON. My Lord will pass this way presently.

BER. A pretty, plump rogue.

AST. A good lusty, bouncing baggage.

BER. Do you know her?

LOD. A pox on her, I was sure her name [110 was in my table-book [17] once. I know not of what cut her die is now, but she has been more common than tobacco ; this is she that had the name of the Honest Whore.

OMNES. Is this she?

LOD. This is the blackamoor that by wash-ing was turned white ; this is the birding-piece [18] new scoured ; this is she that, if any of her religion can be saved, was saved by my Lord Hippolito.   120

AST. She has been a goodly creature.

LOD. She has been ! that's the epitaph of all whores. I'm well acquainted with the poor gentleman her husband. Lord ! what for-tunes that man has overreached ! She knows not me, yet I have been in her company ; I scarce know her, for the beauty of her cheek hath, like the moon, suff'red strange eclipses since I beheld it : but women are like medlars, — no sooner ripe but rotten : [130 A woman last was made, but is spent first ; Yet man is oft proved in performance worst.

OMNES. My Lord is come.

Enter HIPPOLITO, INFELICHE, *and two* Waiting Women.

HIP. We ha' wasted half this morning. Morrow, Lodovico.

LOD. Morrow, madam.

---

[8] Fruit peddlers.   [9] Presumably red.
[10] Handsome.   [11] Brave.
[12] *I.e.*, privateers from that port.
[13] Native ; not = rural.   [14] Handsome wenches.
[15] Mops.
[16] The answer is, of course, the pox ! *i.e.*, syphilis.

[17] Memorandum book.
[18] Fowling-piece, light gun.

HIP. Let's away to horse.

OMNES. Ay, ay, to horse, to horse.

BELL. I do beseech your Lordship, let your eye [19]

Read o'er this wretched paper.

HIP.   I'm in haste;

Pray thee, good woman, take some apter time.

INF. Good woman, do.   141

BELL. Oh, 'las! it does concern a poor man's life.

HIP. Life! — Sweetheart, seat yourself; I'll but read this and come.

LOD. What stockings have you put on this morning, madam? If they be not yellow,[20] change them; that paper is a letter from some wench to your husband.   148

INF. Oh sir, that cannot make me jealous.[21]

       Exeunt [all except HIPPOLITO, BEL-
            LAFRONT, *and* ANTONIO].

HIP. Your business, sir? To me?

ANT.   Yes, my good Lord.

HIP. Presently, sir. — Are you Matheo's wife?

BELL. That most unfortunate woman.

HIP.   I'm sorry
These storms are fallen on him; I love Matheo,
And any good shall do him; he and I
Have sealed two bonds of friendship, which are strong
In me, however Fortune does him wrong.[22]
He speaks here he's condemned. Is't so?

BELL. Too true.

HIP. What was he whom he killed? Oh, his name's here —

Giacomo, son to the Florentine [23]   160
Old Giacomo, a dog, that, to meet profit,
Would to the very eyelids wade in blood
Of his own children. Tell Matheo
The Duke, my father, hardly shall deny
His signed pardon. 'T was fair fight, yes,
If rumor's tongue go true; so writes he here. —
To-morrow morning I return from court;
Pray be you here then. — [*to* ANTONIO] I'll have done, sir, straight : —
But in troth say, are you Matheo's wife?
You have forgot me.

BELL.   No, my Lord.

<hr>

[19] This and other lines of this scene (*e.g.*, 159–166) are printed as prose in Q.

[20] The color of jealousy.

[21] Trisyllabic : jealous.

[22] Injures him.

[23] Mod. eds. supply punctuation here; it is more likely that "old", the first word of this line in Q, should stand as in the present text. "'T was fair fight", which does not fit "Old" Giacomo.

HIP.   Your turner, [170
That made you smooth to run an even bias; [24]
You know I loved you when your very soul
Was full of discord. Art not a good wench still?

BELL. Umph, when I had lost my way to Heaven, you showed it;
I was new born that day.

        Re-enter LODOVICO.

LOD. 'Sfoot, my Lord, your lady asks if you have not left your wench yet? When you get in once, you never have done. Come, come, come, pay your old score, and send her packing; come.   180

HIP. Ride softly [25] on before; I'll o'ertake you.

LOD. Your lady swears she'll have no riding on before, without ye.

HIP. Prithee, good Lodovico.

LOD. My Lord, pray hasten.

HIP. I come.   [*Exit* LODOVICO.]
To-morrow let me see you; fare you well;
Commend me to Matheo. Pray one word more :
Does not your father live about the court?

BELL. I think he does, but such rude spots of shame   190
Stick on my cheek that he scarce knows my name.

HIP. Orlando Friscobaldo, is't not?

BELL.   Yes, my Lord.

HIP. What does he for you?

BELL.   All he should; when children
From duty start, parents from love may swerve.
He nothing does, for nothing I deserve.

HIP. Shall I join him unto you, and restore you
To wonted grace?

BELL.   It is impossible.

HIP. It shall be put to trial; fare you well.
             Exit BELLAFRONT.
The face I would not look on! [26] Sure then 't was rare,   199
When, in despite of grief, 't is still thus fair. —
Now, sir, your business with me.

ANT.   I am bold
To express my love and duty to your Lordship
In these few leaves.

<hr>

[24] The bias of a bowl deflected it from a direct course. Hippolito credits himself with having "turned" Bellafront on his lathe and made her without blemish and capable of direct and chaste conduct.

[25] At a moderate pace.   [26] In *Part I*.

Hɪᴘ.   A book !
Aɴᴛ.   Yes, my good Lord.
Hɪᴘ. Are you a scholar?
Aɴᴛ.   Yes, my Lord, a poor one.
Hɪᴘ. Sir, you honor me.
Kings may be scholars' patrons ; but, faith,
      tell me,
To how many hands besides hath this bird
      flown,
How many partners share with me? [27]
Aɴᴛ.   Not one,
In troth, not one ; your name I held more
      dear.
I'm not, my Lord, of that low character. [210
Hɪᴘ. Your name, I pray?
Aɴᴛ.   Antonio Georgio.
Hɪᴘ. Of Milan?
Aɴᴛ.   Yes, my Lord,
Hɪᴘ.   I'll borrow leave
To read you o'er, and then we'll talk ; till then
Drink up this gold ; good wits should love
      good wine ;
This of your loves, the earnest that of mine. —

Re-enter Bʀʏᴀɴ.

How now, sir, where's your lady? not gone
      yet?
Bʀʏ. I fart di lady is run away from dee, a
mighty deal of ground ; she sent me back for
dine own sweet face. I pray dee come, my
Lord, away ; wu't tow go now?   220
    Hɪᴘ. Is the coach gone? Saddle my horse,
      the sorrel.
Bʀʏ. A pox a' de horse's nose, he is a lousy,
rascally fellow. When I came to gird his
belly, his scurvy guts rumbled ; di horse
farted in my face, and dow knowest an Irishman cannot abide a fart. But I have saddled
de hobbyhorse,[28] di fine hobby is ready. I
pray dee, my good sweet Lord, wi't tow go
now, and I will run to de devil before dee?
    Hɪᴘ. Well, sir. — I pray let's see you,
Master Scholar.   230
Bʀʏ. Come, I pray dee ; wu't come, sweet
face? Go.   *Exeunt.*

[Scᴇɴᴇ II] [29]

Enter Lᴏᴅᴏᴠɪᴄᴏ, Cᴀʀᴏʟᴏ, Aꜱᴛᴏʟꜰᴏ, [*and*]
Bᴇʀᴀʟᴅᴏ.

Lᴏᴅ. Godso, gentlemen, what do we forget?
Oᴍɴᴇꜱ. What?

[27] Books were often dedicated to several patrons.
[28] A horse of small or medium size.
[29] An apartment in the Duke's palace.

Lᴏᴅ. Are not we all enjoined as this day —
Thursday, is't not? ay — as that day to be at
the linen-draper's house at dinner?
Cᴀʀ. Signior Candido, the patient man.
Aꜱᴛ. Afore Jove, true ; upon this day he's
married.
Bᴇʀ. I wonder that, being so stung with a
wasp before, he dares venture again to [10
come about the eaves amongst bees.
Lᴏᴅ. Oh, 't is rare sucking a sweet honeycomb ! Pray Heaven his old wife be buried
deep enough, that she rise not up to call for her
dance ! The poor fiddlers' instruments would
crack for it ; she'd tickle them. At any hand,
let's try what mettle is in his new bride ; if
there be none, we'll put in some. Troth, it's
a very noble citizen ; I pity he should marry
again. I'll walk along, for it is a good old [20
fellow.
Cᴀʀ. I warrant the wives of Milan would
give any fellow twenty thousand ducats, that
could but have the face to beg of the Duke
that all the citizens in Milan might be bound to
the peace of patience, as the linen-draper is.
Lᴏᴅ. Oh, fie upon 't ! 't would undo all us
that are courtiers ; we should have no whoe [30]
with the wenches then.

Enter Hɪᴘᴘᴏʟɪᴛᴏ.

Oᴍɴᴇꜱ. My Lord's come.   30
Hɪᴘ. How now, what news?
Oᴍɴᴇꜱ. None.
Lᴏᴅ. Your lady is with the Duke, her
father.
Hɪᴘ. And we'll to them both presently —
Who's that?

Enter Oʀʟᴀɴᴅᴏ Fʀɪꜱᴄᴏʙᴀʟᴅᴏ.

Aʟʟ. Signior Friscobaldo.
Hɪᴘ. Friscobaldo, oh, pray call him, and
leave me ; we two have business.
Cᴀʀ. Ho, Signior ! Signior Friscobaldo !
The Lord Hippolito.   40
          Exeunt [*all but* Hɪᴘᴘᴏʟɪᴛᴏ *and* Fʀɪꜱ-
              ᴄᴏʙᴀʟᴅᴏ].
Oʀʟ. My noble Lord : my Lord Hippolito !
the Duke's son ! his brave daughter's brave
husband ! how does your honor'd Lordship !
Does your nobility remember so poor a gentle-
man as Signior Orlando Friscobaldo? old, mad
Orlando?
Hɪᴘ. Oh, sir, our friends ! they ought to be
unto us as our jewels, as dearly valued, being
locked up and unseen, as when we wear them

[30] See on *Part I*, V, ii, 144.

in our hands. I see, Friscobaldo, age hath [50
not command of your blood ; for all Time's
sickle has gone over you, you are Orlando still.

ORL. Why, my Lord, are not the fields
mown and cut down, and stripp'd bare, and
yet wear they not pi'd coats again? Though
my head be like a leek, white, may not my
heart be like the blade, green?

HIP. Scarce can I read the stories on your
 brow,
Which age hath writ ; there you look youthful
 still.

ORL. I eat snakes,[31] my Lord, I eat [60
snakes. My heart shall never have a wrinkle
in it, so long as I can cry " Hem," with a clear
voice.

HIP. You are the happier man, sir.

ORL. Happy man? I 'll give you, my Lord,
the true picture of a happy man. I was turning leaves over this morning, and found it ; an
excellent Italian painter drew it ; if I have it in
the right colors, I 'll bestow it on your Lord-
ship.   70

HIP. I stay for it.

ORL. He that makes gold his wife but not
 his whore,
He that at noonday walks by a prison door,
He that i' th' sun is neither beam nor mote,
He that 's not mad after a petticoat,
He for whom poor men's curses dig no grave,
He that is neither lord's nor lawyer's slave,
He that makes this his sea, and that his shore,
He that in 's coffin is richer than before,
He that counts youth his sword and age his
 staff,   80
He whose right hand carves his own epitaph,
He that upon his deathbed is a swan,
And dead no crow — he is a happy man.

HIP. It 's very well ; I thank you for this
 picture.

ORL. After this picture, my Lord, do I strive
to have my face drawn ; for I am not covetous,
am not in debt, sit neither at the Duke's side,
nor lie at his feet. Wenching and I have done ;
no man I wrong, no man I fear, no man I fee ;
I take heed how far I walk, because I know [90
yonder 's my home ; I would not die like a
rich man, to carry nothing away save a winding
sheet, but like a good man, to leave Orlando
behind me. I sowed leaves in my youth, and
I reap now books in my age. I fill this hand,
and empty this ; and when the bell shall toll
for me, if I prove a swan, and go singing to my

nest, why so ! If a crow, throw me out for
carrion, and pick out mine eyes. May not
old Friscobaldo, my Lord, be merry now? [100
ha?

HIP. You may ; would I were partner in
 your mirth.

ORL. I have a little, have all things. I have
nothing ; I have no wife, I have no child, have
no chick ; and why should not I be in my jo-
cundary?[32]

HIP. Is your wife then departed?

ORL. She 's an old dweller in those high
countries, yet not from[33] me. Here, she 's
here ; but, before me, when a knave and a [110
quean are married, they commonly walk like
serjeants together ; but a good couple are
seldom parted.

HIP. You had a daughter, too, sir, had you
 not?

ORL. O my Lord ! this old tree had one
branch, and but one branch growing out of it.
It was young, it was fair, it was straight ; I
pru[n]'d it daily, dress'd it carefully, kept it
from the wind, help'd it to the sun ; yet for
all my skill in planting, it grew crooked, [120
it bore crabs. I hewed it down ; what 's become of it I neither know, nor care.

HIP. Then I can tell you what 's become
 of it ;
That branch is wither'd.

ORL.   So 't was long ago.

HIP. Her name I think was Bellafront ;
 she 's dead.

ORL. Ha? dead?

HIP. Yes ; what of her was left, not worth
 the keeping,
Even in my sight was thrown into a grave.

ORL. Dead ! my last and best peace go with
her ! I see Death 's a good trencherman ; [130
he can eat coarse homely meat, as well as the
daintiest.

HIP. Why, Friscobaldo, was she homely?

ORL. O my Lord ! a strumpet is one of the
Devil's vines ; all the sins, like so many poles,
are stuck upright out of hell, to be her props,
that she may spread upon them. And when
she 's ripe, every slave has a pull at her ; then
must she be press'd. The young, beautiful
grape sets the teeth of lust on edge, yet to [140
taste that lick'rish[34] wine is to drink a man's
own damnation. Is she dead?

---

[31] "A supposed receipt for restoring youth."
(Dyce.)

[32] Jocularity, merriment. Q *Iocundare.*
[33] Apart from.
[34] Tempting ; with a play on the meaning "lustful."

Hip. She's turned to earth.

Orl. Would she were turn'd to Heaven! Umh, is she dead? I am glad the world has lost one of his idols; no whoremonger will at midnight beat at the doors. In her grave sleep all my shame, and her own; and all my sorrows, and all her sins!

Hip. I'm glad you are wax, not marble; you are made   150
Of man's best temper; there are now good hopes
That all these heaps of ice about your heart,
By which a father's love was frozen up,
Are thawed in these sweet showers, fetch'd from your eyes:
We are ne'er like angels till our passion dies.
She is not dead, but lives under worse fate;
I think she's poor; and, more to clip her wings,
Her husband at this hour lies in the jail,
For killing of a man. To save his blood,
Join all your force with mine (mine shall be shown):   160
The getting of his life preserves your own.

Orl. In my daughter, you will say! Does she live then? I am sorry I wasted tears upon a harlot; but the best is I have a handkercher to drink them up; soap can wash them all out again. Is she poor?

Hip. Trust me, I think she is.

Orl. Then she's a right strumpet; I ne'er knew any of their trade rich two years to- gether. Sieves can hold no water, no[r] [170 harlots hoard up money; they have many vents, too many sluices to let it out; taverns, tailors, bawds, panders, fiddlers, swaggerers, fools, and knaves do all wait upon a common harlot's trencher. She is the gallipot to which these drones fly, not for love to the pot, but for the sweet sucket [35] within it, her money, her money.

Hip. I almost dare pawn my word, her bosom gives warmth to no such snakes. [180 When did you see her?

Orl. Not seventeen summers.

Hip. Is your hate so old?

Orl. Older; it has a white head, and shall never die till she be buried; her wrongs shall be my bedfellow.

Hip. Work yet his life, since in it lives her fame.

Orl. No let him hang, and half her infamy departs out of the world. I hate him for her;

[35] Confection.

he taught her first to taste poison. I hate [190 her for herself, because she refused my physic.

Hip. Nay, but Friscobaldo! —

Orl. I detest her, I defy [36] both; she's not mine, she's —

Hip. Hear her but speak.

Orl. I love no mermaids; I'll not be caught with a quail-pipe.[37]

Hip. Y' are now beyond all reason.

Orl. I am then a beast. Sir, I had rather be a beast, and not dishonor my creation, [200 than be a doting father and, like Time, be the destruction of mine own brood.

Hip. Is't dotage to relieve your child, being poor?

Orl. Is't fit for an old man to keep a whore?

Hip. 'T is charity, too.

Orl. 'T is foolery; relieve her! Were her cold limbs stretch'd out upon a bier, I would not sell this dirt under my nails To buy her an hour's breath, nor give this hair, Unless it were to choke her.   210

Hip. Fare you well, for I'll trouble you no more.   *Exit.*

Orl. And fare you well, sir.— Go thy ways; we have few lords of thy making, that love wenches for their honesty.— 'Las my girl! art thou poor? Poverty dwells next door to despair; there's but a wall between them. Despair is one of hell's catchpoles; and lest that devil arrest her, I'll to her. Yet she shall not know me; she shall drink of my wealth, as beggars do of running water, [220 freely, yet never know from what fountain's head it flows. Shall a silly bird pick her own breast to nourish her young ones, and can a father see his child starve? That were hard; the pelican does it, and shall not I? Yes, I will victual the camp for her, but it shall be by some stratagem. That knave there, her hus- band, will be hanged, I fear; I'll keep his neck out of the noose if I can, he shall not know how.

Enter two Serving Men.

How now, knaves? Whither wander [230 you?

1 Serv. To seek your Worship.

Orl. Stay, which of you has my purse? What money have you about you?

2 Serv. Some fifteen or sixteen pounds, sir.

Orl. Give it me. — I think I have some gold about me; yes, it's well. Leave my

[36] Renounce, disown.
[37] Used by fowlers to allure quails. (Dyce.)

lodging at court, and get you home. Come, sir, though I never turned any man out of doors, yet I 'll be so bold as to pull your [240 coat over your ears.

[ORLANDO *exchanges his cloak for the servant's coat.*]

1 SER. What do you mean to do, sir?

ORL. Hold thy tongue, knave ; take thou my cloak. I hope I play not the paltry merchant in this bart'ring. Bid the steward of my house sleep with open eyes in my absence, and to look to all things. Whatsoever I command by letters to be done by you, see it done. So, does it sit well?

2 SER. As if it were made for your [250 Worship.

ORL. You proud varlets, you need not be ashamed to wear blue,[38] when your master is one of your fellows. Away, do not see me.

BOTH. This is excellent.   *Exeunt.*

ORL. I should put on a worse suit, too ; perhaps I will. My vizard is on ; now to this masque. Say 1 should shave off this honor of an old man, or tie it up shorter. Well, I will spoil a good face for once. My beard being off, how should I look? Even like   261
A winter cuckoo, or unfeather'd owl ;
Yet better lose this hair, than lose her soul.
                                        Exit.

[SCENE III] [39]

Enter CANDIDO, LODOVICO, CAROLO, [ASTOLFO], *other* Guests, *and* Bride, *with* [LUKE *and other*] Prentices.

CAND. O gentlemen, so late ! Y' are very welcome ; pray sit down.

LOD. Carolo, didst e'er see such a nest of caps? [40]

AST. Methinks it 's a most civil and most comely sight.

LOD. What does he i' th' middle look like?

AST. Troth, like a spire steeple in a country village overpeering so many thatch'd houses.

LOD. It 's, rather, a long pikestaff [10 against so many bucklers without pikes ; [41] they sit for all the world like a pair of organs,[42] and he 's the tall great roaring pipe i' th' midst.

AST. Ha, ha, ha, ha !

CAND.   What 's that you laugh at, signiors?

LOD. Troth, shall I tell you, and aloud I 'll tell it ;
We laugh to see, yet laugh we not in scorn,
Amongst so many caps that long hat worn.

[1 GUEST.] Mine is as tall a felt [43] as any is this day in Milan, and therefore I love it ; for the block [44] was cleft out for my head, and [20 fits me to a hair.

CAND. Indeed you are good observers ; it shows strange.
But gentlemen, I pray neither contemn,
Nor yet deride a civil ornament ;
I could build so much in the round cap's praise
That 'bove this high roof I this flat [45] would raise.

LOD. Prithee, sweet bridegroom, do 't.

CAND. So [46] all these guests will pardon me, I 'll do 't.

OMNES. With all our hearts.

CAND. Thus, then, in the cap's honor : [30
To every sex and state, both nature, time,
The country's laws, yea, and the very clime,
Do allot distinct habits ; the spruce courtier
Jets [47] up and down in silk ; the warrior
Marches in buff ; the clown plods on in gray ;
But for these upper garments thus I say :
The seaman has his cap, par'd without brim ;
The gallant's head is feather'd — that fits him ;
The soldier has his morion,[48] women ha' tires ; [49]
Beasts have their headpieces, and men ha' theirs.   40

LOD. Proceed.

CAND. Each degree has his fashion ; it 's fit then,
One should be laid by for the citizen ;
And that 's the cap, which you see swells not high,
For caps are emblems of humility.
It is a citizen's badge, and first was worn
By th' Romans ; for when any bondman's turn
Came to be made a freeman, thus 't was said,
He to the cap was call'd, that is, was made
Of Rome a freeman ; but was first close shorn ;
And so a citizen's hair is still short worn. [51

LOD. That close shaving made barbers a company, and now every citizen uses it.

CAND. Of geometric figures the most rare,
And perfect'st, are the circle and the square ;
The city and the school much build upon
These figures, for both love proportion.

---

38 The usual color of servants' livery.
39 A room in Candido's house. — Dyce inquires, " Ought not Beraldo to be of the party?''
40 Citizens. See on *Part I*, III, i, 124.
41 The spikes in the centre of bucklers.
42 A pipe organ.
43 Hat. Q assigns this speech to Lodovico.
44 Mold.   45 Flat cap.   46 If.   47 Struts.
48 Steel hat or helmet.   49 Headdresses.

The city cap is round, the scholar's square,
To show that government and learning are
The perfect'st limbs i' th' body of a state ; [60
For without them, all 's disproportionate.
If the cap had no honor, this might rear it :
The reverend fathers of the law do wear it.
It 's light for summer, and in cold it sits
Close to the skull, [a] warm house for the wits ;
It shows the whole face boldly, 't is not made
As if a man to look [out] [50] were afraid,
Nor like a draper's shop with broad dark shed,
For he 's no citizen that hides his head.
Flat caps as proper are to city gowns   70
As to armors helmets, or to kings their crowns.
Let then the city cap by none be scorn'd,
Since with it princes' heads have been adorn'd.
If more the round cap's honor you would know,
How would this long gown with this steeple [51]
    show?
  ALL. Ha, ha, ha ! most vile, most ugly.
  CAND. Pray, signior, pardon me ; 't was
    done in jest.
  BRIDE. A cup of claret wine there.
  1 [PREN.] Wine? yes, forsooth, wine for the
    bride.
  CAR. You ha' well set out the cap, sir.   80
  LOD. Nay, that 's flat.
  CAND. A health !
  LOD. Since his cap 's round, that shall go
    round. Be bare,
For in the cap's praise all of you have share.
        [*All uncover and drink. As he offers
          the cup to her*] the BRIDE *hits the*
          Prentice [52] *on the lips.*
The bride 's at cuffs.
  CAND. Oh, peace, I pray thee ; thus [53] far
    off I stand —
I spied the error of my servants ;
She call'd for claret, and you fill'd out sack.
That cup give me — 't is for an old man's
    back,
And not for hers. Indeed, 't was but mis-
    taken ;   90
Ask all these else.
  OMNES.   No faith, 't was but mistaken.
  1 [PREN.] Nay, she took it right enough.
  CAND. Good Luke, reach her that glass of
claret. Here Mistress Bride, pledge me there.
  BRIDE. Now I 'll none.   *Exit* Bride.
  CAND. How now?
  LOD. Look what your mistress ails.

[50] Emend. Dyce ; Q *on 't.*
[51] The tall, pointed hat worn by 1 Guest.
[52] Presumably Luke.
[53] Dyce conj. *though.*

  1 [PREN.] Nothing, sir, but about filling a
wrong glass — a scurvy trick.   99
  CAND. I pray you, hold your tongue. — My
servant there tells me she is not well.
  OMNES. Step to her, step to her.
  LOD. A word with you : do ye hear? This
wench, your new wife, will take you down in
your wedding shoes, unless you hang her up in
her wedding garters !
  CAND. How, hang her in her garters !
  LOD. Will you be a tame pigeon still?
Shall your back be like a tortoise shell, to let
carts go over it, yet not to break? This [110
she-cat will have more lives than your last puss
had, and will scratch worse, and mouse you
worse ; look to 't.
  CAND. What would you have me do, sir?
  LOD. What would I have you do ! Swear,
swagger, brawl, fling ! for fighting it 's no matter ; we ha' had knocking pusses [54] enow
already. You know that a woman was made
of the rib of a man, and that rib was crooked.
The moral of which is that a man must [120
from his beginning be crooked to his wife.
Be you like an orange to her : let her cut
you never so fair, be you sour as vinegar.
Will you be ruled by me?
  CAND. In anything that 's civil, honest, and
just.
  LOD. Have you ever a prentice's suit will
fit me?
  CAND. I have the very same which myself
wore.   130
  LOD. I 'll send my man for 't within this
half hour, and within this two hours I 'll be
your prentice. The hen shall not overcrow
the cock ; I 'll sharpen your spurs.
  CAND. It will be but some jest, sir?
  LOD. Only a jest ; farewell. — Come, Ca-
rolo.
        Exeunt [LODOVICO, CAROLO, *and* AS-
          TOLFO].
  OMNES. We 'll take our leaves, sir, too.
  CAND.   Pray conceit not ill
Of my wife's sudden rising. This young
    knight,
Sir Lodovico, is deep seen in physic,   140
And he tells me, the disease, call'd the mother,[55]
Hangs on my wife ; it is a vehement heaving
And beating of the stomach, and that swelling
Did with the pain thereof cramp up her arm,
That hit his lips, and brake the glass — no
    harm ;
It was no harm !

[54] Wenches.   [55] Hysteria.

OMNES.   No, signior, none at all.

CAND. The straightest arrow may fly wide
by chance.

But come, we'll close this brawl up in some
dance.   *Exeunt.*

[ACT II — SCENE I] [1]

Enter BELLAFRONT *and* MATHEO.

BELL. O my sweet husband! wert thou in
thy grave and art alive again? Oh, welcome,
welcome!

MAT. Doest know me? My cloak, prithee,
lay't up. Yes, faith, my winding sheet was
taken out of lavender, to be stuck with rosemary: [2] I lack'd but the knot [3] here, or here;
yet if I had had it, I should ha' made a wry
mouth at the world like a plaice.[4] But,
sweetest villain, I am here now, and I will [10
talk with thee soon.

BELL. And glad am I th' art here.

MAT. Did these heels caper in shackles?
Ah! my little plump rogue, I'll bear up for
all this, and fly high. *Catso, catso!* [5]

BELL. Matheo.

MAT. What sayest, what sayest? O brave
fresh air! A pox on these grates and jingling
of keys, and rattling of iron. I'll bear up;
I'll fly high, wench; hang't off.[6]   20

BELL. Matheo, prithee, make thy prison
thy glass,

And in it view the wrinkles and the scars

By which thou wert disfigured; viewing them,
mend them.

MAT. I'll go visit all the mad rogues now,
and the good roaring boys.[7]

BELL. Thou doest not hear me?

MAT. Yes, faith, do I.

BELL. Thou hast been in the hands of misery,

And ta'en strong physic; prithee now be
sound.

MAT. Yes. 'Sfoot, I wonder how the [30
inside of a tavern looks now. Oh, when shall
I bizzle, bizzle.[8]

[1] A room in Matheo's house.
[2] On the occasion of his funeral, as an emblem
of remembrance.
[3] Of the hangman's noose.
[4] Which was proverbially wry-mouthed.
[5] An obscene expression of contempt. (Ital. *cazzo*.)
[6] Cease this hanging round my neck. Cf. *A Midsummer Night's Dream*, III, ii, 260: "Hang off,
thou cat, thou burr." (Kittredge.)
[7] Roisterers.   [8] Bezzle, drink to excess.

BELL. Nay, see, th' art thirsty still for
poison! Come,

I will not have thee swagger.

MAT.   Honest ape's face!

BELL. 'T is that sharp'ned an axe to cut
thy throat.

Good love, I would not have thee sell thy substance

And time, worth all, in those damned shops of
hell,

Those dicing houses, that stand never well

But when they stand most ill; that four-
squar'd sin [9]

Has almost lodg'd us in the beggar's inn.   40

Besides, to speak which even my soul does
grieve,

A sort [10] of ravens have hung upon thy sleeve,

And fed upon thee. Good Mat, if you please,

Scorn to spread wing amongst so base as
these;

By them thy fame is speckled, yet it shows

Clear amongst them; so crows are fair with
crows.

Custom in sin gives sin a lovely dye;

Blackness in Moors is no deformity.

MAT. Bellafront, Bellafront, I protest to
thee, I swear, as I hope my soul, I will [50
turn over a new leaf. The prison I confess
has bit me; the best man that sails in such a
ship may be lousy.

BELL. One knocks at door.

MAT. I'll be the porter. They shall see
a jail cannot hold a brave spirit; I'll fly high.
                              Exit.

BELL. How wild is his behavior! Oh, I
fear

He's spoil'd by prison; he's half damned
comes there.

But I must sit all storms. When a full sail

His fortunes spread, he lov'd me; being now
poor,   60

I'll beg for him, and no wife can do more.

Re-enter MATHEO, *with* ORLANDO *like a
serving man.*

MAT. Come in, pray! Would you speak
with me, sir?

ORL. Is your name Signior Matheo?

MAT. My name is Signior Matheo.

ORL. Is this gentlewoman your wife, sir?

MAT. This gentlewoman is my wife, sir.

ORL. The Destinies spin a strong and even
thread of both your loves! — The mother's
own face, I ha' not forgot that. — I'm [70

[9] Dicing.   [10] Flock, set.

an old man, sir, and am troubled with a whore-son salt rheum, that I cannot hold my water. — Gentlewoman, the last man I served was your father.

BELL. My father? Any tongue that sounds his name
Speaks music to me ; welcome, good old man !
How does my father? lives he? has he health?
How does my father? — I so much do shame him,
So much do wound him, that I scarce dare name him.

ORL. I can speak no more. 80

MAT. How, old lad, what, doest cry?

ORL. The rheum still, sir, nothing else ; I should be well season'd,[11] for mine eyes lie in brine. Look you, sir, I have a suit to you.

MAT. What is 't, my little white-pate?

ORL. Troth, sir, I have a mind to serve your Worship.

MAT. To serve me? Troth, my friend, my fortunes are, as a man may say —

ORL. Nay, look you, sir, I know, when [90 all sins are old in us and go upon crutches, that covetousness does but then lie in her cradle ;[12] 't is not so with me. Lechery loves to dwell in the fairest lodging, and covetousness in the oldest buildings, that are ready to fall; but my white head, sir, is no inn for such a gossip.[13] If a serving man at my years be not stored with biscuit enough, that has sailed about the world, to serve him the voyage out of his life, and to bring him east [100 home, ill pity but all his days should be fasting days. I care not so much for wages, for I have scraped a handful of gold together. I have a little money, sir, which I would put into your Worship's hands, not so much to make it more —

MAT. No, no, you say well, thou sayest well; but I must tell you — how much is the money, sayest thou?

ORL. About twenty pound, sir. 110

MAT. Twenty pound? Let me see ; that shall bring thee in, after[14] ten *per centum per annum* —

ORL. No, no, no, sir, no ; I cannot abide to have money engender ; fie upon this silver lechery, fie ! If I may have meat to my mouth, and rags to my back, and a flock-bed[15] to

snort[16] upon, when I die the longer liver take all.

MAT. A good old boy, i' faith ! If thou [120 servest me, thou shalt eat as *I* eat, drink as *I* drink, lie as *I* lie, and ride as *I* ride.

ORL. [*aside*] That's if you have money to hire horses.

MAT. Front, what doest thou think on 't? This good old lad here shall serve me.

BELL. Alas, Matheo, wilt thou load a back That is already broke?

MAT. Peace, pox on you, peace. There's a trick in 't ; I fly high ; it shall be so, [130 Front, as I tell you. — Give me thy hand ; thou shalt serve me i' faith : welcome. As for your money —

ORL. Nay, look you, sir, I have it here.

MAT. Pish, keep it thyself, man, and then th'art sure 't is safe.

ORL. Safe ! an 't were ten thousand ducats, your Worship should be my cash-keeper. I have heard what your Worship is — [*aside*] an excellent dunghill cock, to scatter all [140 abroad ; but I 'll venture twenty pounds on 's head. [*Gives money to* MATHEO.]

MAT. And didst thou serve my worshipful father-in-law, Signior Orlando Friscobaldo, that madman, once?

ORL. I served him so long till he turned me out of doors.

MAT. It 's a notable chuff ;[17] I ha' not seen him many a day.

ORL. No matter an you ne'er see him ; [150 it 's an arrant grandee, a churl, and as damn'd a cutthroat.

BELL. Thou villain, curb thy tongue !
Thou art a Judas,
To sell thy master's name to slander thus.

MAT. Away, ass ! He speaks but truth, thy father is a —

BELL. Gentleman.

MAT. And an old knave. There 's more deceit in him than in sixteen 'pothecaries ; it 's a devil. Thou mayst beg, starve, hang, [160 damn ! does he send thee so much as a cheese?

ORL. Or so much as a gammon of bacon? he 'll give it his dogs first.

MAT. A jail, a jail.

ORL. A Jew, a Jew, sir.

MAT. A dog !

ORL. An English mastiff, sir.

MAT. Pox rot out his old stinking garbage !

---

[11] Preserved, pickled.
[12] *I.e.*, covetousness is an old man's vice.
[13] Companion, crony. [14] According to.
[15] *I.e.*, a mattress stuffed with woolen or cotton refuse.

[16] Snore.
[17] Churlish miser.

BELL. Art not ashamed to strike an absent
man thus? 170
Art not ashamed to let this vild [18] dog bark,
And bite my father thus? I'll not endure it.
Out of my doors, base slave!

MAT. Your doors, a vengeance? I shall
live to cut that old rogue's throat, for all you
take his part thus.

ORL. [aside] He shall live to see thee hang'd
first.

Enter HIPPOLITO.

MAT. Gods so, my Lord, your Lordship is
most welcome;
I'm proud of this, my Lord.

HIP. 　　　　Was bold to see you. [180
Is that your wife?

MAT. 　　　Yes, sir.

HIP. 　　　　　I'll borrow her lip.
[Kisses BELLAFRONT *and takes her
aside.*]

MAT. With all my heart, my Lord.

ORL. 　　　　Who's this, I pray, sir.

MAT. My Lord Hippolito; what's thy
name?

ORL. 　　Pacheco.

MAT. Pacheco, fine name; thou seest,
Pacheco, I keep company with no scoundrels,
nor base fellows.

HIP. Came not my footman to you?

BELL. 　　　　Yes, my Lord.

HIP. I sent by him a diamond and a letter.
Did you receive them?

BELL. 　　　　Yes, my Lord, I did.

HIP. Read you the letter?

BELL. 　　O'er and o'er 't is read. [190

HIP. And, faith, your answer?

BELL. 　　　　Now the time's not fit;
You see, my husband's here.

HIP. 　　　　I'll now then leave you,
And choose mine hour; but ere I part away,
Hark you, remember I must have no nay. —
Matheo, I will leave you.

MAT. 　　　　A glass of wine.

HIP. Not now; I'll visit you at other
times.
Y' are come off well, then?

MAT. Excellent well, I thank your Lordship. I owe you my life, my Lord; and will
pay my best blood in any service of yours. [200

HIP. I'll take no such dear payment.
Hark you, Matheo, I know the prison is a
gulf. [19] If money run low with you, my purse
is yours: call for it.

MAT. Faith, my Lord, I thank my stars,
they send me down some; I cannot sink, so
long as these bladders hold.

HIP. I will not see your fortunes ebb;
pray, try.
To starve in full barns were fond [20] modesty.

MAT. Open the door, sirrah. 210

HIP. [aside to FRISCOBALDO] Drink this,
and anon, I pray thee, give thy mistress this.
[HIPPOLITO *gives* FRISCOBALDO *money
and*] exit.

ORL. O noble spirit, if no worse guests here
dwell,
My blue coat sits on my old shoulders well.

MAT. The only royal fellow; he's bounteous as the Indies. What's that he said to
thee, Bellafront?

BELL. Nothing.

MAT. I prithee, good girl.

BELL. Why, I tell you, nothing. 220

MAT. Nothing? It's well. Tricks! That
I must be beholden to a scald, [21] hot-liver'd, [22]
goatish [23] gallant, to stand with my cap in my
hand, and vail [24] bonnet, when I ha' spread
as lofty sails as himself. Would I had been
hanged. Nothing? Pacheco, brush my
cloak.

ORL. Where is't, sir?

MAT. Come, we'll fly high.
Nothing? There's a whore still in thine eye.
Exit.

ORL. [aside] My twenty pounds flies high.
O wretched woman! 231
This varlet's able to make Lucrece com-
mon. —
How now, mistress?
Has my master dy'd you into this sad color?

BELL. Fellow, begone I pray thee; if thy
tongue
Itch after talk so much, seek out thy master.
Th' art a fit instrument for him.

ORL. Zouns, I hope he will not play upon
me!

BELL. Play on thee? No, you two will fly
together,
Because you're roving arrows [25] of one feather.
Would thou wouldst leave my house; thou
ne'er shalt please me! 241
Weave thy nets ne'er so high,
Thou shalt be but a spider in mine eye.

18 Vile.　　19 *I.e.*, it swallows a man's substance.

20 Foolish.　21 Scurfy.　22 Amorous.　23 Lustful.
24 Doff (as a ship dips her flag, or topsail, in
deference).
25 *I.e.*, high fliers. See on *Friar Bacon and Friar
Bungay*, I, ii, 80.

Th' art rank with poison ; poison temper'd well
Is food for health, but thy black tongue doth swell
With venom, to hurt him that gave thee bread.
To wrong men absent is to spurn the dead ;
And so didst thou thy master, and my father.

ORL. You have small reason to take his part ; for I have heard him say five hun- [250 dred times you were as arrant a whore as ever stiff'ned tiffany²⁶ neckcloths in water-starch upon a Saturday i' th' afternoon.

BELL. Let him say worse. When, for the earth's offence,
Hot vengeance through the marble clouds is driven,
Is 't fit earth shoot again those darts at heaven?

ORL. And so if your father call you whore you'll not call him old knave. — [*aside*] Friscobaldo, she carries thy mind up and down ; she 's thine own flesh, blood, and bone. — [260 Troth, Mistress, to tell you true, the fireworks that ran from me upon lines against my good old master, your father, were but to try how my young master, your husband, loved such squibs ; but it 's well known I love your father as myself : I 'll ride for him at midnight, run for you by owl-light ; I 'll die for him, drudge for you ; I 'll fly low, and I 'll fly high, as my master says, to do you good, if you'll forgive me.   270

BELL. I am not made of marble ; I forgive thee.

ORL. Nay, if you were made of marble, a good stone-cutter might cut you. I hope the twenty pound I delivered to my master is in a sure hand.

BELL. In a sure hand, I warrant thee — for spending.

ORL. I see my young master is a madcap, and a *bonus socius*.²⁷ I love him well, Mistress ; yet as well as I love him, I 'll not play the knave with you. Look you, I could [280 cheat you of this purse full of money ; but I am an old lad, and I scorn to cony-catch. Yet I ha' been dog at a cony in my time.
                              [*Gives purse.*]

BELL. A purse? where hadst it?

ORL. The gentleman that went away whisper'd in mine ear, and charged me to give it you.

BELL. The Lord Hippolito?

ORL. Yes, if he be a lord, he gave it me.

²⁶ Thin silk or muslin.   ²⁷ Boon companion.

BELL. 'T is all gold.   290
ORL. 'T is like so. It may be he thinks you want money, and therefore bestows his alms bravely, like a lord.

BELL. He thinks a silver net can catch the poor ;
Here 's bait to choke a nun, and turn her whore.
Wilt thou be honest to me?

ORL. As your nails to your fingers, which I think never deceived you.

BELL. Thou to this lord shalt go ; commend me to him,
And tell him this : the town has held out long,
Because within 't was rather true than strong ;   301
To sell it now were base. Say 't is no hold²⁸
Built of weak stuff, to be blown up with gold.
He shall believe thee by this token, or this ;
If not, by this.
             [*Giving purse, ring, and letters.*]
ORL.   Is this all?
BELL.   This is all.
ORL. [*aside*] Mine own girl still !
BELL.   A star may shoot, not fall.
                              Exit BELLAFRONT.

ORL. A star? nay, thou art more than the moon, for thou hast neither changing quarters, nor a man standing in thy circle with a bush of thorns. Is 't possible the Lord [310 Hippolito, whose face is as civil as the outside of a dedicatory book, should be a muttonmonger?²⁹ A poor man has but one ewe, and this grandee sheep-biter²⁹ leaves whole flocks of fat wethers, whom he may knock down, to devour this. I 'll trust neither lord nor butcher with quick³⁰ flesh for this trick ; the cuckoo, I see now, sings³¹ all the year, though every man cannot hear him ; but I 'll spoil his notes. Can neither love letters, [320 nor the Devil's common picklocks, gold nor precious stones, make my girl draw up her percullis?³² Hold out still, wench.
All are not bawds, I see now, that keep doors,
Nor all good wenches that are mark'd for whores.   *Exit.*

[SCENE II]³³

Enter CANDIDO, [*and*] LODOVICO *like a prentice.*

LOD. Come, come, come, what do ye lack, sir? What do ye lack, sir? What is 't ye

²⁸ Stronghold.   ²⁹ Whoremonger.   ³⁰ Live.
³¹ A note of warning to cuckolds.
³² Portcullis.   ³³ Before Candido's shop.

lack, sir? Is not my Worship well suited?
Did you ever see a gentleman better disguised?

CAND. Never, believe me, signior.

LOD. Yes, but when he has been drunk.
There be prentices would make mad gallants,
for they would spend all, and drink, and whore,
and so forth ; and I see we gallants could [10
make mad prentices. How does thy wife
like me? Nay, I must not be so saucy ; then
I spoil all. Pray you how does my mistress
like me?

CAND. Well; for she takes you for a very
simple fellow.

LOD. And they that are taken for such are
commonly the arrantest knaves ; but to our
comedy, come.

CAND. I shall not act it; chide, you say,
     and fret,   20
And grow impatient : I shall never do 't.

LOD. 'Sblood, cannot you do as all the
world does, counterfeit?

CAND. Were I a painter, that should live
     by drawing
Nothing but pictures of an angry man,
I should not earn my colors ; I cannot do 't.

LOD. Remember y' are a linen-draper, and
that if you give your wife a yard, she 'll take
an ell ; give her not therefore a quarter of your
yard, not a nail.[34]   30

CAND. Say I should turn to ice and nip her
     love,
Now 't is but in the bud.

LOD.   Well, say she 's nipp'd.

CAND. It will so overcha[r]ge her heart with
     grief
That, like a cannon, when her sighs go off,
She in her duty either will recoil,
Or break in pieces and so die ; her death
By my unkindness might be counted murder.

LOD. Die? never, never. I do not bid you
beat her, nor give her black eyes, nor pinch
her sides ; but cross her humors. Are not [40
bakers' arms the scales of justice? Yet is not
their bread light? And may not you, I pray,
bridle her with a sharp bit, yet ride her gently?

CAND. Well, I will try your pills.
Do your faithful service, and be ready
Still at a pinch to help me in this part,
Or else I shall be out clean.[35]

LOD.   Come, come, I 'll prompt you.

CAND. I 'll call her forth now, shall I?

LOD.   Do, do, bravely.

CAND. Luke, I pray, bid your mistress to
     come hither.

LOD.[36] Luke, I pray, bid your mistress to
     come hither.   50

CAND. Sirrah, bid my wife come to me ;
     why, when![37]

LUKE. (*within*) Presently, sir, she comes.

LOD. La, you, there 's the echo : she comes !

            [*Enter*] Bride.

BRIDE. What is your pleasure with me?

CAND.   Marry, Wife,
I have intent, and you see this stripling here ;
He bears good will and liking to my trade,
And means to deal in linen.

LOD. Yes, indeed, sir, I would deal in linen,
if my mistress like me so well as I like her.

CAND. I hope to find him honest ; pray,
     good wife,   60
Look that his bed and chamber be made
     ready.

BRIDE. Y' are best to let him hire me for
     his maid.
I look to his bed? Look to 't yourself.

CAND.   Even so?
I swear to you a great oath —

LOD. [*aside*]   Swear ; cry " Zounds ! " —

CAND. I will not — go to, wife — I will
     not —

LOD. [*aside*] That your great oath?

CAND. Swallow these gudgeons![38]

LOD. [*aside*] Well said !

BRIDE. Then fast ; then you may choose.

CAND.   You know at table
What tricks you played, swagger'd, broke
     glasses, fie !   70
Fie, fie, fie ! and now before my prentice here,
You make an ass of me, thou — what shall I
     call thee?

BRIDE. Even what you will.

LOD. [*aside*]   Call her arrant whore.

CAND. [*aside*] Oh, fie, by no means ! then
     she 'll call me cuckold. —
Sirrah, go look to th' shop. — How does this
     show?

LOD. [*aside*] Excellent well. — I 'll go look
     to the shop, sir. —
Fine cambrics, lawns ; what do you lack?

          Exit LODOVICO [*into the shop*].[39]

CAND. A curst[40] cow's milk I ha' drunk
     once before,

---

[34] A cloth measure of $2\frac{1}{4}$ inches.
[35] Completely at a loss.
[36] Mimicking Candido's mildness.
[37] A common exclamation of impatience.
[38] Be so beguiled.   [39] *I.e.*, the inner stage
[40] Cross.

And 't was so rank in taste I 'll drink no more.
Wife, I 'll tame you.

BRIDE.   You may, sir, if you can ;
But at a wrastling I have seen a fellow   81
Limb'd like an ox, thrown by a little man.

CAND. And so you 'll throw me? — Reach
    me, knaves, a yard !

LOD. A yard for my master.

> [LODOVICO *returns from the shop with a*
> *yardstick and followed by* Prentices.]

1 PREN.   My master is grown valiant.

CAND. I 'll teach you fencing tricks.

OMNES.   Rare, rare ! a prize ! [41]

LOD. What will you do, sir?

CAND.   Marry, my good prentice,
Nothing but breathe [42] my wife.

BRIDE.   Breathe me with your yard?

LOD. No, he 'll but measure you out, for-
    sooth.

BRIDE. Since you 'll needs fence, handle
    your weapon well ;
For if you take a yard, I 'll take an ell. — 90
Reach me an ell !

LOD.   An ell for my mistress. —

> [*Brings one from the shop.*]

Keep the laws of the noble science, sir, and
measure weapons with her ; your yard is a
plain heathenish weapon. 'T is too short ;
she may give you a handful, and yet you 'll
not reach her.

CAND. Yet I ha' the longer arm. — Come,
    fall to 't roundly,
And spare not me, Wife, for I 'll lay 't on
    soundly ;
If o'er husbands their wives will needs be
    masters,   99
We men will have a law to win 't at wasters.[43]

LOD. 'T is for the breeches,[44] is 't not?

CAND.   For the breeches !

BRIDE. Husband, I am for you ; I 'll not
    strike in jest.

CAND. Nor I.

BRIDE. But will you sign to one request?

CAND. What 's that?

BRIDE.   Let me give the first blow.

CAND. The first blow, Wife? — [*aside to*
    LOD.] Shall I? Prompt !

LOD.   Let her ha 't ;
If she strike hard, in to her and break her pate.

CAND. A bargain ; strike !

BRIDE.   Then guard you from this blow ;
For I play all at legs, but 't is thus low.

> *She kneels.*

Behold, I am such a cunning fencer grown, [109
I keep my ground, yet down I will be thrown
With the least blow you give me ; I disdain
The wife that is her husband's sovereign.
She that upon your pillow first did rest,
They say, the breeches wore, which I detest :
The tax which she imposed upon you, I abate
    you ;
If me you make your master, I shall hate you.
The world shall judge who offers fairest play ;
You win the breeches, but I win the day.

CAND. Thou winn'st the day indeed ; give
    me thy hand ;
I 'll challenge thee no more. My patient
    breast   120
Play'd thus the rebel only for a jest.
Here 's the rank rider that breaks colts ; 't is
    he
Can tame the mad folks, and curst wives.

BRIDE.   Who? your man?

CAND. My man ! my master, though his
    head be bare ;
But he 's so courteous he 'll put off his hair.

LOD. Nay, if your service be so hot a man
cannot keep his hair on, I 'll serve you no
longer.   [*Takes off his false hair.*]

BRIDE. Is this your schoolmaster?   129

LOD. Yes, faith, wench ; I taught him to
take thee down. I hope thou canst take him
down without teaching.
You ha' got the conquest, and you both are
    friends.

CAND. Bear witness else.

LOD.   My prenticeship then ends.

CAND. For the good service you to me have
    done,
I give you all your years.[45]

LOD.   I thank you, Master.
I 'll kiss my mistress now, that she may say,
" My man was bound and free, all in one day."

> *Exeunt.*

[ACT III — SCENE I] [1]

Enter ORLANDO [*as* PACHECO], *and* INFELICHE.

INF. From whom, sayest thou?

ORL. From a poor gentlewoman, madam,
whom I serve.

INF. And what 's your business?

ORL. This, madam : my poor mistress has
a waste piece of ground, which is her own by

---

[41] Match, bout.   [42] Exercise.   [43] Cudgels.
[44] Symbol of supremacy in marriage.

[45] *I.e.*, the remaining term of your apprenticeship.
[1] A room in Hippolito's house.

inheritance, and left to her by her mother. There's a lord now that goes about, not to take it clean from her, but to enclose it to himself, and to join it to a piece of his [10 Lordship's.

INF. What would she have me do in this?

ORL. No more, madam, but what one woman should do for another in such a case. My honorable Lord, your husband, would do anything in her behalf, but she had rather put herself into your hands, because you, a woman, may do more with the Duke, your father.

INF. Where lies this land?   20

ORL. Within a stone's cast of this place. My mistress, I think, would be content to let him enjoy it after her decease, if that would serve his turn, so [2] my master would yield too ; but she cannot abide to hear that the lord should meddle with it in her lifetime.

INF. Is she then married? Why stirs not her husband in it?

ORL. Her husband stirs in it underhand ; but because the other is a great rich man, [30 my master is loth to be seen in it too much.

INF. Let her in writing draw the cause at large,

And I will move the Duke.

ORL. 'T is set down, madam, here in black and white already. Work it so, madam, that she may keep her own without disturbance, grievance, molestation, or meddling of any other ; and she bestows this purse of gold on your Ladyship.

INF. Old man, I'll plead for her, but take no fees.   40

Give lawyers them, I swim not in that flood ; I'll touch no gold till I have done her good.

ORL. I would all proctors' clerks were of your mind ; I should law more amongst them than I do, then. Here, madam, is the survey, not only of the manor itself, but of the grange-house, with every meadow, pasture, plough-land, cony-burrow, fish-pond, hedge, ditch, and bush, that stands in it.   [*Gives a letter.*]

INF. My husband's name and hand and seal at arms [3]   50

To a love letter? Where hadst thou this writing?

ORL. From the foresaid party, madam, that would keep the foresaid land out of the foresaid lord's fingers.

INF. My lord turn'd ranger now?

ORL. Y'are a good huntress, lady ; you ha' found your game already. Your lord would fain be a ranger, but my mistress requests you to let him run a course in your own park. If you'll not do't for love, then do't for [60 money! She has no white money,[4] but there's gold ; or else she prays you to ring him by this token, and so you shall be sure his nose will not be rooting other men's pastures.   [*Gives purse and ring.*]

INF. This very purse was woven with mine own hands ;

This diamond, on that very night when he

Untied my virgin girdle, gave I him ;

And must a common harlot share in mine?

Old man, to quit thy pains, take thou the gold.   70

ORL. Not I, madam ; old serving men want no money.

INF. Cupid himself was sure his secretary ; These lines are even the arrows love let flies ; The very ink dropp'd out of Venus' eyes.

ORL. I do not think, madam, but he fetch'd off some poet or other for those lines ; for they are parlous hawks to fly at wenches.

INF. Here's honied poison! To me he ne'er thus writ ;

But lust can set a double edge on wit.   80

ORL. Nay, that's true, madam ; a wench will whet anything, if it be not too dull.

INF. Oaths, promises, preferments, jewels, gold,

What snares should break, if all these cannot hold?

What creature is thy mistress?

ORL. One of those creatures that are contrary to man : a woman.

INF. What manner of woman?

ORL. A little tiny woman, lower than your ladyship by head and shoulders, but as [90 mad a wench as ever unlaced a petticoat ; these things should I indeed have delivered to my Lord, your husband.

INF. They are delivered better.   Why should she

Send back these things?

ORL.   'Ware, 'ware, there's knavery.

INF. Strumpets, like cheating gamesters, will not win

At first ; these are but baits to draw him in.

How might I learn his hunting hours?

ORL. The Irish footman can tell you all his hunting hours, the park he hunts in, the [100

[2] Provided that.
[3] A seal giving the heraldic bearings of its owner.

[4] Silver. The gold is, of course, Hippolito's.

doe he would strike ; that Irish shackatory [5]
beats the bush for him, and knows all ; he
brought that letter, and that ring ; he is the
carrier.

INF. Knowest thou what other gifts have
　　pass'd between them?

ORL. Little Saint Patrick knows all.

INF. Him I 'll examine presently.

ORL. Not whilst I am here, sweet madam.

INF. Begone then, and what lies in me
　　command.　　　　　　*Exit* ORLANDO.

Enter BRYAN.

INF. Come hither, sirrah ; how much cost
　　those satins　　　　　　　　　　　110
And cloth of silver, which my husband sent
By you to a low gentlewoman yonder?

BRY. Faat satins, faat silvers, faat low
gentlefolks? Dow pratest dow knowest not
what, i' faat, la.

INF. She there, to whom you carried letters.

BRY. By dis hand and bod dow say'st true,
if I did so, oh how? I know not a letter a' de
book, i' faat, la.

INF. Did your lord never send you with a
　　ring, sir,　　　　　　　　　　　120
Set with a diamond?

BRY. Never, sa crees sa' me, never ! He
may run at a towsand rings [6] i' faat, and I
never hold his stirrup, till he leap into de
saddle. By St. Patrick, madam, I never touch
my Lord's diamond, nor ever had to do, i' faat,
la, with any of his precious stones.

Enter HIPPOLITO.

INF. Are you so close, [7] you bawd, you pan-
　　d'ring slave?　　　　[*Strikes* BRYAN.]

HIP. How now? Why, Infeliche, what's
　　your quarrel?

INF. Out of my sight, base varlet ! get thee
　　gone.　　　　　　　　　　　130

HIP. Away, you rogue !

BRY. *Slawne loot,* [8] fare de well, fare de
well. *Ah marragh frofat boddah breen !* [9]
　　　　　　　　　　　　　　Exit.

HIP. What, grown a fighter? Prithee
　　what 's the matter?

INF. If you 'll needs know, it was about the
　　clock.

[5] Beater.
[6] Alluding to the knightly sport of riding at the
(suspended) ring, through which the rider attempted
to thrust his lance.
[7] Secret.　　　[8] ? Slán leat ; fare thee well.
[9] ? I m-bárach fromhtha bodach bréan ; on the
day after a feast a churl is fetid.

How works the day, my Lord, pray, by your
　　watch?

HIP. Lest you cuff me, I 'll tell you pres-
　　ently ; [10]
I am near two.

INF.　　　　　How, two? I 'm scarce at one.

HIP. One of us then goes false.

INF.　　　　　　　Then sure 't is you ;
Mine goes by heaven's dial, the sun, and it
　　goes true.　　　　　　　　　　　140

HIP. I think, indeed, mine runs somewhat
　　too fast.

INF. Set it to mine at one then.

HIP.　　　　　　　One? 't is past ;
'T is past one by the sun.

INF.　　　　　　　Faith, then, belike
Neither your clock nor mine does truly strike ;
And, since it is uncertain which goes true,
Better be false at one, than false at two.

HIP. Y' are very pleasant, madam.

INF.　　　　　　　　Yet not merry.

HIP. Why, Infeliche, what should make you
　　sad?

INF. Nothing, my Lord, but my false
　　watch. Pray, tell me —
You see, my clock or yours is out of
　　frame ;　　　　　　　　　　　150
Must we upon the workman lay the blame,
Or on ourselves that keep them?

HIP.　　　　　　Faith, on both.
He may by knavery spoil them, we by sloth.
But why talk you all riddle thus? I read
Strange comments in those margins [11] of your
　　looks.
Your cheeks of late are, like bad printed books,
So dimly charact'red, I scarce can spell
One line of love in them. Sure all 's not well.

INF. All is not well indeed, my dearest
　　Lord ;
Lock up thy gates of hearing, that no
　　sound　　　　　　　　　　　160
Of what I speak may enter.

HIP.　　　　　　What means this?

INF. Or if my own tongue must myself
　　betray,
Count it a dream, or turn thine eyes away,
And think me not thy wife.　　*She kneels.*

HIP.　　　　　Why do you kneel?

INF. Earth is sin's cushion ; when the sick
　　soul feels
Herself growing poor, then she turns beggar,
　　cries,

[10] At once.
[11] Commentary used to be printed, not at the foot
of the page, but in the margin.

And kneels for help.   Hippolito, for husband
I dare not call thee, I have stol'n that jewel
Of my chaste honor, which was only thine,
And given it to a slave.
 Hip.   Ha?
 Inf.   On thy pillow
Adultery and lust have slept ; thy groom [171
Hath climbed the unlawful tree, and pluck'd
 the sweets ;
A villain hath usurped a husband's sheets.
 Hip. 'Sdeath, who? — a cuckold ! — who?
 Inf.   This Irish footman.
 Hip. Worse than damnation ! a wild
 kerne,[12] a frog,
A dog ; whom I 'll scarce spurn.   Longed you
 for shamrock?
Were it my father's father, heart,[13] I 'll kill
 him,
Although I take him on his deathbed gasping
'Twixt Heaven and hell ! A shag-hair'd cur !
 Bold strumpet,
Why hangest thou on me?   Think'st I 'll be a
 bawd   180
To a whore, because she 's noble?
 Inf.   I beg but this,
Set not my shame out to the world's broad
 eye ;
Yet let thy vengeance, like my fault, soar high,
So it be in dark'ned clouds.
 Hip.   Dark'ned ! my horns
Cannot be dark'ned, nor shall my revenge.
A harlot to my slave?   The act is base ;
Common, but foul ; so shall [14] thy disgrace.
Could not I feed your appetite?   O women,
You were created angels, pure and fair ;
But since the first fell, tempting devils you
 are.   190
You should be men's bliss, but you prove their
 rods ;
Were there no women, men might live like
 gods.
You ha' been too much down already ; rise,
Get from my sight, and henceforth shun my
 bed ;
I 'll with no strumpet's breath be poisoned.
As for your Irish lubrican,[15] that spirit
Whom by prepost'rous charms thy lust hath
 raised
In a wrong circle, him I 'll damn more black
Then any tyrant's soul.
 Inf.   Hippolito !

 Hip. Tell me, didst thou bait [hooks] [16] to
 draw him to thee,   200
Or did he bewitch thee?
 Inf.   The slave did woo me.
 Hip. Tu-whoos [17] in that screech-owl's lan-
 guage ! Oh, who would trust
Your cork-heel'd [18] sex?   I think to sate your
 lust
You would love a horse, a bear, a croaking toad,
So your hot itching veins might have their
 bound.
Then the wild Irish dart was thrown? [19]
 Come, how?
The manner of this fight?
 Inf. 'T was thus : he gave me this battery
 first. — Oh, I
Mistake — believe me, all this in beaten gold ;
Yet I held out, but at length th[u]s was
 charm'd.   [*Gives letter, purse, and ring.*]
What, change your diamond, wench?   The
 act is base,   211
Common, but foul, so shall not your disgrace.
Could not I feed your appetite?   O men,
You were created angels, pure and fair,
But since the first fell, worse than devils you
 are.
You should our shields be, but you prove our
 rods.
Were there no men, women might live like
 gods.
Guilty, my Lord?
 Hip.   Yes, guilty, my good Lady.
 Inf. Nay, you may laugh, but henceforth
 shun my bed ;
With no whore's leavings I 'll be poisoned.
           Exit.
 Hip. O'erreached so finely ! 'T is the very
 diamond   221
And letter which I sent.   This villainy
Some spider closely weaves, whose poison'd
 bulk
I must let forth.   Who 's there without?
 Ser. (*within*) My Lord calls.
 Hip. Send me the footman.
 Ser. [*within*] Call the footman to my Lord.
 — Bryan, Bryan !

    Re-enter Bryan.

 Hip. It can be no man else, that Irish
 Judas,

---

[12] Rude peasant.   [13] By God's heart.
[14] Mod. eds., perhaps rightly, insert *not.* See
l. 212.
[15] Leprechaun ; the pigmy sprite of Ireland.

[16] Emend. Dyce. Q *hawkes.*
[17] Note pun on *woo.* Q *Two wooes.*
[18] Addicted to high-heeled shoes ; *i.e.,* light-heeled,
wanton.
[19] An allusion to the darts carried by the Irish
running footmen. (Dyce.)

Bred in a country where no venom prospers
But in the nation's blood, hath thus betray'd
　　me. —　　　　　　　　　　　　　　　230
Slave, get you from your service.

BRY. Faat meanest thou by this now?

HIP. Question me not, nor tempt my fury,
　　villain!
Couldst thou turn all the mountains in the
　　land
To hills of gold, and to give me, here thou
　　stayest not.

BRY. I' faat, I care not.

HIP. Prate not, but get thee gone; I shall
　　send else.[20]

BRY. Ay, do predy; I had rather have
thee make a scabbard of my guts, and let out
all de Irish puddings [21] in my poor belly, [240
den to be a false knave to de, i' faat! I will
never see dine own sweet face more. *A maw-
hid deer a gra*,[22] fare de well, fare de well;
I will go steal cows again in Ireland. *Exit.*

HIP. He's damn'd that rais'd this whirl-
　　wind, which hath blown
Into her eyes this jealousy; yet I'll on,
I'll on, stood armed devils staring in my face.
To be pursued in flight, quickens the race.
Shall my blood-streams by a wife's lust be
　　barr'd?
Fond [23] woman, no; iron grows by strokes
　　more hard;　　　　　　　　　　　　250
Lawless desires are seas scorning all bounds,
Or sulphur, which being ramm'd up, more
　　confounds;
Struggling with madmen madness nothing
　　tames;
Winds wrastling with great fires incense the
　　flames.　　　　　　　　　　　　　　*Exit.*

[SCENE II][24]

Enter BELLAFRONT, *and* ORLANDO [*as*
PACHECO], [*and*] MATHEO, [*who stands aside*].

BELL. How now, what ails your master?

ORL. Has taken a younger brother's purge,
forsooth, and that works with him.

BELL. Where is his cloak and rapier?

ORL. He has given up his cloak, and his
rapier is bound to the peace. If you look a
little higher, you may see that another hath
ent'red into hatband for him too. Six and
four [25] have put him into this sweat.

BELL. Where's all his money?　　　10

ORL. 'T is put over [26] by exchange; his
doublet was going to be translated, but for
me. If any man would ha' lent but half a
ducat on his beard, the hair of it had stuff'd
a pair of breeches by this time. I had but
one poor penny, and that I was glad to niggle
out,[27] and buy a holly wand to grace him
thorough the street. As hap was, his boots
were on, and the[m] I dustied, to make people
think he had been riding, and I had run [20
by him.

BELL. O me! — How does my sweet Ma-
　　theo?

MAT. Oh, rogue, of what devilish stuff are
these dice made of — of the parings of the
Devil's corns of his toes, that they run thus
damnably.

BELL. I prithee, vex not.

MAT. If any handicrafts-man was ever suf-
f'red to keep shop in hell, it will be a dice-
maker; he's able to undo more souls than [30
the Devil; I play'd with mine own dice, yet
lost. Ha' you any money?

BELL. 'Las, I ha' none.

MAT. Must have money, must have some,
must have a cloak, and rapier, and things.
Will you go set your lime-twigs, and get me
some birds, some money?

BELL. What lime-twigs should I set?

MAT. You will not then? Must have cash
and pictures, do ye hear, frailty? Shall I [40
walk in a Plymouth cloak,[28] that's to say,
like a rogue, in my hose [29] and doublet, and a
crabtree cudgel in my hand, and you swim in
your satins? Must have money, come!

　　　　　　　　　　[*Taking off her gown.*]

ORL. Is 't bedtime, master, that you undo
　　my mistress?

BELL. Undo [30] me? Yes, yes, at these
　　riflings I
Have been too often.

MAT.　　　　　　Help to flay, Pacheco.

ORL. Flaying call you it?

MAT. I'll pawn you, by th' Lord, to your
　　very eyebrows.

BELL. With all my heart, since Heaven will
　　have me poor;　　　　　　　　　　50
As good be drown'd at sea, as drown'd at shore.

[20] By stabbing.　　　　[21] Entrails.
[22] A mhaighisdir, a ghrádh; O master, O love.
[23] Foolish.
[24] A room in Matheo's house.
[25] *I.e.*, dicing.

[26] Transferred.　　　[27] Take out, trifling as it was.
[28] *I.e.*, with a staff. According to Thomas Fuller,
a voyager would often land at Plymouth minus
wherewithal to purchase clothing, and cut himself
a stick instead of buying a cloak. "Pictures" (l. 40)
= coins.
[29] Breeches.　　　　　　[30] Ruin.

ORL. Why, hear you, sir? I' faith, do not make away her gown.

MAT. Oh! it's summer, it's summer; your only fashion for a woman now is to be light, to be light.

ORL. Why, pray sir, employ some of that money you have of mine.

MAT. Thine? I'll starve first, I'll beg first; when I touch a penny of that, let [60 these fingers' ends rot.

ORL. [*aside*] So they may, for that's past touching. I saw my twenty pounds fly high.

MAT. Knowest thou never a damn'd broker about the city?

ORL. Damn'd broker? Yes, five hundred.

MAT. The gown stood me in [31] above twenty ducats; borrow ten of [32] it. Cannot live without silver.

ORL. I'll make what I can of it, sir; [70 I'll be your broker, —

[*Aside*] But not your damn'd broker. O thou scurvy knave!

What makes a wife turn whore, but such a slave?

     Exit [*with Bellafront's gown*].

MAT. How now, little chick, what ailest? Weeping for a handful of tailor's shreds? Pox on them, are there not silks enow at mercer's?

BELL. I care not for gay feathers, I.

MAT. What doest care for then? Why doest grieve?

BELL. Why do I grieve? A thousand sor-
     rows strike   80

At one poor heart, and yet it lives. Matheo,
Thou art a gamester; prithee, throw at all,
Set all upon one cast. We kneel and pray,
And struggle for life, yet must be cast away.
Meet misery quickly then, split [33] all, sell all,
And when thou hast sold all, spend it; but, I
     beseech thee,
Build not thy mind on me to coin thee more;
To get it wouldst thou have me play the
     whore?

MAT. 'T was your profession before I married you.   90

BELL. Umh? It was indeed. If all men
     should be branded
For sins long since laid up, who could be
     saved?
The quarter-day's at hand. How will you do
To pay the rent, Matheo?

MAT. Why, do as all of our occupation do
against [34] quarter-days: break up house, re-

move, shift your lodgings; pox a' your quarters!

     Enter LODOVICO.

LOD. Where's this gallant?

MAT. Signior Lodovico? how does my [100 little Mirror of Knighthood? [35] This is kindly done, i' faith; welcome, by my troth.

LOD. And how dost, frolic? — Save you fair
     lady. —
Thou lookest smug [36] and bravely, noble Mat.

MAT. Drink and feed, laugh and lie warm.

LOD. Is this thy wife?

MAT. A poor gentlewoman, sir, whom I make use of a' nights.

LOD. Pay custom to your lips, sweet lady.
     [*Kisses her.*]

MAT. [*aside to* BELLAFRONT] Borrow [110 some shells [37] of him. — Some wine, sweet-heart.

LOD. I'll send for 't then, i' faith.

MAT. You send for 't! — Some wine, I prithee.

BELL. [*aside to* MATHEO] I ha' no money.

MAT. [*aside to* BELLAFRONT] 'Sblood, nor I. — What wine love you, signior?

LOD. Here! [*offering money*] or I'll not stay, I protest; trouble the gentlewoman too [120 much?

     Exit BELLAFRONT.

And what news flies abroad, Matheo?

MAT. Troth, none. Oh, signior, we ha' been merry in our days.

LOD. And no doubt shall again.
The divine powers never shoot darts at men
Mortal, to kill them.

MAT. You say true.

LOD. Why should we grieve at want? Say
     the world made thee
Her minion, that thy head lay in her lap, [130
And that she danc'd thee on her wanton knee:
She could but give thee a whole world; that's
     all,
And that all's nothing; the world's greatest
     part
Cannot fill up one corner of thy heart.
Say the three corners were all fill'd, alas!
Of what art thou possess'd? a thin blown
     glass,
Such as by boys is puff'd into the air!
Were twenty kingdoms thine, thou 'dst live in
     care:

[31] Cost me.   [32] On.   [33] Wreck.
[34] In preparation for.

[35] A well-known romance, translated from the Spanish.
[36] Smart, in good trim.
[37] Money (a cant term).

Thou couldst not sleep the better, nor live
    longer,   139
Nor merrier be, nor healthfuller, nor stronger.
If, then, thou want'st, thus make that want
    thy pleasure ;
No man wants all things, nor has all in meas-
    ure.

MAT. I am the most wretched fellow ; sure
some left-handed priest christ'ned me, I am
so unlucky ; I am never out of one puddle or
another, still falling.

Re-enter BELLAFRONT [*with wine*] *and*
    ORLANDO.

Fill out wine to my little finger. — With my
heart, i' faith.

LOD. Thanks, good Matheo. To your own
sweet self.   150

ORL. All the brokers' hearts, sir, are made
of flint. I can with all my knocking strike
but six sparks of fire out of them ; here's six
ducats, if you'll take them.

MAT. Give me them ! An evil conscience
gnaw them all ! Moths and plagues hang
upon their lousy wardrobes !

LOD. Is this your man, Matheo? An old
serving man !   159

ORL. You may give me tother half too,
sir ; that's the beggar.

LOD. What hast there — gold?

MAT. A sort [38] of rascals are in my debt,
God knows what, and they feed me with bits,
with crumbs, a pox choke them.

LOD. A word, Matheo ; be not angry with
    me :
Believe it that I know the touch of time,
And can part copper, though it be gilded
    o'er,
From the true gold. The sails which thou
    doest spread,   169
Would show well if they were not borrowed.
The sound of thy low fortunes drew me hither ;
I give myself unto thee ; prithee, use me.
I will bestow on you a suit of satin,
And all things else to fit a gentleman,
Because I love you.

MAT.   Thanks, good, noble knight !

LOD. Call on me when you please ; till
    then farewell.   *Exit.*

MAT. Hast angled? Hast cut up this
fresh salmon?

BELL. Wouldst have me be so base?

MAT. It's base to steal, it's base to be a
    whore ;   180

[38] Set.

Thou'lt be more base : I'll make thee keep a
    door.[39]   *Exit.*

ORL. I hope he will not sneak away with
all the money, will he?

BELL. Thou seest he does.

ORL. Nay, then, it's well. I set my brains
upon an upright last ; [40] though my wits be
old, yet they are like a wither'd pippin, wholesome. Look you, Mistress, I told him I had
but six ducats of the knave broker, but I had
eight, and kept these two for you.   190

BELL. Thou shouldst have given him all.

ORL.   What, to fly high?

BELL. Like waves, my misery drives on
    misery.   *Exit.*

ORL. Sell his wife's clothes from her back?
Does any poulterer's wife pull chickens alive?
He riots all abroad, wants all at home ; he
dices, whores, swaggers, swears, cheats, bor-
rows, pawns. I'll give him hook and line, a
little more for all this ;   198
Yet sure i' th' end he'll delude all my hopes,
And show me a French trick danc'd on the
    ropes.[41]   *Exit.*

[SCENE III] [42]

Enter at one door LODOVICO *and* CAROLO ; *at
another* BOTS *and* MISTRESS HORSELEECH.
CANDIDO *and his* Wife *appear in the shop.*

LOD. Hist, hist, Lieutenant Bots ! How
dost, man?

CAR. Whither are you ambling, Madam
Horseleech?

MIS. H. About wordly profit, sir ; how do
your Worships?

BOTS. We want tools, gentlemen, to furnish the trade ; they wear out day and night,
they wear out till no metal [43] be left in their
back. We hear of two or three new [10
wenches are come up [44] with a carrier, and
your old goshawk here is flying at them.

LOD. And, faith, what flesh have you at
home?

MIS. H. Ordinary dishes ; by my troth,
sweet men, there's few good i' th' city. I
am as well furnish'd as any, and, though I
say it, as well custom'd.

BOTS. We have meats of all sorts of dressing ; we have stew'd meat for your French- [20

---

[39] *I.e.*, be a bawd.   [40] I foresaw correctly.
[41] *I.e.*, he will be hanged.
[42] Before Candido's shop.
[43] Mettle ; the words were undistinguished in
spelling.
[44] To London, from the country.

man, pretty light picking meat for your Italian, and that which is rotten roasted for Don Spaniardo.

Lod. A pox on 't.

Bots. We have poulterer's ware for your sweet bloods, as dove, chicken, duck, teal, woodcock, and so forth ; and butcher's meat for the citizen ; yet muttons [45] fall very bad this year.

Lod. Stay, is not that my patient linen- [30 draper yonder, and my fine young smug mistress, his wife?

Car. Sirrah [46] grannam, I 'll give thee for thy fee twenty crowns, if thou canst but procure me the wearing of yon velvet cap.

Mis. H. You 'd wear another thing besides the cap. Y' are a wag.

Bots. Twenty crowns? We 'll share, and I 'll be your pully to draw her on.

Lod. Do 't presently ; we 'll ha' some [40 sport.

Mis. H. Wheel you about, sweet men ; do you see? I 'll cheapen [47] wares of the man, whilst Bots is doing with his wife.

Lod. To 't ; if we come into the shop, to do you grace, we 'll call you madam.

Bots. Pox a' your old face, give it the badge of all scurvy faces, a mask.

[Mistress Horseleech *puts on a mask.*]

Cand. What is 't you lack, gentlewoman? Cambric or lawns, or fine hollands? Pray [50 draw near ; I can sell you a pennyworth.

Bots. Some cambric for my old lady.

Cand. Cambric? you shall, the purest thread in Milan.

Lod. *and* Car. Save you, Signior Candido.

Lod. How does my noble master? How my fair mistress?

Cand. My worshipful good servant. — View it well, for 't is both fine and even.

[*Shows cambric.*]

Car. Cry you mercy, madam ; though [60 mask'd, I thought it should be you by your man. — Pray, signior, show her the best, for she commonly deals for good ware.

Cand. Then this shall fit her. — This is for your Ladyship.

Bots. [*to* Bride] A word, I pray. There is a waiting gentlewoman of my lady's — her name is Ruyna — says she 's your kinswoman, and that you should be one of her aunts.

Bride. One of her aunts? Troth, sir, I [70 know her not.

Bots. If it please you to bestow the poor labor of your legs at any time, I will be your convoy thither.

Bride. I am a snail, sir, seldom leave my house. If 't please her to visit me, she shall be welcome.

Bots. Do you hear? The naked truth is, my lady hath a young knight, her son, who loves you ; y' are made, if you lay hold [80 upon 't ; this jewel he sends you.

Bride. Sir, I return his love and jewel with scorn. Let go my hand, or I shall call my husband. You are an arrant knave.   *Exit.*

Lod. What, will she do?

Bots. Do? They shall all do if Bots sets upon them once. She was as if she had profess'd the trade, squeamish at first ; at last I showed her this jewel, said a knight sent it her.   90

Lod. Is 't gold, and right stones?

Bots. Copper, copper ; I go a-fishing with these baits. She nibbled, but would not swallow the hook, because the conger-head,[48] her husband, was by ; but she bids the gentleman name any afternoon, and she 'll meet him at her garden house,[49] which I know.

Lod. Is this no lie now?

Bots. Damn me, if —

Lod. Oh, prithee, stay [50] there.   100

Bots. The twenty crowns, sir.

Lod. Before he has his work done? — But on my knightly word he shall pay 't thee.

Enter Astolfo, Beraldo, Fontinell, *and the Irish footman* [Bryan].

Ast. I thought thou hadst been gone into thine own country.

Bry. No, faat, la ; I cannot go dis four or tree days.

Ber. Look thee, yonder 's the shop, and that 's the man himself.

Fon. Thou shalt but cheapen, and do [110 as we told thee, to put a jest upon him, to abuse his patience.

Bry. I' faat, I doubt my pate shall be knocked ; but, sa crees sa' me, for your shakes, I will run to any linen-draper in hell. Come, preddy.

Omnes. Save you, gallants.

Lod. *and* Car. Oh, well met !

Cand. You 'll give no more, you say? I cannot take it.

---

[45] Prostitutes.   [46] Formerly used to both sexes.
[47] Chaffer for.

[48] A regular term of abuse.
[49] Summer-houses in suburban gardens were notorious places for clandestine amours.
[50] Stop.

Mis. H. Truly, I'll give no more.

Cand.   It must not fetch it. [120
What would you have, sweet gentlemen?

Ast.   Nay, here's the customer.
            Exeunt Bots *and* [Mistress] Horse-
                    leech.

Lod. The garden house, you say? We'll
bolt [51] out your roguery.

Cand. I will but lay these parcels by —
    my men
Are all at customhouse unloading wares.
If cambric you would deal in, there's the best ;
All Milan cannot sample [52] it.

Lod. Do you hear? one, two, three, —
'sfoot, there came in four gallants! Sure
your wife is slipp'd up,[53] and the fourth [130
man, I hold my life, is grafting your warden [54]
tree.

Cand. Ha, ha, ha! you gentlemen are full
        of jest ;
If she be up, she's gone some wares to show ;
I have above as good wares as below.

Lod. Have you so? Nay, then —

Cand. Now, gentlemen, is 't cambrics?

Bry. I predee now, let me have de best
wares.

Cand. What's that he says, pray, gentle-
        men?   140

Lod. Marry, he says we are like to have
the best wars.

Cand. The best wars? All are bad, yet
        wars do good,
And, like to surgeons, let sick kingdoms blood.

Bry. Faat a devil pratest tow so? a pox
on dee! I preddee, let me see some hollen,
to make linen shirts, for fear my body be
lousy.

Cand. Indeed, I understand no word he
        speaks.

Car. Marry, he says that at the siege in
        Holland   150
There was much bawdry used among the sol-
        diers,
Though they were lousy.

Cand. It may be so ; that's likely. — True,
    indeed ;
In every garden, sir, does grow that weed.

Bry. Pox on de gardens, and de weeds, and
de fool's cap dere, and de clouts! Here, doest
make a hobbyhorse of me?
                    [*Tearing the cambric.*]

Omnes. Oh, fie! he has torn [the] cambric.

Cand.   'T is no matter.

Ast. It frets me to the soul.

Cand.   So does 't not me.
My customers do oft for remnants call :   160
These are two remnants, now, no loss at all.
But let me tell you, were my servants here,
It would ha' cost more. — Thank you, gentle-
    men ;
I use you well, — pray know my shop again.
                                Exit.

Omnes. Ha, ha, ha! come, come, let's go,
    let's go.   *Exeunt.*

[ACT IV — Scene I] [1]

Enter Matheo, *brave*,[2] *and* Bellafront.

Mat. How am I suited, Front? Am I
not gallant, ha?

Bell. Yes, sir, you are suited well.

Mat. Exceeding passing well, and to the
    time.[3]

Bell. The tailor has play'd his part with
you.

Mat. And I have play'd a gentleman's
part with my tailor, for I owe him for the
making of it.

Bell. And why did you so, sir?   10

Mat. To keep the fashion ; it's your only
fashion now, of your best rank of gallants, to
make their tailors wait for their money ; neither were it wisdom indeed to pay them upon
the first edition of a new suit ; for commonly
the suit is owing for when the linings are
worn out, and there's no reason, then, that
the tailor should be paid before the mercer.

Bell. Is this the suit the knight bestowed
upon you?   20

Mat. This is the suit, and I need not shame
to wear it, for better men than I would be
glad to have suits [4] bestowed on them. It's
a generous fellow ; but — pox on him — we
whose pericranions are the very limbecks and
stillatories of good wit, and fly high, must
drive liquor out of stale gaping oysters. Shallow knight, poor squire Tinacheo![5] I'll
make a wild Cataian [6] of forty such! hang
him, he's an ass — he's always sober !   30

---

[1] A room in Matheo's house.   [2] Finely dressed.
[3] In the latest fashion.   [4] At court.
[5] ? For *Tinacrio*, in *Don Quixote* (first published in
1605.)
[6] Dyce quotes Reed: "*i.e.*, forty such shallow
knights, &c. would go to the composition of a dex-
terous thief ;" and adds: "A Cataian came to
signify a sharper, because the people of Cataia
(China) were famous for their thieving."

BELL. This is your fault to wound your friends still.

MAT. No, faith, Front; Lodovico is a noble Slavonian: [7] it's more rare to see him in a woman's company than for a Spaniard to go into England and to challenge the English fencers there. — One knocks, — see. [*Exit* BELLAFRONT.] — La, fa, sol, la, fa, la, rustle in silks and satins! There's music in this, and a taffety petticoat; it makes both fly [40 high! Catso!

Re-enter BELLAFRONT; *after her* ORLANDO, *like himself, with four* Men *after him.*

BELL. Matheo! 't is my father!

MAT. Ha! father? It's no matter, he finds no tatter'd prodigals here.

ORL. Is not the door good enough to hold your blue coats? Away, knaves. — [*Exeunt* Servants.] — Wear not your clothes threadbare at knees for me; beg Heaven's blessing, not mine. — Oh, cry your Worship mercy, sir; was somewhat bold to talk to this gentle- [50 woman, your wife here.

MAT. A poor gentlewoman, sir.

ORL. Stand not, sir, bare to me; I ha' read oft
That serpents who creep low belch ranker poison
Than winged dragons do that fly aloft.

MAT. If it offend you, sir, 't is for my pleasure.

ORL. Your pleasure be 't, sir. Umh, is this your palace?

BELL. Yes, and our kingdom, for 't is our content.

ORL. It 's a very poor kingdom then; what, are all your subjects gone a-sheepshear- [60 ing? Not a maid? not a man? not so much as a cat? You keep a good house belike, just like one of your profession: every room with bare walls, and a half-headed bed to vault upon, as all your bawdyhouses are. Pray who are your upholsters? Oh, the spiders, I see; they bestow hangings upon you.

MAT. Bawdyhouse! Zounds, sir —

BELL. Oh sweet Matheo, peace. — Upon my knees   70
I do beseech you, sir, not to arraign me
For sins which Heaven, I hope, long since hath pardoned!
Those flames, like lightning flashes, are so spent

The heat no more remains than where ships went,
Or where birds cut the air, the print remains.

MAT. Pox on him, kneel to a dog.

BELL.   She that 's a whore,
Lives gallant, fares well, is not, like me, poor.
I ha' now as small acquaintance with that sin,
As if I had never known it, that never been. [8]

ORL. No acquaintance with it? What [80 maintains thee then? How doest live then? Has thy husband any lands, any rents coming in, any stock going, any plows jogging, any ships sailing? Hast thou any wares to turn, [9] so much as to get a single penny by? Yes thou hast ware to sell;
Knaves are thy chapmen, and thy shop is hell.

MAT. Do you hear, sir?

ORL. So, sir, I do hear, sir, more of you than you dream I do.   90

MAT. You fly a little too high, sir.

ORL. Why, sir, too high?

MAT. I ha' suff'red your tongue, like a barr'd cater-tray, [10] to run all this while, and ha' not stopp'd it.

ORL. Well, sir, you talk like a gamester.

MAT. If you come to bark at her because she 's a poor rogue, look you, here 's a fine path, sir, and there, there, there, the door.

BELL. Matheo!   100

MAT. Your blue-coats [11] stay for you, sir. I love a good, honest roaring-boy, and so —

ORL. That 's the devil.

MAT. Sir, sir, I 'll ha' no Joves in my house to thunder avaunt. She shall live and be maintained when you, like a keg of musty sturgeon, shall stink. Where? in your coffin. How? be a musty fellow, and lousy.

ORL. I know she shall be maintained, but how? She like a quean, thou like a [110 knave; she like a whore, thou like a thief.

MAT. Thief? Zounds! thief?

BELL. Good, dearest Mat! — Father!

MAT. Pox on you both! I 'll not be braved. New satin scorns to be put down with bare bawdy velvet. Thief!

ORL. Ay, thief; th' art a murderer, a cheater, a whoremonger, a pot-hunter, a borrower, a beggar —

BELL. Dear Father —   120

MAT. An old ass, a dog, a churl, a chuff, an usurer, a villain, a moth, a mangy mule, with an old velvet footcloth on his back, sir.

---

[8] Or as if the sin had never existed.
[9] Turn over, sell.   [10] A kind of false dice.
[11] Servants.

[7] As meaningless as Simon Eyre's Near-Eastern epithets.

BELL. Oh me!

ORL. Varlet, for this I 'll hang thee.

MAT. Ha, ha, alas!

ORL. Thou keepest a man of mine here, under my nose.

MAT. Under thy beard. 129

ORL. As arrant a smell-smock, for an old muttonmonger [12] as thyself.

MAT. No, as yourself.

ORL. As arrant a purse-taker as ever cried, " Stand ! " yet a good fellow, I confess, and valiant ; but he 'll bring thee to th' gallows. You both have robb'd of late two poor country peddlers.

MAT. How 's this? how 's this? Doest thou fly high? Rob peddlers? — Bear witness, Front — rob peddlers? My man and [140 I a thief?

BELL. Oh, sir, no more.

ORL. Ay, knave, two peddlers. Hue and cry is up, warrants are out, and I shall see thee climb a ladder.[13]

MAT. And come down again as well as a bricklayer or a tiler. — [*aside*] How the vengeance knows he this? — If I be hanged, I 'll tell the people I married old Friscobaldo's daughter ; I 'll frisco you, and your old carcass.

ORL. Tell what you canst ; if I stay [151 here longer, I shall be hang'd too, for being in thy company ; therefore, as I found you, I leave you —

MAT. [*aside to* BELLAFRONT] Kneel, and get money of him.

ORL. A knave and a quean, a thief and a strumpet, a couple of beggars, a brace of baggages.

MAT. [*aside to* BELLAFRONT] Hang [160 upon him. — Ay, ay, sir, fare you well ; we are so. — [*aside*] Follow close. — We are beggars — in satin. — [*aside*] To him.

BELL. Is this your comfort, when so many years
You ha' left me frozen to death?

ORL. Freeze still, starve still !

BELL. Yes, so I shall ; I must ; I must and will.
If, as you say, I 'm poor, relieve me then ;
Let me not sell my body to base men.
You call me strumpet ; Heaven knows I am none.
Your cruelty may drive me to be one ; 170
Let not that sin be yours ; let not the shame
Of common whore live longer than my name.
That cunning bawd, Necessity, night and day

Plots to undo me ; drive that hag away,
Lest being at lowest ebb, as now I am,
I sink for ever.

ORL. Lowest ebb, what ebb?

BELL. So poor, that, though to tell it be
    my shame,
I am not worth a dish to hold my meat ;
I am yet poorer : I want bread to eat.

ORL. It 's not seen by your cheeks. 180

MAT. [*aside*] I think she has read an homily to tickle to the old rogue.

ORL. Want bread ! There 's satin : bake that.

MAT. 'Sblood, make pasties of my clothes?

ORL. A fair new cloak, stew that ; an excellent gilt rapier.

MAT. Will you eat that, sir?

ORL. I could feast ten good fellows with
    those hangers.[14]

MAT. The pox, you shall ! 190

ORL. I shall not, till thou beggest, think
    thou art poor ;
And when thou beggest I 'll feed thee at my
    door,
As I feed dogs, with bones ; till then beg,
    borrow,
Pawn, steal, and hang, turn bawd, when th'
    art no whore. —
[*aside*] My heartstrings sure would crack,
    were they strain'd more. *Exit.*

MAT. This is your father, your damn'd — Confusion light upon all the generation of you ! He can come bragging hither with four white herrings at 's tail in blue coats, without roes in their bellies ; but I may starve ere he give me so much as a cob.[15] 201

BELL. What tell you me of this? alas !

MAT. Go, trot after your dad ; do you capitulate ; I 'll pawn not for you ; I 'll not steal to be hanged for such an hypocritical, close, common harlot. Away, you dog ! — Brave, i' faith ! Udsfoot, give me some meat.

BELL. Yes, sir. *Exit.*

MAT. Goodman slave, my man, too, is gallop'd to the Devil a' the tother [210 side ; Pacheco, I 'll checo you. — Is this your dad's day? England, they say, is the only hell for horses, and only paradise for women ; pray get you to that paradise, because y' are called an honest whore ; there they live none but honest whores, with a pox. Marry, here in our city, all [y]our sex are but foot-cloth

---

[12] Whoremonger.   [13] *I.e.*, be hanged.

[14] The straps, often elaborately ornamented, in which the sword was slung.
[15] Herring's head.

nags : [16] the master no sooner lights but the man leaps into the saddle.

Re-enter BELLAFRONT [*with meat and drink*].

BELL. Will you sit down, I pray, sir? [220
MAT. [*sitting down*] I could tear, by th' Lord, his flesh, and eat his midriff in salt, as I eat this. — Must I choke? [17] — My father Friscobaldo, I shall make a pitiful hog-louse of you, Orlando, if you fall once into my fingers — Here 's the savorest meat ! I ha' got a stomach with chafing.[18] What rogue should tell him of those two peddlers? A plague choke him, and gnaw him to the bare bones ! — Come, fill.　　　　230
BELL. Thou sweatest with very anger, good sweet. Vex not, 'las ; 't is no fault of mine.
MAT. Where didst buy this mutton? I never felt better ribs.
BELL. A neighbor sent it me.

Re-enter ORLANDO [*as* PACHECO].

MAT. Ha! neighbor! Foh, my mouth stinks! You whore, do you beg victuals for me? Is this satin doublet to be bombasted [19] with broken meat?
　　　　　　　　　　　Takes up the stool.
ORL. What will you do, sir?　　　　240
MAT. Beat out the brains of a beggarly —
ORL. Beat out an ass's head of your own. — Away, Mistress ! (*Exit* BELLAFRONT.) Zounds, do but touch one hair of her, and I 'll so quilt your cap with old iron,[20] that your coxcomb shall ache the worse these seven years for 't. Does she look like a roasted rabbit, that you must have the head for [21] the brains?
MAT. Ha, ha! Go out of my doors, you rogue ! Away, four marks ; [22] trudge.　　250
ORL. Four marks? No, sir ; my twenty pound that you ha' made fly high, and I am gone.
MAT. Must I be fed with chippings? You 're best get a clapdish,[23] and say y' are proctor to some spittle-house.[24] — Where hast thou been, Pacheco? Come hither my little turkey-cock.

---

[16] Comparing women, in their long dresses, to horses in long housings that nearly touched the ground.
[17] *I.e.*, why don't you fill my cup?
[18] An appetite by getting angry.
[19] Stuffed out.
[20] My old sword (or dagger).
[21] For the sake of.
[22] Evidently a common wage for servants.
[23] Beggars carried a wooden dish, the cover of which they clapped against it to attract attention.
[24] Hospital.

ORL. I cannot abide, sir, to see a woman wrong'd, not I.　　　　260
MAT. Sirrah, here was my father-in-law to-day.
ORL. Pish, then y' are full of crowns.
MAT. Hang him ! he would ha' thrust crowns upon me, to have fall'n in [25] again ; but I scorn cast clothes, or any man's gold.
ORL. [*aside*] — But mine. — How did he brook that, sir?
MAT. Oh, swore like a dozen of drunken tinkers ; at last growing foul in words, he [270 and four of his men drew upon me, sir.
ORL. In your house? Would I had been by !
MAT. I made no more ado, but fell to my old lock,[26] and so thrashed my blue-coats and old crab-tree-face my father-in-law, and then walk'd like a lion in my grate.[27]
ORL. O noble master !
MAT. Sirrah, he could tell me of the robbing the two peddlers, and that warrants [280 are out for us both.
ORL. Good sir, I like not those crackers.[28]
MAT. Crackhalter,[29] wou't [30] set thy foot to mine?
ORL. How, sir? at drinking?
MAT. We 'll pull that old crow my father, rob thy master. I know the house, thou the servants ; the purchase [31] is rich, the plot to get it easy ; the dog will not part from a bone.　　　　290
ORL. Pluck 't out of his throat, then. I 'll snarl for one, if this [32] can bite.
MAT. Say no more, say no more, old coal ; [33] meet me anon at the sign of the Shipwreck.
ORL. Yes, sir.
MAT. And, dost hear, man? — the Ship-
　　　wreck.　　　　　　　　　　*Exit.*
ORL. Th' art at the shipwreck now, and
　　　like a swimmer,
Bold, but unexpert, with those waves doest
　　　play,
Whose dalliance, whorelike, is to cast thee
　　　away. —

Enter HIPPOLITO *and* BELLAFRONT.

And here 's another vessel, better fraught, [300
But as ill-mann'd ; her sinking will be
　　　wrought,
If rescue come not.　Like a man-of-war

---

[25] Become friends.
[26] Wrestling grip.
[27] Cage.
[28] Liars, braggarts.
[29] Rogue.　　　[30] Wilt thou.　　　[31] Loot.
[32] This sword or dagger.
[33] *I.e.*, still showing fire.

I 'll therefore bravely out ; somewhat I 'll do,
And either save them both or perish, too.
                                    Exit.
  HIP. It is my fate to be bewitched by those
    eyes.
  BELL. Fate ? your folly.
Why should my face thus mad you ? 'Las,
    those colors
Are wound up long ago, which beauty spread ;
The flow'rs that once grew here, are withered.
You turn'd my black soul white, made it look
    new ;   310
And, should I sin, it ne'er should be with you.
  HIP. Your hand ; I 'll offer you fair play.
    When first
We met i' th' lists together, you remember
You were a common rebel ; with one parley
I won you to come in.
  BELL.   You did.
  HIP.   I 'll try
If now I can beat down this chastity
With the same ordnance. Will you yield this
    fort,
If with the power of argument now, as then,
I get of you the conquest : as before
I turn'd you honest, now to turn you
    whore,   320
By force of strong persuasion?
  BELL.   If you can,
I yield.
  HIP.   The alarm 's struck up ; I 'm
    your man.
  BELL. A woman gives defiance.
  HIP.   Sit.
  BELL.   Begin ;
'T is a brave battle to encounter sin.
  HIP. You men that are to fight in the same
    war
To which I 'm press'd, and plead at the same
    bar,
To win a woman, if you would have me speed,[34]
Send all your wishes !
  BELL.   No doubt y' are heard ;[35] proceed.
  HIP. To be a harlot, that you stand upon,[36]
The very name 's a charm to make you one.
Harlot[ta][37] was a dame of so divine   331
And ravishing touch[38] that she was concu-
    bine
To an English king ; her sweet, bewitching
    eye

Did the king's heartstrings in such love knots
    tie
That even the coyest was proud when she
    could hear
Men say, " Behold, another Harlot there ! "
And after her all women that were fair
Were harlots call'd, as to this day some are.
Besides, her dalliance she so well does mix,
That she 's in Latin call'd the *meretrix*.   340
Thus for the name ; for[39] the profession, this :
Who lives in bondage, lives lac'd ; the chief
    bliss
This world below can yield is liberty :
And who, than whores, with looser wings dare
    fly ?
As Juno's proud bird[40] spreads the fairest tail,
So does a strumpet hoist the loftiest sail.
She 's no man's slave ; men are her slaves.
    Her eye
Moves not on wheels screw'd up with jealousy ;
She, hors'd or coach'd, does merry journeys
    make,
Free as the sun in his gilt zodiac ;   350
As bravely does she shine, as fast she 's driven,
But stays not long in any house of heaven,
But shifts from sign to sign, her amorous
    prizes
More rich being when she 's down, than when
    she rises.
In brief, gentlemen haunt them, soldiers fight
    for them,
Few men but know them, few or none abhor
    them.
Thus for sport's sake speak I, as to a woman
Whom, as the worst ground, I would turn to
    common ;
But you I would enclose[41] for mine own bed.
  BELL. So should a husband be dishonored.
  HIP. Dishonored ? Not a whit ; to fall to
    one   361
Besides your husband is to fall to none,
For one no number is.
  BELL.   Faith, should you take
One in your bed, would you that reckoning
    make?
'T is time you sound retreat.
  HIP.   Say, have I won ?
Is the day ours?
  BELL.   The battle 's but half done ;
None but yourself have yet sounded alarms ;
Let us strike too, else you dishonor arms.

----

[34] Succeed.   [35] By some in the audience.
[36] That you consider an important argument.
[37] The mistress of Duke Robert of Normandy,
father of William the Conqueror. The derivation
is, however, fanciful.
[38] Quality.

[39] As for.   [40] The peacock.
[41] The figure is from the practice of enclosing
for private use land formerly common. It was a
cause of much complaint.

HIP. If you can win the day, the glory's
    yours.

BELL. To prove a woman should not be a
    whore :   370

When she was made, she had one man, and no
    more ;

Yet she was tied to laws then, for even than,[42]

'T is said, she was not made for men, but man.

Anon,[43] t' increase earth's brood, the law was
    varied,

Men should take many wives ; and, though
    they married

According to that act, yet 't is not known

But that those wives were only tied to one.

New parliaments were since ;[44] for now one
    woman

Is shared between three hundred, nay she's
    common,

Common ! as spotted leopards, whom for
    sport   380

Men hunt to get the flesh, but care not for 't.

So spread they nets of gold, and tune their
    calls,

To enchant silly women to take falls ;

Swearing they are angels, which, that they
    may win,

They 'll hire the Devil to come with false dice
    in.

Oh Sirens' subtle tunes ! yourselves you flatter,

And our weak sex betray : so men love water ;

It serves to wash their hands, but being once
    foul,

The water down is pour'd, cast out of doors ;

And even of such base use do men make
    whores.   390

A harlot, like a hen, more sweetness reaps,

To pick men one by one up, than in heaps ;

Yet all feeds but confounding.[45] Say[46] you
    should taste me ;

I serve but for the time, and when the day

Of war is done, am cashier'd out of pay ;

If like lame soldiers I could beg, that's all ;

And there's lust's rendezvous, an hospital.

Who then would be a man's slave, a man's
    woman ?

She 's half starv'd the first day that feeds in
    common.

HIP. You should not feed so, but with me
    alone.   400

BELL. If I drink poison by stealth, is 't not
    all one ?

Is 't not rank poison still ? with you alone !

Nay, say you spi'd a courtesan, whose soft side

To touch you 'd sell your birthright, for one
    kiss

Be rack'd ; she 's won, y' are sated : what
    follows this ?

Oh, then you curse that bawd that toll'd[47] you
    in,

The night ; you curse your lust, you loathe
    the sin,

You loathe her very sight ; and, ere the day

Arise, you rise glad when y' are stol'n away.

Even then when you are drunk with all her
    sweets,   410

There 's no true pleasure in a strumpet's sheets.

Women whom lust so prostitutes to sale,

Like dancers upon ropes, once seen, are stale.

HIP. If all the threads of harlots' lives are
    spun

So coarse as you would make them, tell me
    why

You so long loved the trade ?

BELL.   If all the threads

Of harlot's lives be fine as you would make
    them,

Why do not you persuade your wife turn
    whore,

And all dames else to fall before that sin ? [419

Like an ill husband, though I knew the same

To be my undoing, followed I that game.

Oh, when the work of lust had earn'd my
    bread,

To taste it how I trembled, lest each bit,

Ere it went down, should choke me chewing
    it !

My bed seem'd like a cabin hung in hell ;

The bawd, hell's porter ; and the lickerish[48]
    wine

The pander fetch'd was like an easy fine,[49]

For which, methought, I leas'd away my soul ;

And oftentimes, even in my quaffing bowl,

Thus said I to myself, I am a whore,   430

And have drunk down thus much confusion
    more.

HIP. It is a common rule, and 't is most
    true,

Two of one trade never love ; no more do you.

Why are you sharp 'gainst that you once pro-
    fess'd ?

BELL. Why dote you on that which you did
    once detest ?

I cannot, seeing she 's woven of such bad stuff,

Set colors on a harlot base enough.

Nothing did make me, when I loved them best,

---

[42] Then.   [43] Then, soon.
[44] There has been new legislation since then.
[45] Only leads to ruin.   [46] Suppose, let us say.
[47] Enticed.   [48] Tempting, dainty.
[49] Payment, fee.

To loathe them more than this : when in the
    street
A fair young modest damsel I did meet,   440
She seem'd to all a dove, when I pass'd by,
And I to all a raven ; every eye
That followed her went with a bashful glance,
At me each bold and jeering countenance
Darted forth scorn ; to her as if she had been
Some tower unvanquished, would they vail ; [50]
'Gainst me swoln rumor hoisted every sail ;
She, crown'd with reverend praises, pass'd by
    them ;
I, though with face mask'd, could not scape
    the " Hem ! "
For, as if Heaven had set strange marks on
    whores,   450
Because they should be pointing-stocks [51] to
    man,
Dress'd up in civilest shape, a courtesan —
Let her walk saint-like, noteless, [52] and un-
    known —
Yet she 's betray'd by some trick of her own.
Were harlots therefore wise, they 'd be sold
    dear ;
For men account them good but for one
    year,
And then, like almanacs whose dates are
    gone,
They are thrown by and no more look'd
    upon.
Who 'll therefore backward fall, who will
    launch forth   459
In seas so foul, for ventures no more worth?
Lust's voyage hath, if not this course, this
    cross :
Buy ne'er so cheap, your ware comes home
    with loss.
What, shall I sound retreat? The battle 's
    done ;
Let the world judge which of us two have
    won.
    Hip. I !
    Bell.   You? nay then, as cowards
do in fight,
What by blows cannot, shall be saved by
    flight.   *Exit.*
    Hip. Fly to earth's fixed centre, to the
    caves
Of everlasting horror, I 'll pursue thee,
Though loaden with sins, even to hell's brazen
    doors.   469
Thus wisest men turn fools, doting on whores.
                      Exit.

[50] Show deference.
[51] Objects of derision.
[52] Giving no occasion for attention.

[SCENE II] [53]

Enter the Duke, Lodovico, *and* Orlando
[*as* Pacheco] ; *after them* Infeliche, Carolo, Astolfo, Beraldo, [*and*] Fontinell.

    Orl. I beseech your Grace, though your eye
be so piercing as under a poor blue coat to cull
out an honest father from an old serving man,
yet, good my Lord, discover not the plot to
any, but only this gentleman that is now to be
an actor in our ensuing comedy.
    Duke. Thou hast thy wish, Orlando ; pass
    unknown ;
Sforsa shall only go along with thee,
To see that warrant served upon thy son. [54]
    Lod. To attach him upon felony, for [10
two peddlers ; is 't not so?
    Orl. Right, my noble knight. Those ped-
dlers were two knaves [55] of mine ; he fleec'd the
men before, and now he purposes to flay the
master. He will rob me ; his teeth water to
be nibbling at my gold ; but this shall hang
him by th' gills, till I pull him on shore.
    Duke. Away ; ply you the business.
    Orl. Thanks to your Grace ; but, my good
Lord, for my daughter —   20
    Duke. You know what I have said.
    Orl. And remember what I have sworn.
She 's more honest, [56] on my soul, than one of
the Turk's wenches, watch'd by a hundred
eunuchs.
    Lod. So she had need, for the Turks make
them whores.
    Orl. He 's a Turk that makes any woman a
whore ; he 's no true Christian, I 'm sure. I
commit your Grace. [57]   30
    Duke. Infeliche.
    Inf. Here, sir.
            [Duke *and* Infeliche *step aside.*]
    Lod. Signior Friscobaldo.
    Orl. Frisking again? Pacheco !
    Lod. Uds so, Pacheco ! We 'll have some
sport with this warrant ; 't is to apprehend
all suspected persons in the house. Besides,
there 's one Bots, a pander, and one Madam
Horseleech, a bawd, that have abus'd my
friend [58] ; those two conies will we ferret [40
into the pursenet. [59]
    Orl. Let me alone for dabbing [60] them o'
th' neck. Come, come.

[53] An apartment in the Duke's palace.
[54] Son-in-law.   [55] Servants.   [56] Chaste.
[57] To the providence of God ; *i.e.*, adieu.
[58] Deceived Carolo.
[59] A net closed by a draw-string.
[60] Striking.

Lod. Do ye hear, gallants? Meet me anon
at Matheo's.

Omnes. Enough.

    Exeunt Lodovico *and* Orlando.

Duke. Th' old fellow sings that note thou
    didst before,
Only his tunes are that she is no whore,
But that she sent his letters and his gifts,
Out of a noble triumph o'er his lust,   50
To show she trampled his assaults in dust.

Inf. 'T is a good, honest servant, that old
    man.

Duke. I doubt no less.

Inf.   And it may be my husband;
Because, when once this woman was unmask'd,
He levell'd all her thoughts and made them fit,
Now he'd mar all again, to try his wit.

Duke. It may be so, too; for to turn a
    harlot
Honest, it must be by strong antidotes;
'T is rare, as to see panthers change their spots.
And when she's once a star fixed and shines
    bright,   60
Though 't were impiety then to dim her light,
Because we see such tapers seldom burn,
Yet 't is the pride and glory of some men
To change her to a blazing star again;
And it may be Hippolito does no more. —
It cannot be but y' are acquainted all
With that same madness of our son-in-law,
That dotes so on a courtesan.

Omnes.   Yes, my Lord.

Car. All the city thinks he's a whoremonger.   70

Ast. Yet I warrant he'll swear no man
marks [61] him.

Ber. 'T is like so, for when a man goes a-
wenching, is as if he had a strong stinking
breath; every one smells him out, yet he feels
it not, though it be ranker than the sweat of
sixteen bearwarders.

Duke. I doubt then you have all those
    stinking breaths;
You might be all smelt out.

Car. Troth, my Lord, I think we are all [80
as you ha' been in your youth when you went
a-maying; we all love to hear the cuckoo sing
upon other men's trees.[62]

Duke. It's well [that] [63] you confess. But,
    girl, thy bed
Shall not be parted [64] with a courtesan.

---

[61] Observes.
[62] *I.e.*, we all love to make others cuckolds.
[63] Q *yet*, perhaps misreading *y*[t].
[64] Divided, shared.

'T is strange!
No frown of mine; no frown of the poor
    lady,
My abus'd child, his wife; no care of fame,
Of honor, Heaven, or hell; no not that name
Of common strumpet; can affright, or woo
    him   90
To abandon her; the harlot does undo
    him;
She has bewitched him, robb'd him of his
    shape,
Turn'd him into a beast; his reason's lost;
You see he looks wild, does he not?

Car.   I ha' noted
New moons in 's face, my Lord, all full of
    change.

Duke. He's no more like unto Hippolito
Than dead men are to living — never sleeps,
Or if he do, it's dreams; and in those dreams
His arms work; and then cries, "Sweet —
    what's-her-name."
What's the drab's name?

Ast.   In troth, my Lord, I know not;
I know no drabs, not I.

Duke.   Oh, Bellafront! — [101
And, catching her fast, cries, "My Bella-
    front!"

Car. A drench that's able to kill a horse
cannot kill this disease of smock-smelling, my
Lord, if it have once eaten deep.

Duke. I'll try all physic, and this med'cine
    first:
I have directed warrants strong and peremp-
    tory
To purge our city Milan, and to cure
The outward parts, the suburbs, for the at-
    taching [65]
Of all those women, who, like gold, want
    weight;   110
Cities, like ships, should have no idle freight.

Car. No, my Lord; and light wenches are
no idle freight. But what's your Grace's
reach [66] in this?

Duke. This, Carolo: if she whom my son
    dotes on,
Be in that m[u]ster-book enroll'd, he'll shame
Ever t' approach one of such noted name.

Car. But say she be not?

Duke.   Yet on harlots' heads
New laws shall fall so heavy, and such blows
Shall give to those that haunt them, that
    Hippolito   120
If not for fear of law, for love to her,
If he love truly, shall her bed forbear.

---

[65] Arrest.   [66] Purpose.

CAR. Attach all the light heels i' th' city and clap 'em up? Why, my Lord, you dive into a well unsearchable. All the whores within the walls, and without the walls? I would not be he should meddle with them for ten such dukedoms ; the army that you speak on is able to fill all the prisons within this city, and to leave not a drinking-room in any tavern besides.   131

DUKE. Those only shall be caught that are of note ;

Harlots in each street flow.

The fish being thus i' th' net, ourself will sit,

And with eye most severe dispose of it.

Come, girl.   [*Exeunt* DUKE *and* INFELICHE.]

CAR. Arraign the poor whore !

AST. I 'll not miss that sessions.

FONT. Nor I.   139

BER. Nor I, though I hold up my hand [67] there myself.   *Exeunt.*

[SCENE III] [68]

Enter MATHEO, LODOVICO, *and* ORLANDO [*as* PACHECO].

MAT. Let who will come, my noble chevalier ; I can but play the kind host, and bid 'em welcome.

LOD. We 'll trouble your house, Matheo, but as Dutchmen do in taverns : drink, be merry, and be gone.

ORL. Indeed, if you be right Dutchmen, if you fall to drinking you must be gone. [69]

MAT. The worst is, my wife is not at home ; but we 'll fly high, my generous knight, for [10 all that.   There 's no music when a woman is in the consort. [70]

ORL. No ; for she 's like a pair of virginals, [71] Always with jacks at her tail.

Enter ASTOLFO, CAROLO, BERALDO, [*and*] FONTINELL.

LOD. See, the covey is sprung.

OMNES. Save you, gallants.

MAT. Happily encounter'd, sweet bloods.

LOD. Gentlemen, you all know Signior Candido, the linen-draper, he that 's more patient than a brown baker upon the day when he [20 heats his oven, and has forty scolds about him.

OMNES. Yes, we know him all; what of him?

LOD. Would it not be a good fit of mirth, to make a piece of English cloth of him, and to stretch him on the tenters, [72] till the threads of his own natural humor [73] crack, by making him drink healths, tobacco, [74] dance, sing bawdy songs, or to run any bias [75] according as we think good to cast him?

CAR. 'T were a morris dance worth the seeing.   31

AST. But the old fox is so crafty we shall hardly hunt [him] [76] out of his den.

MAT. To that train I ha' given fire already ; and the hook to draw him hither is to see certain pieces of lawn, which I told him I have to sell, and indeed have such ; fetch them down, Pacheco.

ORL. Yes, sir ; I 'm your water-spaniel, and will fetch anything. — [*aside*] But I 'll [40 fetch one dish of meat anon shall turn your stomach, and that 's a constable.   *Exit.*

Enter BOTS, *ushering* MISTRESS HORSELEECH.

OMNES. How now? how now?

CAR. What galley-foist [77] is this?

LOD. Peace, two dishes of stewed prunes [78] : a bawd and a pander. — My worthy Lieutenant Bots ! why, now I see thou 'rt a man of thy word ; welcome. — Welcome Mistress Horseleech. — Pray, gentlemen, salute this reverend matron.   50

MIS. H. Thanks to all your Worships.

LOD. I bade a drawer send in wine, too ; did none come along with thee, grannam, but the Lieutenant?

MIS. H. None came along with me but Bots, if it like your Worship.

BOTS. Who the pox should come along with you but Bots?

Enter two Vintners.

OMNES. Oh brave ! march fair !

LOD. Are you come? That 's well.   60

MAT. Here 's ordnance able to sack [79] a city.

LOD. Come, repeat, read this inventory.

1 VINT. *Imprimis,* a pottle [80] of Greek wine,

---

[72] A frame on which cloth is stretched on hooks to ensure its drying square and without shrinking.
[73] His naturally (placid) disposition.
[74] To drink tobacco was a common expression for smoking.
[75] Take any course.
[76] Om. Q.
[77] A state barge.   Evidently the old harridan sails in, dressed to the nines.
[78] A dish much used in the brothels, since it was supposed to be an aid against infection.
[79] Note the pun.
[80] A two-quart can.

[67] Testify.   [68] A room in Matheo's house.
[69] Get drunk.   [70] Band.
[71] Cf. "a pair of organs" = a single instrument. For "jacks" see on *Part I,* V, ii, 315.

a pottle of Peter-sameene,[81] a pottle of Char-n[e]co,[82] and a pottle of [Leatica].[83]

Lod. Y' are paid?

2 Vint. Yes, Sir. 　　　*Exeunt* Vintners.

Mat. So shall some of us be anon, I fear.

Bots. Here 's a hot day [84] towards ; [85] but, zounds, this is the life out of which a soldier [70 sucks sweetness ! When this artillery goes off roundly, some must drop to the ground : can-non,[86] demi-cannon, saker,[87] and basilisk.[88]

Lod. Give fire, Lieutenant.

Bots. So, so ; must I venture first upon the breach? — To you all, gallants ; Bots sets upon you all.[89] 　　　[*Drinks.*]

Omnes. It 's hard, Bots, if we pepper not you as well as you pepper us.

Enter Candido.

Lod. My noble linen-draper ! — Some [80 wine ! — Welcome, old lad !

Mat. Y' are welcome, signior.

Cand. These lawns, sir?

Mat. Presently ; my man is gone for them. We ha' rigged a fleet, you see here, to sail about the world.

Cand. A dangerous voyage, sailing in such ships.

Bots. There 's no casting [90] overboard yet.

Lod. Because you are an old lady, I will have you be acquainted with this grave [90 citizen. Pray bestow your lips upon him, and bid him welcome.

Mis. H. Any citizen shall be most welcome to me. — I have used to buy ware at your shop.

Cand. It may be so, good madam.

Mis. H. Your prentices know my dealings well ; I trust your good wife be in good case. If it please you, bear her a token from my lips, by word of mouth. 　　　[*Kisses him.*] 100

Cand. I pray, no more ; forsooth, 't is very well ;

Indeed I love no sweetmeats. — [*aside*] Sh 'as a breath

Stinks worse than fifty polecats. — Sir, a word, Is she a lady?

[81] *Pedro-Ximines*, a Malaga wine.
[82] A Portuguese wine.
[83] Aleatico, a red muscatel wine, produced near Siena. Q *Ziattica*.
[84] *I.e.*, a lively skirmish or battle.
[85] Coming, at hand.
[86] Touching in turn each of the four pottles.
[87] A cannon much used on ships and as a siege-gun.
[88] A large cannon, usually of brass.
[89] *I.e.*, challenges you to drink an equal amount.
[90] Note the pun.

Lod. A woman of a good house, and an ancient : she 's a bawd.

Cand. A bawd ! Sir, I 'll steal hence, and see your lawns
Some other time.

Mat. Steal out of such company? Pa-checo, my man, is but gone for 'em. — [110 Lieutenant Bots, drink to this worthy old fellow, and teach him to fly high.

Omnes. Swagger ; and make him do 't on his knees.

Cand. How, Bots? Now bless me, what do I with Bots?
No wine in sooth, no wine, good Master Bots.

Bots. Graybeard, goat's pizzle,[91] 't is a health ; have this in your guts, or this, there [*touching his sword*]. I will sing a bawdy song, sir, because your verjuice [92] face is melan- [120 choly, to make liquor go down glib. Will you fall on your marrowbones, and pledge this health? 'T is to my mistress, a whore.

Cand. Here 's ratsbane upon ratsbane; Master Bots,
I pray, sir, pardon me. You are a soldier ;
Press me not to this service. I am old,
And shoot not in such pot-guns.[93]

Bots. 　　　　　　Cap,[94] I 'll teach you.

Cand. To drink healths is to drink sick-ness. — Gentlemen,
Pray rescue me.

Bots. Zounds, who dare? 　　　130

Omnes. We shall ha' stabbing then?

Cand. I ha' reckonings to cast up,[95] good Master Bots.

Bots. This will make you cast 'em up [96] better.

Lod. Why does your hand shake so?

Cand. The palsy, signiors, danceth in my blood.

Bots. Pipe,[97] with a pox, sir, then, or I 'll make your blood dance —

Cand. Hold, hold, good Master Bots, I drink. 　　　　　　[*Kneels.*]

Omnes. 　　To whom?

Cand. To the old Countess there. [*Drinks.*]

Mis. H. 　　　　　To me, old boy? [140
This is he that never drunk wine ! Once again to 't.

Cand. [*aside*] With much ado the poison is got down,

[91] Penis, used as a whip. Here with reference to Candido's leanness.
[92] Sour, crabbed.
[93] A play upon "pop-guns." (Rhys.)
[94] *I.e.*, citizen.
[95] Figure up. 　　[96] See on l. 88. 　　[97] Drink.

Though I can scarce get up ; never before
Drank I a whore's health, nor will never more.

Re-enter ORLANDO *with lawns.*

MAT. Hast been at gallows?

ORL. Yes, sir, for I make account to suffer
today.

MAT. Look, signior ; here's the commodity.

CAND. Your price? 150

MAT. Thus.[98]

CAND. No, too dear ; thus.

MAT. No. O fie, you must fly higher. Yet
take 'em home ; trifles shall not make us quarrel ; we'll agree ; you shall have them, and a
pennyworth. I'll fetch money at your shop.

CAND. Be it so, good signior ; send me
　　going.

MAT. Going? A deep bowl of wine for
Signior Candido.

ORL. He would be going. 160

CAND. I'll rather stay than go so ; stop
　　your bowl.

Enter Constable *and* Billmen.

LOD. How now?

BOTS. Is't Shrove Tuesday, that these
ghosts walk?[99]

MAT. What's your business, sir?

CONST. From the Duke ; you are the man
we look for, signior. I have warrant here from
the Duke, to apprehend you upon felony for
robbing two peddlers. I charge you i' th'
Duke's name, go quickly. 170

MAT. Is the wind turn'd? Well, this is
that old wolf, my father-in-law. — Seek out
your mistress, sirrah.

ORL. Yes, sir. — [*aside*] As shafts by piec-
　　ing are made strong,
So shall thy life be straight'ned by this wrong.
　　　　　　　　　　　　　　　　Exit.

OMNES. In troth, we are sorry.

MAT. Brave men must be cross'd ; pish, it's
but Fortune's dice roving against me. Come,
sir, pray use me like a gentleman ; let me not
be carried through the streets like a pag- [180
eant.

CONST. If these gentlemen please, you shall
go along with them.

OMNES. Be't so ; come.

CONST. What are you, sir?

BOTS. I, sir? Sometimes a figure, sometimes a cipher, as the State has occasion to cast
up her accounts. I'm a soldier.

CONST. Your name is Bots, is't not?

BOTS. Bots is my name ; Bots is known [190
to this company.

CONST. I know you are, sir ; what's she?

BOTS. A gentlewoman, my mother.

CONST. Take 'em both along.

BOTS. Me, sir?

BILLMEN. [Ay,] [100] sir !

CONST. If he swagger, raise the street.

BOTS. Gentlemen, gentlemen, whither will
you drag us?

LOD. To the garden house.[101] Bots, [200
are we even with you?

CONST. To Bridewell with 'em.

BOTS. You will answer this.

CONST. Better than a challenge. I have
warrant for my work, sir.

　　　　Exeunt [Billmen *with* BOTS *and* MIS-
　　　　　TRESS HORSELEECH].

LOD. We'll go before.

CONST. Pray do. —

　　　　Exeunt [MATHEO, *and* LODOVICO, AS-
　　　　　TOLFO, CARLO, BERALDO, *and* FON-
　　　　　TINELL.]

Who? Signior Candido? a citizen
Of your degree consorted thus, and revelling
In such a house?

CAND. Why, sir? what house, I pray? [210

CONST. Lewd, and defam'd.

CAND. Is't so? Thanks, sir ; I'm gone.

CONST. What have you there?

CAND. Lawns which I bought, sir, of the
　　gentleman
That keeps the house.

CONST. And I have warrant here
To search for such stol'n ware ; these lawns
　　are stol'n,

CAND. Indeed !

CONST. So he's the thief, you the receiver !
I'm sorry for this chance ; I must commit
　　you.

CAND. Me, sir, for what?

CONST. These goods are found upon you,
And you must answer't.

CAND. Must I so?

CONST. Most certain.

CAND. I'll send for bail.

CONST. I dare not ; yet, because [220
You are a citizen of worth, you shall not

[98] "Probably . . . . displaying the fingers."
(Rhys.)
[99] On that day the authorities made a search for
brothels, and the apprentices went about wrecking
them.

[100] Q *And.*
[101] At which Bots had asserted that Candido's
wife would meet Carolo (III, iii).

Be made a pointing-stock, but without guard
Pass only with myself.

CAND.   To Bridewell too?

CONST. No remedy.

CAND.   Yes, patience. Being not mad,
They had me once to Bedlam ; now I 'm drawn
To Bridewell, loving no whores.

CONST.   You will buy lawn ! *Exeunt.*

[ACT V — SCENE I] [1]

Enter at one door HIPPOLITO ; *at another*, Lodovico, ASTOLFO, CAROLO, BERALDO, [*and*]
FONTINELL.

LOD. Yonder 's the Lord Hippolito ; by any
means leave him and me together. Now will I
turn him to a madman.

OMNES. Save you, my Lord.

      Exeunt [*all but* HIPPOLITO *and*
      LODOVICO].

LOD. I ha' strange news to tell you.

HIP. What are they?

LOD. Your mare 's i' th' pound.

HIP. How 's this?

LOD. Your nightingale is in a lime-bush.

HIP. Ha?   10

LOD. Your puritanical " honest whore "
sits in a blue gown.[2]

HIP. Blue gown !

LOD. She 'll chalk out your way to her now ;
she beats chalk.[3]

HIP. Where? who dares? —

LOD. Do you know the brick house of castigation, by the river side that runs by Milan —
the school where they pronounce no letter well
but O?   20

HIP. I know it not.

LOD. Any man that has borne office of constable, or any woman that has fall'n from a
horse-load to a cart-load,[4] or like an old hen
that has had none but rotten eggs in her nest,
can direct you to her ; there you shall see your
punk amongst her backfriends.[5]
There you may have her at your will,
For there she beats chalk, or grinds in the mill ;
With a whip deedle, deedle, deedle, deedle ; [30
Ah, little monkey !

[1] A street.
[2] The garb of the prostitutes in the workhouse.
[3] Crushing chalk was one of the industries of
Bridewell.
[4] Alluding to the public exposure of prostitutes
by carting them through the streets.
[5] False friends.

HIP. What rogue durst serve that warrant,
knowing I loved her?

LOD. Some worshipful rascal, I lay [6] my life.

HIP. I 'll beat the lodgings down about their
ears
That are her keepers.

LOD. So you may bring an old house over
her head.

HIP. I 'll to her —
I 'll to her, stood armed fiends to guard the
doors.
                                          Exit.

LOD. O me ! what monsters are men made
by whores !
If this false fire do kindle him, there 's one [40
faggot more to the bonfire.   Now to my Bridewell birds ; what song will they sing?
                                          Exit.

[SCENE II] [7]

Enter DUKE, CAROLO, ASTOLFO, BERALDO,
FONTINELL, *three or four* Masters of Bridewell, [*and*] INFELICHE.

DUKE. Your Bridewell? that the name?
      For beauty, strength,
Capacity and form of ancient building,
Besides the river's neighborhood, few houses
Wherein we keep our court can better it.

1 MAST. Hither from foreign courts have
princes come,
And with our duke did acts of state commence.
Here that great cardinal had first audience,
The grave Campayne ; that duke dead, his son,
That famous prince,[8] gave free possession
Of this, his palace, to the citizens,   10
To be the poor man's warehouse, and endowed
it
With lands to th' value of seven hundred
mark,
With all the bedding and the furniture, once
proper,[9]
As the lands then were, to an hospital
Belonging to a duke of Savoy.   Thus
Fortune can toss the world ; a prince's court
Is thus a prison now.

DUKE.   'T is Fortune's sport.
These changes common are ; the wheel of fate
Turns kingdoms up, till they fall desolate.[10]

[6] Wager.   [7] A room in Bridewell.
[8] It is really, of course, the London Bridewell that
is here described. The cardinal, duke, and prince
are Campeius, Henry VIII, and Edward VI.
[9] Belonging to.
[10] To the rim of Fortune's wheel the fates of
kingdoms are attached, and they rise or fall in
accordance with its revolutions.

But how are these seven hundred marks by th'
    year   20
Employ'd in this your workhouse?

1 Mast.   War and peace
Feed both upon those lands ; when the iron
    doors
Of wars burst open, from this house are sent
Men furnish'd in all martial complement.
The moon hath thorough her bow scarce drawn
    to th' head,
Like to twelve silver arrows, all the months,
Since sixteen hundred soldiers went aboard.
Here providence and charity play such parts
The house is like a very school of arts ;
For when our soldiers, like ships driven from
    sea,   30
With ribs all broken and with tatter'd sides,
Cast anchor here again, their ragged backs
How often do we cover ! that, like men,
They may be sent to their own homes again.
All here are but one swarm of bees, and strive
To bring with wearied thighs honey to the hive.
The sturdy beggar, and the lazy loon,[11]
Gets here hard hands, or lac'd correction.[12]
The vagabond grows staid and learns t' obey ;
The drone is beaten well, and sent away.   40
As other prisons are, some for the thief,
Some by which undone credit gets relief
From bridled debtors, others for the poor,
So this is for the bawd, the rogue, and whore.

Car. An excellent team of horse !

1 Mast.   Nor is it seen
That the whip draws blood here, to cool the
    spleen
Of any rugged [13] bencher ; [14] nor does offence
Feel smart [15] on spiteful or rash evidence ;
But pregnant [16] testimony forth must stand,
Ere justice leave them in the beadle's hand. [50
As iron on the anvil are they laid,
Not to take blows alone, but to be made
And fashioned to some charitable use.

Duke. Thus wholsom'st laws spring from
    the worst abuse.

Enter Orlando, [*as* Pacheco,] *before*
Bellafront.

Bell. Let mercy touch your heartstrings,
    gracious Lord,
That it may sound like music in the ear
Of a man desperate, being i' th' hands of law.

Duke. His name?

Bell.   Matheo.

[11] Rascal. Q *Lowne.*   [12] Whipping.
[13] Ragged.   [14] Tavern loafer.
[15] Is any offender whipped.   [16] Cogent, clear.

Duke.   For a robbery?
Where is [he] [17]?

Bell.   In this house.

Duke.   Fetch you him hither. —
    [*Exeunt*] Bellafront *and one of the*
    Masters of Bridewell.
Is this the party?   60

Orl. This is the hen, my Lord, that the
cock with the lordly comb, your son-in-law,
would crow over and tread.[18]

Duke. Are your two servants ready?

Orl. My two peddlers are pack'd together,
    my good Lord.

Duke. 'T is well ; this day in judgment
    shall be spent.
Vice, like a wound lanc'd, mends by punish-
    ment.

Inf. Let me be gone, my Lord, or stand un-
    seen ;
'T is rare when a judge strikes and that none
    die,
And 't is unfit then women should be by.   70

1 Mast. We 'll place you, lady, in some
    private room.

Inf. Pray do so.
                    Exit [*with a* Master].

Orl. Thus nice dames swear it is unfit
    their eyes
Should view men carv'd up for anatomies ; [19]
Yet they 'll see all, so [20] they may stand unseen ;
Many women sure will sin behind a screen.

Enter Lodovico.

Lod. Your son, the Lord Hippolito, is
    ent'red.

Duke. Tell him we wish his presence. — A
    word, Sforsa :
On what wings flew he hither?

Lod. These : — I told him his lark [80
whom he loved was a Bridewell-bird ; he 's
mad that this cage should hold her, and is
come to let her out.

Duke. 'T is excellent ; away, go call him
hither.   *Exit* Lodovico.

Re-enter one of the Governors *of the House ;*
Bellafront *after him with* Matheo ; *after
him the* Constable. *Enter at another door*
Lodovico *and* Hippolito. Orlando *steps
forth and brings in two* [Servants *disguised
as*] Peddlers.

Duke. You are to us a stranger, worthy lord ;
'T is strange to see you here.

[17] Q *she.*   [18] *I.e.,* have as his mistress.
[19] Subjects of dissection.   [20] Provided that.

HIP. It is most fit
That where the sun goes, atomies [21] follow it.

DUKE. Atomies neither shape nor honor
bear : 89
Be you yourself, a sunbeam to shine clear.—
Is this the gentleman? Stand forth and hear
Your accusation.

MAT. I 'll hear none ; I fly high in that :
rather than kites shall seize upon me and
pick out mine eyes to my face, I 'll strike my
talons thorough mine own heart first, and spit
my blood in theirs. I am here for shriving
those two fools of their sinful pack. When
those jackdaws have caw'd over me, then must
I cry guilty, or not guilty. The law has [100
work enough already and therefore I 'll put
no work of mine into his hands ; the hangman
shall ha 't first. I did pluck those ganders, did
rob them.

DUKE. 'T is well done to confess.

MAT. Confess and be hanged, and then I fly
high, is 't not so? That for that ! A gallows
is the worst rub [22] that a good bowler can meet
with ; I stumbled against such a post, else this
night I had play'd the part of a true son in [110
these days, undone my father-in-law ; with
him would I ha' run at leap-frog, and come
over his gold, though I had broke his neck
for 't ; but the poor salmon-trout is now in the
net.

HIP. And now the law must teach you to fly
high.

MAT. Right, my Lord, and then may you
fly low ; [23] no more words — a mouse, mum ;
you are stopp'd.

BELL. Be good to my poor husband, dear
my Lords. 120

MAT. Ass !
Why shouldst thou pray them to be good to me,
When no man here is good to one another?

DUKE. Did any hand work in this theft but
yours?

MAT. O yes, my Lord, yes. The hangman
has never one son at a birth ; his children always come by couples. Though I cannot give
the old dog, my father, a bone to gnaw, the
daughter shall be sure of a choke-pear.[24] —
Yes, my Lord, there was one more that [130
fiddled my fine peddlers, and that was my wife.

BELL. Alas, I?

ORL. [*aside*] O everlasting, supernatural,
superlative villain !

OMNES. Your wife, Matheo?

HIP. Sure it cannot be.

MAT. Oh, sir, you love no quarters of mutton that hang up, you love none but whole
mutton.[25] She set [26] the robbery, I perform'd
it ; she spurr'd me on, I gallop'd away. 140

ORL. My Lords, —

BELL. My Lords, — fellow, give me speech,
— if my poor life
May ransom thine, I yield it to the law.
Thou hurt'st thy soul, yet wipest off no offence,
By casting blots upon my innocence.
Let not these spare me, but tell truth ; [now] [27]
see
Who slips his neck out of the misery,
Though not out of the mischief. Let thy
servant
That shared in this base act accuse me here.
Why should my husband perish, he go
clear? 150

ORL. [*aside*] A good child : hang thine own
father !

DUKE. Old fellow, was thy hand in too?

ORL. My hand was in the pie, my Lord, I
confess it. My mistress, I see, will bring me to
the gallows, and so leave me ; but I 'll not leave
her so. I had rather hang in a woman's company than in a man's ; because if we should go
to hell together, I should scarce be letten in,
for all the devils are afraid to have any [160
women come amongst them. As I am true
thief, she neither consented to this felony, nor
knew of it.

DUKE. What fury prompts thee on to kill
thy wife?

MAT. It is my humor, sir ; 't is a foolish
bagpipe that I make myself merry with. Why
should I eat hemp-seed at the hangman's thir-
teen-pence halfpenny [28] ordinary,[29] and have
this whore laugh at me, as I swing, as I totter?

DUKE. Is she a whore? 170

MAT. A sixpenny mutton pasty, for any to
cut up.

ORL. [*aside*] Ah, toad, toad, toad.

MAT. A barber's cittern [30] for every serving
man to play upon ; that lord, your son, knows
it.

HIP. I, sir? Am I her bawd then?

MAT. No, sir ; but she 's your whore then.

---

[21] Atoms, motes. [22] Obstruction.
[23] *I.e.*, stoop to Bellafront.
[24] *I.e.*, something that can hardly be swallowed.

[25] The familiar pun on "mutton" = prostitute.
[26] Planned.
[27] Emend. present Ed. Q *no*.
[28] $.27, the hangman's fee.
[29] Public meal, table d' hôte.
[30] A cittern or lute was part of the appointment
of a barber's shop. (Rhys.)

ORL. [*aside*] Yea, spider; doest catch at great flies?

HIP. My whore?   180

MAT. I cannot talk, sir, and tell of your rems and your rees [31] and your whirligigs and devices; but, my Lord, I found 'em like sparrows in one nest, billing together, and bulling [32] of me. I took 'em in bed, was ready to kill him, was up to stab her —

HIP. Close thy rank jaws! — [*to the* DUKE]
Pardon me, I am vexed. —
Thou art a villain, a malicious devil;
Deep as the place where thou art lost, thou
    liest.
Since I am thus far got into this storm,   190
I'll thorough, and thou shalt see I'll thorough
    untouch'd,
When thou shalt perish in it.

Re-enter INFELICHE.

INF.   'T is my cue
To enter now. — Room! let my prize be
    play'd;
I ha' lurk'd in clouds, yet heard what all have
    said;
What jury more can prove she has wrong'd my
    bed,
Than her own husband? She must be punished.
I challenge law, my Lord; letters and gold
And jewels from my lord that woman took.

HIP. Against that black-mouth'd devil,
    against letters and gold,
And against a jealous wife, I do uphold   200
Thus far her reputation; I could sooner
Shake th' Appenine and crumble rocks to dust
Than, though Jove's show'r [33] rain'd down,
    tempt her to lust.

BELL. What shall I say?

ORL. (*discovers himself.*) Say thou art not a whore, and that's more than fifteen women amongst five hundred dare swear without lying! This shalt thou say — no, let me say 't for thee: — thy husband's a knave; this lord's an honest man; thou art no punk; [210 this lady's a right lady. Pacheco is a thief as his master is, but old Orlando is as true a man as thy father is. I ha' seen you fly high, sir, and I ha' seen you fly low, sir; and to keep you from the gallows, sir, a blue coat have I worn, and a thief did I turn. Mine own men

are the peddlers. My twenty pound did fly high, sir; your wife's gown did fly low, sir: whither fly you now, sir? You ha' scap'd the gallows; to the Devil you fly next, sir. [220 Am I right, my Liege?

DUKE. Your father has the true physician play'd.

MAT. And I am now his patient.

HIP.   And be so still;
'T is a good sign when our cheeks blush at ill.

CONST. The linen-draper, Signior Candido,
He whom the city terms the patient man,
Is likewise here for buying of those lawns
The peddlers lost.

INF.   Alas, good Candido!

DUKE. Fetch him; and when these payments up are cast,   *Exit* Constable.
Weigh out your light gold; [34] but let's have
    them last.   230

Enter CANDIDO *and* Constable, [*who presently goes out*].

DUKE. In Bridewell, Candido?

CAND.   Yes, my good Lord.

DUKE. What make [35] you here?

CAND.   My Lord, what make you here?

DUKE. I'm here to save right, and to drive wrong hence.

CAND. And I to bear wrong here with patience.

DUKE. You ha' bought stol'n goods.

CAND.   So they do say, my Lord;
Yet bought I them upon a gentleman's word,
And I imagine now, as I thought then,
That there be thieves, but no thieves gentlemen.

HIP. Your credit's [36] crack'd, being here.

CAND.   No more than gold,
Being crack'd, which does his [37] estimation
    hold.   240
I was in Bedlam once, but was I mad?
They made me pledge whores' healths, but am
    I bad
Because I'm with bad people?

DUKE.   Well, stand by;
If you take wrong, we'll cure the injury.

Re-enter Constable; *after him* BOTS, *after them two* Beadles, *one with hemp, the other with a beetle.*[38]

DUKE. Stay, stay, what's he? a prisoner?

CONST.   Yes, my Lord.

---

[31] Strumpets. *Rem* = female raven; *re* = female ruff, a bird of the sandpiper family.
[32] Making a horned beast, cuckolding. — After "him" (l. 186) understand "who."
[33] Of gold, when he wooed Danaë.

[34] After we have settled Candido's affairs, produce your prostitutes.
[35] Do.   [36] Reputation.   [37] Its.
[38] A heavy mallet. Q transposes *him* and *them*.

HIP. He seems a soldier.

BOTS. I am what I seem, sir, one of Fortune's bastards, a soldier and a gentleman, and am brought in here with Master Constable's band of billmen, because they face me [39] [250 down that I live, like those that keep bowling alleys, by the sins of the people, in being a squire of the body.[40]

HIP. Oh, an apple-squire.[41]

BOTS. Yes, sir, that degree of scurvy squires ; and that I am maintained by the best part that is commonly in a woman, by the worst players of those parts ; but I am known to all this company.

LOD. My Lord, 't is true, we all know [260 him ; 't is Lieutenant Bots.

DUKE. Bots ; and where ha' you served, Bots?

BOTS. In most of your hottest services in the Low Countries : at the Groyne I was wounded in this thigh, and halted upon 't,[42] but 't is now sound. In Cleveland [43] I miss'd but little, having the bridge of my nose broken down with two great stones,[44] as I was scaling a fort. I ha' been tried, sir, too, in Gelder- [270 land, and scap'd hardly there from being blown up at a breach : I was fired,[45] and lay i' th' surgeon's hands for 't, till the fall of the leaf following.

HIP. All this may be, and yet you no soldier.

BOTS. No soldier, sir? I hope these are services that your proudest commanders do venture upon, and never come off sometimes.

DUKE. Well, sir, because you say you are a soldier,

I 'll use you like a gentleman. — Make room there ; 280

Plant him amongst you. We shall have anon Strange hawks fly here before us. If none light

On you, you shall with freedom take your flight ;
But if you prove a bird of baser wing,
We 'll use you like such birds : here you shall sing.

BOTS. I wish to be tried at no other weapon.

DUKE. Why is he furnish'd with those implements?

1 MASTER. The pander is more dangerous to a state

Than is the common thief ; and though our laws

Lie heavier on the thief, yet that the pander
May know the hangman's ruff should fit him too, 291

Therefore he 's set to beat hemp.

DUKE. This does savor
Of justice ; basest slaves to basest labor.
Now, pray, set open hell, and let us see
The she-devils that are here.

INF. Methinks this place
Should make e'en Lais [46] honest.

1 MAST. Some it turns good ;
But as some men, whose hands are once in blood,

Do in a pride spill more, so some going hence
Are, by being here, lost in more impudence.
Let it not to them, when they come, appear
That anyone does as their judge sit here ; [301
But that as gentlemen you come to see,
And then perhaps their tongues will walk more free.

DUKE. Let them be marshall'd in. —
[*Exeunt* Masters, Constable, *and* Beadles.] — Be cover'd all ;

Fellows, now to make the scene more comical.

CAR. Will not you be smelt out, Bots?

BOTS. No, your bravest [47] whores have the worst noses.[48]

Re-enter two of the Masters ; *a* Constable *after them, then* DOROTHEA TARGET, *brave ;* [49] *after her two* Beadles, *th' one with a wheel, the other with a blue gown.*

LOD. Are not you a bride, forsooth?

DOR. Say ye?

CAR. He would know if these be not [310 your bridemen.

DOR. Uuh ! yes, sir ; and, look ye, do you see? the bride-laces that I give at my wedding will serve to tie rosemary to both your coffins when you come from hanging — scab ! [50]

ORL. Fie,[51] punk, fie, fie, fie !

DOR. Out, you stale, stinking head of garlic ; foh, at my heels.

ORL. My head 's cloven.

HIP. O, let the gentlewoman alone ; [320 she 's going to shrift.

AST. Nay, to do penance.

CAR. Ay, ay, go, punk, go to the cross and be whipp'd.

---

[39] *I.e.*, confront me and put me down, with the charge.
[40] Originally a knight's attendant ; then, as here, = pimp.
[41] Pimp. [42] Limped, as a consequence.
[43] *I.e.*, Cleft-land.
[44] With a pun on "stones" = testes.
[45] Contracted a venereal disease.

[46] The famous courtesan of Corinth.   [47] Finest.
[48] Alluding to the effect of syphilis on the nose.
[49] Finely dressed.   [50] Rogue.
[51] An exclamation of strong reproach, regularly employed by the virtuous on such occasions.

DOR. Marry, mew, marry muff,[52] marry, hang you, Goodman Dog. Whipp'd? do ye take me for a base, spital-whore? [53] — In troth, gentlemen, you wear the clothes of gentlemen, but you carry not the minds of gentlemen, to abuse a gentlewoman of my fashion.   330

LOD. Fashion! Pox a' your fashions! Art not a whore?

DOR. Goodman Slave.

DUKE. O fie, abuse her not; let us two talk. What mought I call your name, pray?

DOR. I'm not ashamed of my name, sir; my name is Mistress Doll Target, a Western gentlewoman.

LOD. Her target against any pike in Milan.

DUKE. Why is this wheel borne after her?   340

1 MAST. She must spin.

DOR. A coarse thread it shall be, as all threads are.

AST. If you spin, then you'll earn money here too?

DOR. I had rather get half-a-crown abroad, than ten crowns here.

ORL. Abroad? I think so.

INF. Doest thou not weep now thou art here?

DOR. Say ye? weep? Yes, forsooth, as you did when you lost your maidenhead. Do you not hear how I weep?   *Sings.* [350

LOD. Farewell, Doll.

DOR. Farewell, dog.   *Exit [with* Beadles].

DUKE. Past shame, past penitence! — Why is that blue gown?

1 MAST. Being stripp'd out of her wanton loose attire,

That garment she puts on, base to the eye,

Only to clothe her in humility.

DUKE. Are all the rest like this?

1 MAST.   No, my good Lord.

You see this drab swells with a wanton rein; [54]

The next that enters has a different strain.

DUKE. Variety is good; let's see the rest.   360

       Exit [1] Master [*with other* Officials].

BOTS. Your Grace sees I'm sound yet, and no bullets hit me.

DUKE. Come off so, and 't is well.

OMNES. Here's the second mess.[55]

Re-enter the two Masters; *after them, the* Constable; *after him,* PENELOPE WHOREHOUND, *like a citizen's wife; after her two* Beadles, *one with a blue gown, another with chalk and a mallet.*

PEN. I ha' worn many a costly gown, but I was never thus guarded [56] with blue coats, and beadles, and constables, and —

CAR. Alas, fair mistress, spoil not thus your eyes.

PEN. Oh, sweet sir, I feel the spoiling of other places about me that are dearer than [370 my eyes; if you be gentlemen, if you be men, or ever came of a woman, pity my case! Stand to me, stick to me, good sir; you are an old man.

ORL. Hang not on me, I prithee; old trees bear no such fruit.

PEN. Will you bail me, gentlemen?

LOD. Bail thee? Art in for debt?

PEN. No; [God] [57] is my judge, sir, I am in for no debts; I paid my tailor, for this [380 gown, the last five shillings a week that was behind, yesterday.

DUKE. What is your name, I pray?

PEN. Penelope Whorehound; I come of the Whorehounds. — How does Lieutenant Bots?

OMNES. Aha, Bots!

BOTS. A very honest woman, as I'm a soldier! — A pox Bots [58] ye.

PEN. I was never in this pickle before; and yet, if I go amongst citizens' wives, they [390 jeer at me; if I go among the loose-bodied gowns,[59] they cry a pox on me because I go civilly attired, and swear their trade was a good trade till such as I am took it out of their hands. Good Lieutenant Bots, speak to these captains to bail me.

1 MAST. Begging for bail still? You are a trim gossip.[60] — Go give her the blue gown, set her to her chare.[61] Work, huswife, for your bread, away.   400

PEN. Out, you dog! — A pox on you all! — Women are born to curse thee! — But I shall live to see twenty such flat-caps [62] shaking dice for a pennyworth of pippins. — Out, you blue-eyed rogue!   *Exit [with* Beadles].

OMNES. Ha, ha, ha!

[52] An expression of contempt.
[53] Presumably = a diseased whore.
[54] *I.e.*, uncurbed by a tight rein.
[55] Course.
[56] Punning on "guarded" = adorned, trimmed.
[57] Q has a dash here, in deference to the statute against profanity.
[58] Infect. Bots disease attacks horses and cattle with worms or maggots.
[59] Prostitutes.   [60] Fine prater.
[61] Chore, set task.
[62] Citizens.

DUKE. Even now she wept, and pray'd;
  now does she curse?

1 MAST. Seeing me; if still she had stay'd,
  this had been worse.

HIP. Was she ever here before?

1 MAST.   Five times at least;
And thus, if men come to her, have her
  eyes   410
Wrung, and wept out her bail.

OMNES.   Bots, you know her?

BOTS. Is there any gentleman here that
knows not a whore, and is he a hair the worse
for that?

DUKE. Is she a city dame? She's so
  attired.

1 MAST. No, my good Lord; that's only
  but the veil
To her loose body. I have seen her here
In gayer masking suits; as several sauces
Give one dish several tastes, so change of habits
In whores is a bewitching art. To-day   420
She's all in colors to besot gallants; then
In modest black, to catch the citizen:
And this from their examination's drawn.
Now shall you see a monster, both in shape
And nature quite from these, that sheds no tear
Nor yet is nice; 't is a plain ramping bear;
Many such whales are cast upon this shore.

OMNES. Let's see her.

1 MAST. Then behold a swaggering whore.
                      Exit [Master *and* Officials].

ORL. Keep your ground, Bots.   429

BOTS. I do but traverse [63] to spy advantage how to arm myself.

Re-enter the two Masters *first; after them the*
  Constable; *after them a* Beadle *beating a*
  basin,[64] *then* CATHERINA BOUNTINALL, *with*
  MISTRESS HORSELEECH; *after them another*
  Beadle *with a blue head* [65] *guarded with yellow.*

CAT. Sirrah, when I cry, "Hold your
hands," hold, you rogue-catcher, hold. —
Bawd, are the French chilblains in your heels,
that you can come no faster? Are not you,
bawd, a whore's ancient,[66] and must not I
follow my colors?

MIS. H. O Mistress Catherine, you do me
wrong to accuse me here as you do, before the
right Worshipful. I am known for a [440
motherly, honest woman, and no bawd.

CAT. Marry, foh, honest? Burnt [67] at fourteen, seven times whipp'd, six times carted,
nine times duck'd, search'd by some hundred
and fifty constables, and yet you are honest?
Honest Mistress Horseleech, is this world a
world to keep bawds and whores honest?
How many times hast thou given gentlemen a
quart of wine in a gallon pot? How many
twelvepenny fees, nay two-shillings fees, [450
nay, when any ambassadors ha' been here, how
many half-crown fees hast thou taken? How
many carriers hast thou bribed for country
wenches? How often have I rins'd your lungs
in *aqua vitae*? [68] And yet you are honest!

DUKE. And what were you the whilst?

CAT. Marry hang you, Master Slave; who
made you an examiner?

LOD. Well said! belike this devil spares no
man.   460

CAT. [*to* BOTS] What art thou, prithee?

BOTS. Nay, what art thou, prithee?

CAT. A whore; art thou a thief?

BOTS. A thief, no; I defy [69] the calling; I
am a soldier, have borne arms in the field, been
in many a hot skirmish, yet come off sound.

CAT. Sound, with a pox to ye, ye abominable rogue! You a soldier? You in skir-
mishes? Where? Amongst pottle-pots in a
bawdyhouse? Look, here, you Madam [470
Worm-eaten, do you not know him?

MIS. H. Lieutenant Bots! where have ye
been this many a day?

BOTS. [*aside to* MISTRESS HORSELEECH] Old
bawd, do not discredit me; seem not to know
me.

MIS. H. Not to know ye, Master Bots?
As long as I have breath, I cannot forget thy
sweet face.

DUKE. Why, do you know him? He says
  he is a soldier.   480

CAT. He a soldier? A pander, a dog that
will lick up sixpence. Do ye hear, you Master
Swine's-snout, how long is 't since you held the
door for me, and cried, "To 't again; nobody
comes!" ye rogue, you?

OMNES. Ha, ha, ha! y' are smelt out again,
Bots.

BOTS. Pox ruin her nose for 't! An I be
not revenged for this — um, ye bitch!   489

LOD. D' ye hear ye, madam? Why does
your Ladyship swagger thus? Y' are very
brave, methinks.

---

[63] March along.
[64] Alluding "to the custom of old, when bawds
and other infamous persons were carted. A mob
of people used to precede them, beating basins."
(Whalley, cited by Dyce.)
[65] Headdress.   [66] Ensign.

[67] Probably = infected with venereal disease.
[68] Spirits.
[69] Reject, despise, disclaim.

Cat. Not at your cost, Master Cod's-
head ; [70]

Is any man here blear-eyed to see me brave?

Ast. Yes, I am ; because good clothes upon
a whore's back is like fair painting upon a
rotten wall.

Cat. Marry muff, Master Whoremaster ;
you come upon me with sentences.[71]   499

Ber. By this light, has small sense for 't.

Lod. O fie, fie, do not vex her ! And yet
methinks a creature of more scurvy conditions
should not know what a good petticoat were.

Cat. Marry, come out ; y' are so busy
about my petticoat, you'll creep up to my
placket,[72] an ye could but attain the honor ;
but, an the outsides offend your Rogue-ships,
look o' the lining — 't is silk.

Duke. Is 't silk 't is lined with, then? 509

Cat. Silk? Ay, silk, Master Slave ! You
would be glad to wipe your nose with the skirt
on 't. This 't is to come among a company of
cod's-heads that know not how to use a gentlewoman.

Duke. Tell her the Duke is here.

1 Mast. Be modest, Kate, the Duke is here.

Cat. If the Devil were here, I care not.
Set forward, ye rogues, and give attendance
according to your places ! Let bawds and
whores be sad, for I 'll sing an the Devil [520
were a-dying.

   [*Exit with* Mistress Horseleech
    and Beadles.]

Duke. Why before her does the basin
ring?

1 Mast. It is an emblem of their revelling.

The whips we use lets forth their wanton
blood,

Making them calm ; and, more to calm their
pride,

Instead of coaches they in carts do ride.

Will your Grace see more of this bad ware?

Duke. No, shut up shop ; we 'll now break
up the fair.

Yet ere we part — you, sir, that take upon
ye

The name of soldier, that true name of
worth,

Which action, not vain boasting, best sets
forth ;   531

To let you know how far a soldier's name

Stands from your title, and to let you see

[70] Blockhead.
[71] Maxims.
[72] The slit in a skirt or petticoat.

Soldiers must not be wrong'd where princes
be,

This be your sentence : —

Omnes. Defend yourself, Bots.

Duke. First, all the private sufferance that
the house

Inflicts upon offenders, you, as the basest,

Shall undergo it double ; after which 539

You shall be whipp'd sir, round about the city,

Then banish'd from the land.

Bots. Beseech, your Grace !

Duke. Away with him ; see it done. —
Panders and whores

Are city plagues, which, being kept alive,

Nothing that looks like goodness ere can
thrive. —

Now good Orlando, what say you to your bad
son-in-law?

Orl. Marry this, my Lord : he is my son-
in-law, and in law will I be his father ; for if
law can pepper him, he shall be so par- [550
boil'd that he shall stink no more i' th' nose
of the commonwealth.

Bell. Be yet more kind and merciful, good
Father.

Orl. Doest thou beg for him, thou precious
man's meat, thou? Has he not beaten thee,
kick'd thee, trod on thee ; and doest thou fawn
on him like his spaniel? Has he not pawn'd
thee to thy petticoat, sold thee to thy smock,
made ye leap at a crust, yet wouldst have me
save him?   560

Bell. Oh, yes, good sir ; women shall learn
of me

To love their husbands in greatest misery ;

Then show him pity, or you wrack myself.

Orl. Have ye eaten pigeons, that y' are
so kindhearted to your mate? Nay, y' are a
couple of wild bears ; I 'll have ye both baited
at one stake. But as for this knave, the gallows is thy due, and the gallows thou shalt
have. I 'll have justice of the Duke ; the law
shall have thy life. — What, doest thou [570
hold him? Let go his hand. If thou doest
not forsake him, a father's everlasting blessing
fall upon both your heads ! Away, go, kiss out
of my sight ; play thou the whore no more, nor
thou the thief again ; my house shall be thine,
my meat shall be thine, and so shall my wine ;
but my money shall be mine, and yet when I
die, so thou doest not fly high, take all.

Yet, good Matheo, mend.   579

Thus for joy weeps Orlando, and doth end.

Duke. Then hear, Matheo : all your woes
are stayed

By your good father-in-law ; all your ills
Are clear purged from you by his working
    pills. —
Come, Signior Candido, these green young
    wits,
We see by circumstance, this plot hath laid
Still to provoke thy patience, which they find

A wall of brass ; no armor 's like the mind.
Thou hast taught the city patience ; now our
    court
Shall be thy sphere, where, from thy good
    report,   589
Rumors this truth unto the world shall sing :
A patient man 's a pattern for a king.   *Exeunt.*

THE
KNIGHT OF
the Burning Peſtle

——————————— *Quod ſi*
Iudicium ſubtile,videndis artibus illud
Ad libros & ad hæc Muſarum dona vocares:
Bæotum in craſſo iurares aere natum.
Horat.in Epiſt.ad Oct.Aug.

LONDON,
Printed for *Walter Burre*, and are to be ſold at the
ſigne of the Crane in Paules Church-yard.
1613.

INTRODUCTORY NOTE

ALMOST everything about this play is a subject of debate except the undisputed fact of its being among the most charming of the Jacobean comedies. It is, indeed, the earliest first-rate and full-length burlesque (or, more strictly, mock heroic) piece of the English stage; and it has remained unequaled in its kind until our own time, save by *The Rehearsal* and, possibly, *The Critic*. Yet the original production was a failure. Perhaps the satire on their critical attainments was resented by the citizens. Perhaps a more sophisticated clientele assembled at the Cockpit in Drury Lane when, in 1635, the play was successfully revived. It was also acted under the Restoration, when the trend of English comedy was aristocratic; but the stages of the eighteenth and nineteenth centuries knew it not.

In a prefatory epistle Walter Burre, its first publisher, declares that the piece was written in eight days and "exposed to the wide world, who . . . utterly rejected it." It was evidently performed by a company of boys, probably the children of the Queen's Revels at the Blackfriars, but exactly when is uncertain. References to other plays agree on the whole with the statement in the induction that "this seven years there hath been plays at this house"; which apparently fixes the date in 1607. But the injunction in IV, i, 77, to read Heywood's play of *The Four Prentices of London*, is troublesome, since its earliest known edition appeared in 1615. There is an entry, however, in the Stationers' Register for 1594 which probably refers to Heywood's play; it may have been available to readers in 1607.

The publisher's epistle mentions the obvious resemblance between *Don Quixote* and *The Knight of the Burning Pestle*, which he calls the "elder above a year." *Don Quixote* was originally published in 1605; there was an edition at Brussels in 1607, on which Shelton's English translation was based. This was not printed till 1612, though it was entered in the Stationers' Register on January 19, 1611, and the preface states that it was actually made five or six years earlier. 1607 seems on the whole a more probable date for *The Knight* than 1610, which some students of the play have argued for. As for its relation to *Don Quixote*, the adventure with the barber and the mistaking of the inn for a castle, as well as the general tone of the satire on the romantic drama, indicate that if Beaumont had not actually read Cervantes he had probably heard a good deal about his book.

The earliest edition of the play fails to mention the author's name; the second and third ascribe it to Beaumont and Fletcher. Recent opinion is strongly inclined to regard it as almost wholly Beaumont's alone. For an elaborate attempt to distinguish the work of the collaborators see E. H. C. Oliphant's *The Plays of Beaumont and Fletcher* (1927). The standard collected editions, none of them very satisfactory, are those of A. Glover and A. R. Waller (1905–1912), A. H. Bullen, general editor (1904–1912 — this does not include *The Knight of the Burning Pestle*), and A. Dyce (1843–1846). *The Knight of the Burning Pestle* has been separately edited by R. M. Alden (with *A King and No King* — 1910), H. S. Murch (1908), and F. W. Moorman (1909). The first edition appeared, in quarto, in 1613 (twice reprinted in 1635). The play is not included in the earliest collected edition of Beaumont and Fletcher, the First Folio, of 1647; it appears in the Second Folio, of 1679. The present text is based on the First Quarto, with a few corrections from the subsequent editions.

THE FAMOUS HISTORY OF THE KNIGHT OF THE BURNING PESTLE

BY

FRANCIS BEAUMONT

THE SPEAKERS' NAMES [1]

The Prologue.
Then a Citizen,
The Citizen's Wife, and
RALPH,[2] her man, [his apprentice,]
[Boys.]
}
sitting below amidst the spectators.

[VENTUREWELL,] a rich merchant.
JASPER, his apprentice, [son to Merrythought].
MASTER HUMPHREY, a friend to the merchant.
Old MASTER MERRYTHOUGHT.
MICHAEL, a second son of Mistress Merrythought.
[TIM, afterwards] a squire,
[GEORGE, afterwards] a dwarf,
} [apprentices].

[WILLIAM HAMMERTON,]
[GEORGE GREENGOOSE,]
} [militiamen.]
An Host.
A Tapster.
A Boy that danceth and singeth.
A Barber.
[Three Men, supposed captives.]
A Captain.
A Sergeant.
Soldiers, [Gentlemen, Attendants, and Servants].

LUCE, merchant's daughter.
MISTRESS MERRYTHOUGHT.
[POMPIONA, daughter to the King of Moldavia.]
[A Woman, supposed captive.]

[THE SCENE — *London and Vicinity;* except Act IV, Scene II, where it is *Moldavia*.]

INDUCTION

[*Several* Gentlemen *sitting on stools upon the stage. The* Citizen, *his* Wife, *and* RALPH *sitting below among the audience.*]

Enter PROLOGUE.

PROL. From all that's near the court, from all that's great,
Within the compass of the city walls
We now have brought our scene —

Citizen [*mounts the stage*].

CIT. Hold your peace, Goodman Boy!
PROL. What do you mean, sir?

CIT. That you have no good meaning: this seven years there hath been plays at this house, I have observed it, you have still [3] girds at citizens; and now you call your play "The London Merchant." Down with [10 your title,[4] boy! down with your title!
PROL. Are you a member of the noble city?
CIT. I am.
PROL. And a freeman? [5]
CIT. Yea, and a grocer.[6]
PROL. So, grocer, then, by your sweet favor, we intend no abuse to the city.
CIT. No, sir! yes, sir! If you were not resolv'd to play the Jacks,[7] what need you study for new subjects, purposely to abuse [20

---

[1] Not in Q₁: based on Q₂, which also contains an address to readers, and a prologue transcribed from the Blackfriars' prologue of Lyly's *Sapho and Phao.*
[2] Old eds. *Raph* or *Rafe,* throughout, the latter indicating the pronunciation.

[3] Always.
[4] The title of the play was announced on a placard.
[5] *I.e.,* a member of one of the companies.
[6] *I.e.,* a member of that company, which was one of the most important.
[7] *I.e.,* play tricks.

your betters? Why could not you be contented, as well as others, with "The Legend of Whittington," [8] or "The Life and Death of Sir Thomas Gresham, with the Building of the Royal Exchange," [9] or "The Story of Queen Eleanor, with the Rearing of London Bridge upon Woolsacks?" [10]

PROL. You seem to be an understanding man; what would you have us do, sir?

CIT. Why present something notably in [30 honor of the commons of the city.

PROL. Why, what do you say to "The Life and Death of Fat Drake, or the Repairing of Fleet Privies?" [11]

CIT. I do not like that; but I will have a citizen, and he shall be of my own trade.

PROL. Oh, you should have told us your mind a month since; our play is ready to begin now.

CIT. 'T is all one for that; [12] I will [40 have a grocer, and he shall do admirable [13] things.

PROL. What will you have him do?

CIT. Marry, I will have him —

WIFE. (*below*) Husband, husband!

RALPH. (*below*) Peace, Mistress.

WIFE. [*below*] Hold thy peace, Ralph; I know what I do, I warrant t' ee.[14] — Husband, husband!

CIT. What say'st thou, cony? [15]   50

WIFE. [*below*] Let him kill a lion with a pestle, husband! Let him kill a lion with a pestle!

CIT. So he shall. — I'll have him kill a lion with a pestle.

WIFE. [*below*] Husband! shall I come up, husband?

CIT. Ay, cony. — Ralph, help your mistress this way. — Pray, gentlemen, make her a little room. — I pray you, sir, lend me [60 your hand to help up my wife; I thank you, sir. — So.

[*Wife comes on the stage.*]

WIFE. By your leave, gentlemen all; I'm something [16] troublesome. I'm a stranger here; I was ne'er at one of these plays, as

they say, before; but I should have seen [17] "Jane Shore" [18] once; and my husband hath promised me, any time this twelvemonth, to carry me to "The Bold Beauchamps," [19] but in truth he did not. I pray you, bear [70 with me.

CIT. Boy, let my wife and I have a couple [of] [20] stools and then begin; and let the grocer do rare things.   [*Stools are brought.*]

PROL. But, sir, we have never a boy to play him: every one hath a part already.

WIFE. Husband, husband, for God's sake, let Ralph play him! Beshrew me, if I do not think he will go beyond them all.

CIT. Well rememb'red, Wife. — Come [80 up, Ralph. — I'll tell you, gentlemen; let them but lend him a suit of reparel [21] and necessaries, and, by gad, if any of them all blow wind in the tail on him,[22] I'll be hang'd.

[RALPH *comes on the stage.*]

WIFE. I pray you, youth, let him have a suit of reparel! — I'll be sworn, gentlemen, my husband tells you true. He will act you sometimes at our house, that [23] all the neighbors cry out on him; he will fetch you up a couraging part so in the garret, that we [90 are all as fear'd, I warrant you, that we quake again: we'll fear [24] our children with him; if they be never so unruly, do but cry, "Ralph comes, Ralph comes!" to them, and they'll be as quiet as lambs. — Hold up thy head, Ralph; show the gentlemen what you canst do; speak a huffing [25] part; I warrant you, the gentlemen will accept of it.

CIT. Do, Ralph, do.

RALPH. " By Heaven, methinks, it were an easy leap   100
To pluck bright honor from the pale-fac'd moon;
Or dive into the bottom of the sea,
Where never fathom-line touch'd any ground,
And pluck up drowned honor from the lake of hell." [26]

CIT. How say you, gentlemen, is it not as I told you?

WIFE. Nay, gentlemen, he hath play'd

---

[8] Entered in the Stationers' Register in 1605, but without mentioning the author. Apparently it was never printed.

[9] *ii If You Know Not Me, You Know Nobody*, by Thomas Heywood, 1606.

[10] Peele's *Edward I* (1593), the phrase about the Bridge, as Dyce notes, being a jocose addition.

[11] A jocose invention. (Dyce.)

[12] That makes no difference.   [13] Wonderful.

[14] To ye; so Q₁; later eds., perhaps rightly, *ye*.

[15] Rabbit; *i.e.*, sweetheart.   [16] Somewhat.

[17] Was to have seen.

[18] Probably Heywood's *Edward IV.*

[19] A lost play, ascribed to Heywood.

[20] Add. Q₂.   [21] Apparel.

[22] *I.e.*, get sufficiently in the lead to be able to perform this action.

[23] So that.   [24] Scare.

[25] Blustering.

[26] Slightly misquoted from Shakespeare's *i Henry IV*, I, iii, 201 ff.

before, my husband says, " Mucedorus," [27] before the wardens of our company.

CIT. Ay, and he should have play'd [110 Jeronimo [28] with a shoemaker for a wager.

PROL. He shall have a suit of apparel, if he will go in.

CIT. In, Ralph, in, Ralph ; and set out the grocery in their kind,[29] if thou lov'st me.

[*Exit* RALPH.]

WIFE. I warrant, our Ralph will look finely when he 's dress'd.

PROL. But what will you have it call'd?

CIT. " The Grocer's Honor."

PROL. Methinks " The Knight of the [120 Burning Pestle " were better.

WIFE. I 'll be sworn, Husband, that 's as good a name as can be.

CIT. Let it be so. — Begin, begin ; my wife and I will sit down.

PROL. I pray you, do.

CIT. What stately music have you? You have shawms? [30]

PROL. Shawms? No.

CIT. No! I 'm a thief if my mind did [130 not give me so. Ralph plays a stately part, and he must needs have shawms. I 'll be at the charge of them myself, rather than we 'll be without them.

PROL. So you are like to be.

CIT. Why, and so I will be : there 's two shillings ; [*giving money*] let 's have the waits [31] of Southwark ; they are as rare fellows as any are in England ; and that will fetch them all o'er the water [32] with a vengeance, as if [140 they were mad.

PROL. You shall have them. Will you sit down then?

CIT. Ay. — Come, Wife.

WIFE. Sit you merry all, gentlemen ; I 'm bold to sit amongst you for my ease.

[Citizen *and* Wife *sit down.*]

PROL. From all that 's near the court, from all that 's great,

Within the compass of the city walls

We now have brought our scene. Fly far from hence

All private taxes,[33] immodest phrases,   150

Whate'er may but show like vicious !

For wicked mirth never true pleasure brings,

But honest minds are pleas'd with honest things. —

Thus much for that we do ; but for Ralph's part you must answer for yourself.

CIT. Take you no care for Ralph ; he 'll discharge himself, I warrant you.

[*Exit* PROLOGUE.]

WIFE. I' faith, gentlemen, I 'll give my word for Ralph.

ACT I — SCENE I [1]

Enter Merchant [2] [VENTUREWELL] *and* JASPER, *his prentice.*

[VENT.] Sirrah, I 'll make you know you are my prentice,

And whom my charitable love redeem'd

Even from the fall of fortune, gave thee heat

And growth to be what now thou art, new-cast thee,

Adding the trust of all I have at home,

In foreign staples,[3] or upon the sea,

To thy direction, ti'd the good opinions

Both of myself and friends to thy endeavors :

So fair were thy beginnings. But with these,

As I remember, you had never charge   10

To love your master's daughter, and even [4] then

When I had found a wealthy husband for her —

I take it, sir, you had not ; but, however,

I 'll break the neck of that commission,

And make you know you are but a merchant's factor.[5]

JASP. Sir, I do liberally confess I am yours,

Bound both by love and duty to your service,

In which my labor hath been all my profit ;

I have not lost in bargain, nor delighted

To wear your honest gains upon my back ; [20

Nor have I given a pension to my blood,[6]

Or lavishly in play [7] consum'd your stock ;

These, and the miseries that do attend them,

I dare with innocence proclaim are strangers

To all my temperate actions. For [8] your daughter,

---

[27] An anonymous comedy of great popularity; (1598).   [28] In *The Spanish Tragedy.*
[29] Exhibit or set forth to advantage the grocers in an appropriate or natural way. For "grocery" F 2 reads *grocers.*
[30] A reed instrument of the oboe family.
[31] Itinerant musicians.
[32] Over the Thames from the Surrey side.
[33] Personal censures.

[1] Not precisely located; presumably a room in Venturewell's house.
[2] So throughout the old eds. in stage directions and speech-tags.
[3] Business centers.   [4] Exactly.   [5] Agent.
[6] Indulged myself sensually.
[7] Gambling.   [8] As for.

If there be any love to my deservings
Borne by her virtuous self, I cannot stop it!
Nor am I able to refrain [9] her wishes.
She's private to herself, and best of knowl-
    edge [10]
Whom she 'll make so happy as to sigh
    for ;   30
Besides, I cannot think you mean to match
    her
Unto a fellow of so lame a presence,[11]
One that hath little left of nature in him.

 VENT. 'T is very well, sir ; I can tell your
    wisdom
How all this shall be cur'd.

 JASP.   Your care becomes you.

 VENT. And thus it must be, sir : I here dis-
    charge you
My house and service ; take your liberty ;
And when I want a son, I 'll send for you.

           Exit.

 JASP. These be the fair rewards of them
    that love!
Oh, you that live in freedom, never prove [12] [40
The travail of a mind led by desire!

     Enter LUCE.

 LUCE. Why, how now, friend? Struck with
    my father's thunder?

 JASP. Struck, and struck dead, unless the
    remedy
Be full of speed and virtue ; [13] I am now,
What I expected long, no more your father's.

 LUCE. But mine.

 JASP. But yours, and only yours, I am ;
That 's all I have to keep me from the statute.[14]
You dare be constant still?

 LUCE.   Oh, fear me not! [15]
In this I dare be better than a woman :
Nor shall his anger nor his offers move me, 50
Were they both equal to a prince's power.

 JASP. You know my rival?

 LUCE. Yes, and love him dearly —
Even as I love an ague or foul weather!
I prithee, Jasper, fear him not.

 JASP.   Oh, no!
I do not mean to do him so much kindness.
But to our own desires ; you know the plot
We both agreed on.

---

 [9] Restrain.
 [10] Is her own confidant, and knows best.
(Neilson.)
 [11] So feeble in his bearing.
 [12] Know from your own experience. [13] Efficacy.
 [14] *I.e.*, to keep me from the penalties provided
in the Statute of Apprentices (1563) for apprentices
who left their masters. (Alden.)
 [15] Don't fear on my account.

 LUCE.   Yes, and will perform
My part exactly.

 JASP.   I desire no more.
Farewell, and keep my heart ; 't is yours.

 LUCE.   I take it ;
He must do miracles makes me forsake it. [60

           Exeunt.

 CIT. Fie upon 'em, little infidels! what a
matter 's here now! Well, I 'll be hang'd for
a halfpenny, if there be not some abomination
knavery in this play. Well ; let 'em look
to 't ; Ralph must come, and if there be any
tricks a-brewing ——

 WIFE. Let 'em brew and bake too, Husband, a' God's name ; Ralph will find all out,
I warrant you, an they were older than they
are. — [*Enter a* Boy.] — I pray, my pretty [70
youth, is Ralph ready?

 BOY. He will be presently.

 WIFE. Now, I pray you, make my commendations unto him, and withal carry him
this stick of licorice. Tell him his mistress
sent it him ; and bid him bite a piece ;
't will open his pipes the better, say.

          [*Exit* Boy.]

     [SCENE II] [16]

Enter Merchant [VENTUREWELL] *and* MASTER
     HUMPHREY.

 VENT. Come, sir, she 's yours ; upon my
    faith, she 's yours ;
You have my hand : for other idle lets [17]
Between your hopes and her, thus with a wind
They are scattered and no more. My wanton
    prentice,
That like a bladder blew himself with love,
I have let out, and sent him to discover
New masters yet unknown.

 HUM.   I thank you, sir,
Indeed, I thank you, sir ; and, ere I stir,
It shall be known, however you do deem,
I am of gentle blood and gentle seem.[18] 10

 VENT. Oh, sir, I know it certain.

 HUM.   Sir, my friend,
Although, as writers say, all things have end,
And that we call a pudding [19] hath his two,
Oh, let it not seem strange, I pray, to you,
If in this bloody simile I put
My love, more endless than frail things or
    gut! [20]

---

 [16] The same.   [17] Hindrances.
 [18] Appearance.
 [19] Sausage.
 [20] Sausages are encased in intestines.

WIFE. Husband, I prithee, sweet lamb, tell me one thing; but tell me truly. — Stay, youths, I beseech you, till I question my husband.   20

CIT. What is it, mouse? [21]

WIFE. Sirrah, didst thou ever see a prettier child? How it behaves itself, I warrant ye, and speaks and looks, and perts up the head! — I pray you, brother, with your favor, were you never none of Master Monkester's [22] scholars?

CIT. Chicken, I prithee heartily, contain thyself: the childer are pretty childer; but when Ralph comes, lamb ——   30

WIFE. Ay, when Ralph comes, cony! — Well, my youth, you may proceed.

VENT. Well, sir, you know my love, and rest, I hope,
Assur'd of my consent; get but my daughter's,
And wed her when you please. You must be bold,
And clap in close unto her; come, I know
You have language good enough to win a wench.

WIFE. A whoreson tyrant! h' as been an old stringer [23] in 's days, I warrant him.

HUM. I take your gentle offer, and withal
Yield love again for love reciprocal.   41
VENT. What, Luce! within there!

Enter LUCE.

LUCE.   Call'd you, sir?
VENT.   I did:
Give entertainment to this gentleman;
And see you be not froward [24] — To her, sir;
My presence will but be an eyesore to you.
                                        Exit.

HUM. Fair Mistress Luce, how do you do?
Are you well?
Give me your hand, and then I pray you tell
How doth your little sister and your brother;
And whether you love me or any other.

LUCE. Sir, these are quickly answered.
HUM.   So they are, [50
Where women are not cruel. But how far
Is it now distant from the place we are in,
Unto that blessed place, your father's warren?

LUCE. What makes you think of that, sir?

HUM.   Even that face;
For, stealing rabbits whilom [25] in that place,
God Cupid, or the keeper, I know not whether, [26]
Unto my cost and charges brought you thither,
And there began ——

LUCE.   Your game, sir.
HUM.   Let no game,
Or anything that tendeth to the same,
Be evermore remem'bred, thou fair killer, [60
For whom I sat me down, and brake my tiller. [27]

WIFE. There's a kind gentleman, I warrant you; when will you do as much for me, George?

LUCE. Beshrew me, sir, I am sorry for your losses;
But, as the proverb says, I cannot cry.
I would you had not seen me!
HUM.   So would I,
Unless you had more maw [28] to do me good.

LUCE. Why, cannot this strange passion be withstood?
Send for a constable, and raise the town.   70
HUM. Oh, no! my valiant love will batter down
Millions of constables, and put to flight
Even that great watch of Midsummer Day at night. [29]

LUCE. Beshrew me, sir, 't were good I yielded, then;
Weak women cannot hope, where valiant men
Have no resistance.
HUM.   Yield, then; I am full
Of pity, though I say it, and can pull
Out of my pocket thus a pair of gloves.
Look, Lucy, look; the dog's tooth nor the dove's
Are not so white as these; and sweet they be,   80
And whipp'd [30] about with silk, as you may see.
If you desire the price, [shoot] [31] from your eye
A beam to this place, and you shall espy
F S, [32] which is to say, my sweetest honey,
They cost me three [33] and twopence, or no money.

[21] A term of endearment.
[22] Richard Mulcaster, formerly headmaster of the Merchant Tailors' School, and at the time of our play of St. Paul's School, whose boys he trained to act.   [23] Libertine.   [24] Obstinate, adverse.
[25] Once.   [26] Which.   [27] Crossbow.
[28] "Stomach", inclination.
[29] The annual military muster of the citizens.
[30] Embroidered.
[31] Old eds. *sute;* cor. ed. 1711.
[32] Either a price mark in code, or (as Murch suggests) a trademark.
[33] Shillings.

LUCE. Well, sir, I take them kindly, and
    I thank you!
What would you more?
HUM.   Nothing.
LUCE.   Why, then, farewell.
HUM. Nor so, nor so ; for, lady, I must tell,
Before we part, for what we met together —
God grant me time and patience and fair
    weather!   90
    LUCE. Speak, and declare your mind in
        terms so brief.
    HUM. I shall : then, first and foremost, for
        relief
I call to you, if that you can afford it ;
I care not at what price, for, on my word, it
Shall be repaid again, although it cost me
More then I'll speak of now ; for love hath
    toss'd me
In furious blanket like a tennis-ball,
And now I rise aloft, and now I fall.
    LUCE. Alas, good gentleman, alas the day!
    HUM. I thank you heartily ; and, as I
        say,   100
Thus do I still continue without rest,
I' th' morning like a man, at night a beast,
Roaring and bellowing mine own disquiet,
That much I fear forsaking of my diet
Will bring me presently to that quandary,
I shall bid all adieu.
    LUCE.   Now, by St. Mary,
That were great pity!
    HUM.   So it were, beshrew me ;
Then, ease me, lusty Luce, and pity show me.
    LUCE. Why, sir, you know my will is noth-
        ing worth
Without my father's grant ; get his consent,
And then you may with assurance try me. [111
    HUM. The Worshipful your sire will not
        deny me ;
For I have ask'd him, and he hath repli'd,
" Sweet Master Humphrey, Luce shall be
    thy bride."
    LUCE. Sweet Master Humphrey, then I am
        content.
    HUM. And so am I, in truth.
    LUCE.   Yet take me with you ; [34]
There is another clause must be annex'd,
And this it is : I swore, and will perform it,
No man shall ever joy [35] me as his wife
But he that stole me hence. If you dare ven-
    ture,   120
I am yours — you need not fear : my father
    loves you —
If not, farewell for ever!

[34] Understand me.   [35] Enjoy.

HUM.   Stay, nymph, stay ;
I have a double gelding, color'd bay,
Sprung by his father from Barbarian [36] kind ;
Another for myself, though somewhat blind,
Yet true as trusty tree.
    LUCE.   I am satisfied ;
And so I give my hand. Our course must lie
Through Waltham Forest,[37] where I have a
    friend
Will entertain us. So, farewell, Sir Hum-
    phrey,
And think upon your business.   *Exit* LUCE.
    HUM.   Though I die, [130
I am resolv'd to venture life and limb
For one so young, so fair, so kind, so trim.
                            Exit HUMPHREY.

WIFE. By my faith and troth, George, and
as I am virtuous, it is e'en the kindest young
man that ever trod on shoe-leather. — Well,
go thy ways ; if thou hast her not, 't is not
thy fault, 'faith.
    CIT. I prithee, mouse, be patient ; 'a shall
have her, or I'll make some of 'em smoke
for 't.   140
    WIFE. That's my good lamb, George. —
Fie, this stinking tobacco kills [me]! [38] would
there were none in England! — Now, I pray,
gentlemen, what good does this stinking tobacco do you? Nothing, I warrant you :
make chimneys a' your faces! — Oh, Husband, Husband, now, now! there's Ralph,
there's Ralph.

[SCENE III]

Enter RALPH, *like a grocer in 's shop, with two*
    Prentices [TIM *and* GEORGE], *reading "Pal-*
    merin of England." [39]

    CIT. Peace, fool! let Ralph alone. — Hark
you, Ralph ; do not strain yourself too much
at the first. — Peace! — Begin, Ralph.

    RALPH. " Then Palmerin and Trineus,
snatching their lances from their dwarfs and
clasping their helmets, gallop'd amain after the
giant ; and Palmerin, having gotten a sight of
him, came posting amain, saying, ' Stay, traitorous thief! for thou mayst not so carry away

[36] *I.e.,* of Barbary, or northern Africa.
[37] Or Epping Forest ; it extended nearly to the
northern gates of the city.
[38] Emend. Sympson ; old eds. *men.*
[39] Both this Spanish (originally Portuguese)
romance and its predecessor, *Palmerin d' Oliva,*
were popular in English translation. The passage
Ralph reads is from *Palmerin d' Oliva,* condensed
and slightly garbled.

her that is worth the greatest lord in the [10 world ; and, with these words, gave him a blow on the shoulder, that he struck him besides [40] his elephant. And Trineus, coming to the knight that had Agricola behind him, set him soon besides his horse, with his neck broken in the fall ; so that the Princess, getting out of the throng, between joy and grief, said, ' All-happy knight, the mirror of all such as follow arms, now may I be well assured of the love thou bearest me.' ' — I wonder why the [20 kings do not raise an army of fourteen or fifteen hundred thousand men, as big as the army that the Prince of Portigo brought against Rosicleer,[41] and destroy these giants ; they do much hurt to wand'ring damsels, that go in quest of their knights.

WIFE. Faith, Husband, and Ralph says true ; for they say the King of Portugal cannot sit at his meat, but the giants and the ettins [42] will come and snatch it from him. [30
CIT. Hold thy tongue. — On, Ralph !

RALPH. And certainly those knights are much to be commended, who, neglecting their possessions, wander with a squire and a dwarf through the deserts to relieve poor ladies.

WIFE. Ay, by my faith, are they, Ralph ; let 'em say what they will, they are indeed. Our knights neglect their possessions well enough, but they do not the rest.

RALPH. There are no such courteous [40 and fair, well-spoken knights in this age : they will call one " the son of a whore " that Palmerin of England would have called " fair sir ; " and one that Rosicleer would have call'd " right beauteous damsel " they will call " damn'd bitch."

WIFE. I 'll be sworn will they, Ralph ; they have call'd me so an hundred times about a scurvy pipe of tobacco.

RALPH. But what brave spirit could be [50 content to sit in his shop, with a flappet of wood [43] and a blue apron before him, selling mithridatum [44] and dragon's-water [44] to visited [45] houses, that might pursue feats of arms, and, through his noble achievements,

procure such a famous history to be written of his heroic prowess?

CIT. Well said, Ralph ; some more of those words, Ralph !
WIFE. They go finely, by my troth.　　60

RALPH. Why should not I, then, pursue this course, both for the credit of myself and our Company ? For amongst all the worthy books of achievements, I do not call to mind that I yet read of a grocer-errant. I will be the said knight. — Have you heard of any that hath wand'red unfurnished of his squire and dwarf ? My elder prentice Tim shall be my trusty squire, and little George my dwarf. Hence, my blue apron ! Yet, in remembrance of [70 my former trade, upon my shield shall be portray'd a Burning Pestle, and I will be call'd the Knight o' th' Burning Pestle.[46]

WIFE. Nay, I dare swear thou wilt not forget thy old trade ; thou wert ever meek.

RALPH. Tim !
TIM. Anon.
RALPH. My beloved squire, and George my dwarf, I charge you that from henceforth you never call me by any other name but " the [80 right courteous and valiant Knight of the Burning Pestle " ; and that you never call any female by the name of a woman or wench, but " fair lady ", if she have her desires, if not, " distressed damsel " ; that you call all forests and heaths " deserts ", and all horses " palfreys."

WIFE. This is very fine, faith. — Do the gentlemen like Ralph, think you, Husband?
CIT. Ay, I warrant thee ; the players would give all the shoes in their shop for him.　　91

RALPH. My beloved squire Tim, stand out. Admit this were a desert, and over it a knight-errant pricking,[47] and I should bid you inquire of his intents, what would you say?
TIM. Sir, my master sent me to know whither you are riding.
RALPH. No, thus : — Fair sir, the right courteous and valiant Knight of the Burning Pestle commanded me to inquire upon [100 what adventure you are bound, whether to relieve some distressed damsels, or otherwise.

[40] Beside ; *i.e.*, off.
[41] Characters in the Spanish romance, *The Mirror of Knighthood*, also popular in England.
[42] Giants.　　　　[43] *I.e.*, a counter.
[44] Used in combating the plague.
[45] *I.e.*, infected.

[46] Eustace, in Heywood's *Four Prentices*, displays the arms of the Grocers on his shield.
[47] Spurring.

Cit. Whoreson blockhead, cannot remember!

Wife. I' faith, and Ralph told him on 't before; all the gentlemen heard him. — Did he not, gentlemen? Did not Ralph tell him on 't?

George. Right courteous and valiant Knight of the Burning Pestle, here is a distressed damsel to have a halfpenny-worth of pepper. 111

Wife. That 's a good boy! See, the little boy can hit it; by my troth, it 's a fine child.

Ralph. Relieve her, with all courteous language. Now shut up shop; no more my prentice, but my trusty squire and dwarf. I must bespeak my shield and arming [48] pestle.

[*Exeunt* Tim *and* George.]

Cit. Go thy ways, Ralph! As I 'm a true [49] man, thou art the best on 'em all.

Wife. Ralph, Ralph! 120

Ralph. What say you, Mistress?

Wife. I prithee, come again quickly, sweet Ralph.

Ralph. By and by.[50] *Exit* Ralph.

[Scene IV] [51]

Enter Jasper *and his mother,* Mistress Merrythought.

Mist. Mer. Give thee my blessing? No, I 'll ne'er give thee my blessing; I 'll see thee hang'd first; it shall ne'er be said I gave thee my blessing. Th' art thy father's own son, of the right blood of the Merrythoughts. I may curse the time that e'er I knew thy father; he hath spent all his own and mine too; and when I tell him of it, he laughs, and dances, and sings, and cries, "A merry heart lives long-a." And thou art a wastethrift, and art run [10 away from thy master that lov'd thee well, and art come to me; and I have laid up a little for my younger son Michael, and thou think'st to bezzle [52] that, but thou shalt never be able to do it. — Come hither, Michael!

Enter Michael.

Come, Michael, down on thy knees; thou shalt have my blessing.

Mich. I pray you, Mother, pray to God to bless me.

Mist. Mer. God bless thee! but Jasper [20 shall never have my blessing; he shall be hang'd first; shall he not, Michael? How say'st thou?

Mich. Yes, forsooth, Mother, and grace of God.

Mist. Mer. That 's a good boy!

Wife. I' faith, it 's a fine-spoken child.

Jasp. Mother, though you forget a parent's love,

I must preserve the duty of a child.

I ran not from my master, nor return 30

To have your stock maintain my idleness.

Wife. Ungracious child, I warrant him; hark, how he chops logic with his mother! — Thou hadst best tell her she lies; do tell her she lies.

Cit. If he were my son, I would hang him up by the heels, and flay him, and salt him, whoreson haltersack.[53]

Jasp. My coming only is to beg your love, Which I must ever, though I never gain it; [40 And, howsoever you esteem of me, There is no drop of blood hid in these veins But, I remember well, belongs to you That brought me forth, and would be glad for you To rip them all again, and let it out.

Mist. Mer. I' faith, I had sorrow enough for thee, God knows; but I 'll hamper thee well enough. Get thee in, thou vagabond, get thee in, and learn of thy brother Michael.

[*Exeunt* Jasper *and* Michael.]

Mer. (*within*)

Nose, nose, jolly red nose, 50
And who gave thee this jolly red nose? [54]

Mist. Mer. Hark, my husband! he 's singing and hoiting; [55] and I 'm fain to cark [56] and care, and all little enough. — Husband! Charles! Charles Merrythought!

Enter old Merrythought.

Mer.

Nutmegs and ginger, cinnamon and cloves;
And they gave me this jolly red nose.

---

[48] Armorial, heraldic.
[49] Honest.   [50] Directly.
[51] Not precisely located; presumably a room in Merrythought's house.
[52] Squander.
[53] Gallows-bird.
[54] The song was preserved in Ravenscroft's *Deuteromelia* (1609).
[55] Indulging in riotous mirth.
[56] Be careful.

MIST. MER. If you would consider your state, you would have little list to sing, iwis.

MER. It should never be considered, [60 while it were an estate, if I thought it would spoil my singing.

MIST. MER. But how wilt thou do, Charles? Thou art an old man, and thou canst not work, and thou hast not forty shillings left, and thou eatest good meat, and drinkest good drink, and laughest!

MER. And will do.

MIST. MER. But how wilt thou come by it, Charles?   70

MER. How! why, how have I done hitherto this forty years? I never came into my dining-room, but, at eleven and six a'clock,[57] I found excellent meat and drink a' th' table; my clothes were never worn out but next morning a tailor brought me a new suit; and without question it will be so ever; use makes perfectness. If all should fail, it is but a little straining myself extraordinary, and laugh myself to death.   80

WIFE. It's a foolish old man this: is not he, George?

CIT. Yes, cony.

WIFE. Give me a penny i' th' purse while I live, George.

CIT. Ay, by Lady,[58] cony, hold thee there.[59]

MIST. MER. Well, Charles; you promis'd to provide for Jasper, and I have laid up for Michael. I pray you, pay Jasper his portion; he's come home, and he shall not consume [90 Michael's stock; he says his master turn'd him away, but, I promise you truly, I think he ran away.

WIFE. No, indeed, Mistress Merrythought; though he be a notable gallows,[60] yet I 'll assure you his master did turn him away, even in this place, 't was; i' faith, within this half-hour, about his daughter; my husband was by.

CIT. Hang him, rogue! he serv'd him well enough: love his master's daughter! By [100 my troth, cony, if there were a thousand boys, thou wouldst spoil them all with taking their parts; let his mother alone with him.

WIFE. Ay, George; but yet truth is truth.

MER. Where is Jasper? He's welcome, however. Call him in; he shall have his portion. Is he merry?

MIST. MER. Ay, foul chive him, [61 he is too merry! — Jasper! Michael!

Re-enter JASPER *and* MICHAEL.

MER. Welcome, Jasper! though thou [110 runn'st away, welcome! God bless thee! 'T is thy mother's mind thou shouldst receive thy portion; thou hast been abroad,[62] and I hope hast learn'd experience enough to govern it; thou art of sufficient years. Hold thy hand — one, two, three, four, five, six, seven, eight, nine, there's ten shillings for thee. Thrust thyself into the world with that, and take some settled course. If fortune cross thee, thou hast a retiring place; come home to me; [120 I have twenty shillings left. Be a good husband;[63] that is, wear ordinary clothes, eat the best meat, and drink the best drink; be merry, and give to the poor, and, believe me, thou hast no end of thy goods.

JASP. Long may you live free from all thought of ill,
And long have cause to be thus merry still!
But, Father ——

MER. No more words, Jasper; get thee gone.
Thou hast my blessing; thy father's spirit upon thee!   130
Farewell, Jasper!   [*Sings.*]

But yet, or ere you part (oh, cruel!)
Kiss me, kiss me, sweeting, mine own dear jewel![64]

So, now begone; no words.   *Exit* JASPER.

MIST. MER. [*aside*] So, Michael, now get thee gone, too.

MICH. [*aside*] Yes, forsooth, Mother; but I 'll have my father's blessing first.

MIST. MER. [*aside*] No, Michael; 't is no matter for his blessing; thou hast my [140 blessing; begone. I 'll fetch my money and jewels, and follow thee; I 'll stay no longer with him, I warrant thee. [*Exit* MICHAEL.] — Truly, Charles, I 'll be gone too.

MER. What! you will not?

MIST. MER. Yes, indeed will I.

MER. [*sings.*]

Heigh-ho, farewell, Nan!
I 'll never trust wench more again, if I can.[65]

MIST. MER. You shall not think, when all your own is gone, to spend that I have [150 been scraping up for Michael.

---

[61] May ill befall him.
[62] Away from home.
[63] Be thrifty.
[64] From a song in John Dowland's *First Book of Songs or Airs* (1597).
[65] Unidentified.

[57] The hours of dinner and supper.
[58] By the Virgin Mary.
[59] Stick to that.   [60] Gallows-bird.

MER. Farewell, good Wife ; I expect it not ; all I have to do in this world is to be merry ; which I shall, if the ground be not taken from me ; and if it be,   [*Sings.*]

When earth and seas from me are reft,
The skies aloft for me are left.[65 a]

Exeunt.

WIFE. I 'll be sworn he 's a merry old gentleman for all that. (*Music.*) Hark, hark, husband, hark ! fiddles, fiddles ! now [160 surely they go finely. They say 't is present death for these fiddlers, to tune their rebecks[66] before the great Turk's Grace ; is 't not, George? (Boy *danceth*.) But, look, look ! here 's a youth dances ! — Now, good youth, do a turn a' th' toe. — Sweetheart, i' faith, I 'll have Ralph come and do some of his gambols. — He 'll ride the wild mare,[67] gentlemen, 't would do your hearts good to see him. — I thank you, kind youth ; pray, bid Ralph [170 come.

CIT. Peace, cony ! — Sirrah, you scurvy boy, bid the players send Ralph ; or, by God's —— an they do not, I 'll tear some of their periwigs beside their heads : this is all riff-raff.[68]   [*Exit* Boy.]

ACT II — SCENE I[1]

Enter Merchant [VENTUREWELL] *and* HUMPHREY.

VENT. And how, faith, how goes it now, son Humphrey?

HUM. Right worshipful, and my beloved friend
And father dear, this matter 's at an end.

VENT. 'T is well ; it should be so. I 'm glad the girl
Is found so tractable.

HUM.   Nay, she must whirl
From hence (and you must wink,[2] for so, I say,
The story tells,) to-morrow before day.

WIFE. George, dost thou think, in thy conscience now, 't will be a match ? Tell me but what thou think'st, sweet rogue. Thou [10 seest the poor gentleman, dear heart, how it labors and throbs, I warrant you, to be at rest ! I 'll go move the father for 't.

CIT. No, no ; I prithee, sit still, honeysuckle ; thou 'lt spoil all. If he deny him, I 'll bring half-a-dozen good fellows myself, and in the shutting[3] of an evening, knock 't up,[4] and there 's an end.

WIFE. I 'll buss[5] thee for that, i' faith, boy. Well, George, well, you have been a wag in [20 your days, I warrant you ; but God forgive you, and I do with all my heart.

VENT. How was it, son? You told me that to-morrow
Before daybreak you must convey her hence.

HUM. I must, I must ; and thus it is agreed :
Your daughter rides upon a brown-bay steed,
I on a sorrel, which I bought of Brian,
The honest host of the Red roaring Lion,
In Waltham situate. Then, if you may,
Consent in seemly sort ; lest, by delay,   30
The Fatal Sisters come, and do the office,
And then you 'll sing another song.

VENT.   Alas,
Why should you be thus full of grief to me,
That do as willing as yourself agree
To anything, so it be good and fair ?
Then, steal her when you will, if such a pleasure
Content you both ; I 'll sleep and never see it,
To make your joys more full. But tell me why
You may not here perform your marriage ?

WIFE. God's blessing a' thy soul, old man !
I' faith, thou art loth to part true hearts. [41
I see 'a has her, George ; and I 'm as glad on 't I
— Well, go thy ways, Humphrey, for a fair-spoken man ; I believe thou hast not thy fellow within the walls of London ; an I should say the suburbs too, I should not lie. — Why dost not rejoice with me, George?

CIT. If I could but see Ralph again, I were as merry as mine host, i' faith.

HUM. The cause you seem to ask, I thus declare —   50
Help me, O Muses nine ! Your daughter sware
A foolish oath, and more it was the pity ;
Yet none but myself within this city
Shall dare to say so, but a bold defiance
Shall meet him, were he of the noble science ;[6]
And yet she sware, and yet why did she swear?

[65 a] Unidentified.
[66] An early form of the violin.
[67] Play at see-saw.   [68] Rubbish.
[1] Presumably a room in Venturewell's house.
[2] Shut your eyes, ignore it.

[3] Close.   [4] Settle the affair, arrange matters.
[5] Kiss.   [6] *I.e.*, an expert fencer.

Truly, I cannot tell, unless it were
For her own ease ; for, sure, sometimes an
    oath,
Being sworn thereafter, is like cordial broth ;
And this it was she swore, never to marry [60
But such a one whose mighty arm could carry
(As meaning me, for I am such a one)
Her bodily away, through stick and stone,
Till both of us arrive, at her request,
Some ten miles off, in the wild Waltham Forest.
    VENT. If this be all, you shall not need to
      fear
Any denial in your love : proceed ;
I 'll neither follow, nor repent the deed.
    HUM. Good night, twenty good nights, and
      twenty more,   69
And twenty more good nights — that makes
    three-score !   *Exeunt.*

[SCENE II] [7]

Enter MISTRESS MERRYTHOUGHT *and her son*
MICHAEL.

    MIST. MER. Come, Michael ; art thou not
weary, boy?
    MICH. No, forsooth, Mother, not I.
    MIST. MER. Where be we now, child?
    MICH. Indeed, forsooth, Mother, I cannot
tell, unless we be at Mile End. [8] Is not all the
world Mile End, Mother?
    MIST. MER. No, Michael, not all the world,
boy ; but I can assure thee, Michael, Mile End
is a goodly matter : there has been a pitch- [10
field, [9] my child, between the naughty Spaniels [10] and the Englishmen ; and the Spaniels
ran away, Michael, and the Englishmen followed. My neighbor Coxstone was there,
boy, and kill'd them all with a birding-piece.[11]
    MICH. Mother, forsooth —
    MIST. MER. What says my white boy? [12]
    MICH. Shall not my father go with us too?
    MIST. MER. No, Michael, let thy father go
snick-up ; [13] he shall never come between a [20
pair of sheets with me again while he lives ; let
him stay at home and sing for his supper, boy.
Come, child, sit down, and I 'll show my boy
fine knacks, indeed. [*They sit down, and she
takes out a casket.*] Look here, Michael ; here 's
a ring, and here 's a brooch, and here 's a

[7] Waltham Forest.
[8] A mile beyond Aldgate. The London train-
bands drilled there.
[9] Evidently the train-bands had recently staged
a sham battle.
[10] Wicked Spaniards.
[11] Fowling-piece.   [12] Darling, pet.
[13] Go hang.

bracelet, and here 's two rings more, and here 's
money and gold by th' eye,[14] my boy.
    MICH. Shall I have all this, Mother?
    MIST. MER. Ay, Michael, thou shalt [30
have all, Michael.

    CIT. How lik'st thou this, wench?
    WIFE. I cannot tell ; I would have Ralph,
George ; I 'll see no more else, indeed, law ;
and I pray you, let the youths understand so
much by word of mouth ; for, I tell you truly,
I 'm afraid a' my boy. Come, come, George,
let 's be merry and wise : the child 's a fatherless child ; and say they should put him into a
strait pair of gaskins,[15] 't were worse than [40
knot-grass ; [16] he would never grow after it.

Enter RALPH, Squire [TIM], *and* Dwarf
[GEORGE].

    CIT. Here 's Ralph, here 's Ralph !
    WIFE. How do you, Ralph? you are wel-
come, Ralph, as I may say. It 's a good boy ;
hold up thy head, and be not afraid ; we are
thy friends, Ralph ; the gentlemen will praise
thee, Ralph, if thou play'st thy part with audacity. Begin, Ralph, a' God's name !

    RALPH. My trusty squire, unlace my helm ;
      give me my hat.
Where are we, or what desert may this be? [50
    GEORGE. Mirror of knighthood, this is, as
I take it, the perilous Waltham Down ; [17] in
whose bottom stands the enchanted valley.
    MIST. MER. Oh, Michael, we are betray'd,
we are betray'd ! Here be giants ! Fly, boy !
fly, boy, fly !   *Exeunt* Mother *and* MICHAEL.
    RALPH. Lace on my helm again. What
      noise is this?
A gentle lady, flying the embrace
Of some uncourteous knight ! I will relieve
      her.
Go, squire, and say the knight that wears this
      pestle   60
In honor of all ladies, swears revenge
Upon that recreant coward that pursues her ;
Go, comfort her, and that same gentle squire
That bears her company.
    TIM.   I go, brave knight. [*Exit.*]
    RALPH. My trusty dwarf and friend, reach
      me my shield ;

[14] In quantities.
[15] A pair of breeches too tight for him.
[16] An infusion of which was supposed to retard
growth.
[17] Upland.

it while I swear. First, by my
⎯⎯⎯⎯⎯uthood ;
Then by the soul of Amadis de Gaul,[18]
My famous ancestor ; then by my sword
The beauteous Brionella [19] girt about me ;
By this bright burning pestle, of mine honor
The living trophy ; and by all respect   71
Due to distressed damsels ; here I vow
Never to end the quest of this fair lady
And that forsaken squire till by my valor
I gain their liberty !

GEORGE.   Heaven bless the knight
That thus relieves poor errant gentlewomen !
                                        [*Exeunt.*]

WIFE. Ay, marry, Ralph, this has some savor in 't ; I would see the proudest of them all
offer to carry his books after him.[20] But,
George, I will not have him go away so [80
soon ; I shall be sick if he go away, that I shall.
Call Ralph again, George, call Ralph again ; I
prithee, sweetheart, let him come fight before
me, and let 's ha' some drums and some trumpets, and let him kill all that comes near him,
an thou lov'st me, George !

CIT. Peace a little, bird ; he shall kill them
all, an they were twenty more on 'em than
there are.

Enter JASPER.

JASP. Now, Fortune, if thou beest not only
        ill,   90
Show me thy better face, and bring about
Thy desperate wheel, that I may climb at
        length,
And stand. This is our place of meeting,
If love have any constancy. O age
Where only wealthy men are counted happy !
How shall I please thee, how deserve thy
        smiles,
When I am only rich in misery ?
My father's blessing and this little coin
Is my inheritance ; a strong revenue ! [21]   99
From earth thou art, and to the earth I give
        thee :   [*Throws away the money.*]
There grow and multiply, whilst fresher air
Breeds me a fresher fortune. — How ! illusion ?
                                Spies the casket.
What, hath the Devil coin'd himself before me ?
'T is metal good, it rings well ; I am waking —

And taking too, I hope. Now, God's dear
        blessing
Upon his heart that left it here ! 'T is mine ;
These pearls, I take it, were not left for swine.
                                        Exit.

WIFE. I do not like that this unthrifty
youth should embezzle away the money ; the
poor gentlewoman his mother will have a
heavy heart for it, God knows.   111

CIT. And reason good, sweetheart.

WIFE. But let him go ; I 'll tell Ralph a
tale in 's ear shall fetch him again with a
wanion,[22] I warrant him, if he be above ground ;
and besides, George, here are a number of sufficient [23] gentlemen can witness, and myself, and
yourself, and the musicians, if we be call'd in
question. But here comes Ralph, George ;
thou shalt hear him speak an [24] he were an
emperal.[25]   121

[SCENE III] [26]

Enter RALPH *and* Dwarf [GEORGE].

RALPH. Comes not Sir Squire again ?
GEORGE.   Right courteous knight,
Your squire doth come, and with him comes
        the lady,

Enter MISTRESS MERRYTHOUGHT *and* MICHAEL
        and Squire [TIM].

For and [27] the squire of damsels, as I take it.
RALPH. Madam, if any service or devoir
Of a poor errant knight may right your
        wrongs —
Command it ; I am prest [28] to give you succor ;
For to that holy end I bear my armor.
MIST. MER. Alas, sir, I am a poor gentle-
woman, and I have lost my money in this
forest !   10
RALPH. Desert, you would say, lady ; and
        not lost
Whilst I have sword and lance. Dry up your
        tears,
Which ill befits the beauty of that face,
And tell the story, if I may request it,
Of your disastrous fortune.
MIST. MER. Out, alas ! I left a thousand
pound, a thousand pound, e'en all the money I
had laid up for this youth, upon the sight of
your Mastership, you look'd so grim, and, as I
may say it, saving your presence, more like
a giant than a mortal man.   21

---

[18] The hero of the romance so entitled. Originally
Portuguese, it came to England from Spain, and
was the most famous of its kind.
[19] In *Palmerin d' Oliva;* the hero's friend Ptolme
wins her.
[20] Try to equal him. [21] Accented on second syllable.

[22] With a vengeance.   [23] Competent.
[24] As if.   [25] Imperial ; *i.e.,* emperor.
[26] The same.   [27] And also.   [28] Ready.

RALPH. I am as you are, lady ; so are they ;
All mortal. But why weeps this gentle
    squire?

MIST. MER. Has he not cause to weep, do
you think, when he hath lost his inheritance?

RALPH. Young hope of valor, weep not ; I
    am here
That will confound thy foe, and pay it dear
Upon his coward head that dares deny
Distressed squires and ladies equity.
I have but one horse, on which shall ride   [30
This lady fair behind me, and before
This courteous squire ; fortune will give us
    more
Upon our next adventure. Fairly speed
Beside us, squire and dwarf, to do us need !

                        Exeunt.

CIT. Did not I tell you, Nell, what your
man would do? By the faith of my body,
wench, for clean action and good delivery, they
may all cast their caps at him.[29]

WIFE. And so they may, i' faith ; for I dare
speak it boldly, the twelve companies [30] of [40
London cannot match him, timber for timber.[31]
Well, George, an he be not inveigled by some
of these paltry players, I ha' much marvel ;
but, George, we ha' done our parts, if the boy
have any grace to be thankful.

CIT. Yes, I warrant thee, duckling.

[SCENE IV] [32]

Enter HUMPHREY *and* LUCE.

HUM. Good Mistress Luce, however I in
    fault am
For your lame horse, you 're welcome unto
    Waltham ;
But which way now to go, or what to say,
I know not truly, till it be broad day.

LUCE. Oh, fear not, Master Humphrey ;
    I am guide
For this place good enough.

HUM.   Then, up and ride ;
Or, if it please you, walk, for your repose ;
Or sit ; or, if you will, go pluck a rose ; [33]
Either of which shall be indifferent
To your good friend and Humphrey, whose
    consent   10

Is so entangled ever to your will,
As the poor, harmless horse is to the mill.

LUCE. Faith, an you say the word, we 'll
    e'en sit down,
And take a nap.

HUM.   'T is better in the town,
Where we may nap together ; for, believe me,
To sleep without a snatch [34] would mickle
    grieve me.

LUCE. You 're merry, Master Humphrey.

HUM.   So I am,
And have been ever merry from my dam.

LUCE. Your nurse had the less labor.

HUM.   Faith, it may be,
Unless it were by chance I did beray me.[35] [20

Enter JASPER.

JASP. Luce ! dear friend Luce !

LUCE.   Here, Jasper.

JASP.   You are mine.

HUM. If it be so, my friend, you use me fine.
What do you think I am?

JASP.   An arrant noddy.[36]

HUM. A word of obloquy ! Now, by God's
    body,
I 'll tell thy master ; for I know thee well.

JASP. Nay, an you be so forward for to tell,
Take that, and that ; and tell him, sir, I gave
    it ;
And say I paid you well.   [*Beats him.*]

HUM.   Oh, sir, I have it,
And do confess the payment ! Pray, be quiet.

JASP. Go, get [you] [37] to your nightcap
    and the diet,   30
To cure your beaten bones.

LUCE.   Alas, poor Humphrey ;
Get thee some wholesome broth, with sage and
    comfrey ; [38]
A little oil of roses and a feather
To 'noint thy back withal.

HUM.   When I came hither,
Would I had gone to Paris with John Dory ! [39]

LUCE. Farewell, my pretty nump ; [40] I am
    very sorry
I cannot bear thee company.

HUM.   Farewell ;
The devil's dam was ne'er so bang'd in hell.

          Exeunt [LUCE *and* JASPER].

---

[29] Salute him as superior. (Moorman.)
[30] They were the Mercers, Grocers, Drapers,
Fishmongers, Goldsmiths, Skinners, Merchant
Tailors, Haberdashers, Salters, Ironmongers, Vintners, and Clothworkers.
[31] *I.e.*, limb for limb, man for man. (Murch.)
[32] The same.   [33] Defecate.

[34] Snack, meal.   [35] Befoul myself.
[36] Simpleton.   [37] Add. Q 2.
[38] A plant used in cough mixtures.
[39] In the song so entitled (preserved in Ravenscroft's *Deuteromelia*) the hero is captured while
on his way to present a captive English crew to the
King of France. (Alden.)
[40] Punning on Numps = Humphrey, and =
blockhead. (Murch.)

WIFE. This young Jasper will prove me another things, a' my conscience, an he [40 may be suffered. George, dost not see, George, how 'a swaggers, and flies at the very heads a' folks, as he were a dragon? Well, if I do not do his lesson [41] for wronging the poor gentleman, I am no true woman. His friends that brought him up might have been better occupied, I wis, than ha' taught him these fegaries; [42] he's e'en in the highway to the gallows, God bless him!

CIT. You're too bitter, cony; the [50 young man may do well enough for all this.

WIFE. Come hither, Master Humphrey; has he hurt you? Now, beshrew his fingers for't! Here, sweetheart, here's some green [43] ginger for thee. Now, beshrew my heart, but 'a has peppernel [44] in 's head, as big as a pullet's egg! Alas, sweet lamb, how thy temples beat! Take the peace on him,[45] sweetheart, take the peace on him.

Enter a Boy.

CIT. No, no; you talk like a foolish [60 woman; I 'll ha' Ralph fight with him, and swinge [46] him up well-favor'dly.[47] — Sirrah boy, come hither. Let Ralph come in and fight with Jasper.

WIFE. Ay, and beat him well; he 's an unhappy [48] boy.

BOY. Sir, you must pardon us; the plot of our play lies contrary; and 't will hazard the spoiling of our play.

CIT. Plot me no plots! I 'll ha' Ralph [70 come out; I 'll make your house too hot for you else.

BOY. Why, sir, he shall; but if anything fall out of order, the gentlemen must pardon us.

CIT. Go your ways, Goodman Boy! [*Exit* Boy.] I 'll hold [49] him a penny, he shall have his bellyful of fighting now. Ho, here comes Ralph! No more! [50]

[SCENE V] [51]

HUMPHREY [*remains*]. *Enter* RALPH, MISTRESS MERRYTHOUGHT, MICHAEL, Squire [TIM], *and* Dwarf [GEORGE].

RALPH. What knight is that, squire? Ask him if he keep

The passage, bound by love of lady fair, Or else but prickant.[52]

HUM.   Sir, I am no knight, But a poor gentleman, that this same night Had stol'n from me, on yonder green, My lovely wife, and suffered (to be seen Yet extant on my shoulders) such a greeting, That whilst I live I shall think of that meeting.

WIFE. Ay, Ralph, he beat him unmercifully, Ralph; an thou spar'st him, [10 Ralph, I would thou wert hang'd.

CIT. No more, wife, no more.

RALPH. Where is the caitiff-wretch hath done this deed? — Lady, your pardon, that I may proceed Upon the quest of this injurious knight. — And thou, fair squire, repute me not the worse, In leaving the great venture of the purse And the rich casket, till some better leisure.

Enter JASPER *and* LUCE.

HUM. Here comes the broker [53] hath purloin'd my treasure.

RALPH. Go, squire, and tell him I am here, An errant knight at arms, to crave delivery Of that fair lady to her own knight's arms. [22 If he deny, bid him take choice of ground, And so defy him.

TIM.   From the knight that bears The golden pestle, I defy thee, knight, Unless thou make fair restitution Of that bright lady.

JASP.   Tell the knight that sent thee He is an ass; and I will keep the wench, And knock his headpiece.

RALPH.   Knight, thou art but dead If thou recall not thy uncourteous terms. [30

WIFE. Break 's pate, Ralph; break 's pate, Ralph, soundly!

JASP. Come, knight; I am ready for you. Now your pestle

                    Snatches away his pestle.

Shall try what temper, sir, your mortar 's of. "With that he stood upright in his stirrups, and gave the knight of the calfskin such a knock [*knocking* RALPH *down*] that he forsook his horse, and down he fell; and then he leaped upon him, and plucking off his helmet ——" [54]   40

---

[41] *I.e.*, teach him a lesson.
[42] Vagaries, pranks.   [43] Raw.
[44] Apparently a lump or swelling. (*N.E.D.*)
[45] Force him to give a bond to keep the peace.
[46] Beat.   [47] Handsomely, soundly.
[48] Naughty.   [49] Bet.   [50] Silence.   [51] The same.

[52] Just riding along.   [53] Pander.
[54] "Quoted or parodied from some romance." (Dyce.)

Hum. Nay, an my noble knight be down so
soon,
Though I can scarcely go,[55] I needs must run.
Exeunt Humphrey *and* Ralph.

Wife. Run, Ralph, run, Ralph; run for
thy life, boy; Jasper comes, Jasper comes!

Jasp. Come Luce, we must have other arms
for you;
Humphrey, and Golden Pestle, both adieu!
Exeunt.

Wife. Sure the Devil (God bless us!) is in
this springald![56] Why, George, didst ever
see such a fire-drake?[57] I am afraid my
boy's miscarried;[58] if he be, though he [50
were Master Merrythought's son a thousand
times, if there be any law in England, I'll
make some of them smart for't.
Cit. No, no; I have found out the matter,
sweetheart; Jasper is enchanted; as sure as
we are here, he is enchanted: he could no
more have stood in Ralph's hands than I can
stand in my Lord Mayor's. I'll have a ring
to discover all enchantments, and Ralph shall
beat him yet. Be no more vex'd, for it [60
shall be so.

[Scene VI][59]

Enter Ralph, Squire [Tim], Dwarf [George],
Mistress Merrythought, *and* Michael.

Wife. Oh, Husband, here's Ralph again!—
Stay, Ralph, let me speak with thee. How
dost thou, Ralph? Art thou not shrewdly [60]
hurt?—The foul great lungies [61] laid unmercifully on thee. There's some sugar-candy
for thee. Proceed; thou shalt have another
bout with him.
Cit. If Ralph had him at the fencing school,
if he did not make a puppy of him, and drive
him up and down the school, he should [10
ne'er come in my shop more.

Mist. Mer. Truly Master Knight of the
Burning Pestle, I am weary.
Mich. Indeed, law, Mother, and I am very
hungry.
Ralph. Take comfort, gentle dame, and
you fair squire;

For in this desert there must needs be plac'd
Many strong castles held by courteous
knights;
And till I bring you safe to one of those,
I swear by this my order ne'er to leave you. [20

Wife. Well said, Ralph!—George, Ralph
was ever comfortable,[62] was he not?
Cit. Yes, duck.
Wife. I shall ne'er forget him. When we
had lost our child, (you know it was stray'd
almost, alone, to Puddle Wharf,[63] and the
criers were abroad for it, and there it had
drown'd itself but for a sculler,[64] Ralph was
the most comfortablest to me: "Peace, Mistress," says he, "let it go; I'll get you [30
another as good." Did he not, George, did
he not say so?
Cit. Yes, indeed did he, mouse.

George. I would we had a mess of pottage
and a pot of drink, squire, and were going to
bed!
Tim. Why, we are at Waltham town's
end, and that's the Bell Inn.
George. Take courage, valiant knight,
damsel, and squire!
I have discovered, not a stone's cast off,   40
An ancient castle, held by the old knight
Of the most holy order of the Bell,
Who gives to all knights-errant entertain.
There plenty is of food, and all prepar'd
By the white hands of his own lady dear.
He hath three squires that welcome all his
guests;
The first hight [65] Chamberlino, who will see
Our beds prepar'd, and bring us snowy sheets,
Where never footman stretch'd his butter'd
hams; [66]
The second hight Tapstero, who will see [50
Our pots full filled, and no froth therein;
The third, a gentle squire, Ostlero hight,
Who will our palfreys slick with wisps of
straw,
And in the manger put them oats enough,
And never grease their teeth with candle-
snuff.[67]

Wife. That same dwarf's a pretty boy,
but the squire's a groutnol.[68]

---

[55] Walk.   [56] Youth.
[57] Fiery dragon.
[58] Perished.
[59] Before the Bell Inn at Waltham.
[60] Severely.
[61] Long, slim fellow; lout.

[62] Comforting.   [63] In Blackfriars.
[64] Waterman.   [65] Is called.
[66] Running footmen greased their legs to keep
them supple.
[67] A trick to keep horses from eating.
[68] Blockhead.

RALPH. Knock at the gates, my squire, with stately lance.

Enter TAPSTER.

TAP. Who's there? — You're welcome, gentlemen ; will you see a room?   60

GEORGE. Right courteous and valiant Knight of the Burning Pestle, this is the Squire Tapstero.

RALPH. Fair Squire Tapstero, I, a wand'ring knight,
Hight of the Burning Pestle, in the quest
Of this fair lady's casket and wrought [69] purse,
Losing myself in this vast wilderness,
Am to this castle well by fortune brought ;
Where, hearing of the goodly entertain
Your knight of holy order of the Bell   70
Gives to all damsels and all errant knights,
I thought to knock, and now am bold to enter.

TAP. An't please you see a chamber, you are very welcome.   *Exeunt.*

WIFE. George, I would have something done, and I cannot tell what it is.

CIT. What is it, Nell?

WIFE. Why, George, shall Ralph beat nobody again? Prithee, sweetheart, let him.

CIT. So he shall, Nell ; and if I join [80 with him, we'll knock them all.

[SCENE VII] [70]

Enter HUMPHREY *and* Merchant [VENTURE-WELL].

WIFE. Oh, George, here's Master Humphrey again now, that lost Mistress Luce, and Mistress Lucie's father. Master Humphrey will do somebody's errant,[71] I'll warrant him.

HUM. Father, it's true in arms I ne'er shall clasp her ;
For she is stol'n away by your man Jasper.

WIFE. I thought he would tell him.

VENT. Unhappy that I am, to lose my child !
Now I begin to think on Jasper's words,
Who oft hath urg'd to me thy foolishness. [10
Why didst thou let her go? Thou lov'st her not,

That wouldst bring home thy life, and not bring her.

HUM. Father, forgive me. Shall I tell you true?
Look on my shoulders : they are black and blue.
Whilst to and fro fair Luce and I were winding,
He came and basted me with a hedge-binding.[72]

VENT. Get men and horses straight ; we will be there
Within this hour. You know the place again?

HUM. I know the place where he my loins did swaddle ; [73]
I'll get six horses, and to each a saddle.   20

VENT. Meantime I'll go talk with Jasper's father.   *Exeunt.*

WIFE. George, what wilt thou lay with me now, that Master Humphrey has not Mistress Luce yet? Speak, George, what wilt thou lay with me?

CIT. No, Nell ; I warrant thee Jasper is at Puckeridge [74] with her by this.

WIFE. Nay, George, you must consider Mistress Lucie's feet are tender ; and besides 't is dark ; and, I promise you truly, I do [30 not see how he should get out of Waltham Forest with her yet.

CIT. Nay, cony, what wilt thou lay with me, that Ralph has her not yet?

WIFE. I will not lay against Ralph, honey, because I have not spoken with him. But look, George, peace ! here comes the merry old gentleman again.

[SCENE VIII] [75]

Enter old MERRYTHOUGHT.

MER. [*sings.*]

> When it was grown to dark midnight,
>   And all were fast asleep,
> In came Margaret's grimly ghost,
>   And stood at William's feet.[76]

I have money, and meat, and drink beforehand, till to-morrow at noon ; why should I be sad? Methinks I have half-a-dozen jovial spirits within me !   [*Sings.*]

I am three merry men, and three merry men ! [77]

---

[69] Embroidered.
[70] Presumably a room in Venturewell's house.
[71] Errand ; *i.e.*, attend to Jasper's affairs for him.

[72] Probably a withe.   [73] Beat.
[74] A dozen miles beyond Waltham.
[75] A room in Merrythought's house.
[76] From the ballad of "Fair Margaret and Sweet William."   [77] From a popular song.

To what end should any man be sad in [10 this world? Give me a man who when he goes to hanging cries,

> Troll the black bowl to me! [78]

and a woman that will sing a catch in her travail! I have seen a man come by my door with a serious face, in a black cloak, without a hatband, carrying his head as if he look'd for pins in the street; I have look'd out of my window half a year after, and have spi'd that man's head upon London Bridge.[79] 'T is [20 vile: never trust a tailor that does not sing at his work; his mind is of nothing but filching.

WIFE. Mark this, George; 't is worth noting: Godfrey my tailor, you know, never sings, and he had fourteen yards to make this gown; and I'll be sworn, Mistress Penistone the draper's wife had one made with twelve.

MER. [*sings.*]

> 'Tis mirth that fills the veins with blood,
> More than wine, or sleep, or food;
> Let each man keep his heart at ease: 30
> No man dies of that disease.
> He that would his body keep
> From diseases, must not weep;
> But whoever laughs and sings,
> Never he his body brings
> Into fevers, gouts, or rheums,
> Or ling'ringly his l[u]ngs consumes,
> Or meets with aches [80] in the bone,
> Or catarrhs or griping stone;
> But contented lives for aye;   40
> The more he laughs, the more he may.[81]

WIFE. Look, George; how say'st thou by this, George? Is't not a fine old man? — Now, God's blessing a' thy sweet lips! — When wilt thou be so merry, George? Faith, thou art the frowning'st little thing, when thou art angry, in a country.

Enter Merchant [VENTUREWELL].

CIT. Peace, cony; thou shalt see him taken down too, I warrant thee. Here's Luce's father come now.   50

MER. [*sings.*]

> As you came from Walsingham,
>   From that holy [82] land,
> There met you not with my true love
>   By the way as you came? [83]

VENT. Oh, Master Merrythought, my daughter's gone!
This mirth becomes you not; my daughter's gone!

MER. [*sings.*]

> Why, an if she be, what care I?
> Or let her come, or go, or tarry.[84]

VENT. Mock not my misery; it is your son
(Whom I have made my own, when all forsook him)   60
Has stol'n my only joy, my child, away.

MER. [*sings.*]

> He set her on a milk-white steed,
>   And himself upon a gray;
> He never turn'd his face again,
>   But he bore her quite away.[85]

VENT. Unworthy of the kindness I have shown
To thee and thine! too late I well perceive
Thou art consenting to my daughter's loss.

MER. Your daughter! what a stir's here wee' yer daughter! Let her go, think no [70 more on her, but sing loud. If both my sons were on the gallows, I would sing,

> Down, down, down they fall;
> Down, and arise they never shall.[86]

VENT. Oh, might I behold her once again,
And she once more embrace her aged sire!

MER. Fie, how scurvily this goes! "And she once more embrace her aged sire?" You'll make a dog [87] on her, will ye? She cares much for her aged sire, I warrant [80 you.   [*Sings.*]

> She cares not for her daddy, nor
>   She cares not for her mammy;
> For she is, she is, she is, she is
>   My lord of Lowgave's lassy.[88]

VENT. For this thy scorn I will pursue that son
Of thine to death.

MER.   Do; and when you ha' kill'd him,   [*Sings.*]

> Give him flowers enow, palmer, give him flowers enow;
> Give him red, and white, and blue, green, and yellow.[88]

---

[78] From a popular song. — "Troll" = circulate, pass.
[79] Where traitors' heads were exposed.
[80] Dissyllabic.
[81] Unidentified; very likely, as Alden suggests, written for the play.
[82] There was a famous shrine of the Virgin in this Norfolk town.   [83] From a well-known ballad.
[84] From a song in Robert Jones's *First Book of Songs and Airs* (1600).
[85] This may be from a variant of the ballad of "The Douglas Tragedy", or of "The Knight and Shepherd's Daughter."
[86] Dyce found these verses in an unprinted masque.
[87] Since we speak of a dog's "sire."
[88] Unidentified; Child suggests that we probably have here a fragment of an old ballad.

VENT. I 'll fetch my daughter —— 90
MER. I 'll hear no more a' your daughter;
it spoils my mirth.
VENT. I say, I 'll fetch my daughter.
MER. [*sings.*]

> Was never man for lady's sake,
>   Down, down,
> Tormented as I, poor Sir Guy,
>   De derry down,
> For Lucy's sake, that lady bright,
>   Down, down,
> As ever men beheld with eye,   100
>   De derry down.[89]

VENT. I 'll be reveng'd, by Heaven!

Exeunt.

Music.

WIFE. How dost thou like this, George?
CIT. Why, this is well, cony; but if Ralph
were hot once, thou shouldst see more.
WIFE. The fiddlers go again, husband.
CIT. Ay, Nell; but this is scurvy music. I
gave the whoreson gallows [90] money, and I
think he has not got me the waits of South-
wark. If I hear 'em not anon, I 'll twinge him
by the ears. — You musicians, play *Baloo!* [91]
WIFE. No, good George, let's ha' *Lach-
    rymae!* [92]   112
CIT. Why, this is it, cony.
WIFE. It 's all the better, George. Now,
sweet lamb, what story is that painted upon
the cloth? [93] The Confutation of St. Paul?
CIT. No, lamb; that 's Ralph and Lu-
crece.[94]
WIFE. Ralph and Lucrece! Which Ralph?
Our Ralph?   120
CIT. No, mouse; that was a Tartarian.[95]
WIFE. A Tartarian! Well, I would the
fiddlers had done, that we might see our
Ralph again!

ACT III — SCENE I [1]

Enter JASPER *and* LUCE.

JASP. Come, my dear dear; though we
    have lost our way,
We have not lost ourselves. Are you not
    weary

With this night's wand'ring, broken from your
    rest,
And frighted with the terror that attends
The darkness of this wild unpeopled place?
    LUCE. No, my best friend; I cannot either
        fear
Or entertain a weary thought, whilst you,
The end of all my full desires, stand by me.
Let them that lose their hopes, and live to lan-
    guish
Amongst the number of forsaken lovers,   10
Tell [2] the long weary steps, and number time,
Start at a shadow, and shrink up their blood,
Whilst I, possess'd with all content and quiet,
Thus take my pretty love, and thus embrace
    him.
    JASP. You have caught me, Luce, so fast
        that, whilst I live,
I shall become your faithful prisoner
And wear these chains for ever. Come, sit
    down,
And rest your body, too, too delicate
For these disturbances. — So; will you sleep?
Come, do not be more able than you are; [20
I know you are not skilful in these watches,
For women are no soldiers. Be not nice,[3]
But take it; [4] sleep, I say.
    LUCE.   I cannot sleep;
Indeed, I cannot, friend.
    JASP.   Why, then we 'll sing,
And try how that will work upon our senses.
    LUCE. I 'll sing, or say, or anything but
        sleep.
    JASP. Come, little mermaid, rob me of my
        heart
With that enchanting voice.
    LUCE.   You mock me, Jasper.

SONG

JASP. Tell me, dearest, what is love?
LUCE. 'T is a lightning from above;   30
    'T is an arrow, 't is a fire,
    'T is a boy they call Desire;
        'T is a smile
        Doth beguile
JASP. The poor hearts of men that prove.[5]

    Tell me more, are women true?
LUCE. Some love change, and so do you.
JASP. Are they fair and never kind?
LUCE. Yes, when men turn with the wind.
JASP.   Are they froward?   40
LUCE.   Ever toward,
    Those that love, to love anew.[6]

[89] From "The Legend of Sir Guy."
[90] Gallows-bird.
[91] A popular tune.
[92] A dance tune by Dowland.
[93] A cheap substitute for tapestry; it served to
curtain off the inner stage.
[94] *I.e.*, the Rape of Lucrece.
[95] Thief; perhaps the Citizen's blunder for *Tarquin.*
[1] Waltham Forest.

[2] Count.
[3] Foolishly fastidious.
[4] Acquiesce.
[5] Experience it.
[6] Those that love are ever disposed to turn to a
new love. This song, as Alden observes, is probably
original.

JASP. Dissemble it no more; I see the god
Of heavy sleep lay on his heavy mace
Upon your eyelids.
    LUCE.   I am very heavy.[7] [*Sleeps.*]
    JASP. Sleep, sleep; and quiet rest crown
        thy sweet thoughts!
Keep from her fair [8] blood distempers, start-
    ings,
Horrors, and fearful shapes! Let all her
    dreams
Be joys, and chaste delights, embraces, wishes,
And such new pleasures as the ravish'd soul [50
Gives to the senses! — So; my charms have
    took. —
Keep her, you powers divine, whilst I contem-
    plate
Upon the wealth and beauty of her mind!
She is only fair and constant, only kind,
And only to thee, Jasper. Oh, my joys!
Whither will you transport me? Let not ful-
    ness
Of my poor buried hopes come up together
And overcharge my spirits! I am weak.
Some say, however ill, the sea and women [59
Are govern'd by the moon; both ebb and
    flow,
Both full of changes; yet to them that know,
And truly judge, these but opinions are,
And heresies, to bring on pleasing war
Between our tempers, that without these were
Both void of a[f]ter-love and present fear;
Which are the best of Cupid. O thou child,
Bred from despair, I dare not entertain thee,
Having a love without the faults of women,
And greater in her perfect goods than men!
Which to make good, and please myself the
    stronger,   70
Though certainly I am certain of her love,
I'll try her, that the world and memory
May sing to aftertimes her constancy. —
                [*Draws his sword.*]
Luce! Luce! awake!
    LUCE.   Why do you fright me, friend,
With those distempered looks? What makes [9]
    your sword
Drawn in your hand? Who hath offended
    you?
I prithee, Jasper, sleep; thou art wild with
    watching.[10]
    JASP. Come, make your way to Heaven,
        and bid the world,
With all the villainies that stick upon it,
Farewell; you're for another life.

    LUCE.   Oh, Jasper, [80
How have my tender years committed evil,
Especially against the man I love,
Thus to be cropp'd untimely?
    JASP.   Foolish girl,
Canst thou imagine I could love his daughter
That flung me from my fortune into nothing?
Discharged me his service, shut the doors
Upon my poverty, and scorn'd my prayers,
Sending me, like a boat without a mast,
To sink or swim? Come; by this hand you
    die;
I must have life and blood, to satisfy   90
Your father's wrongs.

    WIFE. Away, George, away! raise the
watch at Ludgate, and bring a mittimus [11] from
the justice for this desperate villain! — Now, I
charge you, gentlemen, see the King's peace
kept! — Oh, my heart, what a varlet's this
to offer manslaughter upon the harmless gentlewoman!
    CIT. I warrant thee, sweetheart, we'll have
him hampered.[12]   100

    LUCE.   Oh, Jasper, be not cruel!
If thou wilt kill me, smile, and do it quickly,
And let not many deaths appear before me.
I am a woman, made of fear and love,
A weak, weak woman; kill not with thy eyes:
They shoot me through and through. Strike,
    I am ready;
And, dying, still I love thee.

Enter Merchant [VENTUREWELL], HUMPHREY,
          and his Men.

    VENT.   Whereabouts?
    JASP. [*aside*] No more of this; now to
        myself again.
    HUM. There, there he stands, with sword,
        like martial knight,
Drawn in his hand; therefore beware the
    fight,   110
You that be wise; for, were I good Sir Bevis,[13]
I would not stay [14] his coming, by your leaves.
    VENT. Sirrah, restore my daughter!
    JASP.   Sirrah, no.
    VENT. Upon him, then!
        [*They attack* JASPER, *and force* LUCE
        from him.]

    WIFE. So; down with him, down with him,
down with him! Cut him i' th' leg, boys, cut
him i' th' leg!

---

[7] Sleepy.   [8] Dissyllabic.   [9] Does.
[10] Staying awake.

[11] Warrant for arrest.   [12] Confined, jailed.
[13] Hero of the romance of "Bevis of Hampton.'
[14] Await.

VENT. Come your ways, minion ; I 'll pro-
vide a cage
For you, you 're grown so tame. — Horse her
away.
HUM. Truly, I 'm glad your forces have the
day.   *Exeunt [all except]* JASPER.
JASP. They are gone, and I am hurt ; my
love is lost,   121
Never to get again. Oh, me unhappy !
Bleed, bleed and die ! I cannot. O my folly,
Thou hast betray'd me ! Hope, where art
thou fled?
Tell me, if thou beest anywhere remaining,
Shall I but see my love again? Oh, no !
She will not deign to look upon her butcher,
Nor is it fit she should ; yet I must venture.
O Chance, or Fortune, or whate'er thou art,
That men adore for powerful, hear my cry, [130
And let me loving live, or losing die !   *Exit.*

WIFE. Is 'a gone, George?
CIT. Ay, cony.
WIFE. Marry, and let him go, sweetheart.
By the faith a' my body, 'a has put me into
such a fright that I tremble, as they say, as 't
were an aspen-leaf. Look a' my little finger,
George, how it shakes. Now i' truth, every
member of my body is the worse for 't.
CIT. Come, hug in mine arms, sweet
mouse ; he shall not fright thee any more. [141
Alas, mine own dear heart, how it quivers !

[SCENE II] [15]

Enter MISTRESS MERRYTHOUGHT, RALPH,
MICHAEL, Squire [TIM], Dwarf [GEORGE],
Host, *and a* Tapster.

WIFE. Oh, Ralph ! how dost thou, Ralph?
How hast thou slept to-night? [16] Has the
knight us'd thee well?
CIT. Peace, Nell ; let Ralph alone.

TAP. Master, the reckoning is not paid.
RALPH. Right courteous knight, who, for
the order's sake
Which thou hast ta'en, hang'st out the holy
Bell,
As I this flaming pestle bear about,
We render thanks to your puissant [17] self,
Your beauteous lady, and your gentle squires,
For thus refreshing of our wearied limbs,   11
Stiff'ned with hard achievements in wild
desert.

---

[15] Before the Bell Inn, at Waltham.
[16] Last night.   [17] Trisyllabic.

TAP. Sir, there is twelve shillings to pay.
RALPH. Thou merry Squire Tapstero,
thanks to thee
For comforting our souls with double jug ;
And, if advent'rous fortune prick thee forth,
Thou jovial squire, to follow feats of arms,
Take heed thou tender every lady's cause,
Every true knight, and every damsel fair ;
But spill the blood of treacherous Saracens, [20
And false enchanters that with magic spells
Have done to death full many a noble knight.
HOST. Thou valiant Knight of the Burning
Pestle, give ear to me ; there is twelve shillings
to pay, and, as I am a true knight, I will not
bate a penny.

WIFE. George, I pray thee, tell me, must
Ralph pay twelve shillings now?
CIT. No, Nell, no ; nothing but the old
knight is merry with Ralph.   30
WIFE. Oh, is 't nothing else? Ralph will
be as merry as he.

RALPH. Sir Knight, this mirth of yours be-
comes you well ;
But, to requite this liberal courtesy,
If any of your squires will follow arms,
He shall receive from my heroic hand
A knighthood, by the virtue of this pestle.
HOST. Fair knight, I thank you for your
noble offer ;
Therefore, gentle knight,
Twelve shillings you must pay, or I must
cap [18] you.   40

WIFE. Look, George ! did not I tell thee as
much? The knight of the Bell is in earnest.
Ralph shall not be beholding to him : give him
his money, George, and let him go snick up.[19]
CIT. Cap Ralph? No. — Hold your hand,
Sir Knight of the Bell ; there 's your money ;
have you anything to say to Ralph now?
Cap Ralph !
WIFE. I would you should know it, Ralph
has friends that will not suffer him to be [50
capp'd for ten times so much, and ten times
to the end of that. — Now take thy course,
Ralph.

MIST. MER. Come, Michael ; thou and I
will go home to thy father ; he hath enough
left to keep us a day or two, and we 'll set
fellows abroad to cry our purse and our casket ;
shall we, Michael?

---

[18] Arrest ; from *capias.*   [19] Hang.

MICH. Ay, I pray, Mother; in truth my feet are full of chilblains with travelling.   60

WIFE. Faith, and those chilblains are a foul trouble. — Mistress Merrythought, when your youth comes home, let him rub all the soles of his feet, and the heels, and his ankles, with a mouse-skin; or, if none of your people can catch a mouse, when he goes to bed let him roll his feet in the warm embers, and, I warrant you, he shall be well; and you may make him put his fingers between his toes, and smell to them; it 's very sovereign for his head, if [70 he be costive.

MIST. MER. Master Knight of the Burning Pestle, my son Michael and I bid you farewell; I thank your Worship heartily for your kindness.

RALPH. Farewell, fair lady, and your tender
  squire.
If, pricking through these deserts, I do hear
Of any traitorous knight, who through his
  guile
Hath light upon your casket and your purse,
I will despoil him of them, and restore them.
  MIST. MER. I thank your Worship.   81
                    Exit with MICHAEL.
  RALPH. Dwarf, bear my shield; squire, ele-
    vate my lance : —
And now farewell, you Knight of holy Bell.

CIT. Ay, ay, Ralph, all is paid.

RALPH. But yet, before I go, speak, worthy
  knight,
If aught you do of sad [20] adventures know,
Where errant knight [21] may through his
  prowess win
Eternal fame, and free some gentle souls
From endless bonds of steel and ling'ring pain.
  HOST. Sirrah, go to Nick the barber, [90
and bid him prepare himself, as I told you
before, quickly.
  TAP. I am gone, sir.   *Exit* Tapster.
  HOST. Sir Knight, this wilderness affordeth
    none
But the great venture, where full many a
  knight
Hath tri'd his prowess, and come off with
  shame;
And where I would not have you lose your life
Against no man, but furious fiend of hell.

[20] Serious.
[21] Cor. ed. 1711; old eds. *Knights*.

RALPH. Speak on, Sir Knight, tell what he
  is and where;
For here I vow, upon my blazing badge,   100
Never to blaze a day in quietness,
But bread and water will I only eat,
And the green herb and rock shall be my
  couch,
Till I have quell'd [22] that man, or beast, or
  fiend,
That works such damage to all errant knights.
  HOST. Not far from hence, near to a craggy
    cliff,
At the north end of this distressed town,
There doth stand a lowly house,
Ruggedly builded, and in it a cave
In which an ugly giant now doth wone, [23]   110
Y-cleped [24] Barbaroso; in his hand
He shakes a naked lance of purest steel,
With sleeves turn'd up; and him before he
  wears
A motley garment, to preserve his clothes
From blood of those knights which he massa-
  cres,
And ladies gent. [25] Without his door doth
  hang
A copper basin on a prickant [26] spear;
At which no sooner gentle knights can knock,
But the shrill sound fierce Barbaroso hears,
And rushing forth, brings in the errant
  knight   120
And sets him down in an enchanted chair;
Then with an engine, which he hath prepar'd,
With forty teeth, he claws his courtly crown;
Next makes him wink, [27] and underneath his
  chin
He plants a brazen piece of mighty bord [28]
And knocks his bullets [29] round about his
  cheeks;
Whilst with his fingers, and an instrument
With which he snaps his hair off, he doth fill
The wretch's ears with a most hideous noise.
Thus every knight-adventurer he doth trim,
And now no creature dares encounter him. [131
  RALPH. In God's name, I will fight him.
    Kind sir,
Go but before me to this dismal cave,
Where this huge giant Barbaroso dwells,
And, by that virtue that brave Rosicleer
That damned brood of ugly giants slew,

[22] Killed.   [23] Dwell.   [24] Called.
[25] Of gentle blood.
[26] *I.e.*, upward-pointing; the " spear " is, of course, the barber's pole.
[27] Shut his eyes.
[28] Rim, circumference. The " brazen piece " is the basin, which fitted the customer's neck.
[29] *I.e.*, his balls of soap.

And Palmerin Frannarco [30] overthrew,
I doubt not but to curb this traitor foul,
And to the Devil send his guilty soul.

HOST. Brave-sprighted knight, thus far I
   will perform   140
This your request : I 'll bring you within sight
Of this most loathsome place, inhabited
By a more loathsome man ; but dare not stay,
For his main force swoops all he sees away.

RALPH. Saint George, set on before !
   March squire and page !   *Exeunt.*

WIFE. George, dost think Ralph will confound the giant?

CIT. I hold [31] my cap to a farthing he does.
Why, Nell, I saw him wrastle with the great
Dutchman,[32] and hurl him.   150

WIFE. Faith, and that Dutchman was a
goodly man, if all things were answerable to
his bigness. And yet they say there was a
Scotchman higher than he, and that they two
and a knight [33] met, and saw one another for
nothing. But of all the sights that ever were
in London, since I was married, methinks the
little child that was so fair grown about the
members [34] was the prettiest ; that and the
hermaphrodite.   160

CIT. Nay, by your leave, Nell, Ninivy [35]
was better.

WIFE. Ninivie ! Oh, that was the story of
Jone and the wall,[36] was it not, George?

CIT. Yes, lamb.

[SCENE III] [37]

Enter MISTRESS MERRYTHOUGHT.

WIFE. Look, George, here comes Mistress
Merrythought again ! and I would have Ralph
come and fight with the giant ; I tell you true,
I long to see 't.

CIT. Good Mistress Merrythought, begone,
I pray you, for my sake ; I pray you, forbear a
little ; you shall have audience presently ; [38] I
have a little business.

WIFE. Mistress Merrythought, if it please
you to refrain your passion a little, till [10

Ralph have despatch'd the giant out of the
way, we shall think ourselves much bound to
you. I shall thank you, good Mistress Merrythought.

Exit MISTRESS MERRYTHOUGHT.

Enter a Boy.

CIT. Boy, come hither. Send away Ralph
and this whoreson giant quickly.

BOY. In good faith, sir, we cannot ; you 'll
utterly spoil our play, and make it to be hiss'd ;
and it cost money ; you will not suffer us to go
on with our plot. — I pray, gentlemen, [20
rule him.

CIT. Let him come now and despatch this,
and I 'll trouble you no more.

BOY. Will you give me your hand of that?

WIFE. Give him thy hand, George, do ;
and I 'll kiss him. I warrant thee, the youth
means plainly.

BOY. I 'll send him to you presently.[39]

WIFE. [*kissing him*] I thank you, little
youth. (*Exit* Boy.) Faith, the child hath [30
a sweet breath, George ; but I think it be
troubled with the worms ; *carduus benedictus* [40]
and mare's milk were the only thing in the
world for 't.

[SCENE IV] [41]

Enter RALPH, Host, Squire [TIM], *and* Dwarf
[GEORGE].

WIFE. Oh, Ralph 's here, George ! — God
send thee good luck, Ralph !

HOST. Puissant knight, yonder his mansion
   is.
Lo, where the spear and copper basin are !
Behold that string, on which hangs many a
   tooth,
Drawn from the gentle jaw of wand'ring
   knights !
I dare not stay to sound ; he will appear.
           Exit Host.

RALPH. Oh, faint not, heart ! Susan, my
   lady dear,
The cobbler's maid in Milk Street,[42] for whose
   sake   9
I take these arms, oh, let the thought of thee
Carry thy knight through all adventurous
   deeds ;

---

[30] A giant in *Palmerin d' Oliva.*   [31] Bet.
[32] Stowe mentions a gigantic Dutchman in his *Annals.*
[33] Dyce suggests that "and a knight" may have been erroneously transposed from a place directly after *Scotchman.*
[34] The genital organs.
[35] A puppet-show of great popularity.
[36] Jonah and the whale.
[37] Unlocated. When Mrs. Merrythought is able at last to play her scene, it is before her husband's house.   [38] Soon.

[39] At once.
[40] The blessed thistle, a cordial.
[41] Before a barber's shop, in Waltham.
[42] In Cheapside.

And, in the honor of thy beauteous self,
May I destroy this monster Barbaroso! —
Knock, squire, upon the basin, till it break
With the shrill strokes, or till the giant speak.

Enter Barber.

WIFE. Oh, George, the giant, the giant! —
Now, Ralph for thy life!

  BAR. What fond [43] unknowing wight is this,
    that dares
So rudely knock at Barbaros[o]'s cell,
Where no man comes but leaves his fleece be-
  hind?   20
  RALPH. I, traitorous caitiff, who am sent by
    fate
To punish all the sad enormities [44]
Thou hast committed against ladies gent
And errant knights. Traitor to God and men,
Prepare thyself! This is the dismal hour
Appointed for thee to give strict account
Of all thy beastly treacherous villainies.
  BAR. Foolhardy knight, full soon thou shalt
    aby [45]
This fond reproach : thy body will I bang; [29
                He takes down his pole.
And, lo, upon that string thy teeth shall hang!
Prepare thyself, for dead soon shalt thou be.
  RALPH. Saint George for me!   *They fight.*
  BAR.   Gargantua [46] for me!

WIFE. To him, Ralph, to him! hold up the
giant ; set out thy leg before, Ralph!
  CIT. Falsify a blow,[47] Ralph, falsify a blow!
The giant lies open on the left side.
  WIFE. Bear 't off, [48] bear 't off still! there,
boy! — Oh, Ralph's almost down, Ralph's
almost down!

  RALPH. Susan, inspire me! Now have up
    again.   40

WIFE. Up, up, up, up, up! so, Ralph!
down with him, down with him, Ralph!
  CIT. Fetch him o'er the hip, boy!
        [RALPH *knocks down the* Barber.]
  WIFE. There, boy! kill, kill, kill, kill, kill,
    Ralph!
  CIT. No, Ralph; get all [49] out of him first.

  RALPH. Presumptuous man, see to what
    desperate end

Thy treachery hath brought thee! The just
  gods,
Who never prosper those that do despise them,
For all the villainies which thou hast done
To knights and ladies, now have paid thee
  home   50
By my stiff arm, a knight adventurous.
But say, vile wretch, before I send thy soul
To sad Avernus,[50] whither it must go,
What captives holdst thou in thy sable cave?
  BAR. Go in, and free them all ; thou hast
    the day.
  RALPH. Go, squire and dwarf, search in this
    dreadful cave,
And free the wretched prisoners from their
    bonds.   [*Exeunt*] Squire *and* Dwarf.
  BAR. I crave for mercy, as thou art a
    knight,
And scorn'st to spill the blood of those that
    beg.
  RALPH. Thou show'dst no mercy, nor shalt
    thou have any ;   60
Prepare thyself, for thou shalt surely die.

Re-enter Squire [TIM], *leading one winking,*[51]
    with a basin under his chin.

  TIM. Behold, brave knight, here is one
    prisoner,
Whom this wild man hath used as you see.

WIFE. This is the first wise word I heard
the squire speak.

  RALPH. Speak what thou art, and how thou
    hast been us'd,
That I may give him condign punishment.
  1 KN. I am a knight that took my journey
    post
Northward from London ; and in courteous
    wise
This giant train'd [52] me to his loathsome
    den,
Under pretence of killing of the itch ;   71
And all my body with a powder strew'd,
That smarts and stings ; and cut away my
    beard,
And my curl'd locks wherein were ribands ti'd ;
And with a water wash'd my tender eyes,
Whilst up and down about me still he skipp'd ;
Whose virtue is, that, till my eyes be wip'd
With a dry cloth, for this my foul disgrace,[53]
I shall not dare to look a dog i' th' face.

---

[43] Foolish.   [44] Grievous iniquities.
[45] Pay for.   [46] Rabelais's giant hero.
[47] Get in a stroke under cover of a feint.
[48] Parry it.   [49] *I.e.*, all the information you can.

[50] The lake near Naples which was supposed to
be an entrance to Hades.
  [51] With his eyes shut.   [52] Enticed.
  [53] Having his hair and beard cut.

WIFE. Alas, poor knight! — Relieve [80 him, Ralph; relieve poor knights, whilst you live.

RALPH. My trusty squire, convey him to the town,
Where he may find relief. — Adieu, fair knight.
                                    Exit Knight.

Re-enter Dwarf [GEORGE], *leading one with a patch o'er his nose.*[54]

GEORGE. Puissant Knight, of the Burning Pestle hight,
See here another wretch, whom this foul beast
Hath scorch'd [55] and scor'd in this inhuman wise.
RALPH. Speak me thy name, and eke thy place of birth,
And what hath been thy usage in this cave.
    2 KN. I am a knight, Sir Pockhole [56] is my name,   90
And by my birth I am a Londoner,
Free by my copy,[57] but my ancestors
Were Frenchmen [58] all; and riding hard this way
Upon a trotting horse, my bones did ache; [59]
And I, faint knight, to ease my weary limbs,
Light [60] at this cave; when straight this furious fiend,
With sharpest instrument of purest steel,
Did cut the gristle of my nose away,
And in the place this velvet plaster stands. [99
Relieve me, gentle knight, out of his hands!

WIFE. Good Ralph, relieve Sir Pockhole, and send him away; for in truth his breath stinks.

RALPH. Convey him straight after the other knight. —
Sir Pockhole, fare you well.
    2 KN.   Kind sir, good night. *Exit.*
MAN. Deliver us!   *Cries within.*
WOMAN. Deliver us!

WIFE. Hark, George, what a woeful cry there is! I think some woman lies-in there.

MAN. [*within*] Deliver us!   110
WOMAN. [*within*] Deliver us!

[54] Syphilis is apt to attack the nose.
[55] Scotched, scored, cut.
[56] Syphilis was known as the pox.
[57] *I.e.*, he has a certificate of his receiving the freedom of the city.
[58] Syphilis is also known as the French disease.
[59] One of the symptoms of syphilis.
[60] Lit, alighted.

RALPH. What a ghastly noise is this?
    Speak Barbaroso,
Or, by this blazing steel, thy head goes off!
    BAR. Prisoners of mine, whom I in diet [61] keep.
Send lower down into the cave,
And in a tub that's heated smoking hot,[61]
There may they find them, and deliver them.
RALPH. Run, squire and dwarf; deliver them with speed.
                        Exeunt Squire *and* Dwarf.

WIFE. But will not Ralph kill this giant? Surely I am afeard, if he let him go, he will [120 do as much hurt as ever he did.
CIT. Not so, mouse, neither, if he could convert him.
WIFE. Ay, George, if he could convert him; but a giant is not so soon converted as one of us ordinary people. There's a pretty tale of a witch, that had the devil's mark [62] about her (God bless us!), that had a giant to her son, that was call'd Lob-lie-by-the-fire; didst never hear it, George?   130

Re-enter Squire [TIM], *leading a* Man, *with a glass of lotion in his hand, and the* Dwarf [GEORGE], *leading a* Woman, *with diet-bread and drink.*

CIT. Peace, Nell, here comes the prisoners.

GEORGE. Here be these pined wretches, manful knight,
That for this six weeks have not seen a wight.
RALPH. Deliver [63] what you are, and how you came
To this sad cave, and what your usage was.
MAN. I am an errant knight that followed arms
With spear and shield; and in my tender years
I stricken was with Cupid's fiery shaft,
And fell in love with this my lady dear,
And stole her from her friends in Turnbull Street,[64]   140
And bore her up and down from town to town,
Where we did eat and drink, and music hear;
Till at the length at this unhappy town

[61] A feature of the treatment of syphilis.
[62] Brand.   [63] Report.
[64] Notorious for its prostitutes.

We did arrive, and coming to this cave,
This beast us caught, and put us in a tub,
Where we this two months sweat, and should
　　have done
Another month, if you had not reliev'd us.
　　WOMAN. This bread and water hath our
　　　　diet been,
Together with a rib cut from a neck
Of burned mutton ; hard hath been our
　　fare.　　　　　　　　　　　　　　　150
Release us from this ugly giant's snare !
　　MAN. This hath been all the food we have
　　　　receiv'd ;
But only twice a day, for novelty,
He gave a spoonful of this hearty broth
To each of us, through this same slender quill.
　　　　　　　　　　　　Pulls out a syringe.
　　RALPH. From this infernal monster you
　　　　shall go,
That useth knights and gentle ladies so ! —
Convey them hence.
　　　　　　　　　　　Exeunt Man *and* Woman.

　　CIT. Cony, I can tell thee, the gentlemen
like Ralph.　　　　　　　　　　　　　160
　　WIFE. Ay, George, I see it well enough. —
Gentlemen, I thank you all heartily for gracing
my man Ralph ; and I promise you you shall
see him oft'ner.

　　BAR. Mercy, great knight ! I do recant my
　　　　ill,
And henceforth never gentle blood will spill.
　　RALPH. I give thee mercy ; but yet shalt
　　　　thou swear
Upon my burning pestle to perform
Thy promise utter'd.
　　BAR. I swear and kiss.
　　RALPH. Depart, then, and amend. — [170
　　　　　　　　　　　　　　　[*Exit* Barber.]
Come, squire and dwarf ; the sun grows
　　　　towards his set,
And we have many more adventures yet.
　　　　　　　　　　　　　　　Exeunt.

　　CIT. Now Ralph is in this humor, I know he
would ha' beaten all the boys in the house, if
they had been set on him.
　　WIFE. Ay, George, but it is well as it is. I
warrant you, the gentlemen do consider what
it is to overthrow a giant. But, look, George ;
here comes Mistress Merrythought, and her
son Michael. — Now you are welcome, [180
Mistress Merrythought ; now Ralph has done,
you may go on.

[SCENE V] [65]

Enter MISTRESS MERRYTHOUGHT *and*
MICHAEL.

　　MIST. MER. Mick, my boy !
　　MICH. Ay, forsooth, Mother.
　　MIST. MER. Be merry, Mick ; we are at
home now, where, I warrant you, you shall
find the house flung out at the windows.
[*Music within.*] Hark ! hey, dogs, hey ! this
is the old world,[66] i' faith, with my husband.
If I get in among 'em, I 'll play 'em such a
lesson, that they shall have little list to come
scraping [67] hither again. — Why, Master [10
Merrythought ! Husband ! Charles Merrythought !
　　MER. [*appearing above, and singing*]

　　If you will sing, and dance, and laugh,
　　　　And holloa, and laugh again,
　　And then cry, "There, boys, there !" why, then,
　　　　One, two, three, and four,
　　We shall be merry within this hour.[68]

　　MIST. MER. Why, Charles, do you not
know your own natural wife ? I say, open
the door, and turn me out those mangy [20
companions ; [69] 't is more than time that they
were fellow and fellow-like with you. You
are a gentleman, Charles, and an old man,
and father of two children ; and I myself,
(though I say it) by my mother's side niece
to a worshipful gentleman and a conductor ; [70]
he has been three times in his Majesty's service at Chester, and is now the fourth time,
God bless him and his charge, upon his
journey.[71]　　　　　　　　　　　　30
　　MER.

　　　　Go from my window, love, go ;
　　　　Go from my window, my dear !
　　　　　　The wind and the rain
　　　　　　Will drive you back again ;
　　　　You cannot be lodged here.[72]

Hark you, Mistress Merrythought, you that
walk upon adventures, and forsake your husband because he sings with never a penny in
his purse ; what, shall I think myself the
worse ? Faith, no, I 'll be merry. You [40
come not here ; here 's none but lads of
mettle, lives of a hundred years and upwards ;
care never drunk their bloods, nor want made
'em warble " Heigh-ho, my heart is heavy."

[65] Before Merrythought's house.
[66] *I.e.*, it 's the same old story.
[67] *I.e.*, fiddling.　　　[68] Unidentified.
[69] Fellows.　　　[70] Commander.
[71] The point is that his service has not been overseas.
[72] Evidently a popular song, since it is elsewhere
quoted.

MIST. MER. Why, Master Merrythought, what am I, that you should laugh me to scorn thus abruptly? Am I not your fellow-feeler, as we may say, in all our miseries? your comforter in health and sickness? Have I not brought you children? Are they not like [50 you, Charles? look upon thine own image, hard-hearted man! and yet for all this ——

MER.

> Begone, begone, my juggy, my puggy,
> Begone, my love, my dear!
> The weather is warm,
> 'T will do thee no harm;
> Thou canst not be lodged here. —

Be merry, boys! some light music, and more wine! 		[*Exit above.*]

WIFE. He's not in earnest, I hope, [60 George, is he?

CIT. What if he be, sweetheart?

WIFE. Marry, if he be, George, I'll make bold to tell him he's an ingrant [73] old man to use his bedfellow so scurvily.

CIT. What! how does he use her, honey?

WIFE. Marry, come up, sir saucebox! I think you'll take his part, will you not? Lord, how hot you are grown! You are a fine man, an you had a fine dog; [74] it be- [70 comes you sweetly!

CIT. Nay, prithee, Nell, chide not; for, as I am an honest man and a true Christian grocer, I do not like his doings.

WIFE. I cry you mercy,[75] then, George! you know we are all frail and full of infirmities. — D'ee hear, Master Merrythought? May I crave a word with you?

MER. [*appearing above*] Strike up lively, lads! 		80

WIFE. I had not thought, in truth, Master Merrythought, that a man of your age and discretion, as I may say, being a gentleman, and therefore known by your gentle conditions,[76] could have used so little respect to the weakness of his wife; for your wife is your own flesh, the staff of your age, your yoke-fellow, with whose help you draw through the mire of this transitory world; nay, she's your own rib; and again — 		90

MER.

> I come not hither for thee to teach,
> I have no pulpit for thee to preach,

[73] Ignorant.
[74] *I.e.*, it would take the possession of a fine dog to mark you as a fine man; no one would size you up as one by yourself alone.
[75] Beg your pardon.		[76] Character.

> I would thou hadst kiss'd me under the breech,
> As thou art a lady gay.[77]

WIFE. Marry, with a vengeance! I am heartily sorry for the poor gentlewoman; but if I were thy wife, i' faith, greybeard, i' faith —

CIT. I prithee, sweet honeysuckle, be content.

WIFE. Give me such words, that am a [100 gentlewoman born! Hang him, hoary rascal! Get me some drink,[78] George; I am almost molten with fretting; now, beshrew his knave's heart for it!

MER. Play me a light lavolta.[79] Come, be frolic. Fill the good fellows wine.

MIST. MER. Why, Master Merrythought, are you disposed to make me wait here? You'll open, I hope; I'll fetch them that shall open else. 		110

MER. Good woman, if you will sing, I'll give you something; if not ——

SONG

> You are no love for me, Marg'ret,
> I am no love for you. — [80]

Come aloft,[81] boys, aloft! 		[*Exit above.*]

MIST. MER. Now a churl's fart in your teeth, sir! — Come, Mick, we'll not trouble him; 'a shall not ding us i' th' teeth with his bread and his broth, that he shall not. Come, boy; I'll provide for thee, I warrant thee. [120 We'll go to Master Venturewell's, the merchant; I'll get his letter to mine host of the Bell in Waltham; there I'll place thee with the tapster: will not that do well for thee, Mick? And let me alone for that old cuckoldly knave your father; I'll use him in his kind,[82] I warrant ye. 		[*Exeunt.*]

WIFE. Come, George, where's the beer?

CIT. Here, love.

WIFE. This old fornicating fellow will [130 not out of my mind yet. — Gentlemen, I'll begin to you all; and I desire more of your acquaintance with all my heart. [*Drinks.*] Fill the gentlemen some beer, George.

> *Music. Boy danceth.*

[77] Unidentified. Perhaps original, for the nonce.
[78] Along with fruit and other refreshments, it was sold in the house.
[79] A lively dance.
[80] Perhaps a modification of part of the ballad of "Fair Margaret and Sweet William."
[81] Be lively or mirthful.
[82] According to his own nature.

ACT IV — SCENE I [1]

WIFE. Look, George, the little boy's come again : methinks he looks something like the Prince of Orange in his long stocking, if he had a little harness [2] about his neck. George, I will have him dance *Fading*. — *Fading* is a fine jig, I 'll assure you, gentlemen. — Begin, brother. — Now 'a capers, sweetheart ! — Now a turn a' th' toe, and then tumble ! cannot you tumble, youth?

BOY. No, indeed, forsooth.   10

WIFE. Nor eat fire?

BOY. Neither.

WIFE. Why, then, I thank you heartily ; there 's twopence to buy you points [3] withal.

                    [*Exit* Boy.]

Enter JASPER *and* Boy.

JASP. There, boy, deliver this ; [*giving a letter*] but do it well.
Hast thou provided me four lusty fellows,
Able to carry me? and art thou perfect
In all thy business?

BOY.   Sir, you need not fear ;
I have my lesson here, and cannot miss it ;
The men are ready for you, and what else [20
Pertains to this employment.

JASP.   There, my boy ;
Take it, but buy no land.   [*Gives money.*]

BOY.   Faith, sir, 't were rare
To see so young a purchaser. I fly,
And on my wings carry your destiny.   *Exit.*

JASP. Go and be happy ! Now, my latest hope,
Forsake me not, but fling thy anchor out,
And let it hold ! Stand fix'd, thou rolling stone,
Till I enjoy my dearest ! Hear me, all
You powers, that rule in men, celestial !   *Exit.*

WIFE. Go thy ways ; thou art as [30 crooked a sprig as ever grew in London. I warrant him, he 'll come to some naughty end or other ; for his looks say no less. Besides, his father, you know, George, is none of the best ; you heard him take me up like a flirt-gill,[4] and sing bawdy songs upon me ; but i' faith, if I live, George ——

CIT. Let me alone, sweetheart ; I have a trick in my head shall lodge him in the Arches [5]

for one year, and make him sing *peccavi* [40 ere I leave him ; and yet he shall never know who hurt him neither.

WIFE. Do, my good George, do !

CIT. What shall we have Ralph do now, boy?

BOY. You shall have what you will, sir.

CIT. Why, so, sir ; go and fetch me him, then, and let the Sophy of Persia come and christen him a child.[6]

BOY. Believe me, sir, that will not do so [50 well ; 't is stale ; it has been had before at the Red Bull.[7]

WIFE. George, let Ralph travel over great hills, and let him be very weary and come to the King of Cracovia's [8] house, covered with velvet ; and there let the king's daughter stand in her window, all in beaten gold,[9] combing her golden locks with a comb of ivory ; and let her spy Ralph, and fall in love with him, and come down to him, and [60 carry [10] him into her father's house ; and then let Ralph talk with her.

CIT. Well said, Nell ; it shall be so. — Boy, let 's ha 't done quickly.

BOY. Sir, if you will imagine all this to be done already, you shall hear them talk to-gether ; but we cannot present a house cov-ered with black velvet, and a lady in beaten gold.

CIT. Sir boy, let 's ha 't as you can, then. [70

BOY. Besides, it will show ill-favoredly to have a grocer's prentice to court a king's daughter.

CIT. Will it so, sir? You are well read in histories ! [11] I pray you, what was Sir Dago-net? [12] Was not he prentice to a grocer in London? Read the play of *The Four Pren-tices of London*,[13] where they toss their pikes so. I pray you, fetch him in, sir, fetch him in.   80

BOY. It shall be done. — It is not our fault, gentlemen.   *Exit.*

---

[6] In *The Travels of the Three English Brothers* (1607), by Day, Rowley, and Wilkins, the Sophy agrees to further the baptism of the child of his English son-in-law.

[7] A large theatre in Clerkenwell, which catered to the mob.

[8] Cracow's.

[9] *I.e.*, in a gown with gold embroidery.

[10] Take. If this scenario alludes to a romance, it has not been identified.

[11] Tales.

[12] King Arthur's fool ; but aside from his appear-ance in the exhibitions of a society of archers, no connection is known between him and the London citizens.

[13] See introductory note.

---

[1] Unlocated.   [2] Armor.

[3] Tagged laces to keep the breeches up.

[4] A light woman.

[5] Apparently a prison was attached to this court, on which see note on *Bartholomew Fair*, Induction, l. 6.

WIFE. Now we shall see fine doings, I warrant t' ee, George.

[SCENE II] [14]

Enter RALPH, *and the* Lady [POMPIONA], Squire [TIM], *and* Dwarf [GEORGE].

WIFE. Oh, here they come. How prettily the King of Cracovia's daughter is dress'd!

CIT. Ay, Nell, it is the fashion of that country, I warrant t' ee.

POMP. Welcome, Sir Knight, unto my father's court,
King of Moldavia, unto me Pompiona,
His daughter dear! But, sure, you do not like
Your entertainment, that will stay with us
No longer but a night.

RALPH. Damsel right fair,
I am on many sad adventures bound, 10
That call me forth into the wilderness;
Besides, my horse's back is something gall'd,
Which will enforce me ride a sober pace.
But many thanks, fair lady, be to you
For using errant knight with courtesy!

POMP. But say, brave knight, what is your name and birth?

RALPH. My name is Ralph; I am an Englishman,
As true as steel, a hearty Englishman,
And prentice to a grocer in the Strand
By deed indent,[15] of which I have one part; [20
But fortune calling me to follow arms,
On me this holy order I did take
Of Burning Pestle, which in all men's eyes
I bear, confounding ladies' enemies.

POMP. Oft have I heard of your brave countrymen,
And fertile soil, and store of wholesome food;
My father oft will tell me of a drink
In England found, and nipitato [16] call'd,
Which driveth all the sorrow from your hearts.

RALPH. Lady, 't is true; you need not lay your lips 30
To better nipitato than there is.

POMP. And of a wild fowl he will often speak,
Which powd'red [17]-beef-and-mustard called is:

For there have been great wars 'twixt us and you;
But truly, Ralph, it was not 'long of me.
Tell me then, Ralph, could you contented be
To wear a lady's favor in your shield?

RALPH. I am a knight of religious order,
And will not wear a favor of a lady's 39
That trusts in Antichrist and false traditions.

CIT. Well said, Ralph! convert her, if thou canst.

RALPH. Besides, I have a lady of my own
In merry England, for whose virtuous sake
I took these arms; and Susan is her name,
A cobbler's maid in Milk Street; whom I vow
Ne'er to forsake whilst life and pestle last.

POMP. Happy that cobbling dame, whoe'er she be,
That for her own, dear Ralph, hath gotten thee!
Unhappy I, that ne'er shall see the day 50
To see thee more, that bear'st my heart away!

RALPH. Lady, farewell; I needs must take my leave.

POMP. Hard-hearted Ralph, that ladies dost deceive!

CIT. Hark thee, Ralph: there 's money for thee; give something in the King of Cracovia's house; be not beholding to him.

RALPH. Lady, before I go, I must remember
Your father's officers, who, truth to tell,
Have been about me very diligent.
Hold up thy snowy hand, thou princely maid!
There's twelvepence for your father's chamberlain; 61
And another shilling for his cook,
For, by my troth, the goose was roasted well;
And twelvepence for your father's horse-keeper,
For nointing my horse' back, and for his butter [18]
There is another shilling; to the maid
That wash'd my boot-hose [19] there 's an English groat,
And twopence to the boy that wip'd my boots;
And last, fair lady, there is for yourself
Threepence, to buy you pins at Bumbo [20] Fair. 70

---

[14] A room in the palace of the King of Moldavia. The prince of this country, now included in Roumania, but at one time a dependency of Poland, was in London in 1607.
[15] By articles of indenture.
[16] Mock-Latin for the jocose word *nippitate* = strong ale.
[17] Corned, salted.

[18] Used as ointment.
[19] Heavy outer stockings, leggings.
[20] Apparently a jocose invention; "bumbo" = a drink made of rum, sugar, water, and nutmeg.

POMP. Full many thanks ; and I will keep
    them safe
Till all the heads be off, for thy sake, Ralph.
  RALPH. Advance, my squire and dwarf ! I
    cannot stay.
  POMP. Thou kill'st my heart in parting
    thus away.   *Exeunt.*

WIFE. I commend Ralph yet, that he will
not stoop to a Cracovian ; there's properer [21]
women in London than any are there, iwis.
But here comes Master Humphrey and his
love again now, George.
  CIT. Ay, cony ; peace.   80

[SCENE III] [22]

Enter Merchant [VENTUREWELL], HUMPHREY,
    LUCE, *and a* Boy.

VENT. Go, get you up ; [23] I will not be en-
    treated ;
And, gossip mine,[24] I'll keep you sure here-
    after
From gadding out again with boys and un-
    thrifts.
Come, they are women's tears ; I know your
    fashion. —
Go, sirrah, lock her in, and keep the key
Safe as you love your life. —
              [Exeunt] LUCE *and* Boy.
              Now, my son Humphrey,
You may both rest assured of my love
In this, and reap your own desire.
  HUM. I see this love you speak of, through
    your daughter,
Although the hole be little ; and hereafter [10
Will yield the like in all I may or can,
Fitting a Christian and a gentleman.
  VENT. I do believe you, my good son, and
    thank you ;
For 't were an impudence to think you flat-
    tered.
  HUM. It were, indeed : but shall I tell you
    why?
I have been beaten twice about the lie.[25]
  VENT. Well, son, no more of compliment.[26]
    My daughter
Is yours again : appoint the time and take
    her.

[21] Handsomer.
[22] A room in Venturewell's house.
[23] Upstairs.
[24] My dear friend ; said, of course, ironically.
[25] *I.e.,* in some quarrel which involved giving the
lie.
[26] Ceremonious talk.

We'll have no stealing for it ; I myself
And some few of our friends will see you mar-
    ried.   20
  HUM. I would you would, i' faith ! for, be
    it known,
I ever was afraid to lie alone.
  VENT. Some three days hence, then.
  HUM.   Three days ! let me see ;
'T is somewhat of the most ; [27] yet I agree,
Because I mean against [28] the appointed day
To visit all my friends in new array.

Enter Servant.

SERV. Sir, there's a gentlewoman without
would speak with your Worship.
  VENT. What is she?
  SERV. Sir, I ask'd her not.   30
  VENT. Bid her come in.   *[Exit* Servant.]

Enter MISTRESS MERRYTHOUGHT *and* MICHAEL.

MIST. MER. Peace be to your Worship ! I
come as a poor suitor to you, sir, in the behalf
of this child.
  VENT. Are you not wife to Merrythought?
  MIST. MER. Yes, truly. Would I had ne'er
seen his eyes ! He has undone me and himself
and his children ; and there he lives at home,
and sings and hoits [29] and revels among his
drunken companions ! but, I warrant you, [40
where to get a penny to put bread in his mouth
he knows not : and therefore, if it like your
Worship, I would entreat your letter to the
honest host of the Bell in Waltham, that I
may place my child under the protection of
his tapster, in some settled course of life.
  VENT. I'm glad the Heavens have heard
    my prayers. Thy husband,
When I was ripe in sorrows, laugh'd at me ;
Thy son, like an unthankful wretch, I having
Redeem'd him from his fall, and made him
    mine,   50
To show his love again first stole my daughter,
Then wrong'd this gentleman, and, last of all,
Gave me that grief had almost brought me
    down
Unto my grave, had not a stronger hand
Reliev'd my sorrows. Go, and weep as I did,
And be unpitied ; for I here profess
An everlasting hate to all thy name.
  MIST. MER. Will you so, sir ? how say you
by that? — Come, Mick ; let him keep his
wind to cool his porridge. We'll go to [60

[27] Somewhat long.   [28] In anticipation of.
[29] Indulges in riotous mirth.

thy nurse's, Mick: she knits silk stockings, boy; and we'll knit too, boy, and be beholding to none of them all.

Exeunt MICHAEL *and* Mother.

Enter a Boy *with a letter.*

BOY. Sir, I take it you are the master of this house.

VENT. How then, boy?

BOY. Then to yourself, sir, comes this letter.

VENT. From whom, my pretty boy?

BOY. From him that was your servant; but no more

Shall that name ever be, for he is dead;
Grief of your purchas'd anger[30] broke his heart.   70
I saw him die, and from his hand receiv'd
This paper, with a charge to bring it hither:
Read it, and satisfy yourself in all.

VENT. [*reads.*] "Sir, that I have wronged your love I must confess; in which I have purchas'd to myself, besides mine own undoing, the ill opinion of my friends. Let not your anger, good sir, outlive me, but suffer me to rest in peace with your forgiveness; let my body, if a dying man may so much prevail [80 with you, be brought to your daughter, that she may truly know my hot flames are now buried, and withal receive a testimony of the zeal I bore her virtue. Farewell for ever, and be ever happy!   JASPER."
God's hand is great in this. I do forgive him; Yet I am glad he's quiet, where I hope
He will not bite again. — Boy, bring the body, And let him have his will, if that be all.

BOY. 'T is here without, sir.

VENT.   So, sir; if you please, [90 You may conduct it in; I do not fear it.

HUM. I'll be your usher, boy; for, though I say it,
He ow'd me something once, and well did pay it.   *Exeunt.*

[SCENE IV][31]

Enter LUCE *alone.*

LUCE. If there be any punishment inflicted
Upon the miserable, more than yet I feel,
Let it together[32] seize me and at once
Press down my soul! I cannot bear the pain
Of these delaying tortures. — Thou that art

The end of all, and the sweet rest of all,
Come, come, O Death! bring me to thy peace,
And blot out all the memory I nourish
Both of my father and my cruel friend! —
O wretched maid, still living to be wretched, [10
To be a say[33] to Fortune in her changes,
And grow to number times and woes together!
How happy had I been, if, being born,
My grave had been my cradle!

Enter Servant.

SERV.   By your leave,
Young Mistress; here's a boy hath brought a coffin.
What 'a would say, I know not; but your father
Charg'd me to give you notice. Here they come.   [*Exit.*]

Enter Two *bearing a coffin*, JASPER *in it.*

LUCE. For me I hope 't is come, and 't is most welcome.

BOY. Fair Mistress, let me not add greater grief
To that great store you have already. Jasper, That whilst he liv'd was yours, now dead   [21
And here enclos'd, commanded me to bring
His body hither, and to crave a tear
From those fair eyes, though he deserv'd not pity,
To deck his funeral; for so he bid me
Tell her for whom he di'd.

LUCE.   He shall have many. —
Good friends, depart a little, whilst I take
My leave of this dead man, that once I lov'd.—
              Exeunt Coffin-carrier *and* Boy.
Hold yet a little, life! and then I give thee
To thy first Heavenly being. Oh, my friend![34]
Hast thou deceiv'd me thus, and got before me?   31
I shall not long be after. But, believe me, Thou wert too cruel, Jasper, 'gainst thyself, In punishing the fault I could have pardoned, With so untimely death; thou didst not wrong me,
But ever wert most kind, most true, most loving;
And I the most unkind, most false, most cruel!
Didst thou but ask a tear? I'll give thee all, Even all my eyes can pour down, all my sighs, And all myself, before thou goest from me. [40
There[35] are but sparing rites; but if thy soul Be yet about this place, and can behold

---

[30] At having incurred your anger.
[31] Another room.
[32] At the same time seize . . . and press. . . .

[33] A subject of trial.   [34] **Lover.**
[35] Ed. 1711 *these*, perhaps rightly.

And see what I prepare to deck thee with,
It shall go up, borne on the wings of peace,
And satisfied. First will I sing thy dirge,
Then kiss thy pale lips, and then die myself,
And fill one coffin and one grave together.

SONG

Come, you whose loves are dead,
    And, whiles I sing,
       Weep, and wring   50
Every hand, and every head
Bind with cypress and sad yew;
Ribands black and candles blue
For him that was of men most true!

Come with heavy [moaning],[36]
    And on his grave
       Let him have
Sacrifice of sighs and groaning;
Let him have fair flowers enow,
White and purple, green and yellow,   60
For him that was of men most true! [37]

Thou sable cloth, sad cover of my joys,
I lift thee up, and thus I meet with death.
     [*Removes the cloth, and* JASPER *rises
       out of the coffin.*]
   JASP. And thus you meet the living.
   LUCE.   Save me, Heaven!
   JASP. Nay, do not fly me, fair; I am no
     spirit;
Look better on me; do you know me yet?
   LUCE. Oh thou dear shadow of my friend!
   JASP.   Dear substance!
I swear I am no shadow; feel my hand:
It is the same it was; I am your Jasper,
Your Jasper that's yet living, and yet lov-
     ing.   70
Pardon my rash attempt, my foolish proof [38]
I put in practice of your constancy;
For sooner should my sword have drunk my
     blood
And set my soul at liberty, than drawn
The least drop from that body; for which
     boldness
Doom me to anything; if death, I take it,
And willingly.
   LUCE.   This death I'll give you for it;
               [*Kisses him.*]
So; now I am satisfied: you are no spirit,
But my own truest, truest, truest friend.
Why do you come thus to me?
   JASP.   First, to see you;   80
Then, to convey you hence.
   LUCE.   It cannot be;
For I am lock'd up here, and watch'd at all
     hours,
That 't is impossible for me to scape.

---

[36] Cor. ed. 1750; old eds. *mourning*.
[37] Probably original.   [38] Test.

JASP. Nothing more possible. Within this
     coffin
Do you convey yourself. Let me alone; [39]
I have the wits of twenty men about me;
Only I crave the shelter of your closet
A little, and then fear me not.[40] Creep in,
That they may presently convey you hence;
Fear nothing, dearest love; I'll be your
     second;   90
       [LUCE *lies down in the coffin, and*
         JASPER *covers her with the cloth.*]
Lie close; [41] so; all goes well yet. — Boy!

     [*Re-enter* Boy *and* Coffin-carrier.]

   BOY.   At hand, sir.
   JASP. Convey away the coffin, and be wary.
   BOY. 'T is done already.
   JASP.   Now must I go conjure.
           Exit [*into a closet*].

   Enter Merchant [VENTUREWELL].

   VENT. Boy, boy!
   BOY. Your servant, sir.
   VENT. Do me this kindness, boy; hold,
     here's a crown;
Before thou bury the body of this fellow,
Carry it to his old merry father, and salute
     him
From me, and bid him sing; he hath cause.[42]
   BOY.   I will, sir.
   VENT. And then bring me word what tune
     he is in,   100
And have another crown; but do it truly. —
I have fitted him a bargain now will vex him.
   BOY. God bless your Worship's health, sir!
   VENT.   Farewell, boy!   *Exeunt.*

[SCENE V] [43]

Enter MERRYTHOUGHT.

   WIFE. Ah, old Merrythought, art thou
there again? Let's hear some of thy songs.

   MER.

     Who can sing a merrier note
     Than he that cannot change a groat? [44]

Not a denier left, and yet my heart leaps. I
do wonder yet, as old as I am, that any man
will follow a trade, or serve, that may sing and
laugh, and walk the streets. My wife and
both my sons are I know not where; I have

---

[39] Leave it to me.
[40] Don't worry on my account.   [41] Hidden.
[42] Old eds. print this speech as prose.
[43] Before Merrythought's house, or a room therein.
[44] The whole catch was preserved in Ravenscroft's
Pammelia (1609). (Dyce.)

nothing left, nor know I how to come by [10 meat to supper; yet am I merry still, for I know I shall find it upon the table at six a'clock; therefore, hang thought!

> I would not be a serving man
>   To carry the cloak-bag [45] still,
> Nor would I be a falconer
>   The greedy hawks to fill;
> But I would be in a good house,
>   And have a good master too;
> But I would eat and drink of the best,   20
>   And no work would I do.[46]

This is it that keeps life and soul together, — mirth; this is the philosopher's stone that they write so much on, that keeps a man ever young.

Enter a Boy.

BOY. Sir, they say they know all your money is gone, and they will trust you for no more drink.

MER. Will they not? let 'em choose! The best is, I have mirth at home, and need [30 not send abroad for that; let them keep their drink to themselves.

> For Jillian of Berry, she dwells on a hill,
> And she hath good beer and ale to sell,
> And of good fellows she thinks no ill;
>   And thither will we go now, now, now, now,
>   And thither will we go now.
>
> And when you have made a little stay,
> You need not ask what is to pay,
> But kiss your hostess, and go your way;   40
>   And thither, &c.[46]

Enter another Boy.

2 BOY. Sir, I can get no bread for supper.
MER. Hang bread and supper! Let's preserve our mirth, and we shall never feel hunger, I'll warrant you. Let's have a catch; boy, follow me, come.   *Sing this catch.*

> Ho, ho, nobody at home!
> Meat, nor drink, nor money ha' we none.
> Fill the pot, Eedy,
> Never more need I.[46a]   50

MER. So, boys; enough. Follow me; let's change our place, and we shall laugh afresh.   *Exeunt.*

WIFE. Let him go, George; 'a shall not have any countenance from us, nor a good word from any i' th' company, if I may strike stroke [47] in 't.
CIT. No more 'a sha' not, love. But, Nell, I will have Ralph do a very notable matter

now, to the eternal honor and glory of [60 all grocers. — Sirrah! you there, boy! Can none of you hear?

[Enter a Boy.]

BOY. Sir, your pleasure?
CIT. Let Ralph come out on May Day in the morning, and speak upon a conduit,[48] with all his scarfs about him, and his feathers, and his rings, and his knacks.
BOY. Why, sir, you do not think of our plot; what will become of that, then?
CIT. Why, sir, I care not what become [70 on 't; I 'll have him come out, or I 'll fetch him out myself; I 'll have something done in honor of the city. Besides, he hath been long enough upon adventures. Bring him out quickly; or, if I come in amongst you ——
BOY. Well, sir, he shall come out; but if our play miscarry, sir, you are like to pay for 't.
CIT. Bring him away then!   *Exit* Boy.

WIFE. This will be brave, i' faith! George, shall not he dance the morris too, for the [80 credit of the Strand?
CIT. No, sweetheart, it will be too much for the boy. Oh, there he is, Nell! he 's reasonable well in reparel; but he has not rings enough.

[SCENE VI]

Enter RALPH.

RALPH. London, to thee I do present the
            merry month of May;
Let each true subject be content to hear me
            what I say;
For from the top of conduit-head, as plainly
            may appear,
I will both tell my name to you, and wherefore
            I came here.
My name is Ralph,[49] by due descent though
            not ignoble I
Yet far inferior to the flock [50] of gracious gro-
            cery;
And by the common counsel of my fellows in
            the Strand,
With gilded staff and crossed scarf, the May-
            lord here I stand.
Rejoice, O English hearts, rejoice! rejoice,
            O lovers dear!
Rejoice, O city, town, and country! rejoice,
            eke every shire!   10

---

[45] Portmanteau.   [46] Unidentified.
[46a] The whole catch was preserved in Ravenscroft's *Pammelia* (1609). (Dyce.)
[47] If I have anything to say about it.

[48] Fountain, cistern.
[49] Cf. *The Spanish Tragedy*, Act I, Chorus, ll. 5, 6.
[50] Dyce emends *stock*.

For now the fragrant flowers do spring and
    sprout in seemly sort,
The little birds do sit and sing, the lambs do
    make fine sport ;
And now the birchen-tree doth bud, that
    makes the schoolboy cry ;
The morris rings,[51] while hobbyhorse doth
    foot it feateously ;[52]
The lords and ladies now abroad, for their
    disport and play,
Do kiss sometimes upon the grass, and some-
    times in the hay ;
Now butter with a leaf of sage is good to purge
    the blood ;
Fly Venus [53] and phlebotomy,[54] for they are
    neither good ;
Now little fish on tender stone begin to cast
    their bellies,[55]
And sluggish snails, that erst were [mew'd],[56]
    do creep out of their shellies ;   20
The rumbling rivers now do warm, for little
    boys to paddle ;
The sturdy steed now goes to grass, and up
    they hang his saddle ;
The heavy hart, the bellowing buck, the ras-
    cal,[57] and the pricket,[58]
Are now among the yeoman's peas, and leave
    the fearful thicket :
And be like them, oh, you, I say, of this same
    noble town,
And lift aloft your velvet heads,[59] and slipping
    off your gown,
With bells on legs,[60] and napkins clean unto
    your shoulders ti'd,
With scarfs and garters as you please, and
    " Hey for our town ! " cri'd,
March out, and show your willing minds, by
    twenty and by twenty,
To Hogsdon [61] or to Newington,[62] where ale
    and cakes are plenty ;   30
And let it ne'er be said for shame, that we the
    youths of London
Lay thrumming of our caps [63] at home, and
    left our custom undone.
Up, then, I say, both young and old, both
    man and maid a-maying,

51 The morris-dancers wore bells.
52 Elegantly.   53 *I.e.*, venery.
54 Blood-letting.   55 Spawn.
56 Confined ; so ed. 1750 ; old eds. *mute*.
57 A deer not fat enough to be worth hunting.
58 A yearling buck.
59 "A sly allusion to the horns of the citizens."
(Dyce.)
60 For morris dancing.
61 Hoxton.   62 On the Surrey side.
63 Raising a pile on our caps by fingering them ;
i.e., dawdling.

With drums, and guns that bounce [64] aloud,
    and merry tabor playing !
Which to prolong, God save our King, and
    send his country peace,
And root out treason from the land ! and so,
    my friends, I cease.   *Exit.*

ACT V — SCENE I [1]

Enter Merchant [VENTUREWELL], *solus.*

VENT. I will have no great store of company at the wedding ; a couple of neighbors
and their wives ; and we will have a capon in
stewed broth, with marrow, and a good piece
of beef stuck with rosemary.

Enter JASPER [*from the closet*], *his face mealed.*

JASP. Forbear thy pains, fond man ! it is
    too late.
VENT. Heaven bless me ! Jasper !
JASP.   Ay, I am his ghost,
Whom thou hast injur'd for his constant love,
Fond worldly wretch ! who dost not under-
    stand
In death that true hearts cannot parted be. [10
First know, thy daughter is quite borne away
On wings of angels, through the liquid air,
[Too] [2] far out of thy reach, and never more
Shalt thou behold her face ; but she and I
Will in another world enjoy our loves ;
Where neither father's anger, poverty,
Nor any cross that troubles earthly men,
Shall make us sever our united hearts.
And never shalt thou sit or be alone
In any place, but I will visit thee   20
With ghastly looks, and put into thy mind
The great offences which thou didst to me.
When thou art at thy table with thy friends,
Merry in heart, and fill'd with swelling wine,
I 'll come in midst of all thy pride and mirth,
Invisible to all men but thyself,
And whisper such a sad tale in thine ear
Shall make thee let the cup fall from thy hand,
And stand as mute and pale as death itself.[3]
VENT. Forgive me, Jasper ! Oh, what
    might I do,   30
Tell me, to satisfy thy troubled ghost?
JASP. There is no means ; too late thou
    think'st of this.

64 Bang.
1 A room in Venturewell's house.
2 So Qq 2, 3, F. Q 1 *To.*
3 Pretty clearly an allusion to *Macbeth*, **III, iv.**

VENT. But tell me what were best for me to do?

JASP. Repent thy deed, and satisfy my father,

And beat fond Humphrey [4] out of thy doors.
                                    Exit JASPER.

WIFE. Look, George; his very ghost would have folks beaten.

Enter HUMPHREY.

HUM. Father, my bride is gone, fair Mistress Luce;

My soul's the fount of vengeance, mischief's sluice.

VENT. Hence, fool, out of my sight with thy fond passion! [5]   40

Thou hast undone me.   [*Beats him.*]

HUM.   Hold, my father dear,

For Luce thy daughter's sake, that had no peer!

VENT. Thy father, fool! There's some blows more; begone. —   [*Beats him.*]

Jasper, I hope thy ghost be well appeased

To see thy will perform'd. Now will I go

To satisfy thy father for thy wrongs.   *Exit.*

HUM. What shall I do? I have been beaten twice,

And Mistress Luce is gone. Help me, device! [6]

Since my true love is gone, I nevermore,

Whilst I do live, upon the sky will pore;   [50

But in the dark will wear out my shoe-soles

In passion [7] in Saint Faith's Church under Paul's. [8]   *Exit.*

WIFE. George, call Ralph hither; if you love me, call Ralph hither: I have the bravest thing for him to do, George; prithee, call him quickly.

CIT. Ralph! why, Ralph, boy!

Enter RALPH.

RALPH. Here, sir.

CIT. Come hither, Ralph; come to thy mistress, boy.   59

WIFE. Ralph, I would have thee call all the youths together in battle-ray, with drums, and guns, and flags, and march to Mile End in pompous fashion, and there exhort your soldiers to be merry and wise, and to keep their beards from burning, Ralph; and then skirmish, and let your flags fly, and cry, " Kill,

kill, kill! " [9] My husband shall lend you his jerkin, Ralph, and there's a scarf; for the rest, the house shall furnish you, and we'll pay for 't. Do it bravely, Ralph; and think [70 before whom you perform, and what person you represent.

RALPH. I warrant you, Mistress; if I do it not for the honor of the city and the credit of my master, let me never hope for freedom! [10]

WIFE. 'T is well spoken, i' faith. Go thy ways; thou art a spark indeed.

CIT. Ralph, Ralph, double your files bravely, Ralph!

RALPH. I warrant you, sir. *Exit* RALPH. [80

CIT. Let him look narrowly to his service; I shall take [11] him else. I was there myself a pikeman once, in the hottest of the day, wench; had my feather shot sheer away, the fringe [12] of my pike burnt off with powder, my pate broken with a scouring-stick, [13] and yet, I thank God, I am here.   *Drum within.*

WIFE. Hark, George, the drums!

CIT. Ran, tan, tan, tan; ran, tan! Oh, wench, an thou hadst but seen little Ned [90 of Aldgate, Drum Ned, how he made it roar again, and laid on like a tyrant, and then struck softly till the ward [14] came up, and then thund'red again, and together we go! " Sa, sa, sa, bounce! " quoth the guns; " Courage, my hearts! " quoth the captains; " Saint George! " quoth the pikemen; and withal, here they lay, and there they lay; and yet for all this I am here, wench.   99

WIFE. Be thankful for it, George; for indeed 't is wonderful.

[SCENE II] [15]

Enter RALPH *and his company* [*among whom are* WILLIAM HAMMERTON *and* GEORGE GREENGOOSE], *with drums and colors.*

RALPH. March fair, my hearts! Lieutenant, beat the rear up. — Ancient, [16] let your colors fly; but have a great care of the butchers' hooks at Whitechapel; they have been the death of many a fair ancient. [17] — Open your files, that I may take a view both of your

[9] An old battle-cry of the English army. These speeches, and the next scene, ridicule the London train-bands.
[10] Full membership in my company.
[11] ? Remove.
[12] *N.E.D.* cites (1589), " For fustian and fringe . . . trimming up of the town's pikes."
[13] For cleaning the bore of a gun.   [14] Guard.
[15] A street in London; later, Mile End Fields.
[16] Ensign.   [17] Flag.

[4] Trisyllabic.   [5] Silly lamentation.
[6] Ingenuity.   [7] Sorrow.
[8] It was in the crypt of the Cathedral.

persons and munition. — Sergeant, call a muster.

SERG. A stand! — William Hammerton, pewterer!   10

HAM. Here, captain!

RALPH. A corselet and a Spanish pike; 't is well; can you shake it with a terror?

HAM. I hope so, captain.

RALPH. Charge upon me. [*He charges on* RALPH.] — 'T is with the weakest; put more strength, William Hammerton, more strength. As you were again! — Proceed, Sergeant.

SERG. George Greengoose, poulterer!

GREEN. Here!   20

RALPH. Let me see your piece,[18] neighbor Greengoose; when was she shot in?

GREEN. An['t] like you, Master Captain, I made a shot even now, partly to scour her, and partly for audacity.

RALPH. It should seem so certainly, for her breath is yet inflamed; besides, there is a main [19] fault in the touchhole, it runs and stinketh; and I tell you moreover, and believe it, ten such touchholes would breed the [30 pox in the army. Get you a feather, neighbor, get you a feather, sweet oil, and paper, and your piece may do well enough yet. Where 's your powder?

GREEN. Here.

RALPH. What, in a paper! As I am a soldier and a gentleman, it craves a martial court! [20] You ought to die for 't. Where 's your horn? Answer me to that.

GREEN. An 't like you, sir, I was [40 oblivious.

RALPH. It likes me not you should be so; 't is a shame for you, and a scandal to all our neighbors, being a man of worth and estimation, to leave your horn behind you; I am afraid 't will breed example. But let me tell you, no more on 't. — Stand, till I view you all. What 's become o' th' nose of your flask?

1 SOLD. Indeed, law, Captain, 't was blown away with powder.   50

RALPH. Put on a new one at the city's charge. — Where 's the stone [21] of this piece?

2 SOLD. The drummer took it out to light tobacco.

RALPH. 'T is a fault, my friend; put it in again. — You want a nose, — and you a stone.[22] — Sergeant, take a note on 't, for I mean to stop it in the pay. — Remove, and

march! [*They march.*] Soft and fair, gentlemen, soft and fair! Double your files! As [60 you were! Faces about! Now, you with the sodden [23] face, keep in there! Look to your match, sirrah, it will be in your fellow's flask anon. So; make a crescent now; advance your pikes; stand and give ear! — Gentlemen, countrymen, friends, and my fellow-soldiers, I have brought you this day, from the shops of security and the counters of content, to measure out in these furious fields honor by the ell, and prowess by the pound. [70 Let it not, oh, let it not, I say, be told hereafter the noble issue of this city fainted; but bear yourselves in this fair action like men, valiant men, and free men! Fear not the face of the enemy, nor the noise of the guns, for, believe me, brethren, the rude rumbling of a brewer's car is far more terrible, of which you have a daily experience; neither let the stink of powder offend you, since a more valiant stink is nightly with you. To a resolved [24] [80 mind his home is everywhere; I speak not this to take away the hope of your return; for you shall see, I do not doubt it, and that very shortly, your loving wives again and your sweet children, whose care doth bear you company in baskets.[25] Remember, then, whose cause you have in hand, and, like a sort [26] of true-born scavengers, scour me this famous realm of enemies. I have no more to say but this: stand to your tacklings,[27] [90 lads, and show to the world you can as well brandish a sword as shake an apron. Saint George, and on, my hearts!

OMNES. Saint George, Saint George!

Exeunt.

WIFE. 'T was well done, Ralph! I 'll send thee a cold capon afield and a bottle of March beer; and, it may be, come myself to see thee.

CIT. Nell, the boy has deceived me much; I did not think it had been in him. He has performed such a matter, wench, that, [100 if I live, next year I 'll have him captain of the galley-foist [28] or I 'll want my will.

[SCENE III] [29]

Enter old MERRYTHOUGHT.

MER. Yet, I thank God, I break not a wrinkle more than I had. Not a stoup, boys?

---

[18] Gun.   [19] Serious.
[20] Deserves a court-martial.   [21] Flint.
[22] With a play on the meaning "testicle."

[23] Stupid.   [24] Resolute.   [25] Of provisions.
[26] Set.   [27] Weapons.   [28] The lord mayor's barge.
[29] A room in Merrythought's house.

Care, live with cats; I defy thee! My heart is as sound as an oak; and though I want drink to wet my whistle, I can sing:

Come no more there, boys, come no more there;
For we shall never whilst we live come any more there.[30]

Enter a Boy, with a coffin.

BOY. God save you, sir!
MER. It's a brave boy. Canst thou sing?
BOY. Yes, sir, I can sing; but 't is not [10 so necessary at this time.
MER.

Sing we, and chant it;
Whilst love doth grant it.[31]

BOY. Sir, sir, if you knew what I have brought you, you would have little list to sing.
MER.

Oh, the [minion] [32] round!
Full long, long I have thee sought,
And now I have thee found,
And what hast thou here brought? [30]   19

BOY. A coffin, sir, and your dead son Jasper in it.   [*Exit with* Coffin-carrier.]
MER. Dead!

Why, farewell he!
Thou wast a bonny boy,
And I did love thee.[30]

Enter JASPER.

JASP. Then, I pray you, sir, do so still.
MER. Jasper's ghost!

Thou art welcome from Stygian lake so soon;
Declare to me what wondrous things in Pluto's court are done.[30]

JASP. By my troth, sir, I ne'er came there; 't is too hot for me, sir.   31
MER. A merry ghost, a very merry ghost!

And where is your true-love? Oh, where is yours? [30]

JASP. Marry, look you, sir!
      Heaves up the coffin; [LUCE *steps out*].
MER. Ah, ha! art thou good at that, i' faith?

With hey, trixy, terlery-whiskin,
The world it runs on wheels; [33]
When the young man's ——,[34]
Up goes the maiden's heels.[35]   40

MISTRESS MERRYTHOUGHT *and* MICHAEL *within.*

MIST. MER. What, Master Merrythought!

[30] Unidentified.
[31] From Thomas Morley's *First Book of Ballads* (1600). (Dyce.)
[32] Emend. Editor; old eds. *Mimon.* — " Round " = plump. (Kittredge.)
[33] A proverbial expression.
[34] So in old eds.   [35] Unidentified.

will you not let's in? What do you think shall become of us?
MER.

What voice is that, that calleth at our door? [35]

MIST. MER. You know me well enough; I am sure I have not been such a stranger to you.
MER.

And some they whistled, and some they sung,
      Hey, down, down!
   And some did loudly say,   50
   Ever as the Lord Barnet's horn blew,
      Away, Musgrave, away! [36]

MIST. MER. You will not have us starve here, will you, Master Merrythought?
JASP. Nay, good sir, be persuaded; she is my mother. If her offences have been great against you, let your own love remember she is yours; and so forgive her.
LUCE. Good Master Merrythought, let me entreat you; I will not be denied.   60
MIST. MER. Why, Master Merrythought, will you be a vex'd thing still?
MER. Woman, I take you to my love again; but you shall sing before you enter; therefore dispatch your song and so come in.
MIST. MER. Well, you must have your will, when all's done. — Mick, what song canst thou sing, boy?
MICH. I can sing none, forsooth, but " A Lady's Daughter, of Paris properly."   70
MIST. MER.

SONG

It was a lady's daughter, &c.[37]

[MERRYTHOUGHT *opens the door; enter* MISTRESS MERRYTHOUGHT *and* MICHAEL.]
MER. Come, you're welcome home again.

If such danger be in playing,
   And jest must to earnest turn,
   You shall go no more a-maying —— [35]

VENT. (*within*) Are you within, sir? Master Merrythought!
JASP. It is my master's voice! Good sir, go hold him in talk, whilst we convey ourselves into some inward room.   80
                              [*Exit with* LUCE.]
MER. What are you? Are you merry? You must be very merry, if you enter.
VENT. [*within*] I am, sir.
MER.   Sing, then.
VENT. [*within*]   Nay, good sir, open to me.

[36] From the ballad of Little Musgrave and Lady Barnard.
[37] A Protestant ballad, identified by Dyce.

MER. Sing, I say, or, by the merry heart,
You come not in!

VENT. [*within*] Well, sir, I'll sing.

Fortune, my foe, &c.[38]

[MERRYTHOUGHT *opens the door; enter*
VENTUREWELL.]

MER. You are welcome, sir, you are welcome; you see your entertainment; pray you,
be merry. 90

VENT. Oh, Master Merrythought, I am
　　　come to ask you
Forgiveness for the wrongs I offered you
And your most virtuous son! They're in-
　　　finite;
Yet my contrition shall be more than they;
I do confess my hardness broke his heart,
For which just Heaven hath given me punish-
　　　ment
More than my age can carry. His wand'ring
　　　spirit,
Not yet at rest, pursues me everywhere,
Crying, "I'll haunt thee for thy cruelty."
My daughter, she is gone, I know not how, 100
Taken invisible, and whether living
Or in grave, 't is yet uncertain to me.
Oh, Master Merrythought, these are the
　　　weights
Will sink me to my grave! Forgive me, sir.

MER. Why, sir, I do forgive you; and be
　　　merry.
And if the wag in's lifetime play'd the knave.
Can you forgive him too?

VENT. 　　　　　　With all my heart, sir.

MER. Speak it again, and heartily.

VENT. 　　　　　　　　　　I do, sir;
Now, by my soul, I do.

Re-enter LUCE *and* JASPER.

MER.

With that came out his paramour; 110
She was as white as the lily flower;
　　　Hey, troll, trolly, lolly!
With that came out her own dear knight;
He was as true as ever did fight, &c.[39]

Sir, if you will forgive 'em, clap their hands
together; there's no more to be said i' th'
matter.

VENT. I do, I do.

CIT. I do not like this. Peace, boys!
Hear me, one of you! Everybody's part is

[38] One of the most popular songs of the time.
[39] Unidentified; probably, as Child suggests, from
an old ballad.

come to an end but Ralph's, and he's left [121
out.

BOY. 'T is 'long of yourself, sir; we have
nothing to do with his part.

CIT. Ralph, come away!—Make on[40] him,
as you have done of the rest, boys; come.

WIFE. Now, good husband, let him come
out and die.

CIT. He shall, Nell.—Ralph, come away
quickly, and die, boy! 130

BOY. 'T will be very unfit he should die, sir,
upon no occasion—and in a comedy too.

CIT. Take you no care of that, Sir Boy; is
not his part at an end, think you, when he's
dead?—Come away, Ralph!

SCENE IV

Enter RALPH, *with a forked*[41] *arrow through his
head.*[42]

RALPH. When I was mortal, this my costive
　　　corps[43]
Did lap up figs and raisins in the Strand;
Where sitting, I espi'd a lovely dame,
Whose master wrought with lingel[44] and with
　　　awl,
And underground he vamped many a boot.
Straight did her love prick forth me, tender
　　　sprig,
To follow feats of arms in warlike wise
Through Waltham Desert; where I did per-
　　　form
Many achievements, and did lay on ground
Huge Barbaroso, that insulting[45] giant, 10
And all his captives soon set at liberty.
Then honor prick'd me from my native soil
Into Moldavia, where I gain'd the love
Of Pompiona, his beloved daughter;
But yet prov'd constant to the black-
　　　thumb'd[46] maid
Susan, and scorned Pompiona's love;
Yet liberal I was, and gave her pins,
And money for her father's officers.
I then returned home, and thrust myself
In action, and by all men chosen was 20
Lord of the May, where I did flourish it,
With scarfs and rings, and posy[47] in my hand.
After this action I preferred was,

[40] *I.e.*, treat, do by.　　　[41] Barbed.
[42] In ridicule of old plays (*e.g., The True Tragedy
of Richard Duke of York*) in which are introduced
wounded characters with weapons in their wounds.
[43] A burlesque of the opening speech of Andrea's
Ghost in *The Spanish Tragedy.*
[44] Shoemakers' thread.　　　[45] Triumphing.
[46] From the rosined thread of her father's calling.
[47] Nosegay.

And chosen city-captain at Mile End,
With hat and feather, and with leading-staff,[48]
And train'd my men, and brought them all off
    clear,
Save one man that beray'd him with [49] the
    noise.
But all these things I, Ralph, did undertake
Only for my beloved Susan's sake.
Then coming home, and sitting in my shop [30
With apron blue, Death came into my stall
To cheapen [50] *aqua vitae;* but ere I
Could take the bottle down and fill a taste,
Death caught a pound of pepper in his hand,
And sprinkled all my face and body o'er,
And in an instant vanished away.

CIT. 'T is a pretty fiction, i' faith.

RALPH. Then took I up my bow and shaft
    in hand,
And walk'd into Moorfields to cool myself ;
But there grim cruel Death met me again, [40
And shot this forked arrow through my head ;
And now I faint ; therefore be warn'd by me,
My fellows every one, of forked heads ! [51]
Farewell, all you good boys in merry Lon-
    don !
Ne'er shall we more upon Shrove Tuesday
    meet,
And pluck down houses of iniquity.[52]
My pain increaseth ; I shall never more
Hold open, whilst another pumps both legs,
Nor daub a satin gown with rotten eggs ;
Set up a stake, oh, never more I shall !   50
I die ! fly, fly, my soul, to Grocers' Hall !
Oh, oh, oh, &c.[53]

[48] Baton.
[49] Befouled himself as a result of.
[50] Buy, ask the price of.
[51] *I.e.*, the cuckold's horns.
[52] On Shrove Tuesday the municipal authorities made a search for brothels ; that being a great holi-day of theirs, the prentices took it on themselves to wreck such houses.
[53] The actor was now supposed to die — *ad libitum.*

WIFE. Well said, Ralph ! do your obeisance
to the gentlemen, and go your ways ; well said,
Ralph !   *Exit* RALPH.

MER. Methinks all we, thus kindly and unexpectedly reconciled, should not depart [54]
without a song.
VENT. A good motion.
MER. Strike up, then !   60

SONG

Better music ne'er was known
Than a choir of hearts in one.
Let each other, that hath been
Troubled with the gall or spleen,
Learn of us to keep his brow
Smooth and plain, as ours are now ; [55]
Sing, though before the hour of dying ;
He shall rise, and then be crying,
"Hey, ho, 't is naught but mirth
That keeps the body from the earth !" [56]   70

Exeunt omnes.

EPILOGUS

CIT. Come, Nell, shall we go ? The play's
done.
WIFE. Nay, by my faith, George, I have
more manners than so ; I 'll speak to these gentlemen first. — I thank you all, gentlemen, for
your patience and countenance to Ralph, a
poor fatherless child ; and if I might see you at
my house, it should go hard but I would have a
pottle of wine and a pipe of tobacco for you ;
for, truly, I hope you do like the youth, but [80
I would be glad to know the truth ; I refer it to
your own discretions, whether you will applaud
him or no ; for I will wink, and whilst [57] you
shall do what you will. — I thank you with
all my heart. God give you good night ! —
Come, George.   [*Exeunt.*]

[54] Separate.
[55] A final joke on the cuckold's horns.
[56] Very likely, as Alden suggests, this song is original.
[57] In the mean time.

PHILASTER.

OR,

Loue lies a Bleeding.

As it hath beene diuerse times Acted,
at the Globe, and Blacke-Friers, by
his Maiesties Seruants.

Written by {
Francis Beaumont.
and
Iohn Fletcher.
} *Gent.*

The second Impression, corrected, and
amended.

LONDON,

Printed for THOMAS WALKLEY, and are to
be solde at his shoppe, at the signe of the
Eagle and Childe, in *Brittaines Bursse.*
1622.

INTRODUCTORY NOTE

Philaster is mentioned in *The Scourge of Folly* by John Davies of Hereford, which was entered in the Stationers' Register on October 8, 1610. It may have been composed shortly before, or it may date back a year or two. It was acted by the King's Men, Shakespeare's company, at the Globe and the Blackfriars. No source is known, though the maiden disguised as a page and acting as a go-between appears in the tale of Felismena in the *Diana* of Jorge de Montemayor, and in Shakespeare's *Two Gentlemen of Verona* and *Twelfth Night*. (For a review of possible influences see T. P. Harrison, Jr., *Publications of the Modern Language Association*, XLI, 294–303.)

More interesting is *Philaster's* relation to *Cymbeline* (c. 1610). Professor A. H. Thorndike has argued for the priority of Beaumont and Fletcher, and for their strong influence on Shakespeare's final group of dramatic romances. Lacking precise dates, we can not be sure who deserves credit for introducing this type of romantic tragi-comedy. It was destined to be a much practised form of drama; *Philaster* was both influential in establishing the vogue and extremely popular itself, for it was one of the leading items in the London repertory throughout the seventeenth century. In 1695 it was adapted by Elkanah Settle, but in 1711 the original was restored to the boards. In 1763, somewhat altered, it was successfully revived at Drury Lane by the elder Colman; in this version it survived into the nineteenth century.

Despite the coarseness of parts of *Philaster*, there is an aristocratic refinement about this play which is proof that a noble purity could appeal to the same audience that revelled in racy farce and sophisticated comedy. The delicacy of the dramatist's treatment of the disguised Euphrasia, her idealism, her honor, her loyalty to the distressed Arethusa, may be a little artificial and not a little sentimental, but they are very lovely. All that keeps this play from the Shakespearean level is its failure to fuse the real and the ideal, which are here set forth in separate scenes. Shakespeare brings them together, often in the same speech; but that amazing verisimilitude was not consistently achieved by any of his colleagues. Nor must we allow our admiration of the Bellario scenes to blind us to the great, though very different, merits of the portrait of Megra. As for Philaster, romantic heroes are less easily credible than romantic heroines. There has to be a tenor in this kind of drama; Philaster's operatic flourishes in the fourth act are hard to bear with, but his earlier duets with " Bellario " are beautiful, and his Hamlet-like predicament wins our sympathy. The collaboration in this play is so happy that efforts to distinguish the two hands must be regarded with caution. The prevailing opinion is that Beaumont's is the major contribution.

Philaster was first printed, in quarto, in 1620. This edition supplies a generally inferior text; it is, in fact, a distinct version, with a variant beginning and end by another writer. The Second Quarto, of 1622, is the most authoritative and has been followed here, with a few corrections from the other old editions, especially the first, which occasionally preserves original readings garbled by the compositor of Q 2. Later editions appeared in 1628, 1634 (with a revised text, reprinted in subsequent editions), 1639, 1652 (two editions), n.d. [1663], 1687, and 1717. *Philaster* was also printed in the Second Folio, of 1679. It was edited, with *The Maid's Tragedy*, by A. H. Thorndike (1906), for the Bullen *Variorum* by P. A. Daniel (1904), and separately by F. S. Boas (1909).

PHILASTER

OR

LOVE LIES A–BLEEDING

BY

FRANCIS BEAUMONT AND JOHN FLETCHER

[DRAMATIS PERSONAE [1]

THE KING OF SICILY.
PHILASTER, heir to the crown.
PHARAMOND, Prince of Spain.
DION, a lord.
CLEREMONT, } noble gentlemen,
THRASILINE, } his associates.
An old Captain.
Five Citizens.
A Country Fellow.

Two Woodmen.
The King's Guard and Train.

ARETHUSA, the King's daughter.
EUPHRASIA, daughter of Dion, but disguised
    like a page and called BELLARIO.
MEGRA, a lascivious lady.
GALATEA, a wise, modest lady attending the
    Princess.
Two other Ladies.

THE SCENE being in *Sicily*.]

ACT I — SCENE I [2]

Enter DION, CLEREMONT, *and* THRASILINE.

CLER. Here's nor lords nor ladies.

DION. Credit me, gentlemen, I wonder at it. They receiv'd strict charge from the King to attend here ; besides, it was boldly published that no officer should forbid any gentleman that desired to attend and hear.

CLE. Can you guess the cause?

DION. Sir, it is plain, about the Spanish Prince that's come to marry our kingdom's heir and be our sovereign. 10

THRA. Many that will seem to know much say she looks not on him like a maid in love.

DION. Faith, sir, the multitude, that seldom know any thing but their own opinions, speak that they would have ; but the Prince, before his own approach, receiv'd so many confident messages from the state, that I think she's resolv'd to be rul'd.

CLE. Sir, it is thought with her he shall enjoy both these kingdoms of Sicily and [20 Calabria.

DION. Sir, it is without controversy so meant. But 't will be a troublesome labor for him to enjoy both these kingdoms with safety, the right heir to one of them living, and living so virtuously ; especially, the people admiring the bravery of his mind and lamenting his injuries.

CLE. Who? Philaster?

DION. Yes ; whose father, we all know, [30 was by our late King of Calabria unrighteously deposed from his fruitful Sicily. Myself drew some blood in those wars, which I would give my hand to be washed from.

CLE. Sir, my ignorance in state policy will not let me know why, Philaster being heir to one of these kingdoms, the King should suffer him to walk abroad with such free liberty.

DION. Sir, it seems your nature is more constant than to inquire after state news. [40 But the King, of late, made a hazard of both the kingdoms, of Sicily and his own, with offering [3] but to imprison Philaster ; at which the city was in arms, not to be charm'd down [4] by any state order or proclamation, till they saw Philaster ride through the streets pleas'd and without a guard ; at which they threw

[1] Om. Q₂; supplied, slightly altered, from later Qq and F 1679.
[2] The presence chamber in the palace.
[3] By attempting.
[4] Quieted.

799

their hats and their arms from them ; some to make bonfires, some to drink, all for his deliverance ; which, wise men say, is the cause the [50 King labors to bring in the power of a foreign nation to awe his own with.

Enter GALATEA, *a Lady, and* MEGRA.[5]

THRA. See, the ladies ! What's the first?

DION. A wise and modest gentlewoman that attends the Princess.

CLE. The second?

DION. She is one that may stand still discreetly enough and ill-favor'dly dance her measure, simper when she is courted by her friend,[6] and slight her husband. [60

CLE. The last?

DION. Faith, I think she is one whom the state keeps for the agents of our confederate princes ; she'll cog [7] and lie with a whole army, before the league shall break. Her name is common through the kingdom, and the trophies of her dishonor advanced beyond Hercules' Pillars. She loves to try the several constitutions of men's bodies ; and, indeed, has destroyed the worth of her own body [70 by making experiment upon it for the good of the commonwealth.

CLE. She's a profitable member.

MEG. Peace, if you love me ! You shall see these gentlemen stand their ground and not court us.

GAL. What if they should?

LA. What if they should !

MEG. Nay, let her alone. — What if they should ! Why, if they should, I say they [80 were never abroad. What foreigner would do so? It writes them directly untravell'd.

GAL. Why, what if they be?

LA. What if they be !

MEG. Good madam, let her go on. — What if they be ! Why, if they be, I will justify, they cannot maintain discourse with a judicious lady, nor make a leg [8] nor say " Excuse me."

GAL. Ha, ha, ha ! 90

MEG. Do you laugh, madam?

DION. Your desires upon you, ladies !

MEG. Then you must sit beside us.

DION. I shall sit near you then, lady.

MEG. Near me, perhaps ; but there's a lady endures no stranger ; and to me you appear a very strange fellow.

LA. Methinks he's not so strange ; [9] he would quickly be acquainted.

THRA. Peace, the King ! 100

Enter KING, PHARAMOND, ARETHUSA, *and* Train.

KING. To give a stronger testimony of love
Than sickly promises (which commonly
In princes find both birth and burial
In one breath) we have drawn you, worthy sir,
To make your fair endearments to our daughter,
And worthy services known to our subjects,
Now lov'd and wondered at ; next, our intent
To plant you deeply our immediate heir
Both to our blood [10] and kingdoms. For [11] this lady,
(The best part of your life, as you confirm me, 110
And I believe,) though her few years and sex
Yet teach her nothing but her fears and blushes,
Desires without desire, discourse [12] and knowledge
Only of what herself is to herself,
Make her feel moderate health ; and when she sleeps,
In making no ill day, knows no ill dreams.
Think not, dear sir, these undivided parts,
That must mold up a virgin, are put on
To show her so, as borrowed ornaments
To [speak] [13] her perfect love to you, or add [120
An artificial shadow to her nature —
No, sir ; I boldly dare proclaim her yet
No woman.[14] But woo her still, and think her modesty
A sweeter mistress than the offer'd language
Of any dame, were she a queen, whose eye
Speaks common loves and comforts to her servants.[15]
Last, noble son, for so I now must call you,
What I have done thus public is not only
To add [a] [16] comfort in particular
To you or me, but all ; and to confirm [130
The nobles and the gentry of these kingdoms

---

[5] Old eds. erroneously transpose *Lady* and *Megra*, and their speech-tags ; the confusion led to the inclusion of another character in the *dramatis personae* of Q3 *et seq.*: "An old Wanton Lady or Croane."
[6] Lover.
[7] Cajole.
[8] Bow.

[9] Offish.
[10] Family, lineage.
[11] As for.
[12] Reason.
[13] So Q3 *et seq.*; Q2 *talke of.*
[14] *I.e.*, a maiden.
[15] Lovers.
[16] Add. Q3.

By oath to your succession, which shall be
Within this month at most.
 THRA. [*aside*] This will be hardly done.
 CLE. [*aside*] It must be ill done, if it be done.
 DION. [*aside*] When 't is at best, 't will be
   but half done, whilst
So brave a gentleman is wrong'd and flung off.
 THRA. [*aside*] I fear.
 CLE. [*aside*] Who does not?
 DION. [*aside*] I fear not for myself, and yet
   I fear too.   140
Well, we shall see, we shall see.   No more.
 PHA. Kissing your white hand, mistress, I
   take leave
To thank your royal father; and thus far
To be my own free trumpet.   Understand,
Great King, and these your subjects, mine that
   must be,
(For so deserving you have spoke me, sir,
And so deserving I dare speak myself,)
To what a person, of what eminence,
Ripe expectation, of what faculties,
Manners and virtues, you would wed your
   kingdoms;   150
You in me have your wishes.   Oh, this
   country!
By more than all the gods, I hold it happy;
Happy in their dear memories that have been
Kings great and good; happy in yours that is;
And from you, as a chronicle to keep
Your noble name from eating age, do I
Open [17] myself most happy.   Gentlemen,
Believe me in a word, a prince's word,
There shall be nothing to make up a kingdom
Mighty and flourishing, defenced, fear'd, [160
Equal to be commanded and obeyed,
But through the travails of my life I 'll find
   it,
And tie it to this country.   By all the gods,
My reign shall be so easy to the subject
That every man shall be his prince himself,
And his own law — yet I his prince and law.
And dearest lady, to your dearest self,
Dear in the choice of him whose name and
   lustre
Must make you more and mightier, let me say,
You are the blessed'st living; for, sweet Prin-
   cess,   170
You shall enjoy a man of men to be
Your servant; you shall make him yours, for
   whom
Great queens must die.

---

[17] Disclose, declare. F and mod. eds. (except
Colman, 1778) *opine*. See "chronicle" in the preceding line.

 THRA. [*aside*] Miraculous!
 CLE. [*aside*] This speech calls him Spaniard,
being nothing but a large inventory of his own
commendations.
 DION. [*aside*] I wonder what 's his price;
   for certainly
He 'll sell himself, he has so prais'd his shape.

Enter PHILASTER.

But here comes one more worthy those large
   speeches.   180
Than the large speaker of them.
Let me be swallowed quick,[18] if I can find,
In all the anatomy of yon man's virtues,
One sinew sound enough to promise for
   him
He shall be constable.   By this sun,
He 'll ne'er make king, unless it be of trifles,
In my poor judgment.
 PHI. Right noble sir, as low as my obedi-
   ence,
And with a heart as loyal as my knee,
I beg your favor.
 KING.   Rise; you have it, sir.
 DION. [*aside*] Mark but the King, how pale
   he looks!   He fears!   191
Oh, this same whoreson conscience, how it
   jades us!
 KING. Speak your intents, sir.
 PHI.   Shall I speak 'em freely?
Be still my royal sovereign.
 KING.   As a subject,
We give you freedom.
 DION. [*aside*] Now it heats.
 PHI.   Then thus I turn
My language to you, Prince, you foreign
   man!
Ne'er stare nor put on wonder, for you must
Endure me, and you shall.   This earth you
   tread upon
(A dowry, as you hope, with this fair princess),
By my dead father (oh, I had a father,   200
Whose memory I bow to!) was not left [19]
To your inheritance, and I up and living —
Having myself about me and my sword,
The souls of all my name and memories,
These arms and some few friends beside the
   gods —
To part so calmly with it, and sit still
And say, " I might have been."   I tell thee,
   Pharamond,
When thou art king, look I be dead and rotten,

---

[18] Alive.
[19] This line is erroneously transposed with the
preceding in the old eds.

And my name ashes, as I;[20] for, hear me,
  Pharamond!
This very ground thou goest on, this fat earth,
My father's friends made fertile with their
  faiths,[21]   211
Before that day of shame shall gape and swal-
  low
Thee and thy nation, like a hungry grave,
Into her hidden bowels. Prince, it shall;
By the just gods, it shall!
  PHA. He's mad; beyond cure, mad.
  DION. [*aside*] Here is a fellow has some fire
    in 's veins:
The outlandish [22] prince looks like a tooth-
    drawer.[23]
  PHI. Sir Prince of popinjays,[24] I 'll make it
    well
Appear to you I am not mad.
  KING.   You displease us;
You are too bold.
                        No, sir, I am too tame, [220
Too much a turtle,[25] a thing born without pas-
    sion,
A faint shadow, that every drunken cloud
Sails over, and makes nothing.
  KING.   I do not fancy this.
Call our physicians; sure, he's somewhat
    tainted.[26]
  THRA. [*aside*] I do not think 't will prove so.
  DION. [*aside*] H'as given him a general
    purge already,
For all the right he has; and now he means
To let him blood. Be constant, gentlemen;
By Heaven, I 'll run his hazard,
Although I run my name out of the kingdom!
  CLE. [*aside*] Peace, we are all one soul. [231
  PHA. What you have seen in me to stir of-
    fence
I cannot find, unless it be this lady,
Offer'd into mine arms with the succession;
Which I must keep, though it hath pleas'd
    your fury
To mutiny within you, without disputing
Your genealogies, or taking knowledge
Whose branch you are. The King will leave
    it me,
And I dare make it mine. You have your
    answer.

  PHI. If thou wert sole inheritor to him [240
That made the world his,[27] and couldst see no
    sun
Shine upon anything but thine; were Phara-
    mond
As truly valiant as I feel him cold,
And ring'd amongst the choicest of his friends
(Such as would blush to talk such serious
    follies,
Or back such [bellied] [28] commendations),
And from this presence, spite of [all] these
    bugs,[29]
You should hear further from me.
  KING. Sir, you wrong the Prince; I gave
    you not this freedom
To brave our best friends. You deserve our
    frown.   250
Go to; be better temper'd.
  PHI. It must be, sir, when I am nobler us'd.
  GAL. [*aside*] Ladies,
This would have been a pattern of succession,[30]
Had he ne'er met this mischief. By my life,
He is the worthiest the true name of man
This day within my knowledge.
  MEG. [*aside to* GALATEA] I cannot tell what
    you may call your knowledge;
But the other is the man set in mine eye.
Oh, 't is a prince of wax! [31]
  GAL. [*aside*]   A dog it is. 260
  KING. Philaster, tell me
The injuries you aim at [32] in your riddles.
  PHI. If you had my eyes, sir, and suffer-
    ance,[33]
My griefs upon you, and my broken fortunes,
My wants great, and now [nought but] [34]
    hopes and fears,
My wrongs would make ill riddles to be laugh'd
    at.
Dare you be still my king and right me? [35]
  KING. Give me your wrongs in private.
  PHI.   Take them,
And ease me of a load would bow strong Atlas.
                                    They whisper.
  CLE. He dares not stand the shock.   270
  DION. I cannot blame him; there's dan-
ger in 't. Every man in this age has not a

---

[20] Q4 *et seq.* omit *as I;* but the line is not an
Alexandrine, the last two syllables of "Pharamond" being lightly pronounced. Cf. l. 207.
[21] *I.e.*, by shedding their blood. Supply "which"
before "My."
[22] Foreign.
[23] Proverbial for a thin, meagre fellow.
[24] Parrots.
[25] Dove.   [26] Diseased.

[27] Alexander the Great.
[28] Swollen; Qq 1, 2, *belied.*—Q2 omits *all* in the
next line.
[29] Bugbears.
[30] Of what an heir to the throne should be.
[31] A model prince.
[32] Refer to.
[33] Pain.
[34] So Q4 *et seq.*; earlier eds. *nothing.* The text is
probably corrupt.
[35] Q3 *et seq.* add *not.*

soul of crystal, for all men to read their actions through ; men's hearts and faces are so far asunder that they hold no intelligence.[36] Do but view yon stranger well, and you shall see a fever through all his bravery,[37] and feel him shake like a true [truant].[38] If he give not back his crown again upon the report of an elder-gun,[39] I have no augury.[40] 280

KING. Go to ;
Be more yourself, as you respect our favor ;
You 'll stir us else. Sir, I must have you know
That y' are and shall be, at our pleasure, what
    fashion we
Will put upon you. Smooth your brow, or by
    the gods ——
    PHI. I am dead, sir ; y' are my fate. It
        was not I
Said I was wrong'd ; I carry all about me
My weak stars lead me to, all my weak for-
    tunes.
Who dares in all this presence speak, (that is
But man of flesh, and may be mortal,) tell me
I do not most entirely love this prince, 291
And honor his full virtues !
    KING.   Sure, he 's possess'd.
    PHI. Yes, with my father's spirit. It 's
        here, O King,
A dangerous spirit ! Now he tells me, King,
I was a king's heir, bids me be a king,
And whispers to me these are all my subjects.
'T is strange he will not let me sleep, but dives
Into my fancy, and there gives me shapes
That kneel and do me service, cry me king.
But I 'll suppress him ; he 's a factious spirit,
And will undo me. — [*To* PHARAMOND] Noble
        sir, your hand ; 301
I am your servant.
    KING.   Away ! I do not like this ;
I 'll make you tamer, or I 'll dispossess you
Both of[41] life and spirit. For this time
I pardon your wild speech, without so much
As your imprisonment.
        Exeunt KING, PHARAMOND, ARE-
            THUSA, [*and* Train].
    DION. [*aside*] I thank you, sir ; you dare not
        for the people.
    GAL. Ladies, what think you now of this
        brave fellow ?
    MEG. A pretty talking fellow, hot at hand.
But eye yon stranger.[42] Is he not a fine [310

complete gentleman ? Oh, these strangers, I do affect[43] them strangely ! They do the rarest home-things,[44] and please the fullest ! As I live, I could love all the nation over and over for his sake.

    GAL. Gods comfort your poor headpiece, lady ! 't is a weak one, and had need of a nightcap. [*Exeunt*][45] Ladies.

    DION. See, how his fancy labors ! Has he not
Spoke home and bravely ? What a dangerous
        train 320
Did he give fire to ! How he shook the King,
Made his soul melt within him, and his blood
Run into whey ! It stood upon his brow
Like a cold winter dew.
    PHI.   Gentlemen,
You have no suit to me ? I am no minion.[46]
You stand, methinks, like men that would be
        courtiers,
If [I][47] could well be flatter'd at a price,
Not to undo[48] your children. Y' are all
        honest ;
Go, get you home again, and make your coun-
        try
A virtuous court, to which your great ones
        may, 330
In their diseased age, retire and live recluse.
    CLE. How do you, worthy sir ?
    PHI.   Well, very well ;
And so well that, if the King please, I find
I may live many years.
    DION.   The King must please,
Whilst we know what you are and who you are,
Your wrongs and injuries.[49] Shrink not,
        worthy sir,
But add your father to you ; in whose name
We 'll waken all the gods, and conjure up
The rods of vengeance, the abused[50] people,
Who, like to raging torrents, shall swell
        high, 340
And so begirt the dens of these male-dragons,[51]
That, through the strongest safety, they shall
        beg
For mercy at your sword's point.
    PHI.   Friends, no more ;
Our ears may be corrupted ; 't is an age

[36] Communication.
[37] Bravado.
[38] So Q₁ ; other old eds. *tenant.*
[39] *I.e.,* popgun made of elder wood.
[40] *I.e.,* I am no prophet.
[41] Q₁ inserts *your.*   [42] Foreigner.

[43] Like, admire.
[44] Things that thrust home. (Schelling.)
[45] Old eds. *Exit.*
[46] Favorite of the King.
[47] Emend. Weber ; old eds. *you.*
[48] Ruin.
[49] Q₁ *virtues.*
[50] Deceived.
[51] Cf. the heraldic term "male- (*i.e.,* masculine) griffins." (Dyce.)

We dare not trust our wills to. Do you love
   me?
  THRA. Do we love Heaven and Honor?
  PHI.   My Lord Dion, you had
A virtuous gentlewoman call'd you father ;
Is she yet alive?
  DION.   Most honor'd sir, she is ;
And, for the penance but of an idle dream,
Has undertook a tedious pilgrimage.   350

Enter a Lady.

  PHI. Is it to me, or any of these gentlemen,
   you come?
  LADY. To you, brave lord ; the Princess
   would entreat
Your present company.
  PHI. The Princess send for me ! Y' are
   mistaken.
  LADY. If you be call'd Philaster, 't is to you.
  PHI. Kiss her fair hand, and say I will at-
   tend her.   [*Exit* Lady.]
  DION. Do you know what you do?
  PHI. Yes ; go to see a woman.
  CLE. But do you weigh the danger you are
   in?
  PHI. Danger in a sweet face?   360
By Jupiter, I must not fear a woman !
  THRA. But are you sure it was the Princess
   sent?
It may be some foul train [52] to catch your life.
  PHI. I do not think it, gentlemen ; she 's
   noble.
Her eye may shoot me dead, or those true red
And white friends in her face [53] may steal my
   soul out ;
There 's all the danger in 't. But, be what
  may,
Her single name [54] hath arm'd me.
                Exit PHILASTER.
  DION.   Go on,
And be as truly happy as th' art fearless ! —
Come, gentlemen, let 's make our friends
   acquainted,   370
Lest the King prove false.
               [*Exeunt*] Gentlemen.

[SCENE II] [55]

Enter ARETHUSA *and a* Lady.

  ARE. Comes he not?
  LADY.   Madam?
  ARE.   Will Philaster come?

---

[52] Stratagem.   [54] Her name alone.
[53] Q1 *cheekes.*   [55] Arethusa's apartment.

  LADY. Dear madam, you were wont to
   credit me
At first.
  ARE.   But didst thou tell me so?
I am forgetful, and my woman's strength
Is so o'ercharg'd with dangers like to grow
About my marriage, that these under-things
Dare not abide in such a troubled sea.
How look'd he when he told thee he would
   come?
  LADY. Why, well.
  ARE.   And not a little fearful?
  LADY. Fear, madam ! Sure, he knows not
   what it is.   10
  ARE. You all are of his faction ; the whole
   court
Is bold in praise of him ; whilst I
May live neglected, and do noble things
As fools in strife throw gold into the sea,
Drown'd in the doing. But, I know he fears.
  LADY. Fear, madam ! Methought his looks
   hid more
Of love than fear.
  ARE.   Of love ! to whom? to you?
Did you deliver those plain words I sent
With such a winning gesture and quick look
That you have caught him?
  LADY.   Madam, I mean to you. [20
  ARE. Of love to me ! Alas, thy ignorance
Lets thee not see the crosses of our births !
Nature, that loves not to be questioned
Why she did this or that, but has her ends,
And knows she does well, never gave the world
Two things so opposite, so contrary
As he and I am ; if a bowl of blood
Drawn from this arm of mine would poison
   thee,
A draught of his would cure thee. Of love to
   me !
  LADY. Madam, I think I hear him.
  ARE.   Bring him in. [*Exit* Lady.] 30
You gods, that would not have your dooms
   withstood,
Whose holy wisdoms at this time it is
To make the passions of a feeble maid
The way unto your justice, I obey.

[*Re*]-*enter* [Lady *with*] PHILASTER.

  LADY. Here is my Lord Philaster.
  ARE.   Oh, it is well.
Withdraw yourself.   [*Exit* Lady.]
  PHI.   Madam, your messenger
Made me believe you wish'd to speak with me.
  ARE. 'T is true, Philaster ; but the words
   are such

I have to say, and do so ill beseem
The mouth of woman, that I wish them said,
And yet am loth to speak them. Have you
    known   41
That I have aught detracted from your worth?
Have I in person wrong'd you, or have set
My baser instruments to throw disgrace
Upon your virtues?
    PHI.   Never, madam, you.
    ARE. Why, then, should you, in such a pub-
    lic place,
Injure a princess, and a scandal lay
Upon my fortunes, fam'd to be so great,
Calling a great part of my dowry in question?
    PHI. Madam, this truth which I shall speak
    will be   50
Foolish ; but, for your fair and virtuous self,
I could afford myself to have no right
To anything you wish'd.
    ARE.   Philaster, know
I must enjoy these kingdoms.
    PHI.   Madam, both?
    ARE. Both, or I die : by Heaven, I die,
    Philaster,
If I not calmly may enjoy them both.
    PHI. I would do much to save that noble
    life ;
Yet would be loth to have posterity
Find in our stories that Philaster gave
His right unto a sceptre and a crown   60
To save a lady's longing.
    ARE.   Nay, then, hear :
I must and will have them, and more ——
    PHI.   What more?
    ARE. Or lose that little life the gods pre-
    pared
To trouble this poor piece of earth withal.
    PHI. Madam, what more?
    ARE.   Turn, then, away thy face.
    PHI. No.
    ARE. Do.
    PHI. I can endure it. Turn away my face !
I never yet saw enemy that look'd
So dreadfully, but that I thought myself   70
As great a basilisk [56] as he ; or spake
So horrible, but that I thought my tongue
Bore thunder underneath, as much as his ;
Nor beast that I could turn from. Shall I
    then
Begin to fear sweet sounds? A lady's voice,
Whom I do love? Say you would have my
    life ;
Why, I will give it you ; for it is of me
A thing so loath'd, and unto you that ask

    [56] The fabulous serpent, whose look was fatal.

Of so poor use, that I shall make no price :
If you entreat, I will unmov'dly hear.   80
    ARE. Yet, for my sake, a little bend thy
    looks.
    PHI. I do.
    ARE.   Then know, I must have them and
    thee.
    PHI. And me?
    ARE.   Thy love ; without which, all the
    land
Discovered yet will serve me for no use
But to be buried in.
    PHI.   Is 't possible?
    ARE. With it, it were too little to bestow
On thee. Now, though thy breath do strike
    me dead
(Which, know, it may), I have unripp'd my
    breast.
    PHI. Madam, you are too full of noble
    thoughts
To lay a train for this contemned life,   90
Which you may have for asking. To suspect
Were base, where I deserve no ill. Love you !
By all my hopes, I do, above my life !
But how this passion should proceed from you
So violently, would amaze a man
That would be jealous. [57]
    ARE. Another soul into my body shot
Could not have fill'd me with more strength
    and spirit
Than this thy breath. But spend not hasty
    time
In seeking how I came thus : 't is the gods, [100
The gods, that make me so ; and sure our love
Will be the nobler and the better blest,
In that the secret justice of the gods
Is mingled with it. Let us leave, [58] and kiss ;
Lest some unwelcome guest should fall betwixt
    us,
And we should part without it.
    PHI.   'T will be ill
I should abide here long.
    ARE.   'T is true ; and worse
You should come often. How shall we devise
To hold intelligence, that our true loves,
On any new occasion, may agree   110
What path is best to tread?
    PHI.   I have a boy,
Sent by the gods, I hope, to this intent,
Not yet seen in the court. Hunting the buck,
I found him sitting by a fountain's side,
Of which he borrow'd some to quench his
    thirst,

    [57] Suspicious.
    [58] *I.e.*, stop talking.

And paid the nymph again as much in tears.
A garland lay him by, made by himself
Of many several flowers bred in the [vale],[59]
Stuck in that mystic order that the rareness
Delighted me ; but ever when he turn'd   [120]
His tender eyes upon 'em, he would weep,
As if he meant to make 'em grow again.
Seeing such pretty, helpless innocence
Dwell in his face, I ask'd him all his story.
He told me that his parents gentle died,
Leaving him to the mercy of the fields,
Which gave him roots ; and of the crystal
    springs,
Which did not stop their courses ; and the sun,
Which still,[60] he thank'd him, yielded him his
    light.
Then took he up his garland, and did show [130]
What every flower, as country people hold,
Did signify, and how all, ordered thus,
Express'd his grief ; and, to my thoughts, did
    read
The prettiest lecture of his country art
That could be wish'd : so that methought I
    could
Have studied it.   I gladly entertain'd [61]
Him, who was glad to follow ; and have got
The trustiest, loving'st, and the gentlest boy
That ever master kept.   Him will I send
To wait on you, and bear our hidden love. [140]
  ARE. 'T is well ; no more.

Re-enter Lady.

  LADY. Madam, the Prince is come to do
    his service.
  ARE. What will you do, Philaster, with
    yourself ?
  PHI. Why, that which all the gods have
    appointed out for me.[62]
  ARE. Dear, hide thyself. —
Bring in the Prince.   [*Exit* Lady.]
  PHI.   Hide me from Pharamond ![63]
When thunder speaks, which is the voice of
    God,
Though I do reverence, yet I hide me not ;
And shall a stranger prince have leave to brag
Unto a foreign nation that he made   150
Philaster hide himself ?
  ARE.   He cannot know it.

[59] Q₁ *vayle;* other old eds. *bay.*
[60] Constantly.
[61] Took into service.
[62] An "apparent" Alexandrine, the last two syllables being unstressed, and "have" being slurred.
[63] These four words form a metrical line with Arethusa's words to Philaster ; her order to the Lady is an extra-metrical insertion, as Daniel notes.

  PHI. Though it should sleep for ever to the
    world,
It is a simple sin to hide myself,
Which will for ever on my conscience lie.
  ARE. Then, good Philaster, give him scope
    and way
In what he says ; for he is apt to speak
What you are loth to hear.   For my sake, do.
  PHI. I will.

Enter PHARAMOND.

  PHA. My princely mistress, as true lovers
    ought,
I come to kiss these fair hands, and to show,
In outward ceremonies, the dear love   161
Writ in my heart.
  PHI. If I shall have an answer no directlier,
I am gone.
  PHA. To what would he have answer ?
  ARE. To his claim unto the kingdom.
  PHA. Sirrah, I forbare you before the
    King —
  PHI. Good sir, do so still ; I would not talk
    with you.
  PHA. But now the time is fitter.   Do but
    offer
To make mention of right to any kingdom, [170]
Though it be scarce habitable ——
  PHI.   Good sir, let me go.
  PHA. And by the gods —
  PHI.   Peace, Pharamond ! if thou ——
  ARE. Leave us, Philaster.
  PHI.   I have done.   [*Going.*]
  PHA. You are gone ! by Heaven I 'll fetch
    you back.
  PHI. You shall not need.   [*Returning.*]
  PHA.   What now ?
  PHI.   Know, Pharamond,
I loathe to brawl with such a blast as thou,
Who art nought but a valiant voice ; but if
Thou shalt provoke me further, men shall
    say
Thou wert, and not lament it.
  PHA.   Do you slight
My greatness so, and in the chamber of   180
The Princess ?
  PHI. It is a place to which, I must confess,
I owe a reverence ; but were 't the church,
Ay, at the altar, there 's no place so safe,
Where thou dar'st injure me, but I dare kill
    thee.
And for [64] your greatness, know, sir, I can
    grasp

[64] As for.

You and your greatness thus, thus into noth-
　　ing.
Give not a word, not a word back !　Farewell.
　　　　　　　　　　　　　　　Exit.
　PHA.　'T is an odd fellow, madam ; we must
　　stop
His mouth with some office when we are
　　married.　　　　　　　　　　　　　190
　ARE.　You were best make him your con-
　　troller.
　PHA.　I think he would discharge it well.
　　But, madam,
I hope our hearts are knit ; but yet so slow
The ceremonies of state are, that 't will be
　　long
Before our hands be so.　If then you please,
Being agreed in heart, let us not wait
For dreaming form, but take a little stol'n
Delights, and so prevent [65] our joys to come.
　ARE.　If you dare speak such thoughts,
I must withdraw, in honor.　　　　　　200
　　　　　　　　　　　Exit ARETHUSA.
　PHA.　The constitution of my body will
never hold out till the wedding ; I must seek
elsewhere.[66]　　　　　*Exit* PHARAMOND.

ACT II — SCENE I [1]

Enter PHILASTER *and* BELLARIO.

　PHIL.　And thou shalt find her honorable,
　　boy ;
Full of regard unto thy tender youth,
For thine own modesty ; and, for my sake,
Apter to give than thou wilt be to ask,
Ay, or deserve.
　BEL.　　　　　Sir, you did take me up
When I was nothing ; and only yet am some-
　　thing
By being yours.　You trusted me unknown ;
And that which you were apt to conster [2]
A simple innocence in me, perhaps
Might have been craft, the cunning of a boy　10
Hard'ned in lies and theft ; yet ventur'd you
To part my miseries and me ; for which,
I never can expect to serve a lady
That bears more honor in her breast than you.
　PHI.　But, boy, it will prefer [3] thee.　Thou
　　art young,

---

[65] Anticipate.
[66] So arranged in old eds. Dyce suggests lines
of verse ending "withdraw", "body", "elsewhere."
[1] Philaster's apartment.
[2] Construe.
[3] Advance, promote.

And bear'st a childish overflowing love
To them that clap thy cheeks and speak thee
　　fair yet ;
But when thy judgment comes to rule those
　　passions,
Thou wilt remember best those careful friends
That plac'd thee in the noblest way of life. [20
She is a princess I prefer thee to.
　BEL.　In that small time that I have seen
　　the world,
I never knew a man hasty to part
With a servant he thought trusty.　I remem-
　　ber
My father would prefer the boys he kept
To greater men than he ; but did it not
Till they were grown too saucy for himself.
　PHI.　Why, gentle boy, I find no fault at all
In thy behavior.
　BEL.　　　　　Sir, if I have made
A fault of ignorance, instruct my youth :　30
I shall be willing, if not apt, to learn ;
Age and experience will adorn my mind
With larger knowledge ; and if I have done
A wilful fault, think me not past all hope
For once.　What master holds so strict a hand
Over his boy, that he will part with him
Without one warning?　Let me be corrected
To break my stubbornness, if it be so,
Rather than turn me off ; and I shall mend. [39
　PHI.　Thy love doth plead so prettily to stay,
That, trust me, I could weep to part with thee.
Alas, I do not turn thee off !　Thou knowest
It is my business that doth call thee hence ;
And when thou art with her, thou dwell'st
　　with me :
Think so, and 't is so ; and, when time is full,
That thou hast well discharged this heavy
　　trust,
Laid on so weak a one, I will again
With joy receive thee ; as I live, I will !
Nay, weep not, gentle boy.　'T is more than
　　time
Thou didst attend the Princess.
　BEL.　　　　　　　　　I am gone. [50
But since I am to part with you, my Lord,
And none knows whether I shall live to do
More service for you, take this little prayer :
Heaven bless your loves, your fights, all your
　　designs !
May sick men, if they have your wish, be well ;
And Heaven hate those you curse, though I be
　　one !　　　　　　　　　　　　　*Exit.*
　PHI.　The love of boys unto their lords is
　　strange :
I have read wonders of it ; yet this boy

For my sake (if a man may judge by looks
And speech) would out-do story. I may see
A day to pay him for his loyalty.   61

> *Exit* PHILASTER.

[SCENE II] [4]

Enter PHARAMOND.

PHA. Why should these ladies stay so long?
They must come this way. I know the Queen
employs 'em not ; for the reverend mother [5]
sent me word, they would all be for the garden.
If they should all prove honest [6] now, I were
in a fair taking ; [7] I was never so long without
sport in my life, and, in my conscience, 't is not
my fault. Oh, for our country [8] ladies !

Enter GALATEA.

Here's one bolted ; I'll hound at her. —
[Madam !] [9]
GAL. Your Grace !   10
PHA. Shall I not be a trouble?
GAL. [*going*]   Not to me, sir.
PHA. Nay, nay, you are too quick. By
     this sweet hand ——
GAL. You'll be forsworn, sir ; 't is but an
     old glove.
If you will talk at distance, I am for you.
But, good Prince, be not bawdy, nor do not
     brag ;
These two I bar ;
And then, I think, I shall have sense enough
To answer all the weighty apothegms
Your royal blood shall manage.[10]
PHA.   Dear lady, can you love?
GAL. Dear Prince ! how dear? I ne'er [20
cost you a coach yet, nor put you to the dear
repentance of a banquet. Here's no scarlet,
sir, to blush the sin out it was given for. This
wire [11] mine own hair covers ; and this face has
been so far from being dear to any, that it ne'er
cost penny painting ; and, for the rest of my
poor wardrobe, such as you see, it leaves no
hand [12] behind it, to make the jealous mercer's
wife curse our good doings.

[4] Another room in the palace.
[5] The "mother of the maids", who had charge
of the ladies in waiting.
[6] Chaste.
[7] Agitation, distress.
[8] My country's.
[9] So Q1.
[10] Old eds. print this speech as prose ; there are
numerous similar cases in this play, and it is often
impossible to be certain whether the authors intended verse or prose.
[11] It was much used to support the headdress
and the hair.
[12] *I.e.*, no acknowledgment of indebtedness.
(Daniel.)

PHA. You mistake me, lady.   30
GAL. Lord, I do so ; would you or I could
     help it !
[PHA. Y'are very dangerous bitter, like a
     potion.
GAL. No, sir, I do not mean to purge you,
     though
I mean to purge a little time on you.] [13]
PHA. Do ladies of this country use to give
No more respect to men of my full being?
GAL. Full being ! I understand you not,
unless your Grace means growing to fatness ;
and then your only remedy, upon my knowledge, Prince, is, in a morning, a cup of neat [40
white wine brew'd with carduus,[14] then fast till
supper ; about eight you may eat ; use exercise, and keep a sparrow-hawk ; you can shoot
in a tiller ; [15] but, of all, your Grace must fly
phlebotomy,[16] fresh pork, conger,[17] and clari-
fied whey ; they are all dullers of the vital
spirits.
PHA. Lady, you talk of nothing all this
while.
GAL. 'T is very true, sir : I talk of you. [50
PHA. [*aside*] This is a crafty wench ; I like
her wit well ; 't will be rare to stir up a leaden
appetite. She's a Danaë, and must be courted
in a shower of gold. — Madam, look here ; all
these, and more than ——
GAL. What have you there, my Lord?
Gold ! now, as I live, 't is fair gold ! You
would have silver for it, to play [18] with the
pages. You could not have taken me in a
worse time ; but, if you have present use, [60
my Lord, I'll send my man with silver and
keep your gold for you.[19]
PHA. Lady, lady !
GAL. She's coming, sir, behind, will take
     white money.[20] —
[*aside*] Yet for all this I'll match ye.

> *Exit* GALATEA *behind the hangings.*

PHA. If there be but two such more in this
kingdom, and near the court, we may even
hang up our harps. Ten such camphire [21]
constitutions as this will call the golden age
again in question, and teach the old way for [70

[13] Only in Q1.
[14] *Carduus benedictus*, the Blessed Thistle, a cordial.
[15] Crossbow.
[16] Blood-letting.
[17] Conger eel.
[18] Gamble.
[19] Q1 *safe for you.*
[20] Silver ; *i.e.*, she won't set a high price on herself.
[21] Camphor ; it was "anciently classed among
those articles of the *materia medica* which were cold
in an eminent degree." (Weber.)

every ill-fac'd husband to get his own children ;
and what a mischief that would breed, let all
consider !

Enter MEGRA.

Here 's another : if she be of the same last, the
Devil shall pluck her on.[22] — Many fair mornings, lady !

MEG. As many mornings bring as many
days,

Fair, sweet, and hopeful to your Grace !

PHA. [aside] She gives good words yet ; sure
this wench is free. — [23]

If your more serious business do not call
you,   80

Let me hold quarter [24] with you ; we 'll [talk] [25]
An hour out quickly.

MEG.   What would your Grace talk of ?

PHA. Of some such pretty subject as yourself :

I 'll go no further than your eye, or lip ;

There 's theme enough for one man for an age.

MEG. Sir, they stand right, and my lips are
yet even,

Smooth, young enough, ripe enough, and red
enough,

Or my glass wrongs me.

PHA. Oh, they are two twinn'd cherries dy'd
in blushes

Which those fair suns above with their bright
beams   90

Reflect upon and ripen. Sweetest beauty,

Bow down those branches, that the longing
taste

Of the faint looker-on may meet those blessings,

And taste and live.   [They kiss.] [26]

MEG. [aside] Oh, delicate sweet prince !
She that hath snow enough about her heart
To take the wanton spring of ten such lines off,
May be a nun without probation. — Sir,
You have in such neat poetry gathered a kiss,
That if I had but five lines of that number,
Such pretty begging blanks,[27] I should com-
mend   100

Your forehead or your cheeks, and kiss you
too.

PHA. Do it in prose ; you cannot miss it,
madam.

MEG. I shall, I shall.

[22] *I.e.*, the Devil may try to seduce her — I won't.
[23] Liberal.
[24] Have a peaceful interview.
[25] Qq₂, ₆, F, *take.*
[26] So Q₁.
[27] Blank verses.

PHA.   By my life, [but] [26] you shall not ;
I 'll prompt you first. [Kisses her.] Can you
do it now ?

MEG. Methinks 't is easy, now [you] [28] ha'
done 't before [me] ; [29]

But yet I should stick [30] at it.   [Kisses him.]

PHA.   Stick [31] till to-morrow ;
I 'll ne'er part you, sweetest. But we lose
time.

Can you love me ?

MEG. Love you, my Lord ! How would
you have me love you ?

PHA. I 'll teach you in a short sentence, [110
'cause I will not load your memory ; this is all :
love me, and lie with me.

MEG. Was it " lie with you " that you said ?
'T is impossible.

PHA. Not to a willing mind, that will endeavor. If I do not teach you to do it as easily
in one night as you 'll go to bed, I 'll lose my
royal blood for 't.

MEG. Why, Prince, you have a lady of your
own

That yet wants teaching.   120

PHA. I 'll sooner teach a mare the old measures [32] than teach her anything belonging to
the function. She 's afraid to lie with herself
if she have but any masculine imaginations
about her. I know, when we are married, I
must ravish her.

MEG. By mine honor, that 's a foul fault,
indeed ;

But time and your good help will wear it out,
sir.

PHA. And for any other I see, excepting
your dear self, dearest lady, I had rather [130
be Sir Tim the schoolmaster, and leap a dairymaid, madam.

MEG. Has your Grace seen the court-star,
Galatea ?

PHA. Out upon her ! She 's as cold of her
favor [33] as an apoplex ; she sail'd by but now.

MEG. And how do you hold her wit, sir ?

PHA. I hold her wit ? The strength of all
the guard cannot hold it, if they were tied to
it ; she would blow 'em out of the kingdom.
They talk of Jupiter ; he 's but a squib- [140
cracker to her ; look well about you, and you
may find a tongue-bolt.[34] But speak, sweet
lady, shall I be freely welcome ?

[28] So Q₁ ; other old eds. *I.*   [29] Only in Q₁.
[30] Scruple, hesitate.
[31] Remain.
[32] Stately dances.
[33] In her appearance.
[34] *I.e.*, an arrow shot from her tongue.

MEG. Whither?

PHA. To your bed. If you mistrust my faith, you do me the unnoblest wrong.

MEG. I dare not, Prince, I dare not.

PHA. Make your own conditions ; my purse shall seal 'em, and what you dare imagine you can want, I 'll furnish you withal. Give [150 two hours to your thoughts every morning about it. Come I know you are bashful ; Speak in my ear, will you be mine? — Keep this,   [*Gives money.*] [35] And with it, me : soon I will visit you.

MEG. My Lord, my chamber 's most un-safe ; but when 't is night,

I 'll find some means to slip into your lodg-ing ;

Till when ——

PHA.   Till when, this and my heart go with thee !   *Exeunt* [*several ways*].

Re-enter GALATEA *from behind the hangings.*

GAL. Oh, thou pernicious petticoat prince ! are these your virtues? Well, if I do not lay a train to blow your sport up, I am no [160 woman ; and, Lady Towsabel,[36] I 'll fit you for 't.   *Exit* GALATEA.

[SCENE III] [37]

Enter ARETHUSA *and a* Lady.

ARE. Where 's the boy?

LADY. Within, madam.

ARE. Gave you him gold to buy him clothes?

LADY. I did.

ARE. And has he done 't?

LADY. Yes, madam.

ARE. 'T is a pretty sad-talking boy, is it not?

Asked you his name?

LADY. No, madam.

Enter GALATEA.

ARE. Oh, you are welcome. What good news?   10

GAL. As good as anyone can tell your Grace That says she has done that you would have wish'd.

ARE. Hast thou discovered?

GAL. I have strain'd a point of modesty for you.

ARE. I prithee, how?

GAL. In list'ning after bawdry. I see, let a lady live never so modestly, she shall be sure to find a lawful time to hearken after bawdry. Your prince, brave Pharamond, was so hot on 't !   20

ARE. With whom?

GAL. Why, with the lady I suspected. I can tell the time and place.

ARE. Oh, when, and where?

GAL. To-night, his lodging.

ARE. Run thyself into the presence ; mingle there again

With other ladies ; leave the rest to me. —
        [*Exit* GALATEA.]

If destiny (to whom we dare not say,

" Why [didst thou] [38] this? ") have not decreed it so,

In lasting leaves whose smallest characters [30 Was never alter'd, yet [39] this match shall break. —

Where 's the boy?

LADY. Here, madam.

Enter BELLARIO.

ARE. Sir, you are sad to change your serv-ice, is 't not so?

BEL. Madam, I have not chang'd ; I wait on you,

To do him service.

ARE.   Thou disclaim'st in me.[40]

Tell me thy name.

BEL. Bellario.

ARE. Thou canst sing and play?

BEL. If grief will give me leave, madam, I can.   40

ARE. Alas, what kind of grief can thy years know?

Hadst thou a curst [41] master when thou went'st to school?

Thou art not capable of other grief ;

Thy brows and cheeks are smooth as waters be

When no breath troubles them. Believe me, boy,

Care seeks out wrinkled brows and hollow eyes,

And builds himself caves, to abide in them.

Come, sir, tell me truly, doth your lord love me?

BEL. Love, madam ! I know not what it is.

ARE. Canst thou know grief, and never yet knewest love?   50

---

[35] So Thorndike ; other mod. eds. specify a ring.
[36] Sweetheart ; Q₁ *Dowsabell.*
[37] Arethusa's apartment.

[38] Cor. Theobald ; old eds. *thou didst.*
[39] Dyce and other modern eds. include *yet* in the preceding clause.
[40] *I.e.*, any right in me to your service. (Thorn-dike.)   [41] Cross.

Thou art deceived, boy.   Does he speak of me
As if he wish'd me well?
 BEL.   If it be love
To forget all respect to [42] his own friends
With [43] thinking of your face ; if it be love
To sit cross-arm'd and think [44] away the day,
Mingled with starts, crying your name as loud
And hastily as men i' the streets do fire ;
If it be love to weep himself away
When he but hears of any lady dead
Or kill'd, because it might have been your
    chance ;   60
If, when he goes to rest (which will not be),
'Twixt every prayer he says, to name you once,
As others drop a bead, be to be in love,
Then, madam, I dare swear he loves you.
 ARE. Oh y'are a cunning boy, and taught
    to lie
For your lord's credit! But thou knowest a
    lie
That bears this sound is welcomer to me
Than any truth that says he loves me not.
Lead the way, boy. — [*To the* Lady] Do you
    attend me too. —   69
'T is thy lord's business hastes me thus.
Away !   *Exeunt.*

           [SCENE IV] [45]

 Enter DION, CLEREMONT, THRASILINE,
        MEGRA, [*and*] GALATEA.

 DION. Come, ladies, shall we talk a round?
    As men
Do walk a mile, women should talk an hour
After supper : 't is their exercise.
 GAL. 'T is late.
 MEG.   'T is all
My eyes will do to lead me to my bed.
 GAL. [*aside*] I fear they are so heavy you'll
    scarce find
The way to your own lodging with 'em to-
    night.

           Enter PHARAMOND.

 THRA. The Prince !
 PHA. Not abed, ladies? Y' are good sit-
    ters-up.   10
What think you of a pleasant dream, to last
Till morning?
 MEG. I should choose, my Lord, a pleasing
    wake before it.

[42] So Qq₁₋₃; other old eds. *of.*
[43] So Qq₁₋₃; other old eds. *in.*
[44] So Qq₁₋₃; other old eds. *sigh.*
[45] Another room or courtyard, from which stairs
lead up to Pharamond's apartment.

           Enter ARETHUSA *and* BELLARIO.

 ARE. 'T is well, my lord ; y'are courting of
    these ladies. —
Is 't not late, gentlemen?
 CLE. Yes, madam.
 ARE. Wait you there.   *Exit* ARETHUSA.
 MEG. [*Aside*] She's jealous, as I live. —
    Look you, my Lord,
The Princess has a Hylas, an Adonis.
 PHA. His form is angel-like.   20
 MEG. Why this is he must, when you are
    wed,
Sit by your pillow, like young Apollo, with
His hand and voice binding your thoughts in
    sleep ;
The Princess does provide him for you and
    for herself.
 PHA. I find no music in these boys.
 MEG.   Nor I ;
They can do little, and that small they do,
They have not wit to hide.
 DION.   Serves he the Princess?
 THRA. Yes.
 DION.   'T is a sweet boy : how brave [46]
    she keeps him !
 PHA. Ladies all, good rest ; I mean to kill
    a buck
To-morrow morning ere y' have done your
    dreams.   30
 MEG. All happiness attend your Grace ! —
                        [*Exit* PHARAMOND].
                Gentlemen, good rest. —
Come, shall we to bed?
 GAL.   Yes. — All good night.
 DION. May your dreams be true to you ! —
            [*Exeunt*] GALATEA [*and*] MEGRA.
What shall we do, gallants? 'T is late. The
    King
Is up still : see, he comes, a guard along
With him.

        Enter KING, ARETHUSA, *and* Guard.

 KING.   Look your intelligence be true.
 ARE. Upon my life, it is ; and I do hope
Your Highness will not tie me to a man
That in the heat of wooing throws me off,
And takes another.
 DION.   What should this mean? [40
 KING. If it be true,
That lady had been better have embrac'd
Cureless diseases. Get you to your rest :
You shall be righted. —
            Exeunt ARETHUSA [*and*] BELLARIO.
                Gentlemen, draw near :

[46] Finely dressed.

We shall employ you.   Is young Pharamond
Come to his lodging?

DION.   I saw him enter there.

KING. Haste, some of you, and cunningly
discover

If Megra be in her lodging.   [*Exit* DION.]

CLE. Sir,
She parted hence but now, with other ladies.

KING. If she be there, we shall not need to
make   51

A vain discovery of our suspicion. —
[*Aside*] You gods, I see that who unrighteously
Holds wealth or state from others shall be
curs'd

In that which meaner men are bless'd withal :
Ages to come shall know no male of him
Left to inherit, and his name shall be
Blotted from earth ; if he have any child,
It shall be crossly match'd ; the gods them-
selves

Shall sow wild strife betwixt her lord and her.
Yet, if it be your wills, forgive the sin   61
I have committed ; let it not fall
Upon this understanding [47] child of mine !
She has not broke your laws. But how can I
Look to be heard of gods that must be just,
Praying upon the ground I hold by wrong?

Re-enter DION.

DION. Sir, I have asked, and her women
swear she is within ; but they, I think, are
bawds. I told 'em I must speak with her ;
they laugh'd and said their lady lay speech- [70
less. I said my business was important ; they
said their lady was about it. I grew hot, and
cried my business was a matter that concern'd
life and death ; they answered so was sleeping,
at which their lady was. I urg'd again she had
scarce time to be so since last I saw her ; they
smil'd again, and seem'd to instruct me that
sleeping was nothing but lying down and
winking.[48] Answers more direct I could not
get ; in short, sir, I think she is not there. [80

KING. 'T is then no time to dally. — You
o' th' guard,
Wait at the back door of the Prince's lodging,
And see that none pass thence, upon your
lives.   [*Exeunt* Guard.]
Knock, gentlemen ; knock loud ; louder yet. —
What, has their pleasure taken off their hear-
ing ? —
I 'll break your meditations. — Knock
again. —

Not yet?   I do not think he sleeps, having
his [49]

Larum by him. — Once more. — Pharamond !
Prince !

PHARAMOND [*re-enters*] *above.*

PHA. What saucy groom knocks at this
dead of night?
Where be our waiters? [50]   By my vexed soul,
He meets his death that meets me, for this
boldness.   91

KING. Prince, [prince,] [51] you wrong your
thoughts : we are your friends ;
Come down.

PHA.   The King !

KING.   The same, sir. Come down :
We have cause of present counsel with you.

PHA. If your Grace please
To use me, I 'll attend you to your chamber.

[*Re-enter*] PHARAMOND *below.*

KING. No, 't is too late, Prince ; I 'll make
bold with yours.

PHA. I have some private reasons to my-
self
Makes me unmannerly, and say you cannot. —
                [*They press to come in.*] [51]
Nay, press not forward, gentlemen ; he must
Come through my life that comes here.   101

KING. Sir, be resolv'd [52] I must and will
come. — Enter.

PHA. I will not be dishonor'd.
He that enters, enters upon his death.
Sir, 't is a sign you make no stranger of me,
To bring these renegadoes [53] to my chamber
At these unseasoned hours.

KING.   Why do you
Chafe yourself so?   You are not wrong'd nor
shall be ;
Only, I 'll search your lodging, for some cause
To ourself known. — Enter, I say.

PHA.   I say, no. [110

[*Re-enter*] MEGRA *above.*

MEG. Let 'em enter, Prince, let 'em enter ;
I am up and ready ; [54] I know their business ;
'T is the poor breaking of a lady's honor
They hunt so hotly after ; let 'em enjoy it. —
You have your business, gentlemen : I lay
here.

---

[47] Standing under. Q₁ *undeserving.*
[48] Closing one's eyes.

[49] Q₁ *such ;* Q₃–F *this.* The reference is to Megra.
[50] Servants.   [51] Only in Q₁.
[52] Make up your mind.
[53] "Used vaguely as a term of abuse." (*N.E.D.*)
[54] Dressed.

Oh, my Lord the King, this is not noble in you
To make public the weakness of a woman!
    KING. Come down.
    MEG. I dare, my Lord. Your whootings
        and your clamors,
Your private whispers and your broad fleer-
        ings, 120
Can no more vex my soul than this base car-
        riage.[55]
But I have vengeance yet in store for some
Shall, in the most contempt you can have of
        me,
Be joy and nourishment.
    KING.   Will you come down?
    MEG. Yes, to laugh at your worst; but I
        shall wring you,
If my skill fail me not. [*Exit above.*]
    KING. Sir, I must dearly chide you for this
        looseness;
You have wrong'd a worthy lady; but, no
        more. —
Conduct him to my lodging and to bed.
        [*Exeunt* PHARAMOND *and* Attendants.]
    CLE. [*aside*] Get him another wench, [130
and you bring him to bed indeed.
    DION. [*aside*] 'T is strange a man cannot
        ride a stage
Or two, to breathe [56] himself, without a war-
        rant.
If this gear hold,[57] that lodgings be search'd
        thus,
Pray God we may lie with our own wives in
        safety,
That they be not by some trick of state mis-
        taken!

        [*Re-enter*] MEGRA [*below*].

    KING. Now, lady of honor, where 's your
        honor now?
No man can fit your palate but the Prince.
Thou most ill-shrouded rottenness, thou piece
Made by a painter and a pothecary, 140
Thou troubled sea of lust, thou wilderness
Inhabited by wild thoughts, thou swoln cloud
Of infection, thou ripe mine of all diseases,
Thou all-sin, all-hell, and last, all-devils, tell
        me,
Had you none to pull on with your courtesies
But he that must be mine, and wrong my
        daughter?
By all the gods, all these, and all the pages,
And all the court, shall hoot thee through the
        court,

Fling rotten oranges, make ribald rhymes,
And sear thy name with candles upon
        walls! 150
Do you laugh, Lady Venus?
    MEG. Faith, sir, you must pardon me;
I cannot choose but laugh to see you merry.
If you do this, O King! nay, if you dare do it,
By all those gods you swore by, and as many
More of my own, I will have fellows, and such
Fellows in it, as shall make noble mirth!
The Princess, your dear daughter, shall stand
        by me
On walls, and sung in ballads, anything. 159
Urge me no more; I know her and her haunts.
Her lays,[58] leaps, and outlays,[59] and will dis-
        cover all;
Nay, will dishonor her. I know the boy
She keeps; a handsome boy, about eighteen;
Know what she does with him, where, and
        when.
Come, sir, you put me to a woman's madness,
The glory of a fury; and if I do not
Do it to the height ——
    KING.   What boy is this she raves at?
    MEG. Alas! good-minded prince, you know
        not these things!
I am loth to reveal 'em. Keep this fault,
As you would keep your health from the hot
        air 170
Of the corrupted people, or, by Heaven,
I will not fall alone. What I have known
Shall be as public as a print; all tongues
Shall speak it as they do the language they
Are born in, as free and commonly; I 'll set
        it,
Like a prodigious [60] star, for all to gaze at;
And so high and glowing, that other kingdoms
        far and foreign
Shall read it there, nay, travel with it, till they
        find
No tongue to make it more, nor no more
        people;
And then behold the fall of your fair princess!
    KING. Has she a boy? 181
    CLE. So please your Grace, I have seen a
        boy wait on her,
A fair boy.
    KING.   Go, get you to your quarter;
For this time I 'll study to forget you.
    MEG. Do you study to forget me, and I 'll
        study to forget you.
        Exeunt KING, MEGRA, [*and*] Guard.

---

[55] Conduct.   [56] Exercise.
[57] *I.e.*, if this affair should become a precedent.
[58] Lairs.
[59] Out-of-the-way lairs.
[60] Portentous, ominous.

CLE. Why, here's a male spirit fit for Hercules. If ever there be Nine Worthies of women, this wench shall ride astride and be their captain.   189

DION. Sure, she has a garrison of devils in her tongue, she uttered such balls of wildfire. She has so [n]ettled the King, that all the doctors in the country will scarce cure him. That boy was a strange-found-out antidote to cure her infections; that boy, that princess' boy; that brave, chaste, virtuous lady's boy; and a fair boy, a well-spoken boy! All these considered, can make nothing else — but there I leave you, gentlemen.

THRA. Nay, we'll go wander with you. [200
                                      Exeunt.

ACT III — SCENE I [1]

Enter CLEREMONT, DION, [*and*] THRASILINE.

CLE. Nay, doubtless, 't is true.

DION.   Ay; and 't is the gods
That rais'd this punishment, to scourge the
    King
With his own issue. [2] Is it not a shame
For us that should write noble in the land,
For us that should be freemen, to behold
A man that is the bravery [3] of his age,
Philaster, press'd down from his royal right
By this regardless king? and only look
And see the sceptre ready to be cast
Into the hands of that lascivious lady   10
That lives in lust with a smooth boy, now to be
    married
To yon strange prince, who, but that people
    please
To let him be a prince, is born a slave
In that which should be his most noble part,
His mind?

THRA.   That man that would not stir
    with you
To aid Philaster, let the gods forget
That such a creature walks upon the earth!

CLE. Philaster is too backward in't himself.
The gentry do await it, and the people,
Against their nature, [4] are all bent for him, [20
And like a field of standing corn, that's moved
With a stiff gale, their heads bow all one way.

DION. The only cause that draws Philaster
    back
From this attempt is the fair Princess' love,
Which he admires, and we can now confute.

THRA. Perhaps he'll not believe it.

DION. Why, gentlemen, 't is without question so.

CLE. Ay, 't is past speech she lives dishonestly.
But how shall we, if he be curious, [5] work
Upon his faith?   30

THRA. We all are satisfied within ourselves.

DION. Since it is true, and tends to his own
    good,
I'll make this new report to be my knowledge;
I'll say I know it; nay, I'll swear I saw it.

CLE. It will be best.

THRA.   'T will move him.

Enter PHILASTER.

DION.   Here he comes.
Good morrow to your Honor; we have spent
Some time in seeking you.

PHI.   My worthy friends,
You that can keep your memories to know
Your friend in miseries, and cannot frown
On men disgrac'd for virtue, a good day   40
Attend you all! What service may I do
Worthy your acceptation?

DION.   My good Lord,
We come to urge that virtue, which we know
Lives in your breast, forth. Rise, and make a
    head; [6]
The nobles and the people are all dull'd
With this usurping king; and not a man,
That ever heard the word, or known [7] such a
    thing
As virtue, but will second your attempts.

PHI. How honorable is this love in you
To me that have deserv'd none! Know, my
    friends,   50
You that were born to shame your poor Philaster
With too much courtesy, I could afford
To melt myself to thanks; but my designs
Are not yet ripe. Suffice it that ere long
I shall employ your loves; but yet the time
Is short of what I would.

DION. The time is fuller, sir, than you expect; [8]

---

[1] Unlocated; presumably an antechamber to Philaster's apartment.
[2] By his own offspring.
[3] Ornament.
[4] Contrary to their natural lack of unanimity.

[5] Punctilious; *i.e.*, ask for proof.
[6] Raise troops for a rebellion.
[7] Q₁ *knowes;* Q₃, *et seq.*, knew.
[8] Suppose.

That which hereafter will not, perhaps, be
    reach'd
By violence, may now be caught. As for the
    King,
You know the people have long hated him ; [60
But now the Princess, whom they lov'd ——

PHI. Why, what of her?

DION.   Is loath'd as much as he.

PHI. By what strange means?

DION.   She's known a whore.

PHI.   Thou liest.

DION. My Lord ——

PHI. Thou liest,

               Offers to draw and is held.

And thou shalt feel it ! I had thought thy
    mind
Had been of honor. Thus to rob a lady
Of her good name is an infectious sin
Not to be pardon'd. Be it false as hell,
'T will never be redeem'd, if it be sown   70
Amongst the people, fruitful to increase
All evil they shall hear. Let me alone
That I may cut off falsehood whilst it springs !
Set hills on hills betwixt me and the man
That utters this, and I will scale them
    all,
And from the utmost top fall on his neck,
Like thunder from a cloud.

DION.   This is most strange ;
Sure, he does love her.

PHI.   I do love fair truth.
She [9] is my mistress, and who injures her
Draws vengeance from me. Sirs, let go my
    arms.   80

THRA. Nay, good my Lord, be patient.

CLE. Sir, remember this is your honor'd
    friend,
That comes to do his service, and will show you
Why he utter'd this.

PHI.   I ask your pardon, sir ;
My zeal to truth made me unmannerly ;
Should I have heard dishonor spoke of you,
Behind your back, untruly, I had been
As much distemper'd and enrag'd as now.

DION. But this, my Lord, is truth.

PHI.   Oh, say not so !
Good sir, forbear to say so ; 't is then
    truth,   90
That womankind is false ; urge it no more ;
It is impossible. Why should you think
The Princess light?

DION.   Why, she was taken at it.

PHI. 'T is false ! by Heaven, 't is false !
    It cannot be !

[9] Truth.

Can it? Speak, gentlemen ; for God's love,
    speak !
Is 't possible? Can women all be damn'd?

DION. Why, no, my Lord.

PHI.   Why, then, it cannot be.

DION. And she was taken with her boy.

PHI.   What boy?

DION. A page, a boy that serves her.

PHI.   Oh, good gods !
A little boy?

DION. Ay ; know you him my Lord? [100

PHI. [*aside*] Hell and sin know him ! — Sir,
    you are deceiv'd ;
I 'll reason it a little coldly with you.
If she were lustful, would she take a boy,
That knows not yet desire? She would have
    one
Should meet her thoughts and know the sin he
    acts,
Which is the great delight of wickedness.
You are abus'd,[10] and so is she, and I.

DION. How you, my Lord?

PHI.   Why, all the world 's abus'd
In an unjust report.

DION.   Oh, noble sir, your virtues
Cannot look into the subtle thoughts of
    woman !   110
In short, my Lord, I took them ; I myself.

PHI. Now, all the devils, thou didst ! Fly
    from my rage !
Would thou hadst ta'en devils engend'ring
    plagues,
When thou did'st take them ! Hide thee from
    mine eyes !
Would thou hadst [taken] [11] thunder on thy
    breast,
When thou didst take them ; or been strucken
    dumb
For ever ; that this foul deed might have
    slept
In silence !

THRA.   Have you known him so ill-
    temper'd ?

CLE. Never before.

PHI.   The winds that are let loose
From the four several corners of the earth, [120
And spread themselves all over sea and land,
Kiss not a chaste one. What friend bears a
    sword
To run me thorough?

DION.   Why, my Lord, are you
So mov'd at this?

PHI.   When any fall from virtue,

[10] Deluded.
[11] Q₂ *tane.*

I am distracted ; I have an interest in 't.

DION. But, good my Lord, recall yourself,
and think
What 's best to be done.

PHI. I thank you ; I will do it.
Please you to leave me ; I 'll consider of it.
To-morrow I will find your lodging forth,
And give you answer.

DION. All the gods direct you [130
The readiest way !

THRA. He was extreme impatient.

CLE. It was his virtue and his noble mind.

Exeunt DION, CLEREMONT, [*and*]
THRASILINE.

PHI. I had forgot to ask him where he took
them ;
I 'll follow him. Oh, that I had a sea
Within my breast, to quench the fire I feel !
More circumstances [12] will but fan this fire ;
It more afflicts me now, to know by whom
This deed is done, than simply that 't is done ;
And he that tells me this is honorable,
As far from lies as she is far from truth. 140
Oh, that, like beasts, we could not grieve our-
selves
With that we see not ! Bulls and rams will
fight
To keep their females, standing in their
sight ;
But take 'em from them, and you take at
once
Their spleens [13] away ; and they will fall again
Unto their pastures, growing fresh and fat,
And taste the waters of the springs as sweet
As 't was before, finding no start in sleep ;
But miserable man ——

Enter BELLARIO.

See, see, you gods,
He walks still ; and the face you let him
wear 150
When he was innocent is still the same,
Not blasted ! Is this justice ? Do you mean
To entrap mortality, that you allow
Treason so smooth a brow ? I cannot now
Think he is guilty.

BEL. Health to you, my Lord !
The Princess doth commend her love, her life,
And this, unto you.

[*He gives him a letter.*] [14]

PHI. Oh, Bellario,
Now I perceive she loves me : she does show it

[12] *I.e.*, a more circumstantial account.
[13] *I.e.*, their anger.
[14] Only in Q₁.

In loving thee, my boy ; she has made thee
brave.

BEL. My Lord, she has attir'd me past my
wish, 160
Past my desert ; more fit for her attendant,
Though far unfit for me who do attend.

PHI. Thou art grown courtly, boy. —
[*aside*] Oh, let all women,
That love black deeds, learn to dissemble here,
Here, by this paper ! She does write to me
As if her heart were mines of adamant
To all the world besides, but unto me
A maiden-snow that melted with my looks. —
Tell me, my boy, how doth the Princess use
thee ?
For I shall guess her love to me by that. 170

BEL. Scarce like her servant, but as if I
were
Something allied to her, or had preserv'd
Her life three times by my fidelity ;
As mothers fond do use their only sons ;
As I 'd use one that 's left unto my trust,
For whom my life should pay if he met harm ;
So she does use me.

PHI. Why, this is wondrous well :
But what kind language does she feed thee
with ?

BEL. Why, she does tell me she will trust
my youth
With all her loving secrets, and does call
me 180
Her pretty servant ; bids me weep no
more
For leaving you ; she 'll see my services
Regarded : and such words of that soft strain
That I am nearer weeping when she ends
Than ere she spake.

PHI. This is much better still.

BEL. Are you not ill, my Lord ?

PHI. Ill ? No, Bellario.

BEL. Methinks your words
Fall not from off your tongue so evenly,
Nor is there in your looks that quietness
That I was wont to see.

PHI. Thou art deceiv'd, boy : [190
And she strokes thy head ?

BEL. Yes.

PHI. And she does clap thy cheeks ?

BEL. She does, my Lord.

PHI. And she does kiss thee, boy ? ha !

BEL. How, my Lord ?

PHI. She kisses thee ?

BEL. Never, my Lord, by Heaven.

PHI. That 's strange ; I know she does.

BEL. No, by my life.

PHI. Why then she does not love me.
    Come, she does.
I bade her do it ; I charg'd her, by all charms
Of love between us, by the hope of peace
We should enjoy, to yield thee all delights
Naked as to her bed ; I took her oath   200
Thou shouldst enjoy her. Tell me, gentle
    boy,
Is she not [parallelless] [15]? Is not her breath
Sweet as Arabian winds when fruits are ripe?
Are not her breasts two liquid ivory balls?
Is she not all a lasting mine of joy?
    BEL. Ay, now I see why my disturbed
    thoughts
Were so perplex'd. When first I went to her,
My heart held augury. You are abus'd ;
Some villain has abus'd you ; I do see
Whereto you tend. Fall rocks upon his
    head   210
That put this to you ! 'T is some subtle train
To bring that noble frame of yours to naught.
    PHI. Thou think'st I will be angry with
    thee. Come,
Thou shalt know all my drift. I hate her more
Than I love happiness, and placed thee there
To pry with narrow eyes into her deeds.
Hast thou discovered? Is she fall'n to lust,
As I would wish her? Speak some comfort to
    me.
    BEL. My Lord, you did mistake the boy
    you sent.
Had she the lust of sparrows or of goats, [220
Had she a sin that way, hid from the world,
Beyond the name of lust, I would not aid
Her base desires ; but what I came to know
As servant to her, I would not reveal,
To make my life last ages.
    PHI.   Oh, my heart !
This is a salve worse than the main disease. —
Tell me thy thoughts ; for I will know the
    least
That dwells within thee, or will rip thy heart
To know it. I will see thy thoughts as plain
As I do now thy face.
    BEL.   Why, so you do. [230
She is, for aught I know, by all the gods,
As chaste as ice ! But were she foul as hell,
And I did know it thus, the breath of kings,
The points of swords, tortures, nor bulls of
    brass,
Should draw it from me.
    PHI.   Then 't is no time
To dally with thee ; I will take thy life,
For I do hate thee. I could curse thee now.

[15] Cor. Q₄ ; Q₁ *paradise;* Qq₂, ₃, *parrallesse.*

    BEL. If you do hate, you could not curse me
    worse ;
The gods have not a punishment in store
Greater for me than is your hate.
    PHI.   Fie, fie ; [240
So young and so dissembling ! Tell me when
And where thou didst enjoy her, or let plagues
Fall on me, if I destroy thee not !
             [*He draws his sword.*] [15a]
    BEL. By Heaven, I never did ; and when
    I lie
To save my life, may I live long and loath'd !
Hew me asunder, and, whilst I can think,
I 'll love those pieces you have cut away
Better than those that grow, and kiss those
    limbs
Because you made 'em so.
    PHI.   Fear'st thou not death?
Can boys contemn that?
    BEL.   Oh, what boy is he [250
Can be content to live to be a man,
That sees the best of men thus passionate,
Thus without reason?
    PHI.   Oh, but thou doest not know
What 't is to die.
    BEL.   Yes, I do know, my Lord ;
'T is less than to be born, a lasting sleep,
A quiet resting from all jealousy,
A thing we all pursue. I know, besides,
It is but giving over of a game
That must be lost.
    PHI.   But there are pains, false boy,
For perjur'd souls. Think but on those, and
    then   260
Thy heart will melt, and thou wilt utter all.
    BEL. May they fall all upon me whilst
    I live,
If I be perjur'd, or have ever thought
Of that you charge me with ! If I be false,
Send me to suffer in those punishments
You speak of ; kill me !
    PHI. [*aside*]   Oh, what should I do?
Why, who can but believe him? He does swear
So earnestly, that, if it were not true,
The gods would not endure him. — Rise,
    Bellario ;
Thy protestations are so deep, and thou   270
Doest look so truly when thou utt'rest them,
That, though I know 'em false as were my
    hopes,
I cannot urge thee further. But thou wert
To blame to injure me, for I must love
Thy honest looks, and take no revenge upon
Thy tender youth. A love from me to thee

[15a] Only in Q₁.

Is firm, whate'er thou doest ; it troubles me
That I have call'd the blood out of thy cheeks,
That did so well become thee. But, good boy,
Let me not see thee more ; something is
    done   280
That will distract me, that will make me mad,
If I behold thee. If thou tender'st [16] me,
Let me not see thee.
    BEL.   I will fly as far
As there is morning, ere I give distaste
To that most honor'd mind. But through
    these tears,
Shed at my hopeless parting, I can see
A world of treason practis'd upon you,
And her, and me. Farewell for evermore !
If you shall hear that sorrow struck me dead,
And after find me loyal, let there be   290
A tear shed from you in my memory,
And I shall rest at peace.   *Exit* BELLARIO.
    PHI.   Blessing be with thee,
Whatever thou deservest ! Oh, where shall I
Go bathe this body? Nature too unkind,
That made no medicine for a troubled mind !
                    Exit PHILASTER.

[SCENE II] [17]

Enter ARETHUSA.

    ARE. I marvel my boy comes not back
    again ;
But that I know my love will question him
Over and over, — how I slept, wak'd, talk'd,
How I remem'bred him when his dear name
Was last spoke, and how when I sigh'd, wept,
    sung,
And ten thousand such, — I should be angry
    at his stay.

Enter KING.

    KING. What, at your meditations? Who
    attends you?
    ARE. None but my single self. I need no
    guard ;
I do no wrong, nor fear none.
    KING. Tell me, have you not a boy?
    ARE.   Yes, sir. [10
    KING. What kind of boy?
    ARE.   A page, a waiting-boy.
    KING. A handsome boy?
    ARE.   I think he be not ugly ;
Well qualified and dutiful I know him —
I took him not for beauty.
    KING. He speaks and sings and plays?
    ARE.   Yes, sir.

    KING. About eighteen?
    ARE.   I never ask'd his age.
    KING. Is he full of service?
    ARE. By your pardon, why do you ask?
    KING. Put him away.
    ARE.   Sir !
    KING.   Put him away, I say.
H'as done you that good service shames me to
    speak of.   20
    ARE. Good sir, let me understand you.
    KING.   If you fear me,
Show it in duty ; put away that boy.
    ARE. Let me have reason for it, sir, and
    then
Your will is my command.
    KING. Do not you blush to ask it? Cast
    him off,
Or I shall do the same to you. Y' are one
Shame with me, and so near unto myself,
That, by my life, I dare not tell myself
What you, myself, have done.
    ARE. What have I done, my Lord?   30
    KING. 'T is a new language, that all love to
    learn :
The common people speak it well already ;
They need no grammar. Understand me
    well :
There be foul whispers stirring. Cast him off,
And suddenly. Do it ! Farewell.
                    Exit KING.
    ARE. Where may a maiden live securely
    free,
Keeping her honor fair? Not with the living.
They feed upon opinions, errors, dreams,
And make 'em truths ; they draw a nourish-
    ment
Out of defamings, grow upon disgraces,   40
And, when they see a virtue fortified
Strongly above the batt'ry of their tongues,
Oh, how they cast [18] to sink it ! and, defeated,
Soul-sick with poison, strike the monuments
Where noble names lie sleeping, till they sweat,
And the cold marble melt.

Enter PHILASTER.

    PHI. Peace to your fairest thoughts, dear-
    est mistress !
    ARE. Oh, my dearest servant, [19] I have a
    war within me !
    PHI. He must be more than man that makes
    these crystals
Run into rivers. Sweetest fair, the cause? [50
And, as I am your slave, tied to your good-
    ness,

---

[16] Carest for.   [17] Arethusa's apartment.   [18] Plan.   [19] Lover.

Your creature, made again from what I was
And newly-spirited, I'll right your honor.
 ARE. Oh, my best love, that boy!
 PHI.   What boy?
 ARE. The pretty boy you gave me ——
 PHI.   What of him?
 ARE. Must be no more mine.
 PHI.   Why?
 ARE.   They are jealous [20] of him.
 PHI. Jealous! Who?
 ARE.   The King.
 PHI. [*aside*]   Oh, my misfortune!
Then 't is no idle jealousy. — Let him go.
 ARE. Oh, cruel!
Are you hard-hearted too? Who shall now
  tell you   60
How much I lov'd you? who shall swear it to
  you,
And weep the tears I send? Who shall now
  bring you
Letters, rings, bracelets? lose his health in
  service?
Wake tedious nights in stories of your praise?
Who shall [now] [21] sing your crying elegies,
And strike a sad soul into senseless pictures,
And make them mourn? Who shall take up
  his lute,
And touch it till he crown a silent sleep
Upon my eyelids, making me dream, and cry,
" Oh, my dear, dear Philaster! "
 PHI. [*aside*]   Oh, my heart! [70
Would he had broken thee, that made thee
  know
This lady was not loyal! — Mistress,
Forget the boy; I'll get thee a far better.
 ARE. Oh, never, never such a boy again
As my Bellario!
 PHI.   'T is but your fond affection.
 ARE. With thee, my boy, farewell for ever
All secrecy in servants! Farewell, faith,
And all desire to do well for itself!
Let all that shall succeed thee for thy wrongs
Sell and betray chaste love!   80
 PHI. And all this passion [22] for a boy?
 ARE. He was your boy, and you put him
  to me,
And the loss of such must have a mourning
  for.
 PHI. Oh, thou forgetful woman!
 ARE.   How, my Lord?
 PHI. False Arethusa!
Hast thou a medicine to restore my wits,
When I have lost 'em? If not, leave to talk,
And do thus.

 ARE.   Do what, sir? Would you sleep?
 PHI. For ever, Arethusa. Oh, you gods,
Give me a worthy patience! Have I stood, [90
Naked, alone, the shock of many fortunes?
Have I seen mischiefs numberless and mighty
Grow like a sea upon me? Have I taken
Danger as stern as death into my bosom,
And laugh'd upon it, made it but a mirth,
And flung it by? Do I live now like him,
Under this tyrant king, that languishing
Hears his sad bell and sees his mourners?
  Do I
Bear all this bravely, and must sink at length
Under a woman's falsehood? Oh, that boy,
That cursed boy! None but a villain boy [101
To ease your lust?
 ARE.   Nay, then, I am betrayed;
I feel the plot cast for my overthrow.
Oh, I am wretched!
 PHI. Now you may take that little right I
  have
To this poor kingdom. Give it to your joy;
For I have no joy in it. Some far place,
Where never womankind durst set her foot
For [23] bursting with her poisons, must I seek,
And live to curse you;   110
There dig a cave, and preach to birds and
  beasts
What woman is, and help to save them from
  you;
How Heaven is in your eyes, but in your
  hearts
More hell than hell has; how your tongues,
  like scorpions,
Both heal and poison; [24] how your thoughts
  are woven
With thousand changes in one subtle web,
And worn so by you; how that foolish man
That reads the story of a woman's face
And dies believing it, is lost for ever;
How all the good you have is but a shadow,
I' th' morning with you, and at night behind
  you,   121
Past and forgotten; how your vows are frosts,
Fast for a night, and with the next sun gone;
How you are, being taken all together,
A mere confusion, and so dead a chaos,
That love cannot distinguish. These sad
  texts,
Till my last hour, I am bound to utter of you.
So, farewell all my woe, all my delight!
          Exit PHILASTER.

[23] For fear of.
[24] It was an ancient belief that scorpions "being
laid to their own wounds they made, they cure
them."

---

[20] Suspicious.   [21] Only in Q[1].   [22] Sorrow.

ARE. Be merciful, ye gods, and strike me
 dead !
What way have I deserv'd this ? Make my
 breast   130
Transparent as pure crystal, that the world,
Jealous of me, may see the foulest thought
My heart holds. Where shall a woman turn
 her eyes,
To find out constancy ?

    Enter BELLARIO.

       Save me, how black
And guiltily, methinks, that boy looks
 now !
Oh thou dissembler, that, before thou spak'st,
Wert in thy cradle false, sent to make lies
And betray innocents ! Thy lord and thou
May glory in the ashes of a maid
Fool'd by her passion ; but the conquest is [140
Nothing so great as wicked. Fly away !
Let my command force thee to that which
 shame
Would do without it. If thou understood'st
The loathed office thou hast undergone,
Why, thou wouldst hide thee under heaps of
 hills,
Lest men should dig and find thee.
  BEL.   Oh, what god,
Angry with men, hath sent this strange dis-
 ease
Into the noblest minds ! Madam, this grief
You add unto me is no more than drops
To seas, for which they are not seen to
 swell.
My lord hath struck his anger through my
 heart,   151
And let out all the hope of future joys.
You need not bid me fly ; I came to part,
To take my latest leave. Farewell for ever !
I durst not run away in honesty
From such a lady, like a boy that stole
Or made some grievous fault. The power of
 gods
Assist you in your sufferings ! Hasty time
Reveal the truth to your abused lord
And mine, that he may know your worth ;
 whilst I   160
Go seek out some forgotten place to die !
         Exit BELLARIO.
  ARE. Peace guide thee ! Th' ast over-
  thrown me once ;
Yet, if I had another Troy to lose,
Thou, or another villain with thy looks,
Might talk me out of it, and send me naked,
My hair dishevell'd, through the fiery streets.

    Enter a Lady.

LADY. Madam, the King would hunt, and
 calls for you
With earnestness.
  ARE.   I am in tune to hunt !
Diana, if thou canst rage with a maid
As with a man,[25] let me discover thee 170
Bathing, and turn me to a fearful hind,
That I may die pursued by cruel hounds,
And have my story written in my wounds !
             Exeunt.

    ACT IV — SCENE I[1]

Enter KING, PHARAMOND, ARETHUSA, GALA-
 TEA, MEGRA, DION, CLEREMONT, THRASI-
 LINE, *and* Attendants.

  KING. What, are the hounds before, and all
  the woodmen ?[2]
Our horses ready, and our bows bent ?
  DION.   All, sir.
  KING. [*to* PHARAMOND] Y' are cloudy, sir.
  Come, we have forgotten
Your venial trepass ; let not that sit heavy
Upon your spirit ; here 's none dare utter it.
         [*They talk apart.*]
  DION. He looks like an old surfeited stallion, after his leaping, dull as a dormouse.
See how he sinks ! The wench has shot him
between wind and water, and, I hope, sprung
a leak.   10
  THRA. He needs no teaching : he strikes[3]
sure enough. His greatest fault is, he hunts
too much in the purlieus ;[4] would he would
leave off poaching !
  DION. And for his horn, h' as left it at the
lodge where he lay late. Oh, he 's a precious
limehound ![5] Turn him loose upon the pursuit of a lady, and if he lose her, hang him up
i' th' slip.[6] When my fox-bitch Beauty grows
proud, I 'll borrow him.   20
  KING. Is your boy turn'd away ?
  ARE.   You did command, sir,
And I obey'd you.
  KING. [*to* ARETHUSA]   'T is well
  done. Hark ye furder.
          [*They talk apart.*]
  CLE. Is 't possible this fellow should re-

---

[25] Actaeon.
[1] Unlocated ; perhaps before the palace.
[2] Huntsmen. [3] Lowers his flag in surrender.
[4] Disforested lands on the edge of the forest.
[5] Bloodhound. (*Lyam* = leash.)
[6] *I.e.*, strangle him in a noose made of a leash.

pent? Methinks, that were not noble in him ; and yet he looks like a mortified member, as if he had a sick man's salve [7] in 's mouth. If a worse man had done this fault now, some physical [8] justice or other would presently, without the help of an almanac, [9] have opened the obstructions of his liver, [30 and let him blood with a dog-whip.

DION. See, see how modestly yon lady looks, as if she came from churching with her neighbors! Why, what a devil can a man see in her face but that she's honest!

THRA. Faith, no great matter to speak of ; a foolish twinkling with the eye, that spoils her coat ; [10] but he must be a cunning herald that finds it.

DION. See how they muster one an- [40 other! Oh, there's a rank regiment where the Devil carries the colors and his dam drummajor! Now the world and the flesh come behind with the carriage.[11]

CLE. Sure this lady has a good turn done her against her will : before she was common talk ; now none dare say cantharides [12] can stir her. Her face looks like a warrant, willing and commanding all tongues, as they will answer it, to be tied up and bolted when [50 this lady means to let herself loose. As I live, she has got her a goodly protection and a gracious ; and may use her body discreetly for her health's sake, once a week, excepting Lent and dog days. Oh, if they were to be got for money, what a large sum would come out of the city for these licenses!

KING. To horse, to horse! we lose the morning, gentlemen. *Exeunt.*

[SCENE II] [13]

Enter two Woodmen.

1 WOOD. What, have you lodged the deer?

2 WOOD. Yes, they are ready for the bow.

1 WOOD. Who shoots?

2 WOOD. The Princess.

1 WOOD. No, she'll hunt.

2 WOOD. She'll take a stand, I say.

1 WOOD. Who else?

2 WOOD. Why, the young stranger prince.

1 WOOD. He shall shoot in a stone-bow [14] for me.[15] I never lov'd his Beyond-sea- [10 ship since he forsook the say,[16] for paying ten shillings. He was there at the fall of a deer, and would needs (out of his mightiness) give ten groats for the dowcets ; [17] marry, the [18] steward would have the velvet-head [19] into the bargain, to turf [20] his hat withal. I think he should love venery ; he is an old Sir Tristram ; [21] for, if you be remem'b'red, he forsook the stag once to strike a rascal [22] [miching] [23] in a meadow, and her he kill'd in the eye.[24] Who shoots else? 21

2 WOOD. The Lady Galatea.

1 WOOD. That's a good wench, an she would not chide us for tumbling of her women in the brakes. She's liberal, and by the gods, they say she's honest, and whether that be a fault, I have nothing to do. There's all?

2 WOOD. No, one more ; Megra.

1 WOOD. That's a firker,[25] i' faith, boy. There's a wench will ride her haunches [30 as hard after a kennel of hounds as a hunting saddle, and when she comes home, get 'em clapp'd,[26] and all is well again. I have known her lose herself three times in one afternoon, if the woods have been answerable,[27] and it has been work enough for one man to find her, and he has sweat for it. She rides well and she pays well. Hark! let's go. *Exeunt.*

[SCENE III] [28]

Enter PHILASTER.

PHI. Oh, that I had been nourish'd in these woods

With milk of goats and acorns, and not known

[7] Alluding to Thomas Becon's *The Sick Man's Salve,* a pious work first printed in 1561.

[8] Acting as physician.

[9] Which noted the best times for blood-letting.

[10] Coat of arms. "The allusion is to mullets, or stars, introduced into coats of arms, to distinguish the younger branches of a family, which of course denote inferiority." (Mason.)

[11] Baggage.

[12] Spanish fly, used as an aphrodisiac.

[13] A forest.

[14] With a crossbow that shoots stones.

[15] For all of me.

[16] The assay was taken by a man of high rank, to whom the chief huntsman offered his knife for slitting the fallen deer in order to test the quality of the flesh. The huntsman expected a special fee.

[17] Testicles ; they were among the dainties usually presented to the chief person present.

[18] Q1 *his.*

[19] *I.e.,* the velvet-covered horns.

[20] Face, tirve.

[21] Who was a patron of hunting. His name, however, had come to be used as a jocose form of address, vaguely allusive to his fame as an amorist. Cf. Dekker, *Satiromastix,* ed. Pearson, I, 217: "That Lady a' th' Lake is mine, Sir Tristram."

[22] A lean deer, not fit to hunt.

[23] Lurking. Emend. Theobald ; old eds. *milking*

[24] *I.e.,* he made a dead shot of it.

[25] A lively one.

[26] Pounding a saddle softens it.

[27] Suitable.

[28] Another part of the forest.

The right of crowns nor the dissembling trains
Of women's looks ; but digg'd myself a cave
Where I, my fire, my cattle, and my bed,
Might have been shut together in one shed ;
And then had taken me some mountain girl,
Beaten with winds, chaste as the hard'ned
　　rocks
Whereon she dwells,[29] that might have strewed
　　my bed
With leaves and reeds, and with the skins of
　　beasts,　　　　　　　　　　　　　　10
Our neighbors, and have borne at her big
　　breasts
My large coarse issue !   This had been a life
Free from vexation.[30]

Enter BELLARIO.

BEL.　　　　　　　　Oh, wicked men !
An innocent may walk safe among beasts ;
Nothing assaults me here.   See, my griev'd
　　Lord
Sits as [31] his soul were searching out a way
To leave his body ! — Pardon me, that must
Break thy last commandment ; for I must
　　speak.
You that are griev'd can pity ; hear, my Lord !
　PHI. Is there a creature yet so miserable, [20
That I can pity ?
BEL.　　　　　　　Oh, my noble Lord,
View my strange fortune, and bestow on me,
According to your bounty (if my service
Can merit nothing), so much as may serve
To keep that little piece I hold of life
From cold and hunger !
　PHI.　　　　　　　Is it thou?   Begone !
Go, sell those misbeseeming clothes thou
　　wearest,
And feed thyself with them.
　BEL. Alas, my Lord, I can get nothing for
　　them !
The silly country people think 't is treason [30
To touch such gay things.
　PHI.　　　　　　Now, by the gods, this is
Unkindly done, to vex me with thy sight.
Th' art fall'n again to thy dissembling trade ;
How shouldst thou think to cozen me again?
Remains there yet a plague untri'd for me?
Even so thou wep[t]'st, and look'dst, and
　　spok'st when first
I took thee up.
Curse on the time !   If thy commanding tears
Can work on any other, use thy art ;　　　39

[29] Q₁ *dwelt.*
[30] Imitated from the opening of Juvenal's Sixth
Satire. (Dyce.)　　　　[31] As if.

I 'll not betray it.   Which way wilt thou take,
That I may shun thee, for thine eyes are poison
To mine, and I am loth to grow in rage?
This way, or that way?
　BEL. Any will serve ; but I will choose to
　　have
That path in chase that leads unto my grave.
　　　　　Exeunt PHILASTER *and* BELLARIO
　　　　　　severally.

SCENE IV [32]

Enter DION *and the* [*two*] Woodmen.

DION. This is the strangest sudden chance !
　— You, woodman !
1 WOOD. My Lord Dion?
DION. Saw you a lady come this way on a
sable horse studded with stars of white?
2 WOOD. Was she not young and tall?
DION. Yes.   Rode she to the wood or to the
plain?
2 WOOD. Faith, my Lord, we saw none.
　　　　　　　　　　Exeunt Woodmen.
DION. Pox of you[r] questions then !

Enter CLEREMONT.

　　　　　　　　　What, is she found?
CLE. Nor will be, I think.
DION. Let him seek his daughter himself.
She cannot stray about a little necessary [11
natural business, but the whole court must be
in arms.   When she has done, we shall have
peace.
CLE. There 's already a thousand fatherless tales amongst us.   Some say her horse
ran away with her ; some, a wolf pursued her ;
others, 't was a plot to kill her, and that arm'd
men were seen in the wood ; but questionless
she rode away willingly.　　　　　　　20

Enter KING *and* THRASILINE.

KING. Where is she?
CLE.　　　　　　　Sir, I cannot tell.
KING.　　　　　　　How 's that?
Answer me so again !
CLE.　　　　　　　Sir, shall I lie?
KING. Yes, lie and damn, rather than tell
　　me that.
I say again, where is she?   Mutter not !—
Sir, speak you ; where is she?
DION.　　　　　　Sir, I do not know.
KING. Speak that again so boldly, and, by
　　Heaven,

[32] Another part of the forest.

It is thy last! — You, fellows, answer me;
Where is she? Mark me, all; I am your
　　king:
I wish to see my daughter; show her me;
I do command you all, as you are subjects, [30
To show her me! What! am I not your
　　king?
If ay, then am I not to be obeyed?

DION. Yes, if you command things possible
　　and honest.

KING. Things possible and honest! Hear
　　me, thou,
Thou traitor, that dar'st confine thy king to
　　things
Possible and honest! Show her me,
Or, let me perish, if I cover not
All Sicily with blood!

DION.　　　　　　Faith, I cannot,
Unless you tell me where she is.

KING. You have betrayed me; y' have let
　　me lose　　　　　　　　　　　　40
The jewel of my life. Go, bring her me,
And set her here before me. 'T is the King
Will have it so; whose breath can still the
　　winds,
Uncloud the sun, charm down the swelling
　　sea,
And stop the floods of heaven. Speak, can it
　　not?

DION. No.

KING.　　　No! cannot the breath of kings
　　do this?

DION. No; nor smell sweet itself, if once
　　the lungs
Be but corrupted.

KING.　　　　　Is it so? Take heed!

DION. Sir, take you heed how you dare the
　　Powers
That must be just.

KING.　　　　Alas! what are we kings?
Why do you gods place us above the rest, [51
To be serv'd, flatter'd, and ador'd, till we
Believe we hold within our hands your thun-
　　der?
And when we come to try the power we
　　have,
There 's not a leaf shakes at our threat'nings.
I have sinn'd, 't is true, and here stand to be
　　punish'd;
Yet would not thus be punish'd. Let me
　　choose
My way, and lay it on!

DION. [*aside*] He articles with the gods.
Would somebody would draw bonds for [60
the performance of covenants betwixt them!

Enter PHARAMOND, GALATEA, *and* MEGRA.

KING. What, is she found?

PHA.　　　No; we have ta'en her horse;
He gallop'd empty by. There 's some trea-
　　son. —
You, Galatea, rode with her into the wood;
Why left you her?

GAL.　　　　　She did command me.

KING. Command! you should not.

GAL. 'T would ill become my fortunes and
　　my birth
To disobey the daughter of my king.

KING. Y' are all cunning to obey us for our
　　hurts;
But I will have her.

PHA.　　　　　If I have her not,　70
By this hand, there shall be no more Sicily.

DION. [*aside*] What, will he carry it to Spain
　　in 's pocket?

PHA. I will not leave one man alive, but the
　　King,
A cook, and a tailor.

DION. [*aside*] Yes; you may do well to
spare your lady-bedfellow; and her you may
keep for a spawner.

KING. [*aside*] I see the injuries I have done
　　must be reveng'd.

DION. Sir, this is not the way to find her
　　out.

KING. Run all, disperse yourselves. The
　　man that finds her,　　　　　　80
Or, if she be kill'd, the traitor, I 'll make him
　　great.

DION. I know some would give five thou-
　　sand pounds to find her.

PHA. Come, let us seek.

KING. Each man a several way; here I my-
　　self.

DION. Come, gentlemen, we here.

CLE. Lady, you must go search too.

MEG. I had rather be search'd myself.
　　　　　　　　　　　[*Exeunt*] *omnes.*

　　　　　　[SCENE V] [33]

　　　　　Enter ARETHUSA.

ARE. Where am I now? Feet, find me out
　　a way
Without　the　counsel　of　my　troubled
　　head.
I 'll follow you boldly about these woods,
O'er mountains, thorough brambles, pits, and
　　floods.

───────────────
[33] Another part of the forest.

Heaven, I hope, will ease me ; I am sick.
[*She sits down.*] [34]

Enter BELLARIO.

BEL. Yonder's my lady. God knows I
want nothing,
Because I do not wish to live ; yet I
Will try her charity. — Oh, hear, you that
have plenty !
From that flowing store drop some on dry
ground. — See,
The lively red is gone to guard her heart ! [10
I fear she faints. — Madam, look up ! — She
breathes not. —
Open once more those rosy twins, and send
Unto my lord your latest farewell ! — Oh, she
stirs. —
How is it, madam? Speak comfort.
ARE. 'T is not gently done,
To put me in a miserable life,
And hold me there. I prithee, let me go ;
I shall do best without thee ; I am well.

Enter PHILASTER.

PHI. I am to blame to be so much in rage.
I 'll tell her coolly when and where I heard
This killing truth. I will be temperate   20
In speaking, and as just in hearing. ——
Oh, monstrous ! Tempt me not, you gods !
good gods,
Tempt not a frail man ! What's he that has
a heart,
But he must ease it here?
BEL. My Lord, help ! help the Princess !
ARE. I am well ; forbear.
PHI. [*aside*] Let me love lightning, let me
be embrac'd
And kiss'd by scorpions, or adore the eyes
Of basilisks, rather than trust the tongues
Of hell-bred women ! Some good god look
down,   30
And shrink these veins up ! Stick me here a
stone,
Lasting to ages in the memory
Of this damned act ! — Hear me, you wicked
ones !
You have put hills of fire into this breast,
Not to be quench'd with tears ; for which may
guilt
Sit on your bosoms ! At your meals and beds
Despair await you ! What, before my face?
Poison of asps between your lips ! Diseases
Be your best issues ! Nature make a curse,
And throw it on you !

[34] Only in Q1.

ARE. Dear Philaster, leave [40
To be enrag'd, and hear me.
PHI. I have done ;
Forgive my passion. Not the calmed sea,
When Aeolus locks up his windy brood,
Is less disturb'd than I. I 'll make you
know 't.
Dear Arethusa, do but take this sword,
[*Offers his drawn sword.*] [35]
And search how temperate a heart I have ;
Then you and this your boy may live and reign
In lust without control. — Wilt thou, Bel-
lario?
I prithee kill me ; thou art poor, and mayst
Nourish ambitious thoughts ; when I am
dead,   50
[Thy] [36] way were freer. Am I raging now?
If I were mad, I should desire to live.
Sirs,[37] feel my pulse, whether you have known
A man in a more equal tune to die.
BEL. Alas, my Lord, your pulse keeps mad-
man's time !
So does your tongue.
PHI. You will not kill me, then?
ARE. Kill you !
BEL. Not for the world.
PHI. I blame not thee,
Bellario ; thou hast done but that which gods
Would have transform'd themselves to do.
Begone ;
Leave me without reply ; this is the last   60
Of all our meeting.[38] — (*Exit* BELLARIO.) Kill
me with this sword ;
Be wise, or worse will follow : we are two
Earth cannot bear at once. Resolve to do,
Or suffer.
ARE. If my fortune be so good to let me fall
Upon thy hand, I shall have peace in death.
Yet tell me this, will there be no slanders,
No jealousy in the other world, no ill there?
PHI. No.
ARE. Show me, then, the way.   70
PHI. Then guide my feeble hand,
You that have power to do it, for I must
Perform a piece of justice ! — If your youth
Have any way offended Heaven, let prayers
Short and effectual reconcile you to it.
ARE. I am prepared.

Enter a Country Fellow.

C. FELL. I 'll see the King, if he be in the
forest ; I have hunted him these two hours.

[35] Only in Q1.   [36] So Q1 ; later eds. *This.*
[37] Formerly used to both sexes.
[38] Q1 *meetings.*

If I should come home and not see him, my sisters would laugh at me. I can see nothing [80
but people better hors'd than myself, that out-
ride me ; I can hear nothing but shouting.
These kings had need of good brains ; this
whooping is able to put a mean [39] man out of
his wits. There's a courtier with his sword
drawn ; by this hand, upon a woman, I think !

PHI. Are you at peace ?

ARE.   With Heaven and earth.

PHI. May they divide [40] thy soul and body !
                              [PHILASTER *wounds her*.] [41]

C. FELL. Hold, dastard ! strike a woman !
Th'art a craven. I warrant thee, thou [90
wouldst be loth to play half a dozen venies at
wasters [42] with a good fellow for a broken head.

PHI. Leave us, good friend.

ARE. What ill-bred man art thou, to intrude
          thyself
Upon our private sports, our recreation ?

C. FELL. God 'uds [43] me, I understand you
not ; but I know the rogue has hurt [44] you.

PHI. Pursue thy own affairs ; it will be ill
To multiply blood upon my head, which thou
Wilt force me to.   100

C. FELL. I know not your rhetoric ; but I
can lay it on, if you touch the woman.

PHI. Slave, take what thou deservest !
                              They fight.

ARE.   Heaven guard my lord !

C. FELL. Oh, do you breathe ?

PHI. I hear the tread of people. I am hurt.
The gods take part against me : could this
          boor
Have held me thus else ? I must shift for life,
Though I do loathe it. I would find a course
To lose it rather by my will than force.
                              Exit PHILASTER.

C. FELL. I cannot follow the rogue. I pray
thee, wench, come and kiss me now.   111

Enter PHARAMOND, DION, CLEREMONT,
          THRASILINE, *and* Woodmen.

PHA. What art thou ?

C. FELL. Almost kill'd I am for a foolish
woman ; a knave has hurt her.

PHA. The Princess, gentlemen ! — Where's
the wound, madam ! Is it dangerous ?

ARE. He has not hurt me.

C. FELL. By God, she lies ; h' as hurt her in
          the breast ;
Look else.

PHA.   O sacred spring of innocent blood !

DION. 'T is above wonder ! Who should
          dare this ?   120

ARE. I felt it not.

PHA. Speak, villain, who has hurt the Princess ?

C. FELL. Is it the Princess ?

DION. Ay.

C. FELL. Then I have seen something yet.

PHA. But who has hurt her ?

C. FELL. I told you, a rogue ; I ne'er saw
          him before, I.

PHA. Madam, who did it ?

ARE.   Some dishonest wretch ;
Alas, I know him not, and do forgive him !

C. FELL. He's hurt too ; he cannot go
          far ;   130
I made my father's old fox [45] fly about his ears.

PHA. How will you have me kill him ?

ARE. Not at all ; 't is some distracted fellow.

PHA. By this hand, I 'll leave never a piece
of him bigger than a nut, and bring him all to
you in my hat.

ARE. Nay, good sir,
If you do take him, bring him quick [46] to me,
And I will study for a punishment
Great as his fault.   140

PHA. I will.

ARE.   But swear.

PHA.   By all my love, I will. —
Woodmen, conduct the Princess to the King,
And bear that wounded fellow to dressing. —
Come, gentlemen, we 'll follow the chase close.
          [*Exeunt*] ARETHUSA, PHARAMOND,
                    DION, CLEREMONT, THRASILINE,
                    and 1 Woodman.

C. FELL. I pray you, friend, let me see the
King.

2 WOOD. That you shall, and receive
thanks.

C. FELL. If I get clear of this, I 'll go to see
no more gay sights.   *Exeunt.* [150

[SCENE VI] [47]

Enter BELLARIO.

BEL. A heaviness near death sits on my
          brow,
And I must sleep. Bear me, thou gentle bank,
For ever, if thou wilt. You sweet ones all,
                              [*Lies*] *down*.]
Let me unworthy press you ; I could wish

---

[39] Humble, ordinary.   [40] Share.
[41] Only in Q 1.   [42] Bouts at cudgels.
[43] Q 1 *iudge*.   [44] Wounded.
[45] Sword.   [46] Alive.
[47] Another part of the forest.

I rather were a corse strew'd o'er with you
Than quick above you. Dulness shuts mine
     eyes,
And I am giddy ; oh, that I could take
So sound a sleep that I might never wake !
              [*Sleeps.*]

         Enter Philaster.

Phi. I have done ill ; my conscience calls
     me false
To strike at her that would not strike at [10
     me.
When I did fight, methought I heard her pray
The gods to guard me. She may be abus'd,[48]
And I a loathed villain ; if she be,
She will conceal who hurt her. He has wounds
And cannot follow ; neither knows he me.
Who's this ? Bellario sleeping ! If thou beest
Guilty, there is no justice that thy sleep
Should be so sound, and mine, whom thou
     hast wrong'd,
So broken. (*Cry within.*) Hark ! I am pur-
     sued. You gods
I'll take this offer'd means of my escape [20
They have no mark to know me but my
     wounds,[49]
If she be true ; if false, let mischief light
On all the world at once ! Sword, print my
     wounds
Upon this sleeping boy ! I ha' none, I think,
Are mortal, nor would I lay greater on thee.
              Wounds him.
Bel. Oh, death, I hope, is come ! Blest be
     that hand !
It meant me well. Again, for pity's sake !
Phi. I have caught myself ;
            Philaster *falls.*
The loss of blood hath stayed my flight. Here,
     here,
Is he that struck thee : take thy full re-
     venge ;   30
Use me, as I did mean thee, worse than death ;
I'll teach thee to revenge. This luckless hand
Wounded the Princess ; tell my followers [50]
Thou didst receive these hurts in staying
     me,
And I will second thee ; get a reward.
Bel. Fly, fly, my Lord, and save yourself !
Phi.   How's this ?
Wouldst thou I should be safe ?
Bel.   Else were it vain
For me to live. These little wounds I have

[48] Wronged.
[49] Q1 blood.
[50] Pursuers.

Ha' not bled much. Reach me that noble
     hand ;
I'll help to cover you.
Phi.   Art thou [then] [51] true to me? [40
Bel. Or let me perish loath'd ! Come, my
     good Lord,
Creep in amongst those bushes ; who does
     know
But that the gods may save your much-lov'd
     breath ?
Phi. Then I shall die for grief, if not for
     this,
That I have wounded thee. What wilt thou
     do ?
Bel. Shift for myself well. Peace ! I hear
     'em come.
         [Philaster *creeps into a bush.*]
Within. Follow, follow, follow ! that way
     they went.
Bel. With my own wounds I'll bloody my
     own sword.
I need not counterfeit to fall ; Heaven knows
That I can stand no longer.   50
         [Boy *falls down.*] [52]

Enter Pharamond, Dion, Cleremont, *and*
         Thrasiline.

Pha. To this place we have track'd him by
     his blood.
Cle. Yonder, my Lord, creeps one away.
Dion. Stay, sir ! what are you?
Bel. A wretched creature, wounded in
     these woods
By beasts. Relieve me, if your names be men,
Or I shall perish.
Dion.   This is he, my Lord,
Upon my soul, that hurt her. 'T is the boy,
That wicked boy, that serv'd her.
Pha.   Oh, thou damn'd
In thy creation ! What cause couldst thou
     shape
To strike [53] the Princess?
Bel.   Then I am betrayed. [60
Dion. Betrayed ! No, apprehended.
Bel.   I confess,
(Urge it no more) that, big with evil thoughts,
I set upon her, and did make my aim
Her death. For charity let fall at once
The punishment you mean, and do not load
This weary flesh with tortures.
Pha.   I will know
Who hired thee to this deed.
Bel.   Mine own revenge.

[51] Q1 only.   [52] Only in Q1.
[53] Q3, *et seq., hurt.*

PHA. Revenge! for what?

BEL.   It pleas'd her to receive
Me as her page and, when my fortunes ebb'd,
That men strid o'er them careless, she did
   show'r   70
Her welcome graces on me, and did swell
My fortunes till they overflowed their banks,
Threat'ning the men that cross'd 'em; when,
   as swift
As storms arise at sea, she turn'd her eyes
To burning suns upon me, and did dry
The streams she had bestowed, leaving me
   worse
And more contemn'd than other little brooks,
Because I had been great. In short, I knew
I could not live, and therefore did desire
To die reveng'd.

PHA.   If tortures can be found [80
Long as thy natural life, resolve to feel
The utmost rigor.

            PHILASTER *creeps out of a bush.*

CLE.   Help to lead him hence.

PHI. Turn back, you ravishers of inno-
   cence!
Know ye the price of that you bear away
So rudely?

PHA.   Who's that?

DION.   'T is the Lord Philaster.

PHI. 'T is not the treasure of all kings in
   one,
The wealth of Tagus, nor the rocks of pearl
That pave the court of Neptune, can weigh
   down
That virtue. It was I that hurt the Princess.
Place me, some god, upon a pyramis [54]   90
Higher than hills of earth, and lend a voice
Loud as your thunder to me, that from thence
I may discourse to all the underworld
The worth that dwells in him!

PHA.   How's this?

BEL.   My Lord, some man
Weary of life, that would be glad to die.

PHI. Leave these untimely courtesies, Bellario.

BEL. Alas, he's mad! Come, will you lead
   me on?

PHI. By all the oaths that men ought most
   to keep,
And gods to punish most when men do break,
He touch'd her not. — Take heed, Bellario,
How thou dost drown the virtues thou hast
   shown   101
With perjury. — By all the gods, 't was I!
You know she stood betwixt me and my right.

[54] Pyramid.

PHA. Thy own tongue be thy judge!

CLE.   It was Philaster.

DION. Is't not a brave boy?
Well, sirs, I fear me we were all deceived.

PHI. Have I no friend here?

DION.   Yes.

PHI.   Then show it; some
Good body lend a hand to draw us nearer.
Would you have tears shed for you when you
   die?
Then lay me gently on his neck, that there [!10
I may weep floods, and breathe forth my
   spirit. —
'T is not the wealth of Plutus, nor the gold
Lock'd in the heart of earth, can buy away
This armful from me; this had been a ran-
   some
To have redeem'd the great Augustus Cæsar,
Had he been taken. You hard-hearted men,
More stony than these mountains, can you see
Such clear, pure blood drop, and not cut your
   flesh
To stop his life, to bind whose bitter wounds
Queens ought to tear their hair, and with their
   tears   120
Bathe 'em? — Forgive me, thou that art the
   wealth
Of poor Philaster!

   Enter KING, ARETHUSA, *and a* Guard.

KING.   Is the villain ta'en?

PHA. Sir, here be two confess the deed; but
   say [55]
It was Philaster.

PHI.   Question it no more;
It was.

KING.   The fellow that did fight with him
Will tell us that.

ARE.   Aye me! I know he will.

KING. Did not you know him?

ARE.   Sir, if it was he,
He was disguised.

PHI.   I was so. — Oh, my stars,
That I should live still.

KING.   Thou ambitious fool,
Thou that hast laid a train for thy own life! —
Now I do mean to do, I'll leave to talk.   131
Bear [them] [56] to prison.

ARE. Sir, they did plot together to take
   hence
This harmless life; should it pass unreveng'd,

[55] Q_1 *sute*, which Dyce (followed by all but Boas)
emends to *sure*. "Say" may be imperative, or
may = "suppose it is"; in the latter case the
speech should end with a dash.

[56] So Q_1; other old eds., *him*.

I should to earth go weeping.   Grant me, then,
By all the love a father bears his child,
Their custodies, and that I may appoint
Their tortures and their deaths.
  DION. [*aside*] Death ! Soft ; our law will
    not reach that for this fault.
  KING. 'T is granted ; take 'em to you with
    a guard. —   140
Come, princely Pharamond, this business past,
We may with more security go on
To your intended match.
  CLE. [*aside to* DION] I pray that this action
lose not Philaster the hearts of the people.
  DION. [*aside to* CLEREMONT] Fear it not ;
their over-wise heads will think it but a trick.
                                        Exeunt omnes.

                   ACT V — SCENE I [1]

Enter DION, CLEREMONT, [*and*] THRASILINE.

  THRA. Has the King sent for him to death ?
  DION. Yes ; but the King must know 't is
not in his power to war with Heaven.
  CLE. We linger time ; the King sent for
Philaster and the headsman an hour ago.
  THRA. Are all his wounds well ?
  DION. All ; they were but scratches ; but
the loss of blood made him faint.
  CLE. We dally, gentlemen.
  THRA. Away !   10
  DION. We 'll scuffle hard before he perish.
                                        Exeunt.

                   [SCENE II] [2]

Enter PHILASTER, ARETHUSA, [*and*] BELLARIO.

  ARE. Nay, faith, Philaster, grieve not ; we
    are well.
  BEL. Nay, good my Lord, forbear ; we 're
    wondrous well.
  PHI. Oh, Arethusa, oh, Bellario,
Leave to be kind !
I shall be [shut] [3] from Heaven, as now from
    earth,
If you continue so.   I am a man
False to a pair of the most trusty ones
That ever earth bore ; can it bear us all ?
Forgive, and leave me.   But the King hath
    sent
To call me to my death ; oh, show it me,   10
And then forget me !   And for thee, my boy,

  [1] Unlocated.
  [2] A prison.
  [3] So Q1 ; other old eds., *shot.*

I shall deliver words will mollify
The hearts of beasts to spare thy innocence.
  BEL. Alas, my Lord, my life is not a thing
Worthy your noble thoughts !   'T is not a life :
'T is but a piece of childhood thrown away.
Should I outlive you, I should then outlive
Virtue and honor ; and when that day comes,
If ever I shall close these eyes but once,
May I live spotted for my perjury,   20
And waste [by time] [4] to nothing !
  ARE. And I, the woful'st maid that ever
    was,
Forc'd with my hands to bring my lord to
    death,
Do by the honor of a virgin swear
To tell [5] no hours beyond it !
  PHI.   Make me not hated so.
  ARE. Come from this prison all joyful to our
    deaths !
  PHI. People will tear me, when they find
    you true
To such a wretch as I ; I shall die loath'd.
Enjoy your kingdoms peacably, whilst I
For ever sleep forgotten with my faults.   30
Every just servant,[6] every maid in love,
Will have a piece of me, if you be true.
  ARE. My dear Lord, say not so.
  BEL.   A piece of you !
He was not born of [woman] [7] that can cut
It and look on.
  PHI. Take me in tears betwixt you, for my
    heart
Will break with shame and sorrow.
  ARE.   Why, 't is well.
  BEL. Lament no more.
  PHI. [Why,] [8] what would you have done
If you had wrong'd me basely, and had found
My life no price compar'd to yours ? [9]   For
    love, sirs,   40
Deal with me truly.
  BEL.   'T was mistaken, sir.
  PHI. Why, if it were ?
  BEL.   Then, sir, we would have ask'd
Your pardon.
  PHI.   And have hope to enjoy it ?
  ARE. Enjoy it ! ay.
  PHI.   Would you indeed ? Be plain.
  BEL. We would, my Lord.
  PHI.   Forgive me, then.

  [4] So Q1 ; Q2 *by limbs;* other old eds., *my limbs.*
  [5] Number.   [6] Lover.
  [7] So Q1 ; other old eds., *women.*
  [8] Only in Q1.
  [9] Mason (followed by all the later eds.) emends
to read *your life . . . to mine,* which is more logical
but unnecessary and perhaps less dramatic.

ARE.   So, so.
BEL. 'T is as it should be now.
PHI.   Lead to my death.   *Exeunt.*

[SCENE III] [10]

Enter KING, DION, CLEREMONT, THRASILINE,
   [*and* Attendants].

KING. Gentlemen, who saw the Prince?
CLE. So please you, sir, he 's gone to see the
   city
And the new platform,[11] with some gentlemen
Attending on him.
KING.   Is the Princess ready
To bring her prisoner out?
THRA.   She waits your Grace.
KING. Tell her we stay.
            [*Exit* THRASILINE.] [12]
DION. [*aside*]   King, you may be deceiv'd
   yet.
The head you aim at cost more setting on
Than to be lost so lightly. If it must off, —
Like a wild overflow, that s[w]oops before him
A golden stack, and with it shakes down
   bridges,   10
Cracks the strong hearts of pines, whose cable-
   roots
Held out a thousand storms, a thousand thun-
   ders,
And, so made mightier, takes whole villages
Upon his back, and in that heat of pride
Charges strong towns, towers, castles, palaces,
And lays them desolate; so shall thy head,
Thy noble head, bury the lives of thousands,
That must bleed with thee like a sacrifice,
In thy red ruins.

Enter PHILASTER, ARETHUSA, BELLARIO *in a
   robe and garland,* [*and* THRASILINE].

KING.   How now? What masque is this?
BEL. Right royal sir, I should   20
Sing you an epithalamion of these lovers,
But having lost my best airs with my fortunes,
And wanting a celestial harp to strike
This blessed union on, thus in glad story
I give you all. These two fair cedar branches,
The noblest of the mountain where they grew,
Straightest and tallest, under whose still
   shades
The worthier beasts have made their lairs, and
   slept

Free from [the fervor of] [13] the Sirian star [14]
And the fell thunder-stroke, free from the
   clouds   30
When they were big with humor,[15] and de-
   liver'd
In thousand spouts their issues to the earth;
Oh, there was none but silent quiet there!
Till never-pleased Fortune shot up shrubs,
Base under-brambles, to divorce these
   branches;
And for a while they did so, and did reign
Over the mountain, and choke up his beauty
With brakes, rude thorns and thistles, till the
   sun
Scorch'd them even to the roots and dried
   them there.
And now a gentler gale hath blown again, [40
That made these branches meet and twine to-
   gether,
Never to be divided.[16] The god that sings
His holy numbers over marriage beds
Hath knit their noble hearts; and here they
   stand
Your children, mighty King; and I have done.
   KING. How, how?
   ARE.   Sir, if you love it in plain truth,
For now there is no masquing in 't, this gen-
   tleman,
The prisoner that you gave me, is become
My keeper, and through all the bitter throes
Your jealousies and his ill fate have wrought
   him,   50
Thus nobly hath he struggled, and at length
Arrived here my dear husband.
   KING.   Your dear husband! —
Call in the captain of the citadel —
There you shall keep your wedding. I 'll pro-
   vide
A masque shall make your Hymen turn his
   saffron [17]
Into a sullen coat, and sing sad requiems
To your departing souls.
Blood shall put out your torches; and, instead
Of gaudy flowers about your wanton necks,
An axe shall hang, like a prodigious [18] meteor,
Ready to crop your loves' sweets. — Hear,
   you gods!   61
From this time do I shake all title off
Of father to this woman, this base woman;
And what there is of vengeance in a lion

---

[10] Not precisely located; presumably before the
palace, or a room or courtyard in it.
[11] This might mean plan, model, site of a battery,
walk, or terrace.
[12] Only in Q₁.
[13] Q₁ only.
[14] Sirius, the dog-star; supposed to cause heat.
[15] Moisture.
[16] Q₁ *vnarmde.*
[17] Hymen was robed in this color in masques.
[18] Portentous, ominous.

Cha[f]'d among dogs or robb'd of his dear
   young,
The same, enforc'd more terrible, more mighty,
Expect from me !
   ARE. Sir, by that little life I have left to
      swear by,
There's nothing that can stir me from myself.
What I have done, I have done without repent-
   ance,   70
For death can be no bugbear unto me,
So long as Pharamond is not my headsman.
   DION. [*aside*] Sweet peace upon thy soul,
      thou worthy maid,
Whene'er thou diest ! For this time I'll
   excuse thee,
Or be thy prologue.
   PHI.   Sir, let me speak next ;
And let my dying words be better with you
Than my dull living actions. If you aim
At the dear life of this sweet innocent,
Y' are a tyrant and a savage monster,
[That feeds upon the blood you gave a life
   to ;] [19]   80
Your memory shall be as foul behind you,
As you are living ; all your better deeds
Shall be in water writ, but this in marble ;
No chronicle shall speak you, though your
   own,
But for the shame of men. No monument,
Though high and big as Pelion, shall be able
To cover this base murder : make it rich
With brass, with purest gold, and shining jas-
   per,
Like the Pyramids ; lay on epitaphs
Such as make great men gods ; my little
   marble,   90
That only clothes my ashes, not my faults,
Shall far outshine it. And, for after-issues,
Think not so madly of the heavenly wisdoms,
That they will give you more for your mad
   rage
To cut off, unless it be some snake, or some-
   thing
Like yourself, that in his birth shall strangle
   you.
Remember my father, King ! There was a
   fault,
But I forgive it. Let that sin persuade you
To love this lady ; if you have a soul,
Think, save her, and be saved. For myself,
I have so long expected this glad hour,   101
So languish'd under you, and daily withered,
That, Heaven knows, it is a joy to die ;
I find a recreation in 't.

[19] Q₁ only.

Enter a Messenger.

MESS. Where's the King ?
KING.   Here.
MESS.   Get you to your strength,
And rescue the Prince Pharamond from dan-
   ger ;
He's taken prisoner by the citizens,
Fearing [20] the Lord Philaster.
   DION. [*aside*]   Oh, brave followers ! [21]
Mutiny, my fine dear countrymen, mutiny !
Now, my brave valiant foremen, show your
   weapons   110
In honor of your mistresses !

Enter another Messenger.

2 MESS. Arm, arm, arm, arm !
KING. A thousand devils take [these
   citizens !] [22]
DION. [*aside*] A thousand blessings on 'em !
2 MESS. Arm, O King ! The city is in
   mutiny,
Led by an old gray ruffian, who comes on
In rescue of the Lord Philaster.
KING. Away to the citadel ! —
      Exit [Messenger] *with* ARETHUSA,
         PHILASTER, [*and*] BELLARIO.
               I'll see them safe,
And then cope with these burghers. Let the
   guard
And all the gentlemen give strong attend-
   ance.   120
      [*Exeunt all except*] DION, CLERE-
         MONT, [*and*] THRASILINE.
   CLE. The city up ! This was above our
      wishes.
   DION. Ay, and the marriage too. By [all
      the gods,] [23]
This noble lady has deceiv'd us all.
A plague upon myself, a thousand plagues,
For having such unworthy thoughts of her dear
   honor !
Oh, I could beat myself ! Or do you beat me,
And I'll beat you ; for we had all one thought.
   CLE. No, no ; 't will but lose time.
   DION. You say true. Are your swords
sharp ? — Well, my dear countrymen [130
What-ye-lacks,[24] if you continue, and fall not
back upon the first broken shin,[25] I'll have ye
chronicled and chronicled, and cut,[26] and
chronicled, and all-to-be-prais'd and sung in

[20] Fearful for.   [21] Q₁ *fellowes.*
[22] So Q₁ ; Q₂ *et seq.,* um *or* 'em.
[23] So Q₁ ; Q₂ *et seq., my life.*
[24] *I.e.,* shopkeepers.
[25] Q₁ *skin.*   [26] Sculptured.

sonnets, and [bawl'd] [27] in new brave ballads, that all tongues shall troll you in *saecula saeculorum*, my kind can-carriers.

THRA. What if a toy [28] take 'em i' th' heels now, and they run all away, and cry, " The Devil take the hindmost "?   140

DION. Then the same Devil take the foremost too, and souse [29] him for his breakfast ! If they all prove cowards, my curses fly among them, and be speeding ! May they have murrains [30] reign to keep the gentlemen at home unbound [31] in easy frieze ! [32] May the moths branch [33] their velvets, and their silks only be worn before sore eyes ! [34] May their false lights [35] undo 'em, and discover presses,[36] holes, stains, and oldness in their stuffs, and [150 make them shop-rid ! May they keep whores and horses, and break ; [37] and live mewed up with necks of beef and turnips ! May they have many children, and none like the father ! May they know no language but that gibberish they prattle to their parcels, unless it be the goatish [38] Latin they write in their bonds — and may they write that false, and lose their debts !

Re-enter the KING.

KING. Now the vengeance of all the [160 gods confound them ! How they swarm together ! What a hum they raise ! — Devils choke your wild throats ! — If a man had need to use their valors, he must pay a brokage for it, and then bring 'em on, and they will fight like sheep. 'T is Philaster, none but Philaster, must allay this heat. They will not hear me speak, but fling dirt at me and call me tyrant. — Oh, run, dear friend, and bring the Lord Philaster ! Speak him fair ; call him [170 prince ; do him all the courtesy you can ; commend me to him. — Oh, my wits, my wits !

Exit CLEREMONT.

DION. [*aside*] Oh, my brave countrymen ! as I live, I will not buy a pin out of your walls [39] for this. Nay, you shall cozen me, and I 'll thank you, and send you brawn and bacon, and

soil [40] you ever[y] long vacation a brace of foremen,[41] that at Michaelmas shall come up fat and kicking.

KING. What they will do with this poor [180 prince, the gods know, and I fear.

DION. [*aside*] Why, sir, they 'll flay him, and make church-buckets [42] on 's skin, to quench rebellion ; then clap a rivet in 's sconce [43] and hang him up for [a] sign.

Enter CLEREMONT *with* PHILASTER.

KING. Oh, worthy sir, forgive me ! Do not make
Your miseries and my faults meet together,
To bring a greater danger. Be yourself,
Still sound amongst diseases. I have wrong'd you ;
And though I find it last, and beaten to it, [190
Let first your goodness know it. Calm the people,
And be what you were born to. Take your love,
And with her my repentance, all my wishes,
And all my prayers. By the gods, my heart speaks this ;
And if the least fall from me not perform'd,
May I be struck with thunder !

PHI.   Mighty sir,
I will not do your greatness so much wrong,
As not to make your word truth. Free the Princess
And the poor boy, and let me stand the shock
Of this mad sea-breach, which I 'll either turn,   200
Or perish with it.

KING.   Let your own word free them.

PHI. Then thus I take my leave, kissing your hand,
And hanging on your royal word. Be kingly,
And be not mov'd, sir. I shall bring [you] [44] peace
Or never bring myself back.

KING.   All the gods go with thee.

Exeunt omnes.

[SCENE IV] [45]

Enter an old Captain *and* Citizens *with* PHARAMOND.

CAP. Come, my brave myrmidons, let 's fall on.

Let [your] [46] caps swarm, my boys, and your
　　nimble tongues
Forget your mother gibberish of " What do
　　you lack ? "
And set your mouths [ope], [47] children, till
　　your palates
Fall frighted half a fathom past the cure
Of bay-salt and gross pepper, and then cry
" Philaster, brave Philaster ! " Let Philaster
Be deeper in request, my ding-dongs, [48]
My pairs of dear indentures, [49] kings of clubs, [49]
Than your cold-water-camlets, [50] or your paint-
　　ings 　　　　　　　　　　　　　　 10
Spitted with copper. [51] Let not your hasty
　　silks, [52]
Or your branch'd [53] cloth of bodkin, [54] or your
　　tissues,
Dearly beloved of spiced cake and custards,
[You] [55] Robin Hoods, Scarlets, and Johns, tie
　　your affections
In darkness to your shops. No, dainty
　　duckers, [56]
Up with your three-pil'd [57] spirits, your
　　wrought valors ; [58]
And let your uncut cholers [59] make the King
　　feel
The measure of your mightiness. Philaster !
Cry, my rose-nobles, [60] cry !
　　ALL. 　　　　　　　　 Philaster ! Philaster !
　　CAP. How do you like this, my Lord
　　　　Prince ? 　　　　　　　　　　　　 20
These are mad boys, I tell you ; these are
　　things
That will not strike their topsails to a foist, [61]
And let a man-of-war, an argosy, [62]

Hull [63] and cry cockles. [64]
　　PHA. Why, you rude slave, do you know
　　　　what you do ?
　　CAP. My pretty prince of puppets, we do
　　　　know ;
And give your Greatness warning that you talk
No more such bug's-words, [65] or that solder'd [66]
　　crown
Shall be scratch'd with a musket. [67] Dear
　　Prince Pippin,
Down with your noble blood, or, as I live, [30
I 'll have you coddled. [68] — Let him loose, my
　　spirits ;
Make us a round ring with your bills, [69] my
　　Hectors,
And let us see what this trim man dares do.
Now, sir, have at you ! here I lie ;
And with this [s]washing blow (do you see,
　　sweet Prince ?)
I could hulk [70] your Grace, and hang you up
　　cross-legg'd,
Like a hare at a poulter's, and do this with this
　　wiper. [71]
　　PHA. You will not see me murder'd, wicked
　　　　villains ?
　　1 CIT. Yes, indeed, will we, sir ; we have
　　　　not seen one
Fo[r] a great while.
　　CAP. 　　　　　　 He would have weapons,
　　　　would he ? 　　　　　　　　　　　 40
Give him a broadside, [72] my brave boys, with
　　your pikes ;
Branch me his skin in flowers like a satin,
And between every flower a mortal cut. —
Your royalty shall ravel ! [73] — Jag him, gentle-
　　men ;
I 'll have him cut to the kell, [74] then down the
　　seams.
O for a whip to make him galoon-laces ! [75]
I 'll have a coach-whip.

[46] So Q1; other old eds., *our.*
[47] So Q1; other old eds., *up.* 　　 [48] Darlings.
[49] *I.e.*, apprentices; the articles of each apprenticeship were set forth in a pair of indentures, and
their favorite weapon was the club.
[50] Wool and silk cloth watered; *i.e.*, given a
wavy pattern.
[51] "Painted or colored cloths interstitched with
copper." (Thorndike.)
[52] Flimsy silks stiffened with gum.
[53] Embroidered in a figured pattern.
[54] The richest of fabrics, cloth of gold and silk;
"bodkin" is a corruption of "baudkin."
[55] Emend. Theobald ; old eds., *Your.*
[56] Possibly, as Dyce thought, bowers and scrapers
(to customers) ; more probably, as Daniel notes,
in allusion to duck shooting, a great sport of the
citizens.
[57] The best velvet was "three-piled."
[58] Punning on "velures."
[59] Punning on "collars."
[60] Gold coins worth at this time about $4.00 each,
though originally less in value.
[61] A small pleasure boat or barge. The gilded
Pharamond is apparently meant.
[62] A large merchantman, but here evidently
with reference only to size. Philaster is apparently
meant by this and by "man-of-war."

[63] Lie drifting.
[64] Either (1) "be hanged" (according to Grose's
Dict. of the Vulgar Tongue), in which case we must
suppose that the metaphor changes abruptly ; or
(2) "engage in base traffic", suggested by the
reading of Q1: *Stoope to carry coales.*
[65] Hobgoblin's language ; *i.e.*, fearsome or inflated speech. 　　　　　　　　 [66] Patched.
[67] Editors profess to see a pun here on "musket" =
male sparrow-hawk.
[68] Stewed (like an apple). 　 [69] A kind of hooked pike.
[70] Disembowel. Q1 *hock.* 　 [71] Weapon.
[72] Not "spank him with the flat of your halberd"
(Schelling), but merely a jocose order to advance
the pikes and prick him. 　　　 [73] Be frayed.
[74] Caul ; here alluding to the membrane around
the deer's belly.
[75] Narrow, close-woven ribbon or braid used as
trimming ; *i.e.*, as Thorndike notes, "to cut him
into ribbons."

PHA.   Oh, spare me, gentlemen!
CAP. Hold, hold;
The man begins to fear and know himself.
He shall for this time only be seel'd up,[76] [50
With a feather through his nose, that he may
    only
See Heaven, and think whither he 's going,
Nay, my beyond-sea sir, we will proclaim you:
You would [77] be king!
Thou tender heir apparent to a church-ale,[78]
Thou slight prince of single [79] sarcenet,
Thou royal ring-tail,[80] fit to fly at nothing
But poor men's poultry, and have every
    boy
Beat thee from that too with his bread and
    butter![81]   59
    PHA. Gods keep me from these hell-hounds!
    1 CIT. Shall 's geld him, captain?
    CAP. No, you shall spare his dowcets, my
        dear donzels; [82]
As you respect the ladies, let them flourish.
The curses of a longing woman kills
As speedy as a plague, boys.
    1 CIT. I 'll have a leg, that 's certain.
    2 CIT.   I 'll have an arm.
    3 CIT. I 'll have his nose, and at mine own
        charge build
A college and clap 't upon the gate.[83]
    4 CIT. I 'll have his little gut to string a
        kit [84] with;
For certainly a royal gut will sound like
    silver.   70
    PHA. Would they were in thy belly, and I
        past
My pain once!
    5 CIT. Good captain, let me have his liver
        to feed ferrets.
    CAP. Who will have parcels else? Speak.
    PHA. Good gods, consider me! I shall be
        tortur'd.

---

[76] During a hawk's training its eyelids were sewed up with a fine thread; sometimes a small feather was used.   [77] Daniel suggests a hyphen.
[78] Festival at a parish church; such fêtes provided opportunities for licentious conduct; this line is as much as to call Pharamond a bastard.
[79] It also meant "foolish", "weak."—"Sarcenet" was a thin silk.
[80] An inferior member of the falcon family, "between hawk and buzzard."
[81] A boy who, eating bread and butter (a mere puling youngster), sees you attacking the poultry, can scare you off by flourishing his bread and butter at you, even if he hasn't a stick. Nothing could be a more pacific weapon. (Kittredge.)
[82] Alluding to Donzel del Phebo, hero of the Spanish romance translated into English as *The Mirror of Knighthood*; *i.e.*, young gentlemen.
[83] Alluding to Brasenose College, Oxford.
[84] A small fiddle.

1 CIT. Captain, I 'll give you the trimming
    of your two-[85]hand sword,
And let me have his skin to make false scab-
    bards.
    2 CIT. He had no horns, sir, had he?
    CAP. No, sir, he 's a pollard.[86]
What wouldst thou do with horns?
    2 CIT.   Oh, if he had had, [80
I would have made rare hafts and whistles of
    'em;
But his shin bones, if they be sound, shall serve
    me.

            Enter PHILASTER.

    ALL. Long live Philaster, the brave Prince
        Philaster!
    PHI. I thank you, gentlemen. But why are
        these
Rude weapons brought abroad, to teach your
    hands
Uncivil trades?
    CAP.   My royal Rosicleer,[87]
We are thy myrmidons, thy guard, thy roar-
    ers; [88]
And when thy noble body is in durance,
Thus do we clap our musty murrions [89]
    on,
And trace the streets in terror. Is it peace, [90
Thou Mars of men? Is the King sociable,
And bids thee live? Art thou above thy
    foemen,
And free as Phoebus? [90] Speak. If not, this
    stand [91]
Of royal blood shall be abroad, a-tilt,
And run even to the lees of honor.
    PHI. Hold, and be satisfied. I am myself;
Free as my thoughts are; by the gods, I am!
    CAP. Art thou the dainty darling of the
        King?
Art thou the Hylas to our Hercules?   99
Do the lords bow, and the regarded scarlets [92]
Kiss their gumm'd golls,[93] and cry, " We are
    your servants " ?
Is the court navigable and the presence stuck
With flags of friendship? If not, we are thy
    castle,
And this man sleeps.

---

[85] Only in Qq2, 3, where it is *2;* Q8 (cited by Boas), *second.*
[86] Hornless beast.
[87] Brother of Donzel del Phebo. See on l. 62.
[88] Bullies, "roaring boys."
[89] Steel caps, morions.
[90] Probably another allusion to the Knight of the Sun, Donzel del Phebo.
[91] Barrel; *i.e.*, Pharamond.
[92] Scarlet-clad courtiers, the cynosure of all.
[93] Perfumed hands.

PHI. I am what I do desire to be, your
friend;
I am what I was born to be, your prince.

PHA. Sir, there is some humanity in you;
You have a noble soul. Forget my name,
And know my misery; set me safe aboard
From these wild cannibals, and, as I live, [110
I 'll quit this land for ever. There is noth-
ing, —
Perpetual prisonment, cold, hunger, sickness
Of all sorts, of all dangers, and all together,
The worst company of the worst men, madness,
age,
To be as many creatures as a woman,
And do as all they do, nay, to despair, —
But I would rather make it a new nature,
And live with all these, than endure one hour
Amongst these wild dogs.

PHI. I do pity you. — Friends, discharge
your fears: 120
Deliver me the Prince. I 'll warrant you
I shall be old enough to find my safety.

3 CIT. Good sir, take heed he does not hurt
you;
He 's a fierce man, I can tell you, sir.

CAP. Prince, by your leave, I 'll have a sur-
cingle,[94]
And make [95] you like a hawk.

[PHARAMOND] strives.

PHI. Away, away, there is no danger in
him;
Alas, he had rather sleep to shake his fit off!
Look you, friends, how gently he leads! Upon
my word,
He 's tame enough, he need[s] no further
watching.[96]   130
Good my friends, go to your houses,
And by me have your pardons and my love;
And know there shall be nothing in my power
You may deserve, but you shall have your
wishes.
To give you more thanks were to flatter you.
Continue still your love; and, for an earnest,
Drink this.   *[Gives money.]*

ALL. Long mayst thou live, brave Prince,
brave Prince, brave Prince!

[Exeunt] PHILASTER *and* PHARAMOND.

CAP. Go thy ways; thou art the king of
courtesy!
Fall off again, my sweet youths. Come, [140
And every man trace to his house again,

And hang his pewter [97] up; then to the tavern,
And bring your wives in muffs.[98] We will
have music;
And the red grape shall make us dance and
rise, boys.   *Exeunt.*

Enter KING, ARETHUSA, GALATEA, MEGRA,
CLEREMONT, DION, THRASILINE, BELLARIO,
and Attendants.

KING. Is it appeas'd?

DION. Sir, all is quiet as this dead of night,
As peaceable as sleep. My Lord Philaster
Brings on the Prince himself.

KING.   Kind gentlem[a]n![100]
I will not break the least word I have given
In promise to him. I have heap'd a world
Of grief upon his head, which yet I hope
To wash away.

Enter PHILASTER *and* PHARAMOND.

CLE.   My Lord is come.

KING.   My son!
Blest be the time that I have leave to call
Such virtue mine! Now thou art in mine
arms,   10
Methinks I have a salve unto my breast
For all the stings that dwell there. Streams
of grief
That I have [wrong'd] [101] thee, and as much of
joy
That I repent it, issue from mine eyes;
Let them appease thee. Take thy right; take
her;
She is thy right too; and forget to urge
My vexed soul with that I did before.

PHI. Sir, it is blotted from my memory,
Past and forgotten. — For you, Prince of
Spain,
Whom I have thus redeem'd, you have full
leave   20
To make an honorable voyage home.
And if you would go furnish'd to your realm
With fair provision, I do see a lady,
Methinks, would gladly bear you company.
How like you this piece?

MEG.   Sir, he likes it well,
For he hath tried it, and hath found it worth
His princely liking. We were ta'en abed;
I know your meaning. I am not the first

---

[94] Belt, band; probably to prevent the hawk from
spreading wing.
[95] Train.
[96] Waking. One of the methods of taming hawks
was to keep them awake.

[97] Armor.   [98] Then a new fashion.
[99] Presumably a room or courtyard in the palace.
[100] Cor. Theobald; old eds. *gentlemen.*
[101] Cor. Theobald; old eds. *wrought.*

That nature taught to seek a fellow forth ;
Can shame remain perpetually in me,   30
And not in others?   Or have princes salves
To cure ill names, that meaner people want?

PHI. What mean you?

MEG.   You must get another ship,
To bear the Princess and her boy together.

DION. How now !

MEG. Others took me, and I took her and
him
At that all women may be ta'en sometime.
Ship us all four, my Lord ; we can endure
Weather and wind alike.

KING. Clear thou thyself, or know not me
for father.   40

ARE. This earth, how false it is ! What
means is left for me
To clear myself?   It lies in your belief.
My Lords, believe me ; and let all things else
Struggle together to dishonor me.

BEL. Oh, stop your ears, great King, that I
may speak
As freedom would !   Then I will call this lady
As base as are her actions. Hear me, sir ;
Believe your heated blood when it rebels
Against your reason, sooner than this lady.

MEG. By this good light, he bears it handsomely.   50

PHI. This lady !   I will sooner trust the
wind
With feathers, or the troubled sea with pearl,
Than her with anything.   Believe her not.
Why, think you, if I did believe her words,
I would outlive 'em ? — Honor cannot take
Revenge on you ; then what were to be known
But death?

KING.   Forget her, sir, since all is knit
Between us.   But I must request of you
One favor, and will sadly [102] be denied.

PHI. Command, whate'er it be.

KING.   Swear to be true [60
To what you promise.

PHI.   By the Powers above,
Let it not be the death of her or him,
And it is granted !

KING.   Bear away that boy
To torture ; I will have her clear'd or buried.

PHI. Oh, let me call my word back, worthy
sir !
Ask something else ; bury my life and right
In one poor grave ; but do not take away
My life and fame at once.

KING. Away with him !   It stands irrev-
ocable.

[102] It will be a grievous matter if I am denied.

PHI. Turn all your eyes on me.   Here
stands a man,   70
The falsest and the basest of this world.
Set swords against this breast, some honest
man,
For I have liv'd till I am pitied !
My former deeds were hateful ; but this last
Is pitiful, for I unwillingly
Have given the dear preserver of my life
Unto his torture.   Is it in the power
Of flesh and blood to carry this, and live?
                       Offers to kill himself.

ARE. Dear sir, be patient yet ! Oh, stay
that hand !

KING. Sirs, strip that boy.

DION.   Come, sir ; your tender flesh [80
Will [try] [103] your constancy.

BEL.   Oh, kill me, gentlemen !

DION. No. — Help, sirs.

BEL.   Will you torture me?

KING.   Haste there ;
Why stay you?

BEL.   Then I shall not break my vow,
You know, just gods, though I discover all.

KING. How 's that?   Will he confess?

DION.   Sir, so he says.

KING. Speak then.

BEL.   Great King, if you command
This lord to talk with me alone, my tongue,
Urg'd by my heart, shall utter all the thoughts
My youth hath known ; and stranger thing [104]
than these
You hear not often.

KING.   Walk aside with him. [90
       [DION *and* BELLARIO *walk apart.*]

DION. Why speak'st thou not?

BEL.   Know you this face, my Lord?

DION. No.

BEL. Have you not seen it, nor the like?

DION. Yes, I have seen the like, but readily
I know not where.

BEL.   I have been often told
In court of one Euphrasia, a lady,
And daughter to you ; betwixt whom and
me
They that would flatter my bad face would
swear
There was such strange resemblance, that we
two
Could not be known asunder, dress'd alike.

DION. By Heaven, and so there is !

BEL.   For her fair sake, [100
Who now doth spend the springtime of her life

[103] Q [2] *tire.*
[104] So Harvard copy of Q [2] ; later Qq and F [2] *things.*

In holy pilgrimage, move to the King,
That I may scape this torture.

DION.   But thou speak'st
As like Euphrasia as thou dost look.
How came it to thy knowledge that she lives
In pilgrimage?

BEL.   I know it not, my Lord ;
But I have heard it, and do scarce believe it.

DION. Oh, my shame ! is 't possible?
Draw near,
That I may gaze upon thee.   Art thou she,
Or else her murderer? [105]   Where wert thou
born?   110

BEL. In Syracusa.

DION.   What's thy name?

BEL.   Euphrasia.

DION. Oh, 't is just ; [106] 't is she !
Now I do know thee.   Oh, that thou hadst
died,
And I had never seen thee nor my shame !
How shall I own thee?   Shall this tongue of
mine
E'er call thee daughter more?

BEL. Would I had died indeed !   I wish it
too ;
And so I must have done by vow, ere publish'd
What I have told, but that there was no means
To hide it longer.   Yet I joy in this: 120
The Princess is all clear.

KING.   What, have you done?

DION. All 's discovered.

PHI.   Why then hold you me?
All is discovered !   Pray you, let me go.
                         He offers to stab himself.

KING. Stay him.

ARE.   What is discovered?

DION.   Why, my shame.
It is a woman ; let her speak the rest.

PHI. How?   That again !

DION.   It is a woman.

PHI. Bless'd be you powers that favor innocence !

KING. Lay hold upon that lady.
                         [MEGRA *is seized.*]

PHI. It is a woman, sir ! — Hark, gentle-
men,
It is a woman ! — Arethusa, take   130
My soul into thy breast, that would be gone
With joy.   It is a woman !   Thou art fair,
And virtuous still to ages, in despite
Of malice.

KING.   Speak you, where lies his shame?

BEL. I am his daughter.

PHI.   The gods are just.

DION. I dare accuse none ; but, before you
two,
The virtue of our age, I bend my knee
For mercy.

PHI.   Take it freely ; for I know,
Though what thou didst were undiscreetly
done,
'T was meant well.

ARE.   And for me, I have a power [140
To pardon sins, as oft as any man
Has power to wrong me.

CLE.   Noble and worthy !

PHI.   But, Bellario,
(For I must call thee still so,) tell me why
Thou didst conceal thy sex.   It was a fault,
A fault, Bellario, though thy other deeds
Of truth outweigh'd it ; all these jealousies [107]
Had flown to nothing if thou hadst discovered
What now we know.

BEL.   My father oft would speak
Your worth and virtue ; and, as I did grow
More and more apprehensive, [108] I did thirst [150
To see the man so rais'd. [109]   But yet all this
Was but a maiden longing, to be lost
As soon as found ; till, sitting in my window,
Printing my thoughts in lawn, I saw a god,
I thought, (but it was you,) enter our gates.
My blood flew out and back again, as fast
As I had puff'd it forth and suck'd it in
Like breath.   Then was I call'd away in haste
To entertain you.   Never was a man,   159
Heav'd from a sheepcote to a sceptre, rais'd
So high in thoughts as I.   You left a kiss [110]
Upon these lips then, which I mean to keep
From you for ever.   I did hear you talk,
Far above singing.   After you were gone,
I grew acquainted with my heart, and search'd
What stirr'd it so ; alas, I found it love !
Yet far from lust ; for, could I but have liv'd
In presence of you, I had had my end.
For this I did delude my noble father
With a feign'd pilgrimage, and dress'd myself
In habit of a boy ; and, for I knew   171
My birth no match for you, I was past hope
Of having you ; and, understanding well
That when I made discovery of my sex
I could not stay with you, I made a vow,
By all the most religious things a maid

---

[105] "It was the received opinion in some barbarous countries that the murderer was to inherit the qualities and shape of the person he destroyed." (Mason.)
[106] Accurate.

[107] Suspicions.
[108] Capable of understanding.
[109] Ed. 1711 and mod. eds. *prais'd.*
[110] In those times not necessarily more significant than shaking hands.

Could call together, never to be known,
Whilst there was hope to hide me from men's
    eyes,
For other than I seem'd, that I might ever
Abide with you.   Then sat I by the fount,   [180
Where first you took me up.
    KING.   Search out a match
Within our kingdom, where and when thou
    wilt,
And I will pay thy dowry ; and thyself
Wilt well deserve him.
    BEL.   Never, sir, will I
Marry ; it is a thing within my vow ;
But, if I may have leave to serve the Princess,
To see the virtues of her lord and her,
I shall have hope to live.
    ARE.   I, Philaster,
Cannot be jealous, though you had a lady
Dress'd like a page to serve you ; nor will I   [190
Suspect her living here. — Come, live with
    me ;
Live free as I do.   She that loves my lord,
Curs'd be the wife that hates her !
    PHI. I grieve such virtue should be laid in
        earth
Without an heir. — Hear me, my royal father :

Wrong not the freedom of our souls so much,
To think to take revenge of that base woman ;
Her malice cannot hurt us.   Set her free
As she was born, saving from shame and sin.
    KING. Set her at liberty. — But leave the
        court ;   200
This is no place for such. — You, Pharamond,
Shall have free passage, and a conduct home
Worthy so great a prince.   When you come
        there,
Remember 't was your faults that lost you her,
And not my purpos'd will.
    PHA.   I do confess,
Renowned sir.
    KING. Last, join your hands in one. Enjoy,
        Philaster,
This kingdom, which is yours, and, after me,
Whatever I call mine.   My blessing on you !
All happy hours be at your marriage joys,
That you may grow yourselves over all
        lands,   211
And li[v]e to see your plenteous branches spring
Wherever there is sun ! — Let princes learn
By this to rule the passions of their blood ;
For what Heaven wills can never be withstood.
                            Exeunt omnes.

The Maids Tragedie.

AS IT HATH BEENE

diuers times Acted at the *Black-Friers* by
the Kings Maiesties Seruants.

Newly perufed, augmented, and inlarged, This fecond Impreffion.

ASPATIA. AMINTOR.

LONDON,

Printed for *Francis Conftable*, and are
to befold at the White LION in
Pauls Church-yard. 1622.

INTRODUCTORY NOTE

FEW plays in the London repertory achieved the popularity that *The Maid's Tragedy* held throughout the reigns of the Stuarts. Originally acted by the King's Men, it was speedily revived under the Restoration. Hart and Mohun of the new King's Men were celebrated as Amintor and Melantius; and, after the union of the companies in 1682, Thomas Betterton, the most eminent actor of the period, found in the latter one of his greatest rôles. Though it is probable that his performance of several of Shakespeare's heroes has never been surpassed, Betterton chose Melantius for his famous farewell appearance in 1710.

The play has obvious faults, but its power is undeniable. Largely written by the author of *The Knight of the Burning Pestle*, it must none the less be accepted as a sincerely romantic drama, beside which the most exuberant tragedies of Shakespeare's maturity seem almost severely realistic. We miss the Shakesperean care for the integrity of human character, which is here occasionally sacrificed to a theatrical exploitation of situation; but the play tells an absorbing story, contains several confrontation scenes that offer a tragic actor the fullest scope for his art, and is composed in a style of remarkable vigor and, at times, great beauty.

Whether or not *The Maid's Tragedy* was written before *Philaster* we have no means of knowing. It antedates October 31, 1611, when a *Second Maiden's Tragedy*, a play in MS, was so entitled and licensed by Sir George Buck, the Master of the Revels. It was acted at court in 1612–1613. No source for the plot is known. Beaumont's share is supposed to be the greater in this play; Fletcher's hand seems more evident in IV, i, and in V, i, ii, and iii.

The First Quarto, of 1619, presents an inferior text, which is evidently the result of cutting and unauthorized tampering. As in the case of *Philaster*, however, some of its readings are pretty clearly more authentic than variants in the Second Quarto, of 1622, on which, with a few corrections from the other Quartos and the Folio of 1679, the present text is based. The other Quartos appeared in 1630 (with the first ascription of the play to Beaumont and Fletcher), 1638, 1641, 1650, 1661, 1686, 1704, and 1717. It was edited for the Bullen *Variorum* by P. A. Daniel (1904), and with *Philaster* by A. H. Thorndike (1906).

THE MAID'S TRAGEDY

BY

FRANCIS BEAUMONT AND JOHN FLETCHER

SPEAKERS

KING.
LYSIPPUS, brother to the King.
AMINTOR, [a noble gentleman.] [1]
MELANTIUS, } brothers to Evadne.
DIPHILUS,
CALIANAX, an old humorous lord, and father to Aspatia.
CLEON, } gentlemen.
STRATO,
DIAGORAS, a servant.

[Lords, Gentlemen, Servants, etc.]

EVADNE, wife to Amintor.
ASPATIA, troth-plight wife to Amintor.
ANTIPHILA, } waiting gentlewomen to Aspatia.
OLYMPIAS,
DULA, a lady, [attendant on Evadne.]
[Ladies.]

MASQUERS: Night, Cynthia, Neptune, Aeolus, [Sea Gods, Winds].

[THE SCENE — *Rhodes.*]

ACT I — SCENE I [2]

Enter CLEON, STRATO, LYSIPPUS, [*and*] DIPHILUS.

CLE. The rest are making ready, sir.
[LYS.] [3] So let them; there 's time enough.
DIPH. You are the brother to the King, my Lord;
We 'll take your word.
LYS. Strato, thou hast some skill in poetry;
What think'st [thou] [4] of a [5] masque? Will it be well?
STRA. As well as masques can be.
LYS.   As masques can be!
STRA. Yes; they must commend their king, and speak in praise
Of the assembly, bless the bride and bride-groom
In person of some god; they 're tied to rules
Of flattery.
CLE.   See, good my Lord, who is return'd!   11

Enter MELANTIUS.

LYS. Noble Melantius, the land by me
Welcomes thy virtues home to Rhodes;

Thou that with blood abroad buyest our peace!
The breath of kings is like the breath of gods;
My brother wish'd thee here, and thou art here.
He will be too kind, and weary thee
With often welcomes; but the time doth give thee
A welcome above his or all the world's.
MEL. My Lord, my thanks; but these scratch'd limbs of mine   20
Have spoke my love and truth unto my friends,
More than my tongue e'er could. My mind's the same
It [6] ever was to you; where I find worth,
I love the keeper till he let it go,
And then I follow it.
DIPH.   Hail, worthy Brother!
He that rejoices not at your return
In safety is mine enemy for ever.
MEL. I thank thee, Diphilus. But thou art faulty;
I sent for thee to exercise thine arms
With me at Patria; [7] thou cam'st not, Diphilus;   30
'T was ill.

[1] Add. Q₃.   [2] A room in the palace.
[3] So Q₁; other old eds. *Stra.*   [4] Om. Qq₂₋₄.
[5] Mod. eds. unnecessarily emend. to *the.*
[6] Thus far old eds. print scene as prose. Further departures of the present text in rearrangement of lines will not be noted; in general Dyce is followed.
[7] Probably Patras or Patrae, a port in the Morea.

841

DIPH.   My noble Brother, my excuse
Is my King's strict command, which you, my
     Lord,
Can witness with me.
     LYS.   'T is [most] [8] true, Melantius ;
He might not come till the solemnitie[s] [8]
Of this great match were past.
     DIPH.   Have you heard of it?
     MEL. Yes, [and] [9] have given cause to those
          that [here] [10]
Envy my deeds abroad to call me gamesome :
I have no other business here at Rhodes.
     LYS. We have a masque to-night, and you
          must tread
A soldier's measure.[11]   40
     MEL. These soft and silken wars are not
          for me ;
The music must be shrill and all confus'd
That stirs my blood, and then I dance with
     arms.
But is Amintor wed?
     DIPH.   This day.
     MEL. All joys upon him ! for he is my
          friend.
Wonder not that I call a man so young my
     friend :
His worth is great ; valiant he is and temper-
     ate ;
And one that never thinks his life his own,
If his friend need it. When he was a boy,
As oft as I return'd (as, without boast,   50
I brought home conquest), he would gaze
     upon me
And view me round, to find in what one limb
The virtue [12] lay to do those things he heard ;
Then would he wish to see my sword, and feel
The quickness [13] of the edge, and in his hand
Weigh it. He oft would make me smile at
     this.
His youth did promise much, and his ripe years
Will see it all perform'd. —

Enter ASPATIA, *passing by.*

                         Hail, maid and wife !
Thou fair Aspatia, may the holy knot
That thou hast tied to-day last till the hand
Of age undo 't ! Mayst thou bring a race [61
Unto Amintor that may fill the world
Successively with soldiers !
     ASP.   My hard fortunes
Deserve not scorn, for I was never proud
When they were good.   *Exit* ASPATIA.

     MEL.   How 's this?
     LYS.   You are mistaken, for
She is not married.
     MEL.   You said Amintor was.
     DIPH. 'T is true ; but ——
     MEL.   Pardon me ; I did receive
Letters at Patria from my Amintor,
That he should marry her.
     DIPH.   And so it stood
In all opinion long ; but your arrival   70
Made me imagine you had heard the change.
     MEL. Who hath he taken then?
     LYS.   A lady, sir,
That bears the light [above] [14] her, and strikes
     dead
With flashes of her eye : the fair Evadne,
Your virtuous sister.
     MEL.   Peace of heart betwixt them !
But this is strange.
     LYS.   The King, my brother, did it
To honor you ; and these solemnities
Are at his charge.
     MEL. 'T is royal, like himself. But I am
     sad
My speech bears so unfortunate a sound   80
To beautiful Aspatia.   There is rage
Hid in her father's breast, Calianax,
Bent long against me ; and he should not
     think,
If I could call it back, that I would take
So base revenges as to scorn the state
Of his neglected daughter.   Holds he still
His greatness with the King?
     LYS.   Yes. But this lady
Walks discontented, with her wat'ry eyes
Bent on the earth.   The unfrequented woods
Are her delight ; and when she sees a bank [90
Stuck full of flowers, she with a sigh will tell
Her servants what a pretty place it were
To bury lovers in, and make her maids
Pluck 'em and strow her over like a corse.
She carries with her an infectious grief,
That strikes all her beholders ; she will sing
The mournfull'st things that ever ear hath
     heard,
And sigh, and sing again ; and when the rest
Of our young ladies, in their wanton blood,[15]
Tell mirthful tales in course,[16] that fill the
     room   100
With laughter, she will, with so sad a look,
Bring forth a story of the silent death
Of some forsaken virgin, which her grief

---

[8] Only in Q[1].
[10] Only in Q[1].
[12] Power.

[9] So Q[1]; other old eds. *I.*
[11] A stately dance.
[13] Keenness.

[14] Probably = surpasses. (Dyce.) So all the old
eds. except Q[2], which reads *about.* Cf. l. 138.
[15] In a playful frame of mind.   [16] In turn.

Will put in such a phrase that, ere she end,
She 'll send them weeping one by one away.

MEL. She has a brother under my command,[17]
Like her, a face as womanish as hers,
But with a spirit that hath much outgrown
The number of his years.

Enter AMINTOR.

CLE. My Lord [18] the bridegroom!

MEL. I might run fiercely, not more hastily, 110
Upon my foe. I love thee well, Amintor;
My mouth is much too narrow for my heart;
I joy to look upon those eyes of thine;
Thou art my friend, but my disordered speech
Cuts off my love.

AMIN. Thou art Melantius;
All love is spoke in that. — A sacrifice,
To thank the gods Melantius is return'd
In safety! — Victory sits on his sword,
As she was wont. May she build there and dwell;
And may thy armor be, as it hath been, 120
Only thy valor and thine innocence!
What endless treasures would our enemies give,
That I might hold thee still [19] thus!

MEL. I am poor
In words; but credit me, young man, thy mother
Could [do] [20] no more but weep for joy to see thee
After long absence. All the wounds I have [21]
Fetch'd not so much away, nor all the cries
Of widowed mothers. But this is peace,
And that was war.

AMIN. Pardon, thou holy god
Of marriage bed, and frown not, I am forc'd, 131
In answer of such noble tears as those,
To weep upon my wedding day!

MEL. I fear thou art grown too fickle; for I hear
A lady mourns for thee, men say, to death,
Forsaken of thee, on what terms [22] I know not.

AMIN. She had my promise; but the King forbade it,
And made me make this worthy change, thy sister,
Accompanied with graces [above] [23] her;

With whom I long to lose my lusty youth
And grow old in her arms.

MEL. Be prosperous! [140

Enter Messenger.

MESS. My Lord, the masquers rage for you.

LYS. We are gone. —
Cleon, Strato, Diphilus!

AMIN. We 'll all attend you. —
[*Exeunt* LYSIPPUS, CLEON, STRATO,
DIPHILUS] [24] [*and* Messenger].[25]
We shall trouble you
With our solemnities.

MEL. Not so, Amintor;
But if you laugh at my rude carriage
In peace, I 'll do as much for you in war,
When you come thither. Yet I have a mistress
To bring to your delights; rough though I am,
I have a mistress, and she has a heart [149
She says; but, trust me, it is stone, no better;
There is no place that I can challenge [in 't].[26]
But you stand still, and here my way lies.
[*Exeunt.*]

[SCENE II] [27]

Enter CALIANAX *with* DIAGORAS.

CAL. Diagoras, look to the doors better, for shame! You let in all the world, and anon the King will rail at me. — Why, very well said.[28] By Jove, the King will have the show i' th' court!

DIAG. Why do you swear so, my Lord? You know he 'll have it here.

CAL. By this light, if he be wise, he will not.

DIAG. And if he will not be wise, you are forsworn. 10

CAL. One may [sweat] [29] his heart out with swearing, and get thanks on no side. I 'll be gone, look to 't who will.

DIAG. My Lord, I shall never keep them out. Pray, stay; your looks will terrify them.

CAL. My looks terrify them, you coxcombly [30] ass, you! I 'll be judge[d] by all the company whether thou hast not a worse face than I. 20

DIAG. I mean, because they know you and your office.

---

[17] Cf. V, iii, 42. [18] Unpunctuated in old eds.
[19] Ever. [20] Q1 only.
[21] Daniel emends to *gave.*
[22] Under what circumstances.
[23] So Q3 *et seq.;* Qq1, 2, *about;* emend. Theobald *far above,*

[24] Q1 only. [25] Om. old eds.
[26] Add. Q3. [27] Another room.
[28] Good for you, well done.
[29] So Q1; later Qq *sweare;* F *weare.*
[30] Silly.

CAL. Office! [31] I would I could put it off! I am sure I sweat quite through my office.[32] I might have made room at my daughter's wedding; — they ha' near kill'd her amongst them; and now I must do service for him that hath forsaken her. Serve that will!

Exit CALIANAX.

DIAG. He's so humorous [33] since his daughter was forsaken! (*Knock within.*) Hark, [30 hark! there, there! so, so! codes, codes! [34] What now?

MEL. (*within*) Open the door.

DIAG. Who's there?

MEL. [*within*] Melantius.

DIAG. I hope your Lordship brings no troop with you; for, if you do, I must return them.[35] [*Opens the door.*]

Enter MELANTIUS *and a* Lady.

MEL. None but this lady, sir.

DIAG. The ladies are all plac'd above, [40 save those that come in the King's troop; the best of Rhodes sit there, and there's room.

MEL. I thank you, sir. — When I have seen you placed, madam, I must attend the King; but, the masque done, I'll wait on you again.

DIAG. [*opening another door*] Stand back there! — Room for my Lord Melantius! [*Exit* MELANTIUS (*with*) Lady, (*at*) *other door.*] [36] — Pray, bear back — this is no place for [50 such youth and their trulls [37] — let the doors shut again. — Ay, do your heads itch? I'll scratch [38] them for you. [*Shuts the door.*] — So, now thrust and hang. [*Knocking within.*] — Again! who is't now? — I cannot blame my Lord Calianax for going away; would he were here! He would run raging amongst them, and break a dozen wiser heads than his own [39] in the twinkling of an eye. — What's the news now? 60

Within. I pray you, can you help me to the speech of the master-cook?

DIAG. If I open the door, I'll cook some of your calves heads. Peace, rogues! [*Knocking within.*] — Again! who is't?

MEL. (*within*) Melantius.

Re-enter CALIANAX *to* MELANTIUS.

CAL. Let him not in.

DIAG. O, my Lord, 'a must. [*Opens the door.*] — Make room there for my Lord. — Is your lady plac'd? 70

[*Re-enter* MELANTIUS.] [40]

MEL. Yes, sir. I thank you. — My Lord Calianax, well met. Your causeless hate to me I hope is buried.

CAL. Yes, I do service for your sister here, That brings mine own poor child to timeless [41] death. She loves your friend Amintor, such another False-hearted lord as you.

MEL.   You do me wrong, A most unmanly one, and I am slow In taking vengeance; but be well advis'd.

CAL. It may be so. — Who plac'd the lady there 80 So near the presence of the King?

MEL.   I did.

CAL. My Lord, she must not sit there.

MEL.   Why?

CAL. The place is kept for women of more worth.

MEL. More worth than she! It misbecomes your age And place to be thus womanish; forbear! What you have spoke I am content to think The palsy shook your tongue to.

CAL.   Why, 't is well, If I stand here to place men's wenches.

MEL.   I Shall [quite] [42] forget this place, thy age, my safety, And, through [43] all, cut that poor sickly week Thou hast to live away from thee. 91

CAL. Nay, I know you can fight for your whore.

MEL. Bate [44] the King, and, be he flesh and blood, 'A lies that says it! Thy mother at fifteen Was black and sinful to her.

DIAG.   Good my Lord —

MEL. Some god pluck threescore years from that fond man, That I may kill him, and not stain mine honor! It is the curse of soldiers, that in peace

---

[31] "The syllable *off* reminds the testy statesman of his robe, and he carries on the image." (Coleridge, cited by Dyce.)
[32] Official robe.   [33] Temperamental.
[34] Probably a corruption of "God's." An "ejaculation of surprise, no doubt originally profane." (Skeat and Mayhew.)
[35] Turn them back.
[36] Only in Q₁; words in parentheses added by Editor.
[37] Wenches.   [38] *I.e.*, strike, crack.
[39] Weber notes that at a court masque in 1633 Lord Pembroke broke his staff of office over the shoulders of Thomas May, the poet.

[40] Q₁ only.   [41] Untimely.   [42] Only in Q₁.
[43] Dissyllabic.   [44] Bar, except.

They shall be braved by such ignoble men
As, if the land were troubled, would with tears
And knees beg succor from 'em. Would that blood, 101
That sea of blood, that I have lost in fight,
Were running in thy veins, that it might make thee
Apt to say less, or able to maintain
Shouldst thou say more! — This Rhodes, I see, is nought
But a place privileg'd to do men wrong.
　Cal. Ay, you may say your pleasure.

Enter Amintor.

　Amin.　　　　　　What vild injury
Has stirr'd my worthy friend, who is as slow
To fight with words as he is quick of hand?
　Mel. That heap of age, which I should reverence 110
If it were temperate; but testy years
Are most contemptible.
　Amin.　　　　　Good sir, forbear.
　Cal. There is just such another as yourself.
　Amin. He will wrong you, or me, or any man,
And talk as if he had no life to lose,
Since this our match. The King is coming in;
I would not for more wealth than I enjoy
He should perceive you raging. He did hear
You were at difference now, which hast'ned him.　*Hautboys play within.*
　Cal. Make room there! 120

Enter King, Evadne, Aspatia, Lords, *and* Ladies.

　King. Melantius, thou art welcome, and my love
Is with thee still; but this is not a place
To brabble [45] in. — Calianax, join hands.
　Cal. He shall not have mine hand.
　King.　　　　　This is no time
To force you to 't. I do love you both : —
Calianax, you look well to your office; —
And you, Melantius, are welcome home.
Begin the masque.
　Mel. Sister, I joy to see you and your choice;
You look'd with my eyes when you took that man. 130
Be happy in him!　*Recorders [46] [play].*
　Evad.　　　Oh, my dearest Brother,
Your presence is more joyful than this day
Can be unto me.

[45] Brawl.　　　　[46] Flageolets.

Night *rises in mists.* [47]

　Night. Our reign is come; for in the raging [48] sea
The sun is drown'd, and with him fell the Day.
Bright Cynthia, hear my voice! I am the Night,
For whom thou bear'st about thy borrowed light.
Appear! no longer thy pale visage shroud,
But strike thy silver horns quite through a cloud,
And send a beam upon my swarthy face,
By which I may discover all the place
And persons, and how many longing eyes
Are come to wait on our solemnities. 10

Enter Cynthia.

How dull and black am I! I could not find
This beauty [49] without thee, I am so blind:
Methinks they show like to those eastern streaks
That warn us hence before the morning breaks.
Back, my pale servant! for these eyes know how
To shoot far more and quicker rays than thou.
　Cynth. Great Queen, they be a troop for whom alone
One of my clearest moons I have put on;
A troop that looks as if thyself and I
Had pluck'd our reins in and our whips laid by, 20
To gaze upon these mortals, that appear
Brighter than we.
　Night.　　　Then let us keep 'em here,
And never more our chariots drive away,
But hold our places and outshine the Day.
　Cynth. Great Queen of shadows, you are pleas'd to speak
Of more than may be done. We may not break
The gods' decrees; but, when our time is come,
Must drive away, and give the Day our room.
Yet, whilst our reign lasts, let us stretch our power,
To give our servants one contented hour, 30
With such unwonted solemn grace and state
As may forever after force them hate

[47] Perhaps represented by dancers.
[48] Q₁ *quenching.*
[49] With a gesture toward the ladies of the audience

Our brother's glorious beams, and wi[s]h [50]
   the Night
Crown'd with a thousand stars and our cold
   light ;
For almost all the world their service bend
To Phoebus, and in vain my light I lend,
Gaz'd on unto my setting from my rise
Almost of none but of unquiet eyes.
   NIGHT.   Then shine at full, fair Queen, and
    by thy power
Produce a birth, to crown this happy hour, [40]
Of nymphs and shepherds ; let their songs
   discover,
Easy and sweet, who is a happy lover ;
Or, if thou woo 't,[51] then call thine own Endy-
   mion
From the sweet flow'ry bed [52] he lies upon,
On Latmus' [53] top,[54] thy pale beams drawn
   away,
And of [his] [55] long night let him make this [56]
   day.
   CYNTH.   Thou dream'st, dark Queen ; that
    fair boy was not mine,
Nor went I down to kiss him.   Ease and wine
Have bred these bold tales ; poets, when they
   rage,[57]
Turn gods to men, and make an hour an age.
But I will give a greater state and glory, [51]
And raise to time a [nobler] [58] memory
Of what these lovers are. — Rise, rise, I say,
Thou power of deeps, thy surges laid away,
Neptune, great king of waters, and by me
Be proud to be commanded !

         NEPTUNE *rises.*

   NEPT.   Cynthia, see,
Thy word hath fetch'd me hither ; let me
   know
Why I ascend.
   CYNTH.   Doth this majestic show
Give thee no knowledge yet?
   NEPT.   Yes, now I see
Something intended, Cynthia, worthy thee.
Go on ; I 'll be a helper.
   CYNTH.   Hie thee, then,   61
And charge the Wind go [59] from his rocky den,
Let loose his subjects ; only Boreas,
Too foul for our intentions as he was,
Still keep him fast chain'd : we must have
   none here

But vernal blasts and gentle winds appear,
Such as blow flowers, and through the glad
   boughs sing
Many soft welcomes to the lusty spring ;
These are our music.   Next, thy wat'ry race
Bring on in couples we are pleas'd to grace [70
This noble night, each in their richest things
Your own deeps or the broken vessel brings.
Be prodigal, and I shall be as kind
And shine at full upon you.
   NEPT.   Oh, the Wind ! [60]
Commanding Aeolus !

      Enter AEOLUS *out of a rock.*

   AEOL.   Great Neptune !
   NEPT.   He.
   AEOL.   What is thy will?
   NEPT.   We do command thee free
Favonius and thy milder winds, to wait
Upon our Cynthia ; but tie Boreas strait : [61]
He 's too rebellious.
   AEOL.   I shall do it. [*Exit* AEOLUS.]
   NEPT.   Do.
[AEOL., *within.*] Great master of the flood
   and all below,   80
Thy full command has taken. —— Oh, the
   Main !
Neptune !
   NEPT.   Here.

[*Re-enter* AEOLUS, *followed by* FAVONIUS *and
     other* Winds.]

   AEOL.   Boreas has broke his chain,
And, struggling with the rest, has got away.
   NEPT.   Let him alone, I 'll take him up at
    sea ;
He [62] will not long be thence.   Go once
   again,
And call out of the bottoms of the main
Blue [63] Proteus and the rest ; charge them
   put on
Their greatest pearls, and the most sparkling
   stone
The beaten [64] rock breeds : [tell] [65] this night
   is done
By me a solemn honor to the Moon :   90
Fly, like a full sail.
   AEOL.   I am gone.   [*Exit.*]
   CYNTH.   Dark Night,
Strike a full silence, do a thorough right
To this great chorus, that our music may

---

[50] Wish for.   [51] Wilt. Q₁ omits *then call.*
[52] Q₁ *banck.*
[53] The mountain in Caria, the scene of the myth.
[54] Q₁ *brow.*   [55] So Q₁ ; other old eds. *this.*
[56] Q₁ *thy;* Q₃ *et seq., a.*   [57] In their poetic fury.
[58] Trisyllabic. So Q₁ ; other old eds. *noble.*
[59] Q₃ *et seq., fly.*

[60] No punctuation in old eds. ; Theobald supplies
a hyphen, perhaps rightly.
  [61] Tight.   [62] Q₁ *I.*
  [63] For he is sea-god. (Thorndike.)
  [64] Sea-beaten.   [65] Cor. Mason ; old eds. *till.*

Touch high as Heaven, and make the east
　　break day
At midnight.　　　　　　　　　　　*Music.*

[FIRST] SONG

[During which PROTEUS *and other* Sea-deities *enter.]*

Cynthia, to thy power and thee
　　　　We obey.
Joy to this great company!
　　　　And no day
Come to steal this night away,　　　　100
　　Till the rites of love are ended,
And the lusty bridegroom say,
　　"Welcome, light, of all befriended!"

Pace out, you watery powers below;
　　　　Let your feet,
Like the galleys when they row,
　　　　Even beat.
Let your unknown measures, set
　　To the still winds, tell to all
That gods are come, immortal, great,　　110
　　To honor this great nuptial.
　　　　　　　The Measure.[66]

SECOND SONG

Hold back thy hours, dark Night, till we have done;
　　The Day will come too soon;
Young maids will curse thee, if thou steal'st away,
And leav'st their [losses] [67] open to the day;
　　Stay, stay, and hide
　　The blushes of the bride.

Stay, gentle Night, and with thy darkness cover
　　The kisses of her lover;
Stay, and confound her tears and her shrill cryings,
Her weak denials, vows, and often-dyings;　　121
　　Stay, and hide all;
　　But help not, though she call.

NEPT. Great Queen of us and Heaven,
　　hear what I bring
To make this hour a full one.[68]
CYNTH.　　　　　　　　Speak, sea's King.
NEPT. Thy tunes my Amphitrite joys to
　　have,
When [she] [69] will dance upon the rising
　　wave,
And court me as [s]he sails. My Tritons,
　　play
Music to [lay] [70] a storm! I 'll lead the way.
　　[Masquers dance; NEPTUNE *leads it.]* [71]

THIRD SONG

To bed, to bed! Come, Hymen, lead the bride, 130
And lay her by her husband's side;
　　Bring in the virgins every one,
　　That grieve to lie alone,

That they may kiss while they may say a maid;
To-morrow 't will be other kiss'd and said.
　　Hesperus, be long a-shining,
　　Whilst these lovers are a-twining.

AEOL. *[within]* Ho, Neptune!
NEPT.　　　　　　　　　　　　Aeolus!

[Re-enter AEOLUS.]

AEOL.　　　　　　　　　The sea goes high,
Boreas hath rais'd a storm: go and apply
Thy trident; else, I prophesy, ere day　　140
Many a tall ship will be cast away.
Descend with all the [72] gods and all their
　　power,
To strike a calm.
CYNTH.　　　　　　　　[We thank you for this hour:
My favor to you all.] [73]　　To gratulate
So great a service, done at my desire,
Ye shall have many floods, fuller and higher
Than you have wish'd for; [and] [74] no ebb
　　shall dare
To let the Day see where your dwellings are.
Now back unto your government in haste,
Lest your proud charge [75] should swell above
　　the waste,[76]　　150
And win upon the island.
NEPT.　　　　　　　　　　We obey.
　　NEPTUNE *descends and the* Sea-
　　　gods. *[Exeunt* FAVONIUS *and
　　　other* Winds.]
CYNTH. Hold up thy head, dead Night;
　　seest thou not Day?
The east begins to lighten. I must down,
And give my brother place.
NIGHT.　　　　　　　　　　Oh, I could frown
To see the Day, the Day that flings his light
Upon my kingdoms and contemns old Night!
Let him go on and flame! I hope to see
Another wildfire in his axletree,[77]
And all fall drench'd.[78] But I forget. —
　　Speak, Queen:
The Day grows on; I must no more be
　　seen.　　160
CYNTH. Heave up thy drowsy head again
　　and see
A greater light, a greater majesty,
Between our [set] [79] and us! Whip up thy
　　team;

---

[66] A stately dance.
[67] So Q₁; other old eds. *blushes.*
[68] Q₂ *et seq.* add *if not her measure,* which is probably, as Fleay suggests, a misprinted stage direction, *Another measure.*
[69] Emend. Seward; old eds. *they.*
[70] Emend. Heath; old eds. *lead.*
[71] After the second song Q₁ has this stage direction and proceeds with l. 138, omitting what intervenes. Other old eds. *Measure.*

[72] Theobald emends *thy,* perhaps rightly.
[73] So Q₁; other old eds. *A thanks to every one, and.*
[74] Q₁ only.
[75] Q₁ *waters.*
[76] Ocean; *i.e.,* its bed.
[77] Alluding to the myth of Phaethon.
[78] Drowned.
[79] Setting, the west. Emend. Seward; old eds. *sect.*

The Day breaks here, and yon same flashing
　　stream [80]
Shot from the south. Say, which way wilt
　　thou go?

NIGHT. I'll vanish into mists.

CYNTH. 　　　　　　　　I into Day.

　　　　　Exeunt [NIGHT *and* CYNTHIA].

　　　　　Finis Masque.

KING. Take lights there!—Ladies, get
　　the bride to bed.—
We will not see you laid; good night, Amin-
　　tor;
We'll ease you of that tedious ceremony.
Were it my case, I should think time run
　　slow.
If thou beest noble, youth, get me a boy, [171
That may defend my kingdoms from my
　　foes.

AMIN. All happiness to you!

KING. 　　　　　　Good night, Melantius.
　　　　　　　　　　　　　Exeunt.

ACT II — [SCENE I] [1]

Enter EVADNE, ASPATIA, DULA, *and other*
Ladies.

DULA. Madam, shall we undress you for
　　this fight?
The wars are nak'd that you must make
　　to-night.

EVAD. You are very merry, Dula.

DULA. 　　　　　　　　I should be
Far merrier, madam, if it were with me
As it is with you.

[EVAD. 　　　　How's that?

DULA. 　　　　　　　That I might go
To bed with him wi' th' credit that you do.] [2]

EVAD. Why, how now, wench?

DULA. 　　　Come, ladies, will you help?

EVAD. I am soon undone.

DULA. 　　　　　　And as soon done;
Good store of clothes will trouble you at both.

EVAD. Art thou drunk, Dula?

DULA. 　　　Why, here's none but we. [10

EVAD. Thou think'st belike there is no
　　modesty
When we are alone.

DULA. Ay, by my troth, you hit my
　　thoughts aright.

EVAD. You prick me, lady.

1 LADY. 　　　　　　'T is against my will.

DULA. Anon you must endure more and
　　lie still;
You're [3] best to practise.

EVAD. 　　　Sure, this wench is mad.

DULA. No, faith, this is a trick that I have
　　had
Since I was fourteen.

EVAD. 　　　　'T is high time to leave it.

DULA. Nay, now I'll keep it till the trick
　　leave me.
A dozen wanton words put in your head [20
Will make you livelier in your husband's bed.

EVAD. Nay, faith, then take it. [4]

DULA. 　　　Take it, madam! Where?
We all, I hope, will take it that are here.

EVAD. Nay, then I'll give you o'er.

DULA. 　　　　　　So will I make
The ablest man in Rhodes, or his heart ache.

EVAD. Wilt take [5] my place to-night?

DULA. 　　　　　I'll hold your cards
Against any two I know.

EVAD. 　　　　　What wilt thou do?

DULA. Madam, we'll do't, and make 'em
　　leave play too.

EVAD. Aspatia, take her part.

DULA. 　　　　　I will refuse it: [29
She will pluck down a side; [6] she does not
　　use it.

EVAD. Why, do, [I prithee.] [7]

DULA. 　　　　You will find the play
Quickly, because your head lies well that way.

EVAD. I thank thee, Dula. Would thou
　　couldst instil
Some of thy mirth into Aspatia!
Nothing but sad thoughts in her breast do
　　dwell;
Methinks, a mean betwixt you would do well.

DULA. She is in love; hang me, if I were
　　so,
But I could run my country. [8] I love too
To do those things that people in love do.

ASP. It were a timeless [9] smile should prove
　　my cheek. 　　　　　　　　　　40

---

[80] Ray. These lines are another compliment to
the brilliance of the audience, though the ostensible
object of the flattery is the King of the play. "Behold a greater light and majesty than the sun,
intervening between us and the west. The day
breaks, not in the east, but in the south, as a consequence of the beams which emanate from our
audience." Q₁ *yon sun-flaring stream.*
　　[1] An anteroom to Evadne's chamber.
　　[2] Q₁ only.

[3] You were.
[4] Take the trick, as in cards. Antithetical to l. 18.
[5] Q₁ *lie in.*　　　[6] Cause the loss of the game.
[7] Q₁ only.
[8] Drive my country at a hot pace. (Thorndike.)
[9] Untimely.

It were a fitter hour for me to laugh,
When at the altar the religious priest
Were pacifying the offended powers
With sacrifice, than now. This should have been
My [rite]; [10] and all your hands have been employ'd
In giving me a spotless offering
To young Amintor's bed, as we are now
For you. — Pardon, Evadne; would my worth
Were great as yours, or that the King, or he,
Or both, thought so! Perhaps he found me worthless;   50
But till he did so, in these ears of mine,
These credulous ears, he pour'd the sweetest words
That art or love could frame. If he were false,
Pardon it, Heaven! and, if I did want
Virtue, you safely may forgive that too;
For I have lost none that I had from you.
     EVAD. Nay, leave this sad talk, madam.
     ASP.   Would I could!
Then I should leave the cause.
     EVAD. See, if you have not spoil'd all Dula's mirth!
     ASP. Thou think'st thy heart hard; but, if thou beest caught,   60
Remember me; thou shalt perceive a fire
Shot suddenly into thee.
     DULA.   That's not so good;
Let 'em shoot anything but fire, I fear 'em not.
     ASP. Well, wench, thou mayst be taken.
     EVAD. Ladies, good night; I'll do the rest myself.
     DULA. Nay, let your Lord do some.
     ASP. [*singing*]

     Lay a garland on my hearse
       Of the dismal yew —

     EVAD. That's one of your sad songs, madam.
     ASP. Believe me, 't is a very pretty one. [70
     EVAD. How is it, madam?
     ASP.

             SONG

     Lay a garland on my hearse
       Of the dismal yew;
     Maidens, willow branches bear;
       Say I died true.
     My love was false, but I was firm
       From my hour of birth;
     Upon my buried body lay [11]
       Lightly, gentle earth!

     EVAD. Fie on 't, madam! The words are so strange, they   80

Are able to make one dream of hobgoblins. —
" I could never have the power " — sing that, Dula.
     DULA. [*singing*]

     I could never have the power
     To love one above an hour,
     But my heart would prompt mine eye
     On some other man to fly.
       Venus, fix mine eyes fast,
       Or, if not, give me all that I shall see at last!

     EVAD. So; leave me now.
     DULA. Nay, we must see you laid.   90
     ASP. Madam, good night. May all the marriage joys
That longing maids imagine in their beds
Prove so unto you! May no discontent
Grow 'twixt your love and you! but, if there do,
Inquire of me, and I will guide your moan;
And [12] teach you an artificial [13] way to grieve,
To keep your sorrow waking. Love your lord
No worse than I; but, if you love so well,
Alas, you may displease him! so did I.
This is the last time you shall look on me. —
Ladies, farewell. As soon as I am dead, [101
Come all and watch one night about my hearse;
Bring each a mournful story and a tear,
To offer at it when I go to earth;
With flattering ivy clasp my coffin round;
Write on my brow my fortune; let my bier
Be borne by virgins, that shall sing by course [14]
The truth of maids and perjuries of men.
     EVAD. Alas, I pity thee.
     OMNES. Madam, good night.
                     Exit EVADNE.
     1 LADY. Come, we'll let in the bridegroom.
     DULA.   Where's my Lord? [110
     1 LADY. Here, take this light.

           Enter AMINTOR.

     DULA.   You'll find her in the dark.
     1 LADY. Your lady's scarce abed yet; you must help her.
     ASP. Go, and be happy in your lady's love.
May all the wrongs that you have done to me
Be utterly forgotten in my death!
I'll trouble you no more; yet I will take
A parting kiss, and will not be denied.
                [*Kisses* AMINTOR.]
You'll come, my Lord, and see the virgins weep
When I am laid in earth, though you yourself
Can know no pity. Thus I wind myself [120

---

[10] So Dyce; Q₁ *right;* other old eds. *night.*
[11] Lie, and so the mod. eds. read.

[12] Om. Q₃ *et seq.*   [13] Skillful, ingenious.
[14] By turns.

Into this willow garland,[15] and am prouder
That I was once your love, though now refus'd,
Than to have had another true to me.
So with [my][16] prayers I leave you, and must try
Some yet unpractis'd way to grieve and die.

                           Exit ASPATIA.

    DULA. Come, ladies, will you go?
    OMNES.   Good night, my Lord.
    AMIN. Much happiness unto you all!

                           Exeunt Ladies.

I did that lady wrong. Methinks I feel
Her [17] grief shoot suddenly through all my
    veins;
Mine eyes run; [18] this is strange at such a
    time.   130
It was the King first mov'd me to't; but he
Has not my will in keeping. Why do I
Perplex myself thus? Something whispers
    me,
" Go not to bed." My guilt is not so great
As mine own conscience, too sensible,[19]
Would make me think; I only brake a
    promise,
And 't was the King that forc'd me. Timor-
    ous flesh,
Why shak'st thou so? Away, my idle fears!

          Re-enter EVADNE.

Yonder she is, the lustre of whose eye
Can blot away the sad remembrance [20]   140
Of all these things. — Oh, my Evadne, spare
That tender body; let it not take cold!
The vapors of the night will [21] not fall here.
To bed, my love; Hymen will punish us
For being slack performers of his rites.
Cam'st thou to call me?
    EVAD.   No.
    AMIN.   Come, come, my love,
And let us lose ourselves to one another.
Why art thou up so long?
    EVAD.   I am not well.
    AMIN. To bed then; let me wind thee in
    these arms
Till I have banish'd sickness.
    EVAD.   Good my Lord, [150
I cannot sleep.
    AMIN.   Evadne,[22] we 'll watch; [23]
I mean no sleeping.
    EVAD.   I 'll not go to bed.
    AMIN. I prithee, do.
    EVAD.   I will not for the world.

    AMIN. Why, my dear love?
    EVAD.   Why! I have sworn I will not.
    AMIN. Sworn!
    EVAD.   Ay!
    AMIN.   How? Sworn, Evadne!
    EVAD. Yes, sworn, Amintor; and will
    swear again,
If you will wish to hear me.
    AMIN. To whom have you sworn this?
    EVAD. If I should name him, the matter
    were not great.
    AMIN. Come, this is but the coyness of a
    bride.   160
    EVAD. The coyness of a bride!
    AMIN.   How prettily
That frown becomes thee!
    EVAD.   Do you like it so?
    AMIN. Thou canst not dress thy face in such
    a look
But I shall like it.
    EVAD.   What look likes you [24] best?
    AMIN. Why do you ask?
    EVAD. That I may show you one less pleas-
    ing to you.
    AMIN. How 's that?
    EVAD. That I may show you one less pleas-
    ing to you.
    AMIN. I prithee, put thy jests in milder
    looks;
It shows as thou wert angry.
    EVAD.   So perhaps [170
I am indeed.
    AMIN.   Why, who has done thee wrong?
Name me the man, and by thyself I swear,
Thy yet unconquered self, I will revenge thee!
    EVAD. Now I shall try thy truth. If thou
    dost love me,
Thou weigh'st not anything compar'd with me:
Life, honor, joys eternal, all delights
This world can yield, or hopeful people feign,
Or in the life to come, are light as air
To a true lover when his lady frowns,
And bids him, " Do this." Wilt thou kill this
    man?   [180
Swear, my Amintor, and I 'll kiss the sin
Off from thy lips.
    AMIN.   I wo' [25] not swear, sweet love,
Till I do know the cause.
    EVAD.   I would thou wouldst.
Why, it is thou that wrong'st me; I hate thee;
Thou shouldst have kill'd thyself.
    AMIN. If I should know that, I should
    quickly kill
The man you hated.

---

[15] Symbol of rejected love.   [16] Add Q₃.
[17] Q₁ *A*.   [18] Q₁ *raine*.   [19] Sensitive.
[20] Quadrisyllabic.   [21] Q₁ *shall*.
[22] Practically trisyllabic here.   [23] Stay awake.

[24] Is pleasing to you.   [25] Will.

EVAD.   Know it, then, and do 't.

AMIN. Oh, no ! what look soe'er thou shalt
     put on
To try my faith, I shall not think thee false ;
I cannot find one blemish in thy face,   190
Where falsehood should abide. Leave,[26] and
     to bed.
If you have sworn to any of the virgins
That were your old companions, to preserve
Your maidenhead a night, it may be done
Without this means.

EVAD.   A maidenhead, Amintor,
At my years !

AMIN.   Sure she raves ; — this cannot be
[Her] [27] natural temper. — Shall I call thy
     maids ?
Either thy healthful sleep hath left thee long,
Or else some fever rages in thy blood.

EVAD. Neither, Amintor ; think you I am
     mad,   200
Because I speak the truth ?

AMIN.   [Is this the truth ?] [28]
Will you not lie with me to-night ?

EVAD.   To-night !
You talk as if [you thought] [28] I would here-
     after.

AMIN. Hereafter ! yes, I do.

EVAD.   You are deceiv'd.
Put off amazement, and with patience mark
What I shall utter, for the oracle
Knows nothing truer. 'T is not for a night
Or two that I forbear thy bed, but ever.

AMIN. I dream. Awake, Amintor !

EVAD.   You hear right ;
I sooner will find out the beds of snakes, [210
And with my youthful blood warm their cold
     flesh,
Letting them curl themselves about my limbs,
Than sleep one night with thee. This is not
     feign'd,
Nor sounds it like the coyness of a bride.

AMIN. Is flesh so earthly to endure all this ?
Are these the joys of marriage ? Hymen, keep
This story, that will make succeeding youth
Neglect thy ceremonies, from all ears ;
Let it not rise up, for thy shame and mine
To after ages ; we will scorn thy laws,   220
If thou no better bless them. Touch the heart
Of her that thou hast sent me, or the world
Shall know ; there's not an altar that will
     smoke
In praise of thee ; we will adopt us sons ;

Then virtue shall inherit, and not blood.[29]
If we do lust, we 'll take the next we meet,
Serving ourselves as other creatures do ;
And never take note of the female more,
Nor of her issue. — I do rage in vain ;   229
She can but jest. — Oh, pardon me, my love !
So dear the thoughts are that I hold of thee,
That I must break forth. Satisfy my fear ;
It is a pain, beyond the hand of death,
To be in doubt. Confirm it with an oath,
If this be true.

EVAD.   Do you invent the form ;
Let there be in it all the binding words
Devils and conjurers can put together,
And I will take it. I have sworn before,
And here by all things holy do again,
Never to be acquainted with thy bed !   240
Is your doubt over now ?

AMIN. I know too much ; would I had
     doubted still !
Was ever such a marriage night as this ! —
You Powers above, if you did ever mean
Man should be us'd thus, you have thought a
     way
How he may bear himself, and save his honor :
Instruct me in it ; for to my dull eyes
There is no mean, no moderate course to run :
I must live scorn'd, or be a murderer ;
Is there a third ? — Why is this night so calm ?
Why does not Heaven speak in thunder to
     us,   251
And drown her voice ?

EVAD.   This rage will do no good.

AMIN. Evadne, hear me. Thou hast ta'en
     an oath,
But such a rash one that to keep it were
Worse than to swear it. Call it back to thee ;
Such vows as those never ascend the Heaven ;
A tear or two will wash it quite away.
Have mercy on my youth, my hopeful youth,
If thou be pitiful ! for, without boast,
This land was proud of me. What lady was
     there,   260
That men call'd fair and virtuous in this isle,
That would have shunn'd my love ? It is in
     thee
To make me hold this worth. Oh, we vain
     men,
That trust [30] all our reputation
To rest upon the weak and yielding hand
Of feeble woman ! But thou art not stone ;
Thy flesh is soft, and in thine eyes do[th] dwell
The spirit of love ; thy heart cannot be hard.
Come, lead me from the bottom of despair

---

[26] Leave off, stop this.
[27] So Q1 ; other old eds. *Thy.*
[28] Q1 only.
[29] Blood-relationship.   [30] Q2 *et seq.* add *out.*

To all the joys thou hast; I know thou wilt;
And make me careful lest the sudden
  change   271
O'ercome my spirits.
        EVAD.   When I call back this oath,
The pains of hell environ me!
    AMIN. I sleep, and am too temperate.
        Come to bed!
Or by those hairs, which, if thou ha[d]st a soul
Like to thy locks, were threads for kings to
    wear
About their arms ——
        EVAD.   Why, so perhaps they are.
    AMIN. I'll drag thee to my bed, and make
        thy tongue
Undo this wicked oath, or on thy flesh
I'll print a thousand wounds to let out life! [280
    EVAD. I fear thee not; do what thou dar'st
        to me!
Every ill-sounding word or threat'ning look
Thou showest to me will be reveng'd at full.
    AMIN. It will not, sure, Evadne?
    EVAD. Do not you hazard that.
    AMIN.   Ha' ye your champions?
    EVAD. Alas, Amintor, think'st thou I for-
        bear
To sleep with thee because I have put on
A maiden's strictness? Look upon these
    cheeks,
And thou shalt find the hot and rising blood
Unapt for such a vow. No; in this heart [290
There dwells as much desire and as much will
To put that wish'd act in practice as ever yet
Was known to woman; and they have been
    shown
Both. But it was the folly of thy youth
To think this beauty, to what [hand] [31] soe'er
It shall be call'd, shall stoop to any second.
I do enjoy the best, and in that height
Have sworn to stand or die. You guess the
    man.
    AMIN. No; let me know the man that
        wrongs me so,
That I may cut his body into motes,   300
And scatter it before the northern wind.
    EVAD. You dare not strike him.
    AMIN.   Do not wrong me so.
Yes, if his body were a poisonous plant
That it were death to touch, I have a soul
Will throw me on him.
    EVAD.   Why, 't is the King.
    AMIN.   The King!

    EVAD. What will you do now?
    AMIN.   'T is not the King!
    EVAD. What did he make this match for,
        dull Amintor?
    AMIN. Oh, thou hast nam'd a word that
        wipes away
All thoughts revengeful! In that sacred
    name,
"The King," there lies a terror. What frail
    man   310
Dares lift his hand against it? Let the gods
Speak to him when they please; till when, let
    us
Suffer and wait.
    EVAD. Why should you fill yourself so full
        of heat,
And haste so to my bed? I am no virgin.
    AMIN. What devil put it in thy fancy, then,
To marry me?
    EVAD.   Alas, I must have one
To father children, and to bear the name
Of husband to me, that my sin may be   [319
More honorable!
    AMIN.   What a strange thing am I!
    EVAD. A miserable one; one that myself
Am sorry for.
    AMIN.   Why, show it then in this:
If thou hast pity, though thy love be none,
Kill me; and all true lovers, that shall live
In after ages cross'd in their desires
Shall bless thy memory, and call thee good,
Because such mercy in thy heart was found,
To rid [32] a ling'ring wretch.
    EVAD.   I must have one
To fill thy room again, if thou wert dead;
Else, by this night, I would! I pity thee. [330
    AMIN. These strange and sudden injuries
        have fall'n
So thick upon me that I lose all sense
Of what they are. Methinks I am not
    wrong'd;
Nor is it aught, if from the censuring world
I can but hide it. Reputation,
Thou art a word, no more! — But thou hast
    shown
An impudence so high, that to the world
I fear thou wilt betray or shame thyself.
    EVAD. To cover shame, I took thee; never
        fear
That I would blaze [33] myself.
    AMIN.   Nor let the King [340
Know I conceive he wrongs me; then mine
    honor

---

[31] Cor. Bullen; old eds. *land*. The figure is from
hawking; note *stoop* in the next line, and *height* in
the next.

[32] Dispatch.
[33] Blazon, proclaim, publish.

Will thrust me into action ; that [34] my flesh
Could bear with patience.　And it is some ease
To me in these extremes, that I know this
Before I touch'd thee ; else, had all the sins
Of mankind stood betwixt me and the King,
I had gone through 'em to his heart and thine.
I have lost one desire : 't is not his crown
Shall buy me to thy bed, now I resolve [35]
He has dishonor'd thee.　Give me thy hand ;
Be careful of thy credit, and sin close ; [36]　[351
'T is all I wish.　Upon thy chamber floor
I 'll rest to-night, that morning visitors
May think we did as married people use ;
And, prithee, smile upon me when they come,
And seem to toy, as if thou hadst been pleased
With what we did.

　　EVAD.　　　　　Fear not ; I will do this.
　　AMIN. Come, let us practise ; and, as
　　　　wantonly
As ever loving bride and bridegroom met,
Let 's laugh and enter here.

　　EVAD.　　　　　I am content. [360
　　AMIN. Down all the swellings of my
　　　　troubled heart !
When we walk thus entwin'd, let all eyes see
If ever lovers better did agree.　　　*Exeunt.*

　　　　　　[SCENE II] [37]

Enter ASPATIA, ANTIPHILA, [*and*] OLYMPIAS.

　　ASP. Away, you are not sad ! force it no
　　　　further.
Good gods, how well you look !　Such a full
　　　color
Young bashful brides put on ; sure, you are
　　　new married !
　　ANT. Yes, madam, to your grief.
　　ASP.　　　　　Alas, poor wenches !
Go learn to love first ; learn to lose yourselves ;
Learn to be flattered, and believe and bless
The double tongue that did it ; make a faith
Out of the miracles of ancient lovers,
Such as spake [38] truth and died in 't ; and, like
　　me,
Believe all faithful, and be miserable.　　10
Did you ne'er love yet, wenches ?　Speak,
　　Olympias ; [39]
Thou hast an easy temper, fit for stamp.
　　OLYM. Never.

[34] The situation, given that concealment (expressed
in ll. 340, 341).
[35] Am convinced.　　　　[36] Secretly.
[37] Aspatia's apartment.
[38] Modernized by Theobald ; old eds. *speake*, pronounced "spake."
[39] This line was transposed by Theobald from its
place in the old eds., where it follows l. 8 (Q₁ l. 7).

　　ASP.　　　　　Nor you, Antiphila ?
　　ANT.　　　　　Nor I.
　　ASP. Then, my good girls, be more than
　　　　women, wise ;
At least be more than I was ; and be sure
You credit anything the light gives life to,
Before a man.　Rather believe the sea
Weeps for the ruin'd merchant, when he roars ;
Rather, the wind courts but the pregnant sails,
When the strong cordage cracks ; rather, the
　　sun　　　　　　　　　　　　　　　20
Comes but to kiss the fruit in wealthy autumn,
When all falls blasted.　If you needs must
　　love,
Forc'd by ill fate, take to your maiden bosoms
Two dead-cold aspics, [40] and of them make
　　lovers.
They cannot flatter nor forswear ; one kiss
Makes a long peace for all.　But man —
Oh, that beast man !　Come, let 's be sad, my
　　girls :
That downcast of thine eye, Olympias,
Shows a fine sorrow. — Mark, Antiphila ; [29
Just such another was the nymph Oenone's
When Paris brought home Helen. — Now, a
　　tear ;
And then thou art a piece expressing fully
The Carthage queen, [41] when from a cold sea-
　　rock,
Full with her sorrow, she tied fast her eyes
To the fair Trojan ships ; and, having lost
　　them,
Just as thine does, down stole a tear. — An-
　　tiphila,
What would this wench do, if she were
　　Aspatia ?
Here she would stand, till some more pitying
　　god
Turn'd her to marble ! — 'T is enough, my
　　wench !
Show me the piece of needlework you wrought.
　　ANT. Of Ariadne, [42] madam ?
　　ASP.　　　　　Yes, that piece. — [41
This should be Theseus ; h' as a cozening [43]
　　face. —
You meant him for a man ?
　　ANT.　　　　　He was so, madam.
　　ASP. Why, then, 't is well enough. — Never
　　　　look back ;
You have a full wind and a false heart, The-
　　seus. —
Does not the story say his keel was split,

[40] Asps.　　　　　[41] Dido.
[42] Whom Theseus deserted.
[43] Cheating, deceitful.

Or his masts spent, or some kind rock or other
Met with his vessel?

ANT.   Not as I remember.

ASP. It should ha' been so.   Could the gods
    know this,

And not, of all their number, raise a storm? [50
But they are all as ill. — This false smile
Was well express'd; just such another caught
    me. —
You shall not go so.[44] —
Antiphila, in this place work a quicksand,
And over it a shallow, smiling water,
And his ship ploughing it; and then a Fear:
Do that Fear to the life, wench.

ANT.   'T will wrong the story.

ASP. 'T will make the story, wrong'd by
    wanton poets,
Live long and be believ'd.   But where's the
    lady?

ANT. There, madam.

ASP.   Fie, you have miss'd it here,
    Antiphila;   60
You are much mistaken, wench.
These colors are not dull and pale enough
To show a soul so full of misery
As this sad lady's was.   Do it by me,[45]
Do it again by me, the lost Aspatia;
And you shall find all true but the wild island.[46]
I stand upon the sea-breach now, and think[47]
Mine arms thus, and mine hair blown with
    the wind,
Wild as that desert; and let all about me
Tell that I am forsaken.   Do my face,   70
If thou hadst ever feeling of a sorrow,
Thus, thus, Antiphila; strive to make me look
Like Sorrow's monument; and the trees about
    me,
Let them be dry and leafless; let the rocks
Groan with continual surges; and behind me,
Make all a desolation.   Look, look, wenches,
A miserable life[48] of this poor picture!

OLYM. Dear madam!

ASP.   I have done.   Sit down; and let us
Upon that point fix all our eyes, that point there.
Make a dumb[49] silence, till you feel a sudden
    sadness   80
Give us new souls.

Enter CALIANAX

CAL. The King may do this, and he may not
    do it;

My child is wrong'd, disgrac'd. — Well, how
    now, huswives?[50]
What, at your ease!   Is this a time to sit
    still?
Up, you young lazy whores, up, or I'll swinge
    you!

OLYM. Nay, good my Lord —

CAL. You'll lie down shortly.   Get you in,
    and work!
What, are you grown so resty[51] you want
    heats?
We shall have some of the court boys do that
    office.[52]

ANT. My Lord, we do no more than we are
    charg'd;   90
It is the lady's pleasure we be thus
In grief[53] she is forsaken.

CAL.   There's a rogue[54] too,
A young dissembling slave! — Well, get you
    in. —
I'll have a bout with that boy.   'T is high
    time
Now to be valiant; I confess my youth
Was never prone that way.   What, made an
    ass!
A court stale![55]   Well, I will be valiant,
And beat some dozen of these whelps; I
    will!
And there's another of 'em, a trim, cheating
    soldier;[56]
I'll maul that rascal; h' as out-brav'd me
    twice;   100
But now, I thank the gods, I am valiant. —
Go, get you in. — I'll take a course with all.

                 Exeunt omnes.

ACT III — [SCENE I] [1]

Enter CLEON, STRATO, [*and*] DIPHILUS.

CLE. Your sister is not up yet.

DIPH. Oh, brides must take their morning's
rest; the night is troublesome.

STRA. But not tedious.

DIPH. What odds he has not my sister's
maidenhead to-night?

STRA. No; it's odds against any bridegroom living, he ne'er gets it while he lives.

---

[44] Addressed to Theseus in the needlework.
[45] *I.e.,* use me as a model.
[46] Naxos, where Theseus abandoned Ariadne.
[47] Q₁ *Suppose I . . . now.*   [48] Living example.
[49] Q₃ *et seq., dull.*

[50] Hussies.
[51] Inert, sluggish; comparing them "to lazy,
resty mares, that want to be rid so many heats."
(Theobald.)
[52] Q₁ *heat you shortly.*   [53] That, because.
[54] Amintor.   [55] Laughing stock.   [56] Melantius.
[1] The anteroom to Evadne's chamber.

DIPH. Y' are merry with my sister ; you 'll please to allow me the same freedom with [10 your mother.

STRA. She 's at your service.

DIPH. Then she 's merry enough of herself ; she needs no tickling. Knock at the door.

STRA. We shall interrupt them.

DIPH. No matter ; they have the year before them. —
Good morrow, Sister. Spare yourself to-day ;
The night will come again.

Enter AMINTOR.

AMIN. Who 's there ? My brother ! I am no readier [2] yet.   20
Your sister is but now up.

DIPH. You look as you had lost your eyes to-night :
I think you ha' not slept.

AMIN.   I' faith I have not.

DIPH. You have done better, then.

AMIN. We ventured for a boy ; when he is twelve,
'A shall command against the foes of Rhodes.
Shall we be merry ?

STRA. You cannot ; you want sleep.

AMIN.   'T is true. — (*aside*) But she,
As if she had drank Lethe, or had made
Even with Heaven, did fetch so still a sleep, [30
So sweet and sound —

DIPH.   What 's that ?

AMIN.   Your sister frets
This morning, and does turn her eyes upon me
As people on their headsman. She does chafe,
And kiss, and chafe again, and clap my cheeks ;
She 's in another world.

DIPH. Then I had lost ; I was about to lay [3]
You had not got her maidenhead to-night.

AMIN. [*aside*] Ha ! he does [4] not mock me ?
y 'ad lost indeed ;
I do not use [5] to bungle.

CLEO.   You do deserve her.

AMIN. (*aside*) I laid my lips to hers, and that wild breath,   40
That was so rude and rough to me last night,
Was sweet as April. I 'll be guilty too,
If these be the effects.

Enter MELANTIUS.

MEL. Good day, Amintor ; for to me the name
Of brother is too distant : we are friends,
And that is nearer.

AMIN.   Dear Melantius !
Let me behold thee. Is it possible ?

MEL. What sudden gaze is this ?

AMIN.   'T is wondrous strange !

MEL. Why does thine eye desire so strict a view
Of that it knows so well ? There 's nothing here   50
That is not thine.

AMIN.   I wonder much, Melantius,
To see those noble looks, that make me think
How virtuous thou art ; and, on the sudden,
'T is strange to me thou shouldst have worth and honor,
Or not be base and false and treacherous
And every ill. But ——

MEL.   Stay, stay, my friend ,
I fear this sound will not become our loves.
No more ; [6] embrace me.

AMIN.   Oh, mistake me not !
I know thee to be full of all those deeds   59
That we frail men call good ; but by the course
Of nature thou shouldst be as quickly chang'd
As are the winds ; dissembling as the sea,
That now wears brows as smooth as virgins' be,
Tempting the merchant [7] to invade his face,
And in an hour calls his billows up,
And shoots 'em at the sun, destroying all
'A carries on him. — (*aside*) Oh, how near am I
To utter my sick thoughts.

MEL. But why, my friend, should I be so by nature ?

AMIN. I have wed thy sister, who hath virtuous thoughts   70
Enough for one whole family ; and it is strange
That you should feel no want.

MEL. Believe me, this is compliment too cunning for me.

DIPH. What should I be then by the course of nature,
They having both robb'd me of so much virtue ?

STRA. Oh, call the bride, my Lord Amintor,
That we may see her blush, and turn her eyes down.
It is the prettiest sport !

AMIN. Evadne !

EVAD. (*within*)   My Lord ?

AMIN.   Come forth, my love ;
Your brothers do attend to wish you joy. [80

EVAD. [*within*] I am not ready [8] yet.

AMIN.   Enough, enough.

---

[2] No more dressed.   [3] Bet.
[4] Q1 *does he.*   [5] It is not my habit.
[6] F2 has a comma here, Qq no point at all.
[7] Merchantman.   [8] Dressed.

Evad. [*within*] They 'll mock me.

Amin.   Faith, thou shalt come in.

Enter Evadne.

Mel. Good morrow, Sister. He that understands

Whom you have wed, need not to wish you joy ;

You have enough : take heed you be not proud.

Diph. Oh, Sister, what have you done?

Evad. I done ! why, what have I done?

Stra. My Lord Amintor swears you are no maid now.

Evad. Push ! [9]

Stra. I' faith, he does.

Evad.   I knew I should be mock'd. [90

Diph. With a truth.

Evad.   If 't were to do again,

In faith I would not marry.

Amin. (*aside*) Nor I, by Heaven !

Diph.   Sister, Dula swears

She heard you cry two rooms off.

Evad.   Fie, how you talk !

Diph. Let 's see you walk.

Evad.   By my troth, y 'are spoil'd. [10]

Mel.   Amintor. —

Amin. Ha !

Mel.   Thou art sad.

Amin.   Who, I ? I thank you for that.

Shall Diphilus, thou, and I, sing a catch?

Mel. How !

Amin. Prithee, let 's.   99

Mel. Nay, that 's too much the other way.

Amin. I 'm so light'ned with my happiness ! —

How dost thou, love? Kiss me.

Evad. I cannot love you ; you tell tales of me.

Amin. Nothing but what becomes us. — Gentlemen,

Would you had all such wives, and all the world,

That I might be no wonder ! Y' are all sad :

What, do you envy me? I walk, methinks,

On water, and ne'er sink, I am so light.

Mel. 'T is well you are so.

Amin.   Well ! how can I be other,

When she looks thus? — Is there no music there?   110

Let 's dance.

---

[9] Pish.
[10] Some mod. eds. add this to Diphilus's speech, and make a vocative out of *Evadne*. Metrical arrangement here is present Editor's and confirms reading of old texts.

Mel.   Why this is strange, Amintor !

Amin. I do not know myself ; yet I could wish

My joy were less.

Diph. I 'll marry too, if it will make one thus.

Evad. (*aside*) Amintor, hark.

Amin. What says my love? — I must obey.

Evad. You do it scurvily, 't will be perceiv'd.

Cleo. My Lord, the King is here.

Enter King *and* Lysippus.

Amin. Where?

Stra. And his brother.   120

King. Good morrow, all ! —

Amintor, joy on joy fall thick upon thee ! —

And, madam, you are alter'd since I saw you ;

I must salute you ; you are now another's.

How lik'd you your night's rest?

Evad.   Ill, sir.

Amin.   Indeed,

She took but little.

Lys.   You 'll let her take more,

And thank her too, shortly.

King. Amintor, wert thou truly honest [11] till

Thou wert married?

Amin.   Yes, sir.

King.   Tell me, then, how shows

The sport unto thee?

Amin.   Why, well.

King.   What did you do?

Amin. No more, nor less, than other couples use ;   113

You know what 't is ; it has but a coarse name.

King. But, prithee, I should think, by her black eye,

And her red cheek, she should be quick [12] and stirring

In this same business ; ha?

Amin.   I cannot tell ;

I ne'er tried other, sir ; but I perceive

She is as quick as you deliver'd. [13]

King. Well, you 'll trust me then, Amintor, to choose

A wife for you again?

Amin.   No, never, sir.

King. Why, like you this so ill?

Amin.   So well I like her. [140

For this I bow my knee in thanks to you,

And unto Heaven will pay my grateful tribute

Hourly ; and do hope we shall draw out

[11] Chaste.   [12] Lively.   [13] Reported.

A long contented life together here,
And die both, full of gray hairs, in one day :
For which the thanks is yours. But if the
    Powers
That rule us please to call her first away,
Without pride spoke, this world holds not a
    wife
Worthy to take her room.
    KING. [*aside*] I do not like this. — All for-
      bear the room, 150
But you, Amintor, and your lady. —
        [*Exeunt all but the* KING, AMINTOR,
        and EVADNE.]
I have some speech with you, that may
    concern
Your after living well.
    AMIN. [*aside*] 'A will not tell me that he
      lies with her !
If he do, something heavenly stay my heart,
For I shall be apt to thrust this arm of mine
To acts unlawful !
    KING.   You will suffer me
To talk with her, Amintor, and not have
A jealous pang?
    AMIN.   Sir, I dare trust my wife
With whom she dares to talk, and not be jeal-
    ous.   [*Retires.*] 160
    KING. How do you like Amintor?
    EVAD.   As I did, sir.
    KING. How 's that?
    EVAD. As one that, to fulfil your will and
      pleasure,
I have given leave to call me wife and love.
    KING. I see there is no lasting faith in
      sin ;
They that break word with Heaven will break
    again
With all the world, and so dost thou with me.
    EVAD. How, sir?
    KING.   This subtle woman's ignorance
Will not excuse you : thou hast taken oaths,
So great that, methought, they did mis-
    become 170
A woman's mouth, that thou wouldst ne'er
    enjoy
A man but me.
    EVAD.   I never did swear so ;
You do me wrong.
    KING.   Day and night have heard it.
    EVAD. I swore indeed that I would never
      love
A man of lower place ; but, if your fortune
Should throw you from this height, I bade you
    trust
I would forsake you, and would bend to him

That won your throne. I love with my am-
    bition,
Not with my eyes. But, if I ever yet
Touch'd any other, leprosy light here 180
Upon my face ! which for your royalty
I would not stain !
    KING.   Why, thou dissemblest, and
It is in me to punish thee.
    EVAD.   Why, it is in me,
Then, not to love you, which will more afflict
Your body than your punishment can mine.
    KING. But thou hast let Amintor lie with
      thee.
    EVAD. I ha' not.
    KING.   Impudence ! he says himself so.
    EVAD. 'A lies.
    KING.   'A does not.
    EVAD.   By this light, he does,
Strangely and basely ! and I 'll prove it so.
I did not only shun him for a night, 190
But told him I would never close with him.
    KING. Speak lower ; 't is false.
    EVAD.   I am no man
To answer with a blow ; or, if I were,
You are the King. But urge me not ; 't is
    most true.
    KING. Do not I know the uncontrolled
    thoughts
That youth brings with him, when his blood is
    high
With expectation and desire of that
He long hath waited for? Is not his spirit,
Though he be temperate, of a valiant strain
As this our age hath known? What could he
    do, 200
If such a sudden speech had met his blood,
But ruin thee for ever, if he had not kill'd
    thee?
He could not bear it thus ; he is as we,
Or any other wrong'd man.
    EVAD.   It is dissembling.
    KING. Take him ! farewell : henceforth I
      am thy foe ;
And what disgraces I can blot thee with, look
    for.
    EVAD. Stay, sir ! — Amintor ! — You shall
      hear. — Amintor !
    AMIN. [*coming forward*] What, my love.
    EVAD. Amintor, thou hast an ingenious [14]
      look,
And shouldst be virtuous ; it amazeth me [210
That thou canst make such base malicious
    lies !
    AMIN. What, my dear wife?

[14] Ingenuous.

EVAD.　　　　Dear wife! I do despise thee.
Why, nothing can be baser than to sow
Dissension amongst lovers.
　　AMIN.　　　　　　　　Lovers! Who?
　　EVAD. The King and me —
　　AMIN.　　　　　　　　Oh, God!
　　EVAD. Who should live long, and love with-
　　　　out distaste,
Were it not for such pickthanks [15] as thyself.
Did you lie with me? Swear now, and be
　　　　punish'd
In hell for this!
　　AMIN.　　　　The faithless sin I made
To fair Aspatia is not yet reveng'd;　　　220
It follows me. — I will not lose a word
To this [vild] [16] woman; but to you, my King,
The anguish of my soul thrusts out this truth:
Y' are a tyrant! and not so much to wrong
An honest man thus, as to take a pride
In talking with him of it.
　　EVAD.　　　　　　Now, sir, see
How loud this fellow lied!
　　AMIN. You that can know to wrong, should
　　　　know how men
Must right themselves. What punishment is
　　　　due
From me to him that shall abuse my bed? [230
[Is it] [17] not death? Nor can that satisfy,
Unless I send your [limbs] [18] through all the
　　　　land,
To show how nobly I have freed myself.
　　KING. Draw not thy sword; thou know'st
　　　　I cannot fear
A subject's hand; but thou shalt feel the
　　　　weight
Of this, if thou dost rage.
　　AMIN.　　　　　The weight of that!
If you have any worth, for Heaven's sake,
　　　　think
I fear not swords; for, as you are mere man,
I dare as easily kill you for this deed,
As you dare think to do it. But there is [240
Divinity about you that strikes dead
My rising passions; as you are my King,
I fall before you, and present my sword
To cut mine own flesh, if it be your will.
Alas, I am nothing but a multitude
Of walking griefs! Yet, should I murder you,
I might before the world take the excuse
Of madness; for, compare my injuries,
And they will well appear too sad a weight

For reason to endure. But, fall I first　　250
Amongst my sorrows, ere my treacherous hand
Touch holy things! But why (I know not
　　　　what
I have to say), why did you choose out me
To make thus wretched? There were thou-
　　　　sands, fools
Easy to work on, and of state enough,
Within the island.
　　EVAD.　　　　I would not have a fool;
It were not credit for me.
　　AMIN.　　　　　　Worse and worse!
Thou, that dar'st talk unto thy husband thus,
Profess thyself a whore, and, more than so,
Resolve to be so still! — It is my fate　　260
To bear and bow beneath a thousand griefs,
To keep that little credit with the world! —
But there were wise ones too; you might have
　　　　ta'en
Another.
　　KING.　　No: for I believ['d] thee honest,
As thou wert valiant.
　　AMIN.　　　　　All the happiness
Bestow'd upon me turns into disgrace.
Gods, take your honesty again, for I
Am loaden with it! — Good my Lord the
　　　　King,
Be private in it.
　　KING.　　　　Thou mayst live, Amintor,
Free as thy King, if thou wilt wink at this [270
And be a means that we may meet in secret.
　　AMIN. A bawd! Hold, hold, my breast!
　　　　A bitter curse
Seize me, if I forget not all respects [19]
That are religious, on another word
Sounded like that; and through a sea of sins
Will wade to my revenge, though I should
　　　　call
Pains here and after life upon my soul!
　　KING. Well, I am resolute [20] you lay not
　　　　with her;
And so I leave you.　　　　　*Exit* KING.
　　EVAD.　　　　You must needs be prating;
And see what follows!
　　AMIN.　　　　Prithee, vex me not. [280
Leave me; I am afraid some sudden start
Will pull a murder on me.
　　EVAD.　　　　　I am gone;
I love my life well.　　　　*Exit* EVADNE.
　　AMIN.　　　　I hate mine as much.
This 't is to break a troth! I should be
　　　　glad,
If all this tide of grief would make me mad.
　　　　　　　　　　　　　　　Exit.

15 Talebearers, mischief-makers.
16 Old eds. *wild.*
17 So Colman (1778); old eds., *It is.*
18 Emend. Sympson; old eds. *liues* or *lives.*
19 Considerations.　　　　20 Convinced.

[SCENE II] [21]

Enter MELANTIUS.

MEL. I 'll know the cause of all Amintor's
griefs,
Or friendship shall be idle.[22]

Enter CALIANAX.

CAL.   Oh, Melantius,
My daughter will die !
MEL.   Trust me, I am sorry ;
Would thou hadst ta'en her room !
CAL.   Thou art a slave,
A cutthroat slave, a bloody treacherous slave !
MEL. Take heed, old man ; thou wilt be
heard to rave,
And lose thine offices.
CAL.   I am valiant grown
At all these years, and thou art but a slave !
MEL. Leave !
Some company will come, and I respect   10
Thy years, not thee, so much, that I could wish
To laugh at thee alone.
CAL.   I 'll spoil your mirth :
I mean to fight with thee. There lie, my
cloak.
This was my father's sword, and he durst
fight.
Are you prepar'd ?
MEL.   Why wilt thou dote thyself
Out of thy life? Hence, get thee to bed,
Have careful looking-to, and eat warm things,
And trouble not me ; my head is full of
thoughts
More weighty than thy life or death can be.
CAL. You have a name in war, where you
stand safe   20
Amongst a multitude ; but I will try
What you dare do unto a weak old man
In single fight. You 'll give ground, I fear.
Come, draw.
MEL. I will not draw, unless thou pull'st
thy death
Upon thee with a stroke. There 's no one
blow
That thou canst give hath strength enough to
kill me.
Tempt me not so far, then : the power of earth
Shall not redeem thee.
CAL. [*aside*]   I must let him alone ;
He 's stout and able ; and, to say the truth, [30
However I may set a face and talk,
I am not valiant. When I was a youth,

I kept my credit with a testy trick [23]
I had amongst cowards, but durst never fight.
MEL. I will not promise to preserve **your**
life,
If you do stay.
CAL. [*aside*]   I would give half my land
That I durst fight with that proud man **a**
little.
If I had men to hold him, I would beat him
Till he ask [24] me mercy.
MEL.   Sir, will you be gone?
CAL. [*aside*] I dare not stay ; but I will go
home, and beat   40
My servants all over for this.
              Exit CALIANAX.
MEL.   This old fellow haunts me.
But the distracted carriage of mine Amintor
Takes [25] deeply on me. I will find the cause ;
I fear his conscience cries he wrong'd Aspatia.

Enter AMINTOR.

AMIN. [*aside*] Men's eyes are not so subtle
to perceive
My inward misery ; I bear my grief
Hid from the world. How art thou wretched
then?
For aught I know, all husbands are like me ;
And every one I talk with of his wife
Is but a well dissembler of his woes,   50
As I am. Would I knew it ! for the rareness
Afflicts me now.
MEL.   Amintor, we have not
Enjoy'd our friendship of late, for we **were**
wont
To [change] [26] our souls in talk.
AMIN.   Melantius, I can tell thee
A good jest of Strato and a lady the last day.
MEL. How was 't?
AMIN.   Why, such an odd one !
MEL.   I have long'd
To speak with you ; not of an idle jest,
That 's forc'd, but of matter you are bound to
utter to me.[27]
AMIN. What is that, my friend?
MEL.   I have observ'd your words
Fall from your tongue wildly, and all your
carriage   60
Like one that strove to shew his merry mood
When he were ill dispos'd. You were not wont
To put such scorn into your speech, or wear
Upon your face ridiculous jollity.

---

[23] *I.e.*, a trick of showing irascibility.
[24] Q₁ *askt*.   [25] Takes hold, affects.
[26] Emend. Theobald ; old eds. *charge*.
[27] Ll. 52–58 as prose in old eds. ; present arrangement of ll. 52–60 is the Editor's.

[21] Unlocated ; presumably a room in the palace.
[22] *I.e.*, an empty term.

Some sadness sits here, which your cunning would
Cover o'er with smiles, and 't will not be. What is it?

AMIN. A sadness here! What cause
Can fate provide for me to make me so?
Am I not lov'd through all this isle? The King
Rains greatness on me. Have I not received   71
A lady to my bed that in her eye
Keeps mounting fire, and on her tender cheeks
Inevitable [28] color, in her heart
A prison for all virtue? Are not you,
Which is above all joys, my constant friend?
What sadness can I have? No; I am light,
And feel the courses of my blood more warm
And stirring than they were. Faith, marry, too;
And you will feel so unexpress'd [29] a joy
In chaste embraces, that you will indeed   80
Appear another.

MEL.   You may shape, Amintor,
Causes to cozen the whole world withal,
And you yourself too; but 't is not like a friend
To hide your soul from me. 'T is not your nature
To be thus idle. I have seen you stand
As you were blasted 'midst of all your mirth;
Call thrice aloud, and then start, feigning joy
So coldly! — World, what do I here? A friend
Is nothing. Heaven, I would ha' told that man
My secret sins! I'll search an unknown land,   90
And there plant friendship; all is withered here.
Come with a compliment! [30] I would have fought,
Or told my friend 'a lied, ere sooth'd [31] him so. —
Out of my bosom! [32]

AMIN. But there is nothing.

MEL.   Worse and worse! farewell:
From this time have acquaintance, but no friend.

AMIN. Melantius, stay; you shall know what that is.

MEL. See how you play'd with friendship! Be advis'd [33]

How you give cause unto yourself to say
You ha' lost a friend.

AMIN.   Forgive what I ha' done; [100
For I am so o'ergone with injuries
Unheard of, that I lose consideration
Of what I ought to do. Oh, oh!

MEL.   Do not weep.
What is 't? May I once but know the man
Hath turn'd my friend thus!

AMIN.   I had spoke at first,
But that ——

MEL.   But what?

AMIN.   I held it most unfit
For you to know. Faith, do not know it yet.

MEL. Thou seest my love, that will keep company
With thee in tears; hide nothing, then, from me;
For when I know the cause of thy distemper,
With mine old armor I'll adorn myself, [111
My resolution, and cut through thy foes
Unto thy quiet, till I place thy heart
As peaceable as spotless innocence.
What is it?

AMIN.   Why, 't is this — it is too big
To get out — let my tears make way awhile.

MEL. Punish me strangely, Heaven, if he scape
Of life or fame, that brought this youth to this!

AMIN. Your sister —

MEL.   Well said.

AMIN.   You will wish 't unknown,
When you have heard it.

MEL.   No.

AMIN.   Is much to blame, [120
And to the King has given her honor up,
And lives in whoredom with him.

MEL.   How's this?
Thou art run mad with injury indeed;
Thou couldst not utter this else. Speak again;
For I forgive it freely; tell thy griefs.

AMIN. She's wanton: I am loth to say, a whore,
Though it be true.

MEL. Speak yet again, before mine anger grow
Up beyond throwing down. What are thy griefs?

AMIN. By all our friendship, these.

MEL.   What, am I tame? [130
After mine actions, shall the name of friend
Blot all our family, and [strike] [34] the brand

[28] Irresistible.   [29] Inexpressible.
[30] Ceremonious or formal speech.
[31] Blandished.   [32] Intimacy, confidence.
[33] Be warned, consider.
[34] Q₁ *stick.*

Of whore upon my sister, unreveng'd?
My shaking flesh, be thou a witness for me,
With what unwillingness I go to scourge
This railer, whom my folly hath call'd friend.
I will not take thee basely : thy sword
                                   [*Draws his sword.*]
Hangs near thy hand ; draw it, that I may whip
Thy rashness to repentance ; draw thy sword !
    AMIN. Not on thee, did thine anger go as high   140
As troubled waters.[35] Thou shouldst do me ease
Here and eternally, if thy noble hand
Would cut me from my sorrows.
    MEL.   This is base
And fearful.[36] They that use to utter lies
Provide not blows but words to qualify [37]
The men they wrong'd. Thou hast a guilty cause.
    AMIN. Thou pleasest me ; for so much more like this
Will raise my anger up above my griefs,
Which is a passion easier to be borne,
And I shall then be happy.
    MEL.   Take, then, more [150
To raise thine anger : 't is mere cowardice
Makes thee not draw ; and I will leave thee dead,
However. But if thou art so much press'd
With guilt and fear as not to dare to fight,
I 'll make thy memory loath'd, and fix a scandal
Upon thy name forever.
    AMIN. [*drawing his sword*]   Then I draw,
As justly as our magistrates their swords
To cut offenders off. I knew before
'T would grate your ears ; but it was base in you
To urge a weighty secret from your friend, [160
And then rage at it. I shall be at ease,
If I be kill'd ; and, if you fall by me,
I shall not long outlive you.
    MEL.   Stay awhile. —
The name of friend is more than family,
Or all the world besides ; I was a fool. —
Thou searching Human Nature, that didst wake
To do me wrong, thou art inquisitive,
And thrusts [38] me upon questions that will take

My sleep away! Would I had died, ere known
This sad dishonor ! — Pardon me, my friend !
                                   [*Sheathes his sword.*]
If thou wilt strike, here is a faithful heart ; [171
Pierce it, for I will never heave my hand
To thine. Behold the power thou hast in me !
I do believe my sister is a whore,
A leprous one. Put up thy sword, young man.
    AMIN. How should I bear it, then, she being so?
I fear, my friend, that you will lose me shortly ;
                                   [*Sheathes his sword.*]
And I shall do a foul act on myself,
Through these disgraces.
    MEL.   Better half the land
Were buried quick [39] together. No, Amintor ;
Thou shalt have ease. Oh, this adulterous King,   181
That drew her to 't ! Where got he the spirit
To wrong me so?
    AMIN.   What is it, then, to me,
If it be wrong to you?
    MEL.   Why, not so much.
The credit of our house is thrown away.
But from his iron den I 'll waken Death,
And hurl him on this King. My honesty
Shall steel my sword ; and on my [40] horrid point
I 'll wear my cause, that shall amaze the eyes
Of this proud man, and be too glitt'ring [41] [190
For him to look on.
    AMIN. I have quite undone my fame.
    MEL. Dry up thy wat'ry eyes,
And cast a manly look upon my face ;
For nothing is so wild as I, thy friend,
Till I have freed thee. Still this swelling breast.
I go thus from thee, and will never cease
My vengeance till I find [thy] [42] heart at peace.
    AMIN. It must not be so. Stay. Mine eyes would tell
How loth I am to this ; but, love and tears,
Leave me awhile ! for I have hazarded [201
All that this world calls happy. — Thou hast wrought
A secret from me, under name of friend,
Which art could ne'er have found, nor torture wrung
From out my bosom. Give it me again ;
For I will find it, wheresoe'er it lies,
Hid in the mortal'st part. Invent a way
To give it back.

---

[35] So Qq1,2; mod. eds. follow Q3 *et seq., swell as high As the wilde surges.*
[36] Cowardly.   [37] Moderate, mollify.
[38] Thrustest.

[39] Alive.   [40] So Qq1,2; other old eds. *its.*
[41] Trisyllabic.   [42] So Q1; other old eds. *my.*

MEL.   Why would you have it back?
I will to death pursue him with revenge,
   AMIN. Therefore I call it back from thee;
      for I know   210
Thy blood so high, that thou wilt stir in
   this,
And shame me to posterity. Take to thy
   weapon!   [*Draws his sword.*]
   MEL. Hear thy friend, that bears more
      years than thou.
   AMIN. I will not hear; but draw, or I —
   MEL.   Amintor!
   AMIN. Draw, then, for I am full as resolute
As fame and honor can enforce me be;
I cannot linger. Draw!
   MEL. [*drawing his sword*]   I do. But
      is not
My share of credit equal[43] with thine,
If I do stir?
   AMIN.   No; for it will be call'd
Honor in thee to spill thy sister's blood,   220
If she her birth abuse, and on the King
A brave revenge; but on me, that have walk'd
With patience in it, it will fix the name
Of fearful cuckold. — Oh, that word! Be
   quick.
   MEL. Then join with me.
   AMIN.   I dare not do a sin,
Or else I would. Be speedy.
   MEL. Then, dare not fight with me; for
      that's a sin. —
His grief distracts him. — Call thy thoughts
   again,
And to thyself pronounce the name of friend,
And see what that will work. I will not
   fight.   230
   AMIN. You must.
   MEL. [*sheathing his sword*]   I will be
      kill'd first. Though my passions
Offered the like to you, 't is not this earth
Shall buy my reason to it. Think awhile,
For you are (I must weep when I speak that)
Almost besides yourself.
   AMIN. [*sheathing his sword*]   Oh, my soft
      temper!
So many sweet words from thy sister's mouth,
I am afraid, would make me take her to
Embrace and pardon her. I am mad indeed,
And know not what I do. Yet, have a care
Of me in what thou doest.
   MEL.   Why, thinks my friend [240
I will forget his honor? or, to save
The bravery of our house, will lose his fame,
And fear to touch the throne of majesty?

   [43] Almost trisyllabic.

   AMIN. A curse will follow that; but rather
   live
And suffer with me.
   MEL.   I will do what worth
Shall bid me, and no more.
   AMIN.   Faith, I am sick,
And desperately I hope; yet, leaning thus,
I feel a kind of ease.
   MEL.   Come, take again
Your mirth about you.
   AMIN.   I shall never do 't.
   MEL. I warrant you; look up; we 'll walk
      together;   250
Put thine arm here; all shall be well again.
   AMIN. Thy love (oh, wretched!) ay, thy
      love, Melantius;
Why, I have nothing else.
   MEL.   Be merry, then.   *Exeunt.*

Enter MELANTIUS *again.*

   MEL. This worthy young man may do
      violence
Upon himself; but I have cherish'd him
To [my best power],[44] and sent him smiling
   from me,
   To counterfeit again. Sword, hold thine
      edge;
My heart will never fail me.

Enter DIPHILUS.

                    Diphilus!
Thou com'st as[45] sent.
   DIPH.   Yonder has been such laughing.
   MEL. Betwixt whom?
   DIPH.   Why, our sister and the King. [260
I thought their spleens would break; they
      laugh'd us all
Out of the room.
   MEL. They must weep, Diphilus.
   DIPH.   Must they?
   MEL.   They must.
Thou art my brother; and, if I did believe
Thou hadst a base thought, I would rip it out,
Lie where it durst.
   DIPH.   You should not; I would first
Mangle myself and find it.
   MEL.   That was spoke
According to our strain.[46] Come, join thy
      hands to mine,
And swear a firmness to what project I
Shall lay before thee.
   DIPH.   You do wrong us both. [270
People hereafter shall not say there pass'd

   [44] So Qq₃ *et seq.;* Qq₁,₂, *As well as I could.*
   [45] As if.   [46] Stock.

A bond, more than our loves, to tie our lives
And deaths together.

MEL. It is as nobly said as I would wish.
Anon I 'll tell you wonders : we are wrong'd.

DIPH. But I will tell you now, we 'll right
    ourselves.

MEL. Stay not ; prepare the armor in my
    house ;
And what friends you can draw unto our
    side,
Not knowing of the cause, make ready too.
Haste, Diphilus, the time requires it, haste ! —
                          Exit DIPHILUS.
I hope my cause is just ; I know my blood [281
Tells me it is ; and I will credit it.
To take revenge, and lose myself withal,
Were idle ; and to scape impossible,
Without I had the fort, which (misery !)
Remaining in the hands of my old enemy
Calianax — but I must have it.   See

Re-enter CALIANAX.

Where he comes shaking by me ! — Good my
    Lord,
Forget your spleen to me. I never wrong'd
    you,
But would have peace with every man.

CAL.   'T is well ; [290
If I durst fight, your tongue would lie at
    quiet.

MEL. Y' are touchy without all cause.

CAL.   Do, mock me.

MEL. By mine honor, I speak truth.

CAL.   Honor ! where is 't?

MEL. See, what starts you make
Into your [idle] [47] hatred, to my love
And freedom to you. I come with resolution
To obtain a suit of you.

CAL.   A suit of me !
'T is very like it should be granted, sir.

MEL. Nay, go not hence.   299
'T is this : you have the keeping of the fort,
And I would wish you, by the love you ought
To bear unto me, to deliver it
Into my hands.

CAL.   I am in hope thou art mad,
To talk to me thus.

MEL.   But there is a reason
To move you to it : I would kill the King,
That wrong'd you and your daughter.

CAL.   Out, traitor !

MEL. Nay, but stay ; I cannot scape, the
    deed once done,
Without I have this fort.

[47] Q₁ only.

CAL.   And should I help thee?
Now thy treacherous mind betrays itself.

MEL. Come, delay me not ;   310
Give me a sudden answer, or already
Thy last is spoke ! Refuse not offered love
When it comes clad in secrets.

CAL. [*aside*]   If I say
I will not, he will kill me ; I do see 't
Writ in his looks ; and should I say I will,
He 'll run and tell the King. — I do not
    shun
Your friendship, dear Melantius, but this
    cause
Is weighty ; give me but an hour to think.

MEL. Take it. — [*aside*] I know this goes
    unto the King ;
But I am arm'd.   *Exit* MELANTIUS.

CAL.   Methinks I feel myself [320
But twenty now again. This fighting fool
Wants policy ; [48] I shall revenge my girl,
And make her red [49] again. I pray my legs
Will last that pace that I will carry them ;
I shall want breath before I find the King.
                                [*Exit.*]

ACT IV — [SCENE I] [1]

Enter MELANTIUS, [*to*] EVADNE, *and* [Ladies].

MEL. Save you !

EVAD.   Save you, sweet Brother.

MEL. In my blunt eye, methinks, you look,
    Evadne —

EVAD. Come, you would make me blush.

MEL.   I would, Evadne ;
I shall displease my ends else.

EVAD.   You shall, if you
[Commend] [2] me ; I am bashful. Come, sir,
    how do
I look?

MEL.   I would not have your women
    hear me
Break into commendations of you ; 't is not
Seemly.

EVAD. Go wait me in the gallery.
                       Exeunt Ladies.
Now speak.

MEL.   I 'll lock the door first.

EVAD.   Why?

MEL. I will not have your gilded things,
    that dance   10

[48] Lacks sagacity.
[49] Bring the color back into her cheeks.
[1] Evadne's apartment.
[2] Emend. Theobald ; old eds. *Command.*

In visitation with their Milan skins,[3]
Choke up my business.

EVAD. You are strangely dispos'd, sir.

MEL. Good madam, not to make you
merry.

EVAD. No; if you praise me, 't will make
me sad.

MEL. Such a sad commendation I have for
you.

EVAD. Brother,
The court hath made you witty, and learn to
riddle.

MEL. I praise the court for't; has it
learn'd you nothing?

EVAD. Me!

MEL. Ay, Evadne; thou art young
and handsome,
A lady of a sweet complexion,   20
And such a flowing carriage, that it cannot
Choose but inflame a kingdom.

EVAD. Gentle Brother!

MEL. 'T is yet in thy repentance, foolish
woman,
To make me gentle.

EVAD. How is this?

MEL. 'T is base;
And I could blush, at these years, through [4] all
My honor'd scars, to come to such a parley.

EVAD. I understand ye not.

MEL. You dare not, fool!
They that commit thy faults fly the remembrance.

EVAD. My faults, sir! I would have you
know, I care not
If they were written here, here in my forehead.   30

MEL. Thy body is too little for the story;
The lusts [5] of which would fill another woman,
Though [6] she had twins within her.

EVAD. This is saucy;
Look you intrude no more! There's your
way.

MEL. Thou art my way, and I will tread
upon thee,
Till I find truth out.

EVAD. What truth is that you look for?

MEL. Thy long-lost honor. Would the
gods had set me
Rather to grapple with the plague, or stand
One of their loudest bolts! Come, tell me
quickly;
Do it without enforcement, and take heed [40
You swell me not above my temper.

EVAD. How, sir!
Where got you this report?

MEL. Where there was people;
In every place.

EVAD. They and the seconds of it
Are base people; believe them not: they lied.

MEL. Do not play with mine anger; do
not, wretch!   [*Seizes her.*]
I come to know that desperate fool that drew
thee
From thy fair life. Be wise, and lay him
open.

EVAD. Unhand me, and learn manners!
Such another
Forgetfulness forfeits your life.

MEL. Quench me this mighty humor,[7] and
then tell me   50
Whose whore you are; for you are one, I
know it.
Let all mine honors perish but I 'll find him
Though he lie lock'd up in thy blood! Be
sudden;
There is no facing it; [8] and be not flattered.
The burnt air, when the Dog [9] reigns, is not
fouler
Than thy contagious name, till thy repent-
ance
(If the gods grant thee any) purge thy sick-
ness.

EVAD. Begone! you are my brother;
that 's your safety.

MEL. I 'll be a wolf first. 'T is, to be thy
brother,
An infamy below the sin of coward.   60
I am as far from being part of thee
As thou art from thy virtue. Seek a kindred
'Mongst sensual beasts, and make a goat thy
brother;
A goat is cooler. Will you tell me yet?

EVAD. If you stay here and rail thus, I shall
tell you
I 'll ha' you whipp'd! Get you to your command,

---

[3] "Fine gloves manufactured at Milan." (Nares.)
But this is only the literal meaning. Gloves were
often perfumed; *Milan skins* probably means "perfumed skins." Note "choke."
[4] Dissyllabic.   [5] The record of the lusts.
[6] Even if. "Fill" = cover with writing. There
has been much silly annotation at this point, but
the meaning is perfectly clear, as was indeed recognized by Colman. Any woman's whole body, to
say nothing of your little forehead, would afford
insufficient space to write the record of your lusts;
even the distended body of a woman pregnant with
twins would be insufficient.

[7] This whim or affectation of mightiness.
[8] An impudent front on it is impossible; you
can't bluff me.
[9] Sirius, the Dog Star, supposed to be responsible
for the hot weather of the dog days.

And there preach to your sentinels, and tell
     them
What a brave man you are; I shall laugh at
     you.
     MEL. Y' are grown a glorious whore!
          Where be your fighters?
What mortal fool durst raise thee to this
     daring,   70
And I alive! By my just sword, h' ad safer
[Bestrid] a billow when the angry North
Plows up the sea, or made Heaven's fire his
     [foe]! [10]
Work me no higher. Will you discover yet?
     EVAD. The fellow's mad. Sleep, and speak
          sense.
     MEL. Force my swoln heart no further;
          I would save thee.
Your great maintainers are not here; they dare
     not.
Would they were all, and armed! I would
     speak loud;
Here's one should thunder to 'em! Will you
     tell me? —
Thou hast no hope to scape. He that dares
     most,   80
And damns away his soul to do thee service,
Will sooner snatch meat from a hungry lion
Than come to rescue thee. Thou hast death
     about thee.
H 'as undone thine honor, poison'd thy virtue,
And, of a lovely rose, left thee a canker.[11]
     EVAD. Let me consider.
     MEL.   Do, whose child thou wert,
Whose honor thou hast murdered, whose grave
     opened,
And so pull'd on the gods that in their justice
They must restore him flesh again and life,
And raise his dry bones to revenge this scan-
     dal.   90
     EVAD. The gods are not of my mind; they
          had better
Let 'em lie sweet still in the earth; they'll
     stink here.
     MEL. Do you raise mirth out of my easi-
          ness?
Forsake me, then, all weaknesses of nature,
                         [*Draws his sword.*]
That make men women! Speak, you whore,
     speak truth,
Or, by the dear soul of thy sleeping father,
This sword shall be thy lover! Tell, or I'll
     kill thee;

And, when thou hast told all, thou wilt deserve
     it.
     EVAD. You will not murder me?
     MEL. No; 't is a justice, and a noble
          one,   100
To put the light out of such base offenders.
     EVAD. Help!
     MEL. By thy foul self, no human help shall
          help thee,
If thou criest! When I have kill'd thee, as I
Have vow'd to do, if thou confess not, naked
As thou hast left thine honor will I leave thee,
That on thy branded flesh the world may read
Thy black shame and my justice. Wilt thou
     bend yet?
     EVAD. Yes.
     MEL. Up, and begin your story.   110
     EVAD. Oh, I am miserable!
     MEL. 'T is true, thou art. Speak truth
          still.
     EVAD. I have offended; noble sir, forgive
          me!
     MEL. With what secure slave?
     EVAD.   Do not ask me, sir;
Mine own remembrance is a misery
Too mighty for me.
     MEL.   Do not fall back again;
My sword's unsheathed yet.
     EVAD.   What shall I do?
     MEL. Be true, and make your fault less.
     EVAD.   I dare not tell.
     MEL. Tell, or I'll be this day a-killing
          thee.
     EVAD. Will you forgive me, then?   120
     MEL. Stay; I must ask mine honor first.
I have too much foolish nature in me; speak.
     EVAD. Is there none else here?
     MEL. None but a fearful conscience; that's
          too many.
Who is 't?
     EVAD.   Oh, hear me gently! It was the
          King.[12]
     MEL. No more. My worthy father's and
          my services
Are liberally rewarded! King, I thank thee!
For all my dangers and my wounds thou hast
     paid me
In my own metal; these are soldiers'
     thanks! —
How long have you liv'd thus, Evadne?
     EVAD.   Too long. [130

---

[10] So Q$_1$; other old eds. *food.* — For *Bestrid* (l. 72)
Q$_2$ reads *Bestride.*
[11] Cankerworm.

[12] Melantius has already been informed of this:
a good illustration of the authors' tendency to
sacrifice logic and consistency for theatrical effectiveness within a scene.

MEL. Too late you find it. Can you be sorry?

EVAD. Would I were half as blameless!

MEL. Evadne, thou wilt to thy trade again.

EVAD. First to my grave.

MEL. Would gods thou hadst been so blest!

Dost thou not hate this King now? Prithee, hate him;

Couldst thou not curse him? I command thee, curse him;

Curse till the gods hear, and deliver him

To thy just wishes. Yet I fear, Evadne,

You had rather play your game out.

EVAD. No; I feel

Too many sad confusions here, to let in [140

Any loose flame hereafter.

MEL. Dost thou not feel, amongst all those, one brave anger,

That breaks out nobly, and directs thine arm

To kill this base King?

EVAD. All the gods forbid it!

MEL. No, all the gods require it;

They are dishonored in him.

EVAD. 'T is too fearful.

MEL. Y' are valiant in his bed, and bold enough

To be a stale whore, and have your madam's name

Discourse for grooms and pages; and hereafter,

When his cool Majesty hath laid you by, [150

To be at pension with some needy sir

For meat and coarser clothes; thus far you knew

No fear. Come, you shall kill him.

EVAD. Good sir!

MEL. An 't were to kiss him dead, thou 'dst smother him;

Be wise, and kill him. Canst thou live, and know

What noble minds shall make thee, see thyself

Found out with every finger, made the shame

Of all successions,[13] and in this great ruin

Thy brother and thy noble husband broken?

Thou shalt not live thus. Kneel, and swear to help me, 160

When I shall call thee to it; or, by all

Holy in Heaven and earth, thou shalt not live

To breathe a full hour longer; not a thought!

Come 't is a righteous oath. Give me thy [hands],[14]

And, both to Heaven held up, swear, by that wealth

This lustful thief stole from thee, when I say it,

To let his foul soul out.

EVAD. Here I swear it;

And, all you spirits of abused ladies,

Help me in this performance!

MEL. Enough. This must be known to none 170

But you and I, Evadne; not to your lord,

Though he be wise and noble, and a fellow

Dares step as far into a worthy action

As the most daring, ay, as far as justice.

Ask me not why. Farewell.

Exit MELANTIUS.

EVAD. Would I could say so to my black disgrace!

Gods, where have I been all this time? How friended,

That I should lose myself thus desperately,

And none for pity show me how I wand'red?

There is not in the compass of the light [180

A more unhappy creature; sure, I am monstrous;

For I have done those follies, those mad mischiefs,

Would dare [15] a woman. Oh, my loaden soul,

Be not so cruel to me; choke not up

The way to my repentance!

Enter AMINTOR.

Oh, my Lord!

AMIN. How now?

EVAD. My much abused lord! *Kneels.*

AMIN. This cannot be!

EVAD. I do not kneel to live. I dare not hope it;

The wrongs I did are greater. Look upon me,

Though I appear with all my faults.

AMIN. Stand up.

This is [a] [16] new way to beget more sorrow; 190

Heaven knows I have too many. Do not mock me;

Though I am tame, and bred up with my wrongs,

Which are my foster brothers, I may leap,

Like a hand-wolf,[17] into my natural wildness,

And do an outrage. Prithee, do not mock me.

EVAD. My whole life is so leprous, it infects

All my repentance. I would buy your pardon,

Though at the highest set,[18] even with my life;

---

[13] Posterity. [14] Emend. Colman; old eds. *hand.*

[15] Daunt, terrify. [16] So Q1; other old eds. *no.*

[17] Tamed wolf. [18] Stake.

That slight contrition, that['s] [19] no sacrifice
For what I have committed.

AMIN.   Sure, I dazzle ; [20] [200
There cannot be a faith in that foul woman,
That knows no god more mighty than her
     mischiefs. —
Thou dost still worse, still number on thy
     faults,
To press my poor heart thus. Can I believe
There's any seed of virtue in that woman
Left to shoot up, that dares go on in sin
Known, and so known as thine is? Oh,
     Evadne!
Would there were any safety [21] in thy sex,
That I might put a thousand sorrows off,
And credit thy repentance! but I must
     not.   210
Thou hast brought me to that dull calamity,
To that strange misbelief of all the world
And all things that are in it, that I fear
I shall fall like a tree, and find my grave,
Only rememb'ring that I grieve.

EVAD.   My Lord,
Give me your griefs ; you are an innocent,
A soul as white as Heaven ; let not my sins
Perish your noble youth. I do not fall here
To shadow, by dissembling with my tears,
(As all say women can,) or to make less, [220
What my hot will hath done, which Heaven
     and you
Knows to be tougher than the hand of time
Can cut from man's remembrance ; no, I do
     not ;
I do appear the same, the same Evadne,
Dress'd in the shames I liv'd in, the same
     monster.
But these are names of honor to [22] what I am ;
I do present myself the foulest creature,
Most poisonous, dangerous, and despis'd of
     men,
Lerna [23] e'er bred or Nilus. I am hell,
Till you, my dear Lord, shoot your light into
     me,   230
The beams of your forgiveness ; I am soul-
     sick,
And wither with the fear of one condemn'd,
Till I have got your pardon.

AMIN.   Rise, Evadne.
Those heavenly Powers that put this good into
     thee
Grant a continuance of it ! I forgive thee ;

[19] Add. Q3.
[20] Am dazzled.
[21] *I.e.*, any trust to be reposed.
[22] In comparison with.
[23] The marshy home of the Hydra that Hercules
slew.

Make thyself worthy of it ; and take heed,
Take heed, Evadne, this be serious.
Mock not the Powers above, that can and
     dare
Give thee a great example of their justice
To all ensuing eyes,[24] if thou play'st   240
With thy repentance, the best sacrifice.

EVAD. I have done nothing good to win
     belief,
My life hath been so faithless. All the crea-
     tures,
Made for Heaven's honors, have their ends,
     and good ones,
All but the cozening crocodiles, false women.
They reign here like those plagues, those kill-
     ing sores,
Men pray against ; and when they die, like
     tales
Ill told and unbeliev'd, they pass away,
And go to dust forgotten. But, my Lord,
Those short days I shall number to my
     rest   250
(As many must not see me) shall, though too
     late,
Though in my evening, yet perceive a will,
Since I can do no good, because a woman,
Reach constantly at something that is near it ;
I will redeem one minute of my age,
Or, like another Niobe, I'll weep,
Till I am water.

AMIN.   I am now dissolved ;
My frozen soul melts. May each sin thou
     hast,
Find a new mercy ! Rise ; I am at peace. [259
Hadst thou been thus, thus excellently good,
Before that devil-king tempted thy frailty,
Sure thou hadst made a star. Give me thy
     hand :
From this time I will know thee ; and, as far
As honor gives me leave, be thy Amintor.
When we meet next, I will salute thee fairly,
And pray the gods to give thee happy days ;
My charity shall go along with thee,
Though my embraces must be far from thee.
I should ha' kill'd thee, but this sweet repent-
     ance
Locks up my vengeance ; for which thus I
     kiss thee —   270
The last kiss we must take ; and would to
     Heaven
The holy priest that gave our hands together
Had given us equal virtues ! Go, Evadne ;
The gods thus part our bodies. Have a care
My honor falls no further ; I am well, then.

[24] Weber conjectures *ages.*

EVAD. All the dear joys here, and above
hereafter,
Crown thy fair soul! Thus I take leave, my
Lord ;
And never shall you see the foul Evadne,
Till she have tried all honored means that
may
Set her in rest and wash her stains away. [280
Exeunt.

[SCENE II] [25]

*Hautboys play within; a banquet [discovered].
Enter* KING [*and*] CALIANAX.

KING. I cannot tell how I should credit
this
From you, that are his enemy.
CAL.   I am sure
He said it to me ; and I 'll justify it
What way he dares oppose, but [26] with my
sword.
KING. But did he break,[27] without all cir-
cumstance,
To you, his foe, that he would have the fort,
To kill me, and then scape?
CAL.   If he deny it,
I 'll make him blush.
KING.   It sounds incredibly.
CAL. Ay, so does everything I say of late.
KING. Not so, Calianax.
CAL.   Yes, I should sit [10
Mute, whilst a rogue with strong arms cuts
your throat.
KING. Well, I will try him ; and, if this be
true,
I 'll pawn my life I 'll find it ; if 't be false,
And that [28] you clothe your hate in such a
lie,
You shall hereafter dote in your own house,
Not in the court.
CAL.   Why, if it be a lie,
Mine ears are false, for I 'll be sworn I heard
it.
Old men are good for nothing ; you were best
Put me to death for hearing, and free him
For meaning it. You would 'a' trusted me [20
Once, but the time is altered.
KING.   And will still,
Where I may do with justice to the world.
You have no witness.
CAL.   Yes, myself.
KING.   No more,
I mean, there were that heard it.

CAL.   How? no more!
Would you have more? Why, am not I
enough
To hang a thousand rogues?
KING.   But so you may
Hang honest men too, if you please.
CAL.   I may!
'T is like I will do so ; there are a hundred
Will swear it for a need too, if I say it——
KING. Such witnesses we need not.
CAL.   And 't is hard [30
If my word cannot hang a boisterous knave.
KING. Enough. — Where 's Strato?

Enter STRATO.

STRATO.   Sir?
KING. Why, where 's all the company?
Call Amintor in ;
Evadne. Where 's my brother, and Melan-
tius?
Bid him come too ; and Diphilus. Call all
That are without there. —   *Exit* STRATO.
                If he should desire
The combat of you, 't is not in the power
Of all our laws to hinder it, unless
We mean to quit [29] 'em.
CAL.   Why, if you do think
'T is fit an old man and a councillor   40
To fight for what he says, then you may grant
it.

Enter AMINTOR, EVADNE, MELANTIUS, DI-
PHILUS, LYSIPPUS, CLEON, STRATO, [*and*]
DIAGORAS.

KING. Come, sirs! — Amintor, thou art
yet a bridegroom,
And I will use thee so ; thou shalt sit down. —
Evadne, sit ; — and you, Amintor, too ;
This banquet is for you, sir. — Who has
brought
A merry tale about him, to raise laughter
Amongst our wine? Why, Strato, where art
thou?
Thou wilt chop out with them unseasonably,
When I desire 'em not.
STRA. 'T is my ill luck, sir, so to spend
them, then.   50
KING. Reach me a bowl of wine. — Melan-
tius, thou
Art sad.
AMIN.[30] I should be, sir, the merriest here,
But I ha' ne'er a story of mine own
Worth telling at this time.

[25] A hall in the palace.   [26] Except.
[27] Broach the subject.   [28] If.
[29] Abandon.
[30] Q1, incorrectly followed by mod. eds., *Mel.*

KING.   Give me the wine. —
Melantius, I am now considering
How easy 't were for any man we trust
To poison one of us in such a bowl.
    MEL. I think it were not hard, sir, for a
      knave.
    CAL. [*aside*] Such as you are.
    KING. I' faith, 't were easy. It becomes us
      well   60
To get plain-dealing men about ourselves ;
Such as you all are here. — Amintor, to thee
And to thy fair Evadne.   [*Drinks.*]
    MEL. (*aside*)   Have you thought
Of this, Calianax?
    CAL. [*aside*]   Yes, marry, have I.
    MEL. [*aside*] And what's your resolution?
    CAL. [*aside*]   Ye shall have it, —
Soundly, I warrant you.
    KING. Reach to Amintor, Strato.
    AMIN.   Here, my love ;
      [*Drinks and then hands the cup to*
        EVADNE.]
This wine will do thee wrong, for it will set
Blushes upon thy cheeks ; and, till thou dost
A fault, 't were pity.
    KING.   Yet I wonder much [70
Of [31] the strange desperation of these men,
That dare attempt such acts here in our state :
He could not scape that did it.
    MEL.   Were he known,
Unpossible.
    KING.   It would be known, Melantius.
    MEL. It ought to be. If he got then away,
He must wear all our lives upon his sword :
He need not fly the island ; he must leave
No one alive.
    KING.   No ; I should think no man
Could kill me, and scape clear, but that old
      man.
    CAL. But I ! Heaven bless me ! I ! should
      I, my Liege?   80
    KING. I do not think thou wouldst ; but
      yet thou might'st,
For thou hast in thy hands the means to
      scape,
By keeping of the fort. — He has, Melantius,
And he has kept it well.
    MEL.   From cobwebs, sir,
'T is clean swept ; I can find no other art
In keeping of it now. 'T was ne'er besieg'd
Since he commanded.
    CAL.   I shall be sure
Of your good word ; but I have kept it safe
From such as you.

   [31] Theobald emends *at.*

    MEL.   Keep your ill temper in :
I speak no malice ; had my brother kept it,
I should ha' said as much.
    KING.   You are not merry. [91
Brother, drink wine. [KING *rises.*] Sit you
      all still. — (*aside*) Calianax,
I cannot trust [this].[32] I have thrown out
      words
That would have fetch'd warm blood upon
      the cheeks
Of guilty men, and he is never mov'd ;
He knows no such thing.
    CAL. [*aside*]   Impudence may scape,
When feeble virtue is accus'd.
    KING. [*aside*]   'A must,
If he were guilty, feel an alteration
At this our whisper, whilst we point at him ;
You see he does not.
    CAL. [*aside*]   Let him hang himself ; [100
What care I what he does? This he did say.
    KING [*drawing* MELANTIUS *and* CAL-
      IANAX *aside*] Melantius, you can
      easily conceive
What I have meant ; for men that are in fault
Can subtly apprehend when others aim
At what they do amiss ; but I forgive
Freely before this man, — Heaven do so too !
I will not touch thee so much as with shame
Of telling it. Let it be so no more.
    CAL. Why, this is very fine !
    MEL.   I cannot tell
What 't is you mean ; but I am apt enough
Rudely to thrust into [33] ignorant fault. [111
But let me know it. Happily [34] 't is naught
But misconstruction ; and, where I am clear,
I will not take forgiveness of the gods,
Much less of you.
    KING.   Nay, if you stand so stiff,
I shall call back my mercy.
    MEL.   I want smoothness
To thank a man for pardoning of a crime
I never knew.
    KING. Not to instruct your knowledge, but
      to show you
My ears are everywhere : you meant to kill
      me,   120
And get the fort to scape.
    MEL.   Pardon me, sir ;
My bluntness will be pardoned. You pre-
      serve
A race of idle people here about you,
[Facers] [35] and talkers, to defame the worth

   [32] Emend. Dyce ; old eds. *thus.*
   [33] Theobald inserts *an.*   [34] Perhaps.
   [35] Cf. on IV, i, 54. So Q₁ ; other old eds., *Eaters.*

Of those that do things worthy. The man
    that uttered this
Had perish'd without food, be 't who it will,
But for this arm, that fenc'd him from the foe ;
And if I thought you gave a faith to this,
The plainness of my nature would speak more.
Give me a pardon (for you ought to do 't) [130
To kill him that spake this.

    CAL. [*aside*]   Ay, that will be
The end of all ; then I am fairly paid
For all my care and service.

    MEL.   That old man,
Who calls me enemy, and of whom I
(Though I will never match my hate so low)
Have no good thought, would yet, I think, ex-
    cuse me,
And swear he thought me wrong'd in this,

    CAL.   Who, I?
Thou shameless fellow ! didst thou not speak
    to me
Of it thyself?

    MEL.   Oh, then it came from him !

    CAL. From me ! who should it come from
    but from me?   140

    MEL. Nay, I believe your malice is enough ;
But I ha' lost my anger. — Sir, I hope
You are well satisfied.

    KING.   Lysippus, cheer
Amintor and his lady. — There 's no sound
Comes from you ; I will come and do 't my-
    self.

    AMIN. [*aside*] You have done already, sir,
    for me, I thank you.

    KING.[36] Melantius, I do credit this from
    him,
How slight soe'er you make 't.

    MEL.   'T is strange you should.

    CAL. 'T is strange 'a should believe an old
    man's word
That never lied in 's life !

    MEL.   I talk not to thee. — [150
Shall the wild words of this distempered man,
Frantic with age and sorrow, make a breach
Betwixt your Majesty and me ? 'T was wrong
To hearken to him ; but to credit him,
As much at least as I have power to bear.
But pardon me — whilst I speak only truth,
I may commend myself — I have bestow'd
My careless blood with you,[37] and should be
    loth
To think an action that would make me lose

That and my thanks too. When I was a boy,
I thrust myself into my country's cause, [161
And did a deed that pluck'd five years from
    time,
And styl'd me man then. And for you, my
    King,
Your subjects all have fed by virtue of
My arm — this sword of mine hath plough'd
    the ground —
And reap'd[38] the fruit in peace ;
And you yourself have liv'd at home in ease.
So terrible I grew that, without swords,
My name hath fetch'd you conquest ; and my
    heart
And limbs are still the same, my will as great
To do you service. Let me not be paid   [171
With such a strange distrust.

    KING.   Melantius,
I held it great injustice to believe
Thine enemy, and did not ; if I did,
I do not ; let that satisfy. — What, struck
With sadness all? More wine !

    CAL.   A few fine words
Have overthrown my truth. Ah, th' art a
    villain !

    MEL. (*aside*) Why, thou wert better let me
    have the fort :
Dotard, I will disgrace thee thus for ever ;
There shall no credit lie upon thy words. [180
Think better, and deliver it.

    CAL.   My Liege,
He 's at me now again to do it. — Speak ;
Deny it, if thou canst. — Examine him
Whilst he is hot ; for, if he cool again,
He will forswear it.

    KING.   This is lunacy,
I hope, Melantius.

    MEL.   He hath lost himself
Much, since his daughter miss'd the happiness
My sister gain'd ; and, though he call me foe,
I pity him.

    CAL.   Pity ! A pox upon you !

    MEL. Mark his disordered words : and at
    the masque   190
Diagoras knows he rag'd and rail'd at me,
And call'd a lady " whore," so innocent
She understood him not. But it becomes
Both you and me to forgive distraction :
Pardon him, as I do.

---

[26] Apparently the whole colloquy, down to about
l. 196, is not heard by the other guests.

[37] I have spent my blood, taking no care of it, in
your service.

[38] Present punctuation is designed to show that
subjects is the real subject of *reap'd*, though it is
possible that the sense is " My sword hath reaped
the fruit of my actions in the form of the peace we
all enjoy." But the line is short, and Seward's
conjecture may be right : "And *they have* reap'd
the fruit *of it* in peace."

CAL. I 'll not speak for thee,
For all thy cunning. — If you will be safe,
Chop off his head ; for there was never known
So impudent a rascal.
    KING. Some, that love him,
Get him to bed. Why, pity should not let
Age make itself contemptible ; we must be [200
All old. Have him away.
    MEL. Calianax,
The King believes you ; come, you shall go
    home,
And rest ; you ha' done well. — [*aside to him*]
    You 'll give it up,
When I have us'd you thus a month, I hope.
    CAL. Now, now, 't is plain, sir ; he does
    move me still.
He says he knows I 'll give him up the fort,
When he has us'd me thus a month. I am
    mad,
Am I not, still?
    OMNES. Ha, ha, ha !
    CAL. I shall be mad indeed, if you do thus.
Why should you trust a sturdy fellow there
(That has no virtue in him — all 's in his
    sword) 211
Before me? Do but take his weapons from
    him,
And he 's an ass ; and I am a very fool,
Both with ['em] [39] and without ['em],[39] as you
    use me.
    OMNES. Ha, ha, ha !
    KING. 'T is well, Calianax ; but if you use
This once again, I shall entreat some other
To see your offices be well discharg'd. —
Be merry, gentlemen. — It grows somewhat
    late. —
Amintor, thou wouldst be abed again. 220
    AMIN. Yes, sir.
    KING. And you, Evadne. — Let me take
Thee in my arms, Melantius, and believe
Thou art, as thou deservest to be, my friend
Still and for ever. — Good Calianax,
Sleep soundly ; it will bring thee to thyself.
    Exeunt [*all but*] MELANTIUS *and*
        CALIANAX.
    CAL. Sleep soundly ! I sleep soundly now,
    I hope ;
I could not be thus else. — How dar'st thou
    stay
Alone with me, knowing how thou hast used
    me?
    MEL. You cannot blast me with your
    tongue, and that 's
The strongest part you have about you.

[39] Emend. Dyce ; old eds. *him*.

    CAL. I [230
Do look for some great punishment for this ;
For I begin to forget all my hate,
And take 't unkindly that mine enemy
Should use me so extraordinarily scurvily.
    MEL. I shall melt too, if you begin to
    take
Unkindnesses ; I never meant you hurt.
    CAL. Thou 'lt anger me again. Thou
    wretched rogue,
Meant me no hurt ! Disgrace me with the
    King !
Lose all my offices ! This is no hurt,
Is it? I prithee, what dost thou call hurt?
    MEL. To poison men, because they love
    me not ; 241
To call the credit of men's wives in ques-
    tion ;
To murder children,[40] betwixt me and land ;
This I call hurt.
    CAL. All this thou think'st is sport ;
For mine is worse ; but use thy will with
    me,
For betwixt grief and anger I could cry.
    MEL. Be wise, then, and be safe ; thou
    mayst revenge —
    CAL. Ay, o' th' King ; I would revenge of
    thee.
    MEL. That you must plot yourself.
    CAL. I am a fine plotter.
    MEL. The short is, I will hold thee with the
    King 250
In this perplexity, till peevishness
And thy disgrace have laid thee in thy grave.
But if thou wilt deliver up the fort,
I 'll take thy trembling body in my arms,
And bear thee over dangers. Thou shalt
    hold
Thy wonted state.
    CAL. If I should tell the King.
Canst thou deny 't again?
    MEL. Try, and believe.
    CAL. Nay, then, thou canst bring any
    thing about.
[Melantius],[41] thou shalt have the fort.
    MEL. Why, well.
Here let our hate be buried ; and this hand [260
Shall right us both. Give me thy aged breast
To compass.
    CAL. Nay, I do not love thee yet ;
I cannot well endure to look on thee ;
And if I thought it were a courtesy,
Thou shouldst not have it. But I am dis-
    grac'd ;

[40] *I.e.*, heirs who stand.   [41] Q₁ only.

My offices are to be ta'en away ;
And, if I did but hold this fort a day,
I do believe the King would take it from
    me,
And give it thee, things are so strangely car-
    ried.
Ne'er thank me for 't ; but yet the King shall
    know   270
There was some such thing in 't I told him of,
And that I was an honest man.
MEL.   He 'll buy
That knowledge very dearly.

Re-enter DIPHILUS.

                          Diphilus,
What news with thee ?
DIPH.   This were a night indeed
To do it in : the King hath sent for her.
    MEL. She shall perform it then. — Go,
        Diphilus,
And take from this good man, my worthy
    friend,
The fort ; he 'll give it thee.
DIPH.   Ha' you got that ?
    CAL. Art thou of the same breed ? Canst
        thou deny
This to the King too ?
DIPH.   With a confidence [280
As great as his.
    CAL.   Faith, like enough.
    MEL. Away, and use him kindly.
    CAL.   Touch not me ;
I hate the whole strain.[42] If thou follow
    me
A great way off, I 'll give thee up the fort ;
And hang yourselves.
    MEL.   Begone.
    DIPH.   He 's finely wrought.
        Exeunt CALIANAX [*and*] DIPHILUS.
    MEL. This is a night, spite of astronomers,[43]
To do the deed in. I will wash the stain
That rests upon our house off with his blood.

Re-enter AMINTOR.

    AMIN. Melantius, now assist me : if thou
        beest
That which thou say'st, assist me. I have
    lost   290
All my distempers, and have found a rage
So pleasing ! Help me.
    MEL. [*aside*]   Who can see him thus,
And not swear vengeance ? — What 's the
    matter, friend ?

[42] Stock, family.
[43] Astrologers.

AMIN. Out with thy sword ; and, hand in
    hand with me,
Rush to the chamber of this hated King,
And sink him with the weight of all his sins
To hell for ever.
    MEL.   'T were a rash attempt,
Not to be done with safety. Let your reason
Plot your revenge, and not your passion.
    AMIN. If thou refusest me in these ex-
        tremes,   300
Thou art no friend. He sent for her to me ;
By Heaven, to me, myself ! and, I must tell
    ye,
I love her as a stranger : there is worth
In that vild woman, worthy things, Melantius ;
And she repents. I 'll do 't myself alone,
Though I be slain. Farewell.
    MEL. [*aside*]   He 'll overthrow
My whole design with madness. — Amintor,
Think what thou doest ; I dare as much as
    valor ;
But 't is the King, the King, the King,
    Amintor,
With whom thou fightest ! —— (*aside*) I
    know he 's honest [44]   310
And this will work with him.
    AMIN.   I cannot tell
What thou hast said ; but thou hast charm'd
    my sword
Out of my hand, and left me shaking here,
Defenceless.
    MEL.   I will take it up for thee.
    AMIN. What a wild beast is uncollected [45]
    man !
The thing that we call honor bears us all
Headlong unto sin, and yet itself is nothing.
    MEL. Alas, how variable are thy thoughts !
    AMIN. Just like my fortunes. I was run to
    that
I purpos'd to have chid thee for. Some
    plot,   320
I did distrust, thou hadst against the King,
By that old fellow's carriage. But take
    heed ;
There 's not the least limb growing to a
    king
But carries thunder in 't.
    MEL.   I have none
Against him.
    AMIN.   Why, come, then ; and still re-
        member
We may not think revenge.
    MEL.   I will remember. *Exeunt.*

[44] Loyal.
[45] With disordered faculties.

ACT V — [SCENE I] [1]

Enter EVADNE *and a* Gentleman [*of the Bed-chamber*].

EVAD. Sir, is the King abed?
GENT.   Madam, an hour ago.
EVAD. Give me the key, then, and let none
   be near ;
'T is the King's pleasure.
   GENT. I understand you, madam ; would
     't were mine !
I must not wish good rest unto your Ladyship.
   EVAD. You talk, you talk.
   GENT. 'T is all I dare do, madam ; but the
     King
Will wake, and then, [methinks] [2] —
   EVAD. Saving your imagination, pray, good
     night, sir.
   GENT. A good night be it, then, and a long
     one, madam.   10
I am gone.   *Exit.*
   EVAD. The night grows horrible ; and all
     about me
Like my black purpose. Oh, the conscience
Of a lost virgin,[3] whither wilt thou pull me?
To what things dismal as the depth of hell
Wilt thou provoke me? Let no woman dare
From this hour be disloyal, if her heart be flesh,
If she have blood, and can fear. 'T is a dar-
   ing
Above that desperate fool's [4] that left his
   peace,
And went to sea to fight ; 't is so many sins, [20
An age cannot [repent] [5] '[e]m ; and so great,
The gods want mercy for. Yet I must through
   '[e]m :
I have begun a slaughter on my honor,
And I must end it there.
     [*She opens the curtains of the inner stage,*
       discovering the] KING *abed.*[6]
                — 'A sleeps. Good
Heavens ! [7]
Why give you peace to this untemperate
   beast,
That hath so long transgress'd you? I must
   kill him,
And I will do 't bravely ; the mere joy
Tells me I merit in it. Yet I must not

[1] The King's bedchamber.
[2] Q₁ only.   [3] Q₁ *virtue.*
[4] Unidentified ; there may indeed be no special
allusion intended.
[5] So Q₁; other old eds. *prevent.*
[6] In the old eds. *King abed* comes at l. 13, doubtless
from the prompter's warning notation.
[7] Q₁ *Oh God.*

Thus tamely do it as he sleeps — that were
To rock him to another world ; my ven-
   geance   30
Shall take him waking, and then lay before
   him
The number of his wrongs and punishments.
I 'll shape his sins like Furies, till I waken
His evil angel, his sick conscience,
And then I 'll strike him dead. — King, by
   your leave ; — (*Ties his arms to the bed.*)
I dare not trust your strength ; your Grace
   and I
Must grapple upon even terms no more.
So, if he rail me not from my resolution,
I shall be strong enough. — My Lord the
   King !
My Lord ! — 'A sleeps as if he meant to
   wake   40
No more. — My Lord ! — Is he not dead al-
   ready? —
Sir ! My Lord !
   KING. Who 's that?
   EVAD.   Oh, you sleep soundly, sir !
   KING.   My dear Evadne,
I have been dreaming of thee ; come to bed.
   EVAD. I am come at length, sir ; but how
     welcome?
   KING. What pretty new device is this,
     Evadne?
What, do you tie me to you? By my love,
This is a quaint one. Come, my dear, and
   kiss me ;
I 'll be thy Mars ; to bed, my Queen of Love.
Let us be caught together, that the gods   50
May see and envy our embraces.
   EVAD.   Stay, sir, stay ;
You are too hot, and I have brought you
   physic
To temper your high veins.
   KING. Prithee, to bed, then ; let me take it
     warm ;
There thou shalt know the state of my body
   better.
   EVAD. I know you have a surfeited foul
     body ;
And you must bleed.   [*Draws a knife.*]
   KING.   Bleed !
   EVAD. Ay, you shall bleed. Lie still ; and,
     if the devil,
Your lust, will give you leave, repent. This
   steel
Comes to redeem the honor that you stole, [60
King, my fair name, which nothing but thy
   death
Can answer to the world.

KING.   How 's this, Evadne?

EVAD. I am not she ; nor bear I in this breast

So much cold spirit to be call'd a woman :

I am a tiger ; I am anything

That knows not pity. Stir not ! If thou dost,

I 'll take thee unprepar'd, thy fears upon thee,

That make thy sins look double, and so send thee

(By my revenge, I will !) to look [8] those torments

Prepar'd for such black souls.   70

KING. Thou dost not mean this ; 't is impossible ;

Thou art too sweet and gentle.

EVAD.   No, I am not ;

I am as foul as thou art, and can number

As many such hells here. I was once fair,

Once I was lovely ; not a blowing rose

More chastely sweet, till thou, thou, thou, foul canker,[9]

(Stir not !) didst poison me. I was a world of virtue,

Till your curs'd court and you (hell bless you for 't !)

With your temptations on temptations

Made me give up mine honor ; for which, King,   80

I am come to kill thee.

KING.   No !

EVAD.   I am.

KING.   Thou art not !

I prithee speak not these things. Thou art gentle,

And wert not meant thus rugged.

EVAD.   Peace, and hear me.

Stir nothing but your tongue, and that for mercy

To those above us ; by whose lights I vow,

Those blessed fires [10] that shot to see our sin,

If thy hot soul had substance with thy blood,

I would kill that too ; which, being past my steel,

My tongue shall reach. Thou art a shameless villain ;

A thing out of the overcharge of nature   90

Sent, like a thick cloud, to disperse a plague

Upon weak catching [11] women ; such a tyrant

That for his lust would sell away his subjects,

Ay, all his Heaven hereafter !

KING.   Hear, Evadne,

Thou soul of sweetness, hear ! I am thy King.

EVAD. Thou art my shame ! Lie still ; there 's none about you,

Within [12] your cries ; all promises of safety

Are but deluding dreams. Thus, thus, thou foul man,

Thus I begin my vengeance !   *Stabs him.*

KING.   Hold, Evadne !

I do command thee, hold.

EVAD.   I do not mean, sir, [100

To part so fairly with you ; we must change

More of these love-tricks yet.

KING.   What bloody villain

Provok'd thee to this murder?

EVAD.   Thou, thou monster !

KING. Oh !

EVAD. Thou kept'st me brave [13] at court, and whor'd me, King ;

Then married me to a young noble gentleman,

And whor'd me still.

KING.   Evadne, pity me !

EVAD. Hell take me, then ! This for my Lord Amintor.

This for my noble brother ! And this stroke

For the most wrong'd of women !   *Kills him.*

KING.   Oh ! I die. [110

EVAD. Die all our faults together ! I forgive thee.   *Exit.*

Enter two [Gentlemen] *of the Bedchamber.*

1 GENT. Come, now she 's gone, let 's enter ; the King expects it, and will be angry.

2 GENT. 'T is a fine wench ; we 'll have a snap at her one of these nights, as she goes from him.

1 GENT. Content. How quickly he had done with her ! I see kings can do no more that way than other mortal people.

2 GENT. How fast he is ! I cannot hear him breathe.   120

1 GENT. Either the tapers give a feeble light,

Or he looks very pale.

2 GENT.   And so he does :

Pray Heaven he be well ; let 's look. — Alas !

He 's stiff, wounded, and dead ! — Treason, treason !

1 GENT. Run forth and call.

2 GENT. Treason, treason !   *Exit.*

1 GENT.   This will be laid on us :

Who can believe a woman could do this?

Enter CLEON *and* LYSIPPUS.

CLEON. How now ! where 's the traitor?

---

[8] Look for.   [9] See on IV, i, 85.   [10] Meteors.
[11] Susceptible to infection.

[12] Within sound of.
[13] In splendid state.

1 GENT. Fled, fled away; but there her
    woful act
Lies still.
CLEON.   Her act! a woman!
LYS.   Where's the body? [130
1 GENT. There.
LYS. Farewell, thou worthy man! There
    were two bonds
That tied our loves, a brother and a king,
The least of which might fetch a flood of tears;
But such the misery of greatness is,
They have no time to mourn; then, pardon
    me!
Sirs, which way went she?

Enter STRATO.

STRA.   Never follow her;
For she, alas! was but the instrument.
News is now brought in that Melantius
Has got the fort, and stands upon the wall, [140
And with a loud voice calls those few that pass
At this dead time of night, delivering [14]
The innocence of this act.
LYS.   Gentlemen,
I am your King.
STRA.   We do acknowledge it.
LYS. I would I were not! Follow, all;
    for this
Must have a sudden stop.   *Exeunt.*

[SCENE II] [15]

Enter MELANTIUS, DIPHILUS, [*and*] CALIANAX,
    on the walls.[16]

MEL. If the dull people can believe I am
    arm'd,
(Be constant, Diphilus,) now we have time
Either to bring our banish'd honors home,
Or create new ones in our ends.
DIPH.   I fear not;
My spirit lies not that way. — Courage, Cali-
    anax!
CAL. Would I had any! you should quickly
    know it.
MEL. Speak to the people; thou art
    eloquent.
CAL. 'T is a fine eloquence to come to the
    gallows:
You were born to be my end; the Devil take
    you!
Now must I hang for company. 'T is
    strange   10
I should be old, and neither wise nor valiant.

Enter LYSIPPUS, DIAGORAS, CLEON, STRATO,
    [*and*] Guard.

LYS. See where he stands, as boldly confi-
    dent
As if he had his full command about him.
STRA. He looks as if he had the better cause,
    sir,
Under your gracious pardon let me speak it!
Though he be mighty-spirited, and forward
To all great things, to all things of that danger
Worse men shake at the telling of, yet cer-
    tainly
I do believe him noble, and this action
Rather pull'd on than sought; his mind was
    ever   20
As worthy as his hand.
LYS.   'T is my fear, too.
Heaven forgive all! — Summon him, Lord
    Cleon.
CLEON. Ho, from the walls there!
MEL.   Worthy Cleon, welcome:
We could have wish'd you here, Lord; you
    are honest.
CAL. (*aside*) Well, thou art as flattering a
    knave, though
I dare not tell thee so ——
LYS.   Melantius!
MEL.   Sir?
LYS. I am sorry that we meet thus; our
    old love
Never requir'd such distance. Pray [to] [17]
    Heaven,
You have not left yourself, and sought this
    safety
More out of fear than honor! You have
    lost   30
A noble master, which your faith, Melantius,
Some think might have preserved; yet you
    know best.
CAL. [*aside*] When time was,[18] I was mad;
    some that dares fight
I hope will pay this rascal.
MEL. Royal young man, those tears look
    lovely on thee;
Had they been shed for a deserving one,
They had been lasting monuments. Thy
    brother,
Whilst he was good, I call'd him king, and
    serv'd him
With that strong faith, that most unwearied
    valor,
Pull'd people from the farthest sun to seek
    him   40

---

[14] Reporting.   [15] Before the fort.
[16] *I.e.*, on the gallery above the inner stage.

[17] Q₁ only.   [18] From the beginning. (Thorndike.)

And buy his friendship.   I was then his soldier.
But since his hot pride drew him to disgrace
      me,
And brand my noble actions with his lust,
(That never-cur'd dishonor of my sister,
Base stain of whore, and, which is worse, the
      joy
To make it still so,) like myself thus I
Have flung him off with my allegiance ;
And stand here, mine own justice, to revenge
What I have suffered in him, and this old man
Wrong'd almost to lunacy.
    CAL.   Who, I?   50
You would draw me in.   I have had no wrong ;
I do disclaim ye all.
    MEL.   The short is this :
'T is no ambition to lift up myself
Urgeth me thus ; I do desire again
To be a subject, so [19] I may be free ;
If not, I know my strength, and will unbuild
This goodly town.   Be speedy, and be wise,
In a reply.
    STRA.   Be sudden, sir, to tie
All up again.   What 's done is past recall,
And past you to revenge ; and there are
      thousands   60
That wait for such a troubled hour as this.
Throw him the blank.
    LYS.   Melantius, write in that
Thy choice : my seal is at it.
               [*Throws a paper to* MELANTIUS.]
    MEL. It was our honors drew us to this act,
Not gain ; and we will only work our pardons.
    CAL. Put my name in too.
    DIPH.   You disclaim'd us all
But now, Calianax.
    CAL.   That 's all one ; [20]
I 'll not be hang'd hereafter by a trick :
I 'll have it in.
    MEL.   You shall, you shall. —
Come to the back gate, and we 'll call you
      king,   70
And give you up the fort.
    LYS.   Away, away. *Exeunt omnes.*

[SCENE III] [21]

Enter ASPATIA, *in man's apparel.*

    ASP. This is my fatal hour.   Heaven may
      forgive
My rash attempt, that causelessly hath laid
Griefs on me that will never let me rest,
And put a woman's heart into my breast.

It is more honor for you that I die ;
For she that can endure the misery
That I have on me, and be patient too,
May live and laugh at all that you can do.

Enter Servant.

God save you, sir !
    SER.   And you, sir !   What 's your busi-
      ness?
    ASP. With you, sir, now ; to do me the fair
      office   10
To help me to your lord.
    SER.   What, would you serve him?
    ASP. I 'll do him any service ; but, to
      haste, [22]
For my affairs are earnest, I desire
To speak with him.
    SER. Sir, because you are in such haste, I
      would
Be loth to delay you longer : you can not.
    ASP. It shall become you, though, to tell
      your lord.
    SER. Sir, he will speak with nobody ;
[But in particular, I have in charge,
About no weighty matters.] [23]
    ASP.   This is most strange. [20
Art thou gold-proof?   There 's for thee ; help
      me to him.
    SER. Pray be not angry, sir ; I 'll do my
      best.   *Exit.*
    ASP. How stubbornly this fellow answer'd
      me !
There is a vild dishonest trick in man,
More than in women.   All the men I meet
Appear thus to me, are harsh and rude,
And have a subtlety in everything,
Which love could never know ; but we fond
      women
Harbor the easiest and the smoothest thoughts,
And think all shall go so.   It is unjust   30
That men and women should be match'd
      together.

Enter AMINTOR *and his* Man.

    AMIN. Where is he?
    SER.   There, my Lord.
    AMIN.   What would you, sir?
    ASP. Please it your Lordship to command
      your man
Out of the room, I shall deliver things
Worthy your hearing.

---

[19] Provided that.   [20] That makes no difference.
[21] An anteroom to Amintor's apartments.
[22] Make haste.
[23] Q[1] only. "My instructions are that he will
speak with no one, especially if the subject is one
of importance."

AMIN.   Leave us.   [*Exit* Servant.]
ASP. (*aside*)   Oh, that that shape
Should bury falsehood in it !
AMIN.   Now your will, sir.
ASP. When you know me, my Lord, you
    needs must guess
My business ; and I am not hard to know ;
For, till the chance of war mark'd this smooth
    face
With these few blemishes,[24] people would call
    me   40
My sister's picture, and her mine. In short,
I am brother to the wrong'd Aspatia.
    AMIN. The wrong'd Aspatia ! Would thou
         wert so too
Unto the wrong'd Amintor ! Let me kiss
That hand of thine, in honor that I bear
Unto the wrong'd Aspatia. Here I stand
That did it. Would he [25] could not ! [26] Gen-
    tle-youth,
Leave me ; for there is something in thy
    looks
That calls my sins in a most hideous form
Into my mind ; and I have grief enough   50
Without thy help.
    ASP.   I would I could with credit !
Since I was twelve years old, I had not seen
My sister till this hour I now arriv'd ;
She sent for me to see her marriage —
A woful one ! but They that are above
Have ends in everything. She us'd few words,
But yet enough to make me understand
The baseness of the injuries you did her.
That little training I have had is war :
I may behave myself rudely in peace ;   60
I would not, though. I shall not need to tell
    you
I am but young, and would be loth to lose
Honor, that is not easily gain'd again.
Fairly I mean to deal : the age is strict
For single combats ; and we shall be stopp'd,
If it be publish'd. If you like your sword,
Use it ; if mine appear a better to you,
Change ; for the ground is this, and this the
    time,
To end our difference.   [*Draws.*]
    AMIN.   Charitable youth,
If thou beest such, think not I will main-
    tain   70
So strange a wrong ; and, for thy sister's sake,
Know that I could not think that desperate
    thing
I durst not do ; yet, to enjoy this world,

[24] She has evidently painted scars on her face.
[25] That did it.   [26] Stand here.

I would not see her ; for, beholding thee,
I am I know not what. If I have aught
That may content thee, take it, and be-
    gone ;
For death is not so terrible as thou :
Thine eyes shoot guilt into me.
    ASP.   Thus, she swore
Thou wouldst behave thyself, and give me
    words
That would fetch tears into my eyes ; and
    so   80
Thou dost indeed, But yet she bade me watch
Lest I were cozen'd ; and be sure to fight
Ere I return'd.
    AMIN.   That must not be with me.
For her I 'll die directly ; but against her
Will never hazard it.
    ASP.   You must be urg'd.
I do not deal uncivilly with those
That dare to fight ; but such a one as you
Must be us'd thus.   *She strikes him.*
    AMIN.   I prithee, youth, take heed.
Thy sister is a thing to me so much
Above mine honor, that I can endure   90
All this — good gods ! a blow I can endure ;
But stay not, lest thou draw a timeless [27]
    death
Upon thyself.
    ASP.   Thou art some prating fellow ;
One that has studied out a trick to talk,
And move soft-hearted people ; to be kick'd,
                       She kicks him.
Thus to be kick'd. — (*aside*) Why should he
    be so slow
In giving me my death?
    AMIN.   A man can bear
No more, and keep his flesh. Forgive me,
    then !
I would endure yet, if I could. Now show
                       [*Draws.*]
The spirit thou pretendest, and understand
Thou hast no hour to live.
         They fight ; [ASPATIA *is wounded.*]
         What dost thou mean ? [101
Thou canst not fight ; the blows thou mak'st
    at me
Are quite besides ; [28] and those I offer at
    thee,
Thou spread'st thine arms, and tak'st upon
    thy breast,
Alas, defenceless !
    ASP.   I have got enough.
And my desire. There is no place so fit
For me to die as here.   [*Falls.*]
[27] Untimely.   [28] Aside.

Enter EVADNE, *her hands bloody, with a knife.*

EVAD. Amintor, I am loaden with events
That fly to make thee happy ; I have joys
That in a moment can call back thy wrongs
And settle thee in thy free state again.   111
It is Evadne still that follows thee,
But not her mischiefs.

AMIN. Thou canst not fool me to believe
again ;
But thou hast looks and things so full of news,
That I am stay'd.

EVAD. Noble Amintor, put off thy amaze,
Let thine eyes loose, and speak.   Am I not
fair ?
Looks not Evadne beauteous with these rites
now ?
Were those hours half so lovely in thine
eyes   120
When our hands met before the holy man ?
I was too foul within to look fair then ;
Since I knew ill, I was not free till now.

AMIN. There is presage of some important
thing
About thee, which, it seems, thy tongue hath
lost.
Thy hands are bloody, and thou hast a knife.

EVAD. In this consists thy happiness and
mine.
Joy to Amintor ! for the King is dead.

AMIN. Those have most power to hurt us,
that we love ;
We lay our sleeping lives within their arms.
Why, thou hast raised up mischief to his
height,   131
And found one to out-name [29] thy other faults ;
Thou hast no intermission of thy sins,
But all thy life is a continued ill.
Black is thy color now, disease thy nature.
Joy to Amintor !   Thou hast touch'd a life,
The very name of which had power to chain
Up all my rage, and calm my wildest wrongs.

EVAD. 'T is done ; and, since I could not
find a way
To meet thy love so clear as through his
life,   140
I cannot now repent it.

AMIN. Couldst thou procure the gods to
speak to me,
To bid me love this woman and forgive,
I think I should fall out with them.   Behold,
Here lies a youth whose wounds bleed in my
breast,
Sent by a violent fate to fetch his death

[29] Surpass.

From my slow hand !   And, to augment my
woe,
You now are present, stain'd with a king's
blood
Violently shed.   This keeps night here,
And throws an unknown wilderness [30] about
me.   150

ASP. Oh, oh, oh !

AMIN. No more ; pursue me not.

EVAD.   Forgive me, then,
And take me to thy bed ; we may not part.
                                    [*Kneels.*]

AMIN. Forbear ; be wise ; and let my rage
go this way.

EVAD. 'T is you that I would stay, not it.

AMIN.   Take heed ;
It will return with me.

EVAD.   If it must be,
I shall not fear to meet it.   Take me home.

AMIN. Thou monster of cruelty, forbear !

EVAD. For Heaven's sake look more calm !
Thine eyes are sharper
Than thou canst make thy sword.

AMIN.   Away, away ! [160
Thy knees are more to me than violence.
I am worse than sick to see knees follow me
For that I must not grant.   For God's sake,
stand.

EVAD. Receive me, then.

AMIN.   I dare not stay thy language.
In midst of all my anger and my grief,
Thou dost awake something that troubles me,
And says, I lov'd thee once.   I dare not stay ;
There is no end of woman's reasoning.
                                    Leaves her.

EVAD. [*rising*] Amintor, thou shalt love me
now again.
Go ; I am calm.   Farewell, and peace for
ever !   170
Evadne, whom thou hat'st, will die for thee.
                                    Kills herself.

AMIN. (*returns.*) I have a little human
nature yet,
That 's left for thee, that bids me stay thy
hand.

EVAD. Thy hand was welcome, but it came
too late.
Oh, I am lost ! the heavy sleep makes haste.
                                    She dies.

ASP. Oh, oh, oh !

AMIN. This earth of mine doth tremble,
and I feel
A stark affrighted motion in my blood.
My soul grows weary of her house, and I

[30] Wildness.

All over am a trouble to myself.   180
There is some hidden power in these dead
    things,
That calls my flesh unto 'em ; I am cold.
Be resolute and bear 'em company.
There's something yet, which I am loth to
    leave ;
There's man enough in me to meet the fears
That death can bring ; and yet would it were
    done !
I can find nothing in the whole discourse
Of death I durst not meet the boldest way ;
Yet still, betwixt the reason and the act,
The wrong I to Aspatia did stands up ;   [190
I have not such another fault to answer.
Though she may justly arm herself with scorn
And hate of me, my soul will part less troubled
When I have paid to her in tears my sorrow.
I will not leave this act unsatisfied,
If all that's left in me can answer it.

    Asp. Was it a dream? There stands Amin-
      tor still ;
Or I dream still.

    Amin. How dost thou? speak ; receive my
      love and help.
Thy blood climbs up to his old place again ;
There's hope of thy recovery.   201

    Asp. Did you not name Aspatia?
    Amin.   I did.
    Asp. And talk'd of tears and sorrow unto
      her?
    Amin. 'T is true ; and, till these happy
      signs in thee
Stay'd my course, it [31] was thither I was
    going.
    Asp. Thou art there already, and these
      wounds are hers.
Those threats I brought with me sought not
    revenge,
But came to fetch this blessing from thy
    hand ;
I am Aspatia yet.

    Amin. Dare my soul ever look abroad
      again?   210
    Asp. I shall sure live, Amintor ; I am well ;
A kind of healthful joy wanders within me.

    Amin. The world wants [lives] [32] to excuse
      thy loss ;
Come, let me bear thee to some place of
    help.
    Asp. Amintor, thou must stay ; I must
      rest here ;
My strength begins to disobey my will.

How dost thou, my best soul? I would fain
    live
Now, if I could. Wouldst thou have loved
    me, then?
    Amin. Alas,
All that I am 's not worth a hair from thee !
    Asp. Give me thy hand ; mine hands grope
      up and down,   221
And cannot find thee ; I am wondrous sick.
Have I thy hand, Amintor?
    Amin. Thou greatest blessing of the world,
      thou hast.
    Asp. I do believe thee better than my sense.
Oh, I must go ! farewell !   [*Dies.*]
    Amin. She swoons.[33] — Aspatia ! — Help !
      for God's sake, water,
Such as may chain life ever to this frame ! —
Aspatia, speak ! — What, no help? Yet I
    fool !
I 'll chafe her temples. Yet there's nothing
    stirs.   230
Some hidden power tell her Amintor calls,
And let her answer me ! — Aspatia, speak ! —
I have heard, if there be any life, but bow
The body thus, and it will show itself.
Oh, she is gone ! I will not leave her yet.
Since out of justice we must challenge noth-
    ing,
I 'll call it mercy, if you 'll pity me,
You heavenly Powers, and lend for some few
    years
The blessed soul to this fair seat again ! —
No comfort comes ; the gods deny me too. [240
I 'll bow the body once again. — Aspatia ! —
The soul is fled for ever ; and I wrong
Myself, so long to lose her company.
Must I talk now? Here's to be with thee,
    love !   *Kills himself.*

Re-enter Servant.

    Serv. This is a great grace to my Lord, to
have the new king come to him. I must tell
him he is ent'ring. — Oh, God ! — Help, help !

Enter Lysippus, Melantius, Calianax,
    Cleon, Diphilus, [*and*] Strato.

    Lys. Where's Amintor?
    Stra.   Oh, there, there !
    Lys. How strange is this !
    Cal.   What should we do here?
    Mel. These deaths are such acquainted
      things with me,   250
That yet my heart dissolves not. May I
    stand

---

[31] Q₃ *et seq., Did stay . . . 'twas.*
[32] Emend. Seward ; old eds. *lines.*

[33] Old eds. spell *sounds, swounds.*

Stiff here for ever!—Eyes, call up your
    tears!
This is Amintor. Heart, he was my friend ;
Melt ! now it flows. — Amintor, give a word
To call me to thee.
    AMIN. Oh !
    MEL. Melantius calls his friend Amintor.
    Oh,
Thy arms are kinder to me than thy tongue !
Speak, speak !
    AMIN. What?   260
    MEL. That little word was worth all the
        sounds
That ever I shall hear again.
    DIPH.   Oh, Brother,
Here lies your sister slain ! You lose your-
    self
In sorrow there.
    MEL.   Why, Diphilus, it is
A thing to laugh at, in respect of this.
Here was my sister, father, brother, son ;
All that I had. — Speak once again ; what
    youth
Lies slain there by thee?
    AMIN.   'T is Aspatia.
My last is said. Let me give up my soul
Into thy bosom.   [*Dies.*] 270
    CAL. What's that? What's that? Aspa-
    tia !
    MEL.   I never did
Repent the greatness of my heart till now ;
It will not burst at need.
    CAL. My daughter dead here too ! And

you have all fine new tricks to grieve ; but I
ne'er knew any but direct crying.
    MEL. I am a prattler ; but no more.
                        [*Offers* [34] *to kill himself.*]
    DIPH.   Hold, Brother !
    LYS. Stop him.
    DIPH. Fie, how unmanly was this offer in
    you !
Does this become our strain? [35]   280
    CAL. I know not what the matter is, but I
am grown very kind, and am friends with you
[all now].[36] You have given me that among
you will kill me quickly ; but I 'll go home,
and live as long as I can.   [*Exit.*] [36]
    MEL. His spirit is but poor that can be
    kept
From death for want of weapons.
Is not my hands a weapon sharp enough
To stop my breath? or, if you tie down those,
I vow, Amintor, I will never eat,   290
Or drink, or sleep, or have to do with that
That may preserve life ! This I swear to
    keep.
    LYS. Look to him, though, and bear those
    bodies in.
May this a fair example be to me
To rule with temper ; for on lustful kings
Unlook'd-for sudden deaths from God are
    sent ;
But curs'd is he that is their instrument.
                              [*Exeunt.*]

[34] Attempts. Theobald adds this s. D.
[35] Stock, family.   [36] Q 1 only.

THE
Wild-Goose Chase.
A
COMEDIE.

As it hath been Acted with singular
Applause at the *Black-Friers*:

Being the Noble, Last, and Onely *Remaines*
of those Incomparable *Drammatifts*,

$\left\{\begin{array}{c} \textit{FRANCIS BEAUMONT,} \\ \text{AND} \\ \textit{JOHN FLETCHER,} \end{array}\right\}$ Gent:

Retriv'd for the publick delight of all the Ingenious ;

And private Benefit

Of $\left\{\begin{array}{c} \textit{JOHN LOWIN,} \\ \text{And} \\ \textit{JOSEPH TAYLOR,} \end{array}\right\}$ $\left\{\begin{array}{l} \text{Servants to His late} \\ \text{MAJESTIE.} \end{array}\right.$

By a Person of Honour.

Ite bonis avibus ———

LONDON,

Printed for *Humpherey Moseley*, and are to be
sold at the *Princes Armes* in St. *Paules*
Church-yard. 1652.

INTRODUCTORY NOTE

THIS sprightly comedy, wholly the work of Fletcher, was acted at court in 1621, presumably not long after its composition. According to the eminent actors Lowin and Taylor, who introduce the *editio princeps*, it was a particular favorite of the author's : in spite of his " innate modesty " and usual unconcern when he witnessed his plays in performance, he joined " the thronged theatre " in " applauding this rare issue of his brain." " Only we wish," they conclude, " that you may have the same kind of joy in perusing of it as we had in the acting."

Like many another comedy of manners, *The Wild-Goose Chase* is not remarkable for structural excellences. No source of the too episodical plot is known. The play pleases by its very artificiality, its sparkling dialogue, its wit and sophistication, and above all its unforced gaiety. We are on the way, now, from the thoughtful comedy of Jonson to the careless grace of Etherege.

The piece remained in " general received acceptance " up to the closing of the theatres, and when they reopened under the Restoration was one of the first plays to be revived. Farquhar's adaptation, *The Inconstant*, was staged in 1702, but the original was occasionally acted till long after.

The Wild-Goose Chase was not included in the First Folio, of 1647, since, as we learn from the prefatory note of the publisher, the only MS of it had " long been lost, and I fear irrecoverable." He goes on to explain that " a person of quality borrowed it from the actors many years since and, by the negligence of a servant, it was never returned ; therefore now I put up this *Si quis* [advertisement], that whoever happily meets with it shall be thankfully satisfied if he please to send it home." Apparently the *Si quis* turned the trick, and in 1652 the play appeared separately in folio, with eulogistic verses by Richard Lovelace and others. It was reprinted in the Second Folio, of 1679. The present text is based on the first edition, with a few corrections from the second.

THE WILD-GOOSE CHASE

BY

JOHN FLETCHER

DRAMATIS PERSONAE

DE GARD, a noble, staid gentleman, that, being newly lighted from his travels, assists his sister Oriana in her chase of Mirabel the Wild-Goose. Acted by Mr. Robert Benfield.

LA CASTRE, the indulgent father to Mirabel. Acted by Mr. Richard Robinson.

MIRABEL the Wild-Goose, a travell'd Monsieur, and great defier of all ladies in the way of marriage, otherwise their much loose servant,[1] at last caught by the despis'd Oriana. Incomparably acted by Mr. Joseph Taylor.

PINAC, his fellow traveller, of a lively spirit, and servant to the no less sprightly Lillia Bianca. Admirably well acted by Mr. Thomas Pollard.

BELLEUR, companion to both, of a stout blunt humor, in love with Rosalura. Most naturally acted by Mr. John Lowin.

NANTOLET, father to Rosalura and Lillia Bianca. Acted by Mr. William Penn.

LUGIER, the rough and confident tutor to the ladies, and chief engine to entrap the Wild-Goose. Acted by Mr. Hilliard Swanston.

A Young [Man disguised as a] factor. By Mr. John Honyman.

[A Servant to Lillia Bianca.]

[Gentlemen,] Page,[2] Singing-boy, Two [Men disguised as] Merchants, Priest, Servants.

ORIANA, the fair betroth'd of Mirabel, and witty follower of the chase. Acted by Mr. Steph. Hammerton.

ROSALURA, } the airy daughters of Nantolet. William Trigg, Sander Gough.
LILLIA BIANCA, }

PETELLA, their waiting woman.[3] Mr. Shanck.

MARIANA, an English courtesan.

Four Women.

THE SCENE — *Paris.*

ACT I — SCENE I[4]

Enter MONSIEUR DE GARD *and a* Foot-boy.

DE GARD. Sirrah, you know I have rid hard ; stir my horse well,
And let him want no litter.

BOY. I am sure I have run hard ;
Would somebody would walk me, and see me litter'd,
For I think my fellow horse cannot in reason
Desire more rest, nor take up his chamber before me ;
But we are the beasts now, and the beasts are our masters.

DE GARD. When you have done, step to the ten-crown ordinary [5]——

BOY. With all my heart, sir ; for I have [a] twenty-crown stomach.

DE GARD. And there bespeak a dinner.

BOY.   Yes, sir, presently.[6] [10

DE GARD. For whom, I beseech you, sir?

BOY.   For myself, I take it, sir.

DE GARD. In truth, you shall not take it ; 't is not meant for you.
There 's for your provender [*giving money*].
Bespeak a dinner
For Monsieur Mirabel and his companions ;
They 'll be in town within this hour. When you have done, sirrah,
Make ready all things at my lodging for me,
And wait me there.

BOY.   The ten-crown ordinary?

---

[1] Lover.   [2] *I.e.*, the foot-boy.
[3] F₁ adds *Their Servant*. Dyce suggests that this may be the servant to Lillia Bianca, and that Shanck doubled the rôles.
[4] Not precisely located ; in or before the house of La Castre.
[5] Inn, public dining-room.   [6] At once.

883

DE GARD. Yes, sir, if you have not forgot it.
BOY. I'll forget my feet first:
'T is the best part of a footman's faith.
Exit Boy.
DE GARD. These youths, [20
For all they have been in Italy to learn thrift,
And seem to wonder at men's lavish ways,
Yet they cannot rub off old friends, their
French itches;[7]
They must meet sometimes to disport their
bodies
With good wine and good women, and good
store too.
Let 'em be what they will, they are arm'd at
all points,
And then hang saving, let the sea grow high!
This ordinary can fit 'em of all sizes.

Enter LA CASTRE *and* ORIANA.

They must salute their country with old cus-
toms.
ORI. Brother!
DE GARD. My dearest Sister!
ORI. Welcome, welcome! [30
Indeed, ye are welcome home, most welcome!
DE GARD. Thank ye.
You are grown a handsome woman, Oriana —
Blush at your faults! I am wondrous glad to
see ye. —
Monsieur La Castre, let not my affection
To my fair sister make me [be][8] held unman-
nerly;
I am glad to see ye well, to see ye lusty,
Good health about ye, and in fair company;
Believe me, I am proud ——
LA CAST. Fair sir, I thank ye.
Monsieur De Gard, you are welcome from
your journey;
Good men have still good welcome. Give me
your hand, sir. 40
Once more, you are welcome home. You look
still younger.
DE GARD. Time has no leisure to look after
us;
We wander every where; Age cannot find us.
LA CAST. And how does all?
DE GARD. All well, sir, and all lusty.
LA CAST. I hope my son be so. I doubt
not, sir,
But you have often seen him in your journeys,
And bring me some fair news.
DE GARD. Your son is well, sir,
And grown a proper gentleman; he is well
and lusty.
[7] Inclinations. [8] Add F2.

Within this eight hours I took leave of him,
And [over-hied][9] him, having some slight busi-
ness 50
That forc'd me out o' th' way. I can assure
you
He will be here to-night.
LA CAST. Ye make me glad, sir;
For o' my faith, I almost long to see him.
Methinks, he has been away ——
DE GARD. 'T is but your tenderness.
What are three years? A love-sick wench
will allow it.
His friends that went out with him are come
back too,
Belleur and young Pinac. He bid me say little,
Because he means to be his own glad messenger.
LA CAST. I thank ye for this news, sir. He
shall be welcome,
And his friends too; indeed, I thank you
heartily. 60
And how (for I dare say you will not flatter
him)
Has Italy wrought on him? Has he mew'd[10]
yet
His wild fantastic toys?[11] They say that
climate
Is a great purger of those humorous fluxes.[12]
How is he improved, I pray ye?
DE GARD. No doubt, sir, well;
H' as borne himself a full and noble gentle-
man;
To speak him farther is beyond my charter.
LA CAST. I am glad to hear so much good.
Come, I see
You long to enjoy your sister; yet I must
entreat ye,
Before I go, to sup with me to-night, 70
And must not be deni'd.
DE GARD. I am your servant.
LA CAST. Where you shall meet fair, merry,
and noble company;
My neighbor Nantolet and his two fair
daughters.
DE GARD. Your supper's season'd well,
sir; I shall wait upon ye.
LA CAST. Till then I'll leave ye; and y' are
once more welcome. *Exit.*
DE GARD. I thank ye, noble sir! — Now,
Oriana,
How have ye done since I went? Have ye
had your health well?
And your mind free?

[9] Conj. Colman; old eds. *over-ey'd.*
[10] Moulted, shed. [11] Whims, notions.
[12] Changes.

ORI.   You see, I am not bated ; [13]
Merry, and eat my meat.
DE GARD.   A good preservative.
And how have you been us'd? You know,
  Oriana,   80
Upon my going out, at your request
I left your portion in La Castre's hands,
The main means you must stick to. For that
  reason,
And 't is no little one, I ask ye, Sister,
With what humanity he entertains ye,
And how ye find his courtesy?
ORI.   Most ready.
I can assure you, sir, I am us'd most nobly.
  DE GARD. I am glad to hear it ; but, I
    prithee, tell me,
And tell me true, what end had you, Oriana,
In trusting your money here? He is no kins-
  man,   90
Nor any tie upon him of a guardian ;
Nor dare I think ye doubt my prodigality.[14]
  ORI. No, certain, sir ; none of all this pro-
    voked [15] me ;
Another private reason.
  DE GARD.   'T is not private
Nor carried so ; 't is common, my fair Sister ;
Your love to Mirabel : your blushes tell it.
'T is too much known, and spoken of too
  largely ;
And with no little shame I wonder at it.
  ORI. Is it a shame to love?
  DE GARD.   To love undiscreetly ;
A virgin should be tender of her honor,   100
Close,[16] and secure.
  ORI.   I am as close as can be,
And stand upon as strong and honest guards
  too ;
Unless this warlike age need a portcullis ;
Yet, I confess, I love him.
  DE GARD.   Hear the people.
  ORI. Now, I say, hang the people ! He
    that dares
Believe what they say dares be mad, and
  give
His mother, nay, his own wife, up to rumor.
All grounds of truth they build on is a tavern,
And their best censure's [17] sack, sack in abun-
  dance ;
For, as they drink, they think : they ne'er
  speak modestly,   110
Unless the wine be poor, or they want money.
Believe them ! Believe *Amadis de Gaul,*

The *Knight o' th' Sun,* or *Palmerin of Eng-
  land ;* [18]
For these, to them, are modest and true
  stories.
Pray, understand me ; if their tongues be
  truth,
And if *in vino veritas* be an oracle,
What woman is, or has been ever, honest? [19]
Give 'em but ten round cups, they'll swear
  Lucretia
Di'd not for want of power to resist Tarquin,
But want of pleasure, that he stay'd no
  longer ;   120
And Portia,[20] that was famous for her piety
To her lov'd lord, they'll face ye out,[21] died
  o' th' pox.[22]
  DE GARD. Well, there is something, Sister.
  ORI.   If there be, Brother,
'T is none of their things ; 't is not yet so
  monstrous :
My thing is marriage ; and, at his return,
I hope to put their squint eyes right again.
  DE GARD. Marriage? 'T is true his father
    is a rich man,
Rich both in land and money ; he his heir,
A young and handsome man, I must confess,
  too ;
But of such qualities, and such wild flings, [130
Such admirable [23] imperfections, Sister,
For all his travel and bought experience,
I should be loth to own him for my brother.
Methinks, a rich mind in a state indifferent [24]
Would prove the better fortune.
  ORI.   If he be wild,
The reclaiming him to good and honest,
  Brother,
Will make much for my honor ; which, if I
  prosper,
Shall be the study of my love, and life too.
  DE GARD. Ye say well ; would he thought
    as well, and loved too !
He marry ! He 'll be hang'd first. He knows
  no more   140
What the conditions and the ties of love are,
The honest purposes and grounds of marriage,
Nor will know, nor be ever brought t' en-
  deavor,
Than I do how to build a church. He was
  ever
A loose and strong defier of all order ;

[18] Like the others, a hero of romance ; the Knight
o' th' Sun is the hero of *The Mirror of Knighthood.*
[19] Chaste.   [20] Brutus's wife.
[21] Impudently maintain.
[22] Syphilis.   [23] Remarkable.
[24] A moderate estate or rank.

[13] Dwindled.
[14] Fear that I would be a spendthrift.
[15] Instigated.   [16] Secret.   [17] Judgment's.

His loves are wanderers — they knock at each
    door,
And taste each dish, but are no residents.
Or say [25] he may be brought to think of mar-
    riage,
(As 't will be no small labor), thy hopes are
    strangers.
I know there is a labor'd match now follow'd,
Now at this time, for which he was sent for
    home too.   151
Be not abus'd : [26] Nantolet has two fair
    daughters,
And he must take his choice.
    ORI.   Let him take freely.
For all this, I despair not ; my mind tells me
That I, and only I, must make him perfect ;
And in that hope I rest.
    DE GARD.   Since y' are so confident,
Prosper your hope ! I 'll be no adversary ;
Keep [27] yourself fair and right, he shall not
    wrong ye.
    ORI. When I forget my virtue, no man
    know me !   *Exeunt.*

SCENE II [28]

Enter MIRABEL, PINAC, BELLEUR, *and*
    Servants.

    MIR. Welcome to Paris once more, gentle-
    men !
We have had a merry and a lusty ord'nary,
And wine, and good meat, and a bouncing
    reck'ning ; [29]
And let it go for once ; 't is a good physic.
Only, the wenches are not for my diet ;
They are too lean and thin, their embraces
    brawn-fall'n.[30]
Give me the plump Venetian, fat and lusty,
That meets me soft and supple, smiles upon
    me,
As if a cup of full wine leap'd to kiss me ;
These slight things I affect [31] not.
    PIN.   They are ill-built ; [10
Pin-buttock'd,[32] like your dainty Barbaries,[33]
And weak i' th' pasterns ; they 'll endure no
    hardness.
    MIR. There 's nothing good or handsome
    bred amongst us ;

Till we are travell'd, and live abroad, we are
    coxcombs.[34]
Ye talk of France — a slight unseason'd
    country,
Abundance of gross food, which makes us
    blockheads.
We are fair set out indeed, and so are fore-
    horses : [35] —
Men say we are great courtiers — men
    abuse [36] us ;
We are wise, and valiant too — *non credo, si-*
    gnior ;
Our women the best linguists — they are par-
    rots ;   20
O' this side the Alps they are nothing but mere
    drolleries.[37]
Ha ! *Roma la Santa,* Italy for my money !
Their policies, their customs, their frugalities,
Their courtesies so open, yet so reserved too,
As, when ye think y' are known best, ye are
    a stranger.
Their very pick-teeth [38] speak more man than
    we do,
And season of more salt.
    PIN.   'T is a brave [39] country ;
Not pester'd with your stubborn precise [40]
    puppies,
That turn all useful and allow'd contentments
To scabs and scruples [41] — hang 'em, capon-
    worshippers.[42]   36
    BEL. I like that freedom well, and like their
    women too,
And would fain do as others do ; but I am so
    bashful,
So naturally an ass ! Look ye, I can look
    upon 'em,
And very willingly I go to see 'em,
(There 's no man willinger), and I can kiss 'em,
And make a shift —
    MIR.   But, if they chance to flout ye,
Or say, " Ye are too bold ! Fie, sir, remem-
    ber !
I pray, sit farther off — "
    BEL.   'T is true — I am humbled,
I am gone ; I confess ingenuously, I am
    silenced ;
The spirit of amber [43] cannot force me answer.
    PIN. Then would I sing and dance ——
    BEL.   You have wherewithal, sir. [41

---

[25] Assume.   [26] Deceived.
[27] Provided you keep.
[28] Before the house.
[29] Thumping bill.
[30] Lacking in muscular vigor.
[31] Like.
[32] *I.e.,* bony-buttocked ; " pin-bone " = the projecting bone of a horse's hip.
[33] North African horses.

[34] Simpletons.   [35] The "leaders" of a team.
[36] Deceive.   [37] Puppets.
[38] Toothpicks.   [39] Fine.   [40] Puritanical.
[41] *I.e.,* that turn pleasures into questions of the
physical consequences (the scabs of venereal disease)
and of scruples of conscience.
[42] *I.e.,* enemies of sexual freedom.
[43] Highly reputed as an aphrodisiac.

PIN. And charge her up again.

BEL. I can be hang'd first;
Yet, where I fasten well, I am a tyrant.

MIR. Why, thou dar'st fight?

BEL. Yes, certainly, I dare fight,
And fight with any man at any weapon.
Would th' other were no more! But, a pox
on 't!
When I am sometimes in my height of hope,
And reasonable valiant that way, my heart
harden'd,
Some scornful jest or other chops between me
And my desire. What would ye have me to
do, then, gentlemen? 50

MIR. Belleur, ye must be bolder. Travel
three years,
And bring home such a baby to betray ye
As bashfulness! A great fellow, and a soldier!

BEL. You have the gift of impudence; be
thankful.
Every man has not the like talent. I will
study,
And, if it may be reveal'd to me ——

MIR. Learn of me,
And of Pinac. No doubt you'll find employ-
ment;
Ladies will look for courtship.

PIN. 'T is but fleshing,[44]
But standing one good brunt or two. Hast
thou any mind to marriage?
We'll provide thee some soft-natur'd wench,
that's dumb too. 60

MIR. Or an old woman that cannot refuse
thee in charity.

BEL. A dumb woman, or an old woman,
that were eager
And car'd not for discourse, I were excellent
at.

MIR. You must now put on boldness,
— there's no avoiding it —
And stand all hazards, fly at all games bravely;
They'll say you went out like an ox, and
return'd like an ass, else.

BEL. I shall make danger,[45] sure.

MIR. I am sent for home now;
I know it is to marry; but my father shall
pardon me:
Although it be a witty [46] ceremony,
And may concern me hereafter in my gravity,
I will not lose the freedom of a traveller. 71
A new strong lusty bark cannot ride at one
anchor.

Shall I make divers suits to show to the same
eyes?
'T is dull and homespun; — study several
pleasures,
And want employments for 'em? I'll be
hang'd first.
Tie me to one smock? Make my travels
fruitless?
I'll none of that; for every fresh behavior,
By your leave, Father, I must have a fresh
mistress,
And a fresh favor [47] too.

BEL. I like that passingly;
As many as you will, so they be willing, 80
Willing, and gentle, gentle.

PIN. There's no reason
A gentleman, and a traveller, should be
clapp'd up,
(For 't is a kind of b[il]boes [48] to be married),
Before he manifest to the world his good
parts; [49]
Tug ever, like a rascal, at one oar? [50]
Give me the Italian liberty!

MIR. That I study,
And that I will enjoy. Come, go in, gentle-
men;
There mark how I behave myself, and follow,
Exeunt.

SCENE III [51]

Enter LA CASTRE, NANTOLET, LUGIER, ROSA-
LURA, [*and*] LILLIA BIANCA.

LA CAST. You and your beauteous daughters are most welcome.
Beshrew my blood, they are fair ones! — Welcome, beauties,
Welcome, sweet birds.

NANT. They are bound much to your
courtesies.

LA CAST. I hope we shall be nearer acquainted.

NANT. That's my hope too:
For, certain, sir, I much desire your alliance.
You see 'em; they are no gypsies.[52] For their
breeding,
It has not been so coarse but they are able
To rank themselves with women of fair fash-
ion;
Indeed, they have been trained well.

LUG. Thank me.

---

[44] Getting initiated.
[45] Attempt it, risk it. (Lat., *periculum facere*.)
[46] Some mod. eds. emend. *weighty*.
[47] Face.
[48] An iron bar with sliding shackles attached.
[49] Qualities, accomplishments.
[50] Like a galley slave.
[51] A room in the house. [52] Baggages, hussies.

NANT. Fit for the heirs of that state I
    shall leave 'em :   10
To say more, is to sell 'em. They say your
    son,
Now he has travell'd, must be wondrous
    curious [53]
And choice in what he takes ; these are no
    coarse ones.
Sir, here's a merry wench — let him look to
    himself —
All heart, i' faith — may chance to startle
    him ;
For all his care, and travell'd caution,
May creep into his eye. If he love gravity,
Affect a solemn face, there's one will fit him.
    LA CAST. So young and so demure?
    NANT.   She is my daughter,
Else I would tell you, sir, she is a mistress [20
Both of those manners and that modesty
You would wonder at. She is no often-
    speaker,
But, when she does, she speaks well ; nor no
    reveller,
Yet she can dance, and has studied the court
    elements,
And sings, as some say, handsomely ; if a
    woman,
With the decency of her sex, may be a scholar,
I can assure ye, sir, she understands too.
    LA CAST. These are fit garments, sir.
    LUG.   Thank them that cut 'em.
Yes, they are handsome women ; they have
    handsome parts, too,
Pretty becoming parts.
    LA CAST.   'T is like they have, sir. [30
    LUG. Yes, yes, and handsome education
    they have had too,
Had it abundantly ; they need not blush at it.
I taught it : I 'll avouch it.
    LA CAST.   Ye say well, sir.
    LUG. I know what I say, sir, and I say but
    right, sir.
I am no trumpet of their commendations
Before their father ; else I should say farther.
    LA CAST. Pray ye, what's this gentleman?
    NANT.   One that lives with me, sir ;
A man well bred and learn'd, but blunt and
    bitter ;
Yet it offends no wise man ; I take pleasure
    in 't.
Many fair gifts he has, in some of which, [40
That lie most easy to their understandings,
H' as handsomely bred up my girls, I thank
    him.

[53] Particular, finical.

[LUG.] I have put it to 'em, that's my part ;
    I have urg'd it.
It seems they are of years now to take hold
    on 't.
NANT. He 's wondrous blunt.
LA CAST.   By my faith, I was afraid of
    him.
Does he not fall out with the gentlewomen
    sometimes?
    NANT. No, no ; he 's that way moderate
    and discreet, sir.
    Ros. If he did, we should be too hard for
    him.
    LUG.   Well said, sulphur !
Too hard for thy husband's head, if he wear
    not armor.

Enter MIRABEL, PINAC, [BELLEUR], DE GARD,
    and ORIANA.

NANT. Many of these bick'rings, sir.
LA CAST.   I am glad they are no
    oracles.   50
Sure as I live, he beats them, he 's so puis-
    sant.
    ORI. Well, if ye do forget ——
    MIR.   Prithee, hold thy peace.
I know thou art a pretty wench ; I know thou
    lov'st me ;
Preserve it till we have a fit time to discourse
    on 't,
And a fit place. I 'll ease thy heart, I warrant
    thee.
Thou seest I have much to do now.
    ORI.   I am answer'd, sir ;
With me ye shall have nothing on these condi-
    tions.
DE GARD. Your father and your friends.
LA CAST.   You are welcome home, sir ;
Bless ye, ye are very welcome ! Pray, know
    this gentleman,
And these fair ladies.
    NANT.   Monsieur Mirabel, [60
I am much affected with your fair return, sir ;
You bring a general joy.
    MIR.   I bring you service,
And these bright beauties, sir.
    NANT.   Welcome home, gentlemen,
Welcome with all my heart !
    BEL. [&] PIN.   We thank ye, sir.
    LA CAST. Your friends will have their share
    too.
    BEL.   Sir, we hope
They 'll look upon us, though we show like
    strangers.
        [LA CASTRE *and* MIRABEL *talk aside.*]

Nant. Monsieur De Gard, I must salute you also,
And this fair gentlewoman ; you are welcome from your travel too.
All welcome, all.
De Gard.　We render ye our loves, sir.
The best wealth we bring home. — By your favors, beauties. —　70
[*aside to* Oriana] One of these two — you know my meaning.
Ori. [*aside*]　Well, sir ;
They are fair and handsome, I must needs confess it,
And, let it prove the worst, I shall live after it.
Whilst I have meat and drink, love cannot starve me ;
For, if I die o' th' first fit, I am unhappy,
And worthy to be buried with my heels upward.
Mir. To marry, sir?
La Cast.　You know I am an old man,
And every hour declining to my grave,
One foot already in ; more sons I have not,
Nor more I dare not seek whilst you are worthy.　80
In you lies all my hope, and all my name,
The making good or wretched of my memory,
The safety of my state.
Mir.　And you have provided,
Out of this tenderness, [these] handsome [gentlewomen,] 54
Daughters to this rich man, to take my choice of?
La Cast. I have, dear son.
Mir.　'T is true, ye are old and feebled ;
Would ye were young again, and in full vigor !
I love a bounteous father's life, a long one ;
I am none of those that, when they shoot to ripeness,
Do what they can to break the boughs they grew on.　90
I wish ye many years and many riches,
And pleasures to enjoy 'em ; but, for marriage,
I neither yet believe in 't, nor affect it ;
Nor think it fit.
La Cast.　You will render me your reasons?
Mir. Yes, sir, both short and pithy, and these they are :
You would have me marry a maid?
La Cast.　A maid ! what else?
Mir. Yes, there be things called widows, dead men's wills,

54 So F 2; F 1652 *this . . . Gentlewoman.*

I never lov'd to prove those ; nor never long'd yet
To be buried alive in another man's cold monument.
And there be maids-appearing, and maids-being ;　100
The appearing are fantastic things, mere shadows ;
And, if you mark 'em well, they want their heads, too ;
Only the world, to cozen misty eyes,
Has clapp'd 'em on new faces. The maids-being
A man may venture on, if he be so mad to marry,
If he have neither fear before his eyes, nor fortune ;
And let him take heed how he gather these too ;
For, look ye, Father, they are just like melons —
Muskmelons are the emblems of these maids :
Now they are ripe, now cut 'em, they taste pleasantly,　110
And are a dainty fruit, digested easily ;
Neglect this present time, and come to-morrow,
They are so ripe they are rotten gone, their sweetness
Run into humor,55 and their taste to surfeit.
La Cast. Why, these are now ripe, son.
Mir.　I 'll try them presently,
And, if I like their taste——
La Cast.　'Pray ye, please yourself, sir.
Mir. That liberty is my due, and I 'll maintain it. —
Lady, what think you of a handsome man now?
Ros. A wholesome 56 too, sir?
Mir.　That 's as you make your bargain.
A handsome, wholesome man, then, and a kind man,　120
To cheer your heart up, to rejoice ye, lady?
Ros. Yes, sir, I love rejoicing.
Mir.　To lie close to ye?
Close as a cockle? Keep the cold nights from ye?
Ros. That will be look'd for too ; our bodies ask it.
Mir. And get two boys at every birth?
Ros.　That 's nothing ;
I have known a cobbler do it, a poor thin cobbler,

55 Moisture, wateriness.
56 Healthy (alluding to venereal disease).

A cobbler out of mouldy cheese perform it,
Cabbage, and coarse black bread. Methinks,
    a gentleman
Should take foul scorn to have an awl out-
    name [57] him.
Two at a birth! Why, every house-dove
    has it.   130
That man that feeds well, promises as well
    too,
I should expect indeed something of worth
    from.
Ye talk of two!
    Mir. [*aside*]   She would have me get two
    dozen,
Like buttons, at a birth.
    Ros.   You love to brag, sir.
If you proclaim these offers at your marriage,
Ye are a pretty-timber'd man : take heed!
They may be taken hold of, and expected,
Yes, if not hoped for at a higher rate too.
    Mir. I will take heed, and thank ye for
    your counsel.
Father, what think ye?
    La Cast.   'T is a merry gentlewoman ;
Will make, no doubt, a good wife.
    Mir.   Not for me. [141
I marry her, and, happily,[58] get [59] nothing ;
In what a state am I then? Father, I shall
    suffer,
For anything I hear to the contrary, *more ma-
    jorum ;*
I were as sure to be a cuckold, Father,
A gentleman of antler ——
    La Cast.   Away, away, fool!
    Mir. As I am sure to fail her expectation.
I had rather get the pox than get her babies.
    La Cast. Ye are much to blame. If this
    do not affect [60] ye,
Pray, try the other ; she is of a more demure
    way.   150
    Bel. [*aside*] That I had but the audacity
    to talk thus!
I love that plain-spoken gentlewoman admi-
    rably ;
And, certain, I could go as near to please her,
If downright doing — she has a per'lous coun-
    tenance —
If I could meet one that would believe me,
And take my honest meaning without circum-
    stance [61] ——
    Mir. You shall have your will, sir ; I will
    try the other ;

[57] Outdo. For " an awl " F 1652 reads *a Nawl.*
[58] Perhaps.   [59] Beget.   [60] Please.
[61] Circumlocution.

But 't will be to small use. — I hope, fair lady,
(For, methinks, in your eyes I see more
    mercy,)
You will enjoin your lover a less penance ; [160
And though I 'll promise much, as men are
    liberal,
And vow an ample sacrifice of service,
Yet your discretion, and your tenderness,
And thriftiness in love, good housewife's care-
    fulness
To keep the stock entire ——
    Lil.   Good sir, speak louder,
That these may witness, too, ye talk of noth-
    ing.
I should be loth alone to bear the burden
Of so much indiscretion.
    Mir.   Hark ye, hark ye!
'Ods-bobs, you are angry, lady.
    Lil.   Angry! no, sir ;
I never own'd an anger to lose poorly.   170
    Mir. But you can love, for all this ; and
    delight too,
For all your set austerity to hear
Of a good husband, lady?
    Lil.   You say true, sir ;
For, by my troth, I have heard of none these
    ten year,
They are so rare ; and there are so many, sir,
So many longing women on their knees, too,
That pray the dropping down of these good
    husbands —
The dropping down from Heaven ; for they
    are not bred here —
That you may guess at all my hope, but hear-
    ing ——
    Mir. Why may not I be one?
    Lil.   You were near 'em once, sir, [180
When ye came o'er the Alps : those are near
    Heaven!
But since ye miss'd that happiness, there 's no
    hope of ye.
    Mir. Can ye love a man?
    Lil.   Yes, if the man be lovely,
That is, be honest, modest. I would have
    him valiant,
His anger slow, but certain for his honor ;
Travell'd he should be, but through himself
    exactly,
For 't is fairer to know manners well than
    countries.
He must be no vain talker, nor no lover
To hear himself talk ; they are brags of a
    wanderer,
Of one finds no retreat for fair behavior. [190
Would ye learn more?

Mir.   Yes.

Lil.   Learn to hold your peace, then :
Fond [62] girls are got with tongues, women with
    tempers.

Mir.   Women, with I know what ; but let
    that vanish.
Go thy way, Goodwife Bias ! [63]   Sure, thy
    husband
Must have a strong philosopher's stone ; he
    will ne'er please thee else. —
Here's a starch'd piece of austerity ! — Do
    you hear, Father?
Do you hear this moral lecture?

La Cast.   Yes, and like it.

Mir.   Why, there's your judgment now ;
    there's an old bolt shot !
This thing must have the strangest observa-
    tion,[64]
(Do you mark me, Father?), when she is
    married once,   200
The strangest custom too of admiration
On all she does and speaks — 't will be past
    sufferance.
I must not lie with her in common language,
Nor cry, " Have at thee, Kate ! " — I shall be
    hiss'd then ;
Nor eat my meat without the sauce of sen-
    tences,[65]
Your powder'd [66] beef and problems, a rare
    diet !
My first son, Monsieur Aristotle, I know it,
Great master of the metaphysics, or so ;
The second, Solon, and the best law-setter ;
And I must look [67] Egyptian godfathers,   [210
Which will be no small trouble ; my eldest
    daughter,
Sappho, or such a fiddling kind of poetess,
And brought up, *invita Minerva*, at her needle !
My dogs must look their names too, and all
    Spartan :
Lelaps,[68] Melampus ; [69] no more Fox and
    Bawdy[70]-face.
I married to a sullen set of sentences !
To one that weighs her words and her behav-
    iors
In the gold-weights [71] of discretion ! I 'll be
    hang'd first.

[62] Foolish.
[63] Alluding to Bias of Priene, one of the Seven
Sages of Greece.
[64] Attention.   [65] Maxims.   [66] Salted.
[67] Look for, seek out.
[68] Laelaps, the dog of Procris.
[69] The prophet and physician supposed to have
introduced the worship of Dionysus into Greece.
[70] Dirty.
[71] *I.e.*, scrupulously, with extreme precision.

La Cast.   Prithee, reclaim thyself.

Mir.   Pray ye, give me time, then.
If they can set me anything to play at   [220
That seems fit for a gamester, have at the
    fairest,
Till I see more, and try more !

La Cast.   Take your time, then ;
I 'll bar ye no fair liberty. — Come, gentle-
    men ;
And ladies, come ; to all, once more, a wel-
    come !
And, now let's in to supper.

Mir.   [*aside to his friends*]   How dost
    like 'em?

Pin.   They are fair enough, but of so strange
    behaviors ——

Mir.   Too strange for me. I must have
    those have mettle,
And mettle to my mind. Come, let's be
    merry.

Bel.   Bless me from this woman ! I would
    stand the cannon,
Before ten words of hers.

De Gard.   [*aside to* Oriana]   Do you
    find him now?   230
Do you think he will be ever firm?

Ori.   I fear not.   *Exeunt.*

ACT II — Scene I [1]

Enter Mirabel, Pinac, [*and*] Belleur.

Mir.   Ne'er tell me of this happiness ; 't is
    nothing ;
The state they bring with being sought-to,[2]
    scurvy :
I had rather make mine own play, and I
    will do.
My happiness is in mine own content,
And the despising of such glorious [3] trifles,
As I have done a thousand more. For my
    humor,[4]
Give me a good free fellow, that sticks to me,
A jovial fair companion ; there's a beauty !
For [5] women, I can have too many of them ;
Good women too, as the age reckons 'em,   [10
More than I have employment for.

Pin.   You are happy.

[1] The same, though not precisely located. The
scene may be in or before La Castre's house, or.
as mod. eds. specify, in its garden.
[2] Courted, solicited.
[3] Vainglorious, empty.
[4] To my notion.   [5] As for.

MIR. My only fear is, that I must be forced,
Against my nature, to conceal myself ;
Health and an able body are two jewels.

PIN. If either of these two women were
    offer'd to me now,
I would think otherwise, and do accordingly ;
Yes, and recant my heresies ; I would,[6] sir ;
And be more tender of opinion,[7]
And put a little of my travell'd liberty
Out of the way, and look upon 'em seriously.
Methinks, this grave-carried wench ——

BEL.   Methinks, the other, [21
The home-spoken gentlewoman, that desires
    to be fruitful,
That treats of the full manage of the matter,
(For there lies all my aim,) that wench, me-
    thinks,
If I were but well set on, for she is affable,
If I were but hounded right, and one to teach
    me —
She speaks to th' matter, and comes home to
    th' point —
Now do I know I have such a body to please
    her
As all the kingdom cannot fit her with, I am
    sure on 't,
If I could but talk myself into her favor. [30
    MIR. That 's easily done.
BEL.   That 's easily said ; would 't were
    done !
You should see then how I would lay about me.
If I were virtuous, it would never grieve me,
Or anything that might justify my modesty ;
But when my nature is prone to do a charity,
And my calf's tongue will not help me ——
    MIR.   Will ye go to 'em?
They cannot but take it courteously.
    PIN.   I 'll do my part,
Though I am sure 't will be the hardest I e'er
    play'd yet,
A way I never tri'd, too, which will stagger
    me ;
And, if it do not shame me, I am happy. [40
    MIR. Win 'em, and wear 'em ; I give up my
    interest.
PIN. What say you, Monsieur Belleur?
BEL.   Would I could say,
Or sing, or anything that were but handsome !
I would be with her presently ![8]
    PIN.   Yours is no venture :
A merry ready wench.
    BEL.   A vengeance [9] squibber ; [10]
She 'll fleer [11] me out of faith too.

MIR.   I 'll be near thee.
Pluck up thy heart ; I 'll second thee at all
    brunts.[12]
Be angry, if she abuse thee, and beat her a
    little ;
Some women are won that way.
    BEL.   Pray, be quiet,
And let me think : I am resolv'd to go on ; [50
But how I shall get off again ——
    MIR.   I am persuaded
Thou wilt so please her, she will go near to
    ravish thee.
    BEL. I would 't were come to that once !
    Let me pray a little.
    MIR. Now, for thine honor, Pinac, board
    me [13] this modesty ;
Warm but this frozen snowball : 't will be a
    conquest
(Although I know thou art a fortunate
    wencher,
And hast done rarely in thy days) above all thy
    ventures.
    BEL. You will be ever near?
    MIR.   At all necessities ;
And take thee off, and set thee on again, boy,
And cherish thee, and stroke thee.
    BEL.   Help me out too? [60
For I know I shall stick i' th' mire. If you see
    us close once,
Begone, and leave me to my fortune, suddenly,
For I am then determin'd to do wonders.
Farewell, and fling an old shoe.[14] How my
    heart throbs !
Would I were drunk ! Farewell, Pinac ;
    Heaven send us
A joyful and a merry meeting, man !
    PIN.   Farewell,
And cheer thy heart up ; and remember, Bel-
    leur,
They are but women.
    BEL.   I had rather they were lions.
    MIR. About it ; I 'll be with you in-
    stantly. —

            Exeunt [BELLEUR *and* PINAC].

            Enter ORIANA.

[*aside*] Shall I ne'er be at rest? No peace of
    conscience?   70
No quiet for these creatures? Am I ordain'd
To be devour'd quick [15] by these she-can-
    nibals?
Here 's another they call handsome ; I care
    not for her ;

---

[6] F₂ adds *fain*.   [7] Reputation.   [8] At once.
[9] *I.e.*, a devil of a.   [10] Tart-tongued one.   [11] Mock.

[12] In all your onsets.
[13] Accost.   [14] For luck.   [15] Alive.

I ne'er look after her. When I am half-tippled
It may be I should turn [16] her, and peruse her ;
Or, in my want of women, I might call for her ;
But to be haunted when I have no fancy,
No maw [17] to th' matter ! — Now, why do you
follow me ?

ORI. I hope, sir, 't is no blemish to my
virtue ;
Nor need you, out of scruple, ask that question,
If you remember ye, before your travel,   81
The contract you ti'd to me. 'T is my love,
sir,
That makes me seek ye, to confirm your mem-
ory ;
And, that being fair and good, I cannot suffer.
I come to give ye thanks too.

MIR.   For what, prithee ?

ORI. For that fair piece of honesty ye
show'd sir,
That constant nobleness.

MIR.   How? for I am short-headed.[18]

ORI. I 'll tell ye then ; for refusing that free
offer
Of Monsieur Nantolet's, those handsome
beauties,
Those two prime ladies, that might well have
press'd ye   90
If not to have broken, yet to have bow'd your
promise.
I know it was for my sake, for your faith sake,
You slipp'd 'em off ; your honesty compell'd
ye ;
And let me tell ye, sir, it show'd most handsomely.

MIR. And let me tell thee, there was no such
matter ;
Nothing intended that way, of that nature.
I have more to do with my honesty than to
fool it,
Or venture it in such leak barks as women.
I put 'em off because I lov'd 'em not,   99
Because they are too queasy [19] for my temper,
And not for thy sake, nor the contract sake,
Nor vows, nor oaths ; I have made a thou-
sand of 'em ;
They are things indifferent whether kept or
broken ;
Mere venial slips, that grow not near the con-
science ;
Nothing concerns those tender parts ; they
are trifles ;
For, as I think, there was never man yet hop'd
for

Either constancy or secrecy from a woman,
Unless it were an ass ordain'd for sufferance ;
Nor to contract with such can be a tie-all.
So let them know again ; for 't is a justice [110
And a main point of civil policy,
Whate'er we say or swear, they being repro-
bates,
Out of the state of faith, we are clear of all
sides,
And 't is a curious blindness to believe us.

ORI. You do not mean this, sure ?

MIR.   Yes, sure and certain ;
And hold it positively, as a principle,
As ye are strange things, and made of strange
fires and fluxes,
So we are allow'd as strange ways to obtain ye,
But not to hold ; we are all created errant.

ORI. You told me other tales.

MIR.   I not deny it ; [120
I have tales of all sorts for all sorts of women,
And protestations likewise of all sizes,
As they have vanities to make us coxcombs.
If I obtain a good turn, so it is,
I am thankful for it ; if I be made an ass,
The mends are in mine own hands, or the sur-
geon's,[20]
And there 's an end on 't.

ORI.   Do not you love me, then ?

MIR. As I love others ; heartily I love thee ;
When I am high and lusty, I love thee cruelly.
After I have made a plenteous meal, and satis-
fi'd   130
My senses with all delicates, come to me,
And thou shalt see how I love thee.

ORI.   Will not you marry me ?

MIR. No, certain, no, for anything I know
yet.
I must not lose my liberty, dear lady,
And, like a wanton slave, cry for more shackles.
What should I marry for ? Do I want any-
thing ?
Am I an inch the farther from my pleasure ?
Why should I be at charge [21] to keep a wife of
mine own,
When other honest married men will ease me,[22]
And thank me too, and be beholding [23] to me ?
Thou think'st I am mad for a maidenhead ;
thou art cozen'd ;   141
Or, if I were addicted to that diet,
Can you tell me where I should have one ?
Thou art eighteen now,
And, if thou hast thy maidenhead yet extant,

---

[16] Like the leaves of a book.   [17] Appetite.
[18] My memory is so short.   [19] Fastidious, finical.
[20] Alluding to the possibility of contracting a venereal disease.   [21] Expense.
[22] Free me of the charge.   [23] Beholden.

Sure, 't is as big as cod's-head ; and those
    grave dishes
I never love to deal withal. Dost thou see this
    book here?
Look over all these ranks ; all these are
    women,
Maids, and pretenders to maidenheads ; these
    are my conquests ;
All these I swore to marry, as I swore to thee,
With the same reservation, and most right-
    eously ;   150
Which I need not have done neither, for, alas,
    they made no scruple ;
And I enjoy'd 'em at my will, and left 'em.
Some of 'em are married since, and were as
    pure maids again,
Nay, o' my conscience, better than they were
    bred for ;
The rest, fine sober women.
    ORI.   Are ye not asham'd, sir?
    MIR. No, by my troth sir ; there's no
    shame belongs to it ;
I hold it as commendable to be wealthy in
    pleasure
As others do in rotten sheep and pasture.

            Enter DE GARD.

    ORI. Are all my hopes come to this? Is
    there no faith,
No troth, nor modesty, in men?   [*Weeps.*]
    DE GARD.   How now, Sister? [160
Why weeping thus? Did I not prophesy?
Come, tell me why ——
    ORI.   I am not well ; pray ye pardon me.
                             Exit.
    DE GARD. Now, Monsieur Mirabel, what
    ails my sister?
You have been playing the wag with her.
    MIR.   As I take it,
She is crying for a codpiece.[24] Is she gone?
Lord, what an age is this ! I was calling for
    ye ;
For, as I live, I thought she would have
    ravish'd me.
    DE GARD.   Ye are merry, sir.
    MIR. Thou know'st this book, De Gard,
    this inventory.
    DE GARD. The debt-book of your mis-
    tresses ; I remember it.
    MIR. Why, this was it that anger'd her ;
    she was stark mad   170
She found not her name here ; and cri'd down-
    right

Because I would not pity her immediately,
And put her in my list.
    DE GARD.   Sure, she had more modesty.
    MIR. Their modesty is anger to be over-
    done ; [25]
They 'll quarrel sooner for precedence here,
And take it in more dudgeon to be slighted,
Than they will in public meetings : 't is their
    natures ;
And, alas I have so many to dispatch yet,
And to provide myself for my affairs too,
That, in good faith ——
    DE GARD.   Be not too glorious [26] foolish ;
Sum not your travels up with vanities ;   [181
It ill becomes your expectation.[27]
Temper your speech, sir ; whether your loose
    story
Be true or false, (for you are so free,[28] I fear it,)
Name not my sister in 't : I must not hear it.
Upon your danger, name her not ! I hold her
A gentlewoman of those happy parts and car-
    riage,
A good man's tongue may be right proud to
    speak her.
    MIR. Your sister, sir ! D' ye blench [29] at
    that? D' ye cavil?
Do you hold her such a piece she may not be
    play'd withal?   190
I have had a hundred handsomer and nobler
Have su'd to me, too, for such a courtesy ;
Your sister comes i' th' rear. Since ye are so
    angry,
And hold your sister such a strong recusant,[30]
I tell ye, I may do it ; and, it may be, will too ;
It may be, have too ; there's my free con-
    fession ;
Work upon that now !
    DE GARD.   If I thought ye had, I would
    work
And work such stubborn work should make
    your heart ache ;
But I believe ye, as I ever knew ye,
A glorious talker, and a legend-maker   200
Of idle tales and trifles ; a depraver
Of your own truth : their honors fly about [31]
    ye !
And so, I take my leave, but with this caution :

---

[24] The baggy appendage at the front of the breeches of the time.

[25] Outdone, surpassed.
[26] Vaingloriously, boastfully.
[27] The expectation people have of you.
[28] Loose.   [29] Fly off.
[30] Dissenter (from love).
[31] Probably, as Mason suggests, = may such honor attend you as is to be derived from such stories ; possibly, as Dyce holds (emending with Sympson *about* to *above*) = the honors of the ladies in your list are above your reach.

Your sword be surer than your tongue —
you 'll smart else.

MIR. I laugh at thee, so little I respect [32]
thee ;
And I 'll talk louder, and despise thy sister ;
Set up a chambermaid that shall outshine her,
And carry her in my coach too, and that will
kill her.
Go, get thy rents up,[33] go !

DE GARD. Ye are a fine gentleman ! *Exit.*

MIR. Now, have at my two youths ! I 'll
see how they do ; 210
How they behave themselves ; and then I 'll
study
What wench shall love me next, and when I 'll
loose [34] her. *Exit.*

SCENE II [35]

Enter PINAC *and a* Servant.

PIN. Art thou her servant, say'st thou ?
SERV. Her poor creature ;
But servant to her horse, sir.
PIN. Canst thou show me
The way to her chamber, or where I may con-
veniently
See her, or come to talk to her ?
SERV. That I can, sir ;
But the question is, whether I will or no.
PIN. Why, I 'll content thee.
SERV. Why, I 'll content thee, then ; now
ye come to me.
PIN. There 's for your diligence.
[*Gives money.*]
SERV. There 's her chamber, sir,
And this way she comes out ; stand ye but
here, sir,
You have her at your prospect or your
pleasure,
PIN. Is she not very angry ?
SERV. You 'll find that quickly. [10
Maybe she 'll call ye saucy, scurvy fellow,
Or some such familiar name ; maybe she
knows ye
And will fling a pisspot at ye, or a pantofle,[36]
According as ye are in acquaintance. If she
like ye,
Maybe she 'll look upon ye, maybe no,
And two months hence call for ye.
PIN. This is fine.
She is monstrous proud, then ?

[32] Consider.
[33] *I.e.*, go back to the country, where you belong.
[34] Get rid of.
[35] A room in Nantolet's house.
[36] Slipper.

SERV. She is a little haughty ;
Of a small body, she has a mind well mounted.
Can ye speak Greek ?
PIN. No, certain.
SERV. Get ye gone, then ! —
And talk of stars and firmaments and fire-
drakes ? [37] 20
Do you remember who was Adam's school-
master,
And who taught Eve to spin ? She knows all
these,
And will run ye over the beginning o' th' world
As familiar as a fiddler.
Can you sit seven hours together, and say
nothing ?
Which she will do, and, when she speaks, speak
oracles,
Speak things that no man understands, nor
herself neither.
PIN. Thou mak'st me wonder.
SERV. Can ye smile ?
PIN. Yes, willingly ;
For naturally I bear a mirth about me.
SERV. She 'll ne'er endure ye, then ; she is
never merry ; 30
If she see one laugh, she 'll swoon [38] past *aqua
vitae.*
Never come near her, sir ; if ye chance to ven-
ture,
And talk not like a doctor,[39] you are damn'd
too.
I have told ye enough for your crown, and so,
good speed ye ! *Exit.*
PIN. I have a pretty task, if she be thus
curious,[40]
As, sure, it seems she is ! If I fall off now,
I shall be laugh'd at fearfully ; if I go forward,
I can but be abus'd, and that I look for ;
And yet I may hit right, but 't is unlikely.
Stay — in what mood and figure shall I
attempt her ? 40
A careless way ? No, no, that will not waken
her ;
Besides, her gravity will give me line still,
And let me lose myself ; yet this way often
Has hit, and handsomely. A wanton method ?
Ay, if she give it leave to sink into her con-
sideration ;
But there 's the doubt : if it but stir her blood
once,
And creep into the crannies of her fancy,
Set her a-gog ; but, if she chance to slight it,

[37] Meteors.
[38] Spelled in the old eds. *swound.*
[39] Learned man. [40] Finical.

And by the pow'r of her modesty fling it back,
I shall appear the arrant'st rascal to her,   50
The most licentious knave, for I shall [41] talk lewdly.
To bear myself austerely?   Rate [42] my words?
And fling a general gravity about me,
As if I meant to give laws?   But this I cannot do.
This is a way above my understanding;
Or, if I could, 't is odds she 'll think I mock her;
For serious and sad [43] things are ever still suspicious.
Well, I 'll say something;
But learning I have none, and less good manners,
Especially for ladies.   Well I 'll set my best face.   60

Enter LILLIA [BIANCA *and*] PETELLA.

I hear some coming.   This is the first woman
I ever fear'd yet, the first face that shakes me.
                                        [*Retires.*]
    LIL. Give me my hat, Petella; take this veil off,
This sullen cloud; it darkens my delights.
Come, wench, be free, and let the music warble —
Play me some lusty measure.
                    [*Music within;* LILLIA *dances.*]
    PIN. [*aside*]   This is she, sure,
The very same I saw, the very woman,
The gravity I wonder'd at.   Stay, stay;
Let me be sure.   Ne'er trust me, but she danceth!
Summer is in her face now, and she skippeth!
I 'll go a little nearer.
    LIL.   Quicker time, fellows! [71

Enter MIRABEL [*and stands aside*].

I cannot find my legs yet — now Petella!
    PIN. [*aside*] I am amaz'd; I am founder'd [44] in my fancy!
    MIR. [*aside*] Ha! say you so? [45]   Is this your gravity?
This the austerity ye put upon ye?
I 'll see more o' this sport.
    LIL.   A song now!
Call in for a merry and a light song;
And sing it with a liberal spirit.

[41] Will be certain to.
[42] Weigh.   [43] Serious.   [44] Dumfounded.
[45] Do you so?   Is this what you 're up to?

Enter a Man.[46]

MAN.   Yes, madam.
LIL.   And be not amaz'd, sirrah, but take us for your own company. —

[*A song by the* Man, *who then exit.*]

Let 's walk ourselves; come, wench.   Would we had a man or two!   80
    PIN. [*aside*] Sure, she has spi'd me, and will abuse me dreadfully.
She has put on this for the purpose; yet I will try her. —   [*Advances.*]
Madam, I would be loth my rude intrusion,
Which I must crave a pardon for ——
    LIL.   Oh, ye are welcome,
Ye are very welcome, sir!   We want such a one. —
Strike up again! — I dare presume ye dance well;
Quick, quick, sir, quick! the time steals on.
    PIN.   I would talk with ye.
    LIL.   Talk as ye dance.   [*They dance.*]
    MIR. [*aside*]   She 'll beat him off his legs first.
This is the finest masque!
    LIL.   Now, how do ye, sir?
    PIN.   You have given me a shrewd heat.
    LIL.   I 'll give ye a hundred. [90
Come, sing now, sing; for I know ye sing well;
I see ye have a singing face.
    PIN. [*aside*]   A fine modesty!
If I could, she 'd never give me breath. —
    Madam, would
I might sit and recover!
    LIL.   Sit here, and sing now;
Let 's do things quickly, sir, and handsomely. —
Sit close, wench, close. — Begin, begin.
    PIN.   I am lesson'd.

Song [*by* PINAC].

    LIL.   'T is very pretty, i' faith.   Give me some wine now.
    PIN.   I would fain speak to ye.
    LIL.   You shall drink first, believe me.
Here 's to ye a lusty health.   [*They drink.*]
    PIN.   I thank ye, lady. —
[*aside*] Would I were off again!   I smell my misery;   100
I was never put to this rack; I shall be drunk, too.
    MIR. [*aside*] If thou be'st not a right one, I have lost mine aim much;

[46] Possibly the Singing-boy of *Dr. Pers.* and V, vi.

I thank Heaven that I have scap'd thee. To
    her, Pinac!
For thou art as sure to have her, and to groan
    for her. —
I'll see how my other youth does; this speeds
    trimly.
A fine grave gentlewoman, and worth much
    honor!   *Exit.*
  LIL. Now, how do ye like me, sir?
  PIN.   I like ye rarely.
  LIL. Ye see, sir, though sometimes we are
    grave and silent,
And put on sadder dispositions,
Yet we are compounded of free parts, and
    sometimes too   110
Our lighter, airy, and our fiery mettles
Break out, and show themselves: and what
    think you of that, sir?
  PIN. Good lady, sit, for I am very weary;
And then I'll tell ye.
  LIL.   Fie! a young man idle!
Up, and walk; be still in action;
The motions of the body are fair beauties;
Besides, 't is cold. 'Ods me, sir, let's walk
    faster!
What think ye now of the Lady Felicia?
And Bellafronte, the Duke's fair daughter?
    ha?
Are they not handsome things? There is Du-
    arta,   120
And brown Olivia ——
  PIN.   I know none of 'em.
  LIL. But brown must not be cast away,
    sir.[47] If young Lelia
Had kept herself till this day from a husband,
Why, what a beauty, sir! You know Ismena,
The fair gem of Saint Germains?
  PIN.   By my troth, I do not.
  LIL. And, then, I know, you must hear of
    Brisac,
How unlike a gentleman ——
  PIN.   As I live, I have heard nothing.
  LIL. Strike me another galliard![48]
  PIN.   By this light, I cannot!
In troth, I have sprain'd my leg, madam.
  LIL.   Now sit ye down, sir.
And tell me why ye came hither? Why ye
    chose me out?   130
What is your business? Your errand? Dis-
    patch, dispatch!
Maybe, ye are some gentleman's man,[49] and I
    mistook ye,

That have brought me a letter, or a haunch of
    venison,
Sent me from some friend of mine.
  PIN.   Do I look like a carrier?
You might allow me, what I am, a gentleman.
  LIL. Cry ye mercy, sir! I saw ye yester-
    day;
You are new come out of travel; I mistook ye.
And how does all our impudent friends in
    Italy?
  PIN. Madam, I came with duty, and fair
    courtesy,
Service, and honor to ye.
  LIL.   Ye came to jeer me. [140
Ye see I am merry, sir; I have chang'd my
    copy;
None of the sages now: and, pray ye, proclaim
    it.
Fling on me with aspersion you shall please,
    sir,
Of wantonness or wildness: I look for it;
And tell the world I am an hypocrite,
Mask in a forc'd and borrow'd shape: I ex-
    pect it;
But not to have you believ'd; for, mark ye,
    sir,
I have won a nobler estimation,
A stronger tie, by my discretion,
Upon opinion, howe'er you think I forc'd it, [150
Than either tongue or art of yours can slub-
    ber;[50]
And, when I please, I will be what I please,
    sir,
So I exceed not mean;[51] and none shall
    brand it,
Either with scorn or shame, but shall be
    slighted.
  PIN. Lady, I come to love ye.
  LIL.   Love yourself, sir;
And, when I want observers,[52] [I] 'll send for ye.
Heigh-ho! my fit's almost off; for we do all
    by fits, sir.
If ye be weary, sit till I come again to ye.
                    Exit [with PETELLA].
  PIN. This is a wench of a dainty spirit; but
    hang me, if I know yet
Either what to think or make of her. She
    had her will of me,   160
And baited me abundantly, I thank her;
And, I confess, I never was so blurted,[53]
Nor never so abus'd. I must bear mine own
    sins.

---

[47] Proverbial. (Weber.)
[48] A lively dance in triple time.
[49] Servant.

[50] Sully.   [51] Moderation.
[52] Admirers. — " I " is added by F 2.
[53] Contemptuously treated.

Ye talk of travels; here's a curious country!
Yet I will find her out, or forswear my faculty.

　　　　　　　　　　　　　　　　Exit.

Scene III [54]

Enter Rosalura *and* Oriana.

Ros. Ne'er vex yourself, nor grieve; ye
　are a fool, then.
Ori. I am sure I am made so; yet, before I
　suffer
Thus like a girl, and give him leave to tri-
　umph ——
Ros. You say right; for, as long as he per-
　ceives ye
Sink under his proud scornings, he'll laugh
　at ye.
For me, secure yourself; [55] and, for my sister,
I partly know her mind too; howsoever,
To obey my father, we have made a tender
Of our poor beauties to the travell'd monsieur;
Yet, two words to a bargain. He slights us [10
As skittish things, and we shun him as curious.
Maybe my free behavior turns his stomach,
And makes him seem to doubt a loose opinion.[56]
I must be so sometimes, though all the world
　saw it.
Ori. Why should not ye? Are our minds
　only measur'd?
As long as here ye stand secure ——
Ros. 　　　　　　　Ye say true;
As long as mine own conscience makes no
　question,
What care I for report? That woman's miser-
　able
That's good or bad for their tongues' sake.
　Come, let's retire,
And get my veil, wench. By my troth, your
　sorrow,　　　　　　　　　　　　20
And the consideration of men's humorous
　maddings,
Have put me into a serious contemplation.

Enter Mirabel *and* Belleur.

Ori. Come, faith, let's sit and think.
Ros. 　　　　　　That's all my business.
　　　　　　　　　　　　[They retire.]
Mir. Why stand'st thou peeping here?
　Thou great slug, forward!
Bel. She is there; peace!
Mir. 　　　Why stand'st thou here, then,

Sneaking and peeking as thou wouldst steal
　linen?
Hast thou not place and time?
Bel. 　　　　　　I had a rare speech
Studied, and almost ready; and your violence
Has beat it out of my brains.
Mir. 　　　　　　Hang your rare speeches!
Go me on like a man.
Bel. 　　　Let me set my beard up. [30
How has Pinac performed?
Mir. 　　　　　He has won already;
He stands not thrumming [57] of caps thus.
Bel. 　　　　　Lord, what should I ail!
What a cold I have over my stomach! Would
　I had some hum! [58]
Certain I have a great mind to be at her,
A mighty mind.
Mir. 　　On, fool!
Bel. 　　　　　Good words, I beseech ye;
For I will not be abused by both.
Mir. 　　　　　　　　Adieu, then;
I will not trouble you: I see you are valiant,
And work your own way.
Bel. 　　　Hist, hist! I will be rul'd;
I will, i' faith; I will go presently.
Will ye forsake me now, and leave me i' th'
　suds?　　　　　　　　　　　40
You know I am false-hearted this way. I be-
　seech ye,
Good sweet Mirabel — I'll cut your throat, if
　ye leave me,
Indeed I will — sweetheart —
Mir. 　　　　　　I will be ready,
Still at thine elbow. Take a man's heart to
　thee,
And speak thy mind; the plainer still the
　better.
She is a woman of that free behavior,
Indeed, that common courtesy, she cannot
　deny thee.
Go bravely on.
Bel. 　　Madam — keep close about me,
Still at my back — Madam, sweet madam —
Ros. 　　　　　　　　　Ha!
What noise is that? What saucy sound to
　trouble me?　　　　　　　　50
Mir. What said she?
Bel. 　　　　I am saucy.
　　　[Rosalura *and* Oriana *rise and*
　　　　come forward, the former in a veil.]
Mir. 　　　　　　　'T is the better.
Bel. She comes; must I be saucy still?
Mir. 　　　　　　　　More saucy.

---

[54] Probably the same, though not definitely
located.
　[55] As for me, make your mind easy.
　[56] Fear a reputation for looseness.

[57] *I.e.*, idly fingering.
[58] Strong or double ale.

Ros. Still troubled with these vanities?
    Heaven bless us!
What are we born to? — Would ye speak with
    any of my people?
Go in, sir; I am busy.
    Bel.   This is not she, sure;
Is this two children at a birth? I 'll be hang'd,
    then;
Mine was a merry gentlewoman, talk'd
    daintily,
Talk'd of those matters that befitted women;
This is a parcel [59] pray'r-book. I'm serv'd
    sweetly!
And now I am to look to; [60] I was prepar'd
    for th' other way.   60
    Ros. Do you know that man?
    Ori.   Sure, I have seen him, lady.
    Ros. Methinks 't is pity such a lusty fellow
Should wander up and down, and want em-
    ployment.
    Bel. She takes me for a rogue! [61] — You
    may do well, madam,
To stay this wanderer, and set him a-work,
    forsooth;
He can do something that may please your
    Ladyship.
I have heard of women that desire good breed-
    ings,
Two at a birth, or so.
    Ros.   The fellow's impudent.
    Ori. Sure, he is crazed.
    Ros. I have heard of men too that have
    had good manners.   70
Sure, this is want of grace; indeed, 't is great
    pity
The young man has been bred so ill; but this
    lewd age
Is full of such examples.
    Bel.   I am founder'd, [62]
And some shall rue the setting of me on.
    Mir. Ha! so bookish, lady? Is it pos-
    sible?
Turn'd holy at the heart too? I 'll be hang'd
    then;
Why, this is such a feat, such an activity,
Such fast and loose! A veil too for your
    knavery?
O Dio, Dio!
    Ros.   What do you take me for, sir?
    Mir. An hypocrite, a wanton, a dissembler,
Howe'er ye seem; and thus ye are to be han-
    dled! —   81

Mark me, Belleur; — and this you love, I
    know it.   [*Attempts to remove the veil.*]
    Ros. Stand off, bold sir!
    Mir.   You wear good clothes to this end,
Jewels; love feasts and masques.
    Ros.   Ye are monstrous saucy.
    Mir. All this to draw on fools: and thus,
    thus, lady, [*Attempts to remove the veil.*]
Ye are to be lull'd.
    Bel.   Let her alone, I 'll swinge [63] ye else,
I will, i' faith! for, though I cannot skill [64] o'
    this matter
Myself, I will not see another do it before me,
And do it worse.
    Ros.   Away! ye are a vain thing.
You have travell'd far, sir, to return again [90
A windy and poor bladder. You talk of
    women,
That are not worth the favor of a common one,
The grace of her grew in an hospital! [65]
Against a thousand such blown fooleries
I am able to maintain good women's honors,
Their freedoms, and their fames, and I will do
    it. —
    Mir. She has almost struck me dumb too.
    Ros.   And declaim
Against your base malicious tongues, your
    noises,
For they are nothing else. You teach behav-
    iors!
Or touch us for our freedoms! Teach your-
    selves manners,   100
Truth and sobriety, and live so clearly
That our lives may shine in ye; and then
    task [66] us.
It seems ye are hot; the suburbs [67] will supply
    ye:
Good women scorn such gamesters. [68] So;
    I 'll leave ye.
I am sorry to see this; faith, sir, live fairly.
                  Exit [*with* Oriana].
    Mir. This woman, if she hold on, may be
    virtuous;
'T is almost possible: we 'll have a new day.
    Bel. Ye brought me on, ye forced me to
    this foolery.
I am sham'd, I am scorn'd, I am flurted; [69]
    yes, I am so;
Though I cannot talk to a woman like your
    Worship,   110

[59] Partly a.   [60] Need looking after.
[61] Vagabond.
[62] See on II, ii, 73.

[63] Beat.   [64] I lack ability.
[65] The favor of one who was brought up in an
orphan asylum.
[66] Tax, accuse.
[67] Where the brothels were located.
[68] Lewd fellows.   [69] Flouted.

And use my phrases and my learned figures,
Yet I can fight with any man.

MIR.   Fie !

BEL.   I can, sir ;
And I will fight.

MIR.   With whom ?

BEL.   With you ; with any man ;
For all men now will laugh at me.

MIR.   Prithee, be moderate.

BEL. And I 'll beat all men. Come.

MIR.   I love thee dearly.

BEL. I['ll] [70] beat all that love ; love has undone me.
Never tell me ; I will not be a history.

MIR.   Thou art not.

BEL. 'Sfoot, I will not ! Give me room,
And let me see the proudest of ye jeer me ;
And I 'll begin with you first.

MIR.   Prithee, Belleur — [120
If I do not satisfy thee ——

BEL.   Well, look ye do.
But, now I think on 't better, 't is impossible ;
I must beat somebody. I am maul'd myself.
And I ought in justice ——

MIR.   No, no, no ; ye are cozen'd ;
But walk, and let me talk to thee,

BEL.   Talk wisely,
And see that no man laugh, upon no occasion ;
For I shall think then 't is at me.

MIR.   I warrant thee.

BEL. Nor no more talk of this.

MIR.   Dost think I am maddish ?

BEL. I must needs fight yet ; for I find it
concerns me ;
A pox on 't ! I must fight !

MIR.   I' faith, thou shalt not. [130
                              Exeunt.

ACT III — SCENE I [1]

Enter DE GARD *and* LUGIER. [2]

DE GARD. I know ye are a scholar, and can
do wonders.

LUG. There 's no great scholarship belongs
to this, sir ;
What I am, I am. I pity your poor sister,
And heartily I hate these travellers,
These gimcracks, made of mops and motions. [3]
There 's nothing in their houses here but hum-
mings ;

A bee has more brains. I grieve and vex too
The insolent licentious carriage
Of this out-facing [4] fellow Mirabel ;
And I am mad to see him prick his plumes
up.   10

DE GARD. His wrongs you partly know.

LUG.   Do not you stir, sir ;
Since he has begun with wit, let wit revenge
it ;
Keep your sword close ; [5] we 'll cut his throat
a new way.
I am asham'd the gentlewoman should suffer
Such base, lewd wrongs.

DE GARD.   I will be rul'd ; he shall live,
And left to your revenge.

LUG.   Ay, ay, I 'll fit him.
He makes a common scorn of handsome
women ;
Modesty and good manners are his May
games ; [6]
He takes up [7] maidenheads with a new com-
mission —
The church-warrant 's [8] out of date. Follow
my counsel,   20
For I am zealous in the cause.

DE GARD.   I will, sir,
And will be still directed ; for the truth is,
My sword will make my sister seem more
monstrous.
Besides, there is no honor won on reprobates.

LUG. You are i' th' right. The slight he
has show'd my pupils
Sets me afire too. Go ; I 'll prepare your
sister.
And as I told ye ——

DE GARD.   Yes ; all shall be fit, sir.

LUG. And seriously, and handsomely.

DE GARD.   I warrant ye.

LUG. A little counsel more.   [*Whispers.*]

DE GARD.   'T is well.

LUG.   Most stately ;
See that observ'd ; and then ——

DE GARD.   I have ye every way. [30

LUG. Away, then, and be ready.

DE GARD.   With all speed, sir. *Exit.*

Enter LILLIA [BIANCA], ROSALURA, [*and*]
ORIANA.

LUG. We 'll learn to travel too, maybe
beyond him. —
Good day, fair beauties !

---

[70] Om. Ff.
[1] Unlocated ; evidently some public place.
[2] Ff *and Leverdure alias Lugier.*
[3] Grimaces and gestures.
[4] Insolent.
[5] Hidden ; *i.e.,* sheathed.
[6] Spectacles for his mirth.   [7] Collects.
[8] *I.e.,* the permission granted by the church in
the form of holy matrimony.

LIL.   You have beautified us,
We thank ye, sir ; ye have set us off most
    gallantly
With your grave precepts.
    Ros.   We expected husbands
Out of your documents [9] and taught behaviors,
Excellent husbands ; thought men would run
    stark mad on us,
Men of all ages and all states ; we expected
An inundation of desires and offers,
A torrent of trim suitors ; all we did,   40
Or said, or purpos'd, to be spells about us,
Spells to provoke.
    LIL.   Ye have provok'd us finely !
We follow'd your directions, we did rarely,
We were stately, coy, demure, careless, light,
    giddy,
And play'd at all points ; this, you swore,
    would carry.
    Ros. We made love, and contemn'd love ;
    now seem'd holy,
With such a reverent put-on reservation
Which could not miss, according to your
    principles ;
Now gave more hope again ; now close,[10] now
    public,
Still up and down we beat it like a billow ; [50
And ever those behaviors you read to us,
Subtle and new ; but all this will not help
    us.
    LIL. They help to hinder us of all acquaint-
    ance ;
They have frighted off all friends. What am
    I better
For all my learning, if I love a dunce,
A handsome dunce ? To what use serves my
    reading ?
You should have taught me what belongs to
    horses,
Dogs, dice, hawks, banquets, masques, free
    and fair meetings,
To have studied gowns and dressings.
    LUG.   Ye are not mad, sure !
    Ros. We shall be, if we follow your encour-
    agements.   60
I 'll take mine own way now.
    LIL.   And I my fortune ;
We may live maids else till the moon drop
    millstones.
I see, your modest women are taken for mon-
    sters ;
A dowry of good breeding is worth nothing.
    LUG. Since ye take it so to th' heart, pray
    ye, give me leave yet,

Teachings.   [10] Private.

And ye shall see how I 'll convert this heretic.
Mark how this Mirabel ——
    LIL.   Name him no more ;
For, though I long for a husband, I hate
    him,
And would be married sooner to a monkey,
Or to a Jack of Straw,[11] than such a juggler. [70
    Ros. I am of that mind too. He is too
    nimble,
And plays at fast and loose [12] too learnedly
For a plain-meaning woman ; that 's the truth
    on 't.
Here 's one too, that we love well, would be
    angry ;   [*Pointing to* ORIANA.]
And reason why. — No, no, we will not trouble
    ye,
Nor him at this time ; may he make you
    happy !
We 'll turn ourselves loose now to our fair
    fortunes ;
And the downright way ——
    LIL.   The winning way we 'll follow ;
We 'll bait that men may bite fair, and not be
    frighted.
Yet we 'll not be carried so cheap neither ;
    we 'll have some sport,   80
Some mad morris [13] or other for our money,
    tutor.
    LUG. 'T is like enough ; prosper your own
    devices !
Ye are old enough to choose. But, for this
    gentlewoman,
So please her give me leave ——
    ORI.   I shall be glad, sir,
To find a friend whose pity may direct me.
    LUG. I 'll do my best, and faithfully deal
    for ye ;
But then ye must be ruled.
    ORI.   In all, I vow to ye.
    Ros. Do, do ; he has a lucky hand some-
    times, I 'll assure ye,
And hunts the recovery of a lost lover deadly.
    LUG. You must away straight.
    ORI.   Yes.
    LUG.   And I 'll instruct ye ; [90
Here ye can know no more.
    ORI.   By your leave, sweet ladies ;
And all our fortunes arrive at our own wishes !
    LIL. Amen, amen !
    LUG.   I must borrow your man.
    LIL.   Pray, take him ;

[11] Straw man, dummy.
[12] A cheating game played with a leather strap
which the dupe wrongly supposes he has fastened
down.
[13] Morris dance.

He is within.   To do her good, take anything.
Take us and all.

Lug.	No doubt, ye may find takers;
And so, we'll leave ye to your own disposes.

Exit [Lugier *with* Oriana].

Lil. Now, which way, wench?

Ros.	We'll go a brave way, fear not;
A safe and sure way too; and yet a by-way.
I must confess I have a great mind to be married.

Lil. So have I too a grudging [14] of good will
that way,	100
And would as fain be dispatch'd.   But this
Monsieur Quicksilver ——

Ros. No, no; we'll bar him, bye and
main.[15]   Let him trample;
There is no safety in his surquedry.[16]
An army-royal of women are too few for him;
He keeps a journal of his gentleness,
And will go near to print his fair dispatches,
And call it his " Triumph over Time and
Women."
Let him pass out of memory!   What think ye
Of his two companions?

Lil.	Pinac, methinks, is reasonable;
A little modesty he has brought home with
him,	110
And might be taught, in time, some handsome
duty.

Ros. They say he is a wencher too.

Lil.	I like him better;
A free light touch or two becomes a gentleman,
And sets him seemly off; so [17] he exceed not,
But keep his compass [18] clear, he may be
look'd at.
I would not marry a man that must be taught,
And conjur'd up with kisses; the best game
Is play'd still by the best gamesters.

Ros.	Fie upon thee!
What talk hast thou!

Lil.	Are not we alone, and merry?
Why should we be asham'd to speak what we
think? Thy gentleman,	120
The tall, fat fellow, he that came to see
thee ——

Ros. Is 't not a goodly man?

Lil.	A wondrous goodly!
H' as weight enough, I warrant thee.   Mercy
upon me,
What a serpent wilt thou seem under such a
St. George!

Ros. Thou art a fool!   Give me a man
brings mettle,
Brings substance with him, needs no broths
to [lard] [19] him.
These little fellows show like fleas in boxes,
Hop up and down, and keep a stir to vex us.
Give me the puissant pike; take you the
small shot.

Lil. Of a great thing, I have not seen a
duller;	130
Therefore, methinks, sweet Sister ——

Ros.	Peace, he's modest;
A bashfulness; which is a point of grace,
wench;
But, when these fellows come to moulding,
Sister,
To heat, and handling — as I live, I like him;

Enter Mirabel.

And, methinks, I could form him.

Lil.	Peace; the fire-drake.[20]

Mir. Bless ye, sweet beauties, sweet incomparable ladies,
Sweet wits, sweet humors!   Bless you, learned
lady!
And you, most holy nun, bless your devotions!

Lil. And bless your brains, sir, your most
pregnant brains, sir!	139
They are in travail; may they be delivered
Of a most hopeful wild-goose!

Ros.	Bless your manhood!
They say ye are a gentleman of action,
A fair accomplish'd man, and a rare engineer.
You have a trick to blow up maidenheads,
A subtle trick, they say abroad.

Mir.	I have, lady.

Ros. And often glory in their ruins.

Mir.	Yes, forsooth;
I have a speedy trick, please you to try it;
My engine will despatch ye instantly.

Ros. I would I were a woman, sir, fit for
ye!
As there be such, no doubt, may engine you
too;	150
May, with a countermine, blow up your valor;
But, in good faith, sir, we are both too honest,
And the plague is we cannot be persuaded;
For, look ye, if we thought it were a glory
To be the last of all your lovely ladies ——

Mir. Come, come, leave prating; this has
spoil'd your market!
This pride and puff'd up heart will make ye
fast, ladies,
Fast when ye are hungry, too.

---

[14] Secret longing.
[15] Entirely (a dicing phrase).	[16] Arrogance.
[17] Provided that.	[18] Moderation, due limits.
[19] Old eds. *lare*.	[20] Dragon.

Ros.   The more our pain, sir.

Lil. The more our health, I hope, too.

Mir.   Your behaviors
Have made men stand amaz'd; those men
     that lov'd ye,   160
Men of fair states [21] and parts. Your strange
     [conversion][22]
Into I know not what, nor how, nor where-
     fore;
Your scorns of those that came to visit ye;
Your studied whim-whams and your fine set
     faces —
What have these got ye? Proud and harsh
     opinions.
A travell'd monsieur was the strangest crea-
     ture,
The wildest monster to be wond'red at;
His person made a public scoff, his knowledge,
As if he had been bred 'mongst bears or ban-
     dogs,[23]
Shunn'd and avoided; his conversation snuff'd
     at; [24] —   170
What harvest brings all this?

Ros.   I pray ye, proceed, sir.

Mir. Now ye shall see in what esteem a
     traveller,
An understanding gentleman, and a monsieur,
Is to be held; and, to your griefs, confess it,
Both to your griefs and galls.

Lil.   In what, I pray ye, sir?
We would be glad to understand your Excel-
     lence.

Mir. Go on, sweet ladies; it becomes ye
     rarely!
For me, I have bless'd me from ye; scoff on
     seriously,
And note the man ye mock'd. You, Lady
     Learning,   179
Note the poor traveller that came to visit ye,
That flat, unfurnish'd fellow; note him
     throughly;
You may chance to see him anon.

Lil.   'T is very likely.

Mir. And see him courted by a travell'd
     lady,
Held dear and honor'd by a virtuous virgin;
Maybe a beauty not far short of yours neither;
It may be, clearer.

Lil.   Not unlikely.

Mir.   Younger;
As killing eyes as yours, a wit as poignant;

[21] Estates.
[22] Emend. Sympson; Ff *conventions*.
[23] Dogs which were kept chained because of their
fierceness.
[24] Disdained.

Maybe a state, too, that may top your for-
     tune.
Inquire how she thinks of him, how she holds
     him;   189
His good parts, in what precious price already;
Being a stranger to him, how she courts him;
A stranger to his nation, too, how she dotes on
     him.
Inquire of this; be sick to know; curse, lady,
And keep your chamber; cry, and curse: a
     sweet one,
A thousand in yearly land, well bred, well
     friended.
Travell'd, and highly followed for her fashions.

Lil. Bless his good fortune, sir!

Mir.   This scurvy fellow,
I think they call his name Pinac, this serving
     man
That brought ye venison, as I take it, madam,
Note but this scab: [25] 't is strange that this
     coarse creature,   200
That has no more set-off but his jugglings,
His travell'd tricks ——

Lil.   Good sir, I grieve not at him,
Nor envy not his fortune; yet I wonder.
He 's handsome; yet I see no such perfection.

Mir. Would I had his fortune! For 't is a
     woman
Of that sweet-temper'd nature, and that judg-
     ment,
Besides her state, that care, clear understand-
     ing,
And such a wife to bless him ——

Ros.   Pray ye, whence is she?

Mir. Of England, and a most accomplish'd
     lady;
So modest that men's eyes are frighted at
     her,   210
And such a noble carriage —

Enter a Boy.

         How now, sirrah?

Boy. Sir, the great English lady ——

Mir.   What of her, sir?

Boy. Has newly left her coach, and coming
     this way,
Where you may see her plain; Monsieur Pinac
The only man that leads her.

Enter Pinac, Mariana, *and* Attendants.

Mir.   He is much honored;
Would I had such a favor! Now vex, ladies,
Envy, and vex, and rail!

Ros.   You are short of us, sir.

[25] A scurvy fellow.

MIR. Bless your fair fortune, sir!
PIN.   I nobly thank ye.
MIR. Is she married, friend?
PIN.   No, no.
MIR.   A goodly lady;
A sweet and delicate aspect![26] — Mark,
     mark, and wonder! —   220
Hast thou any hope of her?
PIN.   A little.
MIR.   Follow close, then;
Lose not that hope.
PIN.   To you, sir.
     [MARIANA *courtesies to* MIRABEL.]
MIR.   Gentle lady!
Ros. She is fair, indeed.
LIL.   I have seen a fairer; yet
She is well.
Ros.   Her clothes sit handsome too.
LIL.   She dresses prettily.
Ros. And, by my faith, she is rich; she
     looks still sweeter.
A well-bred woman, I warrant her.
LIL.   Do you hear, sir?
May I crave this gentlewoman's name?
PIN.   Mariana, lady.
LIL. I will not say I owe ye a quarrel, mon-
     sieur,
For making me your stale;[27] a noble gentle-
     man
Would have had more courtesy, at least more
     faith,   230
Than to turn off his mistress at first trial.
You know not what respect I might have
     show'd ye;
I find ye have worth.
PIN.   I cannot stay to answer ye;
Ye see my charge. I am beholding to ye
For all your merry tricks ye put upon me,
Your bobs,[28] and base accounts. I came to
     love ye,
To woo ye, and to serve ye; I am much in-
     debted to ye
For dancing me off my legs, and then for walk-
     ing me;
For telling me strange tales I never heard of,
More to abuse me; for mistaking me,   240
When ye both knew I was a gentleman,
And one deserv'd as rich a match as you are.
LIL. Be not so bitter, sir.
PIN.   You see this lady;
She is young enough and fair enough to please
     me;
A woman of a loving mind, a quiet,

And one that weighs the worth of him that
     loves her.
I am content with this, and bless my for-
     tune.
Your curious wits, and beauties ——
LIL.   Faith, see me once more.
PIN. I dare not trouble ye.
LIL.   May I speak to your lady?
PIN. I pray ye, content yourself. I know
     ye are bitter,   250
And, in your bitterness, ye may abuse her;
Which if she comes to know, for she under-
     stands ye not,
It may breed such a quarrel to your kindred,
And such an indiscretion fling on you, too,
For she is nobly friended ——
LIL. [*aside*]   I could eat her
PIN. Rest as ye are, a modest noble gentle-
     woman,
And afford your honest neighbors some of
     your prayers.
          Exit [PINAC, *with* MARIANA *and* At-
               tendants].
MIR. What think you now?
LIL.   Faith, she's a pretty whiting;[29]
She has got a pretty catch too.
MIR.   You are angry,
Monstrous angry now, grievously angry; [260
And the pretty heart does swell now.
LIL.   No, in troth, sir.
MIR. And it will cry anon, "A pox upon
     it!"
And it will curse itself, and eat no meat, lady;
And it will [sigh].[30]
LIL.   Indeed, you are mistaken;
It will be very merry.
Ros.   Why, sir, do you think
There are no more men living, nor no hand-
     somer,
Than he or you? By this light, there be ten
     thousand,
Ten thousand thousand! Comfort yourself,
     dear monsieur;
Faces, and bodies, wits, and all abiliments[31] —
There are so many we regard 'em not.   270

          Enter BELLEUR *and two* Gentlemen.

MIR. That such a noble lady — (*aside*)
     I could burst now! —
So far above such trifles ——
BEL.   You did laugh at me;
And I know why ye laughed.

[26] Accented on the second syllable.
[27] Stalking-horse.   [28] Taunts.
[29] Darling.
[30] Emend. Dyce; old eds. *fight*.
[31] Accomplishments.

1 Gent.   I pray ye, be satisfied ;
If we did laugh, we had some private reason,
And not at you.

2 Gent.   Alas, we know you not, sir !

Bel. I 'll make you know me. Set your
    faces soberly ;
Stand this way, and look sad ;[32] I 'll be no
    May game ;[33]
Sadder, demurer yet.

Ros.   What 's the matter?
What ails this gentleman?

Bel. Go off now backward, that I may
    behold ye ;   279
And not a simper, on your lives !

    [*Exeunt* Gentlemen, *walking back-*
       ward.]

Lil.   He 's mad, sure.

Bel. Do you observe me too?

Mir.   I may look on ye.

Bel. Why do you grin? I know your
    mind.

Mir.   You do not.
You are strangely humorous.[34] Is there no
    mirth nor pleasure
But you must be the object?

Bel. Mark, and observe me. Wherever I
    am nam'd,
The very word shall raise a general sadness,
For the disgrace this scurvy woman did me,
This proud, pert thing. Take heed ye laugh
    not at me,
Provoke me not ; take heed.

Ros.   I would fain please ye, 289
Do anything to keep ye quiet.

Bel.   Hear me.
Till I receive a satisfaction
Equal to the disgrace and scorn ye gave me,
Ye are a wretched woman ; till thou woo'st me,
And I scorn thee as much, as seriously
Jeer and abuse thee ; ask what gill[35] thou art,
Or any baser name ; I will proclaim thee,
I will so sing thy virtue, so be-paint thee ——

Ros. Nay, good sir, be more modest.

Bel.   Do you laugh again? —
Because ye are a woman, ye are lawless,
And out of compass of an honest anger.   300

Ros. Good sir, have a better belief of me.

Lil.   Away, dear Sister !
          Exit [*with* Rosalura].

Mir. Is not this better now, this seeming
    madness,
Than falling out with your friends?

Bel.   Have I not frighted her?

<hr/>

[32] Sober.   [33] See on l. 18.
[34] This is a queer notion of yours.   [35] Wench.

Mir. Into her right wits, I warrant thee.
    Follow this humor,
And thou shalt see how prosperously 't will
    guide thee.

Bel. I am glad I have found a way to woo
    yet ; I was afraid once
I never should have made a civil suitor.
Well, I 'll about it still.   *Exit.*

Mir.   Do, do, and prosper.
What sport do I make with these fools ! What
    pleasure
Feeds me, and fats my sides at their poor
    innocence !   310

    Enter Lugier, [*disguised.*]

Wooing and wiving — hang it ! Give me
    mirth,
Witty and dainty mirth ! I shall grow in love,
    sure,
With mine own happy head. — Who 's this? —
    To me, sir? —
[*aside*] What youth is this?

Lug.   Yes, sir, I would speak with you,
If your name be Monsieur Mirabel.

Mir.   Ye have hit it ;
Your business, I beseech you?

Lug.   This it is, sir :
There is a gentlewoman hath long time affected
    ye,
And lov'd ye dearly.

Mir.   Turn over, and end that story ;
'T is long enough : I have no faith in women,
    sir.

Lug. It seems so, sir. I do not come to
    woo for her,   320
Or sing her praises, though she well deserve
    'em ;
I come to tell ye ye have been cruel to her,
Unkind and cruel, falser of faith, and careless,
Taking more pleasure in abusing her,
Wresting her honor to your wild disposes,
Than noble in requiting her affection ;
Which, as ye are a man, I must desire ye,
A gentleman of rank, not to persist in,
No more to load her fair name with your in-
    juries.

Mir. Why, I beseech ye, sir?

Lug.   Good sir, I 'll tell ye.
And I 'll be short ; I 'll tell ye because I love
    ye,   331
Because I would have you shun the shame
    may follow.
There is a nobleman new come to town, sir,
A noble and a great man, that affects her,
(A countryman of mine, a brave Savoyan)

Nephew to th' Duke, and so much honors her
That 't will be dangerous to pursue your old
    way,
To touch at anything concerns her honor,
Believe, most dangerous. Her name is Ori-
    ana,
And this great man will marry her. Take
    heed, sir ;   340
For howsoe'er her brother, a staid gentleman,
Lets things pass upon better hopes, this lord,
    sir,
Is of that fiery and that poignant mettle,
Especially provok'd on by affection,
That 't will be hard — but you are wise.
    MIR. A lord, sir?
    LUG.   Yes, and a noble lord.
    MIR.   Send her good fortune !
This will not stir her lord. A baroness !
Say ye so? Say ye so? By 'r lady, a brave
    title !
Top and topgallant now ! Save her great
    Ladyship !
I was a poor servant [36] of hers, I must confess,
    sir,   350
And in those days I thought I might be jovy,[37]
And make a little bold to call in to her ;
But *basta*,[38] now ; I know my rules and dis-
    tance ;
Yet, if she want an usher, such an implement,
One that is throughly pac'd, a clean-made
    gentleman,
Can hold a hanging up with approbation,
Plant his hat formally, and wait with patience,
I do beseech you, sir ——
    LUG.   Sir, leave your scoffing,
And, as ye are a gentleman, deal fairly.
I have given ye a friend's counsel ; so, I 'll
    leave ye.   360
    MIR. But, hark ye, hark ye, sir ; is 't
    possible
I may believe what you say?
    LUG.   You may choose, sir.
    MIR. No baits, no fishhooks, sir? No
    gins? no nooses?
No pitfalls to catch puppies?
    LUG.   I tell ye certain :
You may believe ; if not, stand to the danger !
                    Exit.
    MIR. A lord of Savoy, says he? The
    Duke's nephew?
A man so mighty? By Lady, a fair marriage !
By my faith, a handsome fortune ! I must
    leave prating ;
For, to confess the truth, I have abused her,

[36] Lover.   [37] Merry.   [38] Enough (Ital.). Ff *Basto.*

For which I should be sorry, but that will
    seem scurvy.   370
I must confess she was, ever since I knew her,
As modest as she was fair ; I am sure she lov'd
    me ;
Her means good, and her breeding excellent ;
And for my sake she has refus'd fair matches.
I may play the fool finely. — Stay ; who are
    these?

Re-enter DE GARD [*in disguise*], ORIANA, *and*
    Attendants.

[*aside*] 'T is she, I am sure ; and that the lord,
    it should seem.
He carries a fair port, is a handsome man too.
I do begin to feel I am a coxcomb.
    ORI. Good my Lord, choose a nobler ; for I
    know
I am so far below your rank and honor   380
That what ye can say this way I must credit
But spoken to beget yourself sport. Alas, sir,
I am so far off from deserving you,
My beauty so unfit for your affection,
That I am grown the scorn of common railers,
Of such injurious things that, when they can-
    not
Reach at my person, lie with my reputation !
I am poor, besides.
    DE GARD. Ye are all wealth and goodness ;
And none but such as are the scum of men, [390
The ulcers of an honest state, spite-weavers,
That live on poison only, like swoln spiders,
Dare once profane such excellence, such sweet-
    ness.
    MIR. This man speaks loud indeed.
    DE GARD.   Name but the men, lady ;
Let me but know these poor and base depravers,
Lay but to my revenge their persons open,
And you shall see how suddenly, how fully,
For your most beauteous sake, how direfully,
I 'll handle their despites. Is this thing one?
Be what he will ——
    MIR.   Sir?
    DE GARD.   Dare your malicious
    tongue, sir ——   400
    MIR. I know you not, nor what ye mean.
    ORI.   Good my Lord ——
    DE GARD. If he, or any he ——
    ORI.   I beseech your Honor —
This gentleman 's a stranger to my knowl-
    edge ;
And, no doubt, sir, a worthy man.
    DE GARD. [*to* MIRABEL]   Your mercy !
But, had he been [a tainter] [39] of your honor,

[39] Cor. F₂ ; F 1652 *attaint.*

A blaster of those beauties reign within ye —
But we shall find a fitter time.   Dear lady,
As soon as I have freed ye from your guardian,
And done some honor'd offices unto ye,
I'll take ye with those faults the world flings
    on ye,   410
And dearer than the whole world I'll esteem
    ye!

        [*Exeunt* DE GARD, ORIANA, *and*
           Attendants.]

MIR. This is a thund'ring lord; I am glad
    I scap'd him.
How lovingly the wench disclaim'd my vil-
    lainy!
I am vex'd now heartily that he shall have
    her;
Not that I care to marry, or to lose her,
But that this bilbo [40]-lord shall reap that
    maidenhead
That was my due; that he shall rig and top [41]
    her!
I'd give a thousand crowns now, he might miss
    her!

        Enter a Servant.[42]

SERV. [*aside*] Nay, if I bear your blows, and
    keep your counsel,
You have good luck, sir; I'll teach ye to
    strike lighter.   420
MIR. Come hither, honest fellow; canst
    thou tell me
Where this great lord lies, this Savoy lord?
    Thou mett'st him;
He now went by thee, certain.
SERV.   Yes, he did, sir;
I know him, and I know you are fool'd.
MIR.   Come hither;
Here's all this; give me truth. [*Gives money.*]
SERV.   Not for your money,
And yet that may do much; but I have been
    beaten,
And by the worshipful contrivers beaten, and
    I'll tell ye,
This is no lord, no Savoy lord.
MIR.   Go forward.
SERV. This is a trick, and put upon ye
    grossly
By one Lugier.   The lord is Monsieur De
    Gard, sir,   430
An honest gentleman, and a neighbor here;
Their ends you understand better than I, sure.

MIR. Now I know him, know him now
    plain.
SERV. I have discharg'd my [cholers] [43]
    so God by ye, sir!   *Exit.*
MIR. What a purblind [44] puppy was I.
    Now I remember him;
All the whole cast on 's [45] face, though it were
    umber'd,[46]
And mask'd with patches.   What a dunder-
    whelp,[47]
To let him domineer thus!   How he strutted,
And what a load of lord he clapp'd upon him!
Would I had him here again!   I would so
    bounce [48] him,   440
I would so thank his lordship for his lewd
    plot!
Do they think to carry it away,[49] with a great
    band made of bird-pots,[50]
And a pair of pin-buttock'd breeches? — Ha!
    't is he again;
He comes, he comes, he comes! have at him!

Re-enter DE GARD, [*still in disguise*], ORIANA,
    and [Attendants.]

[MIRABEL] *sings.*

My Savoy lord, why dost thou frown on me?
And will that favor never sweeter be?
Wilt thou, I say, for ever play the fool? [51]
De Gard, be wise, and, Savoy, go to school!
My Lord De Gard, I thank you for your antic; [52]
My Lady Bright, that will be [sometimes] [53] frantic;
You worthy train, that wait upon this pair,   [451
Send you more wit, and they a bouncing bair! [54]

And so I take my humble leave of your
    Honors!   *Exit.*
DE GARD. We are discover'd; there's no
    remedy.
Lillia Bianca's man, upon my life,
In stubbornness, because Lugier corrected
    him —
A shameless slave's plague on him for a
    rascal!
ORI. I was in a perfect hope.   The bane
    on 't is now,
He will make mirth on mirth, to persecute us.

[40] Sword; *i.e.*, swashbuckling.
[41] Fix her up and finish her off.   Both verbs em-
body nautical figures, with several double ententes.
[42] The servant of II, ii. See III, i, 93. He re-
appears in IV, i.
[43] Anger.   Emend. Sympson; old eds. *colours.*
[44] Blind.   [45] Of his.   [46] Stained dark.
[47] Dull dog.   [48] Bang, beat.
[49] Carry it off, get away with it.
[50] Apparently a large ruff resembling bird-pots
in shape.   *N.E.D.* gives "pot-birds" = apparatus
for making bird calls by blowing a pipe through
a pot of water.
[51] The first three lines parody the opening lines of
the famous popular song "Fortune, my foe."
[52] Show, performance.
[53] So F2; F 1652 *sometime.*
[54] *I.e.*, bairn, the "n" being omitted for the
rhyme.

DE GARD. We must be patient; I am
vex'd to the proof too. 460
I 'll try once more ; then, if I fail, here 's one
speaks. [*Puts his hand on his sword.*]
ORI. Let me be lost and scorn'd first !
DE GARD. Well, we 'll consider.
Away, and let me shift ; [55] I shall be hooted
else. *Exeunt.*

ACT IV — SCENE I [1]

Enter LUGIER, LILLIA [BIANCA, *and*] [Servant] [2]
[*carrying a willow garland*].

LUG. Faint not, but do as I direct ye ; trust
me ;
Believe me, too ; for what I have told ye, lady,
As true as you are Lillia, is authentic ;
I know it, I have found it ; 't is a poor cour-
age
Flies off for one repulse. These travellers
Shall find, before we have done, a homespun
wit,
A plain French understanding, may cope
with 'em.
They have had the better yet, thank your
sweet squire here !
And let 'em brag. You would be reveng'd ?
LIL. Yes, surely.
LUG. And married too ?
LIL. I think so.
LUG. Then be counsell'd ; [10
You know how to proceed. I have other irons
Heating as well as yours, and I will strike
Three blows with one stone home. Be rul'd,
and happy ;
And so, I leave ye. Now is the time.
LIL. I am ready.
If he do come to [dor] [3] me. [*Exit* LUGIER.]
SERV. Will ye stand here,
And let the people think ye are God knows
what, mistress ?
Let boys and prentices presume upon ye ?
LIL. Prithee, hold thy peace.
SERV. Stand at his door that hates ye ?
LIL. Prithee, leave prating.
SERV. Pray ye, go to the tavern ; I 'll give
ye a pint of wine there.
If any of the madcap gentlemen should come
by, 20

That take up women upon special warrant,
You were in a wise case now.

Enter MIRABEL, PINAC, MARIANA, Priest,
[*and*] Attendants.

LIL. Give me the garland ;
And wait you here.
[*Takes the garland from* Servant,
who retires.]
MIR. She is here to seek thee, sirrah.
I told thee what would follow ; she is mad for
thee.
Show, and advance. — So early stirring,
lady ?
It shows a busy mind, a fancy troubled.
A willow garland, too ? is 't possible ?
'T is pity so much beauty should lie musty ;
But 't is not to be help'd now.
LIL. The more 's my misery. —
Good fortune to ye, lady ! you deserve it ; [30
To me, too-late repentance ! I have sought it.
I do not envy, though I grieve a little,
You are mistress of that happiness, those joys,
That might have been, had I been wise — but
fortune —
PIN. She understands ye not ; pray ye, do
not trouble her ;
And do not cross me like a hare [4] thus ; 't is as
ominous.
LIL. I come not to upbraid your levity
(Though ye made show of love, and though I
lik'd ye),
To claim an interest (we are yet both stran-
gers ;
But what we might have been, had you per-
sever'd, sir !) 40
To be an eyesore to your loving lady.
This garland shows I give myself forsaken
(Yet, she must pardon me, 't is most unwill-
ingly) ;
And all the power and interest I had in ye
(As, I persuade myself, somewhat ye lov'd
me)
Thus patiently I render up, I offer
To her that must enjoy ye ; and so, bless ye ;
Only, I heartily desire this courtesy,
And would not be deni'd, to wait upon ye
This day, to see ye ti'd, then no more trouble
ye. 50
PIN. It [needs] [5] not, lady.
LIL. Good sir, grant me so much.
PIN. 'T is private, and we make no invita-
tion.

[55] Change my clothes.
[1] The same, presumably, though the scene is not
precisely located. Pinac's lodging is evidently near.
[2] Old eds. *Servants.*
[3] Make game of. Emend. Sympson ; Ff *do.*
[4] An evil omen.
[5] Cor F₂ ; F 1652 *need.*

LIL. My presence, sir, shall not proclaim it
public.

PIN. Maybe 't is not in town.

LIL. I have a coach, sir,
And a most ready will to do you service.

MIR. [*aside to* PINAC] Strike now or never ;
make it sure ; I tell thee,
She will hang herself, if she have thee not.

PIN. Pray ye, sir,
Entertain my noble mistress ; only a word or
two
With this importunate woman, and I 'll relieve
ye. —
Now ye see what your flings are, and your fan-
cies, 60
Your states, and your wild stubbornness ; now
ye find
What 't is to gird and kick at men's fair serv-
ices,
To raise your pride to such a pitch and glory
That goodness shows like gnats, scorn'd under
ye.
'T is ugly, naught ; a self-will in a woman,
Chain'd to an overweening thought, is pesti-
lent,
Murders fair fortune first, then fair opinion.
There stands a pattern, a true patient [p]attern,
Humble and sweet.

LIL. I can but grieve my ignorance.
Repentance, some say, too, is the best sacri-
fice ; 70
For, sure, sir, if my chance had been so happy
(As I confess I was mine own destroyer)
As to have arriv'd at you, I will not prophesy ;
But certain, as I think, I should have pleas'd
ye ;
Have made ye as much wonder at my courtesy,
My love, and duty, as I have dishearten'd ye.
Some hours we have of youth, and some of
folly ;
And being free-born maids, we take a liberty,
And, to maintain that, sometimes we strain
highly.

PIN. Now ye talk reason.

LIL. But, being yok'd and govern'd, [80
Married, and those light vanities purg'd from
us,
How fair we grow, how gentle ! and how tender
We twine about those loves that shoot up with
us !
A sullen woman fear, that talks not to ye ;
She has a sad and darken'd soul, loves dully.
A merry and a free wench, give her liberty,
Believe her, in the lightest form she appears
to ye,

Believe her excellent, though she despise ye ;
Let but these fits and flashes pass, she will
show to ye
As jewels rubb'd from dust, or gold new bur-
nish'd : 90
Such had I been, had you believ'd.

PIN. Is 't possible?

LIL. And to your happiness, I dare assure
ye,
If true love be accounted so, your pleasure,
Your will, and your command, had tied my
motions ;
But that hope 's gone. I know you are young
and giddy,
And, till you have a wife can govern with ye,
You sail upon this world-sea light and empty,
Your bark in danger daily. 'T is not the name
neither
Of wife can steer ye, but the noble nature,
The diligence, the care, the love, the patience ;
She makes the pilot, and preserves the hus-
band, 101
That knows and reckons every rib he is built
on.
But this I tell ye, to my shame.

PIN. I admire ye ;
And now am sorry that I aim beyond ye.

MIR. [*aside*] So, so, so ; fair and softly !
She is thine own, boy ;
She comes now without lure.[6]

PIN. But that it must needs
Be reckon'd to me as a wantonness,
Or worse, a madness, to forsake a blessing,
A blessing of that hope ——

LIL. I dare not urge ye ;
And yet, dear sir ——

PIN. 'T is most certain, I had rather, [110
If 't were in mine own choice — for you are
my countrywoman,
A neighbor here, born by me ; she a stranger,[7]
And who knows how her friends ——

LIL. Do as you please, sir ;
If ye be fast, not all the world — I love ye,
'T is most true, and clear, I would persuade
ye ;
And I shall love ye still.

PIN. Go, get before me —
So much ye have won upon me — do it pres-
ently.[8]
Here 's a priest ready — I 'll have you.

LIL. Not now, sir ;
No, you shall pardon me. Advance your
lady ;

6 The falconer's bait for enticing back the hawk.
7 Foreigner.   8 Immediately.

I dare not hinder your most high prefer-
   ment :   120
'T is honor enough for me I have unmask'd
   ye.
  Pin. How 's that?
  Lil.   I have caught ye, sir. Alas, I
   am no stateswoman,
Nor no great traveller, yet I have found ye ;
I have found your lady too, your beauteous
   lady ;
I have found her birth and breeding too, her
   discipline,
Who brought her over, and who kept your
   lady,
And, when he laid her by, what virtuous nun-
   nery
Received her in ; I have found all these. Are
   ye blank now?
Methinks such travell'd wisdoms should not
   fool thus, —
Such excellent indiscretions !
  Mir. *[aside]*   How could she know
   this?   130
  Lil. 'T is true she is English born ; but
   most part French [9] now,
And so I hope you will find her, to your com-
   fort.
Alas, I am ignorant of what she cost ye ;
The price of these hired clothes I do not know,
   gentlemen ;
Those jewels are [10] the broker's, how ye stand
   bound for 'em.
  Pin. Will you make this good?
  Lil.   Yes, yes ; and to her face, sir,
That she is an English whore, a kind of fling-
   dust,[11]
One of your London light-o'-loves, a right
   one ;
Came over in thin pumps and half a petticoat,
One faith, and one smock, with a broken hab-
   erdasher —   140
I know all this without a conjurer.
Her name is Jumping Joan, an ancient sin-
   weaver ;
She was first a lady's chambermaid, there
   slipp'd,
And broke her leg above the knee ; departed,
And set up shop herself ; stood the fierce con-
   flicts
Of many a furious term ; [12] there lost her col-
   ors,
And last shipp'd over hither.

  Mir. *[aside]*   We are betray'd !
  Lil. Do you come to fright me with this
   mystery?
To stir me with a stink none can endure, sir?
I pray ye, proceed ; the wedding will become
   ye !   150
Who gives the lady? you? An excellent
   father !
A careful man, and one that knows a beauty !
Send ye fair shipping, sir ! and so, I 'll leave
   ye.
Be wise and manly ; then I may chance to love
   ye !   *Exit [with* Servant].
  Mir. As I live, I am asham'd this wench
   has reach'd [13] me,
Monstrous asham'd ; but there 's no remedy.
This skew'd-ey'd carrion ——
  Pin.   This I suspected ever. —
Come, come, uncase ; [14] we have no more use
   of ye ;
Your clothes must back again.
  Mari.   Sir, ye shall pardon me ;
'T is not our English use to be degraded. [160
If you will visit me, and take your venture,
You shall have pleasure for your properties.
And so, sweetheart ——   *[Exit.]*
  Mir.   Let her go, and the Devil go
   with her !
We have never better luck with these prelu-
   diums.
Come, be not daunted ; think she is but a
   woman,
And, let her have the Devil's wit, we 'll reach
   her !   *Exit* [Mirabel *with* Pinac].

Scene II [15]

Enter Rosalura *and* Lugier.

  Ros. Ye have now redeem'd my good opin-
   ion, tutor,
And ye stand fair again.
  Lug.   I can but labor
And sweat in your affairs. I am sure Belleur
Will be here instantly, and use his anger,
His wonted harshness.
  Ros.   I hope he will not beat me.
  Lug. No, sure, he has more manners. Be
   you ready.
  Ros. Yes, yes, I am ; and am resolv'd to
   fit him,
With patience to outdo all he can offer.
But how does Oriana?

Lug.   Worse and worse still;
There is a sad house for her; she is now, [10
Poor lady, utterly distracted.
Ros.   Pity,
Infinite pity! 't is a handsome lady.
That Mirabel's a beast, worse than a monster,
If this affliction work not.

Enter Lillia Bianca.

Lil.   Are ye ready?
Belleur is coming on here, hard behind me:
I have no leisure to relate my fortune;
Only I wish you may come off as handsomely.
Upon the sign, you know what.
Ros.   Well, well; leave me.
[*Exeunt* Lillia Bianca *and* Lugier.]

Enter Belleur.

Bel. How now?
Ros.   Ye are welcome, sir.
Bel.   'T is well ye have [manners].[16]
That curtsy again, and hold your counte-
    nance staidly.   20
That look's too light; take heed. So; sit
    ye down now;
And, to confirm me that your gall is gone,
Your bitterness dispers'd (for so I'll have it),
Look on me steadfastly, and, whatsoe'er I
    say to ye,
Move not, nor alter in your face — ye are
    gone, then;
For, if you do express the least distaste,
Or show an angry wrinkle, (mark me, woman!
We are now alone,) I will so conjure thee,
The third part of my execution
Cannot be spoke.
Ros.   I am at your dispose, sir. [30
Bel. Now rise, and woo me a little; let me
    hear that faculty;
But touch me not; nor do not lie, I charge
    ye.
Begin now.
Ros.   If so mean and poor a beauty
May ever hope the grace ——
Bel.   Ye cog, ye flatter
Like a lewd [17] thing; ye lie: " May hope that
    grace! "
Why, what grace canst thou hope for? An-
    swer not;
For, if thou dost, and liest again, I'll swinge
    thee.
Do not I know thee for a pestilent woman?
A proud at both ends? Be not angry,
Nor stir not, o' your life.

16 Cor. F₂; F 1652 *manner*.   17 Wicked.

Ros.   I am [counsell'd,] [18] sir. [40
Bel. Art thou not now (confess, for I'll
    have the truth out)
As much unworthy of a man of merit,
Or any of ye all, nay, of mere man,
Though he were crooked, cold,[19] all wants
    upon him,
Nay, of any dishonest thing that bears that
    figure,
As devils are of mercy?
Ros.   We are unworthy.
Bel. Stick to that truth, and it may chance
    to save thee.
And is it not our bounty that we take ye?
That we are troubled, ve[x]'d, or tortur'd with
    ye,
Our mere and special bounty?
Ros.   Yes.
Bel.   Our pity, [50
That for your wickedness we swinge ye
    soundly;
Your stubbornness and stout hearts, we bela-
    bor ye?
Answer to that!
Ros.   I do confess your pity.
Bel. And dost not thou [20] deserve in thine
    own person,
Thou impudent, thou pert — do not change
    countenance.
Ros. I dare not, sir.
Bel.   For, if ye do ——
Ros.   I am settled.
Bel. Thou wagtail, peacock, puppy, look
    on me:
I am a gentleman.
Ros.   It seems no less, sir,
Bel. And darest thou in thy surquedry —
Ros.   I beseech ye! —
It was my weakness, sir, I did not view ye; [60
I took not notice of your noble parts,
Nor call'd your person nor your fashion
    proper.[21]
Bel. This is some amends yet.
Ros.   I shall mend, sir, daily,
And study to deserve.
Bel.   Come a little nearer.
Canst thou repent thy villainy?
Ros.   Most seriously.
Bel. And be asham'd?
Ros.   I am asham'd.
Bel.   Cry.

18 Cor. F₂; F 1652 *counsel.* — *Out* (next line) may
be misprinted for *on 't*.
19 Dyce suggests, perhaps rightly, *old*.
20 F 1652 inserts *not*.
21 So F₂; F 1652 transposes last two words.

Ros. It will be hard to do, sir.

Bel.   Cry now instantly ;
Cry monstrously, that all the town may hear
     thee ;
Cry seriously, as if thou hadst lost thy mon-
     key ;
And, as I like thy tears ——

Ros.   Now !

Enter Lillia [Bianca] *and four* Women,
laughing.

Bel.   How ! how ! Do ye jeer me ? [70
Have ye broke your bounds again, dame ?

Ros.   Yes, and laugh at ye,
And laugh most heartily.

Bel.   What are these ? whirlwinds ?
Is hell broke loose, and all the Furies flutter'd ?
Am I greas'd [22] once again ?

Ros.   Yes, indeed are ye ;
And once again ye shall be, if ye quarrel.
Do you come to vent your fury on a virgin ?
Is this your manhood, sir ?

1 Wom.   Let him do his best ;
Let 's see the utmost of his indignation ;
I long to see him angry. — Come, proceed,
     sir. —   [*The* Women *display knives.*]
Hang him, he dares not stir ; a man of timber !

2 Wom. Come hither to fright maids with
     thy bull-faces !   81
To threaten gentlewomen ! Thou a man ! A
     Maypole,
A great dry pudding.

3 Wom.   Come, come, do your worst, sir ;
Be angry, if thou dar'st.

Bel.   The Lord deliver me !

4 Wom. Do but look scurvily upon this
     lady,
Or give us one foul word ! — We are all mis-
     taken ;
This is some mighty dairymaid in man's
     clothes.

Lil. I am of that mind too.

Bel. [*aside*]   What will they do to me ?

Lil. And hired to come and abuse us. — A
     man has manners ;
A gentleman, civility and breeding :—   90
Some tinker's trull, with a beard glu'd on.

1 Wom.   Let 's search him,
And, as we find him ——

Bel.   Let me but depart from ye,
Sweet Christian women !

Lil.   Hear the thing speak, neighbors.

Bel. 'T is but a small request : if e'er I
     trouble ye,

[22] Cajoled ; cf. "buttered."

If e'er I talk again of beating women,
Or beating anything that can but turn to me ;
Of ever thinking of a handsome lady
But virtuously and well ; of ever speaking
But to her honor, — this I 'll promise ye :
I will take rhubarb, and purge choler [23]
     mainly ; [24]   100
Abundantly I 'll purge.

Lil.   I 'll send ye broths, sir.

Bel. I will be laugh'd at, and endure it
     patiently ;
I will do anything.

Ros.   I 'll be your bail, then.
When ye come next to woo, pray ye come not
     boist'rously,
And furnish'd like a bearward.[25]

Bel.   No, in truth, forsooth.

Ros. I scented ye long since.

Bel.   I was to blame, sure ;
I will appear a gentleman.

Ros.   'T is the best for ye,
For a true noble gentleman 's a brave [26] thing.
Upon that hope, we quit ye. You fear seri-
     ously ?   109

Bel. Yes, truly do I ; I confess I fear ye,
And honor ye, and anything.

Ros.   Farewell, then.

Wom. And, when ye come to woo next,
     bring more mercy.
          Exeunt [*all except* Belleur].

Bel. A dairymaid ! A tinker's trull !
     Heaven bless me !
Sure, if I had provok'd 'em, they had quarter'd
     me.

Enter two Gentlemen.

I am a most ridiculous ass, now I perceive
     it ;
A coward, and a knave too.

1 Gent.   'T is the mad gentleman ;
Let 's set our faces right.

Bel.   No, no ; laugh at me,
And laugh aloud.

2 Gent.   We are better manner'd, sir.

Bel. I do deserve it ; call me patch [27] and
     puppy,
And beat me, if you please.

1 Gent.   No, indeed ; we know ye. [120

Bel. 'Death, do as I would have ye !

2 Gent.   Ye are an ass, then,
A coxcomb, and a calf !

[23] Bile (which was supposed to predispose one to anger).
[24] Vigorously.
[25] Bear keeper.
[26] Fine.   [27] Fool.

BEL.   I am a great calf.
Kick me a little now. Why, when! [28] [*They kick him.*] Sufficient.
Now laugh aloud, and scorn me. So; good buy ye!
And ever, when ye meet me, laugh.
GENTLEMEN.   We will, sir.
Exeunt.

SCENE III [29]

Enter NANTOLET, LA CASTRE, DE GARD, LUGIER, [*and*] MIRABEL.

MIR. Your patience, gentlemen; why do ye bait me?
NANT. Is't not a shame you are so stubborn-hearted,
So stony and so dull, to such a lady,
Of her perfections and her misery?
LUG. Does she not love ye? Does not her distraction
For your sake only, her most pitied lunacy
Of all but you, show ye? Does it not compel ye?
MIR. Soft and fair, gentlemen; pray ye, proceed temperately.
LUG. If ye have any feeling, any sense in ye,
The least touch of a noble heart ——
LA CAST.   Let him alone;
It is his glory that he can kill beauty. —   [11
Ye bear my stamp, but not my tenderness;
Your wild unsavory courses set [30] that in ye!
For shame, be sorry, though ye cannot cure her;
Show something of a man, of a fair nature.
MIR. Ye make me mad!
DE GARD.   Let me pronounce this to ye:
You take a strange felicity in slighting
And wronging women, which my poor sister feels now;
Heaven's hand be gentle on her! Mark me, sir;
That very hour she dies (there's small hope otherwise),   20
That minute, you and I must grapple for it;
Either your life or mine.
MIR.   Be not so hot, sir;
I am not to be wrought on by these policies,
In truth, I am not; nor do I fear the tricks,
Or the high-sounding threats, of a Savoyan.
I glory not in cruelty, (ye wrong me,)

Nor grow up water'd with the tears of women.
This let me tell ye, howsoe'er I show to ye,
Wild, as you please to call it, or self-will'd,
When I see cause, I can both do and suffer,   [30
Freely and feelingly, as a true gentleman.

Enter ROSALURA *and* LILLIA [BIANCA].

Ros. Oh, pity, pity! thousand, thousand pities!
LIL. Alas, poor soul, she will die! She is grown senseless;
She will not know nor speak now.
Ros.   Die for love!
And love of such a youth! I would die for a dog first;
He that kills me, I'll give him leave to eat me;
I'll know men better, ere I sigh for any of 'em.
LIL. You have done a worthy act, sir, a most famous;
Ye have kill'd a maid the wrong way; ye are a conqueror.
Ros. A conqueror? A cobbler! Hang him, sowter! [31] —   40
Go hide thyself, for shame! Go lose thy memory!
Live not 'mongst men; thou art a beast, a monster,
A blatant beast!
LIL.   If ye have yet any honesty,
Or ever heard of any, take my counsel:
Off with your garters, and seek out a bough,
A handsome bough, for I would have ye hang like a gentleman;
And write some doleful matter to the world,
A warning to hard-hearted men.
MIR.   Out, kitlings! [32]
What caterwauling's here! What gibbing! [33]
Do you think my heart is soft'ned with a black santis? [34]   50
Show me some reason.

Enter ORIANA *on a bed.* [35]

Ros.   Here then, here is a reason.
NANT. Now, if ye be a man, let this sight shake ye!
LA CAST. Alas, poor gentlewoman! — Do ye know me, lady?
LUG. How she looks up, and stares!
ORI.   I know ye very well;
You are my godfather: and that's the monsieur,

---

[28] An exclamation of impatience.
[29] Unlocated; probably a room in La Castre's house.
[30] The reading of the old eds.; we must suppose *that* to refer to Mirabel's glory in killing beauty. Mason emends, perhaps rightly, *let*, = hinder, inhibit.
[31] Cobbler.   [32] Kittens.   [33] Cat-like conduct.
[34] Black sanctus, burlesque hymn, a great discord.
[35] *I.e.*, the curtains before the inner stage are opened, and she is discovered.

DE GARD. And who am I?

ORI. You are Amadis de Gaul, sir. —
Oh, oh, my heart! — Were you never in love,
    sweet lady?
And do you never dream of flow'rs and gar-
    dens?
I dream of walking fires; take heed; it comes
    now.
Who's that? Pray, stand away. I have seen
    that face, sure. —   60
How light my head is!

ROS.   Take some rest.

ORI.   I cannot;
For I must be up to-morrow to go to church,
And I must dress me, put my new gown on,
And be as fine to meet my love! Heigh-ho!
Will not you tell me where my love lies buried?

MIR. He is not dead. — [*aside*] Beshrew my
    heart, she stirs me!

ORI. He is dead to me.

MIR. [*aside*]   Is't possible my nature
Should be so damnable to let her suffer? —
Give me your hand.

ORI.   How soft you feel, how gentle!
I'll tell ye your fortune, friend.

MIR.   How she stares on me! [70

ORI. You have a flatt'ring face, but 't is a
    fine one;
I warrant you may have a hundred sweet-
    hearts.
Will ye pray for me? I shall die to-morrow;
And will ye ring the bells?

MIR.   I am most unworthy,
I do confess, unhappy. Do you know me?

ORI. I would I did!

MIR.   Oh, fair tears, how ye take me!

ORI. Do you weep too? You have not lost
    your lover?
You mock me; I'll go home and pray.

MIR.   Pray ye, pardon me;
Or, if it please ye to consider justly,
Scorn me, for I deserve it; scorn and shame
    me,   80
Sweet Oriana!

LIL.   Let her alone; she trembles;
Her fits will grow more strong, if ye provoke
    her.

LA CAST. Certain she knows ye not, yet
    loves to see ye.
How she smiles now!

Enter BELLEUR.

BEL. Where are ye? Oh, why do not ye
    laugh? Come, laugh at me!
Why a devil art thou sad, and such a subject,

Such a ridiculous subject, as I am,
Before thy face?

MIR.   Prithee, put off this lightness;
This is no time for mirth, nor place; I have
    us'd too much on 't.
I have undone myself and a sweet lady   90
By being too indulgent to my foolery,
Which truly I repent. Look here.

BEL.   What ails she?

MIR. Alas, she is mad!

BEL.   Mad!

MIR.   Yes, too sure; for me, too.

BEL. Dost thou wonder at that? By this
    good light, they are all so;
They are coz'ning-mad, they are brawling-
    mad, they are proud-mad;
They are all, all mad. I came from a world
    of mad women,
Mad as March hares. Get 'em in chains, then
    deal with 'em.
There's one that's mad; she seems well, but
    she is dog-mad.
Is she dead, dost think?

MIR.   Dead! Heaven forbid!

BEL.   Heaven further it!
For, till they be key-cold [36] dead, there's no
    trusting of 'em;   100
Whate'er they seem, or howsoe'er they carry
    it,
Till they be chapfallen, and their tongues at
    peace,
Nail'd in their coffins sure, I'll ne'er believe
    'em.
Shall I talk with her?

MIR.   No, dear friend, be quiet,
And be at peace a while.

BEL.   I'll walk aside,
And come again anon. But take heed to her:
You say she is a woman?

MIR.   Yes.

BEL.   Take great heed;
For, if she do not cozen thee, then hang me;
Let her be mad, or what she will, she'll cheat
    thee!   *Exit.*

MIR. Away, wild fool! — How vild [37] this
    shows in him now! —   110
Now take my faith, (before ye all I speak it,)
And with it my repentant love.

LA CAST.   This seems well.

MIR. Were but this lady clear again, whose
    sorrows
My very heart melts for, were she but perfect,

---

[36] A common comparison, the key in or near the
door being a familiar bit of cold iron.
[37] F₂ *vile.*

(For thus to marry her would be two miseries),
Before the richest and the noblest beauty
France or the world could show me, I would
    take her.
As she is now, my tears and prayers shall wed
    her.
    DE GARD. This makes some small amends.
    ROS.   She beckons to ye ;
To us, too, to go off.
    NANT.   Let 's draw aside all. [120
          [*All retire except* ORIANA *and*
          MIRABEL.]
    ORI. Oh, my best friend ! I would fain ——
    MIR.   What, she speaks well,
And with another voice.
    ORI.   But I am fearful,
And shame a little stops my tongue ——
    MIR.   Speak boldly.
    ORI. Tell ye, I am well. I am perfect well
    (pray ye, mock not) ;
And that I did this to provoke your nature ;
Out of my infinite and restless love,
To win your pity. Pardon me !
    MIR.   Go forward ;
Who set ye on ?
    ORI.   None, as I live, no creature ;
Not any knew or ever dream'd what I meant.
Will ye be mine ?
    MIR.   'T is true, I pity ye ;   130
But, when I marry ye, ye must be wiser.
Nothing but tricks ? devices ?
    ORI.   Will ye shame me ?
    MIR. Yes, marry, will I. — Come near,
    come near ! a miracle !
                [*They come forward.*]
The woman 's well ; she was only mad for
    marriage,
Stark mad to be ston'd [38] to death ; give her
    good counsel.
Will this world never mend ? — Are ye caught,
    damsel ?

          Re-enter BELLEUR.

    BEL. How goes it now ?
    MIR.   Thou art a kind of prophet ;
The woman 's well again, and would have
    gull'd me ;
Well, excellent well, and not a taint upon her.
    BEL. Did not I tell ye ? Let 'em be what
    can be,   140
Saints, devils, anything, they will abuse [39] us ;
Thou wert an ass to believe her so long, a cox-
    comb ;

---

[38] With a play on "stone" = testis.
[39] Deceive.

Give 'em a minute, they 'll abuse whole mil-
    lions.
    MIR. And am not I a rare physician, gentle-
    men,
That can cure desperate mad minds ?
    DE GARD.   Be not insolent.
    MIR. Well, go thy ways ; from this hour I
    disclaim thee,
Unless thou hast a trick above this ; then I 'll
    love thee.
Ye owe me for your cure. — Pray, have a care
    of her,
For fear she fall into relapse. — Come,
    Belleur ;
We 'll set up bills [40] to cure diseased virgins.
    BEL. Shall we be merry ?
    MIR.   Yes.
    BEL.   But I 'll no more projects ; [151
If we could make 'em mad, it were some mas-
    tery.
          Exeunt [MIRABEL *and* BELLEUR].
    LIL. I am glad she is well again.
    ROS.   So am I, certain. —
Be not ashamed.
    ORI.   I shall never see a man more.
    DE GARD. Come, ye are a fool ; had ye but
    told me this trick,
He should not have gloried thus.
    LUG.   He shall not long, neither.
    LA CAST. Be rul'd, and be at peace. Ye
    have my consent,
And what pow'r I can work with.
    NANT.   Come, leave blusbing ;
We are your friends ; an honest way compell'd
    ye ;
Heaven will not see so true a love unrecom-
    pens'd.   160
Come in, and slight him too.
    LUG.   The next shall hit him.   *Exeunt.*

          ACT V — SCENE I [1]

          Enter DE GARD *and* LUGIER.

    DE GARD. 'T will be discover'd.
    LUG.   That 's the worst can happen ;
If there be any way to reach and work upon
    him,
Upon his nature suddenly, and catch him —
    that he loves,

---

[40] Advertisements.
[1] Unlocated, but doubtless an outer room of
La Castre's house or the street before it.

Though he dissemble it, and would show con-
    trary,
And will at length relent, I'll lay [2] my for-
    tune;
Nay, more, my life.
    DE GARD.   Is she won? [3]
    LUG.   Yes, and ready,
And my designments set.
    DE GARD.   They are now for travel;
All for that game again; they have forgot
    wooing.
    LUG. Let 'em; we'll travel with 'em.
    DE GARD.   Where's his father?
    LUG. Within; he knows my mind, too, and
    allows [4] it,   10
Pities your sister's fortune most sincerely,
And has appointed, for our more assistance,
Some of his secret friends.
    DE GARD.   Speed the plough! [5]
    LUG.   Well said!
And be you serious too.
    DE GARD.   I shall be diligent.
    LUG. Let's [6] break the ice for one, the rest
    will drink, too,
Believe me, sir, of the same cup. My young
    gentlewomen
Wait but who sets the game afoot. Though
    they seem stubborn,
Reserv'd, and proud now, yet I know their
    hearts,
Their pulses how they beat, and for what
    cause, sir,
And how they long to venture their abilities [20
In a true quarrel. Husbands they must and
    will have,
Or nunneries and thin collations
To cool their bloods. Let's all about our
    business;
And, if this fail, let nature work.
    DE GARD.   Ye have arm'd me. *Exeunt.*

SCENE II [7]

Enter MIRABEL, NANTOLET, [*and*] LA CASTRE.

    LA CAST. Will ye be wilful, then?
    MIR.   Pray, sir, your pardon;
For I must travel. Lie lazy here,
Bound to a wife! Chain'd to her subtleties,
Her humors, and her wills, which are mere
    fetters!
To have her to-day pleas'd, to-morrow peevish,
The third day mad, the fourth rebellious!

You see before they are married, what moris-
    coes, [8]
What masques and mummeries they put upon
    us.
To be ti'd here, and suffer their lavoltas! [9]
    NANT. 'T is your own seeking.
    MIR.   Yes, to get my freedom. [10
Were they as I could wish 'em ——
    LA CAST.   Fools and meacocks, [10]
To endure what you think fit to put upon 'em!
Come, change your mind.
    MIR.   Not before I have chang'd air,
Father.
When I know women worthy of my company,
I will return again, and wait upon 'em;
Till then, dear sir, I'll amble all the world over,
And run all hazards, misery, and poverty,
So [11] I escape the dangerous bay of matrimony.

Enter PINAC *and* BELLEUR.

    PIN. Are ye resolv'd?
    MIR.   Yes, certain; I will out again.
    PIN. We are for ye, sir; we are your serv-
    ants once more;   20
Once more we'll seek our fortune in strange
    countries;
Ours is too scornful for us.
    BEL.   Is there ne'er a land
That you have read or heard of (for I care not
    how far it be,
Nor under what pestiferous star it lies),
A happy kingdom, where there are no women,
Nor have been ever, nor no mention
Of any such lewd [12] things with lewder quali-
    ties,
(For thither would I travel) where 't is felony
To confess he had a mother; a mistress, trea-
    son?
    LA CAST. Are you for travel too?
    BEL.   For anything, [30
For living in the moon and stopping hedges, [13]
Ere I stay here to be abus'd and baffl'd. [14]
    NANT. Why did ye not break your minds
    to me? They are my daughters;
And, sure, I think I should have that com-
    mand over 'em,
To see 'em well bestow'd. I know ye are
    gentlemen,
Men of fair parts and states; I know your
    parents;

[8] Morris dances.   [9] Lively dances.
[10] Dastards, spiritless creatures.
[11] Provided.   [12] Wicked.
[13] Alluding to the bundle of sticks carried by the
man in the moon.
[14] Disgraced.

[2] Bet.   [3] Persuaded.   [4] Approves.
[5] Proverbial.   [6] *I.e.*, if we.
[7] Unlocated, but presumably some public place.

And, had ye told me of your fair affections —
Make but one trial more, and let me second ye.

BEL. No ; I 'll make hobnails first, and
    mend old kettles.

Can ye lend me an armor of high proof, to
    appear in,   40
And two or three fieldpieces to defend me?
The king's guard are mere pigmies.

NANT.   They will not eat ye.

BEL. Yes, and you too, and twenty fatter
    monsieurs,
If their high stomachs hold.[15] They came
    with chopping-knives,
To cut me into rands [16] and sirloins, and so
    powder [17] me. —
Come, shall we go?

NANT.   You cannot be so discourteous,
If ye intend to go, as not to visit 'em,
And take your leaves.

MIR.   That we dare do, and civilly,
And thank 'em too.

PIN.   Yes, sir, we know that honesty.[18]

BEL. I 'll come i' the rear, forty foot off, I 'll
    assure ye,   50
With a good gun in my hand. I 'll no more
    Amazons ;
I mean, no more of their frights. I 'll make
    my three legs,[19]
Kiss my hand twice, and, if I smell no danger,
If the interview be clear, maybe I 'll speak to
    her ;
I 'll wear a privy coat [20] too, and behind me,
To make those parts secure, a bandog.[21]

LA CAST.   You are
A merry gentleman.

BEL.   A wary gentleman, I do assure
    ye.
I have been warn'd ; and must be arm'd.

LA CAST.   Well, Son,
These are your hasty thoughts ; when I see
    you are bent to it,
Then I 'll believe, and join with ye ; so, we 'll
    leave ye. —   60

[aside] There 's a trick will make ye stay.

NANT. [aside]   I hope so.
    Exeunt [LA CASTRE *and* NANTOLET].

MIR. We have won immortal fame now, if
    we leave 'em.

PIN. You have ; but we have lost.

MIR.   Pinac, thou art cozen'd.
I know they love ye ; and to gain ye hand-
    somely,

15 If their sharp appetites continue.
16 Slices.   17 Pickle, salt, corn.
18 Decency, decorum.   19 Bows.
20 Secret coat of mail.   21 See on III, i, 169

Not to be thought to yield, they would give
    millions.
Their father's willingness, that must needs
    show ye.

PIN. If I thought so ——

MIR.   Ye shall be hang'd, ye recreant !
Would ye turn renegado now?

BEL.   No ; let 's away, boys,
Out of the air and tumult of their villainies.
Though I were married to that grasshopper,
And had her fast by th' legs, I should think
    she would cozen me.   71

Enter a Young [Man, *disguised as a*] Factor.

Y. MAN. Monsieur Mirabel, I take it?

MIR.   Y' are i' th' right, sir.

Y. MAN. I am come to seek ye, sir. I have
    been at your father's,
And, understanding you were here ——

MIR.   Ye are welcome.
May I crave your name?

Y. MAN.   Fosse, sir, and your servant.
That you may know me better, I am factor
To your old merchant, Leverdure.

MIR.   How does he?

Y. MAN. Well, sir, I hope ; he is now at
    Orleans,
About some business.

MIR.   You are once more welcome.
Your master 's a right honest man, and one [80
I am much beholding to, and must very shortly
Trouble his love again.

Y. MAN.   You may be bold, sir.

MIR. Your business, if you please now?

Y. MAN.   This it is, sir.
I know ye well remember in your travel
A Genoa merchant ——

MIR.   I remember many.

Y. MAN. But this man, sir, particularly ;
    your own benefit
Must needs imprint him in ye ; one Alberto,
A gentleman you sav'd from being murder'd
A little from Bologna ; I was then myself
In Italy, and suppli'd ye ; though haply you
    have   90
Forgot me now.

MIR.   No, I remember ye,
And that Alberto too ; a noble gentleman ;
More to remember were to thank myself, sir.
What of that gentleman?

Y. MAN.   He is dead.

MIR.   I am sorry.

Y. MAN. But on his deathbed, leaving to
    his sister
All that he had, beside some certain jewels,

Which, with a ceremony,[22] he bequeath'd to you
In grateful memory, he commanded strictly
His sister, as she lov'd him and his peace, [99
To see those jewels safe and true deliver'd,
And, with them, his last love. She, as tender
To observe [his][23] will, not trusting friend nor
    servant
With such a weight, is come herself to Paris
And at my master's house.

MIR.   You tell me a wonder.

Y. MAN. I tell ye a truth, sir. She is
    young and handsome,
And well attended ; of much state and riches ;
So loving and obedient to her brother,
That, on my conscience, if he had given her
    also,
She would most willingly have made her ten-
    der.[24]

MIR. May not I see her ?

Y. MAN.   She desires it heartily. [110

MIR. And presently ?

Y. MAN. She is now about some business,
Passing accounts of some few debts here
    owing,
And buying jewels of a merchant.

MIR.   Is she wealthy ?

Y. MAN. I would ye had her, sir, at all
    adventure !
Her brother had a main state.[25]

MIR.   And fair too ?

Y. MAN. The prime of all those parts of
    Italy
For beauty and for courtesy.

MIR.   I must needs see her.

Y. MAN. 'T is all her business, sir. Ye
    may now see her ;
But to-morrow will be fitter for your visitation,
For she is not yet prepared.

MIR.   Only her sight, sir ; [120
And, when you shall think fit, for further visit.

Y. MAN. Sir, ye may see her, and I 'll wait
    your coming.

MIR. And I 'll be with ye instantly ; I
    know the house ;
Meantime, my love and thanks, sir.

Y. MAN.   Your poor servant. *Exit.*

PIN. Thou hast the strangest luck ! What
    was that Alberto ?

MIR. An honest, noble merchant 't was my
    chance
To rescue from some rogues had almost slain
    him ;
And he in kindness to remember this !

BEL.   Now we shall have you,
For all your protestations and your forward-
    ness,   129
Find out strange fortunes in this lady's eyes,
And new enticements to put off your
    journey ;
And who shall have honor then ?

MIR.   No, no, never fear it ;
I must needs see her to receive my legacy.

BEL. If it be ti'd up in her smock, Heaven
    help thee !
May not we see too ?

MIR.   Yes, afore we go ;
I must be known myself, ere I be able
To make [thee][26] welcome. Wouldst thou see
    more women ?
I thought you had been out of love with all.

BEL.   I may be
(I find that), with the least encouragement ;
Yet I desire to see whether all countries [140
Are naturally possess'd with the same spirits,
For, if they be, I 'll take a monastery,
And never travel ; for I had rather be a friar,
And live mewed up, than be a fool, and
    flouted.

MIR. Well, well, I 'll meet ye anon, then tell
    you more, boys ;
However, stand prepar'd, prest[27] for our
    journey ;
For certain we shall go, I think, when I have
    seen her
And view'd her well.

PIN.   Go, go, and we 'll wait for ye ;
Your fortune directs ours.

BEL.   You shall find us i' th' tavern,
Lamenting in sack and sugar for our losses. [150
If she be right Italian, and want servants,[28]
You may prefer[29] the properest man. How
    I could
Worry a woman now !

PIN.   Come, come, leave prating ;
Ye may have enough to do, without this
    boasting.   *Exeunt.*

SCENE III[30]

Enter LUGIER, DE GARD, ROSALURA, *and*
LILLIA [BIANCA].

LUG. This is the last adventure.

DE GARD.   And the happiest,
As we hope, too.

[22] By a formal act.   [23] So F₂ ; F 1652 *this*.
[24] Offer of herself.   [25] Large estate.
[26] Cor. F₂ ; Q 1652 *thou*.
[27] Ready.   [28] Lovers.
[29] Recommend, offer.
[30] Unlocated ; presumably a room in Nantolet's house.

Ros.   We should be glad to find it.

Lil. Who shall conduct us thither?

Lug.   Your man is ready,

For I must not be seen; no, nor this gentleman;

That may beget suspicion; all the rest

Are people of no doubt. I would have ye,
ladies,

Keep your old liberties, and as we instruct
ye.

Come, look not pale; you shall not lose your
wishes,

Nor beg 'em neither; but be yourselves and
happy.

Ros. I tell ye true, I cannot hold off
longer,   10

Nor give no more hard language.

De Gard.   You shall not need.

Ros. I love the gentleman, and must now
show it;

Shall I beat a proper man out of heart?

Lug.   There's none advises ye.

Lil. Faith, I repent me too.

Lug.   Repent and spoil all;

Tell what ye know, ye had best!

Lil.   I'll tell what I think;

For, if he ask me now if I can love him,

I'll tell him yes, I can. The man's a kind
man,

And out of his true honesty [affects][31] me.

Although he play'd the fool, which I requited,

Must I still hold him at the stave's end?

Lug.   You are two strange women. [20

Ros. We may be, if we fool still.

Lug.   Dare ye believe me?

Follow but this advice I have set you in
now,

And if ye lose — would ye yield now so
basely?

Give up without your honors sav'd?

De Gard.   Fie, ladies!

Preserve your freedom still.

Lil.   Well, well, for this time.

Lug. And carry that full state —

Ros.   That's as the wind stands;

If it begin to chop about, and scant us,

Hang me, but I know what I'll do! Come,
direct us;

I make no doubt we shall do handsomely.

De Gard. Some part o' th' way we'll wait
upon ye, ladies;   30

The rest your man supplies.

Lug.   Do well, I'll honor ye.   *Exeunt.*

[31] Likes. Cor. F₂; F 1652 *affect*.

SCENE IV [32]

Oriana [*disguised as an Italian lady,*] *and two*
[*persons disguised as*] Merchants, [*discovered
above.*] *Enter,* [*below, the* Young Man *disguised as a*] Factor, *and* Mirabel.

Y. Man. Look ye, sir, there she is; you
see how busy.

Methinks you are infinitely bound to her for
her journey.

Mir. How gloriously she shows! She is a
tall woman.

Y. Man. Of a fair size, sir. My master
not being at home,

I have been so out of my wits to get her company!

I mean, sir, of her own fair sex and fashion —

Mir. Afar off, she is most fair, too.

Y. Man.   Near, most excellent. —

At length, I have entreated two fair ladies

(And happily [33] you know 'em), the young
daughters

Of Monsieur Nantolet.

Mir.   I know 'em well, sir. [10

What are those? Jewels?

Y. Man.   All.

Mir.   They make a rich show!

Y. Man. There is a matter of ten thousand
pounds, too,

Was owing here. You see those merchants
with her;

They have brought it in now.

Mir.   How handsomely her shape shows!

Y. Man. Those are still neat; your
Italians are most curious.[34]

Now she looks this way.

Mir.   She has a goo[d]ly presence;

How full of courtesy! — Well, sir, I'll leave
ye;

And, if I may be bold to bring a friend or two,

Good, noble gentlemen ——

Y. Man.   No doubt, ye may, sir;

For you have most command.

Mir.   I have seen a wonder! *Exit.* [20

Ori. Is he gone?

Y. Man.   Yes.

Ori.   How?

Y. Man.   Taken to the utmost;

A wonder dwells about him.

Ori.   He did not guess at me?

Y. Man. No, be secure; ye show another
woman.

He is gone to fetch his friends.

[32] A room with a gallery in another house.
[33] Perhaps.   [34] Fastidious.

ORI.   Where are the gentlewomen?
Y. MAN. Here, here; now they are come,
Sit still, and let them see ye.

Enter [below] ROSALURA, LILLIA [BIANCA, *and*]
Servant.

ROS.   Pray ye, where's my friend, sir?
Y. MAN. She is within, ladies; but here's
          another gentlewoman,
A stranger to this town; so please you visit
          her,
'T will be well taken.
LIL.   Where is she?
Y. MAN.   There, above, ladies.
SERV. Bless me, what thing is this? Two
          pinnacles   30
Upon her pate! Is't not a glode [35] to catch
          woodcocks?
ROS. Peace, ye rude knave!
SERV. What a bouncing bum she has too!
There's sail enough for a carack.[36]
ROS.   What is this lady?
For, as I live, she's a goodly woman.
Y. MAN. Guess, guess.
LIL.   I have not seen a nobler presence.
SERV. 'T is a lusty wench; now could I
          spend my forty pence,
With all my heart, to have but one fling at
          her,
To give her but a washing blow.[37]
LIL.   Ye rascal!
SERV. Ay, that's all a man has for's good
          will. 'T will be long enough
Before ye cry, " Come, Anthony, and kiss
          me."   40
LIL. I'll have ye whipp'd.
ROS.   Has my friend seen this lady?
Y. MAN. Yes, yes, and is well known to
          her.
ROS. I much admire her presence.
LIL.   So do I, too;
For, I protest, she is the handsomest,
The rarest, and the newest to mine eye,
That ever I saw yet.
ROS.   I long to know her;
My friend shall do that kindness.
ORI.   So she shall, ladies:
Come, pray ye, come up.
ROS.   Oh me!

LIL.   Hang me, if I knew her! —
Were I a man myself, I should now love ye;
Nay, I should dote.
ROS.   I dare not trust mine eyes; [50
For, as I live, ye are the strangest alter'd!
I must come up to know the truth.
SERV.   So must I, lady;
For I am a kind of unbeliever too.
LIL.   Get ye gone, sirrah;
And what ye have seen be secret in; you are
          paid else! [38]
No more of your long tongue.
Y. MAN.   Will ye go in, ladies,
And talk with her? These venturers will
          come straight.
Away with this fellow.
LIL.   There, sirrah; go, disport ye.
SERV. I would the trunk-hos'd [39] woman
          would go with me.   [*Exeunt.*]

SCENE V [40]

Enter MIRABEL, PINAC, [*and*] BELLEUR.

PIN. Is she so glorious handsome?
MIR.   You would wonder;
Our women look like gipsies, like gills [41] to her;
Their clothes and fashions beggarly and bank-
          rupt,
Base, old, and scurvy.
BEL.   How looks her face?
MIR.   Most heavenly;
And the becoming motion of her body
So sets her off!
BEL.   Why then, we shall stay.
MIR.   Pardon me,
That's more than I know. If she be that
          woman
She appears to be ——
BEL.   As 't is impossible.
MIR. I shall then tell ye more.
PIN.   Did ye speak to her?
MIR. No, no; I only saw her; she was
          busy.   10
Now I go for that end; and mark her, gentle-
          men,
If she appear not to ye one of the sweetest,
The handsomest, the fairest in behavior!
We shall meet the two wenches there, too;
          they come to visit her,
To wonder, as we do.

---

[35] Glade; the space between the pinnacles is
compared to an opening in a wood across which
a snare might be set to catch woodcocks, proverbially foolish birds.
[36] Galleon.
[37] Slashing, swashing. Mod. eds. needlessly emend
swashing.

[38] Otherwise you will be beaten.
[39] Trunk-hose were absurdly voluminous; the
servant jocularly compares the extravagant "bum"
of Oriana's dress to them.
[40] The street before the house.
[41] Serving maids.

PIN.   Then we shall meet 'em.

BEL. I had rather meet two bears.

MIR. There you may take your leaves, despatch that business,

And, as ye find their humors ——

PIN.   Is your love there too?

MIR. No, certain; she has no great heart to set out again.

This is the house; I 'll usher ye.

BEL.   I 'll bless me, [20

And take a good heart, if I can.

MIR.   Come, nobly.   *Exeunt.*

SCENE VI [42]

Enter [the Young Man *disguised as a]* Factor, ROSALURA, LILLIA [BIANCA, *and*] ORIANA [*disguised as before*].

Y. MAN. They are come in. Sit you two off, as strangers. —

There, lady. — Where 's the boy?

[*Enter* Boy.]

                    Be ready, sirrah,

And clear your pipes. — The music now; they enter.   *Music.*

Then enter MIRABEL, PINAC, *and* BELLEUR.

PIN. What a state she keeps! How far off they sit from her!

How rich she is! Ay, marry, this shows bravely!

BEL. She is a lusty wench, and may allure a good man;

But, if she have a tongue, I 'll not give twopence for her.

There sits my Fury; how I shake to see her!

Y. MAN. Madam, this is the gentleman.

MIR.   How sweet she kisses!

[MIRABEL *salutes* ORIANA.]

She has a spring dwells on her lips, a paradise!   10

This is the legacy?

Song [by the Boy, *while he presents a casket to* MIRABEL].

From the honor'd dead I bring
Thus his love and last off'ring.
Take it nobly; 't is your due,
From a friendship ever true;
From a faith, &c.

ORI. Most noble sir,

This from my now-dead brother, as his love,

And grateful memory of your great benefit;

From me my thanks, my wishes, and my service.   20

Till I am more acquainted, I am silent;

Only I dare say this: you are truly noble.

MIR. What should I think?

PIN.   Think ye have a handsome fortune;

Would I had such another!

ROS.   Ye are well met, gentlemen;

We hear ye are for travel.

PIN.   Ye hear true, lady;

And come to take our leaves.

LIL.   We 'll along with ye;

We see you are grown so witty by your journey,

We cannot choose but step out too. This lady

We mean to wait upon as far as Italy.

BEL. [*aside*] I 'll travel into Wales, amongst the mountains,   30

In hope they cannot find me.

ROS.   If you go further,

So good and free society we hold ye,

We 'll jog along too.

PIN.   Are ye so valiant, lady?

LIL. And we 'll be merry, sir, and laugh.

PIN.   It may be

We 'll go by sea.

LIL.   Why, 't is the only voyage!

I love a sea-voyage, and a blust'ring tempest;

And let all split!

PIN.   This is a dainty damosel! —

I think 't will tame ye. Can ye ride post? [43]

LIL. Oh, excellently! I am never weary that way;

A hundred mile a day is nothing with me. [40

BEL. [*aside*] I 'll travel underground. — Do you hear, sweet lady?

I find it will be dangerous for a woman.

ROS. No danger, sir, I warrant; I love to be under.

BEL. I see she will abuse me all the world over. —

But say we pass through Germany, and drink hard?

ROS. We 'll learn to drink, and swagger too.

BELL. [*aside*]   She 'll beat me! —

Lady, I 'll live at home.

ROS.   And I 'll live with thee;

And we 'll keep house together.

BEL. [*aside*]   I 'll keep hounds first;

And those I hate right heartily.

---

[42] A room in the house.

[43] Using post-horses, the speediest way of making a journey.

PIN.   I go for Turkey ;
And so, it may be, up into Persia.   50
  LIL. We cannot know too much ; I'll
    travel with ye.
PIN. And you'll abuse me?
LIL.   Like enough.
PIN.   'T is dainty !
BEL. I will live in a bawdyhouse.
ROS.   I dare come to ye.
BEL. Say I am dispos'd to hang myself?
ROS.   There I 'll leave ye.
BEL. I am glad I know how to avoid ye.
MIR.   May I speak yet?
Y. MAN. She beckons to ye.
MIR.   Lady, I could wish I knew to
    recompense,
Even with the service of my life, those pains
And those high favors you have thrown upon
    me ;
Till I be more desertful in your eye,
And till my duty shall make known I honor
    ye,   60
Noblest of women, do me but this favor,
To accept this back again as a poor testimony.
                    [*Offering the casket.*]
  ORI. I must have you too with 'em ; else
    the will,
That says they must rest with ye, is infring'd,
    sir ;
Which, pardon me, I dare not do.
MIR.   Take me then,
And take me with the truest love.
ORI.   'T is certain
My brother lov'd ye dearly, and I ought
As dearly to preserve that love ; but, sir,
Though I were willing, these are but your cere-
    monies.[44]
  MIR. As I have life, I speak my soul !
ORI.   I like ye ; [70
But how you can like me, without I have tes-
    timony,
A stranger to ye ——
MIR.   I 'll marry ye immediately ;
A fair state I dare promise ye.
BEL.   Yet she 'll cozen thee.
ORI. Would some fair [gentleman][45] durst
    promise for ye !
MIR. By all that 's good ——

Enter LA CASTRE, NANTOLET, LUGIER, *and*
    DE GARD.

  ALL.   And we 'll make up the rest,
    lady.

ORI. Then Oriana takes ye ! Nay, she has
    caught ye ;
If ye start now, let all the world cry shame on
    ye !
I have out-travell'd ye.
BEL.   Did not I say she would cheat
    thee?
MIR. I thank ye ; I am pleas'd ye have
    deceived me,
And willingly I swallow it, and joy in 't ;   80
And yet, perhaps, I [knew][46] ye.   Whose plot
    was this?
LUG. He is not asham'd that cast[47] it ; he
    that executed
Followed your father's will.
MIR.   What a world 's this !
Nothing but craft and cozenage !
ORI.   Who begun, sir?
MIR. Well ; I do take thee upon mere com-
    passion ;
And I do think I shall love thee.   As a testi-
    mony,
I 'll burn my book,[48] and turn a new leaf
    over.
But these fine clothes you shall wear still.
ORI.   I obey you, sir, in all.
NANT. And how, how, daughters?   What
    say you to these gentlemen? —
What say ye, gentlemen, to the girls?
PIN.   By my troth — if she can love
    me —   90
LIL. How long?
PIN.   Nay, if once ye love ——
LIL.   Then take me,
And take your chance.
PIN.   Most willingly ; ye are mine, lady ;
And, if I use ye not that ye may love me ——
LIL. A match, i' faith.
PIN.   Why, now ye travel with me.
ROS. How that thing stands !
BEL.   It will, if ye urge it ;
Bless your five wits !
ROS.   Nay, prithee, stay ; I 'll have
    thee.
BEL. You must ask me leave first.
ROS.   Wilt thou use me kindly,
And beat me but once a week?
BEL.   If ye deserve no more.
ROS. And wilt thou get me with child?
BEL.   Dost thou ask me seriously?
ROS. Yes, indeed, do I.
BEL.   Yes, I will get thee with child.
    Come, presently,[49]   100

---

[44] Polite usages.
[45] So F₂; F 1652 *gentlemen.*

[46] Emend. Sympson; old eds. *know.*   [47] Planned.
[48] See II, i, 146.   [49] Immediately, right now.

An 't be but in revenge, I 'll do thee that cour-
    tesy.
Well, if thou wilt fear God and me, have at
    thee !
   Ros. I 'll love ye, and I 'll honor ye.
   Bel.   I am pleas'd, then.
   Mir. This *Wild-Goose Chase* is done ; we
    have won o' both sides.

Brother, your love ; and now to church of all
    hands ;
Let 's lose no time.
   Pin.   Our travelling lay by.
   Bel. No more for Italy ; for the Low
    Countries,[50] [I.] [51]   *Exeunt.*

[50] An obvious double entente.
[51] Supplied by Theobald. F 1652 ends with a
comma.

THE
WHITE DIVEL,

OR,

The Tragedy of *Paulo Giordano Ursini*, Duke of *Brachiano*,

With

The Life and Death of Vittoria Corombona the famous
Venetian Curtizan.

Acted by the Queenes Maiesties Seruants..

Written by IOHN WEBSTER.

Non inferiora secutus.

LONDON,
Printed by *N.O.* for *Thomas Archer*, and are to be sold
at his Shop in Popes head Pallace, neere the
Royall Exchange. 1612.

INTRODUCTORY NOTE

WEBSTER'S reputation rests almost wholly on two plays. Both are passionate dramas of amorous and political intrigue; both are set in Renaissance Italy, where to a contemporary Englishman's notion anything could happen; both are marked by Webster's crabbed but searing commentary on the folly of human complacency and the vanity of human wishes; both are replete with double-entendres, and occasionally condescend to a rude employment of physical horror; and both remain, for all these, romantic tragedies of great power, surpassed only by Shakespeare's in their own time, and since unequalled, except perhaps by Otway's pair of masterpieces, till Ibsen gave Europe a new conception of the tragic drama's function.

Yet none of Shakespeare's colleagues has been more bedevilled in our own day. A "Tussaud laureate", jeers Mr. Shaw, a greater dramatist, a twentieth-century dramatist, but an uncertain and still nineteenth-century critic. Before the second great renascence of the British drama was possible, it was necessary to break the strangle-hold of Shakespeare and the Elizabethans. Shaw's iconoclasm was not only healthy, it was indispensable; but it is so no longer, and is in fact definitely outmoded. Realism and naturalism have run their course, and drama is turning back from the analysis of social problems to the reconstruction of life. Here the Elizabethans have much to teach us, Webster not least. Every word, indeed, in the attacks of Shaw and Archer is hardly less applicable to Shakespeare himself. The differences are vast enough, but they reside in degree, not in kind. The better you like Shakespeare the greater Webster will seem to you.

Comparison between Webster's twin peaks of achievement is inevitable. *The White Devil* has come again to its own within the last few years, and there can be little question that in this play we have one of the supreme heights of the Jacobean range. The magnificent *Duchess of Malfy* is almost as effective till the death of the heroine, which comes rather too early; after that the play falls off. *The White Devil*, however, unlike as it is in most respects to Greek tragedy, comes closer to the best of it than any of the great Elizabethan plays except *Othello* in maintaining the highest tension throughout the entire action. Not once does it slacken: from the bitter protest "Banish'd!" which is the opening word, and Brachiano's "Quite lost, Flamineo", through the great trial scene, the lovers' anguished quarrel, and all the strivings and the agonies, to the Duke's terrible cry, "Vittoria! Vittoria!" and her desperate "O me! this place is hell"; through the cynicism of Flamineo's speeches, which are like salt rubbed in open wounds, and Cornelia's misery ("Call for the robin redbreast and the wren"), to the treachery and bloody horror of the final episode, and Lodovico's black benediction:

> I do glory yet
> That I can call this act mine own. For my part,
> The rack, the gallows, and the torturing wheel
> Shall be but sound sleeps to me; here's my rest:
> I limn'd this night-piece, and it was my best.

The White Devil was published in 1612. It was probably not written before 1609, for the allusion in V, iii, 188, is to Sir Hugh Myddleton's New River, which was begun in that year; and Perseus, in III, ii, 135, comes from Jonson's *Masque of Queens*, which was produced on February 2 of the same year. 1611–1612 is probably correct. The source was the tragic life of Vittoria Accoramboni, which ended with her murder on December 22, 1585. Whether her story reached Webster in written form is unknown. There were several such accounts; but while many details of the play are based on the actual facts, there are so many departures from them, some obviously due to the dramatic adaptation but others apparently unintentional, that Lucas concludes that Webster relied on a circumstantial but oral account. Virginio Orsini, the Giovanni of *The White Devil*, visited England in 1601.

The original reception of the play is described in Webster's address to the reader. It was successfully revived once more under the Restoration. In 1707 Nahum Tate's ridiculous adaptation, *Injured Love,* was published as it was "design'd to be Acted at the Theatre Royal." The standard edition of Webster is that of F. L. Lucas (1928). *The White Devil* and *The Duchess of Malfy* occupy a volume in the Belles Lettres Series, edited by M. W. Sampson (1904). The First Quarto of the former, 1612, was followed by others in 1631, 1665, and 1672. The present text is based on the Harvard copy of Q 1612, which is in agreement with the Garrick copy, cited by Lucas as superior in most signatures to the Dyce copy. It has also been collated with the copy of the Folger Shakespeare Library, which usually, though not invariably, agrees with the Garrick-Harvard State.

THE WHITE DEVIL [1]

OR

VITTORIA COROMBONA

BY

JOHN WEBSTER

To The Reader

In publishing this tragedy I do but challenge to myself that liberty which other men have ta'en before me; not that I affect praise by it, for *nos haec novimus esse nihil:* [2] only, since it was acted in so dull a time of winter, presented in so open and black [3] a theatre, that it wanted that which is the only grace and setting out of a tragedy, a full and understanding auditory; and that since that time I have noted most of the people that come to that playhouse resemble those ignorant asses who, visiting stationers' shops, their use is not to inquire for good books, but new books; I present it to the general view with this confidence:

Nec rhoncos metues maligniorum,
Nec scombris tunicas dabis molestas. [4]   9

If it be objected this is no true dramatic poem, I shall easily confess it: *non potes in nugas dicere plura meas: Ipse ego quam dixi,* [5] willingly and not ignorantly in this kind have I faulted; for should a man present to such an auditory the most sententious tragedy that ever was written, observing all the critical laws, as heighth of style and gravity of person, enrich it with the sententious Chorus, and as it were lifen death in the passionate and weighty Nuntius; [6] yet, after all this divine rapture, *O dura messorum ilia,* [7] the breath that comes from the uncapable multitude is able to poison it; and ere it be acted let the author resolve to fix to every scene this of Horace:

— Haec hodie Porcis comedenda relinques. [8]

To those who report I was a long time in finishing this tragedy, I confess I do not write with a goose quill, winged with two feathers; and if they will needs make it my fault, I must answer [20 them with that of Euripides to Alcestides, [9] a tragic writer: Alcestides objecting that Euripides had only in three days composed three verses, whereas himself had written three hundred, "Thou tell'st truth," quoth he, " but here's the difference: thine shall only be read for three days, whereas mine shall continue three ages."

Detraction is the sworn friend to ignorance; for mine own part I have ever truly cherish'd my good opinion of other men's worthy labors: especially of that full and height'ned style of Master Chapman; the labor'd and understanding works of Master Jonson; the no less worthy composures of the both worthily excellent Master Beaumont and Master Fletcher; and lastly,

---

[1] *I.e.*, a devil disguised under a fair appearance.
[2] We are aware that these things are negligible. (Martial, XIII, 2.)
[3] The Red Bull, a large, partly roofless theatre in Clerkenwell, saw the first performance of *The White Devil*. Toward the end of a winter afternoon it would be getting dark. Malone emends *bleak*. The company was the Queen's Men, formerly the Earl of Worcester's. It seems probable that Webster had severed his connection with them before the publication of this play. His next, *The Duchess of Malfy*, was produced by the King's Men.
[4] You, [my book,] shall not fear the turned-up noses of the malicious, nor shall you provide wrapping-paper for mackerel. (Martial, IV, 86.)

[5] You can not say more against these trifles of mine than I have said myself. (Martial, XIII, 2.)
[6] Give a lively account of the deaths of the characters by means of the . . . classical Messenger.
[7] Oh, the strong stomachs of harvesters. (Horace, *Epodes*, III.)
[8] These you will leave for the swine to eat today. (*Epistles*, I, 7.)
[9] The anecdote is told by Valerius Maximus (III, 7). *Alcestides* is Webster's blunder for *Alcestis*, itself (Lucas suggests) a blunder for the tragic poet *Acestor*. The Latin account specifies one, not three, hundred lines.

without wrong last to be named, the right happy and copious industry of M. Shakespeare, M. Dekker, and M. Heywood; wishing what I write may be read by their light: protesting that, in the strength of mine own judgment, I know them so worthy that, though I rest silent in my own work, yet to most of theirs I dare, without flattery, fix that of Martial: 32

— non norunt, Haec monumenta mori.[10]

[THE PERSONS [11]

MONTICELSO, a cardinal, afterwards Pope Paul the Fourth.[12]

FRANCISCO DE MEDICIS,[13] Duke of Florence; in the fifth act disguis'd for a Moor, under the name of Mulinassar.

BRACHIANO, otherwise PAULO GIORDANO ORSINI,[14] Duke of Brachiano; husband to Isabella, and in love with Vittoria.

GIOVANNI,[15] his son, by Isabella.

LODOVICO,[16] an Italian count, but decay'd.

ANTONELLI, } his friends, and dependents of
GASPARO, }   the Duke of Florence.

CAMILLO,[17] husband to Vittoria.

HORTENSIO, one of Brachiano's officers.

MARCELLO,[18] an attendant of the Duke of Florence, and brother to Vittoria.

FLAMINEO,[19] secretary to Brachiano, brother to Vittoria.

JAQUES, a Moor, servant to Giovanni.

CARDINAL OF ARRAGON.

DOCTOR JULIO.

CHRISTOPHERO, his assistant.

Ambassadors, courtiers, lawyers, officers, physicians, conjuror, armorer, and attendants.

ISABELLA,[20] sister to Francisco de Medicis, and wife to Brachiano.

VITTORIA COROMBONA, a Venetian [21] lady; first marri'd to Camillo, afterwards to Brachiano.

CORNELIA,[22] mother to Vittoria, Flamineo, and Marcello.

ZANCHE, a Moor, servant to Vittoria.

Matron of a house of convertites.

THE SCENE — *Rome and Padua.*]

[ACT I — SCENE I] [1]

Enter COUNT LODOVICO, ANTONELLI, *and* GASPARO.

LOD. Banish'd!

ANT.   It griev'd me much to hear the sentence.

LOD. Ha, ha! O Democritus, thy gods That govern the whole world! courtly reward
And punishment! [2] Fortune's a right whore: If she give aught, she deals it in small parcels,
That she may take away all at one swoop. This 't is to have great enemies: God quit [3] them!
Your wolf no longer seems to be a wolf Than when she's hungry.[4]

GAS.   You term those enemies [5]Are men of princely rank.

LOD.   Oh, I pray for them. [10 The violent thunder is adored by those
Are pash'd in pieces by it.

ANT.   Come, my Lord,
You are justly doom'd: look but a little back Into your former life; you have in three years
Ruin'd the noblest earldom.

GAS.   Your followers

---

[10] These monuments know not how to die. (Martial, X, 2.)

[11] Based on the list first given in Q₃, but with several additions and minor changes.

[12] Historically, Cardinal Montalto, afterwards Sextus V.   [13] Francesco de' Medici.

[14] Bracciano . . . Paolo . . . Orsini; old eds. *Ursini* here, but elsewhere, *Orsini.* Webster's spelling *Brachiano* is intended to indicate the Italian pronunciation, *Bracciano.*

[15] Historically, Virginio.

[16] Historically, Lodovico degli Orsini di Monterotondo, a younger kinsman of Bracciano.

[17] Nephew to the Cardinal; historically, Francesco Peretti.

[18] Younger than the Flamineo of the play; historically, Flamineo.   [19] Historically, Marcello.

[20] The historical Isabella was murdered in revenge for her intrigue with Troilo Orsini.

[21] The historical Vittoria Accoramboni was an Umbrian.

[22] Historically, Tarquinia. She probably planned her son-in-law's assassination.

[1] Rome, but not precisely located.

[2] Opposed to all the known sayings of Democritus. (Sampson.)

[3] Repay, requite.

[4] *I.e.*, prosperous wolves are not regarded as wolves.

[5] The relative is often omitted in this play.

Have swallowed you like mummia,[6] and, being sick
With such unnatural and horrid physic,
Vomit you up i' th' kennel.[7]
　　ANT.　　　　　　All the damnable degrees
Of drinkings have you stagger'd through : one citizen
Is lord of two fair manors call'd you mas-
　　ter,　　　　　　　　　　　　　　20
Only for caviare.[8]
　　GAS.　　　　　　Those noblemen
Which were invited to your prodigal feasts,
Wherein the phoenix scarce could scape your throats,
Laugh at your misery, as fore-deeming you
An idle meteor, which, drawn forth the earth,[9]
Would be soon lost i' th' air.
　　ANT.　　　　　　Jest upon you,
And say you were begotten in an earthquake,
You have ruin'd such fair lordships.
　　LOD.　　　　　　Very good ;
This well goes with two buckets : I must
　　tend [10]
The pouring out of either.
　　GAS.　　　　　　Worse than these : [30
You have acted certain murders [11] here in Rome,
Bloody and full of horror.
　　LOD.　　　　　　'Las ! they were flea-bitings.
Why took they not my head then?
　　GAS.　　　　　　Oh, my Lord,
The law doth sometimes mediate, thinks it good
Not ever to steep violent sins in blood ;
This gentle penance may both end your crimes,
And in the example better these bad times.
　　LOD. So ; but I wonder then some great men scape
This banishment : there's Paulo Giordano Orsini,
The Duke of Brachiano, now lives in Rome,[40
And by close panderism seeks to prostitute
The honor of Vittoria Corombona —
Vittoria, she that might have got my pardon
For one kiss to the Duke.
　　ANT.　　　　　　Have a full man within you.
We see that trees bear no such pleasant fruit

There where they grew first as where they are new set ;
Perfumes, the more they are chaf'd, the more they render
Their pleasing scents ; and so affliction
Expresseth virtue fully, whether true
Or else adulterate.
　　LOD.　　Leave your painted comforts ; [12] [50
I'll make Italian cut-works [13] in their guts,
If ever I return.
　　GAS.　　　　　　Oh, sir !
　　LOD.　　　　　　I am patient.
I have seen some ready to be executed
Give pleasant looks and money, and grown familiar
With the knave hangman ; so do I, I thank them,
And would account them nobly merciful,
Would they dispatch me quickly.
　　ANT.　　　　　　Fare you well ;
We shall find time, I doubt not, to repeal
Your banishment.
　　LOD.　　　　　I am ever bound to you.
This is the world's alms ; pray, make use of it.[14]　　　　　　　　　　60
Great men sell sheep thus, to be cut in pieces
When first they have shorn them bare and sold
　　their fleeces.　　　　　　　*Exeunt.*

SCENE II [1]

Sennet.[2] *Enter* BRACHIANO, CAMILLO, FLA-
MINEO, VITTORIA COROMBONA, [*and* Servants *with torches*].

BRACH. Your best of rest !
VIT.　　　　　　Unto my Lord the Duke
The best of welcome ! — More lights ! at-
tend the Duke.
　　　　　[*Exeunt* CAMILLO *and* VITTORIA.]
BRACH. Flamineo !
FLAM.　　　　　　My Lord?
BRACH.　　　　　　Quite lost, Flamineo !
FLAM. Pursue your noble wishes ; I am prompt
As lightning to your service. Oh, my Lord —
(*whisper*) The fair Vittoria, my happy sister,
Shall give you present audience. — Gentle-
men,
Let the caroche [3] go on ; and 't is his pleasure

---

[6] Mummy was formerly used medicinally.
[7] Gutter.
[8] *I.e.*, you have spent for caviare alone the proceeds of the sale of two of your manors.
[9] Meteors were supposed to be "exhalations"
from the earth, drawn up by the sun.
[10] Await.
[11] The historical Lodovico had murdered Vincenzo
Vitelli.

[12] Specious consolations.
[13] Open-work patterns.
[14] *I.e.*, profit by my experience.
[1] "Vaguely Camillo's house, here perhaps the
entrance-hall, later the banqueting-house." (Lucas.)
[2] Flourish of trumpets. Qq om., but after i, 59,
give the prompter's note : *Enter Senate.*
[3] Coach.

You put out all your torches, and depart.

[*Exeunt* Attendants.]

BRACH. Are we so happy?

FLAM.   Can 't be otherwise? [10
Observ'd you not to-night, my honor'd
Lord,
Which way soe'er you went she threw her
eyes?
I have dealt already with her chambermaid,
Zanche, the Moor; and she is wondrous
proud
To be the agent for so high a spirit.

BRACH. We are happy above thought,
because 'bove merit.

FLAM. 'Bove merit! — we may now talk
freely — 'bove merit! What is 't you doubt? [4]
her coyness? that 's but the superficies of lust
most women have; yet why should ladies [20
blush to hear that nam'd which they do not
fear to handle? Oh, they are politic! They
know our desire is increas'd by the difficulty
of enjoying, where [5] a satiety is a blunt, weary,
and drowsy passion. If the buttery-hatch at
court stood continually open, there would be
nothing so passionate crowding, nor hot suit
after the beverage.

BRACH. Oh, but her jealous husband!

FLAM. Hang him! a gilder that hath [30
his brains perish'd with quicksilver [6] is not
more cold in the liver; [7] the great barriers [8]
moulted not more feathers [9] than he hath shed
hairs, by the confession of his doctor; [10] an
Irish gamester that will play himself naked,
and then wage all downward [11] at hazard, is
not more venturous; so unable to please a
woman, that, like a Dutch doublet,[12] all his
back is shrunk into his breeches.

Shroud you within this closet, good my
Lord: 40
Some trick now must be thought on to divide
My brother-in-law from his fair bedfellow.

BRACH. Oh, should she fail to come —

[4] Fear.
[5] Whereas. Dyce may be right in emending *where*
a to *whereas*.
[6] *I.e.*, from mercurial poisoning. Mercury was
used in the process of gold-plating.
[7] The seat of love.
[8] A form of jousting; the participants fought
across waist-high barriers.
[9] The shorn helmet plumes.
[10] The mercurial treatment of syphilis had this
effect.
[11] Sykes quotes from Stanyhurst's *Description of
Ireland* an account of certain Irish gamesters who
after playing away their clothes would wager their
testes. The imputation is that Camillo's are value-
less, and that his impotence would make him bold
to stake them.
[12] Which, unlike their breeches, was tight-fitting.

FLAM. I must not have your Lordship thus
unwisely amorous. I myself have loved a
lady, and pursued her with a great deal of
under-age protestation,[13] whom some three or
four gallants that have enjoyed would with
all their hearts have been glad to have been
rid of. 'T is just like a summer bird- [50
cage in a garden: the birds that are without
despair to get in, and the birds that are within
despair and are in a consumption for fear they
shall never get out.[14] Away, away, my Lord!

[*Exit* BRACHIANO.]

See, here he comes. This fellow by his ap-
parel
Some men would judge a politician;
But, call his wit in question, you shall find it
Merely an ass in 's footcloth.[15]

Re-enter CAMILLO.

                        How now, Brother?
What, travelling to bed to your kind
wife?

CAM. I assure you, Brother, no; my voy-
age lies   60
More northerly, in a far colder clime;
I do not well remember, I protest,
When I last lay with her.

FLAM. Strange you should lose your count.

CAM. We never lay together, but ere morning
There grew a flaw [16] between us.

FLAM.   'T had been your part
To have made up that flaw.

CAM.   True, but she loathes
I should be seen in 't.

FLAM.   Why, sir, what 's the matter?

CAM. The Duke, your master, visits me,
I thank him;
And I perceive how, like an earnest bowler, [70
He very passionately leans that way
He should have his bowl run.

FLAM.   I hope you do not think —

CAM. That noblemen bowl booty? [17] Faith,
his cheek [18]
Hath a most excellent bias; [19] it would fain

[13] Inexperienced love-making.
[14] From Florio's translation of Montaigne's Essays, "Of Marriage."
[15] A rich cloth laid over a horse's back; it nearly
touched the ground.
[16] Quarrel, with an obvious double entente.
[17] Join with confederates to victimize another
player.
[18] Brachiano's cheek, which, like the round cheek
of a bowl, is trying to touch that of the "mistress."
[19] Bowls were shaped or weighted so as to roll in
a curve (bias) around an object that might bar the
way to the "mistress."

Jump with [20] my mistress.[21]

FLAM.   Will you be an ass,
Despite you[r] Aristotle? or a cuckold,
Contrary to your Ephemerides,[22]
Which shows you under what a smiling planet
You were first swaddled?

CAM.   Pew-wew, sir, tell not me
Of planets nor of Ephemerides;   80
A man may be made cuckold in the daytime,
When the stars' eyes are out.

FLAM.   Sir, God boy you; [23]
I do commit you to your pitiful pillow
Stuff'd with horn-shavings.[24]

CAM.   Brother —

FLAM.   God refuse me!
Might I advise you now, your only course
Were to lock up your wife.

CAM.   'T were very good.

FLAM. Bar her the sight of revels.

CAM.   Excellent.

FLAM. Let her not go to church, but, like
      a hound,
In leon [25] at your heels.

CAM.   'T were for her honor.

FLAM. And so you should be certain in one
      fortnight,   90
Despite her chastity or innocence,
To be cuckolded, which yet is in suspense :
This is my counsel, and I ask no fee for 't.

CAM. Come, you know not where my nightcap wrings me.

FLAM. Wear it a' th' old fashion; let your
large ears come through, it will be more easy.
Nay, I will be bitter. Bar your wife of her
entertainment? Women are more willingly
and more gloriously chaste when they are
least restrained of their liberty. It seems [100
you would be a fine, capricious, mathemati-
cally jealous coxcomb; take the height of
your own horns with a Jacob's staff [26] afore
they are up. These politic inclosures [27] for
paltry mutton [28] makes more rebellion in the
flesh than all the provocative electuaries doctors have uttered [29] since last jubilee.[30]

---

[20] Coincide with, touch.
[21] Or jack, the object-ball at which the bowls were aimed.
[22] Astrological tables.   [23] God be with you, goodbye.
[24] Alluding to the horns of the cuckold.
[25] A variant of *leam* or *lyam* = leash.
[26] An instrument for measuring heights and distances.
[27] An allusion to a grievance of the time, the inclosure of common lands by rich landowners for sheep pasturage.
[28] Slang for "loose women."
[29] Issued, sold.
[30] 1600. The first year of jubilee was proclaimed by Pope Boniface VIII in 1300.

CAM. This doth not physic me.

FLAM. It seems you are jealous; I'll show
you the error of it by a familiar example. [110
I have seen a pair of spectacles fashion'd with
such perspective art, that, lay down but one
twelvepence a' th' board, 't will appear as if
there were twenty; now, should you wear a
pair of these spectacles, and see your wife
tying her shoe, you would imagine twenty
hands were taking up of your wife's clothes,
and this would put you into a horrible causeless fury.

CAM. The fault there, sir, is not in the [120
eyesight.

FLAM. True; but they that have the
yellow jaundice think all objects they look
on to be yellow. Jealousy is worser : her fits
present to a man, like so many bubbles in a
basin of water, twenty several crabbed faces;
many times makes his own shadow his cuckold-maker.

Re-enter [VITTORIA] COROMBONA.

See, she comes. What reason have you to
be jealous of this creature? What an [130
ignorant ass or flattering knave might he be
counted that should write sonnets to her eyes,
or call her brow the snow of Ida or ivory of
Corinth, or compare her hair to the blackbird's bill,[31] when 't is liker the blackbird's
feather! This is all; be wise, I will make you
friends; and you shall go to bed together.
Marry, look you, it shall not be your seeking;
do you stand upon that by any means; [32]
walk you aloof; I would not have you [140
seen in 't. [CAMILLO   *retires.*] — Sister, —
[*aside*] my Lord attends you in the banqueting-house. Your husband is wondrous discontented.

VIT. I did nothing to displease him; I
carved [33] to him at supper-time.

FLAM. [*aside*] You need not have carved [34]
him, in faith : they say he is a capon already.
I must now seemingly fall out with you. —
Shall a gentleman so well descended as [150
Camillo, — [*aside*] a lousy slave, that within
this twenty years rode with the black guard [35]
in the Duke's carriage, 'mongst spits and
dripping-pans. —

CAM. [*aside*] Now he begins to tickle [36] her!

---

[31] Which is yellow. Gentlemen still preferred blondes to brunettes, at any rate theoretically.
[32] Stick to that on any account.
[33] Was courteous.   [34] *I.e.*, gelded.
[35] The lowest menials. "Carriage"=baggage train.
[36] Excite.

FLAM. An excellent scholar, — [*aside*] one that hath a head fill'd with calves' brains without any sage [37] in them, — come crouching in the hams to you for a night's lodging, — [*aside*] that hath an itch in 's hams, which [160 like the fire at the glass-house [38] hath not gone out this seven years? — Is he not a courtly gentleman? — [*aside*] When he wears white satin, one would take him by his black muzzle to be no other creature than a maggot. — You are a goodly foil, I confess, well set out, — [*aside*] but cover'd with a false stone, yon counterfeit diamond.

CAM. [*aside*] He will make her know what is in me.   170

FLAM. Come, my Lord attends you; thou shalt go to bed to my Lord —

CAM. [*aside*] Now he comes to 't.

FLAM. [*aside*] With a relish as curious as a vintner going to taste new wine. — [*to* CAMILLO] I am opening your case hard.

CAM. [*aside*] A virtuous brother, a' my credit!

FLAM. He will give thee a ring with a philosopher's stone in it.   180

CAM. [*aside*] Indeed, I am studying alchemy.

FLAM. [*aside*] Thou shalt lie in a bed stuff'd with turtles' feathers; swoon in perfumed linen, like the fellow was smothered in roses. So perfect shall be thy happiness that, as men at sea think land and trees and ships go that way they go, so both heaven and earth shall seem to go your voyage. Shalt meet him; 't is fix'd with nails of diamonds [190 to inevitable necessity.

VIT. [*aside*] How shall 's rid him hence?

FLAM. [*aside*] I will put brees [39] in 's tail — set him gadding presently.[40] — [*to* CAMILLO] I have almost wrought her to it: I find her coming; [41] but, might I advise you now, for this night I would not lie with her; I would cross her humor,[42] to make her more humble.

CAM. Shall I, shall I?   200

FLAM. It will show in you a supremacy of judgment.

CAM. True, and a mind differing from the

tumultuary [43] opinion; for, *quae negata, grata.*[44]

FLAM. Right; you are the adamant [45] shall draw her to you, though you keep distance off.

CAM. A philosophical reason.

FLAM. Walk by her a' the nobleman's [210 fashion, and tell her you will lie with her at the end of the progress.[46]

CAM. [*coming forward*] Vittoria, I cannot be induc'd, or, as a man would say, incited —

VIT. To do what, sir?

CAM. To lie with you to-night. Your [47] silkworm useth to fast every third day, and the next following spins the better. Tomorrow at night I am for you.   220

VIT. You 'll spin a fair thread, trust to 't.

FLAM. [*aside to* CAMILLO] But, do you hear, I shall have you [48] steal to her chamber about midnight.

CAM. [*aside*] Do you think so? why, look you, Brother, because you shall not think I 'll gull [49] you, take the key, lock me into the chamber, and say [50] you shall be sure of me.

FLAM. [*aside*] In troth, I will; I 'll be your jailer once. But have you ne'er a false [230 door?

CAM. [*aside*] A pox on 't, as I am a Christian! Tell me to-morrow how scurvily she takes my unkind parting.

FLAM. [*aside*] I will.

CAM. [*aside*] Didst thou not [mark] [51] the jest of the silkworm? Good-night. In faith, I will use this trick often.

FLAM. [*aside*] Do, do, do. — *Exit* CAMILLO. So; [52] now you are safe. Ha, ha, ha! [240 thou entanglest thyself in thine own work like a silkworm. — Come, Sister; darkness hides your blush. Women are like curst [53] dogs: civility [54] keeps them tied all daytime, but they are let loose at midnight; then they do most good, or most mischief. — My Lord, my Lord!

---

[37] An obvious pun.
[38] It stood near the Blackfriars Theatre. There are numerous allusions to London in this play, despite its setting.
[39] Gadflies.
[40] At once.
[41] *I.e.*, favorably disposed.
[42] Whim, inclination.

[43] Hurriedly formed, unsystematic.
[44] What is refused is pleasing.
[45] Magnet.
[46] Royal journey to visit various parts of the realm.
[47] The.
[48] I shall find you, I fear you will.
[49] Deceive.
[50] Tate's *Injured Love* reads *so*, perhaps rightly. Daniel proposed the emendation.
[51] So Q₄; earlier Qq *make*.
[52] Locking the door.
[53] Ugly, fierce.
[54] Decency. Q₂, *et seq.*, *cruelty.*

Re-enter BRACHIANO. ZANCHE *brings out a carpet, spreads it, and lays on it two fair cushions.*

BRACH. Give credit I could wish time
        would stand still,
And never end this interview, this hour;
But all delight doth itself soon'st devour. [250

Enter CORNELIA [*behind*].

Let me into your bosom, happy lady,
Pour out, instead of eloquence, my vows.
Loose me not, madam; for, if you forgo
        me,
I am lost eternally.
VIT.   Sir, in the way of pity,
I wish you heart-whole.
BRACH.   You are a sweet physician.
VIT. Sure, sir, a loathed cruelty in ladies
Is as to doctors many funerals :
It takes away their credit.
BRACH.   Excellent creature!
We call the cruel fair; what name for you
That are so merciful?
ZAN.   See, now they close. [260
FLAM. Most happy union!
CORN. [*aside*] My fears are fall'n upon me.
        Oh, my heart!
My son the pander! now I find our house
Sinking to ruin. Earthquakes leave be-
        hind,
Where they have tyrannized, iron or lead or
        stone;
But, woe to ruin, violent lust leaves none!
BRACH. What value is this jewel?
VIT.   'T is the ornament
Of a weak fortune.
BRACH. In sooth, I'll have it; nay, I will
        but change
My jewel for your jewel.
FLAM. [*aside*]   Excellent!   [270
His jewel for her jewel: well put in, Duke.
BRACH. Nay, let me see you wear it.
VIT.   Here, sir?
BRACH. Nay, lower, you shall wear my
        jewel lower.
FLAM. [*aside*] That's better: she must
        wear his jewel lower.
VIT. To pass away the time, I'll tell your
        Grace
A dream I had last night.
BRACH.   Most wishedly.
VIT. A foolish, idle dream.
Methought I walk'd, about the mid of night,
Into a churchyard, where a goodly yew tree

Spread her large root in ground. Under
        that yew,[55]   280
As I sat sadly leaning on a grave
Chequered with cross sticks,[56] there came
        stealing in
Your duchess and my husband; one of them
A pickaxe bore, th' other a rusty spade;
And in rough terms they 'gan to challenge me
About this yew.
BRACH.   That tree?
VIT.   This harmless yew.
They told me my intent was to root up
That well-grown yew, and plant i' th' stead
        of it
A withered blackthorn; and for that they
        vow'd
To bury me alive. My husband straight [290
With pickaxe 'gan to dig, and your fell
        duchess
With shovel, like a Fury, voided out
The earth, and scattered bones. Lord, how
        methought
I trembled; and yet, for all this terror,
I could not pray.
FLAM. [*aside*] No; the Devil was in your
        dream.
VIT. When to my rescue there arose, me-
        thought,
A whirlwind, which let fall a massy arm
From that strong plant;
And both were struck dead by that sacred
        yew,
In that base shallow grave that was their due.
FLAM. [*aside*] Excellent devil! she hath
        taught him in a dream   301
To make away his duchess and her husband.
BRACH. Sweetly shall I interpret this your
        dream.
You are lodged within his arms who shall pro-
        tect you
From all the fevers of a jealous husband,
From the poor envy[57] of our phlegmatic
        duchess.
I'll seat you above law and above scandal;
Give to your thoughts the invention of delight,
And the fruition; nor shall government
Divide me from you longer than a care   310
To keep you great: you shall to me at
        once
Be dukedom, health, wife, children, friends,
        and all.

[55] With a play on "you." Old eds. spell *Eu* or *Ewe*.
[56] Probably, as Sampson suggests, "crosses stuck in the grave."
[57] Malice.

CORN. [*coming forward*] Woe to light
    hearts! they still forerun our fall.
FLAM. What Fury rais'd thee up? —
    Away, away!   *Exit* ZANCHE.
CORN. What make [58] you here, my Lord,
    this dead of night?
Never dropp'd mildew on a flower here
Till now.
FLAM.   I pray, will you go to bed, then,
Lest you be blasted?
CORN.   Oh, that this fair garden
Had [with] [59] all poisoned herbs of Thessaly [60]
At first been planted; made a nursery   320
For witchcraft, rather [than] [59] a burial
    plot
For both your honors!
VIT.   Dearest Mother, hear me.
CORN. Oh, thou dost make my brow bend
    to the earth,
Sooner than nature! See, the curse of chil-
    dren!
In life they keep us frequently [61] in tears;
And in the cold grave leaves us in pale fears.
BRACH. Come, come, I will not hear you.
VIT.   Dear my Lord —
CORN. Where is thy duchess now, adulter-
    ous Duke?
Thou little dream'dst this night she is come to
    Rome.
FLAM. How! come to Rome?
VIT.   The Duchess!
BRACH.   She had been better —
CORN. The lives of princes should like dials
    move,   331
Whose regular example is so strong
They make the times by them go right or
    wrong.
FLAM. So; have you done?
CORN.   Unfortunate Camillo!
VIT. I do protest, if any chaste denial,
If anything but blood could have allayed
His long suit to me —
CORN.   I will join with thee, [62]
To the most woeful end e'er mother kneel'd:
If thou dishonor thus thy husband's bed,
Be thy life short as are the funeral tears   [340
In great men's — [63]
BRACH.   Fie, fie, the woman's mad.
CORN. Be thy act Judas-like — betray in
    kissing!

Mayst thou be envied [64] during his short
    breath,
And pitied like a wretch after [his] [65] death!
VIT. O me accurs'd!   *Exit* VITTORIA.
FLAM.   Are you out of your wits, my
    Lord?
I'll fetch her back again!
BRACH.   No, I'll to bed;
Send Doctor Julio to me presently. —
Uncharitable woman, thy rash tongue
Hath rais'd a fearful and prodigious [66] storm:
Be thou the cause of all ensuing harm.   350
                    Exit BRACHIANO.
FLAM. Now, you that stand so much upon
    your honor,
Is this a fitting time a' night, think you,
To send a duke home without e'er a man? [67]
I would fain know where lies the mass of
    wealth
Which you have hoarded for my maintenance,
That I may bear my beard out of the level
Of my Lord's stirrup. [68]
CORN.   What! because we are poor,
Shall we be vicious?
FLAM.   Pray, what means have you
To keep me from the galleys — or the gal-
    lows?
My father prov'd himself a gentleman — [360
Sold all's land, and, like a fortunate fel-
    low,
Died ere the money was spent. You brought
    me up
At Padua, I confess, where, I protest,
For want of means (the university judge me),
I have been fain to heel my tutor's stock-
    ings, [69]
At least seven years; conspiring with a beard
Made me a graduate; then to this duke's
    service.
I visited the court, whence I return'd
More courteous, more lecherous by far,
But not a suit the richer; and shall I,   370
Having a path so open and so free
To my preferment, still retain your milk
In my pale forehead? [70]   No, this face of mine
I'll arm and fortify with lusty wine,
'Gainst shame and blushing.
CORN. Oh, that I ne'er had borne thee!
FLAM.   So would I;
I would the common'st courtezan in Rome

---

[58] Do.
[59] Add. Q3.
[60] In classical literature a great haunt of witches.
[61] Repeatedly.
[62] In kneeling.
[63] Old eds. have a full stop instead of a dash.

[64] Hated.   [65] Q1 *this*.   [66] Portentous.
[67] An attendant.
[68] *I.e.*, leave off having to run at his stirrup like
a footman.
[69] *I.e.*, act as his servant.
[70] *I.e.*, be womanish.

Had been my mother, rather than thyself.
Nature is very pitiful to whores,
To give them but few children, yet those children   380
Plurality of fathers : they are sure
They shall not want. Go, go,
Complain unto my great Lord Cardinal ;
Yet maybe he will justify the act.
Lycurgus [71] wond'red much men would provide
Good stallions for their mares, and yet would suffer
Their fair wives to be barren.

CORN.   Misery of miseries !
                                        Exit CORNELIA.

FLAM. The Duchess come to court ! I like not that.
We are engag'd to mischief, and must on ;
As rivers, to find out the ocean,   390
Flow with crook bendings beneath forced banks ;
Or as we see, to aspire some mountain's top,
The way ascends not straight, but imitates
The subtle foldings of a winter's snake ;
So who knows policy and her true aspect
Shall find her ways winding and indirect.

[ACT II — SCENE I] [1]

Enter FRANCESCO DE MEDICIS, CARDINAL
MONTICELSO, ISABELLA, *young* GIOVANNI,
with little JAQUES *the Moor.*

FRAN. Have you not seen your husband since you arrived?
ISA. Not yet, sir.
FRAN.   Surely he is wondrous kind.
If I had such a dovehouse as Camillo's,
I would set fire on 't, were 't but to destroy
The polecats [2] that haunt to 't. —

[*Enter* MARCELLO.]

                                        My sweet Cousin ! [3]
GIOV. Lord Uncle, you did promise me a horse
And armor.
FRAN.   That I did, my pretty Cousin. —
Marcello, see it fitted.
MAR.   My Lord, the Duke is here.

FRAN. Sister, away ! you must not yet be seen.
ISA.   I do beseech you,
Entreat him mildly ; let not your rough tongue   10
Set us at louder variance : all my wrongs
Are freely pardoned ; and I do not doubt,
As men, to try the precious unicorn's horn, [4]
Make of the powder a preservative circle
And in it put a spider, [5] so these arms
Shall charm his poison, force it to obeying,
And keep him chaste from an infected straying.
FRAN. I wish it may. Begone.
                    [*Exeunt* ISABELLA, GIOVANNI, *and*
                    JAQUES.]

Enter BRACHIANO *and* FLAMINEO.

                                        Void the chamber. —
                    [*Exeunt* MARCELLO *and* FLAMINEO.]
You are welcome ; will you sit? — I pray, my Lord,
Be you my orator : my heart's too full ;   20
I'll second you anon.
MONT.   Ere I begin,
Let me entreat your Grace forgo all passion
Which may be raised by my free discourse.
BRACH. As silent as i' th' church — [6] you may proceed.
MONT. It is a wonder to your noble friends,
That you, have, [7] as 'twere, ent'red the world
With a free sceptre in your able hand,
And have to th' use of nature well applied
High gifts of learning, should in your prime age
Neglect your awful throne for the soft down [30
Of an insatiate bed. O, my Lord,
The drunkard after all his lavish cups
Is dry, and then is sober ; so at length,
When you awake from this lascivious dream,
Repentance then will follow, like the sting
Plac'd in the adder's tail. Wretched are princes
When fortune blasteth but a petty flower
Of their unwieldly crowns or ravisheth
But one pearl from their scepter ; [8] but, alas,
When they to wilful shipwrack lose good fame,   40
All princely titles perish with their name !
BRACH. You have said, my Lord.
MONT.   Enough to give you taste
How far I am from flattering your greatness !

[71] In Plutarch's Life of him.
[1] A room in Francisco's palace.
[2] Prostitutes.
[3] Here = nephew.

[4] Supposed to be an antidote.
[5] Whose inability to cross the ring of powder would prove its efficacy.   [6] Qq1-3 have no stop.
[7] So Q1 ; Qq2-4 *you having.* Lucas needlessly inserts *that,* but see on I, i, 10.   [8] Qq2-4 *scepters.*

BRACH. Now you that are his second, what say you?

Do not, like young hawks, fetch a course about : [9]

Your game flies fair and for you.

FRAN.   Do not fear it.

I 'll answer you in your own hawking phrase :

Some eagles that should gaze upon the sun

Seldom soar high, but take their lustful ease,

Since they from dunghill birds their prey can seize.   50

You know Vittoria?

BRACH.   Yes.

FRAN.   You shift your shirt there,

When you retire from tennis?

BRACH.   Happily.[10]

FRAN. Her husband is lord of a poor fortune,

Yet she wears cloth of tissue.[11]

BRACH.   What of this? —

Will you urge that, my good Lord Cardinal,

As part of her confession at next shrift,

And know from whence it sails?

FRAN.   She is your strumpet.

BRACH. Uncivil sir, there 's hemlock in thy breath

And that black slander — were she [12] a whore of mine,

All thy loud cannons, and thy borrowed [13] Switzers,   60

Thy galleys, nor thy sworn confederates,

Durst not supplant her.

FRAN.   Let 's not talk on thunder.

Thou hast a wife, our sister ; would I had given

Both her white hands to death, bound and lock'd fast

In her last winding sheet, when I gave thee But one !

BRACH.   Thou hadst given a soul to God, then.

FRAN.   True ;

Thy ghostly father, with all 's absolution,

Shall ne'er do so by thee.

BRACH.   Spit thy poison !

FRAN. I shall not need ; lust carries her sharp whip

At her own girdle. Look to 't, for our anger

Is making thunderbolts.

BRACH.   Thunder? in faith, [71

They are but crackers.

FRAN.   We 'll end this with the cannon.

BRACH. Thou 'lt get naught by it but iron in thy wounds

And gunpowder in thy nostrils.

FRAN.   Better that

Than change perfumes for plasters.[14]

BRACH.   Pity on thee !

'T were good you 'd show your slaves or men condemn'd

Your new-plow'd [15] forehead.[16] Defiance ! and I 'll meet thee,

Even in a thicket of thy ablest men.

MONT. My Lords, you shall not word it any further

Without a milder limit.

FRAN.   Willingly.   80

BRACH. Have you proclaimed a triumph, that you bait

A lion thus?

MONT.   My Lord !

BRACH.   I am tame, I am tame, sir.

FRAN. We send unto the Duke for conference

'Bout levies 'gainst the pirates ; my Lord Duke

Is not at home ; we come ourself in person ;

Still my Lord Duke is busied. But, we fear,

When Tiber to each prowling passenger

Discovers flocks of wild ducks, then, my Lord

('Bout moulting time I mean), we shall be certain

To find you sure enough and speak with you.

BRACH.   Ha ! [90

FRAN. A mere tale of a tub : my words are idle ;

But to express the sonnet [17] by natural reason :

When stags grow melancholic, you 'll find the season.[18]

MONT. No more, my Lord ; here comes a champion [19]

[14] *I.e.*, than endure venereal disease after your amour.   [15] *I.e.*, furrowed in anger.

[16] Old eds. have no stop.   [17] Used of any short poem.

[18] Ll. 86–93 have baffled all the commentators. The sense seems to be that Brachiano's irregularities, to which are now due his absences from home, will eventually infect him with venereal disease, which will lay him up at home. "A tale of a tub" = an empty yarn, a cock and bull story, with a play on "tub" = the tub used in treating syphilis. Perhaps, as Lucas suggests, "wild ducks" = prostitutes, "birds of the game." On "moulting," cf. on I, ii, 34. The melancholy stag may be compared with ll. 329–331, and Monticelso's gloss. In both passages the point seems to be that excessive sexual indulgence will lead to impotence. "Season" may be intended as a play on the meaning "salt", "pickle", and thus be another allusion to "the powdering tub of infamy."

[19] For, as Lucas notes, the boy returns in the armor mentioned in l. 7.

[9] *I.e.*, turn tail.   [10] Perhaps, haply.

[11] A rich cloth, often interwoven with gold or silver.

[12] Even if she were.

[13] *I.e.*, mercenary.

Shall end the difference between you both:

Re-enter GIOVANNI.

Your son, the Prince Giovanni. See, my
    Lords,
What hopes you store in him; this is a cas-
    ket
For both your crowns, and should be held like
    dear.
Now is he apt for knowledge; therefore know
It is a more direct and even way   100
To train to virtue those of princely blood
By examples than by precepts. If by ex-
    amples,
Whom should he rather strive to imitate
Than his own father? Be his pattern, then;
Leave him a stock of virtue that may last,
Should fortune rend his sails and split his mast.
    BRACH. Your hand, boy; growing to [a] [20]
        soldier?
    GIO.   Give me a pike.
    FRAN. What, practising your pike so young,
        fair Coz?
    GIO. Suppose me one of Homer's frogs,[21]
        my Lord,
Tossing my bullrush thus. Pray, sir, tell
    me,   110
Might not a child of good discretion [22]
Be leader to an army?
    FRAN.   Yes, Cousin, a young prince
Of good discretion [22] might.
    GIO.   Say you so?
Indeed, I have heard 't is fit a general
Should not endanger his own person oft;
So [23] that he make a noise when he 's a' horse-
    back,
Like a Dansk [24] drummer. Oh, 't is excel-
    lent!
He need not fight; methinks his horse as well
Might lead an army for him. If I live,
I 'll charge the French foe in the very front [120
Of all my troops, the foremost man.
    FRAN.   What, what!
    GIO. And will not bid my soldiers up and
        follow,
But bid them follow me.
    BRACH.   Forward [25] lapwing!
He flies with the shell on 's head.
    FRAN.   Pretty Cousin!

    GIO. The first year, Uncle, that I go to
        war,
All prisoners that I take I will set free
Without their ransom.
    FRAN.   Ha, without their ransom?
How, then, will you reward your soldiers [26]
That took those prisoners for you?
    GIO.   Thus, my Lord:
I 'll marry them to all the wealthy widows [130
That falls that year.
    FRAN.   Why, then, the next year fol-
        lowing,
You 'll have no men to go with you to war.
    GIO. Why, then, I 'll press the women to
        the war,
And then the men will follow.
    MONT.   Witty prince!
    FRAN. See, a good habit makes a child a
        man;
Whereas a bad one makes a man a beast.
Come, you and I are friends.
    BRACH.   Most wishedly,
Like bones which, broke in sunder and well
    set,
Knit the more strongly.
    FRAN.   Call Camillo hither.[27]
You have received the rumor how Count
    Lodowick   140
Is turn'd a pirate?
    BRACH.   Yes.
    FRAN.   We are now preparing
Some ships, to fetch him in.

    [*Re-enter* ISABELLA.]

        Behold your duchess.
We now will leave you, and expect from you
Nothing but kind entreaty.
    BRACH.   You have charm'd me. —

    Exeunt FRANCISCO, MONTICELSO,
        [*and*] GIOVANNI.
You are in health, we see.
    ISA.   And above health,
To see my Lord well.
    BRACH.   So! [28] I wonder much
What amorous whirlwind hurried you to
    Rome.
    ISA. Devotion,[29] my Lord.
    BRACH.   Devotion? [30]
Is your soul charg'd with any grievous sin?

---

[20] Add Q[2].
[21] In the *Batrachomyomachia* or *Battle of the Frogs
and Mice*, a mock-heroic poem formerly ascribed
to Homer.   [22] Quadrisyllabic.
[23] Provided.   [24] Danish.
[25] Precocious. The lapwing often served as a type
of precocity.

[26] Trisyllabic.
[27] Dyce adds *Exit Marcello*, who might indeed
enter with Giovanni. Lucas notes that Francisco
may simply call off stage.
[28] Qq[1-3] have no stop.
[29] To Brachiano.   [30] To religion.

Isa. 'T is burdened with too many ; and I think 150
The oft'ner that we cast our reckonings up,
Our sleeps will be the sounder.
BRACH.   Take your chamber !
Isa. Nay, my dear Lord, I will not have you angry ;
Doth not my absence from you,[31] two months,
Merit one kiss?
BRACH.   I do not use to kiss.
If that will dispossess your jealousy,
I 'll swear it to you.
Isa.   O my loved Lord,
I do not come to chide.   My jealousy?
I am to learn what that Italian [32] means.
You are as welcome to these longing arms [160
As I to you a virgin.   [*Kisses him.*]
BRACH.   Oh, your breath !
Out upon sweetmeats and continued physic !
The plague is in them !
Isa.   You have oft for these two lips
Neglected cassia or the natural sweets
Of the spring violet : they are not yet much withered.
My Lord, I should be merry : these your frowns
Show in a helmet lovely ; but on me,
In such a peaceful interview, methinks
They are too, too roughly knit.
BRACH.   Oh, dissemblance !
Do you bandy factions 'gainst me? have you learnt 170
The trick of impudent baseness, to complain
Unto your kindred?
Isa.   Never, my dear Lord.
BRACH. Must I be haunted out? or was 't your trick
To meet some amorous gallant here in Rome,
That must supply our discontinuance?
Isa. I pray, sir, burst my heart ; and in my death
Turn to your ancient pity, though not love.
BRACH. Because your brother is the corpulent [33] Duke,

That is, the great Duke,[34] 'sdeath, I shall not shortly
Racket away five hundred crowns at tennis,   180
But it shall rest upon record ! [35] I scorn him
Like a shav'd Polack ; all his reverend wit
Lies in his wardrobe ; he 's a discreet fellow,
When he is made up in his robes of state.
Your brother, the great Duke (because h 'as galleys
And now and then ransacks a Turkish flyboat [36] —
Now all the hellish Furies take his soul !)
First made this match ; accursed be the priest
That sang the wedding mass, and even my issue ! [37]
Isa. O, too, too far you have curs'd !
BRACH.   Your hand I 'll kiss ; [190
This is the latest [38] ceremony of my love.
Henceforth I 'll never lie with thee ; by this,
This wedding ring, I 'll ne'er more lie with thee ;
And this divorce shall be as truly kept
As if the judge had doom'd it. Fare you well :
Our sleeps are sever'd.
Isa.   Forbid it, the sweet union
Of all things blessed ! why, the saints in Heaven
Will knit their brows at that.
BRACH.   Let not thy love
Make me an unbeliever ; this my vow
Shall never, on my soul, be satisfied [39] [200
With my repentance ; let thy brother rage
Beyond a horrid tempest or sea fight,
My vow is fixed.
Isa.   O my winding sheet !
Now shall I need thee shortly. — Dear my Lord,
Let me hear once more what I would not hear :
Never?
BRACH. Never !
Isa. O my unkind Lord ! may your sins find mercy,
As I upon a woeful widowed bed
Shall pray for you, if not to turn your eyes [210
Upon your wretched wife and hopeful son,
Yet that in time you 'll fix them upon Heaven !
BRACH. No more ; go, go complain to the great Duke.
Isa. No, my dear Lord ; you shall have present witness

---

[31] Qq3, 4, followed by Dyce, add *now*, spoiling the emphasis on "two months."
[32] *I.e.*, what that word in our Italian tongue. Cf. *Bussy d'Ambois*, V, iv, 23 : "Murder'd? I know not what that Hebrew means."
[33] Historically it was Bracciano who was fat — monstrously so. Webster may have been adapting his characters to his actors, or may have thought Brachiano's corpulence unromantic, or may have transferred it to Francisco for the sake of this sneer. In any case, he forgot it when he brought the latter in as Mulinassar.
[34] This is a sneer at one of Francisco's titles, that of Grand Duke of Tuscany.
[35] Accented on the second syllable.
[36] A light, fast vessel.   [37] Offspring.
[38] Final.   [39] Discharged.

How I'll work peace between you. I will make
Myself the author of your cursed vow;
I have some cause to do it — you have none.
Conceal it, I beseech you, for the weal
Of both your dukedoms, that you wrought the means
Of such a separation; let the fault   220
Remain with my supposed jealousy,
And think with what a piteous and rent heart
I shall perform this sad ensuing part.

Re-enter FRANCISCO, FLAMINEO, MONTICELSO, [*and*] MARCELLO.

BRACH. Well, take your course.[40] — My honorable Brother!
FRAN. Sister! — This is not well, my Lord. — Why, Sister! —
She merits not this welcome.
BRACH.   Welcome, say?
She hath given a sharp welcome.
FRAN.   Are you foolish?
Come, dry your tears; is this a modest course
To better what is naught, to rail and weep?
Grow to a reconcilement, or, by Heaven, [230
I'll ne'er more deal between you.
ISA.   Sir, you shall not;
No, though Vittoria, upon that condition,
Would become honest.[41]
FRAN.   Was your husband loud,
Since we departed?
ISA.   By my life, sir, no;
I swear by that I do not care to lose.
Are all these ruins of my former beauty
Laid out for a whore's triumph?
FRAN.   Do you hear?
Look upon other women, with what patience
They suffer these slight wrongs; with what justice
They study to requite them: take that course.   240
ISA. Oh, that I were a man, or that I had power
To execute my apprehended wishes!
I would whip some with scorpions.
FRAN.   What! turn'd Fury?
ISA. To dig the strumpet's eyes out; let her lie
Some twenty months a-dying; to cut off
Her nose and lips, pull out her rotten teeth,
Preserve her flesh like mummia, for trophies
Of my just anger! Hell, to my affliction,
Is mere snow-water. By your favor, sir —

Brother, draw near, and my Lord Cardinal —   250
Sir, let me borrow of you but one kiss. —
Henceforth I'll never lie with you, by this,
This wedding ring.
FRAN.   How? ne'er more lie with him?
ISA. And this divorce shall be as truly kept
As if in thronged court a thousand ears
Had heard it and a thousand lawyers' hands
Seal'd to the separation.
BRACH.   Ne'er lie with me?
ISA. Let not my former dotage
Make thee an unbeliever; this my vow
Shall never, on my soul, be satisfied   260
With my repentance; *manet alta mente [repostum].*[42]
FRAN. Now, by my birth, you are a foolish, mad,
And jealous woman.
BRACH.   You see 't is not my seeking.
FRAN. Was this your circle of pure unicorn's horn
You said should charm your lord? Now, horns upon thee,
For jealousy deserves them! Keep your vow,
And take your chamber.
ISA.   No, sir; I'll presently to Padua;
I will not stay a minute.
MONT.   O good madam!
BRACH. 'T were best to let her have her humor:
Some half-day's journey will bring down her stomach,[43]   270
And then she'll turn in post.[44]
FRAN.   To see her come
To my Lord Cardinal for a dispensation
Of her rash vow will beget excellent laughter.
ISA. [*aside*] Unkindness, do thy office; poor heart, break;
Those are the killing griefs which dare not speak.   *Exit.*

Enter CAMILLO.

MAR. Camillo's come, my Lord.
FRAN.   Where's the commission?
MAR. 'T is here.
FRAN.   Give me the signet.
      [FRANCISCO, MONTICELSO, CAMILLO, *and* MARCELLO *retire.*]
FLAM. [*to* BRACHIANO] My Lord, do you mark their whispering? I will compound a medicine, out of their two heads, stronger [280

---

[40] Qq1-3 have no stop.
[41] Chaste.

[42] It shall remain buried deep in my mind. (Virgil, *Aeneid*, I, 26.) Q1 *repositum.*
[43] Anger.   [44] Return in haste.

than garlic, deadlier than stibium ; [45] the cantharides, which are scarce seen to stick upon
the flesh when they work to the heart, shall
not do it with more silence or invisible cunning.

BRACH. About the murder.

FLAM. They are sending him to Naples ;
but I'll send him to Candy.[46]

Enter DOCTOR [JULIO].

Her[e]'s another property too.

BRACH. Oh, the doctor !   290

FLAM. A poor quacksalving knave, my
Lord ; one that should have been lash'd for's
lechery, but that he confess'd a judgment, had
an execution laid upon him, and so put the
whip to a *non plus*.

DOCT. And was cozen'd, my Lord, by an
arranter knave than myself, and made pay all
the colorable [47] execution.

FLAM. He will shoot pills into a man's guts
shall make them have more ventages [300
than a cornet [48] or a lamprey ; [49] he will poison
a kiss ; and was once minded, for his masterpiece, because Ireland breeds no poison, to
have prepared a deadly vapor in a Spaniard's
fart, that should have poison'd all Dublin.[50]

BRACH. Oh, Saint Anthony's fire ! [51]

DOCT. Your secretary is merry, my Lord.

FLAM. O thou cursed antipathy to nature !
— Look, his eye's bloodshed,[52] like a needle a
chirurgeon stitcheth a wound with. — [310
Let me embrace thee, toad, and love thee, O
thou abominable loathsome gargarism,[53] that
will fetch up lungs, lights, heart, and liver, by
scruples ! [54]

BRACH. No more ! — I must employ thee,
honest doctor ;

You must to Padua, and, by the way,
Use some of your skill for us.

DOCT.   Sir, I shall.

BRACH. But, for Camillo?

FLAM. He dies this night, by such a politic
strain,
Men shall suppose him by's own engine
slain.   320
But, for your Duchess' death —

DOCT.   I'll make her sure.

BRACH. Small mischiefs are by greater
made secure.

FLAM. Remember this, you slave ; when
knaves come to preferment, they rise as gal-
lowses [55] are raised i' th' Low Countries, one
upon another['s] shoulders.

Exeunt [BRACHIANO, FLAMINEO, *and*
DOCTOR JULIO].

MONT. Here is an emblem, Nephew ; pray
peruse it :
'T was thrown in at your window.

CAM.   At my window?
Here is a stag, my Lord, hath shed his horns ;
And for the loss of them the poor beast
weeps :   330
The word, " *Inopem me copia fecit.* " [56]

MONT.   That is,
" Plenty of horns hath made him poor of
horns." [57]

CAM. What should this mean?

MONT.   I'll tell you : 't is given out
You are a cuckold.

CAM.   Is it given out so?
I had rather such report as that, my Lord,
Should keep within doors.

FRAN.   Have you any children?

CAM. None, my Lord.

FRAN.   You are the happier.
I'll tell you a tale.

CAM.   Pray, my Lord.

FRAN.   An old tale.
Upon a time, Phoebus, the god of light,
Or him we call the sun, would need be
married.   340
The gods gave their consent ; and Mercury
Was sent to voice it to the general world.
But what a piteous cry there straight arose
Amongst smiths and felt-makers, brewers
and cooks,

---

[45] Antimony.

[46] Crete. Lucas cites, from Nash's *Unfortunate
Traveller :* "He is not fit to travel that cannot with
the Candians live on serpents, make nourishing food
even of poison."

[47] Fictitious. The doctor escaped the lash for
his lechery by conspiring with another rascal who
agreed to charge him with a defaulted debt, to
which the doctor pleaded guilty, thus avoiding
penalty on the other charge. But the supposititious
creditor played him false and made him pay up as
if the debt had been genuine. *Should have* (l. 292) =
would have undoubtedly.

[48] An old wind instrument of the oboe family.

[49] Which has seven branchial openings on each
side behind its head ; they were once supposed to
be eyes.

[50] Alluding to "the Don Diego who made himself
offensive in St. Paul's (some time before 1598)"
(Lucas), and also to the notorious aversion of the
Irish to this practice.

[51] Erysipelas.

[52] Bloodshot.   [53] Gargle.   [54] By minute particles.

[55] Gallows-birds. One was placed on the shoulders
of another, who then stepped aside and left his
predecessor hanging.

[56] Abundance has left me destitute. (Ovid, *Metamorphoses*, III, 466.)

[57] This is obscure. See on ll. 86–93. Probably
both cuckoldry and impotence are glanced at here.

Reapers and butterwomen, amongst fish-
    mongers,
And thousand other trades, which are an-
    noyed
By his excessive heat! 't was lamentable.
They came to Jupiter all in a sweat,
And do forbid the banns. A great fat cook
Was made their speaker, who entreats of
    Jove   350
That Phoebus might be gelded; for, if now,
When there was but one sun, so many men
Were like to perish by his violent heat,
What should they do if he were married,
And should beget more, and those children
Make fireworks like their father? So say I;
Only I will apply it to your wife:
Her issue, should not Providence prevent
    it,
Would make both nature, time, and man
    repent it.
    MONT. Look you, Cousin,   360
Go, change the air,[58] for shame; see if your
    absence
Will blast your cornucopia.[59] Marcello
Is chosen with you joint commissioner
For the relieving our Italian coast
From pirates.
    MAR.   I am much honor'd in 't.
    CAM.   But, sir,
Ere I return, the stag's horns may be sprouted
Greater than these are shed.
    MONT.   Do not fear it:
I 'll be your ranger.
    CAM.   You must watch i' th' nights;
Then 's the most danger.
    FRAN.   Farewell, good Marcello;
All the best fortunes of a soldier's wish   370
Bring you a-shipboard!
    CAM.   Were I not best, now I am
    turn'd soldier,
Ere that I leave my wife, sell all she hath,
And then take leave of her?
    MONT.   I expect good from you,
Your parting is so merry.
    CAM. Merry, my Lord, a' the captain's
    humor right:[60]
I am resolved to be drunk this night.
    [*Exeunt* CAMILLO *and* MARCELLO.]
    FRAN. So! 't was well fitted; now shall we
    discern
How his wish'd absence will give violent way
To Duke Brachiano's lust.

[58] Seek a change of air.
[59] Horn of plenty, another allusion to his cuckoldry.   [60] Precisely.

MONT.   Why, that was it;
To what scorn'd purpose else should we make
    choice   380
Of him for a sea captain? and, besides,
Count Lodowick, which was rumor'd for a
    pirate,
Is now in Padua.
    FRAN.   Is 't true?
    MONT.   Most certain;
I have letters from him, which are suppliant
To work his quick repeal from banishment.
He means to address himself for pension [61]
Unto our sister [62] Duchess.
    FRAN.   Oh, 't was well;
We shall not want his absence past six days.
I fain would have the Duke Brachiano
    run   389
Into notorious scandal; for there 's naught
In such curs'd dotage to repair his name,
Only the deep sense of some deathless shame.
    MONT. It may be objected I am dishonor-
    able
To play thus with my kinsman; but I answer,
For my revenge I 'd stake a brother's life,
That, being wrong'd, durst not avenge himself.
    FRAN. Come, to observe this strumpet.
    MONT.   Curse of greatness!
Sure, he 'll not leave her.
    FRAN.   There 's small pity in 't; [398
Like mistletoe on sear elms spent by weather,
Let him cleave to her, and both rot together.
                    Exeunt.

                [SCENE II] [63]

Enter BRACHIANO, *with one in the habit of a*
                Conjuror.

    BRACH. Now, sir, I claim your promise;
    't is dead midnight,
The time prefix'd to show me, by your art,
How the intended murder of Camillo
And our loathed Duchess grow to action.
    CON. You have won me by your bounty to
    a deed
I do not often practise. Some there are
Which by sophistic tricks aspire that name,
Which I would gladly lose, of nigromancer; [64]
As some that use to juggle upon cards,
Seeming to conjure, when indeed they
    cheat;   10

[61] Trisyllabic.
[62] Greg plausibly suggests that Webster has
momentarily confused with Cardinal Montalto the
Cardinal de' Medici, Isabella's brother.
[63] A room in Camillo's house.   [64] Necromancer.

Others that raise up their confederate spirits
'Bout windmills, and endanger their own
    necks,
For making of a squib ; and some there are
Will keep a curtal [65] to show juggling tricks,
And give out 't is a spirit ; besides these,
Such a whole realm of almanac-makers,
    figure-flingers, [66]
Fellows, indeed, that only live by stealth,
Since they do merely lie about stol'n goods —
They'd make men think the Devil were fast
    and loose, [67]
With speaking fustian [68] Latin. Pray, sit
    down ;   20
Put on this nightcap, sir : 't is charm'd ; and
    now
I 'll show you, by my strong-commanding art,
The circumstance that breaks your Duchess'
    heart.

A Dumb Show [69]

Enter suspiciously JULIO *and* CHRISTOPHERO :
they draw a curtain [70] *where Brachiano's
picture is ; they put on spectacles of glass,
which cover their eyes and noses, and then
burn perfumes afore the picture, and wash
the lips of the picture ; that done, quenching
the fire and putting off their spectacles, they
depart laughing.*
Enter ISABELLA *in her nightgown, as to bedward,
with lights after her,* COUNT LODOVICO, GIO-
VANNI, GUID-ANTONIO, [71] *and others, waiting
on her : she kneels down as to prayers, then
draws the curtain of the picture, does three
reverences to it, and kisses it thrice ; she
faints, and will not suffer them to come near it ;
dies : sorrow express'd in* GIOVANNI *and in*
COUNT LODOVICO ; *she 's convey'd out solemnly.*

BRACH. Excellent ! then she 's dead ?
CON.   She 's poisoned
By the fum'd [72] picture. 'T was her custom
    nightly,
Before she went to bed, to go and visit
Your picture, and to feed her eyes and lips
On the dead shadow.   Doctor Julio,

[65] Docked horse. An allusion to Morocco, the
trained horse of one Banks ; there are many references to them.
[66] Horoscope casters.
[67] See on *The Wild-Goose Chase*, III, i, 72.
[68] Claptrap.
[69] Probably on the inner stage.
[70] Dust-curtains were regularly provided for
portraits.
[71] Sampson suggests *Gasp[aro] Anton[elli].*
[72] Perfumed.

Observing this, infects it with an oil
And other poison'd stuff, which presently   [30
Did suffocate her spirits.
BRACH.   Methought I saw
Count Lodowick there.
CON.   He was ; and by my art
I find he did most passionately dote
Upon your Duchess. Now turn another way,
And view Camillo's far more politic [fate]. [73]
Strike louder, music, from this charmed
    ground,
To yield, as fits the act, a tragic sound.

The Second Dumb Show

Enter FLAMINEO, MARCELLO, CAMILLO, *with
four more as* Captains ; *they drink healths
and dance : a vaulting-horse is brought into the
room :* MARCELLO *and two more whisper'd
out of the room, while* FLAMINEO *and* CAMILLO
*strip themselves into their shirts, as to vault ;
compliment* [74] *who shall begin : as* CAMILLO *is
about to vault,* FLAMINEO *pitcheth him upon
his neck, and, with the help of the rest, writhes
his neck about ; seems to see if it be broke, and
lays him folded double, as 't were under the
horse ; makes shows to call for help ;* MAR-
CELLO *comes in, laments ; sends for the*
CARDINAL *and* DUKE, *who comes forth with
armed men ; wonder[s] at the act, commands
the body to be carried home ; apprehends*
FLAMINEO, MARCELLO, *and the rest, and go,
as 't were to apprehend* VITTORIA.

BRACH. 'T was quaintly [75] done ; but yet
    each circumstance
I taste not fully.
CON.   Oh, 't was most apparent :
You saw them enter, charged with their deep
    healths   40
To their boon voyage ; [76] and, to second that,
Flamineo calls to have a vaulting-horse
Maintain their sport ; the virtuous Marcello
Is innocently plotted forth the room ;
Whilst your eye saw the rest, and can inform
    you
The engine of all.
[BRACH.]   It seems Marcello and Flamineo
Are both committed. [77]
CON.   Yes, you saw them guarded ;
And now they are come with purpose to
    apprehend

[73] So Q₄ ; earlier Qq *face.* "More politic" because
it appeared to be an accident. Historically, Vittoria's
husband was ambushed and shot.
[74] *I.e.,* polite gestures.
[75] Cleverly.
[76] Bon voyage.   [77] Arrested.

Your mistress, fair Vittoria. We are now
Beneath her roof ; 't were fit we instantly [50
Make out by some back-postern.

BRACH.   Noble friend,
You bind me ever to you ; this shall stand
As the firm seal annexed to my hand :
It shall enforce a payment.

CON.   Sir, I thank you. —
                                      Exit BRACHIANO.
Both flowers and weeds spring when the sun
          is warm,
And great men do great good or else great
          harm.   *Exit* Conjuror.

[ACT III — SCENE I] [1]

Enter FRANCISCO *and* MONTICELSO [*with*] *their*
          Chancellor *and* Register.

FRAN. You have dealt discreetly, to obtain
          the presence
Of all the grave lieger [2] ambassadors,
To hear Vittoria's trial.

MONT.   'T was not ill ;
For, sir, you know we have naught but cir-
          cumstances
To charge her with, about her husband's
          death ;
Their approbation, therefore, to the proofs
Of her black lust shall make her infamous
To all our neighboring kingdoms. I wonder
If Brachiano will be here.

FRAN.   Oh, fie !
'T were impudence too palpable.   10
                                      [*Exeunt.*]

Enter FLAMINEO *and* MARCELLO, *guarded, and*
          a Lawyer.

LAW. What, are you in by the week? [3] so ;
I will try now whether thy wit be close prisoner. Methinks none should sit upon thy
sister but old whoremasters.

FLAM. Or cuckolds ; for your cuckold is
your most terrible tickler [4] of lechery. Whoremasters would serve ; for none are judges at
tilting but those that have been old tilters.

LAW. My Lord Duke and she have been
very private. [5]   20

FLAM. You are a dull ass ; 't is threat'ned
they have been very public. [6]

LAW. If it can be proved they have but
kiss'd one another —

FLAM. What then?

LAW. My Lord Cardinal will ferret [7] them.

FLAM. A Cardinal, I hope, will not catch
conies. [8]

LAW. For to sow kisses (mark what I
say), to sow kisses is to reap lechery ; and [30
I am sure, a woman that will endure kissing is
half won.

FLAM. True, her upper part, by that rule ;
if you will win her nether part too, you know
what follows.

LAW. Hark ; the ambassadors are lighted. [9]

FLAM. [*aside*] I do put on this feigned garb
          of mirth
To gull suspicion.

MAR.   Oh, my unfortunate sister !
I would my dagger's point had cleft her heart
When she first saw Brachiano ; you, 't is
          said,   40
Were made his engine and his stalking-horse,
To undo [10] my sister.

FLAM.   I made a kind of path
To her and mine own preferment.

MAR.   Your ruin.

FLAM. Hum ! thou art a soldier,
Followest the great Duke, feedest his victories,
As witches do their serviceable spirits,
Even with thy prodigal blood : what hast got,
But, like the wealth of captains, a poor hand-
          ful,
Which in thy palm thou bear'st as men hold
          water?
Seeking to grip it fast, the frail reward   50
Steals through thy fingers.

MAR.   Sir !

FLAM. Thou hast scarce maintenance
To keep thee in fresh chamois. [11]

MAR.   Brother !

FLAM.   Hear me !
And thus, when we have even poured our-
          selves
Into great fights, for their ambition
Or idle spleen, how shall we find reward?
But, as we seldom find the mistletoe,
Sacred to physic, [on] [12] the builder oak, [13]

---

[1] Unlocated ; perhaps an antechamber or courtyard adjacent to the scene of the examination.
[2] Resident, as distinguished from those sent on
special missions.   [3] Deeply involved.
[4] As Lucas notes, = "castigator", but also
perhaps with a play on the meaning, "instigator."
[5] Intimate.

[6] Lewd.   [7] Hunt them out.
[8] Rabbits, with various plays on other meanings,
e.g., "sweethearts." "To catch conies" = to cheat.
[9] Have alighted.   [10] Ruin.
[11] The chamois jerkin worn under armor. (Lucas.)
[12] Emend. Lucas ; old eds. *or.*
[13] Chaucer and Spenser, as Lucas notes, both
have *builder oak.*

Without a mandrake [14] by it ; so in our quest
    of gain :
Alas, the poorest of their forc'd dislikes   60
At a limb proffers, but at heart it strikes !
This is lamented [15] doctrine.
    MAR.   Come, come.
    FLAM.   When age shall turn thee
White as a blooming hawthorn —
    MAR.   I 'll interrupt you :
For love of virtue bear an honest heart,
And stride o'er every politic respect,[16]
Which, where they most advance, they most
    infect.
Were I your father, as I am your brother,
I should not be ambitious to leave you
A better patrimony.
    FLAM.   I 'll think on 't. —

Enter SAVOY [Ambassador].

The Lord Ambassadors.   [70

Here there is a passage of the lieger Ambassadors *over the stage severally. Enter* French
Ambassador.

    LAW. Oh, my sprightly Frenchman ! — Do
you know him ? he 's an admirable tilter.
    FLAM. I saw him at last tilting : he showed
like a pewter candlestick, fashioned like a man
in armor, holding a tilting-staff in his hand,
little bigger than a candle of twelve i' th'
pound.
    LAW. Oh, but he 's an excellent horseman.
    FLAM. A lame one in his lofty tricks ; he
sleeps a-horseback, like a poulter.[17]   80

Enter English *and* Spanish [Ambassadors].

    LAW. Lo you, my Spaniard !
    FLAM. He carries his face in 's ruff,[18] as I
have seen a serving man carry glasses in a
cypress [19] hatband, monstrous steady, for fear
of breaking ; he looks like the claw of a blackbird, first salted, and then broiled in a candle.
                              Exeunt.

[SCENE II] [20] THE ARRAIGNMENT OF VITTORIA

Enter FRANCISCO, MONTICELSO, *the six lieger*
    Ambassadors, BRACHIANO, [FLAMINEO,
    MARCELLO,] VITTORIA, [ZANCHE], Lawyer,
    and a Guard.

MONT. Forbear, my Lord ; here is no place
    assign'd you :
This business by his Holiness is left
To our examination.
    BRACH.   May it thrive with you !
              Lays a rich gown under him.
    FRAN. A chair there for his Lordship !
    BRACH. Forbear your kindness : an un-
    bidden guest
Should travel as Dutchwomen go to church —
Bear their stools with them.
    MONT.   At your pleasure, sir. —
[*to* VITTORIA] Stand to the table, [gentle-
woman].[21] — Now, signior,
Fall to your plea.
    [LAW.] *Domine judex, converte oculos in* [10
hanc pestem, mulierum corruptissimam.[22]
    VIT. What's he ?
    FRAN. A lawyer that pleads against you.
    VIT. Pray, my Lord, let him speak his
    usual tongue ;
I 'll make no answer else.
    FRAN.   Why ? you understand Latin.
    VIT. I do, sir ; but amongst this auditory
Which come to hear my cause, the half or
    more
May be ignorant in 't.
    MONT.   Go on, sir.
    VIT.   By your favor,
I will not have my accusation clouded
In a strange tongue ; all this assembly   20
Shall hear what you can charge me with.
    FRAN.   Signior,
You need not stand [23] on 't much ; pray,
    change your language.
    MONT. Oh, for God's sake ! — Gentle-
    woman, your credit [24]
Shall be more famous by it.
    LAW.   Well, then, have at you !
    VIT. I am at the mark, sir : I 'll give aim
    to you,
And tell you how near you shoot.[25]
    LAW. Most literated judges, please your
    Lordships
So to connive your judgments [26] to the view
Of this debauch'd and diversivolent [27] woman ;
Who such a black concatenation   30
Of mischief hath effected, that to extirp

---

[14] Supposed to be a sinister plant. The point is
that there is always a fly in the ointment.
  [15] Lamentable ; *i.e.*, this is too bad, but it 's so.
  [16] Consideration of expediency.
  [17] On his way to early market.
  [18] Spanish ruffs were notoriously large.   [19] Crape.
  [20] Unlocated. Probably the curtains of the inner
stage were now opened.

  [21] So Q₄ ; earlier eds. *gentlewomen*, perhaps rightly.
  [22] My Lord Judge, turn your eyes upon this plague,
this most corrupt of women.
  [23] Insist.   [24] Reputation.
  [25] The reference is to archery ; the marker had
the same function as in rifle-practice now.
  [26] Presumably he means "bring your judgments
into a common understanding."
  [27] Desiring or inciting to strife.

The memory of't, must be the consummation
Of her and her projections — [28]
    VIT.   What's all this?
    LAW. Hold your peace ;
Exorbitant [29] sins must have exulceration.[30]
    VIT. Surely, my Lords, this lawyer here
        hath swallowed
Some pothecaries' bills or proclamations ;
And now the hard and undigestible words
Come up, like stones we use give hawks for
    physic ;
Why, this is Welsh to [31] Latin.
    LAW.   My Lords, the woman [40
Knows not her tropes nor figures, nor is per-
    fect
In the academic derivation
Of grammatical elocution.
    FRAN.   Sir, your pains
Shall be well spared, and your deep eloquence
Be worthily applauded amongst those
Which understand you.
    LAW.   My good Lord —
    FRAN. (*speaks this as in scorn.*)   Sir,
Put up your papers in your fustian [32] bag —
Cry mercy, sir ; 't is buckram [33] — and accept
My notion of your learn'd verbosity.
    LAW. I most graduatically [34] thank your
    Lordship ;   50
I shall have use for them elsewhere.   [*Exit.*]
    MONT. I shall be plainer with you, and
    paint out
Your follies in more natural red and white
Than that upon your cheek.
    VIT.   Oh, you mistake ;
You raise a blood as noble in this cheek
As ever was your mother's.
    MONT. I must spare you, till proof cry
    " whore " to that. —
Observe this creature here, my honored Lords,
A woman of a most prodigious spirit,
In her effected.[35]
    VIT.   Honorable my Lord,   60
It doth not suit a reverend cardinal
To play the lawyer thus.
    MONT.   Oh, your trade
Instructs your language. —
You see, my Lords, what goodly fruit she
    seems ;

Yet, like those apples travellers report
To grow where Sodom and Gomorrah stood,
I will but touch her, and you straight shall see
She 'll fall to soot and ashes.
    VIT.   Your envenom'd
Pothecary should do 't.
    MONT.   I am resolved,[36]
Were there a second Paradise to lose,   70
This devil would betray it.
    VIT.   O poor charity !
Thou art seldom found in scarlet.[37]
    MONT. Who knows not how, when several
    night by night
Her gates were chok'd with coaches, and her
    rooms
Outbrav'd the stars with several kind of lights,
When she did counterfeit a prince's court
In music, banquets, and most riotous surfeits,
This whore, forsooth, was holy?
    VIT.   Ha, " whore ? " what 's that?
    MONT. Shall I expound " whore " to you?
    sure, I shall ;
I 'll give their perfect character. They are,
    first,   80
Sweetmeats which rot the eater ; in man's
    nostril,
Poison'd perfumes ; they are coz'ning al-
    chemy ;
Shipwracks in calmest weather ! What are
    whores?
Cold Russian winters, that appear so barren
As if that nature had forgot the spring ;
They are the true material fire of hell ;
Worse than those tributes i' th' Low Countries
    payed,
Exactions upon meat, drink, garments, sleep,
Ay, even on man's perdition,[38] his sin ;
They are those brittle evidences of law   90
Which forfeit all a wretched man's estate
For leaving out one syllable. What are
    whores?
They are those flattering bells have all one
    tune
At weddings and at funerals. Your rich
    whores
Are only treasuries by extortion fill'd,
And empt[i]ed by curs'd riot. They are worse,
Worse than dead bodies which are begg'd at
    gallows,
And wrought upon by surgeons, to teach man
Wherein he is imperfect. What 's a whore?

---

[28] Projects.   [29] Monstrous.
[30] Sores ; but apparently the lawyer means "must be treated like ulcers."
[31] Compared with.
[32] Playing on the meanings : (1) coarse cloth ; (2) claptrap.
[33] Stout linen cloth.
[34] As a graduate should.
[35] Brought to pass.

[36] Convinced.
[37] Alluding to the Cardinal's robe, but also, per- haps, as Sampson suggests, to the color of the legal faculty.
[38] Apparently there was a tax on prostitution.

She's like the guilty counterfeited coin   100
Which, whosoe'er first stamps it, bring[s] in
          trouble
All that receive it.
          VIT.   This character scapes me.
          MONT. You, gentlewoman!
Take from all beasts and from all minerals
Their deadly poison —
          VIT.   Well, what then?
          MONT.   I'll tell thee;
I'll find in thee a pothecary's shop,
To sample them all.
          FR. AMB. [*aside*]   She hath lived ill.
          ENG. AMB. [*aside*] True; but the Cardinal's
                too bitter.
          MONT. You know what "whore" is.   Next
                the devil, adult'ry,
Enters the devil, murder.
          FRAN.   Your unhappy [110
Husband is dead.
          VIT.   Oh, he's a happy husband:
Now he owes nature nothing.[39]
          FRAN. And by a vaulting-engine.
          MONT.   An active plot;
He jump'd into his grave.
          FRAN.   What a prodigy was't
That from some two yards' height a slender
          man
Should break his neck!
          MONT.   I' th' rushes![40]
          FRAN.   And, what's more,
Upon the instant lose all use of speech,
All vital motion, like a man had lain
Wound up[41] three days.   Now mark each
          circumstance.
          MONT. And look upon this creature was
                his wife.   120
She comes not like a widow; she comes
          arm'd
With scorn and impudence.   Is this a mourn-
          ing habit?
          VIT. Had I foreknown his death, as you
                suggest,
I would have bespoke my mourning.
          MONT.   Oh, you are cunning.
          VIT. You shame your wit and judgment,
To call it so.   What, is my just defence
By him that is my judge call'd impudence?
Let me appeal, then, from this Christian
          court
To the uncivil[42] Tartar.

          MONT.   See, my Lords,
She scandals[43] our proceedings.
          VIT.   Humbly thus, [130
Thus low, to the most worthy and respected
Lieger ambassadors, my modesty
And womanhood I tender; but, withal,
So entangled in a cursed accusation,
That my defence, of force,[44] like Perseus',[45]
Must personate masculine virtue.[46] — To the
          point:
Find me but guilty, sever head from body,
We'll part good friends; I scorn to hold my
          life
At yours or any man's entreaty, sir.
          ENG. AMB. She hath a brave spirit.
          MONT.   Well, well, such counterfeit
          jewels   140
Make true on[e]s oft suspected.
          VIT.   You are deceived;
For know that all your strict[47]-combined
          heads,
Which strike against this mine of diamonds,
Shall prove but glassen hammers: they shall
          break.
These are but feigned shadows of my evils:
Terrify babes, my Lord, with painted devils;
I am past such needless palsy.   For your
          names
Of "whore" and "murd'ress," they proceed
          from you
As if a man should spit against the wind;
The filth returns in's face.   150
          MONT. Pray you, mistress, satisfy me one
                question:
Who lodg'd beneath your roof that fatal night
Your husband brake his neck?
          BRACH.   That question
Enforceth me break silence: I was there.
          MONT. Your business?
          BRACH.   Why, I came to comfort her,
And take some course for settling her estate,
Because I heard her husband was in debt
To you, my Lord.
          MONT.   He was.
          BRACH.   And 't was strangely fear'd
That you would cozen her.
          MONT.   Who made you overseer?
          BRACH. Why, my charity, my charity,
                which should flow   160

[39] For he has paid the debt every man owes —
his life, which is but lent him.
[40] With which floors were strewn.
[41] In his winding sheet.
[42] Barbarous.

[43] Defames.
[44] Necessarily.
[45] Perseus appeared for "heroic and masculine
virtue" in Jonson's *Masque of Queens* (1609).
(Simpson.)
[46] Old eds., perhaps rightly, have no stop.
[47] *I.e.*, closely.

From every generous and noble spirit
To orphans and to widows.

MONT.   Your lust.

BRACH. Cowardly dogs bark loudest ; Sir-
    rah Priest,
I 'll talk with you hereafter. Do you hear?
The sword you frame of such an excellent
    temper
I 'll sheathe in your own bowels.
There are a number of thy coat resemble
Your common postboys.

MONT.   Ha?

BRACH.   Your mercenary postboys :
Your letters carry truth, but 't is your guise
To fill your mouths with gross and impudent
    lies.   [*He makes for the door.*] [170

SER. My Lord, your gown.

BRACH.   Thou liest : 't was my stool ;
Bestow't upon thy master, that will chal-
    lenge [48]
The rest a' th' household stuff ; for Brachiano
Was ne'er so beggarly to take a stool
Out of another's lodging : let him make
Valance [49] for his bed on 't, or a demi-footcloth
For his most reverend moil.[50]   Monticelso,
Nemo me impune lacessit.[51]   *Exit* BRACHIANO.

MONT. Your champion's gone.

VIT.   The wolf may prey the better.

FRAN. My Lord, there 's great suspicion
    of the murder,   180
But no sound proof who did it. For my part,
I do not think she hath a soul so black
To act a deed so bloody ; if she have,
As in cold countries husbandmen plant vines,
And with warm blood manure them, even so
One summer she will bear unsavory fruit,
And ere next spring wither both branch and
    root.
The act of blood let pass ; only descend
To matter of incontinence.

VIT. I discern poison under your gilded
    pills.   190

MONT. Now the Duke 's gone, I will pro-
    duce a letter,
Wherein 't was plotted [he] [52] and you should
    meet
At an apothecary's summerhouse,[53]
Down by the river Tiber — view't, my Lords —
Where, after wanton bathing and the heat
Of a lascivious banquet — I pray read it ;
I shame to speak the rest.

VIT.   Grant I was tempted ;
Temptation to lust proves not the act :
Casta est quam nemo rogavit.[54]   199
You read his hot love to me ; but you want
My frosty answer.

MONT.   Frost i' th' dog days !
    strange !

VIT. Condemn you me for that the Duke
    did love me?
So may you blame some fair and crystal river
For that some melancholic distracted man
Hath drown'd himself in 't.

MONT.   Truly drown'd, indeed.

VIT. Sum up my faults, I pray, and you
    shall find
That beauty and gay clothes, a merry heart,
And a good stomach to [a] [55] feast, are all,
All the poor crimes that you can charge me
    with.   209
In faith, my Lord, you might go pistol flies ;
The sport would be more noble.

MONT.   Very good.

VIT. But take you your course ; it seems
    you have beggar'd me first,
And now would fain undo me. I have houses,
Jewels, and a poor remnant of crusadoes.[56]
Would those would make you charitable !

MONT.   If the Devil
Did ever take good shape, behold his picture.

VIT. You have one virtue left : you will
    not flatter me.

FRAN. Who brought this letter?

VIT.   I am not compell'd to tell you.

MONT. My Lord Duke sent to you a
    thousand ducats
The twelfth of August.

VIT.   'T was to keep your cousin [57] [220
From prison : I paid use [58] for 't.

MONT.   I rather think
'T was interest for his lust.

VIT.   Who says so
But yourself? If you be my accuser,
Pray cease to be my judge : come from the
    bench,
Give in your evidence 'gainst me, and let these
Be moderators.[59] My Lord Cardinal,
Were your intelligencing ears as [long] [60]
As to my thoughts, had you an honest tongue,
I would not care though you proclaim'd them
    all.

---

[48] Claim.   [49] Drapery.   [50] Mule.
[51] No one hurts me with impunity.
[52] Cor. Q₃ ; earlier Q**q** *her.*
[53] Such places, in suburban gardens, were notorious as places of assignation in Elizabethan London.
[54] Chaste is she whom none has tempted. (Ovid
Amores, I, viii, 43.)   [55] Add. Dyce.
[56] Portuguese coins worth upwards of half a dollar.
[57] Nephew.
[58] Interest.   [59] Judges.
[60] Emend. Lucas ; old eds. *loving.*

MONT. Go to, go to ! 230
After your goodly and vainglorious banquet,
I 'll give you a choke-pear.[61]
VIT.   A' your own grafting?
MONT. You were born in Venice, honorably
     descended
From the Vittelli ; [62] 't was my cousin's fate —
Ill may I name the hour — to marry you :
He bought you of your father.
VIT.   Ha?
MONT.   He spent there in six months
Twelve thousand ducats, and, to my acquaint-
     ance,[63]
Received in dowry with you not one julio : [64]
'T was a hard pennyworth,[65] the ware being
     so light.
I yet but draw the curtain ; [66] now to your
     picture : 240
You came from thence a most notorious
     strumpet ;
And so you have continued.
VIT.   My Lord —
MONT.   Nay, hear me ;
You shall have time to prate. My Lord
     Brachiano —
Alas, I make but repetition
Of what is ordinary and Rialto talk,[67]
And ballated,[68] and would be played a' th'
     stage,
But that vice many times finds such loud
     friends
That preachers are charm'd silent. —
You gentlemen, Flamineo and Marcello,
The court hath nothing now to charge you
     with ; 250
Only, you must remain upon your sureties
For your appearance.
FRAN.   I stand for Marcello.
FLAM. And my Lord Duke for me.
MONT. For you, Vittoria, your public fault,
Join'd to th' condition of the present time,
Takes from you all the fruits of noble pity.
Such a corrupted trial have you made
Both of your life and beauty, and been styl'd
No less in ominous fate than blazing stars
To princes, here 's your sentence : you are
     confin'd 260
Unto a house of convertites ; and your bawd—
FLAM. [*aside*] Who, I?

MONT.   The Moor —
FLAM. [*aside*] Oh, I am a sound man again.
VIT. A house of convertites ! what 's that?
MONT.   A house
Of penitent whores.
VIT.   Do the noblemen in Rome
Erect it for their wives, that I am sent to
     lodge there?
FRAN. You must have patience.
VIT.   I must first have vengeance.
I fain would know if you have your salva-
     tion
By patent,[69] that you proceed thus.
MONT.   Away with her !
Take her hence. 269
VIT. A rape ! a rape !
MONT. How?
VIT.   Yes, you have ravish'd justice ;
Forc'd her to do your pleasure.
MONT.   Fie, she 's mad !
VIT. Die with these pills in your most
     cursed maws
Should bring you health ! or while you sit a'
     th' bench
Let your own spittle choke you ! —
MONT.   She 's turn'd Fury.
VIT. That the last day of judgment may
     so find you,
And leave you the same devil you were be-
     fore !
Instruct me, some good horse-leech,[70] to speak
     treason ;
For, since you cannot take my life for deeds,
Take it for words ! O woman's poor revenge,
Which dwells but in the tongue ! I will not
     weep ; 280
No, I do scorn to call up one poor tear
To fawn on your injustice. Bear me hence
Unto this house of — what 's your mitigating
     title?
MONT. Of convertites.
VIT. It shall not be a house of convertites ;
My mind shall make it honester to me
Than the Pope's palace, and more peaceable
Than thy soul, though thou art a cardinal.
Know this, and let it somewhat raise your
     spite :
Through darkness diamonds spread their
     richest light. *Exit* VITTORIA. [290

Re-enter BRACHIANO.

BRACH. Now you and I are friends, sir, we 'll
     shake hands

[61] *I.e.*, I 'll give you something to silence you.
[62] This great Roman family had no connection
with Vittoria. But see on I, i, 31.
[63] According to my information.
[64] A papal coin worth about twelve cents.
[65] Bargain.   [66] See on II, ii, 23, Dumb Show.
[67] *I.e.*, town talk ; the Rialto was the exchange
of Venice.   [68] Made into ballads.

[69] In the form of a written warrant or license.
[70] Bloodsucker.

In a friend's grave together : a fit place,
Being the emblem of soft peace, t' atone [71] our
    hatred.
    FRAN. Sir, what 's the matter?
    BRACH. I will not chase more blood from
      that lov'd cheek :
You have lost too much already ; fare you
    well.   [*Exit.*]
    FRAN. How strange these words sound !
      what 's the interpretation?
    FLAM. [*aside*] Good ; this is a preface to
the discovery of the Duchess' death ; he
carries it well. Because now I cannot [300
counterfeit a whining passion for the death of
my Lady, I will feign a mad humor for the
disgrace of my sister ; and that will keep off
idle questions. Treason's tongue hath a villainous palsy in 't ; I will talk to any man,
hear no man, and for a time appear a politic
madman.   [*Exit.*]

Enter GIOVANNI [*and*] COUNT LODOVICO.

    FRAN. How now, my noble Cousin? what,
      in black?
    GIO. Yes, Uncle, I was taught to imitate
      you
In virtue, and you must imitate me   310
In colors for your garments. My sweet
      mother
Is —
    FRAN. How ! where?
    GIO. Is there ; no, yonder ; indeed, sir,
      I 'll not tell you,
For I shall make you weep.
    FRAN.   Is dead?
    GIO.   Do not blame me now ;
I did not tell you so.
    LOD.   She 's dead, my Lord.
    FRAN. Dead !
    MONT.   Blessed lady, thou art now above
      thy woes ! —
Will 't please your Lordships to withdraw
    a little?   [*Exeunt* Ambassadors.]
    GIO. What do the dead do, Uncle? do
      they eat,
Hear music, go a-hunting, and be merry, [320
As we that live?
    FRAN. No, Coz ; they sleep.
    GIO.   Lord, Lord, that I were dead !
I have not slept these six nights. — When
    do they wake?
    FRAN. When God shall please.
    GIO.   Good God, let her sleep ever.

[71] Reconcile.

For I have known her wake an hundred
    nights,
When all the pillow where she laid her head
Was brine-wet with her tears. I am to com-
    plain to you, sir ;
I 'll tell you how they have used her now she 's
    dead :
They wrapp'd her in a cruel fold of lead,
And would not let me kiss her.
    FRAN.   Thou didst love her. [330
    GIO. I have often heard her say she gave
      me suck,
And it should seem by that she dearly lov'd
    me,
Since princes seldom do it.
    FRAN. O all of my poor sister that re-
      mains ! —
Take him away, for God 's sake !
    MONT.   How now, my Lord?
    FRAN. Believe me, I am nothing but her
      grave ;
And I shall keep her blessed memory
Longer than thousand epitaphs.   [*Exeunt.*]

[SCENE III] [72]

Enter FLAMINEO, *as distracted*, [MARCELLO,
    and LODOVICO.]

    FLAM. We endure the strokes like anvils
      or hard steel,
Till pain itself make us no pain to feel.
Who shall do me right now? Is this the end
of service? I 'd rather go weed garlic ; travel
through France, and be mine own ostler ;
wear sheepskin linings, or shoes that stink of
blacking ; be ent'red into the list of the forty
thousand peddlers in Poland.[73]

Enter [*the* Ambassador of] Savoy.

Would I had rotted in some surgeon's house
at Venice, built upon the pox as well as [10
on piles,[74] ere I had serv'd Brachiano !
    SAV. [AMB.]. You must have comfort.
    FLAM. Your comfortable words are like
honey : they relish well in your mouth that 's
whole, but in mine that 's wounded they go

[72] Doubtless the same as III, i. As Lucas observes,
the curtains of the inner stage would probably be
closed here, and Sc. iii would proceed with no other
break.
[73] Sampson notes the prevalence of Scotch and
Irish peddlers there in the seventeenth century,
and that the Lithuanian word for peddler is *szatas* =
Scot.   [74] An obvious pun.

down as if the sting of the bee were in them. Oh, they have wrought their purpose cunningly, as if they would not seem to do it of malice! In this a politician imitates the Devil, as the Devil imitates a cannon: whereso- [20 ever he comes to do mischief, he comes with his backside towards you.

Enter the French [Ambassador].

FRENCH [AMB.] The proofs are evident.

FLAM. Proof! 't was corruption. O gold, what a god art thou! and O man, what a devil art thou to be tempted by that cursed mineral! [Yon][75] diversivolent[76] lawyer, mark him; knaves turn informers, as maggots turn to flies; you may catch gudgeons[77] with either. A cardinal! I would he [30 would hear me: there's nothing so holy but money will corrupt and putrefy it, like victual under the line.[78]

[*Enter the*] English Ambassador.

You are happy in England, my Lord: here they sell justice with those weights they press men to death with.[79] O horrible salary!

ENG. [AMB.]. Fie, fie, Flamineo!

[*Exeunt* Ambassadors.][80]

FLAM. Bells ne'er ring well till they are at their full pitch;[81] and I hope yon cardinal shall never have the grace to pray well till [40 he come to the scaffold. If they were rack'd now to know the confederacy! But your noblemen are privileged from the rack; and well may, for a little thing would pull some of them a-pieces[82] afore they came to their arraignment. Religion, oh, how it is commeddled[83] with policy! The first bloodshed in the world happened about religion.[84] Would I were a Jew!

MAR. Oh, there are too many.   50

FLAM. You are deceiv'd: there are not Jews enough, priests enough, nor gentlemen enough.

MAR. How?

FLAM. I'll prove it: for, if there were

Jews enough, so many Christians would not turn usurers; if priests enough, one should not have six benefices; and, if gentlemen enough, so many early mushrooms, whose best growth sprang from a dunghill, [60 should not aspire to gentility. Farewell; let others live by begging; be thou one of them [85 practice the art of Wolner[86] in England, to swallow all's given thee; and yet let one purgation make thee as hungry again as fellows that work in [a][87] saw-pit. I'll go hear the screech owl.   *Exit.*[88]

LOD. [*aside*] This was Brachiano's pander; and 't is strange
That, in such open and apparent guilt
Of his adulterous sister, he dare utter   70
So scandalous a passion. I must wind him.[89]

Re-enter FLAMINEO.

FLAM. [*aside*] How dares this banish'd count return to Rome,
His pardon not yet purchas'd?[90] I have heard
The deceas'd Duchess gave him pension,
And that he came along from Padua
I' th' train of the young Prince. There's somewhat in 't;
Physicians that cure poisons still do work
With counter-poisons.

MAR. [*aside*]   Mark this strange encounter.

FLAM. [*to* LODOVICO] The god of melancholy turn thy gall to poison,
And let the stigmatic wrinkles in thy face, [80
Like to the boisterous waves in a rough tide,
One still overtake another.

LOD.   I do thank thee,
And I do wish ingeniously[91] for thy sake
The dog days[92] all year long.

FLAM.   How croaks the raven?
Is our good Duchess dead?

LOD.   Dead.

FLAM.   O fate!
Misfortune comes, like the crowner's[93] business,
Huddle[94] upon huddle.

75 Emend. Lucas; Qq1–3 *you;* Q4, and other mod. eds., *your.*
76 See on III, ii, 29.   77 *I.e.*, fools.
78 Below the equator.
79 The fate of those who refused to plead guilty or not guilty.
80 So Dyce, but as Lucas notes they may remain in the background to enhance the pictorial effect.
81 Height.
82 Because of their diseased condition. (Sampson.)
83 Mixed up.
84 Cain's quarrel with Abel about sacrifice. (Lucas.)
85 Understand "that."
86 An early Elizabethan famous for his talent for devouring "iron, glass, oyster shells", etc. In the end, a raw eel was too much for him.
87 Add. Q2.
88 Very likely he merely retires up-stage.
89 Scent him, hunt him down.
90 Got.   91 Ingenuously.   92 *I.e.*, evil days.
93 Coroner's.   94 Heap.

LOD.   Shalt thou and I join housekeeping?

FLAM. Yes, content; let's be unsociably
sociable.

LOD. Sit some three days together, and discourse —

FLAM. Only with making faces; lie in our
clothes.   90

LOD. With faggots for our pillows —

FLAM.   And be lousy.

LOD. In taffeta linings; that's genteel
melancholy;

Sleep all day —

FLAM.   Yes; and, like your melancholic hare,[95]

Feed after midnight.

Enter ANTONELLI [*and* GASPARO, *behind,
laughing.*]

We are observed : see how yon couple grieve!

LOD. What a strange creature is a laughing
fool!

As if man were created to no use
But only to show his teeth.

FLAM.   I'll tell thee what :
It would do well, instead of looking-glasses,
To set one's face each morning by a saucer
Of a witch's congealed blood.

LOD.   Precious [rogue !][96] [101

We'll never part.

FLAM.   Never, till the beggary of courtiers,

The discontent of churchmen, want of soldiers
And all the creatures that hang manacled,
Worse than strappado'd,[97] on the lowest felly
Of Fortune's wheel, be taught, in our two lives,
To scorn that world which life of means de-
prives.

ANT. My Lord, I bring good news. The
Pope, on 's deathbed,

At th' earnest suit of the Great Duke of
Florence,

Hath sign'd your pardon, and restor'd unto
you —   110

  LOD. I thank you for your news. — Look
up again,

Flamineo ; see my pardon.

FLAM.   Why do you laugh?
There was no such condition in our covenant.

LOD.   Why?

FLAM. You shall not seem a happier man
than I ;

You know our vow, sir ; if you will be merry,
Do it i' th' like posture as if some great man
Sat while his enemy were executed ;
Though it be very lechery unto thee,
Do 't with a crabbed politician's face.   119

LOD. Your sister is a damnable whore.

FLAM.   Ha?

LOD. Look you, I spake that laughing.

FLAM. Dost ever think to speak again?

LOD.   Do you hear?

Wilt sell me forty ounces of her blood
To water a mandrake?[98]

FLAM.   Poor Lord, you did vow
To live a lousy creature.

LOD.   Yes.

FLAM.   Like one
That had for ever forfeited the daylight
By being in debt.

LOD. Ha, ha!

FLAM. I do not greatly wonder you do
break ;[99]

Your Lordship learn't[100] long since ; but I'll
tell you —   130

LOD. What?

FLAM.   And 't shall stick by you —

LOD.   I long for it.

FLAM. This laughter scurvily becomes your
face ;

If you will not be melancholy, be angry.

                                           Strikes him.

See, now I laugh too.

MAR. You are to blame : I'll force you
hence.

  LOD. [*to* ANTONELLI *and* GASPARO]
                     Unhand me.

          [*Exeunt*] MARCELLO *and* FLAMINEO.

That e'er I should be forc'd to right myself
Upon a pander !

ANT.   My Lord !

LOD.   H' had been as good
Met with his fist a thunderbolt.

GAS.   How this shows !

LOD. Ud 's death, how did my sword miss
him?   These rogues

That are most weary of their lives still
scape   140

The greatest dangers.

A pox upon him ! all his reputation,

---

[95] Which was proverbially melancholy.

[96] So Qq 3, 4, Lucas ; Q 1 (Garrick) *grine rouge;* Q 1
(Dyce), Q 2, Dyce, Sampson, *gue.*

[97] In torturing by the strappado, the victim's
arms were bound behind his back and by them he
was hauled up on a pulley and dropped, to be brought
up with a dislocating jerk.

[98] Which was supposed to flourish under a gibbet,
from the droppings from the decomposing bodies.

[99] Go bankrupt ; *i.e.,* break your agreement with
me.

[100] For *learn'd't,* which is unpronounceable.

Nay, all the goodness of his family,
Is not worth half this earthquake.
I learnt it of no fencer to shake thus ;
Come, I 'll forget him, and go drink some wine.

                       Exeunt.

[ACT IV — SCENE I] [1]

Enter FRANCISCO *and* MONTICELSO.

MONT. Come, come, my Lord, untie your
     folded thoughts,
And let them dangle loose as a bride's hair : [2]
Your sister 's poisoned.
     FRAN.   Far be it from my thoughts
To seek revenge.
     MONT.   What, are you turn'd all mar-
     ble?
FRAN. Shall I defy him, and impose a war
Most burdensome on my poor subjects' necks,
Which at my will I have not power to end?
You know, for all the murders, rapes, and
     thefts,
Committed in the horrid lust of war,
He that unjustly caus'd it first proceed [10
Shall find it in his grave and in his seed.
     MONT. That 's not the course I 'd wish you ;
     pray, observe me :
We see that undermining more prevails
Than doth the cannon ; bear your wrongs
     conceal'd,
And, patient as the tortoise, let this camel
Stalk o'er your back unbruis'd ; sleep with
     the lion,
And let this brood of secure foolish mice
Play with your nostrils, till the time be ripe
For th' bloody audit and the fatal gripe ;
Aim like a cunning fowler, close one eye, [20
That you the better may your game espy.
     FRAN. Free me, my innocence, from treach-
     erous acts !
I know there 's thunder yonder,[3] and I 'll
     stand
Like a safe valley, which low bends the knee
To some aspiring mountain, since I know
Treason, like spiders weaving nets for flies,
By her foul work is found, and in it dies.
To pass away these thoughts, my honor'd
     Lord,
It is reported you possess a book
Wherein you have quoted, by intelligence,[4]

Lurking about the city.
     MONT.   Sir, I do ;
And some there are which call it my black
     book.
Well may the title hold ; for, though it teach
     not
The art of conjuring, yet in it lurk
The names of many devils.
     FRAN.   Pray, let 's see it.
     MONT. I 'll fetch it to your Lordship.

                  Exit MONTICELSO.
     FRAN.   Monticelso,
I 'll not trust thee ; but in all my plots
I 'll rest as jealous as a town besieg'd.
Thou canst not reach [5] what I intend to
     act.   40
Your flax soon kindles, soon is out again ;
But gold slow heats, and long will hot remain.

Re-enter MONTICELSO.   [*Presents* FRANCISCO
                    with a book.] [6]

     MONT. 'T is here, my Lord.
     FRAN. First, your [7] intelligencers,[8] pray,
     let 's see.
     MONT. Their number rises strangely ; and
     some of them
You 'd take for honest men. Next are pan-
     ders ;
These are your pirates ; and these following
     leaves
For base rogues that undo young gentlemen
By taking up commodities ; [9] for politic bank-
     rupts ;
For fellows that are bawds to their own
     wives,   50
Only to put off [10] horses and slight jewels,
Clocks, defac'd plate, and such commodities,
At birth of their first children.
     FRAN.   Are there such?
     MONT. These are for impudent bawds
That go in men's apparel ; for usurers
That share with scriveners for their good
     reportage ; [11]

---

[1] A room in Francisco's palace.
[2] An old custom of virgin brides.
[3] Above.
[4] By information from your spies.

[5] Comprehend.
[6] Om. Garrick-Harvard copies of Q 1, in signature
G, in which the Dyce copy is superior, as Lucas notes.
[7] The.
[8] Informers.
[9] A reference to the notorious commodity swindle.
A borrower would be required to take the bulk of
the loan in the form of some odd sort of goods for
which there was little or no demand. Then the
lender, through an agent, would buy them back at
an outrageous discount.
[10] On the lover ; *i.e.*, force him to buy "commodities" at absurd prices.
[11] A form of fee-splitting. "Good reportage" =
recommendation.

For lawyers that will antedate their writs ; [12]
And some divines you might find folded
    there,
But that I slip them o'er for conscience'
    sake.
Here is a general catalogue of knaves ;   60
A man might study all the prisons o'er,
Yet never attain this knowledge.
    FRAN.   " Murderers " ! —
Fold down the leaf, I pray.
Good my Lord, let me borrow this strange
    doctrine.
    MONT. Pray, use 't, my Lord.
    FRAN.   I do assure your Lordship,
You are a worthy member of the state,
And have done infinite good in your discovery
Of these offenders.
    MONT.   Somewhat, sir.
    FRAN.   O God !
Better than tribute of wolves paid in Eng-
    land ; [13]
'T will hang their skins o' th' hedge.
    MONT.   I must make bold [70
To leave your Lordship.
    FRAN.   Dearly, sir, I thank you ;
If any ask for me at court, report
You have left me in the company of knaves.
                Exit MONTICELSO.
I gather now by this, some cunning fellow
That's my Lord's officer, [one] [14] that lately
    skipp'd
From a clerk's desk up to a justice' chair,
Hath made this knavish summons, and in-
    tends,
As th' Irish rebels wont were to sell heads,
So to make prize of these.   And thus it hap-
    pens
Your poor rogues pay for 't which have not
    the means   80
To present bribe in fist : the rest o' th' band
Are raz'd out of the knaves' record ; or else
My Lord he winks at them with easy will ;
His man grows rich ; the knaves are the
    knaves still.
But to the use I 'll make of it : it shall serve
To point me out a [list] [15] of murderers,
Agents for any villainy.   Did I want
Ten leash [16] of courtezans, it would furnish
    me ;

Nay, laundress [17] three armies.   That [in] [18]
    so little paper
Should [lie] [19] th' undoing of so many men ! [90
'T is not so big as twenty declarations.[20]
See the corrupted use some make of books ;
Divinity,[21] wrested by some factious blood,
Draws swords, swells battles, and o'erthrows
    all good.
To fashion my revenge more seriously,
Let me remember my dead sister's face ;
[Call] [22] for her picture? no, I 'll close mine
    eyes,
And in a melancholic thought I 'll frame
Her figure 'fore me.

        Enter ISABELLA'S Ghost.

        Now I —d'foot ! [23] how strong
Imagination works ! how she can frame [100
Things which are not ! Methinks she stands
    afore me,
And by the quick idea of my mind,
Were my skill pregnant, I could draw her pic-
    ture.
Thought, as a subtle juggler, makes us deem
Things supernatural, which have cause
Common as sickness.   'T is my melancholy.—
How cam'st thou by thy death? — How idle
    am I
To question mine own idleness ! — Did ever
Man dream awake till now? — Remove this
    object ;
Out of my brain with 't ! What have I to
    do   110
With tombs or deathbeds, funerals or tears,
That have to meditate upon revenge?
              [*Exit* Ghost.]
So, now 't is ended, like an old wife's story.
Statesmen think often they see stranger sights
Than madmen.   Come, to this weighty busi-
    ness ;
My tragedy must have some idle mirth in 't,
Else it will never pass.   I am in love,
In love with Corombona ; and my suit
Thus halts [24] to her in verse. —   *He writes.*
I have done it rarely — oh, the fate of
    princes !   120

---

[12] Lucas suggests an allusion to Dr. Julio's method
of escaping conviction on one charge by trumping
up and pleading guilty to another, perhaps by
falsely dating the second prior to the first.
[13] By the Welsh to King Edgar.
[14] Garrick-Harvard copies of Q 1, *and.*
[15] Garrick-Harvard copies of Q 1, *life.*
[16] Sets of three.
[17] For the women who followed the army and
performed this function were not conspicuous for
their virtue.
[18] Cor. Q 2 ; om. Garrick-Harvard copies of Q 1 ;
Dyce copy bungles the correction : *so in.*
[19] Garrick-Harvard copies of Q 1, *be.*
[20] Statements by plaintiffs of their claims.
[21] Theology.
[22] Garrick-Harvard copies of Q 1, *Looke.*
[23] So Garrick-Harvard copies of Q 1 ; Dyce copy
avoids the oath : *ha't.*
[24] Limps.

I am so us'd to frequent flattery,
That, being alone, I now flatter myself ;
But it will serve ; 't is seal'd. —

Enter Servant.

                                    Bear this
To th' house of convertites, and watch your
    leisure
To give it to the hands of Corombona,
Or to the matron, when some followers
Of Brachiano may be by. Away !
                                    Exit Servant.
He that deals all by strength, his wit is shal-
    low ;
When a man's head goes through, each limb
    will follow.
The engine for my business, bold Count Lodo-
    wick ;   130
'T is gold must such an instrument procure ;
With empty fist no man doth falcons lure.[25]
Brachiano, I am now fit for thy encounter ;
Like the wild Irish, I 'll ne'er think thee dead
Till I can play at football with thy head.
Flectere si nequeo superos, Acheronta movebo.[26]
                                    Exit.[27]

[SCENE II] [28]

Enter the Matron *and* FLAMINEO.

MAT. Should it be known the Duke hath
    such recourse
To your imprison'd sister, I were like
T' incur much damage by it.
    FLAM.   Not a scruple.
The Pope [29] lies on his deathbed, and their
    heads
Are troubled now with other business
Than guarding of a lady.

Enter [*Francisco's*] Servant.

SER. [*aside*] Yonder 's Flamineo in confer-
    ence
With the matrona. — Let me speak with you ;
I would entreat you to deliver for me
This letter to the fair Vittoria.   10
MAT. I shall, sir.

Enter BRACHIANO.

SER.   With all care and secrecy.
Hereafter you shall know me, and receive
Thanks for this courtesy.   [*Exit.*]

[25] The lure was a decoy of feathers to which the
hawk was trained to return.
[26] If the high gods I cannot move, I 'll move the
powers of hell. (Vergil, *Aeneid*, VII, 312.)
[27] Qq₁₋₃ *Exit Mon.*   [28] The house of convertites.
[29] Gregory XIII (d. 1585).

FLAM.   How now ? what 's that
MAT. A letter.
FLAM.   To my sister ? I 'll see 't de-
    livered.   [*Exit* Matron.]
BRACH. What 's that you read, Flamineo ?
FLAM.   Look.
BRACH.   Ha !
" To the most unfortunate, his best respected
    Vittoria." —
Who was the messenger ?
FLAM.   I know not.
BRACH.   No ?
Who sent it ?
FLAM. Ud's foot, you speak as if a man
Should know what fowl is coffin'd in a bak'd
    meat
Afore you cut it up.   20
BRACH. I 'll open 't, were 't her heart.
    What 's here subscribed ?
" Florence ! " this juggling [30] is gross and
    palpable !
I have found out the conveyance.[31] — Read
    it, read it !
FLAM. (*reads the letter.*) " Your tears I 'll
    turn to triumphs, be but mine.
Your prop is fall'n ; I pity that a vine
Which princes heretofore have long'd to
    gather,
Wanting supporters, now should fade and
    wither." —
Wine, i' faith, my Lord, with lees would serve
    his turn.
" Your sad imprisonment I 'll soon uncharm,
And with a princely uncontrolled arm   30
Lead you to Florence, where my love and
    care
Shall hang your wishes in my silver hair." —
A halter on his strange equivocation ! — ·
" Nor for my years return me the sad willow : [32]
Who prefer blossoms before fruit that 's mel-
    low ? " —
Rotten, on my knowledge, with lying too long
    i' th' bed-straw. —
" And all the lines of age this line convinces : [33]
The gods never wax old ; no more do
    princes." —
A pox on 't, tear it ; let 's have no more
    atheists,[34] for God's sake.
BRACH. Ud's death, I 'll cut her into
    atomies,[35]   40
And let th' irregular [36] north wind sweep her up,

[30] Trisyllabic.
[31] Trickery.
[32] Symbol of rejected love.   [33] Overcomes.
[34] *I.e.*, blasphemers; for he has compared princes
to gods.   [35] Atoms.   [36] Wild.

And blow her int' his nostrils! Where's this
   whore?

FLAM. What? what do you call her?

BRACH.   Oh, I could be mad,

Prevent [37] the curs'd disease she'll bring me
   to,

And tear my hair off! [38] Where's this change-
   able stuff? [39]

FLAM. O'er head and ears in water, I
   assure you:

She is not for your wearing.

BRACH.   [In,] [40] you pander!

FLAM. What, me, my Lord? am I your
   dog?

BRACH.   A bloodhound!

Do you brave, do you stand [41] me?

FLAM. Stand you! let those that have diseases run; [42]   50

I need no plasters. [43]

BRACH. Would you be kick'd?

FLAM.   Would you have your neck
   broke?

I tell you, Duke, I am not in Russia;

My shins must be kept whole. [44]

BRACH. Do you know me?

FLAM.   O, my Lord, methodically:

As in this world there are degrees of evils,

So in this world there are degrees of devils;

You're a great duke, I your poor secretary.

I do look now for a Spanish fig or an Italian

sallet [45] daily. [46]   60

BRACH. Pander, ply your convoy, [47] and
   leave your prating.

FLAM. All your kindness to me is like that
miserable courtesy of Polyphemus to Ulysses:
you reserve me to be devour'd last; you
would dig turves out of my grave to feed your
larks; that would be music to you. Come,
I'll lead you to her.   [*Walks backwards.*]

BRACH. Do you face me?

FLAM. [Oh,] [48] sir, I would not go before a
politic enemy with my back towards him, [70
though there were behind me a whirlpool.

[37] Anticipate.
[38] See on I, ii, 34.
[39] With reference to "watered" taffeta or change-
able silk.
[40] So Dyce copy of Q₁; Garrick-Harvard copies,
No; Q₂, *E'en;* Qq₃,₄, omit.
[41] Stand up to, withstand.
[42] Have running sores.
[43] I'm not diseased, and don't intend to run.
[44] Sykes cites Dekker's allusion, in *Seven Deadly
Sins,* to this old Russian method of persuading
debtors to pay up.
[45] Salad; *i.e.,* poison.
[46] Possibly, as Lucas asserts, a "fourteener."
[47] Perform your function.
[48] Om. Garrick-Harvard copies of Q₁.

Enter VITTORIA *to* BRACHIANO *and* FLAMINEO.

BRACH. Can you read, mistress? Look
   upon that letter:

There are no characters [49] nor hieroglyphics;

You need no comment; I am grown your
   receiver. [50]

God's precious! you shall be a brave great
   lady,

A stately and advanced whore.

VIT.   Say, sir?

BRACH. Come, come, let's see your cabinet;
   discover

Your treasury of love letters. Death and
   Furies!

I'll see them all.

VIT.   Sir, upon my soul,

I have not any. Whence was this directed?

BRACH. Confusion on your politic ignorance!   81

You are reclaimed, [51] are you? I'll give you
   the bells,

And let you fly to the Devil.

FLAM.   Ware hawk, [52] my Lord!

VIT. "Florence"! this is some treacherous plot, my Lord;

To me he ne'er was [lovely,] [53] I protest,

So much as in my sleep.

BRACH.   Right! they are plots.

Your beauty! oh, ten thousand curses on't!

How long have I beheld the Devil in crystal! [54]

Thou hast led me, like an heathen sacrifice,

With music and with fatal yokes of flowers,

To my eternal ruin. Woman to man   [91

Is either a god or a wolf.

VIT.   My Lord —

BRACH.   Away!

We'll be as differing as two adamants: [55]

The one shall shun the other. What? dost
   weep?

Procure but ten of thy dissembling trade,

[Ye'd] [56] furnish all the Irish funerals

With howling past wild Irish.

FLAM.   Fie, my Lord!

BRACH. That hand, that cursed hand,
   which I have wearied

With doting kisses! — O my sweetest Duchess,

How lovely art thou now! — Thy loose
   thoughts   [100

[49] Cipher. (Lucas.)   [50] Pimp.
[51] *I.e.,* a tame hawk.   [52] Look out for a trap.
[53] Garrick-Harvard copies of Q₁, *thought on.*
[54] Cf. "white devil." Crystal was used to enclose
spirits.
[55] Magnets.
[56] So Dyce; Q₁ *ee'ld;* other old eds. *Wee'l,* etc.

Scatter like quicksilver! I was bewitch'd;
For all the world speaks ill of thee.

VIT.   No matter;
I'll live so now, I'll make that world recant
And change her speeches. You did name
      your Duchess.

BRACH. Whose death God pardon!

VIT.   Whose death God revenge
On thee, most godless Duke!

FLAM. [*aside*]   Now for two [57]
      whirlwinds!

VIT. What have I gain'd by thee but
      infamy?
Thou hast stain'd the spotless honor of my
      house,
And frighted thence noble society;
Like those which sick [58] o' th' palsy and
      retain   110
Ill-scenting foxes 'bout them, are still shunn'd
By those of choicer nostrils. What do you
      call this house?
Is this your palace? Did not the judge style
      it
A house of penitent whores? Who sent me
      to it?
Who hath the honor to advance Vittoria
To this incontinent college? is't not you?
Is't not your high preferment? Go, go brag
How many ladies you have undone like me.
Fare you well, sir; let me hear no more of you.
I had a limb corrupted to an ulcer;   120
But I have cut it off, and now I'll go
Weeping to Heaven on crutches. For your
      gifts,
I will return them all; and I do wish
That I could make you full executor
To all my sins. Oh, that I could toss myself
Into a grave as quickly! for all thou art worth
I'll not shed one tear more. — I'll burst first.
            She throws herself upon a bed.

BRACH. I have drunk Lethe. — Vittoria!
My dearest happiness! Vittoria!
What do you ail, my love? why do you
      weep?   130

VIT. Yes, I now weep poniards, do you see?

BRACH. Are not those matchless eyes
      mine?

VIT.   I had rather
They were not matches.

BRACH.   Is not this lip mine?

VIT. Yes; thus to bite it off, rather than
      give it thee.

FLAM. Turn to my Lord, good sister.

VIT.   Hence, you pander!

FLAM. Pander! am I the author of your
      sin?

VIT. Yes; he's a base thief that a thief
      lets in.

FLAM. We're blown up, my Lord.

BRACH.   Wilt thou hear me?
Once to be jealous of thee, is't express
That I will love thee everlastingly,   140
And never more be jealous.

VIT.   O thou fool,
Whose greatness hath by much o'ergrown thy
      wit!
What dar'st thou do that I not dare to suffer,
Excepting to be still thy whore? for that,
In the sea's bottom sooner thou shalt make
A bonfire.

FLAM. Oh, no oaths, for God's sake!

BRACH.   Will you hear me?

VIT.   Never.

FLAM. What a damned imposthume [59] is
      a woman's will!
Can nothing break it? — [*aside*] Fie, fie, my
      Lord,
Women are caught as you take tortoises; [150
She must be turn'd on her back. — Sister,
      by this hand,
I am on your side. — Come, come, you have
      wrong'd her.
What a strange credulous man were you, my
      Lord,
To think the Duke of Florence would love
      her!
Will any mercer take another's ware
When once 't is tous'd and sullied? — And
      yet, Sister,
How scurvily this frowardness becomes you!
Young leverets stand [60] not long; and
      women's anger
Should, like their flight, procure a little sport,
A full cry for a quarter of an hour,   160
And then be put to the dead quat.[61]

BRACH.   Shall these eyes,
Which have so long time dwelt upon your
      face,
Be now put out?

FLAM. No cruel landlady i' th' world, which
      lends forth groats
To broom-men and takes use [62] for them,
      would do't. —
Hand her, my Lord, and kiss her; be not
      like

[57] So Dyce; Dyce copy of Q 1, *tow;* Garrick-
Harvard copies, *ten;* other old eds. *the.*
   [58] Probably, as Lucas asserts, = sicken.

[59] Abscess.   [60] Hold out.
[61] Squat.   [62] Interest.

A ferret, to let go your hold with blowing.[63]
    BRACH. Let us renew right hands.
    VIT.   Hence!
    BRACH.   Never shall rage
Or the forgetful wine make me commit
Like fault.   170
    FLAM. [*aside*] Now you are i' th' way on 't,
       follow 't hard.
    BRACH. Be thou [64] at peace with me, let
       all the world
Threaten the cannon.
    FLAM.   Mark his penitence;
Best natures do commit the grossest faults
When they 're giv'n o'er to jealousy, as best
    wine,
Dying, makes strongest vinegar. I 'll tell
    you:
The sea 's more rough and raging than calm
    rivers,
But not so sweet nor wholesome. A quiet
    woman
Is a still water under a great bridge; [65]
A man may shoot her safely.   180
    VIT. Oh, ye dissembling men!
    FLAM.   We suck'd that, Sister,
From women's breasts, in our first infancy.
    VIT. To add misery to misery.
    BRACH.   Sweetest!
    VIT.   Am I not low enough?
Ay, ay, your good heart gathers like a snow-
    ball,
Now your affection 's cold.
    FLAM.   Ud'foot, it shall melt
To a heart again, or all the wine in Rome
Shall run o' th' lees for 't.
    VIT. Your dog or hawk should be rewarded
    better
Than I have been. I 'll speak not one word
    more.
    FLAM. Stop her mouth with a sweet kiss
       my Lord. — [*aside*] So,   190
Now the tide 's turn'd, the vessel 's come
    about.
He 's a sweet armful. Oh, we curl'd-hair'd
    men
Are still most kind to women! This is well.
    BRACH. That you should chide thus!
    FLAM. [*aside*] Oh, sir, your little chim-
       neys
Do ever cast most smoke! I sweat for
    you.

Couple together with as deep a silence
As did the Grecians in their wooden horse. —
My Lord, supply your promises with
    deeds;   199
You know that painted meat no hunger feeds.
    BRACH. Stay — ingrateful Rome —
    FLAM.   Rome! it deserves
To be call'd Barbary for our villainous
    usage.
    BRACH. Soft! the same project which the
       Duke of Florence
(Whether in love or gullery I know not)
Laid down for her escape will I pursue.
    FLAM. And no time fitter than this night,
       my Lord,
The Pope being dead, and all the cardinals
    ent'red
The conclave for th' electing a new pope,
The city in a great confusion.
We may attire her in a page's suit,   210
Lay her post-horse,[66] take shipping, and
    amain
For Padua.
    BRACH. I 'll instantly steal forth the Prince
       Giovanni,
And make for Padua. You two, with your
    old mother,
And young Marcello that attends on Flor-
    ence,
If you can work him to it, follow me;
I will advance you all. — For you, Vittoria,
Think of a duchess' title.
    FLAM.   Lo you,[67] Sister! —
Stay, my Lord; I 'll tell you a tale.[68]
The crocodile, which lives in the river [220
Nilus, hath a worm breeds i' th' teeth of 't,
which puts it to extreme anguish. A little bird,
no bigger than a wren, is barber-surgeon to this
crocodile; flies into the jaws of 't, picks out
the worm, and brings present remedy. The
fish, glad of ease, but ingrateful to her that
did it, that the bird may not talk largely of
her abroad for non-payment, closeth her
chaps, intending to swallow her, and so put
her to perpetual silence; but nature, [230
loathing such ingratitude, hath arm'd this
bird with a quill or prick on the head, top o'
th' which wounds the crocodile i' th' mouth,
forceth her open her bloody prison, and away
flies the pretty toothpicker from her cruel
patient.

---

[63] This, it appears from an anonymous communication cited by Lucas, is only a popular superstition.
[64] If thou art.
[65] Qq₃,₄, *Is like a . . . under London-Bridge.*

[66] Establish relays of post-horses for her.
[67] There you are!, what did I tell you?
[68] Herodotus, Pliny, and others told it, or parts
of it.

BRACH. Your application is, I have not
    rewarded
The service you have done me.[69]
FLAM. No, my Lord. —
You, Sister, are the crocodile : you are blem-
ish'd in your fame ; my Lord cures it ; [240
and though the comparison hold not in every
particle, yet observe, remember what good
the bird with the prick i' th' head hath done
you, and scorn ingratitude. —
[aside] It may appear to some ridiculous
Thus to talk knave and madman, and some-
    times
Come in with a dried sentence, stuff'd with
    sage ;
But this allows my varying of shapes ;
Knaves do grow great by being great men's
    apes. *Exeunt.*

[SCENE III] [70]

Enter LODOVICO, GASPARO, *and six* Ambassadors ; [and,] at another door, FRANCISCO
THE DUKE OF FLORENCE.

FRAN. So, my Lord ; I commend your
    diligence.
Guard well the conclave ; and, as the order is,
Let none have conference with the cardinals.
LOD. I shall, my Lord. — Room for the
    ambassadors !
GAS. They 're wondrous brave [71] to-day.
    Why do they wear
These several habits ?
LOD. Oh, sir, they 're knights
Of several orders : that lord i' th' black cloak
With the silver cross is Knight of Rhodes ; [72]
    the next,
Knight of St. Michael ; that, of the Golden
    Fleece ;
The Frenchman there, Knight of the Holy
    Ghost ; 10
My Lord of Savoy, Knight of th' Annuncia-
    tion ;
The Englishman is Knight of th' honored
    Garter,
Dedicated unto their saint, St. George.
    I could

Describe to you their several institutions,
With the laws annexed to their orders, but
    that time
Permits not such discovery.
FRAN. Where 's Count Lodowick ?
LOD. Here, my Lord.
FRAN. 'T is o' th' point of dinner time ;
Marshal the cardinals' service.
LOD. Sir, I shall.

Enter Servants, *with several dishes covered.*

Stand ! Let me search your dish ; who 's this
    for ?
SER. For my Lord Cardinal Monticelso.
LOD. Whose this ? [20
SER. For my Lord Cardinal of Bourbon.
FRE. [AMB.] Why doth he search the dishes ?
    to observe
What meat is dress'd ?
ENG. [AMB.] No, sir ; but to prevent
Lest any letters should be convey'd in
To bribe or to solicit the advancement
Of any cardinal. When first they enter,
'T is lawful for the ambassadors of princes
To enter with them, and to make their
    suit
For any man their prince affecteth [73] best ;
But after, till a general election, 30
No man may speak with them.
LOD. You that attend on the lord cardinals,
Open the window, and receive their viands !
[SERVANT *(appearing at a window.)*] [74] You
    must return the service : the lord
    cardinals
Are busied 'bout electing of the pope ;
They have given o'er scrutiny,[75] and are
    fallen
To admiration.[76]
LOD. Away, away ! [*Exeunt* Servants.]
FRAN. I 'll lay a thousand ducats you hear
    news
Of a pope presently.
    A Cardinal *on the terrace.*[77]
    — Hark ! sure, he 's elected ;
Behold, my Lord of Arragon appears 40
On the church battlements.
ARR. *Denuntio vobis gaudium magnum.
Reverendissimus Cardinalis Lorenso de Monti-
celso electus est in sedem apostolicam, et elegit
sibi nomen Paulum Quartum.*

---

[69] And so of course it is, even though Flamineo
proceeds to offer another, dictated possibly by fear
that he has gone too far with the Duke, and certainly by the dramatist's inability to resist the
double-entendre that had occurred to him.
[70] Before the Vatican.
[71] Splendidly attired.
[72] *I.e.*, of the order of St. John of Jerusalem ;
their headquarters in 1585 was no longer Rhodes,
but Malta. The cross is the Maltese.

[73] Favors, likes. [74] Old eds. *A Car.*
[75] Balloting.
[76] The proper term is "adoration", *i.e.*, the
homage which followed the new pope's investiture.
[77] Arragon appears on the balcony above the
inner stage.

OMNES. *Vivat sanctus Pater Paulus Quar-*
tus!

[*Enter a* Servant.]

SER. Vittoria, my Lord, —
FRAN.   Well, what of her?
SER. Is fled the city, —
FRAN.   Ha?
SER.   With Duke Brachiano.
FRAN. Fled! Where's the Prince Gio-
vanni?
SER.   Gone with his father.
FRAN. Let the matrona of the convert-
ites   51
Be apprehended. — Fled! oh, damnable! —
[*Exit* Servant.]
[*aside*] How fortunate are my wishes! why!
't was this
I only labored. I did send the letter
T' instruct him what to do. Thy fame, fond [78]
Duke,
I first have poison'd, directed thee the way
To marry a whore; what can be worse?
This follows:
The hand must act to drown the passionate
tongue;
I scorn to wear a sword and prate of wrong.

Enter MONTICELSO *in state.*

MONT. *Concedimus vobis apostolicam bene-*
dictionem et remissionem peccator[u]*m.*   61
[FRANCISCO *whispers to him.*] [79]
My Lord reports Vittoria Corombona
Is stol'n from forth the house of convertites
By Brachiano, and they're fled the city.
Now, though this be the first day of our seat,[80]
We cannot better please the divine Power
Than to sequester from the Holy Church
These cursed persons. Make it therefore
known
We do denounce excommunication
Against them both; all that are theirs in Rome
We likewise banish. — Set on.
Exeunt [*all but* FRANCISCO *and* LODO-
VICO].
FRAN.   Come, dear Lodovico. [71
You have ta'en the sacrament to prosecute
Th' intended murder.
LOD.   With all constancy.
But, sir, I wonder you'll engage yourself
In person, being a great prince.
FRAN.   Divert me not.
Most of his court are of my faction,

And some are of my council. Noble friend,
Our danger shall be 'like in this design;
Give leave part of the glory may be mine.
Exit FRANCISCO.

Re-enter MONTICELSO.

MONT. Why did the Duke of Florence
with such care   80
Labor your pardon? say.
LOD. Italian beggars will resolve you that,
Who, begging of an alms, bid those they beg of
Do good for their own sakes; or, 't may be,
He spreads his bounty with a sowing hand,
Like kings, who many times give out of meas-
ure,
Not for desert so much as for their pleasure.
MONT. I know you're cunning. Come,
what devil was that
That you were raising?
LOD.   Devil, my Lord?
MONT.   I ask you [81]
How doth the Duke employ you, that his
bonnet   90
Fell with such compliment [82] unto his knee
When he departed from you?
LOD.   Why, my Lord,
He told me of a resty [83] Barbary horse
Which he would fain have brought to the
career,[84]
The 'sault,[85] and the ring-galliard; [86] now, my
Lord,
I have a rare French rider.[87]
MONT.   Take you heed
Lest the jade break your neck. Do you put
me off
With your wild horse-tricks? Sirrah, you do
lie.
Oh, thou 'rt a foul, black cloud, and thou dost
threat
A violent storm!
LOD.   Storms are i' th' air, my Lord;
I am too low to storm.
MONT.   Wretched creature! [101
I know that thou art fashion'd for all ill;
Like dogs that once get blood, they'll ever kill.
About some murder? was 't not?
LOD.   I'll not tell you
And yet I care not greatly if I do;

[78] Foolish.   [79] Add. Lucas.
[80] So all old eds. except Dyce (and Folger) copy of
Q 1, which reads *state*.

[81] Qq 1, 2, give to Lodovico.   [82] Politeness.
[83] *I.e.*, untrained; the word could mean either
"restive" or "sluggish."
[84] A rapid run, starting and stopping suddenly.
[85] Bound; horses were trained to leap, curvet,
lash out with the heels, etc. These were all "'saults."
[86] A mixture of bounding forward, curvetting,
and lashing out with the heels.
[87] They had the name of being the best.

Marry, with this preparation : Holy Father,
I come not to you as an intelligencer,[88]
But as a penitent sinner : what I utter
Is in confession merely ; which you know
Must never be reveal'd.
    MONT.   You have o'erta'en [89] me.
    LOD. Sir, I did love Brachiano's Duchess
      dearly,   111
Or rather I pursued her with hot lust,
Though she ne'er knew on 't. She was pois-
    on'd ;
Upon my soul, she was ; for which I have
    sworn
T' avenge her murder.
    MONT.   To the Duke of Florence?
    LOD. To him I have.
    MONT.   Miserable creature !
If thou persist in this, 't is damnable.
Dost thou imagine thou canst slide on blood,
And not be tainted with a shameful fall?
Or, like the black and melancholic yew tree,
Dost think to root thyself in dead men's
    graves,   121
And yet to prosper? Instruction to thee
Comes like sweet showers to overhard'ned
    ground :
They wet, but pierce not deep. And so I
    leave thee,
With all the Furies hanging 'bout thy neck,
Till by thy penitence thou remove this evil,
In conjuring from thy breast that cruel devil.
                     Exit MONTICELSO.
    LOD. I 'll give it o'er ; he says 't is dam-
    nable ;
Besides I did expect his suffrage,[90]
By reason of Camillo's death.   130

      Re-enter Servant *and* FRANCISCO.

    FRAN. Do you know that Count?
    SER.   Yes, my Lord.
    FRAN. Bear him these thousand ducats to
    his lodging ;
Tell him the Pope hath sent them. — [*aside*]
    Happily
That will confirm [him] [91] more than all the rest.
                          [*Exit.*]
    SER. Sir.
    LOD. To me, sir?
    SER.   His Holiness hath sent you
A thousand crowns, and will[s] you, if you
    travel,
To make him your patron for intelligence.

    LOD. His creature ever to be commanded.
                      [*Exit* Servant.]
Why, now 't is come about. He rail'd upon
    me,
And yet these crowns were told [92] out and laid
    ready   140
Before he knew my voyage. Oh, the art,
The modest form of greatness ! [93] that do sit,
Like brides at wedding dinners, with their
    looks turn'd
From the least wanton jests, their puling
    stomach
Sick of the modesty, when their thoughts are
    loose,
Even acting of those hot and lustful sports
Are to ensue about midnight ; such his cun-
    ning !
He sounds my depth thus with a golden
    plummet.
I am doubly arm'd now. Now to th' act of
    blood.
There 's but three Furies found in spacious
    hell ;   150
But in a great man's breast three thousand
    dwell.   [*Exit.*]

         [ACT V — SCENE I] [1]

A passage over the stage of BRACHIANO, FLA-
MINEO, MARCELLO, HORTENSIO, [VITTORIA]
COROMBONA, CORNELIA, ZANCHE, *and others.*
[FLAMINEO, MARCELLO, *and* HORTENSIO
remain.]

    FLAM. In all the weary minutes of my life,
Day ne'er broke up [2] till now. This marriage
Confirms me happy.
    HORT.   'T is a good assurance.
Saw you not yet the Moor that 's come to
    court?
    FLAM. Yes, and conferr'd with him i' th'
    Duke's closet ;
I have not seen a goodlier personage,
Nor ever talk'd with man better experienc'd
In state affairs or rudiments [3] of war.
He hath, by report, serv'd the Venetian [4]
In Candy [5] these twice seven years, and been
    chief   10
In many a bold design.

---

    [88] Informer.   [89] Overreached.
    [90] Trisyllabic.   [91] Add. Dyce.
    [92] Counted.   [93] Great men.
    [1] Padua. A room in Brachiano's palace.
    [2] Dawned.
    [3] Fundamental principles.
    [4] Quadrisyllabic. " He " should be **slurred.**
    [5] Crete.

HORT. What are those two
That bear him company?

FLAM. Two noblemen of Hungary, that,
living in the Emperor's service as commanders,
eight years since, contrary to the expectation
of all the court, ent'red into religion, into the
strict [6] order of Capuchins ; but, being not
well settled in their undertaking, they left
their order, and returned to court ; for which,
being after troubled in conscience, they [20
vowed their service against the enemies of
Christ, went to Malta,[7] were there knighted,
and in their return back, at this great solemnity, they are resolved for ever to forsake the
world, and settle themselves here in a house of
Capuchins in Padua.

HORT. 'T is strange.

FLAM. One thing makes it so : they have
vowed for ever to wear next their bare bodies
those coats of mail they served in. 30

HORT. Hard penance ! Is the Moor a
Christian?

FLAM. He is.

HORT. Why proffers he his service to our
Duke?

FLAM. Because he understands there's
like to grow
Some wars between us and the Duke of Flor-
ence,
In which he hopes employment.[8]
I never saw one in a stern bold look
Wear more command, nor in a lofty phrase
Express more knowing or more deep contempt
Of our slight airy courtiers. He talks
As if he had travell'd all the princes' courts [40
Of Christendom ; in all things strives t' ex-
press,
That all that should dispute with him may
know
Glories, like glowworms, afar off shine bright,
But, look'd to near, have neither heat nor
light. —
The Duke !

Enter BRACHIANO, [FRANCISCO DUKE OF]
FLORENCE (*disguised like* Mulinassar) ; LO-
DOVICO [*disguised as* Carlo], ANTONELLI,
GASPARO [*disguised as* Pedro] ; [*an Officer,*]
FARNESE, *bearing their swords and helmets.*

BRACH. You are nobly welcome. We have
heard at full

[6] At the time when this play was written the
Capuchins were still an austere branch of the Franciscans. [7] See on IV, iii, 8.
[8] Qq1,2, add *Enter Duke Brachiano*, merely the
prompter's warning notation.

Your honorable service 'gainst the Turk.
To you, brave Mulinassar, we assign
A competent pension, and are inly [9] [sorry] [10]
The vows of those two worthy gentlemen [50
Make them incapable of our proffer'd bounty.
Your wish is you may leave your warlike
swords
For monuments in our chapel ; I accept it
As a great honor done me, and must crave
Your leave [11] to furnish out our Duchess'
revels.
Only one thing, as the last vanity
You e'er shall view, deny me not to stay
To see a barriers [12] prepar'd to-night ;
You shall have private standings. It hath
pleas'd
The great ambassadors of several princes, [60
In their return from Rome to their own
countries,
To grace our marriage, and to honor me
With such a kind of sport.

FRAN. I shall persuade them
To stay, my Lord.

[BRACH].[13] Set on there to the presence ! [14]

Exeunt BRACHIANO, FLAMINEO, [HOR-
TENSIO, FARNESE,] *and* MARCELLO.

[LOD.] [15] Noble my Lord, most fortunately
welcome.

The Conspirators *here embrace.*

You have our vows seal'd with the sacrament,
To second your attempts.

[GAS.] [16] And all things ready.
He could not have invented his own ruin,
Had he despair'd, with more propriety.

LOD. You would not take my way.

FRAN. 'T is better ordered. [70

LOD. T' have poison'd his prayer book, or
a pair [17] of beads,
The pommel of his saddle, his looking-glass,
Or th' handle of his racket — Oh, that, that !
That while he had been bandying at tennis,
He might have sworn himself to hell, and
struck
His soul into the hazard ! [18] Oh, my Lord,
I would have our plot be ingenious,
And have it hereafter recorded for example
Rather than borrow example.

FRAN. There's no way
More speeding than this thought on.

[9] Deeply. [10] So Qq2-4; Q1 *sorrow.*
[11] For my absence. [12] See on I, ii, 32.
[13] Cor. Dyce ; old eds. *Fran.* [14] Presence-chamber.
[15] So Qq3,4; Qq1,2, *Car[lo].*
[16] So Qq3,4; Qq1,2, *Ped[ro].* [17] Set.
[18] An inappropriate metaphor, as Lucas notes,
since to hit the ball into a hazard scored a point
for you.

LOD.   On, then. [80

FRAN. And yet methinks that this revenge
is poor,
Because it steals upon him like a thief.
To have ta'en him by the casque in a pitch'd
field —
Led him to Florence!

LOD.   It had been rare. — And there
Have crown'd him with a wreath of stinking
garlic,
T' have shown the sharpness of his government
And rankness of his lust. — Flamineo comes.
    Exeunt LODOVICO, ANTONELLI,[19] [*and*
        GASPARO].

Re-enter FLAMINEO, MARCELLO, *and* ZANCHE.

MAR. [*aside to* FLAMINEO] Why doth this
devil [20] haunt you? say!

FLAM. [*aside to* MARCELLO]   I know not;
For, by this light, I do not conjure for her.
'T is not so great a cunning as men think   90
To raise the devil; for here 's one up already;
The greatest cunning were to lay him down.

MAR. [*aside*] She is your shame.

FLAM. [*aside*]   I prithee, pardon her.
In faith, you see, women are like to burrs:
Where their affection throws them, there
they 'll stick.

ZAN. That is my countryman, a goodly
person;
When he 's at leisure, I 'll discourse with him
In our own language.

FLAM.   I beseech you do. —
                        Exit ZANCHE.
How is 't, brave soldier? Oh, that I had seen
Some of your iron days! I pray, relate   100
Some of your service to us.

FRAN. 'T is a ridiculous thing for a man to
be his own chronicle; I did never wash my
mouth with mine own praise, for fear of getting
a stinking breath.

MAR. You're too stoical. The Duke will
expect other discourse from you.

FRAN. I shall never flatter him; I have
studied man too much to do that. What difference is between the Duke and I? No [110
more than between two bricks, all made of one
clay; only 't may be one is plac'd on the top
of a turret, the other in the bottom of a well,
by mere chance. If I were plac'd as high as
the Duke, I should stick as fast, make as fair
a show, and bear out weather equally.

FLAM. If this soldier had a patent to beg
in churches, then he would tell them stories.

MAR. I have been a soldier too.

FRAN. How have you thriv'd?   120

MAR. Faith, poorly.

FRAN. That 's the misery of peace: only
outsides are then respected. As ships seem
very great upon the river, which show very
little upon the seas; so some men i' th' court
seem colossuses in a chamber, who, if they
came into the field, would appear pitiful pigmies.

FLAM. Give me a fair room yet hung with
arras, and some great cardinal to lug me by th'
ears as his endeared minion.   131

FRAN. And thou mayst do the devil knows
what villainy.

FLAM. And safely.

FRAN. Right; you shall see in the country,
in harvest time, pigeons, though they destroy
never so much corn,[21] the farmer dare not
present the fowling-piece to them! Why?
because they belong to the lord of the manor;
whilst your poor sparrows, that belong to [140
the Lord of Heaven, they go to the pot for 't.

FLAM. I will now give you some politic
instruction. The Duke says he will give you
pension; that 's but bare promise; get it under his hand;[22] for I have known men that
have come from serving against the Turk, for
three or four months they have had pension
to buy them new wooden legs and fresh
plasters; but, after, 't was not to be had; and
this miserable courtesy shows as if a [150
tormentor [23] should give hot cordial drinks
to one three-quarters dead o' th' rack, only to
fetch the miserable soul again to endure more
dog days.[24] —   [*Exit* FRANCISCO.]

Re-enter HORTENSIO, [*with*] a Young Lord,
    ZANCHE, *and* Two *more*.

How now, gallants. What, are they ready for
the barriers?

Y. LORD. Yes; the lords are putting on
their armor.

HORT. [*aside to* FLAMINEO] What 's he?

FLAM. [*aside to* HORTENSIO] A new up- [160
start; one that swears like a falc'ner, and will
lie in the Duke's ear day by day, like a maker
of almanacs; and yet I knew him, since he
came to the court, smell worse of sweat than
an under tennis-court keeper.

HORT. Look, you, yonder 's your sweet mistress.

[19] Perhaps erroneously listed for this scene.
[20] Referring to her complexion.
[21] Grain. This was a common grievance of the
farmers at the time.   [22] In writing.
[23] Torturer, executioner.   [24] See on III, iii, 84.

FLAM. Thou art my sworn brother; I'll tell thee, I do love that Moor, that witch, very constrainedly. She knows some of [170 my villainy. I do love her just as a man holds a wolf by the ears: but for fear of turning upon me and pulling out my throat, I would let her go to the devil.

HORT. I hear she claims marriage of thee.

FLAM. Faith, I made to her some such dark promise; and, in seeking to fly from 't, I run on, like a frighted dog with a bottle at 's tail, that fain would bite it off, and yet dares not look behind him. — Now, my precious gipsy! [25] 181

ZAN. Ay, your love to me rather cools than heats.

FLAM. Marry, I am the sounder lover; we have many wenches about the town heat too fast.

HORT. What do you think of these per-fum'd gallants, then?

FLAM. Their satin cannot save them; I am confident

They have a certain spice of the disease;

For they that sleep with dogs shall rise with fleas.[26]

ZAN. Believe it! A little painting and gay clothes 190

Make you loathe me.

FLAM. How? love a lady for painting or gay apparel? I'll unkennel one example more for thee: Aesop had a foolish dog that let go the flesh to catch the shadow. I would have courtiers be better diners.[27]

ZAN. You remember your oaths?

FLAM. Lovers' oaths are like mariners' prayers, uttered in extremity; but when the tempest is o'er and that [28] the vessel [200 leaves tumbling, they fall from protesting to drinking. And yet, amongst gentlemen, pro-testing and drinking go together, and agree as well as shoemakers and Westphalia bacon.[29] They are both drawers on; for drink draws on protestation and protestation draws on more drink. Is not this discourse better now than the [morality] [30] of your sunburnt gentle-man?

Re-enter CORNELIA.

CORN. Is this your perch, you haggard? [31] fly to th' stews.[32] [*Strikes* ZANCHE].

[25] Wench, baggage.   [26] Proverbial.
[27] Old eds. *Diuers*.   [28] When.
[29] For shoemakers draw shoes onto one's feet, and bacon incites thirst.
[30] So Q₄; earlier eds. *mortality*.
[31] Wild female hawk.   [32] Brothels.

FLAM. You should be clapp'd by the heels now: strike i' th' court! 211
[*Exit* CORNELIA.]

ZAN. She 's good for nothing but to make her maids

Catch cold a-nights: they dare not use a bedstaff [33]

For fear of her light fingers.

MAR. [*kicking* ZANCHE] You 're a strumpet,

An impudent one.

FLAM. Why do you kick her? say, Do you think that she 's like a walnut tree? [34]

Must she be cudgell'd ere she bear good fruit?

MAR. She brags that you shall marry her.

FLAM. What then?

MAR. I had rather she were pitch'd upon a stake 219

In some new-seeded garden, to affright

Her fellow crows thence.

FLAM. You 're a boy, a fool;

Be guardian to your hound; I am of age.

MAR. If I take her near you, I 'll cut her throat.

FLAM. With a fan of feathers?

MAR. And, for you, I 'll whip

This folly from you.

FLAM. Are you choleric?

I 'll purge 't with rhubarb.

HORT. Oh! your brother!

FLAM. Hang him!

He wrongs me most that ought t' offend me least. —

I do suspect my mother play'd foul play

When she conceiv'd thee.

MAR. Now, by all my hopes,

Like the two slaught'red sons [35] of Œdipus,

The very flames of our affection 231

Shall turn [two] [36] ways. Those words I 'll make thee answer

With thy heart-blood.

[33] Defined by Dr. Johnson as "a wooden pin stuck anciently on the sides of the bedstead, to hold the clothes from slipping on either side." The maids dare not use such a pin lest Cornelia snatch it up and beat them with it. And so the clothes slide off, and the maids catch cold.

[34] Alluding to a very old proverb, thus given by Ray (1670):
  "A spaniel, a woman, and a walnut tree,
  The more they're beaten the better still they be."

[35] Eteocles and Polynices, who killed each other fighting for the Theban throne. When their bodies were burned, their hatred was still so violent that the flames turned two ways.

[36] Q₁ *10*.

FLAM. Do like the geese in the progress ; [37]
You know where you shall find me.   [*Exit.*]
MAR.   Very good.
An thou beest a noble,[38] friend, bear him my
    sword,
And bid him fit the length on 't.
YOUNG LORD.   Sir, I shall.
                    [*Exeunt all but* ZANCHE.]
ZAN. He comes. Hence, petty thought of
    my disgrace! —

Re-enter FRANCISCO, *the* DUKE OF FLORENCE.

I ne'er loved my complexion till now,
'Cause I may boldly say, without a blush,
I love you.   240
    [FRAN]. [39] Your love is untimely sown;
there's a spring at Michaelmas,[40] but 't is but
a faint one ; I am sunk in years, and I have
vowed never to marry.
ZAN. Alas! poor maids get more lovers
than husbands. Yet you may mistake my
wealth ; for, as when ambassadors are sent
to congratulate princes, there's commonly
sent along with them a rich present, so that,
though the prince like not the ambassador's
person nor words, yet he likes well of the [251
presentment ; so I may come to you in the
same manner, and be better loved for my
dowry than my virtue.
    [FRAN.] I 'll think on the motion.[41]
ZAN. Do ; I 'll now detain you no longer.
At your better leisure I 'll tell you things shall
startle your blood.
Nor blame me that this passion I reveal :
Lovers die inward that their flames conceal.
    [FRAN.] [*aside*] Of all intelligence this may
    prove the best ;   261
Sure, I shall draw strange fowl from this foul
    nest.   *Exeunt.*

[SCENE II] [42]

Enter MARCELLO *and* CORNELIA [*with a* Page].[43]

CORN. I hear a whispering all about the
    court

You are to fight. Who is your opposite?
What is the quarrel?
MAR.   'T is an idle rumor.
CORN. Will you dissemble? sure, you do
    not well
To fright me thus ; you never look thus pale,
But when you are most angry. I do charge
    you
Upon my blessing — nay, I 'll call the Duke,
And he shall school you.
MAR.   Publish not a fear
Which would convert to laughter ; 't is not so.
Was not this crucifix my father's?
CORN.   Yes. 10
MAR. I have heard you say, giving my
    brother suck,
He took the crucifix between his hands,
And broke a limb off.
CORN.   Yes; but 'tis mended.

Enter FLAMINEO.

FLAM. I have brought your weapon back.
        FLAMINEO *runs* MARCELLO *through.*
CORN.   Ha! Oh, my horror!
MAR. You have brought it home, indeed.
CORN.   Help! Oh, he 's murdered!
FLAM. Do you turn your gall up? I 'll to
    sanctuary,
And send a surgeon to you.   [*Exit.*]

Enter [LODOVICO *as*] Carlo, HORTENSIO, [*and*
    GASPARO *as*] Pedro.

HORT.   How? o' th' ground?
MAR. O Mother, now remember what I
    told
Of breaking off the crucifix ! Farewell.
There are some sins which Heaven doth duly
    punish   20
In a whole family. This it is to rise
By all dishonest means ! Let all men know
That tree shall long time keep a steady foot
Whose branches spread no [wider] [44] than the
    root.   [*Dies.*]
CORN. Oh, my perpetual sorrow !
HORT.   Virtuous Marcello !
He 's dead. — Pray, leave him, lady. —
    Come, you shall.
CORN. Alas! he is not dead ; he 's in a
trance. Why, here 's nobody shall get any-
thing by his death. Let me call him again,
for God's sake !   30
    [LOD.] I would you were deceiv'd.
CORN. Oh, you abuse me, you abuse me,
you abuse me ! How many have gone away

[37] Flamineo rushes off abruptly, flinging back the
jibe, " Do as the geese do in a goose-procession —
follow me, you goose, you! " Cf. Hamlet's exit (IV,
ii, 33) with " Hide, fox, and all after." (Kittredge.)
Cf. also *The Spanish Tragedy*, IV, vi, 301.
[38] Qq 2–4 omit comma.
[39] Old eds. *Fla.* here and in ll. 255, 261.
[40] September 29 ; the allusion is to Indian summer.
[41] Proposal.   [42] The same.
[43] Add. Editor. As Lucas suggests, the Page, for
whom no entrance is provided in S. D. of old eds.,
must witness the murder ; see l. 70.

[44] So Q 4 ; earlier Qq *wilder*.

thus, for lack of tendance! Rear up's head, rear up's head: his bleeding inward will kill him.

HORT. You see he is departed.

CORN. Let me come to him; give me him as he is, if he be turn'd to earth; let me but give him one hearty kiss, and you shall [40 put us both into one coffin. Fetch a looking-glass: see if his breath will not stain it; or pull out some feathers from my pillow, and lay them to his lips. Will you lose him for a little painstaking?

HORT. Your kindest office is to pray for him.

CORN. Alas! I would not pray for him yet. He may live to lay me i' th' ground, and pray for me, if you'll let me come to him.

Enter BRACHIANO, all armed save the beaver, with FLAMINEO, [and FRANCISCO].

BRACH. Was this your handiwork?

FLAM. It was my misfortune. [50

CORN. He lies, he lies; he did not kill him; these have kill'd him that would not let him be better look'd to.

BRACH. Have comfort, my griev'd Mother.

CORN. Oh, you screech owl!

HORT. Forbear, good madam.

CORN. Let me go, let me go.

She runs to FLAMINEO with her knife drawn and coming to him lets it fall.

The God of Heaven forgive thee! Dost not wonder

I pray for thee? I'll tell thee what's the reason:

I have scarce breath to number twenty minutes;

I'd not spend that in cursing. Fare thee well:

Half of thyself lies there; and mayst thou live   60

To fill an hourglass with his mould'red ashes,

To tell how thou shouldst spend the time to come

In blest repentance!

BRACH. Mother, pray tell me

How came he by his death? What was the quarrel?

CORN. Indeed, my younger boy presum'd too much

Upon his manhood, gave him bitter words,

Drew his sword first; and so, I know not how,

For I was out of my wits, he fell with 's head

Just in my bosom.

PAGE. This is not true, madam.

CORN. I pray thee, peace. [70

One arrow's [grass'd] [45] already; it were vain

T' lose this: [46] for that will ne'er be found again.

BRACH. Go, bear the body to Cornelia's lodging;

And we command that none acquaint our Duchess

With this sad accident. For you, Flamineo,

Hark you, I will not grant your pardon.

FLAM. No?

BRACH. Only a lease of your life; and that shall last

But for one day; thou shalt be forc'd each evening

To renew it, or be hang'd.

FLAM. At your pleasure.

LODOVICO sprinkles BRACHIANO'S beaver with a poison.

Your will is law now; I'll not meddle with it.   80

BRACH. You once did brave me in your sister's lodging;

I'll now keep you in awe for't. — Where's our beaver?

FRAN. [aside] He calls for his destruction. — Noble youth,

I pity thy sad fate! — [aside] Now to the barriers.

This shall his passage to the black lake further;

The last good deed he did, he pardon'd murther. *Exeunt.*

[SCENE III] [47]

Charges and shouts. They fight at barriers; first single pairs, then three to three.

Enter BRACHIANO, [FRANCISCO,] and FLAMINEO, with others.

BRACH. An armorer! ud's death, an armorer!

FLAM. Armorer! where's the armorer?

BRACH. Tear off my beaver.

FLAM. Are you hurt, [48] my Lord?

[45] Lost in the grass; spelled *graz'd* in old eds.
[46] Dyce, perhaps rightly, omits the stop.
[47] A courtyard of the palace, changing at l. 86 to Brachiano's cabinet. Lucas thinks the barriers would be fought on the inner stage, and takes *bar* (l. 8) for a part of the helmet. A better arrangement would be to take *bar* as the barrier across which the contestants fought, and to suppose it was set on the outer stage, which Flamineo's order clears, leaving the inner stage for the bed.
[48] Wounded.

Enter Armorer.

BRACH. Oh, my brain's on fire! the helmet is poison'd.

ARM.   My Lord,
Upon my soul —

BRACH.   Away with him to torture!
[*Exit* Armorer, *guarded.*]
There are some great ones that have hand in this,
And near about me.

[*Enter* VITTORIA.]

VIT.   Oh, my loved Lord! poisoned?
FLAM. Remove the bar. — Here's unfortunate revels! —
Call the physicians.

Enter two Physicians.

A plague upon you!
We have too much of your cunning here already;   10
I fear the ambassadors are likewise poison'd.

BRACH. Oh, I am gone already! the infection
Flies to the brain and heart. O thou strong heart!
There's such a covenant 'tween the world and it,
They're loth to break.

[*Enter* GIOVANNI.]

GIO.   Oh, my most loved father!
BRACH. Remove the boy away. —
Where's this good woman? — Had I infinite worlds,
They were too little for thee. Must I leave thee? —
What say yon screech owls? is the venom mortal?
PHY. Most deadly.

BRACH.   Most corrupted politic hangman,   20
You kill without book;[49] but your art to save
Fails you as oft as great men's needy friends.
I that have given life to offending slaves
And wretched murderers, have I not power
To lengthen mine own a twelvemonth? —
[*to* VITTORIA] Do not kiss me,
For I shall poison thee. This unction is sent
From the great Duke of Florence.

FRAN.   Sir, be of comfort.
BRACH. O thou soft natural death, that art joint-twin

[49] By heart; *i.e.*, you are virtuosi.

To sweetest slumber! no rough-bearded comet
Stares on thy mild departure; the dull owl   30
Beats not against thy casement; the hoarse wolf
Scents not thy carrion. Pity winds thy corse,
Whilst horror waits on princes.

VIT.   I am lost for ever.
BRACH. How miserable a thing it is to die
'Mongst women howling!

[*Enter* LODOVICO *and* GASPARO.]

What are those?
FLAM.   Franciscans;[50]
They have brought the extreme[51] unction.

BRACH.   On pain of death,
Let no man name death to me; it is a word
Infinitely terrible. Withdraw into our cabinet.

Exeunt [*all*] *but* FRANCISCO *and* FLAMINEO.

FLAM. To see what solitariness is about dying princes! As heretofore they have [40] unpeopled towns, divorc'd friends, and made great houses unhospitable; so now, O justice! where are their flatterers now? Flatterers are but the shadows of princes' bodies: the least thick cloud makes them invisible.

FRAN. There's great moan made for him.

FLAM. Faith, for some few hours salt water will run most plentifully in every office o' th' court; but, believe it, most of them do but weep over their stepmothers' graves.   50

FRAN. How mean you?

FLAM. Why, they dissemble; as some men do that live within compass o' th' verge.[52]

FRAN. Come, you have thriv'd well under him.

FLAM. Faith, like a wolf[53] in a woman's breast; I have been fed with poultry;[54] but, for money, understand me, I had as good a will to cozen him as e'er an officer of them all; but I had not cunning enough to do it.   60

FRAN. What didst thou think of him? faith, speak freely.

[50] See on V, i, 17.
[51] Accented on first syllable.
[52] The Lord High Steward had jurisdiction over a radius of twelve miles from the court; this area was the verge. The meaning is: as do some men whom I could name, men who live not a thousand miles from court.
[53] Cancer.
[54] The old treatment of cancer was to feed it meat. Bracciano was treated in this fashion for an ulcerous infection of his thigh.

FLAM. He was a kind of statesman that would sooner have reckon'd how many cannon bullets he had discharged against a town, to count his expense that way, than how many of his valiant and deserving subjects he lost before it.

FRAN. Oh, speak well of the Duke.

FLAM. I have done. Wilt hear some of [70 my court wisdom? To reprehend princes is dangerous; and to overcommend some of them is palpable lying.

Re-enter LODOVICO.

FRAN. How is it with the Duke?

LOD. Most deadly ill.
He's fall'n into a strange distraction:
He talks of battles and monopolies,
Levying of taxes; and from that descends
To the most brainsick language. His mind fastens
On twenty several objects, which confound
Deep sense with folly. Such a fearful end
May teach some men that bear too lofty crest,
Though they live happiest, yet they die not best. 82
He hath conferr'd the whole state of the dukedom
Upon your sister, till the Prince arrive
At mature age.

FLAM. There's some good luck in that yet.

FRAN. See, here he comes.

Enter BRACHIANO, *presented in a bed*, VITTORIA, [GASPARO,] *and others.*[55]

There's death in's face already.

VIT. Oh, my good Lord!

BRACH.[56] Away! you have abus'd me:
You have convey'd coin forth our territories,[57]
Bought and sold offices, oppress'd the poor,
And I ne'er dreamt on't. Make up your accounts; [90
I'll now be mine own steward.

FLAM. Sir, have patience.

BRACH. Indeed, I am to blame;
For did you ever hear the dusky raven
Chide blackness? or was't ever known the Devil
Rail'd against cloven creatures?

VIT. Oh, my Lord!

BRACH. Let me have some quails to supper.

FLAM. Sir, you shall.

BRACH. No, some fried dogfish; your quails feed on poison.
That old dog-fox, that politician, Florence —
I'll forswear hunting, and turn dog-killer:
Rare! I'll be friends with him; for, mark you, sir, 100
One dog still sets another a-barking. Peace, peace!
Yonder's a fine slave come in now.

FLAM. Where?

BRACH. Why, there, in a blue bonnet, and a pair
Of breeches with a great codpiece.[58] Ha, ha, ha!
Look you, his codpiece is stuck full of pins,[59]
With pearls o' th' head of them. Do not you know him?

FLAM. No, my Lord.

BRACH. Why, 't is the Devil:
I know him by a great rose [60] he wears on's shoe,
To hide his cloven foot. I'll dispute with him; 109
He's a rare linguist.[61]

VIT. My Lord, here's nothing.

BRACH. Nothing? rare! nothing! When I want money,
Our treasury is empty: there is nothing;
I'll not be us'd thus.

VIT. Oh, lie still, my Lord!

BRACH. See, see; Flamineo, that kill'd his brother,
Is dancing on the ropes [62] there, and he carries
A moneybag in each hand, to keep him even,
For fear of breaking's neck. And there's a lawyer
In a gown whipp'd [63] with velvet, stares and gapes
When the money will fall. How the rogue cuts capers!

[55] Probably the curtains of the inner stage were opened, these characters were "discovered", and the audience at once accepted the whole stage as the Duke's cabinet.
[56] Old eds. note marginally: *These speeches are several kinds of distractions and in the action should appear.*
[57] To do so was often prohibited by statute.
[58] A baggy appendage at the front of the breeches.
[59] "According to the fashion of the time." (Lucas.)
[60] Rosette.
[61] Talker.
[62] Tight-ropes.
[63] Trimmed.

It should have been in a halter.[64] 'T is there;
what's she?   120
FLAM. Vittoria, my Lord.
BRACH.   Ha, ha, ha! Her hair
Is sprinkled with arras-powder,[65] that makes
her look
As if she had sinn'd in the pastry.[66] — What's
he?
FLAM. A divine, my Lord.

> BRACHIANO *seems here near his end;*
> LODOVICO *and* GASPARO, *in the
> habit of Capuchins, present him in
> his bed with a crucifix and hallowed
> candle.*

BRACH.   He will be drunk; avoid him;
Th' argument is fearful, when churchmen
stagger in 't.
Look you, six grey rats that have lost their
tails
Crawl up the pillow; send for a ratcatcher.
I 'll do a miracle. I 'll free the court
From all foul vermin. Where 's Flamineo?
FLAM. [*aside*] I do not like that he names
me so often,   130
Especially on 's deathbed; 't is a sign
I shall not live long. — See, he 's near his
end.
LOD. Pray, give us leave. — *Attende,
Domine Brachiane* —
FLAM. See, see how firmly he doth fix
his eye
Upon the crucifix.
VIT.   Oh, hold it constant!
It settles his wild spirits; and so his eyes
Melt into tears.
LOD.[67] *Domine Brachiane, solebas in bello
tutus esse tuo clypeo; nunc hunc clypeum
hosti tuo opponas infernali.*   140
GAS.[68] *Olim hasta valuisti in bello; nunc
hanc sacram hastam vibrabis contra hostem
animarum.*
LOD. *Attende, Domine Brachiane; si nunc
quoque probas ea quae acta sunt inter nos, flecte
caput in dextrum.*
GAS. *Esto securus, Domine Brachiane;
cogita quantum habeas meritorum; denique
memineris meam animam pro tua oppignora-
tam si quid esset periculi.*   150

LOD. *Si nunc quoque probas ea quae acta
sunt inter nos, flecte caput in l[ae]vum.* — [69]
He is departing; pray, stand all apart,
And let us only whisper in his ears
Some private meditations, which our order
Permits you not to hear.

> *Here, the rest being departed,* LODO-
> VICO *and* GASPARO *discover them-
> selves.*

GAS.   Brachiano!
LOD.   Devil
Brachiano, thou art damn'd!
GAS.   Perpetually!
LOD. A slave condemn'd and given up to
the gallows
Is thy great lord and master!
GAS.   True; for thou
Art given up to the Devil!
LOD.   O you slave!
You that were held the famous politician, [161
Whose art was poison —
GAS.   And whose conscience,
murder!
LOD. That would have broke your wife's
neck down the stairs,
Ere she was poison'd!
GAS.   That had your villainous
sallets — [70]
LOD. And fine embroidered bottles and
perfumes,
Equally mortal with a winter plague!
GAS. Now there 's mercury — [71]
LOD.   And copperas — [72]
GAS.   And quicksilver —
LOD. With other devilish pothecary stuff,
A-melting in your politic brains — dost hear?
GAS. This is Count Lodovico.
LOD.   This, Gasparo; [170
And thou shalt die like a poor rogue.
GAS.   And stink
Like a dead fly-blown dog.
LOD.   And be forgotten

[64] He should have danced at the end of the hang-man's rope.
[65] Powdered orris (iris) root, with which Vittoria had scented her hair.
[66] *I.e.*, the "office" of the pastry; there would be much flour about.
[67] Old eds. note marginally: By the crucifix.
[68] Old eds. note marginally: By the h[a]llowed taper.
[69] Lord Brachiano, safe wert thou wont to be in battle by virtue of thy shield; this shield shalt thou now oppose to thine infernal enemy. . . . Once by the spear wert thou mighty in battle; now shalt thou shake this spear against the enemy of souls. . . . Hearken, Lord Brachiano; if now thou dost approve of these things done between us, incline thine head to the right. . . . Be thou confident, Lord Brachiano; think upon how much of merit thou hast; and finally remember that my soul is a pledge for thine, should there be aught of peril. . . . If now, likewise, thou dost approve of these things done between us, incline thine head to the left.
[70] Salads.
[71] *I.e.*, corrosive sublimate.
[72] Sulphate of copper, iron, or zinc.

Before thy funeral sermon.

BRACH. Vittoria! Vittoria!

LOD.   Oh, the cursed devil!

Come [73] to himself again! We are undone.

GAS. Strangle him in private.

Re-enter VITTORIA *and the* Attendants.

           What, will you call him again

To live in treble torments? For charity,

For Christian charity, avoid the chamber.

     [*Exeunt* VITTORIA *and* Attendants.]

LOD. You would prate, sir? This is a true-love knot

Sent from the Duke of Florence

          BRACHIANO *is strangled.*

GAS.   What, is it done?

LOD. The snuff [74] is out. No woman keeper [75] i' th' world,   181

Though she had practis'd seven year at the pest-house,

Could have done 't quaintlier. [76] — My Lords, he 's dead.

        [*They return.*]

OMNES. Rest to his soul!

VIT.   O me! this place is hell.

           Exit VITTORIA.

[FRAN.] [77] How heavily she takes it!

FLAM.   Oh, yes, yes;

Had women navigable rivers in their eyes,

They would dispend them all. Surely, I wonder

Why we should wish more rivers to the city, [78]

When they sell water so good cheap. [79] I 'll tell thee,

These are but moonish [80] shades of griefs or fears;   190

There 's nothing sooner dry than women's tears.

Why, here 's an end of all my harvest; he [h]as given me nothing.

Court promises! let wise men count them curs'd,

For while you live, [81] he that scores best [82] pays worst.

FRAN. Sure, this was Florence' doing.

---

[73] Qq 2-4, *Comes.*
[74] Of the candle; *i.e.*, of Brachiano's life.
[75] Nurse.
[76] More neatly.
[77] Early eds. confuse *Flo[rence]* and *Fra.* throughout the rest of this scene.
[78] Sir Hugh Myddleton's New River was completed in 1613.
[79] At such a bargain.
[80] Changeable.
[81] Ever.
[82] Runs up the largest account.

FLAM.   Very likely.

Those are found weighty strokes which come from th' hand,

But those are killing strokes which come from th' head.

Oh, the rare tricks of a Machiavellian!

He doth not come like a gross, plodding slave,

And buffet you to death; no, my quaint knave!   200

He tickles you to death, makes you die laughing,

As if you had swallow'd down a pound of saffron.

You see the feat, 't is practis'd in a trice —

To teach court honesty [83] it jumps on ice.

FRAN. Now have the people liberty to talk,

And descant [84] on his vices.

FLAM.   Misery of princes,

That must of force [85] be censur'd by their slaves!

Not only blam'd for doing things are ill,

But for not doing all that all men will: 209

One were better be a thresher. — Ud's death,

I would fain speak with this duke yet.

FRAN.   Now he 's dead?

FLAM. I cannot conjure; but, if prayers or oaths

Will get to th' speech of him, though forty devils

Wait on him in his livery of flames,

I 'll speak to him, and shake him by the hand,

Though I be blasted.   *Exit* FLAMINEO.

FRAN.   Excellent Lodovico!

What, did you terrify him at the last gasp?

LOD. Yes, and so idly, that the Duke had like

T' have terrified us.

FRAN.   How?

LOD.   You shall hear that hereafter.

Enter the Moor [ZANCHE].

See, yon 's the infernal that would make up [86] sport.   220

Now to the revelation of that secret

She promis'd when she fell in love with you.

FRAN. You 're passionately [87] met in this sad world.

ZAN. I would have you look up, sir; these court tears

Claim not your tribute to them; let those weep

---

[83] Understand "that."   [84] Expatiate.
[85] Necessarily.   [86] Q4 *us.*   [87] Sorrowfully.

That guiltily partake in the sad cause.
I knew last night, by a sad dream I had,
Some mischief would ensue ; yet, to say truth,
My dream most concern'd you.
    Lod. Shall's fall a-dreaming?   230
    Fran. Yes ; and for fashion sake I'll dream
    with her.
    Zan. Methought, sir, you came stealing
to my bed.
    Fran. Wilt thou believe me, sweeting?
    by this light,
I was a-dreamt on thee too ; for methought
I saw thee naked.
    Zan.   Fie, sir ! As I told you,
Methought you lay down by me.
    Fran.   So dreamt I ;
And, lest thou shouldst take cold, I cover'd
    thee
With this Irish mantle.
    Zan.   Verily, I did dream
You were somewhat bold with me ; but, to
    come to't —
    Lod. How, how! I hope you will not go
    to it here.   240
    Fran. Nay, you must hear my dream out.
    Zan.   Well, sir, forth !
    Fran. When I threw the mantle o'er thee,
    thou didst laugh
Exceedingly, methought.
    Zan.   Laugh?
    Fran.   And cri'dst out,
The hair did tickle thee.
    Zan.   There was a dream indeed !
    Lod. [aside] Mark her, I prithee ; she sim-
    pers like the suds
A collier hath been wash'd in.
    Zan. Come, sir, good fortune tends you.
    I did tell you
I would reveal a secret : Isabella,
The Duke of Florence' sister, was empoison'd
By a fum'd [88] picture ; and Camillo's neck [250
Was broke by damn'd Flamineo, the mis-
    chance
Laid on a vaulting-horse.
    Fran.   Most strange !
    Zan.   Most true.
    Lod. [aside] The bed [89] of snakes is broke.
    Zan. I sadly do confess I had a hand
In the black deed.
    Fran.   Thou kept's [90] their counsel?
    Zan.   Right ;
For which, urg'd with contrition, I intend
This night to rob Vittoria.

---

[88] See on II, ii, 25.   [89] Knotted mass.
[90] For the unpronounceable *keptst*.

    Lod. [aside]   Excellent penitence !
Usurers dream on't while they sleep out ser-
    mons.
    Zan. To further our escape, I have en-
    treated
Leave to retire me, till the funeral,   260
Unto a friend i' th' country ; that excuse
Will further our escape. In coin and jewels
I shall at least make good unto your use
An hundred thousand crowns.
    Fran.   O noble wench !
    Lod. Those crowns we'll share.
    Zan.   It is a dowry,
Methinks, should make that sunburnt proverb
    false,
" And wash the Ethiop white."
    Fran.   It shall.   Away !
    Zan. Be ready for our flight.
    Fran.   An hour 'fore day.
                 Exit the Moor.
O strange discovery ! why, till now we knew
    not
The circumstance of either of their deaths. [270

Re-enter the Moor.

    Zan. You'll wait about midnight in the
    chapel?
    Fran.   There.   [*Exit* Zanche.]
    Lod. Why, now our action's justified.
    Fran.   Tush for justice !
What harms it justice? We now, like the
    partridge,
Purge the disease with laurel : [91] for the
    fame
Shall crown the enterprise and quit the shame.
                   Exeunt.

[SCENE IV] [92]

Enter Flamineo *and* Gasparo, *at one door ;
another way,* Giovanni, *attended.*

    Gas. The young Duke : did you e'er see a
sweeter prince ?
    Flam. I have known a poor woman's bas-
tard better favor'd. [93] This is behind him.
Now to his face : all comparisons were hateful.
Wise was the courtly peacock that, being a
great minion, and, being compar'd for beauty,
by some dottrels [94] that stood by, to the
kingly eagle, said the eagle was a far fairer bird
than herself, not in respect of her feathers, [10

---

[91] According to Pliny.
[92] A room in the palace.
[93] Better looking.
[94] A kind of plover, supposed to be especially
foolish.

but in respect of her long talons. His will grow out in time. — My gracious Lord !

Gio. I pray, leave me, sir.

Flam. Your Grace must be merry ; 'tis I have cause to mourn ; for, wot you, what said the little boy that rode behind his father on horseback ?

Gio. Why, what said he ?

Flam. " When you are dead, Father," said he, " I hope then I shall ride in the sad- [20 dle." Oh, 't is a brave thing for a man to sit by himself ! He may stretch himself in the stirrups, look about, and see the whole compass of the hemisphere. You 're now, my Lord, i' th' saddle.

Gio. Study your prayers, sir, and be penitent ;
'T were fit you 'd think on what hath former been ; [95]
I have heard grief nam'd the eldest child of sin.   *Exit* Giovanni.

Flam. Study my prayers ! he threatens me divinely ;
I am falling to pieces already. I care not, [30 though, like [Anaxarchus],[96] I were pounded to death in a mortar ; and yet that death were fitter for usurers — gold and themselves to be beaten together, to make a most cordial cullis [97] for the Devil.
He hath his uncle's villainous look already,
In decimo sexto.[98]

Enter Courtier.

Now, sir, what are you ?

Court. It is the pleasure, sir, of the young Duke,   38
That you forbear the presence and all rooms
That owe him reverence.

Flam.   So ; the wolf and the raven
Are very pretty fools when they are young.
Is it your office, sir, to keep me out ?

Court. So the Duke wills.

Flam. Verily, Master Courtier, extremity is not to be used in all offices. Say that a gentlewoman were taken out of her bed about midnight, and committed to Castle Angelo,[99] to the Tower [100] yonder, with nothing about her but her smock, would it not show a cruel part in the gentleman-porter to lay claim [50 to her upper garment, pull it o'er her head and ears, and put her in nak'd ?

Court. Very good ; you are merry. [*Exit.*]

Flam. Doth he make a court ejectment of me ? A flaming firebrand casts more smoke without a chimney than within 't. I 'll smoor [101] some of them.

Enter Florence.

How now ! thou art sad.

Fran. I met even now with the most piteous sight.

Flam. Thou mett'st [102] another here : a pitiful   60
Degraded courtier.

Fran.   Your reverend mother
Is grown a very old woman in two hours.
I found them winding of Marcello's corse ;
And there is such a solemn melody,
'Tween doleful songs, tears, and sad elegies,
Such as old grandams watching by the dead
Were wont t' outwear the nights with, that, believe me,
I had no eyes to guide me forth the room,
They were so o'ercharg'd with water.

Flam.   I will see them.

Fran. 'T were much uncharity in you ; for your sight   70
Will add unto their tears.

Flam.   I will see them ;
They are behind the traverse — I 'll discover
Their superstitious howling.

[*Draws the curtains.*[103]]

Cornelia, *the* Moor [Zanche], *and three other* Ladies *discovered winding* Marcello's *corse.* A *Song.*

Corn. This rosemary is wither'd ; pray get fresh.
I would have these herbs grow up in his grave,
When I am dead and rotten. Reach the bays ;
I 'll tie a garland here about his head ;
'T will keep my boy from lightning.[104] This sheet
I have kept this twenty year, and every day
Hallow'd it with my prayers ; I did not think
He should have wore it.

Zan.   Look you who are yonder. [81

Corn. Oh, reach me the flowers.

Zan. [*aside*] Her Ladyship's foolish.

---

[95] Old eds. spell *bin.*
[96] The Thracian philosopher; his death was at the hands of Nicocreon, tyrant of Cyprus. Emend. Sykes; old eds. *Anacharsis.*
[97] Broth.
[98] *I.e.,* in little, on a small scale.
[99] The Castle of St. Angelo, in Rome.
[100] Referring to the Tower of London, but evidently an explanatory note on "Castle Angelo."
[101] Smother.   [102] Q₄ *meet'st.*
[103] Of the inner stage.
[104] An ancient superstition.

LADY. [aside]   Alas! her grief
Hath turn'd her child again!
CORN.   You're very welcome:
There's rosemary for you; (*to* FLAMINEO) and
    rue for you; —
Heartsease [105] for you; I pray make much of
    it;
I have left more for myself.
    FRAN.   Lady, who's this?
    CORN. You are, I take it, the gravemaker.
    FLAM.   So.
    ZAN.   'T is Flamineo.
    CORN. Will you make me such a fool?
        here's a white hand:
Can blood so soon be wash'd out? Let me
    see;   90
When screech owls croak upon the chimney
    tops,
And the strange cricket i' th' oven sings and
    hops,
When yellow spots do on your hands appear,
Be certain then you of a corse shall hear.
Out upon't, how 't is speckled! h'as handled a toad, sure. Cowslip-water is good
for the memory; pray buy me three ounces
of 't.
    FLAM. [aside] I would I were from hence.
    CORN. Do you hear, sir? I'll give you [100
a saying which my grandmother was wont,
when she heard the bell toll, to sing o'er unto
her lute.
    FLAM. Do, an you will; do.
            CORNELIA *doth this in several forms*
                of distraction.
    CORN.

Call for the robin redbreast and the wren,
    Since o'er shady groves they hover,
    And with leaves and flow'rs do cover
The friendless bodies of unburied men.
    Call unto his funeral dole
    The ant, the fieldmouse, and the mole,   110
To rear him hillocks that shall keep him warm,
And (when gay tombs are robb'd) sustain no harm;
But keep the wolf far thence, that's foe to men;
For with his nails he'll dig them up again.

They would not bury him 'cause he died
    in a quarrel;
But I have an answer for them:
" Let holy Church receive him duly,
Since he paid the church-tithes truly."
His wealth is summ'd; and this is all his
    store:
This poor men get; and great men get no
    more.   120
Now the wares are gone, we may shut up
    shop.
    [105] Pansies.

Bless you all, good people.
            Exeunt CORNELIA, [ZANCHE,] *and*
                Ladies.
    FLAM. I have a strange thing in me, to th'
        which
I cannot give a name, without it be
Compassion. I pray, leave me.
                        Exit FRANCISCO.
This night I'll know the utmost of my
    fate;
I'll be resolv'd what my rich sister means
T' assign me for my service. I have liv'd
Riotously ill, like some that live in court;
And sometimes, when my face was full of
    smiles,   130
Have felt the maze [106] of conscience in my
    breast.
Oft gay and honor'd robes those tortures
    try; [107]
We think cag'd birds sing, when indeed they
    cry.

Enter BRACHIANO's Ghost, *in his leather cassock
    and breeches, boots* [and] *a cowl;* [in his
    hand] *a pot of lily flowers, with a skull in 't.*

Ha! I can stand [108] thee; nearer, nearer yet!
What a mockery hath death made of thee!
    thou look'st sad.
In what place art thou? in yon starry gal-
    lery?
Or in the cursed dungeon? — No? not speak?
Pray, sir, resolve me what religion's best
For a man to die in? Or is it in your knowl-
    edge
To answer me how long I have to live?   140
That's the most necessary question.
Not answer? are you still like some great
    men
That only walk like shadows up and down,
And to no purpose? say: —
            The Ghost *throws earth upon him, and
                shows him the skull.*
What's that? Oh, fatal! he throws earth
    upon me!
A dead man's skull beneath the roots of
    flowers! —
I pray, speak, sir; our Italian churchmen
Make us believe dead men hold conference
With their familiars, and many times
Will come to bed to them, and eat with them.
                        Exit Ghost.

[106] Stupefying effect.
[107] *I.e.*, people whose outward appearance indicates happiness often experience the torments of
conscience.
[108] Stand up to.

He's gone; and see, the skull and earth are
    vanish'd.   151
This is beyond melancholy.[109] I do dare my
    fate
To do its worst. Now to my sister's lodging,
And sum up all these horrors : the disgrace
The Prince threw on me ; next, the piteous
    sight
Of my dead brother ; and my mother's
    dotage ;
And last, this terrible vision — all these
Shall with Vittoria's bounty turn to good,
Or I will drown this weapon in her blood.
                                        Exit.

[SCENE V] [110]

Enter FRANCISCO, LODOVICO, *and* HORTENSIO
    [*following them*].

    LOD. My Lord, upon my soul, you shall no
        further ;
You have most ridiculously engag'd yourself
Too far already. For my part, I have paid
All my debts ; so, if I should chance to fall,
My creditors fall not with me ; and I vow
To quit [111] all in this bold assembly
To the meanest follower. My Lord, leave the
    city ;
Or I 'll forswear the murder.
    FRAN.   Farewell, Lodovico !
If thou dost perish in this glorious act,
I 'll rear unto thy memory that fame   10
Shall in the ashes keep alive thy name.
            [*Exeunt* FRANCISCO *and* LODOVICO.]
    HORT. There's some black deed on foot.
        I 'll presently [112]
Down to the citadel, and raise some force.
These strong court factions, that do brook no
    checks,
In the career [113] oft break the riders' necks.
                                    [*Exit.*]

[SCENE VI] [114]

Enter VITTORIA *with a book in her hand,* [*and*]
    ZANCHE ; FLAMINEO *following them.*

    FLAM. What, are you at your prayers?
        give o'er.
    VIT.   How, ruffian?
    FLAM. I come to you 'bout worldly busi-
        ness ;

Sit down, sit down ; — nay, stay, blowze,[115]
    you may hear it ;
The doors are fast enough.
    VIT.   Ha ! are you drunk?
    FLAM. Yes, yes, with wormwood-water ;
        you shall taste
Some of it presently.
    VIT.   What intends the [116] fury?
    FLAM. You are my Lord's executrix, and I
        claim
Reward for my long service.
    VIT.   For your service?
    FLAM. Come, therefore ; here is pen and
        ink ; set down
What you will give me.   *She writes.*
    VIT.   There !
    FLAM.   Ha ! have you done already? [10
'T is a most short conveyance.
    VIT.   I will read it :
" I give that portion to thee, and no other,
Which Cain groan'd under, having slain his
    brother."
    FLAM. A most courtly patent to beg by ! [117]
    VIT.   You are a villain.
    FLAM. Is 't come to this? The[y] say
        affrights cure agues.
Thou hast a devil in thee ; I will try
If I can scare him from thee. Nay, sit still.
My Lord hath left me yet two case [118] of
    jewels
Shall make me scorn your bounty ; you shall
    see them.   [*Exit.*]
    VIT. Sure, he 's distracted.
    ZAN.   Oh, he 's desperate ; [20
For your own safety give him gentle language.

He enters with two case [118] of pistols.

    FLAM. Look, these are better far at a dead
        lift [119]
Than all your jewel-house.
    VIT.   And yet, methinks,
These stones have no fair lustre, they are ill
    set.
    FLAM. I 'll turn the right side towards you :
        you shall see
How the[y] will sparkle.
    VIT.   Turn this horror from me !
What do you want? What would you have
    me do?
Is not all mine yours? Have I any children?
    FLAM. Pray thee, good woman, do not
        trouble me

---

[109] *I.e.*, this is not an illusion resulting from a
disproportionate amount of black bile.
[110] Unlocated.   [111] Requite.   [112] Immediately.
[113] See on IV, iii, 94.   [114] Vittoria's apartment.

[115] Wench.   [116] Lucas queries *thy.*
[117] Such licenses were often issued.
[118] Pairs.   [119] At a pinch.

With this vain worldly business; say your
　　prayers: 　　　　　　　　　　　　　　30
I made a vow to my deceased lord,
Neither yourself nor I should outlive him
The numbering of four hours.

VIT. 　　　　　　　　　　Did he enjoin it?

FLAM. He did; and 't was a deadly jeal-
　　ousy
Lest any should enjoy thee after him,
That urg'd him vow me to it. For [120] my
　　death,
I did propound it voluntarily, knowing,
If he could not be safe in his own court,
Being a great duke, what hope, then, for us?

VIT. This is your melancholy and despair.

FLAM. Away! Fool thou art to think that
　　politicians 　　　　　　　　　　　41
Do use to kill the effects of injuries,
And let the cause live. Shall we groan in
　　irons,
Or be a shameful and a weighty burden
To a public scaffold? This is my resolve —
I would not live at any man's entreaty,
Nor die at any's bidding.

VIT. 　　　　　　　　Will you hear me?

FLAM. My life hath done service to other
　　men;
My death shall serve mine own turn. Make
　　you ready.

VIT. Do you mean to die indeed?

FLAM. 　　　　With as much pleasure [50
As e'er my father gat me.

VIT. [*aside to* ZANCHE] 　　Are the doors
　　lock'd?

ZAN. [*aside*] Yes, madam.

VIT. Are you grown an atheist? will you
　　turn your body,
Which is the goodly palace of the soul,
To the soul's slaughterhouse? Oh, the cursed
　　Devil,
Which doth present us with all other sins
Thrice-candied o'er — despair with gall and
　　stibium,[121]
Yet we carouse it off [122] — [*aside to* ZANCHE]
　　Cry out for help! —
Makes us forsake that which was made for
　　man,
The world, to sink to that was made for
　　devils, 　　　　　　　　　　　　60
Eternal darkness!

ZAN. 　　　　Help, help!

FLAM. 　　　　　　　I'll stop your throat
With winter plums.

VIT. 　　　　　I prithee, yet remember,
Millions are now in graves, which at last day,
Like mandrakes, shall rise shrieking.[123]

FLAM. 　　　　　Leave your prating,
For these are but grammatical [124] laments,
Feminine arguments; and they move me,
As some in pulpits move their auditory,
More with their exclamation than sense
Of reason or sound doctrine.

ZAN. [*aside to* VITTORIA] 　Gentle madam,
Seem to consent, only persuade him teach [70
The way to death; let him die first.

VIT. [*aside to* ZANCHE] 　　　'T is good.
I apprehend it. —
To kill one's self is meat that we must take
Like pills, not chew 't, but quickly swallow it;
The smart a' th' wound, or weakness of the
　　hand,
May else bring treble torments.

FLAM. 　　　　　I have held it
A wretched and most miserable life
Which is not able to die.

VIT. 　　　　　Oh, but frailty!
Yet I am now resolv'd. Farewell, affliction!
Behold, Brachiano, I, that while you liv'd [80
Did make a flaming altar of my heart
To sacrifice unto you, now am ready
To sacrifice heart and all. — Farewell, Zanche!

ZAN. How, madam! do you think that I'll
　　outlive you;
Especially when my best self, Flamineo,
Goes the same voyage?

FLAM. 　　　　　Oh, most loved Moor!

ZAN. Only by all my love let me entreat
　　you,
Since it is most necessary none [125] of us
Do violence on ourselves, let you or I
Be her sad taster; [126] teach her how to die. [90

FLAM. Thou dost instruct me nobly; take
　　these pistols.
Because my hand is stain'd with blood al-
　　ready,
Two of these you shall level at my breast,

---

[120] As for.

[121] Antimony.

[122] But presents despair (which leads to suicide),
not sugared over, but bitterly; and yet we drink
that potion.

[123] A widespread superstition; the mandrake,
which like several other vegetables sometimes grows
with a forked root somewhat resembling the human
form, was supposed to shriek upon being eradicated.

[124] Rhetorical.

[125] Q2–4, *one*, which mod. eds. adopt, misunderstanding ll. 93, 94. Vittoria and Zanche are to take,
each, a pair of the pistols. One of each pair is
to be aimed at Flamineo; the "other" (*i.e.*, others)
are to be aimed by the women at each other,
Zanche's against Vittoria, Vittoria's against Zanche.
Thus *none* of them does violence to himself.

[126] Continuing the figure of ll. 73, 74.

Th' other 'gainst your own, and so we 'll die
Most equally contented ; but first swear
Not to outlive me.

VIT. AND ZAN.   Most religiously.

FLAM. Then here 's an end of me ; farewell,
    daylight !

And, O contemptible physic, that dost take
So long a study only to preserve
So short a life, I take my leave of thee ! —   100
(*showing the pistols*) These are two cupping-
    glasses [127] that shall draw
All my infected blood out. Are you ready?

BOTH. Ready.

FLAM. Whither shall I go now? O Lu-
cian, thy ridiculous purgatory ! [128] to find
Alexander the Great cobbling shoes, Pompey
tagging points,[129] and Julius Cæsar making
hair-buttons ! Hannibal selling blacking, and
Augustus crying garlic ! Charlemagne sell-
ing lists [130] by the dozen, and King Pepin [110
crying apples in a cart drawn with one horse !
Whether I resolve [131] to fire, earth, water, air,
Or all the elements by scruples, I know not,
Nor greatly care. — Shoot, shoot ;
Of all deaths the violent death is best ;
For from ourselves it steals ourselves so
    fast,
The pain, once apprehended, is quite past.
                   They shoot.

VIT. What, are you dropp'd?

FLAM. I am mix'd with earth already; as
    you are noble,   119
Perform your vows, and bravely follow me.

VIT. Whither? to hell?
    [*They*] *run to him and tread upon him.*

ZAN.   To most assured damnation?

VIT. O thou most cursed devil !

ZAN.   Thou art caught —

VIT. In thine own engine. I tread the fire
    out
That would have been my ruin.

FLAM. Will you be perjur'd? what a
religious oath was Styx, that the gods never
durst swear by, and violate ! Oh, that we had
such an oath to minister, and to be so well kept
in our courts of justice !   129

VIT. Think whither thou art going.

ZAN.   And remember
What villainies thou hast acted.

VIT.   This thy death

Shall make me,[132] like a blazing, ominous star,
Look up and tremble.

FLAM.   Oh, I am caught with a springe ! [133]

VIT. You see the fox comes many times
    short home ;
'T is here prov'd true.

FLAM.   Kill'd with a couple of
    braches ! [134]

VIT. No fitter off'ring for the infernal
    Furies
Than one in whom they reign'd while he was
    living !

FLAM. Oh, the way 's dark and horrid ! I
    cannot see ;
Shall I have no company?

VIT.   Oh, yes, thy sins
Do run before thee to fetch fire from hell, [140
To light thee thither.

FLAM.   Oh, I smell soot,
Most s[t]inking soot ! the chimney is [135] afire :
My liver 's p[a]rboil'd, like Scotch holly-
    bread ; [136]
There 's a plumber laying pipes in my guts ; it
    scalds. —
Wilt thou outlive me?

ZAN.   Yes, and drive a stake
Through [137] thy body ; [138] for we 'll give it out
Thou didst this violence upon thyself.

FLAM. O cunning devils ! now I have tri'd
    your love,
And doubled all your reaches.[139] — I am not
    wounded ;   FLAMINEO *riseth.*
The pistols held no bullets : 't was a plot [150
To prove [140] your kindness to me ; and I live,
To punish your ingratitude. I knew,
One time or other, you would find a way
To give me a strong potion. — O men
That lie upon your deathbeds, and are haunted
With howling wives, ne'er trust them !
    they 'll remarry
Ere the worm pierce your winding sheet, ere
    the spider
Make a thin curtain for your epitaphs. —
How cunning you were to discharge ! do you
practise at the Artillery Yard ? [141] — Trust [160
a woman? never, never ! Brachiano be my
precedent. We lay our souls to pawn to the
Devil for a little pleasure, and a woman makes

---

[127] Vacuum cups for bleeding.
[128] In his dialogue, "Menippos."
[129] Putting the metal points on the laces that
served the Elizabethans for buttons.
[130] Strips of cloth.
[131] Dissolve.

[132] Lucas suggests *men.*
[133] Snare.   [134] By . . . bitches.   [135] Q *chimneis.*
[136] Sampson cites Cotgrave's Dictionary : "*Pain
benist d'Escosse*, a sodden sheep's liver." Holy
Bread, notes Lucas, ordinarily meant the bread
blessed and distributed after the Eucharist.
[137] Dissyllabic.   [138] As a suicide's.
[139] Eluded all your devices.   [140] Test.
[141] Near Bishopsgate Street Without.

the bill of sale. That ever man should marry!
For one Hypermnestra that saved her lord
and husband, forty-nine of her sisters cut their
husbands' throats all in one night;[142] there
was a shoal of virtuous horse-leeches![143] —
[*showing pistols*] Here are two other instru-
    ments.

VIT. Help, help!   170

Enter LODOVICO [*and*] GASPARO [*disguised as*]
    Carlo [*and*] Pedro.

FLAM. What noise is that? Ha! false
    keys i' th' court!

LOD. We have brought you a masque.[144]

FLAM.   A matachin,[145] it seems
By your drawn swords. Churchmen turn'd
    revellers!

[GAS.][146] Isabella! Isabella!

LOD. Do you know us now?

FLAM.   Lodovico and Gasparo!

LOD. Yes; and that Moor the Duke gave
    pension to
Was the great Duke of Florence.

VIT.   Oh, we are lost!

FLAM. You shall not take justice from
    forth my hands.
Oh, let me kill her! — I 'll cut my safety
Through your coats of steel. Fate's a spaniel;
We cannot beat it from us. What remains
    now?   181
Let all that do ill, take this precedent:
Man may his fate foresee, but not prevent;
And, of all axioms, this shall win the prize:
'T is better to be fortunate than wise.

GAS. Bind him to the pillar.[147]

VIT.   Oh, your gentle pity!
I have seen a blackbird that would sooner
    fly
To a man's bosom than to stay the gripe
Of the fierce sparrowhawk.

GAS.   Your hope deceives you.

VIT. If Florence be i' th' court, would he
    would kill me!   190

GAS. Fool! Princes give rewards with
    their own hands,
But death or punishment by the hands of
    others.

---

[142] In the Greek myth of the Danaides.
[143] *I.e.*, lovers of blood.
[144] Which was marked by the appearance of masked strangers.
[145] A sword-dance performed in fantastic costume.
[146] So Qq3,4; Qq1,2, *Con;* perhaps for *Car.*, perhaps for *Conspirators.*
[147] Doubtless one of the columns that supported the "Heavens."

LOD. Sirrah, you once did strike me; I 'll
    strike you
Into the centre.

FLAM.   Thou 'lt do it like a hangman,[148]
A base hangman, not like a noble fellow;
For thou seest I cannot strike again.

LOD.   Dost laugh?

FLAM. Wouldst have me die, as I was born,
    in whining?

GAS. Recommend yourself to Heaven.

FLAM.   No, I will carry
Mine own commendations thither.   199

LOD. Oh, could I kill you forty times a day,
And use 't four year together, 't were too little!
Naught grieves but that you are too few to
    feed
The famine of our vengeance. What dost
    think on?

FLAM. Nothing; of nothing; leave thy
    idle questions.
I am i' th' way to study a long silence;
To prate were idle. I remember nothing.
There 's nothing of so infinite vexation
As man's own thoughts.

LOD.   O thou glorious strumpet!
Could I divide thy breath from this pure air,
When 't leaves thy body, I would suck it up,
And breathe 't upon some dunghill.

VIT.   You my deathsman! [211
Methinks thou doest not look horrid enough;
Thou hast too good a face to be a hangman.
If thou be, do thy office in right form;
Fall down upon thy knees, and ask forgiveness.

LOD. Oh, thou hast been a most prodigious
    comet;
But I 'll cut off your train.[149] — Kill the Moor
    first.

VIT. You shall not kill her first; behold my
    breast:
I will be waited on in death; my servant
Shall never go before me.   220

GAS. Are you so brave?

VIT.   Yes, I shall welcome death
As princes do some great ambassadors;
I 'll meet thy weapon half way.

LOD.   Thou dost tremble.
Methinks fear should dissolve thee into air.

VIT. Oh, thou art deceiv'd, I am too true a
    woman:
Conceit[150] can never kill me. I 'll tell thee
    what:

---

[148] Professional executioner.
[149] Punning on "train" = (1) tail of a comet; (2) retinue.
[150] Punning on "conceit" = (1) vanity; (2) imagination.

I will not in my death shed one base tear;
Or, if look pale, for want of blood, not fear.
[Gives.] [151] Thou art my task, black Fury.

ZAN.   I have blood
As red as either of theirs; wilt drink some?
'T is good for the falling sickness.[152]   I am
    proud   231
Death cannot alter my complexion,
For I shall ne'er look pale.

LOD.   Strike, strike,
With a joint motion!

                [*They strike.* ZANCHE *dies.*]
VIT.   'T was a manly blow!
The next thou giv'st, murder some sucking
    infant;
And then thou wilt be famous.

FLAM.   Oh, what blade is 't?
A Toledo, or an English fox? [153]
I ever thought a cutler should distinguish
The cause of my death, rather than a doctor.
Search my wound deeper; tent [154] it with the
    steel   240
That made it.

VIT.   Oh, my greatest sin lay in my
    blood; [155]
Now my blood pays for 't.

FLAM.   Th' art a noble sister!
I love thee now; if woman do breed man,
She ought to teach him manhood.   Fare thee
    well.
Know many glorious women that are fam'd
For masculine virtue have been vicious;
Only a happier silence did betide them: [156]
She hath no faults who hath the art to hide
    them.

VIT. My soul, like to a ship in a black
    storm,   249
Is driven I know not whither.

FLAM.   Then cast anchor.
Prosperity doth bewitch men, seeming clear;
But seas do laugh, show white, when rocks are
    near.
We cease to grieve, cease to be fortune's slaves,
Nay, cease to die, by dying. — Art thou [157]
    gone?
And thou [158] so near the bottom? — False re-
    port,

Which says that women vie with the nine
    Muses
For nine tough durable lives!   I do not
    look
Who went before, nor who shall follow me;
No, at myself I will begin and end.
While we look up to Heaven, we confound
Knowledge with knowledge.   Oh, I am in a
    mist!   261

VIT. Oh, happy they that never saw the
    court,
Nor ever knew great men but by report.
                              VITTORIA *dies.*

FLAM. I recover like a spent taper, for a
    flash,
And instantly go out.
Let all that belong to great men remember
th' old wives' tradition, to be like the lions
i' th' Tower on Candlemas Day [159]: to mourn
if the sun shine, for fear of the pitiful remainder
of winter to come.   270
'T is well yet there 's some goodness in my
    death;
My life was a black charnel.   I have caught
An everlasting cold; I have lost my voice
Most irrecoverably. — Farewell, glorious vil-
    lains!
This busy trade of life appears most vain,
Since rest breeds rest, where [160] all seek pain
    by pain.
Let no harsh flattering bells resound my
    knell;
Strike, thunder, and strike loud, to my fare-
    well!   *Dies.*

ENG. AM. [*within*] This way, this way!
    break ope the doors! this way!

LOD. Ha! are we betray'd?   280
Why, then let 's constantly die all together,
And, having finish'd this most noble deed,
Defy the worst of fate, not fear to bleed.

Enter AMBASSAD[ORS], GIOVANNI, [*and* Officers].

ENG. [AM.] Keep back the Prince: shoot,
    shoot.

LOD.   Oh, I am wounded!
I fear I shall be ta'en.

GIO.   You bloody villains,
By what authority have you committed
This massacre?

LOD.   By thine.

GIO.   Mine?

LOD.   Yes; thy uncle
Which is a part of thee, enjoin'd us to 't.

---

[151] Old eds. *Car.*
[152] Epilepsy. According to Pliny the blood was
not to be drunk, but smeared on the patient's face.
[153] Sword.
[154] Probe.
[155] Sensual nature.
[156] Let the reader remember it, too. This is
Webster's summing up.
[157] Zanche.
[158] Vittoria.

[159] February 2. Cf. St. Swithin's Day and the
ground hog.   [160] Whereas.

Thou know'st me, I am sure : I am Count
    Lodowick ;
And thy most noble uncle, in disguise,   290
Was last night in thy court.
    GIO.   Ha !
    [GASP.] [161]   Yes, that Moor
Thy father chose his pensioner.
    GIO.   He turn'd murderer ! —
Away with them to prison and to torture ;
All that have hands in this shall taste our jus-
    tice,
As I hope Heaven.
    LOD.   I do glory yet
That I can call this act mine own. For my
    part,
The rack, the gallows, and the torturing wheel

Shall be but sound sleeps to me ; here 's my
    rest :
I limn'd this night-piece, and it was my best.
    GIO. Remove the bodies. — See, my hon-
    ored Lord,   300
What use you ought make of their punish-
    ment.
Let guilty men remember their black deeds
Do lean on crutches made of slender reeds.
                    [*Exeunt.*]

———

Instead of an epilogue only this of Martial
supplies me :

    Haec fuerint nobis praemia, si placui.[162]

    For the action of the play, 't was generally well,[163] and I dare affirm, with the joint testimony of some of their own quality,[164] for the true imitation of life (without striving to make Nature a monster) the best that ever became them ; whereof, as I make a general acknowledgment, so in particular I must remember the well-approved industry of my friend Master Perkins,[165] and confess the worth of his action did crown both the beginning and end.

[161] So Qq 3, 4 ; Qq 1, 2, *Car.*
[162] These things will be our reward, if I have pleased you. (Martial, II, 91.)

[163] Good.   [164] Profession.
[165] Richard Perkins, a leading actor, at this time with the Queen's Men.

A
Tricke to Catch the
Old-one.

As it hath beene often in Action, both
at Paules, and the Black-
Fryers.

Presented before his Maieſtie on
New-yeares night laſt.

Compoſde by T.M.

AT LONDON.
Printed by G: E. and are to be ſold by *Henry Rockytt*,
at the long ſhop in the Poultrie vnder
the Dyall. 1608.

INTRODUCTORY NOTE

LIKE *The Wild-Goose Chase, A Trick to Catch the Old One* illustrates the trend of seventeenth-century comedy toward the school of Etherege and Congreve, and away from on the one hand the romantic narratives of Shakespeare, and on the other the moralistic satires of Jonson. Middleton's play is not so graceful nor so merry as Fletcher's, which moves in a world that after its own fashion is quite as unreal as the Forest of Arden. Money is taken for granted and causes no problem in *The Wild-Goose Chase;* in *A Trick to Catch the Old One* it is very much in the foreground. Fletcher is the aristocrat, concerned with such intangibles as charm and taste and, though comically enough, spiritual compatibility. Middleton frankly devotes his play to the principal interest of the bourgeois mind; and the love story of Witgood and Joyce is not brought very far forward. As story, however, this play is superior to Fletcher's. Manners are of course the prime concern, and taken as a whole Middleton's comedies give us our best picture of his London, or at any rate of its seamier side; but the narrative element forms a sturdy foundation for them, and, though Dampit is evidently written in for a special actor, the plot is admirably shaped.

The heroes of both plays are rakes who, after fifth-act repentances, are dismissed into the bonds of matrimony as if their future could be lived independently of their past. Witgood is actually less coldly heartless than Mirabel, but his past is more visibly before us in the rather appealing figure of the Courtesan. Yet Fletcher's rake, detestable as may be his treatment of Oriana, is after all only trying to exercise every man's right to choose for himself; his antagonist is Oriana, who anticipates the Shavian heroine in her aggressiveness; she wins the duel of sex, and Mirabel capitulates with an easy grace. Witgood's duel is no sham one; it is a fight for existence, and courtesy and sportsmanship have no place in it. The adversaries are not ladies of agreeable charm and duplicity, but rascally skinflints. So despicable are they that we lose our moral balance, as Middleton intends that we shall. We want Witgood to win; and in the sordid atmosphere, not of guilty love, but of financial intrigue, we enlist our sympathies on a very dubious side. It is because our sympathies are enlisted, as they are not in *The Wild-Goose Chase,* that *A Trick to Catch the Old One* seems on sober reflection so amoral. Wit and gaiety, and the subordination of the narrative, keep the former too artificial to raise the moral issue at all. Middleton's realism, even the very solidity of his play's structure, enforces us to abandon that comfortable neutrality in which the moral faculty is able to slumber undisturbed by the world's intrusion or the demands of life.

The exact dates of composition and production are uncertain. C. 1605 is only a conjecture. The play was probably written for the Boys of St. Paul's, and after their disappearance in 1606 or soon after was acted by the children's company at the Blackfriars. It was played at court on January 1, 1609. No source of the plot is known. The play was entered in the Stationers' Register on October 7, 1607. The first edition appeared, in quarto, probably early in 1609; it bears the date of 1608 (presumably, O. S.), but one of the two issues mentions the court performance. It was reprinted in 1616. The present text follows Q 1, with a few corrections from Q 2. The standard editions of Middleton's works are those of A. Dyce (1840), and A. H. Bullen (1885–1886).

A TRICK TO CATCH THE OLD ONE

BY

THOMAS MIDDLETON

[DRAMATIS PERSONAE

THEODORUS WITGOOD.
PECUNIUS LUCRE, his uncle.
WALKADINE HOARD.
ONESIPHORUS HOARD, his brother.
LIMBER,
KIX,[1]
LAMPREY,
SPICHCOCK, } friends to Hoard.
HARRY DAMPIT,
GULF, } usurers.
SAM FREEDOM, son to Mistress Lucre.
MONEYLOVE.
Host.

SIR LAUNCELOT.
GEORGE, servant to Lucre.
ARTHUR, servant to Walkadine Hoard.

Creditors, Gentlemen, Drawer, Boy,
Scrivener, Vintner, Servants, Sergeants,
&c.

JANE, a Courtesan.
MISTRESS LUCRE.
JOYCE, niece to Walkadine Hoard.
LADY FOXSTONE.
AUDREY, servant to Dampit.

THE SCENE — *A country town; then London.*]

[ACT I — SCENE I][2]

Enter WITGOOD, *a gentleman, solus.*

WIT. All's gone! still thou 'rt a gentleman,
that's all; but a poor one, that's nothing.
What milk brings thy meadows forth now?
Where are thy goodly uplands, and thy down-
lands? All sunk into that little pit, lechery!
Why should a gallant pay but two shillings for
his ordinary[3] that nourishes him, and twenty
times two for his brothel[4] that consumes him?
But where's Longacre?[5] In my uncle's conscience, which is three years' voyage about [10
— he that sets out upon his conscience ne'er
finds the way home again — he is either
swallowed in the quicksands of law-quillets,[6]
or splits upon the piles of a *praemunire;*[7] yet
these old fox-brain'd and ox-brow'd[8] uncles
have still[9] defences for their avarice, and

apologies for their practices, and will thus
greet our follies:
" He that doth his youth expose
     To brothel, drink, and danger,   20
Let him that is his nearest kin
     Cheat him before a stranger."
And that's his uncle: 't is a principle in usury.
I dare not visit the city: there I should be too
soon visited by that horrible plague, my debts;
and by that means I lose a virgin's love, her
portion, and her virtues. Well, how should a
man live now that has no living, hum? —
Why, are there not a million of men in the
world that only sojourn upon their brain, [30
and make their wits their mercers;[10] and am
I but one amongst that million, and cannot
thrive upon 't? Any trick, out of the compass[11] of law, now, would come happily to me.

Enter Courtesan.

COUR. My love!
WIT. My loathing! hast thou been the secret consumption of my purse, and now com'st

---

[1] Kex, dried-up stalk.
[2] A public place in a country town.
[3] Meal at a public dining-place.
[4] Prostitute.
[5] Used generally of any estate.
[6] Legal technicalities.
[7] A form of writ; *i.e.*, a legal obstacle.
[8] Cuckoldy.   [9] Always.

[10] *I.e.*, let their wits deal for them, rely on their
wits.
[11] Out of the reach of, and so not punishable

983

to undo my last means, my wits? Wilt leave
no virtue in me, and yet thou ne'er the
better? 40
Hence, courtesan, round-webb'd tarantula,
That dryest the roses in the cheeks of
youth!

Cour. I have been true unto your pleasure;
and all your lands
Thrice rack'd [12] was never worth the jewel
which
I prodigally gave you, my virginity.
Lands mortgag'd may return, and more es-
teem'd;
But honesty [13] once pawn'd is ne'er redeem'd.

Wit. Forgive; I do thee wrong
To make thee sin, and then to chide thee
for 't.

Cour. I know I am your loathing now;
farewell. 50

Wit. Stay, best invention, [14] stay.

Cour. I that have been the secret consumption of your purse, shall I stay now to
undo your last means, your wits? Hence,
courtesan, away!

Wit. I prithee, make me not mad at my
own weapon; stay (a thing [15] few women can
do, I know that, and therefore they had need
wear stays); be not contrary. Dost love me?
Fate has so cast [16] it that all my means [60
I must derive from thee.

Cour. From me? Be happy then;
What lies within the power of my performance
Shall be commanded of thee.

Wit. Spoke like
An honest drab, i' faith. It may prove some-
thing;
What trick is not an embryon at first,
Until a perfect shape come over it?

Cour. Come,
I must help you. Whereabouts left you? I 'll
proceed:
Though you beget, 't is I must help to breed.
Speak, what is 't? I 'd fain conceive it. 70

Wit. So, so, so; thou shalt presently take
the name and form upon thee of a rich country
widow, four hundred a year valiant, [17] in woods,
in bullocks, in barns, and in rye-stacks. We 'll
to London, and to my covetous uncle.

Cour. I begin to applaud thee; our states
being both desperate, they are soon resolute.
But how for horses?

Wit. Mass, that 's true; the jest will be
of some continuance. Let me see; horses [80
now, a bots [18] on 'em! Stay, I have acquaintance with a mad host, never yet bawd [19] to
thee. I have rins'd the whoreson's gums in
mull-sack [20] many a time and often. Put but
a good tale into his ear now, so it come off
cleanly, and there 's horse and man for us, I
dare warrant thee.

Cour. Arm your wits then
Speedily; there shall want nothing in me,
Either in behavior, discourse, or fashion, 90
That shall discredit your intended purpose.
I will so artfully disguise my wants,
And set so good a courage on my state, [21]
That I will be believed.

Wit. Why, then, all 's furnish'd. I shall
go nigh to catch that old fox, mine uncle.
Though he make but some amends for my undoing, [22] yet there 's some comfort in 't, he cannot otherwise choose (though it be but in hope
to cozen [23] me again) but supply any [100
hasty want that I bring to town with me. The
device well and cunningly carried, the name
of a rich widow, and four hundred a year in
good earth, will so conjure up a kind of usurer's
love in him to me, that he will not only desire
my presence — which at first shall scarce be
granted him; I 'll keep off a' purpose, — but
I shall find him so officious to deserve, so
ready to supply! I know the state of an old
man's affection so well: if his nephew be [110
poor indeed, why, he let's God alone with
him [24]; but if he be once rich, then he 'll be
the first man that helps him.

Cour. 'T is right the world; [25] for, in these
days, an old man's love to his kindred is like
his kindness to his wife: 't is always done
before he comes at it.

Wit. I owe thee for that jest. Begone.
Here 's all my wealth; prepare thyself, away!
I 'll to mine host with all possible [120
haste; and with the best art, and most profitable form, pour the sweet circumstance into
his ear, which shall have the gift to turn all
the wax to honey. [*Exit* Courtesan.] — How
no[w]? Oh, the right worshipful signiors of
our country!

[12] Strained to produce as much cash as possible.
[13] Chastity. [14] Plan, device.
[15] *I.e.*, to be staid or steadfast.
[16] Planned. [17] Worth.

[18] A disease of worms; *i.e.*, plague take them.
[19] *I.e.*, he does not know you. Innkeepers were
apt to be procurers.
[20] Sack heated, sweetened, and spiced.
[21] Assume so bold an attitude concerning the
value of my estate.
[22] For ruining me. [23] Cheat.
[24] Leaves it to God to look after him.
[25] Precisely the way of the world.

[*Enter* ONESIPHORUS HOARD, LIMBER, *and* KIX.] [26]

O. HOA. Who's that?

LIM. Oh, the common rioter; [27] take no note of him.

WIT. [*aside*] You will not see me now; the comfort is,

Ere it be long you will scarce see yourselves.   [*Exit.*]   130

O. HOA. I wonder how he breathes; h' as consum'd all

Upon that courtesan.

LIM.   We have heard so much.

O. HOA. You have heard all truth. His uncle and my brother

Have been these three years mortal adversaries:

Two old tough spirits; they seldom meet but fight,

Or quarrel when 't is calmest. I think their anger

Be the very fire that keeps their age alive.

LIM. What was the quarrel, sir?

O. HOA. Faith, about a purchase,[28] fetch-
ing over [29] a young heir. Master Hoard, [140 my brother, having wasted much time in beating the bargain, what did me old Lucre, but as his conscience mov'd him, knowing the poor gentleman, stepp'd in between 'em and cozened him himself.

LIM. And was this all, sir?

O. HOA. This was e'en it, sir; yet for all this, I know no reason but the match might go forward betwixt his wife's son and my niece; what though there be a dissension [150 between the two old men, I see no reason it should put a difference between the two younger; 't is as natural for old folks to fall out, as for young to fall in! A scholar comes a-wooing to my niece; well, he's wise, but he's poor: her son comes a-wooing to my niece; well, he's a fool, but he's rich—

LIM. Ay, marry, sir?

O. HOA. Pray, now, is not a rich fool better than a poor philosopher?   160

LIM. One would think so, i' faith!

O. HOA. She now remains at London with my brother, her second uncle, to learn fashions, practise music; the voice between her lips, and the viol between her legs — she'll be fit

for a consort [30] very speedily. A thousand good pound is her portion; if she marry, we'll ride up and be merry.

KIX. A match, if it be a match!   *Exeunt.*

[SCENE II] [31]

Enter at one door, WITGOOD; *at the other,* Host.

WIT. Mine host!

HOST. Young Master Witgood.

WIT. I have been laying [32] all the town for thee.

HOST. Why, what's the news, bully Had-
land?

WIT. What geldings are in the house, of thine own? Answer me to that first.

HOST. Why, man, why?

WIT. Mark me what I say: I'll tell thee [10 such a tale in thine ear that thou shalt trust me spite of thy teeth, furnish me with some money willy-nilly, and ride up with me thyself *contra voluntatem et professionem.*

HOST. How? Let me see this trick, and I'll say thou hast more art than a conjuror.

WIT. Dost thou joy in my advancement?

HOST. Do I love sack and ginger?

WIT. Comes my prosperity desiredly to thee?   [20

HOST. Come forfeitures to a usurer, fees to an officer, punks [33] to an host, and pigs to a parson desiredly? Why, then, la.

WIT. Will the report of a widow of four hundred a year, boy, make thee leap, and sing, and dance, and come to thy place again?

HOST. Wilt thou command me now? I am thy spirit; conjure me into any shape.

WIT. I ha' brought her from her friends, turn'd back the horses by a sleight; [34] not [30 so much as one amongst her six men, goodly large yeomanly fellows, will she trust with this her purpose: by this light, all unmann'd,[35] regardless of her state, neglectful of vainglorious ceremony, all for my love. Oh 't is a fine little voluble tongue, mine host, that wins a widow!

HOST. No, 't is a tongue with a great [36] T, my boy, that wins a widow.

WIT. Now, sir, the case stands thus: [40 good mine host, if thou lov'st my happiness, assist me.

HOST. Command all my beasts i' th' house.

---

[26] Add. Dyce; om. Qq, which as speech-tags for these characters have *1, 2, 3.*
[27] Notorious profligate.
[28] The acquisition of a piece of property.
[29] Getting the better of.

[30] Punning on "consort" = (1) band of musicians; (2) spouse.
[31] Unlocated; probably the same as Sc. i.
[32] Scouring, searching.   [33] Prostitutes.
[34] Trick.   [35] Unescorted.   [36] Capital.

WIT. Nay, that 's not all neither ; prithee take truce with thy joy, and listen to me. Thou know'st I have a wealthy uncle i' th' city, somewhat the wealthier by [37] my follies. The report of this fortune, well and cunningly carried, might be a means to draw some goodness from the usuring rascal ; for I have [50 put her in hope already of some estate that I have either in land or money. Now, if I be found true in neither, what may I expect but a sudden breach of our love, utter dissolution of the match, and confusion of my fortunes for ever?

HOST. Wilt thou but trust the managing of thy business with me?

WIT. With thee? Why, will I desire to thrive in my purpose? Will I hug four [60 hundred a year, I that know the misery of nothing? Will that man wish a rich widow, that has ne'er a hole to put his head in? With thee, mine host? Why, believe it, sooner with thee than with a covey of counsellors.

HOST. Thank you for your good report, i' faith, sir ; and if I stand you not in stead, why then let an host come off *hic et haec hostis*, a deadly enemy to dice, drink, and venery. Come, where 's this widow? 70

WIT. Hard at Park End.

HOST. I 'll be her servingman for once.

WIT. Why, there we let off together, keep full time ; my thoughts were striking then just the same number.

HOST. I knew 't ; shall we then see our merry days again?

WIT. Our merry nights — [*aside*] which ne'er shall be more seen. *Exeunt.*

[SCENE III] [38]

Enter at several [39] *doors, old* LUCRE *and old* [WALKADINE] HOARD ; [LAMPREY, SPICH-COCK, FREEDOM, *and* MONEYLOVE] *coming between them to pacify 'em.*

LAM. Nay, good Master Lucre, and you, Master Hoard, anger is the wind which you're both too much troubled withal.

HOA. Shall my adversary thus daily affront [40] me, ripping up the old wound of our malice, which three summers could not close up? into which wound the very sight of him drops scalding lead instead of balsamum?

LUC. Why, Hoard, Hoard, Hoard, Hoard, Hoard ! may I not pass in the state of quiet- [10 ness to mine own house? Answer me to that, before witness, and why? I 'll refer the cause to honest, even-minded gentlemen, or require the mere indifferences [41] of the law to decide this matter. I got the purchase, [42] true ; was 't not any man's case? Yes. Will a wise man stand as a bawd, whilst another wipes his nose [43] of the bargain? No ; I answer no in that case.

LAM. Nay, sweet Master Lucre. 20

HOA. Was it the part of a friend — no, rather of a Jew — mark what I say, — when I had beaten the bush to the last bird, or, as I may term it, the price to a pound, then, like a cunning usurer, to come in the evening of the bargain, and glean all my hopes in a minute? to enter, as it were, at the back door of the purchase? for thou ne'er cam'st the right way by it.

LUC. Hast thou the conscience to tell me [30 so without any impeachment to thyself?

HOA. Thou that canst defeat [44] thy own nephew, Lucre, lap his lands into bonds, and take the extremity of thy kindred's forfeitures, because he 's a rioter, a wastethrift, a brothelmaster, [45] and so forth — what may a stranger expect from thee but *vulnera dilacerata*, as the poet says, dilacerate dealing?

LUC. Upbraid'st thou me with nephew? Is all imputation laid upon me? What [40 acquaintance have I with his follies? If he riot, [46] 't is he must want it ; if he surfeit, 't is he must feel it ; if he drab it, 't is he must lie by 't. What 's this to me?

HOA. What 's all to thee? Nothing, nothing ; such is the gulf of thy desire and the wolf of thy conscience : but be assured, old Pecunius Lucre, if ever fortune so bless me that I may be at leisure to vex thee, or any means so favor me that I may have oppor- [50 tunity to mad thee, I will pursue it with that flame of hate, spirit of malice, unrepressed wrath, that I will blast thy comforts.

LUC. Ha, ha, ha !

LAM. Nay, Master Hoard, you 're a wise gentleman ——

HOA. I will so cross thee ——

LUC. And I thee.

HOA. So without mercy fret thee ——

LUC. So monstrously oppose thee —— 60

---

[37] As a consequence of.
[38] London. A public place.
[39] Different.
[40] Confront.

[41] Impartiality.
[43] Cheats him.
[45] Whoremaster.
[42] Plunder, loot.
[44] Ruin.
[46] Waste his substance.

HOA. Dost scoff at my just anger? Oh, that I had as much power as usury has over thee!

LUC. Then thou wouldst have as much power as the Devil has over thee.

HOA. Toad!

LUC. Aspic![47]

HOA. Serpent!

LUC. Viper!

SPI. Nay, gentlemen, then we must [70 divide you perforce.

LAM. When the fire grows too unreasonable hot, there's no better way than to take off the wood.

> *Exeunt* [LAMPREY *and* SPICHCOCK, *drawing off* LUCRE *and* HOARD *different ways*].

FREE. A word, good signior.

MON. How now, what's the news?

FREE. 'T is given me to understand that you are a rival of mine in the love of Mistress Joyce, Master Hoard's niece: say me ay, say me no.   80

MON. Yes, 't is so.

FREE. Then look to yourself: you cannot live long. I'm practising every morning; a month hence I'll challenge you.

MON. Give me your hand upon 't; there's my pledge I'll meet you. *Strikes him. Exit.*

FREE. Oh, oh!—What reason had you for that, sir, to strike before the month? You knew I was not ready for you, and that made you so crank.[48] I am not such a coward [90 to strike again, I warrant you. My ear has the law of her side, for it burns horribly. I will teach him to strike a naked face, the longest day of his life. 'Slid, it shall cost me some money but I'll bring this box into the chancery.   *Exit.*

[SCENE IV][49]

Enter WITGOOD *and the* Host.

HOST. Fear you nothing, sir; I have lodg'd her in a house of credit,[50] I warrant you.

WIT. Hast thou the writings?

HOST. Firm, sir.

WIT. Prithee, stay, and behold two the most prodigious rascals that ever slipp'd into the shape of men: Dampit, sirrah, and young Gulf, his fellow caterpillar.[51]

HOST. Dampit? Sure I have heard of that Dampit.   10

WIT. Heard of him! Why, man, he that has lost both his ears may hear of him: a famous infamous trampler of time[52]—his own phrase. Note him well: that Dampit, sirrah, he in the uneven beard and the serge cloak, is the most notorious, usuring, blasphemous, atheistical, brothel-vomiting rascal that we have in these latter times now extant; whose first beginning was the stealing of a masty[53] dog from a farmer's house.   20

HOST. He look'd as if he would obey the commandment well, when he began first with stealing.

WIT. True. The next town he came at, he set the dogs together by th' ears.

HOST. A sign he should follow the law, by my faith.

WIT. So it followed, indeed; and being destitute of all fortunes, stak'd his masty against a noble,[54] and by great fortune his dog had [30 the day.[55] How he made it up ten shillings, I know not, but his own boast is that he came to town with but ten shillings in his purse, and now is credibly worth ten thousand pound.

HOST. How the Devil came he by it?

[Enter DAMPIT *and* GULF.]

WIT. How the Devil came he not by it? If you put in the Devil once, riches come with a vengeance.[56] H'as been a trampler of the law, sir; and the Devil has a care of his footmen. [40 The rogue has spied me now; he nibbled me finely once, too.—A pox[57] search you!— Oh, Master Dampit!—the very loins of thee! —Cry you mercy, Master Gulf; you walk so low, I promise you I saw you not, sir!

GULF. He that walks low walks safe, the poets tell us.

WIT. [*aside*] And nigher hell by a foot and a half than the rest of his fellows.—But, my old Harry!   50

DAM. My sweet Theodorus!

WIT. 'T was a merry world when thou cam'st to town with ten shillings in thy purse.

DAM. And now worth ten thousand pound, my boy. Report it: Harry Dampit, a trampler of time, say, he would be up in a morning, and be here with his serge gown,

---

[47] Asp.
[48] Lively, cocky.
[49] Unlocated; probably the same as Sc. iii.
[50] Reputable house.
[51] Extortioner.

[52] *I.e.*, one who spends his life trudging about on (law) business. (Kittredge.)   [53] Mastiff.
[54] A gold coin worth 6 *s.* 8 *d.*   [55] Won.
[56] Hastily, violently, in force.   [57] Syphilis.

dash'd up to the hams in a cause ; have his feet stink about Westminster Hall,[58] and come home again ; see the galleons, the galleasses,[59] the great armadas of the law ; then there [61 be hoys [60] and petty vessels, oars and scullers [61] of the time ; there be picklocks of the time too. Then would I be here ; I would trample up and down like a mule : now to the judges, " May it please your reverend-honorable Fatherhoods ; " then to my counsellor, " May it please your worshipful Patience ; " then to the examiner's office, " May it please your Mastership's gentleness ; " then to one of [70 the clerks, " May it please your worshipful Lousiness," — for I find him scrubbing in his codpiece ; [62] then to the Hall again, then to the chamber again —

WIT. And when to the cellar again ?

DAM. E'en when thou wilt again ! Tramplers of time, motions of Fleet Street,[63] and visions of Holborn ; [64] here I have fees of one, there I have fees of another ; my clients come about me, the fooliaminy [65] and coxcombry [66] of the country : I still trash'd [67] and [81 trotted for other men's causes. Thus was poor Harry Dampit made rich by others' laziness, who though they would not follow their own suits, I made 'em follow me with their purses.

WIT. Didst thou so, old Harry ?

DAM. Ay, and I sous'd [68] 'em with bills of charges, i 'faith ; twenty pound a year have I brought in for boat hire, and I ne'er stepp'd into boat in my life.   90

WIT. Tramplers of time !

DAM. Ay, tramplers of time, rascals of time, bull-beggars ! [69]

WIT. Ah, thou'rt a mad old Harry ! — Kind Master Gulf, I am bold to renew my acquaintance.

GULF. I embrace it, sir.   *Exeunt.*

MUSIC

[58] The law courts were held there till 1882.
[59] Heavy galleys.
[60] Coasting vessels.
[61] Wherries.
[62] See on *The White Devil,* V, iii, 104.
[63] *I.e.,* we tramplers of time move along Fleet Street, on our business errands, with the mechanical regularity of puppets. (Kittredge.)
[64] *I.e.,* you may see us tramplers of time also in Holborn, trudging along on business. Hence, we are *visions* of Holborn : we appear there. (Kittredge.) Note that the two streets are mentioned in the song which opens IV, v.
[65] Fools. (A burlesque formation.)
[66] *I.e.,* the fools.
[67] Tramped.
[68] Cf. "soaked."
[69] Bugbears.

ACT II — [SCENE I] [1]

Enter LUCRE.

LUC. My adversary evermore twits me with my nephew, forsooth, my nephew. Why may not a virtuous uncle have a dissolute nephew ? What though he be a brotheller, a wastethrift, a common surfeiter, and, to conclude, a beggar ; must sin in him call up shame in me ? Since we have no part in their follies, why should we have part in their infamies ? For my strict hand toward his mortgage, that I deny not ; I confess I had an uncle's pen'- [10 worth ; [2] let me see, half in half, true. I saw neither hope of his reclaiming, nor comfort in his being ; and was it not then better bestow'd upon his uncle than upon one of his aunts ? — I need not say bawd, for everyone knows what " aunt " stands for in the last translation.

[Enter Servant.]

Now, sir ?

SER. There's a country servingman, sir, attends to speak with your Worship.   20

LUC. I'm at best leisure now ; send him in to me.   *[Exit* Servant.]

Enter HOST *like a servingman.*

HOST. Bless your venerable Worship.

LUC. Welcome, good fellow.

HOST. *[aside]* He calls me thief [3] at first sight, yet he little thinks I am an host.

LUC. What's thy business with me ?

HOST. Faith, sir, I am sent from my mistress, to any sufficient gentleman, indeed, to ask advice upon a doubtful point : 't is [30 indifferent, sir, to whom I come, for I know none, nor did my mistress direct me to any particular man, for she's as mere a stranger here as myself ; only I found your Worship within, and 't is a thing I ever lov'd, sir, to be dispatch'd as soon as I can.

LUC. *[aside]* A good, blunt honesty ; I like him well. — What is thy mistress ?

HOST. Faith, a country gentlewoman, and a widow, sir. Yesterday was the first flight [40 of us ; but now she intends to stay till a little term business [4] be ended.

LUC. Her name, I prithee ?

HOST. It runs there in the writings, sir, among her lands : Widow Medler.

[1] A room in Lucre's house.   [2] Bargain.
[3] "Good fellow" was a canting term for " thief."
[4] Legal business, to be transacted during the court term.

LUC. Medler? Mass, have I ne'er heard of that widow?

HOST. Yes, I warrant you, have you, sir; not the rich widow in Staffordshire?

LUC. Cuds me,[5] there 't is indeed; thou [50 hast put me into memory. There's a widow indeed; ah, that I were a bachelor again!

HOST. No doubt your Worship might do much then; but she's fairly promis'd to a bachelor already.

LUC. Ah, what is he, I prithee?

HOST. A country gentleman too; one of whom your Worship knows not, I'm sure; h'as spent some few follies in his youth, but marriage, by my faith, begins to call him [60 home. My mistress loves him, sir, and love covers faults, you know: one Master Witgood, if ever you have heard of the gentleman.

LUC. Ha? Witgood, say'st thou?

HOST. That's his name indeed, sir; my mistress is like to bring him to a goodly seat yonder; four hundred a year, by my faith.

LUC. But, I pray, take me with you.[6]

HOST. Ay, sir.

LUC. What countryman might this [70 young Witgood be?

HOST. A Leicestershire gentleman, sir.

LUC. [*aside*] My nephew, by th' mass, my nephew! I'll fetch out more of this, i' faith. A simple country fellow — I'll work 't out of him. — And is that gentleman, say'st thou, presently to marry her?

HOST. Faith, he brought her up to town, sir; h'as the best card in all the bunch for 't, her heart; and I know my mistress will [80 be married ere she go down;[7] nay, I'll swear that, for she's none of those widows that will go down first, and be married after; she hates that, I can tell you, sir.

LUC. By my faith, sir, she is like to have a proper[8] gentleman, and a comely; I'll give her that gift.

HOST. Why, does your Worship know him, sir?

LUC. I know him! Does not all the [90 world know him? Can a man of such exquisite qualities be hid under a bushel?

HOST. Then your Worship may save me a labor, for I had charge given me to inquire after him.

LUC. Inquire of him? If I might counsel thee, thou shouldst ne'er trouble thyself further; inquire of him no more but of me; I'll fit thee. I grant he has been youthful; but is he not now reclaim'd? Mark you that, [100 sir; has not your mistress, think you, been wanton in her youth? If men be wags, are there not women wagtails?[9]

HOST. No doubt, sir.

LUC. Does not he return wisest that comes home whipp'd with his own follies?

HOST. Why, very true, sir.

LUC. The worst report you can hear of him, I can tell you, is that he has been a kind gentleman, a liberal, and a worthy; who [110 but lusty Witgood, thrice-noble Witgood!

HOST. Since your Worship has so much knowledge in him, can you resolve[10] me, sir, what his living might be? My duty binds me, sir, to have a care of my mistress' estate; she has been ever a good mistress to me, though I say it. Many wealthy suitors has she nonsuited for his sake; yet, though her love be so fix'd, a man cannot tell whether his non-performance may help to remove it, [120 sir; he makes us believe he has lands and living.

LUC. Who, young Master Witgood? Why, believe it, he has as goodly a fine living out yonder — what do you call the place?

HOST. Nay, I know not, i' faith.

LUC. Hum — see, like a beast, if I have not forgot the name — pooh! and out yonder again, goodly grown woods and fair meadows; pax[11] on 't, I can ne'er hit of that place neither. — He? Why, he's Witgood of Witgood Hall; he an unknown thing! [131

HOST. Is he so, sir? To see how rumor will alter! Trust me, sir, we heard once he had no lands, but all lay mortgag'd to an uncle he has in town here.

LUC. Push![12] 't is a tale, 't is a tale.

HOST. I can assure you, sir, 't was credibly reported to my mistress.

LUC. Why, do you think, i' faith, he was ever so simple to mortgage his lands to [140 his uncle, or his uncle so unnatural to take the extremity of such a mortgage?

HOST. That was my saying still, sir.

LUC.   Pooh, ne'er think it.

HOST. Yet that report goes current.

LUC.   Nay, then you urge me: Cannot I tell that best that am his uncle?

HOST. How, sir? what have I done!

---

[5] An ejaculation of surprise; probably a corruption of "God save me."
[6] Let me understand you, explain yourself.
[7] To the country; with an obvious double-entendre.
[8] Handsome.

[9] Wantons.   [10] Inform.
[11] Pox.   [12] Pish!

Luc. Why, how now! In a swoon, man?

Host. Is your Worship his uncle, sir?

Luc. Can that be any harm to you, sir?

Host. I do beseech you, sir, do me the [150 favor to conceal it. What a beast was I to utter so much! Pray, sir, do me the kindness to keep it in; I shall have my coat pull'd o'er my ears, an't should be known; for the truth is, an't please your Worship, to prevent much rumor and many suitors, they intend to be married very suddenly and privately.

Luc. And dost thou think it stands with my judgment to do them injury? Must I needs say the knowledge of this marriage comes from [160 thee? Am I a fool at fifty-four? Do I lack subtlety now, that have got all my wealth by it? There's a leash of angels [13] for thee: come, let me woo thee speak where lie [14] they?

Host. So [15] I might have no anger, sir ——

Luc. Passion of me, not a jot; prithee, come.

Host. I would not have it known, [sir,] [16] it came by my means.

Luc. Why, am I a man of wisdom?   [170

Host. I dare trust your Worship, sir; but I'm a stranger to your house; and to avoid all intelligencers, I desire your Worship's ear.

Luc. [aside] This fellow's worth a matter of trust. — Come, sir. [Host whispers to him.] Why, now, thou'rt an honest lad. — Ah, sirrah nephew!

Host. Please you, sir, now I have begun with your Worship, when shall I attend for your advice upon that doubtful point? [180 I must come warily now.

Luc. Tut, fear thou nothing;
To-morrow's evening shall resolve [17] the
    doubt.

Host. The time shall cause my attendance.
    Exit.

Luc. Fare thee well. — There's more true honesty in such a country servingman than in a hundred of our cloak companions: [18] I may well call 'em companions, for since blue [19] coats have been turn'd into cloaks, we can scarce know the man from the master. — George! [190

[*Enter* George.]

Geo. Anon, sir.

Luc. List hither: [whispers] — keep the place secret; commend me to my nephew; I

[13] Three gold coins worth about $2.50 each.
[14] Lodge.   [15] If.   [16] Add Q₂.
[17] Dissolve.   [18] Fellows, rascals.
[19] The usual livery for servants.

know no cause, tell him, but he might see his uncle.

Geo. I will, sir.

Luc. And, do you hear, sir?
Take heed you use him with respect and duty.

Geo. [aside] Here's a strange alteration; one day he must be turn'd out like a beg- [200 gar, and now he must be call'd in like a knight.
    Exit.

Luc. Ah, sirrah, that rich widow! — four hundred a year! beside, I hear she lays claim to a title of a hundred more. This falls unhappily that he should bear a grudge to me now, being likely to prove so rich. What is't, trow, [20] that he makes me a stranger for? Hum — I hope he has not so much wit to apprehend that I cozened him: he deceives me then. Good Heaven, who would have [210 thought it would ever have come to this pass! yet he's a proper gentleman, i' faith, give him his due — marry, that's his mortgage; but that I ne'er mean to give him.   I'll make him rich enough in words, if that be good; and if it come to a piece of money, I will not greatly stick for't: there may be hope some of the widow's lands, too, may one day fall upon me, if things be carried wisely.

[*Re-enter* George.]

Now, sir, where is he?   220

Geo. He desires your Worship to hold him excus'd; he has such weighty business it commands him wholly from all men.

Luc. Were those my nephew's words?

Geo. Yes, indeed, sir.

Luc. [aside] When men grow rich, they grow proud too, I perceive that. He would not have sent me such an answer once within this twelvemonth; see what 't is when a man comes to his lands! Return to him again, [230 sir; tell him his uncle desires his company for an hour; I'll trouble him but an hour, say; 't is for his own good, tell him; and, do you hear, sir? put " Worship " upon him. Go to, do as I bid you; he's like to be a gentleman of Worship very shortly.

Geo. [aside] This is good sport, i' faith.
    Exit.

Luc. Troth, he uses his uncle discourteously now. Can he tell what I may do for him? Goodness may come from me in a minute, [240 that comes not in seven year again. He knows my humor; [21] I am not so usually good; 't is no small thing that draws kindness from me, he

[20] Do you suppose.   [21] Disposition.

may know that an he will. The chief cause that invites me to do him most good is the sudden astonishing of old Hoard, my adversary. How pale his malice will look at my nephew's advancement! With what a dejected spirit he will behold his fortunes, whom but last day he proclaim'd a rioter, [250 penurious makeshift, despised brothel-master! Ha, ha! 't will do me more secret joy than my last purchase,[22] more precious comfort than all these widow's revenues.

*[Re-]enter [*GEORGE, *showing in*] WITGOOD.*

Now, sir?

GEO. With much entreaty he's at length come, sir.   *[Exit.]*

LUC. Oh, Nephew, let me salute you, sir! You 're welcome, Nephew.

WIT. Uncle, I thank you.   260

LUC. Y'ave a fault, Nephew; you 're a stranger here. Well, Heaven give you joy!

WIT. Of what, sir?

LUC. Hah, we can hear! You might have known your uncle's house, i' faith, You and your widow; go to, you were to blame, If I may tell you so without offence.

WIT. How could you hear of that, sir?

LUC.   Oh, pardon me! It was your will to have [kept it][23] from me, I perceive now.

WIT. Not for any defect of love, I protest, Uncle.   271

LUC. Oh, 't was unkindness, Nephew! fie, fie, fie.

WIT. I am sorry you take it in that sense, sir.

LUC. Pooh, you cannot color it, i' faith, Nephew.

WIT. Will you but hear what I can say in my just excuse, sir?

LUC. Yes, faith, will I, and welcome.   280

WIT. You that know my danger i' th' city, sir, so well, how great my debts are, and how extreme my creditors, could not out of your pure judgment, sir, have wish'd us hither.

LUC. Mass, a firm reason indeed.

WIT. Else, my uncle's house! why, 't 'ad been the only make-match.

LUC. Nay, and thy credit.

WIT. My credit? Nay, my countenance.[24] Push! nay, I know, Uncle, you would [290

have wrought it so by your wit you would have made her believe in time the whole house had been mine.

LUC. Ay, and most of the goods too.

WIT. La, you there! Well, let 'em all prate what they will, there's nothing like the bringing of a widow to one's uncle's house.

LUC. Nay, let nephews be rul'd as they list, they shall find their uncle's house the most natural place when all's done.   300

WIT. There they may be bold.

LUC. Life, they may do anything there, man, and fear neither beadle nor summ'ner. An uncle's house! a very Cole Harbor.[25] Sirrah, I 'll touch thee near now: hast thou so much interest in thy widow that by a token thou couldst presently send for her?

WIT. Troth, I think I can, Uncle.

LUC. Go to, let me see that.

WIT. Pray, command one of your men hither, Uncle.   311

LUC. George!

[Re-enter GEORGE.]

GEO. Here, sir.

LUC. Attend my nephew. [WITGOOD *whispers to* GEORGE, *who then goes out.*] — *[aside]* I love a' life[26] to prattle with a rich widow; 't is pretty, methinks, when our tongues go together; and then to promise much and perform little. I love that sport a' life, i' faith; yet I am in the mood now to do my nephew some good, if he take me handsomely. — What, have you dispatch'd?   321

WIT. I ha' sent, sir.

LUC. Yet I must condemn you of unkindness, Nephew.

WIT. Heaven forbid, Uncle!

LUC. Yes, faith, must I. Say your debts be many, your creditors importunate, yet the kindness of a thing is all, Nephew; you might have sent me close[27] word on 't, without the least danger or prejudice to your fortunes.

WIT. Troth, I confess it, Uncle; I was [331 to blame there; but, indeed, my intent was to have clapp'd it up suddenly, and so have broke forth like a joy to my friends, and a wonder to the world. Beside, there's a trifle of a forty-pound matter toward the setting of me forth[28]; my friends should ne'er have known on 't: I meant to make shift for that myself.

---

[22] Acquisition.   [23] So Q2; Q1 *it kept.*
[24] Favor, support.

[25] Cold Harbor, a congeries of tenements by the Thames above London Bridge. It was regarded as a sanctuary where debtors and malefactors were safe from the law.
[26] As my life.   [27] Private.   [28] Equipping me.

Luc. How, Nephew? let me not hear such a word again, I beseech you. Shall I be beholding [29] to you?   341

Wit. To me? Alas, what do you mean, Uncle?

Luc. I charge you, upon my love, you trouble nobody but myself.

Wit. Y'ave no reason for that, Uncle.

Luc. Troth, I 'll ne'er be friends with you while you live, an you do.

Wit. Nay, an you say so, Uncle, here 's my hand ; I will not do 't —

Luc. Why, well said! there 's some [351 hope in thee when thou wilt be rul'd. I 'll make it up fifty, faith, because I see thee so reclaim'd. Peace ; here comes my wife with Sam, her tother husband's son.

[*Enter* Mistress Lucre *and* Freedom.]

Wit. Good Aunt.

Free. Cousin Witgood, I rejoice in my salute ; you 're most welcome to this noble city, govern'd with the sword in the scabbard.

Wit. [*aside*] And the wit in the pom- [361 mel. — Good Master Sam Freedom, I return the salute.

Luc. By the mass, she 's coming ; Wife, let me see now how thou wilt entertain [30] her.

Mrs. L. I hope I am not to learn, sir, to entertain a widow ; 't is not so long ago since I was one myself !

[*Enter* Courtesan.]

Wit. Uncle ——

Luc. She 's come indeed !   370

Wit. My Uncle was desirous to see you, widow, and I presum'd to invite you.

Cour. The presumption was nothing, Master Witgood. Is this your uncle, sir?

Luc. Marry am I, sweet widow ; and his good uncle he shall find me ; ay, by this smack that I give thee, thou 'rt welcome. — Wife, bid the widow welcome the same way again.

Free. [*aside*] I am a gentleman now too by my father's occupation, and I see no rea- [380 son but I may kiss a widow by my father's copy ; [31] truly, I think the charter is not against it ; surely these are the words: " The son once a gentleman may revel it, though his father were a dauber ; " [32] 't is about the fifteenth page. I 'll to her.

[*Offers to kiss the* Courtesan, *who repulses him.*]

Luc. Y' are not very busy now ; a word with thee, sweet widow.

Free. [*aside*] Coads-nigs ! [33] I was never so disgrac'd since the hour my mother whipp'd me.   391

Luc. Beside, I have no child of mine own to care for ; she 's my second wife, old, past bearing ; clap sure to him, widow ; he 's like to be my heir, I can tell you.

Cour. Is he so, sir?

Luc. He knows it already, and the knave 's proud on 't ; jolly rich widows have been offer'd him here i' th' city, great merchants' wives ; and do you think he will once look [400 upon 'em ? Forsooth, he 'll none. You are beholding to him i' th' country, then, ere we could be. Nay, I 'll hold a wager, widow, if he were once known to be in town, he would be presently [34] sought after ; nay, and happy were they that could catch him first.

Cour. I think so.

Luc. Oh, there would be such running to and fro, widow ! He should not pass the streets for 'em ; he 'd be took up in one [410 great house or other presently. Fah ! they know he has it, and must have it. You see this house here, widow ; this house and all comes to him ; goodly rooms, ready furnish'd, ceil'd with plaster of Paris, and all hung above [35] with cloth of arras. — Nephew.

Wit. Sir.

Luc. Show the widow your house ; carry her into all the rooms, and bid her welcome. — You shall see, widow. — [*aside to* Witgood] Nephew, strike all sure above an thou [421 beest a good boy, — ah ! —

Wit. Alas, sir, I know not how she would take it !

Luc. The right way, I warrant t'e.[36] A pox! art an ass? Would I were in thy stead ! Get you up ; I am asham'd of you. [*Exeunt* Witgood *and* Courtesan.] — [*aside*] So ; let 'em agree as they will now ; many a match has been struck up in my house a' this [430 fashion: let 'em try all manner of ways, still there 's nothing like an uncle's house to strike the stroke in. I 'll hold my wife in talk a little. — Now Jinny, your son there goes a-wooing to a poor gentlewoman but of a thousand portion ; see my nephew, a lad of less hope, strikes at four hundred a year in good rubbish.

---

[29] Beholden.   [30] Receive.
[31] Certificate of membership in one of the city companies.   [32] Plasterer. — For "fifteenth," Qq *15.*

[33] Cf. on l. 50.   [34] Immediately.
[35] *I.e.,* upstairs. So Q₁ ; Q₂, followed by mod. eds., *about. Above* is required : the stage was certainly not so hung !
[36] To ye.

MRS. L. Well, we must do as we may, sir.

LUC. I 'll have his money ready told [37] for him again [38] he come down. Let me see, [440 too ; — by th' mass, I must present the widow with some jewel, a good piece a' plate, or such a device ; 't will hearten her on well. I have a very fair standing cup ; and a good high standing cup will please a widow above all other pieces. *Exit.*

MRS. L. Do you mock us with your nephew? — I have a plot in my head, Son ; — i' faith, Husband, to cross you.

FREE. Is it a tragedy plot, or a comedy [450 plot, good mother?

MRS. L. 'T is a plot shall vex *him.* I charge you, of my blessing, son Sam, that you presently withdraw the action of your love from Master Hoard's niece.

FREE. How,[39] Mother?

MRS. L. Nay, I have a plot in my head, i' faith. Here, take this chain of gold, and this fair diamond ; dog me the widow home to her lodging, and at thy best opportunity, fasten [460 'em both upon her. Nay, I have a reach ; [40] I can tell you thou art known what thou art, son, among the right Worshipful, all the twelve companies.

FREE. Truly, I thank 'em for it.

MRS. L. He? he 's a scab [41] to thee ; and so certify her thou hast two hundred a year of thyself, beside thy good parts — a proper person and a lovely. If I were a widow, I could find in my heart to have thee myself, son ; ay, from 'em all. [471

FREE. Thank you for your good will, Mother, but indeed I had rather have a stranger ; and if I woo her not in that violent fashion that I will make her be glad to take these gifts ere I leave her, let me never be called the heir of your body.

MRS. L. Nay, I know there 's enough in you, son, if you once come to put it forth. 479

FREE. I 'll quickly make a bolt or a shaft on 't.[42] *Exeunt.*

[SCENE II] [43]

Enter [WALKADINE] HOARD *and* MONEYLOVE.

MON. Faith, Master Hoard, I have bestowed many months in the suit of your niece, such was the dear love I ever bore to her vir-

tues ; but since she hath so extremely denied me, I am to lay out for my fortunes elsewhere.

HOA. Heaven forbid but you should, sir! I ever told you my niece stood otherwise affected.[44]

MON. I must confess you did, sir ; yet, in regard of my great loss of time, and the [10 zeal with which I sought your niece, shall I desire one favor of your Worship?

HOA. In regard of those two, 't is hard but you shall, sir.

MON. I shall rest grateful. 'T is not full three hours, sir, since the happy rumor of a rich country widow came to my hearing.

HOA. How? a rich country widow?

MON. Four hundred a year landed.

HOA. Yea? 20

MON. Most firm, sir ; and I have learnt her lodging. Here my suit begins, sir ; if I might but entreat your Worship to be a countenance for me, and speak a good word (for your words will pass), I nothing doubt but I might set fair for the widow ; nor shall your labor, sir, end altogether in thanks ; two hundred angels——

HOA. So, so ; what suitors has she?

MON. There lies the comfort, sir ; the report of her is yet but a whisper ; and only so- [30 licited by young riotous Witgood, nephew to your mortal adversary.

HOA. Ha! art certain he 's her suitor?

MON. Most certain, sir ; and his uncle very industrious to beguile the widow, and make up the match.

HOA. So! very good!

MON. Now, sir, you know this young Witgood is a spendthrift, dissolute fellow.

HOA. A very rascal. 40

MON. A midnight surfeiter.

HOA. The spume of a brothel-house.

MON. True, sir! which being well told in your Worship's phrase, may both heave him out of her mind, and drive a fair way for me to the widow's affections.

HOA. Attend me about five.

MON. With my best care, sir. *Exit.*

HOA. Fool, thou hast left thy treasure with a thief,

To trust a widower with a suit in love! [50 Happy revenge, I hug thee! I have not only the means laid before me, extremely to cross my adversary and confound the last hopes of his nephew, but thereby to enrich my state, augment my revenues, and build mine own fortunes greater ; ha, ha!

---

[37] Counted.
[38] Against, ready for the time when.
[39] What. [40] Scheme. [41] Scurvy fellow.
[42] I 'll take the risk, whatever the upshot. A bolt was a knobbed arrow, a shaft a sharp one.
[43] A public place.
[44] Inclined, in love.

I 'll mar your phrase, o'erturn your flatteries,
Undo your windings, policies, and plots,
Fall like a secret and dispatchful [45] plague
On your secured comforts. Why, I am able [60
To buy three of Lucre ; thrice outbid him,
Let my out-monies [46] be reckon'd and all.

Enter three [of Witgood's] Creditors.

1 CRED. I am glad of this news.

2 CRED. So are we, by my faith.

3 CRED. Young Witgood will be a gallant
again now.

HOA. [*listening*] Peace !

1 CRED. I promise you, Master Cockpit,
she 's a mighty rich widow.

2 CRED. Why, have you ever heard [70
of her?

1 CRED. Who? Widow Medler? She lies
open [47] to much rumor.

3 CRED. Four hundred a year, they say, in
very good land.

1 CRED. Nay, take 't of my word, if you
believe that, you believe the least.

2 CRED. And to see how close he keeps it !

1 CRED. Oh, sir, there 's policy in that, to
prevent better suitors.   80

3 CRED. He owes me a hundred pound, and
I protest I ne'er look'd for a penny.

1 CRED. He little dreams of our coming ;
he 'll wonder to see his creditors upon him.
　　　　　　　　　　　　　　Exeunt [Creditors].

HOA. Good, his creditors ; I 'll follow.
　　This makes for me.
All know the widow's wealth ; and 't is well
　　known
I can estate her fairly, ay, and will.
In this one chance shines a twice-happy fate :
I both deject my foe and raise my state.[48]
　　　　　　　　　　　　　　　　Exit.

MUSIC

ACT III — [SCENE I] [1]

[*Enter*] WITGOOD *with his* Creditors.

WIT. Why, alas, my creditors, could you
find no other time to undo me but now?
Rather your malice appears in this than the
justness of the debt.

1 CRED. Master Witgood, I have forborne
my money long.

WIT. I pray, speak low, sir ; what do you
mean?

2 CRED. We hear you are to be married
suddenly to a rich country widow.   10

WIT. What can be kept so close but you
creditors hear on 't ! Well, 't is a lamentable
state, that our chiefest afflicters should first
hear of our fortunes. Why, this is no good
course, i' faith, sirs ; if ever you have hope to
be satisfied, why do you seek to confound
the means that should work it? There 's neither piety, no, nor policy in that. Shine
favorably now, why, I may rise and spread
again, to your great comforts.   20

1 CRED. He says true, i' faith.

WIT. Remove me now, and I consume for
　　ever.

2 CRED. Sweet gentleman !

WIT. How can it thrive which from the sun
　　you sever?

3 CRED. It cannot, indeed !

WIT. Oh, then, show patience ! I shall
　　have enough
To satisfy you all.

1 CRED.　　　　　　　Ay, if we could
Be content, a shame take us !

WIT.　　　　　　　　　　　For, look you ;
I am but newly sure [2] yet to the widow,
And what a rend might this discredit make ! [30
Within these three days will I bind you
　　lands
For your securities.

1 CRED.　　　　　　No, good Master Witgood ;
Would 't were as much as we dare trust you
　　with !

WIT. I know you have been kind ; however,
　　now,
Either by wrong report or false incitement,
Your gentleness is injured ; in such
A state as this a man cannot want foes.
If on the sudden he begin to rise,
No man that lives can count his enemies.
You had some intelligence, I warrant ye,   40
From an ill-willer.

2 CRED. Faith, we heard you brought up a
rich widow, sir, and were suddenly to marry
her.

WIT. Ay, why there it was ; I knew 't was
so ; but since you are so well resolv'd [3] of my
faith toward you, let me be so much favor'd
of you, I beseech you all ——

ALL. Oh, it shall not need, i' faith, sir ! ——

WIT. As to lie still awhile, and bury [50
my debts in silence, till I be fully possess'd of

---

[45] Deadly.
[46] *I.e.*, investments not immediately liquid.
[47] See on IV, v, 188.　　　　　[48] Estate.
[1] Witgood's lodgings.
[2] Betrothed.　　　　　[3] Convinced.

the widow ; for the truth is — I may tell you as my friends ——

ALL. Oh, oh, oh ! ——

WIT. I am to raise a little money in the city, toward the setting forth of myself, for my own credit and your comfort. Now, if my former debts should be divulg'd, all hope of my proceedings were quite extinguish'd.

1 CRED. [*aside to* WITGOOD] Do you [60 hear, sir? I may deserve your custom hereafter ; pray let my money be accepted before a stranger's. Here's forty pound I receiv'd as I came to you ; if that may stand you in any stead, make use on 't. — Nay, pray, sir ; 't is at your service.

WIT. [*aside*] You do so ravish me with kindness that

I 'm constrain'd to play the maid, and take it.[4]

1 CRED. [*aside*] Let none of them see it, I beseech you.

WIT. [*aside*]   Fah !

1 CRED. [*aside*] I hope I shall be first in your remembrance   70

After the marriage rites.

WIT. [*aside*]   Believe it firmly.

1 CRED. So. — What, do you walk, sirs?

2 CRED. I go. — [*aside to* WITGOOD] Take no care, sir, for money to furnish you ; within this hour I 'll send you sufficient. — Come, Master Cockpit, we both stay for you.

3 CRED. I ha' lost a ring, i' faith ; I 'll follow you presently ; [*Exeunt* 1 *and* 2 Creditors.] — but you shall find it, sir. I know your youth and expenses have disfurnish'd [80 you of all jewels : there's a ruby of twenty pound price, sir ; bestow it upon your widow. — What, man ! 't will call up her blood to you ; beside, if I might so much work with you, I would not have you beholding to those bloodsuckers for any money.

WIT. Not I, believe it.

3 CRED. Th' are a brace of cutthroats !

WIT. I know 'em.

3 CRED. Send a note of all your wants [90 to my shop, and I 'll supply you instantly.

WIT. Say you so? Why, here 's my hand, then, no man living shall do 't but thyself.

3 CRED. Shall I carry it away from [5] 'em both, then?

WIT. I' faith, shalt thou !

3 CRED. Troth, then, I thank you, sir.

WIT. Welcome, good Master Cockpit ! *Exit* [3 Creditor]. — Ha, ha, ha ! why, is not

this better now than lying abed? I per- [100 ceive there's nothing conjures up wit sooner than poverty, and nothing lays it down sooner than wealth and lechery ! This has some savor yet. Oh, that I had the mortgage from mine uncle as sure in possession as these trifles ! I would forswear brothel at noonday, and muscadine [6] and eggs at midnight.

Enter Courtesan.

COUR. Master Witgood, where are you?

WIT. Holla !

COUR. Rich news !   110

WIT. Would 't were all in plate !

COUR. There's some in chains and jewels. I am so haunted with suitors, Master Witgood, I know not which to dispatch first.

WIT. You have the better term,[7] by my faith.

COUR. Among the number
One Master Hoard, an ancient gentleman.

WIT. Upon my life, my uncle's adversary.

COUR. It may well hold so, for he rails on you,
Speaks shamefully of him.

WIT.   As I could wish it. [120

COUR. I first denied him, but so cunningly,
It rather promis'd him assured hopes
Than any loss of labor.

WIT.   Excellent !

COUR. I expect him every hour with gentlemen,
With whom he labors to make good his words,
To approve [8] you riotous, your state consum'd.
Your uncle ——

WIT. Wench, make up thy own fortunes now ; do thyself a good turn once in thy days. He 's rich in money, movables,[9] and [130 lands ; marry him — he 's an old doting fool, and that 's worth all : marry him. 'T would be a great comfort to me to see thee do well, i' faith : marry him. 'T would ease my conscience well to see thee well bestow'd ; I have a care of thee, i' faith.

COUR. Thanks, sweet Master Witgood.

WIT. I reach at farder happiness : first, I am sure it can be no harm to thee, and there may happen goodness to me by it. [140 Prosecute it well ; let 's send up for our wits,

---

[4] Say no — and acquiesce. (Proverbial.)
[5] Have the victory over.

[6] Muscatel, a sweet wine; it was taken with eggs as an aphrodisiac.
[7] It was in term time, *i.e.*, while the courts were sitting, that London was full of visitors, and the prostitutes were most in demand.
[8] Prove.
[9] Personal property.

now we require their best and most pregnant assistance !

COUR. Step in ; I think I hear 'em. [*Exeunt.*]

Enter HOARD *and* Gentlemen [10] *with the* Host [*as*] *servingman.*

HOA. Art thou the widow's man ? By my faith, sh 'as a company of proper men then.

HOST. I am the worst of six, sir ; good enough for blue coats.[11]

HOA. Hark hither : I hear say thou art in most credit with her.   150

HOST. Not so, sir.

HOA. Come, come, thou 'rt modest. There 's a brace of royals ; [12] prithee, help me to th' speech of her.

HOST. I 'll do what I may, sir, always saving myself harmless.[13]

HOA. Go to ; do 't, I say ; thou shalt hear better from me.

HOST. [*aside*] Is not this a better place than five mark [14] a year standing wages ? Say [160 a man had but three such clients in a day, methinks he might make a poor living on 't ; beside, I was never brought up with so little honesty to refuse any man's money ; never. What gulls [15] there are a' this side the world ! Now know I the widow's mind ; none but my young master comes in her clutches ; ha, ha, ha !   *Exit.*

HOA. Now, my dear gentlemen, stand firmly to me ;
You know his follies and my worth.

1 GENT.   We do, sir. [170

2 GENT. But, Master Hoard, are you sure he is not i' th' house now ?

HOA. Upon my honesty, I chose this time A' purpose, fit ; the spendthrift is abroad. Assist me ; here she comes. —

[*Enter* Courtesan.]

              Now, my sweet widow.

COUR. Y' are welcome, Master Hoard.

HOA. Dispatch, sweet gentlemen, dispatch. —
I am come, widow, to prove those my words Neither of envy [16] sprung nor of false tongues, But such as their [17] deserts and actions

Do merit and bring forth ; all which these gentlemen,   180
Well known and better reputed, will confess.

COUR. I cannot tell
How my affections may dispose of me ;
But surely if they find him so desertless,
They 'll have that reason to withdraw themselves.
And therefore, gentlemen, I do entreat you,
As you are fair in reputation
And in appearing form, so shine in truth.
I am a widow, and, alas, you know,   189
Soon overthrown ! 'T is a very small thing
That we withstand, our weakness is so great ;
Be partial unto neither, but deliver,
Without affection,[18] your opinion.

HOA. And that will drive it home.

COUR. Nay, I beseech your silence, Master Hoard ;
You are a party.

HOA.   Widow, not a word !

1 GENT. The better first to work you to belief,
Know neither of us owe him flattery,
Nor tother malice ; but unbribed censure,[19]
So help us our best fortunes !

COUR.   It suffices. [200

1 GENT. That Witgood is a riotous,[20] undone [21] man,
Imperfect both in fame and in estate,
His debts wealthier than he, and executions
In wait for his due body, we 'll maintain
With our best credit and our dearest blood.

COUR. Nor land nor living, say you ? Pray, take heed
You do not wrong the gentleman !

1 GENT.   What we speak
Our lives and means are ready to make good.

COUR. Alas, how soon are we poor souls beguil'd !

2 GENT. And for his uncle ——

HOA.   Let that come to me. [210
His uncle, a severe extortioner ;
A tyrant at a forfeiture ; greedy of others' Miseries ; one that would undo his brother,
Nay, swallow up his father, if he can,
Within the fathoms of his conscience.

1 GENT. Nay, believe it, widow,
You had not only match'd yourself to wants,
But in an evil and unnatural stock.

HOA. [*aside*] Follow hard, gentlemen, follow hard !

---

[10] Probably, as Dyce notes, Lamprey and Spichcock.
[11] See on II. i. 188.
[12] Gold coins worth about $2.50 each.
[13] Reserving the right to keep out of trouble myself.
[14] A mark was worth two-thirds of £1.
[15] Dupes.   [16] Malice.
[17] Witgood's and his uncle's.

[18] Bias.   [19] Judgment.
[20] Profligate.   [21] Ruined.

Cour. Is my love so deceiv'd? Before
you all   220
I do renounce him ; on my knees I vow
He ne'er shall marry me.
      Wit. [*peeping in*] Heaven knows he never
         meant it !
      Hoa. [*aside to* Gentleman] There take her
         at the bound.
      1 Gent. Then, with a new and pure affec-
         tion,
Behold yon gentleman ; grave, kind, and rich,
A match worthy yourself ; esteeming him,
You do regard your state.
      Hoa. [*aside*]   I 'll make her a jointure,
         say.
      1 Gent. He can join land to land, and will
         possess you
Of what you can desire.
      2 Gent.   Come, widow, come. [230
      Cour. The world is so deceitful !
      1 Gent.   There, 't is deceitful,
Where flattery, want, and imperfection lies ;
But none of these in him ; push !
      Cour.   Pray, sir ——
      1 Gent. Come, you widows are ever most
backward when you should do yourselves
most good ; but were it to marry a chin not
worth a hair now,[22] then you would be for-
ward enough ! Come, clap hands, a match.
      Hoa. With all my heart, widow. [Hoard
         and Courtesan *take hands.*] — Thanks,
         gentlemen ;
I will deserve your labor, and [*to* Courtesan]
         thy love.   240
      Cour. Alas, you love not widows but for
         wealth !
I promise you I ha' nothing, sir.
      Hoa.   Well said, widow,
Well said ; thy love is all I seek, before
These gentlemen.
      Cour.   Now I must hope the best.
      Hoa. My joys are such they want to be
         express'd.
      Cour. But, Master Hoard, one thing I
must remember you of, before these gentlemen, your friends : how shall I suddenly avoid
the loathed soliciting of that perjur'd Witgood, and his tedious, dissembling uncle ? [250
who this very day hath appointed a meeting
for the same purpose too ; where, had not
truth come forth, I had been undone, utterly
undone.
      Hoa. What think you of that, gentlemen ?
      1 Gent. 'T was well devised.

[22] *I.e.,* an impecunious youngster.

      Hoa. Hark thee, widow : train [23] out young
Witgood single ; [24] hasten him thither with
thee, somewhat before the hour ; where, at
the place appointed, these gentlemen and [260
myself will wait the opportunity, when, by
some sleight [25] removing him from thee, we 'll
suddenly enter and surprise thee, carry thee
away by boat to Cole Harbor, have a priest
ready, and there clap it up instantly. How
lik'st it, widow ?
      Cour. In that it pleaseth you, it likes [26]
         me well.
      Hoa. I 'll kiss thee for those words. —
         Come, gentlemen ;
Still must I live a suitor to your favors,
Still to your aid beholding.
      1 Gent.   We 're engag'd, sir ; [270
'T is for our credits now to see 't well ended.
      Hoa. 'T is for your honors, gentlemen ;
         nay, look to 't. —
Not only in joy, but I in wealth excel. —
No more sweet widow, but sweet wife, fare-
      well.
      Cour. Farewell, sir.
         Exeunt [Hoard *and* Gentlemen].

         Re-enter Witgood.

      Wit. Oh, for more scope ! I could laugh
eternally ! Give you joy, Mistress Hoard ;
I promise your fortune was good, forsooth ;
y' ave fell upon wealth enough, and there 's
young gentlemen enow [27] can help you to [280
the rest. Now it requires our wits ; carry thyself but heedfully now, and we are both ——

         [*Re-enter* Host.]

      Host. Master Witgood, your uncle.
      Wit. Cuds me ! remove thyself awhile ;
I 'll serve for him !
         [*Exeunt* Courtesan *and* Host.]

         Enter Lucre.

      Luc. Nephew, good morrow, Nephew.
      Wit. The same to you, kind Uncle.
      Luc. How fares the widow ? Does the
         meeting hold ?
      Wit. Oh, no question of that, sir.
      Luc. I 'll strike the stroke, then, for thee ;
         no more days.[28]   290
      Wit. The sooner the better, Uncle. Oh,
she 's mightily follow'd !
      Luc. And yet so little rumor'd !

[23] Entice.   [24] Alone.   [25] Trick.
[26] Is pleasing to.   [27] Enough.
[28] Postponements, days of grace.

Wɪᴛ. Mightily ! Here comes one old gentle-man, and he 'll make her a jointure of three hundred a year, forsooth ; another wealthy suitor will estate his son in his lifetime, and make him weigh down the widow ; here a merchant's son will possess her with no less than three goodly lordships at once, [300 which were all pawns to his father.

Lᴜᴄ. Peace, Nephew, let me hear no more of 'em ; it mads me. Thou shalt prevent [29] 'em all. No words to the widow of my coming hither. Let me see — 't is now upon nine ; before twelve, Nephew, we will have the bar-gain struck, we will, faith, boy.

Wɪᴛ. Oh, my precious Uncle !　　*[Exeunt.]*

[Sᴄᴇɴᴇ II] [30]

Enter [Wᴀʟᴋᴀᴅɪɴᴇ] Hᴏᴀʀᴅ *and* [Jᴏʏᴄᴇ,] *his* Niece.

Hᴏᴀ. Niece, sweet Niece, prithee, have a care to my house : I leave all to thy discre-tion. Be content to dream awhile ; I 'll have a husband for thee shortly : put that care upon me, wench ; for in choosing wives and husbands I am only fortunate ; I have that gift given me.　　　　　　　　　　　　*Exit.*

Jᴏʏ. But 't is not likely you should choose
　　for me,
Since nephew to your chiefest enemy
Is he whom I affect ; [31] but, oh, forgetful !　10
Why dost thou flatter thy affections so,
With name of him that for a widow's bed
Neglects thy purer love? Can it be so,
Or does report dissemble?

[*Enter* Gᴇᴏʀɢᴇ.]

　　　　　　　　　　How, now, sir?
Gᴇᴏ. A letter, with which came a private
　　charge.
Jᴏʏ. Therein I thank your care.
　　　　　　　　　　　　[Exit Gᴇᴏʀɢᴇ.]
　　　　　— I know this hand —
(*Reads.*) " Dearer than sight, what the world reports of me, yet believe not ; rumor will alter shortly. Be thou constant ; I am still the same that I was in love, and I hope to be [20 the same in fortunes.
　　　　　　Tʜᴇᴏᴅᴏʀᴜs Wɪᴛɢᴏᴏᴅ."
I am resolv'd ; [32] no more shall fear or doubt
Raise their pale powers to keep affection out.
　　　　　　　　　　　　　　　　Exit.

[29] Get ahead of, anticipate.
[30] A room in Walkadine Hoard's house.
[31] Incline to, love.　　　　[32] Convinced.

[Sᴄᴇɴᴇ III] [33]

Enter, with a Drawer, [Wᴀʟᴋᴀᴅɪɴᴇ] Hᴏᴀʀᴅ *and two* Gentlemen.[34]

Dʀᴀ. You 're very welcome, gentlemen. — Dick, show those gentlemen the Pomegran-ate,[35] there.

Hᴏᴀ. Hist !

Dʀᴀ. Up those stairs, gentlemen.

Hᴏᴀ. Pist ! [36] drawer —

Dʀᴀ. Anon, sir !

Hᴏᴀ. Prithee, ask at the bar if a gentle-woman came not in lately.

Dʀᴀ. William, at the bar, did you see [10 any gentlewoman come in lately? Speak you ay, speak you no !

Within. No ; none came in yet, but Mis-tress Florence.

Dʀᴀ. He says none came in yet, sir, but one Mistress Florence.

Hᴏᴀ. What is that Florence? a widow?

Dʀᴀ. Yes, a Dutch widow.

Hᴏᴀ. How?

Dʀᴀ. That 's an English drab, sir ; give [20 your Worship good morrow.　　　*[Exit.]*

Hᴏᴀ. A merry knave, i' faith ! I shall re-member a Dutch widow the longest day of my life.

1 Gᴇɴᴛ. Did not I use most art to win the widow?

2 Gᴇɴᴛ. You shall pardon me for that, sir ; Master Hoard knows I took her at best van-tage.

Hᴏᴀ. What 's that,[37] sweet gentlemen, [30 what 's that?

2 Gᴇɴᴛ. He will needs bear me down, that his art only wrought with the widow most.

Hᴏᴀ. Oh, you did both well, gentlemen, you did both well, I thank you.

1 Gᴇɴᴛ. I was the first that mov'd her.

Hᴏᴀ.　　　　　　　You were, i' faith.

2 Gᴇɴᴛ. But it was I that took her at the bound.

Hᴏᴀ. Ay, that was you ; faith, gentlemen, 't is right.

3 Gᴇɴᴛ. I boasted least, but 't was I join'd their hands.

[33] A tavern.
[34] Probably, as Dyce notes, Lamprey and Spich-cock should be assigned some, at least, of the speeches here. Note assignment of speech, l. 39. The *two* of the entrance direction indicates reduction of personnel in the interest of economy.
[35] Tavern rooms were named instead of numbered.
[36] Q 2 *Hist.*
[37] *I.e.*, the best vantage (though this meaning may not be intended by Hoard).

HOA. By th' mass, I think he did ; you did
all well,   40
Gentlemen, you did all well ; contend no more.

1 GENT. Come, yon room 's fittest.

HOA.   True, 't is next the door !
Ex[eun]t.

Enter WITGOOD, Courtesan, [Drawer,] *and*
Host.

DRA. You 're very welcome ; please you to
walk upstairs, cloth 's laid, sir.

COUR. Upstairs? Troth, I am [38] weary,
Master Witgood.

WIT. Rest yourself here awhile, widow ;
we 'll have a cup of muscadine in this little
room.

DRA. A cup of muscadine? You shall [50
have the best, sir.

WIT. But, do you hear, sirrah?

DRA. Do you call? Anon, sir.

WIT. What is there provided for dinner?

DRA. I cannot readily tell you, sir ; if you
please you may go into the kitchen and see
yourself, sir ; many gentlemen of Worship do
use to do it, I assure you, sir !   [*Exit.*]

HOST. A pretty familiar, priggin[g] [39] rascal ;
he has his part without book ! [40]   60

WIT. Against [41] you are ready to drink to
me, widow, I 'll be present to pledge you.

COUR. Nay, I commend your care ; 't is
done well of you ! [*Exit* WITGOOD.] — ['Las,] [42]
what have I forgot !

HOST. What, mistress?

COUR. I slipp'd my wedding ring off when I
wash'd, and left it at my lodging. Prithee,
run ; I shall be sad without it. [*Exit* Host.] —
So, he 's gone. — Boy !   70

[*Enter* Boy.]

BOY. Anon, forsooth.

COUR. Come hither, sirrah : learn secretly
if one Master Hoard, an ancient gentleman, be
about house.

BOY. I heard such a one nam'd.

COUR. Commend me to him.

Re-enter HOARD *with* Gentlemen.

HOA. [Ay, boy,] [43] do thy commendations !

COUR. Oh, you come well ; away, to boat,
begone !

HOA. Thus wise men are reveng'd ; give
two for one.   *Exeunt.*

[38] Q₂ adds *very*.   [39] Haggling.
[40] By heart.   [41] By the time that.
[42] Old eds. *asse*, but in Q₁ it is evident that a type
has dropped out. Q₂ preserves the space.
[43] Cor. Dyce ; old eds. *I bee*.

Re-enter WITGOOD *and* Vintner.

WIT. I must request   80
You, sir, to show extraordinary care :
My uncle comes with gentlemen, his friends,
And 't is upon a making ! [44]

VIN.   Is it so?
I 'll give a special charge, good Master Wit-
good.
May I be bold to see her?

WIT.   Who? [t]he widow?
With all my heart, i' faith, I 'll bring you to
her !

VIN. If she be a Staffordshire gentlewoman,
't is much
If I know her not —

WIT.   How now? Boy ! drawer !

VIN.   Hie !

[*Re-enter* Boy.]

BOY. Do you call, sir?

WIT.   Went the gentlewoman up that
was here?

BOY. Up, sir? She went out, sir.

WIT.   Out, sir !

BOY.   Out, sir : [90
One Master Hoard, with a guard of gentlemen,
Carried her out at back door, a pretty while
since, sir.

WIT. Hoard ! Death   and   darkness !
Hoard !

Re-enter Host.

HOST. The devil of ring I can find !

WIT.   How now? What news?
Where 's the widow?

HOST.   My mistress? Is she not here, sir?

WIT. More madness yet !

HOST.   She sent me for a ring.

WIT. A plot, a plot ! — To boat ! she 's
stole away.

HOST. What?

Enter LUCRE *with* Gentlemen.

WIT.   Follow ! Inquire old Hoard, my
uncle's adversary.   [*Exit* Host.]

LUC. Nephew, what 's that?

WIT.   Thrice-miserable wretch !

LUC. Why, what 's the matter?

VIN.   The widow 's borne away, sir.

LUC. Ha? passion of me ! — A heavy welcome, gentlemen.   101

1 GENT. The widow gone?

LUC.   Who durst attempt it?

[44] Matchmaking.

WIT. Who but old Hoard, my uncle's adversary?

LUC. How?

WIT.   With his confederates.

LUC.   Hoard,

My deadly enemy? — Gentlemen, stand to me ;

I will not bear it ; 't is in hate of me ;

That villain seeks my shame, nay, [thirsts] [45] my blood ;

He owes me mortal malice.

I 'll spend my wealth on this despiteful plot,

Ere he shall cross me and my nephew thus.

WIT. So maliciously !

Re-enter Host.

LUC.   How now, you treacherous rascal?   111

HOST. That 's none of my name, sir.

WIT.   Poor soul, he knew not on 't !

LUC. I 'm sorry. — I see then 't was a mere plot.

HOST. I trac'd 'em nearly —

LUC.   Well?

HOST.   And hear for certain

They have took Cole Harbor.

LUC.   The Devil's sanctuary !

They shall not rest ; I 'll pluck her from his arms —

Kind and dear gentlemen,

If ever I had seat within your breasts ——

1 GENT. No more, good sir ; it is a wrong to us

To see you injur'd ; in a cause so just   120

We 'll spend our lives but we will right our friends.

LUC. Honest and kind ! come, we have delay'd too long ;

Nephew, take comfort ; a just cause is strong.

              Exeunt [*all but* WITGOOD].

WIT. That 's all my comfort, Uncle. Ha, ha, ha !

Now may events fall luckily and well ;

He that ne'er strives, says wit, shall ne'er excel.

                               [*Exit.*]

[SCENE IV] [46]

Enter DAMPIT, *the usurer, drunk.*

DAM. When did I say my prayers? In anno '88, when the great Armado was coming ; and in anno '99,[47] when the great thunder and lightning was : I pray'd heartily then, i' faith, to overthrow Poovies' [48] new buildings ; I kneeled by my great iron chest, I remember.

[*Enter* AUDREY.]

AUD. Master Dampit, one may hear you before they see you ; you keep sweet hours, Master Dampit ; we were all abed three hours ago.

DAM. Audrey —   10

AUD. O, y' are a fine gentleman !

DAM. So I am i' faith, and a fine scholar. Do you use to go to bed so early, Audrey?

AUD. Call you this early, Master Dampit?

DAM. Why, is 't not one of clock i' th' morning? Is not that early enough? Fetch me a glass of fresh beer.

AUD. Here, I have warm'd your nightcap for you, Master Dampit.

DAM. Draw it on then. I am very [20 weak, truly ; I have not eaten so much as the bulk of an egg these three days.

AUD. You have drunk the more, Master Dampit.

DAM. What 's that?

AUD. You mought,[49] an you would, Master Dampit.

DAM. I answer you, I cannot. Hold your prating ; you prate too much, and understand too little. Are you answered? Give me a [30 glass of beer.

AUD. May I ask you how you do, Master Dampit?

DAM. How do I? I' faith, naught.

AUD. I ne'er knew you do otherwise.

DAM. I ate not one penn'ort' of bread these two years. Give me a glass of fresh beer. I am not sick, nor I am not well.

AUD. Take this warm napkin about your neck, sir, whilst I help to make you un- [40 ready.[50]

DAM. How now, Audrey-prater, with your scurvy devices, what say you now?

AUD. What say I, Master Dampit? I say nothing, but that you are very weak.

DAM. Faith, thou hast more cony-catching [51] devices than all London !

AUD. Why, Master Dampit, I never deceiv'd you in all my life.

DAM. Why was that? Because I never [50 did trust thee.

AUD. I care not what you say, Master Dampit !

---

[45] Old eds. *thrifts.* Dyce silently emends.

[46] A room in Dampit's house.

[47] Probably not, as mod. eds. suggest, an error for '89 (when there *was* a terrific thunderstorm) ; the point is the long lapse of time.

[48] The allusion is unidentified ; the name may indeed be taken at random and intended merely to illustrate Dampit's malevolence.

[49] Might.   [50] Undress you.   [51] Cheating.

DAM. Hold thy prating; I answer thee, thou art a beggar, a quean,[52] and a bawd : are you answer'd?

AUD. Fie, Master Dampit! a gentleman, and have such words?

DAM. Why, thou base drudge of infortunity,[53] thou kitchen-stuff drab of beg- [60 gary, roguery, and coxcombry, thou cavernesed quean of foolery,[54] knavery, and bawd-reaminy,[55] I 'll tell thee what, I will not give a louse for thy fortunes.

AUD. No, Master Dampit? and there 's a gentleman, comes a-wooing to me, and he doubts [56] nothing but that you will get me from him.

DAM. I? If I would either have thee or lie with thee for two thousand pound, would [70 I might be damn'd ! Why, thou base, impudent quean of foolery, flattery, and coxcombry, are you answer'd?

AUD. Come, will you rise and go to bed, sir?

DAM. Rise, and go to bed too, Audrey? How does Mistress Proserpine?

AUD. Fooh !

DAM. She 's as fine a philosopher of a stinkard's wife, as any within the liberties.[57] Fah, fah, Audrey !　　　　　　　　　　　　80

AUD. How now, Master Dampit?

DAM. Fie upon 't, what a choice of stinks here is ! What hast thou done, Audrey? Fie upon 't, here 's a choice of stinks indeed ! Give me a glass of fresh beer, and then I will to bed.

AUD. It waits for you above, sir.

DAM. Foh ! I think they burn horns in Barnard's Inn.[58] If ever I smelt such an abominable stink, usury forsake me,　　[*Exit.*]

AUD. They be the stinking nails of his [90 trampling feet, and he talks of burning of horns.　　　　　　　　　　　　　　*Exit.*

ACT IV — [SCENE I] [1]

Enter, at Cole Harbor, [WALKADINE] HOARD, [Courtesan *as*] the Widow, [LAMPREY, SPICH-COCK,] *and* Gentlemen ; *he married now.*

1 GENT. Join hearts, join hands,
In wedlock's bands,

Never to part
Till death cleave your heart.
You shall forsake all other women ;
You, lords, knights, gentlemen, and yeomen.
What my tongue slips
Make up with your lips.

HOA. Give you joy, Mistress Hoard ; let the kiss come about.[2]

Who knocks? Convey my little pig-eater [3] out.　　　　　　　　　　　　　　　10

LUC. [*within*] Hoard !

HOA. Upon my life, my adversary, gentlemen !

LUC. [*within*] Hoard, open the door, or we will force it ope ;
Give us the widow.

HOA.　　　　Gentlemen, keep 'em out.

LAM. He comes upon his death that enters here.

LUC. [*within*] My friends assist me.

HOA.　　　He has assistants, gentlemen.

LAM. Tut, nor him nor them we in this action fear.

LUC. [*within*] Shall I, in peace, speak one word with the widow?

COUR. Husband, and gentlemen, hear me but a word.

HOA. Freely, sweet wife.

COUR.　　　　Let him in peaceably ; [20
You know we 're sure from any act of his.

HOA. Most true.

[COUR.] [4] You may stand by and smile at his old weakness ;
Let me alone [5] to answer him.

HOA.　　　　　　　　Content ;
'T will be good mirth, i' faith. How think you, gentlemen?

LAM. Good gullery ! [6]

HOA.　　　Upon calm conditions let him in.

LUC. [*within*] All spite and malice —

LAM.　　　Hear me, Master Lucre :
So [7] you will vow a peaceful entrance [8]
With those your friends, and only exercise
Calm conference with the widow, without fury,　　　　　　　　　　　　　　30
The passage shall receive you.

Enter LUCRE, [Gentlemen, *and* Host.]

LUC.　　　　　　　　I do vow it.

LAM. Then enter and talk freely ; here she stands.

---

[52] Hussy.　　　[53] Misfortune, adversity.
[54] *I.e.*, she is like a cavern full of foolery, a vault or cellar stored with foolery. (Kittredge.)
[55] Bawdry. Cf. on I, iv, 80.　　　[56] Fears.
[57] Suburbs, in which the brothels flourished.
[58] One of the inns of court ; it stood in Holborn.
[1] A room in Cold Harbor. See on II, i, 304. Cf. on III, iii, entrance direction.

[2] Circulate.　　　　　　[3] A term of endearment.
[4] Old eds. *Luc.*　　　　[5] Leave it to me.
[6] Trickery.　　　　　　　[7] Provided that.
[8] Trisyllabic.

Luc. Oh, Master Hoard, your spite has watch'd the hour!

You 're excellent at vengeance, Master Hoard.

Hoa. Ha, ha, ha!

Luc.   I am the fool you laugh at;

You are wise, sir, and know the seasons well. —

[Lucre *takes* Courtesan *aside.*]

Come hither, widow; why! is it thus?

Oh, you have done me infinite disgrace,

And your own credit no small injury!

Suffer mine enemy so despitefully   40

To bear you from my nephew? Oh, I had

Rather half my substance had been forfeit

And begg'd by some starv'd rascal!

   Cour. Why, what would you wish me do, sir?

I must not overthrow my state for love;

We have too many precedents for that;

From thousands of our wealthy undone widows

One may derive some wit. I do confess

I lov'd your nephew; nay, I did affect him

Against the mind and liking of my friend[s]; [9]

Believ'd his promises; lay here in hope   51

Of flatter'd living, and the boast of lands.

Coming to touch his wealth and state indeed,

It appears dross; I find him not the man;

Imperfect, mean, scarce furnish'd of his needs;

In words, fair lordships; in performance, hovels.

Can any woman love the thing that is not?

   Luc. Broke you for this?

   Cour.   Was it not cause too much?

Send to inquire his state: most part of it

Lay two years mortgag'd in his uncle's hands.

   Luc. Why, say it did; you might have known my mind;   61

I could have soon restor'd it.

   Cour. Ay, had I but seen any such thing perform'd,

Why, 't would have tied my affection, and contain'd

Me in my first desires. Do you think, i' faith,

That I could twine such a dry oak as this,

Had promise in your nephew took effect?

   Luc. Why, and there 's no time past; and rather than

My adversary should thus thwart my hopes,

I would ——   70

   Cour. Tut, y 'ave been ever full of golden speech;

If words were lands, your nephew would be rich.

[9] Add. Q₂.

Luc. Widow, believe it, I vow by my best bliss,

Before these gentlemen, I will give in

The mortgage to my nephew instantly,

Before I sleep or eat.

   1 Gent. [*of Lucre's party*]   We 'll pawn our credits,

Widow, what he speaks shall be perform'd

In fullness.

   Luc.   Nay, more: I will estate him

In farther blessings; he shall be my heir; —

I have no son —   80

I 'll bind myself to that condition.

   Cour. When I shall hear this done, I shall soon yield

To reasonable terms.

   Luc.   In the mean season,

Will you protest, before these gentlemen,

To keep yourself as you are now at this present?

   Cour. I do protest, before these gentlemen,

I will be as clear then as I am now.

   Luc. I do believe you. Here 's your own honest servant;

I 'll take him along with me.

   Cour.   Ay, with all my heart.

   Luc. He shall see all perform'd, and bring you word.   90

   Cour. That 's all I wait for.

[Lucre *and* Courtesan *rejoin the rest.*]

   Hoa.   What, have you finish'd, Master Lucre?

Ha, ha, ha, ha!

   Luc. So laugh, Hoard, laugh at your poor enemy, do;

The wind may turn, you may be laugh'd at too;

Yes, marry, may you, sir. — Ha, ha, ha!

Exeunt [Lucre, *his party, and* Host].

   Hoa. Ha, ha, ha! if every man that swells in malice

Could be reveng'd as happily as I,

He would choose hate, and forswear amity. —

What did he say, Wife, prithee?

   Cour. Faith, spoke to ease his mind.

   Hoa.   Oh, oh, oh! [100

   Cour. You know now, little to any purpose.

   Hoa.   True, true, true!

   Cour. He would do mountains now.

   Hoa.   Ay, ay, ay, ay.

   Lam. Y 'ave struck him dead, Master Hoard.

   Spi. Ay, and his nephew desperate.

   Hoa.   I know 't, sirs, ay;

Never did man so crush his enemy! *Exeunt.*

[Scene II] [10]

Enter Lucre *with* Gentlemen [*and* Host,] *meeting* Sam Freedom.

Luc. My son-in-law, Sam Freedom! Where's my nephew?

Free. O man in lamentation,[11] Father!

Luc. 　　　　　　　　　　　　How!

Free. He thumps his breast like a gallant dicer that has lost his doublet, and stands in's shirt to do penance.

Luc. Alas, poor gentleman!

Free. I warrant you may hear him sigh in a still evening to your house at Highgate.

Luc. I prithee send him in.

Free. Were it to do a greater matter, I [10 will not stick with [12] you, sir, in regard you married my mother. 　　　　　　　[*Exit.*]

Luc. Sweet gentlemen, cheer him up; I will but fetch the mortgage and return to you instantly. 　　　　　　　　　　*Exit.*

1 Gent. We'll do our best, sir. — See where he comes,

E'en joyless and regardless of all form.

[*Enter* Witgood.]

2 Gent. Why, how [now,] [13] Master Witgood? Fie! you a firm scholar, and an understanding gentleman, and give your [20 best parts to passion? [14]

1 Gent. Come, fie!

Wit. Oh, gentlemen! ——

1 Gent. Sorrow of me, what a sigh was there, sir! Nine such widows are not worth it.

Wit. To be borne from me by that lecher, Hoard!

1 Gent. That vengeance is your uncle's; being done

More in despite to him than wrong to you: [29 But we bring comfort now.

Wit. 　　　　I beseech you, gentlemen ——

2 Gent. Cheer thyself, man; there's hope of her, i' faith!

Wit. Too gladsome to be true.

Re-enter Lucre.

Luc. 　　　　　　Nephew, what cheer? Alas, poor gentleman, how art thou chang'd! Call thy fresh blood into thy cheeks again: She comes —

Wit. 　　　　　Nothing afflicts me so much, But that it is your adversary, Uncle, And merely [15] plotted in despite of you.

Luc. Ay, that's it mads me, spites me! I'll spend my wealth ere he shall carry her so, because I know 't is only to spite me. Ay, [40 this is it. — Here, Nephew [*giving a paper*], before these kind gentlemen, I deliver in your mortgage, my promise to the widow; see, 't is done. Be wise; you're once more master of your own. The widow shall perceive now you are not altogether such a beggar as the world reputes you; you can make shift to bring her to three hundred a year, sir.

1 Gent. Berlady, and that's no toy,[16] sir. 　　　　　　　　　　　　50

Luc. A word, Nephew.

1 Gent. [*to* Host] Now you may certify the widow.

Luc. [*drawing* Witgood *aside*] You must conceive it aright, Nephew, now; To do you good I am content to do this.

Wit. I know it, sir.

Luc. 　　　But your own conscience can tell I had it

Dearly enough of you.

Wit. 　　　　　Ay, that's most certain.

Luc. Much money laid out, beside many a journey

To fetch the rent; I hope you'll think on 't, Nephew.

Wit. I were worse than a beast else, i' faith.

Luc. Although to blind the widow and the world 　　　　　　　　　　　　61

I out of policy do 't, yet there's a conscience, Nephew.

Wit. Heaven forbid else!

Luc. 　　　　　When you are full possess'd, 'T is nothing to return it.

Wit. Alas, a thing quickly done, Uncle!

Luc. Well said! you know I give it you but in trust.

Wit. Pray, let me understand you rightly, Uncle:

You give it me — but in trust?

Luc. No.

Wit. That is, you trust me with it? 　　70

Luc. True, true.

Wit. [*aside*] But if ever I trust you with it again, would I might be truss'd up [17] for my labor!

Luc. You can all witness, gentlemen; and you, sir yeoman?

HOST. My life for yours, sir, now, I know my mistress's mind [so] [18] well toward your nephew; let things be in preparation; and I'll train [19] her hither in most excellent fashion.
                                   Exit.
LUC. A good old boy! — Wife! Jinny! [81

Enter Wife.

MRS. L. What's the news, sir?
LUC. The wedding day's at hand; prithee, sweet wife, express thy housewifery. Thou'rt a fine cook, I know't; thy first husband married thee out of an alderman's kitchen; go to, he rais'd thee for raising of paste. What! here's none but friends; most of our beginnings must be wink'd at. — Gentlemen, I invite you all to my nephew's wedding against Thursday morning.   91
1 GENT. With all our hearts, and we shall joy to see
Your enemy so mock'd.
LUC. He laugh'd at me, gentlemen; ha, ha, ha!   *Exeunt [all but* WITGOOD].
WIT. He has no conscience, faith, would laugh at them: they laugh at one another! Who then can be so cruel? Troth, not I; I rather pity now, than aught envy. [20]   99
I do conceive such joy in mine own happiness, I have no leisure yet to laugh at their follies.
[*To the mortgage*] Thou soul of my estate, I kiss thee!
I miss life's comfort when I miss thee.
O, never will we part again,
Until I leave the sight of men!
We'll ne'er trust conscience of our kin,
Since cozenage brings that title in.   [*Exit.*]

[SCENE III] [21]

Enter three Creditors.

1 CRED. I'll wait these seven hours but I'll see him caught.
2 CRED. Faith, so will I.
3 CRED. Hang him, prodigal! He's stripp'd of the widow.
1 CRED. A' my troth, she's the wiser; she has made the happier choice; and I wonder of what stuff those widows' hearts are made of, that will marry unfledg'd boys before comely thrum [22]-chinn'd gentlemen.   10

Enter a Boy.

BOY. News, news, news!
1 CRED. What, boy?
BOY. The rioter is caught.
1 CRED. So, so, so, so! it warms me at the heart; I love a' life [23] to see dogs upon men. Oh, here he comes.

Enter WITGOOD, *with* Sergeants.

WIT. My last joy was so great it took away the sense of all future afflictions. What a day is here o'ercast! How soon a black tempest rises!   20
1 CRED. Oh, we may speak with you now, sir! What's become of your rich widow? I think you may cast your cap at the widow, may you not, sir?
2 CRED. He a rich widow? Who, a prodigal, a daily rioter, and a nightly vomiter? He, a widow of account? He, a hole [24] i' th' Counter. [25]
WIT. You do well, my masters, to tyrannize over misery, to afflict the afflicted; 't is a [30 custom you have here amongst you; I would wish you never leave it, and I hope you'll do as I bid you.
1 CRED. Come, come, sir; what say you extempore now to your bill of a hundred pound? A sweet debt for frotting [26] your doublets?
2 CRED. Here's mine of forty.
3 CRED. Here's mine of fifty.
WIT. Pray, sirs, — you'll give me [40 breath?
1 CRED. No, sir, we'll keep you out of breath still; then we shall be sure you will not run away from us.
WIT. Will you but hear me speak?
2 CRED. You shall pardon us for that, sir; we know you have too fair a tongue of your own: you overcame us too lately, a shame take you! We are like to lose all that for want of witnesses; we dealt in policy [50 then: always when we strive to be most politic we prove most coxcombs; *non plus ultra* I perceive by us: we're not ordain'd to thrive by wisdom, and therefore we must be content to be tradesmen.
WIT. Give me but reasonable time, and I protest I'll make you ample satisfaction.
1 CRED. Do you talk of reasonable time to us?

[18] Emend. Dyce; Q₁ *to;* Q₂ *too.*
[19] Entice.   [20] Bear malice.
[21] Unlocated; probably a street.
[22] Tufted; the thrum was the waste end of the warp.
[23] See on II, i, 315.
[24] The worst part of a prison.   [25] A city prison.
[26] Rubbing with perfumes. (Skeat and Mayhew.)

WIT. 'T is true, beasts know no reason- [60 able time.

2 CRED. We must have either money or carcass.

WIT. Alas, what good will my carcass do you?

3 CRED. Oh, 't is a secret delight we have amongst us! We that are us'd to keep birds in cages, have the heart to keep men in prison, I warrant you.

WIT. [*aside*] I perceive I must crave a [70 little more aid from my wits. — Do but make shift for me this once, and I 'll forswear ever to trouble you in the like fashion hereafter; I 'll have better employment for you, an I live. — You 'll give me leave, my masters, to make trial of my friends, and raise all means I can?

1 CRED. That 's our desires, sir.

Enter Host.

HOST. Master Witgood.

WIT. Oh, art thou come?

HOST. May I speak one word with you [80 in private, sir?

WIT. No, by my faith, canst thou; I am in hell here, and the devils will not let me come to thee.

CITIZENS.[27] Do you call us devils? You shall find us Puritans. — Bear him away; let 'em talk as they go; we 'll not stand to hear 'em. — Ah, sir, am I a devil? I shall think the better of myself as long as I live — a devil, i' faith!   *Exeunt.* [90

[SCENE IV] [28]

Enter [WALKADINE] HOARD.

HOA. What a sweet blessing hast thou, Master Hoard, above a multitude! Wilt thou never be thankful? How dost thou think to be blest another time? Or dost thou count this the full measure of thy happiness? By my troth, I think thou dost: not only a wife large in possessions, but spacious in content: she 's rich, she 's young, she 's fair, she 's wise. When I wake, I think of her lands — that revives me; when I go to bed, I dream of [10 her beauty — and that 's enough for me; she 's worth four hundred a year in her very smock, if a man knew how to use it. But the journey will be all, in troth, into the country; to ride to her lands in state and order following; my brother, and other worshipful gentlemen, whose companies I ha' sent down for already, to ride along with us in their goodly decorum beards, their broad velvet cassocks, and chains of gold twice or thrice double; against [29] [20 which time I 'll entertain some ten men of mine own into liveries, all of occupations or qualities: I will not keep an idle man about me; the sight of which will so vex my adversary Lucre — for we 'll pass by his door of purpose, make a little stand for [the] nonce,[30] and have our horses curvet before the window — certainly he will never endure it, but run up and hang himself presently!

[*Enter* Servant.]

How now, sirrah, what news? Any that [30 offer their service to me yet?

SER. Yes, sir, there are some i' th' hall that wait for your Worship's liking, and desire to be entertain'd.

HOA. Are they of occupation?

SER. They are men fit for your Worship, sir.

HOA. Say'st so? Send 'em all in! [*Exit* Servant.] — To see ten men ride after me in watchet [31] liveries, with orange-tawny [40 capes, — 't will cut his comb, i' faith.

Enter All [: Tailor, Barber, Perfumer, Falconer, *and* Huntsman].

How now? Of what occupation are you, sir?

TAI. A tailor, an 't please your Worship.

HOA. A tailor? Oh, very good; you shall serve to make all the liveries. — What are you, sir?

BAR. A barber, sir.

HOA. A barber? very needful; you shall shave all the house, and, if need require, stand for a reaper i' th' summer time. — You, [50 sir?

PER. A perfumer.

HOA. I smelt you before. Perfumers, of all men, had need carry themselves uprightly; for if they were once knaves, they would be smelt out quickly. — To you, sir?

FAL. A falc'ner, an 't please your Worship.

HOA. Sa ho, sa ho, sa ho! — And you, sir?

HUNT. A huntsman, sir.

HOA. There, boy, there, boy, there, [60 boy! I am not so old but I have pleasant days to come. I promise, you, my masters, I take such a good liking to you, that I entertain you

---

[27] Old eds. *Cit.;* erroneously altered by mod. eds. to *1 Cred.* They are all talking at once.
[28] A room in Hoard's house.

[29] In preparation for.   [30] Occasion.
[31] Pale blue.

all; I put you already into my countenance,[32] and you shall be shortly in my livery; but especially you two, my jolly falc'ner and my bonny huntsman; we shall have most need of you at my wife's manor houses i' th' country; there's goodly parks and champion [33] grounds for you; we shall have all our [70 sports within ourselves; all the gentlemen a' th' country shall be beholding [34] to us and our pastimes.

FAL. And we'll make your Worship admire,[35] sir.

HOA. Say'st thou so? Do but make me admire, and thou shalt want for nothing. — My tailor!

TAI. Anon, sir.

HOA. Go presently in hand with the [80 liveries.

TAI. I will, sir.

HOA. My barber.

BAR. Here, sir.

HOA. Make 'em all trim fellows, louse 'em well, — especially my huntsman — and cut all their beards of the Polonian [36] fashion. — My perfumer.

PER. Under your nose, sir.

HOA. Cast a better savor upon the [90 knaves, to take away the scent of my tailor's feet, and my barber's lotium-water.[37]

PER. It shall be carefully perform'd, sir.

HOA. But you, my falc'ner and huntsman, the welcom'st men alive, i' faith!

HUNT. And we'll show you that, sir, shall deserve your Worship's favor.

HOA. I prithee, show me that. — Go, you knaves all, and wash your lungs i' th' buttery, go. [*Exeunt* Tailor, Barber, &c.] — By [100 th' mass, and well rememb'red! I'll ask my wife that question. — Wife, Mistress Jane Hoard!

Enter Courtesan, *alter'd in apparel.*

COUR. Sir, would you with me?

HOA. I would but know, sweet Wife, which might stand best to thy liking, to have the wedding dinner kept here or i' th' country?

COUR. Hum! — faith, sir, 't would like me better here; here you were married, here let all rites be ended.   110

HOA. Could a marquesse [38] give a better

answer? Hoard, bear thy head aloft; thou'st a wife will advance it.[39]

[*Enter* Host *with a letter.*]

What haste comes here now? Yea, a letter? Some dreg of my adversary's malice. Come hither; what's the news?

HOST. A thing that concerns my mistress, sir.   [*Gives a letter to* Courtesan.]

HOA. Why then it concerns me, knave!

HOST. Ay, and you, knave, too — cry [120 your Worship mercy. You are both like to come into trouble. I promise you, sir; a precontract.[40]

HOA. How? a precontract, say'st thou?

HOST. I fear they have too much proof on 't, sir; old Lucre, he runs mad up and down, and will to law as fast as he can; young Witgood laid hold on by his creditors, he exclaims upon you a' tother side, says you have wrought his undoing by the injurious de- [130 taining of his contract.

HOA. Body a' me!

HOST. He will have utmost satisfaction; The law shall give him recompense, he says.

COUR. [*aside*] Alas, his creditors so merciless! my state being yet uncertain, I deem it not unconscionable to furder him.

HOST. True, sir, —

HOA. Wife, what says that letter? Let me construe it.   140

COUR. Curs'd be my rash and unadvised words!

      [*Tears the letter and stamps on it.*]

I'll set my foot upon my tongue,
And tread my inconsiderate grant to dust.

HOA. Wife ——

HOST. [*aside*] A pretty shift,[41] i' faith! I commend a woman when she can make away a letter from her husband handsomely, and this was cleanly done, by my troth.

COUR. I did, sir!

Some foolish words I must confess did pass, Which now litigiously he fastens on me. [151

HOA. Of what force? Let me examine 'em.

COUR. Too strong, I fear: would I were well freed of him!

HOA. Shall I compound?

COUR. No, sir, I'd have it done some nobler way

---

[32] Favor.   [33] Champaign.   [34] Beholden.
[35] Wonder.   [36] Polish.
[37] Stale urine, used by barbers as a "lye" for the hair. (*N.E.D.*)
[38] Marchioness.

[39] An unconscious allusion to the horns of the cuckold.
[40] A precontract, only dissoluble by mutual consent, would invalidate a subsequent marriage.
[41] Trick.

Of your side; I 'd have you come off with
    honor;
Let baseness keep with them.   Why, have you
    not
The means, sir?   The occasion 's offer'd you.
    HOA. Where, how, dear Wife?   160
    COUR. He is now caught by his creditors;
the slave 's needy; his debts petty; he 'll
rather bind himself to all inconveniences than
rot in prison; by this only means you may get
a release from him.   'T is not yet come to his
uncle's hearing; send speedily for the creditors; by this time he 's desperate; he 'll set
his hand to anything; take order for his
debts, or discharge 'em quite; a pax on him,
let 's be rid of a rascal!   170
    HOA. Excellent!
Thou dost astonish me. — Go, run, make
    haste;
Bring both the creditors and Witgood hither.
    HOST. [*aside*] This will be some revenge
        yet.   [*Exit.*]
    HOA. In the mean space I 'll have a release
        drawn. — Within there!

        [*Enter* Servant.]

    SER. Sir?
    HOA. Sirrah, come take directions; go to
        my scrivener.
    COUR. [*aside*] I 'm yet like those whose
        riches lie in dreams —
If I be wak'd, they 're false; such is my fate,
Who ventures deeper than the desperate
    state.   180
Though I have sinn'd, yet could I become new;
For where I once vow, I am ever true.
    HOA. Away, dispatch; on my displeasure,
        quickly.   [*Exit* Servant.]
Happy occasion! pray Heaven he be in the
right vein now to set his hand to 't, that noth-
ing alter him; grant that all his follies may
meet in him at once, to besot him enough!
I pray for him, i' faith, and here he comes.

        [*Enter* WITGOOD *and* Creditors.]

    WIT. What would you with me now, my
uncle's spiteful adversary?   190
    HOA. Nay, sir, I am friends.
    WIT.   Ay, when your mischief 's spent.
    HOA. I heard you were arrested.
    WIT.   Well, what then?
You will pay none of my debts, I am sure.
    HOA. A wise man cannot tell;
There may be those conditions 'greed upon
May move me to do much.

    WIT.   Ay, when? —
'T is thou, perjured woman! (Oh, no name
Is vild enough to match thy treachery!)
Thou art the cause of my confusion.
    COUR. Out, you penurious slave!   200
    HOA. Nay, Wife, you are too froward;
Let him alone; give losers leave to talk.
    WIT. Shall I remember thee of another
        promise
Far stronger than the first?
    COUR.   I 'd fain know that.
    WIT. 'T would call shame to thy cheeks.
    COUR.   Shame!
    WIT.   Hark in your ear. —
        [*They converse apart.*]
Will he come off, think'st thou, and pay my
debts roundly?
    COUR. Doubt nothing; there 's a release
a-drawing and all, to which you must set your
hand.   210
    WIT. Excellent!
    COUR. But methinks, i' faith, you might
have made some shift to discharge this yourself, having in the mortgage, and never have
burd'ned my conscience with it.
    WIT. A' my troth, I could not; for my
creditors' cruelties extend to the present.
    COUR. No more. —
Why, do your worst for that, I defy you.
    WIT. Y' are impudent: I 'll call up wit-
        nesses.   220
    COUR. Call up thy wits, for thou hast been
        devoted
To follies a long time.
    HOA.   Wife, y' are too bitter. —
Master Witgood, and you, my masters, you
shall hear a mild speech come from me now,
and this it is: 't 'as been my fortune, gentlemen, to have an extraordinary blessing pour'd
upon me a' late, and here she stands; I have
wedded her, and bedded her, and yet she is
little the worse.   Some foolish words she hath
pass'd to you in the country, and some [230
peevish [42] debts you owe here in the city; set
the hare's head to the goose-giblet: [43] release
you her of her words, and I 'll release you of
your debts, sir.
    WIT. Would you so?   I thank you for that,
sir; I cannot blame you, i' faith.
    HOA. Why, are not debts better than words,
sir?
    WIT. Are not words promises, and are not
promises debts, sir?   240

[42] Silly, ridiculous.
[43] A proverbial expression = tit for tat.

HOA. He plays at back-racket [44] with me.

1 CRED. Come hither, Master Witgood, come hither ; be rul'd by fools once.

[WITGOOD *steps aside with the* Creditors.]

2 CRED. We are citizens, and know what belong to 't.

1 CRED. Take hold of his offer ; pax on her, let her go. If your debts were once discharg'd, I would help you to a widow myself worth ten of her.

3 CRED. Mass, partner, and now you [250 remember me on 't, there 's Master Mulligrub's sister newly fall'n a widow.

1 CRED. Cuds me, as pat as can be ! There 's a widow left for you : ten thousand in money, beside plate, jewels, *et cetera ;* I warrant it a match : we can do all in all with her. Prithee, dispatch ; we 'll carry thee to her presently.

WIT. My uncle will ne'er endure me when he shall hear I set my hand to a release. [260

2 CRED. Hark, I 'll tell thee a trick for that. I have spent five hundred pound in suits in my time ; I should be wise. Thou 'rt now a prisoner ; make a release ; take 't of my word, whatsoever a man makes as long as he is in durance, 't is nothing in law, not thus much.   [*Snaps his fingers.*]

WIT. Say you so, sir ?

3 CRED. I have paid for 't ; I know 't.

WIT. Proceed, then ; I consent.   270

3 CRED. Why, well said.

HOA. How now, my masters ; what, have you done with him ?

1 CRED. With much ado, sir, we have got him to consent.

HOA. Ah — a — a ! and what came his debts to now ?

1 CRED. Some eightscore odd pounds, sir.

HOA. Naw, naw, naw, naw, naw ! tell me the second time ; give me a lighter sum. [280 They are but desperate debts, you know ; ne'er call'd in but upon such an accident ; a poor, needy knave, he would starve and rot in prison. Come, come, you shall have ten shillings in the pound, and the sum down roundly.

1 CRED. You must make it a mark,[45] sir.

HOA. Go to, then ; tell [46] your money in the meantime ; you shall find little less there

[*giving them money*]. — Come, Master [290 Witgood, you are so unwilling to do yourself good now !

[*Enter* Scrivener.]

Welcome, honest scrivener. — Now you shall hear the release read.

SCRI. [*reads.*] " Be it known to all men, by these presents, that I, Theodorus Witgood, gentleman, sole nephew to Pecunius Lucre, having unjustly made title and claim to one Jane Medler, late widow of Anthony Medler, and now wife to Walkadine Hoard, in [300 consideration of a competent sum of money to discharge my debts, do for ever hereafter disclaim any title, right, estate, or interest in or to the said widow, late in the occupation of the said Anthony Medler, and now in the occupation of Walkadine Hoard ; as also neither to lay claim by virtue of any former contract, grant, promise, or demise, to any of her manor[s], manor houses, parks, groves, meadow-grounds, arable lands, barns, stacks, [310 stables, dove-holes, and coney [47]-burrows ; together with all her cattle, money, plate, jewels, borders, chains, bracelets, furnitures, hangings, moveables, or [immoveables].[48] In witness whereof, I, the said Theodorus Witgood, have interchangeably set to my hand and seal before these presents, the day and date above written."

WIT. What a precious fortune hast thou slipp'd [49] here, like a beast as thou art ! [320

HOA. Come, unwilling heart, come.

WIT. Well, Master Hoard, give me the pen ; I see
'T is vain to quarrel with our destiny.

             [*Signs the paper.*]

HOA. Oh, as vain a thing as can be ! you cannot commit a greater absurdity, sir. So, so ; give me that hand now ; before all these presents, I am friends for ever with thee.

WIT. Troth, and it were pity of my heart now, if I should bear you any grudge, i' faith.

HOA. Content ; I 'll send for thy uncle [330 against the wedding dinner ; we will be friends once again.

WIT. I hope to bring it to pass myself, sir !

HOA. How now ? Is 't [50] right, my masters ?

1 CRED. 'T is something wanting, sir ; yet it shall be sufficient.

<hr />

[44] The return of the ball in tennis, a *tu quoque.* (*N.E.D.*)

[45] Two-thirds of a pound ; the creditors make him come up from 50% to 66⅔%.

[46] Count.

[47] Rabbit.

[48] So Q₂ ; Q₁ *immouerables.*

[49] Let slip ; Witgood is addressing himself.

[50] The amount of the money.

HOA. Why, well said; a good conscience makes a fine show nowadays. Come, my masters, you shall all taste of my wine [340 ere you depart.

ALL. We follow you, sir.

[*Exeunt* HOARD *and* Scrivener.]

WIT. [*aside*] I'll try these fellows now. — A word, sir; what, will you carry me to that widow now?

1 CRED. Why, do you think we were in earnest, i' faith? Carry you to a rich widow? We should get much credit by that: a noted rioter! a contemptible prodigal! 'T was a trick we have amongst us to get in our [350 money; fare you well, sir.

Exeunt [Creditors].

WIT. Farewell, and be hang'd, you short pig-hair'd,[51] ram-headed [52] rascals! He that believes in you shall ne'er be sav'd, I warrant him. By this new league I shall have some access unto my love.

She is above.

JOYCE. Master Witgood!

WIT. My life!

JOYCE. Meet me presently; that note directs you [*throwing it down*]; I would [360 not be suspected. Our happiness attends us; farewell.

WIT. A word's enough.   *Exeunt.*

[SCENE V] [53]

DAMPIT, *the usurer, in his bed;* [54] AUDREY *spinning by;* [Boy.]

SONG

Let the usurer cram him, in interest that excel,
There's pits enow to damn him, before he comes to
        hell;
In Holborn some, in Fleet Street some,[55]
Where'er he come there's some, there's some.

DAM. *Trahe, traheto;* draw the curtain; give me a sip of sack more.

Enter [LAMPREY *and* SPICHCOCK].[56]

LAM. Look you; did not I tell you he lay like the Devil in chains, when he was bound for a thousand year? [57]

SPI. But I think the Devil had no steel [10 bedstaffs; [58] he goes beyond him for that.

LAM. Nay, do but mark the conceit [59] of his drinking; one must wipe his mouth for him with a muckinder,[60] do you see, sir?

SPI. Is this the sick trampler? [61] Why, he is only bedrid with drinking.

LAM. True, sir. — He spies us.

DAM. What, Sir Tristram? [62] You come and see a weak man here, a very weak man.

LAM. If you be weak in body, you [20 should be strong in prayer, sir.

DAM. Oh, I have prayed too much, poor man!

LAM. There's a taste of his soul for you!

SPI. Fah, loathsome!

LAM. I come to borrow a hundred pound of you, sir.

DAM. Alas, you come at an ill time! I cannot spare it, i' faith; I ha' but two thousand i' th' house.   30

AUD. Ha, ha, ha!

DAM. Out, you gernative [63] quean, the mullipood of villainy, the spinner of concupiscency!

Enter [SIR LAUNCELOT *and*] *other* Gentlemen.

SIR L. Yea, gentlemen, are you here before us? How is he now?

LAM. Faith, the same man still: the tavern bitch has bit him i' th' head.[64]

SIR L. We shall have the better sport with him; peace! — And how cheers Master [40 Dampit now?

DAM. Oh, my bosom,[65] Sir Launcelot, how cheer I! Thy presence is restorative.

SIR L. But I hear a great complaint of you, Master Dampit, among gallants.

DAM. I am glad of that, i' faith; prithee, what?

SIR L. They say you are wax'd proud a' late, and if a friend visit you in the afternoon, you'll scarce know him.   50

DAM. Fie, fie; proud? I cannot remember any such thing; sure I was drunk then.

SIR L. Think you so, sir?

[51] For the citizens wore their hair short.
[52] Cuckoldy.   [53] Dampit's bedchamber.
[54] "Discovered" on the inner stage.
[55] Cf. on I, iv, 77, 78. The "pits" are the brothels, and the taverns where Dampit is killing himself by drinking. These particular streets are mentioned because he tramps about them on his business, visiting their "pits" *en route.* (Kittredge.)
[56] They enter on the outer stage, which, by virtue of the bed on the opened inner stage, becomes part of the same chamber.   [57] See *Revelation*, xx, 2.

[58] See on *The White Devil*, V, i, 213.
[59] Odd manner.   [60] Handkerchief.
[61] See on I, iv, 13.
[62] *I.e.*, libertine. See on *Philaster*, IV, ii, 18. Professor Kittredge observes that the appellation here supports this interpretation, since lampreys were supposed to be a strong aphrodisiac.
[63] Addicted to "girning" or grumbling. (*N.E.D.*) *Mullipood* is obscure. ? Dirty toad — see *N.E.D.*, "mull" and "pode." (Kittredge.)
[64] Proverbial, = he's drunk.
[65] Best friend, confidant.

DAM. There 't was, i' faith; nothing but the pride of the sack; and so certify 'em. — Fetch sack, sirrah.

BOY. A vengeance sack you once!

[*Exit, and returns presently with sack.*]

AUD. Why, Master Dampit, if you hold on as you begin, and lie a little longer, you need not take care how to dispose your wealth; [60 you 'll make the vintner your heir.

DAM. Out, you babliaminy; [66] you unfeathered, cremitoried [67] quean; you cullisance [68] of scabiosity!

AUD. Good words, Master Dampit, to speak before a maid and a virgin!

DAM. Hang thy virginity upon the pole of carnality!

AUD. Sweet terms! My mistress shall know 'em.   70

LAM. Note but the misery of this usuring slave: here he lies, like a noisome dunghill, full of the poison of his drunken blasphemies; and they to whom he bequeaths all grudge him the very meat that feeds him, the very pillow that eases him. Here may a usurer behold his end. What profits it to be a slave in this world, and a devil i' th' next?

DAM. Sir Launcelot, let me buss [69] thee, Sir Launcelot; thou art the only friend that [80 I honor and respect.

SIR L. I thank you for that, Master Dampit.

DAM. Farewell, my bosom Sir Launcelot.

SIR L. Gentlemen, an you love me, let me step behind you, and one of you fall a-talking of me to him.

LAM. Content. — Master Dampit ——

DAM. So, sir.

LAM. Here came Sir Launcelot to see [90 you e'en now.

DAM. Hang him, rascal!

LAM. Who? Sir Launcelot?

DAM. Pythagorical [70] rascal!

LAM. Pythagorical?

DAM. Ay, he changes his cloak when he meets a sergeant.

SIR L. What a rogue 's this!

LAM. I wonder you can rail at him, sir; he comes in love to see you.   100

DAM. A louse for his love! His father

was a comb-maker; I have no need of his crawling love. He comes to have longer day, [71] the superlative rascal!

SIR L. 'Sfoot, I can no longer endure the rogue! — Master Dampit, I come to take my leave once again, sir.

DAM. Who? my dear and kind Sir Launcelot, the only gentleman of England? Let me hug thee; farewell, and a thousand. [72]

LAM. Compos'd of wrongs and slavish [111 flatteries!

SIR L. Nay, gentlemen, he shall show you more tricks yet; I 'll give you another taste of him.

LAM. Is 't possible?

SIR L. His memory is upon [73] departing.

DAM. Another cup of sack!

SIR L. Mass, then 't will be quite gone! Before he drink that, tell him there 's a [120 country client come up, and here attends for his learned advice.

LAM. Enough.

DAM. One cup more, and then let the bell toll; I hope I shall be weak enough by that time.

LAM. Master Dampit ——

DAM. Is the sack spouting?

LAM. 'T is coming forward, sir. Here 's a countryman, a client of yours, waits for [130 your deep and profound advice, sir.

DAM. A coxcombry; where is he? Let him approach; set me up a peg higher.

LAM. [*to* SIR LAUNCELOT] You must draw near, sir.

DAM. Now, Goodman Fooliaminy, what say you to me now?

SIR L. Please your good Worship, I am a poor man, sir ——

DAM. What make you in my chamber then?

SIR L. I would entreat your Worship's [141 device [74] in a just and honest cause, sir.

DAM. I meddle with no such matters; I refer 'em to Master No-man's office.

SIR L. I had but one house left me in all the world, sir, which was my father's, my grandfather's, my great-grandfather's; and now a villain has unjustly wrung me out, and took possession on 't.

DAM. Has he such feats? Thy best [150 course is to bring thy *ejectione firmae*, and in seven year thou mayst shove him out by the law.

---

[66] Babbler. Cf. on I, iv, 80.
[67] Burnt, syphilitic. (Kittredge.) — "Unfeathered" implies that she has lost her hair from the pox. (Kittredge.)
[68] A corruption of "cognizance" = badge.
[69] Kiss.
[70] Alluding, as Dampit's next observation shows, to the Pythagorean doctrine of metempsychosis.

[71] *I.e.*, period of grace, in which to repay a loan.
[72] Farewells.   [73] On the point of.
[74] An intentional malapropism.

SIR L. Alas, an't please your Worship, I have small friends and less money!

DAM. Hoyday! this gear [75] will fadge well.[76] Hast no money? Why, then, my advice is thou must set fire a' th' house, and so get him out.

LAM. That will break [77] strife, indeed. [160

SIR L. I thank your Worship for your hot counsel, sir. — Alt'ring but my voice a little, you see he knew me not; you may observe by this that a drunkard's memory holds longer in the voice than in the person. But, gentlemen, shall I show you a sight? Behold the little divedapper [78] of damnation, Gulf the usurer, for his time [79] worse than tother.

Enter HOARD *with* GULF.

LAM. What's he comes with him?   170

SIR L. Why, Hoard, that married lately the Widow Medler.

LAM. Oh, I cry you mercy, sir.

HOA. Now, gentlemen visitants, how does Master Dampit?

SIR L. Faith, here he lies, e'en drawing in, sir, good canary as fast as he can, sir; a very weak creature, truly; he is almost past memory.

HOA. Fie, Master Dampit! you lie lazing abed here, and I come to invite you to [181 my wedding dinner; up, up, up!

DAM. Who's this? Master Hoard? Who hast thou married, in the name of foolery?

HOA. A rich widow.

DAM. A Dutch widow! [80]

HOA. A rich widow; one Widow Medler.

DAM. Medler? She keeps open house.[81]

HOA. She did, I can tell you, in her tother husband's days; open house for [190 all comers; horse and man was welcome, and room enough for 'em all.

DAM. There's too much for thee, then; thou mayst let out some to thy neighbors.

GULF. What, hung alive in chains? O spectacle! bedstaffs of steel? *O monstrum horrendum, informe, ingens, cui lumen ademptum!* [82] O Dampit, Dampit, here's a just judgment shown upon usury, extortion, and trampling [83] villainy!   200

SIR L. This is excellent, thief rails upon the thief!

GULF. Is this the end of cutthroat usury, brothel, and blasphemy? Now mayst thou see what race a usurer runs.

DAM. Why, thou rogue of universality, do not I know thee? Thy sound is like the cuckoo, the Welsh ambassador; [84] thou cowardly slave, that offers to fight with a sick man when his weapon's down! Rail [210 upon me in my naked bed? [85] Why, thou great Lucifer's little vicar! I am not so weak but I know a knave at first sight. Thou inconscionable rascal! thou that goest upon Middlesex juries, and will make haste to give up thy verdict because thou wilt not lose thy dinner! Are you answered?

GULF. An't were not for shame ——
                        Draws his dagger.

DAM. Thou wouldst be hang'd then.   219

LAM. Nay, you must exercise patience, Master Gulf, always, in a sick man's chamber.

SIR L. He'll quarrel with none, I warrant you, but those that are bedrid.

DAM. Let him come, gentlemen, I am arm'd; reach my close-stool hither.

SIR L. Here will be a sweet [86] fray anon; I'll leave you, gentlemen.

LAM. Nay, we'll along with you. — Master Gulf ——

GULF. Hang him, usuring rascal!   230

SIR L. Pish, set your strength to his, your wit to his!

AUD. Pray, gentlemen, depart; his hour's come upon him. — Sleep in my bosom, sleep.

SIR L. Nay, we have enough of him, i' faith; keep him for the house.
Now make your best;
For thrice his wealth I would not have his
    breast.

GULF. A little thing would make me beat him now he's asleep.

SIR L. Mass, then 't will be a pitiful [241 day when he wakes; I would be loath to see that day; come.

GULF. You overrule me, gentlemen, i' faith.   *Exeunt.*

---

[75] Matter, affair, business.
[76] Turn out well. Said ironically.
[77] Broach, start.
[78] Didapper, dabchick.
[79] *I.e.*, considering the duration of his activities.
[80] A prostitute.
[81] Another name for medlar, the fruit, was "openarse."
[82] O horrible monster, misshapen, huge, deprived of sight. (Vergil, *Aeneid*, III, 658.)

[83] Cf. on I, iv, 13.
[84] Nares suggests that this title for the cuckoo came from its migrating from the west. There is also, of course, a jocular reflection upon the Welsh nation.
[85] Upon me undressed in my bed.
[86] With reference to its odoriferous possibilities.

ACT V — [SCENE I] [1]

Enter LUCRE *and* WITGOOD.

WIT. Nay, Uncle, let me prevail with you so much ; i' faith, go, now he has invited you.

LUC. I shall have great joy there when he has borne away the widow !

WIT. Why, la, I thought where I should find you presently. — Uncle, a' my troth, 't is nothing so.

LUC. What 's nothing so, sir? Is not he married to the widow?

WIT. No, by my troth, is he not, Uncle. [10

LUC. How?

WIT. Will you have the truth on 't? He is married to a whore, i' faith.

LUC. I should laugh at that.

WIT. Uncle, let me perish in your favor if you find it not so ; and that 't is I that have married the honest woman.

LUC. Ha ! I'd walk ten mile afoot to see that, i' faith.

WIT. And see 't you shall, or I 'll ne'er [20 see you again.

LUC. A quean, i' faith? Ha, ha, ha !

Exeunt.

[SCENE II] [2]

Enter [WALKADINE] HOARD, *tasting wine, the* Host *following in a livery cloak.*

HOA. Pup, pup, pup, pup ; I like not this wine. Is there never a better tierce [3] in the house?

HOST. Yes, sir, there are as good tierce [3] in the house as any are in England.

HOA. Desire your mistress, you knave, to taste 'em all over ; she has better skill.

HOST. [*aside*] Has she so? The better for her, and the worse for you. *Exit.*

HOA. Arthur ! 10

[*Enter* ARTHUR.]

Is the cupboard of plate [4] set out?

ARTH. All 's in order, sir. [*Exit.*]

HOA. I am in love with my liveries every time I think on 'em ; they make a gallant show, by my troth. Niece !

[*Enter* JOYCE.]

JOYCE. Do you call, sir?

---

[1] Unlocated ; perhaps a room in Lucre's house.
[2] A room in Hoard's house.
[3] A plural form. The pun is on the meaning "thrust", in fencing.
[4] A sideboard or cabinet for holding and displaying plate.

HOA. Prithee, show a little diligence, and overlook the knaves a little ; they 'll filch and steal to-day, and send whole pasties home to their wives ; an thou beest a good niece, do [20 not see me purloin'd.

JOYCE. Fear it not, sir — [*aside*] I have cause : though the feast be prepared for you, yet it serves fit for my wedding dinner too.

[*Exit.*]

Enter [LAMPREY *and* SPICHCOCK].

HOA. Master Lamprey and Master Spichcock, two the most welcome gentlemen alive ! Your fathers and mine were all free a' th' fishmongers. [5]

LAM. They were indeed, sir. You see bold guests, sir ; soon entreated. 30

HOA. And that 's best, sir.

[*Enter* Servant.]

How now, sirrah?

SER. There 's a coach come to th' door, sir.

[*Exit.*]

HOA. My Lady Foxstone, a' my life ! — Mistress Jane Hoard ! Wife ! — Mass, 't is her Ladyship indeed !

[*Enter* LADY FOXSTONE.]

Madam, you are welcome to an unfurnish'd house, dearth of cheer, scarcity of attendance.

L. Fox. You are pleas'd to make the worst, sir. 40

HOA. Wife !

[*Enter* Courtesan.]

L. Fox. Is this your bride?

HOA. Yes, madam. — Salute my Lady Foxstone.

COUR. Please you, madam, awhile to taste the air in the garden?

L. Fox. 'T will please us well.

Exeunt [L. FOXSTONE *and* Courtesan].

HOA. Who would not wed? The most delicious life !

No joys are like the comforts of a wife.

LAM. So we bachelors think, that are [50 not troubled with them.

[*Re-enter* Servant.]

SER. Your Worship's brother, with another ancient gentleman, [6] are newly alighted, sir.

[*Exit.*]

---

[5] *I.e.*, members of that one of the great city companies.
[6] Mod. eds. emend *other . . . gentlemen* perhaps rightly. There may have been reduction of personnel here.

HOA. Master Onesiphorus Hoard? Why, now our company begins to come in.

[*Enter* ONESIPHORUS HOARD, LIMBER, *and* KIX.]

My dear and kind Brother, welcome, i' faith.

O. HOA. You see we are men at an hour, Brother.

HOA. Ay, I 'll say that for you, Brother; you keep as good an hour to come to a feast [60 as any gentleman in the shire. — What, old Master Limber and Master Kix! Do we meet, i' faith, jolly gentlemen?

LIM. We hope you lack guests,[7] sir?

HOA. Oh, welcome, welcome! We lack still such guests [7] as your Worships.

O. HOA. Ah, sirrah Brother, have you catch'd up Widow Medler?

HOA. From 'em all, Brother; and I may tell you I had mighty enemies, those that [70 stuck sore; old Lucre is a sore fox, I can tell you, Brother.

O. HOA. Where is she? I 'll go seek her out; I long to have a smack at her lips.

HOA. And most wishfully,[8] Brother, see where she comes.

[*Re-enter* Courtesan *and* LADY FOXSTONE.]

Give her a [smack] [9] now we may hear it all the house over.

[Courtesan *and* ONESIPHORUS HOARD] *turn back.*

COUR. O Heaven, I am betray'd! I know that face. 80

HOA. Ha, ha, ha! Why, how now? Are you both asham'd? — Come, gentlemen, we 'll look another way.

O. HOA. Nay, Brother, hark you: come, y' are dispos'd to be merry.

HOA. Why do we meet else, man?

O. HOA. That 's another matter; I was ne'er so 'fraid in my life but that you had been in earnest.

HOA. How mean you, Brother? 90

O. HOA. You said she was your wife!

HOA. Did I so? By my troth, and so she is.

O. HOA. By your troth, Brother?

HOA. What reason have I to dissemble with my friends, Brother? If marriage can make her mine, she is mine! Why ——

O. HOA. Troth, I am not well of a sudden. I must crave pardon, Brother; I came to see you, but I cannot stay dinner, i' faith.

HOA. I hope you will not serve me so, Brother. 101

LIM. By your leave, Master Hoard ——

HOA. What now? what now? Pray, gentlemen: — you were wont to show yourselves wise men.

LIM. But you have shown your folly too much here.

HOA. How?

KIX. Fie, fie! a man of your repute and name!

You 'll feast your friends, but cloy 'em first with shame.

HOA. This grows too deep; pray, let us reach the sense. 110

LIM. In your old age dote on a courtesan!

HOA. Ha?

KIX. Marry a strumpet!

HOA. Gentlemen!

O. HOA. And Witgood's quean!

HOA. Oh! nor lands nor living?

O. HOA. Living!

HOA. [*to* Courtesan] Speak.

COUR. Alas, you know, at first, sir,

I told you I had nothing. 120

HOA. Out, out! I am cheated; infinitely cozened!

LIM. Nay, Master Hoard ——

Enter WITGOOD *and* LUCRE [*and* JOYCE.]

HOA. A Dutch widow! a Dutch widow! a Dutch widow!

LUC. Why, Nephew, shall I trace thee still a liar?

Wilt make me mad? Is not yon thing the widow?

WIT. Why, la, you are so hard a' belief Uncle!

By my troth, she 's a whore.

LUC. Then thou 'rt a knave.

WIT. *Negatur argumentum*, Uncle. 129

LUC. *Probo tibi*, Nephew: he that knows a woman to be a quean must needs be a knave; thou say'st thou knowest her to be one; *ergo*, if she be a quean, thou 'rt a knave.

WIT. *Negatur sequela majoris*, Uncle: he that knows a woman to be a quean must needs be a knave — I deny that.

HOA. Lucre and Witgood, y' are both villains; get you out of my house!

LUC. Why, didst not invite me to thy wedding dinner? 140

WIT. And are not you and I sworn perpetual friends before witness, sir, and were both drunk upon 't?

[7] Old eds. spell *guesse.*
[8] In response to your wish.   [9] Old eds. *smerck.*

Hoa. Daintily abus'd ! Y 'ave put a junt [10]
upon me !

Luc. Ha, ha, ha !

Hoa.   A common strumpet !

Wit.   Nay, now
You wrong her, sir ; if I were she, I 'd have
The law on you for that ; I durst depose for
her
She ne'er had common use nor common
thought.

  Cour. Despise me, publish me : I am your
wife ;
What shame can I have now but you 'll have
part?   150
If in disgrace you share, I sought not you ;
You pursued me, nay, forc'd me ; had I friends
would follow it,
Less than your action has been prov'd a rape.

  O. Hoa. Brother !

  Cour. Nor did I ever boast of lands unto
you,
Money, or goods ; I took a plainer course,
And told you true, I 'd nothing.
If error were committed, 't was by you ;
Thank your own folly. Nor has my sin been
So odious but worse has been forgiven ; 160
Nor am I so deform'd but I may challenge
The utmost power of any old man's love.
She that tastes not sin before, twenty to one
but she 'll taste it after ; most of you old men
are content to marry young virgins, and take
that which follows ; where,[11] marrying one of
us, you both save a sinner and are quit from a
cuckold for ever.
And more, in brief, let this your best thoughts
win :
She that knows sin, knows best how to hate sin.

  Hoa. Curs'd be all malice ! black are the
fruits of spite,   171
And poison first their owners. Oh, my friends,
I must embrace shame, to be rid of shame !
Conceal'd disgrace prevents a public name.
Ah, Witgood ! ah, Theodorus !

  Wit. Alas, sir, I was prick'd in conscience
to see her well bestow'd, and where could I bestow her better than upon your pitiful Worship? Excepting but myself, I dare swear she 's
a virgin ; and now, by marrying your [180
niece, I have banish'd myself for ever from
her. She 's mine aunt [12] now, by my faith,
and there 's no meddling with mine aunt, you
know — a sin against my nuncle.[13]

Cour. [*kneeling*] Lo, gentlemen, before you
all
In true reclaimed form I fall.
Henceforth for ever I defy [14]
The glances of a sinful eye,
Waving of fans (which some suppose
Tricks of fancy [15]), treading of toes, 190
Wringing of fingers, biting the lip,
The wanton gait, th' alluring trip ;
All secret friends [16] and private meetings,
Close [17]-borne letters and bawds' greetings ;
Feigning excuse to women's labors
When we are sent for to th' next neighbor's ;
Taking false physic, and ne'er start
To be let blood though sign be at heart ; [18]
Removing chambers, shifting beds,
To welcome friends in husbands' steads ; 200
Them to enjoy, and you to marry ;
They first serv'd, while you must tarry ;
They to spend, and you to gather ;
They to get, and you to father : —
These, and thousand, thousand more,
New reclaimed, I now abhor.

  Luc. [*to* Witgood] Ah, here 's a lesson, rioter, for you !

  Wit. [*kneeling*] I must confess my follies :
I 'll down too ;
And here for ever I disclaim
The cause of youth's undoing, game, 210
Chiefly dice, those true outlanders,
That shake out beggars, thieves, and panders :
Soul-wasting surfeits, sinful riots,
Queans' evils, doctors' diets,
Pothecaries' drugs, surgeons' glisters ; [19]
Stabbing of arms [20] for a common mistress ;
Riband favors, ribald speeches ;
Dear perfum'd jackets,[21] penniless breeches ;
Dutch flapdragons,[22] healths in urine ; [23]
Drabs that keep a man too sure in — 220
I do defy you all.
Lend me each honest hand, for here I rise
A reclaim'd man, loathing the general vice.

  Hoa. So, so ; all friends ! the wedding
dinner cools.
Who seem most crafty prove ofttimes most
fools.   [*Exeunt.*]

---

[14] Renounce. [15] Love. [16] Lovers. [17] Secretly.
[18] And therefore unfavorable. "According to the
directions for bleeding in old almanacs, blood was
to be taken from particular parts under particular
planets." (Dyce.)   [19] Clysters, syringes.
[20] And then mixing the blood with wine in a health
to one's mistress.   [21] Cf. on IV, iii, 36.
[22] A flap dragon was a raisin, or similar object, set or
fire and drunk in wine as it flamed. Dutchmen were
supposed to be experts at this variety of drinking.
[23] Another extravagance of the gallants; it was
drunk mixed with wine.

---

[10] Trick.   [11] Whereas.
[12] Playing on "aunt" = "mistress."
[13] Mine uncle.

THE

CHANGELING:

As it was Acted (with great Applause)
at the Privat house in D R U R Y ⸱ L A N E,
and *Salisbury Court.*

Written by $\left\{\begin{array}{c}THOMAS\ MIDLETON,\\ \text{and}\\ WILLIAM\ ROWLEY.\end{array}\right\}$ Gent'.

Never Printed before.

L O N D O N,

Printed for H U M P H R E Y M O S E L E Y, and are to
be sold at his shop at the sign of the *Princes-Arms*
in St *Pauls* Church-yard, 1 6 5 3.

INTRODUCTORY NOTE

The Changeling is sadly marred, to a modern taste, by the lunatic divertissements which were always acceptable to the Elizabethans; yet it is none the less among the most powerful tragedies of the seventeenth century. Beatrice-Joanna and De Flores provide acting rôles of tremendous force. In a series of lurid flashes the lightning-like scenes of the tragic plot reveal their Titanic passions and their indomitable wills, while under a sky lowering with almost Websterian darkness and horror the proud heroine is hunted to her doom.

To Middleton's collaborator the comic portion of the play is due; but Rowley is also credited with the opening and the closing of the main plot. Middleton is doubtless the author of the great tragic episodes. They mark the height of his powers, which he seems only to have reached during the period of his association with Rowley.

The source is the fourth story in Book I of John Reynolds's *Triumphs of God's Revenge against Murder* (1621); but the material is freely handled, the deaths of the principal characters being radically altered. The play was probably written c. 1622; it was acted at court on January 4, 1624, and had a long career on the public stage. It was revived after the Restoration, when the great Betterton was much applauded as De Flores.

No edition, however, is known prior to that of 1653, on which the present text is based. A later issue, in 1668, consists merely of the remaindered sheets of 1653, with a new title page. As Oliphant observes, we can have no confidence that the play has reached us in its original state; the thirty years that elapsed between its production and publication afforded ample scope for stage tampering, which is reflected in the broken metre of many of the lines, and in such inconsistencies as the omission of scenes carefully prepared for — *e.g.*, the quarrel between Antonio and Franciscus (see IV, iii, 168, ff.). It is a grievous commentary on public taste that the title alludes to the leading figure of the foolish underplot.

THE CHANGELING

BY

THOMAS MIDDLETON AND WILLIAM ROWLEY

DRAMATIS PERSONAE

VERMANDERO, [governor of the castle of Alicant,] father to Beatrice.
TOMAZO DE PIRACQUO, a noble lord.
ALONZO DE PIRACQUO, his brother, suitor to Beatrice.
ALSEMERO, a nobleman, afterwards married to Beatrice.
JASPERINO, his friend.
ALIBIUS, a jealous doctor.
LOLLIO, his man.

PEDRO, friend to Antonio.
ANTONIO, the changeling.[1]
FRANCISCUS, the counterfeit madman
DE FLORES, servant to Vermandero.
Madmen.
Servants.

BEATRICE [-JOANNA], daughter to Vermandero.
DIAPHANTA, her waiting woman.
ISABELLA, wife to Alibius.

THE SCENE — *Alicante.*

ACT I — [SCENE I] [2]

Enter ALSEMERO.

ALS. 'T was in the temple where I first beheld her,
And now again the same. What omen yet
Follows of that? None but imaginary.
Why should my hopes or fate be timorous?
The place is holy, so is my intent:
I love her beauties to the holy purpose;
And that, methinks, admits comparison
With man's first creation, the place blest,
And is his right home back, if he achieve it.
The church hath first begun our interview, [10
And that's the place must join us into one;
So there's beginning and perfection too.

Enter JASPERINO.

JAS. Oh, sir, are you here? Come, the wind's fair with you;
Y' are like to have a swift and pleasant passage.
ALS. Sure, y' are deceiv'd, friend, 't is contrary,
In my best judgment.

JAS. What, for Malta? [3]
If you could buy a gale amongst the witches,[4]
They could not serve you such a lucky pennyworth [5]
As comes a' God's name.[6]
ALS. Even now I observ'd
The temple's vane to turn full in my face; [20
I know 't is against me.
JAS. Against you?
Then you know not where you are.
ALS. Not well, indeed.
JAS. Are you not well, sir?
ALS. Yes, Jasperino,
Unless there be some hidden malady
Within me, that I understand not.
JAS. And that
I begin to doubt,[7] sir. I never knew
Your inclinations to travels at a pause
With any cause to hinder it, till now.
Ashore you were wont to call your servants up,
And help to trap your horses for the speed; [8]
At sea I have seen you weigh the anchor with 'em, 31
Hoist sails for fear to lose the foremost breath,
Be in continual prayers for fair winds;
And have you chang'd your orisons?

---

[1] Idiot; with a glance, however, at the meanings: (1) turncoat; (2) child (especially an idiot child), substituted by the fairies for a normal human child which they have stolen from its cradle.
[2] Before a church. — Q *Allegant*, above.

[3] In the source Alsemero was on his way there, hoping to obtain a command against the Turks.
[4] Who had them to sell.
[5] Bargain. [6] *I.e.*, freely. [7] Fear, suspect.
[8] In order to hasten the process.

Als.   No, friend;
I keep the same church, same devotion.

Jas. Lover I'm sure y' are none; the
    stoic was
Found in you long ago; your mother nor
Best friends, who have set snares of beauty, ay,
And choice ones too, could never trap you that
    way.
What might be the cause?

Als.   Lord, how violent [40
Thou art! I was but meditating of
Somewhat I heard within the temple.

Jas.   Is this
Violence? 'T is but idleness compar'd
With your haste yesterday.

Als.   I 'm all this while
A-going, man.

Enter Servants.

Jas.   Backwards, I think, sir. Look,
Your servants.

1 Ser. The seamen call; shall we board
your trunks?

Als. No, not to-day.

Jas. 'T is the critical day, it seems, and the
sign [9] in Aquarius.   51

2 Ser. We must not to sea to-day; this
smoke will bring forth fire.

Als. Keep all on shore; I do not know the
    end,
Which needs I must do, of an affair in hand
Ere I can go to sea.

1 Ser.   Well, your pleasure.

2 Ser. Let him e'en take his leisure too; we
are safer on land.   *Exeunt* Servants.

Enter Beatrice-Joanna, Diaphanta, *and*
Servants; [Alsemero *accosts the lady and
then kisses her.*[10]]

Jas. [*aside*] How now! The laws of the
Medes are chang'd sure; salute a woman! [60
He kisses too; wonderful! Where learnt he
this? and does it perfectly too. In my conscience,[11] he ne'er rehears'd it before. Nay,
go on; this will be stranger and better news at
Valencia than if he had ransom'd half Greece
from the Turk.

Beat. You are a scholar, sir?

Als.   A weak one, lady.

Beat. Which of the sciences is this love you
    speak of?

Als. From your tongue I take it to be
    music.

Beat. You are skilful in 't, can sing at first
    sight.   70

Als. And I have show'd you all my skill at
    once;
I want more words to express me further,
And must be forc'd to repetition:
I love you dearly.

Beat.   Be better advis'd, sir;
Our eyes are sentinels unto our judgments,
And should give certain judgment what they
    see;
But they are rash sometimes, and tell us won-
    ders
Of common things, which when our judgments
    find,
They can then check the eyes, and call them
    blind.

Als. But I am further, lady; yesterday [80
Was mine eyes' employment, and hither
    now
They brought my judgment, where are both
    agreed.
Both houses [12] then consenting, 't is agreed;
Only there wants the confirmation
By the hand royal: that 's your part, lady.

Beat. Oh, there 's one above me,[13] sir. —
    [*aside*] For five days past
To be recall'd! Sure mine eyes were mistaken;
This was the man was meant me. That he
    should come
So near his time, and miss it!

Jas. [*aside*] We might have come by the [90
carriers from Valencia, I see, and sav'd all our
sea-provision; we are at farthest, sure. Methinks I should do something too;
I meant to be a venturer [14] in this voyage.
Yonder 's another vessel, I 'll board [15] her;
If she be lawful prize, down goes her topsail.[16]
                              [*Accosts* Diaphanta.]

Enter De Flores.

De F. Lady, your father ——

Beat.   Is in health, I hope.

De F. Your eye shall instantly instruct you,
    lady;
He 's coming hitherward.

Beat.   What needed then
Your duteous preface? I had rather   100
He had come unexpected; you must stall [17]
A good presence with unnecessary blabbing;

---

[9] In the almanac.
[10] A common salutation then, not necessarily in-
dicative of love.
[11] As far as I know.

[12] Of Parliament.
[13] Her father.   [14] Investor.   [15] Accost.
[16] In token of surrender. — Q *Deflores*, throughout.
[17] Forestall.

And how welcome for your part you are,
I'm sure you know.
    DE F. [*aside*]   Will't never mend, this
        scorn,
One side nor other? Must I be enjoin'd
To follow still [18] whilst she flies from me?
        Well,
Fates, do your worst, I'll please myself with
        sight
Of her at all opportunities,
If but to spite her anger. I know she had
Rather see me dead than living; and yet [110
She knows no cause for't but a peevish will.
    ALS. You seem'd displeas'd, lady, on the
        sudden.
    BEAT. Your pardon, sir; 't is my infirmity;
Nor can I other reason render you
Than his or hers, [of] [19] some particular thing
They must abandon as a deadly poison,
Which to a thousand other tastes were whole-
        some;
Such to mine eyes is that same fellow there,
The same that report speaks of the basilisk.[20]
    ALS. This is a frequent frailty in our
       nature;   120
There's scarce a man amongst a thousand
       found
But hath his imperfection: one distastes
The scent of roses, which to infinites
Most pleasing is and odoriferous;
One, oil, the enemy of poison;
Another, wine, the cheerer of the heart
And lively refresher of the countenance.
Indeed this fault, if so it be, is general;
There's scarce a thing but is both lov'd and
       loath'd;   129
Myself, I must confess, have the same frailty.
    BEAT. And what may be your poison, sir?
        I am bold with you.
    ALS. What [21] might be your desire, perhaps:
        a cherry.
    BEAT. I am no enemy to any creature
My memory has, but yon gentleman.
    ALS. He does ill to tempt your sight, if he
        knew it.
    BEAT. He cannot be ignorant of that, sir,
I have not spar'd to tell him so; and I want [22]
To help myself, since he's a gentleman
In good respect with my father, and follows
        him.

    ALS. He's out of his place then now.
                         [*They talk apart.*]
    JAS.   I am a mad wag, wench. [140
    DIA. So methinks; but for your comfort, I
can tell you, we have a doctor in the city that
undertakes the cure of such.
    JAS. Tush, I know what physic is best for
the state of mine own body.
    DIA. 'T is scarce a well-govern'd state, I be-
lieve.
    JAS. I could show thee such a thing with an
ingredian [23] that we two would compound
together, and if it did not tame the mad- [150
dest blood i' th' town for two hours after, I'll
ne'er profess physic again.
    DIA. A little poppy, sir, were good to cause
you sleep.
    JAS. Poppy? I'll give thee a pop i' th' lips
for that first, and begin there. Poppy is one
simple [24] indeed, and cuckoo (what-you-call't)
another. I'll discover no more now; another
time I'll show thee all.   [*Exit.*] [25]

    Enter VERMANDERO *and* Servants.

    BEAT. My father, sir.
    VER.   Oh, Joanna, I came to meet
        thee.   160
Your devotion's ended?
    BEAT.   For this time, sir. —
[*aside*] I shall change my saint,[26] I fear me; I
    find
A giddy turning in me. — Sir, this while
I am beholding [27] to this gentleman,
Who left his own way to keep me company,
And in discourse I find him much desirous
To see your castle. He hath deserv'd it, sir,
If ye please to grant it.
    VER.   With all my heart, sir.
Yet there's an article between; [28] I must
    know
Your country; we use not to give survey [170
Of our chief strengths [29] to strangers; our
    citadels
Are plac'd conspicuous to outward view,
On promonts' [30] tops, but within are secrets.
    ALS. A Valencian, sir.
    VER.   A Valencian?
That's native, sir. Of what name, I beseech
    you?
    ALS. Alsemero, sir.

---

[18] Always.   [19] Q *or.*
[20] A fabulous serpent, hatched from a cock's egg; it killed with its glance.
[21] Q *And what;* erroneously repeating from the preceding line.
[22] Am unable, lack means.

[23] Ingredient, element.   [24] Remedy.
[25] So Dyce, probably rightly, since Jasperino is not introduced to Vermandero.
[26] *I.e.*, the object of my devotion.
[27] Beholden.   [28] One consideration interposes.
[29] Strongholds.   [30] Promontories'.

VER.   Alsemero? Not the son
Of John de Alsemero?

ALS.   The same, sir.

VER. My best love bids you welcome.

BEAT.   He was wont
To call me so, and then [31] he speaks a most
Unfeigned truth.

VER.   Oh, sir, I knew your father; [180
We two were in acquaintance long ago,
Before our chins were worth iulan [32] down,
And so continued till the stamp of time
Had coin'd us into silver. Well, he's gone;
A good soldier went with him.

ALS. You went together [33] in that, sir.

VER. No, by Saint Jacques, I came behind
     him;
Yet I've done somewhat too. An unhappy
     day
Swallowed him at last at Gibraltar,
In fight with those rebellious Hollanders. [190
Was it not so?

ALS.   Whose death I had reveng'd,
Or followed him in fate, had not the late
     league [34]
Prevented me.

VER.   Ay, ay, 't was time to breathe. —
Oh, Joanna, I should ha' told thee news;
I saw Piracquo lately.

BEAT. [aside]   That's ill news.

VER. He's hot preparing for this day of
     triumph; [35]
Thou must be a bride within this sevennight.

ALS. [aside]   Ha!

BEAT. Nay, good sir, be not so violent;
     with speed
I cannot render satisfaction
Unto the dear companion of my soul,   200
Virginity, whom I thus long have liv'd with,
And part with it so rude and suddenly.
Can such friends divide, never to meet again,
Without a solemn farewell?

VER.   Tush, tush! there's a toy.[36]

ALS. [aside] I must now part, and never
     meet again
With any joy on earth. — Sir, your pardon;
My affairs call on me.

VER.   How, sir? By no means;
Not chang'd so soon, I hope! You must see
     my castle,
And her best entertainment, e'er we part;

I shall think myself unkindly us'd else.   [210
Come, come, let's on; I had good hope your
     stay
Had been awhile with us in Alicant;
I might have bid you to my daughter's wed-
     ding.

ALS. [aside] He means to feast me, and poi-
     sons me beforehand. —
I should be dearly glad to be there, sir,
Did my occasions suit as I could wish.

BEAT. I shall be sorry if you be not there
When it is done, sir; but not so suddenly.

VER. I tell you, sir, the gentleman's com-
     plete,
A courtier and a gallant, enrich'd   220
With many fair and noble ornaments;
I would not change him for a son-in-law
For any he in Spain, the proudest he,
And we have great ones, that you know.

ALS.   He's much
Bound to you, sir.

VER.   He shall be bound to me
As fast as this tie can hold him; I'll want
My will else.

BEAT. [aside]   I shall want mine, if you
     do it.

VER. But come; by the way I'll tell you
more of him.

ALS. [aside] How shall I dare to venture in
     his castle,   229
When he discharges murderers [37] at the gate?
But I must on, for back I cannot go.

BEAT. [aside] Not this serpent gone yet?
                    [Drops a glove.

VER.   Look, girl, thy glove's fallen.
Stay, stay; De Flores, help a little.

DE. F.   Here, lady.   [Offers her the glove.

BEAT. Mischief on your officious forward-
     ness!
Who bade you stoop? They touch my hand
     no more —
There! For tother's sake I part with this;
          [Takes off and throws down the other
          glove.
Take 'em, and draw thine own skin off with
     'em!
                    Exeunt [all but DE FLORES.

DE F. Here's a favor come with a mischief
now! I know
She had rather wear my pelt tann'd in a pair
Of dancing pumps, than I should thrust my
     fingers   240
Into her sockets here. I know she hates me,
Yet cannot choose but love her. No matter;

---

[31] In speaking so.
[32] The first tender down (Gk. ἴουλος). (Dyce.)
[33] Were equal.
[34] A truce existed between the Dutch and the Spaniards from 1609 till 1621.
[35] Joy, festivity.   [36] Trifle.
[37] Cannon used to scatter shot at short ranges.

If but to vex her, I 'll haunt her still ;
Though I get nothing else, I 'll have my will.
                                                    Exit.

[SCENE II] [38]

Enter ALIBIUS *and* LOLLIO.

ALIB. Lollio, I must trust thee with a secret,
But thou must keep it.

LOL. I was ever close [39] to a secret, sir.

ALIB. The diligence that I have found in
        thee,
The care and industry already past,
Assures me of thy good continuance.
Lollio, I have a wife.

LOL. Fie, sir, 't is too late to keep her secret ; she 's known to be married all the town
and country over.   10

ALIB. Thou goest too fast, my Lollio.
        That knowledge
I allow no man can be barr'd it ;
But there is a knowledge which is nearer,
Deeper, and sweeter, Lollio.

LOL. Well, sir, let us handle that between
you and I.

ALIB. 'T is that I go about, man. Lollio,
My wife is young.

LOL. So much the worse to be kept secret,
sir.   20

ALIB. Why, now thou meet'st the substance
        of the point ;
I am old, Lollio.

LOL. No, sir ; 't is I am old Lollio.

ALIB. Yet why may not this concord and
        sympathize ?
Old trees and young plants often grow to-
        gether,
Well enough agreeing.

LOL. Ay, sir, but the old trees raise themselves higher and broader than the young
plants.

ALIB. Shrewd [40] application ! There 's the
        fear, man ;   30
I would wear my ring on my own finger ;
Whilst it is borrowed, it is none of mine,
But his that useth it.

LOL. You must keep it on still [41] then ; if it
but lie by, one or other will be thrusting into 't.

ALIB. Thou conceiv'st [42] me, Lollio ; here
        thy watchful eye
Must have employment ; I cannot always be
At home.

LOL. I dare swear you cannot.

ALIB. I must look out.   40

LOL. I know 't, you must look out ; 't is
        every man's case.

ALIB. Here, I do say, must thy employ-
        ment be ;
To watch her treadings, and in my absence
Supply my place.

LOL. I 'll do my best, sir ; yet surely I cannot see who you should have cause to be jealous of.

ALIB. Thy reason for that, Lollio ? 'T is
A comfortable [43] question.

LOL. We have but two sorts of people in [50
the house, and both under the whip : that 's
fools [44] and madmen ; the one has not wit
enough to be knaves, and the other not knavery enough to be fools.

ALIB. Ay, those are all my patients, Lollio ;
I do profess the cure of either sort ;
My trade, my living 't is ; I thrive by it ;
But here 's the care that mixes with my thrift :
The daily visitants, that come to see
My brainsick patients, I would not have   60
To see my wife. Gallants I do observe
Of quick, enticing eyes, rich in habits,
Of stature and proportion very comely ;
These are most shrewd temptations, Lollio.

LOL. They may be easily answered, sir ; if
they come to see the fools and madmen, you
and I may serve the turn, and let my mistress
alone ; she 's of neither sort.

ALIB. 'T is a good ward ; [45] indeed, come
        they to see   69
Our madmen or our fools, let 'em see no more
Than what they come for ; by that consequent
They must not see her ; I 'm sure she 's no fool.

LOL. And I 'm sure she 's no madman.

ALIB. Hold that buckler fast ; Lollio, my
        trust
Is on thee, and I account it firm and strong.
What hour is 't, Lollio ?

LOL. Towards belly-hour, sir.

ALIB. Dinner time ? Thou mean'st twelve
        a 'clock ?

LOL. Yes, sir, for every part has his hour :
we wake at six and look about us, that 's [80
eye-hour ; at seven we should pray, that 's
knee-hour ; at eight walk, that 's leg-hour ; at
nine gather flowers and pluck a rose, [46] that 's
nose-hour ; at ten we drink, that 's mouth-hour ;
at eleven lay about us for victuals, that 's hand-
hour ; at twelve go to dinner, that 's belly-hour.

---

[38] A room in Alibius's house.   [39] Secret.
[40] Devilish, cursed. Alibius takes the greater
height of the old trees as an allusion to the horns of
the cuckold.
[41] Continuously.   [42] Understandest.

[43] Comforting.   [44] Imbeciles.
[45] Defensive stroke.   [46] Defecate.

ALIB. Profoundly, Lollio! It will be long
Ere all thy scholars learn this lesson, and
I did look to have a new one ent'red ; — stay,
I think my expectation is come home.   90

Enter PEDRO, *and* ANTONIO [*disguised*] *like
an idiot.*

PED. Save you, sir ; my business speaks itself :
This sight takes off the labor of my tongue.

ALIB. Ay, ay, sir, 't is plain enough, you
   mean
Him for my patient.

PED. And if your pains prove but commo-
dious,[47] to give but some little strength to his
sick and weak part of nature in him, these are
[*giving him money*] but patterns to show you
of the whole pieces that will follow to you, beside the charge of diet, washing, and other [100
necessaries, fully defrayed.

ALIB. Believe it, sir, there shall no care be
   wanting.

LOL. Sir, an officer in this place may deserve
something. The trouble will pass through
my hands.

PED. 'T is fit something should come to
your hands then, sir.   [*Gives him money.*]

LOL. Yes, sir, 't is I must keep him sweet,[48]
and read to [49] him. What is his name?

PED. His name is Antonio ; marry, we [110
use but half to him, only Tony.

LOL. Tony, Tony ; 't is enough, and a very
good name for a fool. — What 's your name,
Tony?

ANT. He, he, he ! well, I thank you, cousin ;
he, he, he !

LOL. Good boy ! hold up your head. — He
can laugh ; I perceive by that he is no beast.

PED. Well, sir,
If you can raise him but to any height,   120
Any degree of wit ; might he attain,
As I might say, to creep on but all four
Towards the chair of wit, or walk on crutches,
'T would add an honor to your worthy pains,
And a great family might pray for you,
To which he should be heir, had he discretion
To claim and guide his own. Assure you, sir,
He is a gentleman.

LOL. Nay, there 's nobody doubted that :
at first sight I knew him for a gentleman ; [130
he looks no other yet.

PED. Let him have good attendance and
   sweet lodging.

LOL. As good as my mistress lies in, sir ;
and as you allow us time and means, we can
raise him to the higher degree of discretion.

PED. Nay, there shall no cost want, sir.

LOL. He will hardly be stretch'd up to the
wit of a magnifico.[50]

PED. Oh, no, that 's not to be expected ; far
shorter will be enough.   140

LOL. I 'll warrant you [I 'll] make him fit to
bear office in five weeks ; I 'll undertake to
wind him up to the wit of constable.

PED. If it be lower than that, it might serve
turn.

LOL. No, fie ; to level him with a head-
borough,[51] beadle, or watchman, were but little
better than he is. Constable I 'll able[52] him ;
if he do come to be a justice afterwards, let
him thank the keeper. Or I 'll go further [150
with you ; say I do bring him up to my own
pitch, say I make him as wise as myself.

PED. Why, there I would have it.

LOL. Well, go to ; either I 'll be as errant a
fool as he, or he shall be as wise as I, and then
I think 't will serve his turn.

PED. Nay, I do like thy wit passing well.

LOL. Yes, you may ; yet if I had not been
a fool, I had had more wit than I have too.
Remember what state [53] you find me in. [160

PED. I will, and so leave you. Your best
cares, I beseech you.   *Exit* PEDRO.

ALIB. Take you none with you; leave 'em
all with us.

ANT. Oh, my cousin's gone! cousin,
cousin, oh !

LOL. Peace, peace, Tony ; you must not
cry, child ; you must be whipp'd if you do ;
your cousin is here still ; I am your cousin,
Tony.   170

ANT. He, he ! then I 'll not cry, if thou be'st
my cousin ; he, he, he !

LOL. I were best try his wit a little, that I
may know what form [54] to place him in.

ALIB. Ay, do, Lollio, do.

LOL. I must ask him easy questions at first.
— Tony, how many true [55] fingers has a tailor
on his right hand?

ANT. As many as on his left, cousin.

LOL. Good ; and how many on both?   180

ANT. Two less than a deuce, cousin.

LOL. Very well answered. I come to you
again, cousin Tony ; how many fools goes to [56
a wise man?

---

[47] *I.e.*, serviceable enough.
[48] Clean.   [49] Teach.

[50] Grandee.   [51] A petty parish official.
[52] Vouch for.   [53] Responsible position.
[54] Grade, class.   [55] Honest.   [56] Make.

ANT. Forty in a day sometimes, cousin.

LOL. Forty in a day? How prove you that?

ANT. All that fall out amongst themselves, and go to a lawyer to be made friends.

LOL. A parlous [57] fool! he must sit in [190 the fourth form at least. I perceive that. — I come again, Tony; how many knaves make an honest man?

ANT. I know not that, cousin.

LOL. No, the question is too hard for you. I'll tell you, cousin; there's three knaves may make an honest man: a sergeant, a jailor, and a beadle; the sergeant catches him, the jailor holds him, and the beadle lashes him; and if he be not honest then, the hangman must [200 cure him.

ANT. Ha, ha, ha! that's fine sport, cousin.

ALIB. This was too deep a question for the fool, Lollio.

LOL. Yes, this might have serv'd yourself, though I say 't. — Once more and you shall go play, Tony.

ANT. Ay, play at push-pin,[58] cousin; ha, he!

LOL. So thou shalt; say how many fools are here. — 210

ANT. Two, cousin; thou and I.

LOL. Nay, y'are too forward there, Tony. Mark my question; how many fools and knaves are here; a fool before a knave, a fool behind a knave, between every two fools a knave; how many fools, how many knaves?

ANT. I never learnt so far, cousin.

ALIB. Thou putt'st too hard questions to him, Lollio. 219

LOL. I'll make him understand it easily. — Cousin, stand there.

ANT. Ay, cousin.

LOL. Master, stand you next the fool.

ALIB. Well, Lollio.

LOL. Here's my place. Mark now, Tony, there's a fool before a knave.

ANT. That's I, cousin.

LOL. Here's a fool behind a knave — that's I; and between us two fools there is a knave — that's my master; 't is but " We [230 Three " [59] — that's all.

ANT. We three, we three, cousin.

1 MADMAN. (*within*) Put's head i' th' pillory; the bread's too little.

2 MAD. (*within*) Fly, fly, and he catches the swallow.

3 MAD. (*within*) Give her more onion, or the Devil put the rope about her crag.[60]

LOL. You may hear what time of day it is; the chimes of Bedlam goes. 240

ALIB. Peace, peace, or the wire [61] comes!

3 MAD. (*within*) Cat whore, cat whore! her permasant, her permasant! [62]

ALIB. Peace, I say! — Their hour's come; they must be fed, Lollio.

LOL. There's no hope of recovery of that Welsh madman: was undone by a mouse that spoil'd him a permasant; lost his wits for 't.

ALIB. Go to your charge, Lollio; I'll to mine. 250

LOL. Go you to your madmen's ward; let me alone with your fools.[63]

ALIB. And remember my last charge, Lollio. *Exit.*

LOL. Of which your patients do you think I am? — Come, Tony, you must amongst your schoolfellows now; there's pretty scholars amongst 'em, I can tell you; there's some of 'em at *stultus, stulta, stultum*.[64]

ANT. I would see the madmen, cousin, [260 if they would not bite me.

LOL. No, they shall not bite thee, Tony.

ANT. They bite when they are at dinner, do they not, coz?

LOL. They bite at dinner, indeed, Tony. Well, I hope to get credit by thee; I like thee the best of all the scholars that ever I brought up, and thou shalt prove a wise man, or I'll prove a fool myself. *Exeunt.*

ACT II — [SCENE I] [1]

Enter BEATRICE *and* JASPERINO *severally.*

BEAT. Oh, sir, I'm ready now for that fair service
Which makes the name of friend sit glorious on you!
Good angels and this conduct be your guide!
[*Gives a paper.*]
Fitness of time and place is there set down, sir.

---

[57] Shrewd.
[58] Or put-pin, a child's game, in which each player pushes or fillips his pin with the object of crossing that of another player. (*N.E.D.*)
[59] A stock joke was a picture of two fools, entitled "We Three", the third of course being the spectator.
[60] Neck.   [61] Whip.
[62] Parmesan cheese.
[63] Leave the fools to me.
[64] *I.e.*, so far advanced as to be able to decline *stultus,* = foolish.
[1] Unlocated; presumably a room in the castle.

Jas. The joy I shall return[2] rewards my
     service.   *Exit.*

Beat. How wise is Alsemero in his friend !
It is a sign he makes his choice with judgment ;
Then I appear in nothing more approv'd
Than making choice of him ; for 't is a prin-
     ciple,
He that can choose   10
That bosom well who of his thoughts partakes,
Proves most discreet in every choice he makes.
Methinks I love now with the eyes of judg-
     ment,
And see the way to merit, clearly see it.
A true deserver like a diamond sparkles :
In darkness you may see him — that 's in
     absence,
Which is the greatest darkness falls on love ;
Yet is he best discern'd then
With intellectual eyesight. What 's Piracquo,
My father spends his breath for? And his
     blessing   20
Is only mine as I regard his name,
Else it goes from me, and turns head against
     me,
Transform'd into a curse. Some speedy way
Must be remem'bred. He 's so forward too,
So urgent that way, scarce allows me breath
To speak to my new comforts.

         Enter De Flores.

De F. [*aside*]   Yonder 's she ;
Whatever ails me, now a' late especially,
I can as well be hang'd as refrain seeing her ;
Some twenty times a day, nay, not so little,
Do I force errands, frame ways and excuses,
To come into her sight ; and I 've small reason
     for 't,   31
And less encouragement ; for she baits me
     still
Every time worse than other, does profess
     herself
The cruellest enemy to my face in town,
At no hand can abide the sight of me,
As if danger or ill luck hung in my looks.
I must confess my face is bad enough,
But I know far worse has better fortune,
And not endur'd alone, but doted on ;
And yet such pick-hair'd faces, chins like
     witches',   40
Here and there five hairs whispering in a cor-
     ner,
As if they grew in fear one of another,
Wrinkles like troughs, where swine-deformity
     swills

The tears of perjury, that lie there like wash
Fallen from the slimy and dishonest eye, —
Yet such a one [plucks][3] sweets without
     restraint,
And has the grace of beauty to his sweet.[4]
Though my hard fate has thrust me out to
     servitude,
I tumbled into th' world a gentleman.
She turns her blessed eye upon me now,   50
And I 'll endure all storms before I part with 't.
     Beat. [*aside*] Again?
This ominous ill-fac'd fellow more disturbs me
Than all my other passions.
     De F. [*aside*]   Now 't begins again ;
I 'll stand this storm of hail, though the
     stones pelt me.
     Beat. Thy business? What 's thy busi-
     ness?
     De F. [*aside*]   Soft and fair !
I cannot part so soon now.
     Beat. [*aside*]   The villain 's fix'd. —
Thou standing toad-pool[5] ——
     De F. [*aside*] The show'r falls amain now.
     Beat. Who sent thee? What 's thy er-
     rand? Leave my sight !
     De F. My Lord your father charg'd me
     to deliver   60
A message to you.
     Beat.   What, another since?
Do 't, and be hang'd then ; let me be rid of
     thee.
     De F. True service merits mercy.
     Beat.   What 's thy message?
     De F. Let beauty settle but in patience,
You shall hear all.
     Beat.   A dallying, trifling torment !
     De F. Signior Alonzo de Piracquo, lady,
Sole brother to Tomazo de Piracquo ——
     Beat. Slave, when wilt make an end?
     De F.   Too soon I shall.
     Beat. What all this while of him?
     De F.   The said Alonzo,
With the foresaid Tomazo ——
     Beat.   Yet again? [70
     De F. Is new alighted.
     Beat.   Vengeance strike the news !
Thou thing most loath'd, what cause was
     there in this
To bring thee to my sight?
     De F.   My Lord your father
Charg'd me to seek you out.
     Beat.   Is there no other
To send his errand by?

---

[2] To Alsemero.

[3] Q *pluckt.*   [4] In his sweetheart's eyes.
[5] *I.e.,* frogpond.

De F.　　　　　It seems 't is my luck
To be i' th' way still.
　　Beat.　　　　　Get thee from me !
　　De F.　　　　　So.
[*aside*] Why, am not I an ass to devise ways
Thus to be rail'd at ?　I must see her still !
I shall have a mad qualm within this hour
　　again,
I know 't ; and, like a common Garden[6] bull,
I do but take breath to be lugg'd [7] again. [81
What this may bode I know not ; I 'll despair
　　the less,
Because there 's daily precedents of bad faces
Belov'd beyond all reason.　These foul chops [8]
May come into favor one day 'mongst his [9]
　　fellows.
Wrangling has prov'd the mistress of good
　　pastime ;
As children cry themselves asleep, I ha' seen
Women have chid themselves abed to men.
　　　　　　　　　　Exit De Flores.
　　Beat. I never see this fellow but I think
Of some harm towards me ; danger 's in my
　　mind still ;　　　　　　　　　　90
I scarce leave trembling of an hour after.
The next good mood I find my father in,
I 'll get him quite discarded. — Oh, I was
Lost in this small disturbance, and forgot
Affliction's fiercer torrent that now comes
To bear down all my comforts !

Enter Vermandero, Alonzo, [*and*] Tomazo.

　　Ver.　　　　　Y' are both welcome,
But an especial one belongs to you, sir,
To whose most noble name our love presents
The addition [10] of a son, our son Alonzo.
　　Alon. The treasury of honor cannot bring
　　forth　　　　　　　　　　100
A title I should more rejoice in, sir.
　　Ver. You have improv'd it well. — Daugh-
　　ter, prepare ;
The day will steal upon thee suddenly.
　　Beat. [*aside*] Howe'er, I will be sure to
　　keep [11] the night,
If it should come so near me.
　　　　　[Beatrice *and* Vermandero *talk
　　　　　apart.*]
　　Tom.　　　　　Alonzo.
　　Alon.　　　　　Brother ?
　　Tom. In troth I see small welcome in her eye.

[6] Bulls and bears were baited at Paris Garden,
near the theatres on the Bankside, in Southwark.
[7] Worried by the ear, baited.
[8] *I.e.*, my face.
[9] Its ; referring to his face ; expressed by "foul
chops."　　　　　[10] Title.　　　　[11] Heed.

　　Alon. Fie, you are too severe a censurer [12]
Of love in all points, there 's no bringing on
　　you.
If lovers should mark everything a fault,
Affection would be like an ill-set [13] book, [110
Whose faults [14] might prove as big as half the
　　volume.
　　Beat. That 's all I do entreat.
　　Ver.　　　　　It is but reasonable ;
I 'll see what my son says to 't. — Son Alonzo,
Here is a motion made but to reprieve
A maidenhead three days longer : the request
Is not far out of reason, for indeed
The former time is pinching.
　　Alon.　　　　　Though my joys
Be set back so much time as I could wish
They had been forward, yet since she desires
　　it,
The time is set as pleasing as before ;　　120
I find no gladness wanting.
　　Ver.　　　　　May I ever
Meet it in that point still ! Y' are nobly wel-
　　come, sirs.
　　　　　Exeunt Vermandero *and* Beatrice.
　　Tom. So ; did you mark the dulness of her
　　parting now?
　　Alon. What dulness?　Thou art so excep-
　　tious [15] still !
　　Tom. Why, let it go then ; I am but a fool
To mark your harms so heedfully.
　　Alon.　　　　　Where 's the oversight?
　　Tom. Come, your faith 's cozened [16] in her,
　　strongly cozened.
Unsettle your affection with all speed
Wisdom can bring it to ; your peace is ruin'd
　　else.
Think what a torment 't is to marry one　130
Whose heart is leap'd into another's bosom :
If ever pleasure she receive from thee,
It comes not in thy name, or of thy gift ;
She lies but with another in thine arms,
He the half-father unto all thy children
In the conception ; if he get 'em not,
She helps to get 'em for him ; [17] and how dan-
　　gerous
And shameful her restraint may [grow] [18] in
　　time to,
It is not to be thought on without sufferings.

[12] Judge.
[13] Referring to the setting of the types.
[14] *I.e.*, the list of *errata*.
[15] Captious.
[16] Cheated, deceived.
[17] Q adds *in his passions*. Dyce suggests that
the author wrote the phrase and failed to strike it
out upon revision.
[18] Conj. Bullen ; Q *go*.

ALON. You speak as if she lov'd some other,
    then. 140
TOM. Do you apprehend so slowly?
ALON.   Nay, an that
Be your fear only, I am safe enough.
Preserve your friendship and your counsel,
    Brother,
For times of more distress ; I should depart
An enemy, a dangerous, deadly one,
To any but thyself, that should but think
She knew the meaning of inconstancy,
Much less the use and practice ; yet w' are
    friends.
Pray, let no more be urg'd ; I can endure
Much, till I meet an injury to her ; 150
Then I am not myself. Farewell, sweet
    Brother ;
How much w' are bound to Heaven to depart
    lovingly.   *Exit.*
  TOM. Why, here is love's tame madness ;
    thus a man
Quickly steals into his vexation.   *Exit.*

[SCENE II] [19]

Enter DIAPHANTA *and* ALSEMERO.

DIA. The place is my charge ; you have
    kept your hour,
And the reward of a just meeting bless you !
I hear my lady coming. Complete gentleman,
I dare not be too busy with my praises ;
The' are dangerous things to deal with. *Exit.*
ALS.   This goes well ;
These women are the ladies' cabinets :
Things of most precious trust are lock['d] into
    'em.

Enter BEATRICE.

BEAT. I have within mine eye all my de-
    sires.
Requests that holy prayers ascend Heaven
    for,
And brings 'em down to furnish our defects, [10
Come not more sweet to our necessities
Than thou unto my wishes.
ALS.   W' are so like
In our expressions, lady, that unless I bor-
    row
The same words, I shall never find their
    equals.
  BEAT. How happy were this meeting, this
    embrace,
If it were free from envy ! [20] This poor kiss
It has an enemy, a hateful one,

That wishes poison to 't. How well were I
    now,
If there were none such name known as
    Piracquo !
Nor no such tie as the command of par-
    ents — 20
I should be but too much blessed.
ALS.   One good service
Would strike off both your fears, and I 'll go
    near it too,
Since you are so distress'd. Remove the cause,
The command ceases ; so there 's two fears
    blown out
With one and the same blast.
  BEAT.   Pray, let me find [21] you, sir.
What might that service be, so strangely
    happy ?
  ALS. The honorablest piece 'bout man,
    valor ;
I 'll send a challenge to Piracquo instantly.
  BEAT. How? Call you that extinguishing
    of fear,
When 't is the only way to keep it flaming ? [30
Are not you ventured [22] in the action,
That 's all my joys and comforts ? Pray, no
    more, sir.
Say you prevail'd, you 're danger's and not
    mine then ;
The law would claim you from me, or ob-
    scurity
Be made the grave to bury you alive.
I 'm glad these thoughts come forth ; oh, keep
    not one
Of this condition, sir ! Here was a course
Found to bring sorrow on her way to death ;
The tears would ne'er 'a' dried, till dust had
    chok'd 'em.
Blood-guiltiness becomes a fouler visage ; —
And now I think on one. — [*aside*] I was to
    blame, 41
I ha' marr'd so good a market with my scorn ;
'T had been done questionless ; the ugliest
    creature
Creation fram'd for some use ; yet to see
I could not mark so much where it should
    be !
  ALS. Lady !
  BEAT. [*aside*]   Why, men of art make
    much of poison,
Keep one to expel another. Where was my
    art ?
  ALS. Lady, you hear not me.
  BEAT.   I do especially, sir.
The present times are not so sure of our side

[19] Another room.   [20] Malice.

[21] Understand.   [22] Risked.

As those hereafter may be ; we must use 'em
    then   50
As thrifty folks their wealth, sparingly now,
Till the time opens.
    ALS.   You teach wisdom, lady.
    BEAT. Within there ! Diaphanta !

          Re-enter DIAPHANTA.

    DIA.   Do you call, madam?
    BEAT. Perfect your service, and conduct
    this gentleman
The private way you brought him.
    DIA.   I shall, madam.
    ALS. My love's as firm as love e'er built
    upon.
        Exeunt DIAPHANTA *and* ALSEMERO.

          Enter DE FLORES.

    DE F. [*aside*] I have watch'd this meeting,
    and do wonder much
What shall become of tother ; I'm sure both
Cannot be serv'd unless she transgress ; hap-
    pily [23]
Then I'll put in for one ; for if a woman [60
Fly from one point, from him she makes a
    husband,
She spreads and mounts then like arithmetic :
One, ten, a hundred, a thousand, ten thou-
    sand —
Proves in time sutler to an army royal.
Now do I look to be most richly rail'd at,
Yet I must see her.
    BEAT. [*aside*]   Why, put case [24] I
    loath'd him
As much as youth and beauty hates a sepulchre,
Must I needs show it? Cannot I keep that
    secret,
And serve my turn upon him? See, he's
    here. —
De Flores.
    DE F. [*aside*]   Ha, I shall run mad
    with joy !   70
She call'd me fairly by my name, De Flores,
And neither rogue nor rascal.
    BEAT.   What ha' you done
To your face a' late? Y' ave met with some
    good physician ;
Y' ave prun'd [25] yourself, methinks ; you were
    not wont
To look so amorously.[26]
    DE F.   Not I. —
    [*aside*] 'T is the same physnomy,[27] to a hair
    and pimple,

[23] Perhaps.   [24] Suppose.   [25] Preened.
[26] So like a lover.   [27] Physiognomy.

Which she call'd scurvy scarce an hour ago.
How is this?
    BEAT.   Come hither ; nearer, man.
    DE F. [*aside*] I'm up to the chin in Heaven !
    BEAT.   Turn, let me see ;
Vauh,[28] 't is but the heat of the liver, I per-
    ceive 't ;   80
I thought it had been worse.
    DE F. [*aside*]   Her fingers touch'd me !
She smells all amber.[29]
    BEAT. I'll make a water for you shall
    cleanse this
Within a fortnight.
    DE F.   With your own hands, lady?
    BEAT. Yes, mine own, sir ; in a work of
    cure
I'll trust no other.
    DE F. [*aside*]   'T is half an act of
    pleasure
To hear her talk thus to me.
    BEAT.   When w' are us'd
To a hard face, 't is not so unpleasing ;
It mends still in opinion, hourly mends ;
I see it by experience.
    DE F. [*aside*]   I was blest   90
To light upon this minute ; I'll make use on 't.
    BEAT. Hardness becomes the visage of a
    man well ;
It argues service, resolution, manhood —
If cause were of employment.
    DE F.   'T would be soon seen
If e'er your Ladyship had cause to use it ;
I would but wish the honor of a service
So happy as that mounts to.
    BEAT. [*aside*]   We shall try you. —
O my De Flores !
    DE F. [*aside*]   How's that? She calls
    me hers
Already ! *My* De Flores ! — You were about
To sigh out somewhat, madam?
    BEAT.   No, was I? [100
I forgot, — oh ! ——
    DE F.   There 't is again, the very
Fellow on 't.
    BEAT.   You are too quick, sir.
    DE F. There's no excuse for 't now : I
    heard it twice, madam ;
That sigh would fain have utterance : take
    pity on 't,
And lend it a free word. 'Las, how it labors
For liberty ! I hear the murmur yet
Beat at your bosom.
    BEAT.   Would creation ——
    DE F. Ay, well said, that 's it.

[28] Faugh.   [29] Ambergris.

BEAT.   Had form'd me man!

DE F. Nay, that's not it.

BEAT.   Oh, 't is the soul of freedom!
I should not then be forc'd to marry one [110
I hate beyond all depths; I should have power
Then to oppose my loathings, nay, remove 'em
For ever from my sight.

DE F. [*aside*]   O blest occasion! ——
Without change to your sex you have your
    wishes;
Claim so much man in me.

BEAT.   In thee, De Flores?
There's small cause for that.

DE F.   Put it not from me;
It's a service that I kneel for to you. [*Kneels.*]

BEAT. You are too violent to mean faith-
    fully.
There's horror in my service, blood, and
    danger.
Can those be things to sue for?

DE F.   If you knew [120
How sweet it were to me to be employed
In any act of yours, you would say then
I fail'd, and us'd not reverence enough
When I receive[d] the charge on 't.

BEAT. [*aside*]   This is much,
Methinks; belike his wants are greedy; and,
To such, gold tastes like angel's food. — Rise.

DE F. I'll have the work first.

BEAT. [*aside*]   Possible his need
Is strong upon him. — There's to encourage
    thee;   [*Gives money.*]
As thou art forward, and thy service danger-
    ous,
Thy reward shall be precious.

DE F.   That I have thought on; [130
I have assur'd myself of that beforehand,
And know it will be precious; the thought
    ravishes!

BEAT. Then take him to thy fury!

DE F.   I thirst for him.

BEAT. Alonzo de Piracquo.

DE F. [*rising*]   His end's upon him;
He shall be seen no more.

BEAT.   How lovely now
Dost thou appear to me! Never was man
Dearlier rewarded.

DE F.   I do think of that.

BEAT. Be wondrous careful in the execu-
    tion.

DE F. Why, are not both our lives upon
    the cast? [30]

BEAT. Then I throw all my fears upon thy
    service.   140

[30] Throw of the dice.

DE F. They ne'er shall rise to hurt you.

BEAT.   When the deed's done,
I'll furnish thee with all things for thy flight;
Thou mayst live bravely [31] in another country.

DE F. Ay, ay;
We'll talk of that hereafter.

BEAT. [*aside*]   I shall rid myself
Of two inveterate loathings at one time:
Piracquo, and his dog-face.   *Exit.*

DE F.   O my blood!
Methinks I feel her in mine arms already;
Her wanton fingers combing out this beard,
And, being pleased, praising this bad face. [150
Hunger and pleasure, [32] they'll commend some-
    times
Slovenly dishes, and feed heartily on 'em.
Nay, which is stranger, refuse daintier for 'em.
Some women are odd feeders. — I'm too loud.
Here comes the man goes supperless to bed,
Yet shall not rise to-morrow to his dinner.

Enter ALONZO.

ALON. De Flores.

DE F.   My kind, honorable Lord.

ALON. I am glad I ha' met with thee.

DE F.   Sir.

ALON.   Thou canst show me
The full strength of the castle.

DE F.   That I can, sir.

ALON. I much desire it.

DE F.   And if the ways and straits [160
Of some of the passages be not too tedious for
    you,
I will assure you, worth your time and sight,
    my Lord.

ALON. Pooh, that shall be no hindrance.

DE F.   I'm your servant, then.
'T is now near dinner time; 'gainst [33] your
    Lordship's rising [34]
I'll have the keys about me.

ALON.   Thanks, kind De Flores.

DE F. [*aside*] He's safely thrust upon me,
    beyond hopes.   *Exeunt.*

ACT III — [SCENE I] [1]

Enter ALONZO *and* DE FLORES. (*In the act-*
time [2] DE FLORES *hides a naked rapier.* [3])

DE F. Yes, here are all the keys; I was
    afraid, my Lord,

[31] Splendidly.   [32] Lust.   [33] Before.
[34] From table.   [1] Another room.
[2] *I.e.*, in the interval between the acts.
[3] In the source, behind a door.

I 'd wanted [4] for the postern — this is it.
I 've all, I 've all, my Lord : this for the
    sconce. [5]
    ALON. 'T is a most spacious and impreg-
    nable fort.
    DE F. You 'll tell me more, my Lord. This
    descent
Is somewhat narrow, we shall never pass
Well with our weapons, they 'll but trouble
    us.
    ALON. Thou say'st true.
    DE F.   Pray, let me help your Lordship.
    ALON. 'T is done ; thanks, kind De Flores.
    DE F.   Here are hooks, my Lord,
To hang such things on purpose.
        [*Hanging up his own sword and that*
        of ALONZO.]
    ALON.   Lead, I 'll follow thee. [10
    Exeunt at one door, and enter at the
    other.

[SCENE II] [6]

    DE F. All this is nothing ; you shall see
    anon
A place you little dream on.
    ALON.   I am glad
I have this leisure ; all your master's house
Imagine I ha' taken a gondola.
    DE F. All but myself, sir, — [*aside*] which
    makes up my safety. —
My Lord, I 'll place you at a casement here
Will show you the full strength of all the castle.
Look, spend your eye awhile upon that object.
    ALON. Here 's rich variety, De Flores.
    DE F.   Yes, sir.
    ALON. Goodly munition.
    DE F.   Ay, there 's ordnance, sir, [10
No bastard metal, will ring you a peal like
    bells
At great men's funerals. Keep your eye
    straight, my Lord ;
Take special notice of that sconce before you ;
There you may dwell awhile.
        [*Takes the rapier which he has hidden.*]
    ALON.   I am upon 't.
    DE F. And so am I.   [*Stabs him.*]
    ALON.   De Flores ! O De Flores !
Whose malice hast thou put on ?
    DE F.   Do you question
A work of secrecy ? I must silence you.
        [*Stabs him.*]
    ALON. O, O, O !

[4] I lacked the one.
[5] An isolated redoubt.
[6] In the source, the "vault of the casemate."

    DE F.   I must silence you. [*Stabs him.*]
So ; here 's an undertaking well accomplish'd.
This vault serves to good use now. Ha,
    what 's that   20
Threw sparkles in my eye ? — Oh, 't is a
    diamond
He wears upon his finger ; it was well found ;
This will approve the work. [7] What, so fast
    on ?
Not part in death ? I 'll take a speedy course
    then.
Finger and all shall off. [*Cuts off the finger.*]
    So ; now I 'll clear
The passages from all suspect or fear.
        Exit with body.

[SCENE III] [8]

Enter ISABELLA *and* LOLLIO.

    ISA. Why, sirrah, whence have you com-
    mission
To fetter the doors against me ? If you
Keep me in a cage, pray whistle to me,
Let me be doing something.
    LOL. You shall be doing, if it please you ;
I 'll whistle to you, if you 'll pipe after.
    ISA. Is it your master's pleasure, or your
    own,
To keep me in this pinfold ? [9]
    LOL. 'T is for my master's pleasure, lest
being taken in another man's corn, you [10
might be pounded [10] in another place.
    ISA. 'T is very well, and he 'll prove very
wise.
    LOL. He says you have company enough in
the house, if you please to be sociable, of all
sorts of people.
    ISA. Of all sorts ? Why, here 's none but
fools and madmen.
    LOL. Very well ; and where will you find
any other, if you should go abroad ? [20
There 's my master and I to boot too.
    ISA. Of either sort one, a madman and a
fool.
    LOL. I would ev'n participate of both, then,
if I were as you ; I know y' are half mad already ; be half foolish too.
    ISA. Y' are a brave, [11] saucy rascal ! Come
on, sir,
Afford me then the pleasure of your bedlam. [12]
You were commending once to-day to me

[7] Prove the work was done.
[8] A room in Alibius's house.   [9] Pound.
[10] Put in a pound, with an obvious double-entendre.
[11] Fine.   [12] Madhouse.

Your last-come lunatic ; what a proper [13] [30
Body there was without brains to guide it,
And what a pitiful delight appear'd
In that defect, as if your wisdom had found
A mirth in madness ; pray, sir, let me partake,
If there be such a pleasure.

Lol. If I do not show you the handsomest,
discreetest madman, one that I may call the
understanding madman, then say I am a fool.

Isa. Well, a match ; [14] I will say so.

Lol. When you have a taste of the [40
madman, you shall, if you please, see Fool's
College, o' th' [15] side. I seldom lock there ;
't is but shooting a bolt or two, and you are
amongst 'em. *Exit. Re-enter presently.*[16] —
Come on, sir ; let me see how handsomely
you'll behave yourself now.

Enter Franciscus.

Fran. How sweetly she looks! Oh, but
there's a wrinkle in her brow as deep as philosophy. Anacreon, drink to my mistress'
health ; I'll pledge it. Stay, stay, there's [50
a spider in the cup! No, 't is but a grape-
stone ; swallow it ; fear nothing, poet ; so,
so, lift higher.

Isa. Alack, alack, 't is too full of pity
To be laugh'd at! How fell he mad? Canst
thou tell?

Lol. For love, mistress. He was a pretty
poet, too, and that set him forwards first ; [17]
the Muses then forsook him ; he ran mad for a
chambermaid, yet she was but a dwarf neither.

Fran. Hail, bright Titania!   60
Why stand'st thou idle on these flow'ry
banks?
Oberon is dancing with his Dryades ;
I'll gather daisies, primrose, violets,
And bind them in a verse of poesy.

Lol. [*holding up a whip*] Not too near!
You see your danger.

Fran. Oh, hold thy hand, great Diomede!
Thou feed'st thy horses well ; they shall obey
thee.
Get up, Bucephalus kneels.   [*Kneels.*]

Lol. You see how I awe my flock ; a [70
shepherd has not his dog at more obedience.

Isa. His conscience is unquiet ; sure that
was
The cause of this ; a proper gentleman!

Fran. Come hither, Æsculapius ; hide the
poison.

Lol. Well, 't is hid.   [*Hides the whip.*]

Fran. Didst thou never hear of one Ti-
resias,[18]
A famous poet?

Lol. Yes, that kept tame wild-geese.

Fran. That's he ; I am the man.

Lol. No!   80

Fran. Yes ; but make no words on 't. I
was a man
Seven years ago.

Lol.   A stripling, I think, you might.

Fran. Now I'm a woman, all feminine.

Lol. I would I might see that!

Fran. Juno struck me blind.

Lol. I'll ne'er believe that ; for a woman,
they say, has an eye more than a man.

Fran. I say she struck me blind.

Lol. And Luna made you mad ; you have
two trades to beg with.   90

Fran. Luna is now big-bellied, and there's
room
For both of us to ride with Hecate ;
I'll drag thee up into her silver sphere,
And there we'll kick the dog — and beat the
bush —
That barks against the witches of the night ;
The swift lycanthropi [19] that walks the round,
We'll tear their wolvish skins, and save the
sheep.   [*Attempts to seize* Lollio.]

Lol. Is't come to this? Nay, then, my
poison comes forth again. [*showing the whip*]
Mad slave, indeed ; abuse your keeper! [100

Isa. I prithee, hence with him, now he
grows dangerous.

Fran. (*sing.*)

> Sweet love, pity me ;
> Give me leave to lie with thee.

Lol. No, I'll see you wiser first. To your
own kennel!

Fran. No noise, she sleeps ; draw all the
curtains round ;
Let no soft sound molest the pretty soul
But love, and love creeps in at a mouse-hole.

Lol. I would you would get into your hole!
(*Exit* Franciscus.) — Now, mistress, I will
bring you another sort ; you shall be [110
fool'd another while. [*Exit, and re-enter.*]
— Tony, come hither, Tony : look who's
yonder, Tony.

---

[13] Handsome.   [14] Agreed.
[15] Mod. eds. add *other*.
[16] At once.   [17] Got him started.
[18] The Theban prophet of classical mythology.
According to one version of his story Juno struck
him blind. His sexual metamorphoses are also part
of his myth. The allusion to the geese is presumably mere nonsensical talk to the supposed lunatic.
[19] Here = werewolves.

Enter ANTONIO.

ANT. Cousin, is it not my aunt?[20]

LOL. Yes, 't is one of 'em, Tony.

ANT. He, he! how do you, Uncle?

LOL. Fear him not, mistress; 't is a gentle nidget;[21] you may play with him, as safely with him as with his bauble.[22]

ISA. How long hast thou been a fool?   120

ANT. Ever since I came hither, cousin.

ISA. Cousin? I 'm none of thy cousins, fool.

LOL. Oh, mistress, fools have always so much wit as to claim their kindred.

MADMAN. [*above*] (*within*) Bounce,[23] bounce! he falls, he falls!

ISA. Hark you, your scholars in the upper room
Are out of order.   129

LOL. Must I come amongst you there? — Keep you the fool, mistress; I 'll go up and play left-handed Orlando[24] amongst the madmen.   *Exit.*

ISA. Well, sir.

ANT. 'T is opportuneful now, sweet lady! — nay,
Cast no amazing eye upon this change.

ISA. Ha!

ANT. This shape of folly shrouds your dearest love,
The truest servant to your powerful beauties,
Whose magic had this force thus to transform me.   140

ISA. You are a fine fool indeed!

ANT.   Oh, 't is not strange!
Love has an intellect that runs through all
The scrutinous consciences; and, like a cunning poet,
Catches a quantity of every knowledge,
Yet brings all home into one mystery,
Into one secret that he proceeds in.

ISA. Y' are a parlous fool.

ANT. No danger in me; I bring naught but love
And his soft-wounding shafts to strike you with.
Try but one arrow; if it hurt you, I 'll   150
Stand you twenty back in recompense.
                    [*Kisses her.*][25]

ISA. A forward fool too!

20 The word also meant bawd, mistress, or prostitute.   Q *Ant.*
21 Idiot.   Q *nigget.*
22 The fool's sceptre.   23 Bang.
24 Apparently = "strike terror."
25 Add. Neilson. — *I 'll* stands in Q at beginning of l. 151.   Q frequently mislines verse.

ANT.   This was love's teaching:
A thousand ways [he][26] fashion'd out my way,
And this I found the safest and [the] nearest,
To tread the Galaxia[27] to my star.

ISA. Profound withal! Certain, you dream'd of this;
Love never taught it waking.

ANT.   Take no acquaintance
Of these outward follies; there is within
A gentleman that loves you.

ISA.   When I see him, [159
I 'll speak with him; so, in the meantime, keep
Your habit; it becomes you well enough.
As you are a gentleman, I 'll not discover you;
That 's all the favor that you must expect.
When you are weary, you may leave the school,
For all this while you have but play'd the fool.

Re-enter LOLLIO.

ANT. And must again. — He, he! I thank you, cousin;
I 'll be your valentine to-morrow morning.

LOL. How do you like the fool, mistress?

ISA. Passing well, sir.

LOL. Is he not witty, pretty well, for [170
a fool?

ISA. If he holds on as he begins, he is like to come to something.

LOL. Ay, thank a good tutor. You may put him to 't; he begins to answer pretty hard questions. — Tony, how many is five times six?

ANT. Five times six is six times five.

LOL. What arithmetician could have answer'd better? How many is one hun- [180
dred and seven?

ANT. One hundred and seven is seven hundred and one, cousin.

LOL. This is no wit to speak on! — Will you be rid of the fool now?

ISA. By no means: let him stay a little.

MADMAN (*within*) Catch there; catch the last couple in hell![28]

LOL. Again! Must I come amongst you? — Would my master were come home! [190
I am not able to govern both these wards together.   *Exit.*

ANT. Why should a minute of love 's hour be lost?

26 Q *she.* — Q om. *the,* l. 154.
27 Milky Way.
28 Alluding to the game of barley-break; the last couple was left in "hell", the middle of three compartments.

Isa. Fie, out again! I had rather you kept
Your other posture; you become not your
        tongue
When you speak from [29] your clothes.

Ant.   How can he freeze
Lives near so sweet a warmth? Shall I alone
Walk through the orchard of th' Hesperides,
And, cowardly, not dare to pull an apple?

Re-enter Lollio, *above.*

This with the red cheeks I must venture for.
                        [*Attempts to kiss her.*]
Isa. Take heed, there's giants keep 'em.

Lol. [*aside*] How now, fool, are you [202
good at that? Have you read Lipsius? [30]
He's past *Ars Amandi* [31]; I believe I must
put harder questions to him, I perceive that.

Isa. You are bold without fear too.

Ant.   What should I fear,
Having all joys about me? Do you smile,
And love shall play the wanton on your lip,
Meet and retire, retire and meet again;
Look you but cheerfully, and in your eyes [210
I shall behold mine own deformity,
And dress myself up fairer. I know this shape
Becomes me not, but in those bright mirrors
I shall array me handsomely.

Lol.   Cuckoo, cuckoo! [32]   *Exit.*
        Madmen [*cry*] *above, some as birds,*
                others as beasts.

Ant. What are these?

Isa.   Of fear enough to part us;
Yet are they but our schools of lunatics,
That act their fantasies in any shapes,
Suiting their present thoughts; if sad, they
        cry;
If mirth be their conceit, they laugh again.
Sometimes they imitate the beasts and birds,
Singing or howling, braying, barking, all [221
As their wild fancies prompt 'em.

Re-enter Lollio.

Ant.   These are no fears.

Isa. But here's a large one, my man.

Ant. Ha, he! that's fine sport, indeed,
cousin.

Lol. I would my master were come home!
'T is too much for one shepherd to govern

two of these flocks; nor can I believe that
one churchman can instruct two benefices
at once; there will be some incurable mad [230
of the one side, and very fools on the other.
— Come, Tony.

Ant. Prithee, cousin, let me stay here still.

Lol. No, you must to your book now; you
have play'd sufficiently.

Isa. Your fool is grown wondrous witty.

Lol. Well, I'll say nothing: but I do not
think but he will put you down [33] one of these
days.

                    Exeunt Lollio *and* Antonio.

Isa. Here the restrained current might
        make breach,   240
Spite of the watchful bankers. [34] Would a
        woman stray,
She need not gad abroad to seek her sin:
It would be brought home one ways or other.
The needle's point will to the fixed north;
Such drawing arctics [35] women's beauties
        are.

Re-enter Lollio.

Lol. How dost thou, sweet rogue?

Isa. How now?

Lol. Come, there are degrees; one fool may
be better than another.

Isa. What's the matter?   250

Lol. Nay, if thou giv'st thy mind to fool's
flesh, have at thee!

Isa. You bold slave, you!

Lol. I could follow now as tother fool
did:
" What should I fear,
Having all joys about me? Do you but smile,
And love shall play the wanton on your lip,
Meet and retire, retire and meet again;
Look you but cheerfully, and in your eyes
I shall behold my own deformity,   261
And dress myself up fairer. I know this
        shape
Becomes me not — "
And so as it follows: but is not this the more
foolish way? Come, sweet rogue; kiss
me, my little Lacedaemonian; let me feel
how thy pulses beat. Thou hast a thing
about thee would do a man pleasure, I'll lay [36]
my hand on 't.

Isa. Sirrah, no more! I see you have dis-
        covered   270

---

[29] Apart from, out of keeping with.
[30] "Is it necessary to notice that the name of this
great scholar is introduced merely for the sake of its
first syllable?" (Dyce.) Lipsius was a sixteenth-
century Belgian.
[31] *I.e.*, he is evidently able to tackle harder reading
than Ovid's *Art of Love.*
[32] Alluding to Alibius's apparently imminent
cuckoldom.
[33] Beat you in an argument; with an obvious
double-entendre.
[34] Dike-tenders.
[35] Poles. Q *Articks.*
[36] Bet; with an obvious double-entendre.

This love's knight [e]rrant, who hath made ad-
venture
For purchase of [37] my love. Be silent, mute,
Mute as a statue, or his injunction,
For me enjoying, shall be to cut thy throat ;
I 'll do it, though for no other purpose ; and
Be sure he 'll not refuse it.
  Lol.   My share, that 's all ;
I 'll have my fool's part with you.
  Isa.   No more ! Your master.

Enter Alibius.

  Alib. Sweet, how dost thou ?
  Isa.   Your bounden servant, sir.
  Alib. Fie, fie, sweetheart, no more of that.
  Isa. You were best lock me up. 280
  Alib. In my arms and bosom, my sweet
   Isabella,
I 'll lock thee up most nearly. — Lollio,
We have employment, we have task in hand.
At noble Vermandero's, our castle captain,
There is a nuptial to be solemniz'd —
Beatrice-Joanna, his fair daughter, bride, —
For which the gentleman hath bespoke our
  pains,
A mixture of our madmen and our fools,
To finish, as it were, and make the fag [38]
Of all the revels, the third night from the first ;
Only an unexpected passage over,[39] 291
To make a frightful pleasure, that is all,
But not the all I aim at. Could we so act it,
To teach it in a wild distracted measure,[40]
Though out of form and figure, breaking time's
  head,
It were no matter, 't would be heal'd again
In one age or other, if not in this ;
This, this, Lollio ; there 's a good reward begun,
And will beget a bounty, be it known.

  Lol. This is easy, sir, I 'll warrant you ; [300
you have about you fools and madmen that
can dance very well ; and 't is no wonder, your
best dancers are not in the wisest men ; the
reason is, with often jumping they jolt their
brains down into their feet, that their wits lie
more in their heels than in their heads.
  Alib. Honest Lollio, thou giv'st me a good
  reason,
And a comfort in it.
  Isa.   Y 'ave a fine trade on 't.
Madmen and fools are a staple commodity.
  Alib. Oh, wife, we must eat, wear clothes,
  and live. 310

[37] To acquire, to make booty of.
[38] End. [39] The stage.
[40] Dance.

Just at the lawyer's haven we arrive :
By madmen and by fools we both do thrive.
       Exeunt.

[Scene IV] [41]

Enter Vermandero, Alsemero, Jasperino,
and Beatrice.

  Ver. Valencia speaks so nobly of you, sir,
I wish I had a daughter now for you.
  Als. The fellow of this creature were a part-
  ner
For a king's love.
  Ver.   I had her fellow once, sir ;
But Heaven has married her to joys eternal ;
'T were sin to wish her in this vale again.
Come, sir, your friend and you shall see the
  pleasures
Which my health chiefly joys in.
  Als.   I hear
The beauty of this seat largely [commended].[42]
  Ver. It falls much short of that.
      Exeunt [all but] Beatrice.
  Beat.   So, here 's one step [10
Into my father's favor ; time will fix him.
I 've got him now the liberty of the house.
So wisdom, by degrees, works out her freedom ;
And if that eye be dark'ned that offends me, —
I wait but that eclipse, — this gentleman
Shall soon shine glorious in my father's liking,
Through the refulgent virtue of my love.

Enter De Flores.

  De F. [*aside*] My thoughts are at a ban-
  quet ; for [43] the deed,
I feel no weight in 't ; 't is but light and cheap
For the sweet recompense that I set down
  for 't. [20
  Beat. De Flores.
  De F. Lady.
  Beat.   Thy looks promise cheerfully.
  De F. All things are answerable : time,
  circumstance,
Your wishes, and my service.
  Beat.   Is it done, then ?
  De F. Piracquo is no more.
  Beat. My joys start at mine eyes ; our
  sweet'st delights
Are evermore born weeping.
  De F.   I 've a token for you.
  Beat. For me ?
  De F. But it was sent somewhat unwill-
  ingly ;

[41] A room in the castle.
[42] So Dyce and other mod. eds. Om. Q.
[43] As for.

I could not get the ring without the finger.
                    [*Producing the finger and ring.*]
BEAT. Bless me, what hast thou done?
DE F.   Why, is that more [30
Than killing the whole man? I cut his heart-
    strings ;
A greedy hand thrust in a dish at court,
In a mistake, hath had as much as this.
    BEAT. 'T is the first token my father made
        me send him.
    DE F. And I made him send it back again
For his last token. I was loth to leave it,
And I 'm sure dead men have no use of jewels ;
He was as loth to part with 't, for it stuck
As if the flesh and it were both one substance.
    BEAT. At the stag's fall, the keeper has his
        fees ;   40
'T is [44] soon appli'd : all dead men's fees are
    yours, sir.
I pray, bury the finger ; but the stone
You may make use on shortly ; the true value,
Take 't of my truth, is near three hundred
    ducats.
    DE F. 'T will hardly buy a capcase [45] for
        one's conscience though,
To keep it from the worm, as fine as 't is.
Well, being my fees, I 'll take it ;
Great men have taught me that, or else my
    merit
Would scorn the way on 't.
    BEAT.   It might justly, sir.
Why, thou mistak'st, De Flores ; 't is not
    given   50
In state of [46] recompense.
    DE F.   No, I hope so, lady ;
You should soon witness my contempt to 't
    then.
    BEAT. Prithee — thou look'st as if thou
        wert offended.
    DE F. That were strange, lady ; 't is not
        possible
My service should draw such a cause from
    you.
Offended ! Could you think so? That were
    much
For one of my performance, and so warm
Yet in my service.
    BEAT. 'T were misery in me to give you
        cause, sir.
    DE F. I know so much : it were so ; mis-
        ery   60
In her most sharp condition.

    BEAT.   'T is resolv'd [47] then ;
Look you, sir, here 's three thousand golden
    florins ; [48]
I have not meanly thought upon thy merit.
    DE F. What ! salary? Now you move me.
    BEAT.   How, De Flores?
    DE F. Do you place me in the rank of ver-
        minous fellows,
To destroy things for wages? Offer gold
For the lifeblood of man? Is anything
Valued too precious for my recompense?
    BEAT. I understand thee not.
    DE F.   I could ha' hir'd
A journeyman in murder at this rate,   70
And mine own conscience might have [slept at
    ease],[49]
And have had the work brought home.
    BEAT. [*aside*]   I 'm in a labyrinth ;
What will content him? I 'd fain be rid of
    him. —
I 'll double the sum, sir.
    DE F.   You take a course
To double my vexation, that 's the good you
    do.
    BEAT. [*aside*] Bless me, I am now in worse
        plight than I was ;
I know not what will please him. — For my
    fear's sake,
I prithee, make away with all speed pos-
    sible ;
And if thou be'st so modest not to name
The sum that will content thee, paper blushes
    not :   80
Send thy demand in writing, it shall follow
    thee ;
But, prithee, take thy flight.
    DE F.   You must fly too, then.
    BEAT. I?
    DE F. I 'll not stir a foot else.
    BEAT.   What 's your meaning?
    DE F. Why, are not you as guilty? In,
        I 'm sure,
As deep as I ; and we should stick together.
Come, your fears counsel you but ill ; my ab-
    sence
Would draw suspect upon you instantly ;
There were no rescue for you.
    BEAT. [*aside*]   He speaks home !
    DE F. Nor is it fit we two, engag'd so
        jointly,
Should part and live asunder.

---

[47] Settled.
[48] The English name for various continental coins.
In view of the weight of such a sum in gold Dyce
suggests that Beatrice may hand De Flores a paper.
[49] Add. ed. 1816.

[44] *I.e.*, my remark about the keeper's fees is.
Apparently De Flores makes a gesture of inquiry
or dissent.   [45] Bandbox.   [46] By way of.

BEAT.   How now, sir ! [90
This shows not well.
    DE F.   What makes your lip so strange? [50]
This must not be betwixt us.
    BEAT.   The man talks wildly !
    DE F.   Come, kiss me with a zeal now.
    BEAT. [*aside*]   Heaven, I doubt [51] him !
    DE F.   I will not stand so long to beg 'em
      shortly.
    BEAT.   Take heed, De Flores, of forgetful-
      ness ;
'T will soon betray us.
    DE F.   Take you heed first ;
Faith, y' are grown much forgetful ; y' are
    to blame in 't.
    BEAT. [*aside*] He 's bold, and I am blam'd
    for 't.
    DE F.   I have eas'd you
Of your trouble ; think on 't : I 'm in pain, [99
And must be eas'd of [52] you ; 't is a charity :
Justice invites your blood to understand me.
    BEAT. I dare not.
    DE F.   Quickly !
    BEAT.   Oh, I never shall !
Speak it yet further off, that I may lose
What has been spoken, and no sound remain
    on 't ;
I would not hear so much offence again
For such another deed.
    DE F.   Soft, lady, soft !
The last is not yet paid for. Oh, this act
Has put me into spirit ; I was as greedy
    on 't
As the parch'd earth of moisture, when the
    clouds weep.   109
Did you not mark I wrought myself into 't,
Nay, sued and kneel'd for 't? Why was all
    that pains took?
You see I have thrown contempt upon your
    gold ;
Not that I want it [not], [53] for I do piteously ;
In order I 'll come unto 't, and make use on 't ;
But 't was not held so precious to begin with,
For I place wealth after the heels of pleasure ;
And were not I resolv'd in my belief
That thy virginity were perfect in thee,
I should but take my recompense with grudg-
    ing, [54]   119
As if I had but half my hopes I agreed for.
    BEAT. Why, 't is impossible thou canst be
    so wicked,
Or shelter such a cunning cruelty,
To make his death the murderer of my honor ?

Thy language is so bold and vicious,
I cannot see which way I can forgive it
With any modesty.
    DE F.   Push ! you forget yourself ;
A woman dipp'd in blood, and talk of modesty !
    BEAT. O misery of sin ! would I had been
    bound
Perpetually unto my living hate   129
In that Piracquo, than to hear these words !
Think but upon the distance that creation
Set 'twixt thy blood and mine, and keep thee
    there.
    DE F.   Look but into your conscience ; read
    me there : —
'T is a true book ; you 'll find me there your
    equal.
Push ! fly not to your birth, but settle you
In what the act has made you ; y' are no more
    now.
You must forget your parentage ; [55] to me
Y' are the deed 's creature ; by that name
You lost your first condition, and I challenge
    you,   139
As peace and innocency has turn'd you out,
And made you one with me.
    BEAT.   With thee, foul villain !
    DE F. Yes, my fair murd'ress. Do you
    urge me,
Though thou writ'st maid, thou whore in thy
    affection?
'T was chang'd from thy first love, and that 's
    a kind
Of whoredom in thy heart ; and he 's chang'd
    now
To bring thy second on, thy Alsemero,
Whom, by all sweets that ever darkness
    tasted,
If I enjoy thee not, thou ne'er enjoy'st ?
I 'll blast the hopes and joys of marriage ; [56]
I 'll confess all ; my life I rate at nothing. [150
    BEAT. De Flores !
    DE F.   I shall rest from all lovers'
    plagues then ;
I live in pain now : that shooting eye
Will burn my heart to cinders.
    BEAT.   Oh, sir, hear me !
    DE F. She that in life and love refuses me,
In death and shame my partner she shall be.
    BEAT. [*kneeling*] Stay, hear me once for all ;
    I make thee master
Of all the wealth I have in gold and jewels ;
Let me go poor unto my bed with honor,
And I am rich in all things !

[50] Why do you hold off?   [51] Fear.   [52] By.
[53] Add. mod. eds.; om. Q.   [54] Complaining.   [55] Professor Kittredge places the stop here instead of after " me."   [56] Trisyllabic.

De F.   Let this silence thee :
The wealth of all Valencia shall not buy   [160
My pleasure from me ;
Can you weep Fate from its determin'd pur-
     pose?
So soon may [you] weep me.
     Beat.   Vengeance begins ;
Murder, I see, is followed by more sins.
Was my creation in the womb so curs'd,
It must engender with a viper first?
     De F. Come, rise and shroud your blushes
          in my bosom ;
Silence is one of pleasure's best receipts ; [57]
Thy peace is wrought for ever in this yielding.
'Las ! how the turtle [58] pants ! Thou 'lt love
     anon   170
What thou so fear'st and faint'st to venture on.
                                        Exeunt.

               ACT IV

             [Dumb Show]

Enter Gentlemen, Vermandero *meeting them
with action of wonderment at the flight of
Piracquo. Enter* Alsemero *with* Jasperino
and Gallants : Vermandero *points to him,
the* Gentlemen *seeming to applaud the choice.*
Alsemero, Jasperino, *and* Gentlemen ;
Beatrice *the bride following in great state,
accompanied with* Diaphanta, Isabella,
and other Gentlewomen ; De Flores *after
all, smiling at the accident :* Alonzo's Ghost
appears to De Flores *in the midst of his
smile, startles him, showing him the hand
whose finger he had cut off. They pass over
in great solemnity.*[1]

             [Scene I] [2]

          Enter Beatrice.

     Beat. This fellow has undone me end-
          lessly ;
Never was bride so fearfully distress'd.
The more I think upon th' ensuing night,
And whom I am to cope with in embraces :
One both ennobled [3] in blood and mind,
So clear in understanding — that 's my plague
     now, —
Before whose judgment will my fault appear

───────────────
[57] One of the best recipes for sexual gratification.
[58] Dove.
[1] With pomp and circumstance.
[2] Alsemero's apartment in the castle.
[3] Q *both ennobled both.* " Ennobled " is quadrisyllabic.

Like malefactors' crimes before tribunals.
There is no hiding on 't, the more I dive
Into my own distress. How a wise man [10
Stands for [4] a great calamity ! There 's no ven-
     turing
Into his bed, what course soe'er I light upon,
Without my shame, which may grow up to
     danger.
He cannot but in justice strangle me
As I lie by him — as a cheater use me ;
'T is a precious craft to play with a false die
Before a cunning gamester. Here 's his
     closet ;
The key left in 't, and he abroad i' th' park !
Sure 't was forgot ; I 'll be so bold as look in 't.
                              [*Opens closet.*]
Bless me ! a right [5] physician's closet 't is, [20
Set round with vials ; every one her mark too.
Sure he does practise physic for his own use,
Which may be safely call'd your great man's
     wisdom.[6]
What manuscript lies here? " The Book
     of Experiment,
Call'd Secrets in Nature." So 't is ; 't is so.
[*Reads.*] " How to know whether a woman be
with child or no."
I hope I am not yet, — if he should try
     though !
Let me see [*reads*] " folio forty-five," here 't is,
The leaf tuck'd dow[n] upon 't, the place sus-
     picious.   30
[*Reads.*] " If you would know whether a
woman be with child or not, give her two
spoonfuls of the white water in glass C ——"
Where 's that glass C? Oh, yonder, I see 't
     now —
[*Reads.*] " and if she be with child, she sleeps
full twelve hours after ; if not, not : "
None of that water comes into my belly ;
I 'll know you from a hundred ; I could break
     you now,
Or turn you into milk, and so beguile
The master of the mystery ; but I 'll look to
     you.   40
Ha ! that which is next is ten times worse :
[*Reads.*] " How to know whether a woman be
a maid or not ; "
If that should be appli'd, what would become
     of me?
Belike he has a strong faith of my purity,
That never yet made proof ; [7] but this he calls
[*Reads.*] " A merry sleight,[8] but true experi-

───────────────
[4] Stands open to.   [5] True, actual.
[6] Since it safeguards him against poison.
[7] Trial, test.   [8] Artifice.

ment; the author Antonius Mizaldus.[9] Give the party you suspect the quantity of a spoonful of the water in the glass M, which, [50 upon her that is a maid, makes three several effects: 't will make her incontinently [10] gape, then fall into a sudden sneezing, last into a violent laughing; else, dull, heavy, and lumpish."
Where had I been?
I fear it; yet 't is seven hours to bedtime.

Enter DIAPHANTA.

DIA. Cuds,[11] madam, are you here?
BEAT. [*aside*] Seeing that wench now, A trick comes in my mind; 't is a nice piece [12] Gold cannot purchase. — I come hither, wench, 60
To look my lord.
DIA. Would I had such a cause To look him too! Why, he 's i' th' park, madam.
BEAT. There let him be.
DIA. Ay, madam, let him compass Whole parks and forests, as great rangers do, At roosting time a little lodge can hold 'em. Earth-conquering Alexander, that thought the world
Too narrow for him, in th' end had but his pit-hole.
BEAT. I fear thou art not modest, Diaphanta.
DIA. Your thoughts are so unwilling to be known, madam.
'T is ever the bride's fashion, towards bedtime, 70
To set light by her joys, as if she ow'd [13] 'em not.
BEAT. Her joys? Her fears thou wouldst say.
DIA. Fear of what?
BEAT. Art thou a maid, and talk'st so to a maid?
You leave a blushing business behind; Beshrew your heart for 't!
DIA. Do you mean good sooth, madam?
BEAT. Well, if I 'd thought upon the fear at first,
Man should have been unknown.
DIA. Is 't possible?

BEAT. I will give a thousand ducats to that woman
Would try what my fear were, and tell me true To-morrow, when she gets from 't; as she likes, 80
I might perhaps be drawn to 't.
DIA. Are you in earnest?
BEAT. Do you get the woman, then challenge me,
And see if I 'll fly from 't; but I must tell you This by the way, she must be a true maid.
Else there 's no trial; my fears are not her's else.
DIA. Nay, she that I would put into your hands, madam,
Shall be a maid.
BEAT. You know I should be sham'd else, Because she lies for me.
DIA. 'T is a strange humor! [14]
But are you serious still? Would you resign Your first night's pleasure, and give money too? 90
BEAT. As willingly as live. — [*aside*] Alas, the gold
Is but a by [15]-bet to wedge in the honor!
DIA. I do not know how the world goes abroad
For faith or honesty; there 's both requir'd in this.
Madam, what say you to me, and stray no further?
I 've a good mind, in troth, to earn your money.
BEAT. Y' are too quick,[16] I fear, to be a maid.
DIA. How? not a maid? Nay, then you urge me, madam:
Your honorable self is not a truer, With all your fears upon you ——
BEAT. [*aside*] Bad enough then. [100
DIA. Than I with all my lightsome joys about me.
BEAT. I 'm glad to hear 't. Then you dare put your honesty [17]
Upon an easy trial.
DIA. Easy? — Anything.
BEAT. I 'll come to you straight.
[*Goes to the closet.*]
DIA. She will not search me, will she, Like the forewoman of a female jury?
BEAT. Glass M: ay, this is it. [*Brings vial.*] Look, Diaphanta,
You take no worse than I do. [*Drinks.*]

---

[9] A sixteenth-century French astrologer. According to Sampson, the *De Arcanis Naturae* contains no such experiments; but similar ones are found elsewhere in his works.
[10] Immediately.
[11] Probably a corruption of "God save me." Cf. *codes.*
[12] Scrupulous wench. [13] Possessed.

[14] Whim, notion. [15] Side. (*N.E.D.*)
[16] Lively, impulsive. [17] Chastity.

DIA.   And in so doing,
I will not question what 't is, but take it.
                    [*Drinks.*]
BEAT. [*aside*] Now if th' experiment be
true, 't will praise itself,
And give me noble ease : begins already ;
              [DIAPHANTA *gapes.*]
There's the first symptom ; and what haste it
    makes   111
To fall into the second, there by this time !
             [DIAPHANTA *sneezes.*]
Most admirable secret ! on the contrary,
It stirs not me a whit, which most concerns it.
    DIA. Ha, ha, ha !
    BEAT. [*aside*]   Just in all things, and in
    order
As if 't were circumscrib'd ; one accident [18]
Gives way unto another.
    DIA.   Ha, ha, ha !
    BEAT. How now, wench?
    DIA.   Ha, ha, ha ! I am so, so light
At heart — ha, ha, ha ! — so pleasurable !
But one swig more, sweet madam.
    BEAT.   Ay, to-morrow, [120
We shall have time to sit by 't.
    DIA.   Now I'm sad again.
    BEAT. [*aside*] It lays itself so gently too ! —
    Come, wench.
Most honest [19] Diaphanta I dare call thee now.
    DIA. Pray, tell me, madam, what trick
    call you this?
    BEAT. I'll tell thee all hereafter ; we must
    study
The carriage of this business.
    DIA.   I shall carry 't well,
Because I love the burthen.
    BEAT.   About midnight
You must not fail to steal forth gently,
That I may use the place.
    DIA.   Oh, fear not, madam ;
I shall be cool by that time. The bride's
    place,   130
And with a thousand ducats ! I'm for a jus-
    tice now :
I bring a portion with me ; I scorn small
    fools.[20]   *Exeunt.*

[SCENE II] [21]

Enter VERMANDERO *and* Servant.

VER. I tell thee, knave, mine honor is in
    question,
A thing till now free from suspicion,

Nor ever was there cause. Who of my gentle-
    men
Are absent? Tell me, and truly, how many,
    and who?
    SER. Antonio, sir, and Franciscus.
    VER. When did they leave the castle?
    SER. Some ten days since, sir ; the one
    intending to
Briamata,[22] th' other for Valencia.
    VER. The time accuses 'em ; a charge of
    murder
Is brought within my castle-gate, Piracquo's
    murder ;   10
I dare not answer faithfully their absence.
A strict command of apprehension
Shall pursue 'em suddenly, and either wipe
The stain off clear, or openly discover it.
Provide me winged warrants for the purpose.
                   Exit Servant.
See, I am set on again.

Enter TOMAZO.

    TOM. I claim a brother of you.
    VER.   Y' are too hot ;
Seek him not here.
    TOM.   Yes, 'mongst your dearest bloods,
If my peace find no fairer satisfaction.
This is the place must yield account for
    him,
For here I left him ; and the hasty tie   21
Of this snatch'd marriage gives strong testi-
    mony
Of his most certain ruin.
    VER.   Certain falsehood !
This is the place indeed ; his breach of
    faith
Has too much marr'd both my abused love,
The honorable love I reserv'd for him,
And mock'd my daughter's joy ; the pre-
    par'd morning
Blush'd at his infidelity ; he left
Contempt and scorn to throw upon those
    friends
Whose belief hurt 'em. Oh, 't was most
    ignoble   30
To take his flight so unexpectedly,
And throw such public wrongs on those that
    lov'd him !
    TOM. Then this is all your answer.
    VER.   'T is too fair
For one of his alliance ;[23] and I warn you
That this place no more see you.   *Exit.*

---

[18] Symptom.   [19] Chaste.
[20] *I.e.*, I'm for a big fool, a justice.
[21] Another room in the castle.

[22] The source mentions this "fair house" of Vermandero's, ten leagues from Alicante.
    [23] Related to him.

Enter De Flores.

Tom.   The best is,
There is more ground to meet a man's revenge
    on. —
Honest De Flores.

De F.   That's my name indeed.
Saw you the bride? Good sweet sir, which
    way took she?

Tom. I have bless'd mine eyes from seeing
    such a false one.

De F. [*aside*] I'd fain get off; this man's
    not for my company :   40
I smell his brother's blood when I come near
    him.

Tom. Come hither, kind and true one; I
    remember
My brother lov'd thee well.

De F.   Oh, purely,²⁴ dear sir ! —
[*aside*] Methinks I am now again a-killing on
    him,
He brings it so fresh to me.

Tom.   Thou canst guess, sirrah —
[An] ²⁵ honest friend has an instinct of jeal-
    ousy —
At some foul guilty person.

De F.   'Las! sir,
I am so charitable, I think none
Worse than myself ! — You did not see the
    bride then?

Tom. I prithee, name her not : is she not
    wicked?   50

De F. No, no; a pretty, easy, round-
    pack'd ²⁶ sinner,
As your most ladies are, else you might think
I flatter'd her ; but, sir, at no hand wicked,
Till th' are so old their [chins and noses] ²⁷
    meet,
And they salute witches. I am call'd, I think,
    sir. —
[*aside*] His company ev'n o'erlays my con-
    science.   *Exit.*

Tom. That De Flores has a wondrous hon-
    est heart !
He'll bring it out in time, I'm assur'd on't.
Oh, here's the glorious ²⁸ master of the day's
    joy !
I ²⁹ will not be long till he and I do
    reckon. —   60

Enter Alsemero.

Sir.

Als.   You are most welcome.

²⁴ Utterly.   ²⁵ Emend. Dyce; Q *One.*
²⁶ Presumably = "plump."
²⁷ Conj. Dyce; Q *sins and vices.*   ²⁸ Vainglorious.
²⁹ Dyce emends 'T.

Tom.   You may call that word back ;
I do not think I am, nor wish to be.

Als. 'T is strange you found the way to
    this house, then.

Tom. Would I'd ne'er known the cause !
    I'm none of those, sir,
That come to give you joy, and swill your
    wine ;
'T is a more precious liquor that must lay
The fiery thirst I bring.

Als.   Your words and you
Appear to me great strangers.

Tom.   Time and our swords
May make us more acquainted. This the
    business :
I should have had a brother in your place ; [70
How treachery and malice have dispos'd of
    him
I'm bound to inquire of him which holds his
    right,
Which never could come fairly.

Als.   You must look
To answer for that word, sir.

Tom.   Fear you not,
I'll have it ready drawn at our next meeting.
Keep your day solemn : ³⁰ farewell ; I disturb
    it not ;
I'll bear the smart with patience for a time.
                                    Exit.

Als. 'T is somewhat ominous this ; a
    quarrel ent'red
Upon this day ; my innocence relieves me —

Enter Jasperino.

I should be wondrous sad else. — Jas-
    perino,   80
I have news to tell thee, strange news.

Jasp.   I ha' some too,
I think as strange as yours. Would I might
    keep
Mine, so my faith and friendship might be
    kept in't !
Faith, sir, dispense a little with my zeal,
And let it cool in this.

Als.   This puts me on,³¹
And blames thee for thy slowness.

Jas.   All may prove nothing,
Only a friendly fear that leap'd from me, sir.

Als. No question, it may prove nothing ;
    let's partake it though.

Jas. 'T was Diaphanta's chance — for to
    that wench
I pretend ³² honest love, and she deserves it —

³⁰ Go on celebrating your wedding day.
³¹ Incites me, arouses me.   ³² Offer.

To leave me in a back part of the house,   91
A place we chose for private conference.
She was no sooner gone, but instantly
I heard your bride's voice in the next room to
    me ;
And lending more attention, found De Flores
Louder than she.

ALS.   De Flores ! Thou art out now.

JAS. You 'll tell me more anon.

ALS.   Still I 'll prevent [33] thee :
The very sight of him is poison to her.

JAS. That made me stagger too ; but Dia-
    phanta
At her return confirm'd it.

ALS.   Diaphanta !   100

JAS. Then fell we both to listen, and words
    pass'd
Like those that challenge interest in a woman.

ALS. Peace ! quench thy zeal ; 't is dan-
    gerous to thy bosom.

JAS. Then truth is full of peril.

ALS.   Such truths are.
Oh, were she the sole glory of the earth,
Had eyes that could shoot fire into kings'
    breasts,
And touch'd,[34] she sleeps not here ! Yet I have
    time,
Though night be near, to be resolv'd [35] hereof ;
And, prithee, do not weigh me by my pas-
    sions.[36]

JAS. I never weigh'd friend so.

ALS.   Done charitably ! [110
That key will lead thee to a pretty secret,
                      [*Gives key.*]
By a Chaldean taught me, and I 've
My study upon some. Bring from my closet
A glass inscrib'd there with the letter M,
And question not my purpose.

JAS.   It shall be done, sir. *Exit.*

ALS. How can this hang together ? Not
    an hour since
Her woman came, pleading her lady's fears,
Deliver'd [37] her for the most timorous virgin
That ever shrunk at man's name, and so
    modest
She charg'd her weep out her request to me
That she might come obscurely to my
    bosom.   121

           Enter BEATRICE.

BEAT. [*aside*] All things go well ; my
    woman's preparing yonder

---

[33] Anticipate.   [34] Tainted.
[35] Satisfied, clear.   [36] Show of emotions.
[37] Reported, described.

For her sweet voyage, which grieves me to
    lose ;
Necessity compels it ; I lose all, else.

ALS. [*aside*] Push ! modesty's shrine is set
    in yonder forehead ;
I cannot be too sure, though. — My Joanna !

BEAT. Sir, I was bold to weep a message to
    you ;
Pardon my modest fears.

ALS. [*aside*]   The dove's not meeker ;
She 's abus'd, questionless.

      Re-enter JASPERINO [*with vial*].

                    Oh, are you come, sir ?

BEAT. [*aside*] The glass, upon my life ! I
    see the letter.   130

JAS. Sir, this is M.   [*Giving vial.*]

ALS.   'T [i]s it.

BEAT. [*aside*]   I am suspected.

ALS. How fitly our bride comes to partake
    with us !

BEAT. What is 't, my Lord ?

ALS.   No hurt.

BEAT.   Sir, pardon me,
I seldom taste of any composition.[38]

ALS. But this, upon my warrant, you shall
    venture on.

BEAT. I fear 't will make me ill.

ALS.   Heaven forbid that.

BEAT. [*aside*] I 'm put now to my cunning ;
    th' effects I know,
If I can now but feign 'em handsomely.
                        [*Drinks.*]

ALS. [*aside to* JASPERINO] It has that secret
    virtue, it ne'er miss'd, sir,
Upon a virgin.

JAS.   Treble-qualitied ? [39]   140
    [BEATRICE *gapes and sneezes.*]

ALS. By all that 's virtuous, it takes there !
    proceeds !

JAS. This is the strangest trick to know a
    maid by.

BEAT. Ha, ha, ha !
You have given me joy of heart to drink, my
    Lord.

ALS. No, thou hast given me such joy of
    heart
That never can be blasted.

BEAT.   What 's the matter, sir ?

ALS. [*aside*] See, now 't is settled in a mel-
    ancholy ;
Keep[s] both the time and method. — My
    Joanna,

---

[38] *I.e.*, mixed drink.
[39] Cf. IV, i, 51.

Chaste as the breath of Heaven, or morning's
    womb,
That brings the day forth! thus my love en-
    closes thee.   *Exeunt.* [150

[SCENE III] [40]

Enter ISABELLA *and* LOLLIO.

ISA. O Heaven! is this the [waning] [41]
moon? Does love turn fool, run mad, and all
at once? Sirrah, here's a madman, akin to
the fool too, a lunatic lover.

LOL. No, no, not he I brought the letter
from?

ISA. Compare his inside with his out, and
tell me.

LOL. The out's mad, I'm sure of that;
I had a taste on't. [*Reads letter.*] "To the
bright Andromeda, chief chambermaid to the
Knight of the Sun,[42] at the sign of Scorpio, [10
in the middle region, sent by the bellows-
mender of Aeolus. Pay the post." This is
stark madness!

ISA. Now mark the inside. [*Takes the letter
and reads.*] "Sweet lady, having now cast off
this counterfeit cover of a madman, I appear
to your best judgment a true and faithful
lover of your beauty."

LOL. He is mad still.

ISA. [*reads.*] "If any fault you find, [20
chide those perfections in you which have
made me imperfect; 't is the same sun that
causeth to grow and enforceth to wither, ——"

LOL. O rogue!

ISA. [*reads.*] "Shapes and transhapes, de-
stroys and builds again. I come in winter to
you, dismantled of my proper ornaments; by
the sweet splendor of your cheerful smiles, I
spring and live a lover."

LOL. Mad rascal still!   30

ISA. [*reads.*] "Tread him not under foot
that shall appear an honor to your bounties.
I remain — mad till I speak with you, from
whom I expect my cure, yours all, or one beside himself,   FRANCISCUS."

LOL. You are like to have a fine time on't.
My master and I may give over our profes-
sions; I do not think but you can cure fools
and madmen faster than we, with little pains
too.   40

ISA. Very likely.

LOL. One thing I must tell you, mistress:

you perceive that I am privy to your skill;
if I find you minister once, and set up the
trade, I put in for my thirds; [43] I shall be mad
or fool else.

ISA. The first place is thine, believe it,
    Lollio,
If I do fall.

LOL.   I fall upon you.

ISA.   So.

LOL. Well, I stand to my venture.

ISA.   But thy counsel now;
How shall I deal with 'em?

LOL.   [Why,] [44] do you mean to deal
    with 'em?   50

ISA. Nay, the fair understanding [45] — how
    to use 'em.

LOL. Abuse [46] 'em! That's the way to
mad the fool, and make a fool of the madman,
and then you use 'em kindly.[47]

ISA. 'T is easy, I'll practise; [48] do thou ob-
    serve it.
The key of thy wardrobe.

LOL. There [*giving key*]; fit yourself for
'em, and I'll fit 'em both for you.

ISA. Take thou no further notice than the
    outside.   *Exit.*

LOL. Not an inch; I'll put you to the
inside.   60

Enter ALIBIUS.

ALIB. Lollio, art there? Will all be per-
    fect, think'st thou?
To-morrow night, as if to close up the
Solemnity, Vermandero expects us.

LOL. I mistrust the madmen most; the
fools will do well enough; I have taken
pains with them.

ALIB. Tush! they cannot miss; the more
    absurdity,
The more commends it, so no rough be-
    haviors
Affright the ladies; they're nice [49] things,
    thou know'st.

LOL. You need not fear, sir; so long as [70
we are there with our commanding pizzles,[50]
they'll be as tame as the ladies themselves.

ALIB. I will see them once more rehearse
    before they go.

LOL. I was about it, sir; look you to the
madmen's morris,[51] and let me alone with

---

[43] The other sharers to be her husband and her
lover.   [44] Q *We*.
[45] *I.e.*, don't take my words in an obscene sense.
[46] Deceive.
[47] According to their natures.
[48] Plot.   [49] Finical.   [50] *I.e.*, whips. Q *peesles*.
[51] Morris dance.

---

[40] A room in Alibius's house.
[41] Conj. ed. 1816; Q *waiting*.
[42] Another allusion to the hero of *The Mirror of
Knighthood*.

the other. There is one or two that I mistrust their fooling; [52] I'll instruct them, and then they shall rehearse the whole measure. [53]

ALIB. Do so; I'll see the music prepar'd; but, Lollio,

By the way, how does my wife brook her restraint?   80
Does she not grudge [54] at it?

LOL. So, so; she takes some pleasure in the house; she would abroad else. You must allow her a little more length; she's kept too short.

ALIB. She shall along to Vermandero's with us;

That will serve her for a month's liberty.

LOL. What's that on your face, sir?

ALIB. Where, Lollio? I see nothing.

LOL. Cry you mercy,[55] sir, 't is your [90 nose; it show'd like the trunk of a young elephant.[56]

ALIB. Away, rascal! I'll prepare the music, Lollio.   *Exit* ALIBIUS.

LOL. Do, sir, and I'll dance the whilst. —
Tony, where art thou, Tony?

Enter ANTONIO.

ANT. Here, cousin; where art thou?

LOL. Come, Tony, the footmanship I taught you.

ANT. I had rather ride, cousin.

LOL. Ay, a whip take you! but I'll [100 keep you out; vault in: look you, Tony: fa, la, la, la, la.   [*Dances.*]

ANT. Fa, la, la, la, la.   [*Dances.*]

LOL. There, an honor.[57]

ANT. Is this an honor, coz?

LOL. Yes, an it please your Worship.

ANT. Does honor bend in the hams, coz?

LOL. Marry does it, as low as worship, squireship, nay, yeomanry itself sometimes, from whence it first stiffened: there, rise, a caper.[58]   111

ANT. Caper after an honor, coz?

LOL. Very proper, for honor is but a caper, rise[s] as fast and high, has a knee or two, and falls to th' ground again. You can remember your figure,[59] Tony?   *Exit.*

ANT. Yes, cousin; when I see thy figure, I can remember mine.

Re-enter ISABELLA, [*dressed as a madwoman.*]

ISA. Hey, how [he] [60] treads the air! Shough, shough, tother way! he burns [120 his wings else. Here's wax enough below, Icarus, more than will be cancelled [61] these eighteen moons. He's down, he's down! what a terrible fall he had!
Stand up, thou son of Cretan Daedalus,
And let us tread the lower labyrinth;
I'll bring thee to the clue.

ANT. Prithee, coz, let me alone.

ISA.   Art thou not drown'd?
About thy head I saw a heap of clouds   129
Wrapp'd like a Turkish turban; on thy back
A crook'd chameleon-color'd rainbow hung
Like a tiara down unto thy hams.
Let me suck out those billows in thy belly;
Hark, how they roar and rumble in the [straits]! [62]
Bless thee from the pirates!

ANT.   Pox upon you, let me alone!

ISA. Why shouldst thou mount so high as Mercury,
Unless thou hadst reversion of [63] his place?
Stay in the moon with me, Endymion,
And we will rule these wild rebellious waves,
That would have drown'd my love.

ANT.   I'll kick thee if
Again thou touch me, thou wild unshapen antic;   141
I am no fool, you bedlam!

ISA. But you are, as sure as I am, mad.
Have I put on this habit of a frantic,
With love as full of fury, to beguile
The nimble eye of watchful jealousy,
And am I thus rewarded?

ANT.   Ha! dearest beauty!

ISA. No, I have no beauty now,
Nor never had but what was in my garments.
You a quick-sighted lover! Come not near me: 150
Keep your caparisons, y' are aptly clad;
I came a feigner, to return stark mad.   *Exit.*

ANT. Stay, or I shall change condition,
And become as you are.

Re-enter LOLLIO.

LOL. W[h]y, Tony, whither now? Why, fool!

---

[52] Bullen conj. *footing;* cf. l. 97.
[53] Dance.   [54] Complain.   [55] Beg pardon.
[56] It looks as though someone had been pulling your nose. Professor Kittredge adds, "Perhaps with an allusion to being led by the nose."
[57] Bow.
[58] A leap or frisky hop in dancing.
[59] In the dance.

[60] Emend. Dyce; Q *she.*
[61] In the form of sealing-wax.
[62] Emend. Dyce; Q *streets.*
[63] Promise of succeeding to.

ANT. Whose fool, usher of idiots? You
   coxcomb!
I have fool'd too much.

LOL. You were best be mad another while
then.   160

ANT. So I am, stark mad; I have cause
   enough;
And I could throw the full effects on thee,
And beat thee like a fury.

LOL. Do not, do not; I shall not forbear
the gentleman under the fool, if you do.
Alas! I saw through your fox-skin [64] before
now! Come, I can give you comfort; my
mistress loves you; and there is as arrant a
madman i' th' house as you are a fool, your
rival, whom she loves not. If after the [170
masque we can rid her of him, you earn
her love, she says, and the fool shall ride her.

ANT. May I believe thee?

LOL. Yes, or you may choose whether you
will or no.

ANT. She's eas'd of him; I have a good
   quarrel on 't.

LOL. Well, keep your old station yet, and
be quiet.

ANT. Tell her I will deserve her love.   179
                                     [*Exit.*]

LOL. And you are like to have your desire.[65]

Enter FRANCISCUS.

FRAN. [*sings.*] " Down, down, down, a-
   down a-down," — and then with a
   horse-trick [66]
To kick Latona's [67] forehead, and break her
   bowstring.

LOL. [*aside*] This is tother counterfeit;
I'll put him out of his humor — [*Takes out a
letter and reads.*] " Sweet lady, having now
cast [68] this counterfeit cover of a madman,
I appear to your best judgment a true and
faithful lover of your beauty." This is pretty
well for a madman.

FRAN. Ha! what's that?   190

LOL. [*reads.*] " Chide those perfections in
you which have made me imperfect."

FRAN. [*aside*] I am discover'd to the fool.

LOL. [*aside*] I hope to discover the fool
in you, ere I have done with you. —
[*Reads.*] " Yours all, or one beside himself,
FRANCISCUS." This madman will mend sure.

FRAN. What do you read, sirrah?

LOL. Your destiny, sir; you'll be hang'd
for this trick, and another that I know.   200

FRAN. Art thou of counsel with thy mistress?

LOL. Next her apron-strings.

FRAN. Give me thy hand.

LOL. Stay, let me put yours in my pocket
first. [*Putting letter into his pocket.*] Your
hand is true,[69] is it not? It will not pick?
I partly fear it, because I think it does lie.

FRAN. Not in a syllable.

LOL. So if you love my mistress so well as
you have handled the matter here, you [210
are like to be cur'd of your madness.

FRAN. And none but she can cure it.

LOL. Well, I'll give you over then, and she
shall cast your water [70] next.

FRAN. Take for thy pains past.
                              [*Gives money.*]

LOL. I shall deserve more, sir, I hope. My
mistress loves you, but must have some proof
of your love to her.

FRAN. There I meet my wishes.

LOL. That will not serve; you must [220
meet her enemy and yours.

FRAN. He's dead already.

LOL. Will you tell me that, and I parted
but now with him?

FRAN. Show me the man.

LOL. Ay, that's a right course now; see
him before you kill him, in any case; and yet
it needs not go so far neither. 'T is but a
fool that haunts the house and my mistress
in the shape of an idiot; bang but his [230
fool's coat well-favoredly, and 't is well.

FRAN. Soundly, soundly!

LOL. Only reserve him till the masque be
past; and if you find him not now in the
dance yourself, I'll show you. In, in! my
master!   [*Dancing.*]

FRAN. He handles him like a feather. Hey!

Enter ALIBIUS.

ALIB. Well said; [71] in a readiness, Lollio?

LOL.   Yes, sir.

ALIB. Away then, and guide them in,
   Lollio;
Entreat your mistress to see this sight.   240
Hark, is there not one incurable fool
That might be begg'd? [72] I have friends.

LOL.   I have him for you,
One that shall deserve it too.

---

[64] Disguise.   [65] Dyce conj. *desert.*
[66] Cf. "horseplay."   [67] Diana's.   [68] Cast off.
[69] Honest.
[70] *I.e.,* be your physician.
[71] Well done.
[72] Alluding to the practice of begging the king to
grant the guardianship of a wealthy fool for the
sake of enjoying the income from his property.

ALIB.   Good boy, Lollio !
[*Exit* LOLLIO. *He returns at once*
with] *the madmen and fools,* [*who*]
dance.
'T is perfect ; well, fit but once these strains,
We shall have coin and credit for our pains.
                                        Exeunt.

ACT V — [SCENE I] [1]

Enter BEATRICE : *a clock strikes one.*

BEAT. One struck, and yet she lies by 't !
    O my fears !
This strumpet serves her own ends, 't is appar-
    ent now,
Devours the pleasure with a greedy appetite
And never minds my honor or my peace,
Makes havoc of my right. But she pays
    dearly for 't ;
No trusting of her life with such a secret,
That cannot rule her blood [2] to keep her prom-
    ise ;
Beside, I have some suspicion of her faith to
    me,
Because I was suspected of my lord,
And it must come from her. [*Strike two.*]
    Hark ! by my horrors,   10
Another clock strikes two !

Enter DE FLORES.

DE F.   Pist ! where are you ?
BEAT. De Flores ?
DE F.   Ay. Is she not come from him
    yet ?
BEAT. As I am a living soul, not !
DE F.   Sure the Devil
Hath sow'd his itch [3] within her. Who would
    trust
A waiting woman ?
    BEAT.   I must trust somebody.
DE F. Push ! they are t[e]rmagants ;
Especially when they fall upon their masters
And have their ladies' first fruits ; th' are mad
    whelps :
You cannot stave 'em off from game royal ;
    then
You are so [rash] [4] and hardy, ask no counsel ;
And I could have help'd you to a pothecary's
    daughter   21
Would have fall'n off before eleven, and thank
    you too.

BEAT. O me, not yet ! this whore forgets
    herself.
DE F. The rascal fares so well. Look,
    y ' are undone ;
The day-star, by this hand ! see [Phosphorus] [5]
    plain yonder.
BEAT. Advise me now to fall upon some
    ruin ;
There is no counsel safe else.
DE F.   Peace ! I ha 't now,
For we must force a rising ; there 's no remedy.
    BEAT. How ? take heed of that.
DE F. Tush ! be you quiet, or else give over
    all.   30
BEAT. Prithee, I ha' done then.
DE F.   This is my reach : [6] I 'll set
Some part afire of Diaphanta's chamber.
    BEAT. How ? fire, sir ? That may endan-
    ger the whole house.
DE F. You talk of danger when your fame 's
    on fire.
BEAT. That 's true ; do what thou wilt now.
DE F.   Push ! I aim
At a most rich success [7] strikes all dead sure.
The chimney being afire, and some light par-
    cels
Of the least danger in her chamber only,
If Diaphanta should be met by chance then
Far from her lodging, which is now suspi-
    cious,   40
It would be thought her fears and affrights
    then
Drove her to seek for succor ; if not seen
Or met at all, as that 's the likeliest,
For her own shame she 'll hasten towards her
    lodging ;
I will be ready with a piece [8] high-charg'd,
As 't were to cleanse the chimney ; there 't is
    proper now,
But she shall be the mark.
    BEAT.   I 'm forc'd to love thee now,
'Cause thou provid'st so carefully for my
    honor.
DE F. 'Slid, it concerns the safety of us
    both,
Our pleasure and continuance.
    BEAT.   One word now, [50
Prithee ; how for the servants ?
    DE F.   I 'll dispatch them,
Some one way, some another in the hurry,
For buckets, hooks, ladders ; fear not you,
The deed shall find its time ; and I 've thought
    since

---

[1] A gallery in the castle.   [2] Sensual nature.
[3] Inclination to evil.   [4] Conj. Dyce ; Q *harsh.*
[5] Q *Bosphorus.*   [6] Scheme.
[7] Understand "which."   [8] Gun.

Upon a safe conveyance [9] for the body too!
How this fire purifies wit! Watch you your
  minute.
  BEAT. Fear keeps my soul upon 't, I cannot
    stray from 't.

Enter ALONZO'S Ghost.

  DE F. Ha! what art thou that tak'st away
    the light
  Betwixt that star and me? I dread thee
    not. —
  'T was but a mist of conscience; all 's clear
    again.   *Exit.* [60
  BEAT. Who 's that, De Flores? Bless me,
    it slides by!   [*Exit* Ghost.]
Some ill thing haunts the house; 't has left
  behind it
A shivering sweat upon me; I'm afraid now.
This night hath been so tedious! Oh, this
  strumpet!
Had she a thousand lives, he should not leave
  her
Till he had destroy'd the last. List! O my
  terrors!   *Struck three a'clock.*
Three struck by St. Sebastian's!
  Within.   Fire, fire, fire!
  BEAT. Already? How rare is that man's
    speed!
How heartily he serves me! his face loathes
  one;
But look upon his care, who would not love
  him?   70
The east is not more beauteous than his serv-
  ice.
  Within. Fire, fire, fire!

Re-enter DE FLORES [*and*] Servants: *pass over:*
  ring a bell.

  DE F. Away, dispatch! hooks, buckets,
    ladders! that 's well said.
The fire bell rings; the chimney works, my
  charge;
The piece is ready.   *Exit.*
  BEAT.   Here 's a man worth loving!

Enter DIAPHANTA.

O y' are a jewel!
  DIA.   Pardon frailty, madam;
In troth I was so well, I ev'n forgot myself.
  BEAT. Y' have made trim work!
  DIA.   What?
  BEAT.   Hie quickly to your chamber;
Your reward follows you.

[9] Artifice.

  DIA.   I never made
So sweet a bargain.   *Exit.*

Enter ALSEMERO.

  ALS.   O my dear Joanna,   80
Alas! art thou risen too? I was coming,
My absolute treasure!
  BEAT.   When I miss'd you,
I could not choose but follow.
  ALS.   Th 'art all sweetness;
The fire is not so dangerous.
  BEAT.   Think you so, sir?
  ALS. I prithee, tremble not; believe me,
    't is not.

Enter VERMANDERO [*and*] JASPERINO.

  VER. Oh, bless my house and me!
  ALS.   My Lord your father.

Re-enter DE FLORES *with a piece.*

  VER. Knave, whither goes that piece?
  DE F.   To scour the chimney. *Exit.*
  VER. Oh, well said, well said!
That fellow 's good on all occasions.
  BEAT. A wondrous necessary man, my
    Lord.   90
  VER. He hath a ready wit; he 's worth 'em
    all, sir;
Dog [10] at a house of [11] fire; I ha' seen him
    sing'd ere now. —   *The piece goes off.*
Ha, there he goes!
  BEAT.   'T is done!
  ALS.   Come, sweet, to bed now;
Alas! thou wilt get cold.
  BEAT.   Alas! the fear keeps that out!
My heart will find no quiet till I hear
How Diaphanta, my poor woman, fares;
It is her chamber, sir, her lodging chamber.
  VER. How should the fire come there?
  BEAT. As good a soul as ever lady coun-
    tenanc'd,   99
But in her chamber negligent and heavy [12];
She scap'd a mine twice.
  VER.   Twice?
  BEAT.   Strangely twice, sir.
  VER. Those sleepy sluts are dangerous in a
    house,
An they be ne'er so good.

Re-enter DE FLORES.

  DE F.   O poor virginity,
Thou hast paid dearly for 't!
  VER.   Bless us! What 's that?

[10] Adept.   [11] On.   [12] Sleepy.

DE F. A thing you all knew once, Diaphanta's burnt.

BEAT. My woman! O my woman!

DE F.   Now the flames
Are greedy of her; burnt, burnt, burnt to
death, sir!

BEAT. O my presaging soul!

ALS.   Not a tear more!
I charge you by the last embrace I gave you
In bed, before this rais'd us.

BEAT.   Now you tie me; [110
Were it my sister, now she gets no more.

Enter Servant.

VER. How now?

SER.   All danger's past; you may now
take
Your rests, my Lords; the fire is throughly
quench'd.
Ah, poor gentlewoman, how soon was she
stifled!

BEAT. De Flores, what is left of her inter,
And we as mourners all will follow her.
I will entreat that honor to my servant
Ev'n of my Lord himself.

ALS.   Command it, sweetness.

BEAT. Which of you spied the fire first?

DE F.   'T was I, madam.

BEAT. And took such pains in't too? A
double goodness!   120
'T were well he were rewarded.

VER.   He shall be. —
De Flores, call upon me.

ALS.   And upon me, sir.
         Exeunt [*all but* DE FLORES].

DE F. Rewarded? Precious! here's a
trick beyond me.
I see in all bouts, both of sport and wit,
Always a woman strives for the last hit.
                    Exit.

[SCENE II] [13]

Enter TOMAZO.

TOM. I cannot taste the benefits of life
With the same relish I was wont to do.
Man I grow weary of, and hold his fellowship
A treacherous bloody friendship; and because
I'm ignorant in whom my wrath should settle,
I must think all men villains, and the next
I meet, whoe'er he be, the murderer
Of my most worthy brother. Ha! what's he?
    Enter DE FLORES [*and*] *passes over the stage.*
Oh, the fellow that some call honest De Flores;

But methinks honesty was hard bestead [14] [10
To come there for a lodging; as if a queen
Should make her palace of a pesthouse.
I find a contrariety in nature
Betwixt that face and me; the least occasion
Would give me game upon [15] him; yet he's so
foul
One would scarce touch [16] with a sword he
lov'd
And made account of; so most deadly veno-
mous,
He would go near to poison any weapon
That should draw blood on him; one must re-
solve
Never to use that sword again in fight,   20
In way of honest manhood, that strikes him;
Some river must devour it; 't were not fit
That any man should find it. What, again?

Re-enter DE FLORES.

He walks a' purpose by, sure, to choke me up,
T' infect my blood.

DE F.   My worthy noble Lord!

TOM. Dost offer to come near and breathe
upon me?   [*Strikes him.*]

DE F. A blow!   [*Draws.*]

TOM.   Yea, are you so prepar'd?
I'll rather like a soldier die by th' sword,
Than like a politician by thy poison. [*Draws.*]

DE F. Hold, my Lord, as you are honorable!   30

TOM. All slaves that kill by poison are still [17]
cowards.

DE F. [*aside*] I cannot strike; I see his
brother's wounds
Fresh bleeding in his eye, as in a crystal. —
I will not question this: I know y' are noble;
I take my injury with thanks given, sir,
Like a wise lawyer, and as a favor
Will wear it for the worthy hand that gave
it. —
[*aside*] Why this from him that yesterday ap-
pear'd
So strangely loving to me?
Oh, but instinct [18] is of a subtler strain!   40
Guilt must not walk so near his lodge again;
He came near me now. [19]   *Exit.*

TOM. All league with mankind I renounce
for ever,
Till I find this murderer; not so much
As common courtesy but I'll lock up;

---

[13] Another room in the castle.
[14] Hard up, hard put to it.
[15] Would afford me an occasion to fight.
[16] Mod. eds. insert *him*.   [17] Always.
[18] Accented on second syllable.
[19] He nearly found me out.

For in the state of ignorance I live in,
A brother may salute his brother's murderer,
And wish good speed to th' villain in a greeting.

Enter VERMANDERO, ALIBIUS, *and* ISABELLA.

VER. Noble Piracquo!
TOM.   Pray, keep on your way, sir;
I've nothing to say to you.
VER.   Comforts bless you, sir; [50
TOM. I've forsworn compliment,[20] in troth
    I have, sir;
As you are merely man, I have not left
A good wish for you, nor [21] any here.
VER. Unless you be so far in love with grief
You will not part from 't upon any terms,
We bring that news will make a welcome for us.
TOM. What news can that be?
VER.   Throw no scornful smile
Upon the zeal I bring you; 't is worth more,
    sir.
Two of the chiefest men I kept about me
I hide not from the law or your just ven-
    geance.   60
TOM. Ha!
VER. To give your peace more ample satis-
    faction,
Thank these discoverers.
TOM.   If you bring that calm,
Name but the manner I shall ask forgiveness in
For that contemptuous smile [22] upon you;
I'll perfect it with reverence that belongs
Unto a sacred altar.   [*Kneels.*]
VER.   Good sir, rise;
Why, now you overdo as much a' this hand
As you fell short a' tother. — Speak, Alibius.
ALIB. 'T was my wife's fortune, as she is
    most lucky   70
At a discovery, to find out lately,
Within our hospital of fools and madmen,
Two counterfeits slipp'd into these disguises;
Their names, Franciscus and Antonio.
VER. Both mine, sir, and I ask no favor for
    'em.
ALIB. Now that which draws suspicion to
    their habits,
The time of their disguisings agrees justly [23]
With the day of the murder.
TOM.   O blest revelation!
VER. Nay, more, nay, more, sir — I'll not
    spare mine own
In way of justice — they both feign'd a jour-
    ney   80

[20] Politeness.
[21] Mod. eds. add *for*.
[22] Dyce adds *I threw*, perhaps rightly; cf. l. 57.
[23] Precisely.

To Br[i]amata, and so wrought out their
    leaves [24];
My love was so abus'd [25] in 't.
TOM.   Time's too precious
To run in waste now; you have brought a
    peace
The riches of five kingdoms could not purchase.
Be my most happy conduct; I thirst for 'em;
Like subtle lightning will I wind about 'em,
And melt their marrow in 'em.   *Exeunt.*

[SCENE III] [26]

Enter ALSEMERO *and* JASPERINO.

JAS. Your confidence, I'm sure, is now of
    proof;
The prospect from the garden [27] has show'd
Enough for deep suspicion.
ALS.   The black mask
That so continually was worn upon 't
Condemns the face for ugly ere 't be seen:
Her despite to him, and so seeming bottomless.
JAS. Touch it home then; 't is not a shal-
    low probe
Can search this ulcer soundly; I fear you'll
    find it
Full of corruption. 'T is fit I leave you;
She meets you opportunely from that walk;
She took the back door at his parting with
    her.   *Exit* JASPERINO. [11
ALS. Did my fate wait for this unhappy
    stroke
At my first sight of woman? — She's here.

Enter BEATRICE.

BEAT. Alsemero!
ALS.   How do you?
BEAT.   How do I?
Alas! how do you? You look not well.
ALS. You read me well enough; I am not
    well.
BEAT. Not well, sir? Is 't in my power to
    better you?
ALS. Yes.
BEAT. Nay, then y' are cur'd again.
ALS. Pray, resolve me [28] one question, lady.
BEAT. If I can.   21
ALS. None can so sure. Are you honest? [29]
BEAT. Ha, ha, ha! that's a broad question,
    my Lord.

[24] Obtained their leaves of absence.   [25] Deceived.
[26] Alsemero's apartment. Dyce suggests the loca-
tion of the earlier part elsewhere, on account of
walk in l. 10. But note *door* in l. 11.
[27] Trisyllabic. (Dyce.)
[28] Satisfy me concerning.   [29] Chaste.

ALS. But that's not a modest answer, my Lady.
Do you laugh? My doubts are strong upon me.

BEAT. 'T is innocence that smiles, and no rough brow
Can take away the dimple in her cheek.
Say I should strain a tear to fill the vault,
Which would you give the better faith to?

ALS. 'T were but hypocrisy of a sadder color,   30
But the same stuff; neither your smiles nor tears
Shall move or flatter me from my belief:
You are a whore!

BEAT.   What a horrid sound it hath!
It blasts a beauty to deformity;
Upon what face soever that breath falls,
It strikes it ugly. Oh, you have ruin'd
What you can ne'er repair again.

ALS.   I'll all
Demolish, and seek out truth within you,
If there be any left; let your sweet tongue
Prevent [30] your heart's rifling; there I'll ransack   40
And tear out my suspicion.

BEAT.   You may, sir;
'T is an easy passage; yet, if you please,
Show me the ground whereon you lost your love;
My spotless virtue may but tread on that
Before I perish.

ALS.   Unanswerable;
A ground you cannot stand on; you fall down
Beneath all grace and goodness when you set
Your ticklish heel on't. There was a visor
O'er that cunning face, and that became you;
Now impudence in triumph rides upon't.   50
How comes this tender reconcilement else
'Twixt you and your despite, your rancorous loathing,
De Flores? He that your eye was sore at sight of,
He's now become your arm's supporter, your Lip's saint!

BEAT. Is there the cause?

ALS.   Worse, your lust's devil,
Your adultery!

BEAT.   Would any but yourself say that,
'T would turn him to a villain!

ALS.   'T was witness'd
By the counsel of your bosom,[31] Diaphanta.

BEAT. Is your witness dead then?

ALS.   'T is to be fear'd
It was the wages of her knowledge; poor soul,
She liv'd not long after the discovery.   61

BEAT. Then hear a story of not much less horror
Than this your false suspicion is beguil'd with;
To your bed's scandal I stand up innocence,[32]
Which even the guilt of one black other deed
Will stand for proof of: your love has made me
A cruel murd'ress.

ALS.   Ha!

BEAT.   A bloody one;
I have kiss'd poison for it, strok'd a serpent:
That thing of hate, worthy in my esteem
Of no better employment, and him most worthy   70
To be so employ'd, I caus'd to murder
That innocent Piracquo, having no
Better means than that worst to assure
Yourself to me.

ALS.   Oh, the place itself e'er since
Has crying been for vengeance! the temple,
Where blood and beauty first unlawfully
Fir'd their devotion and quench'd the right one;
'T was in my fears at first, 't will have it now;
Oh, thou art all deform'd!

BEAT.   Forget not, sir,
It for your sake was done. Shall greater dangers   80
Make the less welcome?

ALS.   Oh, thou shouldst have gone
A thousand leagues about to have avoided
This dangerous bridge of blood! Here we are lost.

BEAT. Remember, I am true unto your bed.

ALS. The bed itself's a charnel, the sheets shrouds
For murdered carcasses. It must ask pause
What I must do in this; meantime you shall
Be my prisoner only; enter my closet;[33]
                    Exit BEATRICE [*into closet*].
I'll be your keeper yet. Oh, in what part
Of this sad story shall I first begin? — Ha! [90
This same fellow has put me in.[34] — De Flores!

Enter DE FLORES.

DE F. Noble Alsemero!

ALS.   I can tell you
News, sir; my wife has her commended to you.

DE F. That's news indeed, my Lord; I think she would

---

[30] Forestall.
[31] By your confidante.

[32] I am innocent.   [33] A small private room.
[34] In the way of beginning.

Commend me to the gallows if she could,
She ever lov'd me so well ; I thank her.

ALS. What's this blood upon your band,[35]
De Flores?

DE F. Blood ! no, sure 't was wash'd since.

ALS. 　　　　　Since when, man?

DE F. Since tother day I got a knock
In a sword-and-dagger school ; I think 't is
　　out.　　　　　　　　　　　　　　100

ALS. Yes, 't is almost out, but 't is per-
　　ceiv'd though.

I had forgot my message ; this it is :
What price goes murder?

DE F. 　　　　　How, sir?

ALS. 　　　　　I ask you, sir ;
My wife's behindhand with [36] you, she tells
　　me,
For a brave bloody blow you gave for her sake
Upon Piracquo.

DE F. 　　Upon? 'T was quite through
　　him, sure ;
Has she confess'd it?

ALS. 　　As sure as death to both of you ;
And much more than that.

DE F. 　　　It could not be much more ;
'T was but one thing, and that — she's a
　　whore.

ALS. I[t] could not choose but follow. O
　　cunning devils !　　　　　　　110
How should blind men know you from fair-
　　fac'd saints?

BEAT. (*within*) He lies ! the villain does
　　belie me !

DE F. Let me go to her, sir.

ALS. 　　Nay, you shall to her. —
Peace, crying crocodile, your sounds are heard ;
Take your prey to you. — Get you in to her,
　　sir.　　　*Exit* DE FLORES [*into closet*].
I'll be your pander now ; rehearse again
Your scene of lust, that you may be perfect
When you shall come to act it to the black au-
　　dience,
Where howls and gnashings shall be music to
　　you.
Clip your adult'ress freely ; 't is the pilot [120
Will guide you to the *mare mortuum*,
Where you shall sink to fa[th]oms bottomless.

Enter VERMANDERO, ALIBIUS, ISABELLA, TO-
　　MAZO, FRANCISCUS, *and* ANTONIO.

VER. O Alsemero ! I have a wonder for
　　you.

ALS. No, sir, 't is I, I have a wonder for
　　you.

VER. I have suspicion near as proof itself
For Piracquo's murder.

ALS. 　　　Sir, I have proof,
Beyond suspicion, for Piracquo's murder.

VER. Beseech you, hear me ; these two
　　have been disguis'd
E'er since the deed was done.

ALS. 　　　　I have two other
That were more close disguis'd than your two
　　could be　　　　　　　　　130
E'er since the deed was done.

VER. You'll hear me — these mine own
　　servants ——

ALS. Hear me — those nearer than your
　　servants,
That shall acquit them and prove them guilt-
　　less.

FRAN. That may be done with easy truth,
　　sir.

TOM. How is my cause bandied through
　　your delays !
'T is urgent in [37] blood and calls for haste.
Give me a brother [38] alive or dead ;
Alive, a wife with him ; if dead, for both
A recompense for murder and adultery.　140

BEAT. (*within*) Oh, oh, oh !

ALS. 　　Hark ! 't is coming to you.

DE F. (*within*) Nay, I'll along for company.

BEAT. (*within*) 　　　　Oh, oh !

VER. What horrid sounds are these?

ALS. 　　　Come forth, you twins
Of mischief !

Re-enter DE FLORES, *bringing in* BEATRICE
　　[*wounded*].

DE F. Here we are ; if you have any more
To say to us, speak quickly : I shall not
Give you the hearing else ; I am so stout yet,
And so, I think, that broken rib of mankind.

VER. A host of enemies ent'red my citadel
Could not amaze like this. Joanna ! Beatrice-
　　Joanna !

BEAT. O, come not near me, sir ; I shall
　　defile you !　　　　　　　　150
I am that of your blood [39] was taken from you,
For your better health ; look no more upon 't,
But cast it to the ground regardlessly ;
Let the common sewer take it from distinction
Beneath the stars ; upon yon meteor
　　　　　　[*Points to* DE FLORES.]
Ever hang [40] my fate 'mongst things corrup-
　　tible ;
I ne'er could pluck it from him ; my loathing

Was prophet to the rest, but ne'er believ'd.
Mine honor fell with him, and now my life. —
Alsemero, I am a stranger to your bed ;   160
Your bed was coz'ned on the nuptial night, —
For which your false bride died.

ALS.   Diaphanta!

DE F. Yes, and the while I coupled with
your mate
At barley-break ; now we are left in hell.[41]

VER. We are all there ; it circumscribes [42]
here.

DE F. I lov'd this woman in spite of her
heart ;
Her love I earn'd out of Piracquo's murder.

TOM. Ha ! my brother's murderer ?

DE F.   Yes, and her honor's prize
Was my reward ; I thank life for nothing
But that pleasure ; it was so sweet to me, [170
That I have drunk up all, left none behind
For any man to pledge me.

VER.   Horrid villain !
Keep life in him for future tortures.

DE F.   No !
I can prevent you ; here 's my penknife still ;
It is but one thread more [*stabbing himself*],
and now 't is cut. —
Make haste, Joanna, by that token to thee,
Canst [43] not forget, so lately put in mind ;
I would not go to leave thee far behind. (*Dies.*)

BEAT. Forgive me, Alsemero, all forgive ! [180
'T is time to die when 't is a shame to live.
                              Dies.

VER. Oh, my name is ent'red now in that
record [44]
Where till this fatal hour 't was never read.

ALS. Let it be blotted out ; let your heart
lose it,
And it can never look you in the face,
Nor tell a tale behind the back of life
To your dishonor. Justice hath so right [45]
The guilty hit, that innocence is quit
By proclamation, and may joy again. —
Sir, you are sensible of what truth hath
done ;
'T is the best comfort that your grief can
find.

TOM. Sir, I am satisfied ; my injuries [191
Lie dead before me ; I can exact no more,
Unless my soul were loose, and could o'ertake
Those black fugitives that are fled from
thence,[46]

To take [47] a second vengeance ; but there are
wraths
Deeper than mine, 't is to be fear'd, about 'em.

ALS. What an opacous [48] body had that
moon
That last chang'd on us ! Here 's beauty
chang'd
To ugly whoredom ; here servant-obedience
To a master-sin, imperious murder ;   200
I, a suppos'd husband, chang'd embraces
With wantonness — but that was paid be-
fore.[49] —

[*to* TOMAZO] Your change is come too, from an
ignorant wrath
To knowing friendship. — Are there any more
on 's ?

ANT. Yes, sir, I was chang'd, too, from a
little ass as I was to a great fool as I am ; and
had like to ha' been chang'd to the gallows, but
that you know my innocence [50] always excuses
me.

FRAN. I was chang'd from a little wit to be
stark mad,   210
Almost for the same purpose.

ISA.   Your change is still behind,[51]
But deserve best your transformation ;
You are a jealous coxcomb,[52] keep schools of
folly,
And teach your scholars how to break your
own head.

ALIB. I see all apparent, Wife, and will
change now
Into a better husband, and never keep
Scholars that shall be wiser than myself. [217

ALS. Sir, you have yet a son's duty living ;
Please you, accept it ; let that your sorrow,
As it goes from your eye, go from your heart :
Man and his sorrow at the grave must part.

EPILOGUE

ALS. All we can do to comfort one another,
To stay a brother's sorrow for a brother,
To dry a child from the kind father's eyes,
Is to no purpose ; it rather multiplies :
Your only smiles have power to cause relive
The dead again, or in their rooms to give
Brother a new brother, father a child ;
If these appear, all griefs are reconcil'd.
                           Exeunt omnes.

---

[41] See on III, iii, 188.   [42] Mod. eds. add *us.*
[43] Which thou canst.   [44] Of dishonor.
[45] Precisely.   [46] Dyce needlessly emends *hence.*
[47] Receive.   [48] Opaque.
[49] *I.e.*, Diaphanta paid for that with her life.
[50] With a pun on "innocence" = imbecility.
[51] To come.   [52] Fool.

A NEW WAY TO PAY

OLD DEBTS

A COMOEDIE

As it hath beene often acted at the Phœnix in Drury-Lane, by the Queenes Maiesties seruants.

The Author.

PHILIP MASSINGER.

LONDON,

Printed by *E. P.* for *Henry Seyle*, dwelling in S. *Pauls* Church-yard, at the signe of the Tygers head. Anno. M. DC. XXXIII.

INTRODUCTORY NOTE

THOUGH Massinger is inadequately represented by a single play, the selection of *A New Way to Pay Old Debts* is inevitable. It is the only non-Shakespearean drama prior to *The Beggar's Opera* which has held the English-speaking stage down to the present time. Whatever its literary shortcomings, and it must be conceded that Massinger's poetic merits are negligible, the most recent professional productions, those of the Old Vic in London and Walter Hampden in the United States, testified anew to the remarkable qualities of the principal rôle as an acting vehicle, and to the entertaining nature of Wellborn's trick to catch the old one.

The similarity to Middleton's play of this part of the plot is obvious, but the dramatists' treatment could hardly be more divergent. Massinger is consistently serious, didactic even; his play does not end in forgiveness and a good dinner. Small wonder, then, that *A New Way to Pay Old Debts*, sweating moral earnestness at every pore, seems not to have been brought on the gay stage of Restoration London,[1] where in irresponsible wickedness a purer comedy flourished like the green bay tree. The rising tide of sentimentalism in the eighteenth century carried the piece back into favor; and, of the distinguished actors of the nineteenth, John Philip Kemble, Edmund and Charles Kean, Edwin Forrest, J. B. and Edwin Booth, Samuel Phelps, and Henry Irving all played Sir Giles.

It is of course the monomania of Overreach that gives the play its driving force; character is the mainspring, even though the title is supplied by the intrigue plot. To what extent Sir Giles was studied from life is uncertain. It is not unlikely that the portrait was influenced by the career of a rapacious contemporary, Sir Giles Mompesson, whose extortionate practices as a royal commissioner, monopolist, and patentee were exposed in 1621.

Nor can we be positive when the play was written and produced. 1621–1622 has been suggested, in view of the absence of any record of its licensing in the Astley-Herbert Revels Office book, which began on May 10, 1622. On the other hand, Queen Henrietta's Men began to act at the Phoenix (or Cockpit) in Drury Lane late in 1625; and the fall of Breda, mentioned in I, ii, 28, occurred on July 1 of that year. The allusion may have been added subsequently to the original production; but since it has no appearance of being an insertion, 1625 seems the most likely conclusion.

Whatever the date of composition, the play was not published till 1633. On the Quarto of that year the present text is based. There is as yet no satisfactory edition of Massinger's works. W. Gifford's second and revised edition appeared in 1813. P. Cunningham's was first published in 1867. Among the separate editions of *A New Way to Pay Old Debts* are those of B. Matthews (in vol. III of Gayley's *Representative English Comedies*, 1914), and A. H. Cruikshank (1926).

---

[1] There was, however, a performance at the King's Arms in Norwich by George Jolly's company, probably during the season of 1663–1664. (J. G. McManaway.)

A NEW WAY TO PAY OLD DEBTS

BY

PHILIP MASSINGER

DRAMATIS PERSONAE

LOVELL, an English lord.
SIR GILES OVERREACH, a cruel extortioner.
[FRANK] WELLBORN, a prodigal.
[TOM] ALLWORTH, a young gentleman, page to Lord Lovell.
GREEDY [WOODCOCK], a hungry justice of peace.
[JACK] MARRALL, a term-driver [1]; a creature of Sir Giles Overreach.

ORDER [steward],
AMBLE [usher],   servants to the Lady
FURNACE [cook],   Allworth.
WATCHALL [porter],

WILLDO, a parson.
[TIMOTHY] TAPWELL, an alehouse keeper
Three Creditors, [Servants, etc.]

The LADY ALLWORTH, a rich widow.
MARGARET, Overreach his daughter.
FROTH, Tapwell's wife.
Waiting Woman.
Chambermaid.

[THE SCENE — *The country, near Nottingham.*]

ACT I — SCENE I [2]

[*Enter*] WELLBORN [*in tattered apparel*], TAP-
    WELL, [*and*] FROTH.

WELL. No booze? nor no tobacco?
TAP.   Not a suck, sir;
Nor the remainder of a single can
Left by a drunken porter, all night pall'd [3]
    too.
FROTH. Not the dropping of the tap for your
    morning's draught, sir.
'T is verity, I assure you.
WELL.   Verity, you brach! [4]
The Devil turn'd precisian! [5] Rogue, what
    am I?
TAP. Troth, durst I trust you with a look-
    ing-glass,
To let you see your trim shape, you would quit
    me
And take the name yourself.
WELL.   How, dog!
TAP.   Even so, sir.
And I must tell you, if you but advance   10

Your Plymouth cloak [6] you shall be soon in-
    structed
There dwells, and within call, if it please your
    Worship,
A potent monarch call'd the constable,
That does command a citadel call'd the stocks;
Whose guards are certain files of rusty billmen [7]
Such as with great dexterity will hale
Your tatter'd, lousy ——
WELL.   Rascal! slave!
FROTH.   No rage, sir.
TAP. At his own peril. Do not put your-
    self
In too much heat, there being no water near
To quench your thirst; and sure, for other
    liquor,   20
As mighty ale, or beer, they are things, I take
    it,
You must no more remember; not in a dream,
    sir.
WELL. Why, thou unthankful villain, dar'st
    thou talk thus?
Is not thy house, and all thou hast, my gift?

---

[1] " ? = term-trotter, one who comes up to the law courts for the term." (*N.E.D.*)
[2] Before an alehouse.
[3] Staled. flat.   [4] Bitch.   [5] Puritan.
[6] Cudgel. According to Fuller, a voyager who landed destitute at Plymouth and lacked money for clothes would cut a stick and pretend to be on a walking tour.
[7] Men with rusty halberds.

TAP. I find it not in chalk; and Timothy Tapwell
Does keep no other register.
WELL. Am not I he
Whose riots [8] fed and cloth'd thee? Wert thou not
Born on my father's land, and proud to be
A drudge in his house?
TAP. What I was, sir, it skills [9] not;
What you are, is apparent. Now, for a farewell, 30
Since you talk of father, in my hope it will torment you,
I'll briefly tell your story. Your dead father,
My quondam master, was a man of worship,
Old Sir John Wellborn, justice of peace and *quorum*,[10]
And stood fair to be *custos rotulorum*; [11]
Bare the whole sway of the shire, kept a great house,
Reliev'd the poor, and so forth; but he dying
And the twelve hundred a year coming to you,
Late Master Francis, but now forlorn Wellborn ——
WELL. Slave, stop! or I shall lose myself.
FROTH. Very hardly; [40
You cannot out of your way.[12]
TAP. But to my story:
You were then a lord of acres, the prime gallant,
And I your under-butler. Note the change now.
You had a merry time of 't; hawks and hounds;
With choice of running horses; mistresses
Of all sorts and all sizes, yet so hot
As their embraces made your lordships [13] melt;
Which your uncle, Sir Giles Overreach, observing,
(Resolving not to lose a drop of 'em,)
On foolish mortgages, statutes,[14] and bonds, [50
For a while suppli'd your looseness, and then left you.
WELL. Some curate hath penn'd this invective, mongrel,
And you have studied it.

TAP. I have not done yet.
Your land gone, and your credit not worth a token,[15]
You grew the common borrower; no man scap'd
Your paper pellets,[16] from the gentleman
To the beggars on highways, that sold you switches
In your gallantry.
WELL. I shall switch your brains out.
TAP. Where [17] poor Tim Tapwell, with a little stock,
Some forty pounds or so, bought a small cottage, 60
Humbled myself to marriage with my Froth here,
Gave entertainment ——
WELL. Yes, to whores and canters,[18]
Clubbers by night.[19]
TAP. True, but they brought in profit,
And had a gift to pay for what they call'd for,
And stuck not [20] like your Mastership. The poor income
I glean'd from them hath made me in my parish
Thought worthy to be scavenger, and in time
May rise to be overseer of the poor;
Which if I do, on your petition, Wellborn, [69
I may allow you thirteenpence a quarter,[21]
And you shall thank my Worship.
WELL. Thus, you dogbolt,[22]
And thus —— *Beats and kicks him.*
TAP. [*to* FROTH] Cry out for help!
WELL. Stir, and thou diest;
Your potent prince, the constable, shall not save you.
Hear me, ungrateful hellhound! Did not I
Make purses for you? Then you lick'd my boots,
And thought your holiday cloak too coarse to clean 'em.
'T was I that, when I heard thee swear if ever
Thou couldst arrive at forty pounds thou wouldst
Live like an emperor, 't was I that gave it
In ready gold. Deny this, wretch!
TAP. I must, sir; [80
For, from the tavern to the taphouse, all,

---

[8] Prodigal expenditures.
[9] Matters.
[10] *I.e.*, one of a number of select justices whose presence was required to constitute a bench.
[11] The principal justice of the peace in a county and custodian of the rolls and records of the sessions.
[12] *I.e.*, that 'll be a hard job for you — you have no way!
[13] Estates.
[14] Bonds involving forfeiture of land in case of default.

[15] Tradesmen, especially tavern keepers, issued tokens for small change.
[16] I. O. U.'s. [17] Whereas.
[18] Beggars and vagabonds; their speech is "cant."
[19] Riffraff who gather together in night revels. (Kittredge.)
[20] Grudged not (to pay).
[21] *I.e.*, a dole of a penny a week.
[22] Wretch; literally, a blunt arrow.

On forfeiture of their licenses, stand bound
Never to remember who their best guests were,
If they grew poor like you.

WELL.   They are well rewarded
That beggar themselves to make such cuckolds
    rich.
Thou viper, thankless viper! impudent bawd!
But since you are grown forgetful, I will help
Your memory, and tread thee into mortar:
Not leave one bone unbroken.
                    [*Beats and kicks him again.*]

TAP.   Oh!
FROTH.   Ask mercy.

Enter ALLWORTH.

WELL. 'T will not be granted.
ALL.   Hold — for my sake, hold. [90
Deny me, Frank? They are not worth your
    anger.
WELL. For once thou hast redeem'd them
    from this sceptre; [23]
But let 'em vanish, creeping on their knees,
And, if they grumble, I revoke my pardon.
    FROTH. This comes of your prating, Hus-
    band; you presum'd
On your ambling wit, and must use your glib
    tongue,
Though you are beaten lame for 't.
    TAP.   Patience, Froth;
There's law to cure our bruises.
          They go off on their hands and knees.
WELL.   Sent [24] to your mother?
ALL. My lady, Frank, my patroness, my
    all!
She's such a mourner for my father's death, [100
And, in her love to him, so favors me,
That I cannot pay too much observance to
    her.
There are few such stepdames.
    WELL.   'T is a noble widow,
And keeps her reputation pure, and clear
From the least taint of infamy; her life,
With the splendor of her actions, leaves no
    tongue
To envy or detraction. Prithee tell me,
Has she no suitors?
    ALL.   Even the best of the shire, Frank,
My Lord excepted; such as sue and send,
And send and sue again, but to no purpose; [110
Their frequent visits have not gain'd her pres-
    ence.
Yet she's so far from sullenness and pride
That I dare undertake you shall meet from her

A liberal entertainment. I can give you
A catalogue of her suitors' names.
    WELL.   Forbear it,
While I give you good counsel. I am bound
    to it:
Thy father was my friend, and that affection
I bore to him, in right descends to thee;
Thou art a handsome and a hopeful youth,
Nor will I have the least affront stick on thee,
If I with any danger can prevent it.   121
    ALL. I thank your noble care; but, pray
        you, in what
Do I run the hazard?
    WELL.   Art thou not in love?
Put it not off with wonder.[25]
    ALL.   In love, at my years!
    WELL. You think you walk in clouds, but
        are trans[pa]rent.
I have heard all, and the choice that you have
    made,
And, with my finger, can point out the north
    star
By which the loadstone [26] of your folly's
    guided;
And, to confirm this true, what think you of
Fair Margaret, the only child and heir   130
Of Cormorant Overreach? Does it blush and
    start,
To hear her only nam'd? Blush at your want
Of wit and reason.
    ALL.   You are too bitter, sir.
    WELL. Wounds of this nature are not to be
        cur'd
With balms, but corrosives. I must be
    plain:
Art thou scarce manumiz'd [27] from the porter's
    lodge [28]
And yet sworn servant to the pantofle,[29]
And dar'st thou dream of marriage? I fear
'T will be concluded for impossible
That there is now, nor e'er shall be here-
    after,   140
A handsome page or player's boy of fourteen
But either loves a wench, or drabs love him;
Court-waiters [30] not exempted.
    ALL.   This is madness.
Howe'er you have discover'd my intents,
You know my aims are lawful; and if ever
The queen of flowers, the glory of the spring,

[23] Q notes marginally *His Cudgel.*
[24] *I.e.,* by Lord Lovell.

[25] *I.e.,* don't try to put my question aside by pre-
    tending surprise.
[26] Magnet; here, needle of compass.
[27] Freed, manumitted.
[28] Where servants were punished. (Gifford.)
[29] Slipper (as an instrument of discipline).
[30] Pages.

The sweetest comfort to our smell, the rose,
Sprang from an envious [31] briar, I may infer
There 's such disparity in their conditions [149
Between the goddess of my soul, the daughter,
And the base churl her father.

WELL.   Grant this true,
As I believe it, canst thou ever hope
To enjoy a quiet bed with her whose father
Ruin'd thy state?

ALL.   And yours too.

WELL.   I confess it ;
True, I must tell you as a friend, and freely,
That, where impossibilities are apparent,
'T is indiscretion to nourish hopes.
Canst thou imagine (let not self-love blind
     thee)
That Sir Giles Overreach, that, to make her
     great
In swelling titles, without touch of con-
     science   160
Will [32] cut his neighbor's throat, and I hope his
     own too,
Will e'er consent to make her thine? Give
     o'er,
And think of some course suitable to thy rank,
And prosper in it.

ALL.   You have well advis'd me.
But in the meantime you that are so studi-
     ous
Of my affairs wholly neglect your own.
Remember yourself, and in what plight you
     are.

WELL. No matter, no matter.

ALL.   Yes, 't is much material.
You know my fortune and my means ; yet
     something
I can spare from myself to help your wants.

WELL.   How 's this? [170

ALL. Nay, be not angry ; there 's eight
     pieces [33]
To put you in better fashion.

WELL.   Money from thee?
From a boy? A stipendiary? One that lives
At the devotion of a stepmother
And the uncertain favor of a lord?
I 'll eat my arms first. Howsoe'er blind For-
     tune
Hath spent the utmost of her malice on me ——
Though I am vomited out of an alehouse,
And thus accout'red — know not where to eat,
Or drink, or sleep, but underneath this can-
     opy — [34]   180
Although I thank thee, I despise thy offer ;

And as I in my madness broke my state [35]
Without th' assistance of another's brain,
In my right wits I 'll piece [36] it ; at the worst,
Die thus and be forgotten.

ALL.   A strange humor ! [37]   *Exeunt.*

SCENE II [38]

[Enter] ORDER, AMBLE, FURNACE, *[and]*
WATCHALL.

ORD. Set all things right, or, as my name is
     Order,
And by this staff of office that commands you,
This chain and double ruff, symbols of power,
Whoever misses in his function,
For one whole week makes forfeiture of his
     breakfast
And privilege in the wine cellar.

AMB.   You are merry,
Good Master Steward.

FURN.   Let him ; I 'll be angry.

AMB. Why, fellow Furnace, 't is not twelve
     a'clock yet,
Nor dinner taking up; then, 't is allow'd,
Cooks, by their places, may be choleric.   10

FURN. You think you have spoke wisely,
     Goodman Amble,
My Lady's go-before !

ORD.   Nay, nay, no wrangling.

FURN. Twit me with the authority of the
     kitchen !
At all hours, and all places, I 'll be angry ;
And thus provok'd, when I am at my prayers
I will be angry.

AMB.   There was no hurt meant.

FURN. I am friends with thee ; and yet I
     will be angry.

ORD. With whom?

FURN.   No matter whom ; yet, now I
     think on 't,
I am angry with my Lady.

WATCH.   Heaven forbid, man !

ORD. What cause has she given thee?

FURN. Cause enough, Master Steward. [20
I was entertain'd by her to please her palate ;
And, till she forswore eating, I perform'd it.
Now, since our master, noble Allworth, died,
Though I crack my brains to find out tempting
     sauces,
And raise fortifications in the pastry
Such as might serve for models in the Low
     Countries,

---

[31] Malicious.   [32] Would.
[33] Coins worth about $5 each.   [34] The sky.
[35] Bankrupted my estate.
[36] Mend.   [37] Whim, notion.
[38] A room in Lady Allworth's house.

Which, if they had been practis'd at Breda,
Spinola [39] might have thrown his cap at it, and
    ne'er took it ——

AMB. But you had wanted matter there to
    work on.[40]

FURN. Matter! with six eggs, and a strike [41]
    of rye meal,   30
I had kept the town till doomsday, perhaps
    longer.

ORD. But what's this to your pet against
    my Lady?

FURN. What's this? Marry this: when I
    am three parts roasted
And the fourth part parboil'd to prepare her
    viands,
She keeps her chamber, dines with a panada [42]
Or water-gruel, my sweat never thought on.

ORD. But your art is seen in the dining-
    room.

FURN.   By whom?
By such as pretend love to her, but come
To feed upon her. Yet, of all the harpies
That do devour her, I am out of charity   40
With none so much as the thin-gutted squire
That's stol'n into commission.[43]

ORD.   Justice Greedy?

FURN. The same, the same; meat's cast
    away upon him, —
It never thrives. He holds this paradox:
Who eats not well can ne'er do justice well.
His stomach's as insatiate as the grave,
Or strumpets' ravenous appetites.

WATCH.   One knocks.

ALLWORTH *knocks and enters.*

ORD. Our late young master!

AMB.   Welcome, sir.

FURN.   Your hand;
If you have a stomach, a cold bake-meat's
    ready.

ORD. His father's picture in little.[44]

FURN.   We are all your servants. [50

AMB. In you he lives.

ALL.   At once, my thanks to all;
This is yet some comfort. Is my Lady stir-
    ring?

---

[39] The Marquis of Spinola, commander of the
Spanish forces in the Low Countries. He took
Breda on July 1, 1625, after a siege of ten months.
[40] On account of the scarcity of provisions during
the siege.
[41] A dry measure, usually a bushel, but here evidently less.
[42] Boiled bread flavored with sugar, currants, etc.
[43] Obtained his commission as J. P. by fraudulent
or surreptitious means.
[44] Miniature.

Enter the LADY ALLWORTH, Waiting Woman,
    [*and*] Chambermaid.

ORD. Her presence answer for us.

L. ALL.   Sort those silks well;
I'll take the air alone.
            Exeunt Waiting Woman *and* Cham-
                bermaid.

FURN.   You air and air;
But will you never taste but spoon-meat [45]
    more?
To what use serve I?

L. ALL.   Prithee, be not angry:
I shall ere long; i' the meantime, there is gold
To buy thee aprons, and a summer suit.

FURN. I am appeas'd, and Furnace now
    grows [cool].[46]

L. ALL. And, as I gave directions, if this
    morning   60
I am visited by any, entertain 'em.
As heretofore; but say, in my excuse,
I am indispos'd.

ORD.   I shall, madam.

L. ALL.   Do, and leave me. —
Nay, stay you, Allworth.
        Exeunt ORDER, AMBLE, FURNACE,
            [*and*] WATCHALL.

ALL.   I shall gladly grow here,
To wait on your commands.

L. ALL.   So soon turn'd courtier!

ALL. Style not that courtship, madam,
    which is duty
Purchas'd on your part.

L. ALL.   Well, you shall o'ercome;
I'll not contend in words. How is it with
Your noble master?

ALL.   Ever like himself,
No scruple lessen'd in the full weight of
    honor.   70
He did command me, pardon my presumption,
As his unworthy deputy, to kiss
Your Ladyship's fair hands.

L. ALL.   I am honor'd in
His favor to me. Does he hold his purpose
For the Low Countries?

ALL.   Constantly, good madam;
But he will in person first present his service.

L. ALL. And how approve you of his course?
        You are yet
Like virgin parchment, capable of any
Inscription, vicious or honorable.
I will not force your will, but leave you free [80
To your own election.

---

[45] Liquid or soft diet.
[46] Cor. Coxeter; Q *Cooke.*

ALL.   Any form you please
I will put on ; but, might I make my choice,
With humble emulation I would follow
The path my Lord marks to me.
      L. ALL.   'T is well answer'd,
And I commend your spirit. You had a
      father,
Blest be his memory ! that some few hours
Before the will of Heaven took him from me,
Who did commend you, by the dearest ties
Of perfect love between us, to my charge ;
And, therefore, what I speak you are bound to
      hear   90
With such respect as if he liv'd in me.
He was my husband, and howe'er you are not
Son of my womb, you may be of my love,
Provided you deserve it.
      ALL.   I have found you,
Most honor'd madam, the best mother to
      me ;
And, with my utmost strengths of care and
      service,
Will labor that you never may repent
Your bounties show'r'd upon me.
      L. ALL.   I much hope it.
These were your father's words : " If e'er my
      son
Follow the war, tell him it is a school   100
Where all the principles tending to honor
Are taught, if truly followed ; but for such
As repair thither as a place in which
They do presume they may with license prac-
      tise
Their lusts and riots, they shall never merit
The noble name of soldiers. To dare boldly
In a fair cause, and for their country's safety
To run upon the cannon's mouth undaunted ;
To obey their leaders, and shun mutinies ;
To bear with patience the winter's cold   110
And summer's scorching heat, and not to
      faint,
When plenty of provision fails, with hunger ;
Are the essential parts make up a soldier ;
Not swearing, dice, or drinking."
      ALL.   There 's no syllable
You speak but is to me an oracle,
Which but to doubt were impious.
      L. ALL.   To conclude :
Beware ill company, for often men
Are like to those with whom they do converse ;
And, from one man I warn'd [47] you, and that's
      Wellborn :
Not 'cause he 's poor ; that rather claims your
      pity ;   120

[47] Gifford emends (silently) *warn*.

But that he 's in his manners so debauch'd,
And hath to vicious courses sold himself.
'T is true, your father lov'd him, while he
      was
Worthy the loving ; but if he had liv'd
To have seen him as he is, he had cast him off,
As you must do.
      ALL.   I shall obey in all things.
      L. ALL. Follow [48] me to my chamber, you
      shall have gold
To furnish you like my son, and still [49] sup-
      plied,
As I hear from you.
      ALL.   I am still [49] your creature. *Exeunt.*

SCENE III [50]

[*Enter*] OVERREACH, GREEDY, ORDER, AMBLE,
      FURNACE, WATCHALL, [*and*] MARRALL.

      GREEDY. Not to be seen !
      OVER.   Still cloistered up ! Her reason,
I hope, assures her, though she make herself
Close prisoner ever for her husband's loss,
'T will not recover him.
      ORD.   Sir, it is her will,
Which we, that are her servants, ought to
      serve it,
And not dispute. Howe'er, you are nobly
      welcome ;
And, if you please to stay, that you may think
      so,
There came, not six days since, from Hull, a
      pipe
Of rich Canary, which shall spend itself
For my Lady's honor.
      GREEDY.   Is it of the right race ? [51] [10
      ORD. Yes, Master Greedy.
      AMB. [*aside*]   How his mouth runs o'er !
      FURN. [*aside*] I 'll make it run, and run. —
      Save your good Worship !
      GREEDY. Honest Master Cook, thy hand ;
      again ! how I love thee !
Are the good dishes still in being ? Speak,
      boy.
      FURN. If you have a mind to feed, there is a
      chine
Of beef, well seasoned.
      GREEDY.   Good !
      FURN.   A pheasant, larded.
      GREEDY. That I might now give thanks
      for 't !

[48] Q *You follow.*   [49] Constantly.   [50] The same.
[51] A particular class of wine, or the characteristic
flavor of this, supposed to be due to the soil.
(*N.E.D.*)

FURN.   Other kickshaws.[52]
Besides, there came last [n]ight, from the forest
    of Sherwood,
The fattest stag I ever cook'd.
    GREEDY.   A stag, man?
    FURN. A stag, sir; part of it prepar'd for
        dinner,   20
And bak'd in puff paste.
    GREEDY.   Puff paste too! Sir Giles,
A ponderous chine of beef! a pheasant larded!
And red deer too, Sir Giles, and bak'd in puff
    paste!
All business set aside; let us give thanks here.
    FURN. [*aside*] How the lean skeleton's rapt!
    OVER.   You know we cannot.
    MAR. Your Worships are to sit on a com-
        mission,
And if you fail to come, you lose the cause.
    GREEDY. Cause me no causes. I'll prove 't,
        for such a dinner
We may put off a commission: you shall find it
Henrico decimo quarto.[53]
    OVER.   Fie, Master Greedy! [30
Will you lose me a thousand pounds for a din-
    ner?
No more, for shame! We must forget the belly
When we think of profit.
    GREEDY.   Well, you shall o'errule me;
I could ev'n cry now. — Do you hear, Master
    Cook,
Send but a corner [54] of that immortal pasty,
And I, in thankfulness, will, by your boy,
Send you a brace of threepences.
    FURN.   Will you be so prodigal?

Enter WELLBORN.

    OVER. Remember me to your lady. — Who
        have we here?
    WELL. You know me.
    OVER.   I did once, but now I will not;
Thou art no blood of mine. Avaunt, thou
        beggar!   40
If ever thou presume to own me more,
I'll have thee cag'd and whipp'd.
    GREEDY.   I'll grant the warrant. —
Think of Pie Corner,[55] Furnace!
        Exeunt OVERREACH, GREEDY, [*and*]
                MARRALL.
    WATCH.   Will you out, sir?
I wonder how you durst creep in.

---

[52] Fancy dishes.
[53] *I.e.*, in the statutes of that year.
[54] Triangular piece.
[55] *I.e.*, the piece of pie, but also alluding to the
locality, in West Smithfield; it was noted, according
to Strype, for its cooks' shops.

ORD.   This is rudeness,
And saucy impudence.
    AMB.   Cannot you stay
To be serv'd, among your fellows, from the
        basket,[56]
But you must needs press into the hall?
    FURN.   Prithee, vanish
Into some outhouse, though it be the pigsty;
My scullion shall come to thee.

Enter ALLWORTH.

    WELL.   This is rare.
Oh, here's Tom Allworth. Tom!
    ALL.   We must be strangers; [50
Nor would I have you seen here for a million.
                Exit ALLWORTH.
    WELL. Better and better. He contemns
        me too!

Enter [Waiting] Woman *and* Chambermaid.

    WOMAN. Foh, what a smell's here! What
        thing's this?
    CHAM.   A creature
Made out of the privy; let us hence, for love's
        sake,
Or I shall swoon.
    WOMAN.   I begin to faint already.
        Exeunt [Waiting] Woman *and* Cham-
                bermaid.
    WATCH. Will know your way?
    AMB.   Or shall we teach it you,
By the head and shoulders?
    WELL.   No; I will not stir;
Do you mark, I will not: let me see the wretch
That dares attempt to force me. Why, you
        slaves,
Created only to make legs,[57] and cringe; [60
To carry in a dish, and shift a trencher;
That have not souls only to hope a blessing
Beyond blackjacks [58] or flagons; you that
        were born
Only to consume meat and drink, and batten [59]
Upon reversions [60]! — who advances? who
Shows me the way?
    ORD.   My Lady!

Enter LADY ALLWORTH, [Waiting] Woman,
        [*and*] Chambermaid.

    CHAM.   Here's the monster.
    WOMAN. Sweet madam, keep your glove [61]
        to your nose.

---

[56] The alms-basket of broken meats.
[57] To bow.   [58] Leather jugs for beer.
[59] Feed.   [60] Left-overs.
[61] Gloves were often perfumed.

CHAM.   Or let me
Fetch some perfumes [62] may be predominant ;
You wrong yourself else.
WELL.   Madam, my designs
Bear me to you.
L. ALL.   To me?
WELL.   And though I have met with
But ragged entertainment from your grooms
     here,   71
I hope from you to receive that noble usage
As may become the true friend of your hus-
     band ;
And then I shall forget these.
L. ALL.   I am amaz'd
To see and hear this rudeness.   Dar'st thou
     think,
Though sworn,[63] that it can ever find belief,
That I, who to the best men of this country
Deni'd my presence since my husband's death,
Can fall so low as to change words with thee?
Thou son of infamy, forbear my house,   80
And know and keep the distance that's be-
     tween us ;
Or, though it be against my gentler temper,
I shall take order [64] you no more shall be
An eyesore to me.
WELL.   Scorn me not, good lady ;
But, as in form you are angelical,
Imitate the heavenly natures, and vouchsafe
At the least awhile to hear me.   You will grant
The blood that runs in this arm is as noble
As that which fills your veins ; those costly
     jewels,
And those rich clothes you wear, your men's
     observance   90
And women's flattery, are in you no virtues ;
Nor these rags, with my poverty, in me vices.
You have a fair fame, and, I know, deserve it ;
Yet, lady, I must say, in nothing more
Than in the pious sorrow you have shown
For your late noble husband.
ORD. [*aside*]   How she starts !
FURN. [*aside*] And hardly can keep finger
     from the eye,
To hear him nam'd.
L. ALL.   Have you aught else to say?
WELL. That husband, madam, was once in
     his fortune
Almost as low as I ; want, debts, and
     quarrels   100
Lay heavy on him.   Let it not be thought
A boast in me, though I say I reliev'd him.

'T was I that gave him fashion [65] ; mine the
     sword
That did on all occasions second his ;
I brought him on and off with honor, lady ;
And when in all men's judgments he was sunk,
And, in his own hopes, not to be [buoy'd] [66] up,
I stepp'd unto him, took him by the hand,
And set him upright.
FURN. [*aside*]   Are not we base rogues,
That could forget this?
WELL.   I confess, you made him [110
Master of your estate ; nor could your friends,
Though he brought no wealth with him, blame
     you for 't ;
For he had a shape, and to that shape a mind
Made up of all parts either great or noble ;
So winning a behavior, not to be
Resisted, madam.
L. ALL.   'T is most true, he had.
WELL. For his sake, then, in that I was his
     friend,
Do not contemn me.
L. ALL.   For what's past excuse me ;
I will redeem it.   Order, give the gentleman
A hundred pounds.
WELL.   No, madam, on no terms ; [120
I will nor beg nor borrow sixpence of you,
But be suppli'd elsewhere, or want thus ever.
Only one suit I make, which you deny not
To strangers ; and 't is this. (*Whispers to her.*)
L. ALL.   Fie ! nothing else?
WELL. Nothing, unless you please to charge
     your servants
To throw away a little respect upon me.
L. ALL. What you demand is yours.
WELL.   I thank you, lady.
Now what can be wrought out of such a suit
Is yet in supposition ;   I have said all ;
When you please, you may retire. —
     [*to the* Servants]   Nay, all's forgotten ;
And, for a lucky omen to my project,   131
Shake hands, and end all quarrels in the cellar.
ORD. Agreed, agreed.
FURN.   Still merry Master Wellborn.
                                        Exeunt.

ACT II — SCENE I[1]

Enter OVERREACH [*and*] MARRALL.

OVER. He's gone, I warrant thee ;   this
     commission crush'd him.

---

[62] Understand "which."
[63] Even if the declaration should be made under
oath.   [64] Make arrangements that.

[65] *I.e.*, suitable clothes.
[66] Emend. Dodsley ; Q *bung'd.*
[1] Unlocated ; perhaps a room in Overreach's house.

MAR. Your Worship[s] [2] have the way [on 't],[3] and ne'er miss
To squeeze these unthrifts into air ; and yet,
The chapfallen [4] justice did his part, returning
For your advantage the certificate,
Against his conscience, and his knowledge, too,
With your good favor, to the utter ruin
Of the poor farmer.

OVER.   'T was for these good ends
I made him a justice ; he that bribes his belly
Is certain to command his soul.

MAR.   I wonder,
Still with your license, why your Worship having   11
The power to put this thin-gut in commission,
You are not in 't yourself.

OVER.   Thou art a fool ;
In being out of office I am out of danger ;
Where,[5] if I were a justice, besides the trouble,
I might, or out of wilfulness or error,
Run myself finely into a *praemunire*,[6]
And so become a prey to the informer.
No, I 'll have none of 't ; 't is enough I keep
Greedy at my devotion ; so [7] he serve   20
My purposes, let him hang or damn, I care not ;
Friendship is but a word.

MAR.   You are all wisdom.

OVER. I would be worldly wise ; for the other wisdom,
That does prescribe us a well govern'd life,
And to do right to others as ourselves,
I value not an atom.

MAR.   What course take you,
With your good patience, to hedge in the manor
Of your neighbor, Master Frugal? as 't is said,
He will nor sell, nor borrow, nor exchange ;
And his land, lying in the midst of your many lordships,   30
Is a foul blemish.

OVER.   I have thought on 't, Marrall,
And it shall take. I must have all men sellers,
And I the only purchaser.

MAR.   'T is most fit, sir.

OVER. I 'll therefore buy some cottage near his manor ;

Which done, I 'll make my men break ope his fences,
Ride o'er his standing corn, and in the night
Set fire on his barns, or break his cattle's legs.
These trespasses draw on suits and suits expenses,
Which I can spare, but will soon beggar him.
When I have harried him thus two or three year,   40
Though he sue *in forma pauperis*, in spite
Of all his thrift and care, he 'll grow behindhand.[8]

MAR. The best I ever heard ! I could adore you.

OVER. Then, with the favor of my man of law,
I will pretend some title. Want will force him
To put it to arbitrament ; then, if he sell
For half the value, he shall have ready money,
And I possess his land.

MAR.   'T is above wonder !
Wellborn was apt to sell, and needed not
Those fine arts, sir, to hook him in.

OVER.   Well thought on. [50
This varlet, Marrall, lives too long, to upbraid me
With my close cheat [9] put upon him. Will nor cold
Nor hunger kill him?

MAR.   I know not what to think on 't.
I have us'd all means ; and the last night I caus'd
His host, the tapster, to turn him out of doors ;
And have been since with all your friends and tenants,
And, on the forfeit of your favor, charg'd [them],[10]
Though a crust of mouldy bread would keep him from starving,
Yet they should not relieve him. This is done, sir.

OVER. That was something, Marrall ; but thou must go further,   60
And suddenly, Marrall.

MAR.   Where and when you please, sir.

OVER. I would have thee seek him out, and, if thou canst,
Persuade him that 't is better steal than beg ;
Then, if I prove he has but robb'd a henroost,
Not all the world shall save him from the gallows.
Do anything to work him to despair ;
And 't is thy masterpiece.

MAR.   I will do my best, sir.
OVER. I am now on my main work with
    the Lord Lovell,
The gallant-minded, popular Lord Lovell,
The minion [11] of the people's love. I hear [70
He 's come into the country, and my aims are
To insinuate myself into his knowledge,
And then invite him to my house.
MAR.   I have you ;
This points at my young mistress.
OVER.   She must part with
That humble title, and write Honorable,
Right Honorable, Marrall, my Right Hon-
    orable daughter,
If all I have, or e'er shall get, will do it.
I will have her well attended ; there are ladies
Of errant knights decay'd and brought so low,
That for cast clothes and meat will gladly
    serve her.   80
And 't is my glory, though I come from the
    city,[12]
To have their issue whom [13] I have undone,
To kneel to mine as bondslaves.
MAR.   'T is fit state, sir.
OVER. And therefore, I 'll not have a cham-
    bermaid
That ties her shoes, or any meaner office,
But such whose fathers were Right Worship-
    ful.
'T is a rich man's pride ! there having ever
    been
More than a feud, a strange antipathy,
Between us and true gentry.

Enter WELLBORN.

MAR.   See, who 's here, sir.
OVER. Hence, monster ! prodigy !
WELL.   Sir, your wife's nephew ; [90
She and my father tumbled in one belly.
OVER. Avoid my sight ! thy breath 's in-
    fectious, rogue !
I shun thee as a leprosy, or the plague.
Come hither, Marrall ; — [*aside*] this is the
    time to work him.   *Exit* OVERREACH.
MAR. I warrant you, sir,
WELL.   By this light I think he 's mad.
MAR. Mad ! had you took compassion on
    yourself,
You long since had been mad.
WELL.   You have took a course,
Between you and my venerable uncle,
To make me so.

MAR.   The more pale-spirited you,
That would not be instructed. I swear
    deeply ——   100
WELL. By what?
MAR.   By my religion.
WELL.   Thy religion !
The Devil's creed : — but what would you
    have done?
MAR. Had there been but one tree in all the
    shire,
Nor any hope to compass a penny halter,
Before, like you, I had outliv'd my fortunes,
A withe had serv'd my turn to hang myself.
I am zealous in your cause ; pray you hang
    yourself,
And presently,[14] as you love your credit.[15]
WELL.   I thank you.
MAR. Will you stay till you die in a ditch, or
    lice devour you? ——
Or, if you dare not do the feat yourself,   110
But that [16] you 'll put the state to charge and
    trouble,
Is there no purse to be cut, house to be
    broken,
Or market woman with eggs that you may
    murder,
And so dispatch the business?
WELL.   Here 's variety,
I must confess ; but I 'll accept of none
Of all your gentle offers, I assure you.
MAR. Why, have you hope ever to eat
    again,
Or drink? or be the master of three farthings?
If you like not hanging, drown yourself !
    Take some course
For your reputation.
WELL.   'T will not do, dear tempter, [120
With all the rhetoric the Fiend hath taught
    you.
I am as far as thou art from despair ;
Nay, I have confidence, which is more than
    hope,
To live, and suddenly, better than ever.
MAR. Ha ! ha ! these castles you build in
    the air
Will not persuade me or to give or lend
A token [17] to you.
WELL.   I 'll be more kind to thee.
Come, thou shalt dine with me.
MAR.   With you !
WELL.   Nay more, dine gratis.
MAR. Under what hedge, I pray you? or at
    whose cost?

[11] Darling, favorite.
[12] *I.e.*, am not by birth one of the landed gentry.
[13] The offspring of those whom.

[14] Immediately.
[15] Reputation.   [16] If.   [17] See on I, i, 54.

Are they padders [18] or Abram-men [19] that are
  your consorts? 130
  WELL. Thou art incredulous; but thou
    shalt dine
Not alone at her house, but with a gallant
  lady;
With me, and with a lady.
  MAR. Lady! what lady?
With the Lady of the Lake,[20] or Queen of
  Fairies?
For I know it must be an enchanted dinner.
  WELL. With the Lady Allworth, knave.
  MAR. Nay, now there's hope
Thy brain is crack'd.
  WELL. Mark there, with what respect
I am entertain'd.
  MAR. With choice, no doubt, of dog
    whips.
Why, doest thou ever hope to pass her porter?
  WELL. 'T is not far off; go with me; trust
    thine own eyes. 140
  MAR. Troth, in my hope, or my assurance
    rather,
To see thee curvet [21] and mount like a dog in a
  blanket,
If ever thou presume to pass her threshold,
I will endure thy company.
  WELL. Come along then. *Exeunt.*

SCENE II [22]

[*Enter*] ALLWORTH, Waiting Woman, Chambermaid, ORDER, AMBLE, FURNACE, [*and*]
  WATCHALL.

  WOMAN. Could you not command your lei-
    sure one hour longer?
  CHAM. Or half an hour?
  ALL. I have told you what my haste is;
Besides, being now another's, not mine own,
Howe'er I much desire to enjoy you longer,
My duty suffers, if, to please myself,
I should neglect my Lord.
  WOMAN. Pray you do me the favor
To put these few quince-cakes into your
  pocket;
They are of mine own preserving.
  CHAM. And this marmalade;
'T is comfortable for your stomach.
  WOMAN. And, at parting,
Excuse me if I beg a farewell from you. [10

[18] Footpads.
[19] Abraham-men, vagabond beggars.
[20] In the Arthurian romances.
[21] Bound; *i.e.*, be tossed out.
[22] A room in Lady Allworth's house.

CHAM. You are still before me. I move
  the same suit, sir.
    [ALLWORTH] *kisses 'em severally.*
  FURN. How greedy these chamberers are of
    a beardless chin!
I thin[k] the tits [23] will ravish him.
  ALL. My service
To both.
  WOMAN. Ours waits on you.
  CHAM. And shall do ever.
  ORD. You are my lady's charge; be there-
    fore careful
That you sustain your parts.
  WOMAN. We can bear, I warrant you.
    Exeunt [Waiting] Woman *and* Cham-
      bermaid.
  FURN. Here, drink it off; the ingredients
    are cordial,
And this the true elixir; it hath boil'd
Since midnight for you. 'T is the quintessence
Of five cocks of the game, ten dozen of spar-
  rows, 20
Knuckles of veal, potato-roots and marrow,
Coral, and ambergris. Were you two years
  older,
And I had a wife, or gamesome mistress,
I durst trust you with neither. You need not
  bait [24]
After this, I warrant you, though your jour-
  ney's long;
You may ride on the strength of this till to-
  morrow morning.
  ALL. Your courtesies overwhelm me; I
    much grieve
To part from such true friends; and yet find
  comfort
My attendance on my honorable Lord,
Whose resolution holds to visit my Lady, [30
Will speedily bring me back.
    Knocking at the gate; MARRALL *and*
      WELLBORN *within.*
  MAR. Dar'st thou venture further?
  WELL. Yes, yes, and knock again.
  ORD. 'T is he; disperse!
  AMB. Perform it bravely.
  FURN. I know my cue, ne'er doubt me.
    [*Except* ALLWORTH] *they go off several
      ways.*

[*Re-enter* WATCHALL, *with* WELLBORN *and*
  MARRALL.]

  WATCH. Beast that I was, to make you
    stay! Most welcome;
You were long since expected.

[23] Wenches. [24] Take food on your journey.

WELL.   Say so much
To my friend, I pray you.
     WATCH.   For your sake, I will, sir.
     MAR. For his sake!
     WELL.   Mum; this is nothing.
     MAR.   More than ever
I would have believ'd, though I had found it in
     my primer.
     ALL. When I have giv'n you reasons for
     my late harshness,
You'll pardon and excuse me; for, believe
     me,   40
Though now I part [25] abruptly, in my service
I will deserve it.
     MAR.   Service! with a vengeance!
     WELL. I am satisfied; farewell, Tom.
     ALL.   All joy stay with you!
                         Exit ALLWORTH.

Re-enter AMBLE.

     AMB. You are happily encounter'd; I yet
     never
Presented one so welcome as I know
You will be to my Lady.
     MAR.   This is some vision,
Or, sure, these men are mad, to worship a
     dunghill;
It cannot be a truth.
     WELL.   Be still a pagan,
An unbelieving infidel; be so, miscreant, [49
And meditate on blankets, and on dog whips!

Re-enter FURNACE.

     FURN. I am glad you are come; until I
     know your pleasure
I knew not how to serve up my Lady's din-
     ner.
     MAR. His pleasure! is it possible?
     WELL.   What's thy will?
     FURN. Marry, sir, I have some grouse, and
     turkey chicken,
Some rails and quails, and my Lady will'd me
     ask you,
What kind of sauces best affect your palate,
That I may use my utmost skill to please it.
     MAR. [*aside*] The Devil's enter'd this cook.
     Sauce for his palate!
That, on my knowledge, for almost this twelve-
     month,
Durst wish but cheese-parings and brown
     bread on Sundays.   60
     WELL. That way I like 'em best.
     FURN.   It shall be done, sir.
                       Exit FURNACE.

[25] Depart.

WELL. What think you of the hedge we
     shall dine under?
Shall we feed gratis?
     MAR.   I know not what to think;
Pray you make me not mad.

Re-enter ORDER.

     ORD.   This place becomes you not;
Pray you walk, sir, to the dining-room.
     WELL.   I am well here,
Till her Ladyship quits her chamber.
     MAR.   Well here, say you?
'T is a rare change! But yesterday you
     thought
Yourself well in a barn, wrapp'd up in peas-
     straw.

Re-enter [Waiting] Woman *and* Chambermaid.

     WOMAN. Oh, sir, you are wish'd for.
     CHAM.   My lady dreamt, sir, of you.
     WOMAN. And the first command she gave,
     after she rose,   70
Was (her devotions done) to give her notice
When you approach'd here.
     CHAM.   Which is done, on my virtue.
     MAR. I shall be converted; I begin to grow
Into a new belief, which saints nor angels
Could have won me to have faith in.
     WOMAN.   Sir, my Lady.

Enter LADY [ALLWORTH].

     L. ALL. I come to meet you, and languish'd
     till I saw you.
This first kiss is for form; I allow a second
To such a friend.
     MAR. To such a friend! Heaven bless me!
     WELL. I am wholly yours; yet, madam, if
     you please
To grace this gentleman with a salute —— [80
     MAR. Salute me at his bidding!
     WELL.   I shall receive it
As a most high favor.
     L. ALL.   Sir, you may command me.
         [*Advances to salute* MARRALL, *who*
        retires.]
     WELL. Run backward from a lady! and
     such a lady!
     MAR. To kiss her foot is, to poor me, a
     favor
I am unworthy of.   *Offers* [26] *to kiss her foot.*
     L. ALL.   Nay, pray you rise;
And since you are so humble, I'll exalt you.
You shall dine with me to-day, at mine own
     table.

[26] Tries.

MAR. Your Ladyship's table! I am not good enough
To sit at your steward's board.

L. ALL.   You are too modest;
I will not be deni'd.

Re-enter FURNACE.

FURN.   Will you still be babbling [90
Till your meat freeze on the table? The old trick still;
My art ne'er thought on!

L. ALL.   Your arm, Master Wellborn. —
[*To* MARRALL] Nay, keep us company.

MAR.   I was never so grac'd.
            Exeunt WELLBORN, LADY [ALL-
            WORTH], AMBLE, MARRALL, [Wait-
            ing] Woman, [*and* Chambermaid].

ORD. So! we have play'd our parts, and are come off well;
But if I know the mystery, why my Lady
Consented to it, or why Master Wellborn
Desir'd it, may I perish!

FURN.   Would I had
The roasting of his heart that cheated him,
And forces the poor gentleman to these shifts!
By fire! for cooks are Persians,[27] and swear by it,   100
Of all the griping and extorting tyrants
I ever heard or read of, I ne'er met
A match to Sir Giles Overreach.

WATCH.   What will you take
To tell him so, fellow Furnace?

FURN.   Just as much
As my throat is worth, for that would be the price on 't.
To have a usurer that starves himself,
And wears a cloak of one-and-twenty years
On a suit of fourteen groats,[28] bought of the hangman,[29]
To grow rich, and then purchase, is too common;
But this Sir Giles feeds high, keeps many servants,   110
Who must at his command do any outrage;
Rich in his habit, vast in his expenses;
Yet he to admiration [30] still increases
In wealth and lordships.

ORD.   He frights men out of their estates,
And breaks through all law-nets, made to curb ill men,

As they were cobwebs. No man dares reprove him.
Such a spirit to dare and power to do were never
Lodg'd so unluckily.

Re-enter AMBLE.

AMB.   Ha! ha! I shall burst.

ORD. Contain thyself, man.

FURN.   Or make us partakers
Of your sudden mirth.

AMB.   Ha! ha! my Lady has got [120
Such a guest at her table! — this term-driver,[31] Marrall,
This snip of an attorney ——

FURN.   What of him, man?

AMB. The knave thinks still he's at the cook's shop in Ram Alley,[32]
Where the clerks divide, and the elder is to choose;
And feeds so slovenly!

FURN.   Is this all?

AMB.   My Lady
Drank to him for fashion sake, or to please Master Wellborn;
As I live, he rises, and takes up a dish
In which there were some remnants of a boil'd capon,
And pledges her in white broth![33]

FURN.   Nay, 't is like
The rest of his tribe.

AMB.   And when I brought him wine, [130
He leaves his stool, and, after a leg [34] or two,
Most humbly thanks my Worship.

ORD.   Rose already!

AMB. I shall be chid.

Re-enter LADY [ALLWORTH], WELLBORN, [*and*]
            MARRALL.

FURN.   My Lady frowns.

L. ALL. [*aside to* AMBLE]   You wait well!
Let me have no more of this; I observ'd your jeering.
Sirrah, I'll have you know whom I think worthy
To sit at my table, be he ne'er so mean,
When I am present, is not your companion.[35]

ORD. [*aside*] Nay, she'll preserve what's due to her.

FURN. [*aside*]   This refreshing
Follows your flux of laughter.

---

[27] *I.e.*, fire worshippers.
[28] Small silver coins worth about eight cents each.
[29] The clothes of the condemned went to the executioner.
[30] Wondrously.

[31] See on *Dramatis Personae*.
[32] Off Fleet Street; it was famous for its cooks' shops.
[33] White sauce.
[34] Bow.   [35] Fellow, equal.

L. ALL. [*to* WELLBORN]   You are master
Of your own will. I know so much of
    manners   140
As not to inquire your purposes ; in a word,
To me you are ever welcome, as to a house
That is your own.
    WELL. [*aside to* MARRALL]   Mark that.
    MAR. [*aside*]   With reverence, sir,
An it like your Worship.
    WELL.   Trouble yourself no farther,
Dear madam ; my heart's full of zeal and
    service,
However in my language I am sparing. —
Come, Master Marrall.
    MAR.   I attend your Worship.
         Exeunt WELLBORN [*and*] MARRALL.
    L. ALL. I see in your looks you are sorry,
    and you know me
An easy mistress. Be merry ; I have for-
    got all.
Order and Furnace, come with me ; I must
    give you   150
Further directions.
    ORD.   What you please.
    FURN.   We are ready. [*Exeunt.*]

SCENE III [36]

[*Enter*] WELLBORN [*and*] MARRALL.

    WELL. I think I am in a good way.
    MAR.   Good, sir ! the best way,
The certain best way !
    WELL.   There are casualties
That men are subject to.
    MAR.   You are above 'em ;
And as you are already Worshipful,
I hope ere long you will increase in worship,
And be Right Worshipful.
    WELL.   Prithee do not flout me ;
What I shall be, I shall be. Is 't for your ease,
You keep your hat off?
    MAR.   Ease ! an it like your Worship !
I hope Jack Marrall shall not live so long,
To prove himself such an unmannerly beast,
Though it hail hazel-nuts, as to be cover'd [11
When your Worship's present.
    WELL. (*aside*)   Is not this a true rogue,
That, out of mere hope of a future coz'nage,[37]
Can turn thus suddenly? 'T is rank already.
    MAR. I know your Worship's wise, and
    needs no counsel ;
Yet if, in my desire to do you service,
I humbly offer my advice, (but still [38]

[36] A road.   [37] Fraud, cheating.
[38] Always.

Under correction,) I hope I shall not
Incur your high displeasure.
    WELL.   No ; speak freely.
    MAR. Then, in my judgment, sir, my simple
    judgment,   20
(Still with your Worship's favor,) I could wish
    you
A better habit,[39] for this cannot be
But much distasteful to the noble lady
(I say no more) that loves you ; for, this morn-
    ing,
To me, and I am but a swine to her,
Before th' assurance of her wealth perfum'd
    you,
You savor'd not of amber.[40]
    WELL.   I do now, then?
    MAR. This your batoon hath got a touch of
    it. ——   *Kisses the end of his cudgel.*
Yet, if you please, for change,[41] I have twenty
    pounds here,
Which, out of my true love, I presently   30
Lay down at your Worship's feet ; 't will serve
    to buy you
A riding suit.
    WELL.   But where 's the horse?
    MAR.   My gelding
Is at your service ; nay, you shall ride me,
Before your Worship shall be put to the trouble
To walk afoot. Alas, when you are lord
Of this lady's manor, as I know you will be,
You may with the lease of glebeland called
    Knave's Acre,
A place I would manure,[42] requite your vassal.
    WELL. I thank thy love, but must make
    no use of it ;
What 's twenty pounds?
    MAR.   'T is all that I can make,[43] sir. [40
    WELL. Doest thou think, though I want
    clothes, I could not have 'em,
For one word to my lady?
    MAR.   As [44] I know not that !
    WELL. Come, I 'll tell thee a secret, and so
    leave thee.
I 'll not give her the advantage, though she
    be
A gallant-minded lady, after we are married,
(There being no woman but is sometimes fro-
    ward,)   45
To hit me in the teeth, and say she was forc'd
To buy my wedding clothes, and took me on
With a plain riding suit and an ambling nag.

[39] Suit of clothes.   [40] Ambergris.
[41] *I.e.*, to enable you to buy a change of clothing.
[42] I desire to cultivate ; *i.e.*, occupy as a tenant.
[43] Get together in cash.   [44] As if.
[45] Petulant, refractory.

No, I'll be furnish'd something like myself, [50
And so farewell; for [46] thy suit touching
    Knave's Acre,
When it is mine, 't is thine.
    MAR.   I thank your Worship.
                    Exit WELLBORN.
How was [I] [47] cozen'd in the calculation
Of this man's fortune! My master cozen'd too,
Whose pupil I am in the art of undoing [48] men;
For that is our profession! Well, well, Master
    Wellborn,
You are of a sweet nature, and fit again to be
    cheated;
Which, if the Fates please, when you are pos-
    sess'd
Of the land and lady, you, sans question, shall
    be.
I'll presently think of the means.
                Walk by, mazing.[49]

Enter OVERREACH, [*speaking to a* Servant
    within.]

    OVER.   Sirrah, take my horse. [60
I'll walk to get me an appetite; 't is but a
    mile,
And exercise will keep me from being pursy.[50]
Ha! Marrall! Is he conjuring? Perhaps
The knave has wrought the prodigal to do
Some outrage on himself, and now he feels
Compunction in his conscience for 't; no
    matter,
So it be done.   Marrall!
    MAR.   Sir, —
    OVER.   How succeed we
In our plot on Wellborn?
    MAR.   Never better, sir.
    OVER. Has he hang'd or drown'd himself?
    MAR.   No, sir, he lives;
Lives once more to be made a prey to you, [70
A greater prey than ever.
    OVER.   Art thou in thy wits?
If thou art, reveal this miracle, and briefly.
    MAR. A lady, sir, is fall'n in love with him.
    OVER. With him? What lady?
    MAR.   The rich Lady Allworth.
    OVER. Thou dolt! how dar'st thou speak
    this?
    MAR.   I speak truth;
And I do so but once a year, unless
It be to you, sir. We din'd with her Ladyship,
I thank his Worship.
    OVER.   His Worship!

    MAR.   As I live, sir,
I din'd with him, at the great lady's table,
Simple [51] as I stand here; and saw when she
    kiss'd him,   80
And would, at his request, have kiss'd me too:
But I was not so audacious [as] [52] some youths
    are,
And dare do anything, be it ne'er so absurd,
And sad [53] after performance.
    OVER.   Why, thou rascal!
To tell me these impossibilities.
Dine at her table! and kiss him! or thee! —
Impudent varlet, have not I myself,
To whom great countesses' doors have oft
    flew open,
Ten times attempted, since her husband's
    death,
In vain, to see her, though I came — a suitor?
And yet your good Solicitorship, and rogue
    Wellborn,   91
Were brought into her presence, feasted with
    her! ——
But that I know thee a dog that cannot blush,
This most incredible lie would call up one
On thy buttermilk cheeks.
    MAR.   Shall I not trust my eyes, sir,
Or taste? I feel her good cheer in my belly.
    OVER. You shall feel me, if you give not
    over, sirrah;
Recover your brains again, and be no more
    gull'd
With a beggar's plot, assisted by the aids
Of servingmen and chambermaids — for
    beyond these   100
Thou never saw'st a woman — or I'll quit you
From my employments.
    MAR.   Will you credit this yet?
On my confidence of their marriage, I offer'd
    Wellborn ——
(*aside*) I would give a crown now I durst say
    " his Worship " ——
My nag and twenty pounds.
    OVER.   Did you so, [idiot]! [54]
                  Strikes him down.
Was this the way to work him to despair,
Or rather to cross me?
    MAR.   Will your Worship kill me?
    OVER. No, no; but drive the lying spirit
    out of you.
    MAR. He's gone.
    OVER.   I have done then; now, for-
    getting

---

[46] As for.   [47] Add. Coxeter.   [48] Ruining.
[49] Amazed. Mod. eds. *musing*, perhaps rightly.
Q *masing*.   [50] Short-winded and fat.

[51] As true.
[52] Emend. Dodsley; Q *and*.   [53] Serious.
[54] Cor. Coxeter; Q *I doe* (for *Ideot*.)

Your late imaginary feast and lady,   110
Know my Lord Lovell dines with me to-
    morrow.
Be careful naught be wanting to receive him ;
And bid my daughter's women trim her up ;
Though they paint her, so [55] she catch the
    lord, I'll thank 'em.
There's a piece for my late blows.
    MAR. (*aside*)   I must yet suffer ;
But there may be a time ——
    OVER.   Do you grumble?
    MAR.   No, sir. [*Exeunt.*]

ACT III — SCENE I [1]

[*Enter* LORD] LOVELL, ALLWORTH, [*and*]
Servants.

    LOV. Walk the horses down the hill ; some-
    thing in private
I must impart to Allworth.
                  Exeunt [Servants].[2]
    ALL.   Oh, my Lord,
What sacrifice of reverence, duty, watching,
Although I could put off the use of sleep,
And ever wait on your commands [to] [3]
    serve 'em ;
What dangers, though in ne'er so horrid
    shapes,
Nay death itself, though I should run to meet
    it,
Can I, and with a thankful willingness, suffer !
But still the retribution will fall short
Of your bounties show'r'd upon me.
    LOV.   Loving youth, [10
Till what I purpose be put into act,
Do not o'erprize it ; since you have trusted me
With your soul's nearest, nay, her dearest,
    secret,
Rest confident 't is in a cabinet lock'd
Treachery shall never open. I have found you
(For so much to your face I must profess,
Howe'er you guard [4] your modesty with a
    blush for 't)
More zealous in your love and service to me
Than I have been in my rewards.
    ALL.   Still great ones,
Above my merit.
    LOV. Such your gratitude calls 'em ; [20
Nor am I of that harsh and rugg'd temper

As some great men are tax'd [5] with, who im-
    agine
They part from the respect due to their hon-
    ors
If they use not all such as follow 'em,
Without distinction of their births, like slaves.
I am not so condition'd ; [6] I can make
A fitting difference between my footboy
And a gentleman by want compell'd to serve
    me.
    ALL. 'T is thankfully acknowledg'd ; you
    have been
More like a father to me than a master.   30
Pray you, pardon the comparison.
    LOV.   I allow it ;
And, to give you assurance I am pleas'd in 't,
My carriage and demeanor to your mistress,
Fair Margaret, shall truly witness for me
I can command my passions.
    ALL.   'T is a conquest
Few lords can boast of when they are tempted
    — oh !
    LOV. Why do you sigh? Can you be
    doubtful of me?
By that fair name I in the wars have purchas'd,
And all my actions, hitherto untainted,
I will not be more true to mine own honor [40
Than to my Allworth !
    ALL.   As you are the brave Lord Lovell,
Your bare word only given is an assurance
Of more validity and weight to me
Than all the oaths, bound up with impreca-
    tions,
Which, when they would deceive, most court-
    iers practice ;
Yet being a man, (for, sure, to style you more
Would relish of gross flattery,) I am forc'd,
Against my confidence of your worth and vir-
    tues,
To doubt, nay, more, to fear.
    LOV.   So young, and jealous !
    ALL. Were you to encounter with a single
    foe,   50
The victory were certain ; but to stand
The charge of two such potent enemies,
At once assaulting you, as wealth and beauty,
And those, too, seconded with power, is odds
Too great for Hercules.
    LOV.   Speak your doubts and fears,
Since you will nourish 'em, in plainer language,
That I may understand them.
    ALL.   What's your will,
Though I lend arms against myself, (provided

[55] Provided that.
[1] The same, or another road.
[2] Q *serui.*   [3] Om. Q.   [4] Adorn.
[5] Charged.
[6] Such is not my disposition.

They may advantage you,) must be obeyed.
My much-lov'd Lord, were Margaret only
    fair,   60
The cannon of her more than earthly form,
Though mounted high, commanding all be-
    neath it,
And ramm'd with bullets of her sparkling
    eyes,
Of all the bulwarks that defend your senses
Could batter [none] [7] but that which guards
    your sight.
But when the well-tun'd accents of her tongue
Make music to you, and with numerous [8]
    sounds
Assault your hearing, (such as if Ulysses
Now liv'd again, howe'er he stood the Sirens,
Could not resist,) the combat must grow
    doubtful   70
Between your reason and rebellious passions.
Add this too : when you feel her touch, and
    breath
Like a soft western wind when it glides o'er
Arabia, creating gums and spices ;
And, in the van, the nectar of her lips,
Which you must taste, bring the battalia on,
Well arm'd and strongly li[n]'d [9] with her dis-
    course,
And knowing manners, to give entertain-
    ment —
Hippolytus himself would leave Diana,
To follow such a Venus.[10]
    Lov.   Love hath made you [80
Poetical, Allworth.
    All.   Grant all these beat off,
Which if it be in man to do, you 'll do it ;
Mammon, in Sir Giles Overreach, steps in
With heaps of ill-got gold, and so much land,
To make her more remarkable, as would tire
A falcon's wings in one day to fly over.
O my good Lord ! these powerful aids, which
    would
Make a misshapen negro beautiful,
(Yet are but ornaments to give her lustre,
That in herself is all perfection,) must   90
Prevail for her.   I here release your trust ;
'T is happiness enough for me to serve you
And sometimes, with chaste eyes, to look upon
    her.
    Lov. Why, shall I swear?
    All.   Oh, by no means, my Lord ;
And wrong not so your judgment to the world
As from your fond indulgence to a boy,

Your page, your servant, to refuse a blessing
Divers great men are rivals for.
    Lov.   Suspend
Your judgment till the trial.   How far is it
T' Overreach house?
    All.   At the most, some half hour's rid-
    ing ;   100
You 'll soon be there.
    Lov.   And you the sooner freed
From your jealous fears.
    All.   Oh, that I durst but hope it !
                        Exeunt.

Scene II [11]

[*Enter*] Overreach, Greedy, [*and*] Marrall.

    Over. Spare for no cost ; let my dressers
    crack with the weight
Of curious viands.
    Greedy.   Store indeed 's no sore,[12] sir.
    Over. That proverb fits your stomach,
    Master Greedy.
And let no plate be seen but what 's pure gold,
Or such whose workmanship exceeds the
    matter
That it is made of ; let my choicest linen
Perfume the room, and, when we wash, the
    water,
With precious powders mix'd, so please my
    Lord
That he may with envy wish to bathe so ever.
    Mar. 'T will be very chargeable.[13]
    Over.   Avaunt, you drudge ! [10
Now all my labor'd ends are at the stake,
Is 't a time to think of thrift?   Call in my
    daughter.   [*Exit* Marrall.]
And, Master Justice, since you love choice
    dishes,
And plenty of 'em ——
    Greedy.   As I do, indeed, sir,
Almost as much as to give thanks for 'em.
    Over. I do confer that providence,[14] with
    my power
Of absolute command to have abundance,
To your best care.
    Greedy.   I 'll punctually discharge it,
And give the best directions.   Now am I,
In mine own conceit, a monarch ; at the
    least,   20
Arch-president of the boil'd, the roast, the
    bak'd ;
For which I will eat often, and give thanks

---

[7] Cor. Gifford ; Q *more.*
[8] Rhythmical, metrical.   [9] Reinforced.
[10] See the *Phaedra* of Euripides.

[11] A room in Overreach's house.
[12] Italicized in Q.   [13] Expensive.
[14] Duty of providing.

When my belly's brac'd up like a drum, and
    that's pure justice.   *Exit* GREEDY.
  OVER. [It] [15] must be so. Should the fool-
    ish girl prove modest,
She may spoil all ; she had it not from me,
But from her mother ; I was ever forward,[16]
As she must be, and therefore I'll prepare her.

         [*Enter*] MARGARET.

Alone — and let your women wait without.
  MARG. Your pleasure, sir?
  OVER.   Ha ! this is a neat dressing !
These orient pearls and diamonds well plac'd
    too !   30
The gown affects me not ; [17] it should have
    been
Embroider'd o'er and o'er with flowers of gold ;
But these rich jewels and quaint [18] fashion help
    it.
And how below? since oft the wanton eye,
The face observ'd, descends unto the foot,
Which being well proportion'd, as yours is,
Invites as much as perfect white and red,
Though without art. How like you your new
    woman,
The Lady Downfall'n?
  MARG.   Well, for a companion ;
Not as a servant.
  OVER.   Is she humble, Meg,   40
And careful too, her ladyship forgotten?
  MARG. I pity her fortune.
  OVER.   Pity her ! trample on her !
I took her up in an old tamin [19] gown,
(Even starv'd for want of twopenny chops,) to
    serve thee ;
And if I understand she but repines
To do thee any duty, though ne'er so servile,
I'll pack her to her knight, where I have
    lodg'd him,
Into the Counter [20] and there let 'em howl to-
    gether.
  MARG. You know your own ways ; but for [21]
    me, I blush
When I command her, that was once at-
    tended   50
With persons not inferior to myself
In birth.
  OVER. In birth ! why, art thou not my
    daughter,
The blest child of my industry and wealth?
Why, foolish girl, was't not to make thee great
That I have ran, and still pursue, those ways

That hale down curses on me, which I mind
    not?
Part with these humble thoughts, and apt [22]
    thyself
To the noble state I labor to advance thee ;
Or, by my hopes to see thee Honorable,
I will adopt a stranger to [23] my heir,   60
And throw thee from my care. Do not pro-
    voke me.
  MARG. I will not, sir ; mould me which
    way you please.

         Re-enter GREEDY.

  OVER. How ! Interrupted?
  GREEDY.   'T is matter of importance.
The cook, sir, is self-will'd, and will not learn
From my experience. There's a fawn
    brough[t] in, sir,
And, for my life, I cannot make him roast it
With a Norfolk dumpling [24] in the belly of it ;
And, sir, we wise men know, without the
    dumpling
'T is not worth threepence.
  OVER.   Would it were whole in thy belly,
To stuff it out ! Cook it any way ; prithee,
    leave me.   70
  GREEDY. Without order for the dumpling?
  OVER.   Let it be dumpl'd
Which way thou wilt ; or tell him, I will scald
    him
In his own caldron.
  GREEDY.   I had lost my stomach [25]
Had I lost my mistress dumpling, I'll give
    thanks for.   *Exit* GREEDY.
  OVER. But to our business, Meg ; you have
    heard who dines here?
  MARG. I have, sir.
  OVER.   'T is an honorable man ;
A lord, Meg, and commands a regiment
Of soldiers, and, what's rare, is one himself,
A bold and understanding one ; and to be
A lord and a good leader, in one volume,   80
Is granted unto few but such as rise up
The kingdom's glory.

         Re-enter GREEDY.

  GREEDY.   I'll resign my office,
If I be not better obey'd.
  OVER.   'Slight, art thou frantic?

[15] Q *I*.   [16] Bold, ardent.
[17] I don't care for.
[18] Elegant.   [19] Stamin, a coarse worsted.
[20] One of the city jails.   [21] As for.

[22] Fit.
[23] For, as.
[24] Fuller (*Worthies*) says of this expression, in the
sense of "inhabitant of Norfolk", that it "relates
to the fare they commonly feed on."
[25] Would have lost my appetite. — Punctuation
in next line follows Q. ? Semicolon after "dumpling", and read *for't*.

GREEDY. Frantic! 'T would make me a frantic, and stark mad,
Were I not a justice of peace and quorum [26] too,
Which this rebellious cook cares not a straw for.
There are a dozen of woodcocks ———
OVER.   Make thyself
Thirteen,[27] the baker's dozen.
GREEDY.   I am contented,
So they may be dress'd to my mind; he has found out
A new device for sauce, and will not dish 'em   90
With toasts and butter. My father was a tailor,[28]
And my name, though a justice, Greedy Woodcock;
And, ere I 'll see my lineage so abus'd,
I 'll give up my commission.
OVER. [*calling off stage*] Cook! — Rogue, obey him! —
I have given the word, pray you now remove yourself
To a collar of brawn,[29] and trouble me no farther.
GREEDY. I will, and meditate what to eat at dinner.   *Exit* GREEDY.
OVER. And as I said, Meg, when this gull disturb'd us,
This honorable lord, this colonel,
I would have thy husband.
MARG.   There's too much disparity [100
Between his quality [30] and mine, to hope it.
OVER. I more than hope 't, and doubt not to effect it.
Be thou no enemy to thyself,[31] my wealth
Shall weigh his titles down and make you equals.
Now for the means to assure him thine, observe me:
Remember he's a courtier and a soldier,
And not to be trifl'd with; and, therefore, when
He comes to woo you, see you, do not coy it.
This mincing modesty has spoil'd many a match
By a first refusal, in vain after hop'd for. [110

MAR. You'll have me, sir, preserve the distance that
Confines a virgin?
OVER.   Virgin me no virgins!
I must have you lose that name, or you lose me.
I will have you private [32] — start not — I say, private;
If thou art my true daughter, not a bastard,
Thou wilt venture alone with one man, though he came
Like Jupiter to Semele, and come off,[33] too;
And therefore, when he kisses you, kiss close.
MARG. I have heard this is the strumpet's fashion, sir;
Which I must never learn.
OVER.   Learn anything, [120
And from any creature, that may make thee great;
From the Devil himself.
MARG. [*aside*]   This is but devilish doctrine!
OVER. Or, if his blood grow hot, suppose he offer [34]
Beyond this, do not you stay till it cool,
But meet his ardor; if a couch be near,
Sit down on 't, and invite him.
MARG.   In your house,
Your own house, sir? For Heav'n's sake, what are you then?
Or what shall I be, sir?
OVER.   Stand not on form;
Words are no substances.
MARG.   Though you could dispense
With your own honor, cast aside religion, [130
The hopes of Heaven, or fear of hell, (excuse me,)
In worldly policy this is not the way
To make me his wife; his whore, I grant it may do.
My maiden honor so soon yielded up,
Nay, prostituted, cannot but assure him
I, that am light to him, will not hold weight
When he is [35] tempted by others; so, in judgment,
When to his lust I have given up my honor,
He must and will forsake me.
OVER.   How? forsake thee!
Do I wear a sword for fashion? or is this arm   140

[26] *I.e.*, one of the better qualified justices whose presence was required to constitute a bench. Q *coram*.
[27] "Woodcock" also meant "fool."
[28] "Tailors were supposed to have good appetites." (Cruickshank.)
[29] Neck or roll of pork.
[30] Rank.
[31] *I.e.*, if you acquiesce in my scheme.

[32] Intimate.   [33] Come to an issue.
[34] Attempt.
[35] Gifford (followed by others) emends here, failing to perceive that Margaret fears her easy yielding would decrease her value in Lovell's eyes and encourage *his* infidelity.

Shrunk up or wither'd? Does there live a
    man
Of that large list I have encounter'd with
Can truly say I e'er gave inch of ground
Not purchas'd with his blood that did oppose
    me?
Forsake thee when the thing is done! He
    dares not.
Give me but proof he has enjoy'd thy person:
Though all his captains, echoes to his will,
Stood arm'd by his side to justify the wrong,
And he himself in the head of his bold troop,
Spite of his lordship, and his colonelship, [150
Or the judge's favor, I will make him render
A bloody and a strict account, and force him,
By marrying thee, to cure thy wounded honor!
I have said it.

Re-enter MARRALL.

MAR.   Sir, the man of honor's [36] come,
Newly alighted.
OVER.   In, without reply.
And do as I command, or thou art lost. —
                        Exit MARGARET.
Is the loud music I gave order for
Ready to receive him?
MAR.   'T is, sir.
OVER.   Let 'em sound
A princely welcome. — [*Exit* MARRALL.]
    Roughness awhile leave me;
For fawning now, a stranger to my nature, [160
Must make way for me.

Loud music. Enter [LORD] LOVELL, GREEDY,
    ALLWORTH, [*and*] MARRALL.

LOV.   Sir, you meet your trouble.
OVER. What you are pleas'd to style so is
    an honor
Above my worth and fortunes.
ALL. [*aside*]   Strange, so humble.
OVER. A justice of peace, my Lord.
                Presents GREEDY *to him.*
LOV.   Your hand, good sir.
GREEDY. [*aside*] This is a lord, and some
    think this a favor:
But I had rather have my hand in my dump-
    ling.
OVER. Room for my Lord.
LOV.   I miss, sir, your fair daughter
To crown my welcome.
OVER.   May it please my Lord
To taste a glass of Greek wine first, and sud-
    denly
She shall attend my Lord.

[36] Nobleman's.

LOV.   You 'll be obey'd, sir. [170
           Exeunt [*all but*] OVERREACH.
OVER. 'T is to my wish: as soon as come,
    ask for her!
Why, Meg! Meg Overreach.

[*Re-enter* MARGARET.]

           How! tears in your eyes!
Ha! dry 'em quickly, or I 'll dig 'em out.
Is this a time to whimper? Meet that great-
    ness
That flies into thy bosom; think what 't is
For me to say, "My Honorable daughter;"
And thou, when I stand bare, to say, "Put
    on;"
Or, "Father, you forget yourself." No more;
But be instructed, or expect —— he comes.

Re-enter [LORD] LOVELL, GREEDY, ALLWORTH,
    [*and*] MARRALL.

A black-brow'd [37] girl, my Lord.
LOV.   As I live, a rare one. [180
                     They salute.
ALL. [*aside*] He 's took already: I am lost.
OVER. [*aside*]   That kiss
Came twanging off; I like it. — Quit the
    room.
    [*Exeunt all but* OVERREACH, LOVELL,
        and MARGARET.] [38]
A little bashful, my good Lord, but you,
I hope, will teach her boldness.
LOV.   I am happy
In such a scholar; but ——
OVER.   I am past learning,
And therefore leave you to yourselves. — (*to
    . his daughter*) Remember!
                  Exit OVERREACH.
LOV. You see, fair lady, your father is so-
    licitous
To have you change the barren name of virgin
Into a hopeful wife.
MARG.   [His] [39] haste, my Lord,
Holds no power o'er my will.
LOV.   But o'er your duty. [190
MARG. Which, forc'd too much, may break.
LOV.   Bend rather, sweetest;
Think of your years.
MARG.   Too few to match with yours;
And choicest fruits, too soon plucked, rot and
    wither.
LOV. Do you think I am old?
MARG.   I am sure I am too young.
LOV. I can advance you.

[37] Blondes were preferred.
[38] Q *The rest off.*   [39] Q *He.*

MARG.   To a hill of sorrow,
Where every hour I may expect to fall,
But never hope firm footing. You are noble,
I of a low descent, however rich ;
And tissues match'd with scarlet [40] suit but ill.
Oh, my good Lord, I could say more, but
    that   200
I dare not trust these walls.
    Lov.   Pray you, trust my ear then.

Re-enter OVERREACH [*behind*], *listening.*

    OVER. Close at it ! whispering ! this is ex-
        cellent !
And, by their postures, a consent on both
    parts.

Re-enter GREEDY [*behind*].

    GREEDY. Sir Giles, Sir Giles !
    OVER.   The great Fiend stop that clapper !
    GREEDY. It must ring out, sir, when my
        belly rings noon.
The bak'd meats are run out,[41] the roasts turn'd
    powder.
    OVER. I shall powder you.
    GREEDY.   Beat me to dust, I care not ;
In such a cause as this, I 'll die a martyr.
    OVER. Marry, and shall, you barathrum [42]
        of the shambles !   *Strikes him.*
    GREEDY. How ! strike a justice of peace !
        'T is petty treason,   210
Edwardi quinto ; but that you are my friend,
I could commit you without bail or main-
        prize.[43]
    OVER. Leave your bawling, sir, or I shall
        commit you
Where you shall not dine to-day. Disturb
    my Lord,
When he is in discourse !
    GREEDY.   Is 't a time to talk
When we should be munching?
    Lov.   Ha ! I heard some noise.
    OVER. Mum, villain ; vanish ! Shall we
        break a bargain
Almost made up?   *Thrust* GREEDY *off.*
    Lov.   Lady, I understand you,
And rest most happy in your choice, believe it ;

I 'll be a careful pilot to direct   220
Your yet uncertain bark to a port of safety.
    MARG. So shall your Honor save two lives,
        and bind us
Your slaves for ever.
    Lov.   I am in the act rewarded,
Since it is good ; howe'er, you must put on
An amorous carriage towards me to delude
Your subtle father.
    MARG.   I am prone to that.
    Lov. Now break we off our conference. —
        Sir Giles !
Where is Sir Giles?

Re-enter OVERREACH *and the rest.*

    OVER.   My noble Lord ; and how
Does your Lordship find her ?
    Lov.   Apt, Sir Giles, and coming ;
And I like her the better.
    OVER.   So do I, too. [230
    Lov. Yet, should we take forts at the first
        assault,
'T were poor in the defendant ; I must con-
    firm her
With a love letter or two, which I must have
Deliver'd by my page, and you give way to 't.
    OVER. With all my soul ; a towardly gen-
        tleman !
Your hand, good Master Allworth ; know my
        house
Is ever open to you.
    ALL. (*aside*)   'T was shut till now.
    OVER. Well done, well done, my Honorable
        daughter !
Th' art so already. Know this gentle youth,
And cherish him, my Honorable daughter. [240
    MARG. I shall, with my best care.
                Noise within, as of a coach.
    OVER.   A coach !
    GREEDY.   More stops
Before we go to dinner ! O my guts ![44]

Enter LADY [ALLWORTH] *and* WELLBORN.

    L. ALL. If I find welcome,
You share in it ; if not, I 'll back again,
Now I know your ends ; for I come arm'd for
    all
Can be objected.
    Lov.   How ! the Lady Allworth !
    OVER. And thus attended !
            LOVELL *salutes the* LADY [ALL-
                WORTH] ; *the* LADY [ALLWORTH]
                salutes MARGARET.

---

[40] *Not* the rich silks of the courtier matched with
the red gown of the city fathers. In view of IV, i,
225, where "scarlet" alludes (as it frequently does
in these plays) to the gaily clad courtiers, the antithesis here is not, as Cruickshank suggests, between
"the court and the city", but between the parvenu
and the courtier, the richness of "tissues" standing for the former. Cf. *Philaster,* V, iv, 100.
[41] Of the crust. (Cruickshank.)
[42] Abyss, bottomless pit, devouring gulf.
[43] Surety (for appearance in court).
[44] Massinger's lines are so regular that it seems
likely that this exclamation is an actor's gag, the
line being completed by the present l. 243.

MAR. [*aside to* OVERREACH] No, I am a dolt!

The spirit of lies had ent'red me!

OVER. [*aside to* MARRALL] Peace, patch; [45]
'T is more than wonder! an astonishment
That does possess me wholly!

LOV.   Noble lady, [250]
This is a favor, to prevent [46] my visit,
The service of my life can never equal.

L. ALL. My Lord, I laid wait for you, and much hop'd
You would have made my poor house your first inn;
And therefore, doubting [47] that you might forget me,
Or too long dwell here, having such ample cause
In this unequall'd beauty for your stay,
And fearing to trust any but myself
With the relation [48] of my service to you,
I borrow'd so much from my long restraint [260]
And took the air in person to invite you.

LOV. Your bounties are so great, they rob me, madam,
Of words to give you thanks.

L. ALL.   Good Sir Giles Overreach.
                Salutes him.
— How doest thou, Marrall? Lik'd you my meat so ill,
You'll dine no more with me?

GREEDY.   I will, when you please,
An it like your Ladyship.

L. ALL. When you please, Master Greedy;
If meat can do it, you shall be satisfied.
And now, my Lord, pray take into your knowledge
This gentleman; howe'er his outside's coarse,
            Presents WELLBORN.
His inward linings are as fine and fair   270
As any man's; (wonder not I speak at large; [49])
And howsoe'er his humor carries him
To be thus accout'red, or what taint soever,
For his wild life, hath stuck upon his fame,
He may ere long, with boldness, rank himself
With some that have contemn'd him. Sir Giles Overreach,
If I am welcome, bid him so.

OVER.   My nephew.
He has been too long a stranger. Faith you have;
Pray let it be mended.
      LOVELL *conferring with* WELLBORN.

[45] Fool.   [46] Anticipate.   [47] Fearing.
[48] Report, expression.   [49] Freely, at length.

MAR. [*aside to* OVERREACH]   Why, sir, what do you mean?
This is rogue Wellborn, monster, prodigy, [280]
That should hang or drown himself; no man of worship,
Much less your nephew.

OVER. [*aside*] Well, sirrah, we shall reckon
For this hereafter.

MAR. [*aside*]   I'll not lose my jeer,
Though I be beaten dead for 't.

WELL.   Let my silence plead
In my excuse, my Lord, till better leisure
Offer itself to hear a full relation
Of my poor fortunes.

LOV.   I would hear, and help 'em.

OVER. Your dinner waits you.

LOV.   Pray you lead; we follow.

L. ALL. Nay, you are my guest; come, dear Master Wellborn.
       Exeunt [*all but*] [50] GREEDY.

GREEDY. "Dear Master Wellborn!" so she said. Heav'n! Heav'n!   290
If my belly would give me leave, I could ruminate
All day on this. I have granted twenty warrants
To have him committed, from all prisons in the shire
To Nottingham jail; and now "Dear Master Wellborn!"
And "My good nephew!" — but I play the fool
To stand here prating, and forget my dinner.—

      Re-enter MARRALL.

Are they set, Marrall?

MAR.   Long since; pray you a word, sir.

GREEDY. No wording now.

MAR.   In troth, I must. My master,
Knowing you are his good friend, makes bold with you,
And does entreat you, more guests being come in   300
Than he expected, especially his nephew,
The table being full, too, you would excuse him,
And sup with him on the cold meat.

GREEDY.   How? No dinner,
After all my care?

MAR.   'T is but a penance for
A meal; besides, you broke your fast.

GREEDY.   That was
But a bit to stay my stomach. A man in commission
Give place to a tatterdemalion!

[50] Q *manet.*

MAR.   No bug [51] words, sir;
Should his Worship hear you ——
GREEDY.   Lose my dumpling too,
And butter'd toasts, and woodcocks!
MAR.   Come, have patience.
If you will dispense a little with your wor-
    ship,[52]   310
And sit with the waiting women, you ['ll] [53]
    have dumpling,
Woodcock, and butter'd toasts [54] too.
GREEDY.   This revives me;
I will gorge there sufficiently.
MAR.   This is the way, sir.   *Exeunt.*

SCENE III [55]

[Enter] OVERREACH, as from dinner.

OVER.   She's caught! O women! She neg-
    lects my Lord,
And all her compliment's [56] appli'd to Well-
    born!
The garments of her widowhood laid by,
She now appears as glorious as the spring;
Her eyes fix'd on him, in the wine she drinks,
He being her pledge, she sends him burning
    kisses,
And sits on thorns till she be private with him.
She leaves my meat to feed upon his looks,
And if in our discourse he be but nam'd,
From her a deep sigh follows. But why
    grieve I   10
At this? It makes for me; if she prove his,
All that is hers is mine, as I will work him.

Enter MARRALL.

MAR.   Sir, the whole board is troubled at
    your rising.
OVER.   No matter, I'll excuse it.   Prithee,
    Marrall,
Watch an occasion to invite my nephew
To speak with me in private.
MAR.   Who? the rogue
The lady scorn'd to look on?
OVER.   You are a wag.

Enter LADY [ALLWORTH] and WELLBORN.

MAR.   See, sir, she's come, and cannot be
    without him.

---

[51] Pompous.
[52] *I.e.,* your status as a "worshipful."
[53] Add. Gifford.
[54] All slighting references to women. "Dumpling"
= little plump one; "woodcock" = fool; for "butter'd toasts" cf. *N.E.D.*'s citation of "buttered
bun" = harlot.
[55] The same.
[56] Politeness, courtesy. Q omits apostrophe.

L. ALL.   With your favor, sir, after a plen-
    teous dinner,
I shall make bold to walk a turn or two,   20
In your rare garden.
OVER.   There's an arbor too,
If your Ladyship please to use it.
L. ALL.   Come, Master Wellborn.
        Exeunt LADY [ALLWORTH] *and* WELL-
            BORN.
OVER.   Grosser and grosser!   Now I believe
    the poet [57]
Feign'd not, but was historical, when he wrote
Pasiphaë was enamor'd of a bull:
This lady's lust's more monstrous. — My
    good Lord,

Enter [LORD] LOVELL, MARGARET, and the rest.

Excuse my manners.
LOV.   There needs none, Sir Giles —
I may ere long say "Father," when it pleases
My dearest mistress to give warrant to it.
OVER.   She shall seal to it, my Lord, and
    make me happy.   30

Re-enter WELLBORN and the LADY [ALLWORTH].

MARG.   My Lady is return'd.
L. ALL.   Provide my coach;
I'll instantly away.   My thanks, Sir Giles,
For my entertainment.
OVER.   'T is your nobleness
To think it such.
L. ALL.   I must do you a further wrong
In taking away your honorable guest.
LOV.   I wait on you, madam; farewell, good
    Sir Giles.
L. ALL.   Good Mistress Margaret!   Nay,
    come, Master Wellborn,
I must not leave you behind; in sooth, I must
    not.
OVER.   Rob me not, madam, of all joys at
    once;
Let my nephew stay behind.   He shall have
    my coach,   40
And, after some small conference between
    us,
Soon overtake your Ladyship.
L. ALL.   Stay not long, sir.
LOV.   This parting kiss; [*kisses* MARGARET]
    you shall every day hear from me,
By my faithful page.
ALL.   'T is a service I am proud of.
        Exeunt [LORD] LOVELL, LADY [ALL-
            WORTH,] ALLWORTH, [and] MAR-
            RALL.

---

[57] Ovid (*Metamorphoses* XV, 500 ff.).

OVER. Daughter, to your chamber. —
                [*Exit*] MARGARET.
      — You may wonder, Nephew,
After so long an enmity between us,
I should desire your friendship.
    WELL.   So [58] I do, sir ;
'T is strange to me.
    OVER.   But I 'll make it no wonder ;
And what is more, unfold my nature to you.
We worldly men, when we see friends and
           kinsmen   50
Past hope sunk in their fortunes, lend no hand
To lift 'em up, but rather set our feet
Upon their heads, to press 'em to the bottom ;
As, I must yield,[59] with you I practis'd it.
But now I see you in a way to rise,
I can and will assist you. This rich lady
(And I am glad of 't) is enamor'd of you ;
'T is too apparent, Nephew.
    WELL.   No such thing ;
Compassion rather, sir.
    OVER.   Well, in a word,
Because your stay is short, I 'll have you
           seen   60
No more in this base shape ; [60] nor shall she
           say
She married you like a beggar, or in debt.
    WELL. (*aside*) He 'll run into the noose, and
           save my labor.
    OVER. You have a trunk of rich clothes, not
           far hence,
In pawn ; I will redeem 'em ; and that no
           clamor
May taint your credit for your petty debts,
You shall have a thousand pounds to cut 'em
           off,
And go a freeman to the wealthy lady.
    WELL. This done, sir, out of love, and no
           ends else ——
    OVER. As it is, Nephew.
    WELL.   Binds me still your servant. [70
    OVER. No compliments ; you are stay'd for.
           Ere y' ave supp'd
You shall hear from me. — My coach, knaves,
           for my nephew.
To-morrow I will visit you.
    WELL.   Here 's an uncle
In a man's extremes [61] ! How much they do
           belie you,
That say you are hard-hearted !
    OVER.   My deeds, Nephew,
Shall speak my love ; what men report I weigh
           not.   *Exeunt.*

[58] Q *Well: so.*   [59] Concede, admit.
[60] Costume.   [61] Extremities.

ACT IV — SCENE I [1]

[*Enter* LORD] LOVELL [*and*] ALLWORTH.

    LOV. 'T is well ; give me my cloak ; I now
           discharge you
From further service. Mind your own affairs ;
I hope they will prove successful.
    ALL.   What is blest
With your good wish, my Lord, cannot but
           prosper.
Let aftertimes report, and to your honor,
How much I stand engag'd, for I want lan-
           guage
To speak my debt ; yet if a tear or two
Of joy, for your much goodness, can supply
My tongue's defects, I could ——
    LOV.   Nay, do not melt ;
This ceremonial thanks to me 's superfluous.
    OVER. (*within*) Is my Lord stirring ?   11
    LOV. 'T is he ! oh, here 's your letter. Let
           him in.

Enter OVERREACH, GREEDY, [*and*] MARRALL.

    OVER. A good day to my Lord !
    LOV.   You are an early riser,
Sir Giles.
    OVER.   And reason, to attend your
           Lordship.
    LOV. And you, too, Master Greedy, up so
           soon ?
    GREEDY. In troth, my Lord, after the sun
           is up,
I cannot sleep, for I have a foolish stomach
That croaks for breakfast. With your Lord-
           ship's favor,
I have a serious question to demand
Of my worthy friend Sir Giles.
    LOV.   Pray you use your pleasure. [20
    GREEDY. How far, Sir Giles, and pray you
           answer me
Upon your credit, hold you it to be
From your manor-house, to this of my Lady's
           Allworth's ?
    OVER. Why, some four mile.
    GREEDY.   How ! four mile ? good Sir
           Giles,
Upon your reputation, think better ;
For if you do abate but one half-quarter
Of five, you do yourself the greatest wrong
That can be in the world ; for four miles' rid-
           ing
Could not have rais'd so huge an appetite
As I feel gnawing on me.

[1] A room in Lady Allworth's house.

MAR.　　　　　Wh[e]ther you ride, [30
Or go afoot, you are that way still [2] provided,
An it please your Worship.

OVER.　　　　　How now, sirrah? Prating
Before my Lord! No difference? Go to my
　　nephew;
See all his debts discharg'd, and help his Wor-
　　ship
To fit on his rich suit.

MAR. [*aside*]　　　　　I may fit you too.
Toss'd like a dog still! [3]　　　　　*Exit* MARRALL.

LOV.　　　　　I have writ this morning
A few lines to my mistress, your fair daughter.

OVER. 'T will fire her, for she's wholly
　　yours already. —
Sweet Master Allworth, take my ring: 't will
　　carry you
To her presence, I dare warrant you; and
　　there plead　　　　　40
For my good Lord, if you shall find occasion.
That done, pray ride to Nottingham, get a
　　license,
Still by this token. I'll have it dispatch'd,
And suddenly, my Lord; that I may say,
My Honorable, nay, Right Honorable
　　daughter.

GREEDY. Take my advice, young gentle-
　　man: get your breakfast;
'T is unwholesome to ride fasting. I'll eat
　　with you,
And eat to purpose.

OVER.　　　　　Some Fury's in that gut;
Hungry again! Did you not devour, this
　　morning,
A shield of brawn,[4] and a barrel of Colchester
　　oysters?　　　　　50

GREEDY. Why, that was, sir, only to scour
　　my stomach —
A kind of a preparative. Come, gentleman,
I will not have you feed like the hangman of
　　Flushing,[5]
Alone, while I am here.

LOV.　　　　　Haste your return.

ALL. I will not fail, my Lord.

GREEDY.　　　　　Nor I, to line
My Christmas coffer.[6]

　　　　　Exeunt GREEDY *and* ALLWORTH.

OVER.　　　　　To my wish, we are private.
I come not to make offer with my daughter

A certain portion — that were poor and
　　trivial;
In one word, I pronounce all that is mine,
In lands or leases, ready coin or goods,　　60
With her, my Lord, comes to you; nor shall
　　you have
One motive to induce you to believe
I live too long, since every year I'll add
Something unto the heap, which shall be
　　yours, too.

LOV. You are a right kind father.

OVER.　　　　　You shall have reason
To think me such. How do you like this seat?
It is well wooded, and well water'd, the acres
Fertile and rich; would it not serve for change,
To entertain your friends in a summer prog-
　　ress? [7]
What thinks my noble Lord?

LOV.　　　　　'T is a wholesome air, [70
And well-built pile; and she that's mistress of
　　it,
Worthy the large revenue.[8]

OVER.　　　　　She the mistress!
It may be so for a time; but let my Lord
Say only that he likes it, and would have it,
I say, ere long 't is his.

LOV.　　　　　Impossible.

OVER. You do conclude too fast, not know-
　　ing me,
Nor the engines [9] that I work by. 'T is not
　　alone
The Lady Allworth's lands, for those once
　　Wellborn's
(As by her dotage on him I know they will be,)
Shall soon be mine; but point out any man's
In all the shire, and say they lie convenient [81
And useful for your Lordship, and once more,
I say aloud, they are yours.

LOV.　　　　　I dare not own
What's by unjust and cruel means extorted;
My fame and credit are more dear to me
Than so to expose 'em to be censur'd by
The public voice.

OVER.　　　　　You run, my Lord, no hazard.
Your reputation shall stand as fair,
In all good men's opinions, as now;
Nor can my actions, though condemn'd for
　　ill,　　　　　90
Cast any foul aspersion upon yours.
For, though I do contemn report myself
As a mere sound, I still will be so tender
Of what concerns you, in all points of honor,
That the immaculate whiteness of your fame,

[2] Always.
[3] Cf. II, i, 142.
[4] A piece of a hog's skin was placed inside a cylin-
drical mold and filled with meat, which was then
cooked soft. (*N.E.D.*)
[5] Few would seek a hangman's company at dinner.
But *Flushing* is unexplained. (Q *Vllushing*.)
[6] Cf. "bread-box", "bread-basket."

[7] Tour.　　　[8] Accented on second syllable.
[9] Contrivances.

Nor your unquestion'd integrity,
Shall e'er be sullied with one taint or spot
That may take from your innocence and candor.[10]
All my ambition is to have my daughter
Right Honorable, which my Lord can make
her ;   100
And might I live to dance upon my knee
A young Lord Lovell, borne by her unto you,
I write *nil ultra* to my proudest hopes.
As for possessions and annual rents,
Equivalent to maintain you in the port [11]
Your noble birth and present state requires,
I do remove that burthen from your shoulders,
And take it on mine own ; for, though I ruin
The country to supply your riotous waste,
The scourge of prodigals, want, shall never
find you.   110
   Lov.   Are you not frighted with the imprecations
And curses of whole families, made wretched
By your sinister practices?
   Over.   Yes, as rocks are,
When foamy billows split themselves against
Their flinty ribs ; or as the moon is mov'd
When wolves, with hunger pin'd, hcwl at her
brightness.
I am of a solid temper, and, like these,
Steer on a constant course.   With mine own
sword,
If call'd into the field, I can make that right
Which fearful enemies murmur'd at as
wrong.   120
Now, for these other piddling [12] complaints
Breath'd out in bitterness ; as when they call
me
Extortioner, tyrant, cormorant, or intruder
On my poor neighbor's right, or grand encloser [13]
Of what was common, to my private use ;
Nay, when my ears are pierc'd with widows'
cries,
And undone orphans wash with tears my
threshold,
I only think what 't is to have my daughter
Right Honorable ; and 't is a powerful
charm [14]
Makes me insensible of remorse, or pity,   130
Or the least sting of conscience.
   Lov.   I admire [15]
The toughness of your nature.

   Over.   'T is for you,
My Lord, and for my daughter, I am marble ;
Nay more, if you will have my character
In little, I enjoy more true delight
In my arrival to my wealth these dark
And crooked ways, than you shall e'er take
pleasure
In spending what my industry hath compass'd.
My haste commands me hence ; in one word,
therefore,
Is it a match?
   Lov.   I hope that is past doubt now.   140
   Over.   Then rest secure ; not the hate of
all mankind here,
Nor fear of what can fall on me hereafter,
Shall make me study aught but your advancement
One story higher : an earl ! if gold can do it.
Dispute not my religion, nor my faith ;
Though I am borne thus headlong by my will,
You may make choice of what belief you
please —
To me they are equal ; so, my Lord, good
morrow.   *Exit.*
   Lov.   He 's gone ; I wonder how the earth
can bear
Such a portent ! I, that have liv'd a soldier,
And stood the enemy's violent charge undaunted,   151
To hear this blasphemous beast am bath'd all
over
In a cold sweat ; yet, like a mountain, he,
Confirm'd in atheistical assertions,
Is no more shaken than Olympus [16] is
When angry Boreas loads his double head
With sudden drifts of snow.

Enter Amble, Lady [Allworth,] *and* [Waiting] Woman.

   L. All.   Save you, my Lord !
Disturb I not your privacy?
   Lov.   No, good madam ;
For your own sake I am glad you came no
sooner,
Since this bold bad man, Sir Giles Overreach,   160
Made such a plain discovery of himself,
And read this morning such a devilish matins,
That I should think it a sin next to his
But to repeat it.

---

[10] Spotlessness.   [11] Station.   [12] Trisyllabic.
[13] Enclosures, the fencing off for sheep pasturage of common lands, constituted one of the great grievances of the time.
[14] Understand "which."   [15] Wonder at.

[16] "Either Massinger, or his transcriber, has mistaken Olympus for Parnassus : it may be the former, for, in trusting to their memory, such slips are not unusual in our old writers, who were indeed little solicitous of accuracy in these trivial matters." (Gifford.)

L. ALL.   I ne'er press'd, my Lord,
On others' privacies ; yet, against my will,
Walking, for health' sake, in the gallery
Adjoining to your lodgings, I was made,
So vehement and loud he was, partaker
Of his tempting offers.
    [Lov.]   Please you to command
Your servants hence, and I shall gladly
      hear   170
Your wiser counsel.
    L. ALL.   'T is, my Lord, a woman's,
But true and hearty. — Wait in the next room,
But be within call ; yet not so near to force me
To whisper my intents.
    AMB.   We are taught better
By you, good madam.
    W. WOM.   And well know our distance.
    L. ALL. Do so, and talk not ; 't will be-
      come your breeding. —
     Exeunt AMBLE *and* [Waiting] Woman.
Now, my good Lord ; if I may use my freedom,
As to an honor'd friend ——
    Lov.   You lessen else
Your favor to me.
    L. ALL.   I dare then say thus :
As you are noble (howe'er common men [180
Make sordid wealth the object and sole end
Of their industrious aims), 't will not agree
With those of eminent blood, who are engag'd
More to prefer [17] their honors than to increase
The state [18] left to 'em by their ancestors,
To study large additions to their fortunes,
And quite neglect their births — though I
      must grant,
Riches, well got, to be a useful servant,
But a bad master.
    Lov.   Madam, 't is confessed ,
But what infer you from it?
    L. ALL.   This, my Lord ; [190
That as all wrongs, though thrust into one
      scale,
Slide of themselves off when right fills the
      other,
And cannot bide the trial ; so all wealth,
I mean if ill-acquir'd, cemented to honor
By virtuous ways achiev'd, and bravely pur-
      chas'd,[19]
Is but as rubbage [20] pour'd into a river,
(Howe'er intended to make good [21] the bank,)
Rendering the water, that was pure before,
Polluted and unwholesome. I allow
The heir of Sir Giles Overreach, Margaret, [200
A maid well qualified and the richest match

Our north part can make boast of ; yet she
      cannot,
With all that she brings with her, fill their
      mouths [22]
That never will forget who was her father ;
Or that my husband Allworth's lands, and
      Wellborn's,
(How wrung from both needs now no repeti-
      tion,)
Were real motive that more work'd your
      Lordship
To join your families, than her form and vir-
      tues.
You may conceive [23] the rest.
    Lov.   I do, sweet madam,
And long since have consider'd it. I know
The sum of all that makes a just man
      happy   211
Consists in the well choosing of his wife ;
And there, well to discharge it,[24] does require
Equality of years, of birth, of fortune ;
For beauty being poor, and not cried up [25]
By birth or wealth, can truly mix with neither.
And wealth, where there's such difference in
      years,
And fair descent, must make the yoke uneasy.
But I come nearer.
    L. ALL.   Pray you do, my Lord.
    Lov. Were Overreach' states thrice cen-
      tupl'd, his daughter   220
Millions of degrees much fairer than she is,
Howe'er I might urge precedents to excuse me,
I would not so adulterate my blood
By marrying Margaret, and so leave my issue
Made up of several pieces, one part scarlet,[26]
And the other London blue.   In my own tomb
I will inter my name first.
    L. ALL. *(aside)*   I am glad to hear this. —
Why then, my Lord, pretend you marriage to
      her?
Dissimulation but ties false knots   229
On that straight line by which you, hitherto,
Have measur'd all your actions.
    Lov.   I make answer,
And aptly, with a question. Wherefore have
      you,
That, since your husband's death, have liv'd a
      strict
And chaste nun's life, on the sudden giv'n
      yourself
To visits and entertainments? Think you,
      madam,

---

[17] Promote.   [18] Estate.   [19] Acquired.
[20] Rubbish.   [21] Strengthen.

[22] *I.e.*, stop the talk of those.   [23] Imagine.
[24] The choosing of a wife.
[25] Extolled, enhanced.   [26] Cf. III, ii, 199.

'T is not grow[n] public conference? [27] or the favors

Which you too prodigally have thrown on Wellborn,

Being too reserv'd before, incur not censure?

L. ALL. I am innocent here ; and, on my life, I swear

My ends are good.

LOV.   On my soul, so are mine [240

To Margaret ; but leave both to the event.

And since this friendly privacy does serve

But as an offer'd means unto ourselves

To search each other farther, you having shown

Your care of me, I my respect to you,

Deny me not, but still in chaste words, madam,

An afternoon's discourse.

L. ALL.   So [28] I shall hear you. [*Exeunt.*]

SCENE II [29]

[Enter] TAPWELL *[and]* FROTH.

TAP. Undone, undone! this was your counsel, Froth.

FROTH. Mine! I defy thee! Did not Master Marrall

(He has marr'd all, I am sure) strictly command us,

On pain of Sir Giles Overreach' displeasure,

To turn the gentleman out of doors?

TAP.   'T is true ;

But now he 's his uncle's darling, and has got

Master Justice Greedy, since he fill'd his belly,

At his commandment, to do anything.

Woe, woe to us!

FROTH.   He may prove merciful.

TAP. Troth, we do not deserve it at his hands.   10

Though he knew all the passages [30] of our house,

As the receiving of stol'n goods, and bawdry,

When he was rogue Wellborn no man would believe him,

And then his information could not hurt us ;

But now he is Right Worshipful again,

Who dares but doubt his testimony? Methinks,

I see thee, Froth, already in a cart,[31]

For a close [32] bawd, thine eyes ev'n pelted out

With dirt and rotten eggs ; and my hand hissing,[33]

If I scape the halter, with the letter R [34] [20 Printed upon it.

FROTH.   Would that were the worst!

That were but nine days' wonder. As for credit,[35]

We have none to lose, but we shall lose the money

He owes us, and his custom ; there 's the hell on 't.

TAP. He has summon'd all his creditors by the drum,

And they swarm about him like so many soldiers

On the pay day ; and has found out such a new way

To pay his old debts, as 't is very likely

He shall be chronicl'd for it !

FROTH.   He deserves it   29

More than ten pageants.[36] But   *A cry with-*
are you sure his Worship   *in :* Brave
Comes this way, to my Lady's?   *Master*
TAP.   Yes, I hear him.   *Wellborn!*

FROTH. Be ready with your petition and present it

To his good grace.

Enter WELLBORN *in a rich habit,* [MARRALL,] GREEDY, ORDER, FURNACE, [*and*] *three* Creditors ; TAPWELL, *kneeling, delivers his bill of debt.*

WELL.   How 's this? petition'd to?

But note what miracles the payment of

A little trash, and a rich suit of clothes,

Can work upon these rascals ! I shall be,

I think, Prince Wellborn.

MAR.   When your Worship 's married,

You may be ; I know what I hope to see you.

WELL. Then look thou for advancement.

MAR.   To be known

Your Worship's bailiff is the mark I shoot at.   40

WELL. And thou shalt hit it.

MAR.   Pray you, sir, dispatch

These needy followers, and for my admittance,[37]

Provided you 'll defend me from   *This in-*
Sir Giles,   *terim,*
                              Tapwell
Whose service I am weary of,   *and Froth*
I 'll say something   *flattering*
                            and brib-
You shall give thanks for.   *ing Justice*
WELL.   Fear me [38]   *Greedy.*
not Sir Giles.

---

[27] Talk.   [28] On such terms.   [29] Unlocated.
[30] Doings.
[31] Bawds were punished by being carted through the streets.
[32] Secret.   [33] From the branding iron.

[34] For "Rogue."   [35] Reputation.
[36] Such as the Lord Mayor's Show.
[37] Appointment to office.   [38] The ethical dative

GREEDY. Who, Tapwell? I remember thy
    wife brought me
Last New Year's tide, a couple of fat turkeys.
    TAP. And shall do every Christmas, let
    your Worship
But stand my friend now.
    GREEDY.   How! with Master Wellborn?
I can do anything with him on such
    terms. —   50
See you this honest couple? They are good
    souls
As ever drew out faucet. Have they not
A pair of honest faces?
    WELL.   I o'erheard you,
And the bribe he promis'd. You are cozen'd
    in 'em ;
For, of all the scum that grew rich by my
    riots,
This, for a most unthankful knave, and this,
For a base bawd and whore, have worst de-
    serv'd me :
And therefore speak not for 'em. By your
    place
You are rather to do me justice. Lend me
    your ear. —
[*aside to* GREEDY] Forget his turkeys, and call
    in his license,   60
And, at the next fair, I 'll give you a yoke of
    oxen
Worth all his poultry.
    GREEDY.   I am chang'd on the sudden
In my opinion! — Come near ; nearer, rascal.
And, now I view him better, did you e'er see
One look so like an archknave? His very
    countenance,
Should an understanding judge but look upon
    him,
Would hang him, though he were innocent.
    TAP. [*and*] FROTH.   Worshipful sir.
    GREEDY. No, though the great Turk came,
    instead of turkeys,
To beg my favor, I am inexorable.
Thou hast an ill name : besides thy musty
    ale,   70
That hath destroy'd many of the King's liege
    people,
Thou never hadst in thy house, to stay men's
    stomachs,
A piece of Suffolk cheese or gammon of bacon,
Or any esculent, as the learned call it,
For their emolument, but sheer drink only,
For which gross fault I here do damn thy
    license,
Forbidding thee ever to tap or draw ;
For, instantly, I will, in mine own person,

Command the constable to pull down thy sign,
And do it before I eat.
    FROTH.   No mercy?
    GREEDY.   Vanish ! [80
If I show any, may my promis'd oxen gore me !
    TAP. Unthankful knaves are ever so re-
    warded.
             Exeunt GREEDY, TAPWELL, [*and*]
                       FROTH.
    WELL. Speak, what are you?
    1 CRED.   A decay'd vintner, sir,
That might have thrived, but that your Wor-
    ship broke [39] me
With trusting you with muscadine [40] and eggs,
And five-pound suppers, with your after-
    drinkings,[41]
When you lodg'd upon the Bankside.
    WELL.   [I] [42] remember.
    1 CRED. I have not been hasty, nor e'er
    laid [43] to arrest you ;
And therefore, sir ——
    WELL.   Thou art an honest fellow ;
I 'll set thee up again. — See his bill paid. —
What are you?
    2 CRED.   A tailor once, but now mere
    botcher.[44]   91
I gave you credit for a suit of clothes,
Which was all my stock ; but you failing in
    payment,
I was remov'd from the shopboard, and con-
    fin'd
Under a stall.
    WELL.   See him paid ; — and botch no
    more.
    2 CRED. I ask no interest, sir.
    WELL.   Such tailors need not :
If their bills are paid in one-and-twenty year,
They are seldom losers. — [*to* 3 Creditor]
    Oh, I know thy face :
Thou wert my surgeon.[45] You must tell no
    tales ;
Those days are done. I will pay you in pri-
    vate.   100
    ORD. A royal gentleman !
    FURN.   Royal as an emperor !
He 'll prove a brave master ; my good lady
    knew
To choose a man.
    WELL.   See all men else discharg'd ;
And since [46] old debts are clear'd by a new way,

---

[39] Bankrupted.
[40] Muscatel ; used with eggs as an aphrodisiac.
[41] Between-meals drinks.
[42] Add. Coxeter.   [43] Schemed.   [44] Repairer.
[45] Evidently called in to cure a venereal disease.
[46] Q italicizes the rest of the line.

A little bounty will not misbecome me ;
There 's something, honest cook, for thy good
    breakfasts ; —
And this, for your respect ; take 't, 't is good
    gold,
And I able to spare it.
ORD.   You are too munificent.
FURN. He was ever so.
WELL.   Pray you, on before.
3 CRED.   Heaven bless you !
MAR. At four a'clock the rest know where
    to meet me.   110
        Exeunt ORDER, FURNACE, [*and*]
           Creditors.
WELL. Now, Master Marrall, what 's the
    weighty secret
You promis'd to impart?
MAR.   Sir, time nor place
Allow me to relate each circumstance ;
This only, in a word : I know Sir Giles
Will come upon you for security
For his thousand pounds, which you must not
    consent to.
As he grows in heat, as I am sure he will,
Be you but rough, and say he 's in your debt
Ten times the sum, upon sale of your land ;
I had a hand in 't (I speak it to my shame) 120
When you were defeated [47] of it.
WELL.   That 's forgiven.
MAR. I shall deserve 't. Then urge him
    to produce
The deed in which you pass'd it over to him,
Which I know he 'll have about him, to deliver
To the Lord Lovell, with many other writings,
And present monies ; I 'll instruct you further,
As I wait on your Worship. If I play not my
    prize [48]
To your full content, and your uncle's much
    vexation,
Hang up Jack Marrall.
WELL.   I rely upon thee. *Exeunt.*

SCENE [III] [49]

[*Enter*] ALLWORTH [*and*] MARGARET.

ALL. Wh[e]ther to yield the first praise to
    my Lord's
Unequall'd temperance or your constant
    sweetness
That I yet live, my weak hands fasten'd on

---

[47] Ruined.
[48] Play my part, hold up my end. Literally, engage in a bout, especially of fencing. Q *price.*
[49] A room in Overreach's house. Q *Actus quarti, Scena vltima.*

Hope's anchor, spite of all storms of despair,
I yet rest doubtful.
MARG.   Give it to Lord Lovell ;
For what in him was bounty, in me 's duty.
I make but payment of a debt to which
My vows, in that high office [50] regist'red,
Are faithful witnesses.
ALL.   'T is true, my dearest :
Yet, when I call to mind how many fair ones [10
Make wilful shipwrack of their faiths, and
    oaths
To God and man, to fill the arms of greatness,
And you rise up [no] [51] less than a glorious
    star
To the amazement of the world, that hold out
Against the stern authority of a father,
And spurn at honor when it comes to court
    you ;
I am so tender of your good that faintly,
With your wrong, I can wish myself that right
You yet are pleas'd to do me.
MARG.   Yet, and ever.
To me what 's title, when content is want-
    ing?   20
Or wealth, rak'd up together with much
    care ;
And to be kept with more, when the heart
    pines
In being dispossess'd of what it longs for
Beyond the Indian mines? or the smooth
    brow
Of a pleas'd sire, that slaves me to his will,
And, so his ravenous humor may be feasted
By my obedience, and he see me great,
Leaves to my soul nor faculties nor power
To make her own election?
ALL.   But the dangers
That follow the repulse ——
MARG.   To me they are nothing ; [30
Let Allworth love, I cannot be unhappy.
Suppose the worst, that in his rage he kill me ;
A tear or two, by you dropp'd on my hearse
In sorrow for my fate, will call back life
So far as but to say that I die yours ;
I then shall rest in peace. Or should he prove
So cruel as one death would not suffice
His thirst of vengeance, but with ling'ring tor-
    ments
In mind and body I must waste to air,
In poverty join'd with banishment ; so [52] you
    share   40
In my afflictions, which I dare not wish you,
So high I prize you, I could undergo 'em

---

[50] *I.e.*, above.   [51] Add. Dodsley.
[52] Provided that.

With such a patience as should look down
With scorn on his worst malice.
ALL.   Heaven avert
Such trials of your true affection to me !
Nor will it unto you, that are all mercy,
Show so much rigor ; but since we must run
Such desperate hazards, let us do our best
To steer between 'em.
MARG.   Your lord's ours,[53] and sure ;
And, though but a young actor, second me [50
In doing to the life what he has plotted.

Enter OVERREACH [*behind*].

The end may yet prove happy. Now, my
     Allworth —
ALL. To your letter, and put on a seeming
     anger.
MARG. I 'll pay my Lord all debts due to
     his title ;
And when with terms not taking from his
     honor
He does solicit me, I shall gladly hear him.
But in this peremptory, nay, commanding,
     way,
T' appoint a meeting, and, without my knowl-
     edge,
A priest to tie the knot [54] can ne'er be undone
Till death unloose it, is a confidence   60
In his Lordship [54] will deceive him.
ALL.   I hope better,
Good lady.
MARG.   Hope, sir, what you please :
     for [55] me,
I must take a safe and secure [56] course ; I
     have
A father, and without his full consent,
Though all lords of the land kneel'd for my
     favor,
I can grant nothing.
OVER. [*aside*]   I like this obedience.
But whatso'er my Lord writes, must and shall
     be
Accepted and embrac'd. — [*advancing*] Sweet
     Master Allworth,
You show yourself a true and faithful servant
To your good lord ; he has a jewel of you. —
How ! frowning, Meg? Are these looks to
     receive   71
A messenger from my Lord? What 's this?
     Give me it.
MARG. A piece of arrogant paper, like th'
     inscriptions.
                    OVERREACH *read the letter.*

OVER. " Fair mistress, from your servant
     learn all joys
That we can hope for, if deferr'd, prove
     toys ; [57]
Therefore this instant, and in private, meet
A husband, that will gladly at your feet
Lay down his honors, tend'ring them to you
With all content, the church being paid her
     due."
— Is this the arrogant piece of paper?
     Fool !   80
Will you still be one? In the name of mad-
     ness what
Could his good Honor write more to content
     you?
Is there aught else to be wish'd, after these
     two,
That are already offer'd? Marriage first,
And lawful pleasure after : what would you
     more?
MARG. Why, sir, I would be married like
     your daughter ;
Not hurried away i' th' night I know not
     whither,
Without all ceremony ; no friends invited
To honor the solemnity.
ALL.   An 't please your Honor,
For so before to-morrow I must style you, [90
My Lord desire[s] this privacy, in respect [58]
His honorable kinsmen are afar off,
And his desires to have it done brook not
So long delay as to expect [59] their coming ;
And yet he stands resolv'd, with all due pomp,
As [60] running at the ring,[61] plays, masques, and
     tilting,
To have his marriage at court celebrated,
When he has brought your Honor up to Lon-
     don.
OVER. He tells you true ; 't is the fashion,
     on my knowledge.
Yet the good lord, to please your peevish-
     ness,   100
Must put it off, forsooth ! And lose a night
In which perhaps he might get two boys on
     thee.
Tempt me no farther, if you do, this [goad] [62]
Shall prick you to him. [*Points to his sword.*]
MARG.   I could be contented,
Were you but by, to do a father's part,
And give me in the church.

[53] On our side.   [54] Understand "that."
[55] As for.   [56] Accented on first syllable.

[57] Vain trifles.
[58] Out of regard to the fact that.
[59] Wait for.   [60] Such as.
[61] An exercise of horsemanship, the object being
to thrust a lance through a suspended ring.
[62] So Gifford and others ; Q *good.*

OVER.   So my Lord have you,
What do I care who gives you? Since my Lord
Does purpose to be private, I'll not cross him.
I know not, Master Allworth, how my Lord
May be provided, and therefore there's a
    purse   110
Of gold: 't will serve this night's expense;
    tomorrow
I'll furnish him with any sums. In the mean
    time,
Use my ring to my chaplain; he is benefic'd
At my manor of Gotham,[63] and call'd Parson
    Willdo.
'T is no matter for a license; I'll bear him out
    in 't;
    MARG. With your favor, sir, what warrant
    is your ring?
He may suppose I got that twenty ways,
Without your knowledge; and then to be
    refus'd
Were such a stain upon me! If you pleas'd,
    sir,
Your presence would do better.
    OVER.   Still perverse! [120
I say again, I will not cross my Lord;
Yet I'll prevent you [64] too. — Paper and ink,
    there!
    ALL. I can furnish you.
    OVER.   I thank you; I can write, then.
                              Writes on his book.
    ALL. You may, if you please, put out the
    name of my Lord,
In respect he comes disguis'd, and only write,
" Marry her to this gentleman."
    OVER.   Well advis'd.
'T is done; away. — (MARGARET *kneels*.) My
    blessing, girl? Thou hast it.
Nay, no reply; begone. — Good Master All-
    worth,[65]
This shall be the best night's work you ever
    made.
    ALL. I hope so, sir.
            Exeunt ALLWORTH *and* MARGARET.

    OVER.   Farewell! — Now all's cock-
    sure;[66]   130
Methinks I hear already knights and ladies
Say, " Sir Giles Overreach, how is it with
Your Honorable daughter? Has her Honor

Slept well to-night?"[67] or, " Will her Honor
    please
To accept this monkey, dog, or parrakeet?
(This is state[68] in ladies) or my eldest son
To be her page, and wait upon her trencher?"
My ends, my ends are compass'd! Then for
    Wellborn
And the lands: were he once married to the
    widow,
I have him here. — I can scarce contain my-
    self,   140
I am so full of joy, nay, joy all over.   *Exit.*

ACT V — SCENE [I][1]

[*Enter* LORD] LOVELL, LADY [ALLWORTH, *and*]
    AMBLE.

    L. ALL. By this you know how strong the
    motives were
That did, my Lord, induce me to dispense
A little with my gravity to advance,
In personating some few favors to him,
The plots and projects of the downtrod Well-
    born.
Nor shall I e'er repent, although I suffer
In some few men's opinions for 't, the action;
For he that ventur'd all for my dear hus-
    band
Might justly claim an obligation from me
To pay him such a courtesy; which had I [10
Coyly or over-curiously[2] denied,
It might have argu'd me of little love
To the deceas'd.
    LOV.   What you intended, madam,
For the poor gentleman hath found good suc-
    cess;
For, as I understand, his debts are paid,
And he once more furnish'd for fair employ-
    ment;
But all the arts that I have us'd to raise
The fortunes of your joy and mine, young
    Allworth,
Stand yet in supposition, though I hope well;
For the young lovers are in wit more preg-
    nant   20
Than their years can promise; and for their
    desires,
On my knowledge, they are equal.

---

[63] A village a few miles south of Nottingham.
Q *Gotam:* Stronach suggests a play on "Got 'em."
[64] Anticipate you; *i.e.*, your objections.
[65] Q has (in various copies) a full stop or a comma
here, and a comma after "begone."
[66] Perfectly safe.
[67] Last night.
[68] Stateliness, dignified behavior.
[1] A room in Lady Allworth's house. Q *Scena
quinta.*
[2] Over-scrupulously.

L. ALL.   As my wishes
Are with yours, my Lord ; yet give me leave to
    fear
The building, though well grounded : to de-
    ceive
Sir Giles, that's both a lion and a fox
In his proceedings, were a work beyond
The strongest undertakers, not the trial
Of two weak innocents.
    Lov.   Despair not, madam :
Hard things are compass'd oft by easy means ;
And judgment, being a gift deriv'd from
    Heaven,   30
Though sometimes lodg'd i' th' hearts of
    worldly men,
That ne'er consider from whom they receive it,
Forsakes such as abuse the Giver of it.
Which is the reason that the politic
And cunning statesman, that believes he fath-
    oms
The counsels of all kingdoms on the earth,
Is by simplicity oft overreach['d].[3]
    L. ALL. May he be so ! Yet, in his name [4]
        to express it,
Is a good omen.
    Lov.   May it to myself
Prove so, good lady, in my suit to you !   40
What think you of the motion? [5]
    L. ALL.   Troth, my Lord,
My own unworthiness may answer for me ;
For had you, when that I was in my prime,
My virgin flower uncropp'd, presented me
With this great favor ; looking on my lowness
Not in a glass of self-love, but of truth,
I could not but have thought it as a blessing
Far, far beyond my merit.
    Lov.   You are too modest,
And undervalue that which is above
My title, or whatever I call mine.   50
I grant, were I a Spaniard, to marry
A widow might disparage me ; [6] but being
A true-born Englishman, I cannot find
How it can taint my honor : nay, what's more,
That which you think a blemish is to me
The fairest lustre. You already, madam,
Have given sure proofs how dearly you can
    cherish
A husband that deserves you ; which confirms
    me

That, if I am not wanting in my care
To do you service, you'll be still the same   60
That you were to your Allworth : in a word,
Our years, our states, our births are not un-
    equal,
You being descended nobly, and alli'd so ;
If then you may be won to make me happy,
But join your lips to mine, and that shall be
A solemn contract.
    L. ALL.   I were blind to my own good
Should I refuse it ; [*kisses him*] yet, my Lord,
    receive me
As such a one, the study of whose whole life
Shall know no other object but to please you.
    Lov. If I return not, with all tenderness, [70
Equal respect to you, may I die wretched.
    L. ALL. There needs no protestation, my
    Lord,
To her that cannot doubt —

Enter WELLBORN [*handsomely apparelled*].

                         You are welcome, sir.
Now you look like yourself.
    WELL.   And will continue
Such in my free acknowledgment that I am
Your creature, madam, and will never hold
My life mine own, when you please to com-
    mand it.
    Lov. It is a thankfulness that well becomes
    you.
You could not make choice of a better shape
To dress your mind in.
    L. ALL.   For me, I am happy [80
That my endeavors prosper'd. Saw you of
    late
Sir Giles, your uncle?
    WELL.   I heard of him, madam,
By his minister, Marrall ; he's grown into
    strange passions
About his daughter. This last night he look'd
    for
Your Lordship at his house, but missing you,
And she not yet appearing, his wise head
Is much perplex'd and troubl'd.
    Lov.   It may be,
Sweetheart, my project took.
    L. ALL.   I strongly hope.

Enter OVERREACH, *with distracted looks, driv-
    ing in* MARRALL *before him* [*with a box*].

    OVER. Ha ! find her, booby, thou huge
        lump of nothing ;
I'll bore thine eyes out else.
    WELL. [*aside*]   May it please your Lord-
        ship,   90

For some ends of mine own, but to withdraw
A little out of sight, though not of hearing,
You may, perhaps, have sport.

    Lov.   You shall direct me.   (*Steps aside.*)

    Over.   I shall *sol fa* [7] you, rogue!

    Mar.   Sir, for what cause
Do you use me thus?

    Over.   Cause, slave! Why, I am angry,
And thou a subject only fit for beating,
And so to cool my choler. Look to the writ-
    ing;
Let but the seal be broke upon the box
That has slept in my cabinet these three
    years,
I'll rack thy soul for 't.

    Mar.   (*aside*)   I may yet cry quittance, [100
Though now I suffer, and dare not resist.

    Over.   Lady, by your leave, did you see my
        daughter-lady?
And the lord her husband? Are they in your
    house?
If they are, discover, that I may bid 'em joy,
And, as an entrance to her place of honor,
See your Ladyship on her left hand, and make
    cur[t]sies
When she nods on you, which you must receive
As a special favor.

    L. All.   When I know, Sir Giles,
Her state [8] requires such ceremony, I shall pay
    it;
But in the meantime, as I am myself,   110
I give you to understand, I neither know
Nor care where her Honor is.

    Over.   When you once see her
Supported, and led by the lord her husband,
You 'll be taught better. —— Nephew!

    Well.   Sir.

    Over.   No more? [9]

    Well.   'T is all I owe you.

    Over.   Have your redeem'd rags
Made you thus insolent?

    Well.   (*in scorn*)   Insolent to you!
Why, what are you, sir, unless in your years,
At the best, more than myself?

    Over.   His fortune swells him.
'T is rank [10] he 's married.

    L. All.   This is excellent!

    Over.   Sir, in calm language, though I sel-
        dom use it,   120
I am familiar with the cause that makes you
Bear up thus bravely; there 's a certain buzz
Of a stol'n marriage, do you hear? of a stol'n
    marriage,

In which, 't is said, there 's somebody hath
    been cozen'd;
I name no parties.

    Well.   Well, sir, and what follows?

    Over.   Marry, this; since you are peremp-
        tory. Remember,
Upon mere hope of your great match, I lent
    you
A thousand pounds; put me in good security,
And suddenly, [by] [11] mortgage or by statute [12]
Of some of your new possessions, or I 'll have
    you   130
Dragg'd in your lavender robes [13] to the jail.
    You know me;
And therefore do not trifle.

    Well.   Can you be
So cruel to your nephew, now he 's in
The way to rise? Was this the courtesy
You did me " in pure love, and no ends else? "

    Over.   End me no ends! Engage the
        whole estate
And force your spouse to sign it, you shall
    have
Three or four thousand more, to roar and swag-
    ger
And revel in bawdy taverns.

    Well.   And beg after,
Mean you not so?

    Over.   My thoughts are mine, and
        free.   140
Shall I have security?

    Well.   No, indeed, you shall not,
Nor bond, nor bill, nor bare acknowledgment;
Your great looks fright not me.

    Over.   But my deeds shall.
Outbrav'd?   *They both draw.*

    L. All.   Help, murder! murder!

The Servants *enter.*

    Well.   Let him come on,
With all his wrongs and injuries about him,
Arm'd with his cutthroat practices to guard
    him;
The right that I bring with me will defend me,
And punish his extortion.

    Over.   That I had thee
But single in the field!

    L. All.   You may; but make not
My house your quarrelling scene.

    Over.   Were 't in a church, [150
By Heaven and hell, I 'll do 't!

---

[7] Beat.   [8] Rank.
[9] But this curt form of address.   [10] Obvious.

[11] Cor. Coxeter; Q *my.*
[12] See on I, i, 50.
[13] To "lay up in lavender" was a common eu-
phemism for pawning.

MAR. [*aside to* WELLBORN]   Now put him to
The showing of the deed.
WELL.   This rage is vain, sir ;
For fighting, fear not, you shall have your hands full,
Upon the least incitement ; and whereas
You charge me with a debt of a thousand pounds,
If there be law, (howe'er you have no conscience,)
Either restore my land or I 'll recover
A debt, that 's truly due to me from you,
In value ten times more than what you challenge.[14]
OVER. I in thy debt !   O impudence ! did I not purchase   160
The land left by thy father, that rich land,
That had continued in Wellborn's name
Twenty descents ; which, like a riotous fool,
Thou didst make sale of ?   Is not here inclos'd
The deed that does confirm it mine ?
MAR.   Now, now !
WELL. I do acknowledge none ;   I ne'er pass'd o'er
Any such land.   I grant for a year or two
You had it in trust ; which if you do discharge,
Surrend'ring the possession, you shall ease
Yourself and me of chargeable [15] suits in law,   170
Which, if you prove not honest, as I doubt it,
Must of necessity follow.
L. ALL.   In my judgment,
He does advise you well.
OVER.   Good ! good ! Conspire
With your new husband, lady ; second him
In his dishonest practices ; but when
This manor is extended [16] to my use,
You 'll speak in an humbler key, and sue for favor.
L. ALL. Never ; do not hope it.
WELL.   Let despair first seize me.
OVER. Yet, to shut up thy mouth, and make thee give
Thyself the lie, the loud lie, I draw out   180
The precious evidence ; if thou canst forswear
Thy hand and seal, and make a forfeit of
                     Opens the box.
Thy ears to the pillory, see ! here 's that will make
My interest clear — ha !
L. ALL.   A fair skin of parchment.

[14] Claim.   [15] Costly.   [16] Seized.

WELL. Indented,[17] I confess, and labels [18] too ;
But neither wax [19] nor words. How ! thunderstruck ?
Not a syllable to insult with ?   My wise Uncle,
Is this your precious evidence ? Is this that makes
Your interest clear ?
OVER.   I am o'erwhelm'd with wonder !
What prodigy is this ?   What subtle devil [190
Hath raz'd out the inscription, the wax
Turn'd into dust ?   The rest of my deeds whole
As when they were deliver'd, and this only
Made nothing !   Do you deal with witches, rascal ?
There is a statute [20] for you, which will bring
Your neck in a hempen circle ; yes, there is ;
And now 't is better thought, for, cheater, know
This juggling shall not save you.
WELL.   To save thee
Would beggar the stock of mercy.
OVER.   Marrall !
MAR.   Sir.
OVER. (*flattering him*) Though the witnesses are dead, your testimony   200
Help with an oath or two ; and for thy master,
Thy liberal master, my good honest servant,
I know you will swear anything, to dash
This cunning sleight ; besides, I know thou art
A public notary, and such stand in law
For a dozen witnesses ; the deed being drawn too
By thee, my careful Marrall, and deliver'd
When thou wert present, will make good my title.
Wilt thou not swear this ?
MAR.   I ? no, I assure you ;
I have a conscience not sear'd up like yours ;   210
I know no deeds.
OVER.   Wilt thou betray me ?
MAR.   Keep him
From using of his hands, I 'll use my tongue,
To his no little torment.
OVER.   Mine own varlet
Rebel against me ?
MAR.   Yes, and uncase [21] you too.
The idiot, the patch, the slave, the booby,

[17] Contracts were written in duplicate on the same sheet, which was then divided irregularly ; the indented edges would fit and thus attest the genuineness of the separate copies.
[18] Narrow strips attached to a document to carry the seals.
[19] Seals.   [20] Against witchcraft.   [21] Strip, flay.

The property fit only to be beaten
For your morning exercise, your football, or
Th' unprofitable lump of flesh, your drudge,
Can now anatomize [22] you, and lay open
All your black plots, and level with the
    earth
Your hill of pride, and, with these gabions [23]
    guarded,   221
Unload my great artillery, and shake,
Nay pulverize, the walls you think defend
    you.
  L. ALL. How he foams at the mouth with
    rage !
  WELL.   To him again.
  OVER. Oh, that I had thee in my gripe ; I
    would tear thee
Joint after joint !
  MAR.   I know you are a tearer,
But I 'll have first your fangs par'd off, and
    then
Come nearer to you ; when I have discover'd [24]
And made it good before the judge what
    ways
And devilish practices you us'd to cozen   230
With an army of whole families, who yet
    live,
And, but [25] enroll'd for soldiers, were [26] able
To take in [27] Dunkirk.
  WELL.   All will come out.
  L. ALL.   The better.
  OVER. But that I will live, rogue, to torture
    thee,
And make thee wish, and kneel in vain, to
    die,
These swords that keep thee from me should
    fix here,
Although they made my body but one
    wound,
But I would reach thee.
  LOV. (*aside*)   Heav'n's hand is in this ;
One bandog [28] worry the othc_ r
  OVER.   I play the fool,
And make my anger but ridiculous ;   240
There will be a time and place, there will be,
    cowards,
When you shall feel what I dare do.
  WELL.   I think so :
You dare do any ill, yet want true valor
To be honest, and repent.

[22] Dissect.
[23] Wicker baskets filled with earth, used to
strengthen defensive works and also, evidently,
to protect gunners. Here the gabions are Marrall's
protectors.
[24] Revealed.   [25] If they only were.
[26] Would be.   [27] Capture.
[28] A fierce dog kept chained up.

  OVER.   They are words I know not,
Nor e'er will learn. Patience, the beggar's
    virtue,

Enter GREEDY *and* PARSON WILLDO.

Shall find no harbor here. — After these
    storms
At length a calm appears. Welcome, most
    welcome !
There 's comfort in thy looks. Is the deed done?
Is my daughter married? Say but so, my
    chaplain,
And I am tame.
  WILLDO. Married? Yes, I assure you. [250
  OVER. Then vanish all sad thoughts !
    There 's more gold for thee.
My doubts and fears are in the titles drown'd
Of my Honorable, my Right Honorable
    daughter.
  GREEDY. Here will I be [29] feasting ! At
    least for a month
I am provided. Empty guts, croak no more.
You shall be stuff'd like bagpipes, not with
    wind,
But bearing [30] dishes.
  OVER. (*whispering to* WILLDO)   Instantly
    be here?
To my wish ! to my wish ! Now you that plot
    against me,
And hop'd to trip my heels up, that contemn'd
    me,   259
Think on 't and tremble. They come ! I
    hear the music. —   *Loud music.*
A lane there for my Lord !
  WELL.   This sudden heat
May yet be cool'd, sir.
  OVER.   Make way there for my Lord !

Enter ALLWORTH *and* MARGARET.

  MARG. (*kneeling*) Sir, first your pardon,
    then your blessing, with
Your full allowance of the choice I have
    made.
As ever you could make use of your reason,
Grow not in passion ; since you may as well
Call back the day that 's past, as untie the
    knot
Which is too strongly fasten'd. Not to dwell
Too long on words, this 's my husband.
  OVER.   How !
  ALL. So I assure you ; all the rites of mar-
    riage,   270
With every circumstance, are past. Alas ! sir,

[29] Coxeter *et al.*, perhaps rightly, omit *I*.
[30] Substantial.

Although I am no lord, but a lord's page,
Your daughter and my lov'd wife mourns not
　　　for it ;
And, for Right Honorable son-in-law, you
　　　may say,
Your dutiful daughter.

OVER.　　　　Devil ! are they married ?

WILLDO. Do a father's part, and say,
　　　" Heaven give 'em joy ! "

OVER. Confusion and ruin ! Speak, and
　　　speak quickly,
Or thou art dead.

WILLDO.　　　　They are married.

OVER.　　　　Thou hadst better
Have made a contract with the king of fiends,
Than these — my brain turns !

WILLDO.　　　　Why this rage to me ? [280
Is not this your letter, sir, and these the words,
" Marry her to this gentleman " ?

OVER.　　　　It cannot —
Nor will I e'er believe it ; 'sdeath ! I will not ;
That I, that in all passages I touch'd
At worldly profit have not left a print
Where I have trod for the most curious search
To trace my footsteps, should be gull'd by
　　　children,
Baffl'd and fool'd, and all my hopes and labors
Defeated and made void.

WELL.　　　　As it appears,
You are so, my grave uncle.

OVER.　　　　Village nurses [290
Revenge their wrongs with curses ; I 'll not
　　　waste
A syllable, but thus I take the life
Which, wretched, I gave to thee.
　　　　　　Offers [31] *to kill* MARGARET.

LOV. [*coming forward*]　　Hold, for your
　　　own sake !
Though charity to your daughter hath quite
　　　left you,
Will you do an act, though in your hopes lost
　　　here,
Can leave no hope for peace or rest hereafter ?
Consider ; at the best you are but a man,
And cannot so create your aims but that
They may be cross'd.

OVER.　　　　Lord, thus I spit at thee,
And at thy counsel ; and again desire thee, [300
And as thou art a soldier, if thy valor
Dares show itself where multitude and example
Lead not the way, let 's quit the house, and
　　　change
Six words in private.

LOV.　　　　**I am ready.**

[31] Attempts.

L. ALL.　　　　Stay, sir ;
Contest with one distracted ?

WELL.　　　　You 'll grow like him,
Should you answer his vain challenge.

OVER.　　　　Are you pale ?
Borrow his help, though Hercules call it odds,
I 'll stand against both as I am, hemm'd in
　　　thus.
Since, like [a] [32] Libyan lion in the toil, [33]
My fury cannot reach the coward hunters, [310
And only spends itself, I 'll quit the place.
Alone I can do nothing ; but I have servants
And friends to second me ; and if I make
　　　not
This house a heap of ashes (by my wrongs,
What I have spoke I will make good !) or
　　　[leave] [34]
One throat uncut, — if it be possible,
Hell, add to my afflictions ! *Exit* OVERREACH.

MAR.　　　　Is 't not brave sport ?

GREEDY. Brave sport ! I am sure it has
　　　ta'en away my stomach ;
I do not like the sauce.

ALL.　　　　Nay, weep not, dearest,
Though it express your pity ; what 's de-
　　　creed　　　　　　　　　　　　　320
Above we cannot alter.

L. ALL.　　　　His threats move me
No scruple, madam.

MAR.　　　　Was it not a rare trick,
An it please your Worship, to make the deed
　　　nothing ?
I can do twenty neater, if you please
To purchase and grow rich ; for I will be
Such a solicitor and steward for you,
As never Worshipful had.

WELL.　　　　I do believe thee ;
But first discover the quaint [35] means you
　　　us'd
To raze out the conveyance ?

MAR.　　　　They are mysteries
Not to be spoke in public : certain min-
　　　erals　　　　　　　　　　　　　330
Incorporated in the ink and wax.
Besides, he gave me nothing, but still fed
　　　me
With hopes and blows ; but that was the in-
　　　ducement
To this conun[d]rum. [36]　If it please your Wor-
　　　ship
To call to memory, this mad beast once caus'd
　　　me

[32] Add. Coxeter.
[33] Snare, trap.　　[34] Q *leau'd*.　　[35] Clever.
[36] Whim ; *i.e.*, trick.

To urge you or to drown or hang yourself;
I'll do the like to him, if you command me.

WELL. You are a rascal. He that dares be
    false
To a master, though unjust, will ne'er be true
To any other. Look not for reward   340
Or favor from me; I will shun thy sight
As I would do a basilisk's.[37] Thank my
    pity
If thou keep thy ears; howe'er, I will take
    order [38]
Your practice shall be silenc'd.

GREEDY.   I'll commit him,
If you'll have me, sir.

WELL.   That were to little purpose;
His conscience be his prison. Not a word,
But instantly begone.

ORD.   Take this kick with you.

AMB. And this.

FURN.   If that I had my cleaver here,
I would divide your knave's head,

MAR.   This is the haven
False servants still [39] arrive at.

                        Exit MARRALL.

                Re-enter OVERREACH.

L. ALL.   Come again! [350
LOV. Fear not, I am your guard.

WELL.   His looks are ghastly.

W[I]LLDO. Some little time I have spent,
    under your favors,
In physical studies, and if my judgment err
    not,
He's mad beyond recovery; but [40] observe
    him,
And look to yourselves.

OVER.   Why, is not the whole world
Included in myself? To what use then
Are friends and servants? Say there were a
    squadron
Of pikes,[41] lined [42] through with shot,[43] when I
    am mounted
Upon my injuries, shall I fear to charge 'em?
No, I'll through the battalia, and, that
    routed,   360
        Flourishing his sword [*sheathed*].[44]
I'll fall to execution — ha! I am feeble:
Some undone widow sits upon mine arm,
And takes away the use of 't; and my sword,
Glu'd to my scabbard with wrong'd orphans'
    tears,

Will not be drawn. Ha! what are these?
    Sure, hangmen
That come to bind my hands, and then to drag
    me
Before the judgment seat; now they are new
    shapes,
And do appear like Furies, with steel whips
To scourge my ulcerous soul. Shall I then
    fall
Ingloriously, and yield? No; spite of Fate,
I will be forc'd to hell like to myself.   371
Though you were legions of accursed spirits,
Thus would I fly among you.
        [*Rushes forward and flings himself
            on the ground.*] [45]

WELL.   There's no help;
Disarm him first, then bind him.

GREEDY.   Take a *mittimus* [46]
And carry him to Bedlam.[47]

LOV.   How he foams!

WELL. And bites the earth!

WILLDO.   Carry him to some dark room,[48]
There try what art can do for his recovery.

MARG. O my dear father!
                They force OVERREACH *off.*

ALL.   You must be patient, mistress.

LOV. Here is a precedent to teach wicked
    men
That when they leave religion, and turn athe-
    ists   380
Their own abilities leave 'em. Pray you take
    comfort;
I will endeavor you shall be his guardians
In his distractions; and for your land, Master
    Wellborn,
Be it good or ill in law, I'll be an umpire
Between you, and this, th' undoubted heir
Of Sir Giles Overreach. For me, here's the
    anchor
That I must fix on.

ALL.   What you shall determine,
My Lord, I will allow of.[49]

WELL.   'T is the language
That I speak too; but there is something else
Beside the repossession of my land,   390
And payment of my debts, that I must prac-
    tice.

I had a reputation, but 't was lost
In my loose course; and, till I redeem it
Some noble way, I am but half made up.

---

[37] The fabulous serpent whose glance was deadly.
[38] See to it.   [39] Always.   [40] Merely.
[41] Pikemen.
[42] Strengthened, reinforced.
[43] Musketeers.   [44] Q *vnsheathed.*

[45] So Gifford. Q assigns preceding line to Wellborn.
[46] Warrant of commitment.
[47] Bethlehem Hospital, London's institution for
the insane, and hence any lunatic asylum.
[48] A regular method of treatment then.
[49] Approve.

It is a time of action ; if your Lordship
Will please to confer a company upon me
In your command, I doubt not in my service
To my king and country but I shall do some-
    thing
That may make me right again.
    Lov.   Your suit is granted,
And you lov'd for the motion.[50]
      WELL. [*coming forward*]   Nothing wants
      then   400
But your allowance [51] —

[50] Proposal.   [51] Approval.

THE EPILOGUE

BUT your allowance, and in that our all
Is comprehended ; it being known nor we
Nor he that wrote the comedy can be free
Without your manumission ; which if you
Grant willingly, as a fair favor due
To the poet's and our labors, (as you may,
For we despair not, gentlemen, of the play,)
We jointly shall profess your grace hath might
To teach us action, and him how to write. 410
                            [*Exeunt.*]

THE
BROKEN
HEART.

A Tragedy.

ACTED
By the KINGS Majesties Seruants
at the priuate Houſe in the
BLACK-FRIERS.

Fide Honor.

LONDON:
Printed by I. B. for HVGH BEESTON, and are to
be ſold at his Shop, neere the *Caſtle* in
Corne-hill. 1 6 3 3.

INTRODUCTORY NOTE

FORD's first publication, *Fame's Memorial*, is a long elegiac poem on Charles Blount, Lord Mountjoy and Earl of Devonshire, whose death in 1606 followed by a few months his marriage to Penelope Rich, *née* Devereux, Sidney's Stella. Her wedded life with Robert, Lord Rich, had been a miserable one, and she had long been Devonshire's mistress, without their incurring serious reprobation. Their marriage, however, after her divorce, was regarded as scandalous, and the Earl died heartbroken at the King's displeasure. The youthful Ford, generous and romantic, was deeply moved by the lovers' trials, and throughout his literary career remained a somewhat quixotic idealist and amorist. For him the spiritual union of lovers is an inviolable thing, and wedlock adulterous without a marriage of true minds. To what extent *The Broken Heart* is influenced by the still earlier relations (whatever they may have been) between Penelope and Sir Philip Sidney is very uncertain, despite Sherman's argument (Introduction, Belles Lettres Series) that their predicament was similar to that of Orgilus and Penthea. In any case, the poet's doctrinaire sympathy with lovers as such, his worship of beauty, and his contempt for conventional morality, are constantly reflected in his works.

Ford, then, is not an echo of Shakespeare, Webster, or Fletcher, but the most original of their immediate successors. He is dominated by an idea or mood, which in his best plays he is able to project with remarkable success. To apply to *The Broken Heart* the test of probability, save in the Aristotelian sense, would be as foolish as to reproach Whistler for not delineating in one of his nocturnes every window and chimney pot on the far side of the river. If in this play we are not sensible of the surge of great power, there is a place for sentiment and pathos, especially when they are rendered with such literary distinction. Ford is perhaps a poet first; yet the dramatic effectiveness of *The Broken Heart* is very considerable. Whether there is any justice in the charge that his works are decadent is an interesting question which the Editor hopes soon to discuss elsewhere.

Despite the assertion in lines fifteen and sixteen of the prologue, no source for the plot has been found. The date of composition, and of production by the King's Men at the Blackfriars, has not been precisely determined. Weber (1811) called attention to the citation (IV, ii, 15) of Thomas Deloney's *Garland of Good Will*, of which there was an edition, though it was not the first, in 1631 (Percy Society Reprints, vol. 30, p. viii). The sole quarto of *The Broken Heart* appeared two years later; c. 1632 seems a likely, though quite unsupported, date for its writing. The Quarto of 1633, on which the present text is based, does not carry the author's name on the title page, save in the anagram, *Fide Honor;* but it is signed to the dedication.

The standard edition of Ford's works is still that of W. Gifford, in the revision of A. Dyce (1869). Excellent reprints of the quartos are provided in W. Bang's *Materialen zur Kunde des Älteren Englischen Dramas*, in vol. XXIII, and in vol. I of the " New Series " by H. De Vocht. *The Broken Heart* and *'T is Pity She's a Whore* were also edited by S. P. Sherman (1915).

THE BROKEN HEART

JOHN FORD

THE SPEAKERS' NAMES FITTED TO THEIR QUALITIES

AMYCLAS, *Common to the Kings of Laconia.*
ITHOCLES, *Honor of loveliness,* a favorite.
ORGILUS, *Angry,* son to Crotolon.
BASSANES, *Vexation,* a jealous nobleman.
ARMOSTES, *An Appeaser,* a councillor of state.
CROTOLON, *Noise,* another councillor.
PROPHILUS, *Dear,* friend to Ithocles.
NEARCHUS, *Young Prince,* Prince of Argos.
TECNICUS, *Artist,* a philosopher.
[HEMOPHIL],[1] *Glutton,*
GRONEAS, *Tavern-haunter,* } two courtiers.
AMELUS, *Trusty,* friend to Nearchus.
PHULAS, *Watchful,* servant to Bassanes.
Courtiers, Officers, Attendants, etc.]

CALANTHA, *Flower of beauty,* the King's daughter.
PENTHEA, *Complaint,* sister to Ithocles [and wife to Bassanes].
EUPHRANEA, *Joy,* a maid of honor, [daughter to Crotolon].
CHRISTALLA, *Crystal,*
PHILEMA, *A Kiss,* } maids of honor.
GRAUSIS,[2] *Old Beldam,* overseer of Penthea.

PERSONS INCLUDED

THRASUS, *Fierceness,* father of Ithocles.
APLOTES, *Simplicity,* Orgilus so disguis'd.

[THE SCENE — *Sparta.*]

THE PROLOGUE

OUR scene is Sparta.   He whose best of art
Hath drawn this piece calls it *The Broken Heart.*
The title lends no expectation here
Of apish laughter, or of some lame jeer
At place or persons; no pretended [3] clause
Of jests fit for a brothel courts applause
From vulgar admiration : such low songs,
Tun'd to unchaste ears, suit not modest tongues.
The Virgin Sisters [4] then deserv'd fresh bays
When innocence and sweetness crown'd their lays ;   10
Then vices gasp'd for breath, whose whole commerce
Was whipp'd to exile by unblushing verse.
This law we keep in our presentment now,
Not to take freedom more than we allow ;
What may be here thought a fiction, when Time's youth
Wanted some riper years was known *A Truth:* [5]
In which, if words have cloth'd the subject right,
You may partake a pity with delight.

[1] Q *Lemophil.*
[2] Q *Gransis,* throughout.

[3] Set forth, offered for consideration.
[4] The Muses.
[5] See introductory note.

1095

ACT I — Scene I [6]

Enter Crotolon *and* Orgilus.

Crot. Dally not further; I will know the reason
That speeds thee to this journey.

Org.   Reason? good sir,
I can yield many.

Crot.   Give me one, a good one;
Such I expect, and ere we part must have.
Athens! Pray, why to Athens? You intend not
To kick against the world, turn cynic, stoic,
Or read the logic lecture, or become
An Areopagite,[7] and judge in cases
Touching the commonwealth; for, as I take it,
The budding of your chin cannot prognosticate   10
So grave an honor.

Org.   All this I acknowledge.

Crot. You do! Then, son, if books and love of knowledge
Inflame you to this travel, here in Sparta
You may as freely study.

Org.   'T is not that, sir.

Crot. Not that, sir! As a father, I command thee
To acquaint me with the truth.

Org.   Thus I obey 'ee.
After so many quarrels as dissension,
Fury, and rage had br[oa]ch'd in blood, and sometimes
With death to such confederates as sided
With now-dead Thrasus and yourself, my Lord;   20
Our present king, Amyclas, reconcil'd
Your eager swords and seal'd a gentle peace:
Friends you profess'd yourselves; which to confirm,
A resolution for a lasting league
Betwixt your families was entertain'd,
By joining in a Hymenean bond
Me and the fair Penthea, only daughter
To Thrasus.

Crot.   What of this?

Org.   Much, much, dear sir.
A freedom of converse, an interchange
Of holy and chaste love, so fix'd our souls [30
In a firm growth of union [8] that no time

Can eat into the pledge; we had enjoy'd
The sweets our vows expected, had not cruelty
Prevented all those triumphs we prepar'd for,
By Thrasus his untimely death.

Crot.   Most certain.

Org. From this time sprouted up that poisonous stalk
Of aconite, whose ripened fruit hath ravish'd
All health, all comfort of a happy life;
For Ithocles, her brother, proud of youth,
And prouder in his power, nourish'd closely [9]
The memory of former discontents,   41
To glory in revenge. By cunning partly,
Partly by threats, 'a [10] woos at once and forces
His virtuous sister to admit [11] a marriage
With Bassanes, a nobleman, in honor
And riches, I confess, beyond my fortunes.

Crot. All this is no sound reason to importune
My leave for thy departure.

Org.   Now it follows.
Beauteous Penthea, wedded to this torture
By an insulting [12] brother, being secretly   50
Compell'd to yield her virgin freedom up
To him who never can usurp her heart,
Before contracted mine, is now so yok'd
To a most barbarous thraldom, misery,
Affliction, that he savors not humanity
Whose sorrow melts not into more than pity
In hearing but her name.

Crot.   As how, pray?

Org.   Bassanes,
The man that calls her wife, considers truly
What heaven of perfections he is lord of
By thinking fair Penthea his; this thought [60
Begets a kind of monster-love, which love
Is nurse unto a fear so strong and servile
As brands all dotage with a jealousy:
All eyes who gaze upon that shrine of beauty
He doth resolve [13] do homage to the miracle;
Some one, he is assur'd, may now or then,
If opportunity but sort,[14] prevail.
So much, out of a self-unworthiness,
His fears transport him; not that he finds cause
In her obedience, but his own distrust.   70

Crot. You spin out your discourse.

Org.   My griefs are violent.
For, knowing how the maid was heretofore
Courted by me, his jealousies grow wild
That I should steal again into her favors,

---

[6] Unlocated; presumably a room in Crotolon's house.
[7] A member of the Areopagus, the famous Athenian court.
[8] Some copies of Q *of holy union.* (Dyce. See also De Vocht.)

[9] Secretly.   [10] He.
[11] Consent to.
[12] Arrogant, insolently triumphant.
[13] Is convinced.
[14] Suit.

And undermine her virtues ; which the gods
Know I nor dare nor dream of. Hence, from
   hence
I undertake a voluntary exile ;
First, by my absence to take off the cares
Of jealous Bassanes ; but chiefly, sir,
To free Penthea from a hell on earth ;   80
Lastly, to lose the memory of something
Her presence makes to live in me afresh.
   CROT. Enough, my Orgilus, enough. To
   Athens
I give a full consent. — Alas, good lady ! —
We shall hear from thee often?
   ORG.   Often.
   CROT.   See,
Thy sister comes to give a farewell.

       Enter EUPHRANEA.

   EUPH.   Brother !
   ORG. Euphranea, thus upon thy cheeks I
   print
A brother's kiss ; more careful of thine honor,
Thy health, and thy well-doing than my life.
Before we part, in presence of our father,   90
I must prefer a suit to 'ee.[15]
   EUPH.   You may style it,
My Brother, a command.
   ORG.   That you will promise
To pass never to any man, however
Worthy, your faith, till, with our father's
   leave,
I give a free consent.
   CROT.   An easy motion ![16]
I 'll promise for her, Orgilus.
   ORG.   Your pardon ;
Euphranea's oath must yield me satisfaction.
   EUPH. By Vesta's sacred fires I swear.
   CROT.   And I,
By Great Apollo's beams, join in the vow,
Not without thy allowance [17] to bestow her [100
On any living.
   ORG.   Dear Euphranea,
Mistake me not ; far, far 't is from my thought,
As far from any wish of mine, to hinder
Preferment to an honorable bed
Or fitting fortune ; thou art young and hand-
   some,
And 't were injustice, more, a tyranny,
Not to advance thy merit. Trust me, Sister,
It shall be my first care to see thee match'd
As may become thy choice and our contents.
I have your oath.

   [15] Common for "ye", though here perhaps =
"thee."
   [16] Proposal.   [17] Approval.

   EUPH.   You have. But mean you,
   Brother,   110
To leave us, as you say?
   CROT.   Ay, ay, Euphranea ;
He has just grounds [18] direct him. I will
   prove
A father and a brother to thee.
   EUPH.   Heaven
Does look into the secrets of all hearts. —
Gods, you have mercy with 'ee, else —
   CROT.   Doubt nothing ;
Thy brother will return in safety to us.
   ORG. Souls sunk in sorrows never are with-
   out 'em ;
They change fresh airs, but bear their griefs
   about 'em.   *Exeunt omnes.*

          SCENE II [19]

Flourish. Enter AMYCLAS *the* King, ARMOS-
   TES, PROPHILUS, *and* Attendants.

   AMY. The Spartan gods are gracious ; our
   humility
Shall bend before their altars, and perfume
Their temples with abundant sacrifice.
See, Lords, Amyclas, your old king, is ent'ring
Into his youth again ! I shall shake off
This silver badge of age, and change this snow
For hairs as gay as are Apollo's locks ;
Our heart leaps in new vigor.
   ARM.   May old time
Run back to double your long life, great sir !
   AMY. It will, it must, Armostes : thy bold
   nephew,   10
Death-braving Ithocles, brings to our gates
Triumphs and peace upon his conquering
   sword.
Laconia is a monarchy at length ;
Hath in this latter war trod under foot
Messene's pride ; Messene [20] bows her neck
To Lacedaemon's royalty. Oh, 't was
A glorious victory, and doth deserve
More than a chronicle — a temple, Lords,
A temple to the name of Ithocles. —
Where didst thou leave him, Prophilus?
   PRO.   At Pephon,[21] [20
Most gracious sovereign ; twenty of the no-
   blest
Of the Messenians there attend your pleasure,

   [18] Understand "that."
   [19] Presumably a room in the palace.
   [20] The town of this name was not founded till
after the overthrow of the Spartan supremacy,
but the name was anciently given to Messenia.
   [21] Pephnus, a Laconian town on the eastern shore
of the Messenian Gulf. It was regarded by the
Messenians as the limit of their territories.

For such conditions as you shall propose
In settling peace, and liberty of life.

AMY. When comes your friend, the general?
PRO.   He promis'd
To follow with all speed convenient.

Enter CROTOLON, CALANTHA, CHRISTALLA
[*and*] PHILEMA [*with a garland*], *and* EU-
PHRANEA.

AMY. Our daughter! — Dear Calantha, the
     happy news,
The conquest of Messene, hath already
Enrich'd thy knowledge.
CAL.   With the circumstance
And manner of the fight, related faithfully [30
By Prophilus himself. — But, pray, sir, tell me
How doth the youthful general demean
His actions in these fortunes?
PRO.   Excellent Princess,
Your own fair eyes may soon report a truth
Unto your judgment, with what moderation,
Calmness of nature, measure, bounds, and
     limits
Of thankfulness and joy, 'a doth digest
Such amplitude of his success as would
In others, moulded of a spirit less clear,
Advance 'em to comparison with Heaven; [40
But Ithocles —
CAL.   Your friend —
PRO.   He is so, madam,
In which the period of my fate consists:
He, in this firmament of honor, stands
Like a star fix'd, not mov'd with [22] any thun-
     der
Of popular applause or sudden lightning
Of self-opinion; he hath serv'd his country,
And thinks 't was but his duty.
CROT.   You describe
A miracle of man.
AMY.   Such, Crotolon,
On forfeit of a king's word, thou wilt find
     him. —   *Flourish.*
Hark, warning of his coming! All attend
     him.   50

Enter ITHOCLES, HEMOPHIL, *and* GRONEAS;
the rest of the Lords *ushering him in.*

Return into these arms, thy home, thy sanctu-
     ary,
Delight of Sparta, treasure of my bosom,
Mine own, own Ithocles.
ITH.   Your humblest subject.
ARM. Proud of the blood I claim an interest
     in,

[22] By.

As brother to thy mother, I embrace thee,
Right noble Nephew.
ITH.   Sir, your love's too partial.
CROT. Our country speaks by me, who by
     thy valor,
Wisdom, and service shares in this great ac-
     tion,
Returning thee, in part of thy due merits,
A general welcome.
ITH.   You exceed in bounty. [60
CAL. Christalla, Philema, the chaplet.
     [*Takes it.*] — Ithocles,
Upon the wings of Fame the singular
And chosen fortune of an high attempt
Is borne so past the view of common sight,
That I myself with mine own hands have
     wrought,
To crown thy temples, this provincial gar-
     land: [23]
Accept, wear, and enjoy it as our gift,
Deserv'd, not purchas'd.
ITH.   Y' are a royal maid.
AMY. She is in all our daughter.
ITH.   Let me blush,
Acknowledging how poorly I have serv'd, [70
What nothings I have done, compar'd with th'
     honors
Heap'd on the issue of a willing mind;
In that lay mine ability, that only.
For who is he so sluggish from his birth,
So little worthy of a name or country,
That owes not out of gratitude for life
A debt of service, in what kind soever
Safety or counsel of the commonwealth
Requires, for payment?
CAL.   'A speaks truth.
ITH.   Whom Heaven
Is pleas'd to style victorious, there, to such, [80
Applause runs madding, like the drunken
     priests
In Bacchus' sacrifices, without reason,
Voicing the leader-on a demigod;
Whenas, indeed, each common soldier's blood
Drops down as current coin in that hard pur-
     chase
As his whose much more delicate condition
Hath suck'd the milk of ease: judgment com-
     mands,
But resolution executes. I use not,
Before this royal presence, these fit slights [24]
As in contempt of such as can direct;   90

[23] "The wreath (of laurel) . . . which the
ancients conferred on those who . . . had added
a province to the empire." (Gifford.)
[24] *I.e.*, these appropriate depreciatory expressions.

My speech hath other end : not to attribute
All praise to one man's fortune, which is
    strengthed
By many hands. For instance, here is Pro-
    philus,
A gentleman — I cannot flatter truth —
Of much desert ; and, though in other rank,
Both Hemophil and Groneas were not miss-
    ing
To wish their country's peace ; for, in a word,
All there did strive their best, and 't was our
    duty.
    AMY. Courtiers turn soldiers ! — We vouch-
    safe our hand.   [*They kiss his hand.*]
Observe your great example.
    HEM.   With all diligence. [100
    GRO. Obsequiously and hourly.
    AMY.   Some repose
After these toils are [25] needful. We must
    think on
Conditions for the conquered ; they expect [26]
    'em.
On ! — Come, my Ithocles.
    EUPH. [*to* PROPHILUS]   Sir, with your
    favor,
I need not a supporter.[27]
    PRO.   Fate instructs me.
        Exeunt [all but] HEMOPHIL, [*who*] *stays*
        CHRISTALLA ; [*and*] GRONEAS, [*who*
        stays*] PHILEMA.
    CHRIS. With me?
    PHIL.   Indeed, I dare not stay.
    HEM.   Sweet lady,
Soldiers are blunt — your lip.
    CHRIS.   Fie, this is rudeness ;
You went not hence such creatures.
    GRO.   Spirit of valor
Is of a mounting nature.
    PHIL.   It appears so. —
Pray, in earnest, how many men apiece   110
Have you two been the death of ?
    GRO.   'Faith, not many ;
We were compos'd of mercy.
    HEM.   For our daring,
You heard the general's approbation
Before the King.
    CHRIS.   You " wish'd your coun-
    try's peace ; "
That show'd your charity. Where are your
    spoils,
Such as the soldier fights for ?
    PHIL.   They are coming.

CHRIS. By the next carrier, are they not ?
    GRO.   Sweet Philema,
When I was in the thickest of mine enemies,
Slashing off one man's head, another's nose,
Another's arms and legs —
    PHIL.   And all together. [120
    GRO. Then would I with a sigh remember
    thee,
And cry " Dear Philema, 't is for thy sake
I do these deeds of wonder ! " — Dost not love
    me
With all thy heart now?
    PHIL.   Now as heretofore.
I have not put my love to use ; [28] the principal
Will hardly yield an interest.
    GRO.   By Mars,
I 'll marry thee !
    PHIL.   By Vulcan,[29] y' are forsworn,
Except my mind do alter strangely.
    GRO.   One word.
    CHRIS. You lie beyond all modesty — for-
    bear me.
    HEM. I 'll make thee mistress of a city ;
    't is   130
Mine own by conquest.
    CHRIS.   By petition ; sue for 't
In forma pauperis.[30] — City? kennel ! — Gal-
    lants,
Off with your f[e]athers ; put on aprons, gal-
    lants ;
Learn to reel,[31] thrum,[32] or trim a lady's dog,
And be good, quiet souls of peace, hobgoblins !
    HEM. Christalla !
    CHRIS.   Practise to drill hogs, in hope
To share in the acorns. — Soldiers? corn-
    cutters !
But not so valiant : they ofttimes draw blood,
Which you durst never do. When you have
    practis'd
More wit or more civility, we 'll rank 'ee   140
I' th' list of men : till then, brave things-at-
    arms,
Dare not to speak to us — most potent Gro-
    neas !
    PHIL. And Hemophil the hardy ! — at your
    services.
        Exeunt CHRISTALLA *and* PHILEMA.
    GRO. They scorn us as they did before we
    went.

[25] Mod. eds. *is.*   [26] Are waiting for.
[27] Evidently Prophilus has offered his arm or
hand.

[28] Out at interest ; *i.e.*, I have not lent my love
to anyone, and therefore am not expecting to receive
anything in return.
[29] Who got the better of Mars.
[30] A pauper being entitled to exemption from court
costs and to service of counsel gratis.
[31] Wind yarn or thread.
[32] Make tufts in cloth.

HEM. Hang 'em! let us scorn them, and be
    reveng'd.

GRO. Shall we?

HEM.   We will: and when we slight them
    thus,
Instead of following them, they'll follow us;
It is a woman's nature.

GRO.   'T is a scurvy one. *Exeunt.*

SCENE III [33]

Enter TECNICUS, *a philosopher, and* ORGILUS
    disguised like a scholar of his.

TEC. Tempt not the stars, young man;
    thou canst not play
With the severity of Fate; this change
Of habit [34] and disguise in outward view
Hides not the secrets of thy soul within thee
From their quick-piercing eyes, which dive at
    all times
Down to thy thoughts. In thy aspect I note
A consequence of danger.[35]

ORG.   Give me leave,
Grave Tecnicus, without foredooming destiny,
Under thy roof to ease my silent griefs
By applying to my hidden wounds the balm [10
Of thy oraculous lectures. If my fortune
Run such a crooked byway as to wrest
My steps to ruin, yet thy learned precepts
Shall call me back and set my footings straight.
I will not court the world.

TEC.   Ah, Orgilus,
Neglects in young men of delights and life
Run often to extremities; they care not
For harms to others who contemn their own.

ORG. But I, most learned artist, am not so
    much
At odds with nature that I grudge the thrift [20
Of any true deserver; nor doth malice
Of present hopes [36] so check them with despair
As that I yield to thought of more affliction
Than what is incident to frailty.[37] Wherefore,
Impute not this retired course of living
Some little time to any other cause
Than what I justly render: the information
Of an unsettled mind, as the effect
Must clearly witness.

TEC.   Spirit of truth inspire thee!
On these conditions I conceal thy change, [30
And willingly admit thee for an auditor. —
I 'll to my study.

ORG.   I to contemplations

[33] A grove in the palace grounds.
[34] Clothing.   [35] Dangerous outcome.
[36] Injury to my present hopes.
[37] *I.e.*, the general frailty of men.

In these delightful walks. — [*Exit* TECNICUS.]
    Thus metamorph[o]s'd,
I may without suspicion hearken after
Penthea's usage and Euphranea's faith.
Love, thou art full of mystery! The deities
Themselves are not secure [38] in searching out
The secrets of those flames, which, hidden,
    waste
A breast made tributary to the laws
Of beauty; physic yet hath never found   40
A remedy to cure a lover's wound. —
Ha! who are those that cross yon private walk
Into the shadowing grove in amorous foldings?

PROPHILUS *passeth over, supporting* EUPHRA-
    NEA, *and whispering.*

My sister! Oh, my sister! 't is Euphranea
With Prophilus; supported, too! I would
It were an apparition! Prophilus
Is Ithocles his [39] friend; it strangely puzzles me.
Again? Help me, my book; this scholar's
    habit
Must stand [40] my privilege. My mind is
    busy;
Mine eyes and ears are open.

                Walk by, reading.

Enter again PROPHILUS *and* EUPHRANEA.

PRO.   Do not waste [50
The span of this stol'n time, lent by the gods
For precious use, in niceness! [41] Bright Eu-
    phranea,
Should I repeat old vows, or study new,
For purchase of belief to my desires, —

ORG. [*aside*] Desires!

PRO.   My service, my integrity, —

ORG. [*aside*] That 's better.

PRO.   I should but repeat a lesson
Oft conn'd without a prompter but thine eyes.
My love is honorable.

ORG. [*aside*]   So was mine
To my Penthea, chastely honorable.

PRO. Nor wants there more addition to my
    wish   60
Of happiness than having thee a wife;
Already sure of Ithocles, a friend
Firm and unalterable.

ORG. [*aside*]   But a brother
More cruel than the grave.

EUPH.   What can you look for,
In answer to your noble protestations,
From an unskilful [42] maid, but language suited
To a divided mind?

[38] Free from uncertainty.   [39] Ithocles's.
[40] Be.   [41] Coyness.   [42] Inexperienced.

ORG. [*aside*] Hold out, Euphranea!

EUPH. Know, Prophilus, I never under-
valued,
From the first time you mentioned worthy
love,
Your merit, means, or person; it had been [70
A fault of judgment in me, and a dullness
In my affections, not to weigh and thank
My better stars that offered me the grace
Of so much blissfulness. For, to speak truth,
The law of my desires kept equal pace
With yours, nor have I left that resolution;
But only, in a word, whatever choice
Lives nearest in my heart must first procure
Consent both from my father and my brother,
Ere he can own me his.

ORG. [*aside*] She is forsworn else. [80

PRO. Leave me that task.

EUPH. My brother, ere he parted
To Athens, had my oath.

ORG. [*aside*] Yes, yes, 'a had, sure.

PRO. I doubt not, with the means the court
supplies,
But to prevail at pleasure.

ORG. [*aside*] Very likely!

PRO. Meantime, best, dearest, I may build
my hopes
On the foundation of thy constant suff'rance [43]
In [44] any opposition.

EUPH. Death shall sooner
Divorce life and the joys I have in living
Than my chaste vows from truth.

PRO. On thy fair hand
I seal the like.

ORG. [*aside*] There is no faith in
woman. 90
Passion, oh, be contain'd! My very heartstrings
Are on the tenters.[45]

EUPH. Sir, we are overheard.
Cupid protect us! 'T was a stirring, sir,
Of some one near.

PRO. Your fears are needless, lady;
None have access into these private pleasures [46]
Except some near in court, or bosom-student
From Tecnicus his oratory, granted
By special favor lately from the King
Unto the grave philosopher.

EUPH. Methinks
I hear one talking to himself — I see him. [100

PRO. 'T is a poor scholar, as I told you,
lady.

ORG. [*aside*] I am discovered. — [*as if
studying*] Say it: is it possible,
With a smooth tongue, a leering countenance,
Flattery, or force of reason — I come t' ee
sir —
To turn or to appease the raging sea?
Answer to that. — Your art! what art to
catch
And hold fast in a net the sun's small atoms?
No, no; they 'll out, they 'll out: ye may as
easily
Outrun a cloud driven by a northern blast
As fiddle-faddle so! Peace, or speak sense. [110

EUPH. Call you this thing a scholar? 'Las,
he 's lunatic.

PRO. Observe him, sweet; 't is but his recreation.

ORG. But will you hear a little? You are
so tetchy,
You keep no rule in argument. Philosophy
Works not upon impossibilities,
But natural conclusions. — Mew! — absurd! [47]
The metaphysics are but speculations
Of the celestial bodies, or such accidents
As not mix'd perfectly, in the air engend'red
Appear to us unnatural; that 's all. — 120
Prove it; — yet, with a reverence to your
gravity,
I 'll balk illiterate sauciness, submitting
My sole opinion to the touch of writers.

PRO. Now let us fall in with him.
[*They come forward.*]

ORG. Ha, ha, ha!
These apish boys, when they but taste the
grammates [48]
And principles of theory, imagine
They can oppose their teachers. Confidence
Leads many into errors.

PRO. By your leave, sir.

EUPH. Are you a scholar, friend?

ORG. I am, gay creature,
With pardon of your deities, a mushroom [130
On whom the dew of heaven drops now and
then;
The sun shines on me too, I thank his beams!
Sometime I feel their warmth, and eat and
sleep.

PRO. Does Tecnicus read to [49] thee?

ORG. Yes, forsooth;
He is my master surely; yonder door
Opens upon his study.

[43] Endurance; *i.e.*, fidelity. [44] In the event of.
[45] Hooks for stretching cloth.
[46] Pleasure grounds.

[47] "A term of the schools . . . used when false
conclusions are illogically deduced from the oppo-
nent's premises." (Gifford.)
[48] Rudiments.
[49] Teach.

PRO.   Happy creatures!
Such people toil not, sweet, in heats of state,
Nor sink in thaws of greatness; their affections
Keep order with the limits of their modesty;
Their love is love of virtue. — What's thy
    name?   140
    ORG. Aplotes, sumptuous master, a poor
        wretch.
    EUPH. Dost thou want anything?
    ORG.   Books, Venus, books.
    PRO. Lady, a new conceit 50 comes in my
        thought,
And most available for both our comforts.
    EUPH. My Lord —
    PRO.   Whiles I endeavor to deserve
Your father's blessing to our loves, this scholar
May daily at some certain hours attend 51
What notice I can write of my success,
Here in this grove, and give it to your hands;
The like from you to me: so can we never, [150
Barr'd of our mutual speech, want sure intelli-
    gence,
And thus our hearts may talk when our
    tongues cannot.
    EUPH. Occasion is most favorable; use it.
    PRO. Aplotes, wilt thou wait us twice a day,
At nine i' th' morning and at four at night,
Here in this bower, to convey such letters
As each shall send to other? Do it willingly,
Safely, and secretly, and I will furnish
Thy study, or what else thou canst desire.
    ORG. Jove, make me thankful, thankful, I
        beseech thee,   160
Propitious Jove! I will prove sure and trusty.
You will not fail me books?
    PRO.   Nor aught besides
Thy heart can wish. This lady's name 's Eu-
    phranea,
Mine Prophilus.
    ORG.   I have a pretty memory;
It must prove my best friend. I will not miss
One minute of the hours appointed.
    PRO.   Write
The books thou wouldst have bought thee in a
    note,
Or take thyself some money.
    ORG.   No, no money;
Money to scholars is a spirit invisible —
We dare not finger it: or books or noth-
    ing.   170
    PRO. Books of what sort thou wilt; do not
        forget
Our names.
    ORG.   I warrant 'ee, I warrant 'ee.
---
50 Idea.   51 Wait for.

    PRO. Smile, Hymen, on the growth of our
        desires;
We'll feed thy torches with eternal fires!
            Exeunt [PROPHILUS *and* EUPHRANEA].
    ORG. Put out thy torches, Hymen, or their
        light
Shall meet a darkness of eternal night!
Inspire me, Mercury, with swift deceits.
Ingenious Fate has leap'd into mine arms,
Beyond the compass of my brain. 52   Mortality
Creeps on the dung of earth, and cannot
    reach 53   180
The riddles which are purpos'd by the gods.
Great arts best write themselves in their own
    stories;
They die too basely who outlive their glories.
                                            Exit.

ACT II — SCENE I 1

Enter BASSANES *and* PHULAS.

    BASS. I'll have that window next the street
        damm'd up;
It gives too full a prospect to temptation,
And courts a gazer's glances. There's a lust
Committed by the eye, that sweats and trav-
    ails,
Plots, wakes, contrives, till the deformed bear-
    whelp,2
Adultery, be lick'd into the act,
The very act. That light shall be damm'd up;
D'ee hear, sir?
    PHU.   I do hear, my Lord; a mason
Shall be provided suddenly.3
    BASS.   Some rogue,
Some rogue of your confederacy — factor 4 [10
For slaves and strumpets! — to convey close 5
    packets
From this spruce springal 6 and the tother
    youngster,
That gaudy earwig,7 or my Lord your patron,
Whose pensioner you are. — I'll tear thy
    throat out,
Son of a cat, ill-looking hound's-head — rip up
Thy ulcerous maw, if I but scent a paper,
A scroll, but half as big as what can cover

52 Beyond my capacity to plan.
53 Succeed in understanding.
1 A room in Bassanes's house.
2 Which was supposed to be born a "confused
lump" (*e.g.,* Burton's *Anatomy of Melancholy,* cited
by Sherman), afterwards licked "into form" by
the mother.
3 Immediately.   4 Agent.
5 Secret.   6 Youth.
7 *I.e.,* insinuating person. Q *Eare-wrig.*

A wart upon thy nose, a spot, a pimple,
Directed to my lady : it may prove
A mystical preparative to lewdness.   20
  Phu. Care shall be had ; I will turn every
    thread
About me to an eye. — [*aside*] Here 's a sweet
    life !
  Bass. The city housewives, cunning in the
    traffic
Of chamber merchandise, set all at price
By wholesale ; yet they wipe their mouths
    and simper,
Cull,[8] kiss, and cry " sweetheart," and stroke
    the head
Which they have branch'd ;[9] and all is well
    again !
Dull clods of dirt, who dare not feel the rubs
Stuck on [their][10] foreheads !
  Phu.   'T is a villainous world ;
One cannot hold his own in 't.
  Bass.   Dames at court, [30
Who flaunt in riots, run another bias ;[11]
Their pleasure heaves the patient ass that
    suffers
Up on the stilts of office, titles, incomes ;
Promotion justifies the shame, and sues for 't.
Poor Honor, thou art stabb'd, and bleed'st to
    death
By such unlawful hire ! The country mistress
Is yet more wary, and in blushes hides
Whatever trespass draws her troth to guilt.
But all are false ; on this truth I am bold :
No woman but can fall, and doth or would. —
Now for the newest news about the city ; [41
What blab the voices, sirrah?
  Phu.   O, my Lord,
The rarest, quaintest, strangest, tickling news
That ever —
  Bass. Hey-day ! up and ride me, rascal !
What is 't?
  Phu.   Forsooth, they say the King has
    mew'd[12]
All his gray beard, instead of which is budded
Another of a pure carnation color,
Speckled with green and russet.
  Bass.   Ignorant block ![13]
  Phu. Yes, truly ; and 't is talk'd about
    the streets
That, since Lord Ithocles came home, the
    lions   50
Never left roaring, at which noise the bears
Have danc'd their very hearts out.

  Bass.   Dance out thine too.
  Phu. Besides, Lord Orgilus is fled to Athens
Upon a fiery dragon, and 't is thought
'A never can return.
  Bass.   Grant it, Apollo !
  Phu. Moreover, please your Lordship, 't is
    reported
For certain, that whoever is found jealous
Without apparent proof that 's wife is wanton
Shall be divorc'd ; but this is but she-news —
I had it from a midwife. I have more yet. [60
  Bass. Antic,[14] no more ! Idiots and stupid
    fools
Grate my calamities. Why to be fair
Should yield presumption of a faulty soul —
Look to the doors.
  Phu. [*aside*]   The horn of plenty[15]
    crest him !   *Exit* Phulas.
  Bass. Swarms of confusion huddle in my
    thoughts
In rare distemper. — Beauty ! Oh, it is
An unmatch'd blessing or a horrid curse.

Enter Penthea *and* Grausis, *an old Lady.*

She comes, she comes ! so shoots the morning
    forth,
Spangled with pearls of transparent dew.
The way to poverty is to be rich,   70
As I in her am wealthy ; but for her,
In all contents a bankrupt. — Lov'd Penthea !
How fares my heart's best joy?
  Grau.   In sooth, not well ;
She is so oversad.
  Bass.   Leave chattering, magpie. —
Thy brother is return'd, sweet — safe, and
    honor'd
With a triumphant victory ; thou shalt visit
    him.
We will to court, where, if it be thy pleasure,
Thou shalt appear in such a ravishing lustre
Of jewels above value, that the dames
Who brave[16] it there, in rage to be out-
    shin'd,   80
Shall hide them in their closets, and unseen
Fret in their tears ; whiles every wond'ring
    eye
Shall crave none other brightness but thy
    presence.
Choose thine own recreations ; be a queen
Of what delights thou fanciest best, what com-
    pany,

---

[8] Embrace.   [9] Horned, cuckolded.
[10] Conj. Dyce ; Q *the.*
[11] Course, direction.   [12] Moulted.   [13] Blockhead.

[14] Fool.
[15] Cornucopia ; but allusive to the horns of the
cuckold.
[16] Display their finery.

What place, what times ; do anything, do all
   things
Youth can command, so [17] thou wilt chase
   these clouds
From the pure firmament of thy fair looks.
   GRAU. Now 't is well said, my Lord. —
     What, lady ! laugh,
Be merry ; time is precious.
   BASS. [*aside*]   Furies whip thee ! [90
   PEN. Alas, my Lord, this language to your
     handmaid
Sounds as would music to the deaf ; I need
No braveries nor cost of art to draw
The whiteness of my name into offence.
Let such, if any such there are, who covet
A curiosity of admiration,
By laying out their plenty to full view,
Appear in gaudy outsides ; my attires
Shall suit the inward fashion of my mind ;
From which, if your opinion, nobly plac'd, [100
Change not the livery your words bestow,
My fortunes with my hopes are at the highest.
   BASS. This house, methinks, stands some-
     what too much inward ;
It is too melancholy ; we 'll remove
Nearer the court. Or what thinks my Penthea
Of the delightful island we command ?
Rule me as thou canst wish.
   PEN.   I am no mistress.
Whither you please, I must attend ; all ways
Are alike pleasant to me.
   GRAU.   Island ? prison !
A prison is as gaysome ; we 'll no islands ; [110
Marry, out upon 'em ! Whom shall we see
   there ?
Sea gulls, and porpoises, and water rats,
And crabs, and mews,[18] and dogfish ; goodly
   gear
For a young lady's dealing, or an old one's.
On no terms islands ; I 'll be stew'd first.
   BASS. [*aside to* GRAUSIS]   Grausis,
You are a juggling bawd. — This sadness,
   sweetest,
Becomes not youthful blood. — [*aside to*
   GRAUSIS] I 'll have you pounded. —
For my sake put on a more cheerful mirth ;
Thou 'lt mar thy cheeks, and make me old in
   griefs.—
[*aside to* GRAUSIS] Damnable bitch-fox !
   GRAU.   I am thick of hearing, [120
Still, when the wind blows southerly. — What
   think 'ee
If your fresh lady breed young bones, my
   Lord ?

Would not a chopping boy d 'ee good at
   heart ?
But, as you said —
   BASS. [*aside to* GRAUSIS]   I 'll spit thee
     on a stake,
Or chop thee into collops ! [19]
   GRAU.   Pray, speak louder.
Sure, sure the wind blows south still.
   PEN.   Thou prat'st madly.
   BASS. 'T is very hot ; I sweat extremely.

        Re-enter PHULAS.

                       Now ?
   PHU. A herd of lords, sir.
   BASS.   Ha ?
   PHU.   A flock of ladies.
   BASS. Where ?
   PHU.   Shoals of horses.
   BASS.   Peasant, how ?
   PHU.   Caroches [20]
In drifts ; th' one enter, th' other stand with-
     out, sir ;   130
And now I vanish.   *Exit* PHULAS.

   Enter PROPHILUS, HEMOPHIL, GRONEAS,
     CHRISTALLA, *and* PHILEMA.

   PRO.   Noble Bassanes !
   BASS. Most welcome, Prophilus ; ladies,
     gentlemen,
To all my heart is open ; you all honor me, —
[*aside*] A tympany [21] swells in my head al-
     ready —
Honor me bountifully. — [*aside*] How they
     flutter,
Wagtails [22] and jays together !
   PRO.   From your brother,
By virtue of your love to him, I require
Your instant presence, fairest.
   PEN.   He is well, sir ?
   PRO. The gods preserve him ever ! Yet,
     dear beauty,
I find some alteration in him lately,   140
Since his return to Sparta. — My good
     Lord,
I pray, use no delay.
   BASS.   We had not needed
An invitation, if his sister's health
Had not fallen into question. — Haste, Pen-
     thea,

[17] Provided.   [18] Sea gulls.

[19] Small bits, mincemeat.
[20] Coaches.
[21] Swelling; an allusion to the horns of the
cuckold.
[22] The name of these birds was often applied to
wanton women.

Slack not a minute. — Lead the way, good
  Prophilus ;
I 'll follow step by step.
  PRO.   Your arm, fair madam.
            Exeunt [all but] [23] BASSANES *and*
                  GRAUSIS.
  BASS. One word with your old Bawdship :
        th' hadst been better
Rail'd at the sins [24] thou worshipp'st than
        have thwarted
My will. I 'll use thee cursedly.
  GRAU.   You dote ;
You are beside yourself. A politician   [150
In jealousy ? No, y' are too gross, too vulgar.
Pish, teach not me my trade ; I know my cue.
My crossing you sinks me into her trust,
By which I shall know all ; my trade 's a sure
        one.
  BASS. Forgive me, Grausis ; 't was consid-
        eration
I relish'd not ; [25] but have a care now.
  GRAU.   Fear not ;
I am no new-come-to-'t.
  BASS.   Thy life 's upon it,
And so is mine. My agonies are infinite.
                          Exeunt omnes.

SCENE II [26]

Enter ITHOCLES, *alone.*

  ITH. Ambition ! 't is of vipers' breed : it
        gnaws
A passage through the womb that gave it
        motion.
Ambition, like a seeled [27] dove, mounts up-
        ward,
Higher and higher still, to perch on clouds,
But tumbles headlong down with heavier ruin.
So squibs and crackers fly into the air,
Then, only breaking with a noise, they vanish
In stench and smoke. Morality, appli'd
To timely practice, keeps the soul in tune,
At whose sweet music all our actions dance ; [10
But this is form of books and school [28] tradi-
        tion ;
It physics not the sickness of a mind
Broken with griefs. Strong fevers are not
        eas'd

[23] Q *omnes sed.*
[24] Gifford emends *saints.*
[25] A point I failed to appreciate.
[26] Unlocated ; perhaps a room in the palace.
[27] Temporarily blinded by having had its eyelids
sewed up. The dove would then soar straight up
till its strength was exhausted, when it would fall
at the feet of the " sportsmen."
[28] Scholastic.

With counsel, but with best receipts and
    means ;
Means, speedy means and certain ; that 's the
    cure.

Enter ARMOSTES *and* CROTOLON.

  ARM. You stick, Lord Crotolon, upon a
        point
Too nice [29] and too unnecessary ; Prophilus
Is every way desertful. I am confident
Your wisdom is too ripe to need instruction
From your son's tutelage.
  CROT.   Yet not so ripe,   20
My Lord Armostes, that it dares to dote
Upon the painted meat [30] of smooth persua-
        sion,
Which tempts me to a breach of faith.
  ITH.   Not yet
Resolv'd, my Lord ? Why, if your son's con-
        sent
Be so available, we 'll write to Athens
For his repair to Sparta. The King's hand
Will join with our desires ; he has been mov'd
        to 't.
  ARM. Yes, and the King himself impor-
        tun'd [31] Crotolon
For a dispatch.
  CROT.   Kings may command ; their wills
Are laws not to be questioned.
  ITH.   By this marriage [30
You knit an union so devout, so hearty,
Between your loves to me and mine to yours,
As if mine own blood had an interest in
        it ;
For Prophilus is mine, and I am his.
  CROT. My Lord, my Lord ! —
  ITH.   What, good sir? Speak your
        thought.
  CROT. Had this sincerity been real once,
My Orgilus had not been now unwiv'd,
Nor your lost sister buried in a bride-bed.
Your uncle here, Armostes, knows this truth ;
For had your father Thrasus liv'd, — but
        peace   40
Dwell in his grave ! I have done.
  ARM.   Y' are bold and bitter.
  ITH. *[aside]* 'A presses home the injury ; it
        smarts. —
No reprehensions, Uncle ; I deserve 'em. —
Yet, gentle sir, consider what the heat
Of an unsteady youth, a giddy brain,
Green indiscretion, flattery of greatness,
Rawness of judgment, wilfulness in folly,

[29] Fine, scrupulous.   [30] Gifford conj. *bait.*
[31] Accented on second syllable.

Thoughts vagrant as the wind and as uncer-
tain,
Might lead a boy in years to. 'T was a fault,
A capital fault ; for then I could not dive [50
Into the secrets of commanding love ;
Since when, experience, by the extremities (in
others),
Hath forc'd me collect.[32] And, trust me,
Crotolon,
I will redeem those wrongs with any service
Your satisfaction can require for current.[33]
ARM. Thy acknowledgment is satisfac-
tion. —
What would you more?
CROT. I'm conquer'd ; if Euphranea
Herself admit the motion, let it be so ;
I doubt not my son's liking.
ITH. Use my fortunes,
Life, power, sword, and heart — all are your
own. 60

Enter BASSANES, PROPHILUS, CALANTHA, PEN-
THEA, EUPHRANEA, CHRISTALLA, PHILEMA,
and GRAUSIS.

ARM. The Princess, with your sister.
CAL. I present 'ee
A stranger here in court, my Lord ; for did not
Desire of seeing you draw her abroad,
We had not been made happy in her company.
ITH. You are a gracious princess. — Sister,
wedlock
Holds too severe a passion in your nature,
Which can engross all duty to your husband,
Without attendance on so dear a mistress. —
[*To* BASSANES] 'T is not my brother's pleasure,
I presume,
T' immure her in a chamber.
BASS. 'T is her will ; [70
She governs her own hours. Noble Ithocles,
We thank the gods for your success and welfare.
Our lady has of late been indispos'd,
Else we had waited on you with the first.
ITH. How does Penthea now?
PEN. You best know, Brother,
From whom my health and comforts are
deriv'd.
BASS. [*aside*] I like the answer well ; 't is
sad [34] and modest.
There may be tricks yet, tricks. — Have an
eye, Grausis !
CAL. Now, Crotolon, the suit we join'd in
must not
Fall by too long demur.

[32] Infer, "gather."
[33] As acceptable, to pass current. [34] Sober.

CROT. 'T is granted, Princess, [80
For my part.
ARM. With condition, that his son
Favor the contract.
CAL. Such delay is easy. —
The joys of marriage make thee, Prophilus,
A proud deserver of Euphranea's love,
And her of thy desert !
PRO. Most sweetly gracious !
BASS. The joys of marriage are the Heaven
on earth,
Life's paradise, great Princess, the soul's quiet,
Sinews of concord, earthly immortality,
Eternity of pleasures ; no restoratives
Like to a constant woman ! — [*aside*] but
where is she? 90
'T would puzzle all the gods but to create
Such a new monster. — I can speak by proof,
For I rest in Elysium ; 't is my happiness.
CROT. Euphranea, how are you resolv'd,[35]
speak freely,
In your affections to this gentleman?
EUPH. Nor more nor less than as his love
assures me ;
Which — if your liking with my brother's war-
rants —
I cannot but approve in all points worthy.
CROT. So, so. — [*to* PROPHILUS] I know
your answer.
ITH. 'T had been pity
To sunder hearts so equally consented. 100

Enter HEMOPHIL.

HEM. The King, Lord Ithocles, commands
your presence ; —
And, fairest Princess, yours.
CAL. We will attend him.

Enter GRONEAS.

GRO. Where are the lords? All must unto
the King
Without delay : the Prince of Argos —
CAL. Well, sir?
GRO. Is coming to the court, sweet lady.
CAL. How !
The Prince of Argos?
GRO. 'T was my fortune, madam,
T' enjoy the honor of these happy tidings.
ITH. Penthea ! —
PEN. Brother?
ITH. Let me an hour hence
Meet you alone within the palace grove ;
I have some secret with you. — Prithee,
friend, 110

[35] Decided.

Conduct her thither, and have special care
The walks be clear'd of any to disturb us.
    Pro. I shall.
    Bass. [*aside*]   How 's that?
    Ith.   Alone, pray be alone. —
I am your creature, Princess. — On, my
    Lords!   *Exeunt [all but]* Bassanes.
    Bass. Alone! alone! What means that
    word " alone "?
Why might not I be there? — hum! — he 's
    her brother.
Brothers and sisters are but flesh and blood,
And this same whoreson court-ease is tempta-
    tion
To a rebellion in the veins.[36] — Besides,
His fine friend Prophilus must be her guar-
    dian.   120
Why may not he dispatch a business nimbly
Before the other come? — or — pand'ring,
    pand'ring
For one another, — be 't to sister, mother,
Wife, cousin, anything, — 'mongst youths of
    mettle
Is in request; it is so — stubborn fate!
But if I be a cuckold, and can know it,
I will be fell, and fell.

Re-enter Groneas.

    Gro.   My Lord, y' are call'd for.
    Bas. Most heartily I thank ye. Where 's
    my wife, pray?
    Gro. Retir'd amongst the ladies.
    Bass.   Still I thank 'ee.
There 's an old waiter [37] with her; saw you her
    too?   130
    Gro. She sits i' th' presence-lobby fast
    asleep, sir.
    Bass. Asleep! [a]sleep, sir!
    Gro.   Is your Lordship troubled?
You will not to the King?
    Bass.   Your humblest vassal.
    Gro. Your servant, my good Lord.
    Bass.   I wait your footsteps.
                            Exeunt.

Scene III [38]

[*Enter*] Prophilus [*and*] Penthea.

    Pro. In this walk, lady, will your brother
    find you;
And, with your favor, give me leave a little
To work a preparation. In his fashion
I have observ'd of late some kind of slackness

To such alacrity as nature [39]
And custom took delight in; sadness grows
Upon his recreations, which he hoards
In such a willing silence, that to question
The grounds will argue [little] [40] skill in friend-
    ship,
And less good manners.
    Pen.   Sir, I 'm not inquisitive [10
Of secrecies without an invitation.
    Pro. With pardon, lady, not a syllable
Of mine implies so rude a sense; the drift —

Enter Orgilus, [*disguised as before*].

[*to* Orgilus] Do thy best
To make this lady merry for an hour.   *Exit.*
    Org. Your will shall be a law, sir.
    Pen.   Prithee, leave me;
I have some private thoughts I would account
    with;
Use thou thine own.
    Org.   Speak on, fair nymph; our souls
Can dance as well to music of the spheres
As any's who have feasted with the gods. [20
    Pen. Your school terms are too trouble-
    some.
    Org.   What Heaven
Refines mortality from dross of earth
But such as uncompounded beauty hallows
With glorified perfection?
    Pen.   Set thy wits
In a less wild proportion.
    Org.   Time can never
On the white table of unguilty faith
Write counterfeit dishonor; turn those eyes,
The arrows of pure love, upon that fire
Which once rose to a flame, perfum'd with
    vows
As sweetly scented as the incense smoking [30
On Vesta's [41] [altars]; [42] virgin tears,[43] like
The holiest odors, sprinkled dews to feed 'em
And to increase their fervor.
    Pen.   Be not frantic.
    Org. All pleasures are but mere imagina-
    tion,
Feeding the hungry appetite with steam
And sight of banquet, whilst the body pines,
Not relishing the real [43] taste of food:
Such is the leanness of a heart divided
From intercourse of troth-contracted loves; [39
No horror should deface that precious figure
Seal'd with the lively stamp of equal souls.

---

[36] In the blood; *i.e.*, in the sensual nature.
[37] Servant.   [38] The grove.
[39] Gifford adds *once;* Weber supplies "as *once his*
nature."   [40] Add. Weber.
[41] Q transposes *On Vesta's* and *The holiest.* Cor.
Oliphant.
[42] Q *Artars.*   [43] Dissyllabic.

PEN. Away! some Fury hath bewitch'd
    thy tongue.
The breath of ignorance, that flies from
    thence,
Ripens a knowledge in me of afflictions
Above all suff'rance. — Thing of talk, begone!
Begone, without reply!
    ORG.   Be just, Penthea,
In thy commands; when thou send'st forth a
    doom
Of banishment, know first on whom it lights.
Thus I take off the shroud in which my
    cares
Are folded up from view of common eyes. [50
        [*Throws off his scholar's dress.*]
What is thy sentence next?
    PEN.   Rash man! thou layest
A blemish on mine honor, with the hazard
Of thy too desperate life; yet I profess,
By all the laws of ceremonious wedlock,
I have not given admittance to one thought
Of female change since cruelty enforc'd
Divorce betwixt my body and my heart.
Why would you fall from goodness thus?
    ORG.   Oh, rather
Examine me, how I could live to say
I have been much, much wrong'd. 'T is for
    thy sake   60
I put on this imposture. Dear Penthea,
If thy soft bosom be not turn'd to marble,
Thou 't pity our calamities; my interest
Confirms me thou art mine still.
    PEN.   Lend your hand;
With both of mine I clasp it thus, thus kiss it,
Thus kneel before ye.
    ORG.   You instruct my duty.
    [*They remain for some moments kneel-
        ing, with clasped hands.*]
    PEN. We may stand up. — Have you aught
    else to urge
Of new demand? As for the old, forget it;
'T is buried in an everlasting silence,
And shall be, shall be ever. What more would
    ye?   70
    ORG. I would possess my wife; the equity
Of very reason bids me.
    PEN.   Is that all?
    ORG. Why, 't is the all of me, myself.
    PEN.   Remove
Your steps some distance from me. — At this
    space
A few words I dare change; but first put on
Your borrowed shape.
    ORG.   You are obey'd; 't is done.
        [*He resumes his disguise.*]

PEN. How, Orgilus, by promise I was thine
The Heavens do witness; they can witness too
A rape done on my truth; how I do love thee
Yet, Orgilus, and yet, must best appear   80
In tendering thy freedom; for I find
The constant preservation of thy merit,
By thy not daring to attempt my fame
With injury of any loose conceit,
Which might give deeper wounds to discon-
    tents.
Continue this fair race: [44] then, though I can-
    not
Add to thy comfort, yet I shall more often
Remember from what fortune I am fallen,
And pity mine own ruin. — Live, live
    happy,
Happy in thy next choice, that thou mayst
    people   90
This barren age with virtues in thy issue!
And oh, when thou art married, think on me
With mercy, not contempt! I hope thy wife,
Hearing my story, will not scorn my fall. —
Now let us part.
    ORG.   Part! yet advise thee better;
Penthea is the wife to Orgilus,
And ever shall be.
    PEN.   Never shall nor will.
    ORG. How!
    PEN.   Hear me; in a word I 'll tell
    thee why.
The virgin dowry which my birth bestow'd
Is ravish'd by another; my true love   100
Abhors to think that Orgilus deserv'd
No better favors than a second bed.
    ORG. I must not take this reason.
    PEN.   To confirm it
Should I outlive my bondage, let me meet
Another worse than this and less desir'd,
If, of all the men alive, thou shouldst but
    touch
My lip or hand again!
    ORG.   Penthea, now
I tell 'ee, you grow wanton in my sufferance; [45]
Come, sweet, th' art mine.
    PEN.   Uncivil sir, forbear!
Or I can turn affection into vengeance;   110
Your reputation, if you value any,
Lies bleeding at my feet. Unworthy man,
If ever henceforth thou appear in language,
Message, or letter, to betray my frailty,
I 'll call thy former protestations lust,
And curse my stars for forfeit of my judg-
    ment.

[44] Course.
[45] Reckless in regard to my suffering.

Go thou, fit only for disguise, and [walk],[46]
To hide thy shame ; this once I spare thy life.
I laugh at mine own confidence ; my sor-
    rows
By thee are made inferior to my fortunes. [120
If ever thou didst harbor worthy love,
Dare not to answer. My good genius guide
    me,
That I may never see thee more ! — Go from
    me !
ORG. [I 'll] [47] tear my veil of politic French
    off,
And stand up like a man resolv'd to do :
Action, not words, shall show me. — O
    Penthea !   *Exit* ORGILUS.
PEN. 'A sigh'd my name, sure, as he parted
    from me.
I fear I was too rough. Alas, poor gentleman,
'A look'd not like the ruins of his youth,
But like the ruins of those ruins. Honor, [130
How much we fight with weakness to pre-
    serve thee !   *[Walks aside.]*

Enter BASSANES *and* GRAUSIS.

BASS. Fie on thee ! damn thee, rotten mag-
    got, damn thee !
Sleep? sleep at court? and now? Aches,[48]
    convulsions,
Imposthumes,[49] rheums, gouts, palsies, clog
    thy bones
A dozen years more yet !
    GRAU.   Now y' are in humors.
BASS. She 's by herself : there 's hope of
    that ; she 's sad too ;
She 's in strong contemplation ; yes, and
    fix'd :
The signs are wholesome.
    GRAU.   Very wholesome, truly.
BASS. Hold your chops,[50] nightmare ! —
    Lady, come ; your brother
Is carried to his closet ; you must thither. [140
PEN. Not well, my Lord?
BASS.   A sudden fit ; 't will off !
Some surfeit or disorder. How doest, dearest?
PEN. Your news is none o' th' best.

Re-enter PROPHILUS.

PRO.   The chief of men,
The excellentest Ithocles, desires
Your presence, madam.
    BASS.   We are hasting to him.

PEN. In vain we labor in this course of life
To piece our journey out at length, or crave
Respite of breath ; our home is in the grave.
    BASS. Perfect philosophy ! [51] Then let us
    care   149
To live so, that our reckonings may fall even
When w' are to make account.
    PRO.   He cannot fear
Who builds on noble grounds : sickness or
    pain
Is the deserver's exercise ; [52] and such
Your virtuous brother to the world is known.
Speak comfort to him, lady ; be all gentle.
Stars fall but in the grossness of our sight ;
A good man dying, th' earth doth lose a light.
                  Exeunt omnes.

ACT III — SCENE I [1]

Enter TECNICUS, *and* ORGILUS *in his own*
shape.

TEC. Be well advis'd ; [2] let not a resolution
Of giddy rashness choke the breath of reason.
    ORG. It shall not, most sage master.
    TEC.   I am jealous ; [3]
For if the borrowed shape [4] so late put on
Inferr'd a consequence, we must conclude
Some violent design of sudden nature
Hath shook that shadow [5] off, to fly upon
A new-hatch'd execution. Orgilus,
Take heed thou hast not, under our integrity,
Shrouded unlawful plots ; our mortal eyes [10
Pierce not the secrets of your [heart] : [6] the
    gods
Are only privy to them.
    ORG.   Learned Tecnicus,
Such doubts are causeless ; and, to clear the
    truth
From misconceit,[7] the present state com-
    mands me.
The Prince of Argos comes himself in person
In quest of great Calantha for his bride,
Our kingdom's heir ; besides, mine only sister,
Euphranea, is dispos'd [8] to Prophilus ;
Lastly, the King is sending letters for me
To Athens, for my quick repair to court. [20
Please to accept these reasons.

[46] Emend. Kittredge ; Q *walks. I.e.*, walk ever in
that disguise, to hide thy shameful self.
    [47] Q *I'e.*
    [48] Dissyllabic.
    [49] Abscesses.   [50] Jaws.
    [51] Gifford and Dyce assign the rest of this speech
to Penthea.   [52] Discipline.
    [1] Unlocated ; probably the study of Tecnicus.
    [2] Cautious.   [3] Suspicious.
    [4] Costume, disguise.   [5] Disguise.
    [6] Q *hearts.*   [7] Misconception.
    [8] Disposed of ; *i.e.*, betrothed.

Tec.　　　　　　　Just ones, Orgilus,
Not to be contradicted ; yet beware
Of an unsure foundation ; no fair colors
Can fortify a building faintly jointed.
I have observ'd a growth in thy aspect [9]
Of dangerous extent, sudden, and — look
　　to 't —
I might add, certain —
　　Org.　　　　　My aspect ! [9]　Could art
Run through mine inmost thoughts, it should
　　not sift
An inclination there more than what suited
With justice of mine honor.
　　Tec.　　　　　　I believe it.　30
But know then, Orgilus, what honor is.
Honor consists not in a bare opinion
By doing any act that feeds content,
Brave in appearance, 'cause we think it brave ;
Such honor comes by accident, not nature,
Proceeding from the vices of our passion,
Which makes our reason drunk ; but real
　　honor
Is the reward of virtue, and acquir'd
By justice, or by valor which for basis
Hath justice to uphold it.　He then fails　40
In honor, who for lucre [or] [10] revenge
Commits thefts, murders, treasons, and adul-
　　teries,
With such like, by intrenching on just laws,
Whose sov'reignty is best preserv'd by justice.
Thus, as you see how honor must be grounded
On knowledge, not opinion, — for opinion
Relies on probability and accident,
But knowledge on necessity and truth, —
I leave thee to the fit consideration
Of what becomes the grace of real honor, [50
Wishing success to all thy virtuous meanings.
　　Org.　The gods increase thy wisdom, rever-
　　end oracle,
And in thy precepts make me ever thrifty ! [11]
　　Tec.　I thank thy wish. —　*Exit* Orgilus.
　　　　　　Much mystery of fate
Lies hid in that man's fortunes ; curiosity
May lead his actions into rare attempts.
But let the gods be moderators still ;
No human power can prevent their will.

Enter Armostes [*with a casket*].

From whence come 'ee ?
　　Arm.　　　From King Amyclas — pardon
My interruption of your studies. — Here, [60
In this seal'd box, he sends a treasure dear

To him as his crown.　'A prays your Gravity
You would examine, ponder, sift, and bolt
The pith and circumstance of every tittle
The scroll within contains.
　　Tec.　　　　　What is 't, Armostes ?
　　Arm.　It is the health of Sparta, the King's
　　life,
Sinews and safety of the commonwealth :
The sum of what the oracle deliver'd
When last he visited the prophetic temple
At Delphos.[12]　What his reasons are, for
　　which,　　　　　　　　　　　　　70
After so long a silence, he requires
Your counsel now, grave man, his Majesty
Will soon himself acquaint you with.
　　Tec. [*taking the casket*]　　　　Apollo
Inspire my intellect ! — The Prince of Argos
Is entertain'd ?
　　Arm.　　　　He is ; and has demanded
Our princess for his wife ; which I conceive
One special cause the King importunes you
For resolution of the oracle.
　　Tec.　My duty to the King, good peace to
　　Sparta,
And fair day to Armostes !
　　Arm.　　　Like to Tecnicus !　*Exeunt.* [80

[Scene II] [13]

Soft music.

A Song

Can you paint a thought ? or number
Every fancy in a slumber ?
Can you count soft minutes roving
From a dial's point by moving ?
Can you grasp a sigh ? or, lastly,
Rob a virgin's honor chastely ?
　　No, oh, no ! yet you may
Sooner do both that and this,
This and that, and never miss,
　　Than by any praise display　　　　　10
Beauty's beauty ; such a glory,
As beyond all fate, all story,
　　All arms, all arts,
　　All loves, all hearts,
Greater than those or they,
Do, shall, and must obey.

During which time enters Prophilus, Bassanes, Penthea, Grausis, *passing over the
stage.* Bassanes *and* Grausis *enter again
softly, stealing to several stands, and listen.*

Bass.　All silent, calm, secure. — Grausis,
　　no creaking ?
No noise ?　Dost hear nothing ?

---

[9] Accented on second syllable.
[10] Emend. Gifford ; Q *of.*
[11] To avail myself of them.

[12] Delphi, in Phocis.
[13] Ithocles's apartment.　The outer stage, till s. d.
following l. 32.

GRAU. Not a mouse,
Or whisper of the wind.

BASS. The floor is matted ;
The bedposts sure are steel or marble. — Sol-
    diers 20
Should not affect, methinks, strains so effem-
    inate :
Sounds of such delicacy are but fawnings
Upon the sloth of luxury,[14] they heighten
Cinders of covert lust up to a flame.

GRAU. What do you mean, my Lord ? —
    speak low ; that gabbling
Of yours will but undo us.

BASS. Chamber combats
Are felt, not h[e]ard.

PRO. [*within*] 'A wakes.

BASS. What 's that ?

ITH. [*within*] Who 's there ?
Sister ? — All quit the room else.

BASS. 'T is consented !

Re-enter PROPHILUS.

PRO. Lord Bassanes, your brother would be
    private ;
We must forbear ; his sleep hath newly left
    him. 30
Please 'ee withdraw.

BASS. By any means ;[15] 't is fit.

PRO. Pray, gentlewoman, walk too.

GRAU. Yes, I will, sir. *Exeunt omnes.*

[ITHOCLES *discovered in a chair, and* PENTHEA.

ITH. Sit nearer, Sister, to me ; nearer yet.
We had one father, in one womb took life,
Were brought up twins together, yet have
    liv'd
At distance, like two strangers. I could wish
That the first pillow whereon I was cradl'd
Had prov'd to me a grave.

PEN. You had been happy :
Then had you never known that sin of life
Which blots all following glories with a ven-
    geance, 40
For forfeiting the last will of the dead,
From whom you had your being.

ITH. Sad Penthea,
Thou canst not be too cruel ; my rash spleen
Hath with a violent hand pluck'd from thy
    bosom
A lover-blest [16] heart, to grind it into dust ;
For which mine 's now a-breaking.

PEN. Not yet, Heaven,
I do beseech thee ! First let some wild fires

Scorch, not consume it ! may the heat be cher-
    ish'd
With desires infinite, but hopes impossible !

ITH. Wrong'd soul, thy prayers are heard.

PEN. Here, lo, I breathe, [50
A miserable creature, led to ruin
By an unnatural brother !

ITH. I consume
In languishing affections [17] for that trespass ;
Yet cannot die.

PEN. The handmaid to the wages
Of country toil drinks the untroubled streams [18]
With leaping kids and with the bleating lambs,
And so allays her thirst secure, whiles I
Quench my hot sighs with fleetings [19] of my
    tears.

ITH. The laborer doth eat his coarsest
    bread,
Earn'd with his sweat, and lies him down to
    sleep ; 60
Which [20] every bit I touch turns in disgestion [21]
To gall as bitter as Penthea's curse.
Put me to any penance for my tyranny,
And I will call thee merciful.

PEN. Pray kill me ;
Rid me from living with a jealous husband ;
Then we will join in friendship, be again
Brother and sister. — Kill me, pray ; nay,
    will 'ee ?

ITH. How does thy lord esteem thee ?

PEN. Such an one
As only you have made me : a faith-breaker,
A spotted whore — forgive me : I am one [70
In [act,] [22] not in desires, the gods must wit-
    ness.

ITH. Thou dost belie thy friend.[23]

PEN. I do not, Ithocles ;
For she that 's wife to Orgilus, and lives
In known adultery with Bassanes,
Is at the best a whore. Wilt kill me now ?
The ashes of our parents will assume
Some dreadful figure, and appear to charge
Thy bloody guilt, that hast betray'd their
    name
To infamy in this reproachful match.

ITH. After my victories abroad, at home [80
I meet despair ; ingratitude of nature
Hath made my actions monstrous. Thou
    shalt stand
A deity, my sister, and be worshipp'd

---

[14] Lust.   [15] By all means.
[16] Gifford and Dyce, perhaps rightly, *love-blest.*

[17] Desires.
[18] So Gifford ; Q : *The vntroubled of Country toyle, drinkes streames.*
[19] Flowings ; *i.e.*, streams.
[20] Gifford and Dyce *While.*
[21] Digestion.   [22] Q *art.*   [23] Lover.

For thy resolved martyrdom ; wrong'd maids
And married wives shall to thy hallowed
   shrine
Offer their orisons, and sacrifice
Pure turtles,[24] crown'd with myrtle ; if thy
   pity
Unto a yielding brother's pressure lend
One finger but to ease it.
  PEN.   Oh, no more !
  ITH. Death waits to waft me to the Stygian
   banks   90
And free me from this chaos of my bondage ;
And till thou wilt forgive, I must endure.
  PEN. Who is the saint you serve?
  ITH.   Friendship, or [nearness] [25]
Of birth to any but my sister, durst not
Have mov'd that question, as [26] a secret,
   Sister,
I dare not murmur to myself.
  PEN.   Let me,
By your new protestations I conjure 'ee,
Partake her name.
  ITH. Her name? — 't is — 't is — I dare
   not.
  PEN. All your respects are forg'd.[27]
  ITH.   They are not. — Peace !
Calantha is — the Princess — the King's
   daughter —   100
Sole heir of Sparta. — Me, most miserable,
Do I now love thee? For my injuries
Revenge thyself with bravery, and gossip
My treasons to the King's ears, do. Calantha
Knows it not yet, nor Prophilus, my nearest.
  PEN. Suppose you were contracted to her,
   would it not
Split even your very soul to see her father
Snatch her out of your arms against her will,
And force her on the Prince of Argos?
  ITH.   Trouble not
The fountains of mine eyes with thine own
   story ;   110
I sweat in blood for 't.
  PEN.   We are reconcil'd.
Alas, sir, being children, but two branches
Of one stock, 't is not fit we should divide.
Have comfort ; you may find it.
  ITH.   Yes, in thee ;
Only in thee, Penthea mine.
  PEN.   If sorrows
Have not too much dull'd my infected brain,

I 'll cheer invention for an active strain.[28]
  ITH. Mad man ! why have I wrong'd a
   maid so excellent?

Enter BASSANES *with a poniard ;* PROPHILUS,
 GRONEAS, HEMOPHIL, *and* GRAUSIS.

  BASS. I can forbear no longer ; more, I
   will not.
Keep off your hands, or fall upon my point. —
Patience is tir'd ; for, like a slow-pac'd
   ass,   121
Ye ride my easy nature, and proclaim
My sloth to vengeance a reproach and prop-
   erty.[29]
  ITH. The meaning of this rudeness?
  PRO.   He 's distracted.
  PEN. Oh, my griev'd Lord ! —
  GRAU.   Sweet lady, come not near
   him ;
He holds his perilous weapon in his hand
To prick 'a cares not whom nor where — see,
   see, see !
  BASS. My birth is noble ; though the popu-
   lar blast
Of vanity, as giddy as thy youth,
Hath rear'd thy name up to bestride a cloud,
Or progress in the chariot of the sun, 131
I am no clod of trade, to lackey pride,
Nor, like your slave of expectation,[30] wait
The bawdy hinges of your doors, or whistle
For mystical conveyance to your bed-sports.
  GRO. Fine humors ! they become him.
  HEM.   How 'a stares,
Struts, puffs, and sweats ! Most admirable [31]
   lunacy !
  ITH. But that I may conceive the spirit of
   wine
Has took possession of your soberer custom,
I 'd say you were unmannerly.
  PEN.   Dear Brother ! — [140
  BASS. Unmannerly ! — mew, kitling ! [32] —
   smooth formality
Is usher to the rankness of the blood,
But impudence bears up the train. Indeed,
   sir,
Your fiery mettle, or your springal [33] blaze
Of huge renown, is no sufficient royalty
To print upon my forehead the scorn, " Cuck-
   old."
  ITH. His jealousy has robb'd him of his
   wits ;

---

[24] Doves.
[25] Add. Weber.
[26] Gifford emends *'t is.*
[27] All the considerations you have mentioned are
feigned ; *i.e.,* your new attitude toward me is not
genuine.

[28] *I.e.,* I 'll try to think of something that can be
done.
[29] Personal characteristic.
[30] *I.e.,* attendant slave. [31] Remarkable.
[32] Kitten.   [33] Youthful.

'A talks 'a knows not what.

BASS.   Yes, and 'a knows
To whom 'a talks; to one that franks [34] his
    lust
In swine-security of bestial incest.   150

ITH. Ha, devil!

BASS.   I will halloo 't; though I blush
    more
To name the filthiness than thou to act it.

ITH. Monster!

PRO.   Sir, by our friendship —

PEN.   By our bloods —
Will you quite both undo us, Brother?

GRAU.   Out on him!
These are his megrims,[35] firks,[36] and melan-
    cholies.

HEM. Well said, old touchhole.

GRO.   Kick him out at doors.

PEN. With favor, let me speak. — My
    Lord, what slackness
In my obedience hath deserv'd this rage?
Except humility and silent duty   159
Have drawn on your unquiet, my simplicity
Ne'er studied your vexation.

BASS.   Light of beauty,
Deal not ungently with a desperate wound!
No breach of reason dares make war with
    her
Whose looks are sovereignty, whose breath
    is balm.
Oh, that I could preserve thee in fruition
As in devotion!

PEN.   Sir, may every evil
Lock'd in Pandora's box show'r, in your pres-
    ence,
On my unhappy head, if, since you made me
A partner in your bed, I have been faulty
In one unseemly thought against your
    honor!   170

ITH. Purge not his griefs, Penthea.

BASS.   Yes, say on,
Excellent creature! — [*to* ITHOCLES] Good,[37]
    be not a hindrance
To peace and praise of virtue. — Oh, my
    senses
Are charm'd with sounds celestial! — On,
    dear, on :
I never gave you one ill word; say, did I?
Indeed I did not.

PEN.   Nor, by Juno's forehead,
Was I e'er guilty of a wanton error.

BASS. A goddess! let me kneel.

GRAU.   Alas, kind animal!

ITH. No; but for penance.

BASS.   Noble sir, what is it?
With gladness I embrace it; yet, pray let
    not   180
My rashness teach you to be too unmerci-
    ful.

ITH. When you shall show good proof that
    manly wisdom,
Not oversway'd by passion or opinion,
Knows how to lead [38] judgment, then this
    lady,
Your wife, my sister, shall return in safety
Home, to be guided by you; but, till
    first
I can out of clear evidence approve [39] it,
She shall be my care.

BASS.   Rip my bosom up,
I'll stand the execution with a constancy;
This torture is unsufferable.

ITH.   Well, sir,   190
I dare not trust her to your fury.

BASS.   But
Penthea says not so.

PEN.   She needs no tongue
To plead excuse who never purpos'd wrong.

HEM. Virgin of reverence and antiquity,
Stay you behind.

GRO. [*to* GRAUSIS]   The court wants not
    your diligence.
            Exeunt [*all but*] BASSANES *and*
            GRAUSIS.

GRAU. What will you do, my Lord? My
    Lady's gone;
I am deni'd to follow.

BASS.   I may see her,
Or speak to her once more?

GRAU.   And feel her too, man;
Be of good cheer: she's your own flesh and
    bone.

BASS. Diseases desperate must find cures
    alike.   200
She swore she has been true.

GRAU.   True, on my modesty.

BASS. Let him want truth who credits not
    her vows!
Much wrong I did her, but her brother infinite;
Rumor will voice me the contempt of man-
    hood,
Should I run on thus. Some way I must try
To outdo art, and cry a' [40] jealousy.
                 Exeunt omne[s].

---

[34] Crams, feeds.   [35] Fancies.
[36] Caprices.   [37] *I.e.*, good sir.

[38] Weber conj. the addition of *your*, which Gifford
silently adopts.
[39] Prove, make certain of.
[40] Cry on, exclaim against. Gifford emends *jealousy decry*.

[SCENE III] [41]

Flourish. Enter AMYCLAS, NEARCHUS *leading*
CALANTHA, ARMOSTES, CROTOLON, EU-
PHRANEA, CHRISTALLA, PHILEMA, *and*
AMELUS.

AMY. Cousin of Argos, what the Heavens
    have pleas'd
In their unchanging counsels to conclude
For both our kingdoms' weal, we must submit
    to ;
Nor can we be unthankful to their bounties,
Who, when we were even creeping to our
    [grave], [42]
Sent us a daughter, in whose birth our hope
Continues of succession. As you are
In title next, being grandchild to our aunt,
So we in heart desire you may sit nearest
Calantha's love ; since we have ever vow'd [10
Not to enforce affection by our will,
But by her own choice to confirm it gladly.
    NEAR. You speak the nature of a right just
        father.
I come not hither roughly to demand
My cousin's thralldom, but to free mine own.
Report of great Calantha's beauty, virtue,
Sweetness, and singular perfections, courted
All ears to credit what I find was publish'd
By constant truth ; from which, if any service
Of my desert can purchase fair construc-
    tion,   20
This lady must command it.
    CAL.   Princely sir,
So well you know how to profess observance, [43]
That you instruct your hearers to become
Practitioners in duty ; of which number
I 'll study to be chief.
    NEAR.   Chief, glorious virgin,
In my devotions, as in all men's wonder.
    AMY. Excellent Cousin, we deny no liberty ;
Use thine own opportunities. — Armostes,
We must consult with the philosophers ;
The business is of weight.
    ARM.   Sir, at your pleasure. [30
    AMY. You told me, Crotolon, your son's
        return'd
From Athens. Wherefore comes 'a not to
    court
As we commanded?
    CROT.   He shall soon attend
Your royal will, great sir.
    AMY.   The marriage

Between young Prophilus and Euphranea
Tastes of too much delay.
    CROT.   My Lord, —
    AMY.   Some pleasures
At celebration of it would give life
To th' entertainment of the Prince our kins-
    man ;
Our court wears gravity more than we relish.
    ARM. Yet the Heavens smile on all your
        high attempts,   40
Without a cloud.
    CROT.   So may the gods protect us.
    CAL. A prince a subject?
    NEAR.   Yes, to beauty's sceptre ;
As all hearts kneel, so mine.
    CAL.   You are too courtly.

[*Enter*] *to them* ITHOCLES, ORGILUS, [*and*]
PROPHILUS.

    ITH. Your safe return to Sparta is most
        welcome.
I joy to meet you here, and, as occasion
Shall grant us privacy, will yield you reasons
Why I should covet to deserve the title
Of your respected friend ; for, without com-
    pliment,
Believe it, Orgilus, 't is my ambition.
    ORG. Your Lordship may command me,
        your poor servant.   50
    ITH. [*aside*] So amorously close ! — so
        soon ! — my heart !
    PRO. What sudden change is next?
    ITH.   Life to the King !
To whom I here present this noble gentle-
    man,
New come from Athens. Royal sir, vouch-
    safe
Your gracious hand in favor of his merit.
    CROT. [*aside*] My son preferr'd [44] by
        Ithocles !
    AMY.   Our bounties
Shall open to thee, Orgilus ; for instance, —
Hark in thine ear, — if, out of those inven-
    tions
Which flow in Athens, thou hast there en-
    gross'd [45]
Some rarity of wit, to grace the nuptials   60
Of thy fair sister, and renown our court
In th' eyes of this young prince, we shall be
    debtor
To thy conceit : think on 't.
    ORG.   Your Highness honors me.
    NEAR. My tongue and heart are twins.

41 A room in the palace.
42 Emend. Dyce ; Q *graues.*
43 Courtship.

44 Put forward.
45 Acquired.

CAL. A noble birth,
Becoming such a father. — Worthy Orgilus,
You are a guest most wish'd for.
ORG. May my duty
Still rise in your opinion, sacred Princess !
ITH. Euphranea's brother, sir ; a gentleman
Well worthy of your knowledge.
NEAR. We embrace him,
Proud of so dear acquaintance.
AMY. All prepare [70
For revels and disport ; the joys of Hymen,
Like Phoebus in his lustre, puts to flight
All mists of dullness. Crown the hours with
gladness ;
No sounds but music, no discourse but mirth !
CAL. Thine arm, I prithee, Ithocles. —
Nay, good
My Lord, keep on your way ; I am provided.
NEAR. I dare not disobey.
ITH. Most heavenly lady ! *Exeunt.*

[SCENE IV] [46]

Enter CROTOLON [*and*] ORGILUS.

CROT. The King has spoke his mind.
ORG. His will he hath ;
But were it lawful to hold plea against
The power of greatness, not the reason,
haply
Such undershrubs as subjects sometimes
might
Borrow of nature justice, to inform
That license sovereignty holds without check
Over a meek obedience.
CROT. How resolve you
Touching your sister's marriage ? Prophilus
Is a deserving and a hopeful youth.
ORG. I envy not his merit, but applaud
it ; 10
Could wi[s]h him thrift [47] in all his best desires,
And with a willingness inleague our blood
With his, for purchase of full growth in friend-
ship.
He never touch'd on any wrong that malic'd
The honor of our house nor stirr'd our peace.
Yet, with your favor, let me not forget
Under whose wing he gathers warmth and
comfort,
Whose creature he is bound, made, and must
live so.
CROT. Son, son, I find in thee a harsh condi-
tion ; [48]
No courtesy can win it ; 't is too rancorous. [20

ORG. Good sir, be not severe in your con-
struction ;
I am no stranger to such easy calms
As sit in tender bosoms. Lordly Ithocles
Hath grac'd my entertainment [49] in abun-
dance,
Too humbly hath descended from that height
Of arrogance and spleen which wrought the
rape
On griev'd Penthea's purity ; his scorn
Of my untoward fortunes is reclaim'd
Unto a cou[r]tship, almost to a fawning :
I'll kiss his foot, since you will have it so. [30
CROT. Since I will have it so ! Friend, I will
have it so,
Without our ruin by your politic plots,
Or wolf of hatred snarling in your breast.
You have a spirit, sir, have ye? A familiar [50]
That posts i' th' air for your intelligence?
Some such hobgoblin hurried you from Athens,
For yet you come unsent for.
ORG. If unwelcome,
I might have found a grave there.
CROT. Sure, your business
Was soon dispatch'd, or your mind alter'd
quickly.
ORG. 'T was care, sir, of my health cut
short my journey ; 40
For there a general infection
Threatens a desolation.
CROT. And I fear
Thou hast brought back a worse infection with
thee —
Infection of thy mind, which, as thou say'st,
Threatens the desolation of our family.
ORG. Forbid it, our dear genius ! [51] I will
rather
Be made a sacrifice on Thrasus' monument,
Or kneel to Ithocles, his son, in dust,
Than woo a father's curse. My sister's mar-
riage
With Prophilus is from my heart confirm'd ;
May I live hated, may I die despis'd, 51
If I omit to further it in all
That can concern me !
CROT. I have been too rough.
My duty to my King made me so earnest ;
Excuse it, Orgilus.
ORG. Dear sir ! —

Enter to them PROPHILUS, EUPHRANEA, ITHO-
CLES, GRONEAS, [*and*] HEMOPHIL.

CROT. Here comes
Euphranea with Prophilus and Ithocles.

ORG. Most honored ! — ever famous !

ITH.   Your true friend ;
On earth not any truer. — With smooth
  eyes
Look on this worthy couple ; your consent
Can only make them one.

ORG.   They have it. — Sister, [60
Thou pawn'dst to me an oath, of which engage-
  ment
I never will release thee, if thou aim'st
At any other choice than this.

EUPH.   Dear Brother,
At him, or none.

CROT.   To which my blessing 's added.

ORG. Which, till a greater ceremony per-
  fect, —
Euphranea, lend thy hand, — here, take her,
  Prophilus. —
Live long a happy man and wife ; and further,
That these in presence may conclude an omen,
Thus for a bridal song I close my wishes :

[*Sings*]

> Comforts lasting, loves increasing,   70
> Like soft hours never ceasing ;
> Plenty's pleasure, peace complying,
> Without jars, or tongues' envying ; [52]
> Hearts by holy union wedded,
> More than theirs by custom bedded ;
> Fruitful issues ; life so graced,
> Not by age to be defaced,
> Budding, as the year ensu'th,
> Every spring another youth :
> All what thought can add beside   80
> Crown this bridegroom and this bride.

PRO. You have seal'd joy close to my soul.
  — Euphranea,
Now I may call thee mine.

ITH.   I but exchange
One good friend for another.

ORG.   If these gallants
Will please to grace a poor invention
By joining with me in some slight device,
I 'll venture on a strain my younger days
Have studied for delight.

HEM.   With thankful willingness
I offer my attendance.

GRO.   No endeavor
Of mine shall fail to show itself.

ITH.   We will [90
All join to wait on thy directions, Orgilus.

ORG. Oh, my good Lord, your favors flow
  towards
A too unworthy worm ; but, as you please ;
I am what you will shape me.

ITH.   A fast friend.

[52] Malice.

CROT. I thank thee, son, for this acknowledgment ;
It is a sight of gladness.

ORG.   But my duty.
                         Exeunt omnes.

[SCENE V] [53]

Enter CALANTHA, PENTHEA, CHRISTALLA,
         [*and*] PHILEMA.

CAL. Whoe'er would speak with us, deny
  his entrance ;
Be careful of our charge.

CHRIS.   We shall, madam.

CAL. Except the King himself, give none
  admittance ;
Not any.

PHIL.   Madam, it shall be our care.
           Exeunt [CHRISTALLA *and* PHI-
                     LEMA].

CAL. Being alone, Penthea, you have
  granted
The opportunity you sought, and might
At all times have commanded.

PEN.   'T is a benefit
Which I shall owe your goodness even in death
  for.
My glass of life, sweet Princess, hath few
  minutes
Remaining to run down ; the sands are
  spent ;   10
For by an inward messenger I feel
The summons of departure short and certain.

CAL. You feel too much your melancholy.

PEN.   Glories
Of human greatness are but pleasing dreams
And shadows soon decaying : on the stage
Of my mortality my youth hath acted
Some scenes of vanity, drawn out at length
By varied pleasures, sweet'ned in the mixture,
But tragical in issue. Beauty, pomp,
With every sensuality our giddiness   20
Doth frame an idol, are unconstant friends,
When any troubled passion makes assault
On the unguarded castle of the mind.

CAL. Contemn not your condition for the
  proof
Of bare opinion only. To what end
Reach all these moral texts ?

PEN.   To place before 'ee
A perfect mirror, wherein you may see
How weary I am of a ling'ring life,
Who count the best a misery.

[53] Calantha's apartment in the palace.

CAL. Indeed
You have no little cause ; yet none so great [30
As to distrust a remedy.
PEN. That remedy
Must be a winding sheet, a fold of lead,
And some untrod-on corner in the earth. —
Not to detain your expectation, Princess,
I have an humble suit.
CAL. Speak ; I enjoy [54] it.
PEN. Vouchsafe, then, to be my executrix,
And take that trouble on 'ee to dispose
Such legacies as I bequeath, impartially.
I have not much to give : the pains are easy ;
Heaven will reward your piety, and thank
  it 40
When I am dead ; for sure I must not live —
I hope I cannot.
CAL. Now, beshrew thy sadness,
Thou turn'st me too much woman. [*Weeps.*]
PEN. [*aside*] Her fair eyes
Melt into passion.[55] — Then I have assurance
Encouraging my boldness. In this paper
My will was character'd ; which you, with
  pardon,
Shall now know from mine own mouth.
CAL. Talk on, prithee ;
It is a pretty earnest.
PEN. I have left me
But three poor jewels to bequeath. The first
  is
My youth ; for though I am much old in
  griefs, 50
In years I am a child.
CAL. To whom that [jewel] [56]?
PEN. To virgin wives, such as abuse not
  wedlock
By freedom of desires, but covet chiefly
The pledges of chaste beds for ties of love,
Rather than ranging of their blood ; and next
To married maids, such as prefer the number
Of honorable issue in their virtues
Before the flattery of delights by marriage :
May those be ever young !
CAL. A second jewel
You mean to part with?
PEN. 'T is my fame, I trust [60
By scandal yet untouch'd ; this I bequeath
To Memory, and Time's old daughter, Truth.
If ever my unhappy name find mention
When I am fall'n to dust, may it deserve
Beseeming charity without dishonor !
CAL. How handsomely thou play'st with
  harmless sport

Of mere imagination ! Speak the last.
I strangely like thy will.
PEN. This jewel, madam,
Is dearly precious to me ; you must use
The best of your discretion to employ 70
This gift as I intend it.
CAL. Do not doubt me.
PEN. 'T is long agone since first I lost my
  heart ;
Long I have liv'd without it, else for certain
I should have given that too ; but instead
Of it, to great Calantha, Sparta's heir,
By service bound and by affection vow'd,
I do bequeath, in holiest rites of love,
Mine only brother, Ithocles.
CAL. What said'st thou?
PEN. Impute not, heaven-blest lady, to
  ambition
A faith as humbly perfect as the prayers [80
Of a devoted suppliant can endow it.
Look on him, Princess, with an eye of pity ;
How like the ghost of what he late appear'd
'A moves before you.
CAL. [*aside*] Shall I answer here,
Or lend my ear too grossly?
PEN. First his heart
Shall fall in cinders, scorch'd by your disdain,
Ere he will dare, poor man, to ope an eye
On these divine looks, but with low-bent
  thoughts
Accusing such presumption ; as for words,
'A dares not utter any but of service. 90
Yet this lost creature loves 'ee. — Be a prin-
  cess
In sweetness as in blood ; give him his doom,
Or raise him up to comfort.
CAL. What new change
Appears in my behavior, that thou dar'st
Tempt my displeasure?
PEN. I must leave the world
To revel [in] [57] Elysium, and 't is just
To wish my brother some advantage here ;
Yet, by my best hopes, Ithocles is ignorant
Of this pursuit. But if you please to kill him,
Lend him one angry look or one harsh
  word, 100
And you shall soon conclude how strong a
  power
Your absolute authority holds over
His life and end.
CAL. You have forgot, Penthea,
How still I have a father.
PEN. But remember
I am a sister, though to me this brother

[54] Dyce conj. *enjoin.*
[55] Sorrow.
[56] Add. Gifford.
[57] Add. Weber.

Hath been, you know, unkind, oh, most un-
    kind!
  Cal. Christalla, Philema, where are 'ee? —
    Lady,
Your check lies in my silence.

Re-enter Christalla *and* Philema.

Both.   Madam, here.
  Cal. I think 'ee sleep, 'ee drones; wait on
    Penthea
Unto her lodging. — [*aside*] Ithocles? Wrong'd
    lady!   110
  Pen. My reckonings are made even; death
    or fate
Can now nor strike too soon, nor force too late.
                         Exeunt.

ACT IV — Scene I [1]

Enter Ithocles *and* Armostes.

  Ith. Forbear your inquisition; curiosity
Is of too subtle and too searching nature,
In fears of love too quick, too slow of credit.
I am not what you doubt me.[2]
  Arm.   Nephew, be, then,
As I would wish; — all is not right. — Good
    Heaven
Confirm your resolutions for dependence
On worthy ends, which may advance your
    quiet!
  Ith. I did the noble Orgilus much injury,
But griev'd Penthea more: I now repent it —
Now, Uncle, now; this " now " is now too
    late.   10
So provident is folly in sad issue,
That after-wit, like bankrupts' debts, stand[s]
    tallied,
Without all possibilities of payment.
Sure, he 's an honest, very honest gentle-
    man;
A man of single [3] meaning.
  Arm.   I believe it.
Yet, Nephew, 't is the tongue informs our
    ears;
Our eyes can never pierce into the thoughts,
For they are lodg'd too inward: — but I ques-
    tion
No truth in Orgilus. — The Princess, sir.
  Ith. The Princess? ha!
  Arm.   With her the Prince of Argos. [20

---

[1] Unlocated; presumably a room in the palace.
[2] Suspect me to be.
[3] Simple, sincere.

Enter Nearchus *leading* Calantha, Ame-
    lus, Christalla, [*and*] Philema.

  Near. Great fair one, grace my hopes with
    any instance
Of livery [4] from the allowance of your favor;
This little spark —
    [*Attempts to take a ring from her finger.*]
  Cal.   A toy!
  Near.   Love feasts on toys,
For Cupid is a child; vouchsafe this bounty —
It cannot be [de]ni'd.
  Cal.   You shall not value,
Sweet Cousin, at a price, what I count
    cheap;
So cheap, that let him take it who dares stoop
    for 't,
And give it at next meeting to a mistress;
She 'll thank him for 't, perhaps.
                Casts it to Ithocles.
  Ame.   The ring, sir, is
The Princess's; I could have took it up.   30
  Ith. Learn manners, prithee. — To the
    blessed owner,
Upon my knees —
    [*Kneels and offers it to* Calantha.]
  Near.   Y' are saucy.
  Cal.   This is pretty!
I am, belike, " a mistress " — wondrous
    pretty!
Let the man keep his fortune, since he found
    it;
He 's worthy on 't. — On, Cousin!
  Ith. [*to* Amelus]   Follow, spaniel;
I 'll force 'ee to a fawning else.
  Ame.   You dare not.
    Exeunt [*all but*] Ithocles *and* Armostes.
  Arm. My Lord, you were too forward.
  Ith.   Look 'ee, Uncle,
Some such there are whose liberal contents
Swarm without care in every sort of plenty;
Who after full repasts can lay them down [40
To sleep; and they sleep, Uncle: in which
    silence
Their very dreams present 'em choice of pleas-
    ures,
Pleasures — observe me, Uncle — of rare
    object;
Here heaps of gold, there increments of honors,
Now change of garments, then the votes of
    people;
Anon varieties of beauties, courting,
In flatteries of the night, exchange of dal-
    liance —

Yet these are still but dreams.   Give me felic-
  ity
Of which my senses waking are partakers,
A real, visible, material happiness ;   50
And then, too, when I stagger in expectance
Of the least comfort that can cherish life. ——
I saw it, sir, I saw it ; for it came
From her own hand.
    ARM.   The Princess threw it t 'ee.
    ITH.   True ; and she said — well I remember
      what —
Her cousin prince would beg it.
    ARM.   Yes, and parted
In anger at your taking on 't.
    ITH.   Penthea,
Oh, thou hast pleaded with a powerful lan-
      guage !
I want a fee to gratify [5] thy merit ;
But I will do —
    ARM.   What is 't you say ?
    ITH.   In anger ! [60
In anger let him part ; for could his breath,
Like whirlwinds, toss such servile slaves as lick
The dust his footsteps print into a vapor,
It durst not stir a hair of mine : it should not ;
I 'd rend it up by th' roots first.   To be any-
      thing
Calantha smiles on, is to be a blessing
More sacred than a petty prince of Argos
Can wish to equal, or in worth or title.
    ARM.   Contain yourself, my Lord : Ixion,
      aiming
To embrace Juno, bosom'd but a cloud,   70
And begat centaurs ; 't is an useful moral.
Ambition hatch'd in clouds of mere opinion
Proves but in birth a prodigy.[6]
    ITH.   I thank 'ee ;
Yet, with your licence,[7] I should seem unchari-
      table
To gentler fate, if, relishing the dainties
Of a soul's settled peace, I were so feeble
Not to digest it.
    ARM.   He deserves small trust
Who is not privy-counsellor to himself.

Re-enter NEARCHUS, ORGILUS, *and* AMELUS.

    NEAR.   Brave me !
    ORG.   Your Excellence mistakes his tem-
      per ;
For Ithocles in fashion of his mind   80
Is beautiful, soft, gentle, the clear mirror
Of absolute perfection.

  [5] Reward.
  [6] Monstrosity.
  [7] If you will allow me to say so.

    AME.   Was 't your modesty
Term'd any of the Prince his servants " span-
      iel "?
Your nurse, sure, taught you other language.
    ITH.   Language !
    NEAR.   A gallant man at arms is here, a
      doctor
In feats of chivalry, blunt and rough-spoken,
Vouchsafing not the fustian of civility,
Which [less] [8] rash spirits style good manners !
    ITH.   Manners !
    ORG.   No more, illustrious sir ; 't is match-
      less Ithocles.
    NEAR.   You might have understood who I
      am.
    ITH.   Yes. [90
I did ; else — but the presence [9] calm'd th'
      affront —
Y' are cousin to the Princess.
    NEAR.   To the King, too ;
A certain instrument that lent supportance
To your colossic greatness — to that King, too,
You might have added.
    ITH.   There is more divinity
In beauty than in majesty.
    ARM.   O fie, fie !
    NEAR.   This odd youth's pride turns heretic
      in loyalty.
Sirrah ! low mushrooms never rival cedars.
                    Exeunt NEARCHUS *and* AMELUS.
    ITH.   Come back ! — What pitiful dull thing
      am I
So to be tamely scolded at ! come back ! — [100
Let him come back, and echo once again
That   scornful   sound   of   " mushroom " !
      painted colts —
Like heralds' coats gilt o'er with crowns and
      sceptres — [10]
May bait a muzzled lion.
    ARM.   Cousin, Cousin,
Thy tongue is not thy friend.
    ORG.   In point of honor
Discretion knows no bounds.   Amelus told me
'T was all about a little ring.
    ITH.   A ring
The Princess threw away, and I took up.
Admit she threw 't to me, what arm of brass
Can snatch it hence ?   No ; could 'a grind the
      hoop   110
To powder, 'a might sooner reach my heart

Than steal and wear one dust on 't. — Orgilus,
I am extremely wrong'd.

ORG.   A lady's favor
Is not to be so slighted.

ITH.   Slighted!

ARM.   Quiet
These vain unruly passions, which will render
    ye
Into a madness.

ORG.   Griefs will have their vent.

Enter TECNICUS [*with a scroll*].

ARM. Welcome; thou com'st in season,
    reverend man,
To pour the balsam of a [suppling] [11] patience
Into the festering wound of ill-spent fury.

ORG. [*aside*] What makes he here?

TEC.   The hurts are yet but [12] mortal, [120
Which shortly will prove deadly. To the
    King,
Armostes, see in safety thou deliver
This seal'd-up counsel; bid him with a con-
    stancy
Peruse the secrets of the gods. — O Sparta,
O Lacedaemon! double-nam'd, but one
In fate: when kingdoms reel, — mark well my
    saw, —
Their heads must needs be giddy. Tell the
    King
That henceforth he no more must inquire after
My aged head; Apollo wills it so.
I am for Delphos.

ARM.   Not without some conference [130
With our great master?

TEC.   Nevermore to see him;
A greater prince commands me. — Ithocles,
*When youth is ripe, and age from time doth
    part,*
The lifeless trunk shall wed the broken heart.

ITH. What's this, if understood?

TEC.   List, Orgilus;
Remember what I told thee long before;
These tears shall be my witness.

ARM.   'Las, good man!

TEC. *Let craft with courtesy awhile confer;*
    Revenge proves its own executioner.

ORG. Dark sentences are for Apollo's
    priests;   140
I am not Oedipus.[13]

TEC.   My hour is come;

Cheer up the King; farewell to all. — O
    Sparta,
O Lacedaemon!   *Exit* TECNICUS.

ARM.   If prophetic fire
Have warm'd this old man's bosom, we might
    construe
His words to fatal sense.

ITH.   Leave to the powers
Above us the effects of their decrees;
My burthen lies within me: servile fears
Prevent no great effects. — Divine Calantha!

ARM. The gods be still propitious!

            Exeunt [ITHOCLES *and* ARMOSTES].

ORG.   Something oddly
The book-man prated, yet 'a talk'd it weep-
    ing: 150
Let craft with courtesy a while confer;
Revenge proves its own executioner.
Con it again; for what? It shall not puzzle
    me;
'T is dotage of a withered brain. — Penthea
Forbade me not her presence; I may see her,
And gaze my fill. Why see her, then, I may,
When, if I faint to speak, I must be silent.

            Exit ORGILUS.

[SCENE II] [14]

Enter BASSANES, GRAUSIS, *and* PHULAS.

BASS. Pray, use your recreations, all the
    service
I will expect is quietness amongst 'ee;
Take liberty at home, abroad, at all times,
And in your charities appease the gods,
Whom I, with my distractions, have offended.

GRAU. Fair blessings on thy heart!

PHU. [*aside*]   Here's a rare change!
My Lord, to cure the itch, is surely gelded;
The cuckold in conceit [15] hath cast [16] his horns.

BASS. Betake 'ee to your several occasions;
And wherein I have heretofore been faulty, [10
Let your constructions mildly pass it over.
Henceforth I'll study reformation, — more
I have not for employment.

GRAU.   Oh, sweet man!
Thou art the very Honeycomb of Honesty.[17]

PHU. The Garland of Good-will. — Old
    lady, hold up
Thy reverend snout, and trot behind me
    softly,

---

[11] Emend. Gifford; Weber emends *supple;* Q
supplying.
[12] Gifford conj. *not.* If "but" is right, "mortal"
must = threatening death, and "deadly" = actually
causing death. (Kittredge.)
[13] Who solved the riddle of the Sphinx.

[14] A room in the house of Bassanes.
[15] Imagination.   [16] Shed.
[17] "Like the 'Garland of Good Will' . . . probably one of the popular miscellanies of the day."
(Gifford.) On the former work see introductory
note.

As it becomes a moil [18] of ancient carriage.

Exeunt [GRAUSIS *and* PHULAS].

BASS. Beasts, only capable of sense, enjoy
The benefit of food and ease with thankful-
ness ;
Such silly creatures, with a grudging, kick
not   20
Against the portion nature hath bestow'd :
But men, endow'd with reason and the use
Of reason, to distinguish from the chaff
Of abject scarcity the quintessence,
Soul, and elixir of the earth's abundance,
The treasures of the sea, the air, nay, heaven,
Repining at these glories of creation,
Are verier beasts than beasts ; and of those
beasts
The worst am I : I, who was made a monarch
Of what a heart could wish for, a chaste
wife,   30
Endeavor'd what in me lay to pull down
That temple built for adoration only,
And level 't in the dust of causeless scandal.
But, to redeem a sacrilege so impious,
Humility shall pour before the deities
I have incens'd a [largess] [19] of more patience
Than their displeased altars can require.
No tempests of commotion shall disquiet
The calms of my composure.

Enter ORGILUS.

ORG.   I have found thee,
Thou patron of more horrors than the bulk [40
Of manhood, hoop'd about with ribs of iron,
Can cram within thy breast. Penthea, Bas-
sanes,
Curs'd by thy jealousies, — more, by thy dot-
age, —
Is left a prey to words.

BASS.   Exercise
Your trials for addition to my penance ;
I am resolv'd.

ORG.   Play not with misery
Past cure : some angry minister of fate
Hath depos'd the empress of her soul, her
reason,
From its most proper throne ; but, what's the
miracle
More new, I, I have seen it, and yet live ! [50

BASS. You may delude my senses, not my
judgment ;
'T is anchor'd into a firm resolution ;
Dalliance of mirth or wit can ne'er unfix it :
Practice [20] yet further.

---

[18] Mule.   [19] Emend. Weber ; Q *largenesse.*
[20] *i.e.*, try me.

ORG.   May thy death of love to her
Damn all thy comforts to a lasting fast
From every joy of life ! Thou barren rock,
By thee we have bee[n] split in ken [21] of harbor.

Enter ITHOCLES, PENTHEA *her hair about her
ears,* [ARMOSTES,] PHILEMA, [*and*] CHRIS-
TALLA.

ITH. Sister, look up ; your Ithocles, your
brother,
Speaks t' ee ; why do you weep ? Dear, turn
not from me. —
Here is a killing sight ; lo, Bassanes,   60
A lamentable object !

ORG.   Man, dost see 't ?
Sports are more gamesome ; am I yet in merri-
ment ?
Why dost not laugh ?

BASS.   Divine and best of ladies,
Please to forget my outrage ! Mercy ever
Cannot but lodge under a roo[f] so excellent.
I have cast off that cruelty of frenzy
Which once appear'd, [impostor], [22] and then
juggled
To cheat my sleeps of rest.

ORG.   Was I in earnest ?

PEN. Sure, if we were all Sirens, we should
sing pitifully.
And 't were a comely music, when in parts [70
One sung another's knell. The turtle [23] sighs
When he hath lost his mate ; and yet some say
'A must be dead first. 'T is a fine deceit
To pass away in a dream ; indeed, I 've slept
With mine eyes open a great while. No false-
hood
Equals a broken faith ; there 's not a hair
Sticks on my head but, like a leaden plummet,
It sinks me to the grave. I must creep thither ;
The journey is not long.

ITH.   But, thou, Penthea,
Hast many years, I hope, to number yet, [80
Ere thou canst travel that way.

BASS.   Let the [sun] [24] first
Be wrapp'd up in an everlasting darkness,
Before the light of nature, chiefly form'd
For the whole world's delight, feel an eclipse
So universal !

ORG.   Wisdom, look 'ee, begins
To rave ! — Art thou mad too, antiquity ?

PEN. Since I was first a wife, I might have
been

---

[21] Within sight.
[22] Emend. Weber ; Q *Impostors;* Gifford omits
comma and reads *imposture.*
[23] Dove.
[24] Emend. Weber ; Q *Swan.*

Mother to many pretty prattling babes ;
They would have smil'd when I smil'd, and for certain
I should have cri'd when they cri'd : — truly, Brother,   90
My father would have pick'd me out a husband,
And then my little ones had been no bastards ;
But 't is too late for me to marry now —
I am past childbearing ; 't is not my fault.
    BASS. Fall on me, if there be a burning Aetna,
And bury me in flames ! Sweats hot as sulphur
Boil through my pores ! Affliction hath in store
No torture like to this.
    ORG.   Behold a patience !
Lay by thy whining gray dissimulation :
Do something worth a chronicle ; show justice   100
Upon the author of this mischief ; dig out
The jealousies that hatch'd this thraldom first
With thine own poniard. Every antic rapture
Can roar as thine does.
    ITH.   Orgilus, forbear.
    BASS. Disturb him not ; it is a talking motion [25]
Provided for my torment. What a fool am I
To bawdy [26] passion ! Ere I 'll speak a word,
I will look on and burst.
    PEN. [*to* ORGILUS]   I lov'd you once.
    ORG. Thou didst, wrong'd creature, in despite of malice ;
For it I love thee ever.
    PEN.   Spare your hand ; [110
Believe me, I 'll not hurt it.
    ORG.   Pain my heart too.
[PEN.] [27] Complain not though I wring it hard. I 'll kiss it ;
Oh, 't is a fine soft palm ! — Hark, in thine ear ;
Like whom do I look, prithee ? — Nay, no whispering.
Goodness ! we had been happy ; too much happiness
Will make folk proud, they say — but that is he —   *Points at* ITHOCLES.
And yet he paid for 't home ; alas, his heart
Is crept into the cabinet of the Princess ;
We shall have points [28] and bride-laces.[29] Remember,

<hr>

[25] Puppet.   [26] Dyce emends *bandy*.
[27] Supplied by Weber.
[28] Tagged laces.
[29] Pieces of silk or lace used to tie the sprigs of rosemary in use at weddings.

When we last gather'd roses in the garden, [120
I found my wits ; but truly you lost yours.
That 's he, and still 't is he.
    ITH.   Poor soul, how idly
Her fancies guide her tongue !
    BASS. [*aside*]   Keep in, vexation,
And break not into clamor.
    ORG. [*aside*]   She has tutor'd me :
Some powerful inspiration checks my laziness. —
Now let me kiss your hand, griev'd beauty.
    PEN.   Kiss it. —
Alack, alack, his lips be wondrous cold.
Dear soul, h' as lost his color : have 'ee seen
A straying heart ? All crannies ! every drop
Of blood is turn'd to an amethyst,   130
Which married bachelors hang in their ears.
    ORG. Peace usher her into Elysium ! —
If this be madness, madness is an oracle.
                    Exit ORGILUS.
    ITH. Christalla, Philema, when slept my sister ? —
Her ravings are so wild.
    CHRIS.   Sir, not these ten days.
    PHIL. We watch by her continually ; besides,
We can not any way pray her to eat.
    BASS. Oh, misery of miseries !
    PEN.   Take comfort ;
You may live well, and die a good old man.
By yea and nay, an oath not to be broken, [140
If you had join'd our hands once in the temple, —
'T was since my father di'd, for had he liv'd
He would have done 't, — I must have call'd you father. —
Oh, my wrack'd honor ! ruin'd by those tyrants,
A cruel brother and a desperate dotage !
There is no peace left for a ravish'd wife
Widow'd by lawless marriage ; to all memory
Penthea's, poor Penthea's name is strumpeted.
But since her blood was season'd by the forfeit
Of noble shame with mixtures of pollution, [150
Her blood — 't is just — be henceforth never height'ned
With taste of sustenance ! Starve ; let that fullness
Whose pleurisy [30] hath fever'd faith and modesty —
Forgive me ; oh, I faint !
    ARM.   Be not so wilful,
Sweet Niece, to work thine own destruction.

<hr>

[30] Excess.

ITH.   Nature
Will call her daughter monster ! — What ! not
    eat ?
Refuse the only ordinary means
Which are ordain'd for life ? Be not, my sister,
A murd'ress to thyself. — Hear'st thou this,
    Bassanes ?
    BASS. Fo ! I am busy ; for I have not
       thoughts   160
Enow to think ; all shall be well anon.
'T is tumbling in my head ; there is a mastery
In art to fatten and keep smooth the outside,
Yes, and to comfort up the vital spirits
Without the help of food ; fumes or perfumes,
Perfumes or fumes. Let her alone ; I 'll
    search out
The trick on 't.
    PEN. Lead me gently ; Heavens reward ye.
Griefs are sure friends : they leave without
    control
Nor cure nor comforts for a leprous soul.
         Exeunt the Maids *supporting* PEN-
            THEA.
    BASS. I grant t 'ee ; and will put in practice
       instantly   170
What you shall still admire : 't is wonderful,
'T is super-singular, not to be match'd ;
Yet, when I 've done 't, I 've done 't : — ye
       shall all thank me.   *Exit* BASSANES.
    ARM. The sight is full of terror.
    ITH.   On my soul
Lies such an infinite clog of massy dullness,
As that I have not sense enough to feel it. —
See, Uncle, th' [angry] [31] thing returns again ;
Shall 's welcome him with thunder ? We are
    haunted,
And must use exorcism to conjure down
This spirit of malevolence.
    ARM.   Mildly, Nephew. [180

Enter NEARCHUS *and* AMELUS.

    NEAR. I come not, sir, to chide your late
    disorder,
Admitting that th' inurement to a roughness
In soldiers of your years and fortunes, chiefly,
So lately prosperous, hath not yet shook off
The custom of the war in hours of leisure ;
Nor shall you need excuse, since y' are to ren-
    der
Account to that fair excellence, the Princess,
Who in her private gallery expects it
From your own mouth alone ; I am a mes-
    senger
But to her pleasure.
    [31] Weber ; Q *augury.*

ITH.   Excellent Nearchus, [190
Be prince still of my services, and conquer
Without the combat of dispute ; I honor 'ee.
    NEAR. The King is on a sudden indispos'd ;
Physicians are call'd for ; 't were fit, Armostes,
You should be near him.
    ARM.   Sir, I kiss your hands.
         Exeunt [ITHOCLES *and* ARMOSTES].
    NEAR. Amelus, I perceive Calantha's bosom
Is warm'd with other fires than such as can
Take strength from any fuel of the love
I might address to her. Young Ithocles,
Or ever I mistake, is lord ascendant   200
Of her devotions ; one, to speak him truly,
In every disposition nobly fashioned.
    AME. But can your Highness brook to be so
    rivall'd,
Considering th' inequality of the persons ?
    NEAR. I can, Amelus ; for affections injur'd
By tyranny or rigor of compulsion,
Like tempest-threat'ned trees unfirmly rooted,
Ne'er spring to timely growth. Observe, for
    instance,
Life-spent Penthea and unhappy Orgilus.
    AME. How does your Grace determine ?
    NEAR.   To be jealous [210
In public of what privately I 'll further ;
And though they shall not know, yet they shall
    find it.   *Exeunt omnes.*

[SCENE III] [32]

Enter HEMOPHIL *and* GRONEAS *leading* AMY-
    CLAS, *and placing him in a chair ; followed
    by* ARMOSTES [*with a box*], CROTOLON, *and*
    PROPHILUS.

    AMY. Our daughter is not near ?
    ARM.   She is retired, sir,
Into her gallery.
    AMY.   Where 's the Prince our cousin ?
    PRO. New walk'd into the grove, my Lord.
    AMY.   All leave us
Except Armostes, and you, Crotolon ;
We would be private.
    PRO.   Health unto your Majesty !
         Exeunt PROPHILUS, HEMOPHIL, *and*
            GRONEAS.
    AMY. What ! Tecnicus is gone ?
    ARM.   He is, to Delphos ;
And to your royal hands presents this box.
    AMY. Unseal it, good Armostes ; therein lies
The secrets of the oracle ; out with it.
         [ARMOSTES *takes out the scroll.*]
Apollo live our patron ! Read, Armostes.   10
    [32] A room in the palace.

ARM. [*reads.*] " The plot in which the vine takes root
Begins to dry from head to foot;
The stock soon withering, want of sap
Doth cause to quail [33] the budding grape;
But from the neighboring elm a dew
Shall drop, and feed the plot anew."
AMY. That is the oracle. What exposition
Makes the philosopher?
ARM. This brief one only:
[*Reads.*] " The plot is Sparta, the dri'd vine the King;
The quailing grape his daughter; but the thing 20
Of most importance, not to be reveal'd,
Is a near prince, the elm; the rest conceal'd.
TECNICUS."
AMY. Enough; although the opening [34] of this riddle
Be but itself a riddle, yet we construe
How near our lab'ring age draws to a rest.
But must Calantha quail too, that young grape
Untimely budded? I could mourn for her;
Her tenderness hath yet deserv'd no rigor
So to be cross'd by fate.
ARM. You misapply, sir, — [30
With favor let me speak it, — what Apollo
Hath clouded in hid sense. I here conjecture
Her marriage with some neighb'ring prince, the dew
Of which befriending elm shall ever strengthen
Your subjects with a sovereignty of power.
CROT. Besides, most gracious Lord, the pith of oracles
Is to be then digested when th' events
Expound their truth, not brought as soon to light
As utter'd. Truth is child of Time; and herein
I find no scruple, rather cause of comfort, [40
With unity of kingdoms.
AMY. May it prove so,
For weal of this dear nation! — Where is Ithocles? —
Armostes, Crotolon, when this wither'd vine
Of my frail carcass on the funeral pile
Is fir'd into its ashes, let that young man
Be hedg'd about still with your cares and loves.
Much owe I to his worth, much to his service. —
Let such as wait come in now.
ARM. All attend here!

[33] Wither.   [34] Exposition.

Enter ITHOCLES, CALANTHA, PROPHILUS, ORGILUS, EUPHRANEA, HEMOPHIL, *and* GRONEAS.

CAL. Dear sir! King! Father!
ITH. O my royal master!
AMY. Cleave not my heart, sweet twins of my life's solace, 50
With your forejudging fears; there is no physic
So cunningly restorative to cherish
The fall of age, or call back youth and vigor,
As your consents in duty. I will shake off
This languishing disease of time, to quicken
Fresh pleasures in these drooping hours of sadness.
Is fair Euphranea married yet to Prophilus?
CROT. This morning, gracious Lord.
ORG. This very morning;
Which, with your Highness' leave, you may observe, too.
Our sister looks, methinks, mirthful and sprightly, 60
As if her chaster fancy could already
Expound the riddle of her gain in losing
A trifle maids know only that they know not. —
Pish! prithee, blush not; 't is but honest change
Of fashion in the garment, loose for strait,
And so the modest maid is made a wife.
Shrewd business — is't not, Sister?
EUPH. You are pleasant.
AMY. We thank thee, Orgilus; this mirth becomes thee.
But wherefore sits the court in such a silence?
A wedding without revels is not seemly. 70
CAL. Your late indisposition, sir, forbade it.
AMY. Be it thy charge, Calantha, to set forward
The bridal sports, to which I will be present;
If not, at least consenting. — Mine own Ithocles,
I have done little for thee yet.
ITH. Y' have built me
To the full height I stand in.
CAL. [*aside*] Now or never! — [35
May I propose a suit?
AMY. Demand, and have it.
CAL. Pray, sir, give me this young man, and no further
Account him yours than he deserves in all things

[35] So Weber, *et al.* Q has no punctuation here.

To be thought worthy mine. I will esteem
    him   80
According to his merit.

AMY.   Still th 'art my daughter,
Still grow'st upon my heart. — [to ITHOCLES]
    Give me thine hand. —
Calantha, take thine own ; in noble actions
Thou 'lt find him firm and absolute. — I would
    not
Have parted with thee, Ithocles, to any
But to a mistress who is all what I am.

ITH. A change, great King, most wish'd for,
    'cause the same.

CAL. [*aside to* ITHOCLES] Th' art mine.
    Have I now kept my word ?

ITH. [*aside to* CALANTHA]   Divinely.

ORG. Rich fortunes, guard to favor of a
    princess,[36]
Rock thee, brave man, in ever-crowned
    plenty !   90
Y' are minion [37] of the time ; be thankful for
    it. —
[*aside*] Ho ! here 's a swing in destiny — ap-
    parent !
The youth is up on tiptoe, yet may stumble.

AMY. On to your recreations. — Now con-
    vey me
Unto my bedchamber ; none on his forehead
Wear a distempered look.

OMNES.   The gods preserve 'ee !

CAL. [*aside to* ITHOCLES] Sweet, be not from
    my sight.

ITH. [*aside to* CALANTHA]   My whole fe-
    licity !

Exeunt, carrying out of the King. ORGI-
    LUS *stays* ITHOCLES.

ORG. Shall I be bold, my Lord ?

ITH.   Thou canst not, Orgilus :
Call me thine own ; for Prophilus must hence-
    forth
Be all thy sister's. Friendship, though it cease
    not   100
In marriage, yet is oft at less command
Than when a single freedom can dispose it.

ORG. Most right, my most good Lord, my
    most great Lord,
My gracious princely Lord, I might add, royal.

ITH. Royal ! A subject royal ?

ORG.   Why not, pray, sir ?
The sovereignty of kingdoms in their nonage
Stoop'd to desert, not birth ; there 's as much
    merit

---

[36] So Sherman ; Q omits the comma after *fortunes* ;
Gifford-Dyce : " Rich fortunes guard, *the* favour of
a princess Rock thee . . . ''
[37] Darling, favorite.

In clearness of affection as in puddle
Of generation : you have conquer'd love
Even in the loveliest ; if I greatly err not, [110
The son of Venus hath bequeath'd his
    quiver
To Ithocles his manage,[38] by whose arrows
Calantha's breast is open'd.

ITH.   Can 't be possible ?

ORG. I was myself a piece of suitor once,
And forward in preferment too ; so for-
    ward
That, speaking truth, I may without offence,
    sir,
Presume to whisper that my hopes, and —
    hark 'ee —
My certainty of marriage, stood assured
With as firm footing — by your leave — as
    any's
Now at this very instant — but —

ITH.   'T is granted ; [120
And for a league of privacy between us,
Read o'er my bosom and partake a secret :
The Princess is contracted mine.

ORG.   Still, why not ?
I now applaud her wisdom. When your king-
    dom
Stands seated in your will, secure and set-
    tled,
I dare pronounce you will be a just mon-
    arch ;
Greece must admire and tremble.

ITH.   Then the sweetness
Of so imparadis'd a comfort, Orgilus !
It is to banquet with the gods.

ORG.   The glory
Of numerous children, potency of nobles, [130
Bent knees, hearts pav'd to tread on !

ITH.   With a friendship
So dear, so fast as thine.

ORG.   I am unfitting
For office ; but for service —

ITH.   We 'll distinguish
Our fortunes merely in the title, partners
In all respects else but the bed.

ORG.   The bed !
Forfend it Jove's own jealousy ! — till lastly
We slip down in the common earth together,
And there our beds are equal ; save some
    monument
To show this was the king, and this the sub-
    ject. —   *Soft, sad music.*
List, what sad sounds are these ? — extremely
    sad ones.   140

ITH. Sure, from Penthea's lodgings.

---

[38] Ithocles's management.

ORG. Hark ! a voice too.

A SONG [*within*]

Oh, no more, no more, too late
   Sighs are spent ; the burning tapers
Of a life as chaste as fate,
   Pure as are unwritten papers,
Are burnt out: no heat, no light
Now remains ; 't is ever night.

Love is dead ; let lovers' eyes,
   Lock'd in endless dreams,
     Th' extremes of all extremes,   150
Ope no more, for now Love dies,
   Now Love dies, — implying
Love's martyrs must be ever, ever dying.

ITH. Oh, my misgiving heart !

ORG. A horrid stillness
Succeeds this deathful air ; let 's know the
   reason.
Tread softly ; there is mystery in mourning.
Exeunt.

SCENE [IV] [39]

Enter CHRISTALLA *and* PHILEMA, *bringing in*
PENTHEA *in a chair, veil'd; two other* Servants *placing two chairs, one on the one side,
and the other with an engine* [40] *on the other.
The* Maids *sit down at her feet, mourning.
The* Servants *go out: meet them* ITHOCLES
and ORGILUS.

SER. [*aside to* ORGILUS] 'T is done ; that on
   her right hand.

ORG. Good ; begone.
[*Exeunt* Servants.]

ITH. Soft peace enrich this room !

ORG. How fares the lady ?

PHIL. Dead !

CHRIS. Dead !

PHIL. Starv'd !

CHRIS. Starv'd !

ITH. Me miserable !

ORG. Tell us
How parted she from life.

PHIL. She call'd for music,
And begg'd some gentle voice to tune a fare-
   well
To life and griefs. Christalla touch'd the
   lute ;
I wept the funeral song.

CHRIS. Which scarce was ended
But her last breath seal'd up these hollow
   sounds :
" Oh, cruel Ithocles and injur'd Orgilus ! "
So down she drew her veil, so di'd.

ITH. So di'd ! [10

[39] Penthea's apartment.   [40] Mechanism.

ORG. Up ! you are messengers of death ; go
   from us ;
Here 's woe enough to court without a promp-
   ter.
Away ; and — hark ye — till you see us next,
No syllable that she is dead. — Away,
Keep a smooth brow.
Exeunt PHILEMA *and* CHRISTALLA.
My Lord, —

ITH. Mine only sister !
Another is not left me.

ORG. Take that chair ;
I 'll seat me here in this : between us sits
The object of our sorrows ; some few tears
We 'll part among us. I perhaps can mix
One lamentable story to prepare 'em. —   20
There, there ; sit there, my Lord.

ITH. Yes, as you please.
ITHOCLES *sits down, and is catch'd
in the engine.*
What means this treachery ?

ORG. Caught ! you are caught,
Young master ; 't is thy throne of corona-
   tion,
Thou fool of greatness ! See, I take this veil
   off ;
Survey a beauty wither'd by the flames
Of an insulting [41] Phaëthon, her brother.

ITH. Thou mean'st to kill me basely.

ORG. I foreknew
The last act of her life, and train'd thee hither
To sacrifice a tyrant to a turtle.
You dreamt of kingdoms, did 'ee ? How to
   bosom   30
The delicacies of a youngling princess ;
How with this nod to grace that subtle cour-
   tier,
How with that frown to make this noble trem-
   ble,
And so forth ; whiles Penthea's groans and tor-
   tures,
Her agonies, her miseries, afflictions,
Ne'er touch'd upon your thought. As for my
   injuries,
Alas, they were beneath your royal pity ;
But yet they liv'd, thou proud man, to con-
   found thee.
Behold thy fate ; this steel !

ITH. Strike home ! A courage
As keen as thy revenge shall give it wel-
   come ;   40
But prithee faint not ; if the wound close up,
Tent [42] it with double force, and search it
   deeply.

[41] See on I, i, 50.   [42] Probe.

Thou look'st that I should whine and beg compassion,
As loth to leave the vainness of my glories.
A statelier resolution arms my confidence,
To cozen thee of honor ; neither could I
With equal trial of unequal fortune
By hazard of a duel ; 't were a bravery
Too mighty for a slave intending murder.
On to the execution, and inherit   50
A conflict with thy horrors.

ORG.   By Apollo,
Thou talk'st a goodly language ! for requital
I will report thee to thy mistress richly.
And take this peace along : some few short minutes
Determin'd, my resolves shall quickly follow
Thy wrathful ghost ; then, if we tug for mastery,
Penthea's sacred eyes shall lend new courage.
Give me thy hand : be healthful in thy parting
From lost mortality ! thus, thus I free it.
                             Kills him.

ITH. Yet, yet, I scorn to shrink.

ORG.   Keep up thy spirit : [60
I will be gentle even in blood ; to linger
Pain, which I strive to cure, were to be cruel.
                      [Stabs him again.]

ITH. Nimble in vengeance, I forgive thee. Follow
Safety, with best success : Oh, may it prosper ! —
Penthea, by thy side thy brother bleeds ;
The earnest of his wrongs to thy forc'd faith.
Thoughts of ambition, or delicious banquet
With beauty, youth, and love, together perish
In my last breath, which on the sacred altar
Of a long-look'd-for peace — now — moves —
     to Heaven.   *[Dies.]* [43] [70

ORG. Farewell, fair spring of manhood ! Henceforth welcome
Best expectation of a noble suff'rance.
I 'll lock the bodies safe, till what must follow
Shall be approv'd. — Sweet twins, shine stars for ever ! —
In vain they build their hopes whose life is shame ;
No monument lasts but a happy name. —
                     Exit ORGILUS.

[43] Q *moritur.*

ACT V — SCENE I [1]

Enter BASSANES, *alone.*

BASS. Athens, to Athens I have sent, the nursery
Of Greece for learning and the fount of knowledge ;
For here in Sparta there 's not left amongst us
One wise man to direct ; we 're all turn'd madcaps.
'T is said Apollo is the god of herbs ;
Then certainly he knows the virtue of 'em.
To Delphos I have sent, too. If there can be
A help for nature, we are sure yet.

Enter ORGILUS.

ORG.   Honor
Attend thy counsels ever !

BASS.   I beseech thee
With all my heart, let me go from thee quietly ;   10
I will not aught to do with thee, of all men.
The [doubles] [2] of a hare, or in a morning
Salutes from a splay-footed witch, to drop
Three drops of blood at th' nose just and no more,
Croaking of ravens, or the screech of owls,
Are not so boding mischief as thy crossing
My private meditations. Shun me, prithee ;
And if I cannot love thee heartily,
I 'll love thee as well as I can.

ORG.   Noble Bassanes,
Mistake me not.

BASS.   Phew ! then we shall be troubled.
Thou wert ordain'd my plague — Heaven make me thankful,   21
And give me patience too, Heaven, I beseech thee.

ORG. Accept a league of amity ; for henceforth,
I vow, by my best genius, [3] in a syllable,
Never to speak vexation. I will study
Service and friendship, with a zealous sorrow
For my past incivility towards 'ee.

BASS. Heyday ! good words, good words !
I must believe 'em,
And be a coxcomb [4] for my labor.

ORG.   Use not
So hard a language ; your misdoubt is causeless.   30

[1] Unlocated ; presumably a room in the house of Bassanes.
[2] *I.e.*, the crossing of one's path. Emend. Gifford (silently). Q *doublers.*
[3] See on III, iv, 46.
[4] Fool.

For instance, if you promise to put on
A constancy of patience, such a patience
As chronicle or history ne'er mentioned,
As follows not example, but shall stand
A wonder and theme for imitation,
The first, the index [5] pointing to a second,
I will acquaint 'ee with an unmatch'd secret,
Whose knowledge to your griefs shall set a
    period.
    BASS. Thou canst not, Orgilus ; 't is in the
    power
Of the gods only ; yet, for satisfaction,   40
Because I note an earnest in thine utterance,
Unforc'd and naturally free, be resolute [6]
The virgin bays shall not withstand the light-
    ning
With a more careless danger than my con-
    stancy
The full of thy relation. Could it move
Distraction in a senseless marble statue,
It should find me a rock. I do expect now
Some truth of unheard moment.
    ORG.   To your patience
You must add privacy, as strong in silence
As mysteries lock'd up in Jove's own bosom. [50
    BASS. A skull hid in the earth a treble age
Shall sooner prate.
    ORG.   Lastly, to such direction
As the severity of a glorious action
Deserves to lead your wisdom and your judg-
    ment,
You ought to yield obedience.
    BASS.   With assurance
Of will and thankfulness.
    ORG.   With manly courage
Please, then, to follow me.
    BASS.   Where'er, I fear not.
                      Exeunt omnes.

SCENE II [7]

Loud music. Enter GRONEAS *and* HEMOPHIL,
leading EUPHRANEA ; CHRISTALLA *and* PHI-
LEMA, *leading* PROPHILUS ; NEARCHUS *supporting* CALANTHA ; CROTOLON *and* AMELUS.
Cease loud music ; all make a stand.[8]

    CAL. We miss our servant Ithocles and
    Orgilus ;
On whom attend they?
    CROT.   My son, gracious Princess,
Whisper'd some new device, to which these
    revels

Should be but usher, wherein I conceive
Lord Ithocles and he himself are actors.
    CAL. A fair excuse for absence ; as for
    Bassanes,
Delights to him are troublesome. Armostes
Is with the King?
    CROT.   He is.
    CAL.   On to the dance ! —
Dear Cousin, hand you the bride ; the bride-
    groom must be
Intrusted to my courtship. Be not jealous, [10
Euphranea ; I shall scarcely prove a tempt-
    ress. —
Fall to our dance.

Music

NEARCHUS *dance with* EUPHRANEA, PROPHI-
LUS *with* CALANTHA, CHRISTALLA *with* HEM-
OPHIL, PHILEMA *with* GRONEAS.

Dance the first change, during which enter AR-
MOSTES.

    ARM. (*in* CALANTHA'S *ear*)   The King
    your father's dead.
    CAL. To the other change.
    ARM.   Is 't possible?
                      Dance again.

Enter BASSANES.

    BASS. [*whispering to* CALANTHA]   Oh,
    madam !
Penthea, poor Penthea's starv'd.
    CAL.   Beshrew thee ! —
Lead to the next.
    BASS.   Amazement dulls my senses.
                      Dance again.

Enter ORGILUS.

    ORG. [*whispering to* CALANTHA] Brave Itho-
    cles is murder'd, murder'd cruelly.
    CAL. How dull this music sounds ! Strike
    up more sprightly ;
Our footings are not active like our heart,
Which treads the nimbler measure.
    ORG.   I am thunderstruck.
              Last change. Cease music.
    CAL. So ; let us breathe awhile. — Hath
    not this motion   20
Rais'd fresher color on your [9] cheeks?
    NEAR.   Sweet Princess,
A perfect purity of blood enamels
The beauty of your white.
    CAL.   We all look cheerfully ;
And, Cousin, 't is, methinks, a rare presump-
    tion

---

[5] The printer's "fist" or index-hand.
[6] Assured.
[7] A hall in the palace.   [8] Halt.

[9] Weber, perhaps rightly, emends *our.*

In any who prefer our lawful pleasures
Before their own sour censure, to interrupt
The custom of this ceremony bluntly.

NEAR. None dares, lady.

CAL. Yes, yes ; some hollow voice deliver'd
to me
How that the King was dead.

ARM. The King is dead : [30
That fatal news was mine ; for in mine arms
He breath'd his last, and with his crown be-
queath'd 'ee
Your mother's wedding ring, which here I ten-
der.

CROT. Most strange !

CAL. Peace crown his ashes ! We are
queen, then.

NEAR. Long live Calantha ! Sparta's sovereign queen !

OMNES. Long live the Queen !

CAL. What whispered Bassanes?

BASS. That my Penthea, miserable soul,
Was starv'd to death.

CAL. She 's happy ; she hath finish'd
A long and painful progress. — A third mur-
mur
Pierc'd mine unwilling ears.

ORG. That Ithocles [40
Was murder'd ; — rather butcher'd, had not
bravery
Of an undaunted spirit, conquering terror,
Proclaim'd his last act triumph over ruin.

ARM. How ! murder'd !

CAL. By whose hand?

ORG. By mine : this weapon
Was instrument to my revenge ; the reasons
Are just, and known ; quit him of these, and
then
Never liv'd gentleman of greater merit,
Hope or abiliment [10] to steer a kingdom.

CROT. Fie,[11] Orgilus !

EUPH. Fie, Brother !

CAL. You have done it.

BASS. How it was done let him report, the
forfeit 50
Of whose allegiance to our laws doth covet
Rigor of justice ; but that done it is,
Mine eyes have been an evidence of credit
Too sure to be convine'd.[12] Armostes, rent [13]
not
Thine arteries with hearing the bare circum-
stances
Of these calamities ; thou'st lost a nephew,

A niece, and I a wife : continue man still ;
Make me the pattern of digesting evils,
Who can outlive my mighty ones, not shrink-
ing
At such a pressure as would sink a soul 60
Into what 's most of death, the worst of hor-
rors.
But I have seal'd a covenant with sadness,
And enter'd into bonds without condition,
To stand these tempests calmly ; mark me,
nobles,
I do not shed a tear, not for Penthea !
Excellent misery !

CAL. We begin our reign
With a first act of justice : thy confession,
Unhappy Orgilus, dooms thee a sentence ;
But yet thy father's or thy sister's presence
Shall be excus'd. — Give, Crotolon, a bless-
ing 70
To thy lost son ; — Euphranea, take a fare-
well ; —
And both be gone.

CROT. [*to* ORGILUS] Confirm thee, noble
sorrow,
In worthy resolution !

EUPH. Could my tears speak,
My griefs were slight.

ORG. All good[n]ess dwell amongst ye !
Enjoy my sister, Prophilus ; my vengeance
Aim'd never at thy prejudice.[14]

CAL. Now withdraw. —
Exeunt CROTOLON, PROPHILUS, *and*
EUPHRANEA.
Bloody relater of thy stains in blood,
For that [15] thou hast reported him, whose for-
tunes
And life by thee are both at once snatch'd
from him,
With honorable mention, make thy choice [80
Of what death likes [16] thee best ; there 's all
our bounty. —
But to excuse delays, let me, dear Cousin,
Entreat you and these lords see execution
Instant before 'ee part.

NEAR. Your will commands us.

ORG. One suit, just Queen, my last : vouch-
safe your clemency,
That by no common hand I be divided
From this my humble frailty.

CAL. To their wisdoms
Who are to be spectators of thine end
I make the reference. Those that are dead

Are dead ; had they not now di'd, of neces-
sity   90
They must have paid the debt they ow'd to
nature
One time or other. — Use dispatch,[17] my
Lords ;
We 'll suddenly prepare our coronation.
          Exeunt CALANTHA, PHILEMA, [*and*]
                    CHRISTALLA.
ARM. 'T is strange these tragedies should
never touch on
Her female pity.
BASS.   She has a masculine spirit ;
And wherefore should I pule, and like a girl
Put finger in the eye ?   Let 's be all toughness,
Without distinction betwixt sex and sex.
NEAR. Now, Orgilus, thy choice ?
ORG.   To bleed to death.
ARM. The executioner ?
ORG.   Myself, no surgeon ; [100
I am well skill'd in letting blood.   Bind fast
This arm, that so the pipes may from their
conduits
Convey a full stream ; here 's a skilful instru-
ment.   [*Shows his dagger.*]
Only I am a beggar to some charity
To speed me in this execution
By lending th' other prick to th' tother arm,
When this is bubbling life out.
BASS.   I am for 'ee ;
It most concerns my art, my care, my credit. —
Quick, fillet [18] both [his] [19] arms.
ORG.   Gramercy, friendship !
Such courtesies are real which flow cheerfully
Without an expect[a]tion of requital.   111
Reach me a staff in this hand. — If a prone-
ness
Or custom in my nature from my cradle
Had been inclin'd to fierce and eager blood-
shed,
A coward guilt, hid in a coward quaking,
Would have betray'd fame [20] to ignoble flight
And vagabond pursuit of dreadful [21] safety ;
But look upon my steadiness, and scorn not
The sickness of my fortune, which, since Bas-
sanes
Was husband to Penthea, had lain bedrid. [120
We trifle time in words ; thus I show cunning
In opening of a vein too full, too lively.
                    [*Pierces a vein.*]
ARM. Desperate courage !

[NEAR.] [22]   Honorable infamy !
HEM. I tremble at the sight.
GRO.   Would I were loose !
BASS. It sparkles like a lusty wine new
broach'd ;
The vessel must be sound from which it is-
sues. —
Grasp hard this other stick — I 'll be as nim-
ble —
But prithee, look not pale — have at 'ee !
stretch out
Thine arm with vigor and [23] unshook virtue.
                    [*Opens a vein.*]
Good ! Oh, I envy not a rival, fitted   130
To conquer in extremities.   This pastime
Appears majestical ; some high-tun'd poem
Hereafter shall deliver to posterity
The writer's glory and his subject's triumph.
How is 't, man ?   Droop not yet.
ORG.   I feel no palsies.
On a pair royal do I wait in death :
My sovereign, as his liegeman ; on my mis-
tress,
As a devoted servant ; [24] and on Ithocles,
As if no brave, yet no unworthy enemy.
Nor did I use an engine to entrap   140
His life out of a slavish fear to combat
Youth, strength, or cunning ; [25] but for that I
durst not
Engage the goodness of a cause on fortune,
By which his name might have outfac'd my
vengeance.
O Tecnicus, inspir'd with Phoebus' fire,
I call to mind thy augury ; 't was perfect :
Revenge proves its own executioner.
When feeble man is bending to his mother,
The dust 'a was first fram'd on, thus he tot-
ters.
BASS. Life's fountain is dri'd up.
ORG.   So falls the standards [150
Of my prerogative in being a creature !
A mist hangs o'er mine eyes, the sun's bright
splendor
Is clouded in an everlasting shadow ;
Welcome, thou ice, that sitt'st about my heart :
No heat can ever thaw thee.   *Dies.*
NEAR.   Speech hath left him.
BASS. 'A has shook hands [26] with Time ;
his funeral urn
Shall be my charge.   Remove the bloodless
body.

---

[17] Hasten.
[18] *I.e.*, bind with a narrow strip, to facilitate the
blood-letting.
[19] Q *this.*
[20] *I.e.*, my reputation.   [21] Timorous.

---

[22] Emend. Gifford ; Q *Org.*
[23] Dyce suggests the addition of *with.*
[24] Lover.
[25] Skill.
[26] Said goodbye.

The coronation must require attendance ;
That past, my few days can be but one mourning.   *Exeunt.*

[SCENE III] [27]

*An altar covered with white ; two lights of virgin
wax, during which music of recorders ;* [28] *enter
Four bearing* ITHOCLES *on a hearse, or in a
chair, in a rich robe, and a crown on his head ;
place him on one side of the altar. After him
enter* CALANTHA *in a white robe and crown'd ;*
EUPHRANEA, PHILEMA, [*and*] CHRISTALLA,
in white ; NEARCHUS, ARMOSTES, CROTO-
LON, PROPHILUS, AMELUS, BASSANES, HE-
MOPHIL, *and* GRONEAS.
CALANTHA *goes and kneels before the altar ; the
rest stand off, the* Women *kneeling behind.
Cease recorders during her devotions. Soft
music.* CALANTHA *and the rest rise, doing
obeisance to the altar.*

    CAL. Our orisons are heard ; the gods are
      merciful. —
Now tell me, you whose loyalties pays tribute
To us your lawful sovereign, how unskilful
Your duties or obedience is to render
Subjection to the sceptre of a virgin,
Who have been ever fortunate in princes
Of masculine and stirring composition !
A woman has enough to govern wisely
Her own demeanors, passions, and divisions.[29]
A nation warlike and inur'd to practice   10
Of policy and labor cannot brook
A feminate authority. We therefore
Command your counsel, how you may advise
    us
In choosing of a husband whose abilities
Can better guide this kingdom.
    NEAR.   Royal lady,
Your law is in your will.
    ARM.   We have seen tokens
Of constancy too lately to mistrust it.
    CROT. Yet, if your Highness settle on a
      choice
By your own judgment both allow'd and lik'd
    of,
Sparta may grow in power, and proceed   20
To an increasing height.
    CAL.   Hold you the same mind ?
    BASS. Alas, great mistress, reason is so
      clouded
With the thick darkness of my [infinite] [30] woes,

27 A temple.
28 Flageolets or small flutes.
29 Discords.   30 Q *infinites.*

That I forecast nor dangers, hopes, or safety.
Give me some corner of the world to wear out
The remnant of the minutes I must number,
Where I may hear no sounds but sad com-
    plaints
Of virgins who have lost contracted partners ;
Of husbands howling that their wives were
    ravish'd
By some untimely fate ; of friends divided [30
By churlish opposition ; or of fathers
Weeping upon their children's slaughtered
    carcasses ;
Or daughters groaning o'er their fathers'
    hearses ;
And I can dwell there, and with these keep
    consort
As musical as theirs. What can you look for
From an old, foolish, peevish, doting man
But craziness of age ?
    CAL. Cousin of Argos, —
    NEAR.   Madam ?
    CAL.   Were I presently
To choose you for my lord, I 'll open [31] freely
What articles I would propose to treat on   40
Before our marriage.
    NEAR.   Name them, virtuous lady.
    CAL. I would presume you would retain the
      royalty
Of Sparta in her own bounds ; then in Argos
Armostes might be viceroy ; in Messene
Might Crotolon bear sway ; and Bassanes —
    BASS. I, Queen ! alas, what I ?
    CAL.   Be Sparta's marshal :
The multitudes of high employments could
    not
But set a peace to private griefs. These gen-
    tlemen,
Groneas and Hemophil, with worthy pensions,
Should wait upon your person in your cham-
    ber. —   50
I would bestow Christalla on Amelus.
She 'll prove a constant wife ; and Philema
Should into Vesta's Temple.
    BASS. [*aside*]   This is a testament !
It sounds not like conditions on a marriage.
    NEAR. All this should be perform'd.
    CAL.   Lastly, for Prophilus,
He should be, Cousin, solemnly invested
In all those honors, titles, and preferments
Which his dear friend and my neglected hus-
    band
Too short a time enjoy'd.
    PRO.   I am unworthy
To live in your remembrance.

31 Reveal, explain.

EUPH.   Excellent lady! [60

NEAR. Madam, what means that word,
"neglected husband"?

CAL. Forgive me. — [*to the body of* ITHO-
CLES] Now I turn to thee, thou shadow
Of my contracted lord! — Bear witness all,
I put my mother's wedding ring upon
His finger; 't was my father's last bequest.
Thus I new marry him whose wife I am:
Death shall not separate us. Oh, my Lords,
I but deceiv'd your eyes with antic gesture,
When one news straight came huddling on
    another
Of death! and death! and death! still I
    danced forward;   70
But it struck home, and here, and in an in-
    stant.
Be such mere women, who with shrieks and
    outcries
Can vow a present end to all their sorrows,
Yet live to vow [32] new pleasures, and outlive
    them.
They are the silent griefs which cut the heart-
    strings;
Let me die smiling.

NEAR.   'T is a truth too ominous.

CAL. One kiss on these cold lips, my last!
— Crack, crack! —
Argos now 's Sparta's king. — Command the
    voices
Which wait at th' altar now to sing the song
I fitted for my end.

NEAR.   Sirs, the song!   80

A SONG

ALL. Glories, pleasures, pomps, delights, and ease
        Can but please
[The] [33] outward senses when the mind
    Is not [34] untroubled or by peace refin'd.
1 [VOICE.] Crowns may flourish and decay;
        Beauties shine, but fade away.
2 [VOICE.] Youth may revel; yet it must
        Lie down in a bed of dust.
3 [VOICE.] Earthly honors flow and waste;
        Time alone doth change and last.   90

[32] Gifford emends *court.*
[33] A space in Q makes it clear that a word has
dropped out here.
[34] Gifford emends *or.* But, as Sherman notes,
if "outward" is emphasized the sense is clear
enough: "glories, etc., can please only the *outward*
senses when the mind is troubled or not refined by
peace."

ALL. Sorrows mingled with contents prepare
        Rest for care;
    Love only reigns in death; though art
    Can find no comfort for a broken heart.

                            [CALANTHA *dies.*]

ARM. Look to the Queen!

BASS.   Her heart is broke, indeed.
O royal maid, would thou hadst miss'd this
    part!
Yet 't was a brave one. I must weep to see
Her smile in death.

ARM.   Wise Tecnicus! thus said he:
" When youth is ripe, and age from time doth
    part,
The Lifeless Trunk shall wed the Broken
    Heart."   100
'T is here fulfill'd.

NEAR.   I am your King.

ALL.   Long live
Nearchus, King of Sparta!

NEAR.   Her last will
Shall never be digress'd from: wait in order
Upon these faithful lovers, as becomes us. —
The counsels of the gods are never known
Till men can call th' effects of them their own.

                                [*Exeunt.*]

THE EPILOGUE

WHERE noble judgments and clear eyes are
    fix'd
To grace endeavor, there sits truth, not mix'd
With ignorance; those censures may com-
    mand
Belief which talk not till they understand.
Let some say, " This was flat; " some, " Here
    the scene
Fell from its height; " another, that the mean
Was " ill observ'd " in such a growing passion
As it transcended either state or fashion.
Some few may cry, 't was " pretty well, or
    so,
But — " and there shrug in silence; yet we
    know   10
Our writer's aim was in the whole address'd
Well to deserve of *all*, but please the *best;*
Which granted, by th' allowance of this
    strain
The *Broken Heart* may be piec'd up again.

THE
LADY OF
PLEASVRE.

A
COMEDIE,

As it was Acted by her Majesties Servants, at the private
House in *Drury* Lane.

Written by *James Shirly*.

LONDON,
Printed by *Tho. Cotes*, for *Andrew Crooke,*
and *William Cooke.*
1637.

INTRODUCTORY NOTE

When the Puritans closed the theatres in 1642, Shirley was the leading London dramatist, not only for comedy, but for tragedy and tragi-comedy as well. Alone of the major dramatists he survived the closing and the Commonwealth ; his death in 1666 was due to exposure suffered during the Great Fire. When the theatres reopened at least eight of his plays were speedily revived, but *The Lady of Pleasure* seems not to have been among them.

Nevertheless this amusing piece, while it is no *Way of the World*, shows how Restoration comedy was in the making before the Civil Wars. From Jonson, the great and original source, the stream flows on, through the channels of Middleton, Fletcher, and Shirley, till, mirroring the Merry Monarch and his gaily trivial court, it spreads into the sparkling lake of Etherege, Wycherley, Shadwell, and Congreve. *The Lady of Pleasure* is verbally less coarse than the later comedy, or indeed than many of the earlier plays. In this respect several of Shirley's other works better represent the trend of the times. And there are noble sentiments and considerations of honor in Celestina and her Lord, which are rarely echoed by the more brilliant of Shirley's successors, and may have blocked the play's revival in the '60's.

On the other hand, the cool and calculated intrigue of Aretina is thoroughly typical of the degradation of love in the seventeenth-century comedy of manners, even though we must wait a quarter of a century for the unmixed cynicism of the Restoration masters. The moral note is struck in *The Lady of Pleasure*, but it is not struck very hard. The fifth-act repentances are pretty perfunctory, and the whole play is marked by much the same compromise between wit and conscience as the moral-immoral comedy with which Cibber and Farquhar were to ring the curtain down on Congreve.

The Lady of Pleasure was probably written in 1635, for on October 15 of that year it was licensed for production by the Master of the Revels. It was performed by Queen Henrietta's Men at the Phoenix (or Cockpit in Drury Lane). According to Shirley, in his dedicatory epistle to Richard, Lord Lovelace, it was " fortunate in the scene." No source for the plot is known or needed.

The standard edition of Shirley's works, a most unsatisfactory one, is still that of A. Dyce (1833). *The Lady of Pleasure* was first published, in quarto, in 1637 ; on that edition the present text is based.

THE LADY OF PLEASURE

BY

JAMES SHIRLEY

PERSONS OF THE COMEDY

[A] Lord.
Sir Thomas Bornwell.
Sir William Scentlove.
Master Alexander Kickshaw,[1] } [gallants.]
Master John Littleworth,
Master Haircut, [a barber.]
Master Frederick, [nephew to Lady Bornwell.]
Steward to the Lady Aretina.
Steward to the Lady Celestina.

Secretary [to the Lord].
Servants, etc.

Aretina,[2] Sir Thomas Bornwell's Lady.
Celestina, [Lady Bellamour], a young widow.
Isabella,   } [kinswomen to
Mariana, her sister, } Celestina.]
Madam Decoy, [a procuress.]
[Gentlewoman, servant to Celestina.]

[The] Scene — *The Strand [in London]*.

ACT I — [Scene I][3]

Enter Aretina, *and her* Steward.

Stew. Be patient, madam ; you may have your pleasure.
Are.   'T is that I came to town for. I would not
Endure again the country conversation,
To be the lady of six shires ! The men
So near the primitive making they retain
A sense of nothing but the earth, their brains
And barren heads standing as much in want
Of ploughing as their ground. To hear a fellow
Make himself merry and his horse, with whistling
Sellinger's Round ![4] To observe with what solemnity   10
They keep their wakes,[5] and throw for pewter candlesticks !

How they become the morris, with whose bells
They ring all in to Whitsun-ales ;[5] and sweat,
Through twenty scarfs and napkins, till the hobbyhorse[6]
Tire, and the Maid Marian,[7] dissolv'd to a jelly
Be kept for spoon meat ![8]
Stew.   These, with your pardon, are no argument
To make the country life appear so hateful ;
At least to your particular,[9] who enjoy'd
A blessing in that calm, would you be pleas'd [20
To think so, and the pleasure of a kingdom.
While your own will commanded what should move
Delights, your husband's love and power joined
To give your life more harmony. You liv'd there
Secure, and innocent, beloved of all,
Prais'd for your hospitality, and pray'd for.
You might be envied, but malice knew
Not where you dwelt. I would not prophesy,
But leave to your own apprehension,
What may succeed your change.

---

[1] Gewgaw, trifle. — *Master* is usually abbreviated *Mr.*, throughout.
[2] In allusion to Pietro Aretino, the sixteenth-century dramatist and satirist, the lubricity of whose writings made his name a byword.
[3] A room in Bornwell's house.
[4] See on *A Woman Killed with Kindness*, I, ii, 63, 64.
[5] Festivals.
[6] A performer in the morris dance, who capered about with the figure of a horse fastened to his waist.
[7] A hoydenish character in the morris dance, representing originally Robin Hood's sweetheart.
[8] Soft or liquid diet.   [9] In your case.

ARE.   You do imagine, [30
No doubt, you have talk'd wisely, and confuted
London past all defence. Your master should
Do well to send you back into the country,
With title of superintendent-baili[ff].
    STEW. How, madam!
    ARE.   Even so, sir.
    STEW.   I am a gentleman,
Though now your servant.
    ARE.   A country gentleman,
By your affection to converse with stubble.
His tenants will advance your wit, and plump
        it so
With beef and bag-pudding!
    STEW.   You may say your pleasure;
It becomes not me dispute.
    ARE.   Complain to [40
The lord of the soil, your master.
    STEW.   Y' are a woman
Of an ungovern'd passion, and I pity you.

        Enter Sir THOMAS BORNWELL

    BORN. How now? What 's the matter?
    STEW.   Nothing, sir. [*Exit.*]
    BORN. Angry, sweetheart?
    ARE.   I am angry with myself,
To be so miserably restrained in things
Wherein it doth concern your love and honor
To see me satisfied.
    BORN.   In what, Aretina,
Dost thou accuse me? Have I not obey'd
All thy desires? Against mine own opinion
Quitted the country, and remov'd the hope [50
Of our return, by sale of that fair lordship
We liv'd in? chang'd a calm and retir['d] life
For this wild town, compos'd of noise and
        charge? [10]
    ARE. What charge, more than is necessary
        for
A lady of my birth and education?
    BORN. I am not ignorant how much no-
        bility
Flows in your blood; your kinsmen great and
        powerful
I' th' state; but with this, lose not you mem-
        ory
Of being my wife. I shall be studious,
Madam, to give the dignity of your birth [60
All the best ornaments which become my for-
        tune;
But would not flatter it, to ruin both,
And be the fable of the town, to teach
Other men loss of wit by mine, employ'd
To serve your vast expenses.

    [10] Expense.

    ARE.   Am I then
Brought in the balance? So, sir!
    BORN.   Though you weigh
Me in a partial scale, my heart is honest,
And must take liberty to think you have
Obeyed no modest counsel, to [a]ffect,[11]
Nay, study, ways of pride and costly cere-
        mony: 70
Your change of gaudy furniture, and pictures
Of this Italian master, and that Dutchman's;
Your mighty looking-glasses, like artillery,
Brought [home] [12] on engines; the superfluous
        plate,
Antique and novel; vanities of tires;
Fourscore-pound suppers for my Lord, your
        kinsman,
Banquets for tother Lady Aunt and cousins,
And perfumes that exceed all; train of serv-
        ants,
To stifle us at home, and show abroad
More motley than the French or the Venetian,
About your coach, whose rude postillion   81
Must pester [13] every narrow lane, till passen-
        gers [14]
And tradesmen curse your choking up their
        stalls;
And common cries pursue your Ladyship,
For hind'ring o' their market.
    ARE.   Have you done, sir?
    BORN. I could accuse the gaiety of your
        wardrobe,
And prodigal embroideries, under which
Rich satins, plushes, cloth of silver, dare
Not show their own complexions; your jewels,
Able to burn out the spectators' eyes,   90
And show like bonfires on you by the tapers.
Something might here be spar'd, [with safety] [15]
        of
Your birth and honor, since the truest wealth
Shines from the soul, and draws up just ad-
        mirers.
I could urge something more.
    ARE.   Pray do; I like
Your homily of thrift.
    BORN.   I could wish, madam,
You would not game so much.
    ARE.   A gamester, too?
    BORN. But are not come to that [acquaint-
        ance] [16] yet,
Should teach you skill enough to raise your
        profit.

[11] Hanker for.   Q *effect.*
[12] Q *whom.*   [13] Obstruct.
[14] Pedestrians.
[15] Emend. Dyce; Q *which safely.*
[16] Emend. Dyce; Q *repentance.*

You look not through the subtlety of cards, [100
And mysteries of dice ; nor can you save
Charge with the box,[17] buy petticoats and
    pearls,
And keep your family by the precious income ;
Nor do I wish you should : my poorest servant
Shall not upbraid my tables, nor his hire,
Purchas'd beneath my honor. You make
    play
Not a pastime but a tyranny, and vex
Yourself and my estate by it.
    ARE.   Good ! proceed.
    BORN. Another game you have, which con-
    sumes more
Your fame than purse ; your revels in the
    night,   110
Your meetings call'd the Ball, to which [re-
    pair,] [18]
As to the Court of Pleasure, all your gallants
And ladies, thither bound by a subpoena
Of Venus, and small Cupid's high displeasure ;
'T is but the Family of Love [19] translated
Into more costly sin ! There was a play on 't ;[20]
And had the poet not been brib'd to a modest
Expression of your antic gambols in 't,
Some darks had been discovered, and the deeds
    too.   119
In time he may repent, and make some blush,
To see the second part danc'd on the stage.
My thoughts acquit you for [21] dishonoring me
By any foul act ; but the virtuous know
'T is not enough to clear ourselves, but the
Suspicions of our shame.
    ARE.   Have you concluded
Your lecture?
    BORN.   I ha' done ; and howsoever
My language may appear to you, it carries
No other than my fair and just intent
To your delights, without curb to their mod-
    est [22]
And noble freedom.
    ARE.   I 'll not be so tedious   [130
In my reply ; but, without art or elegance,
Assure you, I keep still my first opinion ;
And though you veil your avaricious meaning
With handsome names of modesty and thrift,
I find you would entrench [23] and wound the
    liberty
I was born with. Were my desires unprivileged

By example, while my judgment thought 'em
    fit,
You ought not to oppose ; but when the prac-
    tice
And trac[k] of every honorable lady [24]
Authorize [25] me, I take it great injustice [140
To have my pleasures circumscribed, and
    taught me.
A narrow-minded husband is a thief
To his own fame, and his preferment,[26] too ;
He shuts his parts [27] and fortunes from the
    world,
While, from the popular vote and knowledge,
    men
Rise to employment in the state.
    BORN.   I have
No great ambition to buy preferment at
So dear a rate.
    ARE.   Nor I to sell my honor,
By living poor and sparingly. I was not
Bred in that ebb of fortune, and my fate [150
Shall not compel me to it.
    BORN.   I know not,
Madam ; but you pursue these ways —
    ARE.   What ways?
    BORN. In the strict sense of honesty, I dare
Make oath they are innocent.
    ARE.   Do not divert,
By busy troubling of your brain, those
    thoughts
That should preserve 'em.
    BORN.   How was that?
    ARE.   'T is English.
    BORN. But carries some unkind sense.

Enter MADAM DECOY.

    DEC. Good morrow, my sweet madam.
    ARE.   Decoy ! welcome ;
This visit is a favor.
    DEC.   Alas, sweet madam,
I cannot stay : I came but to present   160
My service to your Ladyship ; I could not
Pass by your door, but I must take the bold-
    ness
To tender my respects.
    ARE.   You oblige me, madam ;
But I must not dispense so with your absence.
    DEC. Alas, the coach, madam, stays for me
    at the door.
    ARE. Thou sha't command mine ; prithee,
    sweet Decoy —

---

[17] By the dice-box.
[18] Emend. Dyce. Q *appear.*
[19] A sect of religious fanatics popularly credited
with licentious practices.
[20] *The Ball*, by Shirley (1632).
[21] Of, from.   [22] Moderate.
[23] Cut into, infringe upon.

[24] Lady of rank.
[25] Accented on second syllable.
[26] Advancement.
[27] Qualities, accomplishments.

Dec. I would wait on you, madam, but I have many
Visits to make this morning; I beseech —
Are. So you will promise to dine with me.
Dec. I shall 169
Present a guest.
Are. Why, then good morrow, madam.
Dec. A happy day shine on your Ladyship!
Exit.

Re-enter Steward.

Are. What's your news, sir?
Stew. Madam, two gentlemen.
Are. What gentlemen? Have they no names?
Stew. They are
The gentleman with his own head of hair
Whom you commended for his horsemanship
In Hyde Park, and becoming [28] the saddle,
The tother day.
Are. What circumstance is this
To know him by?
Stew. His name's at my tongue's end —
He lik'd the fashion of your pearl chain, madam,
And borrowed it for his jeweller to take 180
A copy by it.
Born. [*aside*] What cheating gallant's this?
Stew. That never walks without a lady's busk,[29]
And plays with fans — Master Alexander Kickshaw! —
I thought I should remember him.
Are. What's the other?
Stew. What an unlucky memory I have!
The gallant that still danceth in the street,
And wears a gross of ribbon in his hat;
That carries oringado [30] in his pocket,
And sugarplums, to sweeten his discourse;
That studies compliment, defies all wit 190
[In] [31] black, and censures plays that are not bawdy —
Master John Littleworth!
Are. They are welcome; but
Pray entertain them a small time, lest I
Be unprovided.
Born. Did they ask for me?
Stew. No, sir.
Born. It matters not, they must be welcome.
Are. Fie! how's this hair disordered? Here's a curl

Straddle[s] most impiously. I must to my closet. *Exit.*
Born. Wait on 'em; my Lady will return again. [*Exit* Steward.]
I have to such a height fulfill'd her humor,[32]
All application's [33] dangerous: these gallants
Must be receiv'd, or she will fall into 201
A tempest, and the house be shook with names
Of all her kindred. 'T is a servitude
I may in time shake off.

Enter Alexander [Kickshaw] *and* Little-worth.

Kick.[34] [*and*] Little. Save you, Sir Thomas!
Born. Save you, gentlemen!
Kick. I kiss your hand.
Born. What [35] day is it abroad?
Little. The morning rises from your lady's eye:
If she look clear, we take the happy omen
Of a fair day.
Born. She'll instantly appear,
To the discredit of your compliment; 210
But you express your wit thus.
Kick. And you modesty,
Not to affect [36] the praises of your own.
Born. Leaving this subject, what game's now on foot?
What exercise carries the general vote
O' th' town now? Nothing moves without your knowledge.
Kick. The cocking now has all the noise; I'll have
A hundred pieces [37] of one battle. Oh,
These birds of Mars!
Little. Venus is Mars his bird too.
Kick. Why, and the pretty doves are Venus's,
To show that kisses draw the chariot. 220
Little. I am for that skirmish.
Born. When shall we have
More booths and bagpipes upon Banstead [38] downs?
No mighty race is expected? — But my lady Returns!

Re-enter Aretina.

Are. Fair morning to you, gentlemen!
You went not late to bed by [39] your early visit.
You do me honor.
Kick. It becomes our service.

[28] Dyce adds *so.* [29] Corset.
[30] Candied orange-peel. [31] Q *On.*
[32] Indulged her caprice. [33] Appeal to her.
[34] Q *Al.,* throughout.
[35] What kind of. [36] Like. Cf. on l. 69.
[37] Coins worth about $5.00 each.
[38] A parish in Surrey. [39] *I.e.,* to judge by.

ARE. What news abroad? You hold precious intelligence.

LITTLE. All tongues are so much busy with your praise
They have not time to frame other discourse.
Will ['t] please you, madam, taste a sugar-
plum?   230

BORN. What does the goldsmith think the pearl is worth
You borrowed of my Lady?

KICK.   'T is a rich one.

BORN. She has many other toys, whose fashion you
Will like extremely. You have no intention
To buy any of her jewels?

KICK.   Understand me —

BORN. You had rather sell, perhaps. But, leaving this,
I hope you 'll dine with us.

KICK.   I came a' purpose.

ARE. And where were you last night?

KICK.   I, madam? Where
I slept not; it had been sin, where so much
Delight and beauty was to keep me waking.
There is a lady, madam, will be worth   241
Your free society; my conversation
Ne'er knew so elegant and brave a soul,
With most incomparable flesh and blood;
So spirited! so courtly! speaks the languages,
Sings, dances, plays o' th' lute to admiration![40]
Is fair, and paints not; games, too, keeps a table,
And talks most witty satire; has a wit
Of a clean [41] Mercury —

LITTLE.   Is she married?

KICK.   No.

ARE. A virgin?

KICK. Neither.

LITTLE.   What, a widow? Something [250
Of this wide commendation might have been
Excus'd. This such a prodigy!

KICK.   Repent,
Before I name her. She did never see
Yet full sixteen, an age, in the opinion
Of wise men, not contemptible. She has
Mourned out her year, too, for the honest knight
That had compassion of her youth, and di'd
So timely. Such a widow is not common;
And now she shines more fresh and tempting
Than any natural virgin.

ARE.   What 's her name?   260

KICK. She was christened Celestina; by her husband,

The Lady Bellamour. This ring was hers.

BORN. You borrowed it to copy out the posy.[42]

KICK. Are they not pretty rubies? 'T was a grace
She was pleas'd to show me, that I might have one
Made of the same fashion; for I love
All pretty forms.

ARE.   And is she glorious?

KICK. She is full of jewels, madam; but I am
Most taken with the bravery [43] of her mind,
Although her garments have all grace and or-
nament.   270

ARE. You have been high in praises.

KICK.   I come short;
No flattery can reach her.

BORN. [*aside*]   Now my lady
Is troubled, as [44] she fear'd to be eclips'd:
This news will cost me somewhat.

ARE.   You deserve
Her favor, for this noble character.[45]

KICK. And I possess it, by my stars' be-
nevolence.

ARE. You must bring us acquainted.

BORN.   I pray do, sir;
I long to see her too. — Madam, I have
Thought upon 't, and corrected my opinion.
Pursue what ways of pleasure your desires
Incline you to; not only with my state,   281
But with my person, I will follow you.
I see the folly of my thrift, and will
Repent in sack and prodigality,
To your own heart's content.

ARE.   But do not mock.

BORN. Take me to your embraces, gentlemen,
And tutor me.

LITTLE.   And will you kiss the ladies?

BORN. And sing and dance. I long to see this beauty;
I would fain lose a hundred pounds at dice now.
Thou sha't have another gown and petticoat
To-morrow. Will you sell my running-
horses?   291
We have no Greek wine in the house, I think;
Pray send one of our footmen to the merchant,
And throw the hogsheads of March beer [46] into
The kennel, to make room for sacks and claret.

[42] Inscription (inside it). The posy was usually a "motto" in verse.
[43] Splendor, ornaments.
[44] As if.   [45] Description of her.
[46] A strong beer brewed in March.

[40] Wonderfully.   [41] Absolute, veritable.

What think you to be drunk yet before dinner?
We will have constant music, and maintain
Them and their fiddles in fantastic liveries;
I 'll tune my voice to catches. I must have
My dining-room enlarg'd, to invite ambassa-
    dors.   300
We 'll feast the parish in the fields, and teach
The military men new discipline,
Who shall charge all their new [47] artillery
With oranges and lemons, boy, to play
All dinner upon our capons.

KICK.   He 's exalted!
BORN. I will do anything to please my lady;
Let that suffice; and kiss o' th' same condi-
    tion.
I am converted; do not you dispute,
But patiently allow the miracle.

ARE. I am glad to hear you, sir, in so good
    tune.   310

Enter Servant.

SERV. Madam, the painter.
ARE.   I am to sit this morning.
BORN. Do, while I give new directions to
    my steward.
KICK. With your favor, we 'll wait on you;
    sitting 's but
A melancholy exercise without
Some company to discourse.

ARE.   It does conclude
A lady's morning work. We rise, make fine,
Sit for our picture, and 't is time to dine.
LITTLE. Praying 's forgot.
KICK.   'T is out of fashion.
                        Exeunt.

[SCENE II] [48]

Enter CELESTINA *and her* Steward.

CEL. Fie! what an air this room has!
STEW.   'T is perfum'd.
CEL. With some cheap stuff. Is it your
    Wisdom's thrift
To infect my nostrils thus? or is 't to favor
The gout in your Worship's hand, you are
    afraid
To exercise your pen in your account book?
Or do you doubt my credit to discharge
Your bills?
STEW.   Madam, I hope you have not
    found
My duty, with the guilt of sloth or jealousy,
Unapt to your command.

CEL.   You can extenuate
Your faults with language, sir; but I ex-
    pect   10
To be obeyed. What hangings have we here!
STEW. They are arras, madam.
CEL.   Impudence! I know 't.
I will have fresher, and more rich; not
    wrought
With faces that may scandalize a Christian,
With Jewish [49] stories stuff'd with corn and
    camels. [50]
You had best wrap all my chambers in wild
    Irish
And make a nursery of monsters here,
To fright the ladies [51] comes to visit me.
STEW. Madam, I hope —
CEL.   I say I will have other,
Good Master Steward, of a finer loom: 20
Some silk and silver, if your Worship please
To let me be at so much cost. I 'll have
Stories to fit the seasons of the year,
And change as often as I please.
STEW.   You shall, madam.
CEL. I am bound to your consent, for-
    sooth! And is
My coach brought home?
STEW.   This morning I expect it.
CEL. The inside, as I gave direction,
Of crimson plush?
STEW.   Of crimson camel [52] plush.
CEL. Ten thousand moths consume 't!
    Shall I ride through
The streets in penance, wrapp'd up round in
    haircloth?   30
Sell 't to an alderman; 't will serve his wife
To go a-feasting to their country-house, [53]
Or fetch a merchant's nurse-child, and come
    home
Laden with fruit and cheese-cakes. I despise
    it!
STEW. The nails adorn it, madam, set in
    method,
And pretty forms.
CEL.   But single gilt, I warrant.
STEW. No, madam, —
CEL.   Another solecism! Oh, fie!
This fellow will bring me to a consumption
With fretting at his ignorance. Some lady
Had rather never pray than go to church
    in 't.   40
The nails not double gilt! To market wo 't? [54]

[47] Dyce emends *great.*
[48] A room in Celestina's house.

[49] *I.e.*, Biblical.
[50] The story of Joseph and his brethren. (Dyce.)
[51] Understand "who."   [52] Camel's hair.
[53] Summerhouse in a suburban garden.
[54] Wilt thou.

'T will hackney out to Mile End,⁵⁵ or convey
Your city tumblers ⁵⁶ to be drunk with cream
And prunes ⁵⁷ at Islington,⁵⁸

STEW.   Good madam, hear me —

CEL. I 'll rather be beholding ⁵⁹ to my aunt,
The Countess, for her mourning coach, than be
Disparag'd so. Shall any juggling tradesman
Be at charge to shoe his running-horse with
     gold,⁶⁰
And shall my coach nails be but single gilt?
How dare these knaves abuse me so !

STEW.   Vouchsafe [50
To hear me speak.

CEL.   Is my sedan yet finish'd,
And liveries for my men-mules,⁶¹ according
As I gave charge?

STEW.   Yes, madam, it is finish'd,
But without tilting-plumes at the four corners ;
The scarlet 's pure, but not embroidered.

CEL. What mischief were it to your con-
     science
Were my coach lin'd with tissue,⁶² and my har-
     ness
Cover'd with needle-work? if my sedan
Had all the story of the prodigal
Embroidered with pearl?

STEW.   Alas, good madam, [60
I know 't is your own cost ; I am but your
     steward,
And would discharge my duty the best way.
You have been pleas'd to hear me ; 't is not for
My profit that I manage your estate
And save expense, but for your honor, madam.

CEL. How, sir ! my honor?

STEW.   Though you hear it not,
Men's tongues are liberal ⁶³ in ⁶⁴ your charac-
     ter,
Since you began to live thus high. I know
Your fame ⁶⁵ is precious to you.

CEL.   I were best
Make you my governor. Audacious var-
     let !   70
How dare you interpose your doting counsel?
Mind your affairs with more obedience,
Or I shall ease you of an office, sir.
Must I be limited to please your Honor,
Or, for the vulgar breath, confine my
     pleasures?

I will pursue 'em in what shapes I fancy,
Here, and abroad ; my entertainments shall
Be oft'ner, and more rich. Who shall con-
     trol me?
I live i' th' Strand, whither few ladies come
To live, and purchase ⁶⁶ more than fame. I
     will   80
Be hospitable then, and spare no cost
That may engage all generous report
To trumpet forth my bounty and my brav-
     ery,
Till the court envy, and remove. I 'll have
My house the academy of wits, who shall
Exalt ⁶⁷ with rich sack and sturgeon,
Write panegyrics of my feasts, and praise
The method of my witty superfluities.
The horses shall be taught, with frequent wait-
     ing
Upon my gates, to stop in their career   90
Toward Charing Cross, spite of the coach-
     man's fury ;
And not a tilter ⁶⁸ but shall strike ⁶⁹ his plume,
When he sails by my window. My balcony
Shall be the courtier's idol, and more gaz'd
     at
Than all the pageantry at Temple Bar,⁷⁰
By country clients.

STEW.   Sure my lady 's mad.

CEL. Take that for your ill manners.
                     [*Strikes him.*]

STEW.   Thank you, madam.
I would there were less quicksilver in your fin-
     gers.   *Exit.*

CEL. There 's more than simple honesty in a
     servant
Requir'd to his full duty ; none should
     dare   100
But with a look, much less a saucy language,
Check at their mistress' pleasure. I'm re-
     solv'd
To pay for some delight : my estate will bear
     it ;
I 'll rein it shorter when I please.

Re-enter Steward.

STEW.   A gentleman
Desires to speak with your Ladyship.

CEL.   His name?

---

⁵⁵ Then a popular resort.   ⁵⁶ Harlots.
⁵⁷ A standard dish in the brothels.
⁵⁸ Then a country village.   ⁵⁹ Beholden.
⁶⁰ In one of the songs in Shirley's *Hyde Park*
(IV, iii) "Toby with his golden shoes" is mentioned
among the horses.
⁶¹ *I.e.*, chairmen.   ⁶² Richly embroidered cloth.
⁶³ Free-spoken, licentious.
⁶⁴ In regard to.   ⁶⁵ Reputation.

⁶⁶ Acquire.
⁶⁷ Dyce adds their *genius*.
⁶⁸ *I.e.*, gentlemen riding out to tilt ; plumes were
regularly worn by tilters.
⁶⁹ Lower, as a ship "strikes" her flag, topsail,
or topmast, as a token of respect or submission.
⁷⁰ Which marked the western limit of the municipal authority. Here the sovereign paused to
receive the sword of the city on visits of state.

STEW. He says you know him not ; he seems to be
Of quality.[71]

CEL.   Admit him.   [*Exit* Steward.]

Enter HAIRCUT.

                                Sir, with me?

HAIR. Madam, I know not how you may receive
This boldness from me ; but my fair intents
Known, will incline you to be charitable. [110

CEL. No doubt, sir.

HAIR.   He must live obscurely, madam,
That hath not heard what virtues you possess ;
And I, a poor admirer of your fame,
Am come to kiss your hand.

CEL.   That all your business?

HAIR. Though it were worth much travel, I have more
In my ambition.

CEL.   Speak it freely, sir.

HAIR. You are a widow.

CLE.   So !

HAIR.   And I a bachelor.

CEL. You come a-wooing, sir, and would perhaps
Show me a way to reconcile the two?

HAIR. And bless my stars for such a happiness.   120

CEL. I like you, sir, the better, that you do not
Wander about, but shoot home to the meaning ;
It is a confidence will make a man
Know sooner what to trust to. But I never
Saw you before, and I believe you come not
With hope to find me desperate [72] upon marriage.
If maids, out of their ignorance of what
Men are, refuse these offers, widows may,
Out of their knowledge, be allow'd some coyness.
And yet I know not how much happiness [130
A peremptory answer may deprive me of.
You may be some young lord, and though I see not
Your footmen and your groom, they may not be
Far off, in conference with your horse. Please you
To instruct me with your title, against which
I would not willingly offend.

HAIR.   I am
A gentleman ; my name is Haircut, madam.

CEL. Sweet Master Haircut, are you a courtier?

HAIR. Yes.

CEL.   I did think so, by your confidence.
Not to detain you, sir, with circumstance,[73] [140
I was not so unhappy in my husband
But that 't is possible I may be a wife
Again ; but I must tell you, he that wins
My affection shall deserve me.

HAIR.   I will hope,
If you can love, I shall not present, madam,
An object to displease you in my person ;
And when time, and your patience, shall possess you
With further knowledge of me, and the truth
Of my devotion, you will not repent
The offer of my service.

CEL.   You say well.   150
How long do you imagine you can love, sir?
Is it a quotidian [74] or will it hold
But every other day?

HAIR.   You are pleasant,[75] madam.

CEL. Does 't take you with a burning at the first,
Or with a cold fit? for you gentlemen
Have both your summer and your winter service.

HAIR. I am ignorant what you mean ; but I shall never
Be cold in my affection to such beauty.

CEL. And 't will be somewhat long ere I be warm in 't.

HAIR. If you vouchsafe me so much honor, madam,   160
That I may wait on you sometimes, I sha' not
Despair to see a change.

CEL.   But now I know
Your mind, you shall not need to tell it when
You come again : I shall remember it.

HAIR. You make me fortunate.

Re-enter Steward.

STEW.   Madam, your kinswomen,
The Lady Novice, and her sister, are
New lighted from their coach.

CEL.   I did expect 'em,
They partly are my pupils. I 'll attend 'em.

HAIR. Madam, I have been too great a trespasser
Upon your patience ; I 'll take my leave. [170

---

[71] Gentility, social position.
[72] *I.e.*, desperately resolved.

[73] Circumlocutions.
[74] An intermittent fever or ague, **recurring daily.**
[75] Jocular.

You have affairs, and I have some employment
Calls me to court ; I shall present again
A servant to you.   *Exit* HAIRCUT.
  CEL.   Sir, you may present,[76]
But not give fire, I hope. — Now to the ladies.
This recreation 's past ; the next must be
To read to them some court philosophy.
                                        Exeunt.

ACT II — [SCENE I] [1]

Enter SIR THOMAS BORNWELL.

  BORN. 'T is a strange humor I have under-
    taken,
To dance and play [2] and spend as fast as she
    does ;
But I am resolv'd : it may do good upon her,
And fright her into thrift.   Nay, I 'll endeavor
To make her jealous too ; if this do not
Allay her gamboling, she 's past a woman,
And only a miracle must tame her.

Enter Steward.

  STEW. 'T is Master Frederick, my Lady's
    nephew.
  BORN.   What of him ?
  STEW. Is come from the university.
  BORN.   By whose directions ?
  STEW. It seems, my Lady's.
  BORN.   Let me speak with him [10
Before he see his aunt. [*Exit* Steward.] — I do
    not like it. —

Re-enter [Steward, *with*] MASTER FREDERICK,
    [*in his college dress.*]

Master Frederick, welcome ! I expected not
So soon your presence ; what 's the hasty
    cause ?
  FRED. These letters, from my tutor, will
    acquaint you.
  STEW. Welcome home, sweet Master Fred-
    erick !
  FRED.   Where 's my aunt ?
  STEW. She 's busy about her painting, in
    her closet ;
The outlandish man of art [3] is copying out
Her countenance.
  FRED.   She is sitting for her picture ?
  STEW. Yes, sir ; and when 't is drawn she
    will be hang'd

[76] "Present arms" is not cited by *N.E.D.* prior
to 1759 ; here "present" appears to mean raise,
level, or aim.
 [1] A room in Bornwell's house.   [2] Game.
 [3] Foreign artist.

Next the French cardinal, in the dining-
    room ;   20
But when she hears you 're come, she will dis-
    miss
The Belgic gentleman, to entertain
Your Worship.
  FRED.   Change of air has made you witty.
                            [*Exit* Steward.]
  BORN. Your tutor gives you a handsome
    character,
Frederick, and is sorry your aunt's pleasure
Commands you from your studies ; but I hope
You have no quarrel to the liberal arts.
Learning is an addition [4] beyond
Nobility of birth.   Honor of blood,
Without the ornament of knowledge, is   30
A glorious [5] ignorance.
  FRED. I never knew more sweet and happy
    hours
Than I employ'd upon my books.   I heard
A part of my philosophy, and was so
Delighted with the harmony of nature,
I could have wasted my whole life upon 't.
  BORN. [*aside*] 'T is pity a rash indulgence
    should corrupt
So fair a genius ! — She 's here ; I 'll observe.

Enter ARETINA, ALEXANDER [KICKSHAW],
    LITTLEWORTH, [*and*] Steward.

  FRED. My most lov'd aunt !
  ARE.   Support me ; I shall faint.
  LITTLE. What ails your Ladyship ?
  ARE.   Is that Frederick, [40
In black ?
  KICK.   Yes, madam ; but the doublet 's
    satin.
  ARE. The boy 's undone ! [6]
  FRED.   Madam, you appear troubled.
  ARE. Have I not cause ?   Was not I
    trusted with
Thy education, boy, and have they sent thee
Home like a very scholar ?
  KICK.   'T was ill done,
Howe'er they us'd him in the university,
To send him to his friends thus.
  FRED.   Why, sir ?   Black,
(For 't is the color that offends your eyesight,)
Is not, within my reading, any blemish :
Sables are no disgrace in heraldry.   50
  KICK. 'T is coming from the college thus,
    that makes it
Dishonorable.   While you w[o]re it for
Your father, it was commendable ; or were
Your aunt dead, you might mourn, and justify.

[4] Title.   [5] Vainglorious.   [6] Ruined.

Are. What luck [7] I did not send him into France !
They would have given him generous education,
Taught him another garb, to wear his lock,[8]
And shape,[9] as gaudy as the summer ; how
To dance, and wag his feather *à la mode*,
To compliment, and cringe ; [10] to talk not modestly,   60
Like, " ay, forsooth," and " no, forsooth " — to blush,
And look so like a chaplain ! — There he might
Have learned a brazen confidence, and observ'd
So well the custom of the country, that
He might, by this time, have invented fashions
For us, and been a benefit to the kingdom ;
Preserv'd our tailors in their wits, and sav'd
The charge of sending into foreign courts
For pride and antic [11] fashions. — Observe
In what a posture he does hold his hat now ! [70
     Fred. Madam, with your pardon, you have practis'd
Another dialect than was taught me when
I was commended to your care and breeding.
I understand not this ; Latin or Greek
Are more familiar to my apprehension :
Logic was not so hard in my first lectures
As your strange language.
     Are.   Some strong waters ; oh !
     Little. Comfits will be as comfortable to your stomach, madam. [*Offers his box.*]
     Are. I fear he 's spoil'd for ever ! He did name
Logic, and may, for aught I know, be gone
So far to understand it. I did always   81
Suspect they would corrupt him in the college. —
Will your Greek saws and sentences discharge [12]
The mercer? [13] Or is Latin a fit language
To court a mistress in? — Master Alexander,
If you have any charity, let me
Commend him to your breeding. — I suspect
I must employ my doctor first, to purge
The university that lies in 's head ;
It alters his complexion.[14]
     Kick.   If you dare   90
Trust me to serve him —
     Are.   Master Littleworth,
Be you join'd in commission.

----

[7] Bad luck.   [8] Lovelock.   [9] Costume.
[10] Derisively for "bow."
[11] Bizarre.   [12] Pay.   [13] The textile dealer.
[14] Constitution.

     Little.   I will teach him
Postures and rudiments.
     Are.   I have no patience
To see him in this shape ; it turns my stomach.
When he has cast his academic skin
He shall be yours. I am bound in conscience
To see him bred ; his own state [15] shall maintain
The charge, while he 's my ward. — Come hither, sir.
     Fred. What does my aunt mean to do with me?
     Stew. To make you a fine gentleman, and translate you   100
Out of your learned language, sir, into
The present Goth and Vandal, which is French.
     Born. [*aside*] Into what mischief will this humor ebb?
She will undo the boy ; I see him ruin'd.
My patience is not manly ; but I must
Use stratagem to reduce her : open ways
Give me no hope.   *Exit.*
     Stew.   You shall be obey'd, madam.
          Exeunt [*all but* Frederick *and* Steward].
     Fred. Master Steward, are you sure we do not dream?
Was 't not my aunt you talk'd to?
     Stew.   One that loves you
Dear as her life. These clothes do not become you ;   110
You must have better, sir —
     Fred.   These are not old.
     Stew. More suitable to the town and time ; we keep
No Lent here, nor is 't my Lady's pleasure you
Should fast from anything you have a mind to ;
Unless it be your learning, which she would have you
Forget with all convenient speed that may be,
For the credit of your noble family.
The case is alter'd since we liv'd i' th' country :
We do not [now] [16] invite the poor o' th' parish
To dinner, keep a table for the tenants ; [120
Our kitchen does not smell of beef ; the cellar
Defies the price of malt and hops : the footmen
And coach-drivers may be drunk like gentlemen,
With wine ; nor will three fiddlers upon holidays,
With aid of bagpipes, that call'd in the country

----

[15] Estate.   [16] Add. Dyce.

To dance, and plough the hall up with their
    hobnails,
Now make my Lady merry. We do feed
Like princes, and feast nothing [else] [17] but
    princes ;
And are these robes fit to be seen amongst
    'em ?
    FRED. My Lady keeps a court then ! Is
      Sir Thomas   130
Affected [18] with this state and cost ?
    STEW.   He was not,
But is converted ; and I hope you wo' [19] not
Persist in heresy, but take a course
Of riot, to content your friends ; you shall
Want nothing, if you can be proud, and spend
    it
For my Lady's honor. Here are a hundred
Pieces, will serve you till you have new clothes ;
I will present you with a nag of mine,
Poor tender of my service ; please you accept ;
My Lady's smile more than rewards me for
    it.   140
I must provide fit servants to attend you,
Monsieurs, for horse and foot.
    FRED.   I shall submit,
If this be my aunt's pleasure, and be rul'd ;
My eyes are open'd with this purse already,
And sack will help to inspire me. I must
    spend it ?
    STEW. What else, sir ?
    FRED.   I 'll begin with you : to encourage
You to have still a special care of me,
There is five pieces — not for your nag.
    STEW. No, sir ; I hope it is not.
    FRED.   Buy a beaver
For thy own block ; [20] I shall be rul'd. Who
    does   150
Command the wine cellar ?
    STEW.   Who command but you, sir ?
    FRED. I 'll try to drink a health or two, my
    aunt's,
Or anybody's ; and if that foundation
Stagger me not too much, I will commence
In all the arts of London.
    STEW.   If you find, sir,
The operation of the wine exalt
Your blood to the desire of any female
Delight, I know your aunt wo' not deny
Any of her chambermaids to practice on ;
She loves you but too well.
    FRED.   I know not how [160
I may be for that exercise. — Farewell, Aris-
    totle ;

Prithee commend me to the library [21]
At Westminster ; my bones I bequeath
    thither,
And to the learned worms that mean to visit
    'em.
I will compose myself ; I begin to think
I have lost time indeed. — Come to the wine
    cellar.   *[Exeunt.]*

[SCENE II] [22]

Enter CELESTINA, MARIANA, [*and*] ISABELLA.

    MAR. But shall we not, madam, expose
    ourselves
To censure for this freedom ?
    CEL.   Let them answer
That dare mistake us. Shall we be so much
Cowards, to be frighted from our pleasure
Because men have malicious tongues, and show
What miserable souls they have ? No, Cousin,
We hold our life and fortunes upon no
Man's charity ; if they dare show so little
Discretion to traduce our fames, we will
Be guilty of so much wit to laugh at 'em.   10
    ISAB. 'T is a becoming fortitude.
    CEL.   My stars
Are yet kind to me ; for, in a happy minute
Be 't spoke, I 'm not in love, and men shall
    never
Make my heart lean with sighing, [23] nor with
    tears
Draw on my eyes the infamy of spectacles.
'T is the chief principle to keep your heart
Under your own obedience ; jest, but love not.
I say my prayers, yet can wear good clothes,
And only satisfy my tailor for 'em.
I wo' not lose my privilege.   20
    MAR. And yet they say your entertain-
    ments are,
Give me your pardon, madam, to proclaim
Yourself a widow, and to get a husband.
    CEL. As if a lady of my years, some beauty,
Left by her husband rich, that had mourn'd
    for him
A twelvemonth too, could live so obscure i' th'
    town
That gallants would not know her, and invite
Themselves, without her chargeable procla-
    mations !
Then we are worse than citizens : no widow
Left wealthy can be throughly warm in
    mourning,   30

---

[17] Add. Dyce.   [18] Favorably disposed toward.
[19] Will.   [20] Head : properly, hat-mould.
[21] Of the Abbey.
[22] A room in Celestina's house.
[23] Every sigh was supposed to cost a drop of **blood.**

But some one noble blood, or lusty kindred,
Claps in, with his gilt coach and Flandrian [24]
  trotters,
And hurries her away to be a countess.
Courtiers have spies, and great ones with
  [large] [25] titles,
Cold in their own estates, would warm them-
  selves
At a rich city bonfire.
    ISAB.   Most true, madam.
    CEL. No matter for corruption of the blood ;
Some undone courtier made her husband rich,[26]
And this new lord receives it back again.
Admit it were my policy, and that   40
My entertainments pointed to acquaint me
With many suitors, that I might be safe
And make the best election, could you blame
  me?
    MAR. Madam, 't is wisdom.
    CEL.   But I should be
In my thoughts miserable, to be fond
Of [27] leaving the sweet freedom I possess,
And court myself into new marriage fetters.
I now observe men's several wits and wind-
  ings,[28]
And can laugh at their follies.
    MAR.   You have given
A most ingenious [29] satisfaction.   50
    CEL. One thing I 'll tell you more, and this
  I give you
Worthy your imitation, from my practice :
You see me merry, full of song and dancing,
Pleasant in language, apt to all delights
That crown a public meeting ; but you cannot
Accuse me of being prodigal of my favors
To any of my guests. I do not summon,
By any wink, a gentleman to follow me
To my withdrawing chamber ; I hear all
Their pleas in court, nor can they boast
  abroad,   60
And do me justice, after a salute,[30]
They have much conversation with my lip.
I hold the kissing of my hand a courtesy,
And he that loves me must, upon the strength
Of that, expect [31] till I renew his favor.
Some ladies are so expensive in their graces
To those that honor 'em, and so prodigal,
That in a little time they have nothing but
The naked sin left to reward their servants ; [32]
Whereas a thrift in our rewards will keep [70

Men long in their devotion, and preserve
Ourselves in stock, to encourage those that
  honor us.
    ISAB. This is an art worthy a lady's practice.
    CEL. It takes not from the freedom of our
  mirth,
But seems to advance it, when we can possess
Our pleasures with security of our honor ;
And, that preserv'd, I welcome all the joys
My fancy can let in. In this I have given
The copy of my mind, nor do I blush
You understand it.
    ISAB.   You have honor'd us.   80

Enter Celestina's Gentlewoman.

    GENTLEW. Madam, Sir William Scentlove 's
  come to wait on you.
    CEL. There 's one would be a client. —
  Make excuse
For a few minutes.   [*Exit* Gentlewoman.]
    MAR.   One that comes a-wooing?
    CEL. Such a thing he would seem ; but in
  his guiltiness
Of little land, his expectation is not
So valiant as it might be. He wears [33] clothes,
And feeds with noblemen ; to some, I hear,
No better than a wanton emissary,
Or scout for Venus' wild fowl ; which made
  tame,
He thinks no shame to stand court sentinel,   90
In hope of the reversion.[34]
    MAR.   I have heard
That some of them are often my Lord's
  tasters :
The first fruits they condition [35] for, and will
Exact as fees, for the promotion.[36]
    CEL. Let them agree ; there 's no account
  shall lie
For me among their traffic.

Re-enter Gentlewoman.

    GENTLEW.   Master Haircut, madam,
Is new come in, to tender you his service.
    CEL. Let him discourse a little with Sir
  William.   *Exit* [Gentlewoman].
    MAR. What is this gentleman, Master
  Haircut, madam?
I note him very gallant, and much courted [100
By gentlemen of quality.
    CEL.   I know not,
More than a trim, gay man ; he has some
  great office,

---

[24] Flemish.   [25] So Dyce ; Q *charge.*
[26] *I.e.*, the deceased citizen made his money by
ruining some courtier.
  [27] Eager for.   [28] Crooked dealings.   [29] Ingenuous.
[30] *I.e.*, the ordinary kiss of greeting.
[31] Wait.   [32] Suitors.

[33] Dyce adds *rich.*
[34] Ultimate possession.   [35] Stipulate.
[36] *I.e.*, their efforts in furthering the affair.

Sure, by his confident behavior.
He would be entertain'd under the title
Of servant to me, and I must confess,
He is the sweetest of all men that visit me.

ISAB. How mean you, madam?

CEL.   He is full of powder;
He will save much in perfume for my chamber,
Were he but constant here. — Give 'em access.

Enter SIR WILLIAM SCENTLOVE [*and*] MASTER
HAIRCUT.

SCENT. Madam, the humblest of your serv-
    ants is   [110
Exalted to a happiness, if you smile
Upon my visit.

HAIR.   I must beg your charity
Upon my rudeness, madam; I shall give
That day up lost to any happiness,
When I forget to tender you my service.

CEL. You practice courtship,[37] gentlemen.

SCENT.   But cannot
Find where with more desert to exercise it.
What lady's this, I pray?

CEL.   A kinswoman
Of mine, Sir William.

SCENT.   I am more her servant.
    [SCENTLOVE *talks apart with the other*
      ladies.]

CEL. You came from court, now, I pre-
    sume?

HAIR.   'T is, madam, [120
The sphere I move in, and my destiny
Was kind to place me there, where I enjoy
All blessings that a mortal can possess
That lives not in your presence; and I should
Fix my ambition, when you would vouch-
    safe
Me so much honor to accept from me
An humble entertainment there.

CEL.   But by
What name shall I be known? In what
    degree
Shall I be of kin[d]red to you?

HAIR.   How mean you, madam?

CEL. Perhaps you'll call me sister: I shall
    take it   130
A special preferment; or it may be
I may pass under title of your mistress,
If I seem rich, and fair enough, to engage
Your confidence to own me.

HAIR.   I would hope —

CEL. But 't is not come to that yet; you
    will, sir,
Excuse my mirth.

   [37] Courtliness.

HAIR.   Sweet madam!

CEL.   Shall I take
Boldness to ask what place you hold in court?
'T is an uncivil curiosity;
But you'll have mercy to a woman's question.

HAIR. My present condition, madam, car-
    ries   140
Honor and profit, though not to be nam'd
With that employment I expect i' th' state,
Which shall discharge the first maturity
Upon your knowledge; until then, I beg
You allow a modest silence.

CEL.   I am charm'd, sir;
And if you scape ambassador, you cannot
Reach a preferment wherein I'm against
    you.
But where's Sir William Scentlove?

HAIR.   Give him leave
To follow his nose, madam, while he hunts
In view — he'll soon be at a fault.[38]

CEL.   You know him? [150

HAIR. Know Scentlove? not a page but
    can decipher him;
The waiting women know him to a scruple;
He's call'd the blister-maker [39] of the town.

CEL. What's that?

[HAIR.] [40]   The laundry ladies can
    resolve [41] you,
And you may guess: an arrant epicure,
As this day lives, born to a pretty wit,
A knight, [too]; [42] but no gentleman. I must
Be plain to you; your Ladyship may have
Use of this knowledge, but conceal the author.

SCENT. [*coming forward, as* HAIRCUT *joins*
     the other ladies] I kiss your fairest hand.

MAR.   You make a difference; [160
Pray reconcile them to an equal whiteness.

SCENT. You wound my meaning, lady.

CEL.   Nay, Sir William
Has the art of compliment.

SCENT.   Madam, you honor me
'Bove my desert of language.

CEL.   Will you please
To enrich me with your knowledge of that
    gentleman?

SCENT. Do you not know him, madam?

CEL.   What is he?

SCENT. A camphire [43] ball; you shall know
    more hereafter;

---

[38] Lose the scent.
[39] Alluding to the Spanish fly, and its provocative
effect. *I.e.*, he is a pimp. Cf. ll. 87–89.
[40] Emend. Dyce; Q *Is.*
[41] Satisfy, convince. *Laundress* was often synonymous with "harlot."
[42] Add. Dyce.
[43] Camphor; balls of it were used by barbers.

He shall tell you himself, and save my character ;
Till then, — you see he 's proud.

CEL.   One thing, gentlemen,
I observe in your behavior, which is rare [170
In two that court one mistress : you pre-
serve
A noble friendship ; there 's no gum within
Your hearts ; you cannot fret,[44] or show an
envy
Of one another's hope ; some would not gov-
ern
Their passions with that temper !

SCENT.   The whole world
Sha' not divorce our friendship, — Master
Haircut !
Would I had lives to serve him ! He is lost
To goodness does not honor him.

HAIR.   My knight !

CEL. [*aside*] This is right playing at court
shuttlecock.[45]

Re-enter Gentlewoman.

GENTLEW. Madam, there is a gentleman
desires   180
To speak w' ee, one Sir Thomas Bornwell.

CEL.   Bornwell?

GENTLEW. He says he is a stranger to your
Ladyship.

SCENT. I know him.

HAIR.   Your neighbor, madam.

SCENT.   Husband to
The lady that so revels in the Strand.

HAIR. He has good parts, they say, but
cannot help
His lady's bias.

CEL.   They have both much fame
I' th' town, for several [46] merits. Pray admit
him.   [*Exit* Gentlewoman.]

HAIR. [*aside*] What comes he for?

Enter Sir THOMAS [BORNWELL].

BORN. Your pardon, noble lady, that I
have
Presum'd, a stranger to your knowledge, —
           [*Salutes* CELESTINA.]

CEL.   Sir, [190
Your worth was here before you, and your per-
son
Cannot be here ungrateful.

BORN.   'T is the bounty

Of your sweet disposition, madam. — Make
me
Your servant, lady, by her fair example,
To favor me. — [ISABELLA *gives him her
cheek.*] [47] I never knew one turn
Her cheek to a gentleman that came to kiss
her,
But sh' ad a stinking breath. — Your servant,
gentlemen.
Will Scentlove, how is 't?

CEL. [*aside to* ISABEL]   I am sorry, Coz,
To accuse you ; we in nothing more betray
Ourselves to censure of ridiculous pride   200
Than answering a fair salute too rudely.
Oh, it shows ill upon a gentlewoman
Not to return the modest lip, if she
Would have the world believe her breath is
not
Offensive.

BORN.   Madam, I have business [48]
With you.

SCENT. [*aside*]   His looks are pleasant.

CEL. [*walking aside with* BORNWELL] With
me, sir?

BORN. I hear you have an exc'llent wit,
madam ;
I see you 're fair.

CEL.   The first is but report ;
And do not trust your eyesight for the last,
'Cause I presume y' are mortal, and may
err.   210

HAIR. He is very gamesome.

BORN.   Y' ave an exc'llent voice,
(They say you catch'd it from a dying swan,)
Which, join'd to the sweet harmony of your
lute,
You ravish all mankind.

CEL.   Ravish mankind?

BORN. With their consent.

CEL.   It were the stranger rape ;
But there 's the less indictment lies against it :
And there is hope your little honesties [49]
Cannot be much the worse, for men do rather
Believe they had a maidenhead, than put
Themselves to th' rack of memory how long
'T is since they left the burden of their inno-
cence.   221

BORN. Why, you are bitter, madam !

CEL.   So is physic ;
I do not know your constitution.

BORN. You shall, if ['t] please you, madam.

CEL.   Y' are too hasty ;

---

[44] Chafe. "Velvet, when stiffened with gum,
quickly rubbed and fretted itself out." (Skeat and
Mayhew.)

[45] *I.e.*, at bandying of compliments.

[46] Different.

[47] Dyce : "offers to salute Isab. who turns from
him." But the point is that she withholds her lips.

[48] Trisyllabic.

[49] Chastities.

I must examine what certificate
You have first, to prefer you.
BORN.   Fine ! certificate?
CEL. Under your lady's hand and seal.
BORN.   Go to ;
I see you are a wag.
CEL.   But take heed how
You trust to 't.
BORN.   I can love you in my wedlock,
As well as that young gallant o' th' first
    hair,   230
Or the knight-bachelor ; and can return
As amorous delight to thy soft bosom.
    CEL. Your person and your language are
        both strangers.
    BORN. But may be more familiar ; I have
        those
That dare make affidavit for my body.
    CEL. D' ee mean your surgeon ? [50]
    BORN.   My surgeon, madam?
I know not how you value my abilities,
But I dare undertake as much, to express
My service to your Ladyship, and with
As fierce ambition fly to your commands, [240
As the most valiant of these [51] lay siege to
    you.
    CEL. You dare not, sir.
    BORN.   How, madam?
    CEL.   I will justify 't.
You dare not marry me ; and I imagine
Some here, should I consent, would fetch a
    priest
Out of the fire.[52]
    BORN.   I have a wife indeed.
    CEL. And there's a statute not repeal'd, I
        take it.
    BORN. Y' are in the right ; I must confess
        y' ave hit
And bled me in a master vein.
    CEL.   You think
I took you on the advantage ; use your best
Skill at defence, I 'll come up to your
    valor,   250
And show another work you dare not do :
You dare not, sir, be virtuous.
    BORN.   I dare,
By this fair hand I dare ; and ask a pardon,
If my rude words offend thy innocence,
Which, in a form so beautiful, would shine
To force a blush in them suspected it,
And from the rest draw wonder.

[50] Who can certify that he is free from venereal
disease.
[51] Understand "who."
[52] *I.e.*, should I consent to marry, not you, but
one of them, would go through fire to fetch a priest.

HAIR.   I like not
Their secret parley ; shall I interrupt 'em?
    ISAB. By no means, sir.
    SCENT.   Sir Thomas was not wont
To show so much a courtier.
    MAR.   He cannot [260
Be prejudicial to you ; suspect not
Your own deserts so much : he 's married.
    BORN. I have other business, madam : you
        keep music ;
I came to try how you can dance.
    CEL. You did ? — [*aside*] I 'll try his humor
        out of breath. —
Although I boast no cunning, sir, in revels,
If you desire to show your art that way,
I can wait on you.
    BORN.   You much honor me ;
Nay, all must join to make a harmony.
                              They dance.
    BORN. I have nothing now, madam, but to
        beseech,   270
After a pardon for my boldness, you
Would give occasion to pay my gratitude.
I have a house will be much honor'd,
If you vouchsafe your presence ; and a wife
Desires to present herself your servant.
I came with the ambition to invite you ;
Deny me not ; your person you shall trust
On fair security.
    CEL.   Sir, although I use not
This freedom with a stranger, you shall have
No cause to hold me obstinate.
    BORN.   You grace me. [280
Sir William Scentlove —
    HAIR.   I must take my leave.
You will excuse me, madam ; court attend-
    ances —
    CEL. By any means.
    BORN.   Ladies, you will vouchsafe
Your company?
    ISAB.   We wait upon you, sir. *Exeunt.*

ACT III — [SCENE I][1]

Table and looking-glass. Enter Lord, *un-
ready;* [2] HAIRCUT *preparing his periwig.*

LORD. What hour is 't?
HAIR.   'Bout three a'clock, my Lord.
LORD. 'T is time to rise.
HAIR.   Your Lordship went but late
To bed last night.
LORD.   'T was early in the morning.

[1] A room in the Lord's house.   [2] Undressed.

SEC. [*within*] Expect [3] awhile; my Lord is busy.

Enter Secretary.

LORD. What's the matter?

SEC. Here is a lady
Desires access to you upon some affairs,
She says, may specially concern your Lordship.

LORD. A lady? What's her name?

SEC. Madam Decoy.

LORD. Decoy? Prithee admit her.

Enter DECOY.

Have you business, madam,
With me?

DEC. And such, I hope, as will not be [10
Offensive to your Lordship.

LORD. I pray speak it.

DEC. I would desire your Lordship's ear
more private.

LORD. Wait i' th' next chamber till I call. —
Exeunt [Secretary *and* HAIRCUT].
Now, madam.

DEC. Although I am a stranger to your
Lordship,
I would not lose a fair occasion offer'd
To show how much I honor and would serve
you.

LORD. Please you to give me the particular,
That I may know the extent of my engagement.
I am ignorant by what desert you should
Be encourag'd to have care of me.

DEC. My Lord, [20
I will take boldness to be plain; beside
Your other excellent parts, you have much
fame
For your sweet inclination to our sex.

LORD. How d' ee mean, madam?

DEC. I' that way your Lordship
Hath honorably practis'd upon some
Not to be nam'd. Your noble constancy
To a mistress hath deserv'd our general vote;
And I, a part of womankind, have thought
How to express my duty.

LORD. In what, madam?

DEC. Be not so strange,[4] my Lord. I
[knew][5] the beauty 30
And pleasures of your eyes, that handsome
creature
With whose fair life all your delight took leave,
And to whose memory you have paid too
much
Sad tribute.

LORD. What's all this?

DEC. This: if your Lordship
Accept my service, in pure zeal to cure
Your melancholy, I could point where you
might
Repair your loss.

LORD. Your Ladyship, I conceive,
Doth traffic in flesh merchandise.

DEC. To men
Of honor, like yourself. I am well known
To some in court, and come not with ambition 40
Now to supplant your officer.[6]

LORD. What is
The lady of pleasure you prefer?

DEC. A lady
Of birth and fortune, one upon whose virtue
I may presume, the Lady Aretina.

LORD. Wife to Sir Thomas Bornwell?

DEC. The same, sir.

LORD. Have you prepar'd her?

DEC. Not for your Lordship, till I have
found your pulse.
I am acquainted with her disposition,
She has a very appliable [7] nature.

LORD. And, madam, when expect you to be
whipp'd [8] 50
For doing these fine favors?

DEC. How, my Lord?
Your Lordship does but jest, I hope; you
make
A difference between a lady that
Does honorable offices, and one
They call a bawd. Your Lordship was not
wont
To have such coarse opinion of our practice.

LORD. The Lady Aretina is my kinswoman.

DEC. What if she be, my Lord? The
nearer blood,
The dearer sympathy.

LORD. I 'll have thee carted.[9]

DEC. Yo' Lordship wo' not so much stain
your honor 60
And education, to use a woman
Of my quality —

LORD. 'T is possible you may
Be sent off with an honorable convoy
Of halberdiers.

DEC. Oh, my good Lord!

LORD. Your ladyship shall be no protection,
If thou but stay'st three minutes.

[6] Here evidently = "pander", "bawd." Cf. l. 160.
[7] Compliant.
[8] A regular punishment of bawds.
[9] Bawds were also punished by being exhibited
through the streets in a cart.

[3] Wait.   [4] Offish.   [5] So Dyce (silently); Q *know.*

Dec.   I am gone. —
When next you find rebellion in your blood,[10]
May all within ten mile o' th' court turn hon-
     est![11]   *Exit.*
    LORD. I do not find that proneness, since
     the fair
Bella Maria died ; my blood is cold,   70
Nor is there beauty enough surviving
To heighten me to wantonness. — Who waits?

    Re-enter HAIRCUT [*and* Secretary].

And what said my Lady?
    HAIR. The silent language of her face, my
     Lord,
Was not so pleasant as it show'd upon
Her entrance.
    LORD.   Would any man that meets
This lady take her for a bawd?
    HAIR.   She does
The trade an honor, credit to the profession.
We may in time see baldness, quarter noses,
And rotten legs[12] to take the wall[13] of foot-
     cloths.[14]   80
    LORD. I ha' thought better ; call the lady
     back. —
I wo' not lose this opportunity. —
Bid her not fear. [*Exit* Secretary.] — The
     favor is not common,
And I 'll reward it. I do wonder much
Will Scentlove was not here to-day.
    HAIR. I heard him say this morning he
     would wait
Upon your Lordship. — She is return'd, sir.

    Re-enter Secretary *and* DECOY.

    SEC. Madam, be confident, my Lord 's not
     angry.
    LORD. You return welcome, madam ; you
     are better
Read in your art, I hope, than to be frighted
With any shape of anger, when you bring [91
Such news to gentlemen. Madam, you shall
Soon understand how I accept the office.
    DEC. You are the first lord, since I studied
     carriage,[15]
That show'd such infidelity and fury
Upon so kind a message. Every gentleman
Will show some breeding ; but if one Right
     Honorable
Should not have noble blood —

    [10] Sensual nature.   [11] Chaste.
    [12] All resulting from syphilis.
    [13] *I.e.*, have precedence.
    [14] Cloths, sometimes embroidered, laid across
horses' backs and hanging almost to the ground.
Their use was a mark of wealth or rank.
    [15] Deportment.

    LORD.   You shall return
My compliment, in a letter, to my Lady
Aretina. Favor me with a little patience. —
Show her that chamber.
    DEC.   I 'll attend your Lordship. [101
     Exeunt [DECOY *and* HAIRCUT].
    LORD. Write : Madam, where your honor
is in danger, my love must not be silent.

    Enter SCENTLOVE *and* KICKSHAW.

Scentlove and Kickshaw!
    KICK.   Your Lordship's busy.
    LORD. Writing a letter ; — nay, it sha' not
     bar
Any discourse.
     [*Walks alternately to the* Secretary
     and to SCENTLOVE *and* KICKSHAW.]
    SEC. " Silent."
    LORD. " Though I be no physician, I may
prevent a fever in your blood." —
And where have you spent the morning's con-
     versation?   110
    SCENT. Where you would have given the
     best barbary
In your stable to have met on honorable
     terms.
    LORD. What new beauty? You acquaint
     yourselves
With none but wonders.
    SCENT.   'T is too low, — a miracle.
    LORD. 'T will require a strong faith.
    SEC. " Your blood."
    LORD. " If you be innocent, preserve your
fame, lest this Decoy-madam betray it, to your
repentance." —   119
By what name is she known?
    SCENT.   Ask Alexander ;
He knows her.
    KICK.   Whom?
    SCENT.   The Lady Celestina.
    LORD. He has a vast knowledge of ladies.
'Las, poor Alexander !
When dost thou mean thy body shall lie fal-
     low?
    KICK. When there is mercy in a petticoat ;
I must turn pilgrim for some breath.
    LORD.   I think
'T were cooler travel, if you examine it,
Upon the hoof through Spain.
    SCENT.   Through Ethiopia.
    LORD. Nay, less laborious to serve a pren-
     ticeship
In Peru, and dig gold out of the mine,
Though all the year were dog days.   130
    SEC. " To repentance."

LORD. " In brief, this lady, could you fall
from virtue, within my knowledge will not
blush to be a bawd."

SCENT. But hang 't, 't is honorable journey-
work ;
Thou art famous by it, and thy name 's up.

KICK.   So, sir !
Let me ask you a question, my dear knight ;
Which is less servile, to bring up the pheasant,
And wait, or sit at table uncontroll'd,   139
And carve to my own appetite?

SCENT.   No more ;
Th 'art witty as I am.

SEC.   " A bawd."

SCENT.   How 's that ?

KICK. Oh, you are famous by 't, and your
name 's up, sir.

LORD. " Be wise, and reward my caution
with timely care of yourself, so I shall not
repent to be known your [loving] [16] kinsman
and servant." —
Gentlemen, the Lady Celestina,
Is she so rare a thing?

KICK.   If you 'll have my
Opinion, my Lord, I never saw
So sweet, so fair, so rich a piece of nature.

LORD. I 'll show thee a fairer presently, to
shame   151
Thy eyes and judgment : look o' that. [*Gives
him a miniature.*] — So ; I 'll subscribe.
                          [*Signs the letter.*]
Seal it ; I 'll excuse your pen for the direction.

KICK. Bella Maria's picture ! she was
handsome.

SCENT. But not to be compar'd —

LORD. Your patience, gentlemen ; I 'll return instantly.   *Exit.*

KICK. Whither is my Lord gone?

SEC. To a lady i' th' next chamber.

SCENT.   What is she ?

SEC. You shall pardon me ; I am his secretary.

SCENT. I was wont to be of his counsel. A
new officer,[17]   160
And I not know 't ? I am resolv'd to batter
All other with the praise of Celestina ;
I must retain [18] him.

                Re-enter LORD.

LORD.   Has not that object
Convinc'd your erring judgments?

KICK.   What ! this picture?

LORD. Were but your thoughts as capable
as mine

Of her idea,[19] you would wish no thought
That were not active in her praise, above
All worth and memory of her sex.

SCENT.   She was fair,
I must confess ; but had your Lordship look'd
With eyes more narrow, and some less affec-
tion,   170
Upon her face, —

KICK. [*returning the miniature*]   I do not
love the copies
Of any dead : they make me dream of goblins ;
Give me a living mistress, with but half
The beauty of Celestina. Come, my Lord,
'T is pity that a lord of so much flesh [20]
Should waste upon a ghost, when they are living
Can give you a more honorable consumption.

SCENT. Why, do you mean, my Lord, to
live an infidel?
Do, and see what will come on 't ; observe [21]
still,
And dote upon your vigils ; build a chamber
Within a rock, a tomb among the worms,
Not far off, where you may, in proof apocry-
phal,   182
Court 'em not devour the pretty pile
Of flesh your mistress carried to the grave.
There are no women in the world ; all eyes,
And tongues, and lips, are buried in her coffin !

LORD. Why, do you think yourselves competent judges
Of beauty, gentlemen ?

BOTH.   What should hinder us ?

KICK. I have seen and tried as many as
another,
With a mortal back.

LORD.   Your eyes are brib'd, [190
And your hearts chain'd to some desires ; you
cannot
Enjoy the freedom of a sense.

KICK.   Your Lordship
Has a clear eyesight, and can judge and penetrate.

LORD. I can, and give a perfect censure [22] of
Each line and point ; distinguish beauty from
A thousand forms, which your corrupted op-
tics
Would pass for natural.

SCENT.   I desire no other
Judge should determine us,[23] and if your Lord-
ship
Dare venture but your eyes upon this lady,
I 'll stand their justice, and be confident 200

---

[16] Q *lovings.*   [17] See on l. 41.
[18] Keep him attached to me.
[19] Image.   [20] Carnality.
[21] Worship, pay your observances.
[22] Judgment.   [23] Decide for us.

You shall give Celestina victory
And triumph o'er all beauties past and living.

KICK. I dare, my Lord, venture a suit of
clothes
You 'll be o'ercome.

LORD.   You do not know my fortit[ude].

SCENT. Nor frailty ; you dare not trust
yourself to see her.

LORD. Think you so, gentlemen ? I dare
see this creature
To make you know your errors, and the differ-
ence
Of her whose memory is my saint. Not trust
My senses ? I dare see, and speak with her. [209
Which holds the best acquaintance to prepare
My visit to her?

SCENT.   I will do 't, my Lord.

KICK. She is a lady free in entertainments.

LORD. I would give this advantage to your
cause :
Bid [her] [24] appear in all the ornaments
Did ever wait on beauty, all the riches
Pride can put on, and teach her face more
charm
Than ever poet dress'd up Venus in ;
Bid her be all the Graces, and the Queen
Of Love in one ; I 'll see her, Scentlove, and
Bring off my heart, arm'd but [with] [25] single
thought   220
Of one that is dead, without a wound ; and
when
I have made your folly prisoner, I 'll laugh at
you.

SCENT. She shall expect you ; trust to me
for knowledge.

LORD. I 'm for the present somewhere else
engag'd.
Let me hear from you.

SCENT.   So ! I am glad he 's yet
So near conversion.

KICK.   I am for Aretina.

SCENT. No mention of my Lord.

KICK.   Prepare his lady :
'T is time he were reduc'd [26] to the old sport ;
One lord like him more would undo the court.
                                        [*Exeunt.*]

[SCENE II] [27]

Enter ARETINA, *with a letter,* [*and*] DECOY.

DEC. He is the ornament of your blood, [28]
madam ;
I am much bound to his Lordship.

ARE.   He gives you
A noble character.

DEC.   'T is his goodness, madam.

ARE. [*aside*] I wanted such an engine. My
Lord has
Done me a courtesy, to disclose her nature ;
I now know one to trust, and will employ
her. —
Touching my Lord, for reasons which I shall
Offer to your Ladyship hereafter, I
Desire you would be silent ; but, to show
How much I dare be confident in your se-
crecy,   10
I pour my bosom forth. I love a gentleman,
One whom there wo' not [need] [29] much con-
juration
To meet. — Your ear.   [*Whispers.*]

DEC.   I apprehend you, and I shall
Be happy to be serviceable. I am sorry
Your Ladyship did not know me before now.
I have done offices ; and not a few
Of the nobility but have done feats
Within my house, which is so convenient
For situation, and artful chambers,
And pretty pictures to provoke the fancy. [20

Enter LITTLEWORTH.

LITTLE. Madam, all pleasures languish in
your absence.

ARE. Your pardon a few minutes, sir. —
You must
Contrive it thus. [*Walks aside with* DECOY.]

LITTLE.   I attend, and shall account it
Honor to wait on your return.

ARE.   He may not
Have the least knowledge of my name or person.

DEC. I have practis'd that already for some
great ones,
And dare again, to satisfy you, madam ;
I have a thousand ways to do sweet offices.

LITTLE. If this Lady Aretina should be
honest,
I ha' lost time. She 's free as air ; I must   30
Have closer conference, and if I have art,
Make her affect me in revenge.

DEC.   This evening?
Leave me to manage things.

ARE.   You will oblige me.

DEC. You shall commend my art, and
thank me after.   *Exit.*

ARE. I hope the revels are maintained
within.

LITTLE. By Sir Thomas and his mistress.

[24] So Dyce ; Q *him.*   [25] Om. Q ; Dyce adds *with a.*
[26] Brought back.   [27] A room in Bornwell's house.
[28] Family, kindred.

[29] So Dyce ; Q *meet.*

ARE. How? His mistress?

LITTLE. The Lady Celestina; I ne'er saw Eyes shoot more amorous interchange.

ARE. Is't so?

LITTLE. He wears her favor with mere [30] pride —

ARE. Her favor?

LITTLE. A feather that he ravish'd from her fan; [40] And is so full of courtship, which she smiles on.

ARE. 'T is well.

LITTLE. And praises her beyond all poetry.

ARE. I'm glad he has so much wit.

LITTLE. [aside] Not jealous!

ARE. [aside] This secures me. What would make other ladies pale With jealousy, gives but a license to my wand'rings. Let him now tax [31] me, if he dare; and yet Her beauty's worth my envy, and I wish Revenge upon it, not because he loves, But that it shines above my own.

Enter ALEXANDER [KICKSHAW].

KICK. Dear madam!

ARE. [aside] I have it. — You two gentlemen profess [50] Much service to me; if I have a way To employ your wit and secrecy? —

BOTH. You'll honor us.

ARE. You gave a high and worthy character Of Celestina.

KICK. I remember, madam.

ARE. Do either of you love her?

KICK. Not I, madam.

LITTLE. I would not, if I might.

ARE. She's now my guest And, by a trick, invited by my husband, To disgrace me. — You, gentlemen, are held Wits of the town, the consuls that do govern The senate here, whose jeers are all authentic. The taverns and the ordinaries are [61] Made academies, where you come, and all Your sins and surfeits made [the] [32] time's example. Your very nods can quell a theatre; No speech or poem good without your seal; You can protect scurrility, and publish; By your authority believ'd, no rapture Ought to have honest meaning.

KICK. Leave our characters.

LITTLE. And name the employment.

ARE. You must exercise The strength of both your wits upon this lady, [70] And talk her into humbleness or anger, Both which are equal, to my thought. If you Dare undertake this slight thing for my sake, My favor shall reward it; but be faithful, And seem to let all spring from your own freedom.

KICK. This all! We can defame her; if you please, My friend shall call her whore, or anything, And never be endanger'd to a duel.

ARE. How's that?

KICK. He can endure a cudgelling, and no man [80] Will fight after so fair a satisfaction; But leave us to our art, and do not limit us.

ARE. They are here; begin not till I whisper you.

Enter SIR THOMAS [BORNWELL], CELESTINA, MARIANA, [and] ISABELLA.

ARE. *Je vous prie, madame, d'excuser l'importunité de mes affaires, qui m'ont fait offenser, par mon absence, une dame de laquelle j'ai reçu tant d'obligation.*

CEL. *Pardonnez-moi, madame; vous me faites trop d'honneur.*

ARE. *C'est bien de la douceur de votre na-* [90] *turel, que vous tenez cette* [33] *langage; mais j'espère que mon mari n'a pas manqué de vous entretenir en mon absence.*

CEL. *En vérité, monsieur nous a fort obligé[es].*

ARE. *Il eût trop failli, s'il n'eût tâché de tout son pouvoir à vous rendre toutes sortes de services.*

CEL. *C'est de sa bonté qu'il nous a tant favorisé[es].*

ARE. *De la vôtre plutôt, madame, qu[i]* [100] *vous fait donner d'interprétation si bénigne à ses efforts.*

CEL. *Je vois bien que la victoire sera toujours à madame, et de langage et de la courtesie.* [33]

ARE. *Vraiment, madame, que* [33] *jamais personne a plus désiré l'honneur de votre compagnie que moi.*

CEL. *Laissons-en, je vous supplie, des complimens, et permettez à votre servante de vous baiser les mains.* [110]

ARE. *Vous m'obligez trop.*

BORN. I have no more patience; let's be merry again

---

[30] Absolute. Dyce *more*.   [31] Accuse, reproach.
[32] Add. Dyce (silently).
[33] *Sic.*

In our own language. Madam, our mirth
    cools. —
Our nephew !

Enter FREDERICK [*drunk, and* Steward].

ARE. Passion of my brain !

FRED. Save you, gentlemen ! save you,
    ladies !

ARE. I am undone.

FRED. I must salute ; no matter at which
end I begin.   [*Salutes* CELESTINA.]

    ARE. There's a compliment !   120

    CEL. Is this your nephew, madam ?

ARE. *Je vous prie, madame, d'excuser les
habits et le rude comportement de mon cousin.
Il est tout fraîchement venu de l'université, où on
l'a tout gâté.*

    CEL. *Excusez-moi, madame, il est bien accom-
pli.*

    FRED. This language should be French by
the motions of your heads and the mirth of
your faces.   130

ARE. I am dishonor'd.

FRED. 'T is one of the finest tongues for
ladies to show their teeth in ; if you'll Latin,
I am for you, or Greek it ; my tailor has not put
me into French yet. *Mille basia, basia mille.*

    CEL. *Je ne vous entends pas, monsieur :* I
understand you not, sir.

FRED. Why, so !
You and I then shall be in charity ,
For though we should be abusive, we ha' the
    benefit   140
Not to understand one another.   Where's my
    aunt?
I did hear music somewhere ; and my brains,
Tun'd with a bottle of your capering claret,
Made haste to show their dancing.

    LITTLE.   Please you, madam,
    [*Offering his box of sweetmeats to*
    CELESTINA.]
They are very comfortable.[34]

    STEW.   Alas, madam,
How would you have me help it ?   I did use
All means I could, after he heard the music,
To make him drunk, in hope so to contain
    him ;
But the wine made him lighter, and his head
Flew hither, ere I miss'd his heels.   150

    KICK. Nay, he spoke Latin to the lady.

ARE. Oh, most unpardonable ! Get him off
Quickly, and discreetly [too] ;[35] or, if I live——

    STEW. It is not in my power ; he swears I
    am

[34] Comforting.   [35] Add. Dyce.

An absurd sober fellow ; and if you keep
A servant in his house to cross his humor,
When the rich sword and belt comes home,
    he'll kill him.

    ARE. What shall I do ?   Try your skill,
    Master Littleworth.

    LITTLE. He has ne'er a sword. — Sweet
    Master Frederick —

    BORN. 'T is pity, madam, such a scion [36]
    should   160
Be lost ; — but you are clouded.

    CEL.   Not I, sir,
I never found myself more clear at heart.

    BORN. I could play with a feather ; your
    fan, lady. —
Gentlemen, Aretina, ta, ra, ra, ra !   Come,
    madam.

    FRED. Why, my good tutor in election !
You might have been a scholar.

    LITTLE.   But I thank
My friends, they brought me up a little better.
Give me the town wits, that deliver jests
Clean from the bow, that whistle in the air,
And cleave the pin [37] at twelvescore !   Ladies
    do   170
But laugh at a gentleman that has any learn-
    ing ;
'T is sin enough to have your clothes suspected.
Leave us, and I will find a time to instruct you.
Come, here are sugarplums ; 't is a good
    Frederick.

    FRED. Why, is not this my aunt's house in
    the Strand ?
The noble rendezvous ?   Who laughs at me ?
Go ! I will root here if I list, and talk
Of rhetoric, logic, Latin, Greek, or anything,
And understand 'em too ; who says the con-
    trary ?
Yet, in a fair way, I contemn all learning,   180
And will be as ignorant as he, or he,
Or any taffeta, satin, scarlet, plush,
Tissue,[38] or cloth a' bodkin [39] gentleman,
Whose manners are most gloriously infected.—
Did you laugh at me, lady ?

    CEL.   Not I, sir ;
But if I did show mirth upon your question,
I hope you would not beat me, little gentle-
    man ?

    FRED. How ! " little gentleman "?   You
    dare not say
These words to my new clothes, and fighting
    sword.

[36] Q *syen.*
[37] In the center of the target at archery.
[38] Rich cloth elaborately embroidered.
[39] Cloth of baudkin, rich brocade.

ARE. Nephew Frederick!

FRED. " Little gentleman ! "
'T is an affront both to my blood and per-
son. 191
I am a gentleman of as tall a birth
As any [boast] [40] nobility ; though my clothes
Smell o' the lamp, my coat [41] is honorable,
Right honorable, full of or and argent. —
A " little gentleman ! "

BORN. Coz, you must be patient ;
My Lady meant you no dishonor, and
You must remember she 's a woman.

FRED. Is she a woman ? That 's another
matter. —
Do you hear ? My uncle tells me what you
are. 200

CEL. So, sir.

FRED. You call'd me " little gentleman."

CEL. I did, sir.

FRED. A little pink [42] has made a lusty ship
Strike her topsail ; the crow may beard the
elephant,
A whelp may tame the tiger ; spite of all
False decks [43] and murderers ; [44] and a " little
gentleman "
Be hard enough to grapple with your Ladyship,
Top and topgallant. — Will you go drink,
Uncle,
Tother enchanted bottle ? You and I 210
Will tipple, and talk philosophy.

BORN. Come, Nephew. —
You will excuse a minute's absence, madam. —
Wait you on us.

STEW. My duty, sir.
Exeunt [Sir THOMAS BORNWELL,
FREDERICK, *and* Steward.]

ARE. Now, gentlemen.

KICK. Madam, I had rather you accuse my
language
For speaking truth, than virtue suffer in
My further silence ; and it is my wonder
That you, whose noble carriage hath deserv'd
All honor and opinion, should now
Be guilty of ill manners.

CEL. What was that
You told me, sir?

LITTLE. Do you not blush, madam, [220
To ask that question?

[40] Emend. Dyce (silently) ; Q *least*.
[41] With a play on coat of arms.
[42] Small sailing vessel.
[43] Frederick returns to his nautical figure. "The
false deck was a slight one raised over the other, as
a defence against boarders, and was sometimes
blown up in action." (Dyce.)
[44] Cannon for short ranges. They fired scattering
shot.

CEL. You amaze rather
My cheek to paleness. What [mean you] [45] by
this?
I am not troubled with the hiccup, gentlemen,
[46] You should bestow this fright upon me.

LITTLE. Then
Pride and ill memory go together.

CEL. How, sir? —

KICK. The gentleman on whom you exer-
cis['d]
Your thin wit, was a nephew to the lady
Whose guest you are ; and though her modesty
Look calm on the abuse of one so near
Her blood, the affront was impious.

LITTLE. I am asham'd on 't. [230
You an ingenious lady, and well manner'd !
I 'll teach a bear as much civility.

CEL. You may be master of the college, sir,
For aught I know.

LITTLE. What college?

[CEL.] [47] Of the bears. [48]
Have you a plot upon me ? D 'ee possess
Your wits, or know me, gentlemen?

Re-enter [Sir THOMAS] BORNWELL [*behind*].

BORN. How 's this?

KICK. Know you ? Yes ; we do know you
to an atom.

LITTLE. Madam, we know what stuff your
soul is made on.

CEL. But do not bark so like a mastiff,
pray. —
Sure they are mad. — Let your brains stand
awhile, 240
And settle, gentlemen ; you know not me ;
What am I?

LITTLE. Th' art a puppet, a thing made
Of clothes and painting, and not half so hand-
some
As that which play'd Susanna in the fair.

CEL. I heard you visited those canvas
tragedies,
One of their constant audience, and so taken
With Susan, that you wish'd yourself a rival
With the two wicked elders.

KICK. You think this
Is wit now. Come, you are —

CEL. What, I beseech you?
Your character [49] will be full of salt and sat-
ire, 250
No doubt. What am I?

[45] Q *you meane*, possibly = "d' you mean."
[46] Understand "that." [47] Om. Q.
[48] *I.e.*, you have the manners of a bearward.
[49] Of me.

Kick.   Why, you are a woman —
Cel. And that's at least a bow wide of
   you[r] knowledge.
Kick. Would be thought handsome, and
   might pass i' th' country
Upon a market day ; but [50] miserably
Forfeit to pride and fashions, that if Heaven
Were a new gown, you'd not stay in 't a fort-
   night.
Cel. It must be miserably out of fashion
   then.
Have I no sin but pride?
Kick.   Hast any virtue,
Or but a good face, to excuse that want?
Cel. You prais'd it yesterday.
Kick.   That made you proud. [260
Cel. More pride !
Kick.   You need not. To close up the
   praise,
I have seen a better countenance in a sybil.
Cel. When you wore spectacles of sack,[51]
   mistook
The painted cloth,[52] and kiss'd it for [53] your
   mistress.
Kick. Let me ask you a question : how
   much
Have you consum'd [54] in expectation
That I would love you?
Cel.   Why, I think as much
As you have paid away in honest debts
This seven year. 'T is a pretty impudence,
But cannot make me angry.
Little.   Is there any [270
Man that will cast away his limbs upon her?
Kick. You do not sing so well as I imag-
   in'd,
Nor dance ; you reel in your coranto,[55] and
   pinch
Your petticoat too hard : y' ave no good ear
To th' music, and incline too much one
   shoulder,
As [56] you were dancing on the rope, and fall-
   ing.
You speak abominable French, and make
A curtsey like a dairymaid. — [*aside*] Not
   mad !
Little. [*aside*] Do we not sting her hand-
   somely?
Born. [*behind*]   A conspiracy !
Kick. Your state [57] is not so much as 't is
   reported,   280

When you confer notes, all your husband's
   debts,
And your own reconcil'd ; but that's not it
Will so much spoil your marriage.
Cel.   As what, sir ?
Let me know all my faults.
Kick.   Some men do whisper
You are not overhonest.[58]
Cel.   All this shall not
Move me to more than laughter, and some
   pity,
Because you have the shapes [59] of gentlemen ;
And though you have been insolent upon me,
I will engage no friend to kick or cudgel you,
To spoil your living and your limbs together.
I leave that to diseases that offend you,   291
And spare my curse, poor silken vermin ! and
Hereafter shall distinguish men from monkeys.
   Born. [*coming forward*] Brave soul ! — You
      brace   of   horseleeches [60] ! - I   have
      heard
Their barbarous language, madam ; y' are too
   merciful.
They shall be silent to your tongue ; pray
   punish 'em.
Cel. They are things not worth my charac-
   ter,[61] nor mention
Of any clean breath ; so lost in honesty,
They cannot satisfy for wrongs enough,
Though they should steal out of the world at
   Tyburn.[62]   300
   Little. We are hang'd already.
Cel. Yet I will talk a little to the pil-
   chards. — [63]
You two, that have not 'twixt you both the
   hundred
Part of a soul, coarse woolen-witted fellows,
Without a nap, with bodies made for burdens !
You, that are only stuffings for apparel,
As you were made but engines [64] for your tail-
   ors
To frame their clothes upon, and get them cus-
   tom,
Until men see you move ; yet, then you dare
   not,
Out of your guilt [65] of being the ignobler
   beast,   310
But give a horse the wall,[66] whom you excel
Only in dancing of the brawls,[67] because

[50] Dyce adds *so*.   [51] *I.e.*, were drunk.
[52] A cheap substitute for tapestry.
[53] Instead of.   [54] Cf. II, ii, 21–23.
[55] A lively dance.   [56] As if.
[57] Estate, fortune.

[58] Chaste.   [59] Garb.   [60] Bloodsuckers.
[61] My characterizing.
[62] Where the gallows stood.
[63] Sardines ; *i.e.*, insignificant fellows.
[64] Devices, contraptions ; *i.e.*, lay figures.
[65] Because of your guilty consciousness.
[66] Cf. on III, i, 80.
[67] A French dance resembling a cotillon.

The horse was not taught the French way.
    Your two faces,
One fat like Christmas, tother lean like
    Candlemas
And prologue to a Lent, both bound together,
Would figure Janus, and do many cures
On agues, and the green disease,[68] by frighting;
But neither can, with all the characters [69]
And conjuring circles, charm a woman, though
Sh'ad fourscore years upon her, and but
    one   320
Tooth in her head, to love or think well of
    you ;
And I were miserable to be at cost
To court such a complexion as your malice
Did impudently insinuate. But I waste time,
And stain my breath in talking to such tad-
    poles.
Go home, and wash your tongues in barley-
    water,
Drink [70] clean tobacco, be not hot i' th' mouth,
And you may scape the beadle ; so I leave you
To shame, and your own garters [71] ! — Sir, I
    must
Entreat you, for my honor, do not penance
    'em ;   330
They are not worth your anger. How shall I [72]
Acquit [73] your lady's silence?
    BORN.   Madam, I
Am sorry to suspect, and dare revenge.
    CEL. No cause of mine.
    BORN. It must become me to attend you
    home.
    CEL. You are noble. — Farewell, mush-
    rooms.
            [*Exit with* SIR THOMAS BORNWELL.]
    ARE.   Is she gone?
    LITTLE. I think we pepper'd her.
    KICK.   I'm glad 't is over;
But I repent no service for you, madam. —

Enter Servant, *with a letter* [*and a jewel, which*
he delivers to KICKSHAW].

To me? from whence? — A jewel! a good
    preface.
Be happy the conclusion. *He smiles upon 't.*
    ARE.   Some love letter. [340
    LITTLE. He has a hundred mistresses ; you
    may
Be charitable, madam ; I ha' none ;
He surfeits, and I fall away i' th' kidneys.

    KICK. I'll meet. —   [*Exit* Servant.]
[*aside*] 'T is some great lady, questionless,
    that has
Taken notice, and would satisfy her appetite.
    ARE. Now, Master Alexander, you look
    bright o' the sudden ;
Another spirit's in your eye.
    KICK.   Not mine, madam ;
Only a summons to meet a friend.
    ARE.   What friend?
    LITTLE. By this jewel, I know her not.
    ARE. 'T is a she-friend. I'll follow, gen-
    tlemen ;   351
We may have a game at cent [74] before you go.
    KICK. I shall attend you, madam.
    LITTLE.   'T is our duty.
           [*Exeunt* KICKSHAW *and* LITTLE-
            WORTH.]
    ARE. I blush while I converse with my own
    thoughts.
Some strange fate governs me, but I must on ;
The ways are cast already, and we thrive
When our sin fears no eye nor perspective.
                   Exit.

        ACT IV — [SCENE I] [1]

Enter two men leading ALEXANDER [KICK-
    SHAW] *blinded, and go off suddenly.*

    KICK. I am not hurt ; my patience to obey
    'em,
Not without fear to ha' my throat cut else,
Did me a courtesy. Whither ha' they brought
    me?   [*Pulls off the bandage.*]
'T is devilish dark ; the bottom of a well
At midnight, with but two stars on the top,
Were broad day to this darkness. I but think
How like a whirlwind these rogues caught me
    up,
And smothered my eyesight. Let me see ;
These may be spirits, and, for aught I know,
Have brought me hither over twenty steeples.
Pray Heaven they were not bailiffs ! — that's
    more worth   11
My fear — and this a prison. All my debts
Reek in my nostril, and my bones begin
To ache with fear to be made dice ; and yet
This is too calm and quiet for a prison. —
What if the riddle prove I am robb'd? And
    yet
I did not feel 'em search me. How now!
    music !

---

[68] Greensickness, chlorosis.
[69] Magic signs and symbols.
[70] Smoke.
[71] To hang yourselves in.
[72] Q *I shall.*   [73] Requite.
[74] It resembled piquet. 100 was "game." Q *Sant.*
[1] A room in the house of Madam Decoy.

Enter Decoy, *like an old woman, with a light.*

And a light! What beldam's this? I can-
　　not pray. —
What art?
　　Dec.　　A friend. Fear not, young man,
　　　　　　I am
No spirit.
　　Kick.　　Off!
　　Dec.　　　　Despise me not for age,　20
Or this coarse outside, which I wear not out
Of poverty. Thy eyes be witness, 't is
No cave, or beggar's cell, th' art brought to;
　　let
That gold speak here's no want, which thou
　　mayst spend,
And find a spring to tire even prodigality,
If thou beest wise.
　　Kick.　　　　The Devil was a coiner
From the beginning; yet the gold looks cur-
　　rent.
　　Dec. Th' art still in wonder; know I am
　　　　mistress of
This house, and of a fortune that shall serve
And feed thee with delights; 't was I sent for
　　thee;　　30
The jewel and the letter came from me.
It was my art thus to contrive our meeting,
Because I would not trust thee with my fame,
Until I found thee worth a woman's honor.
　　Kick. [*aside*] Honor and fame! The Devil
　　　　means to have
A care on 's credit. Though she sent for me,
I hope she has another customer
To do the trick withal; I would not turn
Familiar² to a witch.
　　Dec.　　　　What say'st? Canst thou
Dwell in my arms to-night? Shall we change³
　　kisses,　　40
And entertain the silent hours with pleasure,
Such as old Time shall be delighted with,
And blame the too swift motion of his wings,
While we embrace?
　　Kick. [*aside*]　　Embrace! She has had
　　　　no teeth
This twenty years, and the next violent cough
Brings up her tongue; it cannot possibly
Be sound at root. I do not think but one
Strong sneeze upon her, and well meant, would
　　make
Her quarters fall away; one kick would blow
Her up like gunpowder, and loose all her
　　limbs.　　50
She is so cold an incubus would not heat her;

² A spirit bound to service.　　³ Exchange.

Her phlegm would quench a furnace, and her
　　breath
Would damp a musket bullet.⁴
　　Dec.　　　　　　Have you, sir,
Consider'd?
　　Kick.　　What?
　　Dec.　　　　My proposition.
Canst love?
　　Kick.　　I could have done; whom do you
　　　　mean?
I know you are pleas'd but to make sport.
　　Dec.　　　　　　Thou art not
So dull of soul as thou appear'st.
　　Kick. [*aside*]　　　　This is
But some device; my grannam has some trick
　　in 't. —
Yes, I can love.
　　Dec.　　　But canst thou affect me?
　　Kick. Although to reverence so grave a
　　　　matron　　60
Were an ambitious word in me, yet since
You give me boldness, I do love you.
　　Dec.　　　　　　　　Then
Thou art my own.
　　Kick. [*aside*]　　Has she no cloven foot?
　　Dec. And I am thine, and all that I com-
　　　　mand
Thy servants; from this minute thou art
　　happy,
And fate in thee will crown all my desires.
I griev'd a proper⁵ man should be compell'd
To bring his body to the common market.⁶
My wealth shall make thee glorious; and, the
　　more
To encourage thee, howe'er this form may
　　fright　　70
Thy youthful eyes, yet thou wo't find by light
Of thy own sense, for other light is banish'd
My chamber, when our arms tie lovers' knots
And kisses seal the welcome of our lips,
I shall not there affright thee, nor seem old,
With rivell'd⁷ veins; my skin is smooth and
　　soft
As ermines, with a spirit to meet thine,
Active, and equal to the Queen of Love's
When she did court Adonis.
　　Kick. [*aside*]　　　　This doth more
Confirm she is a devil, and I am　　80
Within his own dominions. I must on,
Or else be torn a' pieces. I have heard
These succubae must not be cross'd.

⁴ *I.e.*, the charge of powder.
⁵ Handsome.
⁶ *I.e.*, patronize professional prostitutes.
⁷ Shriveled, shrunken.

Dec.   We trifle
Too precious time away ; I 'll show you a
    prospect
Of the next chamber, and then out the candle.
    KICK. Have you no sack i' th' house? I
        would go arm'd
Upon this breach.
    DEC.   It sha' not need.
    KICK.   One word,
Mother ; have not you been a cat in your days?
    DEC. I am glad you are so merry, sir. You
        observe
That bed?
    KICK. A very brave one.
    DEC.   When you are [90
Disrob'd, you can come thither in the dark.
You sha' not stay for me. Come, as you wish
For happiness.   *Exit.*
    KICK.   I am preferr'd, if I
Be modest and obey. She cannot have
The heart to do me harm, an she were Hecate
Herself. I will have a strong faith, and think
I march upon a mistress, the less evil.
If I scape fire now, I defy the Devil.   *Exit.*

[SCENE II] [8]

Enter FREDERICK [*gaily dressed,*] LITTLE-
    WORTH, [*and*] Steward.

    FRED. And how d' ee like me now?
    STEW.   Most excellent.
    FRED. Your opinion, Master Littleworth.
    LITTLE.   Your French tailor
Has made you a perfect gentleman ; I may
Converse now with you, and preserve my
    credit.
D' ee find no alteration in your body
With these new clothes?
    FRED.   My body altered? No.
    LITTLE. You are not yet in fashion then.
        That must
Have a new motion, garb, [9] and posture, too,
Or all your pride is cast away ; it is not
The cut of your apparel makes a gallant,   10
But the geometrical wearing of your clothes.
    STEW. Master Littleworth tells you right ;
        you wear your hat
Too like a citizen.
    LITTLE.   'T is like a midwife ;
Place it with best advantage of your hair.
Is half your feather moulted? This does make
No show ; it should spread over, like a canopy ;
Your hot-rein'd [10] monsieur wears it for a shade

And cooler to his back. Your doublet must
Be more unbutton'd hereabouts ; you 'll not
Be a sloven else : a foul shirt is no blemish ; [20
You must be confident, and outface clean
    linen.
Your doublet and your breeches must be al-
    low'd
No private meeting here ; your cloak 's too
    long.
It reaches to your buttock, and doth smell
Too much of Spanish gravity ; the fashion
Is to wear nothing but a cape ; a coat
May be allow'd a covering for one elbow,
And some to avoid the trouble, choose to walk
In cuerpo, [11] thus.
    STEW. [*aside*]   Your coat and cloak 's
        a-brushing
In Long Lane, Lombard. [12]
    FRED.   But what if it rain? [30
    LITTLE. Your belt about your shoulder is
        sufficient
To keep off any storm ; beside, a reed
But wav'd discreetly, has so many pores,
It sucks up all the rain that falls about one.
With this defence, when other men have been
Wet to the skin through all their cloaks, I have
Defied a tempest, and walk'd by the taverns
Dry as a bone.
    STEW. [*aside*]   Because he had no money
To call for wine.
    FRED.   Why, do you walk enchanted?
Have you such pretty charms in town? But
    stay ;   40
Who must I have to attend me?
    LITTLE.   Is not that
Yet thought upon?
    STEW.   I have laid out [13] for servants.
    LITTLE. They are everywhere.
    STEW.   I cannot yet be furnish'd
With such as I would put into his hands.
    FRED. Of what condition must they be, and
        how
Many in number, sir?
    LITTLE.   Beside your fencing,
Your singing, dancing, riding, and French
    master,
Two may serve domestic, to be constant wait-
    ers
Upon a gentleman : a fool, a pimp.
    STEW. For these two officers I have en-
        quir'd,   50
And I am promis'd a convenient whiskin. [14]

---

[8] A room in Bornwell's house.
[9] Bearing.   [10] Hot-loined ; *i.e.*, lustful.
[11] Body (Span.) ; *i.e.*, without the upper garment.
Q *quirpo.*
[12] There were many clothing shops there.
[13] Made a search for.   [14] Pander.

I could save charges, and employ the pie-
wench,
That carries her intelligence in whitepots;[15]
Or 't is but taking order [16] with the woman
That holds [17] the ballads; she could fit him
with
A concubine to any tune; but I
Have a design to place a fellow with him
That has read all Sir Pandarus' works: a Tro-
jan,[18]
That lies conceal'd, and is acquainted with
Both city and suburban fripperies,[19]   60
Can fetch 'em with a spell at midnight to him,
And warrant which are for his turn; can, for
A need, supply the surgeon too.

FRED.   I like thy providence; [20] such a one
deserves
A livery twice a year.

STEW.   It sha' not need; a cast suit of your
Worship's
Will serve; he 'll find a cloak to cover it,
Out of his share with those he brings to bed to
you.

FRED.   But must I call this fellow pimp?

LITTLE.   It is
Not necessary; [21] or Jack, or Harry,   70
Or what he 's known abroad by, will sound bet-
ter,
That men may think he is a Christian.

FRED.   But hear you, Master Littleworth:
is there not
A method, and degrees of title in
Men of this art?

LITTLE.   According to the honor
Of men that do employ 'em. An emperor
May give this office to a duke; a king
May have his viceroy to negotiate for him;
A duke may use a lord; the lord a knight,
A knight may trust a gentleman; and when [80
They are abroad, and merry, gentlemen
May pimp to one another.

FRED.   Good, good fellowship!
But for the fool now, that should wait on me,
And break me jests?

LITTLE.   A fool is necessary.

STEW.   By any [22] means.

FRED.   But which of these two servants
Must now take place? [23]

LITTLE.   That question, Master Fred-
erick,
The school of heraldry should conclude upon;
But if my judgment may be heard, the fool
Is your first man; and it is known a point
Of state to have a fool.

STEW.   But, sir, the other [90
Is held the finer servant; his employments
Are full of trust, his person clean and nimble,
And none so soon can leap into preferment,
Where fools are poor.

LITTLE.   Not all; there 's story [24] for 't;
Princes have been no wiser than they should
be.
Would any nobleman, that were no fool,
Spend all in hope of the philosopher's stone,
To buy new lordships in another country?
Would knights build colleges, or gentlemen
Of good estates challenge the field, and
fight,   100
Because a whore wo' not be honest? [25]   Come,
Fools are a family over all the world;
We do affect [26] one naturally; indeed
The fool is leiger [27] with us.

STEW.   Then the pimp
Is extraordinary.[28]

FRED.   Do not you fall out
About their places. — Here 's my noble aunt!

Enter ARETINA.

LITTLE. How do you like your nephew,
madam, now?

ARE. Well! — Turn about, Frederick. —
Very well!

FRED. Am I not now a proper gentleman?
The virtue of rich clothes! Now could I
take   110
The wall of Julius Caesar,[29] affront
Great Pompey's upper lip, and defy the Senate.
Nay, I can be as proud as your own heart,
madam:
You may take that for your comfort; I put on
That virtue with my clothes, and I doubt not
But in a little time I shall be impudent
As any page, or player's boy. I am
Beholding to this gentleman's good discipline;
But I shall do him credit in my practice.
Your steward has some pretty notions, too, [120
In moral mischief.

ARE.   Your desert in this
Exceeds all other service, and shall bind me
Both to acknowledge and reward.

---

[15] Dishes of boiled milk, eggs, sugar, etc.
[16] Making arrangements.
[17] Dyce, perhaps rightly, emends *trolls*.
[18] Roistering fellow.
[19] *I.e.*, prostitutes.
[20] Either "what thou providest", or "foresight."
[21] Dyce adds *Tom*.
[22] *I.e.*, all.
[23] Have precedence.

[24] Historical example.   [25] Chaste.   [26] Like.
[27] Resident ambassador.
[28] Ambassador extraordinary.
[29] Dyce adds *or*.

LITTLE.   Sweet madam,
Think me but worth your favor ; I would creep
Upon my knees to honor you, and for every
Minute you lend to my reward, I 'll pay
A year of serviceable tribute.
ARE.   You
Can compliment.
     LITTLE. (*aside*)   Thus still she puts me
     off ;
Unless I speak the downright word, she 'll
     never
Understand me. A man would think that
     creeping   130
Upon one 's knees were English to a lady.

Enter ALEXANDER [KICKSHAW, *splendidly
attired*].

KICK. How is 't, Jack ? — Pleasures attend
     you, madam !
How does my plant of honor?
     ARE.   Who is this?
KICK. 'T is Alexander.
     ARE.   Rich and glorious !
LITTLE. 'T is Alexander the Great.
     KICK.   And my Bucephalus
Waits at the door.
     ARE.   Your case [30] is alter'd, sir.
KICK. I cannot help these things ; the
     Fates will have it ;
'T is not my land does this.
     LITTLE.   But thou hast a plough
That brings it in.
     ARE.   Now he looks brave and lovely.
FRED. Welcome, my gallant Macedonian.
KICK. Madam, you gave your nephew for
     my pupil.   141
I read [31] but in a tavern ; if you 'll honor us,
The Bear at the Bridge foot [32] shall entertain
     you.
A drawer [33] is my Ganymede, he shall skink [34]
Brisk nectar to us ; we will only have
A dozen partridge in a dish ; as many pheas-
     ants,
Quails, cocks, and godwits [35] shall come march-
     ing up
Like the train'd band ; [36] a fort [37] of sturgeon
Shall give most bold defiance to an army,
And triumph o'er the table. —
     ARE.   Sir, it will [150
But dull the appetite to hear more, and mine

Must be excus'd.   Another time I may be
Your guest.
     KICK. 'T is grown in fashion now with
     ladies ;
When you please, I 'll attend you. — Little-
     worth. —
Come, Frederick.
     FRED.   We 'll have music ; I love noise.
We will outroar the Thames, and shake the
     bridge, boy.   *Exit* [*with* KICKSHAW].
LITTLE. Madam, I kiss your hand ; would
     you would think
Of your poor servant : flesh and blood is frail,
And troublesome to carry, without help.
     ARE. A coach will easily convey it, or [160
You may take water at Strand Bridge.[38]
     LITTLE.   But I
Have taken fire.
     ARE.   The Thames will cool.[39]
LITTLE. But never quench my heart ; your
     charity
Can only do that !
     ARE.   I will keep it cold
Of purpose.
     LITTLE.   Now you bless me, and I dare
Be drunk in expectation.   [*Exit.*]
     ARE.   I am confident
He knows me not, and I were worse than mad
To be my own betrayer. — Here 's my hus-
     band.

Enter [Sir THOMAS] BORNWELL.

BORN. Why, how now, Aretina? What !
     alone?
The mystery of this solitude?   My house [170
Turn desert o' the sudden !   All the gamesters
Blown up ! Why is the music put to silence?
Or have their instruments caught a cold, since
     we
Gave 'em the last heat? I must know thy
     ground
Of melancholy.
     ARE.   You are merry, as [40]
You came from kissing Celestina.
     BORN.   I
Feel her yet warm upon my lip ; she is
Most excellent company ; I did not think
There was that sweetness in her sex. I must
Acknowledge 't was thy cure to disenchant
     me   180
From a dull husband to an active lover.

---

[30] With a pun on " case " = outside.   [31] Teach.
[32] A famous tavern at the Southwark end of
London Bridge.
[33] Tapster, waiter.   [34] Draw, pour.
[35] Birds of the snipe family.
[36] City militia.   [37] *I.e.*, pasty.

[38] A landing on the Thames, so called because the
way to it was a lane from the bridge on which
the Strand formerly crossed the rivulet from St.
Clement's Well.
[39] Dyce adds *it, sir*.   [40] As if.

With such a lady I could spend more years
Than since my birth my glass hath run soft
    minutes,
And yet be young ; her presence has a spell
To keep off age ; she has an eye would strike
Fire through an adamant.
    ARE.   I have heard as much
Bestow'd upon a dull-fac'd chambermaid,
Whom love and wit would thus commend.
    True beauty
Is mock'd when we compare thus,[41] itself
    being
Above what can be fetch'd [42] to make it
    lovely ;   190
Or,[43] could our thoughts reach something to
    declare
The glories of a face, or body's elegance,
That touches but our sense ; when [44] beauty
    spreads
Over the soul, and calls up understanding
To look [what] [45] thence [46] is offer'd, and
    admire.
In both I must acknowledge Celestina
Most excellently fair, fair above all
The beauties I ha' seen, and one most worthy
Man 's love and wonder.
    BORN.   Do you speak, Aretina,
This with a pure sense to commend? Or
    is 't   200
The mockery of my praise?
    ARE.   Although it shame
Myself, I must be just, and give her all
The excellency of women ; and were I
A man —
    BORN.   What then?
    ARE.   I know not with what loss
I should attempt her love. She is a piece
So angelically moving, I should think
Frailty excus'd to dote upon her form,
And almost virtue to be wicked with her.
                                 Exit.
    BORN. What should this mean? This is no
    jealousy,
Or she believes I counterfeit. I feel   210
Something within me, like a heat, to give
Her cause, would Celestina but consent.
What a frail thing is man ! It is not worth
Our glory to be chaste, while we deny

41 Employ such comparisons.
42 Dragged in by way of comparison.
43 Neilson conj. *Oh,* silently adopted by Schelling-Black. But Aretina is arguing *against* comparisons. Editors have bungled this passage through failure to grasp the antithesis indicated by *when* in l. 193.
44 Whereas.
45 Emend. Dyce ; Q *when.*
46 From the soul.

Mirth and converse with women. He is good
That dares the tempter, yet corrects his blood.
                                 Exit.

[SCENE III] [47]

[*Enter*] CELESTINA, MARIANA, [*and*] ISABELLA.

    CEL. I have told you all my knowledge ;
    since he is pleas'd
To invite himself, he shall be entertain'd,
And you shall be my witnesses.
    MAR.   Who comes with him?
    CEL. Sir William Scentlove, that prepar'd
    me for
The honorable encounter. I expect
His Lordship every minute.

    Enter [SIR WILLIAM] SCENTLOVE.

    SCENT.   My Lord is come.
    CEL. He has honor'd me.

    Enter Lord [*and*] HAIRCUT.

    SCENT.   My Lord, your periwig is awry !
    LORD. You, sir —
        While HAIRCUT *is busy about his hair,*
        SCENTLOVE *goes to* CELESTINA.
    SCENT.   You may guess at the gentleman
    that 's with him.
It is his barber, madam, d' ee observe?
An your Ladyship wants a shaver.
    HAIR.   She is here, sir. — [10
I am betray'd. — Scentlove, your plot. I may
Have opportunity to be reveng'd.   *Exit.*
    SCENT. She in the midst.
    LORD.   She 's fair, I must confess ;
But does she keep this distance out of state? [48]
    CEL. Though I am poor in language to ex-
    press
How much your Lordship honors me, my heart
Is rich and proud in such a guest. I shall
Be out of love with every air abroad,
And for his grace done my unworthy house,
Be a fond prisoner, become anchorite,   20
And spend my hours in prayer, to reward
The blessing and the bounty of this presence.
    LORD. Though you could turn each place
    you move in to
A temple, rather than a wall should hide
So rich a beauty from the world, it were
Less want to lose our piety and your prayer.
A throne were fitter to present you to
Our wonder, whence your eyes, more worth
    than all

47 A room in Celestina's house.
48 Dignity, stateliness.

They look on, should chain every heart a prisoner.

SCENT. 'T was pretty well come off.

LORD. By your example [30 I shall know how to compliment; in this, You more confirm my welcome. [*Kisses her.*]

CEL. I shall love My lips the better, if their silent language Persuade your Lordship but to think so truly.

LORD. You make me smile, madam.

CEL. I hope you came not With fear that any sadness here should shake One blossom from your eye. I should be miserable To present any object should displease you.

LORD. You do not, madam.

CEL. As I should account It no less sorrow, if your Lordship should [40 Lay too severe a censure on my freedom. I wo' not court a prince against his justice, Nor bribe him with a smile to think me honest. Pardon, my Lord, this boldness, and the mirth That may flow from me. I believe my father Thought of no winding sheet when he begot me.

LORD. She has a merry soul. — It will become Me ask your pardon, madam, for my rude Approach, so much a stranger to your knowledge.

CEL. Not, my Lord, so much stranger to my knowledge; 50 Though I have but seen your person afar off, I am acquainted with your character, Which I have heard so often, I can speak it.

LORD. You shall do me an honor.

CEL. If your Lordship will Be patient.

LORD. And glad to hear my faults.

CEL. That as your conscience can agree upon 'em; However, if your Lordship give me privilege, I 'll tell you what 's the opinion of the world.

LORD. You cannot please me better.

CEL. Y 'are a lord Born with as much nobility as would, 60 Divided, serve to make ten noblemen, Without a herald; but with so much spirit And height of soul, as well might furnish twenty. You are learn'd, a thing not compatible now With native honor; and are master of A language that doth chain all [ears],[49] and charm

All hearts, where you persuade; [50] a wit so flowing, And prudence to correct it, that all men Believe they only meet in you, which, with A spacious memory, make up the full wonders. 70 To these you have [join'd] [51] valor, and upon A noble cause know how to use a sword To honor's best advantage, though you [wear][52] none. You are as bountiful as the showers that fall Into the spring's green bosom, as [53] you were Created lord of Fortune, not her steward; So constant to the cause in which you make Yourself an advocate, you dare all dangers; And men had rather you should be their friend, Than justice or the bench bound up together. 80

LORD. But did you hear all this?

CEL. And more, my Lord.

LORD. Pray let me have it, madam.

CEL. To all these virtues there is added one, — (Your Lordship will remember, when I name it, I speak but what I gather from the voice Of others) — it is grown to a full fame That you have lov'd a woman.

LORD. But one, madam?

CEL. Yes, many; give me leave to smile, my Lord, I shall not need to interpret in what sense; But you have show'd yourself right honorable, 90 And, for your love to ladies, have deserv'd, If their vote might prevail, a marble statue. I make no comment [54] on the people's text. — My Lord, I should be sorry to offend.

LORD. You cannot, madam; these are things we owe To nature for.

CEL. And honest men will pay Their debts.

LORD. If they be able, or compound.

CEL. She had a hard heart would be unmerciful, And not give day [55] to men so promising; But you ow'd women nothing.

LORD. Yes, I am [100 Still in their debt, and I must owe them love; It was part of my character.

[49] Emend. Dyce (silently); Q *yeares*.
[50] Expostulate, employ persuasion.
[51] Emend. Dyce; Q *knowne*.
[52] Emend. Dyce, Q *were*.
[53] As if. [54] I add no commentary.
[55] Of grace.

CEL. With your Lordship's
Pardon, I only said you had a fame
For loving women ; but of late, men say
You have, against the imperial laws of love,
Restrain'd the active flowings of your blood,
And with a mistress buried all that is
Hop'd for in love's succession, as all beauty
Had died with her, and left the world be-
   nighted !
In this you more dishonor all our sex   110
Than you did grace a part ; when everywhere
Love tempts your eye to admire a glorious
   harvest,
And everywhere, as full-blown ears submit
Their golden heads, the laden trees bow down
Their willing fruit, and court your amorous
   tasting.
    LORD. I see men would dissect me to a
   fibre ;
But do you believe this?
    CEL. It is my wonder,
I must confess, a man of nobler earth
Than goes to vulgar composition,
(Born and bred high, so unconfin'd, so rich [120
In fortunes, and so read in all that sum
Up human knowledge, to feed gloriously,
And live at court, the only sphere wherein
True beauty moves, nature's most wealthy
   garden,
Where every blossom is more worth than all
The Hesperian fruit by jealous dragon watch'd,
Where all delights do circle appetite,
And pleasures multiply by being tasted,)
Should be so lost with thought of one turn['d]
   ashes.
There's nothing left, my Lord, that can excuse
   you,   130
Unless you plead what I am asham'd to
   prompt
Your wisdom to !
    LORD. What's that?
    CEL. That you have play'd
The surgeon with yourself.
    LORD. And am made eunuch?
    CEL. It were much pity.
    LORD. Trouble not yourself,
I could convince your fears with demonstra-
   tion
That I am man enough, but knew not where,
Until this meeting, beauty dwelt. The court
You talk'd of must be where the Queen of
   Love is,
Which moves but with your person ; in your
   eye
Her glory shines, and only at that flame   140

Her wanton boy doth light his quick'ning
   torch.
    CEL. Nay, now you compliment ; I would
   it did,
My Lord, for your own sake.
    LORD. You would be kind,
And love me then?
    CEL. My Lord, I should be loving,
Where I found worth to invite it, and should
   cherish
A constant man.
    LORD. Then you should me, madam.
    CEL. But is the ice about your heart fallen
   off?
Can you return to do what love commands? —
Cupid, thou shalt have instant sacrifice,
And I dare be the priest.
    LORD. Your hand, your lip ; [150
                  [*Kisses her.*]
Now I am proof 'gainst all temptation.
    CEL. Your meaning, my good Lord?
    LORD. I, that have strength
Against thy voice and beauty, after this
May dare the charms of womankind. — Thou
   art,
Bella Maria, unprofaned yet ;
This magic has no power upon my blood. —
Farewell, madam ! if you durst be the example
Of chaste as well as fair, thou wert a brave one.
    CEL. I hope your Lordship means not this
   for earnest.
Be pleas'd to grace a banquet.
    LORD. Pardon, madam. — [160
Will Scentlove, follow ; I must laugh at you.
    CEL. My Lord, I must beseech you stay,
   for honor,
For her whose memory you love best.
    LORD. Your pleasure.
    CEL. And by that virtue you have now
   profess'd
I charge you to believe me too ; I can
Now glory that you have been worth my trial,
Which, I beseech you, pardon. Had not you
So valiantly recover'd in this conflict,
You had been my triumph, without hope of
   more
Than my just scorn upon your wanton
   flame ;   170
Nor will I think these noble thoughts grew
   first
From melancholy, for some female loss,
As the fantastic world believes, but from
Truth, and your love of innocence, which shine
So bright in the two royal luminaries [56]

[56] Charles I and Queen Henrietta Maria.

At court, you cannot lose your way to chastity.
Proceed, and speak of me as honor guides you.
         Exit Lord.
I am almost tir'd. — Come, ladies, we'll be-
   guile
Dull time, and take the air another while.
         Exeunt.

ACT V — [SCENE I] [1]

Enter ARETINA, *and* Servant [*with a purse*].

ARE. But hath Sir Thomas lost five hun-
   dred pounds
Already?
   SERV.   And five hundred more he borrow'd.
The dice are notable devourers, madam ;
They make no more of pieces [2] than of peb-
   bles,
But thrust their heaps together, to engender.
" Two hundred more the caster ! " [3] cries this
   gentleman.
" I am w' ee." — " I ha' that to nothing, sir.
   The caster
Again." 'T is covered, and the table, too,
With sums that frigh[t]ed me. Here one
   sneaks out,
And with a martyr's patience smiles upon   10
His money's executioner, the dice ;
Commands a pipe of good tobacco, and
I' th' smoke on 't vanishes. Another makes
The bones vault o'er his head, swears that ill-
   throwing
Has put his shoulder out of joint, calls for
A bone-setter. That looks to th' box, to bid
His master send him some more hundred
   pounds,
Which lost, he takes tobacco, and is quiet.
Here a strong arm throws in and in, with which
He brusheth all the table, pays the rooks [4]   [20
That went their smelts [5] apiece upon his
   hand,
Yet swears he has not drawn a stake this seven
   year.
But I was bid make haste ; my master may
Lose this five hundred pounds ere I come
   thither.   *Exit.*
   ARE. If we both waste so fast, we shall
   soon find
Our state [6] is not immortal. Something in
His other ways appear not well already.

[1] A room in Bornwell's house.
[2] See on I, i, 217.
[3] Thrower of the dice.   [4] Simpletons.
[5] Half-guineas.   [6] Estate.

Enter Sir THOMAS [BORNWELL, *and* Servants,
   one with a purse].

BORN. Ye tortoises, why make you no more
   haste ?
Go pay to th' master of the house that money,
And tell the noble gamesters I have another   [30
Superfluous thousand pound ; at night I'll
   visit 'em.
D' ee hear ?
   SERV.   Yes, an[t] please you.
   BORN.   Do 't, ye drudges.
         [*Exeunt* Servants.]
Ta, ra, ra ! — Aretina !
   ARE.   You have a pleasant humor, sir.
   BORN. What ! should a gentleman be sad ?
   ARE.   You have lost —
   BORN. A transitory sum ; as good that way
As another.
   ARE.   Do you not vex within for 't?
   BORN. I had rather lose a thousand more,
   than one
Sad thought come near my heart for 't. Vex
   for trash !
Although it go from other men like drops
Of their lifeblood, we lose with the alacrity   [40
We drink a cup of sack, or kiss a mistress.
No money is considerable with a gamester ;
They have souls more spacious than kings.
   Did two
Gamesters divide the empire of the world,
They'd make one throw for 't all, and he that
   lost
Be no more melancholy than to have play'd
   for
A morning's draught. Vex a rich soul for
   dirt,
The quiet of whose every thought is worth
A province !
   ARE.   But when dice have consum'd all,
Your patience will not pawn for as much
   more.   50
   BORN. Hang pawning ! Sell outright, and
   the fear's over.
   ARE. Say you so ? I'll have another coach
   to-morrow
If there be rich above ground.
   BORN.   I forgot
To bid the fellow ask my jeweller
Whether the chain of diamonds be made up ;
I will present it to my Lady Bellamour,
Fair Celestina.
   ARE.   This gown I have worn
Six days already ; it looks dull, I'll give it
My waiting woman, and have one of cloth

Of gold embroidered ; shoes and pantables [60]
Will show well of the same.

BORN. I have invited
A covey of ladies and as many gentlemen
To-morrow to the Italian ordinary ; [8]
I shall have rarities and regalias [9]
To pay for, madam ; music, wanton songs,
And tunes of silken petticoats to dance to.

ARE. And to-morrow have I invited half
the court
To dine here. What misfortune 't is your
company
And ours should be divided ! After dinner
I entertain 'em with a play.

BORN. By that time [70]
Your play inclines to the epilogue, shall we
Quit our Italian host and whirl in coaches
To the Dutch magazine of sauce, the Steel-
yard,[10]
Where deal,[11] and backrag,[12] and what strange
wine else
They dare but give a name to in the reckon-
ing,[13]
Shall flow into our room, and drown Westpha-
lias,[14]
Tongues, and anchovies, like some little town
Endangered by a sluice, through whose fierce
ebb
We wade, and wash ourselves into a boat,
And bid our coachmen drive their leather
tenements 80
By land, while we sail home, with a fresh tide,
To some new rendezvous.

ARE. If you have not
'Pointed the place, pray bring your ladies
hither ;
I mean to have a ball to-morrow night,
And a rich banquet for 'em, where we 'll dance
Till morning rise, and blush to interrupt us.

BORN. Have you no ladies i' th' next room,
to advance
A present mirth? What a dull house you
govern !
Farewell ! a wife 's no company. — Aretina,
I 've summ'd up my estate, and find we may
have 90
A month good yet.

ARE. What mean you?

BORN. And I 'd rather
Be lord one month of pleasures, to the height

[7] Slippers.
[8] Restaurant.   [9] Dainties.
[10] The headquarters of the German merchants.
[11] Evidently some German wine.
[12] Bacharach, a Rhenish wine.
[13] Bill.   [14] Westphalian hams.

And rapture of our senses, than be years
Consuming what we have in foolish temper-
ance,
Live in the dark, and no fame wait upon us !
I will live so, posterity shall stand
At gaze when I am mentioned.

ARE. A month good !
And what shall be done then?

BORN. I 'll over sea,
And trail a pike. With [15] watching, marching,
lying
In trenches, with enduring cold and hunger,
And taking here and there a musket-shot, [101]
I can earn every week four shillings, madam ;
And if the bullets favor me to snatch
Any superfluous limb, when I return,
With good friends, I despair not to be enroll'd
Poor knight of Windsor.[16] For your course,
madam,
No doubt you may do well ; your friends are
great ;
Or, if your poverty and their pride cannot
Agree, you need not trouble much invention
To find a trade to live by : there are custom-
ers.[17] 110
Farewell ; be frolic, madam ! If I live,
I will feast all my senses, and not fall
Less than a Phaëthon from my throne of pleas-
ure,
Though my estate flame like the world about
me. *Exit.*

ARE. 'T is very pretty ! —

Enter DECOY.

Madam Decoy !

DEC. What ! melancholy,
After so sweet a night's work? Have not I
Show'd myself mistress of my art?

ARE. A lady.

DEC. That title makes the credit of the act
A story higher. Y 'ave not seen him yet?
I wonder what he 'll say.

ARE. He 's here.

Enter ALEXANDER [KICKSHAW] *and* FRED-
ERICK.

KICK. Bear up, [120]
My little myrmidon ; does not Jack Little-
worth
Follow?

FRED. Follow? He fell into the Thames
At landing.

[15] By.
[16] Quarters were provided for a few pensioners
in Windsor Castle.
[17] With a play on the meaning "courtesans."

KICK. The Devil shall dive for him,
Ere I endanger my silk stockings for him.
Let the watermen alone :[18] they have drags
and engines.[19]
When he has drunk his julep, I shall laugh
To see him come in pickl'd the next tide.

FRED. He 'll never sink, he has such a cork
brain.

KICK. Let him be hang'd or drown'd, all 's
one to me ;
Yet he deserves to die by water[20] cannot   130
Bear his wine credibly.[21]

FRED.   Is not this my aunt?

KICK. And another handsome lady ; I must
know her.   [*Goes to* DECOY.]

FRED. My blood is rampant too, I must
court somebody ;
As good my aunt as any other body.

ARE. Where have you been, Cousin?

FRED.   At the Bridge,
At the Bear's foot,[22] where our first health be-
gan
To the fair Aretina, whose sweet company
Was wished by all. We could not get a lay,
A tumbler, a device, a bona roba,[23]
For any money ; drawers were grown dull ; [140
We wanted our true firks,[24] and our vagaries.—
When were you in drink, aunt?

ARE.   How?

FRED.   Do not ladies
Play the good fellows too? There 's no true
mirth
Without 'em. I have now such tickling
fancies !
That doctor of the chair of wit has read
A precious lecture, how I should behave
Myself to ladies ; as now, for example.

ARE. Would you practise upon me?

FRED.   I first salute you ;
You have a soft hand, madam ; are you so
All over?

ARE. Nephew !

FRED.   Nay, you should but smile. 150
And then again I kiss you ; and thus draw
Off your white glove, and start, to see your
hand
More excellently white. I grace my own

[18] Leave it to the watermen.
[19] Contrivances.
[20] Understand "who."   [21] Creditably.
[22] Dyce emends. Cf. IV, ii, 143. But the trans-
position is doubtless intentional.
[23] "Tumbler" and "bona roba" often occur as
slang for "courtesan." "Lay" and "device" evidently have the same meaning here.
[24] Whims, caprices; doubtless both this word and
"vagaries" have here the same meaning as the four
mentioned in the preceding note.

Lip with this touch, and turning gently thus,
Prepare you for my skill in palmistry,
Which, out of curiosity, no lady
But easily applies[25] to. The first line
I [l]ook with most ambition to find out,
Is Venus' girdle, a fair semicircle,
Enclosing both the mount of Sol and Saturn ;
If that appear, she 's for my turn ; a lady [161
Whom nature has prepar'd for the career ;
And, Cupid at my elbow, I put forward ;
You have this very line, Aunt.

ARE.   The boy 's frantic !

FRED. You have a couch or [pallet] :[26] I
can shut
The chamber doo[r]. Enrich a stranger, when
Your nephew 's coming into play !

ARE.   No more.

FRED. Are you so coy to your own flesh and
blood?

KICK. Here, take your playfellow ; I talk of
sport,
And she would have me marry her.

FRED.   Here 's Littleworth. 170

Enter LITTLEWORTH, *wet.*

Why, how now, tutor?

LITTLE.   I ha' been fishing.

FRED. And what ha' you caught?

LITTLE.   My belly full of water.

KICK. Ha, ha ! Where 's thy rapier?

LITTLE.   My rapier is[27] drown'd,
And I am little better. I was up by th' heels,
And out came a tun of water, beside wine.

KICK. 'T has made thee sober.

LITTLE.   Would you have me drunk
With water?

ARE.   I hope your fire is quenched by
this time.

FRED. It is not now, as when your Worship
" walk'd
By all the taverns," Jack, " dry as a bone."

KICK. You had store of fish under water,
Jack.   180

LITTLE. It has made a poor John[28] of me.

FRED. I do not think but if we cast an
angle
Into his belly, we might find some pilchards.

LITTLE. And boil'd, by this time. — Dear
madam, a bed.

KICK. Carry but the water spaniel to a
grassplot,
Where he may roll himself ; let him but shake

[25] Is compliant.
[26] Emend. Dyce ; various copies of Q *palate, palater.*
[27] Q *rapier's is.*   [28] Salt fish.

His ears twice in the sun, and you may grind
  him
Into a posset.[29]
FRED. Come, thou shalt to my bed,
Poor pickerel.
DEC. Alas, sweet gentleman!
LITTLE. I have ill luck an I should smell by
  this time; 190
I am but new ta'en, I am sure. — Sweet gen-
  tlewoman!
DEC. Your servant.
LITTLE. Pray do not pluck off my skin;
It is so wet, unless you have good eyes,
You 'll hardly know it from a shirt.
DEC. Fear nothing.
  Exeunt [all but KICKSHAW *and* ARE-
  TINA].
ARE. [*aside*] He has sack enough, and I
  may find his humor.
KICK. And how is 't with your Ladyship?
  You look
Without a sunshine in your face.
ARE. You are glorious
In mind and habit.
KICKS. Ends of gold and silver!
ARE. Your other clothes were not so rich.
  Who was
Your tailor, sir?
KICK. They were made for me long
  since; 200
They have known but two bright days upon
  my back.
I had a humor, madam, to lay things by;
They will serve two days more: I think I ha'
  gold enough
To go to th' mercer. I 'll now allow myself
A suit a week, as this, with necessary
Dependances, beaver, silk stockings, garters,
And roses,[30] in their due conformity;
Boots are forbid a clean [31] leg, but to ride in.
My linen every morning comes in new,
The old goes to great bellies.[32]
ARE. You are charitable. [210
KICK. I may dine w' ee some time, or at the
  court,
To meet good company, not for the table.
My clerk o' th' kitchen 's here, a witty epi-
  cure,
A spirit that, to please me with what 's rare,
Can fly a hundred mile a day to market,
And make me lord of fish and fowl. I shall
Forget there is a butcher; and to make

My footman nimble, he shall feed on nothing
But wings of wild fowl.
ARE. These ways are costly.
KICK. Therefore I 'll have it so; I ha'
  sprung a mine. 220
ARE. You make me wonder, sir, to see
  this change
Of fortune; your revenue was not late
So plentiful.
KICK. Hang dirty land and lordships!
I wo' not change one lodging I ha' got,
For the chamber [33] of London.
ARE. Strange, of such a sudden,
To rise to this estate! No fortunate hand
At dice could lift you up so, for 't is since
Last night; yesterday, you were no such
  monarch.
KICK. There be more games than dice.
ARE. It cannot be
A mistress, though your person is worth
  love; 230
None possibly are rich enough to feed
As you have cast the method of your riots.
A princess, after all her jewels, must
Be forc'd to sell her provinces.
KICK. Now you talk
Of jewels, what do you think of this?
ARE. A rich one.
KICK. You 'll honor me to wear 't; this
  other toy
I had from you; this chain I borrowed of
  you,
A friend had it in keeping. [*Gives her the jewel
  and chain.*] — If your Ladyship
Want any sum, you know your friend and
  Alexander.
ARE. Dare you trust my security?
KICK. There 's gold; [240
I shall have more to-morrow.
ARE. You astonish me;
Who can supply these?
KICK. A dear friend I have.
She promis'd we should meet again i' th' morn-
  ing.
ARE. Not that I wish to know
More of your happiness than I have already
Heart to congratulate, — be pleas'd to lay
My wonder.
KICK. 'T is a secret —
ARE. Which I 'll die
Ere I 'll betray.
KICK. You have always wish'd me well;
But you shall swear not to reveal the party.
ARE. I 'll lose the benefit of my tongue.

[29] Hot milk curdled with wine or ale.
[30] Rosettes for the shoes.
[31] Well-shaped. [32] *I.e.*, for layettes.
[33] Royal city, capital.

KICK. Nor be [250
Afraid at what I say. What think you first
Of an old witch, a strange ill-favor'd hag,
That, for my company last night, has wrought
This cure upon my fortune? I do sweat
To think upon her name.

ARE. How, sir! a witch?

KICK. I would not fright your Ladyship too
much
At first, but witches are akin to spirits.
The truth is — nay, if you look pale already,
I ha' done.

ARE. Sir, I beseech you.

KICK. If you have
But courage then to know the truth, I 'll tell
you 260
In one word; my chief friend is the Devil!

ARE. What devil? how I tremble!

KICK. Have a heart;
'T was a she-devil too, a most insatiate,
Abominable devil, with a tail
Thus long.

ARE. Goodness defend me! Did you see
her?

KICK. No, 't was i' th' dark; but she ap-
pear'd first to me
I' th' likeness of a be[ld]am, and was brought,
I know not how, nor whither, by two goblins,
More hooded than a hawk.

ARE. But would you venture
Upon a devil!

KICK. Ay, for means.

ARE. [aside] How black [270
An impudence is this! — But are you sure
It was the Devil you enjoy'd?

KICK. Say nothing;
I did the best to please her; but as sure
As you live, 't was a hell-cat.[34]

ARE. D' ee not quake?

KICK. I found myself the very same [35] i' th'
morning,
Where two of her familiars had left me.

Enter Servant.

SERV. My Lord is come to visit you.

KICK. No words,
As you respect my safety. I ha' told tales
Out of the Devil's school; if it be known,
I lose a friend. 'T is now about the time [280
I promis'd her to meet again; at my
Return I 'll tell you wonders. Not a word.
Exit.

ARE. [looking in a mirror] 'T is a false glass;
sure I am more deform'd. —
What have I done? — My soul is miserable.

Enter Lord.

LORD. I sent you a letter, madam.

ARE. You express'd
Your noble care of me, my Lord.

Re-enter [Sir THOMAS] BORNWELL [and]
CELESTINA.

BORN. Your Lordship
Does me an honor.

LORD. Madam, I am glad
To see you here; I meant to have kiss'd your
hand,
Ere my return to court.

CEL. Sir Thomas has
Prevail'd to bring me, to his trouble, hither.

LORD. You do him grace.

BORN. Why, what 's the matter,
madam? 291
Your eyes are tuning *Lachrimae.*[36]

ARE. As you
Do hope for Heaven, withdraw, and give me but
The patience of ten minutes.

BORN. Wonderful!
I will not hear you above that proportion.
She talks of Heaven. — Come, where must we
to counsel?

ARE. You shall conclude me when you
please. [*Exit.*]

BORN. I follow.

LORD. [aside] What alteration is this? I,
that so late
Stood the temptation of her eye and voice,
Boasted a heart 'bove all licentious flame, [300
At second view turn renegade, and think
I was too superstitious, and full
Of phlegm, not to reward her amorous court-
ship
With manly freedom.

CEL. [to BORNWELL] I obey you, sir.

BORN. I 'll wait upon your Lordship presently. [*Exit.*]

LORD. [aside] She could not want a cunning
to seem honest
When I neglected her. I am resolv'd. —
You still look pleasant, madam.

CEL. I have cause,
My Lord, the rather for your presence, which
Hath power to charm all trouble in my
thoughts. 310

[34] Witch, hag.
[35] Dyce emends *myself in the very room.* Q *my
selfe the very same in i' th morning.*

[36] You are about to weep. *Lachrimae* was a
musical composition by John Dowland.

LORD. I must translate that compliment, and owe
All that is cheerful in myself to these
All-quick'ning smiles; and rather than such bright
Eyes should repent their influence upon me,
I would release the aspects, and quit the bounty
Of all the other stars. Did you not think me
A strange and melancholy gentleman,
To use you so unkindly?
CEL.   Me, my Lord?
LORD. I hope you made no loud complaint;
    I would not
Be tri'd by a jury of ladies.
CEL.   For what, my Lord? [320
LORD. I did not meet that noble entertainment
You were late pleas'd to show me.
CEL.   I observ'd
No such defect in your Lordship, but a brave
And noble fortitude.
LORD.   A noble folly!
I bring repentance for 't. I know you have,
Madam, a gentle faith, and wo' not ruin
What you have built to honor you.
CEL.   What 's that?
LORD. If you can love, I 'll tell your Ladyship.
CEL. I have a stubborn soul else.
LORD.   You are all
Compos'd of harmony.
CEL.   What love d' ee mean? [330
LORD. That which doth perfect both.
    Madam, you have heard
I can be constant, and if you consent
To grace it so, there is a spacious dwelling
Prepar'd within my heart for such a mistress.
CEL. Your mistress, my good Lord?
LORD.   Why, my good Lady,
Your sex doth hold it no dishonor
To become mistress to a noble servant
In the now court Platonic way. Consider
Who 't is that pleads to you; my birth and present
Value can be no stain to your embrace;   340
But these are shadows when my love appears,
Which shall, in his first miracle, return
Me in my bloom of youth, and thee a virgin;
When I, within some new Elysium,
Of purpose made and meant for us, shall be
In every thing Adonis, but in his
Contempt of love; and court thee from a Daphne
Hid in the cold rind of a bashful tree,

With such warm language and delight, till thou
Leap from that bays[37] into the Queen of Love,   350
And pay my conquest with composing garlands
Of thy own myrtle[38] for me.
CEL.   What 's all this?
LORD. Consent to be my mistress, Celestina,
And we will have it springtime all the year;
Upon whose invitations, when we walk,
The winds shall play soft descant[39] to our feet,
And breathe rich odors to re-pure the air.
Green bowers on every side shall tempt our stay,
And violets stoop to have us tread upon 'em.
The red rose shall grow pale, being near thy cheek,   360
And the white blush, o'ercome with such a forehead.
Here laid, and measuring with ourselves some bank,
A thousand birds shall from the woods repair,
And place themselves so cunningly behind
The leaves of every tree, that while they pay
[Us][40] tribute of their songs, thou sha't imagine
The very trees bear music, and sweet voices
Do grow in every arbor. Here can we
Embrace and kiss, tell tales, and kiss again,
And none but Heaven our rival.
CEL.   When we are [370
Weary of these, what if we shift our paradise,
And through a grove of tall and even pine,
Descend into a valley, that shall shame
All the delights of Tempe; upon whose
Green plush the Graces shall be call'd to dance
To please us, and maintain their fairy revels,
To the harmonious murmurs of a stream
That gently falls upon a rock of pearl.
Here doth the nymph, forsaken Echo, dwell,
To whom we 'll tell the story of our love, [380
Till at our surfeit and her want of joy,
We break her heart with envy. Not far off,
A grove shall call us to a wanton river,
To see a dying swan give up the ghost,
The fishes shooting up their tears in bubbles,
That they must lose the genius of their waves —
And such love[41] linsey-woolsey,[42] to no purpose.

[37] The laurel, into which Daphne was metamorphosed.
[38] For the myrtle was sacred to Venus, as the bay laurel was to Apollo.
[39] *I.e.*, harmonies.   [40] Q *As*.   [41] Understand "is."
[42] Nonsense, jargon. Literally, a cloth made partly of linen, partly of wool, and therefore neither the one thing nor the other.

LORD. You chide me handsomely; pray tell me how
You like this language.   [*He embraces her.*]
CEL.   Good my Lord, forbear.
LORD. You need not fly out of this circle, madam.   390
These widows are so full of circumstance!
I'll undertake, in this time I ha' courted
Your Ladyship for the toy, to ha' broken ten,
Nay, twenty colts, virgins I mean, and taught 'em
The amble, or what pace I most affected.
     CEL. Y' are not, my Lord, again, the lord I thought you;
And I must tell you now, you do forget
Yourself and me.
     LORD.   You'll not be angry, madam?
     CEL. Nor rude, (though gay men have a privilege,)
It shall appear. — There is a man, my Lord,
Within my acquaintance, rich in worldly fortunes,   401
But cannot boast any descent of blood,
Would buy a coat of arms.
     LORD.   He may, and legs
Booted and spurr'd, to ride into the country.
     CEL. But these will want antiquity, my Lord,
The seal of honor. What's a coat cut out
But yesterday, to make a man a gentleman?
Your family, as old as the first virtue
That merited an escutcheon, doth owe [43]   [409
A glorious coat of arms; if you will sell now
All that your name doth challenge in that ensign,
I'll help you to a chapman [44] that shall pay,
And pour down wealth enough for't.
     LORD.   Sell my arms!
I cannot, madam.
     CEL.   Give but your consent,
You know not how the state may be inclin'd
To dispensation; we may prevail
Upon the Herald's Office afterward.
     LORD. I'll sooner give these arms to th' hangman's axe,
My head, my heart, to twenty executions,
Than sell one atom from my name.
     CEL.   Change that, [420
And answer him would buy my honor from me:
Honor, that is not worn upon a flag
Or pennon, that, without the owner's dangers,
An enemy may ravish, and bear from me;

[43] Own.   [44] Merchant, buyer.

But that which grows and withers with my soul,
Beside the body's stain — think, think, my Lord,
To what you would unworthily betray me,
If you would not, for price of gold, or pleasure
(If that be more your idol), lose the glory
And painted honor of your house. — I ha' done.   430
     LORD. Enough to rectify a satyr's blood.
Obscure my blushes here.

Enter [Sir WILLIAM] SCENTLOVE *and* HAIRCUT.

     HAIR.   Or this or fight with me;
It shall be no exception [45] that I wait
Upon my Lord: I am a gentleman;
You may be less and be a knight; the office
I do my Lord is honest, sir. How many
Such you have been guilty of, Heaven knows.
     SCENT. 'T is no fear of your sword, but that I would not
Break the good laws established against duels.
     HAIR. Off with your periwig, and stand bare.
     [SCENTLOVE *takes off his periwig.*]
     LORD. [*aside to* CELESTINA]   From this   440
Minute I'll be a servant to thy goodness;
A mistress in the wanton sense is common;
I'll honor you with chaste thoughts, and call you so.
     CEL. [*aside to* Lord] I'll study to be worth your fair opinion.
     LORD. Scentlove, your head was us'd to a covering,
Beside a hat; when went the hair away?
     SCENT. I laid a wager, my Lord, with Haircut,
Who thinks I shall catch cold, that I'll stand bare
This half hour.
     HAIR.   Pardon my ambition,
Madam; I told you truth: I am a gentleman,   450
And cannot fear that name is drown'd in my
Relation to my Lord.
     CEL.   I dare not think so.
     HAIR. From henceforth call my service duty, madam.
That pig's-head, [46] that betray'd me to your mirth,
Is doing penance for't.
     SCENT.   Why may not I,
My Lord, begin a fashion of no hair?

[45] Objection.   [46] *I.e.,* closely shorn head.

CEL. Do you sweat, Sir William?

SCENT.   Not with store of nightcaps.

Re-enter ARETINA [*and* SIR THOMAS]
BORNWELL.

ARE. [*aside to* BORNWELL] Heaven has dis-
solv'd the clouds that hung upon
My eyes, and if you can with mercy meet
A penitent, I throw my own will off,   460
And now in all things obey yours, my
     nephew
Send back again to th' college, and myself
To what place you 'll confine me.

BORN. [*aside to* ARETINA]   Dearer now
Than ever to my bosom, thou sha't please
Me best to live at thy own choice. I did
But fright thee with a noise of my expenses ;
The sums are safe, and we have wealth enough,
If yet we use it nobly. — My Lord, — madam,
Pray honor [us] [46] to-night.

ARE.   I beg your presence,
And pardon.

BORN.   I know not how my Aretina [470
May be dispos'd to-morrow for the country.

CEL. You must not go before you have
     done
Me honor to accept an entertainment
Where I have power ; on those terms I 'm your
     guest.

BORN. You grace us, madam.

ARE. [*aside*]   Already
I feel a cure upon my soul, and promise
My after life to virtue. Pardon, Heaven,
My shame, yet hid from the world's eye.

Re-enter DECOY.

DEC.   Sweet madam !

ARE. Not for the world be seen here ! We
     are lost.

[46] Add. Dyce.

I 'll visit you at home. — [*aside*] But not to
     practice   480
What she expects ; my counsel may recover
     her.   [*Exit* DECOY.]

Re-enter ALEXANDER [KICKSHAW].

KICK. Where 's madam ? — [*aside to* ARE-
TINA] Pray lend me a little money ;
My spirit has deceiv'd me ; Proserpine
Has broke her word.

ARE. [*aside to* KICKSHAW]   Do you expect to find
The Devil true to you?

KICK. [*aside*]   Not too loud.

ARE. [*aside*]   I 'll voice it
Louder, to all the world, your horrid sin,
Unless you promise me religiously,
To purge your foul blood by repentance, sir.

KICK. [*aside*] Then I 'm undone.

ARE. [*aside*]   Not while I have power
To encourage you to virtue. I 'll endeavor [490
To find you out some nobler way at court,
To thrive in.

KICK. [*aside*] Do 't and I 'll forsake the
     Devil,
And bring my flesh to obedience. You shall
     steer me, —
My Lord, your servant.

LORD.   You are brave again.

KICK. Madam, your pardon.

BORN.   Your offence requires
Humility.

KICK.   Low as my heart. — Sir Thomas,
I 'll sup with you, a part of satisfaction.

BORN. Our pleasures cool. Music ! and
     when our ladies
Are tir'd with active motion, to give
Them rest, in some new rapture to advance [500
Full mirth, our souls shall leap into a dance.

                       Exeunt.